# PARLIAMENTARY DEBATES

## (HANSARD)

**SIXTH SERIES—VOLUME 155**

# HOUSE OF COMMONS

### OFFICIAL REPORT

SECOND SESSION OF THE FIFTIETH PARLIAMENT
OF THE UNITED KINGDOM OF GREAT BRITAIN
AND NORTHERN IRELAND
THIRTY-EIGHTH YEAR OF THE REIGN OF
HER MAJESTY QUEEN ELIZABETH II

**SESSION 1988-89**

COMPRISING PERIOD
19 JUNE—30 JUNE 1989

*LONDON*
HER MAJESTY'S STATIONERY OFFICE
£68 net

ISBN 0 10 681155 X

# HER MAJESTY'S GOVERNMENT

## MEMBERS OF THE CABINET

(FORMED BY THE RT. HON. MARGARET THATCHER, MP, JULY 1988)

PRIME MINISTER, FIRST LORD OF THE TREASURY AND MINISTER FOR THE CIVIL SERVICE—
The Rt. Hon. Margaret Thatcher, MP
SECRETARY OF STATE FOR FOREIGN AND COMMONWEALTH AFFAIRS—The Rt. Hon. Sir Geoffrey Howe, QC, MP
CHANCELLOR OF THE EXCHEQUER—The Rt. Hon. Nigel Lawson, MP
LORD CHANCELLOR—The Rt. Hon. The Lord Mackay of Clashfern
SECRETARY OF STATE FOR THE HOME DEPARTMENT—The Rt. Hon. Douglas Hurd, CBE, MP
SECRETARY OF STATE FOR WALES—The Rt. Hon. Peter Walker, MBE, MP
SECRETARY OF STATE FOR DEFENCE—The Rt. Hon. George Younger, TD, MP
SECRETARY OF STATE FOR EMPLOYMENT—The Rt. Hon. Norman Fowler, MP
SECRETARY OF STATE FOR NORTHERN IRELAND—The Rt. Hon. Tom King, MP
SECRETARY OF STATE FOR THE ENVIRONMENT—The Rt. Hon. Nicholas Ridley, MP
SECRETARY OF STATE FOR TRADE AND INDUSTRY AND PRESIDENT OF THE BOARD OF TRADE—
The Rt. Hon. The Lord Young of Graffham
SECRETARY OF STATE FOR EDUCATION AND SCIENCE—The Rt. Hon. Kenneth Baker, MP
SECRETARY OF STATE FOR HEALTH—The Rt. Hon. Kenneth Clarke, QC, MP
MINISTER OF AGRICULTURE, FISHERIES AND FOOD—The Rt. Hon. John MacGregor, OBE, MP
SECRETARY OF STATE FOR SCOTLAND—The Rt. Hon. Malcolm Rifkind, QC, MP
SECRETARY OF STATE FOR TRANSPORT—The Rt. Hon. Paul Channon, MP
SECRETARY OF STATE FOR SOCIAL SECURITY—The Rt. Hon. John Moore, MP
LORD PRESIDENT OF THE COUNCIL AND LEADER OF THE HOUSE OF COMMONS—The Rt. Hon. John Wakeham, MP
LORD PRIVY SEAL AND LEADER OF THE HOUSE OF LORDS—The Rt. Hon. The Lord Belstead
SECRETARY OF STATE FOR ENERGY—The Rt. Hon. Cecil Parkinson, MP
CHIEF SECRETARY TO THE TREASURY—The Rt. Hon. John Major, MP
CHANCELLOR OF THE DUCHY OF LANCASTER AND MINISTER OF TRADE AND INDUSTRY—
The Rt. Hon. Antony Newton, OBE, MP

## LAW OFFICERS

ATTORNEY-GENERAL—The Rt. Hon. Sir Patrick Mayhew, QC, MP
LORD ADVOCATE—The Rt. Hon. The Lord Fraser of Carmyllie, QC
SOLICITOR-GENERAL—Sir Nicholas Lyell, QC, MP
SOLICITOR-GENERAL FOR SCOTLAND—Alan Rodger, Esq, QC

## MINISTERS NOT IN THE CABINET

PARLIAMENTARY SECRETARY TO THE TREASURY—The Rt. Hon. David Waddington, QC, MP
MINISTER OF STATE, PRIVY COUNCIL OFFICE, (MINISTER FOR THE ARTS)—The Rt. Hon. Richard Luce, MP
MINISTERS OF STATE, FOREIGN AND COMMONWEALTH OFFICE—
The Rt. Hon. Lynda Chalker, MP
The Hon. William Waldegrave, MP
Minister for Overseas Development—The Rt. Hon. Christopher Patten, MP
The Lord Glenarthur
PAYMASTER GENERAL—The Rt. Hon. Peter Brooke, MP
FINANCIAL SECRETARY TO THE TREASURY—The Rt. Hon. Norman Lamont, MP
MINISTERS OF STATE, HOME OFFICE—
The Rt. Hon. The Earl Ferrers
John Patten, Esq, MP
Tim Renton, Esq, MP
MINISTER OF STATE, WELSH OFFICE—Wyn Roberts, Esq, MP
MINISTERS OF STATE, MINISTRY OF DEFENCE—
Minister of State for Defence Procurement—The Rt. Hon. The Lord Trefgarne
Minister of State for the Armed Forces—The Hon. Archibald Hamilton, MP
MINISTER OF STATE, DEPARTMENT OF EMPLOYMENT—The Rt. Hon. John Cope, MP
MINISTER OF STATE, NORTHERN IRELAND OFFICE—The Rt. Hon. Ian Stewart, RD, MP
MINISTERS OF STATE, DEPARTMENT OF THE ENVIRONMENT—
Minister for Local Government—The Rt. Hon. John Gummer, MP
Minister for Housing, Environment and Countryside—The Earl of Caithness
Minister for Water and Planning—Michael Howard, Esq, QC, MP
MINISTER OF STATE, DEPARTMENT OF TRADE AND INDUSTRY—
Minister for Trade—The Hon. Alan Clark, MP
MINISTER OF STATE, DEPARTMENT OF EDUCATION AND SCIENCE—Mrs. Angela Rumbold, CBE, MP
MINISTER OF STATE, DEPARTMENT OF HEALTH—David Mellor, Esq, QC, MP

MINISTERS OF STATE, SCOTTISH OFFICE—
    Ian Lang, Esq, MP
    The Lord Sanderson of Bowden
MINISTER OF STATE, DEPARTMENT OF TRANSPORT—
    Minister for Public Transport—Michael Portillo, Esq, MP
MINISTER OF STATE, DEPARTMENT OF SOCIAL SECURITY—
    Minister for Social Security—The Rt. Hon. Nicholas Scott, MBE, MP
MINISTER OF STATE, DEPARTMENT OF ENERGY—The Rt. Hon. Peter Morrison, MP

## DEPARTMENTS OF STATE AND MINISTERS

**Agriculture, Fisheries and Food—**
    MINISTER—The Rt. Hon. John MacGregor, OBE, MP
    PARLIAMENTARY SECRETARIES—
    The Baroness Trumpington
    Donald Thompson, Esq, MP
    Richard Ryder, Esq, OBE, MP

**Arts and Libraries, Office of—**
    MINISTER FOR THE ARTS—The Rt. Hon. Richard Luce, MP

**Chancellor of the Duchy of Lancaster and Minister of Trade and Industry—**
    The Rt. Hon. Antony Newton, OBE, MP

**Civil Service, Office of the Minister for the—**
    PRIME MINISTER AND MINISTER FOR THE CIVIL SERVICE—The Rt. Hon. Margaret Thatcher, MP
    MINISTER OF STATE, PRIVY COUNCIL OFFICE (MINISTER FOR THE ARTS)—The Rt. Hon. Richard Luce, MP

**Defence—**
    SECRETARY OF STATE—The Rt. Hon. George Younger, TD, MP
    MINISTER OF STATE FOR DEFENCE PROCUREMENT—The Rt. Hon. The Lord Trefgarne
    MINISTER OF STATE FOR THE ARMED FORCES—The Hon. Archibald Hamilton, MP
    PARLIAMENTARY UNDER-SECRETARY OF STATE FOR THE ARMED FORCES—Michael Neubert, Esq, MP
    PARLIAMENTARY UNDER-SECRETARY OF STATE FOR DEFENCE PROCUREMENT—The Hon. Tim Sainsbury, MP

**Education and Science—**
    SECRETARY OF STATE—The Rt. Hon. Kenneth Baker, MP
    MINISTER OF STATE—Mrs. Angela Rumbold, CBE, MP
    PARLIAMENTARY UNDER-SECRETARIES OF STATE—
    John Butcher, Esq, MP
    Robert Jackson, Esq, MP

**Employment—**
    SECRETARY OF STATE—The Rt. Hon. Norman Fowler, MP
    MINISTER OF STATE—The Rt. Hon. John Cope, MP
    PARLIAMENTARY UNDER-SECRETARIES OF STATE—
    John Lee, Esq, MP
    Patrick Nicholls, Esq, MP

**Energy—**
    SECRETARY OF STATE—The Rt. Hon. Cecil Parkinson, Esq, MP
    MINISTER OF STATE—The Rt. Hon. Peter Morrison, MP
    PARLIAMENTARY UNDER-SECRETARIES OF STATE—
    Michael Spicer, Esq, MP
    The Baroness Hooper

**Environment—**
    SECRETARY OF STATE—The Rt. Hon. Nicholas Ridley, MP
    MINISTERS OF STATE—
    Minister for Local Government—The Rt. Hon. John Gummer, MP
    Minister for Housing, Environment and Countryside—The Earl of Caithness
    Minister for Water and Planning—Michael Howard, Esq, QC, MP
    PARLIAMENTARY UNDER-SECRETARIES OF STATE—
    David Trippier, Esq, RD, MP
    Christopher Chope, Esq, OBE, MP
    Mrs. Virginia Bottomley, MP
    The Hon. Colin Moynihan, MP (Minister for Sport)
    The Lord Hesketh

**Foreign and Commonwealth Affairs—**
    SECRETARY OF STATE—The Rt. Hon. Sir Geoffrey Howe, QC, MP
    MINISTERS OF STATE—
    The Rt. Hon. Lynda Chalker, MP
    The Hon. William Waldegrave, MP
    Minister for Overseas Development—The Rt. Hon. Christopher Patten, MP
    The Lord Glenarthur
    PARLIAMENTARY UNDER-SECRETARY OF STATE—Timothy Eggar, Esq, MP

**Health—**
SECRETARY OF STATE FOR HEALTH—The Rt. Hon. Kenneth Clarke, QC, MP
MINISTER OF STATE—
  David Mellor, Esq, QC, MP
PARLIAMENTARY UNDER-SECRETARY OF STATE—
  Roger Freeman, Esq, MP

**Home Office—**
SECRETARY OF STATE FOR THE HOME DEPARTMENT—The Rt. Hon. Douglas Hurd, CBE, MP
MINISTERS OF STATE—
  The Rt. Hon. The Earl Ferrers
  John Patten, Esq, MP
  Tim Renton, Esq, MP
PARLIAMENTARY UNDER-SECRETARY OF STATE—The Hon. Douglas Hogg, MP

**Law Officers' Department—**
ATTORNEY-GENERAL—The Rt. Hon. Sir Patrick Mayhew, QC, MP
SOLICITOR-GENERAL—Sir Nicholas Lyell, QC, MP

**Lord Advocate's Department—**
LORD-ADVOCATE—The Rt. Hon. The Lord Fraser of Carmyllie, QC
SOLICITOR-GENERAL FOR SCOTLAND—Alan Rodger, Esq, QC

**Lord Chancellor—**
The Rt. Hon. The Lord Mackay of Clashfern

**Northern Ireland Office—**
SECRETARY OF STATE FOR NORTHERN IRELAND—The Rt. Hon. Tom King, MP
MINISTER OF STATE—The Rt. Hon. Ian Stewart, RD, MP
PARLIAMENTARY UNDER-SECRETARIES OF STATE—
  The Lord Lyell
  Richard Needham, Esq, MP
  Dr. Brian Mawhinney, MP
  Peter Viggers, Esq, MP

**Paymaster General—**
The Rt. Hon. Peter Brooke, MP

**Privy Council Office—**
LORD PRESIDENT OF THE COUNCIL AND LEADER OF THE HOUSE OF COMMONS—The Rt. Hon. John Wakeham, MP
LORD PRIVY SEAL AND LEADER OF THE HOUSE OF LORDS—The Rt. Hon. The Lord Belstead
MINISTER OF STATE—The Rt. Hon. Richard Luce, MP

**Scottish Office—**
SECRETARY OF STATE FOR SCOTLAND—The Rt. Hon. Malcolm Rifkind, QC, MP
MINISTERS OF STATE—
  Ian Lang, Esq, MP
  The Lord Sanderson of Bowden
PARLIAMENTARY UNDER-SECRETARIES OF STATE—
  Lord James Douglas-Hamilton, MP
  Michael Forsyth, Esq, MP

**Social Security—**
SECRETARY OF STATE FOR SOCIAL SECURITY—The Rt. Hon. John Moore, MP
MINISTER OF STATE—
  Minister for Social Security—The Rt. Hon. Nicholas Scott, MBE, MP
PARLIAMENTARY UNDER-SECRETARIES OF STATE—
  The Lord Skelmersdale
  Peter Lloyd, Esq, MP

**Trade and Industry—**
SECRETARY OF STATE FOR TRADE AND INDUSTRY AND PRESIDENT OF THE BOARD OF TRADE—
  The Rt. Hon. The Lord Young of Graffham
CHANCELLOR OF THE DUCHY OF LANCASTER AND MINISTER OF TRADE AND INDUSTRY—
  The Rt. Hon. Antony Newton, OBE, MP
MINISTER OF STATE
  Minister for Trade—The Hon. Alan Clark, MP
PARLIAMENTARY UNDER-SECRETARY OF STATE—Robert Atkins, Esq, MP
PARLIAMENTARY UNDER-SECRETARY OF STATE FOR CORPORATE AFFAIRS—The Hon. Francis Maude, MP
PARLIAMENTARY UNDER-SECRETARY OF STATE FOR INDUSTRY AND CONSUMER AFFAIRS—Eric Forth, Esq, MP

**Transport—**
SECRETARY OF STATE FOR TRANSPORT—The Rt. Hon. Paul Channon, MP
MINISTER OF STATE
Minister for Public Transport—Michael Portillo, Esq, MP
PARLIAMENTARY UNDER-SECRETARIES OF STATE—
Minister for Roads and Traffic—Peter Bottomley, Esq, MP
Minister for Aviation and Shipping—The Lord Brabazon of Tara

**Treasury—**
PRIME MINISTER, FIRST LORD OF THE TREASURY AND MINISTER FOR THE CIVIL SERVICE—
The Rt. Hon. Margaret Thatcher, MP
CHANCELLOR OF THE EXCHEQUER—The Rt. Hon. Nigel Lawson, MP
CHIEF SECRETARY—The Rt. Hon. John Major, MP
PAYMASTER GENERAL—The Rt. Hon. Peter Brooke, MP
FINANCIAL SECRETARY TO THE TREASURY—The Rt. Hon. Norman Lamont, MP
ECONOMIC SECRETARY—Peter Lilley, Esq, MP
PARLIAMENTARY SECRETARY TO THE TREASURY—The Rt. Hon. David Waddington, QC, MP
LORDS COMMISSIONERS—
David Lightbown, Esq, MP
Kenneth Carlisle, Esq, MP
Alan Howarth, Esq, CBE, MP
David Maclean, Esq, MP
Stephen Dorrell, Esq, MP
ASSISTANT WHIPS—
John Taylor, Esq, MP
David Heathcoat-Amory, Esq, MP
The Hon. Tom Sackville, MP
Michael Fallon, Esq, MP
Sydney Chapman, Esq, MP

**Welsh Office—**
SECRETARY OF STATE FOR WALES—The Rt. Hon. Peter Walker, MP
MINISTER OF STATE—Wyn Roberts, Esq, MP
PARLIAMENTARY UNDER-SECRETARY OF STATE—Ian Grist, Esq, MP

**Her Majesty's Household—**
LORD CHAMBERLAIN—The Rt. Hon. The Earl of Airlie, KT, GCVO
LORD STEWARD—The Viscount Ridley, TD
MASTER OF THE HORSE—The Rt. Hon. The Earl of Westmorland, KCVO
TREASURER—David Hunt, Esq, MBE, MP
COMPTROLLER—Tristan Garel-Jones, Esq, MP
VICE-CHAMBERLAIN—Tony Durant, Esq, MP
CAPTAIN OF THE HONOURABLE CORPS OF GENTLEMEN-AT-ARMS—The Rt. Hon. The Lord Denham
CAPTAIN OF THE QUEEN'S BODYGUARD OF THE YEOMEN OF THE GUARD—The Viscount Davidson
LORDS IN WAITING—The Viscount Long, The Earl of Dundee, The Earl of Arran, The Lord Strathclyde, The Lord Henley

---

SECOND CHURCH ESTATES COMMISSIONER, REPRESENTING CHURCH COMMISSIONERS—The Rt. Hon. Michael Alison, MP

# HOUSE OF COMMONS

## PRINCIPAL OFFICERS AND OFFICIALS

THE SPEAKER—Rt. Hon. Bernard Weatherill, MP

CHAIRMAN OF WAYS AND MEANS—Rt. Hon. Harold Walker, MP

FIRST DEPUTY CHAIRMAN OF WAYS AND MEANS—Sir Paul Dean, MP
SECOND DEPUTY CHAIRMAN OF WAYS AND MEANS—Miss Betty Boothroyd, MP

CHAIRMEN'S PANEL—

Donald Coleman, Esq, MP, Patrick Cormack, Esq, MP, Stan Crowther, Esq, MP, Dame Janet Fookes, MP, Norman Hogg, Esq, MP, Geraint Howells, Esq, MP, Sir John Hunt, MP, David Knox, Esq, MP, James Lamond, Esq, MP, Michael Latham, Esq, MP, Ted Leadbitter, Esq, MP, Geoffrey Lofthouse, Esq, MP, John McWilliam, Esq, MP, Michael J. Martin, Esq, MP, Sir Anthony Meyer, MP, Michael Morris, Esq, MP, Robert Rhodes James, Esq, MP, Sir Giles Shaw, MP, Sir Michael Shaw, MP, Michael Shersby, Esq, MP, Sir John Stradling Thomas, MP, Nicholas Winterton, Esq, MP

HOUSE OF COMMONS COMMISSION—

Rt. Hon. The Speaker (Chairman), Alan Beith, Esq, MP, Frank Dobson, Esq, MP, Rt. Hon. Sir Barney Hayhoe, MP, Rt. Hon. Peter Shore, MP, Rt. Hon. John Wakeham, MP

SECRETARY OF THE COMMISSION—W. A. Proctor

BOARD OF MANAGEMENT—

C. J. Boulton, CB (Chairman), Sir Victor Le Fanu, KCVO, D. Menhennet, D. Phil., G. A. Roberts, K. S. Morgan, W. J. J. Smillie, FHCIMA, FCFA, ACF

SECRETARY TO THE BOARD OF MANAGEMENT—B. A. Wilson

## OFFICE OF THE SPEAKER

SPEAKER'S SECRETARY—P. J. Kitcatt, CB

SPEAKER'S COUNSEL—H. Knorpel, CB, QC, G. E. Gammie, CB, QC

SPEAKER'S CHAPLAIN—Rev. Canon D. C. Gray, TD, PhD

TRAINBEARER—D. J. Lord

DEPUTY TRAINBEARER—P. L. Warwick

HEO (ADMINISTRATION/DIARY)—Mrs. S. Norvell

HEO (ASSISTANT SECRETARY TO THE SPEAKER)—Miss S. Holt

ASSISTANT TO SPEAKER'S COUNSEL—P. Harvey, CB

## OFFICE OF THE CHAIRMAN OF WAYS AND MEANS

SECRETARY TO THE CHAIRMAN OF WAYS AND MEANS—R. I. S. Phillips

## DEPARTMENT OF THE CLERK OF THE HOUSE

CLERK OF THE HOUSE OF COMMONS—C. J. Boulton, CB

CLERK ASSISTANT—J. F. Sweetman, TD

CLERK OF COMMITTEES—M. T. Ryle

PRINCIPAL CLERKS—
   H. M. Barclay (Public Bills)
   D. W. Limon (Table Office)
   W. R. McKay (Journal Office)
   C. B. Winnifrith (Select Committees)
   R. B. Sands (Overseas Office)
   G. Cubie (Financial Committees)
   A. J. Hastings (Select Committees)
   J. R. Rose (Standing Committees)
   R. J. Willoughby (Private Bills)

DEPUTY PRINCIPAL CLERKS—S. A. L. Panton, M. R. Jack, PhD, D. G. Millar, Mrs. J. Sharpe, Ms. A. Milner-Barry, R. W. G. Wilson, W. A. Proctor, F. A. Cranmer, R. J. Rogers, C. R. M. Ward, PhD, Ms. H. E. Irwin, D. W. N. Doig, A. Sandall, MLitt, D. L. Natzler, E. P. Silk, D. F. Harrison

SENIOR CLERKS—Mrs. S. A. de Ste. Croix, A. R. Kennon, D. W. Robson, L. C. Laurence Smyth, A. R. Gren, S. J. Patrick, D. J. Gerhold, C. J. Poyser, S. J. Priestley, A. H. Doherty, P. A. Evans, R. I. S. Phillips, R. G. James, Miss E. J. Baker, Ms. P. A. Helme, D. R. Lloyd, R. A. Lambert, J. B. Ingram (acting), I. G. Gilbert (acting), J. Darling (acting), J. M. Hope (acting)

CLERK OF SERVICES SUB-COMMITTEES—K. J. Brown

ASSISTANT CLERKS—B. M. Hutton, J. S. Benger, Ms. E. C. Samson, N. P. Walker, M. D. Hamlyn, P. C. Seaward, DPhil, C. G. Lee, C. D. Stanton

SENIOR EXECUTIVE OFFICERS—G. E. Clayton, Miss R. J. Challis, P. G. Moon

HIGHER EXECUTIVE OFFICERS—L. L. Kaye, A. P. Hubner, Miss S. J. Fox, Mrs. P. Fisher, F. McShane, J. D. Whatley, S. D. Barrett, M. Clark, Miss A. M. Loader, Mrs. S. M. Barrett, Miss F. L. Allingham, Mrs. L. M. Nugent, J. A. L. Dresner

SPECIALIST ASSISTANTS—M. P. Hillyard, M. J. Cremin, Ms. A. S. Frost, Dr. L. M. Rosborough, Dr. S. A. Harvey Miss K. Rogers, E. Thompson

EDITORIAL SUPERVISOR OF THE VOTE—G. H. Bright, MBE, DEPUTY—B. Tidball, ASSISTANTS—Miss B. Balcomb, Miss L. Lewis, J. Puricelli, K. B. Wood, P. D. Howlett, Mrs. L. R. Shade

EXAMINERS OF PETITIONS FOR PRIVATE BILLS—R. J. Willoughby, M. G. Pownall

REGISTRAR OF MEMBERS' INTERESTS—A. J. Hastings

TAXING OFFICER—R. J. Willoughby

SUPERINTENDING CLERK—R. A. Broomfield

CHIEF OFFICE CLERKS—M. P. Oxborough, N. P. Wright, Mrs. B. Ward, Miss D. E. Symes, Ms. C. J. D. Quantrell

## DEPARTMENT OF THE SERJEANT AT ARMS

SERJEANT AT ARMS—Sir Victor Le Fanu, KCVO

DEPUTY SERJEANT AT ARMS—P. N. W. Jennings

ASSISTANT SERJEANT AT ARMS—M. J. A. Cummins

DEPUTY ASSISTANT SERJEANTS AT ARMS—P. A. J. Wright, J. F. Collins

CLERK IN CHARGE—Miss S. J. Scott Thomson

ASSISTANT CLERK IN CHARGE—Miss P. Penson

ADMISSION ORDER OFFICE—A. Chipperfield, BEM, Mrs. S. J. Warren, A. J. Spencer

PRINCIPAL DOORKEEPER—G. H. Sargeant

SECOND PRINCIPAL DOORKEEPER—R. T. Warboys

SENIOR DOORKEEPERS—S. E. R. Skinner, R. A. F. Chapman, J. D. Garnett, R. H. Usher, C. Gray, J. C. W. Cooper

HEAD OFFICE KEEPER—W. H. Hazard, MBE

SENIOR OFFICE KEEPERS—M. Bryant, K. R. Kemp, K. R. Dickason

NURSING SISTER—Miss E. Needham

## DEPARTMENT OF THE LIBRARY

LIBRARIAN—D. Menhennet, DPhil

DEPUTY LIBRARIAN—D. J. T. Englefield

LIBRARY AND RESEARCH—

ASSISTANT LIBRARIANS (Heads of Division)—G. F. Lock, Miss J. B. Tanfield

DEPUTY ASSISTANT LIBRARIANS (Heads of Section)—S. Z. Young, Mrs. H. R. Coates, Miss P. J. Baines, BLitt, K. G. Cuninghame, Mrs. J. M. Wainwright, FI InfSc, C. C. Pond, PhD, Mrs. C. B. Andrews, R. C. Clements, Mrs. J. M. Lourie

LIBRARY CLERKS, SENIOR—Ms. F. Poole, Mrs. J. M. Fiddick, C. R. Barclay, Mrs. C. M. Gillie, R. J. Ware, DPhil, Ms. D. Gore, PhD, R. J. Twigger, B. K. Winetrobe, T. N. Edmonds, R. J. Cracknell, Miss O. M. Gay, Miss E. M. McInnes, Mrs. G. L. Allen. ASSISTANT—Miss M. Baber, Ms. A. J. Cook, PhD, E. J. Fishwick, MPhil, Mrs. K. Greener, Miss P. Strickland, A. J. L. Crompton, Miss V. A. Miller, Ms. M. J. Quiney, Ms. S. C. Penfold, Ms. N. R. Donlon, Ms. H. M. Jeffs, J. R. Lunn, PhD, Mrs. P. Carling (temporary)

SENIOR LIBRARY EXECUTIVES—Mrs. S. M. Withers, ALA, Mrs. H. V. Holden, ALA, K. N. H. Parry, ALA, Ms. A. Muir, Miss C. E. Fretten, ALA, Miss I. O. White, ALA (acting)

EDUCATION OFFICER—Mrs. E. R. Stones. ASSISTANT—Mrs. C. C. O'Connor

PROJECT MANAGER, NEW BUILDING—Miss J. Seaton FLA

HIGHER EXECUTIVE OFFICERS—Mrs. P A. Bozdan, S. A. Wise

HIGHER LIBRARY EXECUTIVES—J. A. Prince, MLS, Mrs. P. V. Wiles, Mrs. D. W. Clark, Miss M. H. Fletcher, Mrs. P. E. Cook, ALA, Ms. H. Armstrong, Miss E. J. Jones, ALA, G. Haig, Miss B. Mee, MIInfSc, Miss G. L. Cooper, Mrs. E. H. Riley, ALA, Mrs. F. M. Ward, R. Freebury (acting), Mrs. M. A. Azim, ALA, (acting)

SUPERINTENDING CLERK—J. R. Hutson.

EDITOR, WEEKLY BULLETIN—Miss B. A. Rowlands, ALA

LIBRARY EXECUTIVES—Miss S. Holland, A. D. Parker, ALA, Ms. J. B. Hall, ALA, T. C. Holmes, P. E. M. Ward, Ms. F. Whittle, Mrs. J. M. Smith, ALA, Miss J. Lyall, Miss C. E. Jarrett, Ms. Z. A. Smallwood, C. M. Sear (acting)

CHIEF OFFICE CLERKS—D. J. Plowright, Miss N. Harland

EXECUTIVE OFFICERS—P. R. Davis, J. S. Came, D. B. Inns, Mrs. A. J. H. Mara, D. A. Brown, J. P. Brevitt, M. Greenhill (Head Library Attendant)

VOTE OFFICE—

DELIVERER OF THE VOTE—G. R. Russell

DEPUTY DELIVERER OF THE VOTE—H. C. Foster

ASSISTANT DELIVERER OF THE VOTE—O. B. T. Sweeney

HIGHER EXECUTIVE OFFICER—C. D. Lister

SUPERINTENDING CLERKS—Mrs. S. Fuzio, B. G. Underwood, A. J. Ashton (Sales Office)

VOTE OFFICE ASSISTANTS—T. S. Wilson, G. E. Howard, C. P. Williams, P. Hannett

## ADMINISTRATION DEPARTMENT

HEAD OF DEPARTMENT—G. A. Roberts

FEES OFFICE—

ACCOUNTANT—J. L. G. Dobson

DEPUTY ACCOUNTANT—A. J. Lewis

SENIOR ASSISTANT ACCOUNTANT—G. P. Brown

ASSISTANT ACCOUNTANTS—A. R. Marskell, M. J. Barram, Miss M. M. McColl, M. Fletcher

SENIOR EXECUTIVE OFFICER—K. E. Walton

HIGHER EXECUTIVE OFFICERS—R. Gunn, M. J. H. Caswell, Mrs. P. D. Page, Mrs. N. Norman, Mrs. G. Crowther, Mrs. P. M. Lowther, Mrs. D. Hill, Miss P. Hurford, Mrs. J. S. Peach

EXECUTIVE OFFICERS—Miss D. E. Johnson, D. M. Allen, Miss L. J. F. Clay, Mrs. D. K. Euesden, D. J. D. Woods, Ms. M. R. Morris, Miss R. Harrison, G. L. Turner, Miss P. R. Mills, Mrs. J. D. Mead, Miss G. Bauman, P. F. Dawson, Miss S. E. Flavell, Miss S. A. Weaver, P. H. Olden, A. D. Rowlands, P. J. S. French

ESTABLISHMENTS OFFICE—

HEAD OF OFFICE—B. A. Wilson

DEPUTY HEAD OF OFFICE—J. A. Robb

SENIOR EXECUTIVE OFFICERS—Mrs. R. A. White, V. H. Stocker

HIGHER EXECUTIVE OFFICER—N.P. Crawley

EXECUTIVE OFFICERS—P. C. Kingsley, R. S. Harrison, Miss J. Bremner, M. Page

COMPUTER OFFICE—

COMPUTER OFFICER—R. S. Morgan, FBCS, FIInfSc

ASSISTANT COMPUTER OFFICERS—Mrs. G. S. P. Smith, Mrs. S. C. White

INTERNAL AUDITOR—A. A. Cameron

STAFF INSPECTOR—R. C. Collins

WELFARE OFFICER—Mrs. A. Mossop

## DEPARTMENT OF THE OFFICIAL REPORT

EDITOR—K. S. Morgan

DEPUTY EDITOR—I. D. Church

PRINCIPAL ASSISTANT EDITORS—R. V. Hadlow, J. Gourley, J. Withers, P. Walker

ASSISTANT EDITORS—W. G. Garland, Vee Grainger, J. Ledgerwood, Miss V. A. A. Clarke, Miss H. A. Hales

COMMITTEE SUB-EDITORS—D. Crosswell, Mrs. A. Roberts, Miss L. Sutherland, S. M. Hutchinson, Miss V. A. Widgery, C. Fogarty, Mrs. H. J. G. Natzler, Miss M. Babington, Mrs. A. Street, L. Gilmore, Ms. G. Hardgrave, P. Oglethorpe, P. Hadlow, Miss C. Hanly, M. Watson

REPORTERS—Mrs. E. J. Gregory, Miss J. A. Bradshaw, Miss K. Stewart, Miss E. Morris, Mrs. J. Martin, J. Ransley, Miss J. Goodman, Ms. J. Dall, Mrs. P. Pickford

PRINCIPAL TRANSCRIBER—D. N. Harrington, MBE

DEPUTY PRINCIPAL TRANSCRIBERS—Mrs. M. J. Harding, Miss J. L. Brown

PRINCIPAL HANSARD ASSISTANT—Miss R. Washington

SENIOR HANSARD ASSISTANT—J. Brake

ANNUNCIATOR SUPERINTENDENT—G. Carpenter

## REFRESHMENT DEPARTMENT

GENERAL MANAGER—W. J. J. Smillie, FHCIMA, FCFA, ACF

DEPUTY GENERAL MANAGER—E. J. Nash, MCFA

PERSONNEL ADMINISTRATOR—Mrs. S. M. Nicholls, FHCIMA, MIPM

PERSONAL ASSISTANT TO GENERAL MANAGER—Mrs. A. G. Lunn

BANQUETING MANAGER—C. J. Griffiths

CATERING ACCOUNTANT—D. R. W. Wood, FCA

ASSISTANT CATERING ACCOUNTANT—Mrs. B. A. Langley

EXECUTIVE CHEF—I. Gabay

HEAD CELLARMAN—D. Balcombe

HEAD STOREMAN—A. E. Edmond

---

SHORTHAND WRITER TO THE HOUSE—Mrs. E. M. C. Holland

PARLIAMENTARY WORKS OFFICER (PSA)—B. C. Sewell

HEAD OF SECURITY—Chief Superintendent A. J. Coxon

COMMUNICATIONS MANAGER—Mrs. J. Garbutt

POSTMASTER—J. Arnold

TRANSPORT MANAGER—R. H. Hyde

*19 June 1989*

# THE
# PARLIAMENTARY DEBATES

## OFFICIAL REPORT

IN THE SECOND SESSION OF THE FIFTIETH PARLIAMENT OF THE
UNITED KINGDOM OF GREAT BRITAIN AND NORTHERN IRELAND
[WHICH OPENED 25 JUNE 1987]

### THIRTY-EIGHTH YEAR OF THE REIGN OF
### HER MAJESTY QUEEN ELIZABETH II

---

**SIXTH SERIES**                                   **VOLUME 155**

**FOURTEENTH VOLUME OF SESSION 1988-89**

---

## House of Commons

*Monday 19 June 1989*

*The House met at half-past Two o'clock*

### PRAYERS

[MR. SPEAKER *in the Chair*]

### PRIVATE BUSINESS

KINGSTON UPON HULL CITY COUNCIL BILL *[Lords]*
*Read the Third time and passed, with amendments.*

## Oral Answers to Questions

### WALES

#### Orthopaedic Consultants

1. **Mr. John P. Smith:** To ask the Secretary of State for Wales what is the current waiting time for referrals to orthopaedic consultants in South Glamorgan and Wales as a whole.

**The Parliamentary Under-Secretary of State for Wales (Mr. Ian Grist):** I congratulate the hon. Member for Vale of Glamorgan (Mr. Smith) on drawing pole position for his first Welsh question. However, no figures are available centrally—for South Glamorgan as a whole or for Wales—of the time that patients have to wait for referral to an orthopaedic out-patient clinic. Individual experience varies considerably, with urgent cases being given the priority for treatment that their condition merits.

**Mr. Smith:** I recognise that the Minister and many of his colleagues in Wales will not be with us much longer, and I extend my deep sympathy to them, but what does the Minister intend to do about my constituent Mrs. Julie Froude, aged 35, who has three young children and suffer from a crippling orthopaedic condition? She has been told that she will have to wait 18 months merely to see a specialist, and wait an indefinite time before she receives medical treatment. That is wholly unacceptable and I ask the Minister to intervene.

**Mr. Grist:** If the hon. Gentleman will send me details, I will most certainly intervene. He might like to bear in mind the experience of Fulham and that of a predecessor of his who also graced the Opposition Benches for a very brief time.

**Mr. Denzil Davies:** On the question of orthopaedic consultants, will the Minister ensure that the two new consultants who are to be appointed by the east Dyfed health authority are based in the new Llanelli hospital and not at the west Wales general hospital in Carmarthen? Is he aware that if they are based in Carmarthen, the new operating facilities at Llanelli will be under-used and the waiting list will not be reduced?

**Mr. Grist:** I certainly take very careful note of what the right hon. Gentleman says. When the Llanelli hospital is finished, which I hope will be later this year, I will consider precisely what the situation should be.

**Mr. Ray Powell:** Will the Minister reply to the question? We have had the first question from my new hon. Friend the Member for the Vale of Glamorgan (Mr. Smith). It was on an important matter. Will the Minister talk to the Secretary of State for Wales, who is actually to blame for the result in the Vale of Glamorgan, and his right hon. Friend the Member for Old Bexley and Sidcup (Mr. Heath) who will get the blame for yesterday's disastrous result? The Secretary of State could then raise the matter at this week's Cabinet meeting, get the blame put on the right person's shoulders and ask her to resign because of what is happening to the country and to the Health Service and——

**Mr. Speaker:** Order. The whole House wishes the hon. Gentleman a happy birthday, but his question must relate to orthopaedic consultants.

**Mr. Barry Jones:** Reverting to the question of my hon. Friend the hon. Member for Ogmore (Mr. Powell), does the Minister understand that there is great concern and pain throughout Wales due to the length of waiting lists for hospital treatment? Why does he not admit that our people in Wales want the National Health Service White Paper to be withdrawn and that there is massive electoral evidence for that? I remind him that even the north Wales citadel of his party has fallen. He should take note of that.

**Mr. Grist:** The hon. Gentleman has overlooked the fact that the proposals in our White Paper would actually cut waiting times. Of course, everybody accepts that it is a severe problem, but I seem to remember that when the hon. Gentleman was a Minister matters were often rather worse.

### Advisory Body for Higher Education

2. **Dr. Thomas:** To ask the Secretary of State for Wales, when he last met the Wales Advisory Body for Higher Education and if he will make a statement.

**The Minister of State, Welsh Office (Mr. Wyn Roberts):** The Wales Advisory Body was reconstituted as a single-tier body in March. I chaired the first meeting of the reconstituted body on 7 April.

**Dr. Thomas:** I am grateful to the Minister for explaining to the House how the reconstituted body is operating. Will he tell us something about the relationship between the Wales Advisory Body and the sub-committee of the new Universities Funding Council? Surely it is time for us to plan our education in Wales as one.

**Mr. Roberts:** First, I am sure that many of us would like to welcome the hon. Gentleman back among us after his arduous campaign. Secondly, in answer to his supplementary question, I assure him that there will be a representative of the Wales Advisory Body on the Universities Funding Council subcommittee relating to Wales. I agree with him—and have always thought—that there should be a close link between local authority higher education and universities.

**Mr. Gwilym Jones:** In his next meeting with the advisory body, will my hon. Friend suggest that an appropriate subject for study at the higher education level could be why the Welsh nationalist and Liberal parties were beaten yesterday by the newly emerged version of Militant tendency—the Green party—and why the Conservative vote held up much better in Wales than in almost any other part of Great Britain?

**Mr. Roberts:** Aristotle said that politics was not a proper subject for study for a young man, but I am sure that, as my hon. Friend suggested, it would be interesting for any study to begin with the fact that the Conservative vote in Wales exceeded the combined votes of Plaid Cymru and the Alliance by 40 per cent.

### A55, Gwynedd

4. **Mr. Wigley:** To ask the Secretary of State for Wales what progress has been made with discussions with local authorities and others on the impact of the A55 on Gwynedd; and if he will make a statement.

**Mr. Wyn Roberts:** Tomorrow, my right hon. Friend and I will meet representatives of Gwynedd and the districts within that county. I have already had discussions with Clwyd and the majority of its local authorities. I have been very favourably impressed by the way in which some authorities have planned to secure the enormous potential economic benefits that the new A55 will bring.

**Mr. Wigley:** Some of us are a little surprised that there has been no reference to the fact that one person will no longer be travelling along the A55 to Manchester airport to fly out to Europe, but apparently there are no tears among Conservative Members for the lamented lady.

If the A55 is meant to be the artery which brings economic development to north Wales and especially to Gwynedd, why has there been so much delay in extending it to Holyhead in one direction and Dwyfor in the other, both of which are areas of high unemployment? Will the Minister now seek additional funds to speed up improvements to those connecting roads to ensure that any economic benefit reaches the areas that most need it?

**Mr. Roberts:** From having studied "Roads in Wales 1989" the hon. Gentleman will know that we have co-operated with the counties, and they with us, and that we have devised a strategic road network for Wales, which includes Welsh Office and county roads. We have received a report from consultants about improvements along the A5 in Anglesey and that report is currently under consideration.

**Sir Anthony Meyer:** My hon. Friend will be concerned that some of his constituents and of mine who are anxious to ride their bicycles westwards along the A55 are not allowed under the present arrangements to ride through the Penmaenbach tunnel but have to dismount and carry their bicycles across a dual carriageway. Does my hon. Friend agree that that is an unsafe arrangement and will he carefully reconsider what is involved in the proposal?

**Mr. Roberts:** I can assure my hon. Friend that I am constantly considering that problem which has been brought to our attention recently, but the proper place to air the matter was at the public consultation stage on the tunnel. There are all sorts of difficulties in enabling cyclists either to use the tunnel or to use their bicycles on the path provided for them.

### Severn Barrage

5. **Mr. Stern:** To ask the Secretary of State for Wales which industries in south Wales are the principal users of ports upstream of the proposed Severn barrage.

**Mr. Wyn Roberts:** These ports mainly handle steel, scrap metal, aggregates, agricultural products—including imported fruit and timber—machinery petrochemicals and imported cars.

**Mr. Stern:** I am grateful to my hon. Friend for that reply. Does he agree that the prospects of those industries can only be improved now that the threat of unofficial industrial action in those ports is, I hope, coming to an end? Does he further agree that, now that those ports can look forward to greater prosperity, the threat of a Severn barrage putting an additional barrier between them and their trade becomes even more serious?

**Mr. Roberts:** I agree with the first part of my hon. Friend's question. On the effect on shipping of the Severn barrage, whenever it may come, my right hon. Friend the Secretary of State for Energy has not yet received the final report from the Severn tidal power group, so it would be premature for me to comment at this stage on that aspect.

## Association of District Councils

6. **Mr. Murphy:** To ask the Secretary of State for Wales when he last met the Association of District Councils in Wales; and what matters were discussed.

**The Secretary of State for Wales (Mr. Peter Walker):** I met representatives of the Welsh counties committee and the committee of Welsh district councils at a meeting of the Welsh consultative council on local government finance on 15 June to discuss local government finance matters.

**Mr. Murphy:** The Secretary of State is, of course, aware that the Association of District Councils is in favour of a dog registration scheme. Why, then, does he fly in the face of Welsh public opinion by not agreeing to such a scheme in Wales? Will he give a commitment to the House that he will provide sufficient finance to local authorities in Wales so that there can be proper dog warden schemes in every district in the principality?

**Mr. Walker:** When I met the members of the Welsh counties committee and the committee of Welsh district councils, they did not at any time raise the subject of a dog registration scheme. Perhaps they share my view that although it sounds very nice in theory, in practice it would not work.

**Sir Anthony Meyer:** When my right hon. Friend met the members of the committee of Welsh district councils, did they express to him their delight at the amount of investment in Wales that my right hon. Friend has been able to secure, largely as a result of Britain's membership of the European Community? Did they, like me, share not only the astonishment and delight that the Labour party has at last come round to accepting the idea of Europe, but the incredulity that the conversion campaign should be led by none other than the hon. Member for Dagenham (Mr. Gould)?

**Mr. Walker:** Again, the two committees did not raise those matters as a major topic of our discussion, but I am sure that they are delighted at the very considerable record of inward investment that Wales has enjoyed over the past few years—towards which, if I may say so, they made an important contribution.

**Mrs. Clwyd:** Given the massive public concern about the environment and the decisive rejection of the Government's policies, shown by yesterday's election results, has the right hon. Gentleman discussed with the Association of District Councils the problems posed by the worst industrial polluter in Britain—the Furnacite plant in my constituency? Is he aware that continuing uncertainty about the future of that plant means that people in the Cynon valley are being subjected to unacceptable levels of pollution? Is the right hon. Gentleman also aware that unemployment is still rising there?

**Mr. Walker:** The hon. Lady knows better than anyone else in the House that, since I have been Secretary of State, I have had some rather conflicting advice from political

leadership in the valley as to exactly what it would like to be done about that plant. As the hon. Lady knows, the local authority is currently concerned with certain planning powers on which it has to make judgments.

**Mr. Livsey:** How many proposals has the Secretary of State received from the district councils in the past 12 months about low-cost starter homes and low-cost housing to rent? Are not the district councils pressing him hard on this?

**Mr. Walker:** Obviously, it is a subject that has come up with local authorities and individuals, but I cannot give the number of actual representations. At present, discussions are going on both with the Housing Corporation in Wales and with district councils to see what sensible and practical plans can be developed.

## A55 (Link Roads)

7. **Mr. Raffan:** To ask the Secretary of State for Wales whether he has yet had discussions with Clwyd county council concerning the need to provide link roads to the A55.

**Mr. Wyn Roberts:** I attended a presentation given by the county council on its highway strategy on 14 April. The question of link roads to the A55 was covered.

**Mr. Raffan:** Is my hon. Friend aware of the serious concern in Clwyd among members of all political parties that the county council has got its road priorities wrong and their belief that link roads between the A55 and the A548 should be constructed before a third Dee crossing is even contemplated? If the county council refuses to change its priorities, will my hon. Friend do what the former Secretary of State said that he would do and designate such link roads as trunk roads, so that the Welsh Office can build them?

**Mr. Roberts:** My hon. Friend is right to say that there is some disagreement about priorities on the development of county roads in Clwyd, but it is up to all those concerned to get together with the county council. I visited my hon. Friend's borough council of Delyn last Friday and urged it to have discussions with the county council. We are talking about county roads which, as far as I know, will remain county roads. This is a local matter on which agreement should be reached, just as it has been reached, I believe, on the link from the A55 through the Rhuddlan bypass.

## Welsh Farming Unions

8. **Mr. Martyn Jones:** To ask the Secretary of State for Wales when he last met the Welsh farming unions; and what matters were discussed.

22. **Mr. Ron Davies:** To ask the Secretary of State for Wales when he last met representatives of the Farmers Union of Wales; and what matters were discussed.

**Mr. Peter Walker:** I last met representatives of the Farmers Union of Wales on 20 October 1988 to discuss the hill livestock compensatory review.

**Mr. Jones:** Given the superb result for Labour in north Wales and the massive rejection in Europe of Tory policies, will the right hon. Gentleman make sure that his colleagues in the Council of Ministers ensures that the views of farmers in north Wales are properly represented, as they are not represented among farmers as a whole in Britain?

**Mr. Walker:** Nothing delights the farmers of north Wales more than the sheepmeat premium regime, which I introduced and which they now want to save. When I introduced it, I did not receive great acclaim from the Opposition, but I am glad to say that they are now all eager to defend it. I am delighted to say that the sheepmeat regime is working well, with £56 million of benefits to Welsh farmers last year. We have heard of the great pleasure of the farmers' unions at the considerable increase in the beef suckler cow premium.

**Mr. Ron Davies:** I draw the right hon. Gentleman's attention to the fact that his office did not manage to comply with the normal courtesies and inform me before Question Time that my question was linked with question No. 8.

Will he confirm that every county in Wales has had recorded outbreaks of bovine spongiform encephalopathy? Will he publicly acknowledge that Welsh consumers are eating beef products derived from infected cattle? That statement has been acknowledged by the farmers' unions, the Ministry of Agriculture, Fisheries and Food and the British Veterinary Association. To protect the health of the people of Wales and the economic livelihood of Welsh farmers as stockmen, does the right hon. Gentleman accept that the only effective way of keeping infected animals out of the food chain is by increasing compensation to realistic levels? Will he give an undertaking that he will do just that?

**Mr. Walker:** I do not think that Welsh farmers would be pleased at the way in which the hon. Gentleman has endeavoured, totally without justification, to scare the consuming public about Welsh beef. I regret his exaggerated remarks.

I apologise for the bad mistake that my Office made in failing to inform the hon. Gentleman that his question would be linked. That should have been done.

As for compensatory arrangements, they are constantly under review.

**Mr. Nicholas Bennett:** Is my right hon. Friend aware of the anxiety among potato farmers in Pembrokeshire about the possible abolition of the Potato Marketing Board? Will he confirm that the Welsh Office has made representations to the review being carried out by my right hon. Friend the Minister of Agriculture, Fisheries and Food?

**Mr. Walker:** I can confirm that we have played a full part in the review mechanisms.

**Mr. Geraint Howells:** In his discussions with the leaders of the farmers unions in Wales, did the right hon. Gentleman discuss the Government's proposals for financial cuts in research and development establishments in Wales? Will he give farmers in Wales an assurance that the future of the Trawsgoed and Pwllpeirian experimental farms and the Welsh plant breeding station at Gogerddan, Aberystwyth, will be safeguarded in years to come?

**Mr. Walker:** I assure the hon. Gentleman that the reviews are currently taking place. We have discussed the matter with the farmers' unions in Wales and stressed the importance of ensuring that the grass-growing areas of the United Kingdom, of which Wales is a prominent part, have the appropriate research facilities.

## Labour Statistics

9. **Mr. Roy Hughes:** To ask the Secretary of State for Wales what are the latest unadjusted figures for unemployment in *(a)* Newport, *(b)* Gwent and *(c)* Wales; and if he will give the equivalent figures for 1979 on the most nearly comparable basis.

**Mr. Peter Walker:** On 11 May 1989, the number of unemployed claimants in the Newport district, Gwent and Wales were 5,293, 16,156 and 97,818 respectively. Unadjusted figures for 1979 are not available on a basis which enables a valid comparison to be made. In the last 12 months, Wales has experienced a larger fall in the percentage rate of unemployment than any other region of the United Kingdom.

**Mr. Hughes:** Is this to be the Secretary of State's last hoorah? Does he appreciate that no amount of trumpeting on his part can hide the fact that unemployment in Wales is 8·3 per cent., bottoming out at double the figure that it was under Labour, the country faces a massive balance of payments problem, interest rates are 14 per cent. and the inflation rate is 8·3 per cent. and rising? Surely, far from being a success, the Government's record is a disaster of the first order. That has been recognised by the electorate in the past few days.

**Mr. Walker:** If this were my last appearance, my one regret would be that I should no longer be getting questions from the hon. Gentleman, who is always helpful. I am grateful to him for continuing to ask this question and I hope that he will go on doing so. He considered that unemployment was bottoming out at 150,000, 140,000, 130,000, 120,000, 110,000 and 100,000. I am glad to say that as it goes down to well below the average for the European Community, the hon. Gentleman remains consistent in putting questions which show that last year Wales had the best record in falling unemployment of any region in the United Kingdom.

**Mr. Rowlands:** Is the Secretary of State aware that within the past week there have been announcements in my own community of 150 possible redundancies at Thorne, 600 at the Merthyr Vale colliery and more than 100 at Hoover? According to the company, the job losses at Hoover were as a direct result of interest rates. In those circumstances, what does the Secretary of State say to his Cabinet colleagues about the impact of high interest rates on the mature manufacturing sectors in our communities?

**Mr. Walker:** There is another question on this matter, but if the hon. Gentleman wishes, I can list a set of good announcements which took place last month. In the hon. Gentleman's constituency, there is much investment and expansion——

**Mr. Rowlands:** We are losing more than the new jobs coming.

**Mr. Walker:** That is not true and the hon. Gentleman knows it. Merthyr has a very good record on unemployment, and continues and will continue to do so. The impression that the hon. Gentleman seeks to give that there is some great depression in Merthyr is not the case.

We are about to embark on the biggest derelict land clearance programme in Wales in Merthyr, and the sites are all sites that the local authority wishes to use for further industrial development.

**Mr. Raffan:** Will my right hon. Friend join me in welcoming the dramatic reduction in unemployment in Delyn in the past two years—a fall of 50·1 per cent. between May 1987 and May 1989? Does he agree that this remarkable achievement is due to the fact that the Government gave my constituency the highest development area status, which the Labour party never did, and gave it the Delyn enterprise zone, which the Labour party opposed?

**Mr. Walker:** Yes, I am delighted with the developments in Delyn. I recently visited it and saw what was taking place. I was also delighted the other day to hear the hon. Member for Alyn and Deeside (Mr. Jones) say how staggered he was at the speed of the transformation of the Deeside economy.

**Mr. Wigley:** In view of the possibility of the Toyota engine plant coming to Clwyd, will the Secretary of State take advantage of his opportunity tomorrow to tell Gwynedd county council what steps will be taken to ensure that any spin-off jobs associated with the development, which we greatly welcome, come to areas such as Gwynedd, so that the benefits arising from the scheme are spread as much as possible?

**Mr. Walker:** I never predict investments which may or may not come to an area, and no decisions have been made —[*Interruption.*]—I have never predicted the investments that might come to any part of Wales until the deal is completed and signed because it would be silly to do so. One of the main purposes of my discussions tomorrow will be to see how we can take advantage of all the considerable economic developments in the county.

**Mr. Barry Jones:** The right hon. Gentleman must not be complacent about unemployment in Wales. How will the privatisation of the four remaining skill centres reduce skills shortages in south and north Wales? Does he still believe that the economy has been mismanaged? Does he agree with the hon. Member for Clwyd, North-West (Sir A. Meyer) that the Government's Euro-campaign was disgraceful?

**Mr. Walker:** I am delighted to say that during the course of the next 18 months we shall be getting the new training and enterprise councils into place throughout Wales. They will involve considerable Government investment and will use all the training facilities that are available. So training in Wales in the coming years will, to a greater degree, meet the needs of a new and diversified economy; this will be greatly beneficial to the whole future economy of Wales.

## NHS Reform

10. **Mr. Rogers:** To ask the Secretary of State for Wales what representations he has had welcoming the Government's proposals for reform of the National Health Service.

**Mr. Grist:** My right hon. Friend and I have received a substantial number of representations welcoming the Government's objectives, as outlined in the White Paper

"Working for Patients", to build on the achievement of record levels of patient care which our record levels of investment in the NHS have made possible, so as to bring all areas of the NHS up to the standards of the best and provide even better health care for all.

**Mr. Rogers:** I find it extraordinary that the Secretary of State has received

"a substantial number of representations"

welcoming these proposals. That is almost as vague as his answer to the first question this afternoon, when he said that it was impossible to obtain ordinary statistics within the National Health Service. I wish the Minister would give us a precise figure rather than talking vaguely about "substantial". Opposition Members have received large postbags against these proposals. I want to know who sent these letters to the Minister.

**Mr. Grist:** The hon. Gentleman complains about the weight of letters that he may have received. Like other hon. Members, he has passed many of them on to us. We, too, are constituency Members, and we also receive letters directed to the Welsh Office from members of the public and the various professions involved. To count them all out and dissect them would involve a waste of money which would be better spent elsewhere. Had Opposition Members not wilfully gone around scaring people we should not have had to waste so much time answering so many letters.

**Mr. Gwilym Jones:** Given that the Government spend almost half as much again on the Health Service in Wales in GDP terms as compared with their average European counterparts, does my hon. Friend agree that it is essential that he pursue his discussions on the improvements to the Health Service, so that what we all want to happen will happen and average performances will be brought up to the level of the best?

**Mr. Grist:** I very much agree. Apart from the White Paper, there is also the GPs' contract, the aim of which is to ensure that we in Wales, who do not always receive the best of treatment by certain parts of the Health Service, receive the very best treatment. I should have thought that that was the desire of the constituents of every hon. Member.

**Mr. Win Griffiths:** Would the Minister care to name any doctors or consultants who approve of the Government's proposals? Will he admit that doctors and consultants across Wales are far more typically wholly opposed to them? A doctor wrote to me saying that he believes in three quarters of what the Government are doing and usually votes Conservative in general elections, but he believes that these proposals are, to quote him, "dishonest".

**Mr. Grist:** I think that that doctor will find, as will many other people—perhaps including Opposition Members, as they learn a little more during the passage of the legislation and see the results of the consultations that have taken place—that our proposals will form the basis of the Health Service well into the next century—a modern Health Service, which is not based on the 1940s.

**Mr. John Marshall:** Does my hon. Friend agree that these proposals will lead to greater efficiency and choice in the Health Service and should be warmly welcomed? Does he agree that it is high time that the vicious and misleading propaganda campaign by the BMA was brought to an end?

**Mr. Grist:** My hon. Friend is absolutely right. Our proposals are based on choice for those who work in the Health Service and for its patients. They should all be aware of the opportunities that are open to them as professionals and as patients. At the moment, too many people do not know what is going on and do not have freedom of choice. That is what Conservatives stand for, unlike the blinkered witness of the Opposition.

**Mr. Michael:** Does the Minister not accept that his proposals are based not on choice but on secrecy? Will he tell us what has happened to the papers similar to those for England which the Secretary of State for Wales personally promised during the debate on 1 March? I stress that the word used was "similar" and not "identical". Will he also tell us when we are to have the subsequent papers on specific Welsh proposals which he promised in column 303 during the same debate? When will the Minister start debating the Government's proposals?

**Mr. Grist:** My right hon. Friend the Secretary of State for Wales will shortly make a statement on the detailed programme for implementation in Wales.

**Mr. Nicholas Bennett:** Does my hon. Friend recall that all last year and the year before the Labour party complained that the Health Service was deteriorating and that it was just a matter of spending more money on it? However, when the Government bring forward positive proposals to make the Health Service more businesslike, the Opposition appear to have no policies whatever. If they do not agree with the Government is it not incumbent on them to say what they would do?

**Mr. Grist:** They are an empty vessel making a great deal of sound. That is the truth of the matter.

### Expenditure

11. **Mr. Alan W. Williams:** To ask the Secretary of State for Wales what is the outturn figure for total expenditure within the Secretary of State's responsibility for 1988-89; what was the outturn figure for 1987-88; and what is the growth in the budget (i) in money terms and (ii) in real terms after adjustment for the gross domestic product deflator for 1988-89.

**Mr. Peter Walker:** The outturn for 1987-88 was £3,338 million. The estimated outturn for 1988-89 is £3,658 million. This represents a cash increase of 9·6 per cent. and a real increase of 2·2 per cent.

**Mr. Williams:** I am grateful to the Minister for those figures. He says that there has been a 2·2 per cent. increase in real terms. That bears out what Lord Crickhowell said on the eve of the Vale of Glamorgan by-election, which was that there has been no new policy, no new initiative and little change in the scale of public spending during the right hon. Gentleman's tenure of office. The people of Wales have rumbled that and the Secretary of State has lost both the Conservative seats that he has had to defend during his tenure of office.

**Mr. Walker:** As always, I am grateful to the hon. Gentleman because whether it is a case of statistics or

Conservative posters he is always a great help to my party. An increase in real terms of 2·2 per cent. is in very sharp contrast to a decrease of 3 per cent. per year that took place in the last two years of the last Labour Government.

**Mr. Alan Williams:** Is it not correct to say that that 2·2 per cent. is virtually entirely accounted for by the increase in nurses' pay which applied over the whole country? Is it not a fact that over the rest of the budget for Wales there has at best been standstill and in some cases cuts?

**Mr. Walker:** I am grateful that the right hon. Gentleman of all people should mention nurses' pay. One of the reasons for the 3 per cent. reduction in each of the last two years of the Labour Government was the appalling treatment of nurses' pay by that Government. I hope that the right hon. Gentleman is ashamed of that. I am glad to say that, for example, the budget of the Welsh Development Agency, which has an important economic impact on Wales, has increased by 53 per cent. in the last two years.

### Operations (Waiting Lists)

12. **Mr. Rowlands:** To ask the Secretary of State for Wales whether he will make a statement on the waiting lists for *(a)* hip and *(b)* ear, nose and throat operations in Welsh hospitals.

**Mr. Grist:** I am pleased to note the reduction in the number of people waiting for urgent treatment in the orthopaedic and ear, nose and throat specialties across Wales as a whole, but, naturally, it is disappointing that the number of people waiting for non-urgent treatment has increased slightly. Health authorities have the primary responsibility to reduce waiting times for patients. The Welsh Office is seeking to ensure that district health authorities address the issue through the record level of resources made available to them, by insisting on energetic management action and by specific central funding of particular local initiatives.

**Mr. Rowlands:** Is the Minister not aware that in my community people have to wait for months even to be referred to hospital, let alone receive treatment in them? They have tried the Government's suggestion of looking at neighbouring hospitals only to find that waiting lists there for hip and ENT treatment are equally long. Is not the idea behind all this to drive many of our people into the private health service? As we saw in a dramatic case described in one of the national newspapers, a young child was charged about £800 for treatment for a nose bleed. Is that the sort of Health Service that the Minister wants?

**Mr. Grist:** The hon. Gentleman has overlooked proposals such as treatment centres—He may be aware that one of the health authorities in Wales is likely shortly to bring proposals for one of these to the Welsh Office —the increase in the number of consultants, and the fact that there are shorter waiting times for different areas in Wales. At the moment, many doctors and patients know nothing about such places, and they might be prepared to use them if they knew about them. All these and other aspects of our health proposals will shorten waiting lists and spread choice for patients. The hon. Gentleman should also be aware that there is a problem of referral by doctors even within one health authority, in which one consultant may have a waiting list of a year and another may have one of only three months. Patients should be aware of such knowledge and we want to spread it.

## Cardiff (Manufacturing Industry)

13. **Mr. Morgan:** To ask the Secretary of State for Wales what progress he is able to report on the attraction of new manufacturing industry to the Cardiff employment exchange area.

**Mr. Peter Walker:** Seven manufacturing projects have been secured for the Cardiff travel-to-work area over the past year, compared to three in the previous 12 months. Cardiff will also benefit substantially from the major projects taking place in neighbouring areas by firms such as Ford and Bosch.

**Mr. Morgan:** Is it not a desirable objective that the economy in the Cardiff area should be developed in a balanced way, without an undue preponderance of service industries? Therefore is it not vital that a wide range of training opportunities for young people is provided? One can do that only if there is a healthy spread of manufacturing industry, and it may be necessary to review the development area status of the Cardiff area, to ensure that it can compete fairly to get new manufacturing industry. Since the closure of East Moors in 1978, we have not had one solid, large metal-cutting engineering employer in the area.

**Mr. Walker:** Seven new manufacturing firms coming in over the past year is not a bad record. Having major investments of the magnitude of Ford and Bosch very near is of considerable advantage to Cardiff. I agree that we need a balance, but I know that the hon. Gentleman strongly welcomes the enormous expansion of the financial service industries in Cardiff. Training is required for that as well as for manufacturing industry, so we must see both. I am also pleased to say that the Cardiff bay development programmes are considerable programmes for manufacturing and industry as well as for service industry.

## CHURCH COMMISSIONERS

### Senior Clergy (Programme)

26. **Mr. John Marshall:** To ask the right hon. Member for Selby, as representing the Church Commissioners, whether the Church Commissioners have considered helping to fund and initiate a programme for senior clergy similar to the Industry and Parliamentary Trust.

**Mr. Michael Alison (Second Church Estates Commissioner, representing the Church Commissioners):** The commissioners' funds are not available for in-service training of the clergy. I am, however, passing my hon. Friend's suggestions to the General Synod's board for social responsibility, which is sponsoring a debate in the next month about the Church's ministry in industry, and commerce and to the advisory council for the Church's ministry. My hon. Friend will know that industrial chaplains are the main link between industry and the Church, and already, 57 full-time industrial chaplains are on the commission's payroll.

**Mr. Marshall:** Would it not be useful if the leaders of the Church had a greater understanding of the ethos of the decision-making process by major British companies?

**Mr. Alison:** I agree with my hon. Friend that such inside knowledge would be desirable for the Church that has to have its feet firmly planted in the world. Many of the Church of England's committees connected with the assets of the Church include senior clergy on them. For example, the management of the Church of England's property placed it in the top 10 per cent. of the league table of 43 funds, worth £10 billion or more. In property, it has performed extremely well. As to the stock exchange, in the league table consisting of 1,450 pension funds, the Church of England management of its assets placed it ninth in a percentile scale of 100. That again shows that the Church of England's feet, although other-worldly in many respects, are firmly planted in commercial reality.

### Incumbents (Emoluments)

27. **Mr. Harry Greenway:** To ask the right hon. Member for Selby, as representing the Church Commissioners, what he estimates to be the value of the emoluments of the average incumbent; how these are calculated; and if he will make a statement.

**Mr. Alison:** The present average stipend of an incumbent is estimated to be £9,500 per annum. In addition, an incumbent enjoys free accommodation and a non-contributory pension and death benefit scheme which together are worth on average £5,750 per annum on the most recent estimate.

**Mr. Greenway:** Does my right hon. Friend agree that those figures show that a good clergyman is seriously underpaid? Will he estimate the value to clergymen of the free emolument that has been brought to Britain by the great preaching of Dr. Billy Graham?

**Mr. Alison:** It is difficult to estimate the figure that should be placed upon Dr. Graham's preaching. I am sure, however, that his mission will produce many additions to the occupants of the pews in the Church of England. Unfortunately, the average donation made by those who worship in the Church of England is only £2·19 a week. There is considerable scope for an increase in voluntary giving.

**Mr. Frank Field:** Would not one way of increasing the amount that the laity gives be for the right hon. Gentleman to ask at the next meeting of the board of governors that it sets a timetable for a 50 per cent. increase in clergy pay, and to ascertain how much the laity would have to increase its giving each week to meet that bill? Would not that be an appropriate target to meet over the next five years?

**Mr. Alison:** That is a good and constructive idea. I hope that the hon. Gentleman will bear in mind the extent to which we have succeeded in overtaking inflation in many respects in increasing clergy stipends. On average, and taking emoluments in kind into account, the incumbent receives £15,000 a year, plus help towards, in effect, a free car.

## Office Accommodation

28. **Mr. Thurnham:** To ask the right hon. Member for Selby, as representing the Church Commissioners, if he will list all the office accommodation used by the Church Commissioners in central London.

**Mr. Alison:** The commissioners have one main administrative office at No. 1 Millbank. Apart from this, they have only a small amount of office space integral to the administration of their London residential estates and archive depository.

**Mr. Thurnham:** Given the high valuation of over £25 million that has been placed on No. 1, Millbank, will my right hon. Friend urge the commissioners to see whether they can find cheaper accommodation elsewhere? It occurred to me that there might be a little room at Lambeth palace.

**Mr. Alison:** There is plenty going on already at Lambeth palace without the additional distraction of the lay members of the Church Commissioners. My hon. Friend has raised a serious and constructive issue. We want always to seek the most efficient use of Church resources. If there were evacuation from No. 1, Millbank, the costs of removal and the taking of comparable and reasonably centralised accommodation in London would be likely to be very high.

## HOUSE OF COMMONS COMMISSION

### Sleeping Accommodation

29. **Mr. Barry Field:** To ask the hon. Member for Berwick upon Tweed, as representing the House of Commons Commission, how many beds are available for members of staff in and around the House, how they are allocated; what is the average occupancy rate against the number of sitting days; and what is the total cost of *(a)* attendance, *(b)* laundry and *(c)* cleaning of staff bedrooms.

**Mr. A. J. Beith (On behalf of the House of Commons Commission):** Excluding official residences such as your own Mr. Speaker, there are 94 beds provided for staff of the House whose duties require their attendance for late sittings. These beds are also available for use in emergencies. Of this total, 42 beds are personally allocated and the remainder are available on a first-come-first-served basis. Precise details of occupancy rates and associated costs can be provided only at disproportionate expense.

**Mr. Field:** One is tempted to ask precisely what an emergency would be. Given the considerable amount that is paid out to hon. Members for their accommodation allowance in London, which is over £9,000 a Member, will the hon. Gentleman consider handing over this valuable accommodation either to one of the many seaside landladies in my constituency, who could produce a reasonable profit from it, or to a hotel company that is experienced in managing property of this nature, so that the taxpayer can have full value for money?

**Mr. Beith:** If the hon. Gentleman waits until Wednesday he may get an idea of what constitutes an emergency need for overnight accommodation. The

accommodation is not used by hon. Members, with one or two exceptions such as your Deputies, Mr. Speaker. It is used by members of the staff, some of whom live beyond the mileage limit of late-night transport. The hon. Gentleman raises reasonable questions about how account can be taken of the best way of providing the service and I shall ensure that the Commission is made aware of his comments.

### Crown Immunity

30. **Mr. Allen:** To ask the hon. Member for Berwick upon Tweed, as representing the House of Commons Commission, what assessment he has made of the effect of the application of Crown immunity in the Palace of Westminster on the adequacy of health and safety provision for staff working in the House of Commons; and if he will make a statement.

**Mr. Beith:** Although, as I understand it, neither the enforcement provisions nor those relating to the prosecution of offences in the Health and Safety at Work, etc. Act 1974, apply to the Palace of Westminster, it is nevertheless the policy of the House to endeavour to comply fully with the requirements of the Act and with all other relevant statutory provisions, subject only to such specific exemptions provided for in legislation that arise from the constitutional position of the Crown.

**Mr. Allen:** Is it not outrageous that in this day and age the House of Commons and the Palace of Westminster are not covered effectively by the Health and Safety at Work, etc. Act 1974 and that Crown immunity still exists in respect of people who work and often are injured in this place? Will the hon. Gentleman take steps to ensure that although the Health and Safety Executive is invited into this place on a grace and favour basis, there is a proper monitoring system by the House of Commons Commission to ensure safety conditions affecting people who live and work in the Palace of Westminster are improved to the standards that they would have to meet were the 1974 Act applicable?

**Mr. Beith:** It is misleading to suggest that health and safety at work requirements for the staff working in this place are not covered. It is the object of the authorities of the House to ensure that they are observed in every respect. It is also misleading to suggest that officers of the Health and Safety Executive or other bodies must be invited here. They are admitted at their own request if they wish to come at other times. Nevertheless, it is important that we should be fully satisfied that the House is complying, so far as the limits of this building permit, with the legislation and that its monitoring should take that into account.

**Mr. Alan Williams:** Does not the present situation deprive the people who work here of their rights because under the Health and Safety at Work, etc. Act 1974, in the last resort, they have recourse to law in the event of a dispute between them and the employer? That right is not available to employees here. Our employees are at a disadvantage in relation to people outside this place.

**Mr. Beith:** The right hon. Gentleman will know that it is not possible to prosecute the Crown. However, it is the policy of the House to try to ensure that its employees are not placed at a disadvantage and to meet liabilities where any can be shown. If the right hon. Gentleman is aware of circumstances in which he feels that a dispute has not been properly resolved, I hope that he will draw it to my attention, because I am sure that the House of Commons Commission would not want that to happen.

## HOUSE OF COMMONS

### Chamber (Blinds)

31. **Mr. Harry Greenway:** To ask the Lord President of the Council if he will issue guidance as to when it would be appropriate to draw the blinds in the House of Commons Chamber; and if he will make a statement.

**The Lord President of the Council and Leader of the House of Commons (Mr. John Wakeham):** The blinds on the west side of the Chamber are raised as requested by right hon. and hon. Members, or on the judgment of Officers of the House on duty in the Chamber.

**Mr. Greenway:** Does my right hon. Friend agree that Opposition Members rarely see the light and that to draw the blinds can only make matters worse? Does he also agree that sunlight can only enlighten our proceedings? Can we have much more of it?

**Mr. Wakeham:** I agree with much of what my hon. Friend has said. However, of course my hon. Friend has had no experience of sitting on the Opposition Benches, although he has been a Member of this place for quite a long time. I very much hope that he will not have that experience. I believe that the present system, left to the judgment of right hon. and hon. Members on the Opposition Benches, is the best way to deal with this.

**Mr. Winnick:** Is it the Lord President of the Council's job or that of some other Minister, to draw the blinds on the current Tory electoral anguish?

**Mr. Wakeham:** The hon. Gentleman is always hoping for preferment in the Labour party. One day he may be in charge of deciding whether the blinds should be raised or lowered.

**Sir Geoffrey Finsberg:** Will my right hon. Friend assure the House that future guidelines will not state that the blinds must be drawn to satisfy the requirements of the television authorities?

**Mr. Wakeham:** Obviously, we shall consider how the television experiment will work. I do not believe that the blinds will be any part of a television experiment, but we shall see how we get along.

### Early-day Motions

32. **Mr. Allen:** To ask the Lord President of the Council if he will bring forward proposals to establish a system to allow debate of the early-day motion with the most signatures.

**Mr. Wakeham:** No, Sir.

**Mr. Allen:** The Lord President of the Council will be aware that the original intention of early-day motions was to provide hon. Members with the possibility of debating issues of topical importance and relevance at an early day. Will he seek some reform of the system so that where a number of hon. Members, perhaps a percentage of

Conservative Members and Opposition Members, want to debate a matter, it can be debated perhaps once a week on a Friday morning? On that basis, over the past few weeks, there might have been debates on, for example, the Monopolies and Mergers Commission report on the brewing industry, which is of importance to hon. Members on both sides of the House, the sexual abuse of children and perhaps the legal profession and its current efforts. This week the Lord President of the Council may receive an early-day motion requesting a discussion on the possibilities of an early election. Those debates might be very helpful to the House.

**Mr. Wakeham:** The hon. Gentleman's proposal would fundamentally alter the whole early-day motion system. It is a means of enabling right hon. and hon. Members to express their views on a matter when there is no expectation that time will be available for a debate, and it serves the House well. I do not wish to see motions being touted around for signature, simply to secure a slot for a debate. Other channels are available to right hon. and hon. Members who wish to raise a matter in the House, including Adjournment debates and private Members' motions.

**Mr. Brandon-Bravo:** While I welcome my right hon. Friend's reply to the original question, I might have had some sympathy with the question but for the fact that there is another side to the coin. Motions appear on the Order Paper day after day, week after week and month after month with but one signature—that of the hon. Member for Nottingham, North (Mr. Allen), who wants £100,000 for his own personal publicity campaign. Should not the House find time to debate that outrageous suggestion?

**Mr. Wakeham:** What Leicester did in the last Parliament, Nottingham seems to do in this Parliament. I shall content myself with saying that I spent a very happy day in Nottingham on Friday.

### Palace of Westminster (Map)

33. **Mr. Andrew F. Bennett:** To ask the Lord President of the Council what maps or plans of the Palace of Westminster are available for guidance of new members; and if there is any plan to commission a new map or plan.

**Mr. Wakeham:** A plan of the principal floor is included in the Serjeant at Arms' leaflet "Accommodation and General Facilities for Members, their Private Secretaries and Research Assistants", which is issued to all new hon. Members. Similar plans are included in a variety of other publications and guides. There are no plans at present to commission a new map or plan.

**Mr. Bennett:** Does the Leader of the House accept that the plans that are available are inadequate for any new hon. Member who wants to find his or her way around the four floors of the House and the other buildings? Would it not be a good idea to make available an accurate map, so that right hon. and hon. Members can find all the offices within the House that they need to locate?

**Mr. Wakeham:** Any decision on the need for the House authorities to provide further information for new hon. Members, including the commissioning of maps, would initially be a matter for the Services Committee. I understand that such an approach has already been made to that Committee, which will consider it in due course.

# WALES

## NHS Reform

14. **Mr. Livsey:** To ask the Secretary of State for Wales if he will make a statement on the National Health Service White Paper, "Working for Patients", as it affects Wales.

**The Parliamentary Under-Secretary of State for Wales (Mr. Ian Grist):** Chapter 11 of the "Working for Patients" White Paper describes the detailed programme of action for Wales. Since the publication of the White Paper, my hon. Friend and I have engaged in discussions with key interests to ensure that the programme is implemented so as to secure better health care for all. My right hon. Friend intends to make a statement on the details of the next steps of implementation in the near future.

**Mr. Livsey:** Does the Minister not agree that the NHS White Paper will be disastrous for the rural areas of Wales, that general practitioners will have fewer resources available to cover their areas, and that the creation of NHS hospital trusts will take resources away from community hospitals in rural areas, creating a wholly unacceptable two-tier Health Service?

**Mr. Grist:** The hon. Gentleman overlooks the fact that the rural payments section of the GP's contract is still under consultation, so he is leaping ahead with yet another scare story.

The possibility of having self-governing hospitals, or any other units or doctors, in Wales will rest in the first instance on their choosing to be self-governing and on acceptance by my right hon. Friend the Secretary of State. There will be no second status for anybody under our proposals.

## Lending Rate

15. **Mr. Denzil Davies:** To ask the Secretary of State for Wales what assessment he has made of the effect of the recent increase in the minimum lending rate on the development of the economy of Wales.

**The Secretary of State for Wales (Mr. Peter Walker):** I am pleased to say that since interest rates have been at high levels two recent major surveys have both shown considerable confidence in the level of investment and job creation within the Welsh economy. In the first five months of this year the excellent record of Wales for inward investment continued. As the right hon. Gentleman will know, in 1988 Wales achieved the record both for jobs and for finance for inward investment. Unemployment continues to fall, and last year's 2·5 percentage point reduction in the Welsh rate was the largest of all the United Kingdom regions.

**Mr. Davies:** Does the right hon. Gentleman agree that inward investors might in the short term be able to cope with interest rates of 14 or 15 per cent. but that 95 per cent. of the Welsh economy is indigenous and is not concerned with inward investment, and that that sector has been damaged by high interest rates? Does the Secretary of State agree that it would be better to have a monetary and fiscal mix and to restore some of the cuts made in higher-rate taxes two years ago, thereby taking pressure off interest rates and to some extent redistributing wealth from the more prosperous regions of Britain to the less prosperous, such as Wales?

**Mr. Walker:** A great deal of the investment activity in Wales is very much concerned with the indigenous industries, and that is true in the hon. Gentleman's constituency. A recent survey carried out by the Institute of Directors in Wales showed that the majority of firms there expected an increase of 10 per cent. or more in their labour forces in the coming 12 months. Another factor of considerable importance to Welsh industries is the level of company profits that has enabled those investment programmes to take place.

## Welsh Development Agency (Property Development)

16. **Mr. Knox:** To ask the Secretary of State for Wales what was the level of expenditure in property development by the Welsh Development Agency in 1987-88 and in 1988-89.

**Mr. Peter Walker:** At £45·8 million, the Welsh Development Agency's property-related expenditure in 1988-89 was 43 per cent. higher than the £32·1 million in the previous financial year.

**Mr. Knox:** Does my right hon. Friend agree that that expenditure has played an important part in helping to reduce unemployment in Wales? Does he expect expenditure to be even higher this year?

**Mr. Walker:** I am glad to say that both the agency's factory building programme and its derelict land clearance programme are at record heights.

# Student Top-up Loans

3.30 pm

**The Secretary of State for Education and Science (Mr. Kenneth Baker):** With permission, Mr. Speaker, I wish to make a statement about the arrangements for administering top-up loans for students.

The House will recall that on 9 November I announced the Government's proposals for introducing non-means-tested top-up loans. I said that from 1990, in addition to their grant, all home students in full-time higher education—except postgraduates—would be eligible for a top-up loan averaging over £400 in a full year. I explained that it would be offered at a real interest rate of zero, and that repayments would be deferred when a graduate's income is low.

In that statement, I made clear the Government's view that the top-up loan scheme would be best administered by the financial institutions. The scheme will of course be subject to the necessary legislation and, as I told the House, the Government will bring forward a short Bill to provide legislative authority for it. I am glad to be able to tell the House that, following discussion with representatives of the Committee of London and Scottish Bankers, a scheme has been designed which is agreed to be a cost-effective and feasible means of introducing top-up loans in September 1990 as planned.

Under the scheme there will be a private sector loan admistrator, in the form of a company established and wholly owned by participating financial institutions, under contract to the Government. Participation in the company will be open to a wide range of financial institutions. It is clear from my discussions with members of Committee of London and Scottish Bankers that—subject to the satisfactory outcome of the contractual negotiations—a sufficient number of financial institutions will wish to participate from the outset to ensure that the company will be viable.

Under the arrangements students who wish to benefit from top-up loans will obtain a certificate of entitlement from their university, polytechnic or college. The certificates can be presented to the branches of the banks and other financial institutions that own that company, or to the company itself, which will make the resources available to the student and maintain a record of the transaction. The Government will fund the company for the administrative costs of the scheme and, of course, for the loans themselves.

The Government have carefully considered the repayment system, in the light of the responses to the White Paper "Top-up Loans for Students". We have concluded that repayment should be on the basis of equal amounts, adjusted annually for inflation, being repaid over a standard period. The obligation to repay will be deferred when a graduate's income falls below given levels in relation to average national income. Deferment will be arranged with the company on the basis of self-certification of income and subject to audit. In order to minimise any default on repayments, there will be a financial incentive under which the company will earn a proportion of its fee through securing a high repayment rate.

The Government will meet the costs of detailed preparatory work by the Committee of London and Scottish Bankers and by the company in the period from now onwards. Parliamentary approval will be sought in an additional Supplementary Estimate, to be presented shortly. We shall start immediate negotiations with the interested financial institutions to conclude a contract to cover the operation of the scheme, and that will of course be conditional on the Royal Assent to the Act. The range of costs indicated in the preparatory work is from £8·3 million to £11·5 million for start-up costs, and from £10·4 million to £14 million for annual operating costs. I am glad to say that those are many times smaller than the amounts that I have been reading about in the press over the last few months.

It is right that this scheme should be administered in the private sector, as our financial institutions possess skills in information and banking systems that are not readily available in the public sector. I am satisfied that the arrangements offer an efficient scheme and good value for money, and I commend them to the House.

**Mr. Jack Straw** (Blackburn): If this is good news, as the Secretary of State appears to suggest, why did he hide away this announcement from the voters until after the European elections? Why did he consistently block all our requests for statements and why have the Government welshed on their promise of a debate?

Is the Secretary of State aware that under this grotesquely incompetent scheme the nation ends up with the worst of all worlds, in which the taxpayer pays much more while the student is given much less? Will he confirm that with inflation at 8 per cent., instead of the 3 per cent. forecast in the White Paper, and with the abolition of housing benefit, almost every student will be worse off from next year?

The right hon. Gentleman's statement says, in carefully crafted weasel words, not that there has been an agreement with the financial institutions but that a scheme has been designed

"which is agreed to be a cost-effective and feasible means of introducing top-up loans".

Will the Secretary of State say precisely what has been agreed with the financial institutions, or has nothing bankable been agreed with those institutions?

Will the Secretary of State confirm that he has come close to giving a false impression about costs by specifying costs which relate only to the early years of the scheme when there are relatively few debtors? What will be the cost per student and the cost per outstanding advance once the scheme is fully operational? What figure was advised by Price Waterhouse? Why is there no reference to interest rate subsidy in the statement or, indeed, to its cost, in the White Paper? What are the costs of the preparatory work that the taxpayer is now supposed to meet?

Is the Secretary of State aware that on the most conservative estimates, the administrative set-up and write-off costs, once the scheme is fully operational, will not be less than £100 per debtor? What kind of bloody-mindedness is it that persuades the Secretary of State to give £100 to moneylenders, bureaucrats and bailiffs when instead he could use that £100 per student to restore the real value of the grant? Is he aware that in the United States the cost of defaults on loan schemes such as this is now running at $1·8 billion, one third of the total cost of the scheme? What does the Secretary of State expect the defaults cost of this scheme to be? Will he confirm that it will cost the Exchequer more while giving

[*Mr. Jack Straw*]

students less until decades into the next century and that there is even a prospect of this scheme never breaking even?

Why has the Secretary of State said nothing this afternoon about his earlier grand claims that a loans scheme would increase access and opportunities—I thought that that was the argument in favour of the scheme—or has he now accepted, in the light of the 95 per cent. of representations that he received against the scheme, that it will put students off going into higher education and damage the opportunities of those from low-income homes?

Is the Secretary of State aware that his ministerial career is littered with wheezes and gimmicks which seemed a good idea at the time but which turned out to be half-baked and unworkable? Does he intend to see this barmy loan scheme through, or is he going to cut and run to another Department and leave the mess to someone else —as he did with his previous great invention, the poll tax?

**Mr. Baker:** I am delighted that the spirit of the hustings still survives. I advise the hon. Member for Blackburn (Mr. Straw) not to be too cocky about last Thursday's results. We shall expose the fact that the Labour party, despite its new proposals in its new manifesto, is still Socialist in tooth and claw, and that its proposals on education are totally negative, in that the hon. Gentleman wants to abolish schools and reverse our reforms. [*Interruption.*] I do not know whether this is the first skirmish in the opening campaign for the general election in two or three years' time, but I am quite confident that if it is we shall eventually win. [*Interruption.*]

**Mr. Speaker:** Order. Let us get back to the scheme.

**Mr. Baker:** I was provoked shockingly, Mr. Speaker. The hon. Gentleman said that next year students will be worse off, but that will not be the case. We estimate the disentitlement to benefit next year to be about £65 million and the increased additional resources available through top-up loan schemes will be £167 million. [*Interruption.*] I wish that the hon. Gentleman would listen for a minute. In addition to the £167 million there will be £15 million of access funds.

The hon. Gentleman asked me about bank participation. We have had discussions with a number of banks and other financial institutions. I am clear that there will be substantial interest in participation in the scheme, subject to the negotiation of the final contract. In particular, it is clear that major clearing banks will be ready to participate in the scheme. It is for individual banks and other financial institutions, including building societies, to say whether they will take part in the scheme. That must be their decision, but I am confident, from assurances given personally to me, of substantial interest in participating in the scheme.

The hon. Gentleman talked about those students who will be worse off. As a result of top-up loans, 120,000 students who currently receive no maintenance grant whatsoever, because they are means tested out of it, will have the availability of a top-up loan of about £400 a year on average. Similarly, 160,000 students who receive a reduced grant as a result of parental contribution, but whose parents do not make it up, will also benefit from the top-up loan facility. In addition, some 50,000 students in higher education who have no entitlement to an award at the moment will benefit from top-up loans.

The hon. Gentleman asked me about default. We always include provision for the cost of default in our arithmetic. Annex E of the White Paper on top-up loans shows an illustrative figure of a default rate of 10 per cent. Some default is inevitable, but I do not expect it to be as high as 10 per cent. Some default is inevitable by the nature of the scheme. For example, we will require the loans to be made available to all students who are taking higher degree courses, irrespective of their credit rating. If a graduate unfortunately dies after graduation, the debt of that person will not be taken into his or her estate; it will be written off. Similarly, the scheme allows any outstanding debt to be written off by the age of 50. Those are unusual characteristics of a banking operation, so we have to meet them.

We have always assumed that the Government will have to stand behind the cost of default, as illustrated in the White Paper, but the operating company will earn a proportion of its fee through securing a high repayment rate.

The hon. Gentleman asked about default rates, particularly in America. I remind him that the rate of default in Norway is 1 per cent. and 2 per cent. in Sweden and Japan. In America, the default rate is high for two reasons. First, there are no proposals for deferment while American graduates are earning, so those on low incomes are expected to repay and they default. We are allowing for the obligation to pay to be related to income. Secondly, in America the loan scheme has been extended to those whom we would call further education students and it has proved very difficult to track them as they move all over America.

As I said in my original statement, costs will be between £8 and £12 per student account. In 1995 we estimate that the operating costs will be between £10·5 million and £14 million. That gives the £8 to £12 per student account in 1995. As for what that represents as a percentage of the money outstanding, by 1995 we estimate that there will be an outstanding amount of £1·2 billion and administrative costs of £10 million to £14 million, which is a very small proportion—about 1 per cent. That is all set out in the original White Paper in annex E—[*Interruption.*] I wish that the hon. Gentleman would read the White Paper and be familiar with his figures. Once again he shows that he has not done his homework. He has no ideas; he does not even have ideas about our ideas.

**Mr. James Pawsey** (Rugby and Kenilworth): Does my right hon. Friend accept that his statement will be widely welcomed by Conservative Members and by the country? It will increase the degree of access to higher education by providing a source of cheap funding. Will he confirm that it will be just about the cheapest money in town?

In response to the hon. Member for Blackburn (Mr. Straw), I should like to draw two further points from my right hon. Friend. First, will he confirm that the incidence of default in Scandinavia is between 1 and 2 per cent.? Secondly, on access funds, the original figure quoted in the White Paper was £15 million. Does my right hon. Friend agree that many Conservative Members consider that £15 million is inadequate and would like him to endeavour to improve that figure?

Finally, when we introduce legislation in this matter, is it intended also to have some reference to the funding of student unions and to freedom of speech in higher education and in universities?

**Mr. Baker:** My hon. Friend asked various questions. I can confirm that the default rate in Norway is 1 per cent. It is 2 per cent. in Sweden and 2 per cent. in Japan. My hon. Friend asked also about the level of access funds. The access funds in the White Paper were stated to be about £15 million—that is, £5 million for the universities and polytechnics, £5 million for postgraduates and £5 million for the FE sector. There have been representations during the consultation process that those figures should be higher. I note carefully what my hon. Friend has said. Those decisions will be taken next year in the PES round.

My hon. Friend asked whether it is the cheapest money in town. Certainly, it does not bear a real rate. It is a real rate of zero. It means that the outstanding amount is uprated by the rate of inflation each year. Many students will find that an attractive deal.

My hon. Friend asked about student unions. I recognise the concern on behalf of those students who do not wish, through their own student unions, to be affiliated to the National Union of Students. I am considering various options for change in the present arrangements, and I will bring forward proposals in due course. I will also publish shortly the report of the survey on the student unions and the NUS.

My hon. Friend asked also about freedom of speech. I recognise a real concern that some visiting speakers have been unable to secure a fair hearing, or any hearing at all, on certain campuses. I have consulted the Committee of Vice-Chancellors and Principals, the Committee of Directors of Polytechnics and the Standing Conference of Principals on how best to strengthen the provisions of the 1986 legislation. I am now considering the way forward, and I will bring proposals forward in due course. If necessary, we shall consider further legislation.

**Mr. Simon Hughes** (Southwark and Bermondsey): Does the Secretary of State deny the statement by one of the bank officials whom he met last week to the effect that they were still all at sea about who would pay for the scheme, who would run it, and so on? Does he deny that he cannot say today that anybody has unconditionally agreed to participate in the scheme?

Is it not already the case that, on previously projected figures, it would cost £750 million over 10 years, on the Secretary of State's basis, before the scheme breaks even at the end of the decade? That is on the basis of a 3 per cent. rate of inflation, which is clearly, under his Government's administration, a wildly inaccurate estimate. The additional costs announced today will total at least £150 million. Is it not the reality that the scheme will cost at least £1 billion or more to the Treasury? At the moment, that is not a cost that the Government are having to finance at all, but will involve extra Government money under their scheme of public expenditure.

**Mr. Baker:** The hon. Gentleman must refer to annex E in the White Paper. I am sure that he is familiar with the figures. He will know that it will cost the Government money until the break-even year. As a result of the outlined cost figures that I have given today, it is possible that the break-even year may move about half a year forward, from 2001 to 2002—no more than that. The Government are committed to reducing the rate of inflation. That remains the Government's unremitting target.

**Mr. Robert Rhodes James** (Cambridge): As my right hon. Friend and the House are aware, I am not exactly an enthusiastic supporter of the scheme, either in principle or in practicality. Although, of course, I shall look carefully at my right hon. Friend's statement, in view of what happened last November, I advise the House to look at the statement carefully and to question some of the figures. As it is now grimly evident that the cost of the scheme will primarily be borne by the taxpayer, before drafting legislation will my right hon. Friend consider whether the figures could be rather more precise, whether the implications could be made rather clearer, and whether the House could have a debate on these matters?

**Mr. Baker:** The hon. Member for Blackburn (Mr. Straw) referred earlier to the question of a debate. I should welcome such a debate and I hope that my right hon. Friend the Leader of the House, who is in his place, has registered my expectation that there will be one because it would be helpful. I am happy to give the figures. Indeed, the figures that I put forward this afternoon take us much further forward in our discussions with the banks. Coupled with the figures set out in the "Top-up Loans for Students" White Paper and in annex E, they mean that the figures are before the country and the House. I am happy to consider what my hon. Friend has said. I do not know whether I can convert him to support this scheme, but I believe that he has something of an open mind.

**Mr. Merlyn Rees** (Morley and Leeds, South): Is the Secretary of State aware that I have not needed to read the White Paper or to listen to the statement about this type of loan because it was available before the last war? Indeed, I went to university on such a grant and paid it back out of my gratuity at the end of the war. Therefore I understand the nature of the grant and its effect on students without guessing about it. When I read in the White Paper that the aim is to save public expenditure, that reinforced my view—which is strongly felt because I represent an inner-city area where practically nobody goes into higher education—that all that this will do is to make it doubly difficult for the sort of people that we want to get to university actually to get there. If that is dyed-in-the-wool Socialism, count me a dyed-in-the-wool Socialist.

**Mr. Baker:** It is just as well that the right hon. Gentleman does not live in Australia these days, where the Socialist Government have introduced charging for tuition costs and fees at universities. I am not implying that the hon. Member for Blackburn would seek to follow that, but simply wish to point out that, associated with that proposal in Australia is the graduate tax, a proposal that has won support from some Labour Members. Indeed, the Labour spokesman in the House of Lords favours a graduate tax and I believe that the hon. Member for Durham, North (Mr. Radice), the immediate predecessor of the hon. Member for Blackburn, also favours a graduate tax. There is a lot of new thinking in the Labour party in this area——

**The Parliamentary Under-Secretary of State for Education and Science (Mr. Robert Jackson):** Some new thinking.

**Mr. Baker:** Well, as my hon. Friend has said, there is some new thinking.

The right hon. Member for Morley and Leeds, South (Mr. Rees) raised the question of access. We are the only developed country not to have some form of loans system for students. In the other countries that have top-up loans alongside grants, a higher proportion of the population of young people goes to college, university or the equivalent of polytechnics, especially in America, where there are extensive loans systems. I am often told that such a system will discourage women, but in America women now constitute well over half the student population. The system has not proved a deterrent.

I advise the right hon. Gentleman that I am committed to the expansion of higher education. The Governments of whom he has been a leading member, and Conservative Governments, have always been constrained by the high cost of higher education in our country. The right hon. Gentleman served in the Cabinet that cut higher education significantly, both in numbers and in capital. Student loans will represent a new flow of funds into higher education and will broaden the financial platform.

**Mr. David Madel** (Bedfordshire, South-West): How will discretionary grants fit in when the scheme is under way? Will my right hon. Friend assure me that when all the details have been worked out the greatest care and sensitivity will be exercised towards those students with long courses, such as medicine or veterinary medicine?

**Mr. Baker:** Discretionary grants will, of course, continue, as will the normal mandatory grants. It will be up to the local authorities to decide exactly what the position is and whether they give grants. Those people who are not successful in obtaining a discretionary grant—there are many tens of thousands each year—will be eligible for top-up loans, which will be non-means tested. That represents a guaranteed and assured source of extra available funds.

**Mr. Peter Shore** (Bethnal Green and Stepney): The Secretary of State should know that his announcement will have been greeted with great disappointment, if not dismay, by the great majority of students in British universities who were hoping that the Secretary of State's statement this afternoon would announce that he had had second thoughts about this mean, paltry and damaging scheme.

Is the Secretary of State not aware that medical students, who have five-year courses, three of which are taken up with clinical studies, lasting 46 weeks of the year, have had and will have no opportunity of supplementing their inadequate grants with extra earnings during the long vacation and other periods? Is he not aware that the average medical student today in London is having to borrow from banks up to £3,000 over the length of his course to meet the present deficiencies in his student grant? What effect will this additional burden of loan have upon medical students and especially upon those who have been recruited from rather less affluent circumstances than the Secretary of State normally considers, and on women students, who now form so large a part of our total student intake for medical purposes?

**Mr. Baker:** I will take no lectures on inadequate grants and general expenditure on higher education, from a right hon. Member of the House who was a member of the Labour Cabinet that substantially cut higher education. In general, there were substantial cuts in higher education in 1976, because the Labour Government ran the country so badly. I believe that many students will welcome the proposal for top-up loans. I have already indicated the large numbers of students—the 120,000 who receive no grants at present; the 160,000 who have their grants reduced and the 50,000 who are or who are not on discretionary awards in higher education—who will benefit by having an available source of money, at a cost lower than the costs that the right hon. Gentleman suggested medical students would pay.

Medical students can look foward to a high income but, if they do not achieve that high income, they will be protected by the deferment arrangements. I recognise that the medical students' extra years of study will lead to extra debt, and the repayment term may need to be extended for them.

**Sir Philip Goodhart** (Beckenham): Can I press my right hon. Friend on the question of medical students? In the United States the average doctor starts his medical career with a debt of $50,000. We do not want to see that happening here.

**Mr. Baker:** It is highly unlikely that there will be any figure of that scale. If my hon. Friend looks at the figures, the average loan is £400 a year in the first year, building up slowly over a period of years. We do not, therefore, envisage that scale of indebtedness for medical students. The point I would make again is that, if there is extra debt, the repayment period, which we have envisaged would be five years for a normal student, could be extended to recognise that fact.

**Dr. Dafydd Elis Thomas** (Meirionnydd Nant Conwy): If the Secretary of State was meditating on the statement during his sponsored walk in my constituency on Friday, I doubt whether it has done him any good. Will he address himself specifically to the effect of the scheme on mature students? Is he arguing that the introduction of such a top-up loan scheme will benefit and increase access? Where is the evidence of that in the statement beyond that which he was saying in the White Paper?

**Mr. Baker:** I very much enjoyed going on a sponsored walk in a very beautiful part of the hon. Gentleman's constituency on a lovely day. I thought that it was quite a good day for a leading Conservative politician to be walking in the Welsh hills.

If the hon. Gentleman looks at the availability of student support in other developed countries as compared with this country, he will see that what stands out in this country is its very high level of student support, and that has had an inhibiting effect on the expansion of higher education over the years. In the United Kingdom, for example, in 1984 prices, student support per student is £750; in West Germany £70; in France £180 and in Japan £30. We believe that it is reasonable to expect students to make some contribution towards their upkeep costs while they are studying.

**Mr. Anthony Nelson** (Chichester): In acknowledging that my right hon. Friend has worked extremely hard to come forward with a viable scheme, may I put to him the concern that perhaps some of us have, which is that unless one means-tests the availability of the loans, they may end up as a subsidy to middle class families? The people who will benefit are those parents on good incomes, with high tax rates, who will make sure that their children apply for the grants, which will be at very low cost, because it is money that they would otherwise have to find. Far from encouraging access from students from low-income familes, it could end up being a subsidy for those who, perhaps, have lesser claim.

**Mr. Baker:** I certainly would not introduce means testing for these loans. One of the attractive features of our scheme is that the loans are not means tested. The parents of about one third of students—for example, middle class parents—who have their grants reduced because of means testing do not make up the full entitlement that their children would have if they were not means tested. This system will be of considerable benefit to that group.

**Mr. Win Griffiths** (Bridgend): Will the Secretary of State name the banks and financial institutions that have been in negotiation with him? Exactly what are their terms in respect of the costs that they are prepared to bear in the administration of this scheme? Was the White Paper the basis of their discussion? If so, is not the whole thing bogus, because the inflation rates used in the White Paper were 5 per cent. in 1989-90 and 3·5 per cent. in 1990-91 and the succeeding inflation rate was 3 per cent.? The figures in the report cannot form the basis of a real estimate of the cost of administering the scheme. What is the present estimate of the real inflation rate in the years ahead for the administration of this scheme?

**Mr. Baker:** I have said that the Government's clear intention is to reduce inflation, and we are pursuing economic policies that will secure that end.

The hon. Gentleman asked whether the White Paper was the basis of discussions with the banks. We said that there were certain features that any loan scheme would need to have. One was universal accessibility to all students, irrespective of their position. That is not a normal banking function. We said also that there should be deferment if, after graduation, a graduate has a salary or wage a certain percentage below the national average wage. Again, that is not a characteristic of a normal banking repayment scheme. We have ensured that both factors are built into the scheme as discussed.

I reiterate that it is up to individual banks and other financial institutions, including building societies, to say whether they will participate, but assurances, given personally to me, show that there is substantial interest from the clearing banks in participating in the scheme.

**Several Hon. Members** *rose——*

**Mr. Speaker:** Order. I should like to call all the hon. Members who are now standing. This is an Opposition day, the subject of which has been chosen by the Social and Liberal Democrats. I shall allow questions on the statement to continue until 4.15 pm. If questions are brief, I shall be able to call all those hon. Members who wish to speak.

**Mr. Harry Greenway** (Ealing, North): Will my right hon. Friend confirm that the average student borrows £370 a year and is required to repay it at commercial rates, so this scheme will lighten the load? Will he cost the increase in the number of students in higher education over the past 10 years? There are now 266,000 more

students in higher education, and we are moving towards one in five of the eligible population before the turn of the century.

**Mr. Baker:** I cannot confirm the precise figure, but the average indebtedness of students is of that order. Various surveys on the subject have been carried out. My hon. Friend asked me to cost the increase in the number of students. We have allowed in annex E to the White Paper for the increase in the number of students. Since we have been in office there has been an increase of about 200,000 in the number of students. This has been one of the most rapid periods of expansion, most of which has taken place in the polytechnics, although the universities are begining to expand again. The financial arrangements that I made in respect of universities and polytechnics, and which I announced about a month ago will stimulate polytechnics and universities to expand their numbers. The funding is changing so that it is very much a matter of the money following the students, and that is a demand-led expansion.

**Mr. Dennis Skinner** (Bolsover): Is not today's statement a way for the Secretary of State for Education and Science to try to convince the taxpayer that he will use taxpayers' money to introduce the scheme as a first step so that, later on, the Government can spread the idea abroad that student loans will provide a much greater part of the grant than at present? In other words the Government are using taxpayers' money to get across the idea and will then hammer the students. Will the Secretary of State confirm that Johnson Matthey is one of the banks with which he is having discussions—or is it the Abbey National? When students decide to protest against this evil scheme and come to the House of Commons to do so, will he rejoice in seeing Kate Adie, Brian Barron and other journalists infiltrating picket lines of police who are trying to block the students on Westminster bridge?

**Mr. Baker:** I am sure that if there is a group of militant students waiting to protest, the hon. Gentleman will be at the head gingering them up. I doubt whether his leader would sanction that action. I am not prepared to name any individual bank but neither I nor, as far as I am aware, any of my officials have had discussions with Johnson Matthey.

The hon. Gentleman also said that we were trying to persuade foreign sentiment abroad. I do not follow his argument.

**Mr. Skinner:** No, I did not. I said that a sprat was being used to catch a mackerel.

**Mr. Baker:** I do not follow the hon. Gentleman's argument. It would be foreign sentiment if it were abroad, and I thought he said that. The hon. Gentleman should re-read the White Paper, which makes it clear that from 1990 we shall introduce top-up loans, the grant will be frozen and the loan will go up over a period. We have not disguised our intentions about this, which has been an essential part of the proposals announced in November. Instead of coming in here and shouting at my right hon. and hon. Friends all the time, the hon. Gentleman should do his homework and read the White Paper.

**Mr. Tim Smith** (Beaconsfield): Does my right hon. Friend agree that those student graduates entering the job market in the 1990s will be doing so at a more favourable

[*Mr. Tim Smith*]

time than for many years? In those circumstances, it is not unreasonable to transfer part of the cost of student maintenance from the taxpayer to the employer? Most students will have very little to lose and a great deal to gain from the introduction of the scheme.

**Mr. Baker:** My hon. Friend is right. It is incontrovertible that there is to be what statisticians call a demographic trough and that there will be a dramatic drop in the number of 18, 19 and 21-year-olds in the course of the next five to 10 years. Graduates will find that they are moving into a buyers' market when they leave college. There is very little graduate unemployment today, and there will be even less in the four or five years ahead. My hon. Friend raises the interesting point that in those circumstances, companies may tend to pay off student debts. That is now becoming a regular feature of American schemes in which, if an employer wants to take on a particular person, as part of the employment package he is prepared to write off the debt or provide favourable repayment terms. It may be that various employers in various parts of this country, both in private and public sectors, will want to move towards such arrangements.

**Mr. Donald Anderson** (Swansea, East): Is the Secretary of State going to freeze basic grants or progressively reduce the basic grant using the loan as cover? Has he seriously considered the effect on women? I heard what he said about women's experiences in the United States. The scheme is bound to give women not only a negative dowry, but a disincentive to return to work at a time when the Government are trying to encourage teachers to return to work after basic training. Is the Secretary of State aware that this scheme contradicts other Government policies?

**Mr. Baker:** I do not accept that. Some of the other student loan schemes across the world do not include deferment for a woman graduate who goes off to have a family. It is expected that while she is not earning she will repay some of the debt, but that is not so under our scheme. When people cease to be in employment they fall below the threshold level, so the obligation will be deferred.

As regards the structure of the scheme, I confirm that under the proposals in the White Paper the grant will be increased again next year. Its level will be resolved in the PES round for 1990. It will then be frozen in cash terms over a period of years. It will not be reduced in cash terms. The top-up loan will begin and increase yearly thereafter.

**Mr. Peter Thurnham** (Bolton, North-East): To the extent that disabled students have additional needs, will my right hon. Friend consider adapting his excellent scheme so that they can have extra funds and, when they can earn enough, will he consider helping with easier payments by increasing their thresholds?

**Mr. Baker:** I shall certainly look into that. Disabled students who graduate and take jobs may well qualify for some of the deferment arrangements. There are allowances in the grants for certain aspects of disability.

**Mr. Max Madden** (Bradford, West): How will students be credit-rated in future? Will loans be liable to attachment for non-payment of the poll tax; and will loans be available to students who are overseas nationals?

**Mr. Baker:** The hon. Gentleman's question is about the civil debts of students, not about this particular scheme. A student's credit rating will depend upon whether he repays his debts. We envisage, as I said today, that a loan facility will be available through the loan administrator, a company which will be set up to provide the loan. The banks will be able to bring their considerable expertise, through the branch network, to the recovery of debt.

**Mr. Graham Riddick** (Colne Valley): Despite the fact that loans will not have to be paid back until students have completed their courses and are earning a living, does my right hon. Friend agree that their introduction will have the psychological effect of concentrating the minds of aspiring students on choosing courses which will be useful and worthwhile in later life?

**Mr. Baker:** Yes, one of the things that we discovered when my hon. Friend the Parliamentary Under-Secretary of State and his predecessor visited various countries was that in Sweden, for example—radical, Left-wing Sweden—where there has been a loan scheme like this for years, it was said that the scheme had concentrated students' attention and often increased their motivation.

I agree with my hon. Friend that the scheme will make many students think. I do not believe that it will be harmful to any course of study. More and more young people aged 18 and 19 in the student world recognise the enormous return which they will earn from higher education. There has been great increase in their numbers, about 200,000, in the past 10 years. That encouraging figure is welcomed on all sides of the House.

Economic analyses have shown that the return to a student from higher education is an estimated 25 per cent. on the amount spent on that education. The return to society for that amount is between 5 and 8 per cent. It is a good investment.

**Mr. David Winnick** (Walsall, North): It is not too difficult to know what the Secretary of State would have said about the scheme if he had remained on the Back Benches. Is he aware that this is the sort of Thatcherite discriminatory nonsense that the electorate rejected so decisively on Thursday?

**Mr. Baker:** Is it Thatcherite of Sweden, Norway, Germany and Japan to have a loan scheme? Of course not. That was empty, windbag oratory.

**Mr. Alan W. Williams** (Carmarthen): I was one of seven children from a very modest background; each of us had the benefit of six years in higher education. That was only possible with adequate student grants. Does the right hon. Gentleman realise that the continuing devaluation of the student grant, and his student loan proposals, will cut off millions of people from modest backgrounds who possess the talent that the country needs, and will make higher education more and more a middle class preserve?

**Mr. Baker:** First, there is no evidence abroad that this happens and secondly, as he knows and about which I am constantly chided, the real value of student grants in the United Kingdom has fallen since 1979.

**Mr. Straw:** It has been deliberately cut.

**Mr. Baker:** The hon. Gentleman says that it has been deliberately cut. That confirms what I say, that it has fallen. Since 1979 the number of students has gone up by

200,000. That includes full-time and mature students. If the hon. Gentleman is saying that part-time students are wrong, he has no policy at all for the expansion of higher education.

**Mr. Andrew Smith** (Oxford, East): Does not the patent inadequacy of the Secretary of State's responses show the latest instalment of a saga of breathtaking incompetence concerning the whole scheme? It can only be implemented by a dogmatic determination, not to bring in top-up loans but to destroy the basis of the grant system. Did I hear the Secretary of State right when he said that all students are now to be credit rated as part of the scheme? Will he come clean and tell us the true administrative costs in the later years? On many occasions he referred to annex E. Will he give an undertaking to publish an amended version of annex E showing the true administrative costs, including the default rate cost and the interest rate cost?

Does not his statement unforgivably overlook the effect on those students and institutions whose courses are longer? As my right hon. Friend the Member for Bethnal Green and Stepney (Mr. Shore) said, that applies to medical students. Do the proposals not also deal a body blow to the traditions of Scottish higher education, whose needs have been as contemptuously ignored in the statement as they were in the White Paper itself? What about the effect on teachers and on their training? Is not the statement a body blow to the prospects of successfully addressing the teaching crisis? Above all, will not this shameful statement deny access to higher education to the very students whom we ought to be attracting and who are presently denied that opportunity? Does the Secretary of State realise that his kamikaze determination to go down in history as the man who brought free access to higher education to an end will be opposed with the utmost vigour by the Labour party, the students and, and I am sure, by the public at large?

**Mr. Baker:** Methinks the hon. Gentleman "doth protest too much". The hon. Gentleman should appreciate that under this Government there has been a substantial expansion of higher education. I have proposals to expand it even further. I have provided money for expansion in the last three years and I shall strive to do so in the coming years. The hon. Gentleman asked about teachers. He well knows that I am bringing forward proposals which will probably mean that many teachers will not do the fourth year. I think that the hon. Gentleman has supported a policy which suggests that the course for a bachelor of education degree should no longer be a four-year course, but a three-year course with one term in school. I do not think that I misinterpret the proposals. In that case they stand equal with other students. The hon. Gentleman asked if I would publish a revised version of annex E. I am quite happy to consider that and if it is helpful I shall do so. *[Interruption.]* I am free with information because there are no secrets in my Department. The hon. Gentleman started his attack on me by questioning my competence. I can be accused of many things but I am not usually accused of being incompetent.

## STATUTORY INSTRUMENTS, &C.

*Ordered,*

That the draft Restrictive Trade Practices (Services) (Amendment) Order 1989 be referred to a Standing Committee on Statutory Instruments, &c.—*[Mr. Alan Howarth.]*

## OPPOSITION DAY

[13TH ALLOTTED DAY]

# Transport

**Mr. Speaker:** I must announce to the House that I have selected the amendment in the name of the Prime Minister.

**Mr. Dennis Skinner** (Bolsover): On a point of order. I do not know whether you are aware, Mr. Speaker, but last week when the business statement was made and in subsequent discussions—you know how they talk in this place—people said, "What is on the agenda for Monday?" They were told that it was the SLD Supply day and that its members would decide. They were told, "We can tell you on the record that it is about Hong Kong." I thought, "That sounds attractive and it might mean about 2 million or 3 million votes in the Euro elections if, perhaps, we can bring a few back." Since then, there has been a change and here we are about to discuss transport. I am not knocking that, but this place has to be regulated in a proper fashion.

Very shortly, the television cameras will be coming in and the television people will want to know on Thursday what is to be debated. They will not be satisfied with this "anything will do" approach by people who are disappearing from view. They will want to know. They will ask, "What's on?" They will be told that it is Hong Kong and they will not be very happy when they find that it is transport. I am giving some advice for future debates.

**Mr. Speaker:** That is not a matter for me. As I told the hon. Gentleman last week, we are regulated here by the Order Paper and not by rumour.

4.20 pm

**Mr. Richard Livsey** (Brecon and Radnor): I beg to move,

That this House condemns the lack of adequate investment in public transport, which has resulted in severe congestion and low staff morale leading to the current misery for commuters; and calls for a national transport strategy which invests in the public transport network, encourages a move from road to rail travel and ensures that benefits of new investment in projects such as the Channel Tunnel are shared by the regions and nations of the United Kingdom.

Given the impending chaos that will arise on Wednesday on the public transport system, especially in London, and that the transport crisis with which we are confronted is a major environmental problem, our debate today should be welcome.

The lack of investment by the Government in public transport is deplorable. In particular, the neglect of the rail system in comparison with the investment in the road system beggars belief. In the time that they have been in power, have the Government built any new railway lines? Given their admiration for Victorian values, they should be aware that the Victorians would find the Government's achievements in this respect laughable. What new rolling stock have they provided on the railway lines? What assistance has been given to staff?

This discrimination against the railway system is compounded by the loaded methods of investment criteria against the railway system in comparison with the road system. The Government only started to wake up to the problem of investment in our railways in 1983. Investment was in the doldrums from 1975 to 1983, and, at 1989-90 prices, investment dropped from £546 million in 1975 to

[*Mr. Richard Livsey*]

£347 million in 1983. One result of this failure has been congestion, especially in the south-east, where a massive growth in passenger traffic has resulted in misery for commuters. The Government have failed the nation with their transport policies and the congestion on Britain's roads is a direct result of the Government's failure to invest in public transport.

Daily, harassed commuters travel in overcrowded, tatty rail coaches that are a misery and, in some cases, no better than cattle trucks. These are overloaded, and it is no wonder that staff on the London Underground and Network SouthEast are at their wits' end. Only a massive investment in rail, both in the cities and in main-line electrification, will alleviate these horrendous problems. Meanwhile, behind the wheels of millions of cars and lorries, drivers are stranded in traffic.

**Mr. John Bowis** (Battersea): Will the hon. Gentleman give way?

**Mr. Livsey:** I will give way in a moment. I am trying to say something important.

Drivers are stranded in traffic jams. In London alone, this costs the economy £15 billion a year, and the cost to the environment and people's health is also enormous. My party believes that the Government must plan now for the future, for much more investment in public transport.

**Mr. Bowis:** I agree that it is important to invest in public transport and rail transport in particular, not least in the capital city. However, can the hon. Gentleman tell me which major rail schemes were started and implemented during the period when his party was in cahoots with the then Labour Government? That is the period that he has condemned as having seen no investment whatever.

**Mr. Livsey:** The hon. Gentleman is referring to only two years in that period, and the question is irrelevant in the context of the debate.

I understand that this afternoon British Rail will seek a High Court injunction to outlaw Wednesday's planned 24-hour strike by the National Union of Railwaymen on the ground that the union did not properly conduct its strike ballot. The ballot of 70,000 rail workers turned on the rejected 7 per cent. pay offer and the abolition of national pay bargaining. The NUR will argue that it acted entirely within the law. With inflation running at 8 per cent., the loss of national pay bargaining is an important issue. The case for arbitration is extremely strong.

Last Friday, Mr. Paul Watkinson, British Rail's director of employee relations, said that BR had received information that several hundred of its employees had not had the opportunity to vote in the ballot. That is a claim that requires close examination. There is considerable frustration among British Rail staff, and that is understandable when so many trains are overcrowded. I believe that wiser counsels should resolve the dispute.

**Mr. Donald Anderson** (Swansea, East): Whatever one's views on the merits of the strike, does the hon. Gentleman agree that the action of the British Rail management, in intervening in such a way at such a sensitive time during the course of negotiations, was crass and wholly inept?

**Mr. Livsey:** I agree that its actions were extremely inept and not an example of good personal management. If it was serious about finding a constructive resolution of the dispute, it would not have behaved in such a way.

There is misery for commuters. Our motorways are jammed because of lack of investment in the railway system. It is not surprising that the motorways are overcrowded, because the number of cars on our roads has doubled in the past 12 years. An additional 2 million cars per annum are being sold and driven on British roads and as a result the environment is deteriorating rapidly. Indeed, the countryside has been laid to waste and there is increased air pollution. I understand that delays in the south-east alone cost about £15 billion.

**Mr. Gerrard Neale** (Cornwall, North): Does the hon. Gentleman agree that one of the reasons why considerable disdain has been shown for his party over the past few days is that people such as himself say one thing when it comes to investment in infrastructure and then vote in exactly the opposite way when it comes to activating decisions? Does the hon. Gentleman accept that his late colleague, David Penhaligon, fought tooth and nail to get the road system improved in the west country on a scheme backed by the Government? There was total support for his campaign in Cornwall, as well as support from David Penhaligon's colleagues—candidates and Members alike—but when the issue was brought before us in the Chamber and we were asked to support the scheme, two of his hon. Friends voted against it—the right hon. Member for Tweeddale, Ettrick and Lauderdale (Mr. Steel) and the hon. Member for Southwark and Bermondsey (Mr. Hughes).

**Mr. Livsey:** I accept that the late Member for Truro, Mr. David Penhaligon, campaigned for an improved road system in the west country. I listened to his speeches and I supported him when the issue came to a vote, as did many of my colleagues. It was a good scheme, which led to better access to the west country. That is why I supported it.

This Government, previous Governments and planners have demonstrated over many years a lamentable lack of vision and an inability to diagnose what is happening in the movement of people and goods. Things were done rather better during the previous century. No significant new railway lines have been built during the 20th century.

**Mr. Robert Adley** (Christchurch): Will the hon. Gentleman give way?

**Mr. Livsey:** No, not now. I shall give way to the hon. Gentleman later. I have given way too often already.

We are now entering a new era of investment in our infrastructure, including transport. I have no doubt that the lack of infrastructure will be the biggest internal problem facing Britain over the next 10 years. The decisions taken now will be absolutely crucial.

**Mr. Adley:** The hon. Gentleman has stated that the number of cars has doubled over the past 12 years. Does he believe that that has happened because the economy has been prosperous? He also said that we are building fewer railway lines than the Victorians. Does he believe that the invention of the internal combustion engine has had anything to do with that?

**Mr. Livsey:** I am certain that the invention of the internal combustion engine has everything to do with that.

However, many people are turning to private transport because of the inadequacies of public transport. They are forced to get into their cars because the public transport system is unable to provide a proper, efficient or effective alternative.

The choices in transport confronting us at the moment should be incorporated in the provision of an integrated transport system which would combine rail, road, air and sea transport. We should be planning for a grand design which will link the regions of this country with each other and with the continent. We should cut congestion and pollution.

We need environmentally friendly investment, which means that we must invest more in rail than we are doing at the moment. The statistics show that, of the investment in road and rail, only a quarter goes to rail. I challenge the Minister to give us a commitment today that he will raise the level of rail investment to at least the same level as that on roads.

When we consider infrastructure, we must also consider the integrated approach. Any new road or rail investment should be subjected to an environmental audit. Cost-benefit analysis and the social implications of investment should also be taken into account for both road and rail investment. We should invoke a major 10-year infrastructure programme which should set priorities for roads and rail. The Government have proposed a scheme for a further 900 miles of road investment. Some of that is necessary. However, as we look towards the year 2000, such investment on the roads should be set against similar criteria for investment in rail.

The Government and the Department of Transport are undoubtedly too road-orientated when it comes to transport investment.

**Mr. John Redwood** (Wokingham): Will the hon. Gentleman give way?

**Mr. Livsey:** No, I will not give way now.

Was the £12 billion road investment announced by the Government approximately three weeks ago compared with the possibility of investing that sum in improvements in rail infrastructure? Was that investment appraisal made?

The provision of an additional 900 miles of roads will mean the loss of 25 acres of land for every mile of motorway. That will mean a massive loss of our countryside in certain parts of the country.

**Mr. Redwood:** Is it right that the original intention of this debate on transport was to encourage stronger links to Europe in the light of the federal manifesto of the Social and Liberal Democratic party, and particularly to strengthen the links between the borders of Scotland and central Italy in the light of the election campaign by the right hon. Member for Tweedale, Ettrick and Lauderdale (Mr. Steel)? Is it true that he is now concentrating on national issues because we saw what happened both to the federal manifesto here in England and to his right hon. Friend in Italy?

**Mr. Livsey:** The hon. Gentleman is correct, and I shall refer to 1992 and to the European Community in the latter part of my speech.

Rail is far too low on the list of priorities in respect of new track, rolling stock and staffing. There is no objection in principle—certainly not from us—to private investment in track and to obtaining private finance for our infrastructure if it cannot be obtained from the Treasury. The wrong investment criteria are being used for British Rail. The one-off, return-on-capital criterion of 7 per cent. needs to be questioned.

**Mr. Peter Snape** (West Bromwich, East): Perhaps it will assist the hon. Gentleman if I mention that that figure has been increased from 7 per cent. to 8 per cent.?

**Mr. Livsey:** About a month ago, I participated in a debate in which I said there was a danger that the figure would increase to 9 per cent. Perhaps that debate served at least to reduce the increased figure by 1 per cent.

The calculation must take into account a cost-benefit analysis, which is done as a matter of course on the continent; France uses cost-benefit analysis for its rail system. All main lines should be electrified, yet by the current investment criteria they cannot show the return demanded by the Treasury. Through services must be provided to the Channel tunnel and to such formidable places as Italy. There must be direct links between all regions and countries.

We are living through an era of immense change——

**Mr. Nicholas Soames** (Crawley): Hear, hear.

**Mr. Livsey:** Just because the hon. Gentleman is green with envy.

The United Kingdom will one day be plugged into Moscow, Istanbul, Madrid and Rome by thousands and thousands of miles of rail. That involves a wholly new dimension and requires fresh thinking. As I said in the previous debate, I should like to see a London rail bypass running alongside the M25——

**Mr. Soames:** So would I!

**Mr. Livsey:** ——so that commuters who are stuck in their cars in the constituency of the hon. Member for Crawley (Mr. Soames) will be frustrated to see high-speed trains overtaking them at twice or three times their speed of progress. That would provide a very worthwhile contrast.

The imposition of high fares to fatten up British Rail for privatisation is deplorable. British Rail fares are already the highest in Europe, and are almost double those of SNCF. Clearly, more freight needs to be moved from road to rail and there is a case to be made for repealing section 42 of the Channel Tunnel Act 1987 to allow public investment in some schemes. The priorities must be new rail links for commuters, main line electrification, and direct links with the Channel tunnel.

There must also be direct links between the major London termini, especially from Paddington to King's Cross and to Waterloo, and better use made of the west London line. Links to the Channel tunnel bypassing London via Gatwick and Heathrow are also needed. Roads should be evaluated on the basis of better criteria, and there should be disincentives for people to use cars in cities. My country of Wales has little transport infrastructure and considerable investment is needed, particularly in the electrification of the north and south Wales railway lines.

In 1992 we shall join a single European market of 270 million people on mainland Europe, and we shall have tremendous problems providing transport to and from the Continent. At present, 50 million passengers and 40 million tonnes of freight travel from Britain to the

[*Mr. Livsey*]

continent each year. We need an integrated transport system, and cheaper and more efficient public transport to attract people away from the roads. We need better pay for railway staff, and an immediate settlement of the current disputes. We must create an awareness of bottlenecks, and we need better promotion of the importance of public transport. We need public and private investment in our infrastructure, and an independent assessment and forecast of traffic growth. The woeful inadequacy of such forecasts in the past is the cause of many of our current problems.

**Mr. David Martin** (Portsmouth, South) *rose——*

**Mr. Livsey:** I will not give way: I am about to finish.

We need more investment in the railways: I challenge the Minister to come up with at least a doubling of current investment. The Government must face up to the transport crisis that confronts us. When, in the near future, people are decanted from the Channel tunnel into London, I believe that an already clogged city will come to a complete standstill.

4.41 pm

**The Minister for Public Transport (Mr. Michael Portillo):** I beg to move, to leave out from "House" to the end of the Question and add instead thereof:

"congratulates the Government on the record levels of capital investment in all forms of transport infrastructure since 1979 while at the same time reducing the burden on the taxpayer; welcomes their plans to increase this investment further over coming years with both public and private money to meet the forecast growth in demand which is the result of the economic success of this country under the Conservative Government; welcomes the Government's success in creating the conditions in which the private sector could both finance and build the Channel Tunnel; congratulates the Government on its determination that the whole of the United Kingdom shall share in its benefits; applauds the high priority that they give to all matters of safety on transport; and welcomes their recognition of the importance of environmental conditions in transport policy."

I congratulate the hon. Member for Brecon and Radnor (Mr. Livsey) on his courage in coming to the House today. It is brave indeed to appear on the day after what was described by his hon. Friend the Member for Inverness, Nairn and Lochaber (Sir R. Johnston) as "a blinking awful result".

I was delighted to learn that today's debate was to be about investment in transport—delighted, but slightly puzzled. It is usual on Opposition days for the Opposition to pick a subject on which they can point to their own strength and find something that is embarrassing to the Government. The subject of transport investment, however, does not fall into that category by any stretch of the imagination.

I do not want to pretend that everything in the transport garden is lovely; it is not. We have plenty of problems to contend with. There is the perennial problem of maintaining and improving safety standards. There is the threat posed to air transport by international terrorism. There is the problem of congestion on Europe's air lanes, on our key motorways and in our city centres. There is the problem of catering for rapidly growing demand for transport while respecting our environment. All those are real problems, and the solutions are not easy.

The level of investment, however, is not a problem. There is no question of investment in any form of transport, public or private, being inadequate.

**Mr. Neale:** Can my hon. Friend confirm that he is astonished—his astonishment is reflected on the Conservative Benches—that, having seen the massive exodus from the Social and Liberal Democrats to the Green party in the elections over the past few days, the hon. Member for Brecon and Radnor (Mr. Livsey) did not once mention environmental considerations? Will he also confirm that, whenever a new scheme is launched, the Government take major steps to ensure that the environment is catered for—in terms of tree cover, for instance?

**Mr. Portillo:** My hon. Friend is absolutely right. I intend to make a number of references to the environment, because it is very much at the forefront of our thinking on transport.

The hon. Member for Brecon and Radnor asked me to say something about investment levels. Let me start by giving some of the bald facts. Since 1979 the Department of Transport has completed 264 road schemes, adding 900 miles to the national network. Last year, our expenditure on motorways and trunk roads totalled more than £1 billion. This year we have a budget of £1·3 billion, which represents a real increase of more than 60 per cent. since 1978-79—in other words, a quantum leap in investment since the hon. Gentleman's party last participated in government at the time of the notorious Lib-Lab pact.

**Mr. Anderson:** The Minister has presented the figures for real investment in roads over the past decade as an increase of 60 per cent. Will he give the comparable figures relating to a real increase in rail investment?

**Mr. Portillo:** I shall come to them in due course, and they will be just as uncomfortable for the hon. Gentleman.

The road investment figures take no account of the further increase in investment foreshadowed in our White Paper "Roads for Prosperity", which has proposed more than doubling the roads programme; nor do they take account of our investment in maintenance—making good the backlog of neglect that we inherited—of local authority investment in local road schemes, or of the growing role of the private sector. It simply is not possible to sustain the argument that road investment is being neglected.

The dramatic increase in road investment has been accompanied by increases in other investment. For example, British Rail has invested £2·5 billion over the past five years, and 31 major schemes have been approved since 1983. It plans to spend more than £3·7 billion over the next five years. It is in the middle of the biggest renewal programme since the transfer from steam to diesel, and investment is at the highest level in real terms since 1962 —well above the levels of the late 1970s.

**Mr. Redwood:** Drawing on his experience of the pressures affecting the choice of the new Kent rail link for the Channel tunnel, can my hon. Friend confirm or deny the Liberal suggestion that planning new railway lines across country or near houses is environmentally easy, whereas planning new roads is environmentally difficult? Has he received any submissions from the Liberal party nominating routes across green fields or near people's houses for new railway lines?

**Mr. Portillo:** My hon. Friend has made a good point. As I listened to the speech of the hon. Member for Brecon and Radnor, it passed through my mind that it would be interesting to look at the manifesto commitments of all the SLD candidates in Kent for the county elections. I suspect that we should find that they are not quite so strongly in favour of new railway lines as they would claim when there is a specific proposal before the country.

**Mr. Simon Hughes** (Southwark and Bermondsey): Before the Minister leaves the subject of relative investment in rail and roads, will he confirm that, although there has been substantial investment in the road network, there has been a real decrease in investment in the rail network since 1979? Why is that, and why will the Government not ensure the investment of a similar amount in the rail network?

**Mr. Portillo:** I have already made it clear that we are now investing more than was invested in the late 1970s. There is an upward trend from year to year, and the amounts already earmarked for the years ahead are higher still. The current level of investment in the railways has not been seen since the early 1960s, and certainly far surpasses any amount invested in the late 1970s.

**Mr. Adley:** My hon. Friend will know that I always take a fair and objective stance on these matters. Can he confirm that the figure that he gave for the proposed level of investment for British Rail, over the next five years—sanctioned by the Government, although British Rail will be spending its own money—is about the same as the figure for West Germany's investment this year?

**Mr. Portillo:** I do not have the figure for West Germany. Perhaps I can address that point when I wind up the debate, as I am not sure that my hon. Friend is correct. Certainly our current investment levels are historically extremely high. I have said that they are the highest since the early 1960s, and, as my hon. Friend will know better than anyone else, the rail network at that time was very much larger than it is today. Even the same amount, spread around a smaller system, would today imply a much higher level of investment.

This year, £300 million is being invested in London Underground, which is double the level under the last year of GLC control. There is also investment in the Channel tunnel. Moreover, there is a host of schemes for light rail transit systems up and down the country, to which I shall refer in due course. I do not see how any of that can be represented as under-investment in our infrastructure.

**Mr. Bowis:** Will my hon. Friend be very wary, though, of the suggestion by the hon. Member for Brecon and Radnor (Mr. Livsey) that the west London line should be used increasingly for Channel tunnel freight? Many people in south London will note that that is SLD policy. They would much rather that the freight that is destined for the north-west and elsewhere should go on the Reading line and bypass London altogether.

**Mr. Portillo:** My hon. Friend will no doubt want to point out to his constituents that that is SLD policy. In due course, the Government will see what proposals British Rail makes for its services direct from the regions to the continent.

There is no under-investment, either, in airports. Heathrow has acquired a fourth terminal. Stansted is being developed as London's third airport. New terminal capacity is being added at Birmingham and Manchester airports. The Civil Aviation Authority has a major investment programme to increase air traffic control capacity. There is no shortage of new investment in our ports. Bus operators have also been investing heavily— witness the rapid growth in the total size of their fleets.

Wherever we look, there is no shortage of investment in transport. It is buoyant. The charge of under-investment today is plain silly. Furthermore, in the hand of the hon. Member for Brecon and Radnor, the charge is a boomerang because we are recovering from years of under-investment when the Liberals and the International Monetary Fund shared power with Labour.

However, it is not just the total level of investment that matters: it is also the way in which the money is spent. Our aim is perfectly simple. We want to do all that we can to accommodate the rapidly growing demand for transport —safely, efficiently and with proper respect for the environment.

**Mr. Richard Holt** (Langbaurgh): Does my hon. Friend not agree that our ports are very badly treated by the Government? Light dues are still imposed on them. None of our continental competitors has to pay light dues. It would be far better if we could compete freely with Europe. We could do so if light dues were abolished.

**Mr. Portillo:** I am sure that we should all welcome free competition, but it is a moot point whether we should ask taxpayers to bear charges that really ought to fall on those who make use of the services or whether we should try to persuade our continental partners to come into line with us. I am sure that my hon. Friend welcomes the greatest gift that the Government have given to our ports industry —the abolition of the national dock labour scheme. That will help our ports industry to be competitive.

There are other approaches to transport policy. The Green party, for example, clearly takes the view that environmental considerations must lead us to a shrinking economy, with less for everyone, rather than an expanding economy. The car, the lorry and the plane must go and Britain must become dependent on transport by rail and inland waterway. Even judged on its own terms, the Green party's policy is not very sensible. Anyone who imagines that the construction of a new railway line can be achieved with zero impact on the environment should speak to my hon. Friend the Member for Wokingham (Mr. Redwood) or to any of my hon. Friends with constituencies in Kent. They will quickly put him right about that.

To forgo investment in new infrastructure, with resulting increased congestion, is not an environmentally sensible policy. On our roads, slow-moving, stop-start traffic generates more pollution than free-flowing traffic. If we asked those who suffer from traffic jams day and night outside their homes whether we should close our minds to relieving their plight by building new roads, of course they would say that we should not do so. As I have trespassed into this area, perhaps I should say that the recent European Community decision on vehicle emissions shows that we are determined to reduce the damage to ourselves from vehicle fumes.

It is against that background that I intend to give some practical examples of investment in transport and to explain how they have helped to improve the quality of life. We have targeted expenditure on road schemes that

[*Mr. Portillo*]

bring the maximum benefit to both road users and the local community. In particular, we have concentrated on plugging gaps in the existing motorway network and on schemes to take traffic around built-up areas. These range in scale from short stretches of bypass around small towns and villages to major orbital motorways round London and Manchester. Across the board, every £1 that we spend on roads now yields £2 in measurable benefits to road users and the local community. That has to be a good investment, judged by any standards.

One element in the tally of benefits is the improved safety of new roads. In the recent report on road safety in the European Community, the Belgian Institute for Road Safety cited the high quality of Britain's roads as one reason why we have the best safety record of the 12 member states.

**Mr. Livsey:** If the Minister can quantify the benefits of investment in roads, surely he should be able to do the same for investment in railways and say what the pound-for-pound benefit would be if the rail system were improved.

**Mr. Portillo:** I partly blame myself for this. Over a period, the hon. Gentleman has consistently misunderstood our investment criteria for the railways. I intended to allude to that matter later in my speech. He believes that we apply a commercial rate of return to all investment decisions relating to the railways. That is absolutely untrue. We do not apply a criterion of that sort to investment in the non-profit making and non-commercial sectors, such as the provincial sector. There we are concerned with cost-benefit analysis and with what investment will yield the best results in terms of keeping the railways functional.

We never consider the possibility of closing the railways down. When we assess investment in provincial railways, we give a benefit over and above what we give to roads. Roads have to pass the cost-benefit test, whereas we assume that the provincial railway service will continue. We are simply trying to find a means by which renewal can be achieved most efficiently. In that respect, the railways have a considerable advantage over road schemes.

**Mr. Snape:** I congratulate the Minister on the artful nature of his reply, which covers only a very small proportion of the railway network. Is he unable to tell us whether British Rail has to justify investing its own money in InterCity and freight transport? The hon. Member for Brecon and Radnor (Mr. Livsey) was suggesting that a very different picture would emerge if the same criteria that are applied to roads were to be applied to those two parts of the railways industry.

**Mr. Portillo:** Those sections of the railways that are commercial—including rail freight and InterCity—have to meet, for their new investment, a rate of return criterion, but the hon. Gentleman will recall that I have just said that for every £1 that we spend on roads we get a £2 yield. He will recognise that that is a different order of magnitude from the rates of return that I am talking about on the railways. There is no shortage of road schemes that would qualify, using the cost-benefit basis.

**Mr. Snape:** The £2 benefit for £1 expenditure includes the saving of motorists' time—which is regarded as more important than the saving of time for those who travel on public transport—and also a calculation of the number of road deaths that have been saved as a result of constructing new roads. The problem with the railways is that they do not kill enough passengers to justify expenditure on the same basis as roads.

**Mr. Portillo:** The hon. Gentleman refuses to recognise that roads and railways are different and that they have to be assessed on different bases. However, we try to make the basis of assessment as similar as we possibly can. I believe that we have achieved our aim. The hon. Gentleman's tasteless remark about deaths on railways and roads does not help us forward with that argument.

**Mr. Richard Shepherd** (Aldridge-Brownhills): I am interested in my hon. Friend's argument about orbital or circular routes. Why, after six years, has the Secretary of State thrown into the air the Birmingham north orbital route? Ten million pounds have been spent on engineering investigations and a public inquiry, the report of which has been delayed. Its planning has taken six years. Why has there been this delay when the benefits to be derived from additional roads have been spelt out? When will the Birmingham north orbital route be completed? This is also a cause of concern to the hon. Member for West Bromwich, East (Mr. Snape).

**Mr. Portillo:** I am not convinced that there will be a delay. If there is, I hope that the delay will not be long. The time and effort that have been invested in planning the route will not be wasted. The Birmingham northern relief road, as proposed by the private sector, might easily follow the same route as the one that was proposed at the public inquiry. Although we have received the inspector's report, there is normally a considerable delay before the Department is able to respond to a report. I hope that we can now establish a timetable for the competition for that private sector road to minimise delay and to minimise any nugatory expenditure.

**Mr. Adley:** My hon. Friend is very generous to allow me to intervene again. He takes great trouble to answer questions and the fact that he is taking so many interventions means that we can have a discussion with him on these important matters.

I should like to echo the question asked by the hon. Member for West Bromwich, East (Mr. Snape): why are road and rail assessed in different ways? Can my hon. Friend justify one piece of information that his Department has given me? As he knows, I have pursued the criteria employed by his Department in assessing the costs and benefits of road schemes. I was informed that 7 per cent. of the cost of a traffic warden is assessed as allowable to the cost of building and running our road schemes. Where on earth does the other 93 per cent. go? If a traffic warden is not 100 per cent. costed to the roads, how on earth is the other 93 per cent. costed?

**Mr. Portillo:** My hon. Friend is very generous in his opening remarks. As far as possible, we try to make the criteria equivalent between road and rail. It is not possible to make them 100 per cent. equal because they are different. I do not know the answer to his other question, but I shall write to him about the 7 per cent. and the 93 per cent. of the traffic warden. However, I very much doubt that the costing of a traffic warden is the critical factor in most investment decisions. I had better make progress if I am not to take up too much of the time of the House.

Let me give an example of the way in which road investment can be beneficial. Last summer, we completed the Blackwater, Okehampton and Saltash bypasses, and there are plenty of further improvements to the three trunk roads into Cornwall—the A30, the A38 and the A39. That improvement in road communications is vital for the Cornish economy. That would be appreciated by the hon. Member for Truro (Mr. Taylor) if he were in the Chamber. It has also benefited local communities by taking traffic from town centres—making them cleaner, quieter and safer places in which to live, work and shop. In the case of the controversial Okehampton bypass, for instance, the 1,200 trees which had to be felled to make way for the road are being replaced by 100,000 trees—all of them indigenous species—which will restore the valley to its original splendour, making good the damage done over generations.

There is no doubt in my mind that we must invest in road and rail. There are few cases where one is a direct substitute for the other. It is simply not right for Opposition Members to pretend that there is a realistic prospect of relying on rail transport for the movement of goods and passengers, when over 90 per cent. of passenger transport and 60 per cent. of freight transport is currently carried by road. If we were to assume that, overnight, by some miracle the traffic on our railways doubled, that would remove less than 10 per cent. of traffic from our roads. Given that road traffic increased by 6 per cent. over the past 12 months, it would not take long for that additional road capacity to be used up.

**Mr. Simon Hughes:** Can the Minister give the House his Department's projections for the maximum capacity of the rail network in terms of its percentage of passenger traffic? He said that it is 10 per cent. at the moment and I accept that. What could it be if more investment were made?

**Mr. Portillo:** I suppose that that would depend on what investments were made. Many railway lines are currently very close to capacity, as the hon. Gentleman will know, but, particularly if freight trains were to operate around the clock, there is clearly scope for substantial increases in the amount of freight. Those opportunities will be opened up by the Channel tunnel, and if that comes about it will be interesting to note the attitude of the hon. Gentleman's party.

Congestion in central London is a key target. It has come about because of an unprecedented reversal in the long term declining trend of commuting to London. The economy in our capital has prospered and London has proved to be still one of the most magnetic cities for international business. Curing congestion is expensive, takes a long time and is disruptive. But the Government have not hesitated to set the necessary work in hand. On London's Underground, major station improvements are under way, many more are planned and the Central line is to be upgraded at a cost of more than £700 million. The central London rail study has recommended further renewals to the present system which would cost about £1·5 billion, and new lines running from east to west and north to south. Consultation with affected interests on the east-west crossrail have begun so that a Bill could be presented to Parliament in November.

Another welcome symptom of the attractiveness of London to world business is the development of docklands. Its phenomenal expansion qualifies it to be regarded as a city in its own right. It must have the transport links that such a city merits and we are determined to ensure that it is readily accessible by road and rail and by air and water.

A committee which I chair now co-ordinates the work of the London Docklands development corporation, the London boroughs, the developers, contractors, statutory undertakings, and representatives of local business. We work together with a single purpose to provide the new infrastructure while minimising disruption to traffic, to business or to local communities. Our efforts are presently focused on three objectives: to maintain progress on the Limehouse link and other vital road projects; to improve and to expand the docklands light railway and to see a new Underground line built to docklands and east London.

The east London rail study is in its final stages and we are expecting the consultants' final report shortly. They will be recommending as the best option for improving rail access from central London to docklands an extension of the Jubilee line via London bridge and the Isle of Dogs and ultimately to Stratford. In central London, the study has established that two alternative routes are technically feasible: an extension of the Jubilee line via Westminster and Waterloo, or a continuation of the existing line from Charing Cross via Ludgate Circus.

The Government will be considering that report, and further work will be required before decisions can be taken. Approval of the new line and decisions on its alignment and phasing will depend on how it would be financed and in particular on the negotiation of satisfactory contributions from the developers who stand to benefit. Subject to those considerations, the Government would wish to see a Bill for a new line deposited in November. To facilitate preparation of a Bill, I can announce today that London Regional Transport will, without prejudice to final decisions, begin consultations immediately with local authorities and others directly affected by the alignments being examined.

In case I should be accused of any bias as a London Member, let me add that there are many other city projects up and down the country. The plans for Manchester Metrolink are well advanced. On Friday evening, in the west midlands, I heard more of how the passenger transport executive there is working hard on its proposals for a light rail network centred on Birmingham and the black country. It hopes to obtain powers soon to permit construction of the first line between Snow Hill and Wolverhampton, and I am sure that it will not be long before it is knocking on my door with a proposal for grant towards the new system.

**Mr. Snape:** I am anxious that my colleagues from Birmingham should not embark on yet another wasted journey by being turned away by the Minister when they knock on his door. As he has just changed the rules for urban transport, to get the go-ahead for the Midlands Metro it will be necessary to prove its benefit to non-users of the system, which is directly contradictory to the system that appertained until a few weeks ago. Will the Minister assure the House and those who are responsible for planning the Metro that that last-minute change in the rules will not unduly delay that worthwhile project which has been sought for so long?

**Mr. Portillo:** I cannot make any comment on a scheme that I have not yet received.

**Mr. Snape:** What about the rules?

**Mr. Portillo:** This afternoon, I was able to announce to the House that we have taken a further step forward on the south Yorkshire super-tram project, where the aim is to get the new system in place in time for the world student games in 1991. I have decided to make a 50 per cent. grant available now, so that the evaluation of this project can be completed as quickly as possible. If the evaluation confirms the PTEs' initial calculations, and if the financing and other issues are satisfactorily resolved, I see every hope that this project will benefit from our financial assistance. As many hon. Members will be well aware, there are many other light rail projects in the pipeline.

**Mr. Snape:** Is that the plan?

**Mr. Portillo:** The hon. Gentleman will be able to read in *Hansard* what I have said. I said that there will be a 50 per cent. grant for the feasibility study and that I see every hope that the project will benefit from our financial assistance.

I now turn to rail freight. The key factor is the Channel tunnel. British Rail's Railfreight business has already substantially improved its performance, of course, but the tunnel is the new factor in the freight transport equation which is causing customers to look again at the rail option.

Last Friday, my right hon. Friend was in Cleveland to open a new Railfreight depot—a joint venture between British Rail and ICI. From that depot, the tunnel should allow British Rail to offer a direct freight service to destinations such as Paris and Brussels, taking less than 24 hours. A direct rail service like that, straight to the heart of the European Community, will be an enormous boost to business throughout Britain. So let me, yet again, stress that there is no question of the tunnel being a perk for the south-east, with businesses elsewhere ignored. British Rail estimates that 75 per cent. of the freight carried through the tunnel will originate from points beyond London. As far as freight through the Channel tunnel is concerned, the regions are not the tail but the dog, and the dog will wag the tail.

British Rail is now engaged in detailed consultation on the direct services that it will offer. The British Rail freight network will stand comparison with the best in Europe, and I have no doubt that British Rail will be able to deliver the service that its customers demand. It will publish its plans at the end of the year, as required by law, and I regard that timing as absolutely right.

The area where there is a clear case for a new line is in Kent, where a high-speed rail link will be needed at some stage to ensure that Britain makes the best possible use of our access to the European railway network. That line will be for passenger traffic, but it will, of course, free capacity on other lines to handle freight. The House will have an opportunity to consider the case for this line and British Rail's detailed proposals in due course. I have no wish to pre-empt that debate, but I think that, even now, it is clear that British Rail's proposals show a willingness to spend hundreds of millions of pounds on protecting the environment—vastly more than is being committed on the other side of the Channel.

Nor is British Rail neglecting what may appear to be the less glamorous but important provincial sector. As I said, the SLD sometimes misunderstands the investment criteria that apply. We certainly do not apply the commercial-rate-of-return rule to investments needed to maintain a subsidised service. As a result, the proof of the pudding being in the eating, it is planned that, by 1991, 82 per cent. of provincial rolling stock will have been renewed over an eight-year period. All the moneys that I have talked about are over and above what our two railways are spending on safety.

Over a three-year period, London Underground is spending £226 million on safety matters arising from the Fennell report. British Rail has been considering the installation of automatic train protection for some time. Unfortunately, we cannot buy such a system off the peg, but the Government have approved the installation of pilot schemes. If they are successful, the Government will give sympathetic consideration to a national scheme, if a satisfactory scheme emerges.

Before I leave the subject of railways, let me confirm that the Government are examining how and whether to privatise British Rail, sensibly recognising that decisions on how and whether must be taken together. Our consultant's analysis is progressing well, but that work is not yet at a sufficiently advanced stage for us to reject any options now. All five options set out in speeches made by my right hon. Friend the Secretary of State remain on the table.

It pains me to say that there is a fundamental dishonesty underlying the policy of the SLD. This motion refers to under-investment today and calls for greater investment tomorrow, yet, as every one of my hon. Friends knows, so often, when any specific road or rail scheme is proposed, the local Liberal or SLD candidate is against it and allies himself with any protest group determined to stop the development. If there are roads, railways or runways unbuilt today that are needed, the SLD is probably much to blame.

In transport today, there are clear issues. One is whether we follow policies for economic growth, without which heavy public sector investment is impossible. The second is whether, by relying on ever greater subsidies, we pauperise our transport operators, or whether we encourage them to operate more commercially, to attract passengers and so to generate the revenue for new investment. Between those two clear policy approaches, the SLD vacillates and prevaricates. It is now reaping its just rewards at the polls.

5.13 pm

**Mr. Peter Snape** (West Bromwich, East): The concluding paragraph of the Minister's speech, with its ringing phraseology, was about seven days too late. His speech was obviously written with the European elections in mind. It ended with a ringing plea for support at the polling stations. Regrettably, his speech was no more successful a week later than it would have been last Thursday. I must tell the hon. Gentleman that the election is over. For all the resounding phrases that we heard, on Thursday evening the electors in this country gave a thumbs down with a vengeance to the Government and, sadly, to some of those who are responsible for the motion.

I do not want to intrude on the private grief of the SLD. I do not want to be accused either of promoting or attacking the future career and prospects of the the hon. Member for Brecon and Radnor (Mr. Livsey), but, looking at the motion, I find a lot more relevance coming from the SLD or the alliance, or whatever they call themselves in the wake of Thursday evening's drubbing, than in the amendment tabled by the other losers of the election on Thursday night, Her Majesty's Government. If there are two words that sum up our transport industries after a decade of Thatcherism, they are "chaos" and "congestion". They apply to road, rail and air and, to a certain extent, other problems. Regrettably there is not congestion, but there is certainly plenty of chaos in our merchant shipping fleet.

The air of smug self-congratulation with which the Minister surrounded himself was somewhat unreal. He made great play of what he called the Government's progress in transport over the past decade. He trotted out the usual, largely false, statistics about justification for road building compared with public transport. Opposition Members and, to be fair, one or two more knowledgable Conservative Members will continue to press for fairness in the evaluation of public transport schemes. Not for the first time, we pray in aid the conclusions of the Leitch committee back in 1977, which asked that such schemes be treated in a comparable fashion. It pointed out that there was no real reason why public transport investment should not be treated in exactly the same way as investment in our road network. Nothing that I have heard this afternoon or previously from the Minister shakes my belief that the Leitch committee was right 12 years ago, and it is right now.

The Minister may have felt that my remark about the number of deaths within the railway industry being considerably less than those on our roads was tasteless. That was the word he used. It is a fact, anyway, and it is also a fact that, when putting forward financial justifications for road schemes, the Department of Transport justifiably and understandably points to the reductions that can be made in the number of deaths and serious injuries. Of course it is impossible to put forward similar savings for the rail network. Thankfully, with a few tragic exceptions, some of which have taken place in recent months, travelling by train in this country is probably the safest mode of transport in the world. Therefore, it is impossible to quantify the number of lives that will be saved by increasing the frequency, reliability or number of services of that mode of transport.

British Rail should be given at least a notional financial benefit for its success in carrying passengers millions of miles a year in perfect safety. Without such a notional monetary advance being made to BR, dependence on the newly revised investment rules—the 8 per cent. return on capital—means that all too often British Rail does not put schemes forward. Of course, Ministers—not just this one—and their colleagues in the Department say to the House time and again that there are no investment proposals before them. The Minister's predecessor often said that, under this Government, investment proposals were dealt with and agreed faster than under any previous Government.

We all know that talks take place between the Minister's officials and British Rail's investment committee. It would be a strange world in which British Rail put forward schemes that did not meet the previously laid down criteria of Her Majesty's Government. Life is not like that. If investment schemes were continually put forward and rejected by the Department of Transport because they did not meet those investment criteria, one

could well imagine, at the start, a few irritated telephone calls between the Department of Transport and British Rail headquarters. Following that, there might be a strongly worded missive saying that something was amiss and that the schemes were being put forward without meeting the laid-down investment criteria. Finally, one can imagine an ascerbic telephone call with the demand that someone be fired for being silly enough to put forward such schemes in the first place when the Minister was unable to accept them because they failed to meet the criteria. We all know, accept and acknowledge that. That is how things work in the modern world.

The reality is that many of the more marginal schemes —those that approach the laid-down investment criteria —are not put forward because of British Rail's misgivings that a way will be found to reject them and that if they are rejected odium will somehow fall on those who put them forward. That is amply illustrated by the experience, if I may again be parochial, of my own part of the world and of the Birmingham cross-city railway line. It does not run through my constituency, but it covers the west midlands from Redditch to Lichfield. We have been hearing and have read in regional newspapers for the past two years, that the go-ahead for the electrification of the line is anticipated at any moment. Much of the line, such as the central core around Birmingham New street station, is already electrified. In a written answer only last week the Department told me that no such scheme had been formally presented to it. When asked what discussions had taken place about the scheme, the reply was—it has appeared in *Hansard* and I am paraphrasing it to save time —that unofficial discussions had taken place twice but that the scheme had yet to be formally submitted.

Those unofficial discussions will presumably take place for as long as the Department likes and while they are taking place the Department will repeat its parrot cry, "No formal investment scheme has been submitted." Like many people in the Birmingham area who are concerned about the scheme, I find such conduct unacceptable. I am sure that that example could be repeated for other schemes across the country. It illustrates the difference between two years of unofficial consultation about a railway electrification scheme that is relatively minor in the financial sense but which is significant to us in the west midlands, and the out-of-the-blue £10 billion White Paper "Roads for Prosperity"—its title is a misnomer to many of us—that was produced from under the Secretary of State's desk, a few days ago, much to the surprise of many of us, and probably to him as well.

**Mr. Adley:** Will the hon. Gentleman ask the Minister to comment on the policy of "bustitution", that revolting word? Will he ask the Minister to deny that British Rail has been asked to find 20 or 30 routes where it might be possible to close railways and to replace them with buses? Will he also ask the Minister to deny that, while that is going on, no investment is being put into the lines by British Rail, which means that those lines are becoming less attractive as the weeks go by?

**Mr. Snape:** I would, if I thought that I could ask questions as perceptive as those of the hon. Gentleman. He has asked a relevant and valid series of questions that I am delighted to pass on. We can all guess the reply—that the Government have no intention of demanding that certain lines be put forward for what is meant by that dreadful

[*Mr. Snape*]

word "bustitution". Of course, there is no such intention because what will happen is that the same unofficial talks that have taken place about cross-city electrification will take place about certain railway lines. Across a desk, or perhaps even over a good lunch at L'amico restaurant down the road or at somewhere expensive—certainly not in a Traveller's Fare restaurant in a provincial station—some highly placed person in the Department of Transport will say to someone from British Rail, "Look here, old chap, what about bustitution?" They will order a round of brandies and once the PR man has got over that, he will be told that although the Minister does not want to say anything formally, "We in the Department feel that there is scope for just that sort of thing for some of the less well used routes."

As the hon. Member for Christchurch (Mr. Adley) has just said, while those unofficial discussions and that series of lunches are taking place—costing the taxpayer a great deal of money—there will be no investment of any sort in that line. Indeed, the position might even be worse. Other lines might well see a repeat of the Settle-Carlisle line experience. Although British Rail and the Department will say that no such discussions are taking place, minor adjustments will be made to the timetable to ensure that connections are missed here and there. Early morning trains will be withdrawn because "They're not particularly remunerative, you know" and in no time at all, over yet another lunch, perhaps at Lockets on this occasion if the two participants have become bored with the menu at other restaurants, it will be suggested that the lines are so unprofitable that bustitution may be the only answer because it is not possible to run an economic service on the existing railway line.

**Mr. Peter Fry** (Wellingborough): I am following the hon. Gentleman's argument carefully. As I understand it, like the proposer of the motion, the hon. Member for Brecon and Radnor (Mr. Livsey), he is in favour of an integrated transport system, which would seem to imply that investment should be made where it will have the greatest return. If that is the case, does it not make sense to invest in British Rail routes with more passengers instead of concentrating on routes with few passengers?

**Mr. Snape:** The hon. Gentleman seems really pleased with himself. He has sat back with a wonderfully smug look on his face as if saying mentally, "That has put one over the Opposition."

To a certain extent, the hon. Gentleman is right. The problem about defining the right place for investment is that, like the hon. Gentleman, with whom I have crossed swords on these matters for a good many years, the Government believe that the only place to put money is where the 8 per cent. return is readily achievable. The Opposition believe that investment in public transport, especially in a railway network, brings environmental and energy-saving benefits, as well as the not readily quantifiable benefit of not killing on the roads the number of people that we kill at present. The problem with the hon. Gentleman is that he is obsessed with the contents of his and the Government's wallets rather than with the environmental realities of public transport, which are enormously beneficial in terms of these other not readily quantifiable matters.

**Mr. Anderson:** Does my hon. Friend remember the unhappy precedent of this symbiotic relationship between the Department of Transport and British Rail? When the Department of Transport said that it would like InterCity to break even within five years, British Rail rolled over like a lapdog and said, "No, we can do it in three."

**Mr. Snape:** British Rail's likeness to a lapdog has been referred to in the House many times before, but my hon. Friend is quite right. It is a matter of pride for the InterCity management that it is now running a profitable railway. To an extent, the management of that sector of the railways known as provincial services feel an understandable pride that they are not losing as much money as they used to and that they are expanding some provincial services in a way that I, and I think the House, regard as entirely creditable.

**Mr. Alan Amos** (Hexham): Hear, hear.

**Mr. Snape:** The hon. Gentleman says, "Hear, hear," but the problem with that success is that railwaymen and women want to share in it. They know that the number of passenger journeys is increasing——

**Mr. Portillo:** Privatise.

**Mr. Snape:** The Minister says, "Let us privatise." That is a parrot cry. We have not got round to that yet. His advisers have not yet done their sums. Railwaymen and women must pay today's bills with yesterday's money, without tomorrow's promises coming to reality. Their problem is that they are continually being told how successful the railway network is. It is much more profitable now than it used to be. Then those railwaymen and women say, "We work considerably longer hours than most people." They work considerably longer hours than most people in the House.

**Mr. Amos:** That is not true.

**Mr. Snape:** The hon. Gentleman says that that is not true. I do not know the hon. Gentleman particularly well, but he should be careful. If he clocks up some of the hours that I know are clocked up by signalmen and drivers, he is working far too hard and should go and have a lie down.

Railwaymen and women say, "If we are doing so well, surely we should be allowed to share in the prosperity." Instead, they have been told, "You are taking the 7 per cent." They have been told not to take it or leave it, but that it will be put in their pay packets regardless of the view of their negotiators. They have been told that, before any industrial action, there must be a ballot. They have held a ballot, and a majority—not a massive one, but one larger than that enjoyed by many hon. Members in the popular vote—voted for some sort of industrial action. During supposed last-ditch talks at ACAS only last Saturday, they were told by the same management, which has been boasting of its economic success on running the railway industry, that it would apply for a court injunction to prevent any industrial action next Wednesday.

**Mr. Adley:** Would it help if the hon. Gentleman mentioned his interest?

**Mr. Snape:** If it is necessary, my declaration of interest has been in the Register of Members' Interests since I was elected to the House. I do not think that it is necessary for me to say when I am at the Dispatch Box that I am a member of the National Union of Railwaymen. At this

Box I speak not for the National Union of Railwaymen but for the Labour party—[*Interruption.*] No, it is not the same thing. Conservative Members constantly and deliberately misinterpret the relationship between the Opposition and the trade union movement.

I believe that most fair-minded people would think that those who have delivered in terms of economic performance on the railways deserve a better reward than that offered them at present. The feeling among those who work in the railway industry is one of widespread dissatisfaction with the way they are being treated.

If I might have the attention of the Minister for a moment, I should like to put to him a number of points about the railways. I make no apology for asking him to explain to us once again the reason for the differences in the criteria that he uses to judge the merits of road and rail schemes. Although he attempted partially to answer that point earlier, I ask him to reconsider the recommendations of the Leitch committee in 1977 and, in some subsequent debate, to give us detailed answers as to why the Government have not implemented those recommendations. Before he says that the Labour Government did not either, I should tell him that I asked them to do so at the time. Of course, then the transport team was led by those well-known raving moderates, Messrs. Bill Rodgers and John Horam, who, of course were most highly regarded by the popular press. One of those has since found his rightful home in the Conservative party, by way of the Social Democratic party, and the other has left politics altogether —which is a tragic loss, I must say. I did my best at that time to convince them that the recommendations should be accepted, although they were not.

Will the Minister look again at the cross-city electrification scheme in Birmingham and tell us if and when a decision is likely to be forthcoming? Perhaps he can jog the elbows of those responsible in his Department for the unofficial talks that are taking place about that scheme.

The Minister said a few welcome words about the Channel tunnel and how much the Government wanted to see the benefits of that scheme spread throughout the country. I understand that an investment submission is being prepared for a number of passenger trains to be used in connection with cross-Channel services, which must carry some, if not substantial, accommodation for customs and immigration, depending on agreement finally and belatedly being reached about such matters being dealt with on the trains.

Will there be any leeway in the 8 per cent. investment criterion for those trains, because much will depend, at least initially, on the total number of through services that will be run from the Channel tunnel to provincial cities, such as Birmingham, Newcastle, Manchester and into Scotland? Obviously, if that 8 per cent. criterion is to be adhered to rigidly, there will be a reduced number of train sets, because they are obviously sets that cannot be used for any other purpose. Presumably, the fact that they can be used only for that purpose may weigh against them in terms of investment criteria.

We welcome the fact that the Minister has pointed out the contribution that the Channel tunnel can make, not to transferring existing freight from road to rail—regrettably, at present, there is not much rail freight—but to mopping up some of the projected increase, at least in the next few years, and perhaps making deeper inroads into reducing the number of juggernaut lorries cluttering up the roads in the south of England.

The Minister will be aware of the falling number of section 8 grants in recent years. Will he look again at the criteria for section 8 grants, especially those referring to lorry-sensitive miles? As I understand the system, if it is possible to show that a number of lorries can be taken away from unsuitable roads—however unsuitable roads are defined—obviously it becomes easier for the applicant to receive a contribution towards the provision of private rail sidings. The problem is that the more motorways and dual carriageways we build and the more road improvements we carry out, the fewer lorry-sensitive route miles there will be. I should have thought that, given the problems of congestion, for example, on the M25 and on some of our other motorways, anything that helps to reduce the number of lorries on those motorways— although I accept the fact that that is why motorways were built in the first place—would be welcome.

Will the Minister assure us that he will at least look at the rules on section 8 grants to see whether they can be widened, so that the graph of grants for section 8 private sidings starts to turn up again instead of falling away as dramatically as it has in the past few years?

If we confine our interest to reading the newspapers, we would think that all our roads and motorways are absolutely choked and that the forecasts about road traffic are invariably understated. Of course, in some cases, they are. No one needs reminding of the congestion on the M25. There are those of us, however, in the Opposition who believe that there are better ways of alleviating congestion than spending £10 billion on new motorways or widening existing ones. A transport package would be much more beneficial than the usual behaviour of the Department of Transport, which appears to act more as a Ministry of Transport than as a Department.

Does the Minister agree that many roads are being built on the basis of traffic forecasts that have been greatly overpitched? For many hours of the day and night it is possible to picnic in comparative safety on the outside lane of the M45 from the M1 to Coventry because there is little traffic. The M18 is another road that was built to motorway standard but, for much of the day and night, appears to be under-utilisied. It was built on the basis of projections that have not yet come to fruition and, in the opinion of many, never will.

**Mr. Portillo:** Does the hon. Gentleman think that the case for the Humber bridge was overpitched?

**Mr. Snape:** Of course it was, but for a good reason——

**Mr. Adley:** By-elections.

**Mr. Snape:** Of course. If the Conservative party is trying to tell us that at no time has it produced figures to back up a political necessity, I do not believe it. The Conservative party should reconsider the problems caused by congestion and tolls. I hope that, now that the Minister has made his political pitch, he will agree that the projections that were made to justify building those roads have frequently not come to fruition.

There is a twin problem because, by its nature, traffic forecasting is an inexact science. I ask the Minister about the saga of the M40 from Oxford to Birmingham. In the mid-1970s, under the two moderates to whom I have referred, the Department of Transport decided that no motorway was necessary between those two cities. The Department talked, justifiably, about the need to improve

[*Mr. Snape*]

the existing trunk roads, the A34 and the A41, and to bypass towns and cities such as Banbury and Warwick. The Department costed the exercise and said that it would do all that was necessary to cater for traffic growth in the foreseeable future.

By the early 1980s, it had been decided that that was all a mistake and that a motorway was needed. Because of the traffic projections, it was decided that a two-lane motorway was needed for much of the road's length. It was then decided that the projections were wrong and that a three-lane motorway was necessary. In a decade we have gone from no motorway to a three-lane motorway.

Earlier this year, a public inquiry was set up to consider the possibility of setting up a service area on that road. The inquiry sat for some months, and these things do not come cheap. Recently, the inquiry was adjourned because someone in the Department of Transport decided that the traffic projections were 42 per cent. too low.

This is a saga worthy of the late Mr. Peter Sellers. How does the Department justify such wide fluctuations of opinion between no motorway and a three-lane motorway, the traffic forecasts for which will be exceeded by 42 per cent. by the early 1990s? What kind of computer is used to produce such fluctuating forecasts?

**Mr. Adley:** A Peter Snow swingometer.

**Mr. Snape:** As the hon. Gentleman says, a fairly slow Peter Snow swingometer—with a vengeance. The Minister will forgive me if I sound somewhat cynical about some of the projections from his Department, given the saga, as yet incomplete, of the M40. Is the public inquiry to be resumed later this year? Will the hon. Gentleman give us accurate projections on road traffic between Oxford and Birmingham?

Little mention has been made so far of congestion in the air, or on the ground for those waiting to take to the air. The experiences of last summer and the likely experiences of this summer are no cause for the Government to congratulate themselves. I do not suggest that it is all their fault, but some of it certainly is. Patting themselves on the back when would-be travellers spend hours at airports is no way to impress either the House or the electorate. We need greater investment in our air traffic control facilities and greater involvement in Euro-control. It is a pity that it takes at least one and probably two summers of discontent for air travellers before the myth of sovereignty of the air is dissipated. Euro-control is largely nominal. In addition, there are 42 centres and 22 different control systems in Europe. This makes no sense, and certainly will not make any sense this summer, for those who are sitting in extremely overcrowded airports.

**Mr. Michael Colvin** (Romsey and Waterside): The hon. Gentleman and I have taken an interest in this matter and, in fact, visited Gatwick together to discuss air traffic control, among other matters. He should be gracious enough to acknowledge that the Government have taken the lead during their presidency to persuade the EEC to broaden the scope of Euro-control. There is a good reason for that—the United Kingdom has more to gain from the liberalisation of air services in Europe and the streamlining of air traffic control than any other country, because we have about 20 airlines that provide international services. We are taking the lead in Europe.

I should like the Government to speed up their programme of investment. Expenditure of £600 million in air traffic control sounds like a lot of money, but it is peanuts compared with investment in roads and rail. Failure to make that investment will result in Charles de Gaulle airport becoming a main European hub from which one can travel to London in about two and a half hours. To preserve our lead in civil aviation, we must do more to improve the capacity of our airports in the south-east.

**Mr. Peter Fry** (Wellingborough): On a point of order, Madam Deputy Speaker. Three speeches have been made in an hour and a half and, with the greatest respect to my hon. Friend the Member for Romsey and Waterside (Mr. Colvin), we have had virtually a miniature speech from him. Some of us have been waiting to make our contribution. There is little time for Back Benchers to speak in the debate, so I ask for your protection.

**Madam Deputy Speaker (Miss Betty Boothroyd):** I think that the hon. Member is asking me to make an appeal for shorter speeches so that as many hon. Members as possible can contribute. I gladly accede to that request.

**Mr. Snape:** I gladly accede to it, too. I apologise if we have all been deprived of the doubtless wise words of the hon. Member for Wellingborough (Mr. Fry). Perhaps I allowed myself to be led astray by the number of interventions during my speech.

I agree with much of what the hon. Member for Romsey and Waterside (Mr. Colvin) said. I wish that we could get away from the idea that we have to take the lead over the rest of Europe. That justifiably irritates people. The thought of the Prime Minister appearing through the door of any conference centre brandishing her handbag and threatening to take the lead would be an instant turn-off in many EEC countries. I hope that the hon. Gentleman agrees that, whoever takes the lead, the present system is unacceptable. As he rightly said, £600 million sounds like a great deal of money, but it is peanuts compared with the amount required to do something about the ever-mounting delays and congestion in European air travel.

Bearing in mind your strictures, Madam Deputy Speaker, I shall not produce the statistics to refute some of the Minister's boasts about the level of investment in railways since the Government took office in 1979. It is true that investment for the current year is fairly high, as it was last year, but the early years of the present Administration mark some of the lowest levels of investment within the railway industry for 20 years or so. If one takes the global figure, the public service obligation and investment, the Government are still a long way behind their predecessors. Current expenditure is a fraction of that spent on the railway network throughout Europe. In relation to the more developed countries of the EC, we are eighth out of eight in terms of the proportion of GDP which is spent on railways, which is no cause for self-congratulation.

Our transport system suffers from chaos and congestion, and the sooner the Government lose their air of smug self-satisfaction, which has been typified by the Minister, and the sooner they acknowledge that a deep-rooted problem exists which only money can solve, the better.

5.51 pm

**Mr. Peter Fry** (Wellingborough): I am most grateful, and I only hope that the hon. Member for West Bromwich, East (Mr. Snape) will regard my comments as words of wisdom. I always enjoy listening to his contributions. He is always worth listening to and bullish. I understand why he is so cheerful today. If I were a member of the Labour party and had had his majority at the last two elections, I should be happier than usual today.

The debate has developed in a disappointing way. The hon. Member for Brecon and Radnor (Mr. Livsey) began by giving a blinkered view. One would always think that the only mode of transport worth considering was railway. The debate so far has centred on road investment versus rail investment, but the argument should be opened up.

I came to the House as a member of what was loosely called the road lobby, but I consider myself as good a friend of British Rail as of the British Road Federation, because I have come to the well-thought-out conclusion that as the pressure on transport in this country is increasing, and has been increasing for a number of years, it is pointless to have futile arguments about whether we should invest more in road than rail or more in rail than road when we all realise that, particularly in large urban areas, all modes of transport have a contribution to make if we are to ease the pressure on our cities and means of communication. There is little doubt that today's problem will become considerably worse before it gets better, despite the record levels of investment listed by my hon. Friend the Minister this afternoon.

We are suffering not merely from what the Opposition describe as the neglect of investment in transport infrastructure, which has occurred even during this Administration, but from a lack of investment which goes back 15 or 20 years. A major new road project probably takes 15 years from initial concept to completion. One of the problems of today's debate is that, even if someone in the Department of Transport were to bring forward a wonderful plan and persuade the Treasury that it could be implemented, and even if the finance were advanced, it would take many years to tackle the growing congestion and the tremendous problems that we face. That is why I am sad that the debate so far has concentrated on what has gone before rather than on arguments for the future.

My hon. Friend the Minister and my right hon. Friend the Secretary of State have shown determination and flexibility, which were sadly lacking in the Department of Transport for several years. The team at the Department of Transport is determined that there should be extra investment. One aspect that I particularly commend is that, unlike those of other Administrations, the team is prepared to consider virtually any option if it will improve the overall position.

It is all very well to dismiss spending on roads, but we are told that the number of motor cars is to double by early next century. It is all very well telling people that they should not have a motor car and should travel by public transport, by rail, but once the average person has bought a motor car, he or she will continue to use it and to want to use it because it is the most convenient form of transport. Any Government who fail to recognise that and suggest that people's use of motor cars should be too greatly inhibited will find themselves on the receiving end of public dissatisfaction whenever the next election takes place.

**Mr. Snape:** The hon. Gentleman put a question. I will return it by asking him one. How much money would have to be spent on roads to alleviate the congestion that we see most days in and around our major cities?

**Mr. Fry:** We cannot build our way out of trouble. I have just returned from a visit to the United States, where it is now accepted that it is impossible to build enough roads to satisfy the overwhelming demand. That does not mean, however, that we should do nothing but consider what each mode of transport contributes. We might find that it is best to concentrate on light rail, heavy rail underground, British Rail services or using car sharing more than we do at present. We may need some road improvements or even to build new roads. It would be taking a blinkered view to pass today's motion, as though voting more money for the railways would solve the problem.

As I said earlier, the difficulty arises because the problems are increasing. One interesting aspect of modern travel, particularly travel for work, is how much more complex it is becoming. More and more people travel, not merely in a radial line from outside the city into its centre, but across the city and its suburbs. Yet our public transport systems are nearly all based on radial lines of communication.

**Mr. Simon Hughes:** Does not the hon. Gentleman accept that one measure that should be taken is to charge motorists who insist on driving into towns and city centres unnecessarily, and even to charge those who drive in as a matter of course? A leader in today's *Evening Standard* suggests two methods of doing this in London as the only way of preventing unnecessary congestion from bringing the capital city to a standstill.

**Mr. Fry:** It is possible to use a more rigid parking policy to deter the motorist. The number of commuters coming into London by car is a small percentage of the total number of people coming into the city. Many would argue that that percentage comprises essential users, perhaps Members of Parliament who cannot travel home any other way if the House sits late. It is all very well saying that we should make them pay, but most of them, because they are in business, would pass on the cost to someone else and the charges would hit and therefore penalise people at the lowest end of the income scale.

The problem has been exacerbated recently. Yesterday's *Sunday Telegraph* states:

"Between 1983 and 1988 daily rail journeys into London during the morning rush hour . . . increased from 380,000 to 460,000 . . . During 1981-82 there were 498 million journeys completed on London Underground rising to 798 million in 1987-8".

Increases on this scale have come upon us remarkably quickly, and the decisions needed to deal with them must be made as early as possible because they take so long to implement. The Government, the Secretary of State and the Minister have at least come forward with some imaginative ideas, such as the central London rail study, for which we have been waiting a long time. Even if we agreed all the studies and decided to go ahead with all the projects, the difficulties would continue to multiply.

The Minister and I had an interesting Adjournment debate a few weeks ago about the contribution that private capital can make to transport infrastructure shortages. We differed, in that he felt that private investment could be encouraged to come in without any sweeteners from the

[*Mr. Fry*]

Treasury or the Government. I welcome the Green Paper; I am not entirely sure how the ideas expressed in it will work out in practice, but I remain convinced that many projects, especially road projects, cannot stand on their own without some form of tax relief on the money invested or some sort of payment by way of shadow tolls. I do not especially commend either form of assistance, but something is needed.

The Government have had the courage to think much more adventurously than their predecessors, but if my hon. Friend discovers, as he undoubtedly and unfortunately will, that the considerable investment now being made is insufficient to deal with the congestion, now and in the future, I hope that he can assure me that the Government will keep an open mind when considering alternatives. I am all in favour of my hon. Friend trying to encourage the private sector to come in, as the Green Paper suggested, but it would be wrong to close off all the alternatives.

We are on the verge of a tremendous explosion in the movement of people. It is a fundamental responsibility of any Government to safeguard the freedom of that movement, which is one of our basic liberties. It has taken a long time for Governments in this country to give transport and expenditure on it the high degree of attention that it enjoys today. I am grateful to my right hon. Friend the Secretary of State and to my hon. Friend the Minister for recognising the challenges that transport problems pose. Given the extra expenditure that they have already announced, I am confident that they will have the determination to deal with this problem and to bring relief —if not tomorrow, perhaps in a few years—to the people of this country.

6.3 pm

**Mr. Donald Anderson** (Swansea, East): The hon. Member for Wellingborough (Mr. Fry) asked some basic questions about transport policy and outlined the great explosion in transport use that will happen over the next few years. I wonder whether he and other hon. Members are prepared to face the implications of, for instance, making motorists pay the marginal social costs involved in relieving inner-city congestion. The hon. Gentleman also asked why there had been so much concentration in the debate and in the motion on rail, as opposed to road. He said that transport should be seen as a whole. The answer to the hon. Gentleman's question is that hon. Members have concentrated on rail because its potential contribution to our transport system has been consistently devalued over the years. That is why we seek positively to put the case for rail.

Having heard the Minister's speech I am tempted to ask: if things are so good, why are they so bad? People like me who use public transport in London expect that at least one of the lifts in an Underground station will not work and that, when they change tubes, at least one of the escalators will not work. We expect the honeyed words over the loudspeaker—at least they tell us now why things are wrong—informing us of delays.

International comparisons provide some indication of the Government's neglect. In an editorial on 19 May, *The*

*Independent* said something that might be labelled Marxist by Conservative Members. Under the heading "Neglected transports of horror" it said:

"For nearly 10 years, Margaret Thatcher paid scant attention to transport. Nor did she give any Cabinet Minister a long enough term of office at the Department of Transport to master the subject and push through major reforms. Six men, several of them distinctly second-rate, have succeeded one another during a period which has seen a single Prime Minister and two Chancellors of the Exchequer. This was a sign that Mrs. Thatcher regarded transport as a relatively unimportant portfolio, an error to which her own access to special travel facilities, coupled with her well known antipathy to railways, made her especially prone. The nation is suffering for this lack of interest."

No hon. Member, based on his own experience or on talking to his constituents, can gainsay this lack of interest from on high in transport in this country. Our people travel nowadays. They see the quality of the railways in France and Germany and can compare them with ours. They can compare the glistening newness of the underground in Paris with the squalor and age-old feeling of the Underground in London.

Comparisons of projected investment over the next few years show that West Germany plans to spend £12 billion on major rail programmes. France plans to spend £1 billion a year until the end of the century. These countries display a far more bullish attitude to their railways, and that is reflected in staff morale and usage by passengers. Spain intends to spend £10 billion; Italy proposes investment of up to £18 billion. Even Holland, a small country, is spending £3 billion. The current investment programme of British Rail is £3·8 billion over five years.

Britain is virtually at the bottom of the table of European countries when it comes to building urban railways to relieve inner-city congestion. We plan to build only 1·5 km of such rail, in the form of the Bank extension of the Docklands light railway in London. That is the only domestic urban rail project under construction, and it compares with West Germany's 116·1 km, Italy's 79·7, and France's 62·8. The *Railway Gazette International* year book survey, published in May of this year, showed that the United Kingdom was sandwiched between Finland, with 1·6 km, and Greece, with 0·9. We should be seeking ways of using rail positively to relieve inner-city congestion.

The schemes for 752 km of urban track have been held up because of the Government's insistence that a large proportion of expenditure must come from the private sector—yet it is clearly not providing enough. High-speed railways can fuel the arteries of the new Europe. We have seen a difference of attitude among our European partners in this respect. Rail can also be a major solution to congestion in our inner cities.

I accept that the Government have, in principle, welcomed the central London rail study. I have no doubt that the Minister and his colleagues are seeking additional cash for LRT and British Rail from the Treasury, but, in response to the study, which was published in January, the Treasury has yet to provide additional sums on a scale remotely comparable with what is available for roads.

All in all, the comparisons speak badly for the attitude to rail in this country. Vision is lacking, at a time when our constituents can see increasing squalor in the rail network. The Government's narrow theme is that the passenger must pay. That is rather different from the criteria for investment in roads. They seek to maximise property sales, selling assets as part of their major rail policy.

Environmental and safety considerations have constantly been downgraded. France has certainly shown how high-speed rail can spread growth and investment to the regions and at the same time protect the environment. The result of the Government's policy has been poor staff morale. I invite hon. Members to speak to railwaymen in their constituencies about how they feel about their future. Morale now is very different from what it was under Sir Peter Parker. At that time, ordinary railwaymen felt that at least there was someone fighting their corner—if that is the appropriate word after the European elections. They felt that at least someone was banging the drum for rail.

The uncertainties that derive from privatisation are another major factor affecting morale. Think tanks were at the margins of government a decade ago, but now they are front centre stage and there is talk about bringing back the Great Western and the LMS. The Government's road and rail investment policies are constantly out of balance. Surely a sensible policy would be for the Government to recognise that, even though the railway system cannot make a contribution on the scale that some of the advocates would like, it is there and a major but under-utilised national asset. It could make a major contribution to regional development and could reduce congestion in the cities.

We can anticipate regional demand. For example, in my part of the world in south Wales the heads of the valleys road was built at a time when there was little demand for it. However, we are told that there is no prospect of the electrification of the main line from Paddington to south Wales, because the investment criteria cannot be met. As my hon. Friend the Member for West Bromwich, East (Mr. Snape) showed in his example, although the Government put their hand on their heart and say that they had accepted every project put up, only those projects are proposed by British Rail which they know will satisfy the artificially high criteria imposed by Government.

Government have to take seriously the regional implications of the Channel tunnel. In all their transport policies, they have shown the hallmark that led to their massive defeat in the European elections. They have shown themselves to be out of step with our European partners. They are on their own in a corner in terms of their assessment of the contribution that rail can make to an overall transport policy. They have shown themselves to be environmentally unconscious by failing to understand the contribution that rail can make. One sees in their transport policy, as in their European policy, the personal stamp of the Prime Minister, which proved so disastrous for the Conservatives over the past few days. The Prime Minister never travels by rail and has consistently downgraded the contribution that rail can make. That prevents a serious and sensible policy on rail from being adopted by the Government.

6.13 pm

**Mr. Robert Adley** (Christchurch): It is a pleasure to follow the hon. Member for Swansea, East (Mr. Anderson). I do not disagree with much of what he said. One of the advantages of a transport debate is that it shows the growing consensus—if I am allowed to use that word—not only about the causes but about the need for a solution to many of our transport problems.

The motion moved by the hon. Member for Brecon and Radnor (Mr. Livsey) would have us believe that severe congestion is caused by inadequate investment in public transport. It is actually caused by increasing prosperity. The hon. Gentleman failed to answer my intervention. There is no point in saying to people who have become prosperous that they cannot have cars because there are enough already. Prosperity has created the congestion and we have to find ways to solve it.

I agree with hon. Members who have said that better public transport is the only sane solution to the problem of congestion. At one time it seemed that the motor car would sound the death knell of the railways. However, by its very proliferation the car is the cause of the revitalisation of our railway system. We must take that on board. The Government's economic policies have caused congestion but they need not be ashamed of that because they created the prosperity.

My hon. Friend the Minister of State has been gracious enough to listen to many of my comments about coaches in London. Some of the policies of the Government, such as coach deregulation, have created micro-problems of traffic congestion and pollution in London. That applies especially to commuter coaches which come in and out during rush hours and park all day, often with their engines running and polluting the atmosphere with diesel fumes. We have deprived London's local authorities of the right and duty to designate coach routes. If we had the courage to re-examine some aspects of the deregulation policy, we might be able to deal with small but important parts of the congestion.

I should like to speak about two points made by my hon. Friend the Minister. The first is about the docklands light railway. Yes, we welcome that railway but no, we do not welcome the thinking that caused the Government to insist that the railway be built so cheaply that it was incompatible with the rest of London Regional Transport and British Rail. In a city such as London it is futile to try to save money by building bits of a railway that do not fit in with the rest of the railway system. I hope that we shall not make that mistake again.

When the Minister spoke about Snow Hill to Wolverhampton my heart leapt. There used to be a railway line from Snow Hill to Wolverhampton. It was called the Great Western Railway. A few weeks ago I went to look at Wolverhampton low-level station which had just been saved from destruction and is now being revitalised by Wolverhampton council. I shed tears when I thought of the investment in infrastructure that was put into our railways by our forebears and which we have thrown away.

I make a specific plea to my hon. Friend the Minister, to my hon. Friends and to the Opposition and I hope that the House can unite on it. Because of changing patterns of traffic it may be necessary on occasions to discontinue a rail service. However, there is never a case for destroying the track bed by selling it off, thereby preventing our descendants from reinstating a rail service should condition change. Can we please stop selling off temporarily redundant railway tracks? It was possible to build the docklands light railway only because, by sheer chance, the tracks and land had not been flogged off by British Rail.

There was the old Great Central railway; and the Somerset and Dorset joint railway line which everybody used to laugh at, which stretches forlornly between the

[*Mr. Robert Adley*]

great growth areas of Avon in the north and south-east Dorset in the south. Barbara Castle sanctioned the closure of such lines and if she had not done so we would now be able to reinstate our rail services and see more motions on the Order Paper by my hon. Friends congratulating British Rail on reopening services. There was one recently about the reopening of the line between Burton and Leicester, but that service would never have been reinstated if it had not been for the quirk of fate that kept the track bed in existence.

**Mr. Snape:** May I reassure the hon. Gentleman about the line that moved him to tears? The track bed between Snow Hill and Wolverhampton was preserved by the former and, sadly, now abolished West Midlands county council. In the county structure plan it had the foresight to envisage that that line would reopen in the 1990s—as indeed it will, albeit as a metro line.

**Mr. Adley:** Perhaps that local authority would like to move down to Dorset to give a few lessons to Dorset county council, which believes that transport means roads. The rail infrastructure in and around my constituency were destroyed in the 1960s by the Labour Government. I am not being partisan. One could weep at the opportunities lost then.

There have been references to the European election, if it was an election—a non-election to a non-Parliament.

**Mr. Snape:** Did the Tory party lose in the hon. Gentleman's constituency?

**Mr. Adley:** No, I think that the Conservative candidate in our European constituency increased his share of the vote. That is beside the point.

The substantial vote for the Green party could not and should not be ignored. It was a quiet message to the Conservative party, the Labour party and the Liberal and Alliance party, or whatever it is called this week. That vote is a clear message to all of us that environmental matters are of growing concern to the British electorate. Transport plays a major part in that environmental concern. In a brief debate, it is not possible to go into all the policies that one would like to see pursued but, in California of all places, the home of private enterprise, the state is legislating to ban the internal combustion engine by early in the next century.

Surely we in western Europe must recognise that we have to tell the oil companies and the motor car manufacturers that, if we can send men to the moon, we must be able to develop the electric motor vehicle to a non-polluting form of transport, that we must get on with this and not allow the pace to be dictated by those who have a commercial investment and interest in continuing to provide forms of land transport that fill our air with fumes. It must be technically feasible, and sooner or later Parliament must do something about it.

There is a similar problem about the railways. Electrified railways are clean and they are much the most economical to operate, but they cost a certain amount of money in capital investment. Why do we always have to look longingly across the Channel to see the attitude that our colleagues there take towards public investment in general and in particular towards public investment in their railways? The French provided and built the original train grand vitesse—TGV—to Lyons. They thought that it would be 15 years before there was a return on their investment, but that was achieved in six and a half years. We should take a leaf out of their book, and instead of looking for reasons not to invest in our railway system look at the options available to us and the benefits that can flow from bold decisions. If we did, we would go some way towards alleviating the aggravation and concern felt by many of our fellow citizens.

We have discussed also the vexed question of rail investment versus road investment. My hon. Friend the Minister knows my views on this matter. My right hon. Friend the Secretary of State came here a couple of weeks ago and announced what I can only describe as a roads bonanza. In that beautiful glossy document, among the proposals was a motorway from the Channel tunnel to Southampton. That will be marvellous, except for those who find that the road goes past their front door, but we shall not discuss that aspect of the matter now. However, a railway line already runs between the Channel tunnel and Southampton. A tiny piece of it on the stretch between Ashford and Hastings is the only part not electrified. It is a few miles long, but British Rail is unable to satisfy the Government and meet their investment criteria so as to link up the entire line to through traffic by putting down a third piece of metal to form an electric railway line. It is grotesque that we have these double standards in assessing road versus rail investment criteria.

The hon. Member for West Bromwich, East (Mr. Snape) talked about the unofficial meetings that we all know take place between British Rail and the Department of Transport, and the hon. Member for Swansea, East mentioned this too. I hope that my right hon. Friend the Secretary of State and my hon. Friend the Minister will be honest and straightforward. They must stop pretending that every single piece of new investment that British Rail wants to undertake it can undertake. We all know what that means. It is that when the private meetings have taken place, only when British Rail satisfies the Department's officials does it put in a formal proposition. However, dozens of schemes are thrown out informally. Occasionally, a scheme such as the one between Blackpool and Manchester gets thrown out even after it has been put forward by BR. There can be no justification for a short-sighted decision to throw out a scheme that would complete a whole railway system by electrifying one small section.

The motion refers to the Channel tunnel. I am sure that the hon. Member for Brecon and Radnor will have read my excellent booklet called "Tunnel Vision". In it, I set out to discuss these problems a year or so ago. Have hon. Members thought about what will happen when the Channel tunnel opens? The result will be the M25 in spades. Who realises that all the rail traffic coming to London from the Channel tunnel will, in the initial years, use Waterloo, but will have to operate on a single track of railway line between Vauxhall and Waterloo? It is not even a double track. Hon. Members should think what that means in terms of congestion and delay. If my hon. Friend the Minister thinks that he has difficulties and troubles now with congestion and delay on the railways, to paraphrase a politician on the other side of the Atlantic, "he ain't seen nuthin' yet", because there will be serious problems.

**Mr. Snape:** It was Al Jolson.

**Mr. Adley:** The hon. Gentleman must not distract me!

We are desperately short of experiments in public transport. I shall mention one phrase, which may cause the hon. Member for West Bromwich, East to smile. It is slip coaches. In the old days the Great Western Railway experimented with, and then ran extensively for many years, a system of slip coaches. In it, trains slipped a coach off the back of an express, which then came to a halt at a designated station without causing the main train to stop. That was the only way to do it with a steam engine, but now, with electric tracks and light diesel traction, a whole new world would be opened up by an experiment into powered slip coaches. What people want is the opportunity to travel on a through train without having to change. This applies particularly to the Channel tunnel and to people travelling to airports. Will my hon. Friend the Minister ask British Rail how much it would cost to carry out an experiment into powered slip coaches to see whether they could be used as a way to help to alleviate transport problems?

I shall finish by dealing with railway privatisation. I am afraid that some of my colleagues know more about party politics than public transport. The two make uneasy bedfellows. I am delighted to hear that the confrontation of reality against expectation on the privatisation of the railway has meant that the timetable originally agreed by my reluctant right hon. Friend the Secretary of State for publishing his proposals has now to be delayed. I am prepared to be convinced that somehow we can discover what nobody else in the world has discovered—the way to run a private passenger railway system profitably. There may be reasons why the best railways in the world, in France, West Germany, Switzerland or Italy, are state-controlled and the worst passenger railway system in the world, that of the United States, is owned privately. There may be some hidden message there, which misleads me, and that may be an argument for privatisation.

I am waiting patiently, and I have an open mind about railway privatisation because, as a Conservative, I am in favour of the principle of privatisation. However, I am not prepared to allow political dogma to dictate my view as to whether we should privatise the railways purely for the sake of privatisation. If my hon. Friend the Minister can convince me that the criteria laid down by my right hon. Friend the Secretary of State—that it will provide a better service for the public—will be achieved, I shall support it. Unless and until he does, I shall not.

6.30 pm

**Mr. Gerald Howarth** (Cannock and Burntwood): It is a great pleasure to take up the remarks of the train-spotter's friend, my hon. Friend the Member for Christchurch (Mr. Adley). That term takes me back to the days when I was the chairman of my school's railway society, and the concept of powered slip coaches had us all extremely excited. I am sure that my hon. Friend has done more than probably anyone else in the House to advance the cause of the railways throughout our land. I am only sorry that in his strictures to my hon. Friend the Minister he was not able to congratulate him on having done the decent thing with the Ribblehead viaduct.

**Mr. Adley:** I have done so previously.

**Mr. Howarth:** I am sure that my hon. Friend has congratulated my hon. Friend the Minister on other occasions. For the record, I thank the Minister for what I consider to be a sensible and wise decision.

**Mr. Snape:** There was no private money.

**Mr. Howarth:** The hon. Gentleman may say that, but I think that we are getting used to the idea of private money in the railway system. I think that the privatisation of the railway system will be advantageous when it comes to introducing improved services.

I agree with the Minister that it is astonishing that the "Salads", or whatever they are called, decided on this topic for debate. They are surely on uncertain ground. Almost invariably, those who call for more investment in roads, bypasses and the infrastructure generally are those who organise residents' action committees to prevent developments from taking place. They tend to speak with forked tongue on matters on which my right hon. and hon. Friends have a good story to tell. I know that my hon. Friend the Member for Christchurch feels that more could be done for the railways, but the railways have benefited from the £3,000 million that has been invested in them so far, and they will benefit further from the substantial programme that is to be implemented.

Those of us who use the InterCity services cannot fail to have noticed the vast improvement that has taken place. The services are fast, comfortable and generally punctual. I pay tribute to the friends of the hon. Member for West Bromwich, East (Mr. Snape) who are responsible for manning our railways for what they have done. I warmly welcome the significant improvement that has been made.

**Mr. Snape:** Perhaps the best reward that the hon. Gentleman could give my "friends" is to remove the cloud of uncertainty that is caused by silly privatisation proposals.

**Mr. Howarth:** The hon. Gentleman knows that any change brings in advance of its implementation a degree of uncertainty. If his friends and hon. Friends were to consult those who were employed in nationalised industries and have now been liberated by being brought into the private sector, they would find generally that they are happier in the private sector. They find it more fulfilling and more rewarding than employment within the state sector.

**Mr. Jeremy Corbyn** (Islington, North): Will the hon. Gentleman give way?

**Mr. Howarth:** No, I shall not give way to the hon. Gentleman. I understand that my hon. Friend the Member for Isle of Wight (Mr. Field) wishes to make a contribution to the debate, and I do not wish to impede him.

My hon. Friend the Member for Christchurch will be pleased to know, as will the hon. Member for West Bromwich, East, that after 25 years the Walsall-to-Hednesford line, which runs substantially through my constituency, has recently been reopened. I pay tribute to Staffordshire county council for using the ratepayers' money to back the project, and I hope that ratepayers will support the line and enable it to become a financially viable service. New lines are being opened, and the railways are increasingly responding to the needs of the passenger. Those responsible for the inter-city services have announced that they are running earlier trains from various parts of the country to enable business men to

[*Mr. Howarth*]

arrive in London by 9 am. We are beginning to see a concentration on the needs of the customer and a willingness to respond to those needs.

The deregulation of inter-city and local bus services has led to substantial improvements. The inter-city services are fantastic. The coaches are marvellous—they are fast, efficient and pleasant vehicles in which to ride. Minibuses are in profuse supply throughout the country. They offer frequent and comfortable journeys and are a substitute for using the car.

The Government have tried to grapple with the problems of London's third airport but I do not believe that the solution is entirely adequate. The Civil Aviation Authority's call for another London runway can be answered only by a second runway at Stansted to meet the demand that unquestionably will follow. The nettle had to be grasped in the first place.

Some of my hon. Friends in neighbouring constituencies are concerned about the Birmingham northern relief road. My right hon. Friend the Secretary of State produced a splendid document setting out new proposals for the road system. It referred to the provision of "New Roads by New Means", including the introduction of private finance. It was only when I arrived back in the House about three weeks ago that I picked up the document and found encompassed within it a letter from my right hon. Friend telling me that the relief road was to be what amounts to the first toll motorway project.

Initially, I welcomed the concept. I am not opposed in principle to toll motorways. Most of our fellow citizens who travel on the continent are happy to pay the French Exchequer for the benefit of using the French motorway system, but of course, there is a choice. I usually use N roads to avoid contributing to the French Exchequer. When French motorists come to Britain, I do not see why they should enjoy our fine motorway network without making any contribution to our Exchequer. Toll motorways can make a good contribution.

After five years of deliberation, characterised by the closest consultation between Ministers and the Members of Parliament who represent the affected constituencies, it is distressing that a sudden announcement has had the effect of causing considerable consternation in south Staffordshire. My hon. Friend the Member for Aldridge-Brownhills (Mr. Shepherd) will see his constituency affected by the Birmingham northern relief road. It will suffer particularly because all the options that have been canvassed go through his patch and will upset one section of his constituents or another.

The project has been five years in development. As I have said, there has been substantial consultation with Members of Parliament as well as with local authorities and local people. The Department's preferred route, the so-called green route, was accepted with enthusiasm or resignation by the people in the area, there was a public inquiry and we were awaiting the inspector's report, which would have confirmed the go-ahead. It was then that we were told that all bets were off, and it appears that the issue is to be opened up again. There is to be competition, with tenders invited for an unspecified route. Those who sold their houses under planning blight arrangements could well find that their houses will not come within the new route; there is great uncertainty.

The relief road was widely accepted by my constituents as a necessary development, and the same position was taken by the constituents of my hon. Friends. I have no doubt that the same view was taken by the entire nation. There is no doubt that the part of the M6 which runs through Birmingham is a grossly over-used road. The idea of a diversion was sensible. In my constituency, we can visualise substantial economic benefits deriving from the relief road, and many exciting projects have been put together. For example, the Poplars site—it is owned by Staffordshire county council—has produced a most imaginative scheme in partnership with the private sector. That scheme and others are threatened: everything has been put into the melting pot, and I cannot see what the gain will be.

If I could see that there was to be a clear gain, I would be in favour of it. However, I doubt whether there will be a gain. Many of the new exciting projects are likely to be put at risk. More especially, the Burntwood western bypass is under threat. Similarly, the Cannock eastern bypass is threatened because, unless the new road goes ahead, that bypass will go nowhere. That would be a lot of public sector investment for nothing.

At the very least, my hon. Friend the Minister should tell us that he will confirm the Department's preferred route and ensure that, if there is to be competition, it will be competition on the preferred route. He cannot tell us that there will be no delay. The Birmingham northern relief road is not the same as the Dartford-Thurrock route, which has only two points, one at each end of the river. The Birmingham northern relief road has no fewer than four intersections planned in my constituency. Will a private sector developer have four intersections? I suspect that a private sector developer would be unable to afford four intersections and would have only one mid route. Therefore, we are likely to lose out.

Although my constituents have not expressed this concern yet, they may be concerned that while Londoners have benefited from a great deal of public sector investment in the M25, my constituents may have to pay for the privilege of having a road which elsewhere in the country would have been provided from the public sector.

I understand that time is short, but I hope that I have been able to endorse much of what my hon. Friend the Minister has done and has plans to do. The Government's record on transport has been first class. There is nothing of which we should be ashamed. Unquestionably, more must be done and the Minister must consider air transport. However, I congratulate him and plead that he will have more consultations with his hon. Friends.

6.41 pm

**Mr. Simon Hughes** (Southwark and Bermondsey): During this debate news has reached the House that the Hight Court has ruled in favour of the National Union of Railwaymen, and that Wednesday's rail strike will go ahead at the same time as the strike on the London Underground. The fact that London Transport is coming to a standstill is a reflection of the Government's policy on transport in the capital. Commuter chaos on a regular basis is a continuing capital crisis. The Minister appears to believe that the Government should not interfere with that chaos or even be concerned about it. The Minister hardly referred to the fact that there was any problem on the public transport system.

The Government have that blinkered view because, as my hon. Friend the Member for Brecon and Radnor (Mr. Livsey) said, they assert that they are investing enough on transport. Our motion alleges that the Government are so significantly under-investing in public transport that they are condemning the country to an extremely uncomfortable and precarious economic future. When the Minister replies, we would like him to tell us whether he is prepared to consider some of the advice given to him by his hon. Friend the Member for Christchurch (Mr. Adley), who referred to other countries where the evidence was that privatising and pretending that Government could have a hands-off policy was a receipe for a deteriorating transport system.

It was interesting to note that the hon. Member for Cannock and Burntwood (Mr. Howarth) was in favour of privatisation of roads except where it affected his constituency. The Minister alleged that my hon. Friends and I and our party complain if schemes to invest in transport are proposed in our areas or near our constituencies. That is completely untrue. For example, on a consistent basis, my colleagues have campaigned for the Settle-Carlisle railway. My colleagues have also consistently campaigned for the Cambrian coast railway to remain open, and only today my colleagues are heightening their campaign to keep open the Lewes-Uckfield line.

We must remind the Government that communities comprise people, many of whom do not have private transport. There must be sufficient public transport. That does not mean a service like that which has arisen from deregulating the buses, where the system is fine if someone wants to travel at a peak hour in the morning or afternoon, but no good if someone wants to go off the main route at off-peak hours. There must be sustained investment in a public transport system because that is the only way to deal both with our macro-economic problems and ensure a public service.

**Mr. Gerald Howarth:** I want to help the hon. Gentleman to understand something which he clearly did not understand in my speech. Had it been proposed to us at the outset that the Birmingham northern relief road was to a toll motorway, I would have welcomed it warmly. However, my constituents and I find it difficult to accept, after a public inquiry and five years of agony, that that whole can of worms is to be reopened.

**Mr. Hughes:** The hon. Gentleman cannot have it both ways. If he supports a Government who will land their new ideas for privatised roads somewhere and that somewhere happens to be in his constituency, he cannot really complain about it. If he complains now, I assume that he would complain about something similar happening elsewhere. He cannot expect the rest of the country to put up with something which he would not want in his back yard.

As a proportion of our national expenditure, expenditure on transport has dropped consistently throughout the 10 years of this Government. It was 4·9 per cent. in 1978-79, 4 per cent. in 1986-87 and it is projected to be 3·7 per cent. in 1990-91. The Government are doing that clearly as a matter of policy. In his announcement today about the extension of the Jubilee line through my constituency, the Minister made it clear that the plan would go ahead provided that the private sector invested

in it. I am not against private sector investment, but the idea that we can regularly and consistently reduce as a proportion of our national expenditure the amount of Government money spent on public transport and sustain a decent public transport system is not credible.

**Mr. Adley:** I cannot allow the travesty of truth which the hon. Gentleman has just espoused to remain on the record. He cannot claim that his party led the campaign for the retention of the Settle-Carlisle line. Will he confirm that the formation of the all-party group to retain the line took place entirely as the result of the efforts of Conservative and Labour Members and that not one member of his party joined that group?

**Mr. Hughes:** I did not claim that my party led the campaign. I claimed that my party was involved from the beginning in that campaign with local county councillors and district councillors at both ends of that line on a sustained and regular basis. We have argued the case in this House and outside, as the hon. Gentleman well knows. The record shows that we have consistently argued that the Settle-Carlisle line and others should be retained, while for a very long time the Government have prevaricated. We have had to wait months and years for them to make a decision on what was clearly a crucial matter for the environment and the communities concerned.

My hon. Friend the Member for Brecon and Radnor also made it clear that one of the reasons why it is important to invest substantially more in public transport than we do now is that in only that way would we have an environmentally acceptable transport policy.

Private transport cannot increase at its present rate, with all the inevitable consequences for pollution and congestion, let alone mental illness and frustration, without severely harming the personal and the local environment. It is better by far to invest in the national rail network and, in urban areas, in an underground, a rapid transit network and a bus service. In that way, one maximises transport efficiency, especially if the subsidy system is properly regulated, with the consumption of the minimum amount of fuel and maximum travel occurring at the most convenient times. Encouraging and permitting private transport to grow, building roads to meet that demand, and in so doing automatically increasing demand —the M25 is the best example of that—is an unacceptable solution.

Today's issue of the *Financial Times* makes it clear how ridiculous are present policies. Writing about London Regional Transport in an article headed

"Raising fares and hackles on overcrowded Tube",

Rachel Johnson observes:

"Here's the good news for Tube travellers. London Underground is tackling its biggest problem—overcrowding —which has now reached dangerous levels . . . Now for the bad news. London Underground's proposed solution to the problem, outlined to the Commons transport select committee, is to raise fares to such high levels that people are forced off the system."

Even the Transport Secretary expressed his doubts:

"'I would have to hear convincing arguments from London Underground before I agreed to pricing people off the Underground'."

I am glad to know that even the Secretary of State has doubts.

The reason why our capital will completely clog up is that in a city in which 35 per cent. of commuters use the Underground—which represents a total of 2·6 million

[*Mr. Hughes*]

passengers and a 60 per cent. increase in five years, with a further 30 per cent. increase projected over the next five years—the amount of subsidy and public money being spent on it is being reduced. The new managing director of London Underground seems to think that that is perfectly acceptable:

"We have to get the best out of our troops",
he said, justifying less expenditure, adding:

"McDonald's has shown the way in this. You don't have to have very highly paid and highly educated people to treat the public properly."
Although one often feels like a McDonald's burger squeezed between two halves of a bun when one goes on the Underground, none the less that is no way to treat the travelling public, be they commuters, visitors from other parts of the country, or tourists from abroad.

Comparisons with expenditure in other parts of Europe make it obvious that not enough is being spent. Government funds account for 52 per cent. of public transport costs in Paris. The subsidy in Rome is 82 per cent.; London's subsidy is just 30 per cent. and falling.

The same applies to British Rail, which transports 40 per cent. of London's commuters and which, as with London Underground, has seen a 25 per cent. increase in demand. But has there been increased investment to meet it? No, instead the Government cut investment in British Rail by 25 per cent. over the past seven years, and cuts totalling a further 25 per cent. in the three years 1986-89 were recently announced.

The Minister carefully avoided quoting figures showing a cut in investment in real terms since 1979, though there has been increased expenditure in cash terms. Given the inflation over which the Government preside, it would be difficult for there not to be an increase in cash terms. Presumably increased expenditure in cash terms will continue as inflation endures.

**Mr. A. J. Beith** (Berwick-upon-Tweed): Not necessarily.

**Mr. Hughes:** Not necessarily, as my hon. Friend says —because the Government could continue to cut public expenditure. They always gave the reason for inflation as too much spending from the public purse, yet inflation continues.

The third option of building urban railways to reduce inner-city congestion is also being ignored. Germany and Italy, for example, have substantially more urban railway track than we do. We are at the bottom of the league, with only Finland and Greece having as little urban railway track as we do. I challenge the Minister to deny that the following figures are wrong.

Network SouthEast, which is the most overcrowded sector of the British Rail network serving the capital, had its public subsidy reduced from £350 million in 1983 to £165 million in 1988. It is proposed to cut the subsidy to £85 million in 1992. It is unbelievable that, with demand for some provincial services growing by 50 per cent. and for London commuter services by 25 per cent., the Government respond by spending £7 billion on roads and cutting railway investment from £1 billion in 1983 to half a billion in the last financial year.

Our public transport system problems must be overcome. They include endemic overcrowding, appalling security, and ridiculous safety provisions. In last Wednesday's debate my hon. Friend the Member for Rochdale (Sir C. Smith) demonstrated that, if one happens to be large, overweight, disabled, carrying luggage or accompanied by children, it is impossible to make one's way through the new-style safety gates. The situation is so problematical that there are now more staff supervising the gates than there were before they came into existence.

Massive strategic investment in public transport is required. Only then will we have a safe, cheap, environmentally pleasant and clean public transport system. Without strategic planning, which the Government abolished, it will not work. The transport system has been left to fend for itself, with both London Regional Transport and British Rail left to pay their own way. The Government are willing to announce massive road plans inside or outside the capital, but public money should be spent instead on public transport, to relieve congestion in our capital.

If the Government believe in improving the environment for the majority of British people living in urban areas, they should invest in public transport. The Minister dare not pretend at the Dispatch Box that the Government have been doing that. They cut public expenditure and have heaped misery on the public.

When on Wednesday the public complain about the lack of Tube trains and railway services, they will be criticising not those who are on strike but the Government who imposed that chaos as the penalty for lack of investment over many years.

6.57 pm

**Mr. Portillo:** The complete inability of the hon. Member for Southwark and Bermondsey (Mr. Hughes) to understand the difference between subsidy and investment is depressing. Subsidy is a measure of how much money a railway is losing. Fortunately, our railways lose less money year by year. Investment is a measure of how much money goes into renewing the railways' facilities. The highest figure ever reached in real terms between 1974 and 1979 was £546 million. The figure for 1987-88 was £594 million, for 1988-89 it is £629 million, and for the next four years it will be £781 million, £865 million, £928 million and £865 million.

In contrast, valuable speeches were made by my hon. Friends. I thank my hon. Friend the Member for Wellingborough (Mr. Fry) for pointing out the absurdity of telling the public that at this stage in our economy we can allow no more cars on the roads. That would mean the predominantly white middle class which currently owns cars saying, "Enough is enough," and denying aspiration to car ownership to the working class, to blacks, and to the elderly—all of whom are increasingly the new road users.

My hon. Friend the Member for Wellingborough expressed doubts about getting private finance under way without subsidy. I do not regard private finance as a substitute for the public sector. We made it clear that there will be no scheme by scheme deductions for successful private sector schemes. We are experimenting with private finance and our minds are not closed.

My hon. Friend the Member for Cannock and Burntwood (Mr. Howarth) expressed concern about the Birmingham northern relief road. I can reassure him that the time spent on the public inquiry was not wasted, because the work done will be useful to private sector applicants. We shall establish a short timetable for the competition, and we have every reason to believe that the private sector is likely to follow the route already examined. The public inquiry report can be kept on ice, and that route can be used again in the public sector if the private sector scheme does not bring a result.

I thank my hon. Friend the Member for Christchurch (Mr. Adley) for making a most interesting speech. I shall, of course, bring his point about powered slip coaches to the attention of British Rail. I feel, however, that it is a bit misleading to consider only the initial cost of the docklands light railway. Immense investment has been put into it since, and it is capable of great expansion.

I wish to pick up a couple of points made by the hon. Member for West Bromwich, East (Mr. Snape). The hon. Gentleman mentioned bus substitution. British Rail is using taxpayers' money to subsidise transport services when that is merited on social grounds, and it must be right to test the use of that money against the cost of providing equivalent service by road. There has been only one case of bus substitution so far. I have not requested any particular number of such cases, and I point again to the substantial figures for provincial investment.

As for the cross-city electrification in Birmingham, the rolling stock there is very old. The question is how to replace it. Diesel would be cheaper, but it would be more expensive to maintain and also less reliable, while electric stock, despite its higher capital cost, would provide gains in maintenance and reliability. The sums must be done thoroughly—that is all that we require. I shall be happy to approve the most cost-effective replacement scheme when I receive a submission from British Rail.

The hon. Member for West Bromwich, East also mentioned section 8 grants. He will know that the Freight Transport Association has made a submission recommending an expansion, and I am considering that.

The Government recognise the problems of transport congestion. We have produced plans for investment in roads and public transport. As a Government, we do not wish away the difficulties—we seek to meet them. In particular, we recognise that no project is without its environmental impact, but many projects are beneficial to the environment overall. That is why we are willing to approve them. Our policy is balanced and determined. Of course, any transport policy faces real problems, but the problem today is certainly not any reluctance on the part of the Government to invest in transport. That is why I invite the House to reject the motion.

*Question put,* That the original words stand part of the Question:—

The House Divided: Ayes 65, Noes 213.

**Division No. 246]** **[7.2 pm**

**AYES**

Alton, David
Ashdown, Rt Hon Paddy
Barnes, Harry (Derbyshire NE)
Barnes, Mrs Rosie (Greenwich)
Beith, A. J.
Benn, Rt Hon Tony
Boateng, Paul
Campbell, Menzies (Fife NE)
Campbell-Savours, D. N.
Cartwright, John
Clelland, David
Cohen, Harry
Cook, Frank (Stockton N)
Cook, Robin (Livingston)
Cousins, Jim
Darling, Alistair
Davis, Terry (B'ham Hodge H'l)
Dixon, Don
Duffy, A. E. P.
Eadie, Alexander
Ewing, Harry (Falkirk E)
Fisher, Mark
Foster, Derek
Foulkes, George
Galloway, George
Garrett, Ted (Wallsend)
Golding, Mrs Llin
Gordon, Mildred
Haynes, Frank
Howells, Geraint
Howells, Dr. Kim (Pontypridd)
Hoyle, Doug
Hughes, John (Coventry NE)
Hughes, Simon (Southwark)
Johnston, Sir Russell
Jones, Barry (Alyn & Deeside)
Livingstone, Ken
Livsey, Richard
McCartney, Ian
McFall, John
McKay, Allen (Barnsley West)
Maclennan, Robert
Martlew, Eric
Maxton, John
Meale, Alan
Michie, Mrs Ray (Arg'l & Bute)
Morris, Rt Hon A. (W'shawe)
Owen, Rt Hon Dr David
Pendry, Tom
Pike, Peter L.
Powell, Ray (Ogmore)
Prescott, John
Quin, Ms Joyce
Reid, Dr John
Ruddock, Joan
Salmond, Alex
Sheldon, Rt Hon Robert
Short, Clare
Skinner, Dennis
Snape, Peter
Steel, Rt Hon David
Thomas, Dr Dafydd Elis
Wareing, Robert N.
Welsh, Andrew (Angus E)
Williams, Alan W. (Carm'then)

Tellers for the Ayes:
Mr. Archy Kirkwood and
Mr. Ronnie Fearn.

**NOES**

Alexander, Richard
Alison, Rt Hon Michael
Amess, David
Amos, Alan
Arnold, Jacques (Gravesham)
Arnold, Tom (Hazel Grove)
Ashby, David
Atkins, Robert
Atkinson, David
Baker, Nicholas (Dorset N)
Batiste, Spencer
Beaumont-Dark, Anthony
Bellingham, Henry
Benyon, W.
Bevan, David Gilroy
Blackburn, Dr John G.
Boscawen, Hon Robert
Boswell, Tim
Bowden, Gerald (Dulwich)
Bowis, John
Braine, Rt Hon Sir Bernard
Brandon-Bravo, Martin
Brazier, Julian
Bright, Graham
Brooke, Rt Hon Peter
Brown, Michael (Brigg & Cl't's)
Bruce, Ian (Dorset South)
Butler, Chris
Butterfill, John
Carlisle, John, (Luton N)
Carlisle, Kenneth (Lincoln)
Carrington, Matthew
Chapman, Sydney
Chope, Christopher
Clark, Sir W. (Croydon S)
Conway, Derek
Coombs, Anthony (Wyre F'rest)
Coombs, Simon (Swindon)
Cope, Rt Hon John
Davies, Q. (Stamf'd & Spald'g)
Davis, David (Boothferry)
Dorrell, Stephen
Douglas-Hamilton, Lord James
Durant, Tony
Dykes, Hugh
Evennett, David
Fallon, Michael
Favell, Tony
Fenner, Dame Peggy
Finsberg, Sir Geoffrey
Fishburn, John Dudley
Forman, Nigel
Forth, Eric
Fox, Sir Marcus
Franks, Cecil
French, Douglas
Fry, Peter
Garel-Jones, Tristan
Gill, Christopher
Glyn, Dr Alan
Goodhart, Sir Philip
Goodson-Wickes, Dr Charles
Gorman, Mrs Teresa
Gorst, John
Gow, Ian
Greenway, Harry (Ealing N)
Gregory, Conal
Griffiths, Peter (Portsmouth N)
Ground, Patrick
Grylls, Michael
Gummer, Rt Hon John Selwyn
Hague, William
Hamilton, Neil (Tatton)
Hanley, Jeremy
Hannam, John
Hargreaves, A. (B'ham H'll Gr')
Hargreaves, Ken (Hyndburn)
Harris, David
Hayes, Jerry
Hayhoe, Rt Hon Sir Barney
Hayward, Robert
Heddle, John
Heseltine, Rt Hon Michael
Hicks, Mrs Maureen (Wolv' NE)
Hicks, Robert (Cornwall SE)
Hind, Kenneth
Holt, Richard
Hordern, Sir Peter
Howarth, G. (Cannock & B'wd)
Hughes, Robert G. (Harrow W)
Hunt, David (Wirral W)
Hunt, John (Ravensbourne)
Hunter, Andrew
Irvine, Michael
Jack, Michael
Jackson, Robert
Janman, Tim
Jessel, Toby
Jones, Gwilym (Cardiff N)
Jones, Robert B (Herts W)
Jopling, Rt Hon Michael
Kellett-Bowman, Dame Elaine
Kilfedder, James
Knapman, Roger
Knight, Dame Jill (Edgbaston)
Latham, Michael
Lawrence, Ivan
Lawson, Rt Hon Nigel
Leigh, Edward (Gainsbor'gh)
Lennox-Boyd, Hon Mark
Lightbown, David
Lloyd, Sir Ian (Havant)
Lloyd, Peter (Fareham)
Lord, Michael
Lyell, Sir Nicholas
McCrindle, Robert
Macfarlane, Sir Neil
MacKay, Andrew (E Berkshire)

Maclean, David
McLoughlin, Patrick
McNair-Wilson, P. *(New Forest)*
Mans, Keith
Maples, John
Marlow, Tony
Marshall, John *(Hendon S)*
Martin, David *(Portsmouth S)*
Maude, Hon Francis
Maxwell-Hyslop, Robin
Mayhew, Rt Hon Sir Patrick
Mellor, David
Meyer, Sir Anthony
Miller, Sir Hal
Mills, Iain
Mitchell, Andrew *(Gedling)*
Moate, Roger
Monro, Sir Hector
Montgomery, Sir Fergus
Morrison, Sir Charles
Morrison, Rt Hon P *(Chester)*
Moss, Malcolm
Mudd, David
Neale, Gerrard
Neubert, Michael
Nicholls, Patrick
Nicholson, David *(Taunton)*
Norris, Steve
Onslow, Rt Hon Cranley
Oppenheim, Phillip
Page, Richard
Pattie, Rt Hon Sir Geoffrey
Peacock, Mrs Elizabeth
Porter, Barry *(Wirral S)*
Porter, David *(Waveney)*
Portillo, Michael
Raffan, Keith
Raison, Rt Hon Timothy
Redwood, John
Rhodes James, Robert
Riddick, Graham
Roe, Mrs Marion
Rossi, Sir Hugh
Rowe, Andrew
Sackville, Hon Tom
Scott, Nicholas
Shaw, David *(Dover)*
Shaw, Sir Michael *(Scarb')*
Shephard, Mrs G. *(Norfolk SW)*
Shepherd, Richard *(Aldridge)*

Shersby, Michael
Sims, Roger
Skeet, Sir Trevor
Smith, Tim *(Beaconsfield)*
Speed, Keith
Speller, Tony
Spicer, Sir Jim *(Dorset W)*
Stanbrook, Ivor
Stern, Michael
Stevens, Lewis
Stewart, Andy *(Sherwood)*
Stradling Thomas, Sir John
Summerson, Hugo
Taylor, Ian *(Esher)*
Taylor, John M *(Solihull)*
Taylor, Teddy *(S'end E)*
Temple-Morris, Peter
Thompson, Patrick *(Norwich N)*
Thorne, Neil
Townsend, Cyril D. *(B'heath)*
Tredinnick, David
Trippier, David
Trotter, Neville
Twinn, Dr Ian
Vaughan, Sir Gerard
Waddington, Rt Hon David
Wakeham, Rt Hon John
Walker, Bill *(T'side North)*
Waller, Gary
Walters, Sir Dennis
Wardle, Charles *(Bexhill)*
Warren, Kenneth
Watts, John
Wells, Bowen
Whitney, Ray
Widdecombe, Ann
Wiggin, Jerry
Wilkinson, John
Wilshire, David
Winterton, Mrs Ann
Winterton, Nicholas
Wolfson, Mark
Wood, Timothy
Yeo, Tim
Young, Sir George *(Acton)*

Tellers for the Noes:
    Mr. David Heathcoat-Amory
    and Mr. Alan Howarth.

*Question accordingly negatived.*

*Question,* That the proposed words be there added, *put forthwith pursuant to Standing Order No. 30 (Questions on amendments) and agreed to.*

MR. DEPUTY SPEAKER *forthwith declared the main Question, as amended, to be agreed to.*

*Resolved,*

That this House congratulates the Government on the record levels of capital investment in all forms of transport infrastructure since 1979 while at the same time reducing the burden on the taxpayer; welcomes their plans to increase this investment further over coming years with both public and private money to meet the forecast growth in demand which is the result of the economic success of this country under the Conservative Government; welcomes the Government's success in creating the conditions in which the private sector could both finance and build the Channel Tunnel; congratulates the Government on its determination that the whole of the United Kingdom shall share in its benefits; applauds the high priority that they give to all matters of safety on transport; and welcomes their recognition of the importance of environmental conditions in transport policy.

# Civil Liberties and Bill of Rights

7.14 pm

**Mr. Robert Maclennan** (Caithness and Sutherland): I beg to move,

That this House condemns the erosion over the last decade of civil liberties; believes that such liberties are increasingly under threat through the abuse of public power; and further believes that the rights of the citizen are required to be protected, as in other democracies, by a Bill of Rights.

This year, Parliament celebrated the third centenary of the passage by the Lords and Commons of the Bill of Rights which ushered in the Glorious Revolution. It was the second Act of the reign of William and Mary. Since that Act was passed, the people of this country have looked to Parliament to secure and enlarge their liberties.

It was not the first attempt to ensure that the executive Government would be subject to the law, for in England that was the main thrust of Magna Carta, but from that Bill of Rights stems the modern development of the doctrine of the supremacy of Parliament and the theory that Parliament secures the nation's freedoms.

The House will, I think, acknowledge that that theory has been put to severe test during the past decade. In the eyes of many British people, and of many friendly foreign observers, Parliament seems more the accomplice of an oppressive central Government than a check on overweening power. Liberty is ill in Britain today. A majority Government, elected by a minority of the British people, have contrived to cut down, threaten and abuse institutions and individuals who have dared to raise their voices in dissent or criticism—in local government, in the press, in the broadcasting media, in the universities. In the name of the economy, security or some other reason of state, freedom has come under attack.

The right of public assembly—the means whereby the man in the street has the opportunity to express his dissent —has been hedged around in the name of public order. Proposals have been advanced by the Government to curb jury trials. The presumption of innocence and the freedom from self-incrimination—in the United States, secured by the first amendment to the constitution—are under attack here. Censorship has been reintroduced, not because, as in wartime, careless talk costs lives but because the Government presume to impose standards of taste on the British public. Freedom to disseminate sexual information and advice, at a time when never more needed, has been put at risk by the infamous provisions of section 28 of the Local Government Act 1988.

While the Government pour forth expensive and tendentious propaganda, they seek to stop up all channels of official information, pursuing—like furies—through the courts civil servants and former public servants who have been scandalised by Government evasions and distortions into revealing what they know of the truth.

It is possible, after 10 years, to stand back a little from the sophistries with which each of these invasions of fundamental rights has been justified and to discern a pattern for some, even for several, of these episodes: the Zircon affair; "Death on the Rock"; the Government's rejection of Lord Windlesham's report on that programme without even having read it; the failure to comply with the Brogan judgment of the European Court of Human Rights condemning Britain's detention policy in Northern Ireland without, apparently, a serious attempt to comply with the ruling.

I have tried to approach each of these cases dispassionately and to look at them on their merits, but we have to admit that what we are seeing is a case-by-case compromise of liberty. The Government's amendment to our motion almost admits that. They speak of the balancing of liberty against certain other reasons of state. That is not the thinking one would have anticipated from a Conservative Administration who wrap themselves in the language of liberty. Ronald Dworkin said:

"The essence of liberty is not precise boundaries or mechanical tests but an attitude."

Despite the Government's espousal of economic individualism, there is no sense that in their eyes the fundamental rights and freedoms of the individual are sacrosanct.

We have come to this pass because the Government have exploited the potential of our constitution to allow the concentration of public power in the hands of the Cabinet. Ministers initiate legislation, exercise their broad administrative discretions, control the flow of official information, determine levels of public expenditure and taxation, and appoint the executive heads of the major public authorities. Even to state the theory is to be reminded that in the past decade, Cabinet government has been supplanted by prime ministerial government to an extent unknown in Britain, even in wartime.

Lloyd George and Winston Churchill had as their closest Cabinet colleagues men of other parties with views and opinions widely different from their own. We now have a Prime Minister who brooks no opposition and who does not seek to maintain within her Cabinet any internal balance of views. She admitted before she took office that such a concept was anathema to her and that she sought to do away with Cabinet debate.

I put it to Conservative Members in particular that we have seen the consequences of that dispersal of internal Cabinet debate. If a Government such as ours is not imbued with a sense of the primacy of individual liberty, the British subject has no constitutional safeguard. The will of the majority in Parliament is absolute, and the minority, never mind the individual, can go hang. That constitutional reality understandably embitters the people of Hong Kong, who have seen this Westminster Parliament strip them of their rights as British subjects. We do not hear the call of our own citizens; let us listen to them before it is too late.

In three major respects, the British people suffer constitutional disadvantage in the protection of fundamental rights and freedoms in comparison with the citizens of other democratic countries. First, within our constitution there are no institutional checks and balances such as those which flow from the separation of powers in the United States between the Executive, the legislature and the judiciary. Secondly, although the United Kingdom consists of four nations, we suffer from the most centralised system of government among the major nations of the free world. Thirdly, there is not a transcendent law to which British people may have recourse in the courts of the realm when their fundamental rights and freedoms are attacked. Because of that last weakness, I and other hon. Members have from time to time sought to incorporate into the domestic law of this country the provisions of the European convention on human rights.

The Bill which I introduced in December 1983 was subsequently taken up by Lord Broxbourne in another place, and then introduced with minor modification by Sir Edward Gardner in the House in 1987. On all occasions, it enjoyed considerable cross-party support. The Bills were introduced not as partisan measures but as measures seeking to embody a sense of the inadequacy of our unwritten constitution in the face of the attack on our fundamental rights and freedoms—and not purely by the present Administration, because long before the present Government came to office, successful cases had been brought against its predecessors in the European Court of Human Rights in Strasbourg. In 1987, only 13 Labour Members stayed in the House on a Friday to vote to give the Bill a Second Reading. As a consequence, it failed by six votes to proceed to Committee.

I believe that there is a growing recognition in this country that freedom will be enhanced if the European convention were to be incorporated into our domestic law. That is the policy of my right hon. and hon. Friends. It is a policy favoured by distinguished parliamentarians in all political parties.

**Mr. David Ashbey** (Leicestershire, North-West): Has the hon. Gentleman considered the argument that incorporation of the European convention would restrict human rights in Britain and not increase them, that it would have a restrictive effect, because it would be placed in legislation and nothing would be allowed to go beyond it so that there could be no increased human rights but only restrictions?

**Mr. Maclennan:** I find that a puzzling view. The hon. Gentleman, as a lawyer, will know that not only is it possible to legislate in addition to the provisions of such a charter to amplify the law, but that in the event of a case not being satisfactorily concluded in the eyes of the appellant, the case can be taken further, to the court at Strasbourg. In a short intervention, the hon. Gentleman could scarcely have time to develop his point, but perhaps during the debate he will explain what appears to most of us to be a paradox.

In my view, the Bill and the policy enjoy the support of eminent parliamentarians who have had experience of operating in difficult security circumstances, such as Mr. Roy Mason—as he then was—in Northern Ireland.

**Mr. Richard Shepherd** (Aldrige-Brownhills): The hon. Gentleman will know that I am sympathetic to the drift of his remarks, but given the supremacy of Parliament, what secures the primacy of one piece of legislation over subsequent pieces of legislation?

**Mr. Maclennan:** The Bill would either have to be entrenched by procedures which the House has not hitherto invoked—I do not wholly rule that out in the light of the developments of our constitution—or it would enjoy the kind of primacy which is enjoyed by the European Communities Act 1972, for example, which successive Governments have considered to be the fundament of the law of our country. It is technically possible to repeal it, and there is no doubt that in that sense it does not impair parliamentary sovereignty, but the hon. Gentleman will agree that it is extremely improbable that the European Communities Act would be repealed without a test of public opinion, comparable to the referendum which ensured that it would remain on the statute book. If a Bill of Rights is similarly enacted by the House and enjoys that kind of security, most of us will be satisfied.

[*Mr. Maclennan*]

There remain, however, two obstacles to the enactment of such a Bill—the Prime Minister herself and the right hon. Member for Birmingham, Sparkbrook (Mr. Hattersley) the deputy leader of the Labour party. The opposition of the Prime Minister is of a piece with her general belief in the efficacy of the doctrine of parliamentary sovereignty which she has stuffed down many unwilling throats, not least in her notorious Bruges speech.

However, the opposition of the right hon. Member for Sparkbrook is a little harder to understand, although he has been at pains to seek to explain it in some newspaper articles. Labour's deputy leader appears to acknowledge the attacks on fundamental rights and freedoms that our present constitution allows, and has recommended a constitutional remedy of his own—the reform of the upper House. He talks of some of the difficulties of introducing a Bill of Rights into this place. He will remember the difficulties that were experienced by the Government of 1966 in reforming the upper House, but let that matter lie. He says that the purpose would be to translate the upper House from its current advisory and revising role to that of a body which, in ways not clearly specified, would entrench the freedoms of the British people.

It is clear that what the right hon. Gentleman recommends is insufficient for that purpose, for, as Lord Scarman wrote in *The Independent* newspaper of 19 June:

"Even if the House of Commons could be persuaded to accept the necessity of a second Chamber's assent, a majority of Members of the same party in both Houses could restore the full menace of elected dictatorship. Let us keep in mind that in a pluralistic society many minorities have no real opportunity of acquiring political power and rely on the law's protection against oppression by the majority."

If the right hon. Gentleman's alternative to a Bill of Rights is unsatisfactory, his opposition to incorporation is less than cogent. He appears to take the view that, because a Bill of Rights is not sufficient for his purposes, it is not necessary. I still share many of the right hon. Gentleman's aspirations for the people of this country and acknowledge that what he calls positive liberties must be secured by specific legislation—including, for example, a freedom of information Bill and greatly improved access to legal aid, so that such protection as the law affords is generally available. We shall not, however, by the adoption of a Bill of Rights secure a reordering of our public expenditure priorities, nor shall we effect the redistribution of power from Whitehall and Westminster to the regions and nations of the United Kingdom.

Those are not arguments against such a Bill, for the rights that we espouse for our people by treaty, in affirming our membership of the regime of the European convention, are rights that should be enjoyed through application to our own courts and not alone through the tortuous and expensive route to Strasbourg. They are important rights. This matter is of particular relevance at this time when the House has expressed concern about these matters. They include the right to privacy, the right to freedom of religion—perhaps somewhat reassuring to certain of our ethnic minorities—the right to freedom of expression, a right that has been more tested, than, perhaps, any other fundamental right during the tenure of the present Government.

They include also the right to freedom of peaceful assembly—a right which, as I said, was hedged around by the Public Order Act 1986—and the right to freedom of association, guaranteeing the right to belong to trade unions. Again, many people have wondered whether the Government have it in mind to curb that right still further. They include also the right to enjoy those freedoms without discrimination on many grounds—on any grounds—of status.

**Mr. Graham Riddick** (Colne Valley): I have been listening carefully to the hon. Gentleman's speech to detect any reference to the abuse of trade union power. In passing, he referred to trade union power and suggested that the Conservative Government might be taking too much power from trade unions. The one way in which the Government have enormously extended personal freedom to millions of people was by redressing the abuse of the closed shop. When the hon. Gentleman was a member of the Labour Government, they forced 7·5 million people to belong to trade unions, in many cases against their will. I should have thought that, far from denying freedom to people, we have extended to millions of individuals the freedom either to belong or not to belong to a trade union. Surely that is of great importance to many people.

**Mr. Maclennan:** The hon. Member for Colne Valley (Mr. Riddick) would have been even more secure in the pursuit of his objectives if the European convention had been incorporated into our law. The provisions of that law were tested against the closed shop in the British Rail case. It had to be fought all the way to Strasbourg, whereas those who considered themselves to suffer from the closed shop would have had a right in the domestic courts if my proposals had been accepted by the hon. Gentleman's Government.

**Mr. A. J. Beith** (Berwick-upon-Tweed): I hope that my hon. Friend will not forget also that, when that matter was tested in Strasbourg and those who were aggrieved had to go all the way there, they met the resistance of the Solicitor-General of this Government in advancing a case against them in that court.

**Mr. Maclennan:** I hesitate to rub salt into the wounds of the hon. Member for Colne Valley when I am endeavouring to enlist his support.

**Mr. Riddick:** We must get this right. First, the hon. Member for Caithness and Sutherland (Mr. Maclennan) started his speech by criticising the Conservative Government for taking freedoms from individuals. However, this Government have given back to millions of trade unionists the freedom either to belong or not to belong to a trade union. Secondly, when his party was in government, what did the hon. Gentleman actually do to give individuals that right? He was in the governing party. What did he do about it at the time?

**Mr. Maclennan:** The hon. Gentleman's first point is a repetition of the point that I have already answered. On his second point, the Government to which I belonged, under the leadership of the Home Secretary, the right hon. Roy Jenkins, as he then was, published a White Paper setting forth the proposals that the provisions that I am seeking to have incorporated be incorporated in the law of the land. The hon. Gentleman's own party's opposition to the case of the three British railwaymen is the answer that he needs to bear in mind.

It is important that the Labour party should pay greater attention to support for freedom than it has so far, and not because it is a cure-all. It will not achieve all the objectives that they seek. Neil Ascherson, a journalist who is perceptive and broadly supportive of the Labour party, has put it well. He said:

"By itself a Bill of Rights cannot halt a drift towards authoritarianism and conflicts born of injustice. But it offers a ledge of legal ground on which the injured subject may stand and fight."

That is all that I claim for it, but I claim that it will make a significant difference to the climate in which we live in this country and to the climate of freedom that has been seen to be under threat.

If the Labour party's deputy leader is still seeking to persuade his party that it is better to seek the vindication of those rights in Strasbourg than in Sparkbrook, he cannot be surprised if his point of view seems to some to be perverse. The rights protected by the language of the convention may seem to some to be unduly vague, but the cases that have been dealt with in Strasbourg have covered such precise circumstances as the alleged inhuman treatment of suspected terrorists in Northern Ireland; inadequate safeguarding of personal privacy against telephone tapping by the police; unfair discrimination against British wives of foreign husbands under the immigration rules; alleged inhuman conditions in cases of solitary confinement and segregation; corporal punishment in Scottish schools; ineffective judicial protection for detained mental patients and would-be immigrants; and the dismissal of workers because of the oppressive operation of the closed shop, the case to which I have referred.

They also include the nationalisation of aircraft and shipbuilding companies without adequate compensation —[*Interruption.*] No, a Conservative Government were in office then. Such cases also include the denial of equal citizenship rights to British passport holders from East Africa and interference with free expression by the Law Lords in extending the common law offences of contempt of court and blasphemy. Many other important matters of public law have been brought before the Commission.

When the call to incorporate the European convention was first made 15 years ago, some doubt was expressed about the appropriateness of judges being involved in deciding cases which, of their nature, had a substantial political element. The capacity of British judges to act in such cases was never seriously in question, for the Judicial Committee of the Privy Council had, for many years, fulfilled such a role as the final court of appeal in many Commonwealth countries. That argument was advanced by the Attorney-General the last time this issue was debated in the House—I am glad to see him in his place for this debate—but he must acknowledge that it now seems somewhat dated. In the intervening years we have seen the development by the judiciary, with parliamentary approval, of judicial review of administrative action. Virtually all those cases are of considerable political sensitivity.

We have also seen British judges apply the general provisions of European Community law and find little difficulty in so doing. Indeed, although the European convention has not itself been incorporated into Community law, the European Court of Justice has issued

decisions in the light of it. It therefore follows that, indirectly, the European convention is becoming a part of British law, if only in a limited economic sphere.

Although I have not hitherto proposed that a Bill of Rights should be entrenched under our constitution—to answer the point made by the hon. Member for Aldridge-Brownhills (Mr. Shepherd)—and it is true that its provisions even if incorporated could be rendered null by a simple Act of Parliament, I believe that the political impact of enacting a Bill of Rights would be considerable. Governments would not lightly derogate from its provisions, and the public would be alerted to the potential breach of our freedoms if a Government showed such a purpose.

I recognise that the Prime Minister has argued before now that that is a constitutional matter of the kind that it is right to enact only when there is broad cross-party support. However, notwithstanding her personal view and that of the deputy leader of the Labour party, I believe that such broad cross-party support exists and that it is underpinned by a substantial majority in the country. That is the evidence of opinion polls that have been taken directly on that point.

There is a growing desire for a Bill of Rights in this country. As the matter seems increasingly urgent, I appeal to the Prime Minister to recall the undertaking of the manifesto on which she was first elected, to institute all-party talks. Such a step would go far to give substance to her claim to be concerned for the rights and freedoms of the people. The people of this realm are concerned that they are seeing the erosion of the liberties that they have taken almost for granted, unchecked by this Parliament, which itself is becoming a cipher to be used by an over-mighty Government.

7.44 pm

**The Minister of State, Home Office (Mr. John Patten):** I beg to move, to leave out from "House" to the end of the Question and to add instead thereof:

'welcomes the extension and enhancement of civil liberties over the last decade; believes that the Government has acted fairly to balance the liberties of the individual with the rights of others and of the community as a whole; and considers that these liberties are fully protected by present constitutional arrangements.'.

The hon. Member for Caithness and Sutherland (Mr. Maclennan) made his remarks in a serious tone and gave the House a serious speech. He had obviously thought about what he had to say in some depth and made an interesting speech, on which I congratulate him. Although I did not agree with much of it, it provided a useful text for those of us who wish to examine the arguments of those who, I believe mistakenly, feel that there has been some great erosion of liberties recently, especially in the past 10 years of Conservative government.

Apart from religion and family, to me at least, few things are as important as the protection of basic human rights—I am sure that most hon. Members would agree with that—but the country that the hon. Gentleman described bears little resemblance to the one in which I live and which I know. His suggestion that civil liberties have been eroded in the past 10 years seems to be not only incorrect, but the opposite of the truth. I shall try to demonstrate why I believe that, in what I hope will be the same serious vein as that of the hon. Member for Caithness and Sutherland.

[*Mr. John Patten*]

I should begin by saying that this Government and all the Ministers in it are fully committed to ensuring that the citizen of this country knows his or her rights and that those rights are not violated. That does not mean that liberties are or can ever be under the prescription that we favour or that of the hon. Gentleman's Bill of Rights, of which he sketched a brief plan. It does not mean that those liberties can ever be unqualified because any responsible Government must also take account of the rights of society at large and of the conflicts of rights that exist in society. That is fully recognised in the many international human rights treaties to which we are party.

I will take as an example the right of freedom of expression as defined in the European convention on human rights because

"it carries with it duties and responsibilities".

According to the convention, that right may be limited to the extent necessary in a democratic society in the interests of national security, public safety, the protection of morals, and so on. I do not think that anyone seriously disputes that most freedoms must have some limits. I doubt whether there is any disagreement between the hon. Member for Caithness and Sutherland and myself on that. The disagreement is about where the limits should be drawn.

We should also remember—this was largely ignored in the hon. Gentleman's speech although he was teased into making some references to it, thanks to two excellent interventions by my hon. Friend the Member for Colne Valley (Mr. Riddick)—that political freedom depends to a considerable extent on economic freedom, which is something that Conservative Members hold dear. However much a national constitution may proclaim and purport to guarantee civil rights, those rights will always be limited unless individual citizens have a measure of economic freedom with which they can exercise those rights and within which they can exercise a certain amount of choice.

It is for that reason—not materialism—that the Government have given emphasis to measures which enhance personal freedom—by, for example, returning to people the right not to belong to a trade union. There was precious little freedom at factory gate strike meetings, at picket lines at factory gates or with mass pickets or flying pickets. It is for the same reason that we have given people the opportunity to buy the council house or flat in which they live. Happily, that is now becoming an all-party consensus. The Education (No. 2) Act 1986 and the Education Reform Act 1988 have shifted power away from bureaucracies in the favour of parents, teachers and school governors.

My last point on the necessity to underpin freedom by giving people a measure of improved economic status is that it is no coincidence that the deregulation and freeing of economic life in this country has coincided with increased productivity, lower unemployment, lower taxes and more disposable income in real terms. That bestows freedom, but it also bestows responsibility. That, too, is important.

**Mr. Ashby:** My hon. Friend has missed out one of the most important freedoms that the Government have given us. The reduction of taxation has given individuals the freedom to spend the money for which they have worked hard in the way that they wish rather than the state saying how it should be spent.

**Mr. Patten:** My hon. Friend, characteristically, is absolutely right.

Over the years in which I have been a Member of Parliament, Opposition Members have made much of a supposed diminution of freedom of expression, which I know that some of my hon. Friends also feel. Again, that is a charge that does not stand up to close examination. In this Session, for example, the Government's Official Secrets Act has removed a huge category of Government information from the criminal law. It has also raised new obstacles to bringing prosecutions against journalists in those few areas which still remain within the criminal law. The decision to prosecute in those cases rests no longer with the Government, but with the prosecuting authorities. The test for a journalist is not whether disclosure will cause the Government embarrassment, but whether it will cause specific forms of harm to the national interest, and that the journalist knew that it would. Protection of the national interest will always remain, however, the first priority of the Government, as I hope that it will for all parties in the House.

On the theme of liberty of expression, the Criminal Justice Act 1988 allows the press to challenge specific orders which restrict press reporting. The Police and Criminal Evidence Act 1984 gave judicial protection to journalists' notebooks. Those are three considerable areas in which we have actually improved and not diminished the freedom of journalists to report. I cannot envisage any way in which those matters could restrict the freedom of the press.

**Mr. Michael Stern** (Bristol, North-West): Will my hon. Friend give way on that point?

**Mr. Patten:** Indeed I will. Perhaps my hon. Friend feels that we have gone too far.

**Mr. Stern:** On the contrary, on the question of freedom of expression, does my hon. Friend recall that it was this Government who passed the Education Act 1986, which attempted to guarantee freedom of speech within our universities? Where were the Opposition parties when Professor John Vincent was being beaten up by a mob at Bristol university and when our hon. Friend the Member for Luton, North (Mr. Carlisle) was being forbidden for six months the opportunity to utter a word on every campus in the country?

**Mr. Patten:** I agree with my hon. Friend. I believe that the guarantees of academic freedom are important. I represent a university city. I know that my friend Professor Vincent suffered terribly with those personal attacks, as did his family. That is not the way to conduct free argument.

This Government are committed—as I hope that any Government would be—to the principles which lie behind the idea of open government, but "open government" is an easily turned phrase. The principle is, of course, to make as much information available as possible while preserving the confidentiality that is essential to the effective working of Government. That is, of course, consistent with the principles under which this place works. Ministers are accountable to Parliament for their performance in that respect.

I will cite a few of the many ways in which the Government have made more official information available in the past 10 years. There has been a considerable increase in public consultation, very much more briefing for the media, and publication of research and evaluation papers—*[Interruption.]* No, by Ministers. Tape recorders now operate at every briefing that I give at the Home Office, which I believe is a good way to conduct those matters. There is more publication of research and evaluation papers on the effect of policies and more openness about the processes of Government. There have been cameras inside our prisons and police stations, and Departments consult far more and much more widely. Of course, the Select Committees have developed their role in examining expenditure, administration and policy of the main Departments.

**Mr. Maclennan:** On the subject of Government information and briefings, does the hon. Gentleman not think it significant that at least three major national newspapers and organs of opinion think so little of these as a means of learning the truth about what is going on in the Government that they have declined to participate in the Lobby system?

**Mr. Patten:** The briefings to which I was referring were the kind where journalists with a proper interest want to talk to a Minister on the record, to a Minister's civil servants or to the press department simply to find out information. In my brief experience of Government, there is much more of that now than there was when I started. It is a good thing that, within proper limits, civil servants talk to the press and explain to the press what they are up to and what the bases of policies are without taking on the role of being Ministerial spokesmen.

I believe, however, that the most significant trend of the past 10 years is the fact that the courts have continued to develop and to refine judicial review to supervise the fairness of administrative decisions. I strongly believe that judicial review is far and away the most effective safeguard against the abuse of power. It is a much more effective safeguard than any Bill of Rights could ever be. That is a theme that I shall now try to develop.

**Mr. Richard Shepherd:** The safeguard used to be the House. I wonder what my hon. Friend would say—I think that this is part of the question before the House—to Lord Hailsham's question about the elective dictatorship: what are the institutional safeguards to ensure the continuance of freedom of speech and freedom of assembly? My hon. Friend has not so far addressed that issue, but I hope that he will do so before he concludes.

**Mr. Patten:** Given the parliamentary supremacy, I suppose that theoretically there can be none. I say "theoretically", but we are greatly helped by judicial review. I believe that my noble Friend Lord Hailsham recognises that. Of course, we have public opinion, which underpins so many of our freedoms in this country.

The right of freedom of expression is not absolute, for it is limited to protect the rights of others. Hence, we have laws about racial incitement, libel and blasphemy, as mentioned by the hon. Member for Caithness and Sutherland. The legal framework which protects an individual's rights in this country has been shown in rather starker relief recently as a result of the "Satanic Verses" affair. Hon. Members will be aware of the background to the case, with the demonstration towards the end of May in London and with the lamentable violence in Bradford on Saturday. There are, however, some general points which bear repeating and emphasising before the House.

The first is that our commitment to civil liberties encompasses the rights of freedom of speech, freedom of assembly and freedom of protest, which are three important freedoms. The second is that those freedoms should prevail provided that the criminal law is not broken. That principle underpins those three freedoms. On no account should the freedom to demonstrate be regarded as an opportunity for violent disorder, however passionately held the views of the protesters.

**Mr. Kenneth Hind** (Lancashire, West): On the point made by my hon. Friend the Member for Aldridge-Brownhills (Mr. Shepherd), how does my hon. Friend the Minister view the preservation of those fundamental rights, in the sense that any Government who have a majority in the House can, through that majority, overturn rights that we all accept today as fundamental to our community? They can sweep away those rights purely and simply by means of an elected majority. Are not some rights so fundamental that they should necessarily be over and above that and, if we have a Bill of Rights, should require something like a two-thirds majority to overturn them, as in the United States constitution? We should not, as the hon. Member for Caithness and Sutherland (Mr. Maclennan) suggested, have a temporary Bill of Rights, which would be no rights at all.

**Mr. Patten:** I know that my hon. Friend the Member for Lancashire, West (Mr. Hind) has given much thought to the matter, but I believe that this place, reinforced by public opinion and judicial review, is an adequate safeguard. My hon. Friend went very much further in suggesting how a Bill of Rights should be entrenched and made some suggestions which may be useful to the hon. Member for Caithness and Sutherland, who did not tell us how he would entrench his Bill of Rights.

To return to demonstrations, freedom of assembly and freedom of protest, the whole House will continue to understand and sympathise with the anger and hurt of many Moslems over the contents of "The Satanic Verses". At the same time, our message to Moslem community leaders, although a brief one, must be clear: "By all means meet and voice your protest as British citizens, but do not let your message be lost among, or your reputation be sullied by, the violent actions of a disorderly minority. Do not abuse your freedom to demonstrate by encroaching upon the freedom of others to hold a different view or simply to walk down a usually peaceful shopping street on a Saturday afternoon. Try to impress on young hotheads in your community that pictures of policemen lying on the ground being kicked do nothing to advance the Moslem cause or the cause of ever-improving race relations, which are an important part of our national fabric."

**Mr. Tony Benn** (Chesterfield): Everyone understands why the Minister chose to put that passage in his speech. He referred to blasphemy. There is pressure to extend the law and I have presented a Bill which would abolish the offence of blasphemy. I should like a clear assurance that the Minister stands by the Home Secretary's position that there should be no change in the law. Were an attempt made to assuage those anxieties by extending the law of blasphemy, it would raise serious questions. Hon.

[*Mr. Tony Benn*]

Members on both sides of the House agree that it would be wrong to extend it. Indeed, it would be impossible, because for a Moslem, the Christian faith is blasphemous, and so on.

**Mr. Patten:** I certainly stand by what my right hon. Friend the Home Secretary has said. One of the specific points concerning alleged blasphemy is before the courts, according to a reference on the Press Association tapes this evening.

The motion before the House includes the assertion that civil liberties are increasingly under threat from the abuse of public power. People seem to have short memories. It was this Government who this Session put the Security Service on a statutory footing for the first time. This Government have given redress to citizens who consider that they have a grievance against the security services. The Police and Criminal Evidence Act has strengthened the investigatory powers of the police. If, as is intended, this means that the guilty are more likely to be brought to book, that extends liberty—the liberty to be protected from wrongdoers—while the same Act, with its codes of practice, provides for better safeguards for citizens and those who have not been brought to trial and gives us much more certainty about what powers the police have. As a citizen, I welcome that as much, I hope, as any other hon. Member.

If I disagree with the diagnosis of the hon. Member for Caithness and Sutherland in his thoughtful speech, I find the medicine that he suggests even more unpalatable. He suggests that citizens would enjoy more rights if civil liberties were enshrined in a Bill of Rights. I think that that sums up his argument. Anyone might think, from the way in which this was proposed, that those rights are not protected unless they are codified and set down in a Bill of Rights. That is not so, and the hon. Gentleman knows it.

Those rights are already protected in our common and statute law, although in far more precise terms than is usual in, for example, the European convention on human rights, which most proponents of a Bill of Rights would like to incorporate in our law, and which is couched in much more general terms than much of our statute law. For example, article 6 of the convention specifies in general terms minimum rights for a person charged with a criminal offence but without spelling out details of time limits, cautions, rules of court and police procedures, on which our statute law is increasingly specific, giving greater protection to our citizens.

Arguments for incorporation have been paraded in the national press, although the right hon. Member for Birmingham, Sparkbrook (Mr. Hattersley) in particular has made his opposition clear. I do not often agree with him, and I hope that he will not be alarmed to hear that I agree with some of the things that he has written. He was attacked by the hon. Member for Caithness and Sutherland for being unspecific about the way in which he intended to protect citizens' rights in his scheme. The right hon. Gentleman probably does not need my defence, nor would he welcome it, but I believe that it is unfair for the hon. Member for Caithness and Sutherland to criticise him for not working his ideas out in full when the hon. Gentleman himself did not spell out to the House how he

would entrench his Bill of Rights if it ever reached the statute book, as my hon. Friend the Member for Lancashire, West (Mr. Hind) pointed out.

**Mr. Maclennan:** The Minister has clearly neither heard nor understood what I said, and I apologise if that is my fault. I said that I was not proposing the entrenchment of a Bill of Rights. I was advocating that as with the Bill of Rights of 1689, which not even this Government would contemplate repealing, it should be a simple statute.

**Mr. Patten:** I fully understand what the hon. Gentleman has just said and what he said earlier. He has not explained for the understanding of the House why it is worth going through the exercise if some later Government can turn the whole thing on its head.

**Mr. Hind:** In that case, it is a waste of time.

**Mr. Patten:** It is a complete waste of time, as my hon. Friend comments from a sedentary position. We need to grasp that nettle if we are to get anywhere with the intellectual underpinning of an argument for a Bill of Rights. The hon. Member for Caithness and Sutherland has failed that test.

Incorporating the European convention on human rights would mean that the courts, rather than Parliament, would determine society's needs. That is no reflection on the impartiality of the judiciary. Rather it is a reaffirmation that it is for Parliament, with its sovereignty, to decide. I do not doubt that judges could do the job—of course they could—but I have doubts about what the job would do to the judges. It would politicise them in the public eye. There can be no more powerful exposition of that case than that put forward in the Chamber by my right hon. and learned Friend the Attorney-General in the 1987 debate on the private Member's Bill put forward by our then colleague Sir Edward Gardner.

**Several Hon. Members** *rose*——

**Mr. Patten:** I have given way a great deal. I am anxious not to take up the time of the House because a number of hon. Members wish to contribute.

Our unwritten constitution has served us well, and there is no evidence that a written constitution or Bill of Rights would help us to do it better. Everything depends on how a constitution, written or unwritten, is interpreted and applied in daily life. That is an acid test.

For some people, of course, liberty has been curtailed. The hon. Member for Caithness and Sutherland made threatening statements about the way in which he saw liberty being curtailed. I do not mind the idea that IRA terrorists can travel less easily to and from Great Britain as a result of the powers available to the police, the courts and the Government under the Prevention of Terrorism Act 1974. Those powers are essential for the defence of law-abiding people against terrorism and, alas, they are powers that the Labour party wishes to revoke.

I do not mind that the opportunity for apologists of bombings and shootings to appear on our screens has been curtailed. I do not apologise for the fact that their chances of making propaganda broadcasts have been denied. I certainly do not mind the curtailment of the liberty of a young man to carry a knife in his pocket and the fact that, should he appear in court, the burden of proving why he was carrying that knife now rests with him and not with the prosecution. Those are certainly restrictions on individual liberty, but they are necessary if we are to stop the growth of a knife culture on our streets. I welcomed at the time and I welcome again the support from the Labour Front Bench for that move.

I do not mind that the drug trafficker and the serious criminal know that, when convicted, they may lose not just their liberty but the profits from their crimes, which the courts are now empowered to confiscate. Those curtailments of liberty are extremely important, and few reasonable people would not accept the case for such action.

Ministers and Parliament have a duty to judge the difficult balance between enhancing individual freedom and ensuring proper protection for our nation. All Governments, of whatever colour, will always have that duty. In the past decade, we have looked conscientiously and meticulously at issues of individual freedom. No decision to increase or diminish those powers—I have openly given examples of increasing as well as diminishing powers over individual liberty—has been taken lightly and without clear evidence of need in either direction. Where the protection of the community has needed limited and well-defined reinforcement, we have provided it, and we shall continue to do so. I ask the House to reject the motion.

8.9 pm

**Mr. Alistair Darling** (Edinburgh, Central): Quite understandably, the Minister referred to events in Bradford this weekend. He, like the Home Secretary, has exhibited an unfortunate tendency to lecture Moslems as a whole. We should be mindful of the fact that the majority of Moslems are law-abiding and a minority of people were involved in the trouble at the weekend. Before a Minister imputes blame to the Moslems, he should be careful because it may have unfortunate consequences.

The tragedy is that the reason for the Moslems' hurt and offence has gone undiscussed and undebated in the country because of the trouble on which attention has focused. Unless we are willing to understand and discuss the reasons for the hurt and fromence caused to Moslems we shall be a long way off fostering the mutual understanding and respect needed in this country.

**Mr. Stern** rose——

**Mr. Darling:** No, I shall not give way. I merely wanted to make that remark, and I know that many hon. Members want to speak. I now intend to address the motion before the House.

There is no doubt that a statement of rights in this country is necessary and that, under this Government, the need for a framework of rights has assumed a greater importance and urgency. Who would have thought that a British Government, this Government, would have ordered the seizure of the English language editions of *Pravda* to prevent British people reading about "Spycatcher", when the world already knew all about it?

The Minister said that he did not recognise the country of which the hon. Member for Caithness and Sutherland (Mr. Maclennan) spoke. Perhaps that is where the trouble lies, and perhaps Conservative Members should reflect today that some of the difficulties may be due to the fact that Ministers, particularly the Prime Minister, do not recognise the country which most of us see. The Government are intolerant. They talk of enemies within,

and their record on rights is poor. More than 80 British laws have been amended as a result of decisions in the European Court on Human Rights. No wonder that Conservative Members, particularly the Prime Minister, do not like Europe.

The Government's actions are oppressive, as has been shown by their treatment of broadcasting. We saw the spectacle of police being sent to raid the BBC headquarters in Glasgow in the middle of the night. Who would have thought that that would happen in a British city? We saw the Zircon tapes seized as an elaborate blind, when the real reason for the Government not wanting the Secret Society series to be broadcast was because of the sixth programme in the series, entitled "Cabinet Government", which still languishes in the BBC Scotland offices in Glasgow. That programme was about the election campaign of 1983, and the fact that the Government sought to undermine and spy on the citizens of this country. Their object was to prevent the programme from being shown, and the Zircon affair was a blind.

Other examples of the Government's oppression include the GCHQ and Stalker affairs, the judicial process and the Official Secrets Act 1989, which means that there is now no public interest defence. We have recently seen their blatant attempt to nobble the judiciary in the immigration appeal tribunal system, although, happily, that has now been stopped.

The Government have no concept of citizenship in society, something which is despised by the Prime Minister. She says that every person should be a freeholder, with the implication that being a citizen means that someone also has to own property. Far from setting people free in this country, the Government have climbed on to people's backs and withheld information. They attempt to condition the media, and the Gibraltar affair was an example. To this Government, freedom is not a right but is strictly on loan. The Government's actions and ideology are but one reason for the changing mood sweeping the country. What is to be done about it?

The motion invites us to endorse a Bill of Rights, but the Opposition will not support it for two reasons. First, the main problem with a Bill of Rights in this country is due to the nature of the British constitution, which is unwritten. I think that the hon. Member for Caithness and Sutherland will accept that most countries with a Bill of Rights have a written constitution which can be entrenched, and that there usually is a supreme court to interpret it. In England, there is no such system. Instead, this country's fundamental constitutional doctrine is the supremacy of Parliament, and the fact that no one Parliament can bind its successor. Therefore, it is obvious that a Bill of Rights approved by one Government could be undermined or substantially changed by a subsequent one. The Bill of Rights could not be elevated above other laws and given the status of a super-law.

**Mr. Richard Shepherd:** I am very interested in this argument. At the moment, we are signatories to the treaty on the convention of human rights and the courts are increasingly taking note of it. The Government accept the rulings of the European Court, except for the little derogation before Christmas on the Northern Ireland issues, which the Minister thinks is a great advance for liberty. Therefore, have we not enshrined a Bill of Rights by the mechanisms of the treaty?

**Mr. Darling:** We are a signatory to the treaty, but it is always possible, as the hon. Member for Aldridge-Brownhills (Mr. Shepherd) said, for us to get out of it. At the moment, we do not have a system which allows us to enshrine and elevate any legislation or treaty to the status at which it would be extremely difficult, if not impossible, to completely remove it or so undermine it that it becomes ineffective. It is always open to the Government to legislate themselves out of difficulties with which they may be presented by the courts in this country or elsewhere.

It is a shame that the hon. Member for Caithness and Sutherland did not dwell on the second problem, which involves the contents of a Bill of Rights. There is no doubt that some Governments, particularly this one, would wish to elevate some of their worst political prejudices into constitutional pillars. I doubt that there would be national consensus, and there certainly would not be in the House, about what should be contained in a Bill of Rights.

Difficulties would present themselves when we dealt with the security services, over which there are fundamental differences across the House.

The general problem can be illustrated by the European convention on human rights, to which reference has been made many times this evening. Article 6 states:

"In the determination of his civil rights and obligations or of any criminal charge against him, everyone is entitled to a fair and public hearing within a reasonable time by an independent and impartial tribunal established by law."

As the Minister said, that is all very fine, but unless there are safeguards—for example, involving the time in which someone can be brought to trial—the system is open to abuse.

The Minister sits and nods in agreement, but he may like to reflect that England has no provision comparable with that in Scotland, which requires someone to be brought to trial within 110 days of him being committed for trial. In England, it is possible for someone to remain locked up without trial for a considerable period. The provision in the European convention is all very well as a statement of principle, but without detail and safeguards, it does not have the value imputed to it.

Article 8 of the European convention states:

"1. Everyone has the right to respect for his private and family life, his home and his correspondence.

2. There shall be no interference by a public authority with the exercise of this right".

That is fine, but where does it leave us with regard to phone tapping and so on? General statements, while welcome and sometimes useful are, by themselves, incomplete. It is necessary to specify to a far greater degree than has been done in the European convention or other countries' Bills of Rights, what those rights are. We do not want to have a system of vague rights which can subsequently be undermined by Government action or which allows the judiciary wide room for maneouvre.

The same problem arises in article 12 of the European convention, which states:

"Men and women of marriagable age have the right to marry and to found a family, according to the national laws governing the exercise of this right."

That demonstrates the difficulty faced by some citizens in this country. It is true that men and women of marriageable age have a right to marry, but as we know, this Government and others before them have posed great barriers if a British citizen wants to marry, for example, a Pakistani or Indian citizen. In that case, they have to pass the primary purpose rule. They have to prove that the primary purpose of their marriage is not to gain admission to this country by means of their prospective spouse. So an article such as article 12 can be undermined by the way in which the Government choose to interpret it or to legislate their way out of it.

**Mr. Hind:** How would the hon. Gentleman entrench his Bill of Rights in such a way that it would not be possible for a subsequent Parliament to get round the rights that it contained?

**Mr. Darling:** I say, in the politest possible way, that the hon. Gentleman has been jumping up and down all evening. If he holds on for a little he will hear what we propose.

As I was saying, article 14 deals with discrimination and is also worded in general terms. I emphasise that general rights have only limited value. It is necessary to specify what these rights are and how we might go about enforcing them. Unless it is clear to the courts what remedy Parliament or a convention is proposing, the rights can be undermined.

We should also bear in mind the fact that, unless this detail is enshrined in statute, the issues will be decided not by Parliament, which is supposed to represent the people, but by judges. Ultimately, the Government can still legislate themselves out of awkward difficulties.

Our approach is different, and, I think, practical. It is designed for early implementation and it does not involve writing a constitution for the country. It is designed to fit into the British constitution as it is. The House will be aware that the Labour party proposes major constitutional reform. The reform we have in mind will provide many of the safeguads which, I am sure, the Social and Liberal Democrats—if they are still around—will support, as will a growing number of Conservative Members——

**Mr. Maclennan:** How does the hon. Gentleman propose to entrench these changes?

**Mr. Darling:** If the hon. Gentleman will contain himself, I am just about to get to that point.

We propose that the House of Lords be abolished and replaced by a directly elected second Chamber which will have the power to block for one parliamentary term certain Acts enshrining constitutional reforms and fundamental rights, which I shall refer to in a moment. We aim to provide a clearly stated system of defined rights, a system that can be enforced by citizens in their local courts without having to go to London or Europe. We aim to create rights that provide an immediate remedy.

For example, we consider that a freedom of information Act is essential and long overdue. Citizens have a right to know why decisions were made and who made them. We would repeal the Government's official secrets legislation. We shall enshrine a right to reply Act and a right to privacy, not along the lines proposed by the hon. Member for Winchester (Mr. Browne), but a right not to be interfered with by the state, providing safeguards against the abuse of power by the state.

We believe that the Data Protection Act 1984 needs to be greatly strengthened. Citizens have a right to know what information is held on them and why, so as to avoid abuses. We also believe that a right to equal treatment, regardless of sex, race, sexuality or disability, is essential.

It is worth observing in passing that the regional and national assemblies which we propose will also provide rights and safeguards and will begin to move the balance of power away from Westminster. This Government have abolished councils. The Secretary of State for Education and Science has acquired 415 new powers, and the Secretary of State for the Environment has acquired 315 new powers over local government finance and 100 over housing. Seventy thousand council officials are being barred from the political process. Patronage has been abused. All this must be stopped, and a system of regional and national assemblies can begin to put it right. Decision-making should be handed back to people so that they can see who is making decisions on their behalf. If they do not like what they see, they can replace an assembly with one more to their liking.

The Minister referred to judicial review, but he must know that it is strictly limited. It cannot examine the law or a regulation; it can merely look into the way in which a decision was reached. It is certainly not the answer to the frequent complaints heard in this Chamber——

**Mr. Menzies Campbell** (Fife, North-East): Much of what the hon. Gentleman has just said would probably find agreement in many parts of the House, but he has still not dealt with the point made by my hon. Friend the Member for Caithness and Sutherland (Mr. Maclennan). How would he entrench in his constitutional changes the elements which he regards as so desirable? I find it difficult to imagine that his party will create a constitutional system in which the House of Lords can stop this House legislating in the way in which it has done for many years.

**Mr. Darling:** We propose that the second Chamber will have the power to delay legislation for a whole parliamentary term——

**Mr. Hind:** For one year?

**Mr. Darling:** No, for the length of a Parliament, which could be up to five years. This would force any Government proposing to diminish any of these rights to go to the country with that specific programme in mind. Thus, we shall be able to safeguard rights and the constitutional settlement which we propose—consisting of regional and national assemblies—so as to stop any Government coming to office and tearing them up. A Government would be forced to go back to the country if they wanted to pursue such a programme.

I fully accept that this will not block repeal for all time —under our constitution that would be impossible—but it provides a new safeguard and, as such, it is greatly to be welcomed.

**Mr. Hind:** Does the hon. Gentleman recognise that the public will regard this idea with extreme cynicism? A Labour Government could come to power and pass Acts of Parliament, and then claim that those Acts contained certain fundamental rights. If they were subsequently not elected for a further five years, the system would block the party that came to power from changing the legislation. The Labour Government could then wait until returned to power, and begin again. This will sterilise Parliament for five years and block any progress that is not in line with the hon. Gentleman's point of view.

**Mr. Darling:** Let us take the freedom of information Act as an example. If it incorporated the fundamental right to which I have referred, it would not be possible for a subsequent Government to take away from or seek to

repeal the Act until they had gone back to the country to gain a mandate to do so. That is how we seek to entrench rights that we regard as fundamental.

If an incoming Government were confident of their case, it would be open to them to seek a mandate at a subsequent election to put it into action, and we should have to accept that.

**Mr. Stern:** The hon. Gentleman is making an important point. Once upon a time the Opposition believed in the public ownership of the means of production, distribution and exchange. Should such a Government come to power again and pass legislation to that effect, is not the hon. Gentleman saying that they would regard such action as fundamental, thereby ensuring not only that they could nationalise everything, but that they could prevent a subsequent Government from denationalising?

**Mr. Darling:** The hon. Gentleman is exaggerating. No one is suggesting that every Act passed by a Labour Government would be enshrined in the way I have described. I am talking about a narrow but important range of rights, not about every Bill that would go through the House. The hon. Gentleman must understand the distinction. We shall make it clear in the manifesto on which we fight the next election precisely which rights we propose to enshrine in this way. What I have described does not and could not apply to every piece of legislation that a Government wanted to enact. We propose to provide a framework that will allow remedies that are not possible at present. It is essential to create an open society where freedom is the presumption and where the opportunity of redress is easily available. It is possible to enshrine rights about which there is broad consensus. They should be enshrined in such a way that they cannot easily be overturned by any authoritarian or ruthless Government.

There is no doubt that constitutional change is essential and we propose two planks to such change. First, we propose the reform of the second Chamber in the way that I have described with strong and powerful national assemblies in Scotland and Wales and regional assemblies in England. Side by side with that will be a clear system of fundamental rights. They will be enshrined in such a way that they cannot be overturned with ease. Happily, it will not be long before we see that system in operation.

8.30 pm

**Mr. David Martin** (Portsmouth, South): It is clear from what we have heard in the debate that, when there are proposals to change our constitutional arrangements, we get into grave difficulties. They are difficulties not only of definition but of carrying into practice a system that could not be entrenched in our system of parliamentary representation and of the Queen in Parliament, which is the ultimate repository of power. We have already heard the sort of bickering that would soon break out not only in the Chamber but in cross-party and inter-party disagreements. That would occur when we tried to define what should be put in place of that which we have, imperfect thought it is.

I listened with fascination to the hon. Member for Caithness and Sutherland (Mr. Maclennan). As my hon. Friend the Minister said, the hon. Gentleman made a serious contribution. Undoubtedly, he sincerely believes that in the last 10 years we have seen something happening

[*Mr. David Martin*]

that is very different from what happened before. He believes that there have been compromises with liberty and that the powers of the Cabinet are in some way different. He thinks that the Prime Minister is some kind of dictator, the like of which we have not seen in the House in any generation.

Each of those matters is based on fundamental difficulties faced by the hon. Gentleman. His party has played no serious part in the protection of liberties nor has it had to balance them against the interests of Government. It has not played a serious part in government since the first world war apart from the short period when some members of his party were in the slipstream of the Labour Government during the 1970s. Many of those who were part of that Labour Government would wish to draw a decent veil over their activities, which led directly to the election of my right hon. Friend the Prime Minister and a Conservative Government. That Government were mindful of the trampling of liberties and the seemingly uncheckable and unchecked union activities. The memories of that have played a special part in keeping my right hon. Friend the Prime Minister where she ought to be, in No. 10 Downing street.

Are Cabinet powers any different now from what they were before? Let us look at events this century. Neither Baldwin nor Chamberlain was in any way different from the present Prime Minister in his relations with the Cabinet. Neither Winston Churchill nor Attlee listened any more than any other Prime Minister to fundamental disagreements about the way that Ministers behave or about Cabinet responsibility without expecting a resignation or, as on one famous occasion, suggesting that a period of silence would be beneficial.

Eden had a somewhat weak Government who were short-lived. Macmillan's Cabinet provided an object lesson in dissent because although there were no public disagreements, there were clearly disagreements between Treasury Ministers and the Prime Minister—"little local difficulties" in 1958, when all Macmillan's Treasury Ministers resigned. The Prime Minister of the day went to the country a year later and won a majority of 100. It could be argued that Macmillan's Cabinet was handled with a lighter rein than the Cabinets of many other Prime Ministers, and the same description could be applied to the Cabinet of Sir Alec Douglas-Home.

We can remember times during the Government of Harold Wilson when the whip was cracked. We had references to dog licences, and his Cabinet was very much in control of what went on in Parliament. Harold Wilson dominated Parliament for a time in a way that was no different from any other Prime Minister.

Then we had my right hon. Friend the Member for Old Bexley and Sidcup (Mr. Heath). We remember those halcyon days when everyone was listened to and compromise and consensus were the order of the day. However, we also remember that allegations of dictatorship were levelled against that Government. It was alleged that they were pushing through vast chunks of legislation without listening. Many Opposition Members will remember that time, but now we hear that that Government operated in a way that is wholly different from the way that my right hon. Friend the Prime Minister is operating,

My right hon. Friend the Prime Minister has to come to the House and must go to the country. One cannot blame the British people or those hon. Members who continue to support the Government when they are asked to do so. It is not dictatorship constantly to appeal not only to members of one's own party to support legislation—as has happened for many decades—and also from time to time to have to go to the country. In the end, my right hon. Friend the Prime Minister is as answerable as any Prime Minister before her and as any Prime Minister who follows her.

It is not new for the constitution to be criticised for not giving rights to individuals. It was put in a rather satirical way by Stanley Holloway decades ago, long before the present Prime Minister entered No. 10. He referred to the Magna Carta,

"That was signed by barons of old
That in England today
You can do what you like
So long as you do as you're told."

At that time it was a satirical comment, but people recognised in it a basis in truth.

All Government are faced with the difficulty of striking a balance between the rights of the individual and the interests of the community as a whole. Obviously, we can think of specific cases that occurred in Government's, and we wish that the decisions could have been different. That applies to Governments of all complexions. Hon. Members, rather than judges or anybody else, must have the ultimate power to question Government, and we must jealously guard that right.

**Mr. Maclennan:** The hon. Gentleman has advanced a historical argument about the manner in which Cabinet has been conducted in Labour and previous Conservative Governments. Does he acknowledge that the right hon. Member for Chesterfield (Mr. Benn), who is in the Chamber, was permitted by the Labour Prime Minister to campaign against the Government on the issue of the European Community? Secondly, in terms of the present Government, does he acknowledge that the right hon. Member for Henley (Mr. Heseltine) has blown the gaff and explained all the points about how the present Government work?

**Mr. Martin:** Most certainly not. Several people have left the Government and are now giving commentaries on what happened and what they hope will happen, but that is not necessarily in accordance with reality. The decision whether to go into the Common Market was made on a free vote. It was then followed up, on an idea of the right hon. Member for Chesterfield (Mr. Benn), with a referendum, which confirmed what had been decided in the House. I do not see any difference between what I have been saying, or anything that is inconsistent with what I have been saying, and what the hon. Member for Caithness and Sutherland has said.

I occasionally agree with the right hon. Member for Chesterfield on constitutional issues, and I certainly agreed with his point about blasphemy. I think that Macaulay foresaw him in the character of Sextus in the battle of Lake Regillus, when he said:

"Men said he saw strange visions
Which none beside might see
And that strange sounds were in his ear
Which none might hear but he".

There have sometimes been bizarre lectures from him looking at the historical scene back to the peasants' revolt, well after Magna Carta, through the 17th century, and no doubt we shall hear this evening a contribution from the right hon. Gentleman that is out of the ordinary. I welcome the opportunity to hear what the right hon. Gentleman has to say.

The implementation of a Bill of Rights would be decided not by this place but by judges. That would fundamentally change the constitution that we know and that has grown up over many centuries. Most of the ideas in the European convention on human rights are based on freedoms that have been borrowed from countries such as ours that have had them incorporated for many centuries and that are safeguarded within Parliament. We should jealously guard the powers of this place rather than giving them away to judges or anybody else, because I do not believe that they can be trusted with such a role.

8.41 pm

**Mr. Tony Benn** (Chesterfield): I welcome the debate and the initiative to hold it. We do not often discuss the constitution. Last year, we had a little celebration about the events of 1688, which some said were the basis for our liberties, although some of us take the contrary view about that. "The Rights of Man" by Tom Paine is still banned in the Maze prison. He was one of the greatest democrats in our history and he is still controversial 100 years after his death. I doubt whether I shall achieve that honour. I admire him for having said things of such permanent importance.

I can understand the reasons that the hon. Member for Caithness and Sutherland (Mr. Maclennan) had for introducing this motion because we have had a decade in which many unpleasant things have happened to individuals. Academic freedom in universities has been mentioned, but the Government have banned political discussion on the youth training scheme. If one is on YTS, one cannot discuss why one is unemployed because the Government have said there is to be no such discussion. We have also seen the abolition of the Greater London council, the hamstringing of local government, the banning of unions at GCHQ, the behaviour of the police at Wapping—which I saw myself, and which led to a number of police being charged—"Spycatcher", Zircon, and the "shoot-to-kill" policy.

Yesterday, I sat in Sheffield beside another Member of Parliament the hon. Member for Belfast, West (Mr. Adams). There were television cameras there, which were filming him but those doing the filming knew that if they showed the film, they would be punished. I also knew that the Government could subpoena the film makers if they thought that the film contained any information that would lead to action against him. I have never been more frightened in my life. I was sitting in the heart of this country and seeing a Member of Parliament denied the right to speak to people.

The debate will not be meaningful if we trade party points. Although the use of the powers by different Governments may differ, the problem is the existence of the powers. I can trade many examples about what happened under different Governments, but we cannot remedy this problem without looking at the constitution as a whole. There has been much discussion about a Bill of Rights. Under it, the rights of the people would be set out and monitored by judges appointed by the Prime Minister. They are subservient to the state to the extent that the mere mention of the words "national security" causes them to disregard every other factor. The judges recently disallowed a strike on the ground that it would be inconvenient, which is a contemptible attack on the idea of trade unionism, especially when coupled with sequestration of funds. This cannot be put right by adding one simple ingredient of the kind that the hon. Member for Caithness and Sutherland proposes.

Tom Paine said that the dead cannot control the living. He was right. If the political values of society some years ago had been entrenched, and we could not change them, we should be enslaved by the dead. My hon. Friend the Member for Edinburgh, Central (Mr. Darling) brought forward proposals—not Labour policy—which are to go to the annual conference from the national executive committee. He proposed two things. The first is that we should abolish the House of Lords, although he did not describe how that should be done. I have given some thought to the matter, for reasons into which I shall not go. His second suggestion was that one Government could entrench what they thought important at the expense of the next. What would happen if a Labour Government introduced something that a successor Conservative Government did not like? What would happen if a Conservative Government entrenched things that an incoming Labour Government did not like? There would have to be two elections before any change could be brought about. It is not practical to legislate in that way. These arguments will have to be explored. We need a national constitutional convention, called for the purpose, rather than a discussion on the matter in a three-hour debate on a Supply day for a political party.

The plain fact is that the people of this country have no basic or enforceable civil rights and the reason is simple. We are not citizens living in a democracy, but in law subjects of the Crown, which has immense powers over us and our lives. It has been said that Parliament is supreme, but it is not. Look at the words of the enactment:

"Be it enacted by the Queen's most Excellent Majesty, by and with the advice and consent of the Lords Spiritual and Temporal, and the Commons in the present Parliament assembled".

The Crown enacts the laws. It does not disregard the advice of either House, but we are still, in law, an advisory body. We have no mandatory power over the Crown.

What the Crown is, is an interesting question. The powers of the Crown are exercised now, in the main, by the Prime Minister of the day, personally and often in secret. It has been said that Cabinets are different, and that may be so, but Cabinets are not told what the Prime Minister is doing. Do hon. Members imagine that the Prime Minister discloses to the Cabinet that he or she intends to make somebody a peer or to instruct the security services to do whatever it is he or she wants done?

We do not even have a freedom of information Act for the Cabinet, let alone in Parliament. I would have settled for that in my time.

If people do not know what is going on, they cannot be held accountable. It is all very well for Ministers to come to the House and say that they are accountable, but we do not know what they are up to and the Conservative party did not know what we were up to when we were in Government. If we do not know, the public do not know, and when the truth slips out, the Cabinet Secretary is sent round the world to apply the principles of economy not only to public expenditure, but to the truth.

[*Mr. Tony Benn*]

The prerogative powers that the Prime Minister has at his or her disposal are varied. They include the power to make war without consulting the House of Commons. There was no explicit vote before the Falklands war, as there would have been in the American Congress. The Prime Minister can also sign treaties. The right hon. Member for Old Bexley and Sidcup (Mr. Heath) signed the treaty of accession before it was published. We never saw the treaty of accession until he came home with his signature on it. Ministers can legislate in Brussels by the use of prerogative powers. As a result, Parliament is impotent before Common Market legislation. When, as a Minister, I went to the Council for over five years, I went not with statutory power but with the prerogative power to make treaties, and the prerogative power has nothing whatever to do with the House of Commons.

The corrupting system of patronage extends its tentacles throughout the administration of Government. Is there to be a night of the long knives? That is the Prime Minister deciding whether to sack Ministers. Who is to be put into the other place? The Prime Minister does not consult anyone about that. Who is to be made a judge, a bishop, or chairman of the BBC? These are powers and they are inherent in our constitution. It is all very well saying that we should try to fit a Bill of Rights into our constitution, but let us be serious about the matter. How have we won the rights that we now have? Has any judge ever seriously advanced, on a major front, the rights of the people of this country? There are women who are Members of this place, including one who sits as a Deputy Speaker. Did a judge give those hon. Members their right to vote? Not at all. It was the struggle that did it. Another example is the right to worship.

All our rights have been won by struggle. It annoys some hon. Members—that is why they need to be reminded of the fact—that all our rights were won by breaking the law on the ground of principle. There are many examples, including the Tolpuddle martyrs against the Combination Acts, the suffragettes, the Chartists and the struggle for the right to worship as we think fit. These rights were won by principled people who broke the law, and who may have suffered for doing so. In the end, however, the House had to respond to popular acclaim.

When we ask how rights have been won, I would not put the judges anywhere. If anything, they have been the ones who have tried to punish the people who tried to make these advances.

What rights should we have? One cannot mention a Bill of Rights and assume that everyone will agree. Many will say, "What a good idea," but what rights should there be?

Is the right to work a fundamental right? Is the right to a home a fundamental right? I see people sleeping out on the Embankment every night—in the summer that is more tolerable than at other times of the year. Is there a right to a home? Is that a fundamental right? Is that something that will appear in a Bill of Rights? Is there a right to lifelong education?

Is there a right to health? My father was a member of the Liberal Government of 1910. He told me that the most important thing that that Government did was to make it clear that the nation's health was a national interest. When he told me that in about 1945, I thought that he had made a pretty obvious statement. I thought to myself, "Why did

you mention that?" I realise now why he did so. The right to health is no longer a national interest. The right to free treatment is no longer a national interest. Is the right to dignity in retirement to be in a Bill of Rights? If these rights are to appear in a Bill of Rights, we shall find ourselves in a new arena.

During the 1945 general election, I remember going to Covent Garden with the wife of a Labour candidate, Peggy Ashcroft. I drove around in a loudspeaker van for a fortnight. I remember a man called Knocker O'Connell. He got to the microphone—that was not a good thing to happen during an election because none of us knew when he would let go of it—and produced his political alphabet. He told us "F stands for freedom:"—what Britain brags about. If you can't afford your dinner, you are free to go without." What about President Roosevelt's four freedoms? These included the right to be free from fear, disease and poverty and ignorance. For some people in society the state and trade unions are the enemy, but when we consider the rights to which I have referred, one sees that the state and the trade unions are the friends of many people.

It was the state that gave people the right to health through the National Health Service. Trade unions give people rights. I happened to be speaking in another part of the House today and someone who works within the House told me that her friend, who had worked for 32 years, had been sacked by her employer after she had had to take three or four months off work to look after her dying father. What is she to do? Does that person have rights? If she does, the trade unions and the state are her friends, not her enemies.

If we are to have the rights of which I have been speaking, how shall we monitor them? Will the judges have that role? I think not. Will Parliament be responsible for monitoring them? I think that it must be. Parliament remedies injustice. We are all employed by the public. I stayed up late the other night when the debate on the registration of dogs took place. I was in my place at 3 am. Many people had written to me to express their anxiety about dangerous rottweilers and alsatians. I replied to tell them that I agreed with the feelings that they had set out in their letters. Accordingly, I was in the Chamber to vote at 3 am. Whether we want to do that does not matter, because in the end our constituents will decide whether to return us. There is nothing disreputable about working for our employers if our employers are our constituents. When I travel around the constituency I do not say, "This is my constituency and these are my voters." I am the employee of my constituents.

As I have said, advance always comes from pressure. The Labour party has rediscovered, quite properly, the importance of Scottish devolution following a by-election at Govan. Devolution was not exactly at the top of our agenda a year or two ago. Following the European elections, there will be many Greens emerging from all political parties. That is because the environmental issue has been won. If we are to get the correction of injustice built into the system, we will not be able to use the judges. To use them would be to politicise them, and they are extremely political as things stand. Another mechanism will have to be used, perhaps one that involves the ombudsman. I am not here to make the constitution. Our rights depend for their achievement on struggle and for their maintenance on vigilance.

The issue that we are debating cannot be resolved until we are prepared to examine the constitution afresh from the highest to the most modest levels in our society. When we do so, I think that we shall realise that democracy and monarchical power are completely incompatible. I am not speaking about the royal family, which is a convenient cover for the abuse of Executive power. Instead, I am talking about the principle of monarchial power. I do not think that the British people will ever be free until we have become a Commonwealth, abolished Crown prerogatives —I introduced a Bill on the subject—and embodied Executive power in statute, compelling those who exercise it to be accountable to the elected representatives of the people.

There are already signs in our society of a tremendous popular demand for the basic reforms that I am advocating. There is demand for a Scottish Assembly, and that is a demand for constitutional change. There are demands for the liberation of local authorities from ministerial control. I do not agree with all the provisions of Charter 88, but that is another example of the demands that are being made. Another example is the demand for the disestablishment of the Church of England both within and without the Church, for it is absurd that a bishop can be appointed by a Prime Minister who is not a Christian. It is a strange concept, especially when the Government seem to want conformity on the Bench of bishops.

There is widespread suspicion of the role of the security services. There is opposition to the dangerous doctrine of lifelong confidentiality to the Crown. What an absurd notion that is. There is the idea that someone has an obligation when the Crown itself knows nothing about it. The Prime Minister who gives the order, or his or her minions, may use that doctrine to conceal any revelation of wrongdoing.

The siting of foreign troops in our territory raises constitutional questions. Mr. Attlee, as he then was, brought them in without telling Parliament what he was doing. He was, of course, a Labour Prime Minister. He said that they were on a training mission. They were not on a training mission at all. They were busy building their bases so that 30,000 troops from America could be in Britain, three times as many as there were British troops in India during the time of the Indian empire. There were only about 10,000 British troops in India, apart from the Indian troops. Parliament was not told about the arrival of the American troops. I do not know whether even that Cabinet understood the position.

There was the decision to transfer powers to Brussels. I am making a democratic point, not a national one. The issues that we are discussing will not go away until we examine them more fundamentally. The important question is whether we have a new constitution and a Government of Britain Bill to put to the electorate for endorsement and not whether we should have a Bill of Rights attached to our present undemocratic constitution.

Given the gross abuse of powers of the Crown by successive Governments, few in my judgment now believe in the merits of the so-called unwritten constitution. They are right not to believe in it. It is just a cover for a form of authoritarianism, whichever Prime Minister exercises power. Any sensible political party would be wise to set aside narrow party points and address its mind to the question how we can give to the people of this country a greater right to determine their own future than is possible under the constitution, which we inherited from feudal days and which is now far less democratic than that in any other so-called free country in the world.

8.58 pm

**Mr. Richard Shepherd** (Aldridge-Brownhills): I had not intended to speak in this debate. However, I am grateful to the Social and Liberal Democratic party for raising this subject for discussion this evening. The subject touches on some of the anxieties of thoughtful people in society. What protects us? What defends our liberties, such as the freedom of speech or whatever else we identify as essential liberties?

This debate sounded almost like my school books written by people like Dicey, Wade and Phillip about law and constitution. The old concept was that Parliament, in the last analysis, defended us. Our freedoms were safeguarded here. The simplest and narrowest freedoms, the basic freedoms of expression, conscience, thought and worship, were protected in the House of Commons.

I will not trade insults with my hon. Friend the Minister of State, who cited the Official Secrets Act 1989 as progress in the parliamentary extension of liberty. I need only reflect that that Act introduces the concept of absolute offences, something that this House has campaigned and fought against for 200 or 300 years. The Minister of State believes that that is an advancement of civil liberties. I shall walk on the other side of the street, but I note what he says.

My hon. Friend the Minister of State also referred to the Security Services Act 1989. If I remember that Act correctly, it states that national security is anything that the Secretary of State for the Home Department states that it should be. Furthermore, the Act states that those matters may not go before the courts. My lessons on the constitution referred to the supremacy of Parliament and the rule of law. The courts enacted the laws. That was a test and a bench mark. Freedoms of speech were asserted through the common law.

The courts mention the "treasured" right, but increasingly this century the supremacy of Parliament has enabled the Executive to take upon themselves powers that we never countenanced that decent, reasonable and moderate people would ever think it necessary to assume. It was extraordinary for me as a Conservative Member to listen to my hon. Friend the Minister of State identify as extensions of liberty two of the most oppressive pieces of legislation brought in over the past six months. For the Minister of State to do that really stands matters on their head.

What defends our liberties? I have little confidence in our courts because of the nature of their remit, their acceptance of the supremacy of Parliament and their job to interpret the law, which I do not dispute. How are our freedoms and liberties defended?

Right hon. and hon. Members have identified several issues which have caused me great anxiety. In his final hallelujah, my hon. Friend the Minister of State stated that it was wholly appropriate, without reference to the courts, to prevent free British citizens from moving from one part of this country to another. The European Court of Human Rights, however, found that improper and considered it an invasion of our freedoms. The Government decided to derogate from that and we had 12 months to figure out a way round the European court's ruling. Although the

[Mr. Richard Shepherd]

Government have not found a way round it yet, no doubt they will do so in the next few months. Yet my hon. Friend the Minister of State has been citing those examples as advancements of our civil liberties.

One of my colleagues last January said that Parliament had become a pretty poor defender of our liberties. Given the doctrine of the supremacy of Parliament, and if the Executive can transmit through its party almost any view of the world and enact it into legislation without any correction, it is the duty of the courts to apply that legislation. People who brood on this matter tend to ask whether there is any way in which we can secure certain basic freedoms if they cannot look to Parliament to do so.

The European Court of Human Rights is the mechanism about which we are hearing much today. Incidentally, I opposed it when I first became a Member of this House. I wondered why it was necessary to have a foreign court to oversee our legislative and judicial processes. I regarded that as unnecessary. As a free-born British subject, could I not argue and defend my own rights? But as I watch the growth of Executive power and the exclusion of other centres of balance within our constitution, I become increasingly anxious.

I was elected in 1979. We were told that we were going to have less government and get the Government off people's backs. I remember all those arguments ringing in my head and I still pass them on sometimes to unsuspecting constituents who are not aware of the issues behind them.

We have increasingly concentrated power in the hands of the Executive. In my casualness, I was not mindful of the importance of local government as a balancer. At one time in Walsall, for example, it was important to a large number of residents that the grammar schools there should be maintained. The then Secretary of State for Education, Mrs. Shirley Williams—now of America—did her best to destroy Walsall's grammar schools—but she was unable to do so because the local population offered resistance and exercised its judgment through the council chamber. It happened that Labour was the largest local party and it also wanted to defend the schools, so there the matter rested.

From 1979 until today, I have watched, the Government grasp unto themselves enourmous powers, taking away the rights of local authorities to determine matters which seem wholly appropriate for them to determine. At an earlier stage, and without reflecting, I was happy to see what I thought was in my political interest come to pass. As the right hon. Member for Chesterfield (Mr. Benn) said, however, what is in one's own political interest is not necessarily in the interests of others. I am not the final inheritor of the kingdom on earth. I am merely one of those who pass through, but the powers will endure. What am I creating when I vote for legislation which increases the Executive's powers? I am handing on an instrument to a faceless successor whom I do not know, who may interpret and use those powers aggressively and in a way that will rebound to my party's dishonour and shame.

What disturbed me a little about the speech of my hon. Friend the Minister was that it did not address itself to the constitutional issue. Are our institutions sufficiently strong to protect my right to stand anywhere I like in this country and say what I wish to say? To me, that is a fundamental right. Yet we have passed a Bill that the Law Lords will enact to the effect that, if I have been a member of the security services for 25 years, for example, I cannot talk about them. To do so would be an absolute offence and one for which I could go to prison. I could not even say that I received a gold watch. The Law Lords have the ultimate jurisdiction and the power to apply that law.

Where is the relief from that aggrandisement of government by a Government who have given up the great parliamentary traditions of Burke? Parliamentary democracy is not divided by two plus one—it is the process of argument and discussion. We should all remember that. Such discussion and argument may not win my agreement, but it should secure my acquiescence. Instead, in recent years our parliamentary guillotine has been flipped up and down faster than anything in the French revolution. I believe that this Parliament has seen the operation of about 30 guillotines, seven in the current Session alone. That is all contrary to our traditions.

Where is the instrument of protection? Increasingly, I have seen it in the belated, slow and unhappy process of references to the European Court of Human Rights in respect of rights that we used to take for granted. Britain made one of the major inputs into that system, as one of its original signatories, but unhappily, the aggrandisement of the Executive is causing anxiety. I believe that these are not just the views of a Conservative Back Bencher but are held more widely. During the "Spycatcher" case, I noted constant references to the European Convention on Human Rights. I also observe judges increasingly attempting to align their judgments with the convention, even though there is no question at that stage of a referral to the European Court. Increasingly, I hear free-born British citizens who still have pockets deep enough to challenge the Government and to stand up and fight them saying, "I will go further if necessary."

One day we shall have the European Court's judgments on Northern Ireland. One day we shall get to the bottom of the Stalker affair. One day the European Court will make a judgment on whether or not our official secrets legislation is reasonable. One day we shall have a judgment on the Home Secretary's warrant for investigations which make lawful that which was once unlawful.

Why is it necessary for us to go to a European court? What if the Law Lords are not mindful of the principles and articles of the convention? Is there a device that can strengthen our institutions? The Opposition have talked about reforming the House of Lords, and I suspect that the right hon. Member for Chesterfield can tell us more about its workings as an "inside outsider". I too have come to the conclusion that the sunset home at the other end of the building, with its slight smell of urine, is a pretty poor body. Life support machines are wheeled in and people talk deferentially about one another's magnificent contributions. In fact, half of them are there due to a mere accident of birth, the other half by virtue of having been grand panjandrums in the Civil Service. Yet we hear them telling everyone how wonderful their careers have been. The whiff of liberty and freedom for which I ask is outside their ken. The spirit of the individual is more than a mere accident of birth.

What unique feature makes a man a legislator? The law reform proposals of Lord Mackay are a classic example of the separation of powers in this country. One cannot get into the House of Lords for Law Lords banging on about how we should legislate on law reform. Hon. Members should talk to me about the role of the House of Lords. It is not respectable any more. One cannot look to the present House of Lords—I go along with the hon. Member for Edinburgh, Central (Mr. Darling) to this extent—to act as a block or check because it is representative of no one other than the appointees of the Executive who put them there. That curious arrangement was known as the dignified part of the British constitution. Bagehot said that the cure for the House of Lords was to go and see it. I recommend that those who have listened to our debates on this subject should do just that.

**Mr. Benn:** There is just one charge that the hon. Gentleman has not made against the system. The power of the Prime Minister to give people peerages gives her power over whole sections of society. Many of those people will never receive peerages, but will do anything in the hope that they will. The corruption of patronage—more even than the corruption of inheritance—is a factor that the hon. Gentleman should bring into his denunciation of the other Chamber, which was music to my ears and went further than I would have dared to go.

**Mr. Shepherd:** It is well known that, in church, I can silence two pews on either side of me by my lack of true note.

I have only to sit in this House as a Back Bencher to see how we are humbled by the creative use of the power of patronage. A Cabinet no longer able to raise its voice to speak home truths and to argue its corner generously and courageously is a sight that diminishes us. That is why we are having this debate. Cabinet government has gone by the board. The ability of the House of Commons to hold its Members accountable and to defend liberties is in question. We must therefore examine the institutional arrangements.

The hon. Member for Caithness and Sutherland (Mr. Maclennan) honourably suggested that we could provide a halfway house—a temporary measure to give British citizens more rapid access—by incorporating the European convention. I have concluded that that would be an important contribution to improving the position while we consider more major constitutional reforms.

9.13 pm

**Mr. Harry Barnes** (Derbyshire, North-East): The Government have seriously undermined the democratic, constitutional and civil liberties of the people. A specific example is the recently enacted poll tax legislation, which comes on top of other measures affecting secrecy and freedom. The unfair influence of the poll tax will have a knock-on effect, for instance, on the franchise, which is part of the essential background of the establishment of civil liberties.

As my right hon. Friend the Member for Chesterfield (Mr. Benn) said, it is outside this House that pressure is brought to bear upon us. Pressure groups and other people express their views through the electoral system. It is that which is important. The franchise is being fixed and fiddled by means of the poll tax. One might not think that is the case if one looks at the European election results, when the Government got a bloody nose, but the poll tax is manipulating the franchise.

Since the general election two years ago, the franchise has dropped by more than 4 per cent. in 13 Scottish constituencies. That is not due to major population shifts, or to old people dying and fewer young people becoming eligible to enter, the electoral register. It is due to the impact of the poll tax and to the fear of the connection between the poll tax register and the electoral register. The position is even worse in England. Within a year, the franchise has collapsed by more than 4 per cent. in 17 constituencies, including Finchley, where 2,170 people are missing from the electoral register. In the Liverpool constituencies, 10 per cent. have gone missing from the electoral register within a year.

There have to be explanations, but they cannot be given in traditional terms—that fewer people are registering because no election is due. That does not fit in with what happened in the past after elections. It cannot be argued, either, that the cause is demographic change. The change has been brought about by the introduction of the poll tax. It is a sign to us all of the vast changes that the Government have introduced. The poll tax is the Government's flagship. It is a sign of the principles in which they believe.

In the referendum in Chile on the future of Pinochet, people had to pay, in order to vote and have their names put on the electoral register, the equivalent of a month's wages on an employment scheme, so many working-class people were disfranchised. However, those who voted expressed their need for democratic change.

The same has happened to some extent in this country, although it has not been on so dramatic a scale as in Chile. In Labour areas in particular, where people have the most to fear from the poll tax, between 3 and 4 per cent. of electors are beginning to disappear from the electoral register. The smashing of local government has been going on for a considerable period, but it now appears as though a ton of bricks has finally broken the proverbial camel's back.

The poll tax will interfere seriously with our democratic rights and civil liberties. Even after they have smashed local government, the Government will ensure that they fix the system by means of the poll tax. There will be a sort of Hobson's choice about who is elected. Labour-controlled authorities will be in an invidious position: should they increase the poll tax to provide services, and therefore crucify the very people that they are trying to serve, including many people who are on benefit, or should they cut services for those who need them? If local authorities do not cut the services that they provide, there are others waiting in the wings who will be prepared to cut them. The logic of it all is to tie the electoral register to the poll tax register and to manipulate the results.

The poll tax will lead to centralisation, which will be similar to the centralisation that the Government have introduced by means of many other measures, but it will be all-embracing in terms of the operation of rebate schemes, grants, the uniform business rate and many other matters that are in the hands of a Minister who acts in many respects like a municipal Mussolini in his dealings with local government.

The poll tax makes a vast attack upon civil liberties, by searching out information to ensure that, if someone has been missed off the poll tax register, they will be found on the electoral register and if they are not on the electoral register they can be hunted and searched for in a variety of records that do not exist for poll tax purposes. Today, I received a written parliamentary reply from the Under-Secretary of State for Employment stating:

[*Mr. Harry Barnes*]

"Unemployment Benefit Officers are required to disclose details of the name and address of any person or their partner, aged 18 or over, to a registration officer for a charging authority."

That was in answer to a question about poll tax registration. The answer then makes certain qualifications, but the principle operates in a host of issues in which we would not expect the state and the poll tax registrars to intervene.

That is why, following the pattern set by my right hon. Friend the Member for Chesterfield, I seek to bring two measures before the House—one is before the House and one is on its way. The Re-enfranchisement of the People Bill seeks to separate the electoral register from the poll tax register. There is a doubt in law about the legality of the poll tax legislation. Prior legislation which, thank goodness has never been changed will ensure that it does interfere with electoral registration—the 1275 Statute of Westminster, which guarantees free election; and the Representation of the People Act 1983, which codifies earlier legislation and provides that those free elections will allow people to qualify to vote without duress. Do the Government intend to interfere with that freedom and that right of franchise because they believe that the poll tax is even more important?

The other measure I intend to bring to the House concerns petitions. The Scottish Office has said that petitions to poll tax registrars can quite legitimately be used to place people's names upon poll tax registers, yet the ancient right of petitioning precedes that of franchise in Britain. It is the way in which ordinary people could express their views humbly to their monarch and to their Parliament. It was decided that they should not be put under duress for signing a petition, yet what is it but duress to say that when people sign protests against the poll tax, those protests will be used for the very purpose against which they are protesting?

That is another example of the vast attack on the democratic and constitutional rights of the people which is involved in the poll tax. As we have heard, it is but one of the measures before us and one of the signs that the Government's amendment is an absolute load of rubbish.

9.24 pm

**Mr. Ivan Lawrence** (Burton): The trouble with the word "liberty" is that it means whatever we choose to make it mean. One man's liberty is another man's tyranny. The hon. Member for Derbyshire, North-East (Mr. Barnes) has just affirmed that the community charge, where each person that has a community benefit and can afford to make a contribution shares the burden of the local cost, is the ultimate tyranny. To others it is a much fairer way of imposing a charge upon local services than the rates.

The hon. Member for Caithness and Sutherland (Mr. Maclennan) listed what he considered to be tyrannies. To him the first-past-the-post system of election is a tyranny, but to others the greater tyranny would be to subject our Government to the dictates of the party holding the balance which has attracted the least preferred votes. To him, the Broadcasting Standards Council imposes a tyranny of censorship. Others ask how else we can be expected to protect our children from the pollution of the mind that the television medium could and does inflict upon us without such safeguards. To him, the restriction

upon homosexuals not to proselytise their practices is a tyranny, but to others that most limited of restrictions extends the liberty of those who do not want their children to be brought up in a too liberal environment. It is interesting to recall that the permissive society was propounded in the 1960s by one of the founders of the party that the hon. Gentleman represented.

To the hon. Gentleman, any restriction upon the rights of Crown servants to blow their secrets for money or, by striking, to bring to a standstill the vital communications centre which helps to safeguard the security of the realm, are tyrannies. However, to others such liberties are a greater tyranny and will do far more to destroy our free society than some of the limited restrictions that the Government have considered it necessary to impose.

Like his leader, the hon. Gentleman claims to believe in democracy. Does he really believe that the people of this country actually want to open Britain to the settlement of 3·25 million Chinese people from Hong Kong? If our present society is such a tyranny, is it not immoral to invite so many potential sufferers to such a tyranny for permanent settlement on our shores?

There are many other issues in which one man's liberty is another man's tyranny. What is the hon. Gentleman's view of random breath tests? Is not the restriction of the liberty of the individual the lesser evil than that innocent people should be continuously mowed down by drunk drivers in our streets? What is the hon. Gentleman's view of the firearms legislation? Is it not a safer society with licences and restrictions on the free use of even sporting weapons?

To say that the Government are cutting the overall liberties of people is such manifest nonsense that I am surprised that the hon. Gentleman is not embarrassed about doing so.

Are we not a freer society in which the taxpayer is able to spend more of his own money through lower taxes, and a freer society now with the ability to spend abroad without restriction? Are we not freer if we own our own houses instead of being tenants of a municipality, and, if we are tenants, freer with rights that we never had before? Are we not freer in a society in which workers have a right not to be forced into trade unions, in which trade union leaders are elected and there are secret ballots, and in which the small business man now has a right to tender for contracts and to make his financial and economic way?

Are women not freer in the workplace than they were before the Government took over? Are not parents freer to choose the schools and education of their children? Is not our leisure time freer now that we can go to public houses with flexible licensing hours? In the age of the computer, are we not better protected by data protection laws? Is there not a freer press now that we have *The Independent, Today* and other newspapers that did not exist before, and freer broadcasting with more channels from which to choose?

My hon. Friend the Member for Aldridge-Brownhills (Mr. Shepherd) and other hon. Members have spoken about the official secrets legislation. Although it is perfectly true that Crown servants are no freer than ever they were to publish their secrets for money, are not civil servants far freer under this Government than they were before? Is not a freer society one that has done away with ministerial certificates as the test for criminality and replaced them with the decision of the jury? Is it not a freer society in which the secret service is put on a statutory basis, with rights that are enforceable by the courts?

**Dr. John G. Blackburn** (Dudley, West): My hon. and learned Friend has referred to the Official Secrets Act. On two occasions in my life I have entered a career in which I was subject to the Official Secrets Act and I gave a signed undertaking that I would honour the details of that Act. It was part and parcel of the conditions of my service, and I honoured it. Does he agree that to dishonour an oath, a pledge or a covenant is reprehensible?

**Mr. Lawrence:** What my hon. Friend has just said underlines the extent of his own honour, which I believe all Conservative Members emulate, which is why we supported the legislation when it was introduced.

In the contentious area of police powers, has not liberty been extended by the Police Complaints Authority, by tape-recorded interviews of suspects and by the code of practice in the Police and Criminal Evidence Act 1984 which is daily invoked in our criminal courts?

I could go on for four and half hours or more—but I shall not—listing the steps taken by this Government to safeguard the liberties of the individual. The total weighs heavily in the scale of freedom and far more heavily than the total of the restrictions placed on some individual freedoms to protect the wider freedom of the greater proportion of our people.

I accept the invocation of an Opposition Member not to turn this into a political debate, but when one recalls how things were under the Labour Government who ended their dreary days of individual restriction and restraint with their limitations on spending, on saving and on investment; with the total repression of state control; ever extending its tentacles into our lives; with the bureaucracy of municipal control; with the abuse of trade union power, yet with none of the liberties that I touched on earlier, how can the House pass a motion condemning the erosion of rights under this Government?

Of course we have not been perfect—that is because, as human beings, we are not perfect and because, as many hon. Members have said, our Parliament is a most imperfect institution. As a Government we have been misled into depriving prisoners of certain rights, such as that peremptorily to challenge three members of the jury. We have had our individual liberty unnecessarily restricted by the fluoridation of public drinking water, a matter upon which I could certainly talk for another four and half hours.

As the hon. Member for Edinburgh, Central (Mr. Darling), who spoke for the Labour party, said, it is true that we have been taken to the European Court of Human Rights on many occasions, and more often than some other countries, but that is because we have accepted the right of individual petitions since 1966, compared with that right being accepted by France in 1981; by Greece in 1985; by Spain in 1981; and by Turkey in 1988. As it takes between five and six years for an application to reach the court or the Committee of Ministers, of course we have had more violations. However, it is also because we in the United Kingdom are responsible for legal systems other than that in England, Wales and Scotland. We are responsible for the legal systems of the Isle of Man and of Guernsey, which have themselves been taken to the European Court of Human Rights.

However, the hon. Member for Edinburgh, Central did not tell us that a reference is by no means the same thing as a guilty finding; that some of the issues are by no means serious, and that some are most arguable. In one judgment last year, several complaints were lodged in respect of the opening of personal letters, but only one violation was found. That is a vindication of the civil liberties enshrined in the rules in Scotland. One adverse finding was against the right of the courts to impose a punishment of birching in the Isle of Man, and many people have different views about that matter and about the civil liberties and human rights involved. Another case was the infringement of the freedom of association arising from the closed shop, to which this Government are greatly opposed, but on which they thought that they had the duty to present the arguments fairly in that court. Against that we have, with legal aid, a far more liberal and speedy legal system than many other legal systems in Europe, and our courts, with the civil liberty safeguard of judicial review, are looked upon with admiration by the rest of the world.

Having said all that, I am in favour of incorporating the European convention on human rights into our domestic law, because I believe that we could thereby improve even further our conformity with human rights and civil liberties. I am sad that the various moves to introduce a Bill of Rights in Parliament have for procedural reasons not so far succeeded. I supported such a Bill, and I support it now, because it would be far better if our own alleged violations were to be considered by British courts, with British judges rooted in British traditions, than before foreign courts, with foreign judges rooted in foreign and quite different traditions. Such a Bill would do still more to correct our inevitable lapses and would underline Britain's complete commitment under the Government to the collective enforcement of civil liberties. It would make our efforts to sustain human rights in the world at large even more convincing.

Of course, the passage of such a Bill would not still the nonsense that cascades out of the mouths of the hon. Member for Caithness and Sutherland and his friends and allies, but then, I fear that nothing would do that.

9.35 pm

**Mr. Michael Stern** (Bristol, North-West): I entirely agree with my hon. and learned Friend the Member for Burton (Mr Lawrence) about the extent to which a lack of definition of liberty has informed the debate. That is, perhaps, not surprising, when the director of one of our supposedly foremost educational institutions—the polytechnic of north London—believes that he is supporting liberty and freedom of speech, when he disapproves of a speaker at that institution to such an extent that he throws the whole weight of the administration of that polytechnic behind organising a rival meeting so that people are not encouraged to hear that of which the director disapproves.

The hon. Member for Caithness and Sutherland (Mr. Maclennan), who introduced the debate, listed a number of part-imaginary and part-real areas in which he believed that human rights has suffered in the past 10 years. I should like to put the other side of the case, which has not been entirely explored in the debate so far—the extent to which the Government in the past 10 years have buttressed and extended human rights by their realisation that there can be no liberty and no enforcement of rights without, at

[*Mr. Michael Stern*]

the same time, protecting those rights by ownership of property, and by relating the availability of liberty to that of the right to own and the right to choose.

I cite just a few examples. I am sure that, like me, the hon. Member for Caithness and Sutherland represents a constituency which consists in part of council housing. I am sure that like me, he has discovered over the years that the one area that dominates his constituency surgeries, and which, above all others, creates unhappiness and a feeling that rights have not been given or have been taken away, is that of monopoly municipal housing. That is not surprising. If we consider housing in terms of human rights, the right of the council tenant is the right to take what he or she is given or nothing, whereas the right of the home owner, or of the tenant is a sector where there is nore than one landlord, is the right to choose the type and location of housing appropriate to the individual. That is the fundamental truth. It is this Government who have so extended that right of home ownership and are now in the process of extending the right to choose between landlords. Those are rights which were almost completely forgotten by previous Governments and certainly rights to which Opposition Members are very late converts.

Another example is that until the Government came to power, a person in employment was frequently offered the right to join a pension scheme but that right was not a right —it was a legal obligation. If the person did not want to join the pension scheme because it was wholly inappropriate to his circumstances, under every previous Government the only remedy was to leave the job. The present Government have created the right to say no—the right not to join a wholly inappropriate scheme.

There is another matter that has not been mentioned. I defer to no Opposition Member in looking to the roots of trade unionism and the extent to which in their early days trade unions represented an extension of human rights to the individual, but I hope that the Opposition join me in accepting, at least in part, that in the 1960s and 1970s that form of trade unionism had been subsumed in a trade unionism that was an instrument of repression which took rights from people rather than adding to them.

I have referred to respects in which the Government have extended liberties, but I should like to refer also to aspects where they have reduced the power of the state, thereby extending liberties. One of the Government's first actions was to abolish exchange controls. In so doing, they showed that they had the self-confidence to say to ordinary people, "You have a freedom that was not previously given, at least since the war—if you do not like this country, you have the freedom to go elsewhere and take your property with you." No previous Government had ever dreamed of giving such a freedom because no previous Government had had the self-confidence to know that most people would not want to take it once it was open to them.

It is easy to pick isolated matters on which those who wish to attack our society have, in recent years, lost part of the right to attack it, but under the Government there has been a great extension of freedom for ordinary people.

9.41 pm

**Mr. Menzies Campbell** (Fife, North-East): I start with the proposition that civil liberties are easily removed but difficult to restore. History demonstrates that freedom of speech and of association were rights that had to be won from a protesting and jealous Executive. They are rights which, under our constitution, can easily be removed because the supremacy of Parliament is such that it can override any of the civil liberties that we take for granted. Our constitution provides no protection for the constitution itself. Parliament can as easily legislate to curtail liberty and freedom as to clean up the streets. Alone among the democracies in Europe, we do not have a written constitution or a Bill of Rights.

The United Kingdom was a signatory to the European convention on human rights in 1951. In spite of that, it has never been incorporated into our domestic law. Our courts cannot apply it and aggrieved citizens have to go to Strasbourg. Some have, so it has been established that there should be legal restrictions on telephone tapping and interception of mail, that prisoners should have the right to correspond with their Members of Parliament and that a woman who has the right to live in the United Kingdom may have her foreign husband live with her here. Because of the rulings of the European Court, the law relating to contempt of court has been changed, homosexual rights have been established in Northern Ireland and corporal punishment has been abolished in state schools in Scotland. If our system is so perfect, why is it that citizens have had to have recourse to Strasbourg for those purposes?

In the Minister's speech there was a central thesis that economic freedom was necessary to underpin constitutional freedoms. Put in that form, I have no objection to that principle, but it is not enough. If the only freedom is an economic one, the rich will be more free than the poor. The right to buy council houses, which I support, is a right that can easily be diluted or made more difficult to fulfil if mortgage interest payments increase because of the operation of the economy by the Government of the day.

The Minister also endorsed academic freedom, to which there would be no objection from the Social and Liberal Democrats. In another place, Lord Jenkins of Hillhead moved, and had accepted, an amendment to provide safeguards for academics against threat of dismissal on the grounds of unwelcome opinions. The amendment was resisted by the Government, which proves that there is no monopoly of good sense in relation to the preservation of liberty to be found on the Treasury Bench.

The Minister referred to judicial review as an essential feature of the protection of our liberty. He was quite right, but he omitted to point out that the single most significant feature of judicial review has been the way in which it has developed since the Wednesbury doctrine of 1947, to the Tameside case and beyond. That case is important and if he is not entirely familiar with it, the Minister should have another look at it, because it reflected an important advance in the doctrine of judicial review. It related to selective education, and the court was constrained to review the statement of the Labour Secretary of State at that time. The court's decision was not political, but its consequences were and the court must have been well aware that it would be.

There seems to be some reluctance in the House to rely on judges, but what happens when an individual goes to

Strasbourg? He goes to Strasbourg and enlists the aid of the court to establish the necessary proposition. The right hon. Member for Chesterfield (Mr. Benn) expressed concern about the judges' role. However, in the "Spycatcher" affair they could hardly be said to be the Government's poodles. When the Labour party was endeavouring to clear up a little local difficulty in Liverpool, some of those who were the subjects of the investigations were able to go to the court and obtain an injunction against the executive of their own party to stop it proceeding in a way that would prejudice their rights. In the past, the judges have demonstrated their capacity for making proper decisions.

Much of this debate has turned on the issue whether a Bill of Rights can be entrenched in the constitution. I do not believe that it can unless the sort of wholesale review of the constitution, to which the right hon. Member for Chesterfield referred, takes place. However, neither the Treaty of Union nor the reform Acts by which we gained universal adult suffrage are entrenched in the constitution, although it is unthinkable that any Government would seek to depart or detract from those.

As the hon. Member for Aldridge-Brownhills (Mr. Shepherd) said, since we accept the rulings of the Court of Human Rights, we are, by definition, accepting a restriction on our sovereignty. There seems to be no difference in principle between importing that convention into our own law, and the circumstances in which we accept the court's judgments.

An eminent contemporary jurist said:

"When times are abnormally alive with fear and prejudice the common law is at a disadvantage. It cannot resist the will, however frightened and prejudiced it may be, of Parliament."

In another place, Lord Scarman enjoys a certain reputation in constitutional matters and I would have thought that his opinion was one to which the Government should give some weight. To adopt the convention into United Kingdom domestic law would give common law precisely the advantage that it now lacks.

The hon. Member for Edinburgh, Central (Mr. Darling) who has the privilege of being my Member for Parliament, made a most interesting contribution to the debate in which he seemed to move quickly from the constitutional proposals of the policy review yet to be approved, to the changes which he wanted in society. I am not surprised that he felt it necessary to display a fleetness of academic foot which we have not previously seen from him. His programme cannot be entrenched in law any more than ours. His Act to create a five-year delay using the House of Lords can be repealed like any other. So determined are Labour Front Bench spokesmen—no doubt under the benign influence of the right hon. Member for Birmingham, Sparkbrook (Mr. Hattersley)—to have no truck with a Bill of Rights that they are prepared to propose embracing a constitutional curiosity which many would find repugnant and which is likely to be as easily overcome as any other piece of legislation.

Part of the debate touched on freedom of information. I accept, as the debate showed, that there is an immediate clash of values between those who believe in official secrets and those who believe in freedom of information. The Minister claims that the Government's reform in this area is an advance, a proposition which brought an uncharacteristically inelegant horse laugh from the hon. Member for Aldridge-Brownhills, who went on to display

in his speech that robustness and independence of mind which have earned him the respect of all sections of the House.

The principal concern about the official secrets legislation, which is not yet an Act, is its failure to address what many regard as the real issues. Secrecy has been institutionalised in Britain since 1911 by more than 100 other statutes which make disclosure of information by civil servants or by others a criminal offence, and by strict disciplinary codes. The new official secrets legislation continues the culture of secrecy in Government. Under the new Act there will be no duty to publish information and no provision for a public interest defence for offences of unauthorised disclosure of information. As my hon. Friend the Member for Caithness and Sutherland (Mr. Maclennan) pointed out during the long debates on the Bill, it would be a crime for a civil servant to reveal that his Minister was committing a crime—a most curious consequence of the legislation and a clear insight into the thinking of the Government who prompted it.

There will be no test of harm in relation to certain disclosures such as telephone tapping and surveillance, and no requirement of guilty intent when certain disclosures are made by civil servants. If it was within our power, we would introduce a freedom of information Act to show this clash of cultures. We would establish a public right of access to official information and seek to amend the Official Secrets Bill, if it becomes law. The effect would be to put the onus on the authorities to justify secrecy, instead of on the public to justify access.

Good government depends on the ability to learn from mistakes and to improve policies. In a closed system mistakes remain hidden and no one learns from them. As this debate has shown, it is, in the end, a question of attitude. To judge from some of the contributions today, Conservative Members believe that there has been no infringement of any sort of the liberties of the subjects of the United Kingdom. They believe that from the position of the influence which they enjoy and of the privilege to which, to a certain extent, they have access.

The truth is that in many areas of our lives, public and private, our liberties have been the subject of continued erosion under all Governments since 1945. We do not notice as our liberties are diluted day by day, but eventually a point must be reached at which those who are worried about these matters take a stand, pointing out that the Government have gone so far and must be allowed to go no further. That is why we have introduced this topic for debate and why we shall invite the House to support our motion.

9.54 pm

**Mr. John Patten:** The hon. and learned Member for Fife, North-East (Mr. Campbell) may have explained why he and his right hon. and hon. Friends have introduced this motion, but they certainly have not explained to me exactly what their Bill of Rights would contain or how it would help or hinder. At no stage during the speeches by the hon. Member for Caithness and Sutherland (Mr. Maclennan) or the hon. and learned Member for Fife, North-East did we have any elucidation of exactly what the Bill would contain. They are barking up the wrong tree.

Bills of Rights and written constitutions are not the all-healing prescriptions that they are made out to be. We

[*Mr. John Patten*]

can see that from around the world. No hon. Member has dealt with any authority at all with what such a Bill would contain. [*Interruption.*] It was not stated in the speeches. Secondly, no one has said in the debate how a Bill of Rights could satisfactorily be entrenched. The arguments advanced by the hon. Member for Caithness and Sutherland and by the hon. and learned Member for Fife, North-East were, presumably, arguments of despair. The hon. and learned Member for Fife, North-East is rather unnerving because he looks and sounds like a Tory. It is just that the words do not come out in a Tory way.

**Mr. Menzies Campbell** *rose——*

**Mr. Patten:** I will give way to the hon. and learned Gentleman only on matters of tailoring and asthetics, but not on his political arguments. I will try to make it up to him afterwards.

The hon. Member for Caithness and Sutherland gave no indication at all of how his shadowy Bill of Rights would be entrenched. He and his hon. Friends should have listened much more carefully to my hon. and learned Friend the Member for Burton (Mr. Lawrence), but few SLD Members were in the Chamber when he spoke. He put his finger on the telling dichotomy between liberty and tyranny in this country—that moving frontier where one man's liberty can be another man's tyranny.

I suppose that I must turn briefly to the arguments advanced by the hon. Member for Edinburgh, Central (Mr. Darling). He lifted the veil on the Labour party policy reviews just enough to agitate the right hon. Member for Chesterfield (Mr. Benn), who did not delay for a moment or hold back from attacking his hon. Friend's constitutional prescriptions, which were exceptionally muddled and unclear. The hon. Gentleman was unable to answer any of the questions put by my hon. Friends and was subject to intimidating threats from the right hon. Member for Chesterfield about the new policy review plans needing the endorsement of the next Labour party conference.

There are many hurdles before the plans by the hon. Member for Edinburgh, Central for reform of the House of Lords, regional assemblies and local assemblies, and so on, can be put to the Labour party. The hon. Gentleman mischievously misrepresented what I said about the recent unfortunate demonstrations in Bradford. I certainly did not introduce any overall condemnation of Moslems in this country. I chose my words very carefully, as I hope and believe that he will do in future. I called upon community leaders to try to intervene with the few hotheads who have caused trouble so as to ensure that trouble does not occur in the future. The hon. Gentleman should read the record tomorrow and have the decency to apologise. He should not try to play party politics with sensitive issues about race relations in this country.

My hon. Friend the Member for Portsmouth, South (Mr. Martin) made an interesting speech, as did my hon. Friend the Member for Bristol, North-West (Mr. Stern), who spoke about academic freedom. We all listened carefully to those speeches. My hon. Friend the Member for Portsmouth, South, said that the Liberals, the Alliance, the SDP, the SLD and the Democrats—to name but five —have had no serious experience in government since the first world war and simply do not appreciate how difficult

and demanding it is to balance freedom and security, individiual liberty and national interests. We certainly cannot look to them for guidance. That was made manifestly clear in the last three hours of debate. That is why their motion is so impractical.

This is a poignant day on which to debate an SLD motion. Yesterday's results show that the public do not seem to share that party's preoccupation with its view of civil liberties. Its vote fell to such an extent that it is now in fourth place behind the Greens, which suggests that its manifesto commitment to incorporate the European convention on human rights into Community law was not quite the standard to which the electorate wished to rally. As befits a party that we now see in terminal decline, its arguments are impractical and impossible. That is why I urge my right hon. and hon. Friends to resist the motion in the Lobby.

*Question put,* That the original words stand part of the Question:—

*The House divided:* Ayes 16, Noes 164.

**Division No. 247]**                                             **[10 pm**

### AYES

| | |
|---|---|
| Alton, David | Livsey, Richard |
| Ashdown, Rt Hon Paddy | Maclennan, Robert |
| Barnes, Mrs Rosie *(Greenwich)* | Michie, Mrs Ray *(Arg'l & Bute)* |
| Beith, A. J. | Owen, Rt Hon Dr David |
| Campbell, Menzies *(Fife NE)* | Salmond, Alex |
| Carlile, Alex *(Mont'g)* | Steel, Rt Hon David |
| Howells, Geraint | |
| Hughes, Simon *(Southwark)* | Tellers for the Ayes: |
| Johnston, Sir Russell | Mr. Archy Kirkwood and |
| Kilfedder, James | Mr. Ronnie Fearn. |

### NOES

| | |
|---|---|
| Alexander, Richard | Forman, Nigel |
| Alison, Rt Hon Michael | Forth, Eric |
| Amess, David | Fox, Sir Marcus |
| Amos, Alan | Franks, Cecil |
| Arnold, Jacques *(Gravesham)* | French, Douglas |
| Arnold, Tom *(Hazel Grove)* | Garel-Jones, Tristan |
| Ashby, David | Gill, Christopher |
| Atkins, Robert | Glyn, Dr Alan |
| Atkinson, David | Goodson-Wickes, Dr Charles |
| Baker, Nicholas *(Dorset N)* | Gorman, Mrs Teresa |
| Banks, Robert *(Harrogate)* | Greenway, Harry *(Ealing N)* |
| Batiste, Spencer | Gregory, Conal |
| Benyon, W. | Griffiths, Peter *(Portsmouth N)* |
| Bevan, David Gilroy | Gummer, Rt Hon John Selwyn |
| Blackburn, Dr John G. | Hague, William |
| Boscawen, Hon Robert | Hamilton, Neil *(Tatton)* |
| Boswell, Tim | Hanley, Jeremy |
| Bowis, John | Hargreaves, Ken *(Hyndburn)* |
| Braine, Rt Hon Sir Bernard | Hayes, Jerry |
| Brandon-Bravo, Martin | Hayhoe, Rt Hon Sir Barney |
| Brazier, Julian | Hayward, Robert |
| Bright, Graham | Heathcoat-Amory, David |
| Brooke, Rt Hon Peter | Heseltine, Rt Hon Michael |
| Brown, Michael *(Brigg & Cl't's)* | Hicks, Mrs Maureen *(Wolv' NE)* |
| Bruce, Ian *(Dorset South)* | Hind, Kenneth |
| Butterfill, John | Holt, Richard |
| Carlisle, Kenneth *(Lincoln)* | Howarth, G. *(Cannock & B'wd)* |
| Carrington, Matthew | Hughes, Robert G. *(Harrow W)* |
| Chapman, Sydney | Hunt, David *(Wirral W)* |
| Chope, Christopher | Hunt, John *(Ravensbourne)* |
| Conway, Derek | Hunter, Andrew |
| Cope, Rt Hon John | Irvine, Michael |
| Davis, David *(Boothferry)* | Jack, Michael |
| Dorrell, Stephen | Janman, Tim |
| Douglas-Hamilton, Lord James | Jessel, Toby |
| Durant, Tony | Jones, Gwilym *(Cardiff N)* |
| Evennett, David | Kellett-Bowman, Dame Elaine |
| Fallon, Michael | Knapman, Roger |
| Favell, Tony | Knight, Dame Jill *(Edgbaston)* |
| Fenner, Dame Peggy | Latham, Michael |
| Fishburn, John Dudley | Lawrence, Ivan |

Lawson, Rt Hon Nigel
Lester, Jim *(Broxtowe)*
Lloyd, Peter *(Fareham)*
Lord, Michael
Lyell, Sir Nicholas
McCrindle, Robert
Macfarlane, Sir Neil
MacKay, Andrew *(E Berkshire)*
McLoughlin, Patrick
Mans, Keith
Marlow, Tony
Martin, David *(Portsmouth S)*
Maude, Hon Francis
Maxwell-Hyslop, Robin
Mayhew, Rt Hon Sir Patrick
Mellor, David
Meyer, Sir Anthony
Miller, Sir Hal
Mills, Iain
Mitchell, Sir David
Monro, Sir Hector
Montgomery, Sir Fergus
Morrison, Sir Charles
Moss, Malcolm
Mudd, David
Nelson, Anthony
Neubert, Michael
Nicholls, Patrick
Nicholson, David *(Taunton)*
Norris, Steve
Onslow, Rt Hon Cranley
Page, Richard
Patten, John *(Oxford W)*
Peacock, Mrs Elizabeth
Porter, David *(Waveney)*
Portillo, Michael
Raffan, Keith
Redwood, John
Rhodes James, Robert
Riddick, Graham
Ridsdale, Sir Julian
Roe, Mrs Marion
Ryder, Richard

Sackville, Hon Tom
Shaw, David *(Dover)*
Shaw, Sir Michael *(Scarb')*
Shephard, Mrs G. *(Norfolk SW)*
Skeet, Sir Trevor
Smith, Tim *(Beaconsfield)*
Speed, Keith
Speller, Tony
Spicer, Michael *(S Worcs)*
Stern, Michael
Stevens, Lewis
Stewart, Andy *(Sherwood)*
Stradling Thomas, Sir John
Summerson, Hugo
Taylor, Ian *(Esher)*
Taylor, John M *(Solihull)*
Tebbit, Rt Hon Norman
Thompson, Patrick *(Norwich N)*
Thorne, Neil
Trippier, David
Trotter, Neville
Twinn, Dr Ian
Vaughan, Sir Gerard
Walker, Bill *(T'side North)*
Waller, Gary
Wardle, Charles *(Bexhill)*
Warren, Kenneth
Watts, John
Wells, Bowen
Whitney, Ray
Widdecombe, Ann
Wiggin, Jerry
Wilkinson, John
Wilshire, David
Winterton, Mrs Ann
Winterton, Nicholas
Wolfson, Mark
Wood, Timothy
Young, Sir George *(Acton)*

Tellers for the Noes:
    Mr. Alan Howarth and
    Mr. David Maclean.

*Question accordingly negatived.*

*Question,* That the proposed words be there added, *put forthwith pursuant to Standing Order No. 30 (Questions on amendments), and agreed to.*

**Mr. Speaker** *forthwith declared the main Question, as amended, to be agreed to.*

*Resolved,*

'That this House welcomes the extension and enhancement of civil liberties over the last decade; believes that the Government has acted fairly to balance the liberties of the individual with the rights of others and of the community as a whole; and considers that these liberties are fully protected by present constitutional arrangements.

## BUSINESS OF THE HOUSE

*Resolved,* That, at this day's sitting, the Pesticides (Fees and Enforcement) Bill may be proceeded with, though opposed, until any hour.—*[Mr. Fallon.]*

# Orders of the Day

## Pesticides (Fees and Enforcement) Bill

*As amended (in the Standing Committee), considered. Order for Third Reading read.—Queen's consent, and Prince of Wales's consent, signified.*

10.11 pm

**The Parliamentary Secretary to the Ministry of Agriculture, Fisheries and Food (Mr. Richard Ryder):** I beg to move, That the Bill be now read the Third time.

The Bill is designed to make technical improvements to the Food and Environment Protection Act 1985. Above all, its changes will save taxpayers more than £500,000 a year.

I thank the Opposition, and in particular the hon. Members for Caerphilly (Mr. Davies) and for East Lothian (Mr. Home Robertson) for enabling the Bill to proceed smoothly with their full support Upstairs on Second Reading and in Committee. On the basis of that unanimity, I commend the Bill to the House.

10.13 pm

**Mr. Ron Davies** (Caerphilly): For the sake of accuracy, I should point out that the hon. Members for Caerphilly and East Lothian are actually two different people. I represent Caerphilly and my hon. Friend the Member for East Lothian (Mr. Home Robertson) is unavoidably delayed this evening. The Bill was subject to a brief but interesting debate in Committee. The Opposition supported its central objective, which was to remedy defects in the Food and Environment Protection Act 1985 and to recover the £600,000 which the taxpayer currently pays to evaluate the products of the pesticide industry.

Provision is also made to secure the more effective monitoring of the 1985 Act by local authorities and the Opposition accepted the Minister's assurance in Committee that the local authority associations had been consulted and further accepted that no onerous or unduly costly additional responsibilities were being placed on them.

The Opposition recognise the value of pesticides to agriculture. However, we are determined to ensure that their use is entirely compatible with the health and welfare of the environment, of those who use them, and those who consume products on which they have been used.

The registration and review procedures for which the Bill makes financial provision must be thorough but also speedy. Denise Low, head of the Department's pesticides safety division, is reported in *Farmers Weekly* of 24 March as commenting:

"Resources are not available for us to deal with routine reviews very quickly."

I put to the Minister a question that was asked in Committee. Will he use the Bill to ensure a speedy review of the many pesticides approved prior to 1965 and therefore still subject to no formal testing, and ensure also the registering of new products—some of which may be more environmentally friendly and desirable than those they were designed to replace?

Will the Minister ensure that there is less of the obsessive secrecy that surrounds pesticides, their uses and approvals than currently exists?

[*Mr. Ron Davies*]

Finally, there remains concern in the agricultural industry that the new levies may fall unfairly and disproportionately across the industry. Will the Minister continue his consultations with trade representatives and ensure some form of public reporting, or reporting to Parliament, perhaps annually, on the scheme's operation as amended by the Bill?

My hon. Friend the Member for East Lothian wanted to be present in the House this evening, as he carried the burden of the Bill for the Opposition in Committee. However, he has duties in connection with the European elections, and I am sure that at this moment he is savouring the atmosphere of Tory MEP-free Scotland, just as we do in Wales. However, that matter is contentious but the Bill is not. We did not oppose the Bill's Second Reading or its progress in Committee, and we support its Third Reading.

10.16 pm

**Mr. Geraint Howells** (Ceredigion and Pembroke, North): I agree with the hon. Member for Caerphilly (Mr. Davies) that the Bill is not contentious, and certainly it has our support. As I did not have the privilege of serving on the Committee, I have one or two questions to ask the Minister. I understand that since 1979 1 billion gallons of formulated pesticides have been used per annum. It is a serious matter that the number of health and safety inspectors dropped by 26 between 1977 and 1986.

I am informed that some farms are visited only once every six or eight years, while others have never been visited. I declare an interest, in that I do not believe that an inspector has ever visited my farm. More effective policing of spraying activities is needed, and that view was shared by the Agriculture Select Commitee in its 1987 report. The Government appear to have a lack of commitment to the health and safety inspectorate.

It is reported that, of the 71 incidents reported to the inspectorate in 1986, only 23 were properly investigated, and that inspectors are unable to provide farmers and the public with the information they require about incidents of pesticides poisoning. Although I support the Minister in every way on the pesticides issue, I believe that the Government missed a glorious opportunity to give extra financial aid so that additional inspectors can be appointed to look after the interests both of the public and of the agricultural industry.

10.19 pm

**Mr. Ryder:** I thank the hon. Member for Caerphilly (Mr. Davies) for raising three important points, with which I shall try to deal clearly and concisely.

First, he asked whether the industry would meet the costs, and whether the programme of review and registration would be speeded up. It is no secret that we have recently had some difficulty in completing as many evaluations of both new and old substances as we wished. Industry has a great interest in the rapid processing of new substances, and we are diverting as many resources as possible to deal with the applications. The review of older substances is indirectly in the interests of the companies, but is most immediately a task that we undertake in the public interest to reassure ourselves and the public of their continuing safety. We must balance those private and public interests at all times, and I believe that the Bill, by guaranteeing that the funds will be found, will allow us to progress faster in both cases.

Secondly, the hon. Gentleman asked whether I would seek—in his words—less obsessive secrecy on pesticides. As the hon. Gentleman knows, the work of our advisory committee on pesticides is not restricted by the Official Secrets Act, and industry has said that is not the data but their commercial value that it wishes to protect. We release a great deal of information now, and the issue is really acute only in relation to old pesticides, for which we simply cannot write over 400 evaluations. More resources—and, therefore, the Bill—will help to plug any important gaps in public information that hon. Members may identify. I can reassure the hon. Gentleman that we shall do all that we can to provide as much information as possible. If the information is there and its publication is in the public interest, I think that we should encourage the industry to permit it to go out.

Thirdly, the hon. Gentleman asked whether we would monitor and publish the distribution of resources between companies. The answer is yes. We are conscious of the interest of the industry and the House in the matter. I can assure the hon. Gentleman that consultation is already under way, and I shall inform the House of the outcome as soon as it is available.

The hon. Member for Ceredigion and Pembroke, North (Mr. Howells)—I have always known Pembroke, North as Cardigan, and I suspect that a few people in the hon. Gentleman's constituency do as well—asked me about the availability of resources for enforcement. The strength of the Health and Safety Executive is a matter for my right hon. Friend the Secretary of State for Employment; it does not fall under the aegis of the Ministry of Agriculture. I shall of course pass on the hon. Gentleman's remarks to my right hon. Friend.

Let me paint a broader picture of enforcement for the hon. Gentleman. From the outset, officials in our Department envisaged that environmental health and trading standards officers in local authorities would undertake enforcement of part III of the Food and Environment Protection Act 1985—FEPA—on the type of premises for which they have enforcement powers under the Health and Safety (Enforcing Authorities) Regulations 1977. It was not envisaged that that would entail the provision of additional resources, as such work would largely dovetail and coincide with duties performed under other legislation, and, indeed, would provide local authorities with comprehensive powers to enforce good practice.

Discussions with representatives of local authorities have established that they would not be averse to accepting such an enforcement role, but that such work is not viewed by the associations as devoid of financial resource implications—particularly training and litigation, the cost of neither of which can be readily determined. Local authorities intend to await our decision on the local authority officers to be specified to enforce part III before assessing the extent of the training that is necessary.

The Health and Safety Executive has a well established training scheme as well as a committee—HELA—together with sub-committees for liaison with representatives of local authorities on issues related to enforcement of the Health and Safety at Work etc. Act 1974. My officials, together with those of the Health and Safety Executive, are seeking ways to use the HELA machinery to train authorised local authority officials to discuss the FEPA enforcement issues and to promulgate the kind of advice to which the hon. Member for Caerphilly referred.

Again I thank him for the support that both he and the official Opposition have given to this small though important Bill. I thank also the hon. Member for Ceredigion and Pembroke, North for his support and for that of his party.

*Question put and agreed to.*

*Bill accordingly read the Third time and passed.*

## MEMBERS' INTERESTS

*Ordered,*

That Mr. Rhodri Morgan be discharged from the Select Committee on Members' Interests and Mr. Bob Cryer be added to the Committee.—*[Mr. David Hunt.]*

## STATUTORY INSTRUMENTS, &c.

*Motion made, and Question put forthwith pursuant to Standing Order No. 101(5) (Standing Committees on Statutory Instruments, &c.).*

### AGRICULTURE

That the draft Set-Aside (Amendment) Regulations 1989, which were laid before this House on 18th May, be approved.

### JUDGMENTS

That the draft Civil Jurisdiction and Judgments Act 1982 (Amendment) Order 1989, which was laid before this House on 23rd May, be approved—*[Mr. Fallon.]*

*Question agreed to.*

## Housing (Warrington and Runcorn)

10.25 pm

*Motion made, and Question proposed,* That this House do now adjourn.—*[Mr. Fallon.]*

**Mr. Doug Hoyle** (Warrington, North): This is a subject which affects many of my constituents, particularly those who live in rented property owned by the Warrington and Runcorn development corporation. Some of the matters to which I shall refer do apply not just to the present Minister, the hon. Member for Rossendale and Darwen (Mr. Trippier), but to his predecessor, the hon. Member for Broxbourne (Mrs. Roe).

Oscar Wilde said:

"Democracy means simply the bludgeoning of the people by the people for the people."

In this case, it is not by the people but by the development corporation—aided and abetted by the Department of the Environment and by Ministers.

The history of the matter goes back to 1984 when Warrington borough council first decided to enter into discussions, without prejudice, to see whether it could agree terms with the Warrington and Runcorn development corporation. On 21 March 1985, it formally entered into consultations, which continued until 1986. In July 1986, it was agreed that there was no reason why Warrington borough council should not take over the houses. There were no difficult estates in Warrington; rent arrears worries and vandalism were not a major problem there; the houses owned by the Warrington and Runcorn development corporation were in good condition and of traditional construction; no flat roofs or other structural problems had led to difficulties; staffing levels were low and there was no direct labour organisation.

The proposals were accepted by David Binns, the general manager of Warrington and Runcorn development corporation, who wrote to the Department of the Environment supporting the transfer of the new town housing to Warrington borough council and said:

"Warrington and Runcorn development corporation is in a unique situation in having to organise two housing transfers and two community-related assets transfers, and hence practicality might supersede policy considerations."

There was a problem at that time with Runcorn, too, for he also said:

"Transfer negotiations with Warrington borough council have already reached an advanced stage. Even if Warrington and Runcorn development corporation houses transfer to Warrington borough council, the private housing/public housing ratio in Warrington will still be around 70:30, which is above the national average."

Warrington does not have very large housing estates with demunicipalisation policies designed to break them up.

The negotiations continued, and seemed to be going smoothly until the Peterborough new town tenants were balloted as to who would be their future landlord. In an 83·5 per cent. poll just over 93 per cent. of those entitled to do so opted to transfer to Peterborough city council. At that stage the negotiations appered to come to a halt and difficulties began to arise. Although there was pressure for the negotiations to continue, there was a hiatus and it was finally decided that the best way forward would be for housing associations to come into the picture and for tenants to be able to decide whether they liked the way in which housing associations functioned.

The Minister will probably say that it had nothing whatever to do with the Department of the Environment

[*Mr. Doug Hoyle*]

and that it was purely a matter for Warrington and Runcorn development corporation to decide after consultation with the tenants, but I find that most peculiar. If the Department of the Environment had no role in Warrington and Runcorn development corporation reaching that decision, why were Department of the Environment officials involved in the negotiations for the transfer of the management to the housing association before the Warrington and Runcorn development corporation board considered the decision to transfer? If they had no part in the decision, what were they doing?

The answer was clear from the board's report on 14 May 1988. The Warrington housing association wrote to Mr. Lawton, chief executive of Warrington borough council, as follows:

"Thank you for your letter of 28 September 1988 enclosing a copy of the joint recommendation. Your letter and paper were discussed. Warrington housing association welcomes and supports the paper. It accords very closely with the position that we have taken since being invited to be involved in negotiation.

Indeed, Warrington housing association consistently put the case for the borough council's involvement and real tenant choice in our discussions up to and including ministerial level."

I find it quite amazing to be told it was purely the choice of the development corporation when the Warrington housing association wrote that it had been involved in discussions up to and including ministerial level and had asked that Warrington borough council be involved. It would have made sense for there to be a survey to find out the relative cost of the housing association and the local authority as the managing authority.

The consultation that took place lacked democracy. The tenants were given only about three weeks in which to make a choice. In the Warrington area, 5,000 houses were involved. Warrington and Runcorn development corporation received about 2,000 replies, and 99 per cent. were in favour of the local authority. Unfortunately, the Warrington and Runcorn development corporation chose completely to ignore the wishes of those people, saying that they had been subject to pressure from councillors and had not received all the information.

Our problems today arose from that point. The leader of Warrington borough council and I have written to the Minister about the lack of consultation with the tenants and have asked him to intervene. The Minister has hidden behind the fact that he has no authority to direct a housing authority on a management matter, but that is plainly not true. His Department was involved in the run-up to the decision and it was part and parcel of the decision to hand over to housing associations.

The tenants are upset because they have not been consulted. There is no doubt that the Minister could intervene at any time, particularly as he and the Government always talk about tenants' choice. When we saw the handover to the housing association, no choice was given. The Minister relies on the fact that, at some time in the future, there will be a ballot to decide what the tenants want to do—whether they want to stay with housing associations, be managers, or go to the local authority. It is hardly a level playing field. That could happen at any time. In three years, they will have had experience of housing associations, but they will not have had any experience of being under a democratic authority, with Warrington borough council. That is one reason why the tenants are upset.

The tenants ask why real consultation and the ballot for the managing agent could not take place. It would have made a lot of sense to have relative costs from Warrington borough council and from the housing association so that a real choice could have been made. If necessary, at some time in future they could have another ballot. At least they would have the choice. They had the housing association thrust upon them without any opportunity to choose. I hope that the Minister will deal with that point today.

I refer now to the eventual sale and to the ballot that will take place before it. The Minister will tell us that it cannot happen at the moment because legislation is to go through the House. I note that housing associations presently have a three-year term as management agents, but the agreement allows for an extension. Again, I refer to the board report of 14 May 1988.

Will the Minister give me an assurance that no extension will be permitted and that the ballot will take place as soon as possible within three years? Although the housing association has taken over, I appeal to the Minister to reconsider his decision not to intervene, and to do so in the interests of democracy and tenants' choice, and allow tenants of the Warrington and Runcorn development corporation, even at this stage, to have the proper consultation for which they are pressing, so that they can decide whether they want the managing agent to be the housing association or the Warrington and Runcorn development corporation. There is no legislation that would prevent Warrington borough council from acting as the managing agent.

I welcome the opportunity to discuss this with the Minister. We have had correspondence. I also welcome the expert advice that he has received from the hon. Member for Altrincham and Sale (Sir F. Montgomery), who also has an interest in this matter.

**Sir Fergus Montgomery** (Altrincham and Sale) *indicated dissent.*

**Mr. Hoyle:** A close member of the hon. Gentleman's family has an interest in this matter. Therefore, I have no doubt that the Minister will have received some expert advice from the housing associations.

So that my constituents may arrive at a proper choice, I ask that even at this stage they be given proper consultation.

10.30 pm

**The Parliamentary Under-Secretary of State for the Environment (Mr. David Trippier):** It is customary to congratulate Members on their good fortune in securing an Adjournment debate. However, on this occasion I have to withhold any such benediction. The hon. Member for Warrington, North (Mr. Hoyle) has resorted to this route to continue to noise abroad his misplaced and erroneous views on this matter. It is perfectly fair to say that despite our political differences, he knows that I have always been more than willing to discuss any matter with him. Those discussions have usually been friendly and, I am pleased to say, productive.

However, on this occasion, the hon. Gentleman did not even bother to ask to see me first about this. Instead an early-day motion appeared on the Order Paper, which is not only misleading but also insulting in the way in which it is written. I am glad to say that some of my hon. Friends were also incensed by this action and tabled an amendment to set the record straight.

Now the Gentleman has decided to raise the matter yet again in this debate. It is a most extraordinary way to carry on. I can only assume that it is a temporary mental aberration brought on by the hon. Gentleman's obsessive concern with this subject, which he misunderstands.

The only good thing to come out of this debate is that it gives me the opportunity to let Warrington and Runcorn new town tenants know what will happen in the future, to give them the facts, and to give them the reassurances that they have been seeking.

I shall initially deal with the future of the Warrington new town housing, as that is the hon. Gentleman's principal concern. The most important point, which he seems incapable of grasping—the wording of his early-day motion makes it clear that he is incapable of grasping this important point—is that there is a fundamental difference between management of the housing and the future ownership of the stock. That distinction is absolutely clear, indeed elementary, but it seems to have suited some people to deny it. So I stress again that management and ownership are two quite separate and distinct issues.

Let me turn first to the management of the housing. I have repeatedly made it clear that who the new town development corporation appoints to manage its housing is a matter solely for the corporation. That was the case for the new town housing in Warrington.

The board of Warrington and Runcorn development corporation proposed in May 1988 to appoint four local housing associations to manage its housing. I do not need to remind the hon. Gentleman or the House that several Members of the Labour party serve on that development corporation. When the corporation took that decision it believed that there would be a number of advantages in doing so. It would ensure that a high-quality management service could be maintained as wind-up approached. It would remove the uncertainties affecting the existing housing staff, as they would be offered jobs with the housing associations where possible. It would also meet the Commission for the New Towns' request not to be directly involved in management of the stock when it inherits it from the corporation in October.

Finally, the board believed, quite rightly in my view, that giving tenants the opportunity to experience a housing association must make for a more informed choice of future landlord by tenants in the ballot of ownership. Everyone knows about the council, as they come into contact with it regularly; but who knows as much about housing associations?

Before I forget the point, I must emphasise that, as far as I am aware, the Labour party has said time and time again in the House that it is in favour of housing associations—non-profit making bodies—and I have not heard a single voice of dissent on that matter. I include the hon. Gentleman's right hon. Friend the Member for Halton (Mr. Oakes), who seems to be pleased, or at least satisfied, with the present arrangements.

I am all in favour of any action which makes tenants compare the services offered and rents to be charged by a prospective new landlord, rather than voting for the council on the basis of "the devil you know".

The corporation then consulted tenants on its management proposal as required by law. There is no getting away from the fact that it did consult tenants on

that, and that it did consider tenants' views as required before taking the decision to appoint the housing associations as agents. I am satisfied that the corporation acted quite correctly at all times, and that I am not the only one who believes this.

One of the corporation's tenants complained to the local ombudsman about the way in which the corporation took the decision. Having considered the case, the ombudsman decided in January not to pursue the investigation. The reason given was that there was

"no evidence of maladministration by the corporation leading to injustice".

Obviously, some tenants disagreed with the proposal and others who indicated a preference in the consultation to have the borough council as manager. The corporation carefully considered those views, but decided that there were insufficient objections not to proceed with the proposal. To put the whole matter into context, the House will be interested to know that fewer than 100 responded, out of some 4,222 tenants. In fact, specifically, 65 responded, and of those about half were in favour of the council. Therefore, to be generous, we are talking about 34, or perhaps 35, tenants.

The corporation also considered the representations that it received on a proforma that had been distributed by the borough council. I had hoped that the hon. Member for Warrington, North would have condemned the council for the misleading and incorrect information given on that proforma—but, if he will not, then I will. The proforma, surprisingly enough, failed to distinguish between management and ownership—the same mistake that was made by the hon. Member for Warrington, North in his early-day motion—and that created quite unnecessary confusion and uncertainty among the tenants. I refuse to believe that the council did not know the difference between the two.

The proforma was also misleading on rents, as it gave the impression that the borough council would charge low rents if it managed the stock. As I have told the hon. Gentleman previously, the rent levels remain the responsibility of the development corporation. Whoever manages the housing cannot influence the rent level. The recent increase in rents in Warrington is roughly the same as in all other new towns. There is no connection between the general rent increase and the corporation's decision to appoint the housing associations as managing agents. It obviously follows from that that the agency fee, which must remain commercially confidential information, is such that it can be met from the usual resources available to the corporation. The proforma also contained some rather scurrilous comments about social landlords and plaudits for the council, which were completely irrelevant to the issue of housing management.

This is where I am in some difficulty in understanding the hon. Gentleman's stance on the issue. Perhaps that helps to explain why it is that he has managed, on the one hand, to secure a number of people who appear very happily to have gone ahead and signed the early-day motion, which we have already corrected because factually it was incorrect, but, on the other, does not appear to have gathered any support, particularly from neighbouring parliamentary colleagues.

The proforma is very important because it could—and I have no doubt it did—put the fear of God into a number of people's minds.

*[Mr. David Trippier]*

Overall, having considered the matter carefully on a number of occasions, it seems to me that the corporation has acted quite properly in appointing managing agents, and that decision has been implemented. It is in force now and I have no intention of intervening to change matters.

My personal view is that many tenants will learn a lot about housing associations as a result of that agency agreement. I hope that a similar agency proposal by the Milton Keynes development corporation will also be implemented and do likewise there. As I said earlier, that can only be a good thing in terms of the future ballot on ownership. Tenants will actually be able to choose on the basis of the services and terms offered to them, rather than on the basis of misconception and misinformation. I do not see that that tips the scales in favour of the housing associations when it comes to the vote on ownership; rather, it would seem to ensure fairer competition. I can only think that, if the council is worried about the management agreement, it can only be because it might not have a very good case to put to the new town tenants —why else should it be concerned?

I shall now deal with the separate issue of future ownership of the new town housing. This is by far the most important concern for tenants. Who owns the roof over one's head is a basic and crucial matter for every tenant. We have always recognised that. We therefore decided that, as general policy, if a change of landlord is to take place, tenants must first be given a say in the matter. A change of landlord will have to take place in all the new towns as the remaining new town development corporations, and eventually the Commission for the New Towns, are all due to be wound up. Our intention has always been to offer tenants, whenever possible, a choice about the future ownership of their homes.

In Warrington, we have always said that tenants would be given a ballot on future ownership. As yet, I cannot say exactly when the ballot will take place, but that is our firm intention. The choice is likely to be between the borough council, if the council is interested, and a social landlord, such as a housing association, which would be approved by the housing corporation. The social landlord is likely to be one of the housing associations now managing the housing. We proposed this in our consultation paper on new town housing transfer last year and we have now carried it forward into the Local Government and Housing Bill. Clause 143 of the Bill specifically provides for this choice between the council and the approved landlord. The individual choice of tenants will be respected, so if the tenants want to vote for the council as their future landlord, they will be able to do so and that is what they will get. This is a long-running commitment which we have every intention of honouring.

I should like to take this opportunity to say a few words on the future of the development corporation's other housing stock at Runcorn because it is a topical issue. There are two current issues. The first is the future ownership of the housing at Runcorn. The development corporation has been keen to see this settled before it is wound up at the end of September. It has therefore been discussing with RUNHAG, a group of five local housing associations, the possibility of transferring the stock to it, subject to tenants supporting the idea and a price being agreed for the housing. Tenants have generally supported this proposal and have been expecting to be consulted on it. We also welcomed RUNHAG's involvement and have been keen to see the transfer succeed.

Three weeks ago, just as the development corporation was reaching the conclusion of its negotiations with RUNHAG on price, Halton borough council decided that it might—and I stress might—be interested in acquiring the new town housing and threatened legal action to achieve that end. That interest comes very late in the day. Previously, the council had expressed no interest. I asked the council on no fewer than three occasions in the past eight months to make its intentions clear, but it did not do so.

In the circumstances, I think it quite right that the negotiations with RUNHAG should run their course and the tenants should be consulted on this option. I have therefore told the council that I do not intend to ask the development corporation to open negotiations with the council on future ownership so long as RUNHAG remains in play.

The second issue is the future of the Southgate estate. Proper tenant consultation has now taken place. The board of the development corporation will be considering tenants' views tomorrow and the final decision will be taken on the corporation's proposals for demolishing the existing buildings.

I have made my own views on this well known. I am convinced that demolition is the only sensible answer. We shall then have to consider the future of the site, whether some replacement housing might be provided and the timing of any redevelopment. I hope that Merseyside Improved Houses will continue to discuss the options available with the interested parties and that we can meet as far as possible the wishes of existing Southgate residents expressed in the consultation responses.

I repeat our longstanding commitment to give new town tenants in Warrington a chance to vote for the landlord they want, including the council. In the meantime, they will be managed by the housing associations, which I am certain will be able to prove to many tenants that the hon. Gentleman's concerns are completely misplaced and the council's scare stories unfounded. In Runcorn, I hope that very shortly tenants will be able to be consulted on whether they want RUNHAG to be their landlord. I am sure that it would be the right choice.

*Question put and agreed to.*

*Adjourned accordingly at six minutes to Eleven o'clock.*

# House of Commons

*Tuesday 20 June 1989*

*The House met at half-past Two o'clock*

## PRAYERS

[MR. SPEAKER *in the Chair*]

## PRIVATE BUSINESS

VALE OF GLAMORGAN (BARRY HARBOUR) BILL
*[Lords]*

HAYLE HARBOUR BILL *[Lords]*
*Orders for Second Reading read.*
*To be read a Second time tomorrow.*

# Oral Answers to Questions

## EMPLOYMENT

### Benefit Fraud

1. **Mr. Irvine:** To ask the Secretary of State for Employment if he will make a statement on Operation Grocer recently carried out by employment service fraud investigation in East Anglia and Lincolnshire.

**The Parliamentary Under-Secretary of State for Employment (Mr. Patrick Nicholls):** This operation was one of two concentrated fraud investigations in East Anglia and Lincolnshire into possible cases of benefit fraud involving people working as crop pickers or in packing houses while claiming unemployment benefit. Claims to benefit in more than half of the 800 cases investigated were withdrawn, saving the taxpayer £400,000.

**Mr. Irvine:** Does my hon. Friend agree that carefully targeted unemployment benefit fraud investigations such as Operation Grocer are particularly cost-effective? My hon. Friend has already given the House some figures but can he provide the full figures for 1988-89 of claims for unemployment benefit withdrawn following investigations by his Department and give some indication of the overall savings made?

**Mr. Nicholls:** My hon. Friend is entirely right. Targeting these investigations carefully can produce substantial savings for the taxpayer while ensuring that those who are claiming public funds wrongly are prevented from doing so. The claims withdrawn in the year 1988-89 will be in the region of 869,000.

**Mr. Hardy:** Whilst in no way defending any form of fraud does the Minister accept that if the Government put the same resources into and took the same interest in dealing with tax evasion and tax dodging of all types, the benefit to the country would be enormously greater than that which has followed Operation Grocer?

**Mr. Nicholls:** The second part of the hon. Gentleman's question belies the sentiments that he expressed in the first. This is a question about those who wrongfully claim other people's money. The hon. Gentleman is talking about people who wrongfully try to keep more of their own money. If he is interested in the comparative figures, I can tell him that the cost of investigating Department of Employment fraud in 1987-88 was £15·9 million. The cost of investigating Inland Revenue fraud, which includes individuals and companies, was about £42·4 million.

### Labour Statistics

2. **Mr. Wood:** To ask the Secretary of State for Employment by how much long-term unemployment has fallen during the past year; and if he will make a statement.

7. **Mr. Ken Hargreaves:** To ask the Secretary of State for Employment which regions had the sharpest fall in long-term unemployment during the past year; and if he will make a statement.

**The Secretary of State for Employment (Mr. Norman Fowler):** In the year to April 1989 the number of people unemployed for 12 months or more fell by 28 per cent. Long-term unemployment has fallen even faster than total unemployment and is now at its lowest level for more than six years. Long-term unemployment has fallen in all regions. The biggest falls have been in East Anglia, the south-east and the west midlands.

**Mr. Wood:** I thank my hon. Friend for his reply, which demonstrates that Government policies have meant that many more people are working and producing goods and services that people require than are involved in wasteful Government schemes such as those advocated two years ago by the Opposition. Can my right hon. Friend tell me more about the specifics in terms of particular age groups such as those between 18 and 24, those over 25 and those over 50 who have particular problems in employment?

**Mr. Fowler:** There have been reductions in unemployment in all those age groups. Among 18 to 24-year-olds, long-term unemployment is now down by one third compared to a year ago and has more than halved over the past two years alone. Among the over-25s, long-term unemployment has fallen by a quarter over the past 12 months, and among those aged over 50 there has been a fall of almost 30 per cent. over the past two years.

**Dr. Reid:** I welcome any fall in any form of unemployment. However, will the Minister recognise that the long-term unemployed in my constituency have been among the worst hit by the decision to close part-time benefit offices? May I bring to his attention Cleland and Newmains where there would be no additional cost to his Department if the offices were run since the local club in Cleland offered its premises free, I have offered my parliamentary premises free and the local community has even offered to pay the taxi fares to those offices for Department of Employment employees? Does he think that the closure is a totally unjustifiable imposition on those who are already suffering through long-term unemployment?

**Mr. Fowler:** No, I do not think that. I shall certainly think about the hon. Gentleman's example and consider whether anything can be done. What he said at the beginning of his question was right—that the whole House should welcome the fact that long-term unemployment, which must be regarded as the priority, is falling quickly, and more quickly than unemployment generally.

**Mr. Conway:** I was glad to hear my right hon. Friend's comments about long-term unemployment. Will he debunk the myth put about by Opposition Members that the fall in long-term unemployment has resulted from people taking part-time jobs? Has not about 85 per cent. of the growth in employment been in full-time employment, in contradiction to the myth propagated by the Opposition?

**Mr. Fowler:** During the past 12 months there has been a large increase in full-time employment. However, I do not in any way devalue part-time employment, which many people want. As a purely factual statement, I confirm that full-time employment has increased by more than 80 per cent. during the past 12 months.

**Mr. Corbett:** As the Government have helped to create record unemployment, with the closure of one factory in five in Birmingham, the west midlands and the remainder of the country, can the Secretary of State tell us when unemployment will come down to the level that he inherited in 1979?

**Mr. Fowler:** The hon. Gentleman needs to study the comparisons between Britain and the other western European countries, in all of which the unemployment rate rose in 1979 and in the early 1980s. The significant factor in what is happening in this country, especially in the west midlands, is that unemployment is falling faster than it is in any other western European country.

**Dame Elaine Kellett-Bowman:** Does my right hon. Friend agree that it is not just the fall in long-term unemployment, but the massive rise in employment generally that is very beneficial to citizens of all ages? Is he aware that Lancaster is rapidly running out of industrial land because of the great pressure from businesses wishing to start up? Will he ask his colleagues to assist him in reclaiming what remains of derelict land so that it can be used for industry?

**Mr. Fowler:** I shall certainly consider any proposals put to me by my hon. Friend because I agree with the thrust of her question. She is right to suggest that the figures show that this country's record in creating new jobs is better than that of any other country in western Europe.

**Mr. Fatchett:** Is it not true that the Chancellor's only weapon to fight inflation—pushing up interest rates—is deliberately designed to squeeze activity in the economy, which will reduce the number of jobs and therefore increase unemployment? Will the right hon. Gentleman take this opportunity to say what he expects the unemployment figure to be in 12 months' time? Is he aware that most people suspect that there will be an increase in unemployment and that the figures that he cheerfully announced this afternoon will look very different in 12 months?

**Mr. Fowler:** I will not make such an estimate, and I never have done. At the general election in 1987 the Labour party, in its wildest dreams, said that it would reduce unemployment by 1 million in two years. This Government have reduced unemployment by more than 1

million and there are still more than 600,000 vacancies. There is no reason why unemployment should not continue to fall. The hon. Gentleman cannot bear to hear the good news about unemployment.

## Single Market

3. **Mr. Clelland:** To ask the Secretary of State for Employment what research has been commissioned by his Department into the impact of the single market in the north-east.

**The Minister of State, Department of Employment (Mr. John Cope):** Our department has not commissioned research exactly as described in the hon. Gentleman's question. The impact on particular sectors and regions will depend on how successfully individual firms respond.

**Mr. Clelland:** Should not the Department have conducted such research, given that during the past 10 years of Conservative Government manufacturing industry in the north-east has been reduced massively, with the resultant loss of skills that the Government are doing little or nothing to replace? How can the region be expected to compete on anything like equal terms when more and more people are being employed in service industries and fewer and fewer in making goods to sell outside the region and the country?

**Mr. Cope:** I noticed the report produced by the Northern Development Company the other day which stated that it had just had its most successful year ever in increasing jobs in the north-east and in investment. That is why business confidence in the north-east is now at its highest level for many years, as another recent survey showed.

**Mr. Devlin:** Has my right hon. Friend had a chance to see the projected employment increase for the third quarter of 1989? According to that, the north-east is second only to East Anglia in the projected rate of growth in jobs.

**Mr. Cope:** The north-east is extremely well placed in the country as a whole and for 1992 and the single market. Unemployment in that area has been falling fast.

## Secondary Picketing

4. **Mr. Baldry:** To ask the Secretary of State for Employment if he will introduce legislation to legalise secondary picketing; and if he will make a statement.

**Mr. Fowler:** The Employment Act 1980 removed immunity from all secondary picketing, that is picketing away from a picket's own place of work. I have no intention of changing this legislation.

**Mr. Baldry:** Does my right hon. Friend agree that the possibility of any restoration to the trade unions of the potential of secondary action or secondary picketing would be disastrous for industrial relations, for British competitiveness, British jobs and British exports? Does not the fact that the Labour party is making such proposals demonstrate that it has learnt absolutely nothing during the past 10 years?

**Mr. Fowler:** That is entirely right. Only the hon. Member for Oldham, West (Mr. Meacher) and his Labour colleagues want to see a return to the flying picket. The public regard that as creating indefensible hardship and we are very happy to debate the proposals put forward by the hon. Member for Oldham, West on that.

**Mr. Heffer:** Has the right hon. Gentleman seen the recent pamphlet on industrial relations issued by the Incorporated Catholic Truth Society which states that secondary picketing is a legitimate action on the part of workers to defend themselves from employers who are taking their rights away? Will the right hon. Gentleman look at that pamphlet? If he does, he might learn something and discover that it is not just members of the Labour party who feel strongly about the rights of workers in industry.

**Mr. Fowler:** I shall certainly look at that pamphlet. However, I hope that the hon. Gentleman will equally consider what a former Labour Prime Minister, Lord Callaghan, said about secondary picketing in 1979. He said that he thought that it was entirely wrong that indefensible hardship could be imposed on innocent people. I believe that the great majority of the British public share that view.

**Mr. Batiste:** Does my right hon. Friend agree that the best way forward for industrial relations in the future to build on the steady improvements of the past 10 years is to encourage collaborative attitudes in industry and in particular, no-strike agreements? Does he further agree that to go back to the 1970s with secondary picketing and intimidation, as the Labour party suggests, would be a betrayal of ordinary working people who would not forgive any party which sought to do that?

**Mr. Fowler:** My hon. Friend is right. That would also destroy jobs in this country. The bad industrial relations of the 1970s caused job after job to be exported overseas. That is what the Labour party promises if it is ever returned to office.

**Mr. Meacher:** Is the right hon. Gentleman aware that the International Labour Organisation convention specifically includes a right to sympathetic action and that Britain, under the Thatcherite Government, is the only EC country which now legally bans secondary action? Having distinguished herself in a minority of one over the social charter, will the Prime Minister marginalise herself still further at the Madrid summit in a minority of one over the right to industrial action? When will the Government learn that industrial disputes will not be stopped by ever more repressive legislation or by trying to legalistically to ban the right to strike?

**Mr. Fowler:** The trouble with the hon. Gentleman is that he wants to remove the protection from the public. What he is about is putting the unions above the law. When the hon. Gentleman was interviewed in *The Guardian* he was not arguing for the right to strike; he said that secondary picketing would also be sanctioned by his proposals. That is the situation and it is about time that he came clean on that.

## Small Businesses

5. **Mr. Harris:** To ask the Secretary of State for Employment if he will report on what steps the Government are taking to help small firms; and if he will make a statement.

**Mr. Cope:** There is a wide range of schemes to help small firms gain access to advice, finance and training, and to help those who want to start their own businesses. Those include the small firms service, the loan guarantee scheme, the business expansion scheme, the enterprise allowance scheme and business growth training, launched in April to help small businesses improve their competitiveness and profits through training.

**Mr. Harris:** As about 1,300 small businesses are set up each week, does my right hon. Friend agree that that is an area of considerable success for the Government? However, what help is being made available to those small firms to improve their performance, profitability and skills training under the business growth training scheme announced by his Department in April this year?

**Mr. Cope:** Yes, there is tremendous growth in the small firms sector which reflects the growth in enterprise in the economy generally. Business growth training consists of five broad options to help small businesses improve their competitiveness, starting with small companies, open learning kits, and so on, and working up to seminars and consultancy projects at the higher levels.

**Mr. Cryer:** What effect does the current high level of interest rates have on small firms? Will the rate of bankruptcies among small firms, which has reached an all-time record under the Government, be likely to increase or decrease? Lastly, how many of the 2 million jobs that have been lost in manufacturing industry since the Thatcher Government were elected in 1979 have been in small firms?

**Mr. Cope:** The proportion of small firms in manufacturing is smaller than in the economy generally, but I cannot answer the hon. Gentleman's question precisely without notice. It is sometimes difficult for large as well as small firms to deal with high interest rates, but many business men realise that they are essential to deal with inflation.

**Mr. Brandon-Bravo:** Does my right hon. Friend agree that the establishment and growth of small firms often has its roots in self-employment? I believe that the number of self-employed in Britain has grown by 1 million over the past few years, but Italy, with roughly the same population, has 6 million self-employed people. Can my right hon. Friend assure the House that the help given to small businesses is also given to that seedcorn—the self-employed?

**Mr. Cope:** Yes, it is. Since 1979 the number of self-employed has increased by rather more than 1 million, but, in making international comparisons, one must bear in mind that the definitions are not always the same and to some extent the higher figures reflect the different tax and social security structures in other countries.

**Mr. Ieuan Wyn Jones:** Does the Minister agree that a number of job opportunities in rural areas have been lost because small firms do not have proper access to training? Does he further agree that in rural areas the Government are already finding it difficult to find people to serve on the training and enterprise councils because people are far better off running their businesses and do not want to be bothered about joining such bodies? Is it not time that the Government took their responsibilities seriously and gave the proper resources to training colleges and other educational establishments in order to provide decent training for jobs in rural areas?

**Mr. Cope:** As the hon. Gentleman will find out in a few days' time when we announce the first training and enterprise councils there is no shortage of good people who are only to anxious to contribute to the nation's training effort in that way.

**Sir Anthony Grant:** Is my right hon. Friend aware that the development of the small firms sector has been remarkable since the bleak days when the hon. Member for Bradford, South (Mr. Cryer) was the Minister responsible for small firms and when they were dying like flies? However, will my right hon. Friend bear in mind that high interest rates are beginning to hurt the small firms sector very much and that they will be even more damaging if they go any higher? Will he please ram that point home in his discussions with Treasury Ministers?

**Mr. Cope:** Yes, I will. I shall also reflect on the fact that responsibility for small firms has been held by distinguished right hon. and hon. Members in all parts of the House.

## Industrial Training Boards

6. **Mr. Lofthouse:** To ask the Secretary of State for Employment what steps he is taking to encourage employers to participate in the industrial training boards when these boards no longer raise a statutory levy.

**Mr. Nicholls:** I have asked the chairman of each ITB to bring forward proposals for future arrangements that command the support of employers in the industry.

**Mr. Lofthouse:** Is the Minister satisfied that employers will respond to the voluntary levy? Does he realise that many will rely on other firms to pay the levy and then poach their apprentices, as I remember the Central Electricity Generating Board doing in respect of British Coal employees in the 1960s?

**Mr. Nicholls:** While I appreciate the hon. Gentleman's concern, the evidence is to the contrary, because many non-statutory training organisations have the active support of employers. Over the past couple of years, employers in a number of industries that did not have statutory arrangements before banded together to organise training.

**Mr. Sayeed:** Does my hon. Friend agree that it is absurd to suggest a uniform training levy regardless of the size or needs of the individual company?

**Mr. Nicholls:** My hon. Friend is entirely right to harken to a theme of the White Paper "Employment in the 1990s", in which we made the point that the formalised structure of an industrial training board complete with a levy-raising power does not deliver the goods. That is why we made the proposals we did in the White Paper.

**Mr. Tony Lloyd:** How does the Minister seriously square his assertion that everything in the training garden will be lovely under the voluntary system with the comments of the Federation of Master Builders—hardly a Labour organisation—that the power of ITBs to collect a levy would not have been given at the time that it was had the voluntary system met national training requirements?

If he thinks that that proposition is out of date, how does he square his belief with his own Manpower Services Commission's research showing that 79 per cent. of employers would not contribute more financial resources voluntarily if asked to do so?

**Mr. Nicholls:** If the hon. Gentleman were entirely right in his observations there would be no cause for increasing the number of skilled personnel within the construction industry, because there would be a full complement of trained people willing and available. Clearly that is not the case. We made the point in the White Paper that special circumstances may apply in respect of the construction and engineering industry training boards. Proposals for all ITBs are being received from employers who wish to make particular points, and they will be borne in mind.

## Unions (Funds)

8. **Mr. Carrington:** To ask the Secretary of State for Employment if he will introduce legislation to prevent employers from using the remedy of sequestration of funds against trade unions who refuse to obey court orders; and if he will make a statement.

**Mr. Nicholls:** No, Sir. The remedies available to the court in cases involving contempt are a matter for court procedures and rules, not for my right hon. Friend the Secretary of State for Employment.

**Mr. Carrington:** I am greatly relieved at my hon. Friend's answer. Does he agree that sequestration is frequently the only sanction that the courts have to ensure that trade unions obey the law—[*Interruption.*]—and that any proposal from another political party to abolish sequestration would be a recipe for industrial anarchy? Far from abolishing it, we should consider expanding sequestration to cover the highly organised, so-called unofficial strikes that affected London's transport so badly over the past few months.

**Mr. Nicholls:** My hon. Friend is right in his comments about sequestration—and proof of that was the degree of sedentary heckling to which he was subjected when he made mention of it. Sequestration is not a new, Tory remedy—which is how the hon. Member for Oldham, West (Mr. Meacher) frequently attempts to portray it. It is a remedy that goes back as far as the ecclesiastical courts, as a way of enforcing particular court orders. If they could, the Labour party would ensure that that remedy would be left available for all classes of action except those against trade unions for breaking the law. They are in the business of restoring the power of the trade unions to kick the hell out of the public, and obviously my hon. Friend disapproves of that.

**Mr. Leighton:** Is not the Government's rhetoric about handing the unions back to their members completely misleading, because the draconian step of sequestering union funds has the effect of taking a union away from its members? Is it not the case that British workers have fewer rights than those of any other western industrial nation? Unions find it completely impossible to have lawful disputes, and that is why there is a rash of unofficial action.

**Mr. Nicholls:** The hon. Gentleman is completely wrong. It is not impossible to engage in a lawful dispute: recent events back that up to the hilt. The proposition is perfectly simple. It is that trade unions should not be above the law but should be subject to it as the rest of us are, and, if they disobey it, subject to the same penalties. The hon. Gentleman's policy—to allow the right of sequestration to be used against anyone except trade unions that break the law—clearly appeals to the hon. Gentleman and his friends, but it does not appeal to the public.

**Mr. Greg Knight:** Trade unions should indeed obey the law. Can my hon. Friend think of any reason other than party financial gain for the Labour party to wish to place them above the law?

**Mr. Nicholls:** My hon. Friend is entirely correct. The Labour party tries to present itself as a new, squeaky-clean, moderate party, but it is a creature of the trade union movement and is funded by it.

### Employment Training

9. **Mr. Allen McKay:** To ask the Secretary of State for Employment which local authorities have refused to co-operate with employment training; and what was the date on which his Department received notification in each case.

**Mr. Nicholls:** A comprehensive record is not held centrally of local authorities which have decided not to participate in employment training.

**Mr. McKay:** As the Minister knows, the Conservative-controlled Barnet and Merton authorities have refused to take part in the employment training scheme. Is that not further evidence that the scheme was ill-thought-out and ill-funded from its inception?

**Mr. Nicholls:** I am deeply shocked that the hon. Gentleman should launch an attack on his own Labour-controlled local authority. Barnsley metropolitan borough council is Labour-controlled, a training manager and a member of the main consortium training agency. Moreover, the Barnsley trades council is a training manager as well, in its own right. All the trade unions that were apparently against employment training, including the Transport and General Workers Union, are serving on the trades councils. The decision of two Conservative-controlled authorities not to join the programme, whatever their reasons, is a matter for them. The hon. Gentleman should rejoice at the fact that his Labour-controlled authorities do not see it that way.

**Mrs. Maureen Hicks:** Is my hon. Friend aware of the valuable contribution made by employment trainees to daycare centres for the elderly and handicapped in and around my constituency? Is he also aware of the insecurity that faces those centres—and the trainees—as a result of the spiteful action of the Labour-controlled Wolverhampton council in withdrawing 400 ET places provided by the Government with £700,000?

**Mr. Nicholls:** My hon. Friend is right to deplore the spiteful attitude of certain Labour-controlled authorities. If, however, she hears the hon. Member for Oldham, West (Mr. Meacher) inveighing against employment training, she can take some comfort from the fact that his feelings are not shared by his local authority: Oldham borough council is a training manager under employment training.

**Mr. Meacher:** It is not the Labour authorities or the trade unions that are refusing to co-operate with ET. Is the Minister not aware that only 13 major companies have signed up nationally, and that only two have filled more than half the contracted number of places? Does he know that, according to the Government's own figures, Habitat has filled none of its 200 places, Mothercare has filled none of its 50 and Remploy has filled none of its 456? Worst of all, only 41 per cent. of the Government's national target number of places have been filled. With a record like that in meeting targets, will the Secretary of State be applying for the Chancellorship in the coming reshuffle?

**Mr. Nicholls:** Two points need to be made. First, as always, the hon. Gentleman is entirely wrong. It is difficult to know whether he is wrong because he really does not understand or because he chooses not to. Secondly, if accurate, his scenario is extremely bad news for the unemployed. When faced with giving such an account—wrong though it is—all that the hon. Gentleman can do about the plight of the unemployed is to giggle his way through it.

If the hon. Gentleman really wants to know the position, let me tell him what he knows well enough: in addition to the companies that are part of the large companies unit, a whole range of companies are providing placements instead of being training managers in their own right. The hon. Gentleman makes no mention of that. He has also failed to remind us that the programme is still building up, and that other companies will be joining the LCU shortly. As always, what he cannot stand is good news, even when it comes from his own constituency.

**Mr. Robert G. Hughes:** Does my hon. Friend accept that in Harrow the employment training schemes are regarded as so successful that the problem is not that advanced by the Opposition but the fact that uncertainty is being caused because they do not yet know whether they have a contract for next year, or what the budget will be? Will my hon. Friend confirm that they will be dealt with as soon as possible so that the excellent work of employment training can continue?

**Mr. Nicholls:** Obviously the contracting and recontracting programme has to be done as speedily as possible. However, my hon. Friend is right to make the point that this is an outstandingly successful programme. It is far more successful than any other Government training programme has been and it has given real hope to the unemployed—a great deal more hope than the sour words and diatribes that we hear from the Opposition.

### Restart (Redundant Mineworkers)

10. **Mr. Skinner:** To ask the Secretary of State for Employment if he will now bring forward proposals to amend the restart scheme in respect of redundant mineworkers; and if he will make a statement on the progress of his discussions on this matter.

**Mr. Cope:** The hon. Gentleman will know that there is a draft statutory instrument before the House to modify the terms of the redundant mineworkers payment scheme.

**Mr. Skinner:** Yes, it is No. 43 on the remaining Orders of the Day. With all the Cabinet reshuffles that are being suggested, I want to make sure that the Department of the Employment Minister gives a commitment that the order will be brought before the House during the next 14 sitting days, to stop the harassment that is going on at Department of Employment and Department of Social Security offices. Will he also guarantee that when the amended regulations are brought forward they will include retrospective payment of up to £1,000, for miners who have lost that kind of money during this year-long battle?

**Mr. Cope:** If the hon. Gentleman looks at the order, he will find that it contains a provision for retrospective payment. I think he will find that it is in article 3(d). The order is subject to affirmative resolution, so it will certainly come before the House. The hon. Gentleman will have his opportunity at that stage. There has been no harassment of which I am aware, but if any hon. Member wishes to raise individual cases with me he can do so.

**Mr. Dickens:** Despite the carping by the hon. Member for Bolsover (Mr. Skinner), does my right hon. Friend agree that VAT returns prove conclusively that in every week of the year something like 900 new businesses are started in the United Kingdom? Does that not show— *[Interruption.]*

**Mr. Speaker:** Order. The hon. Gentleman is referring, presumably, to redundant miners' new businesses?

**Mr. Dickens:** Of course. Many of the beneficiaries of these new businesses are miners. Does that not show that the spirit of enterprise is now growing throughout the United Kingdom, and will it not be reflected in the results at the next general election?

**Mr. Cope:** I am sure that it will be. I am also well aware that many redundant mineworkers have taken advantage of the Government's various schemes in order to start small businesses.

**Mr. Eadie:** We certainly welcome the last point that the right hon. Gentleman made about the order that is to come before the House of Commons—that he intends to implement the promise that he made to the miners' parliamentary group that there would be retrospective legislation. Are we also to take it from what the right hon. Gentleman said that if we know of any cases of harassment of miners—I have evidence that some harassment is taking place in the midlands and the north-east—we shall be able to present those cases to him and he will look into them?

**Mr. Cope:** Yes, that is what I have said this afternoon, and it is also what I have said in the past about such cases. So far, they have not been raised with me, but if there are any cases I shall look into them. The hon. Gentleman knows, from when he came to see me with his group, that we take this matter seriously.

## Labour Statistics

11. **Mr. Hayward:** To ask the Secretary of State for Employment what is the rate of fall in unemployment in the United Kingdom and in other comparable European countries; and if he will make a statement.

**Mr. Fowler:** Over the past two years the rate of unemployment has fallen faster in the United Kingdom than in any other major industrialised country. The rate of unemployment in the United Kingdom is now $2\frac{1}{2}$

percentage points below the European Community average and below that of France, Italy, Belgium, Netherlands, Spain, Ireland and Greece.

**Mr. Hayward:** I welcome the figures that my right hon. Friend has given, which clearly demonstrate that future prospects for the unemployed in Britain are better than in most of the rest of Europe. Will my right hon. Friend welcome the enormous order that has been announced today by Rolls-Royce from TWA? It shows that British companies can compete successfully on the world market and guarantee long-term prospects for jobs in high-technology industries.

**Mr. Fowler:** I have just seen the news of that order. I am sure that the whole House will want to congratulate Rolls-Royce. It is yet further evidence of the success and capability of the British aerospace industry, and is extremely good news for jobs.

**Mr. Fearn:** The Secretary of State has just mentioned figures showing the fall in unemployment. Can he say what part tourism is playing in that fall?

**Mr. Fowler:** Tourism is one of the major employment growth sectors in the economy. About $1\frac{1}{2}$ million people are employed in the tourist and leisure industry, which is clearly one of the most important industries in Britain.

**Mr. Roger King:** Is my right hon. Friend aware that every week unemployment levels continue to drop at an ever-increasing rate in the west midlands? We noticed that during the European elections unemployment was not mentioned once by the opposition parties. They can no longer capitalise on it because of our success with it.

**Mr. Fowler:** My hon. Friend is entirely right. The rate of unemployment has fallen faster in the west midlands than in any other part of the country. There are more people now in work in Britain than ever before in our history. *[Interruption.]*

**Mr. Speaker:** Order. I ask the House to settle down.

## Trades Union Congress

12. **Mr. Strang:** To ask the Secretary of State for Employment when he last met the general secretary of the Trades Union Congress to discuss employment issues.

**Mr. Nicholls:** My right hon. Friend the Secretary of State last met the general secretary of the Trades Union Congress on 15 June.

**Mr. Strang:** After the rout of the Conservative party in the Euro-elections, is it not clear that the TUC and the vast majority of British people want the Government to abandon their opposition to the European social charter? Will the Prime Minister be the only one of the 12 in Madrid to stand out against a measure aimed at improving standards for employees and pensioners throughout the Community?

**Mr. Nicholls:** My right hon. Friend will continue to do what she has always done on behalf of Britain—to fight our corner within the European Community. If the hon. Gentleman takes comfort from the result of the European elections, we look forward to seeing whether the smile is on the other side of his face after the next general election.

## Ports

13. **Mrs. Gorman:** To ask the Secretary of State for Employment what representations he has received about the future of scheme ports once the dock labour scheme is abolished; and if he will make a statement.

**Mr. Fowler:** The decision to abolish the dock labour scheme has been widely welcomed.

The Confederation of British Industries, chambers of commerce, and associations representing warehousing and freight transport have all welcomed the ending of the scheme's restrictions and believe that this will result not only in a more competitive ports industry but in more business investment and jobs in scheme port areas.

**Mrs. Gorman:** My right hon. Friend will be aware that despite the £770 million subsidy, the scheme ports already charge 40 per cent. more than the non-scheme ports— [HON. MEMBERS: "Reading."]—and that in order to become competitive with the non-scheme ports and with Rotterdam there has to be agreement between the local employers and the dockers on the way forward—[HON. MEMBERS: "Reading."] People in my constituency who work at the Tilbury docks will be very glad when the Government's new measures are in force.

**Mr. Fowler:** My hon. Friend is right. The business and trade of non-scheme ports has continued to increase over the past 10 or 20 years, and so has employment. I believe that the end of the dock labour scheme will mean that the scheme ports will be able to share in the benefits of the industry.

**Mr. Tony Banks:** As the Government are very much in the pay of the port employers, what sort of contribution does the Secretary of State expect the employers to make to Tory party funds next year?

**Mr. Fowler:** From the ending of the dock labour scheme, we expect a contribution to scheme port areas, which will mean more jobs, and that will mean better prospects for all in those areas and all ports around the country.

## Enterprise Allowance

14. **Mr. Burns:** To ask the Secretary of State for Employment if he will make a further statement on developments in the enterprise allowance scheme.

**Mr. Cope:** Over 440,000 unemployed people have been helped to start their own businesses under the enterprise allowance scheme since it began in 1982. We have provided for 90,000 places this year and about 85,000 people are currently in receipt of the allowance.

**Mr. Burns:** Does my right hon. Friend accept that those figures are extremely welcome, particularly as 9,000 people in Chelmsford have joined the scheme? As 57 per cent. of the businesses involved have lasted for more than three years, does he agree that it is an excellent method of job creation? Will he calculate how much it costs the taxpayer to provide that number of new jobs?

**Mr. Cope:** The net cost per person off the unemployed register is about £1,846, but we are not talking only about people who actually create the businesses; there are also the people whom they employ. For every 100 people who complete the enterprise allowance scheme there are 139 people working two years later.

## PRIME MINISTER

### Engagements

Q1. **Mr. Mans:** To ask the Prime Minister if she will list her official engagements for Tuesday 20 June.

**The Prime Minister: (Mrs. Margaret Thatcher):** This morning I had meetings with ministerial colleagues and others. In addition to my duties in this House, I shall be having further meetings later today.

**Mr. Mans:** Does my right hon. Friend agree that the only way of improving the environment is through increased prosperity? Will she therefore press on with her highly successful policies of the past decade to ensure that this prosperity allows us to continue to meet the aspirations of all our people?

**The Prime Minister:** It is because the Government have created the conditions for a record standard of living that we have been able to spend so much on improving the environment, so much on improving the quality of water —about £1·2 billion this year—and a great deal on improving river cleanliness so that we have the first-equal record of anyone in Europe, far better than any previous Government. Of course, we are spending nearly £2 billion to ensure compliance with the acid rain directive. Altogether, by ensuring prosperity, we have been able to contribute the maximum amount to the environment.

**Mr. Hattersley** *rose—[Interruption.]*

**Mr. Speaker:** Order. I ask the House to settle down.

**Mr. Hattersley:** Last week—last Monday to be exact —the Secretary of State for Social Security explicity rejected the idea that the state pension should provide a "comfortable standard of living". Is that Government policy?

**The Prime Minister:** The basic state pension has always been a basic state pension—never anticipated to create for all the needs of life. That is why we have—[Interruption.] —at the level at which we would and do provide. That is why, even when I was Parliamentary Secretary in the Ministry of Pensions, we started a second pension, the basic pension followed by a second compulsory pension, either a graduated pension financed by the state or an occupational pension scheme. That is why we also have housing benefit. That is why we also have income support and family credit to make up the pension and to make up incomes to a reasonable standard of living beyond that which the basic pension could possibly reach.

**Mr. Hattersley:** Will the Prime Minister make it absolutely explicit—I use the words again—that when the Secretary of State for Social Security says that pensioners living on the basic pension should not expect a "comfortable standard of living", that is Government policy? Yes or no?

**The Prime Minister:** If pensioners have no further income than the basic pension, they will be entitled, as are 2 million, to income support—[Interruption.] The income support for older pensioners will go up this October-November. That, too, was the policy accepted by the Labour Government of which the right hon. Gentleman was a member, if he only knew it.

**Mr. Hattersley:** Will the Prime Minister never learn? Does she not realise that it is the bland statement of such callous policies that encompassed her humiliation last Thursday?

**The Prime Minister:** It is the policy which Labour Governments have had to follow as well, in spite of all their rhetoric. I can remember, as the right hon. Gentleman was Minister of State for Prices and Consumer Protection,—*[Interruption]*—for five years, that in his time—*[Interruption.]*—inflation averaged 12 per cent. a year over five years. I can also remember of that Government, in which he was a Minister—*[Interruption.]*

**Mr. Speaker:** Order. The Prime Minister must have an opportunity to reply.

**The Prime Minister:** I can also remember, when the right hon. Gentleman was the Minister for High Prices—[HON. MEMBERS: "Oh."]—that inflation in 1976 was 21½ per cent., and the then Labour Government could not even make up the pension to that.

**Sir John Hunt:** Will my right hon. Friend give thought today to the Underground strike, which is set to paralyse London tomorrow? In the interests of the long-suffering travelling public in London, is it not time that irresponsible wildcat action of this kind was outlawed by legislation, and when will that be done?

**The Prime Minister:** I wholly and utterly condemn this strike. It is contrary to the public—is against fellow members of the public who rely, and who are entitled to rely, on transport to get to work. It is a typically selfish policy to put themselves first, before those who have to use —*[Interruption.]*—to put themselves first, deliberately causing massive inconvenience to those who have to work. Of course, we do not expect Labour Members ever to think of public service.

Q2. **Mr. Andrew F. Bennett:** To ask the Prime Minister if she will list her official engagements for Tuesday 20 June.

**The Prime Minister:** I refer the hon. Gentleman to the reply that I gave some moments ago.

**Mr. Bennett:** Will the Prime Minister agree that, while the question last Tuesday was when the Chancellor of the Exchequer would need the removal men, the question now is when the right hon. Lady will need the removal men? Does she have the same unequivocal support from the Chancellor and the Foreign Secretary that she gave them last week?

**The Prime Minister:** We are very much together as a Government—*[Interruption.]*—as the hon. Gentleman knows, in spite of tremendous efforts to say to the contrary, and we are very happy with our houses at Nos. 10 and 11 Downing street and in Carlton gardens.

**Sir Richard Body:** When my right hon. Friend is considering whether, at the next meeting of the European Council, the subject of the European social charter is to be raised, will she bear in mind that long ago, the European social charter was established by the Council of Europe,

that this country was one of the first to sign and ratify it and that there are members of the European Community, not least Spain, that have yet to sign and ratify it?

**The Prime Minister:** My hon. Friend makes the point very effectively indeed, and I shall raise it at Madrid. I agree that we signed the charter of the Council of Europe, which is a declaration and is not legally binding. In regard to the proposed social charter for Europe, it is quite absurd to try to impose on very different countries with different social services the same level of social services. It would either mean enormous burdens of extra costs on employers, and therefore more unemployment, or it would mean colossal extra subsidies from this country and Germany to those poorer countries in Europe which could not afford it without our aid. With £2 billion net paid to the European Community, we are paying enough.

Q3. **Mr. McFall:** To ask the Prime Minister if she will list her official engagements for Tuesday 20 June.

**The Prime Minister:** I refer the hon. Gentleman to the reply that I gave some moments ago.

**Mr. McFall:** Now that in European terms both Scotland and Wales are Tory-free zones, and mindful of the voters' verdict in the Vale of Glamorgan, Vauxhall, and Glasgow, Central, does the Prime Minister accept that her nostrums for the country are now as potent and as palatable as a tub of hazelnut yoghurt?

**The Prime Minister:** I am naturally concerned that we have no representation in Scotland, but had Scotland had a Labour Government in the United Kingdom, it would not enjoy a fraction of the prosperity that it now enjoys.

Q5. **Mr. Yeo:** To ask the Prime Minister if she will list her official engagements for Tuesday 20 June.

**The Prime Minister:** I refer my hon. Friend to the reply that I gave some moments ago.

**Mr. Yeo:** Knowing my right hon. Friend's great concern with environmental issues, does she share my sense of shock that every single member of the European Community has been successfully prosecuted for failing to comply with European Commission directives—that is, every single member with one exception, and will she confirm that the one country with an unblemished record of commitment to both the European ideal and the green ideal is the United Kingdom?

**The Prime Minister:** Yes, the United Kingdom is indeed the only one of the main EC countries not to be so prosecuted, because our record on the environment is so good. That is one reason. The second reason is that, as is well known, this Government always play by the rules.

**Mr. Ashdown:** When, on Friday, the Prime Minister meets Dame Lydia Dunn, the most respected and most senior of Hong Kong's politicians, will she pay special attention to the comments that Dame Lydia made yesterday when she said that failure to face up to the nationality problem in Hong Kong could undermine the administration of the colony in the years up to 1997? If the Prime Minister will not herself—*[Interruption.]* If the Prime Minister believes that Britain cannot meet that responsibility itself, will she at least take the lead in ensuring an international solution to these issues?

**The Prime Minister:** The last time that the right hon. Gentleman and other right hon. and hon. Members asked that, I pointed out that we are endeavouring to find increased flexibility, first in the sections of the British Nationality Act 1981 and, secondly, under the broader immigration rules. My right hon. and learned Friend the Foreign Secretary has also pointed out that the British overseas passport does not confer right of abode on people and that right of abode would not enable them to move freely and easily around Europe. That requires citizenship. However, those people can come here for a very brief period with the other passport. If it came to a vital refugee problem, of course, we would wish to garner the help of the whole world to deal with it.

**Q6. Mr. Stanbrook:** To ask the Prime Minister if she will list her official engagements for Tuesday 20 June.

**The Prime Minister:** I refer my hon. Friend to the reply that I gave some moments ago.

**Mr. Stanbrook:** While reflecting on the good as well as the bad things arising out of the Euro-elections, may I ask whether my right hon. Friend agrees that the outgoing President of the European Parliament, Lord Plumb, did a very good job indeed and deserves all our thanks, regardless of party, for the competence, dignity and integrity which he demonstrated over two and a half years as the first British holder of that post?

**The Prime Minister:** Yes, Mr. Speaker. I gladly join my hon. Friend. The noble Lord has been an excellent President of the European Parliament and has given valiant service to it, on which I most earnestly congratulate him. I wish him good luck in the future in his seat in the European Parliament.

**Mr. Sedgemore:** Has the Prime Minister read the unanimous report of the Select Committee on the Treasury and the Civil Service on Delors? If she has read it, has she understood it? If perchance she understood it, does she agree with it?

**The Prime Minister:** The whole report I have not read. I have read the Chancellor's evidence. It is absolutely first-class and points out that he would not think of joining the exchange rate mechanism at present; he believes that the first priority is to get inflation down. I understand that some of the Labour members of the Committee went flatly against the Labour manifesto and voted in favour of joining the exchange rate mechanism.

## NEW MEMBERS

*The following Members took and subscribed the Oath or made the affirmation required by law:*

Catharine Letitia Hoey, for Vauxhall.

Michael Goodall Watson Esq., for Glasgow, Central.

# Public Places (Hygiene)

3.34 pm

**Mrs. Teresa Gorman** (Billericay): I beg to move,

That leave be given to bring in a Bill to control the fouling of public places by dogs.

After the European elections, I can safely say that dogs are the No. 2 subject of the month. The public are rightly concerned about the increasing number of attacks on people by savage dogs, and the Government have responded to that concern. Last week, the Home Secretary promised to strengthen the power of the courts to deal with dangerous animals and with stray dogs and to apply heavier fines to irresponsible dog owners. The Secretary of State for the Environment promised to increase pressure on local authorities to clear up dogs' mess and to charge owners who allow their dogs to stray. Therefore, to some extent, the Government have pre-empted some of the matters that I wanted to deal with in my Bill. I am most especially concerned, however, with the hygiene aspect of the problem.

I decided to introduce this Bill when a mother came to my surgery a few Saturdays ago and pointed out that her small daughter, who had been playing on a grass verge, had slipped into some dog's mess—verges are often used as public latrines by animals—and had been very seriously ill in hospital. It was at that point that I began to discover the number of diseases that are transmitted through dog's mess. It is not just an aesthetic, but a serious hygiene, problem, and, quite rightly, the Government take the problem of public hygiene very seriously.

In addition to the well-known worms, toxocara, which can affect people's spleens and livers and, of course, cause blindness, dogs' faeces also contain salmonella and campylobacter. Those are the diseases with which the child I have mentioned had been afflicted. They can cause serious damage to the intestines of small children and are quite common in adults. There are a number of complaints from which people suffer without realising that the problem stems from dog faeces. Whenever we breathe and smell those faeces, we are taking into our bodies some of the organisms that are present.

A solution to the problem would be privately owned streets. The people who owned their streets would then ensure that they were kept free from dog fouling. As it is, the public own the streets through the local authorities. The Secretary of State has rightly empowered local authorities to take more steps to encourage local councils to introduce pooper-scoop schemes and heavier fines. In Westminster, the fines are up to £100, but that has not entirely persuaded people to do something about this unpleasant problem.

When, in the old days, people had the problem of disposing of soil, they simply threw it out of the window, with the warning of, "Guar-e-loo". Then, when I was a child, the nasty habit of spitting required "do not spit" notices on all the buses. Why do we still tolerate the problem of dogs using the streets as if they were public lavatories?

As I have said, I am concerned about the hygiene problem, as well as how to control dogs on the streets. I draw the House's attention to the situation in several American cities, including the city of Charleston in North Carolina, where there is a dog lead requirement. No dogs are allowed on public streets unless they are on a lead, and that copes with the problem of identifying the person who owns the dog. That is one of the main concerns expressed when we talk about the prospect of legislation in this place. I recommend to the Secretary of State that at some time in the future he thinks about that problem. I am waiting to see, however, how the measures that the Government have recently introduced will affect it.

When there are food poisoning incidents, the Government step in immediately to reassure the public that they are doing all they can to control the problem. They inspect, and they require people preparing food for the public to adopt very high standards. Yet still we allow people with dogs to walk the streets and leave behind them potential disease-causing piles on the pavements.

Next time that we have registration for the community charge we should examine the possibility of people putting their dogs on the community charge form. We could then charge the dog owners for cleaning up after their animals. Meanwhile, my main concern is for health. I should like to propose in my Bill that dog owners be required to obtain a certificate—an MOT of health—from a vet before they are allowed to take their dogs on to the streets.

People will say that that cannot be enforced, but one might as well say that one cannot enforce any sort of public hygiene. Of course it can be enforced, and, last week, the Government stated that they would permit the authorities to introduce more wardens to catch irresponsible people.

We cannot continue to tiptoe around the problem or sweep it under the carpet. It is important that our streets are kept clean and beautiful in the same way as some cities in America. In addition to the current regulations operated in many of our cities and in the Isle of Wight, dog owners in this country should be required to obtain from a vet a certificate that the dog has at least been tested to see that it does not contain worms and other diseases, that it is vaccinated against rabies in addition to the ordinary diseases, and that it cannot cause the problems that currently exist.

*Question put and agreed to.*

Bill ordered to be brought in by Mrs. Teresa Gorman, Mr. Vivian Bendall, Mr. Roger Gale, Mr. Tony Marlow, Mr. Neil Hamilton, Mr. Harry Greenway and Mr. Jerry Hayes.

## PUBLIC PLACES (HYGIENE)

Mrs. Teresa Gorman accordingly presented a Bill to control the fouling of public places by dogs: And the same was read the First time; and ordered to be read a Second time upon Friday 7 July and to be printed. [Bill 161.]

## SELF-GOVERNING SCHOOLS ETC. (SCOTLAND) BILL (ALLOCATION OF TIME)

*Motion made, and Question put forthwith, pursuant to Standing Order No. 80 (Allocation of time to Bills),*

That the Report [19th June] of the Business Committee be now considered.—[*Mr. Sackville.*]

*Question agreed to.*

*Resolved,*

That this House doth agree with the Committee in the said Resolution.

*The following is the report of the Business Committee:*

That the Resolution [24th May] of the Business Committee shall be varied as follows:

(1) The order in which proceedings on consideration of the Bill are taken shall be Amendments to Clauses Nos. 1 to 3, Part I of Schedule No. 1, Clauses Nos. 4 to 7, Part II of Schedule No. 1, Clauses Nos. 8 to 10, Schedule No. 2, Clauses

Nos. 11 to 14, Schedule No. 3, Clauses Nos. 15 to 18, Schedule No. 4, Clause No. 19, Schedule No. 5, Clauses Nos. 20 to 24, Schedule No. 6, Clauses Nos. 25 to 28, Schedule No. 7, Clauses Nos. 29 to 32, Schedule No. 8, Clause No. 33, Schedule No. 9, Clauses Nos. 34 to 74, Schedules Nos. 10 and 11 and Clause No. 75; Government new Clauses; remaining new Clauses.

(2) The following table shall be substituted for the Table set out at the end of that Resolution:

### TABLE

| Proceedings | Time for conclusion of proceedings |
| --- | --- |
| Amendments up to the end of Schedule No. 3 | 5.30 p.m. |
| Amendments up to the end of Clause No. 75 | 6.30 p.m. |
| Government new Clauses | 7.30 p.m. |
| New Clauses Nos. 1 to 10 | 10.00 p.m. |
| Remaining proceedings on consideration | 11.00 p.m. |
| Third Reading | Midnight |

# Orders of the Day

## Self-Governing Schools etc. (Scotland) Bill

*As amended (in the Standing Committee), considered.*

### Clause 1

#### DUTY OF SECRETARY OF STATE TO MAINTAIN SELF-GOVERNING SCHOOLS

3.43 pm

**Mr. Dennis Canavan** (Falkirk, West): I beg to move amendment No. 33, in page 1, line 14, at end insert
'but the Secretary of State shall not, in performing the duty, or exercising the power, distinguish, as regards the benefits or services provided or as regards the terms on which they are provided, between pupils at any self-governing school and pupils at education authority schools in the same area.'.

**Mr. Speaker:** With this, it will be convenient to consider the following Government amendments: No. 72, No. 83, No. 84, No. 91, No. 92; and Government new clause 25 —*Recurrent grant in respect of provision for special educational needs.*

**Mr. Canavan:** As the Bill stands, it is a serious threat to one of the basic principles of comprehensive education, —equality of educational opportunity for all children and young people, irrespective of their ability or aptitude. One of the finest achievements of the 1964-70 Labour Government was the introduction of comprehensive education, and it is worth recalling that it was introduced in Scotland without legislation. The then Secretary of State for Scotland, Willie Ross, simply sent a circular round to all local education authorities in Scotland, and even the few authorities which were Tory-controlled complied with the Secretary of State's request, because it was reasonable and because there was such widespread consensus in Scotland at that time about the fairness of comprehensive education, and particularly the basic principle of equality of educational opportunity. Many people saw through the unfairness and the evils of the two-tier system, under which children were selected or rejected at the ages of 11 or 12 on the result of just one test.

It is greatly to be regretted that the Government have now broken the consensus in favour of comprehensive education, a system for which there is still widespread support in Scotland. Scotland moved towards comprehensive education without the need for legislation, yet the Government are forcing this Bill through the House against the wishes of elected Scottish Members, the majority of those working in education and the majority of parents, all of whom want nothing to do with such an infringement of the basic principle of equality of educational opportunity.

There is an understandable fear of a return to a two-tier system, and without my amendment there will be an increased chance of that happening. The Secretary of State may show bias towards self-governing schools and give them special treatment or unfair advantage over local authority schools. The Government are intent upon eroding the local authority education sector. For political, not educational, reasons, the Secretary of State may try to

[*Mr. Canavan*]

encourage that erosion by giving additional funds to schools that opt for self-governing status, in the hope that that will have a snowball effect, with more parents voting for self-governing status because they want that additional funding for their children.

The Bill will split the local authority education system into two different sorts of school. The self-governing schools will be funded by direct grant from the Secretary of State, with the remainder being funded, as at present, by local authorities. The local authority is dependent upon the Secretary of State, through revenue support grant, for most of the money that it spends on education. It is also dependent upon him for borrowing consent for capital for projects such as the building of new schools or extensions to existing schools. The Secretary of State will have his hands on the purse strings not only of what he hopes will be self-governing schools but, indirectly, of local authority schools. There will be an opportunity for a certain amount of financial manipulation to give unfair advantage to self-governing schools.

The amendment would place upon the Secretary of State a statutory responsibility to be as even-handed as possible between local authority schools and self-governing schools. The Minister may have already noticed that there is a similarity in the wording of my amendment to clause 24, which states:

"the authority shall not, in performing the duty, or exercising the power, distinguish, as regards the benefits or services provided or as regards the terms on which they are provided, between those two categories of pupil."

The two categories of pupils referred to are those at self-governing schools and those at education authority schools.

To refresh the memories of those who were members of the Committee, and the memories of Members present now for Report, clause 24 refers to certain services and benefits for pupils which will continue to be the statutory responsibility of the education authority even for self-governing schools after opting out has taken place. Schedule 6 specifies the obligations which the education authority shall continue to have even after self-governing status has been acquired. Those responsibilities include the responsibility for health and cleanliness of pupils.

Health and cleanliness are important. It is often said that cleanliness is next to godliness. However, educational opportunity is also important. With regard to the important aspect of educational opportunity, which is the prime function of a school, the Secretary of State should have a continuing responsibility to be even-handed in his treatment of education authority schools and any schools which may opt for self-governing status.

If the drafters of the legislation, and presumably the Secretary of State, thought it necessary to write into the Bill a continuing statutory responsibility on education authorities in connection with self-governing schools, I maintain that there is an equally compelling case to place a statutory responsibility on the Secretary of State to be even-handed in his treatment of the two different categories of schools and the two different categories of pupils.

The Secretary of State has some responsibility, directly or indirectly, for the education of all children in Scotland. It is sometimes said that we are all Jock Tamson's bairns. However, in this matter of education, I suppose we are all the Secretary of State's bairns. Just like any good parent who tries to be even-handed with his or her children, if the Secretary of State is to be a responsible and good Secretary of State for education in Scotland, he should have regard to the need for equality of educational opportunity between children attending self-governing schools and those attending education authority schools in the same area.

Unfortunately, the Secretary of State so far, by many of his actions, has failed to live up to his responsibility to be even-handed with pupils, whatever school they attend or whatever category they fall into. That is obvious from the massive cuts in educational provision and the resources provided to education authority schools. Those cuts have been imposed by the Government while at the same time, they can find millions of pounds of taxpayers' money to operate the assisted places scheme in non-education authority schools, which in effect means that millions of pounds of public money are being given out to bolster that privileged sector of education which caters for less than 4 per cent. of Scottish children.

In view of the Secretary of State's track record in being very unfair and using public money to bolster privilege while at the same time denying adequate resources to 96 per cent. of children who attend education authority schools in Scotland, there is a strong need for a statutory responsibility like that proposed in my amendment. It would place the onus on the Secretary of State to give equality of treatment to all children in Scotland, instead of giving an unfair advantage to a privileged minority.

**Mr. Allan Stewart** (Eastwood): The hon. Member for Falkirk, West (Mr. Canavan) made three or four general points in support of the amendment before coming to the point of principle. I accept at the outset that he has a genuine point of principle, but the amendment is unnecessary.

The hon. Gentleman's first point was that the legislation is being passed against the wishes of the majority of parents. It is worth reiterating that nothing will happen at self-governing schools unless the parents wish it to happen. Under the revised provisions before the House, there will, if necessary, be two ballots of parents and, unless they express the wish for their school to have self-governing status, there will be no change. Therefore, this is purely permissive legislation. That is the crucial point against those who have sought to tell the Scottish people that anybody will be forced to do anything under the self-governing clauses.

The hon. Gentleman's second point was that the legislation seeks to undermine the comprehensive system. I have no doubt that we shall return to that point during the debate, but it is not central to the hon. Gentleman's case at this stage. However, it is interesting to note what has been revealed about Opposition Members' view of the objectives of Scotland's comprehensive education system. The hon. Member for Fife, Central (Mr. McLeish) made a remarkable admission in an article in the *Glasgow Herald* this morning. In a number of respects, it was a remarkably honest article, and I commend him on that. He said:

"Before 1979, Education was used by successive governments in an attempt to engineer an even more egalitarian society."

All is revealed. That is what the Labour Government's education policies in Scotland were all about—not according to propaganda from the Adam Smith Institute or the Tory party central office, but according to the Labour party's Front-Bench education spokesman. They were all about social engineering.

**Mr. Dick Douglas** (Dunfermline, West): They did not make a good job of it in my case.

**Mr. Stewart:** I shall not make any personal comment on the hon. Gentleman's education. As he knows, I am a product of the Scottish comprehensive education system, and proud to be so. However, I went through that system rather earlier than the hon. Gentleman.

Dundee high school has been mentioned by the hon. Member for Dundee, East (Mr. McAllion). He will be glad to know, as I am sure the House will be, that this year Dundee high school celebrates its 750th year. Those who sometimes make the most wild assertions about Scottish educational traditions should bear in mind the fact that the tradition of that school has continued in Dundee for three quarters of a millenium.

The third point made by the hon. Member for Falkirk, West related to the assisted places scheme. However, that scheme is about choice, just as the provisions to which the amendment refers are about choice. *[Interruption.]* Let me give the hon. Member for Sheffield, Hillsborough (Mr. Flannery) a quotation, again from the revealing article written by the hon. Member for Fife, Central:

"the hi-jacking and exploitation by the right of parental choice is one of their most significant victories."

I agree. It is a significant and continuing victory.

**Mr. Martin Flannery** (Sheffield, Hillsborough): The hon. Gentleman knows as well as I do that the assisted places scheme is a creaming-off process that attacks comprehensive education, by taking certain children out of it to receive special treatment. The same was done a long time ago. The scheme favours a particular grouping, and the price of it goes up year by year at the expense of comprehensive education.

**Mr. Stewart:** Not at all. The scheme is designed to give those having incomes below a certain level the opportunity to send their children to particular schools. The scheme extends choice and gives parents an opportunity to choose a particular sector of education. It makes no attack on the comprehensive system.

4 pm

**Mr. Harry Ewing** (Falkirk, East): I am sure that the hon. Gentleman does not wish to mislead the House over the way in which the assisted places scheme operates. He seems to suggest that all parents having an income below the level to which he referred have a right to an assisted place for their child, but he knows perfectly well that that is not true. The headmaster of the school operating the scheme has the final say. My hon. Friend the Member for Sheffield, Hillsborough (Mr. Flannery) is right to say that the headmaster—correctly, from his point of view—chooses the cream of the pupils. There are hundreds and hundreds of cases of children of parents who meet the income criteria being refused admission.

**Mr. Stewart:** I am grateful to the hon. Member for Falkirk, East (Mr. Ewing) for confirming that there is a large demand for assisted places. That line was not generally taken by Labour Members in Committee, but the hon. Member for Falkirk, East has more experience and understanding of Scottish education trends than do members of the Labour Front Bench. While the hon. Gentleman is correct to say that not every pupil who wants such an education has an opportunity to receive it, that is not an argument for not extending that opportunity whenever possible.

The hon. Member for Falkirk, West (Mr. Canavan) argues that there should be an equality of treatment as between the Secretary of State's financing of self-governing schools and that which the Secretary of State partly, if not wholly, determines for schools in the local authority sector. The Government's position on that aspect has been stated with great clarity. At the 18th sitting of the First Scottish Standing Committee, my hon. Friend the Minister stated:

"It may help the Committee if I restate the cardinal principle that an individual self-governing school should be neither better nor worse off than it could reasonably have expected if it had remained under local authority management. That phrase has been used many times in Committee and was contained in the descriptive paper that we issued in December, and discussed in response to points made by the hon. Member for Dundee, East (Mr. McAllion)."

I recall that he did so with the brevity to which members of the Committee became accustomed during its proceedings: My hon. Friend continued:

"Therefore, it is right that they should be treated no better and no worse than would be expected for equivalent schools managed by the education authority for the same area."—[*Official Report, First Scottish Standing Committee*, 20 April 1989; c. 854.]

That seems crystal clear to me. I would expect my hon. Friend the Minister to express some sympathy with the general point of principle made by the hon. Member for Falkirk, West—although not with many of his arguments—but I feel that the amendment is unnecessary.

**Mr. John McAllion** (Dundee, East): The hon. Member for Eastwood (Mr. Stewart) referred to the three quarters of a millenium for which Dundee high school has served the people of Dundee. I must point out to him that it has not served them all; it has served only those who could afford the fees. The Opposition are entirely opposed to any link between access to education and ability to pay, which is why we do not rejoice in 750 years of Dundee people being refused education.

**Mr. Alan Stewart:** Logically, then, the hon. Gentleman must wish for the abolition of the independent sector.

**Mr. McAllion:** I look forward to the day when access to education is given freely and equally across the country, irrespective of ability to pay. I certainly support the abolition of public funding for the independent sector. If people want to do their own thing with their own money that is their affair, but they cannot look to public funds from the taxpayer for the indoctrination of elitism in a whole new generation of children.

**Mr. Bill Walker** (Tayside, North) *rose——*

**Mr. McAllion:** I will give way to the hon. Gentleman once, but this is the last time.

**Mr. Walker:** I thank the hon. Gentleman for giving way in his usual courteous manner. Does he agree that pupils from his constituency and mine attend Dundee high school under the assisted placed scheme because of the level of their parents' income and also because they were acceptable, being, in most cases, able and talented? Those

[*Mr. Walker*]

children have been given a unique opportunity. Is the hon. Gentleman saying that children should not be offered such opportunities?

**Mr. McAllion:** The hon. Gentleman entirely misrepresents the scheme. Private fee-paying schools suffer from the same problem experienced for many years by public-sector schools—falling rolls. Because falling rolls meant that the private sector could not maintain its own business, the Government dreamed up the assisted places scheme as a way of filling places with the help of public money. That is why the Labour party will phase out the scheme when they come to office at the next election—as we will; make no mistake about that.

The hon. Member for Eastwood said that he considered the amendment unnecessary. He would think that, because it ties down the Secretary of State for Scotland to treating both sectors fairly. The Conservative party does not want that; it wants to leave the Secretary of State enough room to exercise bias in the allocation of funds.

The hon. Gentleman also said that the Bill was purely permissive. That is not true. Under the clause as it stands, the Secretary of State will clearly favour schools that opt for self-governing status. Parents will quickly get the message: if they want their kids to be educated in a decent school—a decent building with decent equipment and well-paid teachers—they had better opt out of local authority control, because the Secretary of State for Scotland is going to squeeze public-sector funds and force them out. There is nothing permissive about that. My hon. Friend's amendment is right on the ball, and should be supported.

In Committee, the Minister said that self-governing schools would receive exactly the same funding as they might reasonably have expected had they remained under local authority control. Such a proposition is unproblematic only if schools that opt out remain unchanged under the direct rule of the Scottish Office. What will happen when the Government try to apply that principle? What if the roll changes in a school? The funding will then have to change as well. Who will decide how it is to change? The Secretary of State for Scotland.

What if the character of the school changes? That is also permissible under the Bill. A school may go for academic selection or for single-sex status—or, indeed, mixed status—which will obviously have funding implications. Who makes the decision about funding implications? Again, the Secretary of State for Scotland makes it, completely on his own.

What about the capital requirements of a school? It is hard to imagine that the Secretary of State for Scotland will know what the capital funding of any school might have received, had it remained under education authority control. He would need to know the state of the building and the level of priorities in a particular school compared with other schools in the education authority's area, and also where the school would be placed in the programme by the education authority. All that the Secretary of State can do is to put a school at the top of the list and provide it with more capital funding than it might have received from the education authority. I do not know how anyone can say that the Secretary of State will not be allowed to do that.

If the Secretary of State is serious about the principle that there will be no additional funding for self-governing schools that opt out, he must accept the amendment. It writes on to the face of the Bill a restriction that the Secretary of State for Scotland must be fair to both sectors.

**Mr. John McFall** (Dumbarton): On the point about the funding of self-governing schools being the same as that of local authority schools, does not my hon. Friend agree that, for years, Scottish local authorities, particularly Labour-controlled local authorities, have spent more on education than the Government say that they ought to have spent? We have been told by the Government that, although local authorities have spent over the limit during the last 10 years, they will nevertheless be given as much as they have already spent on education because they believed that it was essential to spend that much on education. That holds the key to the debate. The Government will sugar the pill with extra finance and thereby allow self-governing schools to opt out. The Government have given no credible answer on that point.

**Mr. McAllion:** My hon. Friend has made a fair point. that is obvious to everyone in Scotland, particularly since last Thursday's European election results, when the Tories were finally rejected completely in Scotland. To those of us who live in Scotland, it has been obvious for many years that the Government have been squeezing the funds that they have made available to public sector schools. They have squeezed the money that they have made available to education authorities, mostly by controlling what is now called the revenue support grant. They have placed strict limits on education authority spending. The poll tax will now make it virtually impossible for education authorities to raise enough money to spend on schools.

The Government are trying to ensure that the kind of services that are provided by education authorities will be minimal. They have provided them with only minimal funding for those services. At the same time, they have tried to create a new self-governing sector to which the Secretary of State for Scotland, who will have no restrictions placed upon him as the Bill stands, will be able to allocate funds as he likes.

That is the carrot that will be used to tempt parents to take advantage of what was described by the hon. Member for Eastwood as purely permissive legislation, although it is nothing of the kind. It is a carrot to try to save the reputation of the radical, far Right-wing Minister with responsibility for education in Scotland, the hon. Member for Stirling (Mr. Forsyth). He wants to create a two-tier system and also to destroy the local education authority schools sector in Scotland. This is another step down that road.

God knows what will come after this measure. When the School Boards (Scotland) Bill was considered, it was said that it would give power back to the parents. Power was not given back to the parents. Instead, it paved the way for the Self-Governing Schools etc. (Scotland) Bill. This Bill will pave the way for yet another monstrous piece of legislation, behind which there will be only one principle —to attack the public provision of education and to destroy local authority schools. That is why the House, in line with the people of Scotland, should vote for the amendment.

**Mr. Bill Walker:** I welcome the opportunity to speak on the amendment. I am sure that the speech of the hon. Member for Dundee, East (Mr. McAllion) will be read with great interest by his constituents and also by mine, particularly his views on that very fine school, Dundee high school. I did not attend that school, nor did any of my children, but as a Dundonian I believe that it has enhanced the status and position of Dundee, a status and position that sadly, it would not enjoy without the school. It has contributed handsomely in the past to the provision of many leaders in almost every walk of life. However, the hon. Member for Dundee, East, has put it on record that he wishes that school, after 750 years, to be destroyed.

That is not so very surprising. My hon. Friend the Member for Eastwood (Mr. Stewart) referred to the fact that in today's *Glasgow Herald,* there is a most interesting article by the hon. Member for Fife, Central (Mr. McLeish). I am confident that it will be referred to regularly in future and that his attention will be drawn to it on many occasions. There is no question that he has set out clearly what the views of the Labour party are and have been. He wrote:

"Before 1979 Education was used by successive Governments in an attempt to engineer a more egalitarian society."

The hon. Member for Fife, Central is nodding in agreement. He is obviously proud of that. That is good, because I shall find that article very useful in future. I shall also find it useful to quote back to him his comment earlier in the same article that

"privatisation represents a much greater threat than Anglicisation."

There is nothing in the Bill about privatisation. Self-governing schools are not privatised schools.

4.15 pm

The hon. Member for Falkirk, West (Mr. Canavan), to give him credit, is consistent. He found it just as difficult to live with a Labour Government as he does with a Conservative Government. He said that in Scotland today the Conservative Government are putting through legislation which is opposed by the majority of Scottish Members in the House. Of course, that is nothing new. I remind him that the Labour Government passed a Bill through the House to abolish the grammar schools—a fundamental change in English education—without a majority in England. I do not argue with that, because I believe that the unitary Parliament is the right place to take such decisions, but the hon Gentleman and his colleagues cannot have it both ways. They either support the unitary Parliament and what it does or they do not.

In the euphoria since last Thursday—I congratulate the new Member for Glasgow, Central (Mr. Watson) who is obviously a credit to the Labour party and I am sure will be a credit to the House—Labour Members have been very happy with the result and the leaders of the Labour party have been making noises about what they will do in government. If the Labour party was in government, in the same situation as previously, when it had no majority in England, quite properly it would wish to put through legislation affecting England, using its majority in other parts of the United Kingdom—usually Scotland and Wales—to make sure that that legislation got through. The hon. Gentleman is not being even-handed, which is unlike him as he is usually pretty consistent in the way in which he deals with these matters.

The hon. Member for Falkirk, West spoke about cuts in education funds. He and I know that the amount of money contributed by the taxpayer, and previously by the ratepayer, per child in school in Scotland has increased substantially under the Conservative Government, and that the only real reductions occurred under the last Labour Government. The hon. Gentleman should realise that the increase in funding per child has been substantial and has continued under the present Government.

The hon. Member for Falkirk, East (Mr. Ewing) in a fairly lengthy intervention, made it quite clear that, under the assisted places scheme, hundreds were refused acceptance. If that is the case, we can count on his support to increase the funds available so that the hundreds who have been refused places will be able to enjoy the benefits of the scheme. Although those being refused acceptance do not run into large numbers in my constituency, the hon. Gentleman may well be right that hundreds are being refused. We have only his word for it, but if that is the case we look forward to him joining us in the Lobby at some future date when we persuade the Government to increase the funding to make that very fine scheme work effectively.

All hon. Members will realise that the Government and their supporters have never made any secret of the fact that they believe that, when local education authorities are receptive to the needs of local schools and understand the needs of the local community, the likelihood of a school board and the parents wishing to become self-governing would be remote. It will occur only in circumstances in which the parents and the school boards consider that the local authority has not understood, does not wish to understand and does not respond. It is clear that this is permissive legislation.

**Mr. Allan Stewart:** To underline my hon. Friend's point, does he agree that the legislation has already been successful? It was only the threat of self-governing status that caused Strathclyde regional council to change its attitude to the extension to Neilson primary school.

**Mr. Walker:** I thank my hon. Friend the Member for Eastwood for that helpful intervention. I agree with him. What is more important is that, as this legislation is going through the House, we have on the statute book an Act to set up the school boards, and that has produced a dramatic change in attitudes in Strathclyde. Strathclyde is now clearly embracing the setting up of school boards, and it is doing so in a much more positive and aggressive way than the present statute. That can only be encouraging.

It is obvious that the amendment does not reflect Conservative Members' view that this is enabling legislation. That is all it is—it enables; it is permissive; it does nothing more than that. It enables the school boards and the parents, if they feel that the local education authority is not responding to their wishes, to vote for their school to be self-governing, subject to the approval of the Secretary of State.

The hon. Member for Falkirk, West must remember that his amendment has not taken account of the lengthy debates in Committee. He does not accept that Conservative Members believe that there will be no demand for self-governing schools. If Scottish education is everything that the hon. Gentleman and his colleagues claim, there will be no demand for them.

**Mr. Alex Salmond** (Banff and Buchan): I apologise for the absence of my hon. Friend the Member for Moray

*[Mr. Alex Salmond]*

(Mrs. Ewing), who had to return to Scotland this morning because of a serious illness in her family. It is particularly unfortunate because the amendments dealing with special needs and special schools are within my hon. Friend's specialist interest. I will do my best to put her points of view.

I support the arguments put forward by the hon. Member for Falkirk, West (Mr. Canavan). Amendment No. 33 goes to the heart of the fallacy that the Conservative Government are trying to promote in this legislation—the idea that parents will have a free choice between opting out or staying within the state system. However, we all know that there are two situations in which opting out will become a reality, and they are a school closure or a school having reason to believe that it will be more favourably treated in capital allocation by opting out of the state system.

The hon. Member for Tayside, North (Mr. Walker) always makes some remarkable contributions in Scottish debates. He should recognise that this legislation is now being pushed through Parliament by a party that is now the third party in Scotland. It is about 5 per cent. behind the Scottish Nationalist party. The hon. Gentleman should realise also that support for the Scottish Conservative party, as measured by last Thursday's European election, is now less than that for the Green Party in west Surrey. That seems a fragile mandate on which to push forward a piece of legislation that is overwhelmingly rejected by the majority of the Scottish people.

I now refer to what happens to parents when faced with the problems of school closure or the thought that their school might be better funded under the opting-out legislation.

Today's *Glasgow Herald* tells us that the ruling Labour group in Strathclyde

"seems set to proceed with the closure of two secondary schools and eight primaries, despite bitter opposition from parents' groups."

It would be understandable even if parents who opposed the legislation were tempted by the opting-out provisions. I recall a speech by the hon. Member for Falkirk, East (Mr. Ewing) in the Scottish Grand Committee last year when we were discussing the NHS and the opting out of hospitals. He said, as a fierce opponent of the opting-out provisions, that he, as a constituency Member, might be pushed, as an alternative to closure, into considering opting out on the part of a hospital in his area.

I think I see the hon. Member for Tayside, North indicating assent to that proposition. Opting out will not solve the underlying resource and capacity problems in the health or education services. The Tories will have to say exactly which schools they would like to see closed as an alternative to those which stay open as a result of being tempted to opt out. What is proposed will solve nothing. It will simply move the problem, in the education service or in the NHS, to another area. It will also create problems in terms of dividing and fragmenting the education system.

**Mr. Bill Walker:** The hon. Gentleman will appreciate that when this legislation becomes law, the Secretary of State, in the final analysis, will have to agree to a school becoming self-governing. Surely that is the Government taking some responsibility?

**Mr. Salmond:** There is no question but that this is a piece of centralising legislation. It gives enormous power to the Secretary of State over a range of matters. But it does not give parents much power. It would be remarkable if the Minister, desperate to secure some evidence, whatever it might be, of support for opting out, did not grasp at any straw and allowed any school to opt out so that he could claim it as a success for his policy.

It is also difficult to believe that there will not be nods and winks in the direction of certain schools to the effect that if they opt out, they will be exceptionally well treated by way of facilities, new buildings and the like. Parents will face being squeezed between the Strathclyde stick of school closure and the Tory carrot of extra resources. That is not a free choice, and this is not enabling legislation.

**Mr. Allan Stewart:** Will the hon. Gentleman agree that there is a difference between school rationalisation because rationalisation is necessary—which is bound to be unpopular with individual groups of parents—and school rationalisation which is used for other purposes? Consider, for example, the rationalisation carried out in Strathclyde because a majority of the Labour group, against the wishes of the chairman of the Labour group, decided that they did not want single-sex schools in the area. That was an ideological decision. It was different from a straight-forward and sensible rationalisation, even though it might be opposed by individual groups of parents.

**Mr. Salmond:** I have no intention of defending every decision of Strathclyde regional council. Indeed, I do not think that Labour Members would wish to defend every decision of that council on school closures. There is a consensus that the closure programme in many cases was carried out clumsily, to put it no stronger. But at the heart of the argument is the fear that the provision for opting out will tempt people faced with the closure of their school into taking that step, when it will not solve the problem. It will not solve the problem of capacity or offer the additional resources that would be required if more schools in aggregate were to remain open.

The hon. Member for Eastwood (Mr. Stewart) should say which schools in Strathclyde he would close as an alternative to those he would keep open. Unless additional resources are provided for the education service, the take-up of the opting-out provision will be secured by the heavy stick of school closures or the carrot of additional resources.

The amendment tabled by the hon. Member for Falkirk, West goes to the heart of the fallacy that the Tory party is putting forward in this legislation. If Conservative Members wish to claim that there is no intention to treat differently those schools that may be tempted by opting out, they should find no difficulty in accepting the amendment.

**Mr. McFall:** On the issue of single-sex schools, does the hon. Gentleman agree that the Government are flying a kite in relation to Strathclyde? The hon. Gentleman has been consistent in pushing his point without any foundation. There are five single-sex schools in Strathclyde —two are in my constituency and are amalgamating—and I have never heard his argument advanced as a matter of policy. Indeed, I can inform him that it is not a matter of policy because I have contacted the director of education and have raised that point with him. He has said that the abolition of single-sex schools is not a part of Strathclyde's policy. The Government are trying to drive wedges in those areas where there is already pressure because of falling resources and where they have therefore been able to spread discord. That is the real reason.

4.30 pm

**Mr. Salmond:** I accept what the hon. Gentleman says and I hope that he will accept that the reasons that I am giving as to why people might opt out highlight the fallacy of believing that this legislation can be successfully opposed by a general debate about the rights and wrongs of opting out. If we were to have a general debate about those rights and wrongs, Scotland would give an overwhelming majority against opting out. The difficulty with this legislation is that particular pressures may be unfairly imposed on particular groups of parents which may lead them down the road of opting out.

**Mr. Allan Stewart** *rose*——

**Mr. Salmond:** No, I shall not give way to the hon. Gentleman, because I have already done so once.

That is why the SNP made that point so strongly in Committee and said that opting out could not be opposed simply by means of a general debate.

I now turn to the issue of special needs, special schools, special resources and the Government amendments. There were many disreputable and unsatisfactory aspects to the Bill's Committee stage, but the political interchange that led to special schools being included in this legislation was one of the most disreputable of all. I am happy to see the hon. Member for Brigg and Cleethorpes (Mr. Brown) in his place as I say that. As I understand it, special schools were not included in the original legislation. The Labour party made the mistake of tabling an amendment that would have had the effect of including them. However, the English Conservative Members on the Committee then hijacked the amendment and tabled it as their own. That was part of a political game that the Tory members of the Committee were playing.

**Mr. Michael Brown** (Brigg and Cleethorpes): The hon. Gentleman has got it completely wrong. I saw an excellent amendment on the Amendment Paper and felt that it strengthened the Bill. When I serve on a Standing Committee, I read the Bill and the amendments and if I think that they are excellent amendments, I want to show my support for them. Therefore, I approached the Clerk to try to add my signature to that marvellous, extra and wonderful amendment but found that it had disappeared, so I tabled it myself.

**Mr. Salmond:** I am not impressed by the innocence with which the hon. Gentleman puts his case. Although I was not present in the Committee to hear him, I have now read the *Hansard* report of his speeches and it would be difficult not to interpret or detect from his speeches the relish with which he seized on a mistake made by the Labour party. We all play a political game——

**Mr. Brown** *rose*——

**Mr. Salmond:** I have already given way to the hon. Gentleman.

We all play political games—they are the stuff of politics—but we should not play political games with children who need special attention in education.

**Mr. Brown** *rose*——

**Mr. Salmond:** If the Government had carefully considered the question whether special schools sould be included in the opt-out legislation, we can assume that such provisions would have been in the original Bill. This is a serious issue that demands careful consideration. Such provisions should not emerge in the legislation simply as part of a political interchange between Conservative and Labour Members.

**The Parliamentary Under-Secretary of State for Scotland (Mr. Michael Forsyth):** If the hon. Gentleman is telling the House that he has read the *Hansard* of the Committee proceedings, I am surprised that he did not read the strong representations that my hon. Friend the Member for Brigg and Cleethorpes (Mr. Brown) read to the Committee from a lady from Bearsden who has a child with special needs. If the hon. Gentleman has also studied the Bill, he will be aware that, contrary to what he has just told the House, there was a provision in the Bill for the Secretary of State to include special schools by order. The original Opposition amendment, which was then tabled by my hon. Friend the Member for Brigg and Cleethorpes, simply made it automatic that special schools should have that right.

**Mr. Salmond:** Exactly; I thought that that was the point that I had just made.

As to the assurances that the Minister gave in Committee, he changed course as a result of a political interchange that took place in Committee. I do not believe that he can convince us that a great deal of thought had been given to that change of course.

**Mr. Forsyth** *rose*——

**Mr. Salmond:** Perhaps the Minister would listen for a second, and then I shall ask him to answer a specific point about remarks that he made in Committee.

**Mr. Forsyth:** The hon. Gentleman cannot have it both ways. He spent the time in Committee attempting to argue the case for disruption of the House and telling the people of Scotland that the Committee was a waste of time. Is he now criticising the Government because they responded to the arguments that were put in Committee, and amended the Bill accordingly?

**Mr. Salmond:** The Minister's intervention is totally irrelevant. The disruption was to challenge the right of the Government to parachute English Tory Back Benchers into the Committee. I should have thought that the way that the clause emerged in Committee was ample proof that it was unsatisfactory to have a debate on Scottish education dominated by people who had no interest in the Scottish education system.

I trust that the Minister will not dispute assurances that he gave in Committee about consultation with interested groups on special needs children. The Minister may remember—if he cares to pay some attention to the debate —that he gave assurances to the organisations particularly concerned with special needs children that he would engage in a process of proper consultation about the changes that were to take place. I take it that the Minister remembers that assurance.

I now have a copy of a letter about the consultation that took place. A letter from Mr. Cunliffe of the Scottish Education Department was posted on Friday, 2 June. Presumably it reached the organisations on Monday, 5

[*Mr. Salmond*]

June. The organisations were given until Tuesday, 13 June, to submit their opinions to the Government. Given the complexity of special needs education, acknowledged on all sides, does the Minister really believe that a consultation period of a week is enough to consider the full range of issues that were debated in Committee? Should not the Minister have allowed a decent period for the organisations to submit their opinions on the legislation?

If the Minister could not give a proper consultation period, would it not have been proper not to proceed with this aspect of the Bill? If the Government wished to proceed with the opting-out of special schools, could it not have been done later? I would be grateful if the Minister would intervene and confirm that I am correct in saying that only a week was allowed for organisations to submit their opinions on the Government's proposals. I take it that the Minister confirms that that is the case.

Mr. Cunliffe's letter refers to unique problems in trying to assess the resources for recorded children. Then it refers to a dialogue between the education authority on the one hand and an opted-out school on the other as to what degree of resources should be applied to each recorded child. The Minister may call it a dialogue. Having read the letter, I think that complex issues are involved and that these children will be no more than piggies in the middle of a battle between the education authority and the schools that have opted out.

In line with the commitments that the Minister gave in Committee about genuine consultation and considering seriously the range of issues involved, including the resourcing of special schools and the questions that my hon. Friend the Member for Moray raised in Committee, does not the Minister feel that a longer period is required for consultation and reflection? I would be grateful if he would give a constructive response.

**Mr. Michael Forsyth:** It may be helpful if I say something at this point about the Government's amendments Nos. 72, 83, 84, 91 and 92 and new clause 25 and respond to the points made by the hon. Member for Banff and Buchan (Mr. Salmond) in respect of amendment No. 33. We have made it clear all along that, in setting the amount of grant to be paid to a self-governing school, the aim will be to ensure that it is not better off or any worse off than it might reasonably have expected to be under continuing local authority management, as my hon. Friend the Member for Eastwood (Mr. Stewart) pointed out.

The most important consequence is that the recurrent grant paid to a school must reflect the level of spending by the education authority on its own schools. The hon. Member for Banff and Buchan was talking nonsense when he argued that it was a centralising measure. The Secretary of State will not determine the level of funding for a school; that will be determined by the level of funding reflected in the policies of the local authority. The detailed arrangements giving effect to that principle will be a matter for the grant regulations to be made under clause 25. Amendment No. 33 certainly does not achieve any such effect. The Secretary of State is not involved in providing services directly to pupils, whether in a self-governing school or an education authority school. When considering overall levels of resources, what matters is equality of treatment for schools, and that is central to our entire thinking about self-governing schools.

I must say to the hon. Member for Falkirk, West (Mr. Canavan) that, if he reads the report of the Second Reading debate and the quote that my right hon. and learned Friend the Secretary of State used from his right hon. Friend the Member for Birmingham, Sparkbrook (Mr. Hattersley), he will see that we understood the Labour party's position to be that it was against equality of opportunity in education, but was in favour of equality of outcome. That is the difference which separates the two sides of the House. It was extremely helpful for the right hon. Member for Sparkbrook to spell it out so clearly.

The remaining Government amendments are largely concerned with ensuring equity of treatment in resourcing provision for recorded special educational needs in self-governing schools.

I was sorry to hear of the absence from the House of the hon. Member for Moray (Mrs. Ewing) due to family illness. It was a great blessing to the Standing Committee that it was the hon. Lady who participated in our proceedings and not the hon. Member for Banff and Buchan. She approached the matter in an extremely constructive and helpful way, unlike the contribution that we have just heard from the hon. Gentleman. With the hon. Lady's particular experience and interest in special education, we found her advice invaluable in the lengthy discussions that we had on special needs, notably on the changes made in part III to the 1980 Act arrangements for placements of recorded children, and, more generally, on the effect of part I of the Bill on special educational needs. The form of the Bill reflects that influence. I am sorry that the hon. Member for Banff and Buchan did not acknowledge that.

I should acknowledge, too, the many organisations that have given us helpful advice on the proposals in the Bill in relation to special education, for which we were extremely grateful. I express special appreciation to Sense in Scotland, which is concerned with the deaf-blind. It has followed the proceedings in Committee very closely and its main concern was that provision for special educational needs should be both secure and adequately financed. I believe that the amendments that we have tabled today will reassure it on both counts.

Amendment No. 72 reflects the concern on both sides of the Committee that self-governing schools should continue to provide for special educational needs and that there should be a positive duty to encourage and to increase that provision. We have, through clause 28, protected existing levels of provision for special needs. As schools now have a duty to have regard to the need to improve that provision, it is not sensible to require the balloting procedure to apply to improvements that flow from that duty. Amendment No. 92 means that increases in special educational needs provision should not be regarded as a change in the characteristics of a school.

**Mr. Douglas:** If the boards of management of schools that become self-governing are to have this responsibility —I speak with a little interest—who will make the assessment of whether they are adhering to that responsibility? Will the local education authority or the Secretary of State make that assessment?

4.45 pm

**Mr. Forsyth:** The board of governors will be under a duty to do so. If it is failing in any of its duties, there is provision in the Bill for the Secretary of State to take action. If the hon. Gentleman will bear with me a little longer, I think that it will become more evident how we see that process working. Perhaps I could send him a copy of the letter that we sent out, following my undertaking in Committee, when I stressed the problems of the time available. I believe that a copy of the letter would be helpful to the hon. Gentleman.

Amendments Nos. 83 and 84 are made in respect of a further undertaking that I gave in Committee. They deal with the description of a school that is to be provided, along with published proposals relating to that school's application to become self-governing. The amendments would require the description to state what range, or, in other words, the kind, of provisions that the school has for pupils with special eduational needs. Clause 16(4)(b) recognises that all schools should make some provision for special educational needs and requires the extent of that to be stated as a basic characteristic of the school. The amendments, therefore, considerably strengthen the requirement to specify the provision for special educational needs at any school.

When the Committee amended the Bill to make special schools eligible for self-governing status, I agreed to bring before the House on Report amendments that would make any necessary changes to allow for that.

I say to the hon. Member for Banff and Buchan, as I said when I intervened, that it is quite extraordinary for him to take the view that we should not listen to the views expressed in Committee and seek to respond to them. A clearly expressed wish in Committee was that special schools should be eligible in the same way as other schools for that purpose. *[Interruption.]* I am surprised that the hon. Member for Fife, Central (Mr. McLeish) is scoffing, because he tabled the amendment in Committee in the first place.

**Mr. Michael Brown** *rose——*

**Mr. Salmond:** Will the Minister give way?

**Mr. Forsyth:** I shall give way to my hon. Friend the Member for Brigg and Cleethorpes (Mr. Brown) and then to the hon. Member for Banff and Buchan.

**Mr. Michael Brown:** I believe that hon. Members should not forget the 12th sitting of the Committee on Tuesday 11 April, when I read out the letter sent to me by Mrs. Lamont from Bearsden. The House should remember that Mrs. Lamond took the trouble to write a letter to one of the Scottish newspapers putting it clearly on the record that she felt that it was a disgrace that the Opposition were rejecting the possibility of children and parents of children at special schools being offered the same opportunities as those offered in the Bill to other people. If the hon. Member for Banff and Buchan (Mr. Salmond) says that he has read the proceedings of the Committee, he clearly needs to read again the *Hansard* of the 12th sitting of that Committee.

**Mr. Forsyth:** I agree with my hon. Friend. I recall that the substance of the complaint, and of the letter that appeared in one of the Scottish newspapers from Mrs. Lamond, made the point that parents felt aggrieved that

education authorities were able to take policy decisions to close special needs schools and to deprive them of a facility, and that those authorities believed that that would increase parental choice. Of course, the Labour party took its time-honoured position that the local authorities—the politicians—know better than the parents what is needed for their children. That is why the Labour party changed its mind on this matter and withdrew the amendment to which my hon. Friend the Member for Brigg and Cleethorpes had added his name. He then took over the amendment and moved it eloquently during our proceedings.

**Mr. Salmond:** I hesitate to interrupt a reunion of the board of Michael Forsyth Associates, but will the Minister reply to the question that I have asked several times? Does he feel that a week's consultation matches the commitment he gave in Committee to consult the organisations concerned? Given the complexities of the issue, is a week's consultation adequate for organisations to respond? Will he answer directly?

**Mr. Forsyth:** I am finding it increasingly difficult to accept that the hon. Gentleman has read the Committee proceedings. I said that there would be difficulties over consultation, given the time scale involved. The amendment was not moved by the Government, and I accepted it on the basis of the views and arguments expressed.

**Mr. McFall:** On one side.

**Mr. Forsyth:** I was concerned with the side mentioned by my hon. Friend the Member for Brigg and Cleethorpes a few moment ago—the side of the parents of children with special needs who believe that the choice should be available to them in the legislation.

**Mr. Salmond** *rose——*

**Mr. Forsyth:** I will not give way to the hon. Gentleman again.

The Committee was right in its judgment that, if parents of children at a special school wish it to become self-governing, they should be allowed to pursue that objective. I do not agree that special schools are so different from the generality of schools that the parents involved do not wish to participate in ensuring a good education for their children. The hon. Member for Banff and Buchan talked of the compressed timetable, but we have been impressed by the responses we have received and we have received a considerable amount of support for the amendments to which I am speaking.

**Mr. Salmond:** Does the Minister not accept that his argument falls down? If he is saying that the fact that the amendment arose from the Committee caused grave problems over consultation, would that not be an argument for rejecting the amendment in Committee until the Government could carry out proper consultation and think again on the legislation?

**Mr. Forsyth:** The hon. Gentleman seems to have parted company from his hon. Friend the Member for Moray. If the basis of his argument is that we should not have made amendments at this stage in respect of special needs because there should have been a longer time for consultation, none of the commitments I gave to his hon.

[*Mr. Forsyth*]

Friend the Member for Moray would have been possible. I do not think that his hon. Friend would be too pleased with him, but there is nothing new in that.

There are some distinguishing characteristics. Most pupils who go to special schools have records of needs, and they pursue an educational curriculum that is frequently individual and different in content. Therefore, we had to consider how the existence of records of needs might affect the position. Under part 5 of the record, the authorities have a statutory duty to nominate the school to be attended. That nomination must take into account the views of parents and can be subject to the effect of a placing request. It remains the authority's duty to provide for the special educational needs of recorded children and that duty inescapably determines the majority of school placement decisions for such children. That meets the point raised by the hon. Member for Dunfermline, West (Mr. Douglas).

It has been necessary—[*Interruption.*] The hon. Member for Glasgow, Cathcart (Mr. Maxton) is saying that not all recorded children go to special schools. That is not what I said. I said that the authority's duty to provide for the special educational needs of recorded children determines the majority of school placement decisions for such children. That may be in mainstream education or in special schools.

It has been necessary to consider how the authority's role in supplying the special educational needs of recorded children may be fitted into the arrangements for self-governing schools. That aspect is not confined to special schools. Certainly, special schools contain more recorded children, but, where appropriate, recorded children are placed in mainstream schools and the effect of education authority nominations through the record must also be taken into account.

We have concluded that what is needed are not different arrangements for self-governing schools but an approach to the calculation of a separate element of recurrent grant for schools, whether special or mainstream, focused on the provision made for recorded children.

The arrangement I propose for the consideration of the House comprises two essential stages. First, there should be a dialogue and exchange of information between each self-governing school in an area and the education authority. The authority will say what provision it needs to make to fulfil its statutory duty in relation to the education of these children. The schools will tell the authority of the provisions they are able and willing to make to help the authority fulfil that duty. The object of the exchange is that each school and authority should agree on the amount of provision that the school will make and which the authority would take advantage of.

The second phase of the process will be for the school and the authority to estimate the cost of that agreed level of commitment towards recorded pupils and notify that amount to the Secretary of State. Normally, recurrent grant would be set at that level. In the event of agreement not being reached—this concerned the hon. Member for Dunfermline, West—on the level of provision or on its cost or both, the Secretary of State will be able to make a determination. If the Secretary of State cannot accept any aspect of an agreement, he may also make a determination. The recurrent grant calculated under these proposals will be additional to the grant calculated under clause 25 for the generality of functions at a mainstream self-governing school.

For special schools, account must be taken of pupils with special educational needs who may not have a record, either because it is still being prepared or because they have been placed there by children's panels or social work departments. The agreement between the authority and the special school and the recurrent grant will therefore take account of all children and all other costs that arise.

**Mr. Douglas:** Am I interpreting the Minister correctly? Is he saying that it would be in the interest of a special needs school and the education authority in terms of opting out not to reach an agreement but to be in conflict because they would then receive additional resources for special educational needs in a particular area?

**Mr. Forsyth:** No, the hon. Gentleman is not interpreting my words correctly. The additional provision will be made to take account of the needs of the child and an assessment will be made of the best placement for the child. The additional funds provided if the placement is at a self-governing school will be deducted from the education authority's grant in the same way as the provision for self-governing schools in respect of mainstream education. Therefore, there is no incentive to offload the responsibility on to the Secretary of State. That would be undesirable.

I am fairly confident——

**Mr. McFall:** I have considered special needs since the subject was raised in Committee. Taking an empirical case, there are parents with severely mentally handicapped children and parents with profoundly mentally handicapped children. After discussing the issue of special educational needs with those parents, I detect a division in the way they think their children should be educated. Some parents of severely mentally handicapped children have said that they do not want their children to be educated in the same environment as the profoundly mentally handicapped.

The character of a school can change within two or three years and if a school has opted out and the parents of severely mentally handicapped children are dominant, they may make a decision to admit only severely mentally handicapped children. What will happen to children who are profoundly mentally handicapped? If they cannot obtain a place at the school near their locality, will the local authority have to look again at its provision for the mentally handicapped?

**Mr. Forsyth:** The hon. Gentleman is asking me to repeat what I have just told the House at great length. In the case of a particular placement, there will be dialogue between the education authority and the school. If there is disagreement over the needs in terms of provision or resources, the Secretary of State will have a locus. The removal of the requirement to hold a ballot and obtain the Secretary of State's permission to change the characteristics applies only to an improvement in provision for special needs, not to a diminution of it.

5 pm

I am confident that our proposals for special schools mean that they can opt for self-governing status in the certainty that they can continue fully to participate in the provision for special educational needs required for the local education authority's area. Mainstream schools preparing to become self-governing will have the assurance of a continuing role in the education of recorded children. The amendment to clause 25 is technical and consequential.

For all those reasons, I commend the Government amendments to the House. I hope that the hon. Member for Falkirk, West will recognise that his amendment is not necessary and that the commitments on funding that he seeks have already been given in Committee. I am not sure that I can go along with his attitude towards assisted places or his ideas on education, which appear to be concentrated around the concept of equality of outcome. That is best summarised in the remark made by the hon. Member for Fife, Central, that if it is good enough for Henry McLeish's children it is good enough for everyone else. That view was definitely rejected. The clause, although ensuring fairness in the funding of schools, also allows for diversity and an extension of parental choice.

**Mr. Harry Ewing:** I live with the memory of a debate in the Scottish Grand Committee in Edinburgh when the Minister pronounced his belief in cheque-book choice for education. Against that background, I find it not just difficult but absolutely impossible to accept that the Minister is sincerely concerned about Scottish education. Although I am liable to be criticised for apparently criticising my colleagues on the Front Bench, I must say that I can think of nothing more damaging than the opting out of special needs schools. The Minister is not just famous but notorious for running around Scotland telling the doctors and the teachers that they do not understand his proposals. No one except the Minister seems to understand his proposals, although I do not believe that even he understands the damage that will be done to special needs schools. He will live to regret his proposals.

The hon. Member for Tayside, North (Mr. Walker) chided my hon. Friend the Member for Falkirk, West (Mr. Canavan) about a unitary Parliament. The days of centralised Administration have outlived their time. That will soon be the position in this country, as it is already in most other parliamentary democracies. No other developed parliamentary democracy allows a small group of unrepresentative people to impose their unwanted policies on an unwilling population, as is happening in Scotland. The House and the unitary system—of which the hon. Member for Tayside, North is so proud—are being brought into disrepute by the arrogance with which the Minister has proceeded not just with this legislation, but with the legislation on the National Health Service in Scotland. Conservative Members talk about the possibility of schools opting out rather than face closure, but my understanding is that this legislation is exactly the same as that for the NHS and that there will be no possibility of a school opting out simply because the local authority has proposed its closure.

It is worth pausing for a minute to think about what the Government propose for Scottish education. I do not doubt that the Minister will call it choice. Scotland has been forced to accept the assisted places scheme and the grant-aided sector of private education, which is funded largely by taxpayers' money. I cannot understand why Thatcherite Conservatives are in favour of giving taxpayers' money to private schools. I simply do not understand their logic. The Government are withdrawing taxpayers' money from almost every organisation in the United Kingdom, but for some reason the grant-aided sector survives that philosophy.

Scotland will also have the Minister's opting-out system and the local education authority system. All that is designed for one purpose only—to sap the confidence of local authority education in Scotland. Although the Minister will not admit it, he is hoping that the local authority sector will fail and that his opting-out system will flourish. His assisted places scheme has little to do with education and everything to do with filling the empty desks in the grant-aided sector. That is why, in the final analysis, the decision about who should have places under the scheme lies not with the Secretary of State, not with Members of Parliament and not even with local education authorities; it lies with the headmasters of the receiving schools.

Scotland faces a range of education that the Minister will claim means choice, but its purpose is to sap the confidence of the state sector, which is so excellent in Scotland. Every Right-wing Government in any country have always been guilty of promising to the majority what they know only the minority can have. The Government know that this legislation relates only to the minority and that the vast majority will be left with a denuded education system. My hon. Friend the Member for Falkirk, West tabled his amendment in an attempt to prevent the Minister favouring schools that opt out, at the expense of local authority schools.

As most of my colleagues know, I shall not return to the House after the next general election—[*Interruption.*] Unlike the Minister, I am leaving voluntarily. He will be thrown out, and a few more Conservatives with him. In three years' time, when my hon. Friend the Member for Glasgow, Garscadden (Mr. Dewar) is Secretary of State for Scotland and my own Member of Parliament, my hon. Friend the Member for Fife, Central, (Mr. McLeish) is Education Minister, I shall be very disappointed if they do not put an end to the assisted places scheme and all the rubbish that the Minister has proposed today. I do not know what sort of brains in the Scottish Office thought up such rubbish.

I have a feeling that I will not need to express that disappointment, because I have sufficient confidence in my hon. Friends. They know the damage that the Conservative party in Scotland, small though it is, is doing to Scottish education. It will be up to my colleagues to rebuild that system into the proud system it once was before the advent of the Parliamentary Under-Secretary of State for Scotland, the hon. Member for Stirling (Mr. Forsyth).

**Mr. Edward Leigh** (Gainsborough and Horncastle): I will lay a wager with the hon. Member for Falkirk, East (Mr. Ewing). I will wager a bottle of whisky that my hon. Friend the Parliamentary Under-Secretary of State for Scotland, the hon. Member for Stirling (Mr. Forsyth), will be back in the next Parliament.

**Mr. Harry Ewing:** I want to make it absolutely clear that I accept that wager.

**Mr. Leigh:** I am delighted to find a sporting gentleman on the Opposition Benches. Those of us who served on Committee will remember that my hon. Friend the Minister offered us a bottle of whisky if we could answer the Highlands and Islands board's examination of 1890.

[*Mr. Leigh*]

Only four of us took part and I came a very close second only because I had some small historical detail about a battle wrong.

I was interested that the hon. Member for Sheffield, Hillsborough (Mr. Flannery) intervened in the speech made by my hon. Friend the Member for Eastwood (Mr. Stewart). The hon. Member for Hillsborough obviously thinks that English Members have an important contribution to make in these matters. We must have a contribution to make because we can inform Scottish Members about what has been happening in England.

Clearly the hon. Member for Banff and Buchan (Mr. Salmond) has not done his research. If he had read the Committee proceedings or carried out research into what has been happening in England, he would have discovered that far from schools choosing opted-out status because they are in danger of being closed, or because they want increased capital allocations, they have chosen that status because the parents want to run their own schools.

The hon. Member for Banff and Buchan should have considered what has happened in Lincolnshire, in Skegness grammar school, which was the very first school to opt out. If he had considered that, he would have found that Conservative-controlled Lincolnshire county council had not the slightest intention of closing the school or cutting its capital allocation.

**Mrs. Maria Fyfe** (Glasgow, Maryhill): The hon. Gentleman could save himself a great deal of trouble. Due to the benefits of Scottish education, we can read the national newspapers and we can find out what is happening in England.

**Mr. Leigh:** I read national newspapers and Scottish newspapers with great interest. The hon. Lady may have noticed that *The Scotsman* published an article of mine recently about Europe, entitled "The Nightmare and the Dream". I am grateful to *The Scotsman* for giving me the opportunity to make my point.

**Mr. Salmond:** Is it not possible that Scottish and English parents take a different view of these things? Does the hon. Gentleman agree with his right hon. Friend the Member for Kincardine and Deeside (Mr. Buchanan-Smith) that the prosecution of this legislation is a reason why the Conservative vote sank so low in Scotland last Thursday?

**Mr. Leigh:** That is nonsense. The hon. Gentleman knows that that cannot be true. As my right hon. and hon. Friends have made clear, this is permissive legislation. If it is true that this legislation is deeply unpopular among Scottish parents—and I do not know whether it is or not—I am prepared to give them the chance to find out what it is about. In Committee I asked the hon. Member for Fife, Central (Mr. McLeish) time and again whether he thought that any schools would opt out. He refused to answer me. We are facing entirely permissive legislation about which the House should not be too worried.

**Mr. Bill Walker:** In response to the comment made by the hon. Member for Banff and Buchan (Mr. Salmond), is my hon. Friend aware that, in an election in Kirriemuir, the region responsible for education in my constituency, the nationalist candidate was hammered? My constituents have never failed to understand my views or those of my

colleagues in respect of education, and they support me and my hon, Friend the Minister. There is no better way of showing that support than in a regional election where education was an important issue.

**Mr. Leigh:** We should be careful here. Our nationalist friends are still suffering from the result in Glasgow, so they are feeling a little fragile. We should not be too hard on them.

I must reply to the point made by the hon. Member for Falkirk, East about the unitary Parliament. That point has been made again and again in our debates. No doubt he was a Member of the House when the debate was going on, and he must be aware that grammar schools in Lincolnshire were being threatened with closure simply because a Labour-dominated Parliament was trying to force Lincolnshire to close its grammar schools. That Parliament was dominated by Labour Members because of the preponderance of Labour Members from Scotland. The arguments about a unitary Parliament do not hold water.

5.15 pm

These debates have revealed fear among Labour Members. They are afraid that there are Conservative Members who are prepared to take these arguments into the very heartlands of Labour party support in Scotland. We are not trying to ape what the Labour party has done. Our radical ideas will bear fruit. They have already borne fruit with the sale of council houses in giving ordinary people choices and opportunities which they would not have had before.

One point comes out strong and clear from our arguments: this is not an attack on the state sector. If we wanted to attack—and I use that phrase carefully—the state sector, would we not be talking about education vouchers or tax relief for sending children to private schools?

**Mr. Douglas:** That is exactly what the Minister is doing.

**Mr. Leigh:** The hon. Member for Dunfermline, West (Mr. Douglas) should consider what is happening. We are strengthening the state sector. We are talking about creating magnet schools, flagship schools and schools which will provide an opportunity for the whole state sector. This debate is not about destroying the state sector; it is about improving it. I have no doubt that when people look back on these debates, they will see this legislation as a watershed in Scottish politics. They will see that for the first time, we had the courage to go out there and give choice and freedom to the people.

I will not let the hon. Member for Fife, Central forget his article in the *Glasgow Herald*. He stated:

"The new right has temporarily defined the terms of the debate because they are willing to engage—the hijacking and exploitation by the right of parental choice is one of their most significant victories."

Was it not also significant that the hon. Member for Banff and Buchan said that English Members—I presume he meant me, my hon. Friend the Member for Brigg and Cleethorpes (Mr. Brown) or one of my other colleagues who are present—dominated the debate? Perhaps we began to dominate the debate because we are in touch with what people really want. This is not about giving rights to minorities. It is about giving rights, opportunities and choices to people who have not been able to afford them or take those opportunities hitherto. That is why we will find that this legislation is a watershed and why, from this moment on, we go onwards and upwards in Scotland.

**Mr. Michael Brown:** Is it not even more significant that, from what I can detect, the Opposition might not vote against the Government amendments?

**Mr. Leigh:** I think that it is significant that the Opposition might not be prepared to vote on amendment No. 33. I challenge them to vote on their amendment. Are they not going to do that because they realise that the amendment is completely unnecessary and misguided? Perhaps they will not vote against it because my hon. Friend the Minister said in Committee:

"the amount of recurrent grant will be comparable to the provision made for schools still under education authority management . . . self-governing schools will remain in the public sector. Therefore, it is right that they should be treated no better and no worse than would be expected for equivalent schools managed by the education authority".—[*Official Report, First Scottish Standing Committee,* 20 April 1989; c.854.]

Amendment No. 33 is unnecessary and misguided. The hon. Member for Falkirk, West is really worried not about what this narrow technical part of the Bill contains, but that his heartland is being eroded by my hon. Friend the Minister, who will sweep back to power in Scotland in two or three years' time.

**Mr. Henry McLeish** (Fife, Central): We have just heard eloquent testimony to why Scots want some control over affairs such as education. We have endured such speeches for nearly eight weeks in Committee. I am deeply apologetic to my hon. Friends for their having to listen to another two or three minutes.

I assure my hon. Friend the hon. Member for Falkirk, East (Mr. Ewing) that when we take over the Scottish Office in 1991 or 1992 one of our first steps will be to phase out the assisted places scheme because it encourages nothing but privilege and it is a waste of public expenditure. The £10 million that will have been spent on the scheme by that time could be used more productively in the state sector, where I am sure that children get a better education.

**Mr. Michael Forsyth:** I am interested to hear the hon. Gentleman make that promise to the House. Does he recall that in Committee he said:

"Some parts of the Bill might remain, some parts of it might be popular. It would be foolish for anyone to commit any Government of any political party to what they will do in two or three years' time."—[*Official Report, First Scottish Standing Committee;* 18 May 1989, c. 1501.]

Why has the hon. Gentleman changed his mind?

**Mr. McLeish:** The events of the past two or three days may have confirmed in the minds of civil servants and the Government that we are now on course—[*Interruption.*] It would be foolish for any party to give an overall commitment to everything, but let me make it clear that we shall phase out the assisted places scheme, and later on this evening we shall chart what we shall be doing with other parts of the Bill.

The Minister is still playing politics with some of the most sensitive educational issues in Scotland. I bitterly deplore the fact that special needs are still being used as a political football by the Minister and his colleagues on the hard Right, including the hon. Member for Brigg and Cleethorpes (Mr. Brown).

**Mr. Alan Amos** (Hexham): Will the hon. Gentleman give way?

**Mr. McLeish:** No.

The hon. Member for Brigg and Cleethorpes mentioned earlier the letter he had received from Mrs. Lamond. I investigated that letter a bit more effectively than did the hon. Gentleman. Mrs. Lamond wrote to the hon. Gentleman, but on the back of a number of considerations that he has not outlined to the House, the first being essentially political. The lady was advised to write to the hon. Member for Eastwood (Mr. Stewart), but he was regarded as too moderate to do anything purposeful with it. It was then suggested that somone a bit more extreme could deal with it more effectively on the Floor of the Committee. Therefore, the letter was sent to the hon. Member for Brigg and Cleethorpes, allowing him to use it in a most disgraceful fashion by taking one example of a lady with a handicapped child.

Since I have been a Member of the House there have been few occasions when an hon. Member has used a letter in such a way to bring contempt on the Government Benches and to illustrate that they have no policy on special needs. Under the guise of crocodile tears, they are seeking to suggest that they care about the future of Scottish education and special needs.

**Mr. Michael Brown:** Will the hon. Gentleman give way?

**Mr. McLeish:** No.

**Mr. Brown:** On a point of order, Mr. Deputy Speaker. Is it in order for the hon. Member for Fife, Central (Mr. McLeish) to cast aspersions on a lady who has a handicapped son and who wrote to me as a member of the Committee to ask me to commend to the Minister the reason for including special schools within the Bill? Surely you should rule against the hon. Gentleman misusing an ordinary lady with a handicapped child for his political purposes.

**Mr. Deputy Speaker (Sir Paul Dean):** I have heard nothing out of order.

**Mr. McLeish:** At the end of that contribution, Mr. Deputy Speaker, you missed the hon. Gentleman laughing. That was interesting.

Special needs is a sensitive issue and we are worried that special needs schools in Scotland will be eligible to become self-governing schools. I want to put on the record once more that we deplore the decision that was taken in Committee, supported by the hon. Member for Stirling (Mr. Forsyth). The issues involved in special needs schools are far too emotive and sensitive to be divorced from the work of the education authorities which have served them well over many years.

**Mr. Amos:** Will the hon. Gentleman give way?

**Mr. McLeish:** No.

The Minister should put on ice the part of the Bill that deals with special needs until he has engaged in some realistic discussions. The hon. Member for Banff and Buchan (Mr. Salmond) made a good point when he said that there had been no decent discussions with special needs groups in Scotland. It is outrageous that an area of such sensitivity has been treated in such a cavalier way by the Government, especially the Minister.

**Mr. Michael Forsyth:** The hon. Gentleman is making a great deal of the lady from Bearsden. Does he recall that the amendment that he tabled in Committee—*[Interruption.]*—which he withdrew and which we acknowledge was a mistake on his part, was supported by the Scottish Parent Teacher Council? Is he arguing that not only the lady who wrote to my hon. Friend the Member for Brigg and Cleethorpes (Mr. Brown) but the organisation which speaks for parents and parent-teacher councils in Scotland are out of step? Would it not be appropriate to take account of their wishes rather than responding in the prejudiced way that we have heard in the few moments that he has been addressing the House?

**Mr. McLeish:** The SPTC took that decision because the lady was a member of the SPTC and she asked it to write and prepare that amendment.

My third and final point relates to the possibility under clause 28 of the characteristics of a school being changed, which poses a direct and real threat to special needs provisions. Very few Opposition Members feel reassured by the Minister's words or actions on the amendments that have been tabled today. The Government should now take seriously special needs in Scotland, whether it be special needs schools or the integration of children with handicaps into local authority provision.

My hon. Friend the Member for Falkirk, West (Mr. Canavan) has tabled an amendment that has produced a good debate. I sincerely hope that when we call for a Division the Government will support what is a common sense and obvious way of moving forward.

**Mrs. Fyfe:** I support what my hon. Friend the Member for Fife, Central (Mr. McLeish) has just said. There has been a disgraceful lack of consultation with bodies representing children with special needs. The imposition of the guillotine on the debate means that we have had no opportunity tonight to discuss the needs of Gaelic speakers and those adult users of school education who will have no opportunity to have their needs considered.

That is demonstrative of the Government's bullying attitude. They still believe, as we know from listening to the hon. Member for Gainsborough and Horncastle (Mr. Leigh), that they have a right to impose their wishes on the basis of a tiny unrepresentative minority of 10 Scottish Tory Members of Parliament telling Scotland what it will have to suffer. Despite last week's election results, they are still imposing their views on us. They have no European Member of Parliament in Scotland. Glasgow, Central returned a Labour Member to the House, and the Tory candidate lost his deposit yet the Government claim that they have a basis for imposing their views on us.

The Government keep telling us about this being a unitary Parliament, which gives them the right to do what they are doing, but they seem to forget that under no circumstances could England have imposed upon it the views of a number of people who do not even represent one seventh of the Members of that Parliament. That is what happens to us and that is why their conduct risks breaking up the United Kingdom and they are complete fools if they do not realise that this is where this is leading. They should realise that once again last week the Scottish people told them that they do not want the Bill. In our doorstep discussions, a lot of anger was shown by people asking why we were having such a Bill when the vast majority of Scottish people clearly do not want it, any more than they want the poll tax or the Government cuts, and so on. I hope that a Conservative Member will explain to us tonight on what grounds they can do this to the Scottish people.

**Mr. Tony Worthington** (Clydebank and Milngavie): Does my hon. Friend agree that the Government are not only imposing the legislation on the people of Scotland but have not even consulted them about many of its provisions? In Committee, I challenged the Minister in respect of certain matters affecting special schools, asking whether he had consulted any group of parents representing such children. It was obvious that he had consulted none of them.

**Mrs. Fyfe:** My hon. Friend is absolutely right when he says that the Minister failed to consult relevant bodies representing children with special needs. However, why should he bother to do so when he already ignores the needs and wishes of the Scottish electorate as a whole?

*It being half-past Five o'clock,* MR. DEPUTY SPEAKER *proceeded, pursuant to Order [3rd May] and the Resolution this day, to put forthwith the Question already proposed from the Chair.*

*The House divided:* Ayes 193, Noes 266.

**Division No. 248]**    **[5.30 pm**

### AYES

| | |
|---|---|
| Abbott, Ms Diane | Dixon, Don |
| Adams, Allen *(Paisley N)* | Dobson, Frank |
| Allen, Graham | Doran, Frank |
| Alton, David | Douglas, Dick |
| Anderson, Donald | Duffy, A. E. P. |
| Archer, Rt Hon Peter | Dunnachie, Jimmy |
| Armstrong, Hilary | Eadie, Alexander |
| Ashdown, Rt Hon Paddy | Ewing, Harry *(Falkirk E)* |
| Ashley, Rt Hon Jack | Fatchett, Derek |
| Banks, Tony *(Newham NW)* | Fearn, Ronald |
| Barnes, Harry *(Derbyshire NE)* | Field, Frank *(Birkenhead)* |
| Barron, Kevin | Fields, Terry *(L'pool B G'n)* |
| Battle, John | Fisher, Mark |
| Beckett, Margaret | Flannery, Martin |
| Beith, A. J. | Flynn, Paul |
| Bell, Stuart | Foot, Rt Hon Michael |
| Benn, Rt Hon Tony | Foster, Derek |
| Bennett, A. F. *(D'nt'n & R'dish)* | Foulkes, George |
| Bidwell, Sydney | Fraser, John |
| Blair, Tony | Fyfe, Maria |
| Blunkett, David | Galbraith, Sam |
| Boyes, Roland | Galloway, George |
| Bray, Dr Jeremy | Garrett, John *(Norwich South)* |
| Brown, Gordon *(D'mline E)* | Garrett, Ted *(Wallsend)* |
| Brown, Nicholas *(Newcastle E)* | Gilbert, Rt Hon Dr John |
| Brown, Ron *(Edinburgh Leith)* | Godman, Dr Norman A. |
| Buckley, George J. | Golding, Mrs Llin |
| Caborn, Richard | Graham, Thomas |
| Callaghan, Jim | Grant, Bernie *(Tottenham)* |
| Campbell, Menzies *(Fife NE)* | Griffiths, Nigel *(Edinburgh S)* |
| Campbell-Savours, D. N. | Griffiths, Win *(Bridgend)* |
| Canavan, Dennis | Grocott, Bruce |
| Clark, Dr David *(S Shields)* | Hardy, Peter |
| Clarke, Tom *(Monklands W)* | Hattersley, Rt Hon Roy |
| Clay, Bob | Haynes, Frank |
| Clelland, David | Heffer, Eric S. |
| Cohen, Harry | Henderson, Doug |
| Cook, Frank *(Stockton N)* | Hinchliffe, David |
| Cook, Robin *(Livingston)* | Home Robertson, John |
| Corbyn, Jeremy | Hood, Jimmy |
| Cryer, Bob | Howarth, George *(Knowsley N)* |
| Cunliffe, Lawrence | Howells, Geraint |
| Dalyell, Tam | Howells, Dr. Kim (Pontypridd) |
| Darling, Alistair | Hughes, John *(Coventry NE)* |
| Davies, Ron *(Caerphilly)* | Hughes, Robert *(Aberdeen N)* |
| Davis, Terry *(B'ham Hodge H'l)* | Hughes, Roy *(Newport E)* |
| Dewar, Donald | Illsley, Eric |

Ingram, Adam
Janner, Greville
Johnston, Sir Russell
Jones, Barry *(Alyn & Deeside)*
Jones, Ieuan *(Ynys Môn)*
Jones, Martyn *(Clwyd S W)*
Kennedy, Charles
Kirkwood, Archy
Lambie, David
Leighton, Ron
Lestor, Joan *(Eccles)*
Litherland, Robert
Livsey, Richard
Lloyd, Tony *(Stretford)*
Lofthouse, Geoffrey
McAllion, John
McAvoy, Thomas
McCartney, Ian
Macdonald, Calum A.
McFall, John
McKelvey, William
McLeish, Henry
Maclennan, Robert
McNamara, Kevin
McWilliam, John
Madden, Max
Mahon, Mrs Alice
Mallon, Seamus
Marek, Dr John
Marshall, David *(Shettleston)*
Marshall, Jim *(Leicester S)*
Martlew, Eric
Maxton, John
Meale, Alan
Michael, Alun
Michie, Bill *(Sheffield Heeley)*
Michie, Mrs Ray *(Arg'l & Bute)*
Moonie, Dr Lewis
Morgan, Rhodri
Morley, Elliott
Morris, Rt Hon A. *(W'shawe)*
Mowlam, Marjorie
Mullin, Chris
Murphy, Paul
Oakes, Rt Hon Gordon
O'Brien, William
Orme, Rt Hon Stanley
Parry, Robert
Patchett, Terry
Pendry, Tom
Pike, Peter L.
Powell, Ray *(Ogmore)*

Prescott, John
Quin, Ms Joyce
Radice, Giles
Randall, Stuart
Redmond, Martin
Rees, Rt Hon Merlyn
Reid, Dr John
Richardson, Jo
Robinson, Geoffrey
Ross, Ernie *(Dundee W)*
Rowlands, Ted
Ruddock, Joan
Salmond, Alex
Sedgemore, Brian
Sheerman, Barry
Sheldon, Rt Hon Robert
Shore, Rt Hon Peter
Short, Clare
Sillars, Jim
Skinner, Dennis
Smith, Andrew *(Oxford E)*
Smith, C. *(Isl'ton & F'bury)*
Smith, Rt Hon J. *(Monk'ds E)*
Snape, Peter
Spearing, Nigel
Steel, Rt Hon David
Steinberg, Gerry
Stott, Roger
Strang, Gavin
Straw, Jack
Taylor, Mrs Ann *(Dewsbury)*
Taylor, Matthew *(Truro)*
Thompson, Jack *(Wansbeck)*
Turner, Dennis
Wall, Pat
Wardell, Gareth *(Gower)*
Wareing, Robert N.
Watson, Mike *(Glasgow, C)*
Welsh, Michael *(Doncaster N)*
Wigley, Dafydd
Williams, Rt Hon Alan
Williams, Alan W. *(Carm'then)*
Wilson, Brian
Winnick, David
Wise, Mrs Audrey
Wray, Jimmy
Young, David *(Bolton SE)*

Tellers for the Ayes:
    Mr. Allen McKay and
    Mr. Ken Eastham.

### NOES

Adley, Robert
Aitken, Jonathan
Alexander, Richard
Alison, Rt Hon Michael
Allason, Rupert
Amess, David
Amos, Alan
Arbuthnot, James
Arnold, Jacques *(Gravesham)*
Arnold, Tom *(Hazel Grove)*
Ashby, David
Aspinwall, Jack
Atkinson, David
Baker, Rt Hon K. *(Mole Valley)*
Batiste, Spencer
Beaumont-Dark, Anthony
Bellingham, Henry
Bendall, Vivian
Bennett, Nicholas *(Pembroke)*
Benyon, W.
Bevan, David Gilroy
Biffen, Rt Hon John
Blackburn, Dr John G.
Blaker, Rt Hon Sir Peter
Body, Sir Richard
Bonsor, Sir Nicholas

Boscawen, Hon Robert
Boswell, Tim
Bottomley, Mrs Virginia
Bowden, A *(Brighton K'pto'n)*
Bowden, Gerald *(Dulwich)*
Bowis, John
Boyson, Rt Hon Dr Sir Rhodes
Braine, Rt Hon Sir Bernard
Brandon-Bravo, Martin
Brazier, Julian
Bright, Graham
Brooke, Rt Hon Peter
Brown, Michael *(Brigg & Cl't's)*
Browne, John *(Winchester)*
Bruce, Ian *(Dorset South)*
Buchanan-Smith, Rt Hon Alick
Buck, Sir Antony
Budgen, Nicholas
Burns, Simon
Burt, Alistair
Butler, Chris
Carlisle, John, *(Luton N)*
Carlisle, Kenneth *(Lincoln)*
Carrington, Matthew
Chalker, Rt Hon Mrs Lynda
Channon, Rt Hon Paul

Chope, Christopher
Churchill, Mr
Clark, Dr Michael *(Rochford)*
Clark, Sir W. *(Croydon S)*
Colvin, Michael
Conway, Derek
Coombs, Anthony *(Wyre F'rest)*
Coombs, Simon *(Swindon)*
Cope, Rt Hon John
Cormack, Patrick
Couchman, James
Critchley, Julian
Curry, David
Davis, David *(Boothferry)*
Day, Stephen
Devlin, Tim
Dickens, Geoffrey
Dicks, Terry
Douglas-Hamilton, Lord James
Dunn, Bob
Durant, Tony
Dykes, Hugh
Emery, Sir Peter
Evennett, David
Fairbairn, Sir Nicholas
Fallon, Michael
Fenner, Dame Peggy
Forman, Nigel
Forsyth, Michael *(Stirling)*
Fox, Sir Marcus
Freeman, Roger
Fry, Peter
Gill, Christopher
Goodhart, Sir Philip
Gorman, Mrs Teresa
Grant, Sir Anthony *(CambsSW)*
Greenway, Harry *(Ealing N)*
Gregory, Conal
Griffiths, Peter *(Portsmouth N)*
Hague, William
Hamilton, Neil *(Tatton)*
Hampson, Dr Keith
Hanley, Jeremy
Hargreaves, A. *(B'ham H'll Gr')*
Hargreaves, Ken *(Hyndburn)*
Harris, David
Haselhurst, Alan
Hayes, Jerry
Hayhoe, Rt Hon Sir Barney
Hayward, Robert
Heathcoat-Amory, David
Heddle, John
Heseltine, Rt Hon Michael
Hicks, Mrs Maureen *(Wolv' NE)*
Hicks, Robert *(Cornwall SE)*
Higgins, Rt Hon Terence L.
Hill, James
Hind, Kenneth
Hoey, Ms Kate *(Vauxhall)*
Hogg, Hon Douglas *(Gr'th'm)*
Hordern, Sir Peter
Howarth, Alan *(Strat'd-on-A)*
Howarth, G. *(Cannock & B'wd)*
Howell, Rt Hon David *(G'dford)*
Howell, Ralph *(North Norfolk)*
Hughes, Robert G. *(Harrow W)*
Hunt, David *(Wirral W)*
Hunt, Sir John *(Ravensbourne)*
Hunter, Andrew
Irvine, Michael
Irving, Charles
Janman, Tim
Jessel, Toby
Johnson Smith, Sir Geoffrey
Jones, Gwilym *(Cardiff N)*
Jones, Robert B *(Herts W)*
Jopling, Rt Hon Michael
Kellett-Bowman, Dame Elaine
Key, Robert
Kilfedder, James

King, Roger *(B'ham N'thfield)*
Kirkhope, Timothy
Knapman, Roger
Knight, Greg *(Derby North)*
Knight, Dame Jill *(Edgbaston)*
Knox, David
Lamont, Rt Hon Norman
Lang, Ian
Latham, Michael
Lawrence, Ivan
Leigh, Edward *(Gainsbor'gh)*
Lennox-Boyd, Hon Mark
Lester, Jim *(Broxtowe)*
Lightbown, David
Lilley, Peter
Lloyd, Sir Ian *(Havant)*
Lloyd, Peter *(Fareham)*
Lord, Michael
Lyell, Sir Nicholas
McCrindle, Robert
Macfarlane, Sir Neil
MacKay, Andrew *(E Berkshire)*
Maclean, David
McLoughlin, Patrick
McNair-Wilson, Sir Michael
McNair-Wilson, Sir Patrick
Major, Rt Hon John
Mans, Keith
Maples, John
Marland, Paul
Marshall, John *(Hendon S)*
Marshall, Michael *(Arundel)*
Mates, Michael
Maude, Hon Francis
Mayhew, Rt Hon Sir Patrick
Mellor, David
Miller, Sir Hal
Mills, Iain
Mitchell, Andrew *(Gedling)*
Mitchell, Sir David
Moate, Roger
Monro, Sir Hector
Montgomery, Sir Fergus
Moore, Rt Hon John
Morrison, Sir Charles
Morrison, Rt Hon P *(Chester)*
Moss, Malcolm
Moynihan, Hon Colin
Mudd, David
Neale, Gerrard
Nelson, Anthony
Neubert, Michael
Nicholls, Patrick
Nicholson, David *(Taunton)*
Norris, Steve
Onslow, Rt Hon Cranley
Oppenheim, Phillip
Page, Richard
Paice, James
Patnick, Irvine
Pattie, Rt Hon Sir Geoffrey
Peacock, Mrs Elizabeth
Porter, Barry *(Wirral S)*
Porter, David *(Waveney)*
Price, Sir David
Raison, Rt Hon Timothy
Redwood, John
Renton, Tim
Rhodes James, Robert
Riddick, Graham
Ridley, Rt Hon Nicholas
Rifkind, Rt Hon Malcolm
Roe, Mrs Marion
Rossi, Sir Hugh
Rost, Peter
Rumbold, Mrs Angela
Sackville, Hon Tom
Sainsbury, Hon Tim
Sayeed, Jonathan
Scott, Rt Hon Nicholas

Shaw, David (Dover)
Shaw, Sir Michael (Scarb')
Shephard, Mrs G. (Norfolk SW)
Sims, Roger
Skeet, Sir Trevor
Smith, Tim (Beaconsfield)
Soames, Hon Nicholas
Speed, Keith
Speller, Tony
Spicer, Sir Jim (Dorset W)
Spicer, Michael (S Worcs)
Squire, Robin
Stanley, Rt Hon Sir John
Steen, Anthony
Stern, Michael
Stevens, Lewis
Stewart, Allan (Eastwood)
Stewart, Andy (Sherwood)
Stokes, Sir John
Stradling Thomas, Sir John
Summerson, Hugo
Tapsell, Sir Peter
Taylor, Ian (Esher)
Taylor, John M (Solihull)
Tebbit, Rt Hon Norman
Temple-Morris, Peter
Thompson, Patrick (Norwich N)
Thorne, Neil
Thornton, Malcolm
Thurnham, Peter

Townend, John (Bridlington)
Tracey, Richard
Tredinnick, David
Trippier, David
Trotter, Neville
Twinn, Dr Ian
Vaughan, Sir Gerard
Waddington, Rt Hon David
Wakeham, Rt Hon John
Walker, Bill (T'side North)
Waller, Gary
Walters, Sir Dennis
Ward, John
Wardle, Charles (Bexhill)
Watts, John
Wells, Bowen
Whitney, Ray
Widdecombe, Ann
Wiggin, Jerry
Wilshire, David
Winterton, Nicholas
Wolfson, Mark
Wood, Timothy
Yeo, Tim
Young, Sir George (Acton)

Tellers for the Noes:
Mr. Stephen Dorrell and
Mr. Sydney Chapman.

*Question accordingly negatived.*

Mr. DEPUTY SPEAKER *then proceeded to put forthwith the Question on amendments, moved by a Member of the Government, up to the end of schedule 3.*

## Clause 3

### THE BOARD OF MANAGEMENT AND THE ARTICLES OF CONSTITUTION

*Amendments made:* No. 61, in page 2, line 24, leave out
'of the same number as had the school board on the relevant date".

No. 62, in page 2, line 28, leave out
'of the same number as had the school board on that date'.

No. 63, in page 2, line 32, leave out
'of such number, greater than had the school board of co-opted members on that date, as shall be specified in the articles of constitution.'.

No. 64, in page 2, line 34, leave out
'subject to subsection (2) below.'

No. 65, in page 2, line 39, leave out from beginning to end of line 47.

No. 66, in page 3, line 3, leave out 'subsection (5)' and insert 'subsections (5) and (6)'.

No. 67, page 3, line 11, leave out subsection (6) and insert—

'(6) The duty, under subsection (4) above, of an interim board of management shall be construed as a duty to ensure that the election of the parent and staff members who are to succeed them on the board of management takes place as soon as is reasonably practicable and in any event within three months after the incorporation date.'.—*[Mr. Michael Forsyth.]*

## Schedule 1

### THE SCHEME OF GOVERNMENT

*Amendment made:* No. 111, in page 50, line 11, leave out
'and such specification shall accord with section 3(1) of this Act'
and insert
'so however that the first such specification in respect of the board shall require that—

(a) the parent members first elected shall be of greater number than had the school board on the relevant date;

(b) the staff members first elected shall be of the same number as had the school board on that date; and

(c) the appointed members ("appointed" not including persons deemed appointed by virtue of paragraph 1(2) of Schedule 4 to this Act) shall be of greater number than had the school board on that date.

2A. In paragraph 2 above the reference to the relevant date is to the date immediately preceding the incorporation date; and for the purposes of that paragraph numbers shall be determined as if any vacancy in the membership of the school board were filled.'

No. 112, in page 50, line 16, leave out
', or to be an appointed member'.

No. 113, in page 50, line 18, leave out from 'person' to '; and' in line 22 and insert
'who is eligible for election to the board of management shall not be eligible for appointment to the board'.

No. 114, in page 50, line 26, leave out from beginning to end of line 30.—*[Mr. Michael Forsyth.]*

## Clause 4

### MEMBERS' TENURE OF OFFICE

*Amendments made:* No. 68, in page 3, line 16, leave out
'subsection' and insert 'subsections (2) and'.

No. 69, in page 3, line 16, leave out from 'a' to 'shall' in line 18 and insert
'member of a board of management'.

No. 70, in page 3, line 20, leave out subsection (2) and insert—

'(2) Where the parent members first elected to a board of management constitute—

(a) an even number, half;

(b) an odd number, the next whole number less than half,

shall hold office for a term of two years only, the individuals whose term of office is affected by this subsection being determined (in the absence of the agreement of all such members as to who those individuals shall be) by the drawing of lots.'.—*[Mr. Michael Forsyth.]*

## Clause 7

### POWERS AND DUTIES OF BOARD OF MANAGEMENT

*Amendments made:* No. 71, in page 4, line 13, after '(b)', insert
'subject to subsection (2) below and to section (disposal of land by board of management) of this Act,'.

No. 72, in page 4, line 47 at end insert—

'—(5A) The board of management of a self-governing school shall, in the exercise of their functions, have regard to a need to make improvements in the provision which the school makes for pupils with special educational needs.'.—*[Mr. Michael Forsyth.]*

## Clause 13

### INITIATION OF PROCEDURE FOR ACQUISITION OF SELF-GOVERNING STATUS

*Amendments made:* No. 25, in page 6, line 41, after 'are', insert—
'(a) in a case other than that provided for in paragraph (b) below,'.

No. 26 in page 6, line 42, leave out 'a number of' and insert 'at least thirty'.

No. 27, in page 6, line 43, after 'school', insert
'and that the number of such parents so signing must be'.

No. 28, in page 6, line 43, leave out 'parents' and insert 'persons'.

No. 29, in page 6, line 46, after 'maintained', insert
', in respect of the school,'.

No. 30, in page 6, line 47, at end insert
'; and
(b) in a case where the names of fewer than sixty persons so appeared, that the request must be signed by such number of parents of pupils in attendance at the school as would constitute a simple majority of those parents were their total number equal to the number of persons whose names so appeared.'.

No. 31, in page 7, line 2, leave out
'parent had a child who was'
and insert
'person is the parent of'.—[*Mr. Michael Forsyth.*]

## Clause 14

### BALLOT OF PARENTS ON QUESTION OF ACQUISITION OF SELF-GOVERNING STATUS

*Amendments made:* No. 73, in page 8, line 2, after 'section', insert '—(a)'.

No. 74, in page 8, line 3, leave out
'the whole or any part of'.

No. 75, in page 8, line 4, at end insert—
'(not being expenses mentioned in paragraph (b) below); and
(b) the education authority shall pay, or reimburse the school board in respect of, any expenses incurred in connection with, or in contemplation of, legal proceedings (whether or not instituted) arising out of—
(i) the holding of the ballot; or
(ii) the publication under section 16(2) of this Act, following the determination of the result of the ballot, of proposals for acquisition of self-governing status for the school.'.—[*Mr. Michael Forsyth.*]

## Schedule 3

### ARRANGEMENTS IN RESPECT OF BALLOT OF PARENTS REGARDING ACQUISITION OF SELF-GOVERNING STATUS

*Amendments made:* No. 115, in page 56, line 1, after '(a)', insert
'without prejudice to sub-paragraph (b) below,.'.

No. 116, in page 56, line 5, leave out 'other'.

No. 117, in page 56, line 6, leave out 'paragraph' and insert 'sub-paragraph'.

No. 118, in page 56, line 9, leave out 'required by a notice under' and insert 'held by virtue of'.

No. 119, in page 56, line 10, after 'which', insert
'in the case of a ballot required by a notice under subsection (1) of that section'.

No. 120, in page 56, line 21, after '4', insert '(a) and'.
—[*Mr. Michael Forsyth.*]

## Clause 15

### FRESH BALLOT

5.45 pm

**Mr. Michael Forsyth:** I beg to move amendment No. 76, in page 8, line 7, after '15', insert—'(1)'.

**Mr. Deputy Speaker:** With this we may take the following amendments: Government amendment No. 77.

No. 1, in clause 16, page 8, line 24 leave out 'simple' and insert 'two-thirds'.

No. 5, in page 8, line 24 leave out 'simple' and insert '75 per cent.'.

No. 39, in page 8, line 24 leave out 'simple' and insert 'two-thirds'.

No. 59, in page 8, line 24, leave out 'simple' and insert '67 per cent'.

Government amendment No. 78.

No. 6, in page 8, line 24, at end insert,
'provided that the majority represents at least two thirds of all parents eligible to vote.'.

No. 2, in clause 28, page 17, line 41, leave out 'simple' and insert 'two-thirds'.

No. 60, in page 17, line 41, leave out 'simple' and insert '67 per cent'.

**Mr. Alick Buchanan-Smith** (Kincardine and Deeside): On a point of order, Mr. Deputy Speaker. Obviously I accept your selection of amendments, but my hon. Friend the Member for Dumfries (Sir H. Monro) and I have put down our names to amendments Nos. 1 and 2. Will there be an opportunity for us to vote on those amendments, particularly amendment No. 1?

**Mr. Deputy Speaker:** The timing of the guillotine poses a difficulty. This debate must end at 6.30; after that, only Government amendments can be taken. I hope that I have given the right hon. Gentleman enough information for him to be able to judge what he should do.

**Mr. Forsyth:** These amendments take us over some very familiar territory. I feel that I should tell the House just how familiar it is to those of us who served on the Committee, where we discussed a similar group of amendments which had been tabled by the Opposition, providing that, when the turnout for the ballot was less than 50 per cent., there should be a second ballot. Other amendments proposed to replace the simple majority with various more or less sophisticated alternatives. The Opposition again moved that the simple majority be replaced by a two-thirds majority of parents eligible to vote. The hon. Member for Inverness, Nairn and Lochaber (Sir R. Johnston) tabled an amendment that would have replaced the simple majority with a simple majority of those eligible to vote.

We had a brief but constructive discussion, on the basis of which the Government took on board the substance of the Opposition's amendments which would make provision for a second ballot if fewer than 50 per cent. voted. On that basis, the Committee was content to let the amendments be withdrawn. The amendments that we are discussing today honour our commitment in full. I am slightly surprised that various alternative formulae have been brought in. The new proposals in today's amendments are all variations on a theme. We must keep the matter of the ballot in proportion. I cannot emphasise too strongly that it is essentially a test of opinion, carrying no Executive decision.

The process of acquiring self-governing status involves several stages. First, there must be a decision to put the matter to a ballot. That is taken either by a resolution of the school board or by a request by a stated percentage of the parents involved. Then the ballot takes place. The question on which parents are asked to vote is not whether the school shall become self-governing; neither they nor the school board will have the power to decide that. They are asked simply whether they are content that proposals for self-governing status should be put forward. If they are not content, that is the end of the matter. If, however, they return a majority in favour, the school board first has to

[*Mr. Forsyth*]

draw up—[*Interruption.*] I am smiling at the hon. Member for Strathkelvin and Bearsden (Mr. Galbraith) who, having spent so many hours in Committee, seems only now to have realised what these very important provisions are all about. If parents are not content, nothing further can happen. If, however, they return a majority in favour, the school board first has to draw up and publish proposals for self-governing status.

**Mr. McAllion:** The Minister said that, if the majority of parents are not in favour of self-governing status, nothing further can happen, yet the Secretary of State for Education and Science for England and Wales has allowed a school in Birmingham to opt out, although fewer than half the parents at that school voted for it.

**Mr. Forsyth:** The hon. Gentleman will forgive me for pointing out that, contrary to what his party has been saying, the proposals that we have put forward for the reform of education in Scotland are not carbon copies of those for south of the border. He is well aware of the provisions that we have included in the Bill. The amendments that I have tabled provide that, where fewer than half the parents participate in the ballot, there must be a second ballot.

I was explaining the procedure that has to be followed. If the parents return a majority in favour, their school board has to draw up and publish proposals for self-governing status. These are to be sent to the education authority and the Secretary of State for Scotland. They will have to be published in newspapers and otherwise made publicly available. It will then be open to the whole world to make its views known on the proposals. Their representations are to be directed to the Secretary of State. He has to receive them and consider them all. Only in the light of all the representations does he make a decision on whether the school should become self-governing.

It is quite clear that in practice the representations made to the Secretary of State will have to weigh with him; he is not bound to accept a positive ballot result. There will be cases where, notwithstanding the support of the majority in a ballot, the Secretary of State may decide, for good reasons, that the school is not to be allowed to become self governing. He may not be convinced that the school really has a future—for example, if its numbers are in decline. He will have to take those factors into account. He will also have to take account of representations that may be made by the education authority. It will want to apprise him of the full situation in the area—of the other schools and their pupil numbers, of its plans for them, of the implications for the education authority if the school in question should become self-governing. That, I hope, will begin to put the question of a ballot into some kind of perspective.

It is also relevant to look at the kind of ballot results that may be expected, the kind of psychological effect that they may have and the relative weight which the Secretary of State might give to a given result. The hon. Member for Dundee, East (Mr. McAllion) has obviously been studying the question. As he knows, some experience of these matters is building up under the English legislaton. I understand that 64 ballots have already been held on grant-maintained status under the Education Reform Act 1988. Of these, 15 were negative—in some cases quite decisively so—another 40 would have passed the two-thirds majority rule that is proposed by some of the amendments that are before us today. Of those, 36 would have passed the more stringent test of a 75 per cent. majority. It is quite clear that we may therefore expect that, whatever test is set, there will be a clear-cut result in the great majority of cases.

**Mr. John Marshall** (Hendon, South): Does my hon. Friend agree that the opposition of certain Labour Members to these proposals is very strange? Is he aware that the hon. Member for Glasgow, Cathcart (Mr. Maxton) opted into the private sector when he was a teacher?

**Mr. Forsyth:** My hon. Friend is quite right. [*Interruption.*] The hon. Member for Glasgow, Cathcart (Mr. Maxton) says that that is very old. [*Interruption.*] The hon. Gentleman also says that he, too, is very old. We believe in choice in education. We also think that the hon. Member for Cathcart was entitled to teach in the independent sector, if that was his wish. It is a free society.

It is only on the other side of the House that, as we heard from the hon. Member for Fife, Central (Mr. McLeish) the doctrine applies that if it is good enough for Henry McLeish's children it is good enough for everyone else's children. It is only the Opposition who seek to deny choice. [*Interruption.*] I see that the hon. Member for Fife, Central is mouthing, "Privilege." He has made several attacks on the assisted places scheme. He has denounced it as privilege. [*Interruption.*] The hon. Member for Carrick, Cumnock and Doon Valley (Mr. Foulkes) is confirming that. Almost half the total number of pupils on the assisted places scheme come from families with an income of less than £8,500 a year. It is typical of the Labour party that it would limit choice and deny education of that sort to those who would otherwise be unable to afford it.

**Sir Hector Monro** (Dumfries): My hon. Friend gave some interesting statistics, but is he able to say how many of the votes were cast in the face of the likely closure of the school?

**Mr. Forsyth:** I cannot give my hon. Friend the precise figure, but he is mistaken if he believes that the majority of the schools were facing closure. During our discussion of the last set of amendments my hon. Friend the Member for Gainsborough and Horncastle (Mr. Leigh) pointed out that the majority of the schools were not facing closure. The first school in the United Kingdom to go for self-governing status, Skegness grammar school, was not in that position.

I commend to my hon. Friend the Member for Dumfries (Sir H. Monro) a very interesting article in *The Daily Telegraph* some months ago. I shall send a copy of the article to him. It analysed the schools in England that have gone for self-governing status and the reasons for them doing so. It also gave an analysis of the schools that intended to go for self-governing status and showed that the proportion of schools that were not facing some kind of organisational upheaval, such as closure, had been reduced. My hon. Friend the Member for Gainsborough and Horncastle said that the principal motivation would be the belief that, by taking decisions at local level, free of the education authority, schools would be more responsive to the needs of parents and would provide a better service.

That is why it is essential that parents in Scotland should have the same freedom and opportunity as is so clearly sought in England.

It is a mark of the peculiarities of the Labour party in Scotland that it seems to take the view that there is something wrong with Scottish parents—that they are unable to exercise choice and bring about the kind of management of schools that appears to be working so successfully south of the border.

**Sir Hector Monro:** I gave my hon. Friend the figures on Second Reading. Of the 37 schools which, by 6 March, had voted to opt out, 27 faced closure.

**Mr. Forsyth:** I have not checked my hon. Friend's figures. [HON. MEMBERS: "Why not?"] However, he knows now that the measure is even more popular than he might have imagined. He quoted a figure of 37, but there have now been 64 ballots. A proportionately larger number of those schools are not faced with closure. I have just told my hon. Friend that all the evidence from the survey carried out by *The Daily Telegraph* showed that, as more schools came forward for self-governing status, the proportion of schools that were facing some kind of catastrophe had been reduced. I do not believe that there is any difference between the figures that my hon. Friend quoted and the point that I have just made to the House.

I am fairly certain that an opting-out ballot will, in almost all cases, be a matter of such acute interest that it will produce a high turnout and a decisive result. If there is a low turnout, our amendment, which picks up that tabled by the Opposition—I take it that the Opposition tabled their amendment seriously and were committed to it—would give the board one more chance and that would have to be final. If the board failed to organise the second ballot, the matter would go no further, and rightly so. I understand that that has happened in one place in England.

We are concerned about the minority of cases in which there is a positive result but with a smallish majority. The fact that a majority might be relatively slender would have to be taken seriously into account by the Secretary of State. He would have to find out what other evidence there was of genuine parental support for the school and a genuine understanding by the parents of the implications of self-governing status and a genuine will to take on that responsibility. The Secretary of State would need some assurance on these matters in any case, but the strongly positive ballot result would tend to confirm that there was a will and understanding among the parents—but even in that case it would not be absolutely conclusive. Where the majority is more narrow, the Secretary of State will naturally attach proportionately less weight to it.

6 pm

I return to the point that the ballot result itself in no way determines the Secretary of State's decision. In many cases it will be only marginally persuasive to him. A ballot is simply a test, taken at a very early stage, to find out whether the idea of self-governing status should be taken any further. It is only after the ballot result that the school board has to get down to working out full proposals.

Against that background, the House should now consider what the reaction would be if the test were something higher than a simple majority. It would mean that a school might have a ballot in which there was a very high turnout and a majority of 60 per cent. Without further ado, we would then have to say to parents at that school, "I am sorry, but you cannot even apply for self-governing status—your application cannot be considered." In such a case there would be an absolute outcry. People simply would not understand the logic of a law under which, despite a clear majority support in a ballot for the proposition, that proposition could not even reach the stage of being published for wider public views to be sought upon it. That would be perceived as a negation of democracy.

Again, experience in England may be instructive. I am told that there have been nine ballots at which there was a majority for grant-maintained status of less than two thirds. Most of those cases are still pending, so I am not able to comment upon them. However, I note that my right hon. Friend the Secretary of State for Education and Science has rejected one and has approved two others. Are we to say that, when a school can bid for grant-maintained status in England and Wales on the basis of a 56 per cent. majority in a ballot, it can get approval—which is by no means automatic—from the Secretary of State, the same right should be denied to parents of children in schools in Scotland?

**Mr. Leigh:** Does my hon. Friend know of any instance in parliamentary or local government procedure which requires a two-thirds majority?

**Mr. Forsyth:** Opposition Members are referring to constitutional arrangements, but my hon. Friend makes his point very well, and I support him.

The figures that my hon. Friend the Member for Dumfries was seeking have magically come into my possession. I can tell him that, at 9 June, of the 46 schools that have voted in favour of self-governing status, there were 26 to which no change was proposed. Only 10 were facing closure and 10 were facing other significant changes. That updates the information that my hon. Friend reported to the House on Second Reading.

I know that there are fears that the legislation might be used by minority of parents to hijack a school into self-governing status. All such groups thrive on apathy. They rely on getting a vote pushed through when, so to speak, no one is noticing. In short, they rely on a low turnout. I am certainly not in favour of letting unrepresentative groups take control of a school. The best test of that is to see what number of supporters they can muster in a high turnout. That is why we have taken on board the concern expressed by the Opposition and provided the safety net that, where there is a turnout of less than 50 per cent. of those entitled to vote in the ballot, there must be a second ballot forthwith if the matter is to go any further.

I am convinced that the amendments are sensible and are much readily intelligible to the public than any other formula. As my hon. Friend the Member for Gainsborough and Horncastle said, people understand a simple majority and we should stick to it. I commend the Government amendments to the House.

**Mr. Buchanan-Smith:** I am grateful for the opportunity to speak at this stage of the debate. The House will agree that the amendments in my name and that of my hon. Friend the Member for Dumfries (Sir H. Monro) relating to clauses 16 and 28 refer to crucial parts of the Bill. I shall be extremely brief, as I know that other Members wish to speak.

[*Mr. Buchanan-Smith*]

What my hon. Friend the Minister said is all right as far as it goes, and I welcome the change that he has made since Committee—that, in the case of a low turnout, there should be an opportunity to move to a second ballot. But my hon. Friend addressed only the problem of a small turnout. He is right to address that problem and I welcome it, but he has ignored two things: first, when there is a large turnout but only a small majority; secondly, when there is a small turnout on a second ballot. My hon. Friend dealt with neither of those possibilities.

I am delighted that in England and Wales there has been evidence of a large turnout. If there is a large turnout, hopefully the problems will not be so great. However, if there is a small majority, there is the danger of a thoroughly divisive situation. My hon. Friend spoke of hijacking by small groups. That is one danger—if 51 per cent. were in favour and 49 per cent. were against, that would produce a divisive situation in the community served by that particular school. Equally, when there is a small turnout, it is even more important that it should be clear that a large percentage are in favour of the proposal.

That is important in the decision whether to opt out, and it is equally important, if not more so, in any decision to change the character of the school. If a school opted out it might continue in a similar way under different management. I shall not go into all the arguments, but amendment No. 2 in my name and that of my hon. Friend the Member for Dumfries is even more relevant to any decision to change the character of a school.

My hon. Friend the Minister tried to play all that down. He pointed out that we are only triggering off a procedure. I accept that, but he must recognise that the ballot is the last real, open test of public opinion. After that, everything happens not exactly behind closed doors, but at people's discretion to consider one factor or another or to consider representations. It is the last real test of public opinion, and to that extent the numbers voting and the percentage of the vote are absolutely critical in deciding whether a school opts out.

My hon. Friend said that, if my amendment were accepted, and the vote were just below two thirds, it would be a negation of democracy if the proposals were turned down on that basis. That is nonsense. We are talking about a very big change, a total constitutional change as it affects a particular school, either in relation to opting out or in relation to the character of that school. It is not undemocratic to have a test higher than 51 per cent. in constitutional changes, whether they relate to public bodies or private organisations. It is nothing unusual, and it is certainly not a negation of democracy, to look for a test above 51 per cent.

If it is proposed to change the status quo—this is a major change from the status quo in Scottish education—we need a much higher test. Although I welcome what my hon. Friend the Minister proposes in relation to small turn outs, I do not believe that it addresses the main question. The ideal solution is my hon. Friend's amendments, which I welcome, and to have grafted into them the test of a two-thirds majority when the ballot takes place. Unless my hon. Friend the Minister can give some sign that he would be prepared to go further than he is tonight and write the two-thirds majority into the ballot, I shall certainly find it difficult to support it.

**Mr. Donald Dewar** (Glasgow, Garscadden): Hon. Members are in some difficulty because of the timetable motion. This is an important debate. The matter may have been well ventilated in Committee, but, for many hon. Members, it is the one, and unfortunately all too brief, opportunity to debate a central issue. It will be an embittering and unfortunate business if we cannot vote on the amendment moved by the right hon. Member for Kincardine and Deeside (Mr. Buchanan-Smith). It would make a mockery of the procedures of the House and the way in which we conduct our business. Like the right hon. Gentleman, I can only have a very fast run at the arguments. I certainly cannot deploy the kind of case that I would normally wish to deploy in a matter of this importance.

Of course I welcome amendments Nos. 76 and 77. After all, they were originally Opposition amendments in Committee, and they were redrafted for technical reasons and accepted in principle by the Government, and, in response to the Government's promises, they now appear on the Amendment Paper. I welcome them because they ensure a second ballot if less than 50 per cent. of all those eligible to vote are the majority in the first ballot. I agree with the right hon. Gentleman that we must look beyond that and the two-thirds provision. Amendments Nos. 1 and 2 do exactly that. It is simply common sense that, when something as fundamental and radical as opting out of the normal local authority system is suggested, there should be adequate safeguards to ensure a proper basis of support.

It is well known that the Opposition oppose the concept of opting out. We regard it as a fragmentation of the school system. In its wake, it may bring changes in fundamental characteristics that are based on the perceived interests of a small group of children rather than the advantage of the majority. That we are opposed in principle to the opting-out clauses does not mean that safeguards should not be built in where possible, and we should look for sensible improvements. I do not have a great deal of confidence that the Minister will agree with us, but at least he should have the opportunity positively to respond, and the House should have an opportunity to make a considered decision.

I was interested in what the Minister said. We hear a great deal about power to parents and trusting parents. Of course, the Minister is as capable of expediency as everyone else. When it comes to this argument, he hurries to tell us that the ballot is a triggering mechanism, that it does not matter very much and that the power does not lie with the parents, so we do not need to worry too much about how the ballot is conducted or what the safeguards are. He cannot have it both ways. The ballot is important, and it is essential that we get it right. I do not think that it would be safe to leave it as it is in the Bill at the moment, as a simple majority. That is why I support the two-thirds requirement proposed in amendments Nos. 1 and 2.

To use what I understand to be a familiar word in the teaching profession now, we do not want a capricious result. We do not want a situation in which parents, under pressure or in particular circumstances—perhaps in haste, to repent later at leisure—take a decision for the wrong reasons. There has been a statistical argument about the number of schools that have shown interest in the opting-out procedure because of the threat of closure or some other radical change in their boundaries or catchment areas, but I will not bandy statistics.

When he replied to the Second Reading debate, the Minister rather derided my attempt to suggest that this was an important factor, and he produced figures to show that, out of 59 schools that had become, to use his phrase, involved in the process, about 33 were threatened by closure. The figures may have changed since then. No one can deny that that is the kind of situation that will suddenly make opting out look spuriously attractive in a particular set of circumstances.

6.15 pm

That underlines the dangers and the need to make sure that there is a proper basis of support among parents before we go down what we regard as an often dangerous road, and what we all agree is a significant road.

Next there is the technical, perhaps, but important electoral argument. The presence of one child can give rise to a different and varying franchise. I admit to using a little ingenuity, but I am told that one can find cases in which one child can produce—if that is the right word—six votes in the ballot, and certainly not uncommonly three or four votes. Again, 50 per cent. or a simple majority of 50 per cent. plus one, on examination, might turn out to be very different indeed.

I am sorry that I cannot put my argument rather more fully, but if we ignore the right hon. Gentleman's amendments Nos. 1 and 2, we will put an element of risk into the system, and that is unwise. I echo the slogan of another long-off, far-off, battle—there is certainly a case for full-hearted consent in these matters because of the tremendous implications of opting out for individual schools.

Obviously, I did not serve on the Committee, but I can remember the exchanges on Second Reading. The Minister told us that we already have selection in local authority schools, and suggested that anyone who was worried about the introduction of selection because of opting out was jousting at windmills and raising false fears. The Minister went on to explain that what he meant by local authority selection was, for example, a school in my constituency, Knightswood, which has a specialist centre for dance. The more I thought about it, the more curious and odd I found the Minister's argument. The truth is that, in mainstream academic terms, the reintroduction of selection is a possibility further down the road, with an alteration in fundamental characteristics.

That merely underlines the need to make sure that, if parents are to accept this and try to trigger the process, there is a genuine basis on which to proceed. Given all the variations and uncertainties, I do not believe that a simple majority adequately does that. For that reason alone, I commend amendments Nos. 1 and 2 to the House in the genuine hope that we can be sensible enough about the conduct of our business to ensure that the House has a chance to vote on them.

**Sir Hector Monro:** I will add only a few words, as my right hon. Friend the Member for Kincardine and Deeside (Mr. Buchanan-Smith) has clearly put his case and is supported by the Opposition. It is disappointing that my hon. Friend the Minister has taken only a tiny step forward to the position in which he should be, bearing in mind that the Scottish Consumer Council, the Scottish Parent Teacher Council, The Church of Scotland and a

MORI poll are all firmly in favour of the two-thirds majority. My hon. Friend the Minister might have moved a great deal closer towards us.

I feel strongly about this matter. The Minister knows that I am not in favour of opting out. The present structure is perfectly adequate, and there is no need to introduce this measure. I agree with my right hon. Friend that, whatever my hon. Friend the Minister says about this being only a triggering mechanism, it is crucial. It is the key issue in respect of school views on opting out. As my right hon. Friend said, the character of schools is at risk—perhaps the denominational aspect, catchment areas or other issues. I refer in particular to primary school catchment areas, which my hon. Friend the Minister says will be taken into account by consultation. That is not good enough. One wants a clear-cut view. Do the schools actually want to opt out? The only way to get a firm opinion on such a crucial matter is to have a figure substantially above 50 per cent., and that is why my right hon. Friend and I have set two thirds as the required majority.

**Mr. Leigh:** My hon. Friend is on dangerous ground if he is suggesting that on all important constitutional changes, a two-thirds majority is required. For example, should we have a two-thirds majority in a referendum about a Scottish Parliament? He is also in difficulty in addressing his remarks to a situation where, say, six out of 10 parents have voted to govern their own school. He is saying, in effect, "No, under my amendment you cannot do that." My hon. Friend is putting himself in a difficult position.

**Sir Hector Monro:** My hon. Friend may think that; I do not. I know where I stand, and we have had constitutional referendums with various percentages thrown in. My hon. Friend is not on to a good point, and I advise him to come to Scotland and speak to parents who want to opt out. As the Minister said, if they do not want to opt out, they need not do so. It is important that we have a substantial majority, far above 50 per cent., so that the true nature of the vote is brought home to those who must make these decisions.

**Mr. Bill Walker:** While my hon. Friend the Member for Gainsborough and Horncastle (Mr. Leigh) may not be from Scotland, I am, so I hope that my hon. Friend the Member for Dumfries (Sir H. Monro) will appreciate that, while I respect his point of view, it is important for him to understand that there are others who hold a contrary point of view. When schools in my constituency can be closed or fundamentally changed on a simple majority in local government, I cannot see why my hon. Friend is making such an issue of this matter.

**Sir Hector Monro:** My hon. Friend may have a point, but it is wrong in terms of what we are discussing. When, on a majority decision, it is decided to close a school, consider the position in which the Government find themselves in giving away the right for all school closures to be approved by the Secretary of State, albeit in this case in denominational schools and schools in rural areas. Had the Secretary of State retained that right, he could have looked at the whole issue and prevented a school from closing if the parent did not want it to close. Certainly he would have been in a position to prevent more closures than will be the case as the clause is drafted, simply

[*Sir Hector Monro*]

because the option will not rest with him, except for denominational schools and special travelling arrangements applying to schools in rural areas.

**Mr. Michael Forsyth:** If my hon. Friend is arguing that a simple majority is all right for making closure decisions or changes to the character of schools where they are in the control of the education authority—on the basis that approval would be required by the Secretary of State—that is precisely what we have in the Bill for self-governing status, where a simple majority and the consent and approval of the Secretary of State is required. That is the position he is arguing should pertain in cases of school closures where a simple majority is required. There is nothing more fundamental to changing the character of a school than closing it.

**Sir Hector Monro:** I am being accused of adopting a wrong philosophy. My hon. Friend the Member for Tayside, North (Mr. Walker) referred to a simple majority, and I presume he meant a simple majority among parents and in the education authority. I am saying that that whole issue need not have arisen had the Secretary of State retained the right to decide whether a school should or should not be closed, a right which he had until 1980, a right which I exercised frequently when I was a Minister. No school was closed except by the wish of the parents, which I do not think ever occurred.

In other words, hon. Members have been raising issues that are irrelevant to opting out, which is a fundamental and voluntary decision. It is not an action taken under compulsion, like a local authority school closure. For that reason, it is essential that more than 50 per cent. of parents are seen to be in favour.

I am disappointed that the Minister has not come a long way towards accepting the amendment. Unless he is willing to say that in another place he will go a great deal further, I shall not be able to support the Government in this matter.

**Sir Russell Johnston** (Inverness, Nairn and Lochaber): I will not delay the House on this matter. I plead with the Minister to take seriously what the hon. Member for Dumfries (Sir H. Monro) said. The logic and force of the arguments that have been put by hon. Members have been powerful collectively and are important from the Minister's point of view if opting out is to be accepted in the community in which it occurs and is not to be regarded as divisive and narrow. I urge him to reconsider his attitude to the amendment.

**Mr. Bill Walker:** I speak more in sorrow than in anger, having found disappointing the arguments of my hon. Friend the Member for Dumfries (Sir H. Monro) and my right hon. Friend the Member for Kincardine and Deeside (Mr. Buchanan-Smith). I appreciate how strongly they feel about the issue, but I cannot understand how they can be seen to be supporting, and be supported by, the hon. Member for Glasgow, Garscadden (Mr. Dewar), because what he said this evening will be quoted back at him every time he speaks about any sort of assembly in Edinburgh —[*Interruption.*]—in relation to a two-thirds majority.

Equally, I hope that, whenever Labour Members speak in future to Ministers about closure proposals or changes

to schools in their constituencies—changes proposed by a local authority based on a simple majority—they will remember the arguments that were adduced in this debate.

We have been asked to consider what would happen if there was a 51 to 49 per cent. split. Such a vote would cause a division in the local community, it has been said. In fact, divisions in the local community will be caused either way; if it is 49 per cent. one way and 51 per cent. the other or the other way round, divisions will result.

It is important to recognise that an issue such as this cannot be looked at in isolation. It must be viewed against all other activities stemming from legislation that has been passed by this and previous Governments in which we have not stated that, at local authority level, where major decisions are made—not just in education but in many other areas—other than a simple majority basis should apply. To say that there must be a majority of two thirds in all cases, especially at the local level, would require us to change virtually all other legislation, and I doubt whether that is what Labour Members are after.

**Mr. Dewar:** The hon. Gentleman will be aware of the desire on both sides of the House to vote on amendments Nos. 1 and 2. That can happen only if he resumes his seat before 6.30 and allows that vote to take place. I hope he will do that.

**Mr. Walker:** It is not my intention to do anything that would frustrate the wishes of the House, but having listened to my right hon. Friend the Member for Kincardine and Deeside and my hon. Friend the Member for Dumfries speak on this issue, I do not want the people of Scotland, in particular my constituents, to think that they are the only Members with a view in Scotland on this matter. That is vital to me, because I fear that some Members think that the message coming from me and others is not the message that the people of Scotland want to hear. I want to be certain that my voice is heard and that nobody is left in doubt about where I stand on matters requiring a two-thirds majority.

**Mr. Canavan:** On a point of order, Madam Deputy Speaker. Is there nothing you can do to stop this deliberate filibuster—[*Interruption.*]

**Madam Deputy Speaker (Miss Betty Boothroyd):** Order. We are in the middle of a debate and the point that the hon. Member raises is not a matter for the Chair.

**Mr. Allan Stewart:** It must be the first time that an hon. Member who has been speaking for only two or three minutes—I refer to my hon. Friend the Member for Tayside, North (Mr. Walker)—has been accused of filibustering. Will my hon. Friend agree that substantial support for the Bill comes from his and my constituents and from many others?

**Mr. Bill Walker:** I want the House to understand that, if there is a division of views—obviously there is—those of us who support these measures must be seen to be supporting them and to be speaking up in support of them.

**Mr. Dewar:** On a point of order, Madam Deputy Speaker. I would certainly not accuse the hon. Gentleman of filibustering. Like the House, he is the victim of circumstances. However, we are extremely anxious to have a vote on amendments Nos. 1 and 2. Is there any way in which you can help us in this matter?

**Madam Deputy Speaker:** Not unless I can now put the Question.

**Mr. Bill Walker** *rose—[Interruption.]*

**Mr. Canavan:** Sit down and let us have the vote.

**Mr. Bill Walker:** If there has been any filibustering, it has been caused by Opposition interventions. Opposition Members will not allow me even three minutes to speak on a matter about which I feel strongly. The issue of two thirds is important and fundamental, and not just to this piece of legislation because it affects all other legislation. That is why we must think carefully about what we are doing. It is interesting that a simple majority is sufficient in any Committee in this House and that a simple majority is sufficient——

*It being half-past six o'clock,* MADAM DEPUTY SPEAKER *proceeded, pursuant to Order [3rd May] and the Resolution this day, to put forthwith the Question already proposed from the Chair.*

*Amendment agreed to.*

**Madam Deputy Speaker:** I am now required to put all the Questions on amendments moved by the Government up to the end of clause 75——

**Mr. Dewar** *rose——*

**Madam Deputy Speaker:** Does any hon. Member wish to vote against any of those amendments—[HON. MEMBERS: "Yes"] What are those amendments?

**Mr. Dewar** *rose——*

**Madam Deputy Speaker:** Will the hon. Gentleman please number the amendments?

**Mr. Dewar:** It would be useful if the Government amendments could be put individually because we shall certainly now vote against some of them.

**Madam Deputy Speaker** *then proceeded to put forthwith the Question on amendments, moved by a Member of the Government, up to the end of clause 75.*

*Amendment made:* No. 77, in page 8, line 21, at end insert—

'(2) Where in a ballot held in accordance with section 14 or 28 of this Act (other than a ballot held by virtue of this subsection) the total number of votes cast by persons eligible to vote in the ballot is less than fifty per cent. of the persons so eligible, the board shall, in accordance with the said section 14 or as the case may be 28, hold a fresh ballot.'.—*[Mr. Maclean.]*

## Clause 16

#### PROPOSALS FOR ACQUISITION OF SELF-GOVERNING STATUS

*Amendment made:* No. 78, in page 8, line 24, at end insert

'(no declaration having been made under subsection (1) of section 15 of this Act as regards the ballot and no fresh ballot being required by virtue of subsection (2) of that section)'. —*[Mr. Michael Forsyth.]*

*Amendment proposed,* No. 79, in page 8, line 29, leave out 'by regulations'.—*[Mr. Michael Forsyth.]*

*Question put,* That the amendment be made:—

*The House divided:* Ayes 276, Noes 201.

**Division No. 249]** **[6.31 pm**

### AYES

Adley, Robert
Aitken, Jonathan
Alexander, Richard
Alison, Rt Hon Michael
Allason, Rupert
Amess, David
Amos, Alan
Arbuthnot, James
Arnold, Jacques *(Gravesham)*
Ashby, David
Aspinwall, Jack
Atkinson, David
Baker, Nicholas *(Dorset N)*
Batiste, Spencer
Beaumont-Dark, Anthony
Bellingham, Henry
Bendall, Vivian
Bennett, Nicholas *(Pembroke)*
Benyon, W.
Bevan, David Gilroy
Biffen, Rt Hon John
Blackburn, Dr John G.
Blaker, Rt Hon Sir Peter
Body, Sir Richard
Bonsor, Sir Nicholas
Boscawen, Hon Robert
Boswell, Tim
Bottomley, Peter
Bottomley, Mrs Virginia
Bowden, A *(Brighton K'pto'n)*
Bowden, Gerald *(Dulwich)*
Bowis, John
Boyson, Rt Hon Dr Sir Rhodes
Braine, Rt Hon Sir Bernard
Brandon-Bravo, Martin
Brazier, Julian
Bright, Graham
Brown, Michael *(Brigg & Cl't's)*
Browne, John *(Winchester)*
Buchanan-Smith, Rt Hon Alick
Buck, Sir Antony
Budgen, Nicholas
Burns, Simon
Burt, Alistair
Butler, Chris
Butterfill, John
Carlisle, John, *(Luton N)*
Carlisle, Kenneth *(Lincoln)*
Carrington, Matthew
Cash, William
Chalker, Rt Hon Mrs Lynda
Channon, Rt Hon Paul
Chapman, Sydney
Chope, Christopher
Churchill, Mr
Clark, Dr Michael *(Rochford)*
Clark, Sir W. *(Croydon S)*
Colvin, Michael
Conway, Derek
Coombs, Anthony *(Wyre F'rest)*
Coombs, Simon *(Swindon)*
Cope, Rt Hon John
Cormack, Patrick
Couchman, James
Cran, James
Critchley, Julian
Currie, Mrs Edwina
Curry, David
Davis, David *(Boothferry)*
Day, Stephen
Devlin, Tim
Dicks, Terry
Dorrell, Stephen
Douglas-Hamilton, Lord James
Dunn, Bob
Durant, Tony
Dykes, Hugh

Fairbairn, Sir Nicholas
Favell, Tony
Fenner, Dame Peggy
Forman, Nigel
Forsyth, Michael *(Stirling)*
Freeman, Roger
French, Douglas
Gill, Christopher
Goodhart, Sir Philip
Goodson-Wickes, Dr Charles
Grant, Sir Anthony *(CambsSW)*
Greenway, Harry *(Ealing N)*
Gregory, Conal
Griffiths, Peter *(Portsmouth N)*
Hamilton, Neil *(Tatton)*
Hampson, Dr Keith
Hanley, Jeremy
Hannam, John
Hargreaves, A. *(B'ham H'll Gr')*
Hargreaves, Ken *(Hyndburn)*
Harris, David
Haselhurst, Alan
Hayes, Jerry
Hayhoe, Rt Hon Sir Barney
Hayward, Robert
Heathcoat-Amory, David
Heddle, John
Heseltine, Rt Hon Michael
Hicks, Mrs Maureen *(Wolv' NE)*
Hicks, Robert *(Cornwall SE)*
Higgins, Rt Hon Terence L.
Hill, James
Hind, Kenneth
Hogg, Hon Douglas *(Gr'th'm)*
Hordern, Sir Peter
Howarth, Alan *(Strat'd-on-A)*
Howarth, G. *(Cannock & B'wd)*
Howell, Rt Hon David *(G'dford)*
Howell, Ralph *(North Norfolk)*
Hughes, Robert G. *(Harrow W)*
Hunt, David *(Wirral W)*
Hunt, Sir John *(Ravensbourne)*
Hunter, Andrew
Irvine, Michael
Irving, Charles
Jack, Michael
Janman, Tim
Jessel, Toby
Johnson Smith, Sir Geoffrey
Jones, Gwilym *(Cardiff N)*
Jones, Robert B *(Herts W)*
Jopling, Rt Hon Michael
Kellett-Bowman, Dame Elaine
Key, Robert
Kilfedder, James
King, Roger *(B'ham N'thfield)*
Kirkhope, Timothy
Knapman, Roger
Knight, Greg *(Derby North)*
Knight, Dame Jill *(Edgbaston)*
Knox, David
Lamont, Rt Hon Norman
Lang, Ian
Latham, Michael
Lawrence, Ivan
Leigh, Edward *(Gainsbor'gh)*
Lennox-Boyd, Hon Mark
Lester, Jim *(Broxtowe)*
Lightbown, David
Lilley, Peter
Lloyd, Sir Ian *(Havant)*
Lloyd, Peter *(Fareham)*
Lord, Michael
Luce, Rt Hon Richard
McCrindle, Robert
Macfarlane, Sir Neil
MacKay, Andrew *(E Berkshire)*

Maclean, David
McLoughlin, Patrick
McNair-Wilson, Sir Michael
McNair-Wilson, Sir Patrick
Major, Rt Hon John
Mans, Keith
Maples, John
Marland, Paul
Marshall, John (Hendon S)
Marshall, Michael (Arundel)
Mates, Michael
Maude, Hon Francis
Miller, Sir Hal
Mills, Iain
Mitchell, Andrew (Gedling)
Mitchell, Sir David
Moate, Roger
Monro, Sir Hector
Montgomery, Sir Fergus
Moore, Rt Hon John
Morris, M (N'hampton S)
Morrison, Sir Charles
Morrison, Rt Hon P (Chester)
Moss, Malcolm
Moynihan, Hon Colin
Mudd, David
Nelson, Anthony
Neubert, Michael
Nicholls, Patrick
Nicholson, David (Taunton)
Norris, Steve
Onslow, Rt Hon Cranley
Oppenheim, Phillip
Page, Richard
Paice, James
Patnick, Irvine
Patten, John (Oxford W)
Pattie, Rt Hon Sir Geoffrey
Peacock, Mrs Elizabeth
Porter, Barry (Wirral S)
Porter, David (Waveney)
Price, Sir David
Raison, Rt Hon Timothy
Rathbone, Tim
Redwood, John
Renton, Tim
Rhodes James, Robert
Riddick, Graham
Ridley, Rt Hon Nicholas
Ridsdale, Sir Julian
Rifkind, Rt Hon Malcolm
Roe, Mrs Marion
Rossi, Sir Hugh
Rost, Peter
Rumbold, Mrs Angela
Sayeed, Jonathan
Shaw, David (Dover)
Shaw, Sir Michael (Scarb')

Shephard, Mrs G. (Norfolk SW)
Sims, Roger
Skeet, Sir Trevor
Smith, Tim (Beaconsfield)
Soames, Hon Nicholas
Speed, Keith
Speller, Tony
Spicer, Sir Jim (Dorset W)
Spicer, Michael (S Worcs)
Squire, Robin
Stanley, Rt Hon Sir John
Steen, Anthony
Stern, Michael
Stevens, Lewis
Stewart, Allan (Eastwood)
Stewart, Andy (Sherwood)
Stokes, Sir John
Stradling Thomas, Sir John
Summerson, Hugo
Taylor, Ian (Esher)
Taylor, John M (Solihull)
Tebbit, Rt Hon Norman
Temple-Morris, Peter
Thompson, Patrick (Norwich N)
Thorne, Neil
Thornton, Malcolm
Thurnham, Peter
Townend, John (Bridlington)
Tracey, Richard
Tredinnick, David
Trippier, David
Trotter, Neville
Twinn, Dr Ian
Vaughan, Sir Gerard
Waddington, Rt Hon David
Wakeham, Rt Hon John
Walker, Bill (T'side North)
Waller, Gary
Ward, John
Wardle, Charles (Bexhill)
Warren, Kenneth
Watts, John
Wells, Bowen
Whitney, Ray
Widdecombe, Ann
Wiggin, Jerry
Wilkinson, John
Wilshire, David
Winterton, Mrs Ann
Winterton, Nicholas
Wolfson, Mark
Wood, Timothy
Yeo, Tim
Young, Sir George (Acton)

Tellers for the Ayes:
    Mr. Michael Fallon and
    Mr. Tom Sackville.

**NOES**

Abbott, Ms Diane
Adams, Allen (Paisley N)
Allen, Graham
Alton, David
Anderson, Donald
Archer, Rt Hon Peter
Armstrong, Hilary
Ashdown, Rt Hon Paddy
Ashley, Rt Hon Jack
Banks, Tony (Newham NW)
Barnes, Harry (Derbyshire NE)
Barron, Kevin
Battle, John
Beckett, Margaret
Beith, A. J.
Bell, Stuart
Benn, Rt Hon Tony
Bennett, A. F. (D'nt'n & R'dish)
Bidwell, Sydney
Blair, Tony

Blunkett, David
Boateng, Paul
Boyes, Roland
Bray, Dr Jeremy
Brown, Gordon (D'mline E)
Brown, Nicholas (Newcastle E)
Bruce, Malcolm (Gordon)
Buckley, George J.
Caborn, Richard
Callaghan, Jim
Campbell, Menzies (Fife NE)
Campbell-Savours, D. N.
Canavan, Dennis
Clark, Dr David (S Shields)
Clarke, Tom (Monklands W)
Clay, Bob
Clelland, David
Cohen, Harry
Cook, Frank (Stockton N)
Cook, Robin (Livingston)

Corbyn, Jeremy
Cryer, Bob
Cummings, John
Cunliffe, Lawrence
Dalyell, Tam
Darling, Alistair
Davies, Ron (Caerphilly)
Davis, Terry (B'ham Hodge H'l)
Dewar, Donald
Dixon, Don
Dobson, Frank
Doran, Frank
Douglas, Dick
Duffy, A. E. P.
Dunnachie, Jimmy
Eadie, Alexander
Ewing, Harry (Falkirk E)
Fatchett, Derek
Fearn, Ronald
Field, Frank (Birkenhead)
Fields, Terry (L'pool B G'n)
Fisher, Mark
Flannery, Martin
Flynn, Paul
Foot, Rt Hon Michael
Foster, Derek
Foulkes, George
Fraser, John
Fyfe, Maria
Galbraith, Sam
Galloway, George
Garrett, John (Norwich South)
Garrett, Ted (Wallsend)
Gilbert, Rt Hon Dr John
Godman, Dr Norman A.
Golding, Mrs Llin
Graham, Thomas
Grant, Bernie (Tottenham)
Griffiths, Nigel (Edinburgh S)
Griffiths, Win (Bridgend)
Grocott, Bruce
Hardy, Peter
Hattersley, Rt Hon Roy
Haynes, Frank
Heffer, Eric S.
Henderson, Doug
Hinchliffe, David
Home Robertson, John
Hood, Jimmy
Howarth, George (Knowsley N)
Howell, Rt Hon D. (S'heath)
Howells, Geraint
Howells, Dr. Kim (Pontypridd)
Hughes, John (Coventry NE)
Hughes, Robert (Aberdeen N)
Hughes, Roy (Newport E)
Illsley, Eric
Ingram, Adam
Janner, Greville
Johnston, Sir Russell
Jones, Barry (Alyn & Deeside)
Jones, Ieuan (Ynys Môn)
Jones, Martyn (Clwyd S W)
Kennedy, Charles
Kirkwood, Archy
Lambie, David
Leadbitter, Ted
Leighton, Ron
Lestor, Joan (Eccles)
Litherland, Robert
Lloyd, Tony (Stretford)
Lofthouse, Geoffrey
Loyden, Eddie
McAllion, John
McAvoy, Thomas
McCartney, Ian
Macdonald, Calum A.
McFall, John
McKelvey, William

McLeish, Henry
Maclennan, Robert
McNamara, Kevin
McWilliam, John
Madden, Max
Mahon, Mrs Alice
Marek, Dr John
Marshall, David (Shettleston)
Marshall, Jim (Leicester S)
Martlew, Eric
Maxton, John
Meale, Alan
Michael, Alun
Michie, Bill (Sheffield Heeley)
Michie, Mrs Ray (Arg'l & Bute)
Moonie, Dr Lewis
Morgan, Rhodri
Morley, Elliott
Morris, Rt Hon A. (W'shawe)
Mowlam, Marjorie
Mullin, Chris
Murphy, Paul
Oakes, Rt Hon Gordon
O'Brien, William
O'Neill, Martin
Orme, Rt Hon Stanley
Parry, Robert
Patchett, Terry
Pendry, Tom
Pike, Peter L.
Powell, Ray (Ogmore)
Prescott, John
Quin, Ms Joyce
Radice, Giles
Randall, Stuart
Redmond, Martin
Rees, Rt Hon Merlyn
Reid, Dr John
Richardson, Jo
Roberts, Allan (Bootle)
Robinson, Geoffrey
Ross, Ernie (Dundee W)
Rowlands, Ted
Ruddock, Joan
Salmond, Alex
Sedgemore, Brian
Sheerman, Barry
Sheldon, Rt Hon Robert
Shore, Rt Hon Peter
Short, Clare
Sillars, Jim
Skinner, Dennis
Smith, Andrew (Oxford E)
Smith, C. (Isl'ton & F'bury)
Smith, Rt Hon J. (Monk'ds E)
Smith, J. P. (Vale of Glam)
Snape, Peter
Spearing, Nigel
Steinberg, Gerry
Stott, Roger
Strang, Gavin
Straw, Jack
Taylor, Mrs Ann (Dewsbury)
Taylor, Matthew (Truro)
Thompson, Jack (Wansbeck)
Turner, Dennis
Vaz, Keith
Wall, Pat
Wallace, James
Walley, Joan
Wardell, Gareth (Gower)
Wareing, Robert N.
Watson, Mike (Glasgow, C)
Welsh, Michael (Doncaster N)
Wigley, Dafydd
Williams, Rt Hon Alan
Williams, Alan W. (Carm'then)
Wilson, Brian
Winnick, David

Wise, Mrs Audrey
Wray, Jimmy
Young, David *(Bolton SE)*

Tellers for the Noes:
Mr. Ken Eastham and
Mr. Allen McKay.

*Question accordingly agreed to.*

*Amendments made:* No. 80, in page 8, line 37, leave out paragraphs (a) to (c).

No. 81, in page 9, line 5, leave out 'and'.

No. 82, in page 9, line 6, at end insert—
'; and
      (g) give such other information as may be prescribed.'.

No. 83, in page 9, line 15, leave out 'provision, if any' and insert 'range of provisions'.

No. 84, in page 9, line 15, leave out 'makes' and insert 'has'.

No. 85, in page 9, line 41, leave out from second 'the' to end of line 48 and insert—
'persons who are members of the school board shall be constituted as an interim board of management on the school's becoming self-governing but that the interim board shall be succeeded, within three months after the incorporation date, by a board of management the parent members and staff members of which will be elected and on which the parent members will constitute an overall majority.'.—*[Mr. Michael Forsyth.]*

### Clause 18

#### REJECTION OR APPROVAL OF PROPOSALS

*Amendments made:* No. 86, in page 10, line 32, at end insert—
'(initially an interim board of management)'.

No. 87, in page 10, line 41, leave out 'initial'.

No. 88, in page 10, line 42, after first 'of', insert 'interim'.—*[Mr. Michael Forsyth.]*

### Schedule 4

#### INITIAL CONSTITUTION OF BOARD OF MANAGEMENT

*Amendments made:* No. 121, in page 56, line 26, leave out 'Initial Constitution Of' and insert 'Interim'.

No. 122, in page 56, line 27, leave out 'The' and insert 'An interim'.

No. 123, in page 56, line 30, leave out 'Subject to section 3(1) of this Act'.

No. 124, in page 56, line 32, after 'the', insert 'interim'.

No. 125, in page 56, line 34, after 'the', insert 'interim'.

No. 126, in page 56, line 35, leave out sub-paragraph (3) and insert—
      ';
      (c) co-opted members shall become members of the interim board of management being deemed appointed members thereof.'.

No. 127, page 56, line 38, leave out 'sub-paragraph (2)(a) or (b) of'.

No. 128, in page 56, line 39, leave out 'for such period as' and insert—
'until the interim board of management is succeeded by the first board of management to which members are elected, regardless of whether any period which,'.

No. 129, in page 56, line 41, at end insert—
'expires before the date of the relevant election'.

No. 130, in page 56, line 42, leave out paragraphs 3 and 4 and insert—
'3. An interim board of management shall cease to exist on the fulfilment of their duty under section 3(4) of this Act and shall thereupon be succeeded as board of management by the parent members and staff members to whose election that

duty related, together with the person who is for the time being the head teacher of the school.'.—*[Mr. Michael Forsyth.]*

### Schedule 5

#### TRANSITION OF ELIGIBLE SCHOOLS TO SELF-GOVERNING STATUS

*Amendments made:* No. 131, in page 57, line 41, leave out second 'and'.

No. 132, in page 57, line 44, at end insert—
'and
      (e) that without prejudice to the generality of section 10(1)(a) of the 1988 Act (information and reports) and even in so far as that section might not otherwise compel compliance, the education authority shall provide the school board with such information as the board may reasonably request under that section in respect of—
        (i) the administration of the school;
        (ii) the fabric of the school;
        (iii) the staff employed at the school;
        (iv) the pupils in attendance at the school; and
        (v) other children and young persons who would be expected to be pupils in attendance at the school within two years after the incorporation date and of whose existence the authority are aware.'.—*[Mr. Michael Forsyth.]*

### Clause 20

#### EFFECT OF PENDING PROCEDURE FOR ACQUISITION OF SELF-GOVERNING STATUS ON PROPOSALS FOR ALTERATION ETC. OF SCHOOLS

*Amendment proposed:* No. 89, in page 11, line 29, after 'proposal', insert 'shall be'.—*[Mr. Michael Forsyth.]*

*Question put,* That the amendment be made:—
*The House divided:* Ayes 259, Noes 193.

**Division No. 250]**        **[6.46 pm**

**AYES**

Adley, Robert
Aitken, Jonathan
Alexander, Richard
Alison, Rt Hon Michael
Allason, Rupert
Amess, David
Amos, Alan
Arbuthnot, James
Arnold, Jacques *(Gravesham)*
Ashby, David
Aspinwall, Jack
Atkinson, David
Baker, Nicholas *(Dorset N)*
Batiste, Spencer
Beaumont-Dark, Anthony
Bellingham, Henry
Bendall, Vivian
Bennett, Nicholas *(Pembroke)*
Benyon, W.
Bevan, David Gilroy
Biffen, Rt Hon John
Blackburn, Dr John G.
Body, Sir Richard
Bonsor, Sir Nicholas
Boscawen, Hon Robert
Boswell, Tim
Bottomley, Peter
Bottomley, Mrs Virginia
Bowden, A *(Brighton K'pto'n)*
Bowden, Gerald *(Dulwich)*
Bowis, John
Boyson, Rt Hon Dr Sir Rhodes
Braine, Rt Hon Sir Bernard
Brandon-Bravo, Martin

Brazier, Julian
Bright, Graham
Brown, Michael *(Brigg & Cl't's)*
Browne, John *(Winchester)*
Buchanan-Smith, Rt Hon Alick
Buck, Sir Antony
Budgen, Nicholas
Burns, Simon
Burt, Alistair
Butler, Chris
Butterfill, John
Carlisle, John, *(Luton N)*
Carlisle, Kenneth *(Lincoln)*
Carrington, Matthew
Carttiss, Michael
Cash, William
Chalker, Rt Hon Mrs Lynda
Channon, Rt Hon Paul
Chapman, Sydney
Chope, Christopher
Churchill, Mr
Clark, Dr Michael *(Rochford)*
Clark, Sir W. *(Croydon S)*
Colvin, Michael
Conway, Derek
Coombs, Anthony *(Wyre F'rest)*
Coombs, Simon *(Swindon)*
Cope, Rt Hon John
Cormack, Patrick
Couchman, James
Cran, James
Critchley, Julian
Currie, Mrs Edwina
Curry, David

Davis, David *(Boothferry)*
Day, Stephen
Devlin, Tim
Dicks, Terry
Dorrell, Stephen
Douglas-Hamilton, Lord James
Dunn, Bob
Durant, Tony
Dykes, Hugh
Fairbairn, Sir Nicholas
Favell, Tony
Fenner, Dame Peggy
Field, Barry *(Isle of Wight)*
Forman, Nigel
Forsyth, Michael *(Stirling)*
Freeman, Roger
Gill, Christopher
Gilmour, Rt Hon Sir Ian
Goodhart, Sir Philip
Goodson-Wickes, Dr Charles
Grant, Sir Anthony *(CambsSW)*
Greenway, Harry *(Ealing N)*
Gregory, Conal
Hamilton, Neil *(Tatton)*
Hampson, Dr Keith
Hanley, Jeremy
Hannam, John
Hargreaves, A. *(B'ham H'll Gr')*
Hargreaves, Ken *(Hyndburn)*
Harris, David
Haselhurst, Alan
Hayhoe, Rt Hon Sir Barney
Hayward, Robert
Heathcoat-Amory, David
Heddle, John
Heseltine, Rt Hon Michael
Hicks, Mrs Maureen *(Wolv' NE)*
Hicks, Robert *(Cornwall SE)*
Higgins, Rt Hon Terence L.
Hill, James
Hind, Kenneth
Hogg, Hon Douglas *(Gr'th'm)*
Howarth, G. *(Cannock & B'wd)*
Howell, Rt Hon David *(G'dford)*
Howell, Ralph *(North Norfolk)*
Hughes, Robert G. *(Harrow W)*
Hunt, David *(Wirral W)*
Hunt, Sir John *(Ravensbourne)*
Hunter, Andrew
Irvine, Michael
Irving, Charles
Jack, Michael
Janman, Tim
Jessel, Toby
Johnson Smith, Sir Geoffrey
Jones, Gwilym *(Cardiff N)*
Jones, Robert B *(Herts W)*
Jopling, Rt Hon Michael
Kellett-Bowman, Dame Elaine
Key, Robert
Kilfedder, James
King, Roger *(B'ham N'thfield)*
Kirkhope, Timothy
Knapman, Roger
Knight, Greg *(Derby North)*
Knight, Dame Jill *(Edgbaston)*
Knox, David
Lamont, Rt Hon Norman
Lang, Ian
Latham, Michael
Lawrence, Ivan
Leigh, Edward *(Gainsbor'gh)*
Lennox-Boyd, Hon Mark
Lester, Jim *(Broxtowe)*
Lightbown, David
Lilley, Peter
Lloyd, Sir Ian *(Havant)*
Lloyd, Peter *(Fareham)*
Lord, Michael
Lyell, Sir Nicholas

McCrindle, Robert
Macfarlane, Sir Neil
MacKay, Andrew *(E Berkshire)*
Maclean, David
McLoughlin, Patrick
McNair-Wilson, Sir Michael
McNair-Wilson, Sir Patrick
Major, Rt Hon John
Mans, Keith
Maples, John
Marland, Paul
Marshall, John *(Hendon S)*
Mates, Michael
Mayhew, Rt Hon Sir Patrick
Meyer, Sir Anthony
Miller, Sir Hal
Mills, Iain
Mitchell, Andrew *(Gedling)*
Mitchell, Sir David
Moate, Roger
Monro, Sir Hector
Montgomery, Sir Fergus
Moore, Rt Hon John
Morris, M *(N'hampton S)*
Morrison, Sir Charles
Morrison, Rt Hon P *(Chester)*
Moss, Malcolm
Moynihan, Hon Colin
Nelson, Anthony
Neubert, Michael
Nicholls, Patrick
Nicholson, David *(Taunton)*
Norris, Steve
Onslow, Rt Hon Cranley
Oppenheim, Phillip
Page, Richard
Paice, James
Patnick, Irvine
Patten, John *(Oxford W)*
Peacock, Mrs Elizabeth
Porter, Barry *(Wirral S)*
Porter, David *(Waveney)*
Price, Sir David
Raison, Rt Hon Timothy
Rathbone, Tim
Redwood, John
Renton, Tim
Rhodes James, Robert
Riddick, Graham
Ridley, Rt Hon Nicholas
Ridsdale, Sir Julian
Rifkind, Rt Hon Malcolm
Roe, Mrs Marion
Rossi, Sir Hugh
Rost, Peter
Rumbold, Mrs Angela
Sackville, Hon Tom
Sayeed, Jonathan
Shaw, David *(Dover)*
Shaw, Sir Michael *(Scarb')*
Shephard, Mrs G. *(Norfolk SW)*
Skeet, Sir Trevor
Smith, Tim *(Beaconsfield)*
Soames, Hon Nicholas
Speed, Keith
Speller, Tony
Spicer, Sir Jim *(Dorset W)*
Squire, Robin
Stanley, Rt Hon Sir John
Steen, Anthony
Stern, Michael
Stevens, Lewis
Stewart, Allan *(Eastwood)*
Stewart, Andy *(Sherwood)*
Stokes, Sir John
Stradling Thomas, Sir John
Summerson, Hugo
Taylor, Ian *(Esher)*
Taylor, John M *(Solihull)*
Taylor, Teddy *(S'end E)*

Tebbit, Rt Hon Norman
Temple-Morris, Peter
Thompson, Patrick *(Norwich N)*
Thorne, Neil
Thornton, Malcolm
Thurnham, Peter
Townend, John *(Bridlington)*
Tracey, Richard
Tredinnick, David
Trippier, David
Trotter, Neville
Twinn, Dr Ian
Vaughan, Sir Gerard
Waddington, Rt Hon David
Walker, Bill *(T'side North)*
Waller, Gary
Walters, Sir Dennis
Ward, John

Wardle, Charles *(Bexhill)*
Watts, John
Wells, Bowen
Whitney, Ray
Widdecombe, Ann
Wiggin, Jerry
Wilkinson, John
Wilshire, David
Winterton, Mrs Ann
Winterton, Nicholas
Wolfson, Mark
Wood, Timothy
Yeo, Tim

Tellers for the Ayes:
   Mr. Alan Howarth and
   Mr. Michael Fallon.

**NOES**

Abbott, Ms Diane
Adams, Allen *(Paisley N)*
Allen, Graham
Alton, David
Archer, Rt Hon Peter
Armstrong, Hilary
Ashley, Rt Hon Jack
Barnes, Harry *(Derbyshire NE)*
Barron, Kevin
Battle, John
Beckett, Margaret
Beith, A. J.
Bell, Stuart
Benn, Rt Hon Tony
Bennett, A. F. *(D'nt'n & R'dish)*
Bidwell, Sydney
Blair, Tony
Blunkett, David
Boateng, Paul
Boyes, Roland
Bray, Dr Jeremy
Brown, Gordon *(D'mline E)*
Brown, Nicholas *(Newcastle E)*
Brown, Ron *(Edinburgh Leith)*
Bruce, Malcolm *(Gordon)*
Buckley, George J.
Caborn, Richard
Callaghan, Jim
Campbell, Menzies *(Fife NE)*
Campbell-Savours, D. N.
Canavan, Dennis
Clark, Dr David *(S Shields)*
Clarke, Tom *(Monklands W)*
Clay, Bob
Clelland, David
Cohen, Harry
Cook, Frank *(Stockton N)*
Cook, Robin *(Livingston)*
Corbyn, Jeremy
Cryer, Bob
Cummings, John
Cunliffe, Lawrence
Dalyell, Tam
Darling, Alistair
Davies, Ron *(Caerphilly)*
Davis, Terry *(B'ham Hodge H'l)*
Dewar, Donald
Dixon, Don
Dobson, Frank
Doran, Frank
Douglas, Dick
Duffy, A. E. P.
Dunnachie, Jimmy
Eadie, Alexander
Ewing, Harry *(Falkirk E)*
Fearn, Ronald
Field, Frank *(Birkenhead)*
Fields, Terry *(L'pool B G'n)*
Fisher, Mark
Flannery, Martin

Flynn, Paul
Foot, Rt Hon Michael
Foster, Derek
Foulkes, George
Fraser, John
Fyfe, Maria
Galbraith, Sam
Galloway, George
Garrett, John *(Norwich South)*
Garrett, Ted *(Wallsend)*
Gilbert, Rt Hon Dr John
Godman, Dr Norman A.
Golding, Mrs Llin
Graham, Thomas
Grant, Bernie *(Tottenham)*
Griffiths, Nigel *(Edinburgh S)*
Griffiths, Win *(Bridgend)*
Hardy, Peter
Hattersley, Rt Hon Roy
Haynes, Frank
Heffer, Eric S.
Henderson, Doug
Hinchliffe, David
Home Robertson, John
Hood, Jimmy
Howarth, George *(Knowsley N)*
Howell, Rt Hon D. *(S'heath)*
Howells, Geraint
Howells, Dr. Kim *(Pontypridd)*
Hughes, John *(Coventry NE)*
Hughes, Robert *(Aberdeen N)*
Hughes, Roy *(Newport E)*
Illsley, Eric
Ingram, Adam
Janner, Greville
Johnston, Sir Russell
Jones, Barry *(Alyn & Deeside)*
Jones, Ieuan *(Ynys Môn)*
Jones, Martyn *(Clwyd S W)*
Kennedy, Charles
Kirkwood, Archy
Lambie, David
Leadbitter, Ted
Leighton, Ron
Lestor, Joan *(Eccles)*
Litherland, Robert
Lloyd, Tony *(Stretford)*
Lofthouse, Geoffrey
Loyden, Eddie
McAllion, John
McAvoy, Thomas
McCartney, Ian
Macdonald, Calum A.
McFall, John
McKelvey, William
McLeish, Henry
Maclennan, Robert
McNamara, Kevin
McWilliam, John
Madden, Max

Mahon, Mrs Alice
Marek, Dr John
Marshall, David *(Shettleston)*
Marshall, Jim *(Leicester S)*
Martlew, Eric
Maxton, John
Meale, Alan
Michael, Alun
Michie, Bill *(Sheffield Heeley)*
Michie, Mrs Ray *(Arg'l & Bute)*
Moonie, Dr Lewis
Morley, Elliott
Morris, Rt Hon A. *(W'shawe)*
Mowlam, Marjorie
Mullin, Chris
Murphy, Paul
Oakes, Rt Hon Gordon
O'Brien, William
O'Neill, Martin
Orme, Rt Hon Stanley
Parry, Robert
Patchett, Terry
Pendry, Tom
Pike, Peter L.
Powell, Ray *(Ogmore)*
Prescott, John
Quin, Ms Joyce
Radice, Giles
Randall, Stuart
Redmond, Martin
Rees, Rt Hon Merlyn
Reid, Dr John
Richardson, Jo
Roberts, Allan *(Bootle)*
Robinson, Geoffrey
Ross, Ernie *(Dundee W)*
Rowlands, Ted
Ruddock, Joan
Salmond, Alex

Sedgemore, Brian
Sheerman, Barry
Sheldon, Rt Hon Robert
Shore, Rt Hon Peter
Short, Clare
Sillars, Jim
Skinner, Dennis
Smith, C. *(Isl'ton & F'bury)*
Smith, Rt Hon J. *(Monk'ds E)*
Smith, J. P. *(Vale of Glam)*
Snape, Peter
Spearing, Nigel
Steinberg, Gerry
Stott, Roger
Strang, Gavin
Taylor, Mrs Ann *(Dewsbury)*
Taylor, Matthew *(Truro)*
Thompson, Jack *(Wansbeck)*
Turner, Dennis
Vaz, Keith
Wall, Pat
Wallace, James
Walley, Joan
Wardell, Gareth *(Gower)*
Wareing, Robert N.
Watson, Mike *(Glasgow, C)*
Welsh, Michael *(Doncaster N)*
Wigley, Dafydd
Williams, Rt Hon Alan
Williams, Alan W. *(Carm'then)*
Wilson, Brian
Winnick, David
Wise, Mrs Audrey
Wray, Jimmy
Young, David *(Bolton SE)*

Tellers for the Noes:
    Mr. Ken Eastham and
    Mr. Allen McKay.

*Question accordingly agreed to.*

*Amendment made:* No. 90, in page 11, line 30, leave out 'shall be'.—*[Mr. Michael Forsyth.]*

## Schedule 6

### PROVISION OF BENEFITS AND SERVICES FOR PUPILS AT SELF-GOVERNING SCHOOLS ETC.

*Amendment proposed:* No. 133, in page 58, line 46, leave out 'and cleanliness'.—*[Mr. Michael Forsyth.]*

*Question put,* That the amendment be made:—
*The House divided:* Ayes 264, Noes 196.

**Division No. 251]**                    **[6.59 pm**

### AYES

Adley, Robert
Aitken, Jonathan
Alexander, Richard
Alison, Rt Hon Michael
Allason, Rupert
Amess, David
Amos, Alan
Arbuthnot, James
Arnold, Jacques *(Gravesham)*
Ashby, David
Aspinwall, Jack
Atkinson, David
Baker, Nicholas *(Dorset N)*
Batiste, Spencer
Beaumont-Dark, Anthony
Beggs, Roy
Bellingham, Henry
Bendall, Vivian
Bennett, Nicholas *(Pembroke)*
Benyon, W.
Bevan, David Gilroy
Biffen, Rt Hon John

Blackburn, Dr John G.
Blaker, Rt Hon Sir Peter
Body, Sir Richard
Bonsor, Sir Nicholas
Boscawen, Hon Robert
Boswell, Tim
Bottomley, Peter
Bottomley, Mrs Virginia
Bowden, A *(Brighton K'pto'n)*
Bowden, Gerald *(Dulwich)*
Bowis, John
Boyson, Rt Hon Dr Sir Rhodes
Braine, Rt Hon Sir Bernard
Brandon-Bravo, Martin
Brazier, Julian
Bright, Graham
Brown, Michael *(Brigg & Cl't's)*
Browne, John *(Winchester)*
Buchanan-Smith, Rt Hon Alick
Buck, Sir Antony
Budgen, Nicholas
Burns, Simon

Burt, Alistair
Butler, Chris
Butterfill, John
Carlisle, John, *(Luton N)*
Carlisle, Kenneth *(Lincoln)*
Carrington, Matthew
Carttiss, Michael
Cash, William
Channon, Rt Hon Paul
Chapman, Sydney
Chope, Christopher
Clark, Dr Michael *(Rochford)*
Clark, Sir W. *(Croydon S)*
Colvin, Michael
Conway, Derek
Coombs, Anthony *(Wyre F'rest)*
Coombs, Simon *(Swindon)*
Cope, Rt Hon John
Cormack, Patrick
Couchman, James
Cran, James
Currie, Mrs Edwina
Curry, David
Davis, David *(Boothferry)*
Day, Stephen
Devlin, Tim
Dicks, Terry
Dorrell, Stephen
Douglas-Hamilton, Lord James
Dunn, Bob
Durant, Tony
Dykes, Hugh
Fairbairn, Sir Nicholas
Fallon, Michael
Favell, Tony
Fenner, Dame Peggy
Forman, Nigel
Forsyth, Michael *(Stirling)*
Fox, Sir Marcus
Freeman, Roger
Gill, Christopher
Gilmour, Rt Hon Sir Ian
Goodhart, Sir Philip
Goodson-Wickes, Dr Charles
Gorman, Mrs Teresa
Grant, Sir Anthony *(CambsSW)*
Greenway, Harry *(Ealing N)*
Gregory, Conal
Griffiths, Peter *(Portsmouth N)*
Hamilton, Neil *(Tatton)*
Hampson, Dr Keith
Hanley, Jeremy
Hannam, John
Hargreaves, A. *(B'ham H'll Gr')*
Hargreaves, Ken *(Hyndburn)*
Harris, David
Haselhurst, Alan
Hawkins, Christopher
Hayhoe, Rt Hon Sir Barney
Hayward, Robert
Heddle, John
Heseltine, Rt Hon Michael
Hicks, Mrs Maureen *(Wolv' NE)*
Hicks, Robert *(Cornwall SE)*
Higgins, Rt Hon Terence L.
Hill, James
Hind, Kenneth
Hogg, Hon Douglas *(Gr'th'm)*
Howarth, G. *(Cannock & B'wd)*
Howell, Rt Hon David *(G'dford)*
Howell, Ralph *(North Norfolk)*
Hughes, Robert G. *(Harrow W)*
Hunt, David *(Wirral W)*
Hunt, Sir John *(Ravensbourne)*
Hunter, Andrew
Irvine, Michael
Irving, Charles
Jack, Michael
Jackson, Robert
Janman, Tim

Jessel, Toby
Johnson Smith, Sir Geoffrey
Jones, Gwilym *(Cardiff N)*
Jones, Robert B *(Herts W)*
Jopling, Rt Hon Michael
Kellett-Bowman, Dame Elaine
Key, Robert
Kilfedder, James
King, Roger *(B'ham N'thfield)*
Kirkhope, Timothy
Knapman, Roger
Knight, Greg *(Derby North)*
Knight, Dame Jill *(Edgbaston)*
Knox, David
Lamont, Rt Hon Norman
Lang, Ian
Latham, Michael
Lawrence, Ivan
Leigh, Edward *(Gainsbor'gh)*
Lennox-Boyd, Hon Mark
Lester, Jim *(Broxtowe)*
Lightbown, David
Lilley, Peter
Lloyd, Sir Ian *(Havant)*
Lloyd, Peter *(Fareham)*
Lord, Michael
Lyell, Sir Nicholas
McCrindle, Robert
Macfarlane, Sir Neil
MacKay, Andrew *(E Berkshire)*
Maclean, David
McLoughlin, Patrick
McNair-Wilson, Sir Michael
McNair-Wilson, Sir Patrick
Major, Rt Hon John
Mans, Keith
Maples, John
Marland, Paul
Marshall, John *(Hendon S)*
Martin, David *(Portsmouth S)*
Mates, Michael
Mawhinney, Dr Brian
Meyer, Sir Anthony
Miller, Sir Hal
Mills, Iain
Mitchell, Andrew *(Gedling)*
Mitchell, Sir David
Moate, Roger
Monro, Sir Hector
Montgomery, Sir Fergus
Moore, Rt Hon John
Morrison, Sir Charles
Morrison, Rt Hon P *(Chester)*
Moss, Malcolm
Moynihan, Hon Colin
Needham, Richard
Nelson, Anthony
Neubert, Michael
Nicholls, Patrick
Nicholson, David *(Taunton)*
Norris, Steve
Onslow, Rt Hon Cranley
Oppenheim, Phillip
Page, Richard
Paice, James
Patnick, Irvine
Patten, John *(Oxford W)*
Peacock, Mrs Elizabeth
Porter, Barry *(Wirral S)*
Porter, David *(Waveney)*
Price, Sir David
Raison, Rt Hon Timothy
Rathbone, Tim
Redwood, John
Renton, Tim
Rhodes James, Robert
Riddick, Graham
Ridley, Rt Hon Nicholas
Ridsdale, Sir Julian
Rifkind, Rt Hon Malcolm

Roe, Mrs Marion
Rossi, Sir Hugh
Rost, Peter
Rumbold, Mrs Angela
Sackville, Hon Tom
Sayeed, Jonathan
Shaw, David *(Dover)*
Shaw, Sir Michael *(Scarb')*
Shephard, Mrs G. *(Norfolk SW)*
Sims, Roger
Skeet, Sir Trevor
Smith, Tim *(Beaconsfield)*
Soames, Hon Nicholas
Speed, Keith
Speller, Tony
Spicer, Sir Jim *(Dorset W)*
Stanley, Rt Hon Sir John
Steen, Anthony
Stern, Michael
Stevens, Lewis
Stewart, Allan *(Eastwood)*
Stewart, Andy *(Sherwood)*
Stokes, Sir John
Stradling Thomas, Sir John
Summerson, Hugo
Taylor, Ian *(Esher)*
Taylor, John M *(Solihull)*
Taylor, Teddy *(S'end E)*
Tebbit, Rt Hon Norman
Temple-Morris, Peter
Thompson, Patrick *(Norwich N)*
Thorne, Neil

Thornton, Malcolm
Thurnham, Peter
Tracey, Richard
Tredinnick, David
Trippier, David
Trotter, Neville
Twinn, Dr Ian
Vaughan, Sir Gerard
Waddington, Rt Hon David
Wakeham, Rt Hon John
Walker, Bill *(T'side North)*
Waller, Gary
Walters, Sir Dennis
Ward, John
Wardle, Charles *(Bexhill)*
Warren, Kenneth
Watts, John
Wells, Bowen
Whitney, Ray
Widdecombe, Ann
Wiggin, Jerry
Wilkinson, John
Wilshire, David
Winterton, Mrs Ann
Winterton, Nicholas
Wolfson, Mark
Wood, Timothy
Yeo, Tim

Tellers for the Ayes:
    Mr. Alan Howarth and
    Mr. Michael Fallon.

## NOES

Abbott, Ms Diane
Adams, Allen *(Paisley N)*
Allen, Graham
Alton, David
Archer, Rt Hon Peter
Armstrong, Hilary
Ashley, Rt Hon Jack
Barnes, Harry *(Derbyshire NE)*
Barron, Kevin
Battle, John
Beckett, Margaret
Beith, A. J.
Bell, Stuart
Benn, Rt Hon Tony
Bennett, A. F. *(D'nt'n & R'dish)*
Bidwell, Sydney
Blair, Tony
Blunkett, David
Boateng, Paul
Boyes, Roland
Brown, Gordon *(D'mline E)*
Brown, Nicholas *(Newcastle E)*
Brown, Ron *(Edinburgh Leith)*
Bruce, Malcolm *(Gordon)*
Buckley, George J.
Caborn, Richard
Callaghan, Jim
Campbell, Menzies *(Fife NE)*
Campbell-Savours, D. N.
Canavan, Dennis
Clark, Dr David *(S Shields)*
Clarke, Tom *(Monklands W)*
Clay, Bob
Clelland, David
Clwyd, Mrs Ann
Cohen, Harry
Cook, Frank *(Stockton N)*
Cook, Robin *(Livingston)*
Corbyn, Jeremy
Cryer, Bob
Cummings, John
Cunliffe, Lawrence
Dalyell, Tam
Darling, Alistair
Davies, Ron *(Caerphilly)*
Davis, Terry *(B'ham Hodge H'l)*

Dewar, Donald
Dixon, Don
Dobson, Frank
Doran, Frank
Douglas, Dick
Duffy, A. E. P.
Dunnachie, Jimmy
Eadie, Alexander
Ewing, Harry *(Falkirk E)*
Fearn, Ronald
Field, Frank *(Birkenhead)*
Fields, Terry *(L'pool B G'n)*
Fisher, Mark
Flannery, Martin
Flynn, Paul
Foot, Rt Hon Michael
Foster, Derek
Foulkes, George
Fraser, John
Fyfe, Maria
Galbraith, Sam
Galloway, George
Garrett, John *(Norwich South)*
Garrett, Ted *(Wallsend)*
Gilbert, Rt Hon Dr John
Godman, Dr Norman A.
Golding, Mrs Llin
Graham, Thomas
Grant, Bernie *(Tottenham)*
Griffiths, Nigel *(Edinburgh S)*
Griffiths, Win *(Bridgend)*
Grocott, Bruce
Hardy, Peter
Hattersley, Rt Hon Roy
Haynes, Frank
Henderson, Doug
Hinchliffe, David
Home Robertson, John
Hood, Jimmy
Howarth, George *(Knowsley N)*
Howell, Rt Hon D. *(S'heath)*
Howells, Geraint
Howells, Dr. Kim *(Pontypridd)*
Hoyle, Doug
Hughes, John *(Coventry NE)*
Hughes, Robert *(Aberdeen N)*

Hughes, Roy *(Newport E)*
Illsley, Eric
Ingram, Adam
Janner, Greville
Johnston, Sir Russell
Jones, Barry *(Alyn & Deeside)*
Jones, Ieuan *(Ynys Môn)*
Jones, Martyn *(Clwyd S W)*
Kennedy, Charles
Kirkwood, Archy
Lambie, David
Leadbitter, Ted
Leighton, Ron
Lestor, Joan *(Eccles)*
Litherland, Robert
Lloyd, Tony *(Stretford)*
Lofthouse, Geoffrey
Loyden, Eddie
McAllion, John
McAvoy, Thomas
McCartney, Ian
Macdonald, Calum A.
McFall, John
McKelvey, William
McLeish, Henry
Maclennan, Robert
McNamara, Kevin
McWilliam, John
Madden, Max
Mahon, Mrs Alice
Marek, Dr John
Marshall, David *(Shettleston)*
Marshall, Jim *(Leicester S)*
Martlew, Eric
Maxton, John
Meale, Alan
Michael, Alun
Michie, Bill *(Sheffield Heeley)*
Michie, Mrs Ray *(Arg'l & Bute)*
Moonie, Dr Lewis
Morgan, Rhodri
Morris, Rt Hon A. *(W'shawe)*
Mowlam, Marjorie
Mullin, Chris
Murphy, Paul
Oakes, Rt Hon Gordon
O'Brien, William
O'Neill, Martin
Orme, Rt Hon Stanley
Parry, Robert
Patchett, Terry
Pendry, Tom
Pike, Peter L.
Powell, Ray *(Ogmore)*

Radice, Giles
Randall, Stuart
Redmond, Martin
Rees, Rt Hon Merlyn
Reid, Dr John
Richardson, Jo
Roberts, Allan *(Bootle)*
Robertson, George
Robinson, Geoffrey
Ross, Ernie *(Dundee W)*
Rowlands, Ted
Ruddock, Joan
Salmond, Alex
Sedgemore, Brian
Sheerman, Barry
Sheldon, Rt Hon Robert
Shore, Rt Hon Peter
Short, Clare
Sillars, Jim
Skinner, Dennis
Smith, C. *(Isl'ton & F'bury)*
Smith, Rt Hon J. *(Monk'ds E)*
Smith, J. P. *(Vale of Glam)*
Snape, Peter
Spearing, Nigel
Steinberg, Gerry
Stott, Roger
Strang, Gavin
Taylor, Mrs Ann *(Dewsbury)*
Taylor, Matthew *(Truro)*
Thompson, Jack *(Wansbeck)*
Turner, Dennis
Vaz, Keith
Wall, Pat
Wallace, James
Walley, Joan
Wardell, Gareth *(Gower)*
Wareing, Robert N.
Watson, Mike *(Glasgow, C)*
Welsh, Andrew *(Angus E)*
Welsh, Michael *(Doncaster N)*
Wigley, Dafydd
Williams, Rt Hon Alan
Williams, Alan W. *(Carm'then)*
Wilson, Brian
Winnick, David
Wise, Mrs Audrey
Wray, Jimmy
Young, David *(Bolton SE)*

Tellers for the Noes:
    Mr. Ken Eastham and
    Mr. Allen McKay.

*Question accordingly agreed to.*

## Clause 25

### Recurrent grant, capital grants and
### special purpose grant

*Amendment made:* No. 91, in page 14, line 26, after 'shall', insert

'subject to section *Recurrent grant in respect of provision for special educational needs* of this Act,'.—*[Mr. Michael Forsyth.]*

## Clause 28

### Change in characteristics of
### self-governing school

*Amendment made:* No. 92, in page 17, line 27, leave out 'they' and insert

'other than an increase in the range of provisions which the school has for pupils with special educational needs, the board'.—*[Mr. Michael Forsyth.]*

## Schedule 7

ARRANGEMENTS IN RESPECT OF BALLOT OF PARENTS
REGARDING CHANGE IN CHARACTERISTICS OF
SELF-GOVERNING SCHOOL

*Amendment made:* No. 134, in page 60, line 9, leave out
'concerning the ballot' and insert,

'including (without prejudice to the generality of this
sub-paragraph) information—
(i) about the ballot and about the procedure for
changing the characteristics of a self-governing school; and
(ii) in the case of a ballot held by virtue of section
15 of this Act, an explanation (which in the
case of a ballot required by a notice under
subsection (1) of that section shall repeat the
reasons given in the notice by the Secretary of
State for declaring the earlier ballot invalid or
void) as to why a fresh ballot is to be held.'.
—*[Mr. Michael Forsyth.]*

## Clause 29

DISCONTINUANCE BY BOARD OF MANAGEMENT

*Amendment proposed:* No. 93, in page 19, line 5, leave
out
'required by regulations made by the Secretary of State'
and insert 'prescribed'.—*[Mr. Michael Forsyth.]*

*Question put,* That the amendment be made:-
*The House divided:* Ayes 267, Noes 196.

**Division No. 252]**                                   [7.13 pm

### AYES

Adley, Robert
Aitken, Jonathan
Alexander, Richard
Alison, Rt Hon Michael
Allason, Rupert
Amess, David
Amos, Alan
Arbuthnot, James
Arnold, Jacques (Gravesham)
Arnold, Tom (Hazel Grove)
Ashby, David
Aspinwall, Jack
Atkinson, David
Baker, Nicholas (Dorset N)
Batiste, Spencer
Beaumont-Dark, Anthony
Beggs, Roy
Bellingham, Henry
Bendall, Vivian
Bennett, Nicholas (Pembroke)
Benyon, W.
Bevan, David Gilroy
Biffen, Rt Hon John
Blackburn, Dr John G.
Blaker, Rt Hon Sir Peter
Body, Sir Richard
Bonsor, Sir Nicholas
Boscawen, Hon Robert
Boswell, Tim
Bottomley, Peter
Bottomley, Mrs Virginia
Bowden, A (Brighton K'pto'n)
Bowden, Gerald (Dulwich)
Bowis, John
Boyson, Rt Hon Dr Sir Rhodes
Braine, Rt Hon Sir Bernard
Brandon-Bravo, Martin
Brazier, Julian
Bright, Graham
Brown, Michael (Brigg & Cl't's)
Browne, John (Winchester)
Buchanan-Smith, Rt Hon Alick
Buck, Sir Antony

Budgen, Nicholas
Burns, Simon
Burt, Alistair
Butler, Chris
Butterfill, John
Carlisle, John, (Luton N)
Carlisle, Kenneth (Lincoln)
Carrington, Matthew
Carttiss, Michael
Cash, William
Chalker, Rt Hon Mrs Lynda
Chope, Christopher
Churchill, Mr
Clark, Dr Michael (Rochford)
Clark, Sir W. (Croydon S)
Colvin, Michael
Conway, Derek
Coombs, Anthony (Wyre F'rest)
Coombs, Simon (Swindon)
Cope, Rt Hon John
Cormack, Patrick
Couchman, James
Cran, James
Currie, Mrs Edwina
Curry, David
Davis, David (Boothferry)
Day, Stephen
Devlin, Tim
Dicks, Terry
Dorrell, Stephen
Douglas-Hamilton, Lord James
Dover, Den
Dunn, Bob
Durant, Tony
Dykes, Hugh
Fairbairn, Sir Nicholas
Fallon, Michael
Farr, Sir John
Favell, Tony
Fenner, Dame Peggy
Forman, Nigel
Forsyth, Michael (Stirling)
Fox, Sir Marcus

Freeman, Roger
Gill, Christopher
Gilmour, Rt Hon Sir Ian
Goodhart, Sir Philip
Goodson-Wickes, Dr Charles
Gorman, Mrs Teresa
Grant, Sir Anthony (CambsSW)
Greenway, Harry (Ealing N)
Gregory, Conal
Hamilton, Neil (Tatton)
Hampson, Dr Keith
Hanley, Jeremy
Hannam, John
Hargreaves, A. (B'ham H'll Gr')
Hargreaves, Ken (Hyndburn)
Harris, David
Haselhurst, Alan
Hawkins, Christopher
Hayhoe, Rt Hon Sir Barney
Hayward, Robert
Heddle, John
Heseltine, Rt Hon Michael
Hicks, Mrs Maureen (Wolv' NE)
Hicks, Robert (Cornwall SE)
Higgins, Rt Hon Terence L.
Hill, James
Hind, Kenneth
Hogg, Hon Douglas (Gr'th'm)
Howard, Michael
Howarth, Alan (Strat'd-on-A)
Howarth, G. (Cannock & B'wd)
Howell, Rt Hon David (G'dford)
Howell, Ralph (North Norfolk)
Hughes, Robert G. (Harrow W)
Hunt, David (Wirral W)
Hunt, Sir John (Ravensbourne)
Hunter, Andrew
Irvine, Michael
Irving, Charles
Jack, Michael
Jackson, Robert
Janman, Tim
Jessel, Toby
Johnson Smith, Sir Geoffrey
Jones, Gwilym (Cardiff N)
Jones, Robert B (Herts W)
Jopling, Rt Hon Michael
Kellett-Bowman, Dame Elaine
Key, Robert
Kilfedder, James
King, Roger (B'ham N'thfield)
Kirkhope, Timothy
Knapman, Roger
Knight, Greg (Derby North)
Knight, Dame Jill (Edgbaston)
Knox, David
Lamont, Rt Hon Norman
Lang, Ian
Latham, Michael
Lawrence, Ivan
Leigh, Edward (Gainsbor'gh)
Lennox-Boyd, Hon Mark
Lester, Jim (Broxtowe)
Lightbown, David
Lilley, Peter
Lloyd, Sir Ian (Havant)
Lloyd, Peter (Fareham)
Lord, Michael
Luce, Rt Hon Richard
Lyell, Sir Nicholas
McCrindle, Robert
Macfarlane, Sir Neil
Maclean, David
McLoughlin, Patrick
McNair-Wilson, Sir Michael
McNair-Wilson, Sir Patrick
Major, Rt Hon John
Mans, Keith
Maples, John
Marland, Paul

Marshall, John (Hendon S)
Martin, David (Portsmouth S)
Mates, Michael
Mawhinney, Dr Brian
Meyer, Sir Anthony
Miller, Sir Hal
Mills, Iain
Mitchell, Andrew (Gedling)
Mitchell, Sir David
Moate, Roger
Monro, Sir Hector
Montgomery, Sir Fergus
Moore, Rt Hon John
Morrison, Sir Charles
Morrison, Rt Hon P (Chester)
Moss, Malcolm
Moynihan, Hon Colin
Needham, Richard
Nelson, Anthony
Neubert, Michael
Nicholls, Patrick
Nicholson, David (Taunton)
Norris, Steve
Onslow, Rt Hon Cranley
Oppenheim, Phillip
Page, Richard
Paice, James
Patnick, Irvine
Patten, John (Oxford W)
Peacock, Mrs Elizabeth
Porter, Barry (Wirral S)
Porter, David (Waveney)
Price, Sir David
Raison, Rt Hon Timothy
Rathbone, Tim
Redwood, John
Renton, Tim
Rhodes James, Robert
Riddick, Graham
Ridley, Rt Hon Nicholas
Ridsdale, Sir Julian
Rifkind, Rt Hon Malcolm
Roe, Mrs Marion
Rossi, Sir Hugh
Rost, Peter
Rumbold, Mrs Angela
Sackville, Hon Tom
Sayeed, Jonathan
Shaw, David (Dover)
Shaw, Sir Michael (Scarb')
Shephard, Mrs G. (Norfolk SW)
Sims, Roger
Skeet, Sir Trevor
Smith, Tim (Beaconsfield)
Soames, Hon Nicholas
Speed, Keith
Speller, Tony
Spicer, Sir Jim (Dorset W)
Stanley, Rt Hon Sir John
Steen, Anthony
Stern, Michael
Stevens, Lewis
Stewart, Allan (Eastwood)
Stewart, Andy (Sherwood)
Stokes, Sir John
Stradling Thomas, Sir John
Summerson, Hugo
Taylor, Ian (Esher)
Taylor, John M (Solihull)
Tebbit, Rt Hon Norman
Temple-Morris, Peter
Thompson, Patrick (Norwich N)
Thornton, Malcolm
Thurnham, Peter
Townend, John (Bridlington)
Tracey, Richard
Tredinnick, David
Trippier, David
Trotter, Neville
Twinn, Dr Ian

Vaughan, Sir Gerard
Waddington, Rt Hon David
Wakeham, Rt Hon John
Walker, Bill *(T'side North)*
Waller, Gary
Walters, Sir Dennis
Ward, John
Wardle, Charles *(Bexhill)*
Warren, Kenneth
Watts, John
Wells, Bowen
Whitney, Ray
Widdecombe, Ann

Wiggin, Jerry
Wilkinson, John
Wilshire, David
Winterton, Mrs Ann
Winterton, Nicholas
Wolfson, Mark
Wood, Timothy
Yeo, Tim

Tellers for the Ayes:
    Mr. David Heathcoat-Amory
    and Mr. Sidney Chapman.

**NOES**

Abbott, Ms Diane
Adams, Allen *(Paisley N)*
Allen, Graham
Alton, David
Archer, Rt Hon Peter
Armstrong, Hilary
Ashley, Rt Hon Jack
Barnes, Harry *(Derbyshire NE)*
Barron, Kevin
Battle, John
Beckett, Margaret
Beith, A. J.
Bell, Stuart
Benn, Rt Hon Tony
Bidwell, Sydney
Blair, Tony
Blunkett, David
Boateng, Paul
Boyes, Roland
Brown, Gordon *(D'mline E)*
Brown, Nicholas *(Newcastle E)*
Bruce, Malcolm *(Gordon)*
Buckley, George J.
Caborn, Richard
Callaghan, Jim
Campbell, Menzies *(Fife NE)*
Campbell-Savours, D. N.
Canavan, Dennis
Clark, Dr David *(S Shields)*
Clarke, Tom *(Monklands W)*
Clay, Bob
Clelland, David
Cohen, Harry
Cook, Frank *(Stockton N)*
Cook, Robin *(Livingston)*
Cryer, Bob
Cummings, John
Cunliffe, Lawrence
Dalyell, Tam
Darling, Alistair
Davies, Ron *(Caerphilly)*
Davis, Terry *(B'ham Hodge H'l)*
Dewar, Donald
Dixon, Don
Dobson, Frank
Doran, Frank
Douglas, Dick
Duffy, A. E. P.
Dunnachie, Jimmy
Eadie, Alexander
Ewing, Harry *(Falkirk E)*
Fearn, Ronald
Field, Frank *(Birkenhead)*
Fields, Terry *(L'pool B G'n)*
Fisher, Mark
Flannery, Martin
Flynn, Paul
Foot, Rt Hon Michael
Foster, Derek
Foulkes, George
Fraser, John
Fyfe, Maria
Galbraith, Sam
Galloway, George
Garrett, John *(Norwich South)*

Garrett, Ted *(Wallsend)*
Gilbert, Rt Hon Dr John
Godman, Dr Norman A.
Golding, Mrs Llin
Graham, Thomas
Grant, Bernie *(Tottenham)*
Griffiths, Nigel *(Edinburgh S)*
Griffiths, Win *(Bridgend)*
Grocott, Bruce
Hardy, Peter
Hattersley, Rt Hon Roy
Haynes, Frank
Henderson, Doug
Hinchliffe, David
Home Robertson, John
Hood, Jimmy
Howarth, George *(Knowsley N)*
Howell, Rt Hon D. *(S'heath)*
Howells, Geraint
Howells, Dr. Kim *(Pontypridd)*
Hoyle, Doug
Hughes, John *(Coventry NE)*
Hughes, Robert *(Aberdeen N)*
Hughes, Roy *(Newport E)*
Illsley, Eric
Ingram, Adam
Janner, Greville
Johnston, Sir Russell
Jones, Barry *(Alyn & Deeside)*
Jones, Ieuan *(Ynys Môn)*
Jones, Martyn *(Clwyd S W)*
Kennedy, Charles
Kirkwood, Archy
Lambie, David
Leadbitter, Ted
Leighton, Ron
Lestor, Joan *(Eccles)*
Litherland, Robert
Livsey, Richard
Lloyd, Tony *(Stretford)*
Lofthouse, Geoffrey
Loyden, Eddie
McAllion, John
McAvoy, Thomas
McCartney, Ian
Macdonald, Calum A.
McFall, John
McKelvey, William
McLeish, Henry
Maclennan, Robert
McNamara, Kevin
McWilliam, John
Madden, Max
Mahon, Mrs Alice
Marek, Dr John
Marshall, David *(Shettleston)*
Marshall, Jim *(Leicester S)*
Martlew, Eric
Maxton, John
Meale, Alan
Michael, Alun
Michie, Bill *(Sheffield Heeley)*
Michie, Mrs Ray *(Arg'l & Bute)*
Moonie, Dr Lewis
Morgan, Rhodri

Morley, Elliott
Morris, Rt Hon A. *(W'shawe)*
Mowlam, Marjorie
Mullin, Chris
Murphy, Paul
Oakes, Rt Hon Gordon
O'Brien, William
O'Neill, Martin
Orme, Rt Hon Stanley
Parry, Robert
Patchett, Terry
Pendry, Tom
Pike, Peter L.
Powell, Ray *(Ogmore)*
Prescott, John
Quin, Ms Joyce
Radice, Giles
Randall, Stuart
Redmond, Martin
Rees, Rt Hon Merlyn
Reid, Dr John
Richardson, Jo
Roberts, Allan *(Bootle)*
Robertson, George
Robinson, Geoffrey
Ross, Ernie *(Dundee W)*
Rowlands, Ted
Ruddock, Joan
Salmond, Alex
Sedgemore, Brian
Sheerman, Barry
Sheldon, Rt Hon Robert
Shore, Rt Hon Peter
Short, Clare
Sillars, Jim

Skinner, Dennis
Smith, C. *(Isl'ton & F'bury)*
Smith, Rt Hon J. *(Monk'ds E)*
Smith, J. P. *(Vale of Glam)*
Snape, Peter
Spearing, Nigel
Steinberg, Gerry
Stott, Roger
Strang, Gavin
Straw, Jack
Taylor, Mrs Ann *(Dewsbury)*
Taylor, Matthew *(Truro)*
Thompson, Jack *(Wansbeck)*
Turner, Dennis
Vaz, Keith
Wall, Pat
Wallace, James
Walley, Joan
Wardell, Gareth *(Gower)*
Wareing, Robert N.
Watson, Mike *(Glasgow, C)*
Welsh, Andrew *(Angus E)*
Welsh, Michael *(Doncaster N)*
Wigley, Dafydd
Williams, Rt Hon Alan
Williams, Alan W. *(Carm'then)*
Wilson, Brian
Winnick, David
Wise, Mrs Audrey
Wray, Jimmy
Young, David *(Bolton SE)*

Tellers for the Noes:
    Mr. Allen McKay and
    Mr. Ken Eastham.

*Question accordingly agreed to.*

*Amendment made:* No. 94, in page 19, line 6, leave out 'him' and insert 'the Secretary of State'.—*[Mr. Michael Forsyth.]*

### Clause 31

WITHDRAWAL OF GRANT BY SECRETARY OF STATE
*Amendment made:* No. 32, in page 20, line 20, after 'authority,' insert—
'(iia) the parents of the pupils in attendance at the school; '.
—*[Mr. Michael Forsyth.]*

### Clause 32

TRANSFER OF LAND, MOVEABLE PROPERTY AND
OBLIGATIONS TO BOARD OF MANAGEMENT
*Amendment made:* No. 95, in page 22, line 34, at end insert—
'(ba) any obligation or liability under a contract of employment relating to a person previously employed by the education authority to whom section 21 of this Act does not apply; or'.—*[Mr. Michael Forsyth.]*

### Schedule 8

TRANSFER AND APPORTIONMENT OF ASSETS
*Amendments made:* No. 135, in page 60, line 34, at end insert 'and'.

No. 136, in page 62, line 26, at end insert 'and'.—*[Mr. Michael Forsyth.]*

### Schedule 9

COMMISSIONERS FOR SCHOOL ASSETS
*Amendments made:* No. 137, in page 64, line 15, after 'functions', insert 'of a commissioner'.

No. 138, in page 64, line 19, leave out 'paragraph' and insert 'paragraphs 5 and'.—[*Mr. Michael Forsyth.*]

## Clause 35

TRANSFER OF PROPERTY WHERE NO CERTIFICATE ISSUED

*Amendment made:* No. 96, in page 24, line 8, leave out 'become a party to' and insert 'raise or defend'.—[*Mr. Michael Forsyth.*]

## Clause 37

REDUCTION OF DISPOSALS OF PROPERTY BY EDUCATION AUTHORITY

*Amendment made:* No. 97, in page 25, line 5, leave out 'may' and insert 'shall'—[*Mr. Michael Forsyth.*]

## Clause 41

COMMISSIONER FOR SCHOOL ASSETS' RIGHT OF ACTION FOR CONTRAVENTION OF SECTION 38

*Amendment made:* No. 98, in page 27, line 15, after 'may', insert 'seek to'.—[*Mr. Michael Forsyth.*]

## Clause 45

WINDING-UP ORDERS

*Amendments made:* No. 99, in page 28, line 41, after 'may', insert
'after consultation with the education authority and subject to subsection (2A) below,'.

No. 100, in page 28, line 42, at end insert—
'(2A) Where subsection (2)(a) of the said section 31 applies to a notice given under that section the Secretary of State shall not make an order under this section within 5 years of the date on which he gives the said notice.'.

No. 101, in page 28, line 43, after '(2)' insert
'Without prejudice to the generality of subsection (1) above,'.

No. 102, in page 29, line 8, leave out 'or held'.—[*Mr. Michael Forsyth.*]

## Clause 46

DISPOSAL OF PROPERTY ON WINDING UP

*Amendments made:* No. 103, in page 29, line 38, leave out 'or held'.

No. 104, in page 30, line 2, leave out 'or held'.

No. 105, in page 30, line 4, leave out 'which formerly maintained the school'.—[*Mr. Michael Forsyth.*]

## Clause 47

TRANSFER OF SCHOOL FOR ESTABLISHMENT OF NEW SCHOOL

*Amendment made:* No. 106, in page 31, line 12, leave out
'which was formerly responsible for the discontinued school'.—[*Mr. Michael Forsyth.*]

## Clause 48

DISPOSAL OF SURPLUS MONEY ON WINDING-UP

*Amendment made:* No. 107, in page 32, leave out lines 3 to 6 and insert
'shall be paid or, as the case may be, transferred to the Secretary of State, after—

(i) discharge of their liabilities (other than any not required to be discharged before the dissolution date is appointed); and
(ii) payment of all expenses of the winding up.'.—[*Mr. Michael Forsyth.*]

## Clause 49

ESTABLISHMENT OF COLLEGE COUNCILS

*Amendments made:* No. 7, in page 33, line 10, leave out 'industrial.'

No. 8, in page 33, line 21, after first 'by', insert 'employers, or by'.—[*Mr. Michael Forsyth.*]

## Clause 60

POWER OF EDUCATION AUTHORITIES TO FORM COMPANIES TO MANAGE COLLEGES OF FURTHER EDUCATION

*Amendments made:* No. 9, in page 40, line 9, leave out 'An education authority' and insert 'A college council'.

No. 10, in page 40, line 9, after 'of,' insert—
'(a) the education authority; and
(b) '.

No. 11, in page 40, line 11, leave out 'transferring' and insert
'enabling the education authority to transfer.'

No. 12, in page 40, line 33, after 'amend", insert 'or revoke'.

No. 13, in page 40, line 38, at end insert—
'(5) Nothing in this section shall be construed as authorising the carrying on through a college of further education managed by a company formed by virtue of subsection (1) above of any commercial activities which are detrimental to the provision of further education at that college.'.—[*Mr. Michael Forsyth.*]

## Clause 62

ABOLITION OF COMMITTEE TO CONSIDER PAY AND CONDITIONS OF TEACHING STAFF EMPLOYED IN PROVIDING FURTHER EDUCATION

*Amendments made:* No. 14, in page 41, line 40, after first 'or', insert—
', as the case may be, an'.

No. 15, in page 41, line 40, leave out
'subsection (8) or, as the case may be, (9) of'.

No. 16, in page 41, line 42, leave out 'it' and insert 'the order, settlement, determination or award'.

No. 17, in page 42, line 4, leave out 'or determination' and insert 'determination or award'.—[*Mr. Michael Forsyth.*]

## Clause 65

APPRAISAL OF TEACHERS

*Amendments made:* No. 18, in page 44, leave out line 6 to 8 and insert—
'(3) Subject to regulations made under this section, an employer may at any time vary or replace a scheme made in accordance with those regulations and, if such regulations so require, he shall—
  (a) before making, varying or replacing any such scheme, consult any body representing teaching staff who are to be affected by the scheme as proposed to be made, varied or replaced;
  (b) before proceeding with appraisal under any such scheme as so made, varied or replaced, submit it to the Secretary of State'.

No. 19, in page 44, leave out lines 15 to 18.

No. 20, in page 44, line 27, leave out 'any' and insert 'each'.—*[Mr. Michael Forsyth.]*

## Clause 72

### INTERPRETATION

*Amendments made:* No. 108, in page 47, line 30, leave out 'and (2)'.

No. 109, in page 47, line 34, after 'Act', insert ('any such board constituted in accordance with Schedule 4 to this Act being referred to as an "interim board of management")'.

—*[Mr. Michael Forsyth.]*

## Clause 73

### COMMENCEMENT

*Amendment made:* No. 110, in page 49, line 8, leave out '66,'.—*[Mr. Michael Forsyth.]*

## Schedule 10

### MINOR AND CONSEQUENTIAL AMENDMENTS

*Amendment made:* No. 21, in page 65, leave out lines 4 to 16 and insert—

'1. In subsection (5) of section 5 of the Universities (Scotland) Act 1889 (which relates to the constitution of university courts), for the words "the principal" there shall be substituted the words "a vice-chairman elected by the Court from among all its members,".'.

No. 48, in page 69, line 8, at end insert—

'(7A) In section 49 (power of education authorities to assist persons to take advantage of educational facilities), after subsection (2) there shall be inserted the following subsection—

"(2A) In subsection (2) above, references to attending school are to so attending not only where the school is in Scotland, but also where it is in England and Wales or in Northern Ireland ('school education' being construed accordingly).".

(7B) In section 50 (education of pupils in exceptional circumstances)—

(a) in subsection (1), for the words "an appropriate school or college" there shall be substituted the words—

", in any case falling under—

(i) paragraph (a) of this subsection, an appropriate school; and

(ii) paragraph (b) thereof, the particular school.";

(b) after subsection (1) there shall be inserted the following subsection—

"(1A) In subsection (1) above, references to an appropriate school and to a particular school are references not only to schools in Scotland but also to schools in England and Wales or in Northern Ireland ('school education' being construed accordingly)."; and

(c) in subsection (2)(a), for the words "section 51 of this Act" there shall be substituted the words "subsection (1) of section 51 of this Act (for the purposes of this paragraph, any reference in that section to a school being construed as a reference not only to a school in Scotland but also to a school in England and Wales or in Northern Ireland).".'.

No. 22, in page 69, line 44, at end insert—

'(16A) In paragraph (a) of section 97C (interpretation of sections 91 to 97B)—

(a) the words "(i)" and "(or)" and sub-paragraph (ii) shall cease to have effect;

(b) after the word "may" there shall be inserted the words "from time to time"; and

(c) after the word "determine;" there shall be inserted the words "and the provisions of those sections shall accordingly not apply in relation to such teachers or other persons employed by education authorities in Scotland in, or in connection with, the provision of school education as are excluded from, the definition of "teaching staff" by such an order;".'.

—*[Mr. Maclean.]*

## Schedule 11

### REPEALS

*Amendments made:* No. 49, in page 71, line 39, after '(c);' insert 'and'.

No. 50, in page 71, line 41, leave out 'and the words "or college".'.

No. 23, in page 72, line 4, after 'both', insert 'other'.

No. 24, in page 72, line 18, at end insert

'In paragraph (a) of section 97C, the words "(i)" and "or", and sub-paragraph (ii);'.—*[Mr. Maclean.]*

## New Clause 13

### FURTHER PROVISION AS TO APPOINTMENT OF TEACHERS

'After section 87 of the 1980 Act there shall be inserted the following sections—

#### Appointment of principal teachers

87A. Where an education authority intends to fill a post, other than on an acting basis, of a principal teacher in a school, they shall advertise the post in such publications circulating throughout Scotland as they consider appropriate.

#### Selection of teachers

87B. Without prejudice to section 7 of the Local Government and Housing Act 1989 (which provides for the appointment of staff of local authorities to be made on merit) and to any requirement in any other enactment as to the considerations to which they may or may not have regard in making appointments, an education authority who are considering an appointment of a teacher shall not exclude any person from consideration for such an appointment on the ground that—

(a) he is not employed by that education authority; or

(b) he is or is not employed by a particular employer or class of employer; or

(c) he is not currently employed as a teacher.'.

—*[Mr. Michael Forsyth.]*

*Brought up, read the First and Second time, and added to the Bill.*

## New Clause 14

### REMUNERATION OF CERTAIN PERSONS EMPLOYED IN PROVIDING SCHOOL EDUCATION

'(1) This section applies to persons employed by education authorities in Scotland in, or in connection with, the provision of school education in relation to whose remuneration and terms and conditions of employment sections 91 to 97B of the 1980 Act have ceased, by virtue of an order made under section 97C(a) of that Act, to apply.

(2) Where, in relation to the remuneration or terms and conditions of employment of any persons to whom this section applies—

(a) an order made under section 92 of the 1980 Act (as originally enacted and not as substituted by the Education (Scotland) Act 1981); or

(b) a settlement formulated under section 91(1) of the 1980 Act; or

(c) a determination or, as the case may be, an award made under section 97B of the 1980 Act,

is still in force on the date on which such an order as is mentioned in subsection (1) above comes into force, the order, settlement, determination or award shall, subject to subsection (3) below, remain in force after that date.

(3) Where, after this enactment comes into force—

(a) any group of persons to whom this section applies and those employing them agree, whether expressly or impliedly, to an alteration of the remuneration payable to, or the terms and conditions of employment of, that group of persons; or

(b) any such alteration as is mentioned in paragraph (a) above is arrived at in an agreed manner,

that alteration shall, to the extent that it is concerned with the same matters, supersede any such order, settlement, determination or award as is referred to in paragraphs (a), (b) or (c) of subsection (2) above.'.—*[Mr. Michael Forsyth.]*

*Brought up, read the First and Second time, and added to the Bill.*

## New Clause 17

### EDUCATIONAL SERVICES: EXTENSION OF POWER OF SECRETARY OF STATE TO MAKE GRANTS

'In section 73(d) of the 1980 Act (power of Secretary of State to make grants to persons providing education or educational services other than education authorities, universities and managers of educational establishments)—

(a) the word "for" shall be inserted before the words "providing education or educational services" and shall with those words constitute sub-paragraph (i); and

(b) after that sub-paragraph there shall be inserted the word "or" and the following sub-paragraph—

"(ii) in respect of expenditure incurred or to be incurred by them for the purposes of, or in connection with the provision (or proposed provision) of education or educational services.".'.—*[Mr. Michael Forsyth.]*

*Brought up, read the First and Second Time, and added to the Bill.*

## New Clause 22

### REQUIREMENT FOR PROVISION BY EDUCATION AUTHORITY OF ADMINISTRATIVE, PROFESSIONAL OR TECHNICAL SERVICES

'(1) Without prejudice to section 1 of the Local Authorities (Goods and Services) Act 1970 (power of local authority and public body to enter into agreement for certain purposes) the board of management of a self-governing school may require the education authority to provide them with any administrative, professional, technical or other services which the authority provide to or in respect of schools under the authority's management.

(2) An education authority may make such charge as is reasonable for any services which they are required under subsection (1) above to provide; and they shall in determining what charge to make have regard both to the cost of providing the services and to any guidance issued by the Secretary of State in respect of any such charge.

(3) In the event of any dispute arising between the education authority and the board of management as regards the reasonableness of any such charge, the matter may be referred by either party to the Secretary of State, whose decision in that regard shall be final.'.—*[Mr. Michael Forsyth.]*

*Brought up, read the First and Second time, and added to the Bill.*

## New Clause 23

### FUNCTIONS OF SCHOOL BOARD: APPLICATION OF CERTAIN PROVISIONS OF 1988 ACT

'.—(1) In so far as the context admits, functions under this Act of a school board are, for the purposes of—

(a) section 5 of the 1988 Act (advice to boards) matters within the competence of the board;

(b) sections 8(1) (exercise of functions of boards) and 19 (allowances for members) of that Act functions of the board;

(c) section 13 (parents' meetings) of that Act activities of the board.

(2) Subsection (1)(b) of section 17 of the 1988 Act (financing of boards) shall apply in relation to functions of a school board under this Act as it applies to such functions under that Act; and subsection (3) of that section shall be construed accordingly.'.—*[Mr. Michael Forsyth.]*

*Brought up, read the First and Second time, and added to the Bill.*

### Ballot expenses

'    . Subject to section 14(2) of this Act, an education authority who have received written notice under subsection (6) of section 13 of this Act from a school board shall neither pay any sum nor incur any expense, for the purpose of influencing the outcome of the ballot provided for by subsection (1) of the said section 16, in excess of such maximum amount as may be prescribed; and the school board may, for the purposes of the ballot, require the Secretary of State to make payment to them under this section of sums whose total does not exceed that amount in respect of such expenses as they may incur in promoting the acquisition of self-governing status by the school.'.—*[Mr. Michael Forsyth.]*

*Brought up, read the First and Second time, and added to the Bill.*

## New Clause 25

### RECURRENT GRANT IN RESPECT OF PROVISION FOR SPECIAL EDUCATIONAL NEEDS

'    .—(1) For each financial year, recurrent grant payable in respect of any self-governing school—

(a) which is a special school; or

(b) (in the case of a school which is not a special school) in so far as is attributable to expenditure for the purpose of making provision for pupils in attendance at the school who are persons whose needs are recorded by the education authority in implementation of the authority's duty under section 60(2)(b) of the 1980 Act (duty to keep record of needs).

shall be determined having regard to the following provisions of this section.

(2) The education authority and the board of management shall attempt to reach agreement as to—

(a) in the case of a special school, what educational and other provision is to be made in the financial year for the pupils in attendance at the school, the estimated cost of that provision and the estimated expenditure incurred or to be incurred for the purposes of the board's other functions under section 7(1) of this Act in that year;

(b) in any other case, what provision is to be made in that year for such pupils as are mentioned in paragraph (b) of subsection (1) above and the estimated cost of that provision.

and any such agreement, or a failure to reach such agreement, shall be timeously intimated by the board of management to the Secretary of State.

(3) If intimation under subsection (2) above is of a failure to reach agreement or if the Secretary of State does not accept any aspect of an intimated agreement, he shall himself determine the matters mentioned in paragraph (a) or as the case may be (b), of subsection (2) above in determining under section 25(2) of this Act the amount of recurrent grant payable in respect of the school; and his determination as to the said matters shall (without prejudice to the provision made by subsection (2) of section 25 of this Act as to revision) be final.

(4) In determining under section 25(2) of this Act the amount of recurrent grant payable in respect of a school, the Secretary of State shall, where he does not make a determination under subsection (3) above, regard an agreement intimated under subsection (2) above as determining the matters to which it relates.

(5) Grant regulations may prescribe—
(a) what information is to be—
(i) exchanged between an education authority and a board of management for the purposes of their duty under subsection (2) above or for the purposes of subsection (6) below;
(ii) provided to the Secretary of State by the authority and the board for the purposes of his considering any agreement intimated to him under that subsection or subsection (7) below or himself making a determination under subsection (3) above or a variation under subsection (8) below;
(b) the dates by which, in respect of any financial year, such information as is mentioned in paragraph (a) above is to be provided;
(c) the latest date by which, in respect of any financial year, any agreement, or failure to reach agreement, is to be intimated to the Secretary of State under subsection (2) above.

(6) In a case where an amount of recurrent grant payable has been determined in accordance with subsection (4) above, during the course of the financial year the education authority and the board of management—
(a) may agree; and
(b) if the Secretary of State so requires, shall attempt to reach agreement as to, a variation of their agreement under subsection (2) above.

(7) The board of management shall intimate to the Secretary of State any variation agreed, or any failure to reach an agreement, under subsection (6) above; and the Secretary of State shall, if he accepts any agreement reached, vary the amount of recurrent grant payable accordingly.

(8) Where the Secretary of State does not accept an agreed variation intimated under subsection (7) above, or where he has imposed a requirement under subsection (6) above but the education authority and the board of management are unable to agree on a variation of their agreement under subsection (2) above, he may himself vary the amount of recurrent grant payable but he shall not otherwise vary that amount in a case such as is mentioned in subsection (6) above.'.—[*Mr. Michael Forsyth.*]

*Brought up, read the First and Second time, and added to the Bill.*

## New Clause 26

### Disposal of land by board of management

'. —(1) This section applies where a board of management seek the consent of the Secretary of State to the disposal of land which was—
(a) transferred to the board under section 32 of this Act; or
(b) acquired by the board, wholly or partly, with the proceeds of the sale of land which was transferred as mentioned in paragraph (a) above; or
(c) acquired by the board, wholly or partly, with the proceeds of the sale of land which was acquired, wholly or partly—
(i) as mentioned in paragraph (b) above; or
(ii) with the proceeds of any subsequent sale of any such land.

(2) Where the consent of the Secretary of State is sought as mentioned in subsection (1) above, he may—
(a) require the board of management to transfer the land, or any part of it, to the education authority upon payment by the authority to the board of such consideration, if any, as he considers appropriate; or
(b) except in a case where the land is being transferred to the education authority, require the board of management to pay to the authority all, or any part of, the consideration which they receive in respect of the disposal of the land.

(3) Where any land such as is mentioned in subsection (1) above is compulsorily acquired from a board of management, they shall—
(a) not require to seek the consent of the Secretary of State to such disposal; but
(b) inform him that the land is being compulsorily acquired from them; and

(c) pay to the education authority the whole or such part of the compensation which they receive in respect of the compulsory acquisition as the Secretary of State may direct.'.—[*Mr. Michael Forsyth.*]

*Brought up, read the First and Second time, and added to the Bill.*

## New Clause 2

### General academic selection

'A self-governing school shall not introduce general academic selection whereby the admission of pupils to the school or rejection of pupils by the school is made by reference to levels of ability or aptitude.'.—[*Mr. McLeish.*]

*Brought up, and read the First time.*

**Mr. McLeish:** I beg to move, That the clause be read a Second time.

Many concerns were voiced in Committee about the Bill, but none more so than the concern about academic selection. Clauses 16 and 28 seem to include provision for a self-governing school to admit pupils on the basis of academic selection.

In Committee, the Government would not accept that definition of the words "aptitude and ability". But the Opposition clearly felt that aptitude and ability were an euphemism for admission on the basis of academic selection.

Over the past 20 years in Scotland there has been a consensus on the need to build and develop comprehensive education. That has been one of the big success stories of Scottish education over the past 10 to 15 years. The Opposition are alarmed that, under the guise of self-governing status, any school could use academic criteria to admit pupils. As the Committee progressed, the Opposition became less assured of the Government's intent. The Government were keen to suggest that aptitude and ability meant that there could be special provision for the arts and for sports, but the Opposition clearly felt that there was a real threat of academic selection.

7.30 pm

There have been few studies on the impact of comprehensivisation on attainment in Scottish education. One is the work done by the Centre for Educational Sociology in Edinburgh. As usual, the Minister sighs with despair at the mention of that organisation, but it is a reputable, reliable and authoritative source on the benefits of comprehensivisation over the past few years. As my hon. Friend the Member for Glasgow, Garscadden (Mr. Dewar) reminds me, the Scottish Office invests considerable sums of money in tapping its expertise.

Comprehensivisation in Scotland has meant an improvement in overall standards and, equally important, an equalisation of attainment between children of different social backgrounds. That was one of the motivating forces behind the introduction of comprehensive education, not only in England and Wales, but in Scotland.

The Centre for Educational Sociology has produced some interesting statistics on the impact of that change on the two areas of overall improvement and equalisation. In Committee there were few opportunities when the Government could resist the temptation to rubbish the work of the Centre for Educational Sociology, but they failed to provide any evidence to counter the representations that we were making, backed up by the welter of statistics on every educational indicator that we could find.

Clearly, comprehensivisation has been a success in Scotland, and the opposition are worried that that could be threatened by the back-door introduction of selection on the basis of academic criteria.

Scotland has dwelt on the twin aspects of child development—equal worth and equal access. We know that that is anathema to many on the Right wing of the Conservative party who do not believe that a modern progressive education system should have such qualities. Conservative Members like to talk about competition and individual choice, but one of the overriding qualities that comprehensivisation has brought to Scottish education is that children have been treated equally, with access that is not determined at an early age by testing; nor is it dependent, for 98 per cent. of our Scottish schoolchildren, on the ability to pay.

Those are laudable objectives, which the Opposition believe should be nurtured and further developed. But if a self-governing school seeks to introduce academic criteria for admission, not only will the educational clock be put back some 20 years, but it will be educationally divisive. The introduction of admission based on academic criteria would lead to a diminution of choice for the vast majority of Scottish schoolchildren. The wider danger, knowing the Government's track record, is that, at an early date, that very concept could, through legislation, be introduced in education authority schools.

We are talking about more than merely academic selection being used in self-governing schools, but that is the thin edge of the educational wedge in satisfying the lust on the Government Benches in this new Right view of education where everything has to be competitive and children have to be failed at an early stage so that competition comes higher on the education agenda.

That is not the path which other European countries are following. It is widely recognised in education and in training that the countries that are competitive and whose performance greatly outstrips us have a system of education in which all children can develop and take advantage of the education system until the age of 16 or after when they can specialise in training, vocational education and further education. That requires a non-selective system of education at the crucial time in a child's development within a community. That is why the Opposition have sought to make this a key priority in the debate. We have sought to ensure that something that is not wanted in Scotland is adequately dealt with in the House tonight.

It is curious that we have a Bill which, by any stretch of the imagination, is uniquely objectionable to most Scots, and within which are even more objectionable aspects such as academic selection. At one time, when a Government brought legislation before the House, they would have evidence to justify or substantiate what they were seeking to do. The Government have nothing to justify the reintroduction of a method of selecting children for schools, which, as I have said, was smashed by the consensus which has emerged over the past 20 years.

**Mr. Michael Forsyth:** Where does the Bill introduce academic selection, or selection of any kind? Will the hon. Gentleman confirm that the Bill introduces two specific hurdles—the consent of the parents and the consent of the Secretary of State—to make such a change? Will he also confirm that education authority schools will be able to introduce academic selection on the basis of a simple vote by the education committee? There are specific protections and it is wrong for the hon. Gentleman to mislead the House in the way that he has.

**Mr. McLeish:** With the greatest respect to the Minister, it is he who is misleading the House. In Committee, he made great play of the fact that Scottish education authorities could at any time reintroduce academic selection. The real test is that they have no inclination to do so, and that applied when the Conservatives controlled some education authorities in Scotland—an event unlikely to be repeated in the near future. However, it is not true to say that that is a power that local authorities have and would wish to use.

The Minister also asks where in the Bill there is a suggestion of academic selection. It is in clause 16, and there is a reference to aptitude and ability. We cannot accept for a minute that, after two obstacles have been overcome, we should trust the Secretary of State not to decide that a school can change its characteristics and allow academic selection.

**Mr. Bill Walker:** When the hon. Gentleman gets round to reading the statement that he has just made, he may see the conflicting arguments that he has used to present his case. He accepts that it is on the statute book that local authorities can, if they wish, introduce selection, but they have not done so because they did not wish to do so. The Bill simply gives parents and school boards a similar opportunity.

**Mr. McLeish:** I have some respect for the hon. Member for Tayside, North (Mr. Walker), but if he believes that the Bill is permissive and will merely lie on the shelf in schools throughout the country and not be used, he is being extremely naive. The Government introduced assisted places and school boards on the pretext that they would offer parental choice. In truth, they provided the base on which to build self-governing schools. The Bill also reintroduces standardised testing. It all fits together, to allow a school to pit child against child at a very early age. It is very naive of the hon. Member for Tayside, North to assume that the Bill simply provides further parental choice. That is not its purpose. If the hon. Gentleman read some of the Right-wing nonsense in which some of his right hon. and hon. Friends on the Front Bench and Back Benches indulge, he would be more wary of the Minister's overtures about the Bill being only permissive legislation.

Why do the Government wish to see even self-governing schools return to a system that has been massively rejected by the Scottish people and by every other political party in Scotland, and which is repugnant to the majority of parents and educationalists? Even given the Government's comments about aptitude and ability, they must justify such an objectionable measure. In Committee, the Minister wriggled away from giving more precise definitions. I ask him to state tonight whether he believes that selection on the basis of academic ability should be reintroduced in the Scottish education system. I ask him whether he will allow that, as between the primary and comprehensive sector, and cause enormous damage to children?

**Mr. Michael Forsyth:** At the risk of irritating the hon. Member for Glasgow, Garscadden (Mr. Dewar), in Committee I made it clear that I am in favour of schools being selective in their intake. One example is pupils

[*Mr. Michael Forsyth*]

wishing to join a school of dance, such as the Knightswood comprehensive school. In the case of the Douglas academy, selection would apply to children talented in music. In Committee, the hon. Member for Fife, Central (Mr. McLeish) failed to say whether he was against such selection, and whether it was included in the term "general academic selection" in new clause 2.

**Mr. McLeish:** There was nothing very original in that response. The Minister gave the wrong reply to the right question. Setting aside social skills, culture and sport, does the Minister want to see in existence soon the situation in which a self-governing school, after a change in its characteristics, will admit children only on the basis of tests relating to their academic ability at primary school level? Does the Minister support that concept, or will he give an assurance that such a system will not operate?

**Mr. Michael Forsyth:** The Bill allows a self-governing school to make a proposal which, if it receives the endorsement of parents, can go before the Secretary of State for him to take a view. The hon. Gentleman describes music as a social subject whereas it is really an academic subject requiring great skill. Is the hon. Gentleman against schools having specialist departments for music? Is he against specialist departments of classics because of the need for a broad intake to run a successful classics department? Will the hon. Gentleman, like his hon. Friend the Member of Western Isles (Mr. Macdonald) duck the issue of whether there should be selective intake for those whose native language is Gaelic? My view is that such matters are best left to the judgment of parents and to the good sense of the Secretary of State. The hon. Gentleman wants self-governing schools to be more restricted than education authority schools. He should be honest enough to answer the questions that have been asked of him.

7.45 pm

**Mr. McLeish:** Our worry is that, if the Minister were to be sitting in the Scottish Office considering requests from parents, and given that he is ideologically committed to academic selection, he would agree to a school changing its characteristics under the banner of aptitude and ability. The Minister again wriggles away from answering the real question. In Committee, other definitions of ability and aptitude were accepted. Tonight, I ask the Minister whether he wants to see a return to the situation that existed in Scottish schools 15 or 20 years ago, whereby the result of a test set to children in primary schools determined their whole futures. Is that what the Minister wants to achieve in Scottish education?

**Mr. Michael Forsyth:** The hon. Gentleman knows perfectly well that the answer to that question is no. In previous debates, we repeatedly gave assurances that the tests being introduced in primary schools will not be used for the purposes of selection and to rank children, but for giving parents information about their children's academic performance. They will not go as far as the tests run by education authorities such as that in the hon. Gentleman's constituency. His new clause is not about that aspect but about preventing schools from doing what the Douglas academy and Knightswood in the comprehensive sector have done, which is to be selective about particular specialist intakes in meeting a particular specialist need. I

am sorry that the hon. Gentleman's own narrow-minded, ideological bigotry would prevent parents from having the option to vote for or against any change, when he is perfectly content for any education authority to effect changes without consulting parents, other than in the most cursory way.

**Mr. McLeish:** I know that a number of my hon. Friends are keen to participate in the debate, and we are now going over ground that was covered in Committee. However, on a poll of Scottish parents, I know whom they would trust more, given a choice between the Secretary of State and the Minister, and the chairman and responsible members of an education authority.

**Mr. Bill Walker:** Does the hon. Gentleman include and embrace in his new clause physical education and all that it implies? If he does, the hon. Gentleman, with his experience of and background in professional soccer, and one thing or another, must surely agree that parents may want their children to enter a particular school because its staff have a reputation for being particularly experienced in that area of activity.

**Mr. McLeish:** I did not mind the hon. Gentleman's reference to my background in soccer, but his reference to "one thing or another" perplexed me. He follows the line of the Minister. Academic selection relates to admission on the basis of academic ability, which in turn suggests mental rather than physical aptitudes. The Minister nods his head in surprise, but that aspect was covered in Committee, and tonight we have tried to get the Minister to come clean and talk about general academic selection as it is generally interpreted. He has failed to do so. Instead we heard throwaway lines relating to music, dancing and other cultural subjects. My right hon. and hon. Friends will infer from that that the Minister is moving to admission on the basis of academic selection.

**Mr. Michael Forsyth:** The hon. Gentleman asked me to give additional examples, but why did his list ignore the examples of the classics and of Gaelic that I gave? He rode over music as though it were a social skill. Is the hon. Gentleman against schools providing specialist teaching in specialist subjects and being selective about intake? If so, he is against the apparent current practice in comprehensive schools in Strathclyde.

**Mr. McLeish:** The Minister should read new clause 2, which refers to admission criteria on the basis of academic ability. The Minister clearly wishes to ignore our interpretation of that, but most Scots know what is meant by selection between primary and secondary schools. The Minister glibly ignores the reality. Beneath the guise of aptitude and ability, the criteria and characteristics of self-governing schools—established under clause 16—could change over a period, under clause 28. That could include admission on the basis of academic selection.

**Mr. Bill Walker:** As the hon. Gentleman will know, my constituency contains a number of schools. What will he tell primary schools that teach Gaelic? What will he tell parents who wish their children to attend a secondary school that, under the present comprehensive system, offers Gaelic as a subject, if it becomes self-governing because that is wanted locally? Will he say that the school can no longer be selective?

**Mr. McLeish:** I think that that point was covered earlier. Whether or not the Government understand the issue, the people of Scotland will understand it. Most of them fought for a long time to remove academic criteria from the face of Scottish education. Now, in the late 1980s, we see the possibility of a Government's wishing to return to that reactionary and regressive attitude to Scottish education.

We are opposed to such criteria for admission, for the simple reason that we believe that comprehensivisation has shown that we want to invest in every child, with no artificial cut-off point in relation to maturity or ability at any specific age. We do not want to return to a system of investing in failure by rejecting children of 11—or, under this bizarre testing procedure, possibly even younger— when they could move into comprehensive education at the age of 12, 13, 14 or 15, maturing at different stages and combining either academic ability or vocational training with their talents. That is the light that we have tried to cast on the gloom that will surround the future of comprehensive and self-governing schools if the Bill is passed.

We talked earlier about what we wished to do in the future, and I do not want to go into that now. Let me simply say that we see an odious practice seeping through the Bill. We hope that, if it is implemented, self-governing schools in particular will once again, at the earliest opportunity, see equal worth and equal access as an important priority. We ask the House to accept new clause 2, which we think will be widely welcomed in Scotland.

**Mr. Alick Buchanan-Smith:** Let me briefly repeat some of the concerns that I had in Committee. I understand what lies behind new clause 2, although I suspect that some of the fears that prompted it are not as strong as the hon. Member for Fife, Central (Mr. McLeish) makes out.

I am, however, anxious that if any genuine element of selectivity were introduced it could have a dramatic effect on schools in rural areas. As I said in Committee, parents subjected to it might have had no say in the opting out of the secondary school to which their children's primary school was feeding pupils. That in itself is bad enough, but if the parents had no choice because children were being fed to a specific centre, the denial of access to the secondary school that was in the natural position for their area would create horrendous practical and physical problems of, for instance, travel. I freely admit that the problem might not arise in urban areas, as there would be other suitable secondary schools nearby.

My hon. Friend the Minister gave me a strong assurance in Committee that in such circumstances the Secretary of State would on no account allow the introduction of selection on an academic basis. I very much hope that he will repeat that assurance tonight, as it has coloured my attitude to the new clause. I do not support the Bill in any case, but I want to be certain that when it becomes law it will not deny access to the geographically natural secondary school in a rural area because of action taken after the school has become self-governing.

**Sir Russell Johnston:** I strongly agree with what the right hon. Member for Kincardine and Deeside (Mr. Buchanan-Smith) has said. Nevertheless, he cannot say on the one hand, "I am not terribly worried about selectivity; I think that the Opposition are exaggerating," and on the other hand, "Oh dear me, it might happen, and if it happens in a rural context it would be dreadful." The two are not compatible. I share his anxieties for practically the same reasons, however, and consider it entirely right for him to ask for certain assurances.

I strongly support new clause 2, and compliment whoever devised it on the straightforward language in which it is couched: I know that such pellucid simplicity is anathema to the arcane minds of the Minister's advisers, who do not appear to be around at present. The Minister, too, has departed, but no doubt he will be advised by his friendly colleagues. In Committee, he provided a regrettable demonstration that he is the grammatical slave of the obscure and recondite mandarins who write our legislation, and I hope that he will not descend into such arguments this evening.

Let me be more serious. I believe that the hon. Member for Fife, Central (Mr. McLeish) was entirely right in saying that the most important single worry of those of us who oppose the legislation is that it could provide a way of introducing selectivity covertly at an early stage. I thought that the 11-plus argument was long buried, but I fear that it is not.

A long exchange between the hon. Member for Fife, Central and the Minister did not leave me much the wiser, but as I understand the new clause—perhaps the hon. Member for Fife, Central will confirm this—it is designed to prevent general exclusion on academic grounds, but not particular exclusion. For example, if a school wished to concentrate on the various subjects cited by the Minister —dance, classics or Gaelic—I do not think that anything in the new clause could prevent it from doing so.

The new clause is designed to protect the slow developer. I am sorry to sound like an echo of the hon. Member for Tayside, North (Mr. Walker), but I speak as a slow developer myself. I have in my possession a report card. It says that I was 26th in the class in one year and that three years later I was in first position. Some people do not develop as quickly as others, but they are capable of making progress and even becoming Members of Parliament. We want to ensure that this is not a covert way of preventing that happening.

The right hon. Member for Kincardine and Deeside is still very worried and his worries have led him to make the speech that he has just made. He is worried about the Bill being used to prevent people from developing at their own pace,. The new clause will not be used to prevent children from developing at their own pace, so I see no objection to its being accepted. It would not prevent schools from concentrating on the matters to which the Minister referred. That is perfectly proper, understandable and desirable.

8 pm

**Mr. Bill Walker:** It is interesting to hear that the hon. Member for Inverness, Nairn and Lochaber (Sir R. Johnston) was No. 26 in one year and No. 1 the following year.

**Sir Russell Johnston:** No, not in the following year.

**Mr. Walker:** I am wondering whether he was with the same group of 26 students or whether the composition of the group had changed—that from being bottom of the class in one group he moved to another group where he was top of the class.

[*Mr. Walker*]

My concern about the new clause is the inclusion of the word "aptitude." I should have thought that the word "ability" was sufficient. Aptitude is latent and can be developed. For that reason I intervened on a number of occasions during the speech of the hon. Member for Fife, Central (Mr. McLeish). Degrees are now offered in a variety of disciplines, including what I believe to be variations on physical education. Certain schools employ teachers who are particularly good at coaching young people in football, rugby, sailing, skiing, hockey, netball, running and jumping.

The aptitude of a child can be spotted at a fairly early age. If he is provided with the right coaching, he may reach the stage where he can take up a career in which he can use his particular skills. He might be prepared to take a degree of a kind that did not exist 10 or 20 years ago. I do not complain about that. It is right that degrees in other than academic or theoretical subjects are now awarded. Young people are now able to use their great talents and skills to their own advantage and to the advantage of the nation, provided that their aptitude is developed at a sufficiently early age. It would be nice if Scottish people could be seen to be competing with and beating the best simply because they had attended a school where music, dance or drama had been part of the curriculum, due to a member of the staff having the skill to train young people with those aptitudes. The new clause could be used to prevent that from happening.

**Sir Russell Johnston:** Does the hon. Gentleman believe that specialist schools such as he has described could function in sparsely populated rural areas? I can see that happening in urban areas where young people would not have to travel long distances, but it could not happen in sparsely populated areas where general provision has to be made.

**Mr. Walker:** The hon. Gentleman, who has a background in education, ought to know that there have been remarkable developments in some of our rural area schools. Specialist skills are being exercised and used in my area. Local authority schools are encouraging youngsters, even though they live outside the normal catchment area, to travel to them, because they are able to offer specialist training. If a school is fortunate enough to have on its staff individuals, or an individual, with the special talent of being able to develop young people's ability in music, drama, or physical education, it is not surprising that parents encourage their children to travel to that school. In the hon. Gentleman's constituency, as in mine, many children have to travel long distances. Some of them have to live in hostels.

We spend a great deal of time talking about the problems of the inner cities, but we fail to understand the problems, challenges and opportunities that exist in rural schools. The schools in, say, Killiecrankie and the Bridge of Cally, where there is only one teacher, are good schools. Youngsters who are taught in one-teacher schools often excel because they receive tuition of a kind that is not available to youngsters in city schools. Even more important is the fact that they live in communities where learning and education are seen to be a way of improving one's lot and of getting out into the big world and doing things with one's life.

The teaching of Gaelic is growing. A number of schools specialise in the teaching of Gaelic and encourage young people to learn the language, but there is nothing mandatory about it; they learn it by choice. The new clause relates to self-governing schools. It does not relate to local authority schools. Why should schools and parents in my constituency, which covers 2,000 square miles of rural Scotland, be deprived of opportunities simply because at one time the parents and the school board decided that the school should become self-governing? Why should they be any different from secondary schools with vast catchment areas that have remained within local authority control? Why should a school not be able to accept and select pupils because it has become a self-governing school? That is my worry about new clause 2. I do not accept the hon. Gentleman's assessment of it. I believe that it would hit rural schools such as those in my constituency.

I shall use one group of schools as an example as they provide the best illustration. The schools at Blair Atholl and Killiecrankie feed into Pitlochry school and Breadalbane academy, as do many other schools. I have selected those two deliberately because of certain geographical matters. Pitlochry school only goes up to the fourth year so any children wishing to remain in school have to transfer to or begin their secondary education at Breadalbane academy. Breadalbane academy accommodates pupils in the school dormitories, but anyone who has looked at a map of Perthshire will know that it is not the easiest of journeys from Blair Atholl to Breadalbane. One has to go down the A9 and across country to Aberfeldy. The journey from Killiecrankie is just as difficult. Pupils from a number of other schools face fairly tortuous routes.

If Breadalbane academy decides to become a self-governing school, the parents and the school board decide to put forward that proposal and it receives the sanction of the Secretary of State, and if Breadalbane wants to continue to accept pupils to study Gaelic, although they are not from the catchment area, under new clause 2 it may not be able to do so, because it will have become a self-governing school.

**Sir Russell Johnston** *indicated dissent*.

**Mr. Walker:** The hon. Member for Inverness, Nairn and Lochaber shakes his head, but I believe that new clause 2 could have an impact on rural areas. I was impressed by what my hon. Friend the Minister said in earlier debates on the Bill. He drew attention to the fact that those of us representing rural areas would obviously be anxious that children living in the accepted catchment area for a secondary school in a rural area should not be excluded because that school has made a certain choice. My hon. Friend gave a clear assurance, which I am sure he will repeat tonight if necessary, that people will not be left with a lack of choice because of the geographical location of the secondary school. That would be unacceptable to all hon. Members who represent rural constituencies, but my hon. Friend has given his word and has reassured me.

That is not what bothers me about new clause 2. I do not believe that new clause 2 would remove that possibility, but I believe that if it were accepted, it would prevent such a school from accepting from outside its normal catchment area pupils who had aptitudes in the disciplines that I mentioned earlier.

**Sir Russell Johnston:** I understand the hon. Gentleman's argument. If one removed from the new clause the phrase:
"admission of pupils to the school"
the clause would state:
"A self-governing school shall not introduce general academic selection whereby the . . . rejection of pupils by the school is made by reference to levels of ability or aptitude."
I am not particularly interested in preventing pupils from entering a school; I do not want to exclude people because of general matters or to create a situation in which schools are not allowed to accept pupils because of their aptitude.

**Mr. Walker:** The new clause states:
"whereby the admission of pupils to the school or rejection of pupils by the school"—
there are two sides to the coin; I am dealing with the side that worries me—
"is made by reference to levels of ability of aptitude."
I thought that I said at the beginning of my remarks that if the clause is concerned only with academic ability the word "aptitude" is unnecessary. I may be wrong, but it is my judgment that the word "aptitude" embraces anything for which a child has an aptitude. That is why I drew attention to the special disciplines that have been developed in further education and the new degrees that are being offered.

**Mr. McAllion** *indicated dissent.*

**Mr. Walker:** The hon. Member for Dundee, East (Mr McAllion) shakes his head.

8.15 pm

**Mr. McAllion:** I am shaking my head because I cannot believe that the hon. Gentleman is so silly as not to understand the wording of the new clause. If the new clause read, "A self-governing school shall not admit pupils to the school by reference to levels of ability or aptitude," I would understand his argument. But the new clause states that a school
"shall not introduce general academic selection".
That is all the new clause prohibits, so we have wasted about 15 minutes listening to a lot of nonsense about nothing.

**Mr. Walker:** I advise the hon. Gentleman to leave the Chamber and look up the words "general", "academic" and "selection" in the *Oxford English Dictionary*. When he has done so he should come back here and tell me whether I am talking nonsense. The hon. Gentleman should remember that, if the new clause were accepted, it would be on the statute book and it would be judged in terms of law considering what each of those words means separately and collectively. The hon. Gentleman may believe something quite different, but that is what would happen if the new clause became a matter of dispute. We have to consider that when we debate new clause 2.

I understood the argument of the hon. Member for Fife, Central (Mr. McLeish). I doubt whether the way in which the new clause is phrased will produce what he intended. I understood that he objected to any overall assessment such as the 11-plus. He is afraid that youngsters will be selected at a certain age. I believe that the present wording of his new clause will not achieve that. In my view, the important word is "aptitude". I recommend that the hon. Member for Dundee, East should also look up the word "aptitude".

**Mr. Sam Galbraith** (Strathkelvin and Bearsden): The hon. Gentleman seems to be complaining about the wording of the new clause. What does he think about the principle of the new clause?

**Mr. Walker:** I am not in favour of going back to the 11-plus or anything remotely like it, but that does not mean that I am not in favour of individuals with special talents being given the opportunity to attend schools that have facilities for developing those talents. I believe that that would be a sensible use of education. It is happening now in the comprehensive system and I make no complaint about that. It is wise and sensible. Not every school can offer specialist teachers with skills to develop youngsters in particular disciplines. Not every school, and certainly not every rural secondary school, can do so, but some schools today offer specialist skills. Youngsters in my constituency travel fairly long distances to schools that offer specialist disciplines and skills.

That is happening under the existing system of comprehensive education, and it has nothing to do with what the hon. Gentleman and his hon. Friends say. I understand their concern, but the new clause does not achieve what they want to achieve. If it is accepted, it could frustrate schools that are presently able to offer specialist skills under the comprehensive regime. They would be frustrated by the new clause if they were to become self governing. I would have hardly thought that any hon. Member would wish children from within or outwith a catchment area to be excluded because they have an aptitude.

The hon. Member for Fife, Central said that, under the present system, schools can be made selective if the local education authority so wishes—that provision is on the statute book—but they do not do so because the local education authority does not wish it and, thus far, the schools have made no such bids.

All that the Bill does is give self-governing schools the same opportunity as exists for local education authorities. Local education authorities are the final arbiters of these matters. If a local authority decides to make a school selective, the decision must be referred to the Secretary of State. A self-governing school cannot come into being unless the Secretary of State approves. That also is a fundamental change. Both fundamental changes are optional; they are not mandatory. There is no requirement for the education authority, the school board or the parents to decide that a school should become self-governing. No one will force them to do that. However, they have an option and a back-up, with the Secretary of State making the final decision. The case put by the hon. Member for Fife, Central is weakest on that point. Education authorities have had those powers, but they have chosen not to use them. If he is right and there is no demand, there will be no self-governing schools because the option will not be exercised.

**Mr. McLeish:** Is the hon. Gentleman aware that certain education authorities have the power to introduce selection on the basis of academic ability? However, over some years, that practice has fallen into disuse and it is unlikely that it will ever be used again. In relation to self-governing schools, there need have been no reference to student ability. Selection has rightly been removed from

[*Mr. McLeish*]

Scottish education, and the possibility of its returning is advanced by clause 16 and the reference to entry on the basis of ability or aptitude.

**Mr. Walker:** I do not accept the hon. Gentleman's argument, which he has repeated throughout the passage of the Bill, that there is no demand for self-governing schools in Scotland, that there will be no self-governing schools and that, with the passage of time, they will fall into the same category of selection; local education authorities have not exercised their choice, and selection has fallen into disuse. If I am right, there will be some, but not many, self-governing schools, and my local education authority will respond with an understanding of the needs of rural schools.

I have made my case in support of the Bill, and my objection to the new clause is based on what I regard as the likely impact on rural schools in my constituency. Those schools will receive from the local education authority much more sympathetic understanding and treatment of the kind that the parents want for their children. The Bill has already brought about changes in Strathclyde. When it becomes an Act, the Tayside region will be much more responsive and receptive and less oriented to Dundee's many needs. There will be more understanding of the quality of teaching staff in rural areas.

The quality of life is one reason why teachers opt to live in rural areas. We often get good teachers in rural areas —it is true also of doctors and lawyers—and that is why we have high-calibre schools. However, they sometimes feel that the education authority does not fully understand their motivation and why people live in rural areas. The quality of life is probably the most important aspect in their decision to do so.

It is important that, when we examine the Bill and consider what will happen, we should not be dominated by the needs and problems of Scotland's great cities. The Bill, like all the others that pass through this place, will affect rural areas. As my right hon. and hon. Friends have said, those areas must feel that their needs are being satisfied.

I understand why the hon. Member for Moray (Mrs. Ewing) is not present. She has made it clear how she feels about rural schools. That is why my hon. Friend the Minister would be wrong to accept the new clause. Its effect would not be the kind of effect that the hon. Member for Banff and Buchan (Mr. Salmond) for the Democrats —[*Interruption.*] I always think of the hon. Gentleman as being what a Liberal Member of Parliament should be. It is rather sad that not all his colleagues emulate him. His comments are always courteous and generous. He would be an ideal Liberal Member. I do not doubt his concern for rural schools in his constituency, but we have different assessments of what new clause 2 will do. However, our fears are not dissimilar. That is why it is good that we have had this opportunity to put our views on record. For the reasons that I have given, I hope that the Minister will reject the new clause.

**Mr. Tom Clarke** (Monklands, West): I hope that the hon. Member for Tayside, North (Mr. Walker) will forgive me if I do not agree with everything that he said. I will deal with the problems of children with learning difficulties and children with special needs. I support the new clause. As it stands, the Bill does a great disservice to those children. I

have read the Committee debates in some detail, and I have been greatly impressed, as I was this evening, by the speech of my hon. Friend the Member for Fife, Central (Mr. McLeish).

The Government have failed to justify changes that they are attempting to introduce into the Scottish system. Comprehensive education is being turned aside, which means that the kind of elitism that the Scottish people have long since rejected is again being imposed on our educational system. That is bad for the majority of Scottish children, but it is particularly bad for children with special needs whose difficulties and circumstances the House will wish to take into account.

8.30 pm

I do not believe, and have never believed, that Scottish education for the majority of children has been the jewel in the crown of educational provision. Historically, prior to the introduction of comprehensive education, for a small minority it might have been said that we had a splendid system leading, for that small minority, to excellent achievement. But that was the realisation of Jean Brodie's creme de la creme and not of service to the majority of Scottish children.

**Mr. Bill Walker:** Does the hon. Gentleman accept that, in the 200 years before the turn of this century, when Scotland's schools were run substantially by school boards, Scottish education was the envy of the rest of Europe?

**Mr. Clarke:** No, I fear that, in line with my opening remarks, I cannot agree with the hon. Gentleman. I do not believe that for the majority of Scottish children our education system has been the envy of anywhere. Certainly it has not been the envy of those of us who want to see all our children realising their full potential.

I fear that, just as we are seeing an educational system in Scotland contrived so that we are not even having an increase in access to higher education for children from working-class backgrounds, so, once again, we are finding resources thinly spread, and indeed not being spread towards all our children, particularly those in special need.

Access extends to many spheres. My hon. Friends will support my desire to promote the interests of children with special needs, especially as this is Scottish mental handicap week, when voluntary organisations in Scotland such as Barnardo's and the Scottish Society for the Mentally Handicapped are arguing, in their posters and at exhibitions, that those children should be seen as part of our community and have access to good educational opportunities, good housing and a quality of life that has been denied to many of them.

Conservative Members argue about what can be achieved by selection, and it cannot be denied that we are having selection. They speak of children with special aptitudes—for example, children with a special desire to develop their musical talents and so on—and we agree that that is excellent and that provision should be made so that their aptitudes can be reflected in results.

But that type of provision should be widely shared. I have never understood why children who are good musicians should be sent away to special schools, whereas children who may not be so gifted are never able to hear them. Are they not entitled to access to good music, even to hear it, and should that not apply also to children with special needs? Sharing talents should not be in the background of educational provision, but if we have the type of elitism over selection of which we are talking, that is where we will be heading. That seems a particularly selfish approach.

On Second Reading, the Secretary of State, who I regret is temporarily not in his place, said:

"I can state categorically and without equivocation that the Bill is not designed to reintroduce selectivity; nor is it designed to do anything other than to add to the opportunities available to Scottish youngsters and their parents in the educational system."—[*Official Report,* 6 March 1989; Vol. 148, c. 625.]

If that is the intention, it is heavily disguised in the drafting of the Bill, and the proposed new clause would do much to redress the balance—perhaps I should say the imbalance—of provision that the measure will introduce.

With the kind of opting-out provisions that the Minister is recommending, it seems that those who will benefit least are children with special needs. Or are we to introduce elitism in that sphere, too? There was a time when it seemed that hon. Members on both sides of the House were aiming, not overnight but in due course, at integration for all our children. There was a time when I understood that it was felt that the education system and its comprehensive provisions might be made available to all.

I think I see the Parliamentary Under-Secretary looking askance as I make that statement. He knows that I welcome the fact that he has been to the Peto institute and that elsewhere in the Bill he is making provision for local authorities to make use of that service. Although my support for what he has done in that respect is unqualified, I must tell him bluntly that, if he believes in educational provision, he must ask himself why such a service is not being made available today in Scotland. If he goes ahead with opting out, he must ask why the children of whom I speak are being left behind. If all of this should be based on market considerations, he must be wondering whether the Peto institute should exist. Has not the Minister been trying to impose restrictions in Scottish education through his approach?

**Mr. Michael Forsyth:** Uncharacteristically, the hon. Gentleman is contradicting himself. If he is arguing that integration and a move away from special schools should be the way forward, the opportunity for the development of particular techniques and approaches, of which the Peto institute is one, would be diminished. The whole point about allowing for self-governing status in the special needs area is precisely to allow the development of a diversity of approach which the hon. Gentleman and I would probably favour.

**Mr. Clarke:** The Minister will find when he reads my speech that I have been consistent. I am arguing that in the kind of society in which we believe, the time will come when it will not be necessary—although I accept that it is necessary now—for our children to go to Hungary for that type of provision, because it will be available here. Nor will it be necesssary for children to go to schools which have opted out, because our mainstream educational system will be comprehensive enough to respond to their needs and demands.

**Mr. Forsyth:** Yesterday I visited a special school and a number of parents told me that already some education authorities are saying that the powers which will be available to them will not be used by them because they do not believe that the type of provision at the Peto institute is appropriate. The point of allowing for self-governing status for special schools is that it means that it is not then up to one education authority or to one education authority's committee to decide what will be the form of specialist provision; there is an allowance for diversity which follows parental preference.

The hon. Gentleman and I share, on this narrow issue, much in common in terms of our views of the direction in which we should be going. I caution him against going too far down that road, because there are some who are dogmatic about what is right in special needs provision. This provision enables diversity of approach to be retained.

**Mr. Clarke:** I am always prepared to listen carefully to the Minister. He worries about people being dogmatic. I am not sure whether he is the right person to give that sort of lecture, especially in the context of the Bill. Like him, I meet many parents of children with learning difficulties in the special educational sphere. I find even less enthusiasm among those parents for the principle of opting out than among parents of children in mainstream education. I look forward with interest to the development of that debate.

In conclusion, my hon. Friends have established that the Government's departure not just from the principle of comprehensive education, which has already been shown to be successful, but towards, as they see it, embracing elitist education by introducing the principle of opting out, has clearly been rejected by the vast majority of parents in Scotland. The Government are doing a disservice not just to educational traditions—I have already made it clear that I do not believe that those traditions were necessarily in the best interests of all Scottish children—but to children with special needs.

I am not saying that the Government are introducing a Dickensian approach—others might do so, but I am trying to be fair even to the Minister. However, their views are already outdated and are recognised as such by the people of Scotland. What I do say, as Charles Dickens said, is:

"In the little world in which children have their existence, whomsoever brings them up, there is nothing so finely perceived or so finely felt as injustice."

The Bill represents an injustice to the majority of Scotland's children, and especially to those with special needs. For that reason, I support the new clause.

**Mr. Michael Brown:** I listened carefully to the concluding remarks of the hon. Member for Monklands, West (Mr. Clarke), in which he gave the game away. He implied that there will be tremendous parental demand to take advantage of the provisions of the Bill. The logic of the new clause is fundamentally flawed, because it clearly implies that there will be such an overwhelming parental demand to take advantage of the self-governing provisions that it is necessary to circumscribe them and to put restrictions into the Bill at every twist and turn. Those of us who served on the Standing Committee got used to such classic restrictions as this.

Indeed, we come right back to where we started, with the Gainsborough question, which was posed early in our Committee proceedings by my hon. Friend the Member for Gainsborough and Horncastle (Mr. Leigh). My hon. Friend the Minister consistently asked Opposition Members, whenever they made the sort of speeches that they did—I accept, for the best of intentions and reasons—what they were seeking to do. Throughout all the

[*Mr. Michael Brown*]

speeches tonight and all those made in the Standing Committee, Opposition Members have given the game away. Although they know that there will be tremendous parental demand for these provisions they are trying to argue—they have done so tonight—that parents in Scotland will make no such demands. All the amendments and the new clauses—especially new clause 2—make it clear that the Opposition are terrified that there will be considerable demand for these provisions.

I shall dwell first on the way in which I read the Bill and then, as on many previous occasions during the Bill's passage—I shall deal—[*Interruption.*] Does the hon. Member for Glasgow, Garscadden (Mr. Dewar) wish to intervene? He now has the opportunity of challenging directly "the most obnoxious hon. Member in the House" —to use his description. That is what he said about how I conducted myself in Committee. I hope that you Mr. Deputy Speaker, agree that I am taking this new clause seriously. I am speaking tonight in exactly the same way as I spoke in Standing Committee. I found it offensive for the hon. Member for Garscadden to say the things that he did during the guillotine debate about the way in which I conducted myself in Standing Committee. I took the trouble to turn up for virtually every sitting and to take all the debates seriously, whereas he dropped in for only an hour or two on one day of our two or three month-long Committee.

8.45 pm

**Mr. Gerald Howarth** (Cannock and Burntwood): Does my hon. Friend agree that that was born of frustration on the part of the hon. Member for Glasgow, Garscadden (Mr. Dewar)? The hon. Gentleman had completely miscalculated. He had failed to take the lead for the Opposition and had to see my hon. Friend the Minister and the other Conservative Members make complete mincemeat of the Opposition with a measure that will utlimately be very popular with parents in Scotland.

**Mr. Brown:** My hon. Friend is absolutely right. I wonder what, if anything, we shall hear from the hon. Member for Garscadden if he should seek to catch your eye, Mr. Deputy Speaker, later on.

I return to the way in which I interpret the Bill. I shall restate the important point made by my hon. Friend the Minister in Standing Committee at 11.15 pm on 18 April —it is well worth restating—to which the hon. Member for Fife, Central (Mr. McLeish) has referred. The Bill itself introduces two hurdles for self-governing schools and their admissions policy, which do not exist under local education authorities in England, Wales and Scotland at the moment. It is possible for selection to be introduced in local authority schools on the vote of the local education authority committee. I should know because I live about eight miles from the border between—[*Interruption.*] Perhaps Opposition Members will be courteous enough to allow me to finish my sentence. We have heard about obnoxious Conservative Members, and Opposition Members should now allow Conservative Members simply to finish their sentences.

I live just eight miles from the border between Humberside and Lincolnshire. The county of Lincolnshire has a selection policy. Children there can go to grammar or secondary modern schools and take the 11-plus examination. Parents with jobs in my constituency often choose to live the other side of the county boundary so that their children are educated by the Lincolnshire education authority rather than the Humberside education authority. As the House may be aware, a proposal is currently before the Boundary Commission that south Humberside should go into Lincolnshire. I know that many of my constituents will look forward to the opportunities provided by the Lincolnshire education authority.

**Mr. Salmond:** Does the hon. Gentleman accept that other factors might be involved in this mass exodus over the border? Those people might be running away from their Member of Parliament.

**Mr. Brown:** If any are running away, they are certainly not my supporters, because at three successive general elections since 1979 my majority has increased from three figures, to four figures, to five figures. If people are running away, they are not Conservative supporters. Perhaps my political opponents have given up the ghost and are clearing off elsewhere.

To return to the main provisions of the Bill, we need to take the new clause seriously although its logic is fundamentally flawed. The Bill does not alter the current position. All that it does is place two hurdles in the way of self-governing schools which, as I have already said, do not apply to education authority schools. One is the parental ballot and the other is the approval of the Secretary of State. No such hurdles are at present in the way of education authority schools in Scotland or, from my own experience, in England. Lincolnshire is the classic example. If Opposition Members are worried that selection might be introduced into the Scottish education system, they must believe that the vast majority of parents are waiting for self-governing status. Therefore, the wishes of Opposition Members are already protected.

Perhaps I may bring to bear the experience of England. One advantage of having English Members on the Standing Committee was that we already have the Education Reform Act 1988 on the statute book for England; it is not dissimilar to the legislation that I hope will shortly be on the statute book for Scotland. We have had experience of the debate that is taking place in England. As English Members of Parliament, we have been following closely the way in which parents have been taking advantage of the provisions of the Education Reform Act.

I can tell the House of my local experience, for it was just down the road in the seaside resort adjoining the one that I represent, in the constituency of my hon. Friend the Member for East Lindsey (Sir P. Tapsell), that the parents of children at a school in Skegness voted overwhelmingly to take advantage of the provisions of the Education Reform Act. There is no evidence that the introduction of selection is the driving force behind a large number of cases south of the border where parents are voting with their feet very much in favour of self-governing status; in the majority of cases, it is happening where Labour education authorities are in control of education. I am sure that the position will be the same north of the border. We already have the example of Jordanhill school, which was referred to at great length by my hon. Friend the Minister and by a large number of hon. Gentlemen and hon. Ladies who served on the Standing Committee.

The Opposition have deliberately misinterpreted the Bill, which seeks to increase educational opportunity and to raise the standards of education. Parents want their children to go to schools that get results.

**Mr. McLeish:** In Scotland, most children are exposed to education where standards are high, and the standard of education is improving. Standards measured against any other criteria are also improving. What, then, is the problem?

**Mr. Brown:** That is the complacency that we have come to expect of the hon. Gentleman. I remember reading an article by him just before we started our proceedings in Standing Committee. I think that it is worthy of repetition. We were told that what was good enough for Henry McLeish's children was good enough for everybody else. That has been the position taken by the hon. Gentleman from the time that he wrote that article all the way through the proceedings in Committee.

On that basis, I might say that what is good enough for Michael Brown is good enough for everybody else. I failed my 11-plus. I went to a secondary modern school from the age of 11 to the age of 18, but I did not fail my A-levels. I got good grades through the teachers who taught me in that school. I got grade A in English literature, grade B in economics and grade C in history. I accept that I may have failed the 11-plus because I was lazy and probably more concerned with cricket and football.

If I have a criticism of my right hon. Friend and hon. Friends the Ministers, it is that the Bill does not allow enough opportunity for school boards, parents and boards of management to consider their selection policy. It is already circumscribed, as the hon. Gentleman said when he quoted what the Secretary of State said on 6 March in the Second Reading debate in column 625. I believe that there is a case to be made for selection. If I have a small criticism of the Bill, it is that, because of the two hurdles, it circumscribes the opportunities for selection.

If there is a valid criticism of my hon. Friends, it is that once again they have been modest, reasonable and not at all extreme. Once again, as usual, my hon. Friend is the modest Minister. I suggest that there is a case for not making those hurdles as stiff as he and the Secretary of State have made them. I accept the general thesis on where the Government want to be. The Government want to ensure that parents can send their children to schools that get results. I cannot accept the complacent attitude that we have just heard from the hon. Member for Fife, Central. I thought that he gave the game away very effectively. He seemed to suggest that there was nothing wrong anywhere, that every child in Scotland was getting the education he deserved and that there was no room for improvement. I do not accept that. It is always dangerous when politicians sit back complacently, saying that everything is marvellous and there is no need for change.

If everything is marvellous, perhaps it is because of the 25 per cent. increase in expenditure in real terms by the Government on Scottish education in the last 10 years. If the hon. Gentleman thinks that everything in the garden is rosy, perhaps it is because of the tremendous resources that have been put into education. We cannot have it both ways. I am prepared to admit to the parents and children of Scotland, as I am prepared to admit to the parents and children of England, that, notwithstanding the massive increase in financial resources for the education system,

everything in the garden is not yet rosy, but I believe that the Education Reform Act in England and this Bill in Scotland will redress the position.

**Mr. Michael Forsyth:** Has my hon. Friend noticed that the complacency is made altogether worse when there is evidence of declining standards, as has become apparent from the assessment of achievement programme? The hon. Member for Fife, Central (Mr. McLeish) has joined the somewhat irresponsible forces who argue that the evidence is suspect. They adopt a policy of shooting the messenger when they do not like the message.

**Mr. Brown:** My hon. Friend is right. It is worth drawing to the attention of the House some words of the Minister in Committee. In regard to Scottish education he said that the position was like a school report—"Could do better". That is the right and healthy attitude that a Scottish Education Minister should take. It is a credit to my hon. Friend and to the Scottish Office that they recognise that, notwithstanding the massive resources that have been put into Scottish education, there comes a point when money alone does not solve the problem, and we have to raise the standards of education in Scotland.

The purpose of the Bill is to do precisely that. I believe that the new clause would weaken the Bill, which is what the Opposition want to do. They do not want to see the improvements that the Government envisage as a result of the Bill. They want to wreck the Bill, and that is why they have put down such amendments.

As I promised, I shall give way to the hon. Member for Monklands, West (Mr. Clarke).

**Mr. Tom Clarke:** The hon. Gentleman has covered the point.

9 pm

**Mr. Brown:** I am glad to have one satisfied customer from the Opposition.

This may be the last opportunity that I may have to participate in the proceedings on the Bill.

**Mr. McAllion:** I fervently hope so.

**Mr. Brown:** The hon. Gentleman says that he hopes that that is the case. I know that the Opposition have had a rough ride with regard to the English Members serving on the Committee. The Labour party—or it might have been the Scottish National party——

**Mr. Salmond:** Be precise.

**Mr. Brown:** I cannot remember. As far as I am concerned, they are all Socialists—they are all the same.

One or other of the Opposition parties serving on the Committee issued a press release, even before the first sitting, saying what a disgrace it was that there were English Members serving on the Standing Committee. After the first sitting of the Standing Committee, all they did was sit there mute doing their constituency correspondence. From day one they got their comeuppance, because we have considered the proceedings on the Bill responsibly and seriously and we have read up— [*Interruption.*] The problem for Opposition Members is that we have read too many of their articles. We have drawn too much public attention to some of the things that they have said. We have obtained speeches that have been made one day and press releases issued the next day, and we have drawn attention to the inconsistencies.

**Mr. Allan Stewart:** Does my right hon. Friend also agree that we were rather more aware of the views of Councillor Charles Gray than were members of the Opposition?

**Mr. Brown:** That is right. I was upbraided by an hon. Member opposite when I referred incorrectly to councillor Charles Gray as Sir Charles Gray, the chairman of the Strathclyde education committee. I went straight to *The Times* last Saturday to see whether Councillor Gray had been made a knight, because I believed that he should be knighted for his services to Scottish education. In the past few months, Councillor Gray and my hon. Friend the Scottish Education Minister have done a great deal for Scottish education. We are right to pay tribute to the work of Councillor Gray, who I hope will be a "sir" in the not too distant future. They have done a great deal of practical work to raise the standards of education.

I have a shrewd suspicion that the one local councillor who will be waiting with bated breath for the royal assent to the Bill will be Councillor Charles Gray. From some of the statements he has already made, it appears that he actually regrets that the Bill is not yet on the statute book. If he were a Member of the House, he would not be supporting the new clause, because he wants to be where my hon. Friend the Minister is, but he wants to be there a little earlier. Some of the speeches we have heard of Councillor Gray in the press reports during the Committee stage of the Bill indicate that he cannot wait for the Bill to be enacted. We owe it to Councillor Gray—I hope that in the new year's honours list in 1990 he will be Sir Charles —to reject the new clause and to get the Bill on to the statute book as quickly as possible.

**Mr. McAllion:** It was obvious that the hon. Member for Brigg and Cleethorpes (Mr. Brown) had not read the new clause, because he made virtually no reference to it in 20 minutes of drivel similar to that which we heard from him in Committee. At one point the Minister intervened and said that people who did not like the message blamed the messenger. Of course, if anyone is guilty of that sentiment, it is the Minister and his friends in the Scottish Office, because, if they could not get the message last Thursday at the ballot box in Scotland about this Bill and the plans for the National Health Service, they will never get the message.

**Mr. Tom Clarke:** Does my hon. Friend agree that the hon. Member for Brigg and Cleethorpes (Mr. Brown) failed to recognise that the Scottish people liked neither the message nor the messenger?

**Mr. McAllion:** That is precisely the point to which I was coming. The Minister traipses around Scotland speaking to anyone who will listen to him from the media. He says that the doctors and the teachers do not understand the message. However, they understand the message and the messenger, which is why the majority of Scots are represented by Opposition parties.

**Mr. Allan Stewart:** On the swing last Thursday, the Scottish National party would regain Dundee.

**Mr. McAllion:** If the SNP regains Dundee, there will not have been a swing to the Left, which is what the hon. Member for Glasgow, Govan (Mr. Sillars) claimed in Glasgow, Central. If there is a swing to the Left, Labour will hold Dundee easily in the next election.

**Mrs. Fyfe:** Does my hon. Friend agree that it is unwise for Conservative Members to refer to Glasgow, Central considering the pathetic result the Conservative party achieved?

**Mr. McAllion:** That is true. The Tories obviously believe that saving deposits in elections in Scotland constitutes a good performance. It shows the depths to which they have sunk.

The hon. Member for Brigg and Cleethorpes said that one of the advantages of English Members taking part in discussions on the Bill was that they were able to relate their experiences of English education legislation and inform other hon. Members who do not represent English constituencies. There is an element of truth in that, as long as the English Members tell us the truth about the English experience. The hon. Member for Brigg and Cleethorpes talked about the grades he received in school but he did not receive a grade A in truth. He talked about Lincolnshire education authority being a classic example of how an authority provides choice for parents and encourages pupils to come into its area. However, he did not tell us about South Park high school in Lincoln in which 97 per cent. of parents voted in favour of self-governing status in an 88 per cent. turnout. The Secretary of State for Education and Science refused to allow the school to opt out on that basis.

**Mr. McFall:** Does my hon. Friend agree that our objection to English Members is that they know nothing about Scottish education? The hon. Member for Brigg and Cleethorpes (Mr. Brown) mentioned Charles Gray but he did not know whether he had been knighted or not. The hon. Gentleman knew nothing about the issue of the old qualifying examination in Scotland. The English Members were chosen for their ignorance of Scottish education. Many of them knew more about and had more sympathy with South Africa than they did about Scottish education.

**Mr. McAllion:** That is a fair point.

The Secretary of State for Education and Science refused to allow the school in Lincolnshire to opt out because he said:

"I must be satisfied that the school is likely to succeed." In Committee the Minister said:

"We want only good candidates for self-governing status, not lame ducks. We want those schools to be the ones that succeed."—[*Official Report, First Scottish Standing Committee*, 11 April 1989; c. 478.]

If we break through the code in which Tories speak, that means that schools in working-class areas that are full of working-class kids will not have an opportunity to opt out. The Bill is not about giving parents greater choice but about allowing a small elite to opt out into grammar-type schools. That is why the Secretary of State is picking and choosing the schools that can opt out. That is what the Secretary of State for Education and Science and the Minister want and that is why new clauses such as this are essential.

**Mr. Michael Forsyth:** Does the hon. Gentleman not think that he has a cheek to express such an argument when, in Committee, he argued that the Bill ought to be amended, as it was today, to allow for proper consultation with the education authority so that the decision is not taken solely by parents but that the Secretary of State will have other arguments and considerations to take into account? The hon. Gentleman is now condemning my right hon. Friend the Secretary of State for Education and Science because he has taken other factors into account. The hon. Gentleman cannot have it both ways. He simply chooses whatever argument seems most effective to knock the Government. That is why he and his colleagues got into such a mess in Committee.

**Mr. McAllion:** The Minister has made a weak intervention. The only person who decides whether a school may opt out is the Secretary of State. Others may be consulted but Scotland has had 10 years of being consulted by Secretaries of State who represent the Tory Government. They might listen but they do not act upon what they hear. They simply go through the formality of consulting and that is why the ballot procedure is not properly democratic. It does not really matter how the parents vote, it does not matter what the education authority or what the parents of children in the feeder primary schools might say because, ultimately, the Secretary of State makes up his own mind. He wants to wreck the comprehensive system in Scotland and allow schools to opt out if he thinks that they can form the backbone of a new grammar type-school so that such a provision can be put in place across Scotland. That is what the Bill is about. The Minister is not kidding anyone that the Bill is about increasing choice or allowing people to make up their own minds.

It is important that the Minister gives a clear commitment that there will be no reintroduction of general academic selection to secondary schools. The Minister said that he has made the position clear, but nothing could be further from the truth. He has avoided giving anything like the commitment given by the Secretary of State for Scotland on Second Reading, when he categorically rejected the reintroduction of selectivity.

The Minister was pressed time and again in Committee, and again today, to give that commitment, but he refused. He said that the Government had recognised special needs such as dance, music, Gaelic and the classics. He went all round the houses, but he would not give a commitment that there would be no reintroduction of general academic selection. Several Conservative Members suggested that the Minister had given a clear assurance in Committee that no rural schools would be allowed to reintroduce general academic selection that would keep out any children. The Minister did not give any such commitment for urban schools such as those in Dundee, Aberdeen, Glasgow and Edinburgh. Until he gives such a commitment, there will be a deep suspicion that that is what the Bill is all about, no matter what he says.

The hon. Member for Hexham (Mr. Amos) made an honest contribution to our debates in Committee. He was quite open about wanting the reintroduction of general academic selection. He said that he wanted the return of grammar schools in Scotland, in the way that they are now returning in England and Wales. The Minister congratulated his hon. Friend on his effective speech, which he said he appreciated. He surely cannot say that he appreciates his hon. Friend's call for the return of grammar schools and at the same time pretend that the Government will not allow that to happen in Scotland. Either the Minister supports his hon. Friend or he does not. He certainly gave the impression of supporting his hon. Friend in Committee.

The Minister used to belong to the No Turning Back group of Conservative Members, a number of whom are present tonight. That group produced an education pamphlet that clearly attacked the comprehensive system and local authority schools and called for the reintroduction of grammar schools. The hon. Gentleman was not a Minister when he put his name to the pamphlet in 1986. He was careful to withdraw his name when he became a Minister, but he has never taken the opportunity to reject the pamphlet's proposals. I suspect that he still stands by them and awaits the opportunity to bring them into force. The Minister is nodding, so I assume that he intends to reintroduce academic selection.

On 18 April the Minister cited an example from the independent sector, and said:

"Let us consider the variety of schools in the independent sector. Some place a greater emphasis on academic achievement while others emphasise the expressive arts, sport and so on. Parents choose the schools which they believe will be most suited to their children. We wish to see that sort of diversity and choice in the state system and the Bill will deliver that."—[*Official Report, First Scottish Standing Committee,* 18 April 1987; c. 782.]

There are certainly schools in the independent sector that concentrate on academic excellence, but they use selection by academic ability to admit pupils. The Minister was basically saying that he would replicate that system in the state sector. He is all over the place. He will not assure the House that he is opposed to the reintroduction of grammar schools—or senior secondary schools as they are called in Scotland.

The uncertainty and ambiguity of the Minister's answers were reflected even in his description of the way in which a school that opts out will maintain its characteristics. The Minister explained that the school board would have to set out the proposed admissions policy if it was granted self-governing status. Within that policy, it would have to stress any special emphasis which it wanted to characterise the provision of education in the school. Once it had secured a majority in the ballot and gained the approval of the Secretary of State for Scotland, the description of the admissions policy was a binding obligation on the board of management taking over the running of the school. As the Minister said, that would be a guarantee to parents of what the school would be like in future. That is fine, and everyone would support that idea. However, the Minister then, through clause 28, creates the mechanism by which that binding guarantee can be ripped up by the parents if they achieve a simple majority in a ballot.

9.15 pm

The binding agreement to ensure that the school stayed within the characteristics of its proposed admissions policy would be thrown out the window as soon as the board had the simple majority and the Secretary of State's approval to change the characteristic. The Minister said that that would be a significant change which would be of considerable importance to parents, neighbourhood schools and education authorities. That very important change is made possible in clauses 16 and 28. The Minister has studiously avoided any opportunity of saying that the Secretary of State will not allow anyone to use the mechanism to reintroduce general academic selection when a school opts out.

The hon. Member for Brigg and Cleethorpes referred to hurdles. The Secretary of State's permission is certainly

[*Mr. McAllion*]

not a hurdle. At the moment, a Tory Secretary of State for Scotland would be keen to allow any break-up of the comprehensive system.

The Minister has been very careful to restrict the people who are allowed to take part in the ballot of parents. He suggested in Committee that the parents of children in feeder primaries should be given the right to vote, but that was knocked on the head by the Tory majority on the Committee because they wanted to restrict the ballot only to parents who had children at the school. It was suggested that staff should be allowed to participate in the ballot. However, that was also knocked on the head. They will be forcibly transferred from one employer to another. They will have no chance to vote in the ballot. An amendment earlier today would have given adult users of a school the right to take part in a ballot, but the Minister made sure that that amendment was not passed.

The purpose behind all this is to keep the ballot to an absolute minimum. That will create a community of people who might be tempted into voting for something on the basis that they might get something out of it at the expense of the local authority. If the number of people allowed to vote is small enough, they have a good chance of winning.

The hon. Member for Tayside, North (Mr. Walker) made a disgraceful intervention earlier today. He deliberately filibustered on an important amendment which prevented a vote being taken on it. That amendment would have required a two-thirds majority. The Government were careful to ensure that only a simple majority is required to change the characteristics of the school.

**Mr. Bill Walker:** It appears that the term "filibuster" now has a new meaning. A speech lasting less than five minutes is now a filibuster, even when that speech includes a number of lengthy interventions. When the hon. Member for Dundee, East (Mr. McAllion) reads *Hansard,* he will hardly be able to substantiate his charge. I stated very clearly why I supported my colleagues on the Government Front Bench and why I was against the proposal for a two thirds majority. I thought that the debate was very serious and that it was discussed fully and seriously. My constituents will understand why I took that position. It had nothing to do with filibustering.

**Mr. McAllion:** If the hon. Gentleman visits the Library and consults the *Oxford English Dictionary,* he will see that filibustering does not necessarily mean talking for a long time. The hon. Gentleman knew that if he did not stop speaking before 6.30 pm, a vote on the amendment for a two-thirds majority would not be taken. He also was aware that he had made his points very clearly and was talking for no purpose other than to ensure that the vote was not taken. The Government Whip whispered to him and told him to ensure that the amendment was not reached so that the Government could secure the idea that the majority required in the ballots could involve fewer than half the parents voting in favour. The Secretary of State for Scotland agreed with that.

If the hon. Member for Tayside, North doubts that, he should consider what happened last week in England. In a school to which the Minister referred, 56 per cent. of parents voted for opting out and the Secretary of State for Education and Science allowed them to do that. What the Minister did not tell anyone was that the 56 per cent. of parents who voted were a minority of those who were entitled to vote. Therefore, that school was allowed to opt out of education authority control without gaining the support of even half the parents or children at that school for such a move. That is why the Opposition are opposed to the idea. The ballot is simply a hurdle that the Government can manipulate in order to make sure that they get their friends over. If the Secretary of State can achieve that, he will.

**Mr. Allan Stewart:** The hon. Gentleman should withdraw his allegation against my hon. Friend the Member for Tayside, North (Mr. Walker). If he had sat down before half-past six, I would have made my contribution.

**Mr. McAllion:** I saw the Government Whip whisper to the hon. Member for Tayside, North and then go round and whisper into the ear of the hon. Member for Eastwood (Mr. Stewart) to make sure that, if the hon. Member for Tayside, North sat down early, the hon. Member for Eastwood would speak. Both hon. Members took part in a Government ploy and it is a disgrace that hon. Members should be prevented from voting on such an important issue.

**Mr. Bill Walker:** Does the hon. Gentleman realise that he has just referred to decisions made with a two-thirds majority. He and I know that he was elected on considerably less than a 50 per cent. simple majority. But no one disputes—I do not—that he represents Dundee, East, and he does so most effectively. I hope that he continues to do so, but not if he continues to criticise the vote at the school to which he referred and the turnout there.

**Mr. McAllion:** Again, the hon. Gentleman is wrong. The right hon. Member for Kincardine and Deeside (Mr. Buchanan-Smith) dealt clearly with that problem. We are talking about a major institutional change whereby a school is taken out of the education authority's control and given direct funding under the Secretary of State for Scotland. The next step along may be the private sector. Such a decision cannot be taken lightly on the basis of a simple majority. No one would argue that such a decision should be made on a two-thirds majority. A Member of Parliament can be voted out at a general election, but once a school is taken out of the education authority sector it is not easy to return it. The Secretary of State for Scotland makes the decision, and if he says no, nothing can be done about it. Therefore, the hon. Gentleman is drawing a parallel that is wrong and makes no sense.

I know exactly what the Minister is about. He is about wrecking the comprehensive system in Scotland—breaking up education authority schools. In Committee, I remember him describing the introduction of comprehensive education between 1969 and 1974. He said that it was the most fundamental change in the history of Scottish education up to that time and that it had been brought about by the Labour party. The problem is that the Minister and his friends have never accepted that fundamental change and have worked all their lives to reverse it. They started to do it with the School Boards (Scotland) Act 1988 and now they are moving on to the Self-Governing Schools etc. (Scotland) Bill.

**Mr. Leigh:** So what?

**Mr. McAllion:** I will tell the hon. Gentleman so what. Conservative Members should not give us the nonsense that this is all about parental choice. It is about destroying comprehensive education. It is the only thing that it has ever been about and that is why we are here tonight. If the Minister says that it is not about that he must accept the new clause that has been tabled in the name of my hon. Friends. If he does not, he does not have the same candour and honesty as the Secretary of State for Scotland, who at least says what he thinks. He says that he will not allow general selectivity to be reintroduced. The Minister will not allow those words to come out of his mouth and that is why the new clause is important.

**Mr. Gerald Howarth:** The hon. Member for Dundee, East (Mr. McAllion) performed a service in Committee and has also done so on the Floor of the House. Yet again, he has drawn attention to the excellent work of the No Turning Back group, of which I am a member. We enjoyed that contribution of the hon. Gentleman and his earlier contributions to the formulation of English law when he dashed down the Committee Corridor to vote on some English matter. He has certainly played his part in our proceedings.

My hon. Friend the Member for Brigg and Cleethorpes (Mr. Brown) ably pointed out that the Opposition's fears about selectivity were unfounded and that the Bill would open up the positive aspects of selectivity. My hon. Friend was right to reiterate the points made by my hon. Friend the Minister in Committee when, in response to the hon. Member for Dumbarton (Mr. McFall), he stated:

"Nothing can prevent any education authority having a selective intake in any of its schools . . . The Bill does not alter the current position. All it does is to put two hurdles in the way of self-governing schools which do not apply to education authority schools. One is the parental ballot and the other is the approval of the Secretary of State . . . It is possible for selection to be introduced into local authority schools on the vote of the education committee. It will not be possible for selectivity to be introduced into self-governing schools on the vote of the board of management. That is the fundamental difference. It will be much harder to introduce selection into a self-governing school than into a local authority school."—[*Official Report, First Scottish Standing Committee,* 18 April 1989; c. 791-92.]

That makes the position clear.

I understand the concerns of my right hon. Friend the Member for Kincardine and Deeside (Mr. Buchanan-Smith) in respect of local authority schools in rural areas. My hon. Friend the Member for Tayside, North (Mr. Walker) also raised that matter. However, I cannot believe that in a ballot parents will exclude children for whom there is no alternative provision. I am sure that that would not be their wish.

If Opposition Members are correct in saying that schools will not want to become self-governing, my right hon. Friend has no cause for concern. His point is well taken, but he overlooks the Bill's general purpose and why parents are likely to vote for self-governing status. I cannot believe that parents would vote to exclude a minority or even a large number of pupils because they fail to meet the criteria of academic ability, as that would defeat the whole purpose of the Bill. If parents vote for self-government, it will not be to exclude less bright children but to create the ethos they want and which they feel the local education authority has not provided. That is genuine parental choice, and that is what the Bill is all about.

We believe that the Bill will provide parents with greater opportunities to have an input into the type of school that their children attend. It is not true to say that, where schools in England and Wales have voted to opt out, that has provided an opportunity for selectivity. The real reason is best illustrated by the example of Baverstock school in the Maypole area of Birmingham, where the headmaster said:

"Out here, people thought that they had been abandoned"—

and when not abandoned, meddled with. Parents at that school took the opportunity provided by the Government to be in charge of their own destiny. The introduction of selectivity did not enter into it.

That school acquired a bad reputation, suffered from it, and became unpopular. Under the new headmaster and his team, the school was turned around. One of their innovations was to introduce a system whereby the staff are addressed as "Sir" or "Ma'am", uniform is compulsory, and every day begins with assembly. Such a regime was not offered by the local education authority but was wanted by the parents. They voted for self-governing status for that reason, not to introduce selectivity. They wanted to change and protect the ethos of the school in a way that the local education authority would not have permitted.

**Mr. Leigh:** The point must be made that it is not just a matter of pumping more resources into schools. It is also a question of changing their ethos. When schools become self-governing, they may not necessarily be given more resources, but their ethos will alter.

**Mr. Howarth:** That is true. Opposition Members underestimate the desire of parents to bring back some of the old-fashioned virtues and notions in schools where they have been almost driven out.

9.30 pm

**Mr. George Foulkes** (Carrick, Cumnock and Doon Valley): Bring back flogging!

**Mr. Howarth:** As one who was chastised with the cane at school, I can assure the hon. Gentleman that, although other things may have done me harm, that was not one of them. I was very conscious of the need to preserve the discipline of the school.

I know that my hon. Friend the Minister has been under considerable pressure to resist the idea that self-governing schools ought to be able to introduce an element of selectivity. I accept what was said by my right hon. Friend the Member for Kincardine and Deeside about the problems in rural areas, but in densely populated urban areas containing a number of schools, diversity of educational provision could be an advantage. *[Interruption.]* If the hon. Member for Carrick, Cumnock and Doon Valley (Mr. Foulkes) would keep quiet for a moment, he might learn something to his advantage.

**Mr. Foulkes:** I doubt that very much, on the evidence that we have had so far.

**Mr. Howarth:** The hon. Gentleman has had too good a dinner; that is the trouble. As a Douglas from the borders, I am used to hearing the speeches of well-refreshed members of my family from time to time.

It is wrong to suggest that parents now have unlimited choice, despite the parents' charter that the Government

[*Mr. Howarth*]

introduced in Scotland. Throughout the United Kingdom —Scotland is not the only victim—there is rationing by catchment area. As my hon. Friend the Member for Brigg and Cleethorpes pointed out, if people want to opt for the educational provision that exists in Lincolnshire, they must move house. People will often move to a particular area and buy a house there simply to be able to enter the catchment area of a certain school. It is wholly untrue that, in a great Socialist Valhalla, people have been provided with choice by benevolent Socialist councillors and their local education authorities.

I do not see why a school should not be able to set academic criteria when there are alternative schools. To deny that possibility is to imply that academic attainment is all that counts, which is not so. Today sporting ability can lead not only to a fulfilling career but to an extremely lucrative one, and the same applies to artistic and creative abilities. The new clause therefore strikes me as unnecessary.

I believe that, in some instances, academic selection could certainly be entertained by the Secretary of State. If Opposition Members fear that, they should bear it in mind that my right hon. and learned Friend has put it on the record categorically that he is against selection on the basis of academic ability. [*Interruption.*] He has said that; it was mentioned by the hon. Member for Monklands, West (Mr. Clarke).

**Mr. Foulkes** *rose*——

**Mr. Howarth:** I am not sure that I ought to give way to the hon. Gentleman, but as I am in a generous mood I will do so.

**Mr. Foulkes:** Does the hon. Gentleman not remember that the same Secretary of State made an absolute pledge that he would not introduce the provisions of this Bill? That shows how trustworthy his promises are.

**Mr. Howarth:** I do not believe that that is true.

**Mr. Foulkes:** It is true.

**Mr. Howarth:** If it were true, and my right hon. and learned Friend had changed his mind, he must be the most sensible of men, and I am sure that the people of Scotland will be even more grateful for his flexibility of mind.

The Opposition have completely failed to make a case for the amendment. The Bill provides hurdles to ensure that some of their worse fears are confounded. A very good case can be made for academic selection. The Bill does not destroy comprehensive education. Many people believe that a lot of our educational ills can be put down to Mrs. Shirley Williams who compulsorily made education comprehensive. However, this Bill is not the measure to change that.

**Mr. Salmond:** I do not know why the hon. Member for Tayside, North (Mr. Walker) and other hon. Members are in difficulties about the wording of the new clause. It is a model of clarity, if it is compared with many of the amendments and new clauses.

The phrase "general academic selection" is well understood. The hon. Member for Tayside, North agreed with the principle of the new clause but he said that he was worried about its wording. The Under-Secretary of State has it within his power to bring about an historic compromise between the hon. Member for Tayside, North and for Fife, Central (Mr. McLeish) by giving an assurance that he will introduce an appropriately worded amendment in the other place. Such an assurance would, I am sure, be received favourably by the hon. Member for Fife, Central. It would also show whether the Government are serious about not allowing selectivity to creep into Scottish education.

The hon. Members for Brigg and Cleethorpes (Mr. Brown) and for Cannock and Burntwood (Mr. Howarth) often say what the Minister is thinking about educational questions. Both of them, drawing on their exhaustive knowledge of the Scottish education system, have supported academic selection. I have always thought that it is invidious to compare education systems. However, it is appropriate to compare the education system with which the hon. Members for Brigg and Cleethorpes and for Cannock and Burntwood are familiar and the education system in Scotland.

The English system is fragmented. It is partly selective and substantially private. Its achievements should be compared with the Scottish comprehensive system. In Scotland, 21 per cent. of our children gain the necessary qualifications for higher education. In England and Wales, only 15 per cent. of children gain those qualifications. I do not claim that 21 per cent. in Scotland is a remarkable achievement. It should be substantially higher than that.

The hon. Members for Brigg and Cleethorpes and for Cannock and Burntwood have offered us some lessons that they say we in Scotland should learn. They have used the power of their votes in Scottish Standing Committees to push through amendments that they favour, but they should base their offer of the lessons that Scotland should learn on the experience of better international education systems rather than on the experience of an education system that is substantially worse, according to a number of criteria, than the Scottish one.

The right hon. Member for Kincardine and Deeside (Mr. Buchanan-Smith) referred to rural schools. I support his arguments. If selectivity were to be introduced in rural schools, pupils would have to be bussed substantial distances to other schools. The only alternative would be to establish in rural communities schools for pupils with lower attainments. Neither of those possibilities is attractive to any Scottish Member of Parliament who represents a rural constituency. There should be no exclusion on any grounds of a pupil from a rural community school. That view is strongly held by all Scottish Members of Parliament with rural constituencies.

Conservative Members have consistently argued that it would be simpler for an education authority in Scotland to adopt the selective approach than it would be for a school that had opted out and that was awaiting the Secretary of State's decision. There is a fairly substantial difference. Scottish education authorities are democratically elected. They represent, one hopes, the local communities within their area. The same certainly cannot be claimed for the Secretary of State for Scotland. His views of Scottish education are certainly not representative of the Scottish community. Earlier this evening, the Under-Secretary of State, the hon. Member for Stirling (Mr. Forsyth), said that he did not want an unrepresentative minority to grab control of a school in Scotland. The problem we face is that an unrepresentative minority has grabbed control, not of a single school but of the entire education system in Scotland. That was supported by the English battalions in Committee and in the House tonight.

The hon. Member for Dumbarton (Mr. McFall) suggested that the criterion for selecting English Members to serve on the Standing Committee was ignorance of the Scottish education system. I rather suspect that the criterion for selection was familiarity with the Minister responsible for Scottish education. It is clear from the interchange between the surviving members of the No Turning Back group—perhaps the Minister is still a member of such a group—that their purpose was to egg the Minister on to greater and more radical things. Unfortunately the greater and more radical things are not wanted by the vast majority of the Scottish community.

Finally, we are told that we must accept the assurances of the Secretary of State for Scotland. The right hon. Member for Kincardine and Deeside said that he would be prepared to accept such assurances, but I remember the right hon. Gentleman telling the House on a previous occasion that during the last general election he specifically inquired about the possibility of opting out being introduced into Scottish education and had received an assurance from Conservative central office that there were no such plans. That is the credibility of assurances from the Secretary of State and from the Government Front Bench. Had those assurances proved valid in the past, we should not be discussing this legislation this evening.

**Mr. Michael Forsyth:** We have had an interesting debate on new clause 2. Time and again, opponents of our proposals for self-governing schools return to their claim that giving parents the right to seek greater involvement in the running of schools will bring about the return of senior secondary schools, complete with a qualifying examination.

Those opponents claim to base their view on the existence of machinery in clause 28 designed to allow self-governing schools to respond flexibly to future developments by seeking to change their fundamental characteristics. By now they are well aware that any such change requires the support of parents voting in a ballot and the approval of the Secretary of State. The clause 28 machinery exists as a protection for the existing fundamental characteristics of a school that opts for self-governing status. We have deliberately made it difficult to alter those characteristics—more difficult than any parallel changes in an education authority school. It is interesting that the hon. Member for Banff and Buchan (Mr. Salmond) argues that the difference is that local authorities are more democratic. He appears to believe that a local authority education committee is more representative of the wishes of parents.

**Mr. Foulkes:** They are more representative than you are.

**Mr. Forsyth:** The hon. Gentleman has returned from his dinner and has not listened carefully to the arguments in the 15 minutes for which he has graced us with his presence.

The hon. Member for Banff and Buchan is seeking to argue that my right hon. and learned Friend the Secretary of State is not representative of the parents, but although the decision to alter the characteristics of a school is taken by the Secretary of State, it can come to the Secretary of State only when a majority of the parents have voted for it. The process is started by the parents. The hon. Gentleman is seeking to argue that the education authority committees are more representative of the wishes of parents than are the parents themselves.

If we accept the view that self-governing schools will lead to a return of selective schools, our opponents must believe that enough Scottish parents are sufficiently dissatisfied with the present system of secondary schools to support a return to selective schools. What evidence do they have for that? Why do they continue to make those claims? In any secondary school a fair number of parents will have other children still at primary school. They at least are unlikely to be strong supporters of bringing back fully selective entry.

In many parts of the country, a school that aimed to exclude large numbers by a selective entry test would simply find itself unable to attract sufficient pupils to remain viable, and any proposals under clause 28 require the consent of the Secretary of State. He will have regard to the viability of the particular school and any consequences for the wider provision of education for all pupils in the area. On Second Reading my right hon. and learned Friend made it quite clear that there was no question of a return to the selective secondary schools of the past.

My right hon. Friend the Member for Kincardine and Deeside (Mr. Buchanan-Smith) asked me to repeat the assurance that I gave in Committee that there would be no question of allowing selection in any community—rural or otherwise—where the effect would be that children were denied the opportunity of going to the only possible, practical school. I am happy to repeat the undertaking that I clearly gave in Committee.

9.45 pm

I am puzzled why the Opposition should be continually obsessed with that issue. In Committee I made it clear that one use of admission arrangements based on ability or aptitude could be in a school operating a specialist unit of one sort or another. The new clause carries the heading "general academic selection", with the suggestion, perhaps, that particular academic selection would be more acceptable.

In Committee, the hon. Member for Fife, Central (Mr. McLeish) initiated a debate on the concept of giftedness. In the view of Opposition Members, specific provision for giftedness might be seen as acceptable. We still do not know the hon. Gentleman's view on that matter. It appears that the selection of children based on a gift for music or dance is entirely virtuous. We have established that. However, selection for specialist facilities relating to ability in classics or minority foreign languages seems to be a more difficult subject for Opposition Members. They recognise that that might be the most effective and perhaps the only sensible means of making such provision, but such arrangements were clearly coming too close to the bogy of general academic selection. Certainly, any form of selection based on a particular gift with mathematics or mainstream languages was to be ruled out.

What are we to make of all of this? One clue is that Strathclyde regional council makes specialist provision for music at Douglas academy at Milngavie and for dance at Knightswood. By definition, those arrangements must be virtuous, and recognition of special ability in more academic subjects, however, is to be an absolutely no-go area.

[*Mr. Forsyth*]

The drafting of the new clause is less than certain. It is against academic selection in self-governing schools, but it appears to define academic selection by reference to any form of selection based on the ability and aptitude of pupils. I accept that Opposition Members do not intend to exclude the necessary judgments on specialist provision to be made for those with defined special educational needs. They probably did not intend to exclude selection for music or dance units, but the new clause certainly does that. Our view is that the Bill should not rule out such changes It should be open to schools to develop all sorts of specialist provision where they find it possible and valuable to do so. It is for parents in the first instance to vote on whether they consider proposals for such provision acceptable.

Diversity is one of the main themes of our proposals. This new clause is against diversity, and I ask the House to reject it.

**Mr. Galbraith:** The Minister was surprisingly brief in replying to the debate on the new clause.

**Mr. Forsyth:** To enable the hon. Gentleman to have time to respond.

**Mr. Galbraith:** I am grateful to the Minister for his consideration.

I noticed also that the Minister stuck closely to his brief. For example, he did not stray from it to agree with the comments of, for example, his hon. Friends the Members for Brigg and Cleethorpes (Mr. Brown) and for Cannock and Burntwood (Mr. Howarth). Perhaps he thought that, had he strayed from it, he might have let slip the true intentions of the Bill, rather than remaining constrained because of the present political realities in the country.

Although the Minister uttered words of reassurance to his hon. Friend the Member for Kincardine and Deeside (Mr. Buchanan-Smith) about rural schools, he did not reiterate the commitment given by the Secretary of State about not permitting this legislation to be used as a method of reintroducing selection into Scottish education. The Minister did not tonight give such an undertaking. I will resume my seat immediately if the hon. Gentleman wishes to rise to give that undertaking. He simply made a passing reference to the Secretary of State and said that there was no chance of returning to the selective education of the past.

That is a different undertaking from saying that schools which opt out will not be able to reintroduce selection. I accept that not many schools, if any, will opt out, but we want to know—as I say, I will allow him to intervene immediately if he wishes to reassure us—whether those schools will not be able to reintroduce selection of the type that we know we are discussing. I am not talking about a general provision for Scottish education but about the schools in question.

**Mr. Michael Forsyth:** My right hon. Friend gave a clear commitment on Second Reading. He is the Secretary of State. He declared the Government's policy. I support the Government's policy and the hon. Gentleman is wasting the time of the House by seeking to look at nuances of differences of view which do not exist.

**Mr. Galbraith:** The House will have noted that the Minister again failed to give the assurance for which I asked. We are bound to be suspicious when it comes to selection, particularly following the contributions of the hon. Members for Brigg and Cleethorpes, for Cannock and Burntwood and for Hexham (Mr. Amos), who is no longer in his place, in which they clearly said that in their view selection should be reintroduced into the Scottish education system and that that would be their intention if they had their way.

We are now discussing the crux of the Bill. We have so far tonight discussed some important technicalities of the measure, such as ballots, majorities and special needs education. We now discuss what we regard as the main problem, that of the reintroduction of selection into the Scottish education system, a system that got rid of selection many years ago.

We do not want that system reintroduced by the back door. In Committee there was much talk about the Government reintroducing such matters through the front or back doors. Our fear is that they wish to reintroduce selection through the back door. That is why we are totally opposed to the measure. The Minister spoke of hurdles, but they are not very high. Certainly any hurdles of which the Minister spoke would be extremely high if my hon. Friend the Member for Garscadden, (Mr. Dewar) were Secretary of State, as he will be soon.

**Mr. Michael Forsyth:** When the hon. Gentleman says that the hurdles are not very high, he should remember that the first hurdle is to secure the majority of parents in a school for this view. Are we to take it that he believes that there are large numbers of parents in schools in Scotland who will wish to vote for this principle? I do not believe that. If the hon. Gentleman describes that as a small hurdle, he must believe the opposite. Where is his evidence for that view?

**Mr. Galbraith:** The Minister keeps arguing that there is no great demand for this change, that this is simply a piece of enabling legislation and that it will not be required much. Have we spent months listening to rubbish from Conservative Members, wasting the time of Parliament, for a piece of legislation that is irrelevant and that, in the view of the Minister, will hardly ever be used? It beggars belief to hear that sort of rubbish from the Government Benches—[*Interruption.*] One does not wait for murder to be committed before trying to prevent it. That is why we are anxious to deal with this issue properly at this stage.

My hon. Friend the Member for Tayside, North (Mr. Walker)—I deliberately refer to him as my hon. Friend —talked about rural schools, as did a number of other hon. Members. The hon. Gentleman took us on a trip through the Tay valley, on to Killiecrankie and Blair Atholl, and I was waiting, as he moved on, to hear the Uist tramping song. He seemed to think that the trouble with the legislation was that, if one of his local rural schools opted out, it would not be able to offer certain subjects such as Gaelic or specialist sports. If I have misrepresented him, he will correct me.

**Mr. Bill Walker:** My concern—my intervention gives me an opportunity to correct a misapprehension on the part of the hon. Member for Banff and Buchan (Mr. Salmond)—was that the new clause, if accepted, could mean that, if one of my local schools decided to become self-governing, it could not continue to offer the kind of opportunities for selection that are now offered, for example, for Gaelic. In other words, I was concerned about the effect that the new clause could have on schools in my constituency.

**Mr. Galbraith:** The hon. Gentleman is wrong. If rural schools have developed specialist interests in subjects and sports based on their locality, that will always be present.

**Mr. Walker:** Again, the hon. Gentleman either has not heard or has not been listening. I am concerned that schools that become self-governing, which are now offering specialist subjects, for which children travel long distances beyond what would be considered the catchment area, might be prevented from offering such subjects if the new clause were accepted.

**Mr. Galbraith:** I do not think that they would. However, the hon. Gentleman is again introducing a red herring. I do not believe that the new clause could do that technically. Kingussie high school, a rural school, offers shinty. I am sorry that the hon. Member for Inverness, Nairn and Lochaber (Sir R. Johnston) is not in his place. I do not believe that such things would be excluded on the basis of our new clause.

If the hon. Gentleman was honest in saying that he did not wish to reintroduce selection and that the only reason that he was opposing the new clause was that he thought that it was technically unsound——

**Mr. Walker:** I thought that I had made the position even clearer. I said that I had no wish to go back to the 11-plus, and I have not. I believe—I hope that my speech made this clear—that there is room for selection in specialist subjects for which the teachers have specialist aptitudes and abilities which they are offering now. I do not want that position to change.

**Mr. Galbraith:** The more that we debate this—this is the value of debate in the House—the clearer the positions of other hon. Members become. Obviously, the hon. Gentleman wishes to reintroduce selection, although he does not want to reintroduce the 11-plus.

**Mr. Walker** *rose——*

**Mr. Galbraith:** Well, not in the terms that we are talking about.

**Mr. Walker:** Selection already exists.

**Mr. Galbraith:** The hon. Gentleman keeps shouting from a sedentary position that selection exists now, but it does not. That is what we are worried about.

The hon. Member for Brigg and Cleethorpes made it clear that he wanted to reintroduce selection. I believe that I am correct in attributing that view to him. That worries us. He also said that the Opposition are complacent about Scottish education and believe that there is nothing wrong with it. Nothing could be further from the truth. We are all aware that most things in our society could be improved; education certainly could. However, not on Second Reading, in Committee or tonight on Report have we heard exactly how the Bill will improve Scottish education.

We have to take the Minister's assertion and make an act of faith. We have to believe that, if a school is allowed to opt out, there is a de facto reason and some logic that somehow that school will be better. I cannot accept that. We need more and better assurances and some explanation, but they have been missing.

The hon. Member for Cannock and Burntwood made several contributions in Committee and spoke again tonight. We are worried because he said that he wished to reintroduce selection based on academic criteria. I believe that I am correct——

**Mr. Gerald Howarth:** I said that I thought that a strong case could be made for academic selection. I was not specifically calling for it in Scotland. I was simply saying that a strong case could be made, and I should be happy if it could be reintroduced in England and Wales.

**Mr. Galbraith:** It is interesting that the hon. Gentleman has said, "A strong case could be made." Is the hon. Gentleman simply making a debating point, because "a strong case could be made" either for or against? Perhaps the hon. Gentleman has not made his mind up either way, but I suspect that he believes in academic selection.

The other interesting thing that I enjoyed hearing from the hon. Member for Cannock and Burntwood was that the whole purpose of the Bill—and the hon. Gentleman's solution to improve Scottish education—was for the pupils to start calling all teachers "Sir" or "Madam". Many educationists in Scotland will be grateful for that contribution.

Opposition Members oppose the Bill for many reasons, but mainly because it is about introducing selection into the education system by the back door. Many of us remember the 11-plus and the divisions that were created in schools and societies. We remember the mornings when the exam results were made public and the division in classrooms where half the pupils were to go to the senior secondary and other half to the junior secondary, which, for the benefit of the hon. Member for Brigg and Cleethorpes, was the equivalent of a secondary modern school. We do not wish to return to that.

The Minister says that that is not a problem because the sort of testing that he suggests reintroducing into Scottish education will not be used as a method of selection but that the results will be given only to the parents. Is the Minister trying to make us believe that, if a school opts out, he will not ask the parents what results the pupils got in the test? Are we to believe that, somehow, the results that are available from that test will be kept secret from the parents and that they will not be allowed to pass them on through the educational system? No—the results will be used, together with opting out, to damage the comprehensive system within Scottish education.

*It being Ten o'clock,* MR. SPEAKER *proceeded, pursuant to Order, [3rd May] and the Resolution this day, to put forthwith the Question already proposed from the Chair.*

*Question put,* That the clause be read a Second time:—
*The House divided:* Ayes 203, Noes 265.

**Division No. 253]**                                    **[10 pm**

**AYES**

| | |
|---|---|
| Abbott, Ms Diane | Beith, A. J. |
| Adams, Allen *(Paisley N)* | Bell, Stuart |
| Allen, Graham | Benn, Rt Hon Tony |
| Alton, David | Bennett, A. F. *(D'nt'n & R'dish)* |
| Anderson, Donald | Bidwell, Sydney |
| Archer, Rt Hon Peter | Blair, Tony |
| Armstrong, Hilary | Boateng, Paul |
| Ashdown, Rt Hon Paddy | Boyes, Roland |
| Banks, Tony *(Newham NW)* | Bray, Dr Jeremy |
| Barnes, Harry *(Derbyshire NE)* | Brown, Gordon *(D'mline E)* |
| Barron, Kevin | Brown, Nicholas *(Newcastle E)* |
| Battle, John | Brown, Ron *(Edinburgh Leith)* |
| Beckett, Margaret | Bruce, Malcolm *(Gordon)* |

Buckley, George J.
Caborn, Richard
Callaghan, Jim
Campbell, Menzies *(Fife NE)*
Campbell-Savours, D. N.
Canavan, Dennis
Clark, Dr David *(S Shields)*
Clarke, Tom *(Monklands W)*
Clay, Bob
Clelland, David
Cohen, Harry
Cook, Robin *(Livingston)*
Cousins, Jim
Cryer, Bob
Cummings, John
Cunliffe, Lawrence
Dalyell, Tam
Darling, Alistair
Davies, Rt Hon Denzil *(Llanelli)*
Davies, Ron *(Caerphilly)*
Davis, Terry *(B'ham Hodge H'l)*
Dewar, Donald
Dixon, Don
Dobson, Frank
Doran, Frank
Douglas, Dick
Duffy, A. E. P.
Dunnachie, Jimmy
Eadie, Alexander
Eastham, Ken
Ewing, Harry *(Falkirk E)*
Fatchett, Derek
Fearn, Ronald
Field, Frank *(Birkenhead)*
Fields, Terry *(L'pool B G'n)*
Fisher, Mark
Flannery, Martin
Flynn, Paul
Foot, Rt Hon Michael
Foster, Derek
Foulkes, George
Fraser, John
Fyfe, Maria
Galbraith, Sam
Galloway, George
Garrett, John *(Norwich South)*
Garrett, Ted *(Wallsend)*
George, Bruce
Gilbert, Rt Hon Dr John
Godman, Dr Norman A.
Golding, Mrs Llin
Gordon, Mildred
Graham, Thomas
Grant, Bernie *(Tottenham)*
Griffiths, Nigel *(Edinburgh S)*
Griffiths, Win *(Bridgend)*
Grocott, Bruce
Hardy, Peter
Harman, Ms Harriet
Henderson, Doug
Hinchliffe, David
Home Robertson, John
Hood, Jimmy
Howarth, George *(Knowsley N)*
Howell, Rt Hon D. *(S'heath)*
Howells, Geraint
Howells, Dr. Kim *(Pontypridd)*
Hoyle, Doug
Hughes, John *(Coventry NE)*
Hughes, Robert *(Aberdeen N)*
Hughes, Roy *(Newport E)*
Illsley, Eric
Ingram, Adam
Janner, Greville
Johnston, Sir Russell
Jones, Barry *(Alyn & Deeside)*
Jones, Martyn *(Clwyd S W)*
Kennedy, Charles
Kirkwood, Archy
Lambie, David

Leadbitter, Ted
Leighton, Ron
Lestor, Joan *(Eccles)*
Litherland, Robert
Livingstone, Ken
Livsey, Richard
Lloyd, Tony *(Stretford)*
Lofthouse, Geoffrey
Loyden, Eddie
McAllion, John
McAvoy, Thomas
Macdonald, Calum A.
McFall, John
McKay, Allen *(Barnsley West)*
McKelvey, William
McLeish, Henry
McNamara, Kevin
McWilliam, John
Madden, Max
Mahon, Mrs Alice
Marek, Dr John
Marshall, David *(Shettleston)*
Marshall, Jim *(Leicester S)*
Martlew, Eric
Maxton, John
Meale, Alan
Michael, Alun
Michie, Bill *(Sheffield Heeley)*
Michie, Mrs Ray *(Arg'l & Bute)*
Moonie, Dr Lewis
Morgan, Rhodri
Morley, Elliott
Morris, Rt Hon A. *(W'shawe)*
Mowlam, Marjorie
Mullin, Chris
Murphy, Paul
Nellist, Dave
Oakes, Rt Hon Gordon
O'Brien, William
O'Neill, Martin
Orme, Rt Hon Stanley
Patchett, Terry
Pendry, Tom
Pike, Peter L.
Powell, Ray *(Ogmore)*
Prescott, John
Quin, Ms Joyce
Randall, Stuart
Redmond, Martin
Rees, Rt Hon Merlyn
Reid, Dr John
Richardson, Jo
Robertson, George
Robinson, Geoffrey
Ross, Ernie *(Dundee W)*
Rowlands, Ted
Ruddock, Joan
Salmond, Alex
Sedgemore, Brian
Sheerman, Barry
Sheldon, Rt Hon Robert
Shore, Rt Hon Peter
Short, Clare
Sillars, Jim
Skinner, Dennis
Smith, Andrew *(Oxford E)*
Smith, C. *(Isl'ton & F'bury)*
Smith, Rt Hon J. *(Monk'ds E)*
Smith, J. P. *(Vale of Glam)*
Snape, Peter
Spearing, Nigel
Steel, Rt Hon David
Steinberg, Gerry
Stott, Roger
Strang, Gavin
Straw, Jack
Taylor, Mrs Ann *(Dewsbury)*
Taylor, Matthew *(Truro)*
Thompson, Jack *(Wansbeck)*
Turner, Dennis

Vaz, Keith
Wall, Pat
Wallace, James
Walley, Joan
Wardell, Gareth *(Gower)*
Wareing, Robert N.
Watson, Mike *(Glasgow, C)*
Welsh, Andrew *(Angus E)*
Welsh, Michael *(Doncaster N)*
Wigley, Dafydd
Williams, Rt Hon Alan

Williams, Alan W. *(Carm'then)*
Wilson, Brian
Winnick, David
Wise, Mrs Audrey
Wray, Jimmy
Young, David *(Bolton SE)*

Tellers for the Ayes:
Mr. Frank Haynes and
Mr. Frank Cook.

## NOES

Adley, Robert
Aitken, Jonathan
Alexander, Richard
Alison, Rt Hon Michael
Allason, Rupert
Amess, David
Amos, Alan
Arbuthnot, James
Arnold, Jacques *(Gravesham)*
Arnold, Tom *(Hazel Grove)*
Ashby, David
Aspinwall, Jack
Atkins, Robert
Atkinson, David
Baker, Nicholas *(Dorset N)*
Batiste, Spencer
Beaumont-Dark, Anthony
Bellingham, Henry
Bendall, Vivian
Bennett, Nicholas *(Pembroke)*
Benyon, W.
Blackburn, Dr John G.
Blaker, Rt Hon Sir Peter
Body, Sir Richard
Bonsor, Sir Nicholas
Boswell, Tim
Bottomley, Peter
Bottomley, Mrs Virginia
Bowden, A *(Brighton K'pto'n)*
Bowden, Gerald *(Dulwich)*
Bowis, John
Boyson, Rt Hon Dr Sir Rhodes
Braine, Rt Hon Sir Bernard
Brandon-Bravo, Martin
Brazier, Julian
Bright, Graham
Brown, Michael *(Brigg & Cl't's)*
Buchanan-Smith, Rt Hon Alick
Buck, Sir Antony
Budgen, Nicholas
Burns, Simon
Burt, Alistair
Butcher, John
Butler, Chris
Butterfill, John
Carlisle, John, *(Luton N)*
Carlisle, Kenneth *(Lincoln)*
Carrington, Matthew
Cash, William
Chalker, Rt Hon Mrs Lynda
Chope, Christopher
Clark, Dr Michael *(Rochford)*
Clark, Sir W. *(Croydon S)*
Colvin, Michael
Conway, Derek
Coombs, Anthony *(Wyre F'rest)*
Coombs, Simon *(Swindon)*
Cope, Rt Hon John
Cormack, Patrick
Couchman, James
Cran, James
Currie, Mrs Edwina
Curry, David
Davis, David *(Boothferry)*
Day, Stephen
Devlin, Tim
Dicks, Terry

Douglas-Hamilton, Lord James
Dover, Den
Dunn, Bob
Durant, Tony
Dykes, Hugh
Evans, David *(Welwyn Hatf'd)*
Fairbairn, Sir Nicholas
Fallon, Michael
Farr, Sir John
Favell, Tony
Fenner, Dame Peggy
Forman, Nigel
Forsyth, Michael *(Stirling)*
Freeman, Roger
Gill, Christopher
Gorman, Mrs Teresa
Greenway, Harry *(Ealing N)*
Gregory, Conal
Hamilton, Neil *(Tatton)*
Hampson, Dr Keith
Hanley, Jeremy
Hannam, John
Hargreaves, A. *(B'ham H'll Gr')*
Hargreaves, Ken *(Hyndburn)*
Harris, David
Haselhurst, Alan
Hawkins, Christopher
Hayes, Jerry
Hayhoe, Rt Hon Sir Barney
Hayward, Robert
Heathcoat-Amory, David
Heddle, John
Hicks, Mrs Maureen *(Wolv' NE)*
Hicks, Robert *(Cornwall SE)*
Higgins, Rt Hon Terence L.
Hill, James
Hind, Kenneth
Hogg, Hon Douglas *(Gr'th'm)*
Hordern, Sir Peter
Howard, Michael
Howarth, Alan *(Strat'd-on-A)*
Howarth, G. *(Cannock & B'wd)*
Howell, Rt Hon David *(G'dford)*
Howell, Ralph *(North Norfolk)*
Hughes, Robert G. *(Harrow W)*
Hunt, David *(Wirral W)*
Hunt, Sir John *(Ravensbourne)*
Hunter, Andrew
Irvine, Michael
Irving, Charles
Jack, Michael
Jackson, Robert
Janman, Tim
Jessel, Toby
Johnson Smith, Sir Geoffrey
Jones, Gwilym *(Cardiff N)*
Jones, Robert B *(Herts W)*
Jopling, Rt Hon Michael
Kellett-Bowman, Dame Elaine
Key, Robert
Kilfedder, James
King, Roger *(B'ham N'thfield)*
Kirkhope, Timothy
Knapman, Roger
Knight, Greg *(Derby North)*
Knight, Dame Jill *(Edgbaston)*
Knox, David

Lamont, Rt Hon Norman
Lang, Ian
Latham, Michael
Lawrence, Ivan
Lawson, Rt Hon Nigel
Leigh, Edward (Gainsbor'gh)
Lennox-Boyd, Hon Mark
Lester, Jim (Broxtowe)
Lightbown, David
Lilley, Peter
Lloyd, Sir Ian (Havant)
Lloyd, Peter (Fareham)
Lord, Michael
Luce, Rt Hon Richard
Lyell, Sir Nicholas
McCrindle, Robert
Macfarlane, Sir Neil
Maclean, David
McLoughlin, Patrick
McNair-Wilson, Sir Michael
McNair-Wilson, Sir Patrick
Madel, David
Major, Rt Hon John
Mans, Keith
Maples, John
Marland, Paul
Marshall, John (Hendon S)
Marshall, Michael (Arundel)
Martin, David (Portsmouth S)
Mates, Michael
Maude, Hon Francis
Mawhinney, Dr Brian
Mayhew, Rt Hon Sir Patrick
Meyer, Sir Anthony
Miller, Sir Hal
Mills, Iain
Miscampbell, Norman
Mitchell, Andrew (Gedling)
Mitchell, Sir David
Moate, Roger
Monro, Sir Hector
Montgomery, Sir Fergus
Morrison, Sir Charles
Morrison, Rt Hon P (Chester)
Moss, Malcolm
Moynihan, Hon Colin
Neale, Gerrard
Nelson, Anthony
Neubert, Michael
Nicholls, Patrick
Nicholson, David (Taunton)
Norris, Steve
Onslow, Rt Hon Cranley
Page, Richard
Paice, James
Patnick, Irvine
Patten, John (Oxford W)
Peacock, Mrs Elizabeth
Porter, David (Waveney)
Price, Sir David
Raison, Rt Hon Timothy
Rathbone, Tim
Redwood, John
Renton, Tim
Rhodes James, Robert
Riddick, Graham
Ridley, Rt Hon Nicholas
Ridsdale, Sir Julian

Rifkind, Rt Hon Malcolm
Roe, Mrs Marion
Rossi, Sir Hugh
Rost, Peter
Rumbold, Mrs Angela
Sackville, Hon Tom
Sainsbury, Hon Tim
Sayeed, Jonathan
Scott, Rt Hon Nicholas
Shaw, David (Dover)
Shaw, Sir Michael (Scarb')
Shephard, Mrs G. (Norfolk SW)
Sims, Roger
Skeet, Sir Trevor
Smith, Tim (Beaconsfield)
Speed, Keith
Speller, Tony
Spicer, Sir Jim (Dorset W)
Spicer, Michael (S Worcs)
Squire, Robin
Stanley, Rt Hon Sir John
Steen, Anthony
Stern, Michael
Stevens, Lewis
Stewart, Allan (Eastwood)
Stewart, Andy (Sherwood)
Stokes, Sir John
Stradling Thomas, Sir John
Summerson, Hugo
Taylor, Ian (Esher)
Taylor, John M (Solihull)
Taylor, Teddy (S'end E)
Tebbit, Rt Hon Norman
Temple-Morris, Peter
Thompson, Patrick (Norwich N)
Thornton, Malcolm
Thurnham, Peter
Townend, John (Bridlington)
Tracey, Richard
Tredinnick, David
Trippier, David
Trotter, Neville
Twinn, Dr Ian
Vaughan, Sir Gerard
Waddington, Rt Hon David
Walker, Bill (T'side North)
Waller, Gary
Ward, John
Wardle, Charles (Bexhill)
Warren, Kenneth
Watts, John
Wells, Bowen
Whitney, Ray
Widdecombe, Ann
Wiggin, Jerry
Wilkinson, John
Wilshire, David
Winterton, Mrs Ann
Winterton, Nicholas
Wolfson, Mark
Wood, Timothy
Yeo, Tim
Young, Sir George (Acton)

Tellers for the Noes:
Mr. Stephen Dorrell and
Mr. Sydney Chapman.

*Question accordingly negatived.*

## New Clause 12

### Freedom of Speech in Universities, Polytechnics

#### and Colleges

'.—(1) Every individual and body of persons concerned in the government of any establishment to which this section applies shall take such steps as are reasonably practicable to ensure that freedom of speech within the law is secured for members, students and employees of the establishment and for visiting speakers.

(2) The duty imposed by subsection (1) above includes (in particular) the duty to ensure, so far as is reasonably practicable, that the use of any premises of the establishment is not denied to any individual or body of persons on any ground connected with—

(a) the beliefs or views of that individual or of any member of that body; or

(b) the policy or objectives of that body.

(3) The governing body of every such establishment shall, with a view to facilitating the discharge of the duty imposed by subsection (1) above in relation to that establishment, issue and keep up to date a code of practice setting out—

(a) the procedures to be followed by members, students and employees of the establishment in connection with the organisation—

(i) of meetings which are to be held on premises of the establishment and which fall within any class of meeting specified in the code; and

(ii) of other activities which are to take place on those premises and which fall within any class of activity so specified; and

(b) the conduct required of such persons in connection with any such meeting or activity;

and dealing with such other matters as the governing body consider appropriate.

(4) The governing body of every such establishment shall not impose a charge for security on the organisers of any meeting. Any charge for the use of premises shall be in accordance with the established practice of the establishment and shall not in any event be at such a level as to effectively preclude the proposed meeting taking place.

(5) Every individual and body of persons concerned in the government of any such establishment shall take such steps as are reasonably practicable (including where appropriate the initiation of disciplinary measures) to secure that the requirements of the code of practice for that establishment, issued under subsection (3) above, are complied with.

(6) The establishments to which this section applies are—

(a) any university;

(b) any grant-maintained college;

(c) any college of further education; and

(d) any institution for the provision of further education managed by a company formed by virtue of section 60(1) of this Act.

(7) In this section—

"governing body", in relation to any university, means the executive governing body which has responsibility for the management and administration of its revenue and property and the conduct of its affairs;

"university" includes a university college and any college, or institution in the nature of a college, in a university.

(8) Where any of the establishments to which this section applies is maintained by an education authority or authorities or is substantially dependent for its maintenance on assistance from an education authority or authorities, the education authority or authorities maintaining or (as the case may be) assisting the establishment shall, for the purposes of this section, be taken to be concerned in its government.

(9) Where a students' union occupies premises which are not premises of the establishment in connection with which the union is constituted, any reference in this section to the premises of the establishment shall be taken to include a reference to the premises occupied by the students' union.'
—*[Mr. Nicholas Bennett.]*

*Brought up, and read the First time.*

**Mr. Nicholas Bennett** (Pembroke): I beg to move, That the clause be read a Second time.

The purpose of the clause is to insert into the Bill section 43 of the Education (No. 2) Act 1986 but with one new and important subsection which says:

"The governing body of every such establishment shall not impose a charge for security on the organisers of any meeting. Any charge for the use of premises shall be in accordance with

[*Mr. Nicholas Bennett*]

the established practice of the establishment and shall not in any event be at such a level as to effectively preclude the proposed meeting taking place."

10.15 pm

During questions to Scottish Office Ministers on 7 June, my hon. Friends the Members for Hexham (Mr. Amos) and for Eastwood (Mr. Stewart) asked whether our hon. Friend the Under-Secretary would consider extending section 43 to Scotland. He replied:

"It was decided in 1986 not to extend to Scotland the provisions in the 1986 Act which became section 43 as there was little evidence in Scotland of the problems that prompted the legislation south of the border. Since then there has been very little evidence of disruption of free speech in universities or colleges in Scotland."—[*Official Report*, 7 June 1989; Vol. 154, c. 209.]

An important matter of principle is involved. It is that freedom of speech that is enshrined in English and Welsh legislation should also be enshrined in Scottish legislation. I do not understand the Minister's attitude. Knowing his robust views, I cannot believe that he seriously expects the House to accept the principle of freedom of speech in England and Wales but not in Scotland.

**Mr. Tim Devlin** (Stockton, South): Does my hon. Friend agree that should a problem arise in a Scottish university to which those rules would apply, we would not be equipped to deal with it? Are we not denying Scottish students a fairly essential right?

**Mr. Bennett:** My hon. Friend makes a valid point. The Scottish Office is basically saying that, if a fire occurs, it will then take out an insurance policy. I have always believed that the insurance policy should come first. It is not right to suggest that there have not been problems in Scottish universities. Only last year in Aberdeen the South African consul was shouted down——

**Mr. Bill Walker:** Is my hon. Friend aware that Scottish Members—and, indeed, most hon. Members—would abhor any intervention in the principle of freedom of speech in Scotland? We would be appalled if some Right-wing Fascists tried to prevent the hon. Member for Glasgow, Garscadden (Mr. Dewar) speaking in a university. We want to prevent that happening, which is why we want the same legislation for Scotland as for England and Wales. During the passage of the Bill, Opposition Members continually asked for harmonisation between Scotland and England, and we cannot understand why my hon. Friend the Minister refused that.

**Mr. Bennett:** My hon. Friend makes an important point. Of course, race relations legislation is equally applicable to Scotland and England. We want to prevent the shouting down of people in an attempt to stop them expressing their views. The Government appear to be prepared to sit back complacently because Scotland has not suffered quite the same outrages as England.

**Mr. John Redwood** (Wokingham): During debates on the community charge, many Scottish Members said that it was a great pity that Scotland had to be the first to experiment and that England would have it only after it had been proved successful. Do we not now have a marvellous opportunity to show even-handedness in that now, the 1986 Act has proved successful in England and Wales, it should be extended to Scotland?

**Mr. Bennett:** My hon. Friend is right, but with one proviso, because a part of section 43 has not been successful.

**Mr. John Marshall:** Speaking as a former lecturer at Aberdeen university, I wish to ask my Welsh colleague whether he agrees that two things threaten Scotland's reputation—first, the sedentary interventions of the hon. Member for Dunfermline, West (Mr. Douglas) and, secondly, the attempts by individuals to deny freedom of speech in universities? Do not such attempts bring universities into disrepute? My hon. Friend's new clause seeks to safeguard the reputation of Scottish education, which used to be the highest in the United Kingdom.

**Mr. Bennett:** My hon. Friend is right, but my new clause also seeks equality for Scotland with England and Wales. It would also help my hon. Friend the Minister because not so long ago he spoke at Stirling university and attempts were made to shout him down. Being of a robust nature, my hon. Friend managed to continue his speech despite the attempts of the Fascist left to prevent freedom of speech. That shows that there are problems in Scottish universities and it seems that the problems are likely to increase in future. It is important that there should be equality of opportunity and treatment between England, Wales and Scotland. However, Scottish Members have an opportunity to show the way forward to the Departments responsible for education in England and Wales to improve section 43 of the Education (No. 2) Act 1986, because that section is not working at the moment.

**Mr. John Bowis** (Battersea): The Parliamentary Under-Secretary of State for Scotland, my hon. Friend the Member for Stirling (Mr. Forsyth), should be listening to my hon. Friend the Member for Pembroke (Mr. Bennett). Until now, Scotland has always held its head high as one of the leaders in education in the United Kingdom. However, we anticipate a faint-hearted response on this point from the Minister. Should not the Government be considering the problems encountered by England and Wales under the present law and try to go further for Scotland instead of restricting the provision in Scotland to below that applying in England?

**Mr. Bennett:** I find it very difficult to understand the attitude of my hon. Friend the Under-Secretary of State on this. It cannot be in line with what he really believes. He must have been captured by the civil servants in the Scottish Office. If only he could be a free man and speak his mind, there would be a robust approach.

**Mr. Michael Brown:** Is it not a great pleasure to see the Under-Secretary of State for Education and Science, my hon. Friend the Member for Wantage (Mr. Jackson), present in the Chamber? He seems to have the backbone with regard to these matters. Can we not have some backbone in this issue?

**Mr. Bennett:** I hope that my hon. Friend the Under-Secretary of State for Scotland is suitably chastened by the views expressed by my hon. Friend the Member for Brigg and Cleethorpes (Mr. Brown) and that he will take note of the strong views on this issue.

I want to give examples of what has happened in England and Wales since the Education (No. 2) Act 1986 received its Royal Assent. These examples will illustrate the problem which exists in the English and Welsh legislation which we hope to correct and amend in the Bill on student loans later this year. The Under-Secretary of State for Scotland has a golden opportunity to lead the way and accept this new clause, which surmounts the problem which exists in England and Wales.

**Sir Russell Johnston:** Would the hon. Gentleman take an umbrella to the Sahara on the grounds that it might rain?

**Mr. Bennett:** Of course, there is always the chance that it might rain. I would certainly take some water there.

**Mr. Bill Walker:** For the information of my hon. Friend the Member for Pembroke (Mr. Bennett), I have been in the Sahara when it rained very heavily.

**Mr. Bennett:** Looking at the hon. Member for Inverness, Nairn and Lochaber (Sir R. Johnston), it appears that he should take an umbrella because he is obviously suffering from sunstroke and an umbrella could protect him from the sun. The Liberals were soaked in the rain last Thursday and they need an umbrella to protect them, if only to try to show that they are green in some way.

The Conservative Collegiate Forum, the new name given by my right hon. Friend the Member for Chingford (Mr. Tebbit) to the Federation of Conservative Students, which confuses some of us who think it must have something to do with Army cadets in public schools, has examined 97 codes of practice in England and Wales. It considered 49 from universities, 29 from polytechnics and 19 from other places of higher education. Fifty-three of the codes throw on the student body the cost of stewarding the meeting and eight of them demand payments in advance or a deposit.

**Mr. Tim Janman** (Thurrock): I agree with my hon. Friend that it is a priority that we should take action to uphold freedom of speech in Scotland. Does he agree that we should be incorporating section 43 of the Education (No. 2) Act 1986 in this Bill, but that that should be taken as a starting point to make the legislation more embracing in Scotland to prevent the problems that we have seen in England and Wales? The English and Welsh legislation should also be toughened.

**Mr. Bennett:** My hon. Friend has made a very good point which is the purpose of the new clause. I only regret that the new clause tabled by my hon. Friend the Member for Eastwood (Mr. Stewart), about student unions, was not selected for debate. That new clause referred to students being cajoled into being members of student unions whether they wanted to or not which is something about which Conservative Members feel very strongly.

Eight of the codes of practice demand payments in advance or deposits. Those codes mean that, before a meeting can be held, sums of up to £500 must be paid in case the Left wing come along and disrupt the meeting. The onus is not on the Left, who will break up the meeting and cause the damage, but on the organisers. Large sums are demanded by some universities. Aston university, advised by the police that its security barriers would not be sufficient, asked for specially toughened steel barriers and demanded £372·83 from the Conservative students and a further £110 for extra security staff. The Conservative

students did not have that sort of money, and there was a grave danger that the meeting would have to be cancelled. Luckily, part of the charge was waived.

**Mr. Michael Brown:** How can speech be free if it costs £110?

**Mr. Bennett:** My hon. Friend makes a good point. That is why we object to the way in which the English and Welsh legislation has been working.

Nine codes of practice insist that any loss or damage should be made good not by those who caused it but by the organisers of the meeting. Four require the holders of the meeting to bear all or part of the cost of any extra insurance required. Another device used by at least 10 establishments is to limit the number of meetings at which a designated speaker is allowed to appear. Essex university demands six weeks' notice for a meeting. Details must include the name of the speaker, and if the speaker cancels for any reason within those six weeks, the authority can ban the meeting.

Twenty-seven codes of practice state that the meeting may be cancelled if it incites those attending to criminal acts. That is an all-embracing umbrella clause if ever I heard one. I note that the hon. Member for Inverness, Nairn and Lochaber, who raised umbrellas, has now left the Chamber. It seems that any univeristy can say to any association, "I am sorry, but your meeting cannot take place because it might incite the audience to acts of criminal activity." How can anyone guarantee that a meeting will not lead to someone trying to disrupt it or to commit a criminal act? It is an open invitation to a university authority to ban anything it wishes.

**Mr. Bob Dunn** (Dartford): If deposits must be paid, which can be lost in the event of trouble, is that not an open invitation to the Left to cause trouble so that those who organised the meeting will be penalised?

**Mr. Bennett:** That is a valid point. It is all the more valid coming from a former Under-Secretary of State of Education and Science, who speaks with great experience of the matter.

I am especially worried by the behaviour of the director of the polytechnic of north London. I gained my first degree at that polytechnic and was the founder and first chairman of its Conservative association in the troubled times of the early 1970s. To blow my own trumpet, I can say that, standing as the moderate candidate, I led the poll in a ballot for student union president against the Trotskyites. I know how insidious the Left's activities can be in polytechnics and universities and how Left-wing students can intimidate speakers and Conservative students. The director's behaviour is extremely reprehensible. He has demanded the right to vet the subject of the addresses by visiting speakers and to demand that they be changed. If my right hon. Friend the Member for Chingford wished to speak at the north London polytechnic, as he did fairly recently when he was subject to much abuse, the director reserves the right to ask my right hon. Friend to change the subject of his address.

**Mr. Christopher Hawkins** (High Peak): I fully share my hon. Friend's view that the students should not be asked to pay, but the universities fear that, if the students are not asked to pay, the money will have to come from the university's budget for providing education. The taxpayer

[*Mr. Christopher Hawkins*]

generally should pay. We do not tax people who have their houses burgled. The police should protect the freedom of speech at no cost to the universities.

**Mr. Bennett:** My hon. Friend makes a good point. There is a case that the cost of protecting free speech should be borne by the taxpayer generally. But if the student unions, which are usually the cause of the disruption and are usually controlled by the far Left, are seen to be organising the disruption, they should pay for it out of the student union budget, which is provided by the taxpayer.

**Mr. John Marshall:** One problem is that the principals of universities are far too pusillanimous. They should discipline those who behave in an unacademic way and send them down.

10.30 pm

**Mr. Bennett:** My hon. Friend is absolutely right. Bernard Levin made the same point in an excellent article in *The Times* on 1 June. University chancellors and polytechnic directors have been very weak in dealing with student union activists and troublemakers who disrupt meetings. They prefer to ignore and turn their backs on the problem. They are quite happy that disruption should occur, provided that the speakers affected are Conservative or Right-wing.

When Mr. Ray Honeyford was invited to speak at the north London polytechnic, its director felt it necessary to publish a leaflet at the polytechnic's, and therefore, at the taxpayers', expense inviting his students to attend alternative meetings that he organised. He defended his action in a letter to *The Times* recently, to which Mr. Philip Malcolm, national student director of the Conservative Collegiate Forum, responded asking whether the director had ever organised an alternative meeting to one addressed by a Left-wing, Fascist or Communist speaker. Of course he had not. The director of the north London polytechnic only organises alternative meetings to those of Conservative speakers, with whom he happens to disagree. I do not see it as part of the job of the polytechnic authorities to tell students, "We don't want you to listen to this dreadful man because you might be influenced by what he says."

**Mr. John Carlisle** (Luton, North): My hon. Friend may be interested to learn that, a week after my right hon. Friend the Member for Chingford (Mr. Tebbit) spoke, after a fashion, at north London polytechnic, I was invited by its Conservative student association to speak there. Accordingly, I wrote to the polytechnic's principal, Dr. Wagner, asking him to accompany me on the platform and to remain there for the duration of my speech. He refused to do so, presumably because he did not want to witness the abuse from his own students that I would doubtless receive and because he could not discipline them in his own college. He could not guarantee my safety or the freedom of speech that he was ostensibly allowing.

**Mr. Bennett:** My hon. Friend draws attention to the kind of disgraceful behaviour that is exhibited. Although not all right hon. and hon. Members agree with the robust views of my hon. Friend the Member for Luton, North (Mr. Carlisle) on every occasion, I defend his right to

speak at any university or college in this country at which he is invited to speak and to express whatever views he likes, in however robust a manner he chooses. By doing so he upholds the principle of freedom of speech that all my right hon. and hon. Friends deem to be so important and which overrides all other considerations.

**Mr. Norman Tebbit** (Chingford): One must be careful to distinguish—as my hon. Friend does, but he could easily be misinterpreted—between the great mass of university students who want quietly and decently to get on with their studies, and who are content to leave others to hold their own meetings and discussions in a proper and civilised manner, and the minority, whom we see everywhere, and who are mostly Red Fascists and people of that kind. As we know, Fascists are Left-wing, and there is little to distinguish between the National Front's economic policy and that of the Labour Left. We must be careful not to imply that students in Scotland or in any other part of the kingdom are in general of the same kind.

My hon. Friend is also right to emphasise that university authorities are often to blame for disruption. The authorities at the north London polytechnic knowingly employed a man who has a conviction for a serious terrorist offence and placed him in a position of trust among impressionable young people, which is a disgraceful way to behave. If my hon. Friend's new clause would do anything to militate against such conduct by those who are supposed to lead young people, he is well advised to pursue it.

**Mr. Bennett:** I thank my right hon. Friend for his helpful intervention, based on his great experience of public speaking at universities and colleges throughout the country.

I turn to the attitude of the Committee of Vice-Chancellors and Principals.

**Mr. McFall:** Is it not a fact that the Minister did not accept the hon. Gentleman's proposition at Scottish Question Time? The present arrangements are working perfectly well. Hon. Members may not take my word for it, but they should take the Minister's word. On 20 October last year, when he visited Glasgow college of technology, there was something of a fracas; after the meeting, however, he said that the students were to be commended and that he would introduce no legislation. I suggest that some Conservative Members know nothing about it. They come into the Chamber for a debate on Scottish education and filibuster just for the sake of it.

**Mr. Bennett:** I think that the hon. Gentleman has got my hon. Friend's statement slightly wrong. For one thing, he did not preclude future legislation. What he said after that demonstration was that the vast majority of students would not wish to have anything to do with the minority who had caused it. I think that his remarks were indicative of the general Christian attitude that we have come to expect from him: he took a forgiving line.

**Mr. Rupert Allason** (Torquay): I recently conducted a speaking tour of Scottish universities, and spoke at St. Andrews and Edinburgh. It was a very successful tour, and was not marked by the extremism that hon. Members have described.

Let me say a word in support of my right hon. Friend the Member for Chingford (Mr. Tebbit). Most students in Scotland are, in my experience, very keen to get on with their studies and pass their exams; they are not interested in extremism. Those students have nothing to fear from the new clause. Nor, I believe, have the Civil Service, the Scottish Office and our own Front Benches—especially the Opposition. There can be no reason for opposing the new clause, and I warmly support it.

**Mr. Graham Riddick** (Colne Valley): Are not a number of student unions in Scottish universities affiliated to the National Union of Students? Is it not also true that that union still operates a no-platform policy, and that there is therefore an ever-present threat that a minority faction from some university might try to impose such a policy? Is that not why it is so important that the new clause is put on the statute book?

**Mr. Bennett:** My hon. Friend has made a valuable point. What concerns me is that, although there has not been the same level of disruption in Scottish universities —there have been problems at Aberdeen and Stirling—a number of issues have arisen in the past year that could lead to trouble. [Hon. Members: "Where?"] I have just mentioned Stirling and Aberdeen. Hon. Members should open their ears.

We have an opportunity to introduce in Scottish legislation an insurance policy already contained in English and Welsh legislation, so that action can be taken, in the event of disruption, to prevent the problems that we have seen in England and Wales from spreading to Scotland. That seems admirable to me. The principle of free speech ought to be defended.

**Mr. Bill Walker:** I do not wish anyone to misunderstand. There is no doubt that in the past there have been problems at Scottish universities as serious as those that England has experienced. Those of us who have been speaking in Scotland for many decades know that there was a time when we were ashamed by activities that took place—even, in one instance, in the presence of the monarch. That should not be forgotten. I remind my hon. Friend that an umbrella may well be useful: even if it does not rain often, it does so occasionally, and when it does it can be pretty ghastly.

**Mr. Bennett:** I thank my hon. Friend for that helpful intervention. I see that my hon. Friend the Member for Boothferry (Mr. Davis) now wishes to intervene.

**Mr. David Davis** (Boothferry): The hon. Member for Dumbarton raised the question whether there is a problem over freedom of speech in universities. When he and the Minister were at university, the "Red Fascists", as they were called by my right hon. Friend the Member for Chingford (Mr. Tebbit), were very unsubtle: they shouted down psychologists, historians and—as we have heard— even the monarch. That was a very overt form of suppression of freedom of speech. The techniques described by my hon. Friend however, are much subtler and more difficult to detect. The Scottish Office seems to have enfeebled my hon. Friend the Minister—[Hon. Members: "No."] Knowing him now and remembering him 10 years ago, I am quite sure that it has.

The fact that the Scottish Office says that there is no evidence implies that it has investigated the rules that apply in universities to each Conservative association and to each Socialist society and Liberal society and has checked whether they prevent controversial speakers from being able to speak. I hope that my hon. Friend will ask the Minister to justify the statement made by his Department that there has been no suppression of freedom of speech in Scotland and that the Minister will tell us that a positive investigation has taken place. I also hope that he will not reject the new clause.

**Mr. Bennett:** My hon. Friend makes a valuable point. If there has been a survey of Scottish institutions by the Scottish Office, I hope that it was a damned sight better than the one carried out by the Department of Education and Science into the National Union of Students, which wrote the answers for all the constituent unions to send back to the Department.

**Mr. Robert B. Jones** (Hertfordshire, West): Will my hon. Friend follow up the point made by my hon. Friend the Member for Boothferry (Mr. Davis) about the subtle way in which some of the pressures are applied? This does not apply just to political societies—for example, to the policy against Jewish societies by some pro-PLO students. It applies also to the misuse of public funds to finance political societies extravagantly and others in a very discriminatory way that prevents them from offering platforms to visiting speakers. As a former union official at a Scottish university, I have had experience of that.

**Mr. Bennett:** My hon. Friend also makes a valid point. When it referred to the amount of money that it spends on political activities, the National Union of Students interestingly described it as about 0·5 per cent., by which it meant the amount of money spent by Conservative associations and the Communist and Socialist societies. However, it did not mention that most student union officers spend most of their time on politicking, that most student union newspapers are full of Left-wing politics, that most student union meetings spend all their time on Left-wing politics and that between 60 and 70 per cent. of student union funds, paid for by the taxpayer, are spent on Left-wing politics up and down the country.

**Mr. Dunn:** My hon. Friend the Member for Hertfordshire, West (Mr. Jones) made an interesting point about the change in style of the Fascist Left over the years. In the past it was a straightforward attack on those who wished to sing a different tune from that to which they were prepared to listen. Today, many of the vice-chancellors and principals give a lead because of their objection and their hostility to our philosophy. In institutions where vice-chancellors and principals have been prepared to back up freedom of speech, there has been less trouble than has occurred where vice-chancellors and principals have been prepared to give a lead to the trouble.

**Mr. Bennett:** My hon. Friend has made another valid point. He brings me back to the point that I was making a few minutes ago about the letter that all hon. Members have received from the Committee of Vice-Chancellors and Principals of the Universities of the United Kingdom, dated 2 June. Page 1 of the letter says:

"there is no evidence of any institutions placing a limit on the number of meetings that may be organised."

That is simply untrue.

"There may be limitations imposed by virtue only of the unavailability"—

that is an interesting word to use; it is not in my English dictionary—

"of suitable venues at any particular time."

Then it says:

[*Mr. Bennett*]

"With only one or two exceptions, there is no support for the proposal that student unions should be made responsible for meeting security or other costs."

What do we find in the survey by the Conservative Collegiate Forum? We find that 53 codes put an onus on the student bodies. The statements in that letter are untrue. The letter is misleading and covers up the fact that the vast majority of universities, colleges and polytechnics in this country are doing what my hon. Friend the Member for Harborough (Sir J. Farr) said that they would do when he spoke during the Second Reading debate of the Education (No. 2) Bill in 1986. They are finding ways of getting round the code. The purpose of my new clause is to prevent that from happening.

**Mr. Greg Knight** (Derby, North): Is there any reason why a student who, by reason of force or noise, denies freedom of speech to someone at or visiting a place of learning should remain a student?

**Mr. Bennett:** There is absolutely no reason whatsover for that and there is absolutely no reason why the Scottish Office should not accept the new clause, which seeks not only to extend the law that applies to England and Wales to Scotland but to improve it and to give Scotland a lead.

**Mr. Leigh:** Has my hon. Friend noticed that his characteristically able, but lengthy, speech has given rise to a considerable number of interventions from Conservative members who have shown an unprecedented degree of interest in these matters, which is matched only by an unprecedented lack of interest from Opposition Members? Should we not remember the wise words that the only thing necessary for evil to triumph is that good men should do nothing? If Scottish Office Ministers claim that there have been few incidents, they should recall that a lack of freedom anywhere diminishes all our freedom everywhere.

10.45 pm

**Mr. Bennett:** My hon. Friend quotes the words of Edmund Burke which are extremely valuable. They remind us that freedom is indivisible and that we must always defend free speech and not allow the Left to decide who should speak and who should not.

**Mr. Frank Haynes** (Ashfield): The hon. Gentleman probably does not know that the hon. Member for Gainsborough and Horncastle (Mr. Leigh) went to Durham university and became the president of the student union there; but he was not elected: he was appointed by himself. Is that freedom?

**Mr. Bennett:** I find the hon. Gentleman's proposition so astounding that I must let my hon. Friend defend himself.

**Mr. Leigh:** Many things are thrown at one in this House, but that is complete and utter fabrication. I was elected president of the Durham Union Society in a free and popular vote in a secret ballot.

**Mrs. Fyfe:** On a point of order, Madam Deputy Speaker. Given that the debate has to end at 11 o'clock and the Opposition are still not certain whether the Minister intends to accept the new clause, are we to be permitted to make a speech opposing the new clause or is this an example of the free speech to which Conservative Members pretend to adhere?

**Madam Deputy Speaker:** The occupant of the Chair has no control over the amount of time taken by an hon. Member who is moving a motion. This is a Chamber where free speech is allowed and it would be a good idea if other voices from other parts of the Chamber could be heard.

**Mr. Bennett:** I cannot be accused of not giving way to hon. Members who wanted to intervene. I have certainly not restricted the free speech of Opposition Members. I have given way. I shall give way to my hon. Friend the Member for Ipswich (Mr. Irvine), but I want to conclude my speech and hear the Minister's response.

**Mr. Michael Irvine** (Ipswich): I had the honour to serve with the hon. Member for Ashfield (Mr. Haynes) on the Standing Committee considering the Electricity Bill. At regular intervals during the sittings of that Committee, the hon. Member for Ashfield threatened various Conservative Members that he would take them outside. What is more, it is on the record. Is that not exactly the extravagant behaviour from which university vice-chancellors need to be protected when they are standing forth in the name of freedom? Is that not another example of how important it is that the new clause is accepted tonight?

**Mr. Haynes:** On a point of order, Madam Deputy Speaker. I never threatened anybody on that Committee. All I did was ask somebody to come outside so that I could have a word with him, and he happened to be the Minister.

**Madam Deputy Speaker:** I wish that I was in the same position.

**Mr. Bennett:** The deliberations of the Committee considering the Electricity Bill certainly sound more exciting than the debates in some of the Committees on which I have served. However, I wish to finish my speech.

**Mr. Allan Stewart:** Does my hon. Friend agree that, the new clause is also about another principle—the principle of the citizens of the United Kingdom. It is quite clear from her intervention that the hon. Member for Glasgow, Maryhill (Mrs. Fyfe) believes that the rights of freedom of expression of students in England and Wales should not be extended to Scotland. Does he agree that, as the Conservative and Unionist party, we must reject that proposition tonight?

**Mr. Bennett:** Absolutely.

What possible excuse will my hon. Friend the Minister give from his Scottish Office brief for not accepting the new clause? I am minded to push the new clause to a vote unless we get from him an assurance that, even if he is not prepared to accept it tonight because he has a brief, he will take it away and allow his real principles and philosophy and what he really believes in to overcome the Civil Service belief.

I finish by reminding my hon. Friend of what Voltaire said about freedom of speech. We have to defend people's views that we do not believe in and, even until death, defend their right to say it. I hope that my hon. Friend will support the new clause.

**Mr. Douglas:** On a point of order, Madam Deputy Speaker. For about 45 minutes, including interruptions, we have listened to the hon. Member for Pembroke (Mr. Bennett), who moved this new clause, yet he has no intention of pushing it to a vote. *[Interruption.]*

**Madam Deputy Speaker:** Order. That is not a point of order for the Chair.

**Mr. Michael Forsyth:** Perhaps it might help the hon. Member for Glasgow, Maryhill (Mrs. Fyfe) if I were to respond to her at this point, but I inform my hon. Friend the Member for Pembroke (Mr. Bennett) that I know what it must have been like to be the hon. Member for Fife, Central (Mr. McLeish) during our deliberations in Committee. I do not think that I have experienced anything quite like this in the 150 hours or so in which we considered the Bill. There seems to be some strength of feeling on the matter among my hon. Friends. I appreciate my hon. Friend's motives in tabling the new clause. My right hon. and learned Friend has carefully considered whether legislation is necessary for Scotland. I could go on to read the remainder of my speaking note, but I get the distinct impression that my hon. Friends would not find its content palatable.

I advise my hon. Friend the Member for Boothferry (Mr. Davis) that I questioned——

**Mr. Douglas:** The Minister should address the House.

**Mr. Forsyth:** I am addressing a point that was made in an intervention. If the hon. Gentleman will listen, he may learn something about what is going on in Scotland.

My hon. Friend the Member for Boothferry asked what evidence there was for the view that had been expressed by the Scottish Office that there was no problem in Scotland. I asked the Conservative Collegiate Forum to provide me with some examples in Scotland, which it failed to do, apart from he examples that were mentioned by my hon. Friend. The basis of the view that was taken at the time of the Education (No. 2) Act 1986—that this was not a problem in Scotland and that, therefore, the law should not intervene—still stands.

**Mr. Tebbit:** It might help if my hon. Friend the Minister came immediately to the point of whether he is saying that this new clause would be effective if there were those problems but that he does not think that there are those problems, or whether he is saying that this is not an effective clause to guard against such incidents if they should arise. Would he be quite clear about what he is saying?

**Mr. Forsyth:** Yes, I am quite clear; I am saying both. Without getting into the merits of whether the backbone of my hon. Friend the Member for Wantage (Mr. Jackson) is stronger than mine—my hon. Friend the Member for Brigg and Cleethorpes (Mr. Brown) raised this point during the discussion—my hon. Friend the Member for Wantage is looking at the effectiveness of the provisions in the 1986 Act. As my hon. Friend the Member for Pembroke said, there is considerable concern about the operation of those provisions.

Although I had intended to say to the House that there was no prospect of introducing this measure in Scotland, because there has not been a problem, I could go some way towards helping my hon. Friend the Member for Pembroke if I were to give an undertaking that we will look at this matter again on a rather more relaxed timetable in the light of my hon. Friend's review of the

operation of the provisions in England. I am sure that the House would not think it sensible for us to proceed at a breakneck pace without having an opportunity to consult and to take up the suggestion of my hon. Friend the Member for Boothferry. There will be a United Kingdom legislative opportunity shortly to deal with the commitments that have been made in respect of student finance.

**Dame Jill Knight** (Birmingham, Edgbaston): The powerful argument advanced by my hon. Friend the Member for Pembroke (Mr. Bennett) has occasioned an echo of support from the Tory Back Benches. We feel concerned that, while he made an excellent case, the Minister in response simply says that the answers cannot be given because they are unpalatable. I for one would have liked to hear those answers.

**Mr. Forsyth:** The answers are sound, but I do not think that they would meet the views that have been expressed. The argument is that, as there has been no problem in Scotland, it is not necessary to legislate. My hon. Friend the Member for Eastwood (Mr. Stewart) argued that higher education is organised on a United Kingdom basis and that guarantees of freedom of speech should apply on a United Kingdom basis. I am prepared to look at that argument, but only in the context of being certain that the provisions contained in the 1986 Act would be effective and would provide for the security about which my right hon. Friend the Member for Chingford (Mr. Tebbit) asked.

**Mr. Tebbit:** The easy and straightforward course would be for the Minister to accept the new clause; then he would have the leisurely progress of the legislation through the other place to consider the matter. During that time, if it was found not to be quite right, it could be amended. He has not advanced any argument so far to show how it would be harmful. He merely says that he hopes it will never be necessary. I do, too, but it would be jolly good to be in ahead of the problem. If we had had the foresight to have this type of legislation in England and Wales, we would not have had the problems we have there. He owes it to the decent students of this kingdom to legislate in this way, unless he has good reason to show that the proposed clause is defective or in some way would be offensive.

**Mr. Forsyth:** The bulk of the clause has applied in England and Wales and was embodied in the 1986 No. 2 Act. There is great unhappiness about it. I share the views that have been expressed about the imposition of charges on students who have attempted to run meetings, and that is one matter into which the Under-Secretary has looked. I assure my hon. Friend the Member for Pembroke that I will look at the matter again in the light of the review which the Under-Secretary carried out into the operation of the Act and that we will consider whether the judgment that has been made by my right hon. Friend should apply in the future.

**Mr. Dewar:** As we have the unusual spectacle of the Minister at bay—a boy standing on a burning deck—I would inform him that my hon. Friends and I feel that he is right in his initial reaction that what is proposed is unnecessary—*[Interruption.]* We know a little more about student life at Scottish universities than does the right hon. Member for Chingford. I hope the Minister will not

[*Mr. Dewar*]

consider us to be handing him a poisoned chalice when I tell him that he should hold to his present stand of principle and that if he does, he will have our full support.

**Mr. Forsyth:** I am grateful to the hon. Gentleman, although I am surprised that he should regard that as a helpful intervention.

**Mr. Nicholas Bennett:** I am listening carefully to what my hon. Friend the Minister is saying and appreciate that he has thrown away his civil servants' brief, which is a considerable thing for a Minister to do. He is listening to what the House is saying on this issue. However, I am concerned about what my hon. Friend said about the timing and because my hon. Friend talked about "leisurely". Will my hon. Friend give us an undertaking that he will reconsider this matter, in conjunction with the English and Welsh Department of Education and Science, and that the review will take place within the next six to nine months and not within a "leisurely" timetable?

**Mr. Forsyth:** I am happy to give my hon. Friend that undertaking and on that basis I hope that he will not feel inclined to press his new clause to the vote.

**Mr. John Carlisle:** I believe that my hon. Friend should support the new clause because several of us have turned down invitations from Scottish universities because they do not offer the same so-called "protection" that is offered at English and Welsh universities. My hon. Friends and I who receive such invitations do not feel that we can accept them until we can go with the assurance that my hon. Friend and the Government are right behind us in terms of the provisions that apply in England and Wales.

**Mr. Forsyth:** I shall look at that as part of the review and at the time that is taken——

**Madam Deputy Speaker:** Order.

**Mr. Nicholas Bennett:** I beg to ask leave to withdraw the motion.

**Madam Deputy Speaker:** Is it your pleasure that the new clause be withdrawn?

**Hon. Members:** No.
*Question put and negatived.*

*Order for Third Reading read.*

11 pm

**Mr. Michael Forsyth:** I beg to move, That the Bill be now read the Third time.

The deliberations on the Bill have, from time to time, been lively, but none more so than the discussions that we have just had on the last of the new clauses.

One interesting thing about the way in which the Opposition have chosen to oppose the legislation is that they have failed utterly to recognise that the part I provisions are permissive in nature. They simply set up an opportunity for the majority of parents to have the chance to run their schools in a way that meets their needs. The difference between the Government and the Opposition is that we are prepared to trust the parents and that the Opposition are not.

It has been suggested that this legislation is unwanted in Scotland, but as my hon. Friend the Member for Gainsborough and Horncastle (Mr. Leigh) repeatedly pointed out in Committee, the Opposition have refused to state the number of schools in Scotland that they expect to opt for self-governing status. Indeed, the hysteria with which they have greeted part I suggests that they believe that there will be a significant number.

The effectiveness of the legislation, even before it reaches the statute book and before we reached Third Reading, was clear for all to see in the statements made by the secretary of the Educational Institute of Scotland and by people such as the convenor of the education committee of Strathclyde, Malcolm Green. They are saying that the effect of the legislation will be that education authorities will have to take far more account of the wishes of parents and that education authorities will no longer simply be able to follow the view of education headquarters. In the revision of the planning of the delivery of education by authorities such as Strathclyde and others, one can see that even at this stage the legislation is having a salutary effect.

**Mrs. Fyfe:** When confronted with one of his children not wanting to eat his or her dinner, does the Minister open the child's mouth and shove the dinner down that child's throat; and if he does not behave like that with his children, will he explain why he is behaving like that towards the adult electorate of Scotland?

**Mr. Forsyth:** I am grateful to the hon. Lady for her somewhat indelicate analogy. The analogy of forcing things down people's throats is probably better applied to the kind of policies that are pursued by Strathclyde regional council in closing successful schools such as Paisley grammar school and in deciding that single-sex education is anachronistic and a choice that should not be available to parents.

**Mrs. Fyfe:** The Minister should answer my question.

**Mr. Forsyth:** I have answered the hon. Lady's question. No school will become self-governing unless the parents vote for it and unless the Secretary is convinced that they will be able to carry it through. Indeed, the Opposition seem to have been converted during our deliberations in Committee and elsewhere. I was rather struck by the statement that was made by the hon. Member for Fife, Central (Mr. McLeish) to the press today claiming that the Labour party would repeal some of these provisions. He said that they would be swept away. When we were discussing the matter in Committee he said:

"Some parts of the Bill might remain: some parts of it might be popular. It would be foolish for anyone to commit any Government of any political party to what they will do in two or three years' time."—[*Official Report, First Scottish Standing Committee*, 18 May 1989; c. 1501.]

Yet the hon. Gentleman did precisely that today. When I questioned him about it earlier, he said that it was because of the election results in Scotland.

The hon. Gentleman made his commitment in Committee on 18 May. On 19 May the hon. Member for Glasgow, Garscadden (Mr. Dewar) said on Scottish television:

"We will sweep away for ever all the embittering experience of the last 10 years—the poll tax, the schools Bill which were introduced in the face and need and teeth of Scottish public opinion. I think we'll also have a very much stronger assembly".

And so on. So on 18 May the hon. Member for Fife, Central was saying that anyone who made such promises was foolish and on 19 May the hon. Member for Garscadden was making exactly such foolish promises.

The point about self-governing schools is that they break the local authority monopoly. *[Interruption.]* I do not think that the hon. Member for Gordon (Mr. Bruce) is in a position to throw bricks in any direction. The hon. Gentleman will recall the Liberal leader of Strathclyde writing to me, pleading for the powers that are contained in the Bill in order to save Our Lady and Saint Francis school at the same time as the hon. Gentleman was denouncing the principle. When I asked him about the difference in policy between him and the Liberal leader of Strathclyde regional council, he explained that he was speaking on national policy and that the leader of the Liberal group on Strathclyde council was speaking on local matters.

**Mr. Malcolm Bruce** (Gordon): Obviously the election results were better for us than I thought, as the Minister feels the need to attack us. As he well knows, the argument that we put forward is that the Secretary of State would not have needed to introduce any Bill if he had retained his power to review any proposed school closure. That was the power that we wanted. It is reasonable for a local councillor to try to ensure that a school is not closed when he is caught between a Government and a Labour party who will not listen to the local people.

**Mr. Forsyth:** The hon. Gentleman has got it wrong again. The school in question was a denominational school where the Secretary of State retains his power. The difficulty in this case was that the hierarchy did not wish to refer the matter to the Secretary of State. Therefore, self-governing status was the option that was available to the school.

Self-governing schools break the local authority monopoly, create an opportunity for change and have resulted in local authorities being more responsive to the demands and wishes of parents.

The Bill extends choice by the introduction of powers to set up technology academies. Is it not amazing that the Labour party in Strathclyde would rather have school buildings empty in the Gorbals than have brand new, high-tech schools available for the people who voted for them in the Glasgow, Central by-election? I hope that everyone in Glasgow is aware that a brand-new school

[*Mr. Forsyth*]

could be available and that the only education cut that has been made in Glasgow was the cutting out of a brand-new school because of the ideology and fear that dominate the Labour party.

One interesting thing about the progress of our discussions on the Bill is that the use of the word "Anglicisation" has almost disappeared. We do not hear about it any more. That is probably because we have had a succession of amendments from the hon. Member for Fife, Central desperately trying to bring the Bill into line with the legislation in England.

We have had a good example of the transformation of the views of the Opposition as they have had to argue their case against my hon. Friends in Committee. I pay tribute to the effective way in which my hon. Friends conducted themselves in Committee. They astonished even the *Glasgow Herald* which has found it necessary to say that it got it wrong as regards the performance of my hon. Friends. Perhaps the most remarkable conversion of all was the suggestion that the Bill should be amended to create a parental majority for parents on the board of management. The hon. Member for Dundee, East (Mr. McAllion), who was a member of the Committee that considered the School Boards (Scotland) Bill, as it then was, condemned the Government for having a parental majority. He talked about the tyranny of the parental majority. By the time that the Bill that is before us began to be considered in Committee, the hon. Gentleman was arguing for a parental majority. We were happy to oblige the Opposition by introducing provisions for such a majority on Report.

**Mr. McAllion:** Then why is the Minister criticising us?

**Mr. Forsyth:** I am merely surprised that a party that puts so much effort into telling the people of Scotland that a parental majority would be tyranny and that it would be wrong that we should seek to amend the Bill to introduce such a majority.

The hon. Member for Fife, Central asked his colleagues not even to vote against the provisions in the Bill that allow for the introduction of national testing. It seemed that the Opposition accepted the principle of testing but were worried about how it would appear in practice. I was surprised to read the article in today's edition of the *Glasgow Herald* in which the hon. Gentleman stated:

"The Opposition need to form a triple alliance of parents, professionals and politicians. We must develop alternatives to the deeply damaging testing and teaching appraisal proposals contained in the new legislation."

If the testing proposals are so "deeply damaging", why did not the hon. Gentleman vote against them in Committee? He knows, as we all know, that parents want information about the performance of their children. They want that information communicated to them at home. In recognition of that, the Government have struck a popular blow.

In the same article—this is especially touching for those of us who were members of the Committee—the hon. Gentleman states:

"There is a sense of being out-manoeuvred yet no real alternative has emerged."

The hon. Gentleman is there referring to the Labour party. He continues:

"The forces of progressive education in Scotland must not only recapture the agenda and the initiative from the Government. We must once again dominate educational thinking in addition to an effective delivery of the service on the ground."

I have some advice for the hon. Gentleman: vote for the Bill's Third Reading and persuade the people of Scotland that the Opposition look to their interests and not to messages from the Educational Institute of Scotland. If he does that, he will make some progress in seeking to dominate the agenda.

**Mr. Jimmy Dunnachie** (Glasgow, Pollok): There are only 11 Conservative Members left in Scotland.

**Mr. Forsyth:** I was reading the words of the hon. Member for Fife, Central, who has admitted that the Government have set the agenda and have dominated it, and that the Labour party has lost it.

The Bill provides for the introduction of appraisal. What profession should not be subject to scrutiny of performance? What profession is more important than teaching? Opposition Members have found it difficult to work out their position on appraisal, and perhaps that is because the teaching unions are split on the issue. The EIS is against it but the Scottish Secondary Teachers Association, the Professional Association of Teachers and the other unions are supporting it. The hon. Member for Glasgow, Maryhill told us in Committee that the PAT is a union that no responsible teacher should join because it was not prepared to advise its members to go on strike. That says much about the attitude of Labour Members.

The EIS is claiming to be the official opposition. Its leader boasted that that was a sign of how effective it had been. Even the *Glasgow Herald* endorsed that view in an editorial on 12 June. It stated:

"If indeed the institute is the 'official' opposition, that says much for the tenacity and credibility of the union, its officials and members. But it doesn't say much for the performance of the Labour Party in Scotland."

Anyone who was a member of the Committee that considered the Bill would have made that observation. The hon. Member for Garscadden would have done himself more credit if instead of attacking my hon. Friends for their performance he had been in Committee arguing the Opposition's case.

**Mr. Dewar:** Like the Secretary of State!

**Mr. Forsyth:** My right hon. Friend was a member of the Committee. The hon. Gentleman could have been there to argue his party's case. He was not, however, and his party lost.

The Bill also provides for a major extension of the parents' charter which the hon. Member for Fife, Central told us his party now supports. His party opposed it when we proposed it, just as it opposed school boards, which it now supports. We look forward to Labour telling the people of Scotland in a year's time that it supports self-governing schools.

We have also abolished section 88, which even the Convention of Scottish Local Authorities argued was anachronistic, but the Opposition have found it difficult to go along with that. We are liberating the employment of teachers through insistence on the advertising of all posts above principal, and the ending of ring-fencing around official appointments.

The Bill is a major reforming piece of legislation. Much of its provisions have not been discussed in Scotland. Much of it has been presented in terms of the Opposition's myths. It will strengthen the parents' voice, it will strengthen accountability, it will extend choice, it will increase competition and it will raise standards, and I commend it to the House.

11.15 pm

**Mr. McLeish:** We have heard a characteristic and highly personal speech from the Under-Secretary of State with responsibility for education. It is always a grand sight to see him get animated and excited. One of the ingredients that he tends to miss out in his perorations, however, is the fact that the Bill is universally despised in Scotland.

There was no educational argument in the Minister's speech. Rather we had a rich mix of personal animosity and the ideology that we have come to expect from him and his erstwhile colleagues who were recruited on to the Committee to do the job that they enjoy most—being destructive and counter-productive rather than having a sensible debate about education in Scotland.

It is remarkable that, despite suffering electoral casualties at every election in Scotland—we have a Tory MEP-free Scotland and there are only 10 Scottish Tory Members at Westminster—the one thing that the Government will not face is the view of Scottish electors as measured in district and regional council, general and European Parliament elections. I must ask the Secretary of State for Scotland, who I believe is beginning to tune into the fact that he faces a wipe-out of Conservative-held Scottish seats in 1991 or 1992, when he will get a grip on the continuing excesses of his Minister, who is projecting a form of education which is not liked.

The Secretary of State laughs, but why can he go to Wales and suggest there that there should be a triple alliance? He seems to have been converted to regional policies again. He does not argue their case in the Cabinet, though. He goes to Wales and suggests that Wales, the north and Scotland should unite as a triple alliance against the forces of Thatcherism to try to reinstate some sensible regional policy.

The Secretary of State has spoken about trying to put the Scottish scene back on a moderate footing. He has offered glasnost to COSLA. The most important thing that he can do tonight is to distance himself from the Bill and scrap it. At a stroke, that would help the Tories, possibly, to regain some lost ground in Scotland.

The Under-Secretary of State and the Secretary of State would benefit from re-reading the letter that was sent to them by the Church of Scotland on 5 June. Its general assembly passed a motion which was highly critical of the opting-out provisions. On 5 June, Mr. Alasdair Morton, from the Church of Scotland's department of education, sent a letter to the Under-Secretary of State—I know that he does not like this, but I hope that he will listen—which ran:

"Accordingly in the name of the General Assembly of the Church of Scotland I must request the Government to delete Part 1 of the above Bill and to depart from the matters it contains."

That is not an extreme group; it speaks on behalf of Scottish interests—*[Interruption.]* Conservative Members may be disparaging about the Church of Scotland, but it captured in a single sentence the feelings of Scots towards the Bill.

The Under-Secretary spent two or three sessions in Committee attacking the Church of Scotland because it had the temerity to involve itself in political debate. The hon. Gentleman felt that it should concern itself with religious education and religious observance and keep out of politics—[HON. MEMBERS: "Hear, hear."] Hon. Members may applaud that, but the Church of Scotland behaved responsibly and suggested that the Bill be scrapped.

It is interesting that the Prime Minister visited Scotland and addressed the Perth conference on 12 May. She said about Scottish education:

"Excellence has always been part of the Scottish tradition. And when it comes to the Glasgow Vets School, I'm with Malcolm—I support it all the way."

I am sure that she was referring to the Glasgow vets school, not to Malcolm. She continued:

"In a competitive world, Scottish children deserve to be given the very best education and the very best training."

In her distinctive and characteristic style, she then said:

"It's not enough to be just good enough. The Scots need to shine—to be way out in front. And under Conservative Government, they will have the freedom and opportunity to do just that."

That is a rich, rich hypocrisy in view of the Bill and its potential impact on Scottish education during the next two or three years.

The tragedy of the past three months and of tonight's debate is that the Bill is irrelevant to the real needs of Scottish education and to the challenges that Scotland will face in the 1990s with the single European market, the advent of technology and major demographic changes. What does Scotland get?—a Bill that will turn back the education clock 20, 30 or even 40 years. Few, if any, Scots want the Bill to reach the statute book.

I listened to the Minister giving a brief résumé of the Committee stage. He can ignore us and treat us with contempt—that is one of his characteristics—but can he continue to treat the people of Scotland with the same contempt? I said earlier that the Secretary of State appeared to be distancing himself from the excesses and extremism of certain members of the Government, both in the United Kingdom generally and in Scotland. We need some stability in Scottish education.

The Bill, with its technology academies, opting out and testing measures, has the potential to tear Scottish education apart. In whose interests will that be? Will it be in the interests of the children, of the much-vaunted parents about whom the Minister constantly speaks, or of the future of education? The Bill is a miserable, mean and pathetic measure which has been dressed up under the guise of parental choice.

The Scottish people have had no real say in drawing up the Bill. At the last election, from Lord Goold through to senior Ministers, and even the Prime Minister, they all said that there should be opting out for England and Wales but not yet for Scotland. The Bill is not only tragic: it is a total betrayal of what Scotland has been led to expect.

**Mr. Bill Walker:** I would not wish the House to be misled any more than I wished the Committee to be misled. My right hon. Friend the Member for Kincardine and Deeside (Mr. Buchanan-Smith) asked central office in Edinburgh about that matter. He was given an answer that was not in accordance with what I understood the position to be or with the platform on which I stood at the last election. Hon. Members must ask themselves why, then, my result improved. I made my views about this legislation clear—I wanted it, I worked for it and I look forward to its implementation. I said that during 44 speeches in my constituency.

**Mr. McLeish:** I am sure that the right hon. Member for Kincardine and Deeside (Mr. Buchanan-Smith) will want to put on the record what was actually said in the telephone calls between him, the Scottish Office and the hon. Member for Dumfries (Sir H. Monro).

There is a betrayal here, and "betrayal" is one of the dirtiest words in politics. The Ministers here tonight have betrayed the people of Scotland. It was made quite clear in the general election campaign, even to the extent that the Government's principal spokesmen were paraded before *The Scotsman,* that the Government categorically denied that opting out would be on the agenda. However, that is history.

The right hon. Member for Kincardine and Deeside had an excellent piece in this morning's edition of *The Scotsman.* He gave advice to which the Secretary of State for Scotland should listen. It is clear that, after the debacle of the European elections and the impact of Thatcherism in Scotland, where the Tories were completely wiped out, the right hon. Member for Kincardine and Deeside has made some excellent observations. He has offered the Secretary of State and the Conservatives some ideas on the way forward. He stated that, in education, most people regarded the schools opt-out legislation as an irrelevance and continued to be offended by attitudes towards the universities. Those were courageous comments, and it is not for the Opposition to exploit them further.

There is compelling pressure on the Secretary of State for Scotland to listen to the Opposition, to the Scottish people and to the reasoned, rational sane voice of Scottish Conservative politics like that espoused by certain distinguished Tory Back Benchers. The Opposition are listening to those Tory Back Benchers. It is often asked: if that voice is good enough for the Opposition, why can it not be good enough for Conservative Members?

The Government parade choice and parental power. However, this Bill, like education legislation in England, centralises power in a way that we have not seen in Scottish education for many years. For "choice" we should read centralised control. The Minister referred to standards, while my hon. Friend the Member for Dundee, East (Mr. McAllion) spoke about selection. The Bill is not about standards in Scottish education. Most of the Conservative Members who have spoken tonight know nothing about the standards in Scottish schools. All the evidence suggests that Scottish schools are doing extremely well, although they could be doing much better.

We should also be concerned about parents. The involvement of parents was clearly the brainwave of the Minister and of the Prime Minister. They must have asked themselves how they could sell unpalatable policies throughout the length and breadth of the country. They decided to hi-jack parents. For parents we should of course read privatisation.

Scots are not fools and very few Scots will be taken in by this parental nonsense. If the Government were serious about parental choice, they would give every parent the chance to be involved in schools instead of the rather selective situation which will ensue through the school boards, and the more selective approach through self-governing schools.

Earlier in the debate, the Minister chided me for suggesting that we should not be making statements about future education policy. We were buoyed up by last week's results. It is clear that politics is about mood and morale. We look forward with increasing confidence to the day when we can rid the Scottish Office of its present incumbents and bring some sanity back to Scottish education.

The Minister may not like what was said about his precious assisted places scheme. That scheme may disappear on day one when the Opposition regain control of the Scottish Office, but much will have to be done in the rest of the week. The people of Scotland who are considering opting out, or technology academies, should be aware that the Opposition want to ensure that schools which opt out and any technology academies will be reintegrated into the education authority sector.

The reason is simple: both those so-called innovations have nothing to do with extending choice or creating diversity. They are all to do with destroying, step by step, the comprehensive system of education that has been built up by Conservatives, Labour, Scottish nationalists and Liberals during the past few years. When we take office, we shall have none of this nonsense. We shall give back to Scotland investment in education and policies to strengthen the comprehensive system. In the interim, we shall ensure that there is constructive resistance to such education policies.

It is a tragedy that a Bill which is so uniquely despised in Scotland has taken up so much time in the House. We had nearly two months in Committee. The Minister had the cheek to suggest that he had accepted 100 amendments in Committee. Without preaching Anglicisation, may I say that the sad fact is that this shabby Scottish Bill does not even have the safeguards that were included in the English Act. What the Secretary of State for Education and Science thought was good enough for English and Welsh people has not been accepted by the ideologue who is the Under-Secretary of State for Scotland.

This is a disappointing day for Scottish education; but morale in education is high. There will be a struggle against this legislation, and I assure those taking part that the Labour party will be in the forefront of the struggle. I urge my colleagues to vote against Third Reading. This Bill does not deserve it.

11.31 pm

**Mr. Alick Buchanan-Smith:** I need no advice from the hon. Member for Fife, Central (Mr. McLeish) on what I should do or where I may stand. I am grateful to my hon. Friend the Member for Tayside, North (Mr. Walker), but I am perfectly happy to answer for myself. Nothing that has happened in the past few days has given me cause to change my views on this issue or on any others. Hon. Members on both sides of the House will acknowledge that I have consistently been saying the same things about education in Scotland for the past two years.

I am genuinely sad, as we come to the Third Reading of the Bill, that nothing has happened during our consideration of it to convince me that it has merits and should be supported. I still regard it as irrelevant. I do not believe that there is a serious demand for it in Scotland, although, as my hon. Friend the Member for Eastwood (Mr. Stewart) has repeatedly said, there is a demand in some areas. Those to whom I have talked have sensed some confusion over that demand. Is it being demanded for its own sake, or is it being demanded as a way out of problems such as a threatened closure? I acknowledge that there is demand in some areas, but no one can contradict my assertion that there is no general demand for the Bill in Scotland.

My right hon. and learned Friend the Secretary of State and my hon. Friend the Under-Secretary of State have said to me several times, "If it is irrelevant, and if there is no general demand, why worry?" I worry because I believe that the Bill has deep implications for the structure and future development of education in Scotland. I ask them in return, "If it is irrelevant, as I believe it is, and if there is no evidence of great demand, why waste precious parliamentary time in this Session on a Bill which is unnecessary and which has created needless controversy?"

The Bill will change the structure of education in Scotland because it contains the seeds of division for the system generally and, worst of all, for those communities where schools may consider opting out. There is scope in the Bill for extreme groups from any background to exploit problems. The Bill is not in the line of succession of our Scottish educational tradition.

As I said at the outset, in recent years we have witnessed considerable changes in Scottish education—changes in the curriculum and in examinations, for example, and the introduction of school boards, which I supported once the original proposals had been moderated. The Government are imposing far too heavy a diet of change for no clear educational reason or advantage, and in doing that they are wrong. The Bill follows far too closely on the establishment of the school boards. Hon. Members will have addressed parent-teacher association meetings and other school meetings in their constituencies, and will know of the confusion in many people's minds about the establishment of the school boards, which I support, and the opting-out proposals, which follow so closely on it. The Government are doing a disservice to the successful establishment and operation of school boards by introducing the Bill so soon afterwards. The school boards should have been up and working before further change was contemplated.

I am one who believes in evolution, not revolution—as all good Conservatives should. Nowhere in our national life is evolution more important than in education. I am sad that the Government should have proceeded in this way, and equally sad to say that I still cannot support the Bill.

11.36 pm

**Sir Russell Johnston:** The right hon. Member for Kincardine and Deeside (Mr. Buchanan-Smith) has made a speech of clarity and courage. We all know that it is not easy to speak out against one's party, and that must be especially true given the difficult position of the Conservative party in Scotland. The right hon. Gentleman made a straightforward speech, and I agreed with almost everything that he said, although our impression is that the school boards are not proving as acceptable as some claim. But let us leave the school boards aside because they are not the main issue tonight.

The Minister has said that we are wrong to oppose the Bill because it is only permissive—people can choose to opt out or choose not to. We oppose the Bill because, as the right hon. Member for Kincardine and Deeside said, there is no demand for it in Scotland. It is worth repeating that it is passing strange that, while the Government at least accept that more than 50 per cent. of parents should

have to vote for opting-out before it can take place, the Bill stems from a Government with only 25 per cent. of support in Scotland.

The Bill has been rejected throughout Scotland, and its rejection has been coupled with a lack of comprehension of the motivation behind it. People are asking why it is being introduced. As the right hon. Member for Kincardine and Deeside asked, why have we spent all this time putting the Bill through the House?

The Government say that the Bill is about increasing choice. The Scottish Consumer Council, on the other hand, argues:

"Proposals to allow schools to 'opt-out' of education authority control are ill-timed and do not offer parents a significant extension of choice."

The Church of Scotland's education committee says:

"The exercise of powers being proposed by the Bill are likely to be to the disadvantage of children in the sections of the community already suffering most deprivation."

The presbytery of Inverness education committee says:

"The committee is not convinced that the proposals in this paper . . . are to the best interests of Scottish Education."

The great majority of those involved in education seem to be saying that the Bill is not relevant and will not expand educational opportunity. The Minister has attacked the Educational Institute of Scotland; in Committee he did so often. Far be it from me to say that the EIS is a perfect organisation, but its reason for existence is to advance the quality of education and that is what it strives to do. It makes no sense for the Minister responsible for education in Scotland to spend so much time attacking the EIS rather than discussing matters with it and trying to move forward.

Many people feel that the Bill could represent a covert means or reintroducing selectivity, at least in certain areas. That was also in the mind of the right hon. Member for Kincardine and Deeside and it was certainly a view felt by the Scottish Parent Teacher Council which

"believes that comprehensive education might well be compromised by these proposals and that it would have been more honest to have an open and informed debate about its successes and failures, rather than allowing it to be eroded as a consequence of this proposed legislation."

Our view is that unnecessary legislation is being imposed on the people of Scotland by a minority. The Minister referred earlier to something being a travesty of democracy. This is a travesty of democracy in a country that is increasingly becoming the least democratic in the European Community.

11.40 pm

**Mr. Allan Stewart:** With the greatest respect, the hon. Member for Inverness, Nairn and Lochaber (Sir R. Johnston) is not in the strongest position to talk about electoral percentages, following the recent election results. I shall not extend that argument because I would not wish to add any further insult to the injuries that were inflicted upon the Social and Liberal Democrats by the electorate.

I warmly congratulate my hon. Friend the Minister on a masterly presentation of the Government's case throughout the long Committee stage. He was flexible where he felt that there was a case for changing the Government's position. For example, he was flexible on the issue of the chairmanship of the university courts and in providing for a second ballot before self-governing status could be achieved.

It gives me particular pleasure to speak on Third Reading. I had the pleasure last year of tabling a new

[*Mr. Allan Stewart*]

clause to the School Boards (Scotland) Bill which would have provided for self-governing schools. I moved that new clause not because of ideology or any particular philosophical convictions but because of representations from constituents. That is my answer to all the nonsense about manifesto commitments and what was said and what was not said. During my election campaign I did not make a manifesto commitment to support opting out, but that was before the decisions by Strathclyde regional council which persuaded me as a constituency Member to raise this matter in the House. I am delighted that the Bill is to reach the statute book.

In Committee, we heard an enormous amount of nonsense about what are described as Scotland's educational traditions. In the *Glasgow Herald* this morning, we read about what the Labour party believes Scottish educational traditions to be all about. The hon. Member for Fife, Central (Mr. McLeish) has described Scottish education in this way:

"Before 1979 Education was used by successive Governments in an attempt to engineer a more egalitarian society."

That is the kind of Scottish educational tradition in which the Labour party believes, and it should be rejected comprehensively by the Government.

We heard also that the concept of technology academies is alien to Scotland's educational traditions. However, one of the proposed sites for a technology academy agreed by the leader of Strathclyde council and by the chairman of its education committee is Allan Glens. Anyone who knows anything about the history of Allan Glens knows that it was always envisaged as the location of a technology academy.

There has been much discussion about the number of schools that may opt for self-governing status. I may tell my hon. Friend the Minister that he has already won, even before a single school chooses to be self governing, because he has changed the way in which education authorities react to parents' wishes. That is what the Bill is all about.

I have referred, at excessive length in the view of Opposition Members, to the Neilston case and to others I know about. There is no doubt that when Scotland's education leaders take decisions in future, they will be aware of the importance of being responsive to parents, because parents will have the additional choice of opting for self-governing status. That is the key message that goes out from the House to the parents of Scotland.

The Opposition's performance on the Bill has been subject to a certain amount of press comment, and I do not wish to deepen their wounds. However, by far the greatest tribute, if that is the right word, to their lack of performance was that of the general secretary of the Educational Institute of Scotland, who refers to the EIS providing Scotland's official opposition to the Bill. What does that say about the role played by the Labour party in Scotland? The *Glasgow Herald* article, commenting on Mr. Jim Martin, the EIS's new general secretary, stated:

"He has been impressive, partly because he has usurped the political role of the Opposition."

In his surprisingly honest article in the *Glasgow Herald*, the hon. Member for Fife, Central writes:

"There is a sense of being outmanoeuvred, yet no real alternative has emerged."

There can be no better description of the Opposition's performance during the passage of the Bill. That is their epitaph, and they wrote it themselves.

11.47 pm

**Mrs. Fyfe:** When the Scottish public realise tomorrow morning that about 50 Conservative Members wasted a whole hour of the precious little time left for debate to urge freedom for Conservative students, the National Front, contra generals, and the like, and then revealed, by not pressing new clause 12, that they really wanted to store up their views for a future debate, that public will be bitterly angry.

In debates lasting seven hours, no opportunity has been given to debate the needs of adult learners attending schools or colleges of further education, student rectors, Gaelic speakers, trade union rights, negotiating machinery, and the low wages of school workers. The subject of further education received only a brief mention on Second Reading and in Committee, and none at all tonight. Numerous other topics relating to the Bill—it would take too long to mention them all—have not been aired tonight, because Conservative Members thought that it would be more fun to create a diversion for an hour. That is how seriously they treat Scottish legislation, and that is why they are treated with such contempt by the Scottish electorate.

During the recent by-election I spoke at several public meetings on behalf of my hon. Friend the Member for Glasgow, Central (Mr. Watson). With my colleagues I knocked on doors every day for three weeks, and not once did I find anyone who was in favour of the Bill. The local electorate also knew that Allan Glen's school was in Townhead and not in the Gorbals, thereby demonstrating the superiority of their knowledge of education in Glasgow to that of the Minister. Not only did no one ask anything about the Bill, but when I raised it at public meetings not a single member of the audience professed to be in favour of it.

Hon. Members have talked of testing. It is clear that the Tories have failed every electoral test in Scotland, again and again. I remind them that someone with more wisdom than Robert the Bruce said, "If you try, try, try again and still do not succeed, quit: no need to be a damn fool about it!"

11.50 pm

**Mr. McFall:** It gives me great pleasure to speak against the Bill, whose hallmark has been a complete lack of consultation with teachers, education managers or parents in Scotland. There has been more consultation with English Back Benchers than with anyone in Scotland.

For 35 minutes the hon. Member for Pembroke (Mr. Bennett) wittered on, encouraging interventions; yet Scottish Members who were on the Committee, scrutinising the legislation line by line, can get in only two or three minutes at the end of the night. There is something wrong with the system: that is why the frustrations are building up in Scotland, and the Government are so blind that they cannot even see it. The conduct of this Bill shows how out of touch they are with Scottish education, and the narrowness of their view as put forward by the Parliamentary Under-Secretary. Is it the view of the Secretary of State? My interpretation is that Scottish education at present is dictated by a leak in the *Glasgow*

*Herald* and by the hon. Member for Eastwood (Mr. Stewart), who has more power now than he has ever had: he is the Dirty Harry of Scottish politics. Whenever he says anything, it is put forward as education legislation.

I said at the outset of the proceedings on the School Boards (Scotland) Bill 1988 that a two-stage process was involved. I was departing from the view of my Front Bench, which had stated that the Bill represented a climbdown by the Government: my view was that the Bill had been set up to level the playing field between Scotland and England so that the legislation available to England could be introduced. The Parliamentary Under-Secretary said in this very Chamber that the Secretary of State for Education and Science was frit, because he would not go further and completely privatise English education. It was the real Parliamentary Under-Secretary who stood up then, but tonight, in the freedom of speech debate, we did not see him. But we see him in Scotland, however, each and every day, as do the electorate: we see him for all that he is not worth.

Many aspects of the Bill are reprehensible—indeed, every aspect, not least that of academic selection. On Monday 6 March the Secretary of State said that the Bill was not about selectivity. If I were not in the Chamber, I would describe that as a gross mendacity; I am in the Chamber, however, so I shall not. Writ large in the Bill is that it is about academic selection: it is about taking Scottish education back 100 years, and putting it in a Victorian political time warp in which the minority will be satisfied and the majority rejected. The Bill will destroy public education. Some say that it will Anglicise education in Scotland. That is nonsense. It only gives succour to the Scottish National party and others. *[Interruption.]* I am quite happy to say that.

**Mr. Salmond:** I remind the hon. Gentleman that it was the Educational Institute of Scotland that said that the Bill would Anglicise Scottish education.

**Mr. McFall:** The hon. Gentleman is quite right. As a consequence I went to the Educational Institute of Scotland's offices in Edinburgh and told them where it had gone wrong. It cannot be said too often that the Bill is about the destruction of public education in Scotland. It will loosen the links between local education authorities and the electorate. The Under-Secretary of State is loosening the links because for many years Labour-controlled local education authorities have been too successful. This is a naked political attempt to make a breach between electorates and councillors. The Under-Secretary of State knows that. I have asked him about it two or three times and each time he has smiled or smirked at me.

The Minister and the Conservative party in Scotland are ideologues. They have both public and private aspirations. The public aspiration is that the Bill will provide greater choice and freedom. The private aspiration was revealed when the Under-Secretary of State lowered his guard. It is about greed—about cheque-book education. At a meeting of the Scottish Grand Committee in Edinburgh the Under-Secretary of State said that for him education was about people using their cheque books in the way that they want. Education, for him, is a rejection of all that has been good in Scottish education during the last 100 years—an education system which has provided choice and diversity.

The Conservative party has not briefed its candidates or its officers in Scotland. I was on a public platform with a certain Michael Hirst, who used to be a Member of Parliament, but he was rejected by the electors in Strathkelvin and Bearsden. He said that the electorate would be able to get rid of individuals who do not come up to the mark as school board members or officers after four years. But four years is far too long. Scottish education will be destroyed within one or two years. The Minister was clever enough to see that, because he wants to destroy it within a year or two.

The evolution of education in Scotland during the last 100 years has been a painful process. We stand for an egalitarian system and for equality of opportunity for boys and girls. That is why most of the Scottish electorate are behind us. That is why the right hon. Member for Kincardine and Deeside (Mr. Buchanan-Smith) and for Dumfries (Sir H. Monro) are behind us. That is why 40 per cent. of Scottish Tory Back Benchers are against the Bill. They are listening to their constituents. They are not listening, as is the Under-Secretary of State, to the No Turning Back group.

**Mr. McAllion:** Will my hon. Friend comment on what was said by the right hon. Member for Kincardine and Deeside (Mr. Buchanan-Smith)—that, like all decent Scottish Tories, he believed in evolution rather than revolution? Yet in Committee on the School Boards (Scotland) Bill the Minister boasted that he was a revolutionary. Might that not explain the very bad results for the Conservative party last Thursday?

**Mr. McFall:** I entirely agree with my hon. Friend. The right hon. Member for Kincardine and Deeside remarked that the legislation has appeared out of the blue. It is on record in *Hansard* that during the last general election in 1987 the right hon. Member for Kincardine and Deeside phoned Conservative Central Office in Edinburgh and asked, "Is opting-out on the Tory agenda for this election?" He was told loud and clear, "No, there is no such thing as opting-out coming on to the agenda so you can be reassured and you can tell your electorate that we have no such thing on the agenda." But the right hon. Member for Kincardine and Deeside did not consider the hon. Member for Eastwood or the Prime Minister's Private Office——

*It being Twelve o'clock,* MADAM DEPUTY SPEAKER *proceeded, pursuant to order [3rd May] and the Resolution this day to put forthwith the Question already proposed from the Chair.*

*The House divided: Ayes 245, Noes 191.*

**Division No. 254]**                                    **[12 midnight**

### AYES

| | |
|---|---|
| Adley, Robert | Bellingham, Henry |
| Aitken, Jonathan | Bendall, Vivian |
| Alexander, Richard | Bennett, Nicholas *(Pembroke)* |
| Alison, Rt Hon Michael | Benyon, W. |
| Allason, Rupert | Bevan, David Gilroy |
| Amess, David | Biffen, Rt Hon John |
| Amos, Alan | Blackburn, Dr John G. |
| Arbuthnot, James | Blaker, Rt Hon Sir Peter |
| Arnold, Jacques *(Gravesham)* | Body, Sir Richard |
| Arnold, Tom *(Hazel Grove)* | Bonsor, Sir Nicholas |
| Ashby, David | Boscawen, Hon Robert |
| Aspinwall, Jack | Boswell, Tim |
| Atkins, Robert | Bottomley, Peter |
| Atkinson, David | Bowden, A *(Brighton K'pto'n)* |
| Baker, Nicholas *(Dorset N)* | Bowden, Gerald *(Dulwich)* |
| Batiste, Spencer | Bowis, John |

Boyson, Rt Hon Dr Sir Rhodes
Brandon-Bravo, Martin
Brazier, Julian
Bright, Graham
Brown, Michael *(Brigg & Cl't's)*
Burns, Simon
Burt, Alistair
Butcher, John
Butler, Chris
Butterfill, John
Carlisle, John, *(Luton N)*
Carlisle, Kenneth *(Lincoln)*
Carrington, Matthew
Carttiss, Michael
Cash, William
Chalker, Rt Hon Mrs Lynda
Channon, Rt Hon Paul
Chapman, Sydney
Chope, Christopher
Churchill, Mr
Clark, Dr Michael *(Rochford)*
Clarke, Rt Hon K. *(Rushcliffe)*
Colvin, Michael
Conway, Derek
Coombs, Anthony *(Wyre F'rest)*
Coombs, Simon *(Swindon)*
Cope, Rt Hon John
Cormack, Patrick
Couchman, James
Cran, James
Currie, Mrs Edwina
Curry, David
Davis, David *(Boothferry)*
Day, Stephen
Dicks, Terry
Dorrell, Stephen
Douglas-Hamilton, Lord James
Dover, Den
Dunn, Bob
Durant, Tony
Dykes, Hugh
Favell, Tony
Forman, Nigel
Forsyth, Michael *(Stirling)*
Freeman, Roger
Gorman, Mrs Teresa
Greenway, Harry *(Ealing N)*
Gregory, Conal
Hamilton, Neil *(Tatton)*
Hampson, Dr Keith
Hanley, Jeremy
Hannam, John
Hargreaves, A. *(B'ham H'll Gr')*
Hargreaves, Ken *(Hyndburn)*
Harris, David
Haselhurst, Alan
Hawkins, Christopher
Hayes, Jerry
Hayhoe, Rt Hon Sir Barney
Hayward, Robert
Heathcoat-Amory, David
Heddle, John
Hicks, Mrs Maureen *(Wolv' NE)*
Hicks, Robert *(Cornwall SE)*
Higgins, Rt Hon Terence L.
Hill, James
Hind, Kenneth
Hogg, Hon Douglas *(Gr'th'm)*
Hordern, Sir Peter
Howard, Michael
Howarth, Alan *(Strat'd-on-A)*
Howarth, G. *(Cannock & B'wd)*
Howell, Rt Hon David *(G'dford)*
Howell, Ralph *(North Norfolk)*
Hughes, Robert G. *(Harrow W)*
Hunt, David *(Wirral W)*
Hunt, Sir John *(Ravensbourne)*
Hunter, Andrew
Irvine, Michael
Jack, Michael

Jackson, Robert
Janman, Tim
Jessel, Toby
Johnson Smith, Sir Geoffrey
Jones, Gwilym *(Cardiff N)*
Jones, Robert B *(Herts W)*
Key, Robert
King, Roger *(B'ham N'thfield)*
Kirkhope, Timothy
Knapman, Roger
Knight, Greg *(Derby North)*
Knight, Dame Jill *(Edgbaston)*
Knox, David
Lamont, Rt Hon Norman
Lang, Ian
Latham, Michael
Lawrence, Ivan
Lennox-Boyd, Hon Mark
Lester, Jim *(Broxtowe)*
Lightbown, David
Lilley, Peter
Lloyd, Sir Ian *(Havant)*
Lloyd, Peter *(Fareham)*
Lord, Michael
Luce, Rt Hon Richard
Lyell, Sir Nicholas
Macfarlane, Sir Neil
McLoughlin, Patrick
McNair-Wilson, Sir Michael
McNair-Wilson, Sir Patrick
Mans, Keith
Maples, John
Marland, Paul
Marshall, John *(Hendon S)*
Marshall, Michael *(Arundel)*
Martin, David *(Portsmouth S)*
Mates, Michael
Maude, Hon Francis
Mayhew, Rt Hon Sir Patrick
Meyer, Sir Anthony
Miller, Sir Hal
Mills, Iain
Mitchell, Andrew *(Gedling)*
Mitchell, Sir David
Moate, Roger
Montgomery, Sir Fergus
Morrison, Sir Charles
Morrison, Rt Hon P *(Chester)*
Moss, Malcolm
Moynihan, Hon Colin
Neale, Gerrard
Nelson, Anthony
Neubert, Michael
Nicholls, Patrick
Nicholson, David *(Taunton)*
Norris, Steve
Onslow, Rt Hon Cranley
Oppenheim, Phillip
Page, Richard
Paice, James
Patnick, Irvine
Patten, John *(Oxford W)*
Peacock, Mrs Elizabeth
Porter, David *(Waveney)*
Price, Sir David
Raison, Rt Hon Timothy
Rathbone, Tim
Redwood, John
Renton, Tim
Rhodes James, Robert
Ridley, Rt Hon Nicholas
Rifkind, Rt Hon Malcolm
Roe, Mrs Marion
Rossi, Sir Hugh
Rost, Peter
Rumbold, Mrs Angela
Sackville, Hon Tom
Sainsbury, Hon Tim
Sayeed, Jonathan
Shaw, David *(Dover)*

Shaw, Sir Michael *(Scarb')*
Shephard, Mrs G. *(Norfolk SW)*
Sims, Roger
Skeet, Sir Trevor
Smith, Tim *(Beaconsfield)*
Soames, Hon Nicholas
Speed, Keith
Speller, Tony
Spicer, Michael *(S Worcs)*
Squire, Robin
Stanley, Rt Hon Sir John
Steen, Anthony
Stern, Michael
Stevens, Lewis
Stewart, Allan *(Eastwood)*
Stewart, Andy *(Sherwood)*
Stokes, Sir John
Stradling Thomas, Sir John
Summerson, Hugo
Taylor, Ian *(Esher)*
Taylor, John M *(Solihull)*
Taylor, Teddy *(S'end E)*
Temple-Morris, Peter
Thompson, Patrick *(Norwich N)*
Thornton, Malcolm
Thurnham, Peter
Townend, John *(Bridlington)*
Tracey, Richard
Tredinnick, David

Trippier, David
Trotter, Neville
Twinn, Dr Ian
Vaughan, Sir Gerard
Waddington, Rt Hon David
Wakeham, Rt Hon John
Walker, Bill *(T'side North)*
Waller, Gary
Ward, John
Wardle, Charles *(Bexhill)*
Warren, Kenneth
Watts, John
Wells, Bowen
Whitney, Ray
Widdecombe, Ann
Wiggin, Jerry
Wilkinson, John
Wilshire, David
Winterton, Mrs Ann
Winterton, Nicholas
Wolfson, Mark
Wood, Timothy
Yeo, Tim
Young, Sir George *(Acton)*

Tellers for the Ayes:
    Mr. David Maclean and
Mr. Michael Fallon.

## NOES

Abbott, Ms Diane
Adams, Allen *(Paisley N)*
Allen, Graham
Alton, David
Anderson, Donald
Archer, Rt Hon Peter
Armstrong, Hilary
Banks, Tony *(Newham NW)*
Barnes, Harry *(Derbyshire NE)*
Barron, Kevin
Battle, John
Beckett, Margaret
Beith, A. J.
Bell, Stuart
Benn, Rt Hon Tony
Bennett, A. F. *(D'nt'n & R'dish)*
Bidwell, Sydney
Blair, Tony
Blunkett, David
Boateng, Paul
Boyes, Roland
Bray, Dr Jeremy
Brown, Gordon *(D'mline E)*
Brown, Nicholas *(Newcastle E)*
Bruce, Malcolm *(Gordon)*
Buckley, George J.
Caborn, Richard
Callaghan, Jim
Campbell, Menzies *(Fife NE)*
Campbell-Savours, D. N.
Canavan, Dennis
Clark, Dr David *(S Shields)*
Clarke, Tom *(Monklands W)*
Clay, Bob
Clelland, David
Cohen, Harry
Cook, Frank *(Stockton N)*
Cook, Robin *(Livingston)*
Corbyn, Jeremy
Cousins, Jim
Cryer, Bob
Cummings, John
Cunliffe, Lawrence
Dalyell, Tam
Darling, Alistair
Davies, Rt Hon Denzil *(Llanelli)*
Davies, Ron *(Caerphilly)*
Davis, Terry *(B'ham Hodge H'l)*
Dewar, Donald

Dixon, Don
Dobson, Frank
Doran, Frank
Douglas, Dick
Duffy, A. E. P.
Dunnachie, Jimmy
Eadie, Alexander
Eastham, Ken
Ewing, Harry *(Falkirk E)*
Fatchett, Derek
Field, Frank *(Birkenhead)*
Fields, Terry *(L'pool B G'n)*
Fisher, Mark
Flannery, Martin
Flynn, Paul
Foot, Rt Hon Michael
Foster, Derek
Foulkes, George
Fraser, John
Fyfe, Maria
Galbraith, Sam
Galloway, George
Garrett, John *(Norwich South)*
George, Bruce
Gilbert, Rt Hon Dr John
Godman, Dr Norman A.
Golding, Mrs Llin
Gordon, Mildred
Graham, Thomas
Grant, Bernie *(Tottenham)*
Griffiths, Nigel *(Edinburgh S)*
Griffiths, Win *(Bridgend)*
Grocott, Bruce
Hardy, Peter
Harman, Ms Harriet
Henderson, Doug
Hinchliffe, David
Home Robertson, John
Hood, Jimmy
Howarth, George *(Knowsley N)*
Howells, Geraint
Howells, Dr. Kim (Pontypridd)
Hoyle, Doug
Hughes, John *(Coventry NE)*
Hughes, Robert *(Aberdeen N)*
Hughes, Roy *(Newport E)*
Illsley, Eric
Ingram, Adam
Janner, Greville

Johnston, Sir Russell
Jones, Barry *(Alyn & Deeside)*
Jones, Martyn *(Clwyd S W)*
Kennedy, Charles
Kirkwood, Archy
Lambie, David
Leadbitter, Ted
Leighton, Ron
Lestor, Joan *(Eccles)*
Litherland, Robert
Lloyd, Tony *(Stretford)*
Lofthouse, Geoffrey
Loyden, Eddie
McAllion, John
McAvoy, Thomas
Macdonald, Calum A.
McFall, John
McKay, Allen *(Barnsley West)*
McKelvey, William
McLeish, Henry
McNamara, Kevin
McWilliam, John
Madden, Max
Mahon, Mrs Alice
Marek, Dr John
Marshall, David *(Shettleston)*
Marshall, Jim *(Leicester S)*
Martlew, Eric
Maxton, John
Meale, Alan
Michael, Alun
Michie, Bill *(Sheffield Heeley)*
Michie, Mrs Ray *(Arg'l & Bute)*
Moonie, Dr Lewis
Morgan, Rhodri
Morley, Elliott
Morris, Rt Hon A. *(W'shawe)*
Mowlam, Marjorie
Mullin, Chris
Murphy, Paul
Nellist, Dave
O'Brien, William
O'Neill, Martin
Orme, Rt Hon Stanley
Patchett, Terry
Pendry, Tom
Pike, Peter L.
Powell, Ray *(Ogmore)*
Prescott, John

Quin, Ms Joyce
Radice, Giles
Randall, Stuart
Redmond, Martin
Rees, Rt Hon Merlyn
Reid, Dr John
Richardson, Jo
Robertson, George
Robinson, Geoffrey
Rooker, Jeff
Ross, Ernie *(Dundee W)*
Rowlands, Ted
Ruddock, Joan
Salmond, Alex
Sedgemore, Brian
Sheerman, Barry
Sheldon, Rt Hon Robert
Shore, Rt Hon Peter
Short, Clare
Sillars, Jim
Skinner, Dennis
Smith, Andrew *(Oxford E)*
Smith, C. *(Isl'ton & F'bury)*
Smith, J. P. *(Vale of Glam)*
Spearing, Nigel
Steel, Rt Hon David
Steinberg, Gerry
Strang, Gavin
Straw, Jack
Taylor, Mrs Ann *(Dewsbury)*
Turner, Dennis
Vaz, Keith
Wall, Pat
Wallace, James
Walley, Joan
Wardell, Gareth *(Gower)*
Watson, Mike *(Glasgow, C)*
Welsh, Andrew *(Angus E)*
Welsh, Michael *(Doncaster N)*
Williams, Alan W. *(Carm'then)*
Wilson, Brian
Wise, Mrs Audrey
Wray, Jimmy
Young, David *(Bolton SE)*

Tellers for the Noes:
  Mr. Frank Haynes and
  Mr. Robert N. Wareing.

*Question accordingly agreed to.*
*Bill read the Third time, and passed.*

# Immigration

**Mr. Max Madden** (Bradford, West): On a point of order, Madam Deputy Speaker. I wish to raise what I regard as a most serious matter. A document prepared by the head of the immigration and nationality department of the Home Office has been leaked. By arranging an early morning debate on DNA and immigration rule changes, the Government are, according to the leaked Home Office report, seeking to avoid
"two separate rows about immigration issues in quick succession".

Although in his statement last Wednesday the Home Secretary implied that no decision had been taken about the funding of a centrally organised DNA scheme, the document also makes it clear that the Government have made a decision about how they intend to fund a centrally organised DNA scheme. They will do so by a flat-rate increase across all the entry clearance applications. The document also makes it clear that the Government do not intend to allow the House of Commons—*[Interruption.]*

**Madam Deputy Speaker (Miss Betty Boothroyd):** Order. The hon. Gentleman is raising a point of order and I must respond to it. I hope that the House will understand that, but I also hope that the hon. Gentleman will understand that a point of order has to be addressed to the Chair, to be within the Chair's responsibility and to be something that the Chair can answer. I hope that the hon. Gentleman will come to his point of order immediately.

**Mr. Madden:** I am sure that, as the guardian of Back Benchers' rights, Madam Deputy Speaker, you will be concerned that senior Government officials have been advising the Home Secretary and other Ministers, with the knowledge of the Leader of the House and the Prime Minister, that this House should be denied the opportunity of discussing either the principle or the detail of how entry clearance fees are to be increased to pay for a centrally organised DNA scheme.

Lastly, the document also makes it clear that a controversial DNA announcement with the immigration——

**Madam Deputy Speaker:** Order. What has this to do with the Chair? *[Interruption.]* Order. The hon. Gentleman is making a point which should be made in the debate, the time of which he is now usurping. If he is wise, he may catch my eye. I suggest that he raises his points during the debate.

**Mr. Madden:** Further to the point of order, Madam Deputy Speaker. The document makes it clear that the Government's intention in combining a debate on DNA with the immigration rule change is to divert attention from the fact that the Government have no new provisions or promises to make to the people of Hong Kong.
In conclusion——

**Madam Deputy Speaker:** Order. The Chair must, of course, be open and ready to listen to points of order, and I am tolerant. However, the hon. Gentleman is now abusing the Chair and this House. I ask him to come immediately to his point of order, which must be a matter for the Chair, and something that I can answer.

**Mr. Madden:** Indeed. I therefore ask that you, Madam Deputy Speaker, urgently allow the Patronage Secretary,

[*Mr. Madden*]

who is in his place, to make it clear that, in view of the revelations made in this document,, the Government will do what they should have done in the first place, which is to make a statement about the DNA testing scheme and provide a debate at an earlier hour than this to enable the House to debate the scheme. The Government should abandon this debate on immigration changes and provide another debate, but at an earlier hour.

That is my request and in the interests of democracy, of Back Benchers and of the general public, having been found out, the Government should now——

**Madam Deputy Speaker:** Order. These are matters which must be raised in debate.

**Mr. Tam Dalyell** (Linlithgow): On a point of order, Madam Deputy Speaker.

**Madam Deputy Speaker:** Is it a fresh point of order? I have already dealt with the point of order raised by the hon. Member for Bradford, West (Mr. Madden).

**Mr. Dalyell:** It is a fresh point of order. It concerns the abuse of the House of Commons. My hon. Friend the Member for Bradford, West (Mr. Madden) showed me the document, which is signed by a senior civil servant. The point of order for you, Madam Deputy Speaker, is this. Is it right that a senior civil servant, in this case Mr. Stadlen, should produce documents that go into detail about how the House of Commons should be handled? No one quarrels with him producing documents about the substance of the issue, but surely the handling of the House of Commons is not a matter for senior civil servants. It is a matter for the Chair.

In these circumstances, may I make a suggestion, Madam Deputy Speaker? The hour is late. These documents are a disgrace. I suggest that you ask that the document be put before Mr. Speaker and that Mr. Speaker make a ruling at 3.30 pm tomorrow on the propriety towards the House of Commons of this kind of document being produced by a senior civil servant. Some of us think that it is entirely improper.

**Madam Deputy Speaker:** These are matters that should be properly raised in debate. I can assure the hon. Member that Mr. Speaker will certainly read the points of order in the *Official Report*.

12.20 am

**Mr. Alistair Darling** (Edinburgh, Central): I beg to move,

That the Statement of Changes in Immigration Rules (House of Commons Paper No. 388), which was laid before this House on 14th June, be disapproved.

The rules are a reflection of the Government's attitude towards a large number of citizens in this country. They further restrict the ability of people from selected countries to enter the United Kingdom. Sex discrimination persists in the case of female students. No changes are proposed that would facilitate family reunion. Double standards and double-talk are applied throughout the rules and the explanatory memorandum issued by the Home Office. Indeed, the whole thing is summed up by the ridiculous hour at which the House is being invited to discuss this crucial matter—in the early hours of the morning.

The mind of the Government is revealed in the internal memorandum that has already been referred to by my hon. Friends. That memorandum, which has been made available to us, should also have been published alongside the Home Office rules, because it makes it clear what the Government are really about. The rules and the explanatory memorandum are in many ways grossly misleading. I shall refer to the internal memorandum, because it makes clear a number of points of which the House and the public should be aware.

**The Minister of State, Home Office (Mr. Tim Renton):** May I suggest to the hon. Gentleman that he withdraws his remark about the ridiculous hour? These new immigration rules were laid last week. They were prayed against by the Opposition, as is the Opposition's right. The debate could have taken place any time within the next 40 days but was purposely arranged, at the request of the Opposition, at an early time so that it could take place before the imposition of visas on Turkey this coming Friday. That is why the debate is taking place today.

**Mr. Darling:** With respect, I took the opportunity of consulting the Opposition Whips to find out exactly what happened. I would not have made my remarks without first checking the position. It is not the case that the Opposition said that they would accept a debate at this ridiculous hour of the morning. I understand that it was put to the Opposition Whips that we might use Opposition time, but this is Government business and ought to be discussed in Government time. Indeed, the memorandum that has been referred to makes it clear that the Government were keen that there should be a debate earlier than the imposition of visas on Turkey simply to deflect the otherwise understandable opposition if there had been no debate.

**Mr. Renton** *rose*——

**Mr. Darling:** I will give way once more on the point, but I do not think that the House wishes to be detained on this argument when the substance of the rules is far more important.

**Mr. Renton:** Will the hon. Gentleman please accept that we were willing to have the debate yesterday at a reasonable hour? It was at the insistence of the Opposition that it is taking place at an unreasonable hour tonight. Why is it this week rather than next week or the week after? It is because the Opposition wanted to have the debate before the imposition of visas on Turkey this Friday.

**Mr. Darling:** The Minister should know that the Government regulate the business timetable. If the Government had wanted to discuss Government business yesterday, they could have done so. It is disgraceful that they did not want to do so.

The internal Home Office memorandum makes clear what is in the Government's mind. When it refers to the merits of the immigration rules, it refers also to problems facing the Government about an announcement on the future arrangements for citizens within Hong Kong. It talks about the timing of the announcement of the immigration rules. The postponement of tonight's debate was discussed within the Home Office team. The document states:

"postponement would arouse expectations which we cannot at this stage be sure of meeting, leading to possible presentational problems later on. Proceeding with the rules now, by contrast, enables us to say that they have been in the pipe line for some time and are being introduced without prejudice."

It observes—how accurate this is—that new rules

"and a potentially controversial DNA announcement, are quite a handful without the Hong Kong dimension."

It is no wonder that the Government are trying to roll into the one debate the question of DNA and immigration rules.

The document continues:

"The Home Secretary will wish to consider how far he should volunteer to break surface more publicly on Hong Kong: should it be mentioned in the arranged Rules PQ, the Press Notice and the letter to Mr. Darling?"

It was not mentioned in the letter sent to me. We wait to see when it will be mentioned.

The attention that the public have focused on Hong Kong, quite understandably, demonstrates the problems faced by many other people. *The Times* thundered:

"People from Hong Kong should be admitted to this country as a matter of honour."

What about the British men and women who wish to be united with their children or elderly parents, or those who are refused leave to be joined by their spouses because of the primary purpose rule? We read recently of a blatant attempt by the Government to influence the immigration appeals tribunal system against granting admission. The people to whom I have referred want unity with their families like all other citizens. When we consider matters of honour, we should consider those people.

**Mr. Tim Janman** (Thurrock): Will the hon. Gentleman give way?

**Mr. Darling:** I shall not give way now. I have been delayed, and I know that many right hon. and hon. Members wish to contribute to the debate.

**Mr. Janman** rose——

**Madam Deputy Speaker:** Order. The hon. Member for Edinburgh, Central (Mr. Darling) has made it clear that he is not giving way now.

**Mr. Darling:** We have responsibilities also to the east African Asian voucher holders. The Government say that they want to be flexible about Hong Kong. What is to happen? The internal memorandum states:

"As agreed, however, we have set aside for the time being the intention to increase the minimum financial resources required of business men and persons of independent means because of the potential effect that it might have on Hong Kong."

Note the passage

"set aside for the time being".

Does that mean that index-linked compassion is to be limited to Hong Kong? Perhaps it means that the limits are to be raised, but at a less sensitive time—for example, when Parliament has risen for the summer recess. Why is it that the Government are contemplating allowing rich people to buy a place in Britain when the great majority will not have that sort of money, and will apparently be excluded? That solution for the elite is no solution.

**Mr. Janman:** The hon. Gentleman has implied that the Government wish to allow only rich people to leave Hong Kong to come to Britain. Will he tell the House whether the Labour party believes that no one should be allowed in or that everybody should be allowed in?

**Mr. Darling:** With respect, the hon. Gentleman is missing the point. We think that it is thoroughly offensive that a rule should be made for those who are rich, who have assets of more than £150,000, that is different from the rules that will apply to others. The Labour party's position on Hong Kong is clear. We have said that we do not feel able to make promises that we would not be able to fulfil. As the hon. Gentleman knows, we have made that clear time and time again.

The double standards to which I have referred——

**Sir Nicholas Bonsor** (Upminster): Will the hon. Gentleman give way?

**Mr. Darling:** No, I shall not.

The double standards——

**Mr. Renton:** I must take up what the hon. Gentleman has just said. In the Labour party's policy review document, which was published a few weeks ago, the following statement appears:

"We shall hold discussions with the Governments of Malaysia and Hong Kong with the object of providing them with an effective Nationality with the right of abode."

How does that fit in with the hon. Gentleman's remarks?

**Mr. Darling:** The policy review document refers to the 10,000 people, in Hong Kong, in particular, who have no nationality whatever. [HON. MEMBERS: "Come on!"] It does say that. With respect, as I am one of the authors, I know what it says. With due respect, the Minister is trying to muddy the water. What he says has nothing to do with the point at issue.

The double standards that persist throughout the rules are nowhere more clearly illustrated than in the Government's attitude towards the provision of DNA testing. The Government had an opportunity to end the injustices that have been suffered by many people who have been wrongly refused leave to join their families. The Government, instead of abolishing the arbitrary, and frequently wrong, decision-making process based on subjective tests, have elected to allow DNA testing only after the same tests are applied and the entry clearance officer is still not satisfied that relationship exists. As a result, applicants will still have to go through bureaucratic, time-consuming and expensive interviews and be faced with the test if the entry clearance officer is not satisfied. The Government had an opportunity to do away with that red tape and those bureaucratic controls and to introduce a simple test that would prove, once and for all, and quickly, whether people were related.

In this statement, the Government imply that they have not yet reached a decision on costs, yet it is clear from the Home Office memorandum that that is not the case. The Government say in their internal memorandum that the statement

"does not indicate how the scheme will be financed, beyond reiterating that the cost will not be met by the taxpayer. The intention is to make a separate announcement on the funding arrangements shortly before the scheme comes into effect, to avoid a rush of applications aimed at beating the associated increase in settlement fee."

In other words, it is abundantly clear that the Government have already decided to increase settlement fees and that a statement will be made at some quiet time, perhaps during the parliamentary recess.

[*Mr. Darling*]

Will the Minister tell us what he proposes with regard to cost? We have a right to know what is being proposed. The Government know. If the Minister has any respect for the House, he will tell us what the arrangement is to be.

It is no better for applicants who, it now transpires, were wrongly refused permission to come to Britain. The Government have said that they are prepared to consider their cases provided that they pass several subjective hurdles that have been erected in their way. Again the memorandum makes it abundantly clear how limited the Government's compassion is to be. It says:

"we are looking for compassionate features which distinguish the particular case from the generality of average reapplicants. It would be crucial to hold this line to ensure that the concession remains the exception rather than the norm in cases involving overage reapplicants."

In other words, most applicants are effectively being told, "Don't bother. You need not apply because we will not exercise any compassion." These are people who have been wrongly refused as a result of the process that we have set up. They have been denied the right to come and live with their families. If it were happening to white people or anyone else, it would not be tolerated. The Government say one thing in public and another in private.

The double standards that are employed to impose restrictions on people who want to study in the United Kingdom illustrate the point. Under the proposed changes to the immigration rules, visa nationals cannot switch from visitor to student status. Again the memorandum makes interesting reading. It says:

"the changes on admission for study are directed at bogus students, mainly from West Africa."

How on earth can any rational person make such a generalisation? Where is the evidence? Why can a United States visitor decide to study in the United Kingdom when a Nigerian national may not, no matter how powerful his or her case is? Are they not two individuals whose cases ought to be considered on merit rather than on their race? Has a United States visitor never abused the rules?

The same double standards are applied to the visa changes. Visas are now to be imposed against Haiti because, we are told, it is the Government's policy to harmonise visa restrictions in the European Community. Since when? No public announcement has ever been made about it. We know about it because, thanks to some helpful source, we know that the Government have discussed, in secret, with our EC partners the harmonisation of procedures and the erection of a ring fence around Europe. Yet there has been no public announcement; private discussions are the order of the day.

Which country is next? Will it be Jamaica? Jamaican nationals are now experiencing the same problems as were experienced by those countries that now need visas, with increasing numbers of people being refused leave to come to this country. Perhaps the Minister will tell us whether it is to be Jamaica. The Government should think about the hardship caused by visas to those who wish to visit this country for a wedding or a funeral, but are told to come back and reapply at some future date. That is not an option for most people.

Turkey is to be added to the countries requiring visas. What will happen to the Kurdish refugees who are leaving Turkey in growing numbers? The Government look on refugees as a problem, but if they stop them coming to this country they will think that there is no longer a problem. Is it really the case that a man in fear of his life is expected to go to the British embassy in Turkey and queue for a visa in the full view of those he fears? That is not an option, and the Government know it.

The rules are discriminatory and riddled with double standards. The memorandum should leave no one in any doubt that the Government are prepared to treat many of our citizens in a second-class way. It shows that the Government have no scruples. A cynical attempt has been made to mislead the public and hon. Members. To the Government the rules are a matter of presentation, but to parents separated from their children and to husbands separated from their wives it is a matter of decency. That is why we will oppose them in the Lobby tonight.

12.36 am

**Mr. Tim Janman** (Thurrock): I hope to keep my comments brief because I know that a number of hon. Members wish to speak. I congratulate my hon. Friend the Minister on the rule changes, especially that which will prevent people from coming to this country on the false basis of a genuine short-term visit and then switching status to become students on temporary courses. They do one course, complete that, move to another, complete that and so on until they have been here for seven years, after which they can remain permanently. That has happened with large numbers of people. It is morally illegal immigration on a technically legal basis. My hon. Friend is right to introduce changes to close that loophole.

The point made by the hon. Member for Edinburgh, Central (Mr. Darling) about the changes being applied to west Africans but not to Americans was ludicrous. We do not have vast numbers of Americans entering this country on a false basis to secure permanent residency. The whole point of this legislative change is to direct it at where the problem lies—people from west Africa, not from America.

I also congratulate my hon. Friend the Minister on the introduction of visa requirements for Turkish nationals. Many Conservative Members are well aware of the problem of illegal immigration of Turkish nationals. However what will my hon. Friend do in the next decade if Turkey's application to join the European Community is accepted? That would make it difficult to prevent the influx of unrequired, unwanted and unneeded immigration from Turkey that could ensue.

My hon. Friend is also right to make changes in DNA testing. That testing is vital to establish that there is a proper and bona fide relationship between the person wishing to come to this country and the rest of the family who are already here. I cannot for the life of me understand why that testing is not mandatory. It is the only real and genuine way of firmly and scientifically establishing the evidence necessary to prove that there is a bona fide relationship. I cannot understand why it is carried out on a voluntary basis.

As we are debating immigration rule changes, it is appropriate that I should state in this debate that the vast majority of the British people see no need for immigration rule changes vis-à-vis Hong Kong. The British Government's first duty is to the people of this country, not to the people of Hong Kong.

**Sir Nicholas Bonsor:** When I went to Hong Kong a few years ago, I asked vast numbers of people whether they thought of themselves as Chinese or British. They told me with an overwhelming voice that they wished to be Chinese. They wished to follow a Chinese culture, be part of the Chinese community and be part of China. Would it not be ludicrous in those circumstances for the Government to take into this country 3·2 million people who have no wish to be British, no wish to abide by British customs and no wish to be part of our country?

**Mr. Janman:** The point that my hon. Friend the Member for Upminster (Sir N. Bonsor) has made is absolutely right. He reinforces the point that I was making. The danger of making any immigration rule change to accommodate more than 3 million people in Hong Kong is that we might write a blank cheque. If that change were made in the belief that only a few thousand would take it up, we would be powerless in law to prevent the other hundreds of thousands or millions from taking it up if they so wished. The Government would be extremely foolish to write that blank cheque and it seems to be clear from comments made by my right hon. Friend the Prime Minister that that blank cheque will not be written, and that is absolutely right.

**Mr. John Carlisle** (Luton, North): The siren voices from the Opposition Benches about the continuance of Labour's open-door policy—which seems now to extend to 3·25 million Hong Kong Chinese—will not have escaped my hon. Friend's attention. Does he agree that if such a policy were followed the British Government would have an equal duty to tell the 800,000 or so white South Africans that they also have similar rights of abode in this country? With regard to exemptions, is it not interesting to note that the hon. Member for Edinburgh, Central (Mr. Darling) refused to take an intervention asking him whether Labour would impose visas on South Africans? If a policy is applied to the 3·25 million people in Hong Kong, a similar policy must apply to white South Africans and people in other countries.

**Mr. Janman:** I am grateful to my hon. Friend for that very interesting tangential point. His logic and rationale are irrefutable and the House will have taken note of his comments.

When I intervened earlier in the speech of the hon. Member for Edinburgh, Central, he was totally incapable of telling the House what the Opposition's view was on the Hong Kong issue, and whether they were in favour of writing a blank cheque or of taking a more illiberal and tighter view of who should be allowed into this country than that taken by the Government. We are still waiting for the hon. Member for Edinburgh, Central to clarify the Opposition's position. I am sure that the electorate is also waiting to hear the Opposition's views.

Good though the changes are, they are too late. The door is being shut after the immigrants have bolted in. I shall give the House some figures, not from the Home Office but from the National Ethnic Research market research company—a Caribbean company which has done extensive research, for commercial reasons, into the ethnic population of Britain. The figure is not the 2·4 million that the Home Office trots out; it is probably much nearer 4·2 million. The company, which is run by a member of the ethnic community, has produced figures to show that one in three children born in London today is of ethnic origin. Its definition of ethnic origin does not include the Arabs and the Turks: it relates only to Indian, Pakistani, Caribbean and African people.

That is a frightening concept for the country to come to terms with. We have already seen the problems of massive Moslem immigration, with the recent events in Parliament square and in Bradford—*[Interruption.]* I am willing to give way to any hon. Member who stands up and wishes to intervene, but if no one wishes to do so, I suggest that Opposition Members remain silent. That figure of one in three children is true not just of London, but of Leicester, Nottingham, Bradford and many other cities.

I welcome the changes, but I must tell my hon. Friend the Minister that unless we want to create major problems in the decades or the century ahead, we must not only stop immigration but must move to voluntary resettlement to reduce the immigrant population.

**Mr. Robert G. Hughes** (Harrow, West): I fail to understand how my hon. Friend can make a differentiation on the basis of the colour of someone's skin between one person who is British and another person who is British. To do so is patently racist.

**Mr. Janman:** I have made no differentiation. We have not had mass immigration from Canada, Germany or the United States. What we have had, and what many British people, and I suspect the majority of my hon. Friend's constituents, object to, is mass immigration from countries which he knows have caused the immigration—India, Pakistan and the Caribbean. It is fatuous to suggest that we are talking simply about colour. We are talking about country of origin, culture and religion. Those factors are important, and they cause great anxiety to our constituents.

**Mr. Jeremy Corbyn** (Islington, North): On a point of order, Mr. Deputy Speaker. I have been listening closely to the speech of the hon. Member for Thurrock (Mr. Janman). Is it in order for an hon. Member to address the House in such overtly racist terms?

**Mr. Deputy Speaker (Sir Paul Dean):** I have a strong impression that the hon. Gentleman is about to finish.

**Mr. Janman:** You are right, Mr. Deputy Speaker. I would have finished by now had it not been for the intervention of my hon. Friend the Member for Harrow, West (Mr. Hughes).

Those people who defend mass immigration and who are not prepared to find a civilised and practical method of reducing the immigrant population are courting massive civil strife in years to come.

12.49 am

**Mr. John Fraser** (Norwood): We have just heard expressed a vicious streak of racism that hon. Members on both sides of the House had hoped was buried some years ago, for the sake of this country.

**Sir Nicholas Bonsor:** On a point of order, Mr. Deputy Speaker. I find it grossly offensive that Opposition Members should seek to make such a point, given that my hon. Friend the Member for Thurrock (Mr. Janman) was speaking from his heart and in the interests of his constituents—*[Interruption.]*

**Mr. Deputy Speaker:** Order. This subject arouses strong emotions on both sides of the House, but I hope that we shall debate it quietly.

**Mr. Fraser:** In answer to the intervention of the hon. Member for Upminster (Sir N. Bonsor), may I say that that vicious streak of racism to which I referred may be sincere but that that does not excuse it.

**Sir Nicholas Bonsor:** Will the hon. Gentleman give way?

**Mr. Fraser:** No, I——

**Sir Nicholas Bonsor:** Will the hon. Gentleman give way?

**Mr. Fraser:** I was about to say that I believed that many Conservative Members would wish that streak of racism to be buried. It is regrettable that it should have reared its head tonight.

I have only one good thing to say for the Minister. Having pressed him for some time to consolidate the immigration rules, I am glad that he has taken the opportunity to do so. Instead of nine or 10 instruments, we now have a single cat-o'-nine-tails with which to control those who wish to come to the United Kingdom. We thank the Minister, therefore, for the comprehensive nature of the rules, although certainly not for their content.

I suppose that there is a further tribute that one could pay the Minister because under his presidency there has undoubtedly been an increase in the efficiency—and to some extent the courtesy and responsiveness—of Lunar house, not least as a result of the pressure that the Opposition exerted on Ministers last time we debated the immigration rules. That is a good thing, because efficient immigration control is effective immigration control. I do not think that anyone makes any great complaint about that; indeed, long delays and inefficiency can place people in a hopeless position.

What is now happening, however, is that that efficiency, which I welcomed, has gone a stage further, to the point at which it has become a ruthless and summary execution of harsh immigration laws. Immigration officers are using administrative custody to cow prisoners into abandoning their rights and making so-called supervised departures. The Home Office is using methods that attempt to avoid the supervision of judges and magistrates that follows on the bare-faced abrogation of the facilities of Members of Parliament to approach the Minister or his Office. I am surprised that a Minister, who is a Queen's Counsel, should mastermind a policy intended to have the effect of bludgeoning people into leaving the country without access to a judicial system—except by way of judicial review, and that is not easy—or even an immigration appeals system.

The bludgeoning is done by administrative imprisonment—literally detention without trial. One must conclude that the use of detention without trial under the immigration system is a concerted and deliberate Government—directed practice. Let me give two examples of detention without trial. The first involves the use of the notice of intention to deport. Suppose that an immigrant —usually a student—is working part-time. The Government seem to want all the other students to work part-time but not immigrant students. An immigrant student who is found working part-time—a perfectly honourable tradition—*[Interruption.]* Can the hon. Member who has been making a noise return to the bar, Mr. Deputy Speaker? [HON. MEMBERS: "Hear, hear."]

That immigrant will not be charged with any offence. He will not have access to a magistrates' court. Instead, a deportation order will be made with considerable rapidity

and he will be detained in administrative custody. The Immigration Act 1988 will then be applied to him. He will be told that he will have no appeal on the merits of the deportation order but only on the power of the Minister to make that order. He will be given the choice between custody and an unwinnable appeal or what is known, under the immigration rules, as a supervised departure. That is what I describe as a use of administrative custody and detention without trial.

The use of custody in connection with deportation orders should be used only rarely. Before any deportation order is made, full consideration should be given to representations made by the person who is affected. Deportation matters should be treated mercifully and understandably.

Deportation is being used not as a form of immigration control but as a hugely disproportionate——

**Sir Nicholas Bonsor:** Will the hon. Gentleman give way?

**Mr. Fraser:** No, I will not. It is being used as a hugely disproportionate, non-judicial and virtually unappealable punishment and sentence. That practice must stop.

The second form of detention without trial is the use of removal powers, as opposed to deportation, where there is at least the possibility of appeal to an immigration adjudicator. An example is of someone who comes here on a visit and then asks to stay as a student. That is common. Indeed, it has been institutionalised by the changes in the rules. If an immigration officer can get some kind of stated intention from that immigrant that at the back of his mind he thought that he would study when he came here, the leave to enter as a visitor is revoked, irrespective of the merits of the situation. The person is then kept in administrative custody and is removed from this country without any form of appeal, except access to the Divisional Court by way of judicial review. That is an abuse of the powers of removal.

**Mr. Harry Cohen** (Leyton): That is an excellent point. Is not the position worse than that? Is there not an opportunity for entrapment? The immigration officer may ask, "Would you like to study?" The immigrant may reply, "Yes, I would. I would not mind if I had the chance." That person is trapped, whether he intended to study or not.

**Mr. Fraser:** That is exactly what happens.

Recently, I came across the case of a person who was supposed to have made an admission that false representations had been made. When I spoke to the immigrant, it was clear that the command of English was not adequate and the conversation was conducted in Yoruba. Because of that conversation in Yoruba, it became clear that the admissions that were supposed to have been made to the immigration officer in English were unsustainable. If there had not been an intervention on that occasion, the system of supervised departure would have been used and the issue of administrative custody —detention without trial—would have been raised. The system is deliberately geared so that where there has been even a minor criminal offence, no charge is brought because, if it were, the immigrant would at least have access to a magistrates court and an application could be made for bail.

I condemn the heartless and brutal refusal of temporary admission by the Minister of State, except in what he calls exceptional compassionate circumstances. A family in my constituency may have saved for a lifetime to spend thousands of pounds to bring two or three members of the family to this country for a two or three-week holiday. Those people may not be admitted on a temporary basis because the immigration officers say that there are no exceptional compassionate circumstances. That shows heartlessness. In recent changes, the Minister has prevented us, as Members of Parliament, from making direct representations on such matters.

I condemn the failure to humanise the operation of the primary purpose marriage rule, which creates an absurdity. If a spouse wants to remain in the United Kingdom, he or she cannot do so, but if they do not want to remain in the United Kingdom, they can do so. That is the absurdity of the primary purpose rule. The judges cannot make sense of it, and seem to lack the courage to expose its absurdity. However, when Mr. Justice Henry recently eroded the harshness of the primary purpose rule, the Home Office immediately sought to undermine his judgment by writing to the president of the immigration appeal tribunal.

It is clear from the cases now before the courts and the tribunal that incontestably genuine love-match marriages —*[Interruption.]* Right hon. and hon. Members on this side of the House happen to believe that love in marriage should not be the subject of scorn, though it might be the subject of consideration by a future chairman of the Conservative party. Genuine love matches are being frustrated by the artificial residence test. The rules are harsh and increasingly are being heartlessly applied. I shall vote against the motion.

1.1 am

**Mr. Peter Thurnham** (Bolton, North-East): I listened carefully to the speech of the hon. Member for Edinburgh, Central (Mr. Darling) in the hope that he would clear up some of the anomalies and confusions surrounding Labour's immigration policy. We know that Labour are pledged to repeal the legislation that they themselves enforced when in power, when the number of immigrants entering this country was as high as 80,000 per year. However, he neither did so nor answered the questions that were asked of him.

The remarks of the hon. Member for Edinburgh, Central contrast with the Government's action in enforcing existing legislation and with the positive rule changes that are the subject of the debate—which I welcome, and which will reduce abuses and allow genuine applicants to enter the country under a fair and firm policy.

I shall give three examples, two from my own constituency, that demonstrate Government policy in action. I believe that I was the first Member of Parliament to organise the entry into this country of a constituent's son by use of DNA testing. I inherited from my opponent in the 1983 general election a large file on a constituent named Mr. G. M. V. Patel and his son Ishaq. Despite exhaustive inquiries in my constituent's home village in India, no evidence could be found to allow his son's entry to Britain, although Mr. Patel was adamant that he was a true son of the family.

I visited the Home Office and discussed the case at great length with the then Minister of State, Home Office, my right hon. and learned Friend the Member for Ribble Valley (Mr. Waddington), but no decision to enter could

be reached. I then read about the work of Professor Jeffries at Leicester university, and after I wrote to him the Patel family arranged for Ishaq to undergo DNA testing. There was a long wait while the Home Office evaluated the long odds that were arrived at by Professor Jeffries, and then great joy when it was announced on 24 August 1986 that, although Ishaq was over age, he would be allowed entry. I am grateful for the Home Office's handling of that case, which illustrates that it applies policy in a firm and fair way. I thank my hon. Friend the Minister for the way in which other cases have been similarly dealt with.

Although I have had no personal experience of Kurds wishing to enter this country from Turkey, the grandson of one of my constituents, an Iranian, was imprisoned in Turkey. My constituent came to see me because her grandson was about to be returned to Iran, where he would face immediate execution. Less than 30 days remained to deal with that case, but with the help of Prisoners Abroad, whose present director is a former hon. Member of the House, Mr. Keith Best, the case was put to the Home Office sufficiently well to allow that individual to enter Britain and to escape the almost certain execution that would have been his fate in Iran. That is another example of the way that the Home Office implements existing legislation fairly and firmly, and allows entry in genuine cases.

My last example is rather different: it concerns Hong Kong, which must be very much in our minds. We must do all in our power to press for Hong Kong's plight to be treated as an international problem, and urge the international community to bring all possible force to bear on China both to improve its internal policies and to respect the treaty drawn up in 1984. We must, however, adopt towards Hong Kong the same policies that we adopt towards all other aspects of immigration, and keep our minds open to the genuine needs of genuine cases.

I have just received a letter from some people whom I visited when I was in Hong Kong two years ago, at a remarkable establishment known as the Home of Loving Faithfulness Fellowship. It is run by two ladies, Wendy and Valerie, who had set up a home to care for severely handicapped Chinese children whose families were unable to look after them. They had arranged for a number of adoptions so that children could leave Hong Kong and find homes elsewhere. The letter says how worried they are about the present situation. Although they have British passports, they feel guilty about that distinguishing them from others with whom they work. One of them has been away for 27 years, and they feel that they have no home in the United Kingdom.

The letter ends:

"Our own plans are just to go on doing what we have been doing for 24 years here . . . in this beautiful little place called Hong Kong."

I ask my hon. Friend to see that as an example of the need to keep an open mind about what is happening in Hong Kong and to put maximum pressure on all other members of the international community to make the Chinese understand exactly how we feel about their domestic situation, and about the importance of their respecting every line of the 1984 treaty.

1.6 am

**Mr. Pat Wall** (Bradford, North): First, let me join in the protest made at the beginning of the debate about the DNA issue—which has been the subject of much

[*Mr. Pat Wall*]

discussion between many of us and the Minister of State —being lumped in with a general discussion on immigration rules. I think that DNA deserves a separate debate apart from the Adjournment debate that my hon. Friend the Member for Bradford, West (Mr. Madden) has obtained for the early hours of Thursday, and I hope that that can be arranged.

The rule changes that we are discussing mark, in most instances, a further tightening of the screw—a process that began with the introduction of visas for five countries and continued with the provisions of the Immigration Act 1988. Now we see a complete ban on nationals of visa countries switching from temporary admission—mainly as visitors—to student status, which further reduces their rights as against those of non-visa nationals. We also see rules aimed at preventing Turkish citizens of Kurdish origin from obtaining asylum in Britain, although, having been nerve-gassed by Iraq and hounded by Iran and Turkey, they are among the most persecuted peoples in the world, and the most deserving of the right of asylum. Under the rules, only Turkish Kurds who escape to a third country can be considered for asylum in Britain, and that must be a tiny handful of those who need it.

I feel that we have a right to relate these rules to our constituency experience, and I wish to raise two specific issues with the Minister. First—although I feel that the issue of Hong Kong should, and undoubtedly will, be debated separately—let me say that we can have little faith in the Government's ability to deal with the problems of three and a third million Chinese in Hong Kong when a woman in Pakistan can obtain neither consistency, compassion nor speed in her application for a visa to visit a grandchild born in Bradford.

The first of the issues with which I want to deal relates to asylum for Sri Lankan Tamils. Last Wednesday my hon. Friend the Member for Halifax (Mrs. Mahon) asked the Under-Secretary of State for Foreign and Commonwealth Affairs the following question:

"Is the Minister aware that three out of five Tamil refugees who were forcibly returned to Colombo in February 1988 have been tortured? What do the Government intend to do about that?"

The Minister replied:

"I am sure that if the hon. Lady can substantiate her assertion we will draw it to the attention of the Sri Lankan Government."—[*Official Report,* 14 June 1989; Vol. 154, c. 890.]

It is proper to draw the matter to the attention of the Sri Lankan Government, but is it not time that it received the attention of the Foreign and Commonwealth Office and the Home Office? Are we to believe that they are unaware of the circumstances of the case?

Are the Government unaware of the fact that the five male Tamils arrived separately in the first half of 1987, that all five were refused the right of asylum and the right of appeal, that while awaiting deportation their case was taken to judicial review in the High Court on 25 September 1987 and that their appeal was rejected, that on 12 October 1987 their appeal against that decision was upheld in the Court of Appeal but that it was again reversed on 16 December in the House of Lords? The five were then deported. Under the ridiculous rules that now apply, after their deportation they had the right to appeal against the refusal of asylum in this country.

This case—the first of its type—was heard on 16, 17 and 18 January of this year. The appeal of all five was upheld, but they have still not been given the right by the Home Office to come to this country and take up their asylum. The Minister is aware of the fact that Amnesty International has produced conclusive proof that three of the five were tortured. The Government sent them back to Sri Lanka. They would not allow them to appeal here. They are responsible for the torture of those people.

**Mr. Renton:** The hon. Gentleman knows very well that we do not accept the decision of the adjudicator. We have been give permission to apply for a judicial review of the matter. That is taking place. I am very surprised that the hon. Gentleman makes detailed allegations and comments upon the case without waiting for the final decision of the court.

**Mr. Wall:** I am sure that the three Tamils who were tortured in the gaols of Sri Lanka will be as reassured by the Minister's comments as he hopes that hon. Members will be, but I am sure that they have not been reassured.

In a recent judgment Mr. Justice McCowan found that the Home Office had unfairly treated Miss Amarasingham. Mr. Justice McCowan therefore asked the Home Office to review her case. I hope that the same decision—to continue fighting the case until this girl is deported—will not be taken in her case.

One of the most quoted remarks of Karl Marx is that

"History repeats itself, first as tragedy, then as farce."

I am afraid that I must refer to a farcical case in my constituency. A well-known cricket club in my constituency, Undercliffe cricket club, runs an exchange scheme with Australia and New Zealand and brings over to this country young cricketers from those two countries. The scheme is run by three prominent local business men who are connected with the Undercliffe cricket club. They invite teenage youngsters from Australia and New Zealand to Bradford. They stay with them at their expense and play cricket for that club, at a level depending on their ability on arrival.

In April this year they invited an 18-year-old man called Schofield Hewitt from Barbados. Schofield did not understand that he did not need a visas, so went to the consulate in Barbados, and asked for a visa. When he was told that he did not need a visa he became a little uptight and an official stamped his passport, "Visa not granted". When he arrived at Manchester airport, quite reasonably the immigration officer questioned the stamp on his passport. One of the three Bradford business men was called in as Schofield's sponsor. He explained the situation and, quite reasonably, the immigration officer at Manchester airport agreed to grant temporary admission and transferred the case to Leeds-Bradford airport.

Leeds-Bradford airport claimed that he needed a work permit. He is not Leary Constantine, Manny Martindale or Ernest Achone—all West Indian Test cricketers who made the Bradford league, brought enormous pleasure to Bradford people and raised the level of Yorkshire cricket. By bringing young Schofield Hewitt to Bradford, we were only repaying our debt to West Indian cricket. He did not need a work permit and he was deported, despite the fact that he had a return ticket and did not need a visa and despite the fact that Australian and New Zealand youngsters who were white and came from richer backgrounds were allowed to play for the Undercliffe cricket club.

**Mr. Renton:** I thank the hon. Gentleman for giving way to me for the second time. I do not want to delay the House, but it is a very great pity that he did not apply to the Department of Employment for a work permit or come to me for advice. Cricketers coming to Britain temporarily need work permits and are given work permits. We deal with them all the time at the beginning of the cricketing season without any problem.

**Mr. Wall:** My experience as a Member of Parliament was that when I phoned the Home Office and asked for a stop on the case I was told that it was not urgent or important enough. I wrote to the Minister on 25 April and I am still waiting for a reply. When a young, white New Zealander playing rugby for Bradford and Bingley rugby club overstayed, he was told he could stay on without a work permit because he was playing rugby union and he was white.

The case is a mirror of the unfairness of the Home Department and of the completely inefficient way in which it operates. Young Schofield Hewitt was taken to Manchester airport by one of the three members of the Undercliffe cricket club. He was told when to get there and he arrived with his sponsor 10 minutes early, obeying the laws of the land, to discover that the plane had left two hours earlier. That is typical of the way in which the Home Department is run, its inhumanity and its inefficiency.

1.17 am

**Mr. Gary Waller** (Keighley): First, it is welcome that a consolidated version of the rules has been published. It is difficult for practitioners to work with rules which have been amended, sometimes in a quite complicated way, nine separate times. I hope that consolidated rules will be published more often.

I wish to say a few words about over-age applicants and the use of discretion by my hon. Friend. Many applicants who are now over age still reside in Bangladesh. Some of the applicants are over age essentially because their applications were turned down 10 or more years ago. In almost every case, their applications were turned down for reasons of family relationships. As the House knows, documentation in Bangladesh is sparse. To some extent, some applicants or their sponsors brought the problem on themselves because there were false claims for tax purposes for families who did not exist.

Be that as it may, because of DNA testing, it is now possible to prove once and for all whether applications at that time were justified. I understand that, of the DNA tests that have been carried out, 86 per cent. have proved conclusively that the applicants were related as claimed.

It is a matter of natural justice, if a claim failed for that and for no other reason, that those applications should be processed as speedily as possible. In some cases, applicants have waited a long time—many years—for their cases to go through. Even since the DNA test was carried out, they have had to wait a considerable period. Applications should be dealt with in such a way that there is a presumption that discretion will be exercised in their favour unless there are clear reasons why that should not be the case.

I hope, therefore, that, although this matter is not spelt out in the rules, my hon. Friend the Minister will exercise his discretion fairly. I would find it difficult to explain to my constituents why, if a claim failed many years ago because of the lack of DNA testing at that time, they should still be turned down now that it is available. I hope that, when considering such cases in future, my hon. Friend will deal with them compassionately and speedily.

1.19 am

**Mr. Paul Boateng** (Brent, South): The debate has been redeemed by the speech of the hon. Member for Keighley (Mr. Waller) and by the intervention of the hon. Member for Harrow, West (Mr. Hughes). One of the most unpleasant aspects of this measure is the way that it brings to the surface all that is basest in our country, and no baser speech could have been made tonight than that by the hon. Member for Thurrock (Mr. Janman). It was vile and venomous in every respect. To suggest for one moment that the birth of a black child in this country is somehow a cause of concern is contemptible beyond belief. The Minister must reflect on the emotions and attitudes that measures such as this cause to rise to the surface. It is a squalid and unnecessary measure, and it has been introduced in a shroud of subterfuge from the Home Office.

Two aspects of the changes in the immigration rules give rise to particular concern. The first relates to students and the terms and conditions on which they may enter and remain in this country and the proposals that are contained in the rules in respect of them. It is worth looking at them in some detail. Underlying the thought that seems to have gone into this measure, particularly this aspect of it, is a common misconception by the Government and the Home Office, which is that the whole world is just dying to converge on the United Kingdom and that every black, brown and yellow person wants nothing so much as to live in the United Kingdom. *[Interruption.]* One can see from the instant recognition by Conservative Members that that is seriously what they believe. *[Interruption.]* They honestly believe that we are going to be swamped. That phrase is resonant, because it was with that phrase that, at a stroke, the Prime Minister the right hon. Member for Finchley (Mrs. Thatcher) sought to capitalise on the racist vote back in 1979. Ever since, we have been living with the legacy of that. Every so often, with an unerring and knee-jerk reaction, the Home Office feels the need to expel from its bowels measures of this nature. It is particularly unpleasant.

I am glad to see the Minister's nose curl up in distaste. My nose and those of many hon. Members curl up in distaste whenever we have to deal with the immigration rules. That happens whenever we are obliged to deal with the Minister and his officials because all these rules stink and the racism behind them stinks. We have good cause to turn up our noses in the way that we do.

**Mr. Jeremy Hanley** (Richmond and Barnes): The hon. Gentleman talks about the racist Government since 1979. He must admit that since 1979, over 500,000 people have been given permanent settlement in this country, the majority of whom have come from the Indian sub-continent, from the West Indies and from other parts of Asia and Africa, and there have been 30,000 refugees. Is that not a record of which we should be proud? If we were a racist Government, nothing like half a million people would have been allowed permanent settlement since 1979.

**Mr. Boateng:** Our record, sadly, is not one of which we are entitled to be proud. We have cause to be ashamed of

[*Mr. Boateng*]

it in terms of our standing in the world. We must redeem it as a matter of urgency, which is why my hon. Friends and I oppose these rules.

Let us consider the issue of students and the change of status. We say that what is proposed is unfair because of the way in which it discriminates between visa nationals and non-visa nationals. The Government have not produced a shred of evidence to show that there is more likely to be abuse from visa nationals than from non-visa nationals. If there were such evidence, they would be in a position to produce it.

The Minister must know what the impact of these measures will be on genuine students. They will have to leave Britain and return to their countries of origin before being able to apply for entry clearance. They must be aware of the temptation to overstay that that will cause. They must also appreciate the disincentive that measures such as this, being unjust and oppressive, will provide to genuine students to come to this country.

I do not take any heart from the fact that it will be more difficult for students from west Africa and from the Indian sub-continent to come here to study, because all experience—one need only consider the commercial and diplomatic links between our country and those countries, in particular since the movement for colonial freedom began—shows that Britain benefits from students coming here. Despite that, we have imposed a series of increasingly restrictive immigration rules on them, and we have imposed charges in the form of overseas fees that are unconscionable and cause great hardship.

Why have we done that? We have done it to keep out a few—the Home Office does not have the figures—would-be overstayers, a handful of those who would undoubtedly abuse their right and permission for entry. Consider the cost to us of that policy in terms of our reputation overseas, our moral standing and our self-interest resulting from fostering links between students which in turn benefits our commerce and international relations. There is nothing in these measures in relation to students that is in any way warranted. Indeed, the honest student is penalised by the rules. They represent disincentives to comply with them and they are harmful in every way.

**Mr. John Carlisle:** Will the hon. Gentleman agree that the position of honest students who want to come here to study has been prejudiced by those—however few they may be, and I accept what he says about that—who overstay? Will he further agree from his constituency experience, which by now must be considerable, that some stay on and claim to be students, thereby prejudicing the chances of genuine students who want to come here?

**Mr. Boateng:** I do not demur from that in any way, save to say that the scale of the abuse does not warrant the measure and that the measure goes over the top and is not merited by the problem that is faced.

In perpetuating a discriminatory measure between visa and non-visa countries, the Government are identifying certain countries in west Africa and the Indian sub-continent—and everybody who comes from those countries—as a problem. Hon. Members of all parties must have noticed that as a result of that discriminatory tendency more and more countries that are not

visa-national countries are becoming tainted in the same way. In my constituency experience, I have noticed that those who come from Jamaica are treated as though they are visa nationals. There is therefore a quickening of discrimination and disadvantage in the way in which the rules are administered.

I should like a clear undertaking and assurance from the Minister of State that he will look into the experience of Jamaican nationals currently seeking to come to this country, because there is evidence that they are being treated in a discriminatory way by the immigration service and by the Home Office generally.

Another most important matter is the question of the imposition of a visa requirement on people from Turkey.

**Ms. Clare Short** (Birmingham, Ladywood): On the subject of students, has my hon. Friend noticed that the new rules contain a provision that male students are allowed to bring their wives and children to this country, provided that they can all maintain themselves, but that female students are not? Does he agree that it is outrageous that talented women from around the world might win scholarships to our country, but that they are not allowed to live with their spouses and children when men are allowed to do so? Does my hon. Friend not suspect that that is illegal under the European convention on human rights?

**Mr. Boateng:** It is outrageous, sexist and seemingly in contravention of international law. We look forward to hearing from the Minister of State the advice that he has received so that he can assure the House that we are complying with international law in these rules which seem to fly in the face of the relevant convention.

The imposition of visas on people from Turkey has a particular impact on asylum seekers because—this reality is disguised in the Home Office press statement—it is no comfort for people to be told in the statement that

"the imposition of a visa requirement will not stop any Turkish national who qualifies for admission under the Immigration Rules from entering the United Kingdom"

because, as the Minister of State knows, asylum seekers from abroad are not covered by the immigration rules which make no provision for disputed asylum claims other than those made within the United Kingdom.

I see that the Minister of State is anxious to reply to the points that have been made in the debate so perhaps he will answer this one. One has very much in mind the advice that the Minister has received from his officials that he should seek to speak at the end of the debate. That advice was given to let the Minister off the hook. Well, we do not intend to allow him off the hook so easily.

In conclusion, perhaps the Minister will get his mind around the edition of *Echo Sounding,* the newsletter that is circulated to all entry clearance staff overseas, which dealt with the position of refugees and asylum seekers, and tell us in what circumstances it will be possible for someone coming from Turkey successfully to obtain asylum in this country. While he is at it, will he also tell us why all callers to Latchmere house today, who were seeking information about Kurdish asylum seekers, were told that the office was not able to give any information and why they had their queries referred to the press office at the Home Office? Will he make a statement about what Kurdish asylum seekers are experiencing at this time, which their lawyers and friends may not be told? Perhaps he would tell us. It is no use the Minister nodding and smiling benignly because we know what lies behind that face.

In relation to the Hong Kong potential refugees whose fate has been ensnared in the debate, in the past few days Dame Lydia Dunn has said:

"I believe that the British people will wish their Government to do the honourable thing."

I have no doubt that that is what the British people wish their Government to do, but in this measure, as in so much else, the Government have failed to do so.

1.35 am

**The Minister of State, Home Office (Mr. Tim Renton):** Unfortunately, the hon. Member for Brent, South (Mr. Boateng) has left me extraordinarily little time in which to answer either his questions or those asked by other hon. Members. In the eight or nine minutes available to me, I shall do my best to answer the serious questions raised in the debate.

I start by saying that it has been a strange debate. From the protestations of the hon. Members for Edinburgh, Central (Mr. Darling), Norwood (Mr. Fraser) and Brent, South one would have thought that we were introducing earthshaking changes in the immigration rules; we are not. The rule changes that we have laid before the House are modest. They include two extensions of the visa requirement, to Turkey and to Haiti, and two main changes of general application. One represents a tightening of our immigration control—the prohibition on visitors from visa countries switching to being students after entry.

The other change is a relaxation of our immigration control. Needless to say, that has not been mentioned by any Opposition Member in the debate. I refer, of course, to the fact that we are now enabling a woman working here to be joined by her spouse and children under 18, just as wives and children can already come to join a man working in the United Kingdom.

The rule changes that we are introducing in the new consolidated rules will maintain the effectiveness of our immigration control. They are consistent with our policy of operating a system that is both firm and fair.

Doubtless the Opposition will vote against the improvements just as they have voted against all the improvements of the last two years. What then would be their course of action? We now know from the Labour policy review what Labour immigration policy would look like. It would be unfair. It would be full of loopholes. It would encourage bogus applications. It would give comfort to those who are acting illegally and it would lead——

**Mr. Frank Dobson** (Holborn and St. Pancras): On a point of order, Mr. Deputy Speaker. The Minister is speaking, as I understand it, by leave of the House for a second time. [HON. MEMBERS: "No."]

**Mr. Deputy Speaker:** Order. The hon. Gentleman is under a misapprehension. The Minister is speaking for the first time.

**Mr. Renton:** That goes to show the total ignorance on these matters. We have wasting of time through filibustering by the Opposition.

**Mr. Dobson:** Is it not the case that the Minister, in reply to the debate, is supposed to be dealing strictly with the

rules and should not be taking up valuable time that other hon. Members could have used by talking about Labour party policy? He is supposed to be dealing with the rules.

**Mr. Deputy Speaker:** The Minister has very little time. I think that we had better get on.

**Mr. Renton:** This is a disgraceful filibuster by Opposition Members. They know that their immigration policy is full of holes. It would lead to a substantial increase in immigration and they do not want it discussed.

I should like to thank my hon. Friends who have spoken in the debate. I thank my hon. Friend the Member for Thurrock (Mr. Janman) for his support for our immigration rule changes, although he would like them to go further than I would at present.

**Mr. Darling** *rose*——

**Mr. Renton:** I will not give way. I have only six more minutes to speak and I wish to speak about the rule changes.

I thank my hon. Friend the Member for Bolton, North-East (Mr. Thurnham) for his kind remarks about cases that we have dealt with in the Home Office. I thank my hon. Friend the Member for Keighley (Mr. Waller) for his remarks, particularly about the DNA tests. We shall be debating DNA testing tomorrow night in an Adjournment debate that has been initiated by the hon. Member for Bradford, West (Mr. Madden). As the issue does not arise in the rule changes, and as time is short, I propose to leave my remarks about it for tomorrow night.

**Mr. Max Madden** (Bradford, West): On a point of order, Mr. Deputy Speaker.

**Mr. Renton:** I want to talk about our intention to introduce——

**Mr. Madden:** On a point of order, Mr. Deputy Speaker. It is outrageous that the Minister is saying that he is leaving his remarks on the DNA testing scheme, which the Government deliberately made part of this debate, for an Adjournment debate that I shall introduce tomorrow night.

**Mr. Deputy Speaker:** That is not a point of order.

**Mr. Renton:** It would seem—*[Interruption.]*

**Mr. Deputy Speaker:** Order. I remind the House that it is expecting a ministerial reply to the debate. The Minister has little time left.

**Mr. Renton:** I have come to the conclusion that the opposition are interested only in wasting time on immigration. They are not prepared seriously to discuss immigration changes. The hon. Member for Bradford, West is the worst offender. He will introduce an Adjournment debate tomorrow on DNA testing and yet he is insisting on talking about matters that are not in the rule changes that are before the House.

**Mr. Madden:** On a point of order, Mr. Deputy Speaker. The Minister has made a good case for the Government providing further time to debate the DNA testing scheme. The matter is part of this debate—it was deliberately made so by the Government—and the Minister has not responded to the remarks which have been made about the scheme. I ask you, Mr. Deputy Speaker, to consult Mr.

[*Mr. Madden*]

Speaker and to arrange a separate debate at a reasonable hour so that hon. Members can comment on the proposed scheme.

**Mr. Deputy Speaker:** That is not a matter for the Chair.

**Mr. Renton:** What a disgraceful waste of time by the hon. Gentleman. There is no mention of DNA testing in the rule changes, and he knows it.

As for our intention to introduce a visa requirement for nationals of Turkey, I must tell the House——

**Mr. Darling:** On a point of order, Mr. Deputy Speaker.

**Mr. Deputy Speaker:** Order. I appeal to the House. These are not genuine points of order. The debate can continue for only a few more minutes. I hope that in the limited time that is available to it the House will listen to the Minister's reply.

**Mr. Darling:** I would not make a spurious point of order, Mr. Deputy Speaker. At the start of the debate it was said that Mr. Speaker would read *Hansard's* report of the debate and would note that serious allegations were made by the Opposition about the true intentions of the Government as revealed in the confidential internal memorandum, which dealt, among other things, with the Government's proposals for charging for DNA testing. The memorandum makes it clear that a Minister intended tonight to deal with this matter. These matters are crucial——

**Mr. Deputy Speaker:** Order. These are matters for debate. At the beginning of the debate the hon. Gentleman raised a point of order. I doubt whether it is a matter for Mr. Speaker, but the occupant of the Chair at the time undertook to report to Mr. Speaker what he had said.

**Mr. Renton:** The need for introducing visas for Turks has arisen primarily for operational reasons. The number and proportion of Turkish passengers refused leave to enter and removed from the United Kingdom have been rising for several years and have now reached significant levels. We have experienced a sharp rise in the number of Turks claiming asylum at the ports of entry. Today alone we had 243 applications for political asylum by Turks at our airports. That, in one day, is four times the total for 1987.

**Mr. Corbyn:** Will the Minister give way?

**Mr. Renton:** I shall not give way to the hon. Gentleman.

Among the applicants there may be some genuine refugees. Every one of them has to be given a detailed interview, and that takes a great deal of time. Without doubt there are some economic migrants among the new and large total and there is a possibility that the genuine refugees will not have a chance of being examined and interviewed nearly quickly enough.

There are those who say that we should not talk about economic migrants. Since 1 May——

*It being one and a half hours after the commencement of proceedings on the motion,* MR. DEPUTY SPEAKER *put the Question, pursuant to Standing Order No. 14 (Exempted Business).*

*The House divided:* Ayes 113, Noes 170.

**Division No. 255]**                                    **[1.45 am**

### AYES

Abbott, Ms Diane
Archer, Rt Hon Peter
Armstrong, Hilary
Banks, Tony *(Newham NW)*
Barnes, Harry *(Derbyshire NE)*
Barron, Kevin
Battle, John
Beckett, Margaret
Beith, A. J.
Bennett, A. F. *(D'nt'n & R'dish)*
Blair, Tony
Boateng, Paul
Boyes, Roland
Bray, Dr Jeremy
Campbell, Menzies *(Fife NE)*
Campbell-Savours, D. N.
Clay, Bob
Clelland, David
Cohen, Harry
Corbyn, Jeremy
Cousins, Jim
Cryer, Bob
Cummings, John
Cunliffe, Lawrence
Dalyell, Tam
Darling, Alistair
Davies, Ron *(Caerphilly)*
Davis, Terry *(B'ham Hodge H'l)*
Dixon, Don
Dobson, Frank
Dunnachie, Jimmy
Eastham, Ken
Fatchett, Derek
Fields, Terry *(L'pool B G'n)*
Fisher, Mark
Flynn, Paul
Foster, Derek
Fraser, John
Fyfe, Maria
Galbraith, Sam
George, Bruce
Gilbert, Rt Hon Dr John
Godman, Dr Norman A.
Golding, Mrs Llin
Gordon, Mildred
Grant, Bernie *(Tottenham)*
Griffiths, Win *(Bridgend)*
Harman, Ms Harriet
Haynes, Frank
Howarth, George *(Knowsley N)*
Hughes, John *(Coventry NE)*
Illsley, Eric
Ingram, Adam
Janner, Greville
Jones, Barry *(Alyn & Deeside)*
Kennedy, Charles
Leadbitter, Ted
Leighton, Ron
Lloyd, Tony *(Stretford)*

Loyden, Eddie
McAllion, John
McAvoy, Thomas
Macdonald, Calum A.
McFall, John
McKelvey, William
McWilliam, John
Madden, Max
Mahon, Mrs Alice
Marek, Dr John
Marshall, Jim *(Leicester S)*
Martlew, Eric
Meale, Alan
Michael, Alun
Michie, Bill *(Sheffield Heeley)*
Morgan, Rhodri
Morley, Elliott
Mowlam, Marjorie
Mullin, Chris
Murphy, Paul
Nellist, Dave
Patchett, Terry
Pendry, Tom
Pike, Peter L.
Powell, Ray *(Ogmore)*
Quin, Ms Joyce
Redmond, Martin
Rooker, Jeff
Ross, Ernie *(Dundee W)*
Rowlands, Ted
Ruddock, Joan
Salmond, Alex
Sedgemore, Brian
Sheerman, Barry
Shore, Rt Hon Peter
Short, Clare
Skinner, Dennis
Smith, Andrew *(Oxford E)*
Smith, C. *(Isl'ton & F'bury)*
Smith, J. P. *(Vale of Glam)*
Spearing, Nigel
Steel, Rt Hon David
Steinberg, Gerry
Strang, Gavin
Straw, Jack
Taylor, Mrs Ann *(Dewsbury)*
Thompson, Jack *(Wansbeck)*
Turner, Dennis
Vaz, Keith
Wall, Pat
Wallace, James
Walley, Joan
Welsh, Michael *(Doncaster N)*
Wise, Mrs Audrey

Tellers for the Ayes:
    Mr. Allen McKay and
    Mr. Frank Cook.

### NOES

Alexander, Richard
Alison, Rt Hon Michael
Allason, Rupert
Amess, David
Amos, Alan
Arbuthnot, James
Arnold, Jacques *(Gravesham)*
Arnold, Tom *(Hazel Grove)*
Ashby, David
Atkinson, David
Batiste, Spencer
Bellingham, Henry
Bennett, Nicholas *(Pembroke)*
Bevan, David Gilroy
Blackburn, Dr John G.
Bonsor, Sir Nicholas
Boscawen, Hon Robert

Boswell, Tim
Bowden, Gerald *(Dulwich)*
Bowis, John
Boyson, Rt Hon Dr Sir Rhodes
Brandon-Bravo, Martin
Brazier, Julian
Bright, Graham
Burns, Simon
Burt, Alistair
Butcher, John
Butler, Chris
Butterfill, John
Carlisle, John, *(Luton N)*
Carrington, Matthew
Carttiss, Michael
Cash, William
Channon, Rt Hon Paul

Chapman, Sydney
Chope, Christopher
Churchill, Mr
Coombs, Anthony *(Wyre F'rest)*
Coombs, Simon *(Swindon)*
Cope, Rt Hon John
Cormack, Patrick
Couchman, James
Cran, James
Currie, Mrs Edwina
Davis, David *(Boothferry)*
Day, Stephen
Dorrell, Stephen
Douglas-Hamilton, Lord James
Dover, Den
Durant, Tony
Dykes, Hugh
Fallon, Michael
Forman, Nigel
Forsyth, Michael *(Stirling)*
Freeman, Roger
Garel-Jones, Tristan
Gorman, Mrs Teresa
Gregory, Conal
Hanley, Jeremy
Hargreaves, A. *(B'ham H'll Gr')*
Harris, David
Haselhurst, Alan
Hawkins, Christopher
Hayes, Jerry
Hayhoe, Rt Hon Sir Barney
Heddle, John
Hicks, Mrs Maureen *(Wolv' NE)*
Hind, Kenneth
Hogg, Hon Douglas *(Gr'th'm)*
Hordern, Sir Peter
Howard, Michael
Howarth, Alan *(Strat'd-on-A)*
Howarth, G. *(Cannock & B'wd)*
Howell, Ralph *(North Norfolk)*
Hughes, Robert G. *(Harrow W)*
Hunt, David *(Wirral W)*
Hunt, Sir John *(Ravensbourne)*
Hunter, Andrew
Irvine, Michael
Jack, Michael
Janman, Tim
Jessel, Toby
Jones, Gwilym *(Cardiff N)*
Jones, Robert B *(Herts W)*
King, Roger *(B'ham N'thfield)*
Kirkhope, Timothy
Knapman, Roger
Knight, Greg *(Derby North)*
Lamont, Rt Hon Norman
Latham, Michael
Lawrence, Ivan
Lightbown, David
Lilley, Peter
Lloyd, Peter *(Fareham)*
Lord, Michael
Lyell, Sir Nicholas
Maclean, David
McLoughlin, Patrick
Mans, Keith
Maples, John
Martin, David *(Portsmouth S)*
Maude, Hon Francis
Miller, Sir Hal
Mills, Iain

Mitchell, Andrew *(Gedling)*
Mitchell, Sir David
Moate, Roger
Morrison, Sir Charles
Morrison, Rt Hon P *(Chester)*
Moss, Malcolm
Moynihan, Hon Colin
Neubert, Michael
Nicholls, Patrick
Nicholson, David *(Taunton)*
Norris, Steve
Onslow, Rt Hon Cranley
Oppenheim, Phillip
Page, Richard
Paice, James
Patten, John *(Oxford W)*
Peacock, Mrs Elizabeth
Porter, David *(Waveney)*
Raison, Rt Hon Timothy
Redwood, John
Renton, Tim
Ridley, Rt Hon Nicholas
Sackville, Hon Tom
Sayeed, Jonathan
Shaw, David *(Dover)*
Shaw, Sir Michael *(Scarb')*
Shephard, Mrs G. *(Norfolk SW)*
Smith, Tim *(Beaconsfield)*
Speed, Keith
Speller, Tony
Spicer, Michael *(S Worcs)*
Squire, Robin
Steen, Anthony
Stern, Michael
Stevens, Lewis
Stewart, Allan *(Eastwood)*
Stewart, Andy *(Sherwood)*
Stokes, Sir John
Stradling Thomas, Sir John
Summerson, Hugo
Taylor, Ian *(Esher)*
Taylor, John M *(Solihull)*
Taylor, Teddy *(S'end E)*
Temple-Morris, Peter
Thompson, Patrick *(Norwich N)*
Thurnham, Peter
Townend, John *(Bridlington)*
Tracey, Richard
Tredinnick, David
Trippier, David
Twinn, Dr Ian
Vaughan, Sir Gerard
Waddington, Rt Hon David
Walker, Bill *(T'side North)*
Waller, Gary
Ward, John
Wardle, Charles *(Bexhill)*
Watts, John
Wells, Bowen
Whitney, Ray
Widdecombe, Ann
Wiggin, Jerry
Winterton, Mrs Ann
Winterton, Nicholas
Wolfson, Mark
Wood, Timothy

Tellers for the Noes:
    Mr. Kenneth Carlisle and
    Mr. David Heathcoat-Amory.

*Question accordingly negatived.*

# NHS Reform

*Motion made, and Question proposed,* That this House do now adjourn.—*[Mr. Dorrell.]*

1.54 am

**Sir Peter Hordern** (Horsham): During the past 20 years there have been two reforms of the National Health Service—in its administration rather than in its substance. When the Government's proposals for the present reforms were produced, they deserved more serious consideration than they have subsequently received. Judging by some of the hysterical reaction to the Government's proposals, one would think that the Government were out to dismember the NHS completely.

I very much regret the tone as well as the substance of some of the reactions. However, those who are in the front line of the reforms have reacted somewhat differently. A substantial number of hospitals and large practices have expressed interest in going it alone and in accepting proposals. When the nature of the proposals is known and the propaganda has blown over, the proposed reforms will be judged on their merits and found acceptable.

Because the NHS is a national service free at the point of delivery, many people think that it is wrong to attempt reform, because reform represents some kind of threat to the principle of the NHS. However, the shortcomings of the NHS are there for all to see. There are long waiting lists for operations, there are shabby practices and hospitals and overworked general practitioners and hospital doctors. We have only to consider the outcry whenever it is proposed to close an old hospital—even if it is out of date and inefficient—and to open a new one in its place to understand how hard it is to win acceptance for any reform of the NHS which involves change. The general impression seems to be that there is nothing wrong with the system which a lot more money would not put right. That impression is fostered not simply by the Labour party, as we might expect, but by the British Medical Association, which is a professional body manned by professionals.

It is a mistake to expect too much of any trade union which exists for the benefit of its members. However, until I saw its recent advertisement, I had thought that the BMA would conduct itself in a professional manner. Of course, history is against any such hope. We need only remember that the BMA was wholly opposed to the NHS when it was founded. However, by listening to it now, we might think that it had invented it.

Every doctor must take the Hippocratic oath, the most serious professional pledge in existence and one which all doctors aspire to live up to. What was Hippocrates like? Harvey's Oxford Companion to Classical Literature says this of him:

"Hippocrates supported a true scientific spirit, insisted on the permanence of the relation of cause to effect and the necessity of careful observation of medical facts. He was regarded by his contemporaries and successors as a perfect type of physician, learned, humane, calm, pure of mind, grave and reticent."

I do not think that any of those adjectives could be applied to the BMA today.

The BMA's advertisement which appeared in *The Observer* of 4 June states that the Government want the general practitioners' practices with more than 11,000 patients to take over budgets, including the purchase of hospital treatment. It states that GPs would have to

[*Sir Peter Hordern*]

negotiate contracts with hospitals, shop around for the best buys and plan their budgets accordingly. The BMA would not have published that advertisement unless it meant people to think that doctors would be forced to take over budgets and negotiate contracts. Nowhere is there any suggestion that it is entirely up to large practices to run their own practices. Similarly, there is no suggestion that, having done so, they cannot do otherwise. I have never heard of the freedom to adopt an alternative course described as having to negotiate contracts, as though the freedom to escape a centrally controlled system was a challenge to the state.

Perhaps one should dismiss all this talk as hyperbole, but there is worse. The advertisement said:

"Since there is no new money in the system, GPs will be expected to take on the burden of rationing the scarce resources."

That raises a different issue, for there are no qualifying words about real increases, allowing for increases in inflation—just a simple statement that there is no new money in the system.

The House should take this seriously. What is the truth? The public expenditure White Paper states in paragraph 9 on page 5:

"Public expenditure on the NHS is planned to increase in 1989-90 by £1·3 billion compared with the estimated outturn for 1988-89. When the effects of reduced employer's superannuation contributions are taken into account this amounts to a cash increase of nearly £1·6 billion. In addition health authorities' new cost improvement plans are expected to provide a further £25 million. The total increase in resources will thereby amount to some £1·8 billion, equivalent to a cash increase of 9½ per cent."

Paragraph 12 tells us that further increases are planned in 1990-91 and 1991-92, increasing the NHS total gross expenditure to more than £23 billion—an expected 44 per cent. real terms increase on 1978-79. That is all that I need to quote to demolish what the BMA said about there being no increase in cash.

What conclusion can one draw from that deceitful advertisement—for that is what it is? We should remember that the Government have no money of their own. Increases in spending can be made only through increases in revenue from taxation, and that can come only through the hard work and enterprise of the British people. So when the BMA says "no new money" it diminishes us all because it is an especially damaging untruth.

The BMA says that our general practitioners are under pressure and that our young hospital doctors are having to work unreasonably long hours, but that has always been the case. Are there not enough people in the NHS? It is worth reminding ourselves of the progress that has been made. In 1961, 575,000 people were employed in the NHS; in 1988, the figure was 1·22 million. One in 18 families in the land has someone who works for the Health Service. That is a very large figure, and makes the Health Service the largest employer in the western world. We may not have enough general practitioners, but we have 25,000 now compared with 21,000 10 years ago—an increase of nearly 20 per cent. The average list that doctors must manage has decreased from 2,312 to 2,020, which is a 12 per cent. reduction. Last year in our hospitals, 5·3 million patients were treated, which is 1 million more than in 1978. Last year we treated 7·6 million out-patients, as compared with 6·7 million in 1978. On any test, whether immunisation uptake or the continued fall in the standardised mortality ratio for a wide variety of potentially avoidable causes of death, there has been an improvement over the position of 10 years ago.

All the evidence shows a substantial improvement in the services of the NHS. It does not show some of the faults of the system which are inevitable in an organisation as large as the NHS. Although it may be the largest service in the western world, it probably has the longest waiting lists. I speak from the experience of some years as a member of the Public Accounts Committee. I cannot recall a year when the Comptroller and Auditor-General and the National Audit Office did not discover an outstanding example of waste. Until recently, the Department had no idea how many people were recruited for the Health Service or what they did until two years after the event. I can remember an occasion after the review and reform of 1973 when 50,000 administrators were taken on in the space of 18 months, but that was not discovered until two years later.

The National Audit Office's recent reports show that 28 per cent. of operating theatres available during weekdays were unstaffed—23 per cent. because of cancelled sessions. There were wide variations between districts, but when the districts were taken together it was found that only 50 to 60 per cent. of available theatre time was used. Had the theatre time been properly used in the five authorities examined, another 11,000 operations could have taken place. In another report, 20 per cent. of districts confirmed that at least 40 per cent. of the land that they owned could have been disposed of. Another report on the need to evaluate the effectiveness of clinical care showed that there were marked variations between health authorities in the number of deaths due to avoidable factors.

Such faults are inevitable in any large system. They show the need for greater autonomy within the system and greater responsibility, too. I do not believe that anyone reading and understanding those reports could believe that the Health Service is not ripe for review. I deeply regret the fact that the reviews have not been treated as seriously as they should have been, by the BMA in particular.

One has only to consider the cost of drugs, which has increased from £805 million in 1978-79 to £2,167 million in 1987-88—about 10 per cent. of the National Health Service budget. Yet the doctors may not even know the cost of the drugs that they prescribe, which is why prescription costs vary by as much as 50 per cent. from one practice to another. How can that be right? Under the Government's proposals, the district health authorities and the larger practices will be able to make contracts with health authorities outside their own areas, which will make the hospitals increasingly customer-orientated, rather than producer-orientated as they are at present.

It might be better still if GPs could refer their patients wherever they want, but that is less important than the other considerations that I have mentioned.

It is never right to accept waste, especially in a service as large and important as the National Health Service. Yet waste is endemic in the system. The reason why it makes sense to allow some competition for services and to set benchmarks is not that that will save money—because there will be more money—but because it will ensure that the money is spent to better effect. Advances in medicine and the growing number of elderly people will continue to place increasing demands on the Health Service and we must meet those demands as best we can.

We in this House have a duty to ensure that public money is properly spent for the benefit of the public. Forty years after the foundation of the Health Service, it is clear that waste and inefficiency have occurred too often and on too great a scale to allow them to continue unchecked. That is why the Government's proposals should be supported, and the BMA's campaign rejected.

In a day or two, the council of the BMA is to decide whether to accept the proposals for the doctors' contracts. I wish that the decision could have been reached in an atmosphere of calm study of the proposals, rather than being the victim of a thoroughly salacious and disgraceful advertising campaign.

2.8 am

**The Parliamentary Under-Secretary of State for Health (Mr. Roger Freeman):** The House owes a great debt of gratitude to my hon. Friend the Member for Horsham (Sir P. Hordern) for introducing such an excellent debate. The record will show that, at 2 o'clock in the morning, the House was unusually full for an Adjournment debate, because of the presence of my hon. Friends the Members for Hertford and Stortford (Mr. Wells), for Upminster (Sir N. Bonsor), for Basingstoke (Mr. Hunter), for Norwich, North (Mr. Thompson) and for Amber Valley (Mr. Oppenheim)—he has now left the Chamber—and my hon. Friend the Member for Loughborough (Mr. Dorrell), whom I take for granted! This is a sign of how strongly the House feels about this subject.

I agree very much with my hon. Friend the Member for Horsham. Much misunderstanding has been created about "Working for Patients". I agree that some of it has been deliberately created and that it is unhelpful to a constructive and rational discussion of our proposals.

It may help my hon. Friends if I dwell on five basic misunderstandings about the White Paper, two of which were mentioned by my hon. Friend the Member for Horsham. The first is the false claim put about that doctors will have less time to deal with their patients. That cannot be mathematically true in total. There is a fixed number of patients. It seems likely, given the number of doctors in training, that the number of doctors in general practice will increase in the coming years. As my hon. Friend said, there has been a significant increase in the number of doctors. That must mean that, rather than increasing, the average list size may decrease. The implication is that doctors will not have less time on average to deal with patients but will perhaps have a little more. Some doctors will choose to gain more patients and, because of their energy, performance and reputation, will gain more at the margin. That must mean that other doctors in the locality will lose patients. That is right. The contract will soon be discussed by the Conference of Local Medical Committees and it is important that it carefully consider the general principle running through the contract, that we intend to reward hard work and performance in a common aim, which is shared with the Government—better treatment of patients.

Secondly, it is said by some that patients will be sent around the country in search of operations. A member of the British Medical Association used a colourful phrase —he said that patients would be sent around the country in their pyjamas with cheques pinned to their breast pockets: that would be money following the patient. It is nonsense. It is important to change the funding mechanism and the flow of money in the system in such a way that money can follow sensible patient referrals. In other words, the doctor, patient, district health authority and receiving hospital all agree that it is in the best interests of a patient for elective surgery or cold surgery —for example, a hip replacement or operations on varicose veins or a hernia—if that patient is sent a little further than the district general hospital to get the operation done more quickly. We have no intention of sending patients against their will all over the country or excessive distances for urgent operations. This measure in the White Paper is designed to reduce the disparity in waiting times throughout the country and to help patients.

Thirdly, it has been said that patients will be denied drugs that they need from their general practitioner, not only in month 11 or 12 but in month one. That is untrue. My right hon. and learned Friend the Secretary of State has made it plain that we have no intention of cash-limiting general practitioners, either individually or collectively. We will introduce what we call indicative drug budgets. They will provide a guideline for general practitioners as to how much they should prescribe. Our proposals for indicative drug budgets are a sensible way, in co-operation with the general practitioner, of exercising better control, because over-prescribing—particularly of tranquillisers—is not in the best interests of patients.

Fourthly, it is suggested that hospitals will opt out of the Health Service and that the Government are about to dismember the NHS. That too is absolutely untrue. My right hon. Friend the Prime Minister and my right hon. and learned Friend the Secretary of State made it plain that we are not about to privatise the Health Service. It will remain free at the point of delivery and financed mainly by taxation. Hospitals will not opt out by choosing self-governing status but will simply have delegated to them greater responsibility for managing their own affairs.

Earlier today, I attended together with my right hon. and learned Friend the Secretary of State and my hon. Friend the Minister a successful conference at Church house, Westminster, for those interested in self-government. The large audience was drawn from the 200 hospitals and other units that expressed interest in self-government. The conference was designed to allow my right hon. and learned Friend an opportunity to explain his ideas in more detail.

Our proposals are not about opting out or about dismantling the Health Service but concern delegating to those who work most closely with patients, responsibility for employment, pay, and the further development of the service. That must be in the patient's interest. As self-governing hospitals will no longer be subject to interference from regional health authorities or from the Government, they will have no one but themselves to blame if a mistake is made. We want them to develop a sense of responsibility and pride in running their own hospitals. We will finance them with a fair share of taxpayers' money, but we want them to bring their services closer to the community in every sense.

Fifthly, it has been suggested that the Health Service will go in search only of what are called profitable patients, and that unprofitable patients—whatever that might mean —will be denied care by general practitioners or hospitals. That too is nonsense. We are not moving to the American system of cash passing between the patient and the provider of health care. We have set our face against that. As far as the patient is concerned, ours is a cashless system,

[*Mr. Roger Freeman*]

free at the point of delivery and financed from general taxation. Therefore, the concept of a profitable or unprofitable patient is not one that we recognise.

Let me briefly explain why it is nonsense to claim that "unprofitable patients" will be denied proper care. We are so changing the capitation fees payable to general practitioners for providing services to patients that they will rise with the age of the patient. That will encourage GPs to add to their lists and to care for the elderly. Also, the indicative drug budgets, which will affect the majority of general practitioners—those who do not choose to control their own practice budgets—will be specifically tailored to reflect the age profile of the patient list, the relative health of the patients on that list, and their special drug needs and requirements.

Therefore, how can it be claimed that doctors will in any way have a disincentive to take on patients and a real incentive to deny care to those with special health needs? Such a claim is nonsense and a calumny against the medical profession whose own ethics, as my hon. Friend clearly stated, compel the doctor to care for any patient, whatever his or her condition.

As to hospitals, our critics fail to understand or to take on board the exciting concept of dividing responsibility between the purchaser of health care—the district health authority or the general practitioner's practice budget—and the health care provider, which is the hospital. The district health authority, as the guardian of the health requirements of all existing and prospective patients living within its province, will be responsible for the care of every individual. It will be the responsibility of the health authority—properly funded, under our new system of resource allocation—to ensure that hospital care is available locally for the core services that we shall define more carefully and closely in the months to come.

Let me list the issues on which I hope the medical profession and the Department of Health are agreed. First, I hope that we are all agreed on one aim in the reform of the Health Service—which, after all, has not enjoyed as

radical a series of necessary reforms as that which we propose in 40 years. We have a common aim: to improve patient information and choice. We shall do that by giving doctors the right to advertise, ensuring that GPs provide existing and prospective patients with more information and enabling patients to change doctors more easily.

Secondly, we want to improve the quantity and quality of health care. We want to improve the quantity by continuing the rate of growth in real expenditure on the Health Service. My hon. Friend rightly said that the Government had increased expenditure by some 40 per cent., which was reflected in the number of doctors and front-line staff, and the Government will continue to increase the amount of real resources.

Quality is also vitally important. I hope that the medical profession agrees with us that medical audit—and, indeed, the use of contracts between the purchaser and the provider of health care, stipulating the minimum standards required—will serve the patient's interests.

Finally, I hope that the medical profession agrees with our desire for a drive for even greater efficiency, at the same time as an increase in resources. We have a relatively efficient health-care system compared with many other western European nations: we devote a slightly smaller proportion of our GDP to our Health Service than some of those countries devote to theirs, but we provide a good service. We can and should do better, however, and one of the key elements of an improved performance is the delegation of responsibility to self-governing hospitals, GP practice budget-holders and the reformed, slimline, business-like district health authorities and family practitioner committees.

I agree with my hon. Friend. I hope that cooler heads and reason will prevail, and that we will all work together —both sides of the House, the medical profession and the Department of Health—to achieve our long-term and most important aim: to put patients first, and to improve the quantity and quality of health care.

*Question put and agreed to.*

*Adjourned accordingly at twenty-two minutes past Two o'clock.*

# House of Commons

*Wednesday 21 June 1989*

*The House met at half-past Two o'clock*

## PRAYERS

[MR. SPEAKER *in the Chair*]

## PRIVATE BUSINESS

SOUTH YORKSHIRE LIGHT RAIL TRANSIT BILL *[Lords]*
*Read a Second time, and committed.*

VALE OF GLAMORGAN (BARRY HARBOUR) BILL
*[Lords]*

HAYLE HARBOUR BILL *[Lords]*
*Orders for Second Reading read.*
*To be read a Second time tomorrow.*

# Oral Answers to Questions

## TRADE AND INDUSTRY

### Staff Dispersal

1. **Mr. Sayeed:** To ask the Chancellor of the Duchy of Lancaster what is his Department's policy on dispersing staff to the regions; and what proportion of his staff now work outside London.

**The Chancellor of the Duchy of Lancaster (Mr. Anthony Newton):** The Government's policy is that Civil Service work should be located where it can be done most cost-effectively and provide the best service to the public, taking account also of the Government's urban and regional policies.

The Department has some 12,670 staff in post, of whom just over half work outside central London. A further 650 Patents Office posts will move to Newport by 1991, and the location of a number of other units is under review.

**Mr. Sayeed:** I thank my right hon. Friend for that answer. Is the willingness to move outside the south-west evenly distributed across the Civil Service grades or have middle-aged middle management demonstrated greater reluctance to move? If so, what are the implications of that?

**Mr. Newton:** The implications of any differences, whether described by grades or individuals, are that they must be taken into account when considering both whether a move should take place and the arrangements under which it should do so.

**Mr. Ingram:** Has the Minister given any consideration to relocating any of the staff in his Department to Norfolk house in my constituency, which has a long-term lease held by the Property Services Agency at a cost of £166,000 per annum, has lain vacant for a considerable number of years and could accommodate approximately 400 staff?

**Mr. Newton:** As I indicated, there are a number of reviews of possible further relocations taking place. Clearly, we shall bear in mind the availability of office accommodation and the supply of labour in particular locations. I note the hon. Gentleman's point.

**Mr. Harris:** Of the 6,000 or so members of my right hon. Friend the Minister's staff based in central London, how many were able to turn up for work today? Does he agree that the experiences of millions of people in this capital today underline the absolute necessity of dispersing more Whitehall staff to the regions? In that context, will he look at the claims of Cornwall, particularly in this age of modern information technology?

**Mr. Newton:** I cannot give my hon. Friend the exact breakdown that he seeks, but a number of my staff are absent. I also take note, as I hope will the Opposition Front Bench spokesmen, of what my hon. Friend said about the disruption needlessly caused to so many thousands of people by today's events. As always, I shall be mindful of Cornwall's needs.

### Tameside

2. **Mr. Andrew F. Bennett:** To ask the Chancellor of the Duchy of Lancaster what steps his Department is taking to encourage new industries to come to Tameside.

**The Parliamentary Under-Secretary of State for Trade and Industry (Mr. Robert Atkins):** I am tempted to reply, "lots". The north-west is booming economically as a direct result of Her Majesty's Government's policies, and Tameside is no exception. The demand from domestic and foreign companies to invest in the north-west is a true measure of the faith that they have in the British economy.

**Mr. Bennett:** I am sure that the Minister's words will not encourage the large numbers of my constituents who have been out of work for 12 months or more. They particularly resent the way in which the Government invest so many resources in the south-east and, so far as they can see, very few in Tameside. Will the Minister particuarly impress on his Government colleagues the need to complete the motorway around the east side of Manchester and to develop a freight terminal in the Tameside, east side, of Manchester to take full advantage of the Channel tunnel when it is operational, and so as to be prepared for harmonisation in 1992?

**Mr. Atkins:** The hon. Gentleman will be aware that my constituency is further north than his. My hon. Friends who represent northern and north-west constituencies and I find a totally different picture from that painted by the hon. Gentleman. The north-west is doing extremely well at the moment, and long may it continue to do so. As the hon. Gentleman will understand, the points that he raised about infrastructure are matters for my right hon. Friend the Secretary of State for Transport and my right hon. Friend the Secretary of State for the Environment. I will draw their attention to the points that he makes.

**Mr. Jack:** Is not the validity of my hon. Friend's answer borne out when one considers the investment made by companies such as British Aerospace, Fox's Biscuits, Leyland Daf and many others in the Preston area and the capital expansion and employment programmes that they are following?

**Mr. Atkins:** As usual, my hon. Friend is spot on. He will know, as I do, that the local paper in Preston pointed to how the local Labour council had problems because business was booming to such an extent that there was congestion and more space was needed for offices, but that all in all they were problems of success—something that the council recognised even if Labour Members of Parliament do not.

## Trade Deficit

3. **Mr. Alan W. Williams:** To ask the Chancellor of the Duchy of Lancaster with which European Economic Community members Britain's trade is in deficit.

**The Parliamentary Under-Secretary of State for Corporate Affairs (Mr. Francis Maude):** In the 12 months to April the United Kingdom was in deficit on visible trade with Belgium and Luxembourg, Denmark, the Federal Republic of Germany, France, Italy, the Netherlands and Portugal.

**Mr. Williams:** The length of that list is impressive. The Minister scarcely missed out any EC country. How can the Government claim that we have the strongest economy in Europe when we have a trade deficit with virtually every other Community country?

**Mr. Maude:** The question of with which countries we have a deficit is wholly irrelevant. The fact is that three-quarters of the imports into this country are either semi-manufactured capital goods or intermediate goods. They reflect not just increased consumer demand, which is itself an example of the prosperity which pervades this country, but are a consequence of the high investment boom that has been going on. The hon. Gentleman should welcome those signs of strength.

**Mr. Hill:** Is it not nonsense to continue producing figures of deficits with Community countries when we are supposed to become one major trading bloc after 1992? What use are such figures to anybody in the Community, and should we not dispose of them in 1992?

**Mr. Maude:** I find no difficulty in the continued existence of the figures, but many people like figures for their own sake. When we place on businesses the requirement to fill in extremely detailed forms, we have to consider the use for which such information is gathered. As my hon. Friend will know, discussions are going on within Europe about the extent of detail that should be collected after 1992. We take the view that, while it may be right that there should be broad measures of trade between Community members, an excessive amount of detail is unnecessary.

**Mrs. Mahon:** Does the Minister realise that the large part of that deficit which is in textiles—23 per cent.—is worrying people who work in the industry, and that the Government are making things far worse by their policy of high interest rates? People in my constituency are not happy when the Minister trivialises a serious situation.

**Mr. Maude:** I have not trivialised it, but a percentage point on interest rates places only a third of the cost on industry of an extra percentage point on earnings. Those industries which are seeking and working extremely hard to increase their exports are not helped by the prospect of a dock strike, nor by the transport strikes today.

**Sir Anthony Meyer:** Will my hon. Friend confirm that there is no real danger of this country being forced to live on Brussels sprouts and that the advent of the single market in 1992 presents British industry and services with tremendous opportunities?

**Mr. Maude:** My hon. Friend is entirely right. That is why we have mounted a campaign to alert British businesses to the opportunities. However, we have also not sought to hide from British businesses the dangers that may be involved, and the dangers which flow from enhanced competition. The message has been that, for a business to succeed, it must be more competitive, which means containing its costs as best it can and developing its market, services and products to provide what the customer wants.

**Mr. Henderson:** How does the Minister explain what he would no doubt regard as the wholly irrelevant increase in our trade deficit with EC countries from £5·4 billion in 1979 to £18 billion in 1989, and what new steps does he intend to take to continue his economic miracle in Britain's trade with European countries?

**Mr. Maude:** The hon. Gentleman missed out of his potted economic history all the years between those two dates when Britain was in substantial surplus. I do not recall him or his colleagues popping up at every Question Time in those years saying what an economic success that was.

**Mr. Marlow:** There is some debate about joining the European monetary system, I believe. If we were in it, as I understand it, either sterling would be higher or interest rates would be lower, which would mean that either more money would be spent or foreign goods would be cheaper. What would that do to the trade deficit?

**Mr. Maude:** My hon. Friend raises a most interesting question which, as he will realise, falls outside my responsibilities. At this stage of the year it may be unwise for me to venture into that area.

## Departmental Records

4. **Mr. Dalyell:** To ask the Chancellor of the Duchy of Lancaster where Sir Brian Hayes's personal records of the departmental events of January 1986 will be stored on his retirement.

**Mr. Newton:** I understand that Sir Brian Hayes made no personal record of these events.

**Mr. Dalyell:** Are the permanent secretary and the Chancellor still interested in integrity in British public life in the highest echelons of the DTI? As Colette Bowe and John Mogg have both put their accounts of events in bank vaults, would it not be wise and in the interests of posterity for Sir Brian Hayes to make a record and explain why he advised Leon Brittan not to leave the DTI? Did he know that Mr. Powell and Mr. Ingham had approved, quite improperly, the disclosure of the Law Officer's letter? Will Sir Brian reveal his personal view of the Prime Minister's behaviour during the course of those events?

**Mr. Newton:** I hope that the hon. Gentleman will not take the fact that I shall not comment on every part of his question as in any way endorsing the assumptions on which it was based. I can only say, as I have said before, that I have nothing to add to the very full account given to the House by my right hon. Friend the Prime Minister some three years ago.

**Mr. Barry Field:** Does my right hon. Friend agree that it is a long tradition of this House that right hon. and hon. Members do not criticise civil servants, who serve all shades of Government so loyally? In view of the monocular mentality of the hon. Member for Linlithgow (Mr. Dalyell), does my right hon. Friend agree that it would be no bad thing if the hon. Gentleman were placed in storage long before retirement?

**Mr. Newton:** I note what my hon. Friend suggests, and no doubt the hon. Member for Linlithgow (Mr. Dalyell) has also done so.

### ERDF Grant

5. **Mr. Morley:** To ask the Chancellor of the Duchy of Lancaster what are the current figures for ERDF grant in Yorkshire and Humberside in 1988-89.

**Mr. Atkins:** In the financial year 1988-89, ERDF commitments to Yorkshire and Humberside were valued at £26 million.

**Mr. Morley:** Will the Minister join me in congratulating Scunthorpe borough council on creating so many jobs in the borough—more, in fact, than its neighbouring Conservative-controlled authority, even though it has exactly the same access to exactly the same grants? Is the Minister aware of the difficulty facing Yorkshire and Humberside, including Scunthorpe, because of the way in which the integration development operations programme has overrun its plans? Has Commissioner Millan said what help he will give through transitional assistance for current schemes in both Scunthorpe and Bradford borough councils?

**Mr. Atkins:** The hon. Gentleman will be aware that he and two of his colleagues came to discuss this matter. We managed to resolve the misunderstanding that occurred —to his satisfaction, I hope, and to that of his hon. Friends the Members for Rother Valley (Mr. Barron) and for Sheffield, Central (Mr. Caborn). To date, I have no information to give him on what Commissioner Millan is doing, although we are ensuring that the commitment that I honoured in my letter to his hon. Friend will be maintained. I do not wish to be drawn on the comparison between one borough council and another, except to say that I am delighted if any borough is able to create more jobs. After all, whether boroughs are controlled by the Labour party or any other party, it is the Conservative Government's overall economic policy which has provided the environment in which those jobs have been created.

**Mr. Riddick:** Although as a Yorkshire Member I welcome the money coming into Yorkshire from the European Community, may I point out that we need to keep the whole matter in perspective? Are not Yorkshire companies, and British companies generally, making substantial contributions through the tax system to the European Community and helping to fund the £2 billion net contribution that Britain makes each year to the European Community? As we get only £26 million back

through regional funds, does not that pale into insignificance compared with the net contribution that we have to make?

**Mr. Atkins:** My hon. Friend makes his own point in his own way. As a Lancashire Member, I would not wish to be drawn on the subject of the money being given to Yorkshire. In the context of friendly rivalry, I merely hope that Lancashire is doing as well if not better than Yorkshire and Humberside.

### Competitiveness

6. **Mr. Bell:** To ask the Chancellor of the Duchy of Lancaster what has been the change in competitiveness of British industry in the last 10 years.

**Mr. Newton:** Competitiveness involves numerous factors, including quality, reliability, assurance of delivery and after-sales service. In relation to price competitiveness alone, unit labour costs in United Kingdom manufacturing compared with those in other industrial countries, allowing for the effects of exchange rate movements, are thought to have been on average the same in 1988 as in 1979.

**Mr. Bell:** To translate that into real terms, 51,000 jobs were lost on Teesside alone between 1979 and 1981 and although we welcome British Steel's £600 million profit, we should not forget that it was achieved at the cost of the loss of 130,000 jobs, many of them on Teesside. Will the Minister confirm that we have lost about 9 per cent. of world trade since 1979, a loss which has been greater than that of our industrial competitors? Does the Minister think that that reflects a supply side economic failure or success?

**Mr. Newton:** On the specific point raised, the indications are that in recent years the decline in Britain's share of trade has stopped, and may even have been reversed after many years—indeed, decades—in which there was a persistent tendency to decline. With regard to the north-east, there is no doubt that there have been substantial changes in the pattern of employment over the period in question, but they reflect an increase in the competitiveness of the relevant industries, including steel, which means that there are now secure jobs whereas previously there were insecure jobs.

**Mr. Favell:** Is it not a fact that Britain has nothing to fear while the spirit that is obvious today abounds in the many people who have come into London and other industrial cities in the face of the most extraordinary difficulties? An example is the young lady I saw in a baker's in Strutton Ground today, near my London accommodation, who had come into work at 5 am. Despite having had a six-hour journey to reach home last Friday, she is back again today.

**Mr. Newton:** I have not had the opportunity to make that young lady's acquaintance, but I am happy to pay tribute to her efforts and to those of many others who have overcome needless industrial disruption to get to work today.

**Dr. Reid:** On the subject of security in the steel industry, the steel workers of Bellshill will be grateful to the Minister for his assurance that their jobs in the Clydesdale Tube Works are guaranteed. Does the Minister agree that competitiveness is often a function of investment at plant level and that no matter what efforts are made by the work force, in the absence of that investment and technological capital equipment the work force often comes off worst? Is the Minister aware that in the Clydesdale Tube Works at Bellshill over the past two years the workers have increased quality, delivery times and productivity beyond all recognition, but we understand that there is still a threat over their heads due to lack of investment in the mills? How does the Minister intend to ensure that his assurance today that steel jobs are secure will be maintained now that he has privatised the steel industry so that it is outwith our control?

**Mr. Newton:** Eight or nine years ago the steel industry gained a mention in the "Guinness Book of Records" for the largest corporate loss ever made. It has now been privatised, is making substantial profits and has far greater capacity to invest than would have been the case if the previous policy had been allowed to continue.

**Mr. Nicholas Bennett:** Would my right hon. Friend care to speculate about the effect on the competitiveness of British industry if we had a policy of increasing company and personal taxation, imposing import controls, increasing regulation and bureaucracy, and subsidising inefficient industries—all policies that have been espoused by Opposition Members during the past few years?

**Mr. Newton:** The result would have been the same dismal performance that we saw between 1974 and 1979, when Britain's international competitiveness declined by about 25 per cent.

### Enterprise Initiative

7. **Mr. Cash:** To ask the Chancellor of the Duchy of Lancaster how many applications have so far been received for consultancy projects under the enterprise initiative.

**Mr. Newton:** More than 28,000 applications for assisted consultancy projects have been received since the launch of the scheme in January 1988. Building on this success, my right hon. and noble Friend the Secretary of State yesterday announced improvements to make it easier for smaller firms to obtain the advice they need to improve their performance, and to extend the role of enterprise counsellors to cover single market issues.

**Mr. Cash:** Does my right hon. Friend agree that although it is encouraging to see the emphasis being placed on marketing in these consultancy projects, quality seems to be falling back to second in line although it is impossible to sell and market things if they are not of sufficient quality? With regard to the trade deficit and competitiveness, would it not be helpful to put extra emphasis on the importance of quality so as to ensure that we deal with the real reason for the trade deficit, which is that some countries are producing higher quality goods than we are?

**Mr. Newton:** Yes, I agree with my hon. Friend. One of the improvements that my right hon. and noble Friend the Secretary of State announced yesterday was greater emphasis on total quality management in one of the consultancy initiatives.

**Mr. Grocott:** Will the Minister tell us how much the television advertising campaign for the enterprise initiative

has cost? Will he do the arithmetic and tell us how much each successful application has cost as a proportion of total television advertising costs?

**Mr. Newton:** There would be no point in an initiative of this sort if it were not brought extensively to the attention of those at whom it is aimed. The response has been substantial. Our surveys have shown that many of the firms which have acknowledged the benefits that they have gained from the consultancy initiative would not otherwise have sought that advice and help, which is improving the competitiveness and quality of British industry.

**Mr. John Townend:** Is my right hon. Friend aware that in my area several small firms have taken advantage of the scheme and have benefited from the Government-aided consultancy? Does he agree that every effort should be made to increase the take-up among small firms because many are sceptical and some are frightened of consultants? Does he further agree that one way of doing that would be to have a register of small firms which have used the scheme satisfactorily and which would be available to act as referees for other small firms sceptical about the scheme?

**Mr. Newton:** I note and will consider my hon. Friend's suggestion. We are aiming the scheme at small firms. It is satisfactory that of the 28,000 applications to which I have referred, about 90 per cent. have been from firms employing fewer than 100 people. One of the new measures announced in the past two or three days is designed to make the scheme even more user-friendly to small firms.

**Mr. Hoyle:** Will the right hon. Gentleman please answer a direct question and tell us the cost of that television advertising and the cost per application take-up?

**Mr. Newton:** I have already made that clear to the hon. Gentleman's hon. Friend, the hon. Member for The Wrekin (Mr. Grocott). The point about such a scheme is that because of the advantages that it entails we should bring it to the attention of those at whom it is aimed, and that has been achieved.

### Trade Barriers

8. **Mr. Oppenheim:** To ask the Chancellor of the Duchy of Lancaster what action the Government are taking to ensure that the European Economic Community does not erect protectionist trade barriers.

**Mr. Maude:** The United Kingdom is committed to ensuring that our experience of the economic benefits of free markets and deregulation is reflected in Community policy. The Community is also working in the Uruguay round of GATT negotiations to achieve a further substantial liberalisation of international trade.

**Mr. Oppenheim:** Can my hon. Friend confirm that the Government's opposition to protectionist trade runs to opposing vigorously any moves to protectionism emanating from within the Commission, despite recent improvements within the Commission? Can he also confirm that the best way to tackle competition from places like Japan and Korea is to look to our own problems, particularly in education and our attitude to industry, rather than imposing quotas, voluntary restraint agreements and spurious anti-dumping duties, which only push up prices to consumers and compound the inefficiencies of European industry?

**Mr. Maude:** I very much agree with my hon. Friend's sentiments. I am grateful to him for acknowledging that the attitude of the European Commission on these matters is increasingly liberal. Certainly, the new Commission takes the view that free trade is very good and that we should work hard to pursue it. My hon. Friend is also right to say that it is important to open trade in other markets outside the Community. I believe that those markets are opening. It is now up to British businesses to seek to exploit those markets and to get into them and sell hard.

**Mr. Cryer:** Does the Minister agree that after 1992 it will be essential for the survival of the clothing and textile industry that there is a burden-sharing agreement between all 12 member states on the import of textiles and clothing into the Common Market? Does the Minister further agree that the easiest market to penetrate is the United Kingdom market, with six main suppliers supplying every major town and city throughout the United Kingdom? That is not the position in any other member state. Therefore, on the basis of equality, a burden-sharing arrangement should be made. It is vital for the continued success of the British textile industry in areas like mine in Bradford.

**Mr. Maude:** As the hon. Gentleman knows, the multi-fibre arrangement was never intended to be more than a temporary measure to protect industry during a period of disruption and major changes worldwide in the industry. He will know that it is the intention of the Community in the GATT negotiations to consider ways of returning to ordinary trading. He knows also that my hon. Friend the Minister for Trade is well seized of the point that he raised about burden sharing within the Community and is working hard at it. Of course, the hon. Gentleman will want to recognise that the effect of protectionism in textiles—for that is what it is—is to increase the cost of clothing, which affects worst the poorest in society, and to inhibit the industrialisation of developing countries.

**Mr. Aitken:** If we are so opposed to protectionist trade barriers in Europe, can my hon. Friend kindly explain our humiliating acrobatics over the recent EC broadcasting directive? How did it come about that we supported the directive requiring all media companies in this country to take more than 50 per cent. of their programming from EC sources? Having supported that protectionist measure at 2 o'clock in the morning in the House, how did it come about, since we were arguing that it is more communitaire to support the EC party line, that when we got to Brussels the following day, we were out-voted by our communitaire partners and ended up with egg all over our faces?

**Mr. Maude:** I have to tell my hon. Friend that he has got it wrong. We were actually extremely successful in achieving a common position on the broadcasting directive which was very much more liberal than that which was proposed by many of our partners in the Community.

**Mr. Aitken:** Nonsense.

**Mr. Maude:** If my hon. Friend will contain his impatience for a little while, I will tell him that we have by no means lost the agreement. It is of great regret to us, having discussed it in good faith, that two countries in the Community, which pretend perhaps a greater adherence to European idealism than we do, went back on the agreement that they had already reached. But that does not mean that the broadcasting directive will be renegotiated. There is still a numerical majority for the common position that was reached, and I have no doubt that the qualified majority will be reasserted.

## New Businesses

9. **Mr. Amos:** To ask the Chancellor of the Duchy of Lancaster how many new businesses have been established in Northumberland in the past three years; and if he will make a statement.

**Mr. Atkins:** I am tempted to reply yet again, "lots". In the three years 1985 to 1987, the estimated number of new registrations for value added tax in Northumberland was 1,946. The net increase in the VAT-registered businesses in the period was 211—in fact, a 3 per cent. rise.

**Mr. Amos:** I am grateful to my hon. Friend for that excellent news. Does he agree that that is further proof of the Government's economic success in laying permanent foundations for the revival of the north-east, especially for small businesses and for self-employment? That success is now being broadcast far and wide throughout the region by all the media—Tyne-Tees Television, the *Evening Chronicle, The Journal* and the BBC. We are grateful to the Government for their policies.

**Mr. Atkins:** My hon. Friend is well known for his championing of the case which is represented in his constituency. He has summed up succinctly the success story that is Northumberland.

**Mr. Beith:** What practical support is the Minister prepared to give to ensure that European aid goes to businesses in areas of Northumberland to ensure that they benefit after 1992 from more direct communications and other investment projects that will help them to prosper?

**Mr. Atkins:** I paid a visit to the hon. Gentleman's constituency, and I saw just how much is required to be done as well as what is being done to benefit his part of the world. He will continue to put his case and we will seek to reflect his concern within European circles. I know that the hon. Gentleman will agree that the successes of Government policy are being shown even in his part of the world.

## Information Technology

10. **Mr. Ron Brown:** To ask the Chancellor of the Duchy of Lancaster how many of the 52 recommendations of the Select Committee on Trade and Industry report on information technology have been accepted by his Department.

**The Parliamentary Under-Secretary of State for Industry and Consumer Affairs (Mr. Eric Forth):** The Government have broadly accepted 28 of the 52 recommendations of the Trade and Industry Committee's report on IT.

**Mr. Brown:** Is not the Government's record a disgrace, bearing in mind that we still have a very high level of unemployment in this country, which is especially true of Leith where more than 20 per cent. of my constituents cannot get a real job? Can the Minister explain that?

**Mr. Forth:** I confess that the direct connection between employment in the hon. Gentleman's constituency and the Trade and Industry Committee's report on IT escapes me for the moment.

**Mr. Allason:** Is my hon. Friend aware of the growing anxiety about computer hacking in relation to information technology? Is he also aware that, in spite of pressure from various sources about the need for legislation on this subject, it is the view of the police that they are capable of dealing with computer fraud under existing legislation?

**Mr. Forth:** Yes. I am grateful to my hon. Friend. He is obviously aware that there has been a lot of discussion on the subject and much concern has been expressed. The Government, however, are taking a measured view of the problem. They are examining the evidence and they are assessing how far the existing provisions are adequate to meet the problem or how far new measures may be required. I am confident that a decision will be reached shortly, so that we can give the necessary assurances on this important matter. No one will be rushed into a decision. We want to get it right rather than arrive too soon at what may be the wrong decision.

**Mr. Stott:** When looking into the question of information technology, the Select Committee on Trade and Industry considered the deficit in electronic goods. I am sure that the Minister is aware that last year the trade deficit in electronics was £3·9 billion, which is an increase of 15 per cent. on the previous year, and accounts for almost one third of the total trade deficit. In the past four years alone, the deficit in electronic goods—which includes computers, telecommunications and audio equipment—has risen by a staggering 40 per cent. The Minister will be further aware that that pathetic record was remarked upon extensively by the Select Committee. The Government are now involved in negotiating a detailed sector plan with the brewing industry. Is it not time that they got around the table with the IT industry to work out how Britain can begin to remedy that £4 billion trade gap in one of our most important industries?

**Mr. Forth:** The hon. Gentleman exhibits the delight that the Opposition have in producing what they believe is bad news on every possible occasion. But what the hon. Gentleman has not told the House is that—it is important to understand this—every major OECD country, with the exception only of Japan, has an IT trade deficit. He has also not told the House that—this is another important figure—the United Kingdom has a trade surplus with the rest of the EC in IT products; something that the Opposition were trying to portray as an adverse picture not a few moments ago. Rather than fall into the trap that the hon. Gentleman is trying to set for the House in asking whether we shall take action to remedy one particular item that he regards as being bad news, we should acknowledge the excellent work that has been done in the IT industry, acknowledge a success story when we see one and not be driven off course by the sort of selective bad news offered up by the Opposition on these occasions.

## Export Growth

11. **Mr. Beith:** To ask the Chancellor of the Duchy of Lancaster whether he will make a statement on the rate of growth of British exports.

**Mr. Maude:** Since 1979, visible exports have increased in volume—that is in real terms—by 30 per cent., and invisible exports by about 40 per cent. I am sure that the hon. Gentleman will want to join us in congratulating all those businesses that have worked hard to achieve that major success story.

**Mr. Beith:** Is the Minister aware that the Budget prediction that trade will be in balance by 1992 depends upon an annual export growth of 7 per cent. and an import growth 4 per cent. lower than that? By how far are we currently failing to achieve that and has the prediction of the balance of trade by 1992 been revised?

**Mr. Maude:** I am sure that the hon. Gentleman will be reassured to be told that during the three months ending in April 1989, non-oil exports have risen by 7·5 per cent. compared with the equivalent three months a year ago, and that represents the sort of growth in exports about which the hon. Gentleman will be relieved and delighted to hear.

**Mr. Soames:** Does my hon. Friend agree that the Government's work in establishing and promoting the 1992 programme in Europe has been of great benefit to our exporting companies, but is he also aware of the considerable confusion that is caused to British industry by the rather garbled and confused message that appears to have emanated from the Government on European policy since then? Will my hon. Friend clarify to the House what steps the Government intend to take to stabilise the exchange control mechanism and when they will all be singing one song?

**Mr. Maude:** I am sure that if my hon. Friend has been listening carefully he will have heard not only one song but a very good song. We are fully engaged in the EC, we have led in many respects and we have achieved a great many successes. In continuing to improve our exports, nothing can substitute for the ability of firms to produce the goods and services that their customers want, but we have done a great deal in providing the sort of help that is needed to do that.

**Mr. Morgan:** Further to the question asked by the hon. Member for Crawley (Mr. Soames), which did not fully comply with the EEC brown nose directive, unlike the question from the hon. Member for Hexham (Mr. Amos), in what year does the Minister expect our trade to be in balance and to be able to make good the accumulated trade deficit of the past three or four years?

**Mr. Maude:** I see no reason to divert from the most recent forecast of my right hon. Friend the Chancellor of the Exchequer.

**Mr. Page:** While welcoming the increase in the volume of our exports, may I ask what effect a reduction in soft loans will have on their rate of growth, and do any of our foreign competitors intend either to increase or to decrease their support in that respect?

**Mr. Maude:** Clearly, changes in the amount and extent of soft loans available do have an effect. However, that matter is not one with which I deal directly, but no doubt my hon. Friend will receive at some stage a satisfactory reply from my hon. Friend the Minister for Trade. I make no apology for repeating that nothing can substitute for the ability of firms to compete in the market place.

**Mr. John Garrett:** What does the Minister have to say about the Confederation of British Industry survey published this week, which shows that our export prospects are the worst for two and half years? Is not that directly attributable to the Minister's right hon. Friend the one-club Chancellor, whose policies are crippling British exports?

**Mr. Maude:** The hon. Gentleman is wholly wrong. As I said in an earlier answer to one of his hon. Friends, the effect of interest rates on business is considerably less than the effect of unjustified increases in earnings. As to the competitiveness of exchange rates, the hon. Gentleman will recollect that Japan increased exports considerably even when the value of the yen doubled. I say again that it is the ability of businesses to win markets that matters, not what the Government do.

## Monopolies and Mergers Commission (Report)

13. **Mr. Adley:** To ask the Chancellor of the Duchy of Lancaster how many reports produced by the Monopolies and Mergers Commission in the last five years have been prompted by him; and how many have been initiated by the Monopolies and Mergers Commission itself.

**Mr. Maude:** The Monopolies and Mergers Commission has no power to initiate investigations. It can investigate and report only on matters referred to it by Ministers, the Director General of Fair Trading, Director General of Telecommunications, Director General of Gas Supply, or the Civil Aviation Authority. In the last five years some 78 reports by the commission have been published. Of those my right hon. and noble Friend and his predecessors were responsible for initiating 54.

**Mr. Adley:** Does my hon. Friend agree that there should be manifest evidence of widespread discontent before the Monopolies and Mergers Commission decides to investigate matters that are at the heart of our national life? Can my hon. Friend say whether his postbag or his constituency surgeries are bulging with letters or with discontented pub-goers, because mine are not? Is the commission short of work, or is Government policy perhaps dictated by liberal interventionism, as evidenced by my hon. Friend the Under-Secretary of State for Industry and Consumer Affairs?

**Mr. Maude:** As I told my hon. Friend in my original reply, the MMC does not initiate investigations. The inquiry to which my hon. Friend makes oblique reference was referred to it by the Director General of Fair Trading in the belief that certain matters required investigation. The report that the commission produced bears that out. As to the contents of my postbag, I can tell my hon. Friend that I received at least as many representations in favour of implementing the MMC's report as I did against. We are weighing those representations very carefully to arrive at the right answer. When a report containing trenchant findings, as that report did, is produced it is clearly not an option for the Government to do nothing.

**Mr. Holt:** Will my hon. Friend say out of the long list of people that he gave, which of them is the lunatic who referred the merger between William Hill and Mecca to the Monopolies and Mergers Commission? Whatever the outcome may be, the fact remains that William Hill, for which I had the pleasure of working for six years, no longer exists in its previous form. Its directors have either retired or resigned, and anything that the MMC does is now a complete waste of time and money.

**Mr. Maude:** No doubt my hon. Friend will make his observations, in whatever form he feels is appropriate, to the Monopolies and Mergers Commission, which is carrying out that investigation. The reference was made on the very firm advice of the Director General of Fair Trading.

## Information Technology White Paper

14. **Mr. Dunnachie:** To ask the Chancellor of the Duchy of Lancaster what responses his Department has received to the White Paper on information technology (Cm. 646).

**Mr. Forth:** I have received written comments on the White Paper from one firm, a United Kingdom computer manufacturer.

**Mr. Dunnachie:** The Government are now involved in negotiating a detailed sector plan with the breweries. Is it not time for the Government to get around a table with the information technology industry to try to find a way for Britain to reduce the £4 billion trade deficit in this vital industry? Why has the House not debated the White Paper on information technology, and when can we expect to see a trade surplus in IT?

**Mr. Forth:** I do not recall the hon. Gentleman being present for the debate that we had on information technology a couple of months ago. Perhaps he did not notice that there was to be a debate, or perhaps his interest was not as great then as it seems to be now.

The Opposition's record has stuck in a groove. The same phrases and the same prompts have been used twice in fairly quick succession, and, if I may, I shall give the same answer. Of all the major OECD countries, only Japan has a surplus in IT products. The proud record of the United Kingdom is a trade surplus in IT with the rest of the European Community. We shall not contemplate the old-fashioned and time-worn answer of sector plans: we threw that out years ago, and as a result our economy has boomed and become successful.

## Interest Rates

15. **Mr. McAllion:** To ask the Chancellor of the Duchy of Lancaster what is his estimate of the cost to industry of recent rises in interest rates.

**Mr. Newton:** Bank base rates have risen by one percentage point in 1989. The estimated cost to industrial and commercial companies of such an increase is about £0·4 billion in a full year.

**Mr. McAllion:** What is the point of the DTI running a £12 million publicity campaign to raise industry's awareness of 1992 when at the same time the Treasury's high interest rates policy is undermining any investment boom that the Minister thinks that he sees, and crippling the long-term capacity of British industry to compete? In recent months, as we have seen, the Chancellor has been prepared to sing a different song and to stand up even to the Prime Minister. When will the Minister stand up for British industry and take on the Chancellor in the interest rates battle?

**Mr. Newton:** The latest survey of manufacturing industry's investment intentions suggests a further rise of some 15 per cent. in the present year, following a rise of about 15 per cent. last year. That reflects the continuing financial strength of British companies. I have here, and would read out if I had time, a string of investment projects in the hon. Gentleman's own city which, as he must know well, have been announced in recent months or are already going ahead.

**Mr. Gow:** If interest rates were reduced as the Opposition recommend, would not domestic inflation increase and the value of sterling diminish, and would not that in itself add to inflation?

**Mr. Newton:** I see no reason to quarrel with my hon. Friend's analysis. He has made the point well that the real threat to the future of British industry would be a resurgence of inflation, taking it back to the levels run consistently by the last Labour Government.

**Mr. Campbell-Savours:** What factors does the Minister believe will lead to a reduction in inflation, and what is going on now that will result in such a reduction?

**Mr. Newton:** The damping down of the pressure of domestic demand, which is the objective of the Government's policies, has, I think, been acknowledged —for instance, in a number of recent surveys and speeches by the CBI—to be having an effect, not least in the much slower rise in factory-gate prices, which will feed through to the retail prices index in due course.

**Mr. Hind:** My right hon. Friend will no doubt agree that, given the 15 per cent. increase in investment in this country, it ill behoves the Opposition to give us lectures on advances and investment in industry when their own leader, when asked by Mr. Naughtie on BBC radio whether they had any answer to the problem of inflation, replied that he had no such answer. We recognise that interest rates present the only way of curbing inflation.

**Mr. Newton:** Yes, I agree with my hon. Friend.

**Mr. Gould:** In view of the continuing damage done to British industry by the Chancellor's attempt to buck the markets through high interest rates, what representations has the Secretary of State for Trade and Industry made to him on the subject?

**Mr. Newton:** The hon. Gentleman refers to "the continuing damage to British industry". I invite him to explain why we now have a dramatically greater investment boom, a dramatically greater improvement in productivity and a dramatically greater improvement in output than when the Administration that he supported left office. That is the strengthening of the British economy that has taken place.

### Single Market

16. **Mr. Robert G. Hughes:** To ask the Chancellor of the Duchy of Lancaster what monitoring he has undertaken of the level of awareness among business men of the single market achieved by his Department's "Europe—Open for Business" campaign.

**Mr. Maude:** The Department of Trade and Industry carries out a detailed survey of 100 different firms every week. The results show that 90 per cent. of business throughout the country is aware of the single market.

**Mr. Hughes:** Has my hon. Friend had time to look at the CBI survey which shows that three quarters of British companies have taken action on 1992? Surveys in France and Spain show that half the companies have taken action, a survey in Italy shows that a third of companies have taken action and another survey in West Germany shows that one seventh of companies have taken action. Does my hon. Friend take some comfort from the fact that the action that his Department is taking is having some success?

**Mr. Maude:** My hon. Friend is right to draw attention to the CBI survey. He is also right to say that it bodes very well indeed for the future, but that is not to say that British firms can become complacent and relax. The opening of the single market by the end of 1992 will, as I have said before, create much sharper competition. Every firm will have to intensify its activities and increase its cutting edge. However, my hon. Friend is right to draw attention to the extent to which British firms are doing better, and doing it faster, than other firms in the Community.

**Mr. Gould:** Does the hon. Gentleman accept that neither the British people nor British industry are fooled by glossy television advertising? *[Interruption.]* It may have escaped the attention—*[Interruption.]*

**Mr. Speaker:** Order. Interruptions take up a lot of time.

**Mr. Gould:** It may have escaped the attention of Government Members that we are not permitted to advertise during election campaigns in this country. Does the Minister accept, however, that glossy television advertising does not fool either the British people or British industry? They understand very well that the legacy of 10 Tory years has left British industry woefully ill prepared for the single European market. That is one of the major reasons for the Government's disastrous showing in last week's Euro-elections.

**Mr. Maude:** I can think of no better demonstration of the hon. Gentleman's first proposition than the result of the 1987 general election. As for the hon. Gentleman's second proposition, the fact is that British business is now in better shape. It is fitter; productivity is better; output is higher. In every way British business is better fitted than it has been for a generation to take advantage of the opportunities. The one thing that British business does not need is advice from the hon. Gentleman on how to conduct itself.

### Estate Agents

20. **Mr. Martlew:** To ask the Chancellor of the Duchy of Lancaster what progress is being made in the regulation of estate agents.

**Mr. Forth:** After an extensive review of estate agency issues, I have concluded that the best way to achieve a significant improvement in the practices of estate agency is through a combination of self-regulation and statutory provision. I have asked the Director General of Fair Trading to discuss with the industry the introduction of a code of practice for estate agency. He has agreed to report early next year.

We will need to support this code by acting against a number of undesirable practices, including tie-in sales where the agent refuses to pass on bids unless the purchaser agrees to arrange finance or insurance through him. I intend to do this by introducing an order under section 3 of the Act which would define certain practices as "undesirable." I have also asked the director general to review the arguments for extending the Trade Descriptions Act 1968 to misdescriptions of property.

Copies of my report have been placed in the Library and the Vote Office.

**Mr. Martlew:** Does the Minister agree that the people of this country have been ripped off too often by estate agents and that it is time that there were statutory, not voluntary, regulations to curtail the cowboys among estate agents?

**Mr. Forth:** I assure the House that this was not a planted question. I hope that the hon. Gentleman will consider carefully the answer that I have given rather than make a pre-prepared response. I am sure that he will find in my proposals and in the report that I have placed in the Library and Vote Office that I am dealing firmly but fairly with estate agency problems.

**Mr. Latham:** Can my hon. Friend confirm that any legislation that he introduces will contain a provision that

recognises that organisations such as the Royal Institution of Chartered Surveyors are governed by proper professional standards?

**Mr. Forth:** Yes, I am pleased to acknowledge the role that the RICS and many other bodies have played in bringing forward their own positive suggestions to make the property transfer market work as efficiently as possible. Let me make it clear to my hon. Friend that we are not contemplating new legislation. I am using the provisions of the Estate Agents Act 1979 in what I regard as appropriate ways.

**Ms. Quin:** Has the Minister found time to respond to some of the criticisms levelled at the voluntary, self-regulatory approach by some of his hon. Friends, including the hon. Member for Walthamstow (Mr. Summerson) who said that the rules of conduct should be enshrined in law and backed up by full powers of the law? Furthermore, will the Minister's proposals for regulating estate agents deal with the worst abuse at present—estate agents preferring purchasers who are also getting financial services from those estate agents?

**Mr. Forth:** I can confirm that that is precisely one of the matters that will be covered by my invocation of the statutory powers under section 3 of the Estate Agents Act. I am sure that when the hon. Lady and my hon. Friend the Member for Walthamstow (Mr. Summerson) study my proposals in detail, they will find that they are to their entire satisfaction.

# Madrid Summit

3.30 pm

**Mr. Nigel Spearing** (Newham, South): I beg to ask leave to move the Adjournment of the House, under Standing Order No. 20, for the purpose of discussing a specific and important matter that should have urgent consideration, namely,

"the Heads of Government meeting in Madrid, with particular reference to monetary and social policy of the European Community in the light of the fourth report of the Select Committee on the Treasury and Civil Service which was published yesterday."

I raised under Standing Order No. 20 the matter of the agenda of the Heads of Government meeting last Thursday and was also able to set out, on the third Adjournment debate on that day, the parliamentary and procedural reasons why there should be a debate. Since then I have received no communication from the Government concerning a change of business this week which would have permitted a debate, nor have I received any adverse comment on the case that I made.

It is generally agreed that debates on EEC matters recommended by the Select Committee should be held as early as practicable and when the debates in the House can influence Ministers. That principle has been endorsed recently by the Leader of the House in a letter to the Select Committee.

The Committee made a recommendation for debate in respect of the Delors report on economic and monetary union as long ago as 10 May. We reported that

"this debate should be held in good time before the European Council on 26-27 June, when the report is expected to be discussed by the Heads of Government."

Yesterday the Treasury and Civil Service Committee published its report on the Delors proposals, having heard evidence from the Chancellor of the Exchequer and the Governor of the Bank of England. The final paragraph 40 reads:

"We greatly regret that the Government has not accepted the recommendation of the European Legislation Committee that there should be a debate on the Delors Committee's Report before the European Council meeting at Madrid on 26 and 27 June. If the Government attaches significance to arguments about the sovereignty of Parliament it ought not to be selective in its attachment to them. The House must have an early opportunity to debate the far-reaching proposals of the Delors Committee before Her Majesty's Government adopts a position on them at high-level European meetings."

The only way in which the recommendations of those two Select Committees can be followed and a debate can be held is by making to you, Mr Speaker, this submission under Standing Order No. 20.

**Mr. Speaker:** The hon. Member for Newham, South (Mr. Spearing) seeks leave to move the Adjournment of the House under Standing Order No. 20 for the purpose of discussing a specific and important matter that he thinks should have urgent consideration, namely,

"the Heads of Government meeting in Madrid, with particular reference to monetary and social policy of the European Community in the light of the fourth report of the Select Committee on the Treasury and Civil Service which was published yesterday."

As the House knows, under Standing Order No. 20 I have to decide whether this application meets the criteria of the Standing Order and to announce my decision without giving reasons to the House. I have listened with care to what the hon. Member has said but I regret that the matter that he has raised does not meet the criteria of the Standing Order. I cannot therefore submit his application to the House.

# Points of Order

3.35 pm

**Mr. Robin Cook** (Livingston): On a point of order, Mr. Speaker. On 5 May the Secretary of State for Health reported to the House that he had reached agreement with the BMA negotiators over the GPs' contract. He said at the time that that was a sign of agreement by the doctors to his proposals for the Health Service.

This morning, the BMA, meeting in full session, rejected the proposed changes to the GPs' contract. In the light of the earlier statement to the House that the Secretary of State had obtained the BMA's agreement, has there been any application made to you, Mr. Speaker, for a statement now that the contract has been rejected by the BMA?

This must be a matter of particular concern to the House, as it is evident to anyone watching the broadcast media that correspondents are being briefed that it is the intention of the Secretary of State for Health to impose the GPs' contract. Would it not be a courtesy for the House to hear first whether the Government intend to embark on such a confrontation with the Health Service?

**Mr. Speaker:** I have had no application for a statement from the Government.

**Mr. Max Madden** (Bradford, West): On a point of order, Mr. Speaker. You will have been told that at the beginning of last night's debate on the DNA testing scheme and changes in immigration rules I and other hon. Members raised a number of points of order about leaked documents from the head of the immigration and nationality department at the Home Office and about a letter from the Home Secretary to the Leader of the House saying that last night's debate was deliberately arranged by the Government so as to avoid, in the words of the leaked document,

"two separate rows about immigration issues in quick succession".

The leaked documents also made it clear that, contrary to last Wednesday's statement by the Home Secretary that no decisions had been reached on the funding of the centrally organised DNA testing scheme, the Government had decided to increase entry clearance fees on 1 November.

Lastly, and most importantly, it was made clear in the leaked document and the letter that last night's debate was arranged by the Government deliberately to divert attention—in the document's words—from the absence of any new provisions or promises being made by the Government for and to the people of Hong Kong.

Leaked documents are becoming more and more common, but this latest one is serious because it is clear that the Government intend to deny the House any opportunity of debating in principle or in detail whether charges for DNA testing should be introduced and by how much they should be increased——

**Mr. Speaker:** Order. The hon. Gentleman has an Adjournment debate on this matter this evening. What is the point of order for me?

**Mr. Madden:** The point of order is that the documents make it abundantly clear that, rather than announcing a centrally organised DNA testing scheme in a written reply, last Wednesday the Home Secretary——

**Mr. Speaker:** Order. The hon. Gentleman should pursue this matter in his Adjournment debate. I was not present when the points of order were raised yesterday, but I have heard about them. I remind the hon. Gentleman that the debate yesterday arose in the name of the Leader of the Opposition. It was not a Government motion.

**Mr. Madden** *rose*——

**Mr. Speaker:** Order. There is nothing more I can say on this. The hon. Gentleman must pursue the matter in his Adjournment debate tonight.

## BILL PRESENTED

### REPRESENTATION OF THE PEOPLE

Mr. Secretary Hurd, supported by Secretary Sir Geoffrey Howe, Mr. Secretary Walker, Mr. Secretary King, Mr. Secretary Rifkind, Mr. John Wakeham, Mr. Tony Newton and Mr. Douglas Hogg, presented a Bill to amend the law relating to the entitlement of British citizens resident outside the United Kingdom to vote at parliamentary elections and elections to the European Parliament and to increase the maximum amount of candidates' election expenses at parliamentary by-elections: And the same was read the First time; and ordered to be read a Second time tomorrow and to be printed. [Bill 162.]

## WELSH AFFAIRS

*Ordered,*

That the matter of the first year of the Valleys Programme, being a matter relating exclusively to Wales, be referred to the Welsh Grand Committee for its consideration.—*[Mr. Dorrell.]*

# Greyhound Betting Levy

3.40 pm

**Mr. Alan Meale** (Mansfield): I beg to move,

That leave be given to bring in a Bill to extend the functions of the Horserace Betting Levy Board to include the sport of greyhound racing; and to make consequential amendments to the Betting, Gaming and Lotteries Act 1963.

My Bill is designed to end the ridiculously unfair anomaly that currently exists in Britain between the two premier betting sports of horse racing and greyhound racing. Both sports produce billions of pounds in turnover annually, yet they are treated totally differently by the bookmaking industry, particularly in respect of the mechanism which exists under statute to enable moneys to be collected by the industry, which I shall henceforth refer to as a levy.

The bookmaking industry pays over collected amounts produced from bets placed on horse racing, but it refuses to pass on equivalent moneys deducted from punters' winnings in betting shops on greyhound racing.

My Bill seeks to amend the Betting, Gaming and Lotteries Act 1963 and the Horserace Betting Levy Act 1981 to make provision for a levy scheme for greyhound racing similar to that enjoyed for a number of years by horse racing. The measure would be totally self-financing, as off-course bookmakers would pay contributions out of the bets that they take on greyhound racing to the Horserace Betting Levy Board, which would distribute the proceeds to the sport. As a result, membership of the levy board would be increased to include two representatives from the greyhound industry.

The need for such a measure is clear when it is borne in mind that, while betting offices off-course deduct the same amount from winning bets on horse and dog racing, greyhound racing does not receive its share of the revenue from those deductions. Considering that in any one year a turnover of at least £1 billion is involved in off-course greyhound racing bets, the need for such a Bill is obvious.

In practice, the bookmaking industry quietly deducts the extra 2p in the pound on winning bets, not explaining that, unlike horse racing, they keep the money on greyhound bets, a practice with which they have got away for many years. There is no rational argument for continuing with the present system, which is unfair and which borders on deceit of customers by the bookmaking fraternity.

The need for my Bill is clear in view of the level of support for the sport of greyhound racing. According to the 1989 edition of "Social Trends", greyhound racing as a spectator sport came second highest in attendance levels, being surpassed only by football. That survey showed that, in 1987, 4·8 million people attended greyhound racing events in the United Kingdom, compared with 1·38 million who attended rugby league events; 2·5 million for rugby union; 713,000 for test and county cricket; and, more important, only 4·3 million for horse racing.

The need for such legislation is clear. Greyhound racing is popular but is greatly under-financed. That has led to the loss of 13 nationally registered stadiums in the last 10 years. But while those who have made millions of pounds out of the sport—I refer, of course, to the bookmakers—get richer, the sport gets poorer. Standards of stadiums, their facilities for spectators and for racing greyhounds are getting worse.

The owners of greyhounds pay for the maintenance, training and racing of their dogs. Unlike in horse racing, their prize money does not run into thousands of pounds. It is, on average, between £14 and £26, but only if their dog comes first in the race. If they race during the day, the rate of off-course betting on those races can amount to hundreds of thousands of pounds.

At the heart of the problem is the fact that the greyhound racing industry is unable to get a fair price for its services from off-course bookmakers. Because bookmakers can exploit greyhound punters in that way, it makes sense for them to maximise their greyhound racing betting, thereby putting more pressure on the sport. Proof of that can be seen from the fact that between 1977 and 1988 the amount of off-course betting turnover on greyhound racing increased from 17·6 to 26·7 per cent., while betting on horses went down from 82 to 72 per cent. of the total.

The bookmakers argue that they do not pay the levy because most greyhound business is conducted at afternoon meetings. But that does not stop them taking bets from punters in their shops at evening racing. Nor does it stop them continuing to deduct 10p in the pound, rather than 8p, as they should be doing if they did not intend to pass on the money to the sport.

Nor do they argue with the claim that all racing is subject to National Greyhound Racing Club rules relating to stewardship, licensing, discipline and registration. That organisation continually calls for a levy for the sport of greyhound racing. In other words, they are willing to take the service but are unwilling to pay even the dues deducted for the sport.

The purpose of my Bill is to give justice to the sport of greyhound racing. The levy for the sport would not come from the bookmakers, who would merely pass it on, having taken it from the punters. That would be far preferable to allowing them simply to pocket it, as they are doing now. The money generated at current rates would mean at least £10 million per year to the sport and would enable stadiums to obtain loans to better the facilities for spectators, increase prize money in races to acceptable levels, fund necessary veterinary work, and improve security and the sport in general.

The greyhound racing industry, which is supported by millions of people, badly needs such help. Unlike the horse racing industry, it has no Jockey Club to invest, no Racecourse Association, advisory council, equine research centre, Racecourse Security Services or levy board to help it. A levy for greyhound racing would provide the necessary finance to improve the sport and protect the public who support it. The House has already agreed that horse racing needs such a levy. Surely, since it has more supporters than does horse racing, greyhound racing deserves the same treatment as horse racing.

The bookmakers argue that the sport

"has no logical right to a levy and is not entitled to be subsidised by bookmakers."

The aim of this measure is to expose such statements for the nonsense that they are. The purpose of the Bill is to enshrine in law the sport of greyhound racing's undoubted moral right to a levy.

Unless we approve this motion today, we shall allow the punters, spectators, owners and trainers of greyhounds to be further deceived, as they have been so cruelly and unjustly in the past.

*Question put and agreed to.*

Bill ordered to be brought in by Mr. Alan Meale, Mr. Don Dixon, Mr. Menzies Campbell, Mr. Tim Smith, Mr. A. E. P. Duffy, Mr. Richard Alexander, Mr. Frank Cook, Mr. Harry Greenway, Mr. William McKelvey, Mrs. Llin Golding, Mr. Martin Redmond, and Mr. George J. Buckley.

### GREYHOUND BETTING LEVY

Mr. Alan Meale accordingly presented a Bill to extend the functions of the Horserace Betting Levy Board to include the sport of greyhound racing; and to make consequential amendments to the Betting, Gaming and Lotteries Act 1963: And the same was read the First time; and ordered to be read a Second time on Friday 7 July and to be printed. [Bill 163.]

# Opposition Day

## [14TH ALLOTTED DAY, 1ST PART]

## Food Safety, Research and Health

**Mr. Speaker:** I have selected the amendment in the name of the Prime Minister. Fourteen hon. Members have so far expressed an interest in speaking in this debate. If their speeches are brief, most of them, I hope all, will be called.

3.48 pm

**Dr. David Clark** (South Shields): I beg to move,

That this House, noting Her Majesty's Government's failure to address the growing problem of food safety, deplores the decision to close the Institute of Food Research at Langford near Bristol with the corresponding loss of scientific expertise; believes that this will further reduce Her Majesty's Government's ability to protect the health of the British people; regrets that, two years after the Department of Health issued a consultative document on the control of food hygiene, regulations have still not been laid before Parliament; expresses concern at the Ministry of Agriculture, Fisheries and Food's decision to reduce veterinarians in their employ by one quarter and at the national shortage of Environmental Health Officers which leaves many posts unfilled; and calls upon Her Majesty's Government to introduce more effective safety and hygiene regulations, to increase the monitoring of food production and safety and to reverse its short sighted policy of cutting research and development work.

This is a timely debate which, in a sense, is proven by the number of hon. Members who wish to participate in it. It is also timely because, after 10 years of Conservative administration, we have a food poisoning outbreak of epidemic proportions. Only last week, we had the worst outbreak for years of botulism, which is a particular nasty and deadly toxin. Last Wednesday, the Government gave what can only be described as a bizarre response to this immensely serious problem. Their response was to close the Institute of Food Research at Bristol, which ranks among the premier meat research institutes in the world.

**Mr. Robert Key** (Salisbury) *rose*——

**Dr. David Clark:** With respect, Mr. Speaker has asked us to be fairly brief, but I will give way on this point.

**Mr. Key:** I am grateful to the hon. Gentleman, but surely he knows that that particular infection and toxin was not identified at Bristol, but at the public health laboratory service—the centre for applied microbiology and research at Porton Down—which has nothing to do with the closure of which he spoke.

**Dr. Clark:** I will treat the hon. Gentleman's intervention with the disdain that it deserves and ignore it as being absolutely irrelevant. The hon. Gentleman ought to think before he gets to his feet. No one suggested that botulism research was being done at Bristol—those were the hon. Gentleman's words—but I will return to that point in due course.

The act of closing the Bristol institute is typical of Government's response, which is illogical, short-sighted and plain stupid. We should not be surprised that we have these food poisoning epidemics. After all, we have a Government headed by a Prime Minister whose driving philosophy is the enterprise culture and the profit motive.

[*Dr. Clark*]

She has weakened food regulations and opposed modification of them, reduced the number of staff involved in safety monitoring and slashed research into food hygiene and quality. The ethos of her Administration can be summarised in the title of the White Paper that she produced, "Lifting the Burdens". She responded positively to that theme in her speech in Nottingham during the European election campaign.

The folly of that approach can be seen most clearly in connection with food. Experience worldwide has taught us that regulation and controls are vital if food safety standards are to be maintained. As recent elections have shown, the British people have not been fooled by the Tory policy. They recognise that that approach is a recipe for an epidemic of food poisoning and a lowering of standards. That is exactly what we have in Britain in 1989.

**Mr. Tim Boswell** (Daventry): Will the hon. Gentleman give way?

**Dr. Clark:** I have already given way once, after only 30 seconds, and that intervention wasted my time and that of the House.

I know that Conservative Members object to my comments, but the facts speak for themselves. In February of this year, the National Consumer Council commissioned a poll on consumer perception of food safety. The results show that 40 per cent. of those questioned were not confident that they had sufficient information to ensure that the food that they bought was safe. Consumers have every justification for being suspicious. Basic food hygiene regulations have not kept pace with changes in food technology. Most of them were made in the days before microwave ovens, cook-chill and convenience food. The facilities for storing food in retail outlets just cannot cope.

There are horrific stories. In one food manufacturing unit in Birmingham, the owner kept an air rifle to shoot the rats running about the establishment. That is true. Practically the whole of the Royal Air Force strike command in north-east Scotland was laid low after eating oysters. It transpired that these had been supplied not from the Soviet Union but from Japan, and were labelled in Japanese, so no one preparing the oysters could read the instructions. That emphasises the need for more sensible labelling.

Those are interesting, if not amusing anecdotes, but there is a serious aspect to the problem. In 1980, a mere —I use the word advisedly—10,318 cases of food poisoning were notified, while last year that had nearly trebled to over 28,000 cases.

**Dame Elaine Kellett-Bowman** (Lancaster): Will the hon. Gentleman give way?

**Dr. Clark:** I know that the hon. Lady participates in these debates, usually with a great deal of intelligence, but I wish to press ahead because I am conscious of the time.

Already this year, there have been 12,396 cases of food poisoning, while in the same period last year there were 7,930. I know that Tory Members deride statistics, but they are serious and, on occasion, represent deaths.

**Dame Elaine Kellett-Bowman:** I am grateful to the hon. Gentleman for giving way. Many of my constituents are keen on green-top milk, which is unpasteurised and contains a helpful enzyme. They are extremely glad that my hon. Friend the Minister has given way and will allow us to retain green-top milk.

**Dr. Clark:** The hon. Lady has made an ingenious intervention. I am sure that her right hon. Friend the Minister will take on board those plaudits.

The House will recall that the Government's initial response to the salmonella crisis six months ago was to curtail research into salmonella at the Institute of Food Research in Bristol. The Governments folly on that occasion was astounding, but that is not the whole story. The Government were also caught unaware by botulism. They should not have been because the eminent microbiologist Professor Richard Lacey—[HON. MEMBERS: "Oh."] I should tell Conservative Members that Professor Lacey is an official adviser to the Government and to the Ministry of Agriculture, Fisheries and Food. He actually predicted in his book, "Safe Shopping, Safe Cooking and Safe Eating" that botulism

"could return unless the catering industry addresses the problem."

Professor Lacey was not being clairvoyant—he was reading the book, so to speak. Only last year, Europe's biggest botulism outbreak among cattle occurred in the United Kingdom. It was caused by a herd being fed a mixture containing chicken carcasses. Ironically, last year the Government ordered the Institute of Food Research to stop work on a project involving the feeding of chicken carcasses to cattle and the links with botulism. That is why there was no work at Bristol last week to detect the outbreaks of botulism. The Government actually stopped that work. They had learnt nothing—having stopped research into salmonella, they compounded their folly by doing the same with botulism.

What is the Government's response to the food crisis? Deep analysis reveals a twin approach. First, they believe that the interests of the public can be protected, in some perverse way, by cutting research and development and closing research establishments. Secondly, to compensate for the resulting huge gap in public health protection, the Government think that they have discovered a new panacea—irradiation. On both counts the Government are wrong.

—During recent years research projects into food safety and hygience have been axed one after another. Recently the Government decided on further closures and cuts following the so-called Barnes review. The effect of the review is to cut by £30 million the money spent on research and development in agriculture and food. The latest example of that was the closure of the institute at Bristol. That was absolutely incomprehensible. Not only will many excellent projects disappear, but more than 100 scientists will lose their jobs. With those jobs will go the experience and expertise—[HON. MEMBERS: "No".] If that is not true, I hope that the Minister will say so and give us more information. My information is that only six out of more than 100 jobs at Bristol will be relocated. The Minister should deny that if I am wrong.

In an attempt to cover up their folly, the Government have given the impression that jobs and projects will be transferred. That is a travesty of the truth. Only six jobs will be transferred and of the 80-plus projects, many involving food safety and hygiene, not more than a handful will be transferred. If I am wrong, I challenge the Minister to say which projects will be transferred. I am sure that there will not be more than a handful.

We shall lose vital work on meat hygiene. Neither the abattoir at the Bristol institute, which allows practical experiments, nor the highly praised food processing hall are being transferred. Work on refrigeration, which is vital to food hygiene and safety is being terminated. Not only expertise, but facilities which exist nowhere else in the United Kingdom are being lost.

In the long run, the main loser from the Government's obsession with cost-cutting will be the consumer. The closure has been forced by the Government's obsession. On 22 May 1989, the Minister announced, with great pleasure, that he had managed to save £379 million in agricultural spending last year.

**The Minister of Agriculture, Fisheries and Food (Mr. John MacGregor):** In the CAP.

**Dr. Clark:** When one compares that figure with the £111 million expected expenditure on research and development for this financial year, it places Government priorities in perspective. To put it another way, the Minister's annual savings last year would have kept the Bristol institute open for 100 years. That puts the Government's policies in perspective.

The Minister has completely misjudged the position on food irradiation. Does he know that one of the foremost members of his advisory committee on irradiated and novel foods, which produced the report on irradiation in 1986 on which he places so much store, has now changed his mind about the process and has said that it is "unnecessary" and doomed to commercial failure. To quote from a recent interview with Professor Philip James, in *The Press and Journal* Aberdeen:

"The real dilemma now is that people no longer have confidence that a Ministry of Agriculture linked to the producer and processor is going to safeguard the public interest. The public have been overwhelmed by the knowledge that certain companies have been using irradiation to salvage rotten food . . . It is a sad reflection of how the Government and some food manufacturers don't appear to understand how to manage affairs of public interest in the fields of health and safety."

That is a damning indictment of the Ministry by one of its top advisers.

Professor Philip James is not the only person to express concern. Various organisations, including the National Farmers Union, which is dear to the Minister's heart, and the British Medical Association, which is not so dear to the Government's heart, and prominent food retailing companies such as the Co-op, Tesco and Marks and Spencer have also expressed concern about irradiation. People not only now demand to know whether their food is to be irradiated, but why it needs to be irradiated. That is the key question that the Government should answer.

The Labour party does not believe that irradiation is the answer to our food poisoning problems. It is no alternative to ensuring that cleaner food is on sale in the shops. Irradiation would be no incentive to ensure that high hygiene standards are maintained throughout the food chain. Irradiation will leave food more open to subsequent bacteriological contamination. There is no easy and effective method of detecting whether food has been irradiated or, even more importantly, reirradiated.

To return to the recent problem of botulism, perhaps the Minister will confirm that irradiation would have had no effect on wiping out that botulism as it is a toxin.

Another point about irradiation, which has been expressed clearly by Professor James, is that it could be used to make bad food clean. The Minister will be aware, for example, that there have been verified reports of seafood being imported into Britain, mainly from the far east, which has subsequently been found to be substandard. That food has then been exported to Holland, irradiated by Gammaster and then re-imported into Britain and sold illegally—the same food that had been found to be substandard. The incident occurred three years ago, but we have good reason to believe that the trade continues. I have in my possession a letter from Gammaster dated 10 May 1989, agreeing to supply irradiated seafood to Britain. The letter states:

"Our quality assurance include taking samples of each shipment of prawns before irradiation. The Dutch Food Inspectors also take samples before and after irradiation. I would like to emphasize that the irradiation of food products is not yet allowed in the United Kingdom".

However, the letter also suggests the name of the Dutch transport company which would arrange delivery of that food. A telex from the transport company—Allways Transport BV—the following day states:

"in order to enable Gammaster to irradiate this consignment, it is necessary to arrange import of the goods temporarily (without paying duties or VAT of course). Before we can arrange this customs clearance we will have to present a 'health certificate' in acordance with the EEC 'shrimp decree'."

Several of my hon. Friends have tabled an early-day motion on this serious matter. As it is clear from the correspondence that the trade is well organised, I hope that the Minister will pursue the case. Unfortunately, when we passed similar correspondence to his predecessor three years ago, the Government refused to act. I hope that on this occasion the Minister will respond positively.

I know that the Minister is alert to the problem because the research consultative committee residues sub-group of the Ministry of Agriculture revealed in its minutes last year that it was aware of the

"potential for some commodities to arrive in the UK which already have been subjected to irradiation."

I stress that that point was made by one of the Minister's own sub-committees last year.

It is because of such uncertainties that the Labour party opposes the introduction of food irradiation in Britain. It is like using gloss paint to cover rotten window frames.

To sum up, the Government's approach to protecting the nation's health from contaminated food has been abysmal. As we have seen in the past few months, they have adopted a crisis management approach. Indeed, it is hard to understand their actions in recent months. When confronted with a food poisoning epidemic what do they do? They cut the number of staff who monitor and control diseases; they close a food research institute; they introduce food irradiation, which nobody wants; and as a final insult, they produce a leaflet putting the blame for food poisoning where it certainly does not belong—on the consumer. I hope that the House will join us in condemning the Government.

4.7 pm

**The Minister of Agriculture, Fisheries and Food (Mr. John MacGregor):** I beg to move, to leave out from "House" to the end of the Question and add instead thereof:

'commends the Government for implementing a comprehensive range of measures to maintain safety throughout the food chain and to improve the scientific knowledge on which these are based; notes with approval the Agricultural and Food Research Council's decision to strengthen the work of its Institute of Food Research at the Norwich and Reading sites by expanding programmes on food safety and nutrition; endorses the Government's policy of transferring responsibility for near market research and development to industry, enabling more Government funds to be channelled into strategic research; congratulates the Government on the substantial increase in resources for research into food safety during the past ten years; and expresses confidence in the Government's policies on food safety and research and development.'.

The speech of the hon. Member for South Shields (Dr. Clark) was fragmentary in the extreme and extremely fragile in its evidence. I shall demonstrate both those points.

As this is a general debate on food safety, I shall begin by setting out in framework the main elements of the Government's food safety policy. That is necessary because of the hon. Gentleman's spasmodic speech. Indeed, the main elements of our policy are consistent and thorough and are worth restating. I shall do that briefly because the Parliamentary Secretary, my hon. Friend the Member for Mid-Norfolk (Mr. Ryder), dealt with this at length in his speech in the food safety debate earlier this year, on 21 February, and because I have done so on many previous occasions. Furthermore, you, Mr. Speaker, have reminded us that this is a short debate.

The essential elements are, first, a careful and thorough monitoring of the food supply so as to be certain that whatever we do is based on a factual assessment of the situation as a whole; secondly, thorough surveillance to detect any trends that need analysis or policy action of one sort or another; and, thirdly, continuous and in-depth assessment of the facts that emerge using the best possible scientific advice.

In view of the highly selective scientific examples given by the hon. Member for South Shields, I stress that we use the best possible scientific advice over a wide range, using many people.

**Mr. Brian Wilson** (Cunninghame, North) *rose——*

**Mr. MacGregor:** This is a short debate; I will give way once.

**Mr. Wilson:** Does the Minister agree that if he wants the best and most independent scientific advice, by definition any scientists who are also paid by the food industry should not be employed by the Government to give advice?

**Mr. MacGregor:** I shall be able to demonstrate shortly that we use a much wider range of scientific expertise, so that is a feeble attack.

The fourth essential element is decisive action, which could be legislative or advisory on the basis of the expert advice that we have received, and sometimes further research is called for. The fifth essential element is the provision of full information and guidance to the public. Indeed, we publish so much that often the problem is to get even a small proportion of it over. My hon. Friend the Parliamentary Secretary illustrated that graphically in the last debate. The sixth essential element is proper monitoring and enforcement to ensure that legislative obligations are carried out by all in the food chain.

I have available to me substantial resources to carry out these tasks. In my Department I have more than 500 staff engaged in work on policies that relate to consumer protection. Many of them are highly qualified specialists in one branch of science or another. They provide the sound scientific basis to our assessment, enforcement and research activities.

As the House by now will know—this is the answer to the hon. Member for Cunninghame, North (Mr. Wilson) —we are assisted by a wide range of expert committees covering pretty well every area of food matters—to which we have just added the Richmond committee on the microbiological safety of food—to advise us on the many technological developments that are now such an important feature of modern food production. Together we have available some hundreds of independent scientists and experts drawn from the universities, medical schools, research bodies, industry, consumer backgrounds and so on—all leading experts in their particular fields and chosen for their experience and the breadth of knowledge they can bring to bear. They assist us in the assessment of risks of all kinds that are faced by any modern food producing industry, and my colleagues and I rely heavily on their advice. The Opposition keep mentioning one or two scientists. I have been emphasising that we have hundreds of scientists available to us. All aspects of the subject are considered, expertly and in considerable depth, and I stress again the scientists' independence.

The reports that are produced are published. In the case of the steering group on food surveillance there have been no fewer than 25 reports in recent years, covering a wide range of subjects. Each of them is an authoritative scientific document on the subject under consideration. I repeat that the reports are published. But we do not just listen. We act, and we act promptly. In the last six months or so we have announced decisions on salmonella, bovine spongiform encephalopathy, mineral hydrocarbons and aldrin, and given advice on a number of other subjects. Often the action goes comparatively unnoticed in the media, but it is taken notice of by the industry and the consumer is therefore protected.

**Mr. Conal Gregory** (York) *rose——*

**Mr. MacGregor:** This will have to be the last time that I give way.

**Mr. Gregory:** In acknowledging, as the Opposition did not, that some £20 million was spent last year in support of food safety, I think that any hon. Member would accept that there is independent advice which the Department uses skilfully, but that it is implemented at the sharp end by environmental health officers. Will my hon. Friend confirm that he will issue central guidelines to the environmental health officers? Otherwise they will go off at different tangents and will interpret the expert advice in different ways which could be misleading to the public. I know that that is not my right hon. Friend's intention.

**Mr. MacGregor:** We try to give advice and guidance wherever we can. If my hon. Friend has particular points in mind, perhaps he will write to me about them and I shall consider them.

One interesting example of the action that we take relates to certain chemical substances in cling film. Following analysis, our scientists in the Ministry advised that there was a small risk of some leaching to the food contained therein. In immediate consultation with the industries the substances were changed and even any potential slightest risk to the consumer was removed. All this demonstrates that there is no complacency whatever, only constant vigilance.

With the rapid changes in consumer habits these days, including the trend to fast and convenience foods and one-stop weekly shopping on the one hand, and the rapid developments in food technology and processes on the other, there can never be any cause for complacency. I point that out to the hon. Member for South Shields. Most of the Governments of Western Europe, the United States Government and others are finding new salmonella problems with particular types—in the end we are talking about two types out of more than 2,000 strains—with listeria and with campylobacter at present.

As for botulism, with which the hon. Member for South Shields began his speech, if its continued existence is thought to be a sign of failure—the word in the Opposition motion—then it must be said that we in this country have achieved a measure of success that most other countries would be only too pleased to emulate.

The current outbreak, highly regrettable as it is, is nevertheless only the tenth in more than 65 years. The citizens of such countries as the United States, the Federal Republic of Germany, France and the Netherlands—often held up, and rightly, as examples, like ourselves, of countries with high safety records and standards—are many times more likely to suffer from botulism than we are here.

I heard what the hon. Member for South Shields said about Professor Lacey and his book. Professor Lacey did not predict a botulism outbreak. In fact, the evidence to date of the present botulism outbreak points to a canned hazelnut preparation. Professor Lacey stated that "the risk of food poisoning by canned food is tiny."

The action that we have taken on salmonella and BSE is typical of the serious and determined way in which we pursue our responsibilities.

As the House knows, the Government have adopted to date a comprehensive package of 19 measures to tackle this new salmonella problem in order to minimise the potential risk to public health.

**Dr. David Clark:** Seventeen measures.

**Mr. MacGregor:** It was 17, but we are constantly doing what we believe is right to add to them. I am sorry that the hon. Member for South Shields cannot keep up with our pace on this matter.

One of the 19 measures is the food safety guidance leaflet. I was extremely sorry to hear the hon. Member for South Shields, who is normally very responsible in these matters, say that that was shifting the blame—or words to that effect—on to the consumer. He knows that research has shown that, because of the modern developments to which I have referred—such as weekly one-stop shopping —and the new food technologies, much of the risk of food poisoning can take place after the manufacturing process. Therefore, any responsible Government should give advice to consumers as to how, at their end of the food chain, they can protect themselves from food poisoning. I cannot imagine why the hon. Gentleman denigrates our

action of supplying the food safety leaflet. That is a sign of gross irresponsibility. I believe that he has been proved wrong by the fact that it is a best seller, and we shall almost certainly have to reprint it shortly. It shows that we are meeting a positive and, I think, a desirable demand.

**Dr. David Clark:** I noticed that the Minister moved quickly away from the 17 salmonella measures. He knows that he announced 17, but in a written answer, dated 19 June, that I received from the Parliamentary Secretary I was told that two of the key issues still wait to be laid before the House. When will we get the document—three months later?

**Mr. MacGregor:** I have not moved off the subject yet, so I do not know what the hon. Gentleman is talking about. I am still dealing with the 19 measures. We have announced all the measures. We have nearly all of them in place and we are carrying all the others through with all due speed. As he knows, some of them require consultation and then parliamentary action. We have announced that we are taking 19 specific measures on the new salmonella problem.

**Mr. Paul Marland** (Gloucestershire, West): Is my right hon. Friend aware that the latest information from the public health laboratory shows that, despite a recent increase in the consumption of chicken and poultry generally, the incidence of salmonella has dropped considerably? Does that not show that the measures that have been introduced by my right hon. Friend and the industry have been a great success?

**Mr. MacGregor:** As my hon. Friend knows, like other countries, we were faced with a new problem. It is obviously encouraging if there is a change in the trend of cases. We must maintain our vigilance, and the measures remain important. I do not believe that the measures will fully bite for some time—not until they take full effect. I want to be clear about that.

We have taken those 19 measures at all possible stages in the chain from the animal feeding stuffs level, through breeding flocks and hatcheries, to laying flocks and on into the home.

All in all, we are making extremely good progress in introducing those important measures in Britain. No other country in the world has such an impressive range of measures to tackle this exceptionally complex problem.

On the totally new disease of BSE, the moment our veterinary scientists identified what the problem was I set up the Southwood committee; then stopped the feed protein source of the disease, again as soon as our scientists—they were ours—concluded that this was the most likely source; and acted immediately on all the interim and final recommendations of that committee.

Last week I announced that further measures would be taken. Those will ensure that brain and spinal cord, together with certain other bovine offals, cannot be used for human consumption in any way.

I can assure the House that if the scientific evidence and advice suggests that other actions are needed we shall take them. In resource terms the commitment to BSE alone is likely to be in excess of £6 million this year. That, too, is a demonstration of how speedily and responsibly we act.

The emergence of new diseases, like the rapid rate of technological change in the food chain, places increasing demands on the flexibility of the system. It was for that

[*Mr. MacGregor*]

reason among others that we felt that it was desirable to undertake a substantial review of the existing food legislation, which has generally served us well but which needs to be appropriate for all the demands of the 1990s, including developments on the European Community front. I suspect that the hon. Member for South Shields is with me on that.

That is why we have been undertaking a major consultation exercise with over 500 organisations, including many consumer groups, and, as a result, have concluded that the law should be adjusted in the light of changing circumstances. We shall be bringing forward new legislation as soon as the parliamentary timetable permits.

I would expect new legislation to include strengthened controls in the areas of food hygiene—notably powers to require food premises to register with their local authority and powers to require the training of those who handle food; the introduction of emergency control orders to improve our ability to act in food emergencies, although, as the hon. Gentleman knows, we have already taken some action in the Food and Environment Protection Act 1985, introduced by the Government, which enabled me to deal with the Chernobyl situation; and powers to control novel foods and processes as well as a whole range of other changes designed to make food law and its enforcement more effective today to meet any new challenges that may arise.

Just as new technical problems can arise from new processes, so technology can give us new weapons in our armoury to enhance food safety and consumer protection. Let me deal with one such new weapon which the hon. Gentleman has mentioned. I want to begin by stressing that it is only one of many weapons in our armoury; it is not the panacea that the hon. Gentleman claimed it would be. In doing so, I hope that I shall answer all his points on food irradiation.

The House is aware that last year on 4 February we announced that the Government accepted in principle that the ban on irradiated food should be lifted, provided that —this was an important proviso—the proper control framework could be established. Therefore, we set up a working party to consider all the issues related to that control system and to make recommendations, and the House knows that I recently received its report.

I am today publishing that report. Copies are being made available in the Vote Office and in the Library. Based on the recommendations in the report, the Government intend to make available to the consumer and to the food industry the option of that additional measure for protecting certain foods. As I shall elaborate in a moment, there will be a number of opportunities for the House to consider that further in full. But I think it would be helpful if today I outline some of the key points.

First, I want to stress that the Government are basing their decision fundamentally on food safety and consumer grounds—on food safety, that irradiation has a useful contribution to make—a contribution, not the total answer—to the reduction of food—borne disease in certain products, and in some cases better than by other means; and for consumers, provided that we have the proper control and information framework, that it would be wrong to deprive consumers of the freedom to choose

food treated by that safety method if they wish to avail themselves of it. It will not be thrust upon anyone. I repeat, it will not be thrust upon anyone.

**Mr. Eric Martlew** (Carlisle): Will the right hon. Gentleman give way on that point?

**Mr. MacGregor:** No. I have already given way a lot in this short debate.

I know that some have drawn attention to the ability of the process to extend the shelf life of some fruits by delaying their ripening processes. That, too, is a consumer benefit in that what the housewife buys will last longer in the home. But that is not why the Government are proposing to legalise this process, and I wish to underline that. It was considerations of food safety that were predominant in reaching our decision.

It may be helpful if I remind the House of the background to the subject. There is a mistaken impression that food irradiation is something new about which we ought to learn much more before permitting its use in this country, but that is far from being the case. The first patent on food irradiation was taken out as long ago as 1921, so it saw the light of day well before the birth of most current right hon. and hon. Members of this House, myself included. Considerable research on the process has been undertaken over more than 40 years, and scientists tell me that it has been subject to much closer scrutiny worldwide than any other food process.

The safety of the process was established long ago by distinguished authorities of unimpeachable international standing. Top level joint expert committees of the principal international agencies, including the World Health Organisation and the Food and Agriculture Organisation, carried out in-depth safety evaluations over a period of years in the 1970s and confirmed in a report in 1980 that food irradiation up to an overall average dose of 10 kilogray is safe and introduces no special nutritional or microbilogical problems. That report was adopted by the Codex Alimentarius Commission in 1983.

Similar conclusions were reached following full assessments by other national and international bodies. The process's safety, for example, was confirmed by the European Community's Scientific Committee for Food and by the United State's Food and Drugs Administration.

**Mr. David Curry** (Skipton and Ripon): Will my right hon. Friend allow me to intervene?

**Mr. MacGregor:** If my hon. Friend will forgive me, I should like to continue because I know that many other right hon. and hon. Members wish to speak.

Nevertheless, we adopted a thoroughly careful attitude and put in hand our own independent expert assessment. In 1982 we established the Advisory Committee on Irradiated and Novel Foods under the chairmanship of Sir Arnold Burgen, Master of Darwin college, Cambridge. The committee comprised distinguished specialists in all aspects of the subject. Its report, published in 1986, concluded that if correctly applied and up to the level of dose stipulated in the international research of 10 kilogray, irradiation is an effective and efficient form of food preservation treatment.

The committee was satisfied as to the safety and wholesomeness of the food that would result from irradiation and made it clear that for all practical purposes there would be no change in the low level of radioactivity that food naturally contains. In 1987 the committee was reconvened to consider scientific responses to its report and, having done so, reaffirmed its conclusions.

I set out that history to make absolutely clear one basic point—that the safety of food irradiation has been assessed repeatedly over the years by people both in this country and abroad whose highly specialised training and experience best qualifies them to assess all aspects of the technique. The process has been cleared through the most comprehensive set of evaluations.

**Mr. Wilson:** But who is asking for it?

**Mr. MacGregor:** I shall come to that point shortly.

No qualifications have been expressed, and no areas of safety remain outstanding. That is demonstrated by the number of countries that already allow use of the process. It is permitted in 35 countries around the world, and is already in operation in 21 of them. Those countries include the United States and four member states of the European Community. It may come as a surprise that we too permit irradiaton and have done so for the past 20 years or more. Throughout that time, irradiated food has been supplied to a limited number of cancer patients who, by reason of their disease or treatment, are at high risk of infection. We have recognised that those vulnerable members of our society, who require the most carefully controlled and safest diet that we can secure, have found it through irradiated food.

What are the advantages of irradiation for consumers generally? I shall deal shortly with the question of choice but first I must set the important scene of safety as a whole. The World Health Organisation is clear that by killing or greatly reducing the number of micro-organisms naturally present in food, irradiation has a useful contribution to make in reducing some—and I stress some—food-borne disease. Obviously, it cannot be used to treat all food products because in some cases it can affect taste and other qualities. Nevertheless, it is important in reducing some food-borne disease.

Irradiation has, for example, been shown to be effective in dealing with bacteria such as salmonella, listeria and campylobacter. It is not suitable for all foodstuffs, as I have already emphasised, but it has proved its value as a treatment for poultry meat. It is so used already in France and other countries, and the BMA's recent publication "Infection Control" mentions its particular effectiveness for the purpose. Some shellfish can also be successfully treated.

Second, for certain produce such as herbs and spices irradiation can be used to destroy insects, pests and bacterial contamination in place of the existing chemical fumigation methods, about some of which there are concerns on health grounds. For example, the chemical ethylene oxide, which is used for that purpose, is now banned in many countries of the European Community and will shortly no longer be available for use. Manufacturers and consumers need some means of being able to continue to make herbs and spices available without infestation.

All this is extending consumer choice, not damaging it. It is an effective way of dealing with some bacteria and bugs, but of course the essential pre-condition is a proper control mechanism. The Food Act gives the possibility of providing for the registration of irradiation facilities by local authorities. The Government have concluded, however, that it is preferable to have a full licensing system under central Government control, rather than through local authorities. Closer and more specialised supervision will be achieved through the concentration of the powers by central administration than if the responsibility is diffused. This will permit detailed inspection by specialists and the imposition of precise conditions with the granting of licences. It will mean delaying the introduction of food irradiation until we can obtain more extensive powers in the new food Bill, but we think it right to do so.

Conditional upon the licence will be the maintenance of clear and full records, which will be regularly inspected and will allow for the tracing of consignments treated and the verification, through the recording instrument readings, of the dose applied. A further provision will be a requirement that full documentation must accompany each consignment leaving the irradiated plant, so that recipients of irradiated food at any point in the distribution chain are aware of the treatment that has been given.

Apart from inspection of the documentation and of the measuring instruments—the dosimeters—the premises would also be subject to the normal local authority controls on food hygiene. It would be necessary for local authorities to satisfy themselves that good manufacturing practices were being followed and that, in particular, there was proper segregation of treated and untreated foodstuffs and the possibility of contamination after treatment was avoided.

For imported supplies it will be necessary for us to make arrangements to check that the control systems applied and the standards achieved by countries wishing to export to the United Kingdom are equivalent to the controls and standards to be applied in this country. If the European Community's proposal goes ahead, action will of course follow on a Community basis, but, whether Community or national arrangements need to be made, we are quite clear that proper reassurances must be obtained.

As important as the control framework is that consumers should be able to make an informed choice, so that those who do not want irradiated food can be assured that they are not buying it.

**Mr. Martlew:** Will the Minister give way?

**Mr. MacGregor:** I think that I must move on as I must also answer the debate.

**Mr. Martlew:** Will the Minister give way on that specific point?

**Mr. MacGregor:** There will be plenty of opportunities for the hon. Gentleman to speak. In any case, I am about to give the answer: making consumers aware whether they are buying irradiated food means labelling.

**Mr. Martlew:** Will the Minister give way on that point?

**Mr. MacGregor:** The hon. Gentleman can make his contribution during the debate, and there will be many other opportunities.

I assure the House that the Government will insist on a firm requirement for full and clear labelling of all irradiated food and listed ingredients. We want wording that will be clearly understood, and the options that we have in mind, are "irradiated" and "treated with ionising radiation".

[*Mr. MacGregor*]

I am sure that the House will want to debate this issue in full, and as we must seek new powers there will be plenty of opportunities to do so. There may also be a chance to debate it before the summer recess if time can be found to consider European Community document No. 10377/88 on this subject, which the European Community Scrutiny Committee has recommended for debate. There will thus be many occasions to respond to the concerns and to dispel the myths, but today I should like to deal with the two most common ones.

First, it is argued that the treatment should not be allowed in the absence of a detection test that can confirm its use. There are plenty of views to the contrary. The World Health Organisation did not consider that necessary; nor did Codex or the United States Food and Drug Administration. Moreover, our own advisory committee gave particular attention to the point. It concluded that, while a detection test could be a useful supplement to a control system based on licensing and documentation, such as we shall have, it was not necessary for the satisfactory operation of controls. Furthermore, none of the 21 countries already allowing irradiation and operating control systems around the world considered it necessary to wait for the availability of a diagnostic method. The crucial factor is the control system, but given that a diagnostic method could be a useful supplement we shall continue to fund the research work that we are doing on this.

Second, it is argued that irradiation can somehow be misused to make bad food good. I am advised that this is simply nonsense. Irradiation cannot improve appearance, it cannot disguise taste, it cannot mask unpleasant odours. If food is not of acceptable microbiological standard, then these factors will give it away. Food irradiation will not save it.

Moreover, we intend to provide for the examination of food prior to treatment, and we shall be providing that food that does not meet the normal acceptable standards of the industry shall not be irradiated. It will remain an offence to sell or offer for sale unfit food, whether irradiated or not.

Therefore, I commend the working party's report to the House and the Government's decisions upon it. I repeat that irradiation is not a panacea for food safety. I do not, and never will, suggest that it is. It is only one weapon in our large armoury. All the other measures I have talked about today and on other occasions continue to be important parts of the whole surveillance, regulatory and legislative framework that we have to ensure the highest standards of food safety. However, it does offer for certain products a further and successful way of enhancing safety. It can provide clear consumer benefits. In our view, it is now wrong to deprive the food producer and the consumer of the free choice to avail themselves of it, if they wish to do so, and it is on that basis that I am making this announcement today.

Let me underline that point once and for all. Consumers in Britain, under a Conservative Government, enjoy a right to safety, a right to be informed and a right to choose. Irradiated food is safe, irradiated food will be properly labelled and consumers will have the right to buy it and the right to refuse to buy it. Only an irresponsible Government, neglectful of consumer interests, would deny British consumers the same protection as is already afforded to consumers in over 20 other countries. All this demonstrates the responsible and carefully considered approach of the Government to food safety matters. I can hardly say the same about some of the allegations of the Opposition.

The other day the hon. Member for South Shields alleged on "The World this Weekend"—and he has said it again, in part, today—that they have documentary evidence—repeated examples, he said—of seafood coming into this country, being declared as unfit for human consumption and then being exported, irradiated and reimported back here. He said that these companies had actually been flouting the law and that

"the Government has known about it, has turned a blind eye and indeed appear to be encouraging these companies to break the law."

These are serious allegations. I shall therefore be quite fair with the hon. Member for South Shields—and, I hope, quite clear. I should be concerned about any allegations of companies flouting the law. I have therefore checked whether we knew about them. We did not. I have made clear publicly that I would be happy to look at any evidence that the hon. Gentleman can give us.

In the same programme the hon. Gentleman said that he would pass this information on to me. That was 11 days ago. So far I have not received anything from him, but I hope that I shall do so shortly. [*Interruption.*]

**Mr. Frank Cook** (Stockton, North) *rose*——

**Mr. MacGregor:** The hon. Gentleman said that there had been "repeated examples" of seafood coming into this country, and he said that they were recent repeated examples. The only allegations that I can find are in early-day motion 950, signed by a number of his hon. Friends, making allegations about named companies. Is that the evidence that the hon. Gentleman had in mind? I should be very interested to know whether that is the evidence.

**Dr. David Clark:** I did not pass it on to the Minister previously—[*Interruption.*] If hon. Members will be patient for a little longer I shall explain why. Three years ago we passed information to the Minister's predecessor—[*Interruption.*] Hon. Members must let me finish—including the certificates of irradiation from Gammaster. The Minister's predecessor refused to act upon that information. I have the information and I shall pass it on to the Minister. I made it quite clear today that I would pass it on to the Minister, but I wanted to make sure that it was on the record in the House before I did so. Only by doing so could I guarantee a response from the Minister. I think that the Minister will look into the matter seriously in view of the Government's record. That is why I did not pass it on to him.

**Mr. MacGregor:** That is a frightfully feeble answer. With respect to the hon. Gentleman, it suggests that he is more interested in grabbing headlines than in dealing with serious issues responsibly.

Let me tell the hon. Gentleman that there was one case, involving Young's, in January 1985. The company received a severe warning at the time and there is no evidence that anything has happened involving that company since. That is the only case of which I and my Ministry know. That was only one example four years ago and the hon. Gentleman has never suggested otherwise.

The hon. Gentleman said on "The World this Weekend" that we had evidence of repeated examples. We have no such evidence; therefore, I had to turn to the early-day motion.

Some of the companies named are Dutch, and some of the imputed actions referred to in the early-day motion took place in other countries. It is not for me to comment on those since they would be matters for other authorities. But let me tell the hon. Gentleman that if this is his evidence, all three British food importing firms referred to have firmly denied the stories, and indeed my Department's regular contacts with the authorities in the Netherlands have provided no information that would support the Opposition's claims.

I repeat that I am ready to look at any evidence. But I think it is disreputable to name companies in an early-day motion without firm evidence, and I am not surprised that the hon. Member for Great Grimsby (Mr. Mitchell) has firmly, on the Order Paper, rejected the allegation made against one of the firms. I shall look at any evidence, but ultimately the best guarantee of dealing with the issue and ensuring that irradiation is used responsibly and properly is to have the new control system that we have in place.

I ask the House to contrast the difference in the approach of the two parties—the Government's careful, thorough consideration based on the fullest scientific evidence, the establishment of a proper control framework, making a very useful device for food safety available to consumers who want it, and the irresponsible allegations by the Opposition.

I turn briefly to some of the other charges made by the hon. Gentleman in his speech today. My hon. Friend the Parliamentary Under-Secretary will deal with one or two other matters in winding up. I shall turn first to research and development on which the hon. Gentleman concentrated and in which he knows I have a particular interest.

I make no apology for the Government's approach to the funding of near market research and development because I am sure that it makes sense. It is right that the Government should review their priorities on research and development across the board from time to time, and that is what we have been doing. It is right to ask the agrochemical and farming industries to fund the near market development work, that is that which is close to commercial exploitation—as they do in any other industry. That work is to their benefit—they can better assess the commercial possibilities and are more likely that way to carry the results through to full development in the market place—and it avoids duplication. We estimate the industry itself is funding more than £300 million a year of R and D, most of it probably near market.

But that is a different matter from research on food safety, which is not affected. Indeed we are now spending over £10 million a year on food safety and nutrition research, and it has been steadily increasing. It is noteworthy that expenditure on food research has more than doubled in real terms under this Government and since the Opposition left office.

Last week's decision by the Agricultural and Food Research Council to consolidate the work of its Institute of Food Research at its Norwich and Reading sites has to be seen in this context. The near market research from which Government support is being withdrawn at the food research institute is work on eating quality, flavours, shelf life and non-food safety aspects of food processing. That work is of interest to the industry and we hope it will fund it, but it is not related to food safety or other public good issues and I want to be absolutely clear on this point.

So far as food safety is concerned, the decision to restructure the IFR means: more scientists working together on food research at Reading and Norwich, in a more focused way, using the most sophisticated equipment and technology available; an enhanced capacity to deal with a wide range of micro-organisms, including salmonella, listeria and those causing botulism; and increased funding for research in these and other food safety areas.

In Norwich and Reading, the United Kingdom will continue to possess a world-class Institute of Food Research. It will ensure a sound science base which can address and resolve issues of concern to the consumer, the housewife, the man in the street, the producer and industry. For food safety there are real, positive gains.

**Mr. Tam Dalyell** (Linlithgow): It is absolutely wrecking the national fruit variety collections at Brogdale.

**Mr. MacGregor:** I want to move on.

Had time permitted, I should have liked to deal with a number of other issues relating to early-day motions and my hon. Friend will try to deal with some of them when he replies to the debate.

Finally, I want to touch on one matter not raised by the hon. Gentleman this afternoon, pesticides. The Government have taken more action than any other on pesticides. We have a proper statutory system of approval, registration and control for the first time. No one has the right to sell a pesticide, to store it, advertise it or use it unless it has been given safety clearance and approval by Ministers. That is all in the interests of consumers and users.

Before there is any possibility of approval the company has to have tested the safety of the product in terms of health and the environment and its efficacy in use. And there is thorough independent, scientific evaluation.

An independent committee, the Advisory Committee for Pesticides, makes a scientific assessment.

Detailed monitoring takes place thereafter, not least by the working party on pesticides residues. Regular sampling takes place. From time to time concern about pesticides emerges and it is important to set out what we have in place.

Such a control system needs to be completed with an enforcement regime and a policy of public information and guidance in which our agricultural inspectorate plays a crucial part.

Against the background of a control system which is as comprehensive as we can devise and as expert as we can get I have to report to the House an extraordinary incident which occurred last week.

A few days before that, my officials became aware that the Labour party was advertising in one of its magazines two insecticides. My officials established to their satisfaction that the products advertised had no approval, and that the advertisement showed no regard to the legal requirements. Without reference to Ministers my officials did what they would do to any other trader who appeared to be breaking the law, and issued a notice requiring that the Labour party ceased selling non-approved products, and ensured that advertisements observe the established regulations.

[*Mr. MacGregor*]

Imagine my astonishment when the first I heard of this was, via the press, a letter from the general secretary of the Labour party demanding that I repudiate the actions of my officials immediately. So there we have it from the party professing such environmental and safety concern —one law for the Labour party on pesticide regulations and another for everybody else; great moral huffing and puffing as far as everyone else is concerned and unrighteous indignation when the law is applied to the Labour party.

The hon. Gentleman talked about deregulation. It is the Labour party's version of deregulation. For the Labour party it means deregulation beyond the law. That sums it up.

The Opposition spokesman has admitted that his party came to food issues very late. He said that it was a huge field that the Opposition had neglected. The Opposition are willing to throw about wild allegations without proper assessment of the facts and throw their weight about to get me to ask my officials to bend the law in their favour. The Government devote very substantial resources to food safety matters and give them high priority, have a well-established set of mechanisms for obtaining the best scientific evidence and advice, take effective action promptly and give the highest priority to consumer protection and consumer choice. That is why I have no hesitation in commending the Government amendment and urging the House to reject the Opposition motion.

4.49 pm

**Dr. Lewis Moonie** (Kirkcaldy): In a long and dismal procession of incompetent Ministers who have paraded themselves before the House in recent months we have surely heard one of the worst this afternoon. The only "green" thing about the Minister's Department is probably the tie worn by the Parliamentary Secretary.

Two aspects stand out from today's debate: first, the woeful incompetence of the Ministries entrusted with responsibility for public health in this country; secondly, the need to define clearly the objectives that we should be pursuing. The failure of the relevant Ministries is most clearly shown by the disjointed, defensive and reactive approach adopted by the Minister this afternoon. I shall pass over his speech, except for a reference to the irradiation of food, which is a disturbing development.

In passing, I should say that I am sponsored by the Co-operative movement and thus represent the major food producer in this country. It has come out clearly against irradiation. I hope that other hon. Members who speak today will also declare their interests and tell us which of them are in the pockets of big business and which represent the interests of the farmers. People should not imagine for a moment that Conservative Members will not be speaking from prejudice or self-interest, just like the lap dogs in the Ministry who are in the pockets of the agricultural companies and of food production interests. Speaking of lap dogs, the Minister's parliamentary private secretary might be called the rottweiler of big business, although, come to think of it, rottweiler is not a good description of the hon. Member for Sherwood (Mr. Stewart).

We must examine the whole of food policy, not just parts of it. The Minister selected a few non-diseased trees from the wood and concentrated on them, but we must look at the whole picture—the production, distribution, processing and consumption of food, and its impact on our health.

First, let us examine the direct effects which cause illness. The Minister rightly touched on many of the worrying items. Salmonellosis is still the single largest cause of major food poisoning—at least of notified cases, if not of all cases seen in clinical practice. Other conditions are related to the consumption of milk—brucellosis, tuberculosis and campylobacter are all still major causes of ill health. I deprecate any attempt to retain the sale of unpasteurised milk in England and Wales. Such attempts are shameful. We have not had this problem for many years in Scotland and that is exemplified by the much lower incidence of these conditions there. I hope that the Minister will not listen to the more foolish among his hon. Friends—and among mine—who are trying to persuade him that people should be allowed to consume unpasteurised milk. There is compelling evidence that they should not. I know of no public health authority in this country or in any other that would recommend the drinking of unpasteurised milk, which affects not only the health of the individual consumer but can play a part in a chain of infection leading to the infection of innocent people.

There are other direct causes of illness—the contamination of food, the use of hormones in production, the over-use of antibiotics and the largely unknown and ill-defined effects that they may have on the quality of our food. I know that the Government and the EEC are closely examining additives, although perhaps not in as well co-ordinated a way as they might.

I do not blame only the Minister or this Government. This problem has gone on for a long time and is hardly new. The problem of food poisoning did not begin with the rather warped description of a diseased chicken by a former Under-Secretary of State for Health last year. A succession of Ministers and civil servants have failed to protect public health for a long time.

We must also look into the introduction of more sinister elements to the equation. Growth hormones are being used in meat production, not necessarily in this country, but in others from which meat may be imported to this country. The use of irradiation and of new processes such as cook-chill require close attention to detail. I welcome the fact that the Government are introducing a food Bill in the next Session of Parliament and I look forward with interest to reading it, but I still contend that it will not solve the major problem, which is that there is no co-ordinated food policy in this country. Until we have one, problems will continue to arise and need to be dealt with. I grant that some problems have been dealt with promptly, but they were unforeseen. We should look for problems before they arise and try to prevent them from occurring in the first place.

A bad diet indirectly affects people's health. I have mentioned that before and shall go on mentioning it until Ministers of whichever party happens to be in power listen. Bad diet has a sinister, persistent and all-pervasive effect on health. The fat and sugar content of such diets is still far too high. Bad diet can lead to diabetes, heart disease and some forms of cancer. We tend to forget that poverty leads to the inadequate consumption of calories and to an insufficiently balanced diet, and so to ill health. For all their denials, the Government have introduced poverty in full measure to this country over the past few years to an extent that we never thought possible in a civilised society.

From the vast range of problems that I have attempted to outline it must be clear that major improvements in health will only follow action to create a proper food policy which has as its primary objective the improvement of our national diet, not the protection of the interests and well-being of food producers. Confusion reigns at present. Many Ministries are involved—the Department of Health, the Department of Social Security, which deals with aspects of the poverty I have mentioned, the Ministry of Agriculture, Fisheries and Food, the Department of the Environment and the Treasury, which ultimately controls what we are allowed to spend. The Minister, with his familiarity with that Department, is only too well aware of the problems that it can create for the best intentioned of schemes.

All these Departments have conflicting objectives and lack definition and the co-ordination of a common purpose. We have three choices: we can do nothing; we can examine the possibility of setting up a food Ministry —with all the difficulties that that would entail—in an attempt to co-ordinate the work of the different Departments; or we can follow the example that the Government set two years ago when alcohol problems became so manifest. They used the auspices of the Leader of the House to set up a ministerial committee to co-ordinate the efforts of different Departments. That has proved much more successful than I—somewhat sceptical of this type of approach—was at first prepared to admit. Such a committee might be a means of ensuring proper developments.

The Government's record is unsound and is best shown in two areas—first, in their attitude to poverty, of which I shall mention one specific example. Many young pregnant women cannot purchase an adequate diet because they have low incomes. This has been borne out time and again by observers and it is a problem that will not go away. It damages not only the woman's health but the future health of her child. The Government should look into this problem carefully.

The second aspect has already been mentioned by my hon. Friend the Member for South Shields (Dr. Clark). The Institute of Food Research in Bristol is a good example of this. The Minister did not mention it today; perhaps he merely overlooked it and the Parliamentary Secretary will refer to it later. The Government are pursuing the mirage of near-market research. They believe that, merely because something will clearly benefit the public, it will be picked up by commercial organisations, which will perceive it as being of benefit to themselves.

**Miss Emma Nicholson** (Torridge and Devon, West): I am anxious to correct the hon. Gentleman because in what appears to be his peroration he is going from one pinnacle to another without bothering to stop to consider a problem and to find proper solutions. In the last point to which he referred he was wrong, as he has been wrong all along. It is not a question of near-market research meaning that when something is of public benefit it will be taken up by commercial companies. The idea of near-market research is that when something is of commercial benefit companies will take it up and pay for

that research. When it is for the public good and demonstrates no immediate, near commercial benefit, the Government will continue that research.

**Dr. Moonie:** Unfortunately, what the Government define as near-market research and how companies define it are very different, as can be seen from the number of projects that are dropped by the Government and not taken up by the companies concerned, despite a clearly demonstrated value to public health. Companies are in business to make money, not to care for Members of this House and their constituents. The balance sheet at the end of the day is their objective, and that determines their activities, not any altruistic concern for the public health.

Even so, some companies, particularly the one with which I am involved—but also companies such as Marks and Spencer—have gone out of their way to develop sound practices in the handling of food. I accept that, but they have not gone out of their way to share them with any other companies because, obviously, to do so would not be to their commercial advantage.

Not only near-market research is important. The Government are also attempting to cut back on research which is seen by most people to be of limited value to the market but which is of vital importance to the future well-being of, for example, plant research in Britain. I refer to reports that the Government are cutting back on research at several plant stations, particularly at Wellsbourne, Rosemaun and, as my hon. Friend the Member for Linlithgow (Mr. Dalyell) mentioned, Brogdale.

Those stations, Brogdale in particular, contain genetic material which, if not kept, will be lost to the world for ever. This material stretches back to different varieties of fruit and vegetables for centuries, much of which has not been properly explored. Much of it could provide cross-breeding of different varieties of fruit and vegetables which could then be developed for consumption in this country and perhaps improve the quality and variety of food to which we are exposed.

It is shameful that the Government will not maintain research at those plants. The issue has been taken up by the scientific press, in particular recently by the *New Scientist*. Wellsbourne has been described by the International Board for Plant Genetic Resources in Rome as one of the most important temperate vegetable gene banks in the world. Hon. Members will appreciate that it is not simply a matter of my concern. It affects the public generally and it is regrettable that the organisation is not receiving the funds that it needs to keep going.

I have tried to demonstrate how, in a wide variety of areas, the Government have failed to act responsibly. They have failed to perceive that the whole is much greater than the sum of its parts, particularly the few parts to which the Minister referred today. Until the Government accept that principle, we will not develop the type of food policy that our people deserve.

5.3 pm

**Mr. Jerry Wiggin** (Weston-super-Mare): About 10 years ago I found myself with junior ministerial responsibility both for the food industry and for agricultural research. The then Agricultural Research Council was funded equally by the Department of Education and Science and the Ministry of Agriculture, Fisheries and Food.

[*Mr. Jerry Wiggin*]

I took the opportunity at that time of visiting many research institutes to look at their work. I am not a scientist, but as a practical farmer and having visited university and research institutions over the years, I feel practically qualified—I put it no higher than that—to make a judgment about the quality of work being done in, and of the scientists working at, those institutes 10 years ago.

I found that all was not well. Where the scientists were excellent—and there were many—they were grossly underpaid and were reluctant to stay in the employment of the ARC. They were leaving in large numbers to go to industry and into outside research. Where they were elderly and burnt-out, they were being feather-bedded into retirement by an organisation that was well capable of extracting funds from the Government, whether for basic or practical research.

I expressed my concern about that state of affairs over a lengthy period, and although hon. Members will appreciate that two years is too short a time to turn round such a vast ship as a research council, I am sure that those civil servants who were responsible in the Ministry had no doubt of my concern and displeasure. That subsequently was translated by my successor into a welcome change when the ARC became the AFRC, recognising the importance of food and reorganising the way in which it allocated funds for research.

**Mr. Marland:** During his time as a Minister and while visiting laboratories, did my hon. Friend discover much duplication of research? Did it occur to him that there might be possibilities of saving money because one job was being done in two or three different places?

**Mr. Wiggin:** That was the case. For example, the ARC ran two fruit research stations. Given the size of the industry, that did not seem necessary, but many matters of that type have been put right. I am referring to the situation 10 years ago. The recent changes in funding, in the first instance, and, more important, the approach of the AFRC in putting out much of its work to universities and outside institutes, as well as in supporting individuals in the work that they are doing, is to be welcomed, and I totally support the action that the Government have taken.

I hope that in dreaming up projects for near-market application, civil servants will not become too imaginative because there have been some examples where there is no possibility of industry being interested. That is where a common-sense approach must be taken.

The change is deeply traumatic to those who work in the institutes, and the frustration felt and the insecurity in general has frequently meant that many leading scientists in institutes have left, either leaving research altogether or going to work for private industry. When leading scientists leave an institute, that has a demoralising effect on others, and a damaging cycle begins.

Well-informed though they are in the AFRC, the news of closures and changes spreads rapidly. The morale of many employees has been poor for some time, and nowhere worse than at the food research institute at Langford in my constituency. I have always enjoyed excellent relations with the staff of the institute and I have been a visitor there on many occasions. Although

forewarned for a considerable time, I was extremely sad to learn last week of the final decision by the AFRC to close the institute in its present form.

Few of the scientists will be offered jobs elsewhere. Some will be, and naturally I am worried about the local employees—the laboratory assistants and staff who work on the farms and in the abattoir—who will not be able to move. But I feel that I am insufficiently informed—as is the hon. Member for South Shields (Dr. Clark)—to tell the AFRC how to run its business.

That organisation is deliberately at arm's length from Government, and I therefore find the wording of the Opposition motion strange, since it is the responsibility of the AFRC, not of the Government, to administer its funds and to decide to which projects to put its work. Indeed, the Ministry of Agriculture funds its projects through the AFRC as an arm's length operation. I am not qualified to tell that body, in acting with taxpayers' money, how best to operate.

But I am keen to assist those who believe that they can save some of the specialist facilities at Langford. There is a unique opportunity for another organisation to take over the institute's facilities and building. I have in mind Bristol university, the veterinary school of which is world famous and which is also sited at Langford.

There is a possibility that with funding from the Ministry of Agriculture—I hope that the Minister will be in a position to comment positively on this matter—the Meat and Livestock Commission and the AFRC, some of the unique work carried out at the special facilities will be able to continue.

**Ms. Dawn Primarolo** (Bristol, South) *rose*——

**Mr. Wiggin:** I shall not give way to the hon. Lady who last week made no attempt to offer me the most elementary courtesy before she raised in the House the matter of the institute, which is in my constituency. In view of the time, I shall continue.

The obvious merit in being able to carry out this special work is not only that it will continue, but will be conducted in a university atmosphere, which is right and proper. Furthermore, local employees may well be able to find work.

The Opposition's suggestion that there is to be a serious and total change in all food research is patently rubbish. While I accept that some work will cease, who are we as non-scientists and non-experts to decide on this allocation of funds? It is irritating to me that we appoint extremely expert people, indeed we have a fine chairman of the AFRC, but do not then leave them to decide how their funds should be allocated.

I strongly welcome the statement of my right hon. Friend the Minister about the irradiation of food. Much of the original checking of the safety of irradiation was done at Langford and I hope that the expertise will remain within the AFRC. One of our difficulties is that we are approached by scientists whose projects have been terminated and who, naturally, greatly resent that. They have been bound up in the work and believe it to be worthwhile. They resent a committee or outside body saying, "Sorry, it is no longer worth continuing with your research," or "You are not making sufficient progress." Therefore, we sometimes receive a distorted story.

Not however in one case, and I particularly want to mention one aspect of the work at Langford refrigeration.

The House will know that the Low Temperature Research Station was originally set up in Cambridge but moved to Langford, and the expertise contained within that department is very special. I hope that there are plans for continuing work on this facility. If there are, the staff concerned are not aware of them. I hope that the Minister will look with particular care at this aspect. The suggestion that there is nothing further to learn on the subject is patently absurd, and I understand that such work is not being carried out elsewhere.

During the Select Committee's recent inquiry into salmonella in eggs it became clear that, although much is known about food poisoning, the subject is ever changing. The ability of bacteria to change and mutate needs constant vigilance. The dividing line between the responsibility of doctors at the Department of Health, the public health laboratory service and the vets is narrow. It would not be right for me to detain the House by repeating that argument, but those interested may find it worthwhile to study the Committee's report on the subject.

Ensuring the health and cleanliness of our livestock is an expensive business. The poultry industry is counting the cost of recently introduced measures to combat salmonella in eggs. That cost will, unquestionably, be passed on to the consumer. Nevertheless, I believe that the public will be willing to pay. However, it is absurd that other countries in which standards are appreciably lower than ours—this means all other countries because we now lead the world in this matter—can export to this country eggs from flocks which do not meet our health standards. The Government must insist on ending such unfair practices which discriminate against the United Kingdom's egg producers.

Despite all the problems of the past few months, the British public have never enjoyed a wider, more attractive and safer range of foodstuffs than are currently on sale. Some 66 per cent. of all our food is now bought from six main supermarket chains. We have only to see the efforts which they make to confirm the purity of their food to realise that the public is well protected, not just by officials or the Government but by extremely competitive retailers who rely on the quality of their produce to beat the competition down the road.

We shall never totally eliminate food poisoning, any more than disease. Recent events have unquestionably had a salutary effect on all involved, but in the long term we shall have had a most beneficial look at the subject, which must be in the interests of all consumers.

5.16 pm

**Mr. Ronnie Fearn** (Southport): Much of what I said in this House on 21 February during the debate on food safety and water is relevant today. Despite the Government's attempt to dispel fears and to look as though they are taking action by announcing, for example, the appointment of the Food Safety Committee and the ban on bovine offals for human consumption, the fact remains that the Government's prime motivations behind their policy are profit, economic gain and a reduction in public spending.

The order of the day is a menu that is quicker, cheaper and more efficient. Without the ingredients to ensure quality and safety, it is a recipe for disaster. As I said in the previous debate:

"in our rush to progress and our haste to produce food more efficiently and profitably . . . certain people and industries have been allowed to cut corners. Consumers' rights have been neglected and the dangers to their health have become much more prevalent."—[*Official Report*, 21 February 1989; Vol. 147, c, 883.]

Incidences of food poisoning have risen dramatically since that debate. My sources claim that they were investigating at least one and a half times as many cases this spring as last spring. In the second week of May there were 240 reported cases of salmonella poisoning, and everyone is aware that the vast majority of cases of gastric enteritis go unreported. With the prospect of a long hot summer in front of us, as most of us hope, more concerted and organised actions are required from the Government.

At the moment, Government food policy appears to be in a shambles. For example, Ministers cannot make up their minds whether they should ban green top milk. One minute they say that they will and the next that they will not. I welcome the most recent decision that consumers will retain their right of choice to buy untreated milk and I hope that the Government will extend that right to bovine somatotropin-treated milk by bottling separately milk which has been treated with the genetically engineered hormone, and clearly labelling it as such.

New technologies in agriculture, food production and processing make it important for the Government to be aware of the repercussions on consumers' health and the environment in general. That requires research, quality and hygiene standards, regulations and monitoring services. Instead, the Government have decided to cut public spending on food research by as much as 27 per cent. by 1993-94 and to reduce their commitment to experimental husbandry farming.

The closure of the Institute of Food Research at Langford, near Bristol, is part and parcel of the Government's reorganisation of agricultural research and development. The withdrawal of funds for near-market research projects in the belief that the private sector will pick up the tab is naive in the extreme and an example of what blind faith in the market will do. The Government also ignore the fact that many projects cannot be separated, and their attempts to identify near-market research, and to reduce or withdraw their funding, are having a devastating effect.

The Government's action is symptomatic of their entire policy towards research and development. Scientists are leaving Britain on an unprecedented scale. Only last week, a microbiologist involved in food research at one of our universities said to me:

"I do not see any way forward. Research is now seen as a source of income to the institute. If it is left to the private sector, the only research that is likely to be funded is that which follows the goals and objectives of the specific organisation providing the funds."

British industry is not well known for its investment in research and development, and many of the projects which are funded and founded involve pre-marketing research paid for by the sales and marketing departments. Needless to say, their guidelines are fairly stringent. This could be disastrous for the food safety aspect.

What guarantee is there that the findings will ever be published? I note that the large food chains such as Sainsbury's and Tesco's have refused to inform the consumer of the results of their massive testing programmes into chemical contamination of food. Sainsbury's justify this by saying that it considers the information to be confidential to itself and to its suppliers. Surely the consumer, who is the one most likely to be affected, has the right to know what this information is. I

[*Mr. Ronnie Fearn*]

do not see why, if the retailer is doing a good job and is satisfied that the food being sold is safe, it should not want the consumer to know the results of the tests. The consumer has a right to know what pesticides are used on foods. There is a clear case for labelling to give such information—a factor that the Minister hardly mentioned.

The Government's stated objective is to roll back the state. I do not think they have achieved that. All that they have done is to concentrate power at the centre. However, another topic for debate—something that the Government must not forget and must remember in their pursuit of their objectives, whatever they are—is their responsibility to those whom they govern. The Government are responsible for the protection of public safety, which is threatened not only by outside factors, but by all sorts of other hazards. Where there is a threat to public safety or health that any action by the individual cannot remove, it is the Government's responsibility to find the cause and the means to eliminate the danger. The production of a glossy food hygiene booklet aimed at the housewife, at a cost of £750,000, as a response to the recent outbreaks of food poisoning is a poor effort by the Government to carry out their duty, and in many cases is an insult to the consumer.

The consumer, by using proper cooking methods, can kill whatever bacteria are present in the food, but we have to address the question of how the organism got into the food in the first place, and how to prevent it doing so in the future. Prevention can be achieved only through research, detection and control throughout the food chain. The Government must no longer rely on self regulation by the industry. When demands are moving and changing as fast as they are today, with fads coming and going and competition rife, the industry must not and cannot be expected to regulate itself to an extent that ensures safety in food production, processing and retailing. The Government must introduce more regulations and the means to enforce them. Parliamentary time for whatever legislation is necessary to enable sufficient regulation, monitoring and control to take place must be set aside. Self regulation is not the ideal way to ensure safety in food products.

More rather than less research is required. It is no good the Government trotting out statistics and numbers to back up claims that spending in this sector is higher than it ever has been before, because I do not care whether it is or not. I care about whether the amount being spent is adequate to meet health and safety needs. The answer is quite obviously no.

The Government must give food safety top priority. The decision, announced by the Minister today, to allow irradiated food to be sold in Britain without full knowledge of the long-term effects and without other back-up measures to protect the consumer is an example of other considerations having priority. If irradiation is to remain, then the Government should consider such moves as a ban on fractionalised dosage and the proper funding for environmental officers to inspect premises regularly.

I am also concerned about Government action on bovine spongiform encephalopathy, or BSE. Can the Minister assure the House that the banning of cattle offal for human consumption and the move to have all cattle suspected of having BSE slaughtered and destroyed is adequate protection against all aspects of the disease and its human health implications? Can the Government say with confidence that the risk to humans from the disease is remote? Although I am told that the fundamental science on this has not been carried out, can the Minister say that the Government have done all in their power to prevent any such risks? I cannot believe that the Government are so satisfied with the standards of health and animal hygiene that they see their way clear to reducing the complement of veterinary surgeons in the public service. Are the Government content that the standards of hygiene in all abattoirs is safe and something of which we should be proud?

Is the Secretary of State for Health satisfied that the level of environmental officers in post, and even the establishment number, is adequate to do all the follow-up work that is required as a result of the recent outbreaks of food poisoning? Where is the follow-up work that should be done if we wish to ensure that lessons are learnt and mistakes not merely repeated? Does the Secretary of State believe that there are enough officers with enough power to deal with the expansion in the numbers of small manufacturers, retailers and caterers and the many other types of premises that they have to inspect?

The Government must now think in terms of prevention, which is one of the most cost-effective of measures. Food poisoning, other diseases and illness could be avoided with the proper foresight, organisation, co-operation and resources. The cost to the nation as a whole in terms of the costs to the Health Service, to social security and to industry from days off work could easily be avoided.

In the debate last February, I called for the lines of responsibility within and between various Government Departments to be clarified. When various Departments are involved, it is too easy to claim non-responsibility, too tempting to fight one's own corner and too difficult to co-ordinate objectives. Therefore, today I issue a challenge to the Prime Minister. When she reshuffles her Cabinet in the near future, she should set up a Ministry of Food to establish a mechanism to make and carry out a coherent policy on food, and to give the safety and interests of the consumer the utmost priority.

5.27 pm

**Mr. Tim Boswell** (Daventry): I must immediately declare an interest as a council member of the Agricultural and Food Research Council. I attended last week's meeting at which the decision to close the Bristol laboratory was taken. In saying that, I put myself forward neither as a lightning conductor for, nor as a clone of, Government policy. No one need think that the decision was taken lightly, or without consideration of the staff situation, which was sensitively touched on by the constituency Member of Parliament, my hon. Friend the Member for Weston-super-Mare (Mr. Wiggin).

The Opposition motion rests on two fundamental misconceptions. The first and major one is a rehash of the old philosophical confusion about the belief that, because one event follows another, the first must cause the second. For instance, if one believes that night follows day, one ends up believing that day causes night. It is very much the same with food safety. It needs only some accident to happen—accidents in food safety can be extremely unpleasant, as the recent outbreak of botulism has been

—and for there to be the coincidence of that accident with some development in agricultural research for the two to be inevitably put together by the Opposition. I am not quite sure of their view of the direct causation in this matter. For example, I am not sure whether last week was seen as a Government plot to infect their citizenry with botulism or as a plot by the bacillus to embarrass the Government on the eve of the European election. One way or the other, that is the way they see it.

**Mr. Frank Cook:** We infected them, did we?

**Mr. Boswell:** I did not say that.

Sometimes things go wrong with food safety. They have done in the past and they will do in the future. Our interest is in minimising their occurrence. Equally, decisions sometimes need to be taken in food policy and food research. It is inexusable to take those two coincidental happenings and to link them by a chain of causation which does not exist.

My second criticism of the Opposition motion is that for all their efforts, about which we read so much, to modernise and bring themselves up to date for the 1990s, they have not come to terms with the need for restructuring in the wider economy. We would not have made very much progress as a nation in the past 10 years, or even previously, if we had never had to make hard decisions to close a factory or to restructure a business. Anyone with an element of business experience appreciates the central importance of overhead costs. It is a matter of common sense that the number of sites on which an activity takes place, whether it be research or manufacturing, has a close bearing on the level of overhead costs—as, for example, my two district councils found when they consolidated their activities on one site. The larger the number of sites, the higher the overhead costs. That has been a major underlying theme in the decisions that the AFRC has taken to rationalise each of its institutes on one or two sites, and to modernise its operations.

I acknowledge the impact of the withdrawal of the MAFF contribution to near-market research. That could build up to a significant element in the total budget for the AFRC and the IFR during the next three years. However, I must stress that not all the work necessarily has to be done at the same location as the central science activities of the IFR. It need not all be carried out under the same organisation or funding umbrella. Much of it can go to other organisations, whether in the public or private sector. Insufficient attention has been paid to the tremendous increase in funding for AFRC institutes on contracts for the private sector. Much of the work might well be carried out elsewhere or under the funding of other bodies. An example of that is the important work on carcass quality—not that it need necessarily move from Langford—which could appropriately be funded by the industry.

On the public good aspect, I would cite the facilities for the welfare of animals at slaughter—a very sensitive issue —which are sited at Bristol. I understand that MAFF is prepared to continue with that as an item of public good, and so it should.

The result of making such difficult decisions will be a somewhat slimmed down IFR on two sites instead of the current three. The concentration will shift from the somewhat old-fashioned commodity-by-commodity approach, because modern developments have overtaken that, not just in technology but in consumer taste. For example, a TV dinner is not just meat. A number of different items have to be put together and cooked appropriately. With chicken Kiev, different indgredients are mixed, widening the range of consumer choice and taste.

A multi-disciplinary approach is required, looking at the basic science and applying it to all situations. The new institute will concentrate on the disciplines of central science underlying that—safety; the early, rapid and effective diagnosis of bacteria, nutrition, consumer acceptability, the avoidance of taint, and bio-technology.

As an example of the way in which that can be done under the new arrangements, Dr. Roberts and the appropriate members of his microbiology team at Bristol will be transferred to Reading. All the relevant work on food safety can and will continue. It is interesting to note that there were 40 MAFF-funded food safety projects within the research system last year, which is a high number. I have every confidence in the leadership of Professor Georgala at the IFR and a chance for a new, modern activity under the new structure.

This debate concentrates upon the more general aspects of food safety. If nothing else, the events surrounding egg production earlier this year have highlighted the problem, which in general is still growing. However, it is interesting to note that as a result of Government action the salmonella problem has now stabilised. With respect to the hon. Member for Southport (Mr. Fearn), the Government will have to consider a balance of a number of important issues such as consumer safety, consumer confidence and product innovation to meet consumer taste and choice. There is also a need to get the regulatory structure right, as I am confident the Government will do in their forthcoming food legislation.

I call on Ministers to bear three points in mind when preparing this autumn's work. First, they should work actively with their colleagues in the Department of Education and Science to ensure that the necessary funds are available for the full restructuring of the IFR. Secondly, they should ensure that the resources are adequate for the monitoring and regulation of food safety both at national and at environmental health officer level. Thirdly, the campaign for food safety should be applied at all levels so that all the gateways through which bacteria can get in are closed. One that has not been mentioned today, and about which I feel strongly, is food and hygiene training in restaurants.

The bugs that cause food poisoning—which are over, around and within us—are more varied and ingenious than we could ever imagine. We need to close all the possible pathways into the human food chain. Simple slogans and simple assumptions of priority will not work. To take the necessary action, we need the best possible structure for the basic science. I believe that the Government have acted to secure that structure.

5.36 pm

**Mr. Eric Martlew** (Carlisle): Earlier in the debate the Minister would not give way on the question of irradiation of food. It is a pity that he has left the Chamber because he could have put me right. We were given assurances that any irradiated food would be labelled, but what will happen in cafés and restaurants? Will there be labelling on

[*Mr. Eric Martlew*]

the menu or on the restaurant door? That will not happen. Irradiated food brought into this country will end up on the consumer's plate——

**Mr. Frank Cook:** In the Strangers Dining Room.

**Mr. Martlew:** I should be sorry if that happened as it is an excellent Dining Room.

The Government are deliberately misleading the public. If the Minister is prepared to say that irradiated restaurant food will be labelled, I will give way to him.

**Mr. Frank Cook:** The silence is deafening.

**Mr. Martlew:** The record will show that the Minister has refused to give that assurance.

The Government have shown a great deal of complacency today. During the past century consumers have never had a better chance of suffering from food poisoning. The choice is whether it should be from salmonella or campylobacter. The Government's food policy is unfit for human consumption.

I am glad that the problem of salmonella in eggs is improving. A letter from the British Poultry Federation today says that it has improved considerably since the Select Committee's report. The Select Committee can take credit for that, but the Government cannot take any credit because they have done nothing to stop the import of contaminated foreign eggs.

The Government's own chief officer of health said that the worst area in the European Community was Spain. Yet there is no ban on Spanish eggs coming into this country. Only last week, there was a positive test of salmonella in Dutch eggs. Why are the Government doing nothing about that? Those countries do not have our strict standards. They will now undercut us, the consumer will buy foreign eggs and our poultry industry, which has started to put its house in order, will suffer as a result of unfair competition.

Last year, there were 30,000 cases of food poisoning —or so the Government said. There is a question of reporting and whether the figure might be 10 per cent. or 100 per cent. higher. A further 30,000 reported cases of food poisoning did not go into the statistics—the cases of campylobacter which were recorded and blamed on food —so there were really 60,000 recorded cases of food poisoning last year. The problem is worse this year. June and July may be the strawberry season, but it is also the campylobacter season. There is an epidemic at present, which did not happen 10 years ago. Fortunately, it is rarely a fatal disease, but it is unpleasant, as anyone who has suffered from it will testify. What are the Government doing about food safety? The answer is that they are doing very little.

To take the fiasco of green-top milk, last January I asked in a written question whether the Minister intended to ban green-top milk. The answer was that there were no plans to do so. In February, the hon. Member for Newark (Mr. Alexander) asked the same question and the reply was reported in the west Yorkshire evening press. I am sorry that the junior Agriculture Minister is not here.

**Mr. John Home Robertson** (East Lothian): The big one.

**Mr. Martlew:** Yes, the big one. I refer to the Parliamentary Secretary to the Ministry of Agriculture, Fisheries and Food, the hon. Member for Calder Valley (Mr. Thompson). The local paper said:

"MP backs green top milk ban. Plans to ban the sale of green top milk, which will affect the livelihoods of up to 40 Calderdale farmers, have the backing of junior minister Mr. Donald Thompson.

He said the ban was necessary in the interest of public safety. Green top milk"—

[*Interruption.*] This is a serious matter. We should not joke about the next part!

"Green top milk was blamed for the deaths of five elderly people and a baby in Calderdale in 1984".

In fact the figure was seven adults and one baby. That was the year after the Government banned the sale of green-top milk in Scotland. Had they taken action in England at the same time, those people would have lived. The article was written in February. The Minister continued——

**Miss Emma Nicholson:** If the hon. Gentleman follows his train of thought logically, would he want to stop people driving and to close all roads on the ground that 300 people die every week on the roads? The public want the choice to drink green-top milk. With proper consumer labelling, they now have that choice in England and Wales, and I am delighted that that is so.

**Mr. Martlew:** I am sorry that the hon. Lady delights in continuing to advocate a product which has killed people in the past and will kill people in the future. The Government decided that the pressure groups to which the hon. Lady answers——

**Miss Nicholson:** I ask the hon. Gentleman to withdraw that remark.

**Mr. Deputy Speaker (Sir Paul Dean):** Order. I do not think that the hon. Gentleman has given way.

**Mr. Martlew:** Those pressure groups have deceived——

**Miss Nicholson:** On a point of order, Mr. Deputy Speaker. Is it possible for the hon. Gentleman to withdraw that statement? I am answerable to nobody. I assume that the hon. Gentleman means financially answerable, as other Labour Members have made that statement. He is incorrect to say that.

**Mr. Deputy Speaker:** That is not a point of order, but the hon. Lady has got her point on the record.

**Mr. Martlew:** Pressure groups in this country have persuaded the Government to continue to allow the sale of a lethal mixture. I was asked last week whether I would drink green-top milk and I answered that I would not even give it to my cat. It has created terrible problems. The Government are not fit to run a food policy if they do not have the courage to ban green-top milk. The old advertisement said that milk had a lot of bottle. That is certainly more than the Government have.

The Government said that they had no evidence of the irradiation of products. I spoke to local health inspectors who had had a complaint about some prawns which did not smell right. The prawns were sent to the public laboratory in Glasgow, which found there were no bacteria in them, so the only conclusion was that the prawns had been irradiated. The Government have been allowing irradiated food in Britain for years and have given only one warning. They are not in a position to put forward creative policies to protect people from food poisoning. They have failed to do so and, as a result, 2 million people will suffer this year. I have no confidence that the legislation that they intend to propose in the autumn will do anything but continue to protect vested interests.

5.45 pm

**Mr. Robert Key** (Salisbury): It falls to me to bring the debate down to earth. We seem to have been groping in Utopia for the past hour or so. I regret the sharp exchange that I had with the hon. Member for South Shields (Dr. Clark) at the beginning of the debate. It was probably rather uncharacteristic and the hon. Gentleman is far too nice a man for me to treat his remarks with disdain. However, it is important to get the matter into proportion. I ask the hon. Gentleman what is the virtue in not just the duplication but the triplication of scientific procedures which would have resulted if the influence of the Langford institute had remained. I do not wish to dwell on the matter, so I will go on to the important issues facing the consumer. Consumers have not been mentioned much so far. I declare an interest in that I represent many food producers and many food consumers. I also represent the scientific researchers at the Centre for Applied Microbiology and Research at Porton Down.

Shopping is not just a chore. Perhaps the hon. Member for South Shields will accept the challenge to accompany me to seek out the freshest ingredients, the best value for money and the best food for health. If he came to my home in the Wiltshire countryside, which I would be delighted to put at his disposal, he would find that my chest freezer was empty, that the cupboards tended increasingly to be full of beans and that my garden was full of vegetables and rather too many weeds.

I suggest that we need to address ourselves more to the question of whether we, as consumers, are going down the right path. Is it virtuous to be told that more than 60 per cent. of all food is bought in supermarkets in some sort of processed form? Should we not seek instead to extol the virtues of food in season and the value of natural foods, and should we not look rather more seriously at organic farming?

I listened with interest to the hon. Member for Kirkcaldy (Dr. Moonie) and I am sorry that he has had to slip out temporarily. I was interested in and impressed by his comments. I should like to expand on one point that has been missed so far—the role of education of the consumer. It is a matter of health education, which is crucial, and also of good, old-fashioned domestic science, or home economics. I hope that it is taught to boys as well as girls, as all the best chefs in the world are men.

Another point raised was the future of the Centre for Applied Microbiology and Research. We cannot consider the issue before us today without looking at the institutions concerned. The decision to preserve the former microbiological research establishment at the Ministry of Defence was taken by Parliament in 1979 with the full agreement of all parties in the House. The Labour Government took that decision and the Conservative Opposition agreed with it. The management of the renamed Centre for Applied Microbiology and Research

—CAMR—was entrusted to the public health laboratory service and became funded on the health Vote. That point is crucial.

In 1985 CAMR's remit was to generate income. Agreements were signed between CAMR and Porton International and the public health laboratory service board covering the marketing of CAMR products and the building of a much-needed new fermentation pilot plant. The question of building a production centre was also raised, but I regret to say that that was something of a fiasco with severe design failures. That fiasco had nothing to do with either PHLS or CAMR. It was sub-contracted work. I hope that the Under-Secretary of State for Health, my hon. Friend the Member for Kettering (Mr. Freeman), can tell us what is happening about that as there is clearly a role for an expanded CAMR and, indeed, future employment in my constituency could be affected.

There have been many ministerial visits to CAMR in recent years, for which I am grateful. My noble Friend Lord Trefgarne came in 1982 and directed that CAMR should maximise its income generation and aim for economic self-sufficiency, which was the first new trend in research in that area. The second visit was made by my noble Friend Baroness Trumpington in 1987. She gave the centre a new remit. It was to have four corners to its work. The first related to public health laboratory service work, such as AIDS research; the second was work for the then Department of Health and Social Security, such as the development of new vaccines; the third, which has not yet been mentioned, was research for the Department of Trade and Industry into multi-company work; the fourth related to income generation, including money from marketing its scientific expertise.

The present position was outlined both last week and this week in articles in the *Financial Times*. There is much interest and speculation at the moment. It is widely believed that one option is the complete privatisation of CAMR. That would create considerable difficulties in the present contractural arrangements with Porton International in CAMR's other functions and commercial relationships, such as that with Wellcome, and in its remaining public health responsibilities.

There is also the unwelcome possibility that privatisation could close down the centre's work on AIDS and on food poisoning and lead to the destruction of its unique, important and successful European collection of animal cell cultures, as such things would not be attractive to private sector investment companies.

If we are looking for income generation, and since we are increasingly concerned about the destruction of tropical rain forests, not only because of their climatic importance but also because of the loss of genetic diversity, CAMR could be encouraged to set up a new forest cell culture centre which could be internationally self-financing. There could be a number of roles for CAMR in the future, but a key principle must be its ability to retain and develop its multiple relationships with United Kingdom companies, while in no way seeking to derogate from its contractual relationship with Porton International.

The organisation also has a strategic role which can never be divorced from the role of Government, especially in areas such as AIDS research and food poisoning research. One solution could be for the institution to be allowed to become a free-standing agency as part of the Government's review into all their research institutions.

[*Mr. Robert Key*]

As that is feasible, it is possible that CAMR could become financially self-supporting within about five years, so great is its income-generating potential.

Today was supposed to have seen a lobby of Parliament by scientists working in the National Health Service, but it was cancelled because some of their union colleagues decided to have a railway strike instead and the lobby has been rearranged for next month.

When talking about food research, we must remember that we are talking not about a few highly qualified specialist expert scientists but about whole teams including everyone from the scientist to the man in the boiler house. I should take this opportunity to point out that there are two completely separate organisations at Porton Down —the chemical defence establishment and the public health laboratory service, CAMR. There are 700 employees at Porton Down, the vast majority of whom provide support services to scientists. This country faces a demographic problem in relation to man and woman power in the coming years. There is a severe problem with the recruitment and retention of staff, especially at that scientific and technical level in the National Health Service.

Several scientists at Porton Down—and, indeed, representatives of other interests there—have drawn my attention to problems to which I draw the attention of Ministers. The first is the problem of retention and recruitment of younger scientific staff. It is caused by a combination of what I acknowledge is relatively low pay in those institutions and by the high price of housing. I can only conclude that the Whitley Council system of national pay bargaining is serving my constituents badly when the national averages are taken into account in determining pay. It would be very much in the interests of my constituents if an agency for local pay bargaining were established.

The second great difficulty—I suspect that it is faced by many similar institutions throughout the country—is that the people who are employed directly by the National Health Service at CAMR often carry out identical jobs or jobs with nearly identical specifications and requiring identical qualifications, but receive lower pay rates than those employed at Porton International, for example. That means that some people working in the same institution, doing almost the same jobs, receive lower rates of pay. On the other side of the road, scientists who do the same or similar jobs for the Ministry of Defence are on different rates of pay because they are not NHS staff but are civil servants. Furthermore, even within that establishment there are differential pay rates between Army personnel and civil servants. All those differences exist on the one site and present an increasing problem.

Porton Down CAMR is dealing with the important fight against infectious diseases. Salmonella has already been mentioned, but there are also legionella, botulism, bovine spongiform encephalopathy and AIDS.

I should like my hon. Friends to spare a thought for the small poultry producers in my constituency who produce eggs from flocks of just over 25 birds. At the moment— rather ludicrously—Ministry vets are rushing around the country sticking swabs up chickens' backsides to see whether there is any salmonella infection. However, severe doubt has been cast on that test because it is possible for poultry to lay eggs that are infected but for the infection not to show up on a test of the bird, and it is also possible for the reverse to happen and for an egg to be uninfected when the bird is not free from infection. That discrepancy has never been denied by the Government. They have always been completely honest and have said that internationally no test is foolproof. They are right. However, is it worth all the hassle if our small poultry producers have to face the possibility that if infection is discovered their flock will be destroyed and they will be compensated at only one third or one half the market replacement value of their flocks?

In conclusion, it would be to the advantage of the work force at CAMR, which is crucial to food safety in this country because it was there that scientists discovered the source of the hazelnut yoghurt infection within just three hours, if consideration were given to its future within the whole equation of food safety in this country.

5.59 pm

**Mr. Frank Cook** (Stockton, North): The Minister took 41 minutes to respond to the robust and probing opening speech of my hon. Friend the Member for South Shields (Dr. Clark). He devoted 25 minutes to a ministerial statement that should have been made in Government time. I shall not be churlish about that because I was pleased to hear it at long last. We have waited long enough for it. He made one or two challenges that I will answer quickly because many of my colleagues want to speak, despite some of the delaying tactics on the Government Benches.

The Minister referred to early-day motion 950 in my name. I want to alert the House to the fact that after I tabled the motion I did an interview with Central Television. That interview was cut, as interviews are. Part of a leading statement by Central Television last week was that I had said that irradiation could cause illness—I will not quibble with that—and even kill. I have never said that about food irradiation and I never would, because it could not be substantiated. What I said was that there is a huge question mark over the technique and its application.

I hope to outline briefly the nature of that question mark. It is not only I who say that, but the Consumers in the European Community Group which, as the House should know, is made up of 29 voluntary and professional organisations in the United Kingdom, with an interest in the impact of European Community legislation on the British consumer. Irradiation is also opposed by the Retail Consortium, by the Institution of Environmental Health Officers and by the Institute of Trading Standards Administration. So it is not a light-weight reservation that we seek to put on the record.

I want to tackle some of the challenges made by the Minister when he referred to the early-day motion. I am surprised that the Minister should make such efforts to challenge my hon. Friend the Member for South Shields about the nature of an early-day motion that refers to a practice that the Minister seeks to legalise. It is topsy turvy that he should expend so much energy on it.

The Minister asked for evidence. The evidence will be made available. I have always found the Minister to be most candid and I have paid tribute to him on more than one occasion. I have found the Under-Secretary of State for Health, who is to reply to the debate, to be the same, so I expect similar treatment from him.

The investigations that lay behind the early-day motion were set up by people working for a national newspaper. They established a dummy company to import consignments of food that had previously been irradiated —in other words, in contravention of existing legislation. I note that the Minister did not challenge early-day motions 713, 714 and 715 which were tabled in 1986 when we supplied documentary evidence that proved conclusively what was happening, but no action was taken. Further copies of that evidence are available. That explains our lack of confidence in Government action this time.

As I said, a national newspaper set up a dummy company. Contacts were made with Gammaster BV and Hank de Bruijne. Gammaster BV provided the information that Allways Transport could get the consignments into this country and distribute them wherever they were needed, without fail. Not only did the company do that, but it undertook to give a guarantee of bona fides to Allways Transport. In other words, it was prepared to say that the dealer was a good Indian who was not likely to sprag the game or squeal on the practice.

Hank de Bruijne went further. The daughter of the proprietor said that not only would there be no problem with the consignment but that if the intended trader was worried about discovery by port health authorities because the load was too clean bacterially the company had the answer. Instead of giving the consignment the full dose of irradiation, it would apply only a partial dose, irradiating to only 2 kilogray, thereby killing only some bacteria and leaving some creeping and crawling so that the port authorities would be put off the scent, if scent there was to be—an unfortunate phrase in the context.

I doubt whether people will derive any confidence from the controls that the Minister proposed. If we are to be confronted with traders who are likely to adopt practices and subterfuges such as I have outlined, what confidence can we ask the British consumer to have in the measures that the Government propose? In any case, what good will the Government measures do? Everyone agrees that irradiation will kill some bacteria, but I was pleased to hear the Ministr say that it is not a panacea. He said that three times. I hope that he keeps on saying it. It is far from being a panacea. It cannot be used in isolation. The Minister also said that irradiation would not make bad food good. That is right. But it stops bad food from looking and smelling bad. That is the main point that we should emphasise.

I am trying to rush through many points and it is proving difficult. The bacteria that is removed by irradiation will not affect clostridium botulinum because it is not susceptible to irradiation. It is a spore-borne organism which thrives better out of oxygen. That is why the American authorities will not allow irradiation of vacuum-packed meat; that would be the perfect environment for clostridium botulinum. The Minister earlier, and the Secretary of State in his statement on botulism last week, claimed that we have a better resistance to botulism and that the incidence of botulism in other countries is higher.

The Government are trying to claim credit, but I put this riddle to them. If consignments of food are irradiated, the yeasts and moulds that are in competition with clostridium botulinum are killed and clostridium botulinum is allowed free rein to develop even more virulently. There will be more vigorous toxins which may increase the incidence of botulism. The Government cannot have it both ways. They cannot claim better health because of the low incidence of botulism and at the same time seek to introduce a technique which, if used freely, could give botulism free rein.

Consumers want healthy, wholesome food that is produced, prepared, stored, distributed and retailed in healthy and hygienic conditions; there is no substitute for that.

**Mr. Andy Stewart** (Sherwood): That is what they get.

**Mr. Cook:** The hon. Gentleman says that that is what they get. The evidence indicates that that is not what they have been getting. My hon. Friend the Member for Carlisle (Mr. Martlew) has already made an effective point about catering establishments.

My point is that the consumer has a right—not a choice —to expect healthy and wholesome food. Choice is determined by the amount of money in the pocket and the wherewithal. It is all well and good for Government Ministers to tell us that we can go out and buy the food that we want, but they cannot say that to a person living on social security who has a limited income. It is strange that we should be prepared to invoke penalty on social security miscreants when we are not prepared to invoke penalty on people who have transgressed against the rules of food irradiation.

**Dame Elaine Kellett-Bowman:** Pesticide advertisements.

**Mr. Cook:** I am pleased that the hon. Lady has returned to the Chamber in a state of consciousness.

Choice is not an answer to hygienic standards.

I made some points in a letter to the solicitors who are seeking to have a go at me on the basis of the early-day motion, and perhaps this is the right note on which to finish. I said in that letter:

"I note too your unequivocal assertion that your 'clients have never imported or sold any product which has been subjected to the irradiation process'.

Given that there is no reliable method devised as yet to determine whether or not food has been irradiated prior to examination might I counsel the use of the word 'knowingly' after 'never' in any further statements.

One must assume from the content and tone of your letter that"

—until contacted by the reporter—

"your clients were completely ignorant of the practices identified in my EDM. Is this so?

Had you known of them what would have been your reaction?

You will have noted from my interview with Central Television that I act not only for the benefit of the consumer but also at the behest of parties interested in the British food industry who are anxious to ensure that those trading in that sector employ routinely the same proper and effective standards of hygiene as they do themselves in the production, preparation, distribution and retail of healthy and wholesome food for the consumer both in the UK and abroad.

I'm sure that if you . . . feel as concerned for these ends as you are for the standing of . . . in the eyes of the consumer, . . . you will join with me in pursuing energetically measures to eradicate totally such abuse at the earliest date."

If we expect the consumer to choose between irradiated and non-irradiated food, we must at the same time give them a good reason for irradiating it—not the end result but the need for irradiating food in the first place—because at the moment for me there is none.

6.11 pm

**Mr. Christopher Gill** (Ludlow): I support the Government's amendment. My right hon. Friend the Minister has outlined the very positive, professional and responsible aspects of this Government's policy in relation to food safety, which is in sharp contrast to the sparseness of the Opposition policy, as expounded by the hon. Member for South Shields (Dr. Clark). The hon. Gentleman spoke about oysters, and I for one found very few pearls in the oysters to which he referred. Regardless of the language and the country of origin, I must tell the hon. Gentleman that there is no known method of salvaging rotten food, nor of making that food good. It is mischievous and irresponsible of him to suggest otherwise.

Having worked in the food industry for about 30 years, perhaps I should declare an interest. That interest is the same interest that everyone working in the food industry would declare, which is in seeing safe food products of a consistent quality provided for the consuming public. If we do not provide safe consistent products, we will go out of business.

My right hon. Friend referred to the rapid changes in consumer habits. Over the 30 years in which I have been involved in the industry, we have seen food—far from being the major purchase that it once was—relegated to a fairly insignificant part of the family budget. Meals and meal times are also less structured than they were years ago. Above all, 30 years ago ingredients were almost exclusively fresh. Food was prepared in a domestic kitchen, cooked immediately prior to consumption, and eaten at regular times; but that is no longer the case.

First, the food that we eat is no longer fresh; it might be frozen, dehydrated or cooked and chilled. Secondly, less and less food is prepared in a domestic kitchen. More and more of the demand is for convenience food of which there is little or no preparation at home. There has been a dramatic increase in eating out, where the restaurateur or caterer does the preparation and the cooking. All that is quite predictable, having regard to the greater number of housewives and mothers who go out to work, and, indeed, the greater prosperity that people enjoy as a result of 10 years of Conservative government. At this stage I pay tribute to the great British food industry, which has risen to the challenge of satisfying the modern demand for a greater diversity of interesting, wholesome, nutritious, affordable and convenient food.

Thirdly, meals are no longer necessarily cooked immediately prior to consumption. The advent of the microwave and the concept of cook-chill meals means that the cooking process is often remote from the domestic situation. It is remote both in time and place, in the sense that the cooking process has probably taken place in a factory many days or even weeks in advance of consumption.

Fourthly, the notion that meals are taken at regular times is a thing of the past; so too, regrettably, is the notion that meal times are a significant family occasion. We have become a nation of browsers. We eat irregularly in a completely unstructured manner and we eat whatever appeals to us at the time.

As a consequence of those habits—this is the point I wish to underline—we as a nation have a reduced knowledge of buying, preparing, cooking and presenting food. As a nation, we have less understanding of the properties of food, the nutritional values and, specifically, as far as it relates to fresh food, the keeping qualities of food. We have a less than satisfactory understanding of the importance of good hygiene. Indeed, the confidence of consumers in their own ability is so depreciated that in a recent National Consumer Council poll more than half of those interviewed thought that the Government, health education authorities and manufacturers should be "doing the most to provide clear advice and information to consumers on Food Safety."

Never once, for example, was it mentioned that mothers would be the most important influence in guiding families in how they should produce food for their offspring.

The question is what, if anything, those three groups of people, who have been identified in the National Consumer Council poll, should be doing to redress that situation and, especially, what could and what should the Government be doing. There is always a danger—certainly the Opposition would lead us down this dangerous path—of trying to do too much. There is a danger, as a result of trying to do too much, that we will dilute the responsibility of the consumer. There is a danger, too, of being too prescriptive in our legislation. That holds the hazard of stultifying one of the United Kingdom's most successful and innovative industries and, directly following from that, restricting consumer choice and variety.

What should we do? My right hon. Friend the Minister reminded us of the need at all times for constant vigilance —and there is no gainsaying that at all. We must take swift and effective action wherever problems manifest themselves. I fully endorse the Government's policy that we must act only on the basis of the best scientific information available at the time. We must uphold the law which at the moment states that all food should be safe and that all consumers should not be misled. I for one would be happy at the prospect of the Government and the enforcing authorities throwing the book at those who offend those laws. We should continue to publish and disseminate straightforward, simple-to-read common-sense advice to consumers, and I commend to the House the recent booklet on food safety which satisfies all those criteria in good measure.

The hon. Member for Kirkcaldy (Dr. Moonie), who is no longer in his place, spoke about diet, but we should beware the false prophets. A diet industry is becoming prominent which says that some food is good and other food bad. But there is no such thing as bad food, only a bad diet. A good diet is a balanced and varied one. In the words of the old maxim, one might say moderation in all things.

I know that moderation does not always appeal to Opposition Members, but let me leave them with this thought. If, in their estimation, so many things are wrong in Britain today, why do we have a higher proportion of old people than any other country bar one? As they know, as I know and as the Minister knows, it is the old and the young who are most at risk from food poisoning. There cannot be anything terribly wrong with the British diet when so many live to such a ripe old age.

6.20 pm

**Mrs. Ann Clwyd** (Cynon Valley): The Secretary of State said that the Government act quickly to ensure that people eat safe food, but I hope to explode that myth. I have plenty of evidence to show that the Government do not act quickly and that their approach to the problem of food safety is cavalier and irresponsible, particularly on the safety of airline passengers, and, in the next few months, there will be hundreds of those as the holiday traffic increases. It is utterly disgraceful that the Government have not addressed that problem.

In February 1989, the three local authorities responsible for environmental health standards at Heathrow completed a report on airline food safety. They discovered that excessive levels of potentially dangerous bacteria have been found in nearly a quarter of all the meals tested at Heathrow airport—a quarter of the meals on the ground, before they even reach the aircraft.

Only last weekend it was reported that

"air travellers are being exposed to the risk of a 'disastrous outbreak of food poisoning' because of long flight delays and poor hygiene."

The Institution of Environmental Health Officers was reported as saying that

"lack of hygiene training among cabin crew, combined with the rapid increase of bacteria during flight delays, poses a serious threat to passengers' health. It demands new powers to monitor the safety of food on aircraft, which escape controls because the food is given away."

The Under-Secretary of State for Health, the hon. Member for Kettering (Mr. Freeman), was reported as saying that

"he would review regulations in the light of the report."

He said:

"I am looking forward to being briefed further on this to see what can or should be done."

I want to illustrate how, despite having a report from the environmental health officers responsible for environmental health at Heathrow, the Government have ignored those reports and have refused to take any action.

More than 1,000 separate foods were examined by environmental health officers at Heathrow who found some of the worst contamination in paté, appetisers, main courses of beef and rice puddings. The tests were conducted by the airport's local boroughs on freshly made meals which had not even reached the aircraft. By the time that the meals reached passengers, bacteria levels would often be much higher because of poor temperature control.

Most of the foods were prepared by the cook-chill method, which has been implicated in many of the recent cases of food poisoning, but those particular foods were not tested for listeria, which was not looked on as a problem when the tests were carried out. The three London boroughs are beginning a second survey to try to determine whether listeria is present.

Of the foods tested, 24 per cent. harboured 1 million bacteria per gramme—100 times more than the maximum recommended by the Department of Health. E. Coli, the bacteria associated with faecal contamination, was found in 209 separate dishes and salmonella was found in four dishes tested by the environmental health officers.

In case hon. Members think that those are isolated cases, the reported outbreaks of food-borne infections over several years have involved large numbers of people. On one flight from Tokyo to Paris 197 people were affected. On 11 charter flights from Las Palmas, 550 people were affected. In one year on several flights from London 766 people were affected, and on another flight 304 people were affected. This is not a small problem. It is a large problem at the moment and a potentially large problem in the future.

**Mr. Elliot Morley** (Glanford and Scunthorpe): I listened carefully to the figures that my hon. Friend gave of the number of people affected. An outbreak of salmonella in my constituency resulted last week in the tragic death of Benjamin Walker, aged two. One of his friends, also aged two, is currently in hospital, and a third child of the same age from an adjoining village has recently been hospitalised. That is the human face of the tragedy behind those figures.

I have heard much talk of responsibility during the debate, but does my hon. Friend agree that it is not responsible for the Government to cut research programmes into salmonella, including the one led by Dr. Meade in Bristol dealing with eradication programmes? That cut was heavily criticised by the Select Committee's report into salmonella, the members of which were unanimous that the Government should undertake more research into salmonella. The Government cannot be held responsible for that child's death, but a Government who do not face up to their responsibilities to undertake such research will have the deaths of other children and people on their hands.

**Mrs. Clwyd:** I agree with my hon. Friend. It is irresponsible to cut research when, over the past few months, it has been clearly shown that the number of food poisoning cases in Britain is growing rather than decreasing. I thank my hon. Friend for his intervention.

Let me return to the Secretary of State's claim that the Government act quickly. In March, the three environmental health officers responsible for Heathrow sent the Secretary of State for Health a copy of their report. In April, I asked him whether he would make a statement and he said:

"I have just received a copy of the report and I will give it due consideration."—[*Official Report*, 6 April 1989; Vol. 150, c. 290.]

In May, I asked the same question and the Under-Secretary of State said:

"We have recently received a copy of the survey . . . It is still receiving careful consideration within the Department."—[*Official Report*, 2 May 1989; Vol. 152, c. 100.]

In June I asked the same question, and the Under-Secretary of State said:

"I shall let the hon. Member have a reply as soon as possible."

One would think that the Government were studying a massive report, but in fact it is slim and its recommendations are clear. I should not have thought that this urgent problem needed four months' consideration before the Government could make a statement on what they intended to do about it.

Not only that, but as long ago as 1986, at the second world congress of food-borne infections in Berlin, the Government's central public health laboratory service said that the provision of meals on aircraft, particularly on those travelling long distances, posed many food hygiene problems, and that outbreaks of food-borne infections had been reported associated with in-flight meals and had involved a wide range of organisms, including salmonella. It reported the results of that survey at some length. As long ago as that, the Government's own agency had the necessary information, yet the Government refused to take any action.

Heathrow environmental health officers are concerned about the present situation and its potential. The hundreds of thousands of people using Heathrow and other airports throughout Britain are entitled to Government protection. The health officers produced clear reports and suggestions.

[*Mrs. Clwyd*]

They argue that the aviation catering industry ought to adopt a common standard for meal production, which should be the guidelines on pre-cooked and chilled foods published by the Department of Health in 1980. The Department has since issued new guidelines, but how will it compel caterers to observe them? That should not be the responsibility of EHOs, who are already hard pressed.

Heathrow health officers also published a long list of deviations from the required standards. Guideline 2e, for example, states:

"Reheating of the food to be done immediately upon removal from chilled conditions and raised to at least 70°C."

The report comments:

"This raises the question as to whether the food is still in a chilled condition on the aircraft as this depends upon the time of leaving the catering unit, ambient temperature, the length of the flight, any delays . . . There appear to be no international checks on these matters."

Guideline 2g states:

"+10°C is regarded as the critical safety limit for chilled foods."

According to health officers,

"Temperature variances with or without botulism during production, storage and delivery are tremendous."

Recommendation 4 is:

"All raw materials to be of good quality."

The Minister himself stressed the importance of quality control. The deviation noted by health inspectors was:

"Most caterers check out their suppliers, but the degree to which this is done varies enormously. On occasions this is not done at all."

Can the Minister say how the Government will make their new guidelines stick better than the old?

Environmental health officers would like a reply to their report, which the Government have taken so long to consider. The hundreds of thousands of airline passengers who believe that the food they eat is safe should either be advised that fears to the contrary are groundless or that they should take sandwiches for the time being. When the Minister winds up, I hope that he will address himself to the problem of ensuring airline food safety.

6.32 pm

**Mr. Robin Cook** (Livingston): I am glad to follow my hon. Friend the Member for Cynon Valley (Mrs. Clwyd) in her concern about the health hazards posed by airline meals. I have some interest in that subject, as on average I eat two airline meals per week while travelling to and from my constituency. The report to which my hon. Friend drew attention is particularly interesting and provides striking evidence that even in a catering establishment which might be regarded as up-market there is no guarantee that it is free of the health hazards that frequently exist in the food that we buy and eat.

My hon. Friend the Member for Kirkcaldy (Dr. Moonie) made a thoughtful and considered speech, as one would expect of one with his background as a community physician. My hon. Friend the Member for Carlisle (Mr. Martlew) made a forceful case for exploring the Government's contradictory attitudes to green-top milk. As to his observation concerning the Government's reversal on that issue, I was struck by the report that the Government backed down on green-top milk after receiving 1,200 objections. We understand from a written answer that the Department of Agriculture, Fisheries and Food received 6,000 objections to food irradiation.

Unfortunately, it seems that that number of objections —five times the number received in respect of green-top milk—is somehow not so conclusive.

My hon. Friend the Member for Stockton, North (Mr. Cook) fluently put a well-informed case for not regarding food irradiation as a total solution and pointed to the paradox that at this moment irradiation is being offered as a solution when the particular incidence of food poisoning that we currently have in mind was caused by botulism, to which irradiation is almost irrelevant. In so far as it is relevant, it is in the sense that irradiation may contribute to an environment in which the botulinum bacterium will thrive.

The first comment that I have to make is, very sadly, that I understand that during the course of the debate one of the 26 victims of the botulism outbreak in the north-west has died. It is perhaps regrettable that the Secretary of State referred to that outbreak as being one of only nine this century. That may be so, but as many people were affected by the latest outbreak as by all the previous eight outbreaks put together. That is the gravity of the latest occurrence. We must now try to grapple with the serious problem of combating food health hazards.

Throughout the debate there has been a division between Government and Opposition Members. While my right hon. and hon. Friends and I are undoubtedly exercised by the threat, having listened to most of the speeches made by Conservative Members I am not persuaded that they are seized with the gravity of the crisis.

The first step to finding a solution is to admit that a problem exists. The Government's own figures should alarm them. Formal notifications of food poisoning rose from 10,000 in 1978 to more than 20,000 in 1987. Even more alarming than that doubling of cases in a decade is that since 1987 notifications have doubled again. In the first five months of 1989 there were 16,700 recorded cases, giving an annualised rate of more than 40,000.

Fortunately, we have a way of expressing the cost to society of food poisoning in terms that Conservative Members should find easy to grasp. Bradford university's food policy unit conducted a study which concluded that productivity losses from food poisoning cost employers £350 million and that twice as many working days are lost by it as through strikes. The Government's most visible response to date is a consumer leaflet of which we were informed in February. After being briefed by the Government, the press faithfully reported that the Government want housewives to "cook just like mother". The problem is that the Government are still trying to control the food industry with the same regulations that were around at the time when mother went shopping.

Food hygiene regulations for shops effectively date from 1938, although they have been much consolidated. It is breathtaking that while a revolution in food retailing has taken place, with the conversion to open display and self-service, there are no regulations covering the temperature at which such food is stored. We know that the Department of Health is uneasy about that because it produced a consultative document on food hygiene, the background note to which comments:

"In recent years there has been increasing criticism of the absence of regulations on the temperature control of food in retail shops."

The background notes containing that sentence and the consultative document itself were published on 22 June 1987—two years ago tomorrow—but nothing has been heard since. No regulations have been laid before the House in those two years, during which there have been 73,000 recorded cases of food poisoning.

Last February, weary of waiting for the Government to produce regulations, we drafted our own regulations on food hygiene. The response of the Secretary of State at the time was that he was "on the point" of introducing regulations. That was on 15 February. Four months later, the Secretary of State is still ambling around the point, although I was advised in a parliamentary answer received this afternoon that I shall now have to wait at least another four months until the autumn for any draft regulations from the Government.

Instead, the Government have issued a leaflet to shoppers providing advice on what they should do with products after buying them. It seemed reasonable, therefore, to test how shops themselves followed the advice offered to the consumer. One of the key pieces of advice in the leaflet is

"Make sure the fridge is cold enough—and stays below 5 deg C. . . . buy a fridge thermometer to check."

Yesterday I carried out a survey of shops in north London. They were not major supermarkets, but they were not corner shops either—some were parts of local and regional chains or mini-markets. The results of the temperature tests were appalling. Of the seven shops that we inspected, only one was displaying food at less than 10 deg C. One offered tuna paté at 19 deg and was selling chicken pieces at the same temperature. In another the meat pie freezer was running at a temperature of 17·5 deg. In a third, sausages were on sale at 24 deg and ham at 15 deg.

As my hon. Friend the Member for Cynon Valley observed, the most remarkable feature of such tales is that none of the premises is committing an offence or breaking existing regulations, although, in microbiological terms, the temperatures at which the food is offered for sale are hair-raising. There is no point in spending £750,000 on beautifully drawn leaflets advising consumers to store food at temperatures below 5 deg C. if the food bought from the shop is not safe to be put in the fridge, let alone eaten.

There are obvious ways in which the Government could regulate the food industry to provide the consumer with more confidence and safety. Instead, this afternoon we have heard them reach once again for the technical fix—in this case, irradiation. It is extraordinary that the Secretary of State should announce that he is introducing that measure to respond to consumer demand for choice when every opinion poll confirms that consumers do not want their food irradiated. The most recent poll carried out by Marplan found 83 per cent. against it.

Moreover, the irradiation proposal is wildly irrelevant to the problem. Irradiation cannot be applied to fatty foods, because it turns them rancid. It cannot be applied to eggs, although they have been the single most obvious source of concern to the public. Nor can it be applied to yoghurt—if it is, the result is a taste defined by the experts as that of burnt wool. If it is applied to meat of the kind that I found being stored at such high temperatures, the taste is described by the experts as "wet dog smell". It is true that it can be applied to hazelnut purée, but that will not stop botulism—it may destroy the bacteria, but it will not destroy the toxin which causes food poisoning.

The most profound reason to oppose irradiation, however, is that it does not deal with the root causes of the increased incidence of food poisoning. It does not offer a remedy for the results of intensified farming methods and the growing practice—which I, as a layman, find rather bizarre—of recycling one animal's waste as another animal's feedstock. Nor does it address the pressure from the food industry for a longer shelf life, although it is clearly intended as a response to that pressure. It does not address the problem of the varying standards of hygiene in food outlets which have resulted from the explosion in the number of vast fast food chains. It merely provides a technical fix which enables the Government to pretend that it is possible to go on living with all those trends when it is clearly not possible. Food poisoning will continue to increase until we bring in regulations which compel shops to apply the same standards that Ministers are urging on housewives.

We know why the Government dare not do that. It is no accident that they keep putting it off. It is not because the regulations have slipped their mind, or have been put in a file marked "mañana". It is because the present Prime Minister's ideology is flatly opposed to tighter regulations. In her influential intervention in last week's European elections, she denounced what she described as more regulations, more bureaucracy and more state intervention. One of the Ministers present today will have to pluck up courage to explain to the Prime Minister that if the consumer is to be protected adequately from being poisoned by the food on sale in the shops, more regulations will be required, along with more state intervention and—yes—perhaps even a touch more bureaucracy to ensure that the regulations are enforced. I know that it is demanding a good deal of Ministers to ask them to find the courage to storm Downing street with that message, but I offer them a spur, sharpened by the glorious results of last Thursday: if the present Government persist in their refusal to protect consumers, those consumers will increasingly look for a Government who will protect them.

6.45 pm

**The Parliamentary Under-Secretary of State for Health (Mr. Roger Freeman):** I shall answer as many questions as I can. If I cannot deal with all of them today, I shall write to hon. Members.

The Government's policy on food hygiene is to put the consumer first. Hon. Members on both sides of the House agree that the consumer's interests must be our main priority. The hon. Member for Livingston (Mr. Cook) began by referring to botulism, and I shall deal with that first. We have received no reports of any new cases this week; a total of 26 have been reported. I understand that six patients are still on ventilators, and that five are stable and improving. I join the hon. Gentleman in expressing my regret to the family of the 78-year-old lady who, sadly, died of complications this afternoon, and I am sure that the whole House will wish to join in my hope that the remaining patients will make a complete recovery.

My Department is continuing to co-ordinate exhaustive investigations into the outbreak of botulism, in close collaboration with the food industry. The lessons that may be learnt from that investigation will be directly relevant to our review of food legislation. Let me take this opportunity of congratulating all who work in the Health Service, the public health laboratory service, and local authorities which have contributed so magnificently to the investigation and control of the outbreak and the treatment of patients.

[*Mr. Roger Freeman*]

The country's excellent record for rapidly identifying and dealing with food poisoning outbreaks owes much to the work of the public health authority Service and its component bodies. In particular, their pioneering work on the detection and identification of the different kinds of salmonella have formed the scientific foundation that has made it possible for the Government to identify the nature of the problems and introduce the advice and measures necessary to combat the bacteria. The resources available through the laboratory service have increased significantly under the present Government, and this year alone will see a 14 per cent. cash increase. I believe that the service is probably the most efficient and effective of its kind in the world.

The hon. Gentleman went on to deal—by implication —with listeria. New cook-chill and cook-freeze guidelines for catering are to be published tomorrow, 22 June, and copies will be placed in the Library of the House. The guidelines sharpen and clarify existing advice. Copies are also being sent to all health authorities, which are being asked to review their operational procedures to ensure that they conform. We believe that all health authorities conform. We are drawing the publication to the attention of relevant trade organisations, and I hope that all who operate or propose to operate cook-chill or cook-freeze catering systems will follow the principles set out in the guidelines.

The hon. Gentleman referred to the review of the food hygiene regulations. The regulations are statutory, and we are proposing to issue, within two weeks, draft regulations for consultation with the industry and the public. That consultation will take some three months, and we expect to lay regulations before the House in the autumn. The regulations will deal with the temperature controls for food that is required to be kept chilled in the retail distribution system.

We propose to base the legislation on a stratified temperature regime, requiring a maximum of 5 deg C for products where the risk of the growth of pathogenic organisms is high, such as soft cheeses and ready-cooked products intended to be eaten without cooking or reheating, and a maximum of 8 deg C where, although it exists, the risk is lower. In both cases there may need to be a tolerance margin to allow for fluctuations over short periods—for example, during the defrost cycles. We shall need to allow a reasonably brief implementation period to give industry time to re-equip as necessary to meet the new temperature controls. I commend this firm action by the Government as evidence of our determination to protect the consumer, with the co-operation of the food manufacturer, preparer and distributor.

**Mr. Andrew Bowden** (Brighton, Kemptown): Will my hon. Friend confirm that when the regulations come into force environmental health officers will have the power to enter shops and ensure that the regulations are being fully implemented?

**Mr. Freeman:** I can give my hon. Friend that assurance.

Perhaps I may now deal briefly with the points raised by several of my hon. Friends about environmental health officers.

**Ms. Primarolo:** Will the Minister give way?

**Mr. Freeman:** Perhaps I might just explain to the House that, together with the Ministry of Agriculture, Fisheries and Food, my Department is consulting local authorities, which are responsible for recruiting and controlling environmental health officers, about a review of whether their staffing is satisfactory, both now and prospectively, for the changes that are to come.

The hon. Member for Kirkcaldy (Dr. Moonie) referred to a number of matters. I recognise the importance of the gene banks at Brogdale to which he referred. We are taking steps to protect those resources.

My hon. Friend the Member for Weston-super-Mare (Mr. Wiggin), whose important position as Chairman of the Select Committee I respect and understand, asked a number of questions about Bristol, as did a number of hon. Members. We are hoping to transfer not six but 70 posts in food research from Bristol to the other two locations. My right hon. Friend the Minister of Agriculture, Fisheries and Food will write to my hon. Friend the Member for Weston-super-Mare in some detail about Bristol.

My hon. Friend also asked me about current arrangements which he thinks are unfair to United Kingdom producers, who are required to meet the cost of rigorous control measures that do not apply to competing importers. It is a very important subject. Our primary and overriding concern must be to protect the consumer against the risk of infection. Over 97 per cent. of the eggs consumed in the United Kingdom are from domestic production.

The most essential point must, therefore, be to ensure that effective measures are taken at every point in the chain from farmer to consumer. That is what we have done. We cannot just ban imports from other member states, as some people have simplistically assumed. We do not have the power to do so. However, my right hon. Friend the Minister of Agriculture, Fisheries and Food is tackling any possible risk from imports on two fronts. First, we are systematically sampling imports of eggs and testing them for salmonella infection. We shall take up with the member state concerned any case which is found of contamination with salmonella enteritidis. My right hon. Friend has already done so, on the one occasion that we found an infected sample.

Secondly—this is most important—we are working towards the establishment of effective controls at the point of production in other member states. That is the fundamental safeguard for the medium and longer term, but it can be achieved only by agreement on a Community-wide basis, which inevitably takes time.

The hon. Member for Southport (Mr. Fearn) asked me about sell-by dates. The Government intend to phase out sell-by dates and to replace them with the use of use-by dates which will be compulsory for highly perishable foods. I hope that the House will welcome the change.

My hon. Friend the Member for Daventry (Mr. Boswell) asked about environmental health officers. I hope that I have already answered his question, but I shall write to him in greater detail.

The hon. Member for Carlisle (Mr. Martlew) asked about green-top milk. I hope that the House will accept and welcome the Government's decision to permit the sale of green-top milk. That is clearly in accord with the wishes of consumers, but we shall ensure that the milk is properly labelled so that the risks, such as they are, are properly understood.

My hon. Friend the Member for Salisbury (Mr. Key) asked me a detailed question about the Centre for Applied Microbiology and Research. I shall write to him, but may I say to him now that we shall ensure that essential public health and food safety work continues, under Government control. As to the management of the control of the centre, we are still reviewing what to do, but the important point is that we want the centre to continue and to prosper.

The hon. Member for Stockton, North (Mr. Cook) asked about food irradiation and made an interesting contribution, but may I correct him about a point that he made when he intervened during the speech of my right hon. Friend the Minister of Agriculture, Fisheries and Food. Food irradiation is used and has been used within the National Health Service.

**Mr. Frank Cook:** Has been.

**Mr. Freeman:** No. It is being used tonight at the Royal Marsden hospital. Food irradiation makes safe the food that is prepared for patients who are at particular risk.

**Mr. Robert Hughes** (Aberdeen, North): Will the Minister give way?

**Mr. Freeman:** No. I have only four minutes left.

The hon. Member for Cynon Valley (Mrs. Clwyd) asked about airline meals. There are two aspects to her question. I share her concern, and that of other hon. Members, about airline meals. First, are the existing regulations being complied with? We have a range of regulations covering aircraft on the ground and in United Kingdom air space. We expect aircraft flying in international air space to follow the code of practice of the International Air Transport Association. I should be very pleased to meet the hon. Lady and her colleagues, and also environmental health officers, to pursue further her concerns, which I share.

The hon. Member for South Shields (Dr. Clark) opened the debate. His thesis was that changes in food research have led to an increase in food poisoning. There are three reasons why his thesis is false. It deserves good marks for effort but very low marks for logic.

First, food research in this country has not been curtailed. It is running now at twice the level, in real terms, as in 1978-79—at £26 million. We have an excellent record on food research. The difference between the Government and the hon. Gentleman is that we do not share his prejudice towards the near market research that is conducted by the private sector.

Secondly, food poisoning and the increase, which I concede, in the last two years in food poisoning is not unique to the United Kingdom. It is a common factor— *[Interruption.]* The hon. Member for Stockton, North may laugh, but it is common to the countries of western Europe and to the United States. What is unique about this Government is the series of tough measures that my right hon. Friend the Minister of Agriculture, Fisheries and Food has taken to eradicate salmonella.

**Mr. Robert Hughes** *rose——*

**Mr. Freeman:** Thirdly, and finally, the hon. Member for South Shields attempted to draw a conclusion from the change in research into botulism at Bristol and the recent incident. There is absolutely no connection between the

two. The recent outbreak of botulism was due to the lack of heat treatment by the food processor. It had nothing whatsoever to do with research at Bristol.

The Government have taken firm action as regards food safety and food research. I am grateful to my hon. Friend the Member for Ludlow (Mr. Gill) for recognising that. We have set up the Richmond committee, and we have agreed to review food legislation and that review is well in hand. We have an excellent public health laboratory service which is the envy of the world, and we have increased resources for research. We are working in partnership with the private sector.

I urge the House to support the Government amendment and to throw out the Opposition motion.

*Question put,* That the original words stand part of the Question:—

The House divided: Ayes 211, Noes 318.

Division No. 256]    [6.59 pm

**AYES**

| | |
|---|---|
| Abbott, Ms Diane | Dixon, Don |
| Adams, Allen *(Paisley N)* | Dobson, Frank |
| Allen, Graham | Doran, Frank |
| Alton, David | Douglas, Dick |
| Anderson, Donald | Duffy, A. E. P. |
| Archer, Rt Hon Peter | Eadie, Alexander |
| Armstrong, Hilary | Eastham, Ken |
| Ashdown, Rt Hon Paddy | Fatchett, Derek |
| Ashley, Rt Hon Jack | Fearn, Ronald |
| Banks, Tony *(Newham NW)* | Field, Frank *(Birkenhead)* |
| Barnes, Harry *(Derbyshire NE)* | Fields, Terry *(L'pool B G'n)* |
| Barnes, Mrs Rosie *(Greenwich)* | Fisher, Mark |
| Battle, John | Flannery, Martin |
| Beckett, Margaret | Flynn, Paul |
| Beggs, Roy | Foot, Rt Hon Michael |
| Beith, A. J. | Foster, Derek |
| Bell, Stuart | Foulkes, George |
| Benn, Rt Hon Tony | Fraser, John |
| Bennett, A. F. *(D'nt'n & R'dish)* | Galbraith, Sam |
| Bidwell, Sydney | Galloway, George |
| Blair, Tony | Garrett, John *(Norwich South)* |
| Blunkett, David | Garrett, Ted *(Wallsend)* |
| Boateng, Paul | George, Bruce |
| Boyes, Roland | Gilbert, Rt Hon Dr John |
| Bradley, Keith | Godman, Dr Norman A. |
| Brown, Gordon *(D'mline E)* | Golding, Mrs Llin |
| Brown, Nicholas *(Newcastle E)* | Gordon, Mildred |
| Brown, Ron *(Edinburgh Leith)* | Gould, Bryan |
| Bruce, Malcolm *(Gordon)* | Graham, Thomas |
| Buckley, George J. | Grant, Bernie *(Tottenham)* |
| Callaghan, Jim | Griffiths, Win *(Bridgend)* |
| Campbell, Menzies *(Fife NE)* | Grocott, Bruce |
| Campbell-Savours, D. N. | Harman, Ms Harriet |
| Cartwright, John | Hattersley, Rt Hon Roy |
| Clark, Dr David *(S Shields)* | Healey, Rt Hon Denis |
| Clarke, Tom *(Monklands W)* | Heffer, Eric S. |
| Clay, Bob | Henderson, Doug |
| Clelland, David | Hinchliffe, David |
| Clwyd, Mrs Ann | Hoey, Ms Kate *(Vauxhall)* |
| Cohen, Harry | Hogg, N. *(C'nauld & Kilsyth)* |
| Cook, Frank *(Stockton N)* | Home Robertson, John |
| Cook, Robin *(Livingston)* | Hood, Jimmy |
| Corbett, Robin | Howarth, G. *(Cannock & B'wd)* |
| Corbyn, Jeremy | Howells, Geraint |
| Cousins, Jim | Howells, Dr. Kim *(Pontypridd)* |
| Crowther, Stan | Hoyle, Doug |
| Cryer, Bob | Hughes, John *(Coventry NE)* |
| Cummings, John | Hughes, Robert *(Aberdeen N)* |
| Cunliffe, Lawrence | Hughes, Roy *(Newport E)* |
| Cunningham, Dr John | Illsley, Eric |
| Dalyell, Tam | Ingram, Adam |
| Darling, Alistair | Janner, Greville |
| Davies, Rt Hon Denzil *(Llanelli)* | Johnston, Sir Russell |
| Davies, Ron *(Caerphilly)* | Jones, Barry *(Alyn & Deeside)* |
| Davis, Terry *(B'ham Hodge H'l)* | Jones, Ieuan *(Ynys Môn)* |
| Dewar, Donald | Jones, Martyn *(Clwyd S W)* |

Kaufman, Rt Hon Gerald
Kennedy, Charles
Kirkwood, Archy
Leadbitter, Ted
Leighton, Ron
Lestor, Joan (Eccles)
Livingstone, Ken
Livsey, Richard
Lloyd, Tony (Stretford)
Lofthouse, Geoffrey
Loyden, Eddie
McAllion, John
McAvoy, Thomas
Macdonald, Calum A.
McFall, John
McKay, Allen (Barnsley West)
McKelvey, William
McLeish, Henry
Maclennan, Robert
McNamara, Kevin
McWilliam, John
Madden, Max
Mahon, Mrs Alice
Marek, Dr John
Marshall, David (Shettleston)
Martin, Michael J. (Springburn)
Martlew, Eric
Meale, Alan
Michael, Alun
Michie, Bill (Sheffield Heeley)
Michie, Mrs Ray (Arg'l & Bute)
Mitchell, Austin (G't Grimsby)
Moonie, Dr Lewis
Morgan, Rhodri
Morley, Elliott
Morris, Rt Hon A. (W'shawe)
Morris, Rt Hon J. (Aberavon)
Mowlam, Marjorie
Mullin, Chris
Murphy, Paul
Nellist, Dave
O'Brien, William
Orme, Rt Hon Stanley
Owen, Rt Hon Dr David
Patchett, Terry
Pendry, Tom
Pike, Peter L.
Powell, Ray (Ogmore)
Prescott, John
Primarolo, Dawn
Quin, Ms Joyce
Redmond, Martin

Rees, Rt Hon Merlyn
Richardson, Jo
Roberts, Allan (Bootle)
Robertson, George
Robinson, Geoffrey
Rooker, Jeff
Ross, Ernie (Dundee W)
Rowlands, Ted
Ruddock, Joan
Salmond, Alex
Sedgemore, Brian
Sheerman, Barry
Sheldon, Rt Hon Robert
Shore, Rt Hon Peter
Short, Clare
Skinner, Dennis
Smith, Andrew (Oxford E)
Smith, C. (Isl'ton & F'bury)
Smith, Rt Hon J. (Monk'ds E)
Smith, J. P. (Vale of Glam)
Snape, Peter
Spearing, Nigel
Steel, Rt Hon David
Steinberg, Gerry
Stott, Roger
Strang, Gavin
Straw, Jack
Taylor, Mrs Ann (Dewsbury)
Taylor, Rt Hon J. D. (S'ford)
Taylor, Matthew (Truro)
Thompson, Jack (Wansbeck)
Turner, Dennis
Wall, Pat
Wallace, James
Walley, Joan
Wardell, Gareth (Gower)
Wareing, Robert N.
Watson, Mike (Glasgow, C)
Welsh, Andrew (Angus E)
Welsh, Michael (Doncaster N)
Wigley, Dafydd
Williams, Rt Hon Alan
Williams, Alan W. (Carm'then)
Winnick, David
Wise, Mrs Audrey
Wray, Jimmy
Young, David (Bolton SE)

Tellers for the Ayes:
  Mr. Frank Haynes and
  Mr. Jimmy Dunnachie.

## NOES

Adley, Robert
Aitken, Jonathan
Alexander, Richard
Alison, Rt Hon Michael
Allason, Rupert
Amery, Rt Hon Julian
Amess, David
Amos, Alan
Arbuthnot, James
Arnold, Jacques (Gravesham)
Arnold, Tom (Hazel Grove)
Ashby, David
Aspinwall, Jack
Atkinson, David
Baker, Rt Hon K. (Mole Valley)
Baker, Nicholas (Dorset N)
Baldry, Tony
Banks, Robert (Harrogate)
Batiste, Spencer
Beaumont-Dark, Anthony
Bellingham, Henry
Bendall, Vivian
Bennett, Nicholas (Pembroke)
Benyon, W.
Bevan, David Gilroy
Biffen, Rt Hon John

Blackburn, Dr John G.
Body, Sir Richard
Bonsor, Sir Nicholas
Boswell, Tim
Bottomley, Peter
Bottomley, Mrs Virginia
Bowden, A (Brighton K'pto'n)
Bowden, Gerald (Dulwich)
Bowis, John
Boyson, Rt Hon Dr Sir Rhodes
Braine, Rt Hon Sir Bernard
Brandon-Bravo, Martin
Brazier, Julian
Bright, Graham
Brooke, Rt Hon Peter
Brown, Michael (Brigg & Cl't's)
Browne, John (Winchester)
Bruce, Ian (Dorset South)
Buchanan-Smith, Rt Hon Alick
Buck, Sir Antony
Budgen, Nicholas
Burns, Simon
Burt, Alistair
Butcher, John
Butler, Chris
Butterfill, John

Carlisle, John, (Luton N)
Carlisle, Kenneth (Lincoln)
Carrington, Matthew
Carttiss, Michael
Cash, William
Channon, Rt Hon Paul
Chapman, Sydney
Chope, Christopher
Churchill, Mr
Clark, Dr Michael (Rochford)
Clark, Sir W. (Croydon S)
Clarke, Rt Hon K. (Rushcliffe)
Colvin, Michael
Conway, Derek
Coombs, Anthony (Wyre F'rest)
Coombs, Simon (Swindon)
Cope, Rt Hon John
Cormack, Patrick
Couchman, James
Cran, James
Critchley, Julian
Currie, Mrs Edwina
Curry, David
Davies, Q. (Stamf'd & Spald'g)
Davis, David (Boothferry)
Day, Stephen
Devlin, Tim
Dicks, Terry
Dorrell, Stephen
Douglas-Hamilton, Lord James
Dover, Den
Dunn, Bob
Dykes, Hugh
Eggar, Tim
Emery, Sir Peter
Evans, David (Welwyn Hatf'd)
Evennett, David
Fairbairn, Sir Nicholas
Fallon, Michael
Favell, Tony
Field, Barry (Isle of Wight)
Fishburn, John Dudley
Forman, Nigel
Forsyth, Michael (Stirling)
Forth, Eric
Fowler, Rt Hon Norman
Fox, Sir Marcus
Franks, Cecil
Freeman, Roger
French, Douglas
Fry, Peter
Gardiner, George
Garel-Jones, Tristan
Gill, Christopher
Gilmour, Rt Hon Sir Ian
Glyn, Dr Alan
Goodhart, Sir Philip
Goodlad, Alastair
Goodson-Wickes, Dr Charles
Gorman, Mrs Teresa
Gorst, John
Gow, Ian
Grant, Sir Anthony (CambsSW)
Greenway, Harry (Ealing N)
Gregory, Conal
Griffiths, Peter (Portsmouth N)
Grist, Ian
Ground, Patrick
Grylls, Michael
Gummer, Rt Hon John Selwyn
Hague, William
Hamilton, Neil (Tatton)
Hampson, Dr Keith
Hannam, John
Hargreaves, A. (B'ham H'll Gr')
Hargreaves, Ken (Hyndburn)
Harris, David
Haselhurst, Alan
Hawkins, Christopher
Hayes, Jerry

Hayward, Robert
Heddle, John
Heseltine, Rt Hon Michael
Hicks, Mrs Maureen (Wolv' NE)
Hicks, Robert (Cornwall SE)
Higgins, Rt Hon Terence L.
Hill, James
Hind, Kenneth
Holt, Richard
Hordern, Sir Peter
Howard, Michael
Howarth, Alan (Strat'd-on-A)
Howe, Rt Hon Sir Geoffrey
Howell, Rt Hon David (G'dford)
Hughes, Robert G. (Harrow W)
Hunt, Sir John (Ravensbourne)
Hunter, Andrew
Hurd, Rt Hon Douglas
Irvine, Michael
Irving, Charles
Jack, Michael
Jackson, Robert
Janman, Tim
Johnson Smith, Sir Geoffrey
Jones, Gwilym (Cardiff N)
Jones, Robert B (Herts W)
Jopling, Rt Hon Michael
Kellett-Bowman, Dame Elaine
Key, Robert
Kilfedder, James
King, Roger (B'ham N'thfield)
King, Rt Hon Tom (Bridgwater)
Kirkhope, Timothy
Knapman, Roger
Knight, Greg (Derby North)
Knight, Dame Jill (Edgbaston)
Knox, David
Lamont, Rt Hon Norman
Lang, Ian
Latham, Michael
Lawrence, Ivan
Leigh, Edward (Gainsbor'gh)
Lennox-Boyd, Hon Mark
Lester, Jim (Broxtowe)
Lilley, Peter
Lloyd, Sir Ian (Havant)
Lloyd, Peter (Fareham)
Lyell, Sir Nicholas
McCrindle, Robert
Macfarlane, Sir Neil
MacGregor, Rt Hon John
MacKay, Andrew (E Berkshire)
Maclean, David
McLoughlin, Patrick
McNair-Wilson, Sir Michael
McNair-Wilson, Sir Patrick
Madel, David
Major, Rt Hon John
Mans, Keith
Maples, John
Marland, Paul
Marlow, Tony
Marshall, John (Hendon S)
Marshall, Michael (Arundel)
Martin, David (Portsmouth S)
Maude, Hon Francis
Mawhinney, Dr Brian
Mayhew, Rt Hon Sir Patrick
Mellor, David
Meyer, Sir Anthony
Miller, Sir Hal
Mills, Iain
Miscampbell, Norman
Mitchell, Andrew (Gedling)
Mitchell, Sir David
Moate, Roger
Moore, Rt Hon John
Morris, M (N'hampton S)
Morrison, Rt Hon P (Chester)
Moss, Malcolm

Moynihan, Hon Colin
Neale, Gerrard
Needham, Richard
Nelson, Anthony
Neubert, Michael
Newton, Rt Hon Tony
Nicholls, Patrick
Nicholson, David *(Taunton)*
Nicholson, Emma *(Devon West)*
Norris, Steve
Onslow, Rt Hon Cranley
Oppenheim, Phillip
Page, Richard
Paice, James
Patnick, Irvine
Patten, Rt Hon Chris *(Bath)*
Pawsey, James
Peacock, Mrs Elizabeth
Porter, Barry *(Wirral S)*
Porter, David *(Waveney)*
Price, Sir David
Raffan, Keith
Raison, Rt Hon Timothy
Rathbone, Tim
Redwood, John
Renton, Tim
Rhodes James, Robert
Riddick, Graham
Ridley, Rt Hon Nicholas
Ridsdale, Sir Julian
Rifkind, Rt Hon Malcolm
Roberts, Wyn *(Conwy)*
Roe, Mrs Marion
Rossi, Sir Hugh
Rost, Peter
Rumbold, Mrs Angela
Ryder, Richard
Sackville, Hon Tom
Sainsbury, Hon Tim
Sayeed, Jonathan
Scott, Rt Hon Nicholas
Shaw, David *(Dover)*
Shaw, Sir Michael *(Scarb')*
Shelton, Sir William
Shephard, Mrs G. *(Norfolk SW)*
Shepherd, Colin *(Hereford)*
Shepherd, Richard *(Aldridge)*
Sims, Roger
Skeet, Sir Trevor
Soames, Hon Nicholas
Speller, Tony
Spicer, Sir Jim *(Dorset W)*
Spicer, Michael *(S Worcs)*
Squire, Robin
Stanbrook, Ivor

Stanley, Rt Hon Sir John
Steen, Anthony
Stern, Michael
Stevens, Lewis
Stewart, Allan *(Eastwood)*
Stewart, Andy *(Sherwood)*
Stewart, Rt Hon Ian *(Herts N)*
Stokes, Sir John
Stradling Thomas, Sir John
Summerson, Hugo
Tapsell, Sir Peter
Taylor, Ian *(Esher)*
Taylor, John M *(Solihull)*
Taylor, Teddy *(S'end E)*
Tebbit, Rt Hon Norman
Temple-Morris, Peter
Thatcher, Rt Hon Margaret
Thompson, Patrick *(Norwich N)*
Thorne, Neil
Thornton, Malcolm
Thurnham, Peter
Townend, John *(Bridlington)*
Townsend, Cyril D. *(B'heath)*
Tracey, Richard
Tredinnick, David
Trippier, David
Trotter, Neville
Twinn, Dr Ian
Vaughan, Sir Gerard
Viggers, Peter
Waddington, Rt Hon David
Walker, Bill *(T'side North)*
Waller, Gary
Walters, Sir Dennis
Ward, John
Wardle, Charles *(Bexhill)*
Warren, Kenneth
Watts, John
Wells, Bowen
Whitney, Ray
Widdecombe, Ann
Wiggin, Jerry
Wilkinson, John
Wilshire, David
Winterton, Mrs Ann
Winterton, Nicholas
Wolfson, Mark
Wood, Timothy
Yeo, Tim
Young, Sir George *(Acton)*
Younger, Rt Hon George

Tellers for the Noes:
   Mr. Tony Durant and
   Mr. David Lightbown.

*Question accordingly negatived.*
*Main Question, as amended, put and agreed to.*
*Resolved,*

'That this House commends the Government for implementing a comprehensive range of measures to maintain safety throughout the food chain and to improve the scientific knowledge on which these are based; notes with approval the Agricultural and Food Research Council's decision to stengthen the work of its Institute of Food Research at the Norwich and Reading sites by expanding programmes on food safety and nutrition; endorses the Government's policy of transferring responsibility for near market research and development to industry, enabling more Government funds to be channelled into strategic research; congratulates the Government on the substantial increase in resources for research into food safety during the past ten years; and expresses confidence in the Government's policies on food safety and research and development.'.

# Local Government and Housing Bill

*Order for Third Reading read—[Queen's Consent, on behalf of the Crown, signified.]*

7.13 pm

**The Minister for Local Government (Mr. John Gummer):** I beg to move, That the Bill be now read the Third time.

The Government see this as the last of a group of Bills which reform local government, to strengthen it for what will be an increasingly important role for it to play. There has been a tendency for Opposition Members—when there are many of them here—to claim that the Government are less than enthusiastic about local government, and for Conservative Members to point to the extreme examples of the destruction of local government by extremist Labour councils. Neither of those assessments properly represents the whole spectrum of local government. It is the duty of the House to recognise that local government plays a crucial role in the government of the United Kingdom—a role that cannot and ought not to be replaced by any other part of Government.

Secondly, the extremist exceptions rather than the general run of good and well-managed councils have tended to be the focus of attention. The purpose of this Bill is to strengthen the ability of local councils to carry out their role of protecting the people for whom they are responsible and to enable them to provide properly the services that are necessary.

For this reason, we started with the measures that derive from the Widdicombe report. We did not go as far as the committee wanted us to in imposing restrictions on what is known as twin tracking; we were less radical than the committee would have had us be. As most members of it were local government people of real understanding, none of our proposals can undermine local government in the way that the Opposition sometimes suggest that they do.

We sought to strengthen the independence of officers and to ensure that they are seen as non-party political figures. It would be a cause of great sadness if we allowed the efforts of the past 100 years to be overcome. In the middle of the 19th century and thereafter local government officers established their independence at a time when in Birmingham, for instance, Conservative authorities dismissed officers because they were Liberals and Liberal authorities dismissed officers because they were Conservatives. However, we got over that; we grew up and differentiated clearly between the party-political role of elected people and the independent advisory role of officers. That distinction is a crucial part of democracy in Britain——

**Mr. Tony Banks** (Newham, North-West) rose——

**Mr. Gummer:** I shall give way to the hon. Gentleman in a moment.

It was to establish this independence that the Widdicombe committee suggested its reforms which, in large measure, and with certain improvements—in the sense of having softened some of the proposals—we have introduced here.

We have witnessed a remarkable transformation in the Opposition's attitude to the Widdicombe measures during the passage of the Bill. In the early stages of the committee, they tabled a range of amendments which would have

[*Mr. Gummer*]

removed all our requirements and undermined the entire proposal—including the part that referred to chief officers. Many of these amendments were so close to being wrecking amendments that they were not selected for debate.

On Report, a new attitude was expressed. The Opposition now accept that the restrictions on the political activities of chief officers are acceptable and reasonable——

**Dr. John Cunningham** (Copeland): We always did.

**Mr. Gummer:** It is all very well for the hon. Gentleman to say that. If it is true, were the Opposition amendments which were tabled to remove these restrictions tabled with his agreement? If the Opposition always agreed with these restrictions, why did they table the amendments? Why do they not say publicly that it was wrong for the chief executive of a Welsh local authority to be the chairman of the local Labour party at the same time?

**Mr. David Blunkett** (Sheffield, Brightside): Will the Minister acknowledge—he must be aware of this, having examined the evidence given to Widdicombe—that the Labour party placed on record, before Widdicombe reported, its belief in precisely the proposals that were contained in amendments in the names of Labour Members last week, proposing that the restriction should apply to chief officers and their deputies? I know that is so because I gave that evidence to Widdicombe.

**Mr. Gummer:** That makes nonsense of all the amendments that were tabled in Committee. It suggests that originally, while that may have been the position, pressure from——

**Mr. Deputy Speaker (Mr. Harold Walker):** Order. I hope that the Minister is not now seeking to open a debate on amendments that were neither selected nor debated in Committee.

**Mr. Gummer:** I would not dream of doing that, Mr. Deputy Speaker. Now, on Third Reading, we have in the Bill clear distinctions between party political activity and independent advice. Those distinctions should be supported by Members in all parts of the House. They are now more clearly supported than they were at the time of the Committee deliberations. So different is the position that many of us were surprised to hear what was said on Report, but we welcome those who have reformed.

If it is right for chief officers and assistant chief officers to be independent politically, it must also be right for those other officers who give advice to the council, who deal with the public and who are representative of the council. That is what Widdicombe suggested and what we are doing.

**Mr. Tony Banks:** Widdicombe looked at the whole matter of so-called political abuse and could find no evidence to support the various wild allegations that have been made by the Minister and his hon. Friends. If it were a matter of looking at individual officers in local authorities and seeing what they did, and then deciding whether they should be excluded from political activity —because of their position and the advice that they gave —there might have been a meeting of minds on the issue. But the Government have not taken that approach. They have taken the crude approach of salary level without any reference to the functions of the officers concerned.

**Mr. Gummer:** The hon. Gentleman was present for much of the Committee deliberations, but obviously he was not listening if that is what he thinks happened. The Widdicombe committee investigated these matters and suggested that there should be an absolute bar on all local government officers of principal officer level or above. The salary figure merely reflects the level at which that recommendation applies throughout the country.

But we have softened that suggestion by removing the absolute bar and enabling people to appeal to an adjudicator so that he will specifically take into account the type of job done by the individual, which is precisely the point that the hon. Member for Newham, North-West (Mr. Banks) made. I am sad that there was not a meeting of minds. There was no meeting of minds because of the closed minds of Opposition Members, compared with the open minds of Members on the Government Benches.

**Mr. Patrick McLoughlin** (Derbyshire, West): Does my right hon. Friend agree that the Bill will do much to restore the credibility of local government and of some of its officers? Great damage was done to the whole of local government when Derbyshire county council appointed a former Labour MP, who survived in his job for only nine months. That extremely expensive job training scheme did great disservice to the whole system of local goverment in that a chief officer said that he would not work for a Conservative administration.

**Mr. Gummer:** Hence a sadness which could have been overcome in Committee. If the Labour party takes the view that we are told it takes, why did not Opposition Members condemn the appointment of Mr. Race— [*Interruption.*] Why do they want to exclude Mr. Race by supporting the political restrictions on chief officers? They cannot have it both ways.

We wish to ensure that there is a real distinction between those who seek to serve the public party politically and those who seek to serve the public independently in local government. Both are honourable callings, but they are different and there should be no way in which they could be confused. That is the British principle. It may not be the German or French principle, but it is the British one. It has been hard fought and we should be supporting it.

**Mr. William O'Brien** (Normanton): The Minister continues to make wild statements and sweeping references about people who advise councils. Will he now spell out the category and numbers of people involved? The amendments that we tabled in Committee were designed to elicit that information from the right hon. Gentleman. We are still waiting for it.

**Mr. Gummer:** The criteria are not only in the Bill, but we extended the Bill at the hon. Gentleman's request with an amendment which showed that those criteria specifically apply to the terms under which the adjudicator would make individual and group decisions. The hon. Gentleman asked for that to be done and we have done it.

Another way in which the Bill strengthens local government—the first being the way in which it gives real strength to the independence of officers—is that it clarifies the opportunities and powers by which local authorities are able to assist economic regeneration.

**Mr. Nicholas Bennett** (Pembroke): Concern is being expressed by my hon. Friends and others about councillors, being members of authorities, who owe rent as council tenants or rates as ratepayers. Has my right hon. Friend yet had a chance to think about how we might tackle that problem to ensure that when the community charge comes in next year those councillors——

**Mr. Deputy Speaker:** Order. Are those matters within the scope of the Bill?

**Mr. Bennett:** Yes, Mr. Deputy Speaker. They come under Widdicombe—[HON. MEMBERS: "No."] Will councillors who do not pay the charge be brought to account and——

**Mr. George Howarth** (Knowsley, North): On a point of order, Mr. Deputy Speaker. Having already committed the offence of misleading the House into believing that certain things, such as councillors who may or may not owe money, come within the scope of the Bill, is it in order for the hon. Member for Pembroke (Mr. Bennett), having been called to order by you, Mr. Deputy Speaker, then to go on to pretend that such matters come within the scope of the Bill? All those who were members of the Committee know that that is not mentioned anywhere in the Bill.

**Mr. Deputy Speaker:** I must admit that a Bill which contains 164 clauses and 11 schedules is not one that I grasp instantly. However, I find it difficult to discover any reference to these matters in the Bill, and I trust that we shall not have any further references to them in this debate.

**Mr. Gummer:** I was saying——

**Mr. Deputy Speaker:** Order. I hope that hon. Members, including Ministers, will allow the Chair to make some observations on a matter that is before the House.

**Mr. Gummer:** I apologise, Mr. Deputy Speaker. I thought that you were sitting down.

**Mr. Deputy Speaker:** I can well understand the Minister not being certain whether I was sitting down or standing up. I assure him that I was on my feet.

**Mr. Gummer:** I share that problem with you, Mr. Deputy Speaker, and therefore I not only apologise but sympathise. I do not regard the point that has arisen as being part of the Bill. That was the reason, no doubt, why you did not allow a certain amendment to be selected and as the Bill stands there is no reference to that subject. But I am sure, as a matter of general principle, that those who seek to enforce the law should themselves regard the law. It is more difficult to ask people to pay bills if one does not pay them oneself.

**Mr. Allen McKay** (Barnsley, West and Penistone) *rose*——

**Mr. Gummer:** We must get off that subject. I do not wish to court other than the pleasure of Mr. Deputy Speaker, so I will not give way.

Another way in which the Bill supports and strengthens local government is the way in which it increases the clarity with which we are able to use local government powers to encourage economic regeneration. That has been widely supported and is now thought in general to be a useful provision.

The Bill also changes the capital finance scheme so that, in future, more reasonable account can be taken of the needs for capital spending of local authorities, and also their resources. Up to now, there has been a problem because the rules have been laid down so that local authorities with large capital resources have had to have capital allocations similar to those of local authorities with small capital resources. That has militated against directing capital allocations to those with the greatest capital needs. The proposals in the Bill will strengthen local democracy because local authorities with real needs will no longer be unable to get the capital allocations necessary simply because the system makes it so difficult for them to do so.

This Bill also provides additional strengthening for local authorities because of the changes that it makes to local authority companies. It is crucial that the public should know what is going on. The accountability of the electorate is a central part of general democratic accountability. There has been insufficient accountability to the electorate by local authorities for their companies. It has not been clear whether the companies are arm's length organisations or merely a convenient way of carrying out local council decisions through a company structure. In future, that will be made clear and will strengthen accountability.

**Mr. John Battle** (Leeds, West): I welcomed the announcement last Wednesday when the Parliamentary Under-Secretary said that the Government had already exempted from part V of the Bill registered housing associations, which was news to us. Will the Bill be altered in another place to bring that into effect?

**Mr. Gummer:** That is correct. It is a pleasure for Conservative Members to hear the hon. Gentleman welcome that move. I hope that the hon. Gentleman will also accept that, on several occasions during these debates, we have sought to meet one or two—not all, I agree—of his suggestions.

I hope that it will be clear to the local electorate exactly how local authorities organise themselves. If they have an arm's length company, it will be a company. However, if it is not arm's length it will quite properly be seen as part of the local authority's capital structure.

The Bill also strengthens local authorites through the housing finance arrangements. Up to now, the accountability of local authorities has been extremely difficult to unearth because of the way in which the housing is arranged. Some local authorities have taken money from their housing account and used it on the general rate fund. Other local authorities have taken money from the general rate fund and generally supported council tenants with their rents, regardless of whether those tenants were in need. That has made it difficult for the local electorate or tenants to know whether the housing was properly and efficiently run and whether they were getting value for money. The new housing finance arrangements will strengthen local accountability. The Bill will certainly give considerable strength to local authorities by enabling local councils to deal with renewal areas and renovation grants so that they can concentrate the help on those in need, instead of spreading it across larger numbers of people.

[*Mr. Gummer*]

In all those ways, the Bill sets out to be earnest of this Government's support for local councils and local authorities throughout the country. It strengthens officers' independence, cuts away at the politicisation of the independence of advice, gives greater clarity to the discretionary spending of local authorities, brings capital financing much closer to the needs of local authorities, ensures that local authorities' companies are properly controlled and clearly states what sort of companies they are. Its housing finance arrangements ensure that the local authorities' way of dealing with their income is clear to the electorate and their tenants. Above all, it ensures that aids and help are directed to those in need, both through its capital finance changes and in the way in which it deals with housing, renewal areas and renovation grants.

When the Bill is enacted it will be the third of the triumvirate of Acts which will revolutionise the basis on which local authorities operate in this country. There is no easy answer to the problems of local democracy, and no wholesale reorganisation has ever achieved the wonderful results which people seek. We need a new basis upon which local authorities can become better enablers, facilitators and servants of the communities which they are elected. Local authorities will be able to perform those functions all the better because of the passing of this Bill.

7.37 pm

**Mr. William O'Brien** (Normanton): If there is one matter on which we agree with the Minister, it is that there is a difference of attitude between Opposition Members and Conservative Members on the care and development of local government. At least we believe in local government whereas the Minister's contribution suggests that the Government are bent on its demise.

With this Bill, the Government reach their half century of legislation undermining the basic tenets of local democracy. The time is fast approaching when the batsmen of this game of cricket—those people responsible for the demise of local government—should all be sent back to the pavilion and out of the game. In last Thursday's election, the electors gave an overwhelming vote of no confidence to the Prime Minister, and I am sure that that will be repeated to other Ministers, including the Secretary of State for the Environment.

Council tenants and other owner-occupiers who are buying their homes face ever-increasing mortgage rates. On 24 May, interest rates rose to 14 per cent.—the tenth jump in borrowing costs since last summer. This Bill deals with housing. It is significant to note that in the past 12 months people have had to find £40, £50 or £60 per week extra for mortgage repayments. The sum of Tory economic policy has been to make the people who can least pay, pay more. People who got on their bikes to look for work in line with Ministers' suggestions are fortunate if they can afford to purchase a bike shed to live in because of the policies of this Tory Government.

The poll tax bears no relation to people's ability to pay. We do not want the usual tired intervention from the Minister about people in top income brackets paying 15 times as much towards local government costs as the poorest.

**Mr. Deputy Speaker:** As far as I can see, the Bill contains nothing about the community charge. I hope that the hon. Gentleman will stick to what is in the Bill.

**Mr. O'Brien:** I think that if we examine the Bill we will find that there is a reference to the community charge as introduced by the Minister. However, I take your point, Mr. Deputy Speaker. I refer to the Scottish part of the Bill involving legislation which deals with the poll tax.

It is true that the colleague of the Secretary of State for the Environment, the Secretary of State for Social Security, does not believe that there are any poor people. We know perfectly well who has had the greatest benefit from the recent Budgets—Tory supporters who are well off and do not have to worry about inflation.

This is a sorry patchwork of a Bill, a hotch-potch of a Bill. It might as well say, "Whatever the Secretary of State does is deemed to be right and whatever local government does is deemed to be wrong." Local government is always wrong, whether it is in partnership with the private sector to attract business investment and create real jobs or employing an accounts clerk who puts a political poster in his window at home. Local authorities and people who work in local authorities just cannot win.

The Bill gives the Secretary of State for the Environment more than 120 new powers. Perhaps when he cannot get to sleep at night, instead of counting sheep he counts the powers that will accrue to him from the Bill. He can decide by regulation what constitutes political activity or how much a local authority can spend on economic development, or what falls within and what falls without the housing revenue account. The Prime Minister has often said how important it is to trust the people, and that the Government intend to trust the people more and more, but we do not hear much about that nowadays. On the evidence of the Bill, the Prime Minister is saying that we should trust the Secretary of State. Like many people outside this House, we feel that we cannot trust the Secretary of State—he is far too busy taking power away from democratically-elected and accountable local authority councillors and concentrating it in the hands of central Government. That is a result of the Bill.

Part I involves civil liberties and reshapes local government, at least until after the next general election. The Minister has talked at length about the so-called twin-tracking, citing every example as though it were automatically a significant abuse. We do not believe that that is necessarily so. Almost all the examples that the Minister gave involved people at chief executive or chief officer level. We accept that the head of an authority's paid service, its chief officers and its deputies, should not be serving as councillors in another authority and a new clause that we moved in Committee would have ensured that that did not happen. The Minister has not answered the arguments that we put in Committee about the injustice of the proposed restrictions on political activity. He has not even told us what those restrictions will be, although on the basis of the Government's White Paper we can hazard a guess that they could cover everything but the right to belong to a political party, so people employed in local authorities will be prevented from undertaking any activity involving community matters.

We can also guess when the House is likely to have the chance to debate the regulations. Our experience has led us to assume what many Tory Members will have realised —that we shall be debating the regulations on the future of local government at midnight or 2 o'clock in the morning. That is when the Government always introduce regulations to control local government.

**Mr. Allen McKay:** I understand that the starting point for disqualification is a salary of £13,500. As a result of these regulations, many colleagues in the fire service who have helped me will not be able to do so or even put up a window poster. The Government's measures will thus be an abuse of people's civil liberties because they will be denied the right to belong to a political party just because they earn that amount or more.

**Mr. O'Brien:** My hon. Friend is correct, and I shall draw attention to that later.

When the Government allow us to debate these regulations, if we are lucky we shall have one minute of debate per page. When we debated the poll tax regulations, we dealt with 89 pages in 90 minutes. If the Government talk of democracy and freedom of speech, the House is entitled to a better opportunity to discuss these matters, which are important to local government. So much for the parliamentary process, if this is the way the Government treat the future of local government.

The Minister has repeatedly referred to the Government's generosity in providing for an adjudicator, although the amendments that he introduced on Report do not address the civil liberties issue. He said:

"I suspect that large groups of people will be excluded because of the nature of their activities. Many individuals will also be excluded."—[*Official Report*, 13 June 1989; Vol. 154, c. 780.]

We are talking about the rights of ordinary people who work in local authorities to participate in politics and to be the active citizens of whom the Prime Minister speaks so highly.

Under clause 18, a local authority is not just a county, district or London borough council. The phrase includes fire authorities, transport authorities and waste disposal authorities, not to mention the national parks boards. According to the Government, it is acceptable for the chairman of the London residuary body to be a prominent Tory and for the chairman of the Yorkshire regional health authority to be an active Tory and a one-time Tory candidate. It is hypocritical of Conservative Members to vote to suppress the right of local authority employees to play an active part in a political party—especially as senior posts are appointed by the Government—when a fireman of firewoman will not be able to act as treasurer of his or her local Tory party or Labour party because of these restrictions.

What about education staff who are not teachers, lecturers or principals? What about Soulbury advisers, who generally earn more than £13,500, and youth and community service workers? As we saw in Committee, the Government who so blithely take away the rights of council employees are happy for an officer in the Department of Social Security to speak at a National Front rally. To add insult to injury, that civil servant could appeal, as of right, to a tripartite panel including a trade union representative. Only those local government officers caught by the salary restriction can appeal to the adjudicator. We understand that there will be no one adjudicator for England and Wales and, so the Minister says, one for Scotland. Will the Minister spell out the nature of the political restrictions and the groups of people likely to be exempted? People in local government want

answers to those questions. It is grossly unfair to leave thousands of them in suspense simply because the Government will not answer our questions.

I want to spend a little time considering the role of local authority councillors. Double standards apply to them as compared with Members of Parliament.

**Mr. Gummer:** The House would benefit from a little clarification. The hon. Gentleman and I agree about the political activities of chief officers and chief executives. He said that he was not in favour of them serving as elected members of other authorities. He did not say whether he believed that they should not have political affiliations. Will he publicly state that he does not think that a chief executive should also be the chairman of a local political party?

**Mr. O'Brien:** The Labour party submitted evidence to the Widdicombe committee. Those who serve in local government, like those who serve in this House, are entitled to some freedom. They are entitled to please themselves in certain matters. Unlike Conservative Members, we believe that there should be freedom for the individual, including many of those working in local government.

**Mr. Gummer:** Is the House to conclude, therefore, that the hon. Gentleman thinks it perfectly proper for the chief executive of a local authority also to be chairman of the local Labour party?

**Mr. O'Brien:** It is obvious that the Minister was not in the House last night when many Conservative Members were campaigning for freedom of speech in colleges, polytechnics and universities. The House suffered more than 40 minutes of their rhetoric. Tonight the Minister is saying that there should be no freedom for those in local government. How hypocritical can the Government be?

**Mr. Gummer:** It is clear that the hon. Gentleman thinks it perfectly proper for the chief executive of a local authority, who is supposed to advise all parties within that authority, also to be chairman of the local Labour party. The public will be astounded by that and the Society of Local Government Chief Officers will be appalled.

**Mr. O'Brien:** The public will recognise that the Opposition stand square in everything that we do. In contrast, last night Conservative Members campaigned for freedom of speech in colleges, polytechnics and universities, but tonight they do not want freedom of speech for people in local government. Those are the facts on which the public will judge this debate. They will understand that the Tory view of freedom for the individual is that it is right for some but wrong for others.

**Mr. Allan Roberts** (Bootle): Many chief officers and chief executives of local authorities hold strong political opinions. Whether or not they keep their opinions secret is surely a matter for them. I served for some considerable time as a councillor and as chairman of a major committee of a major local authority. I had very good professional advice from chief officers, regardless of their political views. I was happy for chief officers to be members of the political party of their choice—not necessarily the Labour party—because I felt that they were exercising their democratic rights.

**Mr. O'Brien:** When I served in local government we never asked the officers about their political views; we asked for professional views on certain issues. The Government want chief officers to outline their political views before obtaining a position.

Both in Committee and on Report we discussed at length the need for a proper system of remuneration for local authority representatives. The Government would prefer local government to be run by wealthy and retired people. Councils would become elite clubs. Perhaps the Secretary of State envisages councils that meet once a year to hand out contracts, having been given no doubt a good meal. The Opposition attach greater value to local government. Members of Parliament are paid a salary, and those who struggle to live on that salary can line their pockets with lucrative directorships and consultancies. The Government, who have a 100-plus majority, ignore the need for a proper, practical system of remuneration for councillors.

**Mr. McLoughlin:** I understand the hon. Gentleman's point about remuneration. Does he agree that many councils could make it easier for people to attend meetings and not lose money if they held meetings in the evenings? Many councils refuse to do that.

**Mr. O'Brien:** The hon. Gentleman shows his lack of experience. If councils meet in the evening, the officers have to be present. They then take time off in lieu. If they are not at their desks during the day, they are letting down the community and in many instances also their colleagues. Evening meetings are not necessarily good for a local authority.

Under the Bill, councillors could face a £1,000 fine if they fail to declare their direct and indirect pecuniary interests in the form prescribed by the Secretary of State. There is a threat to local authority representatives of a £1,000 fine if they do not declare their interests. There is no doubt that we support accountability and value for money, but councillors already have to register their interests and declare them at meetings when necessary. They can then be barred from speaking and voting and may be required to leave the meeting.

In contrast, Members of Parliament have simply to declare an interest and may then carry on with business as usual. They are not subjected to a £1,000 fine. It is no good the Government and Conservative Members saying that it is the Opposition's responsibility to bring forward appropriate measures. If the Government are really concerned about probity in public life, they should seek to set this House in order and to put the matter straight before they begin to criticise local government.

Consultation is another important issue. Whenever a contentious issue arises, the Government promise that they will consult local authority associations. When they are feeling especially generous, they say that they will also consult the relevant professional bodies. We are not convinced one bit by the Government's protestations on the issue. The Government's new clause on Members' interests was brought forward without proper consultation and at the expense of other key amendments, which had been promised in Committee. Where is the amendment specifying the criteria that the adjudicator will use in hearing appeals? Where is the promised amendment on the question of when the adjudicator will hear appeals? Where is the promised fitness standard for houses in

multiple occupation? What guarantee is there of meaningful consultation on the range of issues that the Bill pretends to address? The Government's attitude to consultation is the same as their attitude to Parliament —a cross between "Nanny knows best" and outright contempt.

The Bill, with all its clauses and schedules, provides once again only for the privileged as opposed to the under-privileged. As a result of the spurious, false and devastating attitude shown in the Bill and by Conservative Members towards local government, we shall be voting against Third Reading, and we ask Conservative Members who have any respect for local government to join us in the Lobby.

8.2 pm

**Mr. David Nicholson** (Taunton): As the first speaker to follow the hon. Member for Normanton (Mr. O'Brien), I should note—and I am sure that it was noted by my right hon. Friend the Minister for Local Government—that no reply was given to his clear challenge.

**Mr. Gummer:** I received a clear reply. The Labour party is committed to the principle that the chief executive of a local authority can be the chairman of a local party.

**Mr. Nicholson:** Indeed, my right hon. Friend did not receive the assurance he requested. That is a point that will be remembered about the speech of the hon. Member for Normanton.

I welcome two of the changes made on Report. Declaring an interest as a consultant for the Association of British Chambers of Commerce, I welcome the concession on amendments and the role played by the hon. Member for Sheffield, Brightside (Mr. Blunkett) last week in ensuring that people who provide their services voluntarily as directors and secretaries to local authority controlled companies will not be regarded as associated with the parent authority by virtue of that connection alone. I welcome the amendments tabled by the Under-Secretary of State for the Environment, my hon. Friend the Member for Surrey, South-West (Mrs. Bottomley).

I also welcome the power introduced on Report, as proposed in the Widdicombe report, to set up a register of local authority members' interests. I tabled a written question on the subject some weeks ago and I can confirm that people in local authorities welcome the protection against the possible abuse of powers. My right hon. Friend the Minister for Local Government made the matter clear last week when he distinguished the considerable powers, especially in planning matters, that local authority councillors have from those of Members of Parliament.

I welcome the general thrust of part I of the Bill on which the hon. Member for Normanton has concentrated much of his attention this evening. In recent weeks, I have become aware that twin tracking has crept in even in areas such as Somerset, both in my own constituency and nearby. To be fair, it is an area where possibly valuable use may be made of the right of appeal to the independent adjudicator, and I welcome that role. However, to use the argument that my hon. Friend the Member for Pembroke (Mr. Bennett) used in the debate on the Self-Governing Schools Etc. (Scotland) Bill last night, it is most important that certain protections should exist, even if the abuse is not currently widely prevalent. We need that protection.

I will give an example to show why that protection is necessary. I note that the Democrat party, or whatever it has decided to be called now, is not represented in the debate. I guess that in southern England the Democrat party is now in a terminal state and I observe, therefore, that in the south-west the Labour party may have passed its electoral nadir. If the Labour party is likely to gain county and district council seats from the Democrat party, we need to be prepared and protected against the use and abuse of twin tracking to which, as shown in the speech by the hon. Member for Normanton, the Labour party is still very much committed.

No speech of mine on this Bill would be complete without a reference to housing. I note that the hon. Member for Normanton referred to housing only in passing. I will speak briefly on the subject because I want to pursue my objectives with my right hon. and hon. Friends by diplomacy. Without claiming any particular virtue, because I may be wrong in my concern on this issue, I must say that, apart from the amendment moved so ably last week by my right hon. Friend the Member for Westmorland and Lonsdale (Mr. Jopling), which was well supported by those who spoke in the debate, I am the only Conservative Member to raise that particular concern during the Bill's progress. When considering my right hon. Friend's proposal and the Government's counter-proposal, I hope that there can be some meeting of minds on the subject in another place. However, I must emphasise that the proposal affects only the margins. We are considering perhaps only dozens of homes per constituency in national parks and similar areas.

I have made it clear all along that my concern has been for those seeking rented accommodation, whether council, private sector or housing association, in the urban areas of constituencies such as mine. I have spoken to the Under-Secretary of State for the Environment, my hon. Friend the Member for Rossendale and Darwen (Mr. Trippier), about this. I do not especially care whether it is the Genghis Khan district council or the St. Francis of Assisi housing association that provides the homes. They are needed at a cost that the tenant, the taxpayer and the community charge payer can afford. I leave that thought with my hon. Friend. However, I believe that he recognises that need and that he also recognises that the position has been made more difficult over the past year by the increase —for which we all understand the reason—in house prices, especially in the south, as a result of which those who originally would have bought into the private sector are now obliged to seek rented accommodation.

Finally, I welcome the measures in the Bill on home improvement grants and renewal areas. I look forward to seeing the ways in which they will help some of my constituents who own their own homes, but whose homes were not traditionally built so that my constituents are now facing problems with resale and mortgageability. I am not referring to the BISF housing that was spoken about in Committee and about which my hon. Friend the Under-Secretary of State was so helpful.

I hope that the Bill will be the foundation for a new, positive and constructive concordat between local government and central Government. I hope that following this Bill and the major Local Government Finance Act 1988, we will allow the waters to settle over the 10 years of what has been an extremely turbulent relationship between central Government and local government over the sharing of powers. I am sure that my right hon. and hon. Friends on the Front Bench know the difficulties that some of those contests have caused to those who seek to serve our party in local government. I support the Bill.

8.10 pm

**Mr. George Howarth** (Knowsley, North): I had not intended to comment on the speech made by the hon. Member for Taunton (Mr. Nicholson) because I always found him to be a reasonable and fair member of the Committee who always had interesting things to say, but when he declared his interest as a consultant to the Association of British Chambers of Commerce—a fine organisation, in my experience, and I have no bones to pick with it—it occurred to me that there was a strong element of hypocrisy in the hon. Gentleman rising to declare his interest and to thank the Government for the concessions that they have made in that direction, while supporting the provisions in the Bill that would take civil liberties away from many people who work in local government. Can the hon. Gentleman not see that there is a direct parallel between the power that he is exercising as a Back-Bench Member of the governing party and the powers being taken away from ordinary individuals who do not seek to peddle any influence, but simply to serve their political beliefs and to serve in local government? I am sure that it was unintentional, but it was hypocritical and mirrored the stinking hypocrisy of what the Government are doing.

**Mr. David Nicholson:** I do not accept that point at all. Would the hon. Gentleman have preferred me not to declare my interest? In doing so, I was paying a tribute to the role played in this matter by his hon. Friend the Member for Sheffield, Brightside (Mr. Blunkett).

**Mr. Howarth:** I was anxious not to make a direct attack on the hon. Gentleman and prefaced my remarks by saying so. I was simply saying that the hon. Gentleman has the freedom to stand up in the House of Commons and to declare an interest in the Association of British Chambers of Commerce. I respect the fact that he made such a declaration. However, he was able to do that at the same time as the House is taking democratic rights away from members or would-be members of local authorities who happen to serve in local government.

The Government seem to have got themselves in an extraordinary mess. They have not sat down rationally and said, "What are we to do about local government? What reforms are necessary? What shall we do about housing policy? What are the problems and how should we proceed?" The Government seem to indulge in policy making not by rational analysis but by the pursuit of prejudice. That prejudice permeates every part of the Bill and all that the Government have done in the past two to four years or in some cases their whole 10-year period in office. That is what I find most alarming and that is why in the long run—it is already starting—the electorate of the British people will decide that they should like something more rational than a Government who operate purely on blind prejudice instead of by serious consideration of any given set of problems.

What we would have liked to see in the Bill, but which does not appear, is a systematic, logical and coherent look at the powers and functions of local government in a modern society. We would have liked consideration of all

[*Mr. Howarth*]

the things that are happening in housing policy and an objective look at the housing needs of the country. But no, there was nothing of the sort. What we got instead were lurid examples from the Minister of State. I notice that he is not in his place—no doubt he has something else to do.

The basis of the provisions on twin tracking did not proceed from any great national outrage or even national concern about what was happening in local government. They proceeded because of a handful of examples of which the Minister of State painted a lurid picture and on the basis of which he then sought to justify his legislation. At no time in our Committee discussions of the relevant clauses did the Minister of State ever give any rational or thoughtful justification for what the Government were doing. It came down to the half dozen individuals in local authorities around the country who the Minister of State, or those who were winding him up, felt should be controlled by legislation. It is extraordinary that a Bill should be placed before Parliament merely because certain people—including the Minister of State—are concerned about what is happening in half a dozen places because of half a dozen people who happen to be local government officers and who happen to serve on local authorities at the same time.

The Bill does not proceed from a consideration of the real problems. It reflects the prejudice not only of the Under-Secretary of State and the Minister of State, but of those other members of the Government who are more vocal and who paint an even more lurid picture than those Ministers do.

I want to speak mainly about the provisions relating to housing. I sat through three and a half months of deliberations on the Housing Act 1988 as it passed through the House and came back from the House of Lords. I recall rising on Third Reading to say that the then Minister, the hon. Member for Bristol, West (Mr. Waldegrave), knew—as did his civil servants and the Secretary of State—that the Bill was irrelevant and would make no difference to any of our housing problems. I spoke again last week on a clause which made exactly the same point about this Bill. The 1988 Act has made no difference whatever to our housing problems. The Ministers know, as their Back Benchers, civil servants and all the experts know, that that Act has been a complete and utter flop. So what did the Government do? Having once legislated on the subject, instead of saying, "Perhaps we got that a bit wrong and should now look at it this way", they are piling on more legislation which is even more defective and which is adding to the problems created by their previous legislation. I hesitate to think where we shall end up. Bad legislation will probably be added to and added to again until ultimately we have a morass of appalling housing legislation.

What does this legislation actually do about the country's housing problems? Over the past 10 years the amount of investment in our housing stock, irrespective of tenure, has reached record low proportions. I grant that the Government have made some alterations in the way in which improvement grants are to be administered and that they have marginally improved the way in which the capital allocations to local authorities are to be

administered. I hope that my constituents will see some benefit from that because I am obviously concerned that there should be some benefit for areas such as Merseyside.

There is no strategy, no framework and no logical approach in the Bill to putting right the major problems of our aged housing, such as the problems that have been stored up because of the system-built techniques of the past. We have major problems of disrepair in our local authority stock because of historical difficulties over repairs, which were largely if not completely to do with resources. The Bill does nothing about the disrepair problem nor about the straitjacket of tenures which is almost unique in Europe and is not to the benefit of those in housing need.

The financial provisions which are supposed to help people are so unequal that tenants get stuck in a tenure type. Any pretence that there is choice in the system goes out of the window. The Government cry freedom, but choice in housing is circumscribed. There is no equality between tenures, nor even within a tenure type. Housing finance should have been reformed. Instead of going along that road, the Government are placing even greater penalties on council tenants. The inevitable consequence will be rent increases because the Government have to make part IV of the 1988 Act work. To do that they have to make council housing ever more unpopular. Unfortunately, that is what it is all about. They have made a mistake and now they have to make somebody pay for it.

What does the legislation do about providing for the homeless? The answer is that it does nothing. We can walk through any major city, not least the capital, any night of the week and see the appalling spectacle of young people sleeping in cardboard boxes under railway arches. Yet we are almost at the end of the 20th century, not in Victorian or Dickensian times.

**Mr. Deputy Speaker:** Order. I remind the hon. Gentleman that Third Reading is not an occasion to debate what might or ought to have been in the Bill. We are debating what is in the Bill.

**Mr. Howarth:** I am grateful for your guidance, Mr. Deputy Speaker. I have strayed, but I think that I have made the point effectively.

The Government have got themselves into a mess on housing. They have offered no solutions to the real problems. They have merely piled predjudice on existing prejudice. The Bill is cheap, shoddy and useless.

**Mr. Tony Banks:** Like the Secretary of State.

**Mr. Howarth:** As my hon. Friend says, it is like the Secretary of State. The Government will pay a sorry price not just for the legislation but for all that it represents and all that goes with it.

8.22 pm

**Mr. Patrick McLoughlin** (Derbyshire, West): I welcome the Bill. Having listened to the hon. Member for Normanton (Mr. O'Brien) one would think that everything was fine in the garden and that there was no need for legislation on the conduct of local authorities. Part I of the Bill has already had quite an effect on some local authorities in regard to representation on committees.

The hon. Member for Normanton told us that basically the Bill said that anything that local government did was wrong and anything that the Secretary of State did was right. If that were the case, we would have needed only a one-clause Bill. In fact, we have a Bill with 164 clauses. We believe in local authorities and in the structure of local government. We want local government to operate fairly under the law.

Some local authorities are deliberately excluding opposition parties from committees. That cannot be justified by anyone, and no one should attempt to justify it, whether it be a Tory or a Labour authority. I want reassurance from my hon. Friend the Minister on clause 15 and the duty of a local authority to allocate seats to political groups.

My hon. Friend may not know that since the county council election in May, Derbyshire county council still refuses to allow any Conservatives to sit on the police authority. I want an assurance from my hon. Friend that when the Bill becomes effective that will not be possible. A Labour-controlled county council should not be able to say that no Conservatives will serve on a police authority. That assurance is important for my constituents and for the people of Derbyshire.

**Mr. Christopher Hawkins** (High Peak): I wish strongly to support what my hon. Friend says. It is a disgrace that a police authority does not represent all political parties and all the people. That is the function of the authority.

**Mr. McLoughlin:** I am grateful to my hon. Friend. It is important that everyone should have confidence in the operations of the police committee and the police authority.

**Mr. O'Brien:** In view of the comment by the hon. Member for High Peak (Mr. Hawkins), will the hon. Member for Derbyshire, West (Mr. McLoughlin) confirm that the views of Tories and other parties can be represented through magistrates who serve on those committees as co-opted members?

**Mr. McLoughlin:** I am amazed by that intervention. The hon. Gentleman is seeking to justify that there should be no elected representatives of minority groups on a police authority. That is absolutely disgraceful. We are talking about elected members of a county council. The intervention by the hon. Member for Normanton portrays the attitude of the official Opposition. He tells us that the Opposition believe in the role of local government. Yet they are justifying the refusal of a local authority to allow minority group representation on a particular committee. I am amazed because I would have thought that there was common ground on that. Obviously there is not. I thought that it was a minor, uncontroversial point, but clearly it is not. Therefore, I am glad that I made it and I hope that I get reassurance later from my hon. Friend.

I also seek reassurance on schedule 1, page 147, line 29, which refers to national parks committees. Derbyshire county council appoints eight people to the Peak Park national planning board. Only one is a Conservative. I want an assurance that there will be greater sharing of the representation.

**Mr. George Howarth:** This is pathetic.

**Mr. McLoughlin:** The hon. Gentleman says that it is pathetic. May I point out that of the eight people appointed by the county council, only one lives in the area of the national park? I do not think that that is a good way of having local representation on the planning board. Can the hon. Gentleman tell me of any other planning authority in the country where a person can serve on the planning authority without being a resident in the area that is covered by that authority?

**Mr. Hawkins** *rose——*

**Mr. McLoughlin:** I shall give way to my hon. Friend because we share the same difficulties.

**Mr. Hawkins:** Again I wish strongly to support my hon. Friend. He has brought up a most important point that I have raised in the House several times. There are a number of national parks where there are very few residents. It is right that a national park is seen as a national asset and that people from outside the area of the park should be on the planning authority. The Peak district national park has a very large population, and it is the planning authority controlling people's day-to-day lives. It is the major planning authority in many areas of my constituency and that of my hon. Friend the Member for Derbyshire, West (Mr. McLoughlin). It is greatly resented that there are so few local representatives on that board.

**Mr. McLoughlin:** My hon. Friend the Member for High Peak (Mr. Hawkins) explained his position on the representation on the board. We both share national park areas and we both know how important this issue is to our areas. I hope that when the Bill becomes an Act it will not be possible for such a small minority representation to be given to opposition parties, and that there will be a fairer distribution.

I do not disagree with everything that the Labour party is saying about local government. This is one area in which I would depart from my hon. Friend the Member for Taunton (Mr. Nicholson), because I agree with the Labour party about something that it has announced in one of its policy documents. The Labour party did quite well in the county council elections in May. The Labour party is so horrified about the antics which its councils get up to in local government that, understandably, it wants to abolish the county councils. I agree with it on that.

**Mr. David Nicholson:** I believe that what inspires those Opposition parties, who are hostile to county councils—I believe it is also true of the Liberals or whatever they call themselves—is that they would like to establish a structure of regional government. Will my hon. Friend tell me from which regional capital he would like his constituency to be governed?

**Mr. McLoughlin:** My hon. Friend tries to send me down an avenue which, I am sure, Madam Deputy Speaker, will cause you to call me to order. I do not support the setting up of regional councils, but I would like to see devolvement down to district councils. I believe that district councils are far better and far more accountable to their local areas.

**Mr. James Couchman** (Gillingham): Does my hon. Friend agree that a perfect model already exists in outer London boroughs—most of them, incidentally, Conservative controlled?

**Madam Deputy Speaker (Miss Betty Boothroyd):** Order. The hon. Gentlemen are now concerning themselves with matters that are not in the Bill.

**Mr. McLoughlin:** I am grateful, Madam Deputy Speaker, for drawing me into line. I was a little worried that we might get drawn down that particular road.

A number of points in part I of the Bill should really have received the almost total support of the House. It is with great regret I say that that they have not. I believe that the structure of local government, and local government operating under certain guidelines, is important for the future of local government. We do not need any lectures about the future of local government and its importance. I go along with the future, the structure and the importance of local government. I do not go along, however, with its abuse.

I was surprised when the hon. Member for Normanton rejected my idea that councils should sit in the evenings. He said that, if councils met in the evenings, the chief officers would not be at their desks the next day, because they would have to take time off in lieu. However, if the councils meet in the day time, those same chief officers will be away from their desks and not available to the public. Some district councils already meet in the evenings and some meet in the mornings. I do not see any difference in the kind of service that they provide to the public. More district councils and county councils meeting in the evenings would mean that many people could stand for local government election who are currently barred from doing so. It is a great shame that there is not a clause in the Bill which positively encourages that to happen.

I warmly welcome the Bill and hope that it gets a Third Reading.

8.33 pm

**Mr. John Battle** (Leeds, West): The Bill is entitled "Local Government and Housing Bill", but our debate on housing, as happened the last time round when we discussed what became the Housing Act 1988, has become marginalised and buried in the rest of the detail of the Bill. After embarking on the major debate on housing last week, we were interrupted by, admittedly, an important debate on dog registration. Just before that debate on dog registration, however, there was a brief debate on shared ownership in rural areas. I believe that the Secretary of State's comments then reveal how out of touch and far off the ground he really is. The Secretary of State was keen to emphasise the principle of shared housing. He said:

"we should allow shared ownership housing in certain rural areas to be retained as low-cost housing for future generations of local people."—[*Official Report,* 14 June 1989; Vol. 154, c. 1032-33.]

He also agreed that we need a way to retain shared ownership housing as low-cost housing once the beneficiary has moved on.

In the Secretary of State's efforts to persuade us that the Government were making arrangements for the passing on of low-cost housing, he produced a sheet of sample calculations which he said would show a typical case. The only problem was that, in real terms, the typical case that he presented was based on a house price exchange value of £174,900, which can hardly be described as a low-cost house. Under that scheme, the new resident's 40 per cent. share would be at least £69,960. The Secretary of State has a fundamental problem. Committed as he is to market values, it is not easy to square basing everything on market

values with subsidising and supporting low-cost initiatives. There is an essential conflict between the market and, as at last the Secretary of State is beginning to acknowledge —under pressure from his Back Benchers in rural areas —the need to treat rural housing as a social policy in Britain. People need decent homes in which to live at prices that they can afford. I believe that that comment was echoed by the hon. Member for Taunton (Mr. Nicholson). It showed that the Secretary of State has no concept of how to square a theory of the free market with the need of people for housing.

My hon. Friend the Member for Knowsley, North (Mr. Howarth) said that here is another Housing Bill—for example, parts V, VI, VII and VIII and 59 clauses—that does not address the issues of homelessness, the absolute shortage of housing for families, house price inflation, and people's problems in having paying their mortgages. It does not improve the chances of people renting a council house, if they are not already in one, but rather it intends to ring-fence. The Minister said that that would strengthen local authority housing. The word "strengthen" should be replaced by the words "squeeze and strangle", because that will be the reality. We can see how that ring-fence account will, as we spelt out last week, include some housing benefit—the rebate payments too—and, that therefore, some of the poorer tenants will have to pay the rent of the poorest through the housing benefit system. Council rents will be forced up and people will be priced out of the right to rent. They will then have to move out of the expensive council housing and into the private deregulated sector in which the landlords have far more power as a result of the 1988 Act to gain repossession and then put up the rents to what the Secretary of State has referred to throughout as "market levels".

In the middle of the debate last week the Secretary of State had the effrontery to make under clause 71 a major statement. He introduced his capital value rents formula, which will again force up rents. He did not grant us the courtesy of a proper statement at the Dispatch Box and at the proper time; he tagged it on to his comments in response to clause 71. His message to council tenants was "Buy or get out, because you will not be able to afford to rent." The only option will be to move into the private rented sector. The Government have been exposed in their attempt to deny people the right to rent. People will not be allowed to rent; they will be priced out by the market. It may come as a surprise to Conservative Members that some people choose to live in council housing. Every week, people visit Opposition Members in an effort to move into council housing. Some of us remember council housing as a dream means of getting out of the appalling and highly priced private rented sector of the past into a decent and affordable home with an inside lavatory and bathroom.

**Mr. Martin M. Brandon-Bravo** (Nottingham, South): It is not often that I have any kind words to say about my Labour-controlled Nottingham city council housing department, but in all fairness to it I must ask whether the hon. Gentleman is saying that a well-run local authority housing department, where there is proper and reasonable maintenance and all the other things that the hon. Gentleman would seek, with a housing revenue account that is in balance, not subsidised, like Nottingham's will be forced falsely and unnecessarily to raise its rents as a result of the Bill. The inquiries and the assurances that I have received show that that will not be the case and that the formula exists only for those councils who, in some way or another, are trying to draw in subsidy in order to charge falsely low rents. Rents in Nottingham do not require that subsidy, so the council will not be forced unreasonably to raise its rents.

**Mr. Battle:** I am grateful to the hon. Gentleman. What he says is a remarkable contrast to those Conservative Members whom I have heard refer to council housing as evil empires. I welcome the hon. Gentleman's comments about Nottingham. He is willing to acknowledge and boast about the situation there. However, I advise him to re-read the Secretary of State's statement because he is introducing capital value rents. Four years ago the Secretary of State said that every council rent in Britain should be at least £35 a week. He has now produced a formula which will nudge rents in that direction.

**The Parliamentary Under-Secretary of State for the Environment (Mr. David Trippier):** The hon. Gentleman should have listened more carefully to my hon. Friend the Member for Nottingham, South (Mr. Brandon-Bravo). It is clear that my right hon. Friend the Secretary of State was talking about a formula to be used in calculating the new housing subsidy which will play a major part in balancing the equation with regard to the ring-fencing of the housing revenue account. In the specific circumstance referred to by my hon. Friend, it is highly likely that rents will remain exactly the same. It is even possible that in his authority, or in some others, they will fall. Surely the hon. Gentleman will not use the scaremongering tactics that we are so used to from the Labour party to suggest that rents will increase substantially. He will look pretty stupid if the rent demands that go to tenants do not substantiate that suggestion.

**Mr. Battle:** In time the truth will out. We have heard the same on property price values, mortgages and private sector rents. The same arguments were put forward for the Housing Act 1988. It was said that private sector rents would not go up, but they are doing so. The Minister's colleagues in the Department of Social Security know that and they are watching them with interest.

The Minister may be able to stand at the Dispatch Box now and pledge that rents will not necessarily go up. We shall have to wait to see what happens, but since the Secretary of State said that he would base rents on capital values, what other option is there when the average value of property is rising? Conservative Members want to finish off council housing. That is the real agenda. The Secretary of State is on record as saying that councillors should not manage local authority housing.

We should reflect on the roots of council housing. Where did it come from in the first instance? My city of Leeds had the highest number of back-to-back houses— 172,000. There were unique reasons for that, not least that the fields were sold off in strips for house building and houses were built along the river. The blocks were then connected and the midden block with the toilet facilities was connected to the drains of the local inns and pubs round about. In other words, corners were cut on sanitation. The result was typhoid and tuberculosis.

Then we had public health legislation which suggested that there should be public housing to give people space, light and sanitation. That was the real history of public housing. The private landlords failed to deliver and everybody suffered. What surprised the councillors—they were not loony Left councillors at the turn of the century —was that the tuberculosis germs did not observe the city boundaries and remain in the poorer areas downtown, but rather moved up the hill on the wind. At that point they decided to introduce legislation to build council housing.

The Government are seeking to price out the public housing sector and send the tenants back to the landlords, weakening conditions and tenants' protections against eviction and repossession. We are entitled to ask why they are so determined to re-run history. Why are they so determined to put the clock back?

The Government have promised a major amendment on standards in the other place. We could not debate that amendment on Report, but a 10-point habitation standard was spelt out. Before the Minister tells us that we were asking for gold taps and the rest, let me say that housing standards were set in the 1930s and we need new standards now to take us into the next century.

The 1986 English house condition survey showed that there has been little improvement in disrepair in recent years. At best the situation is static. There are still well over 1 million unfit houses and houses in a serious state of disrepair. Our housing stock, whether private or public, should not be allowed to deteriorate.

The Minister might do worse than to look at a report published by the Royal Institute of British Architects which says that the Government's drive to get value for money and to achieve private sector funding

"totally disregards achieving the required standard cost in use or long-term maintenance . . . The increase in the number of households has not met with a corresponding increase in house-building. An ever-increasing number of people are being forced into poorly-built or badly-converted accommodation."

We have a long way to go on home improvements before the Government adopt a system of standards. The standards that we set out in the other place should be welcomed and would go some way to tackling the backlog. It remains to be seen whether the Government are committed to improving housing or whether this is simply another tag on to a local government Bill.

The Government may be having second thoughts on the National Health Service, the poll tax and the water proposals. I urge the Government to think again on these proposals in the Local Government and Housing Bill. Some of us remember that in 1983 the Tory party's election manifesto said:

"Our goal is to make Britain the best housed nation in Europe."

That rings hollow now, not only in the light of the Government's significant failure in Europe but their failure towards the nation's housing, witnessed by the hundreds of thousands of people in Britain who are homeless or likely to be homeless because they currently live in overcrowded conditions with no hope for the future.

8.49 pm

**Mr. Tony Marlow** (Northampton, North): I want to make a few brief remarks about a subject which was debated in this House last week, and which I think received as much if not more publicity than anything else that has been debated on this Bill and on which I believe the Government intend to introduce further amendments later on in another place—that is the subject of dogs.

For a long time I have favoured a registration scheme, but no longer.

**Madam Deputy Speaker:** Order. I ask the hon. Gentleman to speak to the Bill, which has nothing to do with dogs.

**Mr. Marlow:** But, Madam Deputy Speaker, clause 138 states that
"a charge may be imposed in respect of anything . . . which is done by any relevant authority."
That is the text to which I refer.

**Madam Deputy Speaker:** Order. The hon. Gentleman may intend to amuse the House, but I insist that he keeps to the subject of the Bill.

**Mr. Marlow:** You put me in great difficulty, Madam Deputy Speaker. Can I perhaps try another text?

**Madam Deputy Speaker:** I think that you better had.

**Mr. Marlow:** Clause 7, on page 10 of the Bill, states:
"Every appointment of a person to a paid office or employment . . . shall be made on merit."
One of the paid offices that would most merit being made by local authorities would be that of a dog warden. Any dog warden so appointed should be appointed on the basis of merit.

**Madam Deputy Speaker:** Order. I am sure that the hon. Gentleman is prepared to amuse us with a very lively speech, but I am serious in suggesting to him that other right hon. and hon. Members wish to speak to the Bill, and he must do likewise.

**Mr. Marlow:** I hear what you say, Madam Deputy Speaker.

Briefly, I believe that my right hon. Friend is quite right in seeking to bring forward amendments at a later stage in another place, which he suggested the other day. There has been a lot of talk about registration on this subject, and I believe that the powers that my right hon. Friend is going to give to local government with regard to this particular nuisance will solve the problem that we are all seeking to solve. I believe that that is the right way to proceed. It gives powers to local people to insist that those powers are used, and it will at a later stage enable the country to be rid of a great nuisance which has been afflicting us and affecting us for a great deal of time. I believe that on this issue my right hon. Friend has got it right.

8.51 pm

**Mr. Tony Banks** (Newham, North-West): I shall come straight to the point. I do not like the Bill. It is like the Secretary of State—brutal, graceless, and almost a complete waste of space. Typical of its kind, it is yet one further turn of the screw in what appears to my right hon. and hon. Friends and me to be the liquidation of local democracy and accountability.

The Bill is also an unholy mess. Any right hon. or hon. Member who sat through the Committee or Report stage will realise just how much of a mess it is. It is the legislative equivalent of a blunderbuss. The only coherence that seems to run through its clauses is one of unalloyed nastiness to local councillors, councils and council tenants. In its generality, the Bill will deprive tens of thousands of council officers of their civic rights. I suspect that that provision will be tested elsewhere, in the European Court of Human Rights. The Bill will also deprive a significant number of councillors of their ability either to earn a living or to remain councillors. It seeks to extend further into the

day-to-day running of local authorities the choking embrace of centralisation, giving ever more powers to the Secretary of State and the faceless grey gnomes of Marsham street.

**Mr. Trippier:** Withdraw!

**Mr. Banks:** I was trying to be complimentary.

I am still waiting for a clue from the Minister as to the political activities that will be off limits to council officers earning more than £13,500 per year. We do not even know how that figure will be calculated, and whether it will include allowances, bonuses or overtime.

The ban on political activities takes no heed of the work that council officers do in giving advice to elected councillors and to the public, and decisions about those activities will be left to the adjudication officer, who will have to exercise the judgment of Solomon. The House is entitled at least to a clue as to the matters that the adjudication officer will take into account when deciding whether or not a council officer's work places him in the category of being a political eunuch.

It is typical of the Government to set a cash limit—democracy with a price tag of £13,500 or more. It is typical of a Government of free market spivs to understand much about money but nothing about values.

The Government say that they are taking this action with the backing of Conservative Members to end so-called abuses in local government, but their evidence is anecdotal. Even Widdicombe, after all the inquiries, could not come up with hard evidence of political abuse in respect of appointments. Much of the anecdotal evidence that Ministers trot out is largely culled from the pages of Right-wing tabloids written by grubby and mendacious hacks.

One appreciates how hypocritical the Bill is, coming as it does from a Government who cannot refrain from abusing power. I refer, for example, to political appointments to public bodies, which are full of Tory stooges these days. The great and the good have been replaced by the stooge, the hack and the lickspittle—all of whom subscribe to Tory values. Such people pack every body to which Ministers have the power to make appointments.

The phrase used by the Government is "Jobs for the boys in local government." Perhaps you, Madam Deputy Speaker, will pardon that sexist phrase. Perhaps it does not bother you, but it does bother me. Such an accusation defies logic. In terms of giving jobs to the boys, local government is like a bunch of political virgins by comparison with this Government of sybarites. When it comes to jobs for the boys and political abuse, no one can teach the Government anything. Nothing in local government remotely approaches the level of political abuse that the present Government practise in public life.

The Government demand a whistle-blower in the town hall. I hope that right hon. and hon. Members in all parts of the House—many Conservative Members have served in local government—agree that our local government system is remarkably free of corruption by comparison with those of other countries, and by comparison even with our own Civil Service. Yet there are to be no statutory whistle-blowers in Whitehall, where there would be a considerable amount of work for them to do—in respect of everything from the overpricing of Ministry of Defence contracts to the Property Services Agency and the out and out corruption of the common agricultural policy. The hypocrisy of the Bill is of staggering proportions.

Ministers speak of the need for impartiality in council officers, but that comes from a Government who have done more than any other in living memory to politicise the Civil Service—to the point where the Government's own information officers protest about the way in which they are used to do party political dirty work on the instructions of Ministers and of No. 10 Downing street. One need only think of Bernard Ingham. Who would retain him once the present Government have gone? My right hon. Friend the next Prime Minister would be mad to retain Mr. Ingham, who has been behaving like a deputy Prime Minister for so long. In view of the things that information officers were getting up to over the Westland letter, how can Conservative Members talk of the abuse of political power in the town halls? How can they talk like that when we can point to their own terrible record?

Conservative Members have mentioned ratepayers' money being used for council newsletters and publicity campaigns. That is a bit much, coming from a Government who spend some £150 million a year of taxpayers' money on politically motivated, party-politically inspired campaigns under the guise of public information.

Finally, let me deal with the aspect of the Bill which will directly affect my people in Newham, especially council tenants. The combining of the rate fund subsidy, rate rebate subsidy and Housing Act 1980 subsidy places that single subsidy wholly within the control of the Secretary of State. The Secretary of State has tried to argue that the inconsistency between the rents of one authority and those of another was an overwhelming argument for them to be evened out. Despite what the Minister has said, we know what will happen. The level will rise rather than fall. I shall be the first to apologise to the Minister if that does not happen, but history points to rents going up rather than down.

There is a simple reason why one local authority should have lower rents than another. Some authorities, at the instigation of their residents, decided to build houses for rent at an early stage. That was a wise investment decision. They did not know that the Secretary of State would come along and expropriate, without compensation, their prudently acquired capital assets. I should like to see what Conservative Members would say if a Labour Government decided to expropriate private resources and assets without compensation. Indeed, I should very much like to see a Labour Government do precisely that.

**Mr. Dave Nellist** (Coventry, South-East): Hear, hear.

**Mr. Banks:** I knew that my good friend the hon. Member for Coventry, South-East (Mr. Nellist) would be on my side, but I suspect that we should be in something of a minority as we are now.

**Mr. Nellist:** An honourable minority.

**Mr. Banks:** Honourable, indeed, but a minority none the less. One day I should like to be in the majority—one does not always want to lose gloriously.

Public housing was first built and let out for rent to supply a need that could not be met in the market place. Even in Victorian times, homes were needed for the working-class families of those who drove the trains,

worked the docks and built the sewers; yet London then, as now, was a high-demand area, so the philanthropists of that age built housing for low rents. Now nurses, cleaners, social workers and teachers cannot afford to buy property in London, and it seems that soon they will not be able to rent it either, because they will always be squeezed out of the market by richer people.

What has become of the Government's economic policy? Countless people are attracted to London by the prospect of work, thus creating a high-demand area, but those are the people least able to afford the higher rents or house prices produced by the Government's proposal to allow rents to reflect house prices—for that is what this proposal amounts to.

Council housing was meant to step in and break the force of the market—to ensure that people were allocated homes according to need rather than ability to pay. That was one of its essential objectives—to ensure that poverty in housing was not passed from one generation to another, and that the poverty of the parents did not mean that the children had to live in squalor, in overcrowded conditions without basic amenities. With this one proposal the Government are twisting the original pure aims of council housing—to house those in greatest need—into a grotesque reflection of that grotesque animal, the house purchase market. No one who has watched with horror the spiralling prices of the past two years—up to August last year, when it became less and less possible for anyone on a modest income to buy the smallest broom cupboard—which displaced people in the cheaper areas such as Newham could possibly wish this to happen to council rents.

The movement of rents towards capital values has an even more dangerous impact on areas such as my borough of Newham, where incomes are lower than the average. Housing benefit is received by 67 per cent. of council tenants in Newham, and 60 per cent. of those tenants are on full income support. The people of Newham suffered significant losses as a result of the changes in the social security regime in April 1988. There were 7,800 transitional payments and, as we all know, only certain categories were entitled to receive transitional protection.

The proposal to move rents towards the market place takes no account of the poverty trap being created and deepened by the significant increase in rents that is likely to ensue. It presupposes that tenants in high-demand areas are likely to be in work, with the benefit of wage increases. What about people on fixed occupational pensions? What about single parents dependent on a mixture of maintenance and low-paid work? What about the unemployed who want to take a job—any job—but find that they are worse off because rents are so high and wages so low? They might be willing themselves to take the risk of being worse off for a time, but can they risk that for their families?

Rent arrears are related purely to poverty and to the level of rents. Despite what we are told about local authorities not collecting their rents, in 1987-88 Newham collected more than 100 per cent. of its rent roll. Rent arrears dropped in that year by 5·6 per cent., but following the massive drop in incomes and the increase in rents that was forced through by the Government, rent arrears inevitably increased in Newham, as elsewhere in the country. In Newham the increase was 30 per cent. It is to the credit of the people of Newham that the increase in rent arrears—from 5·6 per cent. to 30 per cent.—was not

[*Mr. Banks*]

far worse, because the level of poverty to which the people of Newham have been reduced by the benefit changes is absolutely appalling.

Council housing had an honourable beginning. Among the Victorian philanthropists Octavia Hill was a person whom we might have expected the Victorian moralists of today to admire. It is sad to see that council housing has come to a sordid end, mauled by lesser men who do not understand what they are doing. If they did, their sins would be unforgivable.

The Bill is petty and mean minded. It has been put together by a megalomaniac whose only concern seems to be control of local government, without regard to individual merits or faults. I ask my local government colleagues to hang on. In two years' time they will be free from the clutches of this vicious, nasty, mean-minded Government because a Labour Government will set local government and local democracy free. I look forward to the day when I shall greet them from the Government Benches where I shall hold a place of honour, although unfortunately I shall probably still be at the back.

9.6 pm

**Mr. Robert G. Hughes** (Harrow, West): I should like to comment on what was said by the hon. Member for Newham, North-West (Mr. Banks) towards the end of his speech. It contained few facts and it is a great pity that he grievously misquoted a great figure. Miss Octavia Hill opposed the building of council houses. She said that London county council was wrong to build council housing—that there were other ways of providing housing for people. She believed that housing associations ought to do it. If the hon. Gentleman had ever bothered to read her very interesting and important writings, or the biography written by her nephew, he would know that she said that the classic mistake was to mix up the collection of rents and the collection of votes. It is an outrage that the hon Gentleman has had the cheek to misrepresent that great lady.

**Mr. Tony Banks:** The hon. Gentleman is quoting her sister.

**Mr. Hughes:** I shall not even try to answer the hon. Gentleman because I want to make some serious points.

My experience in local government, and of serving on the Standing Committee that considered the Bill, has led me to believe that the Labour party collectively does not understand that there is an important difference between councillors and officers of the council. The Labour party has sought to smudge the dividing line in all the amendments that they have tabled and in all the arguments that they have used. The Opposition have proved beyond any shadow of doubt that it is they who have poisoned the well and made it necessary for the Government to introduce this measure.

It is not surprising that some of the clauses in a 164-clause Bill have not been discussed. As far as I can remember, clause 145, which came out of Committee as clause 155, has not been discussed at all. That is the clause which relates to race relations and the code of practice.

I congratulate the Government on producing clause 155 which will do so much to widen the scope of the Commission for Racial Equality and the Department of the Environment in laying down codes of practice. I apologise if some hon. Members have heard my arguments before but I think that they bear repeating, particularly in the light of some of the remarks in the Chamber during the early hours of this morning.

I do not believe that we know the size of the problem of racial abuse. Some tenants who face harassment report it only when it gets out of hand. Clause 155 will enable a much clearer picture to be produced. The report published last year by the Commission for Racial Equality, entitled "Living in Terror", states that it is not enough to have a vague notion of certain estates where harassment is a problem. When a code of practice has been produced, authorities will need to focus more clearly on the estates where it is happening and ascertain clearly when and where incidents occur. Local authorities should work out a plan of action. They should talk to their tenants, find out where the abuse is coming from and why it happens and decide what to do about it.

I will quote the London borough of Newham, which the hon. Member for Newham, North-West knows much more about and which has been mentioned several times in connection with these matters. Every hour there is an abuse of a black household, and one in four black residents in Newham faces abuse over a 12-month period.

Abuse is not restricted to inner London or to the London borough of Newham. Far too many cases of racial abuse in the London borough of Harrow are reported to me. The problem needs to be tackled, and I am genuinely delighted that the Government have produced clause 155, which will enable them to go further than they could last year. Last year, during the passage of the Housing Bill—now the Housing Act 1988—the Government wanted to go further but were restricted by the long title of the Bill. The Minister of State, Foreign and Commonwealth Office, the hon. Member for Bristol, West (Mr. Waldegrave), who was then the housing Minister, said in Committee:

"I am signalling that the Government are considering the possibility—positively, we shall want to cover all housing . . . I give a commitment today . . . to put the CRE in a position to produce a code with all the implications referred to by my hon. Friend."—[*Official Report, Standing Committee G,* 15 March 1988; c. 1626.]

The Minister was referring to me. I am very grateful to the Government for sticking to their word.

I recognise that it is not easy to put together a code of practice that will work. It is not easy to find out the source of the serious racial abuse to which I have alluded. It is not easy to work out the best solution. Now we have started a process whereby we can start looking seriously at these things and make sure that we do something to help the many black and Asian people who suffer abuse daily on housing estates, in private housing and in owner-occupied property.

Secondly, I wish to discuss the housing revenue changes which seek to prevent councils using ratepayers' or community charge payers' money to underwrite rent arrears or to subsidise artificially low rents. The Labour party has suggested that we are overrating the problem and that it is not happening. I should like to prove that the Bill is necessary and that something has to be done by alluding to what was said by the hon. Member for Normanton (Mr. O'Brien) in the Standing Committee considering the Local Government and Housing Bill.

"In the cities it is just not Labour councils that make rate fund contributions"—

So do

"Kensington and Chelsea, Westminster, Harrow, Barnet"
—[*Official Report, Standing Committtee G,* 18 April 1989; c. 936.]

The hon. Gentleman was challenged about this, but stuck to his guns.

Let us look at the facts behind the hon. Gentleman's allegations. He said that Kensington and Chelsea makes a rate fund contribution. That is not true. Figures produced by the Department of the Environment show a blank in this area; that council makes no rate fund contribution.

The hon. Gentleman sought to put Barnet and Harrow in the same league as Labour councils, which I shall mention in a moment. In Committee, the hon. Gentleman was told that Barnet made a £20,000 rate fund contribution. What we did not know at the time was that Harrow's contribution was much bigger—£24,000, hardly a significant sum.

**Mr. O'Brien:** What about Westminster?

**Mr. Hughes:** Granted, Westminster made a contribution of more than £2 million. I do not comment on Westminster council; it seems to comment on its own problems enough——

**Mr. O'Brien:** It is a Tory council.

**Mr. Hughes:** So it is alleged.

I want to talk about councils which are milking the system—councils in London which are misusing their power in two ways. Let us examine some examples of the budgeted rate fund contributions to the housing revenue account in 1989-90. Camden contributed £39 million, Hackney, £27 million, Islington, £46 million, Lambeth, £32 million, Southwark, £23 million and SLD-controlled Tower Hamlets, £24 million. Brent council contributed £9 million.

Alongside some of these rate fund contributions goes the inability, in some cases, to collect rate arrears. Southwark is the winner in this league, with arrears of £19 million. How can these people say that they seek to make a genuine contribution to good housing in their areas when they run their housing revenue account so badly and milk the ratepayers for a problem that does no good for the provision of decent housing?

In the context of the combination of the housing parts of the Bill with those which implement the Widdicombe report, it is interesting to consider the case of the vice-chairman of Lambeth's housing committee, Miss Josie Byrne. In her case, what the hon. Member for Newham, North-West describes as the gutter press has done a good job. On 8 June she was reported as owing £2,000 in rent arrears, having claimed £20,000 in expenses as a councillor during that year. Magically, within days of the report, she discovered that she could repay those arrears. The *Today* newspaper did a good job in exposing this classic example of the Labour party's misuse of its position to run council housing empires which can be described—I have done so before—as evil.

The Bill will ensure that every council concentrates on running council housing well and on making a contribution to good housing, so that housing will not be merely a political toy of the Labour party.

I welcome the Bill.

9.18 pm

**Mr. David Winnick** (Walsall, North): I agree with the first part of the remarks made by the hon. Member for Harrow, West (Mr. Hughes). He deplored racial abuse and attacks. I and all my right hon. and hon. Friends agree with that. The sort of poisonous rubbish that was heard in an outburst last night from the hon. Member for Thurrock (Mr. Janman) disappointed a number of Conservative Members—I do not know whether a majority—and outrages all Opposition Members. We on the Labour Benches are wholly opposed to racism in all its manifestations. Whether that stance is electorally popular at any given moment makes no difference. We have made our principles clear and we shall stand by them all our lives, in the House and outside it.

This is in essence a thoroughly bad Bill which again shows the malice which the Government feel towards large sections of the community, such as council tenants. One of the Bill's main purposes is greatly to increase council rents. That is the purpose behind the ring-fencing of the housing revenue account. The Secretary of State's statement last week again showed how right we were when we talked of large rent increases to come. They will not come all at once. They will come over a period, but there will be substantial rent increases because the objective of the Government so far as possible is to bring council rents to the level of market rents in the privately rented sector.

Another aim of the Bill is substantially to reduce the existing public sector, which has been reduced substantially already. Normally when we say that Conservative Members laugh and say that that is not their aim. I remind the House of what the Secretary of State said on Second Reading, when responding to an intervention by my hon. Friend the Member for Newham, North-West (Mr. Banks):

"First, I hope that the hon. Gentleman has advised such people that they should have exercised the right to buy and that they can still do so, thereby avoiding the trap of paying rent for a lifetime and ending up owning nothing".—[*Official Report,* 14 February 1989; Vol. 147, c. 175.]

In other words, the right hon. Gentleman wants a substantial reduction in council dwellings arid no replacement by new building. In my borough there has been no new council house building for 10 years, and the same applies to most parts of the country.

Council tenants are to be punished because they wish to remain in that position. The Government say in effect to them, "If you do not like what we are doing, and if you do not like substantial rent increases, the remedy is in your hands. Buy the dwelling." Labour Members say that there will always remain a need for a sizeable public rented sector. There will always be a large number of people—a minority, but a large number nevertheless—who will not be in a position to buy their dwellings, and they have every right to decent accommodation. That can come only from the public sector and genuine housing associations.

Another aspect of the Bill which we find offensive is the part of the ring-fencing of the housing revenue accounts which is designed to ensure that housing benefits, rebates, for poorer council tenants come from the higher rents of other council tenants. The poorer elements will subsidise the even poorer ones, and that is totally offensive to us. The relief of poverty should come of course from central Government. Why should some council tenants pay much higher rents to ensure that those who are less well off are assisted by those higher rents?

[Mr. David Winnick]

The Government refuse to recognise that there remains an acute housing shortage. If it is said that that is only propaganda on the part of Labour Members, consider what was said on Second Reading by the hon. Member for Taunton (Mr. Nicholson), who also spoke today. He said:

"Last Saturday, half my surgery cases had come to me because of housing problems. That was the highest proportion I had encountered in my 18 months as a Member of Parliament. I am finding that it is increasingly difficult to accommodate the housing needs of my constituents—for example, young people, perhaps with a baby, who are living with their parents."[*Official Report,* 14 February 1989; Vol. 147, c. 220.]

I think I see the hon. Member for Cheltenham (Mr. Irving) nodding in agreement with that sentiment. At my surgeries, on the first and last Saturdays each month, the majority of my constituents who come to see me do so over housing problems. The majority of letters that I receive from my constituents are about housing matters. That shows that this is not Labour propaganda or mischief-making. As I said, many people are desperately in need of housing, but as a result of Government policy, with no new council houses being built, we are witnessing a substantial decrease in the public rented sector.

Our fellow citizens in acute housing need are being penalised. That is why we are so opposed to the Government's housing policy. We make no apology for the fact that we believe that we have a duty and responsibility to voice the concern and anger of our constituents with housing difficulties who, as I have said at other times, have as much right to decent accommodation as any hon. Member. If they cannot buy a home because they are on small incomes, why should they be unable to obtain adequate rented accommodation? Why should they be punished?

I am also totally opposed to discrimination against those people employed in local government who, because they earn £13,500 or more, will no longer have the right to be elected to another local authority. That undermines civil liberties. I accept that there can be abuse from time to time; there is no aspect of life, I suppose, in which abuse does not sometimes occur. However, that is no reason why everyone who falls into that earnings bracket should be penalised. I do not wish to defend the indefensible, and if abuse occurs on either side it is wrong. However, I do not want to take away people's democratic rights. As I said only last week, one of the main functions of the House is to defend people's civil liberties.

From time to time Conservative Members make remarks about civil liberties. However, I doubt whether a single Tory Member will tonight rebel against the taking away of the democratic rights of large numbers of people. Perhaps it is wrong to suggest that this would happen to large numbers of people, but the figure does not matter. The important point is that they will no longer be entitled to exercise their democratic right because they happen to work in local government. That is basically wrong. This policy change comes from a Government who have given jobs to all their sympathisers and supporters up and down the country. In the past 10 years, people have been appointed merely because they are members of the Conservative party or closely connected with it.

The right hon. Member for Old Bexley and Sidcup—I am sure that Government Members know to whom I am referring—recently said that the way in which the Government conducts their press office is corrupt. How right he is. My hon. Friend the Member for Newham, North-West referred to the role of Mr. Ingham. I doubt whether there has ever been a Government chief press officer who has so abused his position, and with the direct encouragement of the Prime Minister.

**Mr. Brandon-Bravo:** The House is often given the impression that the only twin tracking which this Bill seeks to eliminate is the kind of outrageous abuse seen in some London boroughs and, occasionally, in Liverpool and one or two other places, but I believe that the abuse is more widespread. In the last county council elections two employees of Nottingham city council were successful. I wish them good luck in their Labour seats on the county council. Will the hon. Member for Walsall, North (Mr. Winnick) comment on the fact that the Labour city council has given consent not just for normal leave to attend to their duties at county hall, but has said that they can have as much time off as they like to carry out whatever length of duties on however many committees of the county council? That permission was granted on the ground that the city would be proud for them to do so. Surely that cannot possibly be right.

**Mr. Winnick:** Even if the hon. Gentleman were right——

**Mr. Martlew:** I was a county councillor for 15 years and I was given as much time off as I liked to carry out my duties, which included two years as chairman of the county council. I worked for a company in the private sector.

**Mr. Winnick:** My hon. Friend's intervention effectively answers the point raised by the hon. Member for Nottingham, South (Mr. Brandon-Bravo). My hon. Friend also implied that those in the public sector should not be given worse treatment than those in the private sector. Even if the hon. Member for Nottingham, South were right, there is no reason to take away everyone else's political rights because of alleged abuse. There is no justification for that.

The Bill helps to explain the deep feeling of revulsion that was demonstrated in last Thursday's vote. Many people believe that the Government have abused their office and that they are completely out of touch with the lives of millions of ordinary people and with the matters that affect them—council rents, the poll tax and many other measures. If Conservative Members do not understand that deep feeling of revulsion, which has brought about such great Labour success in the European elections, I suggest that they study the Bill and much of the other legislation passed in recent years, because it explains only too well why people have come to the conclusion that enough is enough.

9.30 pm

**Mr. Peter L. Pike** (Burnley): I was somewhat surprised when the Minister said that one of the main objectives of the Bill was to strengthen local government. He used that phrase several times. Either he does not understand what "strength" means because he has the wrong dictionary, or he is taking too much note of the current political advisers at the Department of the Environment. The Government are pushing through legislation which curtails the activities of local government and local government employees, but they are doing the opposite with their own Departments.

More political appointees are working in Government Departments than ever before, dealing with matters such as water privatisation and the regulations that will result from the Bill. No other Government have done this to such as extent. We all know the amount of money that the Government are spending on publicising their programmes under the vague notion of public information. Yet when a local authority does the same such information immediately becomes political.

This is another Bill in a long chain of legislation to shackle local government. Ever since they were elected in 1979, the Government have said that they would give freedom to local government, but all that they have done has been to put shackles on local government with legislation such as this and with financial restrictions. The Minister fails to recognise that democracy and freedom in local government are important to many who serve in local government as officers and to local councillors, whether Conservative, SLD or Labour. The Government should recognise the importance of local government.

Because of the way the Bill has been timetabled, last week we had only two days to debate Report stage. It would have been better to have three days, because we could then have had a shorter Third Reading debate. The difficulty with the debate on Third Reading is that we cannot refer to the amendments, whether Government or Opposition, we had insufficient time to debate last week. We can refer only to the Bill as it stands.

My hon. Friend the Member for Newham, North-West (Mr. Banks) said last week that the debate on some important issues was a sham because there was not sufficient time to discuss them. We all know that on Wednesday evening a major debate on the dog registration scheme took place in the early hours of the morning. I hope that the other place will reconsider that issue, because the Government got it wrong. Many other items put into the Bill by amendments and new clauses forced through by the Government have not been properly debated.

My hon. Friends have already mentioned the problems of ring-fencing. The main purpose of some aspects of the Bill is to force people either to buy their council homes or to opt out and thus enhance the private rented sector. Another purpose is to encourage the growing business expansion scheme. While the Bill might, in certain areas, deal with certain problems, it is nevertheless the wrong way to try to solve the housing problems. Rather than giving tax incentives, the Government should make the necessary funding available to deal with the problems.

The current difficulties in both the public and private housing sectors will not be solved by the Bill. The Government are not prepared to allocate sufficient funds to deal with the problems. We are arguing for funds not just for the public sector, but also for the private sector, which suffers from the same problems. The unavailability of land has led to a deterioration of housing standards. The Minister has only to look around his constituency and the neighbouring constituencies in north-east Lancashire, such as mine, to appreciate the problems of decline in the private sector. People cannot improve their homes because their value is so low that they cannot obtain loans. The hon. Member for Taunton (Mr. Nicholson) mentioned defective housing. There are problems with Spooner houses in my area. They are of a wooden frame structure —not all that old—and because of problems with the ties the gable ends need to be rebuilt. Those who bought their council houses in good faith under the right to buy cannot

afford to repair them. Building societies will not lend them any additional money because of the low value of their houses. I hope that the Minister will seriously take on board the problems with housing in north-east Lancashire.

I wish briefly to discuss part I of the Bill and the implications of Widdicombe. They have rightly been dealt with already at some length because the Bill goes far beyond what is required to deal with the minor problem of political involvement by certain key officers. The Bill is a serious erosion of people's rights and civil liberties and of democracy. It moves in the wrong direction and the Government are treading a dangerous path. The arbitrary figure of £13,500 is nonsense and the Government should think again.

Even more important, the Bill gives yet further powers to the Secretary of State to act through regulations. We have been given no idea what will be contained in those regulations, especially the provisions relating to council employees. Will canvassing be forbidden? Will they be prevented from putting up election posters? It is wrong that, time and again, half-baked legislation is pushed through the House without the Government providing crucial information. When the Government introduce regulations they do not allow sufficient time for debate. Of course, they do not want them to be debated, but if they have to be debated they make sure that that happens at a time when they will not receive any publicity. Not only do the Government not believe in local government democracy—they do not really believe in parliamentary democracy.

The Association of District Councils has expressed concern about economic development and discretionary expenditure by local authorities, which is covered in part III. It says:

"The Association wishes to ensure that restrictions to be included in Regulation are kept to a minimum and do not inhibit sensible, constructive and imaginative initiatives."

Again, the association is referring to proposals that will be introduced through regulations, and which are not specified at this stage. The association makes the point that the proposal could result in around 40 per cent. of the 333 non-metropolitan district councils being prevented from giving crucial help to start-ups of small and medium businesses, as they do at present.

Another crucial concern is the companies owned by local authorities and run by local authorities. The Minister is well aware of what I believe is valuable work carried out with Lancashire Enterprise. Many aspects of part III give rise to serious concern about whether the local authorities will be able to continue to provide money and to do all that they wish for such developments.

The Minister for Local Government spoke of the Bill "strengthening" local government. I believe that it will weaken the powers of local government. It could be his swansong as a Minister at the Department of the Environment. Year after year, we have had Bills on housing or local government. Every year, when the Government come back with the next Bill, a different Minister comes forward. Some Ministers have gone sideways, some have gone upwards and some have just gone. Let us hope that whether he goes upwards or not, the present Minister will go and that the Minister who takes his place will look at local government in a more positive and constructive manner.

9.41 pm

**Mr. Dave Nellist** (Coventry, South-East): In the past 10 years, a decade of this Government, we have had 50 Bills on local government. Like the others, this Bill does nothing to widen genuine local democracy and local choice for working people. The twin areas of greatest concern in the Bill are the proposals leading to further substantial rent increases for tenants and the draconian restrictions, about which my hon. Friends have spoken, on the freedom of council workers to participate in political activity. We understand that about 70,000 council workers will be affected, but we do not yet know. The regulations to enact that aspect of the Bill will, undoubtedly, come some months hence in the dead of night. We shall have an hour and a half's debate, as we had a couple of weeks ago when we discussed 96 pages of poll tax regulations.

The hon. Member for Nottingham, South (Mr. Brandon-Bravo) intervened when my hon. Friend the Member for Walsall, North (Mr. Winnick) was speaking, again along the theme of so-called jobs for the boys. He made unsubstantiated allegations about councils in London and the council in Liverpool. He was on very thin ice. He supports a Government half of whose supporters are not just Members of Parliament, but have one, two or 10 other jobs, who often pick up thousands of pounds a year for each of those jobs and for whom Members' wages become pocket money. In the last Parliament, the former right hon. and learned Member for Hexham, Mr. Geoffrey Rippon, was a Member of Parliament, a Queen's counsel and a director or chairman of 45 companies. I will never know how he ever had time to come into this Chamber. The voting record of many of those Tory Members is 10 per cent., 12 per cent. or 15 per cent. In the words of the good book, the hon. Member for Nottingham, South should take the beam out of his own eye before worrying about the mote in somebody else's eye. When it comes to twin tracking, Tory Members in this Tory Government have got it down to a fine art.

We do not know whether exactly 70,000 council workers will be affected, but we understand that it is those who are at present working for local authorities who will be prevented from holding office in political parties, from canvassing at elections—and we can understand that after Sunday's Euro results—or even from commenting publicly on matters of party political controversy, including through letters to newspapers. We can imagine the scenario when a council worker, just as the member of the Campaign for Nuclear Disarmament in Sutton Coldfield some years ago, has a knock at the door from two Special Branch officers because of a letter written to a local newspaper. That is what the Bill will introduce.

As drafted, the Bill gives the Secretary of State—a single individual—the power to prevent 70,000 people in this country from exercising their democratic rights. The Bill is fundamentally anti-democratic. It will not only apply to those people who earn more than £13,500 per year —incidentally, we understand that that figure will be frozen for the future so that more and more people will be caught year after year—it will also apply to many lower-paid council workers who give advice to the council or to its committees or who talk to the media.

The Government are taking the road of Stalin. While ostensibly criticising the lack of democracy in China, Cuba and eastern Europe, they are taking precisely the same powers politically to determine the opinions that this country's working people can hold or, if they do not hold opinions favoured by the Government, the jobs that they are allowed to hold.

I turn now to the clauses relating to housing. The Bill is called a housing Bill, but it does nothing for the housing crisis that has developed in the past 10 years. There has been a 17 per cent. fall in the completion of new houses over that period from 244,000 down to 202,000. Local authorities have a 75 per cent. fall in their completions. Furthermore, at today's prices, local authorities have seen their investment budgets cut from £5,000 million in 1978-79 to £1,000 million in 1988-89. One million council houses have been sold, but over the period 1983 to 1987 the waiting list for those council houses grew by 70 per cent. from 0·75 million to 1·25 million people. Yet this Bill does nothing to redress the problems either of the people who want a house or of those who want their home repaired, improved or modified in some way.

Shelter estimates that 150,000 single young people are homeless in this country. In central London, where this Parliament is situated, over 40,000 young people sleep rough. That is a topic to which I intend to return on an Adjournment debate when I shall refer also to the Vagrancy Act 1824.

Like the Housing Act 1988, this Bill does not mention homelessness, but it will cause it—*[Interruption.]* I am doing my best to ensure that you, Madam Deputy Speaker, can hear what I am saying even if Tory Members are patently not interested in the homelessness of young people or of any other age group, especially the Minister who seems to have much better things to do than to listen to a speech about homelessness. Perhaps I could have his attention for a moment or two.

Part VI will cause homelessness. The housing finance sections of last year's Housing Act did nothing to help. That legislation was an enabling Act. In my six years in this madhouse, I have become less and less worried about enabling Acts and I can see more and more merit in giving a future Labour Secretary of State for Industry an "Industry Bill" to give him the power to nationalise companies and then, at 10 o'clock at night, night after night, I can see no problem in bringing forward the names of the companies that will be taken into public ownership. I have learnt from Bills such as this that enabling legislation gives Ministers powers which are then enacted in future orders.

As my hon. Friends have said, part VI deals with the ring-fencing of housing revenue accounts and receipts from council housing rents to stop cross-subsidisation with the general rate account. In 1987-88, £122 million nationally went from rents into the general rates account and £382 million went in the other direction, from councils' general rate fund accounts towards keeping down rents. I am quite happy for the Government to bring in a law to stop Tory councils from making profits out of council tenants and to stop them from transferring profits from rents into the general rate accounts.

The Government have not, of course, given the major reason why rent and housing revenue accounts have been affected and why rents have doubled in the past few years. The reason is the Government's cut in rent subsidies.

The hon. Member for Harrow, West (Mr. Hughes), whose attention I am seeking to gain, attacked cross-subsidisation and said that it represented bad running of the housing account and that it was the equivalent of milking the ratepayers.

You have been here longer than I have, Madam Deputy Speaker. You can remember that prior to this Government every Government accepted the general premise that support of the poorer sections of the community was a charge on national Governments, not on individual local authorities. It was central Government that had to bear the burden. That premise was established by the battles of councils such as Poplar, and tested in later years by Clay Cross and Liverpool.

The Bill will force councils to fund rent rebates from housing revenue accounts. In Coventry that means that two thirds of council tenants who get housing benefit will have that funded by the one third who do not get housing benefit. That will mean massive rent rises in Coventry and for 5 million council tenants nationally. Rents will rocket to such an extent that the Government's true aim in the Bill will come about and council tenants will be forced to try to buy their homes so that they may get public subsidy —that is, mortgage interest tax relief, which amounts to £5·5 billion nationally, or they will have to accept that their homes be sold to another landlord.

This is where all the legislation starts to be tied together. The Housing Act 1988, which brought in so-called tenants' choice, was extended by the Rent Office (Additional Functions) Order 1989, laid in February and debated on 21 March. It will take effect when part VI of the Bill gets Royal Assent. Part VI will force tenants to consider selling their houses to another landlord, probably a private landlord. When they do so, they will lose the protection of council rents. Their rents will become market rents. If the market rents are different from what the council's rent officer says that the council is allowed to pay, they will lose housing benefit.

I want to give a few examples. Recently we have had 300 cases in Coventry, some of them in my constituency. For a first-floor flat in Hugh road the asking rent is £35 and the market rent assessed by the council rent officer is £23. For a first-floor rear room in North street, just outside my constituency, the asking rent is £51·96 and the assessed market rent is £31. For board and lodging accommodation in Warwick road, in the constituency of the junior Education Minister, the hon. Member for Coventry, South-West (Mr. Butcher), the asking rent is £100·42 and the assessed market rent is £60.

What the 1988 Act, the rent offices order and this Bill, taken together, mean is that my council, in the last example, where the asking rent is £100·42, can claim 97 per cent. of the housing benefit from the Government on the £60 of assessed rent for which it pays housing benefit. It can claim nothing on the £40·42 of the asking rent which is above the assessed rent. The council has two choices. If it does not pay the person claiming for private accommodation the extra money, the result will be that the person will be made homeless. Let us not forget clause 138, as it was when the Bill went into Committee; it discharges all local authorities from having any duty to provide housing. People will be made homeless by the provision. The council's alternative is to pay the extra housing benefit and get nothing from the Government. What will the Minister do? What will his gaffer, who is sitting next to him, do? He will rate-cap Coventry. Coventry would be going outside the regulations. It would be paying housing benefit that the legislation says it should not pay.

I have gone into some detail on the examples because the matter has not been referred to so far in the debate. Hundreds of people in Coventry and tens of thousands nationally could be made homeless because of part VI of the Bill. Councils will not want to risk being rate-capped by the Secretary of State. The Bill does not provide for the building of more houses or for the release of houses for people to rent. It does nothing about the appalling and tragic waste of life on building sites. It is not about housing. It is about further privatisation, shoving up rents and removing the democratic rights of council workers. It is a thieves' charter. The Secretary of State is stealing the democratic rights of 70,000 council workers, and he is stealing too the housing benefit and the very accommodation of tens of thousands of tenants in council and private sector housing. The House should treat the Bill with the contempt that it deserves by kicking it out on Third Reading.

9.54 pm

**Mr. David Blunkett** (Sheffield, Brightside): In the early hours of last Thursday I thought that the longest day had become 14 June, but as today's debate has worn on I realise that this is really the longest day of the year. Coverage of the Bill by the media last week concentrated on dog registration. Much as I have a commitment to that subject and care deeply about it, I hope that the coverage of today's proceedings by the media tomorrow, especially the BBC, which did not cover the debate last Tuesday at all in "Yesterday in Parliament", will acknowledge that what is happening to people's democratic and civil rights, to economic and industrial investment in companies, to the capital investment in our infrastructure and to rents and housing, have some importance even if those who frequent the portals of the Palace of Westminster do not always feel that those matters impinge on them immediately. One day some of those issues will catch them up.

The Minister has an ironic sense of humour which I did not know he had until we were in Committee and he started cracking little jokes. On 28 February, he said:

"We are introducing the Bill because of our commitment to democracy."

In the same debate, he said:

"I am committed to local government".—[*Official Report, Standing Committee G*, 28 February 1989; c. 95.]

In his cheeky little way, he said that again tonight—that he supports local government. Like Dracula offering a blood transfusion, he offers local government a quick way out of what was previously accepted by all parties as local democracy. The purpose of the Bill is clearly to undermine our commitment over generations to the kind of local political democratic system that people have respected.

When the Bill was first introduced, it was described as the 50th Bill dealing with one or more aspects of local government. The Government boasted that it would be their last major local government Bill. I can promise the House that local government is not dead and that it will fight back against the Bill, as it has fought every other major measure introduced by the Government. There is life there, and we shall support our colleagues in local government in retaining and maintaining their commitment to their local electorate.

Only one thread unites the disparate and miscellaneous elements—albeit they are important—encapsulated in the Bill. That is the Government's obsession with replacing representative political democracy with the laws of the market place. The Government are intent on market forces dominating all our lives. That is not the free market, but

[*Mr. David Blunkett*]

a distorted and specially manipulated market that will ensure that the Government's values and ideology are implemented in place of those decided by local people for local people. That is why we are opposing a whole range of measures in three major areas.

First, there is the restriction on basic civil democratic rights. The Government believe that we can have impartiality only if people hide their true political feelings. We believe that independence and impartiality can never be achieved by suppressing the expression of honest political opinions. Democracy can never be safeguarded by undermining basic democratic rights. If, as we said last week, those rights have to be sustained by appeal to the institutions of Europe, people will have to take that road in order to secure, as was described in the House on Monday night, the freedoms that the Government are only too prepared to take away.

It is obvious that anyone who seeks to take away the democratic rights of more than 130,000 people—the rights to speak or to canvas on behalf of a political party—cannot believe in democracy. The Government cannot take away existing rights and replace them with restrictions and at the same time claim that they believe in democracy. That is simply not possible. [*Interruption.*] I understand why those Conservative Members who are braying believe in doing that. If one does not believe in representative political democracy, and if the laws of the market place and the value of one's bank balance are more important than people obtaining their will through the ballot box, one will feel contempt for those institutions and practices which implement that democracy. That is why Conservative Members jeer and show contempt for such rights.

*It being Ten o'clock, the debate stood adjourned.*

## BUSINESS OF THE HOUSE

*Ordered,*

That, at this day's sitting, the Local Government and Housing Bill and the Ways and Means Motions may be proceeded with, though opposed, until any hour.—[*Mr. Maclean.*]

# Local Government and Housing Bill

*Question again proposed,* That the Bill be now read the Third time.

**Mr. Gummer:** Is it democratic for the chief executive of a local authority, who advises all parts of a local council and who is duty bound to give impartial advice to all members of that authority, also to be chairman of the local Labour party?

**Mr. Blunkett:** The Opposition made it clear in new clauses 2, 3 and 4 that we were in favour of a code of practice which differentiated between, first, the restrictions that should be imposed on senior council officers standing for other authorities—what is generally known as twin-tracking—as we made clear again tonight, and, secondly, how people should maintain probity and sensibility in undertaking their tasks outside their working life in pursuing their democratic rights. We said that such a code of practice should be tried for one year.

Many of us would consider it inappropriate for a chief executive to hold a high-profile political position in a political party, but we would not seek to legislate to

remove the rights of 130,000 people in order to prevent that happening. We do not believe in dealing with the worries about the few by removing the rights of the many. That is what we are talking about. [*Interruption.*]

**Madam Deputy Speaker:** Order. The hon. Member for Sheffield, Brightside (Mr. Blunkett) must be heard.

**Mr. Blunkett:** There are some advantages in not being able to see the distorted faces of the Ministers.

It is because we believe that in a democracy there is nothing more fundamental than the right to express a view openly that we are putting forward our view that the Bill is unacceptable. What could be worse than someone asking a fellow member of the council to put a poster in a window, knock on a door or write a letter, only to be told that it is more than his job is worth and that he will be sacked for exercising his democratic right?

The vindictiveness expressed against local authority officers applies equally to councillors. The only suggestion as to how local councillors should carry out their duties under the new regulations is that they should have more evening meetings. Some Conservative Members may have carried out their duties as councillors effectively and understood that, in order to be in touch with their electorate, to have surgeries and to take part in their own political party, they should have evening meetings, while running cities, counties and boroughs during the day. Councillors should be given time off to do that, and they should be properly remunerated—not the £51,000 per year that the chairman of the Yorkshire water authority reaps, nor the £57,000 that the chairman of the London residuary body reaps, but a small and reasonable remuneration to ensure that they can do their job.

We see the same restrictions and market forces implied in respect of economic development, joint companies and capital investment. I am grateful to the hon. Member for Taunton (Mr. Nicholson) for his comments, but he must not be under any illusions. Last week's Government amendments leave very much in the balance joint partnership ventures, economic regeneration and investment in the future. Local authorities will not easily be able to enter into partnerships with the private sector, and voluntary bodies are under threat. The arts lobby is very concerned that the very act of being associated with and receiving investment from local authorities will bring it and the local authorities within the ambit of the Bill's restrictions.

The Bill contains many pernicious provisions, but that which outstrips all the others is the Government's attack on the public rented sector. In Committee, the contribution made by the Minister—I was intrigued to discover that he is a warm-blooded being after all—was to inform right hon. and hon. Members that he did not need central heating because he could wear a woolly vest. That was the Minister's contribution to the issue of public sector housing.

Tonight we have debated the proposition that if market forces do not achieve Government ends, they should be manipulated until they do. The cost of housing in a particular district and the average value of council sales, bearing in mind that the properties being sold are the most expensive, will be interpreted in fixing rents from the centre. The Government will determine rents, and when they have done that they will determine subsidy. When income from rents goes into surplus and the local authority makes a profit, that money must be used to meet the cost of paying housing benefits for other council tenants. The poor will be made to pay for the very poor. Private sector tenants and owner-occupiers enjoy subsidy and tax relief for which we all pay, but local authority tenants will be subsidised by their neighbours and the people on the street.

That twisted logic, which *The Times* described on 3 February as social engineering, will ensure that in high-cost areas rents will increase still further. By increasing rents and, as the Secretary of State described it last week, bringing them in line with the market, the Government will contribute to higher house prices as well. People seeking housing will not be able to afford to rent or to buy. If they are just above the poverty line they will pay full rent, but if they obtain a mortgage they will be hit by the Chancellor's high interest rates. Young people will be hit whichever way they turn. If that is social engineering with the aim of pushing people out of the south-east, the electorate will have none of it.

We want to see a return to affordable, attainable housing so that people can have a decent roof over their heads. Tonight we shall vote on whether we believe that distortion of the market and Government intervention to implement Government values is acceptable to the country, or whether people should determine for themselves local politics, economic development and investment, and be able to ensure affordable rents. We shall vote on whether such matters are to be decided through our system of political democracy or whether the restrictions and laws of the market place should be imposed on everyone from the centre.

Last week we saw the electorate's decision in respect of the European elections. In next year's local council elections and in the next general election, the Bill's provisions will contribute to the downfall of the Conservative Government.

10.9 pm

**The Parliamentary Under-Secretary of State for the Environment (Mr. David Trippier):** Let me begin by saying to the hon. Member for Sheffield, Brightside (Mr. Blunkett) that I am relieved not to have experienced a repeat of the last occasion when there was a major rail strike. The Bill was in Committee, and the hon. Gentleman will recall that at 10.30 am the Conservatives had a full house, while the Opposition Benches were completely empty.

**Mr. Tony Banks:** We were all walking to work, of course.

**Mr. Trippier:** The hon. Member for Newham, North-West (Mr. Banks) certainly was not there. He was probably talking to his parrot at the time.

I felt compelled to jump on to the other side of the Committee, because the hon. Member for Brightside felt a little lonely and I knew that he needed some help and advice. Now the hon. Gentleman has the temerity to accuse Ministers responsible for the Bill of being vindictive. When he stood alone and we bailed him out by delaying discussion, I do not think that our behaviour was vindictive. We could have completed the remaining stages of the Bill in 20 minutes, which would have been a record by any standards; but we chose not to do so.

Having heard the contribution of his hon. Friends tonight, I bet that the hon. Gentleman wishes that some of them had stayed away today as they did then. In particular, I do not think that he would have missed the hon. Members for Walsall, North (Mr. Winnick) and for Coventry, South-East (Mr. Nellist): indeed, I do not think that anyone would miss them.

We have heard from the Opposition the usual mix of exaggeration, half truths and downright misinformation. Of course, they have a huge problem. Apart from the proposals outlined by my right hon. Friend the Minister for Local Government, which stem from the independent Widdicombe committee, the hon. Member for Normanton (Mr. O'Brien) has come up with the revelation—which will be on the record for everyone to see—that the Labour party believes in political chief executives. There is a direct conflict between what he said and what has been said by the hon. Member for Brightside.

The truth is that the Bill will achieve greater accountability, encourage better management and strengthen the local democratic process, as my hon. Friend the Member for Harrow, West (Mr. Hughes) said so clearly in his excellent speech.

The Opposition's other problem is that one of the principal aims of the Bill is to focus resources on those in greatest need. It seeks to direct improvement and repair grants to those on lower incomes, and to give more support to the poorer owner-occupiers. It seeks to focus capital expenditure on the areas of most need, and to relate current subsidies to needs so that authorities in poorer areas with more poor tenants will receive a higher proportion of the available subsidy.

Speaker after speaker this evening has attacked that as unfair. What do they want? What is their policy? Do they want to keep improvement grants for the better off, at the expense of poorer owner-occupiers? Do they want to give fewer resources to the inner cities, and to the poorer authorities of the midlands and the north? Do they really want to retain a central rents system or formula which, by incorporating flat-rate increases regardless of cost, means higher rent increases than necessary in poorer districts and proportionately larger subsidies to richer districts?

**Mr. Battle:** Will the Minister give way?

**Mr. Trippier:** I shall refer specifically to the hon. Gentleman in a few moments. He may wish to intervene then, and I shall certainly give him the opportunity. *[Interruption.]*

**Madam Deputy Speaker:** Order. I hope that the House will have the courtesy to listen to the Minister when he is winding up this important debate.

**Mr. Trippier:** Perhaps Labour Members want all the things that I have mentioned. Perhaps they want to spend more taxpayers' money on everyone. That is a strange thought, however. If it is true, Labour party housing policy is based on taxing poorer people and regions to provide grants for owner-occupiers who do not need them, extra resources for the richer southern authorities that draw in higher capital receipts, and increased subsidies to rents in richer areas with higher average incomes and lower unemployment.

The hon. Member for Leeds, West (Mr. Battle) has returned to his favourite topic, minimum housing standards. He is nothing if not persistent. Let me remind

[*Mr. Trippier*]

the House about his minimum standards. There are 18 of them—enough to keep every environmental health officer in the country busy night and day. It would make the enforcement of income tax seem like a picnic. One of his standards stipulates that

"Any dwelling shall be so located that the immediate environmental factors are tolerable."

What on earth does that mean? Does it mean that if I do not like the view from my kitchen window I can claim that my house is unfit? If the traffic on the road outside my house is heavy at certain times of the day, does that also mean that I can claim that my house is unfit?

Another of the hon. Gentleman's standards is that

"The habitable room of any dwelling shall comprise a minimum size as specified by the Secretary of State."

I see that the hon. Member for Leeds, West is nodding.

**Mr. Battle** *rose——*

**Mr. Trippier:** All this is from a party that claims conversion to consumer choice and that has attacked the Bill throughout its passage as giving the Secretary of State unacceptable powers.

**Mr. Battle:** Will the Minister give way?

**Mr. Trippier:** I shall certainly give way, but the hon. Gentleman must be patient for just a little longer.

The hon. Gentleman suggested in Committee that the Secretary of State is being given unacceptable powers. However, he wants to give the Secretary of State more powers. Is he seriously suggesting that the Secretary of State should prescribe a room size that might condemn thousands of highly desirable houses to unfitness?

I ask the hon. Gentleman this simple question: how many properties in his own constituency would conform to his minimum standards? Would his own house conform to them? Mine certainly does not, nor does the home of my right hon. Friend the Minister for Local Government or of my other ministerial colleague, the hon. Member for Surrey, South-West (Mrs. Bottomley). I give him this undertaking. I shall willingly, on any occasion that is convenient to both of us, visit his home. I know that he is a very hospitable chap. He boasts about Yorkshire hospitality, and I am sure that he will be hospitable, even to a Lancastrian like me. I know that I shall get a cup of tea, or even a little bit more. I am even prepared to bring with me my right hon. Friend the Minister for Local Government and my hon. Friend the Member for Surrey, South-West. I shall enjoy inspecting the hon. Gentleman's home. If it fails any of the standards on the list of 18, I shall ask his local environmental health officer to provide an estimate of how much it would cost to bring his house up to standard and to multiply it by all other houses in a similar condition in his constituency and throughout the land. His proposal sounds reasonable, but it is totally unworkable, impracticable and interventionist in practice.

**Mr. Battle:** I am surprised to hear that the Minister has not heard of the Parker Morris standards which specify area, that there should be no dampness and that there should be adequate natural lighting, all of which are in the catalogue of 18. Will the Minister give an undertaking that he will restore the Parker Morris standards that his Government have removed and that the environmental health officers are calling for?

**Mr. Trippier:** So many additional standards have been laid down by the hon. Gentleman that, if we are not careful, we shall have everything, short of gold taps. It is absolutely ridiculous. The hon. Gentleman and his hon. Friends—[*Interruption.*]

**Mr. Tony Banks:** On a point of order, Madam Deputy Speaker. It may very well be that the Minister is talking rubbish, but we are entitled to hear it. I should be grateful if you would call the House to order.

**Madam Deputy Speaker:** I have already drawn the attention of the House to the fact that far too many conversations are taking place while the Minister is speaking. I appeal to those hon. Members who wish to continue to hold conversations to do so on the other side of the swing doors.

**Mr. Trippier:** Of course until very recently Opposition Members had no alternative but to attack our policy. They had no alternative policy to offer. But the famed Labour party policy review has now been published and the cat is out of the bag. Opposition Members rebutted criticisms a score of times by referring to the clear statement of Labour's housing policy that was to come. It is the alternative to the Bill. Now that we have it all our questions can be answered. Now we learn how more grants for all and more subsidies for all regardless of need will be achieved. Calculating what rents will be under our policy, according to the hon. Member for Brightside, takes only a matter of minutes, and presumably can be worked out on the back of an envelope. So one can assume fairly safely, given the time that Opposition Members spent putting together their alternative to the Bill, which is referred to in their document, that that would be their answer.

**Mr. George Howarth:** On a point of order, Madam Deputy Speaker. I am grateful to the Minister for taking time to publicise the Labour party's excellent housing policy which appears in the review. However, as the Labour party's policy is not contained in the Bill, is the Minister in order?

**Madam Deputy Speaker:** The hon. Gentleman can leave it to the occupant of the Chair to determine whether the Minister is in order.

**Mr. Trippier:** I am most anxious to stay in order.

I have heard a number of Opposition Members refer to their alternative policy, which is precisely what we are discussing.

**Mr. O'Brien:** Will the Minister give way?

**Mr. Trippier:** I shall not give way. I have taken a number of interventions from Opposition Members, and as it is after 10 o'clock I am anxious to wind up.

I hope that Opposition Members will explain to the House and to the rest of the country who will pay for the extra subsidies that they would make available. It is clear that people in the midlands and the north will pay, as the Bill seeks to give fairer treatment to local authorities in the greatest need.

The Labour party's policy is a jumble of vague platitudes, a nod in the direction of every conceivable interest group. It was supposed to have been a review, but it is a recipe that has not changed one jot. It proposes to spend more money on everything and everyone. In direct contrast, the Government are proud to be the champion of greater efficiency in local authorities, greater accountability in housing management and the directing of resources to those in greatest need. The Bill enshrines those policies, and I commend it to the House.

*Question put,* That the Bill be now read the Third time:—

*The House divided:* Ayes 310, Noes 206.

**Division No. 257]**                                    **[10.22 pm**

### AYES

Adley, Robert
Aitken, Jonathan
Alexander, Richard
Alison, Rt Hon Michael
Allason, Rupert
Amess, David
Amos, Alan
Arbuthnot, James
Arnold, Jacques *(Gravesham)*
Arnold, Tom *(Hazel Grove)*
Ashby, David
Aspinwall, Jack
Atkins, Robert
Baker, Rt Hon K. *(Mole Valley)*
Baker, Nicholas *(Dorset N)*
Baldry, Tony
Banks, Robert *(Harrogate)*
Batiste, Spencer
Bellingham, Henry
Bendall, Vivian
Bennett, Nicholas *(Pembroke)*
Benyon, W.
Bevan, David Gilroy
Biffen, Rt Hon John
Blackburn, Dr John G.
Bonsor, Sir Nicholas
Boscawen, Hon Robert
Boswell, Tim
Bottomley, Peter
Bottomley, Mrs Virginia
Bowden, A *(Brighton K'pto'n)*
Bowden, Gerald *(Dulwich)*
Bowis, John
Boyson, Rt Hon Dr Sir Rhodes
Braine, Rt Hon Sir Bernard
Brandon-Bravo, Martin
Brazier, Julian
Bright, Graham
Brooke, Rt Hon Peter
Brown, Michael *(Brigg & Cl't's)*
Browne, John *(Winchester)*
Bruce, Ian *(Dorset South)*
Buchanan-Smith, Rt Hon Alick
Budgen, Nicholas
Burns, Simon
Burt, Alistair
Butcher, John
Butler, Chris
Butterfill, John
Carlisle, John, *(Luton N)*
Carlisle, Kenneth *(Lincoln)*
Carrington, Matthew
Carttiss, Michael
Cash, William
Channon, Rt Hon Paul
Chapman, Sydney
Chope, Christopher
Churchill, Mr
Clark, Dr Michael *(Rochford)*
Clark, Sir W. *(Croydon S)*
Clarke, Rt Hon K. *(Rushcliffe)*
Colvin, Michael
Conway, Derek
Coombs, Anthony *(Wyre F'rest)*
Coombs, Simon *(Swindon)*
Cope, Rt Hon John
Cormack, Patrick
Couchman, James

Cran, James
Critchley, Julian
Currie, Mrs Edwina
Curry, David
Davies, Q. *(Stamf'd & Spald'g)*
Davis, David *(Boothferry)*
Day, Stephen
Devlin, Tim
Dicks, Terry
Dorrell, Stephen
Douglas-Hamilton, Lord James
Dover, Den
Dunn, Bob
Dykes, Hugh
Eggar, Tim
Emery, Sir Peter
Evans, David *(Welwyn Hatf'd)*
Evennett, David
Fairbairn, Sir Nicholas
Fallon, Michael
Favell, Tony
Field, Barry *(Isle of Wight)*
Fishburn, John Dudley
Forman, Nigel
Forsyth, Michael *(Stirling)*
Forth, Eric
Fox, Sir Marcus
Franks, Cecil
Freeman, Roger
French, Douglas
Fry, Peter
Gardiner, George
Garel-Jones, Tristan
Gill, Christopher
Gilmour, Rt Hon Sir Ian
Glyn, Dr Alan
Goodhart, Sir Philip
Goodlad, Alastair
Goodson-Wickes, Dr Charles
Gorman, Mrs Teresa
Gorst, John
Gow, Ian
Grant, Sir Anthony *(CambsSW)*
Greenway, Harry *(Ealing N)*
Gregory, Conal
Griffiths, Peter *(Portsmouth N)*
Grist, Ian
Ground, Patrick
Grylls, Michael
Gummer, Rt Hon John Selwyn
Hague, William
Hamilton, Neil *(Tatton)*
Hampson, Dr Keith
Hanley, Jeremy
Hannam, John
Hargreaves, A. *(B'ham H'll Gr')*
Hargreaves, Ken *(Hyndburn)*
Harris, David
Haselhurst, Alan
Hawkins, Christopher
Hayes, Jerry
Hayward, Robert
Heddle, John
Heseltine, Rt Hon Michael
Hicks, Mrs Maureen *(Wolv' NE)*
Hicks, Robert *(Cornwall SE)*
Higgins, Rt Hon Terence L.
Hill, James

Hind, Kenneth
Hogg, Hon Douglas *(Gr'th'm)*
Holt, Richard
Hordern, Sir Peter
Howard, Michael
Howarth, Alan *(Strat'd-on-A)*
Howarth, G. *(Cannock & B'wd)*
Hughes, Robert G. *(Harrow W)*
Hunt, David *(Wirral W)*
Hunter, Andrew
Hurd, Rt Hon Douglas
Irvine, Michael
Irving, Charles
Jack, Michael
Jackson, Robert
Janman, Tim
Johnson Smith, Sir Geoffrey
Jones, Gwilym *(Cardiff N)*
Jones, Robert B *(Herts W)*
Jopling, Rt Hon Michael
Kellett-Bowman, Dame Elaine
Key, Robert
Kilfedder, James
King, Roger *(B'ham N'thfield)*
King, Rt Hon Tom *(Bridgwater)*
Kirkhope, Timothy
Knapman, Roger
Knight, Greg *(Derby North)*
Knight, Dame Jill *(Edgbaston)*
Knox, David
Lamont, Rt Hon Norman
Lang, Ian
Latham, Michael
Lawrence, Ivan
Leigh, Edward *(Gainsbor'gh)*
Lennox-Boyd, Hon Mark
Lester, Jim *(Broxtowe)*
Lilley, Peter
Lloyd, Sir Ian *(Havant)*
Lloyd, Peter *(Fareham)*
Lyell, Sir Nicholas
McCrindle, Robert
Macfarlane, Sir Neil
MacGregor, Rt Hon John
MacKay, Andrew *(E Berkshire)*
Maclean, David
McLoughlin, Patrick
McNair-Wilson, Sir Michael
McNair-Wilson, Sir Patrick
Madel, David
Major, Rt Hon John
Mans, Keith
Maples, John
Marland, Paul
Marlow, Tony
Marshall, John *(Hendon S)*
Marshall, Michael *(Arundel)*
Martin, David *(Portsmouth S)*
Maude, Hon Francis
Mawhinney, Dr Brian
Mayhew, Rt Hon Sir Patrick
Mellor, David
Miller, Sir Hal
Mills, Iain
Miscampbell, Norman
Mitchell, Andrew *(Gedling)*
Moate, Roger
Moore, Rt Hon John
Morris, M *(N'hampton S)*
Morrison, Rt Hon P *(Chester)*
Moss, Malcolm
Moynihan, Hon Colin
Neale, Gerrard
Needham, Richard
Nelson, Anthony
Neubert, Michael
Newton, Rt Hon Tony
Nicholls, Patrick
Nicholson, David *(Taunton)*
Nicholson, Emma *(Devon West)*

Norris, Steve
Onslow, Rt Hon Cranley
Oppenheim, Phillip
Page, Richard
Paice, James
Patnick, Irvine
Patten, Rt Hon Chris *(Bath)*
Patten, John *(Oxford W)*
Pawsey, James
Peacock, Mrs Elizabeth
Porter, Barry *(Wirral S)*
Porter, David *(Waveney)*
Price, Sir David
Raison, Rt Hon Timothy
Redwood, John
Renton, Tim
Rhodes James, Robert
Riddick, Graham
Ridley, Rt Hon Nicholas
Ridsdale, Sir Julian
Roberts, Wyn *(Conwy)*
Roe, Mrs Marion
Rossi, Sir Hugh
Rost, Peter
Rumbold, Mrs Angela
Sackville, Hon Tom
Sainsbury, Hon Tim
Sayeed, Jonathan
Shaw, David *(Dover)*
Shaw, Sir Michael *(Scarb')*
Shelton, Sir William
Shephard, Mrs G. *(Norfolk SW)*
Shepherd, Colin *(Hereford)*
Shepherd, Richard *(Aldridge)*
Sims, Roger
Skeet, Sir Trevor
Smith, Tim *(Beaconsfield)*
Soames, Hon Nicholas
Speller, Tony
Spicer, Sir Jim *(Dorset W)*
Spicer, Michael *(S Worcs)*
Squire, Robin
Stanbrook, Ivor
Stanley, Rt Hon Sir John
Steen, Anthony
Stern, Michael
Stevens, Lewis
Stewart, Allan *(Eastwood)*
Stewart, Andy *(Sherwood)*
Stewart, Rt Hon Ian *(Herts N)*
Stokes, Sir John
Stradling Thomas, Sir John
Summerson, Hugo
Tapsell, Sir Peter
Taylor, Ian *(Esher)*
Taylor, John M *(Solihull)*
Taylor, Teddy *(S'end E)*
Tebbit, Rt Hon Norman
Temple-Morris, Peter
Thatcher, Rt Hon Margaret
Thompson, Patrick *(Norwich N)*
Thorne, Neil
Thornton, Malcolm
Thurnham, Peter
Townend, John *(Bridlington)*
Townsend, Cyril D. *(B'heath)*
Tracey, Richard
Tredinnick, David
Trippier, David
Trotter, Neville
Twinn, Dr Ian
Vaughan, Sir Gerard
Waddington, Rt Hon David
Wakeham, Rt Hon John
Walker, Bill *(T'side North)*
Waller, Gary
Walters, Sir Dennis
Ward, John
Wardle, Charles *(Bexhill)*
Warren, Kenneth

Watts, John
Wells, Bowen
Whitney, Ray
Widdecombe, Ann
Wiggin, Jerry
Wilkinson, John
Wilshire, David
Winterton, Mrs Ann
Winterton, Nicholas

Wolfson, Mark
Wood, Timothy
Yeo, Tim
Young, Sir George *(Acton)*
Younger, Rt Hon George

Tellers for the Ayes:
   Mr. Tony Durant and
   Mr. David Lightbown.

## NOES

Abbott, Ms Diane
Adams, Allen *(Paisley N)*
Allen, Graham
Alton, David
Anderson, Donald
Archer, Rt Hon Peter
Armstrong, Hilary
Ashdown, Rt Hon Paddy
Ashley, Rt Hon Jack
Banks, Tony *(Newham NW)*
Barnes, Harry *(Derbyshire NE)*
Barnes, Mrs Rosie *(Greenwich)*
Battle, John
Beckett, Margaret
Beith, A. J.
Bell, Stuart
Benn, Rt Hon Tony
Bennett, A. F. *(D'nt'n & R'dish)*
Bidwell, Sydney
Blair, Tony
Blunkett, David
Boateng, Paul
Boyes, Roland
Bradley, Keith
Brown, Gordon *(D'mline E)*
Brown, Nicholas *(Newcastle E)*
Bruce, Malcolm *(Gordon)*
Buckley, George J.
Callaghan, Jim
Campbell, Menzies *(Fife NE)*
Campbell-Savours, D. N.
Cartwright, John
Clark, Dr David *(S Shields)*
Clarke, Tom *(Monklands W)*
Clay, Bob
Clelland, David
Clwyd, Mrs Ann
Cohen, Harry
Cook, Robin *(Livingston)*
Corbett, Robin
Corbyn, Jeremy
Cousins, Jim
Cox, Tom
Crowther, Stan
Cryer, Bob
Cummings, John
Cunliffe, Lawrence
Cunningham, Dr John
Dalyell, Tam

Darling, Alistair
Davies, Rt Hon Denzil *(Llanelli)*
Davies, Ron *(Caerphilly)*
Davis, Terry *(B'ham Hodge H'l)*
Dewar, Donald
Dixon, Don
Dobson, Frank
Doran, Frank
Douglas, Dick
Duffy, A. E. P.
Dunnachie, Jimmy
Eadie, Alexander
Eastham, Ken
Fatchett, Derek
Fearn, Ronald
Field, Frank *(Birkenhead)*
Fields, Terry *(L'pool B G'n)*
Fisher, Mark
Flannery, Martin
Flynn, Paul
Foot, Rt Hon Michael
Foster, Derek
Fraser, John
Fyfe, Maria
Galbraith, Sam
Galloway, George
Garrett, John *(Norwich South)*
Garrett, Ted *(Wallsend)*
George, Bruce
Gilbert, Rt Hon Dr John
Godman, Dr Norman A.
Golding, Mrs Llin
Gordon, Mildred
Gould, Bryan
Graham, Thomas
Grant, Bernie *(Tottenham)*
Griffiths, Win *(Bridgend)*
Grocott, Bruce
Harman, Ms Harriet
Hattersley, Rt Hon Roy
Haynes, Frank
Healey, Rt Hon Denis
Henderson, Doug
Hinchliffe, David
Hoey, Ms Kate *(Vauxhall)*
Hogg, N. *(C'nauld & Kilsyth)*
Home Robertson, John
Hood, Jimmy
Howarth, George *(Knowsley N)*

Howells, Geraint
Howells, Dr. Kim *(Pontypridd)*
Hoyle, Doug
Hughes, John *(Coventry NE)*
Hughes, Robert *(Aberdeen N)*
Hughes, Roy *(Newport E)*
Hughes, Simon *(Southwark)*
Illsley, Eric
Janner, Greville
Jones, Barry *(Alyn & Deeside)*
Jones, Ieuan *(Ynys Môn)*
Jones, Martyn *(Clwyd S W)*
Kaufman, Rt Hon Gerald
Kirkwood, Archy
Leadbitter, Ted
Leighton, Ron
Lestor, Joan *(Eccles)*
Livingstone, Ken
Livsey, Richard
Lloyd, Tony *(Stretford)*
Lofthouse, Geoffrey
Loyden, Eddie
McAllion, John
McAvoy, Thomas
McFall, John
McKay, Allen *(Barnsley West)*
McKelvey, William
McLeish, Henry
Maclennan, Robert
McNamara, Kevin
McWilliam, John
Madden, Max
Mahon, Mrs Alice
Marek, Dr John
Marshall, David *(Shettleston)*
Martin, Michael J. *(Springburn)*
Martlew, Eric
Meale, Alan
Michael, Alun
Michie, Bill *(Sheffield Heeley)*
Michie, Mrs Ray *(Arg'l & Bute)*
Mitchell, Austin *(G't Grimsby)*
Moonie, Dr Lewis
Morgan, Rhodri
Morley, Elliott
Morris, Rt Hon A. *(W'shawe)*
Morris, Rt Hon J. *(Aberavon)*
Mullin, Chris
Murphy, Paul
Nellist, Dave
O'Brien, William
Orme, Rt Hon Stanley
Patchett, Terry
Pendry, Tom
Pike, Peter L.
Powell, Ray *(Ogmore)*

Prescott, John
Primarolo, Dawn
Quin, Ms Joyce
Radice, Giles
Redmond, Martin
Rees, Rt Hon Merlyn
Reid, Dr John
Richardson, Jo
Roberts, Allan *(Bootle)*
Robertson, George
Robinson, Geoffrey
Rooker, Jeff
Ross, Ernie *(Dundee W)*
Rowlands, Ted
Ruddock, Joan
Salmond, Alex
Sedgemore, Brian
Sheerman, Barry
Sheldon, Rt Hon Robert
Shore, Rt Hon Peter
Short, Clare
Skinner, Dennis
Smith, Andrew *(Oxford E)*
Smith, C. *(Isl'ton & F'bury)*
Smith, Rt Hon J. *(Monk'ds E)*
Smith, J. P. *(Vale of Glam)*
Snape, Peter
Spearing, Nigel
Steel, Rt Hon David
Steinberg, Gerry
Stott, Roger
Strang, Gavin
Straw, Jack
Taylor, Mrs Ann *(Dewsbury)*
Taylor, Matthew *(Truro)*
Thompson, Jack *(Wansbeck)*
Turner, Dennis
Vaz, Keith
Wall, Pat
Wallace, James
Walley, Joan
Wardell, Gareth *(Gower)*
Watson, Mike *(Glasgow, C)*
Welsh, Andrew *(Angus E)*
Welsh, Michael *(Doncaster N)*
Wigley, Dafydd
Williams, Rt Hon Alan
Williams, Alan W. *(Carm'then)*
Winnick, David
Wise, Mrs Audrey
Wray, Jimmy
Young, David *(Bolton SE)*

Tellers for the Noes:
   Mr. Frank Cook and
   Mr. Robert N. Wareing.

*Question accordingly agreed to.*

*Bill read the Third time, and passed.*

# Ways and Means

## CAPITAL GAINS (SHARES AND SECURITIES HELD BY COMPANIES)

*Motion made, and Question proposed,*

That provision may be made about the treatment, in determining chargeable gains or allowable losses, of transactions involving the holding of shares in, and securities of, companies by other companies.—*[Mr. Brooke.]*

10.36 pm

**Mr. A. J. Beith** (Berwick-upon-Tweed): The charitable view of these four ways and means resolutions is that they are a sign of the Government's flexibility and their welcome willingness to listen to representations. The uncharitable view is that they illustrate what a mess the Government are in over the Finance Bill. The Government have already voted down three clauses of their own Finance Bill and have had to delay the proceedings on other clauses in order to make time to rewrite other substantial sections of it.

I welcome the fact that the Government have listened to representations, but what they have done has strengthened the argument for having a separate technical Finance Bill in which complicated matters of this kind are dealt with and are the subject of widespread consultation before they are brought to the House, as have been some other parts of the Finance Bill. I hope that the Government will learn that lesson for the future.

*Question put and agreed to.*

## WAYS AND MEANS

### GROUPS OF COMPANIES

*Resolved,*

That provision may be made amending sections 272 and 278 of the Income and Corporation Taxes Act 1970 and section 97 of the Inheritance Tax Act 1984.

### TRUSTEES AND PERSONAL REPRESENTATIVES

*Resolved,*

That provision (including provision having retrospective effect) may be made for the purposes of income tax about trustees and personal representatives.

### TRADING COMPANIES

*Resolved,*

That provision may be made amending the definition of 'trading company' in section 136 of the Capital Gains Tax Act 1979 and section 576 of the Income and Corporation Taxes Act 1988.—*[Mr. Brooke.]*

# Community Charge (Scotland)

10.37 pm

**Mr. Donald Dewar** (Glasgow, Garscadden): I beg to move,

That the Housing Benefit (Community Charge Rebates) (Scotland) Amendment Regulations 1989 (S.I., 1989, No. 361), dated 7th March 1989, a copy of which was laid before this House on 10th March, be revoked.

**Mr. Deputy Speaker (Mr. Harold Walker):** With this it will be convenient to discuss the next two motions:

That the Community Charges (Deductions from Income Support) (Scotland) Regulations 1989 (S.I., 1989, No. 507), dated 15th March 1989, a copy of which was laid before this House on 17th March, be revoked.

That the Community Charges (Information Concerning Social Security) (Scotland) Regulations 1989 (S.I., 1989, No. 476), dated 14th March 1989, a copy of which was laid before this House on 17th March, be revoked.

**Mr. Dewar:** The regulations which we are discussing tonight make unfortunate and unhappy reading. As the House will know, they deal with the poll tax and the enforcement machinery designed to extract an unfair tax from one of the most vulnerable groups in the community, people who have, almost by definition as recipients of income support, suffered under this Government in half a hundred different ways. I am aware that we are not having a general debate about the demerits of the poll tax, and I wish to concentrate fairly briskly on the regulations and some of the salient points which arise from them.

Will the Minister say a word or two about the Housing Benefit (Community Charge Rebates) (Scotland) Amendment Regulations 1989, particularly paragraph 14? This is the paragraph that deals with the 56-day rule. In their doubtful wisdom, the Government decided that the payment of the poll tax would start on 1 April this year, and if an eligible person applied for a rebate within 56 days of the starting point, the rebate—*[Interruption.]*

**Mr. Deputy Speaker:** Order. There is a great deal of distracting sedentary noise. I hope that hon. Members will listen to the hon. Member for Glasgow, Garscadden (Mr. Dewar), as I am seeking to do.

**Mr. Dewar:** I am grateful to you, Mr. Deputy Speaker. I shall now go back to the fascinating subject of the 56-day rule.

I use the word "fascinating" in some seriousness, because it is an illustration of the Government's approach. Let me recapitulate. If one applies within 56 days, one is held to have applied as at 1 April 1989, and any rebate to which one is entitled will be taken from that date. The 56 days have now expired, so anyone who now applies for a rebate will receive one, only from the date of application. As three months have already passed, anyone who failed to apply in that period has already lost three months' worth of rebate. We must not assume that the people who are involved are those entitled to the maximum rebate, but many will lose substantial sums.

The rebate system is a difficult and complicated jungle, and the pain and confusion that have followed its introduction have made it difficult to know exactly how matters stand. I am told by Strathclyde region, which is by far the biggest levying authority in Scotland, that it estimates that around 580,000 people are eligible for rebates. It told me that, on its best estimate, only 480,000 have applied. It looks as though some 100,000 applicants,

many of whom have dependants, will have to suffer because of the 56-day rule. They cannot now catch up, and have lost at least three months' rebate this year. Every day that they delay, mostly because of confusion—there is no doubt about the confusion and misunderstandings that the complexities of the system have produced—means that they will suffer financially even more. That is not an unhappy situation, it is an intolerable one, and one that the Government have consistently refused to remedy, although the remedy was simplicity itself.

I and many of my hon. Friends, and many people who are not politically inclined but know the social realities, have pressed on the Minister the need to extend that 56-day period and to allow a more generous approach towards rebates. We have done so in vain. The Minister of State, Scottish Office, who has borne the brunt of the argument, has reinforced his reputation for not being a man of spontaneous warmth. He is not noted for relating to, and understanding, the problems of the deprived, and he has made it clear that the Government will turn a deaf ear to these proposals. That is a tragedy of which he and his colleagues should be ashamed.

The 56-day rule is formalised in these regulations. If that were the only point at dispute between ourselves and the Government, it would fully justify a vote against them. I hope that the Minister will say something about paragraph 15. For the sake of simplicity, I shall merely quote the explanatory note. It says:

"This paragraph extends the information which may be provided by the Secretary of State to levying authorities to include a person's date of birth."

I mention it because I know that there is a great deal of genuine puzzlement in Scotland as to why the system in England is organised without a person's date of birth being used as part of the poll tax information package, but this has had to be imposed as a statutory requirement in Scotland, and further powers are being taken. This is not the most important point that we shall be debating. It does not have the social implications of the 56-day rule, nor its capacity for damage, but perhaps the Under-Secretary will say a word or two about it.

I do not often face the Under-Secretary across the Dispatch Box, and I do so tonight with an open mind. He will gain valuable brownie points in my eyes if he can provide the explanation that his colleagues in the Scottish Office were unable to provide in the many hours of debate that we had about the machinery of the poll tax.

The real crux of the debate, and the point of particular concern to me and my hon. Friends, is that the main drive of the principal order is to allow the deduction of poll tax arrears from benefit, especially from income support. It is a mean measure that will force the worst off in our community to fall below even the subsistence level of income support as presently calculated by the Government.

We know from recent exchanges with Ministers—and even with the Prime Minister—that the Government do not think that the basic pension is designed to provide comfort or to be an adequate income in itself. If that is true of the pension, it is very much more true of income support, which allows no gracious living, no room for the little luxuries that mean so much to morale and the quality of life of families. I know from constituency experience —as, to be fair, must Conservative Members—that those on income support have to struggle and do not have the decent sufficiency that almost all of us want accorded to those in the greatest difficulty.

It is a shabby proposition to claw back poll tax out of income support. There is no real defence and no social justification for it. I appreciate that the Minister will no doubt advance a number of arguments, one or two of which I can anticipate. He will say that it is perfectly fair because those in receipt of income support have had a special supplement to cover the cost of the minimum poll tax contribution. Of course, the calculation of that is an arcane art, and one that I cannot pretend to have mastered. My understanding is that it is calculated on a United Kingdom basis, which is odd because the poll tax does not yet apply throughout the United Kingdom. It is also odd because in Scotland there are substantial variations, based upon local policy and local needs, in the amount of poll tax to be paid. In a broad-brush approach, everyone apparently has the same supplement—£1·15 this year for a single applicant under the age of 25; £1·30 for those over 25 and, strangely, for a couple it is £2·30, although we might reasonably have expected it to be £2·60.

All that is most unconvincing. I know from conversations with many people that few will believe that it is adequate cover to allow people living at that economic level to meet their poll tax commitments without difficulty or financial embarrassment. I have tried explaining that first, we take the income support personal allowance for the current year, take out the rates element, uprate it by the retail price index less the housing element, arrive at the magic figure of 4·7 per cent.—which sounds suspiciously low compared with the real rise in the cost of living—and then add on the special supplement. There is no credibility in that exercise. Any such argument is blown away by the pressures of reality, the pressures of poverty and the true condition in which those who will be victimised by the rules actually live. No one will think that justifiable, because nothing can justify the tax itself and the basis on which it is levied. There is no doubt in my mind that many people, faced by the clawback authorised in the orders, will find themselves living at a subsistence level that none of us should be prepared to accept.

The Minister may argue that there are many precedents for clawing back from benefit. The main precedent is where there has been overpayment of benefit, and because it must be reclaimed it is taken out of that same benefit in subsequent months. That may have unfortunate financial consequences, but there is a logic in it. It is all in the same benefit payment and there is a rough consistency which most people can understand.

There are occasions on which the South of Scotland Electricity Board or the North of Scotland Hydro-Electric Board, if not too outré or faraway organisations for the Minister to contemplate, have direct deductions to meet debt. It is, of course, theoretically possible for that to be done without the consent of the debtor, as I understand it, although the Minister may want to comment on that. However, in almost all cases in which I have been involved, which must run to many scores, such a step has been taken with negotiation and consent. The debtor is, of course, anxious to reach that consent because he has a specific service—the supply of electricity or gas—that he wants to maintain. There is a logic in that and a benefit for the person concerned, which is understandable.

Under the 1988 regulations for housing benefit, it is possible to deduct an overpayment from income support.

However, talking as I did with a number of local authorities in Scotland, I believe that, very properly, that power has never been used. If it were used, it would lead to bitterness and a lack of confidence in the system, which would do none of us any good. I do not believe that, in terms of precedents or in terms of the financial calculations of income support personal allowances, there is a case for what the Government are doing. I perceived justice, and in term of social impact, there is no case at all.

I recognise that many of my hon. Friends want to contribute, so I will not make a long speech. However, I want to ask a couple of technical questions about the regulations. Perhaps it is my curiosity that is to blame, and there may be simple answers to my questions. I want to draw the Minister's attention to paragraph 2(2)(a), which deals with the issue of a summary warrant in the name of a couple. Perhaps the Minister could give an example of a circumstance in which it would be likely that a summary warrant would be issued in the name of a couple. I understand that a husband and wife living together or a man and a woman living together may be jointly and severally liable for the poll tax debt of each. However, as I understand it, there would be an attempt to recover from both individually and only if one failed to pay would a bill be issued for the debt to the other. It is unlikely, although I may have misunderstood the matter, which is why I am raising it, that summary warrants would go out in the name of both parties, as a couple. Perhaps the Minister could explain when that would happen.

I hope that he will also say a word about the appeal procedure. There will be appeal to the commissioners and in certain circumstances not to one commissioner but to three commissioners, and on a point of law ultimately to the Court of Session. It is an interesting comment on the complexity of the system and on the labyrinth we are constructing that that mass of overlapping and extending appeals is being erected. Perhaps the Minister——

**Mr. Dick Douglas** (Dunfermline, West): There is no Scottish Minister present.

**Mr. Dewar:** Perhaps the Minister could say a few words about the availability of legal aid in such cases.

Perhaps the Minister could also say a few words about deductions, which are the key to the matter. As I understand it, if a single debtor is involved, the deduction is 5 per cent. of the personal allowances for a single claimant aged not less than 25. Although it is not stated, because it may vary from time to time, I believe that it is £1·75 a week at present. For a couple who are both over 18, the relevant allowance is £54·80, I believe that the deduction is rounded up to £2·75. There is a reference to another claim and another test that has to be met. The unfortunate victim of the scheme is left with a minimum of 10p of income support.

I accept immediately—I do not wish to mislead anyone —that if someone is living on income support alone, the £2·75 maximum if he is living as part of a couple will still leave him with quite a significant income, not merely 10p. If someone is left only with 10p, he clearly has a significant amount of other income. However, I repeat the important charge that, even so, many people will be in a difficult situation because they will be living significantly below the very basic level which has been laid down by the Government, who are not noted for their generosity in this area. They are a Government who openly argue that the

[*Mr. Dewar*]

poor need the spur of poverty so that they will better themselves in the market place. If we are driving people below even that standard, all hon. Members, whatever their political convictions, should take time to pause and to consider.

As the Minister no doubt knows, about 150,000 old-age pensioners in Scotland have to supplement their income with income support payments. Some of them will doubtless be driven near to the 10p rule and test by the deductions. In effect, they will then be living on that basic pension which the Prime Minister herself made clear that the Government recognise as not being sufficient for a decent standard of living. Is it right that we should force people into what the Prime Minister has recognised as an inadequate situation simply to recover 20 per cent. of a tax that has no valid basis and that is almost universally seen as unfair and unjust? The answer to that question is a resounding no.

I object strongly to the fact that, typically, it is the local authorities that are being put in the firing line. They are being given the duty of administering a scheme that they neither like nor want. Under the regulations they have to apply in writing to the Department to have the deduction machinery put in motion. As Ministers have doubtless calculated, it will be the local authorities that will be left to take the flak and the burden of the protests.

Having spoken again to the local authorities in my part of the world, which I do frequently, I can report that they have a good record in dealing with those in genuine poverty who find themselves wrestling with the problems of debt to statutory authorities. Strathclyde's record will stand any examination because, sensibly, that authority does not make dilettante political statements about policy, but takes each case on its merits and applies humane and sensible tests, while avoiding the rigours of civil diligence, which is naturally repugnant to public opinion and is a disaster for the individuals concerned.

I expect the same understanding to be applied in this case. However, I believe that on behalf of my hon. Friends I am entitled to protest that local authorities with such records are put again in this embarrassing and difficult position in defence of a system that they regard as an anathema.

Once again, it is a case of the poorest in the community being made to suffer—people who, by definition, are in unfortunate financial circumstances. It is another example of social legislation—because there are important social implications in this—further dividing society and driving a greater and greater wedge between those that have and those that have not.

One third of my constituency—one of my regional wards—has an unemployment rate of over 36 per cent. I am not talking about a couple of streets chosen at random but about large swathes on the west side of the city of Glasgow. Many people there are living in genuine poverty, dependent on benefit. Thoughtless, mean-minded legislation such as this exacerbates that problem, yet Ministers wonder why they face alienation and a level of dislike in Scottish politics that is almost unique in my experience.

Measures such as this are not simply about the mechanics of a collection system. A social principle is involved. A difference of approach is built into this legislation and it shines through the debates and

arguments on this matter. If the regulations are forced through by the Government—I accept they will be tonight, perhaps by many hon. Members who have not had any opportunity of considering them—the House should be ashamed. Even now, the Minister should think about drawing back.

I wish that the Scottish Office was represented on the Treasury Bench to try to defend a system which the vast majority of the people of Scotland regard as unrelated to the ability to pay, which is unjust and which shifts the burden of taxation on to those who can ill afford to bear it. In reinforcing that essentially unjust system, this mechanism has on its shoulders all the disadvantages, all the difficulties and all the shame of the grand design.

10.59 pm

**The Parliamentary Under-Secretary of State for Social Security (Mr. Peter Lloyd):** The hon. Member for Glasgow, Garscadden (Mr. Dewar) raised some points which it seems sensible for me to deal with straight away. He asked particularly about the date of birth. Inclusion of the birth date was requested to make it more convenient and easier for the local authority to distinguish between individuals of the same name—[*Interruption.*] Local authorities may not have asked for it—I do not know—but certainly it is being put in for their additional convenience. That is the reason for it. I am glad to be able to answer one of the first points about which the hon. Gentleman asked.

**Mr. John McAllion** (Dundee, East): Does the Minister agree that the real reason why the date of birth has been made a statutory requirement is that local authorities will have to trace people as they move around the country and every individual in Scotland has been given a computer tag? Does he agree that that is why the date of birth has been made a statutory requirement?

**Mr. Lloyd:** It makes it easier for local authorities to distinguish between people of the same name living in the same household.

The hon. Member for Glasgow, Garscadden asked about appeals. The appeal system is the normal social security appeal system. First the adjudication officer is involved, then the social security appeal tribunal and finally the commissioners on a point of law. It will be exactly the same as in the usual procedure. That is the method with which the social security system and local offices are familiar, and that people on social security who have appealed before know well.

The hon. Gentleman also asked about summary warrants. It will be possible to take out a warrant against one individual when there is a debt in respect of a couple, and it will be possible to proceed against the couple. That is for the local authority to decide.

**Mr. Douglas:** What a lot of dirty work local authorities are being asked to do.

**Mr. Lloyd:** The local authorities will want to recover the community charge owing to them in exactly the same way as they want to recover rates that are owing to them. There is no difference in principle or in the final procedure. On behalf of all its rate or charge payers, the local authority will need to collect what is due. There is nothing new in that.

With regard to the regulations before us, I will begin with the Community Charge (Deductions from Income Support) (Scotland) Regulations 1989 which were laid before Parliament on 17 March and came into force on 8 April. They reflect the intention that there should be equality of treatment, wherever possible, between those in employment and those receiving benefit. The hon. Member for Garscadden rightly made the point that deductions from income support for those receiving benefit represent a parallel and equivalent measure to arrestment of earnings for those in work.

My right hon. Friend the Secretary of State announced in October last year, as part of his uprating statement, that there would be a once-and-for-all adjustment to income support levels to meet the minimum 20 per cent. contribution which recipients will have to make to the community charge. Because this extra amount has been included in income support it is only right to ensure that it is used for its intended purpose.

As it has to with those in work, the levying authority must first obtain a summary warrant, to prove it is owed the money. This will be the trigger for these regulations. Principally, they provide that an authority, having obtained a summary warrant, may apply to the DSS for deductions from income support to meet that debt. In asking for such deductions the authority has to provide sufficient information to enable the local social security office to identify the debtor. Here the birthday date helps. We shall only consider deductions for the amount specified on the warrant or the authority requires.

**Mr. Thomas Graham** (Renfrew, West and Inverclyde): My wife telephoned me tonight and told me that she had a letter saying that the Government want young people in YTS schemes. Such young people would probably receive about £35 per week, and would then be expected to pay 20 per cent. of the poll tax, plus 15 per cent., which exceeds their income support of £27·40. Therefore, a young person who gets, say, £35, which the Government are encouraging, is now expected to pay another £1·14 per week. Does the Minister not think that it is tragic that the Government are encouraging young people to come off the dole and into training schemes for which they will be given some money, but then taking some of that money back? Young people are really being sent to the graveyard, because they will not be able to pay the poll tax. Does the Minister realise that letters have been sent out to the managers running the schemes, and the managers are putting their hands up in horror, because young trainees are expected to live on the trainee allowance? What does the Minister say about that?

**Mr. Lloyd:** The Minister says that the purpose of the community charge is that everybody should make a contribution. The rate will be set by the local authority and there are rebates for those on low incomes. Those who are on YTS obviously come into the category of those on low incomes, and they are likely to get a substantial rebate.

**Mr. Graham:** Does the Minister not realise what I am saying? The Government have implemented a programme to encourage young people to go into employment training schemes—YTS—by saying that, from the guaranteed income support of £27·40, they would be expected to pay a 20 per cent. contribution to the poll tax. The Government are now saying, however, that because they receive additional money for travelling costs, the

Government will take that amount off in poll tax, which comes to a loss of £1·14 a week. Will the Minister answer that? Young people in Scotland will have that amount deducted, while those in England will not have that money deducted until next year. The young people in England will be far better off on the YTS scheme. Will the Minister tell the young people in Scotland what they are expected to live on?

**Mr. Lloyd:** The young people on YTS are earning above the income support rate for their age group, so they have a rebate in exactly the same way as anybody who is on income support, but adjusted for their actual earnings. That appears to be a much fairer system than the one we have now—the one that the hon. Gentleman appears to be defending—where some people pay heavy rates bills and some people pay absolutely nothing. In our system the burden is spread across the whole of the population. It is adjusted for those on lower incomes to suit those incomes. That appears to be basically fair and I should think that the hon. Gentleman would find it very easy to explain that to YTS trainees.

Where there is an outstanding community charge debt and sufficient income support, as decided by the adjudication officer, the rate of deduction will be, as the hon. member for Garscadden said, £1·75 a week for a single person and £2·75 a week for a couple, if both partners are debtors. Those weekly deductions are fixed by the regulations. There is no provision for them to be varied. The adjudication officer will decide that there is sufficient entitlement to income support only—again we come to a point mentioned by the hon. Member for Garscadden—if, after the deduction, the person is left with 10p or more of that part of his income which comes from income support.

This is easy to misrepresent—the hon. Member for Garscadden sailed near to it, but he did not quite go across the line—but this safeguard, which appears in existing provisions for deductions to pay third parties, is there to ensure that we do not extinguish entitlement to benefit. The fixed flat rate deduction for a single person is £1·75 a week, and it is totally wrong to suggest that we propose to make that deduction and leave someone with an income of only 10p. Benefit can be reduced to 10p only if income support was very low to start with and the individual relies mainly on another source of income.

**Mr. Dewar:** I think that the hon. Gentleman would concede that I was very careful not to make that suggestion. If he reads my speech, he will see that I spent some time establishing that point. Will the hon. Gentleman, however, address himself to the example that I cited, which is that of the many thousands of old-age pensioners in Scotland who have the basic pension and income support? Some of them might well be taken down to an income near the basic pension, if not down to 10p above it. We know from the Minister for Social Security and the Prime Minister that it is accepted that that is not sufficient for a comfortable living. Is it necessary that they should be driven into that situation in order to recover the poll tax in the way that is outlined?

**Mr. Lloyd:** My right hon. Friend the Minister for Social Security was referring not just to income support but to housing benefit. The amount taken away will not be more than the income support element of their social security benefits. That is what the hon. Gentleman is asking about.

**Mr. Dewar:** What level could the income be taken down to?

**Mr. Lloyd:** It could get down to a level 10p above the basic pension, but the hon. Gentleman is forgetting that that pensioner may have housing benefit and may well be paying 20 per cent. of the rates now. The point that my hon. Friend was making was that not all the household outgoings have to be met by the single person's pension alone. There are other benefits in addition to income support.

**Mr. Tam Dalyell** (Linlithgow): The Department is about to introduce the scheme into Macclesfield, Scarborough, Cambridge, Bolton and all sorts of other places. With that in view, would it not have some sort of report from the Scottish managers on how matters have worked out in practice? Following the intervention of my hon. Friend the Member for Renfrew, West and Inverclyde (Mr. Graham), is the Minister saying that the managers think that things have worked out as smoothly as he has suggested to the House?

**Mr. Lloyd:** I have not suggested that it has or has not worked out smoothly. I have not reached that issue yet. The community charge has started extraordinarily well in Scotland. It was an enormous change. [*Interruption.*] Hon. Members may laugh, but I have sat in this Chamber listening to Opposition Members explaining how registration would be a complete disaster, how it could not be managed by Scottish local authorities and was administratively impossible. But I understand that Scottish local authorities have done much better than Scottish Members ever believed possible and that the numbers registered range from 99 to 100 per cent.

**Mr. Alex Salmond** (Banff and Buchan): I do not know how familiar the Minister is with recent Scottish newspapers, but is he aware that, in a report in *The Scotsman* last week, local authority finance officers in Scotland estimated that at least 1 million Scots have not paid their poll tax? What does the Minister think about that?

**Mr. Lloyd:** One cannot rely on such figures put out in the newspapers. What I do know is that the expectations for registration have been fulfilled, that many of the bills have been sent out, on time and rebated, but not all of them. There is a large backlog to be made up, as one would expect with any substantial change in a system such as this. Our estimates of the case load for rebates was 780,000, which includes couples and individuals. That means over 1 million individuals. At the end of the 56 days to which the hon. Member for Garscadden referred, we had about one and one third of a million applications. If one grosses that up for the individuals we find that our predictions for the caseload look as though they are being fulfilled.

**Mr. Dewar** *indicated dissent.*

**Mr. Lloyd:** The hon. Gentleman may shake his head, but I am talking about figures that were carefully prepared by my Department for our guidance.

**Mr. Dewar:** I am sorry to intervene again, but this is important. I took the trouble to speak to senior officers of the biggest authority, Strathclyde region, today. Their genuine and best estimate was that the authority was about 100,000 short of its estimate. In other words,

somewhere out there in Strathclyde there are about 100,000 applicants who are probably eligible who have not yet applied. Even if there were only a handful, would there not be a strong case in humane terms for extending the 56-day rule and not penalising those people, particularly in view of the extraordinary confusion that all Scottish Members find in their surgeries every week, when constituents come in with a mass of incomprehensible papers that they do not know what to do with?

**Mr. Lloyd:** The 56-day concession was suggested by Scottish local authorities and we were happy to adopt it, knowing that there would be difficulties at the beginning of the changeover. The total arrangement comprises those 56 days, eight weeks, allowing for two demands for payment, and three spare weeks afterwards. The most vulnerable —those receiving housing benefit—automatically transferred on to the rebate. Those receiving income support were sent a personal letter with a claim form well before 1 April, so they received not a general but a specific notification. Since then there have been television advertising, press advertisements, and a great deal of editorial comment, assisted by the attacks made by Opposition Members, for which I give due credit and for which, in this context at least, I am very grateful.

Applications for rebates not only match but exceed our expectations. The number arriving now is quite small, but one expects applications to continue as people move or become entitled to rebate for the first time. However, from the figures that I have seen and on the basis of our calculations, there is no justification for extending the 56-day period. Other people may produce different calculations, but I am sceptical of the basis on which they were made.

There remains the good cause provision for backdating entitlement, available to those who can show good reason for not having yet made an application. It is for the local authority to judge whether or not the individual had a valid reason for not knowing that application could be made, or for not being able to apply, or was totally confused by wrong information or propaganda—or even by the advice that he should have nothing to do with the community charge.

**Mr. Jeff Rooker** (Birmingham, Perry Barr): As one English Member to another, may I ask the Minister how many Scottish local authorities he has visited to discuss at first hand with officials the difficulties that are arising?

**Mr. Lloyd:** Speaking as one English Member to another, I think that the hon. Gentleman knows the likely answer to his question. Of course I have not visited local authorities in Scotland. I rely, as all Ministers do, on information from not just one, two or three local authorities but, through the system of reporting, from every Scottish local authority. I have information from them all, which is far more valuable and a much sounder basis on which to form a judgment than dashing up on a train or plane to spend a few days in Scotland talking to just one, two or three local authorities.

**Mr. Bill Walker** (Tayside, North): Is my hon. Friend aware that the degree of confusion that exists in Scotland has been brought about by politicians making comments about non-collection of the community charge? I refer particularly to members of the Scottish National party, yet the only district council that it runs is collecting the community charge. Is it surprising that confusion exists?

**Mr. Lloyd:** It is not surprising at all. As I said earlier, local authorities in Scotland have done extraordinarily well to introduce the system with such efficiency and effectiveness, given the tirade of propaganda from Opposition Members. I am certain, however, that those efficient local authorities will be able to judge whether some individuals have been confused—retirement pensioners, for instance—and will take that into account and allow them to backdate their rebates to 1 April.

The Community Charges (Information concerning Social Security) (Scotland) Regulations 1989 permit the Secretary of State, through the staff of DSS local offices, to pass certain specified information to community charge registration officers. As people on income support are receiving additional money to help them pay 20 per cent. of the community charge, it is reasonable that they appear on the community charge register. The purpose of the regulations is to ensure that that happens. I will explain to the House why the regulations take the form that they do.

Community charge registration officers need access to certain sources of information so that their registers are as accurate as possible at any given time. They are able to require the information that they need from the authorities which administer housing benefit and community charge rebate, so they have access to the names, dates of birth and addresses of everyone who has claimed either or both those benefits. If it were not for the regulations, however, the CCROs would not have access to information from DSS offices, as information about income support is held on a confidential basis. That information may be passed to CCROs so that they can check it against their registers and ensure that there are no discrepancies.

I stress that the information that is specified is the minimum necessary for the purpose, and that the CCRO may not use it for any purpose other than for maintaining his register.

The Housing Benefit (Community Charge Rebates) (Scotland) Amendment Regulations 1989 make a number of changes to the arrangements for rebating the community charge in Scotland. Some were necessary to maintain alignment between these regulations and the Housing Benefit (General Amendment) Regulations 1989. It is important that the two schemes should be as closely aligned as possible so that they are as simple as possible for local authorities to administer, and as easy as possible for claimants to understand.

**Mr. John Home Robertson** (East Lothian): The rather dry manner in which the Minister is dragging his way through his brief gives me the impression that he may be having a dummy run for this time next year, when he will be applying the same regulations to England. Will he have a shot at convincing me that he is not simply using Scotland as a guinea pig? Can he also convince me that he knows something about what he is talking about by naming just three local authorities in Scotland which administer the poll tax?

**Mr. Lloyd:** Certainly Scotland is not being used as a guinea pig. As the hon. Gentleman well knows, the reason why legislation was applied to Scotland first was that there

was a larger and earlier demand for a change in the rating system there after the revaluation. That is why Scotland is lucky enough to be experiencing this excellent change first.

If Scotland were being used as a guinea pig, we should have delayed the provision for England and Wales for another year. It might then have been possible to learn some lessons from Scotland—if there are any lessons to be learned. The English legislation is already on the statute book, however, and the preparations are well down the track, so we are treating England in exactly the same way.

The hon. Gentleman asked for three examples of Scottish authorities administering the poll tax. Well, Strathclyde is certainly one. Another is Central. How about that?

**Mr. Bill Walker:** Tayside, Grampian and Fife.

**Mr. Lloyd:** My hon. Friend is quite right. I suspect that if hon. Members asked me to name three English counties now, I should be hard put to do so.

There are a number of other points which might be touched upon, but I have already commented on the main issues that have been raised by Opposition Members, particularly by the hon. Member for Garscadden and I wish to leave time for other hon. Members to make their points, which may be different from those that have already been made. I have confidence, nevertheless, in commending these excellent regulations to the House.

**Several Hon. Members** rose——

**Mr. Deputy Speaker (Mr. Harold Walker):** Order. I appeal for brief speeches in the short time that is left.

11.25 pm

**Mr. Dick Douglas** (Dunfermline, West): I shall, of course, Mr. Deputy Speaker, try to be brief. As you very well know, I tabled a motion on the poll tax that was not taken, for good or bad reasons, on Friday.

I want to take up the point made by my hon. Friend the Member for Glasgow, Garscadden (Mr. Dewar) about the 56-day rule. The Minister was somewhat sceptical about who speaks for Scottish local authorities. It is unfortunate that, once again, no Scottish Minister is on the Treasury Bench to instruct other Ministers about what happens in Scotland. I assume that the Minister knows that the Convention of Scottish Local Authorities and its president speak for Scottish local authorities. Mr. Milligan, the president, made a speech on 12 June in which he said:

"It is extremely likely therefore that a good number of those not paying at that time will be eligible for a rebate which authorities will be unable to backdate as the relevant period for doing so will have expired. These categories of potential claimants plus the general conclusions from our trawl"—
that is, of all local authorities——
"suggests that there may be up to 200,000 or so individuals who will lose out unless the 56-day rule is extended."
That is the view not of one local authority but of all Scottish local authorities, and 200,000 is not an insubstantial number.

The Minister is under an obligation to redress the imbalance. People may not have cottoned on to all the sophisticated advertising. It may be that there has been obfuscation and that people do not understand it. Notwithstanding that, 200,000 people who ought to be receiving benefits that the Government suggest are generous should have their benefits fully backdated.

Those who are really suffering from the poverty trap are just above the income limit for claiming rebate. Scottish

[*Mr. Dick Douglas*]

local authorities have a great deal of sympathy for personal circumstances, but they are required by the legislation to carry out the appropriate debt recovery procedures.

What we are talking about was highlighted yesterday during the Prime Minister's exchanges with my right hon. Friend the Member for Birmingham, Sparkbrook (Mr. Hattersley). We are talking about taking money away from people who are on income support and benefits that provide them not with a luxurious standard of living but with a bare minimum standard of living. By the use of obnoxious procedures, any income support that they receive from the state will be taken away from them, probably leaving them with only 10p. The fact that only a few hon. Members are here this evening demonstrates the lack of knowledge about the subject. Only one Scottish Tory who might know something about it is here this evening. The rest of the Tory Members might know something about the theory, but we are talking about the practice.

**Mr. Bill Walker:** Will the hon. Gentleman give way?

**Mr. Douglas:** I shall not give way. Front-Bench speeches have taken up an hour of our time, so Back Benchers are due their time to speak.

We are talking about taking money back from people who are just above the poverty line to impose a tax that is completely unrelated to ability to pay. The Minister may shake his head, but it is the truth. It is not a charge for local authority services. All hon. Members representing Scottish constituencies could adumbrate their own experiences. I shall give one or two examples of what can happen.

An old woman came to me for advice. She has moved two doors down the road to look after her 90-year-old mother. The local authority deemed her to be living with her mother and so asked her for four lots of poll tax—two because she was living with her mother and two standard charges for the housing that she had vacated. That is not a charge for local authority services; it is a property charge, as it applies to the house that has been vacated. It may be that the multiplier is wrong, but if the multiplier is wrong, why the hell do the Government use that multiplier for the rate support grant?

You know quite a lot about taxation, Mr. Deputy Speaker, so I put it to you that this is the first tax that the Government claim has no anomalies. I suggest that it is riddled with anomalies. The Government will have to bend and review those anomalies, some of which bear most heavily on a section of the population which I have mentioned before and which I make no apologies for mentioning again—the severely mentally impaired.

I have a letter from the Scottish Society for the Mentally Handicapped which has issued a leaflet at a cost of £725. I hope that the Minister will arrange through the Scottish Office for that sum to be reimbursed. The letter states:

"There are also cases where disabled people who are not exempt may be required to pay a Community Charge out of a personal allowance of £10 per week. This has happened in some hostels which have been treated as residential care homes for income support purposes but are classed as domestic homes by Registration Officers."

Why are we removing the burden from those who are most able to pay and putting it on the backs of those who are least able to pay?

I know that I am at odds with some of my hon. Friends in the stance I have taken, but I know what is happening in my area. The position in Scotland is unlike the theories for England and Wales. It does not apply to Northern Ireland where the same social security legislation applies. The Government will not apply the poll tax in the Falls road or the Shankill. Northern Ireland is part of the United Kingdom. They should try it there.

**Mr. Edward Leigh** (Gainsborough and Horncastle): That is because they cannot collect it there.

**Mr. Douglas:** The hon. Gentleman should not intervene from a sedentary position because he is one of the proponents of a united kingdom. If we are a united kingdom, we should all be treated equally.

An explosion is coming in Scotland. It is not that people want to defy the law. They will have no choice.

**Mr. Nicholas Bennett** (Pembroke): Rubbish.

**Mr. Douglas:** Hon. Gentlemen should not say, "Rubbish." If they want to intervene, they should stand up and do so. It is not rubbish: it is fact. People will not be able to meet the obligation. I challenge any of my colleagues who have any responsibility for dealing with local authorities or any communication with them to tell me what is happening to housing debt. I know that it is soaring in Dunfermline, because people cannot meet their obligations. The poll is first call on them. It is automatic. It is an instrument whereby a button is pressed to take away their income support.

The House is empty of Scottish Tories tonight; indeed, Scotland is nearly empty of them. One solitary Scottish Tory is here tonight, and he will vote for this, knowing that many people in his area do not want to defy the law, but will have no alternative, because this is an automatic process. The button is pressed, and income support is taken away. The button is pressed, and warrant sale takes place. It is pressed again, and wage arrestment will follow. The procedure will malign local authorities. If the Government want to implement this, let them take the stick. Let them administer the tax and do the dirty work.

Scottish local authorities cannot stand back another two or three years until the next general election, hoping for a Labour Government then. I dearly want a Labour Government to remove this burden. In the meantime, the people whom I represent will suffer all the more because of the passing of regulations such as these.

11.36 pm

**Mr. Bill Walker** (Tayside, North): At least the hon. Member for Dunfermline, West (Mr. Douglas) had the courtesy to accept that I know something about the situation in Scotland. I do not doubt the integrity with which he looks after his constituents. I hope that he does not doubt the integrity with which I look after mine.

It was interesting to hear the hon. Gentleman highlight the problem of the lady who moved two doors down. I accept his worry on that score. I too am deeply concerned about that aspect of the community charge. I believe that the problem could have been resolved if the local authority had handled it a little more sympathetically. I have had the local authority's decisions reversed in one or two cases in my constituency. In fact, that has happened on four or five occasions. I am not sure of the fifth occasion, because I have not had it confirmed in writing.

When a person moves to stay with a child—as is normal within families—he should not have to pay a double community charge on his usual nearby home. To have to do so is nonsense, as we all know. This anomaly has been created by the way in which some local authorities have handled certain cases. But this is not a long-term criticism. It was inevitable, during this dramatic change, that problems and anomalies would be highlighted. I have shown that many of them can be dealt with at local level.

These regulationss are to do with rebates and clawbacks, and the principles involved in them. The taxpayer is the chap on average income, with two children, who lives next door to someone who is in receipt of public support because his circumstances require that support. The person who pays for that support is the taxpayer. As my hon. Friend the Minister intimated, we should not deviate from the principle that taxpayers' money should be used for the purpose of support for which it was allocated. We have a duty to protect those on low incomes who pay income tax. Many do, and I wish that they did not.

I draw this to the attention of constituents who come to see me. I know where they live, and ask them whether they expect their taxpaying next-door neighbours to pay their dues.

Taxpayers are not the rich and wealthy. Instead, they are average individuals who form the majority. We must protect them, and that is why it is right that clawback powers should be provided in the regulations. We must deal with individuals, and my hon. Friend the Minister told us that each individual would be receiving a letter telling him how the system would operate and how claims could be made. It is right that each individual case should be treated on its merits.

I acknowledge that a small minority will cheat deliberately. We all know who they are. Our constituents come to us to complain about cheats. Those who live near them—perhaps in the same street—know who they are. My constituents tell me about them. When reports have been made to me, I have taken the matter further to the proper authorities. Where necessary, I have ensured that prosecutions follow. That is right and proper.

**Mr. Graham:** Will the hon. Gentleman give way?

**Mr. Walker:** I shall give way in a minute. The hon. Gentleman has had his fair share of the batting—of the evening's activities—and there are others who want to make a contribution.

I do not believe that any hon. Members want those who cheat deliberately, who milk the system, to get away with it, whoever they are and at whatever level they operate. That is why I think it right that, when we use public funds we should——

**Mrs. Maria Fyfe** (Glasgow, Maryhill): Has the hon. Gentleman considered the position of someone such as Lord Vesty, who is famous for cheating the taxpayer out of several thousands of pounds? Lord Vesty will stand to gain huge sums from the introduction and implementation of the poll tax in Cirencester, where he lives. The hon. Gentleman seems to be referring to those on low incomes when he talks about cheats, but he has not yet addressed himself to those who have not paid the poll tax because they cannot afford to do so.

**Mr. Walker:** The hon. Lady protests too loudly. If we live in a civilised society, and I hope that we do, and if there are genuine problems—I have said that individual cases must be examined on their merits—we must recognise them. I deal with each problem as it relates specifically to the individual who has brought it to my attention. I think that all hon. Members adopt that approach. I think also that we all find that not everything is as it is presented to us.

An irate constituent came to me to draw attention to the problems that his mother was facing. He told me that his mother was required to pay the community charge in full. He argued that that was shameful as she was a pensioner, a widow and living alone. I told him that I would examine the circumstances. I did so, and found that the lady had £30,000-worth of equity. When my constituent returned to see me I asked him—I shall not give the names of these people because I am sure that they would not wish me to disclose them—"Do you think that Mr. So-and-So who lives next door, a bus driver with two young children, should pay your mother's community charge? That is effectively what you are saying. You are expecting the taxpayer to pick up the bill." That is why each case must be examined individually.

I have no doubt that in some instances something will have to be done to recognise the special circumstances in which an individual finds himself, possibly as a result of events over which he does not have full control. It is essential that there are provisions within the system to allow for that. We must recognise that there will always be individuals, sadly, who will have to be helped out of the circumstances in which they find themselves.

When the hon. Member for Glasgow, Garscadden (Mr. Dewar) said that there was confusion, I pointedly drew attention in an intervention to the fact that the confusion in my constituency, in Dundee, West and in Dundee, East had been caused by the situation in Tayside. Nobody is in any doubt about where the Labour party stands on this issue. There is confusion in Tayside because the leaders of the Scottish National party are telling the public at large —including those in receipt of housing benefit, those on public support and those who will be affected by the instruments before the House tonight—not to pay the community charge.

But the SNP in office locally—the administration in Angus district—is collecting the community charge. Indeed, additional staff are being taken on to deal with it. So on the one hand SNP members are saying that they will bring in enforcement orders and issue warrants, and on the other, the SNP at the highest level is telling people not to pay. It is no wonder that there is confusion. That is why —for example, in Dundee, East, Dundee, West, Angus, East, Perth and Kinross and in my constituency—we have this problem.

The hon. Member for Garscadden was right to talk about confusion. The people of Tayside have no idea what the SNP—in or out of administration—is telling people, and that is causing the most awful confusion.

**Several Hon. Members** rose——

**Mr. Deputy Speaker (Mr. Harold Walker):** Order. I remind the House of my earlier appeal for brief speeches.

11.47 pm

**Mr. Alex Salmond** (Banff and Buchan): Frequently it seems to be my unfortunate duty to speak following the hon. Member for Tayside, North (Mr. Walker). I hope that the bus driver of whom he spoke is voting for him, after all the hon. Gentleman's heroic efforts on his constituent's behalf.

After examining the instruments Nos. 507 and 476, my hon. Friends and I would like to know why people on income support for their basic income are being asked to pay the poll tax at all. The progenitor of the poll tax, former Councillor Douglas Mason, is quoted in an interesting article in the Aberdeen *Evening Express* of 14 June last—*[Interruption.]* I gather that Conservative Members would rather I called it the community charge. In that article, Mr. Mason revealed that he had called it the poll tax, and he added disarmingly:

"I wish I had thought of calling it the community charge. It sounds so much nicer."

He went on to say that, from the point of view of the poll tax, he had three main criticisms of the measure that the Government had introduced. The report said of his second criticism:

"Secondly, because he designed the tax to make sure local authorities were accountable to the people they serve, he proposed that those who were on benefits should be made to pay the full amount"

of the poll tax. We find, therefore, that ex-Councillor Mason, the progenitor of the poll tax, is disappointed that the Government have gone only as far as making those on income support pay 20 per cent. of the poll tax, plus the community water charge.

It would not have been so bad had the Government arranged matters in such a way that those in receipt of income support and facing the poll tax charge were fully compensated for the amount of poll tax that they must pay. We can only conclude that a Minister who cannot even name three local authorities in Scotland is not aware that in Scotland there are many people whose uprating of income support will not cover the poll tax bill that they face. In my constituency, a single person loses by 31p a week, a married couple by more than 60p a week. In many other areas of Scotland where the poll tax is higher, the loss to those people on income support who face the poll tax is much greater. The Minister must say why, depending on where they live, those on income support in Scotland should find that the poll tax eats into their basic income levels.

This evening we must ask ourselves why the Government are bringing in statutory instruments which require more information and the direct deduction of poll tax from income support. The answer is given in the recent publicity about the 1 million people in Scotland who are not paying the poll tax.

This Sunday's *Observer* contained an interesting comment from the leader of the Labour group on Lothian regional council, Councillor John Mulvey, who said:

"the non-payment campaign is alive and well and going from strength to strength. There is clearly a sizeable number of people who are not prepared to pay the poll tax and their ranks are being swollen by those who cannot afford to pay.

In spite of council officials saying that things are going well, the reality is that they're really quite worried by the scale of opposition that is developing."

Not everyone in the Labour group on Lothian regional council shares his opinion. Councillor Eric Milligan was mentioned earlier in this debate. In the words of Councillor Tony Kinder, the Labour councillor for Broxburn in the Lothian region, Councillor Milligan is the "self-appointed poll tax collector-in-chief to the Conservative Party."

**Mr. George Galloway** (Glasgow, Hillhead): What about Grampian?

**Mr. Salmond:** The hon. Member mentions Grampian region. It is interesting to note that the Scottish National party finance convenor of Grampian region was the one finance convenor in Scotland who was prepared to go to the wall to stop warrant sales in the poll tax, while members of the Labour party in the Grampian region sat on their hands and allowed the Democrats and the Conservatives to vote him out of office. We all know that that is not something which "warrant sale Milligan" is likely to do in the Lothian region.

Statutory instruments Nos. 507 and 476 are signs of Government panic in face of the strength of the non-payment campaign in Scotland. There is no breach of civil liberties which the Government would not be prepared to encounter. There is no imposition on the poorest in the community that the Government would not be willing to consider to try to keep the poll tax show in Scotland on the road. However, the poll tax in Scotland will be ground into the dust of history where it belongs. That will be done by the strength of the non-payment campaign which is under way at the moment.

11.53 pm

**Mr. George Galloway** (Glasgow, Hillhead): We have just heard the red Clydesider from Banff and Buchan talking about the great and stalwart fight which his colleagues in the Grampian region are conducting. His colleague sitting next to him, the hon. Member for Angus, East (Mr. Welsh) comes from the local authority which is one of the most assiduous collectors of the poll tax in Scotland. However, I would be wasting the five minutes available to me if I talked any longer about this farce to my left.

I found none of the farce on the Conservative Benches at all funny this evening. These proceedings have been an outrageous mockery. We were talked down to by a Minister representing the rolling downs of Hampshire, who would not know a Scottish local authority if it hit him in the face. No Scottish Office Minister was present until the Whips went into the back shop and dragged the Minister responsible for the poll tax in Scotland away from his bottle of port. As soon as the Scottish press left the Gallery, the Minister returned to his drinks party in the back shop. Only one Tory Scottish Member of Parliament has sat through this farce from beginning to end, and that is the hon. Member for Tayside, North (Mr. Walker), whom it is not easy to embarrass.

This farce typifies the sad position to which the government of Scotland has been reduced. These regulations will allow the poorest people in Scotland to be hunted down for a few pence and in the name of the community charge. It is only a few pence to Her Majesty's Government, who are sitting atop billions of pounds worth of surplus. The tax, and the farce associated with it, exemplify the reasons why each election and each opinion poll bring home—or ought to—to Her Majesty's

Government the extent to which they are now virtually bereft of popular support in the country of Scotland, which they purport to govern.

The Government, and their comprador in the Scottish Office, are a Government of Scottish Bourbons, who have learnt nothing and are forgetting nothing. There are no prizes for guessing who the Marie Antoinette is. I thought about who the Secretary of State might be, and the only figure I could come up with was Cardinal Rohan, whose patch was Strasbourg, but perhaps that is a delicate subject in these troubled times for the Tory party. The Government, who are implementing their mean-spirited, dire and pathetic regulations, are doing so without the slightest scintilla of popular support. As others have said, they are taking money from people on benefit, which, by definition, gives a level of financial support that is the very lowest that can be accepted in a civilised society of the Prime Minister's type. Even by this Government's standards, that is shameful.

Robin Small of the Low Pay Unit described the regulations as scandalous. He said:

"The whole notion of arresting Income Support which is considered to be subsistence level is scandalous.

How can the Government say they are keeping people off the poverty line by giving them Income Support and then take it away in certain circumstances?"

The *Evening Times* in Glasgow has fought a courageous campaign against the poll tax. It said in an editorial:

"The community charge is a tax without pity. Today we expose how it will be collected from many poor families who won't, or can't afford to pay . . . Is this the sort of heartless society we truly want?"

It describes the Minister's memorandum in this way:

"This is a brutal, oppressive memorandum. It shows how hard-nosed official channels are becoming about poverty. The State will have its pound of flesh, come what may, and never mind if people starve in the process."

There are people in Scotland who are pretty nearly going hungry, and this poll tax and these mean-spirited regulations will make it even harder for people living on the breadline to make ends meet. I hope that that is a pretty sight from the rolling downs of the Minister's constituency, because from where I sit, it is a pretty ugly one.

11.59 pm

**Dr. John Reid** (Motherwell, North): It speaks volumes for the concern of the Scottish National party that, when the hon. Member for Banff and Buchan (Mr. Salmond) is given the opportunity to criticise the perpetrators of the poll tax in Scotland, he instead spends his time attacking the only potential Government, the Labour party.

During my short career in Parliament I have sat through debates on shameful pieces of legislation, but none more shameful than what we are discussing tonight. It might benefit the season ticket holders who have arrived late for the vote, and who were not here to watch the match, if I explained what the legislation is all about. Tonight we are contemplating taking powers to withdraw from essential benefits the anticipated arrears in payment of an unfair tax from those who can least afford to pay it.

If there was ever an admission of the callousness of the poll tax and of the Government who introduced it, this statutory instrument is it. We were told that it was a fair tax, that it took account of ability to pay, that it was designed to encourage individual responsibility and individual dignity. What a sham, what hypocrisy. What is fair about a tax for which arrears can be anticipated and which will deprive the poorest in society of a minimal subsistence benefit designed to keep them not in comfort, not even in the less than comfort of the pension, but just minimally above the poverty line? How can a tax that takes any real account of ability to pay anticipate that the poorest will fall into arrears and inevitably will have to be punished by withdrawal of benefit? How can a tax encourage independence and dignity when, even before it is three months old, the Government are laying regulations that will reduce even further the little economic independence and dignity that anyone on income support can muster?

This is not simply a technical measure. It shows why the poll tax is absolutely rotten to the core. The poll tax already flies in the face of all progressive legislation by treating women as the chattels of their husbands. It stands on its head the Government's claim of individual responsibility by lumping husbands and wives together, even when the wife has only a minimal income. This measure is the most ignominious of all the aspects of the poll tax. It is no wonder that the Scottish Office Ministers did not have the guts to sit on the Front Bench while the Minister defended it.

This is not a tidying-up measure; it is an open admission of the bankruptcy of the Government's social morality. It is an open admission that the poor will fall into arrears and will be punished for it. How much have we heard tonight about the technicalities of the regulations? We heard much about 10p and 56 days. We cannot possibly portray the misery of a family on the poverty line through some chap in a Civil Service office. We cannot possibly understand what families on income support who face the poll tax are going through simply by reading some fancy footnote from the Department of Social Security. We need to live with those families to understand what they face. The Minister's kids do not go to school with the kids of families on income support. The Minister does not have meals with those families. A Minister who cannot name three local authorities in Scotland and cannot name three families in poverty in Scotland has no right to introduce legislation that will so adversely affect them.

I have many criticisms of the poll tax legislation. It is as needed in Scotland, as popular in Scotland and as useful in Scotland as the hon. Member for Stirling (Mr. Forsyth). I have searched all night for a worse criticism, but I cannot find one.

12.3 am

**Mrs. Maria Fyfe** (Glasgow, Maryhill): I am glad to have this opportunity to point out that when the memorandum from the Secretary of State for Social Security was sent to DSS offices in Scotland—it was based on statutory instrument No. 507—it was kept secret from Members of Parliament. When I asked to see a copy, I was told that I could not have one. I asked that it be placed in the Library, but that was refused. Another hon. Member asked whether it would appear in *Hansard,* but was told that it would not, on the grounds that it was only an interim order and that further instructions would be issued at a later date.

The Government were hoping to hide their iniquitous action. They were also hoping to hide the incompetence of the Ministers concerned. I managed to get hold of the memorandum and I have it here with me tonight. On page 2, it says that if a person fails to pay the poll tax, one of

[*Mrs. Maria Fyfe*]

the options open to obtain the poll tax from him is confinement in prison. One point about the poll tax that is well known in Scotland is that people do not go to prison in Scotland for not paying the poll tax. We have the spectacle of the Department of Social Security sending out a memorandum telling officials that people in Scotland go to prison for failing to pay the poll tax although that is clearly wrong. It is hardly surprising——

**Mr. Greg Knight** (Derby, North): Will the hon. Lady give way?

**Mrs. Fyfe:** No.

It is hardly surprising, considering that the Minister could not name three of the Scottish local collecting authorities. It would help if he could at least manage to consult his Scottish Office colleagues to get right the law in Scotland and to avoid the embarrassment of the reaction that rightly came from people when the *Evening Times* exposed the fact that the Government were prepared to leave people in desperate need of money with as little as 10p of their income support. I do not know why they bother to leave 10p. Why not leave nothing, or at least 19p, so that those people can at least put a stamp on a letter to their Members of Parliament to take up their case? There is nothing more to say except that the regulations are one of the main reasons why this Conservative bunch who come in late and hear nothing of the debate——

**Mr. Knight:** Will the hon. Lady give way?

**Hon. Members:** Sit down.

**Mrs. Fyfe:** Those Conservative Members will vote for the regulations. They have nothing but contempt for the people of Scotland.

12.5 am

**Mr. John McAllion** (Dundee, East): I would——

**Mr. Greg Knight:** Will the hon. Gentleman give way?

**Mr. McAllion:** I would consider giving way to the hon. Gentleman if he had had the courtesy to come into the Chamber and listen to the arguments about these regulations and the Scottish response. He has spent his time in the bar or somewhere else. He should go back there now and make no more attempts to intervene in this important debate.

We have seen here tonight the best possible argument for the establishment in Scotland at the earliest possible date of a Scottish Parliament to deal with Scottish matters. Conservative Members have shown an absolute lack of appreciation not only of the Scottish issue——

**Mr. Greg Knight:** On a point of order, Mr. Deputy Speaker. The hon. Gentleman alleged that I have been in the bar. In fact, I have been in the Library, and I hope that he will give way to allow me to answer some of the criticisms that have been made on the subject——

*It being one and a half hours after the motion was entered upon,* MR. DEPUTY SPEAKER *put the Question, pursuant to order [16 June]:*—

*The House divided:* Ayes 193, Noes 280.

**Division No. 258]**           **[12.07 am**

**AYES**

Abbott, Ms Diane
Adams, Allen (Paisley N)
Allen, Graham
Anderson, Donald
Archer, Rt Hon Peter
Armstrong, Hilary
Banks, Tony (Newham NW)
Barnes, Harry (Derbyshire NE)
Battle, John
Beckett, Margaret
Beith, A. J.
Bell, Stuart
Benn, Rt Hon Tony
Bennett, A. F. (D'nt'n & R'dish)
Blair, Tony
Blunkett, David
Boateng, Paul
Boyes, Roland
Bradley, Keith
Brown, Gordon (D'mline E)
Brown, Nicholas (Newcastle E)
Brown, Ron (Edinburgh Leith)
Bruce, Malcolm (Gordon)
Buckley, George J.
Callaghan, Jim
Campbell, Menzies (Fife NE)
Campbell-Savours, D. N.
Clark, Dr David (S Shields)
Clarke, Tom (Monklands W)
Clay, Bob
Clelland, David
Clwyd, Mrs Ann
Cohen, Harry
Corbett, Robin
Corbyn, Jeremy
Cousins, Jim
Cox, Tom
Crowther, Stan
Cryer, Bob
Cummings, John
Cunliffe, Lawrence
Cunningham, Dr John
Dalyell, Tam
Darling, Alistair
Davies, Rt Hon Denzil (Llanelli)
Davies, Ron (Caerphilly)
Davis, Terry (B'ham Hodge H'l)
Dewar, Donald
Dixon, Don
Dobson, Frank
Doran, Frank
Douglas, Dick
Duffy, A. E. P.
Dunnachie, Jimmy
Eadie, Alexander
Eastham, Ken
Fatchett, Derek
Field, Frank (Birkenhead)
Fields, Terry (L'pool B G'n)
Fisher, Mark
Flannery, Martin
Flynn, Paul
Foster, Derek
Foulkes, George
Fraser, John
Fyfe, Maria
Galbraith, Sam
Galloway, George
Garrett, John (Norwich South)
Garrett, Ted (Wallsend)
George, Bruce
Gilbert, Rt Hon Dr John
Godman, Dr Norman A.
Golding, Mrs Llin
Gordon, Mildred
Gould, Bryan
Graham, Thomas

Grant, Bernie (Tottenham)
Griffiths, Win (Bridgend)
Grocott, Bruce
Harman, Ms Harriet
Henderson, Doug
Hinchliffe, David
Hoey, Ms Kate (Vauxhall)
Hogg, N. (C'nauld & Kilsyth)
Home Robertson, John
Hood, Jimmy
Howarth, George (Knowsley N)
Howells, Geraint
Howells, Dr. Kim (Pontypridd)
Hoyle, Doug
Hughes, John (Coventry NE)
Hughes, Robert (Aberdeen N)
Hughes, Roy (Newport E)
Illsley, Eric
Ingram, Adam
Jones, Barry (Alyn & Deeside)
Jones, Martyn (Clwyd S W)
Kaufman, Rt Hon Gerald
Kennedy, Charles
Kirkwood, Archy
Leadbitter, Ted
Leighton, Ron
Lestor, Joan (Eccles)
Livingstone, Ken
Livsey, Richard
Lloyd, Tony (Stretford)
Lofthouse, Geoffrey
Loyden, Eddie
McAllion, John
McAvoy, Thomas
Macdonald, Calum A.
McFall, John
McKay, Allen (Barnsley West)
McKelvey, William
McLeish, Henry
Maclennan, Robert
McNamara, Kevin
McWilliam, John
Madden, Max
Mahon, Mrs Alice
Marek, Dr John
Marshall, David (Shettleston)
Martin, Michael J. (Springburn)
Martlew, Eric
Meale, Alan
Michael, Alun
Michie, Bill (Sheffield Heeley)
Michie, Mrs Ray (Arg'l & Bute)
Mitchell, Austin (G't Grimsby)
Moonie, Dr Lewis
Morgan, Rhodri
Morley, Elliott
Morris, Rt Hon A. (W'shawe)
Mowlam, Marjorie
Mullin, Chris
Murphy, Paul
Nellist, Dave
O'Brien, William
O'Neill, Martin
Patchett, Terry
Pike, Peter L.
Powell, Ray (Ogmore)
Prescott, John
Primarolo, Dawn
Quin, Ms Joyce
Radice, Giles
Redmond, Martin
Rees, Rt Hon Merlyn
Reid, Dr John
Richardson, Jo
Roberts, Allan (Bootle)
Robertson, George
Rooker, Jeff

Ross, Ernie (Dundee W)
Rowlands, Ted
Ruddock, Joan
Salmond, Alex
Sedgemore, Brian
Sheerman, Barry
Sheldon, Rt Hon Robert
Shore, Rt Hon Peter
Short, Clare
Skinner, Dennis
Smith, Andrew (Oxford E)
Smith, C. (Isl'ton & F'bury)
Smith, J. P. (Vale of Glam)
Snape, Peter
Spearing, Nigel
Steel, Rt Hon David
Steinberg, Gerry
Stott, Roger
Strang, Gavin
Straw, Jack
Taylor, Mrs Ann (Dewsbury)
Taylor, Matthew (Truro)

Thompson, Jack (Wansbeck)
Turner, Dennis
Vaz, Keith
Wall, Pat
Wallace, James
Walley, Joan
Wardell, Gareth (Gower)
Wareing, Robert N.
Watson, Mike (Glasgow, C)
Welsh, Andrew (Angus E)
Welsh, Michael (Doncaster N)
Williams, Rt Hon Alan
Williams, Alan W. (Carm'then)
Winnick, David
Wise, Mrs Audrey
Wray, Jimmy
Young, David (Bolton SE)

Tellers for the Ayes:
Mr. Frank Haynes and
Mr. Frank Cook.

## NOES

Alexander, Richard
Alison, Rt Hon Michael
Allason, Rupert
Amess, David
Amos, Alan
Arbuthnot, James
Arnold, Jacques (Gravesham)
Arnold, Tom (Hazel Grove)
Ashby, David
Aspinwall, Jack
Atkins, Robert
Baker, Rt Hon K. (Mole Valley)
Baker, Nicholas (Dorset N)
Baldry, Tony
Banks, Robert (Harrogate)
Batiste, Spencer
Beaumont-Dark, Anthony
Bellingham, Henry
Bendall, Vivian
Bennett, Nicholas (Pembroke)
Bevan, David Gilroy
Biffen, Rt Hon John
Blackburn, Dr John G.
Body, Sir Richard
Boscawen, Hon Robert
Boswell, Tim
Bottomley, Peter
Bottomley, Mrs Virginia
Bowden, A (Brighton K'pto'n)
Bowden, Gerald (Dulwich)
Bowis, John
Boyson, Rt Hon Dr Sir Rhodes
Braine, Rt Hon Sir Bernard
Brandon-Bravo, Martin
Brazier, Julian
Bright, Graham
Brown, Michael (Brigg & Cl't's)
Browne, John (Winchester)
Bruce, Ian (Dorset South)
Buchanan-Smith, Rt Hon Alick
Budgen, Nicholas
Burns, Simon
Burt, Alistair
Butcher, John
Butler, Chris
Butterfill, John
Carlisle, John, (Luton N)
Carlisle, Kenneth (Lincoln)
Carrington, Matthew
Carttiss, Michael
Cash, William
Channon, Rt Hon Paul
Chapman, Sydney
Chope, Christopher
Churchill, Mr
Clark, Dr Michael (Rochford)

Clark, Sir W. (Croydon S)
Clarke, Rt Hon K. (Rushcliffe)
Colvin, Michael
Conway, Derek
Coombs, Anthony (Wyre F'rest)
Coombs, Simon (Swindon)
Cope, Rt Hon John
Couchman, James
Cran, James
Currie, Mrs Edwina
Curry, David
Davies, Q. (Stamf'd & Spald'g)
Davis, David (Boothferry)
Day, Stephen
Dicks, Terry
Dorrell, Stephen
Douglas-Hamilton, Lord James
Dover, Den
Dunn, Bob
Dykes, Hugh
Eggar, Tim
Emery, Sir Peter
Evans, David (Welwyn Hatf'd)
Evennett, David
Fairbairn, Sir Nicholas
Fallon, Michael
Favell, Tony
Field, Barry (Isle of Wight)
Fishburn, John Dudley
Forman, Nigel
Forsyth, Michael (Stirling)
Forth, Eric
Fox, Sir Marcus
Franks, Cecil
Freeman, Roger
French, Douglas
Fry, Peter
Gardiner, George
Garel-Jones, Tristan
Gill, Christopher
Glyn, Dr Alan
Goodlad, Alastair
Goodson-Wickes, Dr Charles
Gorst, John
Gow, Ian
Grant, Sir Anthony (CambsSW)
Greenway, Harry (Ealing N)
Gregory, Conal
Griffiths, Peter (Portsmouth N)
Grist, Ian
Ground, Patrick
Gummer, Rt Hon John Selwyn
Hague, William
Hamilton, Neil (Tatton)
Hampson, Dr Keith
Hanley, Jeremy

Hannam, John
Hargreaves, A. (B'ham H'll Gr')
Hargreaves, Ken (Hyndburn)
Harris, David
Haselhurst, Alan
Hawkins, Christopher
Hayes, Jerry
Hayward, Robert
Heddle, John
Hicks, Mrs Maureen (Wolv' NE)
Hicks, Robert (Cornwall SE)
Higgins, Rt Hon Terence L.
Hill, James
Hind, Kenneth
Hogg, Hon Douglas (Gr'th'm)
Hordern, Sir Peter
Howard, Michael
Howarth, Alan (Strat'd-on-A)
Howarth, G. (Cannock & B'wd)
Hughes, Robert G. (Harrow W)
Hunt, David (Wirral W)
Hunt, Sir John (Ravensbourne)
Hunter, Andrew
Irvine, Michael
Jack, Michael
Jackson, Robert
Janman, Tim
Johnson Smith, Sir Geoffrey
Jones, Gwilym (Cardiff N)
Jopling, Rt Hon Michael
Key, Robert
King, Roger (B'ham N'thfield)
King, Rt Hon Tom (Bridgwater)
Kirkhope, Timothy
Knapman, Roger
Knight, Greg (Derby North)
Knight, Dame Jill (Edgbaston)
Lamont, Rt Hon Norman
Lang, Ian
Latham, Michael
Lawrence, Ivan
Leigh, Edward (Gainsbor'gh)
Lennox-Boyd, Hon Mark
Lilley, Peter
Lloyd, Peter (Fareham)
Lyell, Sir Nicholas
McCrindle, Robert
Macfarlane, Sir Neil
MacGregor, Rt Hon John
MacKay, Andrew (E Berkshire)
Maclean, David
McLoughlin, Patrick
McNair-Wilson, Sir Michael
McNair-Wilson, Sir Patrick
Madel, David
Major, Rt Hon John
Mans, Keith
Maples, John
Marland, Paul
Marshall, John (Hendon S)
Marshall, Michael (Arundel)
Martin, David (Portsmouth S)
Maude, Hon Francis
Mawhinney, Dr Brian
Mayhew, Rt Hon Sir Patrick
Mellor, David
Miller, Sir Hal
Mills, Iain
Mitchell, Andrew (Gedling)
Moate, Roger
Moore, Rt Hon John
Morris, M (N'hampton S)
Morrison, Rt Hon P (Chester)
Moss, Malcolm
Moynihan, Hon Colin
Neale, Gerrard
Needham, Richard
Nelson, Anthony
Neubert, Michael
Newton, Rt Hon Tony

Nicholls, Patrick
Nicholson, David (Taunton)
Nicholson, Emma (Devon West)
Norris, Steve
Onslow, Rt Hon Cranley
Oppenheim, Phillip
Page, Richard
Paice, James
Patnick, Irvine
Patten, Rt Hon Chris (Bath)
Patten, John (Oxford W)
Pawsey, James
Porter, David (Waveney)
Price, Sir David
Raison, Rt Hon Timothy
Redwood, John
Renton, Tim
Rhodes James, Robert
Riddick, Graham
Ridley, Rt Hon Nicholas
Ridsdale, Sir Julian
Rifkind, Rt Hon Malcolm
Roberts, Wyn (Conwy)
Roe, Mrs Marion
Rossi, Sir Hugh
Rost, Peter
Rumbold, Mrs Angela
Sackville, Hon Tom
Sainsbury, Hon Tim
Sayeed, Jonathan
Shaw, David (Dover)
Shaw, Sir Michael (Scarb')
Shelton, Sir William
Shephard, Mrs G. (Norfolk SW)
Shepherd, Colin (Hereford)
Skeet, Sir Trevor
Smith, Tim (Beaconsfield)
Soames, Hon Nicholas
Speller, Tony
Spicer, Sir Jim (Dorset W)
Spicer, Michael (S Worcs)
Stanbrook, Ivor
Stanley, Rt Hon Sir John
Steen, Anthony
Stern, Michael
Stevens, Lewis
Stewart, Andy (Sherwood)
Stewart, Rt Hon Ian (Herts N)
Stokes, Sir John
Stradling Thomas, Sir John
Summerson, Hugo
Tapsell, Sir Peter
Taylor, Ian (Esher)
Taylor, John M (Solihull)
Taylor, Teddy (S'end E)
Thompson, Patrick (Norwich N)
Thorne, Neil
Thornton, Malcolm
Thurnham, Peter
Townend, John (Bridlington)
Townsend, Cyril D. (B'heath)
Tracey, Richard
Tredinnick, David
Trippier, David
Trotter, Neville
Twinn, Dr Ian
Vaughan, Sir Gerard
Viggers, Peter
Waddington, Rt Hon David
Wakeham, Rt Hon John
Walker, Bill (T'side North)
Waller, Gary
Ward, John
Wardle, Charles (Bexhill)
Warren, Kenneth
Watts, John
Wells, Bowen
Whitney, Ray
Widdecombe, Ann
Wiggin, Jerry

Wilkinson, John
Wilshire, David
Winterton, Mrs Ann
Winterton, Nicholas
Wood, Timothy
Yeo, Tim

Younger, Rt Hon George

Tellers for the Noes:
    Mr. Tony Durant and
    Mr. David Lightbown.

*Question accordingly negatived.*

## WELSH GRAND COMMITTEE

*Ordered,*

That during the proceedings on the matter of the first year of the Valleys Programme the Welsh Grand Committee have leave to sit twice on the first day on which it shall meet, and that, notwithstanding the provisions of Standing Order No. 88 (Meetings of standing committees), the second such sitting shall not commence before Four o'clock nor continue after the Committee has considered the matter for two hours at the sitting.—[*Mr. Kenneth Carlisle.*]

## DNA Testing

*Motion made, and Question proposed,* That this House do now adjourn.—[*Mr. Kenneth Carlisle.*]

12.18 am

**Mr. Max Madden** (Bradford, West): Home Office watchers, especially those of us who are closely involved in immigration and nationality matters, never cease to be amazed at the breathtaking arrogance of successive Home Secretaries or at the sustained efforts of their senior officials to manage and manipulate the House and the national news media. But the propensity of Home Secretaries to try to mislead the House at the behest of senior officials has been revealed this week in precise detail. That the issue at the heart of this attempted Home Office deception concerns DNA testing and the immigration rules is all part of a pattern of events concerning immigration and nationality which has unfolded since 1979.

The Government, in concert with senior Home Office officials, have carefully planned and introduced a series of laws, rules, regulations and procedures which, in total, now mean that many black and Asian people find it extremely difficult—even when they have clear rights to live in this country—to enter the United Kingdom, and in recent years even to visit relatives and friends in this country.

The Government's "firm and fair" immigration policy is a euphemism for racist laws which discriminate on the basis of race and colour and against those who suffer the dual misfortune of being black or Asian and poor.

I accuse the Government of trying to mislead the House about a centrally organised DNA testing scheme. Last week, when announcing such a scheme, the Home Secretary said that decisions about how the scheme was to be funded had not been reached. However, a Home Office document, written by the head of the immigration and nationality department, Mr. G. N. Stadlen, makes it clear that a decision on funding has been reached. Indeed, it makes it clear that an increase in entry clearance fees will be introduced on 1 November. It is also clear, from this document and from a draft letter to the Lord President from the Home Secretary, that the Home Secretary has been and is plotting to deny the House any opportunity to debate either the principle of raising entry clearance fees, which are now £60 per person, to fund a centrally organised DNA testing scheme, or, indeed, to debate and

Last night the Government deliberately arranged a debate to discuss DNA testing and changes in the immigration rules together so as to avoid—I quote from the Home Office documents which were leaked this week—

"two separate rows about immigration issues in quick succession."

As is also clear from the draft letter and from Mr. Stadlen's document, the Home Secretary had planned the controversial DNA announcement with the immigration rule changes to "divert some attention" from the absence of any further provisions or promises for the people of Hong Kong.

I believe that all my right hon. and hon. Friends will agree that last night's debate on DNA testing and the immigration rule changes was a shambolic farce. Many hon. Members who wished to participate in that debate had no opportunity to do so and the Minister, who happily is with us again tonight, was left with fewer than 10 minutes to reply to the many questions put to him by hon. Members from all parts of the House.

The Minister said that he would speak about DNA testing in reply to this Adjournment debate. I have many expectations of Adjournment debates, but never before have I witnessed a Minister from a Department which had deliberately contrived to arrange a debate to discuss two issues—DNA testing and the immigration rule changes—tell the House that as he did not have time to talk about DNA testing he would make a statement on it in an Adjournment debate the following evening.

In reply to questions from journalists today, the Home Office has made it clear that the Minister of State will say little about DNA testing tonight, so I am left with no alternative but to believe that the Home Secretary's attempt seriously to mislead the House of Commons has backfired badly. We are left with the Minister of State who, despite all his considerable powers of bluff and bluster, which were fully deployed last night, cannot conceal the Government's embarrassment. He has been left with egg all over his face as a result of the Home Secretary's and the Home Office's attempt to mislead the House of Commons and to arrange the business of the House for their convenience.

**Mr. Deputy Speaker (Mr. Harold Walker):** Order. On previous occasions Mr. Speaker has made it clear that hon. Members must not accuse Ministers of deliberately seeking to mislead the House. That is a reflection on their integrity and honour. I hope that the hon. Gentleman will withdraw that accusation.

**Mr. Madden:** In a moment I shall quote extensively from the document to which I have already referred. Any objective view of that document can only lead one to the inevitable conclusion that the Home Secretary, in concert with other senior Ministers, was actively seeking to mislead the House of Commons.

**Mr. Deputy Speaker:** Order. I have told the hon. Gentleman that Mr. Speaker will not tolerate remarks in the House which reflect on the integrity of hon. Members, whether they be Ministers or otherwise. The hon. Gentleman may well adduce his evidence and leave it for the House to draw its own conclusions, but he must not make that allegation. He must withdraw it.

**Mr. Madden:** I shall gladly do that, Mr. Deputy Speaker.

The Minister of State and his officials should now do what they should have done at the start and make a statement on DNA testing and the centrally organised DNA testing scheme that the Government wish to announce. They should follow that statement with a full debate in the House—I would not dare to say during daylight hours, but at a reasonable hour. Last night we had a non-debate on DNA and a short debate on immigration rule changes in the early hours of the morning, and tonight this debate is taking place well after midnight.

I hope that the Minister of State will readily accept my suggestion, because it would enable the Home Secretary to give full and accurate information about a centrally organised DNA testing scheme which is vital to divided families who desperately want to be reunited in Britain. It would enable all those hon. Members who have many

questions to ask about how the scheme will be funded and operated to put those questions with a reasonable expectation of receiving full and accurate replies.

I quote briefly from the draft letter to the Lord President of the Council for signature by the Home Secretary, which is annex A to the document written by Mr. Stadlen and discusses the timing of last Wednesday's written answer to a parliamentary question on DNA testing. It says:

"I have considered carefully whether there are countervailing Hong Kong factors which justify postponement. My conclusion is that postponement would, if anything, increase speculation on that score rather than diminish it: it will be better to proceed on the basis of 'business as usual' for immediate purposes explaining as necessary that any Hong Kong proposals will be forthcoming separately. Since I shall, with H colleagues' approval, be simultaneously making a possible controversial announcement about the use of DNA in immigration cases, it could well be that that will divert some attention.

I have however removed from the new Rules a measure to increase to £200,000 the minimum sum of £150,000 at present required for entry as a businessman or person of independent means. The current sum has been widely mentioned in recent days in the Hong Kong context, and increasing it now could undermine our current Hong Kong policy.

I attach a copy of the Written Answer and Press Release which have been prepared for the announcement. Our officials have already been in touch about the timing of a debate on the Rules. At that stage, too, it will be very important to consider the Hong Kong dimension and I will, of course, be keeping in close touch with the Foreign Secretary for that purpose.

I am sending copies of this letter to the Prime Minister, the Foreign Secretary, the Secretaries of State for Trade and Industry, for Employment, for Education and Science, and to Sir Robin Butler."

The memorandum from Mr. Stadlen, referring to the timing of last Wednesday's announcement, states in part: "postponement would arouse expectations which we cannot at this stage be sure of meeting, leading to possible presentational problems later on. Proceeding with the rules now, by contrast, enables us to say that they have been in the pipe line for sometime and are being introduced without prejudice to the outcome of the consideration being given to the position of the people of Hong Kong."

**The Minister of State, Home Office (Mr. Tim Renton):** I was under the impression that the hon. Gentleman wanted to talk about DNA. So far he has wasted 13 of the 30 minutes allocated to an Adjournment debate quoting a leaked Home Office document that has very little to do with DNA. Shall we be given a chance to discuss DNA tonight, or is the hon. Gentleman's intention once again frivolously to waste the time of the House, as he did last night?

**Mr. Madden:** I hoped to discuss DNA testing last night. I hoped for an opportunity to ask questions about it after the statement that I had presumed would be made last week, and in a debate in Government time at a reasonable hour. As this is my debate, I shall deploy my arguments and make my speech in my own way. The Minister must contain himself, but if he is so anxious to debate DNA, I hope that he will join me in persuading his right hon. Friends the Home Secretary and the Leader of the House to provide time for a full debate on DNA testing.

The memorandum makes it clear that the immigration rules are not being changed to allow the amount required of business people to be increased to £200,000 because of the Hong Kong dimension. It adds that a later date of laying would enable the Home Secretary
"to develop a defensive line or outline proposals on Hong Kong before the debate. But the Home Secretary's decision to

[*Mr. Madden*]

proceed with the rules changes is premised on our ability to present them as a matter quite separate from Hong Kong, and on the desirability of disposing of the debate before the Government comes under pressure to announce its conclusion. Accordingly, I recommend that the rules be laid on Wednesday."

A section entitled "Handling the announcement" contains the statement:

"The press will now be looking out for the rules changes. I propose therefore that we publish them on the same day as laying, to put us in a position to respond promptly to enquiries and press reports."

In another headed "The debate" there is the comment:

"Because the consolidated rules cover the whole of immigration control, the debate will be wide ranging and we shall prepare briefing accordingly. Mr. Renton will speak at the end. B2 are putting together a draft speech to cover the main rules changes (visas for Turkey and Haiti, students sex discrimination), Hong Kong (briefly) and DNA".

The document goes on to deal with the Government's DNA scheme, which is a serious matter:

"It does not indicate how the scheme will be financed, beyond reiterating that the cost will not be met by the taxpayer. The intention is to make a separate announcement on the funding arrangements shortly before the scheme comes into effect, to avoid a rush of applications aimed at beating the associated increase in the settlement fee.

Although no part of the DNA proposals involves changes in the rules, it is certain that the Opposition and the lobby will use the opportunity offered by the rules changes to argue the case for over-age reapplicants. Consequently we see advantage in combining the two announcements, thus avoiding two separate rows about immigration issues in quick succession."

And so it goes on, in much the same vein.

I know that the Minister is anxious to discuss DNA. May I, therefore, put six questions to him—very quickly —which I very much hope that he will try to answer either tonight or in the debate that I hope we shall be allowed shortly?

First, by how much will entry fees increase on 1 November, as foreshadowed in the internal Home Office document? Secondly, will applicants be required to pay anything for undertaking DNA tests? Thirdly, will there be a flat-rate increase in entry clearance, or a variable increase? Fourthly, what are the projected public expenditure savings to the Home Office and appellate authorities?

Incidentally, I put down two questions for answer today—to the Home Office and Foreign Office—seeking that information, and have as yet received no reply. That is not surprising; obviously the Minister will be falling over himself to give the information tonight.

Fifthly, will the Minister publish full financial details of the operation of entry clearance, bearing in mind that the total cost of an entry clearance officer was given in 1986 as £100,000? Sixthly, will he give a firm assurance that so-called "over-age children" who confirm their application to join their families here by positive DNA tests will be treated sympathetically? Like many other people, I feel that it would be a tragedy if the position set out in the internal Home Office document were translated into reality.

I believe that the way in which the Home Office has sought to deal with the matter raises serious issues. I do not think that anyone who gives a fair and objective interpretation to the Home Office document or to the way in which the Government have sought to orchestrate the announcement of the matter—in my view, there has been a deliberate attempt to mislead and conceal—can feel anything other than grave concern.

This is a crucial matter, to which many divided families have been looking forward for many years. I believe that they deserve better treatment than they have been given by the Home Office and the Government. I hope that the Minister of State will do what he did not do last night and give some clear and full information about the way in which the scheme is to be operated.

12.37 am

**The Minister of State, Home Office (Mr. Tim Renton):** I have rarely known such an abuse of the procedures of the House as we have just heard from the hon. Member for Bradford, West (Mr. Madden). He spoke for 17 of the 30 minutes allocated to an Adjournment debate, simply quoting from a leaked Home Office document which, while it certainly bears on DNA, has very little relevance to it.

In his final remarks the hon. Gentleman described DNA as "a crucially important matter", yet in the rest of his speech he went out of his way to show that his only interest in the subject was to stir up political trouble. He has no real interest in it; if he had, he would have given me time to answer serious questions rather than try to stir a political pot. He talks as though he is simply—in his own words—out to frighten the black, the Asian and the poor.

Why this contemptible attitude? Is the hon. Gentleman so frightened of his own position in his constituency that that is all that he can do? At the end of last night's debate I had only seven minutes in which to answer, rather than the 15 for which I had asked. Why? Because the hon. Member for Brent, South (Mr. Boateng) went on and on talking. When I rose to reply I was constantly interrupted by points of order, not least by the hon. Member for Holborn and St. Pancras (Mr. Dobson), the shadow Leader of the House, who said that I was speaking for the second time in the debate when I had not even spoken for the first time. It showed an extraordinary lack of knowledge of what was happening in the House. By his contempt of the House, the hon. Member for Bradford, West has shown that his only interest in the matter is just to try to stir up a bit of political trouble. I feel sorry for his constituents if that is the only service that they can get from him.

I return to the ludicrous charge by the hon. Gentleman that my right hon. Friend the Home Secretary misled the House about charging for DNA tests. There is no question of that whatsoever. We made it clear from the outset that any DNA scheme will not be funded out of taxpayers' money. Our policy is that the cost of the entry clearance process should be met by the applicants themselves rather than by the taxpayer. I see no reason why the costs of DNA tests should be treated any differently.

We recognise, of course, that the tests are expensive, particularly where several members of the same family are applying. With this in mind, my right hon. Friend made it clear last week that

"The level of the fee to be charged for"
settlement
"applications will need to strike a balance between not imposing too great a burden either on the individual applicant or on the taxpayer."—[*Official Report,* 14 June 1989; Vol. 154, c. *464.*]

If, for one moment, the hon. Member for Bradford, West would unblock his ears and listen I should tell him that, beyond this, no final decision has been taken, whatever he may have read in national newspapers. Once we have worked up the detailed arrangements——

**Mr. Madden:** Will the Minister give way?

**Mr. Renton:** No, I shall not give way to the hon. Gentleman. I have only a few minutes left. He took up a great deal more than half the time and, unlike him, I want to talk about DNA.

Once we have worked out detailed arrangements for financing the DNA scheme, we will of course make a further announcement to the House. That announcement will be made before the scheme is implemented overseas. I can assure the hon. Gentleman that we are conscious of the need to avoid erecting a financial barrier which might constitute a deterrent to genuine family applicants. There has been no deceit whatsoever. Quite the contrary. My right hon. Friend has set out in full the way that we are going. Certain steps now have to be taken. For example, we have to negotiate contracts and prices with commercial suppliers. I repeat that when we have reached a final decision on the matter a further announcement will be made to the House. I hope that for once the hon. Gentleman will give up a little of his sound and fury and that he will go home and think seriously about DNA.

**Mr. Madden:** Will the Minister give way?

**Mr. Renton:** No.

The hon. Gentleman, and other hon. Members, have argued that special consideration should be given to over-age re-applicants who were refused as children on relationship grounds and who do not meet the requirements of the rules relating to adults. I accept that this is a particularly difficult issue. For that reason, we gave it a great deal of thought. I listened very carefully to the points that were made in the debate on the immigration rules last night, but again I say to the hon. Member for Bradford, West that the subject of the debate was not DNA but the immigration rules. DNA is not mentioned in the immigration rules.

**Mr. Madden:** The Minister mentioned it.

**Mr. Renton:** I did not mention it; the hon. Gentleman raised it. In the very short time that was available to me last night I made it absolutely plain that I intended to talk about DNA tonight, not in a debate on the immigration rules.

In particular, I listened to a characteristically thoughtful contribution from my hon. Friend the Member for Keighley (Mr. Waller). However, I cannot agree with my hon. Friend or with the hon. Member for Bradford, West that this is simply a matter of reversing decisions that have turned out to be wrong. It is not as simple as that.

**Mr. Madden:** Why?

**Mr. Renton:** The hon. Gentleman should know, because he studies immigration matters quite carefully, that dependency lies at the heart of the question as to what decides who, other than spouses and fiancés, are allowed to join family units in the United Kingdom. That means that, under normal circumstances, only young children or elderly dependent relatives are given leave to enter.

The immigration rules now make generous provision for the admission of children on the basis that it is desirable for children to spend their formative years with their parents. Once a child has reached the age of 18, however, he is regarded as an independent adult. The rules provide for the admission of children over the age of 18 to join parents or relatives settled here only in the most exceptional compassionate circumstances. It seems to me that a person who once applied as a child cannot automatically be admitted regardless of his present age and circumstances. Many of those involved, after all, have now settled into independent adult life and will have established jobs and families of their own overseas.

This said, and having considered the matter very carefully, we decided that it would be right to relax the requirements of the rules in certain circumstances where a person previously refused entry as a child is now able to establish relationship by means of DNA evidence. A re-applicant will be expected to show that he is still wholly or mainly dependent on his United Kingdom sponsor, as that was the basis of his original application as a child. We will also look for some compassionate circumstances which distinguish the particular case from the generality of over-age re-applicants.

Subject to those requirements, we will be prepared to consider each case on its merits with a view to exercising discretion in suitable cases. I hope that this goes a substantial way towards reassuring my hon. Friend the Member for Keighley, and I hope that it will go some way towards reassuring the hon. Member for Bradford, West —although I doubt it, as his ears are permanently blocked —that we will approach these difficult cases compassionately and sympathetically, while maintaining the basic distinction between children and adults which has been a settled feature of our immigration policy for many years.

DNA is a powerful and important new technique. There is no doubt that it has a good deal to offer in the immigration context. But I believe that the proposals which my right hon. Friend the Home Secretary announced last week and which I have outlined tonight will go a long way towards making disputes about relationships, which have dogged so many immigration cases, a thing of the past. I do not anticipate any immediate reduction in Home Office expenditure, but I remember going on Sylhet village visits with our entry clearance officers from Dacca and I know the great lengths to which they went to establish whether relationships were genuine and as claimed. I hope that, when DNA is rooted and bedded down in our system, some of those village visits will not be necessary in future.

I am sure that most fair-minded people will regard our proposals as a fair and reasonable way forward. I should like to think that even the hon. Member for Bradford, West, with all the bile and anger that he appears to find it inevitable to bring to these difficult immigration matters, on mature reflection will accept the reasonableness of our proposals.

*Question put and agreed to.*

*Adjourned accordingly at thirteen minutes to One o'clock.*

# House of Commons

*Thursday 22 June 1989*

*The House met at half-past Two o'clock*

## PRAYERS

[MR. SPEAKER *in the Chair*]

## PRIVATE BUSINESS

NEW SOUTHGATE CEMETERY AND CREMATORIUM
LIMITED BILL
*Read the Third time, and passed.*

ASSOCIATED BRITISH PORTS (No. 2) BILL.*(By Order)*
*Order read for resumed adjourned debate on Question
—[23 May]—That the Bill be now read the Third time.*

**Hon. Members:** Object.
*Debate to be resumed on Thursday 29 June.*

BRITISH RAILWAYS (PENALTY FARES) BILL *[Lords]*
*(By Order)*

*Order for consideration read.*
*To be considered on Thursday 29 June at Seven o'clock.*

LONDON REGIONAL TRANSPORT (PENALTY FARES) BILL
*[Lords] (By Order)*

*Order for consideration read.*
*To be considered on Wednesday 28 June at Seven
o'clock.*

BUCKINGHAMSHIRE COUNTY COUNCIL BILL *[Lords]*
*(By Order)*

*Order for consideration read.*
*To be considered on Thursday 29 June.*

LONDON UNDERGROUND (VICTORIA) *(By Order)*

BRITISH FILM INSTITUTE SOUTHBANK BILL *(By Order)*

VALE OF GLAMORGAN (BARRY HARBOUR) BILL
*[LORDS] (By Order)*

*Orders for Second Reading read.*
*To be read a Second time on Thursday 29 June.*

HAYLE HARBOUR BILL *[Lords] (By Order)*
*Order for Second Reading read.*
*To be read a Second time on Tuesday 27 June.*

# Oral Answers to Questions

## NORTHERN IRELAND

### EC Structural Funds

1. **Mr. Archer:** To ask the Secretary of State for
Northern Ireland what steps he has taken to maximise the
share of the European Community structural funds
accruing to Northern Ireland.

**The Minister of State, Northern Ireland Office (Mr. Ian
Stewart):** The Government welcome the designation of
Northern Ireland as an objective 1 region for structural aid
from the European Community. Following partnership
consultations, a development plan for the Province was
submitted and negotiations with the Commission on the
Community support framework are under way. Work on
preparing earning measures is well advanced.

**Mr. Archer:** Since the present quota system of
allocation will no longer apply after 1992, will the Minister
ensure that his Department is ready with projects to assure
Northern Ireland of its proper share of the funding? Will
he undertake to ensure that every penny of European
money will go to increase public expenditure and not to
reduce the commitment of the Treasury?

**Mr. Stewart:** We are very anxious to ensure that
Northern Ireland has the maximum opportunity to obtain
the maximum amount of funding for the best possible
projects through the earning measures. Work is already in
hand and my officials are having another meeting with
European Community officials about this next week. With
regard to additionality, to which the right hon. and learned
Gentleman referred, I am fully confident that we shall meet
the European Community additionality requirement. I
understand from Commissioner Millan that any constraint on the availability of funds is more likely to come
from the number of existing commitments in the pipeline
than from any problems on our front.

**Rev. Ian Paisley:** Will the Minister tell the House how
many bodies he consulted in drawing up the strategic plan
that he intends to submit to Brussels for action? How have
the consultations taken place, why was a very important
body—the Institution of Civil Engineers—left out, and are
the discussions still going on?

**Mr. Stewart:** I can tell the hon. Gentleman that
consultations took place between a very large number of
bodies. With regard to the formal consultation process, a
body with a statutory function in relation to the plan or
the earning programme is defined in the Community's
rules as being a partner for specific consultations.
However, the Government consulted much more widely
and included the Confederation of British Industry and the
trade unions. If the particular body to which the hon.
Gentleman referred has views that it wants to put to us on
the use of the programmes and the structural fund we
should be glad to hear from it.

**Mr. John D. Taylor:** As the most important Euro-route
out of Northern Ireland is that between Belfast and Larne
and then out through Scotland, will the Minister assure the
House that the Belfast-Larne road will be improved as a

matter of priority in the development scheme being submitted to the European Community? Will he confirm whether the line of the other Euro-route—from Belfast to Dublin, down to the border—has yet been finalised?

**Mr. Stewart:** The arterial routes which the hon. Gentleman mentions are important parts of the transport infrastructure for Northern Ireland, both to Scotland and to the Irish Republic. Transport proposals have been put to the European Commission in the context of our plan. It will be for the Commission, but in consultation with us, to establish the priorities within that and if those qualify, I will be glad.

**Mr. Hume:** Does the Minister agree that the designation of Northern Ireland as an objective 1 region, and the strategic plan to be based on that, represent a major opportunity substantially to raise living standards in Northern Ireland if the Commission's objectives are met? Does he agree that the Commission stipulates that special interest groups in Northern Ireland must be consulted and that expenditure must be extra and additional to normal Government expenditure? What steps has he taken, first, to ensure that there has been consultation, not just contact, with special interest groups, and, secondly, to assure the Commission that expenditure will be additional?

**Mr. Speaker:** Briefly, please.

**Mr. Hume:** Will the Minister assure the House that the final detailed plan submitted in October will include local development programmes for each part of Northern Ireland?

**Mr. Stewart:** In addition to the consultation and notification that took place before the development plan was permitted, there will be ongoing discussions with interested parties in Northern Ireland. That is in addition to those which have a statutory function and are thus technically partners under the European rules.

The projects for which we are seeking European funding, when they come forward in our public expenditure system, are bids within our overall bid to the Treasury. The mere fact that they are treated in that way for public expenditure purposes does not mean that they are not additional. They would not exist if EC funding was not forthcoming. To separate them out in accounting terms, as some have suggested, would merely put them at risk if for any reason European funding was not forthcoming.

**Mr. Thurnham:** I have just attended a meeting at the Institution of Civil Engineers at which an excellent report was put forward containing a number of proposals for structure investment, a copy of which I will pass to my right hon. Friend. In view of the apparent decline in investment in Northern Ireland compared with the rest of the United Kingdom, I hope that my hon. Friend will consider that report carefully.

**Mr. Stewart:** I am glad to say that investment in Northern Ireland has been improving in an encouraging way in the past year or two, but that does not mean that I shall not be interested to see the document that my hon. Friend mentioned.

**Mr. Jim Marshall:** May I press the Minister a little further on the concept of additionality? He will be aware that there is a difference of view between the Government and the EC Commission. Can he say anything about the Government's thinking on that? More importantly, the Minister's reply to my hon. Friend the Member for Foyle (Mr. Hume) that separating the projects out might put them in jeopardy suggested that they would go ahead irrespective of any EC funding. If that is so, the Minister must accept that they are not additional to existing programmes. We need a cast-iron guarantee that in future any EEC funds will be additional to those approved by the House and the Treasury.

**Mr. Stewart:** Contrary to what the hon. Gentleman suggests, I see no problems in our conforming with the additionality requirements but the matter turns on the subsequent point that he made. I was trying to explain that if those items were taken out of the main public expenditure block for Northern Ireland, as approved by the Treasury and incorporated in our public expenditure plans, any delay in receiving European funds between one financial year and another which meant that the amounts were not forthcoming in full would mean that those projects could not take place. The current arrangement provides some flexibility for the Government in Northern Ireland. I welcome that flexibility and would not want us to be deprived of it.

### Playing Fields

3. **Mr. Harry Greenway:** To ask the Secretary of State for Northern Ireland how many playing fields have been sold for development in the past five years; what was the comparable figure in 1974; and if he will make a statement.

**The Parliamentary Under-Secretary of State for Northern Ireland (Dr. Brian Mawhinney):** Comprehensive records of playing fields in Northern Ireland are not held centrally. Of those grant-aided by the Department of Education, four were sold for development in the past five years. None was sold in 1974.

**Mr. Greenway:** Will my hon. Friend confirm that on principle the Conservative Government will make it a priority not to allow development on school or other playing fields or green spaces? Will he contrast that with the behaviour of Labour-controlled Ealing council, which is promoting a building on the Cayton road playing field in my constituency?

**Mr. Speaker:** Order. That is a bit wide.

**Mr. Cryer:** It is very wide. It is an abuse of Northern Ireland questions.

**Mr. Greenway:** Should not those playing fields be saved for children and for environmental reasons?

**Dr. Mawhinney:** I know that my hon. Friend robustly defends his constituents' interests. I assure him that we consider every possible opportunity to retain playing fields. My hon. Friend will be pleased to know that in the same five years nine major playing field complexes were transferred at no cost to Belfast city council and one to Newtownabbey council.

**Mr. McNamara:** I am sure that we all approve of the Minister's last statement, but will he confirm that the Government have a ratio for the number of playing fields appropriate to the numbers of pupils in a school and that any surplus land has to be sold off for development and that that is the rule in this country? Perhaps the hon. Member for Ealing, North (Mr. Greenway) should find out what the Ministry of Education and Science is doing.

**Dr. Mawhinney:** I am not aware of any ratio. From time to time, due to the decrease in school numbers, land becomes available—*[Interruption.]* It is not a ratio. We try to retain that land in the public sector for public use where there is demand or need, but occasionally land is sold off for development.

**Mr. Peter Robinson:** When land was transferred free of charge to Belfast and to Newtownabbey councils, why were the former playing fields used by the Stranmillis college not transferred to Castlereagh council free of charge?

**Dr. Mawhinney:** The hon. Gentleman, who is a member of that council, knows the answer full well.

### Bill of Rights

4. **Mr. Harry Barnes:** To ask the Secretary of State for Northern Ireland if he will publish a draft Bill of Rights to guarantee human rights and civil liberties in Northern Ireland, for consultation.

**The Secretary of State for Northern Ireland (Mr. Tom King):** Human rights and civil liberties are already well protected by existing legislation in Northern Ireland. I am always willing to consider proposals for strengthening the existing safeguards, but I am not convinced that a Bill of Rights is required.

**Mr. Barnes:** Later today we shall be discussing direct rule and there will be an opportunity for the Minister to elaborate on the points that he has made. I hope that we can discuss the possibility of a Bill of Rights. It is likely that Front Bench spokesmen on both sides will wax lyrical about the need for democracy in Northern Ireland and then, for the fifteenth time, we shall moot the re-establishment of direct rule. Would not a Bill of Rights help to produce the circumstances and the framework in which we could move towards real devolved government in Northern Ireland?

**Mr. King:** I think that if the hon. Gentleman has studied the matter, he will know that there are very real problems about trying to produce a Bill of Rights for Northern Ireland without encompassing a Bill of Rights for the United Kingdom. If the hon. Gentleman is seeking to address the protection of rights, I am certainly determined to ensure that they are properly protected. If that is achieved by separate and individual measures, he will know that one of the rights to which people are entitled is protected from discrimination. The Fair Employment (Northern Ireland) Bill now before Parliament will be a major step forward in that direction.

**Mr. Gow:** Will not the human rights and civil liberties of the people of Northern Ireland be best protected if they are governed in the same way as their fellow citizens in the rest of the United Kingdom? Would their rights not be better protected if Northern Ireland Members could move amendments to proposed legislation and if the system of legislating for the Province by Order in Council ceased?

**Mr. King:** I have always made it clear that I am ready and willing to listen to any ideas for improving the procedures in the House. As the hon. Member for Derbyshire, North-East (Mr. Barnes) has said, we shall shortly be debating the continuance of direct rule. I have made clear on three occasions—the fourth is about to arrive—my concern about direct rule and the fact that it is not a satisfactory long-term solution. I should very much like to find better ways to address some of these issues.

**Mr. McCusker:** Is the Secretary of State aware that a Bill of Rights is one of the few issues which meets his oft-stated criteria for cross-community support in Northern Ireland? Is he aware that members of the Unionist community in Northern Ireland believe that his reluctance to produce a Bill of Rights has more to do with the fact that he could not continue to govern us by the present totally undemocratic methods if there were a Bill of Rights?

**Mr. King:** As that is the first constructive comment that I have heard from the hon. Gentleman, I welcome it. He has made some suggestions, whether I agree with them or not, about how one might address the real issue of the government of Northern Ireland, and he has done so on a cross-community basis, claiming that he has ideas which could command support across the communities. I would welcome hearing any further suggestions that he might like to make.

**Mr. Kilfedder:** It is 15 years or more since I moved a motion urging the establishment of a Bill of Rights for the United Kingdom and, failing that, for Northern Ireland, so there is nothing new in that suggestion, although no doubt it will take the Secretary of State by surprise, as so many other matters take him by surprise. Surely the people of Northern Ireland are entitled to decide this matter by a referendum. Let us have a Bill of Rights based on the United States constitution and the amendments thereto.

**Mr. King:** As the hon. Gentleman made clear, the proposal that he put forward many years ago was on the basis of a Bill of Rights for the United Kingdom. The issue has to be addressed in that way. It is almost impossible to conceive of a separate Bill of Rights which would apply uniquely to Northern Ireland. The issue raises wide concerns and interests. As the hon. Gentleman knows, it is not a new subject and has been widely debated.

**Mr. Maclennan:** Why does the Secretary of State pretend that the hon. Member representing the Ulster Unionists, the hon. Member for Upper Bann (Mr. McCusker), has made a new proposal when his party made the proposal in writing more than two years ago? It has been supported by other parties from Northern Ireland and by the Standing Advisory Commission on Human Rights. Does he not recognise that if he is unwilling to move in this way he will be seen to be governing against the wishes of all parties in Northern Ireland as well as my right hon. and hon. Friends, and he will face the unattractive prospect of being dragged back to Strasbourg time and again as more and more violations of the European convention on human rights occur.

**Mr. King:** Obviously, I did not make myself clear. I was seeking to explain that it is novel to hear constructive proposals from people who until now have preferred to remain silent. I welcome that. I know that this issue has been much discussed. It has been much discussed within my party and there have been long-standing discussions. I recognise that there is scope for serious discussion and I have called times beyond number for constructive suggestions.

**Rev. Ian Paisley:** Is the right hon. Gentleman aware that his remarks to the hon. Member for Upper Bann (Mr. McCusker) about not making constructive remarks in the House will be treated with utter contempt by the people of Northern Ireland in the same way as the contemptuous remark that he made about me during the previous Northern Ireland Question Time? My political demise was greatly exaggerated by the right hon. Gentleman. Will he go back to the pigeonhole and withdraw from it the reports of the Convention and the Assembly which say that we should have a Bill of Rights for Northern Ireland supported across the board? Does he not think that in this centenary year, and with his name being King, he should have his Bill of Rights?

**Mr. King:** I am much distressed by that intervention because I know the deeply sensitive nature of the hon. Gentleman. The thought that anything that I said caused him distress disturbs me beyond measure. I am thinking of charging for the use of my name in the hon. Gentleman's election address as I noticed that it appears considerably more often than his own.

**Mr. Mallon:** Does the Secretary of State agree that a Bill of Rights for the North of Ireland is incompatible with the provisions of the Northern Ireland (Emergency Provisions) Act 1978 and the Prevention of Terrorism (Temporary Provisions) Act 1984 and that until that pernicious legislation is removed from the statute book any positive and constructive discussion about a Bill of Rights is pure pie in the sky?

**Mr. King:** It is not accurate to say that. If the hon. Gentleman studies the European convention, he will realise that there are circumstances in which nations seeking to defend themselves against the evils of terrorism may, on occasions, have to take emergency steps which are consistent with, or recognised under, a convention on human rights because of the particular circumstances at the time. Any Bill of Rights would have to recognise those circumstances. The real attack on the rights of citizens and individual liberty comes from those who seek to murder and maim their fellow citizens.

**Mr. Stanbrook:** Have not the people of Northern Ireland been deprived of the biggest right of all in a democracy—that the will of the majority should prevail, with safeguards for the minority?

**Mr. King:** If my hon. Friend would like to join me, we can debate that subject in much greater detail shortly.

### "Who Framed Colin Wallace"

5. **Mr. Dalyell:** To ask the Secretary of State for Northern Ireland if he has acquired for the Library, "Who Framed Colin Wallace", by Paul Foot, published by the second Earl of Stockton.

**Mr. Ian Stewart:** No, Sir. However, I understand that there are already two copies in the Library.

**Mr. Dalyell:** Why does the Minister suppose that Colin Wallace has come to be believed by the publishing house of Macmillan and its libel lawyers, by the late Airey Neave, who was happy to have information from Colin Wallace, and by raging Left-wingers such as the hereditary Earl Marshall, his grace the Duke of Norfolk?

**Mr. Stewart:** I cannot answer for publishers or many of the other groups of people whom the hon. Gentleman has mentioned. As far as I know, the allegations that have been repeated in the book concerning the conduct of various persons have been fully investigated over a long period in the past. On the responsibilities of my own Department, I am not aware of anything in the book that would justify any further inquiry.

**Mr. Foot:** Does the right hon. Gentleman appreciate, as he might expect from the names on the Order Paper, that the book is first, extremely well published and, secondly, extremely well written and that it will, therefore, be far better than most of the stuff he and his Secretary of State have to submit to during the week? Will he also tell us in detail whether his Department was consulted about the letter that appears in the book which was addressed to the Prime Minister and which set out in detail the reasons why there should have been a proper investigation into the matter and why the demands for an investigation would continue? Was the Prime Minister's failure to reply based on any evidence from his Department?

**Mr. Stewart:** The right hon. Gentleman's reference to the authorship of the book is a form of benevolent nepotism, which he is entitled to use. The contents of the book and all the allegations raised by Mr. Wallace have been investigated separately by the Royal Ulster Constabulary, Sir George Terry and Judge Hughes, and none of the allegations have been found to stand up. Mr. Wallace was given the opportunity to give evidence himself to those inquiries, but despite the fact that he was given assurances that he would not be prosecuted under the Official Secrets Act 1911, he refused to do so. The House can draw its own conclusions from that.

**Mr. McNamara:** Only the conclusions of the Terry report were published—not the evidence. When will the public be allowed to judge whether the conclusions follow from the evidence?

**Mr. Stewart:** I regard that as a serious slur on Sir George Terry.

### Security

6. **Mr. Duffy:** To ask the Secretary of State for Northern Ireland if he will make a statement on the security situation in Northern Ireland.

**Mr. Tom King:** Since I last answered questions on 18 May, there have been no deaths due to terrorist action, but one young soldier was killed in an accidental shooting.

The security threat and incidents remain at a high level, but the determined efforts of the security forces have resulted in 120 people being charged with serious offences, including 13 with murder and 26 with attempted murder since the beginning of the year. A total of 200 weapons, almost 25,000 rounds of ammunition and 435 lbs of explosives have been recovered in Northern Ireland. I understand that the Garda Siochana has recovered 60 weapons, approximately 15,000 rounds of ammunition, and a substantial quantity of explosives.

**Mr. Duffy:** What representations has the Secretary of State received from Ulster Television and the National Union of Journalists about the two soldiers who posed as a television camera crew while filming outside a polling station in Derry on 17 May, during the local government elections?

**Mr. King:** The hon. Gentleman takes an interest in Northern Ireland affairs, but his supplementary question made no mention of the security forces and sought to find immediately a point on which he could seek to criticise, without even a welcome for the fact that, for the first time in my experience, I have been able to tell the House that there have been no security force fatalities in the period since I last reported. On the specific point that he raised, as far as I am aware I have had no representations but I know that that matter is being looked into by headquarters, Northern Ireland.

**Mr. Maginnis:** What value does the Secretary of State attach to maintaining the morale of the RUC? In the words of his right hon. Friend the Prime Minister, may I suggest that it is monstrous under the circumstances that he has failed to deal with the manner in which the deputy chairman of the Police Authority totally devalued her position as a member of that body? It does not matter whether it was at a private dinner party paid for out of public funds, or a public function at which Mrs. Phyllis Bateson behaved in such an outrageous manner. Will the Secretary of State consider whether she should still, after all this time, remain a member of the Police Authority? Will he take to heart the cliché "in vino veritas" or, as my grandfather would have said, "If it is not in when you are sober, it won't come out when you are drunk"?

**Mr. King:** I hope that the hon. Gentleman is thoroughly pleased with that contribution. He would be one of the first to say, "Why don't more Catholics support the RUC? Why don't more Catholics who accept office and serve on the police authority"——

**Mr. Maginnis:** Many do properly.

**Mr. Speaker:** Order.

**Mr. King:** The hon. Gentleman's contribution has been of no value whatsoever. He is simply seeking to repeat a private conversation, of which I have no personal knowledge which, in any case, is the subject of some disagreement. I respect very much indeed, and I hope that the hon. Gentleman and all other hon. Members will support—*[Interruption.]*—yes, the RUC, of course, but also the members of the Police Authority who accept appointment, effectively without reward and at considerable personal risk, especially if they are Catholics and represent the Nationalist community. They do that, and when they are villified in that way it does the hon. Gentleman—*[Interruption.]* There is a nasty stench about the comment and I am not the only person in Northern Ireland who deplores it.

**Rev. William McCrea:** Does the Secretary of State agree that many people in Northern Ireland and throughout the United Kingdom have expressed disquiet about the whole issue of the deputy chairman of the Police Authority? Does he further agree that it is interesting that at no time has the deputy chairman denied that she said those certain things about the former Chief Constable or about the Royal Ulster Constabulary? Without getting the Secretary of State's hackles up, does that not cause him concern, and is he not concerned that people in Northern Ireland should have confidence in those who are guiding the Royal Ulster Constabulary and the Police Authority? One final question—*[Interruption.]* Will the Secretary of State tell the House what embarrassment that said person caused him in the doorway at the end of the night?

**Mr. King:** The first part of the hon. Gentleman's statement was wrong——

**Rev. William McCrea:** No it was not.

**Mr. King:** A denial has been issued by the person concerned——

**Rev. William McCrea:** No.

**Mr. King:** If the hon. Gentleman would do me the courtesy of listening, he would hear me say that the person concerned has issued a denial. It would have been a courtesy for him to have respected that from the start.

**Rev. William McCrea:** That is a false statement.

**Mr. King:** I am not a bit surprised to find the hon. Gentleman joining in; it is exactly what I would have expected of him. I am sure that the House will judge accordingly.

**Mr. Ashdown:** I join the right hon. Gentleman in his repudiation of the distasteful question asked by the hon. Member for Fermanagh and South Tyrone (Mr. Maginnis).

Has the right hon. Gentleman given further consideration to the issuing of plastic bullets to the UDR? Is he aware that if he approved such a measure he would be issuing a highly controversial weapon to what has come to be regarded in Northern Ireland as a highly controversial force?

**Mr. King:** I am grateful to the right hon. Gentleman for his initial comments. The UDR is receiving training in the use of plastic bullets for protection in certain circumstances. No decision has yet been taken about the deployment of those weapons. I want to make it absolutely clear that were a decision to be taken to issue those weapons, there would be no change in the UDR's role or in deployment; it would be decided merely on whether the UDR needed them for its own protection while carrying out its existing tasks.

The alternative—as happened recently—would be to leave the UDR with no option other than to resort to the use of live rounds because it had nothing between either retreat or the use of lethal force. I think that the right hon. Gentleman would understand the problems in that sort of circumstance.

**Sir Michael McNair-Wilson:** Did my right hon. Friend see the "Cook Report" about the various organisations that give commercial backing to the IRA through various devices such as estate agencies? In particular, did he see the footage showing an IRA unit using a general purpose machine gun against an unarmed Lynx helicopter? Can he assure the House that in future helicopters will have proper protection and armament against possible attack?

**Mr. King:** I saw that programme, which I felt underlined something to which I had already drawn the attention of the House on a number of occasions, which is the importance of tackling—as we are seeking to do— gangsterism, extortion and the various illegal fund-raising activities that support and underpin terrorism. On my hon. Friend's latter point, I do not know how genuine the film was, but nevertheless the threat of machine-gun attack against helicopters is real. A number of steps were taken some time ago to give all possible protection to helicopters in the important work that they do.

### International Fund for Ireland

7. **Mr. McCusker:** To ask the Secretary of State for Northern Ireland if he will list all those countries and organisations which have contributed to the International Fund for Ireland, showing the amount each has contributed to date.

**Mr. Ian Stewart:** The United States has contributed $120 million over the period 1986 to 1988 and has committed itself to a contribution of £10 million during 1989. Canada has agreed to provide up to 10 million Canadian dollars over a period of 10 years and New Zealand has contributed a one-off payment of 300,000 New Zealand dollars. The European Community is contributing 15 million ecu this year with the prospect of similar amounts during 1990 and 1991.

**Mr. McClusker:** The right hon. Gentleman appears to have achieved a fair degree of success in that novel way of treating public expenditure priorities in Northern Ireland. Why has he not rattled the begging bowl in Australia, Japan or Korea? Even South Africa might be a reasonable place to try that. In view of the money from charitable sources that we have sent to Ethiopia, why does he not go to Addis Ababa and rattle a begging bowl there? If a begging bowl approach is to be part of the future of Northern Ireland, will the right hon. Gentleman talk to his colleagues about introducing begging as a topic in the education syllabus for Northern Ireland?

**Mr. Stewart:** The hon. Gentleman seems to suggest that there is something undesirable about contributions to the international fund being made available to support the interests of his constituents and those of other Members in Northern Ireland. I find that a difficult proposition to accept. It seems to me that the international fund is an important expression of international support for the British and Irish Governments in what they are trying to do to counter the adverse effects of terrorism in Northern Ireland and in the adjacent areas of the Republic.

**Mr. Nicholas Baker:** As a counterpart to the contributions to the international fund to which my right hon. Friend is referring, may I ask how successful he has been in getting the United States Government to prevent contributions from going to Noraid and similar terrorist support outlets?

**Mr. Stewart:** The answer is that we have made considerable progress. The United States Government, both the present and previous Administrations, have been helpful in that respect.

**Dr. Godman:** The Minister mentioned a European contribution of 15 million United States dollars. Will he give an assurance that where the European Community contribution is used to assist the shipbuilding industry, such purchases of goods and services aided by those funds will be confined to firms in the United Kingdom?

**Mr. Stewart:** I remind the hon. Gentleman that the contribution from the European Community was 15 million ecu, not 15 million dollars. As for the destination of the funds, the board of the fund is independent and I do not think that it would be proper for the board to earmark specific contributions for specific purposes. But its priorities are to stimulate private enterprise in Northern Ireland and to promote economic and social development more generally, rather than being aimed specifically at individual industries in the way in which the hon. Gentleman mentioned.

**Mr. Mallon:** It seems clear to me from what the Minister has said that, like me, he is puzzled by the attitude of the representatives of some parties towards this international fund, even though some of their members, both in the official Unionist party and in the DUP, have benefited enormously from it. Will the Minister assure me that the British Government will make every attempt to ensure that the money goes to the deprived areas where it is most needed, rather than to people who use it to feather their own nests?

**Mr. Stewart:** I assure the hon. Gentleman that it is an important part of the policy of the international fund that priority should be given to areas of greatest need, and I strongly support that.

**Mr. Budgen:** Will my right hon. Friend remind the House that the international fund comes almost entirely from the United States and that it was called the international fund only to try to stave off criticism that once again America was endeavouring to interfere in our affairs at the time of the Anglo-Irish Agreement?

**Mr. Stewart:** That is a rather odd perception of the way in which the fund was established and contributions to it were provided. The United States is a very large economy and the contribution which it makes is most welcome. What my hon. Friend says suggests that contributions from Canada, New Zealand and the European Community are to be disregarded or treated as unwelcome. I welcome them, and if other contributions to the fund were available from other sources overseas, I am sure that we would all welcome those, too.

### Schools (Expenditure)

8. **Mr. Allen:** To ask the Secretary of State for Northern Ireland how much was spent by his Department on *(a)* Catholic schools, *(b)* Protestant schools, *(c)* non-religious schools and *(d)* other categories of schools in the last year, and what is the trend in such expenditures.

**Dr. Mawhinney:** This information is not available in the form requested. As a best estimate, expenditure on controlled schools, which are attended mainly, but not exclusively, by Protestants, was £196·9 million in 1987-88. Expendiure on maintained schools, most of which are under Roman Catholic management, was £158·2 million, and expenditure on voluntary grammar schools, which have a variety of management arrangements, was £59·2 million over the past three years. This represents an increase of 32·9 per cent. for controlled schools, 37·5 per cent. for maintained schools and 31·8 per cent. for voluntary grammar schools.

**Mr. Allen:** The Minister may not agree with me publicly that many children grow up under a curse of religious education, that they would benefit from a secular education and that that would help to resolve the troubles in the Province. Does he agree with me, however, that the cross-contact scheme represents a small flame in trying to get greater understanding between children in the Province and that we should wish it every success? What is he doing to strengthen and encourage that important development?

**Dr. Mawhinney:** I am grateful for the hon. Gentleman's support for the concept of cross-contact between schools in Northern Ireland. He will know that, when I announced the scheme two years ago, the proposed budget for this year was £200,000. He will be pleased to know that the actual budget this year is £650,000, and that is because about 340 schools in the Province, or a quarter of all schools in the Province, have now voluntarily joined the scheme to pursue projects together.

**Mr. McGrady:** Is the Minister aware that his grants to the integrated school sector, to the disadvantage of the voluntary and state sectors, are causing growing concern in Northern Ireland? Will he ensure that the application of educational funds is on an equitable and just basis? Many schools in the voluntary and state sectors have been waiting for capital and development programmes for almost a decade, whereas the integrated school system that he favours seems to be privileged in that respect.

**Dr. Mawhinney:** The hon. Gentleman is right to point out that we are talking simply about capital expenditure. He knows that, for the past 65 years, all Government expenditure in Northern Ireland has been directed either to state schools or to Roman Catholic schools. Parents who wished to have integrated education were discriminated against to the extent that they got no capital provision at all. It seems to the Government a matter of justice that, for a few years, a degree of preference should be given to integrated schools capital programmes to help to redress that imbalance.

## PRIME MINISTER

### Engagements

Q1. **Mr. Gwilym Jones:** To ask the Prime Minister if she will list her official engagements for Thursday 22 June.

**The Prime Minister (Mrs. Margaret Thatcher):** This morning I presided at a meeting of the Cabinet and had meetings with ministerial colleagues and others. In addition to my duties in this House, I shall be having further meetings today, including attendance at the plenary session of the Australia-United Kingdom conference on trade and investment.

**Mr. Jones:** Will my right hon. Friend convey the warm greetings of the whole House to the Prime Minister of Australia on his visit to the United Kingdom? In turn, I congratulate my right hon. Friend on taking the initiative to give renewed vigour to the relationship between our two countries which share so much history and which can achieve so much together in future.

**The Prime Minister:** I gladly take advantage of the opportunity that my hon. Friend presents. Mr. Hawke and his fellow Ministers who have come here for a major consultation between Ministers and Prime Ministers have had very great success. It has been a longer and more extensive visit than usual, and it has been carried out splendidly. The trade and investment conference that is taking place today will also be extremely important. Australia and Britain are vital allies and both are very important to peace in the Pacific and to dealing with the problems that now face us there on a much larger scale than ever before—altogether a very great success.

**Mr. Kinnock:** The Prime Minister has rightly expressed horror and outrage, which we all share, at the barbaric actions of the Chinese Government against their people seeking democracy. Will she take action in support of her condemnation, and, in Madrid next week, urge our partner countries in the European Community to impose economic sanctions against China until the regime stops the killing and the persecution?

**The Prime Minister:** I am among the first to condemn the killing and the execution and the other results that have followed on the latest policy of the Chinese Government. I must say that I think that it would be much too precipitant to do what the right hon. Gentleman proposes, particularly as many of us are very anxious indeed not to precipitate a situation that could cause great panic in Hong Kong.

**Mr. Kinnock:** Would it not be wrong for this democracy and other democracies in the European Community to leave those young people in China with nothing but their own courage to sustain them? Since the kind of people running China simply do not respect words, may I urge the Prime Minister to take a lead now in pressing for combined action against them by the Community?

**The Prime Minister:** May I put this to the right hon. Gentleman—we are responsible right up until 1997 for the five million and more people in Hong Kong. I think that what the right hon. Gentleman proposes could precipitate a very dangerous position. We have been the first to condemn and we have also stopped high level visits and arms contracts. Further measures are being considered, but in my judgment what the right hon. Gentleman proposes could be very dangerous for people for whom we are responsible.

Q2. **Mrs. Gorman:** To ask the Prime Minister if she will list her official engagements for Thursday 22 June.

**The Prime Minister:** I refer my hon. Friend to the reply that I gave some moments ago.

**Mrs. Gorman:** Does my right hon. Friend agree that the best way to improve employment prospects for women throughout Europe is to expand the economy by the kind of measures that the Government have introduced and not to try to force employers—I stress the word "force"—to provide special facilities for women? Will she bear that in mind when considering the social charter in Madrid, which among other things calls ominously for intensification of action against employers on the implementation of equality?

**The Prime Minister:** I agree in the main with what my hon. Friend has said. The Government's policy has been to set conditions to create jobs. We have been outstandingly successful in that, with the highest number ever of people in employment. We have the highest number of jobs that we have ever had. It has worked particularly well for women. The United Kingdom is the only country in the European Community where the unemployment rate is lower for women than for men. We have done excellent work in lowering the rate for men too. The proposed social charter would place additional burdens and restrictions on businesses and so lose jobs rather than create them, especially for women.

**Dr. Owen:** In view of today's findings that more people than ever before support and approve of the National Health Service—90 per cent. of family doctors and 85 per cent. of those in the hospital service—would it not be wiser not to destabilise the NHS but to introduce reform cautiously with development projects, as advocated by the royal colleges, and to evaluate scientifically their success?

**The Prime Minister:** I am very glad that the right hon. Gentleman has at last come round to that view. He could have said it any time, any month, in the last 10 years, but he did not for 10 years, although the Health Service has continuously and steadily been improved by extra resources, extra doctors and extra nurses—*[Interruption.]* —from what it was when his Government left office, when there were strikes, and hospitals and cancer beds were left untended. He has had 10 years to admit that we have done far better. I am delighted now to hear him say it. It is the best service that it has ever been.

**Q3. Mr. Anthony Coombs:** To ask the Prime Minister if she will list her official engagements for Thursday 22 June.

**The Prime Minister:** I refer my hon. Friend to the reply that I gave some moments ago.

**Mr. Coombs:** Will my right hon. Friend join me in welcoming the adoption earlier this week of the European second banking directive which, by allowing banks to operate more freely throughout Europe, will provide a tremendous boost to this very important sector of our economy? Does she also agree that this is further justification of the Government's policy of extending competition and deregulation within the single European market, rather than the grandiose schemes of European economic union and a social market with which the Opposition seem to be so obsessed?

**The Prime Minister:** Yes. We have been negotiating the second banking directive for a very long time. Its passage is very welcome because it will improve greatly our chances of having a free market in financial services which we offer to other people but which they have not always offered to us. So it is a great plus for our people in financial services. Also, we hope that it will soon be followed by an investment services directive. It is, of course, greater prosperity, not only in manufacturing but in the services sector, that enables us to offer higher levels of social services and social protection.

**Mr. Michael:** Now that the Prime Minister has had a little more time to consider the results of the recent European elections, does she not believe that to withdraw the Health Service White Paper would be in the best interests of the health of the people of Britain and of her own political health?

**The Prime Minister:** If the hon. Gentleman reads the White Paper carefully, he will find, as many protesters have found, that it was quite different from the one that he was led to believe. I hope that we shall be able steadily to continue to improve the Health Service in the future, as it is now acknowledged—even on the Opposition Benches —that we have done in the past. We have one of the best Health Services in the whole Community.

**Mr. Robert Banks:** Knowing of the Prime Minister's deep concern and sympathy for the anxieties of the people of Hong Kong, does she agree that we could take an initiative by going to the Commonwealth and asking it to provide rights of abode for all the people of Hong Kong —on the basis that each Commonwealth country took a quota of people—if it became necessary?

**The Prime Minister:** Of course, these matters will be raised at the Commonwealth conference. I do not think that it will be easy to get the results that my hon. Friend seeks, any more than it has been easy to secure other results with other refugees, although it has been very good in taking genuine refugees from Vietnam. It would be a considerable step for the Commonwealth. I have also to report that the Commonwealth—especially Australia and Canada—have been very active in taking in the entrepreneurs from Hong Kong to the advantage— *[Interruption.]* Of course, I do not expect Opposition Members to agree about people who create wealth—they can only spend it. Many of them have gone to Australia and Canada. It has given them peace of mind that they have somewhere to go and they have also brought great comfort to Australia and Canada.

**Mr. John D. Taylor:** Will the recently announced student loan scheme be extended to students from European Community countries who come to the United Kingdom for their higher education?

**The Prime Minister:** No. No more than grants will be extended, unless they are part of the overseas grants service where grants are given to specific people. They will not be given as a general right.

**Q4. Mr. Greg Knight:** To ask the Prime Minister if she will list her official engagements for Thursday 22 June.

**The Prime Minister:** I refer my hon. Friend to the reply that I gave some moments ago.

**Mr. Knight:** Will my right hon. Friend join me in welcoming the fact that the strike at the Liverpool passport office is now over and that, therefore, the threat of disruption to those who wish to holiday abroad has been lifted? However, will my right hon. Friend also join me in condemning the actions of those who wish to prolong the dispute and who have issued a leaflet which says that an all-out strike now, at the beginning of the tourist season, will give the passport workers the chance to give the Tories a bloody nose? Does that not prove that, whatever the place, whatever the issue and whatever packaging is used to try to convince people otherwise, here in Britain Socialists are still the strikers' friends?

**The Prime Minister:** I agree. Those who protest loudly about the greater needs of the public service are the first to say that they do not give tuppence for the public's rights, whether it be to get passports or to come to work. It is undoubtedly the public sector which is serving the public less, and it is such services as the privatised buses that are continuing to run. They genuinely do serve the public.

Q5. **Mr. George Howarth:** To ask the Prime Minister if she will list her official engagements for Thursday 22 June.

**The Prime Minister:** I refer the hon. Gentleman to the reply that I gave some moments ago.

**Mr. Howarth:** The Prime Minister's predecessor, the right hon. Member for Old Bexley and Sidcup (Mr. Heath), dealt very firmly and effectively with racists within his party. In view of the comments made by the hon. Member for Thurrock (Mr. Janman) in the House two nights ago, effectively restoring the old chestnut of repatriation, will the Prime Minister take similar effective action against him?

**The Prime Minister:** I did not hear the first part of the hon. Gentleman's question, but may I make it absolutely clear that there is no racism in this party—*[Interruption.]* —and we utterly and vigorously defend the rights of all people on an equal basis.

**Mr. Quentin Davies:** Does my right hon. Friend agree that the proposed European social charter represents an attempt by other Community countries to impose on us the higher aggregate labour costs from which they currently suffer? To accept that charter in its current form would be to abandon an important competitive advantage which we currently have and, furthermore, the levels of investment, employment and output in this country and in the Community would be lower than they would otherwise be as a result.

**The Prime Minister:** We accept, of course, that there is a social dimension to Community policy. We also accept —*[Interruption.]* Of course, because we were very prominent in our time in trying to steer that social dimension—*[Interruption.]* Oh yes—*[Interruption.]*

**Mr. Speaker:** Order. Interruptions take up a great deal of time.

**The Prime Minister:** —in trying to steer that social dimension, and successfully steering it, to the creation of jobs. Mention any country in the Community that has created more jobs in the past five years than we have. There is not one. We were trying to steer to the creation of a very expensive system of training, because we believe that the most important thing is the creation of jobs.

With regard to the rest of the social dimension, we believe that that is a matter for each country and if that particular charter were made compulsory for many countries, most of them could not afford the social services we have, and they acknowledge that. It would then be said that there would have to be considerable subventions and subsidies paid from other countries, which, of course, the Labour party could not possibly help with because it just spends wealth, it never creates it.

**Several Hon. Members:** On a point of order, Mr. Speaker.

**Mr. Speaker:** Order. I shall take points of order after business questions.

# Business of the House

3.31 pm

**Mr. Frank Dobson** (Holborn and St. Pancras): Will the Leader of the House tell us the business for next week?

**The Lord President of the Council and Leader of the House of Commons (Mr. John Wakeham):** The business for next week will be as follows:

MONDAY 26 JUNE—Opposition Day (15th Allotted Day). Until about seven o'clock there will be a debate on community care. Afterwards there will be a debate on the coal industry. Both debates will arise on Opposition motions.

Remaining stages of the Road Traffic (Driver Licensing and Information Systems) Bill *[Lords]*.

TUESDAY 27 JUNE—Second Reading of the Football Spectators Bill *[Lords]*.

There will be a debate on parliamentary pensions on a motion for the Adjournment of the House.

WEDNESDAY 28 JUNE—Opposition Day (16th Allotted Day). Until seven o'clock there will be a debate on a motion in the name of the Scottish National party entitled "Scotland in Europe".

Motion on the Army, Air Force and Naval Discipline Acts (Continuation) Order.

The Chairman of Ways and Means has named opposed private business for consideration at seven o'clock.

THURSDAY 29 JUNE—Second Reading of the Representation of the People Bill.

The Chairman of Ways and Means has named opposed private business for consideration at seven o'clock.

FRIDAY 30 JUNE—There will be a debate on policing in London on a motion for the Adjournment of the House.

MONDAY 3 JULY—Opposition Day (17th Allotted Day). There will be a debate on an Opposition motion, subject for debate to be announced.

**Mr. Dobson:** Why are the Government insisting on rushing ahead with the Football Spectators Bill next week before the recommendations of the Taylor inquiry into the Hillsborough disaster are known? The Government's Bill is irrelevant to the safety of people in football grounds —so irrelevant that, at present, crowd safety is outside the scope of the Bill. The Prime Minister promised that the Bill would be able to take account of any interim recommendations from the Taylor inquiry. Will the Leader of the House confirm that that could be done only if next week the House passes an instruction requiring the Committee on the Bill to consider safety aspects?

Does not the Leader of the House recognise that the Government's inadequate and partisan proposals are simply not up to the job? If they go ahead with their proposals, the result will be a mess. Surely it would be better for Ministers to get together with everyone concerned and put forward proposals on which everyone can agree as practical solutions to the problems facing football clubs. If he does that, the Opposition can guarantee to give the measure a swift passage through the House.

The present Bill does not produce any practical solutions to the problem, and it is nothing more than a half-baked, partisan product of the Government's machine—[HON. MEMBERS: "Get on with it."] Apparently, Conservative Members want me to get on with it. What we want to get on with, and what we would like the Leader of the House to guarantee, is the opportunity to consider a Bill that will do the job that needs to be done.

Will the Leader of the House note that, although the Opposition have chosen to give up half an Opposition day to debate care in the community, that does not relieve the Government of their obligaton or their promise to have a debate on their response to the Griffiths report on care in the community when that becomes available? The Government received the report as long ago as 12 February 1988.

Why have we not had a statement about—it would appear that we are not to have the opportunity to debate —the general practitioners' contract? The Secretary of State for Health rushed gleefully into the House to announce that the doctors had accepted the contract, but appears to be reluctant to come here now that the GPs' representatives have recommended that the matter should go to a ballot and the GPs should turn it down.

Now that we have received a statement from the Secretary of State for Education and Science, when shall we have the promised debate on the Government's proposal to substitute students loans for students grants?

When will we have an opportunity to debate the Select Committee on the Environment's report on toxic and hazardous waste?

I hope that my final question will meet with approval from both sides of the House: do the Government propose to give the House the opportunity to debate the outcome of the Madrid summit?

**Mr. Wakeham:** The hon. Gentleman asked six questions about next week's business. First, I do not accept for a minute what he said about the Football Spectators Bill. We are not proceeding with indecent haste; the Bill has been before another place since January and was introduced in this House last Monday. I announced a full day's debate for Second Reading, which is appropriate. The policy matters which he raised are best left until Second Reading. I agree that it would be helpful for safety matters to be debated and I shall arrange for an instruction to be tabled, if that is appropriate.

I have indicated that the Government hope to bring forward proposals in relation to the Griffiths report before the summer recess. The question whether we have a further debate would best be considered at that time.

We are, of course, disappointed that the conference of GPs rejected the contract which their own leadership had commended to them. I cannot provide Government time for a debate, but I have just announced three Opposition days. If the hon. Gentleman wishes to raise the matter, perhaps he should consider using Opposition time.

The hon. Gentleman does not seem to understand the Government's policy on top-up loans. My right hon. Friend the Secretary of State for Education and Science made it clear on Monday that he would welcome a debate, and I believe that the timing should best be secured through the usual channels.

I have no immediate plans for a debate on the Select Committee's report on toxic waste, but we can return to that matter.

It is likely that my right hon. Friend the Prime Minister will make a statement about the Madrid summit at the appropriate time next week.

**Sir Bernard Braine** (Castle Point): My right hon. Friend will know from questions to my right hon. Friend the Prime Minister week after week, and from the front pages of our leading journals, of the widespread interest and concern in many international questions—what is happening in China, Hong Kong, Tibet and eastern Europe, and the implications of glasnost and perestroika for all of us in Europe. Can my right hon. Friend find time before we rise for the summer recess for us to turn our attention to these pressing matters?

**Mr. Wakeham:** I agree with my right hon. Friend, and I am extremely conscious of the interest in a general debate on foreign affairs and on some of the specific subjects that my right hon. Friend raised. I shall be looking for a suitable opportunity for a debate soon.

**Mr. Jack Ashley** (Stoke-on-Trent, South): Does not the visit of the Australian Prime Minister provide a timely reminder that nuclear test personnel in Australia are paid compensation while the British Ministry of Defence will not pay a penny in compensation to British nuclear test personnel? Can the Leader of the House explain that discrepancy, and, if not, will he provide time for a debate on this matter next week?

**Mr. Wakeham:** I regret to say that I cannot find time for a debate next week. The right hon. Gentleman has raised this matter with me before. The basic point of difference is that the British Government do not accept the basis of the claims that the victims, or so-called victims, are making.

**Mr. Allan Stewart** (Eastwood): Will my right hon. Friend give us an assurance that the House will be able to consider the Government's domestic airports policy before the summer recess? Is he aware of the continuing anger and puzzlement among the Scottish business community, interested commentators and local authorities such as Glasgow district council at the Secretary of State for Transport's idiosyncratic and irrational refusal to consider the case for allowing transatlantic flights from Glasgow airport?

**Mr. Wakeham:** I cannot promise a debate before the summer recess, but I shall look at the matter and will refer the point to my right hon. Friend the Secretary of State for Transport.

**Mr. David Winnick** (Walsall, North): Has the Leader of the House seen early-day motion 995?

*[That this House pays tribute to the students and workers who demonstrated in Tiananmen Square, Peking, and in other cities in China, for basic democratic rights and reforms; deplores the armed attack by the army on 4th June on the demonstrators in Tiananmen Square which resulted in numerous deaths and injuries; and further calls upon the Chinese authorities to cease the present persecution of anyone considered to have been involved in the demonstrations and not to carry out the sentences of death which have been passed by military courts.]*

Following the remarks of my right hon. Friend the Leader of the Opposition, will there be an opportunity early next week for a statement to be made by the Foreign Secretary on the wave of executions in China? Is the Leader of the House aware of the feeling of revulsion about what is happening? Does he agree that as the leadership of China, these bloodstained murderers, believe that they can get away with what they are doing without any international repercussions, a statement expressing the feelings of the House of Commons and the British people is essential?

**Mr. Wakeham:** We support the feelings expressed in the motion to which the hon. Gentleman refers, as was made absolutely clear by my right hon. Friend the Prime Minister a short time ago and by my right hon. and learned Friend the Foreign Secretary in his statement to the House on 6 June. We deeply deplore the execution of the Shanghai three, in spite of the appeal for clemency made by the EEC Twelve in Peking on 17 June. We regard the death sentences as totally disproportionate to the crimes committed.

**Mr. Robert McCrindle** (Brentwood and Ongar): Although the announcement this week that there is to be a code of conduct for estate agents is welcome, will my right hon. Friend the Leader of the House turn his attention to whether this goes far enough? Bearing in mind the fact that we are dealing here with most people's most important financial transaction of a lifetime, may we have a debate to ascertain whether it is the feeling of the House that for an individual who was a window cleaner or a bus driver last week to be able, without let or hindrance, to be an estate agent this week is not sufficient?

**Mr. Wakeham:** My hon. Friend the Under-Secretary of State for Industry and Consumers Affairs announced yesterday new measures to deal with estate agents who provide an unsatisfactory service. It is proposed to have a voluntary code of conduct, underpinned by the power to ban estate agents who are engaged in undesirable practices. This combination of self-regulation and statutory provision will give consumers protection without reducing competition. I know that my hon. Friend has studied these matters carefully, and if the need for a debate arises I shall look at the matter again.

**Mr. Eddie Loyden** (Liverpool, Garston): In view of the spate of industrial strikes taking place around the country as a result of the Government's role in respect of trade union laws, does the Leader of the House think that it is time we had a debate about restoring the position of the trade union movement so that it can effectively represent its members instead of finding itself constantly before the courts?

**Mr. Wakeham:** The hon. Gentleman has the wrong end of the stick. The trade union reforms which the Government have introduced have helped to improve the position for the public. If the unions had as much regard for the wishes and desires of the public, there might be less industrial action.

**Mr. Ivor Stanbrook** (Orpington): When will my right hon. Friend bring forward proposals in this House to ensure closer co-operation between this House and British Members of the European Parliament to ensure that matters that come before the European Parliament are adequately and thoroughly discussed in this House?

**Mr. Wakeham:** As my hon. Friend is aware, we made a very modest step towards closer co-operation between Members of this House and Members of the European Parliament, which was opposed by the Opposition at the time. I have always sought to make progress by agreement

[*Mr. Wakeham*]

across the Floor of the House and I am always ready to consider matters when I think that I can find agreement to make further progress.

**Mr. A. E. P. Duffy** (Sheffield, Attercliffe): Is the Leader of the House aware that the people of Sheffield are reminded almost daily by the *Sheffield Star*, Radio Sheffield and Radio Hallam and through the proceedings in their own town hall of the horrors of the Hillsborough disaster? Does not the right hon. Gentleman think that the ordinary people are less likely to be impressed by his arguments about the niceties and technicalities of implementation of legislation ultimately than by what now seems to be the Government's determination to push through the Football Spectators Bill while Lord Justice Taylor is still receiving evidence, let alone having had a chance to evaluate it? They will see the Government's action as an act of monumental insensitivity.

**Mr. Wakeham:** I do not think that that is a reasonable assessment of the situation. The Government are bringing forward legislation which will enable us, after the Bill has become an Act, to implement, subject to the approval of this House, any recommendations which will be acceptable in connection with Lord Justice Taylor's recommendations. The hon. Member for Sheffield, Attercliffe (Mr. Duffy) is a caring man, but it is strange that, as he represents Sheffield, he does not want to make all speed to avoid these terrible tragedies which have claimed more than 300 deaths since the war. We should take the first opportunity to try to prevent them. The hon. Member for Holborn and St. Pancras (Mr. Dobson), from the Opposition Front Bench, said that the Opposition would undertake to give a speedy passage to any recommendations from Lord Justice Taylor, whose report we have not seen. However, they would not agree to implement the Popplewell report, which has been published.

**Mr. Geoffrey Dickens** (Littleborough and Saddleworth): We heard earlier that there is to be a debate next week on the coal industry. Will my right hon. Friend find time before the summer recess for a debate on the nuclear power industry? Such a debate would give us an opportunity to show that those who are really concerned about our quality of life and about the protection of the atmosphere should go for a nuclear option.

**Mr. Wakeham:** I recognise that important points can be made. However, as we approach the summer recess I must be very careful about what extra debates I promise my hon. Friend.

**Mr. Robert Hughes** (Aberdeen, North): Does the Leader of the House accept that it is a great disappointment that no statement was made today on yesterday's meeting of the EEC Fisheries Council? The Fisheries Council's failure to act means that the British fleet, and the Scottish fleet in particular, faces a bleak future for the rest of the year. Will the right hon. Gentleman give an undertaking that the Minister of Agriculture, Fisheries and Food will make a statement early next week so that we can press on him the need to take action as sympathetic words are no good for people whose livelihoods are at stake?

Has the Leader of the House seen early-day motion 997 about the visit of F. W. De Klerk?

[*That this House considers the impending visit of F. W. De Klerk to Britain unwelcome, untimely and damaging to the prospects of dismantling apartheid in South Africa and establishing peace in Southern Africa; considers that, as leader of the ruling Nationalist Party and President-in-waiting, F. W. De Klerk has a major responsibility for the continuing repression in South Africa; notes that his government has recently reimposed the state of emergency for the fourth year in succession, resumed the execution of political prisoners, and placed hundreds of ex-detainees under stringent house arrest, concludes that totally committed to ensuring white domination, De Klerk is as unwelcome as was his predecessor P. W. Botha in 1984; also believes that De Klerk's visit is aimed at rehabilating the apartheid régime and easing its foreign debt crisis and has nothing to do with negotiations aimed at ending apartheid; believes that only the release of Nelson Mandela and all other political prisoners and detainees, the ending of the state of emergency and lifting of bans on organisations, as called for by the Commonwealth and the European Community, can begin to create the climate in which the commencement of meaningful negotiations and the dismantling of apartheid become possible, therefore deplores the Prime Minister's invitation to F. W. De Klerk, which can only send the wrong signals to both black and white in South Africa and encourage Pretoria to persist in its current policies; and calls upon the Prime Minister and the Foreign Secretary to cancel their proposed meetings with F. W. De Klerk.*]

Does he accept that it will be wholly obscene for the Prime Minister to sit down tomorrow to talk with the leader of a racist regime which continues to detain its people, which murders and tortures its children and which ought to be the pariah of the international world?

**Mr. Wakeham:** I have in mind having a debate on the fishing industry when the proposals for 1990 are known, but I shall refer the hon. Gentleman's points to my right hon. Friend the Minister of Agriculture, Fisheries and Food.

We reject early-day motion 997. The Government's policy is to maintain contact with all shades of opinion in South Africa. We use such contacts to press the need for change, and that is a sensible policy.

**Mr. Robert Adley** (Christchurch): Is my right hon. Friend aware that information reached me only last night that the British Rail Property Board is putting up for sale by auction on 6 July the last part of the former Great Central railway track bed between Aylesbury and Rugby? Its sale will preclude any future operation of trains on that railway line, which is one of the options being looked at by some of those interested in freight traffic for the Channel tunnel route.

Does my right hon. Friend agree that one of the lessons that we should have learnt in the past few years is that selling redundant railway track bed precludes reintroducing services when transport patterns change? Therefore, will he ask the Secretary of State for Transport to consider the urgency of the matter and to make a statement to the House next week? If he cannot do that, may we at least have an assurance of a debate on the matter before the summer recess?

**Mr. Wakeham:** Without accepting everything that my hon. Friend has said, I give him an undertaking that I shall refer the matter to my right hon. Friend the Secretary of State for Transport.

**Mr. Ron Brown** (Edinburgh, Leith): Before the right hon. Gentleman takes up another job, will he understand that security is important to the House? In particular, will he remember that it was alleged that some Labour Members were involved with the Soviet Union and had been blackmailed? Will he admit now that the source of that misinformation—that smear—came from the south of England, from a former Select Committee employee? Will he comment on that now, because it is so important?

**Mr. Wakeham:** I shall do no such thing. I should have thought that the hon. Gentleman would realise that security matters are so important that they should not be discussed across the Floor of the House.

**Mr. John Watts** (Slough): My right hon. Friend will be aware that a number of Conservative Members are opposed to the Football Spectators Bill, not least because it seems to have no relevance to the central issue of crowd safety, and, as presently drafted, such matters are outside its scope. In reply to the hon. Member for Holborn and St. Pancras (Mr. Dobson), my right hon. Friend said that he would be happy for such issues to be debated on Second Reading on Tuesday. Should the Bill receive a Second Reading, will my right hon. Friend table an instruction to the Committee for it to consider matters of crowd safety?

**Mr. Wakeham:** Yes. If that is required in order to discuss those matters in Committee, I shall see that it is done. I agree that questions of safety go right to the heart of the matters that are of concern.

**Mr. Alex Salmond** (Banff and Buchan): Is it not completely unsatisfactory for the important matter of the Fisheries Council meeting in Luxembourg yesterday to be dealt with by the Government in the form of a written answer? Does not the Leader of the House realise that the jobs of thousands of Scottish fishermen are at stake in the decisions or non-decisions that were made yesterday in Luxembourg? Is not the failure of the Minister of Agriculture, Fisheries and Food to face the House today a sign of the confusion and complacency which mark Government policy towards the fishing industry? When will the Government give the industry the priority to which it is entitled?

**Mr. Wakeham:** My right hon. Friend the Minister of Agriculture, Fisheries and Food has done a good job for the British fishermen, and that should be recognised. Whether statements are written or oral is always a matter of judgment. If we have too many oral statements, there are complaints that debates are curtailed; and if they are written there are complaints because they have not been made orally. I shall refer the matter to my right hon. Friend.

**Mr. Nicholas Bennett** (Pembroke): My right hon. Friend has announced that there is to be an Opposition debate on 3 July and that the subject is to be announced. Will he have discussions through the usual channels to find out whether the Opposition will arrange a debate on their policy on nuclear defence so that the House can discuss the interesting philosophical achievement of the Leader of the Opposition in his twin-track policy of supporting multilateral disarmament and at the same time being a member of CND?

**Mr. Wakeham:** The subject for debate is obviously a matter for the Opposition and not for me, but my hon. Friend makes his point well. He will be aware that we shall soon reach the time of the year when we have a number of debates on defence matters. With his usual ingenuity, he might be able to make his points then.

**Mr. Denis Howell** (Birmingham, Small Heath): The Leader of the House should understand that many people will find it grossly offensive, especially to those who died and to those who were bereaved, for us to press on with the Bill in the way that the Government intend.

**Mr. Dickens:** Which Bill?

**Mr. Howell:** The Football Spectators Bill—I do not have the intellect of the hon. Gentleman.

Is it not a fact that the Government Whips are making it clear to the Opposition that they want to finish the Committee stage of the Bill by the end of July—in one month? Is it not also a fact that whatever Lord Justice Taylor recommends cannot possibly be incorporated in the Bill? What the Government have done in another place, which is a deception, is to allow for an order to debate it here. One has to be in this place for only five minutes to know that orders cannot be amended. That means that the Bill cannot possibly take account of anything that Lord Justice Taylor might tell us about the lessons from Hillsborough. That is absolutely ludicrous. It is offensive to the people who have suffered and to every parliamentary concept that we should not be able to amend a Bill in the light of the recommendations of a very senior High Court judge.

Will the Leader of the House kindly consider those points and tell us how much Committee time we shall have to take on board Lord Justice Taylor's recommendations, whatever they might be?

**Mr. Wakeham:** The right hon. Gentleman has misunderstood the proceedings. This is an enabling Bill. Subsequent to the Bill being passed, there will be debates in the House about setting up any football management authority and about any recommendations. There will be plenty of time for points to be made. The right hon. Gentleman should make his points in Tuesday's debate.

**Mr. John Redwood** (Wokingham): Will my right hon. Friend make time available for an early debate on the relative jurisdictions of the European institutions and this Parliament in the light of the confusion now developing in many areas of Government over who is responsible and which power or body has the necessary control, particularly in the light of the Bill tabled today by my hon. Friend the Member for Stafford (Mr. Cash) setting out clarification of the relative powers under the treaties?

**Mr. Wakeham:** That is obviously an important subject and I should like to find time for a debate. I cannot promise my hon. Friend a debate in the immediate future, but no doubt these matters will be raised under different headings in the near future.

**Ms. Joan Walley** (Stoke-on-Trent, North): Is the Leader of the House aware of the early-day motions which express great concern that there are deadly levels of dioxin

[*Ms. Joan Walley*]

in the food chain and call for the urgent publication of the Government's report? Does he agree that it is deplorable that that report is being publicised by the Department of the Environment and we do not have the opportunity to debate it in the House? Will he arrange for an urgent debate on the report? Does he agree that it is most urgent that we take every possible action to eliminate deadly dioxins from the environment?

**Mr. Wakeham:** As the hon. Lady knows, the purpose of the report is to put before the public the best information available on dioxins in terms of human health and environmental impact. In recent years, there have been considerable reductions in the release of dioxins into the environment, and more are planned. In particular, current plans should reduce emissions from incinerators by 90 per cent. and the use of unleaded petrol should reduce emissions from vehicles by 80 per cent. I recognise that it is an important subject and one that we should find time to debate. However, I cannot promise a debate in the immediate future.

**Mr. Tony Favell** (Stockport): Will my right hon. Friend bear in mind when deciding what to do about the Football Spectators Bill the fact that a great deal of heat is being generated by the football industry about the so-called problems of a national membership scheme? Yet four times as many people each week go to licensed bingo clubs as go to football matches and they have a membership scheme which has not caused any problems.

**Mr. Wakeham:** My hon. Friend has made his point carefully. I shall look forward to the debate next week.

**Mrs. Alice Mahon** (Halifax): Is the Leader of the House aware that the overwhelming responses to the Government's proposals on the National Health Service are hostile? Given that, may we have a special debate on those responses before the end of the parliamentary Session? Is the Leader of the House aware that a ballot conducted in my constituency on Saturday produced 1,020 votes against the proposals and 19 for, with six spoilt papers? It was an independently conducted ballot, and if it was carried out across the country the Government would be in even worse trouble than they were last week with the European elections.

**Mr. Wakeham:** I do not accept the hon. Lady's analysis of the situation. I am interested in the expressions of interest in my right hon. and learned Friend the Secretary of State's proposals for self-governing hospitals. It is an appropriate matter for debate, but I cannot find time for one next week. I suggest that the hon. Lady has a word with her hon. Friend the shadow Leader of the House to see what he wants to do.

**Mr. John Wilkinson** (Ruislip-Northwood): Would it not be a wiser and worthier set of priorities for the Government in the conduct of their business next week if, instead of pushing ahead with the Second Reading of the Football Spectators Bill before the publication of even the interim report of Lord Justice Taylor on the Hillsborough tragedy, they allowed time for a foreign affairs debate on the situation in China? The only hope of the freedom-loving people in China who demonstrated for democracy and the rule of law is the pressure of international opinion on their behalf. Ought not the House to be mobilised to provide that pressure at the earliest possible date?

**Mr. Wakeham:** I agree with my hon. Friend about the importance of a debate on foreign affairs, particularly on the terrible events that have occurred in China. However, I do not agree that the Government can duck their responsibilities with regard to violence and hooliganism at football grounds. We have a clear responsibility to act, and we believe that this is the right time to do so. We will enable any recommendations of Lord Justice Taylor which are appropriate and which the Government accept to be incorporated into the action we take. It is right that we should go ahead with the Bill.

**Mr. Robert N. Wareing** (Liverpool, West Derby): Does the Leader of the House realise that there will be much anguish in Liverpool at the decision to race ahead with the dreadful Football Spectators Bill? If the Leader of the House is adamant that it is an enabling Bill, how does he know, before even the interim report of the Taylor inquiry, that any of its recommendations can be embraced by the Bill? Is it not the case that it enables only a football membership authority to carry out the madcap scheme of the Prime Minister? Is it not time that Ministers ceased to be doormats for every disgraceful whim of the Prime Minister?

**Mr. Wakeham:** The hon. Gentleman has got it wrong. The enabling powers will enable matters wider than those he mentioned to be dealt with. These are matters for discussion when the Bill is before the House. The central point is whether the Government and the House will accept their responsibility to take action.

**Mr. Peter Thurnham** (Bolton, North-East): Now that we are to have a code of practice for estate agents, may we have a debate on the need for a code of practice for property developers? Is there not a breed of rogue elephant property developer who has no respect for covenants and our heritage, who needs no protection and who, at the least, needs his tusks removed?

**Mr. Wakeham:** I guess that there are such cases. I cannot promise my hon. Friend a debate in the near future. There are other ways in which he may raise the matter which he considers to be of concern.

**Mr. John Fraser** (Norwood): Has the Leader of the House seen the reports in *The Independent* today of the threatened resignation of the Attorney-General? Assuming that the resignation is not to make a place for another Queen's Counsel in the Cabinet, does that not underline the importance of debating the Lord Chancellor's Green Paper on legal reforms?

**Mr. Wakeham:** If rumours in newspapers of what will happen to Ministers were the basis for debates in the House, we should be doing nothing but debating the changing scene. I do not take too much notice of what is in the newspapers these days. On the more substantive point of whether we should have a debate on the Green Papers issued by my right hon. Friend the Lord Chancellor, I agree that, ideally, it would be nice to have a debate in the House. We shall, of course, come to those matters at a later stage. I cannot see time for a debate at the moment.

**Mr. Harry Greenway** (Ealing, North): May I support the calls for a debate on events in China so that the hollow calls of the Labour party can be exposed as cries for unworkable sanctions? Labour Members have no proposals for that difficult situation other than simply calling for action that they know they cannot deliver themselves.

May we also have an early debate on the report issued by trade unionists today alleging that there is higher inflation in London than the national average? It is true that parts of London such as Ealing, where the rates have been doubled by the Labour council in two years, have higher inflation.

**Mr. Wakeham:** My hon. Friend is right to add to the calls for a debate on China and to note the slightly strange proposition put to the House by the Leader of the Opposition which will, no doubt, feature in any debate we may have. Rates in Ealing are a disturbing matter. My hon. Friend will have to use his ingenuity to raise the matter, and he will no doubt find a way.

**Mr. Alun Michael** (Cardiff, South and Penarth): Will the Leader of the House find time, if not in the coming week at least before the summer recess, for a debate on the future of the Health Service in Wales? Will he bear in mind the fact that the Secretary of State for Wales said in this Chamber on 1 March that he was about to publish papers parallel to, but different from, those for England setting out the way in which the proposals would be implemented? He has not done so, which places right hon. and hon. Members who represent Welsh constituencies at a considerable disadvantage, as they do not know what he is planning. Will the Leader of the House persuade his right hon. Friend to publish those papers so that we can have an informed debate, especially as the Secretary of State for Wales said in the debate on 1 March that he looked forward to such a debate?

**Mr. Wakeham:** I will do a deal with the hon. Gentleman: I will certainly put the points to my right hon. Friend if the hon. Gentleman will listen to me for one moment. The Opposition had the choice of subject for the last Welsh Grand Committee meeting on 26 April. They did not choose the Health Service in Wales. For the next meeting on 28 June, the choice of subject falls to Conservative Members. It is of great importance to Wales that the Committee should debate the valleys programme in the month of its first anniversary. At the next meeting of the Committee after that, the subject for debate will, once again, be the Opposition's choice. I know that my right hon. Friend the Secretary of State for Wales hopes very much that they will choose to debate the Government's plans for the Health Service. That will provide an opportunity to demonstrate this Government's fine record compared with the disaster of the last Government, when nurses' pay was reduced in real terms, when there were fewer doctors and fewer nurses, and far less was spent on the Health Service.

**Mr. Michael:** Before the recess?

**Mr. Wakeham:** I will do my best.

**Mr. Patrick McLoughlin** (Derbyshire, West): Does my right hon. Friend agree that many people will welcome the introduction next week of the Football Spectators Bill? It would be a grossly missed opportunity if we were to let a parliamentary Session go by without having that enabling legislation. Will my right hon. Friend confirm that, if Lord Justice Taylor produced an interim report saying that the national membership scheme would not be the best way forward, there would be no necessity to use the enabling legislation that we shall be passing through the House?

**Mr. Wakeham:** Business questions are not the right time to discuss the substance of the Bill. Such points can be made in the debate. Like my hon. Friend, I recognise that the basis of the membership scheme was the previous report by Mr. Justice Popplewell.

**Mr. Bob Cryer** (Bradford, South): May we have a debate in the near future on race relations, bearing in mind the serious rioting in Bradford last Saturday in connection with a campaign about the book "The Satanic Verses", and the fact that organisations such as the Bradford Council of Mosques are pursuing that campaign with apparently no regard for the damage being done to race relations? During such a debate, the Home Secretary could elaborate on any links that there might be between groups of Iranians promoting violence and that campaign. We could also emphasise the fact that "The Satanic Verses" is published under the law and that people want the right to read the book and to have that right sustained.

**Mr. Wakeham:** I have some sympathy with part of what the hon. Gentleman has said. Certainly I cannot condone any acts of violence, from wherever they come. I recognise that Iran could do a great deal if it were to renounce publicly the use or the threat of terrorism or violence. It behoves everybody on all sides of the argument to stick strictly within the law and not to resort to violence.

**Mr. Tam Dalyell** (Linlithgow): Has the Leader of the House noticed that you, Mr. Speaker, in your wisdom, have granted my hon. Friend the Member for Brent, East (Mr. Livingstone) an Adjournment debate next week on the conviction of Colin Wallace? Who will answer that debate? May I suggest that it would most properly be answered by the Attorney-General?

May we have an assurance that, whichever Minister answers the debate, he will at least have read the book, which I mentioned during Northern Ireland questions this afternoon, by Paul Foot, "Who Framed Colin Wallace?" Could that Minister politely approach No. 10 Downing street, possibly through the Lord President, to get a comment that can come only from the Prime Minister on what Mr. Foot has written about the late Airey Neave? The best speech that I ever heard the Prime Minister make was from the pulpit of St. Martin-in-the-Fields when she paid tribute to her friend. Some of us believe that what has been said about Airey Neave in the book must be cleared up one way or the other.

**Mr. Wakeham:** I cannot give the hon. Gentleman an answer to the question of who will respond to the debate next Thursday, but I can give him the undertaking that the points that he has made will be drawn to the attention of whichever Minister replies to it and I can assure him that the Minister will give a satisfactory and correct answer.

**Mr. Tony Banks** (Newham, North-West) : Once again, may I ask the Leader of the House for an early debate on animal conservation, especially in the light of the worrying figures that have just been published about the dramatic

[*Mr. Tony Banks*]

decline in the world's whale population? May I draw his attention to my early-day motion 1009 on bull-fighting in Spain?

[*That this House expresses its continuing disgust at the so-called sport of bull-fighting in Spain; believes that the breeding and slaughter of bulls for spectator enjoyment is cruel and uncivilised and should have no place in modern Europe; calls upon the Spanish government to ban bull-fighting; and urges all British tourists concerned about animal welfare not to holiday in Spain until bull-fighting is banned.*]

Does the right hon. Gentleman agree that that is a particularly nasty form of sport? I hope that he will go along with my recommendation about not taking a holiday in Spain, were he to be considering a holiday in Spain in view of the time that he might have on his hands later. We are on his side, and if letters of support from this place can help him, we are ready to write them.

Will the Leader of the House tell the Prime Minister when she goes to the Madrid summit in Spain to make sure that she declines any invitation to a bull fight and that she uses her iron handbag to good effect on the Spanish to try to persuade them to ban that nasty and despicable so-called sport?

**Mr. Wakeham:** With all the hon. Gentleman's charm, I did not know that he also wrote letters. I am glad that I do not receive too many of them. Among all the verbiage, he raised a serious point about bull-fighting in Spain and referred to his early-day motion 1009. We understand the feelings expressed in that early-day motion, but animal welfare in Spain is entirely the responsibility of the Spanish Government. The Spanish authorities are aware of the strength of feeling about bull-fighting among some people in the United Kingdom.

## Question Time

4.15 pm

**Mr. Ken Maginnis** (Fermanagh and South Tyrone): On a point of order, Mr. Speaker. I should be grateful for your guidance. Following the deliberately evasive answer given by the Secretary of State for Northern Ireland to my question during Question Time, I should have liked to give notice that I would seek to raise an Adjournment debate at the earliest possible moment. Is it in order for me to give such notice now?

**Mr. Speaker:** I note what the hon. Gentleman says.

**Mr. Seamus Mallon** (Newry and Armagh): Further to that point of order, Mr. Speaker. Is it not true that informal contacts are a very important part of the political process and that, as such, they should be treated with utter confidentiality? Is there any possibility of the hon. Member for Fermanagh and South Tyrone (Mr. Maginnis) being reminded that the very distasteful way that he related that which was confidential at a dinner hosted by the Secretary of State for Northern Ireland has harmed the political process? Is it not the duty of the House to protect not just what happens on the Floor of the House, but those informal contacts and discussions that are so essential to our lives as politicians?

**Rev. Ian Paisley** (Antrim, North): Further to that point of order, Mr. Speaker.

**Mr. Speaker:** Order. This is an extension of Question Time, when we had a long run on the question——

**Rev. Ian Paisley:** It is to the point.

**Mr. Speaker:** Order. No. I regret that because of that long run we did not get very far down the Order Paper. There are to be two very important debates on Northern Ireland in just a few moments.

## BILL PRESENTED

### European Community (Reaffirmation and Limits of Competence)

Mr. William Cash, supported by Mr. John Redwood, Mr. James Cran, Mr. Roger Knapman, Sir Rhodes Boyson, Sir Marcus Fox, Mr. Christopher Gill, Mr. Graham Riddick, Mr. John Bowis and Mr. Nicholas Bennett, presented a Bill to reaffirm the commitment of the United Kingdom to the European Community; to reaffirm the scope and limits of the competence of the European Community Treaty including the Single European Act; to affirm the rejection by the United Kingdom of the economic and monetary union and of political union within the European Community; to reject the Charter of Fundamental Social Rights proposed by the European Commission; to reaffirm the Luxembourg Accord and the sovereignty of the United Kingdom Parliament; and for other purposes: And the same was read the First time; and ordered to be read a Second time on Friday 7 July and to be printed. [Bill 165.]

## BRUNEI (APPEALS) BILL *[LORDS]*

*Ordered,*

That the Brunei (Appeals) Bill *[Lords]* be referred to a Second Reading Committee.—[*Mr. Sackville.*]

## EUROPEAN COMMUNITY DOCUMENTS]

*Ordered,*

That European Community Document No. 8066/88 on waste be referred to a Standing Committee on European Community Documents.—[*Mr. Sackville*]

## SCOTTISH ESTIMATES:

*Ordered,*

That the Estimates set out hereunder be referred to the Scottish Grand Committee:

Class XVI, Vote 1, Agriculture Support, Scotland
Class XVI, Vote 2, Agricultural Services and Fisheries, Scotland
Class XVI, Vote 3, Regional and General Industrial Support, Scotland
Class XVI, Vote 4, Training Agency, Scotland
Class XVI, Vote 5, Regional Assistance, Scotland
Class XVI, Vote 6, Roads, Transport and Environmental Services, Scotland
Class XVI, Vote 7, Local Transport, Water, Sewerage & Environmental Services, Scotland
Class XVI, Vote 8, Housing Scotland
Class XVI, Vote 9, New Towns and the Urban Programme, Scotland
Class XVI, Vote 10, Privatisation of the Electricity Supply Industry, Scotland
Class XVI, Vote 11, Administration of Justice, Scotland
Class XVI, Vote 12, Police Grant, Legal Aid & Criminal Injuries Compensation, Scotland
Class XVI, Vote 13, Legal Proceedings, Scotland
Class XVI, Vote 14, Prisons, Hospitals and Community Health Services, Etc, Scotland
Class XVI, Vote 15, Education, Arts, Libraries &

Social Work, Scotland
Class XVI, Vote 16, Student Awards, Scotland
Class XVI, Vote 17, Health (Family Practitioner Services), Scotland
Class XVI, Vote 21, Scottish Office Administration
Class XVI, Vote 26, Privatisation of the Scottish Bus Group—[*Mr. Sackville.*]

# Northern Ireland Act 1974

4.17 pm

**The Secretary of State for Northern Ireland (Mr. Tom King):** I beg to move,

That the draft Northern Ireland Act 1974 (Interim Period Extension) Order 1989, which was laid before this House on 13th June, be approved.

This is the fifteenth time that I or my predecessors have come before the House to invite it to renew the system of direct rule that was introduced under the 1974 Act. I noted the comments of the hon. Member for Kingston upon Hull, North (Mr. McNamara) last year, when he described direct rule as patronising, undemocratic, unaccountable, remote and inefficient, and said that it had gone on too long——

**Rev. Ian Paisley** (Antrim, North): Hear, hear.

**Mr. King:** I am delighted to have the hon. Gentleman with me.

Every democrat in this House will endorse the feeling that this is not a satisfactory democratic system. It was intended to be temporary and it is on all our consciences that as yet we have not found a better alternative. I hope that I do not embarrass the hon. Member for Kingston upon Hull, North by referring to him again, but he referred to that as the highest common factor on which there could be agreement for the government of Northern Ireland.

I agree with that assessment, other than in one respect —and this does not condone the system—that being his description of the system as "inefficient". I do not think that it is inefficient and I shall seek to put before the House some of what I believe to be the real achievements of the past year. That is not to say that I am in any way seeking to justify the system. Despite the regrettable absence of a more democratic and accountable system, as far as is possible we are seeking to provide for the Province as efficient, as accountable and as open a system of government as we can—and in that I include not just myself, but my colleagues in the Northern Ireland Office and those with responsibilities in the Northern Ireland departments. I shall, as I did last year, comment on the economic and security aspects and then deal with some of the political issues.

When I opened the equivalent debate last year, I was able to draw the attention of the House to the fact that unemployment in the previous year had fallen by 10,000. I am proud to stand at the Dispatch Box this year and draw the attention of the House to the fact that in the past year the headline total has fallen by a further 10,000.

The Northern Ireland Economic Council said in its 1989 report that the local economy had performed better in the last year than at any time during the 1980s. The figure for investment by Northern Ireland companies was the highest ever last year, at £400 million. That is the mainspring of the improvement in the economy—I shall come to the question of inward investment—because the most important contribution is coming from the success and expansion of companies already located in the Province and from people there starting their own businesses.

We have also had some encouraging new industries. Since we debated this matter last year, I was able to announce the investment by Montupet, which will be

[Mr. King]

moving into the old De Lorean factory. Hon. Members may be aware that the company is now starting recruiting for that important establishment, which will employ 1,100 and which offers an exciting prospect for the future as a major employer in Northern Ireland.

I hold the same view about our first investment by a major company from the far east, which we have achieved in the shape of Daewoo. It is interesting to record, when people wonder how Northern Ireland can perform—I hope that every Northern Ireland Member will take pride in this fact—that it was only in November that I joined in the ceremony of cutting the first turf on a green field site in advance of the construction of that factory.

Since then, 100,000 sq ft of new production facility has been constructed and the first dispatch of video recorders has been made from that factory. Considering that we started from scratch in the middle of November, that is a fair indication of what Northern Ireland can achieve. I hope that that will prove to be the first of a number of valuable new investments.

When I stood at the Dispatch Box last year, my hon. Friend the Member for Newbury (Sir M. McNair-Wilson) intervened to ask if I had anything to say about whether the Government had any intentions over the possible privatisation of Shorts. The House will be aware that it is only a few days since I was able to stand here, after having scarcely embarked on that process at this time last year, to announce what I hope will prove the successful completion of that exercise.

In respect of both Shorts and Harland and Wolff, I had real concern last year lest neither of those companies would be able to continue. It is no secret now—we are able to tell the truth—that Shorts was running losses at a level that were unsustainable. The hon. Member for Belfast, East (Mr. Robinson) will remember that, because he intervened in that debate to urge on me the "ultimate dream", about which we had reservations. I made clear to him at that time my concern for the future of the yard, which faced the prospect of no orders at all and a rapid demise.

I genuinely believe that the acquisition of Shorts, if it is successfully completed by Bombardier of Canada, and the involvement now in Harland and Wolff both of Mr. John Parker and his management and employee buy-out project, together with the crucially important private sector involvement of Mr. Fred Olsen and his investment, offer better prospects for Harland and Wolff—and, with Bombardier, better prospects for Shorts—than have existed for a long time. Far from being concerned about their possible collapse, I now look with considerable optimism at the prospects that they may have before them. Of course nothing can be taken for granted. Many hurdles must be crossed, but the opportunity now exists. If those companies were to start growing, particularly Harland and Wolff after a period of such prolonged contraction, the impact that it would have on the general strength of the Northern Ireland economy can be well understood.

There have been developments in the past year. There was the exciting announcement of a £100 million investment by British Telecom, supported by the European Community, in the new fibre-optic link. It will provide a service to the whole of Northern Ireland and could provide more jobs in the service sector. The Government have announced jobs in the Department of Social Security, and offices in Lewisham, Brixton, Hither Green and in other parts of London will be directly linked to the service in Belfast. That will initially provide 350 jobs and, we hope, in time lead to 500. There may be one or two more interesting announcements shortly, showing the way in which we can take advantage of new technology and obtain jobs for Northern Ireland.

In the past year, we have seen a further expansion in retailing activity. There has been an improvement in retailing facilities, and there have been major construction projects, both outside and inside Belfast, and certainly in the constituency of the hon. Member for Foyle (Mr. Hume). There is new optimism and a new sense of opportunity. Although there is certainly a long way to go and a very big hill to climb, bearing in mind the level of unemployment in certain parts of the Province, perhaps for the first time people are beginning to see a real way of tackling problems. It is against that background that I look with optimism to the economic prospects for the Province.

Those achievements have occurred in spite of and in staunch resistance to the campaign of terror that still seeks to ruin the lives, jobs, hopes and future of many young people in Northern Ireland. That campaign can damage the economic prospects not only of everybody in the Province but of people throughout the island of Ireland.

We must, as we have on other occasions in the House, pay tribute to the security forces' tremendous courage and determination over the past year and the work that they have done in preventing casualties and deaths. This is the first time that I have stood at the Dispatch Box and not had to report any deaths due to terrorism during the period since I last answered questions on security matters. That is not because the danger is over. Hon. Members will have noticed that I drew attention to the fact that the threat still remains, and there is still a need for vigilance and the closest co-operation with the security forces. Through their determination to resist these onslaughts, the people of Northern Ireland have shown where they stand. We shall certainly seek to ensure that they have the sort of support from the security forces to which they are entitled.

The debate last year was just after the summit meeting between the Prime Minister and the Taoiseach. They drew attention in their communiqué to their wish for close co-operation in the fight against terrorism. I want to put on record again our appreciation of the very good relationship between the Royal Ulster Constabulary and the Garda Siochana, and the substantial work that has been done, not least in arms finds and the successful seizure of primed bombs, primed mortars and caches of explosives and weapons by the Garda. Certainly we can look back on real achievements by the security forces.

That is not to say, sadly, that this year has not been marked by some tragic incidents arising from the terrorist campaign. We forget them perhaps all too easily. I have to refresh my memory of Ballygawley; of Benburb where a granddfather and his grandaughter were tragically in the wrong place at the wrong time when coming home from bingo; of the good neighbours in the constituency of the hon. Member for Foyle whose reward from the IRA for concern about a neighbour who might be in distress was their own death; of the tragic murder of Chief Superintendent Breen and Superintendent Buchanan; and of the murder of the young girl in Warrenpoint. Some of those incidents the IRA might have regarded as successful attacks in its awful vocabulary, but others it has recognised as mistakes in its craven apologies, yet all of them show the awfulness of the terrorist campaign.

Against that background, we have sought to ensure that not only the security forces but the instruments of law are fit and proper to enable us to protect the community against the assaults that it faces. We face a sustained attack not merely on the community but on the whole system of justice, whether by the attempts to murder judges, the attempts to murder witnesses, or the attempts to intimidate the whole community so that the terrorists may be above the law. At the centre of my concern has been not only the consideration that in any society it is important that innocent people are not convicted, but the important responsibility of the Government to ensure that guilty people have a reasonable prospect of conviction. We have faced the determined attack on the whole system of justice by trying to ensure that terrorists cannot put themselves beyond the possibility of successful prosecution and conviction.

I mention that merely to put in context the background against which we made changes during the past year. One move was the introduction of genetic fingerprinting to strengthen forensic evidence. We also made changes to allow inferences to be drawn in certain circumstances when people remained silent. We also took steps to ensure that when people are convicted of serious crimes they serve a proper sentence and that if they become reinvolved they will face the full rigours of the law.

Hon. Members will know that a feature of our approach to the prison regime and sentencing in the past year has been to give sympathetic consideration particularly to some who were caught up in the early troubles when very young and who found themselves facing a severe sentence, which meant that effectively they spent all their youth in prison. But that sympathy does not extend to those who become reinvolved after serving a determinate sentence. I have given fair warning to any who think of getting involved again in evil paramilitary terrorist activity that sympathy will not extend to them.

A feature of the past year has been to recognise that in our approach against terrorism we need to use not merely the instruments available to the security forces, but to recognise the need to tackle the evil in every aspect and to deal especially with the terrorists' resources which sustain so much of the terrorism. Some hon. Members have some understanding of the measures that we have taken and the arrangements that we have made to ensure that we are now assembling a much more effective response to gangsterism, smuggling, protection rackets, extortion and intimidation. A feature of the year ahead will be the growing evidence of a more effective counter-attack in those areas, in which we have the very full, active and interested co-operation of the Irish Government, who suffer especially from many of the losses associated with smuggling.

Against that background, I was considerably interested in certain aspects of the recent election results. It is difficult to tackle intimidation when people, with little protection, are understandably, in fear of standing up for what they believe. We can take some real comfort and encouragement from the fact that in the privacy and secrecy of polling booths people are increasingly walking away, especially from the principal party, Sinn Fein, which has been an open advocate and supporter of violence. I note that Mr. Morrison's vote in the European election fell from 91,000 to 49,000—virtually halving. I am encouraged, too, that in the Republic Sinn Fein's pitifully small and inadequate achievement of 1·9 per cent. in the previous general election moved downwards to 1·2 per cent. in the last election. That shows the complete absence of political support throughout the Republic for the evil intentions to which Sinn Fein subscribes.

**Mr. Merlyn Rees** (Morley and Leeds, South): In recent weeks I have been in the middle east, where the point was made to me that there is a comparison between the problems there and those in Northern Ireland. The Secretary of State has just made the point that Sinn Fein, the political wing of the provisional IRA, gets an extraordinarily low vote, and, in the country from where the violence emanates, the SDLP has done so much better. Does that not show what nonsense it is for people in this country to say that we must talk with Sinn Fein, because often in the past we have said that there should be no talks and leaders have become Prime Ministers? Parties must get votes and Sinn Fein has done extremely badly. I hope that the Foreign Office will point that out in many parts of the middle east.

**Mr. King:** I know that that is a favourite analogy that Sinn Fein would seek to make with those, as it were, who have been imprisoned by the British in the past and have then come out to take up respectable democratic positions. There are two fundamental differences. First, they have found themselves in prison because they were leading protest movements in circumstances where they were denied the vote. As we know, in the circumstances of Northern Ireland there is a full opportunity for people to vote for and to support their party. Secondly, not only were those organisations with which Sinn Fein seeks to compare itself denied the vote, but, when they got the vote, they got the majority of the votes. I am on record as saying after the last election that their derisory level of support would not begin to justify a local campaign of civil disobedience, let alone remotely justify the sort of terrorism and violence which Republican terrorists commit. Against that background, we have seen real progress in the economy and in the movement away from support for violence.

I sense that, in Northern Ireland, there is a greater optimism and a real sense of hope. I believe that many others share that feeling. We have sought to reinforce it by a positive campaign aimed to help those areas of real need, particularly in the bigger cities. We have also considered how to help those areas where, undoubtedly, the unemployment levels are far too high and where that optimism and hope have not yet been felt.

In the past year we have made progress elsewhere as well. We have continued our steady work under the Anglo-Irish Agreement and, as I recently reported to the House, we have reviewed the workings of the conference during the past three years. I have published a record of developments since that conference began. The House will have seen that the Anglo-Irish Agreement is not the great dangerous conspiracy that certain people have tried to dress it up as, as though it was a pernicious attempt to undermine the fabric of society, but that it has resulted in steady, useful and co-operative work. There is increasing recognition of areas of common interest between North and South.

[*Mr. King*]

I was struck by the fact that the central issues under debate in the recent Irish elections were, without entering into their merits, unemployment, worries about emigration and the state of the economy. Those are the very issues that are of concern to people in Northern Ireland and, given our level of unemployment, it is extremely understandable. We recognise the need for a stronger economy and both Governments recognise the need to wipe out terrorism, which is such an obstacle to improving the opportunities for people in both our countries.

Stripped away from all the rhetoric and the shouting that accompanies some comments about the Anglo-Irish Agreement, I believe that people increasingly recognise that the conference has not been the greatest bogey suggested by some people. We have worked steadily together. I accept that some Unionists do not particularly like the agreement, but the honest ones say that it has not proved to be the great disaster that they feared and that they can see some benefits deriving from it. Many people in Northern Ireland put the problems of terrorism at the top of their list of concerns, and if the Anglo-Irish Agreement has helped to establish a much better relationship between the RUC and the Garda that is of obvious benefit.

In this debate we are seeking to renew the system of direct rule, but, having recognised the progress that has been made in the past year, I also recognise where progress has been virtually non-existent—in the political arena. In this Chamber now are the only people who can change that. We can easily say that we should just go on as we are. Some people may argue that, in the end, the Government will tell them what they have decided they want to do. Perhaps those people will shout, scream and complain about it, but then say that they do not need to suggest anything themselves.

I have heard one or two stories suggesting that I have some sort of hidden agenda, that there is some secret plan that I have tucked away and that come October, I shall impose it on everyone. Colleagues in this House know me well enough to know that I will tell them straight what the situation is: there is no such plan. I do not believe that there is any point in having a plan unless I have a clearer idea of what the people would be willing to accept and what might provide the basis on which people could move forward. There is no point in the British Government handing down tablets of stone which give the parties an opportunity to squabble and row about them. The right hon. Member for Morley and Leeds, South (Mr. Rees), who has much experience in this matter, knows exactly what I am talking about. I have respect for his experience.

**Sir Michael McNair-Wilson** (Newbury): Surely there is one change as a consequence of the results of the district council elections when there was a high turnout in the Province. It showed that the people of Northern Ireland are concerned about their local government. It is also true, however, that in the past 17 years no attempt has been made to reform the structure of that local government, although in this country we have had no fewer than four local government Acts, one of which went through the House only last night. Why do we expect the political parties to do in their Province that which in this country we do first by an inquiry set up by an independent group, which brings forward proposals that are then debated,

argued about and ultimately made into legislation? Why do we not use the same procedure in Northern Ireland? Why do we always say that the obstacle lies with those of us who have our various party political allegiances, which, of course, limit us anyway, when we could so easily go out to independent people who could undertake the initial task and inquiry for us instead?

**Mr. King:** I am grateful to my hon. Friend because he approaches this matter in a constructive manner and he has put forward proposals as to how we might tackle it. We need to address those issues.

We may now have an opportunity, if people wish to take it, with or without Government, by independent inquiry or in whatever form, to make progress. My hon. Friend the Member for Newbury (Sir M. McNair-Wilson) took one message from the local council elections, and I was equally impressed by another. We are here with Unionist Members who will not talk with any Minister. At the moment, they are still stuck with a situation whereby they are unable to represent their constituents. They were the only people in this House who declined to represent their constituents' concerns about education, health or other issues that are of great importance to every hon. Member.

Those Unionist Members feel paralysed and unable to address such matters on behalf of their constituents, but a new opportunity arose at the local council elections. I was struck by the number of councillors wo have chosen to elect a member of one party as chairman or mayor while also accepting the legitimacy and respectability of another party through their willingness to support a member of that party as vice-chairman, deputy mayor or whatever. I am not sure of the previous situation, but such co-operation is something that can be undertaken across the parties.

At local government level, it seems that people have demonstrated that they are there to serve their electorate's concerns. Without abandoning their own responsibilities and their principles they have shown that they will do their best to serve the interests of the people in their community. I welcome that. If it is possible to do that in local government, is it impossible to do it in the Province as a whole? I know that it is not, because I was much assisted in the difficult issue of Harland and Wolff when the leaders of the parties came together and had meetings with me. I asked those leaders to come with me to talk with the Prime Minister and to represent directly to her the concerns of the people of Northern Ireland about that issue. I make no secret of the fact that those meetings were helpful to me in achieving my desired goal. The Prime Minister was able to hear at first hand some of the concerns about this issue.

It is important to remember that, because of the exercise undertaken, Harland and Wolff saved 2,500 jobs. But we have 105,000 unemployed people in Northern Ireland and we cannot stop there. We need now to address the wider issues. I hope that Unionist leaders will not stand back and say that they were willing to do it for Harland and Wolff, but they will not help if there is a problem in Londonderry or elsewhere. I believe that they are prepared to stand up and say that they will join in discussing such important issues.

The hon. Member for North Down (Mr. Kilfedder) has asked why we cannot get together to promote the Province. The outside world is still trying to represent Northern Ireland as a permanent scene of division and battle, and the hon. Gentleman is right to say that we should show that people can come together and are willing to work together for things that are of benefit to the entire community. I am not saying that I do not want constructive and, at times, pretty strong criticism. I believe that the elected representatives have a role to monitor and to hold the Executive to account. They have a duty to challenge the Secretary of State and to question his actions. At other times, they should come together and work for the Province.

I hope that, following these developments, we can find ways in which we can work together for the benefit of the people in the Province. I hope that hon. Members will take the opportunity to come to me, or my colleagues with responsibility for education, industry or health, to talk through the issues that are of direct concern to them and their constituents.

One interesting point about Northern Ireland which is not sufficiently stressed is the unaccountability of direct rule. Unionist Members nod their heads, but direct rule is not as unaccountable as they seek to make it. Northern Ireland Members have far greater access to the Northern Ireland Ministers who take the decisions than have any other hon. Members. There are about 650 hon. Members and, often, there may be 500 different Members wanting to address a Minister on a particular subject. I hope that the hon. Members feel that the Ministers are pretty quickly available to see them when they wish to do so.

Northern Ireland Members should not say that their constituents are unrepresented. They will be unrepresented only if their representatives are not using the channels which are more accessible to Northern Ireland Members than to any other Members by virtue of the presence of direct rule, which means that there are six Northern Ireland Ministers and only 16 Northern Ireland Members of Parliament. That gives Northern Ireland Members an unequalled opportunity to represent their constituents, particularly with the open door policy, which I want my right hon. and hon. Friends to maintain. However, that opportunity means nothing, and will be of no benefit, if it is not used.

My hon. Friend the Member for Newbury, who takes a keen interest in these matters, said that surely it must be possible to make progress and, of course, he is right. There is absolutely no problem about designing structures and coming up with different concepts for the administration of Northern Ireland. I have deliberately chosen my phrases and, as my hon. Friend knows, I avoid the slogans of the past. I do not talk about power sharing or what is widely acceptable to both communities, but about ideas that might have a chance of working. I am prepared to consider any approaches or options which people want to put forward.

Does the refusal to talk spring from a tremendously strong and firmly held principle or is it a sort of paralysis which comes from not being sure about the way in which anybody wants to go? One issue that worries me is that I have never been convinced that people are clear about what they want to do. If they cannot make up their minds, they will be unable to make any contribution to constructive discussions.

We shall continue to do our best, and I have sought in the account which I have given to show that we have done our best to discharge our responsibilities. Today I have been able to report to the House some measures of achievement, and those, allied to the spirit, courage and determination of the people of Northern Ireland, are the reason why there is a greater sense of optimism and hope in the Province now than there was two or three years ago. However, we must still overcome the problem of finding out how we can establish a more democratic approach.

The solution to the problem lies not in structures or blueprints, but in willingness. I begin to feel that local councils are showing us the way. It would be tragic if Unionists, as Members of this Parliament of the Union, felt that at this level of parliamentary representation we could not reach a level of co-operative and constructive discussion.

I hope that this debate will show that the opportunity will be taken and that we can point a way forward. I have made it clear that I am prepared to discuss any genuinely constructive and helpful approaches which people wish to make which will be of benefit to the people in the Province. If we believe in democracy, we must be prepared to make that effort. Terrorism cannot win, and 20 years on nobody has any excuse for not knowing that terrorism will not win. In the end, democracy must win, and it can do so if it is given the chance. We shall continue to discharge our responsibilities under direct rule.

I look forward to the day when good will and the constructive approach of the elected representatives in the Province will at last offer the prospect, not merely of progress, but of progress with democracy and justice, which is in the interests of everyone in the Province.

4.56 pm

**Mr. Kevin McNamara** (Kingston upon Hull, North): I listened to what the Secretary of State had to say about not having a secret plan for October. I hope that nobody else has a secret plan for him for October because one feature which he has brought to the role of Secretary of State for Northern Ireland, even though I have frequently disagreed with his decisions and actions, has been a dedication and concern for the Province. That must be recognised by people who might find some of his decisions, perhaps because of his ideological background, somewhat surprising.

Nobody in this Chamber today can be satisfied that we are once again discussing the renewal of direct rule over Northern Ireland. If we look at the title of the provision, the Northern Ireland Act 1974 (Interim Period Extension) Order 1989, and think of those 15 years, we could say that rather than an interim measure it has, instead, become the manifestation of our failure to find any democratic solution which is acceptable in Northern Ireland.

I shall not be surprised if, later, the hon. Member for Eastbourne (Mr. Gow) suggests that the interim nature of the 1974 Act is a major factor in the continuing conflict in Northern Ireland.

**Mr. Ian Gow** (Eastbourne) *indicated assent.*

**Mr. McNamara:** The hon. Gentleman nods his head in agreement but his is a mistaken view. The continued necessity for the 1974 Act reflects our failure to find a solution, but is not the source of the conflict.

The problem is that Northern Ireland has never enjoyed any degree of confidence in its future. Legislation on Northern Ireland has always been considered as an interim measure. That has been a constant theme, as shown by the Government of Ireland Act 1920, the permanent crisis atmosphere of the Stormont regime and even the Ireland Act 1949. It is quite clear that few people in Northern

[*Mr. Ian Gow*]

Ireland or the rest of the United Kingdom have ever believed that Northern Ireland's position has been fixed in perpetuity. Direct rule was never intended to be a long-lasting form of government. It was meant to be an instrument for crisis management when the power sharing executive fell. It was hoped that it would allow for the creation of a stable, democratic system of devolved government. However, this has not happened and, because of the absence of purpose, there is a danger that direct rule will simply institutionalise the permanent crisis, as did the Stormont regime.

In many respects, all parties and all Governments have failed to make any advances with Northern Ireland. Perhaps we have stumbled on a more modern and sophisticated system of crisis management, one which is sufficient to secure agreement that it is the best form of government in the worst of all possible worlds.

Today, the Secretary of State expressed a sentiment which I knew he shared with us. He suggested that nobody had any great ambition to preside over a mere system of containment. Northern Ireland will be secure from the threat of political violence and instability only when it has a system of Government which commands the consent of the people of Northern Ireland, not merely their passive and resigned acquiesence.

This debate gives us a useful opportunity to take stock of the extent to which the application of the 1974 Act in the past 12 months has assisted in achieving the objective of a stable and democratic form of Government. I am afraid to say that the record is not too good, as the Secretary of State has said. He referred to economic matters, security matters and the political aspects of the last period of direct rule, and I shall follow his agenda. I shall not say a great deal about the economic situation, as the debate on the appropriation order later this evening will provide an opportunity for some detailed debate. My hon. Friend the Member for Leicester, South (Mr. Marshall) will be less than happy if I shoot all his foxes. The Opposition welcome any sign of improvement in the economic prospects of the Province, particularly in respect of employment. We welcome the fall in unemployment, but at 15·5 per cent. it is still the highest rate in these islands and still higher than it was in June 1979.

The position is not as bright as the Secretary of State would like us to believe. The Government's figures show that, on most of the major economic indicators, Northern Ireland has been lagging behind the rest of the United Kingdom. As the consequences of the mismanagement of the British economy become more and more apparent every day, the impact on Northern Ireland is not conducive to optimism. If we catch a cold on this island, they get pneumonia in Northern Ireland.

The Government have announced the arrival of a number of new industrial projects, and we welcome them, but I cannot help but feel that these efforts would be more successful if the Secretary of State and the Minister responsible for economic development had not been preoccupied with their plans to privatise Shorts and Harland and Wolff. It comes strange from the Government, who are prepared to write off so much in capital debts and capital loans, to claim that those companies were underfunded, when they as the owners had the ability, the strength and the means to supply the

funds and the orders and to make sure of the training and the market. They are now looking to the privatised sector to deal with the problems that they had caused by their lack of investment.

The decision to take powers to prepare the ground for privatisation of the Northern Ireland Electricity Service does not augur well. I wonder how the Government of competition expect to find competition for the NIES in Northern Ireland. Given the high energy costs that prevail in Northern Ireland—higher than in the rest of the kingdom—the Government should be more concerned about preventing a price increase than about increasing profits and, therefore, industrial and domestic consumer costs. Just as night follows day, as NIES is fattened up for a profitable slaughter, prices will increase.

The Secretary of State has paid tribute to the work of the security forces. On behalf of Her Majesty's Opposition, I associate myself with that tribute. He mentioned the happy fact that there had been no deaths to members of the security forces recently. That is to be welcomed, and we hope that it will continue, but there have been serious injuries. A marine from my locality was seriously injured by a bomb last week. The problems are still there. However, the problem for us as democratic politicians is that we have been relying on the security forces to hold the ring while we fail to find the political solution. It is incumbent upon us democratic politicians not to become Lundies but to sit down and try to work out how to prevent such deaths and maimings.

It is also incumbent on us to avoid making the performance of the duties of the security forces more difficult. The Government have a duty to pursue policies to undercut the causes of violence, but they must also ensure that the security forces are sensitive to the difficult environment in which they operate. The real world in Northern Ireland must be recognised in the House. We pay tribute to the police and soldiers who daily risk their lives, but until they are fully accepted in Northern Ireland, the risks will continue. Therefore, it is imperative that the security forces avoid needless friction with local residents, that complaints are speedily dealt with and rumours effectively scotched.

It is also essential that the Government do not undermine the work of the security forces by ill-advised measures. It is not the views of the House that matter so much as those of the citizens of Northern Ireland. It is an undeniable but unfortunate fact that the minority community does not regard the Ulster Defence Regiment as a peace-keeping force. It views it in a less favourable light than the regular Army and the Royal Ulster Constabulary. Therefore, I am concerned about the consideration being given to the extension of the use of plastic bullets by issuing them to the UDR. This would be an unwise move because it would show that the concerns and wishes of the nationalist community, and not simply that decreasing minority who support Sinn Fein, have been ignored. No more should be heard of this foolishness. Neither should the UDR be placed in a situation where it feels the need to use plastic bullets.

Furthermore, if the decision is made, the temptation will be there for the military defence to use the UDR for crowd control and riot control, thus relieving the regular Army of this role at a time when demographic considerations are forcing the Ministry of Defence to re-assess the roles and tasks of the regular Army. It would be a tragedy if that were to happen, and the temptation were to be there. I trust that, even though the Secretary of State has said that training will go ahead, it will be stopped. There are only two possible justifications for direct rule. The first is that it offers a possiblity of tackling a fundamental cause of the conflict in Northern Ireland. The second is that it allows the Government to maintain the initiative. On both counts, the Government have not had a good year.

The Government have introduced a series of violations of civil rights this year. This is not the place to rehearse in detail the arguments for and against the various measures. Suffice it to say that the broadcasting ban, the abolition of the right to silence and the Elected Authorities (Northern Ireland) Act 1989 have not enhanced the Government's reputation. These measures were all attempts to suppress the symptoms of the failure to find a political solution, not constructive efforts to eliminate the causes of conflict and the Government, in those circumstances, have been reacting to an agenda set by the men of violence.

I trust that the Government will not be foolish enough to endorse the claim of Sinn Fein that the broadcasting ban was responsible for the fall in the Sinn Fein vote in the district council and European elections this year. Not only would that be short-term opportunism, but Sinn Fein is already claiming it as its alibi for its disastrous results in both parts of the island in recent elections. It would be foolish of the Government to assist the IRA in its attempts to dismiss its dismal performance on the ground that it was not able to broadcast. The immorality and futility of the murder of its fellow Irishmen and women have cost it its vote. Perhaps the most striking sign of the bankruptcy of the Republican movement is what it is doing to close the Belfast-Dublin railway. In ideological terms, it could not be doing more to copper-fasten partition, and one wonders what it is up to.

The Secretary of State spoke about the legislation that he has introduced. I reiterate the Opposition's stance on Government legislation. We shall examine it carefully, and where we think that it is proper, does not in any way interfere with cherished civil liberties and is not counter-productive and has been properly examined, we shall support it. However, as an Opposition, it is our duty and our right to point out to the Government where we believe that they are making errors in their legislation. We believe that they have made errors in the past year, as we have stated in previous debates.

So far as seizing the initiative is concerned, the Government have clearly run out of ideas, as was clear from the latter part of the Secretary of State's speech. All too often in the past, there has not been enough clearly thought out or articulated policy. Events have decided what the Secretary of State was going to do, not his sense of direction. That was shown by the reaction to the tragic massacre in Ballygawley. The Government do not seem to have a sensible or coherent strategy and they allowed themselves to react to the men of violence in a counter-productive way.

However, the Government have done some things this year which are to their credit. They have not totally lost sight of the need to tackle the sources of conflict. The first step in any solution, no matter what one's views may be about the future of the Province, is to ensure equality between the two communities. Progress has been made on the issue of discrimination in employment. For much of last year the Secretary of State, the Minister responsible at the Department and the Opposition were locked in constructive debate on the terms of the Fair Employment (Northern Ireland) Bill.

It is one thing to pass legislation but another to see that it is implemented and carried forward vigorously and monitored. We will be looking for that and rapid progress in the months ahead. Having passed the legislation, we hope that the Government will not feel that that is all that they must do.

The Minister responsible for the Department of Education in Northern Ireland has taken action on cultural equality, particularly with respect to the Irish language, on education for mutual understanding and in his recent and welcome initiative on community relations. In particular, he has not leaned specifically in the direction of one community. He has said that there are two traditions, two communities and two ideas and concepts which must be savoured, supported and understood. I am sure that that is the proper way for him to act and he must owe much of his success to the advice extended to him by my hon. Friend the Member for Redcar (Ms. Mowlam).

That is the constructive side of direct rule. However, the Opposition hope that the Government have not lost sight of what has too often happened in the past. If we wish to avoid the perpetual cycle of terror and repression, we must place more emphasis on the constructive possibilities of direct rule. The Secretary of State gave some signs of that today.

Having berated the Secretary of State, I now feel an obligation on behalf of the Opposition to offer him some guidance for the future. I hope that the Secretary of State will accept that in the spirit in which it is intended. The Anglo-Irish Agreement can be exploited in a much more constructive way than hitherto, as is shown by the document which emerged from the review which seemed to adopt many of the suggestions put forward by the Labour party. In particular, the agreement can be used to tackle the economic problems of the Province. Given an expansion of Community structural funds, it makes good economic sense for both parts of Ireland to exploit jointly their objective one status and to make joint approaches to the European Commission for joint ventures in the interests and to the benefit of both parts of Ireland. There are large areas of economic and social life where such co-operation can be only beneficial. However, that can happen only if the Government do not try to be too clever by half, as they were this afternoon with regard to the use of additional funds and the concept and doctrine of additionality.

An example of the type of co-operation to which I have referred is that between Northern Ireland Railways and Irish Rail on the scheme to upgrade the Belfast-Dublin rail link to produce faster and more direct communications between the two principal cities of the island. Similar projects could go ahead. We heard earlier this afternoon about arterial roads between the different parts of the islands and their importance to the infrastructure of the islands as a whole. Projects in agriculture, energy and tourism would be eligible for EEC support and objective one status if both Governments can come together. Those projects are of the utmost importance if Ireland is to avoid the isolation with which it is threatened as a result of the Single European Act and the single market in 1992.

Perhaps the Secretary of State's most important comments came at the end of his speech this afternoon. Now that the elections are over and there is a period of

[*Mr. Ian Gow*]

stability in Northern Ireland, the opportunity exists for both communities to come together. That is ultimately desirable and necessary. The Secretary of State referred to decisions that were being taken as a result of direct rule. However, I believe that matters could rightly, properly and more efficiently be dealt with in the Province. Social matters, education, industrial development and similar policies should be decided by the people in Northern Ireland in their own assembly and councils, working together. That would be far better in the interests of the Province and far better for the self-esteem and dignity of the people in Northern Ireland.

While party representatives in this House are so obdurate in their attitude towards a devolved Government, a whole generation is being lost to politics. That generation could come together and learn to compromise. They need not be Lundies, but they could learn to work together and accept other points of view which, on occasions, must be accommodated even if that is not what people want. People from both communities could work together for the good of their communities within Northern Ireland.

Direct rule and the Anglo-Irish Agreement share the characteristic that they fill a vacuum which the party leaders in this House are capable of filling to give their own people in the North of Ireland the opportunity to take part in the positive direction of their political lives and the future of their own Province. I look forward to a time when orders on direct rule will cease and when the parties come together to present the British Government, the Opposition and this House with a scheme which they have been able to work out. The answer lies in the people in the Province, within both parts of Ireland, coming together, working it out and deciding how they want to see their island governed. That will be the decisive factor. Any British Government can act only to hold the ring for a certain length of time. They can try to help to create the circumstances in which the parties can feel that it is to their advantage to come together.

In the long run the Opposition, the Government and the House can hope only that this will be one of the last of the interim orders on direct rule. We can hope only that we can create the conditions and give what help we can to allow the people of Northern Ireland to assume the responsibility for so many things which are now decided for them in this House.

5.18 pm

**Mr. Julian Amery** (Brighton, Pavilion): In his opening remarks, the hon. Member for Kingston upon Hull, North (Mr. McNamara), drew attention to the uncertainty which has hung over the Province since 1920 about its ultimate destination. I hope that he will not think that it is inappropriate for me to state that one of the factors making for that uncertainty has been the attachment of the Labour party, however qualified, to the idea of a united Ireland. That idea has naturally loomed large in the minds of many people in the Province as they naturally feel that, who knows, there may one day be another British Government less attached to the Union than the present Government. I am sure that my right hon. Friend the Secretary of State for Northern Ireland will consider that

when he estimates the value of the practical suggestions put to him by the hon. Member for Kingston upon Hull, North.

It might have been better if the Government had granted our request to hold a debate before the review of the Anglo-Irish Agreement. That request was not granted. The review, prolonged, has taken place. The mountain has moved. I am not sure that it has produced much more than a mouse. Ministers have mainly taken credit for the improvement in relations between the RUC and the Garda. That is welcome news but every Secretary of State for Northern Ireland, from Lord Whitelaw onwards, has give us the same diet of hope. It is difficult for us, as we do not have all the information, to measure how important that improvement is. The conclusion that I find difficult to escape is that, although there has clearly been an improvement in relations between the RUC and the Garda, the IRA has also become a good deal more sophisticated. I am not sure where the balance of advantage lies in dealing with the terrorist situation.

On the economic side, we welcome my right hon. Friend's success in extracting money for Shorts. We trust that that will have a happy ending. I worked for a long time on the side of Shorts when I was Minister of Aviation and there is nothing that I would more gladly wish to see.

I come to the guts of the matter—the political situation. Here there is, as my right hon. Friend said, a stalemate. Dr. Fitzgerald tried to suggest that the SDLP was trying to encourage the minority population to co-operate with the RUC. Lord Fitt shot that down pretty effectively in his letter to *The Times*. From the Unionist party—the majority party—there is clearly no co-operation available for my right hon. Friend.

What is the origin of all this? It is not all that difficult to see. As my right hon. Friend said, he was not using phrases such as power sharing. But for 20 years now the Northern Ireland Office has had a perfectly simple formula —devolved government based on power sharing and an Irish dimension. Without the Irish dimension, the minority population will not co-operate. With the Irish dimension, the majority population will not co-operate.

What conclusion can be drawn? Listening to my right hon. Friend, I felt that I was in a curious time warp. Many years ago I was Under-Secretary of State, Colonial Office, when we still had a Colonial Office. Listening to my right hon. Friend, I could see Oliver Lyttelton and Alan Lennox-Boyd at the Dispatch Box saying, "Look here, our proposals are completely reasonable, but the natives simply won't listen. It is extraordinary. We have put forward what must seem to everybody to be the most sensible possible proposals, from which everybody will benefit. But do you think that they will listen? Not at all." It was exactly the same sort of language. I found it impressive and yet depressing. I remember supporting it as the Under-Secretary of State. It was splendid stuff—the call for power sharing between the Kikuyu and the Masai, the Greeks and the Turks, the Jews and the Arabs. It was much the same, but it never fitted the bill.

The truth is that the longer this colonial situation goes on, the more remote my right hon. Friend must become from the population. He is the governor of a colony. As the governor, he has to be even-handed. Any sign of being more favourable to the Turks than the Greeks, to the minority than to the majority, and his position becomes acutely embarrassing. He has to keep a beady eye on that.

Where do we go from here? I honestly think that the situation cannot long continue. The consequences become more serious as long as we try to pursue a policy that has now failed. It failed at Sunningdale and the "Jim Prior" Assembly; and the Anglo-Irish Agreement has failed.

What is to be done? It is not all that difficult. The first thing is to restore full local government. My right hon. Friend should not be frightened by all the tales about local authorities refusing to collect the rubbish and discriminating against one community or the other. He can suspend local government at any moment if he so wishes. He has all the powers to do that. Twenty years have gone by. He should trust the people a bit more. Let us see how they will repay his trust. That is the first thing.

Secondly, my right hon. Friend called for the representatives of the Province to exercise their rights. But we do not give them the chance to do so. He said that they can all talk to him and his colleagues, but much more important than that would be to have some sort of Northern Ireland Grand Committee. Of course it would have to be staffed by Conservative Members in order to get the business through, but at least Ministers would be forced to debate the arguments at a reasonable time of day with the representatives of the Province. They are here —17 of them. That is really quite a lot. That would be a much more sensible system. At least they could have a debate. So, we need local government, and a Grand Committee here.

Then we come to the Anglo-Irish Agreement. Perhaps we should let it turn into a security agreement between the Garda and ourselves. It does not look as if it will work any other way. But if we want to go further, my hon. Friend the Member for Eastbourne (Mr. Gow) and the "Friends of the Union" have put forward the noble concept of enlarging the Anglo-Irish Agreement to make it a general agreement between the Republic and the United Kingdom so that the Republic would have some oversight of all the United Kingdom, including the large Irish population here, and we would have an oversight of the way in which it handles its affairs—the economy, its neutrality and so on. That is a three-point programme which would not involve any great legislation.

As this is a short debate, I shall conclude with this thought. For 20 years, the Northern Ireland Office has been obsessed with the idea of power sharing and an Irish dimension. That has been attempted on three major occasions. All have failed. My experience of Government Departments, such as it is, is that they will make 20 mistakes to try to prove that they were right the first time that they made a mistake. They will never change their minds on their own. Only a strong Secretary of State can make the break and force his Department to take a new departure. I beg my right hon. Friend to do so while he is still there.

5.27 pm

**Mr. James Molyneaux** (Lagan Valley): The Secretary of State reminded us that this is about the 15th time that we have been called upon to renew what was originally a temporary order. None of us would quarrel with that statement. He was modest enough to avoid going on to draw attention to the fact that that 15th anniversary coincided with the 10th anniversary of the coming into power of the Administration of which he is a distinguished member. If the newspapers are to be believed, he has great things in store for him, but it is not for me to comment on that. I have enough difficulties as it is.

Whatever our political views may be, and wherever in the House we may sit, we have to admit that the Prime Minister and her Administration have been successful in implementing the manifestos and policies that they have adopted, particularly their strategy for the whole of the United Kingdom, not just Northern Ireland, which was set out way back in 1979. Opposition parties do not like those policies, but they cannot deny that, for better or for worse, they have been firmly implemented.

There has been one notable exception. They have failed to implement the policy for Northern Ireland. They have failed not because they have been obstructed or defeated by the warring factions in Northern Ireland or the awkward Northern Irish parties—as our colleagues in the House are inclined to call us—but because they have been defeated by two Departments of State. The right hon. Member for Brighton, Pavilion (Mr. Amery), who has long experience in these matters, drew a clear distinction between the Conservative party and a Conservative Government. The Government have been obstructed by the Northern Ireland Office, aided and abetted by the Foreign Office.

The right hon. Member for Pavilion said that that obstruction was not deliberate, and nor was it muddled thinking. It is something which the two Departments have latched on to, and so far we have not been able to divert them. The right hon. Gentleman was correct to say that only a very strong Secretary of State would be able to do that. I do not think that he was criticising the Secretary of State for Northern Ireland, any more than I am. If the present Secretary of State had the united support of the Government, the understanding, if not the full support, of the Opposition parties and the near-unanimous support of the Conservative party, it could be done.

I am not suggesting that distinguished civil servants in those Departments should be humiliated, but they have to be told that they have tendered advice after advice, submission after submission and drafts for initiative after initiative, and where have they got us? The second state has always been worse than the first. There has always been an obsession with trying something out on the high wire act in the circus when it would be sensible to lay solid foundations and to build a structure brick by brick upon those foundations. There are enough of us in the House representing the parties in Northern Ireland—I am not excluding anyone—who have it in our power to ensure that that structure will endure. I say that with great respect to the Secretary of State and in support of what has been said by the right hon. Member for Pavilion.

The Secretary of State admitted that direct rule is not satisfactory. He went on to make the curious remark that so far it had not been possible to find an alternative. I want to return to what the Conservative party—as opposed to the Government—had in mind all those years ago as a workable alternative. As time goes on, it seems more and more workable. At Question Time today, when we were discussing a Bill of Rights, the Secretary of State asserted that only today for the first time had he received constructive suggestions from the elected representatives of Northern Ireland. I know that he will be generous enough to admit on reflection that his statement was not quite accurate.

[*Mr. James Molyneaux*]

Before the Secretary of State took up his present post in Northern Ireland, we published a document called "The Way Forward", and the hon. Member for Antrim, North (Rev. Ian Paisley) made a parallel suggestion. Our document attracted considerable support and attention at the time. It was hailed as a breakthrough in providing constructive proposals, but it all ran into the sand. Shortly afterwards, the New Ireland Forum report was produced and somehow that was thought to be the bee's knees—something which would resolve all our problems. But that document was not based on reality. With all our faults, we managed to put together a document which, however deficient it may have been in some respects, dealt with political reality.

As the Secretary of State has since discovered, the section of "The Way Forward" dealing with a Bill of Rights occupied the best part of two pages in which we set out the reasons why it should be considered in Northern Ireland. While I share the Secretary of State's view that the objective would be best served by a Bill of Rights embracing the entire United Kingdom, I do not think that that is an insurmountable barrier between us. "The Way Forward" contained constructive proposals for meaningful local government. That point has been raised today by the right hon. Member for Pavilion and the hon. Member for Newbury (Sir. M. McNair-Wilson).

I want to refer to the hon. Members for Newry and Armagh (Mr. Mallon) and for South Down (Mr. McGrady). I know that the SDLP has reservations about the powers of local government. While I do not accept the validity of those reservations, I understand why it feels that way. But with great respect, I ask the hon. Members to remember that there is a whole range of functions which do not involve advantage or disadvantage to any political party or any creed in Northern Ireland. They should also be reassured by the fact that, for the foreseeable future, there will be a Secretary of State for Northern Ireland. Perhaps it will not be the same person, but there will be a Secretary of State for Northern Ireland of whichever party.

An hon. Member said that, if power were given to local government, local councils would not empty bins for people they did not like. Ministers will remember that one council refused to do that on a point of principle. A Minister of the day, who is no longer on the Front Bench, but is still a Member, came to me in a state of anxiety. I asked him what he was going to do. He said, "If they do not carry out their duties, I will have to do the job from the Department of the Environment over their heads. Will you not talk to them to prevent that?" I said, "I shall do no such thing. You are the person who should talk to them." He issued a fairly stiff letter to the council warning that if it refused to carry out its duty the Department would do the job over its head and charge the cost to the council and the ratepayers. Honour was satisfied as the councillors could say, "We have no option. It has to be done, because the Minister has taken a grip on the situation. He is forcing us to do it. What can we do but obey him?" We all know that such situations occur in Great Britain. It is a question of checks and balances and no one but a fool would attempt to deny that it works if the responsibility is shared.

I shall quote briefly from "The Way Forward". Why should anyone fear the devolution of powers to district councils to repair and maintain roads? The document states:

"Roads owe no allegiance to those who travel upon them and, for the traveller, such roads are neither green nor orange but only good or bad. It would be a start if the travellers were given a chance to repair them."

That is an interesting point.

**Mr. Seamus Mallon** (Newry and Armagh): As the right hon. Gentleman is the leader of the majority party and people in Northern Ireland, I thought that he would draw an analogy between the collection of bins and the potholes in roads and a solution to our problems. He may be about to do that. As a representative of the minority community in Northern Ireland, I look forward to hearing his views on the real issue that is at stake today—how we proceed to a solution—rather than how we collect the bins.

**Mr. Molyneaux:** I accept that bins were a facetious example but that is not untypical of the functions to which local government councillors are restricted now. I am saying, give them more power and see whether they can be trusted.

Before the local council elections it was said that if the councils were not restrained, the majority in a given council would grab a monopoly of seats. I accept that that still happens. However, there are many different examples and I think that the Secretary of State had one in mind. My party would usually represent the majority on Armagh council. The hon. Member for Antrim, North will confirm that the chair of the council is held by a member of the Democratic Unionist party and that the vice-chair is held by a member of the Social Democratic and Labour party. That was the point made by the Secretary of State. It may seem to be small beer to some hon. Members, but it points to a happier future.

The hon. Member for Newbury asked in his intervention why, in view of the turnout at the local government election, there was supposed to be widespread frustration over the lack of progress. A total of 59·5 per cent. of the electorate turned out to vote and I seem to remember a parliamentary by-election in Vauxhall not long ago at which there was a staggering turnout of 42 per cent. Given that 59·5 per cent. of the electorate turned out, are those people not entitled to expect that the powers of their newly elected councillors will be increased, not diminished?

The Secretary of State referred to access to Ministers. I remind him that that was made use of in 1985 when the Anglo-Irish Agreement was being drafted. I talked to the present Home Secretary when he was Secretary of State for Northern Ireland and urged him privately to go cautiously and not to follow the route that had been mapped out in the newspapers over eight or nine months. I advised against the course upon which the Government seemed to be embarking. The hon. Member for Antrim, North and I met the Prime Minister late on a Friday night at Downing street at the end of August in that year. We put to her not just our objections—we would have been shirking our duty if we had simply said "no"—but specific proposals as an alternative to those being designed. Our proposals are on the record.

The Secretary of State will remember that when he took office halfway through the operation he was kind enough to arrange a meeting with the Prime Minister. When the hon. Member for Antrim, North and I met the Prime Minister and the Secretary of State we had a lengthy discussion. We elaborated upon the proposals we had put at the previous meeting and pleaded with them to avoid confrontation. They listened politely, but when the agreement appeared in its final form it was clear that our suggestions had been ignored. A civil servant who retired fairly recently from the plush seats explained a few months ago why we had to be ignored, why we could not be further consulted and why we could not be taken into the Government's confidence. He said that they did not consult the Unionists because they might have objected. That is a curious and defective way to conduct democracy.

After the new Parliament was elected at the 1987 general election the hon. Member for Antrim, North and I talked to the Secretary of State and his senior colleagues in the Northern Ireland Office for seven months. The hon. Member for Antrim, North will confirm that we were given the impression that we were getting somewhere and that there was good faith on both sides of the table. At the end of those months we drew our thoughts together and put them down on paper. Even more importantly, we put forward outline proposals for a better and more workable British-Irish agreement and for workable structures within Northern Ireland itself.

I say to the Secretary of State without anger, what good did that do? Why do Her Majesty's Government behave as if we had refused to make constructive suggestions when they know, from the Prime Minister downwards, that those proposals are still on the table?

I have put forward in this debate a proposal on local government. I suggest also that in regard to the Anglo-Irish Agreement Her Majesty's Government should at least match what appears to be the Dublin Government's willingness to consider an alternative agreement. That is not an unreasonable suggestion. Also, significant powers should be given, with safeguards, to the district councils. The Secretary of State and his Ministers will know from experience and from watching the pattern of nominations, elections and so on that unless some progress is made, all the parties in Northern Ireland will find it difficult to recruit competent people to represent the electorate and the ratepayers in the council chambers. We cannot continue in this powerless state for another term.

I want to make another suggestion that has already been touched upon. We should have legislation by Bill rather than by Order in Council. In my simple view that should have been done in 1972. When Stormont was abolished, Her Majesty's Government should have said —it was a Conservative Government, although fortunately not the same Prime Minister—"We have taken power to ourselves and we are now going to legislate for Northern Ireland in the same way as for the rest of the United Kingdom." That is not integration. If it is, the Conservative Government at the time should have realised what they were doing. I do not want to reopen old wounds, but the parties in Northern Ireland that advocated and brought about the abolition of Stormont should have recognised that they were taking a step closer to integration. The move to legislation by Bills was not taken in 1972 and it should have been taken in 1974 when the present Northern Ireland Act was introduced. Fifteen years is far too long.

**Mr. Amery:** I think that the right hon. Gentleman is coming to a point I tried to raise. Would he be in favour of a Northern Ireland Grand Committee where all matters affecting Northern Ireland could be debated? No doubt the Government would have to have a majority on the Committee, but the right hon. Gentleman and his colleagues could debate in detail with Ministers issues affecting Northern Ireland.

**Mr. Molyneaux:** That would be an attractive suggestion, but it would have the same defect as the Northern Ireland Committee which still exists on paper. As long as the Anglo-Irish Agreement remains in force it would be futile to engage in such an operation because, willy-nilly, it would become part of that infernal process. We have been through all this before. Ministers would never come to the Committee and explain precisely why they were introducing certain items of legislation which had already been referred to and foreshadowed in a communiqué from the Anglo-Irish Conference. They cannot say that the Dublin Government do not have an influence when that Government and Her Majesty's Government boast that they have agreed on the promotion of certain legislation in specific areas.

The Secretary of State repeated his request for suggestions and I——

**Mr. Tom King:** I think that the right hon. Gentleman is getting into a bit of a muddle. I thought that he was asking for greater opportunity to debate measures. The suggestion made by my right hon. Friend the Member for Brighton, Pavilion (Sir J. Amery) was that that should take place on the Floor of the House and I thought that the right hon. Gentleman said that he would be willing to participate in such debates. If that is not possible, my right hon. Friend talked about the possibility of some form of Grand Committee and I also thought that the right hon. Gentleman said he would participate in that. I thought that he was looking for more time to debate issues affecting Northern Ireland. However, when another forum is suggested he says that he would not be prepared to participate. That does not seem to be consistent.

**Mr. Molyneaux:** As the Secretary of State will concede, the relevant part of the mechanism, the equivalent of the Floor of the House, is the Committees dealing with Northern Ireland legislation. We and all other parties have representatives on them. The Northern Ireland Committee, as presently constituted, is a toothless body and unless the Northern Ireland Grand Committee were given powers greatly in advance of those of the Scottish Grand Committee, it would not be an attractive idea for the reason I have given. However, it would be at least worth considering.

The Secretary of State repeated honestly and openly a request for suggestions on what we might like to see. I return to my opening sentences. The present Prime Minister and the late Airey Neave, backed by the then Shadow Cabinet, brought forward proposals for a master plan which was set out in brief in the manifesto that was endorsed by the electorate of the whole of the United Kingdom when it elected a Conservative Government in 1979. The manifesto contained firm proposals. It provided for making a start—I stress that it was not an end in itself —on restoring some degree of control and responsibility to elected representatives of the people of Northern Ireland. That was an important objective. Yet that is the only part of the manifesto that has not yet been implemented after 10 years.

[*Mr. Molyneaux*]

Armed as we are with the results of two elections in Northern Ireland, I am not sufficiently arrogant to stand here in the House and demand the implementation of Ulster Unionist policies. I will settle for something far more reasonable and modest than that. I simply ask a Conservative Government to consider getting around to the implementation of Conservative party policies.

5.51 pm

**Mr. Ian Gow** (Eastbourne): I shall not disappoint the hon. Member for Kingston upon Hull, North (Mr. McNamara). I will begin by asserting my belief that the most important single factor in prolonging the tragedy in Northern Ireland is uncertainty about the constitutional future of the Province. I want to follow up a point made by my right hon. Friend the Member for Brighton, Pavilion (Mr. Amery). He referred to the days when he was an Under-Secretary of State at the Colonial Office. He did not remind the House, although he might have done, that he was also Minister of State at the Foreign and Commonwealth Office.

I want to illustrate by example how uncertainty can bring about the very evil it is sought to redress. After the 1979 election, it was clear that the Republic of Argentina was stepping up its claim to the territory of the Falkland islands. It is, of course, the duty of the Foreign and Commonwealth Office to seek to resolve all disputes by peaceful means. Thus, although it was, and remains, the policy and conviction of Her Majesty's Government that sovereignty over the Falkland islands remains lawfully and properly with the Crown, the idea was dreamed up that if one was able to transfer ownership of the islands to Argentina and then take a 99 year leaseback, that would settle the problem of the claim by the Argentine to the British territory of the Falkland islands.

Precisely the wrong signal was sent to the men of violence when that suggestion was made by the British Government. When the junta understood that, although was said that there was no validity in the Argentine claim, nevertheless we would transfer the islands and then lease them back, the Argentine Government believed that we would not be serious in defending the rights of the British people of the Falkland islands.

I will give another example and my right hon. Friend the Member for Brighton, Pavilion may think that I am straying into the world of fantasy. I do not think so. The Republic of Ireland has always claimed—and its constitution still claims—the territory of Northern Ireland. That claim is denied by Her Majesty's Government. The Foreign and Commonwealth Office dreamed up another scheme which was that we would give the Republic a position of special privilege in relation to Northern Ireland; that we would give the Republic the right to put forward views and proposals about how one part of this Kingdom should be governed;, and we laid a duty on Her Majesty's Government, if they disagreed with those views and proposals, to make determined efforts to resolve the differences.

Many people believed that the Anglo-Irish Agreement would never have been signed unless it had been preceded by a prolonged campaign of terrorist violence. What signal was sent by the Anglo-Irish Agreement to the men of violence? I assert that the same signal was sent by the

proposal for a transfer and leaseback of the Falklands to the men of violence in the south Atlantic, as was sent to the men of violence in Ireland by the signing of the AngloIrish Agreement. It added to the constitutional uncertainty of the Province. Northern Ireland has become a bit greener, and it is that perception that has encouraged terrorists to believe that if they can go on a bit longer, they will wring even further concessions from Her Majesty's Ministers.

I want to mark to the House how significant has been the change in policy, even of my own party, in recent years. I want to begin by quoting with approval the words used by my right hon. Friend's friend and mine, Airey Neave. I will quote what he said in Belfast on 7 April 1978, when he was addressing a meeting of the Ulster Unionist Council at which my right hon. Friend the Member for Lagan Valley (Mr. Molyneaux) was present. He said:

"I am able to speak of fundamental principles . . . Foremost of these is the Conservative faith and belief in the Union of Great Britain and Northern Ireland . . . Let no-one in Dublin be under any illusion".

He might have added, "Let no one who is contemplating violence be under any illusion," He continued:

"the Conservative Party stands four-square for the Union of Great Britain and Northern Ireland."

That was a ringing declaration of purpose made in April 1978.

I want now to quote with approval from a speech made only two months later by my right hon. Friend the Prime Minister. She too had gone to address the Ulster Unionist Council in Belfast and, again, my right hon. Friend the Member for Lagan Valley was present. My right hon. Friend the Prime Minister said:

"Our two parties"—

that is, the Ulster Unionist party and the Conservative and Unionist party—

"share one over-riding common purpose—the maintenance and strengthening of the Union of Great Britain and Northern Ireland."

That was said 11 years ago.

I then turned to the manifesto on which my right hon. Friend the Secretary of State and I fought the last election. Do we find a ringing declaration similar to that made by Airey Neave and my right hon. Friend the Prime Minister in that manifesto? We do not. This is what my own party had to say about Northern Ireland:

"There will be no change in the present status of Northern Ireland as part of the United Kingdom unless the people of Northern Ireland so wish it."

I wonder whether the House can mark the contrast between the assertion of our last manifesto, which is without any conviction or declaration of policy and what was said in 1978 by the then Shadow Secretary of State for Northern Ireland and the then Leader of Her Majesty's Opposition.

My right hon. Friend the Member for Pavilion was right when he referred to the policy of the Labour party. The Labour party's manifesto stated:

"We believe in an united Ireland: to be achieved peacefully, democratically, and by consent."

The Labour party has moved its policy objective towards a united Ireland. In the most solemn declaration that one could make—a party manifesto—my own party has abandoned the language that was used in 1978. I believe that the abandonment of that language and of the commitment to maintain and strengthen the Union is prolonging the tragedy in Northern Ireland.

**Mr. Tom King:** I regret the line of argument that my hon. Friend is taking. I do not believe that he is seeking to say to the House that the views of either my right hon. Friend the Prime Minister or of myself have changed in respect of the Union. He knows that that is not true. He knows our policy and he knows where we stand on those matters. He knows that we have made our determination to support the position of the majority in Northern Ireland absolutely clear. I have made no secret of that. I often wonder whether my hon. Friend has reflected on something that worries me, which is that by implying that somehow that determination has changed he perhaps falls into that trap which it was his concern to avoid in raising this matter in the first place.

**Mr. Gow:** I do not follow my right hon. Friend's intervention, but if he is telling the House that there has been no change in the view of the Prime Minister or in the Prime Minister's choice of words, I shall reply by giving him a quotation. On 29 July 1982 my right hon. Friend the Prime Minister said in the House of Commons—I remember it because I was her private secretary at the time—

"no commitment exists for Her Majesty's Government to consult the Irish Government on matters affecting Northern Ireland. That has always been our position. We reiterate and emphasise it, so that everyone is clear about it."—[*Official Report,* 29 July 1982; Vol. 28, c. 1126.]

My right hon. Friend the Secretary of State does not quarrel when I say that those were the words used by the Prime Minister in this place on 29 July 1982, and that those are not words that the Prime Minister would be able to use now. I am simply saying that there is a contrast.

I agree with the suggestions made by my right hon. Friends the Members for Lagan Valley and for Pavilion. However, why has my right hon. Friend the Secretary of State, who is now the longest serving Secretary of State for Northern Ireland ever, abandoned the policy that was worked out so carefully during the four years when Airey Neave was a shadow Secretary of State for Northern Ireland? I have never had a convincing answer from my right hon. Friend about why we abandoned the policy in the manifesto.

Why have we not tried to set up a regional council in Northern Ireland with widely devolved powers over local matters? What is the objection to trying to do that? What is the objection to giving modest additional powers to the 26 district councils and to setting up a regional council? What is the objection to ceasing to legislate for Northern Ireland by Order in Council? When my hon. Friend the Under-Secretary of State replies to the debate, will he tell us why he will not confer modest extra powers on those 26 district councils? Will he tell us why he will not seek to set up a regional council and why he continues to insist on legislating for Northern Ireland by Order in Council?

**Mr. Ken Maginnis** (Fermanagh and South Tyrone): In answer to the hon. Gentleman's questions, I say simply that it is because the Secretary of State for Northern Ireland recognises that we are moving towards 1992 that that process has begun. With the present arrangement between the Irish Republic and the United Kingdom it will, de facto, be possible to absorb Northern Ireland into an administrative all-Ireland arrangement. That is what is satisfying to the Secretary of State for Northern Ireland and that is why he has not given the hon. Gentleman a proper answer to his question.

**Mr. Gow:** I find myself in fundamental, but of course, respectful, disagreement with the hon. Gentleman because

I do not believe that the reasons that he attributed to my right hon. Friend the Secretary of State have ever entered his head. My right hon. Friend can dissent——

**Rev. Ian Paisley:** It may not have entered the head of the Secretary of State, but his partner at the Anglo-Irish conference, Mr. Lenihan, said exactly that and spelt it out in all the newspapers at the election.

**Mr. Gow:** I have expressed my view, which is that the views of the hon. Member for Fermanagh and South Tyrone (Mr. Maginnis) have never entered the head of my right hon. Friend the Secretary of State.

There are many ways in which Her Majesty's subjects living in Northern Ireland are disadvantaged when compared with her subjects living in Brighton, Bridgwater or Eastbourne. In Bridgwater, as in Brighton, people are able to vote for councils with fairly substantial powers—the district councils. The people of Bridgwater and of Brighton are able to vote for county councils. The Members of Parliament for Bridgwater and for Brighton are able to table amendments to legislation affecting their constituents. The people of Bridgwater and of Brighton are to have conferred upon them from 1 April 1990 the inestimable benefits of the community charge. Those benefits are being denied to the constituents of my right hon. Friend the Member for Lagan Valley and to the constituents of my hon. Friend the Member for Fermanagh and South Tyrone. Why those differences? Why treat unequally and disadvantage the people of Northern Ireland.

I was depressed by my right hon. Friend the Member for Pavilion using the colonial analogy and talking about "natives". However, from what my right hon. Friend the Secretary of State seemed to be saying, I advise him that he cannot make any progress in improving the quality of government in Northern Ireland because the Social Democratic and Labour party, the Democratic Unionist party and the Ulster Unionist party either will not talk to him or will not reach agreement with him.

I advise my right hon. Friend the Secretary of State that when those concerned cannot reach agreement, it is the task of statesmen to proceed with the policy and system of government that is best. After all, we have a system of government now which even my right hon. Friend the Secretary of State says is not the best. If the people of Bridgwater are tolerably well governed under the system of district and county councils and by legislation which is amendable, why not treat the people of Northern Ireland in the same way? To say that the people of Northern Ireland are somehow constitutionally different is further to encourage those who believe that if they continue with terror long enough, somehow the resolve of this House and of the British people will weaken. The more that we govern Northern Ireland differently from the remainder of the kingdom, the more we will add to that uncertainty.

My right hon. Friend will not gain agreement among all the parties in Northern Ireland on the right form of government. Indeed, there is no agreement on the present form of government. Why not show leadership and give modest additional powers to the district councils? Why not try a little local government, as Airey Neave recommended? Why not try giving those hon. Members who represent Northern Ireland seats that right to amend prospective legislation that is conferred upon every other hon. Member? What reason can there be for denying them

[*Mr. Gow*]

the rights conferred on us? Why cannot there be a community charge in Northern Ireland? Is it because the Republic does not like it, because my right hon. Friend does not like it, or for other reasons? When my hon. Friend the Minister replies to the debate, I hope that he will tell us why those great advantages are to be denied to the people of Northern Ireland.

This debate is about the government of Northern Ireland. The proposals by the hon. Member for Eastbourne are hardly revolutionary or dramatic. In fact, they add up to giving the 1·5 million people of Northern Ireland those rights that my right hon. Friend believes should properly be conferred upon the people of Somerset, Essex and east Sussex. They are not very dramatic, but they would be a signal to those who believe that the more we govern Northern Ireland differently, the easier it will be to detach Northern Ireland. They will serve as a signal to friend and foe alike.

Two hon. Members represent the Social Democratic and Labour party in this place. To my great regret, their role and the role of the nationalists in Northern Ireland has been undermined by the Anglo-Irish Agreement. It actually confers upon the Republic that duty to represent nationalists that properly rests with the elected national-ists. I honour, acknowledge and respect constitutional nationalists in Northern Ireland, as I acknowledge, honour and respect constitutional nationalists in Scotland and in Wales.

The hon. Members for Foyle (Mr. Hume) and for Newry and Armagh (Mr. Mallon) are as vigilant as ever in the interests of their constituencies in this place, but they have been undermined by the Anglo-Irish Agreement. I say to them that, if we could have equal treatment for the people of Northern Ireland with the people of the remainder of the kingdom, certainly the place of Nationalists would be protected under a just law. If any of the fears of either of those two hon. Members about wrong doing and discrimination by certain district councils should ever come about, blessedly it would be possible —as has been the case with the Local Government and Housing Bill—to build in protections and have a specially empowered ombudsman to protect the interests of the minority.

I hope that, when we next debate this subject, my right hon. Friend the Secretary of State will come to the House with proposals, rather than just saying, "I am paralysed unless and until there is agreement among the political parties in the Province."

6.14 pm

**Mr. Seamus Mallon** (Newry and Armagh): This debate has been in many ways most interesting and in many ways most distressing. From the start, we have listened to the various strands of Unionism in this House propounding their particular form of Unionism—with the notable exception of the hon. Member for Kingston upon Hull, North (Mr. McNamara).

We have listened with great interest—indeed, almost great intrigue—to the Unionism of the time warp, as expressed by the right hon. Member for Brighton, Pavilion (Mr. Amery) and the hon. Member for Eastbourne (Mr. Gow). I hope that no offence will be taken if I say that it reminded me of a line that every nationalist in Ireland has

been aware of since childhood—"The ghost of Roger Casement is knocking at the door." It is almost as if the ghost of Airey Neave, who was very much respected both inside and outside the House, is still knocking at the door of that section of Conservative party Unionism in a way that is now an anachronism. The Unionism that has been expounded by Conservatives today is anachronistic. It is not part of the 1980s and nor will it be part of the 1990s. It is certainly not the basis to take us into a new century.

Another sort of Unionism is that expressed by one section in the North of Ireland. I listened with great interest for something within that that would allow me, as a representative of the nationalist tradition, the opposing tradition, to come out of the debate with the hope that somehow, before our next debate next year, something would allow us to move from the present position. I was disappointed. We did a tour of potholed roads, we did a tour in the dustbin lorry, but we came nowhere near that sign of hope.

The playright Pirandello, who certainly did not run in the European elections for an Italian constituency, once wrote a play entitled "Six Characters in Search of an Author". The North of Ireland is becoming almost analogous to that. It is almost as though the political parties in the North of Ireland are sitting on that stage hoping that someone will write the script for them, put in the stage directions, give them the motivation for the plot and, somehow, somewhere, drop from the skies and provide everything to turn it into the theatrical performance that it would be. We could amend the title of the play to "Six Counties in search of a solution." One of the great advantages—probably the only great advantage —of having two elections one after the other in the North of Ireland is the message heard by everyone involved in the elections about the desire for a solution in the North of Ireland.

Today we should not be discussing what happened in the past, and not become involved in the time warps; we should be recognising that there is now a mood and aclimate within the North of Ireland that wants to solve the problems. Rather than throw theories at each other —which is what we have done so far with local government, regional councils or whatever—we should be trying to lay a basis for a solution, and that basis should be that we are willing to move constructively and substantially towards finding that solution, whatever it may be. Today is not a day for writing into the record the sort of solution that any Unionist or, indeed, any nationalist party might want. Today is a day to get that resolve built into the body politic both in the House and in the North of Ireland. That, somehow, will give those Six Counties at least the beginnings of the solution that they very much crave.

That is essential for a number of reasons. I do not want to go over the recent past or the events of the past year —indeed, I do not want to go over the past at all—but I challenge the assumption inherent in the thesis of the right hon. Member for Pavilion (Mr. Amery) and in the remarks of the hon. Member for Eastbourne and of the right hon. Member for Lagan Valley (Mr. Molyneaux), that others, not us, in Northern Ireland should assume the onus for solving the problems that we face.

They seem to believe that by some means, perhaps by having, say, another Committee upstairs, there should be a different way of considering legislation—but that others, whoever they may be, should bear the brunt of finding the solutions to our problems.

That is a cop-out. It is cowardly, although I accept that it is not meant to be. After all, we are the senior political figures who have been elected in the North of Ireland. To borrow a phrase from President Truman, the buck stops here. It stops with the senior people elected in Northern Ireland, and that means us. It does not mean district councillors, most if not all of whom are part-time political representatives, most of whom do not have the resources or time to do what we have asked of them in relation to this measure. That is an essential fallacy in the time warp proposition that hon. Members have made in the debate.

Our job is to lead in search of that solution, and the only way in which we can start to give that leadership and lay the basis for finding that solution is to start to talk. Is there not something unbelievable, if not obscene, given the violence in the North of Ireland, that the constitutional political parties have not engaged in any dialogue for I forget how many years? Is there not something which will condemn us all in the eyes not just of our opposition but of those whom we represent when we have not sat down at a table together to try to talk about the problem and reach a solution to it? We all stand indicted and condemned for that. If we are to move forward, talking must be the first step.

The comments of the Secretary of State deserve a response. He was right to say that no Secretary of State or anyone else can come to the North of Ireland with a proposition and say, "There is the initiative. There is the solution to the problems." Such a solution does not exist. If we have learnt anything from the past—from the last year or 20 years or 70 years—it is that the single immutable factor which will not change is that, irrespective of what happens here or anywhere else, the people of Northern Ireland—the nationalists, the Unionists, the Catholics and the Protestants—will go on living there cheek by jowl.

They can live in the way they are living now, with violence all around them, in a shaky and unstable political situation and with all the disadvantages which derive from that shaky and dubious type of political situation. Or they can ask, "Why should the world pass us by? Why should we not have all the advantages that we can get? Why should we not take part in the building process as the rest of Europe around us builds? Why must we in the North of Ireland always be the people who get the raw end of every stick?"

Those questions should be asked and answered, and unless we start to answer them—and I am not one for making predictions—we shall see a disintegration of the political process in the North of Ireland.

Take a close look at the results in the urban areas of the local government elections. Let us not forget that in Northern Ireland now there is an enormous divide between the urban and rural areas. The percentages reach 58, but not in the urban areas; in those parts they reach perhaps 32, as in the European elections. That is worrying, because it is the beginning of a lack of confidence in the political process, and I fear that that is writ large on all the gable walls in Belfast, Derry, Newry, Dungannon and everywhere else. If we do not heed that, we shall be putting the future of the North of Ireland in peril.

I said that I did not wish to rake over the past. The past is over. If we want to, we can engage in rhetoric and give examples of why we should or should not do anything. The

past is there and it is our job to create the future. Now there is an opportunity for all political parties in the North of Ireland to respond to the Secretary of State and to say in unequivocal terms, "Yes, we are prepared to enter into discussions with you or without you about the future of the people whom we represent."

We have the opportunity to say that now, and I wish to put on record on behalf of my party that we wish to say, "Yes, the time for talking is now." We wish to see the response to that. We wish to set the time and date for those discussions, however long they may take or difficult they may be. So long as they do not deal in peripheral matters and so long as they are aimed at getting a solution to the problems, we can start talking, and this debate will have been worth while.

But if we do not get a positive response in that way, the message will go out clearly from this House that the age-old quarrel still exists, that the past is that to which we hark, rather than to the future, and that the political process is again about to fail the people of the North of Ireland.

**Mr. Maginnis:** What the hon. Gentleman says sounds fine. The offer, coming from where he stands now, sounds as though it is genuine, but let me ask him a simple question. Is he prepared to disagree with the Fianna Fail manifesto which professed that the only solution to the Northern Ireland problems was within an all-Ireland context? Will he say here and now that he disagrees with that opinion, and hence give us an opportunity, without any veto, to take up his offer?

**Mr. Mallon:** I have not read the Fianna Fail manifesto.

**Mr. Maginnis:** Take my word for it.

**Mr. Mallon:** I will certainly take the hon. Gentleman's word about its contents. I was too busy with two elections in Northern Ireland to be reading Republic of Ireland election manifestos. If the hon. Gentleman wants me to state my political position in relation to the ultimate solution in the island of Ireland, he can have it clearly. He knows well that I and my party believe in working peacefully and constructively towards persuading others that unity within Ireland is the ultimate solution. I believe that to be the ultimate position and that it can be positive and constructive.

**Mr. Maginnis:** Now answer the question I asked.

**Mr. Mallon:** I was kind enough to give way to the hon. Gentleman. I willingly give way to him again if he wishes to restate the question, and he may make a better job of doing so.

**Mr. Maginnis:** Will the hon. Gentleman say that there is a solution, or the possibility of a solution, to the problem in Northern Ireland that does not entail the condition that it must be within an all-Ireland context?

**Mr. Mallon:** I thank the hon. Member for Fermanagh and South Tyrone (Mr. Maginnis) for his intervention. I have made it abundantly clear time after time that I regard the creation of Irish unity as the lasting solution. I am talking today about starting to solve the problems. I have made it clear also that, irrespective of what happens, the people of the North of Ireland will live cheek by jowl with each other, and they will do so for a considerable period. I advise anybody who wishes to wait for the ultimate

[*Mr. Mallon*]

position that I espouse not to hold their breath, or they will be in severe difficulties again. The problems are the challenges of today. We can indulge in debating our political positions, but while we are doing that, the people of the North of Ireland—those on the housing estates, on the small farms and on the streets—are suffering and being neglected, and we are denying them hope. I ask all hon. Members to read *Hansard* tomorrow and, for the first time in a long time, see a glimmer of hope.

I began my speech with an analogy from the theatre. I will go from Pirandello to Shakespeare. We should closely examine the last scene of "Hamlet", when all the protagonists are lying dead on the stage. Who mounts the throne? It is young Fortinbras who had gone off to war. The analogy is stark. If the problem continues, all the protagonists, many of whom are present, will be the victims of the loss of confidence in the political process in the North of Ireland. Who might young Fortinbras be?

6.31 pm

**Rev. Ian Paisley** (Antrim, North): In this debate, an attack was launched against the Ulster Defence Regiment. My first duty in the House, as a representative from Northern Ireland, is to defend that regiment. I will defend it simply by quoting the statistics that were used by the hon. Member for Foyle (Mr. Hume) at his own party conference. They are not doctored, exaggerated Unionist statistics; they are statistics given by the leader of the SDLP. At his conference on 26 November, he was asked:

"Up till last Saturday 2,705 people have died in the 20-year period of the current troubles . . . who killed all these people?"

His answer was:

"The statistics are devastating. 44 per cent. were killed by the provisional IRA and 18 per cent. by their fellow travelling 'republican' paramilitaries. 27 per cent. were killed by Loyalists. 10 per cent. were killed by the British Army. 2 per cent. were killed by the RUC and 0·28 per cent. by the UDR."

So of all the people indicted for killings or responsible for killings, the UDR was responsible for 0·28 per cent. I wonder why such attacks are launched against the Ulster Defence Regiment when it is not responsible for the large number of killings that are included in such statistics.

It is very strange that the spokesman of Her Majesty's loyal Opposition, the hon. Member for Kingston upon Hull, North (Mr. McNamara) should take such an attitude against the Ulster Defence Regiment. It is even stranger for the leader of the Liberal Democrats or Social Democrats, or whatever they like to call themselves, to make such remarks against the Ulster Defence Regiment. I cast those remarks back into his teeth. I strongly consider that the view of the people of Northern Ireland should be stated in the House today. I will leave the matter there.

Hon. Members heard pleas for democracy today, not least from the Secretary of State. I stand appalled that the Secretary of State had the audacity to go to the Dispatch Box and make a plea to the representatives of the majority community in Northern Ireland now to yield to democracy. Let us look at the record of the Anglo-Irish Agreement and at what successive British Governments have done for democracy in Northern Ireland. If ever democracy in Ulster has been slaughtered, it has been slaughtered by politicians on both sides of the House.

The hon. Member for Eastbourne (Mr. Gow) spoke with great feeling. He vividly and dramatically traced the change of attitude, change of face and, to Ulster Unionists, the right about-turn in the Conservative party's commitment to Northern Ireland as an integral part of the United Kingdom. I remember asking the Prime Minister whether she believed that any other Government but her Government, any other Parliament but this Parliament and any other people but the people of Northern Ireland have the right to decide the future government of Northern Ireland. She affirmed that her Government, this Parliament and the people of Northern Ireland were the only people who should be concerned with the government of Northern Ireland.

The Anglo-Irish Agreement was hatched without any effort to deal with Unionist opposition. The right hon. Member for Lagan Valley (Mr. Molyneaux) quoted the words of a prominent civil servant who said that the Government could not just have listened to the words of the Unionists, for they would have objected. What is the Anglo-Irish Agreement? It is an agreement to have a conference at which everything in regard to the government of Northern Ireland is discussed in secrecy by the representatives of Her Majesty's Government and of the Dublin Government. The representatives of this Government have given a clear undertaking that they will seek agreement where there is disagreement. Also, boards in Northern Ireland have some little authority, but the South of Ireland has the right to suggest who should serve on those boards, but representatives in this House from Northern Ireland have no right or authority to do any such thing.

Democracy in Northern Ireland has been killed by the Anglo-Irish Agreement. The hon. Member for Eastbourne is right. It delivered to the Anglo-Irish Conference representatives from Dublin the rights of the nationalist representatives who should have been fighting the case for their own people.

We are told that the Unionists are paralysed, that they have nothing to offer. The Unionists have put their proposals to the Secretary of State. I have a letter from the Prime Minister in which she admits that they are concrete, constructive proposals, yet they are now forgotten. We are not paralysed. The hon. Member for Newry and Armagh (Mr. Mallon) said something that I hope will go to the hearts of all hon. Members. He said that democracy will be destroyed in Northern Ireland if the ballot box is not listened to. The ballot box is not being listened to. The House has tried to destroy the ballot box in Northern Ireland. That is why people are reticent about voting. They ask, "What is the use of voting, when election victories do not bring us any nearer to being listened to?" Those are the facts that the House has to face.

My plea is simple. The Government should say, "We took a wrong turning. We should have consulted the majority. Let us lay aside the Anglo-Irish Agreement and the working of Maryfield. Let the people who really feel that something can be got to satisfy at least the majority of the people on both sides of the divide in Northern Ireland have a say. Let the parties come together and discuss, not in the cage of the Anglo-Irish Agreement but in freedom."

I will not negotiate at any table where the sword is drawn and is hanging over my head. I want to negotiate in freedom. That is all that the Ulster Unionist people ask. I am sorry, Mr. Speaker, that I cannot prolong my speech. I promised to sit down at 20 minutes to 7, and I shall keep my word.

6.41 pm

**Mr. McNamara:** With the leave of the House, I shall be extremely brief. The vision of the Anglo-Irish Agreement being a sword over anyone's head or a threat to anyone in Northern Ireland is a profound travesty of the truth. All the parties within Northern Ireland have the ability to take away from the Anglo-Irish Agreement those elements where the Government of the Republic have the right to intervene. They have the power by agreeing on a form of devolved government and on the powers that it should have. As the parties go to a devolved assembly in the North of Ireland, so they go away from the intergovernmental conference and Maryfield.

Perhaps the hon. Member for Antrim, North (Rev. Ian Paisley) did not listen carefully to what I said about the Ulster Defence Regiment. I said that it is an unfortunate but undeniable fact that the minority community does not regard the UDR as a peace-keeping force; indeed, it views the UDR in a much less favourable light than it does the Regular Army and the RUC. That is a fact. It is not a question whether it is something with which I agree or disagree, or which I purport to support or not to support. It is a tragedy that, when we want people to have confidence in the administration of security matters in Northern Ireland, the UDR is not acceptable. That is part of the challenge faced by the regiment and by the Government.

**Mr. Gow:** I think that it would be helpful if the hon. Gentleman could bring himself to say that he has confidence in the Ulster Defence Regiment.

**Mr. McNamara:** I believe that there is every potential for there being confidence in the UDR. I believe that many members of the regiment go out to do their duty correctly, properly and in a disciplined manner. Indeed, they do their duty courageously on many occasions. I do not deny that, but it does not take away from the fact that there have been bad apples in the barrel or from the fact that is not the way the regiment is seen by the nationalist community. That is the problem to which I was referring.

I shall not delay the House further. The Minister wishes to reply and we wish to know how he has been pursuing his investigations and his discussions with the parties.

6.44 pm

**The Parliamentary Under-Secretary of State for Northern Ireland (Dr. Brian Mawhinney):** In terms of membership of the House, I am among the most junior of those who have taken part in the debate. Yet this is the 11th debate on Northern Ireland in my time here, and I have attended them all. I think that the substance and the tone of the debate have been more constructive than any that I can remember.

The debate is set against a world that has changed since we discussed the subject 12 months ago. Perhaps the greatest change is reflected in the fact that we have had two elections in Northern Ireland in that time. As the debate is about democracy and about the governance of Northern Ireland, I turned to the election manifestos of the three main parties. I noted in the manifesto of the Official Ulster Unionist party that it wanted to give its representatives more control over a variety of matters affecting the day-to-day lives of the people. It went on to say that it wanted

"unrigged devolution of real power—now."

I welcome that statement. The debate has been in part about how we will enable the official Ulster Unionist party to implement that pledge that it made to all the Unionists who voted for it in the local elections.

I turned to the manifesto of the Democratic Unionist party and read:

"The DUP will work towards an alternative to and a replacement of the failed Agreement."

To be fair to the DUP, it went on to lay a precondition on talks, but I welcome the fact that it offered its supporters a commitment to work towards a new future.

Then I turned to the manifesto of the SDLP and I read:

"We believe that there is ample scope and opportunity for all politicians to enter into a dialogue, which can lead to serious negotiations about the creation of future structures that will settle our ancient quarrel. No surrender of principle or loss of face is necessary for that dialogue to take place."

As with the other quotations that I have read, from the Official Unionist manifesto and the DUP manifesto, I welcome that commitment also to the people who support the SDLP.

One thing that has changed since last we debated this subject is that all three major political parties in Northern Ireland have sought the support of the electorate on the basis of statements about the future that are constructive and that lay foundations upon which we can all build.

In a sense, my right hon. Friend the Secretary of State perhaps set the agenda when he said in a speech on 14 February:

"What I want to see is the development of ways in which we can work together for the good of Northern Ireland, and I want to know how people feel we should proceed. We know that it makes sense to talk together, we know we can do it when the issues are important enough."

We come to the direct rule renewal debate in the fortunate position that the three main political parties in Northern Ireland, together with the Government, all recognise that there is a need to project forward, to care for the interests of the people of Northern Ireland and to talk. Perhaps I, above all of the ministerial team, can say that it is ironic that part of the debate has centred on the difficulty of talking, because talking has never been a problem to Ulstermen. Occasionally not talking has been a problem, but talking has never been construed as a difficulty with which Ulstermen have had to grapple. We have a fortunate basis on which to conduct the debate.

Unless it should be thought that manifestos were specially written for the occasion, I turn to something which the hon. Member for Foyle (Mr. Hume) said in a Radio Ulster talkback show on 4 April. He said:

"We can surely talk about matters of life and death without anybody suggesting that they have abandoned their principles."

I agree with him, and I think that the House agrees with him, too. That was the view expressed again by the hon. Member for Newry and Armagh (Mr. Mallon).

The right hon. Member for Lagan Valley (Mr. Molyneaux) made a speech on 18 March to the Unionist Council annual general meeting. He said—I believe that I quote him correctly—

"The three Northern Ireland parties can and do make common cause on matters of common concern to those whom they represent. The latest example was Harland and Wolff when no exotic structures were required to enable us to put our case."

**Mr. Molyneaux:** That is right.

**Mr. Mawhinney:** I am grateful to the right hon. Gentleman for his endorsement that I have quoted him correctly.

**Mr. Molyneaux:** Another outstanding example was when my hon. Friend the Member for Belfast, South (Rev. Martin Smyth) promoted his Bill on disability. On that occasion he had the agreement and support of all the Northern Ireland parties in the House.

**Mr. Mawhinney:** I am grateful to the right hon. Gentleman for reminding me and the House of that fact.

We welcome that view. We welcome the right hon. Member for Lagan Valley stating that view. We understand him when he says that he does not want exotic structures to enable the representatives of the people of Northern Ireland to sit down together, and together with Government, to think ahead. I do not offer the right hon. Gentleman any exotic strucures this evening. However, I offer him the opportunity to sit down and to look at those matters of common concern. I am sure that the right hon. Gentleman would agree that, if the jobs of a section of Northern Ireland were important enough to bring the parties together with Government for the common good —the future governance of Northern Ireland and the future of the people whom he and other hon. Gentlemen represent in Northern Ireland and whom the Government seek to govern fairly and to the best of their ability—surely there is enough concern for that common cause to seek to build constructively on the example that the right hon. Gentleman himself has set.

**Mr. Harry Barnes** (Derbyshire, North-East): Will the hon. Gentleman give way?

**Mr. Mawhinney:** Forgive me, but I will not give way, because I have a number of points to answer.

The right hon. Member for Lagan Valley said that he wanted us to build structures. We want to build structures, but, again, we offer him no exotic structures from which to start. We want him and his colleagues to contribute to that building process. We are ready, if he is. I could not help but notice that part of his speech in which he reflected on many discussions that he has had with Northern Ireland Ministers over the years. He pointed out that they were speeches of a constructive nature. I ask him if the time has not come to start that constructive dialogue again.

I understood the points made by the hon. Member for Antrim, North (Rev. Ian Paisley). I know that he holds strongly to his view. He knows that I do not share it, but I do not disregard the strength or the sincerity of it. However, I must say that the logic of his case should impel him to the table rather than away from it. If he does not believe that democracy is safe in the hands of the Government, without any restraint in Northern Ireland —a proposition which I do not share—the best way in which he can protect the democratic interests of his people is to sit down and see how in his terms that democracy may be bolstered.

The right hon. Member for Lagan Valley said that the Anglo-Irish Agreement was an impediment, and that was a view reflected by my hon. Friend the Member for Eastbourne (Mr. Gow). I must tell the right hon. Gentleman that the Government are fully committed to the agreement and to the principles that it embodies, but we have agreed that, if it were to appear that the objectives of the agreement could be more effectively served by changes in the scope and nature of the working of the conference, consistent with the basic provisions and the spirit of the agreement, the two Governments—not just this Government—would be ready in principle to consider such changes. I believe that, when he reads his and my speeches tomorrow, he will see that I have answered the point that he raised.

The issue is not just about talking, though it is worth noting in passing that since we last met to debate this issue, the Archbishop of Armagh, the Moderator of the Presbyterian church, the Roman Catholic Bishop of Down and Connor and the chairman of the Police Federation have all made their contributions to suggesting that the time for talking has now come. The issue is not about talking. The issue is not even ideas about the future. Those who have said in the debate that there are plenty of ideas about the future governance of Northern Ireland are right. We are coming down with ideas. When we get around the table, it will be weighed down with ideas. Ideas are not the problem.

The problem is political will. Northern Ireland has not got where it is today because the leadership of the main parties took a view similar to that of Mr. Micawber, who simply hung around hoping that something would turn up. Positive leadership was offered—leadership that was designed to effect change and to build and shape a future. I put it to the House that it is that leadership and that political will—or perhaps the absence of it—which are the only things now stopping the people of Northern Ireland being represented around the table so that their future can be considered. That future is at the heart of our debate.

Since we last debated the matter, we have seen politicans of note and ability leaving the Province. Mr. Currie, Mr. Cushnahan and Mr. Millar have left.

**Mr. Seamus Mallon:** What about Vauxhall?

**Mr. Mawhinney:** Ms. Hoey left too.

My general point is that, whatever hon. Members thought of those men, they were all seen as political leaders in Northern Ireland. They were all representatives of the next generation of political leadership. Like those politicans, the young people of Northern Ireland are also leaving. It is not just the political leaders who are leaving, but the future engineers, scientists and entrepreneurs. Young people are leaving because they do not see a future. They look back over the last 20 years and they ask themselves, "Do the next 20 years have to be the same or can they be more constructive?"

The next 20 years can be more constructive. There is a mood in the Province——

**Mr. Mallon:** No word for those who have stayed.

**Dr. Mawhinney:** Those who have stayed are playing their part. They have had their recognition at the ballot box and that recognition from the public is worth more than recognition from me.

The future of the Province concerns all the people of Northern Ireland. The hon. Member for Newry and Armagh (Mr. Mallon) spoke about the need to live together in mutual respect and harmony, cheek by jowl. It is now time to move that process forward and, in the meantime, I commend the order to the House.

*Question put:*—

*The House divided:* Ayes 156, Noes 8.

**Division No. 259]**                                                    **[7 pm**

**AYES**

Abbott, Ms Diane
Amery, Rt Hon Julian
Amos, Alan
Arbuthnot, James
Arnold, Jacques *(Gravesham)*
Arnold, Tom *(Hazel Grove)*
Baker, Nicholas *(Dorset N)*
Banks, Tony *(Newham NW)*
Bidwell, Sydney
Boswell, Tim
Bowden, A *(Brighton K'pto'n)*
Bowis, John
Brazier, Julian
Bruce, Ian *(Dorset South)*
Buck, Sir Antony
Burns, Simon
Burt, Alistair
Butterfill, John
Campbell, Menzies *(Fife NE)*
Carlisle, John, *(Luton N)*
Carlisle, Kenneth *(Lincoln)*
Carrington, Matthew
Cash, William
Channon, Rt Hon Paul
Chapman, Sydney
Clark, Hon Alan *(Plym'th S'n)*
Clark, Sir W. *(Croydon S)*
Clarke, Rt Hon K. *(Rushcliffe)*
Coombs, Anthony *(Wyre F'rest)*
Coombs, Simon *(Swindon)*
Corbett, Robin
Cormack, Patrick
Cousins, Jim
Cran, James
Davies, Q. *(Stamf'd & Spald'g)*
Davis, David *(Boothferry)*
Devlin, Tim
Dixon, Don
Dorrell, Stephen
Dunn, Bob
Durant, Tony
Evennett, David
Favell, Tony
Fearn, Ronald
Field, Barry *(Isle of Wight)*
Fishburn, John Dudley

Forth, Eric
Fox, Sir Marcus
Freeman, Roger
French, Douglas
Gardiner, George
Garel-Jones, Tristan
Garrett, Ted *(Wallsend)*
Gill, Christopher
Gorman, Mrs Teresa
Gow, Ian
Greenway, Harry *(Ealing N)*
Gregory, Conal
Griffiths, Peter *(Portsmouth N)*
Ground, Patrick
Hague, William
Hamilton, Neil *(Tatton)*
Hanley, Jeremy
Hannam, John
Hargreaves, Ken *(Hyndburn)*
Haselhurst, Alan
Heathcoat-Amory, David
Hind, Kenneth
Hordern, Sir Peter
Howarth, Alan *(Strat'd-on-A)*
Howarth, G. *(Cannock & B'wd)*
Hunt, David *(Wirral W)*
Hunter, Andrew
Irvine, Michael
Jack, Michael
Janman, Tim
Johnson Smith, Sir Geoffrey
Jones, Martyn *(Clwyd S W)*
Jones, Robert B *(Herts W)*
King, Rt Hon Tom *(Bridgwater)*
Knapman, Roger
Knight, Greg *(Derby North)*
Knox, David
Lawrence, Ivan
Lester, Jim *(Broxtowe)*
Lightbown, David
Lilley, Peter
Lloyd, Peter *(Fareham)*
McKay, Allen *(Barnsley West)*
MacKay, Andrew *(E Berkshire)*
McLoughlin, Patrick
McNair-Wilson, Sir Michael

McNamara, Kevin
Mans, Keith
Marshall, Jim *(Leicester S)*
Martin, David *(Portsmouth S)*
Mates, Michael
Maude, Hon Francis
Mawhinney, Dr Brian
Maxwell-Hyslop, Robin
Miller, Sir Hal
Mills, Iain
Mitchell, Andrew *(Gedling)*
Mitchell, Sir David
Montgomery, Sir Fergus
Morris, Rt Hon A. *(W'shawe)*
Moss, Malcolm
Nicholls, Patrick
Nicholson, David *(Taunton)*
Norris, Steve
Onslow, Rt Hon Cranley
Page, Richard
Paice, James
Patnick, Irvine
Pattie, Rt Hon Sir Geoffrey
Pike, Peter L.
Porter, David *(Waveney)*
Portillo, Michael
Raison, Rt Hon Timothy
Rhodes James, Robert
Riddick, Graham
Roe, Mrs Marion
Rowe, Andrew
Sackville, Hon Tom
Shaw, David *(Dover)*
Shaw, Sir Michael *(Scarb')*

Shelton, Sir William
Sims, Roger
Smith, Tim *(Beaconsfield)*
Spicer, Sir Jim *(Dorset W)*
Stanbrook, Ivor
Steen, Anthony
Stern, Michael
Stevens, Lewis
Stewart, Andy *(Sherwood)*
Stewart, Rt Hon Ian *(Herts N)*
Stradling Thomas, Sir John
Summerson, Hugo
Taylor, Ian *(Esher)*
Taylor, Matthew *(Truro)*
Tebbit, Rt Hon Norman
Thorne, Neil
Twinn, Dr Ian
Viggers, Peter
Waddington, Rt Hon David
Wakeham, Rt Hon John
Waller, Gary
Wardle, Charles *(Bexhill)*
Wareing, Robert N.
Warren, Kenneth
Watts, John
Widdecombe, Ann
Wilkinson, John
Wilshire, David
Winterton, Mrs Ann
Wood, Timothy

Tellers for the Ayes:
    Mr. David Maclean and
    Mr. John M. Taylor.

**NOES**

Barnes, Harry *(Derbyshire NE)*
Cohen, Harry
Kilfedder, James
Molyneaux, Rt Hon James
Nellist, Dave
Paisley, Rev Ian

Skinner, Dennis
Walker, A. Cecil *(Belfast N)*

Tellers for the Noes:
    Mr. Roy Beggs and
    Mr. Peter Robinson.

*Question accordingly agreed to.*

*Resolved,*

    That the draft Northern Ireland Act 1974 (Interim Period Extension) Order 1989, which was laid before this House on 13th June, be approved.

# Appropriation (Northern Ireland)

**Mr. Speaker:** It might be helpful if I made it clear that the debate on this order may cover all matters for which Northern Ireland Departments, as distinct from the Northern Ireland Office, are responsible. Police and security are the principal excluded subjects.

7.12 pm

**The Minister of State, Northern Ireland Office (Mr. Ian Stewart):** I beg to move,

That the draft Appropriation (No. 2) (Northern Ireland) Order 1989, which was laid before this House on 8th June, be approved.

On 8 March the House voted on account for 1989-90 sums totalling £1,669 million and the present draft order authorises further expenditure totalling £2,195 million. Taken together with the relevant appropriations in aid, these sums constitute the voted elements of Northern Ireland Departments' expenditure total of £4,951 million as shown in the public expenditure White Paper. Expenditure on law and order, amounting to £626 million in 1989-90, is outside this total, being included in Estimates laid for the Northern Ireland Office by the Treasury.

A key objective of the financial expenditure provided by these Estimates is that of strengthening the economy, and during the last year there have been a number of encouraging developments in this respect. Over the last six months unemployment has been falling at an average rate of 600 per month, and growth in employment has been accompanied by growth in output. The latest figures show that output of the production and manufacturing sectors increased by 6 per cent. and 7 per cent. respectively between the fourth quarters of 1987 and 1988. The arrangements announced in recent months for the future of Harland and Wolff and Shorts help to remove uncertainty about major industries in the Province, while substantial new investment by the Korean company Daewoo in Antrim and the French Company Montupet, close to west Belfast, will contribute to reducing the dependence of the Northern Ireland economy on an old and narrow industrial base.

With an ample supply of young people coming into the labour market in the next few years, Northern Ireland provides an excellent opportunity for inward investment which is increasingly being recognised in other parts of the United Kingdom, the European Community and further afield. The public expenditure provision that we are debating is designed to strengthen the foundations on which all the people of Northern Ireland can face the future with greater confidence.

The services to which public expenditure is to be devoted during the current year are, as usual, detailed in the Northern Ireland Estimates. I should, however, like to draw attention to a number of particular matters arising in the case of each department. Provision for agriculture is divided into two-vote 1, relating to support measures which are applied throughout the United Kingdom; and vote 2, in respect of measures that apply to Northern Ireland only. Under the first, provision is being made for expenditure of over £7 million under the recently introduced farm and conservation grant scheme and the farm woodland scheme. I am also pleased to say that

farmers have been responding positively to the investment opportunities provided within vote 2 by the agriculture development programme revived last year.

The three votes for the Department of Economic Development cover a wide range of provision for industry, investment, employment and training. I remind the House of the importance that the Government attach to the promotion of equality of opportunity of employment in Northern Ireland, and our determination that the Fair Employment Bill, which has already completed its passage through this House, should constitute a powerful and effective weapon against discrimination in the work place. This process will be greatly assisted if the number of available jobs increases, and we have taken a number of positive steps towards that end. Some £93 million is being provided through the Industrial Development Board for selective financial assistance to industry and £16 million is required for the provision and maintenance of industrial land and buildings as part of our efforts to attract new inward investment.

I am pleased to say that one third of the total of more than 5,600 new job promotions through the board last year, itself a record number, related to projects involving investment from outside the Province. In the last financial year, the Local Enterprise Development Unit also promoted in excess of 5,000 jobs, bringing to almost 40,000 the total number of such jobs promoted since the unit was established in 1976. An allocation of almost £30 million is now being sought to meet LEDU's job promotion target of 5,500 in the current year.

Vote 3 includes a wide range of measures for the encouragement of enterprise, the provision of training and work experience, and support for the labour market. This year a number of important changes have been made. In order to ensure that every unemployed young person under the age of 18 is guaranteed a training place, £37 million is being sought for the youth training programme to provide a total of approximately 14,000 training places in all. For those in the 18-to-24 age group, the previous qualifying period of 12 months unemployment for entry into the action for community employment scheme, or ACE, has been reduced to six months, and £50 million is accordingly being sought to enable the scheme to provide an average of 10,000 jobs over the current year. For longer-term unemployed adults between the ages of 18 and 60, the job training programme is being expanded to 2,500 places during 1989-90 by the provision of £6·7 million; and 500 of these training places are to be provided within the Making Belfast Work programme. This package should not only offer greater hope to the unemployed, but make an important contribution to the continuing economic recovery through a well-trained work force.

Finally, with regard to DED expenditure, I should explain the situation regarding assistance to the aircraft and ship building industries. The privatisation of Harland and Wolff is now expected in the early autumn. Within vote 2, the £60 million already contained in the public expenditure plans will provide support to the company in the interim and help meet part of the costs of the management buy-out. The full costs will, however, be somewhat higher, and it is our intention to seek additional provision at the Supplementary Estimate stage when the arrangements have been finalised. With regard to Short Brothers, hon. Members will recall that £390 million was provided during March, within the last financial year, but the sale of the company to Bombardier, for which heads of agreement were signed two weeks ago, will require further Government funding, the phasing of which is not yet settled.

Details of the additional provision required in 1989-90 will be put before the House at the earliest opportunity. I am sure that the House will understand that the complexity of the arrangements for Harland and Wolff and for Shorts are such that it has not been possible to achieve full definition in time for provision to be included in these main Estimates, but we are committed to the provision of the necessary funding to enable these two great enterprises to return to private ownership with their finances in a healthy condition.

For the Department of the Environment, an additional £8 million is included under vote 1 this year in the roads programme for extending the structural maintenance of carriageways and footways in the Province. The Belfast cross-harbour road and rail bridges projects are planned to start in 1991, and £5·5 million is accordingly being sought to enable land and property acquisition to proceed.

The Department of the Environment vote 2 covers the important sector of housing, for which £220 million is required, mainly to provide finance for the Northern Ireland Housing Executive and for the voluntary housing movement. The House will recognise that commendable progress has been made in dealing with Northern Ireland's housing problems in recent years, but more needs to be done and this is reflected in the Government's public expenditure contribution to housing of some £310 million this year, within a total gross budget of almost £545 million.

I should also like to draw attention to the fact that £32 million is included in the Department's vote 4 for urban regeneration. These measures are aimed primarily at improving the economic and environmental condition of areas suffering from urban dereliction. An important element of this policy is the encouragement of partnership between Government and the private sector, exemplified by the urban development grant scheme in which each £1 of public money generates approximately £3 of private finance.

Provision for education this year amounts to £891 million. To ensure effective delivery of the education reforms, which are crucially important for young people, as well as for the future economic and social progress of the Province, an additional £30 million is being made available over the next three years, the first tranche of which is included in these Estimates. These enhanced resources will support the implementation of the reforms in a variety of ways, including extra specialist accommodation and equipment for schools. Teachers, too, have an essential part to play in the reforms. The provision in vote 1 is therefore set to cover extra in-service training for teachers, while allowing the pupil-teacher ratio to be maintained at its level of 18.3.

Grants to universities and awards to students are based on the principle of maintaining broad parity of provision with Great Britain, and within education's vote 2 some £109 million covers expenditure on Northern Ireland's two universities, on the Open university and on teacher training. In addition to money for arts and museums, youth, sport and community services, this year an additional £2 million is being provided within this vote for the initiative to help promote community relations in Northern Ireland, which was launched by my hon. Friend the Member for Peterborough (Dr. Mawhinney) in

February. This includes £250,000 to expand the already successful cross-community contact scheme, which brings together young people from the two communities, and £1 million for the cultural traditions programme, announced last week, which will provide support for cultural heritage and traditions through the museums, the Arts Council and local history, heritage and cultural groups. The additional funding will also cover the establishment of the new community relations centre announced by my hon. Friend the Member for Peterborough last Monday, to assist district councils in the development of community relations projects and to enable other bodies to expand their programmes in this sector.

We are also providing for capital expenditure of about £62 million on education projects. This will enable a programme of new building works to commence, and we have already announced the start of nine major school projects in 1989-90. Meanwhile, a contribution of nearly £3 million to the Making Belfast Work initiative will include capital development at White Rock adult education centre, provision of three new nursery schools and a major school-industry links project, all aimed at improving opportunities in the inner city.

The Government have also increased funding to the five education and library boards that are responsible for the main education services in Northern Ireland. This year we are providing £279 million, an increase of 9 per cent. over last year's figure. This includes an important addition of £7 million for spending on school maintenance, bringing the total for maintenance of building and grounds to an estimated £19 million this year. There is also a special injection of £4 million to improve standards of provision in the classroom.

The bulk of the provision of £836 million for vote I in the Department of Health and Social Services this year will be devoted to maintaining existing services. It is also designed to cover some important developments in regional medical services—for example, in respect of neo-natal intensive care, cardiac surgery, frequent treatment for renal failure and additional breast and cervical cancer screening. The £37 million included for capital expenditure will permit the continuation of a substantial programme of works, including development of a major new area hospital at Antrim and completion of the new block at the Mater in Belfast. This funding will also allow work to commence on the construction of a new geriatric unit at Londonderry and on the extension of the cardiology services at the Royal Victoria hospital.

I hope that these comments on the main items of expenditure will have been helpful to hon. Members, and I commend the order to the House.

7.24 pm

**Mr. Jim Marshall** (Leicester, South): I thank the Minister for taking us carefully and thoroughly through the main items of expenditure. I do not intend to follow the path that he has laid out, but it was useful to have those items spelled out so clearly. I am sure that the House will agree with that sentiment.

I noticed that the Minister, like the Secretary of State earlier today, drew attention to the Government's economic achievements. As on previous occasions, I am prepared to concede that there have been economic successes. However, it is as well to remember that the Province remains the most economically deprived and

[*Mr. Jim Marshall*]

backward of any of the regions. No matter which economic indicators one takes, those in Northern Ireland are below the national average.

Because of the economic measures that the Government have had to take to control inflation, throughout the United Kingdom economy in the next year the outlook is less buoyant, and this applies particularly to Northern Ireland. There is no doubt that the expected slowdown in the United Kingdom economy as a result of Government measures will present major economic difficulties in Northern Ireland. This emphasises the vulnerability of the Northern Ireland economy to any downturn in the national economic activity, and highlights the need for the Government and the private sector to consolidate economic achievements and advancements.

Both Ministers and my hon. Friend the Member for Kingston upon Hull, North (Mr. McNamara) spoke about the level of unemployment. The Government praised themselves, and rightly, for the fall in unemployment over the past 18 months or so, but 15·5 per cent. unemployment is still unacceptably high. Male unemployment is even higher, at 19 per cent. Far more has to be done, through public expenditure, private expenditure and attracting further investment to the Province, if we are to make a real and sustained attack on high unemployment.

The Government repeatedly tell us of the triumphs of inward investment. I do not wish to decry that, whether it comes from France, Japan or Canada, but there is a theory, leaving those big industrial investments aside, that many of the smaller investments are creating jobs that are low-scale, part-time, predominantly for female workers and at the bottom of the technology ladder. Nevertheless, they are welcome. If Northern Ireland is to have a prosperous future, it needs above all highly technical jobs for highly skilled people so that it can compete not just in the United Kingdom economy but in the broader European single market economy post-1992.

There is also a fear that the privatisation of Shorts, which the Government consider a triumph, could lead to further job losses, particularly in the high skill sector. If that happens, it will be to the detriment not just of the economy of Belfast but of Northern Ireland as a whole and the island of Ireland.

Having referred briefly to the general economic situation, I want to refer to more specific spending areas. I want to spend some time, but not a great deal of time, in discussing spending programmes in social security, health and housing.

The Minister will know that pensioners in Northern Ireland did not greet the recent statement from the Secretary of State for Social Security with universal acclaim, and the Minister will know the reasons for that. They found it difficult to understand how the Secretary of State could say:

"It is simply no longer true that being a pensioner tends to mean being badly off. For most people retirement is now a time to look forward to with confidence."

I wish that that was so in the North of Ireland. The Minister and his right hon. Friend the Secretary of State for Northern Ireland should remind the Secretary of State for Social Security that in Northern Ireland two thirds of pensioner households still rely on state and other benefits for most of their income.

The Secretary of State for Social Services should also tell pensioners in Northern Ireland that a single pensioner is £10 a week worse off and a married couple £16 a week worse off under this Government than they would have been if the Government had not abolished the link between earnings and pensions. Pensioners in the North of Ireland certainly find it difficult to understand this new-found access to wealth which the Government claim that they have miraculously achieved over the past 10 years.

In an earlier debate my colleagues and I warned the Government that the changes in social security benefits were inadequate to protect living standards. Unfortunately, I must remind the House, although I take no pleasure in saying this, that my prediction has come true. The Minister will be aware that a recent survey by the citizens advice bureaux in Northern Ireland showed the way in which those changes were adversely affecting many people in Northern Ireland. The survey showed clearly that income support is not sufficient to compensate for the loss of additional requirements, single payments and the necessity to pay the first 20 per cent. of rates. It also showed that housing benefit was almost universally reduced for all groups of claimants and that 88 per cent. of those surveyed had lost their entitlement altogether. I believe that the Government's social security policy continues cruelly to pay scant regard to the needs of the least well off members of our community. That is as apparent in Northern Ireland as it is in the rest of the United Kingdom.

I want now to consider health. The estimates provide for an increase of only 3·5 per cent. in health spending on the outturn for 1988-89. If we bear in mind, as I am sure that the House will, the fact that, overall, inflation is running at 8·5 per cent. while internal inflation in the NHS is much higher than that, we do not need to be geniuses to understand the implications of the figures. They mean that the service will come under increased pressure and that more cuts will have to be made.

I reminded the House in an earlier debate that the health profile in the North of Ireland compares unfavourably with all other regions in the United Kingdom. A statistic which underlines that is that Northern Ireland has the worst infant mortality rate in the United Kingdom, with 10·4 deaths per 1,000—that is the figure for 1986, which, I understand, is the last year for which figures are available. That figure and all the other socio-economic indicators of deprivation show that the Government should be providing more money for health in the North of Ireland.

If we consider the fabric of the hospitals in Northern Ireland, it is obvious that many hospitals are in a disgraceful state of disrepair. The Minister and the House will recall that the Ceri Davis report estimated that it would cost between £18 million and £20 million to clear the backlog of maintenance in the Royal group of hospitals alone. Over the past three or four years the Royal group has been able to spend only £1·8 million on maintenance. It is estimated that the Craigavon area hospital requires £1·5 million to be spent on its fabric. I am sure that hon. Members representing constituencies in Northern Ireland can highlight hospitals in their areas which urgently require additional expenditure on repairs and maintenance.

Having made one or two general statements about the Health Service, I want to put several specific questions to the Minister which refer in particular to Belfast city hospital.

Why have two operating theatres at the Belfast city hospital been closed since Monday 5 June, and to my knowledge still remain closed, when the waiting list for operations at the hospital is more than 3,000? That waiting list includes 945 for vascular surgery, 768 for urology, 300 for gynaecology, 817 for ear, nose and throat and 525 for general surgery. Why have the number of intensive care beds at the Belfast city hospital been reduced by 50 per cent.? I understand that there are now four out of eight intensive care beds in use.

I want the Minister to comment next on a rumour, although he may be loth to do so. Will he comment on the rumour that 30 per cent. of the bed complement at the Belfast city general hospital is to close within three months? Rumour has it that two paediatric wards are to close with the loss of 47 beds; two gynaecological wards are to close with the loss of 30 beds; the Jubilee maternity unit is to close with the loss of 64 beds; one neo-natal ward is to close with the loss of 15 beds; and an accident and emergency unit is to close with the loss of 15 beds.

**Mr. Roy Beggs** (Antrim, East): Does the hon. Gentleman agree that, as so many beds appear to be becoming available, it seems nonsense to squander more than £40 million on a new hospital in Antrim?

**Mr. Marshall:** I understand the hon. Gentleman's point, and I have been involved in arguments like that from time to time. However, I do not want that argument to be drawn into the specific questions to which I am seeking answers now. I am sure that the hon. Member for Antrim, East (Mr. Beggs) will put his point to the Minister if he has an opportunity to do so—although hopefully not at too great length. I repeat that I have been referring to a rumour. However, I understand that it is a rumour with solid foundations, and I should like to hear the Minister's reply to my points.

I notice that the Minister praised the Government's achievements in housing. He will recall that in previous debates I have concurred with the praise that has been heaped on the Government's shoulders. But the Estimates show that, good though the progress has been, the funds being made available are still insufficient to meet the demand. If my reading of the Estimates is correct, they show an overall reduction in proposed expenditure of 11 per cent. compared with the 1988-89 provision.

Again, if I have read the Estimates correctly, the housing grant to the Northern Ireland Housing Executive is down 9 per cent. and renovations and enveloping grants are down 29 per cent. This is at a time when the Housing Executive is having additional responsibility imposed upon it by recent legislation to meet the housing needs of the homeless. Further finance is required if we are to bring the general level of the housing stock in the Province up to the standard that is found in England.

A great deal still remains to be done. To put that into perspective, let me remind the Minister of one or two statistics. In Northern Ireland, 8·4 per cent. of dwelling stock is deemed to be unfit compared with 4·9 per cent. in England, and 5·5 per cent. of its dwelling stock lacks one or more basic amenities, compared with 2·5 per cent. in England. Those statistics show that the money needed to rectify the neglect by undertaking repairs and new build is virtually double that required in England.

Having made those general points, let me make two specific points. The first may seem small, but I intend to make it. Why is the grant to the Northern Ireland Federation of Housing Associations and the National Housing Association been reduced from £66,000 to £55,000? That may seem a negligible figure in the overall context of the budget, but it is vital to those two bodies. That reduction seems petty in the light of the Government's commitment to the voluntary housing movement.

Secondly, the Government are giving priority to community care projects in the housing association sector. The Minister will be aware that the Government agreed to provide the bridging finance for such projects until funds were released as a result of the closure of acute beds and other hospital facilities. Those two aspects are no longer synchronised because the finance has not been released from the closure of beds and other facilities. In reality, housing money is being spent on community care projects instead of straight housing. When will that situation be rectified?

Northern Ireland still faces daunting social and economic problems, many of which can be tackled only with continuing and increasing high levels of public expenditure. Ministers in Northern Ireland are, to their credit, more successful than their counterparts in other Departments in obtaining finance, and they are to be congratulated on that. Nevertheless, I urge them to redouble their efforts and to argue more vociferously and stongly with their Treasury colleagues to obtain increased public expenditure for Northern Ireland so that we can begin to take greater steps forward in alleviating the social and economic problems that undoubtedly still exist in the North of Ireland.

7.44 pm

**Mr. James Kilfedder** (North Down): I agree with the hon. Member for Leicester, South (Mr. Marshall), especially on the social and economic problems that face the Province. They can be resolved only by a high level of public expenditure. It is no use the Government saying that they are against massive public expenditure because Northern Ireland, on the periphery of the United Kingdom, needs vast amounts of public money to be invested in it.

I urge the Government to deal without further delay with the appalling number of temporary classrooms which exist in North Down. That is just one example of what is required in Northern Ireland. I am sure that North Down is not unique and that there are plenty of temporary classrooms elsewhere in Northern Ireland.

Every penny spent on our young people is money well spent. We must invest in them and in their future. In doing so, we invest in the future of Northern Ireland and in everybody in the Province, Protestant and Catholic. It is fitting that children should have a proper place in which to receive their education. It is no use their being taught in what I would describe as pre-fab classrooms whose "temporary" existence has, in many cases, lasted a great number of years.

The hon. Gentleman referred to pensioners. There must be more than 10 million pensioners in the United

[*Mr. James Kilfedder*]

Kingdom, about 5 million of whom are below or just above the poverty line. As a result of the Social Security Act 1988, which I opposed in the Division Lobby, millions of pensioners have become even worse off with considerable cuts in their rent and rates rebates.

The recent increase in the retirement pension, amounting to approximately £1·65 a week, was insulting to our senior citizens. The only way to ensure justice for pensioners is to restore the link betweeen pensions and wages. That would mean an increase of at least £10 a week for a single pensioner, bringing the United Kingdom into line with some European countries which pay their pensioners double what is paid to the British pensioner.

The pensioner in Northern Ireland may suffer more than his counterpart elsewhere in Britain. The cost of living in Northern Ireland is higher than in England and electricity is more expensive. Elderly people need heat, so they consume a considerable amount of electricity in order to heat their homes. About two thirds of pensioners in the United Kingdom are women. Many of them are widows and quite a number live alone.

The Government should make every effort to ensure that pensioners can live their retirement years in comfort and dignity. They could ease the lot of women pensioners to some extent by allowing them to have free transport at the age of 60, when they qualify as pensioners, rather than having to wait until their husband retires at the age of 65.

More could be done for pensioners by providing free television licences, or at least by giving them a concessionary rate. I have been raising that matter in the House for the past 21 years. Some pensioners who live in dwellings with a warden pay £5 a year for their colour television licence, while others who may live just a street away have to pay the full £65. That anomaly is unacceptable in this day and age. The only way to deal with the injustice is to give all pensioners a colour television licence, either free or at a greatly reduced cost.

I shall not elaborate on the unemployed in the Province as the hon. Member for Leicester, South has covered the issues so eloquently. He mentioned that employment in Northern Ireland is currently 15·5 per cent. For statisticians, that is just a figure and does not convey any of the hardship involved in the dole queue. More than half the unemployed in Northern Ireland are long-term unemployed. They find it almost impossible to be considered for a job vacancy. The stress and hardship of being unemployed is acute. That is easily discovered by talking to an unemployed person whether he is old, young or has just left school.

I think in particular of the young people in the Province who are full of idealism and eager to become wage earners after they leave school. Many have to endure the dole queue or take a job which in no way provides an opportunity or a challenge to their capabilities. The youth training programme goes some way to soften the blow, but it does not resolve the problem and if one dwells too much on the programme one ignores the problem. We must do more to create jobs in Northern Ireland.

The IRA is waging war which is aimed in part at destroying the economic life of Ulster, and it is partnered in this evil work by Noraid which is campaigning in the United States for the states in America to adopt the MacBride principle. That campaign must have frightened many American investors from investing in Northern Ireland. Of course, its purpose is, jointly with the IRA, to destroy the economic base of Northern Ireland. I am sure that the Minister will agree that not one job has been created in Northern Ireland by the MacBride principle's campaign, but that campaign has robbed a great many Ulster people, young and old, of jobs that could have been created in the Province. That message needs to be conveyed to people in America, especially to state legislatures which adopt the principles as in doing so they are creating hardship in Northern Ireland. They must accept that. The only way to deal with it is to defeat it in the state legislatures and to make sure that money is invested in all parts of Northern Ireland for all people in the Province.

Last week, when the Secretary of State made his statement about Shorts, I repeated the appeal that I made in the House nine months before—according to the Secretary of State he had never heard it before, although I made it in his presence—that instead of English Ministers going to America, there should be an all-party delegation of Members of Parliament representing Northern Ireland who could speak directly to people in America about the jobless in the Province and get jobs for all parts of the Province, including Strabane and other black areas in Northern Ireland.

There are many good aspects of the Province and I am sorry that the media, particularly television, carry an awful image of Northern Ireland abroad. Tourism is essential to Northern Ireland. Fortunately, despite the IRA's vicious campaign of terrorism, many foreigners visit the Province, although not in the numbers who came before the present violence. Perhaps when the Minister replies to the debate, he will deal with the subject. He set up a committee to review tourism in the Province. Perhaps he could say when the report is likely to be published. Everything must be done to enhance the image of the Province. In doing so, not only will we attract tourists from abroad, as well as from England and Scotland, but we will help to improve the prospect of investment in the Province.

Tourism requires good roads. The local people, industry and commerce require good roads especially as 1992 and the single European market approaches and 1993 when the Channel tunnel opens, which will bring the hordes from France, Germany and Spain into Britain. I hope that some of them will come to Northern Ireland. Capital expenditure on roads in Northern Ireland has dropped by 50 per cent. in the past ten years, while it has almost doubled in other parts of the United Kingdom. Although I am sure that he will not be able to answer the question now, perhaps the Minister will look into the matter of the Belfast-Bangor road. When will it be updated? When will it be made into a dual carriageway to take the enormous traffic between Bangor and Belfast.

Mentioning roads is like mentioning trees, because it leads me to talk about dogs. Dog control has caused widespread debate throughout Britain, with more reports of terrible attacks by ferocious animals. In Northern Ireland, the number of stray dogs does not seem to have been affected by the requirement of a dog licence with a substantial fee. The number of stray dogs in Bangor seems to be on the increase and the present law is not being enforced properly. Dog excrement is to be found on pavements everywhere, on the grass where children play, on the beaches and on the piers. It is time for the law to be amended.

Owners should be required to register all dogs by means of a simple injection of a transponder under the skin of the dog which will give a unique number when read by a reading device. Dogs cannot be controlled effectively without such registration. Dogs without a transponder could then be rounded up.

It seems fashionable nowadays to keep ferocious dogs. Perhaps it is part of a macho image which some people wish to project and certainly special attention should be given to the danger presented by such animals to old people and young people. I read in the local paper, the *County Down Spectator,* last week of a couple of young children who were exceedingly frightened by a doberman on the beach at Ballyholme esplanade. The Minister will agree that more people are needed to control dogs. Although it is a matter for local government some guidance helps and perhaps finance will be given and some of the unemployed could be used to round up stray dogs in Bangor.

I turn to one of the problems faced by traders in Bangor and in the North Down borough council area. I urge the Government to investigate the matter of trade waste collection. Traders in the North Down borough council area have been told by the council that they must pay enormous sums to have waste collected from outside their premises. The council states that it is required by the Department of the Environment to make what I regard as exorbitant charges. It says that it has no alternative. My advice to the traders was that they should arrange to have their waste collected privately. I am sure that they could do that for half the cost charged by the council. Traders already pay colossal sums in rates. The rates in the North Down area must be more expensive than in many other parts of Northern Ireland and I do not see why the traders should be further penalised.

As the hon. Member for Leicester, South mentioned, there is an urgent need for additional expenditure on hospitals in the Province. The waiting lists are intolerably long. I receive many complaints of patients waiting for an operation. I refer them to the Eastern health board or to the appropriate Stormont department which then refers them to the health board. Bare figures do not convey the stress imposed on patients waiting for treatment. In fact, there is more than stress because there is often pain and the relatives have to suffer, watching the person in pain and agony.

I must also mention the charge for eye tests introduced by the Government and their proposal for a two-tier eye examination. I received a letter from an optometrist who lives in Bangor in my constituency. He said that he and his colleagues are appalled by what the Government have done. In rebutting what the Secretary of State for Health said a short while ago, he said:

"It is impossible to prescribe spectacles by refraction alone."

The Secretary of State said that is a cheap way of providing an eye test. He goes on to add:

"Around 5 to 10 per cent. of my patients are referred . . . via their family doctor due to suspected ocular or systemic disease. Some may be sight threatening, others life threatening, and in the majority the patient come for routine examination with no symptoms that could be directly related to the cause of referral without further investigation. Many ocular diseases do not affect visual acuity and the patient would be unaware."

Finally, he said:

"it has been suggested that a healthy young man does not need a full eye examination for a pair of spectacles. It is not young men who will take advantage of a cheaper sight test

—it will be the pensioner who is not eligible for a free eye examination but is still on the limits of poverty which account for a high percentage of patients. It is also impossible for a young man to tell whether his eyes are healthy—only the optometrist or ophthalmic medical practitioner can give such assurances."

I mention that subject and quote from the letter so that the Government are made aware of a problem that they have created. I hope that they will review what they have done, because I would hate to think that the eyes and health of people will suffer.

8.4 pm

**Mr. A. Cecil Walker** (Belfast, North): Once again, I take this opportunity to object to the method in which this iniquitous order is imposed upon the Province. In my view, it is morally wrong and completely indefensible that elected representatives cannot subscribe in a tangible way to the needs of their constituents under the terms in which the order is made. To illustrate my concern, I should like to bring to the attention of the Government and the Minister some matters under the various sections outlined in the order.

I have spoken many times in the House during the presentation of the orders of my concern for the Alliance areas in Protestant Ardoyne in north Belfast. The Minister will know that that interface is divided by an unsightly corrugated iron fence. He will also know that there was a proposal to erect an environmental wall to replace that monstrosity. There was also a proposal to carry out some judicious planting in the area and then to have some limited building as a means of restoring confidence and encouraging people to return. That proposal has now been abandoned, as has the proposal to build a sheltered complex in the same area. The proposal came from a well-known housing association and, as far as I am aware, the Government leaned on the association and said that they were not giving permission for building there.

I have heard from sources within the Housing Executive that the area is of low priority. Therefore, I am forced to conclude that a blatant policy of discrimination is being waged against that beleaguered community in the hope that the people will be forced to leave. I request, as a matter of extreme urgency, that the Minister gives the matter his immediate attention and reverses the diabolical decision.

The Minister must also know that there are serious divisions within the Ardoyne community where many killings have taken place. When it is perceived by the Protestant residents there that such discrimination is being practised by the Housing Executive, the stage is set for a full-scale revolt. I know that many would welcome that, particularly those who could then justify a decision to do nothing because of unrest in the area.

I wish also to draw the Minister's attention to the blight that has been allowed to develop in the Cambrai-Ohio street area. I lay that directly at the feet of the civil servants who are supposed to run the housing branch in Stormont, because, as far as I am aware, they do not appear to know what is not being done in the area. The local housing association that has been working there for some years has been trying to obtain action on the project for about five years. It has had no success. There was some limited development by the Minister's predecessors in an effort to inroduce some stability into the area. However, because of the lack of progress since then, the area is now completely blighted.

[*Mr. A. Cecil Walker*]

I know that the Minister responsible is not on the Treasury Bench, but I hope that the Minister who is there will tell him of my plea. He should now leave his ivory tower and visit the two areas to see for himself what is going on. As he looks at the beautiful Catholic housing on the Crumlin road opposite the Ardoyne chapel and sees the excellent new build and rehabilitation schemes that have been provided in Catholic Ardoyne, I have a feeling that he will be forced to agree that there is justification for my accusations of blatant discrimination in the decisions affecting those areas.

I also want to voice the concern of the many reputable housing associations in matters concerning their future. The hon. Member for Leicester, South (Mr. Marshall) touched on this matter. I am concerned that the decision to bring the associations under the control of the Housing Executive was a retrograde step. It gives the executive a role in the affairs of those associations that it should not have. It was evident that this role would be abused. The record of achievement by the associations in respect of price and quality, together with sound design, caused the executive extreme embarrassment. What was predictable has now happened. The executive is now depriving the associations of work in an effort to reduce their effectiveness.

What is more disturbing is that the executive now proposes to carry out this work itself. Department of Health and Social Services and community care programmes are specialised, necessitating high building and architectural skills. Such work was always the domain of the housing associations and cannot be carried out by the executive. Steps should be taken to allow the housing associations to pursue their aim of providing excellent schemes for the benefit of the whole community.

I am also most perturbed about the suggestions to close or amalgamate viable controlled schools in north Belfast. I am sorry that the Parliamentary Under-Secretary of State, the hon. Member for Peterborough (Dr. Mawhinney), who is responsible for education, has now left the Chamber. I was going to say to him that he always prided himself on his adherence to the concept of allowing parents a choice in selecting the schools that their children would attend. How does he square that with any proposals to interfere with the status of the Belfast model schools, where the overwhelming majority of parents have opted for those schools to provide their children's education?

On nursery schools, I noticed that the Minister has authorised the setting up in west Belfast of three of those necessary planks in formative education. That is at a time when the education authorities are withdrawing support for nursery education in my constituency of Belfast, North. I want to make the Minister aware that in one small community in my constituency there are 80 children on the waiting list, but only 26 places available. North Belfast is just as deprived in an educational sense as west Belfast. Its people suffer perhaps more than those in west Belfast from the results of the troubles. Its children have the same rights as those in west Belfast to nursery facilities. I hope that the Minister will take it upon himself to look at the whole question of nursery education as it relates to my constituency, with a view to redressing that glaring imbalance.

I will stay with my constituency and its problems of unemployment and lack of facilities. I am most disturbed about the large allocation of money being given to west Belfast, especially as that area is described incorrectly as north and west Belfast, which gives a completely false impression. I am concerned especially about the vast sums being channelled to community projects headed by Bishop Daly and Father Matt Wallace, when areas such as Black Mountain and Springmartin have been completely ignored.

I am also perturbed that the New Lodge has been given priority treatment when neighbouring Duncairn gardens and York road have been virtually forgotten. The impression in my constituency is that the Government are endeavouring to combat insurrection by throwing money at it and that Protestant north and west Belfast is not being considered seriously for much needed funding. There are many community projects that could be funded by the Belfast action teams or by "making Belfast work" money, and those projects should have immediate attention from those or similar agencies.

Another significant question that must be asked is why the Protestant areas of Ballysillan, Silverstream, Tyndale and Joanmount were deliberately excluded when the action teams drew up their territories, especially when it is recognised by everyone there that those areas are the most deprived. I request that another action team should be set up and appointed to look after those specific areas.

The small units being managed by the Industrial Development Board have proved successful in my constituency because they have given small companies the opportunity to create jobs and to subscribe to the community generally. I am appalled by the decision to increase rents by 40 per cent. If that decision is implemented, some of the units will inevitably be vacated, thereby creating unemployment and encouraging vandalism. The tenants have more than enough with which to contend and many of them are existing on a knife edge. I ask for an immediate investigation into that scandalous proposal, and I ask that steps be taken now to peg the rents at an acceptable level.

I draw the Government's attention to a problem in our Health Service which causes me great concern. I am referring to what are known as magnetic resonance scans, which are necessary to investigate orthopaedic problems. The only machines available to carry out such scans are in London or Dublin. My other area of concern is the lack of lithotrypter machines which can remove kidney and gall stones by high frequency sound waves. The only machines available are in Manchester and Dublin. The pain and suffering caused to patients who are forced to go to London and Dublin must be quite unbearable, apart from the costs involved. In 1988, 48 patients were sent to London for magnetic resonance scans at a cost of £32,015. So far in 1989, 43 patients have been sent and the number of requests is rising steadily. Patients are now being asked to go to London on the 7·15 am flight on Saturdays, as that is the only day available for them to be looked after in London. The irony is that in Belfast we have specially trained operators, but because of cuts in Health Service provision we have not purchased the necessary machines.

**Mr. Kilfedder:** What is the cost of the machine?

**Mr. Walker:** I do not know the exact price of the machines, but I understand that they are fairly expensive.

I was looking at the matter in the light of the suffering caused to people. I was also looking at it in relation to the fact that Dublin always pleads poverty, yet it can afford to have those machines. We also know that London has them. It would, of course, be difficult to send members of the security forces to Dublin for scans. Such scans are often required because of the orthopaedic problems cropping up in the security forces as a result of terrorist activities. I hope that the Minister will at least take my requests on board as an act of compassion. I can assure him that he will be helping many disabled prople to cope with a very painful condition.

On planning, I refer to the new shopping complex at Sprucefield roundabout. As the Minister knows, it was the subject of great controversy between the local planning service public representative and the Minister himself. It resulted in some mixed feelings in the business community, which has loyally supported Lisburn town and its population.

I am now concerned to hear that in an effort to widen the scope of their operations and to attract more customers than shop there now, entrepreneurs have descended on that rural area and are now in the process of considering the provision of small specialised retail units similar to those already existing in the Bow street complex. There is even a suggestion that those same nameless people are approaching landowners in the vicinity and offering to purchase their land at extremely high prices.

If there is any substance in those allegations, the Minister should be aware that such a proposal would be in direct contradiction to what has already been ruled, which is that no development would receive planning permission for a floor area of less than 30,000 sq ft unless it were for a garden centre, when the floor area would be reduced to 10,000 sq ft. I ask the Minister to confirm in his reply that that is the case and that he is not aware of any such proposal which would sound the death knell of the small business community in Lisburn, which is finding it increasingly difficult to make a living in the present economic climate.

8.20 pm

**Mr. Peter Robinson** (Belfast, East): I wish to raise just three issues that arise from the order. I shall speak only briefly on the first. I hope that the Minister will be in a position to throw some light on this subject because it relates to his Department. I trust that if he is listening to my speech he will be able to say something about what progress has been made on the Harland and Wolff buy-out proposition. Many people imagined that because, in a flurry of publicity, the Secretary of State and the Minister announced a heads of agreement arrangement with Mr. Parker and with the Norwegian Mr. Fred Olsen, all the problems were over. However, many other issues remain to be resolved, principally those affecting the work force at Harland and Wolff. It would therefore be valuable if the House could hear an account of what progress has been made since the announcement was made in the House.

The second issue that I wish to raise follows directly from some of the comments made by the hon. Member for Belfast, North (Mr. Walker), whose closing remarks dealt with planning issues. By way of explanation, I should say that planning is dealt with far differently in Northern Ireland than it is in other parts of the United Kingdom. Local government in Northern Ireland has only a consultative role in planning matters. The planning division of the Department of the Environment attends district council meetings with a schedule of planning applications on which it has indicated merely whether it is recommending that approval should be given or that the application should be refused. The district council has the ability to make its opinion known to the planning department.

The planning department then reconsiders its initial recommendation against the backcloth of the council's opinion. It then arrives at a conclusion. Councils frequently ask the planning officer to reconsider the recommended verdict. Consistently in my experience—if experience varies in other parts of the Province I should be interested to hear it—the planning department simply reaffirms its original decision. That shows that the consultative process is merely a rubber-stamp exercise because the department reaches its decision, passes it under the council's nose, and then stamps it with either the approval or the rejection that it had originally intended.

That process also shows that there is only a small role for the elected representative. I must advise the Minister that it is those local elected representatives, most often acting without regard to party and on most occasions acting unanimously, who know what the local community thinks and feels about a planning application and who also know the way in which an application will affect the local community. Even when the planning officer returns, having reaffirmed his original opinion, the council can ask the planning directorate to review that decision.

In my local council I have seen that process eight or nine times and on each of those occasions the planning directorate has simply rubber-stamped the planning department's decision. On no occasion has the planning directorate changed its mind on the issue. That shows that local elected representatives do not have a worthwhile role in planning matters. The planning department must be encouraged to listen to the local elected representatives.

I shall give an example from the most recent meeting of my local council in Castlereagh. A Mr. Ewart, who has premises on the Ballygowan road, leading out towards Ballygowan and Moneyreagh, put in an application for a vehicle sales office. He submitted with his application the views of the local community by way of a petition which showed that the overwhelming feeling in the area was in favour of his proposition. There were no objections to his planning application. Many members of the council viewed the site and recognised that far from detracting from the area, the project would have improved the area and would have offered an added service to its people. If we are to have a planning service, whom is it serving if the local people and the local representatives want a facility, but the Department thinks that it knows better than everybody else?

That is the kind of bureaucracy that we have in Northern Ireland. I do not want to cover ground that should have been covered if we had the time to do so in the previous debate, but I must stress that there is no democracy in Northern Ireland if even the unanimous views of elected representatives can be pushed to one side while the views of faceless bureaucrats enjoy the overwhelming support of the planning department and of the Minister who refuses to change his opinions on such issues.

Also on planning, I must deal with the same subject as the hon. Member for Belfast, North. There has been an

[*Mr. Peter Robinson*]

announcement that in the east Belfast area there is to be a massive retail, recreational, office and industrial complex, covering 35 acres. If I read the proposal properly, it is proposed to knock down the existing Connswater industrial estate. I have been asked about this by its employees. Indeed, I attended a meeting at which the employers of 39 companies on the industrial estate were present. The selling point that was given publicly was that the new project would bring approximately 600 jobs to east Belfast. What a tremendous prospect. The thought of the loss of jobs at Harland and Wolff and at Shorts was swept aside as we thought about the 600 new jobs that would be created by the project.

However, what the blurb did not tell us was that about 500 jobs would be lost as a result of clearing the land to make way for the site of the retail and leisure development. There is great concern in the area that the company should make public its proposition so arbitrarily and without consulting those who are already on site. There is certainly the suggestion that a wink or a nod was given by the planning department before the money was spent on the project.

Will the Minister tell us—I shall be generous in the way that I phrase this—what consultation there was between the planning department and that major company, which is based on this side of the Irish sea? Were any reassurances given to the company? Have the Government considered the impact of that company's proposal on the proposal that they are backing for the Laganside development? It would surely devastate that proposal if there were two similar projects so close to each other. I accept that it is not the Minister's departmental responsibility, so he may not feel able to answer my questions, but I shall be happy to receive answers in writing from the appropriate Minister.

Many of us were led to believe that the Belfast urban area plan would be published in January 1989, but it was not. I now understand that it is unlikely that it will be published before Christmas. That is causing great concern to the construction industry—not just the housing sector —because there is a virtual standstill on major planning applications for housing, industry and recreation. Jobs are already being lost because of the delay. Surely the planning department can get its act together and do rather better than it has done on many past occasions.

Another example is the Carryduff area plan. I do not wish to tread on the territory of the right hon. Member for Lagan Valley (Mr. Molyneaux), but I do not think that he will mind my mentioning this matter. The hearing on the plan took place only last week. It deals with Carryduff's building programme for the years 1987 to 1991. However, it appears that the plan will not be published until the mid-1990s. That is a nonsense. It shows the way that the planning department deals with major inquiries. Surely there could be better programming and better timing so that events come in the right order.

The next issue of concern to me is health. I concur with the remarks of the hon. Member for Leicester, South (Mr. Marshall). I am deeply concerned about the decline in the Health Service in Northern Ireland. As other hon. Members have already said, it is outrageous that there are such long waiting lists for operations and hospital treatment. Although my constituency does not have a major hospital, the Ulster hospital lies on its periphery. That hospital has empty wards because there are no resources to fund the staff necessary to look after patients.

Yesterday, I was part of an all-party delegation that toured the accident and emergency department of the City hospital. The delegation was united in its condemnation of the Eastern health and social services board for what it is contemplating for that department. There have previously been several proposals, but they have all been overridden by the current proposal, which may go before the board some time next week or, if rumour is right, it may be put off until October. The proposal is that the department should close on alternate evenings; that the accident and emergency department at the Mater hospital should close every evening; that the accident and emergency department at the Royal Victoria hospital should remain open; and that the City hospital should alternate with it. The impact of that on the service being provided would be devastating.

Perhaps the Minister could explain how someone in great need—perhaps he has cut off a finger while doing a job in his home—could possibly stop and think, "Do I rush to the Royal Victoria or the City hospital? Which one is open tonight?" He may go to the doors of the City hospital only to find a sign telling him he has it wrong and that he must go to the Royal Victoria hospital. It is complete nonsense.

The proposal does not take any account of the community issue. Whether we like it—and I hope that none of us do—many people in Northern Ireland recognise that there are areas where they are not safe. Many people, especially the security forces, would be loath to go to the Royal Victoria hospital. Indeed, the security bosses would not allow their forces to go there without an armed presence to guard them.

We are told that the reason for the proposal is that the health board might save about £50,000 in heating, lighting and staff wages. How can people be so wrong-headed? Do they think that on alternate nights the hospital can simply turn off the heat and the lights and send the staff away? Perhaps they intend that the staff who will not be required at the City hospital on alternate evenings will instead go and work at the Royal Victoria. We can all imagine the effect of that on the service as the staff try to familiarise themselves with different hospitals on different eveningss. Perhaps they intend to recruit staff to work on, for example, Monday, Wednesday and Friday evening. What would that do to the sleep pattern of doctors and nurses? It is absolute nonsense.

The proposal is also financial nonsense. If the accident and emergency department at the City hospital is closed on alternate evenings, some sort of security would be necessary to look after the empty areas of the hospital where vast quantities of dangerous drugs are stored and where patients' records are kept. Currently there is no need for such security because the nurses and the doctors are always there. If security has to be provided, there will be a need for heat and light, so no savings will be made there. The security staff will have to be paid, so there will be no saving there.

The hospital will have to staff itself on the basis of the unexpected happening. Who will tell someone who comes to casualty desperately needing attention that he must go away, possibly to this death? I cannot believe that anyone will do that. The hospital will have to have some staff as back-up, so where is the financial saving there?

We must contemplate the reality of life in Northern Ireland. What happens if a disaster occurs in the Belfast area? Will the one hospital be able to cope? We may not be talking about a terrorist disaster: it could be an air disaster. One hospital could not adequately cope with such a major event affecting the Belfast area.

I appreciate how people who are not aware of the local circumstances in Northern Ireland might look at a map of Belfast, see three dots close together—representing the Royal Victoria, Mater and City hospitals—and think that some arrangement could be made to save money. In practice, it does not work that way. Not only would such a cut not work, but the results could be disastrous. Ask the nurses.

There will be queues of people waiting for attention, and queues mean violence to nurses. The patience of people in need of attention can become frayed. Many problems will arise, particularly on Friday and Saturday evenings, and there is already great concern among the nursing staff. Many of the nurses I spoke to yesterday made it clear that if this proposal goes through, there will be no place for them in Belfast City hospital. There are plenty of jobs for them in private nursing homes and elsewhere, often at more attractive wages than they are now receiving.

I urge the Minister to bring to bear what influence he has on the members of the board that he appoints to ensure that they do not put through such a perverse proposal to close on alternate evenings the accident and emergency department of Belfast City hospital.

8.42 pm

**Mr. Eddie McGrady** (South Down): I am grateful for this opportunity to participate in the debate. The Minister and the hon. Member for Leicester, South (Mr. Marshall) have dealt with, as it were, the macro-economics of the measure. I shall deal with some of the smaller figures behind the grand millions that appear in the schedule accompanying article 5.

It is appropriate, perhaps, that the first section of that article deals with agriculture, especially as I represent a basically rural and agricultural constituency. I perceive with joy the fact that the Minister of Agriculture, Fisheries and Food has announced that at long last the less-favoured areas submission has been made to the European Commission. In view of the financial consequences of that submission, I urge that as much pressure as possible is brought by the Department of Agriculture on Commissioner Ray McSharry, who is now responsible for that matter in Brussels and who, because of his experience and the similarity of the problems in the North and South, should have a receptive ear to the speedy implementation of the less-favoured areas provision.

One reason why I am anxious to have that issue brought forward as quickly as possible is the inordinate delay that has already taken place. The less-favoured areas were designated in Northern Ireland several years ago, but only yesterday were they submitted to the European Commission despite the fact that in the meantime the agricultural development programme, of which advantage could have been taken by people in the newly designated areas, is already rolling. They have not had the opportunity to enjoy the enhanced support and grant system that the less-favoured areas arrangement would give them.

Because of lack of finance or lack of proper management or administration, a dangerous situation seems to be arising in the administration of the agricultural development programme. When an application is made, an acknowledgement is sent to the farmer giving him permission to start a project, but it does not give him any undertaking that the project will receive grant aid. The substantive reply arrives six or seven months later.

That state of affairs is totally unacceptable. There is sometimes an unfortunate temptation for the local farmer immediately to start a project, to get banking finance and to go ahead with the expenditure, only to find at the end of the day that he will not receive the grant aid which, albeit incorrectly, he thought he would get. That happens either because of lack of funds to ensure proper administrative staff or lack of adequate administrative arrangements. I urge the Minister to examine that point carefully, along with the question of delay in making payments to those whose projects have been approved under the agricultural development programme.

The other form of agriculture is marine agriculture. The Minister will be aware that two of the three major fishing ports in Northern Ireland are in my constituency, at Ardglass and Kilkeel. He will also know that great disadvantage is being caused to the fishing fleet because of the sand bars that have been created by previous governmental expenditure at the entrances to both harbours.

In bad weather, particularly at Kilkeel, boats running for cover cannot pass one another at the entrances to the harbours. There are schemes afoot to have that remedied, but the finance has not been made available.

The severity of the situation can be appreciated by the statistic that out of the possible 98 days' fishing that the fleet could have—thereby providing income and jobs in that sector, including processing, fish sales and exporting—only 47 days are available because of that physical disbarment at the harbour of Kilkeel. A similar problem, because of the silted harbour bar, exists at Ardglass. Could some urgent financial provision be made to eradicate that debilitating situation for the fishing industry in South Down?

I have listened with interest not only to this debate but to the earlier one on direct rule, in which the Secretary of State recited the enormous strides that have been made in employment and Government investment. I envied, but was not jealous of, the hundreds of millions of pounds that have been promised for job preservation in certain parts of Northern Ireland. I should like to think that some of that rich lode could be transferred to my constituency for industrial promotion and that a more active, positive programe from the Industrial Development Board and the Local Enterprise Development Unit could be applied to the development of jobs in local areas.

I have heard arguments to the effect that that would not be financially viable, but in the context of the overall budget that we are discussing—considering the drift to the cities and centres of population, with consequent school, hospital, roads, car parking, environmental pollution and other costs—it would be cheaper to bring the jobs to the workers in rural areas than to take the workers to the jobs in the conurbation.

The second factor that affects the economic development of my constituency is tourism. It is no idle boast that it is the most beautiful part of Ireland in terms of mountain, sea and other scenery and facilities, but it

[Mr. Eddie McGrady]

requires promotion overseas. The Minister's colleague in the Department of the Environment has recently restructured part of the development process, but we need local units with executive functions and finance to promote a concept that is appropriately designed for each area. The Mourne area, not only because of its natural beauty but because it is St. Patrick's country, is a seller, if it can be properly and commercially packaged. That area and Newcastle are the most developed and have the highest tourist input in Northern Ireland. Europe and North America have many links with St. Patrick's country. Most cities in Europe were founded by people from South Down, from the old monasteries of the fourth to the 10th centuries. That connection still exists and should be exploited.

I was pleased to learn a couple of months ago that the fibre-optic link programme was endorsed, signed and proceeded with by the Government. It is the most exciting development that the North of Ireland has seen. 1992 has often been quoted. One of my greatest fears is that the North of Ireland and Ireland as a whole will be marginalised in the European Community because we are on the Atlantic north-west coast of of that Community, and things naturally tend, both commercially and economically, to drift to the centre of any empire. A commercial empire is being created, so we must be more vigilant, ready and properly equipped than anybody else to sustain the onslaught of 1992. I was particularly pleased that the Government have accepted the fibre-optic link in principle and, I hope, in practice.

Will the Minister confirm that the nodes that are attached to those links will be available to small rural towns of South Down and elsewhere? If they are not, the Government will be failing to provide the infrastructure of electronic communications that are so important to our development post-1992. I hope that the Minister's department will examine economic development in the context of bringing industry to workers in rural areas and that sensitive low-level buildings can be provided in advance for the transportation of jobs not only from England but from Europe and North America. That has already happened in Castletown in County Kerry; the New York State Insurance Co. has transferred its entire administrative operation to the little village of Castletown because of the fibre optic links.

I sympathise with the hon. Member for Belfast, north (Mr. Walker), who mentioned the so-called rationalisation of schools. The rationalisation of schools affects the area that I not only represent but live in. I refer to Downpatrick, east Down and Lecale generally. The South-Eastern education and library board intends to close in one fell swoop three secondary—intermediate schools at Crossgar, Downpatrick and Castlewellan and to abolish the grammar school status of what is known as the Down high school at Downpatrick. That was done without any consultation.

I was hoping to get an answer from the Minister at Question Time today. I asked him what consultation took place with the parents of pupils at those schools. He replied that there were statutory development procedures for school reorganisation proposals, that these provided an opportunity for interested parties—including parents

—to make representations to the Department of Education, and that school authorities would normally consult parents before publishing a proposal.

The parents at those schools were not consulted by either the South-Eastern education and library board or anybody else. The board made an on-the-spot decision to close three rural schools that are catering for the education and future of the children of those areas. Schools should be more than establishments for education. They should be allowed to be the social fabric of small towns and villages. I ask the Minister to convey to the Under-Secretary of State the grave concern of parents of children at those four schools that those decisions were taken without consultation.

My area has two further difficulties in education. One is the lack of provision for autistic children. Presumably for financial reasons, the education authority has set its face against providing a modicum of specialist services in normal school provision. That could easily be done with little expenditure. The second difficulty is the provision of veterinary education. There is great concern in rural communities such as mine about the proposal to close the veterinary school in Glasgow to which all veterinary students in Northern Ireland normally go. It would be a great pity if that link between Northern Ireland and Glasgow were abolished.

I now refer to the appropriation for health and social services. I have heard hon. Members talking about £33 million for the Antrim hospital. I do not begrudge that expenditure. It is the second time in my experience that an almost identical amount of money has been allocated to that hospital. Downpatrick hospital must be replaced. A new hospital was to be built in 1956—over a quarter of a century ago—and the money, unfortunately, was diverted to Antrim hospital. I have a sense of déjà vu—It has happened again over a quarter of a century later, without any change.

The amount of expenditure that is required to make Downpatrick a good general hospital, as proposed by consultants and vetted by competent experts, is only about £8 million to £10 million. That would make it a comprehensive, general, geriatric and maternity hospital. Geriatric and maternity facilities have already been put on site.

Perhaps more immediate is the Department's inability to force the Eastern health and social services board to provide a third anaesthetist for the Down hospital. The absence of this anaesthetist is jeopardising the provision of operational services. The board has prevaricated time and again. It uses the excuse of the lack of finance. As the Minister has already indicated his support for the appointment, it is proper that he provides the money for it.

I also wish to draw the Minister's attention to the inadequacy of the staffing of occupational therapy departments. In my area and, I am sure, in many other areas in Northern Ireland there is a two-year wait for the delivery of aids for handicapped people. That is scandalous when such items do not involve a great deal of expenditure. After diagnosis and after assent has been given for the provision of the aid, surely it is not right that physically disabled people should have to wait two years for the provision of an aid.

I echo the comments of the hon. Members for Leicester, South and for North Down (Mr. Kilfedder) about the plight of pensioners following the social security changes.

Pensions were raised in April, but for many pensioners the increases have been completely negatived by the withdrawal of the transitional payment allowance. Many pensioners have less money in their pockets than they had before the pension increases. Surely that was never intended at a time of rising costs. I ask the Minister to consider that point sympathetically.

I congratulate the Minister's colleague in the Department of the Environment on his speedy intervention in the aluminium sulphate scare at Foffany reservoir. He has appointed an independent investigator to find out how the aluminium sulphate got there. The incident is reminiscent of what happened in south-west England, but it is on a much smaller scale. I urge the Minister to expedite the results of the inquiry so as to allay the fears of the local people. To link that with what we are debating, lest you pull me up, Mr. Deputy Speaker, the local feeling is that the withdrawal of workers and the rundown in the number employed at the Foffany works by the Department was probably a contributory factor to the pollution. Aluminium sulphate is a potent toxin in the water supply.

On housing, I draw the Minister's attention to the Policy Studies Institute survey which looked into the disadvantage between Catholic and Protestant in the probability of allocation of housing in Northern Ireland. I do not want to debate the merits and demerits of allocation on a sectarian basis. I simply suggest that the imbalance in allocation of houses on a 2:1 ratio is partly because of the cut of £40 million in the housing budget this year. The Housing Executive has said that, because of these cuts, its modest proposals—I emphasise the word "modest"—cannot be met. In the three-year financial cycle up to 1992 the loss of grant will be £109 million. At a time when there is a downturn in the provision of new build by the private sector, surely the resources of the Housing Executive should not be cut.

Like other hon. Members, I try to make a contribution to the debate, but I would lke a response to the points that I raise. Often for good reasons, in the time available a Minister cannot reply to all the points. If the Minister cannot reply tonight to all hon. Members, I urge him to reply by letter. It is meaningless for us to take part in a debate if we do not get a reply, good or bad, positive or negative, from the Department or from the Minister to whom we have addressed our inquiries.

9.3 pm

**Mr. Roy Beggs** (Antrim, East): Partly as a result of door-to-door canvassing for the recent local government elections and the European elections, some of us have had much closer contact with the people affected by Government decisions than the Ministers who make the decisions or, indeed, by those who advise Ministers in Northern Ireland so badly from time to time. I hope that in future real consideration will be given to the views expressed by those of us who endeavour to represent our constituents.

I realise, as do other right hon. and hon. Members, that nothing we say tonight will change the order. Nevertheless, in order to bring the attention of Ministers and officials issues which have arisen, we do not want to give the impression that we are always on the attack. There are various sections of the order that we recognise as being of value. I welcome the efforts to ensure success of Harland and Wolff and, indeed, Shorts. I congratulate the Department of Economic Development, the Industrial Development Board and the Local Enterprise Development Unit on their achievements to date in job creation.

We all realise that there is still a long way to go and that the level of unemployment in Northern Ireland, including that of some highly skilled young people, is far too great. Only when terrorism is defeated will we see the kind of inflow of inward investment, that will rid us of the scourge of unemployment that has existed for far too long.

Under vote 3, the Department of Economic Development, I welcome the fact that continuing emphasis is being given to the provision of community projects, youth and industrial training and employment schemes and services, including services for the disabled. I am pleased, too, to support the provision of funding for Enterprise Ulster, which serves the whole community of Northern Ireland extremely well, and most communities have benefited from the excellent environment and amenity schemes that have been carried out over the years. Those schemes have given much satisfaction to the long-term unemployed, and we are glad to see them continuing.

We are especially pleased to see the increase from 8,000 to 10,000 places under the Action for Community Employment—known as ACE—provisions. I support the priority that is to be given to those between 18 and 24 years of age. There will be emphasis on structured training to assist those who are fortunate enough to obtain places on that scheme to acquire skills that will enable them to move to more permanent employment and to compete for jobs on the open market. I welcome the steady growth in places under that scheme, but I believe that in future it will have to be further expanded. I trust that funding will be made available for that purpose.

Funding of the Fair Employment Agency and the Equal Opportunities Commission alone will not achieve fair employment or equal opportunity. We hope that we will not see frightened employers, who have been fair employers, blatantly discriminating against Protestants to raise the number of other groups on their list which will have to be furnished to the Fair Employment Agency.

I agree that the unfair attacks by the promoters of the MacBride principles in the United States have done more damage to the prospects of all sections of the unemployed in Northern Ireland. Without their intervention, it is quite possible—in fact one would have expected—that there would have been more inward investment from the United States. We as Unionists have stated clearly that we have no desire to direct employers to specific areas where only Unionists will benefit. We believe that new industry should be located so that all sections of the community can benefit from the job opportunities created on the basis of their own merit. I hope that we will see continuing inward investment and new job opportunities for all to share.

I also hope that those companies that are investing heavily in producing alternative sources of energy will, in the event of the privatisation of the electricity industry, be guaranteed an outlet for the surplus electricity that they can generate and that that will be taken at a fair price. If such a guarantee is not binding, the Government grants that have encouraged the alternative generation of energy will prove to have been a waste of resources.

Under the Department of the Environment vote 1 expenditure, I would like to have seen a greater allocation of funds for upgrading the street lighting system

[*Mr. Roy Beggs*]

throughout east Antrim, and at a faster rate than presently possible. There is also a need to provide more off-street car parking for housing estates. Portland place, Magheramorne, is on the main Larne—Carrickfergus road, an extremely busy road, and householders have to park on that road. There is land available and I am sure that Blue Circle would be more than delighted to negotiate with the Department to make some land available for that purpose.

I regret that I could not identify any planned expenditure to complete the dual carriageway on the Larne-Belfast road from Gingles corner to Corr's corner. We have been waiting nearly 20 years for action to upgrade that Euro-route. I appeal to the Minister to get personal experience of the congestion caused by commercial and private traffic travelling to and from Larne harbour. If it is too much to expect funding to be provided from Europe all at once for the completion of that project, at least the Government should be working towards phasing the work until such time as it is all completed. That would improve overall road safety and traffic flow. I believe that such a decision would command the sympathy and support of those who administer the European regional development fund.

It is many years since the hon. Member for Antrim, North (Rev. Ian Paisley), in his capacity as a Member of the European Parliament, and other colleagues had a European development fund commissioner in Larne. If our Government had proposed the project, we might have good reason to expect support for it. Given the real danger of EC funds drying up in a few years' time, I hope that the project will be completed before then. We are confident that we will obtain the commitment and support of our newly elected European Members of Parliament and of any Commissioner they invite over. With that support, our Government should feel confident enough to get that proposal through.

Glynn village, just outside Larne, was promised a bypass about 10 years ago. It should have been completed by now but, in common with many other projects, it has been put on a long finger. Money has been spent on upgrading the main road through Glynn, but if two articulated lorries were to meet on that road it would be almost impossible for them to pass each other. The narrow footpath there will not accommodate a young mother with a pram on the way to the railway station. I hope that further consideration will be given to the possibility of a Glynn bypass.

Will the Minister look favourably on the recently completed Glenarm village study? We need substantial expenditure on the coastal area between Glenarm and Carnlough where there is high unemployment and great potential for creating employment. Larne borough council has acquired the derelict harbour and funds are urgently needed to enable the Eglinton limeworks to be relocated to the back of the village, where there are new workings. With the proper support, we can encourage entrepreneurs to set up small businesses and improve the general economy for the community.

I was pleased when the Minister said that at long last the cross-city rail link would become a reality. We could look forward to more visitors passing through the Larne harbour area if they were able to travel through Belfast more conveniently.

I emphasise the continuing need to provide funding for renovation and enveloping grants in areas where improvement and redevelopment by the Housing Executive has been agreed. The voluntary housing associations in Northern Ireland continue to be worthy of our fullest support. They should be able to retain their own identity and should not be absorbed and mismanaged by the Northern Ireland Housing Executive, a bureaucratic monster which is far too large to be properly managed.

I recently wrote to Mr. Blease, the chief executive of the Housing Executive. I said:

"I respectfully suggest that the Northern Ireland Housing Executive should seek, if necessary, authority to obtain a deposit in respect of every future allocation of residential accommodation. The deposit should be sufficient to cover the cost of inspection, repair of damage and, where necessary, steam cleaning and fumigation. Where tenants are linked to a trail of filth and vandalism, the public at large should not be held responsible for the cost of putting things right. Inspection reports should be exchanged where transfers between housing districts occur and should have some bearing on whether an exchange or transfer application is approved within a housing district."

I am grateful to the Housing Executive for the prompt response which came within a few days of receipt of my letter. It was properly addressed to me in Larne, except that it was intended for the hon. Member for Upper Bann (Mr. McCusker). I do not know how the mistake had arisen; he must have been on their mind or something. I shall certainly ensure that he receives a copy of the letter in case he has communicated with the executive along the same lines and has not received a reply.

I am concerned because I know from experience that we must take action. The Minister responsible must assist the Northern Ireland Housing Executive to cope with the sort of problems which I have witnessed in my constituency and which no doubt are common in other areas. At the request of pensioners, and young married couples with babies of only a few months old, I have visited properties which have been allocated by the Northern Ireland Housing Executive. If I were to describe some of the conditions left behind, it would provoke illness. It almost makes me sick to think about it again.

I shall give a watered-down report, which I hope will be palatable, which comes from an environmental officer. His description of the property which had just been offered to tenants said:

"Water closet basin insanitary (heavily stained and dirty). The glazed surface to the bath was damaged, normal use of the bath could not account for the small indentations in the bottom of the bath.
Kitchen area:
Rotten woodwork to window frame.
Holes in the floor and in a section of stud wall.
The cupboards were dirty and in a state of disrepair.
The house in general was dirty and strewn with rubbish."

The Housing Executive is naturally interested in getting income, whether the rent is paid by the Department of Health and Social Services or by those young couples who are desperate for accommodation and who will accept accommodation in virtually any condition. It is a disgrace that young people are offered two rent-free weeks to clean the muck and filth left by somebody else. The Minister should take a good walk round sometimes to see the neglect, mismanagement and lack of supervision. He should take steps to give powers to his officials or staff in the Housing Executive to do something about it.

The Housing Executive should not give an existing tenant alternative accommodation until it has inspected the state of the dwelling that the tenant occupies. No dwelling should be reallocated to anyone until it has been inspected, cleaned out, refurbished and repaired where necessary. There should be a thorough inspection of the roof space, the front and rear gardens areas and any other outbuildings. If any tenant has a record with the Housing Executive, the RUC or the environmental health department of causing disturbance or annoyance to adjacent tenants by noise, from whatever source, this record or offence should be taken into account by the Housing Executive if the tenant is being considered for transfer or reallocation either within the district in which he resides or to any other district.

These problems are constantly before us, especially those of us who still serve as elected district councillors. They are the problems being forced on the councils in Northern Ireland, which have few resources, so that the burden of work on the environmental health department is unnecessarily increased. I hope that the Minister will encourage the Housing Executive to take action, and that he will assist it with whatever new powers are needed to improve the situation and to implement some of these suggestions.

I am concerned that I have to raise this next matter in the House. It is a case that has come to light recently, and I trust that there are no other similar cases, although I have suspicions that there are. Under the vote for expenditure for housing, I have reason to call on the Minister as a matter of urgency to stop proceedings in respect of the Cregagh flats phase 2 contract. The Minister should hold an inquiry in the public interest to determine whether certain procedures regarding the action of the executive's consultants have been proper in all respects about the selection and approval of sub-contractors for window supply and installation.

In Larne in east Antrim a company called Sterne Fenster manufactures and markets Starglaze upvc windows. That company was encouraged with support from another Government Department to set up in Northern Ireland. It has successfully tendered and had a verbal indication that its price had been used by the main contractor to win the contract for phase 2 at the Cregagh flats. Starglaze got on to the Northern Ireland Housing Executive approved list on 13 February after, I suspect, ministerial intervention. Obstacles had been placed in the company's way. Starglaze would not join a cartel of manufacturers and be part of a cosy little club which could jack up the prices. Its windows are approved by the British Standards Institution and are made to a very high specification and that is why the company is on the approved list. The windows have been tested for wind resistance and water penetration. Under very high wind loading, no damage, deformation or water penetration occurred to the frames.

Starglaze has been blocked at every stage from supplying windows to the Northern Ireland Housing Executive. For a consultant architect employed by the executive to exert pressure on the main contractor not to use Starglaze frames while saying that, if Starglaze was nominated by the main contractor, its name would go forward to the Housing Executive is quite despicable. To

allege that the company has no track record in Northern Ireland is a deception designed to ensure that the company does not get a contract in Northern Ireland and is put out of business.

Starglaze has installed windows in the Brighton hotel after it was refurbished. It has installed windows in a 14-storey block of flats in the borough of Milton Keynes. It has installed windows in three blocks of 11-storey flats in the metropolitan borough of Stockport. It has installed them in two 14-storey blocks in the metropolitan borough of Sefton and it is scheduled to install its windows in five more blocks in Stockport. Those are but a few examples of the track record behind Starglaze and its high quality windows.

Starglaze has not been fairly treated. It produces high quality windows and doors at keen prices, and that is surely in the public interest. The executive's consultant architect did not give the Starglaze representative a fair hearing. The consultant architect was adamant that Starglaze window frames would not be used. I believe that the main contractor has been frightened off by the consultant architect's attitude.

The Starglaze representative made an appointment with the consultant architect and took a sample of a Starglaze tilt-and-turn window. He waited 40 minutes in the foyer of the consultant's office. Eventually the consultant architect walked past on his way to another appointment with a partner or an employer. He did not give the representative a chance. He was not interested in discussing what was happening.

Starglaze had been increasing its work force in Larne and naturally that is of special interest to me. The contract for Cregagh flats, for which Starglaze submitted the lowest tender, would have created more jobs in my constituency and enabled the company to demonstrate its capability for even larger contracts for its high-quality products delivered on time and at competitive prices.

I have tried to resolve that problem through the proper channels but without success. In a communication from the Housing Executive's acting regional director, I was informed:

"It is the main Contractor's prerogative to nominate any sub-contractors he wishes to use and provided the sub-contractors' products are on the Executive's approved list and there are no other impediments to the ue of the sub-contractor, the Executive will accept the nomination."

The products are on the approved list, so why did the contract not go to Starglaze? What is behind the comment:

"provided . . . there are no other impediments"?

I know of none. The letter goes on to say:

"I have been assured by the Executive's consultants for this scheme that if the main contractor submits his list of nominated sub-contractors, it will be passed to the Executive for approval using the criteria applied in any other scheme."

I want an inquiry. I want the project stopped because justice must be seen to be done. That will be possible only when the practice has been exposed as unfair and the contract has gone back to Starglaze. The power of consultants to obstruct a successful tender by a manufacturer must be examined and diminished.

Who will pay the higher costs incurred by the main contractor who has recently accepted the next lowest suitable tender? Will that result in an extra cost to be paid by the Northern Ireland Housing Executive to the main contractor? We must support fair competition and ensure that there is value for money in all public expenditure.

[*Mr. Roy Beggs*]

The money voted to the Department of the Environment in vote 4 covers expenditure on land registry. Earlier this year the Minister, in a written answer to me, said that a comprehensive review of land registry functions in Northern Ireland would be under way by mid-1989. We have arrived at mid-1989, and I had hoped that the Minister who gave me that reply would have been here to report progress. There are still unreasonable delays in processing transactions, with thousands of queries in a permanent log jam at the land registry office in Belfast.

I have constituent pensioners in Rathcoole, Newtownabbey, paying full rent out of their pensions for the homes that they tried to purchase several months ago. That £22 per week is causing unnecessary hardship. The money to pay for the houses is available on completion of the information that is needed for the transaction from the land registry, and that must be completed as a matter of urgency. I appeal to the Minister to provide additional temporary staff at the land registry in Belfast pending the outcome of the efficiency review that should be under way.

My constituents in east Antrim and those elsewhere whose homes were built nearly 30 years ago can reasonably expect funding for rewiring, central heating, improvements to old-fashioned and inadequate kitchens and the replacement of warped metal window frames which cannot be permanently straightened. In the interests of energy conservation alone, it would make a lot of sense to replace those metal framed windows immediately in all Housing Executive houses.

Will the Minister also bear in mind the many people who were encouraged to buy their homes from the Housing Executive? As first-time buyers they knew nothing about caveat emptor. The executive in my area has been replacing thousands of faulty flues. First-time buyers are committed to mortgage repayments and cannot raise another £600 to replace a faulty flue. Surely it would not be unreasonable to devise an entry point into the grants scheme which would enable people who have bought faulty homes from the Housing Executive at least to have some grant aid and assistance to replace a faulty flue. We still have a responsibility to those who have purchased properties which could put their health at risk and we should not duck out of it.

Vote 6 on page 4 of the order makes provision to fund the Northern Ireland fire authority. I and my constituents appreciate that the Northern Ireland fire authority serves all sections of the community well. There are limited numbers of full-time firemen in Northern Ireland, so the service is dependent on volunteer, part-time firemen who are on either 24-hour or 12-hour call. I should like to make an appeal to the Secretary of State through the Minister that suitable provision should be made to enable all the trained, part-time firemen who are employed in Government Departments, education and health boards, district councils and the private sector to respond to call-outs for the fire service during normal working hours. Employers should encourage that, provided that no one in their place of work is endangered if they respond to a fire call.

I trust that none of the money voted in the order is planned for capital work in connection with the proposed residential fire training depot at Old Manse road, Jordanstown, in Newtownabbey, in my constituency. The peace and privacy of that residential area would be adversely affected if such a proposal were to go through on appeal in future. There are much more suitable sites for a residential training establishment for the Northern Ireland fire authority. I hope that the Minister will use his influence and will be seen to support the residents in their objections, the views of Newtownabbey council and the objections that I have lodged, and encourage the Northern Ireland fire authority to withdraw the appeal which is pending with the Department of the Environment or seek to have the application refused.

I join other hon. Members who register concern about the long waiting list for urgent treatment in our hospitals. Long waiting lists are not acceptable and should not be condoned, especially by the representatives of a Government who endeavour to project themselves as a caring Government.

One of my constituents, a pensioner, a lady who had had a hip replacement operation nearly 18 months ago, has been waiting to have her other hip replacement. Her husband pleaded with me to do something. She refused to say at which hospital she had been treated and she refused to name the consultant, as she said that she appreciated what they did for her so much that she did not want to get anyone into trouble. She suffers discomfort and some bad pain, and there must be many others who could be relieved of pain if it were possible to shorten the waiting lists. I hope that that will be possible. No hon. Member could sit idly by and look at his mother or a relative in the same circumstances without urging that something be done quickly. Not everyone can afford private medicine and those who are in genuine need and cannot afford private treatment should not have to wait 18 months for necessary medical attention.

We in Larne are well served by Moyle hospital. The Moyle action committee has been endeavouring to persuade the Minister and the Prime Minister that the grand hospital plan for Antrim is not in the best interests of the people of east Antrim and is not necessary. The Estimates, according to my interpretation, show that at present rates over £40 million could be spent on the Antrim hospital. I want the people of Antrim to have adequate hospital facilities, but we have heard tonight about the closure of wards in existing hospitals. How can we justify spending millions of pounds to build new hospitals when existing facilities are not being fully utilised? Like the hon. Member for South Down (Mr. McGrady), I think that small expenditure on Moyle hospital would provide us with adequate hospital facilities for a lifetime. Proper use of the teaching hospitals and facilities in Belfast would be a much better use of public money.

Over the past 15 years successive Ministers, goaded on by officials, have supported that out-of-date proposal. The Ministers and the Ministers' nominees on the health boards—they are not elected and are not accountable to anybody—are the main supporters, together with a few who will benefit directly from new specialist employment and major posts created at Antrim.

I wish to record my opposition to the running down of Moyle hospital in Larne and to state clearly that the expenditure proposed for the Antrim site will not provide value for money. Unfortunately, the Public Accounts Committee cannot investigate the expenditure until it has taken place. It is a pity that its powers could not be extended to examine some of the proposals being made.

I know that other hon. Members wish to make a contribution, so I shall conclude. I welcome the provision that has been made for expenditure at Larne high school in my constituency. I regret that there is no mention of the funding for the final development at Larne grammar school. It is a pity that, when the contractors were on the site and the parents had raised the money to complete the project, the work could not be finished. I suspect that it will now be on the long finger.

With respect to the moneys voted to the Department of Health and Social Services and the Department of Education, I ask the Minister to take a chance and bank on the fact that in Northern Ireland we tend to underspend, so the Minister should anticipate sufficient underspend to allow for the provision of an additional speech therapist at Hillcroft special school in Newtownabbey. The parents of handicapped children there have been greatly distressed because more children were enrolled and statemented because they required speech therapy. To cope with that transitional problem, many of those who have been receiving speech therapy and who have no other means of communication and so are dependent on the help of speech therapists no longer have that benefit because time has been allocated to the younger handicapped children.

To provide an extra therapist would not be a major item of expenditure. It is a safe bet that more than the salary of one speech therapist will be left behind in the underspend before the end of the year. If even one additional child is statemented as requiring speech therapy in another special school in my constituency, additional staffing will be required there. It would be appropriate for the Minister to authorise the appointment of one additional speech therapist in east Antrim. If necessary, that speech therapist could be peripatetic and employed between the special schools where definite needs have been established.

Other hon. Members have already referred tonight to the long list of children awaiting the opportunity to receive even limited nursery education. Carrickfergus and other parts of my constituency have the same problems as those to which other hon. Members have referred. The principals of nursery schools are embarrassed. They have 90 or 100 children on the waiting list, but they are allowed to enrol only just over 20 children. Of those 20, they have to accept six or so because they have been recommended by health visitors or others for good reasons. The education and library boards cannot deal with that matter on their own because of cuts in successive years. They do not have the funds to provide sufficient nursery places. Surely such education could be provided at less cost if it were possible to utilise existing vacant classrooms in our primary schools. Where that is not possible, a definite commitment in the east of the Province would be welcome. The Government could signal to the North Eastern education and library board that money could be used to provide nursery school places, and I hope that that will be possible.

I also ask the Minister to deal sensitively with the proposals put forward by the South Eastern education and library board. The hon. Member for South Down earlier referred to the problems associated with state education in that area. I gladly and wholeheartedly support his comments. If the Minister accepts the proposals coming from the South Eastern education and library board and refuses to take account of the opinions of parents and teachers in the area, there will be a greater exodus, so great that they will need no state schools in South Down. That is happening at a time when the Minister is saying that parents must have choice. I therefore appeal to him to listen to what they are saying.

South Down also experiences high unemployment. If the status of Down high school is destroyed, it will be difficult to encourage into the area the young executives who we hope will set up new industries. If Down high school's status is changed from that of a grammar school, many parents will be forced to send their children far beyond the area of the school. That school has a good history, a good tradition and an excellent record, and should be retained as the grammar school for the area.

I hope that the Minister responsible for education in Northern Ireland will not contribute to driving out the people who maintain an interest in Down high school and who represent a diminishing group in the state sector in that area.

9.50 pm

**Rev. Ian Paisley** (Antrim, North): I begin by giving my full backing to what the hon. Member for Antrim, East (Mr. Beggs) has just said about Down high school and to the other hon. Members who spoke earlier when, unfortunately, I was not able to be present.

This is a serious matter. I have raised it in the House previously and I do so again tonight because that grammar school is the only gramar school for the Protestant community in that area. If it disappears, the Roman Catholic children will still have the opportunity of a grammar school education, but Protestant children will not. Working-class protestants will be bereft of grammar school schooling while those who are wealthy will be sent to schools in Belfast where they will have to be resident. Working-class children will not have that opportunity.

As the hon. Member for Antrim, East has just said, there will be an exodus from the area. That is not only my view; it has been put to me by the governors of the school and the residents of Downpatrick. The Minister must take that view on board because, if he does not, as one governor said to me, we shall be forced to come to the conclusion that there is deliberate discrimination against one section of the community whose children will not be offered proper schooling. I trust that the Minister will take on board the other issues raised about school closures. He must pay careful attention to this serious matter.

This is a tragedy, because the small schools in the rural areas of Northern Ireland have been a cement in the community. We talk about keeping the community together, but the cement is being removed and the fabric destroyed. The community will be without the facilities that keep it together and that contribute to a whole society.

I turn now to the equally serious matter of Mitchell House school which provides residence for severely physically handicapped children. Recently, without notice to any of the parents, the staff were suddenly told that they would all be made redundant and that the resident part of the school would be closed. Physically handicapped children will no longer have the opportunity to reside there. Indeed, the parents have now been told that the children who were resident will be sent back to their homes. The facilities to give respite to the parents of

[*Rev. Ian Paisley*]

seriously physically handicapped children will be taken away. It is a terrible indictment of the Government that, in this age, such facilities are to be taken away.

I want additional facilities made available so that those parents can have the break that they need. I hope that tonight the Minister will give some ray of hope to them. He should talk to them and recognise their frustrations and the problems that they are up against. He should understand the condition of their children and the necessity for them to be treated humanely. The Government should take quick action in this matter.

Some 20 or so years ago the Northern Ireland roads system was second to none. Many good improvements were made and the Province was moving forward. Now, because of the deterioration in the infrastructure, many strategic roads are outdated and capital funding has been over-restricted for many years. I have had a peep at the pamphlet "Roads for Prosperity" that covers roads in England. I trust that a similar document will be prepared for Northern Ireland.

A strategic plan for Northern Ireland has been proposed, and I hope that it will show what will happen to the roads in the Province. I am greatly disturbed by the proposal that all the main traffic to the Channel tunnel should go over the border and via Holyhead to Wales. Associations within Northern Ireland local government have made representations about that. I hope that the Minister will tell us about his plans. There appears to be a dragging of feet on the subject of the roads to Larne. If the Larne port is to retain its prosperity—something that has been helpful to the whole east Antrim district—we need to know what is in the Government's mind for the extension of proper road facilities in that area. I trust that the people of Northern Ireland will soon be told what the Government intend to do.

There is congestion on the west link to Belfast, which will be further increased with the construction of the New Cross harbour bridges. What does the Minister intend to do about relief work to deal with the congestion?

Will the Government consider the construction of lengths of dual carriageway or climbing lanes on the roads to ports which support heavy lorry traffic? I understand that a large grant is going to the Irish Republic for the culverting of roads that are out of date. If so, and if the Irish Republic is to receive a large grant to update its roads, may we be assured that Her Majesty's Government have made application to ensure that, when heavier traffic comes on to the roads of Northern Ireland, we will be able to take advantage of EEC grants?

When is it expected that the dual carriageway into Ballymena will be completed? Will it take 10 years, the time stated at the inquiry? I have also been asked to mention the concern of many people about the Newry bypass. When will that be completed?

I am reliably informed that it will cost £200 million to bring the water service in Northern Ireland up to EEC standards. Is that money available? Is it a fact that when that work is done, £200 million having been spent on it, there will be no more water available than is available now? Will there be reserve capacity to take account of future industrial expansion in Northern Ireland? Has that been taken into account in forward planning? New industry and more jobs in Northern Ireland will require a good reserve capacity of water.

I confirm what was said by the hon. Member for Antrim, East about the Housing Executive. Why does it not have a plan to bring all the houses under its control, when they are being rehabilitated, up to a common standard? I have in mind houses in Ballymena with old steel windows. It seems strange that the Executive puts new wooden windows into some houses, and then argues with the tenants of other houses that their old steel windows are fine, that the wind and rain does not get through them and that they must be content to live with them.

The Minister had better consider this issue. I regularly go into houses and see, for example, newspapers stuffed between the brickwork and the steel windows, and the tenants tell me that the housing executive intends to take the old windows out, straighten them and put them back again. I can think of one area, Wilson avenue in Ballymena, where there has been almost civil commotion about the fact that the management will not renew the windows properly. The time has come for the Housing Executive to accept that a common standard should apply to all houses.

Matters of this kind cause great concern to tenants, especially when they have the upheaval of the Housing Executive moving in to do rehabilitation work. Hon. Members who represent Northern Ireland constituencies will appreciate the commotion that occurs when that happens, with people being forced to live in one bedroom. I visited a house recently in which all the floorboards had been taken up, with only two boards being left to enable the tenants to cross the floor to get to bed.

In other places, the Housing Executive moved the people out and made other provisions so that they could be outside while the work was being done. We have heard about the repair of flues. I have been in houses in my area when people have been called in to repair flues, and they have almost destroyed the whole house. I have seen the mess that they have made with soot and so on. The Housing Executive said, "We will not give you a new carpet even though the carpet has been destroyed." Suits of clothes hanging in wardrobes were completely destroyed, and then there was an argument about compensation. Housing Executive tenants must be dealt with humanely. There must be an opportunity for them to have their rights. Those matters have concerned hon. Members in our constituency work.

Why can the University Grants Committee back-up scheme, which is available in the rest of the United Kingdom, not be made available to Northern Ireland so that Northern Ireland students can benefit from it? Hon. Members will know that, apart from all the other troubles in Northern Ireland, basic matters concern the well-being and life of the community. They must have priority. The Government and the Northern Ireland Office must take those matters into account.

It is impossible for the Minister to answer all the questions that have been raised tonight, but we would appreciate a written answer to those questions that he cannot answer tonight so that we can go back to our constituents and say, "This matter was raised in the House; here is the answer," and then take it further.

10.2 pm

**Mr. Harry Barnes** (Derbyshire, North-East): My approach to the appropriations is similar to the approach that I would have taken if there had been time to call me in the debate on direct rule, although what I want to say now is different from what I would have said in that debate.

I see Socialism and democracy or aspects of Socialism and democracy as essential in resolving major problems faced by working people, whether they be Catholic, Protestant or of any other denomination or loyalty. Democratic and Socialist solutions seem to me to be appropriate. I see Socialism and democracy as interlinked concepts. Socialism without democracy becomes bureaucratic abuse. Democracy without Socialism, as we experience it throughout the United Kingdom, is shallow and inadequate. Just as devolved government with a Bill of Rights could allow the healthy development of non-sectarian politics in Northern Ireland, we need an economic and social transformation in Northern Ireland on Socialist and democratic terms, with the democratic and participative transformation of the economy, or at least we need to do what we can about nudging it in that important direction.

How can the Protestant and Irish working class co-operate and aid one another if they are expected to be passive recipients or victims of the economic process? If they are expected to be victims of a system that operates cut-throat enterprise activities and a cut-throat enterprise culture, those are not the conditions and circumstances in which the co-operation that is required in the Province can be nurtured and extended.

The voting patterns of hon. Members from Northern Ireland on the Government's enterprise culture initiatives is likely to prove instructive. It is something that in future we might look at closely in terms of debates concerning appropriations.

Let us look at the economic plight of Northern Ireland which these appropriations and Government policy do nothing to improve. Like Wales and the north-east of England, Northern Ireland is an area of industrial decline, shipbuilding and textiles being at the centre of the loss of its manufacturing base. Northern Ireland has shared little in the claimed recovery of the British economy, having a low GDP per head of the population. It is not seen by overseas investors and many others as an attractive area for capital location, and has little inward investment.

There was a rise of foreign investment in the 1960s, especially from the USA, with movements at a peak in the mid-1970s, with transnationals concentrated in mechanical engineering and textiles. Following the 1973 oil crisis, energy costs soared in the Province and areas such as artificial fibres went into terminal decline. Previous gains were often lost. In 1981, transnationals accounted for 23 per cent. of manufacturing jobs; by 1983, that was down to 16 per cent.

Bombardier—a most unfortunately named firm to come to Northern Ireland—is being given Short Brothers, with Government funding, without appropriate public control of the equity that is being provided. Most of Northern Ireland's economic problems rest on a change of direction in the United Kingdom economy, and perhaps in the world economy, away from closures, contractions, mergers and movements of high finance and corporate

headquarters to the south of England, away from tax and benefit cuts which open up the inequality gap, and away from the enterprise culture.

Economically, socially and politically, Northern Ireland needs something like the popular planning models that are recommended in a publication by the Transport and General Workers Union, which calls for a regional development bank to co-ordinate investment and target funds, with local authorities drawing up structure plans in association with their communities and trade unions, conducting job audits of the impact of total public sector activity and identifying business opportunities. Local projects would be integrated into an overall strategy, supported by community education and training programmes, with roles for bodies such as trade union resource centres similar to the Belfast unemployment centres project under the EEC's anti-poverty programme.

Essential for such measures of economic democracy is a context of political democracy, a devolved government with a Bill of Rights giving some scope for socialist policies, and interests which require that conflicts of race, gender, religion, sectional interests and sectarianism are overcome. Economic and political aspects of Socialism and democracy are appropriate to handling the problems within Northern Ireland. Those are the principles that I would have propounded in the earlier debate, had time been available. I have given some indication of what economic and social advances can be made within the Province. I would associate them with similar political developments of a constitutional nature that are required.

10.14 pm

**Mr. Ken Maginnis** (Fermanagh and South Tyrone): I apologise for the fact that I was not in the House for the beginning of the debate. I sat through the last debate without being called and I feel that I have an opportunity to say now some of the things that I had wished to say then.

Rather than deal with the specifics of the appropriations, I shall deal with the generalities and, to some extent, with our problems. Those problems are not caused by the lack of finance—I doubt if anyone taking part in the debate has complained that Northern Ireland is under-financed—but by the fact that the administration of the affairs of the various departments in Northern Ireland leaves so much to be desired that the finance is to a large extent wasted. The reason for that is partly the direct rule system, which, when influenced by the Anglo-Irish Agreement, means that Ministers are constantly junketing around Northern Ireland, almost begging for approval from the populace for the way in which they administer the area.

Two Ministers are especially adept at that. The Ministers with responsibility for educational matters and for health and environmental matters are for ever junketing around the Province telling us about the money that they have found for this and for that project. However, what they are really doing is distributing in a belated manner money that has already been allocated to Northern Ireland. They are distributing that funding in a piecemeal fashion, and that makes it difficult for civil servants to plan ahead.

Most hon. Members will know that last week the Public Accounts Committee suddenly found that the Northern

[*Mr. Ken Maginnis*]

Ireland Housing Executive had valued certain horticultural stock at more than £500,000, when, in fact, the true value of that stock was £45,000. We would be making a grave mistake if we put the blame squarely on the shoulders of those working with the Northern Ireland Housing Executive. The problem is that Ministers do not allow their departmental staff the scope to plan ahead to ensure that such errors do not occur.

I am not suggesting that all is well within the Civil Service. When one has the sort of direct rule system that we have had in the past 15 years—with, for example, the Secretary of State attempting to rule almost like a viceroy, and his junior Ministers following his example—of course we will find much the same problem or attitude permeating the Civil Service. The belief is that there is no accountability and no need for accountability in Northern Ireland. As an elected Member I probably suffer more directly than my constituents in trying to deal with that attitude.

That attitude permeates right down to the girl on the switchboard. Only yesterday at about three minutes to 1 o'clock I phoned one office and asked the girl on the switchboard to put me through to the head of the department. While I was doing something else I listened as the telephone rang, rang and rang. I suddenly realised that it was now five minutes past 1 o'clock and I set the telephone down and phoned back immediately only to be answered by the porter. I complained to him that I had not been put through to the head of the department and he said, "Ah well, he has probably gone to lunch." That was reasonable, but I thought that it was unreasonable that the young lady on the switchboard had plugged the telephone in but had then left her post to go to lunch and left me hanging on the other end. Her attitude appeared to be that if the person was there he would answer.

I had identified myself when I first telephoned and if such treatment is given to a Member of Parliament, what on earth happens to my constituents who try to get a service from that department or other departments? Where does the blame lie? I believe that it lies fairly and squarely with Ministers, although there is no doubt that senior civil servants should ensure that their departments are properly administered.

A more poignant, tragic example of what happens to my constituents involves a man who suffers from multiple sclerosis. By December 1988 he found it necessary to write to the Housing Executive to suggest that he needed an entrance into his little Orlit house so that a car could drive in rather than his being wheeled out to the roadway to get into a vehicle.

That matter was dealt with by the district housing manager, who got a report from a hospital consultant. She was unable, however, to make a decision and had to refer the matter to a welfare officer in her department. A further process had to be gone through and the welfare officer had to refer the matter to an occupational therapist. That therapist eventually managed to get a report together and by March of this year the district office had approval, as far as that went, for a roadway into the side of that man's house. It was then necessary for the district officer to refer the proposal to an engineer at regional level for approval. The regional officer approved it, but then had to pass the matter on to the road service department, a different

section within the Department of the Environment. Once again it was deemed to be necessary that the alteration should be made to the entrance and the work was regarded as feasible, but that was not enough, as the matter then had to be referred to the planning department. It was at that stage that it arrived with me; meanwhile there had been a seven-month delay.

When I rang the planners they promised that the matter would be attended to within a week. I thought it reasonable therefore that I should ring the regional engineer and suggest to him that he could go ahead quickly and begin to get things in hand. Imagine my surprise when he told me that he would be unable to deal with it because there was no direct labour organisation within his department to do a job which was worth slightly less than £1,000. He said that when he had received approval from the planning department he would have to refer the matter to an outside consultant because it would have to go to public tender. Therefore, a £1,000 job had now become a £5,000, £6,000, £7,000 or even £8,000 job. It was likely that at least a year would have elapsed before my unfortunate constituent would be able to drive, or have a car driven, up to the side of his house so that he could travel around.

I apologise for boring the House with that story, but it was worth the few minutes that it has taken to demonstrate the frustration faced by hon. Members such as myself when trying to ensure that our constituents' needs are given proper attention. The problem is not due to lack of funding, but to the bureaucratic machine which grinds slowly and, sometimes, not so surely. If we are to make the best use of the funding assigned to the Province, we must trim down the bureaucratic process under which we have suffered for the past 15 years. That process is destroying the opportunity for many good things to take place within the Province.

Earlier today, I listened to the Secretary of State talk about the need for good relations between the two communities in Northern Ireland. In the district council area in which I live, work and serve as a district councillor, very reasonable working arrangements exist between the two communities. Indeed, I would not be exaggerating if I said that we might be a little ahead of 25 other councils. Be that as it may, what reward do we receive for our efforts to share responsibility within the community?

Dungannon district council, along with Larne district council, is one of the two councils that do not have a proper leisure centre. Over the years, we made plans to provide a leisure centre that would be comparatively modest and would adjoin our present swimming pool. Initially, the Department of Education for Northern Ireland suggested that we were being too ambitious. Therefore, we went back to the drawing board and came up with a modest project costing £1·1 million.

Just as we had arranged with the permanent secretary at the Department of Education that we could begin to think about moving ahead and providing the leisure centre, the Minister responsible sent us a letter, the first two paragraphs of which read:

"You will be aware that in the course of the last few months the Minister has made a number of announcements about specific capital projects—mainly in the schools sector —which have been given approval to start in 1989/90."

Those were the various projects that had motivated a junket out to a certain part of the Province where he told us that he had found money to enable them to go ahead. The letter went on:

"I have to inform you that, apart from these projects, the Department will be unable to facilitate any other new starts in this financial year.

On the District Council front this means that the Department is unable to offer grant-aid on current applications in respect of sporting, recreational, community and arts facilities provision under the recreation and Youth Service".

In other words, the Minister had indulged in a con game. He had pretended to have extra money. He had gone out and distributed this money, and then promptly returned to his office to write to the rest of us and tell us that there was no money left for us—that to a council which was under-provided for, and one that provided good cross-community provision for its people.

Is it any wonder if I am sceptical when the Secretary of State says piously from the Dispatch Box that, if only the communities would come together and work more agreeably together, the problems of Northern Ireland would be sorted out? I am inclined to think that the Minister looked at Dungannon district council and said, "What a peaceable bunch. We can cut them out at this stage. We will send the money to somewhere that is slightly less agreeable."

It is not just the Minister with responsibility for education who acts in this high-handed and arrogant way. Recently, an organisation called the Goodman organisation sought planning permission to build a meat factory in my constituency, on a roundabout which is on the main route from the M1 to Omagh and Enniskillen, so it is busy. The factory was planned to go outside a village and adjacent to a voluntary secondary school, a housing estate and a number of private houses. Immediately, there was local opposition to the proposal, and I conveyed that opposition to every department involved in the decision to allow planning permission to go ahead. Initially, I was assured by the planners, the roads people, the water people, and the Department of Agriculture drainage division that there was no difficulty. They were opposed to a project in the area, but the whole matter had to be referred to an article 22 inquiry.

The ordinary objectors to the project did not have the finance to engage a barrister, and finance is not made available to such people. The organisation was able to bring along a high-powered team and senior counsel to represent it. Some of us, realising that we were in difficulty, went along to the inquiry and drew to the attention of the commissioner the danger of building a factory on that site. One of the matters that we drew to his attention was that if the organisation were allowed to build a factory in that location, it would be creating a monopoly—something to which the Government are supposed to be opposed.

The commissioner agreed with us in his findings. With regard to roads he said:

"I share and support these apprehensions about the advisability of introducing this access at this point, in spite of the Road Service's stated acceptance of it."

The road service had told me earlier that it was opposed to the proposal.

In terms of water, the commissioner said:

"the effect on the natural habitat of the river by the abstraction of such a percentage at low river flows has not been investigated. It would seem to me that such an abstraction rate was bound to have some effects downstream."

The commissioner was equally derogatory about effluent:

"The effluent treatment plant, skin shed and stomach content storage area will also be visible from the Omagh Road. I have noticed that at all the plants that I have visited there is some area for dumping unwanted waste. I am sure that it is required for emergency use, if not the normal running of the plant. In the case of this site it would have to be close to the river, at the lowest part of the site, or in a prominent position by the A4 or A5."

He concluded by rejecting the planning application.

In terms of employment, the commissioner recognised that the claims that the factory would provide 200 new jobs were false. As a result of the factory being built beside Ballygawley, 80 jobs in the same firm proposing the new factory would be lost in Enniskillen. The claimed 200 jobs would be reduced to 120. I was able to tell the commissioner that another plan to build a small boning factory providing 40 jobs would have to be abandoned if a monopoly developed. Therefore, the claimed 200 jobs were really only 80.

Members of the Ulster Farmers Union and other informed sources went further and suggested that Mid-Ulster Meats with 50 or 60 jobs, the council abattoir in Dungannon with a considerable number of jobs and other meat factories would ultimately be forced out of business. The Goodman Meats project would actually cause a net loss of jobs.

When the Minister was approached about this matter, he informed people that he did not know anything about it. He said that it had not arrived on his desk. For months it appeared that it had not arrived on his desk. Then the district councillors in Dungannon caught on. As soon as we approached the council elections, we realised that the announcement was going to be made and there would be no one there to object. We decided to try to stop that happening. A senior person in the planning department was telephoned and asked to state that that would not happen. A very clever assurance was given. We were told that it would not happen before the election. We should perhaps have understood that we would be misled. It did not happen before the election; it happened the day after, before we got back to our councils. That is the sort of trickery that we have to live with day by day, week by week and year by year.

There are many—I hope that I am one of them—who try to be reasonable. *[Interruption.]* I did not make it clear that the announcement was that planning permission would be given for the firm.

There are not many hon. Members here today, but those who read *Hansard* tomorrow might well look at Goodman International's background. It is based in the Irish Republic. There is nothing wrong with that: we do a great deal of business with the Irish Republic. But the firm is reported to be close to certain members of the Fianna Fail Government. In fact, it is supposed to subscribe heavily to that party's election expenses. No doubt it was able to bring influence to bear through the Anglo-Irish Conference or through other connections to circumvent the recommendations of the commissioner who investigated the planning application.

Let me quote from the *Irish Farmers Monthly* of April 1989. It says that the Goodman outfit

"has the ability to house over 25,000 cattle on nearly 50 acres of concrete."

The important part says:

"The cattle are fed on what is probably the cheapest feed in Ireland with usual ingredients including imported corn, gluten, meat and bone meal from his own factories, molasses and the inclusion of chicken litter at up to 20 per cent. of the diet. A recent visitor to the feed lots expressed surprise at the

[*Mr. Ken Maginnis*]

feeding of such a high level of chicken litter. But he was told, in a matter of fact way, that over a third of the diet had comprised of chicken litter on occasion".

That is the entrepreneur whom our administrative team is inviting into Northern Ireland to create a monopoly which will put our other abattoirs out of business, and which will ultimately result in the backbone of our economy, the farming industry, getting lower prices for its cattle. That is the irresponsibility that we have to face week after week, month after month, year after year.

But there is more. A FEOGA grant—processed through the Department of Agriculture at Stormont—worth £750,000 was agreed for that project long before planning permission was even considered. Because I insisted on an answer at the inquiry I managed to extract a letter that had been sent to the Department of Agriculture from the Goodman organisation saying that it had been confidently assured that planning permission would be agreed in May or June 1988. Yet the inquiry was not due to take place until September or October. To enlighten hon. Members, let me say that on no previous occasion have I ever found a FEOGA grant being awarded to any organisation until it could prove that it had planning permission to go ahead with a project in a specific place.

We shall have to deal not only with the £750,000 FEOGA grant but with a large grant from the Industrial Development Board—none of us will be told for how much—to put our other abattoirs out of business, to create a monopoly and to undermine our agricultural industry with an organisation that uses 20 per cent. chicken litter and bonemeal in cattle feed. What would the Minister responsible for environmental and health matters have to say about that? It is a pity that he is not in the House tonight to hear what we have to say.

While a massive organisation can ride roughshod over the interests of the community I represent—and Ministers at the Northern Ireland Office allow it to happen—the little fellow——

**Mr. Sydney Chapman** (Chipping Barnet): Disgraceful.

**Mr. Maginnis:** It is disgraceful. I am glad to have an accord with the Government Whip. I hope that he will advise his right hon. and hon. Friends in the Northern Ireland Office of his feelings on the matter.

The little fellow who tries to run a bus and coach hire firm and wants to provide an adequate service for my constituents—a firm such as Lakeland Tours in County Fermanagh—is balked every step of the way. Ulster Bus is allowed to prevent the development of a service for my constituents. The Department of the Environment road transport licensing branch permits that to happen. In an effort to provide an express service for students travelling the 90 miles from Belfast to Enniskillen each weekend, going out on a Friday and returning on a Sunday night, a group of enterprising constituents decided to set up a travel club and hoped to engage Lakeland Tours to provide that service.

The road transport licensing branch sent them a letter warning them that it would be irregular, that Ulster Bus provided an adequate service, that they should not cut across that service and to do so would be in contravention of regulations. But what happened a week or two later?

Ulster Bus announced a special weekend commuter fare and a new service on exactly the lines that had been proposed by the private operator—Lakeland Tours.

The little man is neither cared for nor cared about. I have example after example of that type of irregularity in dealing with the affairs of Northern Ireland. That irregularity means that the people I represent are getting neither value for the money that is there to be spent nor any opportunity to make proper representations, and I do not have the opportunity to make day-to-day representations on their behalf.

I am not allowed to have meetings with permanent secretaries by order of Ministers, one of whom is sitting in the Chamber now. He forbids his permanent secretary and senior civil servants to see me and other colleagues unless we agree to talk to him. That is the disgraceful way in which we are treated and I want it to be put on the record fairly and squarely. I want the Minister, if he disputes that, to stand up and do so as fairly and squarely as I have made my comments. We will then know where we stand in the future. I will know that there is a means whereby I can properly represent the interests of my constituents without having to submit to the bully-boy intimidation I have suffered for the past three and a half years.

**The Parliamentary Under-Secretary of State for Northern Ireland (Mr. Peter Viggers):** I would be happy to see the hon. Gentleman and any other Member of Parliament at any time, because that is the normal etiquette observed between Members of Parliament and Ministers. As for the hon. Gentleman saying that it is not possible for him to put his point of view across, he has done so for the past 36 minutes. If he continues for much longer, there will not be an opportunity for me to reply to the debate.

**Mr. Maginnis:** I certainly will not——

**Rev. Ian Paisley:** On a point of order, Mr. Deputy Speaker. Can you tell us when the debate has to end?

**Mr. Deputy Speaker (Sir Paul Dean):** The debate has to end at 11.30 pm at the latest.

**Mr. Maginnis:** I am grateful for that advice. I do not intend to take any of the time available to the Minister. I believe that he and his colleagues have a great deal to answer for.

As I said at the beginning, the people I represent do not suggest that they are underfunded or that they are not properly catered for financially. I could make many more points but——

**Rev. Ian Paisley:** Can the hon. Gentleman tell the House why the ban on Members of Parliament seeing permanent secretaries does not extend throughout the entire Northern Ireland Office? For example, I can meet the permanent secretary at the Department of Agriculture. When an attempt was made by the Minister, Lord Lyell, to stop that meeting, I received a personal apology from the permanent secretary who said that he would meet me at any time to discuss the matters I wanted to raise.

**Mr. Maginnis:** I do not know the answer to the hon. Gentleman's point. Perhaps the Minister will explain why he and some of his colleagues are so adamant that we have to meet him and only him and why we cannot discuss with senior civil servants issues that should not and would not normally take up the time of a Minister. I will say frankly to the Minister that some of his senior officers are willing to meet me and my colleagues but are keen that the Minister does not know that they have infringed his directive.

I will take the Minister's hint. Obviously, he will make amends. He is about to explain why we have such a bureaucratically inefficient system and why the firms from outside, one of which I have mentioned at length and which may turn out to be another De Lorean, are dealt with in a privileged manner and why some of the smaller firms—the backbone of our community and economy— are treated in such a despicable and offhand way.

I am grateful for the opportunity to have brought those facts before the House. I can stand by those facts. Let the Minister, when he replies, contradict me if he dares. Let him tell me that I cannot stand by those facts. He knows that that is not true.

10.54 pm

**The Parliamentary Under-Secretary of State for Northern Ireland (Mr. Peter Viggers):** Northern Ireland appropriation debates, especially those on main Estimates, are always wide-ranging. Hon. Members have raised many points on the spending plans and policies for particular services. I am anxious to have an opportunity to deal with as many of those as possible. I noted that earlier in the debate, which I have sat through for the past four hours, there was a comment that Ministers have not always found it possible to deal with points at the end of the debate. I accept that comment. On previous occasions, I have found that I have been squeezed out of the debate because hon. Members from Northern Ireland were so anxious to take part that it seemed right to give way to them. However, I was anxious to deal with as many points as possible.

The hon. Member for Antrim, North (Rev. Ian Paisley) was good enough to say that he recognised that it would not be possible to deal with all the points raised. Indeed, the number has been so many that it will not be possible to deal with them all. However, I give the House the assurance that I will deal with as many as possible and I will ensure that the points cannot be dealt with in debate are drawn to the attention of my ministerial colleagues as they relate to their Departments and letters will be written to hon. Members accordingly.

Before I deal with specific points arising from the debate, I want to add briefly to the comments that my right hon. Friend made in his opening remarks on the broader economic and public expenditure context within which the estimate provisions are framed, especially the industrial and economic areas for which I have responsibility.

Hon. Members will be aware that, when giving details of the outcome of the 1988 public expenditure round for Northern Ireland, my right hon. Friend the Secretary of State reaffirmed the priority within public expenditure that we attach to strengthening the economy. That objective is second only to the overriding priority of combating terrorism through the programme on law and order and I am pleased to say that there are clear signs that our public expenditure strategy is contributing to improvements in the economy.

It is also the case, of course, that Northern Ireland has benefited from the high levels of growth on the United Kingdom mainland and future prospects will be similarly linked to developments at national level. The combined effect of national economic growth and our public expenditure strategy has been reflected in, for example, the growth of output over recent years in the textile and clothing industries. There is also evidence of current growth and strong growth potential in a number of other sectors such as plastics, plastic packaging, information technology, electronics, including software production, and certain sectors of the food processing industry.

Another notable feature of the Northern Ireland economy in recent years has been the buoyancy of the retail sector. In the year to December 1988, the number of employees in retail distribution rose by some 1,300 or 2·7 per cent. and further increases can be expected. We are looking forward to welcoming the new Debenham store which is to open in Belfast city centre, and which will create 500 new full and part-time jobs.

Employment in manufacturing industries has also risen, from 100,530 in March 1987 to 102,190 by March 1989, with nearly all major sectors experiencing growth. Overall, the total number of employees in Northern Ireland increased by 6,370 during the same period.

Comments were made during the debate, notably by the hon. Members for Leicester, South (Mr. Marshall) and Derbyshire, North-East (Mr. Barnes), that some of those jobs were not necessarily of high quality and that they were, perhaps, low-tech jobs. I must say in parenthesis that I know that the hon. Member for Leicester, South wished to be here for the end of the debate, but it was simply not possible. He wishes to tender his apologies and he was good enough to say so to me.

**Mr. Kevin McNamara** (Kingston upon Hull, North): He has to attend the funeral of a close friend early in the morning.

**Mr. Viggers:** I am grateful to the hon. Gentleman for pointing that out. I am sure that the hon. Member for Leicester, South will be grateful that that is on the record.

I must say to the two hon. Gentlemen who raised the point about the quality of jobs that that opinion would not be shared by those at Standard Telephones and Cables and Du Pont and by those now working at the Antrim technology park. I am proud of the quality of the jobs created across the sector of employment, from the large companies through to the small companies. There has been substantial growth on a long-term, viable basis. As my right hon. Friend said in his introductory remarks, at the same time the trend in unemployment is downward. Since January 1987, the seasonally adjusted figure has fallen by almost 17,000. Moreover, the prospects for continuing economic improvement are good. The latest survey from the Confederation of British Industry reports a positive balance in business confidence in all sectors of the economy.

Notwithstanding this background of economic improvement, we recognise the need for public expenditure allocations which address Northern Ireland's comparatively high levels of need, within the necessary constraint of national economic policy. The hon. Member for Leicester, South made a substantial point of that in his introductory remarks. We recognise that, although falling, unemployment levels are still around twice the national average; and even that disguises much higher rates of unemployment in certain areas, with male unemployment posing a particular challenge. Similarly, housing unfitness was still over 8 per cent., though again declining, in the

*[Mr. Viggers]*

1987 housing survey; and Northern Ireland has a proportionately larger school population to educate than other parts of the United Kingdom.

Therefore, I advise hon. Members representing other parts of the United Kingdom, who may feel that special and perhaps excessive provision is given to Northern Ireland, that it is right and proper that public expenditure should continue to run at a higher level per capita than the United Kingdom average. Indeed, it runs at about 40 per cent. above the average for the rest of the United Kingdom, although one would not necessarily recognise that fact when one hears the complaints from hon. Members representing Northern Ireland constituencies.

Reflecting those needs, the main estimates before the House tonight incorporate a number of important increases over the previous plans for 1989-90. These include an additional £24 million to the Industrial Development Board for its job promotion activities; and an additional £25 million for Action for Community Employment and job training.

I must advise the hon. Member for Antrim, East (Mr. Beggs) who commented on the tragedy of highly trained people being unemployed, that 70 per cent. of the long-term unemployed have no educational qualifications, which is why we are now switching so many extra resources to the link between training and employment and why we are seeking to promote the training elements in our schemes including the Action for Community Employment scheme, which now has a 20 per cent. training element.

We have also found an extra £23 million for priority roads, education and health programmes and an extra £15 million to continue the "Making Belfast Work" initiative as part of a £55 million overall programme.

The hon. Member for Belfast, East (Mr. Robinson) asked about progress on Harland and Wolff and on Shorts —a most important subject. My right hon. Friend said in his introductory remarks that additional provision will be sought through Supplementary Estimates for the full 1989-90 costs of the privatisations. We are convinced that the future of those companies lies in the private sector, and we are happy with the heads of agreement that have been exchanged in each case. They provide a real chance for a much brighter future for those who work for the companies. However, more remains to be done before the privatisations are fully concluded, but I am confident that it will be achieved.

As to Harland and Wolff, since the signing of the heads of agreement with the management buy-out team and Mr. Olsen, significant progress has been made in preparation for the formal completion of the sale. Discussions between my officials and the MEBO-Olsen team and their respective advisers are continuing to finalise the legal contracts and other matters associated with the sale of the company. A formal notification of the terms of the disposal has been submitted to the European Commission and I am hopeful that we shall receive an early and positive response.

Mr. John Parker, the chairman of Harland and Wolff, and his senior management team have held a series of what I understand to have been constructive meetings with the work force and we await the outcome of his negotiations. Subject to EC Commission approval and the satisfactory

conclusion of the other pre-contract conditions and procedures, I would expect that the sale would be completed in September as planned.

We have been working consistently to achieve moving Shorts to the private sector since my statement to the House on 21 July last year. My right hon. Friend the Secretary of State made a statement on 7 June about the heads of agreement for the sale of Short Brothers to Bombardier of Canada. There will be a further opportunity for hon. Members to consider further the details of the privatisation agreement with Bombardier when Supplementary Estimate provision is sought. The agreement with Bombardier has opened the way for the transfer of Shorts from public ownership to the private sector, and we believe that this will give the company the best possible opportunity for a bright commercial future. We are satisfied with Bombardier's commitment to making a success of Shorts as a single company in Northern Ireland. We believe that during the next few years developments will prove exciting both for Shorts and for Northern Ireland. We look to the company to make a major contribution to the Northern Ireland economy.

The hon. Member for Leicester, South commented on the low percentage increase in spending on health and personal social services. Total expenditure will amount to £946 million, including £7·7 million for the 1989 review body pay awards for which Supplementary Estimates will be taken later. I think that perhaps the hon. Gentleman had not taken account of the fact that a reduction from 1 April 1989 in the rate of employers superannuation contributions has created savings of some £15 million. Together with the health and social services boards' cost improvement programmes yielding some £6·5 million, those savings mean that effective spending on the programme will be about 8·5 per cent. above last year's level, and not the figure that the hon. Gentleman quoted.

The hon. Gentleman also asked about bed closures in hospitals. During the past year the Eastern health and social services board has closed a number of acute beds, but that is in line with targets in the regional strategy for 1987 to 1992. I have been assured that services to patients have not been reduced as a result. Indeed, I understand that the number of patients receiving treatment continues to rise, reflecting a more efficient use of the resources available.

The hon. Gentleman asked about theatre closures at the Belfast City hospital. The recent theatre closures are a temporary measure brought about by a nursing shortage that arises from sickness and unexpected difficulties in recruitment. The normal theatre nursing complement of 62 has been reduced to 47, with the result that there are only four theatre teams instead of the usual six—that is, one to cover each theatre. The six theatres are used in rotation; no theatre has actually been closed. It is hoped that a fifth theatre nursing team will be available in two or three weeks and that a return to normal will follow in the near future.

The hon. Gentleman commented on hospital waiting lists. Of course, we are very concerned about that. The Department has recently had discussions with four health and social services boards about the validation and medical management of waiting lists and waiting times. Departmental guidance on the completion of waiting list returns has been reissued and a clinicians' guide to waiting list management will be published to promote better practice.

The hon. Gentleman referred to expenditure on the Health Service at large, to Northern Ireland's health profile and to the need to provide resources to deal with the health problems in the region. I draw the attention of the House to the fact that the Government have recognised the special needs of Northern Ireland, which is why programme costs are more than 20 per cent. higher per capita than in England and Wales. That is precisely in recognition of Northern Ireland's higher needs.

The hon. Member for North Down (Mr. Kilfedder) raised the issue of temporary classrooms. As my hon. Friend mentioned in his opening speech, nine new school projects with a total cost of £11 million have been allocated resources to enable them to start in 1989. A major aspect of that programme is the replacement of substandard facilities to meet the needs of the modern curriculum and to rationalise the existing stock of school buildings. I hope that, on the basis of what I have said, the hon. Gentleman recognises that matters are moving in the right direction.

The hon. Member also asked, as did the hon. Member for South Down (Mr. McGrady), about the tourism review that I commissioned in October of last year and which I received at the end of April. It will be published soon. I can give the hon. Gentlemen a preview by saying that the review has recognised that a comparatively small proportion of those who come to Northern Ireland do so as genuine holidaymakers or tourists. We believe that much more can be done to promote Northern Ireland as a tourist location and we intend to pursue that policy vigorously. As I say, the policy document will be published soon. We recognise the great importance of this area and agree that much more can be done.

The hon. Members for North Down (Mr. Kilfedder) and for Antrim, North referred to the level of roads expenditure. As I travel around Northern Ireland, I am surprised by the number of roads that are being improved and built. I appreciate that that is casual comment, and on one recent long journey it seemed that almost every paving stone was being replaced along the length of the road.

As my right hon. Friend said in his opening remarks, an additional £8 million is included in this year's roads programme for extending the programme of structural maintenance of carriageways and footways. The total provision for roads in 1989-90 is about £129 million, which the House will agree is a substantial allocation indeed.

The hon. Member for Belfast, North (Mr. Walker) raised the question of the rationalisation of controlled secondary schools in his constituency. I hope he will accept that some further rationalisation is necessary. Some of the schools in question are already too small to provide a properly balanced curriculum for their pupils. The Belfast education and library board is currently considering how best the rationalisation might be achieved, but has not yet reached a final conclusion. When the board reaches firm proposals, they will be subject to the statutory development proposal procedures, which will give all interested parties an opportunity to comment on them before decisions are taken.

The hon. Gentleman also referred to the resources that have been allocated under the "Making Belfast Work" initiative and suggested that certain parts of his constituency had been unfairly treated. I would not wish to minimise the problems in his constituency, but the Government are confident that the allocations for deprived areas of Belfast have been made in good faith.

We have tried to direct them to the areas of greatest need, and I believe that they are being effective in achieving their results.

The hon. Member for Belfast, North also raised a point about MRI, and I have in the last hour or so learned more about magnetic resonance imaging than I ever thought would be necessary for me. The provision of MRI remains an objective in the current regional strategy. I understand that the clinical efficacy of this equipment is still undergoing evaluation. A number of studies are in progress and the results of a major evaluation being carried out by the Medical Research Council are expected to be made available later this year. Also, the technology is rapidly changing and I understand that, as development progresses, new models are likely to become available which will be considerably cheaper to install and run and which will offer a wider range of clinical applications. The significant investment of resources required for MRI will also be a factor in the timing of its introduction.

By pointing out that resources were available in Dublin and London, the hon. Gentleman asked, as it were by implication, why no such resources were available in Northern Ireland. The capital costs per MRI installation are currently about £1 million, and revenue costs are estimated at £275,000 per year. If, as he said, it is possible for his constituents and others in Northern Ireland to enjoy the benefit of these resources by travelling to London or Dublin, as they wish, that appears to be a sensible use of resources at this stage, although obviously the matter will be kept under review.

The hon. Member for Belfast, North also spoke about the increase in IDB rents—I think he referred to Industrial Development Board rents rather than to Local Enterprise Development Unit rents—for small businesses. He said that some small businesses were being driven out of business by rent increases. If that is the case, I would wish to know about it, and I shall institute an inquiry and see what can be done. I hope I shall discover that the increases are fair and reasonable, but I shall take note of the point and ensure that no firm is driven out of business by such increases in rent.

**Mr. A. Cecil Walker:** I will identify to the Minister within the next day or so the business about which I was speaking.

**Mr. Viggers:** I am grateful to the hon. Gentleman. Without more information, I cannot comment further, but obviously I want to know the details, and I shall pursue the matter myself.

The hon. Member for Belfast, East asked about the Belfast urban area plan. The plan was published on 17 November 1987, and the closing date for submitting objections was 15 January 1988. The number of objections received was 2,400, and a public local inquiry into them by the Planning Appeals Commission was held in mid-1988, as I am sure that the hon. Gentleman will know. The commission is expected to report to the Department later this year and, after considering the report, the Department will issue its response and adoption statement. Although it is hoped that the plan will be adopted in late 1989, it depends on the date on which the commission reports to the Department and on the issues raised by the report.

The hon. Gentleman asked also about planning consultation, and expressed concern about the lack of consideration given to representations made to planning

*[Mr. Viggers]*

officials. Any planning applicant has the right to appeal to the Planning Appeals Commission if he or she is not satisfied with the Department's decision to refuse planning permission for a project.

The hon. Member for South Down raised further points about school rationalisation. For some time, the South Eastern education and library board has been considering the future of controlled secondary grammar school provision in South Down, as the hon. Gentleman knows. It has, however, suspended further consideration of the matter until it is in a position to take into account the effects of the education reform proposals that were recently announced by my hon. Friend the Minister of State, Department of Education and Science. When the board comes to a final decision on the matter, it will have to publish a development proposal outlining its proposals. There will be ample opportunity for all interested parties to comment on the proposal during the statutory consultation period, and the Department will take those comments into account before either approving or rejecting the proposal. There is no action which the Department can take until a proposal is published by the board.

The hon. Gentleman expressed some dissatisfaction that it had taken so long to submit the United Kingdom case for the less-favoured areas extension to Brussels. As he is probably aware, the criteria for designation of land are strict, and tests are necessarily time-consuming, and there is a significant extraction process in the presentation of statistical data relating to various economic and demographic tests. However, the matter is now in the hands of the EC Commission, and we hope that it will be able to reach a decision quickly.

The hon. Gentleman referred also to the Policy Studies Institute report on housing. I noted his comments. It is no surprise that, among its other findings, the PSI study finds no evidence of any sort of discrimination against Catholics. We welcome that.

The hon. Gentleman referred also to the star fibre optics programme, which we regard as an important element in selling high technology investment into Northern Ireland. He asked whether the star programme will apply to all areas of Northern Ireland. I confirm that that will be the case, because spurs from the fibre-optic ring will run into different regions. However, the hon. Gentleman does not need to rely on the spur in his own constituency, because the ring runs through the hon. Gentleman's constituency. He will be among those who are most able to take most advantage of the star programme.

The hon. Member for Belfast, East referred to accident and emergency services. The recommendations arising from a complementary study, carried out by a number of members of the eastern board into all the services provided at the Belfast City hospital, the Mater hospital and the Royal Victoria hospital, were included in the eastern board's draft operational plan as a basis for consultation. Proposals to implement some of the recommendations of the report are expected to go before the board shortly. My hon. Friend the Minister responsible for health matters will want to discuss the proposals with the board chairman when the board has come to a decision.

The hon. Member for Antrim, East asked about delays at the land registry. There is still a backlog of registrations. We are aware of the difficulties caused by delays in registration, and an efficiency scrutiny under the auspices of the efficiency unit is due to issue its report on the operation of the land registry on 31 August 1989, which I think is the date that the hon. Gentleman was seeking.

The hon. Gentleman referred also to window contracts at the Cregagh flats. He will appreciate that I am not in a position to respond to his concerns tonight, but I will ensure that his points are drawn to the attention of my hon. Friend the Under-Secretary of State for the Environment.

The hon. Member for Antrim, East expressed concern about the future of Moyle hospital at Larne. There are no proposals from the Northern health and social services board to close the hospital. The opening of the new hospital at Antrim will, however, necessitate a realignment of acute service, particularly those currently provided at the Moyle and at Waveney hospital in Ballymena. The role of these hospitals will change to that of supporting the new hospital. The precise range of services to be provided at the Moyle is a matter for the Northern board. The board's proposals will ultimately have to be approved by the Department of Health and Social Services.

The hon. Member for Antrim, North raised the issue of Mitchell House school. I am advised that this is a far from simple issue. My hon. Friend will note the points that have been made by the hon. Gentleman and I undertake that he will write to him.

The hon. Gentleman also asked about the cost of complying with the EC water directive. We take our obligations under the directive seriously and we will be assessing the resource implications in the context of public expenditure planning arrangements. The hon. Gentleman will appreciate that it is too early to be specific about the allocations which will be made for this purpose.

The effect of the Channel tunnel on road communication and transportation, particularly of freight, was also referred to by the hon. Gentleman. I would find it most surprising to discover that the normal pattern whereby transport companies in the Republic of Ireland use the ports of Northern Ireland, because of their increased and better efficiency, would be reversed as a result of the Channel tunnel. I will arrange for the hon. Gentleman to receive a letter on the subject when we have given it careful consideration.

The hon. Member for Fermanagh and South Tyrone (Mr. Maginnis) made a speech which I thought fell below his normal standards of objectivity. He commented on the service by the Northern Ireland Civil Service and told a horror story about a telephonist who had left him hanging on at lunchtime because it was her lunchtime and she was going off. I was shocked by the hon. Gentleman's story because I know it to be so unfair to the standard of service provided in Northern Ireland. If he comes across a case of inefficiency or lack of courtesy, I hope that he will draw it to the attention of Ministers because we would wish to pursue it.

We have the privilege of knowing the very high standard of service provided by the Northern Ireland Civil Service. The levels of courtesy and industry are exceptional. As one who comes from outside Northern Ireland, I have been greatly impressed by the Northern Ireland Civil Service. I believe that, man for man and woman for woman, it provides a better service than is provided in any other part of the United Kingdom. I say too that it ill becomes the hon. Gentleman, if he is seeking to assist in promoting the interests of Northern Ireland, to talk down the people who seek to serve Northern Ireland. By comparing the service provided, for instance, by the Passport Office, by the DHSS and by telecommunications in Northern Ireland with the service provided elsewhere, we know that the people of Northern Ireland are very well served.

I have sought to deal with the points that were raised during the debate. I recognise that it has not been possible to deal with everything. I repeat——

**Mr. Maginnis** *rose*——

**Mr. Viggers:** I am sorry; I do not wish to give way at this point.

**Mr. Maginnis:** On a point of order, Mr. Deputy Speaker. I am not sure that there is a great deal that you can do about it, but you will recall that the Minister asked for time to respond to the serious allegations which I made. I immediately gave way so that he could do so. I should like you and the House to note that he has not answered one single point about the administration in Northern Ireland.

**Mr. Viggers:** I was coming to a conclusion. I will simply say that I have tried to deal with the various points raised during the debate. I am grateful to hon. Gentlemen for the concern that they have expressed on behalf of their constituents which enables us to seek to provide a better service in return.

*Question put and agreed to.*

*Resolved,*

That the draft Appropriation (No. 2) (Northern Ireland) Order 1989, which was laid before this House on 8th June, be approved.

# Peak National Park (Flood Damage)

## STATUTORY INSTRUMENTS &c.

*Motion made, and Question put forthwith pursuant to Standing Order No. 101(5) (Standing Committees on Statutory Instruments, &c.).*

### DESIGNS

That the draft Design Right (Semiconductor Topographies) Regulations 1989, which were laid before this House on 6th June, be approved.

### RESTRICTIVE TRADE PRACTICES

That the draft Restrictive Trade Practices (Sale and Purchase and Share Subscription Agreements) (Goods) Order 1989, which was laid before this House on 22nd May, be approved.

That the draft Restrictive Trade Practices (Services) (Amendment) Order 1989, which was laid before this House on 12th June, be approved—[*Mr. Garel-Jones.*]

*Question agreed to.*

## Peak National Park (Flood Damage)

*Motion made, and Question proposed,* That this House do now adjourn.—[*Mr. Garel-Jones.*]

11.24 pm

**Mr. Nicholas Winterton** (Macclesfield): I am most grateful for the opportunity to raise the pressing need for urgent action to be taken to repair the damage that was suffered in the Wildboarclough valley and in a limited number of other areas in my constituency as a result of the devastating cloud burst and flash floods of 24 May. The exceptionally heavy rainfall on the dry baked mountain sides poured off into Todd Brook, which runs north through Kettleshulme and south into Clough Brook which runs through the Wildboarclough valley.

The floods left one man dead, Dr. Donald Hatch, when his car hit a swirling flood of water near Todd Brook and Kettleshulme on the A5002, and was swept into the raging brook. Two brave firemen built a make-shift bridge from three ladders and, with the help of passing drivers, lowered it across the water to the car. Using what I can only describe as that precarious device, the firemen eventually reached the car, sadly, only to find the driver drowned and pinned beneath his car. I am sure that the whole House will wish to join me in expressing our sympathy to the family and friends of Dr. Hatch.

The main disaster, however, was in the Wildboarclough valley and the effect of the floods upon the area involved was dramatic. Seven road bridges were extensively damaged and two miles of highway were virtually destroyed. It is too early as yet to assess the full impact of the disaster upon the local community, but it is important that we begin now to plan for the future to ensure that the unique character of the beautiful area of the Peak district national park can be properly and fully restored.

The intensity of the rainfall over a period of just 40 minutes caused extensive damage; the total list of which, in fact, includes 13 highway bridges, an unknown number of footbridges, substantial lengths of retaining walls, sections of the highway and hundreds of dry-stone walls. Local farmers, householders and businesses have suffered severe damage not just to the fabric of their buildings, but to their incomes and, what is more, to their whole environment.

Whatever additional resources are offered, it will take many months—perhaps a year or two—before the scars of this freak storm are removed. It was a once-in-a-hundred years storm.

I have visited the affected area and met not just with local residents, farmers and others in business, but with the local councillors and the Cheshire county council director of highways and transportation, whose responsibility it is to co-ordinate much of the response to the damage and to carry out the necessary repairs.

The county will be approaching the Government, with my full support, to ask for special grant aid to help it cope with a repair bill which could, if the valley is to be returned to its former state, come to a staggering £2 million or more. I hope that the Minister will listen sympathetically not just to the request for additional resouces to make good the roads and bridges which have been damaged, but also to repair the dry-stone walls and other damaged property in such a manner as is in keeping with the character of this most scenic and valuable of areas. The dry-stone walling in particular is a hallmark of the countryside of the Peak national park and to replace it, for example, with wire fencing, timber fencing or other more modern materials would be to lose for ever one more piece of our rural heritage, and a piece which is a major tourist feature of the Peak park and east Cheshire.

I am sure that my hon. Friend will take that point and do what he can to reassure local people, and those many thousands more who visit this beautiful area, that every possible step will be taken to restore Wildboarclough to its former state.

I accept quite willingly that some of this assistance may be channelled through the Peak Park joint planning board, not least the grants for the restoration of the dry-stone walling. I make no pretence, however, that I am asking for anything other than a major commitment from the Government. I also understand that it may be necessary, or perhaps wise, to seek additional emergency assistance from the European Community. I am sure that my hon. Friend will do all that he can to advise local authority representatives on the best way to make such an approach and that he will do all that he can to support such an application should it be made at some time in the near future.

So far, however, I have done no more than paint a broad-brush scenario of the situation that has arisen in an important small village in my constituency and the adjoining areas since 24 May. The House will appreciate that such a general picture is nothing compared to the impact upon the individuals who live there and their way of life.

Hill farmers, already facing difficulties, have been seriously affected, Mr. Lionel Belfield of Chambers farm, Macclesfield forest, saw his access drive and the bridge that supported it swept away almost in their entirety. Mr. Mike Richardson of High Ash farm, Wildboarclough, saw many of his trees washed away and his approach road swept away, Mr. John Eardley of Clough house farm saw one of his access roads and bridges completely destroyed. Mr. Derek Wild, a resident and the owner of Edinboro cottages in the centre of Wildboarclough, a superb terrace of stone cottages, saw them awash with flood water which left a legacy of mud and slime.

Mr. Fred Bailey of Brough farm lost a hard core road, the land drains that he had just installed as well as stock. Mr. Will Eardley of School cottage lost a number of ewes and lambs. Mr. Robert Webberley, who had just purchased Dingers Hollow farm from Piers Holmes Smith, who is moving to Scotland, found the flood pouring through his house and farm buildings. Mr. John Bowler found his dry-stone walls demolished, and he lost 34 ewes and 19 lambs from his farm, Torgate.

For local businesses the difficulties have not finished there. With the damage to local roads has come an interruption to the passing trade which was the lifeblood of many local men and women. The Crag inn, run by Mr. and Mrs. Woodward, has had virtually no custom since the disaster struck. Through no fault of their own—their customers—ramblers, sightseers, lovers of the countryside —simply do not pass through the village any more and their trade joins them in their absence. The Higton family of the Brookside cafe are suffering the same fate as is the landlord of the Stanley Arms inn. I have sampled the hospitality of all three places, and I can recommend their hospitality and their fare to anyone who would call.

With road signs saying "Road closed" on all approach roads to the village and valley, business is now almost non-existent except for the locals, who account for no more than 20 per cent. of usual trade.

Throughout the crisis the people of Wildboarclough have stood together and have sought to help each other. The local parish council, chaired by Mr. John Bowler, a much-respected local farmer—I have already mentioned the losses he has sustained—supported by the clerk of the parish council, Mr. Robert Ashley, has served as an excellent co-ordinating body. It has ensured that the problems experienced by local people have been drawn urgently to the attention of the officers of the Cheshire county council and the Macclesfield borough council, which are the responsible local authorities. It has also drawn those problems to the attention of the Peak Park joint planning board. The local branch of the National Farmers Union and its secretary, Mrs. Sally Hodgson, have done their best to advise and to help all the farmers who have been affected.

I must tonight make mention of Mr. Bill Livesley, the local borough councillor, and Mr. David Palmer, the local county councillor, both of whom I have worked with closely. They have visited Wildboarclough to see first hand the damage which has been done, and we have arranged a public meeting tomorrow evening in the Old School Room in Wildboarclough at which all those involved in the many different roles can exchange information about the precise work which needs to be done, its likely cost, the period during which it will be carried out and the possible sources of financial assistance. I am sure that, this evening, my hon. Friend will want to send a clear message and indication to that meeting that he is aware of the problems and that all possible action will be taken to provide the necessary financial and technical assistance to restore life to its normal pattern.

The list of those to whom special acknowledgement is due would not be complete without reference to the local police force, the fire brigade, and the officers and men of the two local authorities, the Cheshire county council and the Macclesfield borough council. I wish to pay particular tribute to the officers and councillors of Cheshire county council under the chairmanship of their newly installed chairman, because they made a thorough site inspection a few days after the disaster to see for themselves precisely what had happened in that valley.

I am sure that the House will be interested if I refer briefly to the extract from the report prepared for the county council and me by the director of highways and transportation, Mr. Brian Nielson, for whom I have the greatest regard and who has certainly left no stone unturned to try to help the people of Wildboarclough. His report states:

"On Wednesday 24th May at approximately 14.15 hours a radio call was received at the Macclesfield Area Office from an Area Supervisor in the Wincle area"

—Wincle is an adjoining village—

"that heavy rainfall was occurring and causing extensive flooding in Wincle and Wildboarclough and that assistance would be required to clear these floods from the carriageway.

Up to lunchtime of 24th May the weather had been hot, dry and sunny and this type of weather pattern had been existing in this area since 27th April and therefore ground conditions on the hillsides at the time of the storm were exceedingly dry . . .

Further reports were received from members of the public that severe storm damage had occurred in the

[*Mr. Nicholas Winterton*]

Wildboarclough area and it was becoming apparent that damage to highways, culverts and bridge structures had occurred.

At 15.50 hours a report was received from the Cheshire police that severe flooding was occurring at Reed Bridge, Kettleshulme, some miles from Wildboarclough and that a car had been swept off the carriageway into adjoining farmland by the severity of the flood at this location. Acting on this information from the Police the B5470 was temporarily closed. Immediately Direct Labour Organisation personnel were instructed to proceed to Kettleshulme area to erect suitable barriers to warn traffic of the road closure at this location."

The report continues:

"Reports were now being received by radio from County personnel that extreme severe storm damage had occurred in the Wilboarclough area and that extensive damage to bridge structures, culverts and carriageways had occurred. Also on the A537 in the area of Shining Tor, landslides had taken place partially closing the carriageway.

At approximately 16.30 hours the Bridges Section of the County Highways Department were informed of damage which had occurred to structures and a request was made for Bridge Engineers to be despatched to the Macclesfield area immediately. Direct Labour had been put on to full mobility for providing barriers to roads in the Macclesfield Forest, Wildboarclough, Saltersford and Kettleshulme areas as these roads were impassable.

All the bridges crossing the Clough stream had been extensively damaged. It was also noticed that culvert head walls, highway boundary walls and the highway structure had either been severely damaged or washed away completely.

At 22.00 hours a sweeper from Macclesfield Borough Council was organised to commence clearing up heavy deposits of gravel from the main A537 Buxton Road and Old Buxton Road, Macclesfield Forest. DLO gangs were deployed to commence clearing roads of heavy deposits of stone walling particularly in the Clough road from the Stanley Arms Public House to High Ash Farm where extensive flooding had occurred. Contact was also made with the residents of Edinboro Cottages who requested assistance in clearing up flood damage to their premises."

That is a record of some of the action taken by the end of that first day, 24 May. The work continued over the following days and was matched by sterling efforts from the police, the fire brigade and the borough council.

The severity of the storm and the extensive damage which occurred has had a devastating effect on the local community, especially the farmers within the area. Several have land on either side of bridges which are now impassable and are having to do a considerable mileage in detours to be able to feed and attend to their livestock, tend their land and receive winter feed and other deliveries. One farmer in particular, Mr. George Turnock of Lower Barn farm, Wildboarclough, is experiencing difficulties in gaining access to his premises as the only road in at the present time is alongside the Clough stream which is very narrow and in a dangerous condition in many places and exposed to any further flooding which may occur. Unless access is facilitated in the very near future for his winter fodder and to enable him to transport his beasts to market, he will suffer severe financial loss.

Wildboarclough was a picturesque valley in the Peak national park, and is a popular area for visitors, for walkers, for cyclists, for school parties and many others who love the beautiful countryside of the Peak Park and east Cheshire. The devastation caused by the flash flood has to some extent been exacerbated because of the environmental need to restore the valley, including the highway, to its former condition. Rebuilding the highway does not present major engineering difficulties, but the cost

will be substantial if the retaining walls, culverts and so on are to be restored, as I hope that they will be, to their original character and specification.

It is in this major task that the people of Wildboarclough, few in number but important none the less, need the assistance of Government at all levels, perhaps from the European Community, from the Countryside Commission, from the North-West water board and from the Groundwork Trust, in addition to the many bodies to which I have already referred. Wildboarclough and the Clough valley may be unknown to many people, but to the people of Cheshire and the north-west it is a delightful spot. We want to restore it. I hope that the Government will respond positively to my request on behalf of my constituents.

11.40 pm

**The Parliamentary Secretary to the Ministry of Agriculture, Fisheries and Food (Mr. Richard Ryder):** I am grateful to my hon. Friend the Member for Macclesfield (Mr. Winterton) for initiating this short debate. He has most movingly and clearly described the extent of the devastation caused by the flash floods in Wildboarclough valley on 24 May, I have seen his photographs and those taken by my officials of the devastation caused on that day.

Let me first offer my most sincere condolences to him and to the family and friends of Dr. Hatch who was so tragically killed in this disaster. Clearly the effect of this sudden storm on the local community has been devastating and I offer it all my sympathy in the difficulties that it now faces. I must also say that the initiatives that the local community has taken to itemise the damage and seek assistance in repairing it are first class. I would particularly like to single out the contribution of Mr. John Bowler, the chairman of the parish council who has personally suffered a good deal but who has, none the less, given a lead in the recovery effort.

My hon. Friend underlined that point. I have the impression of a strong and compassionate local community which has responded with great fortitude and speed to an entirely unforeseen disaster. It has my admiration as well as my sympathy and the promise that Government will do what they can within their powers to help put right the damage.

Clearly, a great responsibility here rests on the local community, the local authority and other organisations in the area as well as a number of Departments of State. Though I shall want to concentrate tonight on the assistance that my Department can offer and on its involvement so far in advising farmers, perhaps I can first address myself to the question of local authority assistance and repairs to the damaged highway. As my hon. Friend has said, there has been significant damage to the main access road through the valley. I know that he has already written to my right hon. Friend, the Secretary of State for Transport, to bring to his attention the sad events in Wildboarclough. He has now, I believe, received a reply to his letter. The position on this, as I understand it, is as follows.

The primary responsibility for dealing with emergencies like the devastation in Kettleshulme and Wildboarclough and, in particular, damage to major roads, lies with the local authorities. They have wide discretionary powers to spend money for such purposes under section 138 of the Local Government Act 1972 and normally include an amount in their budgets for such contingencies.

At the same time, however, the Government recognise that it would be unreasonable to expect the entire burden of this extra local authority expenditure to fall on the ratepayer.

Under a model scheme designed to deal with extraordinary costs arising from emergencies, known as "the Bellwin Scheme", my right hon. Friend the Secretary of State for the Environment can in certain circumstances, provide special financial assistance to local authorities. These circumstances include a situation where, as a consequence of an emergency, authorities would otherwise incur an undue financial burden in carrying out immediate works to safeguard life and property or prevent suffering and severe inconvenience to affected communities. That burden is defined as expenditure above and beyond a threshold which represents what the local authority might normally be expected to budget for.

The Bellwin scheme has been used only twice so far. Once, following the emergencies created by the severe weather during the winter of 1986-87 and, again, after the great storm of 1987. If the county council considers it has a case for assistance of this kind, then I am sure that my right hon. Friend the Secretary of State for the Environment would be prepared to look at a detailed and fully costed application.

Clearly, in an emergency of this kind, it is essential to be able to make an early estimate of the extent of the damage and disruption and to identify all those organisations which may be able to assist in putting things right. My hon. Friend has already told us that a meeting has been arranged for tomorrow evening in Wildboarclough. I understand that representatives of the county council, the borough council, the Peak Park board, the Countryside Commission, the North West water authority rivers division, and the Groundwork Trust have been invited together with my hon. Friend and a representative from Lord Derby's estate. I shall be very happy to ensure that a record of our debate tonight goes to the chairmen of these organisations. I am also delighted to say that officials from my own Department will be attending tomorrow's meeting as will representatives of the National Farmers Union. I look forward to seeing a full report from my officials. I would here echo my hon. Friend's tribute to the role which Mrs. Sally Hodgson the secretary of the Macclesfield branch of the NFU has played in advising and helping farmers in the wake of catastrophe.

My own officials have also been deeply involved. They have already written to all the farmers concerned asking them to state exactly the amount of the damage which they have experienced. They have also ensured that all these farmers are fully familiar with the farm and conservation grant scheme provisions since we believe that under this scheme a good deal of useful assistance will be available towards repairing the damage.

My hon. Friend has already said that this is an area of particular beauty and that the dry-stone walling which is a characteristic feature of the landscape contributes greatly to its beauty. The floods have wrought particular devastation here. My hon. Friend has said that to replace those dry stone walls with wire or timber fencing would mean the loss of a precious part of our rural heritage. I am entirely at one with him on this. As he will know, we as a

Government, attach very high importance to assisting farmers to build and maintain traditional stone walls and to plant and lay hedges. That is why the highest rates of grant available under our new farm and conservation grant scheme are precisely for this kind of work. Fencing, by comparison, attracts a very much lower rate of grant.

Because Wildboarclough is in a less favoured area we are able to offer grants to the farmers concerned of 50 per cent. of the costs involved in reinstating the stone walls. Those grants may also cover incidental items such as gates, stiles and footbridges. It is also possible under our capital grant arrangements for farmers, if they wish, to charge for the cost of their own labour in rebuilding the stone walls. I am sure that this facility to charge at a standard cost rate will prove helpful to those concerned.

In addition to the grants which we are able to offer, the national park authorities have discretion to top-up the amount available to a maximum of 80 per cent. of the full cost of the work. We have been holding exploratory discussions with the Peak Park board to see whether it is able to contribute in this way and I very much hope that these will be successful. We understand from the local NFU that there may be some concern that the farmers involved will have already exhausted their entitlement to grant-aidable investment work. My officials have looked into this aspect and I am pleased to be able to tell my hon. Friend that we do not expect any difficulty on this score. If I may, I would like then to advise all the farmers concerned to contact the ministry as soon as they can with a full survey of the rebuilding work which is necessary. It is of course important that they seek Ministry advice before embarking upon significant expenditure on which they hope to get grant.

There is one other aspect of the capital grant arrangements where I trust that we may be able to offer some flexibility to assist the farmers concerned. This relates to farmers who hold an improvement plan qualifying for Ministry grant aid. In ordinary circumstances, the content of such plans constitutes a contract between the farmer and the Ministry. The work in the plan may not be significantly varied and the farmer is obliged to complete all the investments set out in that plan. In these exceptional circumstances, however we shall look sympathetically at any individual cases in which a farmer is now unable to complete his approved plan because of the effect of the floods. The farmer will then be free to withdraw from his plan without penalty, or to change it to include new investments made necessary as a result of the impact of the flood damage. For farmers holding plans under the agriculture and horticulture development scheme or the agriculture improvement scheme, this could include some work on the rebuilding of farm roads and related items. Again, if there are any farmers who may stand to benefit from this flexibility, I urge them to seek advice and help from local Ministry staff as soon as possible.

I hope that I have been able to demonstrate to my hon. Friend that we are anxious to play the fullest part that we can in a co-ordinated effort to remedy the devastation caused in one of our most beautiful areas.

My hon. Friend has also suggested that an application should be made to the European Community for assistance from its disaster fund. On this I have to say that I am rather less sanguine. The Commission's criteria for offering assistance are extremely tight. It is generally prepared to intervene only in cases of very large-scale

*[Mr. Richard Ryder]*

damage rendering many people homeless. For example, in 1987 we received some limited funding from the Community in the aftermath of the October storms. However, that was allocated to individuals and families, and to the Red Cross for emergency feeding and housing. In other cases, such as the Arkengarthdale floods in 1986, where the damage was similar to that in Wildboarclough but much more widespread, we were unable to attract Commission assistance. I can give my hon. Friend the commitment that we will help if we can on this, but we must not raise our hopes too high.

I am sure that my hon. Friend is aware that the Government are unable to intervene to pay compensation towards losses which could have been insured. That would, I fear, rule out compensation for the loss of livestock and damage to private housing.

However, that said, there are a number of other ways in which Government can help through other departments, and I have outlined some of those this evening. I am happy to assure my hon. Friend that we will work closely at the local level with those affected and with all other organisations involved in the repair work. I again extend my sympathies to all those who have been adversely affected and my congratulations on the positive way in which the local community has responded. My Department will do everything within its powers to contribute to the vital task of restoring this area and to reinstating it as a place much loved, not only by those who live there but, as my hon. Friend pointed out, by the many visitors there too. My hon. Friend has, as ever, done a great service to his constituents by raising this issue in the House tonight.

*Question put and agreed to.*

*Adjourned accordingly at eight minutes to Twelve o'clock.*

# House of Commons

*Friday 23 June 1989*

*The House met at half-past Nine o'clock*

PRAYERS

[MR. SPEAKER *in the Chair*]

### PETITIONS

## London Assessment Studies

9.36 am

**Mr. Gerald Bowden** (Dulwich): I beg leave to present two petitions on behalf of my constituents. The first is from Nunhead Action on Road and Rail, signed by representative members of community groups including Nunhead Residents' Association, the Peckham Society and South Circular Alert, who are all concerned that the road assessment study proposals now being considered will destroy open spaces and the lives and homes of their communities.

The second petition is from the Camberwell Society and is signed by 1,000 or more members, who also express their anxiety about the new road proposals and the view that if bigger roads are built, they will only attract more traffic —a view that I heartily endorse.

*To lie upon the Table.*

## Litter

9.37 am

**Mr. Simon Burns** (Chelmsford): I beg to call attention to the growing and unacceptable problem of litter; and to move,

That this House welcomes the Government's commitment to taking decisive measures to tackle the problem of litter; urges all those responsible for land in cities, towns and countryside to take account of widespread public concern at littering and discharge effectively their responsibility to keep that land free of litter; calls for urgent new measures to discourage littering, to assist those who are already taking seriously their responsibilities and to ensure that those who do not are obliged to do so; and supports the Government's proposal to place a duty on local authorities to keep their areas clean and to publish a code of practice.

I am extremely grateful to my hon. Friend the Member for Thanet, North (Mr. Gale) for the opportunity to raise an important issue this morning. I regard the litter problem in this country as being a non-party policitical issue that cuts across the political divide. However, I was bitterly disappointed that on two occasions my non-contentious, non-political Control of Litter (Fines) Bill was objected to by two Labour Members. When in future I hear Labour supporters claiming that they care about the environment and about litter-related problems, not only will I take their remarks with a pinch of salt but half the salt in Siberia.

I shall not dwell on the past but will look to the future and try to analyse what constructive measures can be taken to eliminate the litter problem, which is becoming such a blot on our landscape. My right hon. Friend the Prime Minister has rightly expressed her disgust at the state of our towns and countryside, and my hon. Friend the Under-Secretary of State for the Environment has won widespread praise for the vigour with which she tackles the problem and seeks to find relevant solutions that will meet the problem. Their concern is reflected by worries expressed throughout the country about declining standards of cleanliness in public places.

A recent Department of the Environment poll showed that almost 75 per cent. of people surveyed are worried about litter. Similarly, a poll by FDS Market Research revealed that 76 per cent. of British people think that there is more litter about now than there was 10 years ago. Sadly, Britain is in danger of becoming the dustbin of Europe.

Our inner cities and towns are riddled with litter abandoned by thoughtless, selfish litter louts. Our countryside also suffers from the dumping of litter, and the sides of motorways and major roads are a national disgrace. No longer is our nation a green and pleasant land. Fast food packaging, crisp bags, disposable drinks cans and cigarette stubs mar our environment: we are a nation that wallows in filth.

Why are we such a dirty nation when so many people express genuine concern and disgust at the sad state to which we have reduced ourselves? I believe that there are three answers. First, it is a question of attitude. Recently I visited Japan to study its litter laws, and was amazed to be told that the main thrust of that country's actions to deal with the problem was related to attitudes, rather than taking the form of a battery of laws and regulations. I was astonished by this revelation. Not only are Japan's streets infinitely cleaner than ours, but we could not possible rely on the attitudes of individuals. The attitude of the average

*[Mr. Simon Burns]*

person in this country is clearly entirely wrong and negative. Stand in any high street or drive behind any car and it is the same dismal story—people thoughtlessly abandoning their litter on the pavement or spilling it out of car windows.

It is just as amazing that few people who witness such spectacles have the courage to speak to the culprits, not only to tell them what they think of such actions but to try to chivvy them into picking up their litter. There seems to be complete apathy and lack of interest.

We need a complete change in attitude, and I believe that most of that change can be brought about by parents. Just as children are told from an early age that it is wrong to steal or lie, so they should be instructed not to drop litter. As a second step, parents should educate their children and lead by example. Sadly, however, the current initiatives in schools will probably mean that the children will start educating their parents rather than the other way about.

Another way of quickening the pace of changing attitudes is to alter the general perception of the problem, just as smoking has changed in the public's perception from a harmless, glamorous habit to an anti-social and disgusting one. People should not turn a blind eye, but should go up to those who drop litter and tell them exactly how selfishly and anti-socially they are behaving. It will be a long process, but that is no excuse for doing nothing.

Secondly, legislation has a key role to play. Laws encourage cleanliness and establish a deterrent against the more slovenly and selfish members of society. In his "Notes on Paris", Baudelaire wrote:

"Everyone's washing pavements. Even when it is pouring with rain. It's a national obsession."

Paris and other major European cities require people by law to keep the pavements in front of shops and houses clean. Every morning, and again in the afternoon, elderly ladies can be seen along with staff of retail outlets, scrubbing down the pavements in front of their homes and shops and making their contribution to keeping the law.

In West Germany people can be prosecuted if the streets in front of their houses are grubby, or even if their house fronts are not up to standard. In Australia litter droppers can be fined up to £240 on the spot. Something must do done in this country to strengthen existing legislation and to give local authorities real powers— powers that they are crying out for—to enforce anti-litter legislation.

The major anti-litter legislation—the Litter Act 1983 —is a national joke. It is ineffective because it is rarely used, and it is rarely used because the police are far busier carrying out more important tasks in combating crime: not unnaturally, the enforcement of litter laws is fairly low on their list of priorities. Even when litter louts are charged, the law is so complex that it is difficult to secure a successful prosecution. To prosecute successfully involves first seeing the offence being committed and secondly proving that the offender intended to drop litter. It is difficult to obtain evidence, and the derisory fines imposed by magistrates do not help.

The difficulty of enforcing the legislation is highlighted by the number of prosecutions between 1983 and 1988. They amounted to a mere 5,901, in a country with a population of over 50 million. Taken on a county or police-authority basis the figures are even more depressing.

In 1987 the county with the best record was Cumbria, with 296 prosecutions; the next highest figure, however, was 88, showing a drop of more than 200 in a single year. Greater London, with a population of between 7 and 8 million, boasted a figure of 18 prosecutions in that year, and in my county of Essex only 39 people were prosecuted. Of the 42 shire counties, 27, or about 65 per cent., prosecuted fewer than 40 people. Seven areas, including London and Merseyside—two places where it might be argued that the problem is at its greatest—prosecuted fewer than 20 people, and Cambridgeshire prosecuted only nine.

The punishments meted out by magistrates were equally depressing, thus establishing a general feeling that people can commit offences almost with impunity. Even if they are caught and successfully prosecuted—which, as those figures show, is fairly unlikely—the punishment will be very minor. The maximum fine under the 1983 Act is £400; the average fine actually imposed is £32.

The 1987 figures highlight the problem. In that year 1,628 people were fined a total of £57,407, an average of £35 per person. The majority of those—962—were given an average fine of only £19, while 475 were fined an average of £41, 154 were fined an average of £86 and only 37 were fined over £100, with an average fine of £183.

Those figures show that no deterrent is being built up. I believe that my hon. Friend the Minister should have a quiet word with the Lord Chancellor and encourage him to make known to magistrates the maximum fines under the 1983 Act, and to point out tactfully that the present level of fines is unacceptably low and is not helping to solve the problem. People are treating the fines as a joke, and will continue to offend with impunity.

The 1983 Act should be amended so that merely dropping litter becomes an absolute offence without the requirement to prove intent. However, but more must also be done on the legislative front to reinforce existing laws. I certainly do not advocate the repeal of the 1983 Act. We should keep it on the statute book, but should bring in further legislation to give local authorities the powers that they need and want to enforce the law effectively. Another way in which the Act should be strengthened is the removal from the police of the powers and requirements to enforce the Act. The police do not have the time to enforce it. They are overburdened. It is more important that they should reduce the level of serious crime rather than have to enforce the Litter Act. That power should be given by law to local authorities. They want it, and because they want it they will ensure that it is used to maximum effect.

Local authorities should also be allowed to give designated officers the power to impose on-the-spot litter fines. The example of Westminster city council shines like a beacon. It has shown the Government how to tackle the problem. Last year, by private legislation Westminster city council secured the right to allow designated council officials to impose on-the-spot fines, or issue fixed penalty tickets. Dozens of local authorities are carefully watching the Westminster experiment. They desperately want the powers that Westminster has taken for itself by means of private legislation, but the only way in which to obtain them is to introduce a private Bill, which is time consuming. Each local authority would have to use the private Bill procedure, which would cost a not inconsiderable sum of money. The Government could get round the problem by introducing legislation that would automatically give to all local authorities the power to use the legislation, if they so wish.

I am confident that the legislation would work and would help to solve the problem. Westminster city council has been given the power to designate local authority workers and officials as people who have the power to issue fixed penalty tickets to litter louts. Between 50 and 60 people have been designated as able to use that power. That is in addition to their existing work. Many of them also check building regulations and scaffolding. No additional employees would be needed, thus leading to a greater burden on ratepayers. The litter work would dovetail with their existing functions. I suspect that in the case of certain smaller local authorities—including, possibly, Chelmsford borough council—there may be a problem. They do not employ as many staff as Westminster city council, so they might have to take on additional staff. However, I do not believe that community charge payers in the smaller local authorities would be averse to paying for additional staff, provided that their streets and town centres were cleaned up.

If Westminster officials see that people are dropping litter, they have the power to go up to them and ask them to pick it up and either deposit it in a rubbish bin or take it away with them. If they meet with a refusal, they have the power to issue a fixed penalty ticket, in just the same way as traffic wardens issue parking tickets. A person who is given a fixed penalty ticket has two weeks in which to go to a magistrates court if he disagrees and thinks that he should not have been issued with a ticket. Either he can contest it in court, or he can pay the fine. Such a power is badly needed by all local authorities.

Early results in Westminster show that it is an effective power in the war against litter. Between April 1988 and April 1989, 727 people were approached in Westminster, and 723 of them either picked up their rubbish and deposited it in a rubbish bin or took it away with them. Four of them were issued with a ticket. The first successful prosecution took place two weeks ago. Somebody was taken to court under the Litter Act, having been issued with a fixed penalty ticket, was fined £40, and £35 costs were awarded against him.

Some may argue that the fact that only four people were issued with fixed penalty tickets is minimal, but that is to miss the point, because the other 723 people who dropped litter in Westminster picked it up. When they are next in Westminster I am quite sure that they will think twice about dropping litter again. If local authorities used the power properly, they would build up a reputation for being hot on litter, in just the same way as London has a reputation for being hot on people who park their cars illegally and then find that their cars have been wheel-clamped. People do not like having to spend relatively large sums of money on getting their cars back. Similarly, they would not like to suffer a penalty for dropping litter. If local authorities were known to be hot on little louts, people would think twice before discarding their empty fag packets, sweet papers or fish and chip packaging. That is the crux of the matter.

Cash dispenser wall units in banks, which are such a boon to people on Sundays when they have no money, are also a nuisance. Time after time the little slips of paper that come shooting out are abandoned. At the end of the day the pavement around any bank is awash with them. Banks realise that this is a problem and they are taking steps to counteract it by installing litter bins near dispensers. Sadly, however, for far too many lazy people it is just too easy to drop the slip rather than to walk a few feet and deposit it in a bin.

Food outlets, banks and retail shops should be made responsible for keeping the pavement outside their premises litter free, just as businesses in European cities have to take on that responsibility. Yesterday I received a letter from the Retail Consortium. It said that it believes that this is a valid point and that it is trying to encourage its members to get their staff to keep the pavements in front of their premises clean. Sadly, however, legislation is needed so that businesses are required to do that. Public-spirited companies and businesses are prepared to do it, but far too many of them either do not think about it, or they cannot be bothered, or they think up every excuse under the sun for not doing it because, they say, it will increase costs and therefore prices to the customer, or they will have taken on additional staff. That is nonsense but they will not see it like that until it is staring them in the face and they have to do something about it.

A good case can also be made for extending the legislation to the owners of private dwellings. They, too, should be made responsible for keeping their front gardens and the pavements outside their front gates clean. It is not just the Government or local authorities who should be made responsible for keeping our streets, towns and countryside litter free. The Government and legislation provide important leads, encouragement and deterrence, but all of us, as responsible citizens, must play our part. There would be moaning and complaining and barrack room lawyers and wide boys would try to think up every excuse under the sun as to why the legislation would not work. They would say that it is an infringement of civil liberties and they would trot out all kinds of other rubbish. But that is not necessarily true. Such initiatives should be given a chance to work, because after a number of years, when the problems have been dramatically reduced, people will welcome the fact that their pavements are much cleaner and they will wonder why on earth they had not taken the initiative years before. The moaning and groaning will be long forgotten because there will have been an improvement to the environment in which we live and that will be welcomed.

I welcome the possibility that the Government will place a duty on local authorities to keep their areas clean. The publication of a strict code of practice would ensure that positive action results in cleaner streets, roads and countryside. Obviously I cannot anticipate any announcement that my hon. Friend's Department may make and the battery of initiatives and powers that it may suggest to clear up the problem, but I hope that it will announce that provision. Local authorities should have a greater duty to keep their streets clean. I know that some excellent local authorities spend a great deal of time and money on rubbish collection and road sweepers, but other local authorities fail in that respect. I believe that all local authorities should look again at the practices and procedures that they employ to keep their areas clean. Some of them are failing in that duty and they need prodding by central Government to ensure that they raise their standards. I suspect that a code of practice is the only way to achieve that as individual ratepayers and community charge payers will have the right to appeal to a court to make sure that their local authority fulfils its duties.

[*Mr. Simon Burns*]

Local authorities could and should do more to review the frequency of street cleaning and rubbish collection, espcially in shopping areas. They should also ensure that there are sufficient litter bins in public places and that they are emptied frequently. All too often litter bins are cascading with litter that has not been collected. Sometimes black dustbin liners remain on the streets for too long before being collected. They get damaged and litter spews out all over the highway and the pavements. If local authorities are worried about the provision of litter bins in towns, villages and cities they should do more to involve local business men. Local business men should be encouraged to sponsor the placing of more litter bins in the high street. Retailers will welcome the opportunity to spend money on more litter bins, and, as a quid pro quo, no one would object if they put their names on the sides of the bins as a form of advertising so that people know that the entire community, including the business community is involved in solving the problem.

It is important to harness public good will towards combating litter. I do not think that any hon. Member from any political party, can underestimate the depth of feeling and the magnificent work that many people do throughout the country to try to address the litter problem and persuade people to behave in a cleaner, more social way. Sadly, until relatively recently, they were like an echo in the dark. They were considered by some to be a minority special interest group—the litter nuts who banged on about a single issue. They had no success and it was a waste of time. I pay tribute to their perseverance and their dedication. They were not litter nuts, they had identified a problem that many politicians have recognised far too late. At least politicians now recognise the problem, but only due to the dedication and work of those people.

Far too many people are litter louts. It seems to be ingrained in the British subconscious. But there is another brighter side to the coin. Up and down the country many public-spirited people are prepared to help by going out on litter picks and by going to schools, talking to children, highlighting the problem and trying to make them appreciate what will happen to our environment if it is allowed to continue. They try to enthuse youngsters so that they can play their part and educate their parents out of their anti-social behaviour. Those people have spent many long, thankless hours seeking solutions to the problem.

In Chelmsford, we are fortunate to have an ad hoc "Cleaner Chelmsford Committee" led by the former mayor of Chelmsford, Councillor Phillip Firth and comprising councillors, business men and concerned individuals who have done much sterling and recognised work over many years to try to address the problems in that town. Their efforts are reinforced throughout the country where, in other local authority areas, town and villages, concerned individuals have grouped together to do something rather than simply to moan about the problem. National organisations such as Keep Britain Tidy are doing tremendous work by highlighting problems, publicising the need for action and trying to co-ordinate individuals and the private sector. All that is going on at a subconscious level, below Government through individual initiatives which are appealing to people's sense of civic pride, almost shaming them into changing their habits and doing something positive to clean up.

That approach can be extended from private groups into the education system. I welcome the anti-litter campaigns in our schools that have been initiated by my hon. Friend the Under-Secretary of State for Education and Science, the hon. Member for Coventry, South-West (Mr. Butcher). It is important to get youngsters actively involved and interested in the subject and so that, one hopes, that will lead to a change in attitude and as they grow up they will instil in their children that one does not drop litter.

More should be done to encourage the recycling of rubbish. Sheffield, about which my hon. Friend the Member for Sheffield, Hallam (Mr. Patnick) knows a great deal more, is engaged in an exciting project involving central Government, the local authority, industry and volunteers, with the aim, over the next three years of showing that there are better ways of using rubbish than merely throwing it away. I believe that that project plans to cash in on up to 50 per cent. of the city's 250,000 tonnes of annual domestic waste output. It is an ambitious project and I wish it success because it will encourage other local authorities to expand their modest plans for recycling, through bottle banks and waste recycling programmes. If there is a success story in one part of the country and it is shown that local authorities can make money out of rubbish it will be a great incentive for other areas to follow that example or to expand their own projects to maximise the benefits which, we hope, will come to Sheffield.

Similarly, manufacturers have a role to play. I welcome that fact that one of the major soft drinks manufacturers in Britain is looking into ways of redesigning cans of soft drinks because those irritating ring pulls are always thrown away and create litter everywhere. It is looking at ways of redesigning those cans so that the spikes, for want of a better word, remain stuck to the can. Perhaps manufacturers could reconsider, on a purely voluntary basis—the Government cannot direct through legislation —reintroducing the old refundable deposit system for bottles and cans. I remember when I was a child that it was a source of extra pocket money to collect the bottles, take them back to the retail outlet and receive perhaps an old tuppence or threepence. If that was reintroduced, it would encourage people to save their bottles rather than just abandon them. The individual would get money back and the material from which the bottles or cans are made could be re-used. Manufacturers should give that serious consideration.

Manufacturers should also ensure that more take-away food is packaged in bio-degradable material. Most hon. Members will accept that one of the most depressing sights in our towns is the litter outside the fast food outlets at about 11 o'clock or 12 o'clock at night. Fish and chip papers are strewn all over the street together with hamburgers, fried chicken and so on. Rubbish is just abandoned everywhere. Manufacturers could and should do more to look into the use of bio-degradable packaging for fast food. It is excellent that Kentucky Fried Chicken is in the process of changing its methods so that shortly 80 per cent. of its packaging will be bio-degradable. Also, Wimpy is to be praised because it too has moved away from plastic packaging to bio-degradable packaging. That is a step in the right direction but far more manufacturers and fast food producers could move in that way.

**Mr. Irvine Patnick** (Sheffield, Hallam): Does my hon. Friend agree that a condition of planning permission should be that people who are given fast food agencies —I accept that they are a good way of obtaining staple food—have to agree to a litter-cleaning clause so that they have to employ people to clean around their area? Will he also consider flyposting and graffiti, which I also think of as a form of litter?

**Mr. Burns:** My hon. Friend's first point is extremely valid. If the Government were prepared to introduce rules and regulations to make retail outlets, fast food outlets and banks responsible for the pavement outside their premises, I hope that we would not have to go so far with the planning legislation. However, if it is felt that making retail outlets responsible for the pavement would not be enforceable, it would be worth looking into the planning aspect to see whether the problem can be tackled in that way.

I could not agree more with my hon. Friend's point about graffiti, which I also see as a form of litter. I should like to see greater parental control. I suspect that much of the graffiti is done by young children in their early or mid-teens who, at 9 o'clock or 10 o'clock at night should not be allowed to wander our streets bored out of their brains and taking aerosol cans to walls because they have nothing better to do. They should be under their parents' control at home. Greater parental control would see a reduction in the problem. Also, if people are caught flyposting or spraying graffiti on walls, they should be made to clean it up. They would find that a particularly unpleasant job and would not want to repeat it in a hurry.

The current litter problems are totally unacceptable. Once the situation has deteriorated to a certain level lethargy and apathy take a grip and it is much more difficult to improve matters. If people are used to living in filth and litter, instead of trying to do something about it they will accept it, become immune to it and contribute to it. If they are walking down a street which is covered in litter, they will not bother to make the effort to throw their rubbish away in a bin or take it home with them. Therefore, it is difficult to pull people out of their lethargy. We have to ensure that action is proposed to improve the problem and give further enthusiasm to those who are concerned and want to find a solution. Also, people who complain about the problem at present would see that improvements can be made and they will become enthusiastic and everyone will make a conscious effort.

I welcome the Government's commitment to tackling the problem and I look forward to the announcement in the Queen's Speech and the publication of the green Bill. The Bill is widely and eagerly awaited. I am confident that the work being carried out by the Department of the Environment will result in concrete proposals which will meet the expectations that have been raised. As my right hon. Friend the Prime Minister said, if we bag it and bin it, we really will win it.

10.17 am

**Mr. David Amess** (Basildon): I congratulate my hon. Friend the Member for Chelmsford (Mr. Burns) on bringing the subject of litter to the attention of the House. There is no doubt that he has been tireless in his efforts to try to persuade the House to take the matter seriously. The

hon. Member for Wallsend (Mr. Garrett), who unfortunately could not be here today, has also made many speeches on the subject of litter.

There is some irony in the fact that the hon. Member for Basildon should follow the hon. Member for Chelmsford. My hon. Friend the Member for Chelmsford will be aware of some modest rivalry over the county town of Essex. Of course, Chelmsford is the county town but, over the past few years, since the Liberal party has taken control of the district authority, there has been a deterioration in the general well-being of the environment in Chelmsford. It was that which prompted me to say that perhaps we should break away from the tradition of Chelmsford as the county town and move it to Basildon, which has undergone many improvements in the past few years. However, I believe that the political balance in Chelmsford has been somewhat redressed and on recent visits to Chelmsford I have noticed some improvements.

Does my hon. Friend agree that it is extraordinary that there is not one member of the Democrats or SDP present? At local level we have to put up with bits of paper being pushed through our doors saying that they are against litter. They are in favour of sunshine and people behaving themselves, but, above all, they are against litter. Surely the representatives of those parties could have organised themselves so that at least one hon. Member would be present today.

**Mr. Burns:** It is extremely interesting that the Democrat Benches are completely empty. Does my hon. Friend agree that one of the reasons for that is that in Chelmsford and throughout the nation the lights are going out for that party?

**Mr. Amess:** My hon. Friend's remarks are most apt. Liberals keep putting bits of paper through letter boxes saying that they are opposed to litter. Today is a golden opportunity to debate the subject in the House, but not one Social and Liberal Democrat Member is present.

A few weeks ago, I was privileged to participate in a debate with a cross-section of young people. It clearly emerged that they were concerned about environmental issues. They raised with me issues such as lead-free petrol, the Amazon rain forests, the ozone layer and all sorts of other environmental problems. My raising the subject of litter was a hoot. They said, "Who's bothered about litter? Cans and bits of paper do not matter." Following last week's substantial vote in favour of a party that has expressed concern about our environment, the problem of litter should be No. 1 on the list of priorities. It is within everyone's power to do something about it, but it is symptomatic of the problem that insufficient young people take it seriously enough at present.

As my hon. Friend the Member for Chelmsford said, litter is a nationwide problem, although I am sure that some Opposition Members would say that the north and midlands are tidier that the south. However, that probably has something to do with the general split of the population.

I do not wish my remarks to be construed as an attack on the people who try to keep our streets, highways and byways clean. I applaud the work of dustmen—as, no doubt, SLD members would were they present—and those who sweep our streets. They have a rotten and difficult job.

[*Mr. Amess*]

They cannot keep up with the amount of refuse that is chucked on the ground by people who take it for granted that someone else will pick it up.

The problem of litter should be at the top of the agenda and the political debate that we are enjoying. I shall briefly tell hon. Members how we are tackling the problem in Basildon.

My hon. Friend the Parliamentary Under-Secretary of State for the Environment responded to an Adjournment debate at the end of January and is therefore only too well aware of what we are trying to do in Basildon, but other hon. Members may be interested to learn about our general approach. Last year, we launched the "I love Basildon" campaign, which was a public declaration stating that we are building and creating a fine town and that we wish to keep it that way. We are tackling the problems of litter, graffiti—which was mentioned by my hon. Friend the Member for Sheffield, Hallam (Mr. Patnick)—and vandalism. On a cross-party basis, the community is working together to ensure that our town is the cleanest in the country. None of our ideas is original; they have all been tried before. Local businesses and fast food chains are sponsoring litter bins, and we are installing anti-litter bins.

We are trying something in Basildon that has not been tried before. Tonight, unannounced—although I suppose that I am announcing it now—I am going on a midnight patrol through the town to see at first hand what is going on. I shall ask young people of 13, 14 and 15 why they are standing on street corners, perhaps creating some sort of disturbance. I am sick to death of people saying that they are bored. It is different if someone is not well or is having a breakdown, but how people in 1989, with all the problems that we face, can say that they are bored is beyond me. There are many activities to occupy all minds, regardless of age. I shall be going on my midnight patrol tonight to find out about vandalism and to tackle the problems of graffiti and litter.

**Mr. Tony Banks** (Newham, North-West): I applaud the hon. Gentleman's initiative. I hope that nothing ill befalls him when he is patrolling around at midnight. Is it not a rather odd time to be patrolling, or was the hon. Gentleman just using a catchphrase? If people are hanging around on street corners in Basildon at midnight, I suspect that it will not be because they are bored but because they are up to no good. It might rebound on the hon. Gentleman when they find out who is asking them questions.

**Mr. Amess:** I shall tackle the problems regardless of the consequences. The hon. Gentleman is right; I was using a phrase, because the patrol will begin at 9 pm and finish at midnight. I should probably have some difficulty in seeing litter at midnight.

**Mr. Harry Greenway** (Ealing, North): My hon. Friend's announcement of his unannounced visit will interest everyone. A man in my constituency is a great contributor to various causes. He is a very nice man and I am not trying to belittle him, but if a list of donations to a cause is shown he always takes me to it and says, "Do you see where it says 'anonymous'? That is me."

**Mr. Amess:** I do not have an appropriate answer to my hon. Friend's intervention, but I thank him for making it.

Basildon is holding a front and back garden competition to decide who has the nicest garden. The general purpose is to highlight our aim of making Basildon as attactive as possible.

My hon. Friend the Member for Chelmsford said that there is money to be made out of rubbish. How right he is, and we shall certainly make money out of rubbish in Basildon. We have an excellent company called the Basildon Waste Paper Company and local businesses have invited Scouts, Guides and others to do what was always done in the past—to collect newspapers, cans, can rings and other refuse, with all the proceeds going to local charities.

Basildon has the largest covered shopping centre in Europe. I am trying to encourage the people who run it to play a looped tape that will welcome people, thank them for shopping in Basildon and entreat them not to drop their litter.

My hon. Friend the Member for Chelmsford said that litter should not be a party political subject. Unfortunately, politics is slightly involved in Basildon because there is a never-ending argument about who is responsible for cleaning up a green. Basildon has a new town commission, a district council and falls under the control of Essex county council. I am not bothered who clears litter; I just want Basildon kept clean and tidy. We should not fight over who will earn brownie points for cleaning up the place, which is why I am calling on the Guardian Angels. I know that there is some controversy about the Guardian Angels, whose logo quotes the words of Edmund Burke. It says:

"All that is required for the triumph of evil is that good men remain silent and do nothing."

I am not prepared to become involved in the argument about the merits of what the Guardian Angels have tried to do, but the House may be interested to know that the Guardian Angels have a branch that is prepared, free of charge, to try to clean up areas. I am inviting them to come to Basildon to clean up some areas about which constituents have written to me. We contacted the appropriate authorities, but nothing happened. In one part of London, the Guardian Angels have issued on excellent traders' charter, and local businesses have rallied round. I applaud the efforts of the Guardian Angels, and if they can clean up Basildon, I would welcome it.

Those who know Basildon well will have noticed the signs saying that Basildon is a nuclear-free zone. I do not want to become involved in the U-turn on nuclear energy in which the Labour party has engaged, but I believe that there should be big signs at the entrances to our town saying, "Welcome to Beautiful Basildon." I want everyone in Basildon to be proud of the area in which they live.

I agree with my hon. Friend the Member for Chelmsford that we need a national solution to the litter problem. I praise the Government's efforts to clean up our highways and byways. My right hon. Friend the Prime Minister wants the problem to be taken seriously. I applaud the efforts of the Keep Britain Tidy campaign and Project 2000 and last week's announcement on what we will do to educate people to read signs so that their dogs no longer foul footpaths. We must be positive about the issue and get people to take it much more seriously.

There are two sides to tackling the problem—education and penalties. Through the national curriculum we must ensure that little children are educated on the subject. That is why I was pleased to receive this morning a handwritten letter from schoolchildren in Basildon, saying:

"My friends and I at Lee Chapel Primary school have collected these milk bottle tops in response to the appeal to keep Basildon tidy. We do hope that this effort will go some way to make this possible.
                    Yours Sincerely
          Mary, Karen, Jo-Anne and Emily."
The letter was accompanied by a beautiful drawing of one animal saying to another,

"I wish they would keep Basildon tidy".
That is a profound message.

We must ensure that young people are educated so that they can embarrass their parents and stop them dropping litter. Yesterday, I was driving behind someone in a brand new BMW who must have had pots of money. He pressed a button so that the electric window came down and then calmly chucked out cigarette ends and packets and crisp bags—that from a supposedly well-educated member of the public. Who does he think will pick up the rubbish?

I agree with what my hon. Friend the Member for Chelmsford said about the project in Westminster. I am delighted that one of my constituents is working on it. I am sure that my hon. Friend the Member for Chelmsford is aware of the zip patrols which highlight particular areas in Westminster and have been very effective. It is sad that we must resort to the tactics of imposing on-the-spot litter fines. Those efforts are necessary until the effects of radical changes in education are felt.

I congratulate my hon. Friend the Member for Chelmsford on giving the House the opportunity to air our litter problems. I hope that the House and the nation will take this matter seriously so that, in years to come, we will be proud of the Government's achievements and will have ensured that Britain is the cleanest country in the world.

10.34 am

**Mr. Harry Greenway** (Ealing, North): I, too, warmly congratulate my hon. Friend the Member for Chelmsford (Mr. Burns) on initiating this important debate. Nothing does more to damage a community's morale than litter scattered about and the dirt that it causes. I remember when, as a young national service man doing basic training, a sergeant-major picked up a colleague's spoon from a pile of litter. He said, "Do you see this, soldier? What is that?" The soldier said, "It looks like grease." The sergeant-major replied, "Yes, it is grease. Grease draws dirt. Dirt kills soldiers!" That was one of the most dramatic pieces of discipline that I have ever seen. I have always remembered that sequence of thought—grease draws dirt, dirt draws germs and germs kill people. That is why litter is such a serious matter. That is why my hon. Friend has done the House such a service in introducing this important debate.

The thoughts of the House will be with my hon. Friend the Member for Basildon (Mr. Amess) tonight following his announcement of his unannounced visit to the street corners of Basildon. We wish him well in his noble endeavours. I hope that the friend who always tells me about his anonymous donations will not be hurt if I say that he sometimes asks, "Do you think that you could announce at the next meeting that I made another anonymous donation?" Anonymous kindnesses should be flushed out and announced. Likewise, my hon. Friend's unannounced visit should be known. It will be awaited with great interest.

Nothing does more to damage the environment than litter. We are becoming increasingly conscious of the environment. I wonder whether the House is aware that, by recycling a skipful of newspapers and other paper, 50 trees would be saved. Half the world's trees are used for pulp to make paper and other material. It is tragic if that paper is wasted. In addition, trees take in carbon dioxide and give out oxygen. We should remind ourselves every day of their positive contribution to the environment. The beauty of growing trees, even strugglers, shows the hand of God upon our environment.

My hon. Friend the Member for Basildon implied in the middle of his speech that litter starts to become a problem in schools. It is my experience, as one who served in schools for 23 years and finally ran a school of 2,200 for seven years, that the school leadership needs to keep firm control over litter. There is nothing more demoralising than children walking about scuffing paper in the corridors, yard, playgrounds or sports fields. That happens in some schools. It happens largely because ice cream vans, crisp-selling vans and the like are sometimes allowed to park inside the school grounds without the vendors accepting any responsibility for collecting the litter that is created by the products they sell. I know from my own experience that children very much want tuck such as crisps, but I also know that the difficulties I have described often result. The vendors of crisps and ice creams often make handsome contributions to school funds. That is valuable and positive, but would be lost by my proposal, which I ask my hon. Friend the Minister to consider in her reply.

Would it not be possible for all ice cream vans, crisp-selling vans and other vehicles which sell such items to school children to be kept at least 100 yards away from the school gates? That is necessary for reasons both of litter and of discipline. If a school is attempting to control children during the lunch hour, as is its responsibility, there is often indiscipline with children breaking school bounds and rushing out to the ice cream or crisp-selling vans to make purchases. Either the vans must be brought into school, so that there is no question of school discipline being broken, or they must be taken right away. I would prefer them to be taken right away unless, by coming inside the school premises to sell their wares—and people make considerable sums from such sales—the sellers accept the responsibility of assisting the staff to persuade children to put litter into bins, which they should provide, and they should also clear up the area where children have been eating food.

Heaven knows that teachers have enough to do, but it would help greatly if they got into the practice of tapping the shoulders of children who drop a piece of paper and asking them to pick it up and put it in a bin. That should always be done. Schools should also have litter squads. Sometimes children drop litter and are not apprehended and told to put it in the bin. Schools should set up squads of children, perhaps defaulters, for we no longer have the cane and some sort of sanction must be found for children who misbehave. Collecting litter is not a bad sanction and I used it from time to time when I was a teacher. Children who have misbehaved could be formed into litter squads and at the end of the morning, the beginning of the afternoon or the end of the day, they could pick up any litter around the school so that it is always spotless. If schools are spotless, they are attractive. If they are derelict and strewn with litter, morale goes quickly.

**Mr. Tony Banks:** Is the hon. Gentleman not wrong? Is he not encouraging the wrong philosophy by saying, as I think I heard him say, that children who misbehave should be formed into litter squads? In his initiative as a teacher, he linked punishment with collecting litter. That does not encourage and foster the attitude that the collection of litter is a matter of pride in a school. Making litter collection a sanction associates it with being punished by one of the teachers.

**Mr. Greenway:** The hon. Gentleman makes an interesting point. I said that I thought the first way to induce a good anti-litter attitude in children was by teachers asking them to pick up litter. I said then that it could be a useful disciplinary procedure to form litter squads, and there have to be disciplinary procedures. It is no good saying otherwise.

**Mr. Tony Banks:** I did not say that.

**Mr. Greenway:** I myself also organised squads positively by inviting children to join squads and saying, "Come on, let's clean up the school. Look at the mess." I used to collect the litter with them. If head teachers and deputy head teachers are helping as well, although heaven knows, they have enough to do running institutions of 2,200 children, the job will be done as it should be.

It is imperative that children leave school at 16 or later dedicated to the idea that they should not throw litter in schools, on pavements, or anywhere else and that they should always find a receptacle for litter. My old grandmother, who lived to be 95 years of age, always carried a bit bag in her handbag when she became an old lady. If any mess was incurred, such as when she read a letter and wanted to get rid of it while sitting on the bus, she would tear it up and put it in the bit bag. Perhaps the hon. Member for Newham, North-West should carry a bit bag round with him.

**Mr. Tony Banks:** I thought that the Prime Minister was doing that.

**Mr. Greenway:** I am not suggesting that the bit bag would be for his speeches—or for mine. There is nothing wrong with the idea of a bit bag and it is a fair tip, especially for people who are immobile and who cannot get to a rubbish bin. If they are carrying something like a big bag, they can put the bits into it.

One must applaud the efforts of the Westminster city council in its anti-litter drive, but nationally, we must try to reach the standards of other countries, even Spain, where there is a daily litter collection. That happens in some parts of this country as well. In very hot parts of Spain, if there were not a daily collection of litter, diseases would quickly spread. We have to extend that principle to this country, even though it will cost more.

**Mr. Patnick:** One of the odd things about litter and waste disposal in Spain is that waste disposal is carried out by private contractors. Also, litter is collected during the hours of darkness. Would my hon. Friend care to consider those points?

**Mr. Tony Banks:** We should get the hon. Member for Basildon (Mr. Amess) to do it.

**Mr. Greenway:** That is another task for my hon. Friend the Member for Basildon (Mr. Amess). My hon. Friend the Member for Sheffield, Hallam (Mr. Patnick) makes a most telling point when he says that litter in Spain is collected during the hours of darkness. It is collected at 3 am or 4 am and, no doubt, account is taken of that in the wages paid to the refuse collectors. The fact that it is collected by private enterprise organisations must mean that there is great efficiency.

**Mr. Tony Banks:** There are far more practical reasons why that is done in Spain and in Greece as well. First, it is a damn sight cooler at night. Collecting rubbish is not a nice job anyway, but collecting it in the heat of the day in Mediterranean countries would not be at all pleasant. Secondly, it is necessary, in the heat, to have far more collections because of the obvious effect of heat on food rubbish in particular.

**Mr. Greenway:** I made my point about Spain because, at present, it is as hot here as it is in Spain and we must take account of that, although I know that such heat is only too rare here. However, the hon. Gentleman makes his own point effectively.

I must speak briefly of the situation in Ealing. My hon. Friend the Member for Basildon said that he did not like to bring politics into this matter. I do not either, but I must point out that this year, there have been serious reductions in street cleansing and refuse collection in the London borough of Ealing, although the rates have increased by 32 per cent. and, two years ago, they increased by 65 per cent. People are concerned that they are paying far more in rates, yet the streets are not being cleaned as regularly as before and refuse is not being collected as regularly as before. That is serious. Public cleansing and refuse collection services should not be cut but should be at the top of the list of priorities because of the dangers to health.

Our foolish and politically unwise council made a serious mistake. Over Christmas and the New Year we had no refuse collection for 10 to 14 days. There were bags of litter everywhere: outside people's houses and in the street. That led to a plague of rats, which was extremely serious. Once rodents establish themselves—and nowhere is it easier for them to do so than where litter is lying around as it was on the streets of Ealing at the turn of the year —they are tenacious.

Some people say that in one year two rats can produce 1,200. Once a rat plague is established it is immensely difficult to put a stop to it. That was the problem facing the borough of Ealing as a result of the council's foolish and wicked failure to collect refuse over the Christmas and New Year period.

I am not saying that refuse collectors and street cleaners are not entitled to proper Christmas holidays like everyone else, but we cannot say to them, "Off you go boys, all of you, for a fortnight's holiday and forget about the rubbish" because of the possible results. Proper services must continue to be provided. We cannot expect people to carry them out for peanuts. They will have to be paid more for working at a time of year when they could expect to be on holiday, or they should be allowed extra time off at another time of the year when there is less pressure.

There is no doubt that the events of last Christmas must not happen again. Next Christmas I look forward to proper street cleansing and refuse collection in Ealing without fear or favour. We do not want rats back in Ealing, or people slipping and falling into rubbish bags for weeks after the festival. Once a large amount of litter has accumulated it takes ages to clear the backlog. Litter must not be allowed to pile up.

There is a serious problem of litter and smoking in many public places, caused notably by visitors to churches, cathedrals and museums. I saw somebody smoking in Westminster Abbey last week and it took me back 20 years to when I last saw somebody smoking in a cathedral in St John's Cathedral in Warsaw. I have never forgotten the offence I felt at that. If people smoke and throw their cigarettes on the floor of a beautiful cathedral, it is a great offence to other people and affects law and order. When the incident occurred in Warsaw cathedral, an old lady rushed at the individual concerned and had to be restrained because she was so hurt by the action. When I saw the smoker in Westminster Abbey last week I also wanted to rush at him, but I did not. I had a word with one of the bedesmen who received a pack of cheek from the individual for asking him not to smoke.

Does the Minister agree that people smoking and throwing litter about in our beautiful churches, cathedrals and abbeys should be fined £1,000 on the spot or if, quite sensibly, they do not carry such amounts, be asked to pay as soon as possible?

Perhaps even more severe penalties should be imposed. Such offences must not be allowed under any circumstances. They amount to a desecration of God's house, are wholly and grossly offensive to other individuals and produce litter, with all the knock-on effects which I have described. The practice of dropping litter is growing. Officials of the abbey and of other cathedrals have told me that more people are coming into churches and cathedrals on a casual basis. They do not have a religious background of any kind and, with the sad weakening of religious education in schools, they do not even respect God's house and do not realise that what they are doing is offensive.

We may be reaching the point where we must have in Westminster Abbey, St Paul's Cathedral and other such great and fine institutions, notices declaring, "No smoking under any circumstances. Offenders will be fined at least £1,000 if they do so." That would be a sad day but we may be approaching it.

10.55 am

**Miss Ann Widdecombe** (Maidstone): I am grateful for the opportunity to speak in this debate. I, too, wish to congratulate my hon. Friend the Member for Chelmsford (Mr. Burns), not only on securing the debate, but on the considerable tenacity with which he has pursued the subject. He has placed an excellent Bill before us, and has been extremely tenacious, despite the unexpected cries of objection from Opposition Members every time the matter comes up. I look forward to the Bill having a better fate in the future. I also congratulate him on the wide-ranging and comprehensive nature of his speech and the way in which he looked at almost every aspect of litter.

It ill-behoves this place to lecture the nation on its litter habits. Ever since I came to this place I have been disgusted by the scenes of devastation which can be seen after any Committee meeting or any normal day in the Chamber. Leaving Committee, we crunch across a sea of litter which is much less pleasant and less elevating than crunching across a sea of autumn leaves. I hope that when television finally comes to the Chamber, some panning shots will be shown of the scenes in the Chamber when we have finished for the day. Sadly, once the people of this country have seen those shots I do not think they will take our strictures on litter terribly seriously. Some of the powers given to Westminster city council could well be given to the Serjeant at Arms and others in the House to enforce better conduct.

I recently took one of my hon. Friends, certainly not anyone present today, to task for his litterous habits in Committee when my feet had literally sunk into the litter being dropped from the neighbouring seat. I asked him what he expected to happen to the litter, and he replied that there were people to pick it up. His reply was horribly reminiscent of the philosophy of those who say, "Oh, dear, the servants will do it." I also thought that his reply might contain implications that he expected women to clear it up. I have noticed that those who do not throw down litter in Committee or the Chamber are the 41, now 42, female Members.

On the Committee on which I serve, my right hon. Friend the Member for Norfolk, South (Mr. MacGregor) and I are the two who regularly take our litter away with us. I do not see why everyone else cannot do the same. When we look at Committee rooms and the Chamber at the end of a lengthy debate we cannot, realistically, turn round and talk about the disgusting habits of litter louts and others.

**Mr. Patnick:** Does my hon. Friend think that litter bins in the House of Commons would be any less decorous? Could we not have more litter bins to encourage Members to place their waste papers in them?

**Miss Widdecombe:** I thoroughly support the comments of my hon. Friend. However, we are not all entirely geriatric. It is a short step from the Committee rooms to the Committee room corridor where bins are placed at fairly regular intervals. I cannot believe that it would be a vast strain, even at the somewhat anti-social hours at which we sometimes leave Committee and the Chamber, to walk to one of the receptacles and place our litter in it.

**Mr. Harry Greenway:** Perhaps my hon. Friend would be interested in my suggestion that each hon. Member should carry a bit bag.

**Miss Widdecombe:** Yes, indeed I am. My hon. Friend the Member for Ealing, North (Mr. Greenway) could be quite enterprising. He could come in with a supply of bit bags and sell them at 5p a time for some worthy cause. Hon. Members could collect them from the Lobby as they came into the Chamber. All that is required is a little self-restraint, which is what we are asking the general public to practice.

On the more serious question of how we enforce tidiness, I entirely agree that we need adequate penalties and, perhaps more important, that those penalties should be backed by an adequate will to solve the problem. I am rather sorry that the 741 people in Westminster were merely asked to pick up their litter. It would have had a more deterrent effect and would have caught the popular imagination far more if those 741 people had been issued with fixed penalty tickets. I do not say that vindictively because I cannot believe that a fixed penalty ticket for litter will create a terrible stigma; it is not likely to blight a

[*Miss Widdecombe*]

person's life, any more than a parking ticket is. It would have made the point more effectively had those people been issued with fixed penalty tickets.

If there are to be penalties for litter dropping, they ought to be enforced vigorously, at least initially, to get the message home that dropping litter is an offence, and involves more than merely being asked to pick the litter up if one is unlucky enough to be caught. We must make it clear to people that they will have to pay the penalty.

If that practice were adopted more widely and if there were fines nationwide along the lines of the Westminster scheme, take-away food containers, fish and chip wrappings and other common causes of litter, including cash dispenser receipts, could have warnings stamped on them to the effect that a fine was likely to be imposed if they were dropped. At the moment there is no immediate warning to the person who is thinking carelessly of throwing something away that by doing so he may incur a fine. Dropping litter is rarely a deliberate action; it is a careless and uneducated action.

**Mr. Burns:** It has just occurred to me that all slips that come out of cash dispensing machines carry a number identifying the owner. In 99 per cent. of cases the person using the card to obtain money at a cash dispensing unit is the legal owner of this slip. Would there not be a case for the police to collect up the slips of paper left in the street and start to prosecute the guilty parties? That would surely have a deterrent effect?

**Miss Widdecombe:** The police simply do not have the time, but litter wardens or council officials could perhaps trace a random sample of guilty parties. If that process were accompaniesd by a great deal of publicity, it might be effective. A more effective way of solving the problem would be to educate people from a very young age not to drop litter. It would then be an automatic response.

The sponsored picking-up of litter is one good way of making the whole process fun rather than making it seem like punishment. The hon. Member for Newham, North-West (Mr. Banks) had a good point when he said that people should regard picking up litter not as punishment but as natural, worthy and—from the school child's point of view—fun. There are few sadder sights than a playground strewn with litter, which reminds us that we are not teaching our children to respect their environment. Ultimately the success of our attempts will depend on the will with which the arrangements are enforced and on the deterrent effect.

A couple of years ago I returned to Singapore, where I spent many happy years as a child. That country has very strict litter rules, and one does not see litter on the streets of the main city of Singapore. In the surrounding areas, however, the streets are every bit as dirty as London's streets. The reason is obvious. In the city, litter laws are enforced vigorously. The clean streets are something of a showpiece and a matter of national pride. Outside in the residential areas, the laws are not strictly enforced, so there is no deterrent and people continue to drop litter.

It is not just a matter of having strict laws; they have to be enforced universally. That is why my hon. Friend the Member for Chelmsford was so right to talk about front gardens and back gardens. We have a lovely garden in front of the block of flats in which I live in London but the hydrangea bushes fail to be enhanced by the crisp packets, Coke tins and so on carelessly tossed in from the street. We need laws to prevent that from happening. It is a deliberate act; it is not the same as someone happening to drop his chewing gum packet on the ground. People ask themselves, "Where can I put this?" and then throw the object away in the most convenient place. We must inculcate the right attitudes in people at a very early age. At the same time, we need realistic penalties and the will to impose them. Such penalties could be an attractive source of revenue to councils.

I commend the Westminster example but in particular I commend the Bill introduced by my hon. Friend the Member for Chelmsford and wish it a better fate in the few weeks left to us.

11.7 am

**Mr. Keith Mans** (Wyre): I am grateful for the opportunity to say a few words in support of my hon. Friend the Member for Chelmsford (Mr. Burns) in this excellent and long overdue debate.

We are all becoming increasingly aware of our environment. Over the past year a number of issues have hit the headlines and the amount of media attention that is being given to the environment is increasing day by day. That concern is encouraging, the more so because it comes from the younger generation. But our concern for the environment is still not sufficiently well targeted. Most of us want the environment in which we live to be improved but we do not have a clear idea of what we could do and what ought to be done or of what principles should lie behind our concern. Some people worry about global warming, some about planning applications and the urbanisation of our countryside while others worry about noise. Many of the environmental groups are in conflict with each other, but one thread runs through all their concern—the idea that it is someone else's job to solve the problem, and that the Government, local authorities or local businesses should be responsible for solving environmental problems.

The debate is especially relevant because we can all improve our environment by solving the problem of litter. Litter is one aspect of pollution. We need to have a few general principles to apply in dealing with pollution and in ensuring that the world is a cleaner place. The first principle should be the principle of minimising waste. In future the way in which we produce things—from motor cars to hamburgers—should involve keeping by-products to a minimum and, wherever possible, those by-products should be re-used. If that is impossible, we should ensure that what is left over is recycled. That applies particularly to litter. If we are to minimise waste and the amount of wastepaper and other items left around our towns and countryside, we must encourage industry to examine more closely the way in which it operates and, specifically, the way in which it packages its goods. Increasingly over the years we have become a consumer society and in the process we have increased the volume and content of packaging at the expense of the volume and content of the product itself. Packaging, which now accounts for an increased percentage of the whole product, ends up in our litter bins—it is to be hoped—or lying around somewhere for someone else to collect.

The other day I read about the extreme example of an American company that produced a potato peeler the same colour as potato peelings. The idea behind that rather shrewd marketing tool was that when the housewife peeled the potatoes she would throw away the peeler as well and would have to buy another one. However, the company found that the potato peeler was not selling very well because no one could see it on the shelves. It decided to surround it with a large, brightly coloured and expensive package, and as a result it sold like hot cakes. That is not the direction that we should follow when producing items for sale because it would not encourage waste minimisation. We must ensure that those involved in marketing and retailing present their products for the public to see and to buy without including a huge amount of packaging. After all, packaging does not add value to the product; indeed, it simply costs the customer more.

Having reduced waste to a minimum, there will still be a great deal left over about which we must do something. With litter, that should mean recycling. Earlier this year I introduced a Bill under the ten-minute Bill procedure to encourage the recycling of wastepaper. I did that partly because of the problem mentioned by my hon. Friend the Member for Ealing, North (Mr. Greenway), of the number of trees being chopped down each year to meet our demand for paper, but also because of the problems with litter generally.

The amount of raw pulp that we import each year adds £716 million to our import bill. What is even more significant is that we also import £9 million of wastepaper for use in the various production processes in the paper mills. We do that despite the fact that there is a surplus quantity of wastepaper lying around in our towns and in the countryside. There is a strong incentive to ensure that increasing amounts of wastepaper and other products are recycled. In the process used to produce items for sale, any remaining waste should be recycled. It may be bottles, batteries or wastepaper. Litter is a prime candidate for recycling.

Of course, hon. Members are not entirely innocent of leaving litter around the House. The Committee Rooms always contain huge amounts of paper that hon. Members have had to leave on the floor because there are so few litter bins in the rooms.

**Miss Widdecombe:** Hon. Members do not have to leave litter on the floor. They have a choice between that and picking it up and carrying it to a bin. They are under no compulsion to choose the former. It is a dirty, filthy habit in which, unfortunately, too many hon. Members indulge.

**Mr. Mans:** I was simply painting the picture as it stands, and not suggesting——

**Mr. Tony Banks:** I want to make this a pincer movement on the hon. Gentleman. I, too, am absolutely disgusted by the filthy habits of Members of Parliament, both in Committee Rooms and in the Chamber. One of the advantages of there not being very many hon. Members in the Chamber today is that at least it will remain tidy. Hon. Members should not use the excuse that because there is no litter bin they have to put their rubbish on the floor, because members of the public will then use exactly that excuse when they are on trains or in the street. They will say, "I couldn't find a bin, so I threw it on the floor." It is exercising double standards to lecture members of the public while setting such a terrible example in this place.

**Mr. Mans:** Both my hon. Friend the Member for Maidstone (Miss Widdecombe) and the hon. Member for Newham, North-West (Mr. Banks) jumped in rather too quickly. I was trying to paint a picture of what actually happens now. Of course, it is absolutely right that we should lead rather than follow and that we set the public a good example. I think that more litter bins would help, but of course that is by no means the whole argument. I agree that it is perfectly reasonable to expect hon. Members to take their litter out of Committee rooms and put it in a bin. Nevertheless, it would improve matters if there were more litter bins in the rooms, although that is not a panacea in itself and we need to do more.

Although the Chamber is rather thinly populated today, I am glad that the hon. Members present feel so strongly about the amount of litter that we leave around. One of the points that I made when I introduced my Bill was that we should encourage the Palace of Westminster to recycle the wastepaper collected. I regret to say that I have not had a great deal of success with the authorities in trying to ensure that that happens.

**Mr. Patnick:** I am sure that my hon. Friend the Minister will tell the House that the Department of the Environment uses recycled paper. She said during a recent debate that that was being promoted within her Department. I hope that other Departments follow suit.

**Mr. Mans:** I, too, wish that that would happen. After introducing my Bill I wrote to every Secretary of State asking what they were doing about using recycled paper. The responses varied tremendously, and many of them lapsed into a form of officialese that said very little, but took an awfully long time to say. Even more depressing was that many of the replies contained photocopies of those replies. I am not sure why they did that, but perhaps they were for me to send to some mythical constituent on whose behalf I was supposedly raising the issue. In fact, my letters made it perfectly clear that I wanted to know exactly how many Departments were using recycled paper. The Palace of Westminster and Government Departments could do a great deal more, by way of example, to encourage the recycling of paper products, which in itself would generate the demand for more recycled paper and would encourage the collection of litter.

The world's natural resources are ever-diminishing. We cannot afford simply to dispose of everything. We must try to recycle it and so minimise the amount of raw materials used to produce products. We face a huge challenge in ensuring that we maintain and increase our standard of living, yet at the same time design products that ensure minimum use of our natural resources. We must ensure that products contain little waste, but, where they do, that waste must be collected and recycled.

I am grateful to my hon. Friend the Member for Chelmsford for giving us the opportunity to debate this important subject. As I said earlier, this debate is long overdue. I hope that some concrete proposals come out of it.

11.18 am

**Mr. Tom Cox** (Tooting): This debate is crucial, but like so many of our Friday debates it makes me wonder how much coverage it will receive in the media. Reference has already been made to the fact that when the television cameras are introduced we will have to smarten up or our

[*Mr. Tom Cox*]

electorate will complain. We must question whether this is the sort of debate that television producers will want to show. It is certainly a very important debate. I congratulate the hon. Member for Chelmsford (Mr. Burns) on moving the motion.

The hon. Member for Wyre (Mr. Mans) made a valid point about recycling. Sadly, we live in a throwaway society, and big companies encourage it. I am sure that many hon. Members can remember that, when something went wrong with our household appliances, we could get them repaired. Hon. Members should try to get even the smallest component for something. People in big companies or in small family shops say, "Sorry, they do not make them any more. You will have to buy the entire unit."

I am sure that, every week, hon. Members get several letters from their constituents complaining about these very issues. Britain is often called a dirty country. That refers to many aspects of the environment in which we live. There are grounds for saying that, certainly in large cities. Hon. Members have referred to other cities in the world. Those of us who travel find that many large European cities are far more advanced than our own in trying to keep areas clean. When I have attended Council of Europe meetings in Paris, I have seen the Paris municipal authority motorcyclist whose job is to clean up dog mess. That is a superb idea. It is a means of showing people that it is wrong to allow dogs to foul pavements and that the Paris local authority is concerned about it.

We have been talking about crisp-packet litter and so on. I do not dispute that it is a problem, but it is only one aspect of the overall problem. The condition of streets is obviously of great concern, but, one wonders—when one can find them—how often rubbish bins are emptied. We see them overflowing with crisp packets, drink cans and so on. That is no encouragement for people to say. "I should take my litter away." People tend to add their litter to the pile.

What about the number of abandoned motor cars that no one seems to do anything about? After a week or so, it is obvious that some cars are abandoned, and we must take up the matter with the police. They say, "It is not really anything to do with us. You had better get in touch with the local council." The matter then drags on for a month or so. I am sure that all hon. Members have seen mattresses and old furniture dumped in the streets for days on end.

My hon. Friend the Member for Lewisham, Deptford (Ms. Ruddock) recently introduced a Bill to control fly tipping. Fly tipping is an enormous problem in parts of London and, I am sure, in many large cities. It may even be a problem in some small towns. The Minister is concerned about that problem.

I saw someone in a van dumping rubbish in the London borough of Wandsworth. I took down the registration number and a description of the van and of the person driving it. That was on a Sunday afternoon. On the Monday morning, I referred the matter to the technical services director of the London borough of Wandsworth, who was concerned and said, "Thank you very much for informing us of this. If we catch this person will you be prepared to appear in court?" I said, "Certainly." After a couple of weeks, I rang up and asked, "How are you

progressing?" He said, "We are terribly sorry to tell you, but we now find that that van, like so many, had false licence plates on it." The Minister is aware that some individuals make enormous sums of money by removing rubbish. Sadly, because they have false number plates on their vehicles, nothing happens to them. We must introduce much stricter laws as soon as possible.

One sees lorries travelling around carrying materials with no cover over them. I have often seen loads being shed as lorries swing around to Vauxhall bridge. The Minister may say that loads should be covered if the material can come off the back of a lorry, but that requirement does not seem to be enforced often.

The motion calls for the introduction of new measures. I do not think that any hon. Member would disagree with that. However, I take some exception to the last two lines of the motion, which state:

"and supports the Government's proposal to place a duty on local authorities to keep their areas clean and to publish a code of practice."

I do not disagree with the principle of that, but many hon. Members have served in local government and know that, because of the Government's rate-capping policies, many local authorities whether Labour or Conservative-controlled, face enormous problems in administering their services. I realise that the occupant of the Chair cannot comment on hon. Members' speeches, but, in Adjournment debates, Conservative Members often call for things to be done on the very measures that they have supported in the Lobby. They call for extra funding for certain things to be done.

**Mr. Patnick:** I am sad that we have got into a party political debate on a subject that I thought would cross party boundaries. It is possible for councils to save large sums of money by competitive tendering for the services that the hon. Gentleman has mentioned. If we are to put the matter into the political arena, let us start from point one.

**Mr. Cox:** I am glad that the hon. Gentleman has raised that point. I was about to refer to that very issue.

Local authorities were once responsible for cleaning their areas. I served on the metropolitan borough of Fulham. Our road sweepers took great pride in their job. They had their patch. By God, if anyone dropped rubbish on their patch and they saw them doing it, they would chase them and tell them to pick it up. I saw that happen in the Fulham Broadway area. After the road sweeper had cleaned the place, someone walked along and dropped some rubbish. Also, according to poeople who work in hospitals and schools, that pride does not exist because contractors now clean hospitals and schools.

One of the largest hospitals in the country, St. George's hospital, is located in Tooting. Staff there complain bitterly about the conditions after contractors have been in, supposedly to clean. There is no pride in or continuity of work. Contractors work in one area for a few days and they know that they will be somewhere else next week or the following week, so there is not the pride that there was. That is sad.

While acknowledging that the problem is of great importance and that the public generally must be encouraged to keep the environment much cleaner, we should also exhibit far more concern about the pay and conditions of those responsible for providing cleaning services. The comment about competitive tendering made by the hon. Member for Sheffield, Hallam (Mr. Patnick) sounded wonderful, as do so many of the things that we hear from the Government, until we see them working in practice. If one talks to those responsible for cleaning services in Wandsworth, for example, one learns that overall conditions of employment and pay are much worse under private contractors than they were when the local authority was the employer. Poor pay and conditions will not encourage into those jobs people with the kind of commitment that existed when cleaners were answerable to their local authority and related to their local community.

It is said that local councils should provide more recycling amenities in the form of bottle banks and paper reception centres, for example. Although local authorities are not hostile to such initiatives, they ask where they fit the budgets that they must now observe.

**Mr. Mans:** The hon. Gentleman appears to believe that everything must fit a budget. However, in the case of recycling there are perfectly good schemes in operation in other parts of the country, particularly in the north-west, whereby companies are happy to site wastepaper igloos and other recycling devices in car parks and elsewhere free of charge. Also, county councils will refund money to local authorities that free them from the dumping of that rubbish on their tips. Local councils who examine such possibilities more closely will see that the implications are positive, not negative.

**Mr. Cox:** The hon. Gentleman makes an interesting comment. However, investment is still needed. I acknowledge that if such policies are pursued, they can generate a great deal of money for the benefit of ratepayers and the community as a whole, as my hon. Friend the Member for Newham, North-West (Mr. Banks) can testify from his experience as a member of the Greater London council. I am not arguing that only local authorities should finance the necessary facilities, but they should at least be up front in setting an example. However, many are unable to do so because of the Government's rate-capping policies.

**Mr. Mans:** Nonsense.

**Mr. Cox:** With great respect, it is not nonsense. If Conservative Members ask council officers about the problems that confront them, they will be told—as I have been, by a Conservative-controlled borough that I serve as a Member of Parliament—that rate-capping is one of them.

If fines are to be imposed, they must have a truly deterrent effect. In this day and age, it is no use fining people £5 or £10, because they may consider that to be a laughing matter. In other parts of the world, people pay very dearly if they are caught littering the environment. Greater emphasis must also be placed on education. The hon. Member for Ealing, North (Mr. Greenway) mentioned the education of children, but that of adults must not be overlooked. It is not children who empty cigarette ends into the road or who throw rubbish from car windows. Perhaps the Government, together with local authorities, will consider a programme of education and the imposition of more severe penalties.

Some boroughs provide skips in certain areas at weekends, and that service is properly publicised. There will always be people wondering what to do with an old mattress or piece of furniture. They should be made aware that it is only necessary to take it to a nearby council skip for it to be disposed of. Very often, refuse collectors will say—and I do not criticise them for this—that it is not their job to take away mattresses or old pieces of furniture. All local authorities should give far greater publicity to skip and other clearance services, so that such items will not be dumped.

The hon. Member for Chelmsford has done a first-class job in introducing his motion, which I hope will have the Government's full support and receive the publicity that it deserves. I was once a Government Whip, and on many occasions I sat on the Government Front Bench listening to debates about measures that I thought were long overdue, yet a month or so later one would ask oneself, "Whatever happened to that idea?" I hope that that does not happen to the motion tabled by the hon. Member for Chelmsford.

11.37 am

**Mr. Tony Banks** (Newham, North-West): I, too, believe that the hon. Member for Chelmsford (Mr. Burns) is to be congratulated on introducing the motion. It was noted by the hon. Member for Wyre (Mr. Mans) that, despite the small number of hon. Members present in the Chamber, a great deal of feeling has been generated, and I underline that point. I become positively homicidal when walking around areas of Forest Gate in my constituency that seem to be particularly filthy, observing people drop litter, and seeing the result. The cleaners do a good job in that area, but in a matter of 20 minutes, half an hour or one hour after they have finished, the place is filthy again.

We all agree that dropping rubbish in the street is socially offensive. It is also environmentally and economically wasteful. It does not give me any great pride to say that I have not come up with any initiatives such as that of the hon. Member for Basildon (Mr. Amess), who proposes walking around his constituency at midnight. I certainly would not go walking around Newham at midnight—not that I am anything but a much-loved Member of Parliament. Nevertheless, I do not fancy trying to have a rational discussion on Marxist philosophy with the kind of people who hang around street corners in Newham at midnight after they have had a skinful in the local pub.

My borough is one of the filthiest in the whole of London, and London is one of the filthiest cities in Europe, if not the filthiest city. My hon. Friend the Member for Tooting (Mr. Cox) mentioned how Paris copes. What is that city's secret? It is no secret. The authorities in Paris devote a considerable amount of public money to maintaining services. The secret, such as it is, is a combination of resources, political will and the determination to see a project carried through to its conclusion.

Paris's infrastructure, too, is more favourable to street cleansing, its wider boulevards making for easier access, and there is more space to store rubbish from the streets. Moreover, as my hon. Friend the Member for Tooting will know, street cleansing methods there are very different from those employed in London. The streets are washed down daily, and mechanised cleansing and "poop scoops" are much more widely used. Similarly, the Paris metro is much better than the London Underground system; again, it is a matter of resources and political will. We can will the

[*Mr. Tony Banks*]

end, but we must also provide the means. Plenty of people in this country are prepared to say what is desirable, but when they are asked to devote resources to achieving that desirable objective the resources somehow are not there. That is certainly true of the Government's attitude to litter.

I receive many complaints about litter from my constituents, who blame the council for this problem, along with so many others. "What is the council going to do about it?" is the question that they usually ask. While I share people's concern about the level of services provided in any borough, I must point out that it is not councillors or council officers who go around throwing litter on the ground; it is the dirty people in the area. Rather than fulminating against Newham council or storing up their anger to visit on me when I happen to be walking in the streets, my constituents would do better to direct that anger against some of those who are perpetrating this social nuisance.

We must ask ourselves why we in this country, and in London, are so filthy. As my hon. Friend the Member for Tooting has said, we live in a "chuck-away" society, existing on a diet of fast food. It is considered a mark of progress no longer to sell bottles on which a deposit is charged, providing an incentive to take them back to the shop. When I was much younger, I was quite a budding little capitalist: I used to do quite well from collecting bottles, taking them back to the off-licence and getting the money. Now, however, we have the throwaway bottle, replaced in many instances by the can. There is a lot to be earned from recycling aluminum cans, but schemes are needed to encouage people to take bottles and cans to bottle and can banks.

The hon. Member for Wyre (Mr. Mans) mentioned packaging. Nowadays everything is contained in increasingly attractive and increasingly useless packaging. Products seem to be sold on the basis of the packaging rather than the contents. That is where so much of the competition comes. Vast quantities of paper litter are generated, and, as the hon. Gentleman pointed out, it is also a waste of trees. Hon. Members are among the worst offenders because of the amount of paper that we generate and receive in our post bags, much of which ends up in the rubbish bin. I hasten to add that that does not include letters from constituents—I had to put that in! Most of it is mail shots.

My hon. Friend the Member for Livingston (Mr Cook) was on a train one day, having gone through a vast quantity of post. Some of the organisations that had written to him had helpfully put their names on the envelopes, so he was able to throw some of the post away without even opening it; and a number of unopened letters went straight into the bin. As he was getting off the train my hon. Friend was chased by the guard, who called after him, "Mr. Cook, you seem to have left all these unopened letters." My hon. Friend was faced with the embarrassment of having to accept all the unopened letters—and, no doubt, the unspoken criticisms of many of his fellow travellers, who obviously believed that that was the sort of things that Members of Parliament did.

I tell that story to make the point that Members of Parliament receive huge amounts of unecessary and unwanted mail, as, indeed, do householders generally. The

increase in the amount of "rubbish mail" that comes through the door every day is generating a litter problem and wasting resources. Another contributory factor is the upsurge in fast food chains. I remember the days when the only fast food shops around were the fish and chip shops: now every shopping street in the country has any number of fast food outlets.

In the inner-city areas in particular, the sense of community has been all but destroyed. I remember that when my mother or my father, of course, had finished cleaning the path—ours was not a sexist household, Madam Deputy Speaker, as you can well imagine—they would put down the bucket of water and sweep the pavement and gutter outside. Some old people in the east end can still be seen doing precisely that, but I do not see many people doing it. Such practices date back to earlier days when there was clearly a much stronger sense of community spirit and community pride. The destruction of that sense of community is, of course, partly the fault of planners, the new brutalism of 1960s architecture the building of those appalling tower blocks.

At the last count, Newham had about 110 tower blocks —I say "at the last count" because the odd tower block is always being blown up when it is found, after only 25 years, that it was rendered unsafe by the method employed in its construction. As well as being an undesirable living unit, a tower block may prove structurally unsound. Although inhabitants of tower blocks, stacked as they are in vertical "streets", live in dense concentrations, they are isolated at the same time because there is access only on each floor. Such tower blocks are nasty, unpleasant, brutalising places in which to live, and it is not surprising that so much filth, graffiti and violence builds up. There is a depressing downward cycle: the more violent and unpleasant the environment in which people live, the more they want to go inside, close the door and allow whatever is happening outside to go on. It is nothing to do with them; they are glad to get away from it.

The central problem, however, is one of social attitudes. While I join hands with Conservative Members on the foulness of litter on the streets, I part company with them on the causes of the problem. I think that there is a very political element in it. Life in Britain, in my view, is now brutal, greedy, selfish and increasingly violent.

**Mr. Patnick:** The hon. Gentleman referred to high-rise and high-density flats. Will he cast his mind back to who decided to institute such close living conditions?

**Ms. Diane Abbott** (Hackney, North and Stoke Newington): Macmillan.

**Mr. Patnick:** The hon. Lady has just arrived in the Chamber. I was speaking to the organ grinder.

Can the hon. Gentleman remember who instigated that, who continued it and what ensuing Governments did to try to stop some of the projects that were under way?

**Mr. Banks:** As a matter of fact, I am a ventriloquist; I was speaking without moving my lips. My hon. Friend the Member for Hackney, North and Stoke Newington (Ms. Abbott) is absolutely correct, but I would prefer to put the hon. Gentleman down myself, rather than leaving the privilege to her. In the 1950s and 1960s, Governments, both Conservative and Labour, encouraged that sort of building. Unfortunately, it is today's generation, today's councillors and today's politicians who have to try to clear up the mess. I am making no narrow party political point over the building of tower blocks. It is down to the planners and politicians of the day.

When I was a member of Lambeth borough council there was a scheme to build more and more tower blocks. The planners talked in glowing terms about the kind of communities that they would create. When one looks back, one can almost see that those people thought that they were acting in the best interests of the people. They were going to do away with the back-to-backs and insanitary houses that had no proper facilities; instead they would provide nice, modern flats. They were absolutely wrong.

That is why, among all the occupations that I hate the most, the long-term planners head the list because they always manage to get it wrong. I should like to find the planners and the politicians who decided to put up those tower blocks, put them on the 22nd floor, have the doors nailed up and leave them there for a while. Those who designed tower blocks and pushed for their construction were not the people who ended up having to live in them. I shall always condemn the decisions that were taken in the 1960s. I can also say with a clear conscience that when I was on Lambeth council I was bitterly opposed to the building of tower blocks. In that respect both my conscience and my hands are clean.

I have already said that life today in Britain is brutal, greedy, selfish and increasingly violent. The blame for that combination of nastiness lies squarely with the philosophies and policies of the Government, and in particular with the Prime Minister. She is the person behind it. The Prime Minister denies that there is anything called society. She says that there is just a collection of families and individuals. In her daily utterances the emphasis is on the individual, not on the community—it is all right to be selfish and greedy. That is the essence of Thatcherism today.

**Miss Widdecombe:** Will my hon. Friend give way?

**Mr. Banks:** I am not the hon. Lady's Friend, but I shall still give way.

**Miss Widdecombe:** The hon. Gentleman is quite right; he is not my hon. Friend. Is it not the case that society's habits as a whole are dictated by those of the individual and that the Prime Minister's message is about the responsibility of the individual to contribute to society? The kind of matters that we have been discussing this morning are the responsibility of individuals. If individuals picked up their litter, did their social duty and played their part as active citizens, that would make for a decent society. So it is down to the individual.

**Mr. Banks:** But society is more than just the aggregate of the individuals who live within it. Society collectively sets the norms and the values that are then translated into the action—social or anti-social—of individuals within society. That is the way it works; it cannot work the other way round. We cannot say that society is merely a collection of unrelated individuals. That is where the Conservative party gets it completely wrong. It says that society is no more than the market and that, if we allow individuals to act on their own, there is, somehow, a secret means by which they will all end up acting responsibly.

**Mr. Mans:** Will the hon. Gentleman give way?

**Mr. Harry Greenway:** Will the hon. Gentleman give way?

**Mr. Banks:** I shall give way to all Conservative Members who wish to take me on.

**Mr. Greenway:** I apologise to my hon. Friend the Member for Wyre (Mr. Mans). As he is sitting behind me, I did not realise that he had risen to his feet.

There is a fundamental division between us. I believe, and so do my colleagues, that we achieve progress only if individuals work together. The collectivist, Marxist approach—which believes in progress on the back of an amorphous thing called society—is inadmissible because it does not work. That is not to say that I do not believe strongly in a sense of community. But a community is a collection of individuals, not a mass.

**Mr. Banks:** Obviously a community is made up of individuals, but the sense of community is larger than the sum of its parts. That is why Conservative Members cannot grasp the concept.

**Mr. Mans:** Am I right in saying, therefore, that the hon. Gentleman's vision of what society should be like is the sort that existed in this country in the late 1970s, which resulted in the winter of discontent, waste paper and rubbish not being collected and even the grave diggers going on strike?

**Mr. Banks:** No, because there was a capitalist, individualist society in the 1970s.

**Mr. Mans:** The hon. Gentleman's party was in power.

**Mr. Banks:** The mere fact that a Labour Government were in power does not alter the fact that it was also a capitalist society. One of the problems with the Labour party is that it still thinks that it can administer capitalism better than the capitalists. I do not believe that to be so. Socialism, for me, is not a fringe benefit of an efficient, capitalist system. Socialism for me is completely and utterly opposed to capitalism. That is where I part company with some of my colleagues. I believe in Socialism and collectivism. That is the big difference between me and Conservative Members, and, indeed, between me and some of my hon. Friends.

**Ms. Abbott:** Conservative Members deny the efficacy of collectivist solutions to problems, but they would be the first to argue for collectivist solutions in some areas. They do not argue that people should have their own private armies. They believe that there should be a collectivist solution to the defence of the realm. If collectivism works in defence, it ought to work in relation to litter. If Conservative Members reject collectivist solutions to the litter problem but accept them for defence, may it not be that they take the defence of the realm much more seriously than the environment and litter? Collectivism does work. There are certain areas in which collectivism is the only successful way in which to organise affairs. To look at the increasing litter menace in London, particularly in Hackney, and then to say that there is not a role for the state by means of a collectivist solution is absurd.

**Mr. Banks:** I agree entirely with my hon. Friend.

To return to social attitudes towards litter, it does not necessarily follow that the only socially responsible societies are to be found in Socialist countries. It is far

[*Mr. Banks*]

more likely that they will be found in Socialist countries, but Sweden, Denmark and Switzerland are capitalist countries, where there is a much more socially responsible attitude towards street cleanliness and litter because society in those countries is much more socially and economically cohesive. There is less disparity of wealth and opportunity in Sweden, Switzerland, Norway and Denmark than one finds in this country. One does not necessarily have to live in a Socialist society, but one has to be living in a society that is a damned sight more fair and just than this society is under this Government.

Public property in this country is treated as second rate and with contempt by the Prime Minister. She dislikes anything that is public. For all I know, she might even hate public lavatories. Anything that is public is second rate and must be sold off, given away or, even worse than that, allowed to become run down. That is what has happened to far too many public services. It has to be set against her attitude, and that of the Government, towards private property. That is sacred and sacrosanct. This attitude goes right the way through our society because that is the example which has been set at the top.

Tenants on council estates are made to feel second-class citizens by a Government who put all the emphasis on the economic benefits of owner-occupation. I travel around London a great deal on public transport. People in London seem to regard buses and the train carriages as mobile litter bins. They do not consider that the trains or the streets belong to them. That is because of the philosophy promoted by the Government—from the very top—that public property is second rate. People would not drop rubbish in their own living rooms, they would not stick chewing gum on their own sofas and chairs, but they certainly do that on the Underground in London. They would not scrawl artless graffiti on the outside walls of their homes as they do in streets and on trains. They would not let their dogs crap on the carpet as they do outside the home. They do not recognise streets and public places as belonging to them and I blame the Government for that attitude.

**Mr. Burns:** I know that the hon. Gentleman has a great reputation as a wit, but surely he is stretching the bounds of belief by trying to claim that the unfortunate habit of sticking chewing gum under the seats on public transport, dogs fouling public places and graffiti started on 3 May 1979. Regrettably, society has had to suffer those problems under Conservative and Labour Governments. I suspect that some of those problems in a more prehistoric form were suffered under Liberal Governments many decades ago.

**Mr. Banks:** I am not trying to suggest that in this highly sophisticated forum. I am delighted that the hon. Member for Littleborough and Saddleworth (Mr. Dickens) has managed to totter into the Chamber. His presence always adds something extra. A frisson goes through us all as we see him lower his bulky frame into the seat. I hope that he will make a speech, if he can prop himself up. I notice that he carries a stick and I wish him well, but I notice that it has not stopped him leaping up with an alacrity that is certainly denied slimmer and less agile Conservative Members. I welcome him to our proceedings, late though his presence is.

In reply to the hon. Member for Chelmsford, I am not blaming the Government entirely. However, those trends have been increasing as it is all part of capitalism; but I have done that one already. All those tendencies have become worse since 1979. That is because of the philosophy of the Government and the attitude struck at No. 10 Downing street and throughout the Cabinet.

**Miss Widdecombe:** The hon. Gentleman gave very loud support to my deploring the habits of Members of Parliament. Does he attribute the disgusting habit of Labour Members to the philosophy of the Conservative Government? If that is so, how can we influence them in other matters?

**Mr. Banks:** I blame the Prime Minister for what happens on Labour Benches. Members of Parliament are no different from other members of society. They may be slightly madder than most, or even slightly more anti-social than many ordinary members of the public, but they are still subject to the same attitudes and influences because they are members of society. In a sense, the Prime Minister's attitude must permeate through the Labour party as well as through the Conservative party.

**Mr. Harry Greenway** *rose*——

**Mr. Banks:** I shall give way for the last time. Although I am quite enjoying this, I have a feeling that other hon. Members may wish to speak.

**Mr. Greenway:** The hon. Gentleman is making a serious point when he says that his colleagues in the Labour party do not have the character to maintain their Socialist way of life without being knocked off it by anyone else. As the hon. Gentleman is making so many political points, which he is quite entitled to do, I point out that the borough that he represents has had a Labour council for 60 or 70 years, yet has more litter and graffiti than almost anywhere else, except perhaps Tower Hamlets which also had a Labour council for the past 60 or 70 years, except for the past two or three years when it has had an equally bad Liberal council. The Labour council in Ealing has cut street cleansing and litter collection, but has put up the rates by 32 per cent. and has increased staff substantially in the gay and lesbian unit for homosexuals.

**Mr. Banks:** The hon. Member for Ealing, North (Mr. Greenway) is well known for his antipathy towards his local council. The hon. Gentleman, who represents one of the constituencies under that council, could be of more assistance by arguing in favour of more resources for his borough to deal with many of the pressing problems that exist there rather than producing his usual anecdotes about gay and lesbian groups. When I check up on what the hon. Member says about his borough, and I always do that, I often find that his "facts" and reality do not always coincide. I suspect that was another example.

It is not down simply to the boroughs. I am talking about attitudes that affect everyone, even Labour Members. People do not consider dropping litter as a particularly heinous crime. It is part of the attitude on both sides of the House. The hon. Member for Maidstone (Miss Widdecombe) rightly attacked all hon. Members. We are not isolated from the attitudes of people outside the House of Commons. When I asked other hon. Members why they drop rubbish, one hon. Friend replied, "If I collected it up, they would probably sack the cleaner." He considered that he was part of a job creation scheme trying to foster employment among cleaners. Perhaps under latter-day Tories, that is precisely the case and perhaps my hon. Friend had a far more sophisticated political attitude than I do. Perhaps he knows that, under the Government, if everyone stops dropping litter they will not encourage services and re-employ the people who were picking up the litter: they will sack them. Perhaps my hon. Friend had a point, but because of my background I could not go around dropping litter even if it were part of an extended job creation programme.

Let me say something nice about the Government—I can probably do that for the next 30 seconds or so. 1990 is to be Tidy Britain Year. I welcome that initiative. I must say to the Minister that every year should be Tidy Britain Year. However, I trust that it will not be a year of silly gimmicks such as those from the Prime Minister in the past. For example, the Prime Minister's interest in litter and the state of London streets seem to date precisely from June 1986 when she was coming back from Heathrow airport to No. 10 Downing street in her bullet-proof Daimler—she does not travel on the train—having visited Israel where she was particularly impressed by the cleanliness of the streets. It was a shame about the dead bodies on the West Bank, but the streets were nice and clean. That obviously impressed her so she decided to call in another of her initiatives.

We had that ludicrous photo-opportunity in St. James's park when specially placed, no doubt sanitised, litter was put down for the Prime Minister to spike and put into a black plastic bag which was being held by a very sullen and embarrassed-looking Secretary of State. However, he always looks sullen. If someone told him that he had won £1 million on the pools he would manage to look miserable about it. However, he looked particularly miserable and sullen and embarrassed on that ludicrous occasion. If the Prime Minister had been collecting a few choice dog turds, I might have applauded her and thought that at least she had the courage of her convictions, but very nice clean litter was put down for her to stick in a bag. It made her look extraordinarily silly, almost as silly as the hon. Member for Littleborough and Saddleworth, who is rising to his feet.

**Mr. Geoffrey Dickens** (Littleborough and Saddleworth): I have sat here for quite some time listening to the hon. Gentleman. Although I am hobbling, at least I am not at home watching the Test match and have come here to do my duty in Parliament. I have listened for quite some time to the hon. Gentleman's insults to our Prime Minister. He has forgotten that when the Prime Minister came to office she wanted to change people's attitudes. She felt that if they owned the properties in which they lived they would start to take pride in them. They would not send a card to the council if they had a draught under a door or if a cupboard would not fit; they would start to mend it themselves. They would not throw litter into their own front gardens and then phone the council to come and clear it up because, in trying to enable everyone to become a home owner, the Prime Minister was trying to build character. I like to think that it is the same character that has brought me here today.

**Mr. Banks:** As I have said, I welcome the hon. Gentleman. He is wise to be here rather than watching England being slaughtered in the Test match. I am sure that he is here because of his civic duty rather than wanting to close his eyes to yet another English massacre.

I do not think that the Prime Minister has brought about the pride or spirit about which the hon. Gentleman spoke. As I have said, she has encouraged selfishness and greed and stress on the individual. As long as the individual is doing fine, devil take the hindmost. That is the Government's philosophy. It does not build community spirit. It makes those who are doing OK feel good, but it makes a large number of people who are casualties of the system feel that they are pariahs or that there is something wrong with them. Litter is symptomatic of the attitude that the Prime Minister has spent so much time encouraging.

The hon. Member for Littleborough and Saddleworth is a valiant defender of the Prime Minister. I hope that sooner or later he will be suitably rewarded either with political office or some honour. He is a champion in his ability to defend the indefensible.

I was talking about 1990 and Tidy Britain Year. I trust that it will not consist of yet more ineffective initiatives and photo-opportunities for the Prime Minister and Ministers. For example, UK 2000 was an initiative launched in 1986 under the chairmanship of Richard Branson—Mr. Rubbish as he became known. That has not worked. It was launched with an enormous amount of shouting by the Prime Minister and Conservative politicians, but its litter programme has disappeared.

At the invitation of the Department of the Environment the Tidy Britain Group, formerly the Keep Britain Tidy Group, reviewed its strategy and approach in 1987. The result was a clean-90s programme launched by the Prime Minister and the Secretary of State in March 1988. As I have said, that was when we had the ludicrous photo-opportunity with the Prime Minister picking up litter.

The Tidy Britain Group became the sole Government agent in litter matters from April 1988. It took on a more active campaigning role. Government funding for the group increased in 1988-89 from £560,000 to £1·2 million to finance the clean-90s campaign. The funding was further increased by an announcement on 15 December last year saying that the grant would be pushed up to £3 million for 1989-90. That is pathetic. That is a Britainwide initiative yet the Government are providing only £3 million at a time when the Chancellor of the Exchequer is bragging about the kitty being awash with money. Of course, he cannot spend any of it because of the problem that would cause for inflation and, although the figures are appalling now, they could get worse. The Chancellor could spend more of that money on providing additional resources for the Tidy Britain Group and for the initiatives that the Government keep saying they want to deal with litter.

It is noticeable that the Tidy Britain Group has been looking at the litter problems around motorway service stations and beside major trunk roads. One of the service stations it has opted to study is near Grantham. I wondered why it chose a service station near Grantham when it could have picked any service station on any motorway. Of course, even Conservative Members can grasp the reason for that. It is a gimmick with no resources behind it. It is a chance for a good photo-opportunity for the Prime Minister or Ministers and will provide a few more television slots. Ultimately, it does not amount to

[*Mr. Banks*]

anything. If the Government cannot be judged by actions rather than words and gimmicks, the Minister—I have a high regard for her as a person—and her colleagues cannot be serious about the problems of litter in this country.

We need a series of proposals and we need to change the law in respect of litter dropping. Police enforcement of the Litter Act 1983 has been described by the Tidy Britain Group as pathetic. In 1987 the Metropolitan police made 18 prosecutions—one for every 1,500 officers. The average fine in 1987 was £35, which is less than the cost of bringing the prosecution. The possible maximum fine available is £400. Fines as low as £5 do not encourage police officers to recognise that enforcement of the litter law is important or act as a deterrent against dropping litter. The police say that the requirement to prove intent causes difficulties.

There needs to be a strengthening of the law, and dropping litter should be an absolute offence without having to prove intent to leave it behind. It is ludicrous. Someone can drop a cigarette packet and when challenged by a police officer say that they intended to go back for it later. In that way, they have not committed a crime. That reduces the law to an absurdity and that is why niether enforcement officers nor members of the public take it seriously.

The police force's current commitment to policing by objectives and priorities may have inhibited police officers in their enforcement of the litter laws, considering that they have little priority and it is not a cost-effective task. When we complain to the police, when the London group of Labour Members of Parliament meets the Metropolitan police Commissioner, he says that he does not have the bodies to be able to do anything about it. He says, "Would you rather I reduced the number of crimes of violence, car thefts and burglaries or chased litter louts?" Of course, there is only one answer. If it means that we have to provide more resources for the police, so be it. That is what the Government should do. That would be willing the means to fulfil the ends.

It is a question of enforcement and the resources to carry it out. If the police had to pay the bill for clearing up the massive amounts of litter dropped on our streets, they might change their views on whether it is cost-effective to stop the rubbish being deposited in the first place. The best approach is to devolve the responsibility to local authorities together with responsibilities for traffic wardens, on which negotiations are currently taking place.

There has been mention of the Westminster initiative and the City of Westminster Act 1988. That gave the local authority employees power to issue fixed penalty tickets for litter offenders. In practice, some 70 to 80 employees, while engaged on their normal duties, are given that power. They have approached about 700 people in the past year. They always give the offender an opportunity to pick up the litter before issuing the ticket. Only four people have refused to pick up the litter and were issued with a ticket. One refused to pay the £10 fixed penalty and was subsequently fined £40 with £35 costs.

The scheme has not had a major impact but it may have started a change of attitude in the areas in which it operates. That is why the local authorities, the Association of London Authorities and the London Boroughs Association have asked for the powers to be given to all local authorities. I hope that the Minister will say something about that.

On the matter of enforcement, the Government must strengthen and simplify the litter laws and specify a higher minimum penalty with an absolute offence for dropping litter. They must ensure that the police are aware that enforcement of the litter laws is a priority. They must also ensure that the magistrates impose realistic fines on those convicted of littering. Also, they must give all local authorities power to enforce the litter laws.

The hon. Member for Sheffield, Hallam (Mr. Patnick) talked about privatisation. The Government find it easy to lay the duty of care for a clean environment on the local authorities. That is what the Secretary of State has said. At the same time, they tie hands of local authorities with legislation on competitive tendering.

I do not believe that competition will improve cleansing services. Accepting the lowest quote will not ensure clean streets, but will involve local authorities in a constant round of performance monitoring and of imposing penalties, as they have had to do in Wandsworth and Merton. When those penalties mount up to such an extent that the private company must default, the local authority will still be responsible for clearing up the streets. However, it will no longer have the resources or the work force to do the job. Placing responsibility entirely on a local authority and allowing ratepayers to take it to court is wholly misdirected. I have tried to make the case for increased resources for local authorities.

The London borough of Newham is divided by the A11 and the A13. We must tolerate the environmental pollution of hundreds of thousands of vehicles screaming through the borough. In fact, vehicles do not scream through the borough, because if hon. Members know what the A11 and A13 are like they will be aware that it is quicker to walk over the roofs of the cars rather than drive. Further problems are caused by people throwing their litter out of car windows, and their cars' exhaust fumes pollute our environment.

Commuter parking in the borough makes street cleansing more difficult. Cleaners cannot get into gulleys, which leads to the need for night and weekend cleansing. However, that involves more resources for the local authority because it demands higher wage rates and better conditions for the people who do that filthy but vital work.

I should like to make a firm proposal. All hon. Members have their own proposals, and earlier the hon. Member for Basildon suggested a good proposal. I wish him well tonight on his midnight patrol. After close examination, we now understand that his patrol will begin at 9 pm. I hope that he manages to survive. If he does not, as Basildon is a marginal seat another Labour Member of Parliament will be elected. I shall not tell any of my friends in the east end to hang around in Basildon from 9 pm onwards, but at least the hon. Member for Basildon has some pride in his local community. I recommend the hon. Member for Basildon's attitude to his local authority to the hon. Member for Ealing, North, because if he was as supportive of his local authority as the hon. Member for Basildon is of his council, Ealing would be a much nicer place to live.

**Mr. Harry Greenway:** If I supported my local authority I should be supporting cuts in refuse collection and street cleansing. My duty is to oppose such cuts and achieve proper cleaning of our streets to get rid of the epidemic of rats and litter.

**Mr. Banks:** Since 1983, I have never heard the hon. Gentleman say a nice word about his borough, and he should examine his conscience carefully in that regard. He should argue for more resources for the London borough of Ealing, instead of continually asking for it to be rate capped. He should take a leaf out of the book of the hon. Member for Basildon.

I should like the London borough of Newham and other areas to have street wardens, who could deal with the range of street problems such as illegal parking, litter, unlicensed vehicles, and owners who allow their dogs to foul streets and paths. They should have the power to enforce socially responsible attitudes on our streets. However, that would deal only with the symptoms of the problem; its core goes deep into the philosophy of this Government and the social attitudes that they encourage. Those attitudes will not change until the Government change.

All shops should be required by law to provide bins outside their premises. The hon. Member for Chelmsford mentioned cash dispensers. The Midland bank has installed a cash dispenser at Forest Gate that provides receipts. People who use it leave their receipts all over the ground. The Midland bank should be required to put a litter bin immediately under its cash dispenser. It certainly makes enough money from the overdraft that I have with it to provide bins below cash dispensers throughout the country. Indeed, it could probably finance the cost of every bin from my overdraft.

Fast food chains should be required to collect litter within a quarter mile radius of their shops. Most people who use such shops dump their litter within 400 yd of the shop. McDonalds, Wimpy, Kentucky Fried Chicken and other such shops that purvey fairly disgusting food should collect litter within a quarter mile radius of their shops.

We cannot deal with the problems of litter by gimmick or exhortation, even if the gimmick and exhortation emanate from 10 Downing street. We need legal remedies such as those that I have specified and investment in infrastructure and cleansing services. Above all, if we are to achieve a long-term solution to litter and mess in our streets, we need a change in social attitudes. We need to restore pride in public ownership and the community, which we will never get from the Prime Minister or the Government. However, we certainly shall get it from a Socialist Government led by my right hon. Friend the Member for Islwyn (Mr. Kinnock).

12.26 pm

**Mr. Irvine Patnick** (Sheffield, Hallam): It is always a pleasure to follow the hon. Member for Newham, North-West (Mr. Banks). What he lacks in content he makes up for in noise.

I did not expect my motion to be called today as originally it was number three in the ballot. Although, fortunately, my motion now appears second on the Order Paper, I am aware, from my 20 years of opposition in Sheffield and on South Yorkshire county council, that people such as myself are unable to control time. I note that Opposition Members keep entering the Chamber and preparing to make speeches.

I am sad to see that no other hon. Members representing Sheffield constituencies are present to discuss regeneration of Sheffield.

**Mr. Tony Banks:** They knew that the debate would not be reached.

**Mr. Patnick:** We know not yet; miracles have happened before.

The hon. Member for Newham, North-West, in his own inimitable manner, attacked my hon. Friend the Member for Littleborough and Saddleworth (Mr. Dickens), who is a thin, shy, unassuming and quiet person. He was upset by the attacks made by the hon. Member for Newham, North-West, and on his behalf I spring to his defence. The hon. Member for Newham, North-West is a man of few words, which are often spoken at great length. His attacks on my right hon. Friends the Prime Minister and the Secretary of State for the Environment were not only in bad taste but were unwarranted, and I do not understand why he had to make them. There is plenty of scope for debate on litter without a need to make personal attacks.

On 1 November 1988, my right hon. Friend the Prime Minister congratulated the Keep Britain Tidy efforts and said that she was ready to use the law. She said that if necessary, individuals would be forced to take responsibility for the areas immediately in front of their premises. My right hon. Friend called for a new clean-up campaign which should be supported actively by every individual. She said:

"There could be a major improvement in the appearance of our towns and cities if people did not throw down litter". —[*Official Report,* 1 November 1988; Vol. 139, c. 820.]

She said that if litter were thrown down, people should pick it up.

The hon. Member for Newham, North-West nearly fooled me. I thought that he had become the invisible man, but he had merely moved around the Chamber. The hon. Gentleman said that we should use the arm of the law and referred to the police. I envisage a new arm of law enforcement, similar to the lollipop ladies and gentlemen, which would have a specific responsibility to deal with litter and graffiti. Although those who throw litter and spray graffiti on the walls are breaking the law, we should not use the police to deal with them. It is wrong, too, that traffic wardens are responsible to the police, although they deal with road traffic offences. I believe that an establishment within the bodies involved in law enforcement could be created to ensure that those who drop litter, spray paint on walls and put up posters illegally feel the force of the law.

The Tube, railway and bus stations, the airports and railway carriages are natural and national litter magnets. It is odd that the cleanest spots in London are the platforms at Westminster Tube station. Spain, to which my hon. Friend the Member for Ealing, North (Mr. Greenway) referred, is litter-strewn. Footpaths are paved for only part of their length. The most litter-strewn country that I have ever seen is Gibraltar.

Litter is a phenomenon that I have come to know. When I was a member of Sheffield city council, it was normal for members to throw all the papers that they did not need on the floor. When I asked why, I was told that if the papers were left on the desks, the cleaners would put them into the members' lockers, so the next time the members opened them, they would see all the papers that

[*Mr. Patnick*]

they wanted disposed of. The Sheffield city council chamber is a quaint place in which to work. It now has an ample number of litter baskets.

As my hon. Friend the Member for Maidstone (Miss Widdecombe) and the hon. Member for Newham, Noth-West pointed out, there is nowhere in the Chamber to put papers, save for the slots in front of the Benches. It is normal for Members to throw their papers on the Floor. Those who look into the Chamber when television is with us will be able to see the way in which we generate paper and what we do with it. We must set an example. Something needs to be done about the paper bombardment. Recently, I was a member of the Committee on the local Government and Housing Bill. My hon. Friend the Member for Ealing, Acton (Sir G. Young) had a good idea. He placed a large paper sack at the back of the Committee room, into which we were able to throw all our waste paper.

The battle against litter is never-ending. Litter reflects a lack of civic pride and says more about a place than any publicity machine. Residents require clean streets and pavements, grass verges to be cut and cars not to be parked on grass verges or pavements. The first step in dereliction is the growth of litter, which is followed by the growth of graffiti, followed by fly-posting.

Sheffield, where I have lived all my life and which I represent, built an incinerator to burn rubbish at Bernard road in Sheffield. The idea was that the heat produced would be used to give some local council dwellings hot water and central heating. In the mess that resulted from the Local Government Act 1972—which I accept was introduced by my Government—when better was thought to be greater, the monster of the South Yorkshire county council was set up. One stupidity was that Sheffield city council collected the waste and South Yorkshire county council disposed of it. The incinerator at Bernard road no longer belonged to Sheffield city council but belonged to South Yorkshire county council. The waste was collected by the city council, taken to the county council for disposal, the county council burnt it and produced heat. It was not Sheffield city council's heat; it had to be sold to it. It was nonsense. We were generating rubbish, having the rubbish collected and taking the rubbish to the incinerator, but it was burnt there and we had to buy the heat from the power station. If ever Topsy ruled and if ever bureaucracy went mad, that was an example, and if there was ever a reason for getting rid of the metropolitan county councils, that was a good reason, if not the only one.

In South Yorkshire, we had a catchment area of 1·3 million people, as opposed to the 600,000-odd in Sheffield. We did not manufacture enough waste. There was not sufficient rubbish for the power station to burn. Sadly, an alteration had to be made at times to the incinerator to allow it to generate heat and give hot water in periods when rubbish was not available throughout the county. Imagine the hoo-ha when the huge district heating system broke down. I subscribe to the theory that the larger and more complicated something is, the greater the likelihood of it going wrong. Sure enough, the system used to go wrong and the problems had to be seen to be believed. There was a shortage of rubbish despite the increase in packaging.

When one buys a shirt from one of the major stores, one has to remove the pins, the collar stiffeners, the lovely little piece of plastic in the front, the pieces of cardboard and, depending on how up-market or down-market the shirt is, a lovely piece of tissue paper. There is always a plastic bag surrounding all the other packaging. If the shirt is really up-market, it will be inside a box that has to be thrown away. I have no shares in Marks and Spencer, but I have seen sweaters hanging up there with only a little label with the size printed on it. That is a good step forward. However, despite the increase in packaging, we were short of rubbish to burn in South Yorkshire.

Sheffield also uses a combined heat and power and recycling process. It was pioneered in Sheffield and my hon. Friend the Minister was there recently to open the project. We build housing away from the incinerators and disposal areas because nobody wants to be near an industrial area, and I agree with that. None the less, industry is a source of power. We can all remember the cooling towers that seemed to give off sufficient heat. Surely there must be some way to use that heat. Sheffield has pioneered that project, among others.

As I said in an intervention in the speech of my hon. Friend the hon. Member for Chelmsford (Mr. Burns), litter, fly-posting and graffiti are one and the same problem and when combined with vandalism, the decline of our area begins.

I listened to the hon. Member for Newham, North-West when he was talking about the piece of paper that comes out when one goes to a cash dispenser. Some banks give a choice about whether one wants a printed receipt. Banks could—and I am not referring to the hon. Member for Newham, North-West—take action to eliminate that piece of paper. I am sure that few people know where to put the piece of paper when they take it out of the machine. I have heard that only multi-millionaires do not have to worry about money. Most of us when we take money out of a cash dispenser are pleased when something comes out and most cross when there is nothing there. We are shocked when the machine shows our balance. I have said, "Oh God", a number of times when I have read the balance figure. We could be positive and ask banks to get rid of those slips of paper.

Posters are stuck on anything which does not move: shop windows, walls, telephone kiosks and any bit of street furniture. Fly-posting brings down the tone of an area. It is highly likely that the perpetrators of these blemishes on the landscape are totally unaware of their contravention of the law and the risk of prosecution. Like general litterers, fly-posters leave their trademark. They probably would not do so if they had even a basic knowledge of the law. they may have a good reason for believing that nothing drastic will happen to them if they flout the law.

Many authorities take great pride in the smart appearance of their area. However, it must be admitted that vast areas have some increasingly tatty and uncared for parts, and fly-posting contributes a great deal to that. Usually, the advertisements give sufficient detail to track down those who have stuck them up.

My understanding of the law is that the person putting up the poster is the one who is prosecuted. That is wrong; I believe that the advertisers should be stopped from fly-posting. We have all seen the posters advertising anything from pop concerts and records to political fringe party meetings. Those posters are stuck on telephone kiosks and any piece of street furniture which does not move. I have even seen them on traffic lights, nailed to telegraph poles and put around lamp stands. Something should be done about that.

I do not wish to advocate legal action on a large scale, but warnings by letter of the consequences of further breaches of the law to the more obvious and persistent offenders, together with the help of local newspapers, might do the trick. There is an increasing number of environmental interest groups. The deterioration of the urban and, to a lesser degree, the rural scene, by litter of all types, including fly-posting, is the subject of much complaint. Extensive powers have already been given to public bodies to tackle fly-posting. There is sufficient legislation to do so, but there must be a willingness to take action.

An article in *The Times* in 1987 said that a bus company was considering suing vandals who had caused £2 million worth of damage to its vehicles with spray cans. Such actions of vandalism are the worst type. Stiffer sentences were urged in an article on graffiti vandals which appeared in a publication in Sheffield more than a year ago, on 10 June 1988. It said that the battle against graffiti was costing the council £250,000 per year.

Something must be done about the subways, which are a part of town and city life. They should be for traffic, not people. Pedestrian subways are a breeding ground for litter, graffiti, fly-posting and vandalism. They should be closed, and alternative ways found to enable people to go about their daily business. The underpass between King's Cross and St. Pancras, an area I know well, is not a nice place, late at night, but it is the only way to cross that area. There are subways in Sheffield permeated by a similar atmosphere.

One feature I have noticed since becoming a Member of Parliament and travelling to London is the fly-tipping and tipping of waste that takes place in London on roadsides, near roundabouts and underneath motorways. All sorts of places seem to be a magnet for people who want to get rid of a load of rubbish. If they do so, they are not only committing a prosecutable offence but damaging the environment.

I live next to countryside in Sheffield and I see many respectable people wheeling barrows full of clippings and rubbish to tip in the beautiful bluebell woods, which are one of Sheffield's features. They would not leave a pile of rubbish on their own carpet, yet they are prepared to leave it on the carpet which belongs to everyone, of grass and the natural environment.

As I explained, I was a leading member of the opposition in Sheffield council. Sheffield has some quite innovative schemes in place. For example, we have a collection scheme for garden refuse and large, strong plastic sacks are provided. We also have an abandoned car collection scheme, which I greatly admire. One of the greatest things that Sheffield has done in the fight against litter and pollution was to be among the first cities to enforce the clean air legislation. That cost a lot of money. Everyone used to think of Sheffield as a blackened city but now it is clean and attractive. One of our great problems is created by starlings, pigeons and now, seagulls, which seem suddenly to have found that the city is better than their normal habitat.

Sheffield also has a furniture collection scheme. One can ring up and a van or lorry will arrive on which one can load one's rubbish. Like other cities, we have bottle banks. I agree with the hon. Member for Newham, North-West

and my hon. Friend the Member for Chelmsford that we should reimpose a deposit system for bottles. At the moment, we put bottles in bins or bags and they add to the volume of waste. It is a waste of our natural resources to have a firm churning out bottles only for them to be thrown away. That does not seem sensible. Bottle banks should be placed outside large stores. They should be obliged to provide such a facility. Many stores are into the environment. As part of that environmental kick they could provide bottle banks. Some stores put waste paper bins outside. There is a branch of McDonald's in Victoria, not far from where I live. McDonald's is one of the firms that employs people to pick up the litter round their premises and sweep the pavements. The larger stores have an obligation to do something to help people dispose of bottles. It would be progress indeed if companies were prepared to do that.

I thoroughly enjoy reading newspapers but they are the bane of my life. My late father used to keep newspapers around so that eventually one could not get near him without pulling a newspaper away. I inherited that tendency. It was in my genes. I discovered that I was doing it at home. My wife used to throw the papers in the bin and I could be seen at midnight with a torch searching for a newspaper that I considered vital. It was a beautiful sight. I always found the wrong newspaper and, in any case, it was never as important as it seemed. I now realise that following in my father's footsteps and hoarding newspapers in not a way forward. In Sheffield I take about four newspapers a day. We have to do something with them. We can burn them, or throw them in the bin, which means that they will be tipped but there seems to be no collection service. We have bottle banks so why do we not have newspaper banks in which to throw newspaper for recycling?

As I said earlier, we do not use our resources very well. We should give people an incentive to take their litter to a given point in the fear that they will pay a penalty if they do not. The police have far too much to do in maintaining law and order on the large scale, but although litter offences may be minor offences they can cause great upset. We should find a way of imposing a penalty on those who leave litter. I agree with the hon. Member for Newham, North-West that we do not want a £10 or a £5 fine, but we could have an on-the-spot fine.

**Mr. Dickens:** My hon. Friend has been telling us some of Sheffield's success stories. He may be pleased to hear that in one of the villages in my constituency we have a road cleaner called Raymond Watkins. He is such a good road cleaner that he will do anything at any hour of the day to keep the village clean. Such is his reputation that people no longer throw rubbish away because they know that poor old Raymond will have to deal with it. The local authority has suggested that Raymond Watkins should move to another place, and 300 people have signed a petition pleading with it not to move him.

We should not forget that much can be achieved by example. It is a question of attitude, although we tend to forget that. It is terribly important that we should set a good example at home and at school.

**Mr. Patnick:** I accept what my hon. Friend says about street cleaners taking pride in their work. I usually meet one in the mornings because his beat is close to where I collect some of my four daily newspapers. He is always

[*Mr. Patnick*]

smiling and happy. There is a very good fish and chip shop near where I live, but unfortunately the birds take the fish and chip wrappings out of the bins and strew them over the pavements. That street cleaner's first job is to clear up the mess left by those birds.

I recently wrote to my hon. Friend the Minister of State, Home Office asking whether anything could be done about fly-posting. It appears that, as ever, there is a strong law on that, but no one wants to enforce it. Under section 6 of the Town and Country Planning Act 1984 any advertisement must receive either the deemed or the express consent of the local planning authority or the Secretary of State. A condition of that consent is that before any advertisement is displayed, the permission of the owner of the site must be obtained. We all know that those who put up fly posters do not bother to do that. If they see a nice stretch of wall, a shop window boarded-up or a "To Let" sign, they stick their posters all over it. It is cumulative, because someone else then puts his poster over that poster and then another person puts another one over that. It looks so tatty. Sheffield city council actually employs men with steam guns—they are masked and look as though they come from Mars—to remove fly posters.

Believe it or not, Sheffield city council leases premises to the very people who put up fly posters. If there is to be a concert in council-owned premises and fly posters advertising that concert are put up, the council should take action against those who perpetrate that crime on the environment. Unfortunately, that just does not happen. It is surely not difficult to discover who is running the concert, who is appearing, where one can buy tickets and so on.

There are statutory fines for offenders who paint graffiti on walls. One of the problems with graffiti, especially that done with spray paint cans, is that there does not appear to be any way of obliterating the paint once it has been sprayed on. Some of that graffiti is not only racist, it is obscene. Some of it is just childish in the extreme. It makes me wonder what sort of intelligent person uses a spray can. Some of the graffiti appears to be quite professional.

Many hon. Members have said that the people who use spray cans to write graffiti are artists. As one comes by train to London one sees graffiti on the walls of various buildings, but graffiti is another sin or crime against the environment. We need graffiti-proof paint. One thing that I have noticed since I have been a Member of the House is that Tube trains have had to have graffiti removed from them. I do not know which is worse, graffiti or the marks that remain when it is removed. Surely it is not beyond the wit of man to come up with a spray-paint-proof treatment for railway train carriages. Somebody could say, "The next thing that they will do is spray-paint the walls." That is not where it is done. It is obviously done in sidings where trains are parked.

The Criminal Damage Act 1971 provides that

"A person who without lawful excuse destroys or damages any property belonging to another intending to destroy or damage"—

It is always hard when one reads legal expressions; they never make sense except to lawyers—

"any such property or being reckless as to whether any such property would be destroyed or damaged shall be guilty of an offence."

In my language, it is an offence to damage somebody else's property. When an hon. Member puts down a resolution in the House, it needs either a semicolon or a colon to make it read.

The maximum sentence, covering a wide range of activities, is 10 years' imprisonment, if the offender is convicted on indictment—that is, after a trial by judge and jury in a Crown court rather than before a magistrate. Graffiti writing will invariably be regarded as one of the less serious forms of criminal damage, and offenders are likely to be dealt with by a magistrate.

The Public Order Act 1986 also covers several relevant offences. Graffiti that is likely or intended to stir up racial hatred may render the writer liable to prosecution under section 18 of the Act. The Attorney-General's consent is required before proceedings for an offence under that section can be brought. The maximum penalty for a person convicted on indictment is two years' imprisonment, a fine, or both. If the person is convicted summarily by a magistrate, the maximum penalty is six months, a fine or both. There is little case law on either of those provisions, but it seems likely that, in certain circumstances, they extend to graffiti writers.

Obviously, the police will take the first steps in the process leading to trial. The new enforcement arm that I continue to advocate should be responsible for that. Whether an offender is reported, arrested or merely cautioned is a discretionary matter for the police officers concerned. When the process is started, it is for the Crown prosecution service to decide to bring charges. If it decides to charge someone, it will also choose the offence with which that person is to be charged. The Crown prosecution service examines two sets of criteria— evidential sufficiency and public interest—as the Crown prosecutors' code explains.

If a person is tried and convicted of criminal damage or of an offence under the Public Order Act 1986, a variety of penalties will be available within the statutory maximum. The Home Office has provided a guide book summarising the penalties for offenders in different age groups.

The Criminal Justice Act 1988 replaces youth custody and detention centre orders with unified custodial sentences. Parents can be ordered to pay any fines, costs or compensatory orders imposed on their children, and the Act extends that provision to fines imposed when juveniles breach supervision or community service orders.

Vandalism is a key factor in parliamentary debates on the subject of litter. There are discussions with people working in Government Departments, local authorities, the police and the academic world, but there has been little if any systematic research into vandalism nationally, so my remarks illustrate only one small part of the subject. It is important not to get vandalism out of proportion. Although a great deal of damage is done to property such as buses, trains and telephone kiosks, it is not really vandalism—in the sense that public telephones, for example are not wrenched from their mountings and thrown away.

I shall bear in mind the remarks of the hon. Member for Newham, North-West about the right housing policies being axiomatic in solving many problems. The current trend of devising more humane designs and layouts will help, particularly if special attention is paid to eliminating features known to encourage vandalism.

The move away from smaller housing units was started in the 1960s by a Conservative Government, even though the shortcomings of such property were capable of being overcome. In those days it was thought that plumbing was the yardstick by which the fitness of a house should be measured. The criteria were an inside toilet, hot water and a bathroom, as well as a ventilated food cupboard. The layout of rooms was another factor. Many is the time that I have appeared either at a public inquiry in connection with a compulsory purchase or clearance order to decide on the fitness of certain housing. However, there is now a move back to smaller houses and away from flats, and there is increasing recognition among local authorities that there is a need for private housing. Nevertheless, there are certain difficult policy areas where a firm steer by central Government would be useful. They include the importance of maintenance as opposed to new building.

**Mr. Deputy Speaker (Sir Paul Dean):** Order. I realise from listening to the hon. Gentleman that litter covers a multitude of sins, but his present remarks are wide of the motion.

**Mr. Patnick:** Thank you for your guidance, Mr. Deputy Speaker.

Litter is more than just a question of the indiscriminate throwing away of rubbish. It is also about the way in which people live. It has to do, as was said by my hon. Friend the Member for Littleborough and Saddleworth with the way that people are brought up. The blind spots often occur at semi-public spaces on housing estates. Litter can be not only pieces of paper but beds and furniture. When I visited Vauxhall for the recent by-election, I saw dumped there beds, settees and bags of rubbish, as did my hon. Friend the Under-Secretary of State for the Environment who accompanied me. We saw also black plastic sacks that had not been collected by the local authority.

Litter accumulates even in unoccupied buildings; people seem to break in and put it there. There is also the rubbish that is put through letter boxes. When householders have gone away, free newspapers and so forth are still delivered. In derelict areas that are being redeveloped or rehabilitated, we must ensure that what remains is tidied up. Old retaining walls, for instance, are breeding grounds for litter and graffiti, and old fireplaces and bathroom suites are also thrown on to vacant land.

We must keep the streets clean and tidy. A street should not look its worst immediately after the dustmen have called. More provision must be made for the disposal of household rubbish, and rubble should not be left lying around building sites. The hon. Member for Tooting (Mr. Cox) made the important point that lorries are loaded with rubbish that does not seem to be fastened down or covered with a net. It blows all over the street, with the driver unaware of what is happening.

I welcome the hon. Member for Hackney, North and Stoke Newington (Ms. Abbott) to the Opposition Front Bench, where I hope she spends many a happy year.

Maintenance is vital, and we must ensure that the councils catch up with the problem. I thank my hon. Friend the Member for Chelmsford (Mr. Burns) for giving us the opportunity to debate it. We must persevere. We also have a duty to set an example. The Benches today are rather a pleasant sight without the litter that we see at 2 or 3 am.

Litter was one of the subjects that I wanted to raise when I first came to the House, and I hope that my hon. Friend the Minister will tell us that a new enforcement officer—a "litter lady" or "litter-pop man"—can be appointed to deal with the first stage in prosecutions and to make people aware of the penalties.

1.17 pm

**Mr. Harry Barnes** (Derbyshire, North-East): The speech of the hon. Member for Sheffield, Hallam (Mr. Patnick) was something of an occasion. He spoke for 41 minutes. As he told us at the outset, the hon. Gentleman has second place on the Order Paper with a subject of his own—Sheffield—and I am rather pleased that he has spoken at such length, because I, as a neighbour of Sheffield, cannot now be accused of attempting to stop him speaking. Although he is obviously interested in the subject of litter, I found it interesting that he should make it more difficult for himself to speak in a later debate.

**Mr. Patnick:** It was pretty obvious to me that, with so few Opposition Members present, the Opposition would not allow an opportunity for the second debate

**Mr. Barnes:** As the hon. Gentleman said earlier, we have yet to see what happens. I understand his frustration, however. Last week I drew second place for a debate on the poll tax but did not get the opportunity to speak, and last Friday a Scottish Member had the same experience with a debate on the same subject.

Another interesting feature of the hon. Gentleman's speech was the number of references that he made to Sheffield. He mentioned bottle banks, patrols and other services. I had the feeling that he was beginning to miss Sheffield very much. Perhaps he has discovered that the council is not as obnoxious as he sometimes claimed when he was leader of the opposition there, and has decided it is more fruitful to be involved in local politics. I hope that he will have that opportunity again after the next general election.

I understand that advances have already been made by the district council into the Hallam area. Strangely enough, the hon. Member for Hallam is waxing lyrical about Sheffield council, although I, as a member of the same political party that runs Sheffield, object to a number of things that the council is doing, not least its plans to extend its boundaries and take over the northern part of my constituency. If I survive the next general election, that will make me a Member of Parliament for a Sheffield constituency. Therefore, if we had the second debate on the Order Paper, a Member of Parliament would be here to respond to points made by the hon. Member for Hallam.

I hope that the hon. Gentleman will correct one statement that he made. In a long speech, it is difficult to be as precise as one would wish, but he referred to graffiti connected with racism and suggested that there was much worse graffiti than that, including obscenities. I believe that racism is the worst possible type of obscenity. I hope that the hon. Member for Hallam agrees with me.

The procedures of the House are very strange. Yesterday, I tried desperately to speak in the debates on Northern Ireland, especially in the debate about direct rule. I sat patiently waiting to speak but was unable even to intervene during the Minister's speech. Today, I came to listen to a debate on litter and found that a big ideological battle was going on, allowing hon. Members to refer to many concerns about the direction of party politics. Many

[*Mr. Barnes*]

of us who object to the characteristics of an increasingly crass, capitalist society believe that litter is the mark of a capitalist society and that if we move in a different political direction we shall solve the litter problem and other problems that are associated with it.

I intend, therefore, to refer to issues that might be considered to be of an ideological nature, just as I had intended to do yesterday in the debates on Northern Ireland. It is time that the ideological case for democracy and Socialism was put forward at all opportunities, just as Conservative Members put forward the ideological case for the enterprise culture at every opportunity. Democracy and Socialism would be able to tackle many of the problems that we face.

Associated problems connected with litter are dog mess, noise, lack of care for one's neighbours, queue jumping and other anti-social activities. The throwing around of rubbish adds to the nuisance. Many of the problems were referred to by the hon. Member for Hallam, but he provided no analysis. Therefore, the earlier ideological debate vanished. A much more pragmatic view was put forward by the hon. Gentleman, and he drew considerably on Sheffield council's experience.

A sea change in social attitudes is needed. During the war, and in post-war Britain, there was a much more collectivist response by people to litter, noise and anti-social activities. People believed that it was their public duty to behave in a reasonable and decent manner towards their neighbours. That attitude is breaking down, though it has not broken down entirely. Many people still behave in a perfectly reasonable and decent way. If it were not for that, there would be nothing for Socialists and democrats to build upon and we would be in a desperate situation. The whole basis of an enterprise culture is that people should advance themselves, live their own lives and follow their individual concerns without bothering about anyone else. That means that people's lives are affected by others who are simply acting selfishly. We have to revert to the position that came out of war-time experiences and was built upon in the post-war consensus but is now seriously under attack.

That is not to say that everything is down to the Prime Minister and everything is a consequence of Thatcherism. She did not build a grasping capitalist society or create the get-rich-quick mentality. That already existed. She has simply unleashed the political expression of that which was already there in the economic and social nature of society.

In earlier times, many Conservatives believed in the values of civic duty and responsibility. It appears in some of the older Conservative Members who still reflect the traditional Conservative values, but it is beginning to disappear. Conservatives such as Disraeli felt that there should be training and education which, although it was elitist, meant that the leaders that it produced would have some responsibility towards the rest of society and would try to spread the values of civic duty and responsibility throughout society. The Macmillan set of values has bitten the dust and the crudest form of free-enterprise advocacy imaginable has developed in Britain. It was rife in certain Right-wing circles in Europe and has always existed in America. American society is not particularly adept at handling problems such as litter and noise. It is an aggressive, self-assertive attitude in which people say,

"Give me my rights and don't give anyone else theirs." It is asserting itself in Britain and has been mentioned by several Conservative Members, including the hon. Member for Chelmsford (Mr. Burns). Obviously, he has a different response to such problems.

Personal responsibility is a matter of arguing with people—not just lecturing them and telling them that they should behave and respond in a certain way or they will become totally disgusting. It may be that the law needs to be changed, as has been suggested. We need a sea change in attitudes that currently reflect the commercialised values that have bounded forth from the United States of America to be grabbed by political forces in the Conservative party. There has been a coup, those attitudes have taken over and the old guard has disappeared. All that needs to be changed dramatically as it is based on the silliest notions of human behaviour, assuming that people are out for what they can grasp for themselves and must be considered in terms of their competitiveness and that the best of all worlds would be to have a regulatory system in politics, economics and social affairs, although it would retain the existing low levels of behaviour. It assumes that people are incapable of co-operating and working together and assisting each other, yet those qualities come to the fore in a crisis, difficulty and disaster. We need to nurture those attitudes and responsibilities.

We need to get rid of the Government and advance in an entirely different direction so that Socialist and democratic values can be linked together. Socialism without democracy becomes bureaucratic abuse such as the current nonsense in China and is highly dangerous. Democracy without Socialism is what we have in Britain and although it has advantages over the dictatorial regime, is a low-level, sham philosophy that does not try to raise anyone's horizons or get them to behave responsibly towards the needs of others and seek to assist them, as is illustrated by the mess and corruption that exists in economics and is reflected in problems such as litter which is associated with economic issues.

Everything our society produces has an inbuilt obsolescence. The hon. Member for Hallam talked about shopping for a shirt. As he said, one does not buy only a shirt because it comes with all sorts of status symbols, pins, bags and so on. That unnecessary rubbish has to be dumped. If society is already uncaring and all that unnecessary rubbish is forced on it, the rubbish will not be disposed of correctly.

That occurs throughout our society. For example, I will be catching the train later to travel to Sheffield. Having been busy in the House one may be in need for sustenance during the journey. The only thing one can obtain on trains is plastic cups of coffee. There is now a new procedure whereby one plastic cup is placed inside another. Sugar is provided in a packet, milk comes in a container and one is given a disposable spoon. Therefore, simply having a cup of coffee generates a great deal of rubbish.

I will probably need a rubbishy microwaved cheeseburger, which will be served in a container. If I want sandwiches as well, all sorts of mess will come from the wrappings. Within a short time my table will be covered with rubbish.

Last weekend, following a debate in the House on coal mining subsidence, I travelled back on the train to Sheffield with my hon. Friend the Member for Mansfield (Mr. Meale). We had a whole host of material on the table before us. We intended to dispose of it correctly because we are responsible, but before we had an opportunity to do so, somebody passed by, looked at us and said, "Thatcherite thugs." That is what we were considered to be in today's society. We are part of society because we have to live within it. That is why, when Socialism is achieved, Socialists will be a lost generation. We will have been built on past generations. Socialism is for the future. We must begin to build on our values and transcend some of the inadequacies of our behaviour.

The hon. Member for Hallam also mentioned newspapers. When one buys a newspaper it is full of material that one does not want. It is all associated with advertising and commercialisation. It is entirely unnecessary. One has to sort out the interesting bits. Therefore, newspapers bought on trains or while travelling generally may finish up on the streets rather than in rubbish bins.

Councils face great problems in collecting rubbish because of the lack of resources. Often, socially responsible people who wish to place their rubbish in bins find that it is impossible to do so because the bins are overflowing. Such people then have to be additionally responsible and buy more rubbish bins, or another plastic bag in which to put their debris and take it home to place in their dustbin. However, that cannot be done if the dustbin is already overflowing from rubbish collected on previous occasions.

Litter reveals to me some of the massive and serious problems that exist within our society. We leave local authorities to collect rubbish. Local authorities have been hammered and bashed by the Minister and the Department for the Environment. The Government have passed 50 measures directed against local authorities since 1979 and have hampered their tackling problems such as litter. I could mention other problems that have been created by legislation, but you, Mr. Deputy Speaker, would rule me out of order.

The poll tax will increase the financial problems of local authorities and will cause more mess and rubbish on our streets. Private interests will be encouraged to tender for cleansing services, but they will be interested not in refuse collection but in increasing profits. The contracts that they will sign will probably be so lengthy and detailed that they will contribute to the litter and rubbish that is thrown around.

I am sure that my hon. Friend the Member for Stoke-on-Trent, North (Ms. Walley) will mention unnecessary packaging materials. Hon. Members receive much correspondence, much of which calls for a reply. The Halifax building society sent hon. Members a big glossy publication. Most hon. Members threw it straight into the wastepaper basket because they did not have time to read all the nonsense contained in it. Probably only hon. Members who have a particular interest in the subject read it.

Some controls must be placed on what is sent to people and we must increasingly use recycled material. The amount of rubbish and waste material that is thrown away in the House is criminal. The House is only one institution in this country and if commerce is taken into account the amount of rubbish that is thrown away could be multiplied. Fax machines and new technology will not contain or control the problem of litter but will lead to more paper and rubbish and many difficulties.

We need a sea change in our attitudes. Such a change is beginning. The Prime Minister is taking action to control litter. In St James's Park she was involved in a charade in which some sanitised litter was thrown down for her to pick up. The consequences of the sudden change in her attitude to litter will be the same as the consequences of her change to green politics. Her lack of answers on green policies led to the advance of the Labour party and the Green party. Perhaps someone should set themselves up as a litter control party, or perhaps parties should include a litter policy in their manifestos. They will find a ready response in society to such policies.

An individual cannot control litter, but collectively we can begin to transform and change our society. At the next general election, it must be clearly seen that the Labour party has policies to deal with social problems. I hope that Conservative Members will act to undermine the nonsense that is being put about by their party.

1.28 pm

**Ms. Diane Abbott** (Hackney, North and Stoke Newington): I am proud to represent the constituency of Hackney, North and Stoke Newington. Hackney has much of which to be proud—the energy and self-organisation of the people and the extent to which many colours and creeds live happily together. Last weekend, the Hackney show, which is the equivalent of a village fair, took place on Hackney downs. It was a happy event, with the young and old, people of all colours and creeds, enjoying themselves in the sunshine. It showed the best of Hackney, but rubbish and litter are serious problems which are a blight on the borough.

I should like to outline what the Government should do. There are many specific rubbish problems in Hackney. Two famous markets, Petticoat lane and Ridley road, draw people from all over London. They are marvellous places to visit, but they generate a lot of rubbish. In common with the rest of London, Hackney has many problems because of commercial rubbish, especially from shops. Not all of the 10,000 shops in Hackney make sufficient arrangements to dispose of their rubbish and not all are willing to pay the council to take it away. Only 3,000 have a contract with the council to take rubbish away, so 7,000 shops are putting out their rubbish and, presumably, waiting for the fairies to take it away. The shops put their rubbish in black bags which are placed on the pavement. They burst or are mauled by dogs and the rubbish is scattered all over the pavement. There is a problem also because of irresponsible parents whose children drop their sweet papers, cigarette packs and crisp packets. We need to encourage a more responsible attitude among the old and the young, especially children, towards dropping litter.

Another problem is the menace of stray dogs and dogs that are not on a leash in public. Like many Opposition Members and some Conservative Members, I would support a dog registration scheme in line with the proposals of the Royal Society for the Prevention of Cruelty to Animals. That scheme would lead to a more responsible attitude by dog owners and reduce the number of dogs roaming the streets, thereby decreasing the amount of dog dirt on the pavements, which is a health risk as well as unsightly. It would reduce the number of strays that tear up the black plastic bags of rubbish.

The efforts of planners have contributed to Hackney's rubbish problems. Like many other inner-city areas, Hackney has several estates laid out in such a way that they provide communal areas for which no one in

[*Ms. Diane Abbott*]

particular has responsibility. Whether they are patches of grass in the centre of estates, walkways or landings in tower blocks, they tend to collect rubbish. The old terraces may have been slums, but they had a certain spirit and people took responsibility for their front doorstep and bit of pavement. Soulless slab blocks as a result of soulless planning have replaced the slum terraces, and people do not take responsibility for the common areas, where rubbish collects.

The consumer society causes rubbish in Hackney, too. In the past decade we have seen the explosion in the consumption of take-away food—for example, hamburgers and kebabs—in their throw-away containers. They generate an enormous amount of rubbish in Hackney and all over Britain.

Rubbish is a serious problem in Hackney, for the reasons that I have outlined. At this time of the year, when the sun is shining and the blossom is on trees, the rubbish is a particular eyesore. In many ways, Hackney is a gay, vibrant and delightful place to be. Many people have written to me about the rubbish on the streets. Certain roads have terrible problems with rubbish, especially Gunton road, Shakespeare walk, Church walk and Stoke Newington high street. It is a blight and an eyesore which is making people angry.

Hackney council is well aware of people's feelings about rubbish and litter and it is doing all that it can. It is in the process of introducing some changes that it hopes may improve matters. It is trying to introduce night collections of rubbish as well as the ordinary day-time collections. Rubbish collectors will collect rubbish at night so, it is hoped, we shall wake up in the morning to a clean and sparkling borough. The council will be tougher with shopkeepers who do not make proper arrangements for the disposal of their rubbish and who are not prepared to enter into contracts with the council for disposal. The council is trying to raise the morale of its work force generally and to make the public aware of when rubbish is supposed to be collected, so if it is not collected at the correct time, the public have a number they can ring to compalin. The council is doing all that it can to deliver what the people of Hackney want, but the council cannot do everything by itself. It is fighting the trend in society, as I have said.

We face specific problems in the borough. Although all in the borough who are concerned about rubbish—of whom I am one—urge the council to continue with all it is doing and to try even harder in the future, there is no doubt that we must look to the Government eventually. What are they going to do about rubbish, litter and the environment in the inner cities, especially in boroughs such as Hackney? We do not want Britain to become like cities in America, such as New York, where the inner cities are no-go areas, sewers and dumps and the divide between the haves and have-nots becomes impossibly great? I am happy to live in a mixed community such as Hackney, and I want it to remain a mixed community where people are happy to live and to bring up their children side by side.

What can the Government do? First and foremost, if the Government are serious about rubbish, litter and, above all, the environment, they must provide local authorities with the resources to deal with the problem. They must give the resources to provide enough street sweepers, to employ enough dustmen, to buy the most up-to-date cleaning, sweeping and rubbish collecting equipment and to allow communal skips and special bins for shops to be made easily available. They must provide more resources so that boroughs such as Hackney can do all that they want in clearing up litter.

The Government must change their mind on the dog registration scheme. An effective system of dog registration would encourage dog owners to be more responsible and would do much to cure the problem of dogs roaming the streets. There would be less mess on pavements and fewer dogs tearing open black bags full of rubbish and scattering the contents on the streets. The Government should also consider whether we need harsher penalties for shopkeepers who do not take seriously their responsibility to dispose of rubbish. We need more resources for environmental health so that inspectors can go round to inspect shops.

Above all, we need a change in attitude by the Government. When we have a Government who despise the public sector, who say that anything done by the private sector is better simply by virtue of the fact that it is done by the private sector and who are determined to see the public sector wither away, services that can only be carried out collectively, such as keeping clean the streets of inner cities, are bound to suffer. A Government who despise the public sector will neglect the staff and starve the sector of money. We have seen the results in the environment of London, especially in the rubbish problem. It does no good for the Prime Minister to carry out publicity stunts and to be photographed picking up rubbish in the street. What is needed is a real commitment by the Government, and more resources for local authorities for their cleansing departments and environmental health departments. We also need to consider legislation on dogs, and on shop keepers in connection with what they do with their rubbish. We need to consider the penalties that can be enforced in dealing with people who drop litter. We need legislation, but also money. The Government must put money where their mouth is to tackle the problem of rubbish.

I am grateful to have been able to bring to the attention of the House the important issue of rubbish in Hackney, about which many thousands of my constituents are concerned. Rubbish is an environmental blight on a borough which otherwise has much to be proud of. We know that the council is doing its best, and we support it in that, but urge it to do even more, and we look to the Government to take the matter seriously. Despite what Conservative Members say the rubbish problem can best be solved by local councils and the Government, and cannot be dealt with by private enterprise. We have seen boroughs which have brought in private enterprise to collect bins and deal with rubbish, and the rubbish collection has almost collapsed.

My fellow Labour party Members and I take the matter extremely seriously. Conservative Members could be accused of hypocrisy because they never talk about making the resources and money available to enable councils such as Hackney to do the job. When I talk about the importance of solving the problem of litter, I know that I speak not only for many thousands of people in Hackney, many of whom have written to me, but for many millions of people in the country.

If Conservative Members and the Minister do not believe me when I talk about the rubbish menace in

Hackney, the piles of litter in Stoke Newington high street and on Stamford hill street corners, and the problem facing the cleansing department, I invite the Minister and the Prime Minister to come to Hackney to visit the streets which I mentioned and the cleansing department, and to talk to the dustmen, street cleaners and, above all, local residents. If the Prime Minister and the Under-Secretary were to come to Hackney and see the rubbish menace with their own eyes, instead of returning to their palatial houses in the salubrious suburbs, I believe that the money—and we need money—to deal with the rubbish in Hackney would be forthcoming the next day. The Government should put money where their mouth is to tackle the problem of rubbish in the environment.

1.43 pm

**Ms. Joan Walley** (Stoke-on-Trent, North): I too welcome the opportunity this morning to debate this important issue. My hon. Friend the Member for Hackney, North and Stoke Newington (Ms. Abbott) was right when she said that the public rightly perceive this as a most important issue, not just for those living in Hackney. I listened most carefully and I hope that the Parliamentary Under-Secretary of State will take up the invitation offered by my hon. Friend. I am sure that people all over the country would also wish to extend that invitation and I fear that the Prime Minister and the Under-Secretary will have to make many visits if they are to obtain some grasp of the extent of the litter problem which exists throughout the streets of our towns and countryside.

The fact that for the past 10 years the Government have avoided taking any action to deal with this important issue other than, as we have heard so clearly this morning, cutting back on local authority expenditure, is an indication of the political priority which they give to the issue. I welcome the move made by the hon. Member for Chelmsford (Mr. Burns) to provide the Chamber with an opportunity to discuss this issue. I only wish that his example had been followed much earlier by the Prime Minister and the Secretary of State for the Environment.

During the debate we have heard much about head teachers, their role and the way in which they have set an example in schools. I pay tribute to my own head teacher whom I have not seen for 22 years, Mr. E. S. Kelly, who instilled in all his pupils the idea that it was wrong to drop litter. He told us that sweets were bad for our teeth, and he was right, but he also told us that we should never drop wrappers or rubbish in the street. He told us to put it in our pockets and take it away or to put it in the bin. He was such a good teacher that his words of wisdom have stayed with me and no doubt they will continue to do so.

I only wish that the Prime Minister had the same commitment to dealing with the problem. The Prime Minister should not lecture members of the public about picking up rubbish when she so contrived it that officials from the Department of the Environment dropped the rubbish that she picked up in the first place. Many people who are concerned about the environment know only too well how hollow the Prime Minister's calls for action are.

We have heard about the so-called shining example set by Westminster council which came to the House for powers to do something about litter. But Westminster had to take the initiative, just as this opportunity to discuss the subject has arisen on the initiative of a private Member.

We cannot deal with the matter in isolation or look at the example of one local authority, even if that authority is doing well, which I doubt. The Government should introduce well thought-out plans and strategies and provide the necessary resources to do something about the problem. I draw the attention of the House also to the grave problems in the City of Westminster; so far from being concerned about the problem of rubbish, the council was not even charging traders for the disposal of commercial rubbish. That is an important omission.

For 10 years now, our towns and cities have played host to a consumer society in which it is all too easy to throw things away. I agree with what William Morris said—that one should look carefully at material objects and decide whether they are useful or beautiful. If they are neither, one should not create consumer demand for them. A great deal of work needs to be done and I have no doubt that consumers will start to vote with their feet and will not go out and buy unnecessary goods in unnecessary packaging. Consumers have an important part to play in conveying the message that much of what is produced is not necessary—that it is a waste of resources and a waste of the energy to produce it.

Given that there is a huge problem and that rubbish is strewn across our countrysides and roads, what have the Government done and what do they propose to do in future? I hope that the Minister will tell us what the Department's strategy is. It certainly has not had a strategy for the past 10 years. It is difficult to see what the Secretary of State for the Environment has done since the Prime Minister hauled him in following her visit to Israel back in 1986 to point out that beautiful Britain was beautiful no more because of the large amount of rubbish.

Consumers have responsibilities and, like schools and head teachers, could do much to improve matters, by changing their lifestyle. Unless that is backed by effective legislation, effective deterrents to the dropping of litter, properly resourced local authorities and the sort of initiatives already taken by Sheffield, the contributions of individuals will be lost in the sea of rubbish. I congratulate those hon. Members who have put the issue of litter and rubbish into the wider context, because no discussion can be effective without considering the need for waste minimisation, waste reduction and recycling.

It is important that the Minister tells us what the Government intend to do about recycling. What is the Government's position on the European directives relating to the recycling and re-use of glass containers? What discussions is the Minister having with her colleagues in the Department of Trade and Industry? Why is there no concerted Government action? Why are any policies on recycling being lost between the bureaucracies of the Department of Trade and Industry and the Department of the Environment? Despite the good example set by the Minister's own Department, why does not the Serjeant at Arms have any authority to provide recycled paper in the Palace of Westminster? That is the Government's responsibility. It is a nonsense that hon. Members are still sending out correspondence about recycling on non-recycled paper. If it is all right for the Department of the Environment to decide to use recycled paper, why is it not all right for the Palace of Westminster? Why are hon. Members suffering the long-standing penalty of having to write letters on non-recycled paper when they are trying to get some action on the issue? The Government have the

[*Ms. Joan Walley*]

responsibility to direct and lead and their failure to do so is indicative of their lack of adequate policies during the past 10 years.

When the much-heralded green Bill finally appears before the House, what commitments will it contain on recycling? I hope that the Minister can tell us that today. The Department of the Environment published a Green Paper on the role of waste disposal authorities, but it contained nothing of significance on the issue of recycling.

Following the earlier conclusion caused by the failure to distinguish clearly between waste and reclaimable materials when sections 12 to 14 of the Control of Pollution Act 1974 were enacted, the worrying impression has been created that the importance of the role of recycling is not yet fully recognised by the Department of the Environment. We must be told whether, in the reorganisation of the waste disposal functions of local authorities, the importance of recycling will be recognised. Certainly no reference to that appears in the Green Paper. Why not? Will the Minister assure the House that she will include recycling.

Has the Minister any plans to impose a duty on local authorities to set up recycling facilities? Such an important function should not be left to market forces and introduced only if a profit can be made from it. The Opposition are concerned about the environment and we believe that the environmental costs of different policies are equally as important as the economic costs—which are so often the only costs taken into account in the Government's policies.

Has the Minister any plans to license and regulate recycling facilities? What plans are there for each local authority to publish annual recycling plans? For the past 10 years, there has been a responsibility on waste disposal authorities to produce a strategic plan for dealing with waste management. Even after 10 years, some authorities have not produced those plans. It is doubly important that the Government should require each authority with responsibility for waste management to publish an annual recycling plan.

Will the Minister allow any financial surplus from consumer-aided recycling schemes to be reapplied to the benefit of the local environment? If individuals are to do their bit to conserve resources, they need to know that they can reap the benefits.

The Minister should realise that any recycling policy will cost money. As we have heard many times today, local councils have been badly affected by rate-capping policies and prevented from initiating and even maintaining their varied range of services to deal with all aspects of waste, including litter and rubbish.

Salaries have been cut for people who clean and sweep the streets and empty rubbish bins, and their conditions of employment have worsened. There has also been a reduction in the provision of rubbish bins. We have seen the examples that were referred to by the hon. Member for Ealing, North (Mr. Greenway), who talked about getting people to pick up litter as punishment. There has been a growth of community schemes, funded by the Manpower Services Commission, doing work that should rightly have been done by local authorities on a regular daily, weekly and monthly basis. The result is that, even in the voluntary sector, the work of projects such as UK 2000, which have

important ideas to introduce, has been marginalised. It has been possible to do that work only on the cheap. We want the Government to give a commitment that they will make available to local councils the money that will enable them to take full advantage of important pilot projects such as UK 2000 under its present leadership.

It is important to know whether the Minister has any plans, when dealing with rubbish and litter in a co-ordinated way, to give planning authorities extra powers to require and provide resources for clearing derelict land—to give derelict land a facelift—so that people can have a sense of pride in the community. Unless that is done, it will be difficult for individuals to recognise what they can achieve through their own actions if all they see around them is decay, neglect and dereliction as a result of cuts in local authority services.

Local councils provide bottle banks and opportunities for recycling and are the only ones who empty rubbish bins. They have many imaginative schemes for bulky household refuse collections, which prevents fly tipping on the streets, and for regular street cleaning. Local authorities also provide money for school education projects, and local councils should be encouraged to take the initiative of employing more officers to promote a dialogue with local industry so that partnership schemes might be introduced. They should also have greater scope to remove the abandoned cars that clutter our streets.

All such services cost money, and often they are provided by the same councils that have been worst hit by 50 legislative changes made over the past 10 years, such as rate capping. I hope that the Minister will give an undertaking that money will be available for a wide range of projects.

The Department of the Environment together with other Departments should take the lead. Does the Minister have any plans to discuss with the Home Secretary the whole inadequacy of current legislation relating to litter? Reference has been made to prosecutions and I have a table showing prosecutions ranging from 296 in Cumbria to a mere nine in Cambridgeshire. However, it does not show that in some areas there were no prosecutions whatsover. Comments by Graham Ashworth of the Keep Britain Tidy Group show only too clearly that the Litter Act 1983 is not working. Why has section 4 never been enacted, and what proposals do the Government have to update that legislation so that fines and penalties will serve as an effective deterrent, or be incorporated into the green Bill—not just as an isolated piece of legislation such as the Control of Litter (Fines) Bill of the hon. Member for Chelmsford (Mr. Burns), but as part of an overall and concerted approach to the problems of litter and rubbish?

Other issues to be addressed include the need for higher standards of transport. The Minister for Roads and Traffic produced £1 million to improve trunk roads, but at the same time reduced cleansing standards. What is the use of coming up with a little money once a year when councils no longer have the resources every day of the year? We heard from the Home Secretary the role that litter played in the tragic Bradford stadium fire. What laws exist to control litter in places such as football stadiums? The answer is that they are not covered by existing legislation.

Mention has been made in the debate of fly tipping, but the Government have made no proposals for introducing a remedy. It was left to my hon. Friend the Member for Lewisham, Deptford (Ms. Ruddock) to introduce legislation for dealing with that offence—but I congratulate the Minister on ensuring that both part I and part II will reach the statute book regardless of the views of her right hon. Friend the Secretary of State for the Environment.

For the past 10 years, Government policy on litter has been non-existent. The Prime Minister pays lip service to the need to clean up our dirty streets, towns, parks and countryside. But lip service is all that there has been. There is no place in the debate for lip service and double standards, but there is a place for concerted and co-ordinated action by the Government. The public will not follow the example set out by Ministers who drop litter in this Chamber, or by a Prime Minister who instructs that rubbish should be dropped in St. James's park so that she may make a hollow political point. The Prime Minister's hypocritical action in instructing Department of the Environment officials to drop rubbish so that she could be publicly seen to pick it up was not lost on the environmentally conscious public.

People in towns, in rural areas and in the countryside generally want to be able to take pride in their communities. They want to play their part. They want their councils to take a lead, and they want those councils to have the resources. They want properly funded cleansing services; they do not want gimmicks. They want more than £3 million to be spent on the initiatives that the voluntary sector has introduced. They want to be involved in all that is going on, and they want a commitment to waste reduction and recycling.

People desperately want the green Bill to take the wider issues on board, and, rightly, they fear that under the present Government it will be based entirely on subservience to market forces. They want the existing legislation to be updated so that it is a real deterrent and dropping litter a real offence. After last week, they know that only a Labour Government can to that. Those of us who are genuinely concerned know that "bagging and binning it" will not change anything. Conservative Members may laugh, but their day of reckoning will come, and on the record of the past 10 years their policies will win nothing.

Local authorities need power and resources. As has been said, litter is a public health problem, and the Institution of Environmental Health Officers is rightly concerned about it. More than anything else, it is an indication of the extent to which we have become a throw-away society. The public pressure to clean up our towns and cities is there. Real action is needed. So far we have had only lip service, and I hope that the Parliamentary Under-Secretary will give us a firmer commitment today.

2.6 pm

**The Parliamentary Under-Secretary of State for the Environment (Mrs. Virginia Bottomley):** I join others in warmly congratulating my hon. Friend the Member for Chelmsford (Mr. Burns) on his initiative in raising a subject that is of crucial importance to all hon. Members and, I believe, to all members of the public.

The Government are determined to take decisive action to deal with the problem. We have had a strong lead from the Prime Minister, who, long before other green campaigners jumped on to the bandwagon, made it abundantly clear that it was time to wage war on litter and to see action—and that is what the Government intend to do.

The contributions to today's debate have been noticeably constructive, realistic and practical, and have shown considerable knowledge of a complex and detailed subject. Litter relates to waste disposal, refuse collection and street-cleansing systems, and has strong implications for householders, business operators and individual citizens. It is of course important that our proposals take account of the way in which litter abatement can be properly effected in that wider context, and, as is generally known, we shall be introducing an environment protection Bill at the earliest opportunity. The Bill will update waste disposal regulations. We want the waste operation authorities to discharge their responsibilities properly, and we want waste to be dealt with properly from its origin to its disposal. We shall also make provision for longer-term disposal.

Litter is not a trivial subject but one of great importance to us all, and it plays its part in the many other environmental concerns with which the Government have rightly dealt. We have a proud record in giving a lead on a range of subjects. Deservedly, the Government and the Prime Minister have received much credit for the "saving the ozone layer" conference, for the moves towards establishing a framework convention on climate change and for doing so much to tackle the problem of acid rain, to clean up our rivers and to ensure that throughout the spectrum—at global, national, regional and individual levels—we are taking all the proper steps to improve our environment and to ensure that Britain is a beautiful country in which we can justly take pride.

Conservative Members believe that remarkable achievements have taken place in the bid to restore Britain's place in the world. We are committed to ensuring that we can show the same lead on the environmental front, and nothing prompts more concern than the offensive, unsightly and needless phenomenon of litter. We are not prepared to put up with dirty streets and squalid housing estates, or with our beautiful buildings and lovely countryside being despoiled by people's discarded refuse. That is why we so welcome the motion of my hon. Friend the Member for Chelmsford which identifies so many of these important subjects.

The green consumer is on the warpath. He is demanding that businesses put their house in order. Many hon. Members have referred to packaging. Businesses have already begun to respond to consumer demand by reducing the amount of packaging. Similarly, manufacturers responded to the need to remove chlorofluorocarbons from their products as soon as they realised that that was rightly and properly being demanded.

Many years ago the litter lout was seen for what he was and for what he should again be seen to be: an offensive individual who ought to be ashamed of committing such an offence. I shall say more about the powers that we hope will strengthen the litter laws. We are committed to a programme of Government action, but it must go hand in hand with a profound change of attitude.

There have been many examples in recent years of changes in attitude. Smoking is one example; the wearing of seat belts is another. During the last 10 years people's attitudes towards the wearing of seat belts have changed completely. Moreover, to give credit to the Under-Secretary of State for Transport, my hon. Friend the Member for

[*Mrs. Virginia Bottomley*]

Eltham (Mr. Bottomley), I ought to point out that the enforcement of the law on drinking and driving has led to a profound change in people's behaviour. We are determined that people's attitude towards litter should also change profoundly.

Many hon. Members have given examples of how people have responded to the need to clean up litter. My hon. Friend the Member for Littleborough and Saddleworth (Mr. Dickens) mentioned Raymond Watkins. There are people like Raymond Watkins throughout the country who are busily and eagerly playing their part in the war against litter. A co-ordinated and comprehensive strategy must be worked out.

Mention has been made of the excellent steps that have been taken by Westminster city council, which has to deal with particular problems. There are only 180,000 residents, but there is a daily commuter population of 750,000 and there are about 23 million tourists a year, about 9 million of whom come from overseas.

I spent a day with the Westminster group that deals with street cleaning and refuse collecting. It has a professional and profoundly dedicated approach to ensuring that the job is properly done. There are 8,500 litter bins, with 450 in Oxford street alone. It is no use Opposition Members saying that it is just a question of Government resources being needed. Many of the bins have been provided by sponsors. The group has been working with, not against the grain and has persuaded the fast food operators to come on to its side. The business community now realises that it is in its own best interests to ensure that the consumer can shop in good surroundings and not be surrounded by debris.

Westminster city council has adopted new technology and innovative methods. It has also used appropriate and helpful publicity and implemented the experimental fixed penalty scheme.

My hon. Friend the member for Basildon (Mr. Amess) —the "I love Basildon" supporter—referred again to the work that is being done in his area. Croydon's achievements are also magnificent. The Cleaner Chelmsford committee to which my hon. Friend the Member for Chelmsford referred is another example. It works best when there is a partnership between local residents, the business community, the local authority and schools—all those who, rightly and properly, have an interest in the matter.

Only yesterday I was in the constituency of my hon. Friend the Member for Hendon, South (Mr. Marshall) and was told about Hendon's scheme. Local residents do not say that they want a nuclear-free zone and all the other cheap Opposition gimmicks. Instead they want a litter-free zone. In Hampstead garden suburb individual residents have taken over responsibility for the stretch of road outside their house. The organiser, Peter Loyd, has taken time and trouble to ensure that the task is done and that people feel involved and committed. There are similar schemes throughout the country, such as Spring Clean Day, organised by the Civic Trust and the Tidy Britain Group.

There have been a multiplicity of projects raising public awareness because so often people litter without being aware of it. Those projects are bringing people together and making sure that local authorities are playing their full part. I pay special tribute to the wife of my hon. Friend the Member for Ealing, Acton (Sir G. Young) who is turning Cookham into a green village, the group at Chalfont St. Peter and many others throughout the country.

Businesses are also facing their responsibilities. There is more to be done. Many hon. Members have referred to the paper from cash dispensers and there are other specific problems. We shall look for ways of tackling them all.

At the root of the solution is a fundamental change in attitudes. Many hon. Members, including the hon. Member for Stoke-on-Trent, North (Ms. Walley) and my hon. Friends the Members for Ealing, North (Mr. Greenway) and for Chelmsford have referred to the importance of educating youngsters and working in schools. My hon. Friend the Under-Secretary of State for Education and Science has recently raised the subject with local education authorities.

Children are not natural litterers. All too often they learn the habit from their parents. We must mobilise them as our advocates and ambassadors. Many people have told me that they changed to using unleaded petrol because of the persuasive powers of their children. Youngsters can do a great deal about litter and we shall encourage schools to work with us. My hon. Friend the Member for Chelmsford referred to the importance of education and example and that should not be overlooked.

However, we have to look at the carrot and the stick, so we must consider enforcement which has been mentioned by many hon. Members. Littering is a crime. Under the Litter Act 1983 it is an offence which currently attracts a fine of up to £400. Hon. Members have referred to the variability of prosecution. Although the maximum fine is £400, the average is between £32 and £35. We are concerned about that. Some groups have already taken steps to make sure that magistrates realise that littering is often the first step in the general decay of an area— delinquency, vandalism and petty crime—and should be recognised as serious in terms of punishment and in every other way.

Points have been raised about the absolute offence. There are difficulties because it is a general principle that simple actions should not in themselves be an offence unless accompanied by an indication of intent. In the Westminster fixed penalty scheme the litter wardens and others first advised the individual to pick up the piece of litter, before issuing a fixed penalty. It is important that enforcement works with some persuasion. We want to clean up Britain and clean up our streets.

We are looking very carefully at the Westminster scheme. Many other local authorities have asked for similar powers. In many ways it seems to have worked effectively and has been a useful tool for the local authority in enabling it to fulfil its responsibilities.

In his private Member's Bill my hon. Friend the Member for Chelmsford suggested that other local authorities should be able to adopt similar schemes. Unfortunately, his Bill has not made progress, but it may be that before long he will receive some encouragement on that part of it.

We have mentioned many examples of forward-looking and imaginative local authorities. But we have to accept that other local authorities have singularly failed in their responsibilities to clean streets regularly, effectively and efficiently. They are not giving the citizens the service that they want. Too often people see dirty streets when they want cleans ones. People want clean streets and pavements, parks, playing fields, car parks, shopping centres, roadside verges and roundabouts. They are entitled to them. The Government will take action to ensure that in future, all local authorities deliver what the best already do, permanently. As the House is aware, we have proposed a new duty on local authorities to keep their land clean. This will clarify and codify their present range of duties and responsibilities.

We are also proposing a code of practice to which local authorities must have regard in carrying out their duty. For the first time, this will set clear objective standards. Local authorities will be required to meet these standards and will be certain of what they must aim for, and local residents will be able to see when an authority is not reaching the standard, and call it to account.

I must emphasise that the code is to be a reasonable document. It will be a tool for local authorities to use, taking account of practicalities in the task of cleaning up as well as the high standards that local residents are entitled to expect. It will spell out specific requirements on particular problems and will give clear advice. It will be a vehicle for recommending the best means of achieving those standards.

In drawing up the code, on which we shall be consulting local authorities, businesses and all interested parties, we have taken care to learn from the lessons of the Tidy Britain Group. The House is aware that my right hon. Friend the Prime Minister launched the group's forward-looking, anti-litter initiative—the 27 pilot projects examining major problem areas such as high streets, tourist areas, transport and special events. In each case, it is not simply a global wish that the place should be cleaned up but a scientific, analytical study of the methods that work and not of the best way of hoping that something will happen.

Before and after studies have been incorporated to assess the effectiveness. The intention is to establish the best ways of cleaning particular areas and getting all sectors involved in keeping them clean. We want to spread the lessons learnt to other areas so that all can benefit. The group will be drawing up practical guidelines on how to tackle particular problem areas.

There has been excellent co-operation between local authorities, chambers of commerce, voluntary groups and others. I have been lucky enough to launch a number of projects. The Government are providing a grant of £3 million for the Tidy Britain Group. It will be used to pioneer the group's schemes. Often the delivery and organisation is a matter for local authorities, businesses and all others who are partners in the campaign against litter.

The local authorities have already embarked, rightly, on contracting out and competitive tendering for a number of services under the Local Government Act 1988. Some Opposition Members have bleated about resources in the context of local authorities being required more effectively to fulfil the responsibility they already have. The Government have provided more resources for local authorities in terms of grant this year and we all know that there is great scope for savings in competitive tendering and in using the private sector. The Audit Commission report entitled "Preparing for Compulsory Competition" makes it clear that savings of 20 per cent. or more can be achieved in contract prices. That is an undeniable opportunity for local authorities.

Local authorities will also have an opportunity to specify the service they want and the quality they want and to ensure that there are penalty points in the contract so that local residents obtain good value for money and high-quality services, and the best have done that very well. All must be joined in the campaign against litter.

The hon. Member for Hackney, North and Stoke Newington (Ms. Abbott) talked about dogs. Local authorities already have powers to make byelaws on fouling. We have made it clear that the new duty to keep land clean will extend to dog mess. That will complement our further proposals announced last week, including a duty on local authorities to deal with strays and the power to charge for kennelling in the meantime. The Home Secretary has announced his plan to introduce powers to control dangerous dogs. The proposals are the right way of tackling dog fouling, straying and attacks by dangerous dogs. They will make an important impact.

No one can tackle the problem of litter alone, and no one will achieve a litter-free Britain overnight. However, the job must be done, and the Government are firmly committed to ensuring that it is. As Minister with special responsibility for litter, I want to make it clear how urgent the task is. It is clear that people have the energy and the will to take it on, but we must mobilise every section of society into playing its part.

Next year is Tidy Britain Year. It marks the beginning of a long-term campaign—the clean-90s campaign—to change fundamentally and permanently our attitude to litter and the way in which we cope with it. The Government give the campaign full backing. We shall provide the tools and ensure that those responsible are properly equipped and motivated to do the job.

Litter is not only a matter of legislation. It is a task for everyone working together, above all, in the local community. We need energy, co-operation and enthusiasm from politicians, officials, business and commerce, schools and voluntary groups and, above all, from individuals. We need people who are prepared to show an example—to bend down and pick up litter. Local authorities must fulfil their responsibilities and give individuals the power to take action when they are dissatisfied with what local authorities are achieving.

We need energy, enthusiasm, education, enforcement and example. We shall not hesitate to set an example. We shall shortly be bringing forward our clear proposals for our campaign against litter. We shall not hesitate to take the decisive action that is necessary to tackle this unacceptable and offensive scourge once and for all.

2.26 pm

**Mr. Geoffrey Dickens** (Littleborough and Saddleworth): I join other hon. Members in congratulating my hon. Friend the Member for Chelmsford (Mr. Burns) on raising this issue. He did so, as he always does on behalf of his constituents, with great dedication. He puts many hon. Members to shame by the amount of work that he does in this place.

It is peculiar speaking after my hon. Friend the Minister. It is a long time since I heard a junior Minister make such a wonderful speech, making the Government's case clear to the country. All who listen to broadcasts of her speech or read reports of it tomorrow will be encouraged by the efforts that she and her officials are making to ensure that once again Britain can take pride in

[*Mr. Geoffrey Dickens*]

being clean and sparkling for visitors and people who live here. One often returns from foreign countries and enviously says, "I wish that our towns were as clean as some of those that I visited." As my hon. Friend the Minister said, the difference between us and other countries is our attitude. Parents, teachers and headmasters should teach children not to drop litter. If street cleaners do their work well, they set an example, and people will not add to their task by throwing litter and rubbish everywhere.

Westminster city council was mentioned earlier. Westminster must almost be the dustbin of the world. It is one of the greatest tourist attractions in the world. It is faced with a huge task, because overseas visitors are not always as careful in our city as they are in their own.

The hon. Member for Hackney, North and Stoke Newington (Ms. Abbott) mentioned Hackney. The rubbish in Hackney does not result from visitors dropping it there. The rubbish in Hackney is probably the people of Hackney. The hon. Member for Hackney, North and Stoke Newington, like me, must set an example. I must conclude and allow my hon. Friend the Member for Chelmsford to sum up the debate.

2.29 pm

**Mr. Burns:** I am pleased that we have had the opportunity to debate this important matter and I thank hon. Members for their valid contributions. I am reassured by the Minister's statement that the Government are determined to beat the litter louts and to get Britain clean again in the next few years.

*Question put and agreed to.*

*Resolved,*

That this House welcomes the Government's commitment to taking decisive measures to tackle the problem of litter; urges all those responsible for land in cities, towns and countryside to take account of widespread public concern at littering and discharge effectively their responsibility to keep that land free of litter; calls for urgent new measures to discourage littering, to assist those who are already taking seriously their responsibilities and to ensure that those who do not are obliged to do so; and supports the Government's proposal to place a duty on local authorities to keep their areas clean and to publish a code of practice.

# Orders of the Day

## Private Members' Bills

### ELIMINATION OF POVERTY IN RETIREMENT BILL

*Order for Second Reading read.*

**Hon. Members:** Object.
*Second Reading deferred till 7 July.*

2.30 pm

**Mr. Jeremy Corbyn** (Islington, North): On a point of order, Mr. Deputy Speaker. I mean no disrespect, but I detected some tardiness in the Clerk getting to his feet. I was on the point of moving, That the Bill be read a Second time. Yesterday, 500 London pensioners came to the House to lobby in support of the Bill. Only one Tory Member agreed to meet them. They will be disappointed that the Bill was not discussed.

**Mr. Deputy Speaker (Sir Paul Dean):** Objection has been made to the Bill and the hon. Member has given a date for Second Reading.

### ITINERANTS (CONTROL) BILL

*Order for Second Reading read.*

**Hon. Members:** Object.
*Second Reading deferred till 30 June.*

### FIRE SAFETY INFORMATION BILL

*Order for Second Reading read.*

**Hon. Members:** Object.
*Second Reading deferred till 7 July.*

### PUBLIC SAFETY INFORMATION BILL

*Order for Second Reading read.*

**Hon. Members:** Object.
*Second Reading deferred till 7 July.*

### PROTECTION OF RESIDENTS IN RETIREMENT HOMES BILL

*Order for Second Reading read.*

**Hon. Members:** Object.
*Second Reading deferred till 7 July.*

### GAMING MACHINES (PROHIBITION ON USE BY PERSONS UNDER EIGHTEEN) BILL

*Order for Second Reading read.*

**Hon. Members:** Object.
*Second Reading deferred till 7 July.*

### RE-ENFRANCHISEMENT OF THE PEOPLE BILL

*Order for Second Reading read.*

**Hon. Members:** Object.
*Second Reading deferred till 7 July.*

### COAL MINING SUBSIDENCE (DAMAGE, ARBITRATION, PREVENTION AND PUBLIC AWARENESS) BILL

*Order for Second Reading read.*

Hon. Members: Object.

*Second Reading deferred till 7 July.*

## BRITISH RACING COMMISSION BILL

*Order for Second Reading read.*

Hon. Members: Object.

*Second Reading deferred till 7 July.*

## FOOTBALL SPECTATORS (No. 2) BILL

*Order for Second Reading read.*

Hon. Members: Object.

*Second Reading deferred till 7 July.*

# Enfield Royal Ordnance Factory

*Motion made, and Question proposed,* That this House do now adjourn.—*[Mr. Maclean]*

2.32 pm

**Mr. John Hughes** (Coventry, North-East): I am grateful for the opportunity to raise a matter of great importance —new evidence which has been presented to me about the sale of the Royal Ordnance factories by the Ministry of Defence to British Aerospace and, in particular, the sale of the former Royal Ordnance factory at Enfield, north London.

The Enfield factory, which opened in 1811, was one of the best-known rifle factories in the world and its highly skilled work force produced one of the Army's best-known weapons in the Lee Enfield rifle. It was a tragedy when the closure of the Enfield factory, with the loss of 1,200 jobs, was announced in August 1987, four months after British Aerospace had purchased Royal Ordnance for £190 million. At the time, the Enfield factory was valued by the Ministry of Defence at just £1·5 million. However, estimates of its redevelopment value have since ranged from £50 million to £125 million. It is a prime 100-acre site just within the M25, which has become a natural boundary for the green belt. Plans to develop the site for industry, commerce, housing and leisure were announced in May this year.

In a report published last year, the Public Accounts Committee said that it was concerned that the Ministry of Defence did not explore the possibility of redevelopment at Enfield or obtain an alternative valuation of the site based on the assumption that redevelopment might be approved in the future. The report of the Public Accounts Committee warned that British Aerospace could make a substantial gain on the site's sale or development without benefits accuring to taxpayers. Opposition Members and even some Conservative Members believe that these events are an indictment of the Government who have given away Royal Ordnance at a knock-down price and closed their eyes to the development potential at Enfield.

However, new evidence has been passed to me which suggests that the Government actively connived at the closure of the Enfield factory because they knew that the site would be closed and redeveloped before they sold Royal Ordnance to British Aerospace. The evidence also suggests that the Government engaged in a charade of competition in which other companies as well as British Aerospace were supposedly bidding for Royal Ordnance, while the Government had already made up their mind to hand the factories to British Aerospace.

The managing director of an engineering firm which used to make parts for the Enfield factory has informed me that about 30 subcontracting firms were called by the Ministry of Defence to a meeting at the Enfield factory in the autumn of 1986, about seven months before the sale to British Aerospace was announced. During interviews which lasted about four hours, the managing director told me that the subcontractors were told at the meeting that British Aerospace would be purchasing Royal Ordnance and would be closing the Enfield factory because the site was worth a great deal which would cover the cost of the purchase of Royal Ordnance.

All the 30 subcontractors present were asked under no circumstances to report that information and not to allow the closure plan to be known. According to the managing

[*Mr. John Hughes*]

director, British Aerospace officials were present at the meeting. Indeed, they openly discussed the terms and conditions under which the subcontractors would work once British Aerospace had bought Royal Ordnance. British Aerospace officials also had with them full specifications and samples of the SA80 rifle, production of which was to be transferred from Enfield to the Royal Ordnance factory at Nottingham as part of the closure plan.

The Minister may wonder why I have not revealed the name of the engineering firm or the managing director who has told me about the Enfield meeting. The reason is that he passed on the information in confidence although his firm no longer works for the Ministry of Defence. He has no axe to grind with the Ministry because the company decided to expand into other sectors. He wishes to remain anonymous because he fears that going public could jeopardise his chances of winning orders not from the Ministry of Defence, but from other big companies. I can understand his reluctance to allow his name to be made public. Look what happened at the Coventry Webster Machine Tool factory, which was drawn to the attention of the House on 18 June 1980 by my hon. Friend the Member for Birmingham, Perry Barr (Mr. Rooker). I am aware that on that occasion the John Brown company brought pressure to bear on the individuals involved with threats of closure and redundancies. Ironically, it has suffered the same fate earmarked for Enfield. In Coventry, a housing estate now exists where the factory once stood.

I cannot overstress the vulnerability of that company director and I repeat that I understand his reluctance to allow his name to be made public. Can Ministers who use their office to carry out this form of grand larceny, and who culpably devalue the parliamentary rights of every hon. Member and the democratic rights of every British citizen, be trusted to protect the trading position of this public-spirited individual and his employees? I must tell the House that I fully believe the managing director's assertions that such a meeting took place at the Enfield factory. All the evidence points to the fact that the Government, who supposedly believe in market forces, stitched up a deal with British Aerospace to ease the company's cash flow problem and to rob the taxpayers of millions of pounds.

The Enfield case is not an isolated one. Last November, a leaked memo from Warburg Securities revealed that British Aerospace was sitting on a land bank worth £1·1 billion, much of which it acquired when Austin Rover and Royal Ordnance were privatised and sold to British Aerospace. The report valued Enfield and the nearby Waltham Abbey Royal Ordnance factories at a total of £450 million. Royal Ordnance had already decided to close the Waltham Abbey site before it was sold to British Aerospace. Despite that, it was still valued at only £2 million.

The leaked Warburg memo gets to the heart of the matter and suggests that British Aerospace should

"move out of the southern sites where possible"

and

"move into cheaper labour northern areas."

It says that

"unemployment in the south is not a political issue"

and that

"redundancy costs are more than covered by land sales and pension fund surplus."

British Aerospace and the Government have connived in nothing less than naked asset-stripping on a massive scale. Yet Ministers at the Ministry of Defence have not been held responsible for deliberately cheating the taxpayer out of millions of pounds and allowing British Aerospace to make a killing. If a local authority had become involved in a scandal remotely like this one, I am pretty sure that the Government and the district auditor would have intervened and the councillors responsible would have been surcharged, disqualified and even sent to prison.

Ministers are fond of talking about local authorities' alleged abuse of power. The Government are currently pushing through Parliament a Bill supposedly designed to tackle the minuscule problem by banning 130,000 council officers from political activity. That is hypocrisy of the highest order because the real abuse of power is carried out by central Government. Nowhere has that been done more openly than with the sale of the Royal Ordnance factories to British Aerospace.

Ministers often say that legislation is needed to reform local government but not central Government because Ministers are accountable to Parliament. That has been exposed as nonsense by the Royal Ordnance sale. Yesterday's National Audit Office report clearly established that the foundation for the privatisation of Royal Ordnance was laid down in 1984. It also established that the Ministry of Defence's degree of commitment for the Government's privatisation philosophy was such that it no longer recognised its responsibility to the House of Commons. The comptroller's report pointed to the blatant contempt which was shown when, having set up a meeting of 30 subcontractors in September 1986, the Ministry then issued an information memorandum to supposed prospective purchasers in October 1986. That is conclusive evidence that the Government, through their Ministries were involved in asset-stripping.

Enfield originally made 115 of the rifle's 140 parts, and only 25 were out-sourced. Since production was transferred to Nottingham, only 12 parts are manufactured in house and 138 are manufactured by the vultures who, in 1986, sat down and tore to pieces the process and the Enfield work force. It is about time that questions were asked inside the Ministry of Defence, which was responsible for the give-away sale, and connived in a plan to close Enfield, which put 1,200 workers out of a job, and redeveloped the factory site. This is a matter of the gravest public concern and warrants an urgent investigation into the conduct of the Government and the Minister.

2.43 pm

**The Parliamentary Under-Secretary of State for Defence Procurement (Mr. Tim Sainsbury):** Any disinterested observer who had not read the National Audit Office report but who read the varying press comment on it might be forgiven for believing that at least two—perhaps even more—reports had been published yesterday. He would have been still more confused if he had heard the hon. Member for Clackmannan (Mr. O'Neill) during the Army debate claiming that the Enfield site had already been sold for between £300 and £400 million.

There is just one report, and the accounting officer, Sir Michael Quinlan, will be giving evidence on it on Monday. We do not of course wish to pre-empt the Public Accounts

Committee's study, but the report repays careful study. Indeed, I am tempted to read it aloud, the better to inform those who have apparently not bothered to study it.

It may be of help if I explain the background to the sale.

The first point, and one which seems to be constantly overlooked by critics, is that the sale was not of a piece of land, but of a business. As the report says, it was the Government's aim to sell Royal Ordnance as a going concern; it was sold with a number of assets but also with all its liabilities. The net worth of the company reflects both those elements.

Before any increase in the value of the sites at Enfield and Waltham Abbey can be realised, high costs will have to be incurred. I shall say more about that in a moment. As an illustration, Royal Ordnance provided £100 million in its 1987 accounts for rationalisation and restructuring. Against that background, it is completely unrealistic to look at only one side of the balance sheet.

I must make it quite clear yet again that the Ministry of Defence did not sell the Enfield site for £1·5 million or any other figure: we sold a business which was, and remains, one of our main defence suppliers.

It may help the House if I describe the history of the valuations of the Enfield site. In preparation for the privatisation of Royal Ordnance, the Department commissioned a valuation of all the company's land holdings, from a highly reputable firm of chartered surveyors. That company valued the company's sites on two bases—their existing use value, based on the open market value of the land itself and the depreciated replacement cost of the buildings and other works, and their alternative use value, based on the open market value of the sites taking into account the possibility of use for other purposes. The existing use valuation of Enfield, as at 31 December 1985, was £4·1 million. The alternative use valuation taking into account the possibility of use for other purposes was £2 million—that is, less than half the existing use valuation. The higher, existing use, valuation was made available to prospective purchasers of Royal Ordnance.

For those who are familiar with neither the complexities of property development, nor the site and the difficulities, risks, delays and uncertainties which would be involved in developing it—I fear that they include many of those who commented on the transaction—perhaps I should explain why the alternative use valuation was apparently so low.

In arriving at their valuation, our surveyors took into account a number of factors that seem to have been completely ignored by those who have simply assumed that the entire site would be capable of maximum development and would therefore command a high price for every one of its acres.

First and most important, the assumption ignores the fact that the site is within the metropolitan green belt, and at that time had no planning permission for development. Indeed, it still has no planning permission—nor is any planning application outstanding. It therefore remains to be seen whether permission will be granted, and if so, on what terms, and for what parts of the site.

Secondly, in valuing the site, one has to take into account the likelihood that any planning consents would be restricted as to the type of development which might be permitted.

Thirdly, there are the substantial restructuring and redundancy costs. Enfield was, after all, a manufacturing site, and British Aerospace has estimated that there will be a £40 million cost in closing it and providing the facilities at Nottingham.

Fourthly, there are likely to be significant decontamination costs, particularly at the Waltham Abbey site, although the full extent of these is not yet clear. That is a typical example of the uncertainties that surround any development proposals.

Fifthly, other substantial costs will be involved in preparing the site for development, and for example, in site clearance.

As the report says:

"The National Audit Office's consultants considered it likely that a developer would be required, as a condition of planning permission, to carry out an abnormal amount of landscaping over an extensive area and to undertake other costly works."

Suitable access is a particular problem at Enfield, where there appears to be only one means of access. In such cases, where a specific piece of land has to be purchased for access to an otherwise land-locked site, it is known in the trade as "ransom land". Ransom land is well named. It is commonly the case that its owner can negotiate a price with those who hope to purchase it based on a share of the development value of the entire site to which it gives access. That share can be up to 50 per cent. of the development value in cases such as Enfield, where there is only one possible means of access.

Finally, there is the delay in receiving any returns on all this investment. It is already more than two years since the sale, and no receipts are yet in prospect.

There has been reference to whether there should have been a clawback provision in the sale. Clearly we will be looking carefully at what the report has to say on clawback, both in general and with reference to this case. All clawback arrangements have about them an element of swings and roundabouts. The possibility of more later not surprisingly usually means less now. However, when the sale is just of a piece of land, the inclusion of a clawback provision is relatively straightforward and the advantages and disadvantages comparatively easy to evaluate. The sale of Royal Ordnance was not like that. Nor is there evidence that clawback is at all common when businesses, as distinct from land as such, are sold. That is the view of Rothschild, our merchant bank advisers for the sale, which has wide experience in such matters.

One of the aims of privatisation was to put Royal Ordnance on a full commercial footing, as free as possible from Government restraints on the way it conducted its business. A clawback provision would have had the undesirable result of a continuing involvement by the Department in the rationalisation of the company, because manufacturing facilities would have to be relocated before the site was fully available for redevelopment. Furthermore the Ministry of Defence is its main customer.

As I have said, when selling a business as a going concern a number of judgments have to be made—for example, what land potential purchasers of the company might consider to be surplus to their overall requirements, and different purchasers might have different views on that, depending on the requirements of other parts of their business; what type of redevelopment might maximise the value of such land; and how likely it is that planning permission for that could be obtained. It can take years to

[*Mr. Tim Sainsbury*]

obtain a final decision on planning permission, which would inevitably prolong uncertainty and delay the achievement of the wider aims of privatisation.

There may well be some gain to be made from developing the sites, but that would only occur after substantial hurdles in the way of development have been overcome. Given all the risks, uncertainties, delays and costs that will be involved, it is clear that the allegations of enormous windfall profits from such development simply do not stand up to close examination.

**Mr. Steve Norris** (Epping Forest): I represent one of the significant sites involved, so I am grateful to my hon. Friend for giving way in such a short debate. Does he agree that contrary to all the ludicrous speculation about values amounting to hundreds of millions of pounds attributed to those sites, the NAO report in fact clearly states:

"The NAO noted that they valued these sites as at 31 March 1989 at no more than 8·3 per cent. of the figures reported by the media in 1988."

Does my hon. Friend agree that as the most ludicrous of all those figures was probably about £400 million, the NAO is basically saying that the actual value of those sites has never been more than about £25 million to £30 million —exactly as we assumed when the original sale of Royal Ordnance was made?

**Mr. Sainsbury:** I know that my hon. Friend takes a close interest in those matters, as does our hon. Friend the Member for Enfield, North (Mr. Eggar), in whose constituency lies the Enfield site. The figure that my hon. Friend quotes from the NAO report is the latest valuation, some two years after the date of the sale, since when there has been an increase in property values. The figure of 8·3 per cent. puts the matter in perspective.

The suggestion that in all this the Department neglected to obtain good value for money for the taxpayer from the sale of Royal Ordnance, and was somehow misled into parting with valuable assets at less than their real value, is particularly misguided.

The allegation that appears in the press from time to time that we sold individual sites for their existing use values of a few million is nonsense. At the time of the sale, we were fully aware of the low value of the sites which the National Audit Office's equally expert surveyors have now confirmed, and of the substantial risks and costs of developing them which our surveyors had identified. We withheld from bidders for the company details of the alternative use valuations of the sites precisely because they were lower than the existing use valuations. In fact, the total alternative use valuations of the Royal Ordnance sites was a negative figure.

The hon. Gentleman made allegations about decisions to close taken before the sale. I firmly reject any suggestion that the closure of the Enfield factory was decided before the sale. Although the company had decided before the sale to apply to develop the Waltham Abbey site and the surplus piece of land within the boundaries of the adjacent Enfield site, no decision had been taken to close the Enfield operation. That decision was made after the sale by the new owners, and was announced in August 1987. We have no record of any meeting involving the Ministry of Defence at which the future ownership of Royal Ordnance was discussed with Royal Ordnance subcontractors, as the hon. Gentleman has suggested.

At that time, Royal Ordnance Enfield would have been involved in preparing its tender for the second tranche of SA80 production. Tenders were invited in June 1986 for reply by November 1986, and the decision to accept the Royal Ordnance tender, subject to confirmation by the new owners of the company, was made in February 1987. No doubt, Royal Ordnance would be able to say whether it had held any meetings with subcontractors at which the future ownership of the company was raised.

The essential point is that, at no time before the sale of Royal Ordnance was agreed on 2 April 1987, was anyone in a position to make any authoritative statement about the future ownership of the company—neither anyone connected with the Department nor anyone at Royal Ordnance, since that company was not even a party to the sale negotiations.

It is unfortuate that the new evidence that the hon. Gentleman claims to have had in his possession for nearly two weeks, as of yesterday was still not in the hands of the Public Accounts Committee. I hope that he will bring it forward. I assure the hon. Gentleman that neither his constituent nor his business has anything to fear if he does so.

**Mr. John Hughes:** I have already written to the Chairman of the Public Accounts Committee and supplied him with the information.

**Mr. Sainsbury:** I am glad to hear that. As of yesterday, it was not in the hands of the Public Accounts Committee.

In conclusion, I repeat that the various allegations which have been made about the sale of Royal Ordnance are completely unfounded. The company was sold for £190 million in an open and wide-ranging competition to the bidder who made the highest offer—a highly satisfactory return for the taxpayer. The valuations that were made at the time of the sale have been generally endorsed by the surveyors commissioned by the National Audit Office. The company, in its new ownership, has already begun the process of rationalisation and restructuring, which we expect to be of great benefit to the Department and hence to the taxpayer in fostering a more competitive ammunition industry.

The most important point is that it is now absolutely clear that the sale of Royal Ordnance was no "rip-off" of the taxpayer. There was not and is not a "pot of gold" which the Ministry of Defence virtually gave away. The Enfield site has not been sold, has no planning permission and has had no development carried out upon it. The site values that have been quoted by some Opposition Members are nonsense. The reports that appeared in the press about likely development profits were, it is now clear, plainly inaccurate and unjustified.

None of them came from responsible valuers in possession of all the facts. Indeed, I note that, in the case of the figure quoted in the Warburgs report, the company itself, in a statement to the National Audit Office, acknowledges that

" . . . there was no suggestion in the report on British Aerospace that the values ascribed to properties represented professional valuations arrived at after examination of the sites and upon the basis of particular assumptions."

It was recognised that a proper professional valuation had not been made, that the sites had not been examined and that the necessary assumptions had not been made.

This transaction has been subjected to an unusual degree of scrutiny. The various investigations have concluded that all proper procedures were followed and that due regard for the taxpayers' position was taken. In the words of the National Audit Office report,

"The National Audit Office recognise that the Department and their advisers took account of the relevant considerations in reaching their decisions and arranging for the sale of the company."

*Question put and agreed to.*

*Adjourned accordingly at one minute to Three o'clock.*

# House of Commons

*Monday 26 June 1989*

*The House met at half-past Two o'clock*

PRAYERS

[MR. SPEAKER *in the Chair*]

# Oral Answers to Questions

## ENERGY

### Sacked Miners

1. **Mr. Skinner:** To ask the Secretary of State for Energy whether he will meet the chairman of British Coal with a view to discussing the re-employment of the miners sacked during the mining dispute; and if he will make a statement.

**The Parliamentary Under-Secretary of State for Energy (Mr. Michael Spicer):** Since this is the ninth time that the hon. Gentleman has asked the same parliamentary question, he will be aware that the dismissal and re-employment of dismissed miners is a matter entirely for the management of British Coal. Of the 1,014 miners who were dismissed 663 have been taken back.

**Mr. Skinner:** The Secretary of State for Energy did not have to ask nine times to get his job back. Is he aware that a fortnight ago Geoff Almond was killed in Betteshanger colliery when he was crushed to death? John Moyle, president of the Kent area and a local inspector, went to the colliery. He is a victimised miner, because British Coal refused to give him his job back. Upon trying to find out the events which led to that tragic death, he was ordered off the premises because he was a sacked miner. It is high time that the Secretary of State for Energy or any of his accomplices had a word with British Coal. When victimised miners who are trying to resolve and find out the cause of such tragic accidents are ordered off the premises, it shows that it is high time that British Coal and all its allies gave up this lust for revenge.

**Mr. Spicer:** Perhaps I can help the hon. Gentleman by once and for all setting this matter in its proper context and giving further details of some of the charges brought during the miners' strike. There were three charges of murder, five of threat to kill, three for explosives offences——

**Mr. Hood:** Answer the question.

**Mr. Spicer:** This is exactly answering the question. There were 49 charges involving offensive weapons, 15 for arson, 1,019 for criminal damage, 13 for conspiracy to cause damage, 39 assaults, 360 for assault on the police, 429 for assault causing bodily harm, 19 for resisting arrest, 31 for burglary and 352 for theft. That is merely the beginning of the list of charges. There were 201 custodial sentences handed out. Perhaps that explains why British Coal cannot take back all the miners.

**Mr. Dickens:** Does the Minister agree that there is not a private employer in this country who would be expected to take back on his staff someone who had beaten another member of staff with a baseball bat? Offences involving miners included incidents such as concrete slabs being dropped off bridges. Why should the hon. Member for Bolsover (Mr. Skinner) come to the House time and time again to suggest to the Government that they should encourage the chairman of a nationalised industry to do something which no private employer would dream of doing?

**Mr. Spicer:** I agree with my hon. Friend, and as I said in my opening comments, I could have listed further charges which were brought and sentences passed.

**Mr. Patchett:** The Minister read out a list of charges. Will he list the number of charges dropped after the dispute?

**Mr. Spicer:** Of course, not all charges were proceeded with. We are talking about 201 custodial sentences. Only 333 miners were, in the end, not reinstated.

### Office of Electricity Regulation

2. **Mr. Mullin:** To ask the Secretary of State for Energy what discussions he has had with the director-general-designate of the Office of Electricity Regulation since his appointment.

**The Secretary of State for Energy (Mr. Cecil Parkinson):** Discussions are taking place between my Department and Professor Littlechild on a wide range of issues.

**Mr. Mullin:** Is it not wholly improper to appoint Professor Littlechild to a job which requires independence, given his association with a number of Conservative party think-tanks and his former role as a political adviser?

**Mr. Parkinson:** First, Professor Littlechild has never been a political adviser. He has been an adviser to the Government, which is quite different from being an adviser to the party. I have never heard any Labour Members suggest that Sir Gordon Borrie is unfit to hold his job as the Director General of Fair Trading because he stood as a Labour candidate in a parliamentary election. He has turned out to be a distinguished public servant, as will Professor Littlechild.

**Mr. Rost:** When is the grid company likely to be able to announce the basis on which it will charge for transmission? Until that is announced, no contracts can get under way, either between the newly independent producers or between the distributors and existing producers.

**Mr. Parkinson:** We are making good progress on a range of issues. I hope that these figures will be available by the end of July.

## Central Electricity Generating Board

**3. Mr. Jack Thompson:** To ask the Secretary of State for Energy when he last met the chairman of the Central Electricity Generating Board; and what matters were discussed.

**Mr. Parkinson:** I regularly meet the chairman of the Central Electricity Generating Board.

**Mr. Thompson:** Following recent reports that the European Commission is to investigate the legality of the electricity privatisation Bill, whose provisions concerning the protection of the nuclear industry are under question, did the Secretary of State discuss with the chairman of the CEGB the future prospects for National Power and its marketability if the European Commission makes an adverse decision?

**Mr. Parkinson:** We shall clear all our plans with the European Commission, with which we have had preliminary discussions. The Commission recognises that at the end of this privatisation we shall have the most open electricity supply industry in Europe. Broadly speaking, it is strongly in favour of our proposals and we expect to be able to satisfy it about the details of the fossil fuel levy.

**Sir Trevor Skeet:** Is my right hon. Friend aware that negotiations are taking place between the generators and the large industrial users about the direct buying of electricity, which comes under clause 6? Will he accelerate that process and ensure that the CEGB's successor will have the right to do just that?

**Mr. Parkinson:** The industry is settling a range of complex issues at the moment. They arise from the fact that we shall be changing the whole basis on which the industry operates. At present, it is producer-dominated and the producer—the generator—has the last word in disputes. In future, producers and users will have to negotiate a settlement between themselves—that is what they are in the process of doing.

**Mr. Maclennan:** Given the expressed view of the chairman that, following the removal of the duty to supply from the Central Electricity Generating Board to the consumer, responsibility for maintaining medium and long-term research fell, upon whose shoulders does the Secretary of State intend that that financing should fall?

**Mr. Parkinson:** My Advisory Committee on Research and Development—ACORD—has been looking at the entire range of research that is carried out in the electricity supply industry. The successor companies have already made it clear that they will carry on with a range of operational and medium-term research. ACORD is advising me whether there are any areas that the companies do not want to pursue which, in ACORD's opinion, should be pursued. The Government would then take those on.

**Mr. Colvin:** Has my right hon. Friend discussed with the chairman of the CEGB the problems of research and development following privatisation? Following his decision to sanction the closure of Marchwood engineering laboratories and the allocation of their R and D capacity to Berkeley and Ratcliffe-upon-Soar, it seems that the plans that the Government have in mind favour National Power and Power Gen, which will draw on the resources of those two research establishments. If any other bodies such as the distribution companies choose to generate power after privatisation, which they will be empowered to do, to whom will they go to get research and development done? Surely a case can be made for the privatisation of the CEGB's research and development facilities in a single company which can contract its resources to anyone who may want to generate, rather than for making these facilities the exclusive preserve of National Power and Power Gen.

**Mr. Parkinson:** We considered the privatisation of the research facilities as a separate research company, and came to the conclusion that that was not practicable. Private generators would be able to approach these research establishments and seek to place contracts. Other research establishments are available. The main fact was that after the most careful examination there was no justification for maintaining Marchwood. The work being done there can be transferred to Ratcliffe and Berkeley. Marchwood is simply not necessary.

**Mr. Morgan:** Following press reports last week that the Government have done a U-turn in their relations with the CEGB and National Power, in respect of the full indemnity that we understand will now be given for nuclear waste reprocessing disposal and decommissioning, as distinct from merely the unforeseeable costs of those three categories of the CEGB's and National Power's expenditure, will the Secretary of State tell the House whether he agrees that that is a thoroughly undignified chapter in the breaking of a promise made at the Committee stage? Does he agree that he is now reduced to shovelling the shares off the back of a lorry before he finally shovels the Department of Energy into oblivion?

**Mr. Parkinson:** My advice to the hon. Gentleman would be quite different. He should stop believing as gospel everything that he reads in the newspapers. There has been no change in Government policy. The policy as set out during the Committee stage is the policy that we are maintaining. We are advised that clause 93 in its present form did not achieve the aims that we had for it when we put it to the Committee.

If Opposition Members wish to quote either my hon. Friend the Under-Secretary of State or myself, I hope that they will quote *Hansard* accurately instead of misrepresenting what we say.

## Electricity Privatisation

**4. Mrs. Clwyd:** To ask the Secretary of State for Energy what is his current estimate of the total costs of advertising and other expenditure to be incurred in the flotation of the electricity supply industry.

**5. Mr. Redmond:** To ask the Secretary of State for Energy what is the total cost incurred to date by his Department on advice on public relations and advertising aspects of the privatisation of the electricity supply industry.

**Mr. Michael Spicer:** No advertising expenditure by Government will take place before the Electricity Bill receives Royal Assent. It is therefore too early to provide estimates of costs.

**Mrs. Clwyd:** It is perhaps not surprising that the Minister ducks the question. Will he confirm or deny that the cost of pursuing the Government's half-baked dogma will be between £200 million and £370 million? Does he agree that that kind of money would be better spent on the Energy Efficiency Office—instead of halving its budget—so that it can help people to save energy, to reduce pollution and to cut fuel poverty and wastage? That would be a much better use of the money than electricity privatisation.

**Mr. Spicer:** I assure the hon. Lady that whatever costs are incurred will achieve value for money for the taxpayer. We cannot help it if the Labour party does not like wider share ownership. We do, and we will continue to back it.

**Mr. Redmond:** Does the Minister agree that the money that will be spent flogging off the industry would be better spent reducing standard charges for old-age pensioners —or is it party dogma against old-age pensioners?

**Mr. Spicer:** The Government are absolutely committed to the privatisation of the electricity industry, because we believe that it will achieve much better standards for the consumer, will put a downward pressure on the prices for the consumer and will achieve things that the Labour party would never have achieved in its wildest dreams by keeping the industry nationalised.

**Mr. Marlow:** Will my hon. Friend explain to the mixture of simpletons and troublemakers on the Opposition Benches that if, in privatising an industry, the advertising cost is more than recouped by an increase in the price that the Government get, it is a jolly good idea for the taxpayer? Will he also point out that companies like Unilever, ICI and other people spend money on advertising, and they do so because they feel that it is commercially beneficial?

**Mr. Spicer:** My hon. Friend is absolutely right. The net benefits to the taxpayer are precisely as he states them.

**Mr. Dykes:** Will my hon. Friend re-examine the consumer advertising, both before and after flotation, of the area boards now and the area plcs afterwards, in view of the still prevailing serious allegations of unfair competition against the private sector retailers, notably in the form of the latest advertisements of the Eastern electricity board—"£50-worth of free current if you buy a cooker from us"?

**Mr. Spicer:** My hon. Friend has for some time been a champion of the independent sector. The Bill and the restructured industry will recognise the anxieties that he and others have expressed by making certain that the retailing aspects of the privatised industry will be ring-fenced, kept entirely independent, and will not be able to trade in that unfair way.

**Mr. James Lamond:** Although we understand that it is Tory party policy and dogma to spread share ownership much wider, is it right to use public money to publish propaganda for that purpose?

**Mr. Spicer:** We are absolutely committed to a policy which since 1979 has resulted in an increase in private shareholders from 3 million to 9 million. We absolutely agree with that and think that it is right in every possible

sense, not least because it provides a great incentive to greater efficiency within the industry. The process of privatisation involves projecting the industry to the public.

## Greenhouse Effect

6. **Mr. Favell:** To ask the Secretary of State for Energy when he last had discussions with other European Community Energy Ministers on the greenhouse effect.

**The Minister of State, Department of Energy (Mr. Peter Morrison):** Although not specifically discussed by Community Energy Ministers, the greenhouse effect is borne in mind in the Council's consideration of energy issues.

**Mr. Favell:** In view of the threat to the earth's atmosphere from the burning of fossil fuels, are not those Greens who advocate the abandonment of the nuclear option foolish in the extreme? Is that generally recognised throughout Europe?

**Mr. Morrison:** That is generally recognised throughout Europe, and the environmental Council of Ministers made precisely that point in a recent resolution. It is sad that the Greens are pursuing a route which presumably will achieve the opposite to what they desire.

**Mr. Campbell-Savours:** For each therm of energy output, which fuel cycle has the least impact on the greenhouse effect—coal, oil or nuclear?

**Mr. Morrison:** Nuclear.

**Mr. John Marshall:** Does my right hon. Friend agree that it is high time that the Labour party learned from President Mitterrand that nuclear power is the friend of the environment?

**Mr. Morrison:** My hon. Friend is entirely correct. I notice from the Labour party's latest policy review that the ultimate conclusion of its policy will be to phase out all nuclear power stations. That will have a very harmful impact on the greenhouse effect.

## British Coal

8. **Mr. Haynes:** To ask the Secretary of State for Energy when he last met the chairman of British Coal; and what matters were discussed.

13. **Mr. Hood:** To ask the Secretary of State for Energy when he next expects to meet the chairman of British Coal; and what matters he expects to discuss.

**Mr. Parkinson:** I meet the chairman of British Coal regularly to discuss all aspects of the coal industry.

**Mr. Haynes:** It is time that the Secretary of State discussed with the chairman of British Coal the amount of coal which the Central Electricity Generating Board is to take on. I have serious reason to believe that the CEGB and British Coal have done a dirty deal which will affect the Nottinghamshire miners whom the Secretary of State defends in this Chamber. The take has been reduced from 75 million tonnes to 60 million tonnes. What will the Secretary of State say at the Dispatch Box on behalf of the Nottinghamshire miners now?

**Mr. Parkinson:** If I catch your eye later today, Mr. Speaker, I will tell the House that that allegation is complete and utter rubbish. British Coal and the two generators are in the process of negotiation about the quantity of coal and the term for which they will take it. We have made the Government's position absolutely clear. We believe that we have put the industry in a strong position to get the lion's share of that business. That is what we would like to happen.

**Mr. Hood:** When the Secretary of State next meets the chairman of British Coal, will he ask him how much it cost to pay off the private coal companies in Bilston Glen as a result of the closure of that colliery? How much pay-off to the private contractors was made in compensation?

**Mr. Parkinson:** I will ask the chairman of British Coal that when I next meet him. However, I volunteer some information to the hon. Gentleman in the hope that it will help him. As the hon. Gentleman is aware, Bilston Glen lost £20 million in the last financial year in addition to £50 million of accumulated losses that it had made before then. That is why the colliery had to close.

**Mr. Andy Stewart:** When my right hon. Friend next meets the chairman of British Coal, will he congratulate him and his working miners on achieving increased profits of £500 million this year? Fifty per cent. of deep-mined coal comes from Nottinghamshire, which is something of which the people there are very proud.

**Mr. Parkinson:** I shall certainly do as my hon. Friend asks, and I will remind the chairman that Nottinghamshire miners find the attitude of the Labour party towards them totally hypocritical. That party gave those miners no support when they needed it but is trying to exploit them now.

**Mr. Ashby:** I hope that my right hon. Friend will discuss with the chairman of British Coal a problem affecting my constituency concerning jobs at the new mine at Asfordby near Rutland. Undertakings were given that Leicestershire miners would be offered jobs there. My right hon. Friend will know that a number of Leicestershire mines will shortly close, and jobs at Asfordby are very necessary for those affected. Will my right hon. Friend remind the chairman of undertakings that jobs at Asfordby would be made available to Leicestershire miners?

**Mr. Parkinson:** I shall do as my hon. Friend asks, but I point out that although more than 100,000 miners have left the industry since the end of the strike, not one was refused a job if he wanted to stay in the industry. Every one who left did so voluntarily, with a substantial redundancy payment.

**Mr. Hardy:** Does the Secretary of State accept that the jobs of many miners in Leicestershire and elsewhere are at stake as a consequence of the short-sighted consideration that sees the importing of South African and other coal as being economical? Does the right hon. Gentleman accept that many of his right hon. and hon. Friends are more interested in the future of the South African coal mining industry than in our own?

**Mr. Parkinson:** The hon. Gentleman delivers a good old emotive sentence but one which has no basis in fact, as he knows. Imports represent about 10 per cent. of our total coal burn, and some of those imports are very necessary because we do not produce all the qualities of coal that we

need. Of that 10 per cent., less than 2 per cent. is South African. There is no sign that there will be substantial imports from South Africa.

## Electricity (Carbon Dioxide Emissions)

9. **Mr. Wood:** To ask the Secretary of State for Energy what is the reduction in the amount of $CO_2$ emitted per unit of electricity supplied between 1959 and the present day.

**Mr. Peter Morrison:** $CO_2$ emissions per unit of electricity supplied have reduced by 33 per cent. over the period 1959 to the present day.

**Mr. Wood:** I thank my right hon. Friend for his encouraging response. Can he give an indication of future trends and how they would be affected if nuclear energy was no longer part of the country's total energy production?

**Mr. Peter Morrison:** It is very important to continue our nuclear programme. If we do not, $CO_2$ emissions will increase. Of the 33 per cent. reduction to which I referred, about one third is attributable to nuclear-generated electricity, so its abolition—which the Opposition propose should ultimately occur—would have a very deleterious effect.

**Dr. Kim Howells:** Given the Government's obvious enthusiasm for the production of energy from non-fossil fuel sources, why have the West German Government abandoned plans to build a nuclear reprocessing plant at Wackersdorf, and why have the Siemens electricity company and the America firm Acro decided to establish Europe's first thin layer solar cell factory at Wackersdorf? Will Government money be invested in similar technology in this country?

**Mr. Morrison:** I may have many responsibilities, but I was not aware that the European Community had extended them to Germany's energy policies, so I cannot answer the hon. Gentleman.

**Mr. Hind:** Has my right hon. Friend seen today's press reports that in generating sufficient electricity to centrally heat the average-sized home, coal causes three times as much environmental damage as gas? Is not the message from that that the way forward for Britain's energy requirements must be the use of energy sources that do not damage the ozone layer and contribute to the greenhouse effect, and that nuclear and gas are two ways of achieving that objective?

**Mr. Morrison:** As my hon. Friend is probably aware, the gas burn directive does not prohibit the generation of electricity by gas, but does not encourage it. The United Kingdom takes a very positive stance on that and we are doing our best to have that directive repealed.

## Office of Electricity Regulation

10. **Mr. Illsley:** To ask the Secretary of State for Energy what discussions he has had with the director general-designate of the Office of Electricity Regulation on the possibility of a fossil-fuel combustion tax.

**Mr. Parkinson:** None, Sir.

**Mr. Illsley:** In view of the speculation hanging over the future of the Department of Energy, and the recent publication by the Secretary of State for the Environment of a document advocating a carbon or coal tax, will the Secretary of State tell us who would be responsible for bringing in such a tax? Would it not be better to introduce energy efficiency measures rather than hitting the coal industry again?

**Mr. Parkinson:** My right hon. Friend made it clear the next day at a press conference that the views that he had expressed in that pamphlet were personal views. He was talking about discussions that are going on in international fora. He also made it clear that we had no plans to introduce a carbon tax here.

**Mr. Mans:** Does my right hon. Friend agree that, for many years now, the taxpayer has subsidised the production of electricity from coal, and that in view of that there is no question of a tax being levied on fossil fuel?

**Mr. Parkinson:** As I have said, there are no plans for such a tax. We and previous Governments have favoured coal strongly: far from penalising it, we have subsidised it.

**Mr. Barron:** In the constituency of the Secretary of State for the Environment, the right hon. Member for Cirencester and Tewkesbury (Mr. Ridley), is the Coal Research Establishment, which is a centre of excellence for research and development relating to clean coal burn, not just in this country but in Europe. Would the Secretary of State for Energy mind taking his right hon. Friend to visit that establishment to see how we can really start to talk about getting rid of greenhouse gases in the world?

**Mr. Parkinson:** I shall mention that to my right hon. Friend. He always welcomes helpful suggestions, and I am sure that he will welcome this one.

The hon. Gentleman is right to emphasise clean coal burn technology. We shall have to change the way in which we produce electricity from coal; coal is the great pollutant, and the way forward is more efficient cleanburn technology.

### Energy Conservation

11. **Mr. Ray Powell:** To ask the Secretary of State for Energy by what proportion he estimates the national demand for electricity will be diminished through energy conservation measures in the years 1995, 2000, 2005 and 2010.

**Mr. Peter Morrison:** I cannot make such an estimate, because improved energy efficiency does not automatically lead to reduced consumption of electricity. However, it is worth noting that the energy used to produce one unit of GDP in 1987 was 7 per cent. lower than in 1983. This represents a saving of over £2 billion.

**Mr. Powell:** Following the 50 per cent. reduction in the Government's conservation expenditure, is it not time that the Government started to talk about an energy policy instead of a privatisation policy? Is the Minister not concerned about the industrialists—particularly at Rockwell International in my constituency—who produce for conservation and yet are continually bombarded with Government cuts, with the result that their programme is miles behind? Is it not about time that the right hon. Gentleman began altering his policy?

**Mr. Morrison:** If the hon. Gentleman looks carefully at the figures, he will see that the reduction is nothing like 50 per cent. If he also looks at where the reduction is being made, he will find that the programmes involved have come to the end of their lives. He will also find, on reflection, that the large advertising budget of the previous two years has had precisely the desired effect: energy efficiency is now very much at the forefront of most people's minds.

**Mr. Dickens:** Is it not a fact that although we are conserving energy, at the same time we are living in an electronic age? Most of our offices are now using a good deal of electronic equipment, and, because of our great economy, industries are taking off and are therefore using more electricity than they did a few years ago. Although we are encouraging energy conservation, we are also trying to match the demands of industry, trade and commerce, as it is sensible for us to do.

**Mr. Morrison:** I agree entirely with my hon. Friend. If we pursued the policies advocated by some, though not necessarily by Opposition Members, the economy would not grow and that is not what most hon. Members want.

**Mr. Alan W. Williams:** Will the Government learn the lessons of the European elections—the performance of the Green party and the tragic results for their own party? Is it not clear that the people of Britain totally reject nuclear power and that they want far more investment in energy conservation and in renewable sources of energy?

**Mr. Morrison:** If the hon. Gentleman were to ask many of the people who supported the Green party at the European elections, I think he would find that many of them had not read the Green party's manifesto. Had they read what it said about the nuclear aspect, they may well not have voted Green in the elections.

**Mr. Blair:** Is there not a growing consensus that the best means of combating the greenhouse effect and of promoting environmental protection is through energy efficiency and conservation, which is precisely what the Lords amendments to the Electricity Bill set out to achieve? Why does the right hon. Gentleman not say that the Government will accept those amendments and, for once, put the public interest before privatisation?

**Mr. Morrison:** I quite agree with what the hon. Gentleman says about energy efficiency. I wish, though, that he would look at his own party's policy towards coal, which he might find also has a greenhouse effect. If he looked at the Lord's amendments, he would see that they are unworkable. He, of all people, I am sure, would not wish unworkable clauses to be included in an Act of Parliament.

### Nuclear Power

12. **Mr. Hannam:** To ask the Secretary of State for Energy what is the total number of jobs in the United Kingdom dependent on the nuclear power industry.

**Mr. Michael Spicer:** The total number of jobs in the United Kingdom dependent on the nuclear power industry is estimated at about 180,000.

**Mr. Hannam:** Does my hon. Friend agree that this figure shows that one in every 144 jobs in this country is dependent upon the nuclear power industry? Does that not demonstrate that the Labour party's commitment to phase out nuclear power by the year 2000 makes absolutely no sense at all when one is considering future employment in this country?

**Mr. Spicer:** I agree with my hon. Friend. I should have thought that the hon. Member for Sedgefield (Mr. Blair) would be particularly concerned about the threat to his party's fortunes if his party's policy, which does not favour the nuclear industry, were to be implemented. While I was researching the answer to my hon. Friend's question, I discovered the interesting fact that close to the constituency of the hon. Member for Sedgefield, 1,000 people are employed on a £9·5 million contract for Sizewell B and that in Stockton, South, which is also close to the hon. Gentleman's constituency, there is a £31 million contract for Sizewell B. One of the people who would be extremely worried, I should have thought—if the Labour party's policy on nuclear power were to be implemented —would be the official energy spokesman for the Labour party.

**Mr. Eadie:** Since the hon. Gentleman is giving statistics relating to the nuclear power industry, and the energy industry in particular, will he confirm that in the last seven or eight years between 150,000 and 155,000 jobs have been lost in the mining industry?

**Mr. Spicer:** I confirm that—or at least around those figures. However, the output from the mining industry in that period was almost identical to what it was before, when there was all that extra employment. We very nearly doubled productivity in that period. That is one of the reasons why our coal mining industry will be able to compete against the rest of the world.

**Mr. Douglas:** Following that answer, do the Minister's figures include those for employment in the South of Scotland electricity board's nuclear capacity? Will he compare and contrast that with the figures relating to coal production for electricity in Scotland? When will an agreement be concluded to safeguard the remaining jobs in the coal mining industry between the South of Scotland electricity board and British Coal so that we may retain some jobs in the coal industry in Scotland?

**Mr. Spicer:** I think that the hon. Gentleman is straying away from the question, which relates to jobs in the nuclear industry. However, I confirm that the figures that I gave are for the United Kingdom as a whole. As to the specific point that he raised, that is currently the subject of negotiations. The Government very much hope that the result of the negotiations will be to the benefit of the coal industry and of electricity consumers. That has to be part of the equation.

## Offshore Licensing

17. **Mr. Carrington:** To ask the Secretary of State for Energy when he expects to announce the awards as a result of the applications for the 11th offshore licensing round.

**Mr. Peter Morrison:** I hope to be in a position to make the announcement within the next week or so.

**Mr. Carrington:** Will my right hon. Friend confirm that there is still a very high level of interest in North sea exploration which is a vindication of the Government's policies for the development of the North sea and has led to the massive extension of the proven reserves in our part of the North sea?

**Mr. Morrison:** I can confirm to my hon. Friend that there is a very high level of interest in the North sea. I hope that when we are able to announce the 11th round it will prove very successful. That means that we can look forward with more than hope to North sea oil and gas for longer than people had orginally thought.

**Mr. Doran:** The Minister paints a very rosy picture, and I share some of his optimism, but there is a cloud on the horizon—the serious skill shortage in the North sea which threatens future development and possibly current production. What steps does the Minister propose to take to encourage the oil industry to improve its lamentable training record?

**Mr. Morrison:** The hon. Gentleman will perhaps be pleased to hear that the matter was discussed at the most recent meeting that I had with Oilco—the oil industry liaison committee—attended by the employers and the trade unions and further discussions will take place. I agree that the manpower in the North sea is vital for its further development. Its success has been achieved because of that manpower.

## THE ARTS

### Arts Education

56. **Mr. Harry Greenway:** To ask the Minister for the Arts what steps he is taking to ensure that the arts form part of children's education.

**The Minister for the Arts (Mr. Richard Luce):** The Secretary of State for Education and Science and I support the place of the arts in education. The national curriculum ensures this. As I announced in the House on 23 May, my right hon. Friend and I are funding research into good practice to demonstrate the range of educational opportunities available in the contemporary arts, museums and galleries, and public libraries.

**Mr. Greenway:** Will my right hon. Friend note that it has taken this Conservative Government to make art and music a compulsory part of the school curriculum for all children, and that the previous philistinic Labour Governments never did anything but talk about it? Where do art and education come together specifically for the benefit of London children?

**Mr. Luce:** It is, of course, a matter for my right hon. Friend the Secretary of State for Education and Science, who should be given credit for ensuring that for the first time music is a compulsory subject in school. The new curriculum makes it possible to include almost every facet of art in one form or another and I hope that teachers will take advantage of that. In regard to my hon. Friend's second question, there are a number of examples of good practice in London. The national maritime museum has an excellent scheme for children through the Armada exhibition; the royal opera house has workshops and works with schools, as does the English National Opera, and the London Mozart Players have an excellent education scheme in Croydon.

**Mr. Cohen:** The Minister will recall his answer to me which showed that an increasing number of museums are beginning to charge for school parties. Will the Minister condemn that as bad practice? Will he confirm that by charging for school parties the heritage and the important educational value of items in those museums are no longer accessible to many school children?

**Mr. Luce:** The hon. Gentleman is referring to the new guidelines on school activities within school hours. My right hon. Friend the Secretary of State for Education and Science has already pointed out that parents can make voluntary contributions. However, I have undertaken with my right hon. Friend carefully to monitor the progress on this because we are anxious to ensure that the access of schools to important centres of art and to museums is not only maintained, but strengthened.

**Mr. Fisher:** Is the Minister aware that the number of school visits to theatres, dance performances, museums and concerts has fallen dramatically in recent weeks as a direct result of Government changes in funding school visits through the Education Reform Act? Is he aware that the national theatre's excellent production of Adrian Mitchell's play "The Pied Piper" had to cancel a week's performances because of Government changes making it extremely difficult for schools to make out-of-school visits? How is that helping arts companies or arts education in schools? Is that good practice?

**Mr. Luce:** As I said earlier, I have undertaken to monitor progress and to ensure that there is no setback in terms of the number of schools visiting arts institutions. There is no overwhelming evidence to suggest that what the hon. Gentleman says is right. In one or two examples, much of the misunderstanding has been about the guidelines. Those guidelines are clear. My right hon. Friend the Secretary of State for Education and Science has set out what schools can do to ensure that they maintain contact with arts organisations.

## Business Sponsorship

57. **Mr. John Marshall:** To ask the Minister for the Arts if he will make a statement about the level of business sponsorship of the arts.

**Mr. Luce:** I am pleased to say that business sponsorship has increased from £500,000 a year in 1976 to over £30 million today. The Government's business sponsorship incentive scheme has brought nearly £25 million new money to the arts and to museums.

**Mr. Marshall:** How many sponsors under the BSIS are new arts sponsors? How many have renewed their generous sponsorship?

**Mr. Luce:** It is interesting that the Association for Business Sponsorship of the Arts has undertaken research which demonstrates that about 90 per cent. of all the organisations that become first-time sponsors decide to remain sponsors because they regard it as a good investment. That is most encouraging. For the first time under our scheme, we have had 1,000 first-time sponsors, so the House can see the scale of the increase in support through sponsorship.

**Mr. Maclennan:** I welcome that increase, but what is the Minister's view on the deficit in sponsorship in respect of the innovative and experimental arts, which, by their nature, attract small audiences?

**Mr. Luce:** There are increasing examples of sponsorship to support creativity and innovation. I do not remember whether the hon. Gentleman was in the Chamber during the debate on the arts some 10 days ago, when I announced that the Arts Council had established an endowment scheme designed especially to give support through the private sector—although it is managed by the Arts Council—for innovation and experimentation. Of course, the Arts Council already does that with the taxpayer's money, and that is partly the role of the taxpayer.

**Mr. Fishburn:** Is my right hon. Friend aware that English National Ballet, of which I am a director, has taken the lead in business sponsorship? None the less, this cannot possibly enable the company to survive, unless the Government find a way of providing an adequate subsidy from their pocket after the community charge is introduced. Is my right hon. Friend aware that, as a director, I have a responsibility under the Insolvency Act 1986 to suggest that that ballet company should close if that money is not forthcoming soon?

**Mr. Luce:** I am very much aware of the important role that my hon. Friend plays in English National Ballet. I acknowledge his point that there is considerable concern about the possible effect of the introduction of the community charge, especially with respect to Westminster city council, on English National Opera and English National Ballet. I am in touch with the chairman and will keep in touch with my hon. Friend about this matter.

**Mr. Pike:** I recognise that the amateur sector is vital in the performing arts. How much money is allocated to it?

**Mr. Luce:** It is difficult to give a figure. The Arts Council's main efforts are directed towards supporting professional organisations. I shall write to the hon. Gentleman to clarify the point.

## Opera

58. **Mr. John Greenway:** To ask the Minister for the Arts how many people attended *(a)* subsidised and *(b)* unsubsidised performances of opera in the 12 months to 14 June 1989.

**Mr. Luce:** The latest figures available for subsidised performances show that 1,080,000 people visited the opera in 1987-88. No figures are available for privately funded opera companies.

**Mr. Greenway:** I am sure that my right hon. Friend welcomes the recent success of the "Carmen" production at Earl's Court, given that the two London opera companies receive the lion's share of the Arts Council's support for opera. Does my right hon. Friend agree that, for the regional opera companies, Arts Council and local authority funding is vital to their existence and to achieving a wider audience? Is he aware that, in its 10th anniversary season, Opera North achieved 90 per cent. audience penetration?

**Mr. Luce:** I am aware of my hon. Friend's close interest in Opera North, which is based in Leeds and sets high standards. Regional opera has been able to achieve the highest possible quality only through a measure of taxpayers' support. My hon. Friend rightly drew attention to other private sector activities, such as Carmen at Earl's Court. I understand that recent performances attracted audiences of 95,000. Other companies in the private sector, such as D'Oyly Carte opera company, are attracting large audiences.

**Mr. Wilson:** Is the Minister aware that Opera North receives money from local government? I congratulate him on being the first Minister whom I have heard express a squeak of concern about the implications of the community charge. I suggest that as well as addressing those concerns to the chairmen of various boards, he addresses them forcefully to his colleagues in Government, who have been oblivious to the effects of the poll tax on local authorities' ability to raise and spend money at their discretion on projects, including the arts, that benefit the community.

**Mr. Luce:** My earlier answer on the community charge was related especially to Westminster city council, which has indicated that it has particular problems, unlike other authorities. I hope that borough councils in London will play their part in supporting the important English National Ballet and English National Opera.

### Local Museums and Galleries

**59. Mr. Soames:** To ask the Minister for the Arts what steps he is taking to encourage national institutions to send artefacts to local museums and galleries.

**Mr. Luce:** National museums and galleries are active in lending artefacts to local museums and galleries. I am specifically encouraging further such activity through my funding provided to the Museums and Galleries Commission's travelling exhibitions unit.

**Mr. Soames:** I thank my right hon. Friend for that good news. Is he aware that the high cost of insuring art exhibits is one of the reasons why borough councils and others are deterred from making full use of the increased facilities that the Department has offered? What steps will my right hon. Friend take to make the procedure easier and to assist them with insurances?

**Mr. Luce:** My hon. Friend has put his finger on what was the problem in the past. He might be interested to know that in 1988-89 no less than £1 billion of Government indemnity has been provided. That is a record figure and has saved the national museums and galleries £5 million in commercial insurance. The scheme plays a leading role in facilitating lending.

## CIVIL SERVICE

### National Union of Civil and Public Servants

**74. Mr. Allen:** To ask the Minister for the Civil Service when he will next meet representatives of the NUCPS; and what matters he expects to discuss.

**The Minister of State, Privy Council Office (Mr. Richard Luce):** I have meetings from time to time with representatives of Civil Service trade unions both centrally and during visits to Departments. Matters of mutual interest are discussed.

**Mr. Allen:** Is the Minister aware that the senior civil servant in every Government Department has been replaced since the Prime Minister took office? That treatment is almost as ruthless as her treatment of the 1979 Cabinet. Does the Minister support that policy? If not, what steps will he take to restore some impartiality to the senior Civil Service?

**Mr. Luce:** I do not understand what the hon. Gentleman means by every senior civil servant. If he is talking about permanent secretaries, perhaps he needs reminding that we have been in office since 1979. It is not surprising that many permanent secretaries have changed and that many of them have retired. To suggest that any of our senior civil servants are not impartial but partial is a serious allegation.

### Civil Servants (Greater Manchester)

**75. Mr. Andrew F. Bennett:** To ask the Minister for the Civil Service what was the total number of civil servants in Greater Manchester in 1979; and what was the most recent figure.

**Mr. Luce:** For the administrative area of Greater Manchester, the number of non-industrial civil servants on 1 January 1979 was 19,270. The most recent figure at 1 January 1989 is 16,720.

**Mr. Bennett:** From those figures do we take it that the Government's policy to disperse civil servants from London and the south-east to the regions has stopped? Does he accept that there is still a strong argument for encouraging civil servants and Government Departments to move to the north-west, which has a far more attractive environment than London and the south-east?

**Mr. Luce:** There is no question of stopping the policy of relocation; on the contrary, my right hon. Friend the Secretary of State for Social Security recently announced that 1,000 jobs will be relocated out of London to Glasgow, Belfast and Wigan. Wigan, which is part of Greater Manchester, will get another 260 civil servants. The hon. Gentleman should also take note of the fact that my right hon. Friend the Paymaster General recently announced that no less than 34,000 Civil Service jobs are under review with the possibility of relocation in other areas. I think that the motive for doing so is getting stronger every day.

### Civil Service Agencies

**76. Mr. Harry Greenway:** To ask the Minister for the Civil Service how many Civil Service jobs in the London area have been agencified; how many are expected to be agencified during the next two years; and if he will make a statement.

**Mr. Luce:** This information is not readily available to my Department. The location of staff in agencies is a matter for the Departments and agencies concerned. But I hope very much that, like other Government activities, they will continue to review the location of their work, including localities which are the focus of the Government's regional and urban policies.

**Mr. Greenway:** I hope that my right hon. Friend will find the new logistic terms "agencified" and "agencification" expressive if somewhat ugly. If civil servant jobs are agencified will my right hon. Friend ensure that it is done sensitively and that it pays regard to the morale of the people who are moved of such a scheme? Will he seek an early agencification of passport office jobs with a view to ending all the trouble that we have had there and getting the half a million passports that people are seeking for their holidays out to them?

**Mr. Luce:** On the latter point about the passport office, my hon. Friend may recall that my right hon. Friend the Home Secretary has made it plain that the passport office is a serious candidate to become an agency as soon as possible—that is now being studied. All the evidence so far suggests that morale is good in the seven agencies already established. They know precisely what their targets and objectives are. That is something that helps the management of the Civil Service and helps morale.

**Mr. Maclennan:** Will the Minister please acknowledge that he makes it more difficult for the Secretary of State for Education and Science to introduce a core curriculum in English if he accepts, without comment, the ugly and incomprehensible word "agencified"?

**Mr. Luce:** I have not used that word. I am partly responsible for plain English in the Civil Service and I shall take the hon. Gentleman's point on board.

77. **Mr. Simon Coombs:** To ask the Minister for the Civil Service how many Civil Service agencies he expects to be set up in the next 12 months.

**Mr. Luce:** Seven executive agencies have already been set up, and Departments are working on more than 30 other proposals. Those include the whole social security operation and, in my own Department, the Civil Service recruitment agency and the occupational health service.

**Mr. Coombs:** Is my right hon. Friend aware that his commitment to continue the relocation of civil servants out of London will be widely welcomed on the Conservative Benches? Will he couple that with a commitment to a continuing reduction in the total number of civil servants, in particular those who must work in London and are therefore held to ransom to Mr. Jimmy Knapp who has recently replaced his better rail campaign with a no rail campaign?

**Mr. Luce:** In the past 10 years, the size of the Civil Service has been reduced by roughly 21 per cent. and now it is certainly a slimmed-down and professional service. It is worth noting that four out of five civil servants are employed outside the Greater London area, and with the policy for relocation, that number is expected to increase.

**Mr. Janner:** Does the Minister recognise that many agencies, whether they are in public or in private hands, have been responsible for much of the unlawful discrimination against people on grounds of sex and race? His Department is now to meet that problem through the action programme, which the Labour party welcomed when he announced it. What will he now do with the agencies to see that they do not discriminate in a way that is unlawful and wrong?

**Mr. Luce:** It will, of course, be exactly the same for the agencies because they are all part of the Civil Service and those who serve in agencies continue to be civil servants. The hon. and learned Gentleman is, therefore, right to stress that the agencies will have the same objective. Objectives and targets are set under the framework agreements formed in the agencies. I envisage that in the setting up of all agencies it will be a clear intention that the principle of equality of opportunity in every area should be clearly established.

**Mr. John Greenway:** When considering agencies over the next year or so, will my right hon. Friend take the opportunity to move more Civil Service jobs out of London into the provinces, especially the north? Is he aware that there is a symposium tomorrow by York city council supported by other local authorities in north Yorkshire for that very purpose?

**Mr. Luce:** I am grateful to my hon. Friend for drawing that to my attention. It is worth repeating that my right hon. Friend the Paymaster General has made it plain that 34,000 Civil Service jobs are now under review with a view to considering whether they should be relocated in other parts of the country. If even part of that relocation takes place, it will be a substantial addition to the 12,000 people who have moved out of London since 1979.

### Civil Service Unions

78. **Mr. Fisher:** To ask the Minister for the Civil Service what discussions he has had with the Civil Service unions about improving the service to the public.

**Mr. Luce:** None, Sir. But my officials have held discussions with representatives of the Council of Civil Service Unions on the Office for the Minister for the Civil Service study "Service to the Public" and on training in this area.

**Mr. Fisher:** Does the Minister agree that the service to the public in both the passport office and the Department of Social Security might be improved by employing more civil servants? If more civil servants had been employed, many of the problems in the passport office this summer would not have existed. If there were more civil servants in the Department of Social Security, rather than simply having to administer, they could give welfare advice to claimants who need the benefits that they are not getting at the moment.

**Mr. Luce:** I am glad, of course, that an agreement has now been reached in the passport office and, as the hon. Gentleman probably knows, it will lead to an increase in the number of civil servants there. With regard to the passport office and to the Department of Social Security, I come back to the establishment of agencies for which clear performance targets and objectives can be set, including objectives on the quality of service to the public. The House will have noted that my right hon. Friend the Chief Secretary to the Treasury made an admirable speech last week, drawing attention to the importance of the quality of Government services to the public.

79. **Mr. Soames:** To ask the Minister for the Civil Service what recent progress has been made in the establishment of Civil Service agencies.

**Mr. Luce:** On 24 May, the resettlement agency in the Department of Social Security was launched. On 6 June, I launched the Civil Service college in my own Department as an executive agency. That takes the total of agencies that have been set up to seven with over 30 further activities announced as candidates.

**Mr. Soames:** In view of the considerable success of the agencies, especially in respect to the motivation of those who work for them, will my right hon. Friend confirm that he intends to press ahead with the agencies as quickly as possible and across the board?

**Mr. Luce:** I can say without hesitation that that is the case. The fact that my right hon. Friend the Secretary of State for Social Security announced last month his plan to establish an agency for the Department of Social Security, which includes 87,000 civil servants, is an indication of the importance that we attach to this reform.

**Mr. Tam Dalyell** (Linlithgow): On a point of order, Mr. Speaker. Could we have injury time for Civil Service questions? We did start late.

**Mr. Speaker:** We did, and I gave it.

# Edinburgh University Dental School

3.32 pm

**Mr. Alistair Darling** (Edinburgh, Central): I beg to ask leave to move the Adjournment of the House under Standing Order No. 20, for the purpose of discussing a specific and important matter that should have urgent consideration, namely,
"the closure of Edinburgh university dental school."

The matter is urgent because the decision was leaked through a detailed press briefing last Thursday evening. The university was told of its fate when it saw the television cameras filming outside. The matter is important because three years ago, Edinburgh was promised a new dental hospital with teaching facilities. Last year, it was told that the dental school would expand. Now it is told that the school is to be shut, with its final admission of students only three months away. The Secretary of State for Scotland has recycled an old promise of a new hospital and he claims it as an achievement.

The leak has all the hallmarks of a Scottish Office briefing. How typical it is of this Government that if there is dirty work afoot, they use a leak to carry it out. If a decision is bad or unpopular, they blame someone else. Edinburgh has been told that it will lose its school. It is told that it will have instead a post graduate institute, if you please. It is not told who will pay for the institute, where it will be or when the hospital will be built. Many believe that the car park that is on the site at present will remain there for a considerable time.

The university is entitled to make its case. It was never warned of the closure. It is no use the Secretary of State blaming the Universities Funding Council. The right hon. and learned Gentleman is an Edinburgh Member himself and he was also rightly quick to save the Glasgow veterinary school. The decision to close the Edinburgh dental school stands in stark contrast.

If we cannot have a debate today, we need a statement —not further press briefings. Edinburgh university and the public, who value their education and their dental health, are entitled to something better than this shabby treatment at the hands of the Secretary of State and the Government.

**Mr. Speaker:** The hon. Gentleman asks leave to move the Adjournment of the House for the purpose of discussing a specific and important matter that he believes should have urgent consideration, namely,
"the closure of Edinburgh university dental school."

I listened with concern to what the hon. Gentleman said but, as he knows, my sole duty in considering an application under Standing Order No. 20 is to decide whether it should be given precedence over the business already set down for today or for tomorrow. I regret that the matter he has raised does not meet the criteria of the Standing Order, and I cannot, therefore, submit his application to the House.

**Mr. Nigel Griffiths** (Edinburgh, South): On a point of order, Mr. Speaker. I accept the ruling that you have just given, but can you use any influence on the Government to ensure that we have an early debate on university education, so that this matter, which has so incensed the Edinburgh community, can be fully aired and debated?

**Mr. Speaker:** That is not a matter for me, but no doubt there may be other opportunities.

**Mr. Jeremy Corbyn** (Islington, North): On a point of order, Mr. Speaker. Yesterday's edition of *The Observer* carried reports about the behaviour of the immigration service, on the instruction of the Home Office, in attempting to deny Kurdish refugees from Turkey the right to apply for political asylum.

**Mr. Richard Holt** (Langbaurgh): What is the point of order?

**Mr. Corbyn:** My point of order is that this is a serious matter and serious allegations were made in that newspaper article, so I wonder whether you, Mr. Speaker, have had any application or request from Home Office Ministers to make a statement about that behaviour and what instructions they have given.

**Mr. Speaker:** I have not had such a request.

**Several Hon. Members** *rose*——

**Mr. Speaker:** Order. I remind the House that this is an Opposition Day.

**Mr. D. N. Campbell-Savours:** On a point of order, Mr. Speaker. I wish to raise with you the question of what is published on the Order Paper. You may be aware that I have been running a campaign to get Mr. Tiny Rowland to divest himself of his interest in *The Observer*. Over the past two months I have tabled 21 motions drawing attention to his conflict of interests and to the pressure that is being exerted on journalists of that newspaper in a number of ways. The motions relate to the tapping by Mr. Rowland of the Al-Fayed telephones, to allegations made by Donald Trelford against Mr. Mark Thatcher, which are untrue and which have been firmly denied, and to other allegations about the Tornado contract and the activities of Lonrho in the Bahamas.

Under our new procedures, these motions only surface on the Order Paper on Thursdays. Those of us who campaign on various matters rely on our motions being published, particularly if our campaigns involve a great deal of extra work. Last Thursday, I added signatures to 21 motions and briefed people to the effect that all the motions that I had tabled would be available for scrutiny. Thursday's Order Paper did not carry all the motions, however, and I am told that there is confusion in the system. Five of the motions did not end up on the Order Paper as a result.

Something must be done about this new rule, which undermines the position of campaigners. It has been done to save money, but there are other ways of saving money which have not been pursued. Will you, Mr. Speaker, personally review this matter and give a ruling on why my motions did not appear on the Order Paper, when I was assured that they would?

**Mr. Speaker:** I shall certainly look into that. The hon. Gentleman is correct in saying that motions appear in full on Thursdays. The matter has been confirmed by the Services Committee, and if the hon. Gentleman wishes to have a change made, he should make his representations to that Committee.

**Mr. Dennis Skinner** (Bolsover): On a point of order, Mr. Speaker. Have you received any notice of a possible statement by the Prime Minister, who is proposing to use taxpayers' money to subsidise Ministers whom she sacks? Are you aware that it could involve yourself, Mr. Speaker?

**Mr. Speaker:** I am not a Minister.

**Mr. Skinner:** Yes, Mr. Speaker, but let me finish. Will the new order extend as wide as the sacking of Mr. Speaker? I do not know, and I do not know whether you have been informed of that.

There is also the question whether Ministers will in future wish to resign. What will be the point of Ministers sending resignation letters if they can be sacked and pick up 7,000 quid? What will happen before a general election when it looks as though the whole of the Cabinet will be cleaned out through a Labour victory? It is conceivable that some of them might use taxpayers' money to get out before the ship sinks. We should know all the facts.

**Mr. Speaker:** The hon. Gentleman will have to pursue that matter in a different way—*[Interruption.]* Order. As far as I am concerned, I think that I can only be sacked by the House.

# Opposition Day

[15TH ALLOTTED DAY]

## Community Care

**Mr. Speaker:** I must announce to the House that I have selected the amendment in the name of the Prime Minister.

**Mr. Tim Rathbone** (Lewes): On a point of order, Mr. Speaker. Have the Government given you notice of any intention to announce today what they intend to do to mark the United Nations designated International Day against Drug Abuse and Trafficking? If not, and as there is a full string of the Leader of the House, the Chief Whip and the Secretary of State for Health presently on the Front Bench, perhaps they could incorporate that information in the reply to the debate.

**Mr. Speaker:** That is a matter for the Front Bench. The hon. Member for Workington (Mr. Campbell-Savours) drew attention to matters contained in early-day motions, and that might be an admirable subject.

3.41 pm

**Mr. Robin Cook** (Livingston): I beg to move,

That this House condemns the continuing failure of Her Majesty's Government to ensure that community services are expanded at a rate which matches the closure of mental health hospitals or the growth in the population of the very elderly; expresses concern that the sole focus on the acute sector of the White Paper Working for Patients will further divert resources from chronic care; regrets that, in the year since Ministers received the Griffiths Report on Community Care, they have failed to respond to a single recommendation; accepts its central conclusion that social service authorities should be the lead agency for community care; and rejects proposals that would confine local authorities to being purchasers rather than providers of services for the elderly and handicapped in their communities.

The whole House will know that, more than one year ago, Sir Roy Griffiths presented a blueprint to rationalise and develop care in the community. The Government's enthusiasm both for that problem and for Sir Roy's solution can be gauged by the fact that they chose to publish his report on the day after Budget day in 1988, which made sure that it never disturbed the conscience of a single sub-editor.

Last week we passed another milestone in the history of the Griffiths report, because as of then, Ministers have spent longer ruminating over their response to Griffiths than it took Sir Roy to research, write and print the entire report. There is a stark contrast to that delay. In the same period that Ministers sat on Sir Roy's recommendations, the Secretary of State found the time to write a White Paper that turns upside down the entire acute sector of the National Health Service. It was published at the end of January, consultation on it finished four months later, and we are threatened with a Bill on that White Paper in five months' time.

The contrast between the breakneck pace of the Government's White Paper and the tardy progress in response to the Griffiths report is that no one wants the Secretary of State to force through his eccentric plans for our hospitals—even his Back Benchers are now praying that it will fade away and stop terrifying them in their constituencies—while everyone involved in delivering community care has pleaded with the Secretary of State to respond positively to the Griffiths report.

I understand that the House will not hear the Secretary of State's response today—[HON. MEMBERS: "Why not?"] He has been kind enough to write to me to apologise because he will not be taking part in the debate. I understand that the Government will be represented in both the opening and closing of the debate by the Parliamentary Under-Secretary, whose name unfortunately does not even appear on the Government's amendment. Of course, I welcome the Under-Secretary to our debate. He is a gentleman of both courtesy and candour. I shall not try to get him into trouble with his superiors by arguing whether in those qualities he compares favourably or not with them. It is not a criticism of the Parliamentary Under-Secretary when I say that the House might have expected the Secretary of State to participate in this debate.

**The Secretary of State for Health (Mr. Kenneth Clarke):** I am grateful to the hon. Gentleman for giving way, but I am surprised that he has raised this point. He shadows no fewer than two Departments of State and invariably participates in every debate on any subject arising from either Department. If he were a football player, he would be described as a greedy player. I believe that there are members of his team who are more than competent, but he often seems unwilling to give them an airing. My hon. friend the Parliamentary Under-Secretary of State is extremely competent to answer the hon. Gentleman's attacks on this or any other subject, particularly when the hon. Gentleman has chosen to raise a subject which he knows perfectly well will be addressed in a few weeks' time when there is to be a statement on the Griffiths report.

**Mr. Cook:** As I understand the Secretary of State's intervention, he is explaining why the Parliamentary Under-Secretary should be Secretary of State rather than himself. He chose to refer to my experience of Supply day debates. I have been to the House of Commons Library and checked on the 54 Supply day debates which have been held since the last general election. Of those 54 motions tabled by the Labour party, on only seven out of the 54 occasions, were the debates not replied to by a Cabinet member. Of those seven, there was only one occasion on which the speech from the Government Bench was made by a Parliamentary Under-Secretary rather than a Minister of State; that was when, unfortunately, the Minister of State, Agriculture, Fisheries and Food was taken ill in Brussels and replaced by a Parliamentary Secretary. Although the House may not have fully appreciated his speech, we well understood why the Parliamentary Secretary made it.

The clear conclusion is that the only time when a healthy team of Ministers has left a Parliamentary Under-Secretary to reply to the debate is when the topic under discussion was care in the community. Those outside the House who are concerned about community care and try to make it work, will note that this demonstrates where community care comes in terms of this Government's priorities. Unfortunately, outsiders reading this debate will feel particularly aggrieved as they struggle to maintain services for community care which are in constant danger of being washed away by an ever-rising tide of need.

Since the publication of the Griffiths report, another 40,000 elderly people have been added to the total number of those aged over 85. I recently received a parliamentary answer which showed how the provisions to support those people living at home have failed to keep pace with the increase in numbers. The number of those attending day hospitals per thousand of elderly over 75 has fallen from 552 in 1983 to 498 in 1987. That is a 10 per cent. drop, although such provision can be vital in enabling the elderly to be supported when living at home.

At least central Government can choose how many resources they put into the problem. Local authorities, when providing their services, find that they are ground between the lower millstone of ever-rising demand and the upper millstone of ever-decreasing resources. Sir Roy Griffiths states:

"many social services departments and voluntary groups grappling with the problems at local level certainly felt that the Israelites faced with the requirement to make bricks without straw had a comparatively routine task."

Those people left to take the strain are those officially designated informal carers, by which is normally meant the nearest available female relative. In reality, they provide the great bulk of care in the community. It is an outrage that we leave them to get on with it with minimal support. Nursing is a skilled job. Those in the profession receive three years' training and are then expected to work eight-hour shifts at a stretch. Time and again we ask informal carers to provide 24-hour constant nursing without training, respite or help, and often without sleep. It is hardly surprising that study after study shows that people left in constant attendance without a break are in poorer physical and mental health than the rest of the population.

One development since the Griffiths report clearly shows the Government's indifference to these carers. In April last year, people caring for a disabled relative were the only group on long-term supplementary benefit who received no premium on transfer to income support. As a result, 150,000 carers found that they were £5 a week worse off in entitlement. We owe this group an immense debt; to reward that debt by cutting still further an income that is already pathetic beggars belief.

What makes the Government's meanness towards relatives who care for the elderly at home all the more unjust is the Government's willingness to tolerate dramatic rises in payments of social security to the proprietors of private homes. In 1980, the Government made social security payable to cover residential fees of private and voluntary homes, and presumably intended thereby to stimulate the private sector in residential care. That, certainly, was the dramatic effect.

Unfortunately, as happens so often when the Government are faced with the financial consequences of their own policies, they then rebelled at the bill. In 1985, they stopped paying the fees and imposed a national limit on each category. I have received figures in parliamentary answers which show that the limits on these categories have been lowered in real terms since their introduction in 1985. For elderly people in nursing homes, the money has fallen from £199 to £190 a week; for the mentally ill, it has fallen from £211 to £195; for the mentally handicapped, it has fallen from £234 to £205. The cost of such homes, however, is not falling in real terms: it is rising. In between, a real gap is emerging between what they charge and what the social security system will pay, with the result that a

[*Mr. Cook*]

growing number of elderly and handicapped people cannot meet their bills and face the real risk of being put out on the street.

We condemn the Government's irresponsible policy of allowing this sector to grow unplanned and uncontrolled. Some, at least, of the payments that go to elderly people in residential care could have been used to sustain them in the community if local authorities had been given half the resources that the Government are willing to pay the proprietors of private homes. Having created this problem, Ministers cannot justify the cynical response of capping expenditure and leaving vulnerable and elderly patients to face the consequences of being unable to pay their bills.

From the elderly, I turn to services for those decanted from mental health hospitals, where we find the same picture of rising demand overwhelming inadequate provision. The Government have certainly pursued a vigorous programme of hospital closures, nowhere more markedly than in the case of mental health hospitals. The closure programme has been so rapid that Ministers seem to have difficulty keeping abreast of it. Last year I tabled a parliamentary Question inviting Ministers to list the mental health hospitals for which there were no closure plans. A subsequent survey of the list published in *Hansard* discovered that it included four mental health hospitals which had already closed at the time of the answer and two others which closed during the time that it took to carry out the survey. When I wrote to Ministers drawing their attention to this inaccuracy, I received a letter which had the breath to advise me:

"the majority of the information in the reply was correct." Apparently it is sufficient for Ministers these days to aim at only a pass mark in a parliamentary answer.

Since then, I have received figures which confirm how badly the expansion of community care has failed to match the contraction of institutional care. Between 1979 and 1986, 28,500 long-stay patients were discharged from mental health hospitals into the community. In that same period, only 2,230 extra places were provided in day centres for the mentally ill. In other words, fewer than one in 10 of those discharged to the community had the opportunity of a place which could provide them with support and the opportunity of comfort. One can, of course, find excellent cases of an integrated range of community care facilities right across the country, from Dorset to Lambeth. It is all the more lamentable that, given those illustrations of what is possible, the majority of cases fall so far short.

A number of studies now confirm that, for most of those leaving care in an institution, care in the community is a myth. For starters, if the statutory authorities are going to deliver care in the community, they must know where to find the former patients who will receive that care. One study of 50 patients discharged from Claybury mental hospitals could trace only 26. Of those 26 who were traced, only six had a place at any day centure. A study of 150 patients discharged from mental hospitals in Essex could trace only 100. Two thirds of those traced had received no help since leaving hospital.

That is not just a problem for the authorities: it is a source of distress for the relatives. A son—perhaps even a wife—may have a serious mental health condition, but his parents may not know where he is—whether he is in accommodation, whether he is being fed or whether he is going through an acute episode or is in a stable condition.

The reality is that, although we may not know where any one patient might be, we have an accurate idea of where they turn up. Hon. Members can find some of them under railway arches within strolling distance of the House. One medical study of the homeless who attended the Crisis at Christmas venue last year discovered that more than half of them had a history of psychotic disorder, and one third displayed psychotic symptoms that very night; yet two thirds of them had no contact with any medical centre.

They also turn up in our remand centres, because it is more convenient for our society to label their behaviour as criminal than to respond to their medical or social needs. At the time of the Rampton disorders, I tabled a parliamentary Question to the Government, from the answer to which I discovered that one in six of those who were inmates at the Rampton remand centre at the time were formerly in-patients at psychiatric hospitals. As Dr. Kilgour, the director of medical services of Her Majesty's prisons, has said:

"My colleagues and I find ourselves having to handle people who are inappropriately committed to custodial sentence due, to put it bluntly, to the failure of the community to provide suitable facilities for them."

I read in *The Daily Telegraph* last week that this problem has now surfaced in the consciousness of the Prime Minister. Confronted with the closure of Friern Barnet hospital in her constituency, the Prime Minister has ordered plans for further hospital closures to be frozen. I am glad that someone in the Government has recognised the problem, but that emphatically cannot be a permanent solution. Many of our present stock of mental health hospitals were built by the Victorians. Some of them were built as the local poorhouses—places of punishment and detention rather than of medical treatment. The solution is not to perpetuate those conditions indefinitely, but to make a reality of community care by providing the services that are needed to support the patients who leave the hospitals—to provide them with small-scale residential communities, with day hospitals and drop-in centres, and with sheltered employment opportunities, because many of those leaving hospital want to work.

This morning, West Lothian Poverty Action Forum in my constituency published an excellent report that allows claimants to speak in their own voices. I was much struck by the observation of one disabled claimant about the trap in which he found himself. He had no experience; therefore he could get no job. He could get no job; therefore he could obtain no experience. Only community provision can help him to break out of that trap.

That brings me back to the Government's failure to respond to Sir Roy's recommendations to improve care in the community. There are plenty of reasons why we should treat the report with caution. Indeed, if I suspected that that was why the Government were taking so long to respond to the report, I would treat the delay with more understanding and tolerance. Sir Roy's report contains no commitment to extra resources to make community care work. There is nothing about enabling users to participate in the planning of services or to contribute to the management of those services when they are up and running. For all the rhetoric about consumerism in the report, Sir Roy has produced a design intended to improve lines of managerial accountability, not to make the services accountable to the users.

**Mr. Peter Thurnham** (Bolton, North-East): The hon. Gentleman has criticised the Government for the length of time in responding to the Griffiths report. As I understand it, the Labour party policy review did not agree with Griffiths, in so far as Griffiths calls for local authorities to be more the organisers and purchasers of services instead of the providers. Why is the Labour party so keen on the local authority being the provider? Is that because of the continued obeisance of the Labour party to the trade unions?

**Mr. Cook:** It is true that one reason why the Labour party remains committed to public provision is that public provision overwhelmingly provides better working conditions for those who provide the service. We do not believe that a caring and compassionate service can be provided for those in need if it is based on the exploitation of the workers in the service.

It is certainly not the case that we have failed to respond to Griffiths. We have produced major documents in response to the Griffiths report. We have differences with Griffiths. We believe that in many respects he was in error partly because of the remit that he was given by Treasury Ministers and that that explains why he was unable to recommend extra resources. We believe that it is inexcusable that the Government will not tell us whether they agree with Griffiths and, if they fail to agree with him, what they will put in place of Griffiths.

The hon. Member for Bolton, North-East (Mr. Thurnham) has put his finger on the major reason why Ministers have been delaying a response to Griffiths. That has not happened because Griffiths failed to recommend extra resources—that must commend the report, rather than be a handicap in the Government's eyes. Ministers have behaved like paralysed rabbits for the past year as a result of the sheer horror that they must feel at Griffiths's central recommendation. As the hon. Member for Bolton, North-East said, the central recommendation is that if we are serious about care in the community, more responsibility and control of resources will have to be given to local authorities which provide the services in the community. That message is as welcome to No. 10 as telling the Prime Minister that Labour has a 14-point lead in the opinion polls.

The Prime Minister has presided over a sustained strategy of undermining local government, which has abolished the local authorities which she liked least, which has cribbed and confined with restrictions the right to express political opinions of those local authorities which remain, and which is currently compelling the authorities to hand over many of their services to private contractors.

After a decade of running down local government, the Prime Minister and her Ministers have received a report which advises them that, in this matter at least, they cannot do without local government. It tells them that, if they are serious about caring for the elderly and providing for the mentally ill and mentally handicapped, they need local government. Rumours are surfacing in the press that a compromise has been worked out in the Cabinet and that local authorities will be designated as the lead agencies in community care, but that they are to be denied any

opportunity to demonstrate leadership because they will be stripped of all responsibility for direct provision of services.

The Adam Smith Institute recently threw a party to celebrate its 100th proposal to be accepted by the Government. It has produced a document along the lines that I have just described. It justifies preventing local authorities from making direct provision on the following grounds:

"Government's priority should be to encourage the growth of the private sector. No initiative by Government should undermine that independent sector or attempt to compete with it."

There is a remarkable double standard there. Local authorities are to be obliged to put all their services out to competitive tendering, but the private sector is protected from competition by the local authority. Given the Adam Smith solution to the Hong Kong problem, we should all be grateful that it is not proposing that we should sweep up the mentally ill and put them down on the Mull of Kintyre.

It cannot be emphasised too strongly that local authorities are the largest single providers of residential and domicillary care; they understand the needs of people requiring community care; that they have acquired unrivalled experience and professional skills in running community care; and that it would be pure ideological vandalism to break up that service—and we shall fight any proposals to do so.

In the meantime, scandalous examples of the failure of community care continue to accumulate. I mentioned that former patients can be found in hostels for the homeless and in remand centres. Tragically, they also turn up as the subjects of inquests, such as that currently being held into the death of Beverley Lewis. Deaf, blind and handicapped from rubella, and unable to demand help herself, she starved to death in the community in the year since Griffiths. Tragic though her case is, it does not compare with the much greater scandal of the delay and indifference with which Ministers treated Griffiths over that same year. We have already lost a whole year. It is because we believe that there is no more time to lose that we shall vote tonight for an urgent response from the Government.

4.5 pm

**The Parliamentary Under-Secretary of State for Health (Mr. Roger Freeman):** I beg to move, to leave out from "House" to the end of the Question and add instead thereof:

"commends the Government's record on the development and funding of community services for all people in need of care; reaffirms its support for the policy of community care; believes that it will be complemented and strengthened by the proposals contained in the Government's White Paper, 'Working for Patients'; and looks forward to an announcement of the Government's conclusions on Sir Roy Griffiths' report, 'Community Care: Agenda for Action', in the near future."

I am grateful to the hon. Member for Livingston (Mr. Cook) for making out an excellent case for my early preferment. However, I do not believe that his recommendation will be entirely productive.

I apologise for the absence of my hon. Friend the Minister of State, Department of Health, who is chairing a conference of the Council of Europe in Strasbourg, which is an important and long-standing engagement. My response will be as brief as possible, because I know that many right hon. and hon. Members wish to speak. If I

[*Mr. Roger Freeman*]

catch your eye later, Mr. Speaker, and with the leave of the House, I shall seek to answer some of the questions that will arise.

What do we mean by care in the community? For the mentally ill and the mentally handicapped, we mean providing care away from the large, isolated and inhumane Victorian institutions that for so long have been the hallmark of institutional care. That policy has existed for 20 years, shared with differential rates of fervour by right hon. and hon. Members on both sides of the House. We want to move away from a regime that involves long-stay facilities, hostels, houses—[*Interruption.*] Perhaps the hon. Member for Peckham (Ms. Harman) will pay me the courtesy, as she usually does, of listening to my arguments——

**Mr. Nigel Griffiths** (Edinburgh, South): It is not worth it.

**Mr. Freeman:** The hon. Gentleman's remark is a little premature. If he will listen to what I have to say, I shall do him the courtesy of listening to his contribution.

We want to move away from a regime of institutional care in isolated, Victorian institutions to a system whereby we provide a range of facilities much closer to the community.

We want to enable more elderly people to stay in their own homes for as long as possible before institutional care becomes necessary and unavoidable. I quote from the report of the Public Accounts Committee laid on 25 April 1988, which I am sure the hon. Member for Livingston read:

"We draw attention to the fact that up to 23 per cent. of claimants"—

that is claimants of income support——

"entering residential homes could have stayed in their own homes for longer periods had appropriate community support services been made available."

Although not all right hon. and hon. Members may agree with that figure, I am sure that they accept the broad thrust of the Committee's argument.

The Government want to ensure that a greater proportion of the elderly can stay in their own homes for as long as possible, and we fully appreciate that that requires proper domiciliary support. If the elderly are allowed to remain in their own homes they retain their dignity and independence, and are closer to their friends and families. It is a more effective use of taxpayers' money to care for the elderly in their own homes, which is where they want to receive care, rather than in institutions.

**Dame Elaine Kellett-Bowman** (Lancaster): Is my hon. Friend aware that the Lancaster health authority was the first in the country to provide round-the-clock nursing care for those who stay in their own homes? We have two large institutions, and we pioneered the kind of service to which my hon. Friend has referred.

**Mr. Freeman:** My hon. Friend is right, and I pay tribute to Lancaster. There are many examples of excellent community care facilities, although I regret to say that there are also many areas where they are not excellent. I shall deal with that a little later.

**Ms. Harriet Harman** (Peckham): I support what the Minister has said about the importance of people being able to stay independent in their own homes. Does he not recognise, however, that one of the recruiting sergeants for residential care—both public and, increasingly, private—is the present difficulty of obtaining home helps and meals on wheels, compared with 10 years ago? Local authority social service and voluntary sector provision have not kept pace with the growing number of people who need such services.

**Mr. Freeman:** One of the challenges in any review of community care provision is the need to look carefully at how taxpayers' money is spent. I agree that there is a strong case for using taxpayers' money for the care of the elderly in their own homes—and the hon. Lady listed a range of services—rather than in hospital, if they are cured, or in nursing or residential homes. There must be a case for providing proper support for those who wish to stay in their own homes.

What was Sir Roy asked to do in his report? He was not asked, as the hon. Member for Livingston (Mr. Cook) said, to consider the level of resources; he was asked to consider how we should decide which elderly and handicapped people should be cared for in the community, what help should be provided and who should make the necessary judgment. What did he suggest? As we all know, he suggested that the social services authorities should have prime responsibility for assessing and arranging, although they should not necessarily have monopoly in the provision of services. As my hon. Friend the Member for Bolton, North-East (Mr. Thurnham) said in an intervention, Sir Roy recommended a range of provision.

The Government will be making a statement about our response to the Griffiths report before the summer recess, but there will also be a debate in Government time at a suitable point thereafter. A substantial amount of time has been devoted to considering the implications of the report, and I remind the House that different Departments are involved: the Department of the Environment, the Department of Social Security, the Treasury and, of course, the Department of Health. It is very complicated to work through all the implications, and it would be much better to get the analysis right than to rush it.

The hon. Member for Livingston said that this was the third debate on community care in seven months. It will probably be the last occasion for the Government to listen to comments and advice from the House before we announce our conclusions.

**Mr. John Battle** (Leeds, West): The Minister has given the impression that existing facilities and services were being supported. Is not the Treasury at this very moment discussing with the Department of the Environment reductions in local authority provision, which means that next year authorities will not be able to spend as much on home and meals at home for the elderly? While we are discussing the matter, the service is being reduced. Is that not the reality?

**Mr. Freeman:** No, it is not the reality. If the hon. Gentleman will be patient, I shall deal shortly with social services provision and the resources devoted to local authorities.

I am puzzled by the Opposition motion. It

"expresses concern that the sole focus on the acute sector of the White Paper Working for Patients will further divert resources from chronic care".

The hon. Member for Livingston has obviously given some careful thought to the wording of the motion.

Provision for care in the community was deliberately omitted from the White Paper. We wanted sufficient time in which to prepare a proper response. That will come shortly. There are two reasons why the hon. Member for Livingston needs further time in which to reflect on the phrasing of an appropriate motion. He knows that the White Paper "Working for Patients" does not have as its sole focus acute care. Many of the proposals concern primary care.

The responsibility for providing a comprehensive range of health services for all people, including those in the community—the elderly, the mentally handicapped and the mentally ill—will rest firmly under our proposals with the district health authority. It will be the purchaser of care. Who that care is provided for will depend on a variety of circumstances. The district health authority will be responsible for the balance and range of services that are required and for the care of everyone, including those in the community. By definition, a community health service must be provided locally. The district health authority will have the primary responsibility for ensuring that it is provided.

**Ms. Hilary Armstrong** (Durham, North-West): The Government say that they have not yet responded to Griffiths because they are considering the whole range of responses and want to consider them all carefully. Why, therefore, have the Government not held a debate so that hon. Members could give their responses to Griffiths, which could also be considered by the Government?

**Mr. Freeman:** We are having a debate on Griffiths today.

**Ms. Armstrong:** But in our time.

**Mr. Freeman:** I have already said that when the Government respond to the Griffiths report there will, at a suitable time, be a debate in Government time.

**Mr. Tim Devlin** (Stockton, South): Will my hon. Friend remind hon. Members how many debates we have had on the subject in the last two years?

**Mr. Freeman:** I have already said that this is the third debate within six months.

The hon. Member for Livingston implied that the Treasury was cutting the resources that are made available to local authorities. He should know that personal social services are provided through the local authority. Expenditure in real terms on personal social services increased by 25 per cent. between 1980 and 1989. The provision for personal social services in 1989-90 has increased by 10 per cent. in cash terms. National Health Service provision for community heath services, such as district nurses, health visitors, chiropody, occupational therapy and community psychiatric nurses increased by 27 per cent. in real terms between 1979-80 and 1986-87. There has been real growth in the amount of resources devoted to community health services. Income support for the elderly in residential and nursing homes has increased substantially, to approximately £1 billion of taxpayers' money.

**Mr. Tony Worthington** (Clydebank and Milngavie): Unlike many of my colleagues, I think that the Government have responded to the Griffiths report. They have done so by setting up a structure in "Working for Patients" that makes community care very difficult indeed.

The assumption is that most health care is of the "wheel them in horizontal and wheel them out vertical" kind, rather than of a continuing nature, which is what is required by many patients. Is the Minister able to say how many times mental health is mentioned in "Working for Patients"?

**Mr. Freeman:** I hope that I have made it plain that "Working for Patients" was directed at reforms in primary care and the hospital service and that we shall be responding shortly as to community care for the mentally ill, handicapped and elderly. The district health authorities will be responsible for ensuring that there is a complete range of provision for all those patients.

Turning to mental illness, the hon. Member for Livingston was perfectly fair on the House, and I agree with him, about the rundown in the number of beds in mental hospitals. Between 1977 and 1987, patient numbers have reduced from some 84,000 to some 60,000—a reduction of about 24,000. Over the same 10 years, local authorities and the Health Service have provided about 11,000 places. Day hospital places have increased by 5,000 to 18,000, residential places have increased by 4,000 to 9,000 and places at day centres have increased by 2,000 to 6,000. Between 1981 and 1986, the number of community psychiatric nurses doubled.

Hon. Members who contribute to the debate will share the hon. Gentleman's concern and mine that in the past there has not been adequate provision for those discharged from large psychiatric hospitals. There is no question about that. However, I must make two points. First, any discharge from a mental institution, in the past, or today, is a clinical decision and is not taken by administrators or politicians. Secondly, some of those patients go home where they are properly cared for. Nevertheless, the hon. Gentleman made a fair point. I agree with him that the provision of facilities in the community is not uniformly adequate and in the past some authorities have discharged patients from mental hospitals without ensuring that there was proper and adequate care. That is one issue that we shall address in our response to Griffiths.

I shall make one final point about hospital closures. At a recent Question Time, my hon. Friend the Member for Macclesfield (Mr. Winterton) asked me a question, and perhaps my answer was not as clear as it should have been. Let me make it quite plain that we have pursued the policy, and shall continue to pursue it with great vigour, of ensuring that a hospital closes only as a consequence of adequate facilities being available in the community and not for financial reasons. I give the House that very clear assurance.

**Mr. Chris Mullin** (Sunderland, South): In my constituency there is a large psychiatric hospital from which large numbers of people have been discharged. As any hon. Member in that position will know, one receives a constant stream of complaints from neighbours, relatives, staff who work in the hospital or patients themselves that people are being discharged into the community for financial reasons. The most extreme case that has come to my notice involved three people who were discharged into the community, and two of them committed suicide.

**Mr. Freeman:** I want to make it quite plain that discharge from psychiatric hospitals is a matter of clinical judgment. It is not for administrators, politicians or

[*Mr. Freeman*]

ministerial judgment. Hospitals will not close for financial reasons. In future, hospitals will close only when we are satisfied that there are adequate facilities in the community. That has been Government policy. I am not announcing or stating new policy, I am simply emphasising existing policy.

**Mr. Nicholas Winterton** (Macclesfield): Is my hon. Friend aware that considerable pressure is being brought by managers on consultants to discharge patients because they want to empty the hospital to realise its capital value for development? I hope that my right hon. and learned Friend the Secretary of State for Health and my hon. Friend the Minister—I know that my hon. Friend is deeply committed to the problems of the mentally handicapped, mentally ill and elderly—are aware that great pressure is being brought on consultants which inevitably could affect their clinical decisions.

**Mr. Freeman:** I do not deny that that pressure exists. Intelligent ways to ensure the release now of the capital value of sites that are under-utilised are already being pursued in the Health Service. Before a hospital is closed, residential facilities must already be in place. I draw my hon. Friend's attention to the practice in the Oxford and East Anglian regions, which have excellent bridging finance schemes, and the practice in Yorkshire——

**Ms. Harman:** Not enough is done.

**Mr. Freeman:** The bridging schemes work well in the Oxford and East Anglian regions; perhaps other regions should learn lessons from them. In Yorkshire, where only part of the mental hospital site which I have in mind is used, there has been an imaginative sale and lease-back of facilities, so that all the present patients are properly cared for in existing facilities but substantial capital is released now to construct new facilities. Other measures which the Government have under consideration must await the response to the Griffiths report.

**Mr. Tom Clarke** (Monklands, West): We know of the importance of the timetable as we discussed these matters. I should like to ask the Minister, as we do not have the benefit of hearing from the Secretary of State for Health, about the press reports last week that the famous committee E, which is apparently considering this matter, received evidence. As the Secretary of State is here, perhaps he will take the opportunity to try to catch your eye, Mr. Speaker. I am sure that no one would object. Is it true that the Adam Smith Institute has submitted a paper to that committee and that it will submit a revised paper in two weeks' time?

**Mr. Freeman:** The newspaper reports are inaccurate.

**Ms. Harman:** In what respect?

**Mr. Freeman:** The hon. Member for Monklands, West (Mr. Clarke) asked me whether there was a moratorium on the closure of hospitals. I have told him that those newspaper reports are inaccurate. I have described the Government's policy on mental hospitals. When the hon. Gentleman has a chance to contribute in greater detail, I shall be happy to respond.

**Mrs. Alice Mahon** (Halifax): My hon. Friend the Member for Livingston (Mr. Cook) referred to mentally ill people who are languishing in prison and on remand. Does the hon. Gentleman have plans to monitor how many people who previously had serious psychiatric disorders are in prison? What does he intend to do to ensure that this tragic business stops once and for all?

**Mr. Freeman:** The Home Office has commissioned a study of all patients in remand centres and long-stay prisons to ascertain how many are suffering from a form of mental illness. As I am sure the hon. Lady knows, the estimates of prisoners who have some form of mental illness range from 3 per cent. to 30 per cent. Undoubtedly, a number of prisoners in the prison service should not be in prisons but should be either in special hospitals or in mental institutions with some form of security. We are working closely with the Home Office to ascertain the numbers and to work out how initially those people can avoid the criminal system and how those who go through it can be moved, with proper security, to mental institutions.

We have already laid it down that by 1991 all district health authorities should have comprehensive care programmes for the mentally ill. We shall issue guidelines shortly to those health authorities to show how they should put those care programmes in place and what form they should take. The Royal College of Psychiatrists is drawing up guidelines on standards to assess patients before discharge and to ensure that there is proper follow-up thereafter. I assure the House that, when my right hon. and learned Friend the Secretary of State for Health and his Cabinet colleagues are reaching a conclusion on the Griffiths report, they will cover the important aspect of mental illness.

**Mr. Nigel Griffiths:** Does the hon. Gentleman realise that comprehensive care programmes and plans are not worth the paper they are written on if they are not backed up by comprehensive funding? Does he realise that the constituents who write to me are caught between the Scylla of seeing their relatives in mental hospitals with declining levels of care and others under increasing pressure as funding becomes tighter and the Charybdis of having their relatives in the community, with cuts in the number of home helps, meals-on-wheels services and in the general level of funding and provision in the community? We want to see some action on finance, not merely vague programmes.

**Mr. Freeman:** I shall deal with the elderly shortly. I commend the arrangements that Oxford region has put in place to transfer capital and revenue funding from large hospitals that are slowly being run down into proper provision, facilities and staffing in the community for mentally handicapped people. We should like such a model to be applied throughout the Health Service.

Between 1976 and 1986 there was a fall of 15,000 in the number of mentally handicapped patients being cared for in larger institutions. All those patients have returned to the community. Some have returned to their homes, but about 8,000 are using day and residential care facilities. Our closure policy for mental-handicap institutions is the same as that for mental-illness institutions.

Residental or village communities may be part of the new range of facilities that will be built in the future. As long as those village or residential communities for mentally handicapped people are not isolated or inward looking, they will have an important role to play. Hon. Members have a duty to explain to our local communities the importance of caring for mentally handicapped people in the community. Too often, we learn of community groups' opposition and of planning permission for the purchase and construction of small homes in the community for mentally handicapped people being contested.

**Mr. Worthington:** The Minister said that 15,000 fewer people are being catered for in hospitals for the mentally handicapped. The way in which he gave the figure was unintentionally deceptive. Those figures have fallen because, first, local authorities have prevented people from entering hospital, despite their lack of resources, and, secondly, because people are dying in those hospitals. Only a minority are being discharged into the community.

**Mr. Freeman:** By and large, local authorities have done an extremely good job caring for mentally handicapped people in the community.

**Mr. Tony Favell** (Stockport): My hon. Friend said that the community has a responsibility to look after people who are less fortunate, especially mentally handicapped people. My hon. Friend will be interested to learn that recently a survey was held in Stockport of patients who had been discharged from Offerton House hospital. Every one of them said that they would prefer to be in the community rather than to return from whence they came. The local authority and the local community take their responsibility seriously. I am president of Stockport Mencap, and I accept that it has a responsibility to people who are less fortunate.

**Mr. Freeman:** I pay tribute to Stockport, which is renowned for its care of mentally ill and mentally handicapped people.

Between 1980 and 1986, the Government spent about £11 million on 40 schemes to move 340 children out of long-stay institutional care into the community. That represents a cost of £30,000 per place. I do not begrudge —neither, I am sure, does the hon. Member for Livingston —a penny of that money. They are immensely expensive but immensely valuable schemes. The Government do not want any mentally handicapped children to be looked after in the larger, isolated long-stay institutions. The number of children currently in such institutions is less than 400 and we want that figure to be reduced to nil.

We are well aware of the demographic pressures and their effect on care of the elderly. The over-65 population has gone up by some 6·7 per cent. between 1980-87. The number of the very elderly will substantially increase. With regard to the National Health Service, it is important that we do not keep the elderly who are medically cured in hospital beds for longer than necessary. They consume a lot of medical and nursing care and, once medically cured, many of them prefer to be back in their homes or in the community under some form of rehabilitation care.

The elderly have benefited enormously from the NHS. Some 40,000 hip replacements are now performed each year compared with some 5,000 undertaken 20 years ago. Such operations bring great relief to a number of elderly people.

The hon. Member for Edinburgh, South asked me about assistance in the home. There has been a significant expansion in such assistance between 1980-87 and in real terms home help expenditure has gone up by 28 per cent., meals-on-wheels expenditure by——

**Ms. Harman:** What about resourcing?

**Mr. Freeman:** If the hon. Lady will permit, I will come to resourcing in a moment.

Expenditure on meals-on-wheels has gone up by 11 per cent., on nursing care by 14 per cent. and day centre expenditure is up by 16 per cent. In our review of Griffiths, we are tackling the issue of how to spend taxpayers' money wisely and efficiently. As I have already said, we spend £1 billion through income support on care for the elderly in residential and nursing homes. Clearly, it is right for the majority of those elderly people to be in such homes, but we are considering how care can also be given in the home to ensure that elderly people remain in their homes for as long as possible.

**Mr. Ieuan Wyn Jones** (Ynys Môn): Perhaps I could tempt the Minister into giving us some idea of the Government's thinking on this issue. Is he suggesting that the Government have shifted the emphasis away from ploughing money into providing care in residential and nursing homes back towards care in the community? Will the Government's response to Griffiths be the provision of resources for people in their own homes—the Minister has already said that 25 per cent. of such cases could be cared for in their own homes if they were provided with resources. Is the Minister saying that the inevitable additional resources will be given to a public body, either the local authority or the district health authority, or will they be given to the local authorities to buy in care from private or voluntary concerns?

**Mr. Freeman:** The hon. Gentleman is trying to tempt me into foreshadowing our response to Griffiths. I have noted what he has said and, if he can be patient, I am sure that he will be able to contribute to the debate on Griffiths that will come in Government time.

It is important to consider the role of the family and the private and voluntary sectors in giving support to those living in the community. We have no philosophical objections, unlike, I suspect, the hon. Member for Livingston (Mr. Cook) to the private sector providing care for the mentally ill and the mentally handicapped. Over the past few years, some local authorities have pioneered the private sector care of such people under the quality control of the NHS and themselves. So long as there is a proper contract and proper quality control, we want to see such care expanded.

Care in residential and nursing homes is provided largely by the private sector, although local authorities and the NHS play an important role. Lady Wagner made some important recommendations about residential care in her report. We have started a three-year programme to improve quality. We are looking at projects that encourage better contacts with the local community, better information about what is offered, training for care staff and a complaints procedure. We are taking Lady Wagner's other recommendations as part and parcel of our overall review of care in the community. I shall make a statement about some of her other recommendations shortly.

In 1988, we increased the fees for registration and inspection to help local authorities to inspect. We have laid down a minimum inspection rate of two a year. As I have

[*Mr. Freeman*]

said, we need to consider the other matters that fall to central Government, although many of the recommendations in the Wagner report were for local authorities and there is no reason for them to delay in implementing the recommendations that were addressed to them.

This Government believe that the voluntary sector has a vital role to play. The Department of Health contributes £36 million a year to voluntary organisations, much of it to those involved in care. Districts and regions provide £25 million a year locally. I pay tribute to the work of the voluntary sector whch is so vital, especially for the carers. As the House will know, we launched the "Helping the Community to Care" initiative with about £10 million of funding and a separate initiative, "Care in the Community", which has evaluated about 28 pilot projects, including one in Bolton for the care of those coming out of institutions for the mentally handicapped, as my hon. Friend the Member for Bolton, North-East (Mr. Thurnham) will know. We have funded the voluntary sector, which has a vital role to play.

I want to deal with the role of family and friends. It is important that we do not seek, as Members of Parliament or members of society, to shuffle off wholly to the state responsibility for caring for those in the community. Families, siblings and friends have an important role to play. They must be involved and we all have a responsibility. It is true that we are a more fragmented society. Children live much further from their parents than they did 20, 30 or 40 years ago. It is most important that family and friends retain and build on their responsibility to care for relatives when they come out of institutions.

**Mr. Dennis Turner** (Wolverhampton, South-East): The Minister talked about fragmentation. The Government have it in their hands to resolve that and that is the essence of this debate. The Minister talked about the voluntary sector and the service it provides. Yet there is a crisis of resources in the voluntary sector at present. The Government are not facing up to that. How can the Minister tell us that he is responding positively to the needs of the voluntary sector when the Government are reducing the amount of income for the voluntary sector to meet the needs of the mentally handicapped, the mentally ill, the homeless and those in despair? We know that the Government are not doing that and that is why we are having this debate today.

**Mr. Freeman:** The hon. Gentleman is misinformed about the voluntary sector. The total income of voluntary organisations has risen substantially and the level of support provided by this Government has also increased.

Care in the community is a vitally important subject. It touches the lives of most of us through our relatives and friends. It is the mark of a civilised society that we provide high quality care in community. The Government take that seriously and we shall bring proposals forward shortly. I commend the amendment to the motion.

4.42 pm

**Mr. Andrew Smith** (Oxford, East): I welcome the opportunity to take part in this debate, which addresses the most important social challenge facing us for the next 50 years. I do not envy the task of the Under-Secretary of State who has been put up this afternoon to defend the indefensible. Although one can agree with what he said generally about the need for humane treatment for mentally ill people and for support for elderly people who want to remain in their homes, it was all rhetoric. His lofty sentiments were not backed up by one jot of a concrete proposal for action to address the needs of people who are suffering now and who have been suffering during the long period during which the Government have scandalously not responded to the Griffiths report.

I remind the House that the report is subtitled "Agenda for Action". For the Government, it has been nothing more than an agenda for prevarication. We are at last promised a statement and a debate on the matter before the recess. I ask the Minister whether that statement will set out in full and practical terms how care in the community is to be delivered in line with the Griffiths report, or whether it will be a holding statement which merely promises a White Paper later in the year after more months of delay and prevarication. I shall gladly give way to the Minister if he wants to answer the question. Shall we have a definitive statement before the recess, or will the White Paper come later? Evidently the Minister does not want to take this opportunity to answer that question. I strongly advise him to do so by the end of the debate, because millions of people cannot afford to wait any longer for the answer.

When the Government make their statement, I hope that they will take full account of the extensive consideration of the matter by voluntary associations, professional bodies, the trade unions, local authorities and the Select Committee on Social Services. Policy on this matter is far too important and too long-lasting in its implications and inevitably involves too many parties in delivery to be tackled successfully on a blinkered or partisan basis. The framework for community care must command sufficient general support to be administered and developed by Governments and local authorities of different political persuasions. The vulnerable people whose needs the policy must address deserve better than the political shuttlecock treatment. The overriding objective must be to place their needs and preferences at the centre of the system; to that end, the key problems that must be addressed are clear.

First, the range of community care options and services is such that there is an enormous premium on effective co-ordination, which does not exist at present and which can clearly be delivered only by local authorities working under a comprehensive and coherent policy, organised centrally through Government, with people of sufficient standing in the Cabinet sufficiently committed to making of a success of it for us to know that resources will be available to enable the local authorities and other carers to do the job.

Secondly, this is an area of policy where services must be demand led. We must not have a system in which people's needs are perpetually bashed against cash ceilings which bear no relation to the real level of need and the cost of delivering services. Thirdly, we are considering people who, inevitably, are dependent to some degree or other. It is all the more important that they have a degree of choice open to them and a meaningful voice in the way in which services are delivered. Fourthly, that applies very much to the carers in families, as it does to those for whom they care.

In the limited time available, I want to concentrate on the implications for local authorities and resourcing and the implications of that for choice. The present financing of community care is chaotic to the point of imminent breakdown. Oxfordshire illustrates that well. I was interested that the Under-Secretary of state should praise the Oxford region bridging scheme. If the situation in Oxfordshire is good, I dread to think what it is like in the rest of the country. If things are so marvellous in Oxfordshire and if there is bridging finance, why was Oxfordshire faced with the imminent closure of a hospital for the mentally handicapped, which had been known about for a year in advance?

Why was I in the district health authority manager's office, one week before the closure was due to take place, with tearful and angry parents, who still did not know where their mentally handicapped son was going to go? If it had not been for my intervention, what would have happened to that young man? That story of personal tragedy is repeated thousands of times throughout the country as a result of the inadequacy of the way in which the system works at present.

The position on costs and the finance available for meeting them is no better in relation to residential care. A survey undertaken by Oxfordshire Welfare Rights of local residential care homes and nursing homes showed, on a 69 per cent. response rate, that more than 200 elderly residents in Oxfordshire had to contend with a gap between the cost of home care charges and what they received in income support, with an average shortfall being made up either by the elderly person, who was often exhausting his or her savings, or by relatives. I am sure that I am not the only hon. Member to have received heart-breaking letters from people who can no longer meet the difference and make up the shortfall in the cost of their relatives' care. Some of those letters come from people who are themselves elderly and who are trying to find the money out of their pension or inadequate income.

In the other half of cases in the survey, people could not make up the shortfall at all, and were being subsidised either by the homes or by the other residents. How did homes respond to that state of affairs? The survey quoted the remarks of representatives of two private residential and nursing homes. One said:

"We are not now accepting any DHSS funded residents unless the top-up is made. Existing residents we are still caring for, but as you can see at great cost. The private sector cannot continue to sustain these losses."

The second home said:

"Moved two back to hospital"—

that is not to say that the residents needed on medical grounds to go back to hospital; they were merely moved back to hospital—

"rest are in the nursing home by our generosity but it is jeopardising the business."

I am sure that hon. Members—especially those who represent southern constituencies—will be no strangers to this alarming state of affairs.

**Ms. Armstrong:** It is the same everywhere.

**Mr. Smith:** My hon. Friend tells me that the problem is equally bad in other parts of the country. We cannot allow it to continue.

The Minister rightly said that those who stay in their own homes need support if they are to remain as independent as possible. Clearly, they need a much better co-ordinated policy on domiciliary support services. At present, the rhetoric has it that independent elderly people are receiving support in their own homes, but in reality

many of those people have been dumped and neglected. They are isolated and alone and do not receive the support they need. If they are to receive that support, and if local authorities are to be able to undertake the key co-ordinating role that Griffiths prescribed for them, we shall need nothing short of a revolution in the organisation of local authority finances.

In Oxfordshire, the cost of upgrading old people's homes to the standard that the authority requires the private sector to maintain and of providing effective community care services for elderly people alone would require an additional £7 million revenue over the next five years, while the capital costs would run up to £17 million gross. Those are not extravagant sums in relation to the needs to be met, but we have to remember that, in common with other authorities, Oxfordshire faces severe restrictions on its revenue budgets and the massacre of its capital programme as a result of reductions in capital receipts and the changes in the rules for capital financing under the Local Government Finance Act 1988.

While the Department of Health says that it is actively promoting care in the community and is attempting to push people out of long-stay institutions and hospitals—a fact to which the hon. Member for Macclesfield (Mr. Winterton) referred—we have an unco-ordinated, exploding but inadequate Department of Social Security budget and the cuts and restrictions imposed by the Department of the Environment make it quite impossible for local authorities to pick up the pieces.

That illustrates two great dangers of the Griffiths recommendations, especially in the hands of this Government. First, it would be disastrous if local authorities were given the prime responsibility for community care while at the same time being denied the powers or resources to meet those responsibilities. Secondly, if the Government specify that local authorities should not, in the main, be the deliverers of care but merely the planning and contracting agents for the voluntary and private sectors, those in need of care will be denied an important degree of choice, and those planning the provision will be denied the most direct means of ensuring that needs can be met at the quality standard that the community rightly expects. Everyone knows what a disaster the contracting out of hospital cleaning, for example, has been, and we do not want the same to happen to domiciliary services.

As many of us have said throughout, care in the community is not a cheap option. If it is to work at all satisfactorily, it requires a large injection of resources, as well as the very best and most efficient management of those resources. That cannot be achieved through any private insurance scheme proposed by the Adam Smith Institute, any more than such schemes can act as a substitute for the National Health Service.

We are talking about a common public obligation which must be met by all contributing to the cost in proportion to their means and receiving care in proportion to their needs. I believe that that is what the public wants.

As we bring such a system into operation, let us remember that we have a terrific commitment to caring for other people—in the local authorities, health authorities, social service departments, home help service, council housing departments, housing associations and voluntary associations and among private providers, as well as within families. People go into such jobs because they want to help other people and spread a bit of human happiness.

[*Mr. Smith*]

Let us—and let the Government—harness that energy and commitment to caring so that people's eyes can be lifted from the demoralisation of knowing that they cannot give of their best because they do not have the wherewithal to do so. Let us set our sights on a civilised society in which carers have the resources and support necessary to do their job and in which all those in need of community care can help themselves to some of the dignity that should be everybody's right.

Planned provision, adequately funded and properly co-ordinated, with a variety of client choice in delivery, is the key to success in that endeavour. I hope that those aims will command the support of the whole House and that the Government will take notice. If they do not, millions in need of care will pay a terrible price in the years to come.

4.58 pm

**Mr. Nicholas Winterton** (Macclesfield): I am pleased to be able to make a brief contribution to this very important debate. First, let me make it clear to my hon. Friend the Minister that I think that it is a great pity that the Government did not make a statement on the Griffiths report before they issued the White Paper "Working for Patients" because the two go so closely together. It is difficult to make a proper assessment and analysis of the many radical proposals in the White Paper without knowing precisely where the Government stand in relation to the Griffiths report.

We are dealing with three main categories of people—the mentally ill, the mentally handicapped and the elderly and infirm who require some form of special care or accommodation. I intend to direct my remarks mainly to the care of the mentally ill. I know that my hon. Friend the Minister is aware of my deep concern for and interest in that matter. It is appropriate to look after most of those who suffer from mental handicap through care in the community—that is desirable, humane and compassionate. There is one caveat, however, and it is that when people with mental handicap also suffer from mental illness, some of them should be looked after in long-stay hospitals because of the complexity of their condition.

In respect of the elderly, the infirm, and those requiring special accommodation or care in the community, and not in an institution or a hospital, it would be wrong to put all our eggs into the one basket of private provision. I served on a county council which had responsibility for social services and the provision of part III accommodation. Since I entered Parliament 18 years ago, I have taken a great interest in that subject and have regularly visited all the part III homes in my constituency and virtually all the private and independent homes—some of which I opened with great pleasure. It would be wrong and very damaging to put all our eggs into one basket and hand over the care of the elderly to the private sector. Indeed, from the representations from people operating wonderful caring homes in the independent sector, I do not think that even the private sector wants that.

My main concern is for the mentally ill. I generally support the policy of care in the community. However, unlike a number of people in my hon. Friend's Department, and unlike organisations such as MIND, my long interest and service in this area make me believe that there is a permanent need for long-stay hospital places for many mentally ill people, especially those suffering from schizophrenia. It is a tragedy that for purely commercial reasons some magnificent hospitals are being closed and their sites redeveloped. Part of the treatment of the mentally ill is the environment in which they live—the refuge and the asylum aspects of hospital care. Again, speaking from some knowledge, I know that although some of the hospitals for the mentally ill may be the Victorian institutions that some have described, built when buildings were intended to last virtually for ever, many can be altered, upgraded, rehabilitated and turned into the most attractive accommodation for the modern care of the mentally ill. Those hospitals are often sited in wonderful parkland, woodland and gardens.

I was a member of the Select Committee on Social Services which carried out an in-depth and very lengthy inquiry into care in the community for the mentally ill and mentally handicapped. Many of those who treat them believe that their environment—that refuge, asylum, quiet and tranquility—is part of the treatment and care that they require. I view with deep concern the rapid closure of those hospitals, with the patients being discharged into the community and often inadequately catered for in accommodation or in the number of skilled and qualified personnel available to look after them.

As the hon. Member for Livingston (Mr. Cook) said, it is tragic that hundreds of mentally ill people frequently end up in prisons. Some hon. Members may ask how I know that. It is because as a member of the Select Committee, having completed and reported on our inquiry into care in the community for the mentally ill and mentally handicapped, we carried out an inquiry into the prison medical service. We visited at least 20 prisons in Scotland, England and Northern Ireland, where we came across many dozens of prisoners who should never have been there; more appropriately, they should have been receiving treatment and care in a mental hospital. When discharged into the community they had committed minor offences, although some were, perhaps, a little more serious. They had not done so intentionally, but because of their mental condition. When they appeared before the courts either the hospitals were not prepared to take them back or there was no hospital place available, so they were put into prisons. That is a tragedy not only because they are not receiving the care and treatment that they need either to contain their condition or, as one would hope, to make them better, but because their condition is being exacerbated and they are receiving no meaningful treatment.

I am pleased that my hon. Friend the Minister said that his Department was carrying out some form of survey. He was kind enough to allow me to bring a delegation from the National Schizophrenia Fellowship to see him a few weeks ago. I wonder whether he has now had time to consider whether his Department can financially assist Professor Kathleen Jones of York university, who is an expert in that area and is embarking on an inquiry into the whereabouts of a specific number of people who have been discharged from mental illness hospitals.

One of the tragedies of what has happened since we put the policy of care in the community into practice is that those who have been discharged have not been followed up and monitored. I hate to quote yet again the hon. Member for Livingston, but I accept what he said about many of those sad people now sleeping in cardboard boxes, on streets not many yards from this Palace of Westminster or under the arches at Waterloo.

**Mr. James Couchman** (Gillingham): My hon. Friend and I shared the Select Committee investigation into care in the community. Does he agree that although we saw some appalling examples of deinstitutionalisation from here to the west coast of America, we also saw some extremely good examples of people who had been discharged into the community being supported in very good circumstances?

I agree with my hon. Friend that there are a number of patients for whom the asylum offers by far the best remedy. Does he agree that we should be seeking a continuum of care from informal accommodation within the community right through to something similar to the existing mental hospitals?

**Mr. Winterton:** I am happy to agree strongly with my hon. Friend's remarks. When my hon. Friend the Minister responded to the hon. Member for Livingston, he said that he felt that at least two health authorities provided excellent facilities within the community and that those examples should be followed elsewhere. I agree with my hon. Friend the Member for Gillingham (Mr. Couchman) that in America we saw the extremes of absolutely superb facilities in some areas and absolutely grotesque, horrible facilities, of the sort we just would not want to think about, in other areas. We need to strike a balance and achieve a continuum of care.

I hope that my hon. Friend the Under-Secretary will confirm when he winds up that, in the immediate future, the Government will recommend to health authorities not to close or dispose of any additional psychiatric, mental illness hospitals. It is vital that we review the position to see exactly where we stand before we dispose of any more valuable sites.

I know that my hon. Friend would not expect me to sit down without mentioning Parkside hospital in my own constituency. Sad to say, some of the Mersey and Macclesfield regional and district health authorities' senior management appears more interested in realising capital assets than in caring and treating people with mental illness and mental handicap. Parkside hospital, Macclesfield which is renowned for its care of the mentally ill, is not isolated in the middle of some bleak moor. It is in the community, in the heart of Macclesfield and situated in magnificent parkland and gardens which, as I have said, constitute part of the therapy of caring and treating the mentally ill.

The Mersey regional health authority and the Macclesfield district health authority are seeking to dispose of more than 80 per cent. of the site for housing and other development. That would be a rich capital harvest for the health authority, but what of the environment for those still requiring treatment and care for their mental illness? Will any of the gardens, parkland, asylum or refuge, which are such a valuable part of the treatment and care of the mentally ill, remain? No. All that will go under bricks, concrete, pipes and road. That should not happen.

On behalf of the community I am fighting what is almost a last ditch battle to try to persuade the health authority to rethink. As my hon. Friend the Under-Secretary knows, I invited him to visit Parkside hospital and the nearby young persons' unit and am pleased to say that, in principle, he has accepted. I urge him to come before too long if he does not want to see a hospital that has been closed and facilities that are no longer available.

It is vital that the Government realise what is being done in their name up and down the country. I know from the work which I do on the Select Committee on Social Services that Parkside hospital is not an isolated case, and the Under-Secretary should come to Macclesfield as soon as possible. The future welfare of those suffering from mental illness and mental handicap, as well as the elderly requiring specialist accommodation, is at stake and these groups should be able to look to a Government of any political view for the care, humanity and compassion which I believe all hon. Members would wish to give them.

As many of my hon. Friends are aware, I feel deeply about this matter. The lengthy inquiry that we had into care in the community just a few years ago opened my eyes. I went into it with an open mind and I came out realising that we have to do a lot for the elderly and particularly for the mentally ill and handicapped and that we would not serve their future welfare and well-being if, for the wrong reasons, we disposed of valuable hospital sites. Why not bring the community into those hospitals, where necessary? Why not build care and cluster group dwellings for the mentally ill on those sites?

One aspect which I am afraid my hon. Friend and, dare I say it, Sir Roy Griffiths do not fully appreciate is that the facilities that exist for the mentally ill and handicapped within their respective hospitals are such that it would be difficult to replicate them within the community. Such facilities include sheltered workshops, hydrotherapy pools and all the specialist facilities that are so important to the well-being and meaningful life of these people.

Is it not stupid and crazy that dozens of people from Parkside hospital in Macclesfield have been discharged into the community and are now being collected every day in buses and minivans to be brought back to the hospital? Facilities should have been built within the wonderful grounds and areas surrounding the hospital which are so treasured by the people of Macclesfield. The hospital is a valuable community facility which, by the way, in essence cost the Health Service next to nothing because it was vested in the Health Service when it was formed so superbly in 1948.

I believe that I heard my right hon. and learned Friend the Secretary of State for Health say in an earlier intervention that the Government's pronouncement on the Griffiths report would come within two weeks. Perhaps my hon. Friend the Under-Secretary will tell me whether I am right when he winds up the debate. The Government's statement on that report is urgently awaited and it is so important that the Government should get it right.

5.16 pm

**Mr. Ronnie Fearn** (Southport): On numerous occasions in this House during the past two years I have experienced a phenomenon known as deja vu when we have debated serious issues, such as that we debate today. There may be many reasons for that. One is that the Government never listen to the pleas of the public or the Opposition, no matter how forceful their case may be.

When I first entered the House in May 1987, I did not expect to participate in so many debates on care, of which I believe this is the seventh. I am not sure whether the hon.

[*Mr. Ronnie Fearn*]

Member for Livingston (Mr. Cook) feels the same, but the House has heard a great deal from him on the subject in recent months. I note that he did not speak in the care in the community debate which I introduced on 19 April and which covered many of the points raised so far today. That aside, I cannot deny that I welcome this opportunity to discuss the subject and to highlight the plight, suffering and degradation of many of our citizens.

When I opened the previous debate on this matter, I pointed out the critical position in which many thousands of mental health patients found themselves as a consequence of pressures on health authorities and hospitals. Those pressures resulted in many mental health facilities closing and patients being discharged from units without being found alternative arrangements and with no provision for their care being made in the community.

In that debate, I also highlighted the difficulties faced by numerous elderly people who were unable to care for themselves and were not receiving the services they needed because health authorities and social services departments did not have the resources—this was true of those in my own constituency. The authorities were not receiving the resources or the financial or manpower help to cope with their needs.

I also referred to the effect that demographic changes and the great increase in the number of elderly people would have on services in the future, and of the increasing number of elderly people who would be totally dependent and in need of 24-hour care. I also mentioned the direct and disturbing effect which the proposals in the National Health Service White Paper—I refrain from using its title because I believe that it works against patients, particularly those in need of chronic care, rather than for them—would have on community services.

I am sorry to say that everything I said then still applies today and, because of the nature of the subject, the numbers in need of care and support services will have multiplied, and the distress and anxiety felt by those individuals and their carers will already have taken its toll. It is an absolute disgrace that so many vulnerable people should be left without the support services that they so desperately need—some of them, such as the mental health patients who are discharged into the community, without even a roof over their heads.

Even worse, it is obvious that the Government are aware of the difficulties and the disorganisation which confront all who are involved. It is also obvious that the reason for the Government's lack of action is purely ideological. Words fail me when I contemplate the possibility that the major stumbling block is not Conservative ideology but the stubbornness and idiosyncrasy of one person—the Prime Minister.

I was pleased to hear the Leader of the House say last Thursday that he hoped that the Government would bring forward proposals about the Griffiths report before the summer recess. The Minister confirmed that today, although I did not hear the "two weeks" mentioned by the hon. Member for Macclesfield (Mr. Winterton). I was a little worried to hear him say, however, that the question whether to hold a further debate on the matter would best be considered then. I should have hoped that, once the Government had announced their proposals, we should have the opportunity to debate them in full.

We must ensure that all the consequences of the Government's proposals are clearly worked out and that no area of community need is ignored. Reports that the Cabinet Committee will now recommend that local authorities play the major role in managing community services are welcome up to a point. Not so welcome is the report that a hard-fought battle is being waged about the amount of control that the Government are to have, with the likely result that councils will be forced to contract out services to the private sector.

I would have some trouble accepting these proposals in their totality. The Social and Liberal Democrats' green paper, "Prescription for Health", states that we would

"implement the Griffiths proposal for making local authorities the lead agency for co-ordination of delivery and development of services, but with certain additional safeguards and modifications."

Hon. Members will find our green paper comprehensive and interesting. Should they want to read it without purchasing a copy, I should certainly let them have one. I shall not quote it in full, but no doubt hon. Members will read its contents soon.

One of the safeguards that we want would be an increase in the statutory obligations of local authorities to ensure that certain client groups who are not covered by present legislation—the elderly, for instance—are not given lower priority. We should like the introduction of a general-management style organisation, with clear functional responsibility, delegated authority and budgets. Above all, we recognise the need to tackle present inadequacies of funding and to provide the additional resources that Griffiths implies. This is necessary if care in the community is to work well.

Although we see many of the attractions of a puralist approach to the provision of care, under which local authorities are the enablers, we would have difficulty supporting enforced contracting out. The local authority should decide that. If voluntary organisations were given security of funding they would make a valuable contribution to community care, and in some cases the private sector would have a part to play, too. I know the Minister mentioned £36 million being put into the voluntary sector, but to my knowledge no authority has the security of knowing that funding will be forthcoming year after year, or that it will increase.

It cannot be stressed too much that there will never be an adequate alternative to public provision in all types of services. Public provision must remain an option for the individual and must always be available as a last resort. Local authorities must be given the means and the power to provide systems of services based on individual clients and their carers' needs—ideally, systems selected by those in need of the services.

One of the most serious consequences of the Government's drive to reduce public spending regardless of the human cost is the appalling state in which social services departments find themselves. There are serious shortages of all groups of staff across the country, and alarming shortages in some areas. Needless to say, they tend to be in the most deprived areas and in places in which housing is virtually impossible to find or its cost is out of most people's reach. At a time when reported child abuse cases are at their highest ever level—as we heard in the Standing Committee considering the Children Bill—and when the number of mentally ill and elderly people in need of care is on the increase, it is imperative that social services departments be given the means to rectify the problem. Many of them are collapsing under the pressure, and it is now up to central Government to do something about that.

I hope that before any new enterprise resulting from the Griffiths recommendations is embarked upon, the problems being faced by social workers and other social services groups will be well and truly ironed out. Unless they are, the smooth implementation and success of any scheme is doubtful.

Many organisations involved in health and community care services are worried about the lack of reference in the recent proposals to the responsibility of health authorities in relation to community care services; perhaps general practice services should be included in this context. Doubtless the Minister will mention them. Some medical and health services are inextricably linked to community care services—for example, geriatric psychiatry, various out-patient services, discharge procedures and many community health services. I hope that the Government have something in mind which will ensure that the services required by community care clients are available and within easy reach.

I am convinced that the present proposals are nowhere near adequate to cover these needs. In the last debate on this topic, I pointed to the valuable service with which the millions of informal carers provided the country. At that time, I did not say that it is estimated that 100,000 children carry some of the burden of this care. Although it is right that young people should be taught responsibility and care for others, they should not bear the brunt of our failure to provide the resources that are necessary. Youngsters facing difficulties must not be overburdened and must be as free as possible to pursue a course that will lead to self-fulfilment and independence.

The current approach to informal carers in general is in danger of creating an ever increasing circle of dependency. It would be far more sensible and cost-effective in the long term to take more care of our carers by providing them with the financial and support services which they undoubtedly need and by ensuring that we do not hasten the day when the informal carers themselves become dependent on the care of others.

The long-term aim of any policy for care in the community should be to enable people to lead their lives as independently as possible and to ensure that the quality of their lives is as good as it can reasonably be expected to be. Community care and health care are not appropriate services to be subjected to market forces. Too many customers will be left defenceless. Two-tier systems will develop. A person in need of such care should not have to fight to receive it. For the common good, it is part of the Government's duty on behalf of us all, who may well need these services one day, to enable the individual to live life as fully and independently as possible by ensuring the provision of comprehensive and good quality care services for all.

5.29 pm

**Mrs. Gillian Shephard** (Norfolk, South-West): The hon. Member for Southport (Mr. Fearn) has confessed to a feeling of deja vu in this debate. It is true that two points always emerge from debates on community care. First, the policy has been around for a long time. Indeed, it has been pursued by Governments of different hues for at least a

quarter of a century. Secondly, although, and even to judge by this debate, it is clear that there is no absolute consensus on what is meant by successful community care, some useful principles over that period have—as is to be expected and hoped—emerged to govern what can and cannot work in care in the community.

A most useful contribution to the debate was the Audit Commission's report "Making a Reality of Community Care" which was published in 1986. That identified the following principles: strong and committed local champions of change; a focus on action, not bureaucratic machinery; locally integrated services cutting across agency boundaries; a focus on the local neighbourhood; a multidisciplinary team approach; and a partnership between statutory and voluntary organisations.

I would add another principle to those of the Audit Commission, which is that residential and institutional care should remain part of the spectrum of care in the community to cope with crises, and with respite care when it is needed. That is not just for the mentally ill, but for the elderly who can suffer crises of illness or of chronic difficulties and need to be admitted to hospital for a time but can then be returned safely to the community, and for people with a mental handicap who, from time to time, can cope well in the community but who, perhaps for a short period, need to be returned to institutional care— sometimes to help those who are caring for them. A wide range of principles are established on which community care can operate. I believe that there has been a recognition in the Department of Health, which has been underlined by my hon. Friend the Minister this afternoon, that there is a need to retain some inpatient care within the full range of community care.

While all those of us who are concerned with health and social service issues are eagerly awaiting the Government's response to the Griffiths report, those who know the practical difficulties involved in community care provision sincerely hope that the response, when it comes, will draw heavily on experience in the field. I hope, too—here I am not in agreement with the hon. Member for Oxford, East (Mr. Smith), who has left the Chamber—that ample time will be allowed for discussion and consultation, especially bearing in mind the criticisms that have come from a not dissimilar quarter about the so-called lack of time for discussion and consultation on the National Health Service White Paper. We need time to draw together experience from those working in the field. It is most important that consultation is taken seriously and built most thoroughly into the White Paper.

I make those points specifically because, if there is one comment to make about community care it could be that there is a multiplicity of ways of making it successful. Some of those ways have emerged from the Government's own pilot projects which were begun in 1984-85 and which were generously funded with a large sum of money from joint financing allocations. Twenty-eight projects were selected and every health region and every client group was represented. The university of Kent was commissioned to assess the projects, and I believe that a final report on its assessment is awaited. Perhaps my hon. Friend can refer to that in his final comments.

Other ways of providing community care will certainly emerge from the private sector and will be supported from this side of the House. Experiments with sheltered housing and care provided on a continuum in the private sector, not to mention some valuable work and experiments done

[*Mrs. Gillian Shephard*]

by the Federation of Private Residential Home Owners, provide interesting examples of partnerships between the statutory and voluntary sectors, which should be developed and followed up.

In that connection, it is worth mentioning that for many people who will be in their 80s after the turn of the century money may not necessarily be the main problem. The main problem for those people, who may have access to the income from the disposal of their homes, will be personal security and the knowledge that they will be cared for to the end of their lives. Those will be the most important considerations in the minds of such people and the private sector should be, and I believe will be, ready to face that challenge. Indeed, it is the least that we can expect of it, given that £1 billion of taxpayers' money is currently going directly from social security funds to finance people in private residential homes. While the vast majority of those homes are well run, the response to Griffiths must suggest ways in which the use of that £1 billion is effectively monitored and targeted.

Although there is a clear need for a strong Government policy framework in community care, there is an equally strong case for that policy to be interpreted locally and in accordance with local needs. That was, indeed, the thrust of the recommendations emerging from the Audit Commission. That may seem an obvious point, but it needs making because on the ground there is a such a wide diversity of provision and problems across the country. For example, Surrey has the problem of a number of clusters of large psychiatric hospitals and hospitals for the mentally handicapped. The solutions for Surrey will not be the same as, for example, those for west Norfolk, where the health authority is in the fortunate position of building up from scratch the provision of community care for the mentally handicapped and the mentally ill. There are similar clusters of large hospitals and institutions in the north-west of England, which no doubt give particular point to the remarks of my hon. Friend the Member Macclesfield (Mr. Winterton).

**Mrs. Ann Winterton** (Congleton): On the question of large community homes, is my hon. Friend aware that in the north-west of England in my constituency, there is one specific home called Cranage Hall hospital, which is an excellent example of what could happen? That hospital could turn into a village-type community, with a revolving door principle, so that people who are already in the community can go back into the hospital home for specific respite care and to use the facilities. It is set in beautiful grounds. It has not only been supported by the local community for some considerable time, but the community has contributed to many of its facilities. The Congleton Lions, for example, have recently contributed a rumpus room. Is my hon. Friend also aware that parents and relatives of mentally handicapped people in residential care are often concerned that homes may be closed and that their children may be moved elsewhere, rather like a pound of carrots, without being fully consulted?

**Mrs. Shephard:** I was not aware of the particular examples that my hon. Friend drew to the attention of the House, but, knowing her excellent record and her

knowledge of her area, I am sure that the House will wish to give the fullest possible credence to her praise of the work of those particular institutions.

It is worth remembering, when one is talking about institutional care, that the people who are least enthusiastic about it, are those who are consigned to it. That must be borne in mind, too, when one is considering a balanced spectrum of care for the mentally ill and the mentally handicapped.

Other variations in what already exists on the gound can be centred on the number of private residential homes and the amount of private residential accommodation which is available, and that varies enormously across the country. In the south-coast resorts and in parts of Norfolk, there is an enormous concentration of such provision. In parts of northern England, Wales and Scotland, clients and patients do not have the same range of choice.

Sir Roy Griffiths's report laid emphasis on the important role of social services departments as providers, organisers and enablers for community care. He saw them as facilitators. However, that is not a very revolutionary concept, because in the best-run authorities that is a role that they already fulfil. They, together with health authorities, organise joint financing for community care, they grant aid to the voluntary sector, either directly or through joint finance, they co-operate with the private sector and, for example, in Norfolk they are actively involved in training provision with the private sector. They must inspect and monitor standards in the private sector.

I am assured that there is now no resistance to the concept of direct and specific funding to local authorities from central Government. I hope that, when the Government's response to the Griffiths report is announced, it will take account of the current role of social services departments and note that their attitudes and activities have changed greatly and become extremely realistic over the past five years.

I want to consider briefly community care for the mentally ill—a matter which I have raised several times in this House. As my hon. Friend the Minister said in an earlier debate:

"hospital closures should be occurring only as a consequence of the development of better alternative forms of provision. The closure of hospitals per se is in no sense a primary aim of Government policy."—[*Official Report,* 1 February 1989; Vol. 146, c. 406.]

I know that my hon. Friend has been visiting as many health regions as possible to see what is happening at the grass roots. I am sure that as a result of that, he will sympathise with the frustration felt by many people working with the mentally ill that huge sums of money are currently locked up in keeping open large, old-fashioned hospitals when, if that money could only be released before the closures, it could be used to provide a range of suitable alternatives, including in-patient care, as part of the spectrum. My hon. Friend referred to that in his opening remarks. He referred to the East Anglian health region where bridging finance has been used to good account.

Despite that, a mechanical problem remains which concerns not principle or resources, but the budgeting procedures which make the co-ordination of the closure of large hospitals—which, in so many places, are totally unsuitable to the needs of the modern day patient—and their replacement almost impossible to achieve. I raised that matter with my hon. Friend in an earlier debate and he assured me that the Government would be exploring actively ways to work with the private sector to release capital as bridging finance from old, unsatisfactory, crumbling, uncomfortable psychiatric hospitals which were destined for closure. I hope that my hon. Friend will be able to say something in his reply about any progress which may have been made in that respect.

The sheer complexity of the joint financing mechanism is most off-putting and a sure way of discouraging health authorities, local government, voluntary organisations and the private sector from working together. Whatever else comes from the Government's response to the Griffiths report, I hope that there will be a radical simplification of the current mechanism of joint financing. That mechanism is the greatest possible disincentive to the kind of working together between the authorities concerned that we all want to see.

5.42 pm

**Mr. David Hinchliffe** (Wakefield): If there is anyone left in this country who still does not understand the reasons for the opposition to the Government's proposals in their White Paper on the National Health Service to running the NHS on market principles, he need only consider the current state of free-market community care. That shows precisely what will happen if we allow our caring services to be run on the lines of market principles.

Today's debate is not simply about the Government's political indifference and incompetence: it is about the appalling human consequences of leaving the care of dependent and vulnerable people to the marketplace. It is about the human tragedy of a care policy which has led to insecurity and fear for thousands of elderly and handicapped people who are victims of a system that is geared nowadays primarily to business interests instead of to properly thought out social care.

The current shambles which is described as community care arises directly as a result of the Government allowing provision to be determined primarily by the free market. For the past 10 years or so, decisions on policy have been determined primarily by business motives and not by the needs of individuals. In effect, the Government have freed the market, but conveniently they have ignored the fact that many potential consumers of care have no real choice, in many instances have no purchasing power and often do not want or need the product of institutional care which is being forced on them.

In his opening remarks, the Minister referred to £1 billion being poured through income support into private residential care. I want to draw the Minister's attention to the report from the Public Accounts Committee, which stated that nearly a quarter of the individuals in private institutional care who receive income support could have remained independent in their own homes in the community had proper community support been available. We are talking about £250 million a year of income support which is used for people in private institutional care who do not want or need to be in institutional care. That is very worrying.

I have been interested in community care since I entered social work in the late 1960s. The Government's record on community care is one of turning the clock back generations, away from genuine community provision and back to institutional care as the main response to elderly and mentally handicapped people who are in need. I reject that policy, because it belongs to the dark ages. It has no place in the latter part of the 20th century.

The Minister talked about getting people out of isolated Victorian institutions. In many areas, the isolated Victorian institutions which have been used by the NHS over many generations, which I admit are totally unsuitable for care, are being closed. However, they are being re-opened privately to provide the same kind of care.

I hope that the Minister will visit my constituency soon and see Snapethorpe hospital for which closure has been proposed. That is the most modern hospital in my constituency. I will show the Minister Sandal Grange, an isolated Victorian institution which was closed 10 years ago because it was deemed unsuitable for the care of elderly people. The people were moved to Snapethorpe hospital. Sandal Grange was sold off and re-opened for precisely the same function in the private sector. Vast numbers of mentally handicapped people are being moved from outdated Victorian public institutions into outdated private institutions. That policy is a non-starter.

The Government have not only concentrated resourcing on the creation of institutional care; they have cut resources to fund preventive networks and support services. I challenge the Minister to tell us in his reply how he has increased the resources. We all know that there has been a huge growth in need in terms of the number of elderly people who are dependent on support, while the funding for that support has not been increased relative to the growth in need. The Government have created an incentive to enter institutional care by attacking local authorities' abilities to provide real community provision.

I noticed a letter in the *British Medical Journal* on 9 January last year from Dr. Bennett, a geriatrician at the London hospital. He referred to problems he has encountered when families refuse to take back an elderly relative from hospital care because they cannot cope with caring for the elderly relative in the community. Dr. Bennett stated:

"The patients are alone and frail, and they and their carers are desperate. All have experienced failings in the health and social services—a home help sick and no replacement available, day centre waiting lists of many months, faster and faster discharges from hospitals into community 'support' despite mental and physical frailty . . .

Places in old people's homes are diminishing rapidly and waiting lists grow. Increasing pressure is put on all concerned to consider private care. For my patients this means leaving a community they have known for 80 or more years and moving 80 kilometres away for an affordable place, beyond reasonable visiting reach for most relatives."

That is what is happening in hospitals. That problem probably confronts geriatricians throughout the country, with families saying, "We cannot go on caring for our elderly dependant because there is no support."

There is a desperately urgent need to examine also the ease with which the present system allows the individual's independence to be removed. Under Government policy, families who have been struggling to care for their elderly, physically or mentally handicapped relatives are told, "Sorry, their condition is not bad enough to merit the provision of a telephone. Sorry, we can provide a home help only two hours a week. Sorry, we can provide meals on wheels only twice a week. Sorry, we can provide respite care, so that you can have a break, only one week of the year. Sorry, we have no day care facilities but we will put you on the waiting list for day care once a week."

[Mr. David Hinchliffe]

When relatives finally give up the ghost and say, "We have had enough," what is on offer? There is a no-questions-asked offer of £140 a week if the relative concerned is packed off to private institutional care. That is not on. A similar level of financial support should be available to relatives who are struggling to care for their dependants in the community. There should be no incentive for them to wash their hands and say, "Let us put them into an institution, wash our hands of them, and make our lives much easier and happier."

My experience is that Government policy makes it as difficult as possible for the elderly to remain independent in their communities, and as easy as possible to slip them away into private institutional care, which is in no way humane. There are people in institutional care who do not want or need it, and who would be happier receiving support in the community. It is an indictment of Government policy—this has been admitted by hon. Members in all parts of the House—that people are placed in private institutions because of a lack of appropriate Health Service or local authority provision.

For many elderly people, entering private care may be just the start of their problems. Apart from losing their independence and having to move from the place where they have lived all their lives, there are the financial consequences, to which my hon. Friend the Member for Oxford, East (Mr. Smith) referred. In many cases their capital dries up and their home has to be sold. There is evidence from Age Concern, which I know has written to the Minister for Social Security, that homes have been sold when the carer is still living there, so that the person who gave so much care over the years suddenly finds himself homeless. That is a consequence of the person entering private care requiring the capital from the sale of their property to pay for their fees. Subsequently, the resident may have to move to a cheaper home, and could ultimately end up in a local authority part III accommodation.

A number of people who have lived in my constituency all their lives, and who were compelled to enter private care because Health Service provision dried up, were moved 20 or 30 miles away. Six weeks later, under the provisions of current legislation, they were deemed residents of that new area, and were unable to secure local authority funding to return to part III accommodation in the locality in which they lived all their lives. It is scandalous to shunt people miles away from their natural homes when they are at their most vulnerable and need help and support of the kind that should be available in the final years of their lives.

I am sure that my hon. Friend the Member for Oxford, East is familiar with the recent work of the Oxford welfare rights group on income support as it relates to private residential care in Oxford. It found recently that 69 per cent. of those living in private homes cannot meet their fees but depend on top-ups from relatives or outside agencies to meet them. In Oxford, there is an average shortfall of £37 per resident per week. I have no reason to believe that that situation is not to be found elsewhere.

Evidence from registered homes tribunals reveals the way in which many elderly or handicapped people become pawns in the operation of free market care. There is proof —some of it published by my hon. Friend the Member for Peckham (Ms. Harman)—that private homes, many of which operate on a very tight profit margin, cut standards to keep down their costs. Research by the north London polytechnic published in 1985 also revealed that private residential homes cut staffing levels to save money, to the detriment of their residents.

I could speak at length about the problems of provision for the elderly, particularly in the private sector. However, I am not anti-private sector. Rather, I am concerned that the Government allow the fate of vulnerable people to be placed in the hands of individuals who are preoccupied only with profits, and when the elderly or handicapped person's income dries up, they are sent down the road. That is the point at which private care finishes, and that is my grievance against the profit-based system, which is an unsuitable basis for health and social care.

The present system cries out for urgent changes, far beyond those that Griffiths has on offer. The Griffiths report makes a very conservative response when radical changes in community care are needed. We must address all needs, and public investment must be concentrated on preventing, not creating, the institutional dependence that the existing system so often creates. The Government's free market experiment in community care is an abysmal failure, at the cost of billions and billions of pounds. More importantly, it has failed at great personal cost to many elderly and handicapped people, who have endured great misery as a result of the Government's policies.

5.56 pm

**Mr. Peter Thurnham** (Bolton, North-East): The hon. Member for Wakefield (Mr. Hinchliffe) claims that he is not anti-private sector, but most of his speech comprised a long diatribe against it. My experience is that it performs in a much better way than the public sector.

I support Griffiths's recommendations, and particularly paragraphs 1.3.3 and 1.3.4, which go to the heart of the debate. They refer to
"building first on the available contribution of informal carers and neighbourhood support."
They add that local authorities should act as the
"designers, organisers and purchasers of non-health care services, and not primarily as direct providers, making the maximum possible use of voluntary and private sector bodies to widen consumer choice, stimulate innovation and encourage efficiency."
The hon. Member for Wakefield cast doubt on the role of the private sector, claiming that only the public sector can meet the needs of the community, whereas I believe that the whole essence of care in the community is building on and reinforcing private and voluntary efforts. Our response to the Griffiths report should reinforce and enhance private and voluntary work. Although, obviously, no payment is made for voluntary work, a recent report valued its contribution at £11 billion by comparison with the £6 billion at which the Audit Commission valued public sector provision. Therefore, two thirds of the effort is currently made by voluntary workers, and that sector should be reinforced.

The Government are right to deliberate carefully over the Griffiths report. Obviously the National Health Service White Paper had to be published first because provision there is of a different order, amounting to a cost of about £24 billion. It was only right and proper that the NHS review should be conducted first, before the Government turned their attention to community care. We all look forward to the Government's response, which I know will pay full care and attention to the way in which informal carers can work with voluntary bodies such as Crossroads, which perform a very effective role and provide greater value for money in the provision of care and services to people needing help at home than the public sector can now, or could ever do in the future.

I was disappointed by the speech of the hon. Member for Livingston (Mr. Cook). The Opposition are engaged in a flirtation with popularity in the opinion polls at present, and I imagined that that might lead to some new thinking and, perhaps, a more statesmanlike approach in today's Opposition debate. I heard no new thinking, however; the Opposition's only solution appears to be more expenditure, although the present Government have provided more money than Labour.

**Mr. Favell:** Given the number of mentally ill, mentally and physically handicapped and elderly people who we all hope will live in the community, it is surely stupid to expect local authorities to provide everything. To denigrate the efforts of the voluntary bodies is sheer stupidity.

**Mr. Thurnham:** It is significant that the Labour party's review disagreed with Griffiths on that very point, suggesting that local authorities should be the providers. That is the heart of the difference between us.

The recipients of services—the patients and the carers —want a greater say. I thought that I was beginning to agree with the hon. Member for Livingston when he said that he wanted a policy that would enable users to play their part, but he did not go on to explain how he thought that that could be achieved. My hon. Friend the Member for Norfolk, South-West (Mrs. Shephard) said that the answer lay in a multiplicity of services, but the Opposition seem to think that there is a simple bureaucratic answer to the problem of providing such massive amounts of care for such vast numbers of people, most of whom want to be cared for at home rather than in institutions.

I can speak from personal experience, having fostered and then adopted a handicapped child who had been in care for six years. That is an example of how the best care is—and, I believe, should be—provided in the family home. Every child should have the love of a family. One of the most surprising statistics that I have seen recently appears in the survey by the Office of Population Censuses and Surveys on the prevalence of disability in children, which states that 5,500 children in England, Wales and Scotland are in institutional care. My inquiries had suggested that there might be as many as 3,000, including those in Northern Ireland; the OPCS figure is nearly twice that, and shows how much more should be done to help families to continue to care for their own children and to foster and adopt children.

An OPCS survey on disability in adults states that about 50 per cent. of the 210,000 people in category 10 —the most severely handicapped—are being cared for in private households. If the most disabled people can be cared for at home that is where our efforts should be directed, and I support the calls for more respite care and home helps.

**Mr. Andrew Rowe** (Mid Kent): Does my hon. Friend agree that one of the most striking features of community care is the smallness of the amount required by the many people who want to continue to care? The reason why we are all so anxious to hear the Government's response to Griffiths is that Griffiths has made a real attempt to find a way of co-ordinating the finance available so that it is possible for consumers to demand the small amounts that they want, rather than waiting for ages to receive the large amount imposed on them.

**Mr. Thurnham:** I agree. It is not just a question of the smallness of the amount, however; it is also a question of the type of help required. One of the current difficulties with local authority provision is that people must take what is on offer, and if what they want and need does not coincide with that it is too bad. They may be told that their child is too handicapped for anyone to be able to help.

Bolton council, which I believe has done more than most councils in this respect, has just produced a report called "Goal 2000". One of its conclusions is that there is "virtually no service provision specific to the needs of people with challenging behaviour."
That shows how far local authorities' current provision falls short of what is needed. I want carers and committed individuals to play a part in the direction of public funds, so that those funds reinforce the massive contribution made by informal carers and voluntary groups. I shall be interested to learn what mechanisms the Government can devise to achieve that. The Department of Employment has set up new training and enterprise councils to take charge of a £3,000 million training budget. The private sector will have two thirds of those councils, and will play a leading role in the direction of public spending. I hope that we can look to such models in this context.

I was amazed at the number of people who came up to me in Bolton during the general election and said that they could not cope any longer with their children—who, in some instances, were well into their twenties—and wanted help. After the election I called a meeting of those people, who then formed a handicap action group. I was astonished at their commitment. A report was produced stating their needs and explaining how far local authority provision fell short of what was required. Under the excellent chairmanship of Mr. John Seddon, they put forward proposals which have been largely accepted by the local authority and the health authority.

Bolton has been the subject of a number or reports; it has been at the forefront of most of the thinking on care in the community. A report by the local district audit committee called for more co-operation between the local authority and the health authority, and we shall look closely at the Government's proposals in that regard.

I agree with the Opposition calls for more expenditure. We do need more money, but it must be spent much more in accordance with the wishes of patients and carers, and it must reinforce the £11 billion of voluntary care that is currently being provided, without being seen as a substitute for private care. Private and voluntary care is an excellent medium, and it should be helped and enhanced in every possible way by Government policy.

6.8 pm

**Mrs. Alice Mahon** (Halifax): I intend to concentrate on the care of the elderly. Over the past 10 years we have witnessed the wholesale privatisation of care, at great and unnecessary cost to the taxpayer and with tragic results for many elderly people. My hon. Friend the Member for Wakefield (Mr. Hinchliffe) was right to draw attention to that.

It is no good the Minister or anyone else hiding behind clinical decisions. As hospitals have emptied beds for the elderly and mentally ill, consultants have had no choice

[*Mrs. Alice Mahon*]

but to go around the wards with lists of private accommodation. At the same time cuts have been made in social service budgets, and local authorities have not been able to make up the shortfall. Approximately £10 million was provided in 1980 for the care of the elderly in the private sector. It is now well over £10 million each year. It is no use the Government trying to justify their decision by using value for money arguments, because that is a massive waste of resources.

I criticise the private sector, and I admit to having a vested interest in the matter. As a Member of Parliament, as a councillor for five years before that and as a spokeswoman for social services I came into close contact with the elderly in many private homes. Many of those homes are very pretty, with chintzy furnishings and Laura Ashley decor, but that is only to attract people to them. The fact is that they offer little dignified care to the elderly. Most elderly people have no contract with the home, so their position is very insecure. I heard recently of an elderly person in my constituency having to be moved out of a private home, purely for cash reasons. There is no complaints procedure. There is no one to put forward their case if elderly people feel that they are being treated unfairly.

My other major complaint about private homes is that when old people apply for admission there is only a perfunctory evaluation of their financial assets. It has led to wholesale institutionalisation. The Public Accounts Committee reported that a quarter of those in care need not be in care. That is right. The Government were warned about that in the early 1980s when they deliberately moved towards the privatisation of care for the elderly.

I had to smile during the Euro-elections. I canvassed in an area where the number of private homes has gone up significantly. It is a Conservative ward. Nearly all those private homes were exhibiting Tory party stickers. I think that they were saying "Thank you" to the Conservative party for the lucrative cash handouts that they had received for caring for the elderly. However, some do not care properly for the elderly. Many of them employ low-paid, untrained staff, many of whom were YTS trainees. No occupational therapy is provided in most of the homes. Even in homes where occupational therapy is provided, the amount is small. Some homes do not provide a planned programme of orientation, but it is provided in local authority homes where the staff are trained to ensure that elderly people remain very much in touch with what is going on. The staff in local authority homes take training courses. I have yet to come across a private home that sends its staff on training courses.

**Mr. Couchman:** Is the hon. Lady saying that all is well with local authority old people's homes? As a councillor, I chaired the social services committee for five years and my experience was that local authority homes are among some of the most institutionalised establishments that can be found. They institutionalise old people in the same way as the large, long-stay hospitals institutionalise the mentally ill and the mentally handicapped. Does the hon. Lady not agree?

**Mrs. Mahon:** No, I do not. That has not been my experience. We have moved away from rigid, institutionalised care in large hospitals. My experience is that local authority homes can be monitored and that, if necessary, the management can be changed. That cannot be done in private homes. There is very little monitoring. Only two officers in my local authority are trying to monitor hundreds of places. That cannot be done properly.

**Mr. Favell:** Will the hon. Lady give way?

**Mrs. Mahon:** No. I should like to finish this point.

I have been told recently about a private home in my constituency where residents are put to bed at 6 o'clock. Some of them are drugged. It is a case of out of sight, out of mind. When I went to that home they told me that they dared not complain. There is a lack of control and accountability of private homes and it is impossible to monitor them.

**Mr. Favell:** I agree with the hon. Lady that the worst thing to do with the elderly or the mentally handicapped or mentally ill is to institutionalise them, but is it not true that we are learning all the time? Local authorities are learning and the private sector is learning. It is important to give the elderly plenty to do. Does she agree that sheltered accommodation should be provided for as long as possible? People are then able to cook for themselves, make their own beds and look after themselves generally. That is very much better for the elderly than providing them with a bedroom and then sticking them in an awful rectangular room where they all gaze into the middle of the room. There is no more certain recipe for misery. Whether it is local authority or private sector care, we must ensure that we provide sheltered accommodation for the elderly.

**Mrs. Mahon:** I wish that the hon. Gentleman had put that point to his Government about 10 years ago. Then the £10 billion which I believe has been wasted on the private sector could have been used to provide an intensive care package for the elderly, which would have meant that they did not have to go into care.

Institutionalised care destroys independence and murders the mind. Care in the private sector is often provided only for the money that it brings in. There is a great need for much more humane care of the elderly.

When the Minister referred to carers, families and friends playing a major role in the care of the elderly I thought that he had no idea of the size and seriousness of the problem. The Equal Opportunities Commission estimates that there are 1·25 million carers, most of them women, looking after the elderly and the disabled in the community, but the Carers Association believes that there are many more. There has been a huge growth in the number of elderly people. I have a vested interest, because my constituency contains a large number of elderly people and ranks third in the country. Therefore I have a great deal of experience of talking to carers.

There are now more women caring for elderly dependants than there are women caring for children. It is estimated that between the ages of 35 and 65, over 50 per cent. of all women can expect at some time to provide care for the elderly or the infirm. It is often provided at great cost to themselves. People who give up work to care for the elderly are immediately put at a financial disadvantage. They receive a pittance in benefits. Their benefits have been cut during the last few years, particularly last year. Many of the carers are elderly, too. An elderly couple in my constituency is trying to look after a violent, mentally ill son. He is twice as big as they are and he weighs more than they do. They find it very difficult to care for him. A growing problem is mental stress and granny bashing. We have not paid enough attention to that problem but it causes heartbreak on all sides.

Recently I visited a constituent who told me that she never goes out, because no one will sit with an incontinent granny, and that she spends her life washing and cleaning. She went on to say, "I love my mother dearly, but I am waiting for her to die." She was at the end of her tether. Then she said, "I haven't had a holiday for five years." She told me that she had given up a very good job and that she had not had a full night's sleep for a very long time. Finally she told me, "I don't like asking people to the house because it smells like a toilet." That woman had received very little help from the local authority or anyone else. The £10 billion that has been provided for the private sector could have given her a great deal of respite. Good hospitals and other kinds of good care have been closed down, purely on economic grounds, during the last 10 years.

The Government say that they want to provide choice, but that woman has not been given any choice. She has had to sacrifice her own life to look after her elderly mother. The majority of the 1·25 million carers have not been given any choice, either. It is hell on earth for some of the carers who are trying to cope.

The Minister replied to my intervention about mentally ill people in prison by saying that the Home Office was carrying out a survey. That is too little and too late. Warnings have been flooding in to the Government about what is happening in the prison service and about what is happening to people sleeping under bridges and in cardboard boxes. The Government have been responsible for closing hospitals prematurely throughout the country without making sure that there is somewhere where those vulnerable people can go. The Government have taken 10 years to initiate a Home Office inquiry and they should be ashamed of themselves.

I very much welcome the debate, but I shall welcome even more a debate in Government time. I hope that they will come to the House with some humane and decent proposals for caring for the elderly, the mentally ill and the mentally handicapped.

6.20 pm

**Mr. Tony Favell** (Stockport): I am an enthusiastic supporter of the mentally disabled, the mentally ill, the physically disabled and the elderly leading as full a life as possible in the community. I am very glad that, throughout the debate, hon. Members on both sides of the House have supported that view. That is what the disabled want. They do not want to be institutionalised; they want to lead as full a life as possible in the community. From time to time that can be a disadvantage to them and possibly embarrassing to those of us who are not disadvantaged.

Dorothy Birch, a lady in my constituency who is disabled and who does an enormous amount for disabled people in Stockport, visited West Germany recently. When she came back she said, "You do not see any disabled people in West Germany." I said, "Is that a good thing or a bad thing?", and she replied, "It is a bad thing. If no disabled people are seen, that means they are kept out of sight and out of mind." It is to the credit of our community that disabled people are not kept out of sight and out of mind.

However, from time to time we have to provide respite care for disabled people who require help. I strongly urge my hon. Friend to look very carefully into the funding of sheltered accommodation instead of the more traditional caring accommodation. According to housing associations such as the Anchor housing association and the Collingwood housing association, it need be no more expensive to provide sheltered accommodation for elderly and handicapped people than to provide 24-hour care.

It is so much better for disabled people to have a little privacy—perhaps their own bedsit where they can invite friends—to be able to cook their breakfast and make their own bed, although it may take a long time, than to be got up, have their beds made for them and their breakfast provided and then to sit in a rectangle gazing at each other for the rest of the day. Many hon. Members will have had the awful experience of visiting such places and seeing people who in many cases have absolutely nothing to look forward to but death. That is disgraceful. It should be investigated, and the sooner something is done the better.

Many hon. Members have commented on the Griffiths report. I agree with paragraph 1.3.1 which states that local authorities should

"assess the community care needs of their locality, set local priorities and service objectives, and develop local plans in consultation with health authorities. . ."

Ultimately, the local authority will have to ensure that there is provision for disabled people within its boundaries. However, I disagree with paragraph 1.3.2 which states that local authorities should

"identify and assess individuals' needs, taking full account of personal preferences (and those of informal carers), and design packages of care best suited to enabling the consumer."

It is far better to divide the roles. It is fair enough that a local authority should ensure that there is overall provision for disabled people within their town, city or locality, but it is better for someone else to identify individual needs. I suggest that the best person to do that is the general practitioner, who has a full list of all his patients. The new contract, which contains many good things, as Conservative Members recognise, insists that every general practitioner sees each elderly person on his list at least once a year. General practitioners in my constituency do that more often. Many insist upon seeing elderly people at least once every six months. General practitioners are in touch with families and understand their needs over many years. They know whether a disability is transitory or permanent and they are the best people to assess what should be done, and of course the facilities exist already.

**Mr. John Marshall** (Hendon, South): Does my hon. Friend accept that schizophrenics are mentally ill people who have not been helped by community care? They are frequently so aggressive that they lose their doctors and they often do not agree to carry out the treatment that has been prescribed for them. Does he agree that, if they are to be cared for within the community, they need far greater supervision than they have had until now?

**Mr. Favell:** I understand my hon. Friend's point, but most mental illness does arise from schizophrenia. As he will know, one in 10 people require some kind of mental treatment at some time in their lives. It has to be the general practitioner's responsibility as it would be impossible for the local authority to supervise one in 10 people living within its boundaries.

[*Mr. Favell*]

I suggest that my hon. Friend the Minister looks very carefully into the possibility of general practitioners assessing individual needs while the town hall is responsible for ensuring that there is provision for people who require the help that general practitioners consider their patients need.

6.27 pm

**Mr. John Marshall** (Hendon, South): I believe that one aspect of mental health policy has been a gigantic failure—the treatment of schizophrenics. I went to a meeting of my National Schizophrenia Fellowship branch, where one lady told me that her daughter had been released into the community. What did release into the community mean? It meant that that night, she was sleeping somewhere in one of the parks in London. Her mother did not know which park it was, only that she was sleeping rough and that she was not using the treatment that had been prescribed for her.

This morning I received a letter about a particular patient:

"He returned to his flat . . . on 5 June and since then he has been arrested by the local police a few times, they have called the crisis team who do nothing and next morning Hendon Magistrates court discharge him. The residents . . . live in fear of his verbal abuse, loud music played day and night through his open windows and at times violent behaviour—then the police are called and arrest him and so the pattern repeats itself—I could write for hours. He has no doctor in Barnet . . . Doctor . . . struck him off for bad behaviour and no one else will accept him. What can you do to help us?"

Such individuals are not calling for care within the community. I suspect that we have to accept that, if certain schizophrenics are cared for within the community, they will refuse to accept the treatment prescribed for them. There is quite inadequate supervision of their lifestyles, and as a result they, their parents and the community suffer. I believe that we should do much more for them. Sometimes, the mentally ill are treated as the Cinderellas of the social services.

**Mr. Rowe:** My hon. Friend is making a very powerful point. Does he agree that it is part of a larger, extremely difficult problem—that of how far we should allow self-determination to people whom we are trying to treat in a much more mature and adult way? My hon. Friend is talking about one extreme, but the problem runs right through community care.

**Mr. Marshall:** I accept that the problem of self-determination has existed for a long time. I suspect that we may have moved from one extreme to the other.

I shall quote two examples of people who have come to my surgery for advice. One man came to me without an appointment saying that he had a terrible problem. He had received a telephone call from Marseilles. His son had walked out of the local mental hospital, emptied his account at the local building society and gone to Marseilles. The phone call was asking for money to enable him to come back home. That is an example of self-determination, someone walking out of treatment that he should have.

It is all very well talking about the philosophical advantages of self-determination, but I am talking about the practical disadvantages to the patient, the community and parents. I shall always remember a group of people who came to me in my constituency and said, "You must help us. Mr. X has been given a flat in our block and he plays music 16 hours a day. He starts at 8 pm and carries on through the night." That course of action is not benefiting him, his family or the community. I hope that the Government will do something about it.

6.30 pm

**Mr. Tom Clarke** (Monklands, West): My hon. Friend the Member for Livingston (Mr. Cook) introduced this excellent debate, which reflects the importance of this crucial subject at a time when so many expect so much from the Government. Alas, they must have been disappointed by events this afternoon. In many ways, this has been a remarkable debate. The Secretary of State for Health appeared, albeit briefly, and made one short intervention. He accused my hon. Friend of being greedy in a team sense. When the right hon. and learned Gentleman occasionally looks at an egg and reflects on his hon. Friend the Member for Derbyshire, South (Mrs. Currie), he might regret not employing the tactics that he wrongly attributed to my hon. Friend.

If ever there were a debate involving Hamlet without the grave digger, this is it. There is no doubt that the Secretary of State should have been present throughout and should have told us the Government's thinking on these crucial matters. It is true that we have had three debates on community care recently—one was introduced by my hon. Friend the Member for Bristol, South (Ms. Primarolo) in a Consolidated Fund Bill debate; one was introduced by the Social and Liberal Democrats through the hon. Member for Southport (Mr. Fearn), who spoke earlier; and today we have this debate introduced by the Labour party in Opposition time. It is not enough, fifteen months after the report by Sir Roy Griffiths, for the Government to say again that they will make a statement, giving every sign that it will be a holding statement. If this trailer means that, after a long delay, a White Paper will be published during the recess and there will be inadequate debate before the Government rush through legislation, the Government can expect the utmost vigilance from the Opposition.

Now that the Minister has had time to consult the Secretary of State, I shall press him on one matter. In this crucial matter, the House has to depend for its information almost exclusively on rumour. What is happening with the famous E committee? Is a Cabinet committee considering the Griffiths report? If so, what have been the influences during its deliberations? We are told that the committee has been largely influenced by the Right-wing think tank, the Adam Smith Institute. We are told that the Secretary of State has been handbagged by the Prime Minister who, once again, finds herself at odds with one of her senior Ministers. If, as the Minister said in reply to me, these are mere rumours, why does he not take the opportunity to tell us the precise facts? This is a mature Chamber. There are many hon. Members on both sides whose input to our debate has been particularly helpful, who are well informed, who have tried to encourage mature input into the debate and who expect better than we have had from the Government so far.

We expect better because we were told that we should wait for the Government's White Paper on health, "Working for Patients". There was little in it about community care and what there was, as we have heard from virtually every general practitioner in our constituencies, was extremely unhelpful. As my hon. Friend the Member for Wakefield (Mr. Hinchliffe) rightly said, the problem remains. As hon. Members have insisted, within a few minutes' walk of the House of Commons there are people living in cardboard boxes. As the hon. Member for Macclesfield (Mr. Winterton) said in a thoughtful speech and as my hon. Friend the Member for Halifax (Mrs. Mahon) said in a telling speech, far too many people who are mentally ill or mentally handicapped are being sent to prison because the courts do not know where to put them.

This morning in *The Times*, in an article dealing with the problems of prisons, we read almost as an afterthought the comment:

"The board of Canterbury Prison, Kent, says: 'The problem will become worse as mental hospitals devolve their inmates into the community without adequate support services and because changes in the rules governing housing benefit seem likely to lead to a reduction in hostel places'.".

All that is happening when, as my hon. Friends have said, public money is being spent, but as a contribution to the unplanned explosion of private residential homes. Sir Roy Griffiths has asked why that is happening, and we are entitled to know the Government's thinking. The Public Accounts Committee has said that the sum involved is about £250 million. With that money, we could do much in a planned way for the aspirations of community care that have been expressed in the debate.

The Government still offer no strategy for community care—worse, while we have been waiting all this time for a response to the Griffiths report, we have seen fragmentation in various Departments, including the Department of Health. We have seen Departments acting independently and Departments imposing policies that appear to be in conflict with the strategies in which, we are told, the Government believe, including the poll tax. If ever there was a perverse incentive for community care, that is it.

The Department of Health and Social Security has been split into two Departments, without an explanation of how that may influence our attitudes to community care. We have seen the impact of social security cuts. The hon. Member for Bolton, North-East (Mr. Thurnham) referred to Crossroads. The Labour party accepts that there is a role for voluntary organisations and that the private sector often fulfils a useful function. Why should a Government and their supporters who are so committed to voluntarism appear to ignore the views of the voluntary organisations? If ever there was a crisis, it was on the funding of Crossroads, as we know from our constituency correspondence. Again, as part of fragmentation, Lord Young interfered in these matters. We know that employment training schemes have an impact on what is happening in the community.

As for my constituency, I shall merely tell the story of a man who was involved with Crossroads. His wife suffers from Alzheimer's disease. He was given some help, which he very much appreciated, in visits two or three days a week which were ordered by Crossroads. Because of the argument about funding, which has not been wholly resolved, he was told that that help would be taken away. He came in tears to see me. We should remember that his wife will not be exempt from the poll tax. If people are contributing to local authority services, it ill behoves those who impose their ideology to argue, as many do, that the role of local authorities should be reduced.

There are strong suspicions that, as the Government think these matters out, there are influences on their thinking that are not necessarily helpful and are almost wholly based on ideology. I note that the Secretary of State for Social Security is sitting on the Front Bench. His presence late in the debate confirms my point.

We are told that the Under-Secretary of State for Scotland, the hon. Member for Stirling (Mr. Forsyth), had considerable influence on Government thinking, about which we shall hear when they have concluded their long deliberations.

**Mr. Dick Douglas** (Dunfermline, West): Lord help us.

**Mr. Clarke:** My hon. Friend the Member for Dunfermline, West (Mr. Douglas) says, "Lord help us". The influence of the hon. Member for Stirling has caused many problems in Scotland. If he has as much influence on the United Kingdom, we are in trouble.

I mentioned the fragmentation of and contradictions in Government policy. I remind the House of what occurred with Lennox Castle hospital. I am sorry that a Minister from the Scottish Office is not present; perhaps they have more important matters to deal with. The hon. Member for Stirling was aware of the many valid criticisms of conditions at Lennox Castle hospital. He was further aware of the television programme that told the world of some of the outrageous conditions there. What did he do? Did he involve himself in consultation? Did he say, "Yes, we are committed to community care, so let us consult"? Did he consult the Confederation of Health Service Employees or the consumers about whom we have heard so much? Did he consult those involved in joint planning, however inadequate it is in Scotland? No, he did not.

The hon. Member for Stirling, who is the most monetarist of monetarists, threw money at the problem by announcing £9 million of expenditure over the next two years without saying whether it was part of a strategy for community care—a policy which would be welcomed by the people of Scotland and, given the main stream of the debate, elsewhere. That proves that, if there is the will, the Government can find the necessary resources, which is why my hon. Friends were right to emphasise the importance of resources.

The Disabled Persons (Services, Consultation and Representation) Act 1986—I make no apology for returning to it—offers the Government an opportunity, if only they would grab it, of a framework for community care. It deals with citizens who have special needs and their right of access to information and it makes agencies, social services, housing and health departments accessible. We shall never solve the problem of people being discharged from hospitals, about which we have heard much today, including from my hon. Friend the Member for Oxford, East (Mr. Smith), until we realise that there is a role for bridging, preparation and assessment. It is scandalous that many people are leaving the community to go into community care that does not exist.

Many hon. Members, including my hon. Friend the Member for Livingston, referred to carers. We owe much to carers, who do so much work 24 hours a day. That commitment should not be exploited. The social security changes, which have worked to the considerable

[Mr. Clarke]

disadvantage of carers of disabled people, should not be allowed to continue without review. The changes are false economy, because no one is helped, least of all the Treasury, if the relationship between the carer and the person they are caring for breaks down and both become institutionalised.

The Audit Commission has said that it is gravely worried about the way in which the Government have organised the changes. It mentioned a lack of planning, strategy and auditing of expenditure of public money, with drastic consequences for the people involved. The Salvation Army estimates that up to three quarters of its hostels' inmates may be suffering from mental illness. Such problems must be taken on board by the Government. They cannot ignore the appalling problem, which was brought to the notice of the Standing Committee considering the Children Bill, of older children, who have no parents or other family, leaving care and facing the difficulties of community life. In many cases, they are being trapped into crime, drugs and prostitution because the Government are not prepared to accept the responsibility that parents would accept for their children. That is the responsibility of a caring Government.

The Government's delays and lack of commitment owe more to ideology than an appraisal of the problems. They are influenced by people who believe that we should consider only consumers, as explained by Mr. Norman Flynn, who in an article entitled "The 'New Right' and Social Policy" said:

"If possible, individuals should manage without help from institutions of any sort, except their own families."

The Minister made that point, as though, collectively, the state had no responsibility. What does that attitude mean in reality? What did the National Council for Voluntary Organisations—volunteers expressing their views and pleading to the Government—say about the family and its input? It said:

"One woman, aged 73, who suffered from a stroke in 1986, is currently in hospital following a further stroke. The sheltered housing scheme where she now lives have said that her care needs are now too great for her to remain a resident there. Nursing home fees in the area—Berkshire—are around £300 per week and the woman concerned would be reliant on income support of £185. As the widow of a milk roundsman who died in 1959 this woman has only a small amount of capital which would soon be eroded by the need to 'top up' her own fees; her children both have financial family commitments of their own and would not be able to assist."

I fear that that problem is reflected throughout many parts of the country.

We cannot dismiss such problems by saying that they must be dealt with by distant families or friends and that the Government have no responsibility. However, that would be the view of the Adam Smith Institute. I have had the benefit of reading the paper that we understand has been before Cabinet committee E. It shows the conflict in philosophy between the Government and the Opposition. The paper says:

"Government can, by providing very modest encouragement to the private sector, help it to grow with that rising demand. It can, by means of incentives to personal saving and personal provision, make it easier for most people to provide for their own care needs in retirement."

In other words, the choice is artificial, because without good planning and services there is no option.

If local authorities are to be underfunded and denied essential resources, where is the choice? According to the mentality displayed in the paper of the Adam Smith institute, we shall have to rely on people who can afford to pay for services. What will happen to the rest? Are they not entitled to advocacy and consultation on what happens to services? Of course they are, but the overwhelming evidence before the House confirms the view of the Audit Commission that community care is in disarray and Sir Roy Griffiths's view that it remains in chaos.

For that reason, Opposition Members have a responsibility to promote the needs, demands and requirements for services of millions of elderly, vulnerable and disabled people and their carers. We do not believe that the Government have placed on such matters the priority which the British people would rightly demand. That is why the Government offer a proper suspicion of any scrutiny from Europe. They know that, if Europe is looking for best practice from central Government, it will not find it in Great Britain. For that reason we believe that the Government have failed the nation. We shall reflect our repugnance and our despair at their policies by voting in the Lobby tonight.

6.50 pm

**Mr. Freeman:** The hon. Members for Monklands, West (Mr. Clarke) and for Oxford, East (Mr. Smith) asked again about our response to Griffiths. As I made plain at the outset of the debate, we shall make a statement before the summer recess on our response to it, and there will be a debate in Government time at the appropriate time thereafter.

The hon. Member for Monklands, West is tilting at windmills that he has created in his own mind when he refers to the Adam Smith Institute.

**Mr. George Foulkes** (Carrick, Cumnock and Doon Valley): Let us hear from the Secretary of State.

**Madam Deputy Speaker (Miss Betty Boothroyd):** Order. The Minister is at the Dispatch Box, and he must be heard.

**Mr. Freeman:** We are carefully considering all the evidence and the results of our review of Griffiths. We shall make our announcement before the summer recess.

**Mr. Andrew Smith** rose——

**Mr. Freeman:** I am about to answer the hon. Gentleman's point, if he will listen to me.

The hon. Member of Oxford, East asked me about the cost of upgrading local authority residential care homes to home life standard. Since 1978 local authority personal social services capital outturn expenditure has gone up by 22 per cent. in real terms under this Government. It was cut by two thirds by the previous Labour Administration.

My hon. Friend the Member for Macclesfield (Mr. Winterton) made a thoughtful, wide-ranging speech in which he raised a number of points about mental illness with which I shall try to deal. There is no moratorium on the closure of hospitals for those suffering from mental illness or a mental handicap, but no hospital will close until or unless there are adequate facilities in the community. I hope that I made that clear earlier.

My hon. Friend talked about the need for long-stay care and asylum care. My hon. Friend is right that there is a need for long-term facilities for those suffering from mental illness or a mental handicap. Certainly existing buildings can and should be re-used. At the beginning of this debate, I said that we were well aware that such institutions should not be isolated or too large, but should be part of the community. I accept that some of the institutions that are being run down currently are physically in the community and I am sure that some of those facilities can be re-used.

My hon. Friend also asked about discharged patients in prisons. Part of the problem is that the courts do not in all cases use their present powers to send potential prisoners to hospital for mental illness care. We would encourage the courts so to do. It is also important that consultants should visit prisoners and especially those on remand awaiting trial as promptly as possible. We are in close liaison with the Home Office to ensure that that happens. My hon. Friend also asked about the inquiry undertaken by Professor Kathleen Jones and I shall respond to that shortly.

My hon. Friend, in common with several other hon. Members, also spoke about those living under the arches at Waterloo. I have also visited those who are living in cardboard homes, not only under the arches of Waterloo but elsewhere. Those poor unfortunate people and their existence are a blot on society, but I must tell the House that those people have access to medical care; general practitioners visit those people. One cannot simply shovel all those who are living rough into institutions against their will.

**Mr. Battle** *rose——*

**Mr. Freeman:** No, I shall not give way.

My hon. Friend the Member for Macclesfield also asked me about visiting Parkside hospital. I assure my hon. Friend that I shall visit that hospital with him and I plan to do so as quickly as possible—in September, I hope.

The hon. Member for Southport (Mr. Fearn) properly reminded us about the importance of the voluntary sector. He was also right to emphasise the importance of long-term funding for voluntary organisations. It can be counter-productive for those organising voluntary societies to spend too much of their time chasing for money, whether it comes from the public purse or from other sources. It is important that those societies should be given some form of funding security, perhaps over three to five years. The Department of Health is carefully reviewing how it provides assistance through statutory means—we provide about £15 million a year. I am sympathetic to the hon. Gentleman's suggestion of extending the guarantee of funding, so long as that does not hamper our ability to provide new finance to new organisations when submissions are made.

My hon. Friend the Member for Norfolk, South-West (Mrs. Shephard), with all her experience in such matters, made a number of relevant points. She was right to talk about the multiplicity of ways in which to make community care work. There are a multiplicity of facilities, professions and authorities that provide such care, which represents a partnership between the NHS, the local authorities, the private sector and voluntary organisations. My hon. Friend asked about the evaluation of the pilot projects on care in the community. The university of Kent is evaluating the 28 pilot projects and the results should be available at the end of the year. The interim results suggest that the initiative has been successful. I will write to my

hon. Friend—if I forget, I am sure that I shall be prodded —at the end of the year, and I shall send her a copy of the final report.

My hon. Friend also spoke about money being locked up in mental illness and mental handicap hospital sites. My hon. Friend is absolutely right that we need the necessary facilities now, in advance of those hospitals' closure. I repeat that they shall be closed only when there are adequate facilities in the community. We are looking at a number of imaginative ways in which existing capital and revenue can be released. When we respond to Griffiths shortly, I hope that my hon. Friend will be satisfied that we are pursuing a number of initiatives in that connection.

The hon. Member for Wakefield (Mr. Hinchliffe), in common with me, drew attention to the Public Accounts Committee report. He rightly reminded us that some 23 per cent. of those in residential care wanted to be at home. I believe that that is relevant; I would not necessarily agree with the percentage quoted by the hon. Gentleman, but the thrust of his remarks was correct. Our review of the Griffiths report has meant that we have carefully considered how resources should be devoted to help the elderly frail stay in their own homes.

My hon. Friend the Member for Bolton, North-East (Mr. Thurnham) again stressed the crucial role of the voluntary sector. Since 1978, we have increased funding to the voluntary sector by 130 per cent. in real terms. I share my hon. Friend's views about the importance of that sector. My hon. Friend also spoke about adoption, and I draw his attention and that of the House to the family placement scheme for the mentally ill. Under that scheme, mentally ill people are placed with families, outside institutions, and adequate financial resources are made available either from the social services as appropriate or from the Health Service. That scheme is in its infancy, but it is working well and I commend it to the House.

My hon. Friend also spoke about the services provided for those who are mentally handicapped or who display challenging behaviour. My hon. Friend may not know that, this week, we published a new report, the short title of which is "Needs and Responses". I hope that he will find it helpful. I also hope that local authorities and NHS district authorities will find it helpful in outlining the best practice to deal with those with challenging behaviour.

The hon. Member for Halifax (Mrs. Mahon) spoke of the resources available for local authorities and local authority homes. I must correct a statement that I made earlier about the increase in the resources available to the personal social services sector. I understated that expenditure increase, which represents 25 per cent. in real terms between 1980-88. The numbers of those who have been helped by nursing care during that time is up by 14 per cent. The number of day centres has increased by 16 per cent., the number of home helps by 28 per cent. and the number of meals on wheels by 11 per cent. The hon. Lady also asked me about consultants going round wards with lists of private accommodation. We have made it clear several times that elderly people should not be moved to private homes against their will if it means that they have to take responsibility for the fees.

My hon. Friend the Member for Stockport (Mr. Favell) talked about sheltered accommodation, which is extremely important, and I commend local authorities that have concentrated on the provision of sheltered accommodation for elderly people. It provides dignity and security in old age. He also suggested that the general practitioner

[*Mr. Freeman*]

should have a greater role in assessing care for the elderly. I am glad that he supports the new contracts that my right hon. and learned Friend the Secretary of State negotiated with the General Medical Services Committee. Under the new contract, every doctor is encouraged—indeed urged —to visit every elderly person in the practice each year, and higher capitation fees are paid for those over 75. We are ensuring that general practitioners care especially for the very elderly.

My hon. Friend the Member for Hendon, South (Mr. Marshall) talked about schizophrenics in the community. It is important to keep track of those discharged from hospital, or those who never reached hospital in the first place, who are suffering from schizophrenia. The Royal College of Psychiatrists is introducing an initiative on that, which I mentioned at the beginning of the debate. I hope that we shall make a further statement on that in due course.

The Labour party has talked tonight about the need for extra resources for care in the community, yet if one studies its proposals for the reform of the NHS and for care in the community, one sees at least three that are counter-productive for resources. The Labour party has said that it is utterly opposed to private practice in the Health Service. That will mean £60 million less, because of the loss of private beds. The Labour party has said that it will end compulsory tendering, which will mean the loss of £100 million a year. It has said that it will put local councillors and union representatives on health authorities. Nothing could be more calculated to make the management of resources in the Health Service more inefficient.

This has been a constructive debate on a vital matter. As Conservatives, we care deeply about care in the community for the mentally ill, the mentally handicapped and the elderly. The Government have increased resources over the past 10 years. We are in partnership with local government, the private sector and the voluntary sector. We will bring forward our proposals shortly. I invite the House to support the amendment in the name of my right hon. Friend the Prime Minister.

*Question put,* That the original words stand part of the Question:—

*The House divided:* Ayes 197, Noes 281.

**Division No. 260]**                                    **[7.02 pm**

### AYES

Abbott, Ms Diane
Adams, Allen *(Paisley N)*
Allen, Graham
Alton, David
Anderson, Donald
Archer, Rt Hon Peter
Armstrong, Hilary
Ashdown, Rt Hon Paddy
Banks, Tony *(Newham NW)*
Barnes, Harry *(Derbyshire NE)*
Barnes, Mrs Rosie *(Greenwich)*
Barron, Kevin
Battle, John
Beckett, Margaret
Bennett, A. F. *(D'nt'n & R'dish)*
Bermingham, Gerald
Bidwell, Sydney
Blair, Tony
Blunkett, David
Boateng, Paul
Bradley, Keith
Brown, Gordon *(D'mline E)*
Brown, Nicholas *(Newcastle E)*
Brown, Ron *(Edinburgh Leith)*
Buckley, George J.
Caborn, Richard
Callaghan, Jim
Campbell, Menzies *(Fife NE)*
Campbell-Savours, D. N.
Canavan, Dennis
Carlile, Alex *(Mont'g)*
Cartwright, John
Clarke, Tom *(Monklands W)*
Clay, Bob
Clwyd, Mrs Ann
Cohen, Harry
Coleman, Donald
Cook, Robin *(Livingston)*
Corbett, Robin
Corbyn, Jeremy
Cousins, Jim
Cox, Tom
Crowther, Stan
Cryer, Bob
Cummings, John
Cunliffe, Lawrence
Cunningham, Dr John
Darling, Alistair
Davies, Rt Hon Denzil *(Llanelli)*
Davies, Ron *(Caerphilly)*
Dixon, Don
Dobson, Frank
Doran, Frank
Douglas, Dick
Duffy, A. E. P.
Dunnachie, Jimmy
Dunwoody, Hon Mrs Gwyneth
Eadie, Alexander
Eastham, Ken
Evans, John *(St Helens N)*
Ewing, Harry *(Falkirk E)*
Fatchett, Derek
Fearn, Ronald
Field, Frank *(Birkenhead)*
Fisher, Mark
Flynn, Paul
Foot, Rt Hon Michael
Foster, Derek
Foulkes, George
Fraser, John
Fyfe, Maria
Garrett, John *(Norwich South)*
Garrett, Ted *(Wallsend)*
George, Bruce
Gilbert, Rt Hon Dr John
Gordon, Mildred
Gould, Bryan
Graham, Thomas
Grant, Bernie *(Tottenham)*
Griffiths, Win *(Bridgend)*
Grocott, Bruce
Hardy, Peter
Harman, Ms Harriet
Hattersley, Rt Hon Roy
Haynes, Frank
Healey, Rt Hon Denis
Heffer, Eric S.
Henderson, Doug
Hinchliffe, David
Hoey, Ms Kate *(Vauxhall)*
Hogg, N. *(C'nauld & Kilsyth)*
Home Robertson, John
Hood, Jimmy
Howarth, George *(Knowsley N)*
Howell, Rt Hon D. *(S'heath)*
Howells, Dr. Kim *(Pontypridd)*
Hughes, John *(Coventry NE)*
Hughes, Robert *(Aberdeen N)*
Hughes, Roy *(Newport E)*
Hughes, Simon *(Southwark)*
Illsley, Eric
Ingram, Adam
Janner, Greville
Jones, Barry *(Alyn & Deeside)*
Jones, Ieuan *(Ynys Môn)*
Jones, Martyn *(Clwyd S W)*
Kaufman, Rt Hon Gerald
Kinnock, Rt Hon Neil
Kirkwood, Archy
Lambie, David
Lamond, James
Leadbitter, Ted
Leighton, Ron
Lestor, Joan *(Eccles)*
Litherland, Robert
Lloyd, Tony *(Stretford)*
Lofthouse, Geoffrey
Loyden, Eddie
McAvoy, Thomas
Macdonald, Calum A.
McFall, John
McKay, Allen *(Barnsley West)*
McKelvey, William
McLeish, Henry
Maclennan, Robert
McWilliam, John
Madden, Max
Mahon, Mrs Alice
Marshall, David *(Shettleston)*
Marshall, Jim *(Leicester S)*
Martin, Michael J. *(Springburn)*
Martlew, Eric
Meacher, Michael
Meale, Alan
Michael, Alun
Michie, Bill *(Sheffield Heeley)*
Mitchell, Austin *(G't Grimsby)*
Moonie, Dr Lewis
Morgan, Rhodri
Morley, Elliott
Morris, Rt Hon A. *(W'shawe)*
Morris, Rt Hon J. *(Aberavon)*
Mowlam, Marjorie
Mullin, Chris
Murphy, Paul
Oakes, Rt Hon Gordon
O'Brien, William
O'Neill, Martin
Orme, Rt Hon Stanley
Patchett, Terry
Pendry, Tom
Pike, Peter L.
Powell, Ray *(Ogmore)*
Prescott, John
Primarolo, Dawn
Quin, Ms Joyce
Randall, Stuart
Redmond, Martin
Rees, Rt Hon Merlyn
Reid, Dr John
Richardson, Jo
Robertson, George
Robinson, Geoffrey
Rogers, Allan
Ross, Ernie *(Dundee W)*
Rowlands, Ted
Ruddock, Joan
Sedgemore, Brian
Sheerman, Barry
Sheldon, Rt Hon Robert
Shore, Rt Hon Peter
Skinner, Dennis
Smith, Andrew *(Oxford E)*
Smith, C. *(Isl'ton & F'bury)*
Smith, Rt Hon J. *(Monk'ds E)*
Smith, J. P. *(Vale of Glam)*
Spearing, Nigel
Steel, Rt Hon David
Steinberg, Gerry
Stott, Roger
Strang, Gavin
Straw, Jack
Taylor, Matthew *(Truro)*
Thompson, Jack *(Wansbeck)*
Turner, Dennis
Vaz, Keith
Wall, Pat
Wareing, Robert N.
Watson, Mike *(Glasgow, C)*
Welsh, Michael *(Doncaster N)*
Williams, Rt Hon Alan
Williams, Alan W. *(Carm'then)*
Wilson, Brian
Winnick, David

Wise, Mrs Audrey
Worthington, Tony
Young, David *(Bolton SE)*

Tellers for the Ayes:
   Mr. Nigel Griffiths and
   Mr. Frank Cook.

## NOES

Adley, Robert
Aitken, Jonathan
Alison, Rt Hon Michael
Allason, Rupert
Amess, David
Amos, Alan
Arbuthnot, James
Arnold, Jacques *(Gravesham)*
Arnold, Tom *(Hazel Grove)*
Ashby, David
Aspinwall, Jack
Atkins, Robert
Baker, Rt Hon K. *(Mole Valley)*
Baker, Nicholas *(Dorset N)*
Baldry, Tony
Banks, Robert *(Harrogate)*
Batiste, Spencer
Beaumont-Dark, Anthony
Bendall, Vivian
Bennett, Nicholas *(Pembroke)*
Benyon, W.
Biffen, Rt Hon John
Blackburn, Dr John G.
Bonsor, Sir Nicholas
Boscawen, Hon Robert
Boswell, Tim
Bottomley, Peter
Bottomley, Mrs Virginia
Bowden, A *(Brighton K'pto'n)*
Bowden, Gerald *(Dulwich)*
Bowis, John
Boyson, Rt Hon Dr Sir Rhodes
Braine, Rt Hon Sir Bernard
Brandon-Bravo, Martin
Brazier, Julian
Brooke, Rt Hon Peter
Brown, Michael *(Brigg & Cl't's)*
Browne, John *(Winchester)*
Bruce, Ian *(Dorset South)*
Buchanan-Smith, Rt Hon Alick
Budgen, Nicholas
Burns, Simon
Butcher, John
Butler, Chris
Butterfill, John
Carlisle, John, *(Luton N)*
Carlisle, Kenneth *(Lincoln)*
Carrington, Matthew
Cash, William
Channon, Rt Hon Paul
Chapman, Sydney
Chope, Christopher
Churchill, Mr
Clark, Hon Alan *(Plym'th S'n)*
Clark, Dr Michael *(Rochford)*
Clark, Sir W. *(Croydon S)*
Clarke, Rt Hon K. *(Rushcliffe)*
Colvin, Michael
Conway, Derek
Coombs, Anthony *(Wyre F'rest)*
Coombs, Simon *(Swindon)*
Cope, Rt Hon John
Couchman, James
Cran, James
Critchley, Julian
Currie, Mrs Edwina
Curry, David
Davies, Q. *(Stamf'd & Spald'g)*
Davis, David *(Boothferry)*
Day, Stephen
Devlin, Tim
Dicks, Terry
Dorrell, Stephen
Douglas-Hamilton, Lord James

Dover, Den
Dunn, Bob
Durant, Tony
Dykes, Hugh
Eggar, Tim
Emery, Sir Peter
Evennett, David
Fallon, Michael
Favell, Tony
Fenner, Dame Peggy
Field, Barry *(Isle of Wight)*
Finsberg, Sir Geoffrey
Fishburn, John Dudley
Fookes, Dame Janet
Forman, Nigel
Forth, Eric
Fowler, Rt Hon Norman
Fox, Sir Marcus
Franks, Cecil
Freeman, Roger
French, Douglas
Fry, Peter
Gale, Roger
Gardiner, George
Garel-Jones, Tristan
Gill, Christopher
Gilmour, Rt Hon Sir Ian
Glyn, Dr Alan
Goodhart, Sir Philip
Goodlad, Alastair
Goodson-Wickes, Dr Charles
Gorman, Mrs Teresa
Gow, Ian
Grant, Sir Anthony *(CambsSW)*
Greenway, Harry *(Ealing N)*
Greenway, John *(Ryedale)*
Gregory, Conal
Griffiths, Peter *(Portsmouth N)*
Ground, Patrick
Grylls, Michael
Gummer, Rt Hon John Selwyn
Hague, William
Hamilton, Hon Archie *(Epsom)*
Hamilton, Neil *(Tatton)*
Hanley, Jeremy
Hannam, John
Hargreaves, A. *(B'ham H'll Gr')*
Hargreaves, Ken *(Hyndburn)*
Harris, David
Hayes, Jerry
Hayhoe, Rt Hon Sir Barney
Hayward, Robert
Heathcoat-Amory, David
Hicks, Mrs Maureen *(Wolv' NE)*
Hicks, Robert *(Cornwall SE)*
Hind, Kenneth
Hogg, Hon Douglas *(Gr'th'm)*
Holt, Richard
Hordern, Sir Peter
Howarth, Alan *(Strat'd-on-A)*
Howarth, G. *(Cannock & B'wd)*
Howell, Rt Hon David *(G'dford)*
Howell, Ralph *(North Norfolk)*
Hughes, Robert G. *(Harrow W)*
Hunt, Sir John *(Ravensbourne)*
Hurd, Rt Hon Douglas
Irvine, Michael
Irving, Charles
Jack, Michael
Jackson, Robert
Janman, Tim
Jessel, Toby
Johnson Smith, Sir Geoffrey
Jones, Gwilym *(Cardiff N)*

Jones, Robert B *(Herts W)*
Jopling, Rt Hon Michael
Kellett-Bowman, Dame Elaine
Key, Robert
King, Roger *(B'ham N'thfield)*
Knight, Greg *(Derby North)*
Knight, Dame Jill *(Edgbaston)*
Lawson, Rt Hon Nigel
Lennox-Boyd, Hon Mark
Lightbown, David
Lloyd, Sir Ian *(Havant)*
Lloyd, Peter *(Fareham)*
Lord, Michael
McCrindle, Robert
McNair-Wilson, Sir Michael
Marshall, John *(Hendon S)*
Marshall, Michael *(Arundel)*
Martin, David *(Portsmouth S)*
Maude, Hon Francis
Maxwell-Hyslop, Robin
Miller, Sir Hal
Miscampbell, Norman
Mitchell, Andrew *(Gedling)*
Mitchell, Sir David
Moate, Roger
Monro, Sir Hector
Montgomery, Sir Fergus
Moore, Rt Hon John
Morrison, Sir Charles
Moss, Malcolm
Moynihan, Hon Colin
Mudd, David
Neale, Gerrard
Nelson, Anthony
Neubert, Michael
Newton, Rt Hon Tony
Nicholls, Patrick
Nicholson, David *(Taunton)*
Norris, Steve
Onslow, Rt Hon Cranley
Oppenheim, Phillip
Page, Richard
Paice, James
Parkinson, Rt Hon Cecil
Patnick, Irvine
Patten, John *(Oxford W)*
Pattie, Rt Hon Sir Geoffrey
Pawsey, James
Peacock, Mrs Elizabeth
Porter, Barry *(Wirral S)*
Porter, David *(Waveney)*
Portillo, Michael
Powell, William *(Corby)*
Price, Sir David
Raison, Rt Hon Timothy
Redwood, John
Renton, Tim
Rhodes James, Robert
Ridley, Rt Hon Nicholas
Ridsdale, Sir Julian
Roberts, Wyn *(Conwy)*
Roe, Mrs Marion
Rossi, Sir Hugh
Rost, Peter
Rowe, Andrew
Sackville, Hon Tom
Sainsbury, Hon Tim
Sayeed, Jonathan
Scott, Rt Hon Nicholas

Shaw, David *(Dover)*
Shaw, Sir Giles *(Pudsey)*
Shaw, Sir Michael *(Scarb')*
Shelton, Sir William
Shephard, Mrs G. *(Norfolk SW)*
Shepherd, Colin *(Hereford)*
Shepherd, Richard *(Aldridge)*
Sims, Roger
Skeet, Sir Trevor
Smith, Sir Dudley *(Warwick)*
Soames, Hon Nicholas
Speed, Keith
Spicer, Sir Jim *(Dorset W)*
Spicer, Michael *(S Worcs)*
Squire, Robin
Stanbrook, Ivor
Steen, Anthony
Stevens, Lewis
Stewart, Allan *(Eastwood)*
Stewart, Andy *(Sherwood)*
Stokes, Sir John
Stradling Thomas, Sir John
Sumberg, David
Summerson, Hugo
Tapsell, Sir Peter
Taylor, Ian *(Esher)*
Taylor, Teddy *(S'end E)*
Temple-Morris, Peter
Thompson, D. *(Calder Valley)*
Thompson, Patrick *(Norwich N)*
Thornton, Malcolm
Thurnham, Peter
Townend, John *(Bridlington)*
Townsend, Cyril D. *(B'heath)*
Tracey, Richard
Tredinnick, David
Trippier, David
Twinn, Dr Ian
Vaughan, Sir Gerard
Waddington, Rt Hon David
Wakeham, Rt Hon John
Waldegrave, Hon William
Walden, George
Walker, Bill *(T'side North)*
Waller, Gary
Walters, Sir Dennis
Ward, John
Wardle, Charles *(Bexhill)*
Warren, Kenneth
Watts, John
Wells, Bowen
Wheeler, John
Whitney, Ray
Widdecombe, Ann
Wiggin, Jerry
Wilkinson, John
Wilshire, David
Winterton, Mrs Ann
Winterton, Nicholas
Wolfson, Mark
Wood, Timothy
Yeo, Tim
Young, Sir George *(Acton)*
Younger, Rt Hon George

Tellers for the Noes:
   Mr. John M. Taylor and
   Mr. David Maclean.

*Question accordingly negatived.*

*Question,* That the proposed words be there added, *put forthwith pursuant to Standing Order No. 30 (Questions on amendments), and agreed to.*

Madam Deputy Speaker *forthwith declared the Main Question, as amended, to be agreed to.*

*Resolved,*

That this House commends the Government's record on the development and funding of community services for all people in need of care; reaffirms its support for the policy of community care; believes that it will be complemented and strengthened by the proposals contained in the Government's White Paper, Working for Patients; and looks forward to an announcement of the Government's conclusions on Sir Roy Griffiths' report, Community Care: Agenda for Action, in the near future.'

# Coal Industry

**Madam Deputy Speaker (Miss Betty Boothroyd):** I must tell the House that Mr. Speaker has selected the amendment in the name of the Prime Minister.

7.14 pm

**Mr. Tony Blair** (Sedgefield): I beg to move,

That this House believes that the future of a resource as important as coal should not be left to market forces; opposes reliance on imported coal to meet Britain's energy needs; and calls upon Her Majesty's Government to intervene in the negotiations between British Coal and the electricity supply industry in order to ensure the long-term contracts for production which are necessary for the coal industry to fulfil its duties to the country, the consumer, the environment and those that work in it.

We have debated the coal industry many times, but rarely in the context of such pressing and urgent developments. We are not talking this time about whether we should close so-called non-economic pits or save them in the interests of mining communities. This is not a debate about whether the coal industry can make itself efficient, because the industry has recorded a 35 per cent. reduction in costs in three and a half years, and such a record would be the envy of any private sector company. It is not a debate about productivity, as it is generally acknowledged that no other group of workers could rival the 75 per cent. increase in productivity that the miners have achieved in recent years. We have peeled away the outer layer of arguments about Britain's coal industry and we are down to the core.

The focus of our debate may be the coal industry but the issue concerns the whole future of the nation's energy needs. The question is whether a modern energy policy should be dictated by short-term market forces, as Conservatives believe, or whether—as the Labour party declares—it should be the product of industry and Government acting together to balance the long-term interests of the country against the vested interests of the market.

Whether in meeting the traditional concerns of the consumer or the fresh challenge of the environment, we say, without hesitation, that energy policy is too vital to our future, too critical in its effects on our quality of life and too fundamental in its strategic importance for industry and the consumer to be left to the vagaries of the market. The essential truth, which the Government seem incapable of recognising, is that what the marketplace wants is not necessarily what the country needs.

This is not an abstract argument. It arises today in an acute practical form. We know that British Coal is in the process of negotiating new contracts with National Power and PowerGen—the duopoly created by privatisation of the generation of electricity. At the moment, the two bodies take about 75 per cent. of British Coal's output and are thus pivotal to its survival.

In turn, National Power and PowerGen are negotiating contracts to supply power to area boards or distributors. That is supposed to happen under the new contract system that is central to the privatisation process, whereby each of the area boards negotiates for separate parts of the generating capacity. That was the original plan. With more than 70 different power stations and 12 area boards, the nightmarish complexity of the contractual arrangements —to be superimposed on the merit order system which, by common consent, has worked well for decades—is only now becoming apparent. When I visit power stations and ask about the new contract system I find that the response varies between despair and hysteria. So complex is the new computer system that it alone will add £60 million to consumers' bills.

As I said, that was the original plan. Yet the *Financial Weekly* of 22 June says:

"Government advisers on the privatisation of the electricity industry have proposed scrapping the horrendously complicated intra-industry billing and charging system planned for the sell-off. The advisers are said to have told ministers that the system won't work".

In other words, the negotiation for the carve-up of power station contracts, which was at the heart of the case for privatisation that the Secretary of State advanced, is in a complete mess. At least it is now easier to make sense of each day's press as it speculates on the future of the Cabinet in general and of the Secretary of State in particular. As the right hon. Gentleman's plans for privatisation come step-by-step closer to terminal chaos, so does his anxiety to flee his Department, or even to abolish it, become ever more frenzied.

We are now witnessing a rather undignified race between the reshuffle and the day of reckoning; between the right hon. Gentleman's future ambitions and his past mistakes. He has at least one unrivalled talent—he is always the first to abandon the sinking ship. Nothing in politics is closer to a gale warning than the sight of the right hon. Gentleman trying to climb on board one new Department after another. The Opposition have a very firm view of his prospects—a view which, I have no doubt, is endorsed by his Cabinet colleagues—that he should stay where he is and stick with what he started. If a critical element of his privatisation process is failing between National Power and PowerGen, the pressure will become all the greater to put the squeeze on short-term fuel costs to provide some fig leaf of justification for continuing with the privatisation proposals.

During the past few years British Coal has reduced the cost of coal supply to the electricity industry by some £650 million. That has not been passed on to the electricity consumer because the Secretary of State has been fattening up the industry's profit sheet to pave the way for privatisation. None the less, it has happened. The contracts between British Coal and the electricity industry amount to 75 million tonnes. We have heard reports that the electricity industry is now thinking of contracting for only 60 million tonnes, which would lose the country 15 million tonnes, 15,000 jobs and 15 pits.

When the matter was first raised a few weeks ago, the Under-Secretary gave one of his memorable interviews on the "Today" programme. He was asked seven times whether the reports were correct, and as each answer or non-answer became longer and more incoherent, we were reminded of what Lord Byron said about his mother-in-law:

"She has lost the art of communication but not, alas, the gift of speech."

If the Under-Secretary, who is charged with responsibility for the coal industry, does not know the state of the negotiations, we are entitled to ask who does. If it is true that the electricity industry wishes to import more coal or heavy fuel oil, and if that is brought into the southern ports, it will reduce the need for power sent south from the midlands power stations and therefore reduce the need for midlands coal. Conservative Members should reflect on that when they vote tonight, because a 15 million

tonne reduction in coal is not at the margin of energy policy: it is fundamental. It would mean a significant fundamental shift in energy supply.

Today we have prepared an analysis of what the international coal market might look like over the next few years. If we consider all the main centres used to import coal into Britain, it is difficult to understand how any sensible Energy Secretary could be justified in relying upon imported coal to meet the country's future energy needs. The latest "International Coal Report", published just a week ago said, for example, about Australia:

"Australian exporters are suffering acute shortage."

It said:

"The supply situation is so tight that the world's largest exporter of seaborne coal is about to become an importer."

We know that the new Australian pits to be opened during the next few years are intended to supply Pacific basin countries, and in particular Japan, which is constantly opening up new coal markets.

The home market in the United States is growing, and its new acid rain controls are estimated to put $2 to $5 a tonne on the price of its coal, so there is no succour for us there. What about Poland, Colombia or South Africa? Are we to make our energy needs dependent upon supplies from those countries? What about the great hope mentioned a few years ago by many Conservative Members, that to meet future energy needs we should look to coal produced by China? According to our figures, in the first quarter of this year China's coal exports declined by 11 per cent., and according to the most recent reports, China is now importing coal.

**Mr. Nicholas Bennett** (Pembroke): I have been listening with fascination to the hon. Gentleman's speech. He mentioned both oil and coal, but not nuclear power, which provides the second largest percentage of generated electricity. What representations did he receive from the National Union of Mineworkers and from sponsored Labour Members when they discovered that the new pro-nuclear policy of the Labour party was pushed through while they were out of the room?

**Mr. Blair:** In a debate about the price of fuel and how to reduce costs to the consumer, it is rather peculiar for an hon. Member to make a statement in favour of nuclear power. I am grateful that he has raised the matter, because, if the privatisation process has taught us anything, if it has brought us any benefit, it is that it has exploded once and for all the notion that we should go nuclear because it is cheaper.

Is the Secretary of State aware of, and has he studied, recent history which, for example, shows that in 1981 imported coal was 20 per cent. more expensive than indigenous coal because of industrial unrest in Poland? Does he know that every 20 cents change in the sterling-dollar exchange rate makes a £6 per tonne difference one way or the other? Does he know that the world market for steam coal is so small that, if an extra buyer goes into the market for as much as 15 million tonnes, that will, of necessity, drive up the price of imported coal?

If the Secretary of State thinks that that is all the imagination of the Labour party, he should study the recent report by James Capel's international mining department—hardly a body sympathetic to the Labour party—which said about the electricity supply industry in its analysis of the coal industry:

[*Mr. Blair*]

"A privatised ESI will aim to minimise fuel costs: imports, in the short term, will be the answer . . . In the long term, international prices will go up. The British coal industry could be competitive with world markets by 1990 and could be restricting imports to peripheral power stations by 1995. A free-for-all policy on imports would close many mines which could be competitive."

That is the risk that we take.

If National Power and PowerGen decide, for their own strategic reasons—to second-source coal, as has been reported; if they want imports as a matter of principle irrespective of price competitiveness; if they believe that to be in their commercial interests, surely it is the job of the Secretary of State to ask whether it is not in the interests of the public to secure supply and whether it is not in the interests of the balance of payments that we do not suffer losses as a result of imported coal. Should not those interests be weighed in the balance against those of the private sector?

We have sought in vain to discover the Government's exact energy policy on coal imports. The junior Minister said in another place a short time ago—and perhaps it is the belief of the Secretary of State:

"We believe that the purchase of coal, whether imported or indigenous, is a matter for the commercial judgment of individual customers."—[*Official Report, House of Lords*, 4 April 1989; Vol. 505, c. 1006.]

We are entitled to know the state of the negotiations between the industries, for both of which the Secretary of State is still absolutely responsible under his statutory duties. When we weigh the sacrifices of miners and mining communities, with almost one third fewer employed today than 10 years ago—many of my hon. Friends can bear testimony to the appalling levels of unemployment that still exist in the mining communities—we are at least entitled to know the Government's energy policy on coal imports. It is said that the strategic interests of this privatised duopoly may differ from those of the country, but why should we put those interests above the country's interests? Why should this be treated as if it were some private concern between the Coal Board and the privatised electricity industry, without involving the Government acting on behalf of the public interest?

It is not as if the Government are unable or unprepared to recognise strategic considerations when it suits them to do so. The Secretary of State has talked about coal meeting what he calls, fair competition. How do the proposals on nuclear power square with that proposition? Nuclear power will be ring-fenced from the market with 20 per cent. of all fuel being bought from what are primarily nuclear sources. It was said in the other place that the industry will be given a guarantee against future costs on decommissioning, reprocessing and disposing of nuclear waste if they arise from factors outside the industry's control.

If coal has greater duties imposed upon it in relation to the environment, they will not be subsidised by the taxpayer. The Government may say that the reason they are prepared to offer this unique public guarantee to a private sector company, which is what it will be, is because of the importance of nuclear power. But is coal any less important than nuclear energy? If the Government recognise the market's limitations and the wisdom of taking a long-term view of nuclear power, why do they insist that these matters are of no account with regard to

coal? If the test to be applied were whether this would provide fair competition, I can tell the Government that fair competition with the nuclear industry is all that the coal industry demands.

In order to understand why these policies have come about, we must ask: what is the Government's overriding priority? It is simply privatisation and nothing else. The Secretary of State has been told that nuclear power cannot be sold without these unprecedented public guarantees against commercial risk. We are to have private profit and public liability, and in this grotesque contradiction of everything which the Conservatives avowedly stand for, we can clearly see the simple fact that they have no principle of policy, no motive and no objective in view, save to sell the nation's assets as quickly as legislation will allow and as cheaply as they dare. The message is privatisation first, public interest last.

The long-term future of the coal industry, the pressing demands of environmental protection, which require not the maximising of profit, but its control in the public interest, are to be sacrificed to the idol, the mixture of ideology and vested interest. It is the Secretary of State's peculiar misfortune to be in charge of the largest privatisation in history, just when privatisation has gone out of fashion.

Today, there is a new political agenda which is not about selling off the nation's public services, but about improving them. It is not about the old game of extracting profit from captive consumers, but about new ways of ensuring that consumers, and the society in which they live, can control the profit makers in the interests of the people. It is because the Government are out of date and out of touch that we believe with increasing confidence that, at the next election, they will be out of office as well.

7.35 pm

**The Secretary of State for Energy (Mr. Cecil Parkinson):** I beg to move, to leave out from "House" to the end of the Question and add instead thereof:

'congratulates the management and workforce of British Coal on their achievements in increasing productivity and reducing costs; welcomes the Government's continuing financial support for the industry which is enabling it to move towards profitability and a viable future; recognises that the only secure long term future for the industry lies in becoming an efficient and competitive supplier of coal; rejects the proposition that British Coal can only sell if its customers are forced to buy, and, has confidence that British Coal, on the basis of its own performance and not of Government dictat, will become the supplier of choice to the privatised electricity industry.'

I very much welcome the opportunity to debate the coal industry, but I must say straight away that I am disappointed by the shallow terms of the Opposition's motion. I wish to start by breaking some bad news to the hon. Member for Sedgefield (Mr. Blair): the contracts negotiations are going extremely well. In spite of snippets which he may read in the *Financial Weekly,* I assure him that the new system will be in place and working by 1 October, and all the signs are that we are ahead in our arrangements, rather than behind.

**Mr. Blair** *rose——*

**Mr. Parkinson:** No, I shall not give way at the moment.

The industry is going through a period of enormous change. Twenty-five years ago, coal had many customers. Most people heated their homes with coal, our trains and ships were largely fuelled by coal, which provided our gas and virtually all our electricity. Today the industry has only one major customer: the electricity supply industry, which is being privatised.

**Mr. John Cummings** (Easington) *rose*——

**Mr. Parkinson:** I shall give way in a moment, if the hon. Gentleman will allow me to make a start.

We have made it very clear that the privatised electricity industry, like any other business, will be free to choose its suppliers, and that includes its coal suppliers, but we have also made it clear that we want British Coal to win the bulk of the business and we believe that, on the basis of its own performance, it can. These are not just empty words. It is a sign of our confidence in coal's future that we have committed ourselves to the privatisation of the coal industry after the next election. That is not a commitment which we would make unless we believed that we were going to have something large, successful and worthwhile to sell. We will have a large, successful and worthwhile coal industry after the privatisation of the electricity industry, and after the next election.

Our confidence is firmly based on the industry's performance since the strike. In the year before the strike British Coal produced 105 million tonnes of coal at a productivity of 2·43 tonnes per man shift. Last year, 1988-89, British Coal produced 103 million tonnes at a productivity of 4·14 tonnes. Therefore, output fell by less than 2 per cent. over this five-year period, while productivity rose by over 70 per cent., and productivity is continuing to rise. So far this year it has been running at levels over 9 per cent., above the same period last year. At the end of last month British Coal achieved a new productivity record of 4·63 tonnes—that is nearly 12 per cent., up on the average for last year.

**Mr. Dennis Skinner** (Bolsover) *rose*——

**Mr. Parkinson:** I shall give way in a moment.

I pay full tribute to Sir Robert Haslam and his team for what has, by any standards, been a superb performance over the last few years.

**Mr. Blair** *rose*——

**Mr. Parkinson:** I shall give way in a moment.

I believe that it also reflects the Government's record of unwavering support for the industry, not just since the strike but before as well. Over the 10 years since 1979, we have put over £6·5 billion of capital investment into the industry. The investment in low-cost capacity and in modern mining equipment has been a crucial factor in what the industry has achieved. This Conservative Government have provided the taxpayers' money to fund that huge investment.

**Mr. Blair:** Perhaps I could ask the Secretary of State a specific question. Are these contracts which are presently being negotiated, and which he says are going so well, for the full 75 million tonnes at present taken at British Coal?

**Mr. Parkinson:** The contract arrangements of which I spoke involved the contracts between the generators and the distributors which, as the hon. Gentleman said, lead on to the coal contracts—*[Interruption.]* The centre of my speech deals with why I believe the hon. Gentleman has a wrong-minded approach.

It is not just the capital investment itself, but the financing of the industry to which I should like to draw

hon. Members' attention. We hear a great deal from the Opposition about the industry's financial burdens, but if they took the trouble to look at the figures for themselves they would see that British Coal's debt has actually fallen over the last five years from £4·2 billion to under £4 billion. As the House knows, I shall be coming forward in due course with proposals for restructuring the industry's capital, but I must point out that the massive investments we have made have been financed very largely at no cost to the industry, by grant which carries no interest.

Altogether, since 1979 we have injected nearly £10 billion of grant finance. Going back even further and taking into account previous grants and debt write-offs, our coal industry has received almost £20 billion at current prices since nationalisation, all of which has been written off and none of which bears a penny of interest.

**Mr. Skinner:** If, since nationalisation, the industry had received as much pro rata as the farmers have received we would be selling coal all around the world.

The Secretary of State referred to the massive productivity increases that the miners have achieved during the past few years. If that is correct—and it is—will he lend his weight to the NUM resolution that will be passed next week, which will state that NUM members want to recoup some of that massive productivity increase in the form of a substantial increase in wages of at least double digits—I hope as much as the 26 per cent. that the top directors got last year?

**Mr. Parkinson:** The hon. Gentleman consistently speaks up for and cares about the industry, but one of the problems is that he advocates the very policies that would destroy it.

I should like to repeat the last figures that I gave. The taxpayer has provided this industry with more than £20 billion of grant and loans, every penny of which has been written off as loss and not a penny of which bears interest.

Apart from deficit grant we have also provided restructuring grant support. Since the strike the number of men on colliery books has fallen from 170,000 to about 75,000 today. The House will note with satisfaction British Coal's achievement of being able to offer alternative jobs to all who wish to remain in the industry, even in coalfields such as those of Scotland, in which I recognise that the contraction has been especially severe.

No other industry has received such support, but for those who want to leave the industry the grants that we have provided have allowed British Coal to offer redundancy terms that are second to none. We have also made available £60 million of funding for British Coal Enterprise, thereby enabling the creation of more than 40,000 new job opportunities in Britain's coalfields. This is an impressive record by any standards. Our support for the industry has been consistent, generous and effective, and I bitterly resent snide remarks from the Opposition to the effect that the Government are somehow hostile to the coal industry. The facts give the lie to that assertion.

**Sir Trevor Skeet** (Bedfordshire, North): My right hon. Friend's figures are impressive—he mentioned a £20 billion write-off since nationalisation. How much additional assistance has been granted to the industry in the form of social credits?

**Mr. Parkinson:** As I have said, the £20 billion includes all grants under all headings, plus the capital injected into the industry by the taxpayer and subsequently written off as lost.

I turn now to British Coal's relationship with the privatised generators. As I said earlier, there is no tripartite agreement between the Government, the generators and British Coal to reduce coal purchases by 15 million tonnes or by any other figure. The generators and British Coal are about to embark on the final stage of their negotiations, and those negotiations will settle the level of future purchases. I must make it clear that the Government will not force customers into long-term contracts for British coal in order to provide artificial support for the industry. I am confident that if British Coal continues to restructure its operations, to cut costs and to introduce new and more flexible working practices, the generators will choose to retain British Coal as their major supplier. They are hard-headed business men and they know the dangers to their business of being over-reliant on foreign suppliers, just as they have learnt from hard experience, four times in the past 20 years, the dangers of total dependence on a single United Kingdom supplier.

I listened to the sudden discovery by the hon. Member for Sedgefield that coal prices in world markets could go up, that Australia is quite a long way from the United Kingdom and that China is not planning to be a major supplier. I am glad the hon. Gentleman is finally catching on; these things have been known to me and to other members of the industry for years and they will form part of the considerations which will affect the attitudes of the generators as they come to place their business. The idea that the hon. Gentleman and his juvenile team of researchers have just stumbled on an amazing truth shows how naive and ill-informed he has been to date——

**Mr. Blair:** I find it difficult to see whether that amounts to a confession or a denial of our principal charge. I shall put the question to the right hon. Gentleman again. I do not doubt that the electricity suppliers are looking at this matter from their commercial viewpoint. I have asked the right hon. Gentleman a specific factual question. He is the Secretary of State in charge of both industries. Have they or have they not been talking about a contract for the entire 75 million tonnes or for a lesser amount of 60 million tonnes?

**Mr. Parkinson:** The hon. Gentleman is trying to get me to issue some form of instruction to the negotiators. The two sides are in negotiation, seeking to arrive at an agreement. The generators do not want to be over-dependent on a single United Kingdom supplier— they have been bitten by that bug four times in the past 20 years. They also know that there is an enormous advantage in having a secure, reliable, home-based supplier, and that being over-dependent, or dependent to any major extent, on imports can be dangerous. They do not need the hon. Gentleman to remind them of that. I trust both sides to negotiate sensibly and to come to a sensible arrangement.

All sorts of figures have been bandied about in the past. The only ones that matter are those which emerge from the final negotiations which are about to get under way——

**Mr. Blair:** Let us get this straight. If the privatised electricity industry decides that it wants to second-source its supply—to look to imports for a substantial, not the main, chunk of its coal supply—are we to take it that the right hon. Gentleman will not stand in the industry's way? If it wants to make an agreement for 60 million tonnes, 60 million tonnes it will be?

**Mr. Parkinson:** Once again, the hon. Gentleman is trying to get me to predetermine the negotiations. I have already made it clear that we have put the industry in a position to protect itself. We expect it, on the basis of its new competitiveness, to land the lion's share of the business, but I am not prepared to put a figure on what it will or will not achieve. It must negotiate——

**Mr. Dick Douglas** (Dunfermline, West): Will the right hon. Gentleman give way?

**Mr. Parkinson:** In a moment.

As I told the UDM annual conference earlier this month, I am sure that the generators are well aware of the reputation of particular pits and coalfields for good industrial relations and for reliability of supply. The UDM pits have and deserve that reputation; others have not, and do not.

The hon. Member for Sedgefield asked why British Coal, having obtained a core contract, should not be allowed a first option to sell additional coal at the lowest price quoted by its competitors. That is what the hon. Gentleman demanded the other day. He does not suggest in any way that British Coal can win this business. The hon. Gentleman wants me to give it permission to buy the business with taxpayers' money. Volume for volume's sake is a recipe for bankruptcy, not security. I am not prepared to intervene on such an option.

The Opposition motion refers to the duty that the coal industry owes to the environment and I agree with that. We have to recognise that even so-called "clean" coal-burning technologies have damaging environmental effects. We cannot wish away the environmental advantages of other fuels such as gas, but we can help to reduce the disadvantages of coal, and particularly of British Coal.

As many hon. Members will know, British coal is relatively high in sulphur—I believe the average figure is around $1.5$ per cent. but it ranges from less than $0.5$ per cent. in some Scottish coalfields to 3 per cent. or so in Yorkshire. To reduce sulphur emissions to more acceptable levels, generators have essentially two choices: they can either burn low-sulphur coal or they can install fluegas desulphurisation equipment.

I am able to confirm today that we have asked the privatised generators to continue to plan on the basis of installing 12,000 MW of FGD capacity during the 1990s. That represents a very large cost indeed—about £1.6 billion. The first of those installations at Drax should come on stream by 1993-94, and should provide a secure outlet for up to 10 million tonnes of indigenous coal, and should substantially eliminate the need for low sulphur imports.

**Mr. John Home Robertson** (East Lothian): The Secretary of State has acknowledged that Scottish coal has one of the lowest sulphur contents in the United Kingdom. Why has he stood back and allowed the last of the Lothian coalfields to be mothballed, in spite of the fact that we have more than 100 million tonnes of good quality and low-sulphur reserves in that coalfield?

**Mr. Parkinson:** I am glad that the hon. Gentleman has pointed out to the House that the capacity has been mothballed and can be opened up if it becomes economic. The plain fact is that the Scottish pits are far and away our most uneconomic. We are seeking to ensure that there continues to be a market for high-sulphur British coal. I should have thought that the hon. Gentleman— *[Interruption.]* If we were to revert to low-sulphur coal, we would have to import massive quantities from overseas. The fitting of Drax and other stations with FGD equipment will ensure that there is a substantial market for British Coal, which would otherwise have been at a major disadvantage.

We have also agreed that British Coal should pursue a joint venture with the private sector to construct a pithead power station in Nottinghamshire, using a modern and efficient boiler design, and we are encouraging the next stage of the Grimethorpe topping cycle experiment, which holds out the possibility of much higher efficiencies than in conventional boilers. All these developments will help British Coal to compete more effectively and fairly against imported coal in the power station markets of the 1990s.

The Government have shown in many ways their commitment to coal. By its own performance and with the taxpayers' support, British Coal has put itself in a position to win the major share of the electricity industry's coal business.

By contrast, the "new pragmatists" in the Opposition are as ready as ever to revert to type and to the failed policies of the past. When the young lion roared today, what we heard was exactly the same noise as the old lion of Chesterfield used to make—protect, subsidise, interfere, direct, ban competition. They claim to care about the environment, but they plan to make us almost totally dependent on the most polluting fuel. They claim to care about the workers, but they back the most reactionary union in Britain, the NUM, and reject one of the most progressive.

I invite the House to reject the Opposition's defensive and defeatist motion and to support the Government amendment.

7.54 pm

**Mr. John Cummings** (Easington): I am extremely grateful for the opportunity to address the House on an issue which is very near to my heart and the hearts of all my constituents. I speak as someone who has worked in the industry for 29 years. My father worked in the industry for 51 years, so between the two of us we have 80 years' service. I am a sixth generation coal miner. For six generations, the colliery in which I worked has supported not just my family, but the families of many thousands of hard-working people. After hearing the Secretary of State's remarks, I believe that the Government no longer have faith in the mining industry of Great Britain. Since 1985 we have had from British Coal false promises about the north-east area, followed by half promises, lies and deceit.

We have had closures, which became restructuring, which in turn became reorganisation and then rationalisation. All of them had the same result—the redundancies of a valued and precious work force, who require work and the dignity of being able to work. However, the Government and British Coal have denied them that dignity.

The Government and British Coal are not just selling short a very valued work force; they are selling short the British nation. The Secretary of State has sold short the nation's most precious assets—assets which the Japanese would give their eye teeth for and assets which could take this nation forward well into the next millenium. However, the Government are prepared to sell now for a quick buck and to hell with the future. I believe that that is a disgrace of national proportions.

There are now seven deep coal mines in the north-east. Capacity in those mines has been reduced, while there has been expansion in opencast mining in west Durham. The countryside has been raped and pillaged in a way that has never been seen in the north-east.

The Government are supporting the production of coal by means of slave labour in such countries as Colombia, South Africa and Poland in the eastern European bloc. There has been rape and pillage, too, of those nations. Such coal production is, however, supported by the British Government against the interests of miners in the north-east, who are producing coal economically and profitably and with greater productivity than ever before. That filthy Colombian coal—won on the backs of slave and child labour—is being imported into the ports of Sunderland, Middlesbrough and Hartlepool. That is a disgraceful affair, of which any proud Englishman would be ashamed.

I want to consider industrial relations in British Coal. I was a lodge secretary for 20 years at my colliery, and I sat on a consultative committee for close on 30 years. We engaged in consultation and conciliation. We knew the manager, the under-manager and the officials. We entered freely into conciliation week in and week out to improve safety and industrial relations. There was understanding and agreement between people who had a common love of the industry. What is happening now? The industry is managed by silhouettes from British Coal headquarters. They are the marionettes of the Secretary of State and his cronies in the Department of Energy.

The finest consultation and conciliation process within any industry in Great Britain has been subjected to the manipulation of the Secretary of State and people who have neither love nor understanding of the industry. For example, my forefathers and I worked at Murton colliery which is 150 years old this year. The lodge secretaries are very anxious about C seam—the old yard seam. They wrote to the area board asking for a meeting of the Murton Mining Federation. They received the reply, "What is the mining federation?" That federation has been in existence since 1890 and it has dealt with manager after manager from the days of the South Hetton Coal Company, through the managers and agents of the National Coal Board, to British Coal. However, British Coal had the impudence to ask, "What is the Murton Mining Federation?"

The Murton Mining Federation has existed for the benefit of the community, through the provision of colliery housing, swimming pools, welfare parks and welfare of the elderly. It has also existed for the benefit of management. Management has been able to discuss matters with all the unions from Murton colliery for nearly 100 years, but the gen boys at British Coal have had the impudence to come in and ask, "What is the Murton Mining Federation?"

In the north-east area of British Coal, as in other areas, we have undergone change. We have freely accepted mechanisation, and we accepted computerisation with enthusiasm. We did that freely, without agreements or seeking financial remuneration. We accepted those things

[*Mr. John Cummings*]

for the good and the benefit of the industry. Where has it got us? Spite and vindictiveness of a kind which we have never seen before—not even from the South Hetton Coal Company, the Landonderrys or other private enterprise —has been levied at us by the Government and the corporation. The Secretary of State has announced a sell-out of treacherous proportions today and that will be remembered by this and by future generations.

8.4 pm

**Mr. Andy Stewart** (Sherwood): Today's debate on the coal industry gives the House the opportunity to review the Government's commitment and to contemplate the future of Britain's major source of energy in the new green environment and privatised power generating industry. The British Coal industry exists only if there is a market for its product. The cost of coal in a free market determines whether it succeeds or loses out to other carbon fuels. We must remember that the consumption of coal is now only half what it was 50 years ago. The consequence has been pit closures under both Labour and Conservative Governments, although from what we hear from Opposition Members, one would think that closures happened only under a Conservative Government.

During the Labour Administrations between 1964-70 and 1974-79, a total of 295 collieries were closed, of which 32 were closed by the right hon. Member for Chesterfield (Mr. Benn) when he was Secretary of State for Energy.

When I became the Member for Sherwood in 1983, my constituency had 10 collieries employing 12,000 men and producing 7·5 million tonnes of coal. After losing Hucknall and Linby pits as their reserves ran out, and Newstead which joined the nearby Annesley complex, only Blidworth, which closed in March 1989, was closed because production was uneconomical under British Coal management.

With coal reserves at 30 million tonnes, many miners believed that with different management the tragedy at Blidworth could have been avoided. Many of the miners facing redundancy at Blidworth were convinced and prepared to put their money into forming a company to keep the pit open. However, at the time of the closure announcement, a British company carried out a feasibility study and was convinced that it could make Blidworth colliery a success. It offered to manage the pit from British Coal under the Coal Industry Act 1947, at no cost to British Coal or to the taxpayer. Sadly, that offer was rejected out of hand.

Today, there are six highly productive and efficient collieries in Sherwood which employ 6,000 men and produce 7 million tonnes of coal. That streamlining of the industry has take palce without the need for any compulsory redundancies. Nevertheless, I have always publicly urged miners who must face the choice of taking redundancy to stay with the coal industry unless they were satisfied that they had a marketable skill which was in demand locally. Those who have stayed have seen another year of improved earnings and conditions. It is ironic that those conditions which were skilfully negotiated by the Union of Democratic Mineworkers benefit all mine-workers throughout the industry.

I want to thank my right hon. Friends the Secretaries of State for Energy and for Employment on behalf of my retired miners who rightly took advantage of the enhanced redundant mineworkers payments scheme, for accepting the miners representation through Roy Lynk, the president of the UDM, and for meeting my hon. Friends the Members for Broxtowe (Mr. Lester), for Nottingham, South (Mr. Brandon-Bravo), Nottingham, East (Mr. Knowles), Newark (Mr. Alexander), Gedling (Mr. Mitchell) and myself, to put their case.

**Mr. William O'Brien** (Normanton): Will the hon. Gentleman give way?

**Mr. Stewart:** No, many hon. Members want to speak. I will give way later if I do not answer the hon. Gentleman's points.

The prompt response from my right hon. Friend the Secretary of State for Employment that he would change the unemployment benefit rules to meet those circum-stances was greatly appreciated. However, I was puzzled, because during that time we heard numerous allegations from Opposition Members of miners being harassed and intimidated by staff working in employment offices to sign up for work at restart interviews or their benefits would stop. Only last week, the hon. Member for Bolsover (Mr. Skinner) during Employment Question Time was still running the Labour party line of alleged harassment.

I contend that, for political gain, Labour Members sat on their hands, allowing rumour to escalate and thus causing unnecessary alarm before they did anything about it. I may be asked what proof I have of that. I need say only that complaints of that nature came from Labour Members. In my constituency, which the House knows has more miners than any other, 1,500 men used the redundant mineworkers payments scheme to retire permanently.

In the week after the Second Reading of the Employment Bill last January, I received two telephone calls and three letters drawing attention to a letter from the unemployment benefits office in Arnold concerning restart and benefits. One telephone call made by me to the employment deputy manager for the Nottingham area clarified the position, and my statement to the local press reassured my constituents that there was no need for alarm. I suggest that, when Opposition Members are confronted by a similar situation in future, instead of making mischief they should give their constituents the service that they deserve.

**Mr. O'Brien** *rose——*

**Mr. Stewart:** No, I shall not give way. I have too many important things left to say.

Overall, Nottinghamshire's super-miners clocked up an operating profit for British Coal in the financial year 1988-89 of £65 million, which represents half of British Coal's profits from deep mining—a record that no other coalfield area can match. British Coal's total operating profit of £500 million is the highest figure since the industry was nationalised in 1947. However, the downside to that achievement is that the industry carries an interest burden of £430 million, representing a charge of approximately £5 per tonne of coal sold. That highlights the need for restructuring British Coal's finances.

I ask my right hon. Friend urgently to consider giving British Coal the same preferential treatment as that afforded to British Steel in the early 1980s. Although

British Steel's profits are similar to those of British Coal, as a consequence of restructuring, its interest charges amount to only £17 million.

We hear a lot about the past in coal industry debates. Unfortunately, we cannot turn back the clock but should use the past as a guide to the future, in meeting the challenges that face the industry after the electricity industry is privatised in 1990. National Power and PowerGen—the two successor companies to the Central Electricity Generating Board—will require coal at a price that will provide the nation with its primary source of energy at a cost that will make our industrial goods more internationally competitive, and one that will not be considered a luxury.

Competition for annual contracts of 75 million tonnes must be fair, and British Coal must not be subjected during negotiations to pressure from the new companies, with the threat of cheap, subsidised imports. If allowed, that would exacerbate the nation's already stretched balance of payments. British Coal's ability to continue as the supplier of choice rather than of necessity is well demonstrated by its progress over the past four years. Productivity is up by more than 90 per cent., while costs are down 32 per cent.

**Mr. Terry Patchett** (Barnsley, East): The hon. Gentleman has spoken at great length about colliery closures and the necessity for them, and about the beautiful redundancy terms that were offered. Is it not the case that the hon. Gentleman was one of the Conservative Members who, during the 1984 strike, assured the Union of Democratic Mineworkers that it was no part of British Coal's programme to close pits? What changed his mind?

**Mr. Stewart:** I can tell the hon. Gentleman what changed my mind, and I thank him for asking the question that I deliberately prompted. *Hansard* of 4 December 1978 quotes the then Secretary of State for Energy, the right hon. Member for Chesterfield as stating:

"I have never found the NUM in any way unreasonable where closures are necessary because of exhaustion or because pits are out of line in economic terms."—[*Official Report*, 4 December 1978; Vol. 959, c. 1015-1016.]

I believe that that answers the hon. Gentleman's question.

Of paramount importance is a reduction in coal prices of 22 per cent. in real terms, representing a loss in sales realisations for British Coal of £900 million per year. Collieries continue to improve their performance. In Nottinghamshire, there is a big switch to retreat mining. This year, 52 miles of underground roadways will be completed. Leading the way are Thoresby and Rufford collieries, with record-breaking performances of 130 m per week. Bilsthorpe pit is about to begin a £10 million underground motorway 4,000 m long.

**Mr. O'Brien:** Will the hon. Gentleman give way now?

**Mr. Stewart:** It seems that every Opposition Member wants to intervene, but I am not giving way again. I have done so once, and that is enough.

A further £18 million will be spent on heavy duty coal face equipment in the coming year. Some of that machinery will be fitted with British Coal's new automatic steering systems, which reduce the amount of dirt mined by up to 40 per cent. and give better roof control, enabling productivity to increase by a further 30 per cent. Such improvements will make the industry highly competitive by 1992. However, before then, many collieries will be vulnerable to subsidised imports. It would be tragic to

threaten their progress for the very short-term gains to be made from importing coal. By 1995, any savings made by an all-out import policy in 1990 would have disappeared and the electricity supply industry will be paying millions of pounds more for imported coal than if it had bought British.

There is a risk that many deep mines that could compete with imported coal in 1995 will be closed by 1990 if the Government encourage an early free-for-all on imports. Perhaps my right hon. Friend will dispel rumours that British Coal can compete for only 60 million tonnes of the new companies' total requirements of about 75 million tonnes, even if it agrees to meet the last tranche of 15 million tonnes at world prices.

The Union of Democratic Mineworkers has always accepted fair and unfettered competition, but the threat posed to Nottinghamshire by imported coal is potentially catastrophic. Restructuring has already seen 15,000 men leave the industry. Recently, the UDM president proposed a five-year honeymoon period after electricity privatisation, and I hope that my right hon. Friend will seriously consider that suggestion. It is not a case of special pleading. As the Nottingham *Evening Post* commented, the UDM's attitude is the stuff of realism. The union is forward-looking, prepared to modernise agreements and to adopt working practices that relate to the reality of highly capitalised mining technology—without which the coal industry would be hopelessly ill prepared for the 1990s.

Decisions affecting the next decade will be governed by the environmental debate on the greenhouse effect. Misleadingly, that is being equated with the operation of coal-fired power stations. Although coal burning is responsible for 15 per cent. of the global greenhouse effect, coal-fired power generating contributes only 7 per cent.

**Mr. Cummings:** How does the hon. Gentleman know? Who says so?

**Mr. Stewart:** That is not the basis on which to base a switch to nuclear power, which was once seen as the panacea in providing cheaper electricity, but which is now accepted both by the Government and by the CEGB as costing about 40 per cent. more. To have any significant effect on emissions would require a worldwide nuclear programme of impracticable dimensions. Action in Britain alone, or action concentrated only on coal, would be ineffective. Annual consumption of coal in Britain is 115 million tonnes, from a worldwide total of more than 3 billion tonnes. The United Kingdom coal-fired power stations contribute less than 0·5 per cent. to the global greenhouse effect. Remedial action must be on an international scale. Already, all are agreed that increased efficiency in the use of energy would be an effective way in which to lessen the greenhouse effect.

Leading the way is British Coal's new system, called the topping cycle, which will allow new coal-fired stations to generate electricity at 45 per cent. efficiency rather than the 37 per cent. from standard stations now in use. It would be clean in terms of sulphur and nitrogen oxide, and would reduce electricity costs and carbon dioxide output. A miniature high-tech station based on the system is planned in my constituency—where else?—at Bilsthorpe colliery. It is the joint project of British Coal and the east midlands

[*Mr. Stewart*]

electricity board. The principal reason for the choice of site is the excellent industrial relations in the Nottinghamshire coalfield.

A unique feature of the project is that mineworkers will be offered shares at preferential prices. Their opinions were echoed by their president, who said, "It is a chance of a lifetime for the working miner to have a financial stake in his future, and we are very enthusiastic about the project and its prospects."

I share that optimism. The technological revolution has arrived. In a debate in 1984, I said:

"Every day we hear of the sunrise industries. The greatest of these is the coal industry. It will be here when the others have gone".—[*Official Report,* 7 June 1984; Vol. 61, c. 474.]

I have neither heard nor seen anything since then to change my statement. Come 1992 and the single European market, the British coal industry will be ready and able to supply the home market and the highly protected European markets, particularly those of France and Germany.

**Several Hon. Members** *rose——*

**Mr. Deputy Speaker (Mr. Harold Walker):** Unless speeches are brief, I am afraid that some hon. Members will be disappointed.

8.22 pm

**Mr. Geoffrey Lofthouse** (Pontefract and Castleford): I follow what appeared to be a brief written by the Democractic Union of Mineworkers and the Department of Energy——

**Mr. Martin Brandon-Bravo** (Nottingham, South): What is wrong with that?

**Mr. Lofthouse:** It depends on which side of the issue we stand.

This evening, however, we have listened to what amounted to nothing less than NUM-bashing from the Secretary of State. We have come to expect it from the hon. Member for Sherwood (Mr. Stewart), who always has a prepared brief—probably from the UDM, but we do not know. Personally bashing a major union, however, does the Secretary of State no credit. I should have thought that it would be wiser to leave that subject well alone.

As my hon. Friend the Member for Sedgefield (Mr. Blair) said, the debate is not about market forces; it is a continuation of the bashing of miners and the mining industry that began in 1984. As the Secretary of State knows, I have spent many hours over the years on the Select Committee on Energy, listening to many expert witnesses, including the right hon. Gentleman. At no time have I heard any evidence that the Government's policy was not deliberately to run down the mining industry purely for reasons of dogma and revenge.

The Secretary of State will recall that in his evidence to the Committee he said that the increased import of coal posed no fears, because the capacity of the ports could not cope with it: that was his defence when he was challenged. Of course, it was part of the plan to increase port capacity to enable more coal to come into the country. His permanent secretary does not really agree with the proposals: only a fortnight ago he told the Select Committee that there were no plans to interfere with the free market, and suggested that his Department was sitting on the sidelines. It is fairly obvious this evening, however, that the Secretary of State is prepared to accept a much lower percentage of fuel for the CEGB than is guaranteed by the agreement now in operation, which can mean only that there will be more imports.

Sir Peter Gregson—the permanent secretary to whom I have referred—told the Select Committee on the same occasion that the £311 million in the Department's estimate for the restructuring grant was equivalent to 15,000 miners' jobs in the current financial year. Given that the overspill from the previous year was 5,000 jobs, we are talking about the loss of 20,000 jobs. If Sir Peter Gregson is wrong, I invite the Secretary of State or the Minister to say so. If he is right, however, I remind the Secretary of State that the same Select Committee, in its 1987 report on the coal industry, said that never again must this or any other industry be run down so rapidly without consideration of the social consequences.

Those consequences have been pointed out in the House time and again, but the only reply that we have received from the Secretary of State and his hon. Friends is a reminder of the attractive redundancy terms enjoyed by miners. Not once have they been able to give an instance of measures to encourage alternative employment in the mining communities. In areas such as mine—the Wakefield area, which has lost 11,000 jobs since 1984—there is no evidence of that to this day.

I hope that the Secretary of State accepts the figures that I have given, and will tell us whether his Department, the Department of Employment and the Department of Trade and Industry are taking part in discussions to try to solve the problems of communities that have been devastated by the rundown of the coal industry.

**Mr. Parkinson:** Let me clear up that point. What Sir Peter Gregson said was that the total available provision was £311 million. We do not know how many redundancies there will be, because we are not in charge of the closure programme. Last year we under-provided and had to come back to the House for a supplementary estimate. This is not a prediction; it is a provision which may or may not be needed. If it is not needed, it will be carried forward into the next year.

**Mr. Lofthouse:** Sir Peter Gregson made it clear that the figure might also be an under-estimate. If that is the case, we are talking about more than 20,000 miners.

Hon Members have referred to attractive redundancy terms, and I do not deny that men over 50 received reasonable compensation in the form of lump sums and weekly payments, which some of them welcomed. But it is a different ball game now: the average age of miners is 34, and they have no weekly payments to cushion the blow. Young men have nowhere else to go. One of the schemes guaranteed that a further payment would be made if men took redundancy, based on so many years' service. The agreement expires in August, in the same financial year as about 20,000 job losses in the mining industry. Does the Secretary of State plan to extend the redundancy payments scheme for mineworkers, bearing in mind that a devastatingly large number of men will be made redundant? If he does not do so, the mining communities will suffer even greater hardship than they have experienced hitherto.

The Government's policy is deliberately to encourage coal imports. Lord Marshall has repeatedly told the Select Committee that he will shop in the cheapest market. He made no bones about it. If that happens, profitable pits will have to be closed. The miners have been congratulated on their wonderful achievements since the miners' strike, but 20,000 of the miners who have done such wonderful things will lose their jobs this year. That is on record. Only a fortnight ago Sir Peter Gregson told the Select Committee on Energy that 20,000 miners would lose their jobs this year.

I am convinced that the CEGB, or its successor, will not take the same amount of coal from British Coal as it has taken hitherto. There will be even more coal imports. It is economic lunacy to run down the coal industry and close profitable pits. In 1987 the Select Committee on Energy said that the industry would be down to 67,000 men by 1990. The then Secretary of State for Energy pooh-poohed that forecast. However, it is now forecast that the industry will be down to 50,000 men by the end of this financial year. When the industry is run down to the extent that it cannot meet demand, how much cheap coal will there then be? Kids in primary schools in my constituency know the answer to that question. When we cannot meet demand from our own resources, the price of coal will spiral. That will be the effect of the Government's policy.

I hope that the Secretary of State will note the comments of Sir Robert Haslam. In his evidence to the Select Committee, Sir Robert made it clear that he does not share all the views of the Secretary of State. I hope that the Secretary of State saw the press statement issued by British Coal on 14 June in which Sir Robert expressed his concern about the future of the coal industry and about the unfairness of the Government's policy regarding nuclear power. The Secretary of State's policy is to cut the aid that is given to British Coal, but at the same time he is introducing legislation that will featherbed the nuclear industry.

In his press statement Sir Robert Haslam

"expressed great surprise that nuclear power—with costs for producing electricity at least 40 per cent. more than coal—is now being justified as the 'environmentally friendly' fuel resource."

Sir Robert went on to say that the United States does not think that nuclear power is environmentally friendly because nuclear power stations are to be closed, partly for economic reasons but also because of the views of people in the United States. They have found that nuclear power stations are not the great economic success that they had hoped for; they do not result in the production of cheap fuel, the argument that is used against coal.

The Secretary of State took over from his predecessors the job that the Prime Minister began during the miners' strike—to destroy the miners, to get revenge on them and damn the consequences to the country's major source of energy.

8.36 pm

**Sir Geoffrey Finsberg** (Hampstead and Highgate): A notable feature of the debate is the total absence of Liberals, SDPs, nationalists—all those who claim to be interested in the environment. The last two speeches by Opposition Members to which I have listened were very similar to those that I heard when I entered the House some 20 years ago. They were genuine, from the heart and full of understanding. They reminded me of what I call the old mining group of the Labour party. They were in sharp contrast to the speech by the hon. Member for Sedgefield (Mr. Blair), which was full of entertainment value but very short of understanding.

I, too, heard the radio interview that my hon. Friend the Under-Secretary of State for Energy gave. I should have been very angry if he had said what the figures would be, because it is not his job to carry out the negotiations. As my right hon. Friend the Secretary of State made clear, negotiations are now taking place and we shall have to await the results. It is not for Ministers to interfere in negotiations of that kind.

I am probably the last remaining Conservative Member who has worked underground for more than two years in the pits, mainly as a back ripper. I remember my very happy association with the mining industry. For a couple of years I was on the national committee of the Bevin boy movement. I did my training in Nottinghamshire and I worked in Derbyshire. My one claim to fame is that in those days I worked at the same pit as Cliff Gladwin who is, of course, in "The Guinness Book of Records". I, probably, never shall be. Perhaps we could do with Cliff Gladwin in the England team today, if he was able to score runs now as he did in that particular match, with one leg bye off a certain part of his anatomy.

It cannot be right that the electricity industry, whether under nationalised or private control, should be forced to buy from any particular source. The industry has to provide a service to the consumer. It is the consumer who in the end decides whether he is satisfied. He is entitled to expect that those who supply him are buying in the best market in terms of both calorific and monetary value. I would place my reliance on the common sense of those who are carrying out the negotiations. I only wish that my right hon. Friend the Secretary of State could knock a few heads together to stop unnecessary legal fees being accumulated in a certain dispute between part of the coal industry and part of the electricity industry north of the border. That is a total waste of money and I only wish I could persuade my right hon. Friend—I have failed so far —to give a direction to stop that nonsense.

My second point may not command as much support as what I have said already. The Labour party seems to have learnt virtually nothing in 40 years. It is still blinkered by outdated ideas. I recall a speech on this subject. I had to do a lot of research to find it and I should quote from it briefly:

"The coal situation is one of the gravest and most complex in the whole of our affairs to-day and one which will have its repercussions on every sector of national life. With the formation of the National Coal Board, the middleman will be eliminated, but this will not mean cheaper coal".

How right that was.

"Lord Hyndley has already indicated that the price of coal will almost certainly rise."

The speaker opposed the formulated policy of the National Coal Board because, he said, it ignored technical improvement; it would not stop the fall in production or help our export trade. It had no recruiting policy, and would be one of the worst monopolies in the country. It would impair the freedom of the miner; there would be no impartiality in price fixing and no protection of the public.

That speech was made on 10 January 1947, and according to the press report it was given by a certain Mr. Geoffrey Finsberg. I stand by every word that I uttered 42

[*Sir Geoffrey Finsberg*]

years ago. I said then, as I say tonight, that in the end it is the consumer who matters and the National Coal Board grossly let down the consumer.

**Mr. Allen McKay** (Barnsley, West and Penistone): As one Bevin boy to another, does the hon. Gentleman agree that we would never have been Bevin boys had the system of market forces not ruined the coal industry to such an extent that it has to be privatised because it could not supply coal when it was wanted?

**Sir Geoffrey Finsberg:** I do not agree with the hon. Gentleman, who in circles outside the House I would call a friend. He omits the facts at the time. I shall not take a long time to answer his point because we have been asked for short speeches.

The industry could have found the capital to have re-equipped the industry without the taxpayer being called upon as a result of nationalisation.

I saw the flag of the NCB being raised to immense cheers from miners who thought that a new world was beginning. Sadly, that new world never came about because they were let down by those who ran the industry and those who ran the National Coal Board.

**Mr. Jack Thompson** (Wansbeck): Does the hon. Gentleman recognise that many of the people who took over the industry in 1947 were the same people who ran the industry before 1 January 1947?

**Sir Geoffrey Finsberg:** I agree with the hon. Gentleman. That was how most of the miners for whom I had and have immense admiration were duped. They thought that a new panacea was being created by the raising of that flag. They were duped by the Labour party which was then in government. The hon. Gentleman knows that that is true.

I believe that the sooner the coal industry is in private hands the better it will suit the miners who work in it and the customers who buy its products. If what my right hon. Friend the Secretary of State is doing to speed up the denationalisation of the electricity industry will help that, I give him not three cheers but four cheers.

8.45 pm

**Mr. Jimmy Hood** (Clydesdale): First, I should like to comment briefly on the speech by the hon. Member for Sherwood (Mr. Stewart). I shall not say too much about the parrot nature of his written speech in case I embarrass him, but Opposition Members well know who must have written it. The hon. Member for Sherwood told us quite a lot about Bilsthorpe. Bilsthorpe has a Labour parish council, a Labour district council, a Labour county council and, as of last week, a Labour MEP. The only link that is missing is a Labour Member of Parliament.

**Mr. Andy Stewart:** The hon. Member for Clydesdale (Mr. Hood), who was one of my constituents before he left for greener pastures, should see the letter which I received from the Bilsthorpe parish council in 1983. The nine Labour party councillors wrote congratulating me on winning the election to Westminster above the Labour candidate.

**Mr. Hood:** I wonder whether the hon. Gentleman received a letter from Blidworth parish council.

In the tenth year of Conservative government, known to many of us in the mining industry as the decade of shame, it is important to remember that we are discussing the mining industry ten years on. I listened with amazement to the Secretary of State tonight boasting about the wonderful job that the Government have done for the mining industry. If getting rid of 150,000 miners is doing a good job, that shows how much the Government care about the mining industry and the mining communities. Why did they run down the mining industry? Why are they so against miners, their families and their communities? Is it because coal stocks are declining? there has been no such decline in coal reserves. Is it because there is a drop in demand for coal? That is certainly not enough to justify running down the mining industry. Is it not a livid hatred of miners and their unions, particularly the National Union of Mineworkers?

The hon. Member for Sherwood told us that the UDM is such a responsible organisation. It is so responsible that it has negotiated the smallest percentage increase in basic rates in the history of mining unions in the past 20 years. That is how good a union it is. Let me give the hon. Member for Sherwood one piece of advice to help him in his good fortunes, or his misfortunes, in the next general election. If he honestly thinks that wrapping his arms around Roy Lynk will help him get re-elected, I can tell him that that is like wrapping his arms around the captain of the Titanic.

I wish to make a brief reference to the Under-Secretary of State who is on the Government Front Bench. I was a bit annoyed, to say the least, at some of his out-of-character and disgraceful comments earlier today in answer to my hon. Friend the Member for Bolsover (Mr. Skinner) about the sacked miners. We heard him display all the old hatred and expose the Government's attitude towards the miners once again. I wish to clear up a few matters. The Minister did not tell us about the thousands of miners who were charged with standing on picket lines, standing up in a village or sitting on a summer seat and who were taken to court, found innocent but still not given their jobs back.

The hon. Member for Sherwood spoke about the great work that the UDM is doing in a new rejuvenated industry. He did not tell us about Paul Gallant who is on the area executive of the UDM who was charged with GBH for assaulting a striking miner and his retired father. Nothing was done against that individual, who is now welcoming the Secretary of State to UDM conferences wherever it has them now. There was no fair hand in considering the problems of miners and administering justice to miners at that time. Is it not a fact that of all the atrocities that were committed against miners who were on strike, not one working miner found guilty of any offence was sacked? Can the Secretary of State tell us what happened to the working miner who petrol-bombed my car because I was a striking miner during the miner's strike? Can he tell me what happened to the working miner who bombed my garage because I was a striking miner during the miners' strike? The answer is, nothing.

The hon. Member for Sherwood (Mr. Stewart) talked about the green pastures to which I have gone. He is so right. I am now among my ain folk, as we say in Scotland, where I was born and bred and I am proud to represent them. Before I moved, the hon. Member for Sherwood was my Member of Parliament, but there has been a 100 per cent. improvement in the quality of my life because I represent myself, because I live in my constituency.

The number of Scottish miners has decreased during this decade of shame. Ten years ago, there were 21,000; five years ago, there were 14,000; and now there are 1,600. A shadow is hanging over the Scottish deep-mine industry. On 2 February 1989, in a press release, British Coal praised the Scottish miners for their 15 per cent. increase in productivity. There was a special reference to Longannet:

"At Longannet coal face teams have established a new record for a week's output from a single coal face of 31,228 tonnes"—

a record that improved on the previous 1957 record of 25,000 tonnes. British Coal praised the Scottish miners with one hand and put the knife into them with the other.

**Mr. Ted Leadbitter** (Hartlepool): I hope that my hon. Friend will remind the House that Shell, an international company, is bringing coal—in small boats, not bulk carriers—into small ports in Scotland. It is a loss leader. It is not making a profit on that exercise, in the hope that, when it wins the market, it will be able to get the contract and then up the price.

My hon. Friend the Member for Pontefract and Castleford (Mr. Lofthouse) made a suggestion about redundancies that affect Scotland. Should not what Sir Peter Gregson said on 14 June to the Select Committee on Energy be put on the record? He said that the £311 million for restructuring grant should be able to cover, first, the redundancies that spilled over from last year, in addition to the 15,000 redundancies in the current year.

**Mr. Hood:** My hon. Friend is right. We have been given horrific figures showing by how much coal has been subsidised when transported by Shell to capture the so-called market. I was pleased to hear my hon. Friend's helpful intervention, because it takes me to my next point.

To add insult to injury for miners, Ministers have acted against them. I remember the Prime Minister introducing a Bill to allow for up to £40 million of imported coal. I remember Nottinghamshire Conservative Members opposing that Bill, obviously because of a certain self-interest.

The Secretary of State has said today that the Government will not be so foolish as to put the market into the hands of foreign importers. I see no evidence to support that. We have been told that only 2 million tonnes of coal comes from South Africa. That sounds fine, but how much South African coal is dumped in places such as Rotterdam and enters Britain through the back door? We know that South African coal has been moved in lorries from Nottingham in the midlands and blended with Durham coal, but that coal is not recorded in the figures.

We might not know the true figures, but we know that there are Conservative Members who willingly support the closure of the mining industry. One Conservative Member —I doubt that he will speak tonight—would probably want to tell us that we should bring all our coal in from South Africa. The South African bovver boys are here, and I see one. They would love to bring in South African coal, selling our natural reserves short.

Britain's natural resources are the envy of the world. We all know what happened in the 1960s and 1970s. I shall not defend the actions of other Governments who fell into the trap of accepting cheap oil but who, when the market was captured and the coal industry started to run down,

pulled the rope in and quadrupled prices, almost destroying many western economies. That is the danger that we face. We must recognise that it is a trap into which no Government, regardless of party, should fall. I am not convinced that the Government are sincere in saying that they will not fall into that trap.

The Government support the idea of using coal from China, South Africa or Colombia. As my hon. Friend the Member for Easington (Mr. Cummings) said, that coal comes from child labour. The Government would sooner have that than British coal. The Government who whinge about Parliament's sovereignty support the idea of placing our energy requirements in the hands of foreign importers.

The Government are on their way out, are they not? [Hon. Members: "Hear, hear."] Are they behind 12 per cent. or 14 per cent. this week? [Hon. Members: "It is 14 per cent."] We will soon have a Tory-free Scotland and a Tory-free Nottingham. This country needs its coal produced by British miners. The Government will not achieve that—only a Labour Government will.

8.56 pm

**Mr. Andrew Mitchell** (Gedling): I am grateful for the chance to speak in the debate. I recognise the sincerity with which Labour Members prosecute any debate on the coal industry. There is a sort of agelessness about the way in which it is conducted. For many Labour Members it is clearly a measure of success if miners are kept in jobs, whereas Conservative Members believe in promoting a successful industry that can produce economically and sell what it produces.

I want to make three general points. The first is about the tremendous progress that has been made in the industry in Nottinghamshire. It is a pity that Labour Members do not look more carefully at that aspect. Secondly, in one or two tangential ways, I have some sympathy with the hon. Member for Sedgefield (Mr. Blair) about the coal industry's difficulties in the negotiation of contracts. Thirdly, I emphasise the critical need for the industry to be returned to the private sector as swiftly as possible.

I read the motion moved by the hon. Member for Sedgefield with some surprise, because it did not acknowledge the tremendous progress that has been made by the mining industry. It does not show the sort of support for the industry—which Conservative Members would have expected following the review of Labour policy—or the new brand of trade unionism represented by the Union of Democratic Mineworkers which so well fights for its members' interests. The hon. Gentleman may have failed to show his motion in advance of the debate to the latterday Machiavelli who plays such an important role in the Labour party—Peter Mandelson.

In a hitherto adverse market, the mining industry has made much progress, and it is important to recognise that. Its operating profit this year at £500 million is twice as much as last year, as my hon. Friend the Member for Sherwood (Mr. Stewart) said in his excellent speech. It is not for nothing that my hon. Friend is known in Nottinghamshire as the miners' friend—a title to which he is justly entitled.

Tremendous price reductions have been made in the industry, saving its customers £500 million in the past year alone. Operating costs have been reduced by over 20 per cent. in real terms. Deep-mine profits of £125 million have

[*Mr. Andrew Mitchell*]

been made, whereas the comparable figure for last year was a loss of £112 million. Accidents in the industry have reduced by no less than two thirds since the strike, from 93 per 100,000 man shifts to 29·4. Conservative Members would have liked to hear Labour Members acknowledge how well the industry has done over recent years.

Deep mine operating profits of £73 million were achieved in Nottinghamshire last year. Even after capital charges of £55 million, an overall profit of £34 million was made. Productivity in Nottinghamshire has increased by nearly 12 per cent., which represents 4·35 tonnes per man shift and an increase of nearly 40 per cent. in three years. So far this year, productivity is running ahead of those levels. Those are significant statistics.

Nottinghamshire provides well over half of British Coal's deep-mine profits. I ask my hon. Friend the Minister what possible commercial justification he sees for British Coal having its headquarters in London, miles from the nearest pit. It is an extremely valuable piece of real estate. For those who work there, it is a nice, gentle location overlooking the walls of Buckingham palace, but there can be no possible commercial justification for it. Even if there were some economic justification for it, it is bad for management to be so far removed from its area of commercial activity.

Given that nearly 60 per cent of British Coal's deep-mine profits come from Nottinghamshire, will my hon. Friend the Minister, in the run-up to privatisation, encourage its chairman and board to locate near its most profitable area? I agree to take British Coal's chairman to see the excellent office sites in Nottingham so that he can see how congenial it would be to locate there. Many people believe that such a move would send out highly desirable signals to the industry and the generators who buy from it.

Pressure on the industry remains intense, and nowhere more so than in my constituency. Earlier this year, Gedling colliery underwent massive restructuring. It will never be enormously profitable because its seams are too thin, but it sells almost all the coal that it produces, because its quality is so high. Heavy losses were made last year, and this year, following the costs of major restructuring, it has been set a new target of 12,500 tonnes a week. I am glad to be able to tell the House that last week, for the first time, the much reduced work force managed to reach that target. Excellent progress has been made and we should congratulate its men and management on what has been achieved and express the hope that it continues.

The need to achieve viability is generally recognised, but not by all Labour Members. However, there is a glimmer of hope that recognition is coming. The Secretary of State spoke about British Coal being a supplier of choice and said that it is important that there is a free market in coal. I was extremely surprised, therefore, to hear that generators have said, and I think that I have heard right, that they do not intend to buy exclusively from British Coal, regardless of economics. Surely what is sauce for the goose is sauce for the gander. If they intend to achieve the best value for money, they must allow British Coal that same opportunity. This correct approach for British Coal has been endorsed by the electricity supply industry. I am sure that that approach will be supported by the chairman of the East Midlands electricity board.

A policy of the carrot and the stick is required. Turning round an unprofitable, unproductive and demoralised industry takes much time, but as long as that turnround is being achieved, the industry deserves to be given the time for which it has asked. It must know roughly how much coal will be needed by generators over the next five years. After that, the UDM calculates that the industry will be sufficiently reformed, productive and successful to take on all comers and have no fear of foreign competition.

In supporting my right hon. Friend's excellent amendment to the neanderthal Opposition motion, I do not ask him to intervene in commercial negotiations, but I hope that he will point out that, just as we expect British Coal to compete on its merits, so we expect it to be allowed to compete for all generators' coal requirements and not be frozen out of a part of their market. That is required in order to ensure the future stability of the distributors, the generators, the coal industry and the public.

In addition, the desirability of any form of dependence on foreign coal is now looking particularly shaky, for the reasons expressed on both sides of the House. There is no such thing as an organised market in foreign coal. The Amsterdam-Rotterdam-Antwerp market is not a true spot market. Coal is traded in dollars and at the moment the dollar is, to say the least, a fluctuating currency.

China has been mentioned. It has taken on some long-term contracts, but it has failed to deliver. That country has major infrastructure problems and there are also tremendous problems with its port handling. Later this year it may even have to import coal.

Currently the United States industry is suffering major industrial disruption and it may be hard pressed to meet its internal demands.

British Coal was riddled with political involvement, strikes, appalling industrial relations and a complete lack of commercialism. Since the strike it has produced the same tonnage with roughly half the manpower. The cost per gigajoule in Nottinghamshire is £1·42; it has come down from nearly £2. Those arguments, quite apart from a debt of loyalty that the country owes to the UDM, underline the desirability of a soft landing for the industry and a defined period of time for continuing reconstruction and adjustment.

Recently, the Secretary of State addressed the UDM annual conference. He cannot have failed to notice that the UDM fights just as hard for its members as any other union, but it looks forward to the future and not back to the past. I regret that the union is opposed to privatisation, as nationalisation has been the curse of the industry. I hope that miners will talk to their colleagues in the steel industry before making up their minds about the merits of privatisation. The leadership of the UDM is, nevertheless, determined to ensure that its members get an outstanding deal if privatisation goes ahead.

I wonder whether my hon. Friend noticed the agenda at that conference, which dealt with matters such as the importance of free shares for miners if privatisation takes place; pensions payable with a lump sum at 50 years old; creative schemes such as that at Bilsthorpe; and plans to develop a mothballed pit with the creation of nearly 1,000 new jobs.

Did my right hon. Friend hear the words of the president of the UDM following its deal with British Coal last autumn concerning six-day working? His words are most important. He said:

"This agreement is necessary and in my opinion will protect the jobs of many miners and the future of the mining industry. The agreement will allow us to compete with any foreign competition and is yet another demonstration that the UDM are working for, the future while other unions are living in the past".

But the NUM remains immune to common sense and refuses to accept six-day working.

British Coal and the UDM face great challenges and great difficulties. They need to achieve economic viability, to adapt to electricity privatisation and to face up to the environmental problems about which we have heard. They must also face up to the privatisation of the industry. The men whom I met on my recent visit to the Gedling pit are not interested in the politics of coal mining or in the past. They want a healthy industry where their hard work and skill wins them a secure future and a decent wage.

I hope that we shall soon see a fair deal between British Coal and the generators based on some of the realities that I have raised tonight.

**Several Hon. Members** rose——

**Mr. Deputy Speaker:** Order. I can see six hon. Members seeking to catch my eye. I understand that the Front Bench spokesmen will seek to wind up the debate at 9.30. The arithmetic will be obvious to those hon. Members.

9.8 pm

**Mr. Peter Hardy** (Wentworth): I shall be brief. The thing that concerns me about the speeches of the hon. Members for Gedling (Mr. Mitchell) and for Sherwood (Mr. Stewart) is that they do not share my view that the industry is contracted to the point where the sooner there is one union for mineworkers the better. That would certainly not suit either their own or their political book.

I want to contribute partly because I represent the National Association of Colliery Overmen, Deputies and Shotfirers, which has its conference in Cardiff this week. That association is extremely anxious because, although it has heard the platitudes from Ministers, it knows that, despite the fact that large sums of public money have been invested in the industry, that is no guarantee that the Government will manage the industry in the national interest, no guarantee that the Government will ensure that taxpayers' money is properly safeguarded, and no guarantee that the Government will try to persuade the electricity industry to use British Coal in which they have invested large sums of money. That is no guarantee that this country would not be exposed to the consequences of a dependence on coal imports. Apart from the retention of jobs and self-sufficiency, we have an obligation to sustain industrial capacity, and our mining engineering and equipment industry could be greater and more important. However, it requires a substantial home base and I fear that that home base is contracting.

That base has contracted in my area. The Minister will boast that not a man has been made compulsorily redundant. That is so. Their morale has been destroyed deliberately, so that they have wanted to get out because they have felt fearful that, no matter how successful their pit, it will close and they may as well take the money now. The operation of the time scale of redundancy payments was engineered and structured to secure that. While the individual has been cushioned against the shock of redundancy, the communities in which the mining industry was of enormous importance have been simply ignored.

We are supposed to be having an economic miracle. A few areas appear to have experienced it, but the coalfields of Britain have not. They were the areas with the highest level of unemployment even before the policies inflicted on them in the past three or four years.

The hon. Member for Sherwood talked about representing many pits. When I entered the House, there were more collieries in my constituency than in any other. As my hon. Friend the Member for Rother Valley (Mr. Barron) will be aware, the Boundary Commission removed quite a few of them, but this Government have reduced the number further. Some pits that I lost as a result of the Boundary Commission changes of 1983 remain, but their life expectancy may be reduced, and the work force has contracted.

There is one colliery left in my constituency. It is one of the most successful and profitable in the country, but even that colliery, with a potential for profit and a record of achievement of which the men should be proud and of which I, as their Member of Parliament, am proud, the men are still fearful for the future. That is a ridiculous situation and a comment on the farcical policies now followed.

I see that the hon. Member for Tatton (Mr. Hamilton) is in his place. Some Conservative Members seem to be far more interested in the South African industry than in the British industry. Forty-two Conservative Members have signed an early-day motion about the South African coal industry and 16 of them have probably been on free trips to the South African coal industry in the past two years. Perhaps that early-day motion accompanied the return to work of the Passport Office and those Conservative Members have now realised that they have an opportunity to go abroad on holiday.

It would be interesting if some of those 42 Conservative Members were to visit a pit in the United Kingdom, especially one of the pits with heavy duty faces which result from the substantial investment about which the Minister boasted. If they make such a visit, perhaps it will dawn on them that it would be remarkably foolish and feckless for us to embark on the course of action that they want to pursue.

You will be aware, Mr. Deputy Speaker, that many of us from mining areas became green long before it was politically fashionable. We were green because we objected to the disfigurement and destruction of our environment. We became concerned about the lust of Conservative Members to see as much opencast mining as possible, in the hope that it would be followed by privatisation, so that profits would be made in other parts of the country from the rape and exploitation of areas such as mine. The removal of our publicly owned enterprise should persuade the Minister that, if the Government are concerned to be a Government of one nation, they will have to recognise the bitterness and anxiety about future opencast mining, which we would be expected to tolerate. If the Government close our deep mines, they should not expect the people of the coalfields of Britain to tolerate their surface environment being destroyed as well. We were prepared to support the national interest. We are not prepared to support the profit-seeking greed of a few Conservative Members.

The hon. Member for Hampstead and Highgate (Sir G. Finsberg) appeared to question the approach, tactic and values of nationalisation, and read us the speech that he made in 1947. I know that the hon. Gentleman is

[*Mr. Peter Hardy*]

fair-minded so I ask him to bear in mind the industry's achievements since 1949. It became the safest deep-mine industry in the world, with more and better industrial training than any other mining industry in the world. Relationships within the mining community developed patchily but sometimes superbly. Imperfect though the nationalisation of the industry may have proved to be, it served this country's interests, not least because 90 per cent. of British Coal's purchases came from British commerce and British business. That would go out of the window with the loss of the market about which hon. Members have been expressing their fears tonight.

I urge the Government to renew their endeavours to ensure that the electricity industry maintains its satisfactory and viable level of purchase of British coal. I ask the Minister to accept the argument advanced by my hon. Friend the Member for Sedgefield (Mr. Blair) who said that sterling will certainly not remain at its present level as a result of industrial devastation and the reduction of oil exports. If the Minister accepts that Governments should look beyond the end of their noses, he will recognise the worth and the wit of the Opposition's motions.

9.17 pm

**Mr. Neil Hamilton** (Tatton): I am grateful to the hon. Member for Wentworth (Mr. Hardy) and to the other Opposition Members who trailed my speech so generously, although, unfortunately, they do not seem to have been very successful in attracting my hon. Friends into the Chamber.

I am sorry that the hon. Member for Sedgefield (Mr. Blair) has temporarily left his place. He imparted the most unusual flavour to the debate by introducing some literary references—for example, to Lord Byron. That suggests to me that his speech was vetted by the right hon. Member for Blaenau Gwent (Mr. Foot), who is known to be one of the foremost experts on that great poet. The hon. Gentleman's speech certainly had all the characteristic vagueness of the speeches of the right hon. Gentleman, but without the romance.

In reflecting on the hon. Gentleman's speech I was reminded of Byron's description of Don Juan:

"He was the mildest manner'd man
That ever scuttled ship or cut a throat,
With such true breeding of a gentleman,
You never could divine his real thought."

I thought that that was particularly relevant to the hon. Gentleman's speech. We heard nothing from him about the Opposition's ideas for the future of the industry. He had the gall to accuse the Conservative party of looking to ideology and vested interest in its policy on coal. If there is one charge that could not be laid at our feet, it is that we take an ideological view or seek to protect vested interests. That is precisely the Labour party's policy on coal.

The hon. Gentleman also had the gall to accuse us of seeking to put the industry in a position to grasp profit from captive consumers. But what happened in the 40 years of nationalisation? The legal structure of the industry, coupled with successive Governments who were unwilling to grapple with its problems have allowed it to extract huge sums from the taxpayers and consumers—unwillingly, and by way of taxation and higher prices than were necessary. In our privatisation policy, which I greatly welcome, we seek to restore to the coal industry the freedom of the market so that consumers, rather than vested interests, can rule the day.

Several Opposition Members, including the hon. Member for Pontefract and Castleford (Mr. Lofthouse), accused us of seeking to bash the coal industry. If we have been bashing the coal industry for the past 10 years, we have been using the most extraordinary weapon to do it. Our weapon has been the cheque book. Have we really damaged the coal industry by giving it £10 billion in grants and £6·5 billion in investment? It is the most massive investment programme for the industry during the post war period. If a crime has been committed by successive Governments, it has been to demand money with menaces from the taxpayer and the consumer. The end of that criminal activity, through privatisation, will massively benefit the people of this country.

The truth is that 40 years of nationalisation have proved a disastrous failure. It has not been in the interests of the miners, because the number of men employed in the industry is now a small fraction of what it was in the immediate post-war period. It has not protected the industry against the inevitability of contraction of output, because output is very much smaller than it was in the immediate post-war period.

I wish that Opposition Members would come to grips with the realities of the international energy market, because that is the only way in which the future of the industry and the jobs that go with it can be sustained. Coal is a fossil fuel—and, unfortunately, the industry and the country have been faced with a fossil union in the National Union of Mineworkers, which over the years has set its face against every beneficial change that would have been in the interests of both the miners and the industry. Even now, after the most disastrous strike—during which, because of its irresponsible activities, it virtually destroyed itself and many pits that might otherwise have survived —it is still opposing such forward-looking policies as flexible working and the six-day week, upon which the profitability of some pits and the opening of new pits depend.

There has been a fossil party in the form of the Opposition, who have danced to the tune piped by Arthur Scargill and, it seems, still do so—[*Interruption.*] Opposition Members sit here tonight trying to defend their vested interests. They are certainly not defending the vested interests of those who, over generations, have supported the Labour party in the belief that in so doing they were supporting the interests of the coal industry.

We are not here simply to debate what is in the best interests of a particular section of the population or a particular section of British industry. We should be debating the national interest, which depends on the cheapest possible source of energy consistent with strategic requirements. There has been a sense of unreality in the speeches of Opposition Members. They spoke about the freeing of the energy industry, especially electricity generation, as tolling the death knell of the industry, as though it will import all its coal requirements, regardless of the strategic and long-term implications. No sensible company, which is in business in the long term and must make a profit to survive, will base its decisions on such short-term considerations. The importance of the freedom to import is that, at the margin, it will exercise a considerable discipline on the British industry to ensure that its costs are as low as possible so that it can be competitive.

I rise to the bait put in front of me by the hon. Member for Wentworth (Mr. Hardy) about South African coal. There is nothing horrific in the fact that we may import some South African coal. If, by doing so, we reduce the energy costs of British industry and, in the process, provide jobs for black workers in South Africa, there is surely nothing wrong in that. I am not suggesting that those imports will amount to anything very much in comparison with the total coal burn in this country. They will always be marginal. However, if they amount to even 10 or 15 per cent. of our total coal burn, the beneficial effects will be widely felt.

Privatisation offers enormous scope to improve the position of the coal industry and to remove the constraints of political interference from which it has suffered so much during the past 40 years. I hope that my hon. Friend the Under-Secretary will agree that it is a shame that we have to wait until after the next general election, which we certainly intend to win, in order to implement our privatisation policy. Action can be taken in advance of privatisation without prejudicing the public sector.

**Mr. Alan Meale** (Mansfield) *rose*——

**Mr. Hamilton:** As it is 9.24 pm, I do not have time to give way, because I hope that one other hon. Member, perhaps the hon. Member for Mansfield (Mr. Meale), may be able to make a speech.

Opencast production is constrained by legislation. The licensed opencast producers are limited in what they can produce, both by tonnage limits and other controls, principally because British Coal is both the regulator and a competitor in the market. I should like my hon. Friend the Under-Secretary to invest coal in the Crown before the next general election so that British Coal no longer has the inevitable conflict of interest of deciding who will produce, and at what price the royalty should be set. That would be an important fillip to a part of the British opencast industry which will wish to be a major player in the market after privatisation.

Therefore, the coal industry has nothing to fear from privatisation so long as the miners who work in it, their union representatives and their other representatives of different political persuasions look to the future of the industry as being based on satisfying the demands of the consumers. That is the surest foundation on which to base a successful industry. After privatisation, the coal industry's future will be good and, therefore, I congratulate my right hon. Friend the Secretary of State and my hon. Friend the Under-Secretary on having had the vision and courage to bring forth this, the greatest of all privatisations.

9.27 pm

**Mr. Alan Meale** (Mansfield): I wish to talk about Conservative Members' constant references to the Government's good work in relation to the coal industry. I represent a constituency which is at the heartland of the coal mining industry—Mansfield, Nottinghamshire—in which the headquarters of the Union of Democratic Mineworkers and the National Union of Mineworkers are located. It is about time that Conservative Members,

particularly those who are from Nottinghamshire, stopped rubbishing the miners of both unions in the Nottinghamshire area.

Those miners know at first hand exactly what the Government have done to the mining industry and they know that every time Conservative Members open their mouths as they have been, all they do is to conjure up fires between the different groups of workers. It is no good Conservative Members saying that they know and understand what is happening, and even smile about it.

We in the Nottingham area are currently spending tens of thousands of pounds via social and other services throughout the county, and in education programmes both voluntary and statutory, to try to douse the flames created by the mining strike of the early 1980s. It is about time that Conservative Members stopped rekindling those flames just for the sake of political votes at election times. Instead, we should be concerned about the people from those mining communities and what we can do to help them obtain and retain jobs in their communities.

Today, the Secretary of State mentioned the mining strike. He is the least qualified to come forward with such arguments. If he is concerned about Nottinghamshire, he should do more than visit it once in a blue moon, and call in at Nottingham to speak to those at the chamber of trade who represent a minority of people in the county.

The Secretary of State raised the subject of the Government's good housekeeping. Conservative Members also mentioned harassment, which occurred throughout the Nottinghamshire coalfields in the form of the loss of 16,000 mining jobs, the closure of pits, the rundown of communities and the lack of investment because there was no structural plan for investment in new jobs throughout the county.

Speaking of good housekeeping, today I received a reply from the Minister responsible for coal. I had asked him how much the Government had spent on the privatisation of electricity supply. In 1987-88 they spent £0·8 million on financial advice in connection with the privatisation. In 1988-89 that rose to £5·5 million, and this year the Government have set aside £26·5 million for outside advice on the privatisation of a public industry. It is a disgrace that there should have been a 3,000 per cent. increase in the spending of public money on the privatisation of a public asset.

Finally, Conservative Members representing the Nottinghamshire area should stop their party political battles and should stop putting out press releases asking where particular Labour Members were when there were votes on the Associated British Ports (No. 2) Bill and on similar legislation. In votes on motions such as tonight's, they should vote with the Opposition and support the mining communities in Nottinghamshire.

9.31 pm

**Mr. Kevin Barron** (Rother Valley): I must tell my hon. Friend the Member for Mansfield (Mr. Meale) that I hope that many hon. Members on both sides will take to heart what he said about the prevailing social conditions in the Nottinghamshire coalfield, which stem from the industrial dispute of 1984-85. All of us can learn lessons from the problems that still exist in that area.

I must tell the hon. Member for Sherwood (Mr. Stewart) that he was out-jumped on the restart scheme —his claim to fame—because a few months before he

[*Mr. Kevin Barron*]

mentioned it in the House, Opposition Members had already—last July—brought up restart in the context of British coalfields. If he can derive any comfort from this, we intend to look into an extension of the restart scheme to cover ex-Tory Members of Parliament in the Nottinghamshire area in years to come.

My hon. Friend the Member for Pontefract and Castleford (Mr. Lofthouse) touched a nerve earlier tonight when he mentioned what the Minister's civil servant said said when giving evidence to the Select Committee on Energy two weeks ago. The Secretary of State jumped up and tried to explain in detail what the restructuring grant meant. I was present to hear the evidence, and what it meant was plain: at least 15,000, to judge from last year, when the figure given was 2,000 or 3,000 and we ended up with almost 8,000. Who knows what this year's amount will be? The events of the next few weeks will determine it.

The hon. Member for Hampstead and Highgate (Sir G. Finsberg) was quite right to read us his speech of 1947. It showed what has happened in the intervening years since the time when he worked for two years in the industry. There have been massive changes in the past 40 years. I was pleased to be part of the industry for 20 of those years —a time in which the industry, within the public sector, became one of the best respected deep coal-mining industries in the world.

These reflections shatter the arguments of the hon. Member for Tatton (Mr. Hamilton), who brought us his customary historical view of the industry—nothing in the past 40 years has been good because the industry has not been in the private sector. On both occasions this century when this country was attacked from outside, the first thing that the Government did was to nationalise the coal industry so that we could fight those who threatened our existence.

The implicit question behind the motion tabled by my right hand hon. Friends and myself is whether this country will begin once again to import large amounts of its energy supplies or whether it has learnt the lessons of the past and will support an indigenous coal industry—one that not only supplies coal securely and at the right price but protects the balance of payments and, despite the job losses of the past few years, still provides direct employment for some 100,000 people.

Throughout the world, coal producers negotiate long-term contracts with their electricity generators. Obviously, that makes good sense on both sides. If one wants to see the real world of privatised electricity, one need only go to the United States. Companies there own the generators and the coal mines. Companies will not build generators or sink mines unless they have contracts of 20 to 30 years. In this country, people thought that the privatisation of the electricity supply industry would replicate the real privatised generators of the world—and that could have happened.

British Coal was able to make an unsurpassable offer to the successor companies of 10-year contracts within the retail price index. People will remember that such a contract was sounded out in January. However, between January, when that 10-year contract was offered—perhaps the best on the energy market—and now, there has been an intervention by the Department of Trade and Industry and the Prime Minister about what was then thought to be the

correct lifeline of a contract between the generators and the fuel suppliers. The Prime Minister put an end to those contracts.

It was first of all thought that the Prime Minister and the DTI had insisted that coal supply contracts should be signed for only between six months and three years. Even the generators, fighting their corners, thought that that was nonsense. The Prime Minister, however, had to be appeased, so the compromise was reached that the contracts should be between one and five years.

The Secretary of State has recently made a number of statements about the Government wanting to see free market negotiations. It is all very well for him to talk about free market negotiations, but the stipulation by a Government Department, and I understand by the Prime Minister, is that contracts should be for between one and five years. In fact, the Secretary of State said that he would not force customers into long-term contracts with British Coal. That is true, because the Government are stopping British Coal negotiating what anybody would call long-term contracts for the supply of fuel into the generation companies.

What appears to be missing from the Government's calculations is an understanding of the realities of the coal-mining industry. If contracts with British Coal should run for only five years, on what criteria could the industry make judgments about future investment? The Secretary of State and many Conservative Members have made great play of the £6·5 billion capital investment in British Coal in the past 10 years. Will the Secretary of State tell us whether any industry or the Government would have made the investment in Selby or Asfordby without a predetermined market for that coal?

What will happen in future when the only contract possible will be for five years, but it can take anywhere between five or 10 years before a fuel source is brought on in such massive mines as Selby or Asfordby? The Government's imposition of short-term contracts on the industry is to enable the fulfilment of the Prime Minister's dream of a Britain without coal mines or miners. It is to give time to those who would replace British coal—as my hon. Friend the Member for Easington (Mr. Cummings) said—with coal mined in Colombia, South Africa, Australia or Poland, and to prepare the facilities for its large-scale importation. That is the reason for the five-year contracts.

The recent fall in sterling against the dollar has meant that international coal prices are increasing. It can no longer be asserted that British Coal cannot compete in the international market, and many experts say that it could and does now. By encouraging the myth that imported coal is cheaper, the Government are doing a great disservice to the British coal industry and to the country as a whole. We know that the international energy markets are wildly unpredictable and that that can put Britain's industrial competitiveness at risk—or what is left of it since the Government came to office 10 years ago.

British Steel now imports seven out of every eight tonnes of coal that it uses. That did not use to happen. Ten years ago, it imported hardly any coal except when that was necessary. It took a determined line and now imports seven out of every eight tonnes of coal. How will the change in the pound-dollar rate affect British Steel now? For how long are its supplies assured? Are the Government prepared to allow the uncertainty of supply which results from transferring from home-produced coal to imported coal to affect the electricity supply industry in the way that it will surely affect British Steel?

Despite the Government's amendment, the Secretary of State has shown that he will take no steps to secure the long-term future of the coal industry. He was quite embarrassed today when it was revealed in the debate that 60 million tonnes is the figure for the future market for British Coal in this country. I challenge the Secretary of State now. I will give way to him if he will tell us that British Coal will be allowed to fight evenly and competitively for every tonne of coal in the market for electricity generation over the next six months. The Secretary of State will not rise to that challenge. The generators, British Coal and everyone else know that the Government are determined to take markets away from British Coal no matter how much imported coal costs. The Secretary of State's silence speaks volumes about this.

I have quite taken to the hon. Member for Gedling (Mr. Mitchell) since he became a Member of the House. I hope that he does not feel that this compliment will be followed by an attack on his local Conservative association. He made a good contribution to the debate; he referred to the positive aspects of what is happening in British Coal, and many hon. Members on both sides of the House share his feelings about them.

The hon. Member for Gedling has evidence in the Secretary of State's refusal to rise to my challenge that the Government are deeply involved in ensuring that British Coal loses its contract irrespective of the price for the 10 million tonnes or 15 million tonnes to which I have referred.

Instead of awarding the British Coal work force a Queen's award for industry for their 90 per cent. productivity increases, the Government appear to be rewarding them with the prospect of more job losses. Instead of applauding British Coal's contract, which offered coal for 10 years at prices related to the RPI—an offer which is not matched anywhere else in the world for any form of energy—the Secretary of State voted for the construction of port facilities designed specifically to import coal into this country.

**Mr. Parkinson** *indicated dissent*.

**Mr. Barron:** The Secretary of State may shake his head. I was a teller when he walked through the Aye Lobby with the Prime Minister to vote in favour for the Bill for the ports on the Humber. I will send the Secretary of State a copy of *Hansard* if he has forgotten what he did that night.

Opposition Members and the whole of the British coal-mining industry will not be unaware of the kind of support that they have received from the Government over the past six months or so. No matter what words they utter or what they do, it is clear that the Government's policy towards the coal industry is determined by a mixture of their ideological idiocy and political prejudice.

The prejudice between British coal miners and Tory Governments is well known. It has been evident in the 1980s, and it was evident in the 1970s in my generation. However, it was clear also in the 1920s when the arguments between Labour and capitalism were rehearsed in the mining communities between the coal owners and the mining unions. We know where Conservatism has stood for generations.

Nothing more could have been asked of the British coal industry over the past four years than that which it has delivered. For the industry to be confronted by a Government who are prepared to work against it in the winning of contracts so that foreign coal will come into this country is a stab in the back for the people who work so hard. That shows where the Government's loyalties really lie. There is nothing of flag waving in the Government's attitude. Now we can see who really wants to protect British interests and who does not. If British Coal does not win the contracts that it deserves, that will go down as one of the most tragic stabs in the back that the industry has ever suffered from the current Government.

9.45 pm

**The Parliamentary Under-Secretary of State for Energy (Mr. Michael Spicer):** As my hon. Friends the Members for Tatton (Mr. Hamilton) and for Hampstead and Highgate (Sir G. Finsberg) so shrewdly noted, there can be no doubt that the debate has been a terrible personal embarrassment for the hon. Member for Sedgefield (Mr. Blair) who opened it. I noticed that he kept his head down throughout his speech like a Chinese news-reader. He hardly mentioned coal at all, except to say that the international coal market is so tight that logically we have nothing to worry about from imports.

My right hon. and hon. Friends and I do not go that far, but the hon. Gentleman is on the right lines. My advice is that he should talk occasionally to his hon. Friend the Member for Rother Valley (Mr. Barron), who is petrified, like most of his right hon. and hon. Friends, at the prospect of coal imports. I shall return to that subject shortly.

The future of coal poses the hon. Member for Sedgefield a ghastly dilemma. On the one hand, he and his new-style Socialists see the coal industry as baggage that they would like to discard. It reminds them of Mr. Arthur Scargill, who for obvious reasons they are trying to put back under wraps, but not very successfully. Labour understand that coal pollutes the very atmosphere that they want to clear up, and generally it does not fit well with their adman's image of sweet-smelling roses and jolly music that is their particular manifestation of Socialism.

On the other hand, Labour have to contend with the hon. Member for Bolsover (Mr. Skinner) and with other Opposition Members who have spoken tonight, telling them that coal lies at the very foundation of the Labour movement, and that for Labour to turn its back on it is to turn its back on years of struggle and disruption. So good is coal, say the hon. Member for Bolsover and his hon. Friends, that one day it must triumph again and replace most other sources of energy—notably nuclear power.

The important question in assessing the significance of the Opposition motion is who is winning the power struggle within the Labour party over the future of coal. If one looks at the Opposition's recent policy review, the answer is clear. Despite all the charm of the hon. Member for Sedgefield, the hon. Member for Bolsover and his hon. Friends have won the argument. That is why Labour is committed unequivocally to phasing out nuclear power, why it chooses motions such as that before the House tonight to debate in the Opposition's own time, and why the hon. Member for Sedgefield leaves coal matters to his hon. Friend the Member for Rother Valley whenever he

[*Mr. Michael Spicer*]

can, hoping himself to be moved to other pastures as soon as the Electricity Bill has passed safely through Parliament. [*Interruption.*] Opposition Members have made remarks about my right hon. Friend the Secretary of State, and I am returning the compliment.

That is also why the hon. Member for Sedgefield employs every diversion that he can muster to avoid addressing the essential question of how we are to meet the increased demand for electricity that everyone—probably even the hon. Gentleman in his heart of hearts—acknowledges will come about, even if we allow for measures to increase efficiency, while at the same time cutting carbon dioxide emissions and abolishing the nuclear industry.

One of the hon. Gentleman's recent diversions was to issue another of his famous press releases on 20 June. Its primary purpose was to attack our policy on the nuclear industry. At the bottom of the first page, in quotation marks, was an extract from a speech that I was alleged to have made to the House on 10 April this year. I am supposed to have said that the schedule in the Electricity Bill that provides for making grants to the nuclear industry would be activated

"only if there is a change in environmental policies that the industry could not have foreseen."

What I actually said—it is column 667 of *Hansard*—was:

"We are clear about the policy. The industry, and therefore the consumer, will pay for decommissioning unless something happens that was not capable of being foreseen—such as"—

not "only"—

"the regulations concerning the environment being changed —and proper provision could not therefore have been made in the accounts."—[*Official Report*, 10 April 1989; Vol. 150, c. 667.]

That is virtually the opposite of what was attributed to me by the hon. Member for Sedgefield.

I have laboured the point partly to illustrate the diversionary tactics employed by the hon. Gentlemen to disguise his embarrassment about his energy policies—particularly those concerned with coal—but partly because I think it scandalous behaviour on the part of Labour's official energy spokesman to distort totally what I said to the House of Commons and then to attack it.

**Mr. Blair:** I take it as an enormous compliment that nearly half the Minister's speech so far has been taken up by an attack on me. May I set the record straight? In column 677 of *Hansard* for 10 April 1989 appear the following words—the very words that the Minister has just denied using:

"Because we do not want that to persist"—

that is, the comments that would be made by Opposition Members—

"we are making it clear that the schedule will be activated only if there is a change in environmental policies that the industry could not have forseen."—[*Official Report*, 10 April 1989; Vol. 150, c. 667.]

All that I did was quote those words.

**Mr. Spicer:** I assure the hon. Gentleman that he has completely distorted the position as given in the quotations that I have given him and the speeches that I have placed on the record, and he knows it.

**Mr. Blair** *rose*——

**Mr. Spicer:** No, I shall not give way.

Some of his hon. Friends have tried to help the hon. Gentleman out of his embarrassment—it has happened again tonight—by trying to focus the argument on clean coal technology. Of course we all agree that the methods of producing electricity with reduced carbon dioxide emissions are a good thing, but do not let us kid ourselves. The building of a nuclear power station results in a 100 per cent. reduction in carbon dioxide emissions, while a coal-fired power station using the topping cycle —which is yet to be fully developed—is likely to produce a reduction of only about 20 per cent. The Labour party, in its attack on the nuclear industry, seems to be incapable of recognising that. Even a modern gas-fired station will reduce carbon dioxide emissions by up to 40 per cent.

Perhaps it is because we do not have the cultural hang-up about the coal industry that is so deeply rooted in the Labour party that we have a clear policy on its future. It is precisely that policy which was spelt out by my right hon. Friend the Secretary of State for Energy at the beginning of the debate. Through the massive investment of capital in modern machinery, which is still running at £2 million every working day, we intend to exploit the nation's best reserves of coal in such a way as to allow the industry to stand on its own feet, to beat off foreign competition as the supplier of choice to the electricity industry and ultimately—to answer my hon. Friends the Members for Gedling (Mr. Mitchell) and for Tatton and others who have raised the matter—to place it once more in the private sector.

**Mr. Barron:** The Minister said that he is prepared to see British Coal beat off foreign competition. Will he now answer the question that twice today the Secretary of State has refused to answer: whether British Coal will be able to negotiate to supply the generating industry with more than the 60 million tonnes of coal that is the sticking point at present? Will he answer yes or no?

**Mr. Spicer:** The hon. Gentleman has asked that question—[HON. MEMBERS: "Answer the question."]—and I shall answer it in my own way. The hon. Gentleman knows exactly what our position is—that it is not our policy to order any industry to do anything at the expense of another part of the community. My hon. Friend the Member for Tatton made that point when he said that we have to represent not exclusively the coal industry but the entire nation, including those who use electricity. They have the right to buy their electricity as cheaply as possible. Opposition Members are not concerned about that. We have never hidden our aim that there should be free trade in coal. I have said time and again to the House of Commons that there is no question of the Government preventing anyone from negotiating a price for the import of coal. The question, however, is which side of the House has the confidence to back the industry's ability to fight off coal imports.

The hon. Member for Sedgefield made the point, quite fairly, that the world market for steam coal is not particularly bright. British Coal is in an extraordinarily powerful position, partly because of the difficulties over importing coal, partly because of the problems in the world coal market and partly because—a point which the Opposition are never prepared to accept and concede—of the massive investment by the Government in the coal industry. The only question that Opposition Members should answer is whether those who work in the mining industry are prepared to back the massive investment, largely by the taxpayer, in the industry by adopting the manning procedures and efficient mining methods that are required if the industry is to beat off competition, something which all hon. Members hope will take place.

**Mr. Barron:** If I accepted all the Minister's arguments about the cost of foreign coal and all his other arguments, would he answer the question whether British Coal is free to negotiate every tonne of coal—74 million or 75 million tonnes—that is currently being burnt in generating stations?

**Mr. Spicer:** Of course it is free to negotiate. What a stupid question, if I may be discourteous to the hon. Gentleman. That is precisely what we have been saying all along. Of course British Coal is allowed to negotiate whatever it thinks that it can sell. The question, however, is whether the coal industry will take advantage of the massive investment by the Government in the industry. It has responded in many respects. It has nearly doubled its rate of productivity. There are good things. The reason that the industry is in its present state—a potentially powerful position—has everything to do with what this Government have done for the industry and nothing to do with the carping and griping which has come from the Opposition throughout the whole process. That is why I ask the House to discard the motion and treat it with the distain that it deserves.

*Question put,* That the original words stand part of the Question:

*The House divided:* Ayes 195, Noes 272.

**Division No. 261]**                                           **[10.00 pm**

### AYES

Abbott, Ms Diane
Adams, Allen *(Paisley N)*
Allen, Graham
Alton, David
Anderson, Donald
Archer, Rt Hon Peter
Armstrong, Hilary
Ashdown, Rt Hon Paddy
Banks, Tony *(Newham NW)*
Barnes, Harry *(Derbyshire NE)*
Barron, Kevin
Battle, John
Beckett, Margaret
Bennett, A. F. *(D'nt'n & R'dish)*
Bermingham, Gerald
Bidwell, Sydney
Blair, Tony
Blunkett, David
Boateng, Paul
Boyes, Roland
Bradley, Keith
Brown, Gordon *(D'mline E)*
Brown, Nicholas *(Newcastle E)*
Brown, Ron *(Edinburgh Leith)*
Buckley, George J.
Caborn, Richard
Callaghan, Jim
Campbell, Menzies *(Fife NE)*
Campbell-Savours, D. N.
Canavan, Dennis
Carlile, Alex *(Mont'g)*
Clay, Bob
Clwyd, Mrs Ann
Cohen, Harry
Coleman, Donald
Cook, Frank *(Stockton N)*
Cook, Robin *(Livingston)*
Corbett, Robin
Corbyn, Jeremy
Cousins, Jim
Cox, Tom
Crowther, Stan
Cryer, Bob
Cummings, John
Cunliffe, Lawrence
Cunningham, Dr John
Darling, Alistair
Davies, Rt Hon Denzil *(Llanelli)*
Davies, Ron *(Caerphilly)*
Dewar, Donald
Dixon, Don
Dobson, Frank
Doran, Frank
Douglas, Dick
Duffy, A. E. P.
Dunnachie, Jimmy
Dunwoody, Hon Mrs Gwyneth
Evans, John *(St Helens N)*
Ewing, Harry *(Falkirk E)*
Fatchett, Derek
Fearn, Ronald
Field, Frank *(Birkenhead)*
Fisher, Mark
Flynn, Paul
Foot, Rt Hon Michael
Foster, Derek
Foulkes, George
Fraser, John
Fyfe, Maria
Garrett, John *(Norwich South)*
Garrett, Ted *(Wallsend)*
George, Bruce
Gilbert, Rt Hon Dr John
Gordon, Mildred
Gould, Bryan
Graham, Thomas

Grant, Bernie *(Tottenham)*
Griffiths, Nigel *(Edinburgh S)*
Griffiths, Win *(Bridgend)*
Grocott, Bruce
Hardy, Peter
Harman, Ms Harriet
Hattersley, Rt Hon Roy
Haynes, Frank
Healey, Rt Hon Denis
Henderson, Doug
Hinchliffe, David
Hoey, Ms Kate *(Vauxhall)*
Hogg, N. *(C'nauld & Kilsyth)*
Home Robertson, John
Hood, Jimmy
Howarth, George *(Knowsley N)*
Howell, Rt Hon D. *(S'heath)*
Howells, Dr. Kim (Pontypridd)
Hoyle, Doug
Hughes, John *(Coventry NE)*
Hughes, Robert *(Aberdeen N)*
Hughes, Roy *(Newport E)*
Illsley, Eric
Ingram, Adam
Janner, Greville
Jones, Barry *(Alyn & Deeside)*
Jones, Martyn *(Clwyd S W)*
Kaufman, Rt Hon Gerald
Kirkwood, Archy
Lambie, David
Lamond, James
Leadbitter, Ted
Leighton, Ron
Lestor, Joan *(Eccles)*
Litherland, Robert
Livsey, Richard
Lloyd, Tony *(Stretford)*
Lofthouse, Geoffrey
Loyden, Eddie
McAvoy, Thomas
Macdonald, Calum A.
McFall, John
McKay, Allen *(Barnsley West)*
McKelvey, William
McLeish, Henry
McWilliam, John
Madden, Max
Mahon, Mrs Alice
Marshall, David *(Shettleston)*
Marshall, Jim *(Leicester S)*
Martin, Michael J. *(Springburn)*
Martlew, Eric
Meacher, Michael
Meale, Alan
Michael, Alun
Michie, Bill *(Sheffield Heeley)*
Mitchell, Austin *(G't Grimsby)*
Moonie, Dr Lewis
Morgan, Rhodri
Morley, Elliott
Morris, Rt Hon A. *(W'shawe)*
Morris, Rt Hon J. *(Aberavon)*

Mowlam, Marjorie
Mullin, Chris
Murphy, Paul
Oakes, Rt Hon Gordon
O'Brien, William
O'Neill, Martin
Orme, Rt Hon Stanley
Parry, Robert
Patchett, Terry
Pendry, Tom
Pike, Peter L.
Powell, Ray *(Ogmore)*
Prescott, John
Primarolo, Dawn
Quin, Ms Joyce
Randall, Stuart
Redmond, Martin
Rees, Rt Hon Merlyn
Reid, Dr John
Richardson, Jo
Robertson, George
Robinson, Geoffrey
Rogers, Allan
Ross, Ernie *(Dundee W)*
Rowlands, Ted
Ruddock, Joan
Sedgemore, Brian
Sheerman, Barry
Sheldon, Rt Hon Robert
Shore, Rt Hon Peter
Short, Clare
Skinner, Dennis
Smith, Andrew *(Oxford E)*
Smith, C. *(Isl'ton & F'bury)*
Smith, Rt Hon J. *(Monk'ds E)*
Smith, J. P. *(Vale of Glam)*
Spearing, Nigel
Steel, Rt Hon David
Steinberg, Gerry
Stott, Roger
Strang, Gavin
Straw, Jack
Taylor, Matthew *(Truro)*
Thompson, Jack *(Wansbeck)*
Turner, Dennis
Vaz, Keith
Wall, Pat
Wallace, James
Watson, Mike *(Glasgow, C)*
Welsh, Michael *(Doncaster N)*
Williams, Rt Hon Alan
Williams, Alan W. *(Carm'then)*
Wilson, Brian
Winnick, David
Wise, Mrs Audrey
Worthington, Tony
Young, David *(Bolton SE)*

Tellers for the Ayes:
  Mr. Robert N. Wareing and
  Mr. Ken Eastham.

### NOES

Adley, Robert
Aitken, Jonathan
Alexander, Richard
Alison, Rt Hon Michael
Allason, Rupert
Amess, David
Amos, Alan
Arbuthnot, James
Arnold, Jacques *(Gravesham)*
Arnold, Tom *(Hazel Grove)*
Ashby, David
Aspinwall, Jack
Atkins, Robert
Baker, Nicholas *(Dorset N)*
Baldry, Tony
Banks, Robert *(Harrogate)*

Batiste, Spencer
Beaumont-Dark, Anthony
Bendall, Vivian
Bennett, Nicholas *(Pembroke)*
Benyon, W.
Bevan, David Gilroy
Biffen, Rt Hon John
Blackburn, Dr John G.
Body, Sir Richard
Bonsor, Sir Nicholas
Boscawen, Hon Robert
Boswell, Tim
Bottomley, Peter
Bottomley, Mrs Virginia
Bowden, Gerald *(Dulwich)*
Bowis, John

Boyson, Rt Hon Dr Sir Rhodes
Braine, Rt Hon Sir Bernard
Brandon-Bravo, Martin
Brazier, Julian
Brooke, Rt Hon Peter
Brown, Michael *(Brigg & Cl't's)*
Browne, John *(Winchester)*
Bruce, Ian *(Dorset South)*
Buchanan-Smith, Rt Hon Alick
Buck, Sir Antony
Budgen, Nicholas
Burns, Simon
Butcher, John
Butler, Chris
Butterfill, John
Carlisle, John, *(Luton N)*
Carlisle, Kenneth *(Lincoln)*
Carrington, Matthew
Cash, William
Channon, Rt Hon Paul
Chapman, Sydney
Chope, Christopher
Churchill, Mr
Clark, Hon Alan *(Plym'th S'n)*
Clark, Dr Michael *(Rochford)*
Clark, Sir W. *(Croydon S)*
Clarke, Rt Hon K. *(Rushcliffe)*
Colvin, Michael
Conway, Derek
Coombs, Anthony *(Wyre F'rest)*
Coombs, Simon *(Swindon)*
Cope, Rt Hon John
Couchman, James
Cran, James
Currie, Mrs Edwina
Curry, David
Davies, Q. *(Stamf'd & Spald'g)*
Davis, David *(Boothferry)*
Day, Stephen
Devlin, Tim
Dicks, Terry
Dorrell, Stephen
Douglas-Hamilton, Lord James
Dover, Den
Dunn, Bob
Durant, Tony
Dykes, Hugh
Eggar, Tim
Emery, Sir Peter
Evans, David *(Welwyn Hatf'd)*
Evennett, David
Fallon, Michael
Favell, Tony
Fenner, Dame Peggy
Field, Barry *(Isle of Wight)*
Finsberg, Sir Geoffrey
Fishburn, John Dudley
Fookes, Dame Janet
Forman, Nigel
Forth, Eric
Fowler, Rt Hon Norman
Fox, Sir Marcus
Franks, Cecil
Freeman, Roger
French, Douglas
Fry, Peter
Gale, Roger
Gardiner, George
Garel-Jones, Tristan
Gill, Christopher
Gilmour, Rt Hon Sir Ian
Glyn, Dr Alan
Goodhart, Sir Philip
Goodlad, Alastair
Goodson-Wickes, Dr Charles

Gorman, Mrs Teresa
Gow, Ian
Grant, Sir Anthony *(CambsSW)*
Greenway, Harry *(Ealing N)*
Greenway, John *(Ryedale)*
Gregory, Conal
Griffiths, Peter *(Portsmouth N)*
Grylls, Michael
Gummer, Rt Hon John Selwyn
Hague, William
Hamilton, Hon Archie *(Epsom)*
Hamilton, Neil *(Tatton)*
Hampson, Dr Keith
Hanley, Jeremy
Hannam, John
Hargreaves, A. *(B'ham H'll Gr')*
Hargreaves, Ken *(Hyndburn)*
Harris, David
Hayes, Jerry
Hayhoe, Rt Hon Sir Barney
Hayward, Robert
Hicks, Mrs Maureen *(Wolv' NE)*
Hicks, Robert *(Cornwall SE)*
Higgins, Rt Hon Terence L.
Hill, James
Hind, Kenneth
Hogg, Hon Douglas *(Gr'th'm)*
Hordern, Sir Peter
Howarth, Alan *(Strat'd-on-A)*
Howarth, G. *(Cannock & B'wd)*
Howell, Ralph *(North Norfolk)*
Hughes, Robert G. *(Harrow W)*
Hunt, Sir John *(Ravensbourne)*
Irvine, Michael
Irving, Charles
Jack, Michael
Jackson, Robert
Janman, Tim
Jessel, Toby
Johnson Smith, Sir Geoffrey
Jones, Gwilym *(Cardiff N)*
Jones, Robert B *(Herts W)*
Jopling, Rt Hon Michael
Kellett-Bowman, Dame Elaine
Key, Robert
Kilfedder, James
King, Roger *(B'ham N'thfield)*
Knight, Greg *(Derby North)*
Lawson, Rt Hon Nigel
Lord, Michael
Maclean, David
Martin, David *(Portsmouth S)*
Maude, Hon Francis
Maxwell-Hyslop, Robin
Miller, Sir Hal
Miscampbell, Norman
Mitchell, Andrew *(Gedling)*
Mitchell, Sir David
Moate, Roger
Monro, Sir Hector
Montgomery, Sir Fergus
Moore, Rt Hon John
Morrison, Sir Charles
Moss, Malcolm
Moynihan, Hon Colin
Mudd, David
Neale, Gerrard
Nelson, Anthony
Neubert, Michael
Newton, Rt Hon Tony
Nicholls, Patrick
Nicholson, David *(Taunton)*
Norris, Steve
Onslow, Rt Hon Cranley
Page, Richard

Paice, James
Parkinson, Rt Hon Cecil
Patnick, Irvine
Patten, John *(Oxford W)*
Pattie, Rt Hon Sir Geoffrey
Pawsey, James
Peacock, Mrs Elizabeth
Porter, Barry *(Wirral S)*
Porter, David *(Waveney)*
Portillo, Michael
Powell, William *(Corby)*
Price, Sir David
Raison, Rt Hon Timothy
Redwood, John
Renton, Tim
Rhodes James, Robert
Ridley, Rt Hon Nicholas
Ridsdale, Sir Julian
Roberts, Wyn *(Conwy)*
Roe, Mrs Marion
Rost, Peter
Rowe, Andrew
Sackville, Hon Tom
Sainsbury, Hon Tim
Sayeed, Jonathan
Scott, Rt Hon Nicholas
Shaw, David *(Dover)*
Shaw, Sir Giles *(Pudsey)*
Shaw, Sir Michael *(Scarb')*
Shelton, Sir William
Shephard, Mrs G. *(Norfolk SW)*
Shepherd, Colin *(Hereford)*
Shepherd, Richard *(Aldridge)*
Shersby, Michael
Skeet, Sir Trevor
Smith, Sir Dudley *(Warwick)*
Soames, Hon Nicholas
Speed, Keith
Spicer, Sir Jim *(Dorset W)*
Spicer, Michael *(S Worcs)*
Squire, Robin
Stanbrook, Ivor
Stanley, Rt Hon Sir John
Steen, Anthony
Stevens, Lewis
Stewart, Allan *(Eastwood)*
Stewart, Andy *(Sherwood)*

Stokes, Sir John
Stradling Thomas, Sir John
Sumberg, David
Summerson, Hugo
Taylor, Ian *(Esher)*
Taylor, John M *(Solihull)*
Taylor, Teddy *(S'end E)*
Temple-Morris, Peter
Thompson, D. *(Calder Valley)*
Thompson, Patrick *(Norwich N)*
Thorne, Neil
Thornton, Malcolm
Thurnham, Peter
Townend, John *(Bridlington)*
Tracey, Richard
Tredinnick, David
Trippier, David
Twinn, Dr Ian
Vaughan, Sir Gerard
Waddington, Rt Hon David
Wakeham, Rt Hon John
Waldegrave, Hon William
Walden, George
Walker, Bill *(T'side North)*
Waller, Gary
Ward, John
Wardle, Charles *(Bexhill)*
Warren, Kenneth
Watts, John
Wells, Bowen
Wheeler, John
Whitney, Ray
Widdecombe, Ann
Wiggin, Jerry
Wilkinson, John
Wilshire, David
Winterton, Mrs Ann
Winterton, Nicholas
Wolfson, Mark
Wood, Timothy
Yeo, Tim
Young, Sir George *(Acton)*
Younger, Rt Hon George

Tellers for the Noes
  Mr. David Lightbown and
  Mr. David Heathcoat-Amory.

*Question accordingly negatived.*

*Question,* That the proposed words be there added, *put forthwith pursuant to Standing Order No. 30 (Questions on amendments), and agreed to.*

Mr. Speaker *forthwith declared the main Question, as amended, to be agreed to.*

*Resolved,*

That this House congratulates the management and workforce of British Coal on their achievements in increasing productivity and reducing costs; welcomes the Government's continuing financial support for the industry which is enabling it to move towards profitability and a viable future; recognises that the only secure long term future for the industry lies in becoming an efficient and competitive supplier of coal; rejects the proposition that British Coal can only sell if its customers are forced to buy, and, has confidence that British Coal, on the basis of its own performance and not of the Government's dictat, will become the supplier of choice to the privatised electricity industry.

## BUSINESS OF THE HOUSE

*Ordered,*

That, at this day's sitting, the Road Traffic (Driver Licensing and Information Systems) Bill *[Lords]* may be proceeded with, though opposed, until any hour.—*[Mr. Chapman.]*

# Road Traffic (Driver Licensing and Information Systems) Bill *[Lords]*

*(As amended in Standing Committee) considered.*

### New Clause 1

#### SIGHT TESTING

'It shall be a condition of the validity of any driving licence that the eyesight of the holder has been tested within a period and to a standard which shall be prescribed by a statutory instrument subject to approval by both Houses of Parliament.'.—*[Mr. Cohen.]*

*Brought up, and read the First time.*

10.15 pm

**Mr. Harry Cohen** (Leyton): I beg to move, That the clause be read a Second Time.

This is a sensible new clause as it would improve the current practice for testing the eyesight of a driver. At the moment a would-be driver has a one-off test just before his driving test when he must look at a number plate X yards away. After that test he may drive for life without a further eyesight test and it is assumed that his eyesight is satisfactory.

In Committee the Minister said that, each day, 60 cases of eyesight problems were reported to the driver and vehicle licensing centre. I pointed out to him that that meant that there were about 22,000 such cases a year—and that does not take into account the cases that are not reported. The Minister tried to justify his case by arguing that only 300 cases were subject to prosecution because of eyesight deficiencies. The other people, however, would be picked up for all sorts of reasons such as dangerous driving, but in each case poor eyesight would be a factor.

In Committee the Minister argued that eyesight was not important enough to warrant regular eye tests——

**The Minister for Roads and Traffic (Mr. Peter Bottomley):** Will the hon. Gentleman give way?

**Mr. Cohen:** I shall give way in a minute.

To an extent I agree with the Minister, as medical fitness is not just good eyesight, but it was wrong for him to say that eyesight was not important.

**Mr. Bottomley:** The point I was making was that the people who are most likely to be involved in injury crashes are those who have the best eyesight. I did not say that eyesight was not important.

**Mr. Cohen:** I take that point. There are some people who are too cocky and who cause accidents although they have all their faculties. Nevertheless, eyesight is an important factor. I appreciate the Minister's intervention, because he is now acknowledging that eyesight is important. As he has acknowledged that, eyesight should be tested regularly. People with poor eyesight may not only be involved in an accident, but may cause an accident, despite not being involved in it themselves. It is important for others that drivers have tests even if they believe that their sight is good.

**Mr. Frank Haynes** (Ashfield): My hon. Friend is correct. I welcome the Minister's comment about perfect eyesight and people having accidents, but he is doing nothing about it. My hon. Friend is aware that I am conscious of drivers passing me who are on the telephone. They have accidents although their eyesight is perfect, as the Minister says.

**Mr. Cohen:** My hon. Friend is right and my hon. Friend the Member for Islington, North (Mr. Corbyn) raised in Committee the point about car telephones and people's attention being distracted when they were supposed to be driving. Again, the Minister said that that was wrong and that he thought some action should be taken against such people. However, no amendment has been tabled on Report. It is an ideal opportunity for the Minister to act after making his comments in Committee, yet we have seen no action.

**Mr. Jeremy Corbyn** (Islington, North): I was reluctant to intervene in my hon. Friend's speech because he was just warming up. Is he aware that during our numerous debates in Committee about the misuse of car phones and their inherent danger, and about the lack of eyesight testing, the Minister largely conceded all our arguments? One would have thought that, having done so, he would table amendments to deal with the problem of drivers with poor eyesight and with drivers who persist in driving and talking on the telephone at the same time and who cannot, therefore, control the car properly. He has not done so. Does my hon. Friend not think that that is strange? The Minister seems to believe in a laissez-faire approach or perhaps he believes that road safety problems will be solved by some honeyed words from him at a suitable time on Radio 4.

**Mr. Cohen:** My hon. Friend makes a good point. The Bill seeks to reduce accidents, so there must be action on eyesight testing. My hon. Friend is right to say that the Minister spoke honeyed words in Committee about car telephones, but he did not make commitments about eyesight tests. He was shaky in his comments on eyesight tests and I suspect that the reason was that his Government had brought in charges for eye tests for the general public. We saw a report at the weekend that the average charge is now about £10·40 and that there has been a massive slump of 50 per cent. in the number of people taking that test. The Minister's Government have caused that. If the Minister were to take action on eyesight tests so that there were fewer road accidents, that would mean that the charge should be scrapped. The Minister is afraid to cross the Prime Minister because he is afraid that he would be sacked, so he will not speak up for the people who will be the victims.

The Minister should take action on eyesight tests, and a proper test should be free. There should be an element of compulsion and the test should be carried out regularly. Many drivers would welcome that. Those who failed the test would welcome finding out that they were unfit to drive because they would realise that they were a risk to themselves. Nobody should have anything to fear from having a proper eyesight test to see whether he is fit to drive. In addition to being compulsory, the test should be free—*[Interruption.]*

**Mr. Speaker:** Order. May I ask hon. Members not to indulge in private conversations.

**Mr. Cohen:** Thank you, Mr. Speaker. I appreciate your support. I am pleased to be given a hearing on this

[*Mr. Cohen*]

important matter. People's lives are at stake and the House should give due weight and proper consideration to my very serious proposal.

Sight tests are sometimes taken at the scene of an accident, and I have referred to the prosecutions that take place—about 300 a year. However, by then it is too late; the accident has already occurred and there may have been injuries or a death.

I asked the Minister what is the total number of people required to take regular eyesight tests to retain their driving licence and what proportion fail every year. I am talking not about the general public but about those who drive heavy goods vehicles and so on. The Minister replied:

"There is no information about the number of people required to take regular eyesight tests."

That is scandalous. If people are required to take regular tests, the information should be kept.

We were told in Committee that there was not enough evidence to justify a change. I dispute that, and I shall present a great deal of evidence from people who say that there should be regular tests. Yet the Minister requires some categories of people to take eyesight tests by law but then does not keep the information so that he can establish whether the tests are relevant or should be extended.

In his reply to me, the Minister said:

"In 1988-89 the total number of people required to take a prescribed eyesight test to determine their fitness to drive was 2,981.

Eyesight problems account for around 8 per cent. of the medical declarations on applications and notifications (during the currency of the licence), and around 8 per cent. of referrals and revocations relate to eyesight.

In 1987-88 there were 10,442 revocations refusals in all and in 1988-89 there were 10,891 revocations refusals in all, resulting in over 800 revocations refusals on eyesight grounds"—[*Official Report,* 18 May 1989; Vol. 153, c. *277*.]

Eight per cent. is not an insignificant proportion. If we extrapolate from that figure, we may conclude that there are a lot of people driving around with bad eyesight, whose sight will not have been tested since they passed the number plate test perhaps 20 years ago.

**Mr. Corbyn:** Does my friend agree—[HON. MEMBERS: "Your friend?"] Yes, he is a good friend of mine and an old friend——

**Mr. Tony Banks** (Newham, North-West): An excellent friend.

**Mr. Corbyn:** And an excellent friend. My hon. Friend has shown that in the majority of cases poor sight is voluntarily reported by more responsible drivers who feel that they may be a danger to other road users. That shows that there is a problem and that it is recognised by some drivers.

My hon. Friend's new clause would ensure that all drivers would be forced to have eyesight tests. That would mean that irresponsible drivers or those who did not believe that their sight was deteriorating would be forced to take a sight test and the roads would be much safer.

**Mr. Cohen:** I agree with my hon. Friend. I am not saying that everybody should take a sight test every week or even every year, but there should be a system for regular testing of drivers for their own benefit as well as everyone else's.

The Minister was kind enough to the Committee that considered the Bill to set up a meeting to which he brought along departmental experts. They sent shivers down my spine, however, when they argued for no change. That was especially my feeling when they said that most drivers drive by intuition and that it would not matter whether some of them were blindfolded. They did not quite say that, but they reached that position. I would hate to be driving a car if I were blindfolded or if a driver coming towards me were blindfolded.

10.30 pm

**Mr. Bob Cryer** (Bradford, South): My hon. Friend's words confirm what I thought the Minister said: that drivers with perfect eyesight are more likely to be involved in accidents. The Minister has presented us with a curious form of logic. On that basis, those with good eyesight would, under the regulations, be prescribed with glasses that would make their eyesight worse so as to make them immune from accidents. Surely that is a topsy-turvy approach. Perhaps my hon. Friend will comment upon that.

**Mr. Cohen:** That is self-explanatory.

**Mr. Peter Bottomley:** Will the hon. Gentleman give way?

**Mr. Cohen:** Yes, of course.

**Mr. Bottomley:** I think that the hon. Gentleman was right to say, "That is self-explanatory." He was presented with the sort of logic that would seem better in "Alice Through the Looking-glass" than in this place. The hon. Gentleman may be having a good deal of fun, but he should not say that the experts on eyesight and eye testing declared that individuals can drive better when they are blindfolded. He may say that I said that; it would not be true, although it would perhaps be acceptable. If he made the assertion, it would not be true, but it would be less unlikely. The same can be said of the hon. Member for Bradford, South (Mr. Cryer). The hon. Member for Leyton (Mr. Cohen) should not attribute such a comment to medical experts.

The truth is that those of us who are most concerned about eyesight put 60 motorists a day on report to Swansea while some put themselves on report. Fourteen out of 15 can continue driving. If those are the most likely to have eyesight troubles, and if most of them continue driving, it is worth accepting that drivers are right, if they have any concern, to ask those at Swansea, "Should I continue driving?" That presentation provides the reassurance that many should. The real problem comes, as the hon. Gentleman knows—he has probably experienced it himself, as most of us have—when we are young and our eyesight is at its best. That is when our involvement in injury accidents is at is greatest.

**Mr. Cohen:** I appreciate that. It should be said that the experts retreated when we started talking about the possibility of drivers being safer when they drove blindfolded. The main point, however, was that eye tests were not so relevant as driving by intuition. I disagreed with that.

The Minister is right about voluntary tests and drivers expressing worries and revoking their licences. In many instances, however, they are told that they can receive treatment, and that if they do so they can continue to drive. That is the position once they know that their eyesight is deficient in some way. I am saying that that should apply to the general public. The average motorist should know that his eyesight has become deficient. If he has that knowledge, he can receive treatment and, probably, continue to drive. It is far better that he continues to drive after treatment than to continue to drive without having had the benefit of any treatment.

**Mr. Cryer:** Perhaps my hon. Friend will comment on the Minister's assumption that our eyesight is best when we are young. People normally develop short-sightedness in their teens. That eyesight deficiency, which is easily and accurately corrected to produce perfect vision, stays with an individual until middle age. The assumption that at a certain age we are all provided with perfect or near-perfect eyesight that does not need correction, and that we do not need the tests that are provided for in the new clause, seems to be completely misplaced.

**Mr. Cohen:** I agree. Eyesight deficiencies can occur at any time. My eyesight deficiency occurred while I was at school, when I suddenly required glasses. My sister's eyesight deficiency occurred during her working life, when she was a teenager. It can happen at any time. Individuals can develop various eye ailments at different times. It is not only a problem of old age. That is why tests should be general for all drivers at regular intervals. I said that I would not delay the House too long, but various reports have recommended regular eyesight tests.

**Mr. Tony Banks:** The rate of eye testing is down by about 50 per cent., because of the Government-imposed charges. I take it that my hon. Friend has made that point. He should stress it again and again because it goes completely against the arguments of Conservative Members who supported the imposition of additional charges. The number of eye tests has fallen by 50 per cent. because of the charges imposed by short-sighted Conservative Members—in political terms, that is.

**Mr. Cohen:** I thought that my hon. Friend had made a Freudian slip, but it was a relevant one. The fact that the number of eye tests is down means that there will be more drivers with eyesight deficiencies who, in the normal course of events, would have had an eye test. Those drivers who, like me, wear glasses, probably went for an eye test every two years. That has been the average length of time between my check-ups up to now, but now that a charge has been introduced the length of time taken between visits is bound to be extended. Such people will be on the road with eyesight defeciencies when, formerly, they would have had a test. The 50 per cent. drop in the number of eye tests is appalling, and it will create more injuries, accidents and deaths. The Government must take responsibility for that policy.

**Mr. Corbyn:** I thank my hon. Friend for giving way again. Surely further research into the cause of road accidents is required. It is clear that many people drive who ought to have an eye test, and my hon. Friend's proposal would help to reduce the numbers who do so. Is my hon. Friend also aware that the real victims of those who drive with inadequate eyesight on a dark night, a wet day or in a poorly illuminated area are likely to be pedestrians and cyclists, rather than other motorised road users? Those victims are in no position to speak up about this. I cannot understand why the Minister does not realise the force of our argument that we need proper eyesight testing for all drivers to ensure that they can see properly and drive safely.

**Mr. Cohen:** My hon. Friend is absolutely right, and it is too late to do anything once the accident has occurred.

Another point was made by Lord Lucas in the other place.

**Mr. John Home Robertson** (East Lothian): Lord Lucan?

**Mr. Cohen:** Lord Lucan has disappeared; perhaps he was in an accident because he had an eyesight problem. I do not know, but he has not been seen for a long time.

In the other place, Lord Lucas said that as far as he was aware there had been no research because Stats 19, the police form reporting an accident, includes no requirement whatsoever to note physical health, whether general physical health or eyesight. Therefore, no evidence has been collected to show whether it was a contributory factor.

As my hon. Friend the Member for Islington, North said, when an accident occurs we do not know whether bad eyesight was a contributory factor. It may well have occurred because of eyesight deficiency, yet that will not be shown in the official forms. The figures to which I referred earlier show that, even so, many such cases are reported in which eyesight problems are a factor.

Plenty of people have called for higher standards, and one organisation to do so was one which I am sure that Conservative Members would hold in the highest regard: the police. They called for drivers' eyesight to be of a higher standard, and for compulsory regular testing. The Minister is ignoring the police. We know that his party——

**Ms. Mildred Gordon** (Bow and Poplar): Will my hon. Friend agree that under this Government's policies the cost of glasses and frames has gone up and up, and therefore in addition to the fact that there is now a charge for testing, as he rightly says, people will put off having their eyes tested and changing their glasses——

**Madam Deputy Speaker:** Order. We are dealing with new clause 1, which relates to sight testing and driving licences.

**Mr. Cohen:** I shall not go down the road suggested by my hon. Friend, as I have already dealt with it. Certainly, these high charges put drivers off having tests.

**Mr. Peter Bottomley:** How much did the hon. Gentleman pay for his glasses? Are they private or National Health?

**Mr. Cohen:** They are private glasses, bought cheaply at the Baker's Arms. As far as I can remember, they cost me about £20 a long time ago——

**Mr. Corbyn:** How near is that to the Green Man roundabout? Could my hon. Friend see that roundabout when he came out of the optician's? What has been the effect of the Government's road building madness on that roundabout?

**Mr. Cohen:** I can certainly see that the Government are giving Leyton and Leytonstone a bad deal with their road plan. I do not need my £20 glasses to see that—all the facts and figures go to prove it.

[*Mr. Cohen*]

There have been other reports in support of eyesight testing. Lord Lucas also quoted the report by McKean and Edington, of Southampton university, on the incidence of glaucoma. Admittedly, it was a small survey, but it showed that many people had not realised that they could not see to the left or the right, and that that led to their accidents. A test would show up that problem. The Minister should have taken that evidence into account.

I know that some of my hon. Friends are not too happy about the Common Market, but in the recent European elections the people said that they want the best European practices here. There are obviously bad practices in Europe, but the social charter, for instance, is an example of best practice. So is eyesight testing for drivers. Belgium, Denmark, Ireland and Luxembourg all impose far better requirements for testing than we do. In the European Community, the minimum static acuity for a two-eyed person is 0·4 in the better eye and 0·2 in the worse eye, and 0·5 for both eyes together. For a one-eyed person, it is 0·8.

**Mr. Cryer:** What about a three-eyed person?

**Mr. Cohen:** I shall not take that up, lest we come on to four-eyed people like me in my glasses.

I have mentioned one of five tests required by EC policy. We have a once-in-a-lifetime test, the number plate test, and it is not even a very good one. Surveys of large numbers of people have provided clear evidence of defects of eyesight. The evidence is there. The Government will get into trouble again with their policy for the EEC, because there is a Council directive on driving licences. It is number 10357/1/88, entitled "Minimum Standards of Physical and Mental Fitness for Driving a Motor Vehicle". There are two groups, one for driving heavy vehicles and one for general capacity vehicles. It says for group 1:

"applicants shall be required to undergo a medical examination if it becomes apparent, when the necessary formularies are being completed or during the tests which they have to undergo prior to obtaining a driving licence, that they have one or more of the medical disabilities mentioned in this Annex."

That, of course, includes an eyesight test. The directive further says that they

"shall undergo such periodic medical examinations as may be prescribed by national laws".

The implication in the directive is that there shall be periodic tests, not just a one-off test as we have in this country. It says under group 2:

"applicants shall undergo a medical examination before a driving licence is first granted to them and thereafter drivers shall undergo such periodic examinations as may be prescribed by national laws".

That implies regularity. It does not say that there will not be any tests after the initial one. Indeed, it says:

"The standards set by member states for issuing driving licences may be stricter than those set out in this Annex."

That is showing that the Government are well out of tune with the rest of Europe.

The directive goes on:

"All applicants for a driving licence should undergo an appropriate investigation to ensure that they have adequate visual acuity for driving motor vehicles. Where there is reason to doubt that the applicant's vision is adequate, he should be examined by a competent medical authority. At this examination attention should be paid to the following in particular: visual acuity, field of vision, twilight vision and progressive eye diseases."

None of these is investigated in our number-plate test.

**Mr. Cryer:** I am sure that when my hon. Friend refers to Europe, he is referring to that section of Europe that is called the Common Market. He should make that distinction clear.

Will my hon. Friend address his mind to regulations that will give the Minister the power to ensure that—for example, where eyesight tests are carried out and driving licences are submitted to Swansea for certification that the test has been approved and carried out—the legislation referring to the production of licences within five days is suitably modified so that those people whose licences are caught up in the log-jam at Swansea are not prosecuted? Because they have taken the test and their licences have gone to Swansea for approval and certification, they are open to another offence. As my hon. Friend knows, the failure to produce a licence within five days can be treated by the police as an offence even though there are good reasons, such as that the licence is at Swansea. For instance, diabetics have medical checks every three years.

**Mr. Cohen:** I should have thought that that would be a reasonable course to adopt. Of course, it is incumbent upon Swansea to process the licences rapidly, or at least to provide some evidence to the driver of the fact that his licence is being processed in Swansea. My hon. Friend has made a good point.

It is not just the European Community countries; many other countries around the world require more stringent eye tests for drivers than we do—in fact, it would be difficult to have worse than our system of a one-off test. The Community proposal in document 10357/1/88 says of corrective lenses:

"correction must be well tolerated. Driving licences shall not be issued to or renewed for applicants or drivers without a normal field of vision or suffering from diplopia."

How can that be tested for if there are no regular tests?

When the EEC produces these documents there is a ministerial response stating the Government's attitude. I hurried to the Library to get a copy of the response, which was contained in an explanatory memorandum. It stated:

"The Commission now proposes that the process of harmonisation should be taken a stage further . . . allowing residents"

of other member states to drive in the United Kingdom and vice versa. Our non-conformity with the other states will cease if the proposal goes through.

It also states that drivers of minibuses and light goods vehicles would have to meet higher medical standards. That would be difficult because they are volunteers and they might be deterrred by the costs involved. The Government should help voluntary drivers in those circumstances to pass a better quality test. Those drivers would want that because they are driving people for whom they care and they would want a higher standard of driving. The Department of Transport should help those organisations.

**Mr. Cryer:** The additional requirements for minibus drivers are not connected with the eyesight tests. They are part of the unnecessary and superfluous harmonisation proposals that pour from an over-eager and zealous Commission that wants to reduce us all to the same level of conformity. While I accept my hon. Friend's point that is is desirable to increase the standards of eyesight testing, the directive to which my hon Friend is referring—if it is the one that I have in mind—would make it very difficult for voluntary organisations to maintan their minibus services for the disabled.

**Mr. Cohen:** That is why I referred to the drivers in voluntary organisations and said that the Government should help them directly perhaps by giving them priority in tests. I am not in favour of harmonisation of everything under the sun, but I am in favour of better standards for driving and eyesight tests. At the moment we have the worst such tests in Europe.

The memorandum states:

"An acceptable driving licence will benefit United Kingdom drivers in other Community countries . . . and would cut the costs of British licensing arrangements."
That takes away aother of the Government's arguments.

The startling point about the explanatory memorandum, which is about a proposal which refers to eyesight tests, is that the Government avoid the issue of eyesight tests. They are not mentioned in the Government's memorandum. That shows the Government's guilt over that issue.

I rest my case on that. The Minister has been shown to be guilty of not coming forward with proper standards for eyesight tests of drivers. I think that an eyesight test should be included in a general medical fitness test for drivers. That may be difficult to implement. However, at the very least, this sensible new clause should be accepted to allow a statutory instrument to come before the House to provide for regular eyesight tests. That would save many lives and a great number of injuries. Such testing should also be free.

The Government should stand ashamed of the charge for eye tests that they imposed, of the consequential 50 per cent. reduction in the number of people taking eye tests, and of the increasing incidence of poor eyesight among drivers and the public in general. I commend my very sensible new clause, and I hope that House will see sense and that the Minister will recognise his guilt and accept it.

*Motion made, and Question proposed,* That the debate be now adjourned.—[*Mr. Garel-Jones.*]

*Question put:—*
*The House divided:* Ayes 128, Noes 46.

**Division No. 262]**             **[10.55 pm**

### AYES

| | |
|---|---|
| Alexander, Richard | Cash, William |
| Alison, Rt Hon Michael | Channon, Rt Hon Paul |
| Allason, Rupert | Chapman, Sydney |
| Amess, David | Chope, Christopher |
| Amos, Alan | Clarke, Rt Hon K. (Rushcliffe) |
| Arbuthnot, James | Coombs, Anthony (Wyre F'rest) |
| Arnold, Jacques (Gravesham) | Coombs, Simon (Swindon) |
| Arnold, Tom (Hazel Grove) | Cran, James |
| Ashby, David | Currie, Mrs Edwina |
| Batiste, Spencer | Davies, Q. (Stamf'd & Spald'g) |
| Bennett, Nicholas (Pembroke) | Davis, David (Boothferry) |
| Bevan, David Gilroy | Day, Stephen |
| Blackburn, Dr John G. | Devlin, Tim |
| Boswell, Tim | Dorrell, Stephen |
| Bottomley, Peter | Douglas-Hamilton, Lord James |
| Bowis, John | Dunn, Bob |
| Brazier, Julian | Durant, Tony |
| Brooke, Rt Hon Peter | Fallon, Michael |
| Buck, Sir Antony | Favell, Tony |
| Burns, Simon | Fenner, Dame Peggy |
| Butcher, John | Fishburn, John Dudley |
| Butterfill, John | Forman, Nigel |
| Carrington, Matthew | Forth, Eric |

| | |
|---|---|
| Franks, Cecil | Neubert, Michael |
| Freeman, Roger | Nicholls, Patrick |
| French, Douglas | Nicholson, David (Taunton) |
| Gale, Roger | Norris, Steve |
| Garel-Jones, Tristan | Paice, James |
| Gill, Christopher | Pawsey, James |
| Goodhart, Sir Philip | Porter, David (Waveney) |
| Gow, Ian | Powell, William (Corby) |
| Greenway, John (Ryedale) | Redwood, John |
| Gregory, Conal | Rhodes James, Robert |
| Griffiths, Peter (Portsmouth N) | Sackville, Hon Tom |
| Gummer, Rt Hon John Selwyn | Sayeed, Jonathan |
| Hague, William | Shaw, David (Dover) |
| Hampson, Dr Keith | Shaw, Sir Michael (Scarb') |
| Hanley, Jeremy | Shephard, Mrs G. (Norfolk SW) |
| Hannam, John | Shersby, Michael |
| Hargreaves, A. (B'ham H'll Gr') | Skeet, Sir Trevor |
| Hargreaves, Ken (Hyndburn) | Squire, Robin |
| Harris, David | Stanbrook, Ivor |
| Heathcoat-Amory, David | Stevens, Lewis |
| Hill, James | Stewart, Andy (Sherwood) |
| Hind, Kenneth | Stradling Thomas, Sir John |
| Howarth, Alan (Strat'd-on-A) | Summerson, Hugo |
| Howarth, G. (Cannock & B'wd) | Taylor, Ian (Esher) |
| Howell, Ralph (North Norfolk) | Taylor, John M (Solihull) |
| Hunt, Sir John (Ravensbourne) | Thompson, Patrick (Norwich N) |
| Irvine, Michael | Thorne, Neil |
| Jack, Michael | Thurnham, Peter |
| Jessel, Toby | Townend, John (Bridlington) |
| Jones, Gwilym (Cardiff N) | Twinn, Dr Ian |
| Jopling, Rt Hon Michael | Waddington, Rt Hon David |
| King, Roger (B'ham N'thfield) | Walden, George |
| Knight, Greg (Derby North) | Waller, Gary |
| Lightbown, David | Wardle, Charles (Bexhill) |
| Lord, Michael | Wheeler, John |
| Martin, David (Portsmouth S) | Widdecombe, Ann |
| Maude, Hon Francis | Winterton, Mrs Ann |
| Maxwell-Hyslop, Robin | Winterton, Nicholas |
| Mitchell, Sir David | Wood, Timothy |
| Moate, Roger | |
| Morrison, Sir Charles | Tellers for the Ayes: |
| Moss, Malcolm | Mr. Kenneth Carlisle and |
| Nelson, Anthony | Mr. David Maclean. |

### NOES

| | |
|---|---|
| Abbott, Ms Diane | Livsey, Richard |
| Ashdown, Rt Hon Paddy | Loyden, Eddie |
| Banks, Tony (Newham NW) | McAvoy, Thomas |
| Barnes, Harry (Derbyshire NE) | McKay, Allen (Barnsley West) |
| Bradley, Keith | Mahon, Mrs Alice |
| Brown, Ron (Edinburgh Leith) | Parry, Robert |
| Buckley, George J. | Patchett, Terry |
| Cohen, Harry | Pike, Peter L. |
| Cook, Frank (Stockton N) | Powell, Ray (Ogmore) |
| Cousins, Jim | Prescott, John |
| Cox, Tom | Primarolo, Dawn |
| Cryer, Bob | Ruddock, Joan |
| Cummings, John | Sheerman, Barry |
| Cunliffe, Lawrence | Skinner, Dennis |
| Dixon, Don | Spearing, Nigel |
| Duffy, A. E. P. | Taylor, Matthew (Truro) |
| Dunnachie, Jimmy | Wallace, James |
| Foster, Derek | Wareing, Robert N. |
| Gordon, Mildred | Watson, Mike (Glasgow, C) |
| Haynes, Frank | Welsh, Michael (Doncaster N) |
| Hinchliffe, David | Wise, Mrs Audrey |
| Howarth, George (Knowsley N) | |
| Illsley, Eric | Tellers for the Noes: |
| Jones, Martyn (Clwyd S W) | Mr. Martin Redmond and |
| Kirkwood, Archy | Mr. Jeremy Corbyn. |

*Question accordingly agreed to.*
*Debate to be resumed tomorrow.*

# Enterprise Education Initiative

*Motion made, and Question proposed,* That this House do now adjourn.—[*Mr. Sackville.*]

11.6 pm

**Mrs. Gillian Shephard** (Norfolk, South-West): I am grateful to have the opportunity to raise in the House the important matter of co-operation between industry and education. The demographic decline in the number of young people, combined with rapid technological advances in all areas of industry and commerce, means that effective collaboration between business and education is vital if we are to maximise the potential of our young people.

The importance of collaboration between industry and education was perceived and tackled in Norfolk, of which my constituency is a part, some 12 years ago. The idea of a Norfolk schools and industry group first emerged as long ago as 1977. The group itself, now called the Norfolk education, industry and commerce group, was formally incorporated in 1981, since when industry and schools in Norfolk have greatly benefited from the partnership.

Everyone closely involved in education has had cause in the past to be concerned about the gap between the education system and business employers. Those in education have traditionally complained that employers are not interested in the broad aims and achievements of the education system, while employers, equally traditionally, have complained that schools are incapable of turning out young people who can read and write.

A particular instance of the gap in mutual understanding was the old certificate of secondary education examination which had many excellent features, such as its emphasis on course work, steady achievement and relevant study material, which have now been incorporated into the general certificate of secondary education. However, despite its excellence, many employers never understood the CSE, never wanted it, preferred the general certificate of education—often because they had taken it—and always regarded the CSE as second best. As one head teacher put it to me:

"Megaphone diplomacy to bridge that sort of gap doesn't work. What's needed is a consistent long-term working together so we can see what the other is trying to achieve."

That was the aim of the Norfolk education, industry and commerce group when it was set up in 1981. At that time a major problem facing schools and industry was unemployment. Clearly the group's main role was to prepare young people for the demands of industry in a world where jobs were scarce and where their knowledge and skills needed to be as closely matched as possible to the jobs that there were. Now, thanks to the success of the Government's economic policy, the reverse is the case. With excellent employment prospects and a 20 per cent. drop in the number of young people, the need for close links between education and employers is just as great because employers will be competing for the right young recruits for their businesses. That competition will be given even greater point as we approach the challenges of 1992.

The aims of the group are to form links between business and education; to develop an understanding of business and its importance to the nation's prosperity; to affirm the importance of wealth creation in society and its social consequences; to present business as a stimulating environment offering fulfilling and creative careers; to

discover how the needs of an industrial society are being met within the constraints of our education system and to provide a resource directory, a copy of which I have in the House, and which is a model of its kind, listing 140 different companies which are linked with the scheme. They include manufacturers, retailers, distributors, professional services and other services such as removals businesses, Anglia Television, oil companies, Norwich airport and catering concerns and, especially important in Norfolk, a farm-school link.

The group is a company limited by guarantee and with charitable status. Its executive committee includes the British Institute of Management, the careers service, chambers of commerce and trade, college principals, the Confederation of British Industry, the local education authority, the Engineering Employers Federation, head teachers, Her Majesty's inspectors, industrial training boards, the Institute of Directors, the Institute of Industrial Directors, junior chambers, the National Farmers Union, Understanding British Industry and the University of East Anglia. I go into some detail because I believe that the group is a model of its kind.

Clearly its work has developed over the years, but by any standards it is impressive as 6,000 sixth-form students have been involved in conferences and discussions, and 3,000 fifth-form students have been involved in seminars. Each year, 200 young people take part in young enterprise projects with prizes from industry. In 1988-89 alone, 29 school-based conferences were held and eight conferences for teachers and representatives of industry and commerce. The work for the young people is carefully structured and I have first-class examples of the material used in seminars and discussion groups. That material is jointly prepared by industry and education. One especially important event was a conference on education business partnerships held last January and arising from the CBI business education task force initiative.

The philosophy underlying that initiative could well serve as an inspiration for the Department of Trade and Industry enterprise education initiative. The brief for that business education task force states:

"Without an effective partnership developing between business and education the prospects for an internationally competitive United Kingdom economy in the 21st century will become remote. The issues have to be high on the agenda, both of the business community and of educationalists. We will all fail if answers cannot be found and applied."

The consciousness of the need for education, among other things, to produce young people who can meet the challenges of today's and tomorrow's business and industry has been developing in education as part of the Government's education policy. Norfolk was fortunate to be chosen as a pilot area for the technical and vocational education initiative some years ago. That new approach to learning for 14 to 18-year-olds was Government-funded so that lessons could become more practical and relevant to adult life and work. Over the next few years, £10 million will be spent in Norfolk to extend the benefit of TVEI to all secondary schools. The Norfolk education industry and commerce group had agreed through its contacts and the network that it had built up to provide two weeks' work experience for every school leaver as part of TVEI—an offer now superseded by the developments that my hon. Friend will describe. But he will agree that it is to the group's credit that it was able to provide that much-needed extension of TVEI out of its own local initiative.

Other developments in various job-related courses for young people include work experience and lead to qualifications from organisations such as the Business and Technician Education council, the City and guilds and the Royal Society of Arts. Moreover, the national curriculum builds in a number of improvements which, although good in themselves, are also helpful to employers. A common curriculum leading to a common examination means, obviously, that employers can easily understand the standards that young people have reached, from whichever part of the country they come. The inclusion and encouragement of technology as part of the national curriculum are also vital not only for the education of young people but for needs of industry and business. Regular testing and assessment built into the Education Reform Act 1988 mean that records of a pupil's achievement when presented to employers can give a meaningful description of a young person's ability. That should be in place by 1990.

Other changes in the Education Reform Act, such as the inclusion of a business representative on every governing body, have been helpful in promoting integration between education and the business and industrial world. Many counties, including Norfolk, already have such representation, but now that governing bodies have such a close relationship with the way that schools are run—because of local financial management—practical interaction between business and education expertise will prove invaluable.

At the heart of education and industry links lies the need for two different cultures to understand one another. Industry Year in 1986 was a recognition that the two cultures were interdependent and that, in turn, on their co-operation depends the success of the economy. The feeling in the industrial world that somehow education might be anti-industry or anti-business caused schools to be the chief target for Industry Year—happily, with fruitful results. It is my experience that schools, far from finding the attentions of business and industry a nuisance, welcome them as a source of practical and almost moral support. Since 1986, demand for industrial involvement in schools has outstripped supply. I hope that we shall hear from my hon. Friend the Minister about the response of the Department of Trade and Industry to that demand.

I hope that my hon. Friend the Minister can respond to a number of specific concerns on school-industry links. First, there is a need for the benefits that I have described, arising from the Norfolk group's work for Norfolk youngsters, to be spread nationwide, for the benefit of everybody else's youngsters. The combination of the demographic decline in the number of young people and the need for a well-trained and flexible work force in the national interest means that such benefits are far too valuable to be available only where local enthusiasm has seen fit to develop them.

Secondly, a careful look should be taken at the particular difficulties of rural areas and small businesses. It is one thing for a large company to allow time for its managers to devote to learning about the educational system; it is another for a small, developing company to have to do the same—yet it is small business which is providing the fastest growing sector in our economy, which will employ many young people and which most precisely needs the help of flexibly trained employees.

Thirdly, real resources must be put into the development of a Government-inspired scheme on an ongoing basis. An excellent beginning has been made, but we have gone beyond the stage, if we are serious about school and business links, of expecting the education service simply to absorb that extra task with no help. The programme needs to run for a realistic time. There needs to be proper input into teacher education. The programme must be properly structured and should take account of the work that is already done by counties such as Norfolk.

This is an important subject, but it is an unsocial hour. I am grateful to my hon. Friend the Minister for his patience in listening to me. I know that he too regards the link between education and industry and business as very important. I look forward to hearing his response.

11.19 pm

**The Parliamentary Under-Secretary of State for Industry and Consumer Affairs (Mr. Eric Forth):** I congratulate my hon. Friend the Member for Norfolk, South-West (Mrs. Shephard) not only on bringing this important subject to the attention of the House but on her good fortune in being able to do so. I shall endeavour to reply to the points that she made and give the House the up-to-date picture in the important subject of communication and understanding between education and industry.

I was most impressed—I think that anyone would be—by the detail that my hon. Friend gave the House of the initiatives and impressive work that has been done in Norfolk. I doubt whether many other local education authorities could match Norfolk's dedication and involvement. I hope that others will be made aware of the progress in Norfolk and will attempt to emulate it.

In the light of my hon. Friend's comments, I should like to draw attention to two important developments in the past week. I shall describe how they fit into a Governmentwide strategy to encourage enterprising attitudes in schools.

In preparing our plans, we have taken into account many of the points made by my hon. Friend. We have been determined to build on existing good practice and the experience of counties such as Norfolk and to avoid the reinvention of wheels. We therefore mounted a national initiative—the enterprise and education initiative—under which lessons learned throughout the country are shared by all local education authorities and spread throughout the business community and education world. It has a clear and simple structure and a sensible time scale. It will certainly meet two of the criteria that my hon. Friend mentioned. I assure her that it is well resourced; we currently plan to spend £32 million on it over the next four years.

My hon. Friend has already drawn attention to the need to ensure that trainee teachers gain appreciation of the needs of employers and of the importance of links between schools and employers. I am glad to be able to tell the House that part of the initiative of the Department of Trade and Industry will be a programme in initial teacher training. We will be committing £3·5 million to this work.

We have decided to help employers find their way round the education service and to help teachers find helpful employers. My hon. Friend has already drawn attention to the need to support and encourage the involvement of small businesses and those in rural areas: not only will smaller enterprises be able to benefit most from having future employers who are versatile and

[*Mr. Eric Forth*]

enterprising in their attitudes, but they are most likely to be able to offer teachers an understanding of economic management in miniature.

The Confederation of British Industry found in its survey that one factor stopping companies getting involved is confusion about who they should approach. The Society of Education Officers has told us that what is stopping many schools is that they do not have the time or organisation to make individual approaches to smaller local businesses. The Department has put in place a network of local enterprise and education advisers whose sole job is to encourage local partnership activity, in particular by marketing to employers the benefits of links with schools and persuading them to become involved. There are 147 advisers in place, whose work is costing the Department £8 million over two years. We are putting this considerable sum of money into this work because we believe that it is essential to the thrust of the initiative. By deploying this marketing force, we can help the uncommitted employer find his or her way through the multiplicity of organisations that operate in this sector, and continue to help the education service.

We recognise that it is not sufficient to ask employers to get involved with schools. We need to suggest specific activities, preferably offering deepening involvement as the employer gains experience. We have therefore set two demanding targets for our advisers, and, indeed, for employers.

First, we have asked the advisers to find work experience places for all pupils. Work experience does not mean offering a permanent job to young people. It means giving them a chance to find out what work is like. All that companies are being asked to do is take one or two children at a time and let them do a job for a week or two or, if that is not possible, to let them shadow a member of staff actually doing the job.

I am delighted to announce that in only the first five months of this year our advisers have found 67,000 additional work experience places. That is an impressive figure and I take this opportunity to commend the advisers who have found those places. I am sure that my hon. Friend welcomes that figure. I would not be surprised if she found that her county is taking a leading part in the scheme along the lines that she outlined. I am also delighted to report to the House the positive attitude that has been found among many of the companies that have been approached. We are very encouraged by that.

Partnership, however, does not stop at work experience for young people. Teachers, too, need personal experience of business especially if they are to deliver effectively the new national curriculum. Our second target, therefore, is to offer 10 per cent. of teachers each year the opportunity to gain some personal experience of the world of business.

Ten per cent. of teachers is a challenging target, particularly as many schools will be unable to spare the teachers in term time, so a high proportion of the placements will take place in school holidays. But we know that many employers are keen to arrange interesting placements for local teachers. They want to tell teachers about their industries. So, with the help of employers, we are determined to offer such an attractive programme to teachers that they will be keen to take part. We are committing £14 million over five years to ensure that that happens.

I have so far described how employers can help the local education service by giving work experience to a young person, and then graduating to giving business experience to a teacher, but there are many other ways in which employers can work with schools. Our advisers stand ready to help both employers and teachers to get involved in such activities, and we expect that they will give greater attention to these activities over the coming months. The national nature of the adviser service also means that good practice can quickly be shared around the country—as, indeed, can lessons about how to involve employers in rural areas.

I also emphasise that all this activity has been designed to complement the work of the Department of Education and Science and the Department of Employment. My right hon. Friends the Secretary of State for Employment and the Secretary of State for Education and Science joined my right hon. Friend the Secretary of State, in launching the DTI's enterprise and education initiative. I shall touch on the roles of the other two Departments in this area.

The Department of Employment, and in particular the Training Agency, are particularly concerned with easing the transition from school to work. It is vital that education and training should smoothly bridge the transition from school to work. TVEI, mentioned by my hon. Friend, compacts and work-related further education initiatives help that to happen, in conjunction of course with the work of the careers service and YTS programmes.

The main task of the Department of Education and Science is to improve the structure and relevance of the curriculum. Last week that led to an important development in the form of the publication of the report of the national curriculum working group on design and technology. I sincerely compliment the group on its report which will present an exciting challenge to both teachers and their pupils. In the past, we have taught craft subjects by telling pupils what to make, and how to make them. In the future, pupils will be asked to think for themselves about the design of what they make, the time available to make it, the choice of materials, and indeed the cost. If the report is accepted, pupils will in future be taught to take account of the needs and preferences of consumers, and to prepare a simple business plan, including a cash forecast and budget, and to monitor performance against it. They will consider the importance of people as a resource, and the need to bring together, train and organise teams.

Where do we go from here? First, the various industry-education link bodies are beginning to respond to the curricular developments that I outlined earlier. They know that there is now little need for trail blazing. They instead need to advise and support teachers as they get to grips with the new design and technology curriculum, and in due course with the need to teach economic and industrial understanding within the whole curriculum. I am considering ways in which the DTI might support the link bodies as they set about this challenging and important task.

Second, I see signs that our support for local partnership activity, such as the adviser and teacher placement services, will lead to the creation of strong local partnerships between the education service and employers. For instance, we have already heard how, in Norfolk, the education, industry and commerce group is setting many fine examples to the rest of the country in promoting partnership activity. That organisation acts as host for both the DTI adviser and the teacher placement organiser.

I believe that every local community needs to create a strong and effective body which will promote partnership activity. The DTI has sought to encourage this process by generally appointing one local host organisation only to run both the adviser and teacher placement services. Last week in another important development we announced that we are taking this process one step further. We intend to give the new training and enterprise councils the chance to provide both the adviser and teacher placement services, but only, of course, if the existing local host bodies agree that their local TEC can take over this role. Local TECs will then be able to take a strategic overview of the whole work-related education and training provision in their area.

We must also review, before the end of next year, whether individual advisers and their hosts have offered good value for money to the taxpayer and to the local community. If they have, we shall need to consider whether the Department of Trade and Industry should offer further limited financial support to help individual communities to take over and develop the adviser service in a way that makes it even more responsive to local needs. I hope that my hon. Friend will be reassured, therefore,

not only that we have put in place substantial resources to meet the immediate perceived demand, but that we shall keep a close eye on how matters develop and then hope that the burden can be gradually transferred from the taxpayer to local community efforts tailored in a way that most suits local needs.

I appreciate the spirit in which my hon. Friend has raised this subject. I have been impressed by what she has said about the efforts being made in her county of Norfolk. I hope that, from the few comments I have been able to make, my hon. Friend has been reassured that the Department of Trade and Industry is sensitive not only to needs nationally, but to the needs in Norfolk that she has described. I hope that what I have said will be good news in Norfolk and in the rest of the country and that people will realise the extreme seriousness with which we take the issue, the extent of the resources that we are committing to it and the great importance that Ministers at the Department of Trade and Industry and other Departments give to it. I hope that my hon. Friend will take that message back to Norfolk and give people there thanks for the work they have done and encouragement for the work that I am sure they will do in the future.

*Question put and agreed to.*

*Adjourned accordingly at twenty-nine minutes to Twelve o'clock.*

# House of Commons

*Tuesday 27 June 1989*

*The House met at half-past Two o'clock*

## PRAYERS

[MR. SPEAKER *in the Chair*]

## PRIVATE BUSINESS

### HAYLE HARBOUR BILL *[Lords]*

*Order for Second Reading read.*
*To be read a Second time on Thursday 29 June.*

### KING'S CROSS RAILWAYS BILL

*Motion made,*
That the petitions of Eileen Tegg and Nicholas Holliman be referred back to the Court of Referees.—*[Mr. Chris Smith.]*

**Hon. Members:** Object.

# Oral Answers to Questions

## HEALTH

### NHS Reform

1. **Mr. Day:** To ask the Secretary of State for Health whether the intention of the new general practitioners' contract is to increase doctors' list sizes.

**The Secretary of State for Health (Mr. Kenneth Clarke):** No, Sir. The sole aim of the new contract is to raise the standard of care patients receive from the family doctor service. There is no possibility that it will lead to any increase in average list size.

**Mr. Day:** Is my right hon. and learned Friend aware that, in 1965, the British Medical Association, which was in dispute with the then Labour Government, recommended that general practitioners resign from the National Health Service? Is he further aware that the main point of dispute between the then Government and the BMA at the time was seniority payments, to which the Labour Government were opposed? Does he agree that the Opposition's present position is therefore rather hypocritical?

**Mr. Clarke:** My hon. Friend is right. There was a serious dispute between the former Labour Government and general practitioners on the last occasion when the general practitioners' contract was being revised. Obviously, the attitude of today's Labour party is rather different from that of its predecessor. The hon. Member for Livingston (Mr. Cook) would simply write a letter to the BMA asking what it wants the Labour party to agree to. That was not the practice in former times.

**Mr. Fearn:** Does the Secretary of State agree that a general practitioner should have a maximum number of patients? If there is to be a maximum, is it to be categorised according to elderly, young, indifferent, or what?

**Mr. Clarke:** Nothing that I propose will increase a doctor's average list size. Obviously, patients will join the practice of a doctor whom they think gives them the right quality of care and the right amount of time. I would be most reluctant to contemplate a maximum. It would mean telling patients that they have to leave the list of a doctor whom they think is giving satisfactory service. That is not the way of going about it.

**Mr. Nicholas Winterton:** Does my right hon. and learned Friend agree that increasing the capitation percentage of a doctor's remuneration could reduce the amount of time that a doctor can spend with each patient and that that could be counterproductive for health care?

**Mr. Clarke:** No. Although I do not regard myself as a mathematical genius, I believe that most of those arguments are nonsense. A doctor's average list size is determined by the number of doctors and patients. I have no control over either of those things. Because more general practitioners keep joining the National Health Service, the average list sizes keep dropping, and I imagine that they will continue to do so. Patients will not join the list of someone who has taken on so many patients that he starts cutting the time that he spends with each patient. There is no way that anybody should or will react to the new contract by trying artifically to inflate a practice list over the average size.

**Mr. Robin Cook:** Does the Secretary of State appreciate that the simple and straightforward way by which GPs can increase the average list size is by not appointing new partners? Is he aware of complaints, particularly by women graduates, that since he published his White Paper adverts for new partners have dried up and adverts for part-time partners have practically vanished? How can he possibly pretend that a contract that will make it more difficult for women to become established as general practitioners is likely to encourage more women to come forward for cervical smears?

**Mr. Clarke:** It is an astonishing allegation that, for purely financial reasons, doctors will reduce the time that they can give patients just by not taking on another partner, and thereby willingly taking on more patients for themselves. The financial advantage to a partner in the average practice would be quite minor. I do not think that many doctors would be so irresponsible as to do that, and I do not think that patients would stay with practices that do that. I do not accept that anything in the new contract is any deterrent to women becoming full partners in general practice. I expect many more women to do so. For the first time, we are making provision for part-time principals, job sharing and so on to recognise that more women are likely to go into practice and have family commitments during some part of their careers.

### NHS Reform (Yorkshire)

2. **Mr. John Greenway:** To ask the Secretary of State for Health what assessment he has made of the prospects for self-governing hospitals in the Yorkshire region.

**Mr. Kenneth Clarke:** I am very pleased to have received so far 10 expressions of interest in self-governing status in the Yorkshire region. I cannot yet comment in detail on the prospects for particular hospitals and units in the region.

**Mr. Greenway:** Although I recognise that hospitals facing the threat of closure might not achieve self-government, does my right hon. and learned Friend agree that hospitals that have expressed an interest in self-government should not have their hopes dashed by rationalisation plans formulated by health authorities since his White Paper proposals were published? In particular, will he consider the case of Malton, where the local general practitioner practice, supported by the family practitioner committee, is keen to take on a practice budget in conjunction with Malton community hospital achieving self-governing status, towards which maintaining general practitioner beds and other services is essential for improved patient care and convenience?

**Mr. Clarke:** I have made it clear that self-government cannot be considered as an alternative to necessary closure and that health authorities must continue with planning their services as now. Nevertheless, I see prospects of a combination of self-government for a community hospital and of practice budgets for some local general practitioner practices leading to an increased use and better financing of popular general practitioner beds in community hospitals. If any expressions of interest come from Malton, I shall, of course, consider them with interest and on their merits.

**Mr. Duffy:** Earlier this month the Secretary of State announced the regional conference for Leeds on 11 July for the hospitals that he has in mind for self-government and that are showing interest in the idea. As some hospitals in Sheffield, Doncaster and north Nottinghamshire, which fall, as he knows, within the area of the Trent regional health authority, are showing similar interest, will he consider arranging a separate conference to be located in, say, Sheffield for the same purpose?

**Mr. Clarke:** I shall consider that helpful suggestion. We are not so rigid about regional boundaries as to insist that people attend a centre that is less convenient for their hospital. The meetings that I have attended so far with people from the units where interest has been expressed have been extremely successful, and I am sure that we shall have a full series of such meetings.

**Mr. Kirkhope:** Will my right hon. and learned Friend accept from me that there is considerable excitement in Leeds at the prospect of self-government for hospitals, and positive and great interest in the possibilities for the future? However, will he join me in condemning the scurrilous scaremongering of the unions and other politically motivated people in Leeds to try to prevent self-government?

**Mr. Clarke:** Local people are extremely interested in the idea of doctors, nurses and hospital managers having more autonomy over how their hospital is run. When I attend meetings with those interested, there is considerable interest as we explain in more detail how our proposals will work in financial and personnel terms and how they will be able to develop their own services. I agree with my hon. Friend. All that is happening despite the daft campaign in

some locations where people are still claiming that the proposals will lead to hospitals leaving the Health Service or to disruptions in the service. That argument is simply not sustainable when one considers the details of our proposals.

**Mr. Crowther:** Is the Secretary of State aware that some consultants in the Yorkshire region are privately expressing fears that a hospital that does not become self governing may suffer a hidden penalty in the allocation of resources? Will he give the House a cast-iron assurance that that will not happen?

**Mr. Clarke:** Under the new system, resources will be allocated to the health authorities and to general practitioners who hold practice budgets. They will decide the hospitals with which to have an agreement for the provision of the services that they need. The fear that the hon. Gentleman has described is based on a fundamental misunderstanding of how the new arrangement will work.

## NHS Reform

3. **Mr. Cousins:** To ask the Secretary of State for Health whether he intends that reduction in length-of-stay targets should form part of hospital contracts.

**The Parliamentary Under-Secretary of State for Health (Mr. Roger Freeman):** Length of stay could be one element which health authorities might discuss with hospitals when reaching an agreement on a contract as it might be an important factor in determining how many patients could be treated within the resources available. The contract itself need not, however, specify how long a patient should stay in hospital.

**Mr. Cousins:** Does the Minister accept that it would be disgraceful to build into a system for hospital contracts financial pressures that could lead to patients being discharged before their social circumstances in the community are right and before their medical needs are correct? Does he agree that that would simply be shifting the cash responsibility from the hospital contract on to social and community service—another sector of the budget?

**Mr. Freeman:** The quality of care available in hospital is not related to and cannot be correlated with the length of stay of patients. The average length of stay of patients over the past 10 years has decreased from 13 days to 10 days. That is a reflection of the substantial increase in day surgery and of advance in medical technology.

**Mr. Redwood:** How serious is the Minister about improving quality of treatment? Will he use the contracts as one way of improving quality? What progress is being made with the appointments systems as part of that package? Could those also be enforced through the contracts?

**Mr. Freeman:** Quality is extremely important in hospital care. I commend to my hon. Friend and the House the new document published by my right hon. and learned Friend the Secretary of State for Health on 20 June entitled "Self-governing Hospitals", which goes into some detail about the importance of quality in contracts for care of patients in hospital.

**4. Mr. Roy Hughes:** To ask the Secretary of State for Health what representations he has received from professional bodies and trade unions concerning the Government's review of the National Health Service.

**5. Mr. Knox:** To ask the Secretary of State for Health how many representations he has received from members of the public about the White Paper "Working for Patients".

**Mr. Kenneth Clarke:** I have received in total about 8,000 representations so far.

**Mr. Hughes:** Would it not be wiser if the Secretary of State were more candid with the House and admitted that all those bodies have been positively hostile to his proposals, believing that they can cause serious damage to patient care? If he did so, he could scrap his proposals and go back to the drawing board. Certainly many of his Back-Bench Members would be relieved.

**Mr. Clarke:** I fear that if I say anything of the kind, it will be a long way from the truth. Although there is a great deal of public campaigning, I am having extremely helpful and constructive meetings not only with those who lead the professional organisations, but with large numbers of their members. It is obvious that the process of implementing the reforms is already under way, because the great bulk of them have been readily accepted by the majority of the medical profession and others.

**Mr. Knox:** Will my right hon. and learned Friend confirm that he is giving serious consideration to all constructive representations made to him?

**Mr. Clarke:** I can. The whole basis on which we have proceeded is to issue a White Paper and working documents inviting constructive contributions. We intend to work out in detail matters such as self-governing hospitals and general practitioners' practice budgets with willing volunteers. I keep telling my organised critics that they must choose whether they wish to remain spectators on the sidelines, merely shouting abuse, or to take part in constructive and sensible discussion on how the Health Service might be improved.

**Mr. Grocott:** If it is true that the Minister is listening to constructive criticism, which some of us have reason to doubt, can he give the House one or two concrete examples of the way in which his proposals have changed as a result of the almost universal objections that he has received?

**Mr. Clarke:** I spent 10 hours in the time-honoured method of beer and sandwiches in an almost locked room resolving difficulties over the general practitioners' contract and bringing to an end a very protracted period of negotiation.

If the hon. Gentleman would look at our latest documents for those interested in self-government, he will find that there is an overall statement and a working paper describing financial and contractual difficulties, and that thinking has moved on quite a lot. Since we produced the White Paper we have put in much more detail, precisely in response to the detailed questions that have been put to us.

**Dr. Reid:** I congratulate the Minister on being more restrained in his comments about doctors than he was at the previous Question Time. A careful reading of *Hansard* for the previous Question Time will reveal that he and his hon. Friends branded the medical profession and doctors

as being unscrupulous, misleading and liars. Will the Minister take the opportunity to dissociate himself from the comments that were made on that occasion about the medical profession?

**Mr. Clarke:** I would normally rely on the hon. Gentleman to read *Hansard* with a little more care than he appears to have been doing. Both I and many of my hon. Friends have made strong comments about some of the advertising material put out by the British Medical Association. We believe that it is an extremely unscrupulous campaign. We have made no attacks on the medical profession or on individual doctors, except on those doctors who are misleading their patients and are making wild allegations that they know to be untrue. As I said in reply to a previous question, there is an enormous gulf between some of the public protestations on behalf of the associations and what is said in private discussion with the leaders of the BMA and others. The BMA is obviously in favour of better financial management systems, medical audit and money following the patient. We should build on that and ignore all the rather silly propaganda that appears in the newspapers.

**Dame Jill Knight:** Will my right hon. and learned Friend always bear it in mind that the reactions to the review from the medical profession, especially the BMA, are as predictable as Pavlov's dogs? It has always rejected every suggestion for reform in the National Health Service. Does he agree that, if he had listened to it and had not pressed through the reform of the limited list, we would have had £73 million per annum less to spend on patients?

**Mr. Clarke:** My hon. Friend and I can remember many such campaigns that the BMA has run, under successive Governments, against suggestions for reform. On the strength of my latest meeting with the BMA leadership I am more hopeful on this occasion. The BMA began by accepting our aims and various features of the reforms, but it has not yet been able to put forward any positive proposals of its own that might further those aims. However, the initial outright rejection that is customary from the BMA has already begun to modify.

**Mr. Robin Cook:** May I give the Secretary of State the thanks of the official Opposition who, since the publication of his White Paper, had our best election results for 20 years? It is about time that he started listening to what the electorate is trying to tell him. Having told my hon. Friend the Member for Newport, East (Mr. Hughes) that he has received 8,000 representations, will he now share with the House the breakdown of those representations and tell us how many supported his White Paper and how many wanted him to drop the whole idea and get back to the real problems of axed beds and closed wards?

**Mr. Clarke:** I am afraid that I do not see my role in life as a good Samaritan to the Labour party. My principal duty is to carry through a process of reform that will produce a better National Health Service. Sooner or later, the Labour party must decide what it is saying rather than maintain its present outright opposition to everything that we propose.

I am glad to say that many of the 8,000 representations that I have received deal with the serious detail of the White Paper and, for that reason, they do not break down into yes and no answers. It is only the Labour party which is continuing to reject outright each suggestion that happens to come from the Government.

**Sir Peter Hordern:** Has not the unscrupulous and misleading campaign carried out by the BMA so confused the doctors that they do not know whether to sign the contracts that have been placed before them and which the BMA has recommended?

**Mr. Clarke:** I fear that that is the case. The BMA has run a strident campaign, but when it called a conference to endorse the deal that its leaders had negotiated with me it was unable to get consent. Now, no doubt, it is trying to explain it to many doctors who mistakenly fear that they will lose income as a result of the changes, and who also feel that they should be left to decide entirely for themselves what they do and how and when they do it. That is not the basis on which we should proceed given that the BMA began by agreeing with me that a new and better contract was required by April 1990.

6. **Mr. Cox:** To ask the Secretary of State for Health what financial help is to be given by his Department to those hospitals that are seeking to explain to local communities the Government's White Paper on the National Health Service; and if he will make a statement.

**The Minister of State, Department of Health (Mr. David Mellor):** No specific financial allocation has been made to health authorities for this purpose. However, health authority chairmen and senior National Health Service managers have attended national and regional conferences, and received written material and visual aids to help them to explain the proposals and their implications to NHS staff and the public. This commitment to communication will continue throughout the period of the implementation process.

**Mr. Cox:** Is the Minister aware that the document entitled "Working for Patients" contains an obligation to explain to patients the implication of the White Paper? Today we have repeatedly heard the Secretary of State bitterly condemning doctors who are seeking to do that because he does not like the points that they are making to their patients. Wandsworth health authority, whose area the hon. and learned Gentlemen and I represent, wants to explain the White Paper, but it cannot do so because it does not have the money. Therefore, the very people whom the White Paper is supposed to be about will not have the opportunity to have it explained to them or to have their queries answered. That is a typical example of the Government imposing decisions on the very people who will not be given any opportunity to voice their objections to them.

**Mr. Mellor:** A shortened version of "Working for Patients" has been made widely available to the public and there is ample opportunity for lively debates on the merits of the White Paper to be conducted in the local press. The hon. Gentleman knows that that is happening in our local press.

The hon. Gentleman knows that we have been working for patients in his constituency by building a new 700-bed, £35 million hospital—something inconceivable in the decade when the Labour party was in power, when capital spending was slashed to the bone. We shall continue to work in that constructive way for patients in Tooting.

**Dame Elaine Kellett-Bowman:** Does my hon. and learned Friend agree with the leading article in my local paper which pointed out that local communities would have to be deaf, daft, or both, if they were not already well aware of the Government's proposals? Does he accept that excellent hospitals such as that at Lancaster and outstandingly good general practitioners, who are already providing many of the services for which they are not yet paid, will benefit enormously, as will their patients?

**Mr. Mellor:** I am sure that what my hon. Friend says is right. The danger of a public debate arises if some people choose to use a debate about a great national service merely to spread propaganda, rather than truth, which means that the public debate becomes muddy. However, I am sure that the fact that the Government have proposals for improving patient care will stand us in good stead in the next decade when, as we all know, there will be unprecedented pressures on the NHS. It is better that we do that rather than act like those who throw mud around, but have no constructive proposals of their own.

**Ms. Harman:** Why is it that although local communities receive an unwelcome dose of Government propaganda about their Health Service proposals, they have no say as to whether their local hospitals should be opted out of their local health authorities? If the Minister really believes, as he says, that more Health Service decisions should be taken locally, why does he not give local people a ballot before their local hospital is opted out?

**Mr. Mellor:** There is a lack of coherence in the criticism from the Opposition. The Government were criticised by the hon. Member for Tooting (Mr. Cox) for apparently not having made money available to tell local people about the proposals and are now being accused of putting forward a barrage of propaganda. The hon. Lady knows that no National Health Service hospital will opt out of anything; it is simply a matter of whether it becomes self governing within the NHS. Parroting slogans like demented mynah birds does the Opposition no good because people will realise that self-governing status is quite different from opting out. The decision as to whether a hospital should have self-governing status, like other decisions made within the NHS, will depend on whether, having taken account of the different voices, there is a good management case for doing so. The NHS has never been run by ballot, and it will not be in the future.

7. **Mr. Colin Shepherd:** To ask the Secretary of State for Health what will be the effects of the proposals for medical audit outlined in the White Paper "Working for Patients".

16. **Mr. Butterfill:** To ask the Secretary of State for Health if he will explain the intended effects of the White Paper proposals for medical audit.

**Mr. Mellor:** The objective of the comprehensive system of medical audit proposed in the White Paper is to provide necessary reassurance to doctors, patients and management that the quality of medical care is under continual examination, and that clinical outcomes are being measured and thereby the best possible service provided for patients.

**Mr. Shepherd:** Does my hon. and learned Friend recall that at the outset there was considerable hostility to the concept of medical audit, but that with further understanding there has been near-universal acceptance, and even welcome, of this valuable concept? Does my hon. and learned Friend think that, with careful consideration, the BMA might find some useful pointers for the future conduct of its campaign?

**Mr. Mellor:** My hon. Friend makes an interesting point. Clinical audit was pioneered by doctors and we are merely proposing to systematise it. As I made clear in an announcement to the House earlier this month, we made available £1 million for pilot projects, for which we have had enthusiastic applications across the length and breadth of the country. As my right hon. and learned Friend made clear at our last meeting with the BMA there was a welcome not only for that part of the White Paper, but for improved information systems, the concept of money following patients and so on. I hope that the public propaganda battle will soon come into line with the obvious measure of agreement which exists on a number of key points in the document.

**Rev. Martin Smyth:** Will nurses be included in the medical audit programme and how much money have the Government targeted to put the system into operation to provide the back-up to the National Health Service?

**Mr. Mellor:** The measurement of clinical outcomes will show the effectiveness of all parts of the clinical process. So far, the sum of money made available for pilot studies is in excess of £1 million. We shall obviously move forward and ensure that as this becomes systematised, fresh resources will be made available at every stage.

**Mr. Hayes:** I am sure that my right hon. and learned Friend the Secretary of State is not at all surprised that medical audit, which is about quality control, has been welcomed by all the medical professions. Is he encouraged by the fact that not only medical audit but money travelling with patients and resource management have been accepted by the BMA and other bodies? Does that not explode the myth that the medical profession is wholly opposed to the White Paper?

**Mr. Mellor:** I hope that that also demonstrates that a barrage of inaccurate propaganda will not drive the Government off the reforms. Then we can have more sensible discussion of the merits and the detailed application of the proposals, and less propaganda calculated to mislead rather than to shed light on what everyone knows to be the vital necessity to change the service to fit the 1990s, when it will be subjected to unprecedented pressure. I believe that as time goes on more and more people will be compelled to admit that there is much merit in our proposals.

**Mrs. Mahon:** When the Minister goes on his round of regional consultations with management, will he discuss medical audit in detail? Will he also tell us where his meeting with management in Leeds at 10 am on 11 July will take place? When I contacted his Department last week I could not find out.

**Mr. Mellor:** I shall communicate that to the hon. Lady willingly. The meeting is about self-governing hospitals, but there will be plenty of opportunities to discuss other key proposals in the White Paper.

## Handicapped Children

8. **Mr. Thurnham:** To ask the Secretary of State for Health whether he has received any representations about the number of handicapped children in institutional care; and if he will make a statement.

**Mr. Freeman:** My right hon. and learned Friend the Secretary of State met a deputation from Exodus earlier this year to discuss mentally handicapped children in hospital care. We have not received any representations about other groups of handicapped or disabled children in recent times.

**Mr. Thurnham:** Will my hon. Friend do all in his power to assist British Agencies for Adoption and Fostering, and other such bodies, to find homes for handicapped children when they are needed? Does he accept that the figure of 5,500 handicapped children in institutional care, shown in the the first-ever survey by the Office of Population Censuses and Surveys, is far too high—about twice as high as previous estimates?

**Mr. Freeman:** About three in 100 children are born with some disability—that is, about 360,000—and about 5,500 are in institutional care. I share my hon. Friend's enthusiasm for putting as many of them as possible into proper family care: we provide the agency to which he refers with about £300,000 a year, and support it strongly.

**Mr. Ashley:** Is the Minister aware of the staggering increase in the number of children and adults in short-term institutional care—from 11,000 in 1975 to 36,000 in 1985, according to the Audit Commission? Is there any way in which he can avoid the charge that those figures are an absolute condemnation of the level of support services in the community?

**Mr. Freeman:** The right hon. Gentleman is certainly right that the number of children undergoing short-term care in institutions has risen. That is partly a reflection of the fall in the number of children in long-term institutional care. Most children going into temporary care are there for between one and three months.

**Mr. Favell:** The Griffiths report recommends that each social services department should ensure that adequate facilities exist for handicapped people in the community in each local authority area. That is fair enough, but is it sensible to suggest that social workers should assess the individual needs of each handicapped person? Would it not be far better for general practitioners to do that, and to take responsibility for their patients? After all, primary health care teams have doubled in size in recent years, and there are adequate facilities to deal with the problem.

**Mr. Freeman:** I agree with my hon. Friend's sentiments. Doctors have an important role to play, and we shall keep his suggestion under careful review.

**Mr. Alfred Morris:** Is it not an affront to handicapped children in institutional care, and also outrageous, that many of the most important sections of the all-party Disabled Persons Services, Consultation and Representation Act 1986 are still awaiting implementation three years after Royal Assent? Does that not diminish the standing of the House? Is the Minister aware that local authorities of all persuasions now complain about a lack of resources with which to provide services under the parent Act, the Chronically Sick and Disabled Persons Act 1970? When will he respond to the just demands of disabled people and their organisations?

**Mr. Freeman:** The Government announced yesterday that there would be a response to Griffiths before the summer recess, and that there will be a debate, in Government time, at the appropriate time thereafter. The issues that the right hon. Gentleman raises will be addressed then.

### Electoral Registration

9. **Mr. Harry Barnes:** To ask the Secretary of State for Health in how many constituencies in England electoral registration has fallen by 1,000 and more in the last year and if he will make a statement.

**Mr. Freeman:** The Office of Population Censuses and Surveys is responsible for statistics relating to electoral registers. A volume entitled "Electoral Statistics 1989" is available in the Library. This indicates that the electoral register fell by 1,000 or more in 76 English constituencies between 1988 and 1989, and there were increases of 1,000 or more potential voters in 63 constituencies.

**Mr. Barnes:** The report by the Office of Population Censuses and Surveys shows also that there was a decline in England of 82,491, and offered as a reason for this that, as it could not be demographic changes or migration, it could have something to do with registration or with the postal strike of 1988. Unfortunately, the postal strike does not account for a similar collapse in Scotland between 1987 and 1988. Who is fiddling the franchise in Finchley and another 75 constituencies in England? Is this the only way that the Government feel that they can hold on to seats?

**Mr. Freeman:** I am somewhat baffled by that supplementary question. My right hon. Friend the Home Secretary is responsible for the electoral registration procedures and the franchise is not being fiddled.

**Mr. Jessel:** As to demographic aspects of the electoral register, has my hon. Friend any information about how many centenarians are on the electoral register? Are they not tending to increase in number, and does this not show an improvement in the nation's health?

**Mr. Freeman:** Yes. What is more, the doctors' contract makes specific provision for improving care for the very elderly through doctors visiting the over-75s on an annual basis and through higher capitation fees for the elderly.

### NHS Reform

10. **Mr. Andrew Smith:** To ask the Secretary of State for Health what further representations he has received in respect of his proposals to cash-limit general practitioners' budgets.

**Mr. Mellor:** General practice budgets are not to be cash limited.

**Mr. Smith:** Under the White Paper proposals, both the larger practices that become budget holders and all the rest, through the indicative budgets set for family practitioner committees on drugs costs, will be subjected to cash limits. Is it not the case that that can only have the effect of undermining the confidence of patients in the

doctor-patient relationship, as the cash considerations threaten to displace medical considerations? As a result, patients will increasingly fear that the cost of their treatment rather than the medical need for their treatment will take priority. Will this not damage the most valuable part of the NHS?

**Mr. Mellor:** The hon. Gentleman builds a house on sand because his basic premises are completely wrong. First, in terms of large practices, anyone who chooses to have a practice budget will choose to do so because he believes that he can operate effectively within it. That is quite different from an imposed cash limit. Secondly, if the hon. Gentleman really thinks that an indicative drug budget is the same as a cash limit, he is being misleading. He should know that an indicative budget is a way to show general practitioners where their prescribing practices place them compared with others. I am happy to repeat that once again. Every patient will get the drugs that he needs, and that is a pledge.

**Mr. McCrindle:** In view of the predictable opposition to indicative drug budgeting by the pharmaceutical companies, will my hon. and learned Friend the Minister take this opportunity to restate what he sees as the benefits to patient care of the Government's proposals?

**Mr. Mellor:** It will be in the interests of patients who really need drugs, particularly expensive drugs, and there should be proper control of budgets to allow us in future to pay for the drugs that patients need. I know of no other enterprise for which £2,000 million of expenditure would be treated on the basis that those who sign the prescription forms can do anything they like. There is no threat to patients because doctors are being put under some pressure to prescribe generically instead of prescribing branded drugs which are twice as expensive. If we are to find the elbow room to afford the wonder drugs of the future, we must be sensible about not paying excessively for less than wonderful drugs which are merely branded instead of generic.

11. **Mr. Tony Lloyd:** To ask the Secretary of State for Health if he will make a statement on reaction in the North Western regional health authority to his recent White Paper.

**Mr. Mellor:** Reaction from the authority has been most positive. Members of the authority had an opportunity to consider the Government's White Paper "Working For Patients" at a seminar arranged in the region on 17 April. Since then the authority has forwarded to the Department expressions of interest in self-governing status from eight hospitals and one community unit, and in doing so they drew attention to the need, which we fully accept, to protect medical education and research.

**Mr. Lloyd:** Will the Minister take into account the fact that of the eight hospitals in the north-west region, four of them—Christies, Manchester royal infirmary, St. Mary's and the royal eye hospital—are not simply district-based services, but provide regional specialties? Does the Minister recognise that the medical professionals, the ordinary people in the street and the whole of public opinion in the north-west is hostile or suspicious of the Government's proposals? Why will the Government not agree to some form of consultation, or even ballots, outside the districts directly affected? The proposals affect the whole of the north-west region.

**Mr. Mellor:** With respect to the hon. Gentleman, it is not true to say that all the groups to which he referred are opposed to the expressions of interest in self-governing status. I can show that there is substantial support already for self-governing status in those hospitals that have expressed an interest.

Regional specialties will continue to be provided and we are aware of the need to ensure that regional specialties are protected. There will also be ample opportunity for people to make their views known before the Secretary of State has to take any decision on self-governing status. Indeed, an expression of interest is not the same as a formal application and none of those hospitals have been invited to, or have made, formal applications.

**Mr. Hind:** My hon. and learned Friend will have noticed in the response of the North Western regional health authority to the White Paper "Working for Patients" three expressions of interest to form National Health Service hospital trusts. In Wrightington hospital in the West Lancashire district health authority 95 per cent. of the patients come from all over the region and from the rest of the country. Does my hon. and learned Friend accept that his proposal for money following the patient is ideal for that hospital as it will provide better care and more independence for the doctors at that hospital?

**Mr. Mellor:** I entirely agree with my hon. Friend and I am glad that he referred to Wrightington hospital. The senior medical staff at Wrightington have been the driving force behind the expression of interest from that hospital for, I suspect, precisely the reasons that my hon. Friend has given.

### Tuberculosis Vaccinations

13. **Mrs. Dunwoody:** To ask the Secretary of State for Health when it was decided to discontinue the routine vaccination of pre-school children against tuberculosis.

**Mr. Freeman:** Pre-school children are not routinely vaccinated against tuberculosis. The BCG vaccine is currently recommended for children generally at aged 13 and for infants born to immigrants from developing countries, or where there is a family history of the disease. It is only the school vaccination programme at aged 13 that has had to be postponed due to a temporary shortage of the BCG vaccine.

**Mrs. Dunwoody:** Is the Minister aware that preventive health care works only when it is in use and that this programme is tremendously important particularly for immigrant families which suffer from active tuberculosis? Does he agree that it is quite likely that the disease will again become the real difficulty that it used to be in my youth unless the programme is reinstated as rapidly as possible? Is what is happening now a demonstration of how much the Government care about preventive health care?

**Mr. Freeman:** I agree with the hon. Lady about the importance of preventive health care. Vaccination of the priority groups is continuing; it has not been stopped. Britain now has some 4,000 cases of tuberculosis a year

compared with some 40,000 in 1948. That is still too many and I agree with the hon. Lady about the importance of that programme for the immigrant population.

### Midwives

14. **Mr. Andrew F. Bennett:** To ask the Secretary of State for Health what is the total number of midwives currently working in the National Health Service.

**Mr. Mellor:** At 30 September 1987, 19,320 whole-time equivalent midwives were employed in the National Health Service in England.

**Mr. Bennett:** Will the Minister explain to the House why morale among midwives working in hospitals is so low, why the numbers leaving the profession are steadily increasing and why recruitment is proving so difficult?

**Mr. Mellor:** I do not accept the premise of the hon. Gentleman's question. There are 20 per cent. more midwives today than there were a decade ago and never have midwives been better paid than they are now. In the past 12 months their pay has increased on average by some 20 per cent. There is absolutely no reason for midwives' morale to be anything other than high.

## PRIME MINISTER

### Engagements

Q1. **Mr. Wood:** To ask the Prime Minister if she will list her official engagements for Tuesday 27 June.

**The Lord President of the Council and Leader of the House of Commons (Mr. John Wakeham):** I have been asked to reply.

My right hon. Friend the Prime Minister is attending the European Council meeting in Madrid.

**Mr. Wood:** I thank my right hon. Friend for that reply. Bearing in mind the continuing importance of a sound defence policy, is my right hon. Friend not relieved that the Government can rely on friends who believe in nuclear deterrence rather than nuclear disarmers such as Mr. Ron Todd?

**Mr. Wakeham:** Yes, I agree. However much the Opposition try to hide it, with their present defence policy they could not sign up to NATO's excellent comprehensive concept which my right hon. Friend the Prime Minister and the 15 other NATO leaders agreed last month.

**Mr. Hattersley:** What is the Government's revised forecast for the annual deficit on current account?

**Mr. Wakeham:** It is not my job to give revised forecasts at the Dispatch Box at this time. It is also unwise to draw conclusions from one month's figures. The May current account figure of £1·3 billion is the lowest monthly figure since last September and the signs that import growth has been slowing down in recent months suggest that the tightening of monetary policy may be starting to influence recorded trade.

**Mr. Hattersley:** What sort of an economic policy is it that rejoices, as the right hon. Gentleman has just rejoiced, at the worst balance of payments figure—worst except for eight previous months in our history—a forecast for the current year which would be infinitely worse than the

Treasury predicted at Budget time, and a balance of payments which produces interest rates which continue to impose intolerable burdens on home owners? What sort of an achievement is that and what sort of a triumph is it that the Leader of the House boasts about?

**Mr. Wakeham:** The right hon. Gentleman is so fond of working out his supplementary questions that he does not listen to the answers. I started my answer by saying that it is unwise to draw conclusions from one month's figures, and that is not boasting about figures. The Government's policies, which have successfully brought down inflation in the past, will do so again.

**Mr. Teddy Taylor:** Will the Leader of the House have time in his busy day to send a message of congratulation to my right hon. Friend the Prime Minister for fighting so hard for common sense and stopping Britain being sucked into the kind of bureaucratic Socialist nonsenses that we had at the time of George Brown and Harold Wilson's national plan?

**Mr. Wakeham:** I shall certainly do as my hon. Friend asks. My right hon. Friend the Prime Minister will be making a statement to the House when she returns, but things look pretty good to me.

**Q2. Ms. Abbott:** To ask the Prime Minister if she will list her official engagements for Tuesday 27 June.

**Mr. Wakeham:** I have been asked to reply.
I refer the hon. Lady to the reply that I gave some moments ago.

**Ms. Abbott:** When will the Government meet the very real grievances and concerns of people throughout the country, and particularly of general practitioners, about the Government's proposals for the Health Service?

**Mr. Wakeham:** My right hon. and learned Friend the Secretary of State for Health is negotiating—as would have been apparent to any right hon. or hon. Member present in the Chamber for health questions—to reach a satisfactory solution over doctors' contracts. I have no doubt that satisfactory arrangements will ultimately be made.

**Q3. Sir William Clark:** To ask the Prime Minister if she will list her official engagements for Tuesday 27 June.

**Mr. Wakeham:** I have been asked to reply.
I refer my hon. Friend to the reply that I gave some moments ago.

**Sir William Clark:** Will my right hon. Friend join me in welcoming the fact that since 1983 employment in this country has increased by nearly 3 million and is running at an all-time record high? Does he agree that that economic achievement and success has been made possible only because of sound financial policy, encouragement and enterprise that the Government have persistently pursued?

**Mr. Wakeham:** Yes. More people are in work than ever before. Between 1983 and 1987 as many new jobs were created in this country as in the whole of the rest of the European Community put together. Over the past decade, self-employment has risen by more than 1 million as people have responded to Government policies of deregulation and of encouraging enterprise and initiative. A 1 million fall in unemployment since the last general

election was achieved in less than the two years that Labour claimed their reckless policies of high spending and phoney jobs would take to produce the same result.

**Mr. Winnick:** Now that the Prime Minister is out of the country, will the Leader of the House say whether Cabinet Ministers are haunted by the date of 13 July 1962—the night of the long knives—when seven members of the then Cabinet were sacked by Harold Macmillan? If this is the right hon. Gentleman's last appearance in the House deputising for the Prime Minister, may I express my regret that he has served under a leader who blames everyone but herself for failures and wish him every success for the future—with or without redundancy money?

**Mr. Wakeham:** The hon. Gentleman has more experience of losing elections than I have. In my judgment he must get ready to lose a few more.

**Q4. Mrs. Gorman:** To ask the Prime Minister if she will list her official engagements for Tuesday 27 June.

**Mr. Wakeham:** I have been asked to reply.
I refer my hon. Friend to the reply that I gave some moments ago.

**Mrs. Gorman:** Does my right hon. Friend, and through him my right hon. Friend the Prime Minister, agree that a necessary precondition of our joining the European monetary system is the abolition of exchange controls by the other member nations, which is something that we did with great success in 1979?

**Mr. Wakeham:** I agree with my hon. Friend that it is highly desirable that all our European partners should follow our lead in abolishing exchange controls. As to the outcome of the Madrid summit, my hon. Friend should await the statement by my right hon. Friend the Prime Minister on her return.

**Sir Russell Johnston:** As it is now clear, and has been remarked upon by the Treasury Select Committee, that the Government signed the Single European Act without believing in it, can the right hon. Gentleman give an assurance that his right hon. Friend the Prime Minister is not about the same sort of business in Madrid?

**Mr. Wakeham:** I am not responsible for Select Committee reports, except for that which the House approved the other day. However, I give the hon. Gentleman a categorical undertaking that my right hon. Friend the Prime Minister would not sign a communiqué with which she did not agree.

**Q5. Mr. Watts:** To ask the Prime Minister if she will list her official engagements for Tuesday 27 June.

**Mr. Wakeham:** I have been asked to reply.
I refer my hon. Friend to the reply that I gave some moments ago.

**Mr. Watts:** Will my right hon. Friend, in support of the action taken by my hon. Friend the Member for Windsor and Maidenhead (Dr. Glyn), find time to discuss with our right hon. Friend the Home Secretary the alarming reports of an acid house party in Berkshire at the weekend and to consider with him whether adequate powers exist in current legislation to deal with such menaces or whether fresh legislation is required to protect young people from being ensnared in the vicious circle of drug abuse?

**Mr. Wakeham:** I agree with my hon. Friend that press reports of drug taking at the events at White Waltham are deeply disturbing. A police investigation is in progress. The Home Secretary has asked the police for a full report. The wider implications will be considered when the report has been received. The police already have tough powers to tackle the misuse of drugs and the menace of drug dealing. They have powers to trace, freeze and confiscate the assets of those involved in the evil trade of drug trafficking.

**Mr. Skinner:** Will the Leader of the House remind the SLD——

**Hon. Members:** Who?

**Mr. Speaker:** Order. The hon. Gentleman is very experienced. He cannot ask the Leader of the House to undertake anything for which he is not responsible.

**Mr. Skinner:** The Leader of the House is responsible, Mr. Speaker, in his capacity as Leader of the House, if the Short money is being paid to parties that have a specific name. *[Interruption.]* Will he therefore recall the correspondence that we had last year when that party was in the throes of changing its name? He ought kindly to remind it that it got the Short money under one name and that if it intends to change its name again it had better be careful or it will lose the lot.

**Mr. Wakeham:** On this particular issue, I think that the Members of the party who sit behind the hon. Gentleman had better take notice of him, because he is one of the greatest living experts on this matter. I treasure very much the letter that he wrote to me in his own fair hand some time ago setting out the whole position.

Q6. **Mr. Oppenheim:** To ask the Prime Minister if she will list her official engagements for Tuesday 27 June.

**Mr. Wakeham:** I have been asked to reply.
I refer my hon. Friend to the reply that I gave some moments ago.

**Mr. Oppenheim:** Bearing in mind the Government's economic policies, will my right hon. Friend consider recent comments that nationalisation is no solution to social ills and that free markets are the best way to signal the desires of consumers and to encourage innovation? Those remarks were made by Willy Brandt, the president of the Socialist International, to which the British Labour party still subscribes.

**Mr. Wakeham:** I agree that nationalisation is no answer to anything. The Labour party purports to be a convert to the market and to a partnership between Government and industry, but its notion of a partnership is like the walrus and the oysters.

Q7. **Mr. Fraser:** To ask the Prime Minister if she will list her official engagements for Tuesday 27 June.

**Mr. Wakeham:** I have been asked to reply.
I refer the hon. Gentleman to the reply that I gave some moments ago.

**Mr. Fraser:** Will the Leader of the House obtain immediate instructions from the Prime Minister to withdraw amendments in the other place that would give privatised water companies immunity from prosecution and allow untreated sewage to be released into our rivers? The fact the Prime Minister feeds us that stuff, with authority, about the economy is no reason for releasing it into our rivers.

**Mr. Wakeham:** The House will have an opportunity to consider the Bill which is now in another place when it returns here. I have no intention of taking the hon. Gentleman's advice. When the Bill returns here we shall be able to debate any changes that are made in the other place. I believe that our record is better than that of virtually any other country in the European community.

**Dr. Glyn** *rose——*

**Hon. Members:** Hear, hear.

**Mr. Speaker:** Order.

**Dr. Glyn:** Contrary to suggestions, I missed the party by half an hour. I have impressed on the Home Secretary that it is necessary to tighten the law that relates to these sort of events which are held on private property with the consent of the owner. At the moment there is only one sanction—a £1,000 fine. The amount of money that was made on that occasion was enormous with 11,000 present at up to £40 a ticket. No provision whatsoever had been made for proper hygiene, but the police had no power to intervene because the party was held on private property.

**Mr. Wakeham:** I am grateful—*[Interruption.]*

**Mr. Speaker:** Order. Interruptions take up a lot of time.

**Mr. Wakeham:** I am grateful to my hon. Friend for what he just said and I know that the Home Secretary will be interested in hearing his views on the matter. As I said, my right hon. Friend has called for a report, and he will consider the issues involved after that.

Q10. **Mr. Loyden:** To ask the Prime Minister if she will list her official engagements for Tuesday 27 June.

**Mr. Wakeham:** I have been asked to reply.
I refer the hon. Gentleman to the reply that I gave some moments ago.

**Mr. Loyden:** Will the Leader of the House reconsider his previous answer relating to the subject of unemployment? Is he aware that, despite the figures that he gave, hardcore unemployment in this country remains virtually unchanged and that only by massaging and fiddling the figures are the Government able to paint a picture which suggests that the whole problem of unemployment is now off the agenda? Is he aware that unemployment is still causing great hardship among families, who consider that such steps as the Government have taken represent a policy of complete disregard?

**Mr. Wakeham:** That supplementary question is just not a reasonable analysis of the situation. The Government's policies have created a great many jobs in Britain. Of course there are still problems, but we shall tackle them vigorously with the policies that have been so successfully pursued over the last 10 years.

# Wang Laboratories (Plant Closure)

3.31 pm

**Mr. Donald Dewar** (Glasgow, Garscadden) *(by private notice)*: To ask the Secretary of State for Scotland, if he will make a statement on the closure of the Wang corporation's electronics plant at Stirling and on his Department's recent negotiations with the company.

**The Secretary of State for Scotland (Mr. Malcolm Rifkind):** I am deeply concerned at the decision by Wang Laboratories to close its Stirling plant. The decision appears to have been forced on the company by commercial pressures worldwide and in no way reflects on the excellent work force at Stirling.

My immediate concerns are to ensure continuity of employment for the work force and to ensure that the skills and facilities which have been developed at the plant are not lost to Scotland. I have had discussions with senior representatives of the company with a view to achieving this end. The Government stand ready to co-operate with the company and others in seeking the productive use of this plant and of its fine work force.

**Mr. Dewar:** Will the Secretary of State accept that the closure of the Wang plant is a bitter blow, particularly because it was so flamboyantly advertised by Ministers as a showpiece of the new technology built into the Stirling campus and promising at least 700 jobs that will now not materialise? Does this not underline the importance of attracting industry which has decision-making power and is based on substantial research and development capacity?

Will the right hon. and learned Gentleman note that, while we accept that risks are inherent in the attraction of inward investment, it is equally important that we learn what went wrong in this case? Will he answer the following questions? What public funds have gone to Wang, and in particular what funding has been sunk in the £3·5 million extension for which he cut the first sod only in March 1987? When was the last instalment paid and what steps are being taken to recover the money? Are steps being taken to alter the system, given the similar and harrowing experience that we had with the Caterpillar company?

Judging from the right hon. and learned Gentleman's press statements, the Scottish Office learned of the closure only a week ago. That suggests either a failure in monitoring what was happening in a company in receipt of substantial funds or a lack of frankness on the part of Wang. Will he give his views on that?

Will the right hon. and learned Gentleman say more about the prospects of the plant being sold as a going concern, so saving the jobs? Has Wang given any assurances that it will take a realistic and helpful view of the transfer of the plant, if there is such a possibility?

I come to possibly the most discouraging aspect of the matter. Wang has chosen to concentrate its European operations in Limerick and not in Stirling. Can the Secretary of State throw any light on the reasons why that decision was taken? Are we not entitled to an explanation, given that the Secretary of State was quoted, when inaugurating the recent extension, as urging

"Scots to have as much faith in their country as Americans"—

and particularly Wang—

"had in it as an ideal location in which to invest"?

**Mr. Rifkind:** I shall deal with the specific points raised by the hon. Gentleman. On his final point, the explanation given by Wang is that its plant in Limerick is much larger than its Stirling plant—which it undoubtedly is—and has excess capacity. Because of its poor global economic position, it intends to concentrate its activities at one European plant, and it has chosen the larger plant at Limerick, which has excess capacity and can absorb a certain amount of the work done at Stirling.

Wang has said that it intends to be extremely helpful in seeking an alternative user for the plant. It is in its interests to do so, and I have every reason to assume that that will be a priority. We shall obviously keep in close contact with Wang on that matter.

A total of £3·7 million has been paid to Wang since 1982, and the last payment was due in February of this year. Under the rules that operated in 1982, no company is bound by the offer letter to repay grant, but in specific circumstances there may be grounds to seek to reclaim money paid, and we are studying that.

On the question of any change in the system, I have to inform the hon. Gentleman that, when the negotiations with Wang took place in 1982, the system then in force was that applied under the previous Labour Government. Since then we have changed the rules, and all offers of regional selective assistance on applications submitted since November 1984 have specific clauses to ensure that the Government can reclaim part or all of any money paid in the event that the recipient company runs into difficulties within three years of the final payment. In addition, since 1984 any sums paid to a company investing in the United Kingdom are related not to the capital that that company has invested but to the number of jobs created as opposed simply to the number of jobs that it had promised to create.

I can assure the hon. Gentleman and the House that since 1984 the rules applied have been much stricter and enable clawback. Had the current rules been in force at the time of the original negotiation with Wang, every penny paid to it could have been required to have been repaid to the Government in the circumstances that have now developed.

**Mr. Allan Stewart** (Eastwood): Does my right hon. and learned Friend agree that the sad decision by Wang was made because worldwide it has been laying off employees because of the advance of workstation networks in the market at the expense of mini-computers? Does he further agree that the electronics industry in Scotland remains in extremely good health, as has been shown by Compaq's recent announcement at Renfrew? Has not by far the most important decision relating to the Scottish economy during the last few days been the announcement of a plan for a £1,000 million additional investment and 35,000 new jobs in Strathclyde?

**Mr. Rifkind:** New investment coming into Scotland is encouraging, both in the electronics industry and elsewhere. Not only are there the 500 additional jobs announced by Compaq at Erskine in the electronics industry, but there has recently been a decision by Sun Microsystems to establish a plant at Linlithgow. In the non-electronics sphere, only this morning the Crusader company announced its intention to relocate 380 jobs, most of which will be transferred from Reigate to Greenock in the enterprise zone in Inverclyde.

Scotland clearly remains a very attractive place for investment, both for the electronics industry and for other industries. The electronics industry in Scotland employs some 43,000 people, so the investment by Wang—useful and important though it was—represents only a tiny proportion of the total.

**Mr. Martin O'Neill** (Clackmannan): Is the Secretary of State aware that my constituency abuts the Stirling plant and that the travel-to-work area of Alloa has an employment rate of 20 per cent? Is he further aware that it is especially disappointing for the Central region that Wang was the only electronics firm that has ever been attracted to it? Does not the difficulty that the region has experienced in securing such employment make it doubly difficult for us to believe that there will be any great enthusiasm on the part of any other company to come to the region? Will not the right hon. and learned Gentleman make full use of all the assistance and attraction that he can provide to prevent future employment draining off to the new towns, which seem to be obtaining the bulk of hi-tech employment in Scotland?

**Mr. Rifkind:** I am not sure that the hon. Gentleman will have the agreement of all his colleagues on that observation. The Wang plant in Stirling remains a very attractive building, with an existing, trained, highly qualified work force. I do not share his inherent pessimism as to the ability to attract a company to use the excellent work force and the excellent plant in Stirling. Of course, none of us can guarantee what the outcome will be, but I think that the hon. Gentleman would do a service to his constituents if he sought to maximise the attractions of Stirling rather than to suggest the opposite.

**Mr. Kenneth Warren** (Hastings and Rye): Is it not reprehensible that the management of Wang did not consult Her Majesty's Government before it took its precipitate decision, bearing in mind that the Government are a substantial investor in the company? May I be assured that the Secretary of State for Trade and Industry will try to make sure that clauses are built into all investments to ensure that consultation takes place before such decisions are made and that payback will be required at all times?

**Mr. Rifkind:** It is certainly desirable that there should be maximum consultation with Government when decisions of this kind are contemplated. I assure my hon. Friend that in all offers of regional selective assistance since 1984 the possibility of clawback has been written into the conditions of offer. That is a substantial improvement on the position that existed for a good number of years before that.

**Mr. James Wallace** (Orkney and Shetland): The Government have set great store by their inward investment policy. The decision must come as a great blow to them. What implications for the future of that policy does the Minister think the announcement has, following the decision of Caterpillar? In regard to future projects, what will be done to try to ensure that they have some research and development and design component, together with managerial functions, so that we do not become vulnerable to branch factory closures?

**Mr. Rifkind:** There have been a vast number of decisions on inward investment into Scotland over the years and only a tiny fraction have withdrawn subsequently.

As to the second part of the hon. Gentleman's comments, I have seen suggestions, both in his question and elsewhere, that we should be disinterested in possible investment that is only of an assembly plant nature. I countenance strongly against that. If one considers the experience in Scotland, one sees that many plants that began as assembly plants go on to much greater things. IBM began as an assembly plant, as did Digital and Hewlett-Packard, but in each case we see the company as a major operation going far beyond pure assembly; they are production centres and sources of research and development in Scotland at present. So the fact that a company may be first attracted to Scotland or any other part of the United Kingdom for a limited purpose is in itself not a reason for dissuading it. I assure the hon. Gentleman that many other parts of Europe would be only too happy to step into the breach if we showed disinterest in possible investment on such grounds.

**Mr. Spencer Batiste** (Elmet): Does my right hon. and learned Friend agree that the announcement by Wang underlines the inherent unreliability of a system which, by use of cash grants of public money, encourages companies to set up business in places that they might not otherwise choose, with that business, on any downturn, becoming the most vulnerable? How would he react to what must be the inevitable conclusion to be drawn from the criticisms of the hon. Member for Glasgow, Garscadden (Mr. Dewar)—that the practice should be discontinued in future?

**Mr. Rifkind:** I certainly think that the old system was less satisfactory because it did not explicitly and directly tie any grant to the number of jobs created and it did not allow for a specific right of clawback if within a certain period the jobs ceased to exist or the economic activity ceased. Clearly that made it easier in the past for companies to consider withdrawal from the United Kingdom in the event of any problems developing. That is why the Government decided to address themselves to the problem and in 1984 changed the rules substantially, which makes withdrawal much less likely in future.

**Mr. Harry Ewing** (Falkirk, East): Is the Secretary of State aware that I have reason vividly to remember Wang coming to Stirling because I happened to be the Member of Parliament for Stirling when the company was attracted there? Whatever the Secretary of State says about the old system employed by the Labour Government, the fact is that his predecessor, now the Secretary of State for Defence, negotiated the deal in 1982, three years after his Government came to power, under the terms and conditions that prevailed at that time. The Tories had three years to change the system if they were worried about it, but they did not lift a finger.

I deeply resent what Wang has done to my former constituents over the last few days and the disgraceful way in which the people of Stirling have been treated. *[Interruption.]* Why should the Secretary of State be surprised? I have a 1982 Scottish Office press notice in which his predecessor, the then Secretary of State, said:

[*Mr. Harry Ewing*]

"We offer investors a climate in which they can make money supplying a Europe-wide market, keep it out of the hands of the tax collector and repatriate it at will".
That is exactly what Wang has done, and the Tories are as culpable as Wang.

**Mr. Rifkind:** I thought that the hon. Gentleman was going to conclude his question by saying that the Tories are as culpable as the last Labour Government. When my right hon. Friend made that announcement in 1982, the hon. Gentleman was the first to welcome it. [*Interruption.*] The hon. Gentleman was the first to welcome it. He went on record at the time, saying how delighted he was that Wang had been persuaded to go to Stirling, and he congratulated the Government on what they had achieved. The hon. Gentleman must not apply double standards. He should acknowledge that the Government came to their conclusion about five years ago, under my right hon. Friend who was then Secretary of State for Scotland, and that the terms under which these matters have been negotiated, both under the previous Government and in the first few years of this Administration, were too lax in respect of the requirements they expected from overseas investors. That is why that has been changed, and that is why it should be applauded by the hon. Gentleman.

**Mr. Phillip Oppenheim** (Amber Valley): Surely it is obvious that there can be no guarantee that grant-aided plants will succeed, which is why we welcome putting in the provision for clawback in the 1984 legislation. That was never done by previous Governments. Will my right hon. and learned Friend remind Opposition Members of the closure of Linwood, into which huge sums of money were pumped by the previous Labour Government? They got virtually none of it back when a multinational replaced it a few years ago.

**Mr. Speaker:** Order. I ask the hon. Members to stick to the main question. We have a heavy day in front of us.

**Mr. Rifkind:** We would all take the view, as my hon. Friend implies, that it was sensible to introduce the changes that were announced in 1984. They ensure that, in certain circumstances, public funds that have gone to a company can be returned to the public Exchequer if the basis on which they were granted does not turn out to have been fulfilled.

**Mr. Jim Sillars** (Glasgow, Govan): Does the Secretary of State appreciate that, after a long effort with the electronics industry in Scotland, only one tenth of employed people are employed by indigenous Scottish companies and the other 90 per cent. are controlled by external capital? Does that not lead him, along with the Scottish Development Agency and Locate in Scotland, to look for a fundamental review of strategy in the electronics industry? The Wang episode is only one example; there are other potentials along the line. The right hon. and learned Gentleman must know that I am telling the truth.

In the review, will the Secretary of State consider the clawback, not only in relation to Government money but the enhanced capital asset of the plant, so that the clawback should rightly go back to the people of Scotland? It would be much easier to find an alternative tenant for the Wang factor if Wang were not selling the factory on the open market at a price dictated by it.

**Mr. Rifkind:** I note what the hon. Gentleman says. If the Scottish National party is hostile to 90 per cent. of the electronics industry in Scotland, which he says is controlled from outside Scotland, he has just suggested signing the death warrant for about 40,000 jobs. If that is the view and objective of his party, I am sure that very few people in Scotland will be prepared to agree with it.

**Mr. Ernie Ross** (Dundee, West): The Secretary of State cannot ignore the fact that, for Wang, he is the public representative of the taxpayer and the people of Scotland. Why, once again, was he caught with his trousers down? He is our public representative. He should tell us why Wang could take its decision with so much Government money in the plant and why he did nothing about it. He will be unable to do anything about it once it has been made.

**Mr. Rifkind:** The hon. Gentleman obviously lives in a totally different world from that of the rest of the British public if he believes that a Government can forbid an overseas company from deciding to withdraw its investment. As the hon. Gentleman is presumably now well aware, under the conditions that were introduced by this Government, any decision announced since 1984 has an automatic right to clawback of any public funds. On Wang, there may indeed be grounds to seek to reclaim moneys paid, and we are studying them at present.

**Several Hon. Members** *rose——*

**Mr. Speaker:** Order. I am bound to have regard to the business for today. We have an important debate ahead of us in which many right hon. and hon. Members wish to take part. I shall take two questions from each side of the House.

**Mr. John Marshall** (Hendon, South): Does my right hon. and learned Friend agree that the Government have had substantial success in attracting new companies into the Scottish economy and that that task could be made more difficult by the crusade against multinational companies by Opposition Members? Is my right hon. and learned Friend aware of the possibility that that company may have decided to concentrate its European production at Limerick because of the excessive subsidies given by the Irish Government——

**Mr. Speaker:** Order. That is not the point. The hon. Gentleman should stick to the question. This is not a debate.

**Mr. Marshall:** I had hoped that I was sticking to the question, Mr. Speaker. I was talking about Wang concentrating its European production at Limerick and asking my right hon. and learned Friend to ensure that that was not due to excessive subsidies, and, if it was, whether he will make representations to Sir Leon Brittan.

**Mr. Rifkind:** I understand that the company's main consideration was to concentrate its European activities in one plant. If the company had decided to concentrate its European activities in Stirling, major new investment would have been required. However, by concentrating it at Limerick, the company has been able to use the unused capacity in its plant in that country.

**Mr. Dennis Canavan** (Falkirk, West): What was the size of the payment that the Government made to the Wang corporation in February this year? Why do the

Government try to claim all the credit when companies such as Wang come to Scotland and yet try to disclaim virtually all responsibility when they pull out? Is not this case indicative of a basic failure in the Government's industrial strategy, whereby billions of pounds of public money can be handed out to multinational companies which are here today and gone tomorrow precisely because the Government refuse to impose stringent conditions to make multinational companies accountable to their work forces and to the communities in which they are located?

**Mr. Rifkind:** The sum paid at the beginning of this year —the last tranche—was approximately £250,000, but I shall check that figure. In answer to the hon. Gentleman's final remarks, this Government, unlike his own, have begun to introduce the sort of stringent conditions that the last Labour Government did not think were necessary.

**Mr. Christopher Gill** (Ludlow): Does my right hon. and learned Friend agree that it is not the role of Government to try to pick winners and that this case demonstrates the hazards of trying to do that? Will he remind the House of the Government's successful history in creating the climate and environment for investment which alone can lead to permanent, sustainable jobs? In so doing, will he remind the House that one man's grant is another man's tax bill?

**Mr. Rifkind:** Regional selective assistance is not paid automatically to any applicant. Before any grant is paid, an application would normally have had to be considered and approved by the Scottish Industrial Development Advisory Board or by the similar boards that serve England and Wales. Therefore, an assessment of the viability of a project is made by an independent body that gives advice to the Secretary of State and to the Government Department concerned.

**Mr. Tam Dalyell** (Linlithgow): As one with dismayed constituents working at Wang and who has visited the factory on two occasions, may I say that it is difficult to have good foresight in an industry in which investment decisions may be extremely tricky and where products change. I express certain sympathy with the company; it may well have done its best. May I ask two factual questions?

**Mr. Speaker:** Just one, please.

**Mr. Dalyell:** Since October of last year, how much Government money has gone into Wang and—this is a related issue—why did Wang give the Scottish Office only one week's notice of what it was going to do? It must have known that there would be difficulty because it was receiving considerable sums of public money.

**Mr. Rifkind:** In answer to the first part of the hon. Gentleman's question, since October or November of last year, just the final tranche of the sum originally agreed in 1982 has been paid. That was the sum to which I referred in answer to the hon. Member for Falkirk, West (Mr. Canavan). On the question of a period of notice, I agree with the hon. Gentleman that it would have been desirable if direct contact had been made at an earlier stage. The company has apologised to the Scottish Office for that. It is a most regrettable fact that that did not happen. Naturally, I must accept its apology, but it would have been better if it had not been needed in the first place.

**Several Hon. Members** *rose——*

**Mr. Speaker:** I am sorry that I have been unable to call the three hon. Gentlemen, but I shall certainly bear in mind their claims when we return to the matter.

**Mr. Edward Leigh** (Gainsborough and Horncastle): On a point of order, Mr. Speaker.

**Mr. Speaker:** It is a very heavy day.

**Mr. Leigh:** If this country created more jobs than the rest of the EEC together, how much parliamentary time would there be available to discuss other issues if every time 300 jobs were lost at a factory you, Mr. Speaker, allowed 25 minutes to discuss it?

**Mr. Speaker:** The granting of a private notice Question is a matter for the Chair, as the hon. Gentleman well knows.

## BILLS PRESENTED

### BAIL (AMENDMENT)

Mr. Ieuan Wyn Jones, supported by Mr. Peter Archer, Mr. Gerald Bermingham, Mr. Alex Carlile, Mrs. Llin Golding, Mr. Harry Greenway and Mr. Keith Vaz, presented a Bill to make further provision in relation to bail in or in connection with criminal proceedings in England and Wales; and for connected purposes: And the same was read the First time; and ordered to be read a Second time upon Friday 7 July and to be printed. [Bill 169.]

### NATIONAL HEALTH SERVICE (IMPROVED PROVISION OF SERVICES)

Mrs. Alice Mahon, supported by Mrs. Maria Fyfe, Mr. John Battle, Mr. Dave Nellist, Mr. David Hinchliffe, Ms. Dawn Primarolo, Mrs. Audrey Wise, Mr. Jeremy Corbyn, Mr. Eric Illsley, Mr. Bob Cryer, Mr. Max Madden and Ms. Mildred Gordon, presented a Bill to require improved provision of services in all aspects of the National Health Service; and for connected purposes: And the same was read the First time; and ordered to be read a Second time upon Friday 7 July and to be printed. [Bill 170.]

# Ban of Useless Animal Experiments

3.56 pm

**Mr. Harry Cohen** (Leyton): I beg to move,

That leave be given to bring in a Bill to ban experiments upon animals of dubious or unproven value, including tests for cosmetic and warfare purposes, certain LD50 and Draize eye tests; to empower the Home Secretary to ban further categories and types of animal experiments; to amend the Animals (Scientific Procedures) Act 1986 to ensure that all proposed animal experiments are subject to independent scrutiny to determine their worth and to specific approval by the Home Secretary; and for connected purposes.

The continuance of so many useless animal experiments in this country is a public scandal and is against the wishes of the British people. Many of the tests are unnecessary and obsolete. The Government published figures that showed that in 1987 the overall number of scientific procedures was 3,631,393, and that more than 70 per cent. of those were carried out without anaesthetic. That worked out at about 10,000 a day. There will be 70 such procedures in the 10 minutes that I shall address the House. In 1986 there were 3,112,100. The Government decided to adjust seasonally their figures for scientific procedures down to 2,953,900, which is a 5 per cent. reduction on 1986. The House can see, however, that the number is still about 3 million. Therefore, the project system that was introduced in the Animal (Scientific Procedures) Act 1986 has not significantly reduced the number of animals used. In the Committee on that Bill, I proposed bans on useless tests. That is still the most relevant and humane way forward.

My Bill proposes to introduce a ban on cosmetic tests which are useless. In 1987 there were 14,534 such tests. The EEC definition of a cosmetic product is

"any substance or preparation intended for placing in contact with the various external parts of the human body (epidermis, hair system, nails, lips and external genital organs) or with the teeth and the mucous membranes of the oral cavity with a view exclusively or principally to cleansing them, perfuming them or protecting them in order to keep them in good condition, change their appearance or correct body odours."

Those products are designed to beautify the hair or skin or to improve the appearance generally. They are products such as creams, lotions, oils, face masks, toilet soaps, perfumes, toilet waters, bath and shower preparations, shaving products, lipsticks, make-up and cleansers, shampoos and sunbathing products. There is a long list of them. However, the public overwhelmingly want a ban on those tests. They see them as being unnecessary, especially as there are already enormous numbers of ingredients capable of doing that work. There does not need to be wholesale new slaughter.

I welcomed Avon's decision last week to ban animal tests in its laboratories. It admitted that that decision was influenced by the consumer boycott. The public want beauty without cruelty. The Home Office is a long way behind the public. It has issued six project licences. However, in a written reply to a question on 24 January about what restraints the animal procedures committee had imposed on those licensees, it was said that that information could be found in a detailed statistical return. That will not stop a single test.

The truth of the matter is that the Home Office has set broad parameters for the granting of project licences, which are being granted to testing laboratories such as Toxical and Hazelton. It is left to the discretion of a laboratory whether the test commissioned by the cosmetic company is justifiable. The APC—the animal procedures committee—is not evaluating each procedure, so the current situation is virtually the same as it was before the Animal (Scientific Procedures) Bill was introduced. It has already been acknowledged that at least two APC members want a ban on such tests. The ingredients for the cosmetic products have been long established and tested through human-experience and there is no need for new tests on animals.

My Bill also calls for a ban on warfare experiments on animals. The Government refuse to provide the number of such tests carried out on animals, but, since 1916, when Porton Down was established, they must have run into millions. Such tests are the most ghastly and cruel experiments ever undertaken in Britain, but the details of them and their number are rarely published, so there is no justification for them. What is even worse is that Porton Down has Crown immunity so that it can get away with what it likes. It was even referred to in "Spycatcher", by Peter Wright, who said:

"On one occasion I went down to Porton to see a demonstration of a cigarette packet which had been modified by the Explosives Research and Development Establishment to fire a dart tipped with poison."

A sheep was bumped off and Peter Wright said:

"I knew also then that assassination was no policy for peacetime".

Animals at Porton Down are being used for such experiments.

Chris Fisher of the British Union for the Abolition of Vivisection, in an excellent article, also says that such tests are unjustified and states:

"The official justification for continuing with this kind of research goes something like this—in order to be able to defend ourselves against chemical or biological attack, we must first invent the weapon to be used against us so that we can develop a defensive response! This strategy, if it is to be believed, is the equivalent of developing a drug to combat a disease which does not exist yet."

In those circumstances, such tests are of no use to the public. Mr. Fisher concludes:

"the close co-operation between the scientists at Porton and their counterparts in the US and other allied countries meant that they were partners to an offensive research programme."

They are not involved in a defensive programme. We should also remember that we have signed treaties to the effect that we will not undertake chemical and biological warfare.

It is also morally indefensible to carry out ballistic tests on animals. The armed forces should use alternatives such as gelatin for still target tests.

My Bill also tackles toxicology experiments such as LD50 and Draize eye tests. It has already been shown that animals are bad models for humans in such tests as unexpected side effects are displayed in humans. Fewer than 50 per cent. of such tests are shown to be accurate. In 1987, 111,313 classical LD50 tests were carried out on animals. Animals were dosed with a substance to determine the level that would kill 50 per cent. of them. The Zurich Institute of Toxicity has said:

"For the recognition of symptomatology of acute poisoning in man, and for the determination of the human lethal dose, the LD50 in animals is of very little use."

FRAME—the Fund for the Replacement of Animals in Medical Experiments—has said:

"it is now widely recognised that the precise LD50 value this method is supposed to provide is an unobtainable illusion, because of a variety of uncontrollable biological variables.

Moreover, it has been used to place chemicals in a small number of broad categories (such as very potent, potent, marginal and no significant effect)."

Such categories are useless, yet animals are being killed in such tests. FRAME has also referred to the former Minister at the Home Office, the hon. and learned Member for Putney (Mr. Mellor), who said on 11 March 1986 that the LD50 classical test was rarely used in the United Kingdom, yet more than 111,000 such tests are carried out. So much for its rare use.

In 1987, there were 24,314 Draize tests, in which a substance is dripped into the eye of an animal and left for seven days to that the amount of swelling, soreness and ulceration can be assessed. We could ban Draize immediately. Many companies, such as Health Designs Incorporated and the Noxell corporation, have already developed alternative testing. One alternative is not to do the tests if they are not worth while in the first place. Other alternatives include the use of cell cultures, computer modelling, mild tests on human volunteers and constant and more extensive surveillance of medicines after they have been made available for general prescription. FRAME has produced a long list of alternatives. The Government have put up a mere £60,000, a pathetic amount for studies of alternatives. My Bill would shift the burden of proof to the experimenter.

The Minister and the Government have shown themselves to be uncaring. They will not even label products to show whether tests have been done on animals to allow people to make a choice for themselves. That attitude is morally reprehensible and scientifically dubious. As FRAME said:

"Animal experiments that are unnecessary use unnecessarily large numbers of animals or are unnecessarily painful"—

**Mr. Speaker:** Order. The hon. Gentleman has spoken for 10 minutes.

*Question put and agreed to.*

Bill ordered to be brought in by Mr. Harry Cohen, Ms. Diane Abbott, Mr. Tony Banks, Mr. Harry Barnes, Mr. Gerald Bermingham, Mrs. Ann Clwyd, Mr. Frank Cook, Mr. Don Dixon, Mr. David Hinchliffe, Miss Joan Lestor, Mr. Eddie Loyden, and Mr. Robert N. Wareing.

### Ban of Useless Animal Experiments:

Mr. Harry Cohen accordingly presented a Bill to ban experiments upon animals of dubious or unproven value, including tests for cosmetic and warfare purposes, certain LD 50 and Draize eye tests; to empower the Home Secretary to ban further categories and types of animal experiments; to amend the Animals (Scientific Procedures) Act 1986 to ensure that all proposed animal experiments are subject to independent scrutiny to determine their worth and to specific approval by the Home Secretary; and for connected purposes. *And the same was read the First time; and ordered to be read a Second time upon Friday 7 July and to be printed. [Bill 168.]*

## Football Spectators Bill *[Lords]*

*Order for Second Reading read.*

**Mr. Speaker:** I have selected the motion for an instruction in the name of the Secretary of State and am prepared to allow it to be referred to during the Second Reading debate. Is the House agreeable to the two motions being debated together?

**Dr. John Cunningham** (Copeland): No.

**Mr. Speaker:** In that case the motion for the instruction will be debated separately. However, I am still prepared to allow it to be referred to on Second Reading. I warn those who may be called to speak on the instruction that the scope of that debate is much narrower than that on Second Reading.

In view of the large number of right hon. and hon. Members who wish to speak in the debate, I propose to limit speeches to 10 minutes between 7 and 9 o'clock. I make a special appeal to those who may be called before that time to bear in mind that limit, because it would be inequitable if they spoke at greater length.

4.8 pm

**The Secretary of State for the Environment (Mr. Nicholas Ridley):** I beg to move, That the Bill be now read a Second time.

As the House will know, the Bill is addressed to the continuing problems of hooliganism associated with football, both in this country and abroad. Part I of the Bill provides a framework for a national membership scheme for spectators at designated football matches in England and Wales. Part II gives the courts powers to impose restriction orders on convicted hooligans to prevent them from travelling to English and Welsh matches abroad.

This Bill comes to us having completed its passage in another place. As the House is aware, the Government felt it right to delay the Bill for two months following the terrible events at Hillsborough stadium on Saturday 15 April. Before I go on to talk about the Bill, I should like to add my personal sympathy to those bereaved and injured at Hillsborough, and to the people of Liverpool as a whole. As my noble Friend Lord Hesketh said in another place on Third Reading of the Bill on 16 June, we must all share the hope that this, the latest in a long line of tragedies that British football has suffered in the past 40 years, will also be the last.

Following the Hillsborough disaster, my right hon. Friend the Home Secretary invited Lord Justice Taylor to chair an inquiry into what happened there, and

"to make recommendations about the needs of crowd control and safety at sports grounds".—[*Official Report,* 17 April 1989; Vol. 151, c. 19.]

His is an independent inquiry, and the content and timing of his report are entirely a matter for him. I stress, however, that the Bill was amended on Third Reading in the other place not to anticipate in anyway, but to allow Parliament to take account of Lord Justice Taylor's eventual report. Parliament will now have two opportunities to debate the national membership scheme following receipt of Lord Justice Taylor's final report: the first before a football membership authority is appointed, and the second after the scheme has been submitted, and approved by me.

**Dr. Cunningham:** Does that mean that the Secretary of State will bring to the House a scheme that will not be amendable in any way?

**Mr. Ridley:** The House can reject the scheme if it wishes. Furthermore, the original Bill is there not to enable a scheme to be debated in every detail by Parliament, but to allow football to have the authority of Parliament to introduce such a scheme. By proceeding with the Bill now, we can put the framework for the national membership scheme on the statute book and be ready to proceed rapidly if Parliament so decides in the light of any comments that Lord Justice Taylor may make. The final decision to implement the scheme will not, however, be made until it has been debated twice more.

**Sir Ian Gilmour** (Chesham and Amersham): Would not my right hon. Friend very much increase support for part I if he gave an unequivocal undertaking now that if Lord Justice Taylor expressed serious doubts about, or opposition to, an identity card scheme he would not proceed with part I?

**Mr. Ridley:** I do not think that we can prejudge what Lord Justice Taylor may say. We have deliberately amended the Bill so that—on not one occasion but two —not only the Government but both Houses of Parliament will have the opportunity to give their views on whether the scheme as proposed by the Football Membership Authority should proceed. Surely my right hon. Friend would not want to fetter Parliament's decision on whether it wished to proceed with the scheme, whatever Lord Justice Taylor may or may not say. I am sure that he would not suggest that we should abnegate our responsibilities to someone whose report we have not yet seen.

**Several Hon. Members** *rose——*

**Mr. Ridley:** I can see that a number of hon. Members wish me to give way. I shall give way to the hon. Member for Liverpool, Walton (Mr. Heffer), but after that I am sure that the House would prefer me to make a little progress, as many hon. Members wish to speak.

**Mr. Eric S. Heffer** (Liverpool, Walton): The right hon. Gentleman said that the scheme would be debated in the House twice. Can he tell us when and at what time? Will it be in the middle of the night, or can we have a proper debate for some hours? Even at this late stage, will the right hon. Gentleman agree to the House being allowed to amend the scheme? It is ludicrous that the arrangements should be on a negative basis—that we should vote either for or against the scheme without any opportunity to amend it.

**Mr. Ridley:** The debate will not take place until Lord Justice Taylor has delivered his final report, but I shall invite the House to consider the proposal that I appoint the Football Membership Authority, which will then design the scheme. When it has done so, it will be for me to consent to it. There will then be another debate in which the House will have a further opportunity to give its views.

I think that, even in his absence, I can give an assurance on behalf of my right hon. Friend the Leader of the House that adequate time will be provided for the two debates, which will take place at times agreed between the usual channels. There is no question of our trying to confine them to the small hours or to a Friday morning.

**Dr. Cunningham:** Does not the Secretary of State see the hopeless position that he is portraying when the centrepiece of the legislation, the scheme that is supposed to deal with the problems, will never be debated in detail in Parliament, and Parliament will never have the chance to influence it?

**Mr. Ridley:** Does not the hon. Gentleman see the point that this is a highly technical scheme, which will be produced by the football industry and the people in it? It has never been proposed, and is not proposed now, that the details of the scheme should be amended according to the votes in Parliament.

The hon. Member for Holborn and St. Pancras (Mr. Dobson) asked in business questions last Thursday whether the Bill's scope would allow for amendments on safety matters. In response to that question, I am proposing that the House should instruct the Standing Committee that will consider the Bill that it has the power to make provision in the Bill relating to any aspect of the safety of spectators at designated football matches.

The Government do not intend to bring forward wide-ranging amendments on new safety measures in this Bill. Under the Safety of Sports Grounds Act 1975, as amended by the Fire Safety and Places of Sport Act 1987, the Home Secretary already has the powers to make orders that, for example, could contain a provision requiring local authorities to include certain terms and conditions in safety certificates for a sports ground. The existing legislation does not, however, give the Home Secretary any enforcement functions. We have it in mind to propose an amendment to this Bill to provide a power to give the Bill's licensing authority a monitoring and enforcement role, to back up the Home Secretary's existing powers under the safety of sports grounds legislation—although only in relation to designated football matches in England and Wales. This will add to the Bill powers to enable us to deal with safety matters, on receipt of Lord Justice Taylor's report.

**Mr. Denis Howell** (Birmingham, Small Heath): The Secretary of State will be aware that, immediately after the Hillsborough disaster, the Home Secretary drew attention to the need for all-seater stadiums. The Minister for Sport has made some statements about that which will no doubt be referred to in the debate. Will the proposals dealing with safety take that on board? How will the powers to enforce that be provided? What funds, if any, will be available if the Government go down that road?

**Mr. Ridley:** I am delighted to confirm what my right hon. Friend the Home Secretary said when he made the statement about the Hillsborough disaster. My hon. Friend the Minister for Sport has already had one meeting with the football authorities to discuss the possibility of all-seater stadiums. There is considerable support in the House for the concept, provided that it is adapted to the most suitable grounds and limited to those grounds where it is considered necessary. This matter will take some time to resolve, but it is right that the Bill and the instruction to the Committee should be wide enough to enable my right hon. Friend the Home Secretary to use his powers to make any such provision if that is decided to be the right way forward. I cannot at this point commit the Government to providing finance for such hypothetical situations.

It seems to me desirable that the Committee should be enabled to consider amendments concerning safety generally. The intention is not to anticipate Lord Justice Taylor's report, but to enable us to deal with his recommendations, just as the amendments that we made in another place—to provide for parliamentary debates on the scheme after Royal Assent—allow the House to consider any comments that Lord Justice Taylor may make on the membership scheme in his final report.

The Hillsborough disaster and Lord Justice Taylor's inquiry are rightly very much on all our minds. That is why I have explained today how we have taken account of them. However, the Hillsborough tragedy does not remove the need for the anti-hooliganism measures provided for in parts I and II to proceed in this Session of Parliament.

Hooliganism has been a fact of football life for all too many years. Since the mid-1960s, it has deterred millions of genuine football supporters from attending matches. Attendances fell from 35 million in 1967-68 to 21 million in 1987-88. Football hooliganism has made life very unpleasant for those who live or trade near football grounds, and the behaviour of England football supporters abroad has brought only shame to this country.

However, the Opposition may tell us, and I have heard mumblings from the Opposition Front Bench already, that all this is changing, that attendances are beginning to rise —so they are, very slowly. We may be told that a number of valuable measures have been taken in the past few years to tackle the problem, and so they have—restrictions on the sale of alcohol at football grounds; powers for the courts to impose exclusion orders on convicted hooligans, all as a result of Government legislation; stronger police co-ordination both nationally and internationally; more co-operation between the police and football clubs; effective segregation of rival groups of supporters inside grounds and the introduction of closed-circuit television.

These measures have been worth while, I agree. They have been taken very largely as a result of pressure from the public and from Government rather than at the voluntary initiative of the football authorities. Unfortunately, although they have been worth while, the measures taken so far have not been enough. They have just about contained the problem. They have not cured it. We still need about 5,000 police to control football crowds every weekend of the football season—largely at the expense of the taxpayer and the ratepayer.

Violence continues. The 1987-88 domestic season ended with a number of serious incidents of violence and was followed by the disgraceful scenes involving English football followers in West Germany in June last year. The season which finished last month has seen regular outbreaks of trouble both at and away from football grounds, culminating in a number of serious incidents on 13 May, less than a month after Hillsborough.

On that day, there was a pitch invasion at Crystal Palace football ground by Birmingham City football supporters, in which 16 people were injured, including a stabbing. At the match between Bristol City and Sheffield United, fighting between rival groups of supporters spilled over on to the pitch and held up the game. There were disturbances up and down the country—in Sheffield, in Cheshire, at Southampton railway station and at the Toddington service station on the M1. In all, more than 300 people were arrested on the weekend of 13 May at or on their way to or from football matches.

The claim that football hooliganism has ceased to be a problem inside football grounds is simply not borne out by the facts.

**Mr. Robert N. Wareing** (Liverpool, West Derby): Had this Bill been on the statute book at the time of the disturbances in West Germany which were attributed to British fans, how many of those British fans would have been subjected to restriction orders? Is it not the case that there was not one conviction then?

**Mr. Ridley:** If this Bill had been enacted and had been in force for a few years, a large number of hooligans would have been banned from membership schemes and we could have prevented them from travelling to the overseas matches. I do not claim that this would work in a very short time, because it is necessary to have the bans on those who would commit——

**Mr. Denis Howell:** Will the Secretary of State give way?

**Mr. Ridley:** I have already given way to the right hon. Gentleman once. If I give way now, it will be for the last time.

**Mr. Howell:** The Secretary of State is very generous. He is now considering a very important matter. It is not the practice of continental policy authorities to charge those offenders, as we saw during the competition in Germany. They keep the fans overnight and then get them out of the country as fast as they can. They are not brought before the courts in Europe. My hon. Friend the Member for Liverpool, West Derby (Mr. Wareing) is right: in those circumstances, there will be no offence to proceed against in this country under the terms of this Bill.

**Mr. Ridley:** The right hon. Gentleman misses the point. If they were hooligans, they would have been brought before the British courts and would have had to report during major overseas matches under part II of the Bill.

**Dr. Cunningham** rose——

**Mr. Ridley:** I am being interrupted by the hon. Gentleman who is about to make a speech. Could he not develop his points when it comes to his turn? However, I shall give way.

**Dr. Cunningham:** Will the Secretary of State explain in a little more detail exactly what he has just said? With what will those people who have been detained overnight in police cells in European countries before being returned to Britain be charged? Since they are not charged abroad, and will not be charged here, how can they be excluded from travelling in the future?

**Mr. Ridley:** The hon. Gentleman holds the record for missing the point. He has done so during the past three years that he has been shadowing me, and today is no exception. The point is that those who are convicted of hooliganism in British courts will be required to report here and so will not be able to travel abroad. Does he not realise that the sooner that the Bill is on the statute book the sooner those people will be caught in the way that I have described? The longer that we delay, the more will be free to go to Europe to make a nuisance of themselves.

**Mr. John Carlisle** (Luton, North): Does my right hon. Friend agree that it is remarkable that what he has accurately described—arrests, hooliganism and the peace and quiet of towns and cities being shattered—surrounds a game of sport? Is it not a fact that those in Britain who have no interest in football—the vast majority—are desperately seeking an assurance from the Government

*[Mr. John Carlisle]*

that something will be done, and the Bill is one way of correcting the terrible problems that Britain's towns and cities have suffered for many years?

**Mr. Ridley:** I never understand why the hooligans on the Opposition Benches associate themselves with the hooligans in the football grounds. They should be aware that public opinion polls show that some 80 per cent. of the population want the problem dealt with.

**Several Hon. Members** *rose——*

**Mr. Ridley:** I shall not give way.

When the Government bring forward measures to deal with the problem, the Opposition should be more——

**Several Hon. Members** *rose——*

**Mr. Speaker:** Order. I have already told the House that a great number of hon. Members wish to participate in the debate, some of whom are rising now. It will be difficult to call them if the Secretary of State is not allowed to continue.

**Mr. Ridley:** I must comply with your request, Mr. Speaker, and make a little more progress.

The truth is that the measures in place so far are simply not enough to put a stop to football hooliganism. Even the chairman of the Football Association reacted to the events of 13 May by calling for a ban on all away supporters —a significantly more restrictive control than we have proposed. His own organisation promptly came up with another proposal for a membership scheme of a different kind.

Football has had many opportunities to put its own house in order. It has failed to take them. Before the decision to introduce the Bill was taken last year, my right hon. Friend the Prime Minister asked the president of the Football League and the chairman of the Football Association, at a meeting on 6 July, if they would voluntarily introduce a national membership scheme. They said that they would not, and the Government subsequently introduced the Bill. The continuing incidence of football violence since then has demonstrated just how right we were.

Part I provides a statutory framework for a national membership scheme for football spectators and for the licensing of football grounds in relation to the scheme. It provides for me to designate the matches to which the scheme will apply, to appoint a Football Membership Authority to draw up the scheme and for the Football Membership Authority to submit it to me for approval. On each of those three key points, my powers are exercisable only by statutory instrument, subject to the negative resolution procedure. In each case, the House will be able to debate and vote on the issue. It is our intention, and that of the football authorities, that they should set up and run the FMA. As a result of an amendment moved in another place, both the FMA and I are required to consider the possibility of phasing the introduction of the scheme.

Clause 5 lays down requirements that the scheme must satisfy and others with which it may deal. Its contents have been expanded a little as a result of amendments made in another place to specify exemptions for disabled people and accompanied children in designated areas and to provide for temporary membership arrangements for the clubs to use. Those amendments meet the genuine concerns of clubs about the practical application of the scheme without weakening its basic purpose, which is to limit admission to spectators who are members of the scheme or who are authorised by it.

Clause 5 provides also for the Football Membership Authority to disqualify people from membership of the scheme at its discretion, and its powers to do so were clarified by amendments made in another place. The clause specifically provides that the full protection of the Data Protection Act 1984 will be available to applicants and to members of the scheme.

People who are convicted of an offence that is among those listed as relevant in the schedule to the Bill will be banned from membership of the scheme for a fixed period of either two or five years. It will be an offence to attend or to attempt to attend a designated football match for anyone who is not a member of or otherwise authorised by the scheme. It will also be an offence for a club or anyone else to admit spectators to a designated football match without a licence for the ground. The powers of the licensing authority are set out in clauses 8 to 11.

The licensing authority will be the Secretary of State or a body appointed by me.

**Mr. Tony Banks** (Newham, North-West): He is worse than Hitler.

**Mr. Ridley:** The authority's job will be to ensure that clubs have the equipment and are following the procedures required to enable the national membership scheme to work. If a club deliberately ignores the conditions of its licence it will run the risk of conviction for a criminal offence. If it is seriously or persistently in breach of its licence the Bill provides for the licence to be suspended or revoked.

A final decision to go ahead with the scheme will depend on parliamentary approval, when we have had the chance to consider Lord Justice Taylor's report. Even then it will, of course, take time to put the scheme in place. We shall not introduce it until we are confident that it will work effectively and safely. Subject to appropriate technology, we hope to see implementation achieved in the early months of the 1990-91 football season.

**Mr. Michael Foot** (Blaenau Gwent): If the right hon. Gentleman has followed previous debates, he will recall that one of the main criticisms of the plan as previously presented, and which the details that he has given today confirm, is that it will harm the position of many smaller clubs. Clubs will see the size of their crowds persistently reduced, which will put many of them out of business. What is the Government's best calculation of the number of clubs that will be injured by the scheme in that way?

**Mr. Ridley:** My present estimate is zero. Nothing could have done more damage to football than hooliganism, which has reduced the size of gates from 35 million people to 21 million. If football can regain only half those lost spectators that will transform not only the sport's finances but the fortunes of some smaller clubs. Would the right hon. Gentleman argue after a serious hotel fire that we should not introduce new regulations on hotel safety because that might bankrupt some smaller establishments? Is that the line that the right hon. Gentleman is taking?

**Mr. Foot:** Will the right hon. Gentleman be good enough to answer the question that I and many others have put? What is the Government's calculation, irrespective of other matters, of the harm done by the Bill to the number of people attending football matches? What will be its effect on many of the smaller clubs, and is it the Government's firm intention to proceed with a plan that will drive many of them out of business?

**Mr. Ridley:** I have already answered that question. My answer was zero.

Part II deals directly with the problem of football hooligans abroad. The behaviour of such people has been a national disgrace for years. I do not think that there is any argument about the need for these provisions.

**Mr. Terry Dicks** (Hayes and Harlington): Will my right hon. Friend give way?

**Mr. Ridley:** No, I really must get on.

Clauses 12 to 16 provide that when someone is convicted of a relevant offence, as defined in the Bill, the court may also impose a restriction order requiring him, or her, to report to an agency when certain matches take place abroad. Restriction orders will run for the same periods as automatic disqualification from membership of the scheme in this country—two years or five, depending on the severity of the sentence.

**Mr. Dicks:** Will my right hon. Friend give way?

**Mr. Ridley:** No.

**Hon. Members:** Give way.

**Mr. Speaker:** Order. It is clear that the Secretary of State does not intend to give way.

**Mr. Ridley:** The court must be satisfied that a restriction order would help to prevent or reduce violence or disorder at matches abroad.

Clauses 17 to 19 govern the operation of reporting agencies. The reporting agency will set the time at which someone subject to an order must report, so as to ensure that he cannot attend the match. Offenders will have rights of appeal against the court's decision to impose restriction orders, but once the order is made, failure to report when required will itself be a criminal offence.

Clause 20 allows for an application to be made for a restriction order in cases where someone resident here has been convicted of an offence outside England and Wales.

**Mr. Dicks:** As I understand my right hon. Friend, he has said that if the restriction on hooligans travelling abroad had been in operation two years ago, some of the offences that have been committed abroad would not have happened. Does my right hon. Friend know that I received a letter from the Home Secretary just over a year ago in which he told me that it was impossible to introduce any measure that would prevent people from going abroad? What has happened between then and now to alter the position?

**Mr. Ridley:** The question related to taking away people's passports, which my right hon. Friend could not possibly do. However, this measure will solve the problem to the satisfaction, I hope, of my right hon. Friend the Home Secretary, my hon. Friend the Member for Hayes and Harlington (Mr. Dicks) and myself.

I recognise that there has been controversy about the Government's proposals, in the police service and in football itself. Of course, the police are rightly concerned that the national membership scheme should not be introduced until the technology is ready. So are we. It is our intention that the Association of Chief Police Officers should continue to be consulted closely as the scheme is drawn up. The football authorities will be drawing up the scheme themselves. It will be their responsibility to produce a scheme that best suits the needs of football, within the framework of the Bill. If they and the clubs will take a positive rather than a negative approach to the scheme, they and their supporters will benefit from it. Individual clubs should see this as an opportunity to develop closer links with their supporters—as their members—not to put them off.

I began by referring to Lord Justice Taylor's inquiry. I will emphasise again now what I said at the beginning: Parliament will have not one but two opportunities to debate and vote on the national membership scheme after we have received the report and in the light of any comments that Justice Taylor may make on the scheme. By proceeding with the Bill now, we can put the framework for the scheme in place and make it possible to move on rapidly with the scheme, if Parliament agrees that we should do so when it has seen what Lord Justice Taylor has to say.

It would be irresponsible to throw away the progress that we have already made on this Bill by delaying it for one year. The case for both parts I and II remains conclusive. Events since Hillsborough have shown only too clearly that hooligans continues to infect football. The national membership scheme offers the prospect of removing that infection in the interests both of genuine football supporters and of others whose lives are damaged by the behaviour of football hooligans. We should not hesitate to put the framework for the scheme in place.

4.40 pm

**Dr. John Cunningham** (Copeland): I agreed with the Secretary of State when he again reiterated on behalf of Government Members the sorrow that people felt about the tragedy at Hillsborough. We on the Opposition Benches shared his expressions at least on that, if on little else, in what seemed to be the speech of a team member bound for relegation.

The preparation and promotion of the Bill have all the familiar trademarks of the domineering attitudes of the Prime Minister. The Bill epitomises all that is wrong with the Government and with many Conservative Members. As with the poll tax and water privatisation, the Secretary of State promotes the Bill only because the Prime Minister says so. She is determined to impose a national membership scheme and identity cards on hundreds of thousands of law-abiding football supporters. She is determined to do that against the advice of soccer administrators and the Police Federation and against all the evidence that her scheme is irrelevant to the problems of hooliganism and violence which have grown dramatically under her Administration.

This is not simply the wrong Bill at the wrong time. It is the wrong Bill at any time. Every team has its strikers and its specialists for dead ball situations and corner kicks, and the Thatcher team is no exception. Today we heard from the Secretary of State, her special own goal specialist,

[*Dr. John Cunningham*]

and as with previous speeches of the right hon. Gentleman on many occasions, the majority of his colleagues in the Cabinet have an arranged away fixture, while he is at the Dispatch Box. The right hon. Gentleman reminds me of the old Robin Hall and Jimmy McGregor song:

"Fitba' crazy, fitba' mad.
It's the fitba' that's robbed him of the wee bit of sense he had."

In January of this year, the Secretary of State said in a press release that the Bill would

"break the link between violence and football."

He said that knowing—if he did not know, he should have been aware—that the majority of incidents of violence, hooliganism and arrests already take place outside football grounds. The tragedies at Bradford and Sheffield were not caused by violence or hooliganism.

The Popplewell report did not recommend the proposals in this measure, which is being unnecessarily pushed through Parliament in the middle of the Taylor inquiry, which is specifically charged with making recommendations about the needs of crowd control and safety at sports grounds. It simple does not bear examination for the Secretary of State to say that the House should proceed to reach conclusions on legislation before what should be, and almost certainly will be, a watershed report about the circumstances and situations in and near sports grounds in this country. It is, frankly, ridiculous to ask Parliament to legislate in advance of that vitally important investigation, and the conclusions that it will take many more months to formulate.

The overwhelming majority of spectators of course want better standards of behaviour on and off the pitch, and the Professional Footballers Association, fan clubs, the Football Association and the Football League all recognise the need to go on working to improve those standards. But requiring all football supporters—law-abiding citizens overwhelmingly—to carry identity cards is irrelevant to those aims and objectives.

There is a clear and urgent need for soccer stadium facilities to be fundamentally improved, but far from bringing extra financial resources and essential investment into football clubs, the Bill is likely to reduce attendances and income, redirect existing and often inadequate cash to the equipment and administration necessary to operate a compulsory national indentity card scheme and bring many clubs in the lower divisions in England and Wales, despite what the Secretary of State said, into serious financial difficulties, if not into insolvency.

The Government's proposals are far more likely to deter decent football supporters than they are to deter hooligans. Once more we see the Government ignoring the advice, opinions and evidence of the people on the spot —the police, club administrators and those responsible for managing the situation—and imposing yet another central Government regime, another quango.

The Secretary of State recognised that the situation outside grounds, on trains and on public transport generally, was where the major problems existed when he said, in his 17 January press statement, and repeated today when talking about motorway service stations:

"Outside football grounds the behaviour of rival groups of supporters"—

although I believe that to be a misuse of the word——

"makes life intolerable both for law-abiding football supporters and for those who live or trade nearby, or wish to travel by train on the same day as a football match."

We share the right hon. Gentleman's view on those points, but the possession, or lack of a compulsory identity card will not prevent the incidents which are all too common in Britain today, whether or not football is the focus. Indeed, it could make the situation worse by requiring people to leave home or work earlier to ensure entry on time.

It could lead to more people spending more time in town and city centres before games, thus increasing the potential for disputes and disturbances—[HON. MEMBERS: "Why?"]—because people do not want to queue up and miss the beginning of a game. They want to ensure that they get into the ground, and therefore they will travel earlier. [*Interruption.*] If Conservative Members went to a few more football matches, they would know all about it.

For several years, under pressure, it is true, from fans, from public opinion, from Parliament and—I agree with the Secretary of State—from the Government, football clubs have taken, and are continuing to take, action to improve the situation inside grounds. The effective segregation of fans, family enclosures, close co-operation with the police and the installation of closed-circuit television have all been important and beneficial advances.

Local community schemes and, increasingly, good co-operation between clubs and local councils are also making a positive contribution to improving the situation. This essential progress must continue and that financial support from the Football Trust and from central and local government should be increased wherever possible.

The Bill, however, is irrelevant to all of those issues. It simply does not touch them. The Football Association, the Football League, the overwhelming majority of football clubs in England and Wales, the Police Federation and football supporters share that view. The evidence available to the House supports our conclusions and not those of the Secretary of State.

Nobody in football would deny that there is a problem of hooligan behaviour which attaches itself to the game, more regularly in some places than in others, but it is not unique to football. Other sports and society at large are afflicted by public disorder and violent crime.

The nature of the problem which attaches itself to football has altered significantly. Although there are still incidents of violence and disorder within grounds, those have been contained and trouble-makers are quickly identified and dealt with by improved policing, aided especially by closed-circuit television, now present at all league grounds.

The 6,147 arrests during the 1987-88 season represented a tiny proportion, 0·03 per cent., of the 18 million attendances at games in that season. That compared with arrest figures for the population at large of 3·9 per cent. The number of arrests is, of course, a measure of the effectiveness of club and police control, and as it gets more effective, the purpose is to weed people out and get them out of the grounds. Many of the offences included in that total occurred away from the grounds and would not be directly dealt with by a mandatory identity card scheme. Indeed, two thirds of those offences occurred outside the grounds and only about 2,000 arrests were made within them. Of the 6,147 arrests during the season, in only 1,089 cases did conviction result in exclusion orders—a sign, at least, that a considerable number of those arrests were not for violence or serious disorder.

**Mr. Alistair Burt** (Bury, North): Given the scale of policing at football matches, the fact that football matches take place under close scrutiny and the fact that police officers are in large-scale attendance in the towns before matches, is it not remarkable that the scale of offences is so high? It is no point comparing that with what happens with the public at large, who are not subject to closed-circuit television or close scrutiny. It is remarkable that the scale of offences at matches is so high when there is such close scrutiny.

**Dr. Cunningham:** The hon. Gentleman has missed the point. With 18 million attendances, the scale is not high compared with other aspects of crowd behaviour in other circumstances.

**Mr. Ridley:** The hon. Gentleman appears to be reaching the conclusion that all is well and that there is no need to do anything—[HON. MEMBERS: "No."] That is the impression that the hon. Gentleman is giving. He will be laughed out of court if he persists with his complacent and stupid attitude.

**Dr. Cunningham:** The Secretary of State is more dozy and dim than I had thought. It is clear that he has not been listening, but if he reads *Hansard* tomorrow he will realise that I said that all is not well, that we all recognise that and that we want further improvement. We do not think that his proposals are relevant to the problems.

With the help of the Football Trust, all league clubs now have closed-circuit television at their grounds. In addition, a further £500,000 has been allocated by the Football Trust this season to provide the police with 45 portable systems to improve evidence gathering, which will enable them to take more positive action against troublemakers. That is the measure that the football authorities and the police believe will deal most effectively with the problem within the grounds, by deterring people from committing offences and by more quickly identifying those who have committed them. With one exception, all league clubs have voluntarily introduced partial membership schemes in the home areas of their grounds. All the clubs have comprehensive local plans to deal with the safety and control of spectators, which have been drawn up in consultation with the local police and local authorities. The vast majority of league clubs have family enclosures at their grounds, and they are now attracting more and more families to the game. Indeed, as the Secretary of State rightly said, attendances have been rising over the last three seasons.

The football-in-the-community scheme co-ordinated by the league and the Professional Footballers Association has proved effective in bringing clubs closer to their local communities. Some 34 clubs are involved and there are plans for extending it throughout the league. Many of the clubs not involved in the scheme have introduced a community programme on their own initiative. At 93 per cent. of clubs with a PFA scheme for the 1987-88 season, arrest levels were below their divisional average.

**Mr. Kenneth Hind** (Lancashire, West): The hon. Gentleman said that most grounds now have closed-circuit television to help the police. Does he accept that at Selhurst park on 19 May there was a pitch invasion during which 16 fans were arrested and one was stabbed? As there was closed-circuit television available on that occasion, does he now accept that it was obviously inadequate to

deal with the problem? Many people involved in offences on that day were beyond the policing available and so got away with them. Are not the hon. Gentleman's proposals inadequate to deal with the problems?

**Dr. Cunningham:** I do not accept any of what the hon. Gentleman says, other than that there was a serious disturbance at Selhurst park. However, I am not yet sure of the reasons for that disturbance and I am not sure that the hon. Gentleman is sure either.

**Mr. John Fraser** (Norwood): I was at that match. One of the problems was that the fences had been taken down because of the recent Hillsborough disaster—a problem now facing many grounds. If the police had tried to arrest all those who invaded the pitch—they had no support from the majority of supporters—there would have been a major incident. I do not in any way excuse what happened at Selhurst park—it mainly involved Birmingham supporters—but it was caused partly by the taking down of fences as a consequence of Hillsborough. There would have had to be mass arrests for the Bill to have been of any consequence.

**Dr. Cunningham:** In December last year, the Police Federation said about the proposed national membership scheme:

"Think again, Mr. Moynihan. The report of Sports Minister Mr. Colin Moynihan's working party on a national membership scheme for football has come in for almost universal condemnation. Sadly the strictures are deserved, for this is an extraordinary mish mash of good intentions and half-baked nostrums. If the Government insists on using its majority to steamroller this scheme through Parliament, the results could be disastrous."

Those were the comments of the police about the proposals. The Police Federation continued:

"When the scheme breaks down, it will do so on match days and give rise to the threat of even worse disorder than it seeks to suppress."

**Mr. Michael Shersby** (Uxbridge): The hon. Gentleman is quoting views that the Police Federation expressed some months ago. Is he sure that they are the same today? He may find that they are not.

**Dr. Cunningham:** I am sure that the police do not support the proposals in the Bill.

The Bill is riddled with inconsistencies and contradictions and is full of holes. It is merely an enabling Bill; the heart of the Government's proposals—the so-called national membership scheme—is missing. That is to be left to a football membership authority. The Bill, however, makes no reference to the football membership authority recommended by the Minister's working party. Instead, it says the Secretary of State will appoint an administrator —who may, or may not, be the football membership authority. We do not know.

Whatever the House decides—not only today but in Committee—in advance of the Taylor inquiry report, the House cannot in any way influence the details of the heart of the proposals. The Secretary of State will determine that and bring it to the House on a take-it-or-leave-it basis. That is a wholly unsatisfactory way for the House to be asked to deal with such a matter, and in their heart of hearts Conservative Members know that to be so. The House is being asked to give the Secretary of State for the Environment a blank cheque for the proposals, and it should not do so.

*[Dr. Cunningham]*

I say to Conservative Members who have misgivings about the Bill—as many had misgivings about previous legislation such as the poll tax and water privatisation—that it is no good looking to the House of Lords to amend the Bill; it has already been in the House of Lords. Conservative Members cannot fall back on that excuse. If they intend to influence these matters, they must do so here and now through their vote in the Lobby tonight. There is no other way.

**Mr. David Evans** (Welwyn Hatfield): Will the hon. Gentleman answer a simple question? Is his answer to the problem more police, more dogs, more horses and more fences? If, as I suspect, it is, will that continue until there are more police than there are spectators? Does he agree that it is about time that the Government and the House protected the vast majority of people who go in trepidation every Saturday in areas where football matches are being played?

**Dr. Cunningham:** Since my answer to the hon. Gentleman's unsimple question is no, all his supplementary questions fall. I do not agree that the answer is more police, more dogs and more horses. I think that he knows that very well. Nor do I say, incidentally, that the answer is the scheme that he and others have pioneered in the football club with which he has had a long association. That seeks to ban away supporters altogether.

**Mr. Joseph Ashton** (Bassetlaw): Will my hon. Friend point out a major hole in the Bill that has been brought out by the Football League—that it is the custom at football matches to open the gates for people to leave 15 minutes from time? If the gates were locked until the 90th minute, there would be chaos. When the gates are opened 15 minutes from time, what is there to stop anyone walking in free, without a membership card? People do it now. Anyone could walk in without a card and cause a riot.

**Dr. Cunningham:** My hon. Friend is right. That is a problem that again is not addressed by the Secretary of State's proposals.

Unlike many of the existing voluntary schemes, the Government scheme comes without any real benefit to members. No entitlements or rights will flow from being forced to have an identity card. It is nothing less than compulsory identity cards for up to perhaps 4 per cent. of the population of England and Wales.

The Government have rightly excluded Scotland from the provisions of the Bill. The Bill is nonsense for England and Wales. We support the exclusion of Scotland but at present Scottish and Welsh teams compete in European tournaments. Under the Government proposals Welsh fans will be required to carry identity cards; Scottish fans will not. English fans travelling to Scotland will be required to carry identity cards but Scottish fans travelling to England will not.

What will happen, for example, at an England versus Scotland match at Wembley, with Scottish supporters travelling down for the day, and Scots men and women who live in England claiming that they are just down for the day as well? Will a Scottish person living and working temporarily in England be required to have an identity card? Ministers have no answers to these questions. If the Secretary of State has got an answer, I will be happy to

give way. I think in football parlance that is called a set-up pass; selling one's team mates short would, I think, describe the Secretary of State's behaviour in pointing to his hon. Friend.

To admit people without identity cards to a designated game will be a criminal offence, punishable by a prison sentence. What will be the position, and who will be responsible for order and for taking decisions if, in the interest of safety and public order, the police instruct ground authorities to open the gates and admit people, whether or not they have tickets and cards? That is exactly what happens from time to time every season. Who will be responsible? Who will be in charge? There is no answer to those questions either.

**Mr. Brian Wilson** (Cunninghame, North): Before my hon. Friend goes too far away from the Scotland versus England example, may I point out that there was a lot of trouble associated with the recent international at Hampden. All that trouble took place in the streets and in the city centre. If the Government would do something to stop marauding Fascists who have nothing to do with football attaching themselves to football crowds, they would be getting to the core of the problem. The proposed scheme would have been utterly irrelevant to everything that happened in Glasgow that day.

**Dr. Cunningham:** I agree with my hon. Friend, although we might not agree about the outcome of the match.

Part I of the Bill is totally unacceptable and clause 5 is particularly obnoxious. Does the House really believe that pensioners, who will have to carry identity cards, are a threat to public order? Are women a major cause of hooliganism? I understand from debates in another place that the Government insist that women cannot be excluded because male troublemakers would dress up and pose as women to gain entry. On such stupidities do the Government rest their vacuous case. All unaccompanied children aged 10 years and over will be required to have identity cards. There is no evidence to support the need for that draconian proposal. Season ticket holders who pay large sums to guarantee their seats and their comfort at every home game will also be required to carry identity cards.

A major anxiety occasioned by the proposal to introduce a compulsory scheme is the prospect that fooball will lose a great many casual spectators, estimated at 20 per cent. of attendances and probably including a great many hon. Members. These people may go to matches two, three or half-a-dozen times a season. They and we often have no particular club allegiance, although I have; I say it quietly—Newcastle United.

In London and other major cities such as Birmingham and Liverpool many people may go to different grounds. The Government should recognise the problem posed by the potentially damaging loss of income which is worrying dozens of football administrators. How will the proposals cater for the spectator who decides at short notice to attend a match? Football clubs need flexibility to be able to issue cards on match days even for a single fixture. At larger clubs that attract much casual support the proposed scheme will lead to considerable administrative difficulty, delays, frustration and even anger.

Similar arguments apply to foreign visitors. Large numbers of spectators living in Europe, particularly Holland and Scandinavia, visit London clubs frequently, if not regularly in some cases. Similarly, Irish spectators travel to watch Liverpool and Everton in particular. The European and Irish spectators may in future have to present their passports at football club offices to obtain a one-match membership card and a ticket. The proposal is preposterous.

In its independent report on the Government's proposed scheme, Arthur Young stated that it had examined the technology available and had identified six options. The review showed:

"No one supplier was able to demonstrate conclusively at this stage that their technology or approach could satisfy the total requirements of the national membership scheme."

We have only to go into London Underground at rush hour to see what happens. When there is a crush, the barriers are opened and everyone is allowed through. It is exactly such hold-ups, delays and aggravation that the Secretary of State proposes to impose on football spectators and clubs.

The problem that continues to cause football authorities, clubs and the police the greatest anxiety is the possibility that the technology will fail on a match day at more than one club, just before the start of the match, when thousands may be waiting to be admitted. What will happen then? The police will advise the club to open the gates. They will break the law by asking someone to commit a criminal offence and render himself liable to a gaol sentence.

At the briefing meeting for club chairmen on 17 January, the Secretary of State apparently said that local police will not have overriding powers to instruct clubs to suspend the operation of the membership scheme in order to admit spectators without checking cards. However, we know that, in the past, when all-ticket matches have been played, the police have done just that—admitted spectators without tickets, in the interests of public safety and order. The Secretary of State says that he will stop that. He will be responsible for the problems that result or, alternatively, for the fact that thousands of people, who want to see a match, have tickets and are members, will have to be turned away. That is a recipe for civil disturbance outside football grounds.

I see that the Secretary of State has written to all Tory Members pleading for loyalty in the Lobby tonight. One of his loyal and hon. Friends has kindly sent the Opposition a copy of that letter. It would be interesting to see the loyal reply from the right hon. Member for Old Bexley and Sidcup (Mr. Heath). In any event, as I am sure that right hon. Gentleman would say, the best form of loyalty to one's friends is to tell them the truth, however unpalatable it might be. No amount of fudging can cover the huge inadequacies of the Secretary of State's proposals. He is fudging.

Typically, the Secretary of State is deliberately inaccurate and misleading in his letter to all Conservative Members. In his letter, he claims:

"The FA made a significant change of direction on 18th May in a statement which embraced the principle of a membership scheme."

The Secretary of State appears to be referring to off-the-cuff remarks by Mr. Bert Millichip, but the FA and the Football League, in a brief to the House today, continue their opposition to part I of the Bill, which they describe as "seriously flawed".

They go on to say that it

"should not be considered in detail before full account has been taken of the recommendations of Lord Justice Taylor."

We share their views.

**Mr. Nigel Spearing** (Newham, South): Is my hon. Friend aware that the letter was sent not only privately to Conservative Members but to all hon. Members—at least to other hon. Members—including myself on 21 December? The Minister with responsibility for sport said:

"The Government, police and the football authorities were represented on the working party and agreed its recommendations."

Quite clearly, they did not. The Football League told me that that was misrepresentation. Later, on 23 February, the Minister wrote:

"I recognise that the football authorities have made clear all along their opposition to the principle of the scheme."

Therefore, is there not only dubiety in the Government's letter to Conservative Members but a calculated intention to mislead?

**Dr. Cunningham:** My hon. Friend's comments are borne out by the letter that he received, of which I have a copy, from Mr. J. D. Dent, the secretary of the Football League Ltd., dated 28 February this year. Mr. Dent wrote:

"Dear Mr. Spearing"—

I will not read the whole letter—

"It is good of you to take up with the Minister his misrepresentation of the football authorities' views and I am most grateful to you for this."

There we have it—the football authorities themselves saying that the Minister with responsibility for sport was misrepresenting their position.

We can at least agree the principle of part II of the Bill and the intention to restrict people convicted of a football-related offence from travelling to matches abroad. That proposal rightly enjoys general support, but, again, there are weaknesses in the detail of the Bill. Police in Europe often do not charge detained troublemakers but simply return them to Britain as soon as possible. As they stand, the proposals simply cannot deal with those people —there will be nothing to exclude them for. In addition, exclusion will require a very large administrative effort by the police effectively to implement the reporting scheme nationwide when matches abroad are designated.

This Bill is the imposition of central Government control upon a single sport. It is unprecedented in its implications for civil liberties, and it has no parallel in Europe. Once again, it gives the Secretary of State powers that effectively prevent proper Parliamentary scrutiny of his proposals. It would punish football and the game's supporters for the hooliganism and public disorder that are endemic in Tory Britain. As the Association of Chief Police Officers reported last year:

"From Petersfield to Penrith, from Barnstaple to Bridlington, come reports of unprovoked attacks on property, public and police".

The chief officers referred to 251 incidents, involving 36,000 people, in which over 2,000 arrests were made. That is, 2,000 arrests from 36,000 people in towns and cities around the country. That is as many as the arrests from 18 million football supporters in a whole season, and Conservative Members say that they are dealing with the right problem. They are not even aiming at the right target. There were 1,700 arrests at race meetings alone in this country last year—600 at Royal Ascot in one week. *[Laughter.]*

**Mr. Richard Holt** (Langbaurgh): Will the hon. Gentleman give way?

**Dr. Cunningham:** I will not give way.

**Mr. Holt** *rose*——

**Madam Deputy Speaker (Miss Betty Boothroyd):** Order. The hon. Member for Copeland (Dr. Cunningham) has made it clear that he is not giving way. I call Dr. Cunningham.

**Dr. Cunningham:** The hon. Gentleman— *[Interruption.]* Pardon?

**Mr. Holt** *rose*——

**Madam Deputy Speaker:** Order. I heard the hon. Gentleman use the word "liar".

**Mr. Holt:** I will withdraw the word "liar". The hon. Gentleman is misleading the House, and he is afraid to give way.

**Madam Deputy Speaker:** Order. I call Dr. Cunningham.

**Dr. Cunningham:** The hon. Gentleman flatters himself.

**Mr. Holt:** Give way—see if you can give way.

**Dr. Cunningham:** After his behaviour, I am certainly not giving way to the hon. Gentleman.

Regrettably but true, it is the case in this country, that, wherever and whenever large numbers of people gather, there are always some arrests. As the figures show, to single out soccer is misguided and plainly wrong, especially when the situation in soccer grounds is improving because of the actions that are being taken.

In early 1988, the Association of Chief Police Officers commissioned the centre for football research at Leicester university to undertake a survey of senior police officers with responsibility for policing Football League grounds. In all, the centre received replies from officers at 90 of the 92 Football League grounds. The survey covers a wide range of issues involving contemporary policing methods at football, but there is particular focus on a compulsory national scheme. The results of the survey—the most comprehensive one that we are aware of—show that the senior officers were divided about the Government's proposed scheme. A large proportion of them believed that hooliganism inside grounds is decreasing—the evidence bears that out—and four out of five of those senior police officers believed that hooliganism outside grounds was not worsening.

There is growing violence in all aspects of British life. It is more dangerous than ever before in our streets and on our public transport systems because of the increase in crimes of violence under this Government. To single out soccer grounds ignores where most violence takes place. Because of better crowd control, closed circuit television cameras and improved policing, football grounds are actually safer places to be than the average high street on a Saturday afternoon. The Labour party has supported the measures that were put into action by the Football League and the Football Association in their fight against violence associated with football. These actions have been successful in reducing the percentage of those arrested for any offences related to football to 0·03 per cent. of spectators, while the national average for criminal offences is 3·9 per cent. of the population. Football has done that, at a cost of £15 million to itself. A compulsory identity card scheme will cost many more millions and again the Government are inconsistent.

Let us consider the Secretary of State's performance in the House two weeks ago. The latest figures show that in 1985, 1,200 people were treated in hospital after being attacked by dogs. The Post Office unions claim that there are 5,000 dog attacks on postmen and women every year. It is estimated that about 1 million people in Britain are bitten by dogs every year. Yet this same Secretary of State rejected a dog owner registration scheme as

"complicated, bureaucratic and expensive to administer".— [*Official Report*, 14 June 1989; Vol. 154, c. 1076.]

**Mr. Tony Banks:** The score must be 6:0 now.

**Dr. Cunningham:** The Bill is not based on ideology, but on idolatory. The Prime Minister must have it, however stupid and however nonsensical. This is the Prime Minister who, on 18 May, was the subject of a four-page spread in the *Daily Mail*—a typical *Daily Mail* hagiography. Its banner headline reads:

"My European Nightmare by Maggie".

Well, that was one of her dreams that certainly came true. If we read beyond the headline, the Prime Minister is quoted as saying:

"As I said in my Bruges speech, we are practical. They have identity cards, but can you imagine compulsory identity cards in this country? We recoil from it."

That was what the Prime Minister said barely one month ago, but today we have a three-line Whip on all her Ministers who are being dragooned into the Lobbies in favour of compulsory identity cards for football supporters.

The Bill is based on blind support for that increasingly isolated and erratic Prime Minister. It should not proceed before Lord Justice Taylor——

**Mr. Ridley** *rose*—*[Interruption.]*

**Dr. Cunningham:** I shall give way in a moment.

It should not proceed before Lord Justice Taylor reports and it should be referred to the special statutory committee procedure so that witnesses can be called to give evidence and to answer questions from the Committee; so that we can have the football authorities, the police and, if necessary, Lord Justice Taylor here to comment before the legislation goes through. The Government's decision to press ahead with the Bill at this time and in this way, while the inquiry is still sitting, is not rational.

**Mr. Ridley:** Half an hour after I last intervened in the hon. Gentleman's speech—after half an hour of absolute twaddle—it is now clear that the hon. Gentleman does not think that anything is wrong and does not think that anything should be done.

**Dr. Cunningham:** I advise the right hon. Gentleman to quit and to think about his goal difference because it is getting worse all the time——

**Mr. Tony Banks:** It is time for the yellow card.

**Dr. Cunningham:** I unreservedly offer the support of the Labour party for any Bill which is genuinely and effectively concerned with football safety and the enhancement of a great national game. These are not and should not be matters of party political dispute. But this Bill does not meet those requirements. As drafted it can never do so. That is why we are opposing it tonight.

5.24 pm

**Mr. John Carlisle** (Luton, North): Inevitably the House has been treated to a certain amount of humour from the hon. Member for Copeland (Dr. Cunningham) and, I suppose, to a certain amount of factual evidence that supports his party's opposition to this excellent Bill. However, what he was short on, as my right hon. Friend the Secretary of State rightly pointed out in his two interventions, was any type of answer to the terrible problems not only that we face as a country, but which football itself faces.

Much of the hon. Gentleman's argument was flawed. In his defence he quoted the Police Federation's opposition to the Bill, omitting to mention, of course, that just four or five weeks ago it reversed its opposition and said that it was in favour of the "no away supporters scheme" as exemplified at Luton. The hon. Gentleman quoted the Football Association in his favour, not mentioning of course, the words of Mr. Bert Millichip who has been described in a sedentary intervention as "a 68-year-old nonentity". He said:

"I do not know where we go from here. I just do not know what course of action we can take, but something has got to be done."

The problem with the hon. Gentleman's speech was that he did not give the House any fresh ideas. The complacent attitude of the hon. Gentleman and of his right hon. and hon. Friends belies the fact that they have understood the fundamental principle of the Bill.

Conservative Members appreciate that the problem exists. We shall not sit idly by and watch hooliganism spread throughout the greatest of our national games. Perhaps in the minds of some of my hon. Friends we are attempting to deal only inadequately with the problem, but the hon. Member for Copeland gave no answers in his speech.

When my right hon. Friend the Secretary of State referred to the Sporting Events (Control of Alcohol etc.) Act 1985, which was supported by the right hon. Member for Birmingham, Small Heath (Mr. Howell), the right hon. Gentleman said that we should never have enacted that legislation.

**Mr. Denis Howell** *rose——*

**Mr. Carlisle:** I shall give way to the right hon. Gentleman in a moment. The right hon. Gentleman said that we should never have done it, but he supported the Bill. The right hon. Gentleman and I served on the Committee on that Bill. He knows that it was rushed through this and another place in a day and a half with the full support of the right hon. Gentleman and his party. However, he is now saying that that Bill was a mistake, and saying, "We should not have supported it," and, "I have no other answer."

**Mr. Howell:** The Opposition have never supported the proposal that drinks should not be sold inside grounds —*[Interruption.]* No, we have always said that the problem was drinking outside grounds. If the hon. Member for Luton, North (Mr. Carlisle) will consider Hillsborough and if he will look at the police report on Crystal Palace, he will find considerable evidence—I am sure that Lord Justice Taylor will tell us this—of people arriving late because they had been drinking outside the ground. One effect of that legislation has been to aggravate the late arrival of people who cannot get a drink inside the ground. That has caused additional difficulties, which we predicted at the time.

**Mr. Carlisle:** I advise the right hon. Gentleman to go back to *Hansard* and to read the record and the surrounding press comments of the time. The measure was supported by almost all hon. Members. If I recall correctly, there was little division between us. The right hon. Gentleman would be wise to remember that at times he has supported certain measures and at others he has not.

None of that alters the fact that throughout this argument, no Opposition Member—on either the Front or the Back Benches—and no member of the Football League or the Football Association has come up with any real solution to the terrible problem that we face.

Although the speech of the hon. Member for Copeland was humorous at times, Conservative Members consider this to be a serious problem. Perhaps the hon. Gentleman lives in an ivory tower away from the problem on Saturday afternoons, but if he lived near any of the football grounds where nearby residents have suffered terrible afflictions because of football hooliganism, his attitude would be somewhat less light-hearted and more serious.

**Dr. Cunningham:** I am sorry that the hon. Gentleman does not have a sense of humour, but I am grateful to him for giving way. I never said that this is a laughing matter. What I said was laughable was the performance and proposals of the Secretary of State.

As the hon. Member for Luton, North has made an allegation, I should make it clear that I am very familiar with the conditions and the circumstances around many soccer gronds—for example, St James's park, Roker park and Elland road—and rugby grounds, too. I am a regular —although, unfortunately, not as frequent as I would like —attender at sports occasions. I watch Sunday soccer and a lot of schoolboy soccer. My greatest pleasure is watching my son play centre forward for his comprehensive school team.

**Mr. Carlisle:** The hon. Gentleman says that, but he still does not answer the basic problem, or perhaps even acknowledge that there is a problem.

**Mr. Tom Pendry** (Stalybridge and Hyde): Will the hon. Gentleman give way?

**Mr. Carlisle:** I shall give way to the hon. Gentleman a little later, because I know that he will probably want to intervene.

For many of us the Bill has been a long time coming. Inevitably, there was a right and seemly delay after Hillsborough. I am grateful to my right hon. Friend for listening to those of my hon. Friends who thought that we should sit back and wait for some interim comments from Lord Justice Taylor, and as my right hon. Friend has pointed out, at the end of the day to take into account the findings of Lord Justice Taylor.

Over the years, this game—I remind the House that, after all, it is only a game—has attracted an element of hooliganism and criminality which has resulted in deaths and injuries, in towns and cities on Saturday afternoons being turned, by military operation, into no-go areas, and in public transport being completely unsafe for those who wish either to travel to the match or to the area of the match. Those living around football grounds have suffered

[*Mr. Carlisle*]

the desecration of their gardens, broken windows and abuse. Regrettably, all those matters are associated with football. It is a fact that the crowds have halved in about 20 years and that the disgraceful behaviour of our so-called soccer fans abroad has brought shame and disgrace on the name of this country and on many of our towns and cities. That is why I salute what the Government are doing. They will not sit back and let the problem continue.

The saddest night of my life was in March 1985 when I attended the FA cup quarter final. My club, Luton Town —just outside my constituency—was playing Millwall. I say to my right hon. and hon. Friends, who may be worrying about the Bill, that had they been with me that night—some of them may have experience of what football hooliganism really means—they would have seen the way in which people behaved. Half-crazed with drink and with the knowledge that their team was losing, those hooligans took vengeance on my club by ripping out the seats, by tearing down the goal posts, by bursting through the fences and by injuring people. The situation was so bad that the young cadets of the St. John's ambulance, who were there to help those who needed help, were not allowed out on to the pitch. The police were attacked with iron bars and seats. On that night the whole area around the ground was devastated by the damage inflicted by those hooligans.

My hon. Friends say to me, "Yes, but is this the answer? Have we really come to the stage where we must force people to have membership cards?" I tell them that, if they had seen those scenes—which have sadly been repeated in and out of football grounds throughout the country—they would perhaps have some sympathy with the arguments of my constituents.

**Mr. Ashton:** Is it not a fact that Luton Town was very much to blame on that night? First, it did not print any replay tickets and did not have them ready to give to Millwall supporters on the previous Saturday, which has been standard practice for many years; secondly, it let 8,000 people into a section of the ground which probably would hold only 5,000; and, thirdly, the Bedford police were not ready, despite warnings sent from St. Pancras station, and had no experience of such trouble. The crowd had to invade the pitch to save themselves. When Luton Town and the police realised what a massive clanger they had dropped, to save itself from an investigation, Luton Town brought in its scheme. Much of the problem was due to bad organisation. Luton Town let far too many into the ground and was not able to police it.

**Mr. Carlisle:** I am sure that the hon. Gentleman's words, if expressed to my constituents in the Luton and Dunstable hospital the following morning, would have been of great comfort. Of course people say that it was not the fault of anybody, bar those in authority. It was not the fault of football fans: it was because Luton town did not allow enough police for the ground and it let too many supporters into the ground. I can tell the hon. Member for Bassetlaw (Mr. Ashton), because I was there, that it did not let them into the ground—they burst through the gate a la Hillsborough style. His attitude is the same as that of other Opposition Members—it is always someone else's fault, but never the fault of—[*Interruption.*]

**Mr. Terry Fields** (Liverpool, Broadgreen): On a point of order, Madam Deputy Speaker. The hon. Member for Luton, North (Mr. Carlisle) has clearly stated that people burst into the Hillsborough football ground. That is a lie. It is a distortion of the truth.

**Madame Deputy Speaker:** I am sure that, if that is incorrect, the hon. Member for Luton, North (Mr. Carlisle) may reflect on it and make some correction. I shall just say to the entire House that a number of hon. Members wish to speak in this debate, and that it may be counter-productive for too many hon. Members to approach the Chair and to show their interest in speaking.

**Mr. Carlisle:** I say to the hon. Member for Liverpool, Broadgreen (Mr. Field) that it would be presumptuous of anybody to state what happened at Hillsborough. He will know, however, that the facts suggest that those gates were left open or, as I said about Luton, they were burst open. I did not say that they were burst open at Hillsborough. —[*Interruption.*] Will the hon. Member for Broadgreen stop wagging his finger at me? The problem at Hillsborough was similar to the one at Luton. The difference, as the hon. Member for Bassetlaw said, was that the crowd spilled on to the field at Luton.

Those sad events left deep scars on my local club and on my town. My hon friend the Member for Welwyn Hatfield (Mr. Evans) and his colleagues on the board of directors of Luton Town took the sensible, necessary and drastic step of saying that that would not happen again and that they would pursue the experiment of a "no away supporters" scheme. In the three years or so since that scheme was introduced, we have had one arrest. The police go home at half-time. Families have returned to the ground. It is a delight to see young children there. Perhaps more important than anything, those who come to the town to shop and visit relatives, who probably outnumber the football supporters by four or five to one, know that they can come in peace and quiet.

**Mr. Wareing:** Will the hon. Gentleman give way?

**Mr. Carlisle:** No, I have given way enough.

Those people come with the absolute assurance that, because the football crowd has been controlled by our system, they can come to the town and enjoy the sort of Saturday afternoon that the majority of the country would wish for them.

**Mr. Wareing:** Will the hon. Gentleman give way?

**Mr. Carlisle:** No, I will not, because of the time.

I am proud to represent a constituency that has been the leader in correcting a terrible problem that has afflicted this country and has brought football into disrepute.

**Mr. Wareing:** Will the hon. Gentleman give way?

**Madam Deputy Speaker:** Order. The hon. Gentleman has made it clear that he is not ready to give way at this time.

**Mr. Carlisle:** I will not give way on the basis that many hon. Members on both sides wish to make a contribution. I know that the hon. Member for Liverpool, West Derby (Mr. Wareing) is keen on the subject land may wish to catch your eye, Madam Deputy Speaker, a little later.

We have seen such a change in our town in the past three years that we are bound to say to our hon. Friends and those hon. Members who listen from the Opposition,

"Why not try our system?" People say to me, "But yours is a 'no away supporters' scheme." Our scheme is exactly the same as that envisaged in the Bill. One has to be a member to come to our ground. If, however, the hon. Member for West Derby wished to watch the Luton versus Liverpool game at Kenilworth road, he would be entitled at the start of the season, for a cost of £1, to apply for membership and, provided that he is a good and upstanding citizen, which I know him to be, there would be no reason to refuse him membership. His problem would be that, because our scheme has been so popular, we have a waiting list.

**Mr. Wareing:** Will the hon. Gentleman give way?

**Mr. Carlisle:** I shall reluctantly give way to the hon. Gentleman.

**Mr. Wareing:** I am much obliged, because the hon. Gentleman has mentioned me. On 21 January this year I attended Luton Town football ground to see Everton. On that occasion, between 2.20 and 2.25 pm., I stood at a turnstile watching people use their membership cards to gain entry. Forty people entered in five minutes; 10 of them had great difficulty with their cards, and four entered with the help of the card of the person standing behind them.

**Mr. Carlisle:** I have heard the hon. Gentleman say that before and I am grateful for the information. New technology is now available which was conveniently forgotten by the hon. Member for Copeland who has seen the demonstrations, and I hope—I stress "hope", as the Bill is full of hope—that it will correct the problem. Luton pioneered the scheme and I am sure that, if my hon. Friend the Member for Welwyn Hatfield has the opportunity to speak, he will enlarge on what I have said.

In June 1986 my right hon. Friend the Prime Minister invited representatives of the Football Association to come to No. 10 to discuss the problem of football hooliganism. I do not like to use that phrase, but it is convenient today. The former secretary of the Football Association, Mr. Ted Croker, told my right hon. Friend to "take your tanks off my lawn" when she suggested that the Government, together with the Football Association, the Football League and others, might try to do something about the terrible problem inflicted on the game.

The remarkable thing about the opposition to the Bill from both sides of the House is that it fails to recognise that that is the intention of the legislation. It is unique for legislation to be passed for one specific sport. The Bill is an attempt—at this stage it may be nothing more than that—to take the problem away from football. Where that problem goes is, of course, the problem—[*Laughter.*] Opposition Members may laugh, but if I was in football I do not believe that I would reject something from a Government who said that they would try to take the problem away from me as they believe that it is also partly their problem.

The Bill is an attempt, and nothing more, to try to correct a problem. It may or may not work, but many of us hope that it will. We cannot ignore the problem. The hon. Member for Copeland may quote figures to show that the number of arrests is going down. We may argue that closed-circuit television and segregation have helped to deal with the problem. I do not deny that matters have improved, but there is still no corrective treatment. There

is no way in which to distinguish between those who go to a game to enjoy it and the tiny minority who want to wreck it. The tragedy of all legislation is that it is framed for the minority, not for the majority.

**Mr. Alan Meale** (Mansfield): Will the hon. Gentleman give way?

**Mr. Carlisle:** No, I will not.

The hon. Member for West Derby has spoken about the practicalities of the proposed scheme. Many hon. Members have taken the trouble to see what different systems are available, be it a smart card, a voucher system or whatever. The new technology will not suffer the same problems as those outlined by the hon. Gentleman.

We believe that every match should be an all-ticket game. There is nothing wrong with that and I do not believe that that represents an erosion of civil liberties. If a man wants to go to a game once or three times a season, what is wrong with asking him to make some small sacrifice by going along to his local post office or football club to buy a ticket to enable him to go to that game or games for up to five years? The card would not limit his entry to one ground; he would be permitted entry to any of the 92 grounds in the Football League. That is why the proposed scheme runs parallel with the Luton scheme.

When the Luton scheme was thought out, we always envisaged that it would be part of a total membership scheme. On that basis, the good guys will buy tickets and the bad guys will fall foul of the law, once established. We want to support those who are well-behaved. We ask them to make a small sacrifice by purchasing a ticket, probably once every five years, for a minimal cost. It would be extraordinary if such people said they would have nothing to do with it because it would erode their civil liberties. People may ask why they should buy a ticket, but hon. Members know that if they wish to attend any major sporting event, be it at Twickenham or Lords, where I have been for the past few days, one must buy a ticket to gain entry to the ground. I do not consider that the purchase of that ticket represents an erosion of my civil liberties. All that we are trying to do is to correct the existing problem.

I hope that the Bill will receive the full support of my hon. Friends. Originally I was against a compulsory membership scheme. I did not like the thought that one had to buy a ticket and that one must be identified. But we cannot go on as we are. The events after Hillsborough are crucial, as they suggest that some elements in the football crowd could not care tuppence about the game and are intent on wrecking it.

The Bill tries to correct what has been going wrong. It will act as a deterrent. It will ensure that those who go to football grounds do so with the intention of watching the match and of behaving, or they will lose their cards. The Bill will enable the police and the stewards to monitor and to filter fans who are going to matches when they arrive at railway stations, bus stations and on the roads leading up to the grounds. That would have helped at Hillsborough. People will have to have not only a ticket, as at Hillsborough, but a membership card.

The Bill must act as a deterrent, but it will not deter the genuine football supporter who wants to ensure the well-being of the game. I count myself in that category and that is why I support the Bill.

5.46 pm

**Mr. Stanley Orme** (Salford, East): What are the alternatives to the Government's Bill? What is the answer to the problem? Nobody denies that a problem exists. Following Hillsborough the Government set up an inquiry under Lord Justice Taylor. That inquiry was given wider powers of examination than those given to Popplewell. The Government set up that inquiry so that a report could be made. They stopped the progress of their Bill in the House of Lords and gave it a breathing space. Therefore, why on earth are the Government going ahead now before we have that report before us?

We accept that a problem exists and it is right that, given the expertise and experience in this House, it should be discussed here. However, we should have Lord Justice Taylor's report before us. Surely we should know what he has to say, or are the Government afraid that he will come up with some proposals that run counter to their own? Surely that is what the Secretary of State apparently fears.

I am a football supporter. I have played and watched soccer all my life and, when I have the time to do so, I watch Manchester United. I have studied the record of that particular club and it is worth repeating it to the House tonight. Manchester United is among the best supported football clubs in Britain. Its average home gate is more than 40,000. In 1987-88 it attracted about 750,000 spectators and there were 38 arrests.

**Mr. David Evans:** Will the right hon. Gentleman confirm that Manchester United has a 50 per cent. membership scheme and that it was the one club that followed the Government's directive three years ago.

**Mr. Orme:** Yes, it has a membership scheme of which I am in favour, but I am not in favour of backing it up with the identity card nonsense. It is nonsense because it would not work.

There are genuine football supporters and football supporters' clubs. Those people deal with this problem on the ground week in, week out; they oppose violence and want it to be eradicated. They are in the front line of this battle and may be in a membership scheme involving 50 per cent. of spectators. I would welcome a 100 per cent. membership scheme. I am talking about a club which has 40,000 spectators per home match. In 1984-85 there were 124 arrests, so in the past three or four years there has been a reduction of about 50 per cent. in the number of arrests.

**Mr. David Evans** *rose*——

**Mr. Orme:** No I shall not give way again.

The club has worked hard to reduce the levels of violence at Old Trafford and spent a huge amount of time and money on creating an environment which is both safe and comfortable for spectators. The family stand is a positive step against violence, and youth groups and other organisations are always welcomed. The club has one of the best safety records in Europe. It has the most up-to-date equipment and a willingness to co-operate with the authorities in an effort to deal with the area's relatively small hooliganism problem. It has closed circuit television and various other facilities.

I have seen the club in operation. I have been on the popular side and in the stand, and I have seen the police surveillance system. Do we want to transfer existing problems from inside to outside the grounds? Do we want to create a problem when spectators arrive late, the system breaks down and people are anxious to get in? Those are the sort of problems related to a sport which is watched by millions of people every week.

There has been an increase in violence but, as my hon. Friend the Member for Copeland (Dr. Cunningham) said, there has been an increase in violence at other sports. That has occurred in boxing and, particularly, at horse racing. That is a classic example of the media closing ranks and not revealing the problems in those sports in the same way as they have revealed them at football matches.

What about the problems which exist in county towns? What about the yuppie influence and the lager louts? Many of the areas in which these problems occur are miles away from football grounds and are never in any way connected with football. As has been said, the increasing violent crime in Britain—recent Home Office figures show that there has been an 11 per cent. increase—is not to be found in football grounds or connected with football, in which there has been a reduction in violence in recent years.

The Minister has said that football will foot the bill for the scheme. The financial implications of the scheme are catastrophic. The Arthur Young study forecast that the scheme would cost about £70 million to implement over the first five years. The projected 20 per cent. loss in gate revenue will result in a £34 million loss in the first year alone.

As my right hon. Friend the Member for Blaenau Gwent (Mr. Foot) said, there is a very real concern about clubs in the third and fourth divisions. Many clubs will go to the wall because they will be unable to finance the scheme or obtain support to do so. Therefore, the scheme will have a detrimental effect on our national sport.

Improved stands within the grounds are needed, and I acknowledge that football clubs have not done enough in the past. More money must be spent and we must bring together the people within the game and those who have to administer it, such as the police and local authorities. My hon. Friend the Member for Copeland said that this should not be a party matter and we should try to resolve the problem on an all-party basis. However, the Government have made no attempt to do so. While they wait for Lord Justice Taylor's report, the Government should call together the football clubs, supporters, the police, local authorities and the Opposition and suggest that they all examine a way of dealing with the problem. We should analyse the problem without sweeping anything under the carpet and, at the same time—[HON. MEMBERS:"Talk."] No, we should not just talk but should come forward with proposals. We should consider what Lord Justice Taylor says because the Secretary of State's proposals will not succeed. They will drive people away from the game and those who create problems at football matches will feel that they have scored a victory and will exploit the position.

We should set up a body which could be the start of an implementation of a statutory body which would contain the interests of the managers, players, supporters, police, transport officials and local authorities. It should be given teeth and powers to intervene to call to account clubs and other authorities. It should have the correct power to act when appropriate and should be based on Lord Justice Taylor's report, when it is completed. Why do we not put such proposals to Lord Justice Taylor? We should also tell the Government that this enabling Bill will not resolve the problems as they say it will.

As my hon. Friend the Member for Copeland has clearly shown this afternoon, the identity card scheme is riddled with contradictions and has no basic support. The Bill is a wholly inappropriate way of dealing with the problems associated with football and should be scrapped or, at the very least, delayed until we have digested Lord Justice Taylor's report.

5.58 pm

**Sir Neil Macfarlane** (Sutton and Cheam): I shall not detain the House too long or follow too closely the speech of the right hon. Member for Salford, East (Mr. Orme). I listened closely to the speeches from the Front Bench spokesmen and I shall listen even more closely to the speech of my hon. Friend the Minister for Sport when he winds up the debate. He will have to catch up on many of the points raised in the debate, because there were a number of crucial pointers and factors which should be carried along with momentum.

I have not fully made up my mind about the Bill and shall be open to persuasion during the next few hours. It is most important that we consider the manner of the problem of the past 20 years or so. I must make it perfectly clear that I, like the right hon. Member for Salford, East, have always been an enthusiastic supporter of a membership scheme. It has been well chronicled elsewhere that, a few years ago, I had one or two differences of opinion with some former colleagues about the efficacy of this way of approaching the problem. However, I shall not digress.

I had always hoped, in the numerous meetings that I attended with many of my colleagues four or five years ago, that the football authorities would encourage a membership scheme. The right hon. Member for Salford, East referred to Manchester United; I can confirm that earlier this year I saw an effective range of card schemes in operation at Carrow road, Norwich City's ground, when my own famous Sutton United played there earlier in the year. I could not help feeling that if all the 92 clubs in the League, and others, had followed that model and the model proposed by my hon. Friend the Member for Welwyn Hatfield (Mr. Evans)—who has chaired Luton Town football club so successfully for so many years—we should not be where we are now.

In September 1985 the Football League set up a working party to study the question of membership cards, largely in the wake of the inquiry by Mr. Justice Popplewell—who, incidentally, brushed aside in his interim report the fact that he was advocating a national identity card system, because such a system was, he said, likely to prove impractical at the turnstiles.

**Mr. David Evans:** Is my hon. Friend aware that the only club that embraced the Popplewell report—which, as he may know, recommended home fans only—was Luton Town?

**Sir Neil Macfarlane:** I do not want a clash of minds or personalities with my hon. Friend—we go back a long way—but we are talking about a wholly different dimension of the problems of numbers and techology. In principle, however, I agree with him.

The Football League working party recommended that all clubs should have a membership scheme, the basic principles of which should be common to all of them. Some of those principles may well have been implemented;

in some instances, however, the desirability of such a scheme may have been ignored. My hon. Friend the Member for Luton, North (Mr. Carlisle) underlined the problems of the failure of the football authorities to do very much: if they have done much, they have kept very quite about it in recent years.

It is depressing to note that—having written to all 92 clubs in the Football League inviting those interested in the very difficult problems of football to let him have their views on every, or any one subject—Mr. Justice Popplewell noted in the report:

"I have rather sadly to record that over 50 out of the 92 league clubs did not even take the trouble to acknowledge receipt of my letter".

I was closely involved with the Popplewell inquiry, along with my hon. Friends in the Home Office and other Departments, and I found it staggering that only 50 clubs out of 92 took the trouble to reply. It makes me wonder what the world of football is doing, or what it is perceived to be doing by those who have loved football for 30 or 40 years. I want to try to find out what hon. Members think that the football world has done to try to enhance its reputation, and to restore its rightful place in the life of our nation.

Why have so many thousands of people stopped going to League matches? I used to go in the early 1950s when I was living in Essex, in outer north-east London. Those games were attended by more than 40 million people, but since then the numbers have gone down and down. I know that we are now a nation of participators, and that there are alternative activities in which people can indulge. The fact remains, however, that they have stopped going to matches—although in recent years there has been a slight increase, which I welcome.

Why has the improvement of stadiums been given such low priority by and large throughout the 92 clubs? What about the poor old football fan and the facilities that he or she has had to suffer? Why has so little money been spent, other than by the Football Trust? What effect has the easy availability of alchohol had on some spectators' behaviour, and why do people consider that going to a football match poses a risk to their well being?

Doubtless many factors led to the decline in spectator attendance at football matches, but the fact of that decline is beyond argument: all the evidence shows that fewer and fewer people are attending.

I find myself in difficulties over the proposals in the Bill, taking them against the backcloth of the tragedy at Hillsborough. I fear that not enough research has been conducted by the police, the Department of the Environment or the Football Association. Hillsborough graphically illustrated Oliver Popplewell's reservations about the practicality of an identity card system at the turnstiles, and, I understand, is the reason why the police dislike many of the Bill's proposals. Their worst fear has always been the excessive accumulation of spectators at the point of entry.

I am also concerned at the rush to proceed with the legislation. Perhaps my hon. Friend the Minister can allay my concern. I should have thought that even Lord Justice Taylor's interim report would have presented a golden opportunity for us to latch on to: it might well have provided the golden research which I think that we need, and which I hope we shall be able to implement. I believe that many involved in football would wish the Government to wait until the report is to hand. I also fully

[*Sir Neil Macfarlane*]

accept the points made in the letter from my right hon. Friend the Secretary of State for the Environment—quoted by the hon. Member for Copeland (Dr. Cunningham)—about the need for action, although I am not entirely happy about his interpretation of future timing. The wording of the letter was skilful, especially the penultimate paragraph.

I am profoundly unhappy that we are proceeding to Third Reading before Parliament has had a chance to review the Taylor report. On the other hand, we have now sat for the better part of 10 years with nothing being done. We face a dilemma: we are up against a timetable.The World Cup takes place next year, and clearly an important dimension of necessary provision is in the Bill. We cannot tolerate the gratuitous violence that football, more than any other sport, seems to encourage. We are all acquainted with the catalogue of violence caused by our people on both sides of the Channel—and sometimes on the Channel—over the past 20 years or so. When he was Minister for Sport, the right hon. Member for Birmingham, Small Heath (Mr. Howell) had to apologise to the head of the French Government in 1974 in the Parc des Princes. He knows exactly what went on; he knows the problem.

Above all, I believe that over the past 10 years we have failed, not only at home but abroad, to secure prosecutions and convictions. Far too many people have got away with it, time and again. We have seen it happen in London, Cambridge, Leeds and elsewhere. In effect, this is a failure of our law and order, and that is what I find so depressing.

I shall wait with interest to hear what my hon. Friend the Minister has to say about the problem. Clearly we cannot continue as we have for the past decade or so. Urgent action is needed. Even after Hillsborough, violence has taken place inside the ground. Everyone is sick and tired of it. The country expects us to do something, and I hope that my hon. Friend will answer many of our questions when he winds up the debate.

6.7 pm

**Mr. Menzies Campbell** (Fife, North-East): I find myself substantially in agreement with much of what has been said by the hon. Member for Sutton and Cheam (Sir N. Macfarlane), who speaks with the authority of a previous Minister for Sport. The reasonableness of his approach was self-evident.

After hearing the Secretary of State trying to justify the Bill, I find myself driven to the conclusion that it is shoddy in its conception, inept in its timing, and wholly lacking in merit. Before I deal with that in more detail, let me say to the hon. Member for Luton, North (Mr. Carlisle)—whose sincerity I recognise—that anyone with any interest in football must be concerned about the way in which it is stained with hooliganism and violence. Concern about the problem, however, does not justify the embracing of measures that are likely to be ineffective, and there is a real risk of raising expectations based on part I of the Bill which are unlikely to be justified. It has already been said in the debate that this should not be a party political issue. I fear that the Government are making it such by their determination to press ahead at this stage.

Those of us who oppose part I do not do so out of any complacency about the problem that faces football, nor are we here as uncritical defenders of the Football League

or the Football Association. Certain criticisms can be made of both these bodies, but equally a proposal as flawed as this one should not obtain the support of the House.

Three conclusions may be reached by Lord Justice Taylor. First, he may say that the football membership scheme in part I would have prevented or ameliorated some of the events of Hillsborough. If he said that, many of us opposed to the Bill now would find it persuasive. Secondly, he may say that the football membership scheme, as proposed, would have no effect. If that happened, we should have to consider what is the proper attitude to take, after seeing the report. However, if he says that, after careful review of the evidence and careful consideration of what has been said to him, it is his belief that a national membership scheme would have aggravated the problems at Hillsborough, what justification could there be for the Government proceeding in the teeth of that conclusion, resulting from an impartial examination of the circumstances? In what conceivable circumstances would the Government reject the impartial review of someone who was chosen because he was thought to be entirely suitable to bring the necessary intellectual objectivity to what happened at Hillsborough and make the kind of recommendations that the Government would regard as valid?

**Mr. James Couchman** (Gillingham): The converse of what the hon. and learned Gentleman has just said is that, if Lord Justice Taylor recommends that a national membership scheme is just what is needed, he should then endorse such a scheme.

**Mr. Campbell:** I did my best to say just that. Perhaps I did not express myself in sufficiently trenchant terms, but no doubt the hon. Gentleman will accept that if that is Lord Justice Taylor's recommendation it will be extremely persuasive. It will persuade me and I will recommend that my right hon. and hon. Friends should support such a scheme.

That issue was not properly addressed in the Secretary of State's speech. In a sense, as other speeches have demonstrated, that lies at the heart of our debate. A public inquiry by a respected judge is still to report on issues that are directly germane to what we are considering today. Notwithstanding that, the Government still intend to proceed apace with this legislation.

It is not unreasonable to describe such a course of action as a Gadarene rush to judgment. Sensitivity has hardly been the hallmark of this Government, and on this occasion they have excelled themselves. The people of Liverpool are still awaiting Lord Justice Taylor's report. Some of them are still nursing their grief and the Government's decision to press ahead after what some of us regard as far too short a period is a demonstration of insensitivity that many of these people will find difficult to understand. The Government may win the vote this evening, although, as we have heard, many have reservations about the Bill. I wonder what prospects the Government would have of winning that vote if they were to take off the Whip and allow hon. Members to vote according to their consciences. [*Interruption.*]

**Mr. Deputy Speaker (Mr. Harold Walker):** Order. The convention of the House is that hon. Members do not pass between the hon. Member addressing the House and the Chair.

**Mr. Campbell:** Thank you, Mr. Deputy Speaker. The hon. Member for Cunninghame, North (Mr. Wilson) is a close friend of mine, and I am sure that his movement was no reflection either on me or on the strength of my argument.

There is some legitimate concern about the nature of the powers that would be given to the Secretary of State were the Bill to be enacted. There is a divergence between what Ministers say and the powers conferred on them by the Bill. The whole process of the scheme lies under the direct control of the Secretary of State and not of Parliament. Under clause 1(2), the Secretary of State will designate matches. He may need a statutory instrument to alter that designation, but that is subject to annulment by either House of Parliament. Furthermore, such a statutory instrument would not be capable of amendment. Once annulled, it would be a simple matter to bring forward another. Clause 3(2) provides that the Secretary of State is to designate the football membership authority. Therefore, it will be his creature. He will be responsible for its constitution and its powers. Its very existence will be at his pleasure. If he wishes to withdraw his designation of the Football Membership Authority, he can do so under clause 3(3) without any statutory instrument.

We do not yet know everything that the scheme will contain. Clause 5(2) says what the scheme must contain, but clause 5(3) says what it may contain. There are mandatory provisions and permissive provisions, but these are not exclusive, and this uncertainty causes much concern about the nature of the powers that the Bill would confer on the Secretary of State. The scheme as finally approved may contain a whole raft of provisions that are not included in clause 5(2) or clause 5(3).

The alleged purpose of this legislation is to improve behaviour at football matches and in the surrounding areas. One is entitled to ask where is the evidence that it will do just that. Evidence is necessary when one embarks on a restriction of what would otherwise be a lawful activity. When one imposes on a huge majority of law-abiding citizens a restriction in their freedom because of the abhorrent and aberrant behaviour of a small number of people, such a restriction should be justified by clear and unequivocal evidence that what is proposed will provide the required solution.

**Mr. John Carlisle:** The evidence of Luton is there for all to see. I remind the hon. and learned Gentleman that there has been one arrest in three years and there is peace and quiet in the town and in and around the ground. That is the one pilot scheme with a 100 per cent. system that has been put into effect, and it has been extremely successful.

**Mr. Campbell:** Yes, but the Luton scheme is not the scheme in part I, a point made by the hon. Member for Sutton and Cheam. If the Luton scheme were exactly on all fours with part I, some of us might be more impressed by the scheme than we are. We cannot ignore the fact that the numbers of people attending Luton football matches have not grown recently, while it is acknowledged that elsewhere there has been a growth in attendence.

**Mr. David Evans:** Is the hon. Gentleman aware that last year, because the team is now in the first division, the attendance at Luton Town increased by 21 per cent.? That increase was the fourth highest in the division.

**Mr. Campbell:** A long run in the cup tends to have that effect, but, in any event, I should have been much more impressed by the figures if we had those for the past five years.

**Mr. Denis Howell:** The House should be accurately informed. The attendance before the Luton experiment averaged 11,000 per match. The average is now 9,000 per match, having risen in the past year from 8,000. If the same attendance figures applied to every other ground, football would be bankrupt.

**Mr. Campbell:** Both the right hon. Member for Birmingham, Small Heath (Mr. Howell) and the hon. Member for Welwyn Hatfield (Mr. Evans) are capable of catching your eye, Mr. Deputy Speaker, so I shall leave them to their 15-round contest.

**Mr. Deputy Speaker:** Order. I remind the House that hon. Members cannot have it both ways: they cannot make both interventions and speeches in a debate in which a very large number of hon. Members wish to speak.

**Mr. Campbell:** The need to show evidence as to why the scheme is justified is made all the more acute by the fact that the football authorities have taken steps to deal with disorder at football matches. Reference has already been made to the use of closed-circuit television, to the segregation of supporters, to the encouragement of families to spectate and to closer integration with the community. We must ask ourselves whether the scheme in the Bill can have any material effect to improve behaviour. I rather fancy that better stadiums, better facilities, all-seated stadia and a recognition that football fans are entitled to a proper standard when they visit football matches are more likely to be persuasive of good behaviour. In that regard, the activities of the Football Trust are to be commended. Some of us have open minds about the idea of a football levy board.

It seems to me that the most effective deterrent against criminal behaviour at football matches and elsewhere is the belief that one is likely to be apprehended. Resources and efforts to that end should now be pressed instead of pressing a proposal which is misconceived, has no merit and which appears to have very considerable disadvantages for football. The proposals also have substantial potential costs for clubs. How are third and fourth division clubs to meet those expenses? If we consider their balance sheets, it is a miracle that some of them can keep their doors open. The proposal will discourage casual spectators. The truth is that unfashionable football clubs will be put substantially at risk.

The Government have been disingenous in the use of statistical information. We have been told on many occasions that there were 6,147 arrests last year. However, we have not been given accurate information about how many convictions followed those arrests. So far we have not yet reached the stage in the United Kingdom when arrests equal convictions. We have not heard how many of those arrests related to events inside football grounds and how many outside. We know that some of the arrests relate to pickpocketing, drugs offences and car thefts. Those are thoroughly undesirable, but it is difficult to justify the view that they are football-related crimes.

The Government had an opportunity arising from the tragic events at Hillsborough for mature reflection and reconsideration. They had an opportunity to consider an

[*Mr. Campbell*]

external and impartial judgment on their proposals through Lord Justice Taylor's inquiry. By their precipitate desire to proceed with this measure, the Government have rejected that opportunity, and the House in turn should reject the Bill.

6.22 pm

**Sir Rhodes Boyson** (Brent, North): I grew up in soccer territory in the Rossendale valley. Within five or six miles of where I lived there were Blackburn Rovers, Bolton, Bury and even Accrington Stanley in those days. It was not until I joined the Royal Navy during the second world war that I ever saw a rugger ball. I thought that the equipment in the Royal Navy must be worse than that in the Haslingden grammar school because the ball was such a funny shape. I stood amazed.

From the beginning I have been imbued with the football culture. The one thing that I despair about—although despair may be too strong a word—is the fact that as a boy I could travel on the tram and then on the bus with a set of people from the little village in which I lived to watch Blackburn Rovers without any worry to my parents or anyone else. We went to see matches, the hymns were sung, people behaved and there was no obscene chanting. It was part of a culture that I respected and it helped to make me, no matter what values I hold now.

**Mr. David Martin** (Portsmouth, South): As with rugby today.

**Sir Rhodes Boyson:** Yes, but they still do not play rugby in the Rossendale valley. There is one team now, so there has been a decline in the valley. It is called Bacup and Rawtenstall grammar school old boys.

I believe that we are discussing a non-party matter. We are considering order and discipline. We are not considering free enterprise or Socialism. There is a breakdown of law and order in adolescent behaviour which at the moment is revealing itself more in football than anything else. However, like water in the bowels of a ship, it will move from one side to the other. If the troublemakers leave football, they will go somewhere else, until we solve the adolescent problems in society.

This Bill dealt with symptoms, not causes. Even if it is successful, we will still be left with a massive problem and there is no sign of it going away. In recent years Tory and Labour Governments have suffered from legislative hyperactivity. When anything happens, there must be another Bill. We spend our time day after day here discussing not first principles, but Bills to clear up what we got wrong in Bills last year. Almost every Department has one of these. Perhaps we should spend six months in this place without debating any Bills and we could discuss what we should really be here for. That may come as a shock and some hon. Members may disappear because they cannot decide what to do.

We are facing a major breakdown of law and order in this country which, as I have said, has little to do with Socialism or free enterprise. It is caused by the disappearance of community ties which once held people together. Although Edmund Burke was never a member of the Tory party, he called certain groups of people "little platoons". Unless people believe that they belong to little platoons, they will create their own at war with society.

The family is breaking down and we no longer see three generations together. There is no trouble at rugby league where three generations of family watch the game. However, once adolescents and peer groups get together, there is trouble. We are separating the old people into sheltered accommodation so another generation is being isolated. The second generation must move 20 or 200 miles away to gain economic prosperity. There is nothing wrong with that, but it makes it difficult for the children and the three-generation family breaks down.

The churches are relatively empty and the local government reorganisations of 1964 and 1972—which I opposed at the time and still oppose—put people into units to which they did not want to belong and in which they had no history. In most cases we do not even know where those places are now.

There is a breakdown in security and behaviour in many of our homes, schools, and in large areas of our towns. A rootless adolescent generation has grown up and it is almost ungovernable. It accepts no standards apart from its own immediate egoistic satisfaction. That is basically the problem.

A survey carried out in 1988 by the National Union of Teachers, of which I used to be a district committee member in my trade union days, showed that one in three teachers expected a major disruption in the school year at some stage. Half the teachers surveyed said that there was frequent indiscipline in their schools. A National Association of Schoolmasters/Union of Women Teachers survey in 1986 showed that 4 per cent. of teachers had been physically attacked in the previous six months and 25 per cent. had been threatened with physical attack. Worst of all, the National Association of Head Teachers' survey of nursery schools showed that one in five schools for three and four-year-olds was out of control. If we cannot control children at the age of three or four, how can we control them when they are adolescents?

All that assumes that the children go to school. A survey of a well-run Labour borough—this applies to other boroughs; I am not making any political points here because there is a deep sickness which both Labour and Conservative must deal with—showed that in three big comprehensive schools the attendance of 15 to 16-year-old boys was 47 per cent., 48 per cent. and 52 per cent. That means that half the 15 to 16-year-old boys did not attend school that year or they did so on a rota system. They would come in on alternate days while another boy worked on the market. If we cannot get children into school, how can we get them to behave? If they are living on the fringes of society, at war with society, getting mixed up with all sorts of things outside, they will be undisciplined and there is no solution to that.

These pupils will be uncontrollable in adolescence. No matter whether we have plastic, wooden or golden football identity cards, it will make no difference to those adolescents because they have got away with it for years and they will get away with it again. They are at war with our values in society. The Children and Young Persons Act 1969 caused untold harm by not making young people liable for their actions, particularly when we consider how young people grow up more quickly these days.

School breakdown, family breakdown and schools giving pupils little or no faith in past or present-day society, with little knowledge of our history and literature, mean that we have prepared what we called during the second world war a Molotov cocktail for adolescents, which will blow up under us.

The Education Reform Act 1988, which I supported, is an attempt to introduce some sense and control. I understand that the national curriculum will be retained whichever party is in control in Parliament in the future. But in addition, we have television, videos and magazines glorifying brutality. Those magazines can be picked up in all the newspaper shops. There are no restraints. Self-fulfilment becomes self-gratification. Self-expression becomes self-absorption and we reap the dastardly flowers of a permissive age gone mad.

All that applies to 10 to 20-year-olds, from whom the violence comes. The average age of the male criminal today is 14 years and seven months. Violence is happening not just at our football matches, but in society generally. If we have football identity cards, are we to have cards for those who riot outside pubs? The licensed victuallers have sent out 500,000 applications for cards to prove that people who drink are of the age of 18. Are we then to have a card for those who visit public houses? There will soon be more cards than there are bankers' cards.

On new year's eve last year 128 people were arrested in Trafalgar square. Are we to have cards to admit people into Trafalgar square on new year's eve? More were arrested on that occasion than at most football matches. At Pilton pop festival in Somerset 106 people were arrested recently. Are we to have pop festival cards? Will all the cards be different colours—if enough colours exist?

Only this weekend two policemen were hurt and 13 youths were arrested after a one-hour running battle in Andover in Hampshire. According to newspaper reports 11 "tanked up" youths were arrested at Blandford in Dorset last week. Are we to have cards for "tanked up" youths as well?

I support compulsory identity cards. Some hon. Members would not go along with me on that. However, I am trying to carry people with me, so if I lose some on the way I shall try to rope them in again later. I know that the wild libertarians on the Conservative Benches do not support compulsory identity cards. I am glad that we have Members such as my hon. Friend the Member for Pembroke (Mr. Bennett) who makes me look like a moderate. Long may he remain here. I am a middle-ground man compared with him. I must introduce him to my wife. Such a card should carry a photograph, fingerprints, blood group, a section to say whether the bearer wants to leave his kidneys as a donor and a national insurance number. If freedom of information means that we know what the Government are doing, it should also mean that the Government should know what the individual is doing. It should work both ways in our society.

I wonder whether the Bill is necessary and whether it will work. According to my figures, there was one arrest for every 5,000 attending a first division match last year, and one arrest for every 3,233 attending all division matches. Last year, 25 times as many people were arrested in London for offences against the person committed well away from football grounds as for offences committed in or near the grounds. More than 75 per cent. of the 92 teams had fewer than five arrests last year, yet they will all be landed with the scheme. If ever there was a case of burning villages in Cyprus, this is it. If one person misbehaved, the lot had to be destroyed and everybody

was lined up and shot. I thought that we had passed that stage, given the respect for the individual that we are supposed to have now.

As for turnstiles, I should like those who wrote the Bill to travel on the underground with me. We would have to travel for only two hours before one broke down. They are a form of all-in wrestling. They are certainly good for muscle development. Turnstiles do not work on the Underground, so why should they work at the football grounds? As hon. Members have already said, if they break down, people will riot and move in.

If the cards do not carry the owner's photograph, many people who set out for the game will not arrive there. A mile away from the match they will be locked into the nearest cupboard—I trust that they will live through the experience—and somebody else will go to the match with their card. However, it will be a clever machine that can read a photograph. We do not yet have such a machine on the Underground, but I look forward to the day that we do.

The four tribes that make up these islands have always been difficult to discipline. We talk about them being law-abiding, but only those who have not read history can believe that. They are law-abiding only when the law has been enforced from above. Let me give just one illustration of English youth, without referring to the Irish, Scots or Welsh. Remember the 6,000 London apprentices whom Taine reminded us formed the garrison of Calais and tyrannised the countryside for miles around. When they succumbed to superior numbers they died to a man, fighting savagely to the last. That is why the English are such brilliant infantry. We have the only Army in the world which prefers the bayonet to the bullet. Those who say that the British are law-abiding do not know what they are about.

Look at the early industrial revolution. Those of us from Lancashire and the north know what happened in its early years. The situation is complicated by the new industrial revolution. I agree with the Government's economic policy. I might lose any friends that I have on the Opposition Benches by saying so. There is a heavy price to pay for our new economic prosperity. That price is being uprooted from one's community. Fathers are away from their children. Just like the industrial revolution, it will impose a great penalty on adoloscents growing up.

I would support a Bill that returned caning to schools so that we could have order in our schools; heavier punishment for hooligans; enforced rather than the voluntary attendance at school that exists in many local authorities; identity cards for all; that said that three generations should meet at least once a week—perhaps, for the Jewish, on a Friday night—so that grandparents could recognise their grandchildren, and vice versa.

**Mr. Nicholas Bennett** (Pembroke): At a seance.

**Sir Rhodes Boyson:** I do not mind where they meet. They can even meet at a football match and watch Luton play. However, we must bring them together at least once a week.

Such a Bill would shut any school that did not have a 95 per cent. attendance rate, and change the management immediately. If I catch Mr. Speaker's eye in the debate on Friday on policing in London, I may also be able to put forward my thoughts on some form of local national service which would be a cross between dad's army and an

*[Sir Rhodes Boyson]*

Outward Bound school. Unless we organise people, they will organise themselves. That is what is happening. People are at war with us.

Let me return to what I said at the beginning on legislative hyperactivity—the greatest disease in Britain at the moment—and the need to debate the major problems of our society. We need to debate why crime is so high in our society. It should not be so high. We should debate why 250,000 people are unemployed in London despite there being plenty of jobs in my area; why there is such a huge number of family breakdowns; why there is such a dependence on drugs and drinking among people growing up; why many parts of London are so seedy; and why we have so many dropouts. These are not problems of capitalism or Socialism. They are signs of a breakdown not just among adolescents, but in the unity of our society. We will not solve those problems by throwing accusations across the Floor of the House.

On 2 July it will be the 500th anniversary of the birth of Cranmer, whose Book of Common Prayer is one of the finest pieces of the English language. I am not suggesting that by returning to religion everyone will learn to behave. I am not saying that an agnostic or an atheist cannot behave. But we have lost a means of establishing standards.

The Bill deals with symptoms, not causes. The symptoms are a sign that there is something seriously wrong with the way in which we in Britain are bringing up our adolescents. We need more debates on such matters in the Chamber rather than on the continual legislation which exhausts those who debate it throughout the night. In that way, we may start objective thinking again, which would be a good thing.

6.38 pm

**Ms. Kate Hoey** (Vauxhall): I am very pleased to make my maiden speech in a debate on a subject about which not only I but millions of people throughout the country feel passionately. I begin by thanking all right hon. and hon. Members and the staff of the House for their kindness in welcoming me as a new Member of Parliament. I have been offered everything from tours of the House and rundowns of right hon. and hon. Members to avoid, to advice on rules to obey and not to obey. I have also been inundated with offers to pair.

I have reached the conclusion that there are some drawbacks in being a new Member of Parliament. Perhaps I may misquote Oscar Wilde, who in the circumstances in which I find myself might have said, "A lady without a desk may be considered unfortunate but a lady without a desk, a telephone or a chair to call her own may be called careless." I do not wish to appear to be a person who is the victim either of misfortune or of carelessness, because I want to be earnest, but at the moment I have nothing to call my own in this House. Nevertheless, I shall not dwell on that but will move on to speak about happier matters.

My predecessor, Stuart Holland, worked conscientiously for all his constituents. His case-load was huge and he was held in great regard by the people of Vauxhall. I am sure that the House wishes him every success in his new responsibilities in Europe. I thank him for the support that he gave me over the past few weeks.

I am also honoured to succeed another hon. Member who was well known to the House, George Strauss, who spent so many years here. If there is one thing of which I am certain, it is that there is no way that I could spend the number of years in this House that he did, because to do so I would have to reach a very, very old age.

I am fortunate that there are in my constituency many of London's famous landmarks. They include Lambeth palace, the south bank centre, St. Thomas's hospital and the Oval cricket ground. I was most disappointed that the Government missed an opportunity to provide a community sports centre at the Oval, and I only hope that in the next few weeks it will bring better news of England's cricketers in the final Test.

On a more serious note, I remind the House that every night in my constituency, and within a mile of this Chamber, between 1,000 and 2,000 men and women sleep out in cardboard city on the south bank. Many of them are young people without any hope of ever having a roof over their heads. Most feel totally alienated from politicians and from everything that we do in this House. The population of my constituency comprises a disproportionate number of young people aged between 16 and 24, and it is those very young people whom the Bill's provisions will directly affect. The Government cannot provide them with homes, the Government cannot provide them with jobs, and now the Government want to alienate them even further.

Most right hon. and hon. Members probably remember their first visit to a football match. I can vividly. I recall being taken by my father to Windsor park in Belfast, where I unfolded my stool and happily watched the match from the terraces. Existing supporters are very much the vital link in the marketing of football, for they create the customers of the future. Sponsorship and the income that derives from it can never replace supporters and the income from them.

We are all aware that football has attached to it an element that we would all like to see removed, and that hooligans in football colours have vandalised trains and stations. However, a vicious circle has been created whereby the precautionary measures taken by British Rail, civil and transport police and the clubs feed the negative image of soccer fans so that they are all treated, carte blanche, as potential hooligans, and are herded and hounded in an unnecessarily provocative way. When fans are marched through the streets and forced on to already scruffy and vandalised special trains, it breeds a resentment that can, sadly, manifest itself in more unsocial behaviour.

Conservative Members must be continually reminded that the overwhelming majority of men, women and children who attend football matches are peaceful, law-abiding supporters, yet the Bill treats them all as potential hooligans. What angers me most about the Football Spectators Bill is that the only relevant people who were not consulted were the spectators themselves. Where were the supporters' organisations on the working party? They did not serve on it, and they were not consulted. Why is there no place for the supporters' organisations on the Football Membership Authority?

The Football Supporters Association, of which I am proud to be a founder member, produced excellently researched evidence. Part II of the Bill contains a proposal to prevent convicted hooligans from travelling abroad when English teams or clubs are playing there by making them report to attendance centres. That was urged by the FSA a number of years ago. Why not direct a similar effort at the home-based problem and leave the rest of the supporters alone? Why does no one want to listen to those who most want to see football thrive—its supporters?

Let us make supporters real members of their clubs, with all the privileges as well as responsibilities that membership traditionally confers—especially the right to be properly represented. Why is the Minister for Sport not pushing through a genuine membership scheme? Does anyone really believe that the FMA, made up as it will be of members of the Football League and of the Football Association, will ever force clubs to adopt genuine membership? The Government failed dismally to exploit the opportunity with which they were presented.

The Minister for Sport cannot possibly believe that compulsory identity cards will solve the problem of football hooliganism. They will create a nightmare of bureaucracy that will do nothing to stop the hooligan element but much to prevent the genuine football lover from attending matches. If a person's ID card is taken away from him, he will simply borrow one from another member of his family. If he cannot do that, the genuine hooligan will go out and mug a 10-year-old on his way to a match. Ticket touting will be replaced by ID card touting. Stan Flashmans of the ID card will be springing up all over the country.

It is sad that after the Hillsborough tragedy the Minister for Sport did not have the courage to take on the Prime Minister, because everyone in football, from board chairmen and players to the authorities and spectators, realise that it is not the Minister for Sport who is pushing through the Bill but the Prime Minister.

Football supporters are the greatest asset that the professional game has, but it has taken the football authorities a long time to acknowledge that. Recently a quarter of a million people signed their opposition to the Bill, and at last there is co-operation between the FA, clubs and supporters. In Committee, my right hon. and hon. Friends will build on that co-operation to ensure that, whatever may be the outcome, football's relationship with its supporters will never be the same.

There is still time for the Government to think again. I was encouraged to hear the hon. Member for Sutton and Cheam (Sir N. Macfarlane) say that he has not yet made up his mind about the Bill. If the Minister for Sport is not convinced by his hon. Friend's opinion or by me, perhaps I will be able to convince his predecessor. We should build on the opportunity created by the spirit that came out of Hillsborough, which we all felt. There are so many good examples of football clubs working to involve their supporters. The hon. Member for Luton, North (Mr. Carlisle) mentioned the hooligan problem at Millwall. I remind him that this year Millwall won the award for being the club that has done most to solve the problem of hooliganism.

I believe that sport in its wider context is crucial to the future of our young people. I hope to play my part in its development in this House. Above all, it is to the people of Vauxhall that I pledge my time in the House in working to represent them, and I hope to continue to do that for a number of years.

6.49 pm

**Mr. Jim Lester** (Broxtowe):It is a great privilege to follow the hon. Member for Vauxhall (Ms. Hoey) and to be the first to congratulate her on the quality of her maiden speech. As I live in her constituency, I take a great interest in her activities. I make a public offer to pair with her. I have never succeeded in finding a pair, even though I have been a Member of Parliament for 15 years.

The hon. Lady's involvement with Arsenal football club makes her well qualified to comment on our national game and to take part in the debate in the informed, concerned and lucid way that she demonstrated in her maiden speech. She has also demonstrated the energy that is necessary to achieve a seat, a telephone and a desk, the raw materials that would enable her to perform her task well. I am confident that she will make her mark. I am also delighted to say that I agree with the broad thrust of her speech, especially her recognition of the value of football supporters in our national game.

I approach the debate with considerable sadness. For the whole of my life I have been a keen football supporter. I am also a great supporter of my hon. Friend the Minister for Sport. It gives me no pleasure whatsoever to be in disagreement with him and the Government over the Football Spectators Bill. We all recognise that there is a problem but many of us find it amazing, following Hillsborough and all that has been said, that this should be regarded as a party political issue. Concern about football hooliganism ought to unite both sides of the House.

My right hon. Friend the Secretary of State for the Environment insists that Parliament must take a decision tonight. Many of us know that all sorts of things—the European election results, loyalty to party, which the Secretary of State has referred to in a letter, a three-line Whip and considerable persuasion—have brought that about. It leads me to believe that it is not the quality of the argument that will prevail. The fact is that the Government want the Bill, willy-nilly. We shall force through a Bill for a national scheme in a relatively short time, despite the reservations of many of those who are affected, including Conservative Members as well as Opposition Members who know something about football.

I find it difficult to understand why we need to pass the Bill at this time. The argument is that, if the Bill is not passed now, 12 months will be lost. We are already committed to debating Lord Justice Taylor's conclusions, although we have not had an assurance that they will be taken into account. That is a grave weakness in what has been said so far by Ministers. There is little prospect of those conclusions being published until the New Year. We have been told that we shall be able to debate them in the New Year. We should base our views on the conclusions and on the work that we can do between then and now, not on what we think at this moment.

My right hon. Friend the Secretary of State, whose integrity I respect, has also assured me that he will not introduce or approve any scheme until he is satisfied that it is workable. I should like to know the basis on which he will decide that a scheme is workable. What tests and what criteria will there be? The very professional Arthur Young report includes all sorts of bar charts as to what must and must not be done. It came to the conclusion that, even if the Bill had been passed within the original time scale, the

[*Mr. Jim Lester*]

scheme could not be implemented before 1991-92. What, therefore, is the reason for the inordinate hurry to pass the Bill at this time, with all this pressure?

I object in principle to the Bill. I question the Government's purpose. They say that it is not to deal with hooliganism but to separate hooliganism from football. I am a great supporter of my hon. Friend the Member for Brent, North (Sir R. Boyson) who has talked about the problems of hooliganism. The general public are not concerned simply about hooliganism connected with football; they are concerned about hooliganism, wherever it takes place. I regard the Bill as social engineering. We are trying to break away the working-class football hooligan from football so that it is a better game for those of us who are not broken away from it. That is a very grave legislative principle.

Football is a national game and a national activity, just as going to the theatre or watching cricket and rugby are national activities. At Saturday lunchtime during the winter, people make a choice about what they would like to do. That happens in families. It also happens in my surgery. I might say to a councillor who has sat with me all through the morning surgery, "Would you like to go and watch a football match this afternoon?" About 5 million out of the 18·5 million who attend football matches go on a casual basis, and about 25 per cent. of those who attend football matches go to only four matches a year.

People have the right to make a spontaneous decision to take part in a lawful activity. It will be a grave attack on that right if their names have to be registered on a central computer and if they have to carry an identity card simply to attend a football match. To do that, just to isolate over 1,089 people who have committed football-related offences, needs to be argued with greater force than it has been so far.

I support a national ID scheme. It would bring great benefits in terms of both international security, fraud and other matters. However, my right hon. Friend the Prime Minister regards it as anathema to the British people. One of my colleagues could not understand why football supporters feel even more strongly, simply because they will be required to carry an identity card, for no other reason than to go to football matches. However, it causes grave offence to many of my constituents. They feel that it means that they are such a risk to others that they will have to carry an identity card, on top of their season ticket and their membership ticket for their club. It is a grave infringement of people's liberty.

A great deal has been said about the number of police who are required to attend football matches. I define what we are trying to do in part I of the Bill as the fruit machine approach or the needle in the haystack approach. The reason for such complicated access through many turnstiles on a Saturday afternoon by means of an identity card is because, suddenly, one of the many thousand turnstiles will flash red, since one of the 1,089 people who has been accused of a football-related offence has tried to cheat. I wonder how many police will be required to man every turnstile at every football match, in every division, in case there is a flashing red light? It is the needle in the haystack, the fruit machine, the chance approach.

If people do not want to be dissociated from football and do not intend to practise their hooliganism elsewhere,

they will play the game of beating the system. Therefore 500,000 people will have to watch those going through the turnstiles. There will be endless nil returns every week. however, the system will have to be operated in case one of the 1,089 people tries to cheat and to get into the ground against the rules.

That is a tremendous overreaction to a relatively simple problem to solve. Having said that, I appreciate the need to provide a constructive alternative, and there has been a shortage of those in the debate. In seeking such alternatives, it is necessary to spend more time in the short term considering carefully the way forward.

Other hon. Members have spoken of the way in which people will be convicted and will not be able to travel to games abroad. In part II of the Bill we deal with the exclusion of people who have committed a football-related offence. We assume, in that part of the Bill, that they had been charged with some offence, and there is an assumption that people who are hooligans in this country wish to be hooligans overseas. I suspect that that is not a genuine assumption to make. For example, I recall that many of those who offended us all in West Germany went there wearing T-shirts emblazoned with the slogan, "England's invasion of Germany 1988." That had nothing to do with football. Nor did it mean that they had been hooligans in this country. That aside, since 1987, since exclusion orders were introduced, there have been 1,889 such orders. Considering that 18·5 million people attend football matches each year, that is a tiny number of exclusion orders.

It would make more sense to have attendance orders, not exclusion orders. Let us focus on those who cause the problems rather than on the 999·97 in 1,000 who do not. I propose that we examine the Bill carefully, abolish part I and amend part II so that anyone who has committed a football-related offence would be required to attend on the Saturday when there is a match.

If I were a chief constable, I would rather be responsible for looking after the 1,889 attending a police station than search through 500,000 people—on the fruit machine principle—in case a red light flickered and they were trying to get in. That would be a more sensible way of targeting on those who cause the problem rather than on the vast majority who do not.

Reference has been made to inconsistency. I shall not rub that in. There is an inconsistency in relation to, say, a dog registration where a dog is required to be registered only once in its lifetime. That scheme was regarded as costly, complicated and bureaucratic. The scheme proposed for football fans would mean people registering every week. That would prove more costly and complicated and even more bureaucratic.

It is also a mistake to think that other options have not been considered. The Dutch and Germans, for example, have a problem of football hooliganism. They have approached it on a more sensible basis, by targeting on clubs where offences are committed—six out of 34 clubs—and requiring them to implement an away members' scheme.

I have in my pocket the card which members are required to carry. At least, I had the card in my pocket and I proposed to display it to the House, but I seem to have mislaid it. That is one of the problems with the football scheme as proposed in the Bill; if one cannot find the card, one cannot get in. I have now found the card in my pocket, and as I hold it up, hon. Members can see what it looks like.

In other words, another country with similar problems is adopting a more selective and sensible approach. It does not require all the 34 clubs—in our case it would be 92 clubs—to go through this enormously complicated and bureaucratic procedure. It targets on those clubs where there is a problem, and we could easily do the same.

**Mr. Wilson:** Is the hon. Gentleman aware that even with such a reduced scheme, during a recent Netherlands-West Germany international game, alleged supporters of those clubs, through contempt for a membership scheme of any kind, did not apply for membership cards, were therefore unable to get tickets for the international and instead of going near the ground, waged a running battle with police through the streets of the city while the game was being played?

**Mr. Lester:** I am trying to demonstrate that we could take one of several different approaches, instead of running away with the idea that we must do something in a hurry because we have a problem, saying, "We are doing something. We are taking this action. Therefore you should vote for it." In my view, it is not the only answer. There are other constructive ways to approach the problem and I am putting some of them forward as best I can.

There is a great deal of research going on in this country which I believe shows, for example, that 52 per cent. of arrests—bearing in mind that we are talking about arrests and not charges—occur at 21 per cent. of grounds. The idea that we must lump all 92 clubs together in one scheme, when the problems affect a much smaller number of clubs, offends my principles, and I should have thought that that offended the principles of many of my hon. Friends.

We must also consider the political consequences, an issue that people might like to wish away. I judge from the community where I live and where I have lived all my life, that the party that I support and represent is not entirely popular. It has been said that the message we are trying to put over is not being presented properly. I get the feeling that the problem is not the way in which the message is being put across but the fact that the message is being well understood, and the Bill epitomises much of what people are beginning to dislike about my party.

It has been pointed out that football supporters have not been involved in the discussion of the scheme. Indeed, Conservative Members have not been involved in the scheme's evolution. There have been no policy discussions other than a rather scrappy working party report.

Despite that, we seem to be certain that we have the answer, and that is why, the Government say, they are going ahead with the scheme. They are going ahead whoever objects, be they football supporters, the industry or the police. "We shall impose it," they say. That arrogance—of saying "We know best," whatever the subject—is starting to get reaction from our traditional supporters.

I warn my hon. Friends, especially those who represent marginal seats—I have two good hon. Friends in Nottingham in marginal seats; we also have two good football clubs there—that we must think carefully about what is proposed and the effect that it will have on marginals. People do not like their liberties being

challenged. They do not like schemes being imposed on them against their better judgment. In other words, we should think carefully about what we are doing before we proceed further.

I hope that hon. Members in all parts of the House believe in the rule of law. If we impose a law on people who do not understand it and who resent it, we challenge the rule of law. Remember, there appear to be constructive alternatives to what is being proposed. To impose fines and create criminal offences in the way proposed in the Bill will, I fear, defeat, or at least challenge, the rule of law.

Bearing that in mind, I have a last plea to make to the Government. I have been involved with several measures by way of the special Standing Committee procedure. For hon. Members who are not aware of that procedure, it means that the Standing Committee for the first three sessions—I would be happy if, in this case, it could be done in a week—turns itself into a special Standing Committee. On the basis of the legislation, the members of that Committeee, chaired by the Chairman of the relevant Committee, hear evidence from all sources on the impact of the legislation in question. That has a salutary effect on legislators, for they are in a position to hear and challenge the view of those most affected and who wish to give evidence.

To cool the temperature and make better legislation than we have before us, but in particular to show that we are interested in the views of those concerned and are not trying to impose a measure on them against their will, we should support the principle of adopting the special Standing Committee procedure in this case.

**Several Hon. Members** *rose*—

**Mr. Deputy Speaker:** Order. We are now into the 10-minute time zone. I hope that speakers will not feel obliged to take the whole of their 10 minutes.

7.8 pm

**Mr. Joseph Ashton** (Bassetlaw): With the exception of the contribution of the Secretary of State, we have heard some excellent speeches this afternoon. But none was better than that of my hon. Friend the Member for Vauxhall (Ms. Hoey), who I am glad to welcome to our deliberations. I lived for 16 years in the constituency that she represents and I am aware of some of the problems with which she must contend. She made an admirable speech, a pearl among maiden speeches, and it is refreshing to have a woman colleague taking part in a debate on a subject such as football and contributing with such expertise and knowledge of the subject. If she is selected to be a member of the Standing Committee, she will be a great asset to the deliberations.

We are witnessing the Government attempting to use the King Herod principle. Throughout 2,000 years of history it has been proved that King Herod-type legislation does not work. Under such legislation, the whole community is punished to catch the 1 per cent. of people who are causing the problem. Invariably, such legislation fails. It failed to impose prohibition in America in the 1920s and 1930s and it failed when the Labour party tried to introduce a prices and incomes policy to govern everybody's pay rises. Such legislations usually ends in tears, and that will be the fate of this Bill, under which 99

[*Mr. Joseph Ashton*]

per cent. of innocent spectators will be punished in an effort to catch the fewer than 1 per cent. of the guilty who will indulge in crime and vandalism wherever they go.

I was at Hillsborough two months ago and witnessed the disaster. Although booze was a factor, the membership card system would only have made the problems worse. It would have meant people queueing for longer to get into the ground, it would have been more difficult to gain admission and the riots would have occurred earlier.

Many hon. Members have received an excellent brief from the Football League committee pointing out that, at the Arsenal-Liverpool match a few months ago, when 51,000 people were trying to get into the ground, the membership card system would have meant an additional 37 minutes queueing, on the assumption that it takes four seconds to produce a card to get through the turnstile. That would have caused more panic, more annoyance, more problems and more riots.

Hillsborough proved how easy it was to bribe the man at the turnstile. In many instances, he takes £10 to allow people to climb over the turnstile and not go through the existing apparatus. As I understand it—at least, it is what the Minister said on television—the Minister is proposing a simple card that will be pressed flat against a disc, which will light up if the card is genuine. If the light does not appear, a steward and a policeman will have to apprehend that person and throw him out. Grounds such as Manchester United and Hillsborough have about 80 turnstiles, so that will mean 80 stewards and 80 policemen.

I assure the House that the fans will just do what we did when I was in the Royal Air Force. If we did not have train tickets, when we arrived at the station four of us would line up and the first person would give the ticket collector a used ticket and then run. Those behind would say to the ticket collector, "Don't worry mate, we'll catch him," and we went through the barrier as well. It was all timed to coincide with the arrival of the train, and away we all went. The same will happen with membership cards. The guy who does not have one obviously knows that he does not have one and the guys behind him probably do not have one either. They will either pay or not pay according to how they feel at the time. There could be 51,000 people trying to get into the ground at 7 o'clock on a dark, wet, January night for a mid-week cup tie replay, and the computer will probably be frozen because it has been standing unused all week. It will be chaos.

It was wrong of the Secretary of State to suggest that the Opposition were trying to make political capital out of the problems and were supporting hooliganism. He should not have suggested that we would not support sensible measures; we would. If he agreed to adapt the scheme so that it applied only to away supporters, I would vote for it because it would work. We should seriously consider that possibility when we reach the Committee stage. The right hon. Gentleman should understand that every team has away supporters, who would not object to carrying identity cards. They are proud to be identified with their clubs. It should be a voluntary membership scheme, and priority should be given to those voluntary members. They could have certain concessions—for example, season ticket holders could have 10 per cent. knocked off the price

of their tickets. I am sure that in those circumstances many supporters would voluntarily become members of the scheme.

Under such a scheme, away supporters could be segregated at the home ground. I am sure that they would accept the need to park in specific areas. They could be given maps showing how to reach the ground. A voluntary scheme would solve 98 per cent. of the problems because every ground would be required to designate an area for scheme members. I am not sugesting anything similar to the Luton scheme where away supporters are banned. That is an infringement of civil liberties and it stops me watching Sheffield Wednesday playing at Luton, as it also stops thousands of people who should never be excluded from matches.

I am certainly not a football hooligan. Why should Luton Town have the right to tell me that I cannot go there to watch my team playing? That is not fair; there is nothing clever about that. Perhaps the club now has fewer problems, but it is denying football supporters their basic right to watch their team—and I am one of them. That is not right. I do not wish to be personal, but the chairman of Luton Town—the hon. Member for Welwyn Hatfield (Mr. Evans)—is sitting on the Conservative Benches. He should not have the right to tell me that I cannot go to the Luton ground to watch Sheffield Wednesday. He is exceeding his powers—

**Mr. David Evans** *rose*——

**Mr. Ashton:** I cannot give way, as I am running out of time.

No one has mentioned the cost of the scheme to third and fourth division clubs. The Secretary of State and the Prime Minister continually throw out the suggestion that there is plenty of money in football because of the transfer fees. It is not that they do not understand the system, it is that they deliberately refuse to accept that the transfer money goes round in a circle within the game. It is not like money spent on bricks and mortar, on stands or on seating, which is money gone for ever. One club buys a player from another and so the money goes round and perhaps dwindles from Liverpool paying £1 million to Hartlepool, for which £20,000 would be a large sum, as my hon. Friend the Member for Houghton and Washington (Mr. Boyes) knows because he is a director of Hartlepool. Let the Government tell Hartlepool supporters that their club will be put out of action, and watch their reaction.

One of my local football clubs is being put out of action because the ground is being sold over its head to provide a site for a supermarket. There is a gut feeling among supporters of the small clubs. I am a shareholder in Sheffield Wednesday and we are surrounded by clubs such as Mansfield, Barnsley, Doncaster, Rotherham, Leeds and a host more. Every one of those clubs has the right to exist, but the Bill will knock them sideways because they cannot afford to lose their 20 per cent. casual support.

I did a Central Television interview with the chief culprits of the problems in Germany. They were proud of what they had done. They were not football supporters; they openly admitted that not one of them had ever been to a match. Indeed, they could not afford to go to the match because they had travelled overnight, boozing all the way on £20 spending money. They were not interested in watching football, just in fighting world war 3. I am as keen as anyone to stop those people causing trouble, but the Bill will not do that.

Last week I was part of a Select Committee trip to Washington to study the problem of drugs. We saw 12-year-old kids being arrested and put into handcuffs for selling crack. We visited a huge place in Washington which reminded me of "Oliver Twist". Those kids were being organised to sell drugs, whereas Fagin taught his to steal handkerchiefs. It was a step back to 100 years ago. Those kids have no other outlet.

Football is the opium of our people, and we must not kid ourselves about that. It releases an enormous amount of tension, energy and aggression among teenagers, which used to be dissipated by national service, by carrying bricks on a hod up a ladder or by working in a rolling mill or a coal mine. Those means to release tension no longer exist, so football is a wonderful safety valve. Countries such as America, which do not have that safety valve, instead have drug pushers on the corners peddling crack at $5 a time to give some euphoria, some release or some high kick that our teenagers get from going to football matches and cheering their teams when they have the ecstasy of seeing them score goals or win the cup.

If we curtail that activity and deter supporters from attending football matches, we shall simply build up the social problems. It is no coincidence that a great deal of lager lout violence occurs in towns that do not hold football matches, such as Aylesbury, Stroud and Amersham. They have affluent lager louts. They do not have football teams——

**Mr. Deputy Speaker:** Order.

**Mr. Ashton:** I must conclude, as I have been called to order. I hope that some of the points that I have made will hit home. I also hope that I will be chosen to serve on the Committee, because I am sure that this Bill is not the way to solve the problems.

7.19 pm

**Mr. David Evans** (Welwyn Hatfield): I shall not take up time answering some of the unfair comments and criticisms that have been made about Luton Town football club, but I will point out that Luton Town is a privately owned club and that we choose whom we like to have in it.

The issue that we are discussing today is not narrow and parochial. It has to be seen in the context of Britain's international standing. The problem addressed by the Bill is crucial. The Bill constitutes a serious attempt to deal with the problem. I contend that the problem is too important to permit delay.

Football is the traditional national game of the country. It used to be a matter of national pride. Each Saturday, thousands of spectators, integrated, would pack the terraces. Fathers were accompanied by their children and there was little trouble. When there was overcrowding or over-enthusiasm, spectators did as directed by police officers. Hon. Members may remember the famous occasion of the single officer on a white horse who served as a potent symbol of the good order and humour that characterised sport at that time.

Today, unfortunately, the game is a matter not of national pride but of national shame. Football hooliganism on the terraces and on the streets is seen overseas as part of the English disease. It has led to the fortification of our football stadiums and the banning of English clubs from European competition, and it has contributed to the general perception abroad of the British as a nation of thugs, exemplified by the hooligan on the terrace and the lager lout in the bar of the foreign holiday resort.

The disease can no longer be ignored. Much of the problem arises from a lack of discipline. When there is no self-discipline, it has to be imposed, ideally by the family, but ultimately by society itself. Imposing discipline by law is the least preferable method, but when other methods have failed, as they surely have, we must resort to it. Hence the Bill.

The demise of our national game, on and off the field, is not a recent phenomenon. Indeed, the game has been in steady decline for almost the entire post-war period. I suggest, however, that 1966, the year when England last won the World Cup, marked a watershed in the recent history of the game. Since then, attendances have fallen by over one third, from 34·5 million a season to about 20 million. There has also been a sharp decline in the number of professional footballers in the game.

It was about that time that sponsorship became a significant feature of the game. Winning became all-important if clubs were to attract much-coveted sponsors. Freedom of contract brought higher salaries but fewer players. Certain teams began to interpret the rules of the game in a way that had never been envisaged. The professional foul, time wasting, the questioning of decisions and other forms of cheating became the accepted norm. Combined with the use of the offside tactic and the increasing exodus of our best players to foreign clubs, the game became much less interesting to watch.

The lack of sportsmanship and the increased hostility among players on the pitch soon became a feature of behaviour on the terraces. The so-called fans began to chant obscenities and to fight among each other on the terraces, and, whenever possible, on the pitch. Some found themselves segregated and later penned in by fences. The result is that today football matches are played in an almost warlike atmosphere. Fans are herded to grounds with the help of dogs and horses. They are frog-marched. Then they are caged in like animals and watched over by video surveillance. It takes 5,000 police officers, at a cost of about £300,000 per-Saturday, to control their activities.

Not surprisingly, a significant proportion of the decent, law-abiding, football-going public has abandoned the game. The position is not getting any better, as some would have us believe. In the 1987-88 season, there were no fewer than 6,147 arrests at football grounds, an increase of 11 per cent. on the previous season. In April of this year, just a week after the Hillsborough tragedy, 94 were arrested at Chelsea and 24 at West Ham. The last Saturday of the season witnessed trouble up and down the country, including a pitch invasion by Birmingham fans at Crystal Palace that put 16 people in hospital. Not by any means for the first time, the England-Scotland game was marred by the antics of the mindless minority, with 150 of them being arrested.

What then have those responsible for the game, the football administrators, done to try to stem the steady flow of deteriorating standards of the national game? The answer is, not a lot. The game is run by hooligans for hooligans. Not only have the administrators failed to come up with any effective solution, but they have constantly discredited constructive suggestions put forward by the Government.

Just a few years ago, for example, the Government asked football to put its own house in order by introducing

[*Mr. David Evans*]

a 50 per cent. voluntary membership scheme. Only one big club, Manchester United, made a serious attempt to introduce such a scheme; within weeks it had a voluntary membership of some 40,000. Most clubs chose to ignore the Government. Because of the incompetence of the Football Association and the self-interest of the twits in the management of the Football League—it has had three presidents in the last year, which shows the contribution that it can make—the Government's request went almost completely unheeded. The reaction of the football authorities fulfilled in no way the Government's intentions in respect of the scheme.

It is primarily because of the ineptness and lack of effective leadership by the football authorities that the Government have found it necessary to introduce the Bill. As for the clubs themselves, they have been happy to spend millions on transfer fees and exorbitant fees, but they plead poverty when it comes to spending money on improving safety and facilities at their grounds.

The Bill is essential to the very survival of the game. A comprehensive, computerised national membership scheme, drawn up and implemented by the football membership authority, will discourage the yobbo from attending matches. Those that attend and continue to indulge their anti-social behaviour will find that they wait a very long time—five years—before they can attend another match. The benefits of the scheme may not become apparent overnight, but I believe that in time we will rid ourselves of the scourge of hooliganism and entice back the millions of football-loving families.

The members-only scheme that we introduced at Luton Town football club in 1986 is often used as a yardstick against which to measure the Government's proposals. However, it needs to be remembered that ours is a members-only scheme for Luton supporters; under the Government's proposals, all fans will belong to a national scheme. That makes strict comparisons difficult. Nevertheless, contrary to some of the wild and inaccurate reporting, the scheme at Luton provides some useful pointers.

In the 1985-86 season, the last season before the scheme was introduced, there were 104 arrests, four of them for stabbing offences. During the subsequent three seasons, the police at Luton have had to make just one arrest. Those encouraging statistics have not been achieved at the expense of the club's finances or support. The scheme was closed last December with 20,000 members. A waiting list now applies. The average attendance last season of just under 10,000 per match represents an increase of 21 per cent., the fourth highest increase in the first division. The club is in a healthy financial state, thanks in part to additional sponsorship and to the fact that 28 companies have prepaid for the construction of executive boxes. Those companies and our sponsors have made it clear that they are happy and indeed keen to be associated with a club free of hooliganism.

Despite the success at Luton and the obvious benefits inherent in the Government's proposals, there are many who oppose the Bill. They claim that it encroaches on our civil liberties, that it will force small clubs out of business, that it is unworkable in practice and that it fails to address the problem of trouble outside the ground.

**Mr. Deputy Speaker:** Order.

**Mr. Evans:** It will only be——

**Mr. Deputy Speaker:** Order. I am sorry, but I have to implement the rule to which the House agreed.

7.29 pm

**Mr. Eric. S. Heffer** (Liverpool, Walton): Nobody can say that there has been no hooliganism and that there has not been or is not a problem. There is. However, some Conservative Members have failed to recognise the problems with which we must deal. Let me quote an example of hooliganism. Until the tragedy at Heysel, the Liverpool team travelled around, playing football in just about every large city on the continent. When the team went to Rome, a group of Liverpool supporters were set upon by some supporters, and at least two of my constituents were stabbed. The Italian authorities were extremely helpful in ensuring that they were properly looked after and helped to get them back to our country. The Liverpool people got tremendous support throughout the continent. The one great blot was the Heysel stadium tragedy. There is no simple answer to what happened at Heysel.

What happened at Hillsborough was not the result of hooliganism. The hon. Member for Luton, North (Mr. Carlisle), who said that fans had burst through the gates, was not telling the truth. Everybody knows that, rightly or wrongly, a policeman gave instructions for the gate to be opened. I said at the time that I did not argue with the decision. There are several views about it, but there was no hooliganism. There was a great tragedy, just as there was a tragedy at Heysel.

I should like to point out what Liverpool supporters say about the Bill. On Friday 7 April, I presented a petition to the House. It was signed by 26,411 supporters from Liverpool—the Liverpool football supporters. I am not talking about supporters of the club that I support, Everton. Their petition reads:

"That we condemn the proposed legislation to force football supporters to carry identification cards, and we believe that a system of identity cards will have little impact on the problem of football-related violence, will hinder football's attempt to attract a new generation of supporters and will lead to the eventual demise of the game as a spectator sport."—[*Official Report,* 7 April 1989; Vol. 150, c. 471.]

That is absolutely right. They enthusiastically gave me that petition on the night that Liverpool played Derby County. It was an evening match at which 40,000 people were present.

My old friend Lord Sefton of Garston—we were great mates in the Liverpool trades council and Labour party, before he took a slightly wrong path and went to the House of Lords—made an excellent speech in which he said that he had written to the chief constable of Liverpool requesting some figures relating to how many people were injured or arrested at matches at Liverpool and Everton in one year. The chief constable said that there was a total attendance of 1,812,000 people at the two football grounds in one season. He gave figures relating to crimes committed two hours before the game, during the game and after the game, as laid down in the Bill. At Everton there were four cases of theft from the person and 15 woundings—not a happy scene. At Liverpool there were 10 thefts and no woundings. The figures included thefts from motor cars and so on. Out of the 1,812,000 people who had gone to those matches, about 30 people were arrested, and most of the offences took place outside the pitch.

Ministers often give us figures relating to arrests and so on. We are told that there were 6,147 arrests during the 1987-88 season, but we are not told that those arrests represent 0·03 per cent. of the 18 million people who attend games throughout the season. I invite all hon. Members to read the excellent brief from the Football League and the Football Association.

There have been some excellent speeches in the House today. One or two were made by Conservative Members —those who support our opposition to the Bill. We heard an excellent speech by my hon. Friend the Member for Copeland (Dr. Cunningham) and, in particular, an excellent speech by my new hon. Friend the hon. Member for Vauxhall (Ms. Hoey). I hope that she makes many more such speeches. I say that as somebody who was not happy about the way in which she was picked, but she is here and she has made an excellent speech. I am sure that she will make a good contribution to our proceedings.

It is interesting that, apart from one or two hon. Members who go to football matches and, for some reason, get a bit crackpot about it, other Conservative Members who attend football matches are opposed to the Bill. The overwhelming majority of people who go to football matches and even those who do not are opposed to the Bill. Let us deal with hooliganism and other problems, but let us deal with them in a different way from that which has been suggested. I appeal to Conservative Members to be bold and to be like myself and others have been over the years when we have disagreed with our Governments. I ask them to go into the Lobby and vote according to their consciences and, if their consciences say say no, vote no. If enough of them do that, we will defeat the Bill tonight.

7.38 pm

**Mr. Michael Shersby** (Uxbridge): I declare an outside interest as parliamentary adviser to the Police Federation,. In contributing to the debate, I should like to express the most recent considered views of the Police Federation as well as those of my constituents. Hon. Members who have been here for some time will know that the position I occupy has been occupied by several distinguished hon. Members, and it provides an opportunity for the Police Federation's view to be made known.

The extent of football violence and of violence associated with the game of football has caused considerable concern during the past few years to all hon. Members and to many members of the public for reasons of which we are all well aware. Such events have generated widespread agreement about the need for some sort of action. However, there is much less agreement about the sort of action that is necessary.

My right hon. Friend the Secretary of State has suggested to his colleagues that there is agreement by the Police Federation and the Football Association on the principle of a membership scheme. That is true, but I must inform the House that the Police Federation would prefer a 100 per cent. home-supporters-only scheme, which is not proposed in the Bill. As I understand it, the Football Association argues for an away club membership scheme, which is not proposed in the Bill either. Such a scheme was referred to in a fine speech by the hon. Member for

Bassetlaw (Mr. Ashton), to whom I always listen with great attention. Neither the Police Federation nor the Football Association is in favour of my right hon. Friend's precise proposals, although they have both expressed their preference for a different type of national membership scheme.

The prime concern of the Police Federation is the injury and loss of life suffered by football supporters at matches during the past few years. Naturally, the federation is also concerned about the real difficulties that police officers have to face when policing the often large crowds of supporters who arrive late at football grounds and who are anxious to gain admission quickly. Sometimes those supporters do not have tickets. Sometimes they are excitable and may well have been drinking on their way to the match. Nevertheless, the federation has serious reservations about the type of national membership scheme that may be proposed by the Football Membership Authority. It is not convinced that, when enacted, the Bill will stop hooliganism outside football grounds, although it may well make a contribution towards achieving that end.

The federation has carefully considered the position in recent days as a responsible staff federation. It would much prefer a 100 per cent. home supporters scheme, such as is operated at Luton, but it recognises that that may be difficult to achieve, especially because many fans regularly support clubs that are many hundreds of miles from their home town and yet regard that team as their home club. The overriding consideration of the federation is to support action that will stop the spiralling violence and hooliganism that is connected with the game of football. For that reason above all, the federation is prepared to accept that there should be a membership scheme.

I should prefer any scheme brought forward to be approved by affirmative resolution of this House so that we would all have a chance to debate and approve it. However, I realise that technical difficulties may be associated with, for example, the question of hybridity because some clubs will be treated differently from others. I am glad that, at the very least, after Lord Justice Taylor has reported, the House will have two opportunities to debate both the constitution of the FMA before it is set up, and the final scheme that is submitted to the Secretary of State for approval, subject to the agreement of the House on his approval.

Hon. Members will therefore have two opportunities, if they so wish, to vote against either the constitution of the FMA and to defeat it, or to vote against the proposed membership scheme. Every hon. Member who was present on the night when the Shops Bill failed, will know that even in a House in which the Government have a large majority, such measures can be defeated. If the Bill were to fail on either of those counts, both the membership scheme and the Bill would probably be dropped. It is now clear that if the House does not approve the constitution of the FMA or my right hon. Friend's approval of the scheme, the measure will not go ahead. That was made clear in my right hon. Friend's speech this afternoon.

I hope that my hon. Friend the Minister responsible for sport will give a firm undertaking to consult the Police Federation on the scheme to be recommended by the FMA if the Bill is passed. I hope that he will give that assurance this evening. I stress the need for my right hon. and hon. Friends to agree to consult the Police Federation as well as the chief constables. My right hon. Friend knows that the federation is a staff association that was set up by

[*Mr. Michael Shersby*]

an Act of Parliament 70 years ago. So, it has a special place in the scheme of things. That is the basis for its request to be consulted. In my view, it could make a practical input that will help to make whatever scheme may be recommended more acceptable and more workable.

The federation also considers that the scheme outlined in the Bill should be administered by an independent statutory authority rather than by an authority formed by the Football Association and the Football League. It takes that view because it considers that in the past those bodies have not exercised sufficient influence to ensure that the money from admissions has been used to improve football grounds and to provide proper facilities for supporters. If, however, the FMA is to be constituted as proposed in the Bill, the federation would like it to be headed by an independent chairman who should be a national figure, widely acceptable to both the football world and the police. I suggest that there should be a commissioner of football and that the chairman of the FMA should be known as that commissioner. He should have specific responsibility for ensuring the safety of football grounds, in addition to being the independent head of the FMA. That would be a useful move forward.

The federation wishes to make another proposal—that the FMA should have the power to recommend to the Secretary of State that there should be a ban on away supporters at certain grounds for an appropriate period, should that prove necessary. Furthermore, the federation believes that a good opportunity now exists to exclude convicted child molesters and pickpockets from any membership scheme that may be approved.

My constituents who have written to me about the Bill have expressed their concern about the introduction of identity cards for attendance at football matches. They will be relieved to know that this is an enabling Bill—[*Interruption.*]—yes, and that I, as their representative, will have two further opportunities, if I so wish, to vote against either the FMA or the scheme that it proposes. I give notice to the House that I shall exercise that privilege if I judge it right to do so.

When my hon. Friend the Minister for Sport replies to the debate, I should be grateful if he would state whether the Government will agree to formal consultation with the Police Federation when the scheme is produced by the FMA and before it is approved by my right hon. Friend. I should also be grateful if he would comment on the proposal that there should be an independent chairman of the FMA, perhaps styled the "commissioner of football" as I have suggested.

**Mr. Meale** *rose*——

**Mr. Shersby:** I hope that the hon. Gentleman will forgive me if I do not give way, but I am up against the time constraints.

If my hon. Friend gives me those assurances tonight, I shall give him this assurance—I shall not oppose the Second Reading of the Bill, but I shall reserve my position and that of the federation with regard either to the constitution of the FMA or to any scheme that it may recommend for approval to my right hon. Friend the Secretary of State.

7.48 pm

**Mr. Tom Pendry** (Stalybridge and Hyde): I should like to add my voice to those who have congratulated my hon. Friend the Member for Vauxhall (Ms. Hoey) on an excellent maiden speech. Those of us who know her know of her love for sport and are not surprised that she made such a speech. We know that she is a great champion of football and of all sports and we look forward to hearing from her in the future. Some hon. Members may not know that my hon. Friend was once a high-jumper for Northern Ireland. On the basis of her speech tonight, she is well on the way to becoming a parliamentary high-flyer. I think that she was a little unfair on the Minister for Sport in asking him to take on the Prime Minister; no one else on the Government Benches would dare.

This is a sad day for association football and for those millions who follow it. It is a sad day, too, for the Government, but most of all it is a sad day for the House. Almost certainly, if we had had a free vote tonight, a majority of hon. Members would vote against the legislation. Instead of attempting to enact the Football Spectators Bill, which is irrelevant to the real problems that the game faces, the Government should be listening to those who care about, love and understand the game. As has already been said, the real tragedy, following the sad loss of life at Hillsborough, is that we——

**Mr. Ridley:** Will the hon. Gentleman give way?

**Mr. Pendry:** I am pushed for time, but for the Secretary of State I will give way.

**Mr. Ridley:** Is there a free vote among Opposition Members? Certain Labour Members would dearly like to vote for the Bill. We all know who they are, and so does the hon. Gentleman.

**Mr. Pendry:** That is another of the Secretary of State's red herrings. Of course, one or two of my hon. Friends were doubtful until they heard the informed voices of the rest of us. We are all united.

I was about to say that the House and the football authorities are missing out on a great opportunity, following the disaster at Hillsborough, to sort out the myriad of problems that affect our game. Why are we discussing this legislation before the Taylor report, either interim or final? The report is crucial because the inquiry's remit is the safety of crowd control, which is bound to impinge on the relevance of ID cards. We still do not know when Lord Justice Taylor will report, either in the interim or finally. Why, therefore, did the Minister for Sport assure the House, in a written answer:

"The timetable for the Football Spectators Bill will allow the House, in considering the Bill, to take account of relevant recommendations from Lord Justice Taylor's inquiry into the Hillsborough disaster."—[*Official Report*, 24 April 1989; Vol. 151, c. 415.]

Why does not the Secretary of State come clean? The Government are determined to railroad this legislation through. There is no way that we can amend it at any stage —and he knows that. I am sure that the country is in no doubt as to the Government's intentions. It is the Prime Minister's baby. She wants the Bill through, and that lot over there will in the main support it.

Lord Justice Taylor will certainly not report next week when we go into Committee. The Government should not legislate on an interim report—there are dangers in that course—but should wait for the final one. Legislation should not be based on the interim report, because the Popplewell inquiry, following the Bradford tragedy, clearly showed that interim reports can be dangerous. In his interim report, Lord Justice Popplewell said:

"Urgent consideration should be given to introducing a membership system in England and Wales so as to exclude visiting fans."

Although that was his interim report, it is the one that is often thought of as the pioneer of this legislation. However, in his final report in January 1986—six months into the football season—Lord Justice Popplewell, amended it to

"a partial membership scheme which still allows casuals to enter the ground."

That is a gross distortion of the Government's claim that the ID card scheme is built on the recommendations of the Popplewell report—the interim report, perhaps; but the final report, certainly not.

The Minister for Sport and the Secretary of State have got it completely wrong. It would be morally wrong, and dangerous, for the Government to put pressure on Lord Justice Taylor to report early to fit in with the compressed legislative timetable, rather than to report accurately.

Football is now in an impossible position. The more the game tries to clear itself and make it attractive and safe, the more the Government attack it. The Bill was originally conceived in another place. It has 22 clauses—Catch 22. The ultimate relevance of the Bill is that it can destroy so-called football hooliganism but, as seems likely, football will be destroyed in the process. It is Catch 22 indeed.

The legislation is bad. As chairman of the all-party football committee, I have received hundreds of letters —as no doubt other hon. Members have—but I want to quote just one, written to me on 3 March. It says:

"Dear Mr. Pendry,

As a life long supporter of Blackpool FC and football generally, I am very concerned about the Government's plans to introduce a national football membership scheme . . . More seriously, I feel that football can only be harmed by such an intervention. I have taken up the issue with my local MPs both in Fleetwood and Hull but obviously the Conservative MPs have toed the party line in their replies."

He concludes by saying:

"I would also be grateful if you could provide me with any information which supports the case against the scheme. I look forward to hearing from you.

N. Hodgson. (On behalf of Hull University Conservative and Unionist Association)."

If the Tories' own party members are up in arms, as they are, the Bill will have a rough passage. Following the Euro-elections, many Labour candidates with football grounds in or near their constituencies cannot wait for the next general election.

We have heard about the Home Office's belief that fewer police will be needed if the legislation goes through.

**Mr. Denis Howell:** Rubbish.

**Mr. Pendry:** I agree with my right hon. Friend that it is rubbish. I shall just mention one fact, which I believe has already been mentioned. There are more than 1,800 turnstiles in the 92 league clubs. If the proposed scheme goes through, there will be at least one policeman, if not more, at the end of every turnstile on the wrong side of the ground. It means that extra police officers will be needed to police queues. That must clearly be thought through.

We heard today from my pair, who represent, the Police Federation, that the Police Federation has changed its mind. I believe that it has changed its mind only since the

hon. Member for Uxbridge (Mr. Shersby) became its parliamentary adviser. As I have heard that there is an hon. Member who is very close to the Opposition who wishes to have a pair, I shall reflect on my position.

**Mr. Meale:** Does not my hon. Friend find it strange that a Member of Parliament who has taken on this new position should be promoting or supporting legislation while the organisation which he represents does not argue for a similar system to combat violence in other sports, such as horse racing, where there have been 17,000 incidents—three times the number for football—or Henley, where stabbings have occurred, or rowing, in which the Minister for Sport participates?

**Mr. Pendry:** I thank my hon. Friend for that intervention—*[Laughter.]* I hope, Madam Deputy Speaker, that you will have compassion on me for that.

ID cards will punish the majority of the 99·99 per cent. of those who have nothing to do with hooliganism. We all know that similar problems exist on Benidorm's beach, in the home counties or in our city centres. Those same hooligans are attaching themselves to football. The legislation will not stop the fights at Euston station. There will be no closed-circuit cameras positioned there. We need tough and planned sentencing of convicted criminals. The law is already in place—we have the Public Order Act 1986 —but it is not being used. If exclusion orders were imposed on those who cause trouble, preferably with a rider to make criminals sign on on Saturday afternoons, hooliganism could be divorced from football.

I quote from *Hansard:*

"An exclusion order scheme . . . will enable the courts to ban convicted hooligans from attending football matches. The purpose of this scheme is to exclude the troublemakers, and especially the ringleaders who instigate much of the violence."—[*Official Report*, 13 January 1986; Vol. 89, c. 799.] Those are not my words but the words of the Home Secretary. Why is that legislation not being used? Why do fewer than one in six of those supposedly arrested for football-related incidents receive exclusion orders? Why, two and a half years into the scheme, is it being dumped in favour of the ID scheme? The Bill shows that the Government are out of touch with our national game. With the exception of those hon. Members who regularly attend games—they are being gagged tonight, but some brave ones will come through the Lobby—Conservative Members do not understand the problems facing football.

I cite the problems of a small club like Colchester United. In 1986-87, its average gate was 2,740. In 1987-88 it introduced a 100 per cent. membership scheme. When it introduced the Luton-type scheme, its gate dropped enormously. Even though it was heading for promotion at Christmas, it had to sell players, and the club slumped to ninth. The scheme was abandoned midway through that season, but the average gate for the season was just 1,754 —36 per cent. down on the previous year. This season, even though Colchester has been fighting for its life, having abandoned the scheme, its gate rose by 65 per cent. Its gate is up to 2,893. That is what will happen to many clubs similar to Colchester if this legislation is passed.

The Dutch FA listened to the Dutch Government and the Dutch Government listened to it——

**Madam Deputy Speaker (Miss Betty Boothroyd):** Order.

**Mr. Pendry:** I am sure that in Committee——

**Madam Deputy Speaker:** Order. I am a hard woman.

7.59 pm

**Mr. Gwilym Jones** (Cardiff, North): I join other hon. Members in adding my welcome to the hon. Member for Vauxhall (Ms. Hoey) and my congratulations on her excellent maiden speech. It was a pleasure to be in the Chamber to listen to her speech, and I am sure that we shall hear much more from her in the future, not least on the subject of football in which she has obvious expertise.

I offer a somewhat guarded welcome to the Bill because I imagine that it is hardly likely that many will have a real enthusiasm for it. I cannot say that I believe that the Bill is desirable, but I appreciate that it is most necessary.

Some reference has already been made to the emotion that regards football as our national game. As I come from Wales, I shall not claim that football is my national game. Those who know Wales will appreciate that rugby is far more likely to be our national game. If I was honest I would say that it is our religion rather than our national game.

Only a few weeks ago in Arms Park, the spiritual home of international rugby, an important soccer match was played. It was an all-seated football match, which appeared to be carried off successfully and which stood up well to comparison with other football matches. That example could help us to contemplate the ideal to which we are all striving. Another example of that ideal is American football matches. In the United States, American football is not just a game but an entertainment. As far as I am aware, that game is regarded as extremely safe for all the family to attend.

Surely that is the way in which all sports should be going. They should be much more of a family entertainment. Ideally, there should be good parking provision so as not to cause a nuisance to anyone else, and even space for picnics and barbecues. Football should be played in seated stadiums where spectators and fans could enjoy services, including the sale of alcoholic drink, during the game and the entertainment. I appreciate that that proposition would not be encouraged now, but in the future it could be. That is the ideal to which we should strive as we have not reached that ideal now.

At the moment many of us would be afraid to take our younger children to most of our professional football clubs. We do not regard such clubs as the venues of traditional family entertainment. Those grounds are preceived to be home to large tribal warfare, inside and outside the ground. People perceive that major action is necessary to deal with the problem. I know that the opponents of the Bill argue that the numbers involved in such trouble are small and that it is only public perception that the problem is major.

The hon. Member for Copeland (Dr. Cunningham) tried to quote figures to show that the number arrested at football matches was small and decreasing in comparison with the total number attending. I noticed, however, that he did not respond to a pertinent intervention from my hon. Friend the Member for Bury, North (Mr. Burt), who sought to point out that there is already close supervision by the police and the stewards and closed-circuit television, but that the current number of arrests are still being made.

We must not underestimate or ignore the public perception of the problem. I do not agree with the claim that the problem is not major. The public perceive it as a problem and we must not ignore their concern.

**Mr. John P. Smith** (Vale of Glamorgan): Does the hon. Gentleman perceive the problem among Welsh clubs. If so, would he care to name the Welsh league clubs where that problem prevails?

**Mr. Jones:** I am afraid that I must tell my new colleague from south Wales that I do not believe that the Welsh clubs are innocent. I am sorry to admit that Cardiff City football club does not have the highest reputation and it must aim for a much higher standard of behaviour among its fans. The problem is not peculiar to English clubs.

The problem is not new. About 15 years ago I remember trying to organise a function in Cardiff. I tried to encourage people to go into the centre of Cardiff one Saturday evening. When it came out that Manchester United was playing in Cardiff that day, the overwhelming consensus was that Cardiff would not be the appropriate place for the function to be held. That was the attitude 15 years ago and it has not changed now; in fact, it is perceived that the problem is just as bad or much worse now.

We must respond to the public's perception of the problem. If we asked the public whether they thought that the problem was getting worse, the answer would be yes. If we asked whether they thought that action should be taken, the answer would be yes. The Bill is currently the best way forward. The overwhelming public opinion is that there is no case for doing nothing about the problem, but that appears to be the attitude conveyed by the Opposition.

Although I said that this Bill does not relate to the national game of Wales, there are two Welsh aspects to it. The hon. Member for Vale of Glamorgan (Mr. Smith) might have been trying to prompt the question about Welsh clubs being excluded from the Bill's provisions. I do not believe that that is a practical suggestion. For that to happen the three Welsh clubs would have to be eliminated from the Football League and from the Football Association cup. Almost everyone in Wales would regard that as undesirable.

The second Welsh aspect relates to one of the foremost, if not the first, advocates of a national membership scheme, the former Member of Parliament for Cardiff, West, Mr. Stefan Terlezki. He was tireless in lobbying for such a membership card scheme. He had good experience on which to base his case, as he had previously been the chairman of Cardiff City and therefore had first-hand experience of the problems encountered inside and outside that ground. Cardiff City football ground, Ninian Park, was also in the constituency of Stefan Terlezki. He knew better than anyone the apprehension felt by residents near that football club when they knew that an important football match, or, in many cases, any football match, was being played.

The residents of Canton and Leckwith, which are close to Ninian Park, or those of Grangetown and Riverside, which are further afield, see the litter in their streets as a result of football matches. They see indiscriminate parking which adds to the existing congestion and traffic problems. They see take-away meals, half consumed, being deposited on the streets or in their gardens. They see vomit and worse being deposited on their streets and in their gardens. They suffer vandalism to their gardens and houses and, especially, they suffer intimidation at any of their attempts to remonstrate with those who cause the problems. "Terrorised" is not too strong a word to describe how many residents feel who live close to football grounds, be they in Cardiff or in other cities and towns. That feeling, above all others, is justification for making progress with the problem.

However much we abhor the scenes on the pitches or terraces, however great our anxiety to stop violence and the suffering caused by it, our determination should be, above all, to protect the innocent. Who are more innocent than the people who live close to football grounds? Consider what they must put up with.

**Mrs. Ann Winterton** (Congleton): Can my hon. Friend tell the House what is contained in the Bill that will help those people living close to football grounds? For the life of me I cannot see what it is, and I would be interested to hear what my hon. Friend has to say.

**Mr. Jones:** I must disagree with my hon. Friend, as I believe that the Bill strives to do the all-important thing —to break the link between violence and football. That violence is not football's responsibility, but it is its problem.

Football is the focal point for the hooligans that presently associate with it. Any convicted hooligan, however, would have no incentive to travel to a football ground as he would be denied admission and therefore the focal point of his violence would be removed. Violence is the prime cause of the problem for residents around football grounds. I believe that it is one of the prime reasons why we should make progress with the Bill, and I hope that we shall give it a Second Reading tonight.

8.8 pm

**Mr. Gerald Bermingham** (St. Helens, South): I shall make a brief contribution.

Tonight some have argued that nothing can be done about the problem, while others have argued that something can be done. The argument has rolled back and forth, but we all agree that there is a problem in the sporting world and we all want a solution to it. I have never yet come across a situation, however, in which, while discussions are going on and the evidence is being taken, the decision is being made. The hon. Member for Broxtowe (Mr. Lester), in a brave speech, put his finger on it when he spoke about the arrogance of deciding before one knows and the danger of making a decision before all the evidence is collected.

The Hillsborough tragedy was awful. Mr. Justice Taylor's inquiry is sifting the evidence with great care. We are told that when he reports we will be given two opportunities to discuss the matter. Sadly, that statement misleads the House. The first opportunity that we shall be given will be when the Football Membership Authority is set up, which will be done by the Secretary of State. We shall know little about the membership authority until we are told. The decision will have been made. Whatever Mr. Justice Taylor has to say, the membership scheme will already exist and the decision will have been taken. What arrogance—the Government allow us to discuss the matter and consider the evidence after the decision has been taken.

We have been told that we shall be given a second opportunity to discuss the membership scheme when the Secretary of State has approved the Football Membership Authority's decision on the scheme. When all the decisions have been taken, we shall be told that we can consider Mr. Justice Taylor's report, but the decision will have been taken. What arrogance. How small are we now and how tiny is our judgment. Why do not the Government have the courage and wisdom to say, "We shall listen to the arguments and evaluate the evidence."

The Leader of the Opposition has suggested that we should have a special Standing Committee. That would be a second best suggestion. The best suggestion would be to put the Bill on the back burner until we have the evidence. However, if we cannot persuade the House to do that tonight, perhaps we can persuade hon. Members to have a special Standing Committee which could at least call for the evidence and hear the arguments. At least then the decisions taken by the Committee would be in the knowledge of all the available evidence, not on the grounds of dogma, arrogance and pride which dictate that the Bill must go through.

Many years ago when I was a young lawyer I was told to remember one great maxim: one is not always right. I tender that piece of advice to the Minister tonight. What is being suggested is a bit like asking the jury to call in the verdict before being allowed to hear the evidence. The problem we face is as simple as that, and I hope that the House will show more sense than has been shown so far in the debate by some Conservative Members.

8.15 pm

**Mr. Anthony Coombs** (Wyre Forest): I strongly support the Bill, not only as someone who recognises the fear, crime and damage to the national reputation which is too often focused on our football grounds, is totally unacceptable and cannot be merely shrugged off as a manifestation of violence in society, but as someone who is passionate about the game. I still play a bit and have watched professional football at least twice a week for 25 years. A member of my family had the honour, some may say the misfortune, to be chairman of a first division football club for 20 years.

I am convinced that anyone with any imagination will see the Bill as an opportunity to make football the great national spectator sport which it once was. That something is rotten in the state of football must be obvious to everybody who is not a purblind member of the league management committee. Last year alone, arrests in the football league increased by 11 per cent. to 6,000, and that figure was doubled by the amount of ejections for bad behaviour at football grounds, which amounted to another 6,000.

It takes 5,000 policemen, who could be performing more constructive tasks, to police football matches every weekend of the season. This is at a time when the majority of league clubs are technically near insolvency and shored up only by their asset values and the activites of property developers who wish to develop their grounds. This at a time when the concentration in the Football League in the top five clubs is becoming greater than ever, as witnessed by the fiasco when the chairman of one first division football club tried to bargain with both ITV and the BBC

[*Mr. Anthony Coombs*]

at the same time during the recent television negotiations. The standards of behaviour on the pitch reflect the falling standards of behaviour on the terraces.

The Football Trust figures show that in 1970-71 there were 37 sendings off and 906 cautions, and by 1987 there were 215 sendings off and 4,037 cautions. These problems demand immediate action, and are compounded by the apparent acceptance of violence as an integral part of football shown in the statements of breathtaking complacency made by the chairman of first division football clubs, such as Ken Bates of Chelsea. In a letter to his supporters on 4 January this year he said:

"We must be careful that our rational feelings are not carried away by reaction to media comment. At our match with Middlesborough last season we had 53 arrests within the ground and this was described as a riot".

Surprise, surprise!—How should the media describe it, as some sort of teddy bears' picnic? A certain divine retribution was shown, and that complacency was exposed when, the Saturday after the Hillsborough tragedy, there were no less than 94 arrests at Stamford Bridge, the home of Chelsea football club.

That is not to say that the Football League's problems are ignored. We have heard about the initiatives including the Sporting Events (Control of Alcohol etc.) Act 1985 and the Criminal Justice Act 1988, the public order act on the statutory front. We have heard that, to a certain extent, clubs have taken initiatives in closed-circuit television, partial membership schemes, segregation and in some inconsistent efforts to improve player behaviour.

However, violence continues to increase. Only a few weeks ago, my old club, Birmingham City, and Crystal Palace were involved in appalling pitched battles following a football match. We still see spectators running amok in town centres. By December, there were no less than 300 incidents last season alone involving British football fans on public transport. There is some evidence, as adduced by the Football Trust, that the pattern of arrests per match is spreading from the first and second divisions right across the Football League.

The result of all this is that the game which was the gentleman's game of Matt Busby, Johnny Haynes, Gil Merrick and Trevor Brooking now too often reflects, in the 10 men behind the ball, the zonal marking and the 135 per cent. effort on the pitch, the sort of hard, talentless attitudes seen off it.

It does not take an enormous effort of imagination, for which football administrators are rarely noted, to see that the Bill provides an opportunity to break out of that cycle. The membership scheme will provide an opportunity to raise the image, appeal and dignity of the game and gradually exclude those elements who organise and are involved in violence, and who drag the name of football through the mud. As a result, we could attract back to the game the 12 million fans who have been lost during the past 20 years.

It is significant that a poll conducted by the *Mail on Sunday* between 21 and 23 November last year showed that 61 per cent. of people said that they would regularly watch a football match on television, but 48 per cent. never went to a football match. However, 80 per cent. of that 48 per cent. had been to a football match during the past four or five years. Of those polled, 56 per cent. thought that a

membership scheme was a good idea, which indicates their loyalty to the game and the fact that they are hungry for a lead to protect the sport and ensure its revival.

Any scheme which leads to the revival of football will not be without difficulties. Of course clubs are worried about the decline in casual support. However, support for Luton recovered quickly in one season, following the introduction of a membership scheme. We have already heard that Manchester United managed on a voluntary basis to recruit no less than 40,000 members to its membership scheme during the past two or three years.

If we consider the problems of entry, only a minority of clubs are faced with 650 to 1,000 fans entering per minute, and smart cards will accommodate those numbers. It should not be beyond the wit of the larger clubs to have the necessary stewarding to deal with such numbers. Equally, it should not be beyond the wit of many clubs to provide sufficient pre-match entertainment so that more than 40 per cent. of fans—the number quoted by Manchester United—get into the grounds up to 10 minutes before kick-off.

As for the costs, although the Arthur Young study group talked about ridiculous figures of between £33 million and £36 million net, its projections of profit per supporter over five years were ridiculously low, at about £2 per member. It made no projection for the increased support that I believe the membership scheme will bring in the long term. It is very significant that, of the 90 companies that originally showed an interest, at least five or six are now prepared to proceed with such a scheme on a totally free basis for football clubs. [HON. MEMBERS: "Which ones?"] I think that that will be borne out later in debate.

Of course there will be practical difficulties, but they can be overcome. As for the principle, the Government are right to insist that the problem must be dealt with as a matter of urgency, and equally right to lay down a framework for implementaton of the scheme. The rewards will be great. Not only will cities, towns and suburbs which have too often been shuttered and fearful on match days no longer be a focus for the violence for which football has provided too many opportunities, but—equally important —our national game will be saved as a spectator sport for fathers and sons and for young and old alike. It will be made respectable. Entertainment, not blind confrontation, will be encouraged, and the Bill will do much to restore our national sporting reputation.

8.21 pm

**Mr. John P. Smith** (Vale of Glamorgan): Not only is the Bill unacceptable to the people of this country; not only is it typical of an attitude which, especially over the past six to nine months, has cost the Government dear in votes—not least in my election to the Vale of Glamorgan seat; it is typical of legislation that shows the Government to be out of touch with the attitudes and views of the people.

The Bill is particularly insulting to the people of Wales. There is, in fact, no reason for it to apply to them, as Welsh league teams do not suffer from the problems that we have seen in England. As the hon. Member for Welwyn Hatfield (Mr. Evans) pointed out, this is a particularly English disease.

**Mr. Couchman:** Does that mean that the hon. Gentleman does not wish Welsh clubs to play English clubs in the leagues that they share? He is suggesting that Welsh club supporters should be able to arrive without identity cards to watch league games in England—that there should be differentiation between the two sets of supporters. That is an odd suggestion.

**Mr. Smith:** It highlights the problems in the Bill. Not only will it not work—not only will it penalise the vast majority of decent football spectators, such as my family —but it will penalise Welsh football clubs, which do not share the problem.

I disagree with the hon. Member for Cardiff, North (Mr. Jones), who drew attention to the sad plight of Cardiff and the problems associated with violence there. The situation in Cardiff has improved dramatically over the past decade. Of more concern to those living in the vicinity of Cardiff City's ground, Ninian park, are the crimes of violence committed on the streets after dark, which have made many women and elderly people afraid to go out at night. That is what frightens people in the area, especially since the present Government came to power—much more than isolated problems of violence at football matches.

I share with the hon. Member for Cardiff, North a love of our country's national sport, rugby, but I also love soccer. I enjoy taking my two boys to matches, accompanying my nine-year-old but allowing my teenage son to go alone, in the knowledge that there will be no trouble and that they will come away from a good day's entertainment with no risk of violence. On the day of a major rugby international in Cardiff, however, the city is almost a war zone. Does the Minister mean to extend the identity card system to include our much-loved national sport? According to Conservative arguments, there is a greater case for applying the system to rugby in Wales than there is for applying it to soccer. We were not banned from Europe after the Heysel stadium disaster.

**Mr. Gwilym Jones:** The hon. Gentleman has almost invited me to respond. I challenge him to produce any statistics concerning arrests or other information from the police to suggest that international rugby matches in Cardiff have generated the same problem as soccer matches. I think, however, that the hon. Gentleman is agreeing with me that we should warn people in advance that if a problem developed with rugby matches we should need to take appropriate action.

**Mr. Smith:** Let me draw the attention of the House to the statement made by the director of our local football club, David Sylvester. Although the club is not in the league, he—as a lay person—is committed to the great sport of soccer. He said that there is a problem; and that the reputation of soccer as a whole has been affected by isolated offences perpetrated by a few people. He also said what every sensible person in the country is saying: that an identity card system would be utter nonsense.

8.26 pm

**Mr. Kenneth Hind** (Lancashire, West): After the Hillsborough disaster, in which many of the large number of Liverpool supporters whom I represent were injured and two were killed, I thought that there was hope for the game of football: that it would be shaken into reality, that behaviour would improve and that we would see change.

When the Government decided to suspend consideration of the Bill, I imagined that we would see a new dawn; but we have seen anything but a new dawn.

Four weeks later, on the day of the game between Crystal Palace and Birmingham City, 300 people were arrested at football matches, 16 of them at that game, where the pitch was invaded and one person was stabbed. The message was clear: nothing had been learnt by football supporters since Hillsborough.

We have a duty to look at the history of football over the past few years, and to establish what has been achieved and what we can do to improve standards of behaviour. I have been a football supporter since the age of about eight, when I started to go regularly with my father to see Manchester United play. I have been to semi-finals, European cup semi-finals and European cup finals at Old Trafford, and since that young age I have seen the standard of football spectators' behaviour deteriorate continuously.

Before I was elected I earned my living in the courts, and defended football supporters day by day. Many came back to my office to be represented time and again. The situation needed to be taken in hand. It got to the stage where I could trace the grounds at which a client's local team played by looking at his record of court appearances. That sort of thing must stop.

By 13 May, four weeks after Hillsborough, the minority of football supporters had learnt nothing. I agree that they are a minority, but we cannot operate the law on the basis that because only a minority cause the trouble, we should do nothing about it. That would result in anarchy. Although these people are in a minority, thousands of them get into trouble at football matches. We must take action that will allow football matches to be enjoyed by the majority so that it becomes a family sport, free from fear and violence. The Bill sets out to achieve that.

The hon. Member for Copeland (Dr. Cunningham) said that the scheme is without precedent in Europe. It is, but it is without precedent in Europe that one country —England—is banned from competition in Europe because of the behaviour of its supporters. A problem without precedent needs serious and tenacious measures to deal with it, and the Bill does that.

I do not regard a national membership scheme as a breach of civil liberty. Nobody has the right to go everywhere. Nobody can go into private premises, which is what a football ground is, as of right. My hon. Friend the Member for Welwyn Hatfield (Mr. Evans), who is the chairman of Luton, said that he and his directors reserve the right to deny entry to their grounds. Football authorities generally should do the same but they cannot because, under the powers of the courts and the law as it stands, the mechanism is not there. The Bill will allow them to do that through banning orders.

It has been said that the Bill will not deal with the problem outside the grounds. However, Luton Town does not have trouble outside the grounds. There has been only one arrest there recently. There is no trouble because people know that if they turn up at Luton Town without a ticket, they will not get into the grounds. Therefore, they do not turn up. I accept that the Hillsborough situation was different, and we can deal with that when we have Lord Justice Taylor's report, which will make recommendations about the problem of ticket touts. However, if

[*Mr. Kenneth Hind*]

fans know that they will not get into grounds without tickets, they will not travel long distances to get to such grounds.

**Mr. Eric Illsley** (Barnsley, Central): Will the hon. Gentleman give way?

**Mr. Hind:** I would normally, but many hon. Members wish to speak.

Football is a business, and the Government have told those who are making money out of it that they should put their house in order. The football authorities achieved a certain amount, but they have not achieved enough. If they had achieved more, the events of 13 May at Crystal Palace would not have occurred. Three hundred fans would not have been arrested around the country on that date. Therefore, the Government must step in to lay the foundations of a scheme to sort out the problem.

I know that there is a lot of strong feeling about it, but this is an enabling Bill, and the public must realise that. This is not the end of the matter. We have two further chances to consider the details. Before we next debate the matter, we shall probably have in our hands a report from Lord Justice Taylor. I know of people who died at Hillsborough and we owe them detailed consideration of that report before we take the next step. However, if we do not take the opportunity to put this enabling Bill on the statute book, it would be two years before we could introduce such a scheme, if we decided in those two further debates that that was the appropriate way to deal with the matter. The football authorities have not put their house in order, so we must do it for them. Therefore, I shall have no hesitation in supporting the Government and voting in favour of the Bill.

8.35 pm

**Mr. John Fraser** (Norwood): I start by declaring an interest as a Crystal Palace supporter. I had better do that because, under the provisions of the Bill, if I give the wrong allegiance when I apply for an ID card, I shall be committing a criminal offence. That shows the bureaucracy of the scheme. Both Crystal Palace and Charlton Athletic play on the same ground, but if people are forced to choose allegiances, those who will be put off are those who support football rather than supporting a particular team. There can be no doubt that most football fans want to see an end to pitch invasions and violence. They want to see a game, to see good football. The chants of "Off, off, off" that come from ordinary supporters when there is bad behaviour at a ground proves that point.

I object to the Bill on principle. Being a football supporter does not make me a member of a feral species. I do not need to be licensed like a wild animal. I do not want my name being put on a computer and I do not want to opt for a team preference. When I go to the north of England on holiday, I want to go to see Manchester United. Because I am a registered Crystal Palace supporter, I do not want to be forced, when I go to Old Trafford, to go to the Millwall end rather than to the Manchester United end.

My main objection to the Bill is on the grounds of practice. The House of Commons has an ID scheme for all staff, including research assistants. The Minister for Sport knows one or two things about this. If our ID scheme

cannot keep out undesirable people, how will a scheme that is supposed to operate for 20 million people, rather than a few hundred research assistants, keep the hooligans off the terraces? People will make false applications for membership. There will be a good deal of crime as people will be robbed of their membership cards so that others can get into the ground. There will be many other practical difficulties.

We shall do terrible damage to the game, and I can illustrate the truth of that statement by applying it to my local team. On 19 November last year, Crystal Palace stood ninth in the league. In the 16th game, it won by four goals to two against Leicester, and the attendance was 8,843. By 3 December, the team had dropped to 13th, when it drew 0:0 against Manchester City, although the attendance was rather better at 12,444. By 17 December, when the team drew 0:0 against Leeds, it was 14th in the league and there was an attendance of 9,847.

I am reminded of a colleague of mine, a former hon. Member for Vauxhall—not the present incumbent my hon. Friend the Member for Vauxhall (Ms. Hoey) whose speech I commend, but the former Member, Mr. George Strauss, who saw me going down to the constituency night after night during the municipal elections which I am afraid we lost heavily. He said to me, "You know the mistake you made, John? You peaked too early." Crystal Palace did not peak too early. It was 14th with an attendance of 9,800.

Crystal Palace suddenly had a run of wins. By the time it reached the second leg of the play-off against Swindon Town, which Palace won 2:0, the crowd had risen to 23,000. At the final match of the play-offs, when Palace played Blackburn and miraculously won one of the most exciting football matches that I have seen in my life, there was a capacity crowd of 30,000. That is what the scheme will kill.

The Bill will kill that great surge of support for football teams which do well in the league or the cup. In some cases attendances swell far in excess of the usual 8,000 or 9,000. That is the problem with Luton Town. Any examination of the attendances at Luton Town will confirm that.

The identity card scheme will act as a massive disincentive to supporters who swell into a ground when a team is doing well. That is part of the magic of football. A team doing badly during the season and then having a good run in the cup will suddenly have a surge in attendance and people who do not support the team all the time will go to watch it play. That is the great thing about football. That is what the Bill will kill. This Bill will not prevent people being killed at football matches: it will kill football.

I want to consider what happened at Selhurst park when Crystal Palace played Birmingham City. None of us wants to tolerate the kind of behaviour shown by Birmingham City fans on that occasion. It arose from frustration because Birmingham City had just been relegated. If Crystal Palace had won that game, it might have been promoted if Manchester City had lost against Bury.

Hundreds of fans invaded the pitch at Selhurst park, but nothing in the proposed scheme could have prevented that. If the proposed scheme is to work, that game would not simply have been delayed for 15 minutes or so; it would have been delayed for hours or abandoned so that the fans who had invaded the pitch could be arrested to ensure that they lost their membership cards. The cause of that pitch invasion was due to too much alcohol and a certain amount of frustration about the relegation of Birmingham City. However, it also occurred because the barriers had been taken down, quite sensibly and prudently, immediately after the Hillsborough disaster.

One of the problems in our football grounds is that there are V-shaped, or funnel-shaped, enclosures for away fans. There is the same problem of crush in those enclosures as that which occurs in the bay of Bengal when the wind comes up. Because of the V-shaped nature of the enclosure, a surge can take place, resulting in death and injuries. That is a problem of crowd organisation and it will not be solved by this Bill.

The problem with the Bill is that it is devised in the main by the greatest hooligan and vandal of them all. It has been devised by that woman who incidentally is not having much support in playing in an away match in Madrid. The Prime Minister is the political vandal who is now becoming a football vandal. I hope that the House will express its true view about the Bill. I am sure that there must be massive reservations among Conservative Members and I hope that the Bill can be defeated. We all want to defeat football hooliganism and violence. This Bill is not the way to do that. If there is ever a huge surge in a crowd at a cup final or at a major league match and people cannot get into the game as the computer has broken down because the scheme cannot work physically, those who have introduced this Bill may have many lives and injuries on their hands.

8.43 pm

**Mr. John Greenway** (Ryedale): In his autobiography "Arsenal from the Heart", Bob Wall, the former Arsenal secretary, devoted a whole chapter to the problems of football hooliganism. That book was published more than 20 years ago. The hooligans of the 1960s are now the parents of the hooligans of the 1980s. Problems of hooliganism and yobbish behaviour are endemic in our society. The tragedy about this debate is that we are being asked to vote on a Bill which holds out a utopian solution for the ills of football, but we cannot reflect on Lord Justice Taylor's report into the worst tragedy in the history of football.

I must declare an interest. I am a lifelong football enthusiast, having been associated with York City football club of which I am now president, and I am also a very keen follower of Arsenal football club. It would not be inopportune of me now to congratulate Arsenal on winning the first division championship. I mention that because 10 million people watched that final exciting televised match at Anfield which showed the reasons why so many of us are so enthusiastic about our exciting game of football.

Following two football teams can lead to divided loyalties, such as when York City beat Arsenal 1:0 in the FA cup four or five years ago. Emotions and loyalties are also strained by the Bill. The Government have come in for a great deal of criticism over this measure, much of it unjustified. The Bill is not born out of malice for football, it is born out of malice for football hooligans and those mindless yobs who besmirch the name of their country, their town, their city or the club that they purport to represent.

My argument with the Government is not about whether more action may be needed. It is about whether this is the right measure. I do not believe that it is, and I regret to say that I cannot support it in the Lobby tonight. I am opposed to the principle of what almost everyone associated with football as well as the police have rejected and criticised—the requirement that every fan may enter a soccer ground only by means of an identity card which in effect is nothing more than an electronic key. That is not club membership: it is a gross violation of the dignity and freedom of the law-abiding individual which would not be tolerated by the public in any other part of society. That is a recipe for yet more disasters outside football stadiums on match days. The tragic irony is that every fan at Leppings lane, Hillsborough, would have been a member of the proposed membership scheme.

The recent events at Crystal Palace and Bristol on the last day of the soccer season serve as a reminder of the worst features of soccer violence which the Bill is trying to resolve. Those events reinforce the view of the police that away supporters are most often at the centre of violent incidents. Unless the problem caused by away fans can be resolved, football will ultimately face the unenviable choice of an enforced 100 per cent. membership scheme, which the Government have in mind, or a ban on away fans.

I believe that the full membership scheme for away supporters only, which was originally suggested by the House of Commons all-party football committee and which was recently endorsed and embraced by the FA secretary Graham Kelly in his working paper, offers a realistic and practical alternative. There is little difficulty in segregating fans on match days. That is already a regular feature of match policing and it is helped in no small measure by the determination of young travelling fans to join their pals and occupy the terraces allocated to away supporters. Many clubs achieve that through their travel clubs whereby only members of that travel club can gain tickets and therefore access to those terraces.

If those terraces were designated for away clubs only, we could achieve the desired objectives of discouraging misbehaviour and the easy identification of any troublemakers. Most matches in the lower divisions—between third and fouth division clubs which face the prospect of going out of business if the Bill is enacted—attract a relatively small number of away supporters. If by accepting a membership scheme for them we can avoid the more damaging consequences of a 100 per cent. scheme for everyone else, such a proposal would be a worth while addition to the current soccer scene.

For home supporters, clubs should promote meaningful membership of the kind originally envisaged by Lord Justice Popplewell. "Members only" turnstiles could facilitate discounts to home supporters and allow police and stewards, as now, to concentrate supervision on the remaining turnstiles to ensure that young hooligans following the away team or belonging to another club do not infiltrate home supporters to cause trouble. Regular fans could be encouraged to become members by providing benefits, not an electronic key for entry. Casual fans and visitors could still attend matches without difficulty. The Government have already accepted in the other place that arrangements will have to be made for non-members.

When I put those proposals to the 48 chairmen of the third and fourth division clubs at their annual general meeting two weeks ago, they unanimously agreed to support them. That shows that some elements of the

[*Mr. John Greenway*]

football world can speak with one voice and respond favourably to the fact that more needs to be done to deal with the hooligan element associated with football.

Understandably, the first and second division clubs, facing larger crowds, have not yet endorsed them and can see some difficulties. I hope that when my hon. Friend the Minister replies he will be able to say that the Government are still willing to consider how the football membership scheme should be drawn up, perhaps to embrace such proposals so that we can avoid the damaging consequences of yet more trouble outside football grounds which seems likely to result from the scheme, and to protect the interests of particularly the smaller clubs.

Let there be no glib solutions to the control of large crowds. The terrors of what can occur provide every justification for the harshest punishment of the minority who cause the trouble, without which neither football nor society will ever be rid of the yob element.

The Bill is a lost opportunity. The public are rightly asking: why stop at football? Violent and drunken behaviour is seen all round us, not only in our cities, but in our towns and, I regret, even in our villages. We need a charter for hooligans wherever and whenever it occurs. The Government have embodied a workable solution in part II by requiring convicted hooligans to report to attendance centres. But why stop at international matches? Why not extend that principle to domestic matches, too?

In his letter to colleagues, my right hon. Friend the Secretary of State for the Environment implied that the reason why the right of exclusion orders under the Public Order Act 1986 had not stamped out hooliganism is that, if one club bans hooligans from its ground, they can travel to another club to cause trouble. The Government's solution is to police them out with these electronic keys, but what is to stop hooligans causing trouble outside or somewhere else? What is to prevent the 18-year-old thug who has been banned from football from robbing a younger fan of his card to gain admission to that match? That is what happens now with all-ticket games. What is to stop multiple card applications? There is only one certain way in which to stop the hooligan causing trouble, and that is by policing him out of society and making him go somewhere else. Those are matters we shall no doubt wish to debate further in Committee.

The enactment of penal legislation in Parliament can never guarantee universal success in coercing elements of society into behaving in a particular way. If it could, we would not have drunk drivers, drug addicts or a host of others whose personal behaviour the majority find unacceptable. The core proposal in part I will not end all hooligan behaviour inside and outside football grounds. Measures already taken, for which the Government deserve credit, should be built upon, not by restricting the freedom of law-abiding fans, but by imposing proper harsh restrictions and punishments on those who cause the trouble.

8.53 pm

**Mr. Keith Vaz** (Leicester, East): I add my congratulations to my hon. Friend the Member for Vauxhall (Ms. Hoey) on her fine speech. In a recent newspaper article, she said that she wished to be the first woman Minister for Sport. After the recent European election results, she may

get her wish sooner than she thinks. I also pay tribute to the law-abiding football supporters in Britain, and, specifically, in my constituency of Leicester, East.

The Bill represents the most sustained attack on the game of football by any Government in our history. The hooligan who is currently playing away in Madrid—to borrow an image from my hon. Friend the Member for Norwood (Mr. Fraser)—has achieved something unique. She has united the football clubs and the national supporters groups as they seek to reclaim the game not from the hooligans but from the Government. I and many other hon. Members have had numerous letters from supporters representing a cross-section of our constituencies opposing the scheme.

I have to declare an interest as the president of two local football clubs—Hillcroft football club in Netherhall, and Thurnby Lodge football club in the Thurnby Lodge estate. I had the pleasure of meeting both those clubs at the end of last week and they both urged me to voice their opposition here and, on their behalf, the opposition of millions of other football supporters to the Bill.

The Bill will do nothing to improve the game's image. It will do nothing to improve the safety of football grounds. It will do nothing to improve the ability of football spectators to enjoy the game. It will do nothing to increase the number of spectators at games. It will do nothing to end the violence that has afflicted society over the past decade.

Last Friday, the Home Secretary came to Leicester and I and others presented him with a petition of some 10,000 signatures from pensioners and others who were desperate as the result of the high level of crime in Leicestershire. It is wrong that the Goverment should be obsessed merely by the small incidence of football hooliganism. Lawlessness has increased enormously over the past decade.

The Bill will increase the risk of violence outside grounds. It will decrease the number of football supporters and it will cause the decline and closure of many clubs. So much could be done by the Government and the Minister for Sport to improve the image of football and to ensure that football becomes a truly recreational facility. They could remove the current restrictions on local authorities, such as my own in Leicester, enabling them to enhance a partnership with private football clubs. The hon. Member for Luton (Mr. Carlisle) said that his was a private club and that he could decide who entered it.

My local authority would be keen to assist local football clubs to develop recreational facilities, but they need the spending power that the Government do not allow them. I recently visited my local football club, Leicester City, and I commend its scheme to the House. That is a voluntary, not a compulsory scheme, with a current membership of 61 per cent. That club has a good relationship with its supporters and with supporters of visiting teams. It also has a good relationship with the police. When I visited, I went into the police control box and I know, in contrast to what the hon. Member for Uxbridge (Mr. Shersby), the paid consultant for the Police Federation, said, that the police in Leicester would be opposed to a compulsory scheme.

Recently, my right hon. Friend the Member for Birmingham, Small Heath (Mr. Howell) visited Leicester City football club and was given a tremendous reception by the supporters. We went on to the pitch and presented him with a certificate for his many years of service to sport, along with a compulsory identity card. The reaction of the football supporters showed that they were completely against the scheme. Recently, in a football magazine, the secretary of Leicester City football club, Alan Bennett, said:

"we do not believe such a scheme will help the problem that we all face of bad behaviour, and it would be suicidal for soccer to voluntarily introduce a scheme which we believe is unlikely to work and certainly is likely to reduce our attendances drastically."

Alan Bennett, a man of considerable experience, described it as suicidal.

I now refer to the civil liberties implication of the scheme. It is a back-door attempt by the Government to impose a compulsory identity scheme on every citizen of the country. Those who disagree must look at the Government's record and the restrictive legislation on civil liberties that has poured out of the Home Office. I refer to the Police and Criminal Evidence Act 1984, the Public Order Act 1986 and other such pieces of legislation. If the Government impose a compulsory membership scheme on football supporters, it will be imposed on other sports and on all citizens. We will have the absurd scenario of citizens' cards being removed because those citizens have behaved in a particular way. We will all bitterly oppose that.

I echo the sentiments that have been expressed by many hon. and right hon. Members who urge the Government to wait for the outcome of the Taylor inquiry. Ministers should wait, because that inquiry will contain a great deal of information that will be of direct benefit to the House when considering what needs to be done. The Government are hell-bent on a strategy that will increase disorder, not decrease it. They want to destroy the game of football, and this horrible measure is their means of doing it. The verdict of sporting history will be harsh.

9 pm

**Mr. Matthew Carrington** (Fulham): The right hon. Member for Birmingham, Small Heath (Mr. Howell) wishes to start his speech fairly soon, so I shall be brief. He and I have one thing in common in this debate: we are the two hon. Members who have two league football grounds in our constituencies. *[Interruption.]* I apologise to the hon. Member for Liverpool, Walton (Mr. Heffer). There are three hon. Members with that considerable honour. However, the two football grounds that I have the great honour to have in my constituency—Fulham and Chelsea —exemplify some of the problems from which football has suffered in recent years. As has been said, over the past 20 years, attendance at football games has dropped from about 34 million to about 21 million. That is a drop of about 40 per cent., which is a problem from which football suffers in a way that is hard to explain. Undoubtedly the problem does not arise from a single source.

Without question, violence plays a serious role in the problems in which football clubs find themselves. Clubs have done a great deal to tackle the problems. They have taken considerable measures inside their grounds, and some clubs—Fulham is one—now claim not to have any problems with their own fans. However, Fulham and Chelsea in particular have problems with away fans who travel to watch grames and are outside their control. They cause problems inside the grounds and even more difficult problems outside the grounds. Problems outside the grounds have not been successfully tackled, even though there has been massive policing at many football matches. Local residents have suffered considerably, particularly near urban football grounds where there is little parking and where it has proved extremely difficult to get fans into the grounds. Local residents have suffered violence, vandalism, racial abuse and sexual harassment. All the problems are associated with crowds getting out of control, and they have led to the difficulties in which football now finds itself. The Bill addresses those problems.

The Bill is far from anti-football. In many ways, it will be the saviour of football. It will enable football to return to the family sport and the violence-free experience that families can enjoy. It will allow football to be as popular as it was immediately after the war. The police have been tackling problems associated with violence. That in itself has caused considerable problems. The cost of policing football matches is astronomical and only partly offset by the clubs. The three clubs within the borough of Hammersmith and Fulham pay less than 20 per cent. of the costs incurred by the police in providing residents with the type of protection from fans that they need. That hides most of the problems.

It has been rightly said that, if one wishes to commit a crime, one picks an area in which a home football match is going on. One is able to get away, as there are no police on the streets. One knows full well where they are likely to be. Residents have suffered badly.

I believe that the scheme will iron out many of the problems by ensuring that those who attend football matches are identified as committed football supporters. It will keep out those people who are known troublemakers —those who are known to the courts and also those who are known to the clubs. They will be identified as they try to go through the gates and they will be kept out, whether or not there is a court order against them.

One of the most important aspects of the Bill that has not figured largely in the debate is the licensing of grounds. The Secretary of State will be able to impose conditions that will enable football clubs to treat their fans like human beings. Fans are treated like animals far too often. If people are treated like animals, either they stay away or a small minority start to behave like animals. It is unreasonable of any club nowadays to expect fans to stand. Even if some fans claim that they derive a kind of macho enjoyment from standing to watch a match, stadiums ought to provide seating throughout the ground. Fans should not be forced to suffer for their football.

There are positive aspects to the membership scheme for clubs. The problem that faces Fulham football club best exemplifies them. Its average gate for each home match is about 4,000. The club admits that it is losing about £500,000 a year. The losses are made up by rich benefactors. However, it is unreasonable to expect a league club to survive indefinitely if it makes losses of that size. The club also faces enormous problems over its ground, which, for a variety of historical reasons, was sold.

If one assumes that the 4,000 gate does not consist only of regular supporters, those who actually support Fulham on a half-regular basis will number between 12,000 and 15,000. If most of those people joined the membership scheme, Fulham football club would be able to identify 12,000 or even 15,000 people who claim to be Fulham football club supporters. The scheme would enable them to appeal for money to their real supporters, whom at the moment they do not know. It would also enable the club to market many of the things that a modern football fan might wish to have. For example, if only 4,000 out of

[*Mr. Matthew Carrington*]

12,000 to 15,000 supporters have seen a match, the other 8,000 or 11,000 might like to buy a video recording of the match. That could be done quite cheaply. Fans would be able to see a match that otherwise they would not have seen because it was not shown on television.

The scheme will provide small clubs with the opportunity to get themselves out of their financial plight. It would identify their supporters and rally their support. It would enable clubs to become part of the entertainment industry, which is what football really is. The details of the scheme need to be worked out. Success or failure will depend on whether the scheme is able to tackle violence outside the ground. Many of my constituents say that they do not care if the fans kill themselves inside the ground, as long as they behave themselves outside the ground. If the scheme manages to sort out the problem of violence outside the ground, it will be widely supported and will lead to the regeneration of league football.

9.8 pm

**Mr. Denis Howell** (Birmingham, Small Heath): We have had a fascinating debate. Not the least of our delights has been the maiden speech of my hon. Friend the Member for Vauxhall (Ms. Hoey). She is an international sportswoman in her own right and gave an international performance for us all today. She spoke with feeling, particularly about supporters' rights, and asked why they have not been consulted by the Minister for Sport and why he continues to insult them, with all their collective wisdom, by not having them on his working party.

**The Under-Secretary of State for the Environment (Mr. Colin Moynihan):** Will the right hon. Gentleman give way?

**Mr. Howell:** In just a minute. Keep calm.

The Minister will not have them on his working party. They will not be allowed to serve on the Football Membership Authority. The Minister is not prepared to listen to their collective wisdom. That is one of the reasons why the Government are getting into such difficulties over the scheme.

**Mr. Moynihan:** So far, so bad. Will the right hon. Gentleman now inform the House correctly, first that I consulted the football supporters on two occasions, and secondly that there is no decision about who should constitute the FMA? I think it eminently sensible to consider whether supporters' representatives should be considered in due course as possible members of the Football Membership Authority.

**Mr. Howell:** The Minister wants 20 minutes in which to reply to the debate. Perhaps I may take some injury time to deal with his intervention. I am patron of the National Association of Football Supporters Clubs and I have been in close touch with the Football Supporters Association. They both tell me——

**Mr. Moynihan:** Will the right hon. Gentleman answer my question?

**Mr. Howell:** I wish you would listen for a moment.

**Madam Deputy Speaker:** Order. I assure the right hon. Gentleman that I am listening.

**Mr. Howell:** You always listen, Madam Deputy Speaker, and I apologise for that slip of the tongue. In any event, you would never be the sort of Minister who would sit on the Front Bench interrupting almost before the Opposition spokesman has begun his comments.

The supporters' association tell me that they went to see the Minister, that he did not stop talking from the moment they got into his office and that he did not listen to anything they had to say. That is the trouble with the hon. Gentleman. He does not listen. He just talks, and that is one of the troubles to which the football people draw our attention. They say that the Government will not listen. "They talk at us all the time," they say. Nobody would object if they talked sense, but they keep talking nonsense. My hon. Friend the Member for Vauxhall, who precipitated this crisis in my speech, put her finger exactly on the point when she said that the football supporters' association have a good deal to say.

The only justification for the measure I could find in the remarks of the Secretary of State was that we must deal with football because of violence in society. The Government describe it as football hooliganism. I confess that I do not believe there is any such thing as football hooliganism. There is criminality in society and there is violence——

**Mr. Ridley:** Whitewash.

**Mr. Howell:** I will come to the question of whitewash, the word that the Secretary of State shouts at me from a sedentary position.

This is the promise that the Conservatives made in 1979, the rule of law with which they said they would deal:

"The most disturbing threat to our freedom and security is the growing disrespect for the rule of law. In government as in opposition, Labour have undermined it. Yet respect for the rule of law if the basis of a free and civilised society. We will restore it".

That having been the promise, let us look at the facts so that we can put the matter in perspective.

The number of crimes of violence against the person in 1979, when that promise was made, was 94,960. In 1988, the last recorded figures available, the number was 158,248. There has been an increase in violence under the Conservatives of 67 per cent. The Government should be dealing with that today. That is where their priorities should lie. They issued figures last week showing that the number of crimes of violence in the first quarter of this year went up by a further 11 per cent.

There has been nothing like an increase of that magnitude in violence on football grounds or in football, as despicable as any violence is on football grounds. That is why the Government have chosen football violence, so-called, for this measure. They have totally failed to deal with violence in society and they want a scapegoat. The scapegoat is football, and that is why we have the Bill today.

The Secretary of State asked for examples of what we should be doing. We should be having a more intelligent policy to deal with violence as it exists in football. That should be done by targeting the place where the violence is likely to occur, not by having a blanket restriction on civil liberties applying to everybody who is likely to go to a football match.

The Minister might like to comment on some figures that I obtained from the Sir Norman Chester centre for football research at the university of Leicester. They are as available to the Government as they are to me. About 52 per cent. of arrests occur at 21 per cent. of the grounds; 35 per cent. of the grounds are responsible for 8 per cent. of arrests; 26 clubs have less than one arrest per match. yet all the fans, all the civilised supporters going to the grounds, will be subject to a massive restriction on their civil liberties even though the problems can be targeted and should be dealt with by the Government. Last year, seven clubs had fewer than 10 arrests during the whole season. We need an intelligent approach to the problem. Although 10 grounds had more than 2,000 arrests, 82 clubs had only two arrests. To produce a blanket solution to such a disparate problem is a monumental abuse of government and of civil liberty.

We all know that the problems stem from a small number of fixtures that produce a large proportion of arrests. If the Government concentrated on them we would support that sort of policing. It would be sensible to deal with the criminals where they are active—and as I said, it is criminality rather than hooliganism. As the hon. Member for York—[HON. MEMBERS: "Ryedale."] Of course, I meant the hon. Member for Ryedale (Mr. Greenway), who represents York City. He said that it would make more sense to apply the principle of part II of the Bill—which has a little merit—to part I by identifying people and making them appear at attendance centres. However, that solution does not find favour with the Government.

**Mr. John Carlisle** *rose——*

**Mr. Howell:** I am sorry, but there are many points to which I wish to reply.

**Mr. Carlisle** *rose——*

**Mr. Howell:** I shall give way if the hon. Gentleman promises to be very brief.

**Mr. Carlisle:** The right hon. Gentleman suggested that the Labour party would support certain measures for certain games on the basis that they could be picked out as potential troublemakers. I have some sympathy with that view. The right hon. Gentleman must also understand, however, that unsolicited violence does occur at games, such as at Selhurst park earlier this month and during the opening game at Scarborough two years ago. How can he say that there should be one rule for some games but not for all of them?

**Mr. Howell:** I have a great deal of experience of dealing with these matters. As the Minister knows, a great deal of intelligence about games where there is likely to be trouble comes in from the police, and that intelligence should be used. It is certainly not being used very well at the moment.

I presided over a committee that represented all football interests, such as the coach operators, the railways and the police, but it has never been mentioned since the day that I went out of office. One of the problems is that the Government know it all; they can do it all on their own. That is certainly not the way to solve the problems.

There are two problems of great importance about which not a word was said by the Secretary of State in that most lamentable speech that he inflicted on the House— civil liberties and the practicality of the scheme. We know why we did not hear a word about those from the Secretary of State—because no man or woman living in this country has ever seen the Secretary of State at a football match. We would all be interested if we ever saw the Secretary of State at a sporting event. He has never been to a football match. That is why he is the repository of all wisdom on the subject that he wishes to inflict upon us.

Millions of football supporters are decent people who have never been in trouble in their life; 99·9 per cent. of all the people who go to football matches are peaceful, law-abiding citizens. The Government and the Secretary of State propose that those law-abiding citizens shall be registered, photographed, computerised and processed. That is Conservatism today. Those who believe in civil liberty and the value of freedom reject that entirely. Of course, those innocent citizens will not be allowed to take a member of their family to a football match without that person being registered.

**Mr. Couchman** *rose——*

**Mr. Howell:** I am sorry, but I am not giving way.

One interesting fact that emerges from the university of Leicester is that the largest crowds occur at holiday time because fathers, mothers, brothers and sisters visit their families and they all go together to a match as a family. That should be encouraged, but it will be actively discouraged by the Bill.

The Bill will outlaw neutrality in football. It will impose segregation for ever. That is outrageous. We should be moving away from segregation back to the days when people living next to each other who supported rival teams could sit next to each other to enjoy the sporting encounter. That will never happen under the Bill. That traditional sporting joy of the British people is being killed.

I move to the practical objections, on which we have not heard one word from the Minister. If the scheme is imposed, it will aggravate the very problem that it is supposed to deal with at the turnstiles.

**Mr. Moynihan:** No.

**Mr. Howell:** The Minister says no. Those of us who were at Hillsborough, and every sensible, intelligent person, know what will happen. The Minister arrived at Hillsborough by helicopter at midnight. Had he been there earlier he would have known what would have happened if the turnstile operators, beleaguered as they were that day, had been required to take cards and process them through a computer, as well as taking money. The problem would have been aggravated.

Under the procedure that is proposed we cannot amend the orders that will come before us; we will have to take them or leave them. It is inconceivable that Lord Justice Taylor will tell us that the membership scheme could have assisted at Hillsborough.

**Mr. Graham Riddick** (Colne Valley) *rose——*

**Mr. Howell:** No, I am not giving way.

**Mr. Couchman** *rose——*

**Mr. Howell:** I will not give way. I am dealing with the situation that is facing Lord Justice Taylor. He has been put in an impossible position by the Government. The Secretary of State is forcing through his scheme and putting Lord Justice Taylor in an impossible situation, which is a most undignified state of affairs. That is something of which we must take account. We all know——

**Mr. Riddick:** Will the hon. Gentleman give way now?

**Mr. Speaker:** Order. There will possibly be an opportunity for the hon. Gentleman to make his point in the debate on the instruction.

**Mr. Howell:** Peat Marwick's investigations showed an estimated 25 per cent. loss of gate, representing some 700,000 spectators—which is an outrageous imposition.

**Mr. Moynihan** *indicated dissent.*

**Mr. Howell:** The Minister will have an opportunity to prove that his knowledge of accountancy is superior to that of Peat Marwick, and we shall listen with great interest.

For the past six months the Minister for Sport has been telling us that football can make a profit out of the legislation because clubs will be able to sell their mailing lists to cover their costs. There has not been one word about that from the Secretary of State. Why is that? It is because not one of the firms that expressed interest can operate a scheme free of charge to the Football League. Not one. They all know that they cannot profitably operate a mailing list. One reason why they cannot do so is because the Minister has had to agree, under the provisions of the Data Protection Act 1984, that members can put a cross in a square if they do not want their names and addresses passed on to a mailing company. The football authorities, football supporters and certainly the Opposition will advise every supporter to exercise that right. There is no reason why supporters should be flooded with advertising about double glazing or second hand cars —apparently all that is okay by the Government, although not in respect of the poll tax.

The Bill has many other deficiencies.

**Mr. Ridley:** If I were the right hon. Gentleman, I would pack it in.

**Mr. Howell:** The Secretary of State packed in football 50 years ago. He has never been seen at a football ground since. I wish that he would not make insulting remarks after his own speech earlier today.

**Mr. Ridley:** Having listened to the right hon. Gentleman's flannel so far, I think he is saying that there is a general increase in violence and that football should be allowed to keep its share of it—because he is not prepared to do anything about it and has no ideas. The right hon. Gentleman's complacency is revolting to those of us who really care.

**Mr. Howell:** I accepted the challenge by the Secretary of State to my hon. Friend the Member for Copeland (Dr. Cunningham) to say what should be done. I have said what should be done. Violence should be identified and targeted and then dealt with. I do not want to waste any more time on puerile interventions.

I turn to a matter of equal importance. We are in favour of the principle enshrined in part II of the Bill but we are concerned about its application. As I said earlier, unless the Minister can tell the House tonight that arrangements are being made with other European Ministers not only to apprehend troublemakers but to bring them to justice in the European courts, which has not happened so far, he will have no names to feed into his computer when he comes to implement part II. *[Interruption.]* The Minister may say that that is absolute nonsense but I shall give him two examples.

**Mr. Moynihan:** The right hon. Gentleman has stated that if we do not have such arrangements with overseas countries, we would not be able to ban anybody under part II. He is totally wrong because, as he knows, anyone convicted of a football hooligan offence by the courts in this country, with appropriate action being taken by the court, will be banned under part II from going to overseas matches for either two or five years.

**Mr. Howell:** I am obliged to the Minister, but he will now tell the House—[Hon. Members: "Withdraw".] I am not withdrawing because I am going to justify it. The Minister will now tell the House why, in these circumstances, not one of the 300 people arrested in West Germany has ever been dealt with in courts in this country. Perhaps he will also tell the House why he has not done anything about the members of the National Front who went with the England team to Albania and to Iceland and behaved disgracefully. I am informed—*[Interruption.]* this is all part of part II—I am informed by representatives of the Football Association and of Leicester university that there was the most appalling behaviour. Those people arrived in those countries appallingly dressed and assaulted other supporters. They gave the Nazi salute during the British national anthem and then left the ground before the match had started. That is the essence of the matter, but the Minister has nothing whatsoever to say about it and no proposals whatsoever for dealing with it. It is a scandal. He should join us in denouncing it and say that he will take action.

I turn now to the Football Membership Authority itself. It is ridiculous that a Football Membership Authority is to be appointed and accepted by the Secretary of State without any opportunity for the House to discuss it. I agree with the hon. Member for Ryedale that it is wrong that the Bill as drafted does not provide for any consultation about membership with the supporters, or even with the police.

The Football Membership Authority will be a figleaf organisation, provided by the Government to give them a figleaf of respectability. It will have no powers apart from those which the Secretary of State decides that it shall have. It will make no decisions except those of which the Secretary of State approves. It is not a free-standing organisation. It cannot take its own decisions. It cannot determine its own policy. It will be bound hand and foot at absolutely every turn. It must register and computerise. It cannot exempt other categories of supporters.

We know that guests, disabled people and children accompanied by adults will be exempted, but the FMA has already been told that even if it wants to, it cannot exempt old-age pensioners and women. There are hardly any examples of old-age pensioners or women acting as football hooligans. The whole thing is ludicrous, yet a great attack is being made on the civil liberties of a mass of people, including old age pensioners and women.

Perhaps the most ludicrous of all the proposals is that dealing with overseas visitors. Those who want to attend football matches will be allowed to do so on the production of their passports. Where will the gates be located at our football grounds such as Wembley at which passports can be produced? Stealing passports is one of the most lucrative businesses in our society, but the Government's proposals will encourage it.

The Government have totally rejected all the proposals and objections that have been made. In my judgment, the scheme cannot possibly work. It will create aggravation at the turnstiles and deep resentment throughout the country. I say to my friends in football that, if they have any sense, they will have nothing to do with the scheme. We all know that those whom the gods wish to destroy, they first make mad. The Government are mad. There is no need for the football authorities to prove that lunacy is infectious. They should therefore have nothing to do with the scheme.

To show how irrelevant the scheme is, I shall cite the recent remarks of Judge Dennis Clark in Liverpool, who was dealing with people who had committed offences away from football grounds.

**Mr. Roger King** (Birmingham, Northfield): The right hon. Gentleman's time is up.

**Mr. Howell:** No, it is not; I have another five minutes.

Judge Clark noted that most of the violence described in the cases before him took place away from soccer grounds and so could not have been prevented by the Government's identification card scheme, which he described as futile and cosmetic.

The judge was absolutely right on all counts. People who vote for the scheme today will vote for a scheme which certainly is futile and cosmetic.

We must spend a few minutes on all-seater stadiums, but, Mr. Speaker, due to your ruling, we may be able to return to it. All-seater stadiums are the new panacea. We all want to work towards all-seater stadiums, but I have a relevant question to which the Secretary of State has not yet addressed himself. Do the Government intend to make it a criminal offence to stand up? Unless we have an answer to that question, we will not know whether we can enforce all-seater stadiums. The Minister has obviously not contemplated that question, but I must tell him that at many grounds this year I have seen people who have been allocated seats—at Manchester city and Leeds especially—refusing to sit down. We must not believe that an all-seater stadium is a panacea, because it is not. We must know how we can force people to sit down in such stadiums.

I have already objected strongly to the proposal that we should approve the scheme by orders. It is a monstrous proposition to Parliament. Most of us in the House have never heard of an order being defeated, as that rarely happens. The orders are to be brought before us after we have Lord Justice Taylor's report. We then either have to accept them or the Government have to withdraw them. The reality is that no Government will withdraw an order and admit that they have made a monumental misjudgment of such an important situation.

We hope that the House will vote for the special procedure resolution, which will at least give us the opportunity to have witnesses called and to hear what they have to say, because the views of such witnesses were silent in the Minister's statement.

This is a Bill conceived by the prejudice of the Prime Minister—a reservoir of prejudice so deep that no man can plumb it. It is a Bill that owes its intellectual content to the Minister for Sport about whom no more need be said. It is a Bill about law and order throughout the realm, yet the Home Secretary has not taken part in the debate. It is a Bill that removes the rights of citizens.

The Bill will not work. I cannot understand why the Government want to accept responsibility for it. The Government are saying that the Bill is the answer to all the football problems. The very first time that there are problems, as there will be when the Bill is on the statute book, the Government will have to accept full responsibility for them.

The Bill cannot be brought into effect until 1990-91 —that is its timetable. That year will be an exciting one in which to bring in the Bill. If the House forces the Bill on the country today, 1991 will be the year when football constituencies and others will show their contempt for the Government. They will restore to themselves the dignity and the civil rights that have long been theirs.

9.40 pm

**The Parliamentary Under-Secretary of State for the Environment (Mr. Colin Moynihan):** Before I comment on the points that have been made during this debate I would like to say how much I share the sympathy which hon. Members have expressed for those affected by the Hillsborough disaster. My visit to the stadium following the tragedy will remain with me as an occasion of great sadness. It was correct in every sense to pause for a decent period to mark our respect for those who died and who were injured and to have allowed time to consider additional measures to ensure that such an event never happens again.

This has been a productive and interesting debate, not least because of the contribution from the hon. Member for Vauxhall (Ms. Hoey). I congratulate her on an outstanding maiden speech. I listened carefully to what she said and I am glad that I can meet her at least on the principal point that she raised with regard to supporters. I agree with the hon. Lady that supporters must be "real members", to use her phrase, of their clubs. There is a major onus on football clubs to respond in that manner. I would like to see the European initiative of bringing them on to the boards of football clubs followed much more closely in this country. When the right hon. Member for Birmingham, Small Heath (Mr. Howell) began his speech I said that I thought that it was important for us to consider carefully the case for supporters or for a supporters' organisation representative to be represented on the Football Membership Authority.

We heard a predictably long-winded speech from the right hon. Member for Small Heath. It was long on criticism of our plan to tackle football hooliganism and precious short of ideas and constructive proposals. He made six or seven points, all of them inaccurate. First he talked about the appalling behaviour of our fans in Germany and Iceland and asked why those fans were not dealt with at home. Under the present law such hooligans have committed no offence known to our courts. Under the provisions of the Bill, however, hooligans convicted of corresponding offences abroad can be subject to restriction orders and prevented from attending designated matches outside England and Wales. I am sure that, when the right hon. Gentleman reads the Bill he will welcome that move forward.

**Mr. Wareing** rose——

**Mr. Wilson** rose——

**Mr. Moynihan:** No, I shall not give way. I have less than 20 minutes in which to respond. I purposely kept to 20

[*Mr. Moynihan*]

minutes in the expectation that the right hon. Member for Small Heath would do likewise so that other hon. Members could make their contribution to this debate.

The right hon. Gentleman also spoke about people being required to hand over cards to turnstile operators so that they could look at them. That is totally unnecessary. The right hon. Gentleman knows that the technology is available to ensure that individual members do not have to hand over cards to turnstile operators. Therefore, there need be no additional delay at the turnstile if the appropriate technology is chosen.

The right hon. Gentleman went on to talk about the "national membership association". The right hon. Gentleman could go right through the Bill without finding a mention of any national membership association. I am well aware of what he was talking about but if he was referring to the Football Membership Authority he should also be aware that there are provisions within the membership scheme that can be deployed to allow the FMA to tackle incitement to violence, racial abuse at grounds and any incident that brings the game into disrepute which does not lead to action by the courts.

Those various abject and abhorrent practices can be handled under the discretionary powers of the Football Membership Authority, which can ban individual members for two years, and there is also an appeal mechanism therein. For the first time, many of the incidents at grounds which rightly cause anger and annoyance among law-abiding citizens or—I emphasise this—any similar incident away from grounds which brings the game into disrepute, can lead the Football Membership Authority to use its discretionary powers to ban those people from becoming members of the football membership scheme and thus from attending matches for two years. The right hon. Member for Small Heath should take a little time to look at that important provision, which he should welcome.

I was surprised that the right hon. Gentleman advocated that members of the national membership scheme who join through their clubs should place a cross in the box to show that they do not wish to receive correspondence. Of the 92 clubs in Britain, 90 have partial membership schemes. Those clubs appreciate the opportunity to communicate with members so that they can keep them in touch with what is happening and inform them, not only about the success of the club but about sponsorship deals. Many such deals are associated with the cards. For example, British Rail sponsorship is associated with Reading football club's card.

The clubs appreciate being able to keep their supporters informed, because their members benefit when the club is financed by the sponsors. Yet here, the right hon. Gentleman stands at the Dispatch Box and tells clubs to stop communicating with their supporters and to put a cross in the box. That is an appalling derogation of his responsibility.

**Mr. Denis Howell:** I said nothing of the sort. I said that I would advise supporters to put a cross so that they would not receive an avalanche of unwanted mail. It is an entirely different matter for the football club of which they are members. Obviously, the supporters want to hear from their football club but do not want their club to disclose their names and addresses.

**Mr. Moynihan:** That is yet another fascinating revelation: there is a distinction in Labour party thinking between the members of a football scheme or club and the supporters of a club. It was very much our thinking that they were one and the same group of people. We thought that if clubs had an opportunity to encourage as many members as possible, they would want to find as many supporters as possible to watch their games.

The six points made by the right hon. Gentleman were all, regrettably, inaccurate. It has been made crystal clear to the right hon. Gentleman and other hon. Members that even with the most advanced technology available and with no commercial opportunities whatsoever, the cost would be £3·30 per annum if the card was to last three years, and possibly less if the FMA decided that it should last for four or five years.

We consider that to be a small price to pay for individual football supporters to be able to go to and from clubs safely. If the commercial opportunities are developed, it is possible that the card will not cost the football clubs anything but, in practice, will be an income stream to them. That is an important consideration which should motivate clubs to ensure that as many members as possible come to their ground.

The contribution of my right hon. Friend the Member for Brent, North (Sir R. Boyson) was thought-provoking and relevant, particularly to the wider debate of the problems of adolescent law and order. We have a duty to tackle the problems of law and order wherever they exist in society. That was the background for much of the Public Order Act 1986 and the Education Reform Act 1988 to which my right hon. Friend referred. However, no one would deny that there is a major problem of disorder, violence and hooliganism associated with football which must be tackled. The best way forward is to put deterrents in place, which is precisely what we intend to do by divorcing once and for all true football supporters—the vast majority of supporters—from the hooligans.

I cannot accept the claim by the right hon. Gentleman that there was a problem in only a limited number of grounds. The very first day of last season saw problems with the newest club in the fourth division—Scarborough —and, regrettably, only three weeks after a glowing recommendation of Aldershot's record in a BBC television documentary, there was trouble there.

**Mr. Kevin Barron** (Rother Valley): Will the Minister give way?

**Mr. Moynihan:** No.
We must take action to tackle hooliganism wherever it may occur, and I regret to say that there is no guarantee that it is not equally likely to occur at Hartlepool, Chelsea, Aldershot or Scarborough.

**Mr. Barron** *rose——*

**Mr. Moynihan:** The hon. Gentleman has not been present throughout the debate. Some of my hon. Friends have been, and I think that it is important that I should respond to what they have said.

My hon. Friend the Member for Uxbridge (Mr. Shersby) made some pertinent comments about the view of the Police Federation, whose view he put very clearly. I welcome the federation's responsible approach to our proposals, and I am happy to give an assurance that, along with the Association of Chief Police Officers, the federation will be consulted about the scheme. My officials and I discussed the proposals with the federation at an early stage, and I am also happy to repeat the Government's agreement to the concept of an independent chairman for the FMA. Other hon. Members have raised the same point, and we may return to it in Committee.

Hon. Members have raised the important issue of the displacement of violence. I refer them to the 100 per cent. home-only scheme that operated extremely successfully at Luton. I also refer them to the view of the Bedfordshire police:

> "To suggest that football hooligans have been forced out of the ground and are now committing violent offences within the community is totally without foundation. The groups of hooligans who used to attend home matches are well known to the police, and had they been responsible for an increase in local violence this would have been quickly recognised and appropriate action taken."

The hon. Member for Copeland (Dr. Cunningham) wrongly said that none of the police had come down in support of the concept of the scheme. Not only has it been made clear today that the Police Federation has expressed a strong preference for a home-only membership scheme, under which all away team supporters would be banned; but the federation wishes to impose a much more radical new measure than that proposed by the Government. There was no evidence in the hon. Gentleman's speech that he wanted to pursue any new measure.

**Dr. Cunningham:** I am grateful to the Minister for giving way so late in his speech. I accept what he has said about the police, but the fact is that none of the police organisations supports the proposals in the Bill.

**Mr. Moynihan:** That was a timely intervention—for I am about to quote from the Police Superintendents Association of England and Wales. The association has written:

> "I am pleased to inform you that this Association is broadly in agreement with the Summary of Conclusions".

All last summer was spent in consideration of a proposal which had the agreement of the working party members —the FA, the Football League and police representatives —and which formed the nucleus of the Bill. The hon. Member for Copeland would have difficulty finding a distinction between those proposals and the present ones —and the superintendents agreed with the main proposals. His was, in fact, a very untimely intervention.

**Mr. Holt:** My hon. Friend will recall that earlier I rather inadvisedly and unwisely called the hon. Member for Copeland (Dr. Cunningham) a liar. I withdrew that and said that he had been inaccurate to say that 600 people had been arrested at Ascot over three days. I have taken the trouble to ring the assistant chief constable of the Thames Valley Police, Mr. Dunn, who told me that over the four days of Royal Ascot, 32 people were arrested.

**Mr. Speaker:** We are debating football.

**Mr. Moynihan:** My hon. Friend has spoken for himself. If the hon. Member for Copeland wishes to withdraw, I shall give way.

**Dr. Cunningham:** I do not wish to withdraw. If the hon. Member for Langbaurgh (Mr. Holt) had been listening instead of bellowing abuse, as he was continuously, he would have heard that I said "last year".

**Mr. Speaker:** The two hon. Members are about equal.

**Mr. Moynihan:** It is clear that the Jockey Club has made a dramatic improvement.

The hon. Member for Copeland also made comparisons about crime statistics. I find it surprising that he comes to the Dispatch Box to make such false and fatuous comparisons between apples and cheese. The crimes committed outside the grounds are different from those committed inside. After all, no driving or speeding offences are committed inside the grounds. The most relevant and comprehensive comparison would be between the number of arrests against equivalent numbers of police hours. I doubt whether there would be any disagreement about making that comparison, and I see that the hon. Gentleman agrees. The comparison of the number of arrests against the equivalent number of police hours is six of notifiable offences in society and 130 at football matches. That appalling number of incidents is permitted despite 5,000 police being on duty—police whom my constituents, and I hope every other hon. Members' constituents, would prefer to be downtown tackling crime.

It is vital that the House recognises that the most significant step in recent weeks is the decision by the Government, accepted by the other place, that there should be two debates after Lord Justice Taylor has reported. It is vital that the House recognises, before it votes, that after Royal Assent for the Bill, no action will be taken on the membership scheme, or even on the establishment of the Football Membership Authority, until the Government come back to the House and every hon. Member has had the opportunity to consider Lord Justice Taylor's report. Then the House will have the opportunity to vote. Furthermore, once the scheme is prepared, the House will have another opportunity to look at it and decide whether it wishes to give approval to the decision by my right hon. Friend the Secretary of State to implement that scheme.

All this will happen after Lord Justice Taylor's final report, whenever it is published. It would be wrong and inappropriate to take action on the details of the scheme or the composition of the Football Membership Authority until we have his final report. Hon. Members on both sides of the House have expressed understandable concerns. I hope that as they decide how to vote, they will reflect that they will have the opportunity to look in detail at that report and to consider all its implications before the FMA is set up or the scheme approved.

*Question put,* That the Bill be now read a Second time:—

*The House divided:* Ayes 330, Noes 252.

**Division No.263]** **[10.00 pm**

### AYES

| | |
|---|---|
| Adley, Robert | Baldry, Tony |
| Aitken, Jonathan | Banks, Robert *(Harrogate)* |
| Alexander, Richard | Batiste, Spencer |
| Alison, Rt Hon Michael | Beaumont-Dark, Anthony |
| Allason, Rupert | Bellingham, Henry |
| Amery, Rt Hon Julian | Bendall, Vivian |
| Amess, David | Bennett, Nicholas *(Pembroke)* |
| Amos, Alan | Bevan, David Gilroy |
| Arbuthnot, James | Blackburn, Dr John G. |
| Arnold, Jacques *(Gravesham)* | Blaker, Rt Hon Sir Peter |
| Arnold, Tom *(Hazel Grove)* | Bonsor, Sir Nicholas |
| Ashby, David | Boscawen, Hon Robert |
| Aspinwall, Jack | Boswell, Tim |
| Atkins, Robert | Bottomley, Peter |
| Atkinson, David | Bottomley, Mrs Virginia |
| Baker, Rt Hon K. *(Mole Valley)* | Bowden, A *(Brighton K'pto'n)* |
| Baker, Nicholas *(Dorset N)* | Bowden, Gerald *(Dulwich)* |

Braine, Rt Hon Sir Bernard
Brandon-Bravo, Martin
Brazier, Julian
Bright, Graham
Brooke, Rt Hon Peter
Brown, Michael *(Brigg & Cl't's)*
Browne, John *(Winchester)*
Bruce, Ian *(Dorset South)*
Buchanan-Smith, Rt Hon Alick
Budgen, Nicholas
Burns, Simon
Burt, Alistair
Butcher, John
Butler, Chris
Butterfill, John
Carlisle, John, *(Luton N)*
Carlisle, Kenneth *(Lincoln)*
Carrington, Matthew
Cash, William
Chalker, Rt Hon Mrs Lynda
Channon, Rt Hon Paul
Chapman, Sydney
Chope, Christopher
Churchill, Mr
Clark, Hon Alan *(Plym'th S'n)*
Clark, Dr Michael *(Rochford)*
Clark, Sir W. *(Croydon S)*
Clarke, Rt Hon K. *(Rushcliffe)*
Colvin, Michael
Conway, Derek
Coombs, Anthony *(Wyre F'rest)*
Coombs, Simon *(Swindon)*
Cope, Rt Hon John
Cormack, Patrick
Couchman, James
Cran, James
Currie, Mrs Edwina
Curry, David
Davies, Q. *(Stamf'd & Spald'g)*
Davis, David *(Boothferry)*
Day, Stephen
Devlin, Tim
Dorrell, Stephen
Douglas-Hamilton, Lord James
Dover, Den
Dykes, Hugh
Eggar, Tim
Emery, Sir Peter
Evans, David *(Welwyn Hatf'd)*
Evennett, David
Ewing, Mrs Margaret *(Moray)*
Fairbairn, Sir Nicholas
Fallon, Michael
Farr, Sir John
Favell, Tony
Fenner, Dame Peggy
Field, Barry *(Isle of Wight)*
Finsberg, Sir Geoffrey
Fishburn, John Dudley
Fookes, Dame Janet
Forman, Nigel
Forsyth, Michael *(Stirling)*
Forth, Eric
Fowler, Rt Hon Norman
Fox, Sir Marcus
Franks, Cecil
Freeman, Roger
French, Douglas
Fry, Peter
Gale, Roger
Gardiner, George
Gill, Christopher
Glyn, Dr Alan
Goodhart, Sir Philip
Goodlad, Alastair
Goodson-Wickes, Dr Charles
Gorst, John
Gow, Ian
Greenway, Harry *(Ealing N)*
Griffiths, Peter *(Portsmouth N)*

Grist, Ian
Ground, Patrick
Grylls, Michael
Gummer, Rt Hon John Selwyn
Hague, William
Hamilton, Hon Archie *(Epsom)*
Hamilton, Neil *(Tatton)*
Hampson, Dr Keith
Hanley, Jeremy
Hannam, John
Hargreaves, A. *(B'ham H'll Gr')*
Harris, David
Haselhurst, Alan
Hawkins, Christopher
Hayes, Jerry
Hayward, Robert
Heathcoat-Amory, David
Heddle, John
Heseltine, Rt Hon Michael
Hicks, Mrs Maureen *(Wolv' NE)*
Higgins, Rt Hon Terence L.
Hill, James
Hind, Kenneth
Hogg, Hon Douglas *(Gr'th'm)*
Holt, Richard
Hordern, Sir Peter
Howard, Michael
Howarth, Alan *(Strat'd-on-A)*
Howarth, G. *(Cannock & B'wd)*
Howe, Rt Hon Sir Geoffrey
Howell, Rt Hon David *(G'dford)*
Howell, Ralph *(North Norfolk)*
Hughes, Robert G. *(Harrow W)*
Hunt, David *(Wirral W)*
Hunt, Sir John *(Ravensbourne)*
Hunter, Andrew
Hurd, Rt Hon Douglas
Irving, Charles
Jack, Michael
Jackson, Robert
Janman, Tim
Jessel, Toby
Johnson Smith, Sir Geoffrey
Jones, Gwilym *(Cardiff N)*
Jones, Robert B *(Herts W)*
Jopling, Rt Hon Michael
Kellett-Bowman, Dame Elaine
Key, Robert
King, Roger *(B'ham N'thfield)*
King, Rt Hon Tom *(Bridgwater)*
Kirkhope, Timothy
Knapman, Roger
Knight, Greg *(Derby North)*
Knight, Dame Jill *(Edgbaston)*
Lamont, Rt Hon Norman
Lang, Ian
Lawrence, Ivan
Lawson, Rt Hon Nigel
Lee, John *(Pendle)*
Leigh, Edward *(Gainsbor'gh)*
Lennox-Boyd, Hon Mark
Lightbown, David
Lilley, Peter
Lloyd, Sir Ian *(Havant)*
Lloyd, Peter *(Fareham)*
Lord, Michael
Luce, Rt Hon Richard
Lyell, Sir Nicholas
McCrindle, Robert
Macfarlane, Sir Neil
MacGregor, Rt Hon John
MacKay, Andrew *(E Berkshire)*
Maclean, David
McLoughlin, Patrick
McNair-Wilson, Sir Michael
McNair-Wilson, Sir Patrick
Madel, David
Major, Rt Hon John
Malins, Humfrey
Mans, Keith

Maples, John
Marland, Paul
Marshall, Michael *(Arundel)*
Martin, David *(Portsmouth S)*
Mates, Michael
Maude, Hon Francis
Mawhinney, Dr Brian
Maxwell-Hyslop, Robin
Mellor, David
Meyer, Sir Anthony
Miller, Sir Hal
Mills, Iain
Miscampbell, Norman
Mitchell, Andrew *(Gedling)*
Mitchell, Sir David
Moate, Roger
Monro, Sir Hector
Moore, Rt Hon John
Morris, M *(N'hampton S)*
Morrison, Sir Charles
Morrison, Rt Hon P *(Chester)*
Moss, Malcolm
Moynihan, Hon Colin
Mudd, David
Neale, Gerrard
Needham, Richard
Nelson, Anthony
Neubert, Michael
Newton, Rt Hon Tony
Nicholls, Patrick
Nicholson, David *(Taunton)*
Nicholson, Emma *(Devon West)*
Norris, Steve
Onslow, Rt Hon Cranley
Oppenheim, Phillip
Paice, James
Parkinson, Rt Hon Cecil
Patnick, Irvine
Patten, Rt Hon Chris *(Bath)*
Patten, John *(Oxford W)*
Pattie, Rt Hon Sir Geoffrey
Peacock, Mrs Elizabeth
Porter, Barry *(Wirral S)*
Porter, David *(Waveney)*
Portillo, Michael
Powell, William *(Corby)*
Price, Sir David
Raffan, Keith
Raison, Rt Hon Timothy
Rathbone, Tim
Redwood, John
Renton, Tim
Rhodes James, Robert
Riddick, Graham
Ridley, Rt Hon Nicholas
Ridsdale, Sir Julian
Rifkind, Rt Hon Malcolm
Roberts, Wyn *(Conwy)*
Roe, Mrs Marion
Rossi, Sir Hugh
Rost, Peter
Rowe, Andrew
Rumbold, Mrs Angela
Sackville, Hon Tom
Sainsbury, Hon Tim
Sayeed, Jonathan
Scott, Rt Hon Nicholas
Shaw, David *(Dover)*
Shaw, Sir Giles *(Pudsey)*
Shaw, Sir Michael *(Scarb')*

Shelton, Sir William
Shephard, Mrs G. *(Norfolk SW)*
Shepherd, Colin *(Hereford)*
Shersby, Michael
Sims, Roger
Skeet, Sir Trevor
Smith, Sir Dudley *(Warwick)*
Smith, Tim *(Beaconsfield)*
Soames, Hon Nicholas
Speed, Keith
Speller, Tony
Spicer, Sir Jim *(Dorset W)*
Spicer, Michael *(S Worcs)*
Squire, Robin
Stanbrook, Ivor
Stanley, Rt Hon Sir John
Steen, Anthony
Stern, Michael
Stevens, Lewis
Stewart, Allan *(Eastwood)*
Stewart, Andy *(Sherwood)*
Stewart, Rt Hon Ian *(Herts N)*
Stokes, Sir John
Stradling Thomas, Sir John
Sumberg, David
Tapsell, Sir Peter
Taylor, Ian *(Esher)*
Taylor, John M *(Solihull)*
Taylor, Teddy *(S'end E)*
Tebbit, Rt Hon Norman
Temple-Morris, Peter
Thatcher, Rt Hon Margaret
Thompson, D. *(Calder Valley)*
Thompson, Patrick *(Norwich N)*
Thorne, Neil
Thornton, Malcolm
Thurnham, Peter
Townend, John *(Bridlington)*
Townsend, Cyril D. *(B'heath)*
Tracey, Richard
Tredinnick, David
Trippier, David
Trotter, Neville
Twinn, Dr Ian
Vaughan, Sir Gerard
Viggers, Peter
Waddington, Rt Hon David
Wakeham, Rt Hon John
Waldegrave, Hon William
Walden, George
Walker, Bill *(T'side North)*
Walker, Rt Hon P. *(W'cester)*
Waller, Gary
Walters, Sir Dennis
Ward, John
Wardle, Charles *(Bexhill)*
Warren, Kenneth
Wells, Bowen
Wheeler, John
Widdecombe, Ann
Wiggin, Jerry
Wilshire, David
Wolfson, Mark
Wood, Timothy
Yeo, Tim
Young, Sir George *(Acton)*

Tellers for the Ayes:
   Mr. Tristan Garel-Jones and
   Mr. Tony Durant.

## NOES

Abbott, Ms Diane
Adams, Allen *(Paisley N)*
Allen, Graham
Alton, David
Anderson, Donald
Archer, Rt Hon Peter
Armstrong, Hilary
Ashley, Rt Hon Jack

Ashton, Joe
Banks, Tony *(Newham NW)*
Barnes, Harry *(Derbyshire NE)*
Barnes, Mrs Rosie *(Greenwich)*
Barron, Kevin
Battle, John
Beckett, Margaret
Beggs, Roy

Beith, A. J.
Bell, Stuart
Benn, Rt Hon Tony
Bennett, A. F. *(D'nt'n & R'dish)*
Benyon, W.
Bermingham, Gerald
Bidwell, Sydney
Blair, Tony
Blunkett, David
Boateng, Paul
Boyes, Roland
Boyson, Rt Hon Dr Sir Rhodes
Bradley, Keith
Bray, Dr Jeremy
Brown, Gordon *(D'mline E)*
Brown, Nicholas *(Newcastle E)*
Brown, Ron *(Edinburgh Leith)*
Bruce, Malcolm *(Gordon)*
Buckley, George J.
Caborn, Richard
Callaghan, Jim
Campbell, Menzies *(Fife NE)*
Campbell-Savours, D. N.
Canavan, Dennis
Cartwright, John
Clark, Dr David *(S Shields)*
Clarke, Tom *(Monklands W)*
Clay, Bob
Clelland, David
Clwyd, Mrs Ann
Cohen, Harry
Coleman, Donald
Cook, Frank *(Stockton N)*
Cook, Robin *(Livingston)*
Corbett, Robin
Corbyn, Jeremy
Cousins, Jim
Cox, Tom
Crowther, Stan
Cryer, Bob
Cummings, John
Cunliffe, Lawrence
Cunningham, Dr John
Dalyell, Tam
Darling, Alistair
Davies, Rt Hon Denzil *(Llanelli)*
Davies, Ron *(Caerphilly)*
Davis, Terry *(B'ham Hodge H'l)*
Dewar, Donald
Dicks, Terry
Dixon, Don
Dobson, Frank
Doran, Frank
Douglas, Dick
Duffy, A. E. P.
Dunnachie, Jimmy
Dunwoody, Hon Mrs Gwyneth
Eadie, Alexander
Eastham, Ken
Evans, John *(St Helens N)*
Ewing, Harry *(Falkirk E)*
Fatchett, Derek
Fearn, Ronald
Field, Frank *(Birkenhead)*
Fields, Terry *(L'pool B G'n)*
Fisher, Mark
Flannery, Martin
Flynn, Paul
Foot, Rt Hon Michael
Forsythe, Clifford *(Antrim S)*
Foster, Derek
Foulkes, George
Fraser, John
Fyfe, Maria
Galbraith, Sam
Galloway, George
Garrett, John *(Norwich South)*
Garrett, Ted *(Wallsend)*
George, Bruce
Gilbert, Rt Hon Dr John

Gilmour, Rt Hon Sir Ian
Godman, Dr Norman A.
Golding, Mrs Llin
Gordon, Mildred
Gould, Bryan
Graham, Thomas
Grant, Bernie *(Tottenham)*
Greenway, John *(Ryedale)*
Griffiths, Nigel *(Edinburgh S)*
Griffiths, Win *(Bridgend)*
Grocott, Bruce
Hardy, Peter
Harman, Ms Harriet
Hattersley, Rt Hon Roy
Healey, Rt Hon Denis
Heffer, Eric S.
Henderson, Doug
Hicks, Robert *(Cornwall SE)*
Hinchliffe, David
Hoey, Ms Kate *(Vauxhall)*
Home Robertson, John
Hood, Jimmy
Howarth, George *(Knowsley N)*
Howell, Rt Hon D. *(S'heath)*
Howells, Dr. Kim (Pontypridd)
Hughes, John *(Coventry NE)*
Hughes, Roy *(Newport E)*
Hughes, Simon *(Southwark)*
Illsley, Eric
Ingram, Adam
Irvine, Michael
Janner, Greville
Johnston, Sir Russell
Jones, Barry *(Alyn & Deeside)*
Jones, Ieuan *(Ynys Môn)*
Jones, Martyn *(Clwyd S W)*
Kaufman, Rt Hon Gerald
Kilfedder, James
Kinnock, Rt Hon Neil
Kirkwood, Archy
Knox, David
Lambie, David
Lamond, James
Leadbitter, Ted
Leighton, Ron
Lester, Jim *(Broxtowe)*
Lestor, Joan *(Eccles)*
Litherland, Robert
Livsey, Richard
Lloyd, Tony *(Stretford)*
Lofthouse, Geoffrey
Loyden, Eddie
McAvoy, Thomas
McCartney, Ian
Macdonald, Calum A.
McFall, John
McKay, Allen *(Barnsley West)*
McKelvey, William
McLeish, Henry
McNamara, Kevin
McWilliam, John
Madden, Max
Mahon, Mrs Alice
Marek, Dr John
Marshall, David *(Shettleston)*
Marshall, Jim *(Leicester S)*
Martin, Michael J. *(Springburn)*
Martlew, Eric
Maxton, John
Meacher, Michael
Meale, Alan
Michael, Alun
Michie, Bill *(Sheffield Heeley)*
Michie, Mrs Ray *(Arg'l & Bute)*
Mitchell, Austin *(G't Grimsby)*
Molyneaux, Rt Hon James
Moonie, Dr Lewis
Morgan, Rhodri
Morley, Elliott
Morris, Rt Hon A. *(W'shawe)*

Morris, Rt Hon J. *(Aberavon)*
Mowlam, Marjorie
Mullin, Chris
Murphy, Paul
Nellist, Dave
Oakes, Rt Hon Gordon
O'Brien, William
O'Neill, Martin
Orme, Rt Hon Stanley
Owen, Rt Hon Dr David
Patchett, Terry
Pawsey, James
Pendry, Tom
Pike, Peter L.
Powell, Ray *(Ogmore)*
Prescott, John
Primarolo, Dawn
Quin, Ms Joyce
Radice, Giles
Randall, Stuart
Redmond, Martin
Reid, Dr John
Richardson, Jo
Roberts, Allan *(Bootle)*
Robertson, George
Robinson, Geoffrey
Rogers, Allan
Rooker, Jeff
Rowlands, Ted
Ruddock, Joan
Salmond, Alex
Sedgemore, Brian
Sheerman, Barry
Sheldon, Rt Hon Robert
Shore, Rt Hon Peter
Short, Clare
Sillars, Jim
Skinner, Dennis
Smith, Andrew *(Oxford E)*
Smith, C. *(Isl'ton & F'bury)*

Smith, Rt Hon J. *(Monk'ds E)*
Smith, J. P. *(Vale of Glam)*
Snape, Peter
Spearing, Nigel
Steel, Rt Hon David
Steinberg, Gerry
Stott, Roger
Strang, Gavin
Straw, Jack
Summerson, Hugo
Taylor, Mrs Ann *(Dewsbury)*
Thomas, Dr Dafydd Elis
Thompson, Jack *(Wansbeck)*
Turner, Dennis
Vaz, Keith
Walker, A. Cecil *(Belfast N)*
Wall, Pat
Wallace, James
Walley, Joan
Watson, Mike *(Glasgow, C)*
Watts, John
Welsh, Andrew *(Angus E)*
Welsh, Michael *(Doncaster N)*
Whitney, Ray
Wigley, Dafydd
Wilkinson, John
Williams, Rt Hon Alan
Williams, Alan W. *(Carm'then)*
Wilson, Brian
Winnick, David
Winterton, Nicholas
Wise, Mrs Audrey
Worthington, Tony
Wray, Jimmy
Young, David *(Bolton SE)*

Tellers for the Noes:
  Mr. Frank Haynes and
  Mr. Robert N. Wareing.

*Question accordingly agreed to.*

*Motion made—[Dr. Cunningham.]—and Question put,*
That the Bill be committed to a Special Standing
Committee:—

*The House divided: Ayes 234, Noes 326.*

**Division No. 264]**                                  **[10.14 pm**

**AYES**

Abbott, Ms Diane
Adams, Allen *(Paisley N)*
Allen, Graham
Alton, David
Anderson, Donald
Archer, Rt Hon Peter
Armstrong, Hilary
Ashley, Rt Hon Jack
Ashton, Joe
Banks, Tony *(Newham NW)*
Barnes, Harry *(Derbyshire NE)*
Barnes, Mrs Rosie *(Greenwich)*
Barron, Kevin
Battle, John
Beckett, Margaret
Beggs, Roy
Beith, A. J.
Bell, Stuart
Benn, Rt Hon Tony
Bennett, A. F. *(D'nt'n & R'dish)*
Bermingham, Gerald
Bidwell, Sydney
Blair, Tony
Blunkett, David
Boateng, Paul
Boyes, Roland
Bradley, Keith
Bray, Dr Jeremy
Brown, Gordon *(D'mline E)*
Brown, Nicholas *(Newcastle E)*

Bruce, Malcolm *(Gordon)*
Buckley, George J.
Caborn, Richard
Callaghan, Jim
Campbell, Menzies *(Fife NE)*
Campbell-Savours, D. N.
Canavan, Dennis
Cartwright, John
Clark, Dr David *(S Shields)*
Clarke, Tom *(Monklands W)*
Clay, Bob
Clelland, David
Clwyd, Mrs Ann
Cohen, Harry
Coleman, Donald
Cook, Frank *(Stockton N)*
Cook, Robin *(Livingston)*
Corbett, Robin
Corbyn, Jeremy
Cousins, Jim
Cox, Tom
Crowther, Stan
Cryer, Bob
Cummings, John
Cunliffe, Lawrence
Cunningham, Dr John
Dalyell, Tam
Darling, Alistair
Davies, Rt Hon Denzil *(Llanelli)*
Davies, Ron *(Caerphilly)*

Davis, Terry (B'ham Hodge H'l)
Dewar, Donald
Dixon, Don
Dobson, Frank
Doran, Frank
Douglas, Dick
Duffy, A. E. P.
Dunnachie, Jimmy
Dunwoody, Hon Mrs Gwyneth
Eadie, Alexander
Eastham, Ken
Evans, John (St Helens N)
Ewing, Harry (Falkirk E)
Fatchett, Derek
Fearn, Ronald
Field, Frank (Birkenhead)
Fields, Terry (L'pool B G'n)
Fisher, Mark
Flannery, Martin
Flynn, Paul
Foot, Rt Hon Michael
Forsythe, Clifford (Antrim S)
Foster, Derek
Foulkes, George
Fraser, John
Fyfe, Maria
Galbraith, Sam
Galloway, George
Garrett, John (Norwich South)
Garrett, Ted (Wallsend)
George, Bruce
Gilbert, Rt Hon Dr John
Godman, Dr Norman A.
Golding, Mrs Llin
Gordon, Mildred
Gould, Bryan
Graham, Thomas
Grant, Bernie (Tottenham)
Griffiths, Win (Bridgend)
Grocott, Bruce
Hardy, Peter
Harman, Ms Harriet
Hattersley, Rt Hon Roy
Heffer, Eric S.
Henderson, Doug
Hinchliffe, David
Hoey, Ms Kate (Vauxhall)
Hogg, N. (C'nauld & Kilsyth)
Home Robertson, John
Hood, Jimmy
Howarth, George (Knowsley N)
Howell, Rt Hon D. (S'heath)
Howells, Dr. Kim (Pontypridd)
Hughes, John (Coventry NE)
Hughes, Roy (Newport E)
Hughes, Simon (Southwark)
Illsley, Eric
Ingram, Adam
Janner, Greville
Johnston, Sir Russell
Jones, Barry (Alyn & Deeside)
Jones, Ieuan (Ynys Môn)
Jones, Martyn (Clwyd S W)
Kaufman, Rt Hon Gerald
Kilfedder, James
Kinnock, Rt Hon Neil
Kirkwood, Archy
Lambie, David
Lamond, James
Leadbitter, Ted
Leighton, Ron
Lestor, Joan (Eccles)
Litherland, Robert
Livsey, Richard
Lloyd, Tony (Stretford)
Lofthouse, Geoffrey
Loyden, Eddie
McAvoy, Thomas
McCartney, Ian
Macdonald, Calum A.

McFall, John
McKay, Allen (Barnsley West)
McKelvey, William
McLeish, Henry
McNamara, Kevin
McWilliam, John
Madden, Max
Mahon, Mrs Alice
Marek, Dr John
Marshall, David (Shettleston)
Marshall, Jim (Leicester S)
Martin, Michael J. (Springburn)
Martlew, Eric
Maxton, John
Meacher, Michael
Meale, Alan
Michael, Alun
Michie, Bill (Sheffield Heeley)
Michie, Mrs Ray (Arg'l & Bute)
Mitchell, Austin (G't Grimsby)
Molyneaux, Rt Hon James
Moonie, Dr Lewis
Morgan, Rhodri
Morley, Elliott
Morris, Rt Hon A. (W'shawe)
Morris, Rt Hon J. (Aberavon)
Mowlam, Marjorie
Mullin, Chris
Murphy, Paul
Nellist, Dave
Oakes, Rt Hon Gordon
O'Brien, William
Orme, Rt Hon Stanley
Owen, Rt Hon Dr David
Patchett, Terry
Pendry, Tom
Pike, Peter L.
Powell, Ray (Ogmore)
Prescott, John
Primarolo, Dawn
Quin, Ms Joyce
Radice, Giles
Randall, Stuart
Redmond, Martin
Rees, Rt Hon Merlyn
Reid, Dr John
Richardson, Jo
Roberts, Allan (Bootle)
Robertson, George
Robinson, Geoffrey
Rogers, Allan
Rooker, Jeff
Rowlands, Ted
Ruddock, Joan
Salmond, Alex
Sedgemore, Brian
Sheerman, Barry
Sheldon, Rt Hon Robert
Shore, Rt Hon Peter
Short, Clare
Skinner, Dennis
Smith, Andrew (Oxford E)
Smith, C. (Isl'ton & F'bury)
Smith, Rt Hon J. (Monk'ds E)
Smith, J. P. (Vale of Glam)
Snape, Peter
Spearing, Nigel
Steel, Rt Hon David
Steinberg, Gerry
Stott, Roger
Strang, Gavin
Straw, Jack
Taylor, Mrs Ann (Dewsbury)
Thomas, Dr Dafydd Elis
Thompson, Jack (Wansbeck)
Turner, Dennis
Vaz, Keith
Walker, A. Cecil (Belfast N)
Wall, Pat
Wallace, James

Walley, Joan
Wareing, Robert N.
Watson, Mike (Glasgow, C)
Welsh, Andrew (Angus E)
Welsh, Michael (Doncaster N)
Wigley, Dafydd
Williams, Rt Hon Alan
Williams, Alan W. (Carm'then)
Wilson, Brian

Winnick, David
Wise, Mrs Audrey
Worthington, Tony
Wray, Jimmy

Tellers for the Ayes:
  Mr. Frank Haynes and
  Mr. Nigel Griffiths.

## NOES

Adley, Robert
Aitken, Jonathan
Alexander, Richard
Alison, Rt Hon Michael
Allason, Rupert
Amery, Rt Hon Julian
Amess, David
Amos, Alan
Arbuthnot, James
Arnold, Jacques (Gravesham)
Arnold, Tom (Hazel Grove)
Ashby, David
Aspinwall, Jack
Atkins, Robert
Atkinson, David
Baker, Rt Hon K. (Mole Valley)
Baker, Nicholas (Dorset N)
Baldry, Tony
Banks, Robert (Harrogate)
Batiste, Spencer
Beaumont-Dark, Anthony
Bellingham, Henry
Bendall, Vivian
Bennett, Nicholas (Pembroke)
Bevan, David Gilroy
Blackburn, Dr John G.
Blaker, Rt Hon Sir Peter
Bonsor, Sir Nicholas
Boscawen, Hon Robert
Boswell, Tim
Bottomley, Peter
Bottomley, Mrs Virginia
Bowden, A (Brighton K'pto'n)
Bowden, Gerald (Dulwich)
Braine, Rt Hon Sir Bernard
Brandon-Bravo, Martin
Brazier, Julian
Bright, Graham
Brooke, Rt Hon Peter
Brown, Michael (Brigg & Cl't's)
Browne, John (Winchester)
Bruce, Ian (Dorset South)
Buchanan-Smith, Rt Hon Alick
Budgen, Nicholas
Burns, Simon
Burt, Alistair
Butcher, John
Butler, Chris
Butterfill, John
Carlisle, John, (Luton N)
Carlisle, Kenneth (Lincoln)
Carrington, Matthew
Cash, William
Chalker, Rt Hon Mrs Lynda
Channon, Rt Hon Paul
Chapman, Sydney
Chope, Christopher
Churchill, Mr
Clark, Hon Alan (Plym'th S'n)
Clark, Dr Michael (Rochford)
Clark, Sir W. (Croydon S)
Clarke, Rt Hon K. (Rushcliffe)
Colvin, Michael
Conway, Derek
Coombs, Anthony (Wyre F'rest)
Coombs, Simon (Swindon)
Cope, Rt Hon John
Cormack, Patrick
Couchman, James

Cran, James
Currie, Mrs Edwina
Curry, David
Davies, Q. (Stamf'd & Spald'g)
Davis, David (Boothferry)
Day, Stephen
Devlin, Tim
Dorrell, Stephen
Douglas-Hamilton, Lord James
Dover, Den
Dykes, Hugh
Eggar, Tim
Emery, Sir Peter
Evans, David (Welwyn Hatf'd)
Evennett, David
Fairbairn, Sir Nicholas
Fallon, Michael
Farr, Sir John
Favell, Tony
Fenner, Dame Peggy
Field, Barry (Isle of Wight)
Finsberg, Sir Geoffrey
Fishburn, John Dudley
Fookes, Dame Janet
Forman, Nigel
Forsyth, Michael (Stirling)
Forth, Eric
Fowler, Rt Hon Norman
Fox, Sir Marcus
Franks, Cecil
Freeman, Roger
French, Douglas
Fry, Peter
Gale, Roger
Gardiner, George
Gill, Christopher
Glyn, Dr Alan
Goodlad, Alastair
Goodson-Wickes, Dr Charles
Gorst, John
Gow, Ian
Greenway, Harry (Ealing N)
Griffiths, Peter (Portsmouth N)
Grist, Ian
Ground, Patrick
Grylls, Michael
Gummer, Rt Hon John Selwyn
Hague, William
Hamilton, Hon Archie (Epsom)
Hamilton, Neil (Tatton)
Hampson, Dr Keith
Hanley, Jeremy
Hannam, John
Hargreaves, A. (B'ham H'll Gr')
Harris, David
Haselhurst, Alan
Hawkins, Christopher
Hayes, Jerry
Hayward, Robert
Heathcoat-Amory, David
Heddle, John
Heseltine, Rt Hon Michael
Hicks, Mrs Maureen (Wolv' NE)
Higgins, Rt Hon Terence L.
Hill, James
Hind, Kenneth
Hogg, Hon Douglas (Gr'th'm)
Holt, Richard
Hordern, Sir Peter

Howard, Michael
Howarth, Alan (Strat'd-on-A)
Howarth, G. (Cannock & B'wd)
Howell, Rt Hon David (G'dford)
Howell, Ralph (North Norfolk)
Hughes, Robert G. (Harrow W)
Hunt, David (Wirral W)
Hunt, Sir John (Ravensbourne)
Hunter, Andrew
Hurd, Rt Hon Douglas
Irvine, Michael
Irving, Charles
Jack, Michael
Jackson, Robert
Janman, Tim
Jessel, Toby
Johnson Smith, Sir Geoffrey
Jones, Gwilym (Cardiff N)
Jones, Robert B (Herts W)
Jopling, Rt Hon Michael
Kellett-Bowman, Dame Elaine
Key, Robert
King, Roger (B'ham N'thfield)
King, Rt Hon Tom (Bridgwater)
Kirkhope, Timothy
Knapman, Roger
Knight, Greg (Derby North)
Knight, Dame Jill (Edgbaston)
Lamont, Rt Hon Norman
Lang, Ian
Lawrence, Ivan
Lee, John (Pendle)
Leigh, Edward (Gainsbor'gh)
Lennox-Boyd, Hon Mark
Lightbown, David
Lilley, Peter
Lloyd, Sir Ian (Havant)
Lloyd, Peter (Fareham)
Lord, Michael
Luce, Rt Hon Richard
Lyell, Sir Nicholas
McCrindle, Robert
Macfarlane, Sir Neil
MacGregor, Rt Hon John
MacKay, Andrew (E Berkshire)
Maclean, David
McLoughlin, Patrick
McNair-Wilson, Sir Michael
McNair-Wilson, Sir Patrick
Madel, David
Major, Rt Hon John
Malins, Humfrey
Mans, Keith
Maples, John
Marland, Paul

Marshall, Michael (Arundel)
Martin, David (Portsmouth S)
Mates, Michael
Maude, Hon Francis
Mawhinney, Dr Brian
Maxwell-Hyslop, Robin
Mellor, David
Meyer, Sir Anthony
Miller, Sir Hal
Mills, Iain
Miscampbell, Norman
Mitchell, Andrew (Gedling)
Mitchell, Sir David
Moate, Roger
Monro, Sir Hector
Moore, Rt Hon John
Morris, M (N'hampton S)
Morrison, Sir Charles
Morrison, Rt Hon P (Chester)
Moss, Malcolm
Moynihan, Hon Colin
Neale, Gerrard
Needham, Richard
Nelson, Anthony
Neubert, Michael
Newton, Rt Hon Tony
Nicholls, Patrick
Nicholson, David (Taunton)
Nicholson, Emma (Devon West)
Norris, Steve
Onslow, Rt Hon Cranley
Oppenheim, Phillip
Paice, James
Parkinson, Rt Hon Cecil
Patnick, Irvine
Patten, Rt Hon Chris (Bath)
Patten, John (Oxford W)
Pattie, Rt Hon Sir Geoffrey
Peacock, Mrs Elizabeth
Porter, Barry (Wirral S)
Porter, David (Waveney)
Portillo, Michael
Powell, William (Corby)
Price, Sir David
Raffan, Keith
Raison, Rt Hon Timothy
Rathbone, Tim
Redwood, John
Renton, Tim
Rhodes James, Robert
Riddick, Graham
Ridley, Rt Hon Nicholas
Ridsdale, Sir Julian
Rifkind, Rt Hon Malcolm
Roberts, Wyn (Conwy)

Roe, Mrs Marion
Rossi, Sir Hugh
Rost, Peter
Rowe, Andrew
Rumbold, Mrs Angela
Sackville, Hon Tom
Sainsbury, Hon Tim
Sayeed, Jonathan
Scott, Rt Hon Nicholas
Shaw, David (Dover)
Shaw, Sir Giles (Pudsey)
Shaw, Sir Michael (Scarb')
Shelton, Sir William
Shephard, Mrs G. (Norfolk SW)
Shepherd, Colin (Hereford)
Shersby, Michael
Sims, Roger
Skeet, Sir Trevor
Smith, Sir Dudley (Warwick)
Smith, Tim (Beaconsfield)
Soames, Hon Nicholas
Speed, Keith
Speller, Tony
Spicer, Sir Jim (Dorset W)
Spicer, Michael (S Worcs)
Squire, Robin
Stanbrook, Ivor
Stanley, Rt Hon Sir John
Steen, Anthony
Stern, Michael
Stevens, Lewis
Stewart, Allan (Eastwood)
Stewart, Andy (Sherwood)
Stewart, Rt Hon Ian (Herts N)
Stokes, Sir John
Stradling Thomas, Sir John
Sumberg, David
Tapsell, Sir Peter
Taylor, Ian (Esher)
Taylor, John M (Solihull)
Taylor, Teddy (S'end E)

Tebbit, Rt Hon Norman
Temple-Morris, Peter
Thatcher, Rt Hon Margaret
Thompson, D. (Calder Valley)
Thompson, Patrick (Norwich N)
Thorne, Neil
Thornton, Malcolm
Thurnham, Peter
Townend, John (Bridlington)
Townsend, Cyril D. (B'heath)
Tracey, Richard
Tredinnick, David
Trippier, David
Trotter, Neville
Twinn, Dr Ian
Vaughan, Sir Gerard
Viggers, Peter
Waddington, Rt Hon David
Wakeham, Rt Hon John
Waldegrave, Hon William
Walden, George
Walker, Bill (T'side North)
Walker, Rt Hon P. (W'cester)
Waller, Gary
Walters, Sir Dennis
Ward, John
Wardle, Charles (Bexhill)
Warren, Kenneth
Wells, Bowen
Wheeler, John
Widdecombe, Ann
Wiggin, Jerry
Wilshire, David
Wolfson, Mark
Wood, Timothy
Yeo, Tim
Young, Sir George (Acton)

Tellers for the Noes:
    Mr. Tristan Garel-Jones and
    Mr. Tony Durant.

*Question accordingly negatived.*
*Bill accordingly committed to a Standing Committee.*

## BUSINESS OF THE HOUSE

*Ordered,*

That, at this day's sitting, the Motion in the name of Mr. Secretary Ridley relating to the Football Spectators Bill *[Lords]* may be proceeded with, though opposed, until any hour; and the Motion in the name of the Prime Minister for the Adjournment of the House may be proceeded with, though opposed, until One o'clock, or for three hours after it has been entered upon, whichever is the later.—*[Mr. Chapman.]*

# Football Spectators Bill [Lords]

10.27 pm

**The Secretary of State for the Environment (Mr. Nicholas Ridley):** I beg to move,

That it be an Instruction to the Committee on the Football Spectators Bill [Lords] that it have power to make provision in the Bill relating to any aspect of the safety of spectators at designated football matches.

This motion was tabled at the suggestion of the hon. Member for Holborn and St. Pancras (Mr. Dobson). I have already explained its meaning and purpose and the use to which the Government might seek to put it by moving an amendment in Committee. I do not think that I need to add anything to what I said earlier.

10.28 pm

**Mr. Denis Howell** (Birmingham, Small Heath): I do not wish to detain the House, but I think that the Secretary of State should give us a little more explanation of his motion because it might cause considerable problems to the Committee. I have already referred to all-seater stadiums, which is a desirable aim towards which we hope to move.

The purpose of the Government's proposal is to allow us to amend the Safety of Sports Grounds Act 1975, although that is not the legislation that we will be discussing. It raises questions about the powers of local authorities, the rights of football grounds and the cost of implementing any of the schemes. Can the Secretary of State assure us that all those matters can be debated in Committee under his proposal? If so, we shall be satisfied.

We do not wish to resist anything that will improve the safety of grounds and, wherever possible, we shall support the Government. Nevertheless, there are questions of cost and convenience for the football authorities and the local authorities, and we need to be satisfied on those matters before approving the motion.

10.29 pm

**Mr. Robert N. Wareing** (Liverpool, West Derby): I am pleased that at least the Government have decided that it will be possible to introduce measures through the Bill which will enable the whole question of safety at football grounds to be properly considered. This precipitate legislation still needs major amendment if there is a real desire to do something about safety at football grounds.

My hon. Friend the Member for Stalybridge and Hyde (Mr. Pendry) referred to what had happened in relation to violence at football grounds in Holland. They set up an advisory board to consider not just hooliganism but safety and crowd control. I hope that the Government will listen to what other people have to say. It is a forlorn hope because, as we know, the Government never make mistakes. So they will decide what to do and they will not listen to anybody else.

I appeal to reasonable hon. Members on the Government Benches to support any move for which we press to try to ensure that the Government consult the people who know about football stadiums. I mean the football authorities, the police and, most of all, the people who tend to be ignored time and again by Government Members—the football supporters' associations. We want real safety. We want conditions in which Hillsboroughs do

not occur again. The people of Liverpool are extremely concerned that all that we will get is sympathy but no real action.

We should consider the experience of other countries. In Germany after the second world war, when they had the advantage of being able to build from scratch, the great stadiums were not built in urban areas, where so many of our grounds are. That is why we have problems on the streets outside grounds, why there is annoyance to people in their residences and why, incidentally, if the scheme is forced on us, we may have Luton copied everywhere else.

At one time the Anglican Church was regarded as the Tory party at prayer, but now Luton Town football club is taking on the pose of the Tory party at play. When I attended that ground on 21 January, in the directors' room there were no fewer than four Tory Members, including two members of the Cabinet, the right hon. Members for Huntingdon (Mr. Major) and for Hertsmere (Mr. Parkinson). Obviously they are impressed with the position at Luton.

Of course, safety does not extend outside the ground. During the 1987-88 football season there were no fewer than 262 cases of criminal damage in Luton town centre and 13 assaults on the police. Luton is not a Tory paradise; it is not a place of peace and tranquillity, no matter what people say.

**Mr. John Carlisle** (Luton, North): As the hon. Gentleman has spoken of my constituency as a place of peace and tranquillity, which it is, will he give the House the figures of arrests in the town for the previous year and the figures for the year before the membership scheme was introduced?

**Mr. Speaker:** Order. I hope that the hon. Member for Liverpool, West Derby (Mr. Wareing) will not be tempted to do that. He must confine his remarks to the instruction on the Order Paper.

**Mr. Wareing:** I will not be dragged along that road, Mr. Speaker.

If we are serious about safety in our football grounds, the Committee will have to consider the provision of more football grounds. When cup semi-finals and other large matches are being played, it should be possible for the Football Association and the Football League to use stadiums such as Wembley. We need four or five more such stadiums, but that requires public finance. It cannot be done by private finance. Football grounds in West Germany and Holland are provided by municipalities.

The Secretary of State should think about getting the people who know to advise him and about setting up an advisory body upon which football organisations, football supporters and the police will be represented. There should be an attempt to examine the structure of existing football grounds.

If identity cards are to be shown at every match in the country—each year, hundreds of matches are played at the 92 Football League grounds, at Wembley and at other stadiums—it will be necessary to examine turnstiles and access to grounds. Many football stands are built on main roads. For example, the Kop end of Liverpool football ground abuts the main road. Liverpool football club has solved most of the problem by ensuring that only season ticket holders and people with special discretionary match-day tickets go through the turnstiles. If identity cards are introduced, there will have to be structural changes at Liverpool football ground to accommodate people going through the turnstiles. The Government must be able to give financial assistance to football clubs.

We must also consider Tottenham Hotspur football club. A high street is adjacent to that ground. There must be major structural changes to ensure safety in that ground, and even to deal with the problem of showing identity cards.

The Committee will examine not only overall safety, the problems that we have had in the past and the problem at Hillsborough and other grounds, but the increased danger as a result of large crowds, very often on Wednesday or Tuesday nights, queueing in our main streets to get into football grounds. Safety will be imperilled by the Bill, and that is yet another reason it should be the priority in Committee.

10.38 pm

**Mr. Peter L. Pike** (Burnley): One thing that unites hon. Members is that none of us wishes to see a repeat of the Hillsborough, Bradford or Heysel tragedies. We should do everything possible to secure safety in our football grounds. Whatever our views may have been in the previous debate, we all welcome the safety instruction that was given to the Committee.

Having due regard to the Secretary of State's record in ensuring that certain matters are fulfilled, I hope that he will assure hon. Members that we are to have a proper opportunity to discuss important safety aspects when the proposals come forward. I hope that he will assure us that there will be full consultation with football clubs, spectators, local authorities and the police who have to implement the proposals. The Government have set themselves a tight timetable. If they want to deal properly with the problem, it is important that they do not push legislation through hastily. Legislation in haste can be bad legislation. The Government should ensure that they get things right.

To some extent, the Taylor inquiry was predetermined because it had to issue an interim report. Many people are afraid that inquiries have to rush their investigations to meet the Government's requirement that they publish an interim report. As was said in the previous debate, the Popplewell final report differed considerably from the interim report.

All of us—Government, Opposition, police, local authorities, football club management and spectators— have a responsibility to ensure that our football grounds are safe. I hope that the Secretary of State will give an assurance that he will take account of the fears of many people that a membership scheme will cause safety problems at gates—but we cannot go into that debate now.

I hope that the Secretary of State will not push us towards having all-seating stadiums. We should not necessarily accept that that is the only way to solve the problem. I do not accept that standing stadiums cannot be made safe. As my hon. Friend the Member for Liverpool, West Derby (Mr. Wareing) said on a similar point, there are often safety problems outside the grounds—at Underground stations and on the roads. I hope that the Secretary of State will make a commitment to provide from public funds the resources necessary to ensure that spectators outside grounds are safe, just as we are trying to ensure that spectators inside grounds are safe.

10.42 pm

**Mr. Alan Meale** (Mansfield): A number of aspects of the motion worry me greatly. It is outrageous that the Secretary of State has moved such a motion at this time. We have just spent hours talking about the fact that we will have two more opportunities to debate the safety issue. Why, therefore, is the right hon. Gentleman trying to impose this on the Committee? Even on the Government's tight time scale, it will take until 1991, or thereabouts, before the requirements are made law.

Who will pay for the extra safety requirements that will be imposed? We have heard that computerisation of membership details will cost individual clubs £50,000-plus. The Minister outlined ways in which some of that money could be raised, but what happens if it is not raised? Imposition of £50,000 in the first year on a club such as Mansfield, which I represent, would have disastrous effects. It cannot afford to lose that amount. As it is, it is struggling to get by week by week through the season.

Will the Government give a commitment to put extra resources into the clubs? I hope that the Secretary of State will comment on that matter. In fact, there will be greater financial imposition on the clubs on top of that £50,000. In my area a local newspaper and British Coal have sponsored our local club, Mansfield Town. They, with the help of the Football Ground Improvements Trust, have enabled us to open one side of the ground. That has made the ground safe, and will encourage families to attend and greater support for the club. Such clubs cannot afford to spend more money.

I do not know how far the Secretary of State will take note, but I want to mention to him the police charges for extra security, which must go with safety at football grounds. Already many third and fourth division clubs have faced severe problems because of the extra police charges imposed in recent years.

We want some answers before the motion is approved. It is no good the House willy-nilly approving such a clause, sending it to Committee, the Committee endorsing it, and it then becoming part of the Bill without a proper debate. We need to be told that more money will be guaranteed for the clubs in the lower divisions to ensure that they can comply with the security and safety requirements that will be imposed by this measure.

10.47 pm

**Mr. Harry Barnes** (Derbyshire, North-East): Now we have passed the Second Reading of the Football Spectators Bill, we are in something of a mess, and we should not be tacking on to the end of it considerations about safety. The Bill itself has strong safety implications. We are also awaiting the report of the Taylor inquiry. The Committee, therefore, will be placed in an awkward position when it considers the Bill. We will be facing great difficulties unless the Bill is considered at great length in Committee, so that the Taylor report can be taken into account and its recommendations used to shape the amendments, which could provide for identification cards in special areas or membership schemes in connection with safety provisions.

We have put the cart before the horse with a vengeance. It is horrific that safety matters should be considered as a secondary item and that in some way they must find their way into the identity card proposals that we have just been discussing. It is too big an issue to be dealt with as an

[*Mr. Harry Barnes*]

afterthought. What may be needed in Committee is a fundamental rethink, to which the Taylor report would be relevant. It would help to put some shape into the Bill. Perhaps, as was said on Second Reading, part II will emerge as the part of the Bill that controls the entire operation of the provisions for football clubs.

10.48 pm

**Mr. Brian Wilson** (Cunninghame, North): I want to make one substantive point relating to safety. The bottom line of the legislation is what happens on a wet Wednesday night in the middle of December outside a football ground, when 50,000 people are trying to gain entry, perhaps in the space of little more than one hour. If the Government cannot answer that question, they should abandon the legislation. I believe that such legislation can be put forward only by people who are profoundly ignorant of the real circumstances outside football grounds in such conditions.

Just before Christmas I met a woman at a lunch, who was the No. 10 representative of the working party which came up with these proposals. She had never been to a football match in her life and was proud to admit it. That is the basis of knowledge represented in the entire measure.

I see the same mentality, from largely the same Conservative Members, as that which rammed the poll tax through Parliament. They knew very little of what they were doing, but they were prepared to nod through legislation on the basis of an ideological obsession. The same mentality has been displayed tonight.

In all earnestness, the Secretary of State is playing with human life tonight. If 50,000 people are trying to get into a football ground in the conditions that I have described and the apparatus breaks down, there will be major problems. We have been told that, in such circumstances, the gates would probably be opened. That might suffice, although the example of Hillsborough is not encouraging. What is even more dangerous than such a breakdown is the rumour that that apparatus has broken down. Imagine that tens of thousands of people are trying to get into the ground and are pressing forward to do so when the word goes round, as rumours always spreads in crowds, that the apparatus has broken down. The ensuing pressures could create mayhem at the football ground. The Secretary of State is taking the responsibility for such action by pushing through this nonsense tonight.

To put this instruction before the House at this stage adds insult to injury to Lord Justice Taylor and his investigation. By pushing it through the House, the Secretary of State recognises that safety considerations must be taken into account. If that is so, safety considerations should be incorporated in legislation, but what possible sense or consistency is there in pressing ahead with that legislation while Lord Justice Taylor is still taking evidence? It would be better to wait until he has taken evidence and reported before introducing legislation that reflects his recommendations and takes into account ground safety. Such legislation would be based on public need and good rather than on the ridiculous obsession with an ID card scheme. That scheme will not solve any of the problems, but it will add to the problems experienced in the cities outside the football grounds as well as, arguably, those inside them.

The instruction adds insult to injury and it cures nothing. The Bill is a disaster and the human life put at risk by its implications will be the personal responsibility of the Secretary of State.

10.51 pm

**Mr. Ridley:** The hon. Member for Cunninghame, North (Mr. Wilson) was discussing the contents of the Bill, but I must confine myself to the instruction to the Committee. However, he made one relevant point. We are expressly moving this instruction to the Committee so that any recommendations that Lord Justice Taylor may eventually make can be taken on board and implemented quickly as a result of the Bill. That is the main point of asking the Committee to consider safety.

Under the Safety of Sports Ground Act 1975, my right hon. Friend the Home Secretary has the power to make directives that apply to local authorities, as the licensing authorities for football grounds, concerning changes that might have to be made because of new safety requirements, possibly to do with turnstiles, perimeter fences or, certainly, all-seater stadiums. I was glad to hear what the right hon. Member for Birmingham, Small Heath (Mr. Howell) had to say about such stadiums and we hope to make some progress on that subject. That could be the subject of a directive.

All those powers are already in place under statute and all that we seek to do is to move an amendment in Committee that will give us the power to ensure that we can monitor the performance of local authorities in insisting on common standards in all football grounds. At the same time it will ensure that my right hon. Friend has the power, although I am sure that it will not be necessary, to enforce any decision that he makes about something that is currently absent.

**Mr. Meale** *rose——*

**Mr. Ridley:** I shall give way in a moment.

Apart from the existing powers, all that we seek to do is to ensure that these powers are sufficient to enforce anything that Lord Justice Taylor may require through the present system. There is nothing draconian about them.

The hon. Members for Liverpool, West Derby (Mr. Wareing), for Burnley (Mr. Pike), for Mansfield (Mr. Meale) and for Derbyshire, North-East (Mr. Barnes) seemed to believe that we were talking about the money resolution and were concerned that this resolution made it possible to pay money towards improvements on grounds for safety reasons. We are debating not the money resolution, but the instruction. Neither the money resolution nor the Bill contains powers for the Government to make any financial provision towards the cost of improvements to safety on grounds. This debate cannot cover the points which they made.

*Question put and agreed to.*

*Ordered,*

That it be an Instruction to the Committee on the Football Spectators Bill [*Lords*] that it have power to make provision in the Bill relating to any aspect of the safety of spectators at designated football matches.

## FOOTBALL SPECTATORS BILL *[LORDS]*
## [MONEY]

*Queen's Recommendation having been signified—*
*Resolved,*

That, for the purposes of any Act resulting from the Football Spectators Bill [*Lords*] it is expedient to authorise the payment out of moneys provided by Parliament of any expenses incurred by the Secretary of State in consequence of the Act—[*Mr. Garel-Jones.*]

## ESTIMATES

*Resolved,*

That this House agrees with the Report [20th June] of the Liaison Committee—[*Mr. Garel-Jones.*]

# Colin Wallace (Manslaughter Conviction)

*Motion made, and Question proposed,* That this House do now adjourn.—[*Mr. Garel-Jones.*]

10.55 pm

**Mr. Ken Livingstone** (Brent, East): I rise to raise an issue which has been the subject of a recent book by the journalist Paul Foot: the framing for murder of Colin Wallace, a former employee in the security services of Northern Ireland. In his book, Paul Foot decisively proves that Wallace was framed for a crime which he did not commit in order to ensure that there was no exposure of Wallace's knowledge of the seditious activities of members of the security services.

I am not alone in believing this explanation. Wallace's case has gathered support across the political spectrum, within the media, and from past and serving members of the security services.

The story begins in Northern Ireland in the early 1970s when a separate information unit within the Army information service was set up. Wallace, a central figure in this unit, was required to engage in secret black propaganda disinformation activities. This was a co-ordinated operation to discredit and smear elected politicians using psychological warfare, forgeries, hoax bombings, and the buggery of young boys in the Kincora boys' home for blackmail purposes. Details of these activities were published in "The Pencourt File" and later Peter Wright's "Spycatcher" and David Leigh's "The Wilson Plot".

Wallace's knowledge was political dynamite, and when he began to question these activities, those in power clearly felt that he had to be gagged. He knew too much and had to be discredited. Conviction for murder would clearly achieve that purpose.

Referring to the high-level meetings which took place in the Ministry of Defence, Clive Ponting said in *The Sunday Times,* 17 May:

"By 1983 the case(s) of Wallace (and Holroyd) had been a long-running internal problem and a great effort had gone into contingency action if and when Holroyd got the story into the Press. The task was to try to ensure (their) stories were contained."

On 25 June 1987, on Channel 4 News, Ponting was quoted as follows:

"There was never any suspicion that Wallace was making these stories up or that it was totally unfounded and very easy to rubbish. It was very much a matter that, OK the story was being contained at the moment because he was in jail, but that in a few years' time he would be back out again and could be expected to start making the allegations again and then that would be a serious problem."

That is the background to Wallace's conviction. He did not kill Mr. Jonathan Lewis and an honest investigation would have discovered this. It would have proved beyond doubt that members of the security services compromised senior politicians and perverted our judicial system.

From 1983 to 1987 Wallace was in correspondence with the Home Office and his local Member of Parliament, the hon. Member for Arundel (Mr. Marshall). On three occasions, Wallace petitioned the Home Office over the inadequate Sussex police force investigation and the disturbing conduct of the police during his trial.

When Wallace appealed to the Court of Appeal, one of the three judges that rejected his appeal was Mr. Justice Stocker, who had worked with Wallace on the Widgery inquiry into bloody Sunday. Wallace knew that the

Secretary of State could intervene only if there was new evidence which had not already been aired. Therefore, on 21 August 1983, his petition detailed: the failure to interview and take further statements from key witnesses with new information; new evidence questioning the time of death; new evidence concerning the use of a car important to the case and irregular police conduct in communicating with jurors.

Wallace listed 30 features of the forensic, medical and other evidence that conflicted with the prosecution case. In his petition of 15 March 1983, he submitted conclusive forensic information challenging crucial evidence on blood groupings, alcohol content, the time of death and the injuries inflicted on Lewis. He demonstrated that the police had omitted important information from the statements by the deceased's wife, Mrs. Jane Lewis, and had concealed details that were important to the defence, and suggested other factors that explained the death of Jonathan Lewis. In addition, he asked why police officers had told potential witnesses that he had kidnapped a child when they knew that that was completely untrue.

After Wallace had waited for over a year for a reply to his petitions, on 17 August 1984 the then Parliamentary Under-Secretary of State wrote to Lord Avebury stating that there were no grounds for action to be taken on the conviction. Responding to that, Wallace petitioned the Home Secretary again on 27 August 1984, demolishing point by point the reply to the Under-Secretary. In a letter to the hon. Member for Arundel on 1 September 1984, Wallace claimed:

"the numerous independent people who have examined all the papers relating to my case appear to agree that the evidence presented just does not fit the Prosecution's case and that there are glaring inconsistencies in many parts. It is, therefore, a little odd that the Home Office should show such apparent indifference to the matter—unless there are political reasons for doing so."

Wallace also requested that the Secretary of State arrange a separate investigation of the links between the case and the investigation into the Kincora boys' home. The Minister replied that the Sussex police had found no links between the two; yet no police officer or other official had contacted him or his solicitor to discover what information should have been investigated.

Following the naming of Wallace in the House as a key witness in the Kincora affair, the then chief constable of the Sussex police, Sir George Terry, was appointed with general oversight of the RUC investigation into Kincora. The Sussex officer in charge of the Wallace murder inquiry, Detective Superintendent Harrison, was then appointed to head the new Sussex police team. Harrison was later promoted.

On 18 October 1988 and 16 January this year I wrote to the current chief constable of Sussex, Mr. Birch, about discrepancies and irregularities in the Wallace investigation. They involved press conferences given by police officers during the trial concerning Wallace's activities in Ireland; interviews between journalists and jurors during the trial; statements written by two Sussex officers which contained identical sections; and the failure to follow up important new evidence capable of proving Wallace's innocence.

**Mr. Tam Dalyell** (Linlithgow): Before my hon. Friend leaves the subject of Terry, may I ask whether he recollects the occasion on 22 June when, during Northern Ireland questions, my hon. Friend the Member for Kingston upon Hull, North (Mr. McNamara) said in a supplementary on my main question:

"Only the conclusions of the Terry report were published —not the evidence. When will the public be allowed to judge whether the conclusions follow from the evidence?"

The Minister of State replied to that very civil question with a non sequitur:

"I regard that a serious slur on Sir George Terry."— [*Official Report*, 22 June 1989; Vol. 155, c. 482.]

It was not a slur on Sir George Terry; it was a perfectly civil and proper inquiry.

**Mr. Livingstone:** The problem with so much of the case, as it has developed, has been our inability to get a straight answer out of Government representatives or from the members of the security forces who have been involved in the investigations. We are constantly told that the matter has been investigated in the past, but no one has ever produced any details of those investigations.

Chief Constable Birch claimed that the issues had been raised through a variety of legal and political channels but that no information had come to light in respect of any of the matters raised, and refused to assist me further. In a reply on 24 February this year, I stated that I was unable to find any record of their being raised before. I then asked 10 specific questions about the case. After I had waited for more than three months, the assistant chief constable replied on 9 June:

"the circumstances surrounding Mr. Wallace's conviction had been exhaustively examined on a number of occasions, and I do not propose to carry out any further enquiries into the matter."

Chief Constable Birch's office has refused to answer my questions, because if it does it will be further incriminated in the cover-up. Unusually, the Sussex police consulted the Director of Public Prosecutions before replying to my letter.

The role of the Sussex police can only be described as disgraceful. The evidence suggests collusion between the security services implicated in the Kincora affair and the Sussex police. Responding to a letter written on 22 January 1988 by the Under-Secretary, Wallace claimed that it was full of inaccuracies and misunderstandings, and suggested that the Under-Secretary had not read the relevant correspondence, nor carried out inquiries as he had claimed. In reply to a specific forensic point about the diatoms in Mr. Lewis's body, which challenged police evidence over the location of the death, the Minister said that Mr. Wallace's solicitors would have to prove this. But how? The Metropolitan police forensic laboratory continually refused to make the material available to Wallace's solicitors.

In addition, Wallace asked why photographs of him in an SAS uniform and posing beside captured weapons were made available at the trial. Was it to create the impression that he had connections with paramilitary organisations in Northern Ireland?

It was also incorrect for the Under-Secretary of State to claim that any irregularities in the conduct of police officers had already been considered by the courts. I challenge the Minister to say tonight when these matters were considered by any court. They had been raised in petitions to the Home Secretary as far back as 1983 by Wallace, but not one of those concerns has been dealt with. It was because the Home Office failed to investigate these issues that Wallace wrote to the Police Complaints Authority and the Sussex chief constable. The Sussex police refused to accept the complaints or to enter into any correspondence with him, and the Police Complaints Authority said that it could not deal with the issues because it had arisen before the authority came into being. Wallace was led a merry dance between one official body and another, constantly being fobbed off as he attempted to pursue the case.

More recently, the Minister of State, Northern Ireland Office assured the House, when challenged on the content of the Foot book, that all the allegations concerning the conduct of persons had been "fully investigated" over a long period. What investigation? Who was involved? Who was interviewed? When did it begin and end? These are the same questions I have put to the Prime Minister and other Government Ministers. In reply, the House is constantly assured that all evidence concerning the allegations have been fully investigated and that there is not a shred of evidence to support them.

The Prime Minister, in a letter on 23 June 1988, stated that Mr. Wallace had failed to take the opportunity to contribute to these investigations. How can this be equated with the fact that Wallace sent a detailed dossier to the Prime Minister in November 1984, although not a single person approached him about the contents? On 10 August 1988 I asked the Prime Minister the precise nature of these "careful investigations". Once again I got no reply.

Named individuals have gone on record in the Foot book supporting Wallace's allegations. The book names Mike Taylor, who accompanied Wallace in placing hoax bombs, also Chris Whitehead and Wendy Austin, who substantiate these allegations. Those are three named individuals. Will they now be interviewed? Why have they never been interviewed before?

The Government's determination not to answer these questions proves that there was never any determined effort to establish the truth. Had the Sussex police properly and thoroughly investigated the death of Mr. Lewis they would have established that Wallace had nothing whatever to do with his death.

The Home Office has recently stated that it is in the process of seeing whether Paul Foot's book contains any evidence that might call into question the safety of the conviction of Colin Wallace. From experience, I have no confidence in their ability to do this.

What is the motive for such a cover-up? The answer can only be to protect the reputation of Airey Neave. For four years he was the shadow Cabinet spokesperson on Ireland, adviser to the then Leader of the Opposition on the intelligence services and head of her private office—the filter between her and the rest of the world. In reality he was the second most important person in the Tory party during that period of the Prime Minister's leadership of the Opposition. There was another side to Airey Neave that neither the public nor even most of his parliamentary colleagues knew about. He kept in close touch with the MI5 dissidents who were involved in treasonable activities.

After Colin Wallace left his job in Army headquarters in Northern Ireland, he was approached by Neave. Although he had never met Neave before, Neave obviously knew that Wallace had been an agent of MI5 and that he had been involved in the disinformation and propaganda campaigns against both the IRA and the Labour Government.

**The Minister of State, Home Office (Mr. John Patten):** I do not know how the hon. Member for Linlithgow (Mr. Dalyell) can associate himself with this.

**Mr. Livingstone:** Neave's proposal to Wallace was simple: continue the same work but do it directly for Neave. Wallace agreed and over the following months prepared background papers and speeches for Airey Neave which dealt with the growing strength of the British Left and its alleged links with the IRA and the Soviet Union. Those were taken up in a series of speeches which were widely reported. Proof of Neave's involvement with Wallace lies in the fact that Wallace has retained the correspondence in Airey Neave's handwriting and that is in our possession to produce——*[Interruption.]*

**Mr. Dalyell:** The Minister has said that I should stop my hon. Friend. On the contrary, I have seen the letters. I knew the late Airey Neave very well and these questions must be answered. Part of the trouble is that Ministers have never faced up to the fact that these questions must be answered.

**Mr. Livingstone:** When questioned about this on the Floor of the House, the Leader of the House was unable to explain how Airey Neave would have known that Wallace was working for MI5 or how he had been so well informed about the nature of Wallace's work. The Prime Minister simply refuses to answer those questions.

When all the evidence and witnesses are assembled, the full-scale conspiracy aimed at the heart of our democracy is truly shocking. Taken together, they prove beyond a shadow of a doubt that during the 1970s a substantial and powerful minority of the British establishment was involved in activities which in any other country would be called treason. Airey Neave knew of the treason: how much he knew is a secret that he took to the grave. From his contacts with Peter Wright and Colin Wallace, we can presume that he was most probably quite well aware of what was happening. Neave alone was in a position to change the course of events, and Peter Wright was not. Neave was in a position to choose, promote and organise the election of the present Prime Minister as leader of the Tory party.

Is that the reason why the Prime Minister blocks every attempt to inquire into the Wallace frame-up and the dirty war? Is that why such a vast effort was expended to try to prevent the publication of "Spycatcher"? Is that why all the questions in Parliament are met with evasive and stonewalling answers? There is no reason why the Government should try to cover up scandals that took place during the time of a Labour Government unless it is to protect the reputation of old and faithful supporters.

A full independent inquiry into the Wallace frame-up would inevitably lead to the question of how much did Airey Neave know and what was his role in those events. Once that question is asked, it inevitably leads to another. As I have said, Airey Neave was the Prime Minister's closest friend and adviser. As head of her private office, he decided who saw her, and as her unofficial security adviser he personally introduced her to the world of MI5 and MI6.

Are we to believe that in all that time he never once indicated to her, even in the barest or most general outline, the treason in which he was involved? If the answer to that question is no, then did she not once ever suspect that the man who ran her private office and stood like a praetorian guard at her door was involved in some very unparliamentary activities?

11.12 pm

**The Minister of State, Home Office (Mr. John Patten):** I have the honour to represent the constituency of Oxford, West and Abingdon. Abingdon was the constituency represented by the late Airey Neave whose memory and whose record as an hon. Member of this House we have just heard subjected to the vilest attack imaginable. I have never in the decade during which I have been a Member of this place heard such a monstrous attack, and on a man who died within the precincts of the Palace of Westminster. The hon. Member for Brent, East (Mr. Livingstone), without any evidence at all, accused the late Airey Neave of involvement in treason.

**Mr. Dalyell** *rose*——

**Mr. Livingstone** *rose*——

**Mr. Patten:** Under no circumstances will I give way. I thought that the hon. Member for Linlithgow (Mr. Dalyell) had some grip on reality. I thought that he would have tried to intervene to persuade his hon. Friend the Member for Brent, East to cease his vile attacks on an honourable man who was murdered by IRA terrorists— IRA terrorists whom the hon. Member for Brent, East never condemns and whose activities I suppose he supports. Those are the activities of the hon. Member for Brent, East.

To launch an attack on Airey Neave in that way has lowered the standards of debate in this House to unparalleled depths. Over the years, the hon. Member for Brent, East will reflect, if he ever reflects on anything, on the appalling things that he has said tonight and learn to regret them.

The hon. Member of Linlithgow, whom I have held in great respect over the past 10 years, will also learn to regret joining in the attack on the memory of Airey Neave. I have to call both hon. Members honourable Gentlemen, but representing the people of Abingdon as well as Her Majesty's Government, I have to say that what has been said in the Chamber tonight will be deeply, persistently and permanently resented by those who still mourn a great patriot and a great servant of the House, whose coat of arms remains at the end of the Chamber, illuminated as a permanent memorial to a man who gave his blood so that freedom in this place could be maintained.

The hon. Member for Brent, East is an honourable Gentleman within the terms of the House. I have had to listen to what he has had to say, but in the two years that I have been in the Home Office I have been struck by the extraordinary care with which on every occasion allegations and suggestions of a miscarriage of justice are treated by officials within the Home Office. Those papers go through many hands, and the tradition of the exhaustive and exhausting examination of all allegations goes back to the days when Home Office officials had to prepare the papers that went to the Home Secretary of the day faced with the decision of whether to proceed with the capital sentence. That tradition is still there in the Home Office and the meticulous care that is given to all cases is a remarkable tribute to those who advise Home Office Ministers on such cases.

**Mr. Dalyell** rose——

**Mr. Patten:** I shall not give way to the hon. Gentleman under any circumstances. He has besmirched his reputation by his support for the attack on Airey Neave.

**Mr. Harry Barnes** (Derbyshire, North-East) rose——

**Mr. Patten:** I shall certainly not give way. The hon. Gentleman did not intervene, so he has equally associated himself with that vile attack on Airey Neave. I cannot believe what I have seen and heard tonight in the Chamber.

It is important to begin with the facts of the case. They are that, on 20 March 1981, at Lewes Crown court, Mr. Colin Wallace was convicted of manslaughter after having been indicted for murder, and was sentenced to 10 years' imprisonment. He applied for leave to appeal against conviction and sentence on 12 February 1982. His application was refused by the full Court of Appeal. At the time of the offence, Mr. Wallace was employed by the Arun district council as its information and liaison officer, and his assistant was Jane Lewis, the wife of the victim, Mr. Jonathan Lewis.

The prosecution alleged that Mr. Wallace and Mrs. Lewis had been having an affair while they were working on the preparation for a BBC television programme in the series "It's a Knockout" held at Arundel in July 1980 and that Mr. Lewis had been suspicious of their association.

The prosecution stated that the two men met on 5 August. Mr. Lewis was rendered unconscious, placed in the boot of Mr. Wallace's motor car and dumped in the River Arun, where he died from drowning. In his defence, Mr. Wallace admitted that there was a meeting but maintained that the two men had parted on good terms. The case rested largely on the circumstantial evidence, although it included some scientific evidence on tests on spots and splashes of blood found in the boot of the car on that sad occasion.

Since 1983, a number of representations have been made claiming that Mr. Wallace is innocent of the offence of manslaughter. The House may find it helpful if I outline the position of my right hon. Friend the Secretary of State for the Home Department in relation to cases such as that of Mr. Wallace. Constitutionally, the duty of administering justice in individual cases is placed on the courts. The Home Secretary has certain advisory and statutory powers to intervene in a criminal case, and from time to time he does so. He may use, for example, the powers conferred on him by section 17 of the Criminal Appeal Act 1968 to refer a case tried on indictment to the Court of Appeal. The Home Office, in the person of the Home Secretary, does that from time to time.

My right hon. Friend must take every care to ensure that he does not exercise those powers in any way that might tend to usurp the functions of the court. In practice, that means that he can consider intervening only if significant new evidence or another consideration of substance comes to light that has already been aired in the courts. That is the basic and fundamental principle. It must be new evidence or a new matter of substance that appears to cast doubt on the safety of the conviction.

Under no circumstances can my right hon. Friend the Secretary of State review the decisions of the courts on the basis of facts or arguments that they have already considered, or seek in any way to act as a further court of appeal. That would amount to political interference in the proper work of the courts.

Mr. Wallace's claims of innocence were carefully considered on a number of occasions in the past and found to consist of arguments about matters that have already been considered in the courts. Therefore, they have not been seen by us as evidence of a kind that might justify my right hon. Friend's intervention. In those circumstances no grounds have been found on which to justify any interference with Mr. Wallace's conviction.

In tonight's debate we heard of a book by Mr. Paul Foot entitled "Who Framed Colin Wallace?"—a number of copies of which we have secured within the Home Office.

**Mr. Dalyell:** Has the Minister read it?

**Mr. Patten:** As I explained to the hon. Member for Brent, East on 14 June, we are carefully considering the material contained in Mr. Foot's book. When I say carefully, I mean very carefully. When that process is completed, we shall decide whether any action is called for in respect of Mr. Wallace's conviction. I must emphasise that every case in which a miscarriage of justice is alleged is given the most careful and detailed consideration.

All sorts of allegations have been made about evidence in Mr. Foot's book concerning the Kincora boys' home and the alleged conduct of the security forces. Such allegations are certainly not new. Following Mr. Wallace's conviction for manslaughter in 1981, he turned his attention to the investigation in 1982 by Sir George Terry. Mr. Wallace alleged that both the Army and the intelligence services knew of the homosexual activities at Kincora long before the matter became public and that, rather than reporting those activities, they sought to use that information for their own ends.

All I can do, and all I shall do, is repeat the statement made by ministerial colleagues on numerous occasions, as recently as during Northern Ireland questions on 22 June. All the allegations raised by Mr. Wallace about the conduct of the security forces in Northern Ireland have been fully and carefully investigated not only by the Royal Ulster Constabulary but by Sir George Terry and Judge Hughes, in 1984. No evidence was discovered as a result of those investigations to substantiate any of the allegations of criminal activity.

It must be said also that Mr. Wallace was given every opportunity to give evidence during those inquiries. However, despite assurances being given to him that he would not be prosecuted for any breach of the Official Secrets Act in respect of any information that he communicated concerning those matters, Mr. Wallace refused to do so. And despite every obstacle being removed from his path, he consistently refused to substantiate any part of his allegations. It is very important that the House realises that.

All the points made in tonight's debate will of course be taken into account, because an allegation of a miscarriage of justice is an extremely serious matter, and the Home Office takes such cases extremely seriously. What a tragedy that a debate on a serious issue, an allegation that there has been a miscarriage of justice, should have been so distorted and blackened by a bizarre, absurd and ridiculous attack on the memory—the hon. Member for Brent, East is smirking. He cares nothing about any decent human

[*Mr. Patten*]

values. All he has done, supported by the hon. Member for Linlithgow, is to attack the memory of a brave colleague who gave his life so that freedom in this country and the freedom that we enjoy in this Chamber might continue to be enjoyed in the face of an IRA threat which, as far as I can see, the hon. Member for Brent, East supports. The hon. Gentleman has lowered himself not only in the eyes of this House but also in the eyes of all British people by his dreadful, dreadful allegations during the debate. Nothing will ever take away the smear on his reputation which he has planted there.

All hon Members agree that Airey Neave gave his life for our freedom.

**Mr. Dalyell** *rose*——

**Mr. Patten:** That is something——

*The motion having been made after Ten o'clock, and the debate having continued for half an hour,* MR. DEPUTY SPEAKER *adjourned the House without Question put, pursuant to the Standing Order.*

*Adjourned at twenty-five minutes past Eleven o'clock.*

# House of Commons

*Wednesday 28 June 1989*

*The House met at half-past Two o'clock*

## PRAYERS

[MR. SPEAKER *in the Chair*]

## PRIVATE BUSINESS

LONDON LOCAL AUTHORITIES BILL *[Lords]*
*Order for consideration, as amended, read.*
*To be considered tomorrow.*

QUEEN MARY AND WESTFIELD COLLEGE BILL *[Lords]*
*Order for Second Reading read.*
*To be read a Second time tomorrow.*

# Oral Answers to Questions

## ENVIRONMENT

### Home Insulation

1. **Mr. Buckley:** To ask the Secretary of State for the Environment what advice he is giving to local authorities that wish to help low-income households with draught-proofing, insulation and other means to keep warm in cold homes; and if he will make a statement.

**The Parliamentary Under-Secretary of State for the Environment (Mr. David Trippier):** Advice to local authorities on the availability of Government-funded loft insulation grants under the homes insulation scheme 1987 is contained in Department of the Environment circulars 29/87 and 17/88, and advice on the extent to which energy-related works may be funded by home improvement grants is included in Department of the Environment circulars 21/80 and 16/88.

**Mr. Buckley:** In view of the retraining scheme, which has stopped local authorities using charitable organisations to deal with the problem, will the Minister consider improving the allocation to local authorities under the housing investment programme? In my local authority area pensioners face continuing and increasing problems because of the coldness of their homes.

**Mr. Trippier:** We are certainly prepared to consider a more flexible attitude towards the HIP allocation for public housing. I had the opportunity to mention that in the Standing Committee that considered the Local Government and Housing Bill. We must consider the difference between public housing and private rented housing. We have brought forward a scheme in the legislation currently before Parliament that will cover the points that the hon. Gentleman has made on the Order Paper. It will be much wider ranging and will meet the requirements that he specified.

**Mr. Holt:** Recently I asked my right hon. Friend the Secretary of State for Energy why we do not change the law and prevent builders from equipping new houses with ordinary windows instead of with double glazing or triple glazing. That would save the need for insulation later and a great deal of harassment from cowboy operators. It would make buildings warm and proper as soon as they were built without messing around later. Is it not time that the Government woke up to a technological innovation that has been with us for 50 years?

**Mr. Trippier:** I am certainly prepared to liaise with my right hon. Friend the Secretary of State for Energy, but my principal concern and that of the Department of the Environment is building regulations. Rather than stipulating what everyone should have in their homes, we should preserve freedom of choice.

**Mr. O'Brien:** Is the Minister aware of the reply that the Minister for Local Government gave when the matter was mentioned in a debate on the Local Government and Housing Bill? In his wisdom, the Minister for Local Government advised people to wear an extra jumper to keep warm in the winter months. My hon. Friend the Member for Hemsworth (Mr. Buckley) suggested that additional HIP resources should be provided, covering local authority and private housing, to stop draughts and keep houses warm. Will the Minister take note of that?

**Mr. Trippier:** As the hon. Gentleman knows, my right hon. Friend the Minister for Local Government has a superb sense of humour which emerged many times in Committee. Speaking in my capacity as his vicar here on earth, I can confirm that it was said in precisely that spirit. The Local Government and Housing Bill allows a wider qualification for the receipt of improvement grants, which I seem to remember the Opposition welcoming. We did not divide on the issue in Committee.

### North Sea (Pollution)

2. **Mr. Brandon-Bravo:** To ask the Secretary of State for the Environment what proportion of pollution in the North sea comes from the Rhine.

**The Secretary of State for the Environment (Mr. Nicholas Ridley):** According to the North sea quality status report of November 1987, about 50 per cent. of contaminant inputs from rivers to the North sea are accounted for by the Rhine and the Meuse together.

**Mr. Brandon-Bravo:** The public will be surprised and shocked by what my right hon. Friend has told the House. They will be surprised because Britain is supposed to be the dirty man of Europe, and they will be shocked to learn of the damage done to the environment by German rivers. They are entitled to be angry at the lecturing we get from Europe. On a more positive note, will my right hon. Friend look to the future? Does he agree that it is not just a question of money and how deep our purse is, but of the long period that will be necessary to do what we can on this side of the Channel to improve the environment and our rivers?

**Mr. Ridley:** My hon. Friend is right and I will give him further details. Of the nitrogen entering the North sea, the eastern North sea receives 768,000 tonnes from the continent as opposed to 75,000 tonnes from Britain. The continental contries discharge 14·6 tonnes of mercury into the North sea, as opposed to 1·9 tonnes from Britain. On cadmium, the figures are 31·6 tonnes against 5·8 tonnes. For industrial waste, the figures are 1·2 million tonnes as opposed to 0·2 million tonnes from Britain. For incineration, the figure for Britain is 2 per cent. and for continental countries it is 55 per cent. It is questionable who is the dirty man of the North sea.

**Mr. Malcolm Bruce:** Does the Secretary of State accept that it is invidious to come to the House and pass blame on to the continental countries for the pollution that we are causing? Will he acknowledge that the Irish sea is the most radioactive sea in the world as a result of pollution from this country——

**Mr. Speaker:** Order. This question relates to the Rhine.

**Mr. Ridley:** I never know why Opposition Members want to knock this country and its excellent record. The Irish sea is not the most radioactive sea by any means. It is 80 times more dangerous to live in Cornwall than in the constituency of Copeland because of natural radiation from radon.

**Mr. Devlin:** It would be of great interest to the House and to people in the north-east if my right hon. Friend would give us some idea of how much industrial waste is put into the North sea by Britain and West Germany respectively. How much waste is incinerated at sea? As my right hon. Friend will know, the ash and other contaminants that are not incinerated fall into the sea, thus polluting it.

**Mr. Ridley:** I shall give my hon. Friend the figures on industrial waste. Germany puts in 1·2 million tonnes per annum, which is 60 per cent. of the total. The United Kingdom puts in 0·2 million tonnes, which is 10 per cent. For incineration, the figure for Germany is 58,000 tonnes, whereas for Britain the figure is 2,000 tonnes per annum. I want merely to establish the facts in this matter.

**Mrs. Ann Taylor:** Does the Secretary of State accept that his criticisms of other countries would carry more force if we put our own house in order? What is the cost to the United Kingdom of stopping the pollution of the North sea by sewage sludge, which is expected to be banned by next year's North sea conference, and the cost of stopping the dumping of raw sewage from coastal outflows into the North sea? Should not the Government disclose the costs of those developments, especially as the European Commission is preparing the directive on sewage, or will the Secretary of State suggest that this is another directive on pollution prevention that will be flouted by the Government?

**Mr. Ridley:** I do not know why the hon. Lady continues to knock the United Kingdom in the face of the figures that I have just given—*[Interruption.]* I am not knocking anybody; I am merely giving her the figures, which she does not seem to like very much. I dispute the hon. Lady's view on sewage sludge. Putting sewage sludge into the sea may be the best way to deal with it. No doubt the hon. Lady has seen the recently published report on dioxins, of which one of the main sources is the incineration of sewage sludge. Incineration may be the worst environmental option. The hon. Lady should get her science right; she is ill-founded in science. Furthermore, the hon. Lady does not seem to realise that the Royal Commission on

Environmental Pollution has recommended that long sea outfalls are the best way of dealing with sewage from coastal towns.

## City Grant Initiative

3. **Mr. Heddle:** To ask the Secretary of State for the Environment how many jobs the city grant initiative is currently creating.

**Mr. Trippier:** Projects approved since May last year are expected to provide over 8,500 permanent jobs and about 4,600 temporary construction jobs.

**Mr. Heddle:** Although I welcome those encouraging figures, how many derelict acres have been recovered, how many new homes and factories have been built and, most important, how much private sector investment has been brought in on the back of the city grant initiative?

**Mr. Trippier:** The answer to the latter question is that for every pound of taxpayer's money that we have invested through city grant, we have attracted four times that figure from the private sector, which is most impressive. About 1,200 homes have been built, 230 acres of derelict and rundown land have been brought back into use, and approximately 3·5 million sq ft of industrial and commercial floor space will be created as a result of city grant.

**Mr. O'Brien:** What is the Minister doing to ensure that city grants are not used as a vehicle to generate greater tax dodges, as is happening with property enterprise trusts? When will the Minister make available to the House the details of the city grants that are given to private developers so that we can investigate where the money is going and how it is being spent? The reply that the Minister has given to the hon. Member for Mid-Staffordshire (Mr. Heddle) does nothing to encourage the availability of information or accountability for the money that is spent through city grant. When will the House be given the information about where the money is going?

**Mr. Trippier:** That question is outrageous. I have never heard an hon. Member of any party ever say that city grant has been used for a dubious purpose. It has been widely recognised as a successor to the urban regeneration grant and to the urban development grant, but it is a much more efficient system. I have made clear to local authorities their significant part in this, because I will not accept an application for city grant unless the project has received planning permission. Therefore, it has been widely welcomed by the local authorities. I am only too happy to give the details to the hon. Gentleman and to the House and to answer any specific questions that he might table. We have absolutely nothing to hide and a great deal of which to be proud.

## Association of County Councils

4. **Mr. Oppenheim:** To ask the Secretary of State for the Environment when he last met the Association of County Councils; and what was discussed.

**Mr. Ridley:** On 29 November last, to discuss local authority capital finance and local authority interests in companies.

**Mr. Oppenheim:** Does my right hon. Friend agree that many of the duties carried out by county councils could be devolved down to district authorities and be more effectively carried out by them? Does he further agree that the policy of abolishing county councils would command almost universal support, bearing in mind that even the Opposition have come out in favour of abolition, perhaps in recognition of the damage done to them by the leader of Derbyshire county council?

**Mr. Ridley:** A short month after we regained control of one of the major local authority associations—the Association of County Councils—it would be strange for me to say that we should abolish them. In that context, I congratulate John Chatfield on becoming the Conservative chairman of the Association of County Councils. I invite the Opposition to consider how they think they will ever win an election when they cannot even hold a local authority association of that importance in mid-term. I advise my hon. Friend that we have no plans to abolish the county councils.

**Mr. Pike:** When the Secretary of State discussed capital finance with the county authorities, did he recognise that many counties have a problem meeting the large capital costs of developing new waste disposal sites that meet adequate safety levels? Does he recognise that that is an important problem, and will he ensure that the county authorities receive sufficient allocations in future years to meet that need?

**Mr. Ridley:** I realise the importance of that. As the hon. Gentleman may know, we hope to have early legislation on the counties' responsibilities in relation to waste disposal. We must ensure that the capital allocations follow the policy that we will lay down. If county councils are short of capital, one option is to ensure that the disposal operations are carried out by the private sector and that they are properly regulated by the county councils.

**Mr. Raison:** Is my right hon. Friend aware that many people, including my constituents in Buckinghamshire, believe that they are well served by their county councils? Will he accept my thanks for the fact that he does not at present intend to introduce further changes in the structure of local government?

**Mr. Ridley:** I agree with my right hon. Friend. The Government have in many respects carried out a major reform of local authorities. We should give them a period to adjust to the new circumstances, which they are beginning to do. They are also beginning to perform much more in the interests of their electors and chargepayers-to-be. We should allow them a period to consolidate.

**Mr. Michael:** Is the Secretary of State aware of the county councils' concern for the elderly for whom they are responsible? They are especially worried about the way in which the cold affects old people. Is he aware that the reply of the Under-Secretary of State for the Environment was entirely unsatisfactory, because what is needed to improve insulation is not only more flexibility, but more money? The amount of money available has been slashed because the Government have reduced the number of people in training places. They were doing a tremendous amount of good work in that area.

**Mr. Ridley:** The hon. Gentleman cannot ask a supplementary to question No. 1 on question No. 4, which refers to county councils. We are not responsible for the matters with which my hon. Friend the Under-Secretary of State was dealing.

## Local Government Finance

5. **Mr. Hind:** To ask the Secretary of State for the Environment what representations he has had from tenant groups in favour of a system of local government finance based on capital value rates.

10. **Mr. Burt:** To ask the Secretary of State for the Environment what representations he has had from tenant groups in favour of a system of local government finance based on capital value rates and local income tax.

**Mr. Ridley:** Not surprisingly, I have received hardly any representations in favour of a system of local government finance based on capital value rates or a local income tax.

**Mr. Hind:** Does my right hon. Friend agree that it would be monstrous for tenants to have capital value rates based on the value of their properties? Does he agree that about 20,000 people living in council houses in my constituency would consider it a major injustice if they had to pay rates based on the price of a house in which they have no financial interest?

**Mr. Ridley:** It is impossible to contemplate basing local authority payments, of whatever description, on the capital value of the houses of those who rent them. It is inexplicably unfair. Council property in central London will be up to four or five times more valuable than council property in, say, my hon. Friend's constituency. Why should those council tenants be expected to pay four or five times more for the same services? Our system is based on the cost of the services that are provided, and is infinitely fairer. The community charge in Lancashire, West, if it had been in place last year, would have been £230 in total. But if there had been a system of local income tax, a single person earning £11,000 a year—about the national average wage—would have paid a tax bill of £495.

**Mr. Burt:** Does my right hon. Friend agree that he has received no representations from tenant groups because they have been working out—as they have been in my constituency—how badly stung they would be by a system of double taxation, not only in the extra burden of the ridiculous administration costs needed to run two tax systems, but in their failure to control their local authority spending, because local income tax would make the local authorities less accountable? Is that not why they have not been pestering him with demands to bring in that outrageous system?

**Mr. Ridley:** To be fair, my hon. Friend should admit that they never dreamt that it could happen because they could not contemplate the nightmare of a Labour Government. Just in case they should have that nightmare, I should reinforce what my hon. Friend has said. A system based on capital value rates and local income tax would cost up to four times as much to administer as the present rating system. In my hon. Friend's constituency the local income tax rate alone, if that was the system adopted, would be 6·4p in the pound, which is about as much as my right hon. Friend the Chancellor of the Exchequer has knocked off national income tax.

**Mr. Rooker:** Does the Secretary of State appreciate that he cannot back up with factual background analytical material a single figure that he has quoted from the Dispatch Box today? Will he explain to the House how it is that, up to now, he has defended the idea that, among domestic ratepayers, owner-occupiers should pay a tax on occupancy based on rental values, and that it will continue for business men as a tax on the rental value of the property that they own as a means of collecting local authority rates? The right hon. Gentleman has mixed those two up, and the way in which he has answered the question is disgraceful. Capital value taxes or rental value taxes are a tax on occupancy, not a tax on ownership. It is simply a means of raising the revenue. Does not the Secretary of State appreciate that? The revenue should be raised in a fairer way than through a flat-rate poll tax.

**Mr. Ridley:** I know that it hurts the hon. Gentleman, but I am going to rub his nose in it. The other day he was talking about the iniquities of capital value rents. Why does he support a party that advocates capital value taxes for local authorities based on the capital value of a tenant's house? By advocating that policy rather than the community charge he is selling his constituents down the river.

**Mr. Campbell-Savours:** Why will not the Secretary of State stop misrepresenting Labour policy? Why does he not look at what it says as against what he wants to believe it says? Does he understand that that policy is eminently more sensible than the poll tax? The simple truth is that the right hon. Gentleman is on his backside with the poll tax. The Cabinet is considering paying an extra subsidy to local authorities so that they can reduce the poll tax by £30 per man and woman because the Cabinet knows that it is unpopular. Is that not the truth?

**Mr. Ridley:** I say to the hon. Gentleman in all humility —[*Interruption.*]—that if I have made any false assumption in working out the figures that I have given this afternoon it is because I have written three times to the hon. Member for Copeland (Dr. Cunningham) asking for full details of what the Labour party proposes, but on none of those occasions have I had an acknowledgement, let alone a reply. If the hon. Gentleman would like to write to me to tell me on what assumptions he bases his twin-tax horror regime—his twin-tax nightmare—I will rework the examples and take the hon. Gentleman through them so that he is satisfied about the enormous havoc that his party's policy would wreak on his constituents. I will not hesitate to tell his constituents on every possible occasion the horrors of the policy that he has advocated.

**Mr. Norris:** Does my right hon. Friend agree that it is appalling that the Labour party should make such outrageous suggestions when it is well known that one of the groups most likely to benefit under the community charge arrangements is the single elderly who live on their own? Are not the people who live in that poverty trap among those to whom any party pledged to care for the less fortunate should pay attention?

**Mr. Ridley:** My hon. Friend is right. When opposition for opposition's sake is at an end, our system will be seen to be far fairer to people who deserve help and relief than anything that has come from the Labour party.

**Dr. Cunningham:** Humility is a facet of the right hon. Gentleman's character which he has hitherto kept well disguised. I fear that its sudden emergence is rather late to save his skin. If he checks the records of his correspondence he will find that he has received a reply to his letters. Since he appears to be so concerned about the financial well-being of council house tenants, perhaps he should explain to them and to the House why he and his right hon. Friend the Minister for Local Government plan to increase tenants' rents to make them pay the rents of those who do not pay. Why is he planning to increase council house tenants' rents to make them subsidise the poll tax of those who are much better off? Since, as a scientist, the right hon. Gentleman says that he is always interested in evidence, why does he not consult the records and studies of the Institute for Fiscal Studies and the Rating and Valuation Association, both of which show that a system of capital values will not only be more efficient, but fairer.

**Mr. Ridley:** Openness is not a facet of the hon. Gentleman's character which he has ever failed to disguise. Please may we be told what proportion of new local authority revenue will come from capital revenue rates and how much from local income tax? Does the hon. Gentleman plan resource equalisation and is there any system of rebates? Will he answer any of the questions about the Labour party's system? I shall not desist from exposing the figures implied by his system until he gives the proper data to change the figures, and when he does so I will change the figures, and he will not like them either. —[*Interruption.*]

**Mr. Speaker:** Order. Perhaps we can now settle down to question No. 6.

## Community Charge

6. **Dr. Goodson-Wickes:** To ask the Secretary of State for the Environment if he has any plans to harmonise the design of community charge registration forms.

**The Minister for Local Government (Mr. John Gummer):** My right hon. Friend produced a model form in consultation with local authority associations last autumn. He has no powers to prescribe the form.

**Dr. Goodson-Wickes:** Does my right hon. Friend agree that several local authorities have, by ignoring the guidelines issued by his own Department, fallen foul of the Data Protection Act 1984? Who is expected to pick up the bill for those forms which will now have to be processed manually?

**Mr. Gummer:** My hon. Friend is right in saying that local authorities have the right and the powers to produce their own forms, which is perfectly proper. Local authorities often say that they want more independence and this is one area in which they have it. If they decide to do differently they must also take the advice of the Department which is that they should check whether their forms comply with the Data Protection Act. If they do not, that is their responsibility and they must pay the bill.

**Mr. Nellist:** Is not the Minister deluding himself if he thinks that any cosmetic changes made to the forms will minimise the hatred of the poll tax felt throughout the country? Is it not a fact that despite any design changes which his hon. Friend the Member for Wimbledon (Dr. Goodson-Wickes) may propose, the tax is a savage attack on the living standards of the low paid, young, old and women who are presently living in low-rated properties? Almost 1 million people in Scotland have not paid the poll tax and it is likely that by next April, four or five times that number will not be paying the poll tax in England and Wales, notwithstanding any suggestions from the hon. Member for Wimbledon.

**Mr. Gummer:** No. The facts are that first, the poorest group of the population will pay 25 per cent. less towards the community charge than they presently pay towards the rates, so there will be a cut in the cost of rates or community charge to the poorest. Secondly, the top 10 per cent. of earners will pay 15 times as much towards local authority costs than the bottom 10 per cent. Thirdly, one in four of the population will receive a rebate. Fourthly, 5 million people will, in effect, not pay the community charge because they will receive an 80 per cent. rebate and sufficient to cover a sensible community charge in their area. The policy of the hon. Member for Coventry, South-East (Mr. Nellist), which was originally to support the rates, would hit the poorest much more than the community charge.

**Mr. Dykes:** Would it not be a good idea to have different coloured forms for the three different kinds of tax? We could have a blue form for the personal community charge, a green form for the standard community charge, which is a classic property tax, and a red form for the collective community charge.

**Mr. Gummer:** I prefer to keep the red form for any area that tries to bring in the Labour party's two-tax proposals.

**Mr. Blunkett:** As the Minister has already said this afternoon that poll tax registration officers have already breached the Data Protection Act 1984 with the intrusive and non-statutory questions that they have asked, what advice would he give to people who think that they have a form that includes intrusive questions?

Does the right hon. Gentleman accept that these officers are not responsible to local authorities but are directed under the Act by the Minister? Is it not time that the Government accepted responsibility for the chaos in registration?

**Mr. Gummer:** I know that the hon. Gentleman wants to create chaos out of a system that is working rather well. Labour authorities are saying how well it is working, in the sense that they are getting the forms back. I was in Ipswich —a Labour-controlled authority—only last week. The council there compliments itself on the degree to which it is obtaining results—*[Interruption.]* The hon. Gentleman can take it from me—*[Interruption.]*

**Mr. Speaker:** Order. This all very entertaining but it takes up a great deal of time. We are making very slow progress.

**Mr. Gummer:** Anyone who is asked a question for which there is no statutory backing need not respond to it and if he does not want to answer it he should not.

## Global Warming

7. **Mr. Wallace:** To ask the Secretary of State for the Environment if he will make a statement on the effects of global warming.

**Mr. Ridley:** I hope that global warming will reduce Chamber warming.

The potential impacts of global warming and climate change are currently being reviewed and assessed by the intergovernmental panel on climate change, established under the United Nations environment programme and the World Meteorological Organisation last November. The panel will report in the autumn of 1990.

**Mr. Wallace:** I am sure the Secretary of State will agree that one of the important factors contributing to global warming is the destruction of many tropical rain forests. Is his Department encouraging and helping local authorities —many of them controlled by my party—that are trying to adopt purchasing policies to find alternatives to tropical hardwoods from non-sustainable sources?

**Mr. Ridley:** We must take this problem extremely seriously, and internationally. That is why we have proposed in the United Nations and in the United Nations environment programme general council that there should be a global framework convention on climate change, under which various protocols can be negotiated, including one on tropical rain forests. The right way forward is to involve all the nations of the world; our initiative in this field has been taken very seriously and has received a great deal of support. We cannot do this at only the national level, let alone at the local authority level.

**Mr. Squire:** I support what my right hon. Friend says about the inevitable international impact of this issue, but does he agree that the problem of carbon dioxide, which is not covered by the steps that have already been taken to control power station emissions, and which will be exacerbated by the catalyst solution for cars, remains one of the single most pressing problems?

**Mr. Ridley:** My hon. Friend is right. One of the worries is that the drive to improve nitrogen oxide emissions from motor vehicles and to reduce sulphur dioxide emissions from coal-fired power stations has the result of increased fuel consumption and hence increased emissions of carbon dioxide. I am afraid that carbon dioxide, which is the most important greenhouse gas, has become the Cinderella of environmental policies, and we must watch out and make sure that our policies have the effect of reducing, not increasing, carbon dioxide.

**Mr. Allan Roberts:** Does the Minister agree that only two thirds of the 50 per cent. of the $CO_2$ that goes into the environment comes from burning fossil fuel and that methane, chlorofluorocarbons, nitrous oxide and surface ozone are also significant contributory factors? Will he admit that the experts who attended the Prime Minister's special seminar on the greenhouse effect pointed out that a 15 per cent. reduction in carbon dioxide emissions, which a change of emphasis to nuclear power stations would produce, is three times less than the reduction that would take place from the major energy conservation initiatives that the Government not only refuse to contemplate but are cutting back on?

**Mr. Ridley:** The hon. Gentleman says that only two thirds of carbon dioxide comes from burning fossil fuels. Therefore, one would have thought that that would be the area where one would start to seek to make reductions. Secondly, since I was at the Prime Minister's seminar and he was not, may I tell him that his account of it is far from accurate.

## Unleaded Petrol

8. **Mr. Jacques Arnold:** To ask the Secretary of State for the Environment what percentage of garages now stock unleaded petrol.

**The Parliamentary Under-Secretary of State for the Environment (Mrs. Virginia Bottomley):** It is estimated that well over 50 per cent. of petrol stations are now selling the fuel, and that two out of three refuellings take place at a petrol station where unleaded is available.

**Mr. Arnold:** Does that not show the effect that the Government's green policies are having both on environmental pollution and on public health? Can my hon. Friend tell us what further progress has been made as a result of the Budget provisions?

**Mrs. Bottomley:** Certainly the uptake of unleaded petrol is a clear indication of action, not words, in regard to environmental protection. The Chancellor increased the differential in the Budget. It is now the second highest in the European Community. Since then the uptake of unleaded petrol has risen threefold. It was 6·4 per cent. in March and it is now approaching 20 per cent. This is an indication of the popularity of environmental policies and the success of the Chancellor's differential.

**Mrs. Maureen Hicks:** Is my hon. Friend aware that in addition to the lead that Wolverhampton has taken with its recent highly successful lead-free campaign, the town can now proudly boast that 98 per cent. of its garages stock unleaded petrol?

**Mrs. Bottomley:** I think that the entire House would like to pay tribute to the success of Wolverhampton's initiative. In one day alone mechanics managed to adjust the magnificent total of 1,126 motor vehicles. As a result it is now able to enter the "Guinness Book of Records". I hope that others will follow Wolverhampton's example.

**Dr. Kim Howells:** Does the Minister agree that the important measurement is the percentage of unleaded petrol that is used in cars and not necessarily what is stocked in garages? Can she tell the House how that percentage compares with West Germany's progress?

**Mrs. Bottomley:** West Germany is already making greater progress than we are in the uptake of unleaded petrol. We have made rapid and fast progress. We want others who have cars that can be adjusted to get that done. Several million cars that could use unleaded petrol still need adjustment. It is an area where helping the wallet also helps the environment. The Government are committed to take all possible opportunities to promote and encourage the uptake of unleaded petrol. We hope that environment-alists will take steps that are already within their power and use unleaded petrol which protects the environment.

**Mr. Adley:** Welcome though the progress in unleaded petrol is, does my hon. Friend agree that if we are seriously concerned to deal with the major environmental problem called the internal combustion engine, we should look at the Californian example? Will my hon. Friend, therefore, please obtain from the state government of California full details of their proposal to eliminate completely the internal combustion engine by the early years of the next century? Will she put those details in the Library and give the Government of which she is a member a target of achieving the same objective here?

**Mrs. Bottomley:** Perhaps I should ask my right hon. Friend the Secretary of State whether I can go on a ministerial visit to California to look at the arrangements there. I shall look into this matter further. Already, people can avoid churning the equivalent of 300 double-decker bus loads of lead into the environment every year. Lead is a cumulative poison, which is potentially damaging to children's health and development, and it is time that people made sure that they were not unnecessarily polluting the environment.

## Rent and Rate Arrears

9. **Mr. Simon Hughes:** To ask the Secretary of State for the Environment if he will make a statement on the level of rent and rate arrears in London.

**Mr. Gummer:** At 1 April 1988, the rent and rate arrears of London authorities amounted to £350 million—just under half the total for England. Arrears ranged from less than 5 per cent. of the annual rent and rates due for such authorities as Hillingdon and Barking and Dagenham, to some 20 per cent. or more for Brent, Lambeth and Southwark. High arrears can be attributed only to the boroughs' poor management. It is for authorities to see that rent and rates are collected, but the measures that I announced last Monday should encourage greater financial discipline.

**Mr. Hughes:** Does the Minister recognise, as many authorities including Tory authorities do, that the massive increases in rent arrears result, substantially, from the Government's £650 million housing benefit cuts last year? Does the Minister accept that, as the Government's policy unfolds next year, with the poll tax and rent increases, the tenants who pay their rents regularly will be picking up the tab for the barrage of Government policies that, increasingly, penalise the poor?

**Mr. Gummer:** That cannot possibly be true, because if it were, the rent and rate arrears in the Labour-run authorities of Hillingdon, Dagenham and Barking would be similar to those in Labour-run Brent, Lambeth and Southwark, but they are not. Arrears in Brent are bad because, until recently, it did not even have a list of its tenants and the keys to its council houses were being sold in Nigeria. It is not surprising that it cannot collect the rents.

**Mr. Bowis:** Are not the biggest lists for rent arrears, rate arrears and squatted properties in London in the Labour-run boroughs? Are not such boroughs cheating on the homeless and on those who desperately need repairs to their homes? Is it not high time for those who, loyally and legally, pay their rates and rents to have some recompense from such dissolute councils?

**Mr. Gummer:** My hon. Friend is right. If rents are not collected, other people have to pay for them, whether they are the ratepayers or other tenants. In those authorities that already do not subsidise their rent from ratepayers, the other tenants have already been contributing. Some boroughs do not collect the rents because their system of rent collection is extremely inefficient, and they have no intention of collecting it. When a borough has on its arrears committee a councillor who is herself in considerable arrears, it is not surprising that people do not pay their rents.

**Dr. Cunningham:** I believe that the Minister is aware that the leaders of Brent borough council in particular recognise the force of what he is saying and have made it clear to him that they are making strenuous new efforts to resolve the problems of rent arrears, as they should be doing. Will the Minister reflect again on the answer that he has just given to the hon. Member for Battersea (Mr. Bowis), who was asking for protection for tenants who pay their rents? Is the hon. Gentleman aware, as the Minister is because he announced it, that the Government are planning additionally to place burdens on those tenants by making them pay for that shortfall?

**Mr. Gummer:** The hon. Gentleman should look carefully at the programme that was announced by Brent. I have done some work on the more detailed programme produced by the Labour-controlled London borough of Southwark. If it proceeds with its new tougher policy, it should have started before the Spanish Armada had arrived if it wanted to collect its rent arrears by today. The borough will collect only a tiny proportion—£78,000 a year—of rent arrears of £37 million.

**Mrs. Ann Taylor:** Treat this seriously.

**Mr. Gummer:** It is all right for the hon. Lady, but the people who pay for those rent arrears are the tenants and the ratepayers who pay their rents and rates. Why should the tenants of Barking and Dagenham pay for the inefficency of the Labour council in Southwark? Why should the tenants of Hillingdon pay for the inefficiency of the Labour party in Brent? We must have an efficient system, and if Brent collected its rents the paying tenants would not have to suffer. Because of the Opposition's rottweiler tendency, they are determined not to listen to the facts—*[Interruption.]*

**Mr. Speaker:** Order. It is very unseemly to make animal noises.

**Mr. Gummer:** Because the Opposition do not want to hear the facts—which are that the tenants and the ratepayers who pay their rent and rates have to carry the cost of those who do not—the rottweiler tendency wins again.

## Sports Council

11. **Mr. Menzies Campbell:** To ask the Secretary of State for the Environment when he last met the chairman of the Sports Council; and what matters were discussed.

**The Parliamentary Under-Secretary of State for the Environment (Mr. Colin Moynihan):** I have met the chairman of the Sports Council on a number of informal occasions since his appointment on 20 May. My first formal meeting with him will be on 3 July when we will discuss the council's corporate plan.

**Mr. Campbell:** During the Minister's meetings with the chairman of the Sports Council, did he discuss the potential damage to the Commonwealth games next year if rugby players from the United Kingdom accept invitations to play in centenary matches in South Africa? In particular, did he discuss with Mr. Yarranton the potential conflict between his two positions as chairman of the Sports Council and vice-chairman of the Rugby Football Union?

Is the Minister satisfied that all the members of the Sports Council support the Gleneagles agreement, which is the policy of Her Majesty's Government and which, with a few erratic exceptions, is supported by all proper-minded Members of this House?

**Mr. Moynihan:** If the hon. and learned Gentleman had listened to my answer, he would have heard me say that I have yet to meet the new chairman of the Sports Council formally. As the hon. and learned Gentleman knows, the chairman's views on apartheid are quite clear. In a press statement on 12 June he said:

"I abhor the apartheid system of South Africa as I do all forms of racialism. As chairman of the Sports Council I shall do my utmost to support the Gleneagles agreement."

**Mr. Redwood:** Does my hon. Friend agree that many users of watersports facilities on rivers and lakes would not want consent levels for sewage works to be relaxed because that might pollute rivers unnecessarily? Has he received any representations from the Sports Council on that matter?

**Mr. Moynihan:** I have indeed discussed that subject with the Sports Council, although not yet with the new chairman. One point that he has welcomed in the water privatisation measures is the fact that we are going further than we have ever gone before to protect and enhance the use of our water courses for sport and recreation. I am sure that my hon. Friend will warmly welcome that.

**Mr. Denis Howell:** Does the Minister appreciate that press statements or letters on the very important subject of apartheid and the involvement of British sportsmen in South African sport are inadequate? Is he aware that the Gleneagles agreement calls upon him and Government Ministers, as a duty, urgently to combat those evils

"by taking every practical step to discourage contact or competition"?

What urgent and practical steps has the hon. Gentleman taken and how does he intend to protect not only the Commonwealth games in Auckland but the world student games in Sheffield and the Manchester Olympic bid, all of which are at great risk because of the Government's inactivity on such a desperately important subject?

**Mr. Moynihan:** I wrote to the president of the Rugby Football Union on 17 May drawing attention to the Government's commitment to the Gleneagles agreement and the implications that such a tour may have for other sports. I strongly discouraged the passing on of invitations to players to compete in South Africa. I have also spoken to the RFU and colleagues in Scotland and Wales have written in similar terms to their respective unions. The

Government are fully committed to the Gleneagles agreement, but in a free society such as ours their role is limited to giving advice and seeking to persuade.

## Ivory

12. **Mr. Andy Stewart** : To ask the Secretary of State for the Environment what measures were agreed at the recent meeting of European Community Environment Ministers to ban trade in ivory.

**Mrs. Virginia Bottomley:** The Environment Council strongly supported the United Kingdom Government's proposal for an immediate ban on the import into the Community of raw and worked ivory.

**Mr. Stewart:** I thank my hon. Friend for that positive result. Is she aware that the British people are delighted by the Government's strong lead in trying to stamp out that evil trade? One could say that we are in a position to blow our trumpet. What success has my hon. Friend had in persuading other countries to follow our example?

**Mrs. Bottomley:** I thank my hon. Friend for his tribute. My noble Friend the Minister for Housing, Environment and Countryside visited Kenya and was most successful with the initiative taken at the Environment Council. All members of the Community now ban raw and worked ivory, Hong Kong has taken further steps to ban imports, Japan is strengthening its controls, and the United Arab Emirates have announced their intention to become parties once again to the CITES agreement.

**Mr. Hardy:** Is the Minister aware that elephant tusks from east Africa tend to be shaped differently from those originating in central and southern Africa, yet photographs of tusks imported into Britain and Europe over the past few months supposedly from central and southern Africa clearly originated from the Kenya national parks and are a result of the serious poaching there? In view of the corrupt, irresponsible and illegal nature of such activities in east Africa, will the Minister ensure not only that a ban is enforced by Britain and Europe but that there is a great deal more international effort to stop that particularly disgraceful trade?

**Mrs. Bottomley:** Very great care was taken to control such legitimate trade as was allowed through the ivory trade monitoring unit at CITES, which has worked closely with our Customs and with our managing agents in the countries concerned. As a result of concern about the species, we decided that the African elephant should be included in appendix I of CITES, which will outlaw all ivory trade.

**Mr. Nicholas Winterton:** While warmly welcoming my hon. Friend's reply and the very fine example set by the United Kingdom, is she not afraid that by banning ivory we could drive that evil trade underground? Is she aware that South Africa and Namibia have found ways of cutting out illegal poaching, though both countries are so openly criticised by Opposition Members?

**Mrs. Bottomley:** I am well aware of the steps taken by the countries that my hon. Friend mentions to control the ivory trade. Our primary concern must be the conservation of the species, and we have decided that the time is right

for the African elephant to be included in appendix I of CITES together with the Indian elephant, and to outlaw trade in its ivory.

## Football Identity Cards

14. **Mr. Cunliffe:** To ask the Secretary of State for the Environment what discussions he has had with fellow European Ministers of Sport on producing a common European football identity card.

**Mr. Moynihan:** None. I gave a report on developments on a national membership scheme for England and Wales at the sixth conference of European Ministers with responsibility for sport in Reykjavik from 30 May to 1 June during the discussion on spectator violence. European Governments are kept informed about the scheme through our membership of the Council of Europe standing committee on spectator violence.

**Mr. Cunliffe:** Is it not a fact that European Ministers laughed out of court the Minister for Sport's proposal for a common European football identity card, which was also condemned by the European Football Association? It is their belief and ours that it would militate against genuine football supporters as against the hooligan element. Can the Minister explain why Britain is once again out of step with Europe?

**Mr. Moynihan:** The answer to all the hon. Gentleman's questions is no. At Reykjavik European Ministers warmly supported our determination to stamp out football hooliganism and the package of measures, including the Football Spectators Bill, that we are putting in place. That may be the reason why Holland and Spain are considering their own membership schemes—which will, rightly, be drawn up as appropriate for the problems that those countries face.

**Mr. Latham:** Will my hon. Friend waste no more time on the European dimension? It will be difficult enough for us to operate the scheme here without worrying about what they do in Italy.

**Mr Moynihan:** As my hon. Friend will know, I am merely answering the question tabled for my response, and that covers Europe. Suffice it to say that I disagree with my hon. Friend about the practicality of the scheme in this country. The strong commitment of the Government and the vote last night has shown not only that we shall see the scheme in place, but that it will prove a very important measure in ending the problems of violence associated with football in this country.

## Calls Development Area, Leeds

15. **Mr. Fatchett:** To ask the Secretary of State for the Environment what representations he has received over the decision by the Leeds development corporation to use its compulsory purchase powers to acquire riverside land in the Calls development area in Leeds; and if he will make a statement.

**Mr. Trippier:** None, Sir, other than those from the hon. Gentleman.

**Mr. Fatchett:** Does the Minister recognise that the use of compulsory powers by Leeds development corporation has caused considerable consternation among local businesses? When will this Government-appointed body —made up entirely of place men responsible to the Secretary of State—take account of the wishes of local business, and when will it recognise that its chairman has now completely lost the confidence of local business and will soon lose that of the local chamber of commerce as well?

**Mr. Trippier:** I entirely reject the hon. Gentleman's final comment. As for his substantive question, no compulsory purchase order has been laid for the area that he mentions. The Leeds development corporation will proceed in exactly the same way as local councils which prefer to negotiate without the use of the CPO.

I find it amazing that the hon. Gentleman loses no opportunity to attack the Leeds development corporation simply because it was the present Government's idea. The truth is that the corporation is doing a tremendous amount of good for Leeds, and I think that the hon. Gentleman should join with it to try to achieve its objectives.

# Points of Order

3.31 pm

**Sir Bernard Braine** (Castle Point): On a point of order, Mr. Speaker. Although they have not yet been printed in *Hansard,* I wonder whether your attention has been drawn to remarks made last night by the hon. Member for Brent, East (Mr. Livingstone) about our late colleague Mr. Airey Neave. In the course of his speech, the hon. Gentleman asserted that Mr. Neave had been involved in treason.

You will know, Mr. Speaker, that Mr. Neave was more than a personal friend to those of us who were old enough to serve in the second world war and then together in this House. You will also know that outside this place he was one of the most admired and courageous of all our war heroes. The hon. Member's remarks, which are now widely current, have deeply wounded not only Conservative Members, but many Opposition Members who knew Mr. Neave's qualities.

My question to you, Sir, is twofold. First, was it in order for the hon. Gentleman to make such an infamous charge, and, if not, what action can you take? Secondly, if by some strange quirk it was in order for the hon. Gentleman to use the privilege of this place to make such an assertion, in the light of the hurt that it will cause not merely to hon. Members but to the family of our late colleague—whose arms are here to remind us of his significance to our country in its hour of danger—have you received any indication from the Leader of the Opposition, or from anyone speaking on his behalf, that his attention has been drawn to the matter and that he has reprimanded the hon. Gentleman and repudiates what he has said?

**Mr. Speaker:** The matter has been drawn to my attention. Of course, I have not had an opportunity, nor has the House, of reading it in *Hansard*. What was said was in order in terms of free speech in this place, but I must say to the whole House that successive Committees of Privileges and Procedure have drawn attention to the obligation on hon. Members to use their freedom of speech with responsibility. The Chair makes no comment on individual speeches that are in breach of no rule of the House, but I trust that there will be general support throughout the House for the proposition that hon. Members should avoid expressing themselves in ways that are bound to cause deep offence.

**Mr. Harry Barnes** (Derbyshire, North-East): Further to the point of order, Mr. Speaker. I was one of six hon. Members who were in the House when the statement was made by my hon. Friend the Member for Brent, East (Mr. Livingstone). I am bound to wonder whether my hon. Friend was informed that this point of order would be raised so that he could have been in the Chamber on this occasion.

**Mr. Speaker:** I am not aware of that.

**Mr. Ian Gow** (Eastbourne): Further to the point of order, Mr. Speaker. The late Mr. Airey Neave had been mentioned in dispatches for gallantry and had been awarded the military OBE, the Military Cross and the Distinguished Service Order, yet last evening it was alleged in the House that he was involved in treason.

There are few people of whom it can be said that he could never do anything dishonourable, but one of those few of whom it could be said is Airey Neave. He served his country in war with exemplary courage, and this House in peace with exemplary fidelity. Airey Neave is not able to be here to defend himself, but his friends wish to defend him.

Is it in order, Mr. Speaker, to attack a former Member of the House who cannot defend himself, and would it be in order for you to give a ruling that assaults on the dead involving a charge of treason should in future be out of order?

**Several Hon. Members** *rose*——

**Mr. Speaker:** Order. I will take together all the points of order on this subject.

**Sir Hector Monro** (Dumfries): On a point of order, Mr. Speaker. I wish to be associated with the remarks of my hon. Friends who have spoken on behalf of Airey Neave. I have read, as I am sure many other hon. Members have, the reports in the Library of last night's Adjournment debate, and I confirm that the wording of what was said was disgraceful. On no fewer than three occasions was Airey Neave accused of treason.

I do not believe that we can leave matters as they are and simply say that what was said was in order and that nothing more can be done about it. I suggest that we must call on the shadow Leader of the House or the Leader of the Opposition to come to the House and apologise on behalf of the hon. Member for Brent, East (Mr. Livingstone), who behaved in a quite disgraceful way. Such lack of courtesy should not be accepted by the House.

**Mr. Dennis Skinner** (Bolsover): On a point of order, Mr. Speaker. If what the hon. Member for Dumfries (Sir H. Monro) has said were to be the case, you might decide that it would be a good idea for an inquiry to be held into the facts surrounding the allegations that were made by my hon. Friend the Member for Brent, East (Mr. Livingstone) last night.

While you are about it, Mr. Speaker, it might be a good idea for that inquiry to call on the Minister of State, Foreign and Commonwealth Office to substantiate the allegations that he made against all Labour Members recently about their connections with the KGB. If it is good enough for an issue such as that to be raised, let us have a wholesale inquiry into all the allegations that are made by the Tories.

**Mr. Nicholas Soames** (Crawley): On a point of order, Mr. Speaker. I support what was said by my hon. Friend the Member for Dumfries (Sir H. Monro). Surely it cannot be proper for the holder of two of the greatest awards for gallantry in the field, who was murdered within the precincts of the House by the INLA and who was a much loved and respected Member of the House to be slandered in such a grotesque and contemptible manner. If there is no provision for you to make a ruling, Mr. Speaker, let the House decide that such allegations should never be made about an hon. Member ever again.

**Mr. Ron Brown** (Edinburgh, Leith): Further to the point of order, Mr. Speaker. I did not know Airey Neave —perhaps it is better that way—so I will not speak ill of the dead. Whether or not he was involved with the security forces I cannot tell. However, if we talk about the living and about this House, it is interesting to note that at no time, or certainly rarely, does it rise to the occasion and protect Socialist Members who are on the Left and who speak about certain issues, when repeatedly we are libelled and slandered. That has been going on for some time.

As my good comrade, if I may call him that, the hon. Member for Bolsover (Mr. Skinner) has said, a certain individual in the south of England has made allegations that have been used by the Foreign Office against myself and others. If anyone ought to be investigated, that person ought to be investigated. The Foreign Office and the Government should be investigated, too, because they are totally corrupt.

**Mr. Harry Ewing** (Falkirk, East): I am not in favour of attacks on the dead, but I wish to make my position perfectly clear. It was a great pity that the Father of the House did not stop his point of order before he reached the stage where he turned it into a political issue. The key point is whether it was an insult to the late Airey Neave to say what my hon. Friend the Member for Brent, East (Mr. Livingstone) said about him during the Adjournment debate last night. Adjournment debates are the responsibility of the individual Member who is allocated half an hour at the end of the day's proceedings. It had nothing whatever to do with any political party in the House. *[Interruption.]* It is all right for Conservative Members to snigger and laugh. The hon. Member for Stirling (Mr. Forsyth) is standing there sniggering.

However, I say to them, particularly to the Father of the House and the hon. Member for Dumfries (Sir H. Monro), that if they intend to turn this into the kind of political issue that they are in danger of turning it into they are just as guilty—*[Interruption.]*

**Mr. Speaker:** Order.

**Mr. Ewing:** I want this point to be heard, Mr. Speaker. They are just as guilty of besmirching the memory of Airey Neave as any other hon. Member who attacks him, now that he is no longer with us.

**Several Hon. Members** rose——

**Mr. Speaker:** Order. I do not think that we can pursue the matter any further. We have freedom of speech in this place, as all hon. Members know. Every right hon. and hon. Member must take responsibility for what he says here. What was said last night I personally deprecate, naturally, since I also knew Airey Neave. I think that the whole House accepts that he was a patriot in the true sense of the word. However, what was said by the hon. Member concerned was his responsibility and it was in breach of no rule of the House.

**Mr. Bill Walker** (Tayside, North): Further to that point of order, Mr. Speaker.

**Mr. Speaker:** We cannot pursue the matter, but go on.

**Mr. Walker:** I am sorry if you feel, Mr. Speaker, that in some way I am taking advantage of the House, but those of us who have service backgrounds are conscious of the fact that some individuals who served their country during the second world war did so under appalling conditions, particularly those in prison camps. There are generations living today who do not understand the emotions and the feelings of those who were involved in those circumstances and situations. That is why it is important that hon. Members who make speeches about

individuals who lived through those circumstances should bear in mind the record of the individual, as against the allegations.

**Mr. Richard Holt** (Langbaurgh): On a point of order, Mr. Speaker, of which I have already given you notice. You will recall that during yesterday's debate on the Football Spectators Bills the hon. Member for Copeland (Dr. Cunningham) tried to besmirch the good name of racing by saying that there were 600 arrests at Ascot. Subsequently, I ascertained from the assistant chief constable of Thames Valley that in fact there were only 32 arrests. The hon. Gentleman, who is here to defend him-self——

**Mr. Speaker:** Order. We cannot return to that debate. Please raise the point of order with me.

**Mr. Holt:** The hon. Gentleman, who is here to defend himself, then said that he did not say last week; he said last year. I then checked on the number of arrests last year. The figure was not 600 then, either; it was a similar figure to that for last week.

I did not wish to raise the matter today, because I should have liked to have the opportunity to ascertain exactly what the hon. Member for Copeland said in the debate late last night. I am told by *Hansard* that I am not allowed to look at the speech of any other hon. Member until it has been printed, in the same way as you, Mr. Speaker, said that you cannot see what the hon. Member for Brent, East (Mr. Livingstone) said until it has been printed. However, the hon. Member for Copeland is able to check what he said before it is printed. Last night I was told by *Hansard* that if the hon. Gentleman had wanted to check what he had said and correct the false information that he, as a Front-Bench spokesman in a major debate had given to the House, he could have cleared his name and that of horse racing.

**Mr. John Cunningham** (Copeland) rose——

**Mr. Speaker:** Order. I had better have the first bite.

The hon. Member for Langbaurgh (Mr. Holt) did me the courtesy of informing me that he would raise this matter. Page 264 of "Erskine May" states:

"It is not in order for a Member to obtain or to quote during a current sitting the record made for the Official Report of the remarks of any other Member."

That is a long-standing rule. If the hon. Gentleman wishes to have it changed, he must draw it to the attention of the Procedure Committee.

**Dr. Cunningham:** Further to that point of order, Mr. Speaker. If the hon. Member for Langbaurgh (Mr. Holt) were not so unpleasant, boorish and graceless in his approach to debates, the matter could have been settled quite simply yesterday evening and we need not have detained the House today. The hon. Gentleman could have had the text of my speech, which was lying on the Table of the House.

I used figures that were used in the Second Reading debate in the House of Lords on 2 February 1989. Those figures were obtained by my noble Friend Lord Graham of Edmonton. He obtained them for Ascot week last year. They relate to all arrests in and around the vicinity of Ascot and the racecourse, including public transport to and from the course. The figures were provided by the local police.

**Mr. Holt:** Further to that point of order——

**Mr. Speaker:** Order. I am not taking any further points of order. We cannot have a continuation of last night's debate.

## STATUTORY INSTRUMENTS, &c.

**Mr. Speaker:** With permission, I shall put together the two motions on statutory instruments.

*Ordered,*

That the draft Solicitors (Amendment) (Northern Ireland) Order 1989 be referred to a Standing Committee on Statutory Instruments, &c.

That the draft Limitation (Northern Ireland) Order 1989 be referred to a Standing Committee on Statutory Instruments, &c.—*[Mr. Chapman.]*

# Postal Services (Reform)

3.47 pm

**Mr. Anthony Coombs** (Wyre Forest): I beg to move,

That leave be given to bring in a Bill to empower organisations other than the Royal Mail to provide a postal service; and for connected purposes.

The Bill seeks to abolish the Post Office's exclusive privileges to carry letters around the United Kingdom under section 66 of the British Telecommunications Act 1981, to promote competition, encouraging incentive and new services to improve efficiency and thus to improve standards of services to customers of the Royal Mail and existing costs.

The Bill follows two Bills proposed by my hon. Friends the Members for Battersea (Mr. Bowis) and for Billericay (Mrs. Gorman) in January and February this year and an Adjournment debate on the subject last month. The hon. Member for Falkirk, East (Mr. Ewing) called the matter a "hardy annual". It is now becoming a triannual and reflects the urgency felt in the House and by the public at large about the declining standards of service in the Post Office and the urgent action required to remedy it.

The Royal Mail service will soon be a 21st-century service with a 17th-century pedigree. In 1657, Cromwell put the existing monopoly on a statutory basis, not for reasons of efficiency or economies of scale, but because of the use of the post for

"many and wicked designs which have been and are daily contrived against the peace and welfare of the Commonwealth."

That paranoia about security and absence of objective thinking seems to have been extended down the ages to many who unthinkingly oppose the abolition of the monopoly to this day.

However, it does not take much objectivity to identify the present concern about standards. The Post Office itself does so in its annual reports and accounts. In 1979, it identified "unsatisfactory postal services". In 1986, it said:

"Quality of services falls short of target."

In 1987, it said:

"Continuing traffic growth and considerable industrial unrest made it difficult to meet the quality of service targets."

In 1988 it talked of 213 unofficial disputes, 63,500 working days lost and no fewer than 126 million letters being delayed. In its report this year, the Post Office will no doubt reveal that last year's postal strike caused the loss of 1·2 million working days and that delivery standards declined.

Further afield, evidence comes from the London School of Economics, which said:

"The quality of services is probably no better, and may be worse, than in 1971".

In May this year, the Post Office Users National Council talked about its dismay about the delay in introducing improvements designed as part of last year's tariff package and it declared itself far from satisfied with the quality of service figures resulting from the new basis of measurement, which was a realistic door-to-door basis of measurement. Colleagues no doubt have anecdotal evidence from their constituencies which would amplify the problems many times over.

The Post Office argues that its volumes increased by 30 per cent. over five years, that it has created 18,000 jobs and that it will invest about £620 million over the next three years. However, one might ask why, if volumes are increasing so much and if economies of scale are so important, there are no improvements in service. Equally, the Post Office might argue that a monopoly guarantees through a national service a quality of service that is expected by the general public. In the past five years, there have been many interruptions. Last year, one sixth of all days lost through strikes and stoppages were in the Post Office. That contradicts the Post Office assertions. The Post Office might argue that a monopoly is necessary to protect services in rural areas, although it agrees that there is no reason why those costs could not be made explicit and the Post Office compensated by potential competitors for the diseconomies of scale that might be revealed.

Irrespective of those arguments, the Post Office monopoly is not delivering a sufficient standard of service. As *The Times* said last September:

"In return for accepting the monopoly, the customer does require that the service should be reliable".

Sadly, it is not and delivery standards appear to be declining. The Post Office Users National Council carried out a door-to-door survey in February and found that only 79 per cent. of first-class mail reached the doorstep by the following working day. The target is 100 per cent. By May, that proportion had declined to 72 per cent. In some districts, such as Peterborough, only half the first-class service reached districts regarded as distant the next day and only 61 per cent. reached districts next door to the home district the next day.

The results of a survey by the Mail Users Association are even worse. Over a period of 18 months, from June 1987 to March 1989, fewer than two thirds of first-class letters reached their destinations the following day. The second-class service has become a fairly unfunny joke. The so-called standards maintained by the Post Office are maintained at 90 per cent. only by continually moving the goalposts. In 1975, the target was moved from delivery on the second day after posting to the third day after posting. In 1978, that became the third day after the letters were collected, as opposed to after they were posted.

The present position is totally unsatisfactory. My argument is that, as in every other area of human economic endeavour, be it clothing, foods or utilities, competition forces the economy to respond to the needs of the consumer. That will apply in the case of this monopoly also.

It is significant that, in 1987, my right hon. and learned Friend the Member for Rushcliffe (Mr. Clarke), then the Chancellor of the Duchy of Lancaster, pointing to a bad year for industrial relations in the Post Office, said:

"We must consider whether it is secure as a monopoly carrier."

In 1988, the situation was considerably worse, and he was still considering. The present Chancellor of the Duchy of Lancaster voted in 1976 and 1979 for the abolition of the monopoly. Even Alan Tuffin has said:

"We accept that we may have to live with competition. We will take it on and beat it."

The Post Office Board and the Mail Users Association are both in favour of competition. Indeed, my right hon. Friend the Prime Minister recently stated:

"I agree that greater competition would be good, and we may have to consider ending the monopoly on the postal letter service, which would bring welcome competition."—[*Official Report*, 6 June 1989; Vol. 154, c. 15.]

If any further evidence were needed, I offer the fact that, since the parcel service was opened to competition, its turnover has increased dramatically, as have its profits, to £32·2 million this year. It has extended its services and it is providing a better quality of service for the public.

There are a number of suggestions about the form that such competition should take. I do not believe that there should be a free-for-all, achieved by reducing the minimum charge from the present £1 to a nominal amount, because there would be problems of supervision and other complex problems and no significant competition except in specialist areas. Equally, trying to duplicate what has happened with British Telecom and having a Mercury-type competitor on a national basis would unnecessarily restrict entry to the market, involve huge infrastructure costs and mean that competition was unrealistic in the short term.

Two scenarios have the informal agreement of the Post Office as pragmatic and viable. They would give uniform pricing for a nominal service and guarantee deliveries in any particular area. They would also be co-operative and would use the existing Post Office infrastructure. One scenario involved companies being given licences on a regional and district basis for collection, sorting and local delivery. The other, which is supported by many people in the Post Office and by the Mail Users Association——

**Madam Deputy Speaker (Miss Betty Boothroyd):** Order. The hon. Gentleman would remain in good order if he now concluded.

**Mr. Coombs:** The last word should be left to Roland Hill, who was born in my constituency and who was the father of the penny post. When advocating the abolition of the Post Office monopoly, which he called an offence to our statute book, he said that abolition would allow the "probable rise of a wholesome competition wherever the service is performed with less than the greatest efficiency and cheapness".

The British public deserve greater efficiency and cheapness. I commend my Bill to the House.

3.58 pm

**Mr. Harry Ewing** (Falkirk, East): Fortunately, Roland Hill was born before the hon. Member for Wyre Forest (Mr. Coombs) became the Member for Parliament for that constituency, which is something for which we must be thankful.

Speeches on this issue never change. I should declare my interest right at the beginning of my opposition to this ten-minute Bill. I am sponsored by the Union of Communication Workers.

When the hon. Gentleman said that the public wanted urgency in the privatisation or liberalisation of the Post Office, call it what one will, he was failing to take account of recent surveys and public opinion polls. The morning after the Prime Minister gave her broad hint that she was in favour of breaching the monopoly, Derek Jameson had a phone-in on his BBC radio programme. It went on until the Friday morning and showed that 68 per cent. of people in this country are in favour of maintaining the monopoly and that only 32 per cent. are in favour of breaching it. In anybody's language that is a substantial majority in favour of retaining the status quo, and there are, of course, good reasons for that, especially for people living in rural areas.

I shall repeat what I said in January and again in February. For the time being—I emphasise "for the time being"—rural areas are represented by Conservative Members of Parliament. It therefore always astonishes me

[*Mr. Harry Ewing*]

that Conservative Members are prepared to come to the House and present ten-minute Bills that would put their constituents at a most serious disadvantage in terms of the postal services. I am convinced that most constituents do not know what their Members of Parliament are up to when they come to the House. It is well known that all the surveys and costings have shown that in the rural areas the cost of sending a letter would be at least £1. The great advantage of the monopoly and the universal postal system is that there is a universal postal rate. Whether a letter is posted in Orkney or in Shetland and sent down to St. Ives in Cornwall, or vice versa, it costs the same as a letter posted in London to another address in London.

The Post Office workers accept that the monopoly places upon them a responsibility to deliver a service. I agree with the hon. Member for Wyre Forest that there is always room for improvement. Those who work in the service are just as keen as—if not keener—than the hon. Gentleman to improve the service. To bring about the improvements that my colleagues in the Post Office want would be more difficult than the difficulty the hon. Gentleman has had in presenting his rather silly Bill.

I say to the hon. Member for Wyre Forest as kindly as I can that he does not understand some of the problems that the Post Office has to put up with. One major problem is the concentration of postings at 5 o'clock at night. Big businesses do not post twice or three times a day; they post only once a day. If big businesses could discipline themselves to post two or three times a day, many of the Post Office's problems would be removed.

Another major problem is envelopes that are put through meters to be franked. I advise Conservative Members to do as I do and to check the date on the letter against the date on the envelope. I receive letters repeatedly, especially from Government Departments, on which the date is five days previous to that on the envelope. That has nothing to do with the Post Office, but is the fault of those who process the meters.

As kindly and as gently as I can, I point out to Conservative Members that, after the tragic incident at Lockerbie, the Secretary of State for Transport protested that he had posted a letter and he blamed the Post Office for the fact that it had not been received. It was disgraceful that it was said that the letter was posted on 19 December and was lost in the Christmas mail, although it was later discovered that it was not posted until 20 January. That is is how easy it is for people to blame the Post Office.

The Abbey National building society, when it was changing its status, did exactly the same. It blamed the Post Office when its shareholders had not received their letters, but it had not even put the letters in the mail.

When Conservative Members begin to understand the Post Office's problems, especially those that I have highlighted, they can talk about inefficiency. Until that time, we should continue to throw out such Bills.

*Question put, pursuant to Standing Order No. 19 (Motions for leave to bring in Bills and nomination of Select Committees at commencement of public business):—*

The House divided: Ayes 77, Noes 161.

**Division No. 265]**        **[4.03 pm**

### AYES

Adley, Robert
Arnold, Jacques *(Gravesham)*
Atkinson, David
Beaumont-Dark, Anthony
Braine, Rt Hon Sir Bernard
Brazier, Julian
Brown, Michael *(Brigg & Cl't's)*
Budgen, Nicholas
Burns, Simon
Carrington, Matthew
Cash, William
Clark, Sir W. *(Croydon S)*
Colvin, Michael
Coombs, Anthony *(Wyre F'rest)*
Coombs, Simon *(Swindon)*
Currie, Mrs Edwina
Curry, David
Day, Stephen
Evans, David *(Welwyn Hatf'd)*
Evennett, David
Fairbairn, Sir Nicholas
Favell, Tony
Fenner, Dame Peggy
Forman, Nigel
Fry, Peter
Gill, Christopher
Goodhart, Sir Philip
Goodson-Wickes, Dr Charles
Gow, Ian
Greenway, Harry *(Ealing N)*
Gregory, Conal
Hague, William
Hamilton, Neil *(Tatton)*
Hargreaves, Ken *(Hyndburn)*
Hicks, Mrs Maureen *(Wolv' NE)*
Holt, Richard
Howarth, G. *(Cannock & B'wd)*
Hughes, Robert G. *(Harrow W)*
Irvine, Michael
Janman, Tim
Jones, Gwilym *(Cardiff N)*
Jones, Robert B *(Herts W)*
King, Roger *(B'ham N'thfield)*
Kirkhope, Timothy
Lawrence, Ivan
Leigh, Edward *(Gainsbor'gh)*
Mans, Keith
Mills, Iain
Montgomery, Sir Fergus
Morris, M *(N'hampton S)*
Oppenheim, Phillip
Paice, James
Patnick, Irvine
Pawsey, James
Peacock, Mrs Elizabeth
Porter, David *(Waveney)*
Raison, Rt Hon Timothy
Redwood, John
Riddick, Graham
Sayeed, Jonathan
Shaw, Sir Giles *(Pudsey)*
Skeet, Sir Trevor
Smith, Tim *(Beaconsfield)*
Spicer, Sir Jim *(Dorset W)*
Stanley, Rt Hon Sir John
Stewart, Allan *(Eastwood)*
Stradling Thomas, Sir John
Summerson, Hugo
Taylor, Ian *(Esher)*
Thorne, Neil
Tredinnick, David
Vaughan, Sir Gerard
Warren, Kenneth
Watts, John
Widdecombe, Ann
Wilshire, David
Winterton, Nicholas

Tellers for the Ayes:
    Mr. Nicholas Bennett and
    Mr. John Bowis.

### NOES

Abbott, Ms Diane
Adams, Allen *(Paisley N)*
Allen, Graham
Alton, David
Anderson, Donald
Armstrong, Hilary
Ashdown, Rt Hon Paddy
Ashton, Joe
Barnes, Harry *(Derbyshire NE)*
Barron, Kevin
Battle, John
Beggs, Roy
Bell, Stuart
Benn, Rt Hon Tony
Benyon, W.
Bermingham, Gerald
Boateng, Paul
Brown, Gordon *(D'mline E)*
Brown, Nicholas *(Newcastle E)*
Brown, Ron *(Edinburgh Leith)*
Bruce, Malcolm *(Gordon)*
Buckley, George J.
Caborn, Richard
Callaghan, Jim
Campbell, Menzies *(Fife NE)*
Campbell-Savours, D. N.
Clark, Dr David *(S Shields)*
Clay, Bob
Clwyd, Mrs Ann
Coleman, Donald
Cook, Frank *(Stockton N)*
Corbyn, Jeremy
Cousins, Jim
Cox, Tom
Crowther, Stan
Cryer, Bob
Cunliffe, Lawrence
Cunningham, Dr John
Darling, Alistair
Davies, Ron *(Caerphilly)*
Davis, Terry *(B'ham Hodge H'l)*
Dewar, Donald
Dixon, Don
Dobson, Frank
Doran, Frank
Douglas, Dick
Duffy, A. E. P.
Dunnachie, Jimmy
Eadie, Alexander
Eastham, Ken
Evans, John *(St Helens N)*
Ewing, Harry *(Falkirk E)*
Ewing, Mrs Margaret *(Moray)*
Fatchett, Derek
Fields, Terry *(L'pool B G'n)*
Flannery, Martin
Foot, Rt Hon Michael
Forsythe, Clifford *(Antrim S)*
Fraser, John
Fyfe, Maria
Galbraith, Sam
Galloway, George
Garrett, John *(Norwich South)*
Godman, Dr Norman A.
Gould, Bryan
Graham, Thomas
Griffiths, Nigel *(Edinburgh S)*
Griffiths, Win *(Bridgend)*
Hardy, Peter
Haynes, Frank
Hinchliffe, David
Home Robertson, John
Howarth, George *(Knowsley N)*
Howells, Dr. Kim (Pontypridd)
Hoyle, Doug
Hughes, John *(Coventry NE)*
Hughes, Roy *(Newport E)*
Illsley, Eric

Janner, Greville
Jones, Ieuan *(Ynys Môn)*
Jones, Martyn *(Clwyd S W)*
Kaufman, Rt Hon Gerald
Kennedy, Charles
Kilfedder, James
Kinnock, Rt Hon Neil
Lambie, David
Leadbitter, Ted
Leighton, Ron
Livingstone, Ken
Lloyd, Tony *(Stretford)*
Lofthouse, Geoffrey
Loyden, Eddie
McAvoy, Thomas
McKay, Allen *(Barnsley West)*
McKelvey, William
McLeish, Henry
Maclennan, Robert
McWilliam, John
Madden, Max
Marshall, David *(Shettleston)*
Martin, Michael J. *(Springburn)*
Maxton, John
Meale, Alan
Michael, Alun
Michie, Bill *(Sheffield Heeley)*
Michie, Mrs Ray *(Arg'l & Bute)*
Molyneaux, Rt Hon James
Moonie, Dr Lewis
Morgan, Rhodri
Mullin, Chris
Murphy, Paul
Oakes, Rt Hon Gordon
O'Brien, William
Orme, Rt Hon Stanley
Patchett, Terry
Pike, Peter L.
Powell, Ray *(Ogmore)*
Prescott, John
Radice, Giles
Redmond, Martin
Rees, Rt Hon Merlyn
Reid, Dr John

Richardson, Jo
Robertson, George
Rogers, Allan
Rooker, Jeff
Rowlands, Ted
Ruddock, Joan
Salmond, Alex
Sedgemore, Brian
Sheerman, Barry
Sheldon, Rt Hon Robert
Short, Clare
Sillars, Jim
Skinner, Dennis
Smith, C. *(Isl'ton & F'bury)*
Smith, Rt Hon J. *(Monk'ds E)*
Smith, J. P. *(Vale of Glam)*
Snape, Peter
Steel, Rt Hon David
Steinberg, Gerry
Stott, Roger
Strang, Gavin
Straw, Jack
Taylor, Mrs Ann *(Dewsbury)*
Thomas, Dr Dafydd Elis
Thompson, Jack *(Wansbeck)*
Turner, Dennis
Vaz, Keith
Wallace, James
Wareing, Robert N.
Welsh, Andrew *(Angus E)*
Welsh, Michael *(Doncaster N)*
Wigley, Dafydd
Williams, Alan W. *(Carm'then)*
Wilson, Brian
Winnick, David
Worthington, Tony
Wray, Jimmy
Young, David *(Bolton SE)*
Young, Sir George *(Acton)*

Tellers for the Noes:
    Mr. Norman Hogg and
    Mr. Dave Nellist.

*Question accordingly negatived.*

## OPPOSITION DAY

[17th Allotted Day] [*Second Part*]

# Scotland in Europe

**Madam Deputy Speaker (Miss Betty Boothroyd):** Mr. Speaker has selected the amendment standing in the name of the Prime Minister.

4.15 pm

**Mr. Alex Salmond** (Banff and Buchan): I beg to move,
That this House notes the continued and overwhelming rejection of the Conservative Party's colonial régime in Scotland, the willingness of the Labour Party leadership to place Trident submarines on the Clyde against the wishes of the Scottish Labour Conference and majority Scottish opinion, the results of the European elections which saw the Scottish National Party gain 26 per cent. of the vote and move into a clear second place in Scottish politics, the continued alienation of the United Kingdom from its European partners and the obstruction to European Community co-operation presented by the Prime Minister's little Englander attitudes; and recognises that the only constitutional change which can meet fully the need for economic and social progress in Scotland is independence as a full and equal partner within the European Community.

The House will note that our motion refers to the Government's colonial attitude to Scotland. I know that his description of their policy programme has caused some anxiety to the Tory party in the past, and particularly to the Secretary of State for Scotland, who has been anxious to disavow a quotation of 8 March attributed to him by the *Scottish Field:*
"In fact the powers of the Secretary of State for Scotland are not unlike those of a colonial governor."
If the Secretary of State maintains that he did not say that, the House will have to accept his word, although I am still perplexed about why the *Scottish Field* of all magazines should want to make up the quotation. However, the case for saying that the Tory party treats Scotland like a colony does not depend on quotations, accurate or otherwise: it rests on actions and facts.

The case rests on the actions of this Government in a range of policies, from the poll tax, to opting out in education, to the review of the National Health Service. In these areas the Government's policy programme is being imposed against the overwhelming body of Scottish opinion, using what the Secretary of State used to call—he does so less now—the "Gatling gun" of the Tory majority in this place and the army of political appointees north of the border who do the Tory bidding.

I was struck on Monday of this week by the irony in Brian Meek's column in the *Glasgow Herald.* He is something of a soulmate or confidant of the Secretary of State for Scotland, more so perhaps than is the hon. Member for Stirling (Mr. Forsyth). Councillor Meek complained in the column about being bumped off the Lothian and Borders police board. He complained that the Tory party representatives on that board were being reduced from three to one, and said that it was disgraceful that the Labour party majority on the committee should abuse its powers in that way.

Councillor Meek may have a point in this case. The majority party on a committee should not use its powers to reduce the representation of minorities. The irony lies in the fact that I cannot remember Councillor Meek ever having written a column in the *Glasgow Herald* or

[*Mr. Alex Salmond*]

anywhere else in which he noted the complexion of, for example, the health boards in Scotland. Trade union representation and opposition party representation on those boards has been systematically reduced by this Government. We look forward to Councillor Meek regaling Scotland on the unfairness of this——

**Mr. Harry Ewing** (Falkirk, East): Is the hon. Gentleman aware that 10 of the 15 members of the Forth Valley health board live in the constituency of the hon. Member for Stirling (Mr. Forsyth)? Not one comes from the highly industrialised constituency of Falkirk, East and of the others, a small number are shared between Falkirk, West and Clackmannan. Is that the sort of bias to which he is referring?

**Mr. Salmond:** I am grateful to the hon. Gentleman and aware of what he says. My colleagues and I recently met a Scottish Trades Union Congress delegation, which gave us the facts and figures of how this pattern is being replicated all over Scotland. So it was ironic that Councillor Meek mentioned the Lothian and Borders police board but did not refer to anywhere else in Scotland —or even to his own appointment as a prominent member of Livingston development corporation. I do not think that the new town of Livingston has ever elected a Conservative councillor in its electoral history. So throughout Scotland there is a colonial system of government imposed by the Tory majority.

**Mr. George Robertson** (Hamilton): I was somewhat puzzled when I read the Order Paper because it says:

"This Opposition Day is at the disposal of the leader of the Ulster Unionist Party, pursuant to Standing Order No. 13. The selection of the matter to be debated has been made by the Scottish National Party."

I cannot help wondering whether there is a quid pro quo involved in the right hon. Member for Lagan Valley (Mr. Molyneaux) giving up this day. May I ask the hon. Member for Banff and Buchan (Mr. Salmond) a question? We know that the SNP is in favour of an independent Scotland in Europe and that it is also in favour of an independent Wales in Europe. Will the hon. Gentleman tell the House whether it is in favour of an independent Ulster in Europe?

**Mr. Salmond:** The hon. Gentleman demonstrates his ignorance of House procedures. I know that he has been here for some time but he has learnt very little. As I understand it, under Standing Order No. 13 the second Opposition party in the House is the Ulster Unionist party because of the name change and the disintegration of the alliance parties after the election. Just as in the previous Parliament it was the prerogative of the alliance to allocate the second party Opposition day, that is now the prerogative of the Ulster Unionist party. I must disappoint the hon. Gentleman. There is nothing more sinister in the Supply day than that. [*Interruption.*]

As the hon. Gentleman knows, I am a great believer in the self-determination of nations. I believe in self-determination for the Scottish nation, the Welsh nation and the Irish nation. I should be interested to hear at some time from the hon. Gentleman how he squares his support for self-determination for peoples across five continents with his refusal to accept it in the one country, Scotland, where he has any influence.

I was making the point that there is a colonial system of government in Scotland, imposed by Tory votes south of the border and implemented by Tory bagmen north of the border. In the argument about a colonial system of government, I can claim support from some sources in the Conservative party. Speaking in warning against colonial attitudes towards Scotland, the right hon. Member for Shropshire, North (Mr. Biffen), said on Channel 4 on 18 March that he found it quite insulting that anybody should say of Scotland:

"'Oh, they can't possibly be a nation, they can't possibly have a national Government, they haven't got the population or the size',—it is an absolute nonsense of an argument, it is a patronising argument and on the lips of Englishmen it really is quite disgraceful because it's almost a proconsular argument, as though we were colonial peoples who hadn't yet got the resources for independence and that is complete and utter rubbish."

Those were wise words that will stand the test of time. They were wise words not just for the English Conservative party but also for the Scottish Labour party because increasingly it is taking its agenda from politics south of the border.

A couple of months ago, in an idle moment, I turned on my television. There at Inverness was the Scottish Labour party in full flight in conference. The motion on the agenda was on unilateral nuclear disarmament. I expected a strong debate. Given the fundamental reassessment that is taking place in Labour ranks I expected a spirited exchange of views. No, there was not. So great was the unanimity within the Scottish Labour party that that motion—a hard motion in favour of unilateral nuclear disarmament—was passed without opposition, or at least overwhelmingly. That may reflect the consensus that exists in the Scottish Labour party. More realistically perhaps, the hon. Member for Clackmannan (Mr. O'Neill) did not think it worth while to argue the case at a Scottish Labour conference. For whatever reason, the Scottish Labour party reflected the consensus that exists in Scotland both for unilateral nuclear disarmament and against the Trident missile system.

The Labour party leadership in this place will not reflect that consensus. It will reflect the consensus between the two Front Benches, where the major differences are whether we shall have four or three Trident submarines stationed on the Clyde, whether the nuclear strike force will be increased by a factor of eight or four, or whether, as one delegate said yesterday at the Transport and General Workers Union conference, it is a Labour or a Tory finger on the nuclear button.

Presumably there are still left among Scottish Labour Members of Parliament some real unilateralists as well as some gut ones. Perhaps they should reflect on the Labour party's attempt to out-yuppie the Tory party. Just like the Tory party, Labour party policies are relegating the Scottish dimension to accommodate the requirements of an electoral system south of the border.

The Tory amendment to our motion makes the point that the SNP is also a minority party in Scotland. Perhaps there is no great difference between achieving 20 per cent., or a fifth, of the vote, which is what the Tory party achieved in Scotland last Thursday, and achieving 26 per cent., or a quarter, of the vote, which is what the SNP achieved in the Euro-elections. We feel that there are fairly substantial differences between us and them. One is that the SNP claims no mandate to run or govern Scotland until it obtains a majority of the seats and has a mandate to negotiate independence. That is in clear contrast with the Tory party, which claims its mandate to run Scotland on a basis of 10 parliamentary seats, no European seats and a vote now reduced to 20 per cent.

Another substantive difference between the position of the SNP and the Tory party can be seen in the detail of Scottish opinion polls. Even at 20 per cent. of the vote, the Conservative party can at least claim that it is out-performing the support for the constitutional status quo in Scotland, which the latest MORI poll, in June, put at no more than 15 per cent. across Scotland. However, that is not the position of the SNP. Even with our vote rising to 26 per cent., we are under-performing when measured against the support for Scottish independence, shown in that poll to be 35 per cent., and when measured against the between 51 per cent. and 62 per cent. support for independence in Europe, shown in other polls.

**Mr. Donald Dewar** (Glasgow, Garscadden): I know that the hon. Gentleman is fastidious in these matters, so I make this point for the sake of accuracy. Is not the support for a Scotland independent in Europe at 22 per cent. in the latest MORI poll? The hon. Gentleman has added another factor—Scotland independent outwith the EEC—to get his 35 per cent.

**Mr. Salmond:** I wonder whether the hon. Gentleman appreciates where his argument is leading him. Will he differentiate, in the devolution element of the poll, between his policy of independence from the United Kingdom, the Democrats' policy of quasi-federalism, the old devolution policy of the Labour party and the policy of David Martin, which is quite different from that of any of the other policies? We were given a choice between independence, devolution and the status quo. The figures that I have quoted are those recorded in the poll. I suspect that even the hon. Gentleman will not deny the figures of between 52 per cent. and 61 per cent. saying yes to a direct question of yes or no to independence in Europe, in three successive opinion polls.

**Mr. Alistair Darling** (Edinburgh, Central): May I pursue the hon. Gentleman on the question of independence for Scotland inside or outside Europe? As I understand it, the nationalists see much of their appeal coming from the fact that they are offering Scotland independence within the European Community. If the terms for Scotland remaining in the EEC are renegotiated and found to be unsatisfactory, do I take it that the nationalist line is independence outside Europe, come what may?

**Mr. Salmond:** I shall be dealing with that matter later in my speech.

The SNP policy is absolutely clear. If we obtain a majority of seats in Scotland at the next general election, we will have a mandate to negotiate independence with Westminster—

**Mr. Darling** *rose*—

**Mr. Salmond:** If the hon. Gentleman will contain himself, I shall answer his question.

The SNP will have a mandate to negotiate independence with Westminster and simultaneously to negotiate with the EEC. The constitutional settlement resulting from that will be put to the Scottish people in a referendum, so the Scottish people will decide. I do not

understand how, as a democrat, the hon. Member for Edinburgh, Central (Mr. Darling) could possibly object to that process—

**Mr. Darling** *rose*—

**Mr. Salmond:** I hope that the hon. Gentleman will allow me to continue.

Despite the SNP's improvement to 26 per cent. of the vote, it is substantially under-performing, the support for independence shown in successive opinion polls. The SNP may not yet be winning the elections in Scotland, but it is winning the arguments—

**Several Hon. Members** *rose*—

**Mr. Salmond:** I wish that hon. Members would contain themselves.

When one wins the argument—

**Mr. John Home Robertson** (East Lothian) *rose*—

**Mr. Salmond:** The hon. Gentleman must contain himself.

**Mr. Home Robertson** *rose*—

**Mr. Salmond:** I have been very generous in giving way. to Labour Members. I shall give way to the hon. Gentleman later if he allows me to develop a few more points.

During the European election campaign I was struck by the similarities—as I will no doubt be similarly struck in this debate—in the arguments of the two main Unionist parties—the Tory party and the Labour party, Tweedledum and Tweedledee. The response to the independence in Europe argument makes that especially evident. Both Labour and Tory spokesmen have claimed that Scotland would not be allowed to be independent in Europe; that somehow the nasty foreigners would keep out Scotland—

**Several Hon. Members** *rose*—

**Mr. Salmond:** If hon. Members will allow me to develop a few points, I might be generous enough to give way later.

During the European election, the SNP published substantive legal opinion from Professor Victor McKinnon and the French advocate Maitre De Roux pointing out that the conventions of state succession and the treaty of Rome—*[Interruption.]* I cannot understand why Labour Members are laughing, because we published legal opinion from other Europeans. I should have thought that the views of other Europeans on this issue were very important.

Both those substantive legal opinions pointed out that the laws of state succession and the treaty of Rome would keep Scotland within the Community during the negotiations. There was an intervention in the debate by Professor Emile Noel who, until 1987, was the Secretary-General of the European Commission. Indeed, he held that position for more than 20 years and is probably the greatest living authority on Community rules and procedures. As far as I know, he has no axe to grind on Scottish politics. On 5 March he said about Scotland:

"There is no precedent or provision for the expulsion of a member state, therefore Scottish independence would create two member states out of one . . . They would have equal status with each other and the other eleven states. The remainder of the UK would not be in a more powerful position than Scotland."

[*Mr. Salmond*]

Professor Noel expanded on those remarks in an article in *The Scotsman* on 12 June. At the same time, *The Scotsman* revealed what had happened to the Conservative party legal opinion threatened to be commissioned by Mr. James Proven, who had promised to make it the centrepiece of his re-election campaign in the north-east of Scotland. *The Scotsman* revealed that senior Tory sources said that the Conservative party had decided not to publish that opinion because it was "ambiguous" and could be "misinterpreted".

The greatest living authority on EEC procedures—[*Interruption.*] I am surprised by the laughter that greets the credentials of Professor Emile Noel——

**Several Hon. Members** *rose*——

**Madam Deputy Speaker:** Order. The hon. Member for Banff and Buchan (Mr. Salmond) need give way only if he chooses to do so.

**Mr. Salmond:** The position is that the greatest living authority on EC procedures volunteers support for the argument advanced by the SNP, while the Tory party cannot even pay someone to make their particular argument.

**Sir Nicholas Fairbairn** (Perth and Kinross): If, without payment, another living authority on that subject may comment—if the greatest living authority in France pronounces the concept that Scotland is already a member state, in order to make the point that there could be no objection to its being a separate member state, the whole basis of that opinion is false.

**Mr. Salmond:** The hon. and learned Gentleman should have read Professor Noel's article, for I am certain that he is well aware of Scotland's status and, having been the European Commission's Secretary-General for 20 years, of the procedures, regulations and likely reactions of the European Community.

**Mr. David Curry** (Skipton and Ripon): Does the hon. Gentleman distinguish between legal opinion—all those whose views he quoted are either lawyers or officials—and political reality? How many years does he envisage that the negotiations would take to complete? Does he accept that the last thing that countries such as Spain and France, with their separatist problems, want is to see the principle of separatism introduced into the Community? Negotiations would be long, painful and difficult—and the hon. Gentleman might not be in power by the time that they were completed.

**Mr. Salmond:** If the hon. Gentleman had familiarised himself with the subject of today's debate, he would know that Professor Noel's article dealt with that aspect. Professor Noel wrote that Scotland's membership of the Community would be accepted, and that any negotiations would concern only matters of detail. I quote again from the article about Professor Noel in *The Scotsman,* stating that he

"has confirmed his view that an independent Scotland would be entitled to EEC membership, with negotiation on the detail and not on the principle."

The suggestion by the hon. Member for Skipton and Ripon (Mr Curry) is deeply insulting, because it implies that Scotland has nothing of value that the Community would find attractive—such as 80 per cent. of Europe's oil reserves and 40 per cent. of its fish reserves. Even more insulting—to other Europeans also—is the argument, made against all available evidence, that other member states would somehow want to flout the democratic will of the Scottish people.

Today's debate is about how Scotland's interests can best be represented in Europe and how Scotland can best be governed at home.

**Mr. Home Robertson:** I am grateful to the hon. Gentleman for introducing to the House the important views of Professor Noel, although I must confess that I had not heard of him before. Why is the hon. Gentleman making those important arguments in this "colonial" Parliament, as he refers to it, when he has an opportunity to make them instead before a body that does represent the people of Scotland—the Scottish Constitutional Convention?

**Mr. Salmond:** If I were the hon. Member for East Lothian (Mr. Home Robertson), I would not boast about not knowing the name of the person who has been Secretary-General of the European Commission for 20 years, for that displays his ignorance of European politics.

**Several Hon. Members** *rose*——

**Madam Deputy Speaker:** Order. This is not "Mastermind".

**Mr. Salmond:** The hon. Member for East Lothian knows very well that the Scottish National party is willing to have its arguments judged by the Scottish people, but it is not prepared to have a veto placed on them by the hon. Member for Glasgow, Garscadden (Mr. Dewar).

The case made in Scotland by the Tories is remarkable. They say that somehow Scotland is better represented by English Tory Ministers chosen by the Prime Minister than by Scottish Ministers chosen by the people of Scotland. In reality, in most cases Scotland has no representation in Europe. In the two years to the end of 1988, out of 151 Council of Ministers meetings, representatives of the Scottish Office attended only five—and then in a junior capacity. Of the 95 major ministerial speeches made over the same period on Community topics, Scottish Office Ministers managed none at all. That is how influential the Scottish Office is in European policy determination.

Perhaps, as Member of Parliament for a constituency in north-east Scotland, I can take some consolation from the fact that the five meetings that Scottish Office Ministers managed to sneak into were all concerned with the fishing industry. In the House last week, however, we were given a working example of the priority that the Government allocate to that industry. The mid-year Council meeting made some fundamental decisions affecting the future finances of the Scottish fleet, and refused to act on the low Scottish North sea haddock quotas. The Government did not even consider it worth while to make an oral statement to the House, substituting a written answer in which the Scottish case was dismissed in two sentences. The fact is that Scotland is not represented at the top table where the real decisions are made. We are not represented but misrepresented by Tory Ministers who share neither our political values nor our industrial priorities: that is the reality of our provincial position in the Community.

When we had a similar debate last year, the Secretary of State for Scotland was unwise enough to unload some of his prejudices on to the House. He told us that the small countries of Europe rarely, if ever, had

"a decisive role to play in the major issues that affect the Community."—[*Official Report,* 6 July 1988, Vol. 136, c. 1089.]

I found those remarks interesting and later in the year I tested them by putting down some questions to the junior Foreign Office Minister, whose post was formerly held by the Secretary of State for Scotland. I received entirely different answers to similar questions.

This is what the junior Foreign Office Minister said about the role of small countries in Europe:

"All member states, irrespective of their size, play an important role in the process of development of the Community."

She also said:

"The treaties . . . provide for all member states to contribute on an equitable basis to Community decision-making."—[*Official Report,* 31 October 1989; Vol. 139, c. 483-484.]

There we have it. The official position of the Government is that small countries have an important role to play—except, of course, Scotland. We have the opportunity to build a consensus with our European partners, as all Community states must do, but that is something of which the Prime Minister is manifestly incapable.

Within the European Community, Scotland would have twice as many MEPs as at present, a Commissioner as of right, votes on the Council and a turn to lead the European Community through the presidency of the Council as a full and equal partner. We would have real influence in Europe to match real power in Scotland. That is the other side of the "Scotland in Europe" argument, and the argument for independence.

**Mr. Nigel Griffiths** (Edinburgh, South): If Scottish representation were expanded, would the new representatives sit with the current Scottish MEP, Mrs. Ewing, with the Gaullists and others on the Right wing? Why has Mrs. Ewing not resigned from that grouping?

**Mr. Salmond:** The hon. Gentleman is manifestly out of date. The groupings in the European Parliament are currently being negotiated, and I am sure that Mrs. Ewing will continue to represent Scotland's interests. The hon. Gentleman will find that she has a superb voting record across a range of social and economic issues in the European Community. Clearly his lack of confidence in her is not shared by the electorate of the Highlands and Islands, who returned her to the European Parliament with a resounding majority.

I want to examine three examples of the domestic power that independence in Europe would give. At present the United Kingdom is pursuing policies that are not in Scotland's interest. The first example is monetary policy—the interaction between interest rate and exchange rate policy. No one in Scotland—not even, I suspect, the Secretary of State at his most effusive—would claim that the Scottish economy was overheating; the best that can be said is that it has undergone a slow recovery from the oil recession of 1986. Yet the monetary policy being applied in Scotland is designed to combat an overheated economy.

Can the Secretary of State tell us how inflationary pressures on the south-east of England will be eased by the imposition of penal interest rates on fishermen in the north-east of Scotland? How will a cost squeeze on Scottish industry help the problems of the balance of payments? For Scotland, a high interest rate is not just a blunt instrument; it is the cure for a disease from which we do not suffer.

A recent paper from the Scottish Centre for Economic and Social Research pointed out that an independent Scotland we could look forward to low interest rates and a stable exchange rate regime as part of the exchange rate mechanism of the EMS, regardless of whether sterling decided to join.

My second example is that of Wang leaving Stirling. Let me say to the Secretary of State that there seems little point in throwing a tantrum at Wang executives: I suspect that lecturing them will be as effective as lecturing Caterpillar executives has been in the past. Clearly the relationship between a country and multinational companies has little to do with size. The strength of a bargaining position depends not on the size of the economy—otherwise Wang would not be on its way to Limerick—but on the strength of the overall economy. [*Interruption.*] I see that Conservative Members do not take my point. Let us take the example of Norway in the 1970s—a country of 4·5 million people which managed by general agreement to negotiate a deal with the international oil companies far superior to that negotiated by the United Kingdom. The bargaining position of the Norwegian Government was helped by the strength of the country's economy.

**Dr. John Reid** (Motherwell, North): The hon. Gentleman might also reflect on Ireland in the 1960s. Through massive tax handouts, Ireland was able to bring in multinational companies for about 10 years; they disappeared as soon as the 10 years were up. The issue is related to size and economic muscle as well as to the wealth of the Government.

Can the hon. Gentleman answer a simple question? I have been wondering since I came into the Chamber why the hon. Gentleman moved the motion, rather than the leader of his party. Until now I had assumed that it was because the hon. Gentleman was considered to be better equipped to outline the intellectual basis for independence, but—knowing the attributes of the party leader, and having heard the hon. Gentleman's speech—I have had to abandon that assumption. Will he explain why he moved the motion?

**Mr. Salmond:** The hon. Gentleman may not know that the duties of my hon. Friend the Member for Moray (Mrs. Ewing) have been curtailed over the past week by illness in the family. I shall not take the matter any further than that.

**Dr. Reid:** I did not know.

**Mr. Salmond:** No one would argue that multinational investment is not an important factor; it can be extremely valuable. The question is whether it is the sole arm of economic strategy, as it appears to be in Scotland at present. The key to a robust economic policy is building on resource strength, skill strength, areas of natural advantage and the promotion of indigenous companies. Those are exactly the economic policies that would be open to a Scottish Government.

If we had a Scottish Government this year it would be faced with a substantial budget surplus. Even hon. Members who suffer from the most dependent mentalities

[*Mr. Salmond*]

should not be surprised at that: after all, the United Kingdom Treasury is awash with funds at present. But there is a substantial difference. The United Kingdom Treasury is boxed in by inflationary and balance of payments constraints. Those constraints would not be faced to the same extent by an independent Scotland.

The Scottish National party has published our proposals for the economic regeneration of Scotland. I look forward to the Labour party publishing similar proposals, or indeed any precise programme. The SNP's policy proposals would create 78,000 jobs in the first year as we embark on a regeneration strategy for the Scottish economy, projecting Scotland on to a higher rate of growth and employment.

**Mr. Dewar:** Will the hon. Gentleman, who has been talking about the budget that he has done for an independent Scotland in Europe, comment on the letter dated 14 June 1989 which appeared in *The Scotsman* from a well-known supporter of the SNP, Professor Malcolm Slessor, in which he said:

"In fact, a financial forecast of what Scotland would be like as an independent country is about as meaningless as one of Chancellor Lawson's pieces of star-gazing."

**Mr. Salmond:** I commend the hon. Gentleman to read the SNP's economic plans for an independent Scotland.

**Mr. Dewar:** I have read them.

**Mr. Salmond:** In that case, he may have obtained some useful ideas and will now give us a clue about what the Labour party proposes for its first year in government for Scotland. I recall the Labour party's programme at the last general election, when it worked out its jobs plan for Scotland by dividing by 10 the figure that it promoted for the United Kingdom as a whole.

**Mr. William Cash** (Stafford) *rose——*

**Mr. Salmond:** The alternative to the economic regeneration of Scotland through independence is to continue at the lower end of United Kingdom growth and to fail to provide decent employment for all our people and a decent living for that one third of the Scottish population who currently live in poverty. Labour Members in particular should reflect on the fact that the working people of Scotland are those who pay the economic price of the union.

This debate is a platform for the SNP, building on the substantial case that has already been promulgated for independence in Europe. For the Unionist parties, it should serve as a warning. Some of us, a growing number, have a broader ambition for our people than shoehorning Scottish priorities into the requirements of the English electoral system. The economic and political union with England has served its purpose. It will come under increasing pressure. It offers nothing which can stand comparison with the challenge and opportunity of independence within the wider Community of Europe.

4.52 pm

**The Secretary of State for Scotland (Mr. Malcolm Rifkind):** I beg to move, to leave out from "House" to the end of the Question and add instead thereof:

"notes the continued success of the present Government's policies in securing for Scotland record living standards and

the advantages of membership of the European Community within the United Kingdom, alongside a strong defence of the United Kingdom's essential interests, and the rejection of the Scottish National Party's policy of independence in Europe by the overwhelming majority of voters in Scotland at the European elections; and recognises the potential damage to the real interests of Scotland underlying the constitutional change advocated by opposition parties."

The hon. Member for Banff and Buchan (Mr. Salmond) made it clear in the early substantive part of his speech that he accepts that the European elections were a severe rebuff for the central political strategy of the SNP over the last year—that is, the policy of independence in Europe.

During the election campaign, Mrs. Winnie Ewing was quoted as saying that Scotland's relationship with the European Community

"is the central issue in this election campaign."

As the hon. Member for Banff and Buchan was frank enough to admit, about three quarters of the electorate refused to support the policy that his party had said was the fundamental and most important element in its whole political strategy.

In the motion, the hon. Gentleman and his hon. Friends refer to the change of policy that the Labour party is contemplating in regard to unilateral disarmament. I say as an aside that it is a matter of considerable interest that the only parties in Scotland nowadays that appear to be prepared to advocate support for CND and unilateral disarmament are the SNP, the Communist party and the Greens. I am sure that that is an aspect that the hon. Member for Banff and Buchan proclaims as loudly and clearly in Banff and Buchan as he does in Glasgow or in the House.

I have noted that he and his hon. Friend the Member for Moray (Mrs. Ewing) are sometimes less euphoric in the north-east of Scotland about their belief in unilateralism than they would suggest when they proudly present themselves as the new Clydesiders when they are campaigning in Glasgow Central, but I pass that by.

It is not appropriate for the hon. Gentleman to attack the Labour party for a change in policy, and certainly not during a debate on the European Community. We might have had some reference from the hon. Gentleman to the fact that for many years he and his hon. Friends were not the ardent enthusiasts for the European Community that they now present themselves as being. He and his hon. Friends bitterly opposed "Scotland in the European Community" and they spent the whole period of the referendum on the European Community advocating, unsuccessfully, that the people of Scotland should vote no.

**Mr. Michael J. Martin** (Glasgow, Springburn): Does the right hon. and learned Gentleman recall that at the time of the referendum, the hon. Member for Glasgow, Govan (Mr. Sillars), Margo MacDonald, who had just left the House, and the hon. Member for Southend, East (Mr. Taylor) campaigned all over Scotland saying that the European Community was undemocratic and that this country should have no part of it?

**Mr. Rifkind:** That is absolutely correct.

**Mr. Jim Sillars** (Glasgow, Govan): I have no objection to anyone reminding the House or any other forum that I campaigned against entry to the European Community. It was not, however, on the basis that it was undemocratic but on entirely different grounds—for example, that it would be injurious to the economic situation of the United Kingdom at that time, and therefore injurious to Scotland,

and it is easy to prove that. Is the Secretary of State aware that at that time people such as I said that if we went into the European Community, we would have to accept that a page of history had turned and that there would be no going back from that position?

**Mr. Rifkind:** Let us explore that, because the hon. Gentleman makes an interesting observation. I have been reading the document he published entitled "No Turning Back"—[*Interruption.*] More than one document has been published under that title, I hasten to assure my hon. Friends—at least, I hope that is the case, because otherwise this is even more sinister than one might have imagined.

In the alternative version of "No Turning Back", the hon. Member for Govan invites his readership to consider what has changed. We are entitled to ask why he and his hon. Friends, who were passionately hostile to the European Community in the past, have now seen the Community as the salvation of all of Scotland's interests. Is it a change brought about by conviction or by opportunism? He says in that document:

"Bitter though the pill may be to swallow, it is quite irrelevant whether in 1972 and again in 1975 we were correct in opposing entry. We are 16 years down a very different road than any ever travelled before. There is no turning back."

Later he says:

"Like it or not, we are in the European Community."

If that is the principle—that after 16 years it is now irrevocable and there is no turning back—on what basis does he say after 250 years that it is appropriate to try to disintegrate the United Kingdom?

If, as a matter of principle, the hon. Gentleman believes that Scotland's membership of the United Kingdom after 250 years is fundamentally against Scotland's interests and that it is right and proper, as a matter of principle, to campaign for the dissolution of the United Kingdom, why is he so willing to accept that after a mere 16 years, his position of principle has ceased to be relevant and that he must accept, however reluctantly, that Scotland should be in the Community?

Why will he not campaign for an independent Scotland outside the Community, as that is what he and his party were campaigning for at that time? The reality is that the conversion to Europe has nothing whatever to do with the European Community.

**Mr. Ron Brown** (Edinburgh, Leith) *rose*——

**Mr. Rifkind:** No, I will not give way.

The reason for the conversion is also outlined in the same document by the hon. Member for Govan. Saying that they must deal with the charge of separatism, he comments:

"It is the label which Unionist parties stuck upon the SNP."

He goes on:

"The SNP was never able to overcome the problem. It was forced into ever more sophisticated rebuttals of the separatist charge, but in a sense the more it explained, the more convincing the label appeared."

The hon. Gentleman is correct in his view, and the attempt to present some new doctrine of independence in Europe is no more than a weak and flabby attempt to suggest that our membership of the Community has somehow changed the fundamental realities of the situation.

Logically, the Scottish National party must be against both the United Kingdom and the European Community. The basis of that party's policy during the first 40 years of its existence was that for any alternative Government or Parliament to take decisions in the name of the Scottish people that were outwith Scotland's control was against Scottish interests. On that basis, the hon. Member for Govan and his hon. Friends seek to dismember the United Kingdom. They do not seek to reorganise the United Kingdom. They wish this Parliament at Westminster to have no power over Scottish interests and to be unable to legislate or determine policies that would apply to Scotland. Therefore I have to ask the hon. Gentleman and his hon. Friends why they believe that a United Kingdom Parliament must inevitably act against Scottish interests, whereas the Parliament in Strasbourg or the Commission in Brussels will be the new salvation for Scotland and its destiny.

**Mr. Sillars:** I should have thought that the right hon. and learned Gentleman, of all people, given his minority position inside the British Cabinet, would understand the clear difference between this place and Strasbourg. This place exercises legislative control over Scotland. Strasbourg does not. [*Interruption.*] Strasbourg exercises no legislative control over—[*Interruption.*] Before the hon. Member for Glasgow, Garscadden (Mr. Dewar) gets too worked up, let me tell him that I have not finished the sentence. There is nothing comparable to this place in the power that it exercises over Scotland. The hon. Gentleman knows that full well.

**Mr. Rifkind:** I advise the hon. Gentleman to re-read his own document in which, under a chapter headed

"Increasing the powers and influences of the Parliament",

he calls for the European Parliament to be given fiscal powers to impose new taxation on the peoples of the Community. Will he explain that, in the light of his earlier comments? I shall gladly give way to the hon. Gentleman.

**Mr. Sillars:** If the right hon. and learned Gentleman reads it out, which he has not done, he will see that that is a suggestion for developing the powers of the European Parliament at the margins, on the basis that——

**Mr. Michael Brown** (Brigg and Cleethorpes): On the margins?

**Mr. Sillars:** Yes, of course on the margins. The hon. Gentleman has not read the document, either. Why he interjects without having read it is beyond me. [*Interruption.*]

**Madam Deputy Speaker:** Order.

**Mr. Sillars:** It would be a means of increasing the powers of the European Parliament. Even if that were accepted, because it is not party policy—[*Interruption.*] The last people who should laugh are Labour Members. The Labour party frequently publishes the equivalent of Green Papers and pamphlets and says that the ideas contained in them are the personal points of view of this group, that group or that individual and that they do not bind the Labour party. If it is good enough for the Labour party, why is it not good enough for other parties? The fact remains that 99 per cent. of the power that the right hon. and learned Gentleman's Government wields in Scotland comes from this place and from no other part of western Europe.

**Mr. Rifkind:** The hon. Gentleman invites me to read out what is in the document. I cannot resist the invitation. On page 19 he says that the European Parliament

"should have a tax raising ability used to supplement the budget allocation for policy initiatives. In its earliest days this could be a limited power."

Elsewhere in the document he says:

"Of course an increase in the powers of the"

European

"Parliament means a decrease in the powers of the member states."

What the hon. Gentleman, in this brave new world, is suggesting is that Scotland should withdraw from the United Kingdom Parliament because that has the power to legislate for and to tax the people of Scotland and that the United Kingdom Parliament should be replaced by the European Parliament which would have a comparable power—a power which would grow over the years to come.

The hon. Gentleman believes that Scottish interests, because we are a minority in the House, have not been well represented over the years. We have over 10 per cent. of the membership of the House and our population is 5 million in a country of 55 million. He is suggesting that a Scottish Government and the Scottish people—representing 5 million people out of a European Community of over 320 million people where, on the basis of their population, their representation would amount to only 1·5 per cent.—would have more power in the European Parliament and that that would provide better protection for Scottish interests. It shows that the hon. Gentleman is living in a land of dreams and mystery that bears no relationship to the world in which the rest of us live.

Another factor that the House should be aware of and that the hon. Gentleman will have to live with——

**Mr. Andrew Welsh** (Angus, East): Will the right hon. and learned Gentleman give way?

**Mr. Rifkind:** I shall give way in a moment.

The hon. Gentleman and his hon. Friends present a case that is based on the proposition that, somehow, Scotland is in a unique position as a national minority without full rights within the European Community. They know perfectly well, however, that there is a multitude of peoples with their own national identity throughout western Europe who do not have representation on the Council of Ministers, who do not have the power of veto that he is so anxious to obtain and who are not full, individual member states of the European Community.

The hon. Gentleman is proposing no less than the fragmentation of western Europe and the European Community. He believes that the French, the Germans and the Italians would be prepared to accept the fragmentation of the United Kingdom, with each state becoming a member of the European Community. He does not see the implications of such a proposition for each of the national minorities—for the Basques, the Catalans, the Corsicans and the Bavarians. National minorities exist in virtually every state of the European Community. The hon. Gentleman and his hon. Friends can be seen once again to be living in a land of total unreality.

**Mr. Andrew Welsh:** As the right hon. and learned Gentleman is speaking for all those Governments, he should well understand that Scotland is in a very different position. I should like to know from the Secretary of State for Scotland, in his great defence of the Scottish people, how many times he has attended the Council of Ministers.

**Mr. Rifkind:** The hon. Gentleman seems to be unaware of the fact that our political philosophy is different from his. When I was a British Minister in the Foreign and Commonwealth Office I attended the Council of Ministers on numerous occasions. If ever I believe that it is appropriate for the Secretary of State for Scotland to attend a Council of Ministers meeting I shall do so. We are Unionists because we believe that Scottish interests, and those of the rest of the United Kingdom, are best served by a strong United Kingdom Government who can bring about major achievements for the United Kingdom as a whole. I do not expect the hon. Gentleman either to believe or to accept that proposition, but that is the basis of our philosophical differences.

**Mr. Welsh:** Has there been no appropriate occasion to defend the Scottish fishing industry and Scottish industry in general? Were those occasions not appropriate? Is that why the Secretary of State never attended such a meeting?

**Mr. Rifkind:** Only last Thursday I met the Scottish Fishing Federation. At no stage did it make any of the carping comments that the hon. Gentleman likes to make—far from it. It welcomes the opportunity to have close and continuing co-operation with the Scottish Office. That point is well recognised.

**Mr. Bill Walker** (Tayside, North): Does not my right hon. and learned Friend agree that the humbug and hypocrisy of "No Turning Back" is fully exposed when one looks at article I of the Act of Union, which says:

"That the two kingdoms of England and Scotland shall upon the first day of May which shall be in the year one thousand seven hundred and seven, and for ever after, be united into one kingdom by the name of Great Britain"?

The words are "for ever after." That, surely, is no turning back.

**Mr. Rifkind:** My hon. Friend is correct. It is not just Conservatives or Unionists who are quite successfully able to rubbish the arguments of the hon. Member for Banff and Buchan (Mr. Salmond). I think of the remarks that have been made by Mrs. Isobel Lindsay, a senior member of the hon. Gentleman's own party.

**Mr. Salmond:** Will the right hon. and learned Gentleman give way?

**Mr. Rifkind:** Perhaps I may quote her remarks before I give way to the hon. Gentleman, when he will seek to distance himself from them. In September of last year, Mrs. Isobel Lindsay said:

"In the new weighted voting system for the Commission which applies to many vital decisions Scotland would only have three votes out of 79. We would also of course be on the outmost periphery. Anyone who talks in glowing terms of Scotland's capacity to influence key economic decisions in the European Community is being more than a little unrealistic."

I now give way to someone who is a little unrealistic.

**Mr. Salmond:** The House missed the Secretary of State's answer to the fundamental point raised by the hon. Member for Tayside, North (Mr. Walker). Perhaps he will repeat it in a moment. In regard to the quotation, I am sure that the right hon. and learned Gentleman has studied majority voting procedures. He will realise that neither the large states nor the small states operating together can have majority voting on the Council of Ministers. I am sure that the people of Scotland would rather have three votes on the Council of Europe working for us than 10 votes working against us.

**Mr. Rifkind:** The people of Scotland did not think that when three quarters of them voted against that policy in the European elections.

**Mr. Ron Brown** *rose*——

**Mr. Dick Douglas** (Dunfermline, West) *rose*——

**Mr. Rifkind:** As many hon. Members wish to take part in the debate, I hope that hon. Gentlemen will excuse me if I do not give way.

Members of the Scottish National party put a lot of effort into the European policy that they thought would save them. Mr. Gordon Wilson, the chairman, said:

"The SNP believes that the Scots will choose independence in Europe. But let the people decide."

The people have rejected that overwhelmingly.

**Mr. Douglas** *rose*——

**Mr. Rifkind:** I shall not give way. No doubt the hon. Gentleman will wish to make his own remarks.

While hon. Gentlemen representing the SNP have been the subject of some ridicule because of their independence in Europe policy, in one way I am sympathetic to them. If there is anything more absurd than independence in Europe it is "Independence in the United Kingdom"—the slogan of the Labour party. That policy has not only caused some mystery, concern and curiosity among my right hon. and hon. Friends, but I understand that the shadow Foreign Secretary, the right hon. Member for Manchester, Gorton (Mr. Kaufman) has also found that extraordinary new policy a source of mystery. When he was asked his views on independence in the United Kingdom, he was quoted as saying,

"It seems to be an irrelevant fantasy. Perhaps someone would be kind enough to explain it to me."

I hope that when he is taken into a corner and it is explained to him——

**Mr. Ron Brown** *rose*——

**Mr. Douglas** *rose*——

**Madam Deputy Speaker:** Order. The Secretary of State has indicated that he is not giving way.

**Mr. Rifkind:** When one of my hon. Friends was trying to intervene earlier, the hon. Member for Edinburgh, Leith (Mr. Brown) kept barracking him and told him to seek an opportunity to speak in the debate. He should practise what he preaches.

In the gentlest possible way, I hope that, when Labour's interesting new policy has been explained in a way that is comprehensible to the right hon. Member for Gorton, it may also be explained to the House. The hon. Member for Glasgow, Garscadden (Mr. Dewar) is usually a careful user of words. He does not normally indulge in tautological nonsense. He does not normally invite Conservative or Opposition Members to accept a policy which is a grammatical absurdity and a political nonsense. If this is to be an exception we are entitled to know why.

5.13 pm

**Mr. Donald Dewar** (Glasgow, Garscadden): We are all agreed that Europe is important, our links with Europe matter and our developing role is also of vital importance. I suspect that that is not necessarily true in other parts of the Conservative party.

I cannot resist giving the Secretary of State a quotation which he will say I should not take too seriously, but it comes from a good source, *Scottish Tory News,* and it has a splendid photograph of Lord Goold looking masterful on the front page. On the back page it has an account of

"The Scottish Conservative Party's Annual European Educational Trip, affectionately known as Bob Balfour's Bus Tours (and nick-named 'The Daughters of the Revolution Give Loathsome Johnny European One in the Teeth') . . . The Tour, the purpose of which is to educate Party members about the functions of the European Parliament, . . . is heavily subsidised by both the EC and the German Christian Democratic Union".

The tour included

"Visits to SHAPE headquarters, the European Parliament buildings in Strasbourg, and numerous Bier-Kellers".

It was "very informative" and had

"only . . . one minor setback, when a mad Frenchman crashed his car into the back of a bus. But slight casualties apart"—

that must be a reference to Mr. Alasdair Hutton and Mr. James Provan—

"the trip was immensely successful, churning out many a born-again European amongst the Scottish Tories."

It then invites people to apply to 3 Chester street for the next trip later this summer.

The opening paragraph was:

"They came. They saw. They couldn't muster up the strength to conquer, so they went away again."

That is a perfectly fair comment on the Scottish Conservative party.

There is some reason for the lack of enthusiasm in Conservative circles about 1992 and the integrated market. After 10 years of Conservative rule and after many years of an apparent economic miracle, so we are told, the United Kingdom has a visible trade deficit with the other 11 members of the EC, which in 1988 was £13,500 million —an unprecedented record of failure, representing more than two thirds of our visible trade deficit. I make that point at the outset, because when we talk about the structures, the theories and the constitutional arguments, we cannot ignore the simple fact that under the Conservative Government we have had a disastrous time in Europe and we are at the wrong end of every piece of European economic arithmetic.

The motion is no more than a worthless swirl of unconnected ideas and prejudices. It is tempting to ask people to examine not what the SNP says but what it does, but that assumes a certain consistency, at least in its aims, which is becoming harder to justify. In a quote which will certainly be familiar to hon. Members representing the SNP, I wish to refer to the views of Dr. Flora Isles, the group secretary of the SNP group on Tayside regional council. She said:

"The Party has apparently no firm policy on anything, and frequently changes it to suit the circumstances at any one time: or sometimes it appears to have several different policies on one issue."

I could not identify or define the problem more succinctly if I spent some time on the drafting.

I cannot talk about it at any great length, but there are interesting parallels between the European situation and

[*Mr. Donald Dewar*]

Dr. Flora Isles's problems over the poll tax. I hope that SNP Members will answer the relevant question put by Dr. Isles when she said:

"The Party had better decide now whether it wishes to continue to have councillors. It certainly cannot beg people to stand as candidates and then expect them to plunge themselves and their families into a state of financial disaster."

I understand from the chairman of the group, Councillor Frances Duncan, that the SNP policy supremo, Mr. MacAskill urged them that they

"must not go down the surcharge road."

The gap between rhetoric and reality is one of the problems in Europe and in the SNP stance.

Apparently the great turning point on Europe was the much heralded SNP conference this year at Inverness. It was much heralded. Mr. Gordon Wilson, who one or two of us may remember is the leader of the SNP, said of his policy:

"This is a bridge and what we are seeing is a narrowing, rushing stream now broadening out."

He continued:

"Rather than grasp a nettle, the party has grasped a thistle."

That must have been rather an uncomfortable experience, but I am not sure whether it explains with any great clarity why the SNP has changed its position.

It is interesting that it was reported that at the SNP conference

"Many doubters were won over by an amendment that any Scottish government would put the terms of entry to the EC to the Scottish people in a referendum."

That has been acknowledged today by the hon. Member for Banff and Buchan (Mr. Salmond), but it is a little odd that a party which is banking everything on the total irresponsibility of suggesting that there is solution for the country except as an independent nation in Europe has to buy support at its own party conference by promising a referendum on a self-evident truth. That suggests a certain dash of expediency which is difficult to justify.

We then have the saga with which we are all familiar of the seats where the SNP MEP—that used to be a plural concept—will sit. The hon. Member for Glasgow, Govan (Mr. Sillars), in a BBC programme on 2 June was pressed by me, among others. He made it clear that Mrs. Winifred Ewing had been wrong for all these years and would be dropped overboard without a backward glance. She would have to decamp and she would be told so. He also made it clear that he would not sit with the Socialists. He said that he would not sit with the British Labour group and that he would not sit with the French Socialists because they were soft on terrorism and were not worthy of his support or friendship.

He then said:

"Our executive are actually going to discuss this. [Laughter.] Oh yes, oh yes. We are going to review our position."

The implication was that it would be reviewed so that when people put crosses on ballot papers, they would know exactly what was happening. Matters have not worked out that way. We still do not know about the SNP's position, although we may hear a little more about it in the rest of the debate. We cannot claim to know where the SNP stands on Europe if we cannot find out even where its members are going to sit in the European Parliament.

"Scotland independent in Europe" is not a simple slogan but an exercise in expediency. I agree with the Secretary of State to the extent that I believe that separatism has now been recognised as a desperate problem for a separatist party. That was frankly set out in August 1988 in the "No Turning Back" pamphlet written by the hon. Member for Govan. I do not want to bother the House with further quotations so I will say merely that it was in an extended passage entitled:

"A sharp reminder about separatism."

It was clear from what the hon. Gentleman said that he felt that the SNP would not be able to remove people's doubts about separatism, about the self-interest it represents and about the destruction and dislocation that would come with it unless the SNP could find some way to persuade people that the party was an animal that had changed to a wholly different position.

What made the idea of Scotland being independent in Europe attractive was not the merits of the argument, but the fact that it could be camouflage and used for electoral advantage and to get over what the hon. Member for Govan clearly recognised were the major intellectual and political disadvantages of being seen as a separatist party. That is not the right basis on which a major shift in policy should be taken.

I do not know what the practical problems or possibilities of Scotland negotiating its entry would be if the people of Scotland decided that they wished to follow the advice of the SNP and, frankly, I shall not spend a great deal of time on the matter. I am glad that today we have not had the usual obscure arguments about the Greenland precedent and that we have not had to watch the hon. Member for Govan and his hon. Friends dancing on the head of a pin—a rather inelegant exercise. We heard about an eminent authority—indeed, the greatest living authority in the world. It came as a considerable relief to Labour Members that that person turned out not to be the hon. Member for Govan. There is normally an arrogant certainty about his views which suggests that he has at least convinced his friends and colleagues that he falls into that category.

Whether Scotland gets into the EC or not, it is obviously important that Scotland remains within the market which is the United Kingdom, whether that market is part of the European Community or not. Even the substantial number of SNP supporters who wish to be independent, but outside the EC, would agree that we have to have those arrangements. The reason is the dislocation and disruption to which I have referred. This week, there has been a great deal of concern about Wang and about the branch factory phenonemon. I believe that there would be a genuine problem even within the EC if we were an independent country which had deliberately distanced itself economically and politically from the rest of the United Kingdom, which could be a positive action of dissociation.

Presumably there would be a danger, for example, that any English company with factories in Scotland might see those factories as the first likely victims in the case of recession. We must also consider the dismemberment of social services and public utilities. What would happen to families in different parts of the United Kingdom who would suddenly be faced with a choice between competing nationalities? Although the pace of European integration may proceed, that would be the position for a long time.

What trust can we put in a budget that depends on optimistic assumptions about oil revenues? If oil revenues are a key factor, we are entitled to ask what would happen if they went. The budget does not add up and assumes cuts in housing, local government and education. If one is launching an independent, separate state, one does not do so on special factors that will have only a limited life. One does not do so on a prospectus of 30 or 40 years.

The hon. Member for Banff and Buchan referred to Professor Malcolm Slesser, who is a well-known member of the Scottish Nationalists.

**Mr. Sillars:** He is a nice fellow.

**Mr. Dewar:** The hon. Member for Govan describes Professor Slesser, rather patronisingly, as a nice fellow. I will repeat what Professor Slesser said:

"In fact, a financial forecast of what Scotland would be like as an independent country is about as meaningless as one of Chancellor Lawson's pieces of star-gazing."

That is a pretty harsh judgment on the exercise in which the hon. Member for Banff and Buchan has been engaged for the past 12 months, but it is perhaps a good dose of reality when looking at that piece of make-believe.

**Mr. Salmond:** The hon. Gentleman and I have debated this subject before, not least on a "Left, Right and Centre" programme two months ago. The hon. Gentleman stumped off after the programme saying that it would never happen again. I do not know what would never happen again. I do not know whether he meant he would never discuss again the economics of an independent Scotland or would not appear on "Left, Right and Centre" to do so. On that programme, the hon. Gentleman failed wholly to discredit the view that there would be substantial economic opportunities for an independent Scotland. Perhaps the hon. Gentleman will move on to tell us what areas of economic policy his new concept of independence within the United Kingdom would provide. Would it, for example, provide any control over monetary policy in Scotland?

**Mr. Dewar:** That was not exactly a ringing defence of the hon. Gentleman's budget and its problems. It was more a case of someone in a tight corner trying to counter-attack. All I can say to the hon. Gentleman—and I hope that he is not disappointed by this—is that I cannot remember the context of that conversation, but I must also say that I do not normally remember conversations with him.

It is intellectually bizarre to find a group of politicians who argue for Socialism in one country, as some members of the SNP have done honourably for some time, and who now embrace the Single European Act with an enthusiasm that makes Lord Cockfield look like a foot-dragger. One cannot rely on Scotland as a nation state with a fast-fading veto for protection in the European Community. One certainly cannot rely on Scotland being able to hold up the pace of change by using a veto in terms of the Luxembourg compromise. If that is the basis on which the SNP is arguing its case, it is out of touch with the times, and it is no more than a bad joke.

In its policy document in June 1989, the SNP produced what it described as the way in which one measures a nation's independence. It said that it is measured

"by whether it controls its own economy through legislation and a range of economic powers."

It said that the chief of the essential tests of independence were:

"monetary and fiscal policy; exchange rate policy; overall public expenditure; trade policy".

I do not agree because I think that that is too simplistic an approach, but if that is the test, it seems that we are in the business of what the report itself in the heading to that chapter called "bogus independence" in the light of what is happening in Madrid and in the European Community at present. It is also not sensible in terms of the tests that the SNP itself has set, let alone by the tests that others may have set.

I am genuinely surprised—and I say this with respect —to hear the hon. Member for Govan apparently arguing that of course he wants independence in Europe, as long as the European Parliament does not have any power, control or legislative authority over Scotland or any other part of the member state. I will, of course, read the *Hansard* report of his comments. That view is wholly incompatible with his own pamphlet a few months ago. He dismissed the pamphlet as a personal point of view, so if his comments today are the official policy of the SNP, which I presume they are, they are an extraordinary mockery of many of the points that the SNP has been arguing in recent debates and of its whole European stance.

**Mr. Kenneth Hind** (Lancashire, West): Will the hon. Gentleman give way?

**Mr. Dewar:** No, because I must hurry on.

**Mr. Hind:** I want to answer the hon. Gentleman's question.

**Mr. Dewar:** I do not want my question answered from the Conservative Benches.

**Mr. Hind:** What about an independent Scotland in the United Kingdom? Tell us what that idea is all about.

**Mr. Dewar:** I will not give way. I want to bother the House with one more important quotation, in which the hon. Member for Lancashire, West (Mr. Hind) may be interested. It is from an authority that the Secretary of State also used, which is a respectable authority in nationalist terms. Mrs. Isobel Lindsay spoke at the Inverness conference of the SNP against the "Scotland independent in Europe" motion. She said that the resolution was dishonest because it implied that the single European market would have devastating effects under the status quo, but not for an independent Scotland. The conference report states:

"'This is a nonsense,' she insisted".

That is the problem that the SNP faces. Isobel Lindsay has been my unwilling ally in this debate, but nevertheless she is an honest witness and records the matter fairly.

**Mr. Sillars:** Is the hon. Gentleman going to deal with another area of enormous interest to Isobel Lindsay, who has been as consistent on this issue as on the European issue, and consider that part of our motion dealing with the contradiction of the Labour party in Scotland saying "No Trident" when the hon. Gentleman is imposing Trident on Scotland because his right hon. Friend the Leader of the Opposition and the national executive have said that Trident will come to Scotland?

**Mr. Dewar:** I am not going to discuss defence policy today—*[Interruption.]*—because it is not the main thrust

[*Mr. Dewar*]

of this argument. However, I shall be delighted to discuss it on other occasions and I do not doubt that I shall have the opportunity.

Experience in Europe proves that one must be in the big league if one is to survive effectively. If I went around the 11 European Community countries—apart from Denmark—and asked, "Who is representing Denmark in Madrid?", I expect that the answer would be many blank expressions. Perhaps that is a cheap way of making the point, but it is an effective way. We must recognise that small countries do not have much clout or leverage.

The hon. Member for Banff and Buchan was being dishonest when he suggested that the recent MORI poll showed 35 per cent. support for the SNP's position, because on the issue of independence in Europe there was just 22 per cent. support—less than the Conservative party polled at the last general election. I should have thought that nothing could be more telling about the SNP's position. The Scottish National party will not win this argument because argument and information are the enemies of its case. It is asking the Scots to grasp at the appearance and trappings of power, but to surrender the reality of influence.

**Mr. Hind:** Will the hon. Gentleman give way?

**Mr. Dewar:** No, I shall not give way because I am just coming to an end.

**Mr. Hind** *rose——*

**Mr. Dewar:** No, I have said that I shall not give way.

**Mr. Hind** *rose——*

**Madam Deputy Speaker:** Order. I call Mr. Dewar.

**Mr. Dewar:** Opposition Members do not join the Government in defending the status quo. A great deal is happening in Europe at the moment to which we in Scotland could relate effectively. Alliances are being built and contacts made. New power structures are beginning to emerge within the EEC. If one talks to the West Germans and to the men who are in the Länder, to the Basques and to the Catalans, one realises that their presence is now being felt and that they are now beginning to build their own methods of working together and in partnership with national Governments to influence events. If we in Scotland are to do that, our system must be reformed and we must be given the opportunity.

As is well known, the next Labour Government will establish a Scottish Parliament, which I hope will take advantage of those opportunities. The Scottish National party belittles that and calls it "the Bavarian solution". But having looked at the Bavarian economy and experience, I can only say that I should not mind seeing it repeated in Scotland in terms of employment and economic opportunity. The Scottish National party belittles that, but they would, wouldn't they? We should talk to those who are setting the pace in Europe. We should recognise the markedly greater powers—greater than the Länder and greater than those of the regions of Spain—that a Scottish Parliament would have within the framework of the United Kingdom.

When I make such points, I am accused of trying to have the best of both worlds, but why should we not have the best, if it is available? There is nothing wrong with that.

Scotland should have the strength of being in full partnership with the United Kingdom. It should have the strength of proper independence within the framework of the United Kingdom. It should have the strength of being able to work with the rest of the United Kingdom within Europe, but it should also have the flexibility and the potential of a developing role, directly affecting European policy.

Our reforms and policies would give Scotland all that. They are right on the merits of the argument. I believe that they have the support of most Scots. We are determined to deliver and we shall do so at an early date.

5.33 pm

**Mr. Allan Stewart** (Eastwood): The hon. Member for Banff and Buchan (Mr. Salmond) made a predictable speech, except in one regard. We shall have to check in *Hansard* and read precisely what he said, but I understood him to say that his party supported the Irish nation's right of self-determination. If he said that, I must advise him that that is precisely the policy of Sinn Fein and that it is something that we shall have to consider further.

I turn to the speech of the hon. Member for Glasgow, Garscadden (Mr. Dewar)——

**Mr. Ron Brown** *rose——*

**Mr. Stewart:** I cannot give way to the hon. Gentleman because I must get on. Time is limited.

At the end of his speech the hon. Member for Garscadden referred briefly to the concept of independence in the United Kingdom, but he did not explain it. It was a ringing slogan, but his speech did not address its inherent contradictions in any way. He propounded the need for some kind of what he referred to as a "Parliament", although his amendment refers to a "Parliament or Assembly". It is clear that his party cannot decide even on the name of that great body.

During the Glasgow, Central by-election a grand meeting of all the candidates was called by the Campaign for a Scottish Assembly. It was attended by all the parties, except for the Scottish National party, which presumably was, not unnaturally, reluctant to subject its policy to sustained and public scrutiny. Then, as now, the proponents yet again disagreed on all the fundamentals.

**Mr. Hind** *rose——*

**Mr. Stewart:** I shall give way later to my hon. Friend.

All those attending disagreed on the powers, on the taxation system and on the voting system for such a body. At the end of the proceedings, there was the usual Laurel and Hardy act, featuring two of the leading, self-appointed, non-elected great men of the constitutional convention movement, Canon Kenyon Wright and Mr. Bob McCreadie, the candidate of the Scottish Social and Liberal Democratic party, who subsequently became one of the most spectacularly non-elected candidates of recent British political history. When there was a vote——

**Mr. Thomas Graham** (Renfrew, West and Inverclyde) *rose——*

**Mr. Stewart:** I shall give way to the hon. Gentleman later, after I have given way to my hon. Friend the Member for Lancashire, West (Mr. Hind).

At the end of the proceedings the vote was in favour of the position of the Scottish National party—although the party was not there. At that point, Mr. McCreadie stormed off the platform, abusing Canon Kenyon Wright, the chairman of the meeting. Indeed, Mr. McCreadie almost went as far as demanding that the canon be fired —*[Laughter.]* Yes, we are the party of the awfully good bad puns. That is yet another example of the more that one goes to the root of the slogans that we hear from the Labour party and from those who advocate an assembly, a parliament or whatever it should be called, the more the disagreements come through——

**Mr. Graham** *rose*——

**Mr. Stewart:** I have said that I shall give way first to my hon. Friend the Member for Lancashire, West.

**Mr. Hind:** I am obliged to my hon. Friend, who will no doubt be aware that Conservative Members who believe in the United Kingdom and who feel that Scotland has an important part to play in it might consider the Act of Union in terms of a Scottish Parliament and question why an hon. Member such as myself, representing an English constituency, should have over 85,000 constituents, when many constituencies in Scotland are much smaller. I refer especially to the Tweeddale, Ettrick and Lauderdale constituency, which has just over 38,500 constituents. Will the Labour party's policy include trading some of the seats in this Parliament for some in the Scottish Parliament so that the United Kingdom as a whole could be more equally represented in this House?

**Mr. Stewart:** My hon. Friend has made a valid point. I hope that the Labour party will answer that question. Of course, Opposition Members will not endeavour to answer the more fundamental questions. I am not referring simply to those about numbers, but also the West Lothian question, which is wholly unanswerable.

Both my right hon. and learned Friend the Secretary of State and the hon. Member for Garscadden gave the House some interesting quotations——

**Mr. Graham** *rose*——

**Mr. Stewart:** I shall give way to the hon. Gentleman, but then I must complete my speech.

**Mr. Graham:** The hon. Gentleman referred earlier to the Constitutional Convention. I can assure the hon. Gentleman that the people of Scotland would prefer to see the Scottish National party and the Conservative party and their representatives playing a meaningful role in the Constitutional Convention. However, it is well known throughout Scotland that Scottish National party councillors have no hesitation in entering into deals and agreements with Conservative members to run the council. As the hon. Gentleman knows, on Renfrew district council the Scottish National party formed a coalition with the Conservative party. The same happened in Glasgow district council. In nearly every authority in which the Scottish National party has councillors, those councillors have no hesitation in doing deals with the Conservatives so that they can run the council and implement near-Conservative proposals. I find it strange for a Conservative Member not to agree at least to work in the Constitutional Convention along with SNPs, Liberals and everyone else. We would welcome it.

**Mr. Stewart:** The hon. Member for Renfrew, West and Inverclyde (Mr. Graham) has raised the interesting point

of the policy of the Scottish National party. The hon. Member for Garscadden has quoted rightly and properly from Dr. Flora Isles on the great Tayside controversy. No doubt, when winding up, the Scottish National party representative will wish to refute the allegation that it has put forward different policies in different parts of the country. All four hon. Members representing the SNP in the House will wish to proclaim from the rooftops how much they agree with Mr. Alex Neill, its candidate in the by-election, that it is the party of the Red Clydesiders, and that the mantle of Clydeside Socialist, Left-wing philosophy correctly belongs to the Scottish National party. Let that ring out around the hedgerows of Perthshire, Angus and Banff and Buchan.

**Mr. Bill Walker:** Does my hon. Friend agree that probably the SNP did so badly in Angus and Perthshire in the recent elections because the people did not believe that it was the inheritor of Red Clydesiders?

**Mr. Stewart:** I am sure that my hon. Friend is right. The advantage of the Conservative party, or for that matter the Labour party, is that we can pursue our policies and we do not have to remember which constituency we are in at the time. We have a consistent philosophy.

**Mr. Ron Brown:** Will the hon. Gentleman give way?

**Mr. Stewart:** I shall give way for the last time to the hon. Gentleman.

**Mr. Brown:** It is interesting to hear the chit-chat between the nationalists and the Conservatives, bearing in mind that it is almost like when auld freens fa' oot—as they say in Scotland. We should remember that in 1979 the nationalists were supporting the Tories. *[Interruption.]* Perhaps they have learnt something, but they have not learnt enough about Europe. Europe is much larger than the area of the EEC. If the hon. Member for Glasgow, Govan (Mr. Sillars) wants independence in Europe, he will not get it in Strasbourg, but he will get it within that part of the world that can respond to Socialist policies.

I can say also to the Labour party, which is important to me, that if we back-track on the basic policies in Scotland, particularly on the poll tax, and kid people on——

**Madam Deputy Speaker:** Order. I must remind the hon. Gentleman that an intervention has to be a question and a pertinent comment, not a speech.

**Mr. Stewart:** The question of the hon. Member for Edinburgh, Leith (Mr. Brown) would be better directed to the representatives of the Scottish National party than to me. In the Glasgow, Central by-election, day after day the Scottish National party reassured the people that it was a Socialist party and the party that had inherited the mantle of the Red Clydesiders. I hope that that makes the hon. Gentleman a little happier.

The Scottish National party has been, first, split on the issue of Europe and, secondly, has taken its current position for electoral expediency. There have been quotations from Isobel Lindsay. I shall quote another distinguished SNP figure, a former senior vice-chairman of the SNP, who said on 17 September 1988 in *The Scotsman:* "1992 is about the free market economy. To those of you who think of yourselves as Socialists, have you given any thought to what you are being asked to give up?"

[*Mr. Stewart*]

The truth is that it has adopted its slogan of independence in Europe purely because, as the hon. Member for Govan said in one of his books or pamphlets,

"the charge of separation disappears."

**Mr. Graham:** Will the hon. Gentleman give way?

**Mr. Stewart:** No, because so many other hon. Members wish to speak.

It has been put forward solely for electoral expediency. It raises, as a policy, two key questions: is it deliverable, and is it desirable? The argument put forward by the hon. Member for Banff and Buchan that it is deliverable rests on two assertions. The first assertion is correct. He is correct in saying that, if the Scottish National party gained a majority of Scottish seats, in practice it would have the right to withdraw and to negotiate to take Scotland out of the United Kingdom. Of course, Parliament can repeal the Act of Union at any time, but, in practice, if that happened, Parliament would say that the people of Scotland had elected a majority of representatives of the party whose objective, purpose and the reason for its very existence was to break up the Union. I believe that that is precisely what would happen.

I do not believe that the second assertion on deliverability is correct. It is no good quoting lawyers, however expert. The question is what the Council of Ministers would do. What would happen is that there would be the continuing member—the successor state to the United Kingdom—and Scotland would have an application on the table. It has been pointed out that there is a freeze on applications until 1993. I shall quote from the 1989 report of an independent Scottish institute, the Fraser of Allander Institute, which is not normally especially favourable to the Conservative cause. It said:

"the negotiations will take several years and Scotland would be lucky to join the European Community this century."

That is the reality.

**Mr. Salmond:** Will the hon. Gentleman give way?

**Mr. Stewart:** No. I have already said that I will not give way again.

The second question is: is it desirable? My right hon. and learned Friend the Secretary of State has spelt out the case against that very clearly this afternoon. My position has always been clear. Given the choice between the devil of a unilateral Scottish Assembly and the deep blue sea of an independent Scotland, I would give unequivocal support to an independent Scotland. A unilateral Assembly would lead to decades of constitutional chaos and then the break-up of the United Kingdom.

Scotland faces in practice a three-way choice at the next election. The choice is between the Conservative and Unionist party, which is for private enterprise and a stable economy; the Labour party, putting forward whatever brand of yuppie Socialism is then in current vogue and a constitutional hotch-potch which would lead to chaos; and the Scottish National party. If people believe in a Socialist Scotland outside the United Kingdom—I repeat, with an uncertain relationship with the European Community—of course they should vote for it, but not otherwise.

**Mr. Ron Brown:** John Maclean.

**Mr. Stewart:** John Maclean will not be an elector at the next general election. It will be no good people saying afterwards, "We did not mean it; it was just a wee protest about the Health Service," or complaining because the road was up outside their house. If people vote for the Scottish National party and for this slogan in sufficient numbers, the Act of Union will be broken. Let no one be unclear about that. I hope and believe that it will not happen. We should steadily and confidently counter the propaganda against the Union by those who argue that the Union does not work to the benefit of Scotland.

At the beginning of this Parliament the Labour party adopted the language and gestures of nationalism. I believe that it has initiated a partial retreat from that stance as it has begun to realise the dangers of that policy. Let us hope that that retreat into common sense continues.

5.49 pm

**Mr. Michael J. Martin** (Glasgow, Springburn): I am concerned at the way in which the SNP can present its case to the electorate one year and execute a complete U-turn the following year.

My intervention in the Secretary of State's speech was important as it is worth reminding the hon. Member for Glasgow, Govan (Mr. Sillars) that he visited the Rolls-Royce factory with Margo MacDonald and the hon. Member for Southend, East (Mr. Taylor). My hon. Friend the Member for Edinburgh, Leith (Mr. Brown) was right to say that we are not just talking about Europe, but the European Economic Community. The hon. Member for Govan once argued that the EEC is undemocratic and that Members of the European Parliament do not have any power and that that power rests with the Commissioners and the Council of Ministers. Why is it then that the only time we heard about independence within Europe from that hon. Gentleman was during the campaign in Glasgow, Govan?

**Mr. Sillars** rose——

**Mr. Martin:** I shall not give way, as the hon. Gentleman will have an opportunity to reply later.

Why did the SNP not use the slogan "Independence within the European Community" rather than "Independence within Europe" given that the hon. Member for Govan argued that we were not talking about Europe, but the Community? The SNP has been dishonest. There are aspects of the EEC that I do not like, but I firmly believe that if we are part of Europe, Scotland is stronger as part of the United Kingdom than as a separate state.

The SNP is also dishonest because its policy is not just about independence, but is anti-English. Everything it does and everything it stands for is directed by a hatred of the English. Why should we seek to break away from a country with which we have a common border and which is part of a small island? The SNP wants to fragment the United Kingdom, but Scotland would not have a chance as a single entity within the EEC. It would be out-voted by the more powerful nations and it would mean that England and Wales would become weaker.

The SNP reminds me of the party with which it claims to have links, the party of Quebec in Canada. The provinces of Canda are autonomous, but the party of Quebec wants to separate that province from Canada. It believes that such separation would make the province stronger, but the real motive for that separation is its hatred for the people it describes as the "Anglophones". The party of Quebec is more interested in fining a tobacconist because he refused to put a French sign up on his door than in anything else.

**Mr. Salmond:** What has that got to do with us?

**Mr. Martin:** There is plenty on the record to prove that the SNP and members of the party of Quebec have met and regard themselves as fraternal bodies. If the SNP gets any power in Scotland the racial elements displayed by the party of Quebec will become apparent in Scotland.

**Mr. Andrew Welsh** rose——

**Mr. Martin:** I will not give way as the hon. Gentleman will have his own opportunity later.

We have already seen what happened when the SNP got some power in the city of Glasgow. In Glasgow we have a lot for which to thank the Salvation Army as it looks after the destitute, young children and many other needy people. The first thing that the SNP did when it won seats on the Glasgow district council—the proposal came from Mr. Stewart Ewing, the husband of the European Member of Parliament representing the Highlands—was to refuse a modest grant to the Salvation Army. At that time the SNP had wards in Easterhouse, Provan and the Drumchapel areas and it said that it would not vote for any proposals that would improve the lot of those who voted Labour. There is a piece of land still lying in my ward on which houses could have been built had it not been for the Nats aligning themselves with the Tories and refusing to build council houses in the Eastfield district of Springburn.

There is also a Fascist element within the SNP which the leadership will do absolutely nothing about. Consider the great victory won by my hon. Friend the Member for Glasgow, Central (Mr. Watson) and let us remember what the SNP did. I have witnesses to prove that in Royston hill SNP workers encouraged young children to throw stones at Labour cars.

**Mr. Andrew Welsh** rose——

**Mr. Martin:** I will not give way, as I want this to go on the record to prove what type of people the SNP are.

**Mr. Welsh:** On a point of order, Madam Deputy Speaker. If it is in order for the hon. Gentleman to place this nonsense on record, is it also in order to ask him whether he complained to the police about it? That was the proper course of action if such an incident took place.

**Mr. Martin:** I have already said that I have witnesses to the events that took place and I am willing to obtain statements from them.

There is a convent in Royston hill that looks after elderly people. It asked for Labour workers to come up to take elderly people who had a postal vote to the polling station. Those people were in their 80s—we have them in every constituency—and they value their votes. As they were being taken into the polling station, SNP workers insulted them by saying that the Labour party had robbed them from the grave to get them to vote. That was the type of insult that they hurled at people who wanted to exercise their democratic rights.

**Mr. John Maxton** (Glasgow, Cathcart): My hon. Friend, unlike myself, was not present at the count at Glasgow, Central. First, my hon. Friend the new Member for Glasgow, Central (Mr. Watson) had to be brought in

at a side door because the police could not guarantee his safety from the SNP mob outside. Some of us had to leave that count and we suffered racist abuse from that mob and were spat upon by people from the SNP.

**Mr. Martin:** I am glad that my hon. Friend mentioned that, because such things did not happen only at the Glasgow, Central by-election. Back in Margo MacDonald's time in Govan, when I was a young councillor, the agent for the Labour party had to be given police protection. Margo MacDonald came into the count bedecked with four big Highlanders in full Highland regalia as if they were her praetorian guard. Such actions demonstrate the type of people with which we are dealing, but the SNP leadership will do nothing about them.

If, God forbid, a majority of SNP Members are elected, the type of element seen at Glasgow, Central is bound to be elected. Such elections will be damaging to democracy in Scotland as well as damaging to the people of Glasgow and——

**Mr. Sillars:** Corrupt Labour.

**Mr. Martin:** It was a form of corruption for the hon. Member for Govan to hold an anti-poll tax meeting on the borders of my constituency and that of the late Bob McTaggart when he told the people not to pay their poll tax when he knew full well that the Angus local authority, controlled by the SNP, was recruiting labour to implement that poll tax. It is corrupt and dishonest to attack Strathclyde regional council for its redundancies because it gave one of the best redundancy agreements I have seen in a long time—whereas, in Tayside, 900 cleaners lost their jobs.

**Mr. Brian Wilson** (Cunninghame, North): Would my hon. Friend agree that, in any election campaign, the dishonesty of a leaflet is compounded when the leaflet's publisher does not have the guts to put on it the name of its party or its symbol, and that party is identifiable only in the tiniest print?

**Madam Deputy Speaker:** Order. I must caution the hon. Gentleman that we are straying a long way from the motion on the Order Paper.

**Mr. Martin:** I saw that leaflet. The last piece of dishonesty that I want to mention——

**Mr. Graham** rose——

**Mr. Martin:** I shall not give way.

It is dishonest to tell the people of Scotland that the SNP wants to fight to have more power in Europe when the SNP Euro-candidate in Glasgow could not get in quickly enough to fight to get into Westminster after the death of the previous Member. That shows how dishonest the SNP is.

I am glad to be able to put on record the type of element which the hon. Member for Govan joined when he deserted the Labour party. I am glad that he deserted the Labour party because we do not want his kind in the party. I hope that, at the very least, the media will take note of the type of people running around the streets af Scotland saying, "Vote SNP".

6.3 pm

**Mr. Bill Walker** (Tayside, North): It is always a pleasure to follow the honest approach of the hon. Member for Glasgow, Springburn (Mr. Martin). Too often in these debates we listen to intellectual exchanges, but do not hear nearly enough said from the heart, and the Scottish people understand the feelings of the heart. I am sure that the hon. Member for Springburn is always respected by his electorate because he speaks from the heart.

I understood why the hon. Member for Springburn felt as he did about the SNP's attitude and the unsavoury elements which, sadly, exist within that party. There is no doubt that it has practised intimidation and lies, not only in his constituency, but in mine. It was asked whether such matters had been reported to the police; everything of which I speak has been reported to the police and has been dealt with.

At the last general election there was an SNP member at one of the polling stations in my constituency with massive badges and many credentials to show that he was entitled to be there—and with a shotgun. If ever there was evidence of intimidation, surely that was it. It was unfortunate for him that one of the first people to arrive at the polling station was an off-duty policeman who dealt summarily with the intimidator. Such practices are fairly common.

Anyone who has studied the SNP's position on independence in relation to anything must recognise that it is basically a separatist party which wants to break up the United Kingdom. It is asking the people of Scotland to give up all the benefits of belonging to Great Britain. We could spend a long time discussing the economic benefits, whether real, imagined or invented. However, I do not wish to spend too much time doing so. Like the hon. Member for Springburn, I wish to deal with other aspects of what it means to be part of the United Kingdom.

Since 1707, Scotland has retained its identity, history and culture, yet it has always played a massive part in the creation of British history, identity and culture. That is what the SNP wishes to rupture and destroy. Conservative and Labour Members and the Democrats, or whatever identity they have these days, have made it clear that we are parties of the Union. We may have different views about how we see the Union progressing, but we do not differ on the fact that we wish to retain the Union and this unitary Parliament.

In an intervention I drew attention to the wording of the Act of Union. People in Scotland constantly remind me about this Act, but I usually find that they have never read it. I do not think that any Act passed by this House is cast in stone because anyone who believes, as I do, in our democracy recognises that its cornerstone is that no Parliament is bound by decisions made by a previous one. This Parliament is paramount and, in conjunction with the other place, we can change the law as it affects the United Kingdom. Nothing is permanent.

However, in his intervention, comments and writing the hon. Member for Govan has made it quite clear that entry into the European Community is cast in stone, and there is no turning back. If that is his view of our relationship with Europe, surely that cannot also be the view of a man who wants to be a separatist and destroy the Act which created the Union.

**Sir Nicholas Fairbairn:** Secession from Britain inevitably means secession from Europe which would give the Scottish Nationalists the Scotland which they had before 1907—in Europe, but outside the market of the United Kingdom and, consequently, outside the market of Europe. Scotland was the poorest area because it was isolated at its own choice.

**Mr. Walker:** I thank my hon. and learned Friend for his helpful intervention, which neatly encapsulated the fundamental flaws in the arguments put forward by the separatist Nationalists.

We all know that the SNP's Govan by-election slogan, which should have read, "Separation in Europe" because, effectively, that is what it was asking for, was a policy put forward on the basis that the SNP has inherited Red Clydeside. Anyone who has made any attempt to win elections north of Perth will know that the Labour party has difficulty in doing so. In the mountain areas of the Highlands its members are lucky to save their deposits. Therefore, it would seem odd to suggest that the Red Clydeside flag should be flown by the nationalists north of Perth.

**Mr. Graham** *rose——*

**Mr. Walker:** No, I shall not give way. The hon. Gentleman has already made about three speeches.

The SNP row that we see in Angus and Tayside at the moment has its origins in the fact that the SNP in the north of Scotland, certainly in my constituency and Tayside, has always tried to present itself as the party of the middle or middle Right, certainly of the Right. It finds it difficult to accept that it is now the party of the Red Clydeside inheritance.

**Mr. Graham** *rose——*

**Mr. Walker:** Will the hon. Gentleman allow me to complete what I am saying?

That is why Dr. Flora Isles and other SNP members including one of my constituents, Councillor Francis Duncan, are so concerned. It has been said that, in a letter, Dr. Flora Isles made it clear that she did not understand the SNP's policies because it did not have any and seemed to have different policies for different places at different times. That has been put on the record by one of the leading SNP activists in Tayside.

Anyone who has studied the activities of SNP district councils will realise that the SNP believes that it can be selective about its policies in Europe or anywhere else. Its Members of Parliament in Europe can say there whether they agree with the legislation emerging from the European Parliament, the European Commission and the Council of Ministers. They will pick the policies that they like, just as they try to do here. Members of the SNP tell people in Scotland and elsewhere to reject the community charge, but in office it is a different story. The administration in Angus is busy collecting the charge and, more importantly, it is taking on more staff to ensure that it gets the money. That is the source of the confusion. The SNP is the party of all the people all the time with any policy, so long as it gives SNP members the chance to appear to be winning.

I am delighted to see the hon. Member for Glasgow, Central (Mr. Watson) in his place; he put a stop to this nonsense. I do not agree with Labour party policy, but at least Labour Members told the people of Scotland what their policy was—in Glasgow, Aberdeen, Wick, Thurso and the Western Isles. Their policy is the same everywhere. The nationalists want to be all things to all people.

I am not depressed by the recent European election results, which we have carefully analysed in my constituency. They show that I would be returned with a comfortable majority. *[Interruption.]* I make no apology for saying that the first thing I do after every election is to analyse how the results will affect me. If other hon. Members were honest, they would admit to doing the same. Analysis is possible because the people who vote give us little green cards—hon. Members know about the different ways of doing this. Tayside, North had the highest turnout in the north-east and, as we know, in north Tayside the higher the poll, the better it is for the sitting Member. In parts of my constituency the turnout was higher than 50 per cent., and it was largely a Tory turnout. That is why I speak so happily this evening.

The election result came about largely because of the confusion, chaos, misrepresentation and downright lies and intimidation developed by the SNP in recent years. Now it is all coming home to roost. SNP Members are a sorry lot; they will have to live with what they have done and said and with what their supporters have done and said. I invite the Red Clydesiders to come to my constituency to speak every week, because they will push up my majority——

**Mr. Graham:** Does the hon. Gentleman agree that the Red Clydesiders would probably turn in their graves at the thought that this lot—the SNP—are claiming to be the new breed of Red Clydesiders? Not long ago the SNP tore up the telegram from the Red Clydeside ship workers. Red Clydesiders must be appalled—their ancestors got results by voting Labour.

**Mr. Walker:** That needs no response from me.

I have mentioned history, identity and culture. Many people in Scotland who have connections with the Royal Navy, the Royal Air Force, the Army and the Royal Marines do not want their regiments, squadrons and ships disbanded and thrown away. How marketable in Perth and Perthshire would be the suggestion that we disband the Black Watch? What utter nonsense! Our British history, identity and culture are much more important than all the nonsense and fraudulent economic packages of which we have heard from the SNP.

6.16 pm

**Mrs. Ray Michie** (Argyll and Bute): I congratulate the Scottish National party on bringing this motion to the House, and on having consulted higher authority and taken advice that it should do so, so that we can all know what SNP Members mean by an independent Scotland in Europe. I want to concentrate on the constitutional aspects, not on personal matters. I hate nothing more than to hear Scots shouting at other Scots.

The SNP's argument for an independent Scotland in Europe is interesting, but fundamentally different from how my party sees Scotland's role in Europe. We view the Community as a group of interdependent states sharing a common political and economic structure, but largely composed of families of interdependent nations and regions.

There is no independence in the Community. On the contrary, when a state joins, it gives up some of its sovereignty to the institutions of the Community—to an extent, it "trades in" its independence, or part of it, for membership. The SNP plans to prise Scotland free from England, yet have it cede its newly won sovereignty to a body that would give England a continuing say in Scottish affairs. I hope that the SNP realises that whatever the merits of its case it could not be implemented without the majority consent of the Scottish people. I know that SNP Members have said that they would hold a referendum, but I am not yet clear about how they will become independent from the United Kingdom and then seek independence in Europe.

The SNP must remember what people in Scotland believe. The majority want to control their own affairs through a Scottish Parliament, but they do not want to sever their links and ties with the United Kingdom.

I have always been interested in the Labour party's slogan about an independent Scotland in the United Kingdom, but I am not sure whether it has yet explained what that means. We have yet to see full commitment by the Labour party to strong home rule. Historically, the Labour party has been lukewarm, if not actively hostile, to the idea of giving people greater constitutional control over their own affairs, particularly in Scotland.

I welcome the fact that the Opposition are now at last, after difficulties of their own, acknowledging the merits of the Liberal party's radical home rule policy, and that the hon. Member for Glasgow, Garscadden (Mr. Dewar) has been, if not on the road to Damascus, at least on the road to Bavaria. No doubt all will be revealed during the deliberations of the Constitutional Convention. If the Opposition can be converted to the overwhelming case for a fair electoral system, the Scottish people can be assured that their Parliament will not become a vehicle for imposing Socialism on Scotland. Those outwith the central belt would have no confidence in a system that produced simply Strathclyde writ large.

**Mr. Wilson:** Strathclyde has done okay by Argyll.

**Mrs. Michie:** I could dispute that, but I will not.

My party is the only true home rule party. Its policy is for a federal United Kingdom, with Scotland leading the way with the transfer of power from this place to a Scottish Parliament in Edinburgh. Unlike unionism or separatism, federalism is not a dogma. There is no federal model or blueprint that must be applied regardless of circumstances. The aim is to find the right balance between the states of the federation and between them and the centre.

With the restoration of the Scottish state within a federal United Kingdom the Scottish people would recover control of all their own affairs except those that they chose to leave to a federal Government, such as foreign affairs and defence. The division of function would be entrenched. Any disputes would be referred to a constitutional court for decision. There would be single-tier, all-purpose local authorities in order to avoid top-heavy costly Government structures.

Members of those authorities and of a Scottish Parliament would be elected by a modern electoral system of proportional representation that would reflect the diversity of views within Scotland. The first-past-the-post system is a dinosaur of a prehistoric constitutional era. We can see it here. The Government govern the United Kingdom with only 42 per cent. of the vote, yet they have

[*Mrs. Michie*]

a majority of 100-plus seats. In Scotland the Labour party has only 42 per cent. of the vote, yet it has 70 per cent. of the seats.

On home rule and Europe, it would be essential for a Scottish Government to have direct links with the European Community. At the level of the Council of Ministers that would mean that, on all matters affecting Scotland, a Scottish Minister would accompany the United Kingdom Minister and would be entitled to speak on Scotland's behalf. On matters that affected Scotland alone, the Scottish Minister would take the lead in negotiations and would be entitled to cast the United Kingdom vote.

**Dr. Norman A. Godman** (Greenock and Port Glasgow): With growing monetary union, surely domestic Parliaments will have no control over the deliberations of the Council of Ministers. Over the next few years that must inevitably mean that more power will accrue to the European Parliament and this place will lose power.

**Mrs. Michie:** I agree with the hon. Gentleman that this place will lose power. We have seen how horrified hon. Conservative Members are about that possibility. I was referring to a Scottish Parliament and to the European Community. Fishing is an example which I believe should be in the control of the Scottish Office or of a Scottish Parliament rather than the United Kingdom Parliament. A Minister from Scotland should be responsible for fishery negotiations in Europe.

Local authorities and others are ahead of the Government's lethargic approach to Europe. I give it to Strathclyde region that it has had a representative in Brussels for the last five years. We have just heard the announcement of £400 million for Strathclyde. We shall have to consider the fact that the Argyll and Bute region is not to benefit.

**Mr. Michael J. Martin:** Surely the hon. Lady must admit that every local authority worker in Argyll was over the moon when that region came into Strathclyde because rates of pay went up. That is all the workers shouted about when they came into Strathclyde. At least they had something to aim for.

**Mrs. Michie:** The local authority workers may have shouted with joy, but I and my party are in favour of single-tier local authorities. Strathclyde has done well, but there are many things that it does not do. It is unfortunate that we are not sharing in the £400 million of expenditure. On roads, for example, Strathclyde region decided in 1976 that it would not adopt any roads in Argyll and Bute that had not been kept up previously by the council. That is bad for the development of business. I am still trying to persuade Strathclyde region to reverse that policy.

It is interesting to compare the antiquated regional policy of the Government with the more progressive and enlightened federalism of other European countries. In West Germany the 11 Länder have modern information offices and lobby centres. They also have two observers who attend European Community ministerial meetings. At least five Spanish areas, including Catalonia and the Basque region, have representation in Europe. That is what I want to see for Scotland when it has its own Parliament.

The continued refusal of the Government and the Tory party in Scotland to acknowledge the wish of the Scottish people to control their own affairs never ceases to amaze me. The Conservative party has to answer some simple questions. Does the party recognise that Scotland is a nation? Does it accept that the Scottish people are entitled to determine their own affairs and that their wishes should be paramount? Is there not a great inconsistency when the Government proudly give self-determination to 1,800 islanders 3,000 miles away, yet arrogantly deny it to 5 million people 400 miles up the road?

The only sensible way of governing this country is to have a federal United Kingdom. The Secretary of State is a professed federalist, yet he has said that there is no demand for federalism. If we want out into the highways and byways of England and asked the people if they cared whether Scotland had its own Parliament, they would say, "Great; why should it not?" Some hon. Members representing constituencies south of the border think that we have over-representation. I am sure that many hon. Members would be delighted to see the back of us if we went to our own Scottish Parliament in Edinburgh. They would have much more time to debate their own affairs and we would not have to debate our affairs more often than not at midnight.

Where does all this leave Scotland? We are being governed without consent. The Government always claim to act in the name of freedom and choice, but it is they who decide what the choices are to be. It was put very well in the document "A Claim of Right for Scotland":

> "There is a profound hypocrisy in saying that the Scots should stand on their own feet while simultaneously denying them management of their own political affairs, and that denial is a clear deprivation of choice for Scots. Scots can stand on their own feet only by refusing to accept the constitution which denies them the power to do so."

I wish that the Government would understand these words.

The Tory Government claim, and say in their amendment, that they are bringing prosperity to Scotland. Even if that were the case, that is not an argument for denying the Scottish people the right to have a say in their affairs. It is as though the Government think that it is sufficient to offer us financial carrots while beating us with a constitutional stick. The case for home rule is not solely or predominantly an economic one and no one should be misled into thinking that this is now the case. We cannot be bought and sold.

The most pernicious suggestion that I have heard is that the only options for Scotland are the status quo and independence. That is a dangerous game to play. Polarisation of the debate into one of unionism and independence may result in many people being pushed against their will and interest into the separatist camp. The Secretary of State would be gambling that the voters will decide that they are British first and Scottish second. That is a bet which he would not win.

6.31 pm

**Sir Hector Monro** (Dumfries): It is not often that I follow a ghost party, but I am doing so now. I commiserate with the hon. Member for Argyll and Bute (Mrs. Michie), who has been abandoned, not only in the election, but by her party tonight. It is not often that we have a Scottish debate at which none of the SLD Members or Democrats turns up. That shows that the proud words that she has been delivering about the Scottish nation do not hold true for her colleagues.

I am enjoying tonight because, from both sides of the House, we have had the best demolition job that I have ever seen. The SNP must rue the moment that it chose the subject for this debate and coerced the Ulstermen into giving it the opportunity to hold it. Throughout the evening, holes have been drilled into its policies, where it has a united one at all. Throughout its existence it has been a party of isolation with a determination to break up the United Kingdom. This slogan of independence in Europe is but a facade. Even in late 1987, it was recommending a referendum so that it could get out of Europe if possible.

The hon. Member for Glasgow, Springburn (Mr. Martin) mentioned the SNP's brash attitude to electioneering. Those of us who have been involved in elections over many years have been saddened by the attitude of the SNP and its workers. There has always been civility in Scottish electioneering, and the rudeness, incivility and near-riot attitude of the SNP supporters do it no good. Much of this has been activated by the hon. Member for Glasgow, Govan (Mr. Sillars). He changed his party three times. He has written a book called "No Turning Back", but that is because nobody will have him back.

The SNP staked all on, and crowed like a rooster about, independence in Europe in the latest election. The ploy fooled no one and failed miserably.

**Mr. Home Robertson:** The Tory party did badly as well.

**Sir Hector Monro:** Touché. We increased our vote substantially.

**Mr. Home Robertson:** Not enough.

**Sir Hector Monro:** I accept that. One cannot win them all all the time.

We are coming to 1992, which is all about free trade and enterprise. Like the Labour party, the SNP has a Socialist doctrine in favour of Government controls and is opposed to the objective of Europe. During the 1974-79 period, the Labour Government had a great opportunity to take us into Europe with some enthusiasm, but they did not. They mucked up the common agricultural policy and did not get back one penny in rebates—something that we managed to achieve later.

We have not yet had an explanation of the Labour party's policy of independence in the United Kingdom, but I do not want to spoil our slightly more friendly relationship tonight.

In the European elections, the SNP flagship was the policy of independence in Europe, on which it hoped to win more seats, but it did not. The Scottish people did not endorse its policies. They were not taken in by the SNP budget, which was manifestly inaccurate. The income was grossly overstated and the expenditure was inaccurate. No person who thinks about the Scottish economy could do so without including in any policy the use of nuclear power. However, the SNP is dead against anything to do with nuclear energy, and so is against a nuclear deterrent, without which the United Kingdom and Scotland would be open to threats from another country. The SNP's opposition to that shows that it does not have its basic priorities right in terms of peace and defence.

The Scotland about which the SNP talks seems to be different from the country in which we all live. It is difficult to recognise the reality of the picture of Scotland that it paints. The SNP runs it down and makes no allowance for great achievements by the Secretary of State for Scotland and the Prime Minister. Let us take the example of unemployment. In May 1987, 337,000 people were unemployed—13·6 per cent. of the working population. Today, 239,000 are unemployed—9·6 per cent. The figure has reduced by nearly 100,000 in two years, and by four percentage points. My constituency has seen a 40 per cent. drop in unemployment in those two years, which shows that the economy is working.

**Mr. Home Robertson:** The hon. Gentleman's majority has gone down even more.

**Sir Hector Monro:** The Labour party came a rather bad second at the last election in Dumfries. I am not in the least bit worried about that.

There is no complacency in Scotland about unemployment. We have the Industry Department for Scotland, the enterprise trusts, the Scottish Development Agency, Government initiatives and employment training. All this is good for Scotland, but it is decried by the SNP. It is time that both that party and the Labour party made some effort to look at the good news in Scotland and how successful economic policies for the future of our country have been.

**Mr. Wilson:** The Tories lost two seats—that is good news.

**Sir Hector Monro:** Do not spoil it.

The Opposition parties fail to notice the dramatic improvements such as the development of roads like the M74, which is starting soon, the A75 and the roads in the north-east, and new hospital buildings and home ownership, which is going like a bomb. The quality of life, which is so important in Scotland, is improving rapidly. Company profits are the highest that they have been for 20 years in the United Kingdom and it is from there that we get the investment to provide jobs for Scotland. All this is good news, but it would be destroyed by the SNP's policy of independence.

There is Unionism and cohesion in Scotland. It does not want to be over-governed, whether by an assembly, by independence or by breaking up the United Kingdom. We want consolidation and confidence for the future, a climate of expansion and an ever-improving standard of living. We are producing that. The SNP, the Socialists and the Democrats will destroy it.

6.39 pm

**Mr. Jim Sillars** (Glasgow, Govan): Earlier in the debate the governor-general asked me to explain why my party argues for membership of the European Community as distinct from the old Union, when Scotland has been part of the Union for a long time but part of the European Community for only a short time. The right hon. Member for Henley (Mr. Heseltine) put it rather well. He said:

"It is important that we understand the changing definition of sovereignty. If one changes the definition of sovereignty, power moves from old concentrations to new, which is a source of resentment. How could it be otherwise? We are at the heart of that dilemma because power is moving from this place, which causes a growing and legitimate concern."—[*Official Report,* 18 May 1989; Vol. 153, c. 536.]

[*Mr. Jim Sillars*]

Indeed, it was in recognition of that change that I first spoke about independence in Europe on 3 May 1972, as reported in *Hansard* at column 531.

Leaving aside the SLD, at first sight there appear to be three options: independence in Europe, the status quo and Labour party policy. In fact, there are just two options: first, independence in Europe and, secondly, the two variants of Unionism. We must compare one with the other. I shall first discuss the Tory variant of Unionism. It requires us to accept a continued legislative incorporation in an integrated political system.

The hon. Member for Tayside, North (Mr. Walker) kept talking about the unitary state. Under the Tory party, that political system subordinates Scottish policy to that of England, as we are currently witnessing with the Government's policy of high interest rates to cool down the south-east. Scotland certainly does not need cooling down in the economic circumstances north of the border.

Scottish political power is non-existent within that Tory system. The governor-general is not Scotland's man in the Cabinet; he is Thatcher's man in Scotland, and the majority of people in Scotland recognise that. The power structure of the United Kingdom makes that quite obvious. The Secretary of State for Scotland—and I do not intend to be offensive—is a placeman. He does not command his position in the Cabinet from a Scottish power base. He does not tell the Cabinet what to do on Scottish policy; he is told what the policy will be and it is "Scottified" by the Scottish Office. He has no veto ability. He could resign and be replaced by the hon. Member for Stirling (Mr. Forsyth), then the hon. Member for Edinburgh, West (Lord James Douglas-Hamilton) and then, ultimately, the hon. Member for Tayside, North.

The Secretary of State needs to develop a lobbying skill. It has always been the case that those who can lobby best make the best Secretaries of State. Of course, in European policy Scotland is not even quoted. I can sum up the Tory attitude to Scotland within the United Kingdom in a simple sentence—no power, little influence, a lobbying outfit; and within the European Community—Scotland cannot exercise any power.

The Labour party variant is slightly different. Its amendment contains the words "within the United Kingdom", which makes it clear that, like the Tories, its main purpose is to preserve the Union. It thinks that the best way to do that is through devolution—the devolving of power to a Scottish assembly. We must strip the Labour party of its camouflage of the slogan "Independence in the United Kingdom". It is no wonder that the hon. Member for Glasgow, Garscadden (Mr. Dewar) would not give way to any hon. Member wanting to question him on that slogan.

Stripped of that camouflage, Labour's policy involves a mechanism for the distribution of resources between health, education, housing, roads, local government, administration of regional funds—not the policy decision on how the funds should be created—and control of the Scottish Development Agency and the Highlands and Islands Development Board, which are currently within the Secretary of State's remit. Labour party policy contains no wealth-creation measures inherent in macro-economic decisions such as how to allocate resources between consumption and investment, interest rate policy, fiscal policy, oil policy, and depletion of oil policy.

Rumour has it that the hon. Member for Garscadden recently went abroad for the first time in 10 years and discovered the Bavarian solution, which is a bureau of information lobby, once again inside Brussels. In reality, the Labour party envisages a subservient role for Scotland within the United Kingdom. That becomes most evident in its defence policy. It is no wonder that the hon. Member for Garscadden did not want to refer to the part of our motion dealing with the question of Trident.

*Scotland on Sunday* on 12 March stated:

"Labour's defence review, due to be published in May, has run into trouble with the party in Scotland, which pledged unswerving support yesterday for unilateral disarmament. With Shadow defence spokesman Mr. Martin O'Neill listening, a succession of delegates demanded retention of unilateralism in the crucial review document which is expected to move the party into a flexible position on nuclear defence . . .

In a clear warning to the leadership not to change course, the Inverness conference voted overwhelmingly to maintain the present defence policy. The unequivocal position backed by the Scottish Executive leaves leader Mr. Neil Kinnock and Mr. O'Neill in no doubt that a softening on unilateralism will be resisted in Scotland."

That was the decision of the Labour party's Scottish conference in March, but we still await the resistance in Scotland. When it comes to a division of policy within the Unionist context set by the Labour party, there is no question who is the boss—he who lies south of the border.

We were told by the Labour party that it would entrench a Scottish Assembly and that once it was established there would be no possibility of this Parliament overturning it. We have seen the spectacle of Labour Members of Parliament going to the Scottish Constitutional Convention and signing documents stating that they supported Scottish sovereignty. That is very strange because on 19 June, when dealing with an SLD motion on civil liberties and a Bill of Rights, the hon. Member for Edinburgh, Central (Mr. Darling) attacked the idea of a Bill of Rights and said that the Opposition would not support the motion for two reasons:

"First, the main problem with a Bill of Rights in this country is due to the nature of the British constitution, which is unwritten . . . In England"—

he does not pretend that it is the United Kingdom—

"there is no such system. Instead, this country's fundamental constitutional doctrine is the supremacy of Parliament."—[*Official Report,* 19 June 1989; vol. 155, c. 90.]

The deputy leader of the Labour party attacked Charter 88 in an article in *The Guardian* in December 1988. He said:

"The attractions of a written constitution are obvious enough. Entrenched clauses"—

which I thought was Labour party policy on an assembly—

"—which can only be changed by complicated and protracted constitutional amendment—limit the power of government. It is impossible to incorporate those attractions into our system. British democracy is—for better or for worse—based on the absolute sovereignty of parliament."

In other words, what Parliament gives, Parliament can take away.

Of course, the Labour party sings a different song north of the border, and says that the Scottish people are sovereign. Down here, when speaking to the bosses in London, it parrots the English constitutional view.

**Mr. Darling:** Will the hon. Gentleman give way?

**Mr. Sillars:** No, I will not give way. [Hon. Members: "Give way."] Oh, all right then.

**Mr. Darling:** The hon. Gentleman has criticised an observation of mine about the British constitution and the doctrine of the supremacy of Parliament. I do not understand why he should criticise a statement of fact, whether or not he agrees with it. I note that in "Dod's Companion" he lists that he once studied law. He did not say that he had actually completed the course. I advise him to do so, because he will find that that is exactly what the British constitution states, whether or not he likes it. He cannot criticise people who simply set out the facts.

Perhaps the hon. Gentleman will now answer the question that his hon. Friend the Member for Banff and Buchan (Mr. Salmond) would not answer: what will the nationalists do if they find that the terms for remaining in —or for entering—Europe are unacceptable? Is he advocating independence for Scotland alone with Greenland?

**Mr. Sillars:** The hon. Gentleman wishes to divert attention from the fact that the Labour party signed a declaration of sovereignty at the Scottish Constitutional Convention. I have read the policy review. It is reasonable for the Labour party to say that it will alter the British constitution, but it is not reasonable for it to say to the Scots, "We will alter it for you," but then come to Westminster and say that it cannot be altered and repeat time and again that the sovereignty of this Parliament is a constitutional fact of life. They cannot endlessly repeat that the sovereignty of this Parliament is a constitutional fact of life. The hon. Member for Edinburgh, Central cannot get out of that.

**Mr. Harry Ewing** rose——

**Mr. Sillars:** I am sorry, but I am not prepared to allow the hon. Gentleman to intervene. The hon. Gentleman was always a good trade union leader, but he never had to negotiate with me.

There is a problem in delivering the Labour party's variant of Unionism, because it is fundamentally a Unionist party. It accepts the sovereignty of Parliament. It may tell the Scottish people, "We have conceived the idea of a Scottish Assembly, which we believe has great merit. We believe that it is essential for the Scottish people, but unless we can carry the vote south of the border we cannot guarantee to deliver it." That is the Labour party's position as a Unionist party. It made the same argument in respect of Trident, saying, "We do not want it, but if the Government say we must accept it, we must."

**Mr. Ewing** rose——

**Mr. Sillars:** No, I shall not give way, but I am reminded that the hon. Member for Falkirk, East (Mr. Ewing), who claims to be an old friend of mine, made the public statement that, come what may, there will be a Scottish Assembly after the next general election. When I wrote a nice letter asking what he meant by that, he replied that he would tell lots of people but would not tell me. On the basis of that old friendship, I shall not give way to the hon. Gentleman.

**Mr. Ewing** rose——

**Mr. Sillars:** No. I am reaching the end of my speech.

Tonight, we have heard a defence of the Union from Conservative and Labour Members.

**Mr. David Lambie** (Cunninghame, South): The hon. Gentleman did not serve in this House for 13 years.

**Mr. Sillars:** The hon. Member for Cunninghame, South (Mr. Lambie) has not spoken in this House for 13 years.

What is so good about that Union? Is it a paradise that we are supposed to be defending? A report entitled "The State of the Nation" claims that in Scotland homelessness has doubled, annual housebuilding has dropped from 9,000 new starts to 4,000, NHS beds have been cut by 3,000, while the waiting lists stand at 77,000, unemployment is up by 85 per cent., manufacturing jobs have been cut by one third, and 18,000 teenagers have lost income support because of social security changes.

The report also claims that the number of Scottish families that have had their gas cut off for being unable to pay their bills has risen by 20 per cent. Wages too have suffered. In 1979 Scottish workers were paid on average £7·30 a week less than those in the south-east of England. It has since risen to £39·50 a week. That is what the Labour party says in its document, "The State of the Nation". That is what the Labour party in Scotland has been defending.

The epitaph of the Labour party in Scotland came through very clearly in the debate. At the end of the day, when Labour is boiled down to its Unionist essence, it would rather have a Tory Government elected in England governing Scotland than an independent Scottish Labour Government in an independent Scotland. That is Labour's epitaph.

6.53 pm

**The Minister of State, Scottish Office (Mr. Ian Lang):** I must confess that I thought the debate would be somewhat pointless, based as it was on the fraudulent and meaningless slogan of independence in Europe—which is almost as meaningless as talking about divorce within marriage. However, the debate turned out to be worth while because it succeeded in extracting one substantive fact from the hon. Member for Glasgow, Govan (Mr. Sillars)—that his view is that after Scotland's separation from the rest of the United Kingdom, and after that curious sleight of hand whereby Scotland will somehow find itself to have become a fully fledged member of the European Community, the power of taxation over the people of Scotland should be in the hands of a European Parliament. Regardless of the Council of Ministers and of the view of a Scottish Parliament, the hon. Member for Govan seeks to impose the power of taxation on Scotland not from Westminster but from Strasbourg, giving it a greater power over Scotland than Westminster would have. The power to tax is one of the most important there is and clearly the slogan "subservience in Europe" is more appropriate than "independence in Europe" on that basis.

I am happy to talk about Scotland in Europe because I welcome comparisons between it and other European countries. Since 1980, Scotland has enjoyed faster growth than any other country in Europe. The Fraser of Allander Institute forecasts that the Scottish economy will grow faster than that of the United Kingdom in the next year. Its manufacturing productivity has grown in the current decade faster not only than in Europe but in the United

[*Mr. Ian Lang*]

States and Japan. Our exports grew again last year, to 50 per cent. of the total compared with 25 per cent. since we first joined the Community.

Scotland's manufacturing exports are higher per head not only than those of other countries in Europe but of Germany and Japan. Scotland enjoys lower unemployment than France, Italy, Belgium, Holland, Spain and Ireland, and it is falling faster. Scotland is playing a full part in Europe and is well able to stand comparison.

Scotland is also benefiting enormously from Europe. Although there is a 35 per cent. work force restriction on assisted areas under the rules of the European Community, in Scotland 65 per cent. of the working population are accounted for in development areas. More than one quarter of all European aid to the United Kingdom comes to Scotland. Over the past decade it has received about £730 million from the European regional development fund, £250 million from the social fund, £1·5 billion in loans from the European investment bank and from the European Coal and Steel Community.

More than £3 billion has been invested in infrastructure and in industrial regeneration. Under a succession of initiatives in recent years, special help has been given through the Glasgow programme to Tayside, West Lothian and the Western Isles, and through the agricultural development programme to the other islands. More recently, the £12 million RENAVAL programme has been established for the shipbuilding areas of the Clyde, and another £73 million is being provided for an integrated operation in the Highlands and Islands. That is the biggest operation of its kind ever in Scotland or in Europe.

Under the Strathclyde programme, £1 billion of European money, United Kingdom taxpayers' money and private sector money will be brought together in a carefully targeted and integrated programme to help the Strathclyde economy through training, infrastructure, technology, innovation, and its environment. All that has been achieved through the activities of the Scottish Office with the assistance of the United Kingdom's negotiating power in Brussels.

Scottish National party Members are always keen to compare Scotland with other small countries in Europe, but if they look to Denmark, they will see that Scotland has received six times as much from the European regional development fund since it was founded than has Denmark. We are preparing for the next major European event, with the arrival of the single European market in 1992. Scotland will benefit from that also as it's companies prepare for Europe. In 1979, only one thing was binding the European Community together—our money and a lot of red tape.

The British Government have helped to develop the Single European Act, deregulate Europe and open up new opportunities for Scotland, as for the rest of the United Kingdom. Just as the single British Act of 1707 benefited Scotland, so too will the Single European Act. The SNP's single Scottish Act would change all that, and overnight Scotland would become a small, irrelevant country left out in the cold. When Scotland came to seek admission to the European Community, the resounding answer from the other member states would be "Nein", "Non", "Nunta", "Niemals", and "No di certo".

Interdependence is the key to the future of Scotland and of Europe—not independence, but the coming together of nations that our Conservative Government have persistently espoused and helped to develop. Scottish independence in Europe is a fraudulent conception. The Scottish National party is not internationalist but the party of little Scotlanders. Scottish nationalists are not free marketeers but Socialists. For years they fought tooth and nail against membership of the European Community, and now they are enjoying a death-bed conversion that carries no conviction. I urge the House to throw out the motion.

*Question put,* That the original words stand part of the Question:—

*The House divided:* Ayes 5, Noes 297.

**Division No. 266]** [6.59 pm

### AYES

Jones, Ieuan *(Ynys Môn)*
Salmond, Alex
Sillars, Jim
Thomas, Dr Dafydd Elis
Wigley, Dafydd

Tellers for the Ayes:
Mr. Andrew Welsh and
Mrs. Margaret Ewing.

### NOES

| | |
|---|---|
| Abbott, Ms Diane | Clark, Hon Alan *(Plym'th S'n)* |
| Adams, Allen *(Paisley N)* | Clark, Dr David *(S Shields)* |
| Alton, David | Clark, Dr Michael *(Rochford)* |
| Amess, David | Clarke, Rt Hon K. *(Rushcliffe)* |
| Amos, Alan | Clwyd, Mrs Ann |
| Arbuthnot, James | Cohen, Harry |
| Armstrong, Hilary | Colvin, Michael |
| Arnold, Jacques *(Gravesham)* | Cook, Frank *(Stockton N)* |
| Arnold, Tom *(Hazel Grove)* | Coombs, Anthony *(Wyre F'rest)* |
| Ashby, David | Coombs, Simon *(Swindon)* |
| Ashdown, Rt Hon Paddy | Cope, Rt Hon John |
| Atkins, Robert | Cormack, Patrick |
| Atkinson, David | Cox, Tom |
| Baker, Nicholas *(Dorset N)* | Cran, James |
| Baldry, Tony | Currie, Mrs Edwina |
| Batiste, Spencer | Darling, Alistair |
| Battle, John | Davies, Q. *(Stamf'd & Spald'g)* |
| Beaumont-Dark, Anthony | Davis, David *(Boothferry)* |
| Bennett, Nicholas *(Pembroke)* | Day, Stephen |
| Benyon, W. | Dewar, Donald |
| Bermingham, Gerald | Dixon, Don |
| Bevan, David Gilroy | Doran, Frank |
| Blackburn, Dr John G. | Dorrell, Stephen |
| Boscawen, Hon Robert | Douglas-Hamilton, Lord James |
| Bottomley, Peter | Dover, Den |
| Bottomley, Mrs Virginia | Duffy, A. E. P. |
| Bowden, A *(Brighton K'pto'n)* | Dunnachie, Jimmy |
| Bowis, John | Durant, Tony |
| Boyes, Roland | Dykes, Hugh |
| Braine, Rt Hon Sir Bernard | Eadie, Alexander |
| Brazier, Julian | Eastham, Ken |
| Bright, Graham | Emery, Sir Peter |
| Brooke, Rt Hon Peter | Evennett, David |
| Brown, Gordon *(D'mline E)* | Ewing, Harry *(Falkirk E)* |
| Brown, Michael *(Brigg & Cl't's)* | Fairbairn, Sir Nicholas |
| Browne, John *(Winchester)* | Fallon, Michael |
| Bruce, Ian *(Dorset South)* | Fatchett, Derek |
| Bruce, Malcolm *(Gordon)* | Favell, Tony |
| Buchanan-Smith, Rt Hon Alick | Fenner, Dame Peggy |
| Buck, Sir Antony | Fields, Terry *(L'pool B G'n)* |
| Budgen, Nicholas | Fishburn, John Dudley |
| Burns, Simon | Flannery, Martin |
| Burt, Alistair | Fookes, Dame Janet |
| Butler, Chris | Forman, Nigel |
| Butterfill, John | Forsyth, Michael *(Stirling)* |
| Callaghan, Jim | Forth, Eric |
| Campbell, Menzies *(Fife NE)* | Foster, Derek |
| Carlisle, Kenneth *(Lincoln)* | Fowler, Rt Hon Norman |
| Carrington, Matthew | Franks, Cecil |
| Cash, William | French, Douglas |
| Channon, Rt Hon Paul | Fry, Peter |
| Chapman, Sydney | Fyfe, Maria |

Galbraith, Sam
Gale, Roger
Galloway, George
Gardiner, George
Garel-Jones, Tristan
Gill, Christopher
Gilmour, Rt Hon Sir Ian
Goodhart, Sir Philip
Gow, Ian
Greenway, Harry *(Ealing N)*
Greenway, John *(Ryedale)*
Gregory, Conal
Griffiths, Nigel *(Edinburgh S)*
Griffiths, Peter *(Portsmouth N)*
Griffiths, Win *(Bridgend)*
Grist, Ian
Gummer, Rt Hon John Selwyn
Hague, William
Hamilton, Neil *(Tatton)*
Hanley, Jeremy
Hannam, John
Hardy, Peter
Hargreaves, Ken *(Hyndburn)*
Harris, David
Haselhurst, Alan
Hayes, Jerry
Hayhoe, Rt Hon Sir Barney
Haynes, Frank
Hayward, Robert
Heathcoat-Amory, David
Heddle, John
Heseltine, Rt Hon Michael
Hicks, Robert *(Cornwall SE)*
Hill, James
Hinchliffe, David
Hind, Kenneth
Hogg, N. *(C'nauld & Kilsyth)*
Home Robertson, John
Howarth, Alan *(Strat'd-on-A)*
Howarth, George *(Knowsley N)*
Howarth, G. *(Cannock & B'wd)*
Hughes, Robert *(Aberdeen N)*
Hughes, Robert G. *(Harrow W)*
Hughes, Simon *(Southwark)*
Hunt, David *(Wirral W)*
Hunt, Sir John *(Ravensbourne)*
Hunter, Andrew
Hurd, Rt Hon Douglas
Ingram, Adam
Irvine, Michael
Jack, Michael
Janman, Tim
Johnson Smith, Sir Geoffrey
Johnston, Sir Russell
Jones, Gwilym *(Cardiff N)*
Jones, Robert B *(Herts W)*
Jopling, Rt Hon Michael
Kellett-Bowman, Dame Elaine
Kennedy, Charles
King, Roger *(B'ham N'thfield)*
King, Rt Hon Tom *(Bridgwater)*
Kirkhope, Timothy
Kirkwood, Archy
Knight, Dame Jill *(Edgbaston)*
Knox, David
Lambie, David
Lang, Ian
Latham, Michael
Lawrence, Ivan
Lee, John *(Pendle)*
Lennox-Boyd, Hon Mark
Lilley, Peter
Lloyd, Peter *(Fareham)*
Lord, Michael
McAvoy, Thomas
McCrindle, Robert
Macfarlane, Sir Neil
MacKay, Andrew *(E Berkshire)*
McKelvey, William
McLeish, Henry

Maclennan, Robert
McLoughlin, Patrick
McNair-Wilson, Sir Michael
McNair-Wilson, Sir Patrick
Madden, Max
Major, Rt Hon John
Malins, Humfrey
Mans, Keith
Maples, John
Marshall, David *(Shettleston)*
Marshall, John *(Hendon S)*
Marshall, Michael *(Arundel)*
Martin, David *(Portsmouth S)*
Martin, Michael J. *(Springburn)*
Maude, Hon Francis
Mawhinney, Dr Brian
Maxton, John
Maxwell-Hyslop, Robin
Meyer, Sir Anthony
Michie, Bill *(Sheffield Heeley)*
Miller, Sir Hal
Mills, Iain
Mitchell, Andrew *(Gedling)*
Mitchell, Sir David
Moate, Roger
Monro, Sir Hector
Moonie, Dr Lewis
Morris, M *(N'hampton S)*
Morrison, Sir Charles
Moss, Malcolm
Neale, Gerrard
Neubert, Michael
Nicholls, Patrick
Nicholson, David *(Taunton)*
Norris, Steve
Oakes, Rt Hon Gordon
Onslow, Rt Hon Cranley
Oppenheim, Phillip
Owen, Rt Hon Dr David
Page, Richard
Paice, James
Patchett, Terry
Pattie, Rt Hon Sir Geoffrey
Peacock, Mrs Elizabeth
Pike, Peter L.
Porter, David *(Waveney)*
Portillo, Michael
Powell, William *(Corby)*
Prescott, John
Raffan, Keith
Raison, Rt Hon Timothy
Redwood, John
Rees, Rt Hon Merlyn
Reid, Dr John
Renton, Tim
Rhodes James, Robert
Riddick, Graham
Rifkind, Rt Hon Malcolm
Robertson, George
Sackville, Hon Tom
Shaw, Sir Giles *(Pudsey)*
Sheldon, Rt Hon Robert
Shepherd, Colin *(Hereford)*
Shersby, Michael
Skinner, Dennis
Smith, Rt Hon J. *(Monk'ds E)*
Smith, Tim *(Beaconsfield)*
Snape, Peter
Speed, Keith
Steel, Rt Hon David
Stevens, Lewis
Stewart, Allan *(Eastwood)*
Stewart, Andy *(Sherwood)*
Stradling Thomas, Sir John
Strang, Gavin
Sumberg, David
Taylor, Ian *(Esher)*
Taylor, John M *(Solihull)*
Tebbit, Rt Hon Norman
Thompson, D. *(Calder Valley)*

Thompson, Patrick *(Norwich N)*
Thorne, Neil
Thurnham, Peter
Tredinnick, David
Trippier, David
Trotter, Neville
Waddington, Rt Hon David
Wakeham, Rt Hon John
Walden, George
Walker, Bill *(T'side North)*
Walker, Rt Hon P. *(W'cester)*
Wallace, James
Waller, Gary
Wardle, Charles *(Bexhill)*
Warren, Kenneth
Watson, Mike *(Glasgow, C)*
Watts, John
Wheeler, John

Whitney, Ray
Widdecombe, Ann
Wilkinson, John
Wilshire, David
Wilson, Brian
Winterton, Mrs Ann
Winterton, Nicholas
Wise, Mrs Audrey
Wolfson, Mark
Wood, Timothy
Worthington, Tony
Wray, Jimmy
Yeo, Tim
Young, Sir George *(Acton)*

Tellers for the Noes:
　　Mr. David Maclean and
　　Mr. David Lightbown.

*Question accordingly negatived.*

*Question,* That the proposed words be there added, *put forthwith pursuant to Standing Order No. 30 (Questions on amendments):—*

The House divided: Ayes 203, Noes 98.

**Division No. 267]**　　　　　　　　　　　　　　　　**[7.11 pm**

**AYES**

Amess, David
Amos, Alan
Arbuthnot, James
Arnold, Jacques *(Gravesham)*
Arnold, Tom *(Hazel Grove)*
Ashby, David
Atkins, Robert
Atkinson, David
Baker, Nicholas *(Dorset N)*
Baldry, Tony
Batiste, Spencer
Beaumont-Dark, Anthony
Bennett, Nicholas *(Pembroke)*
Benyon, W.
Bevan, David Gilroy
Boscawen, Hon Robert
Bottomley, Peter
Bottomley, Mrs Virginia
Bowden, A *(Brighton K'pto'n)*
Bowis, John
Braine, Rt Hon Sir Bernard
Brazier, Julian
Bright, Graham
Brown, Michael *(Brigg & Cl't's)*
Browne, John *(Winchester)*
Bruce, Ian *(Dorset South)*
Buchanan-Smith, Rt Hon Alick
Buck, Sir Antony
Budgen, Nicholas
Burns, Simon
Burt, Alistair
Butler, Chris
Butterfill, John
Carlisle, Kenneth *(Lincoln)*
Carrington, Matthew
Cash, William
Channon, Rt Hon Paul
Chapman, Sydney
Clark, Hon Alan *(Plym'th S'n)*
Clarke, Rt Hon K. *(Rushcliffe)*
Colvin, Michael
Coombs, Anthony *(Wyre F'rest)*
Coombs, Simon *(Swindon)*
Cope, Rt Hon John
Cormack, Patrick
Cran, James
Currie, Mrs Edwina
Davies, Q. *(Stamf'd & Spald'g)*
Day, Stephen
Dorrell, Stephen
Douglas-Hamilton, Lord James
Dover, Den

Durant, Tony
Dykes, Hugh
Emery, Sir Peter
Evennett, David
Fallon, Michael
Favell, Tony
Fenner, Dame Peggy
Fookes, Dame Janet
Forsyth, Michael *(Stirling)*
Forth, Eric
Fowler, Rt Hon Norman
French, Douglas
Gale, Roger
Gardiner, George
Garel-Jones, Tristan
Gill, Christopher
Goodhart, Sir Philip
Gow, Ian
Greenway, Harry *(Ealing N)*
Greenway, John *(Ryedale)*
Gregory, Conal
Griffiths, Peter *(Portsmouth N)*
Grist, Ian
Gummer, Rt Hon John Selwyn
Hague, William
Hamilton, Neil *(Tatton)*
Hanley, Jeremy
Hannam, John
Hargreaves, Ken *(Hyndburn)*
Harris, David
Haselhurst, Alan
Hayes, Jerry
Hayhoe, Rt Hon Sir Barney
Hayward, Robert
Heddle, John
Heseltine, Rt Hon Michael
Hicks, Robert *(Cornwall SE)*
Hind, Kenneth
Howarth, Alan *(Strat'd-on-A)*
Hughes, Robert G. *(Harrow W)*
Hunt, David *(Wirral W)*
Hunt, Sir John *(Ravensbourne)*
Hunter, Andrew
Irvine, Michael
Jack, Michael
Janman, Tim
Johnson Smith, Sir Geoffrey
Jones, Gwilym *(Cardiff N)*
Jones, Robert B *(Herts W)*
Jopling, Rt Hon Michael
Kellett-Bowman, Dame Elaine
King, Roger *(B'ham N'thfield)*

King, Rt Hon Tom *(Bridgwater)*
Kirkhope, Timothy
Knight, Dame Jill *(Edgbaston)*
Knox, David
Lang, Ian
Latham, Michael
Lawrence, Ivan
Lee, John *(Pendle)*
Lennox-Boyd, Hon Mark
Lester, Jim *(Broxtowe)*
Lightbown, David
Lilley, Peter
Lloyd, Peter *(Fareham)*
Lord, Michael
McCrindle, Robert
Macfarlane, Sir Neil
MacKay, Andrew *(E Berkshire)*
McLoughlin, Patrick
McNair-Wilson, Sir Michael
McNair-Wilson, Sir Patrick
Major, Rt Hon John
Malins, Humfrey
Mans, Keith
Maples, John
Marshall, John *(Hendon S)*
Marshall, Michael *(Arundel)*
Martin, David *(Portsmouth S)*
Maude, Hon Francis
Mawhinney, Dr Brian
Maxwell-Hyslop, Robin
Meyer, Sir Anthony
Miller, Sir Hal
Mills, Iain
Mitchell, Andrew *(Gedling)*
Mitchell, Sir David
Moate, Roger
Monro, Sir Hector
Morris, M *(N'hampton S)*
Morrison, Sir Charles
Moss, Malcolm
Neale, Gerrard
Neubert, Michael
Nicholls, Patrick
Nicholson, David *(Taunton)*
Norris, Steve
Onslow, Rt Hon Cranley
Oppenheim, Phillip
Page, Richard
Paice, James
Pattie, Rt Hon Sir Geoffrey
Peacock, Mrs Elizabeth
Porter, David *(Waveney)*

Portillo, Michael
Powell, William *(Corby)*
Raffan, Keith
Raison, Rt Hon Timothy
Redwood, John
Renton, Tim
Riddick, Graham
Rifkind, Rt Hon Malcolm
Sackville, Hon Tom
Shaw, Sir Giles *(Pudsey)*
Shepherd, Colin *(Hereford)*
Shersby, Michael
Smith, Tim *(Beaconsfield)*
Speed, Keith
Stevens, Lewis
Stewart, Allan *(Eastwood)*
Stewart, Andy *(Sherwood)*
Stradling Thomas, Sir John
Sumberg, David
Taylor, Ian *(Esher)*
Taylor, John M *(Solihull)*
Tebbit, Rt Hon Norman
Thompson, D. *(Calder Valley)*
Thompson, Patrick *(Norwich N)*
Thorne, Neil
Thurnham, Peter
Trippier, David
Trotter, Neville
Waddington, Rt Hon David
Walden, George
Walker, Bill *(T'side North)*
Walker, Rt Hon P. *(W'cester)*
Waller, Gary
Wardle, Charles *(Bexhill)*
Warren, Kenneth
Watts, John
Wells, Bowen
Wheeler, John
Widdecombe, Ann
Wilkinson, John
Wilshire, David
Winterton, Mrs Ann
Winterton, Nicholas
Wolfson, Mark
Wood, Timothy
Yeo, Tim
Young, Sir George *(Acton)*

Tellers for the Ayes:
    Mr. David Maclean and
    Mr. David Heathcoat-Amory.

**NOES**

Allen, Graham
Alton, David
Armstrong, Hilary
Ashdown, Rt Hon Paddy
Barnes, Harry *(Derbyshire NE)*
Barron, Kevin
Bennett, A. F. *(D'nt'n & R'dish)*

Bermingham, Gerald
Boateng, Paul
Boyes, Roland
Brown, Gordon *(D'mline E)*
Brown, Nicholas *(Newcastle E)*
Bruce, Malcolm *(Gordon)*
Buckley, George J.

Callaghan, Jim
Campbell, Menzies *(Fife NE)*
Campbell-Savours, D. N.
Clark, Dr David *(S Shields)*
Clwyd, Mrs Ann
Cohen, Harry
Cook, Frank *(Stockton N)*
Cook, Robin *(Livingston)*
Cox, Tom
Cryer, Bob
Dewar, Donald
Dixon, Don
Dobson, Frank
Douglas, Dick
Eadie, Alexander
Eastham, Ken
Ewing, Harry *(Falkirk E)*
Ewing, Mrs Margaret *(Moray)*
Flannery, Martin
Foster, Derek
Fyfe, Maria
Galbraith, Sam
Galloway, George
Garrett, John *(Norwich South)*
Garrett, Ted *(Wallsend)*
Godman, Dr Norman A.
Gordon, Mildred
Griffiths, Win *(Bridgend)*
Haynes, Frank
Hogg, N. *(C'nauld & Kilsyth)*
Home Robertson, John
Howarth, George *(Knowsley N)*
Hughes, Robert *(Aberdeen N)*
Hughes, Simon *(Southwark)*
Illsley, Eric
Ingram, Adam
Johnston, Sir Russell
Jones, Barry *(Alyn & Deeside)*
Kennedy, Charles
Kirkwood, Archy
Lambie, David
Lestor, Joan *(Eccles)*
Livsey, Richard
Loyden, Eddie

McAvoy, Thomas
McKelvey, William
McLeish, Henry
Maclennan, Robert
Madden, Max
Mahon, Mrs Alice
Martin, Michael J. *(Springburn)*
Maxton, John
Michael, Alun
Michie, Bill *(Sheffield Heeley)*
Michie, Mrs Ray *(Arg'l & Bute)*
Moonie, Dr Lewis
Nellist, Dave
Oakes, Rt Hon Gordon
Patchett, Terry
Pike, Peter L.
Powell, Ray *(Ogmore)*
Redmond, Martin
Reid, Dr John
Robertson, George
Salmond, Alex
Sheldon, Rt Hon Robert
Sillars, Jim
Skinner, Dennis
Snape, Peter
Spearing, Nigel
Steel, Rt Hon David
Strang, Gavin
Thomas, Dr Dafydd Elis
Vaz, Keith
Wallace, James
Wareing, Robert N.
Watson, Mike *(Glasgow, C)*
Welsh, Andrew *(Angus E)*
Wigley, Dafydd
Williams, Alan W. *(Carm'then)*
Wilson, Brian
Wise, Mrs Audrey
Worthington, Tony
Wray, Jimmy

Tellers for the Noes:
    Mr. Allen Adams and
    Mr. Nigel Griffiths.

*Question accordingly agreed to.*

MR. DEPUTY SPEAKER *forthwith declared the main Question, as amended, to be agreed to.*

*Resolved,*

That this House notes the continued success of the present Government's policies in securing for Scotland record living standards and the advantages of membership of the European Community within the United Kingdom, alongside a strong defence of the United Kingdom's essential interests, and the rejection of the Scottish National Party's policy of independence in Europe by the overwhelming majority of voters in Scotland at the European elections; and recognises the potential damage to the real interests of Scotland underlying the constitutional change advocated by opposition parties.

# London Regional Transport (Penalty Fares) Bill *[Lords] (By Order)*

*Order for consideration, as amended, read.*

*Motion made, and Question proposed,* That the Bill, as amended, be now considered.—*[Mr. Thorne.]*

7.22 pm

**Mr. Andrew F. Bennett** (Denton and Reddish): On a point of order, Mr. Deputy Speaker. You will be aware that towards the end of the Second Reading debate Opposition Members pressed the hon. Member for Ilford, South (Mr. Thorne), who is responsible for the Bill, for an undertaking that when the new ticket barriers were introduced on London Underground and the penalty fares scheme came into effect, people would not be forced to use the mechanical ticket barriers. The hon. Gentleman gave that undertaking. I asked:

"Will the hon. Gentleman confirm that there will always be an alternative to using the mechanical ticket barriers?"
He replied:

"The intention is that there will always be that option available."—[*Official Report,* 6 February 1989; Vol. 146, c. 762.]

That undertaking has not been carried out. That is fairly serious, particularly when private Bills are involved. There is a procedure by means of which undertakings are given, either in writing or orally in Committee or in the House, that something will happen. If that does not happen, the principle of the private Bill procedure is defeated.

About three weeks ago I took up with the hon. Member for Ilford, South the fact that he had given this undertaking. It had become obvious at Westminster Underground station that people were being forced to go through the mechanical barriers. He asked for more information and eventually sent to me a copy of a letter which says:

"The procedure at all stations where automatic gates are in operation is that a member of staff is available to give assistance if persons have difficulty using those gates and he may invite the passenger to use an alternative gate which he operates manually."

It is quite clear from a meeting that I had yesterday morning with the hon. Gentleman that the individual passenger does not have the right, for which I asked and about which I was given an assurance, not to go through the automatic gates. He can ask the London Regional Transport representative at the barrier, but if that individual decides that he must go through the gates he is denied that choice.

It is quite clear that the House was misled. Apart from making that statement, the agents for the Bill had the privilege of being in the Box. I understand that London Regional Transport representatives were also present. They made no attempt between 6 February when the Bill had its Second Reading and the point at which I took it up with them, three weeks ago, to correct that mistake.

**Mr. Deputy Speaker (Mr. Harold Walker):** Order. What is the point of order for me?

**Mr. Bennett:** I am coming to that. The point of order is that since all the rules of procedure have been broken the hon. Gentleman ought to get up and apologise to the House, on his own behalf and on behalf of the agents and London Regional Transport, for misleading the House, or you ought to rule that because there has been a gross breach of procedure we should not proceed with the Bill at this stage. It should be withdrawn and then reintroduced so that, having broken the conventions of the House since they gave an undertaking on a private Bill, the hon. Gentleman and——

**Mr. Deputy Speaker:** Order. I am responsible only for what happens in the Chamber. Whatever anyone—be they agents or anybody else—does outside the Chamber is not my responsibility. They do not take part in our proceedings. The hon. Gentleman complains that words were used in the House that constituted an undertaking or an assurance, that it has not been fulfilled and that it shows a lack of credibility or sincerity. The responsibility for that rests not with me but with the hon. Member for Ilford, South (Mr. Thorne), who gave the undertaking, and the House. The hon. Member for Ilford, South has heard what has been said. He may wish during the debate to comment on the remarks of the hon. Member for Denton and Reddish (Mr. Bennett). They are not, however, matters for me, nor are they matters upon which I can make a judgment or take action.

**Mr. Bob Cryer** (Bradford, South): Further to that point of order, Mr. Deputy Speaker. There is a point of order upon which you can give guidance to the House. Hon. Members promote private Bills and we rely on other hon. Members to give assurances. One expects such assurances to be honoured. However, this assurance was given on behalf of an entirely separate organisation that is seeking additional powers. I seek your guidance on whether the House should adjourn for a few minutes while an assurance is sought, or find some means by which clarification can be sought. If that does not happen, there is no opportunity for the hon. Member to seek guidance from the agents or the promoters, who are in the Box for that very purpose. They do not sit there just to have an overview of our procedures.

**Mr. Deputy Speaker:** The hon. Gentleman knows perfectly well that whatever takes place on the other side of the Bar of the House has nothing to do with me or with our proceedings in the Chamber. That is something that we do not recognise.

The hon. Gentleman suggests that when assurances are given in the Chamber the House ought to adjourn to check the validity or the strength of those assurances.

**Mr. Cryer:** No, that is not what I said.

**Mr. Deputy Speaker:** I thought that that was what the hon. Gentleman was suggesting to me.

**Mr. Cryer:** Let me guide you, Mr. Deputy Speaker. I was suggesting that, when an hon. Member is asked for an assurance, either he can produce a bland platitude which does not mean anything, or he can consult the sponsors, who may be beyond your knowledge or understanding according to the conventions of the House. I was suggesting that to allow the sponsor of a Bill to seek guidance, surely the occupant of the Chair has powers to adjourn the House to allow discussions to take place on an assurance requested by hon. Members, in view of discrepancies between the assurance solemnly given in the House and the outcome. There appears to be such a chasm between the two that there should be some means in our procedures of making sure that an hon. Member is not placed in the difficult and embarrassing position of being

[*Mr. Cryer*]

accused of letting down the standards of the House by not allowing or giving credence to the assurances that he has given. That is what I am seeking from you, Mr. Deputy Speaker.

7.30 pm

**Mr. Deputy Speaker:** I understand the hon. Gentleman's point. He has been in the House long enough to know that our procedures usually allow sufficient time for hon. Members in charge of a Bill, or those giving assurances, to reflect or perhaps seek guidance before the debate is concluded so that they may give the House a more mature and considered view. That is why we usually have an interval between a motion or amendment being tabled and finally responded to in the light of what has been said in a debate. The hon. Gentleman knows perfectly well that I do not have the power, nor would it be practical for the occupant of the Chair, to adjourn the House in circumstances that may fit the situation described by the hon. Gentleman. He knows as well as I do that on many occasions assurances have been given by Members in charge of a Bill, whether or not they were Ministers, and subsequently doubt has been cast on the validity or exact interpretation of those assurances.

**Mr. Kevin Barron** (Rother Valley): Further to that point of order, Mr. Deputy Speaker. If a Committee considering a private Bill makes a special report asking for assurances from a Government Department—which may not be the Department sponsoring the Bill—in those circumstances can the occupant of the Chair make a ruling to bring the matter back to Committee so that assurances can be sought on the Committee's special report?

**Mr. Deputy Speaker:** That does not apply to present circumstances. I shall not seek to rule on a hypothesis or on proceedings on another Bill.

**Mr. Andrew F. Bennett:** Will you reconsider the points that you made a few moments ago on two bases, Mr. Deputy Speaker? A private Bill is totally different from Government legislation. Traditionally, Ministers try to get Government legislation through and the onus is on Opposition and Conservative Members to press the Minister in charge of the Bill to make sure any undertaking given is absolutely clear.

I understand that the tradition for private Bills is rather different. Normally assurances are given by the agents or by the hon. Member in charge of the Bill in the House on behalf of the agents and are treated rather differently. I realise that the private Bill procedure has become discredited and the sooner that we manage to implement the procedures to get rid of them from the Floor of the House the better. Surely the principle that any undertaking given is upheld should be adhered to.

As I understand it, you have a responsibility as Chairman of Ways and Means to vet names which are put forward to be included on the A list of parliamentary agents. I understand that that vetting is to ensure that those agents are people of honour who will adhere to the tradition on private Bills that undertakings given are carried out.

If the House allows an undertaking to be breached tonight without any apology or any other action being taken, and if the agents do not come forward——

**Mr. Deputy Speaker:** Order. I am not prepared to allow a debate or a discussion about the credentials of agents. They do not take part in our proceedings, nor do they speak in the Chamber. Any assurances given in the Chamber have been given by an hon. Member or hon. Members, and they are responsible for their words to the House. It is not for me to question the bases of their assurances.

I have been rather more forthcoming than I might normally have been in seeking to explain the basis of a ruling that I have given. The hon. Gentleman is now coming dangerously near to seeking to debate my ruling, and I cannot tolerate that. If the hon. Gentleman wishes to address the motion before the House, the House will hear him.

**Mr. Andrew F. Bennett:** I would not want to question your ruling, Mr. Deputy Speaker. I wish merely to make the point that procedures on private Bills are being discredited. That means that hon. Members who are regularly approached by agents asking them to withdraw blocking motions will no longer be able to accept the word of those agents. That is deplorable. I hoped that you could take steps to ensure speedy action on the breach that has occurred with this particular agent.

**Mr. Deputy Speaker:** Once again the hon. Gentleman is making allegations the foundation and substance of which I am not in a position to judge. The assurance which he claims to have been breached was given by an hon. Member in the Chamber. That hon. Member alone is responsible for the credibility or sincerity with which that assurance was given.

I am most reluctant to enter into a debate on my ruling, but surely in the course of a debate, if hon. Members are dissatisfied with a provision of a Bill before the House, they seek an assurance about it on the basis of which they are then prepared to allow the Bill to make progress. If they subsequently find that that assurance has not been fulfilled or was given without sincerity or credibility, they will take that into account in deciding whether the Bill should be allowed to proceed further. It is a matter on which the House will exercise its judgment in the course of our proceedings. I very much hope that we can now get on.

**Dr. John Marek** (Wrexham): Perhaps it would be helpful if you Mr. Deputy Speaker, were to allow the hon. Member for Ilford, South (Mr. Thorne) to explain whether an assurance was given and the reasons for it later when we debate the Bill? Were he to do that we could make progress, as many hon. Members are slightly bemused as to exactly what is going on.

**Mr. Neil Thorne** (Ilford, South): I have been waiting for 10 minutes to get in and now I am pleased to do so.

**Mr. Deputy Speaker:** Order. May I draw the hon. Gentleman's attention to the fact that if he is pursuing the point of order and satisfying the point that has been raised by the Opposition, he should bear it in mind that if he turns his remarks into a speech he may pre-empt his right to speak later? I am glad to allow the House to hear him on the point of order, but if he wishes to reserve the right to reply to any debate on the motion before the House, he would be wise to consider his remarks and perhaps to save them until the end.

**Mr. Thorne:** Perhaps I should take your advice, Mr. Deputy Speaker. If you think that I am likely to transgress that rule perhaps you will be kind enough to tell me and I will resume my seat immediately.

I shall try to encapsulate the position. I am grateful to the hon. Member for Denton and Reddish (Mr. Bennett) for warning me that he would raise the matter. I would be grateful if he would refer to the paragraph before those from which he quoted. I said:

"The hon. Member for Denton and Reddish (Mr. Bennett) mentioned inoperative machinery and I have answered that point. Passengers pushing prams will be able to pass through the manned barrier."—[*Official Report,* 6 February 1989; Vol. 146, c. 762.]

I was referring primarily to the manual barrier for those who push prams or have other difficulties. That is the basis on which I was speaking.

**Mr. Andrew F. Bennett:** That is ridiculous. The hon. Gentleman should read out my intervention.

**Mr. Thorne:** It has already been read. I confirm that I was talking primarily about people who have difficulty in getting through the automatic barriers. I should like to make that absolutely clear. I understand that the hon. Gentleman is also concerned that people should have some freedom to choose whether they go through the automatic barriers. That is a rather different matter. People have their tickets checked far more efficiently through the automatic barriers and should therefore be encouraged to use those.

**Mr. Harry Cohen** (Leyton): On a point of order, Mr. Deputy Speaker. Dubiety was raised by the last comments of the hon. Member for Ilford, South (Mr. Thorne). I was in the House on that day and the assurance was not taken as relating only to people pushing prams. It was taken as an assurance that everyone would have the choice of using the manual barriers. I will now come to my point of order, as I can see that you are getting very itchy, Mr. Deputy Speaker.

It must be a matter of serious concern that the House was misled in that way. I am not saying that the House was misled deliberately, but I and other hon. Members who were present on that day thought that the assurance was a general assurance for passengers using the barriers. In view of the point that the hon. Member for Ilford, South has just made, the House was misled. The Bill might not have received its Second Reading if we had been given a limited assurance, rather than the general assurance we believed had been given.

In view of the seriousness of the matter and the fact that the assurance goes to the heart of the Bill, our proceedings should be put back from tonight so that the matter can be considered again.

**Mr. Deputy Speaker:** I have made it clear that no matter how strong, weak, credible or otherwise an assurance given by an hon. Member, it is not a matter for the Chair, but a matter for the House to take into account in forming its judgment about the Question before the House or that may be before the House. It is not a matter for me, as I have made clear several times. We can now move on to debate the Question before the House.

**Mr. Andrew F. Bennett:** I am appalled by the behaviour of the hon. Member for Ilford, South (Mr. Thorne). Obviously, I cannot call him a liar in the House and I shall not do so, but his statement was the most outrageous I have ever heard in the House of Commons. I wrote to him three weeks ago on this point. At no time did he put forward the alibi that he has tried to claim today about prams. His argument was always that there was an alternative available in the present operation, which was that people could ask to go through the manual barriers. If he was really an honourable gentleman, and if he really believed that his undertaking related only to people with prams, he would have made that point to me during the three weeks since we had that correspondence. I am utterly amazed that he should now have made his statement. I am also amazed by the behaviour of the agents, and I will put down a motion for the firm of Sherwood and Co. to be removed from the list of parliamentary agents.

**Mr. Cryer:** My hon. Friend is now saying that the promoter of the Bill had three weeks in which to make his position clear, and he was extremely reluctant to get to his feet tonight to produce his off-the-cuff remark. My hon. Friend is telling the House that the promoter has failed for three weeks to clarify the solemn assurance on the barriers he gave to the House. Like my hon. Friend, I am amazed that he chose the last possible moment to open his mouth and produce an explanation that is wholly contrary to that clearly implied in *Hansard.*

7.45 pm

**Mr. Bennett:** I must make it clear that I am not saying that the hon. Member for Ilford, South did not reply to me in those three weeks, but I am saying that he never brought forward the alibi that he was referring only to prams. This evening is the first time he has mentioned that.

When I had a meeting with London Regional Transport about Westminster station and Victoria station, London Regional Transport never made that point. I find it amazing that the hon. Gentleman should have said what he said tonight. He is responsible for his words in this House, but the parliamentary agents are responsible for the way in which private Bills go through the House. Parliamentary agents who feel that they can treat the House in such a way are not fit to serve as parliamentary agents. I shall table a motion to have Sherwood removed from the list of parliamentary agents who enjoy privileges in the House. The failure of Sherwood to ask the hon. Gentleman to apologise to the House is outrageous and brings into disrepute the way in which we proceed on private Bills.

We rise regularly to object to private Bills. The agents immediately get on to us, find out our reasons for objecting and often, as a result of negotiations, we accept their word as honourable individuals and remove our block. In due course, letters go backwards and forwards, amendments are tabled and other procedures take place in the House. If agents can see an undertaking being given to the House and then broken, we can have no faith in them. The rest of the parliamentary agents on the A list must have a strong interest in having a company such as Sherwood removed from the list as soon as possible, because Sherwood has brought the whole system into disrepute.

I was hoping to talk on Report about the wider issues of the Bill. Most of us have watched the major deterioration of the London Underground system once it was taken away from London Transport, which was made up of elected representatives. Were London Regional Transport accountable to democratically elected individuals, the present industrial dispute would not be

[*Mr. Bennett*]

taking place and there would not be an attempt to introduce the ticket barriers, which are so degrading to human beings. People who are rather larger than will fit comfortably through the barriers are forced to make a special request to have the gates opened so that they can go through. I am also certain that an elected body would not have presided over the gross inefficiency and lack of safety that have developed on London Underground.

An elected body would not have come forward with proposals for a penalty fares scheme when it had so obviously alienated the public that it had itself created a situation in which many people felt that they could get their own back on bureaucratic organisation by not paying their fares. London Regional Transport has brought that upon itself. An elected body would also not have behaved so autocratically to the trade unions.

If the penalty fares scheme is to be operated effectively, some of the people collecting penalty fares on trains will collect a considerable amount. If they collect a considerable amount, they have every reason, as a result of the way in which the London Underground has developed, to feel that they may be subject to attack and they can ask legitimately for protection. I believe that the unions have asked for negotiations and for assurances that people collecting penalty fares will be properly protected, but they have not been given those assurances. London Regional Transport, as it is now constituted, feels that it can take no notice of anyone who has a problem and that it can simply push the Bill through the House of Commons with phoney assurances and the hope that the payroll vote will carry the Bill through.

I suggest to London Regional Transport that it should tackle the problem of non-payment differently. It ought to abandon the Bill and put its own house in order. Once it has done that, it can then make a true assessment of how far there is really a major loss of revenue as a result of people not paying their fares.

London Regional Transport should deal first with the question of the morale of people who work on the Underground. I have spoken to two or three people who have been instructed to operate the new gates and their morale has deteriorated further because they have received many complaints and much hassle from the general public, who are upset about them. The total failure to treat reasonably the people working on the stations, issuing tickets and collecting fares, has led to much indifference among those people. A reasonable employer would have considered staff morale first. I am sure that if London Regional Transport had done something to raise the morale of those who issue and collect the tickets on the stations, the number of people not paying fares would have reduced dramatically.

London Regional Transport should also consider passenger morale. As long as passengers feel that London Regional Transport cares very little for them and is simply concerned to make a profit out of them rather than to provide a service, they will feel that they can take it out on London Regional Transport by not paying their fares. Unfortunately, in the end they do not take it out on London Regional Transport; they take it out on other farepayers because either the service deteriorates or the other farepayers have to increase their contributions.

I am certain that if LRT were running a service of which Londoners and the country as a whole could be proud in our capital, there would be a great deal less fare evasion. People would be much happier to pay if they thought that they were getting a good service and good value for money and if they saw that the money that they were paying was being invested to improve the quality of the service and that it was not being used for draconian measures to stop people avoiding paying their fares.

It might solve some of the problems if London Regional Transport also considered the fare structure and the ticket system. It is clear that the multiplicity of tickets is one of the problems. The introduction of the new automatic barriers and their failure to adjust to all the tickets has caused a great deal of difficulty. One would have thought that since London Regional Transport was planning to introduce those barriers it might have been sensible to adapt the tickets so that they could all be used in the barriers before the barriers were introduced rather than afterwards. If hon. Members visit the Thomas Cook transport office in the House, they will find that the tickets issued for hon. Members wishing to go to Heathrow cannot be used in the machines. If London Regional Transport cannot get simple things like that right, one must question its competence to run the service at all. The ticket system and the complexity of the fares clearly add to the difficulties because other European countries with simpler fare structures have a much lower incidence of fares evasion.

London Regional Transport could legitimately have adopted one of two approaches. It could either have encouraged passengers to pay by having tickets checked on the trains, or it could have checked tickets at station exits. Tomorrow night the House will be debating the British Railways (Penalty Fares) Bill. At least British Rail seems to have found a logical solution. It has said, "Let's improve the service to passengers by having free exit from stations with no checks on people entering and leaving the stations. Instead, let's have a system of travelling ticket collectors to check on-train whether the passengers have tickets. Let's then ask for a penalty fare system for those travelling without tickets." That seems a perfectly logical proposal, but London Regional Transport has gone for another approach. It wants a system of penalty fares and travelling ticket collectors, with all the hassle that that will involve on the trains for both the individual passengers and the collectors, and it also wants to take the draconian step of imposing these barriers.

Anyone who has travelled via Westminster station and the other stations where the barrier system is fully implemented can see for themselves the chaos that has been caused. Any train arriving at Westminster from about 8 o'clock in the morning until about 10 o'clock at night produces a substantial number of people. When they come up the steps, they are faced with one barrier that does not work very well and with about three others through which they can pass. When the passengers push their tickets through, some get through the barriers successfully but others get halfway through when the doors come back on them. It can be quite unpleasant when the doors bang against the person. Those people who have tickets without a magnetic strip have to ask one of the station staff standing by the barrier to operate it as though the ticket had a magnetic strip. Those people who find it difficult to pass through the barriers have to ask one of the station operatives to open them.

If someone is built like the hon. Member for Rochdale (Sir C. Smith), it might not be difficult to ask the person at the ticket barrier whether he or she would mind opening the gate because if one is the hon. Member for Rochdale, it is fairly obvious that one will not get through the barriers. However, I find it undignified that anyone who is sufficiently large as to find it uncomfortable to go through the barrier should have to ask a gate operative to let him through. We now discover from the hon. Member for Ilford, South that people do not have a right to go through an open gate. Someone pushing a pram will be allowed through and, at the discretion of London Underground, those of a large size might be allowed to go through.

If an individual asks to be allowed through the gate, and shows a valid ticket, I should have thought that at the very least that person should be allowed through. However, London Underground is not prepared to do that because if everybody who asked to walk through were allowed to do so it would become clear that about 95 per cent. of passengers would prefer to go through the gates rather than through the barriers. London Underground is trying to intimidate people. It is certainly humiliating one group of people.

I am sure that most hon. Members can think of people who are rather large and who are not too happy about the fact. Such people will not want to have to ask someone operating the barrier for permission to go through the gates simply because of their size. Pregnant women might also be unhappy about going through the gates, with the chance that, because of the way in which they malfunction, the gate doors will come back on them as they are passing through.

It is unreasonable that any of those individuals should have to explain to a station operative the reason why they do not want to go through the barriers. It is completely unacceptable in a civilised society. It would have been far better if London Underground had accepted that, if it wanted to impose the barriers, as at Westminster, it should at least have given every individual the absolute right to go through a gate rather than through one of the barriers if those individuals do not wish to do so.

From my own observations of the Underground at Euston and at other stations, and from my observations yesterday when London Underground showed me the system, I have noticed that at most stations the system is working reasonably well in that the barriers are there but there is an alternative and people can walk past them at the side. The majority of passengers are choosing to walk through the open gate. The slight reduction in the flow from allowing people to go through the barriers only if they want to do so means that the station operatives can carry out efficient physical checks on the tickets. When I watched what was happening at Victoria station the other morning in the company of people from London Regional Transport, there seemed little evidence of people avoiding paying their fares by passing through the open gate. My observations at Notting Hill and Euston stations reinforce my belief that people are showing valid tickets.

It is a little odd for London Regional Transport to say that it is difficult for the people in the traditional ticket offices to stop and check someone showing a wrong ticket because it is London Regional Transport that has put those people in those little huts. Obviously, it is difficult for them to get out and to try to apprehend somebody who has offered a wrong ticket. If that member of the station staff were not standing in a hut the position would be much more reasonable.

Until London Regional Transport can provide an efficient service that is not disrupted as a result of industrial action, until it can improve the safety and the cleanliness of the Underground, and until it can sort out the appalling mess created by the introduction of the barriers, the House should not allow the Bill to proceed and should insist that undertakings given in the House are adhered to.

8 pm

**Mr. Cohen:** I, too, believe that we should not proceed further with the Bill tonight. I know that a number of clauses and amendments are before the House. I shall try not to stray on to those but hope to catch your eye, Mr. Deputy Speaker, later, especially on new clauses 1 and 2, dealing with industrial action.

New clause 1 says:
"No penalty fare scheme shall apply on any day when the operations of the Corporation are subject to industrial action."
That would strike me as a sensible clause, because we all know the chaos that can arise during industrial action.

New clause 2 says:
"No penalty fare scheme may apply to any station where there is not a readily available alternative exit or entrance to the automatic barriers."
I am especially keen to discuss those two clauses. However, we are only debating whether the Bill should again be considered by the House. I do not think that it should, because of the whole business of the assurances that we were given at Second Reading. I spoke in that debate and pointed out the great public unrest about the automatic ticket barriers. I mentioned a number of categories of people who had problems going through the barriers. It was not just women with prams, but pensioners, women with children, whether or not they had prams, who found it difficult to see their children through the barriers and would rather have the freer access, pregnant women and people with luggage.

I mentioned too, the problem of congestion and the fact that the barriers cause even greater queues. There is a serious problem of overcrowding on the Underground anyway. Because London Regional Transport has implemented the Government's policy of forcing fares up, season tickets are very expensive and people are not happy to put them into the barrier and risk losing them.

I draw to the House's attention a letter that was sent to my hon. Friend the Member for Islington South and Finsbury (Mr. Smith) by his constituent, a Ms. S. P. Barnard. She said:
"Dear Mr. Smith,
I wish to bring to your attention yet another hazard of travelling by underground. Last Tuesday lunchtime I was returning to work from visiting Waterloo station and on leaving the Northern line ticket gates my travel-card was stolen.
I was in a hurry and as usual there was a backlog of passengers trying to get out of those death-trap gates. I put my card in after the person in front of me and one card popped up and the man in front took it. I stood there waiting for mine and of course it was too late to do anything when I realised what had happened.
He'd taken mine and his single yellow ticket was in the machine. At first I'd thought my ticket was stuck and after some reluctance, the staff on duty checked the collection box, to no avail. Then they admitted it now happened quite often with these new gates. I was very angry, as you can imagine.

[*Mr. Cohen*]

After being given the run around about who to see for a refund. L.T. have promised to re-imburse all the tickets I need to buy between now and when it was due to run out, (The following Monday).

But what I think should now be done, is that passengers be made aware of the fact that this is a new crime to be aware of when travelling by tube. And not have all the hassle I've had. Why hasn't this crime already been publicised?"

My hon. Friend the Member for Islington, South and Finsbury immediately wrote to LRT to take up that matter. The barriers were supposed to reduce crime, but this is a new crime arising from their installation.

**Mr. Andrew F. Bennett:** The problem is that one cannot be certain whether it is deliberate or accidental. The worst of it is that it will be very difficult to prosecute a person, because one must prove that that individual did not think that it was his ticket coming back. It makes it a most difficult crime to pursue. It is extremely worrying that it will be a growing crime in London.

**Mr. Cohen:** That is right. It would be virtually impossible to prove it if the person who ended up with the ticket denied that he had stolen it and insisted that it was a mistake. That is a new point, but season tickets were considered at Second Reading. It was in the context of people being worried to put their tickets in the machine for fear of losing them. Pressure was put on for passengers to have freedom of choice in the use of the barriers or the manual gate.

My hon. Friend the Member for Denton and Reddish (Mr. Bennett) said:

"Will the hon. Gentleman confirm that there will always be an alternative to using the mechanical ticket barriers?"

The hon. Member for Ilford, South (Mr. Thorne), on behalf of the promoters said:

"The intention is that there will always be that option available."—[*Official Report*, 6 February 1989; Vol. 146, c. 762.

The hon. Gentleman was unequivocal about that. However, for the first time today we have heard the hon. Gentleman saying that that only applies to women with prams, which was not the view gained by the House when it gave its approval for the Bill to proceed at Second Reading.

If hon. Members had realised that the choice was being taken away from travellers in that blunt manner, I am not sure that they would have given the Bill a Second Reading. After all, I have stood at elections where the Conservative party kept telling the electorate that it is the party of choice. To be fair to Conservative Members, I believe that many of them are honourable. They actually believe that they are the party of choice, although all the time they are taking money and public services away from people, which reduces choice. They are putting a burden on the people as opposed to giving them choice. I believe that many Conservative Members are in favour of giving people choice and, if they had known that choice was being taken away, I wonder whether they would have been so keen to go through the Lobby.

**Dr. Marek:** Will my hon. Friend give his opinion on the system used on the Tyne and Wear Metro, where there are turnstiles, but there are no automatic ticket barriers or controls? There is free exit and entry to the Metro, but there is an efficient on-train ad hoc ticket inspection system. Does he feel that the Bill is going about the problem of evasion in the wrong way and that perhaps a system such as that established on the Tyne and Wear metro might be preferable?

**Mr. Cohen:** That is right. There should be that choice available. By all means let London Transport have efficient systems for people to get in and out of the stations, if people are prepared to use them, but there should be a choice. London Regional Transport is going about it the wrong way and has not learnt lessons from the Tyne and Wear Metro and other systems around the world which have sensible systems.

My hon. Friend the Member for Denton and Reddish mentioned that on 5 June at Westminster station the choice to use the barriers or not had been taken away. On 2 June at Euston station staff were brought together almost like a would-be police force to man the ticket barriers and to force passengers to use them, giving them no choice. It is ironic that the staff should be used in that way, because barriers were brought in to cut the number of staff required. It is like the staff being asked to dig their own graves or sign their own redundancy notices. About 12 staff were sent down to the barriers and they stopped everybody and said, "You must use the barriers, you cannot use the manual barrier." That is what happened at Euston on 2 June between 6 and 7 o'clock at night. I had cause to complain to LRT about that.

One respectable passenger—I can vouch for her respectability as she is chairman of the Leyton Labour party—was passing through Euston and she told the staff that she wanted to use the manual barrier. That was a reasonable request, but she was stopped from doing so. The staff demanded of her the reason for her request. She told them that she felt safer and more comfortable going through that manual barrier, but they told her that that was not good enough. The staff told her that if she were disabled they would allow her to go through. Later in their discussions, however, it came out that the disabled are not allowed to travel on the Underground unless they have obtained permission in the first place. I shall be asking questions about that. Clearly the disabled are faced with a Catch-22 situation. LRT has forced the use of the automatic barriers by dismissing every reason suggested for not using them. It has taken away passengers' choice.

I do not believe that we should consider the Bill, as LRT has got its priorities wrong by spending so much money on promoting it. I came across a cutting this week from the publication of the London Hazards Centre, "The Daily Hazard", which said:

"In 1987 we reported on the absurd similarity between the penalties imposed for fare dodging on London Underground and the average fine for employers whose negligence causes the death of a worker—both around £400."

We all know that, increasingly, the safety of LRT is at risk. LRT's priority should be to ensure that safety is improved and it should provide a compensation scheme for accidents to its staff. There should be more important priorities than fare dodgers.

Nobody supports people who dodge paying their fares, which is a criminal offence, but it appears that LRT has got its priorities wrong. About 300 British Transport police operate on LRT and they are immensely overstretched because of crimes of all kinds, particularly serious crimes of violence. Often the police are not on hand to deal with such crimes, because there are not enough of them.

I have chased up the Minister to find out the cost of the barriers, but I have been given some evasive answers. Originally the Minister told me that they cost £22 million, but I am now told that various items relating to the computers were not included in that cost. I am now told that it is LRT's responsibility to say how much the barriers cost. I am still awaiting that information from LRT although the national press has reported that the cost is in the region of £165 million. That money would have provided 550 British Transport police for 10 years. Rather than waste any more money on the Bill, that money should be spent on the transport police so that fare dodgers and other more violent criminals on the Tube are caught.

8.15 pm

I agree with my hon. Friend the Member for Denton and Reddish that money should be spent on making the stations spick and span and a pleasure to visit. If people consider that the transport system is cheap, squalid and nasty they will try to evade paying for it. To clean up the existing squalor would be an incentive to people to pay their fares. The money should also be spent on staffing for the benefit of passengers and the service. It would have been far better if LRT had made safety its priority instead of the nonsense of a Bill before us.

I have studied the statement given by the promoters of the Bill and it does not refer to the trade unions being consulted. The trade unionists, however, are the front line in fare collection. They have not been consulted, but it is they who face violence if they confront someone on the tube and say that that person has not paid his fare.

**Dr. Marek:** I am a Member sponsored by the National Union of Railwaymen and, as far as I am aware, that union has not been consulted by LRT on any aspect of the Bill, even though it intimated to the management of LRT its worries about attacks on the staff. That is why the Bill is unsatisfactory.

**Mr. Cohen:** Yes, it is my understanding that the trade unions have not been consulted.

If such penalty fare collection is to become part of the job of the staff, one would think that, at the very least, they would receive additional pay, but, in its statement, LRT has not said that it is prepared to pay staff more for their extra onerous task. That is not surpising, as we are already in the middle of industrial action because of the meanness of LRT. It has sought to impose the Government's wage-cut policy on its staff. We all know that the current dispute has been caused because LRT has only offered its staff 7 per cent. while inflation is 8 per cent. and rising. That wage offer is on top of the staff reductions that have been faced year after year and the worsening conditions under which staff must work. Many guards have been taken off trains so the other staff must now take the blame if anything goes wrong, but they receive nothing extra for that.

The workers' industrial action is justified and they have common cause with the passengers who have suffered from worsening conditions and increasing risks to safety. We should support the workers of LRT and put pressure on the Government to settle their justifiable claim so that they receive wages for their onerous extra tasks. Those staff will have to collect the penalty fares and they will undoubtedly risk violence, but the mean LRT board has not offered them a penny for doing so.

The House will recall that the chairman of LRT has described the strike action as "ungodly", but that term can also be used to describe LRT. The LRT management is trying to screw down the workers without paying them properly for their onerous extra tasks and it has caused passengers to suffer because of the increasingly squalid conditions. That management policy can only be described as "ungodly". The House should not agree to such a policy, especially as there has been no consultaion with the trade unions. There has also been no consultation with hon. Members.

When we discussed the Bill in the last Session I raised the problem of the possibility of violence to staff. I said then that I had not been consulted and that nobody from LRT had talked to me, a London Member of Parliament. From that day to this, nobody from LRT has told me about the proposals and the fact that they may lead to violence on staff.

**Dr. Marek:** It would be extremely useful if my hon. Friend would agree that the hon. Member for Ilford, South (Mr. Thorne) should seek to catch Mr. Deputy Speaker's eye so that he can explain these matters, rather than the Opposition talking in a vacuum without knowing exactly what is taking place behind the scenes. The hon. Member for Ilford, South may be able to assure us on some of these points and confirm where the division lies between those of us who have caveats about the Bill going ahead and those of us who do not.

**Mr. Cohen:** I agree with my hon. Friend, and I am about to conclude my remarks to give the hon. Member for Ilford, South that opportunity.

I have given a number of reasons for opposing the Bill: the public, hon. Members and trade unions have not been consulted; there is the problem of the barriers; and LRT has the wrong priorities. My hon. Friend the Member for Denton and Reddish said that when the GLC controlled public transport in London it acted as a democratic channel so that the public could be involved. Now, they are not involved at all. We should consider that factor.

The Bill, like the ticket barriers, is an enormous waste of money and the time of the House, particularly when we bear in mind the real problems facing the Underground. I shall be interested to hear how the hon. Member for Ilford, South can justify the inaction of LRT in those circumstances. I have given a powerful set of reasons why we should abandon the Bill.

**Mr. Nigel Spearing** (Newham, South): I am sure that in a few moments the hon. Member for Ilford, South (Mr. Thorne) will take up the request of my hon. Friend the Member for Leyton (Mr. Cohen).

It is a happy accident that the three London Members come from east London because public transport there is even more important to ordinary people than it is in other parts of the conurbation. That is not surprising because car ownership in our boroughs—Walthamstow, Newham and, possibly, Redbridge—may be lower than elsewhere.

It is also a happy accident that the sponsor of the Bill, the hon. Member for Ilford, South, and I served on the traffic and transport committee of the Greater London council. I know that the hon. Gentleman takes an interest in these matters and has a practical grasp of them. I hope that he will concede, even if he does not always agree with me, that I also try to have a practical grasp of them.

[*Mr. Nigel Spearing*]

It is an anomaly that, due to the excellence of the private Bill procedure of this House, which permits us to consider on the Floor of the House whether a Bill should go further after being in Committee, this Bill is being debated at a proper time and in a proper way, whereas the Government denied the House the opportunity even to discuss the proposals considered at Madrid last week. It is a democratic anomaly which puts the Government in a poor light.

It is also due to the Government's actions that hon. Members present this evening, and no less a person than the Minister of State, Department of Transport, are dealing with a subject that should be considered in the GLC county hall across the river. As I think the hon. Member for Ilford, South would agree, this is the sort of issue which was dealt with in a morning's Committee meeting, or maybe over a series of several meetings months, perhaps, after informal presentations from officers of London Regional Transport, questions from committee members and other members of the Greater London Council.

The sort of problems involving barriers and the practicalities of penalty fares, which have been described by my hon. Friend, were dealt with by representatives of London in county hall in a way which did not impinge upon the legislature of the nation. It is extraordinary that we have to bring the Secretary of State for Transport and my hon. Friend the Member for West Bromwich, East (Mr. Snape) to the Front Bench in the national legislature to talk about practical and important matters relating to London Regional Transport. I am glad that we have the opportunity to do so but I wish that it could be done in county hall, where it should be, and that the time of the House was not being taken up with this matter tonight. However, we have no alternative, so my remarks tonight will be similar to those which I might have made had I been sitting in that committee as I did 20 years ago.

Is this Bill necessary? I would question LRT officials if they brought such proposals before a committee in county hall. The claim is that London Regional Transport is losing up to £26 million a year through fare evasion. I accede that it may be losing money and the matter may have been dealt with on Second Reading. I hope that the hon. Member for Ilford, South will tell us the basis of that calculation.

If the barriers and the new ticket system are as good as London Regional Transport has claimed, will the loss be reduced by that system—partially effective and offensive though it may be? One would have thought that if LRT were losing that amount of money, the electronic system which it installed would be designed to reduce it without recourse to legislation. Therefore, what is the necessity for the Bill, as well as the barriers? Must we have both? Apparently, both London Regional Transport and the Government say that we should. As a representative of the citizens of London and of the legislators here, I do not see why we should. If the barriers did their job, we would not need the Bill. This matter should be explained.

We also need an explanation of the interpretation of the word "penalty". We are soon to have a different sort of penalty fare in London: penalty fares for those who want to travel at peak times. The Government have endorsed that principle. The Prime Minister, from the very seat in which the Minister of State is now sitting, endorsed that principle when asked a question by my hon. Friend the Member for Leyton only 10 days ago. She said that travellers would have to pay more at peak times to pay for better services in general. However, those who pay peak fares will not receive better services, and we object to that.

**Mr. Andrew F. Bennett:** Does my hon. Friend accept that the introduction of such penalties for people who travel at peak times will cause resentment? That is the sort of thing which motivates people to take out their resentment on the system, either by defacing stations or by trying to cheat on tickets. If the Government behaved in a responsible way and carried the travelling public with them they could do a great deal to encourage people to look after property and dissuade them from trying to evade fares.

**Mr. Spearing:** My hon. Friend makes an important point, particularly in relation to incipient violence—I am not talking about theft. People's attitude to the transport system is to ask whether it is user-friendly, designed for their convenience and delight or to oppress them. That is an important psychological factor.

I was brought up in the middle and late 1930s when London Regional Transport was a delight to the eye and an exemplar throughout the world of good transport management. That is not so today. The existence of penal fares at peak hours, or penalty fares for alleged fare dodging, will tighten that psychological screw. That is another reason why I ask: should we have this Bill? If London Regional Transport is going to apply penalty fares at peak hours, should we let them have this Bill as part of the general package? We do not have much control over that because the Secretary of State has taken statutory powers relating to the fares structure of London Regional Transport. However, at least the House and representatives of London have some powers over this miserable piece of legislation.

**Mr. Cohen:** Has my hon. Friend thought about one of the implications of the Government's policy of loading extra fares on people who travel at peak times—the effect on the cost of living index? The increase in fares will be absorbed in the prices index as only a small rise, but this will be an enormous extra burden on people who use the system to travel in peak times, and that will be reflected in their pay claims. The Government will then say that the prices index has risen by only a little and ask these people why they are claiming a great deal more. Is not that a recipe for trouble?

8.30 pm

**Mr. Spearing:** Indeed. It is penal in the broadest sense. The original instruction that the former Secretary of State for Transport gave LRT was that fares should generally rise in relation to the cost of living index. That policy has now changed because they rose last time by 12 per cent., roughly double the general increase in prices. We do not know the size of the increase being planned by LRT now. Perhaps the Secretary of State will not agree to it, although recently Mr. Wilfrid Newton told London Labour Members of Parliament in reply to my question about whether the principle had been agreed and it was now merely a matter of method, amount and timing, that that was exactly so. I hope that he was wrong. The Minister of State is also a London Member; I hope that he and the Secretary of State will not permit these penal fares.

As my hon. Friend the Member for Leyton said, public transport costs in London are already leaping ahead of inflation, which itself is too high, and that is inflationary. The Government claim that they believe in fighting inflation, yet they produce it by doubling LRT fares.

In the middle of the last century, the heyday of Victorian probity and enterprise, Parliament in its wisdom laid down the maximum fares for private railway companies. LRT is still a public transport concern—we have not yet privatised it and I hope that we never shall. Although the railway companies may have run only one train a day at these fares, it was called the parliamentary train because there was a maximum fare. Are the Government going back on that relatively enlightened Victorian policy? I suggest that their public transport policy shows that they are.

Will these proposals stop evasion? For the past few moments I may have spoken controversially, but I shall now revert to what I might have said in a county hall committee. We all have a vested interest in stopping fare evasion even if we disagree with the fare structure. The psychology of LRT's anti-fare-dodging measures is not right. Recently LRT produced machines that authorise people to travel, but I am not sure that they are in operation everywhere. If there is no ticket man at a station —I do not blame the staff for that: there are severe shortages—we press a button and receive authority to travel. At our destination, the ticket collectors know where we got on. This good idea has only just been introduced and I do not know whether it is yet fully effective. I hope that the hon. Member for Ilford, South will tell us whether it is. Properly used, the system could cut down some evasion.

The chance of detection also cuts down evasion, as we all know from experience of other areas. The Post Office is a past master of this game. It sends a little van with a revolving aerial around the streets. It does not matter what is inside the van—there might just be a man turning a handle. What matters is that in the next two days people queue up at the Post Office to pay their telly licenses. That is a cost-effective form of ensuring that people do not evade their responsibilities. I have detected nothing like it on London Underground—quite the reverse.

We have argued before that there must be more staff on the platforms and stations. This is one of the reasons why the motormen are going on strike. They know that Government policy is going in the opposite direction of public opinion, and no wonder they get wild and annoyed. As a result the atmosphere is soured and industrial action takes place. There must be more people to check up. The possibility of detection will ensure that people pay their fares or carry the right pass.

I must confess to having been stopped by inspectors on LRT three times in the past year. Curiously enough, it always happened on a Sunday morning. I have only once seen someone checking tickets on a train on a weekday. Inspectors should check tickets at the big interchange stations, just as we pick up people going through Customs. A spot check is cost-effective, time-effective and person power-effective. Under the present system, people on the Underground do not know whether they will be stopped.

I have with me my London Regional Transport pass for three zones. When they were first introduced, the passes showed large numbers which could be easily read. Inspectors or conductors could see at a glance whether the pass holder was eligible to travel. The new passes need fairly close scrutiny to determine the zones. That does not inspire me with confidence in the management, although there may be an explanation for it. The poor chap driving the bus or at the ticket barrier would have to be very good to read the zone numbers. Employees of LRT say that one of their problems is that the new pass is not easily inspected. It is difficult for them if they have to stop people for a while to read the pass, because passengers get annoyed.

Last Sunday week I was on a bus and showed my pass, whereupon I was told that I was out of my zone. I said that the zone had been zone 3 last year, but I was told that the zones had now changed and the one I was in was zone 3a. The conductor told me that the zones had changed last December, so I paid up, and fair enough—up to a point. Confusion in the system does not give people confidence. I have had a complaint from Beckton in my constituency, which contains many new people and houses. The train station, North Woolwich, is in zone 3, but to judge from the boundaries the area is zone 4 for buses. I have written to LRT about this anomaly and no doubt it will provide a curious explanation.

This sort of thing helps neither the passengers nor the poor staff. If they do their job, they get the kickback from the customer; if they do not do their job, under the present management of London Regional Transport, which is pretty tight on some people, they may be jumped on by a spot—someone in plain clothes—for not doing their job. So the poor old lady or gent who is operating the bus is squeezed. Those are the problems in industrial relations today.

**Dr. Marek:** I deplore as much as my hon. Friend does the system of different zones and different fares. I wonder whether it is all part of a plan to destabilise a simple, straightforward fare system in London so that the structure may be amenable to privatisation in the unlikely event that the Tory party wins the next election.

**Mr. Spearing:** I hope not. I have a reputation for seeing under stones things that are not there. My hon. Friend's thesis may be true but I fear that the problems are caused by inefficiency, lack of imagination and an inability to see things from the point of view of the passengers, who happen to be the owners. We talk about customers but the citizens of London are not just customers of London Underground Ltd. or of London Buses; they are the owners. The Minister is not the owner.

Bus passes do not apply universally as they used to. Under the Transport Act 1985 the traffic commissioners gave permission for minibuses to run through east London; they do not accept passes, including pensioners' passes. We are beginning to see the break-up of the system. I do not think that the administrative cock-up over zones was deliberate but Government policy on pensioners not being allowed to travel free on certain minibuses is deliberate and is part of the scheme for privatisation. Therefore, old-age pensioners are penalised. If the break-up of the bus system does not allow for universal ticketing, there is discrimination and people are penalised in terms of convenience if not on fares.

**The Minister for Public Transport (Mr. Michael Portillo):** If the hon. Gentleman's thesis were correct, why

*[Mr. Michael Portillo]*

would I have written to the London boroughs concerned to ask them to extend concessionary fares to privately operated minibuses?

**Mr. Spearing:** I am glad that the Minister asked that question. Being a relatively new Member, perhaps he does not remember the history of concessionary fares in London. Originally, London boroughs decided whether to give passes to their residents. Some did, mainly the Labour boroughs, and some did not. There was an outcry throughout London, with people saying that it was ridiculous that concessionary fares depended on which side of the road someone lived or on which party was in the majority in a borough; everyone demanded that concessionary fares should be issued Londonwide. It may be news to Government Members that that was not the case originally. The responsibility was transferred from the London boroughs to the Greater London council, which was established by the Conservative party as a strategic transport and planning authority for London, and pensioner passes were applicable throughout London.

**Mr. Cohen:** My hon. Friend is right; the Greater London council was established by the Tory party but I remind him that concessionary fares were established by a Labour GLC.

**Mr. Spearing:** I am grateful to my hon. Friend for pointing that out, but the fares could not have applied on an all-London basis without the existence of a body that was strategically necessary for transport and planning, something that the Government denied subsequently. We wanted concessionary fares to remain on an all-London basis but the Conservative party has now produced the anomaly, as the Minister admitted. Route D16 runs through Tower Hamlets and Newham. Does the Minister expect Newham council to provide concessionary fares while others do not?

**Mr. Cryer:** I am sure my hon. Friend will agree that the Minister's intervention was interesting and revealing. No announcement has been made about the secret letters that the Minister has been touting round London. The Minister has been trying to remedy in secret the damage that the legislation abolishing the GLC achieved in public. The Government are trying to remedy the very policies that the GLC was carrying out amicably until a group of extreme Right wingers tabled a clause to abolish the GLC.

8.45 pm

**Mr. Spearing:** I agree with my hon. Friend. The position is even worse. Because the Government abolished the GLC for all the wrong reasons—we now see the results in the transport and traffic chaos in London—we have a patchwork system. The minibuses which the Government have encouraged and which are outside the remit of London Buses—probably the public do not know that —have to apply to individual boroughs, as the Minister has admitted, if they want pensioners' passes. That is ridiculous. The Minister is encouraging boroughs which suffer from an unfair rate system to remedy an anomaly that the Government created. That is yet another example of the fares and transport chaos in London.

Whatever the need for dealing with fare dodgers, this penalty fares Bill is ill-fitted for the job. It should be drafted in a way that satisfies the psychology and pride of the people of London, the well-being of those who work on the system and, above all, those who use it daily to travel to work.

**Mr. Cryer:** It is a pleasure to say a few words on the Bill. I am particularly interested in the statement that the promoters circulated to hon. Members. It sets out the origination of the Bill which was a report of a working group of officials from the Home Office, the Lord Chancellor's Department, London Regional Transport and the Department of Transport.

The group was considering the principles that should apply to a penalty fares scheme on public transport. Unfortunately the report is not in the Vote Office or we could have had ready reference to it. The Library is obtaining a copy for me. My hon. Friend the Member for West Bromwich, East (Mr. Snape) has a copy. I sought information from the Vote Office. Unfortunately the promoters have not arranged for copies of the report to be in the Vote Office. The Vote Office tells me it may be several days before it can get copies.

**Mr. Peter Snape** (West Bromwich, East): I fear that inadvertently I may have caused the problem. Like my hon. Friend, I read the promoters' statement. I went first to the Vote Office, as he did, and then to the Library to find out whether the report was available. The Library staff kindly and efficiently produced the report for me. Alas, it is the only one available in the building. That explains why my hon. Friend is subject to delay in its provision.

**Mr. Cryer:** That shows that the promoters have not been as assiduous as they might have been in providing hon. Members with information.

I was interested to note that the Bill started off with a working group of officials. Officials are not elected, directly or indirectly. They are appointees within the Civil Service career structure and it might be argued that they are not the most democratically minded individuals.

I looked again at the promoters' statement to see whether there were, for example, representatives of the people who operate services and who turn out at 4 or 5 in the morning, go down, open the trains, get on the stations, rather than dealing with high quality decisions with cups of Civil Service tea to hand in comfortable rooms with furniture that is well upholstered, like some members of the working party. I cannot see that any representatives of the workers who operate the railway system or the buses —those who start up the Routemasters at 4.30 am, get out the ticket machines and start the gritty business of meeting the travelling public in the morning and late at night— were involved.

The lack of such people in the working party is a matter of regret. Paragraph 7 in the promoters' statement says :

"The Bill has the support of the Department of Transport and there has been consultation with the Unions representing those who would have to implement the penalty fares scheme."

I am interested to know—I am sure that the hon. Member for Ilford, South (Mr. Thorne) will tell us—the result of those consultations. I wonder why the promoters are so shy about it. Perhaps the result was glorious and the trade union representatives fell on the necks of the administrators of the scheme and said, "What a wonderful idea. We like meeting angry people in crowded trains to try to impose penalty fares, and this is a challenge." That is the sort of gobbledegook yuppie language that the

Government so often use in such circumstances. If that had happened, I should have thought that it would be included in the statement. If it had happened but the promoters had not included it, they would have been remiss. No doubt the hon. Member for Ilford, South will reveal all to us in due course.

**Dr. Marek:** I do not think that there have been consultations. There certainly were none with the NUR. I am aware of what the promoters' statement says. The hon. Member for Ilford, South (Mr. Thorne) is refusing to explain these things to us. Would it not have been better if these things had been explained to us in advance?

**Mr. Cryer:** My hon. Friend is right. The sentence
"The Bill has the support of the Department of Transport and there has been consultation with the Unions representing those who would have to implement the penalty fares scheme" requires some elucidation. It could refer to those who are to be on the trains, who will have to say to people on a crowded tube train in the morning, "You've not got your ticket and I want a penalty fare, chum"—the conversation that would ensue would be interesting and possibly difficult. It could refer to the people who get the paperwork from the people on the trains, implement it, and record the penalty fare payments, docket them and transfer them to the accounting department. It is not clear, and there would be a difference of view between those two unions.

I suspect that the people who go on the trains to collect the penalty fares do not view the task with relish. I suspect that those who merely administer the scheme would do it simply as another administrative exercise. After all, they are nicely insulated from the public, who will be protesting their innocence and so on. It is possible that that statement covers administrators but not the people who carry out the scheme. I am eagerly anticipating the explanation of the hon. Member for Ilford, South about why that elliptical sentence is included in the statement.

It is a matter of deep regret that the Government chose not to involve the people who are running the services in helping to draw up the scheme. It is an unfortunate characteristic of our society that the people who work, day in day out, at something and spend their lives working to provide a service—in this case, transport—are so rarely consulted on how it should be run. My hon. Friend the Member for West Bromwich, East has many years' experience of the railways and knows that that is the case. Those who operate the service are always the last to be consulted about changes that affect the operation that they are running.

The promoters should be aware that 99·9 per cent. of those who operate the services have an affection for them, a devotion to the cause of providing a service, an ability and talent to do so and a contribution to make. I am afraid that one of the adversities that we face is a hierarchical system. People appointed by the Secretary of State produce a report in insulated offices in Whitehall and then hand it on to be imposed on the people who are working the system to ensure that it provides a service, and often to cover up the deficiencies of management.

One of the reasons why there is industrial action today is that there has not been adequate consultation because there is a belief in the noxious phrase that the management must manage. That means that management must be able to impose its views on the work force, whatever the views of the majority, and those who do the routine tasks are always the majority. That is not an adequate way to work

any system, whether it is a transport system, a factory or anything else. Jimmy Knapp, the NUR leadership and ASLEF are demonstrating that they will not have their negotiating rights trampled on by an arrogant management elite and that they want meaningful consultation rights, and wage negotiations, and decent working conditions negotiated under a proper, democratic and humane system. That is what the argument is about, and it is reflected in an interesting way in the Bill and the statement on behalf of the promoters in support of consideration of the Bill.

The system about which we are talking was imposed from on high—if we consider administrative rooms in Whitehall as being on high. Some people would refer to the ideas they produce as coming from the bowels of the earth. That is the origin of this legislation, so it has some deficiencies. The basic one is that, like all management people, they see their task as "increasing efficiency", which to them means getting rid of people. People are our national asset. They have the ability and the talent to design, to improve and to give value, yet they are the very people that the working party decided should be removed and ticket machines put in their place. There are a number of severe disadvantages in that.

My hon. Friend the Member for Denton and Reddish (Mr. Bennett) mentioned the breach of faith by the hon. Member for Ilford, South. As will be clear in *Hansard,* an assurance was given that there would be some access to platforms without having to pass through ticket barriers. Those of us who use London Regional Transport know that that is not the case. When the ticket machines were first installed a gate was always left open, but that usually does not happen now. Quite often all the barriers are in operation and there is no alternative to passing through those barriers. That is very difficult for people with children, prams, pushchairs or baggage.

There used to be porters at railway stations, but now, other than at major mainline stations, they have disappeared from the face of the earth. However, there are still ticket collectors and they can give assistance and advice. The change machines do not always work. In my experience the machines that require exact fares work more often than those that give change. That is another inconvenience for travellers. People working at stations can give advice about fares, travel, connections and so on, but the report ignores all that.

9 pm

**Dr. Marek:** I do not know how the machines work, but I suspect that they are all of the same type. When a machine does not have enough change, the light-emitting diode on top of the machine will change to "exact fare only". My experience is that most machines, and certainly those at Euston, say "exact fare only". It is lucky to find a machine that gives change. We would have more confidence in LRT if it could assure us that all its machines and barriers would be foolproof. If experience of current machines is anything to go by, they are inadequate—indeed, anything that LRT does appears to be inadequate in some way.

**Mr. Cryer:** The machines will have to be extremely robust. They have been installed and in general use for only a few weeks. There may have been pilot projects, but I have not seen one. With the vast range of LRT stations, it is possible that there has been a pilot project somewhere.

[*Mr. Cryer*]

The machines must withstand one of the most intensive underground systems in the world, so their margin of safety must be very great if they are to survive the onslaught of such massive use. Like my hon. Friends, I have my reservations about the safety of ticket barriers. If a fire breaks out, such as the tragic and horrible incident at King's Cross, the barriers need to be removed rapidly. The machines and barriers physically reduce the amount of space available for people to get out in an emergency. There is only a matter of seconds, perhaps 120 to 180, to evacuate people from a station.

The fire at King's Cross started at the bottom of an escalator, which acted as a chimney. The draught of air flowing through that chimney rapidly spread the fire. The barriers had to be opened rapidly to allow the people to get out. I wonder whether the new ticket barriers can be rapidly opened or whether they will impede evacuation. King's Cross now has monitors and video cameras surveying the whole of the ticket area. The station also has a central ticket cubicle that is, I suppose, manned while the station is open, as well as a ticket cubicle that is often staffed.

I imagine that London Transport keeps a continuing eye on King's Cross because of the seriousness of the fire that occurred there, which made it the focus of worldwide attention. But we must bear in mind every station, including those at the end of branch lines and which are used much less than King's Cross. I have not seen at those stations the same degree of video monitoring as is in evidence at King's Cross.

Provision must be made for the worst possible case, where there is no supervision and no ticket collectors. Nevertheless, I suppose that with the advent of the Bill, even the last vestiges of that staffing will disappear, and I have severe reservations about the substitution of staff by machines.

The report that started the current trend to automation was published before the King's Cross fire. It is clear that the Bill is a Government measure, one stage removed through London Regional Transport. My guess is that if the King's Cross fire had occurred when the working party report was being prepared, the Bill would not have been produced, the working party would have changed the principles on which it was founded, and the House would not have been required to consider such legislation. It concerns me that LRT is so obdurate and pig-headed that it is not prepared to take into account the lessons learnt from King's Cross and to defer any proposals for several years, until the situation is comprehensively understood.

It would be interesting to know from the hon. Member for Ilford, South whether there have been any pilot schemes to assess the reliability of the machinery involved. As I said, it will be subject to a great deal of use, and all machinery wears out. What provision is to be made—on the basis of experience that, of necessity, must be limited —for dismantling, maintaining and overhauling ticket barriers and other equipment? What are London Underground's plans? Will ticket barriers, for example, be removed for routine overhauls or will some be overhauled in situ? If the latter, they must inevitably be taken out of use, which will reduce access to and egress from stations —and egress is the most significant consideration in respect of accidents.

The principle on which the Bill is based will make it incumbent on London Transport to install ticket barriers at all stations so that staff can be concentrated on the trains, to collect penalty fares.

Once the Bill is enacted, there will no longer be an opportunity to raise questions. One may write a letter to the chairman of London Regional Transport, who is an appointee, and seek information, but it will not be possible to raise matters in public, in the way that we can now on the Floor of this House.

Health and safety hazards also give food for thought. The report of the working party produced in May 1986 was designed to get rid of ticket attendants. We should be told by the sponsor—who, I suspect, does not know—how many ticket attendants will be displaced and put on to trains to collect penalty fares, how many people will be made redundant and what additional maintenance requirement will be imposed on London Regional Transport for the ticket machines.

The maintenance task is likely to be enormous. Every station probably has half a dozen machines; multiplied by several hundred, that will pose a task of exceptional stringency. Every machine must be working if health and safety standards are to be maintained. If the machines are to be replaced to guarantee maximum access, a given number of machines must be kept in store, overhauled and maintained ready for immediate replacement. If the machines are to be repaired in situ, that is an entirely different matter: a potentially serious hazard will be posed to health and safety at work and to passenger safety, and we should be told about that as well.

The linking of public with private legislation has social implications. This is essentially a Government Bill; its origin was in the Government working party set up in 1986. Its report was approved by the Secretary of State, who then told London Transport and British Rail to go ahead. Meanwhile, the Government have introduced legislation which provides further hazards.

We know that since the present Government came to office in 1979 violence has increased. Inadequate street lighting caused by cuts in local authority expenditure has caused women to be worried about walking in the streets late at night. I know of no woman who would say that our city streets are safe at all times of day and night. Many women to whom I have spoken have mentioned their fear of walking in the city streets in the dark, especially late at night.

Let us suppose that a woman is going to her station and hears footfalls behind her. She must walk along a subway to reach the station: it is ill lit and covered with graffiti. The Elephant and Castle is a case in point. The subway could be seen as a dangerous area—I do not say that it is; I merely say that it could be. When she reaches the station, the woman may seek safety in the form of a ticket collector or cashier, and find that the station is deserted and devoid of fellow passengers.

There is a machine, but it requires the exact money, and she does not have the right change. That means that she cannot get on the train because a penalty fare is involved. So she turns back and sees the ill-lit corridors behind her with potential danger lurking there.

9.15 pm

That woman might have been obliged to take night work because, by the Employment Bill, the Government have removed protection for women against working at night. When a woman applies for a job and is offered night work, she may say, " I do not like night work because I am afraid of walking about late at night, and the shift finishes at 10 pm, when the streets are empty and stations are deserted. The buses do not run frequently because of cuts by the Conservative Government." The employer replies, "That is the job. Take it or leave it."

There may be no union at the factory to which the woman can appeal for aid and support, because the Government have been working against trade unions and they want to reduce union membership as much as possible. The woman goes to the Department of Employment saying that she turned the job down. "That is a superficial reason for turning the job down. You are not demonstrating that you are actively seeking work," the official at the Department replies. "I have been for a job," she says. The official says, "Yes, but you turned it down for reasons which do not sound good to us, so we are stopping your benefit under the new Social Security Act."

In other words, women are placed in peril by a combination of events, a third of which we are discussing tonight. It cannot be denied that Government legislation affects millions of women. The removal of protection against night work and the requirement actively to be seeking work are two of the events. The Bill—and British Rail penalty fare proposals on which I hope to speak tomorrow in the House—remove the friendly help and advice of staff at stations in our great city of London.

British Rail management hopes to take the same action at every station throughout the country, so these steps are of universal application. We are debating a measure applying only to LRT, but it is all part of a pattern by which women will become more vulnerable, although men, too, will suffer.

Even if not by design, and even though disparate Departments may be promulgating their own ideas, all this legislation links up. Even if there is no plan for a wholesale reduction in facilities, representing an attack on the standards of protection afforded to the work force, that is the effect of what is being done.

The hon. Member for Ilford, South should agree to halt further consideration of the measure. He should inform those involved that, in the light of circumstances in society, the Bill should be withdrawn and the whole principle enshrined in the 1986 report—of replacing people on stations with machines—reconsidered. People, rather than machines, should be retained.

Considering further the position of women at stations, imagine the plight of a woman with small children, one in a pushchair and the other a toddler. She has the problem of getting through the wretched automatic barriers. She must try to find somebody who can help her, and hope that somebody will be in evidence to come to her aid.

My guess is that late at night management will not be all that scrupulous about ensuring that staff are there to open locked gates. Before that lady reaches the gate she will have had to find the exact change for a ticket because the machine that gives change will have broken down and the sign "exact fare only" will be flashing on the screen. As a result of all the flurry and the difficulty she may go on to the train without a ticket. London Regional Transport officials will then say to her, "You haven't got a ticket, so you will have to pay a penalty fare." Meanwhile, her children will be tugging at her skirt. One will have fallen out of its pram and an ice cream will be slithering down the new dress of the toddler who is walking. The mother will

have to explain the circumstances to a railway official who, during his walk down the corridor of a crowded train, has had a bit of abuse from two or three people. It is most unsatisfactory.

No hon. Member would dispute that that could happen, yet this is the system that London Regional Transport considers an improvement. At the moment, a woman in that position can say to the ticket collector, "Can you help me with my pushchair?" and he will tell her, "Yes, I'll give you a hand." That happens day in, day out. That will disappear.

It will be a wretched system. It is objectionable that a group of highly placed people in Whitehall should have decided that this is good for people. I wonder how many mothers were members of the working party. Do those members take their children regularly on the Underground or on buses? I suspect that not many mothers were on the working party. How many of its members were trade unionists? According to the promoters' statement, it does not appear that any of them were trade unionists. Neither women with young children nor disabled people were represented on the working party which established this wretched principle that machines should be used instead of people.

The scheme is replete with difficulties for the travelling public. The elite who run London Regional Transport ought to pay more attention to the travelling public. My guess is that the elite—the management of London Regional Transport—are provided with chauffeur-driven cars. The Secretary of State for Transport who established the working group and, when it reported, gave his approval and authority for the scheme to go ahead, goes around in a chauffeur-driven car. He is not given a set of tickets or tokens for the Underground and asked to exchange them for tickets and, when he has time, to use them. I am not sure who is on the working group as they are not listed here.

**Mr. Snape:** Before my hon. Friend leaves that interesting scenario of the Secretary of State travelling on London Underground, given the problems with the machines that my hon. Friend has outlined so graphically, would the right hon. Gentleman be capable of feeding a ticket into the right slot and making his way through the ticket barrier?

**Mr. Cryer:** My guess is that in order not to reveal his lack of knowledge of these machines, the Secretary of State would get his private secretary to go ahead and demonstrate that it was all right so that the photographers could make it appear that the Secretary of State for Transport knew what he was doing.

The Secretary of State for Transport has established a working group of officials. If the permanent secretary or a deputy secretary at the Department of Transport were involved, official cars would be available for their use. The permanent secretary will have an official car to take him from his residence to the Department and home again every day. That is a rather cosseted existence for the person who supervises the working group of officials. If all the officials on the working group were permanent secretaries—and I doubt that—they would all be cosseted in that way. We all know that the Secretary of State has a chauffeur-driven Rover. We all know that it is a big Rover for a Secretary of State, a lesser model, probably a Montego, for a Minister of State and a Mini for an

[*Mr. Cryer*]

Under-Secretary. None the less, they all have chauffeurs. They are supervised by the Prime Minister, who has not set foot inside a railway carriage for years, and who likes to be driven around exclusively in her chauffeur-driven Jaguar.

**Dr. Marek:** I used to ask an annual question about whether the Prime Minister travelled by British Rail in her official duties. The answer always used to be no. However, two or three years ago the answer was yes. There had been one instance, and it may be that there has been another since then.

**Mr. Cryer:** Here we are examining whether the Prime Minister has been on a railway once or twice in the past five years.

**Mr. Andrew F. Bennett:** Or down to Finchley on the tube.

**Mr. Cryer:** I suspect that she does not often go down to Finchley on the tube. Although strictly speaking she should not use the official car for going to Finchley on constituency journeys, my guess is that she fiddles it by arranging an official engagement just beyond Finchley each month so that she can get out, spend 20 minutes there and then get back into the official car and go on to her official engagement. The Prime Minister is still not using the tube or the bus to Finchley. Were she to do so, she would get involved in conversations such as those in which many penalty fare collectors will take part—very heated and bitter discussions—because she would meet the people who are being adversely affected by the legislation and she does not want to do that. She is not facing up to the difficulties which her legislation encompasses and the specific transport difficulties that are now being created.

It is extremely unfair that the elite in our society should be imposing a system on people claiming that it will recoup some of the fares that are estimated to be lost through fraud each year. The note from the promoters makes that justification. It says that, with all the massive investment of many millions of pounds in new ticket equipment, they will now reduce the millions of pounds lost each year in fare evasion. One of the best ways of reducing fare evasion would be to employ more ticket collectors and to have more spot checks. That would have been better than this massive investment. As I have said several times before —it bears repeating—people are our greatest asset.

The figures for the losses can at the most be estimates. By virtue of the fact that the figures are for fare evasion, we have no guaranteed knowledge that they are accurate.

9.30 pm

**Mr. Snape:** I apologise for interrupting my hon. Friend yet again. I know that he is not aware of what I am about to say because he was unable to obtain the relevant document. I can tell him that the figure given in the document for fare evasion in May 1986 was £19·5 million. Remarkably, by February 1989, when the hon. Member for Ilford, South (Mr. Thorne) first moved the Second Reading, the figure had grown to £26 million. Are not those figures remarkably accurate when, by the very nature of fare evasion, the figures can only be guessed at?

**Mr. Cryer:** My hon. Friend is right. It is a remarkable chance that the figures have risen, as he said, from the 1986 figure of £19·5 million to the latest figure of £26 million.

People may be driven to the conclusion that those guesses —which is all that they are—have been inflated to justify the Bill, which must be one of the worst bases on which to propose legislation. The working party guessed the scale of evasion and as it was attempting to justify the imposition of the new machinery and the removal of people, it had to produce rather high figures. When this legislation was introduced, instead of providing a complete rationale with considerable information and copies of the report, it decided that it would produce yet another inflated figure. It probably decided to increase the figure by the level of inflation. That was no justification for the figure.

**Dr. Marek:** My hon. Friend is on to an important point. A failing of our system of government is that the Minister will say that the level of evasion is £26 million and we shall have to take his word for it. I am not blaming him, because that would be true of whoever was the Minister. In a better system of government, the Minister would have asked whether we would like to come round to his office and would have ensured that London Regional Transport would have its expert there and that all the figures would be available for us or our assistants to peruse. He would have said that there was nothing to hide. In this place, we never have such offers and my hon. Friend is right.

**Mr. Cryer:** I agree with what my hon. Friend has said. I would be interested to learn whether there are any detailed calculations relating to the £19·5 million in the document, which was not provided in the Vote Office tonight, or whether it was merely a bald figure. I suspect the latter, because if the working party had produced detailed statistical justification, it would be subject to more challenge. The less detail one provides, the more difficult it is to challenge. We must say that we reject the figure because it has been plucked from the air. Perhaps the Treasury gave advice on that, because the Treasury is rather fond of plucking figures from the air. The figure is fallacious and until the promoters produce information based on the calculations produced by the 1986 working party report, I fear that we shall have to reject the figure.

However, the hon. Member for Ilford, South does not seem very interested. He is busy trying to fix things with the Government Whip and since this is essentially a Government Bill, that is understandable. I am pleading for the promoter to provide us with the detailed figures on which the alleged loss of fares revenue is based. I hope that the hon. Member for Ilford, South will have time to reply to the debate. I do not wish to take too long because I know that my hon. Friend the Member for West Bromwich, East wishes to participate.

**Dr. Marek** *rose——*

**Mr. Cryer:** I give way to my hon. Friend with pleasure, although this will have to be the last time.

**Dr. Marek:** I am grateful to my hon. Friend, who has once again made an important point. We must decide whether the Bill is the right way to stop fare evasion, which we are all against. Perhaps my hon. Friend will couple his plea for the provision of figures about evasion in the London system with a plea for the figures on evasion in the Tyne and Wear Metro system, which is an open system. If we could compare the evasion in the two different systems, we would be in a better position to judge the merits of this Bill.

**Mr. Cryer:** I am sure that the sponsor, who has been plotting with the Government Whip, has been taking an interest in our affairs. I hope that he can provide the information that I require.

**Mr. Thorne:** The hon. Gentleman has asked me many questions and I am looking forward to having the time to answer them.

**Mr. Cryer:** I am most grateful to the hon. Gentleman and should like to ask him another question because I am not sure whether his attention was firmly fixed on the point raised by my hon. Friend the Member for Wrexham (Dr. Marek). My hon. Friend referred to comparisons with the Tyne and Wear Metro. As the hon. Gentleman knows, that is a recently constructed, virtually new metropolitan railway system, which has proved extremely successful. It would be interesting to know the comparative levels of fare evasion.

I have now said enough to express my views and my strong reservations about the proposed legislation. I hope that the promoter can answer some if not all of the points that I have raised. In view of the welter of questions, the preferable option would be to withdraw the Bill for more mature consideration.

**Mr. Portillo:** I had the opportunity of speaking at an earlier stage of the Bill's progress to express the Government's view. Therefore, I need not take up much of the House's time tonight, except to say that the Government support the Bill.

Both London Regional Transport and British Rail lose considerable amounts of money from people travelling on their services without having paid the correct fare or any fare at all. That simply increases the costs of travel for the honest passenger. Penalty fare arrangements are widely used abroad and we believe that LRT and BR should be allowed the opportunity of introducing similar systems in this country.

Although a penalty fares scheme based on existing legislation operates on the docklands light railway, it is true to say that penalty fares will be largely unfamiliar to the British travelling public. It is therefore right that the Committees of both Houses should have spent some time discussing the details of the Bill.

I know that my hon. Friend the Member for Ilford, South (Mr. Thorne) will seek to respond to the specific points that have been raised tonight. However, I stress that it will not be possible for LRT to introduce a penalty fares scheme on any of its services unless an activating order is issued by my right hon. Friend the Secretary of State for Transport. Before an activating order is issued we will need to be convinced that the system proposed by LRT is completely fair to passengers and that it is likely to work effectively. In order for penalty fares to work, a passenger must have a reasonable opportunity to buy the correct ticket for the journey and it follows that the operator must provide adequate opportunities for the passenger to buy a ticket at the start of his journey. That is the crux of any penalty fares scheme and we shall be paying particular attention to that in considering any request for an activating order that is put to us by London Regional Transport.

**Mr. Snape:** The Minister's contribution was illuminating and on this occasion he certainly did not detain the House for too long. I do not know whether the absence of his advisers from their usual place had anything to do with the brevity of his contribution, but he made no attempt to tackle any of the points or questions raised this evening. I hope that the hon. Member for Ilford, South (Mr. Thorne) will spend considerably longer replying to these important matters than did the Minister.

My hon. Friends, who have been the main contributors to the debate, have rightly subjected the Bill to considerable scrutiny. My immediate criticism of it is that it represents yet another worsening of conditions for the travelling public.

My hon. Friend the Member for Bradford, South (Mr. Cryer), who is not at present in the Chamber, asked about the compensation of the working party from whose recommendations the Bill flows. Before informing the House of the composition of that working party, it might be helpful if I informed my hon. Friends, and, indeed, the sponsor of the Bill, of some background to its introduction.

The Opposition remember that the penalty fares provisions first appeared in the London Regional Transport Act 1984. That was a not inappropriate year for that legislation, because prior to the abolition of the Greater London council, the right hon. Member for Cirencester and Tewkesbury (Mr. Ridley), who was at that time Secretary of State for Transport, was determined to strip the GLC of its principal function, which was that of responsibility for transport matters in London. The right hon. Gentleman was asked during the Committee stage of the Bill about those penalty fares provisions and how they would work. Being the broad-brush man that he is—and the water-colour expert that he is to prove it—he predictably urged us to wait until the outline was filled in. He promised us—truthfully as it turned out—that legislation would eventually appear.

In 1986 Ministers set up the working party to which my hon. Friend the Member for Bradford, South referred. I should have thought that that was indicative of their desire to see machines issue tickets and collect them at the end of the journey. It has been a consistent thread of the Government's policy that demanning, especially in public sector industries, is what government is about, and that any standard or concept of service for the travelling public is very much a back number—if it is considered at all.

I must tell my hon. Friend the Member for Bradford, South that there were no permanent secretary's in the working party—they being far too grand to serve on working parties investigating matters affecting the travelling public. However, the Department of Transport was represented by three members of the public transport, London division, and a legal adviser; the Home Office by someone from CI division; the Lord Chancellor's Department by a gentleman from the private and international law division and London Regional Transport by two representatives, a solicitor and the group planning manager.

It is difficult to imagine that members of that working party had much experience of the problems of rush hour travel or, indeed, any other sort of travel on London Underground. The Home Office representative was the only woman member of the team, but we do not know whether she was qualified in the way in which my hon. Friend the Member for Bradford, South starkly outlined, in that she had experienced some of the difficulties faced by

*[Mr. Snape]*

women travelling on London Underground. Appendix 1 of the working party report makes no mention of her grade or circumstances.

An indication of the thinking behind the report can be readily gleaned from the preamble, which states:

"This report has been prepared by an inter-Departmental Working Group on Penalty Fares set up by Ministers in May 1986."

Its terms of reference and membership are set out in appendix I, which I have already mentioned.

In paragraph B of the report, £19·5 million is given as the amount lost due to fare evasion on the London Underground. It also refers to a further £9 million lost due to fare evasion on the buses and states that the trend is rising. That is the sort of unquantifiable statement so beloved by interdepartmental working parties anxious to justify the inevitable conclusions and anxious to please their political masters. I must tell my hon. Friend the Member for Bradford, South that no detailed figures or explanation was given as to how the original figure was arrived at.

9.45 pm

Perhaps I could add to the ever-increasing burden of the hon. Member for Ilford, South by asking him to tell the House how that £19·5 million has grown to £26 million and whether the promoters have provided him with any detailed figures to justify that second and higher figure.

In paragraph B(4) reference is made to the

"substantial reduction in operating costs"

We should insert in brackets "that means manpower costs".

The report states that London Underground is investing £135 million in a new, highly automated ticket system. Bearing in mind the impact that inflation has had on the supposed figure lost through fare evasion, does the hon. Member for Ilford, South have any information as to the impact of inflation on the £135 million investment laid out in the 1986 report?

A suggestion of the report's lack of credibility can be found in the preamble where reference is made to

"the need for a penalty fares scheme on the buses is much less pressing since it is more difficult to travel on a bus without buying or showing a ticket"

It goes on to point out that on one-person-operated buses the ticket is purchased from the driver, but from conductors in other circumstances. That was written before the Chinese and others were lucky enough to benefit from the virtual gift of Routemaster buses from London Buses Ltd., or whatever fancy name it calls itself these days.

Those of us who travel regularly on public transport will be aware that there is widespread fare evasion on buses, particularly on OPO buses where the top deck is a no-go area for the driver. My hon. Friend the Member for Bradford, South is right that the top deck is, all too often, a no-go area at night for women or anyone else who does not fancy a broken nose. Among certain regular bus users it is customary to pay the minimum fare and then to retire to the top deck knowing full well that the driver has too much to do to ascertain whether people have gone beyond the stage for which they paid. The possibility of an inspector boarding a bus to check whether the correct fare has been paid is, particularly late at night, almost

non-existent. Such is the credibility that the working party must bridge, but it appears from a couple of hours' reading of its report that it has singularly failed to do that.

In paragraph G of the report the working party outlines the major issues of principle and asks:

"Should lack of reasonable opportunity to buy a ticket be the sole valid excuse for not having one?"

What is a valid excuse for not having a ticket? Most of us travel on public transport, except, of course, Ministers who never have to worry about that. Reference has already been made to the new ticket machines, part of the £135 million plus inflation investment designed to strip London Underground of any human presence.

We are all aware that in their new and pristine condition these machines do everything except play pop records on Radio 2 or Capital Gold. The theory is that someone puts his money into a slot and, depending on the type of machine, chooses his destination or ticket price and receives not only a ticket, but change. As my hon. Friends have indicated, all too often the machine's light emitting diode display shows that it will accept only the correct change.

In what should be a showpiece station, Westminster —of course, in London Underground's opinion it is not, because its showcase station is St. James's park where the top brass work—many, sometimes most of the fairly newly-installed machines display the legend, "correct change only".

My hon. Friend the Member for Bradford, South graphically illustrated the dilemma of a woman with two small children, perhaps in a fractious mood, with a pram, trolley or shopping basket. Under the general statement of principles, could such a passenger claim lack of reasonable opportunity because of the deficiency of these machines and the fact that a proportion, perhaps the majority, of them will accept only the correct change? Perhaps the hon. Member for Ilford, South could answer that question.

All of us can envisage the scenario, whether at Westminster or any other well-used tube station, in which the ticket window is surrounded by a considerable number of people. The window is supposed to be manned until at least 7 or 8 o'clock in the evening, although I can record a number of occasions in recent years when the supposed showpiece station next door was not manned at all after 7, 8 or 9 o'clock in the evening, which is an indictment of the incompetence and general lack of interest of London Underground management. In a city which prides itself in attracting tourists, it is likely that language and currency difficulties would be experienced at the station ticket window. The patience of those standing in the queue would be rapidly exhausted by the sort of exchanges which we can imagine taking place between the passengers and the ticket clerk.

Given that combination of by no means unlikely circumstances, the passenger may decide to take her fractious children, shopping basket and trolley to a London Underground train without buying a ticket. She would have to do so single-handed, because the demanning of stations means that she would have to lever her children, shopping basket and trolley on to the train herself. Guards and assistance for people in those circumstances are an old-fashioned concept of the past. If she decided to travel without a ticket, would the hon. Member for Ilford, South consider that she had had a reasonable opportunity to buy a ticket? If not, would she, under the terms of the Bill, be liable for a penalty fare?

The second issue of principle in this section of the Bill——

**Mr. Barry Sheerman** (Huddersfield): The Minister was deep in conversation during some of the important points made by my hon. Friend. Of course, we know that he is reluctant to use public transport; otherwise, he would not have been late for the Pavarotti concert the Sunday before last when he tried to get there by car and arrived after the concert had begun, which must have been disconcerting both for him and for Mr. Pavarotti. The lady with the children would have been warned by the Labour Member from her constituency not only to have the right change, but against travelling on the tube in the first place because so many passengers passing through the new turnstiles have had their tickets munched up by the ticket machines. The ticket would never come out the other side. If she was waiting for a British Rail train at the other end, she might force her way through and get on the train with no ticket, through no fault of her own. If she were a constituent of mine, she might miss her train to Huddersfield if she did not. She would never have got the pushchair through the barrier in the first place, though.

**Mr. Snape:** I am torn between considering Pavarotti halting in mid-note to greet the exalted personage who, alas, is no longer with us, and my hon. Friend's constituent going all the way to Huddersfield on London Underground. Neither scenario is particularly likely, but my hon. Friend painted a graphic picture which must have placed yet another question mark in the mind of the hon. Member for Ilford, South, who is responsible for piloting this shabby piece of legislation through the House.

I was referring to the major issues of principle laid down in the report which generated this piece of legislation. The second principle is as follows:

"To what extent should inspectors retain the discretion to waive penalty fares or to institute prosecution procedures as an alternative to levying a penalty fare?"

I have never had the dubious pleasure of working for London Underground in the days of a Conservative Government, but I am probably the only Member who has been a guard on the railway and travelled on extremely crowded trains. My heart goes out to the inspectors charged with collecting the penalty fares. Twenty-one years ago——

**Mr. Thorne:** Does the hon. Gentleman want me to answer his questions? If so, he is giving me very little time in which to do so.

**Mr. Snape:** I do not want to appear to be lecturing the hon. Gentleman on procedure, but I am sure that provision will be made through the usual channels, which

I note are conferring even now, for him to reply at some unspecified future time. Once we have discussed the many amendments that appear on the Paper, we look forward to hearing from the hon. Gentleman.

I hope I may be permitted a little trip down memory lane as I ask the House to come back with me to 1968, the era of flower power and San Francisco, when the hon. Member who now represents West Bromwich, East was a passenger guard at Manchester's Victoria station. One of the trains on which I sometimes worked then was the 23.30 from Manchester to Rochdale via Oldham, which called at all stations. Sometimes on a Saturday night some of the passengers on that train were a little boisterous. Since coming here I have learnt that the phrase is, "They had dined well," but I should not have thought——

**Mr. Speaker:** Order. The whole House is fascinated by this, but does the Underground go up there?

**Mr. Snape:** It does not, but the same principle applies, Mr. Speaker. I sense a certain frisson among those charged with the heavy responsibility of advising you from time to time on these matters——

**Mr. Thorne:** I beg to move, That the Question be now put——

**Mr. Cryer:** The hon. Member for Ilford, South has not replied yet.

**Mr. Speaker:** Order. The hon. Gentleman must have an opportunity to reply before I grant the closure.

**Mr. Snape:** I am grateful to you, Mr. Speaker.

I conclude my reminiscences by pointing out that the dilemma faced by the inspector on the Underground when collecting penalty fares would be as great——

**Dr. Marek** *rose*——

**Mr. Snape:** Let me finish my reminiscences; I can scarcely bring myself to stop again. Already I feel a wave of nostalgia sweeping over me. My point is that the inspector charged with these onerous responsibilities would face enormous difficulties if he had to tackle a similar crowd of people to those with whom I had the problem of dealing in 1968. My last word about 1968 is that it was an era of flower power when no one ever resorted to physical violence. That was the theory. Things are very different in brutal Britain in 1989. I fear that an inspector charged with collecting penalty fares on a Saturday night on London Underground would need at least some protection before he embarked on the journey——

*It being Ten o'clock, the debate stood adjourned.*
*Debate to be resumed tomorrow.*

## Services Discipline

10 pm

**The Parliamentary Under-Secretary of State for the Armed Forces (Mr. Michael Neubert):** I beg to move,

That the draft Army, Air Force and Naval Discipline Acts (Continuation) Order 1989, which was laid before this House on 12th June, be approved.

The purpose of this order is to continue in force for a further year the Army Act 1955, the Air Force Act 1955 and the Naval Discipline Act 1957, which together provide the statutory basis for discipline in the three services.

Annual parliamentary approval for the special legal status of the service man or woman whereby he or she is subject to the constraints of military discipline as well the rule of civil law is a long-established constitutional concept. The Select Committee examining the last Armed Forces Bill in 1986 recommended that the current system for a five-yearly Armed Forces Act and annual extension of the service discipline Acts by Order in Council be continued.

We shall, of course, be giving further consideration to some of the areas highlighted by the 1986 Select Committee in considering proposals for the next quinquennial Bill. The House will, I am sure, understand that I am not able to anticipate the provisions of the Bill. However, I think that this may be an appropriate time to review some of the further progress we have made in response to the Select Committee. My hon. Friend the then Under-Secretary of State, the Member for Kettering (Mr. Freeman), gave our response to the recommendations of the Select Committee in July 1987. Since then, and in particular, enabling provisions have been made in the Criminal Justice Act 1988 for standing civilian courts and courts martial to suspend sentences of imprisonment imposed on civilians subject to the service discipline Acts. Although the number of cases likely to be involved is very small, it is a sensible and useful provision.

We also, of course, continue to keep the provisions of civilian legislation generally under review so that they are mirrored in service legislation to the extent that it is practical and sensible. This review is part of the balance we seek to maintain between the rights of service men and women as citizens on the one hand and the extra constraints necessarily imposed on them by service discipline on the other.

Making service personnel aware of their rights and responsibilities is therefore of great importance. In line with the Select Committee's recommendation, all the three service leaflets given to those charged with offences under the service discipline Acts have been reviewed and revised and updated where appropriate. I am also pleased to be able to tell the House that the general leaflet on rights and responsibilities which was introduced last year for all new recruits is being updated and expanded.

I am conscious, too, that a fair and equitable system of discipline is essential to the maintenance of good morale and effectiveness in the armed forces. The conditions of service we offer will be ever more important in recruiting and retaining the personnel we need to sustain the nation's defences.

Inevitably, perhaps, one hears about breaches of discipline which occur and this can distract from a recognition of the overwhelming adherence that there is to it. Service men and women recognise that service discipline is a critical protection for themselves in the fast-moving, highly skilled and sometimes dangerous job that they do. Anybody who chooses to breach that discipline can be a liability not only to himself but to his colleagues and even civilians. We therefore owe it to those who serve in the armed forces with such professionalism, skill and dedication, and to whom I pay wholehearted tribute tonight, to ensure that the system of discipline is upheld. Accordingly, I invite the House to approve the order.

10.4 pm

**Mr. Allan Rogers** (Rhondda): On behalf of the Opposition, I also pay tribute to our service men and women, who as the Minister said, in their dedication and discipline give such great service to the country.

The Minister referred to the pamphlet on rights and responsibilities that is given to new recruits. Last year, my hon. Friend the Member for Knowsley, South (Mr. Hughes), who cannot be with us because of illness—I am sure that the House would like to send him our best wishes —suggested that the pamphlet should be distributed to all members of the forces. I should have thought that the Minister could take that idea on board.

My hon. Friend the Member for Knowsley, South also referred last year to the problem of bullying, both informal and formalised, in often brutal initiation ceremonies. Unfortunately, what we see in the media and what has been reported to us shows that the problem has not diminished. Even today, people accused of these outlawed offences are being prosecuted. I appreciate that the Minister is doing his best, but unfortunately his best is not good enough. Will he once again emphasise to senior officers that this sadistic behaviour is not to be tolerated in our armed services? Will he tell them that the prevalence of this behaviour in the units under their command shows their inability to command? Will he consider taking action against such senior officers, because that would go a long way to solving the problem and stamping out these sadistic practices?

**Sir Antony Buck** (Colchester, North): The hon. Gentleman, who knows a lot about armed forces establishments, used the word "prevalence". Will he agree that that was not the right word to use, because only a small minority go in for this awful practice of bullying? Furthermore, senior officers in all the forces are determined to see that it is stopped, just as we all are.

**Mr. Rogers:** I agree. I used the word "prevalence" in its literal sense rather than in any quantifiable sense. Perhaps the word "occurrence" might be better, as I was not intending to show any specific numbers or to suggest that there were large numbers of offences.

We should remember that the cases of bullying and initiation ceremonies that come to the fore are but the tip of the iceberg. As the hon. and learned Gentleman will acknowledge, those of us who have served in armed forces know that this sort of thing used to be much more widespread, but, because of the efforts of various Ministers and senior officers, it has been cut substantially. I still do not like the idea that it exists in our armed services. It is difficult enough for people to train in what is, by necessity, a tough and disciplined profession. Bullying has no place in training tough soldiers, sailors and airmen.

We welcome the report on the ethnic origins of applicants for entry into the regular forces, which is part of the Defence Estimates this year. I am still trying to wade through the statistical morass of this report, but I accept the broad conclusion of the substantial under-representation of the ethnic minorities in our armed forces. The Royal Air Force, because of different recruiting techniques, appears to be more successful than the other services in dealing with that problem. Will the Minister urge all services to consider methods used in other branches and then adopt a universal approach based on the best practice?

Until we can integrate our ethnic minorities into all institutions of public life, whether the armed services, the police or whatever, there will not be a truly integrated society. A career in the armed services is a good opportunity for ethnic minorities to become fully integrated.

The subject of AIDS was mentioned in both the 1987 and 1988 continuation order debates. Last year the Ministry of Defence said that it had recognised the seriousness of the problem and had played a full part in the AIDS education campaign. How successful does the Minister believe the campaign to have been? Has his Department kept central records of the number of personnel tested HIV-positive? If so, what are the results of those records? *The Independent* reported on 19 June that the rate of HIV infection in the US Army, while lower than in the civilian population, was higher than expected on previous estimates. Can the Minister assure the House that all reasonable steps are being taken to monitor the British position?

Another matter raised in previous debates was the increasing use of private contractors for services such as cleaning and catering. Concern was expressed about the use of service personnel to complete work that the contractors had left unfinished. Has that practice now ended?

We are concerned about the MOD's management of its housing stock. It has been criticised by the Public Accounts Committee, which noted that the MOD had said that it recognised the need to do much better in its management of married quarters. The question is whether better management is, in itself, sufficient. The 18th report of the Review Body on Armed Forces Pay, Cmnd. 579, referred to the poor quality of much service accommodation and said that better management arrangements would not, in themselves, make more money available.

There has been considerable criticism from hon. Members on both sides of the House of the Government's overall policy towards service accommodation. In the Army debate on 8 June the hon. Member for Canterbury (Mr. Brazier), who I am sure will participate in this debate, devoted considerable time to detailing the terrible problems of Army personnel when attempting to become owner-occupiers. It was clear that he had considerable support from many of his hon. Friends. The provision of appropriate housing for service personnel is one of the main determinants of morale, but it is evident that the Government are failing to deal with the problem.

A scheme must be evolved to ensure that service families have homes on leaving the service. That has been discussed for many years, but we have not yet achieved a resolution of that peculiar and difficult problem. Even for those who can afford it, house purchase during armed service and its consequent absentee landlordism does not work, especially for those who now face seven-year tours of duty in Germany. Every garrison has its crop of horror stories about experiences of letting houses in Britain. The families have to carry a double burden of mortgage and rent, usually on a single income. They cannot bear those risks for long.

I am sure that Conservative Members wish to contribute to the debate, as they have in previous defence debates, so I shall not speak at length. However, the problem is serious and must be resolved. I understand that the hon. Member for Canterbury tabled an amendment to the Finance Bill. I do not know whether it was accepted or rejected because I have not followed that Bill in all its gory detail.

**Mr. Julian Brazier** (Canterbury): My amendment was firmly rejected by members of both Front Benches. However, constructive discussions with my right hon. and hon. Friends continue. I hope that the hon. Member for Rhondda (Mr. Rogers) will extend the constructive views that he has expressed over the past minute or so to members of the shadow Treasury team.

**Mr. Rogers:** Yes, and I understand the problems of right hon. and hon. Members on both Front Benches. I feel sure that they wish to consider sympathetically other proposals, which could include direct assistance from the Ministry of Defence, which currently feels that fiscal relief within the Finance Bill is not the answer, and that such an arrangement would create all sorts of problems in respect of tax relief extended to purchasers in other peculiar situations. There can be no doubt that at present there are instances of premature voluntary retirement among skilled NCOs, for example, who are encouraged by their wives to leave early as they seek security for their family when a suitable house and job becomes available.

I know that the Ministry of Defence is sympathetic and recognises that problem, and if it cannot be resolved in the Finance Bill perhaps it can be sorted out within the Ministry. We shall do all that we can to help the Minister to resolve that problem.

10.16 pm

**Miss Ann Widdecombe** (Maidstone): I am grateful for an opportunity to participate in the debate, because I am also very concerned about incidents of bullying. My hon. Friend the Minister will be aware of extremely serious allegations of bullying of one of my constituents, who ended up in hospital with a split kidney. I cannot go into any detail on those allegations, or even name my constituent or his regiment, as I understand that the matter is now sub judice and that a court martial is proceeding. Nevertheless, one or two aspects surrounding that case, but not directly connected with it, are of particular concern.

In case there may be any doubt, I should say at the start that the case to which I refer does not involve my local regiment, the 36th Engineers, which has an extremely proud record on that score and about which I have never heard even the slightest whisper of any bullying.

My concern is that recruiting policies are at fault, and that people are being recruited who are liable to engage in a sustained campaign of bullying. Whether or not it is proved that there was such a campaign in the case of my constituent, cases have been proven at courts martial over the 12 months since our previous debate. In other words, one is not dealing always with an NCO who momentarily lost his temper and hit a subordinate. No matter how

*[Miss Ann Widdecombe]*

deplorable such an incident may be, it is at least an impulsive action and not part of a campaign of sustained and cruel bullying, which is a sign of a deeply flawed character.

I ask myself how people capable of such behaviour manage to get through the recruiting process. It seems that there is a need for it to be tightened up. We must ask also why such bullying is more prevalent in the Army—and I use the word "prevalent" in exactly the same sense as it was used by the hon. Member for Rhondda (Mr. Rogers)—than in the other two services.

I am concerned also about the remedy available to young soldiers who are the victims of bullying. The case to which I referred involves a 17-year-old recruit who had only just joined up and who was away from home for the first time. What measures has the Army taken to ensure that young recruits can report what they are having to endure without fear of reprisal? The questions that I asked that recruit included why he did not go to his commanding officer or telephone home. The answer was that there was direct intimidation against doing so.

Surely the Army can devise a foolproof means of dealing with the matter, similar to the recognised grievance procedure used by any employee in a civilian occupation. When a recruit alleges bullying and his allegation appears to stand up, he should be protected immediately from whatever intimidation has been threatened, and his allegations should be considered seriously from the start in the recruit's base. In the case that I encountered, the parent had to go to the barracks before any justice was won.

I am also concerned about the role played by NCOs. It is now generally acknowledged that many NCOs have to spend so much time on paperwork—indeed, they are taken on specifically for the purpose—that they are no longer spending as much time as they used to on training their men and, above all, looking after their welfare. That is a negation of the role that we expect them to be drafted and promoted to carry out.

For those three reasons—particularly my concern about recruits' recourse on base once the bullying has started, and the role of NCOs—I would welcome a response from the Minister. When my constituent's case has been decided by a court martial and any appeals have been dealt with, I hope to raise the matter in much more detail, because I believe that it has many worrying implications.

10.21 pm

**Mr. Menzies Campbell** (Fife, North-East): Like others who have spoken, I pay tribute to the men and women in our armed forces. I suspect that discipline and morale are inextricably linked: if discipline is right morale will almost certainly be right, and if morale is right the punishing effects of discipline will almost inevitably be unnecessary.

Although conducted in a rather low-key way—in a spirit of bipartisanship, or even tripartisanship—the debate is of some constitutional significance. The 1689 Bill of Rights provided that an army could not be maintained without the consent of Parliament. Although this is in some respects a symbolic occasion, it none the less reflects the fact that Parliament retains an important constitutional control over those who serve in our armed forces and the system of discipline imposed on them.

I was heartened to hear the Minister say that the procedures were being kept under constant review, particularly in the light of the developments in criminal procedure for civilians. My experience of military discipline is rather limited, being confined to appearing as civilian defence counsel in a naval court martial. My recollection of the event—which was spread over three or four days—is of the extraordinary lengths to which the naval authorities went to ensure that I, as a civilian lawyer, was in no way disadvantaged or inhibited. I also recall the lengths to which the judge advocate's representative went to ensure that, in that capacity, I was made familiar with the procedures that were adoped. If anecdotal evidence can be relied on in a debate such as this, let me say that my direct experience of these matters has been entirely favourable.

I can also speak from experience of a case of someone —I must protect his anonymity—who was originally sentenced to seven years for an offence which, again, I should not reveal. After a variety of appeal procedures, his sentence was reduced to six months. That gave rise, not surprisingly, to some sense of relief on the part of the individual concerned and his family, but it raised in my mind the question whether the way in which the original sentence had been imposed was in accordance with the principles we would all think necessary to attend on a case of that kind.

If we face a demographic trend which will make it more difficult to recruit people to the armed services, we shall have to ensure that their conditions, once they join up, encourage them to go on being members of the armed services. Also, if we must rely on more female members of the armed services, that may have some consequence for the nature of the discipline employed in all three services.

May we be assured that the constant review to which the Minister referred will be tailored to take account of those trends and of the alteration, to some extent, in the character of the three services with which the order is concerned?

I shall say little about bullying. There must be a point at which robust training—that which is necessary to discover the character of an individual who presents himself or herself for the demanding tasks which service men and women perform—moves from what is legitimate to what is sadistic, and that must sometimes be a narrow issue. But systematic bullying should never be permitted.

Reference has been made to commanding officers. In my judgment, a commanding officer who does not know that systematic bullying is taking place in a unit for which he or she has responsibility is not fulfilling those responsibilities. I have no doubt that the Minister will assure the House that the Ministry of Defence brings this responsibility home to those who are in command of units where there may be a risk of the kind of unacceptable behaviour which the whole House would condemn and which, if publicised—even if involving only minor incidents—brings nothing but harm to the reputation of the three services to which hon. Members have paid justifiable tribute.

10.27 pm

**Mr. Julian Brazier** (Canterbury): I shall raise three points. The first concerns the issues raised by the hon. Member for Rhondda (Mr. Rogers) about the need for a new approach to the problem of service men leaving the services and wanting to buy homes.

The House generally was encouraged by the constructive response from the Parliamentary Under-Secretary of State for the Armed Forces at the end of the recent debate on the Army. I was also encouraged by the fact that, although the Chief Secretary to the Treasury was not happy with proposals that were put to him when we discussed the Finance Bill, in particular about tax relief on rent, he clearly acknowledged that a serious problem existed, and he agreed to discuss possible solutions to it.

While I appreciate that the Minister is seeking solutions, the final solution must not be based on the concept of two households. It has been shown time and again not to work. The concept of trying to persuade a sergeant or corporal, or even a junior officer, in Germany or Ulster to try to run two households—to be paying rent at one end and a mortgage at the other—does not work.

There must be a scheme which is linked to the eventual purchase of a house so that a man can feel confident that he will be able to afford a home at the end of his service without attempting to run two households while is serving. This problem applies particularly to the Army, because soldiers principally serve abroad, although it applies also to some sections of the RAF.

**Mr. David Nicholson** (Taunton): I pay tribute to my hon. Friend's efforts relating to the matter that he has just mentioned. I have had constituency cases involving service men seeking to buy houses, so I hope that he will eventually achieve a successful solution to the problem. It would be odd if a Conservative Government, who are promoting so vigorously the concept of home ownership in all other sections of society, did not remove the obstacles that face service men.

**Mr. Brazier:** I am most grateful for my hon. Friend's comments.

My second point affects the Royal Navy in particular and to a much lesser extent other members of the armed forces. It is most important to maintain morale. Mobility is not the problem in the Royal Navy; the problem is separation. The fact that those who serve in the Royal Navy spend so much time away from their wives is extremely bad for morale. Ships are now spending more time at sea than at any time since the second world war. For financial reasons, we have reduced the numbers of service men in shore postings, where we have introduced civilianisation.

My hon. Friend the Under-Secretary of State for the Armed Forces referred briefly to conditions of service. In last year's review of allowances a quite reasonable change was made as it applied to the other services but it has had a most serious effect on those who serve in the Royal Navy. Moreover, I was told in a written answer a few weeks ago that it has saved almost no money. I refer to the change in the arrangements for the payment of boarding school allowances.

Justification for the payment of boarding school allowances to members of the other two services has always been that it was the only means by which the child of a soldier or an airman could enjoy a continuous education, now that the state boarding schools have disappeared. It has been ruled that service men whose wives and families do not accompany them will lose the allowance. Those who are coming towards the end of their service have always had rather a raw deal, but it has always been most unfair on those who serve in the Royal Navy. In their case, the main problem is separation from their families. The allowance provided some means of taking some of the strain off their wives.

It has now been ruled that the wife has to follow the husband if he happens to have a shore posting between two sea-going ones. That will lead to all the mobility problems from which the two other services already suffer, on top of the extraordinary strain of separation. The Royal Navy's case is special. It is by far the smallest service. The cost of the boarding school allowances is only £24 million a year. The sharp increase during the last 12 months of premature voluntary release, particularly among officers, is a direct result of that policy.

My third and last point is about how to attract more members of the ethnic minority communities into the armed forces. If we are to become a united society, we must attract more of them into the armed forces. I hope that the suggestion I am about to make will be taken constructively. It is a chicken and egg situation. Members of the ethnic communities are in a small minority in the armed forces. One hears that in some instances they feel threatened, not so much by bullying but by the general feeling that they are being ostracised.

A means of attracting people from the ethnic communities into the services might be to build on the experience that we already have of the regimental structure. There is a London Scottish regiment. It is not confined to Scotsmen and it is very successful. I have a friend in it. There is a London Irish regiment and, of course, there are the Gurkha regiments. They are all historic regiments with a tremendous war record. If we were to experiment, perhaps in the territorial army with a London Sikh regiment—the Sikhs have a fine military tradition—one unit that provided a focus for excellence could act as a flagship for attracting members of ethnic minorities into the armed forces. However, that is just a thought. I shall conclude, having made my three points.

10.35 pm

**Mr. Harry Cohen** (Leyton): I shall be brief. I wish to discuss service men who contract HIV infections or AIDS. I echo the point made by my hon. Friend the Member for Rhondda (Mr. Rogers) in asking the Minister to provide the figures for those in the armed forces who contract the HIV virus and AIDS and to tell us whether the position is being properly monitored by his Department.

I raised the subject in last year's debate on the armed forces. Some of the points that I made then are still relevant. I said:

"a television programme . . . concerned with the United States forces in Thailand . . . showed that the Thai Government were most irresponsible in relation to visiting troops. That might apply, too, to countries that our troops visit. For example, in some of the African countries as many as 90 per cent. of prostitutes have the HIV virus. If our soldiers frequent such establishments, perhaps in a fit of drunkenness or a deliberate act on their part, they take a grave —grave is the right word in this context—risk.

The Minister should not only promote health education, which is vital, but put pressure on the Governments of the countries which our troops visit to behave responsibly and clean up those areas where AIDS can be spread."

[*Mr. Harry Cohen*]

My final point was:

"The Government should be examining ways of making it easy for those in the armed forces who contract AIDS to acknowledge it, leave the armed forces and receive proper care. They need to be able to do that without fear, without shame and stigma and, especially, without severe financial hardship. If that does not happen, they will stay in the armed forces and try to cover it up and suffer."—[*Official Report,* 14 July 1988; Vol. 137, c. 681-82.]

Those points are still relevant, but the Minister's predecessor did not reply to them. Unfortunately, there is no sign that they have received any consideration since.

The Government should put pressure on countries where our troops could be at risk. Health education should be undertaken on a large scale by all the armed forces on a regular basis and should include the availability of condoms. Those who contract the HIV virus should be given the opportunity to leave quietly without financial loss and with access to follow-up care.

Contracting HIV or AIDS should not be a disciplinary offence or a cover for another disciplinary offence to get those who are infected out of the armed forces. The Ministry of Defence has to deal with the matter properly.

10.38 pm

**Mr. Keith Mans** (Wyre): I am grateful for the opportunity to speak briefly in this debate on Army, Navy and Air Force discipline and morale. I apologise to my hon. Friend the Minister for not being here for all his speech. I should be grateful if he would address one or two of my comments in his winding-up speech.

One of the first speeches that I made in the House concerned personnel shortages in the armed forces. More specifically, I dealt with pilots in the Air Force. I was assured then that such shortages did not exist and that no shortages were projected. We can see 18 months later that such shortages exist and are becoming worse. They are spreading to many sectors of all three services. Previously, shortages were confined to specific trades and specific qualifications, but we now see infantry battalions, for example, especially in Germany, under strength simply because they cannot meet their recruiting targets. The problem that should have been addressed 18 months ago has clearly not been addressed, and we now face an even bigger problem as a result. I hope that we shall do something about that quickly.

The latest allowance package has been at best neutral and at worst counter-productive in terms of encouraging people to stay in the three services and discouraging people from leaving. The proposal of my hon. Friend the Member for Canterbury (Mr. Brazier) to help people in the armed forces to buy their own property has had some success at least in the Finance Bill. I am disappointed by the response of the Ministry of Defence to that initiative. It should have been able to react more quickly to some of the points made and to come up with other proposals in house, as it were. I hope that now, when it is clear to all that a problem exists, we shall come up with some proposals.

I have a few ideas for such proposals. We need to act quickly on recruiting, beyond the advertising campaigns used at present. I want to take up one of the points made on the recruitment of women. We have talked about that for far too long, especially in relation to training women pilots in the Air Force, as I said in the House 18 months ago. I was assured there that thre was no need for such a proposal. Six months ago, a study was being carried out, but nothing has happened since.

We are very short of pilots in the Royal Air Force, yet we have a potential supply of highly qualified pilots outside. Women who are training at present with university air squadrons and who want to come into the Royal Air Force are being denied the opportunity to do so and are going into civilian airlines instead. Will my hon. Friend the Minister tell us why we do not get on with the matter and start up a scheme to allow women to beome pilots in the Royal Air Force? I am not suggesting a huge scheme to allow women to fly all types of aircraft.

**Mr. Frank Cook** (Stockton, North): A pilot scheme.

**Mr. Mans:** I just want to see a pilot scheme to allow women——

**Mr. Cook:** It should get off the ground.

**Mr. Mans:** I want to see a scheme to allow women to train initially at least for certain types of aircraft. I should have thought that that could be done by the end of this year, rather than having to wait two or three years.

We must solve the recruiting problem and we must also solve the rentention problem. People are leaving the service at too high a rate. As recently as a year ago, one set of figures said that there would be a surplus of 60 pilots in the Air Force. Within six months, that had changed to a deficit of 265. I can assume only that the people compiling the figures were working too much on historical data and were not projecting the figures far enough forward, bearing in mind the competition now posed by the airlines for the recruitment of people who can be trained as pilots. The way in which statistics are compiled has gone wrong in other areas as well, so we must produce schemes such as the one suggested by my hon. Friend the Member for Canterbury for retaining people.

I should also like to see, as I have said previously in the House, that those who reach the end of their engagement receive their gratuity if they stay in the service, as well as if they leave. It seems odd that an organisation that is trying to retain people is paying them large sums of money to leave.

Equally, we must do something about the rents that service personnel pay for their accommodation and quarters. We could reduce the rents to significantly below their present levels so that service men would then have the opportunity to save up to buy their own homes for when they leave the service, perhaps using the sort of scheme that my hon. Friend the Member for Canterbury has suggested.

The matter is now of great urgency and I sincerely hope that the Ministry of Defence will look closely and quickly at ways of remedying the shortage of personnel in all three of our armed services.

10.45 pm

**Mr. Frank Cook** (Stockton, North): I am tempted to follow the hon. Member for Wyre (Mr. Mans) down a few of his back lanes, but I feel that I must confine my main comments to the order. However, to offer the hon. Gentleman a crumb of consolation, he may be interested to know that the Army Air Corps has already earmarked its first female candidate for a pilot's course. However, it has done so on the basis that that lady is a doctor and is finishing her military training. As a military doctor, she may have to render medical attention to casualties and be left without a pilot and she may need to get herself and the casualty out of that situation—and the pilot as well, if he is merely incapacitated. That seems a strange, singular and selective logic to apply to warfare. Although it may be a useful scenario for television situation comedies, it is less so for the hard life with which we expect our trained service men and women to cope.

I remind the Minister and the House that my position as Opposition defence Whip and as an active participant in the parliamentary armed services scheme has meant that in the past two years I have visited many service units in all arms of the services. I also remind the House that I am a member of the independent board of visitors of both the Royal Naval detention quarters at Portsmouth and of the military corrective training centre at Colchester. It is with particular reference to what I have experienced there and to what I have discussed right across the board with commissioned ranks, commanding officers and senior non-commissioned officers that I want to address two main issues tonight.

However, I begin with an issue that has been mentioned by several hon. Members, including the hon. Member for Wyre, the hon. and learned Member for Fife, North-East (Mr. Campbell) and my hon. Friend the Member for Leyton (Mr. Cohen). I refer to the level of training that we invest and the amount of attention and effort that we put into ensuring that our service men and women have adequate training of a high standard. It is no longer sufficient to shove a musket with a bayonet on the end of it into somebody's mitt and to tell him to get into the front line, because this is very much a high-tech activity in all regards, and we must try to ensure that we retain as much of that investment as we can.

From my visits to Colchester and to Pompey, I have learnt that one of the most common offences that invites detention is absence without leave. It was ever thus. However, that is quickly followed by another two classes of offence. The first relates to cash, and the second to drugs. I suppose that the problems for the young service man—I can speak only from experience as a service man in the Airborne Regiment because I was not in the WRAF, so if any of my female colleagues are here, they must forgive me.

**Miss Widdecombe:** What about me?

**Mr. Cook:** I apologise to the hon. Lady. I was referring to Opposition Members.

In my day, it was always a problem trying to manage and control negotiable assets. I vividly recall the shenanigans that went on after a pay parade, when we saluted with our right hand, and seized in our left hand a book and a quantity of money, and screamed, "Pay and book correct, sir." We never had the temerity to look at it to see whether that statement was correct; we were not allowed to. Having marched out of the pay parade, there was always a melee, with people saying, "Here is the pound I owe you," or, "There is the 25 bob you have been waiting for." Debts were then settled until the next night, when in the billet there was always the plea, "Lend us a quid." There was a kind of usury, willingly entered into by both lender and borrower.

Those were the days when "credit rating" was a term that still had to be invented. "Creditworthiness" had not been heard of. To get a £20 overdraft, one had to have three guarantors and more than five hostages. I make light of it, but that is not the case now. We are in the times of instant credit, with nothing more than a plastic identification and a PIN number needed to unlock anybody's assets. A young person may be sent to a cash-point by a buddy or a girl friend with a plastic card and a PIN number with the instruction, "Get me 25 quid." When there, he finds it so easy to get that £25 out that he withdraws £30, with no effort and with almost a pat on the head for doing it, because the friend or girl friend is grateful to him for going. It is so easy to get into the situation of obtaining money by false pretences, fraudulent behaviour or thieving. We have made those offences much easier.

I know that there is cash and credit counselling, but it appears to come after the service man's record has been besmirched. It comes as a form of redemption rather than of prevention. I am seeking an assurance that emphasis will be put on this problem not only during the basic training periods and the early pastoral care that is necessary for service personnel, but as a continuing service, given not only to service men or women but to their families.

I realise that drugs are a delicate subject. Hon. Members should recall my points about the amount invested in training and in bringing service personnel up to scratch when considering drug offences. Most drug offences in the forces involve soft drugs. All of them at the end of the day invite dishonourable discharge. Inevitably, there will be some cases where serving individuals have possibly been caught in possession of a minimal amount of cannabis, have served a fairly lengthy stretch of detention and then find themselves decanted into civvy street with the type of skill which is difficult to replace in the services and impossible to use in civvy street. There are many such people.

From time to time informed commentators—I freely admit that I am not one of them—within the armed forces, the medical profession and on civvy street express the opinion that perhaps we should consider a change of attitude to the use of soft drugs. I do not make that plea. I simply remind the Minister that we have heard about the demographic trough, about the difficulties in recruitment and about the investment in training. Our allies who find that their personnel are taking soft drugs do not operate such stringent rules as ours. If we are to believe Fleet street, or rather its replacement, our enemies' service personnel are apparently using drugs left, right and centre.

I do not plead any case, but if unofficial discussions about this matter are taking place and if senior people are quietly expressing their views, perhaps there is a case for a discreet examination of the statistics vis a vis ourselves and our NATO allies. Perhaps we could then consider alternative treatment and action in such drugs cases as opposed to automatic discharge.

10.56 pm

**Mr. Neubert:** This has been a relatively succinct and significant debate on matters of importance. It is my intention to endeavour to respond to the best of my ability to the majority of the points that have been raised tonight. I welcome hon. Members' interest in the well-being of Her Majesty's armed forces.

[*Mr. Neubert*]

First, I thank the hon. Member for Rhondda (Mr. Rogers) for his welcome to the introduction of the leaflet for new recruits on their rights and responsibilities. I assure him that, in deference to the undertaking given by my predecessor last year, we considered making that leaflet available to all members of the services. That suggestion was made by the hon. Member for Knowsley, South (Mr. Hughes) whose absence we regret and to whom we wish a speedy return to the House.

Having considered the hon. Gentleman's suggestion, however, we came to the conclusion that that would mean issuing some 300,000 copies of the leaflet, which, in general terms, covers a number of subjects. That information is already widely available to units, notices are posted and members of the armed forces have access to advice on all the issues covered. We therefore believe that it would not be to the advantage of the armed forces to distribute the leaflet as widely as suggested. We suspect that, in common with so much literature that is sent to us, it might end up in the bin. That would not be an effective use of resources. We understand, however, the need for members of the services to have proper advice on their rights.

It is a matter of regret, but also of reality, that in such a short debate hon. Members have concentrated, naturally, not on the overwhelming adherence to discipline that applies in the armed forces, but on those examples that hit the headlines and naturally cause concern. I shall respond to that concern, but I hope that it will be seen in the perspective of generally good morale, first-class discipline and dedication among our armed services.

The subject of bullying once again played a prominent part in this debate, with more than one Member mentioning it. We have made clear more than once, and shall continue to do so, that bullying and ill-treatment have no place in service life and will not be tolerated. Each allegation is viewed most seriously and is thoroughly investigated. Progress has been made in implementing the range of measures announced by my hon. Friend the Member for Kettering (Mr. Freeman) on 7 June last year. I have set them out in a letter to the hon. Member for Clackmann (Mr. O'Neill) dated 23 June this year, a copy of which has been placed in the Library.

It may be as well to list some of the measures taken. All levels in the chain of command have been reminded that bullying and ill-treatment will not be tolerated and, as I have said, such allegations will be thoroughly investigated and, if they are substantiated, firm disciplinary action will be taken. Specific measures included 102 extra posts in the training organisation which have been re-established and filled to allow officers and NCOs more time for their supervisory roles. That relates to the paperwork point made by my hon. Friend the Member for Maidstone (Miss Widdecombe).

The enhanced role given to the Women's Royal Voluntary Service has been well received. An additional 92 posts are being established to improve welfare arrangements for single personnel and, so far, 24 of those posts have been filled in the United Kingdom. We intend to concentrate next on filling posts in Germany. Districts have implemented arrangements for providing additional training for civilian doctors engaged in recruiting to ensure that they are aware of the specific requirements of the army.

The full man-management training package for instructors is being developed and the content and scope of man-management training for junior officers and NCOs has also been reviewed and increased. The revised pamphlet with further guidance on the importance of out-of-hours supervision has been issued, and an instructive document on alcohol abuse has also been revised and issued.

Although it is early days to assess the success of these measures, we believe that substantiated allegations of bullying appear to be declining. I have figures to show this. I do not wish to be complacent, but I hope that they may place the matter in proper perspective. There were 15 substantiated cases in 1986, 31 cases in 1987, which naturally gave rise to concern, and only 12 cases last year. So far this year there have been six cases. To that extent, they are encouraging.

Having outlined the measures that we have taken and have yet to see come into effect, I shall address the issue of initiation ceremonies to which the hon. Member for Rhondda referred. The services have been concerned that so-called initiation ceremonies may have had a link with bullying. Last year, my hon. Friend the Member for Kettering told the House that initiation ceremonies in the Army had been abolished. Similar action has been taken in the Royal Air Force, by standing orders prohibiting all such ceremonies. The Royal Navy, while by no means complacent, is not aware that initiation ceremonies play a significant part in Navy life.

My hon. Friend the Member for Maidstone was concerned about a case which involved a constituent. She was constrained in what she could say tonight because she believed that this was still a matter before courts martial. I shall not use the name of the constituent involved, but I will use the case as an illustration. It shows that we cannot be sure of the facts of the matter from evidence from one source. The purpose of the judicial process is to examine in a court all points of view and reach a reasonable man's conclusion based on them. The case demonstrates how seriously the Army takes all allegations of bullying.

All complaints, however minor, are thoroughly investigated by the special investigation branch. This alleged case of bullying involved three recruits and four non-commissioned officers, and was investigated. All the non-commissioned officers were court-martialled this month. To ensure fairness, four separate trials were held, each with a different court, but each, to ensure continuity, was legally advised by the same representative of the Lord Chancellor's Office.

After the cases against the accused had been heard, all were acquitted by their respective courts martial. Before any hon. Member rushes to conclusions, I add by way of background that a key witness failed to appear in court, so charges were dropped against two non-commissioned officers. In other cases, one witness has admitted to lying, and in general the witnesses were unconvincing. I should not want my hon. Friend the Member for Maidstone to leave the House not knowing that these cases have been the subject of completed courts martial. One has to take time to consider all aspects of these matters, and to hope that the British system of justice, which is world renowned, is upheld in such courts as well as elsewhere——

**Miss. Widdecombe:** I am grateful for that detailed account. I should point out that we contacted my hon. Friend's office only today and were told that this was still sub judice and that I should therefore be careful what I said about it. So I am surprised to learn that decisions have already been taken.

Will my hon. Friend confirm that this young soldier left the Army with an exemplary discharge and was offered the opportunity to re-enlist, which is not consistent with his having given any false evidence?

**Mr. Neubert:** I did not allege that he had given false evidence; I merely gave some details of the case. It is perhaps not appropriate for a matter of this complexity and seriousness to be discussed on the Floor of the House. I just wanted to counter one or two of the points that my hon. Friend made. I hope that my hon. Friend will agree that it would be better to discuss this further elsewhere. I shall be happy to hear all she has to say in writing or in person.

The subject of ethnic minorities in the services is also very serious. At the risk of being repetitive, I make it absolutely plain that the armed services are fully integrated, non-discriminatory organisations, in which no discrimination is tolerated. As we said in the "Statement on the Defence Estimates", the results of the first year's monitoring of applicants and recruits by ethnic origin revealed that the ethnic minorities were greatly under-represented among applicants for the armed forces, and that their success rate was lower than that of white applicants. Naturally, we cannot leave that unexamined. We have commissioned a study by outside consultants on what can be done to improve the situation. They are due to submit their report shortly, so at this stage I can say nothing more on this subject.

**Mr. Rogers:** Speaking from memory, I think that the success rate for applicants to the Air Force was about 85 per cent., which was 20 per cent. higher than in the Army. I suggested that the Minister should try to find the best practice in the services and then urge the other services to adopt a similar recruiting technique. Will he consider that?

**Mr. Neubert:** Yes, of course. That is still an open question. That is exactly the kind of consideration that we shall give following the submission and evaluation of the report.

On the point of my hon. Friend the Member for Canterbury (Mr. Brazier) about the formation of ethnic minority regiments, we believe that that would be divisive and contrary to the position of the armed forces which I described as a fully integrated, non-discriminatory organisation. We wish to encourage ethnic minority recruitment and we have commissioned a report to that end. I hope before much longer to have more to report to the House on that.

We seem to go from one serious issue to another. A point mentioned by more than one hon. Member, and particularly by the hon. Members for Rhondda and for Leyton (Mr. Cohen) was AIDS. The Ministry of Defence recognises the seriousness of AIDS. We have taken a full part in the education campaign. All new recruits and those in service are subject to lectures, briefings, videos and other instruction. Personnel deployed overseas are clearly and specifically briefed on the cause of the disease and the actions necessary to reduce the risk of infection. On returning from overseas, personnel are advised on the danger of passing on the infection. Those at risk are encouraged to consult their medical officer confidentially, to undergo counselling and, if necessary, voluntary testing for HIV infections.

The services continue to employ HIV carriers and AIDS sufferers until their health deteriorates to a point where discharge on medical grounds becomes appropriate. They will be given medical advice and treatment. As regards numbers, it may be some reassurance to the House to hear that currently there are only three known HIV-positive individuals and two AIDS cases in the armed services. I was asked whether we are properly monitoring the position: yes, we are. Otherwise, our policy is the same as Government policy in general towards AIDS.

The hon. Member for Leyton asked about discharges. The services take a compassionate view of the AIDS sufferer. It is our policy to continue to employ sufferers in the armed forces for as long as possible. If a service man has to be discharged on medical grounds he will be treated humanely and allowed to leave with dignity, as would anyone leaving on any health ground.

The hon. Member for Rhondda picked up the point from last year about private contractors. The undertaking that my predecessor gave, which was to ensure that work not done adequately by private contractors would not be done by serving soldiers, still stands. Commands have been reminded not to assist private contractors or re-do their work. I hope that that point is accepted.

Several hon. Members spoke on housing. I tried hard, but I could not see the connection with discipline, unless occupation of our poorer quarters is regarded as a form of punishment. Housing is a matter of considerable concern. Not surprisingly, my hon. Friend the Member for Canterbury was here to make his point again. He suggested that the solution should not be two households.

I think that that is a little sweeping, because for some people it will be two households. There are many who have two households.

We are aware of the needs of those who do not have homes of their own. We are endeavouring to work a scheme which we hope will be brought in and which will meet the need. While this endeavour continues, we are discouraged if my hon. Friend the Member for Wyre (Mr. Mans) should think that the Ministry of Defence has been laggard. He will acknowledge that in the debate in Committee on the Finance Bill the Treasury Minister said that contacts had been made with him by Ministers in the Ministry of Defence and that the door was still open for further discussion. That is where the matter stands. The judgment of my hon. Friend the Member for Canterbury was right.

We have very much in mind the need to recruit and retain service personnel. I hesitate to say how much work is going on in the Ministry of Defence, because it might alarm hon. Members to know how many are under way. We are acutely aware of the need not only to maintain recruitment but to retain those who are presently serving, who are valuable, highly skilled and dedicated personnel whom we do not wish to lose. We are constantly seeking ways to ensure that they are happy in their work and wish to continue.

Hon. Members have not paid sufficient attention to the success that the Government have had in providing employment. The 34th successive monthly fall in unemployment has just been announced. As my right hon. Friend the Prime Minister made clear last Thursday, the Government have been outstandingly successful in

[*Mr. Neubert*]

creating new jobs. This makes the employment scene highly competitive, and the services cannot escape that. However, we are by no means complacent, and have a whole range of matters under review. They include the points mentioned tonight.

We wish to see to a wider role for women. I remind the House that it was the Chief of the Air Staff who gave impetus to the campaign for the wider use of women in the Royal Air Force, by his interview in a magazine earlier in the year. We are also seeking ways to offer greater promotion possibilities to women.

The hon. Member for Stockton, North (Mr. Cook) spoke about two matters that deserve the attention of the House. The first was drug abuse. I can assure him that, as I am sure he would expect, that is taken seriously, wherever and when ever it occurs. All ranks are made aware of the hazards of abuse through a comprehensive education package and, depending on the seriousness of the offence, may be discharged. This is the right way to proceed. I cannot agree with the hon. Gentleman's request for leniency in such cases simply to solve our manning difficulties. That would be inimical to the image and prestige of our professional armed services.

As to the instance of drug abuse, although I am aware of the concern, I do not accept that it is a major problem. I hope that that will not make the hon. Gentleman think that we are complacent about it, but there has been a drop in the number of drug-related offences committed by service men since 1984, when the figure was 370. By last year, that was down to 91. That is a testimony to the approach adopted by the services. They are aware of the need for constant vigilance. Moreover, steps have been taken to improve both the detection and prevention of drug abuse. I made a special visit to RAF Rudloe Manor to see the RAF police who are engaged in such work, among other things.

Secondly, the hon. Gentleman for Stockton, North spoke about the need for debt and credit counselling, and anticipated my rather general reply. All three services are aware of the need to provide advice and information on personal and financial matters, including credit counselling. Advice is available to all service personnel within units, and they can be directed to outside financial advisers if necessary. Where cases occur, they are always followed up with further counselling and advice. The hon. Gentleman's point was that prevention was better than cure, and we take that to heart and will consider what he said about that.

I have endeavoured to cover the majority of the issues raised during the debate. I am grateful to the House for bearing with me as I did so. I am pleased with the general support that the House has given, which will be appreciated by the armed forces as well as by the Minister responsible.

*Question put and agreed to.*

*Resolved,*

That the draft Army, Air Force and Naval Discipline Acts (Continuation) Order 1989, which was laid before this House on 12th June, be approved.

## MEMBERS' INTERESTS

*Ordered,*

That leave be given to the Select Committee on Members' Interests to visit Canada, in pursuance of its inquiry into parliamentary lobbying.—[*Mr. Alan Howarth.*]

## PETITIONS

## Stranmillis College of Education

11.20 pm

**Rev. Martin Smyth** (Belfast, South): I have a petition, Mr. Deputy Speaker, which has been signed by 164 students from the Stranmillis college of education. The college is in my constituency but the students come from throughout Northern Ireland. They oppose the proposed top-up loans system that is set out in the White Paper. I sympathise with them and support the petition and their prayer.

The petition reads:

Wherefore your Petitioners pray that your Honourable House will retain the present system of student grants. And your petitioners, as in duty bound, will ever pray.

This morning I spoke to two senior academics and they said that they would be happy with loans because they would save them having to borrow for their children, but they felt that poorer families would be penalised.

*To lie upon the Table.*

## Gipsy Sites (Leicester)

11.21 pm

**Mr. Keith Vaz** (Leicester, East): I beg leave, Mr. Deputy Speaker, to present three petitions that have been signed by more than 1,450 of my constituents. All three petitions relate to the proposal by the environmental health department of Leicester city council to establish gipsy and traveller sites in densely populated areas of the eastern part of the city. The proposal affects directly the residents of Humberstone, West Humberstone and Rushey Mead. The residents are opposed to the proposals and call on the council to consult them first before any action is taken. They further call on the House to make it clear to the Secretary of State for the Environment that should the matter come before him he must take appropriate action to prevent the sites being used for these purposes.

The first petition is presented on behalf of councillor Mike Preston, Mr. Keith Newcombe, Mr. Steve Marston, Mrs. Sue Chapman and 547 residents from Netherhall and Humberstone. The second petition is presented on behalf of Mrs. Margaret Ayers of 40 Lanesborough road, Rushey Mead, Leicester and 403 other residents of Rushey Mead. The third petition is presented on behalf of Mrs. Bird and 501 other residents of Old Humberstone.

The petitions state that the local residents oppose the proposals of the environmental health department of the city council for gipsy sites on the plots of land at Rushey Mead, Keyham lane and north of Keyham lane west respectively.

Wherefore your petitioners pray that your honourable House encourage the Secretary of State for the Environment to take action to prevent the gipsy site from gaining permission.

*To lie upon the Table.*

## West London (Road Building)

11.24 pm

**Mr. Matthew Carrington** (Fulham): I beg leave to present a petition, Mr. Deputy Speaker, on behalf of my constituents and those of the hon. Member for Hammersmith (Mr. Soley). It is from the association of the residents of Sands End and West London RoadWatch. It is signed by 4,095 residents of the borough of Hammersmith and Fulham, who express their justified concern about the proposed road called the western environmental improvement route and the view, which I strongly support, that the road will cause immense damage to their environment without solving west London's traffic problem.

The petition urges my right hon. Friend the Secretary of State for Transport

to take note of the environmental destruction, damage to the social fabric and deterioration in the quality of life which will result from his proposed road-building plans for London, and to abandon the Assessment Studies in their present form, delete major road-building options, particularly the 'Western Environmental Improvement Route' invest public money in public transport to serve the needs of all Londoners and preserve our environment.

*To lie upon the Table.*

# EC Anti-dumping Duties

*Motion made, and Question proposed.* That this House do now adjourn.—[*Mr. Lightbown.*]

11·24 pm

**Mr. Phillip Oppenheim** (Amber Valley): I start by apologising to my hon. Friend the Minister for keeping him up so late. He is already familiar with the general drift of my arguments, but nevertheless I am glad that he will be replying to the debate, because no one else can defend the indefensible better than he can.

I have always found the concept of dumping rather strange. The idea that companies persistently and consistently sell products into export markets at an uneconomical price, perhaps subsidised by their Governments, in order to drive home industries out of business and subsequently to cream the market with high prices stretches one's credulity. Nevertheless, anti-dumping cases have become increasingly popular recently. That is partly because they make the initiators of such actions appear to be the friends of free trade, especially in an area in which direct and overt forms of protectionism such as quotas and tariff barriers are becoming increasingly popular.

I argue that regulations and laws against dumping are perfectly all right provided that they are fairly drafted. Unfortunately, the European Community's anti-dumping laws are patently unfair and unjust. Those laws as they stand allow the Commission to fine companies involved in so-called dumping even when that clearly has not occurred. The Community's regulations are complex and convoluted, but I shall touch on two of the ways in which they can make it appear that a company or industry has engaged in dumping when it has not.

The first is by so-called price construction. When the Commission investigates supposed cases of dumping, it does not compare the exporting company's domestic price with that charged in the export market. Instead, for a variety of reasons, the Commission constructs prices artificially, and not on a like-for-like basis. When the Commission considers the price charged domestically in Japan, for example, it includes all overheads and marketing costs—but virtualy excludes them in respect of the European market price. The result is that almost inevitably dumping appears to have occurred when it has not.

The second way in which the Commission makes it appear that dumping has occurred is by including in the regulations a provision that a start-up industry that is selling its products at a loss—perhaps because its plant has not yet reached economical capacity—can be found guilty of dumping and have duties imposed upon it even though its export prices may be well above those prevailing on its home market. That is a major disincentive for start-up factories abroad attempting to sell into the European market. Such injustices explain why companies in the colony of Hong Kong, for example, can be said to be guilty of dumping.

It may be thought strange that Hong Kong companies can be accused of dumping. After all, its economy is one of the most open, free and liberated in the world. It is subject to no Government policy, there is little intervention in industry, and virtually no subsidies. The question may be asked as to how small and medium-sized Hong Kong companies can afford persistently to dump their goods on to the European market. I do not think that they can, yet in recent years the Commission found Hong Kong manufacturers of video tapes, for example, guilty of supposed dumping. It now proposes to investigate imports of denim cloth from Hong Kong, even though they are already heavily protected by the multi-fibre arrangement and Community quotas.

I know that my hon. Friend the Minister will adduce in his defence of the Commission and its anti-dumping regulations the information that the European Court of Justice has ruled in the Commission's favour. Let me point out that all the European Court of Justice has done is say that the Commission has imposed those regulations to the letter. It has not judged the matter on the basis of the justice or otherwise of the regulations.

I suspect that my hon. Friend will also adduce in the Commission's defence the fact that the GATT code supposedly endorses the European anti-dumping regulations. The GATT code is a very vague and broadly drafted document: in many ways it is the lowest common denominator of agreement between GATT members. The fact that it seems to enshrine the concept of the EC regulations in no way makes those regulations just.

Some people would say, "After all, the Japanese have traded unfairly against us in the past; why should we mind if we are putting up a few barriers against them now?". I do not want to dwell on the subject of supposed Japanese protectionism, except to say that in my experience it has often been heavily exaggerated in the west, especially by industrialists and business men, who have not made proper efforts to sell into the Japanese market and who often have not been selling goods of sufficient quality to succeed.

It is also worth reminding ourselves that we in the west are ourselves guilty of large-scale protectionism, not just in Europe but in the United States, which often tries to present itself as the great land of free trade. We have a range of voluntary restraint agreements, export restraint agreements, quotas, tariff barriers and a variety of other mechanisms which, over the years, have spun an entangling web that to a large extent prevents the free movement of goods into our market and the American market.

Those barriers cover goods ranging from textiles—which, of course, are bought by almost everyone in the EEC and America—to high-tech goods such as microchips, computers and cars. Moreover, we in Europe and America have intervened in our own industries, and have subsidised the shipbuilding and car industries particularly heavily. We should remember that when we consider imposing slightly unfair regulations on the Japanese.

The range of protectionist instruments currently in the EEC armoury do not even help our home industries. By protecting industry, we not only reduce competition on our home market—which makes our own companies concentrate on that market to the expense of export markets—but compound the inefficiencies of our industries, and make it far less likely that they will be able to compete on equal terms with Japan and other East Asian countries on the world markets. Such protectionism is a recipe for slow decline.

Anti-dumping duties, in imposing heavy price rises, are effectively a tax on European consumers to the benefit of the industrial lobbies and special interests that are unable to keep up with overseas competition. That, of course, adds considerably to European prices. I cannot say to what extent anti-dumping duties have added to the price of articles such as photocopiers or electronic typewriters, because the EEC Commissioners are unfortunately less than forthcoming. In fact, they have consistently refused to give any details of the amount of duties that they have raised, notwithstanding the fact that the entire amount goes into the Commission's pocket. I feel that the House has a right to expect the Commission to reveal that information. Its stonewalling attitude makes British Government Departments look profligate with the truth.

The EEC is very much in the news just now. It is being used as a stick by some new converts to the EEC with which to beat our Prime Minister. Some of us who have for long been supporters of the concept of the European Community find that odd. We also dread to think what would happen if the EEC ever got control of many of our national areas of government, such as social policy. If it did, and if it introduced legislation as patently unjust—and released as little information about it—as it does about anti-dumping duties, that would make a complete farce of government, and people would rapidly lose confidence in the EEC.

It is also ironic that many people in Europe are accusing Britain of being anti-European and uncommunautaire. After all, Britain is the most liberal of the EEC trading partners, notwithstanding some remaining trade barriers. Indeed, some Europeans have a bit of a cheek lecturing us on being un-European, when they maintain a whole range of non-tariff barriers against British products such as telecommunications equipment. They should look to liberalising their own markets and creating genuinely internal European markets. If they had made the progress that we have made in the last few years in liberalising our market, they would be on stronger ground when criticising us for being non-European.

I wish to inject some optimism into the debate. There is good news in that the new Commission includes some liberal-minded politicians, particularly Mr. Bangemann, Sir Leon Brittan and Mr. Andriessen, who seems to be standing out against the creation of a fortress Europe—or, rather, a ghetto Europe, as it would become. I understand that they are currently fighting a battle against European industrial interests such as Fiat to try to ensure that there is no EEC-wide car quota after 1992, and I wish them well in their efforts.

Her Majesty's Government have been at the forefront in trying to liberalise trade and reduce tariff and non-tariff barriers and all types of trade barriers. I hope that the Minister will not think me remiss when I say that perhaps we could do a little more to try to push the Commission away from imposing what are patently anti-dumping duties on a whole range of products which do not give any protection or benefit to our industry in the long term and which only impose large price rises on EEC consumers.

11.37 pm

**The Minister for Trade (Mr. Alan Clark):** I congratulate my hon. Friend the Member for Amber Valley (Mr. Oppenheim) on the force and clarity with which he put forward his views. He did so in a manner which we have come to expect from him, being among my hon. Friends the most articulate of the exponents of free trade in its purest form. He pursued his arguments in tonight's debate, as he did in the debate in October of last year, and he loses

no opportunity to draw attention to the strength of his case each month when my Department is scheduled to answer at Question Time.

I welcome the opportunity to clarify the position both regarding the Community's policy in this sphere and the views of Her Majesty's Government. My hon. Friend will agree that an Adjournment debate is not the place or time at which to embark on a detailed critique of anti-dumping policy, but I am ready to do my best to respond to some of the points my hon. Friend made.

As for the Community's legislation, it is appropriate for me to put on record the basis for the Community's present approach, which is regulation 2423/88, which consolidated the earlier legislation. This reflects the principle of GATT article VI and incorporates the interpretive and other requirements of the code.

In a number of respects the regulation is more liberal than GATT requires. Particular examples are the way in which a limit is fixed on the duration of duties and the requirement that they should be set at less than full dumping margin where the injury margin is lower. This is in contrast to United States practice, but of course I am not responsible for American policy and I would not be expected to defend it here. My hon. Friend is right to draw attention to the increasing signs of protectionism in a number of sectors. The United States is edging away from the principle of free trade and moving towards a quite naked and flagrant protectionism in some sectors.

Perhaps the most significant departure of Community legislation from the GATT code is the introduction of the concept of the Community interest which certainly, in our view, allows the likely impact on consumers and industrial users, as well as wider economic aspects, to be taken into account before any duty or other remedy is decided upon.

The regulation is a detailed document which lays down the internal Community procedures to be followed. It prescribes at some length the way in which a dumping margin is to be calculated and the factors which are to be taken into account in determining injury. Competence in this field is reserved to the Community under the treaty of Rome. Thus the main responsibility for carrying out the main procedures, including investigations and the determination of dumping and injury margins, is placed upon the Commission. It can also decide on its own authority to impose provisional duties, which are not, however, collected until a definitive duty has been fixed. But at the end of the process it is for the Council of Ministers, on the basis of qualified majority voting, to take the decision whether remedial duties should be applied.

My hon. Friend made a number of general points about anti-dumping cases where the justification is unreal and he implied that some aspects of the evidence are rigged. I use that word in a non-pejorative sense. He made no specific allegations. He referred to examples of goods originating in Hong Kong, but his case would have been stronger had he been able to cite particular examples and to subject the figures to more detailed scrutiny. He has referred to examples that are causing him disquiet. They are being considered by the Community. I hope that he will refer them to my Department where we shall look into them closely.

Over the years the Commission has investigated a steady stream of anti-dumping cases, the majority of which have involved basic or intermediate industrial goods. A significant proportion has concerned imports from state trading countries. My hon. Friend concentrated on

[*Mr. Alan Clark*]

imports from the far east, but the state trading countries are the principal culprits. Price and market disciplines do not operate there, as they do in the liberal Western economies. There has been no major increase in the number of investigations, although that is sometimes alleged. I have a detailed table of figures with which I shall not weary the House, but I shall forward it to my hon. Friend.

**Mr. Oppenheim:** I did not go into great detail about facts and figures, because this is only a short debate. However, I point my hon. Friend in the direction of the photocopier case, the electronic typewriter case and the computer printer case where there are problems with constructive pricing and with the asymmetry of price determination in the exporting and the importing market. Those are three specific cases where regulations have been imposed unjustly.

It is certainly true that there has been no overall increase in the number of cases, but there has been a substantial increase since the mid-1980s in the number of cases against east Asian countries that do not have state trading organisations. Nevertheless, I accept that there has been a reduction in the number of cases against state trading types of organisations and centrally controlled economies.

**Mr. Clark:** That reminds me of a point that is not covered in the text of my reply. My hon. Friend showed a little naivety in his argument. He could not comprehend how an exporter could deliberately target a market, sell under the going rate to achieve market share and ultimately eliminate competition, get a free rate and then adjust prices upwards. That is an accepted commercial strategy. The most notable example was the destruction of the motor cycle industry in parts of the Community, notably the United Kingdom, which was followed by considerable increases in the prices of the predator exporter. However, I do not want to get involved in detailed arguments at this stage. I accept what my hon. Friend says about office equipment. I shall send him more detailed figures and look forward to his further comments.

Anti-dumping is a legal and technical instrument and not a discretionary measure which can be used at will to achieve wider policy aims in the Community context, although some countries, notably the United States, tend to use it in a discretionary way to achieve wider trade policy or protectionist objectives.

The Government's approach has been to subject the Commission's findings to careful examination and, where necessary, to raise questions about the degree of dumping and injury established. We have given particular attention to the remedies proposed and their impact on consumers. We follow the principle, which no doubt my hon. Friend would approve, that GATT provides an instrument for use in defined circumstances: it does not require that action should be taken unless on economic grounds it is justified. Where we disagree with the Commission's proposals, we are fully prepared to say so and, if necessary, to register our vote against them in the Council, as we have done on a number of occasions in the past year.

Whatever may be said about the present GATT framework and the Community's policy, there will continue to be a need for an effective internationally agreed instrument to deal with unfair trading practicies. It will not be sufficient to rely solely on national competition laws. The majority of OECD countries do not, at this time, appear to see the need for any radical change in the present anti-dumping instrument or in its application. We believe that useful work can be done in the OECD in examining the concept of unfair trading and the relevance of present trade policy instruments, but that will take time to bring to completion.

In the meantime, the Uruguay round will, as I have said, provide an opportunity for addressing some of the criticisms and the proposals made by Japan, Korea and certain other newly industrialised economies which feel that the present system needs to be subjected to tighter rules and disciplines. It is unlikely that the Community will wish to amend its legislation until those negotiations in GATT have been concluded.

*Question put and agreed to.*

*Adjourned accordingly at twelve minutes to Twelve o'clock.*

# House of Commons

*Thursday 29 June 1989*

*The House met at half-past Two o'clock*

## PRAYERS

[MR. SPEAKER *in the Chair*]

## PRIVATE BUSINESS

ASSOCIATED BRITISH PORTS (No. 2) BILL *By Order*
*Order read for resuming adjourned debate on Question*
—*[23 May]*—That the Bill be now read the Third time.
*Debate to be resumed on Thursday 6 July.*

### BRITISH RAILWAYS BILL

### LONDON REGIONAL TRANSPORT (No. 2) BILL

### BROMLEY LONDON BOROUGH COUNCIL (CRYSTAL PALACE) BILL
*Orders for consideration read.*
*To be considered on Thursday 6 July.*

### BUCKINGHAMSHIRE COUNTY COUNCIL BILL *[Lords]* (*By Order*)

### LONDON LOCAL AUTHORITIES BILL *[Lords]* (*By Order*)
*Orders for consideration read.*
*To be considered on Thursday 6 July.*

### LONDON REGIONAL TRANSPORT (PENALTY FARES) BILL *[Lords]* (*By Order*)
*Order read for resuming debate on Question*—*[28 June]*
—That the Bill be now considered.
*Debate to be resumed on Thursday 6 July.*

### LONDON UNDERGROUND (VICTORIA) BILL (*By Order*)

### BRITISH FILM INSTITUTE SOUTHBANK BILL (*By Order*)

### VALE OF GLAMORGAN (BARRY HARBOUR) BILL *[Lords]* (*By Order*)

### HAYLE HARBOUR BILL *[Lords]* (*By Order*)

### QUEEN MARY AND WESTFIELD COLLEGE BILL *[Lords]*
*Orders for Second Reading read.*
*To be read a Second time on Thursday 6 July.*

### KING'S CROSS RAILWAYS BILL
*Ordered,*

That the Committee on the King's Cross Railways Bill have leave to visit and inspect the areas affected by the proposed works, provided that no evidence shall be taken in the course of such visit and that any party who has made an appearance before the Committee be permitted to attend by his Counsel, agent or other representative.—*[The Chairman of Ways and Means.]*

# Oral Answers to Questions

## AGRICULTURE, FISHERIES AND FOOD

### Fur Farming

1. **Dr. Kim Howells:** To ask the Minister of Agriculture, Fisheries and Food when he last discussed with representatives of the Council of Europe the deliberations of that body on fur farming.

3. **Mrs. Mahon:** To ask the Minister of Agriculture, Fisheries and Food whether he proposes to raise in the EC Council of Ministers the issue of fur farming and regulations relating thereto.

5. **Ms. Primarolo:** To ask the Minister of Agriculture, Fisheries and Food what is his response to the Farm Animal Welfare Council's statement on mink and fox farming.

**The Parliamentary Secretary to the Ministry of Agriculture, Fisheries and Food (Mr. Donald Thompson):** I discussed the Council of Europe recommendations with my officials before the last meeting in April and asked them to take account of the Farm Animal Welfare Council's recent statement. Until this work is complete, there would be little point in raising the matter in the Council of Ministers. In the meantime, I have asked the state veterinary service to continue its monitoring of fur farms, as recommended by the Farm Animal Welfare Council.

**Dr. Howells:** Will the Minister put to the Council of Europe the case for phasing out fur farms, as it is clear from a wide range of evidence that fur farms do not and cannot meet the basic requirements of farm animal welfare?

**Mr. Thompson:** The Farm Animal Welfare Council did not recommend that I should ban fur farms. The Council of Europe is a good forum in which to discuss fur farming. The British are well down the league of people who farm for fur. The Danes farm 10 million animals, the Swedes 2 million, the Dutch 1·5 million and the French 500,000, compared with 250,000 in the United Kingdom.

**Mrs. Mahon:** Will the Minister acknowledge that there has not been proper research into fur farming? Will he instruct his officials not to support any recommendations until there has been research into this sort of farming? Will he undertake to publish that research? Fur farming worries many people. The animals are in great distress and often self-mutilate. This is a very serious issue.

**Mr. Thompson:** The hon. Lady is right to be worried. About 25 per cent. of fur produced in the United Kingdom comes from Calderdale. We have asked the Farm Animal Welfare Council to investigate fur farming. The council always publishes its conclusions in full. We in no way restrain the council in who it calls to give evidence, nor in any way do we restrict what it does with that evidence afterwards.

**Ms. Primarolo:** What action will the Minister take on the farming of arctic foxes in breach of the Berne convention, to which we are signatory? Farming animals for their fur is abhorrent. We should stick clearly to the conventions that we have signed. What steps will the hon. Gentleman take to reinforce our commitment to the Berne convention?

**Mr. Thompson:** We shall follow the guidelines of the Council of Europe and those laid down by the Farm Animal Welfare Council. There seems to be much more emotion about the farming of foxes than about the farming of mink, although the hon. Lady probably feels as emotional about both. We are considering all aspects, and we undertake to publish all our research.

**Mr. Jessel:** Has my hon. Friend noticed that some of those who complain about fur farming wear leather shoes?

**Mr. Thompson:** My hon. Friend is right. Most people wear leather shoes. Hon. Members are saying that to rear an animal purely for one purpose, but not for meat, is abhorrent. The Government well understand that point, but I am not undertaking to restrict mink farming. I pledge that we shall ensure that mink farming observes the most hygienic and proper codes. The Fur Breeders Association of Great Britain is to be commended for its code of practice, which its members follow closely.

**Mr. Colvin:** Will my hon. Friend confirm that he accepts the 1984 ruling of the Royal Society for the Prevention of Cruelty to Animals that animals in fur farms are semi-domesticated, not wild? Will he further confirm that before he returns to the Council of Ministers for more discussions, and on receipt of recommendations from his officials when they have completed their work, he will discuss the matter with fur farmers' representatives before reaching any conclusions?

**Mr. Thompson:** I often meet the Farm Animal Welfare Council, the RSPCA, fur farmers and others. My hon. Friend rightly said that animals in fur farms are semi-domesticated, which is why it is abhorrent for people to release them into the wild. I am sure that no hon. Member agrees with that practice, which in the past has destroyed the ecology of valleys. I shall consult the relevant bodies before taking further steps.

## Irradiated Food

2. **Mr. Nigel Griffiths:** To ask the Minister of Agriculture, Fisheries and Food when he expects to discuss food irradiation with other EC Agriculture Ministers.

**The Minister of Agriculture, Fisheries and Food (Mr. John MacGregor):** I expect discussions on the draft directive on food irradiation to start later this year.

**Mr. Griffiths:** Has the Minister had an opportunity to study the report of the Consumers Association on food irradiation in this month's "Which?", which warns that food irradiation removes nutrients from food but increases the likelihood of toxins and radiolytic products being left in it? Does he agree that we need firm Government action to improve standards throughout the food chain and not irradiation?

**Mr. MacGregor:** On the latter point, over the past few months we have taken a number of steps, where necessary, to deal with food safety and standards throughout the food chain. One should not take decisions on food

irradiation on the ground that it will solve all food safety problems. Food irradiation has a part, but only a part, to play in the total process of dealing with food safety. It is right to give consumers and manufacturers freedom of choice on that process, given the beneficial effects that it can have for some food products. As to the report of the Consumers Association, food irradiation has been studied by more scientists than almost every other food process. It has no greater effect on nutrition than the other processes through which food goes, including cooking. Food irradiation is neutral in its effect on toxins.

**Miss Emma Nicholson:** Will my right hon. Friend confirm that, contrary to the scare stories put forward by the Opposition, food irradiation cannot by some extraordinary miracle turn bad food good? It leaves bad food bad, but gives good food a longer shelf life, thereby increasing the housewife's freedom of choice.

**Mr. MacGregor:** As so often on these matters, my hon. Friend talks good sense. I agree with everything that she said.

**Dr. David Clark:** Does the Minister recall telling the House last week that if he introduced irradiation he would ensure that the public were made aware of whether food had been irradiated? As the majority of irradiated food will be sold in restaurants, will he give a categorical guarantee that restaurants will be required to display a notice in a prominent position stating that they sell irradiated food? Alternatively, it should be clearly stated on the menu that they are selling irradiated food.

**Mr. MacGregor:** As the hon. Gentleman knows, it will be some time before the ban on food irradiation in this country can be lifted.

**Mr. Home Robertson:** Answer the question.

**Mr. MacGregor:** I am coming to the point. This is relevant. It will be some time before the ban is lifted. We will wish to consult and take decisions on a range of details including precisely what is included on labels. The point made by the hon. Gentleman is one of those details. Precisely how we ensure that the consumer knows that food in restaurants has been irradiated will be a matter for detailed consultation and consideration. I assure the hon. Gentleman that I firmly believe that consumers must have informed freedom of choice. His point will be dealt with.

**Mr. David Martin:** When was food irradiation first patented? How much scientific evidence has been accumulated since then?

**Mr. MacGregor:** From memory, I think that the first food irradiation process was permitted in 1921.

**Dr. Moonie:** The Minister remembers that, does he?

**Mr. MacGregor:** I do not have to be alive to remember everything that I have read. From my historical education, I can remember other things.

For more than 40 years food irradiation has been studied by scientists. Provided that the proper control framework is operated and the right levels are used, the safety aspects have been fully approved by scientists internationally in many scientific bodies and by many organisations that have considered food irradiation, including the advisory committee in this country.

### Forestry

6. **Mr. Ron Davies:** To ask the Minister of Agriculture, Fisheries and Food what estimates his Department makes of future demand for nursery-grown trees for commercial forestry in England and Wales.

**Mr. MacGregor:** The Forestry Commission estimates its own needs which it meets largely from its own nurseries, while the horticultural trade makes separate assessments of the likely demand from the private forestry sector. The Horticultural Trades Association meets the commission periodically to discuss likely planting trends.

**Mr. Davies:** Is the Minister aware of the research undertaken at the university of Suffolk which has shown unacceptably high levels of lead in food crops grown adjacent to motorways? Would it make more sense in terms of protecting public health, enhancing the environment and giving a much-needed boost to the forestry industry if corridors of land adjacent to motorways could be taken out of agricultural production and given over to forestry?

**Mr. MacGregor:** That is a much wider question than the main question before us. I am aware of some of the research, although I have not had the opportunity to study it. I would have to know the basis of the research and be sure of it before I acted on it. Moving from that to the solution that the hon. Gentleman has suggested is a very different matter and raises much wider considerations. I cannot give him the assurance that he seeks.

**Mr. Lord:** My right hon. Friend will be aware of the serious effects of the tax change in the 1988 Budget on the supply of nursery trees. He will know that millions of those trees have been burnt this year because they were not required. He will also know that young trees cannot be kept indefinitely and that when they are nearly three years old they must be disposed of if not required. I appreciate that this may be difficult to organise, but will my right hon. Friend do his best to ensure that supply and demand in this difficult area are kept in reasonable balance so that we can plant the trees which we need to plant and so that nursery businesses do not suffer such shocks in the future?

**Mr. MacGregor:** The Forestry Commission makes its own estimates of its demand and, on the whole, it supplies its own trees. My hon. Friend must recognise that it is much more difficult to do that in the private sector when the demand involves thousands of landowners and others who may want to decide which trees to plant. It is difficult for the Government to make that kind of estimate. I am aware of the immediate downturn in planting following last year's Budget. That always happens when there are major changes in the way in which regimes are financed. However, there has been a general welcome for the change from tax reliefs to grants. I hope that there will be a pick-up following the period of uncertainty—the time that people must take to assess the new regime. My hon. Friend will be pleased to know of the response in the first eight months to the farm woodlands scheme, which involves the planting of 10 million new trees in the next three years, many of which are broadleaf trees. I am sure that he will have noticed also that, in the first 10 months of the scheme, applications under the woodland grant scheme have been encouraging, with applications for nearly 36,000 hectares.

**Mr. Mallon:** Is the Minister aware of the deep concern among officials in the North of Ireland about the possible sale of some public forests into private hands? Does he agree that, because of the small acreage of forests in the North of Ireland, that would be to the detriment of a service that has made a tremendous input to the industry? Will he have discussions with his colleagues in the Northern Ireland Office to ensure that those fears are dispelled as soon as possible?

**Mr. MacGregor:** I have no responsibility for forestry matters in Northern Ireland, but I will make sure that the hon. Gentleman's remarks are passed on to my right hon. Friend the Secretary of State for Northern Ireland. However, over the past eight years, disposals have been extremely successful in dealing with the rationalisation of the public estate. I strongly support the announcement by my right hon. and learned Friend the Secretary of State for Scotland on 16 June about the programme for the next 10 years. It gives a considerable and timely boost to the private forestry sector and enables the commission's estate to be further rationalised.

**Mr. Greg Knight:** Is my right hon. Friend aware that many Conservative Members warmly welcome the farm woodlands scheme? He has mentioned the number of trees being planted. Will any of them be oaks and, if so, how many?

**Mr. MacGregor:** Yes. I am grateful for my hon. Friend's question. Farmers' responses to the scheme in the early months of its introduction have been extremely encouraging. It is noticeable how many applications have been received for farmland in lowland areas, most notably perhaps in East Anglia, which is leading the way. I am particularly pleased to note that about 2 million oak trees are involved in the overall figures.

7. **Mr. Tony Lloyd:** To ask the Minister of Agriculture, Fisheries and Food if he will make a statement on European forestry policy and its impact on English forestry.

**Mr. MacGregor:** There is no common forestry policy as such. However, the Council of Agriculture Ministers recently agreed a package of voluntary measures making up a forestry action programme. The main effect of this programme from the United Kingdom's point of view is that we shall be able to obtain some reimbursement of our expenditure on the afforestation of agricultural land.

**Mr. Lloyd:** The Minister admitted that forestry nurseymen have had a hard time since last year's changes in forestry policy. Will he make sure that some of the European money from the forestry package is devoted to easing forestry nurserymen's problems? The Minister responsible refused to meet the nurserymen. Will the Minister reverse the decision, with a view to meeting the nurserymen to discuss how the money could be used to assist their problems?

**Mr. MacGregor:** It is important to understand what the European forestry programme does. We were successful in achieving our objectives in the negotiations. One of them was to ensure that, in future, the schemes that we have been pioneering in this country will be eligible for some European funding. Depending on the response to our current schemes, about £6 million is likely to come from the European Community for the kind of schemes that we are introducing. It will depend on the uptake of the schemes, and nurserymen will obviously have to take that into account.

**Mr. John Greenway:** With regard to the uptake of the schemes, how many hectares are likely to be planted under existing applications for the farm woodlands grant? What interest has been shown by tenants and what arrangements can be made to ensure that they can profit from this excellent arrangement?

**Mr. MacGregor:** For the first eight months, the figure is about 6,200 hectares. I have obviously been keen for opportunities to be extended to tenants. The schemes are long term, so tenants need to secure their landlords' agreement. I am pleased to say that, so far, about 15 per cent. of applications have been granted to tenants. That is not far short of the total number of tenanted holdings. It appears that there is a reasonable response by landlords to tenants.

**Mr. Geraint Howells:** After listening to the Minister's reply, is it right for me to assume that his friends in Europe are unwilling to give money to the public sector—the Forestry Commission—in this country?

**Mr. MacGregor:** The main schemes in the forestry programme about which we were talking do not affect the Forestry Commission or public authorities.

**Mr. Home Robertson:** Now that the crisis in woodland nurseries has been referred to by hon. Members from both sides of the House, does the Minister accept that it is proof positive that forestry speculators do not give a damn about the long-term benefit and welfare of Britain's woodlands, and that all they ever wanted was access to a lucrative tax dodge? Will he further accept that the Forestry Commission has by far the best record of public accountability and giving the public access to British woodland? Therefore, will he repudiate the proposals recently made by the Secretary of State for Scotland to force the Forestry Commission to privatise a further 250,000 acres of our forests, so putting even more woodlands behind closed gates?

**Mr. MacGregor:** On the second question, the hon. Gentleman was obviously not listening. I have already warmly supported the comments made by my right hon. and learned Friend the Secretary of State for Scotland in answer to a previous question, and I do so again. My right hon. and learned Friend also made it clear that public access is a matter that we are considering further in relation to the programme over the next 10 years.

On the first question, I repeat that when the system of taxes or grants is changed, there is always a period during which people will wish to reflect before they make a decision about future planning. There was an even sharper decline in planting when the capital transfer tax was introduced by the Labour Government in the 1970s. The hon. Gentleman and his party supported the main thrust of the changes made last year, so I am not at all clear exactly what he is complaining about.

## Farm Livestock (Slaughtering)

9. **Mr. John P. Smith:** To ask the Minister of Agriculture, Fisheries and Food if his Department will consider introducing legislation to ensure that farm livestock are slaughtered as close to the farm of origin as possible.

**Mr. Donald Thompson:** No, Sir. There are already extensive controls protecting the welfare of animals during transport.

**Mr. Smith:** Bearing in mind the fact that there has been a huge increase in the export of livestock to the continent for slaughter, that there are proposals to reduce the number of stops for water and food—which means that livestock can be in transit for up to 24 hours or more, which is particularly cruel and unnecessary—and that there are good economic benefits to the farming community and slaughtering industries in encouraging domestic slaughter, may I ask the Minister to consider these arguments when he and his colleagues examine livestock transport arrangements?

**Mr. Thompson:** The hon. Gentleman does well to mention this matter, especially in relation to Welsh sheep which are exported throughout the continent, both dead and alive. I always consult my colleagues about the transport of animals. The controls laid down in the United Kingdom are, in some respects, even more stringent than those broadly laid down by the EC. All animals leaving this country have to be rested for at least 10 hours on this side of the water in approved lairages.

**Mr. Ron Davies:** At the moment.

**Mr. Thompson:** The hon. Gentleman says "at the moment". I understood that the purport of the question was that we should keep a watch on Europe where the distances involved are much greater. Animals emanating from this country are at an advantage, not a disadvantage.

**Mr. Knapman:** Does my hon. Friend agree that we cannot have it both ways? If more meat is to be slaughtered in big, modern abattoirs which are licensed to export meat to other countries, it logically follows that less meat will be slaughtered close to the farm gate.

**Mr. Thompson:** That is a good point which I fully understand and shall explain to Opposition Front-Bench spokesmen because obviously they do not. They have been pressing for licensed abbatoirs—export abattoirs—which, of necessity, will be bigger and more efficient, but will also have to be further away from the farm. Animals will have to be taken to those export-approved slaughterhouses. There is a good trade in live animals abroad because once a live animal is abroad it can be killed as a French or German animal would be killed. That is an attraction to the countries that import our animals. We take a great deal of trouble to ensure that those animals are taken abroad in the best possible way and that their welfare is safeguarded.

**Mr. Andrew F. Bennett:** Can the Minister confirm that there has been a steady increase in the number of sheep exported live? Surely it is much kinder to slaughter sheep in this country rather than abroad, and also much better for British jobs.

**Mr. Thompson:** There has been an increase in the amount of sheepmeat going abroad, both dead and alive, and the number of live exports has increased in proportion with that. If the sheep are properly conducted, housed, lairaged and transported, they travel very well.

## Food Safety

10. **Mr. Thurnham:** To ask the Minister of Agriculture, Fisheries and Food what recent measures he has taken to improve food safety in the United Kingdom; and if he will make a statement.

**Mr. MacGregor:** I have recently introduced several measures at all stages in the food chain, from production of animal feed right through to storage and handling of food in the home.

**Mr. Thurnham:** Does my right hon. Friend agree that the major British food firms lead the world in safety standards? Does he also agree that the difference between the Government and the Opposition in this regard is that whereas my right hon. Friend, with his scientific advisers, works closely with those firms to establish new standards and research priorities, the Opposition listen to spurious advice and call for inefficiently used local authority environmental health officers?

**Mr. MacGregor:** I agree that our food industry has a very good record, in both range and quality of provision and in food safety. I well know how much the industry is investing in new plant and facilities to enable it constantly to improve food safety. After all, unless it does so it will not continue to expand and sell its products, both at home and in the export market, and its export record shows how successful it has been.

I also agree that it is extremely important for Government action to be based on the best available scientific advice. We have many scientists from all disciplines, both independent and in the Ministry, to advise us and maintain constant surveillance. It is on that basis that we are able to act promptly to protect the consumer.

**Mr. Robert Hughes:** Does the Minister accept that there is a close connection between food hygiene—and food safety—and preparation? Is he aware that in Aberdeen there is great concern at the decision announced yesterday to go ahead with the cut in the research budget at the Torry research station? When the Minister saw a deputation of Members of Parliament the day before, we put it to him that the research being done in collaboration with the EEC was under threat, and he promised to consider the matter. Has he done so, and if so, what decision has he reached?

**Mr. MacGregor:** It is important to remember that Torry's research, and the research that the Government have said from the outset that they will not continue to fund, is of a commercial nature, close to the development end—near-market research that is appropriate for commercial exploitation if companies wish to take up the opportunity. That is precisely the kind of research which we feel should be funded by the industry. My hon. Friend the Parliamentary Secretary has had extensive discussions with the industry, and I regret to say that the industry does not wish to fund those particular projects. As for the proposed European Community projects, my hon. Friend is currently considering them and will write to the hon. Gentleman shortly.

**Mr. Hill:** Is my right hon. Friend as concerned as I am about the latest report by health inspectors on food being taken out of the country by air? The report said that one in four aircraft meals was dangerous to passengers. Will my right hon. Friend look into the matter? Could not the food be subjected to irradiation? Surely the problem needs more scrutiny. Like many of my colleagues, I travel frequently in aircraft.

**Mr. MacGregor:** I suspect that at present I travel in aircraft as much as anyone, as I spend so much of my time negotiating beyond these shores. I am aware of some of the recent research reports. Indeed, we debated the subject in the House last Wednesday, and my hon. Friend the Parliamentary Under-Secretary of State for Health, whose primary responsibility it is, said that he was examining the situation closely to see whether any action was required from him.

If and when the ban on irradiation is lifted—obviously, such action will require parliamentary approval—it will apply only to products for which it is appropriate. It will then be for the industry involved—in this case, the airline—and for consumers themselves to decide whether they wish to make use of irradiated food.

**Mr. Ron Davies:** Does the Minister realise that the Labour party's policy to create an independent food standards agency has now been endorsed by the National Consumer Council and the Institute of Trading Standards Administration? Given the growing concern that exists about the quality and wholesomeness of food that is available to the British consumer, does the right hon. Gentleman agree that this would be an ideal opportunity for him to set to one side his political interests and include our proposal for an independent agency in the food Bill which he is currently considering?

**Mr. MacGregor:** I have had a quick look at the National Consumer Council report and obviously I shall wish to read it further. From that quick look, it seems to me that there are criticisms, as I know from when I have been to the United States, of the way in which that country organises these matters. There are criticisms of the way in which the Food and Drug Administration has operated, just as there are criticisms in other countries. Every country must decide how it wishes to deal with food safety, and there is no perfect answer. It is interesting to note, however, that the majority of countries, certainly in the European Community, organise these matters in the way that we do. I understand that the paper in question has been produced as a consultative document. I have no doubt that there will be much discussion about the pros and cons, and there are clearly a number of cons listed in the document in that respect.

**Mr. Jack:** Can my right hon. Friend confirm that the Ministry will continue to take a strong line in rebutting spurious and unscientifically sponsored claims about food safety, such as the recent comments made about the chemical Alar?

**Mr. MacGregor:** It is extremely important that scientific advice and evidence, not emotion and scary headlines, are the guide in these matters from the point of view of Government action. It is important for all parties in the House not to respond to immediate pressures from interest groups and scare stories but to consider the evidence and listen to responsible scientists. That is what

I do and on that basis we asked our advisory committee recently to look again at the evidence on Alar. The committee made a clear recommendation and we have stuck with that.

### Farm Animals

11. **Mr. John Hughes:** To ask the Minister of Agriculture, Fisheries and Food whether his Department has responded to the call from Compassion in World Farming for farm animals to be accorded the status of sentient animals; and if he will make a statement.

**Mr. Donald Thompson:** I have told Compassion in World Farming that the Government see no need to press for a change in the status of farm animals under European law because the treaty of Rome already provides all the necessary powers to protect the welfare of farm animals.

**Mr. Hughes:** Is the Minister aware that the conditions in which many animals travel when they are exported are nothing short of barbaric, causing the animals a great deal of unnecessary suffering? If the new Common Market transport regulations fail to eliminate that suffering, what steps will he take to press for improved standards?

**Mr. Thompson:** I do not agree that animals being transported in and from the United Kingdom are caused suffering anywhere near the description that the hon. Gentleman gave. This is the fifth question about animal welfare today, and it is a credit to the House that we take the matter so seriously. I have before me our clear statement of policy detailing how we expect animals to be carried when they travel in this country and to other countries. We shall press the European Commission to maintain rigorously the standards that we have set and which seem to be operating successfully in this country.

**Mr. Charles Wardle:** Will the Minister accept that lofty strictures about the treatment of farm animals are an insult to the vast majority of British farmers, who look after their livestock in a humane fashion and have quite enough to do making a living from the land without interference from politically motivated animal rights protestors?

**Mr. Thompson:** I agree with my hon. Friend that the vast majority of our farmers deal with their farming business and the welfare of their animals in an exemplary way. In Parliament, however, we are concerned with the villain in all sorts of ways and we cannot tolerate villainy in regard to animals.

### Food (Contamination)

12. **Dr. Moonie:** To ask the Minister of Agriculture, Fisheries and Food if he will make a statement about the future of research into microbiological contamination of food.

**Mr. MacGregor:** My Department is firmly committed to providing support for food safety research, on which substantial resources are already being spent. For example, I announced earlier this year that my Department plans to spend £1 million annually on new research on salmonella in poultry and £4·5 million over the next five years on a new strategic research initiative designed to predict the growth of food poisoning organisms in a wide variety of food environments and processes.

**Dr. Moonie:** What specific steps will the Minister take to monitor the possible adverse effects of the continuing consumption of raw milk?

**Mr. MacGregor:** Where any cases of food poisoning arise from that source, as from any other, we have the evidence put to us and we shall be monitoring it.

### Bovine Spongiform Encephalopathy

13. **Mr. Pike:** To ask the Minister of Agriculture, Fisheries and Food if he will include a statement on the current incidence of bovine spongiform encephalopathy.

**Mr. MacGregor:** On average, about 150 suspect cases of BSE are being reported each week.

**Mr. Pike:** Will the Minister confirm that cases of BSE have been reported in every county in England and Wales? Would it not be sensible, therefore, to introduce compulsory inspection by vets at slaughterhouses now rather than wait to be compelled to do so by the EEC in 1991?

**Mr. MacGregor:** The actions that we have properly taken—first, from the moment when we knew and could diagnose what the disease was, secondly from the moment when we thought that we knew with a fair degree of certainty what the source was, and finally from the report of the Southwood committee—are designed fully to deal with this problem and to protect the consumer. The Southwood report said that the risk to human health was extremely remote, but to be absolutely sure we have taken steps, including the one that I recently announced, to make sure that infected material does not enter the food chain. I think that that is the right way to tackle the matter.

**Dr. David Clark:** The Minister has acknowledged that the Southwood report admits the possibility, albeit remote, that this terrible disease could be transmitted to humans. To ensure that there is no temptation for farmers to send dubious animals to market, will the Government stop shilly-shallying and offer farmers 100 per cent. compensation for BSE-infected animals sent to slaughter?

**Mr. MacGregor:** It appears that there is still a great deal of misunderstanding about the compensation that we are offering. Such animals are not worth very much in the market, but the compensation is 50 per cent. of the original market value, which is well above what they would now be worth. The other important point is that the action that I have recently announced—to deal with susceptible offals and ensure that they do not enter the food chain—deals with this problem.

### Nitrates

14. **Mr. Cran:** To ask the Minister of Agriculture, Fisheries and Food what representations he has received in response to his consultation document "Nitrate Sensitive Areas Scheme".

**Mr. MacGregor:** The closing date for responses to the nitrate consultation document is 30 June. It has therefore not yet been possible to assess all the responses because that date has not been reached. Replies are still being received and assessed.

**Mr. Cran:** My right hon. Friend is to be congratulated on a consultative document that is undoubtedly in the public interest and illustrates how environmentally aware the Government are. As my right hon. Friend moves towards his conclusions, will he consider consulting farmers about compensation in those cases in which restrictions go beyond good farming practice?

**Mr. MacGregor:** I am grateful for my hon. Friend's praise. It is not necessary to consult farmers on that point because we have already announced that there will be compensation for restrictions that go beyond good agricultural practice. We shall be consulting farmers on the pilot areas, which I hope to announce in the autumn. It will be then that we shall begin to get the full scheme into operation.

### Whaling

15. **Mr. Haynes:** To ask the Minister of Agriculture, Fisheries and Food if he intends to discuss with other European Community Fisheries Ministers the recommendations made at the 41st annual meeting of the International Whaling Commission; and if he will make a statement.

**Mr. Donald Thompson:** The European Community does not have competence on whaling matters as such, but those members with interests in whaling are members of the International Whaling Commission and we consult them in that forum. At the recent annual meeting of the commission, resolutions were passed calling upon Japan, Norway and Iceland to reconsider their whaling research plans, and Japan's request for its small coastal whaling boats to take 320 minke whales was rejected. I welcome those decisions.

**Mr. Haynes:** Is the Minister aware that I have switched my interest from my furry friends to those massive whatever they are? Is the Minister aware that Japan will kill 400 whales this year and Iceland 68 and does he accept the sham that that killing is for "research"? When will there be sanctuary for these beautiful beasts? Come on, Minister, and let us know.

**Mr. Thompson:** The hon. Gentleman deserves an answer. We were instrumental in persuading Iceland not to take 10 sei whales next year and we reduced the number of whales to be taken by the Japanese to 320. We are not interested in spurious scientific whaling. We shall continue to press our case and the case for the whale.

## PRIME MINISTER

### Engagements

Q1. **Mr. Canavan:** To ask the Prime Minister if she will list her official engagements for Thursday 29 June.

**The Prime Minister (Mrs. Margaret Thatcher):** This morning I presided at a meeting of the Cabinet and had meetings with ministerial colleagues and others. In addition to my duties in the House, I shall be having further meetings later today.

**Mr. Canavan:** Does the Prime Minister recall that only a few years ago when the Wang Corporation announced that it was bringing 700 jobs to Scotland, she tried to take much of the credit for it personally, hailing it as splendid news on her birthday and a shot in the arm for Scotland?

If the Minister is to avoid shooting herself in the foot with £4 million of taxpayers' money being lost and, more seriously, shooting down the jobs of 240 Scottish workers, will she renew her personal interest in the case and demand an urgent meeting with company representatives with a view to discussing every possible means of Government intervention to stop the closure and to keep the jobs in Scotland where more than 250,000 people are still unemployed?

**The Prime Minister:** As the hon. Gentleman probably knows, my right hon. and learned Friend the Secretary of State for Scotland answered a private notice question on Tuesday about the closure. The closure comes as a shock because it is a comparatively new factory. The company has come across great market difficulties in selling its product and it has to rationalise. The company made it clear in the closure notice that the work force in Scotland has performed excellently. It also made it clear that it would do everything possible to assist in selling the factory to another occupant perhaps, to have as many jobs continuing there as possible. My right hon. and learned Friend the Secretary of State for Scotland pointed out that in 1982 we were under the Labour system of grants. We had not changed the system then, so we are not in a position to demand part of the grant back. The system of grants was changed in 1984. Had the grant been given later, we would have been in a position to get some of it back.

**Mr. Bill Walker:** Has my right hon. Friend been informed of the situation in the National Union of Railwaymen, where delegates attending the conference about the strike are paid £70 per day, plus expenses, while the ordinary railwaymen who are on strike are paid £2 per day? Does that not show the cynicism within that organisation, with no care for the workers and even less care for the travellers?

**The Prime Minister:** I think that it is utterly deplorable —the inconvenience to which the travelling public are being put by the strikes. Many people are making splendid efforts to get to work because they will not be put off by such strikes. The double tragedy is that British Rail is virtually advertising, "We will not get you to your destination." That is what a strike means for passengers and freight. More people will make other arrangements to get to work and more manufacturers will make other arrangements to transport their freight. It is a double tragedy of gross inconvenience for the public and for the future of British Rail.

Q2. **Mr. Wray:** To ask the Prime Minister if she will list her official engagements for Thursday 29 June.

**The Prime Minister:** I refer the hon. Gentleman to the reply that I gave some moments ago.

**Mr. Wray:** Is the Prime Minister aware that of the 10 million pensioners in Britain, 6 million are living below the poverty line? Does she realise that since 1986, when pensioners had their first increase, they have had increases of 40p, 85p and £1·65p, which amounts to less than £3 in three years? Is she also aware that thousands of pensioners are losing out because of Government guidelines which mean that if their date of birth falls after the first pay day they will lose a week's pension?

**The Prime Minister:** As the hon. Gentleman is aware, under this Government the basic pension has been inflation-proof, whereas the Labour Government were unable to stick to their promise to keep the pension in line with prices because when in 1976 prices went up by 21·5 per cent. the pension went up by only 15 per cent.

Q3. **Mr. Riddick:** To ask the Prime Minister if she will list her official engagements for Thursday 29 June.

**The Prime Minister:** I refer my hon. Friend to the reply that I gave some moments ago.

**Mr. Riddick:** Does my right hon. Friend agree that in the light of the present rail strikes we should be moving towards privatisation of the rail network and the removal of legal immunities in relation to strike action, particularly in public monopoly services? My right hon. Friend has already condemned the National Union of Railwaymen for holding the travelling public to ransom. Can she give any explanation for the failure of the Leader of the Opposition to condemn the NUR?

**The Prime Minister:** I hope that the Leader of the Opposition will condemn the strike, which has given so much inconvenience to thousands of citizens, thousands of trade unionists and thousands of other people who seek conscientiously to get to work to carry out their duties. Privatisation is not an effective response to the situation. It is justified on its own as a policy. When the buses were on strike we saw that the privatised buses still ran. We are not yet ready to bring forward proposals for the privatisation of British Rail, which would require careful preparation, but I shall take my hon. Friend's comments on board. Privatised services are less likely to strike than public ones.

**Mr. Ashdown:** Has the Prime Minister noticed that last week President Gorbachev established for the Soviet Parliament just that system of scrutiny over the KGB which she refused this Parliament in relation to our secret services? *[Interruption.]*

**Mr. Speaker:** Order. Such interruptions take up a great deal of time, which is to no one's benefit.

**Mr. Ashdown:** If such scrutiny is good enough for the Soviet Parliament, why is it regarded as a dangerous over-extension of democracy here?

**The Prime Minister:** I had no idea that the right hon. Gentleman was so utterly naive. I shall take such comments from that direction with a sackful of salt.

**Mr. Gow:** Will my right hon. Friend mark the contrast between the nobility of character and patriotism of the late Airey Neave and the squalid opportunism of his critics?

**The Prime Minister:** Yes, and I gladly pay tribute to the late Airey Neave for his patriotism, his sense of duty, and his honour. The loss of his life was a tragedy for this country.

Q4. **Dr. Reid:** To ask the Prime Minister if she will list her official engagements for Thursday 29 June.

**The Prime Minister:** I refer the hon. Gentleman to the reply that I gave some moments ago.

**Dr. Reid:** Will the Prime Minister confirm the information that I have obtained from the Library that a 63-year-old pensioner on a net income of £70·01p per week living in Southwark will pay exactly the same poll tax as a 63-year-old professional lady earning £1,000 per week who is married to a millionaire and living in Dulwich? Why does the right hon. Lady so strongly support such an unfair tax?

**The Prime Minister:** As the hon. Gentleman knows, the community charge meets about 25 per cent. of local government expenditure. About another 25 per cent. is met by the business tax, and the remaining 50 per cent. is met by the taxpayer. Higher-rate taxpayers will, of course, contribute very much more to local authority expenditure than those paying a lesser rate.

Q5. **Miss Nicholson:** To ask the Prime Minister if she will list her official engagements for Thursday 29 June.

**The Prime Minister:** I refer my hon. Friend to the reply that I gave some moments ago.

**Miss Nicholson:** In her busy day, has my right hon. Friend had time to reflect on the current excellent provision of health care and, in particular, on the major investment in hospital building projects, 401 of which have been completed since 1979 at a cost of more than £1 milion per project, with a further 144 projects nearing completion? Will my right hon. Friend give an assurance that that excellent momentum will be continued?

**The Prime Minister:** Yes, and I am delighted to hear my hon. Friend's comments. Labour's policies would cut expenditure on hospital building, whereas ours have greatly increased it. Our policy is one of trying to improve the Health Service in places where it was not so good, by constructing excellent new hospitals. A number of right hon. and hon. Members who represent London constituencies have had to stand back while that was done elsewhere, but we look forward to having new hospitals, too, under a Conservative Government.

**Mr. Kinnock:** Will the Prime Minister explain why Britain's inflation rate is nearly twice the European average?

**The Prime Minister:** It is at about the same level to which the last Labour Government would have loved to keep it down.

**Mr. Kinnock:** When does the Prime Minister expect Britain's inflation rate to fall to the European average?

**The Prime Minister:** My right hon. Friend the Chancellor of the Exchequer will get the inflation rate down, and it will come down over the rest of the lifetime of this Parliament.

**Mr. Kinnock:** Does the Prime Minister recall saying that Britain's rate of inflation started to rise because we were following the deutschmark? During her recent visit to Madrid, did she not agree that her objective was to return to shadowing the deutschmark?

**The Prime Minister:** No, not shadowing the deutschmark, but joining the exchange rate mechanism when certain conditions are fulfilled. Does the right hon. Gentleman recall that Labour holds the record for inflation this century? Under Labour, it reached 27 per cent.—more than one quarter of the value of the pound —in one year. That was Labour's record when the right hon. Gentleman was a Member of this House.

Q6. **Mr. Thurnham:** To ask the Prime Minister if she will list her official engagements for Thursday 29 June.

**The Prime Minister:** I refer my hon. Friend to the reply that I gave some moments ago.

**Mr. Thurnham:** Does my right hon. Friend agree with others that the standard of English in this country and the whole education of our children must be improved? Should not everyone support the Government's important reforms, which are designed to achieve that objective?

**The Prime Minister:** It is important that the standard of both English teaching and English education should be improved. We have set out specific curricular demands and attainment tests for that purpose. They will shortly be introduced in primary schools and then in secondary schools,to the great benefit of the children of this country.

Q8. **Mr. Madden:** To ask the Prime Minister if she will list her official engagements for Thursday 29 June.

**The Prime Minister:** I refer the hon. Gentleman to the reply that I gave some moments ago.

**Mr. Madden:** Will the Prime Minister take urgent action today to help industry in Yorkshire? Will she ask Sir David Alliance, the chairman of Coats Viyella to keep open CV Carpets in Batley, which is now threatened with closure and the loss of 140 jobs? Will she also have a word with her hon. Friend the Member for Sheffield, Hallam (Mr. Patnick), who is a director of Eversure Curtains where the staff are currently on strke in pursuit of trade union recognition? Will she urge him to grant recognition to that trade union and also to do something about increasing the wages of the machinists whom he employs, who are currently paid £61 for a 38-hour week?

**The Prime Minister:** On the hon. Gentleman's first question, no—closures are inevitably a matter for commercial judgment. *[Interruption.]* Yes, of course they are. The hon. Gentleman should be the first to recognise that Alliance Coats Viyella has done a very great deal to bring the textile industry right up to the latest best possible standards, both in investment and in design. We owe a great deal to it. It would be very good if some of those who criticise industry started up something themselves and made it succeed.

# European Council (Madrid)

3.31 pm

**The Prime Minister (Mrs. Margaret Thatcher):** With permission, Mr. Speaker, I should like to make a statement about the meeting of the European Council in Madrid on 26 and 27 June which I attended with my right hon. and learned Friend the Secretary of State for Foreign and Commonwealth Affairs.

The full conclusions of the Council have been placed in the Library of the House. Economic and monetary matters were the main item on the Council's agenda. Agreement was reached on four points.

First, the objective of progressive realisation of economic and monetary union was reaffirmed. This objective was first set in 1972 before Britain joined the Community and has subsequently been reaffirmed on numerous occasions, including in the Single European Act passed by this House, but no definition of it was agreed in Madrid.

Second, the report of the Delors committee, which sets out an approach to economic and monetary union by stages, was accepted as a basis for further work, but not the only basis. It will be possible to bring in other ideas and other approaches.

Third, the Council agreed that the measures necessary to achieve the first stage of progressive realisation of economic and monetary union will be implemented from 1 July 1990. These include completion of the single market, abolition of all foreign exchange controls, a free market in financial services and strengthening of the Community's competition policy by reducing state aids. They are all matters for which the United Kingdom has campaigned strongly and where we are well ahead of the great majority of our European partners.

No decisions were reached on what should follow this first stage, and stages 2 and 3 of the Delors report were not endorsed. Indeed, several delegations—not only the United Kingdom—made clear that they had substantial difficulties with them.

Fourth, it was agreed to carry out the preparatory work for the organisation of an eventual intergovernmental conference to lay down subsequent stages, but such a conference would meet only after implementation of the first stage has begun and when there has been full and adequate preparation. Its decisions would have to be reached by unanimity and would require ratification by this House.

In short, we made as much progress as can be made at this stage while leaving longer-term issues for further discussion by Finance Ministers and central bank workers over the months and years ahead. We have ensured that there is nothing automatic about the move to subsequent stages.

Very difficult issues remain to be resolved. As my right hon. Friend the Chancellor of the Exchequer has made clear, stages 2 and 3 of the Delors report would involve a massive transfer of sovereignty which I do not believe would be acceptable to this House. They would also mean, in practice, the creation of a federal Europe.

The Government support the objective of closer monetary co-operation, but will work for solutions which leave crucial economic decisions in our own hands. Although Britain's membership of the exchange rate mechanism of the European monetary system was not an issue at this Council, I reaffirmed our intention to join the ERM, but we must first get our inflation down. We shall look for satisfactory implementation of other aspects of the first phase of the Delors report, including free movement of capital and abolition of foreign exchange control.

The Council also discussed what is called the social dimension. On this the United Kingdom's record is very good, and I took with me to Madrid our own document setting out our substantial achievements in this field. We have also ratified the Council of Europe's social charter, unlike some of our Community colleagues. The Council's conclusions on this subject recognise that the highest priority is to create the conditions for more jobs. The Government do not believe that the Community's proposed social charter would help to achieve this aim. Indeed, we believe that imposing extra burdens on industry would make the Community less competitive. That is the main reason why my right hon. Friend the Secretary of State for Employment was unable to accept the conclusions of the June Social Affairs Council, and I confirmed that refusal in Madrid.

But the conclusions of the European Council brought out a very important point, raised by many Governments during the discussion: that national legislation and voluntary agreements have a legitimate role in achieving the Community's social dimension, and not everything has to be the subject of directives from the European Community. We shall be putting that view very strongly in the further discussions which will take place.

I shall summarise very briefly the outcome of the Council's discussions on the other main issues. The Council reaffirmed the priority task of completing the single market with the emphasis on the areas of particular importance for the United Kingdom—financial services, technical standards, transport and public purchasing. The Council's discussions demonstrated that there will not be a withholding tax on savings—a proposal which the United Kingdom has consistently opposed. The Council welcomed the progress being made in the fight against fraud in relation to the Community budget. The Council showed that there is wide acceptance of our need to keep checks at frontiers against drugs, terrorism and criminals while making free movement of ordinary, law-abiding citizens a greater reality.

In political co-operation, the Heads of State and Government expressed their utter condemnation of what has happened in China and agreed a series of measures which match those that the United Kingdom is already taking. The Council also expressed its understanding of the anxiety which has been caused in Hong Kong by the atrocious happenings in China.

I would like to congratulate the Spanish Government on their presidency of the EC over the past six months, and in particular on the progress made on the single market, with over 60 directives agreed. I also congratulate the Spanish Prime Minister, Señor Gonzales on bringing a difficult European Council to a successful conclusion.

The main outcome of the Council—agreement to implement a first phase of economic and monetary union —is very much in the interests of British industry and the City of London, while fully protecting the powers of this House. Far from being isolated, as some have claimed, the United Kingdom was able to play an important role in bringing the Council to these sensible and practical conclusions. It is in the same spirit of determination to strengthen co-operation with other members of the European Community, while arguing always for cutting constraints on enterprise and free competition and leaving to member states those decisions which properly belong to them, that we shall approach the undoubtedly difficult discussions of the Community's future which lie ahead.

**Mr. Neil Kinnock** (Islwyn): I am grateful to the Prime Minister for her statement.

On the important question of British participation in the exchange rate mechanism of the European monetary system, first, do the main conditions for entry into the exchange rate mechanism set down by the Prime Minister mean that she now accepts that exchange rate management must be the essential basis of monetary policy, as her Chancellor of the Exchequer believes?

Secondly, does she concur with her Chancellor's publicly stated view that he is
"certain that participation in the Exchange Rate Mechanism would strengthen both the stability of the pound and efforts to bring down inflation?"
If she does, would not membership of the ERM assist with efforts to bring down the present rate of inflation to European averages?

Thirdly, does the Prime Minister agree with the view of some of her right hon. Friends that participation in the exchange rate mechanism and the exercise of constructive influence in any development of stages 2 and 3 of the Delors report are essential if London is to remain a major financial centre? Does she accept that Britain would be in a better position to modify or remove less acceptable features of stages 2 and 3 if the pound were put into the ERM at an early date?

Fourthly, are not the conditions that the Prime Minister has laid down for participation in the exchange rate mechanism, most notably the condition that British inflation must be at the European average, just her way of saying that under her policies the pound will never join the exchange rate mechanism?

On the social charter, will the Prime Minister tell us why she is the only one of all the Community's Conservative leaders who rejects completely the proposals of the social charter? Does not the support for the charter by so many Governments right across the political spectrum in the Community reveal the Prime Minister's position as being isolationist, backward and disadvantageous to the British people?

Does the Prime Minister recall that after the NATO summit a month ago she said of the communiqué:
"wriggle as some people may, that is what they have signed up to"?
As at Madrid she was forced to accept a process that she had set out to stop, will she make an exception to her own rule and, just for once, try not to wriggle out of the commitments she has made?

**The Prime Minister:** On the exchange rate mechanism, our promise has been that we would go in when the time was right. I put conditions on that and made it much clearer that when those conditions were met we should be able to go in. One condition depends on us, which is that we get inflation well down, but some of the other conditions depend on the other members of the Community. Some of them belong to the exchange rate mechanism, but still protect their currencies by not having freedom of capital movements and by keeping foreign exchange control. It is quite different to stay in an exchange rate mechanism when one has foreign exchange control from when has abolished that foreign exchange control.

We shall see how the exchange rate mechanism holds up. I hope that it holds up reasonably well. The bands are very different for the particular currencies, but the abolition of foreign exchange controls will be a major event for the exchange rate mechanism.

On stages 2 and 3, many other people share our view that the——

**Mr. Tony Banks** (Newham, North-West): Name them.

**The Prime Minister:** Other people share our view that the stages set out in the Delors report are not the right stages.

I will name a person. I gladly respond to the hon. Gentleman's shouting. Karl Otto Poehl, the governor of the Bundesbank, in a speech on 22 June, said:
"I myself doubt whether the time has come for such a comprehensive renunciation of sovereignty, namely the transfer of monetary powers to supranational institutions. I can only repeat what I said a little while ago. Neither a single currency nor a European central bank is necessary for an economic and monetary union to function. What is more important is that the member states pursue a consistent policy."
That is a very effective demonstration.

On the social charter, as I have said, some of the people round that table had not yet ratified the Council of Europe social charter, which we have signed and ratified, and which is here. They also pointed out that if they were to have anything like as good social services as we have they would require large subsidies of money from the bigger nations in the European Community. They again pointed out that the history of social services and membership of trade unions was totally different in many different countries. Therefore, the principle of what was called subsidiarity should come into play—the central Commission should not take unto itself powers that could quite well be carried out at national level—and that was included in the communiqué. We were instrumental in creating that communiqué and we shall be instrumental in carrying it out.

**Mr. Julian Amery** (Brighton, Pavilion): Does my right hon. Friend agree that one of the most important decisions taken at Madrid was that, in the preparations for the eventual intergovernmental conference, the Delors report, valuable though it is, would not be the only document considered?

Will my right hon. Friend instruct the Treasury and the Bank of England to carry out a detailed review of the operation of the sterling area between 1931 and the 1960s? Sterling was never a single currency; it was a reserve currency. The Bank of England was its heart, but it was never its central bank. The Governments of other countries that were part of the sterling area continued to retain their own central banks and, of course, their own control of budgetary and fiscal policy. Is it not important that the Government should put forward proposals that reflect the British vision of a united Europe?

**The Prime Minister:** My right hon. Friend is absolutely right. The Delors report will not be the only document taken into account in considering how to come to closer monetary and economic union. We shall be able to put up alternative schemes. It is clear that the governor of the Bundesbank thought that there were alternative schemes.

[*The Prime Minister*]

Our way is to co-operate through voluntary action, which we believe will achieve the same objective. We will, of course, look at the sterling area, in which this country has unique experience, because it could be valuable in the next stage of the Community's deliberations. I am grateful to my right hon. Friend.

**Mr. Paddy Ashdown** (Yeovil): The right hon. Lady would be amazed if the rest of us were so naive as to believe her description of events. Anyone who listened to it would be bound to take it with, to coin a phrase, a large "sackful of salt". When will the Prime Minister realise that Britain's long-term best interests will be served by Britain helping to shape and being part of European integration rather than always being seen to be a block and barrier to it? Is it not odd that the line on economic and monetary integration which she defended in Madrid is almost exactly the same little Englander line that was put forward in the Labour party's European manifesto?

**The Prime Minister:** I should have thought that the right hon. Gentleman could do better than that. Twelve nations signed the communiqué. The right hon. Gentleman seems to despise them all—nearly the whole of Europe.

Stage 1 of the Delors report is agreed. That is a quantum leap. It includes many other aspects of work that we' must do in the Community, for example, on the internal market—which will be a quantum leap when it has been completed by 1992—the freedom of capital movement, abolition of foreign exchange controls and reduction of subsidies, so that there is much freer competition throughout the Community. That is a major step forward. I should have thought that the right hon. Gentleman could at least welcome it.

**Sir Bernard Braine** (Castle Point): Will my right hon. Friend accept the warm congratulations of Conservative Members and, I suspect, many people elsewhere on her remarkable achievement in Madrid, especially on rallying the support of some member states which, like us, are not enamoured of the idea of a bureaucratically controlled Community which would reduce national Parliaments to rubber-stamping machines? Does not Britain now have an opportunity to shape the future economic and social patterns of the Community in accordance with the wishes of all the people?

**The Prime Minister:** My right hon. Friend is absolutely right. Several members of the Community are deeply disturbed by the transfer of sovereignty in stages 2 and 3, especially those whose Parliaments are central to their democratic processes. Parliaments have a varying significance to several nations of the Community. Many expressed doubts similar to those that we expressed; others do not want to be under the domination of a German-French axis, and therefore wish to develop different mechanisms. We shall do exactly what my right hon. Friend said—develop a system that is right for all members of the Community so that they can go forward on a voluntary and fully agreed basis which we can bring before the House for approval.

**Dr. David Owen** (Plymouth, Devonport): Is the Prime Minister against any system of European central banks, especially a system that has the same anti-inflationary

pressures as witnessed by the Bundesbank? Does she rule out even parallel currencies? If she is as anxious as many hon. Members about a creeping movement towards a federal Europe—[Hon. Members: "Oh."] Yes, against a federal Europe. The central principle is to preserve the right of the House to fix rates of direct taxation and of the House and the Government to fix their own borrowing requirements.

**The Prime Minister:** Under stages 2 and 3 of the Delors report, we should lose some of the rights to which the right hon. Gentleman refers. That just would not be acceptable to the House, for which such rights are central to the control of Parliament over the Executive.

With regard to the other points which the right hon. Gentleman made, we look for a way forward by voluntary agreement and co-operation to which we can gladly give our support steadily to work together more closely. That is the way forward.

**Mr. Teddy Taylor** (Southend, East): Is the Prime Minister aware that people of all opinions about the EEC greatly admire her courage in trying to make the Common Market more workable and sensible and less bureaucratic? Does she think that it is a tragedy for our democracy that a party that at one time claimed to represent working people, who gave their lives and guts to fight for democracy and for people to be able to control decisions, is now prepared to pass that to bureaucrats? That party is led by someone who is little more than a Jacques Delors stooge.

**The Prime Minister:** One of the most worrying features of following stages 2 and 3 of the Delors report would be that the Council of Twelve, or the central bank governors, would have the deciding say in the guidelines to which the rest of us would have to agree. Those central bank governors would not be democratically accountable in any way.

**Mr. Frank Dobson** (Holborn and St. Pancras): But the right hon. Lady just quoted the boss of the Bundesbank with approval.

**The Prime Minister:** Certainly they would not. They would be much less democratically accountable than the Bundesbank is under the exchange rate mechanism as it currently operates. It is usual for the Government to be practical in their approach to Europe and to sort things out. That was our approach to the common agricultural policy—where surpluses are now right down—to the European budget, which is now on a reasonable basis, and to the internal market, with which we are steadily going ahead. Although it was right in the treaty of Rome at the beginning, it has not yet been achieved. It will be achieved by 1992 largely because we sought to make it one of our top priorities.

**Mr. Nigel Spearing** (Newham, South): Will the Prime Minister confirm that successive Conservative Prime Ministers signed the treaty of accession to the European Community and the Single European Act without an electoral mandate or the prior permission of the House? Is it not also true that initially the Government opposed the Single European Act? What is to prevent a similar reversal on a treaty to bring in economic and monetary union? Is it not clear that the acts and aspirations of the Prime Minister and of the right hon. Members for Old Bexley and Sidcup (Mr. Heath) and for Henley (Mr. Heseltine) have stripped the powers of this House and therefore have denied the British people the right to determine their own legislation, their own taxation and—under economic and monetary union—their own effective Government?

**The Prime Minister:** The hon. Gentleman is quite correct in that successive Labour and Conservative Governments have gone ahead and negotiated with Europe and have signed communiqués with Europe and that is part of the duty of Governments in negotiating with other Governments within the European Community. I refer the hon. Gentleman to the conclusions of The Hague European Council meeting held in November 1976— which he will recognise took place during the time of a Labour Government:

"The achievement of economic and monetary union is basic to the consolidation of Community solidarity and the establishment of European union."

There were similar references at European Councils in December 1974, July 1978 and December 1978. Yes, we have both been carrying out the duties of Government in negotiating with other Governments. Usually we have included in our manifesto the kind of Europe that we wish to see, and the hon. Gentleman is aware of the Europe that we wish to see. I had thought that we could get to a proper Common Market without a Single European Act. The hon. Gentleman is aware that the Single European Act, for the purposes of achieving a single market, made more of the directives subject to majority voting, but kept certain of the essential features, such as taxation, subject to unanimous voting, and I think that that was absolutely vital.

**Mr. Cranley Onslow** (Woking): Is my right hon. Friend aware that there will be as warm a welcome in the country as there has been in this House for her reaffirmation that any transfer of sovereignty to implement Delors stages 2 and 3 would be totally unacceptable? There will also be a welcome for what she said about progress in Europe not depending on EEC directives alone. May I congratulate my right hon. Friend on one particular achievement out of many in Madrid, and that is her skill in succeeding in getting the French Government to commit themselves unequivocally and unconditionally to the objectives for 1990 which we have supported for so long.

**The Prime Minister:** The communiqué makes it quite clear that stage 1 of the Delors report must begin to be implemented by July 1990. We have already done many of those things, and when we are arguing in Europe one of our great strengths is that in practical terms we are way ahead of many of our European partners in what we have actually done as distinct from what we say. We keep our promises. We have freedom of capital movement and we have abolished exchange controls. We actually deal in the ecu and we have issued securities in the ecu. We are quite prepared to have—and indeed have—various European currencies in our reserve. That is way ahead of many countries.

**Mr. Peter Shore** (Bethnal Green and Stepney): There is uncertainty and anxiety about what precisely the Prime Minister agreed to in Madrid. Will she confirm that her conditional acceptance of stage 1 in no way commits us to acceptance of stage 2 or stage 3? Will she also pledge herself to oppose strenuously any proposal for economic

or monetary union, as the Delors plan envisages, which would transfer from Britain and its Parliament powers that are essential to economic self-government?

**The Prime Minister:** I thought that I had made it clear in my statement, although it is a complicated statement because we were dealing with a very complicated subject, that we have accepted stage 1 of the Delors report, which will not surprise the right hon. Gentleman. He knows that we accept the completion of the single market in any event. We accept abolition of foreign exchange controls—indeed, we have already done it—and we have been the first in seeking to get subsidies reduced across Europe. We have accepted all of those and are starting to implement them. That is stage 1.

We have not accepted stage 2 or stage 3. I was the only one really to refer to paragraph 39 in the Delors report —the hon. Gentleman will realise the significance of that —because I said that we did not accept that. Paragraph 39 attempted to say that, if one accepts any part of the report, one must be taken as accepting the whole. We totally and utterly rejected that, and so did the final communiqué. It was just an attempt to coerce us, and we would have nothing of it.

I hope that I also indicated that major derogations of national sovereignty of the kind in the Delors report, in which we give up fundamental functions with regard to monetary, fiscal economic policy to a group of central bank governors who are not democratically accountable, would not be acceptable to this House or to me in any way. I hope, therefore, that we can get further by co-operation. What matters is following consistent policies and not handing over responsibility to other bodies.

**Mr. David Curry** (Skipton and Ripon): Will my right hon. Friend accept Conservative Members' congratulations on demoting the status of holy writ that was attached to the Delors report and on making it clear that economic and monetary union are not the same things? Does she agree that, until there are further documents on the table, discussion is bound to centre on the Delors report? Therefore, will it not be in the interests of the United Kingdom for my right hon. Friend to put on the table her own proposals on how to enhance monetary co-operation so that countries that are deeply disturbed by the Delors report and people such as the president of the Bundesbank have an alternative paper on which discussions can be focused? That practice worked successfully in the case of fiscal harmonisation.

**The Prime Minister:** My hon. Friend is absolutely right. We shall be working out alternative proposals, and I hope that other people will do so, too, so that they are on the table to be considered during this interim stage. Other economists will be working upon it. It is very different from the approach of the Delors report, which seems to start from federation and then work backwards and pass major rights of national sovereignty to a kind of federated body. We will follow my hon. Friend's advice.

**Dr. Dafydd Elis Thomas** (Meirionnydd Nant Conwy): When she reports back to the House on European Council meetings, why does the Prime Minister refer to discussions of social policy in terms of what is called the social dimension? Will she now confirm or deny whether she believes that the social dimension of Community policy exists as a linguistic and socio-economic reality? Does she

[*Dr. Dafydd Elis Thomas*]

now accept that, for all other members of the Community, the social dimension is as much a part of European reality as the economic drive to the single market?

**The Prime Minister:** Yes. The most important aspect of the social dimension—the hon. Gentleman will find it in the communiqué—is development and job creation. This country has outshone any other in the European Community in the number of jobs that we have created in the past three years. It has been absolutely at the top of the scale on social dimension.

With regard to the social charter, many other countries would wish that they had social policies, social security policies, national health services and housing benefits as good as ours, and they openly admit that they could not possibly afford them without massive subventions from the rest of us. As we have already paid £2 billion this year to the Community, I do not think that we can undertake any more.

**Mr. Terence L. Higgins** (Worthing): In the further difficult negotiations that lie ahead, will my right hon. Friend stress that, over the centuries, the power of this House has rested on the control of money, both taxation and public expenditure, and that, contrary to the suggestion in the Delors report, the mass of expert evidence published by the Treasury Committee makes it clear that monetary union would not require countries to abdicate control over fiscal policy? Will my right hon. Friend make sure that that point is made clear in the forthcoming document as an alternative to the Delors report, which she has just promised?

**The Prime Minister:** I agree with my right hon. Friend. One of the problems of the Delors report was that, instead of defining several different ways of having European monetary and economic union, it set out on just one particular formula, and then set out the stages to that. Normally, if one commissions a report, one expects several options to be given, and the benefits and disadvantages of each to be weighed. That is what we must achieve.

**Ms. Joyce Quin** (Gateshead, East): The communiqué states that social aspects should clearly be given the same importance as economic aspects in the creation of a single market. Given that statement, which of the social methods that the Prime Minister has hitherto blocked is she now prepared to agree to so that some progress many be made?

**The Prime Minister:** Yes, that is in the communiqué. If the hon. Lady looks at it she will also find that the most important issue in the social aspect is job creation and development, without which we would not have the wealth to create the rest of the social services. That is more or less understood by the people round the table. In the communiqué they also said that they thought that both voluntary agreement and national legislation had a great part to play in the social aspect of the Community, and should not be centralised through the Commission.

**Mr. John Marshall** (Hendon, South): Does my right hon. Friend agree that it ill behoves the Socialist President of France to lecture this country on progress towards European monetary union when he imposes restrictions on the ability of his fellow citizens to move their money across Europe? What would be the impact of the Madrid

agreement if attempts were made to reintroduce exchange controls into this country, as recommended by the Labour party?

**The Prime Minister:** The whole future of the internal market, free market, free movement of capital and one of the central parts of the European Community would go. It is designed for freer movement of money, goods and people, and that cannot be achieved unless we abolish foreign exchange control in all its forms. That has yet to be done by France and Italy, which are members of the European exchange rate mechanism. I hope that when they abolish their exchange controls, the European exchange rate mechanism will hold. It will be a considerable step forward.

**Mr. Jack Ashley** (Stoke-on-Trent, South): Is the Prime Minister aware that her attitude towards the Community's proposed social charter is a logical extension of her attitude in Britain towards workers, wages, conditions and trade union rights, and that that is reflected in the hard line being adopted by many public service employers is Britain? There can be no doubt where responsibility lies for the wave of strikes and industrial unrest. It lies in No. 10 Downing street.

**The Prime Minister:** Nonsense. Perhaps the right hon. Gentleman did not hear me earlier when I said that I had taken full accounts of our social policies, and handed them out. Far from there being any criticism of our social policy, there was a good deal of acclamation for the work that we had undertaken, and a good deal of agreement that social policy is right for the national Parliament to legislate upon and not right for the Commission to have major directives upon. There was also a good deal of agreement that the membership of people in trade unions varied enormously across the Community—from about 15 per cent. in one country to more than 50 per cent. in others—the history and legal systems were different and it was not a right and proper matter for the Community to legislate on. There was no criticism whatever of Britain's position, nor should there be because we are already operating many things in the charter to a far higher level than are some other countries.

**Mr. David Howell** (Guildford): Bearing in mind what my right hon. Friend says about Britain being well ahead in many of these matters, did she have a chance to raise with Chancellor Kohl in Madrid the issue of the inward looking and anti-competitive structure of German industrial ownership, particularly in financial services? Is not that a matter in which majority voting, which has served this country well on many matters, could be used to crack open this cartelised criss-cross of holdings which works directly against the emergence of a single free market in Europe, which we want?

**The Prime Minister:** I agree with my right hon. Friend. The German insurance and investment industries, for example, are very much more protected than ours; ours are much more open. Considerable restrictions are placed on investment of German insurance and pension funds. Again, we tend to be much more open.

I did not mention the matter to Herr Kohl on this occasion, but it is well known, and it is one of the reasons for our difficulties in getting some of the financial services directives approved. I know that my right hon. Friend will be very pleased that the second banking directive has now been approved, and we have made financial services one of the top priorities for going ahead with the next six months of directives.

**Mr. Brian Sedgemore** (Hackney, South and Shoreditch): Why is the Prime Minister so reluctant to allow the British people to benefit from Europe's renaissance and play a part in the next European revolution? Does she not understand that the 20th-century notion of a nation state is becoming as irrelevant, tired and tiresome as she is?

**The Prime Minister:** It took us a long time to get rid of the effects of the French revolution 200 years ago, and we do not want another.

**Sir Peter Tapsell** (East Lindsey): Was not the clear indication of the recent remarks of the governor of the Bundesbank about the exchange rate mechansim—quoted by my right hon. Friend—that he feared that, contrary to widespread popular belief, it might turn out to be an instrument for inflation rather than deflation? Does not that bear out the unwisdom of treating technical and practical matters as though they had some theological significance?

**The Prime Minister:** My hon. Friend is absolutely right. The exchange rate mechanism is, of course, anchored to the deutschmark. For historic reasons, the German people's greatest fear is and always has been inflation, just as for years ours was unemployment. Inflation has led them to have an independent Bundesbank and to keep inflation right down, and others are therefore geared to that as well. If we were to proceed to Delors stages 2 and 3, that would be determined not by a nation whose policies are so anchored in nil inflation but by a number of nations that might find it easier to have higher inflation. I think, therefore, that the Bundesbank governor is right to be a bit fearful of the consequences.

**Mr. Win Griffiths** (Bridgend): Can the Prime Minister confirm that anyone who read the full text of the declaration of economic and monetary union and the conclusions of the presidency will find that, along with the 11 other Heads of Government, she agreed that the Delors report was a good basis for further work on economic and monetary union, that it fulfilled the obligations laid down at Hanover, that it agreed that stage 1 should be launched on 1 July 1990 and that there would subsequently be an intergovernmental agreement to carry on with the second and third stages? Can the Prime Minister rebut the press reports of her comments that she would vote against such a conference and that the move to the second and third stages was not automatic?

**The Prime Minister:** As I said in my statement, the Delors report is one basis for further work, but not the only basis. That was recognised, and that is why it was put into the communiqué in such a way. We fully agree that stage 1 should start on 1 July 1990. As the hon. Gentleman knows, we are already well ahead and already operating a good deal of the Delors report.

The preamble of the Single European Act refers to the original

"objective of the progressive realization of Economic and Monetary Union,"

which goes right back to the conference in Paris on 19 to 21 October 1972. We are not talking just about economic and monetary union; we are talking about its progressive realisation, which allows a much more measured time so that we get each stage right before we go on the next.

Later in the Single European Act—passed by this House—there is a heading:

"Co-operation in Economic and Monetary policy (Economic and Monetary Union)".

That seems to indicate that economic and monetary union consists of co-operation in economic and monetary policy, which suggest that there will be ways of achieving it other than the one in the Delors report.

**Mr. Nicholas Budgen** (Wolverhampton, South-West): Will my right hon. Friend confirm that when, in 1979, foreign exchange controls were abolished in this country it was in anticipation that the pound would freely float for the foreseeable future? Will she further anticipate that the French and other countries in the EEC may be somewhat reluctant to abolish their foreign exchange controls in a fixed rate mechanism and that therefore, sadly, our pound may not go into the exchange rate mechanism as early as some of our friends in the EEC had hoped?

**The Prime Minister:** I accept that the abolition of foreign exchange controls will be a very important event for those big currencies in the exchange rate mechanism which still rely on foreign exchange controls to keep within the relevant bands to which they have agreed. I also agree with my hon. Friend that if one goes to an absolutely fixed rate, which is proposed by the Delors report, without any latitude, I think that many of my other colleagues in the European Community would not like that and would feel that it put in a rigid rate which could create distortions elsewhere.

As often happens in the Community, we get such reports and generally people say, "We will consider them further." When they come to look at the detail, they too realise that they could not carry them out in some of the particular details that are mentioned in that report. I think that the fixed exchange rate is one that would come under considerable criticism and people could not do it; they prefer much wider bands, similar to those available at present.

**Mr. Ron Leighton** (Newham, North-East): Does the Prime Minister ever read the small print of what she agrees to? She agreed to the Single European Act. We did not. She agreed at Hanover to the setting up of the Delors committee to work out the details of economic and monetary union. Why does she always bluff and bluster before conferences, and then give way when it comes to the crunch? If there is to be a central bank, to whom will it be responsible and accountable? What is the point of electing Members of Parliament to this place if economic policy is to be decided somewhere else? Is not the truth that, although the right hon. Lady is kicking and screaming, she is nevertheless being dragged along?

**The Prime Minister:** I am not sure from what the hon. Gentleman said whether he is for or against the view that I have taken. He was not exactly clear in his remarks. If anyone was kicking and screaming, that was not happening from this Dispatch Box but from the Opposition Benches.

I agree with the hon. Gentleman about a central bank. It is described briefly in the Delors report. It is not accountable to anyone, and that was precisely one of my great complaints. It has no democratic accountability, far

[*The Prime Minister*]

less than the Bundesbank has at present, and I did not think that that would be acceptable to the British parliamentary system. So we are agreed on that.

When it comes to an intergovernmental conference, then I must say, as happened over the Single European Act, that one learns by experience that an intergovernmental conference can be called by a simple majority of countries there, and it can be called at any time that one can get a simple majority. Hence such a conference could be called.

Its conclusions would have to be agreed by unanimity, but before that happened the great effort that we made, and made successfully, was to throw enough doubt on the Delors report—in which we were assisted by many other colleagues—to make it clear that other ways forward must be considered. There are other ways of going progressively and steadily towards a different definition of monetary and economic union by, as Karl Otto Poehl says, consistently following similar policies but without direction.

**Sir Anthony Meyer** (Clwyd, North-West): The Liverpool *Daily Post* on Monday carried a headline saying "PM into battle with Europe." Will my right hon. Friend take this opportunity to make it plain that it was not in that spirit that she set out in Madrid to advance British interests in the Community?

**The Prime Minister:** My right hon. Friends and I had spent a considerable time studying the Delors report. The Chancellor of the Exchequer had set out his views extremely clearly in two speeches, one at Chatham house and one to the Institute of Directors. We went there to do as much as we could to try to get our viewpoint over to others and to try to get them along with us. Right at the beginning we had some people with us, and between us we convinced others that it would not be right to accept stages 2 and 3 of the Delors report. Nor would it be right just to consider that as one way only towards monetary and economic union. It was by steady study of the report and by steady and consistent argument that we won the day, and we have, as a result, the communiqué.

**Mrs. Ann Clwyd** (Cynon Valley): Given that one of the main aims of the treaty of Rome is to reduce the gap between the rich and the poor, and that the recently published Office of Population Censuses and Surveys study on population trends in Britain shows that the gap is substantial and getting bigger, is this one of the aims of the treaty that the Prime Minister would like to see amended? If not, what proposals has she to reduce the gap between the rich and the poor, both in Britain and in the Community?

**The Prime Minister:** There is only one way, and that is, as the communiqué puts it, by steady development and job creation. We do it not by speeches but by having a system of enterprise and incentive, which enables the creation of wealth, which enables much better and greatly improved social services. Many there were impressed by the social services that we have. The new report from the OPCS, shows that the statistics on infant mortality have again considerably improved all over the United Kingdom.

**Mr. James Kilfedder** (North Down): As a committed European, I congratulate the Prime Minister on the skill and tenacity that she showed at the Madrid conference.

This brought about a successful conclusion, which may lead to greater co-operation between European nations without further loss of national sovereignty. Are the other European leaders aware of the danger posed by terrorists using the freedom of movement of people between member states? What steps are being taken to deal with the issue?

**The Prime Minister:** My hon. Friend put it rightly when he said that we wish to have closer co-operation by voluntary means without surrendering national sovereignty to bodies that would not be democratically accountable. I notice that the 1971 White Paper, upon which the European Communities Act, through which we joined the Community, was founded, said:

"Like any other treaty, the Treaty of Rome commits its signatories to support agreed aims: but the commitment represents the voluntary undertaking of a sovereign state to observe policies which it has helped to form. There is no question of any erosion of essential national sovereignty".

As to frontiers, the removal of certain physical barriers, terrorism, drugs and criminal activity, I remind my hon. Friend that at the end of the Single European Act there is a general declaration, which all member states signed, saying:

"Nothing in these provisions shall affect the right of member states to take such measures as they consider necessary for the purpose of controlling immigration from third countries, and to combat terrorism, crime, the traffic in drugs and illicit trading in works of art and antiques." Once again, I drew the attention of European colleagues to that solemn general declaration which was made at the same time as the Single European Act was passed.

**Several Hon. Members** *rose——*

**Mr. Speaker:** Order. I remind the House that after this we have a further statement—the business statement—the Second Reading of a Bill and then opposed private business at 7 o'clock. I shall take three more questions from each side and then we must move on.

**Mr. Dick Douglas** (Dunfermline, West): We accept that what the Prime Minister has done has bought a little time in which she can learn some of the lessons of history. They show that, in the management of currency, any international organisation set up to do this will manage it in the interests of the dominant currency or country. For example, the gold standard was managed in the interests of sterling, Bretton Woods was managed in the interests of the dollar and the European monetary system is managed in the interests of the deutschmark. If we repeatedly stand on the side, we shall be held continuously at a competitive disadvantage. Will the Prime Minister accept that her strictures about democratic control in relation to macroeconomic policy and fiscal policy would carry much more weight if she showed greater respect for this institution, the House of Commons? Does she accept that her negotiating posture is a wasting asset in relation to Europe?

**Mr. Speaker:** Briefly, please.

**Mr. Douglas:** Will she give time in the coming recess to thinking of moving over and being replaced by somebody much more suitable?

**The Prime Minister:** I will not take lessons from anyone about respect for the House of Commons. I think that the hon. Gentleman will find that my record of attending on Tuesdays and Thursdays has exceeded that of any other

Prime Minister. Also, if he looks throughout the Community, I think that he will find that there are not many who are making statements in their own Parliaments about what happened in Madrid. There is a statement in the Danish Parliament and possibly in the Netherlands Parliament, but others do not have their Prime Ministers under the kind of cross-examination that I welcome because it enables one to get several facts across to the Opposition.

**Sir Peter Hordern** (Horsham): May I congratulate my right hon. Friend most warmly on her firm commitment to join the exchange rate mechanism? Is she aware that one of the conditions that she has set out lies not fully within our control—the abolition of exchange controls? Will she therefore have a word with Mr. Mitterrand and tell him that life in the Community without exchange controls is very agreeable and that it is most unlikely that there will be a flood of money leaving France as a result of abolishing exchange controls since the French people will pursue their timeless custom of keeping their gold under their beds no matter what Government are in power?

**The Prime Minister:** I thank my hon. Friend. The French are now committed to abolition of exchange controls in 1990. As my hon. Friend is aware, they tried to impose certain capital taxes on others before they would agree to abolition. We put up a tremendous fight, as did others, and we were successful. The French did not get the imposition of an extra capital tax or the withholding of tax on capital. They are now committed to 1990. I think that Spain is committed to 1992. It will be an important step when they take it, but I agree that it is a vital one for them to take.

**Ms. Marjorie Mowlam** (Redcar): In view of the comments of the Prime Minister in the House this afternoon about the Delors report—that it is a way forward and that parts of it are now acceptable—will she tell us whether she still considers it to be Marxist, or has she mellowed since Madrid?

**The Prime Minister:** I do not think that anyone has ever said that it was Marxist. What we have said is that it transfers a fundamental part of the sovereignty of a sovereign Parliament to a group of people, which is a great centralising feature where there is no democratic control. That is totally and utterly wrong, whatever one calls it.

**Mr. Jonathan Aitken** (Thanet, South): May I congratulate my right hon. Friend on her very nimble footwork in Madrid which seems to have led her to moving away from the previously preferred menu of Europe à la carte into serving up an interesting new dish of good old British fudge which will take the EC a very long time to digest? Can she confirm that none of the Delors proposals which survived into this superbly fudged Madrid communiqué is irresistible or irreversible?

**The Prime Minister:** I can only confirm that we did not accept stages 2 and 3, that they are to be considered along with other proposals, that it was clear from the speeches that were made that many other colleagues did not accept the details of stages 2 and 3 and did not like the very great transfer of sovereignty that would be involved in their Parliaments, and that those Parliaments that did not like it were those where the democratic process is at its most obvious. I do not think that it is necessarily a fudge. My hon. Friend is right that it has bought time to do a lot more work on how to co-operate on the next stage. That is the way that I would put it.

**Mr. John P. Smith** (Vale of Glamorgan): Will the Prime Minister tell the House and the country precisely what it is in the social charter that she finds so objectionable? Is it the right to fair pay, the right to clean, safe and decent working conditions, equal rights for men and women, or what?

**The Prime Minister:** No. It is the imposition of many things upon which we already have our own national legislation or our own national policy, derived from our history and from our particular kind of law, which is very different from the law in the Community, and the feeling that if each and every country is to have imposed upon it some of the ways of other countries in addition to their own we shall have maximum costs on industry and finish up with a highly protected Europe which would suit some people, but not us.

**Mr. Ian Taylor** (Esher): Will my right hon. Friend accept my congratulations on her positive statement this afternoon and on the fact that in Madrid 10 of our fellow partners in the EC were very much on our side in adopting our step-by-step approach to commitment to economic and monetary union—an approach which was well prepared by the Chancellor of the Exchequer at a meeting a few weeks earlier? During the period that we have to prepare for stage 1 of the Delors report, will the Government do their utmost to ensure that we meet the conditions that are imposed and that we put maximum pressure on our partners in the Community to meet the conditions that we believe should be imposed on them so that we are more than ready to join the exchange rate mechanism at the earliest possible date?

**The Prime Minister:** Yes. I hope that stage 1 will go well because the completion of the internal market on its own is in all our interests and was one of the things that we joined the Community for in the first place. We still have to meet some of the directives, some of which are the most difficult, but I hope that we shall get well ahead with that. I hope that the foreign exchange controls will be abolished in 1990 and that we shall see the steady removal of subsidies in industries across Europe because while they exist there cannot be fair competition. We shall attempt to carry out our part of the bargain and to persuade others to carry out theirs.

We have agreed to the progressive realisation of economic and monetary union. It is not a sudden thing. We shall go steadily towards it taking one step at a time and in that way achieve a much more certain future than we would if we were pressured into something in which we did not believe.

# Business of the House

4.33 pm

**The Lord President of the Council and Leader of the House of Commons (Mr. John Wakeham):** With permission, Mr. Speaker, I should like to make a statement about the business for next week.

MONDAY 3 JULY—Supplemental timetable motion on and progress on consideration of Lords amendments to the Water Bill.

TUESDAY 4 JULY—Until seven o'clock, completion of consideration of Lords amendments to the Water Bill.

Second Reading of the Antarctic Minerals Bill *[Lords]*.

Completion of remaining stages of the Road Traffic (Driver Licensing and Information Systems) Bill *[Lords]*.

WEDNESDAY 5 JULY—Opposition Day (17th Allotted Day). Until about seven o'clock there will be a debate entitled "The Crisis in Training". Afterwards there will be a debate entitled "The Immigration Rules and DNA Testing." Both debates will arise on Opposition motions.

Committee and remaining stages of the Representation of the People Bill.

THURSDAY 6 JULY—Estimates Day (2nd Allotted Day). There will be debates on common police services and expenditure on information technology. Details of the Estimates concerned and the relevant Select Committee reports will be given in the *Official Report*.

Remaining stages of the Human Organ Transplants Bill.

FRIDAY 7 JULY—Private Members' Bills.

MONDAY 10 JULY—Estimates Day (3rd Allotted Day). There will be debates on Department of Energy administration and civil aviation services. Details of the Estimates concerned and the relevant Select Committee reports will be given in the *Official Report*.

*[Thursday 6 July*

*Estimate:*

*Class XI, Vote 3 (Home Office administration, immigration and police support services, England and Wales), so far as it relates to common police services.*

*Relevant Select Committee Reports:*

*Home Affairs Committee 1st Report, Session 1988-89 on the Forensic Science Service (HC 26) and the Government's response (CM 699).*

*Home Affairs Committee 3rd Report, Session 1988-89 on Higher Police Training and the Police Staff College (HC 110).*

*Home Affairs Committee 4th Report, Session 1988-89 on Home Office Expenditure (HC 314).*

*Estimate:*

*Class V, Vote 2 (Department of Trade and Industry: support for industry), so far as it relates to expenditure on information technology.*

*Relevant Select Committee Reports:*

*Trade and Industry Committee 1st Report, Session 1988-89 on Information Technology (HC 25), and the Oral Evidence given on 26 April (HC 338).]*

**Mr. Frank Dobson** (Holborn and St. Pancras): I thank the Leader of the House for his statement. I start by thanking the Government for accepting the Opposition's arguments that the Antarctic Minerals Bill is of such significance, not just to us but to the future of the planet, that it is sensible to debate it at a reasonable hour.

Having expressed my thanks, I must express my concern at the proposal to dispose of the Water Bill in a further day and a half. The Bill is currently 416 pages long and there are 55 pages of Lords amendments to be considered. I understand that the Government have put down a further 300 amendments, though they are not yet available in the Vote Office for anyone who wants to know what they are about. That means that, at best, each amendment will receive less than one minute's scrutiny.

In view of the importance that the Prime Minister said today she attaches to parliamentary scrutiny and sovereignty, does the Leader of the House agree that it would be better to devote a little more time to the Water Bill, particularly as to do so might relieve his right hon. Friend the Secretary of State for the Environment of future appearances in the courts? Even his short measures usually end up with him losing cases in the High Court. We believe that it is right and proper that more than one and a half days should be devoted to that very important legislation.

I hope there is support from right hon. and hon. Members in all parts of the House for a debate before the recess on the situation in China and in Hong Kong, in the light of recent events and of the recent visits by the Foreign Secretary and by my right hon. Friend the shadow Foreign Secretary to Hong Kong.

Finally, I return to my two old chestnuts. When is there likely to be a statement by the Government on the Griffiths report "Care in the Community", and shall we have an opportunity to debate their response before the recess? When may we expect the long-promised debate on the proposal to substitute student grants by student loans? Will there be one before the recess, or will the right hon. Gentleman wait until the students return to their studies in the autumn?

**Mr. Wakeham:** The hon. Gentleman asked five questions in relation to next week's business. I thank him for his remark about the Antarctic Minerals Bill. That is an important measure, and I believe that the time we have found is satisfactory to all concerned.

The time we have allocated to the Water Bill is more than adequate for dealing with the amendments, as the majority of them are technical. As to the hon. Gentleman's reference to my right hon. Friend the Secretary of State for the Environment, I seem to remember him winning court cases rather than losing them.

**Mr. Dobson:** He loses more than he wins.

**Mr. Wakeham:** My right hon. Friend has had a winning streak recently, which is more than can be said for the hon. Gentleman.

As to the important question of China and Hong Kong, I recognise the need for at least a foreign affairs debate shortly. I hope to find time for one in the relatively near future, and that matter will be discussed through the usual channels.

The Government intend to make a statement about the Griffiths proposals before the summer recess, and there will be a debate in Government time at a suitable opportunity thereafter. I cannot promise exactly when that will be.

Although the hon. Gentleman asks me about student top-up loans every week, it seems that he still does not understand our proposals—which is a very good reason for a debate. My right hon. Friend the Secretary of State for Education and Science and I have both made it clear already that we would welcome such a debate, but its timing is best discussed through the usual channels.

**Sir Fergus Montgomery** (Altrincham and Sale): I draw my right hon. Friend's attention to early-day motion 1038.

*[That this House deplores the remarks of the honourable Member for Brent, East during the adjournment debate on Tuesday 27th June in which he alleged that the late Airey Neave was involved in treason; notes that Airey Neave had been decorated for gallantry on four occasions, and had served his country with honour in war and peace; and calls on the honourable Member for Brent, East to apologise to the House and to withdraw his disgraceful remarks.]*

That early-day motion concerns the Adjournment debate on 27 June and the remarks of the hon. Member for Brent, East (Mr. Livingstone), who said that the late Airey Neave was involved in terrorism. [HON. MEMBERS: "Treason."] Rather, that the late Airey Neave was involved in treason. If those remarks had been made about any existing right hon. or hon. Member, the hon. Member for Brent, East would have had to withdraw them immediately. Will my right hon. Friend consider whether there is any way to prevent such a thing happening again? Airey Neave had a war record of great bravery, gave great service to this House, and was killed by cowards. Surely there is some way of protecting his reputation from political pygmies.

**Mr. Wakeham:** The question of order is one for you, Mr. Speaker, not me—though I may say that I very much agree with your remarks last night. I agree also with the comments of my hon. Friend. I totally deprecate the remarks of the hon. Member for Brent, East (Mr. Livingstone) and believe that he should withdraw them.

**Mr. James Wallace** (Orkney and Shetland): Does the Leader of the House intend to have a debate on the Procedure Committee's report on the ten-minute Bill procedure? We welcome the fact that there is to be an early debate on foreign affairs, but does not the Leader of the House accept that on both sides of the House there is considerable concern about the position in China, in particular about the plight of British passport holders in Hong Kong? Those matters should not be relegated to a general debate on foreign affairs. Could the Leader of the House not think again about holding a debate that relates specifically to Hong Kong and China?

**Mr. Wakeham:** I cannot promise an early debate on the ten-minute Bill procedure. Some of our new arrangements are working better than the previous arrangements, but we shall have to look into the matter again and I shall be in touch with the hon. Gentleman.

I agree that Hong Kong is a particularly important matter. The Foreign Affairs Select Committee report on Hong Kong is expected to be published tomorrow. I hope to be able to arrange a debate in due course after its publication, but we must await the report.

**Mr. Michael Marshall** (Arundel): On the day that marks the centenary of the Inter-Parliamentary Union, and following the unveiling earlier today by you, Mr. Speaker, of the bust of the Back Bencher who founded the Inter-Parliamentary Union, may I ask my right hon. Friend, in view of what he said a moment or two ago, whether the foreign affairs debate that he has in mind might encompass—perhaps in terms of the motion that is tabled—recognition and appraisal of the work of the Inter-Parliamentary Union, embodying, as it does, important contributions from both sides of the House?

**Mr. Wakeham:** I shall consider carefully my hon. Friend's suggestion which, if it could be incorporated, would be appropriate. I am sure that in its debate on foreign affairs the House would want to pay tribute to the work of the IPU.

**Mr. Eric S. Heffer** (Liverpool, Walton): May we have a two-day debate on foreign affairs? Apart from the question of China and Hong Kong, there is also the confused situation in Europe. I have been a Member of this House for a long time and I have heard many of my hon. Friends talk about Europe. For example, my right hon. Friend the Member for Leeds, East (Mr. Healey) argued quite strongly when he was Chancellor of the Exchequer that we ought not to join the European monetary system, or rush into it. I have also heard my right hon. and learned Friend the Member for Monklands, East (Mr. Smith) who now speaks on economic matters say recently on radio that we ought not to rush into the EMS. I am a little confused. We ought, therefore, to have a serious debate about Europe, when we could discuss the implications of a wider Europe rather than just the Common Market.

Increasingly, the nation state is being discussed, even in the Soviet Union where it was not discussed before. There are so many serious issues of great importance—not yah-boo politics—that need to be properly debated here. The future of Europe and our position in Europe are among the matters that ought to be debated. I ask the right hon. Gentleman to take on board what I have said and to consider holding a two-day debate so that on one of those days we may discuss Europe seriously, not on the basis of yah-booism.

**Mr. Wakeham:** I agree with the hon. Gentleman that there are some serious issues to be discussed, but I hope that he recognises the difficulties I am in. I have already had requests for debates on foreign affairs and Hong Kong, and now I have had a request for a debate on Europe. With the best will in the world, it will be impossible to meet all those demands in the immediate future. May I ask the hon. Gentleman, who I know raises the matter seriously, to have a word with his right hon. Friend the Leader of the Opposition and see whether he can help me to find one of the three days.

**Mr. Rupert Allason** (Torbay): Having had an involuntary swim in the River Thames yesterday during the course of the annual dinghy race between this House and another place, I can bear witness to the cleanliness of the water in the Thames. However, the same cannot be said of the state of cleanliness of the waters off our coastline, in particular off south Devon. Will my right hon. Friend assure the House that he will give full time for a debate that will cover not just the technical points in the Lords amendments to the Water Bill but the very important issue of pumping raw sewage into the English Channel?

**Mr. Wakeham:** I agree that these are important matters, and that we must make time to debate them and get across the message that, whatever shortcomings there may be, our record is considerably better than that of a great many other parts of Europe. Although I am

[*Mr. Wakeham*]

responsible for finding the bulk of the time for the Lords amendments to the Water Bill, others will have a say in how best to allocate that time. No doubt, however, my hon. Friend's point will be borne in mind.

**Mr. Jeff Rooker** (Birmingham, Perry Barr): I draw the attention of the Leader of the House to early-day motion 1003 about the crisis in Sylvan high school in Croydon.

[*That this House deplores the proposal of Croydon Council to close Sylvan High School, an 11-16 years mixed comprehensive, and establish a city technology college in its place against the wishes of parents, school governors and staff; notes that parents voted 97 per cent. against the proposal, on a 57 per cent. turnout, despite Croydon Council circulating 13,907 copies of a consultation document and refused the Save Sylvan Campaign facilities to circulate a one-page response; believes Sir Phillip Harris, who heads the sponsors, is misguided in his desire to change the school and deeply regrets that the proposal has led to uncertainty which has gravely damaged the school, leading to the loss of staff which according to the Times Educational Supplement will mean that in September the school has the prospect of no drama, music or full-time commitment to humanities, and two-thirds of the craft design technology staff missing; reminds the Secretary of State of his visit to Sylvan High School in 1986, following which he wrote to the school saying he found the dedication of the Head and staff to be impressive, was delighted to see so much enthusiasm by the pupils and was reassured to know of such worthwhile and rewarding work; and therefore calls upon the Right honourable and honourable Members who constituencies are affected to make vigorous representations to the Secretary of State for Education and Science to take account of the vote of parents expressing parental choice, which should be paramount.*]

Could we have an early debate before the Secretary of State reaches a decision on the application of that school to become a city technology college, bearing in mind that 97 per cent. of the parents, in a 57 per cent. turnout, voted against? In September, because of the massive loss of staff, it is likely that the children will be unable to take a whole range of courses. All Croydon Members have been asked to make representations. I know that parents of all political persuasions are extremely grateful for the action that you have taken, Mr. Speaker—the school is in your constituency, although it serves the borough—and they have asked me to say how grateful they are to you and to do so at as early an opportunity as possible. I met them, together with my hon. Friend the Member for Blackburn (Mr. Straw). However, the parents are not so keen on what the other three right hon. and hon. Members for Croydon have been doing. Before the school is damaged beyond recall, so that parents take their children away from it, it is crucial that we have an early debate so that the Secretary of State for Education and Science can get the real feelings of parents in Croydon, which he is unable to get in the House at present.

**Mr. Wakeham:** Let me put the record straight. Croydon council's proposal to close Sylvan high school is now before my right hon. Friend the Secretary of State for Education and Science. He will reach a decision on the proposal, strictly on its merits, and will take into account the views of those who have an interest in the matter. I do not believe that I should say anything in advance of his decision.

**Sir Peter Hordern** (Horsham): May I ask my right hon. Friend to hold a two-day debate on foreign affairs? I support what was said by the hon. Member for Liverpool, Walton (Mr. Heffer). One of the days should be devoted to European affairs, perhaps with the co-operation of the Opposition. Is my right hon. Friend able to say what has happened to the debate which was to take place on parliamentary pensions?

**Mr. Wakeham:** It seemed to me that the time at which the debate on parliamentary pensions would have taken place the other night was sufficiently late to have made it difficult for hon. Members to grasp some of the complexities, and that the speeches might be better if we managed to hold the debate a little earlier in the evening.

As for my hon. Friend's request for a two-day debate on foreign affairs, I know that he will have some sympathy for me at this time of the year. Seeking to find one day, let alone two days, for a foreign affairs debate is difficult enough. I shall do my best, but I really cannot give any firm undertaking.

**Mr. Bob Cryer** (Bradford, South): I support the appeal of many hon. Members for sufficient time to be devoted to a foreign affairs debate so that some of us can express our very strong support for the Transport and General Workers Union in passing a resolution that Britain should get rid of nuclear weapons. We could then invite support for the United Nations nuclear non-proliferation treaty which is supported by 133 nations that have refused either to manufacture or deploy nuclear weapons. Then we could adopt a morally superior attitude which I hope would be more acceptable to my hon. Friends. It would be useful to have time to debate that matter.

**Mr. Wakeham:** I do not often get upset with the hon. Gentleman but he seems to have dished my ploy of trying to persuade the Leader of the Opposition to find a day, if that is the basis on which he wants to have a debate. I shall have to struggle on as best I can.

**Mr. Ivan Lawrence** (Burton): Now that the importance of Europe is beginning to dawn on Members of Parliament, even though it has not dawned upon the two out of three electors who stayed at home during the Euro-elections, and as it is becoming more and more obvious that this place will have to exercise a bit more parliamentary control over what the Government are doing in that connection, is it not time to consider the totally deplorable way in which the House considers European measures and to institute a review that leads to an improvement of the way in which we consider what goes on in Europe?

**Mr. Wakeham:** As my hon. and learned Friend knows, the Select Committee on Procedure is considering that matter. A number of people, including myself, have given evidence to it. We are still considering some of the issues. I hope that some further constructive proposals may be put to the Select Committee in the not-too-distant future so that we can find a better way of dealing with these important issues, which I fully agree with my hon. Friend are not dealt with adequately at present.

**Mr. Jack Ashley** (Stoke-on-Trent, South): Is the Leader of the House aware that a number of people, including me, have been infuriated by the refusal of an orange badge parking permit to a woman suffering from thalidomide who has no arms although she can walk? That decision is insensitive, stupid, unjustified and bureaucratic. Will he tell the Minister for the disabled that a deputation of Opposition Members wishes to see him next week to complain about that individual case and, because there is evidence that the Minister is now considering decisions which would rob thousands of disabled people of their orange badges, we want to talk to him before any decision is made? May we also have a debate next week?

**Mr. Wakeham:** The answer to the last part of the question is that I am sorry but I cannot find time for a debate next week. However, the answer to the first part of the right hon. Gentleman's question is that these are matters for my hon. Friend the Minister for Roads and Traffic and I shall refer them to him. As I understand it, the difficulty has been that there has been a very great increase in the number of parking permits given to people who have difficulty in walking. The parking concessions are primarily for those disabled people who have difficulty in walking. Other concessions and help may be more appropriate to people with other disabilities. I know that my hon. Friend is considering these matters and I have no doubt that he will find the best possible solution.

**Mr. Michael Latham** (Rutland and Melton): As my right hon. Friend is shortly to bring the clergy ordination measure before the House, as it has been narrowly approved by the ecclesiastical committee, will he consider bringing before the House proposals to get rid of that committee altogether? Is he aware that some of us who have served on that committee for 15 years believe that that type of parliamentary control is completely out of date?

**Mr. Wakeham:** The measure to which my hon. Friend refers is now before another place. I shall await its passage there before bringing it forward here. I do not want to answer the wider question off the cuff. I have no views on the matter or on any changes, but if my hon. Friend would like to write to me or talk to me, I should be happy to discuss the matter further.

**Mr. Greville Janner** (Leicester, West): May we please have an early debate on the anxieties of teachers in my constituency in Leicester, and I am sure throughout the country, at the growing shortage of resources which is making life more difficult in all schools, but especially in schools in disadvantaged areas, and the shortage of speech therapists and other experts to help people not to suffer from unnecessary disablement? As our schools go into their holidays tomorrow, can they please have some hope of returning to better news?

**Mr. Wakeham:** I am sure that the hon. and learned Gentleman will recognise first that the teacher-pupil ratio at present is substantially better than it was under the Government that he supported. I recognise that it is not perfect and that there are shortages, particularly in certain areas. He will also agree that my right hon. Friend the Secretary of State for Education and Science has taken steps to improve the position, particularly in certain specialised subjects. I cannot promise an early debate,

although I note that my right hon. Friend is answering questions on Tuesday, so perhaps the hon. and learned Gentleman will make his points then.

**Sir John Stokes** (Halesowen and Stourbridge): While we all enjoy hard work, will my right hon. Friend soon be in a position to announce the date of the summer recess, which might possibly be earlier this year, so that we can give our full attention to important matters like cricket and eschew politics for a while?

**Mr. Wakeham:** I promise my hon. Friend that I shall announce the date of the summer recess as early as I can manage. I promise my hon. Friend that it will be for as long as I can manage, but I am afraid I cannot tell him the date yet.

**Mr. Dennis Skinner** (Bolsover): In view of what the Prime Minister had to say about the Common Market, and her attitude to current issues such as the EMS, perhaps we could get rid of the Water Bill next week and have a debate on the Common Market. Then the Prime Minister could explain whether it is true that she said to the other leaders in Madrid when she was explaining Britain's social charter that she had introduced a new measure—£7,000 for sacked Ministers. She could also explain whether the holding position on the Common Market will last only until she leaves the stage, let us say during the next 12 months, and hands over to another Tory leader. Perhaps we can then finish off with a Bill—the Single European Bill mark 2—so that some of us can vote it down. If that is what the Prime Minister wants, we shall give her a chuck on.

**Mr. Wakeham:** I had better delay before having such a debate. In that delaying time, I wonder whether the hon. Gentleman might have a word with his hon. Friend the Member for Hackney, South and Shoreditch (Mr. Sedgemore) who seems to have become a Euro-fanatic in recent weeks to see whether he can sort him out. Then we would have a consistent line from the Opposition who seem to have changed their tune.

**Mr. Roger King** (Birmingham, Northfield): I am aware of the replies from my right hon. Friend about the lack of time for debates, but will he bring pressure to bear on my right hon. Friend the Secretary of State for Transport to make a statement to the House on the rail strike? It is causing widespread dismay among people in all parts of the kingdom. We could look for some answers and some solutions to the future problems of the rail industry, and ascertain the views of Opposition Members who have remained absolutely silent on this highly difficult situation.

**Mr. Wakeham:** I agree with my hon. Friend that the situation requires us to consider policies, as my right hon. Friend the Prime Minister said at Prime Minister's Question Time. However, I do not believe that it is the right moment for my right hon. Friend the Secretary of State for Transport to make a statement to the House about the strike. It is a matter for those who are on strike and the management to resolve. I should have thought that many of the strikers would think carefully about whether they want to continue to inflict unnecessary suffering on so many commuters.

**Mr. Max Madden** (Bradford, West): As the Government refused to make a statement or provide a Government debate on the DNA centrally organised

[*Mr. Max Madden*]

testing scheme, and as the Labour party is now providing a three-hour debate on the subject next week, will the Leader of the House consider adding some Government time so that many unanswered questions can be resolved?

Secondly, before the right hon. Gentleman decides the date of the summer recess, will he arrange for a debate on the plight of British pensioners, particularly those who have to live on the basic pension? That would enable the Government to consider introducing a summer bonus to help pensioners cope with the increasing prices in the shops and water, electricity and gas charges and announcing that the Christmas bonus will be increased in line with the inflation that has occurred since it was first introduced. It is a scandal that British pensioners are living at the lowest standards of any pensioners in Europe. When will the Government provide time for us to discuss their plight and do something about it?

**Mr. Wakeham:** It is neither a scandal nor accurate. The hon. Gentleman does not understand what is going on. No pensioner in Britain is expected to live on the basic pension alone. Of course, 80 per cent. of all pensioners have income from private sources and the Government provide help for those on low incomes through income support and housing benefit. In October, 2·5 million pensioners will gain from the £200 million poorer pensioners' package. Therefore, what the hon. Gentleman says is just not correct. Perhaps he should do his homework before we have any such debate.

With regard to the debate on immigration rules and DNA testing on the day next week that I have allocated as an Opposition day, I find it rather strange that any important subject that the Opposition choose to debate on an Opposition day should be considered unreasonable. Opposition days are for debating matters that the Opposition want to debate. We provide the day and they provide the subject for debate. That is perfectly proper.

**Mr. Nicholas Bennett** (Pembroke): To return to the subject raised by my hon. Friend the Member for Birmingham, Northfield (Mr. King), has my right hon. Friend seen early-day motion No. 1023, which is headed:
"Industrial Action on British Rail"?
[*That this House deplores the continuing misery and disruption to British Rail customers, notes that during last week's bus strike in London those bus services which have been put out to tender by L.R.T. and which are now run by private operators continued to run; and therefore calls upon the Government to bring forward early proposals to denationalise British Rail and to consider also introducing legislation to ban strikes in essential public services.*]
Does my right hon. Friend not agree that there is a need for an early debate on the subject because, as my hon. Friend the Member for Northfield said, there has been a deafening silence from the Opposition and we want to know whether the Leader of the Opposition is the strikers' friend on this issue as well?

**Mr. Wakeham:** I appreciate my hon. Friend's understandable curiosity on these matters. Yesterday's rail strike was quite unnecessary and caused disruption for millions, especially in London. Such industrial action is pointless and, once again, I urge the rail unions to accept British Rail's offer of talks.

**Mr. Peter L. Pike** (Burnley): Does the Leader of the House recall that he has often promised that we would have a debate on the report of the Select Committee on the Environment on toxic waste and the Government's response to it? As the Government are intending to introduce legislation later this year and there is increasing concern within county councils, will he give an assurance that he will hold the debate before the summer recess? In recognising the problems on that and to save him having to answer the same question every week, will he give a firm promise that a debate will be provided before the Government introduce legislation affecting waste disposal?

**Mr. Wakeham:** No, I will not give any such undertaking. The Committee reported on 8 March and the Government published a full response as a Command Paper on 27 April. The response described in detail the measures already in hand to meet most of the Committee's recommendations and firmly rebuffed the remaining recommendations. We have discussed many environmental issues in recent weeks. At this stage in the year, it is difficult to find additional time, so I cannot promise the hon. Gentleman a further debate in the immediate future.

**Mr. Ian Bruce** (Dorset, South): Will my right hon. Friend find time for a debate and the opportunity to vote on the procedures of the House and on the facilities available to hon. Members to do their job in representing their constituents? I am sure that my right hon. Friend knows that when new Members arrive in this place and declare it a silly way to run a country and Parliament, we are told that after a couple of years we shall get used to it and like it. I have now been here a couple of years and I would not run a country in the way in which we do now. May we have the opportunity to change our procedures?

**Mr. Wakeham:** My hon. Friend is doing a great job in running the country and I congratulate him on his efforts. I am not sure that additional debates on improving the facilities of this place would get us very far. There are many steps being taken and we are doing our best to improve the facilities. I do not want to sound like an old hand, but the facilities are far better than they were when I came into the House and many hon. Members have been here far longer than I have. We are making some progress.

We had a debate the other day on procedure matters. It was not very well attended and only a few hon. Members were anxious to contribute. Those who did were mostly members of the Select Committee on Procedure, with a few others. However, it was a good debate and we shall come back to procedure debates later on for sure. There are several reports on procedure, but I cannot promise an early debate on them at present.

**Mr. Tony Banks** (Newham, North-West): I want to take the Leader of the House back to the point raised by my hon. Friend the Member for Bolsover (Mr. Skinner) about ministerial hand-outs. Will the Leader of the House tell us whether it is true that Ministers will receive redundancy payments? If so, will that money go to Ministers who jump as well as those who are pushed? If that is so, and something nasty happens to the right hon. Gentleman, will he opt to take the money or to go with dignity?

**Mr. Wakeham:** I do not know whether the hon. Gentleman is quite as innocent as he would like us to believe sometimes. I shall do my best to explain the position to him. The Top Salaries Review Body considered the question of ministerial severance pay carefully, following support for its introduction from hon. Members of all parties. I told the House in May 1988 that the Government proposed to implement the TSRB recommendations when parliamentary time allowed.

I suppose that the hon. Gentleman might be singing a different song if he thought that he had a chance of ever becoming a Minister, so his comments are understandable. The position has not changed one iota since May 1988.

**Mr. James Cran** (Beverley): Will my right hon. Friend find some time for us to discuss the important ramifications of the report into the brewing industry by the Monopolies and Mergers Commission, especially against the background of the extravagant campaign being conducted, I believe, by the Brewers Society and some of the major brewers and also against the background that some people are trying to turn logic on its head by suggesting that it is not monopolistic for six large brewers to control 75 per cent. of beer production, 74 per cent. of brewers' tied houses and 86 per cent. of loan ties? Does my right hon. Friend agree that there are some important ramifications for monopoly policy in that area and that the House should discuss them?

**Mr. Wakeham:** My noble Friend the Secretary of State for Trade and Industry is continuing to discuss the issues with the national brewers and we should await the outcome of those discussions before we think about having a debate.

**Mr. D. N. Campbell-Savours** (Workington): Is the Leader of the House aware that I am having great difficulty in winning the ballot for private Members' motions so that I can raise the question of the proprietorial control of *The Observer* newspaper by Tiny Rowland? Has the right hon. Gentleman had a chance to read the report of the independent directors of *The Observer* who were critical of *The Observer's* coverage of the takeover of House of Fraser, but equally whitewashed the activities of Mr. Donald Trelford, Mr. Adam Raphael, Mr. Rowland and his colleagues on the publication in *The Observer* of articles relating to Tornado? Is he aware that when the independent directors went in they did not interview the journalists? If they had done so, the report might have been very different. Should not Parliament be allowed the right to debate these matters, which are important to the freedom of the press?

**Mr. Wakeham:** I am not sure that I can help the hon. Gentleman very much. He may not be lucky in winning the private Members' ballot. If I were able to enter it and I won it, I should let him have my ticket, but unfortunately I am not allowed to do so, so I cannot help him this week.

**Mr. Greg Knight** (Derby, North): My right hon. Friend is a reasonable man. May I ask him, therefore, to think again about providing time for a debate on the rail strike, in view of the strength of feeling among Conservative Members? Is it not important that Conservative Members are able to place on record their views on the troglodyte behaviour of Mr. Jimmy Knapp? Is it not equally important that the House and the country have the opportunity to learn the views of the Leader of the Opposition on this matter? As a result of his silence, if he is not the strikers' friend on this issue, he is certainly the invisible man.

**Mr. Wakeham:** My hon. Friend makes his point well. If I were able to find time, the subject would make an interesting debate.

# Points of Order

5.8 pm

**Mr. Tony Marlow** (Northampton, North): On a point of order, Mr. Speaker. It is the usual whinge. We had a very important statement today. Given the great forest of people who sought to catch your eye, it was quite impossible that they could all do so. All I ask is whether, the next time we have a very important statement by my right hon. Friend the Prime Minister after a Council of Europe meeting, it would be possible to take some sort of list of those who sought to get in today, but who, quite understandably, were unfortunate in not being able to catch your eye.

**Mr. Speaker:** I well understand the hon. Gentleman's concern and distress about the matter. I do keep a list and I looked at it today. I will certainly continue to do so.

**Mr. Dennis Skinner** (Bolsover): Further to that point of order, Mr. Speaker. You cannot call every hon. Member. I was not called and I am not whingeing. I used a bit of ingenuity and raised the matter in business questions. The hon. Member for Northampton, North (Mr. Marlow) could have done the same if he had been smart enough.

On another point of order, Mr. Speaker. I have not raised the matter of the Rose theatre before because it has been left to others who deal with such cultural matters. It has been brought to my attention that it is high time that we had another statement from the Secretary of State for the Environment.

**Mr. Tony Banks** (Newham, North-West): Hear, hear.

**Mr. Skinner:** I hear my hon. Friend saying, "Hear, hear." He knows about this. It is important that we have a statement, because there are possibly some connections which are a little unsavoury, to say the least, namely——

**Mr. Speaker:** Order. The hon. Member should have raised this matter with the Leader of the House. I can arrange neither statements nor debates.

**Mr. Skinner:** It is a constitutional matter, Mr. Speaker. I want to know in what way I, or someone else, can raise this matter. A Member of the House of Lords, Lord McAlpine of West Green, treasurer of the Tory party and non-executive director of Imry Merchant Developers, may well be catching the ear of the Secretary of State for the Environment more than anyone else in this matter. Can I raise the matter here or should it be raised somewhere else? Is it a matter of privilege?

**Mr. Speaker:** The hon. Member should not raise the matter with me.

**Mr. Tony Banks:** On a point of order, Mr. Speaker. I will not whinge either about the ministerial statement. The Select Committee on Procedure is considering the scrutiny of EEC legislation and EEC matters. I know that, if there are complaints about timing, you will say that the business of the House is not your concern. It is, however, your prerogative to determine how long you will allow questions on a statement to continue. As the summits come up only once every six months, would not the ability of the House to scrutinise EEC matters be enhanced by allowing questions on those statements to continue for a sufficiently long time to enable all hon. Members—apart from me, of course—to ask the Prime Minister a question?

**Mr. Speaker:** The hon. Member knows that on this occasion I allowed questions on the Prime Minister's statement to continue for an hour. There was then another statement, on which questions ran for 50 minutes. We are about to consider the Second Reading of a Bill. As the hon. Member for Bolsover (Mr. Skinner) correctly stated, it is impossible for every Member to be called. I do my best to be utterly fair. I do not think that the hon. Member for Newham, North-West (Mr. Banks) is a deprived citizen.

## Statutory Instruments, &c.

**Mr. Speaker:** With the leave of the House, I will put together the six motions relating to statutory instruments.

*Ordered,*

That the draft Motor Vehicles (Wearing of Seat Belts by Children in Rear Seats) Regulations 1989 be referred to a Standing Committee on Statutory Instruments, &c.

That the Education (National Curriculum) (Modern Foreign Languages) Order 1989 (S.I., 1989, No. 825) be referred to a Standing Committee on Statutory Instruments, &c.

That the Education (National Curriculum) (Attainment Targets and Programmes of Study in English) Order 1989 (S.I., 1989, No. 907) be referred to a Standing Committee on Statutory Instruments, &c.

That the Offshore Installations (Safety Representatives and Safety Committees) Regulations 1989 (S.I., 1989, No. 971) be referred to a Standing Committee on Statutory Instruments, &c.

That the Offshore Installations (Emergency Pipe-line Valve) Regulations 1989 (S.I., 1989, No. 1029) be referred to a Standing Committee on Statutory Instruments, &c.

That the Education (School Hours and Policies) (Information) Regulations 1989 (S.I., 1989, No. 398) be referred to a Standing Committee on Statutory Instruments, &c.—*[Mr. Lightbown.]*

### SCOTTISH AFFAIRS

*Ordered,*

That the matter of Broadcasting in Scotland, being a matter relating exclusively to Scotland, be referred to the Scottish Grand Committee for its consideration.—*[Mr. Lightbown.]*

# Orders of the Day

## Representation of the People Bill

*Order for Second Reading read.*

5.12 pm

**The Secretary of State for the Home Department (Mr. Douglas Hurd):** I beg to move, That the Bill be now read a Second time.

I apologise for the fact that I cannot be here for the wind-up speeches because of a commitment that I found difficult to escape. I have informed the hon. Member for Kingston upon Hull, West (Mr. Randall) of my proposed absence.

The purpose of this Bill is to extend the existing franchise for British citizens overseas and to set a new limit on candidates' election expenses at a United Kingdom parliamentary by-election.

In 1985, the House decided that the right to vote for Britons abroad should no longer be confined just to members of the forces and other servants of the Crown. In building on those existing arrangements, as we did in the Representation of the People Act 1985, we showed, I hope, that our electoral arrangements can evolve and adapt, in a sensible and practical way, to changing social circumstances without losing their essential character and continuity. The House is rightly cautious in new legislation on the franchise. We set an initial time limit of five years on the period during which a British citizen resident abroad may register to vote. We also imposed, both in the Act and in regulations made later, a number of restrictions and conditions on the extension we were making.

The Government made a commitment, at the time that we agreed to these restrictions and conditions, that we would review them in the light of their operation. My predecessor said:

"as time goes on, many of the objections that have been voiced will be seen to be invalid. It is likely that a case for a further extension will be made out."—*[Official Report,* 29 January 1985; Vol. 72, c. 217.]

After three years' experience of the overseas franchise, the time has come to make that case.

The arrangements made in 1985 have not proved attractive to our citizens abroad. Only 12,000 overseas British citizens worldwide were registered to vote in 1987, the first year of operation, and also a general election year. In 1988 the numbers registered in the whole of the United Kingdom fell sharply to just over 2,000. There has been little improvement this year, despite the opportunity for registered overseas electors to vote in the recent European parliamentary elections. There are 2,832 overseas electors on the register for England and Wales, 132 in Scotland and just six for the whole of Northern Ireland—a total of only 2,970 for the United Kingdom. We must, I believe, ask ourselves why this franchise is used by less than 1 per cent. of those of our overseas citizens eligible to vote here. Do the arrangements made in 1985 offer a fair deal to our citizens overseas?

**Mr. Tony Banks** (Newham, North-West): Voting is a voluntary activity. If overseas citizens are not voting, that is their right. Perhaps the Home Secretary will start looking at the number of people in this country who do not

[*Mr. Tony Banks*]

vote and change the way in which our voting procedures are organised. Perhaps he will think about supporting my idea for compulsory voting.

**Mr. Hurd:** That is not the issue. The question is whether, because of our caution, we have hemmed in these new overseas voters so that they are reluctant, because of restrictions, to exercise their right. We need to examine that question, just as the Bill does.

**Mr. Robert B. Jones** (Hertfordshire, West): Will my right hon. Friend confirm that there is a difference between registration and voting and that the Opposition parties have consistently and rightly supported drives against under-registration in the United Kingdom as a whole, so logically they should also support attempts to make registration easier for United Kingdom citizens abroad, too?

**Mr. Hurd:** My hon. Friend is right. He has made his point neatly.

We have received emphatic replies on the question whether the existing restrictions are excessive. Much of what the overseas voters say is borne out by the full response that I received to the consultation paper issued on the subject last spring.

Change is needed in two basic respects. The first is the discouraging five-year cut-off, with its automatic denial of democratic rights after an arbitrary period. The second is the cumbersome bureaucracy which, as a result of our caution in 1985, we have imposed on our citizens abroad who want to vote in our elections. Some of those bureacratic burdens, notably the requirement to seek attestation of all first applications from a British consular office, are in secondary legislation. We shall in due course seek the consent of the House to reduce those burdens and, where practicable, to remove them altogether. Where we can help our citizens abroad, for example, by sending them annual reminders of the need to register, rather as is done for domestic electors, we shall do so, and clause 5 would enable me and my right hon. Friends to require electoral registration officers to do that.

**Mr. Robert Maclennan** (Caithness and Sutherland): Has the right hon. Gentleman estimated the cost of imposing that duty on electoral registration officers? What is the basis of his assertion about the number of those people who might be entitled to vote if they registered?

**Mr. Hurd:** I shall ask my hon. Friend the Under-Secretary of State to deal with the hon. Gentleman's second point. On the first point, we have made a calculation—but it may not be exact. If the hon. Gentleman wishes to question it, he should do so. I doubt that he would seriously be able to undermine our estimate.

I turn to the main provisions of the Bill and the fundamental question of where the cut-off for overseas voting should be set: for how many years should a British citizen be able to reside overseas and still be able to cast his vote in our parliamentary elections? I readily acknowledge that there cannot be a precise or objective answer. A balance must be struck between the claims and interests of those who have been abroad for a long time but have retained close and continuing connections with Britain and those who cut adrift from such links much earlier.

In 1985, we took an ultra cautious, tentative approach and set the limit of five years. Following our experience of the system, we can now see that many of the fears expressed at that time were misconceived. Perhaps they overlooked the extent to which a system requiring annual registration is self-regulating. Some hon. Members,. especially on this side of the House, who responded to our consultation paper strongly argued that there should be no time limit, as is the case in several other major democracies. That is an arguable point of view with which I have much sympathy. We should try to get a reasonable view after listening to as many opinions as possible. We should not ram through legislation against such strongly held views. I recognise the strength and sincerity of the view that we must draw the line somewhere and that the constituency link is not infinitely elastic.

The Bill proposes a limit of 25 years, which would enfranchise citizens working on longer-term contracts abroad who intend, as many do, to retire to the United Kingdom. The Bill will include, by and large, citizens who, encouraged by successive Governments, have gone abroad to work for international and world development organisations, to advance British economic interests as private business men or to pursue careers in European Community institutions. It will recognise the rights of thousands of British citizens across the globe who, through modern communications, cheaper air fares and a genuine affection for their country, maintain strong links with the United Kingdom. Many of them have family and friends, property, children at school and are often liable for payment of taxes here. They may be business men, journalists, teachers or officials, voluntary workers, missionaries or church workers.

I remember the first debate that I attended on this subject, when the Labour party held the view that such people were lotus eaters. I remember the former Labour Leader of the House, now Lord Glenamara, using that phrase. I hope that we have moved on and that Labour Members will not argue that the people whom we have enfranchised in a rather timid and tentative manner should be described and denounced as lotus eaters.

**Mr. Jeff Rooker** (Birmingham, Perry Barr): The Secretary of State said that the limit is to be increased from five to 25 years. Given that within 25 years there will probably be at least two boundary changes in a constituency, is the Secretary of State satisfied that people living abroad will have sufficient links with constituencies to know in which constituency to register? Registration by overseas citizens is voluntary, contrary to the answer that the Secretary of State gave to the hon. Member for Hertfordshire, West (Mr. Jones), whereas registration for people living in Britain is not. It is illegal not to register to vote in this country, so therefore there is a distinction. I accept the generality of the Secretary of State's argument for the 25-year limit, but will electoral rolls be accurate, bearing in mind the fact that registration officers do not keep them for 25 years?

**Mr. Hurd:** Registers are available. The hon. Gentleman is neglecting the fact that overseas citizens will have to register every year. The extent of contact will vary from case to case, but I do not think that the hon. Gentleman's objection is sound because they will be maintaining contact by registering every year. We should not disenfranchise them because they have lived abroad for 15 or 20 years rather than five years.

**Mr. Tony Banks** rose——

**Mr. Hurd:** I have already given way to the hon. Gentleman.

I can understand the argument for having no time limit. I used to accept the argument for a tight limit, which was the mood of the House four years ago. I hope that we have moved on and that the House will agree, in the light of experience, that clause 1 strikes the right balance. I hope that it will be accepted in that spirit.

**Mr. David Winnick** (Walsall, North): Many hon. Members believe that it is absurd that anyone who has been away from Britain for 25 years should be able to vote. Is there not also the question of their commitment to the United Kingdom? Under the law as it currently stands, for them to be able to vote they must show that they do not intend permanently to live outside Britain. That provision is to be dropped. Such people pay no taxes to the Exchequer, so why should they be entitled to vote here?

**Mr. Hurd:** The hon. Member has returned to the lotus-eating argument, which I hoped had been disposed of many years ago. His approach is deeply old-fashioned because it does not take into account changes in society. Thousands of people have been encouraged to move abroad by the Government and for business reasons. In the old days, it was thought that the only people who should be allowed to vote were diplomats and soldiers of the British Army of the Rhine. That is the old-fashioned concept to which the hon. Gentleman is sticking. Most overseas citizens have links here and will return to Britain at the end of their working lives. The world has moved on, and in future people will increasingly work overseas. To dismiss such people as having lost their connections with or loyalty to Britain is a deeply obscure and reactionary point of view.

**Mr. Richard Shepherd** (Aldridge-Brownhills): For tax purposes, what will happen if people sell their businesses overseas, thereby escaping capital gains tax? Has a determination been made regarding their tax liabilities or responsibilities? Does not the Bill have implications for final estate duties? Does registering to vote determine where one's heart or one's residence is?

**Mr. Hurd:** I shall not follow my hon. Friend down that byway. We made it perfectly clear in 1985, and we do so again now, that there is no connection between British tax laws and the provisions of the Bill.

I mentioned earlier the denial of democracy that is inherent in the present arrangements. That denial is especially obvious—I think that this is a quirk—in the exclusion from the right to vote of young people who, through no fault of their own, were not registered to vote when they went abroad or were taken abroad by their parents. It was clear from the consultation exercise that it is common ground that we can and should enfranchise that group of people. Clauses 2 and 3 seek to do just that.

Clause 4 deals with a matter that has already been mentioned in interventions—the requirement for the applicant to make a statutory declaration about his future place of residence. Many of our citizens abroad have objected, understandably, to making such a declaration. It

was never connected with tax, but many of them thought that it was. That view was reflected by my hon. Friend the Member for Aldridge-Brownhills (Mr. Shepherd). In the light of experience, we cannot see much point in having that declaration. It cannot be verified one way or the other by the person considering the application. It is a symbolic gesture, and if it has any effect at all, it is only that it might allow a dishonest person to vote while preventing an honest person from doing so. It adds only nuisance value to the procedures, and the Bill would abolish it.

**Mr. Tony Banks:** I am grateful to the Home Secretary for giving way because he will not be here at the end of the debate and I am anxious to push him on these points. Taxation is crucial. Ministers and the Prime Minister have stood at the Dispatch Box and, with regard to local government changes, have said that whether someone pays rates influences the policies for which he votes at local elections. One justification for the poll tax was the fact that so many people are out of the rating system. In other words, voting must accompany the payment of taxes. The Home Secretary's argument today is the reverse of that. People who do not pay taxes will still be able to vote for policies to which they will be making no financial contribution. That is a complete reversal of what Ministers have insisted should apply in local government and it is now to be applied to central Government.

**Mr. Hurd:** The hon. Gentleman is attacking the whole concept of overseas voting. But that concept has been established for several years and it is not seriously contested in the House. The hon. Gentleman is mounting a rearguard and reactionary opposition to something that has been on the statute books for some time. There has never been a connection between the existence of this franchise since 1985 and the taxation laws. The hon. Gentleman would be the first to object if we tried to make such a connection. That connection has not existed and the Opposition are not about to propose one. We are talking not about a new principle today, but about the ramifications and restrictions which in the past have hedged in the principle of the overseas franchise.

**Mr. Stuart Randall** (Kingston upon Hull, West): I am grateful to the Home Secretary for giving way as he will not be here for the wind-up.

The Home Secretary referred to democracy and extending the franchise. Why will he not come clean with the House? Under the existing legislation, there are 500,000 target voters overseas. Under the new proposals in this Bill, there will be 2 million target voters. That is what the Bill is all about. The Government want to enhance the number of votes that the Conservative party will get at the next and subsequent general elections. All this stuff about democracy is a charade. Why will not the Home Secretary come clean?

**Mr. Hurd:** That is not worthy of the hon. Gentleman. I do not know why he is so defeatist. I thought that the Labour party was in a rather more confident mood. The assumption that Labour is going to lose, or fail to gain all the votes of the officials in the Commission, is strange. I thought that the Commission was now Labour's particular buddy. I advise the hon. Member for Kingston upon Hull, West (Mr. Randall) to have a little more confidence in his prospects and his capacity to enlist the votes of

[*Mr. Hurd*]

Commission officials and the children of missionaries. The hon. Gentleman's intervention has not really edified the House.

The other main purpose of the Bill is contained in clause 6, which sets a new limit on candidates' expenses at by-elections for seats in this House. I gave an assurance in a written answer on the day that I presented this Bill that the new limit is without prejudice to the outcome of a longer-term review that I have set in hand, and I repeat that assurance now. I also repeat, as I said in the written answer that appears in *Hansard* of 21 June, that the review will cover general election expenses as well as by-election expenses. I am preparing a consultation paper which will enable me to seek the views of political parties and election registration officers on the question of election expenses at general elections, by-elections and European elections. We will need a little time to glean views and bring forward sensible proposals.

Meanwhile, the Bill recognises what all hon. Members recognise: the intensity of campaigning at modern parliamentary by-elections and the need to set realistic limits for them. The Bill does that. It applies to parliamentary elections throughout the United Kingdom. As I said earlier, proposals for some easing of the regulations covering consular attestation of overseas electors' declarations will be brought before the House in due course. At the same time, we will try to meet another point and seek the consent of the House to lighten the burden of attestation—*[Interruption.]* I hope that the hon. Member for Kingston upon Hull, West is listening—which three years ago we placed on holidaymakers and others applying for the absent voting facilities provided by the Representation of the People Act 1985.

On those terms, I commend the Bill to the House.

5.34 pm

**Mr. Stuart Randall** (Kingston upon Hull, West): This Representation of the People Bill is short and contains only six clauses. However, it is important. What is the Government's motive in introducing the Bill now? There is a commitment to the Bill in the Conservative party manifesto. In addition, the Bill's title suggests that it is about improving the representation of the people. In part, I believe that that is true. However, I believe that the Government's main purpose is very party political. As I said in an intervention earlier, they want to increase the number of votes cast for the Tory party at the next and subsequent general elections.

In the Bill, the Government extend the franchise for British citizens, many of whom have lived outside the United Kingdom for some considerable time and do not have any intention of returning to live here. Many of them do not pay British taxes and their links with the United Kingdom are minimal. I believe that many of them are out of touch with the political situation in this country.

The Conservative party believes that many of the expatriates intend to vote Conservative instead of Labour. If we accept that assumption, then it is clearly in the interests of the Conservative party to maximise the number of British citizens living overseas who are eligible to vote.

In the Representation of the People Act 1985, arrangements were made for British citizens to vote while they are out of the country on holiday. Again, the thinking conveyed by many Conservatives at that time was that better-off people tend to vote Conservative and better-off people tend to go overseas for their summer holidays. Therefore, a drive to get absent voters to vote in a general election was seen by many people to be a net vote winner for the Conservative party.

I believe that there are two major elements to the Bill. It extends the period that a British citizen may live overseas and qualify as an elector from five years to 25 years. Not only may those citizens have lived out of the country for much of their lives, they will also no longer be expected to demonstrate that they ever intend to return to live in the United Kingdom. Clearly that will embrace a number of people, many of whom will have severed their links with Britain. Many will be married to nationals of the country in which they reside and will perhaps have children who may be receiving education in that country. Their children may be married themselves, and there may be grandchildren. Similarly, those British citizens' children may have careers in the other country. Those citizens will feel locked in for good in the other country and they will never return to Britain. I have friends who are in that position.

Those people have made their choice of life styles. I cannot see why we should extend a franchise, as the Bill suggests, to all those people, without exception, which will enable them possibly to determine the type of Government in this country when to all intents and purposes their lives are unaffected by the type of Government in this country.

I believe in principle that the British citizens who reside in this country and who must put up with the consequences of the policies of a Government—Labour or Conservative—should determine the political complexion of the Government who are elected as a result of a general election. At the same time, I believe that British citizens who live abroad temporarily—for a limited period—should have the right to vote.

The other main element of the Bill is the extension of the franchise to young people who, when they resided in the United Kingdom, were unable to have their names added to the electoral register because they were too young to vote. A possible consequence of that measure is that many young people who might have resided in the United Kingdom only for a matter of weeks or even days and who can know very little about the United Kingdom will now be entitled to vote and determine the kind of Government that we have in this country. Many young people live in countries in which local newspapers report only what the British Government do and rarely report on Opposition parties in any detail. Such young people would invariably vote in the same way as their parents, and that is what the Tory party is banking on.

We should take account of two criteria when considering political representation for British citizens. First, as a fervent democrat, I believe that we should always do all that we can to encourage people to vote. We have fought for our democratic system for hundreds of years. We must protect it, reform it and nurture it to take account of changes in our society and the world about us. I am sure that all hon. Members would support that objective.

The second criterion is that those who are granted a vote should intend to reside in the United Kingdom after their stay overseas. Why should we do what the Bill seems to propose—which is to give the vote to people who have, perhaps, emigrated for good and are probably out of touch with what is going on, or people who abuse Britain by becoming tax exiles? Why should we spend public money encouraging such people to have their names included on the electoral register? There are exceptions—perhaps not many—to the general rule laid down in the Bill. I hope that the details will be carefully looked at in Committee.

As a result of the Representation of the People Act 1985, the number of people throughout the world who registered in 1987 reached only about 11,000 or 12,000, as the Home Secretary said. Clearly, that number is not very high, and it certainly fell short of the 500,000 target for which some Conservatives hoped.

I should be grateful if the Minister would tell us the Government's estimate of the number of people throughout the world who will be enfranchised by the Bill. Will he confirm that his Department is using an estimate based on the international passenger survey of 2 million people who now become eligible to register as a result of the Bill? If the number of people who are enfranchised by the Bill were substantially to increase, it is possible that our general election campaigns will no longer be limited to the British Isles.

It has been reported that the Conservative party bought a mailing list as part of a drive to persuade 100,000 people living abroad to register in 1987, in time for the last general election. However, that measure fell flat and only a small number of people registered as a result of the Conservative party's appeal. After 1992, when we can expect many more British people to live in EEC countries, the demand for absentee voting will certainly increase. If the Government increase the number of possible voters further still by extending the franchise, both the Labour and Conservative parties could be supported by their sister political parties on the continent in canvassing political voters. In some ways, that may sound fanciful, but, if the number of registered voters is sufficiently large—perhaps about 2 million—it is possible that campaigning for a general election might have that new emphasis. I am not sure whether that is a desirable trend. Do the Government wish to encourage it?

The extended franchise in the Bill could result in new methods of campaigning for votes in a country such as the United States. A large number of British citizens emigrated to the United States of America over a considerable number of years. Many of them have retained their British citizenship and would be able to register to vote in British general elections. One can envisage certain United States or international businesses based in the United States contacting potential voters to encourage them to vote in a certain way. Do we as politicians wish to encourage that kind of external interference in our political and democratic processes? The data bases exist and the mail-shot technology is well-established. Does the Minister agree that such interference could be a consequence of the Bill? I should be interested to know whether the Conservative party wishes to encourage it. Clearly, there are two sides of the coin, and I wonder whether the Conservative party has fully thought them through.

As the Home Secretary suggested, clause 1 extends to 25 years the period during which British citizens may be registered as voters under the 1985 Act. Why have the Government introduced such a jump from five to 25 years? What does the Minister regard as the quantitative and qualitative benefits of such changes? Clause 2 extends the franchise to British citizens overseas who could not register in the United Kingdom because they were under age. Clause 2(1) states that a condition for being able to vote is that

"he was last resident in the United Kingdom within the period of twenty-five years"

What does that mean? The Minister is a lawyer and he is well versed in these matters. A woman could come to the United Kingdom, have a baby and then, a few weeks or months later, return overseas. Would the baby have resided here? Would he eventually qualify to vote? In the context of the Bill, what is a resident? The Representation of the People Act 1918 states that a resident should be ordinarily resident. If the parents are on the electoral register, does it mean that the baby could be regarded as ordinarily resident?

Electoral law relies on discretion. Therefore, we must tighten up that important part of the Bill so that we make it absolutely clear what residence means. There are no definitions in the Bill. Clearly, that is a matter to which the Standing Committee will give attention. That is especially important as electoral law is rarely tested in the courts.

One question that arises from extending the franchise for overseas people is how the Tory party will stimulate the latent vote. I hope that the Minister will confirm that the Government will not abuse their position by producing more so-called Government information leaflets to encourage people overseas to vote Conservative. If the Government are so keen on extending the franchise, did the Minister consider giving the vote to certain aliens who are settled in the United Kingdom? At least they know what is going on politically and they can make value judgments before casting a vote.

Clause 4 abolishes the requirement for British citizens overseas to declare that they intend to return to the United Kingdom so that they can register to vote. That means that the vote will be given to people who have left the United Kingdom and, perhaps, intend never to return. When people live overseas for long periods they usually do not pay United Kingdom income tax. Should we take a leaf out of the book of the Americans who, during the war of independence in 1776, said that there should be no taxation without representation? Does the Minister consider that for many of the tax exiles who have given up Britain to live overseas there should be no representation without taxation? If these tax exiles pay tax they should, by right, have a vote. Does not the Minister agree that this is a reasonable criterion for extending the representation of these people?

Clause 5 enables ——

**Mr. Maclennan:** I am listening with growing disbelief to the Labour party spokesman suggesting that there should be some kind of property qualifications for the British citizen. Is that really his intention? Obviously, only those with property worth a certain amount will be in a position to pay taxes.

**Mr. Randall:** I am saying that the way in which this Bill is worded makes it open ended, with loose definitions. I am suggesting that we should considerably tighten up the Bill's wording. The point which I have just made about residency is one good example of a massive loophole. If we do not tighten it up, it will create great difficulties in this kind of electoral law.

Clause 5 enables annual reminders to be sent to overseas electors. I presume that these would be similar to

[*Mr. Randall*]

the forms that we receive in the United Kingdom from our individual returning officers. In principle, we must support that notion, but will the Parliamentary Under-Secretary give the House the cost of doing so?

The Home Secretary did not respond to the intervention of the hon. Member for Caithness and Sutherland (Mr. Maclennan). Will he give us the cost of implementing this proposal? Will officials chase up people to return their forms as they do in the United Kingdom, and what will be the cost?

Clause 6 increases the limit on candidates' election expenses for by-elections, In principle, we welcome the increased level for three reasons. First, by-elections have tended to become national events, not merely to do with a particular constituency. Clearly, that implies extra costs for political parties. Secondly, the growing sophistication of campaigning in by-elections—for example, the extensive use of computer data banks—means that all parties incur greater costs during the highly competitive by-elections which must be catered for. Thirdly, and perhaps most important, the political parties must remain within the electoral law at all times. We must not create pressures for parties to adopt imaginative accounting methods in order to keep within the strict financial limits.

The increase is a stop-gap measure. I hope that the Government will carry out a much more comprehensive review of election expenses at by-elections.

5.52 pm

**Mr. Robert B. Jones** (Hertfordshire, West): I have known the hon. Member for Kingston upon Hull, West (Mr. Randall) for a number of years, and I never expected to hear from him one of the most reactionary and fuddy-duddy speeches I have ever heard in the Chamber. It was quite apparent, even from his comments about it being primarily Conservative voters who take overseas holidays, that he is probably not even in touch with his own constituents who, I bet my bottom dollar, go to Spain, Italy and France for their holidays. Good luck to them.

I was hardly surprised that the new-found internationalism of the Labour party lasted not one minute beyond 15 June. It has suddenly developed an antipathy to people from our country who choose to work overseas to create wealth for this country and jobs for the hon. Gentleman's constituents. I am sure that he has many manufacturing companies in his constituency which are proud of their exports. Those exports could not be successfully competed for abroad if there were no salesmen and technical back-up teams overseas. This, above all, is one of the arguments against the five-year rule.

There is a logical argument which says that once people have retired they may not have the vote. However, anyone who works and lives overseas for five, 25 or 30 years has an important link with the United Kingdom. When talking to many of our citizens overseas, I find that they keep closely in touch with home and many of them subscribe to local papers. Sometimes, they are more informed about events at home than many people in this country.

I certainly welcome the Bill. It also helps to rectify the unjustified distinction that currently exists between Crown servants and people working in the European Commission, the European patent office or private

business. It is plainly absurd that someone who has spent a lifetime in the diplomatic service overseas is, under current legislation, regarded as having close links and a permanent vote in the United Kingdom, while someone working in the European patent office is not.

A number of British citizens abroad pay taxes to the United Kingdom. That is particularly true of those who have retired from local government, the police and the Civil Service who have their tax deducted at source. The hon. Member for Kingston upon Hull, West seems to make no distinction between the groups, and I find that strange.

**Mr. Randall:** I accept that those people pay taxes and in my speech I attempted to clarify that. The Bill is worded in such a way as to convey a blanket statement which embraces all people. In Committee we must introduce amendments to make it clear so that those people to whom the hon. Member for Caithness and Sutherland (Mr. Maclennan) referred will not be penalised.

**Mr. Jones:** I do not accept that there should be a link between paying taxes and voting. I simply refute what the hon. Gentleman and some of his hon. Friends said, in apparently disparaging terms, about many of our citizens who live overseas and have various connections with the United Kingdom.

I am conscious that other Members wish to speak so I shall not detain the House too long. I wish to refer to the remarks made by my right hon. Friend about postal votes in the United Kingdom. They are important and the present arrangements are unsatisfactory in a number of regards. I hope that my right hon. Friend will look at ways to make the attestation much simpler. There is no doubt that people have found it difficult to understand and it has imposed an incredible burden on returning officers who, to all intents and purposes, have been unable to make checks. I hope that my right hon. Friend will look at other problems in the postal voting system at the same time.

There are far too many acting returning officers and registration officers who insist on absent voters in the elderly or incapacitated category having to declare from exactly which illness or condition they are suffering, rather than simply allowing them to state that they are unable to travel to the polling station because they have difficulty walking. That approach is too intrusive because some people may be suffering from diseases some of which may be terminal and would not want them disclosed on the forms that are available to the political parties and registration officers. It would be to everyone's benefit if we could create a much simpler system of postal vote applications.

We have a unique opportunity to try to bring our citizens in line with those of many of the other European countries and beyond. Socialist Governments in France and elsewhere seem to have no difficulty in allowing such an approach to be taken towards their citizens abroad. It seems extraordinarily insular for some Opposition Members, though not all, to take an entirely different view.

5.58 pm

**Mr. Robert Maclennan** (Caithness and Sutherland): This debate has certainly given us an extraordinary indication of how far the Labour party has strayed from its original desire to see adult suffrage extended throughout this country. We listened to an appalling statement from the hon. Member for Kingston upon Hull, West (Mr. Randall) which showed not only a total lack of knowledge of the historical roots of the Labour party, but of the present day world in which we live. To suggest that expatriates are ignorant of what is going on in this country shows a lack of awareness of the modern means of communication and is a slur on many of our citizens who are great patriots and live abroad in the service of this country. Many of them take a closer interest in what is happening here than do a number of citizens living closer to home.

The suggestion by the hon. Member for Kingston upon Hull, West that it was in some way undesirable to conduct a domestic election abroad, or to inform British citizens about the issues on which a general election was being fought, is surely unworthy of serious support. Labour policy as expressed by the hon. Gentleman seems to be to encourage a tax connection between overseas voters and this country, but many people who live overseas are not particularly well off, and the nexus between tax and voting in parliamentary elections has never had the Labour party's support before. The hon. Gentleman has made an appalling, reactionary statement, which I think would come to public notice were it not for the apparent lack of press interest in the debate, notwithstanding its importance.

That leads me back to a question that I put—perhaps not very clearly—to the Home Secretary in an intervention. How important will the extension of the franchise be? There has been a broad variation in the estimates of the number of people who will be affected, which have ranged from half a million to 2 million.

**The Parliamentary Under-Secretary of State for the Home Department (Mr. Douglas Hogg):** Our estimate is that the number will not exceed 2 million, although we are not sure of the precise figure.

**Mr. Maclennan:** That is very significant: it suggests a substantial addition to the electoral roll, and I consider that highly desirable if the voters are citizens of this country. It is bound to have cost implications, however, and the Minister will probably want to mention those when he winds up the debate.

The 1985 Act was a cautious Act. The rule requiring citizens to have lived abroad for no longer than five years was particularly restrictive, and did not reflect the fact that many people who work abroad do so in cycles lasting considerably longer than that. The Government were right to extend the period, but any such restriction is bound to be somewhat arbitrary, and the choice of 25 years is clearly that. The Home Secretary said that he had toyed with the idea of imposing no such temporal restriction, and I feel that there is a good case for that, as people who fall on the wrong side of the 25-year boundary may have just as good a claim to be registered as voters as those who fall just on the right side. The drawing of such lines is certain to create anomalies.

**Mr. Tony Banks:** Does the hon. Gentleman want retrospective votes?

**Mr. Maclennan:** The hon. Gentleman will have an opportunity to contribute: I do not intend to speak for long.

The Government's decision to simplify the procedures is sensible, as procedures were partly responsible for

defeating the intent of the earlier Bill. The declaration of intention to return to this country strikes me as a particularly pointless requirement, which we do well to dispense with. It would be fairly simple for someone who was sufficiently keen to vote to make such a declaration, and it would be impossible to judge whether it was valid.

I entirely support the Government's proposals relating to those who leave the United Kingdom before they are old enough to vote. The general principle of extending the franchise in this manner is, I believe, right and just. I do not consider most people who live abroad to be parasites; in my view, they are hard working, and many contribute to the promotion of this country's commercial and diplomatic objectives. Without their work the United Kingdom would be more insular and out of touch with the rest of the world than any of us would wish. There are lotus eaters living on these islands, but no one suggests that they should be subjected to a test of whether they serve the nation. Many of us could nominate categories of such people, but it would be intolerable to do so, and it is equally nonsensical to categorise people living abroad in the same way.

The increase in parliamentary by-election expenses takes account of the considerable pressures faced by all political parties fighting such elections, which have become increasingly national events. The risk of a formal breach of the law is very great, and legislation should take account of that. I hope that this measure will enable the law to be enforced more severely than it has been on occasions in the past.

Broadly speaking, I welcome the Government's proposals.

6.7 pm

**Mr. Jeff Rooker** (Birmingham, Perry Barr): Let me start at the end of the Bill with clause 6, which deals with by-elections. I do not believe that anyone who has been within 100 miles of the organisation of a by-election in the last decade can say with hand on heart that the law has been observed in relation to the expenses of virtually any serious candidate. Raising the limit will not cost the parties a penny more. The money has already been spent, and we all know it. This measure is long overdue.

I am disappointed, however, that the Government have not taken the opportunity to rectify a problem that we thought we had got rid of by raising the deposit for parliamentary candidates. I do not agree with such deposits in any case—I think that signatures should be used instead—but one of the reasons for raising the deposits was to cut out the non-serious candidates. Winning a seat in the House is not a game; its purpose should not be publicity for stunts and organisations. Raising the deposit, however, has not stopped the nonsense at by-elections, where numerous candidates for different parties simply abuse the system for free national publicity.

I think that we could have taken the opportunity to abolish the requirement for a deposit and instead demand a minimum of 500 signatures for the nomination of candidates. Personally, I would go for 1,000; 500 is a compromise. I am serious about this. Anybody who claims to be a serious candidate for this place and who cannot find 500 signatures is, frankly, playing games with the electorate. We should cut out the monetary problems facing minor parties that are serious but are bereft of

[Mr. Jeff Rooker]

financial support. Although I am due to be in Birmingham on Wednesday evening, I should like to be here to move an amendment to clause 6 to that effect, if I would be in order in doing so.

My intervention earlier led the Home Secretary to believe that I was against the Bill. That is not the case, and I made my position clear when we debated the subject previously. I presume that the 25-year period will date from Royal Assent. To the best of my knowledge, electoral registers have not been kept by registration officers for 25 years. That means that the information going back that far will not be available.

**Mr. Douglas Hogg:** The hon. Gentleman is right in some respects, but the problem to which he refers can be met because most county or district council archives have the information. Where they have not, the registers can be obtained from the British library or from the national library of Scotland.

**Mr. Rooker:** I am pleased to hear that. I am happy so long as they are available. The local authority in Birmingham does not keep registers that far back, although I am aware that they are available at the central reference library or at the local studies department of the university, but one has to go through a process to obtain them. It is important that the registers are available so that the registrations can be checked. This is a serious matter concerning the right of people to vote in a constituency, and there must be a degree of certainty in the matter.

The electoral register is notoriously inaccurate. We do not debate election law and matters affecting the representation of the people often enough. Indeed, we do so only when we are obliged to do so or when there is a highly partisan issue following a change. That has not prompted this debate, but let us be clear that we are not adequately debating the Bill.

The measure has not yet been published for two clear weekends between its date of printing and Second Reading. It is being rushed through Parliament. Our normal conventions and Standing Orders are not being followed. That is by agreement, so I make no complaint, but it means that the Bill will not be scrutinised line by line and will not have a Standing Committee stage upstairs. We shall not have the chance that we would otherwise have to consider fully the way in which the electoral register works.

The electoral register can be described as a snapshot of one day. As I say, it is highly inaccurate. The poll tax register, on the other hand, is a rolling register; once one is on it, one stays on it. There is no requirement for an annual re-registration for the poll tax register. It changes only if the person's address changes.

I do not understand why our electoral registration system cannot follow the system in other western democracies. Under their system, once registered, a person remains registered until or unless there is a change of address. In Britain, particularly in the inner cities, there are enormous registration difficulties. There is massive under-registration, particularly for that one day, and that causes people to lose their vote.

I appreciate that it is easier nowadays for people to get back on to the register—if, say, somebody failed to fill in the form on the day in question—but administrative hurdles must still be surmounted. That involves getting the necessary form, filling it in and taking it to the electoral registration office. There would be no need for that if we adopted the rolling register so that, once registered, one remained on it. Other countries do it and there is no reason why we should not do the same.

Time permits me to make only a brief reference to the question of stateless persons living in this country. Consider, for example, people who came here from the Baltic states in the late 1940s and early 1950s. Many of them have never taken British nationality. Some of them could not even pass the naturalisation test; even today their command of the English language is not that good. But they have struggled and managed to survive in this country. They will not take Soviet citizenship because they are not Soviet citizens. So they find it difficult to obtain a passport, although the Home Office goes out of its way to issue such people with special documents.

While I would not think of linking taxes with votes, we should bear in mind that those stateless persons pay their taxes in this country, and they will have to pay the poll tax because they pay rates now. They will be on the rolling register for poll tax purposes. They have lived here perhaps for decades and I do not see why provision cannot be made for them to vote in British parliamentary elections.

We in this House—by "we" I mean the two major parties—are so conservative in making electoral arrangements that it beggars belief. Why is there no provision in the Bill to get rid of the necessity for voting to occur on a Thursday? Why not allow voting at weekends? The Thursday rule is a throwback to market days when constituencies were bought and sold.

Why is there no provision in the Bill for compulsory attendance at polling stations? I refer, of course, to compulsory attendance, not to compulsory voting. In recent weeks we have seen pictures of tanks trundling over people who were fighting for the right to have a proper vote and voice in the way their country is run. People in Britian gave their lives for the vote. It is people's civic duty and responsibility at least to get off their backsides and go to the polling station. Even if they do not like the candidates on offer, they should at least register their attendance at the polling station.

If time permitted, I would explain in detail how our system of voting is archiac, unfair and undemocratic. It is long overdue for reform to bring us in line with the more modern and democratic systems that are used in most other countries. We have not exported our voting system to, say, Poland or the Soviet Union. They do not use the first-past-the-post method. By their system, a single candidate can be defeated. In Britain, a single candidate gets elected without even the need for an election.

There should be a provision in the Bill to tidy up the rules applying to the description, the six words, on the ballot paper. I was astonished to discover during the Euro-elections that Members of the European Parliament remain MEPs, in the way local councillors remain in office, up to and beyond the day of the election and are able legally to describe themselves on the ballot paper as, "Member, European Parliament". That gives an unfair advantage to certain candidates, and the rule applying to the words that may be used needs tidying up.

When I inquired into that matter, I was surprised to learn that at the last general election the Prime Minister actually had "Prime Minister" on the ballot paper. The words read, "The Conservative candidate, Prime Minister." In the five general elections that I have fought, and reached this place, the Prime Minister in only one of them described herself as the Conservative party candidate. That was in 1983. In the two elections in 1974 and in the 1979 election she did not even describe herself as "The Conservative candidate". She described herself as the "Finchley and Friern Barnet Conservative candidate" —distancing herself at that time, when she was a member of the Cabinet, from the then Leader of the Conservative party. In those six words, no former Member of Parliament who holds a ministerial office should be entitled to display ministerial office on the ballot paper. I hope that an amendment to that effect will be made to the Bill when it is debated again next Wednesday.

6.17 pm

**Mr. David Winnick** (Walsall, North): I agreed with some of the points made by my hon. Friend the Member for Birmingham, Perry Barr (Mr. Rooker), and certainly democracy should be more valued in Britain than it is. My hon. Friend said that everyone should be under a legal obligation to attend a polling station at election time even if they did not wish to vote. I agree, and I confess that I am often disappointed when people tell me, "We never vote." Sometimes they say it almost with pride.

One thinks not only of what happened in China a few weeks ago but of the intense struggle that was fought in Britain by men and women to obtain the vote. Women went to prison and on hunger strike for the elementary right to vote. No wonder we on the Labour Benches take a different view from some people about the need to preserve, defend and value our system of parliamentary democracy. We need no lectures from the hon. Member for Caithness and Sutherland (Mr. Maclennan) and the Members of his party about our commitment to parliamentary democracy and civil liberties.

I also agreed with the remarks of my hon. Friend the Member for Perry Barr about the need for tighter restrictions at by-elections. I see no reason why such elections should become a kind of circus. The restrictions could be tighter without denying anybody the right to stand for election to Parliament. It is well known that a number of people stand at by-elections who would not dream of standing at general elections. They do so because they obtain the publicity that they would never get at a general election.

The Bill devalues democracy. I accept that many people who go abroad on contracts or with the armed services or to the EEC in Brussels have every right to retain their vote. I would be the last person to wish to take away that right to vote in national elections. We have made that clear on a number of occasions, and when the Representation of the People Act 1985 was passing through the House. The basic questions concern the number of years abroad, continued commitment to this country and whether the person intends to return to Britain. Before a Conservative Member mocks that, it should be borne in mind that that was precisely what the Government brought forward and what now exists in law. Before a person who lives abroad can vote, he must sign a declaration that he does not intend to reside permanently outside the country. The Home Secretary did not give any reason that I can accept why that should be abolished.

The hon. Member for Caithness and Sutherland gave the impression that everybody who goes abroad, for no matter how many years, does so for the best of reasons, in the interests of Britain, but we know that that is not always so. Some of these people go to escape the law and many others to escape paying tax here. Even now, they believe that it is far better to go abroad where their tax liability will be much less than if they stayed in Britain. Have they gone abroad for the best of reasons? Should we congratulate them on that?

The Bill proposes that people who go abroad can stay for up to 25 years without any evidence of their continuing commitment to the United Kingdom or that they will ever return, and still have the vote. However, the Government argued about local elections that it was necessary to have some kind of financial commitment, through paying rates or the poll tax, before one could have the vote. They laid that down in the law. Even the poorest people, those on income support, have to pay 20 per cent. of the poll tax before they have the right to vote. That was a new commitment that the Government introduced, against which we strongly argued.

The Government now propose that those who go abroad for many years, and therefore pay no tax in the United Kingdom, will still be able to vote in a general election even if they have no intention of returning. As my hon. Friend the Member for Kingston upon Hull, West (Mr. Randall) rightly said, if a child leaves the country with his parents, when he comes of voting age, he will be able to vote even if he has never been back to the United Kingdom. The Minister will no doubt correct me if I am wrong on this.

**Mr. Rupert Allason** (Torbay): I draw the hon. Gentleman's attention to the position of expatriate workers who live in a British colony. I am thinking in particular of those in Bermuda. They may have given an undertaking or signed a document saying that they have no intention of coming back to the United Kingdom, but they do not have a vote in that British colony. After they have fulfilled the residential qualifications in Bermuda they may not obtain the Bermudian status that gives them the right to vote. Many expatriates would like to continue their long-term interest in the United Kingdom and vote in United Kingdom elections but cannot do so, and the tax disincentives for them are considerable.

**Mr. Winnick:** The hon. Gentleman will no doubt be able to pursue that point in Committee. I have noted what he said, but he did not convince me that our opposition to the Bill is wrong.

I am convinced that if Conservative central office thought that the Tories would lose as a result of this measure, it would not be before us now. The Tory party has come to the cynical conclusion that it will get votes from the provisions of the Bill. It may be right, and I will not challenge that. To maximise the votes that they can get from abroad, the Government have decided on this measure. The Tories would gain far more votes than the Democrats. The hon. Member for Caithness and Sutherland is being naive if he does not understand why the Bill is before us.

**Mr. Maclennan:** I am grateful to the hon. Gentleman for giving way and for drawing attention to my principled opposition to the Labour party's view.

**Mr. Winnick:** I am willing to concede that the hon. Gentleman has made a principled stand, but his principle is misplaced. There is no reason to take such a stand. The

[*Mr. Winnick*]

points that we have made are far more principled and are far more concerned with preserving our democracy, and with our commitment to this country and its political process. This is a shabby scheme. It is understandable that the Conservative party should introduce it, but those of us who vote against it will do so with every justification.

6.25 pm

**Mr. Tony Banks** (Newham, North-West): I agree entirely with my hon. Friend the Member for Walsall, North (Mr. Winnick). I do not support the Bill, which smacks of international gerrymandering. The Home Secretary tried to dress it up in the language of the extended franchise, but we know that the instincts and intentions of the Government are base. They think that the Bill will extend the trawl. They will be going out looking for the international redneck vote to supplement the miserable performance that they are fully expected to have at the next general election.

I listened carefully to the Home Secretary, who said that not enough people were voting under the existing system for overseas voters introduced by the Representation of the People Act 1985. Roughly 500,000 people overseas are eligible to vote. Something like 13,000 of them voted in the 1987 election. As I said to the Home Secretary, voting is a voluntary act. I do not know why 500,000 people minus 13,000 did not turn up to vote.

**Mr. Rooker:** Is my hon. Friend aware that, out of the 500,000 who registered, only about 2,000 actually voted?

**Mr. Banks:** The statistic that I saw in the Library a little while ago suggested that the 13,000 voted. Let us not quibble. If 500,000 people were registered, only a small number decided to vote under the existing system. One would have thought that the Home Secretary would try to get the additional people to register and vote instead of saying that he will make it easier for people to register by having fewer restraints. There are no restraints on up to 500,000 voting anyway, so we are now looking for the greater number of up to 2 million who may register as a result of the changes proposed in the Bill, and thus be eligible to vote. We do not know how many will vote.

This is absurd. If we looked at this logically, we would be asking about the franchise here and about the 30 per cent. of people who were eligible to vote at the last general election but did not. Why do we not lower the voting age, or declare a public holiday on polling day? Why do we not try to get through the House compulsory voting? Why do we not change the voting procedures? Why do we not have run-off campaigns between the candidates so that whoever ends up as Member of Parliament speaks for over 50 per cent. of the constituency? Why do we not have postal votes for everybody? One could go on talking about the way to tap into the extra 30 per cent. of people who do not vote in a general election, but no Conservative Member makes that proposal.

I support the proposal that British citizens overseas in the diplomatic service, in the armed services or on short-term contracts should have their right to vote while working overseas because they are showing a continuing long-term commitment to this country. When people have effectively emigrated and have not the slightest intention of coming back, I do not see why I should be expected to

support their right to vote for a Government whose economic and social policies will not affect them. We are talking about tax exiles. We are talking about people who have put two fingers up to this country because they do not want to have anything to do with it. They have said, "We are clearing off. We will go abroad and live off our ill-gotten gains." Those are the sort of people who will be in the extended categories.

Taxation is crucial if one is living overseas. It is not crucial here. If someone lives in this country, he is living under the laws that have been passed by the Government. Taxation is not crucial in this country but a person who lives overseas, with no intention of coming back, and who pays no taxes in this country should not have the right to vote for policies which will never cost him anything and which will never affect him economically or socially.

**Mr. Allason** *rose*——

**Mr. Banks:** I will not give way. I will be sitting down in a few moments so that we may vote by 7 o'clock.

The Prime Minister herself has said that, unless people are contributing to local taxes and rates, they will not act responsibly in the way that they vote at local elections. If it is good enough for the Prime Minister to use that argument, to which we are opposed, I do not see how the Government can try to take the reverse position in regard to those who live overseas, who have no intention of coming back to this country and who pay no taxes or rates here.

I agree with my hon. Friend the Member for Walsall, North. I am no narrow-minded nationalist, but I am damned if I will support the right of tax exiles to vote for policies in this country. The Government see this as a way of trawling round the country looking for the redneck vote. It will not do them any good at the next election. In the meantime, I am opposed root and branch to the proposals in the Bill.

6.31 pm

**Mr. Harry Barnes** (Derbyshire, North-East): The importance of the measure was displayed by the Minister who stated that potentially there were 2 million votes involved. That means that over 3,000 votes might be involved per constituency at a time when the electoral register is in collapse because of the poll tax. There are 76 constituencies in England where the electorate has dropped by more than 1,000 in the last year, including a drop of 2,170 in Finchley which, according to the Office of Population Censuses and Surveys, is not due to demographic reasons, but must have something to do with registration. In a letter to me the only explanation offered by the Prime Minister for the registration figures not being as high as they should be is the September 1988 postal strike. That is an unfortunate explanation which does not apply to the position in Scotland where there was a similar collapse in registration in the major cities between the general election of 1987 and 1988. Therefore, the poll tax is relevant to the Bill.

I am concerned about the low priority that is being given to this important legislation. It is not just, as the hon. Member for Caithness and Sutherland (Mr. Maclennan), the representative of the SLD, said, that the press are not here; many hon. Members are not here either. The Bill is being rushed through, hopefully for some, in less than two hours. We are not giving it the consideration that major constitutional legislation should have. The Secretary of State, who introduced the Bill, has left the House. With all respect to my hon. Friend the Member for Kingston upon Hull, West (Mr. Randall), we are leading with the reserves. It is an important measure which should be discussed in prime time.

The Representation of the People Act 1985 was discussed at considerable length during 1984 and 1985. It was of wider scope than the present measure but Labour voted against it on Second Reading. Considerable time was spent on it in a Committee of the whole House. Only when certain amendments were introduced was there agreement not to vote against it on Third Reading. All the concessions made at that stage for overseas voters are being overridden. The position is even worse. Clause 1 extends from five years to 25 years the period during which people can pick up electoral registration overseas. The original proposal in 1984 was seven years, but it was amended to five years; now it is to be 25 years.

Under existing legislation people who were under 18 when they left this country are excluded. That condition is being removed. A person who left the country as a babe in arms may, 18 years later, qualify for registration and may vote in English elections, yet some people in this country will be excluded from their birthright by the operation of the poll tax which deters them from being not just on the poll tax register but on the linked electoral register.

The minimal requirement of a declaration that a person did not intend to reside permanently outside the United Kingdom is being abolished. People will not even have to say that they intend to return here at some stage. We should ask who should be on the electoral register and what principles should be involved. People should be involved with the nation and should participate in its affairs. They should be concerned about the services that are provided because they benefit from them.

I do not accept the principle of no representation without taxation which operates in regard to the poll tax. Everybody within a society should be entitled to vote as a birthright, but we have to decide what a society is. Society does not mean that a person leaves the country, settles in another area and devotes himself to that nation where he will develop interests distinct from his interests here. Someone who settles overseas is bound to become more involved with the interests of the country where his children are growing up.

The explanatory and financial memorandum refers to the costs of registering overseas electors. If there was a decent principle, I would not quibble about the cost because we cannot put too high a price on democracy. We should be willing to spend any amount to ensure that people have the franchise. It will cost £1·72 to register an overseas elector and 62p each year to maintain registration. That expenditure can be contrasted with the failure of the Government to try to stimulate electoral registration in this country through advertising.

Expenditure on advertising by the Home Office to encourage electoral registration amounted to 0·31 per cent. of total Government advertising expenditure in the past year. We should contrast that with the expenditure of more than £6 million by Abbey National in its campaign to encourage people to exercise their vote on the society becoming a plc. Abbey National was not allowed to ask people to vote yes, but it encouraged full use of the franchise. Should we not encourage full registration of electors? Should we not get rid of poll tax legislation which

for the first time has introduced the principle of no registration without taxation? That principle applies in Chile where, at the recent referendum, in order to register people had to pay an amount equivalent to one month's money on an employment scheme, as a result of which many of the Chilean working class did not have a vote. The vote against Pinochet would have been much greater but for the financial constraints on people.

The poll tax is creating a similar situation in Britain. For the first time since the franchise was extended universally—in 1918 for all men and in 1928 for all women —there will be a tax on those who qualify to vote. A similar situation applied in the 19th century and before 1918 when we had the 40 shilling vote and other fancy franchises.

Those are the types of measures that we should be considering in a Bill such as this. We should be discussing my Re-enfranchisement of the People Bill, which would detach the poll tax register from the electoral register, rather than the nonsense before us today.

6.40 pm

**Mr. Jeremy Corbyn** (Islington, North): I am shocked that we should be debating a Bill such as this which basically shows the Tory party's deep concern for its future. It has to scrabble round the world looking for tax dodgers, crooks, thieves and wastrels, anywhere that it can, in order to get a Tory Government re-elected in two years' time. That is what the Bill is about. It has nothing to do with democracy.

The Home Secretary has given us an eloquent testimony of his commitment to democracy by clearing off the minute that he finished his speech. He may have gone abroad; I do not know. Perhaps he has gone to see a tax exile. There is something disgraceful and distasteful about the Bill.

If the Government were serious about ensuring that democracy in Britain worked properly, they would not have pushed through the poll tax which has taken thousands of people off the register. The London Central European constituency had 40,000 fewer voters two weeks ago than it had in 1984. That was the result not of the migration of people from central London, but of fear of the poll tax. That was the reason behind the poll tax.

Local authorities are spending less and less money on voter registration and canvassing follow-ups. The voter registration system is less accurate than it used to be. The Housing Act 1988 and the activities of dodgy landlords further discourage people from registering. That has always been a problem and will continue to be one.

The Government's only answer to all the problems of non-participation in elections is to threaten people with the poll tax and offer the vote to tax dodgers living abroad. A baby born in Britain today and taken out of the country tomorrow would, after its birth had been registered and a passport issued—if that were possible in the time—be eligible to vote in British elections from 2007 until 2014, having played no part in Britain's political or economic life.

Thousands of people are denied the right to vote who are legally resident in Britain as asylum-seekers or refugees, or who have another nationality but are legally resident and work in Britain, making their contribution to society. It is not just those who pay tax who should have the vote. Those political exiles are making their

[*Mr. Jeremy Corbyn*]

contribution to society, but they are denied the right to vote here and in their country of origin. It is monstrously unfair for us to preach democracy while denying such people the right to participate in elections.

About 15 million people across Europe, often the poorest, are suffering the ravages of economic policies pursued by Governments such as ours and are being denied any participation in a democratic process that can influence their lives. That is distasteful, and the Home Office should examine the ways in which the electoral register and the franchise in Britain could be extended to people living and contributing to society here rather than scrabbling round the world looking for tax exiles to vote for them.

The raising of the parliamentary limit on by-election campaigns is nonsense. Parliamentary by-elections have been turned into a circus by the activities of the Front-Bench spokesmen of all parties in the House and by media exposure. There is an increasing antipathy towards all political parties in by-elections because people feel that they are being taken for a ride. They feel that they are spectators in their own electoral process.

Raising the limit to about £14,000 for by-elections, plus the unit cost increase for each vote of 16·4p for every entry on the electoral register, means that by-election campaigns will cost about £20,000 or more per candidate. Multiply that by five or six candidates, and we are talking about £100,000 worth of political publicity being pushed out, often during a two-week by-election campaign. That is not a promotion of democracy, but a way of squashing and squeezing smaller third parties.

I am happy and proud to be a member of one of the two largest parties in Britain, but, as a Member of the House, I have a duty, as others have, to ensure that democracy is fair and that everyone has a right to express their point of view.

The Bill seems to be a bit obsessed with money all round. We heard at the beginning that the Government estimate an expenditure of £1·72 per overseas voter to be registered, but there is no increase for voter registration in Britain. We must consider that.

We must also consider the electoral deposit. There is a general feeling that if we increased the electoral deposit we would reduce the number of candidates and get away from irritants from third, fourth, fifth, sixth, 10th and 12th parties; that is wrong. We should not prevent people from contesting elections or submitting their name for election as a result of their inability to pay a cash deposit. If there is to be a limit, it should be based on the number of signatures in support of a candidature. At the moment that is only 10, but there is no reason why it should not be substantially increased and the parliamentary election deposit abolished at the same time.

Many hon. Members have put forward different proposals for extending and improving participation in democracy in Britain. The Bill does nothing towards that. It helps not one jot to improve democracy in Britain; it only enfranchises those who, in effect, have emigrated.

**Mr. Tony Banks:** Someone said earlier that he did not know where the 25-year rule came from. We know that it comes from the 1964 general election when many people upped and left the country because a Labour Government were elected. The 25-year rule was a way of enfranchising all those who have left Britain since 1964. It is no mere coincidence.

**Mr. Corbyn:** There were those who, under the previous Labour Government, were paid large sums of money to write articles in the Sunday newspapers saying that they could not afford to live in Britain because of what they considered to be the penal rates of tax. I do not consider that to be a basis for re-enfranchising them. They should show some commitment to Britain by living here and contributing to our society.

I hope that when the Under-Secretary of State replies he will at least show that the Home Office has considered the points that have been made tonight. I hope that the Bill will not go forward and that we shall not extend the franchise in the way that the Government want, but that we shall extend democratic participation in Britain.

6.48 pm

**The Parliamentary Under-Secretary of State for the Home Department (Mr. Douglas Hogg):** In the course of the debate a number of hon. Members have outlined their own views about defects that they perceive to exist in our electoral system. I acknowledge that many of the problems they mentioned are not addressed by the Bill, which is narrowly focused and is intended to be so. That is why we have not sought to address the points made, for example, by the hon. Member for Birmingham, Perry Barr (Mr. Rooker) regarding the deposit and eligibility to stand.

In short, we are seeking to extend the franchise to people who hitherto have been deprived of it. The broad principle by which I stand—and I am glad that the hon. Member for Caithness and Sutherland (Mr. Maclennan) stands by it as well—is that British citizens should, unless there are persuasive reasons to the contrary, have the right to vote. That seems to me to be an admirable principle. We should not deprive British citizens of the right to vote unless there is an obvious and compelling reason why we should do so. That approach is adopted by most developed countries.

We live in a world in which citzens of Britain and of every other country must live abroad, or choose to do so, to work, or for an increasing number of other purposes or reasons.

**Mr. Tony Banks:** Will the Minister give way?

**Mr. Hogg:** No, I shall not give way for the moment —and perhaps not at all, because my time is extremely limited.

The hon. Member for Islington, North (Mr. Corbyn) launched an attack on tax exiles. It is possible that among those to whom the franchise will be extended by the Bill will be people whom the hon. Gentleman calls tax exiles. However, the fact that some unworthy people may be caught in the net is not a good reason for denying a franchise to the very many worthy people who are presently denied it. People now go abroad for long periods for a whole variety of reasons. They work in international agencies, commerce and business, and they serve as missionaries or educationists. The list is endless. To describe the people who may be given a franchise by the Bill in the way that the hon. Member for Islington, North described them, as

"tax dodgers, crooks, thieves and wastrels",

is deeply offensive to the many people who go abroad for wholly legitimate reasons.

**Mr. Banks** *rose*——

**Mr. Hogg:** I shall give way in a moment, but I must finish this point.

The hon. Member for Caithness and Sutherland made the important point that the Labour party is, in its attitude to the Bill, departing from the standards that it has set itself for many years. Labour is saying in effect that people should not have the right to vote unless they pay tax. That argument was explicitly deployed by the hon. Member for Kingston upon Hull, West (Mr. Randall)—he nods assent. If that policy were adopted, the huge majority of students who are currently entitled to vote would be denied that right. If we were to adopt the argument of the hon. Member for Kingston upon Hull, West, millions of old-age pensioners who do not pay tax would also be denied the right to vote. That would be the consequence of the proposal made by the right hon. Gentleman from the Labour Front Bench.

**Mr. Randall:** When the Minister reads the *Official Report* tomorrow, he will learn that I referred only to tax exiles.

**Mr. Hogg:** We heard otherwise from some Opposition Members, and those honourable exceptions included the hon. Member for Perry Barr. Nevertheless, the Opposition's argument against the Bill is that there should be some linkage between the obligation and the fact of paying tax and the franchise, which I do not accept in respect of parliamentary elections.

**Mr. Tony Banks:** Will the Minister give way now?

**Mr. Hogg:** No, not at this moment. I gave way to the hon. Member for Kingston upon Hull, West. I have enjoyed the many interventions of the hon. Member for Newham, North-West (Mr. Banks), but he had ample opportunity to put his point of view.

The hon. Member for Caithness and Sutherland asked a number of questions, which I shall try to answer. We do not know the number of persons who will be eligible to vote. Our best estimate is that the total will be of the order of 2 million. If you, Madam Deputy Speaker, were to ask me how many people we estimate will take up the franchise, I would reply that our broad calculation is 60,000. That is the figure we have in mind. In 1987, 12,000 overseas citizens registered to vote in the general election that year, but we do not know how many did so.

The hon. Member for Kingston upon Hull, West made a defeatist speech in suggesting that the purpose of the Bill is to increase the number of Conservative votes. I have two comments to make on that point. First, we are taking the high moral ground that British citizens are, prima facie, entitled to vote even when they live abroad. Secondly, it is extraordinary that the Labour party should suggest that its policies are so unattractive that it will not have supporters among those living abroad. That may be right, but such a view tells us something about the Labour party. When I hear the hon. Member for Islington, North describe British citizens overseas as

"tax dodgers, crooks, thieves and wastrels"

I am not in the least surprised why he supposes that Labour will not receive many votes from them.

The explanatory memorandum gives information about the important aspect of costs. For local government, the cost will be £1·72p per voter initially and thereafter 62p per year. The calculations are set out in the annex to our second consultation paper that is now in the Library. Those figures have been made available to local authorities in good time, and I am pleased to report that there was no particular criticism of them. I do not claim that those figures are 100 per cent. accurate, but the order of the estimate is correct.

Hon. Members who attacked our abolition of the declaration fail to grasp what we are about. The declaration in its present form requires people to assert that they do not intend to live permanently outside the United Kingdom. No honest man can put his name to such a declaration, because such a circumstance is unverifiable. More importantly, any honest man considering whether he is capable of making such a declaration truthfully must bear in mind that his intentions may change. There is no reason why a person who is essentially honest and recognises the basic facts of life should be penalised in the way that the Opposition suggest.

The criteria affecting children are clearly set out in the Bill. Young persons will be entitled to apply to register if they were resident in the constituency during the relevant time period—and residency is a matter of fact, meaning a permanent connection—and their parent or guardian was also registered at a relevant address within the appropriate constituency. I see no lacuna in that situation.

I shall bring my remarks to a conclusion. I have not answered every hon. Member who has spoken, but I propose to do so in writing instead. The justification for the Bill is an appropriate extension of the franchise to people who should not be denied it. On that basis, I commend the Bill to the House.

*Question put,* That the Bill be now read a Second time:—

*The House divided:* Ayes 162, Noes 19.

**Division No. 268]**                                  **[6.58 pm**

## AYES

Alexander, Richard
Allason, Rupert
Amess, David
Amos, Alan
Arbuthnot, James
Arnold, Jacques *(Gravesham)*
Arnold, Tom *(Hazel Grove)*
Ashby, David
Aspinwall, Jack
Atkins, Robert
Atkinson, David
Baker, Nicholas *(Dorset N)*
Bennett, Nicholas *(Pembroke)*
Bevan, David Gilroy
Boscawen, Hon Robert
Boswell, Tim
Bottomley, Mrs Virginia
Bowis, John
Braine, Rt Hon Sir Bernard
Bright, Graham
Brooke, Rt Hon Peter
Browne, John *(Winchester)*
Bruce, Ian *(Dorset South)*
Buck, Sir Antony
Budgen, Nicholas
Burt, Alistair
Butler, Chris
Carlisle, John, *(Luton N)*
Carlisle, Kenneth *(Lincoln)*
Carrington, Matthew

Carttiss, Michael
Channon, Rt Hon Paul
Chope, Christopher
Colvin, Michael
Coombs, Anthony *(Wyre F'rest)*
Cran, James
Davies, Q. *(Stamf'd & Spald'g)*
Davis, David *(Boothferry)*
Dorrell, Stephen
Dunn, Bob
Dykes, Hugh
Emery, Sir Peter
Fallon, Michael
Fenner, Dame Peggy
Field, Barry *(Isle of Wight)*
Forth, Eric
Fox, Sir Marcus
Freeman, Roger
Fry, Peter
Gale, Roger
Garel-Jones, Tristan
Gill, Christopher
Gow, Ian
Greenway, John *(Ryedale)*
Gregory, Conal
Griffiths, Peter *(Portsmouth N)*
Ground, Patrick
Grylls, Michael
Gummer, Rt Hon John Selwyn
Hague, William

Hamilton, Neil *(Tatton)*
Hampson, Dr Keith
Hanley, Jeremy
Hannam, John
Hargreaves, Ken *(Hyndburn)*
Harris, David
Hawkins, Christopher
Hayward, Robert
Higgins, Rt Hon Terence L.
Hogg, Hon Douglas *(Gr'th'm)*
Hordern, Sir Peter
Howarth, Alan *(Strat'd-on-A)*
Howarth, G. *(Cannock & B'wd)*
Howells, Geraint
Hunt, David *(Wirral W)*
Hunt, Sir John *(Ravensbourne)*
Hunter, Andrew
Hurd, Rt Hon Douglas
Irvine, Michael
Jack, Michael
Janman, Tim
Johnson Smith, Sir Geoffrey
Jones, Robert B *(Herts W)*
Jopling, Rt Hon Michael
Kilfedder, James
King, Roger *(B'ham N'thfield)*
Knapman, Roger
Knight, Greg *(Derby North)*
Knight, Dame Jill *(Edgbaston)*
Latham, Michael
Lawrence, Ivan
Lester, Jim *(Broxtowe)*
Lightbown, David
Lilley, Peter
Lloyd, Peter *(Fareham)*
Lord, Michael
Lyell, Sir Nicholas
McCrindle, Robert
Macfarlane, Sir Neil
MacKay, Andrew *(E Berkshire)*
Maclean, David
Maclennan, Robert
McLoughlin, Patrick
McNair-Wilson, Sir Michael
McNair-Wilson, Sir Patrick
Malins, Humfrey
Mans, Keith
Maples, John
Marshall, John *(Hendon S)*
Marshall, Michael *(Arundel)*
Martin, David *(Portsmouth S)*
Mates, Michael
Maude, Hon Francis

Miller, Sir Hal
Mills, Iain
Mitchell, Andrew *(Gedling)*
Mitchell, Sir David
Moate, Roger
Moss, Malcolm
Moynihan, Hon Colin
Neubert, Michael
Nicholson, David *(Taunton)*
Norris, Steve
Onslow, Rt Hon Cranley
Oppenheim, Phillip
Page, Richard
Pattie, Rt Hon Sir Geoffrey
Peacock, Mrs Elizabeth
Porter, David *(Waveney)*
Portillo, Michael
Powell, William *(Corby)*
Raffan, Keith
Redwood, John
Renton, Tim
Rhodes James, Robert
Roe, Mrs Marion
Sackville, Hon Tom
Shaw, David *(Dover)*
Shaw, Sir Giles *(Pudsey)*
Shaw, Sir Michael *(Scarb')*
Shepherd, Colin *(Hereford)*
Shepherd, Richard *(Aldridge)*
Shersby, Michael
Sims, Roger
Speed, Keith
Stanbrook, Ivor
Stevens, Lewis
Stewart, Andy *(Sherwood)*
Stradling Thomas, Sir John
Summerson, Hugo
Tapsell, Sir Peter
Taylor, Ian *(Esher)*
Tebbit, Rt Hon Norman
Thurnham, Peter
Trotter, Neville
Waddington, Rt Hon David
Wardle, Charles *(Bexhill)*
Wheeler, John
Widdecombe, Ann
Winterton, Mrs Ann
Wood, Timothy
Yeo, Tim

Tellers for the Ayes:
  Mr. John M. Taylor and
  Mr. Sydney Chapman.

**NOES**

Banks, Tony *(Newham NW)*
Clwyd, Mrs Ann
Cohen, Harry
Cousins, Jim
Cryer, Bob
Douglas, Dick
Godman, Dr Norman A.
Hinchliffe, David
Madden, Max
Mahon, Mrs Alice
Mitchell, Austin *(G't Grimsby)*
Nellist, Dave

Pendry, Tom
Pike, Peter L.
Sheldon, Rt Hon Robert
Skinner, Dennis
Spearing, Nigel
Winnick, David
Wise, Mrs Audrey

Tellers for the Noes:
  Mr. Harry Barnes and
  Mr. Jeremy Corbyn.

*Question accordingly agreed to.*
*Bill read a Second time.*
Bill committed to a Committee of the whole House.
—*[Mr. Maclean.]*
*Committee tomorrow.*

# British Railways (Penalty Fares) Bill
## *[Lords]* (By Order)

7.13 pm

**Sir Patrick McNair-Wilson** (New Forest): I beg to move, That the Bill, as amended, be now considered.

**Dr. John Marek** (Wrexham): On a point of order, Madam Deputy Speaker. I was wondering whether the hon. Member for New Forest (Sir P. McNair-Wilson) will delay his comments so that he can reply to questions from Opposition Members. Of course it is in his hands.

**Sir Patrick McNair-Wilson** *indicated assent.*

**Madam Deputy Speaker (Miss Betty Boothroyd):** That seems to have been accepted by the hon. Gentleman.

**Mr. Bob Cryer** (Bradford, South): In many respects the Bill is similar to the London Regional Transport (Penalty Fares) Bill that we debated last night. The statement produced by the promoters refers to the working party report that we discussed last night. That report made it clear that British Rail was working on a scheme for penalty fares based on the report. Therefore, some of the ground that we cover will be identical.

It is important to draw the attention of the House to the fact that the report which forms the basis of the legislation was drawn-up by people who may not meet the difficulties that a penalty fares scheme may produce. It was extremely difficult to get hold of a copy of the report as no copies are available in the Vote Office—although I have ordered one —and there are only two copies in the Library. That seems to be less than adequate when the Bill being debated by the House is based on that report.

The report deals with the terms of reference to examine London Regional Transport's concerns about penalty fares provisions. The working party consisted of four members of the Department of Transport, one representative from the Home Office, a representative of the Lord Chancellor's Department—curiously enough from the private and international law division—and two representatives of London Regional Transport, the solicitor and the group planning manager. It would be interesting to know whether the members of that committee travel on British Rail because the report was the basis of British Rail's calculations in making its proposals, so it is a very important document for us to consider.

7.15 pm

One of my deep regrets is that the Department of Transport did not think it fit to include in that working party any representatives of the trade unions involved. The Minister might argue that it is not usual for outsiders to be included in departmental or interdepartmental working parties. It may not be usual, but it has occurred. When the previous Labour Government were establishing the Co-operative Development Agency Act 1978, they established a departmental working party which included members from various strands of the co-operative movement, including representatives from working co-operatives organised through the industrial common ownership movement, and from the Co-operative Union. It included a very good cross-section of experience and ability.

As it was done on that occasion, I see no reason why the working party that produced the report on penalty fares could not have been similarly extended to include representatives of the Transport Salaried Staffs' Association to represent the people who will administer the scheme, the NUR to represent the people in the ticket offices who will be made redundant, and ASLEF as train drivers will also be involved. If disputes occur on driver-only trains, when the travelling inspector gets on a train to check whether people have paid their fares, inevitably the communication cord may be pulled and the driver may be drawn into the argument.

It would have been useful for the working party to have included all the trade unions representing those who work for British Rail. The fact that the Government did not take the trouble to do that and chose instead to use a group of civil servants and some representatives of the management of London Regional Transport points to the deficiency in the basis of the legislation. It is also a pointer to the Government's heavy-handed attitude in imposing a scheme on British Rail.

It is a sad reflection on the managements of British Rail and London Regional Transport, who are so subservient that they cannot set their faces against those badly thought-out and designed proposals. It is an example of the way in which such schemes are imposed, just as British Rail management is attempting to impose the removal of the national negotiating rights that the NUR and ASLEF have built up over many years. The workers do not want to accept that. That is the kernel of the present dispute, which has been created entirely by the intransigence, obduracy and arrogance of the management of British Rail. Passengers who are inconvenienced should remember that it takes two sides to make a dispute, and although the weight of the press is heavily aimed against the ordinary workers on the railway system, it is the people in the offices and in the executive suites who have chauffeur-driven cars and who seldom use the railways who are creating the difficulties, the confrontation and the strike action.

That brings me back to the membership of the working party and the people who produced the scheme which has been so eagerly taken up by the British Rail management. The people who have taken up the scheme sometimes do not appear to care very much for railways. The management élite of British Rail are provided with chauffeur-driven cars, although I do not know why they should be when they are running a transport system. I suspect that they rarely travel on the system as ordinary fare-paying passengers and that they use only main-line services and the first-class section of trains when they travel on the railways, which is rare. They do not seem to be the best persons to judge what is best for the travelling passenger.

The reason for this proposal is that when the report was produced in May 1986 it was claimed that £19·5 million was lost in fare revenue, and the figure has now increased to £26 million. The promoters of the Bill will be only too keen to provide the House with information about how the calculations were made. As I understand it, the calculations relate to London Regional Transport, because the report was based on London Regional Transport, but I have no doubt that British Rail will be anxious to provide figures and the basis of the calculations of the amount lost through fare dodgers.

**Sir Patrick McNair-Wilson:** If I heard the hon. Gentleman correctly, he used the figure of £26 million. I must correct him and point out that the figure was £36 million for Network SouthEast alone.

**Mr. Cryer:** I am grateful to the hon. Gentleman. I have made a note that the figure is £36 million for Network SouthEast alone. But where has the figure come from? I used the figure of £26 million for London Regional Transport, although, as I said, I recognise that that figure does not apply to British Rail, which covers a larger area than London Regional Transport. I am concerned about the basis on which this legislation, which will make a massive change, is put forward. We have not so far had an explanation about either London Regional Transport or British Rail. If the figure for Network SouthEast is £36 million, we should know the basis on which that figure was calculated.

The hundreds of millions of pounds of investment nationwide, the redundancies and the difficulties in collecting the penalty fares are all connected with the amount that is being dodged. I hold no brief for people who evade fares. Clearly, we want to maximise the revenue of all public passenger services to provide a better service. That means that everyone is contributing and Labour Members believe strongly in collective provision. However, having identified the problem, the Bill is not necessarily the correct solution; it may be the worst because it gives rise to a number of problems.

**Mr. Harry Cohen** (Leyton): I agree with my hon. Friend. No Labour Member favours fare evasion and we want to see firm action taken against it. My hon. Friend is also right to say that British Rail has produced no proof for the figure of £36 million lost on Network SouthEast alone. Has my hon. Friend any information about that figure? Does he not think that British Rail should have substantiated it? The figure is big for so small an area. British Rail is almost accusing many people in the south-east of being crooks. That is an appalling insult and a slur on people in the south-east for which British Rail has provided no detailed information.

**Mr. Cryer:** I refer my hon. Friend to clause 7 of the statement on behalf of the promoters in support of consideration of the Bill, as amended in Committee. The figure quoted is £36 million, to which the hon. Member for New Forest (Sir P. McNair-Wilson) drew attention. The figure refers to Network SouthEast alone. Unfortunately, it is given no credence and seems to have been plucked from the air by British Rail officials, who are keen that this legislation should go through so that British Rail can dispense with the services of a number of employees. British Rail management sees employment not as a valuable asset, but as a nuisance to be dispensed with at every conceivable opportunity. For several years, its policy has been to introduce driver-only trains—and it has removed signal boxes and installed automatic crossings. In every case where that has been done there have been problems, and in some cases lives have been lost.

**Mr. Peter L. Pike** (Burnley): Is not British Rail making it increasingly difficult to pay one's fare because of reductions in manning? My hon. Friend knows well the East Lancashire line and the Roses line, where most of the stations are unmanned. If one is catching a train to London, it is difficult to pay for a ticket and one often finds

[*Mr. Peter L. Pike*]

that one does not have enough time at Preston to pay for a long-distance fare. British Rail has also reduced manning on many trains, so one often does not have one's ticket checked. People who have no tickets do not have to pay. I have a handful of tickets that have not been clipped either because there has been no ticket collecter on the train or because he has not reached me as there are too many passengers on the train.

**Mr. Cryer:** As my hon. Friend knows, my wife comes from Darwen in Lancashire, so we frequently make visits across the Pennines. Colne station, which used to be staffed, has been reduced by some high-quality decision of British Rail management to a pile of rubble with a bus shelter in the middle of the platform as the only sign that there is a railway there. There are no staff to sell tickets and people have to buy their tickets on the train. That is often difficult because on crowded trains the ticket dispenser, checker and collecter cannot always get round all the coaches.

Quite apart from the basis of this legislation and the dubious claims put forward, I should have thought that if there was a national scandal of people avoiding fares, the promoters would have made available details of the number of people chased, where they came from and where they were going and the number of prosecutions for the amount of money lost. All that information should have been provided to substantiate British Rail's claims. However, we have been provided with nothing but a bald figure. That shows a certain contempt for the House because the promoters seem to assume that the Bill will be passed as a matter of course so they need not take too much trouble to delve out the information. It is possible, of course, that the promoters do not have that information and are trying, metaphorically, to bluster their way through.

**Mr. Cohen:** I bring my hon. Friend back to the point about the £36 million a year that British Rail claims is lost through fare evasion on Network SouthEast alone. The hon. Member for New Forest (Sir P. McNair-Wilson) represents a constituency that is in Network SouthEast, but right at the edge. Is British Rail saying that there are many crooks and thieves in the New Forest who refuse to pay their fares? Perhaps they voted for the hon. Member for New Forest. Should not the hon. Gentleman put his house in order in terms of his constituents? That appalling slur on those people has meant that it has fallen to the Opposition to defend them and say that they are basically honest.

**Mr. Deputy Speaker (Sir Paul Dean):** Order. I am sure that the hon. Member for Bradford, South (Mr. Cryer) will bear it in mind that the debate is on the motion, That the Bill, as amended, be now considered. His remarks must relate to that motion.

7.30 pm

**Mr. Cryer:** Yes, Mr. Deputy Speaker. I am keen to consider the Bill.

British Rail should provide figures for our consideration. I am grateful to you, Mr. Deputy Speaker, for pointing out that we are considering the Bill. British Rail has employed sponsors—who, no doubt, are more generously provided for than British Rail employees—to promote the Bill for our consideration. The sponsors and British Rail have not put the necessary information before us. My hon. Friend the Member for Leyton (Mr. Cohen) has made a good point, which no doubt the hon. Member for New Forest is bearing in mind so that he can give us information about the basis for the £36 million loss.

Labour Members believe in collective provision. We want to ensure that everyone contributes and that there are no fare dodgers. They place a bigger burden on other users of the railway service and the reduction in revenue diminishes the opportunity for investment. Naturally, we are keen that fare dodgers are caught, but is this the right way to go about it? It is not.

I do not want to go too much into the details of the King's Cross disaster because we dealt with that last night in the debate on the London Regional Transport (Penalty Fares) Bill. King's Cross was an example of how fire can rapidly take hold, causing loss of life and scarring. It stunned even the most experienced and hardened fire officers. I am sure that there are British Rail stations with similar characteristics—underground passages which can act as chimneys, causing draughts that lead to potential dangers for passengers.

**Dr. Marek:** I wonder whether the Waterloo-City line is such an example.

**Mr. Cryer:** My hon. Friend is right to draw the attention of the House to that line. Wherever there are large passageways rising at an angle potential fire traps are created.

We are talking about the installation of automatic ticket barriers. If they cannot be opened immediately fire breaks out, will passengers be in danger? British Rail may say, "That is unlikely. We have heeded all the warnings after King's Cross." No one expected the King's Cross disaster. Health and safety reports on London Underground had been ignored. ASLEF members who drew attention in a leaflet to the danger of underground fires and the hazards of travel were threatened with the sack by British Rail management. That management has introduced a new rule under which any BR employee who publicly criticises BR faces the penalty of sacking. If all those circumstances are compounded, we may find that fires start because of defective machinery and dangers arise because passengers are impeded when leaving railway premises.

**Mr. Peter Snape** (West Bromwich, East): I apologise for interrupting my hon. Friend at an early stage in his interesting analysis of this measure. Is he aware that the circumstances surrounding disciplinary action may soon be worse than he envisaged? Under the proposals, in the brave new Britain of 1989, to abolish national negotiations in the railway industry, an employee who has the temerity to speak to the press about safety or any other matter could face dismissal by his area manager and have no right of appeal.

**Mr. Deputy Speaker:** Order. I again remind the House that the debate is on the motion, That the Bill, as amended, be now considered. If it is decided in the affirmative, the House will go on to consider the amendments. I remind the House that we cannot have a broad debate on railway policy. Hon. Members can discuss whether we should debate what is in the Bill and the amendments that are to come. A broad debate would be out of order.

**Mr. Cryer:** I am grateful to you, Mr. Deputy Speaker. We are debating whether the Bill should be further considered and in deploying those arguments we must consider, to some extent, the Bill's contents. I was making the point that the Bill's contents are so important that they should be further considered.

One characteristic of the Bill is the installation of automatic machinery that may impede the egress of passengers in a period of potential danger. My hon. Friend the Member for West Bromwich, East (Mr. Snape) said that British Rail employees could not draw to the public's attention information about dangerous circumstances, even though they might have drawn it to the attention of various layers of British Rail management. An employee would be sacked it he said to a local newspaper, "This escalator is dangerous. It smokes every now and then. We have put the fires out four or five times. Something should be done about it."

In debating the motion, we should consider whether British Rail management would attempt to interfere if a British Rail employee wanted to raise these issues with his or her Member of Parliament. We must send a clear message that British Rail employee's rights should in no way be curtailed by British Rail management. They should not be prevented from going to their Member of Parliament with information about potentially dangerous circumstances placing passengers in jeopardy or about any other railway matter. Hon. Members will agree that if British Rail management attempted to intimidate employees it would be a potentially serious breach of privilege, and the House would deal with it accordingly.

**Dr. Marek:** My hon. Friend has made a good point about safety on the railways. There are differences between the London Regional Transport (Penalty Fares) Bill, which we considered yesterday, and this motion. I remind my hon. Friend of Mersey Rail, which is a British Rail system. It has a tunnel going right round Liverpool, escalators going up to ground level and gates. I do not think that automatic gates will be installed there. Does my hon. Friend accept that penalty fares introduce a greater risk to safety, because of the associated hassles and controls? Does he agree that, when debating whether we should consider the Bill, one important question is whether under the Bill's provisions the railways will be safe? Will my hon. Friend address himself to that point in due course?

**Mr. Cryer:** The ramifications of the Bill are enormous. I wonder why the working party produced a solution for our national railway system when we have a well-tried system, to which people are accustomed, that has stood the test of time.

British Rail is using the Bill as an opportunity to get rid of employees. People are our greatest asset. We should have people on platforms checking tickets rather than automatic ticket machines. We are unclear to what extent British Rail will use the powers in the Bill, but once the legislation has been passed the necessary powers will be handed to it. We should therefore be provided with more detailed information than is contained in this sheet and a half of nine scant clauses.

We cannot leave the application of the Bill's powers to the vagaries of British Rail management, which has not always made the right decisions. I recall the introduction of automatic lights on level crossings without barriers. For many years previously, the system was to have manned barriers at level crossings, which physically kept traffic off railways. An early consequence of the introduction of automatic lights was the Hixson level crossing disaster, which occurred because the instructions for the operation of the barriers were defective. A large transformer was caught on the level crossing by a diesel-electric locomotive, thereby causing a serious accident. I use that example to show that, when we are deciding whether the Bill should be considered further, its safety ramifications are enormous and cannot be dismissed lightly.

**Dr. Marek:** My hon. Friend is on to an extremely good point. When deciding whether the Bill should be further considered, we must be guided by experience. Will my hon. Friend bear in mind the fact that the Government relaxed restrictions on level crossings about 10 years ago? That did not lead to the Hixson disaster, but it led to a disaster at Lockington. Through their policies, the Government were responsible for the deaths of innocent people. Only recently have they realised the follies of their policy and introduced more barriers. We should know why the Government support the Bill. Do they believe that it will lead to public expenditure savings?

**Mr. Cryer:** In deciding whether we should further consider the Bill, such safety considerations must be paramount.

The policy of successive British Rail managements has been to get rid of employees. British Rail is now introducing rigid, anti-democratic rules to prevent employees from becoming involved in developing the railways. The Bill is based on the 1986 report of the working party. My hon. Friend the Member for West Bromwich, East has much experience of working on the railways and is a railway enthusiast. If he were still a British Rail employee, he could not have access to the press without being threatened with dismissal. That British Rail management would not be seeking his advice and experience of many years in different operating capacities is scandalous. Thousands of British Rail employees want to provide a proper public service. They want adequate and improving standards on the railways, yet they are not being consulted.

7.45 pm

We must consider the people who will operate under the Bill. The trains on which inspectors will be checking tickets will often be crowded. Inspectors will be involved in heated arguments and there will be difficulties and divisions. Far from improving the image of the railway network, inspectors will be facing enormous difficulties. In my area, trains on the service between Bradford interchange and Leeds and Shipley and Leeds—a station that I frequently use—are always crowded at busy times. People stand in aisles, yet British Rail is seeking powers to employ inspectors to argue with people about whether they have tickets.

The annex to the working party's report gives guidance to inspectors about how to deal with such difficulties. It is nonsense for half a dozen people in a lush room of the bureaucracy in Whitehall to discuss academically how railmen will deal amiably with fraught, anxious passengers. It does not reflect well on British Rail that it is seeking such powers.

I should like to mention how some stations are laid out. One of the platforms at Shipley, which is a triangular

[*Mr. Cryer*]

station, is a considerable distance from the ticket office. Will machines be placed on all platforms or at a central booking office, such as at Shipley? If people cannot obtain a ticket because the machine is broken or because they do not have the right change, will they miss the train because they are frightened that they may be interrogated by an inspector for not having a ticket? Will British Rail operate a fairly liberal policy and readily accept people's excuses? Will it impose on passengers the same arrogant restrictive nonsense that it imposes on its employees by not allowing them to talk to local newspapers?

It is important that staff are encouraged to take a pride in the railway, and a majority of them do. I speak not as a casual observer but as the founder of the Keighley and Worth Valley railway in Yorkshire. I called its first meeting and did every aspect of work on it from plate laying to firing engines, driving engines and maintenance. I did that from 1961 and negotiated with British Rail until 1982 when pressure of public duties—alack, alas—forced me off the footplate.

I know the details involved in operating railways. I have come across many hundreds and probably thousands of railwaymen and women who exhibit enthusiasm for their network. However, under the terms of this Bill, they would be removed from stations and replaced by ticket machines. It would be preferable if we put all the ticket machines in British Rail's boardroom and got the board of British Rail out on to the stations to deal with the public. Then we might get better decisions from management.

**Mr. Snape:** We might get trains on Wednesdays as well.

**Mr. Cryer:** Yes. The National Union of Railwaymen might be able to negotiate a decent agreement which, after all, is all that it is trying to do.

In considering whether we should give further consideration to the Bill, we must bear in mind the removal of staff from stations. In our further consideration of the Bill, we cannot exclude other legislation because all this links together. For example, the Social Security Bill contains new regulations requiring people to show that they are actively seeking work. The Opposition argued against that and said it would be difficult to show that someone was actively seeking work. We thought that the proposal was unreasonable and that the test of availability for work, which has operated for many years, was entirely adequate.

**Mr. Deputy Speaker:** Order. I remind the hon. Gentleman once more that the Bill has had its Second Reading. It has been amended in Committee and we are now discussing whether it should be further considered. The hon. Gentleman's points about the Social Security Bill do not arise on this Bill and he would be out of order if he were to discuss them now.

**Mr. Cryer:** My point is related directly to the Bill. This Bill allows penalties to be imposed on passengers who do not have tickets. I understand that British Rail will introduce automatic ticket machines throughout the length and breadth of the land and will have more open stations. Passengers will be obliged to obtain tickets.

In discussing whether the Bill should have further consideration, we must bear in mind a woman who is offered a night job which she cannot refuse because of the

legislation to which I have just referred, but which I will not mention again. It would be dangerous for a woman to work at night if she had to travel on British Rail. The recent employment legislation has removed the protection that prevented women from being employed at night.

I understand why you objected to my previous line of argument, Mr. Deputy Speaker. At first sight, the legislation to which I referred and this Bill do not appear to be linked. However, further consideration of the Bill must involve other legislation because its effects might mean that a woman who had finished night work might require assistance on a station platform late at night. She might hear footfalls in the dark and be afraid. I know that you, Mr. Deputy Speaker, are as concerned as I am about the increase in violence since the Government came to office in 1979. Many women are worried about it. A woman coming off night duty might seek assistance and could expect help in a staffed station. However, this Bill will remove staff from stations.

Occasionally staff are not helpful. However, in the main, 99·9 per cent. of staff will help passengers. They help women with prams. They help passengers on to and off trains and they open gates. They also help disabled people. But they are going to be replaced by ticket machines.

I believe that the Bill should be deferred. Having been over the pros and cons of the Bill for only a relatively brief time, I believe that it would probably be better if the sponsor went back to British Rail and said, "I do not think the time is right for a wholesale change in the operation of British Rail."

The Bill gives powers to British Rail management. However, that management has been inconsistent in its operation and has shown itself—even before the present dispute—to be arrogant and prepared to impose its views, whatever their merits, on the rank and file staff—the train drivers, cleaners and station operators. The management's attitude has resulted in the present confrontation and strike action and I lay the responsibility for that entirely at the door of BR management—*[Interruption.]* As my hon. Friend the Member for West Bromwich, East has just said from a sedentary position, the Government are leaning on the management. I am always worried by the way in which BR management gives in so easily to the Government and does not exercise its independent——

**Mr. Deputy Speaker:** Order. The hon. Gentleman is a very experienced Member. We want to get the debate off to a good start. I remind him and the House again that the Bill is concerned solely with penalty fares for people without a valid ticket. We are now considering whether this comparatively narrow Bill should be considered and whether we should get on to the amendments that have been tabled mostly by the hon. Member for Wrexham (Dr. Marek). As the hon. Gentleman knows, it is quite out of order to extend the debate beyond those comparatively narrow issues.

**Mr. Cryer:** I am grateful to you, Mr. Deputy Speaker, for taking so much time to give me guidance. I was tempted by my hon. Friend the Member for West Bromwich, East who muttered something from a sedentary position. I wanted that point to be in *Hansard* and I am sure that you appreciate that.

**Mr. Cohen:** Does my hon. Friend accept that one reason why the Bill should not be considered tonight is that British Rail is out of date in respect of modern management trends? I draw my hon. Friend's attention to British Telecom, which has recently adopted a scheme whereby if it does not provide a service, its customers can claim a refund. In effect, that is a penalty fare in the opposite direction. Should that not apply to British Rail management? Should it not be in the Bill? Should not the sponsor take the Bill back? If British Rail wants to impose penalty fares on people who avoid buying tickets, the management should pay a penalty to the customer when it is wrong.

**Mr. Cryer:** My hon. Friend's argument boils down to the idea that we should give further consideration to the Bill because he suggests an amendment to reverse the concept of penalty fares so that if trains do not arrive a bonus voucher should be given to passengers. That is a very good idea. However, having considered the pros and cons of whether we should further examine the Bill, and bearing in mind my hon. Friend's ingenious proposal, I believe that it may be better if the promoter took the Bill back and suggested that my hon. Friend's ideas would be useful in highlighting the unfair burden which the Bill proposes for passengers. On those grounds, I would have reservations about giving the Bill further consideration.

**Dr. Marek:** My hon. Friend the Member for Leyton (Mr. Cohen) made another good point about the negative penalty fare that could be imposed upon management. Will my hon. Friend the Member for Bradford, South (Mr. Cryer) take that idea on board? A few years ago, I travelled on the TGV between Paris and Lyon. A striking steward blocked the line, and the train had to be diverted. When that happened, the conductor came around handing the equivalent of a fiver back to everybody on the train because of the delay. Such things can be done. Penalty fares should be considered with that in mind.

**Mr. Deputy Speaker:** There is nothing about penalty fares for management in the Bill. The Bill deals with penalty fares for passengers. The hon. Gentleman's remark would have been perfectly in order on Second Reading, but it is not in order in this debate. We must deal with the Bill as it is, as amended, whether it should be further considered and whether we should discuss the amendments.

8 pm

**Mr. Cryer:** On whether the Bill should be further considered, which is what we are debating—it is an important item—the question asked by my hon. Friend the Member for Wrexham (Dr. Marek) is outside the terms of the Bill, as you, Mr. Deputy Speaker, as helpfully as always, have pointed out. That reinforces my belief that we should give the Bill further consideration. My hon. Friend's point about refunds to passengers on the TGV should be incorporated in the Bill so that we can give it proper consideration. The Bill is stunted. Unfortunately, no amendment has been tabled to cover that point. That demonstrates the advantages of discussing such issues and of several minds coming together.

Second Reading is some time away, and the Bill will go to a private Bill Committee which, as we know, is not like a Committee that deals with a public Bill where Bills are scrutinised by, perhaps, 20 or 30 hon. Members in Committees that are open to the public. Private Bill Committees consist of a handful of people—say four or five—so we do not get the same sort of input as we do with public Bills.

Although I cannot discuss the details of the TGV experience, when the conductor handed out refunds, I believe that we should incorporate an amendment to balance the Bill so that passengers have some quid pro quo for the additional difficulties. We accept that the penalties should be imposed; the question is how. Additional penalties are being faced by passengers in difficult circumstances. Innocent people are harassed if they do not have a ticket. Additional powers will be given. My hon. Friends argue that the Bill should not be given further consideration. British Rail is seeking these powers too early and without proper consideration. It should be able to take advantage of our debates, and, one would hope, reintroduce the Bill in a new form. Therefore, it might be better if we did not give the Bill further consideration at this stage.

**Dr. Marek:** I was interested in what my hon. Friend the Member for Bradford, South (Mr. Cryer) had to say. He made some useful points that we should consider before deciding to consider the Bill. This Bill is better than the one that we had before us yesterday.

**Mr. Cohen:** It could not be worse.

**Dr. Marek:** There may be something in that.

There are mitigating circumstances in the Bill. By and large, there are no automatic barriers at British Rail stations—or, rather, I cannot remember whether there are any. I hope that my hon. Friend the Member for West Bromwich, East (Mr. Snape) will contradict me if I am wrong. British Rail may want to introduce automatic barriers at some stage, and it may be possible to do so without further legislation—London Regional Transport was able to introduce automatic barriers without legislation—and most people would then consider this Bill as bad as the one that we considered yesterday.

**Mr. Cohen:** My hon. Friend will know that I have strongly objected to automatic ticket barriers for several reasons, some of which I explained yesterday. I should be greatly concerned if, as my hon. Friend said, British Rail is considering such barriers. Has he heard any hint that that is the case? Many people have said that such barriers do not work and are a waste of money. The public deplore them. On behalf of the House, will my hon. Friend say to British Rail management, "No barriers"?

**Dr. Marek:** We do not want barriers on British Rail. I assure my hon. Friend that we do not need them. British Rail tickets now pass through London Regional Transport barriers. This matter is directly related to penalty fares, safety and whether the installation of barriers is a proper provision of service. Would barriers make British Rail—whether it is underground, as in Merseyside, or above ground, as in most other parts of the country—safer or less safe? That is the central question that we should address.

As I said, British Rail tickets now go through London Regional Transport barriers. If those tickets have a magnetic strip, they will open the gates. It is not inconceivable that, in three or four years, tickets may have an implanted code on the back, showing whether they are blue saver tickets, white saver tickets, first-class tickets, or single or return tickets. All sorts of information could be implanted on the back of a ticket. There may be proposals

[*Dr. Marek*]

for ticket collecting at King's Cross, Euston, Paddington, Waterloo and other major stations to be done by automatic ticket machines. I would not expect the sponsor of the Bill, the hon. Member for New Forest (Sir P. McNair-Wilson), to have an answer to that at his fingertips, but the matter must be considered. I fear that, if that procedure is introduced, it will place this Bill on a par with the one that we considered yesterday.

I compliment the hon. Member for New Forest on being assiduous in his duty and, on more than one occasion, going to his advisers outside the House. Of course we cannot take any notice of them inside the House. I hope that he will reply to the debate before time runs out in a couple of hours. If he can do that, it would compare favourably with the performance of the sponsor of yesterday's Bill, who did not consult his advisers. Perhaps he knew all the answers anyway. He moved the closure of the debate to which he did not reply. This Bill is on a happier path than the Bill that we discussed last night.

Several amendments have been tabled. If we decide to consider the Bill, we will be able to consider them. My hon. Friend the Member for Bradford, South talked about the impact of one or two amendments. I thoroughly approve of the amendment to be moved by the Bill's promoters. If permission is given to go into a restricted area or not to have a current ticket, it should be given not by the person providing the service, but by the person "controlling". That is the word used in the amendment, which is extremely sensible and would enable the Bill to work that little bit better if the House decides to give it its blessing and send it on its way.

Unfortunately, my favourable comments cannot be directed towards the Minister's performance. He is writing and I hope that he is writing something suitable about the Bill and about the debate that has taken place so far. I hope that he will be able to respond positively, or even negatively, this evening. Whether or not he agrees with us is a different matter. What is important is that he should give a constructive response. Certainly, he did not do that yesterday and I would hate him to repeat his performance tonight. I think that he spoke for one minute——

**Mr. Cohen:** One minute.

**Dr. Marek:** My hon. Friend said that the Minister spoke for one minute.

In yesterday's debate, the level of fare evasion was raised, and it has already been raised tonight. That is another central theme in the Bill, and if we are to consider the Bill——

**The Minister for Public Transport (Mr. Michael Portillo):** I want to be entirely sure that the hon. Gentleman realises that I am not the Bill's sponsor. I have already expressed the Government's general support for the Bill and I said that the matters raised during last night's debate were matters for the Bill's sponsor, not the Minister. The Minister had little to add on whether the Bill should be considered further.

**Dr. Marek:** I welcome that response, for which I am grateful. It may be that the point that I wish to raise this evening and which I raised last night will be answered. It

certainly was not answered yesterday. The Minister, perhaps quite rightly, did not answer it and the Bill's sponsor did not seek to speak.

I wish to take up the issue of the level of fare evasion. If the level is not great, it is hardly worth considering the Bill any further. Equally, if the level of evasion is such that considerable extra expenditure would be incurred in combating it and bringing it down to what the sponsor would deem an acceptable level, it would not make economic or any other sense for the promoters to pursue the Bill. The costs involved would exceed the likely return and it would not be worth our while to give further consideration to the Bill. I hope that the hon. Member for New Forest will reply, and that when he does he will address this matter.

How were the figures showing the level of evasion arrived at? What sampling techniques were used? These questions must be answered so that the House is able to make a judgment. It was on this point that I criticised the Minister. I apologise if my criticism was wrongly directed and should have been aimed at the sponsor, whose duty it was to respond. The Minister said:

"Both London Regional Transport and British Rail lose considerable amounts of money from people travelling on their services without having paid the correct fare or any fare at all"—[*Official Report,* 28 June 1989; Vol. 155, c. 1057.] However, he did not amplify that statement.

8.15 pm

**Mr. Cohen:** It is not just the amounts, and the proof of how they were arrived at, which we need to know before we can give consideration to the Bill; we also need to know the reasons for the evasion. The promoters' statement contains no attempt to consider the possible reasons for the amounts, let alone proof of whether they are correct. Does my hon. Friend consider that we should have received more information before considering the matter in a more detailed way?

**Dr. Marek:** Yes, my hon. Friend is right. I was going to address this issue later in my remarks. There is a lack of information. The promoters' statement gives a background to the Bill and we have received the working party's reports. I do not know whether my hon. Friend the Member for Bradford, South has left his report here for the rest of us to consider. I should certainly like to see it at some stage, although I have a rough idea of what it contains.

We must consider whether the House is able to give a judgment on the Bill which is good enough for the average man in the street to rely on. At the end of the day, we are here to represent our constituents and the public who must be able to rely on us and to know that we have the information on which to base our judgment, and then be able to use our judgment in the most constructive way.

I shall return to the central issue of evasion. The Minister did not spend much time justifying the need for the Bill on the grounds of the amount of evasion. I hope that either the Minister or the hon. Member for New Forest will spend more time tonight giving us the statistics on which the Bill is founded.

Yesterday, I said that one problem of this form of Government was that it was oppositional, in that we face each other and have to try to score points off each other. It would be a great advantage to the country if, instead of doing that at the consideration stage of a private Bill, which is not a completely political measure—I can think of other measures which are more political—the Minister could ask British Rail and London Regional Transport for the statistics. We must satisfy ourselves about the statistics before we support the Bill and ensure that there is nothing secret about them. I would have been delighted if the Minister had invited us or our agents to come to the Department of Transport, where we would be given every opportunity to see the figures. We would then have been able to exercise our judgment when we spoke in the House.

Unfortunately, the Minister did not take up my request, and did not even reply to it. It may be, as the Minister said, that I should have asked the sponsor of the Bill. It would be useful if the hon. Member for New Forest could persuade British Rail to open the books and show us the sampling techniques used, how the statistics were acquired, over how many days, on which lines and how accurate the estimate was. I think that it was estimated that £36 million was lost in revenue every year. That is a lot of money and if it is the correct estimate it shows that we have a society that we would not wish for. It would be far better for everyone to be honest and to get into the habit of being honest. One way of getting into that habit is to realise that if we are dishonest we are likely to be caught and will have to pay a penalty fare. Bearing that in mind, it would seem that we would all want to speed the Bill on its way. However, it is not as simple as that, because there are disadvantages to it.

**Mr. Cohen:** Advertisements put out regularly by British Rail refer to fare evaders getting a criminal record. Would someone who paid a penalty fare automatically gain such a record? Is there not a danger of information going awry, and would not the possibility of a court appearance be a more effective deterrent than on-the-spot penalties?

**Dr. Marek:** My hon. Friend raises an interesting point, but I am not sure that I am able to answer it with authority. A system of prosecution might be more effective, but I saw the penalty-fare system working on the excellent Tyne and Wear Metro when I was in Newcastle upon Tyne earlier this week, with spot checks being made on the trains. Although the system is called the Metro, the trains travel overground and the system, which is run by the local authority, is to all intents and purposes a railway system.

Perhaps there is a lesson to be learnt from Newcastle. The carriages of the Metro trains contained large notices saying that anyone caught by an inspector without having paid the proper fare would face a penalty of, I believe, £5 if the fare was paid within seven days and £10 if it was not. No doubt offenders could subsequently be prosecuted; they were certainly asked for their names and addresses. I have not enough experience to know whether the system works: perhaps the Minister knows, and my hon. Friend the Member for West Bromwich, East (Mr. Snape), who is an expert in such matters, may also be able to help.

There are ticket machines on the Tyne and Wear Metro, and passengers are, to an extent, honour bound to travel with a valid ticket. There is, of course, a limit to how far the system could be translated to British Rail. The maximum fare on the Tyne and Wear Metro is £1 or £2, and there are ample opportunities for the purchase of day tickets and, no doubt, tickets for a longer period. The fare structure on British Rail is a different matter: a single first-class ticket from Newcastle to London, for instance,

costs nearly £70, and a second-class ticket nearly £50. It is worth bearing in mind, however, that the penalty-fare system is working on the Tyne and Wear Metro.

My hon. Friend the Member for Bradford, South said that the working party had not consulted the railway unions. It is sad that those who control the service should have felt that they could decide on the best way of introducing a penalty-fare system without consulting those who would have to operate it. That is one of the faults of British industry in general—but I am sure that I should be ruled out of order if I dwelt on any other aspect of British industry. It is a pity that the consultative document did not benefit from the experience and active participation of employees. I should add that I speak as a Member sponsored by the National Union of Railwaymen.

The difference between this Bill and the London Regional Transport (Penalty Fares) Bill is that in the last month or so there has been some consultation—late in the day, but none the less welcome—between British Rail management and the unions. I have a copy of a letter written a few days ago to the general secretary of the NUR by the director of Network SouthEast. As it is not confidential, I may read extracts from it to help hon. Members make up their minds about the Bill. It shows that there has been an attempt at consultation, although it may be too little too late. Other matters, of course, are currently worrying the NUR and British Rail management—but I shall not stray on to that ground either.

If employees can be brought into the consultation—even at this late stage—if an undertaking can be given that the system will operate in a certain way, although there is no such undertaking in the Bill, and if in the end the NUR is satisfied, I am sure that it will say the same as us: "If the Bill cuts down on evasion and leads to a better society, we are for it."

**Mr. Cohen:** I am sure that the railwaymen would say that, but would they not also say that if they are to be responsible for the collection of penalty fares they will expect to be paid for that responsibility, and also that they do not want any redundancies? Is that, perhaps, one of the reasons why British Rail embarked on consultation so late in the day—because it would have to give a commitment on both counts? Does my hon. Friend think that that is why London Regional Transport and London Underground did not consult at all—because they are even meaner in those respects?

**Dr. Marek:** My hon. Friend may well be right; I do not know. I am not saying that I expect the hon. Member for New Forest to be able to answer such questions, but if he happens to know the answer it would be useful to hear it.

It may not be just management that is meaner. There is a paymaster whose representatives sit on the Conservative Benches. They may say that the 7 per cent. is not a magic figure that has come out of a hat, but has been arrived at independently by various bodies. Many hon. Members, however, believe the facts to be slightly different from those presented by the Government or in the faithful press, which renders whatever the Government may say as absolute truth. We are a little cleverer than that in the House.

I am placing the most favourable possible construction on recent events. If the consultation is successful, I shall be happy to withdraw even amendments that I feel, with good

[*Dr. Marek*]

reason, should be made. I shall do so later rather than now, because I hope that we shall consider the Bill and that in time I shall be able to speak to my amendments.

I must, however, get some points straight if the Bill is to be considered. Not only London Underground but British Rail has automatic ticket machines. We must consider the whole issue of the reliability of equipment provided in the past by British Rail and assess whether —should the Bill be passed and an activating order made by the Minister for certain lines—the automatic ticket machines that are to be installed will be maintained to the high degree promised by BR. If they fail to work, will maintenance staff be on hand within a few minutes, failing which will automatic "permission to travel" machines be on hand?

**Mr. Pike:** My hon. Friend will be aware of the number of occasions on the Underground and at other LRT facilities when machines display "No change given" signs. That often puts all the machines out of use, unless the traveller is prepared to pay well in excess of the fare for the journey. Frequently the offices at BR stations will not be open to enable the traveller to buy a ticket.

**Dr. Marek:** My hon. Friend makes an important point. LRT might say that the ticket office will always be open, and that might be the case. Unfortunately, however, one could find Murphy's law in operation, and at the very time when the machines break down, the official in the ticket office has three or four Americans and one or two Japanese visitors wishing to purchase tourist cards for the week, and the traveller knows that there will be no chance for perhaps 15 minutes of his obtaining a ticket. There are usually several ticket machines in operation in LRT locations. With BR, on the other hand—my hon. Friend the Member for West Bromwich, East will correct me if I am wrong —there will be only one machine at a station vending tickets automatically.

I appreciate that BR sets service standards. BR says that ticket offices must be open and that people should be able to buy tickets within a few minutes. Can we, using our judgment, say that British Rail will—if the Bill becomes law—service and maintain the machines to a standard which will ensure that any departure from total availability will be so rare that not I nor my hon. Friends the Members for Burnley (Mr. Pike) and for Leyton (Mr. Cohen) will have reason to complain?

I fear that LRT and BR would fail that test now. Certainly the Underground ticket machines would fail the test because, as my hon. Friend the Member for Burnley pointed out, "Exact fare only" is a sign which the machines display all too frequently. That means that they have not been serviced properly in that they do not have sufficient change in them.

**Mr. Cohen:** The Government insist that the lowest tender for maintenance must be accepted. BR might find itself, in this privatised world, with a cowboy contractor servicing and maintaining its machines. In those circumstances, the automatic machines could not possibly be in operation for 99 per cent., let alone 100 per cent., of the time.

**Dr. Marek:** My hon. Friend makes a valuable point, even if it does not apply to BR's willingness to maintain

the ticket machines so that they are available all the time. If the machines are not working, the passenger who turns up at a station with only a few minutes to spare before his train is due to depart will face a dilemma. If the machine is not working and the authority to travel machine has not been installed or has run out of paper, he must consider whether to board the train and risk having to convince an authorised person—with an explanation that he must deliver within 10 or 20 days, as the Bill lays down—that he had no alternative, with the possibility of being landed with a penalty fare and, even worse, a criminal record.

**Mr. Cohen:** A person in that position might decide to jump on the train because he has a pressing appointment. With the cuts in service that are being made, there could be a long delay before his next train. That passenger may have the intention of paying at the other end. He may have no intention of evading the fare. That raises a whole new implication for the penalty fare concept because it implies an assumption on the part of the traveller to pay at the other end. Should that not be recognised in the Bill?

**Dr. Marek:** I tabled an amendment to that effect, but because it would have involved BR proving an intention it was not selected for debate. I was not surprised at that, because it is difficult to prove an intention. Usually such an issue has to be decided by the Court of Appeal. At the lower level with which we are concerned, the traveller is in a dilemma. He may be in a hurry—in the south-east people are, generally speaking, in more of a hurry than they are elsewhere—and he is faced with the awful decision whether or not to get on the train.

Let us not forget that with InterCity trains the guard will have an awful job trying to get through the whole train to check tickets. If one has jumped on to an InterCity train and is at the back end of a second class, or in a first class compartment—depending, of course, on which way through the train the guard is going—one may get away without paying any fare.

But suppose one has an authority-to-travel ticket or, even worse, no ticket and one must provide an explanation to an authorised person, the guard in the case I am citing. The job of the guard going through a crowded train to check tickets will be almost impossible. On occasions it is impossible already. I cannot imagine how, on crowded trains, that type of situation can be avoided.

Deadlock will occur if there are, say, half a dozen people with authority-to-travel tickets and other people explaining how there were numbers of people at the ticket office or that the automatic machine did not work, or that there was some emergency involving the staff, so that they simply got on the train. Some travellers might want blue saver return tickets, others might want executive tickets, while others might want tickets to proceed to the continent. I do not see how a guard, faced with his other duties, will be able to cope with all that ticket writing and explanation assessing.

How will these issues be addressed by BR on crowded InterCity services, let alone if there has been a breakdown at some starter stations where there have been a dozen or more people wanting tickets and they have been unable to obtain them before commencing their journeys?

**Mr. Pike:** Another problem with the Bill is the increasing use by British Rail of what it calls open stations. I believe that Preston station is to be made open. British Rail is gradually removing ticket barriers, opening up shopping areas and encouraging people to use the refreshment facilities on the station. Will not such open stations encourage people to get on trains without tickets?

**Dr. Marek:** I cannot see that, although it is another difficult point. It is possible to have open stations. Germany has many open stations so that one can get on any train without a ticket. My hon Friend may view that with dismay, but within three or four minutes a guard comes along asking for a ticket. He is not left by himself —I have seen four guards on some of these trains, and they provide a proper service. However, if there are to be open stations—I am aghast by what my hon. Friend has just said—will the trains be properly staffed and serviced by British Rail employees? I need a lot of convincing.

**Mr. Cohen:** My hon. Friend spoke about the various types of ticket and I can see the problems involved in that. Did my hon. Friend see the article by my right hon. Friend the Member for Birmingham, Sparkbrook (Mr. Hattersley), the deputy leader of the Opposition, in *The Guardian* last weekend? My right hon. Friend asked for toast and was told by a British Rail employee, "Sorry, sir, you are not a first-class passenger." My right hon. Friend replied, "Actually I am." The British Rail employee said, "You still can't have toast because you are not having the full breakfast."

**Mr. Deputy Speaker:** Order. I find it difficult to see what toast and breakfast have to do with whether the House should consider the Bill.

**Dr. Marek:** My hon. Friend's example shows the inability of the privatised service to provide proper facilities for passengers. Trusthouse Forte now runs the catering service, so questions about that should be addressed to the Minister.

The employees of British Rail must be sure about the ticket machines. Will they be properly serviced? Will they be functioning? Will "permission to travel" machines issue tickets and will tickets, which should be available all the time, be unavailable not less than 0·0001 per cent. of the working year? If we could be satisfied of that, that would overcome the first of the 12 problems that we have to consider before we decide whether to consider the Bill.

Automatic ticket machines are often inoperative. This must happen, because nobody can expect a 100 per cent. operating rate for any ticket machine or "permission to travel" machine or even 100 per cent. availability of booking staff behind the booking window, because emergencies happen. It would be wrong to insist that British Rail has a standard of 100 per cent., although it must have a standard close to that. If something goes wrong, will booking staff be available immediately to be drafted in to where the problem is, to keep the sale of tickets going? It is vital that the answer to that is yes, because if it were not, that would raise many problems and many people would have to make decisions about whether to travel without valid tickets and be liable to penalty fares, or miss their train.

I should like the hon. Member for New Forest to say something about that. What will happen if an emergency affects the availability of booking hall staff? Many stations have only one person in the booking office. My station of Wrexham has only one little window and usually only one person is there issuing tickets. That employee might not be able to get to the office, perhaps for a silly reason such as

oversleeping—we have all done that. What will happen if he does not open the booking hall and the "permission to travel" machine happens to jam at the same time?

8.45 pm

The hon. Member for New Forest must assure me that such problems will occur only 0·0001 per cent. of the time, and justify that record. One needs a bit more than just an assurance. Too often British Rail has said that it will do certain things, or the Secretary of State for Transport has said that he is setting passenger service standards for British Rail, but years go by and they are not achieved. That is not necessarily because British Rail does not want to achieve them, but it is under the constraints of finance. Therefore, we need a commitment that booking staff will be drafted in and people will not have to make such difficult decisions.

The phrase "authorised person" is dotted about throughout the Bill and it would be interesting to know who an authorised person is. Is it a guard, a booking clerk, an inspector, or anybody else working on the railway? All could be an authorised person, but they will need extra training. When staff have to deal with the public, training is important, and British Rail must realise that. The authorised person must have on-the-job training to help him to decide how to handle these issues. British Rail will give him authority, but training is another important aspect.

Let us take the example of a person waiting, with only three or four minutes left before his train is due and the ticket machine is not working and the booking clerk is not available. That person has to decide whether to risk a penalty fare. However, if an authorised person were available he could make the decision. He could say, "Hang on, you've got three minutes before the train goes and the booking clerk will be back in one minute and will be able to give you a ticket, and I shall make sure that the train does not go." On the other hand, the authorised person should also have the power and authority to say, "Four or five people are waiting and the platform is over the bridge and 50 yards down the track so you'd better go now because I can't guarantee that you'll get a ticket. However, you've been here for a few minutes and in those circumstances, it is reasonable to say that it is our failure and I give you authorisation to go. I will make sure that the authorisation I've given is logged properly at the station so that if you are asked by another authorised person why you do not have a 'permission to travel ticket' you can make the relevant statement and it will be backed up by the log that I shall make and the permission that I am giving you." If the Bill is passed an amendment to allow that will have to be made to it.

Not every railway employee is trained to deal with members of the public. Some stations have only a few railway employees and they have to deal with many things. I should like an assurance from the hon. Member for New Forest that on-the-job training will be given so that staff are taught how to handle the public and to minimise aggravating circumstances.

It is also important that a different type of on-the-job training is given to authorised persons who control tickets on trains or in restricted areas to make sure that they know how to minimise violence should a person be found not to be travelling with valid authority to travel. It is not unknown for people who have had too much to drink to be on certain trains on certain lines at certain times of the

[*Dr. Marek*]

week. Guards need training to cope with such people. If any British Rail employee thinks that there is even a remote risk of violence as a result of asking for a ticket, I would advise that employee not to ask for the ticket but to leave it to the British Transport police to sort out the matter at the next station

If a guard asks a person for his authority to travel, if it is not produced and if the guard has to levy a penalty fare, he must be trained on the best way to do it. I think that the guards should work in pairs rather than singly. I am not sure that I am competent at this stage of the debate to judge the issue. I should be grateful if the hon. Member for New Forest could tell us something about that.

If the Bill goes through and penalty fares are to be charged, there should be radio communication between guards or authorised persons who have to exact the penalty fares. There will be a real threat to British Rail employees. There should be a panic button so that British Rail employees would be assured that the train would stop at the next station where there would be an adequate complement of British Transport police to deal with trouble. I am not saying that we are a violent nation and that there will be trouble all the time, but if people who may be violent, perhaps because of alcohol addiction, do not have at the back of their minds the knowledge that they will be caught, put in a cell overnight and perhaps charged, they will take liberties with British Rail staff. No one wants that to happen. An important way of ensuring that it does not happen is to have radio-controlled equipment, panic buttons and a proper complement of British Transport police available to go to stations where trouble may occur. If publicity were given to such incidents, the number would decline.

At this stage I need to have confidence that British Rail would have the equipment and the people available. I do not have that confidence. We need more than an assurance. We need to know the detailed plans that British Rail has for the employment of extra British Transport police, for on-the-job training and for radios and panic buttons to be provided. I welcome the fact that such equipment is being introduced, but more detail is needed.

Wages and salaries are also important. I am not referring to the 7 per cent. pay dispute, but if staff are to be given extra duties they will expect to be remunerated accordingly. I am not asking staff to hold British Rail or the travelling public to ransom by saying that they will not operate the penalty fare scheme unless they get an astronomical amount for doing so. The staff are not asking for that, but they are asking for a little more simply because the job will result in more hassle since people do not like paying penalty fares.

Staff will have to do more on trains in checking tickets and authorities to travel, and in issuing tickets if passengers have a valid explanation. Depending on which side of the bed people get out of in the morning, they are more likely to argue the toss. That will put an extra burden on staff. I shall not dwell too long on the need for extra remuneration. No doubt the hon. Member for New Forest cannot say that everything has been agreed, but I hope that he will go back to British Rail management to point out that that is another central issue which has to be solved. The staff must have confidence that if the Bill becomes an Act they will get a fair day's pay for a fair day's work. No one can ask for more. That is all that the railway employees are asking for.

The next point has already been partly covered. I do not want to delay the House too long, but authorised persons should be conversant with the full range of operating duties. As time goes on there are fewer and fewer employees on British Rail. Because of that, the job that any person has to do multiplies. Any person on a station will have to understand and cope with the new scheme. This fits in with the requirement for on-the-job training. I do not want to repeat what I have said, but British Rail staff will have to be conversant with many more things.

A person who works on the platform of a station may not know all the intricacies of tickets; he may not know whether a ticket machine has broken down or why the booking office is not manned. The ticket office is not always near the gate to the area where a person will be liable to a penalty fare if he is found without valid authority to travel. A lot of education and training will be necessary. I hope that British Rail will make sure that its staff know exactly what they are doing.

We need more British Transport police. I suspect that over the years the number of British Transport police has been reduced. It is only recently that the number has increased. The number of British Transport police in Holyhead has been cut, yet those men serve the line all the way to Crewe. That cannot be right. The certainty or the near-certainty of transgressors being caught—those who are anti-social, violent or who cheat—is the best deterrent. I should like to have some assurances from the hon. Member for New Forest that British Rail takes that matter seriously.

**Mr. Cohen:** This is an important point. The public's perception of safety and fare evasion is bad. Is my hon. Friend aware that the British Transport police undertook a survey at Fenchurch street of the public's perception of those matters, but that has been covered up. The British Rail board has refused to publish that information. Is not that a scandal? Unless that information comes out into the open, such matters cannot be dealt with, and we will not be able to take the necessary steps, such as having more police, to make sure that the system is safer. That has repercussions for the Bill. If the British Rail board is so secretive on such an important matter, how do we know that its figures and its rationale are right in relation to penalty fares?

9 pm

**Dr. Marek:** My hon. Friend is right. I criticised the Government earlier for not being open about their statistics, and British Rail falls into the same category. There is nothing to hide. The British travelling public are not second-class passengers. British voters are not second-class citizens until the day comes to vote. They should be treated with respect and given the information. There should be nothing secret. The hon. Member for New Forest has heard what my hon. Friend the Member for Leyton has said. I hope that such information will be released in the interests of better discussion and a better judgment of the Bill.

Another matter that should be in the Bill but is not is a provision for the review of penalties for fare evasion. I am no expert on Home Office matters, but violent members of the public who assault someone often seem to receive only a minor penalty. In contrast, a person who fraudulently fiddles £1 million from the City of London usually gets off and goes to Majorca or the Bahamas. I had better not insult any country, so I withdraw those names. Some—not any of us—may say, "If you can get away with it, good luck to you." We should try to inculcate into people the belief that they should be social and not try to get away with it.

Extra staff would mean a greater certainty of detection. But it is no good if, at the end of the day, those who are caught only get a scolding from the judge or magistrate who says, "Naughty lad, go away and don't come back again." They will know that they can do the same again with impunity. Such a sentence does not deter a certain type of person. It may be that I am wrong about that. I shall take advice to see whether anybody has any experience of that, but it will be useful to consider that when we debate the amendments.

Another important matter is publicity. Many members of the public will not know about the Bill, despite our having considered it in Committee and its having passed all its stages in the House, perhaps leaving this Chamber with one small amendment to go to the other place.

The Bill says something about notices being prominently displayed. I should like an assurance that such notices will not only be displayed and be visible to the public but be comprehensible. In the past, private railway companies and even British Rail were very good at producing notices packed with small print about rules and regulations affecting people intending to travel on the railway, and nobody ever read them. Nevertheless, if anyone transgressed, the rules and regulations were pointed out—but by then it was too late, because ignorance is no defence in law.

If the Bill is to make progress, it must provide for such notices to be easily understood not only by the public at large but by those who are not as conversant with reading as others, or the traveller in a hurry who only has time to glance at the information once or twice. The promoters of the Bill should explain what types of notices will be produced, how many will be displayed, and where, so that we may be convinced that no one can truthfully say, "I did not know the rules. I did not see any notice. I am innocent. How dare you ask me for a penalty fare." I can imagine such arguments being made, but we should try to avoid that likelihood. The promoters should say something about the publicity that will be given at every station to which an activating order will apply.

I suggest to the promoters that any person convicted of assault should be banned from travelling on the railways for five years or some other appropriate period. Such a provision might cut down the number of assaults, particularly if convictions are given widespread publicity. If that is done, I suspect that we shall have a better Bill, a better railway system, and a better society.

I turn to the positive aspects of the Bill, and quote from a letter from Mr. Chris Green, director of Network SouthEast, to Mr. Jimmy Knapp, general secretary of the National Union of Railwaymen:

"As you may know, this Bill comes up for consideration in the House of Commons on Thursday evening this week, 29 June. The Bill was reported from the Unopposed Bills Committee on 19 April with a few minor amendments to the drafting, following points made earlier in the Commons debate.

Dr. Marek has tabled a number of further amendments to the Bill, with the likely effect of delaying or blocking its progress, or disabling its provisions."

I certainly do not wish to do that. I hope that I have made my position clear.

Although we may not have time tonight to consider the Bill, I hope that my remarks will be taken seriously. As we all know, private Bills can be considered at 2.30 pm in the afternoon very expeditiously. I hope that my points will be satisfactorily dealt with, so that British Rail's employees will not be confronted by any problems. If so, I shall do my utmost to ensure that the Bill gets a fair wind, even if it cannot be entirely dealt with tonight.

The letter continues:

"I recognise that this reflects the concerns of your Union about the possible implications for the legislation on members engaged in revenue protection work."

That is right, but I have tabled amendments because I believe that they should be made. The letter then says:

"We have had earlier discussions on the Network SouthEast strategy for revenue protection, in which Penalty Fares form an essential part, and I regret that it has not, in present circumstances, been possible to resume or conclude such discussions, but it would be our intention to do so as soon as the climate is favourable."

I welcome unreservedly that statement. It is generous. All hon. Members want the Bill to become law. Nobody should be able to evade paying the proper fare. Mr. Chris Green then says:

"I should like to reemphasise the purpose of the legislation as we see it. The aims are i) to recover a significant proportion of the revenue currently lost through fare evasion for lack of a proper ticketing discipline."

If that is one of the purposes of the Bill, that is right. We ought to be told how much money is being lost, whether the estimates we have heard about tonight are accurate and whether there will be a proper ticketing discipline. Many of the points that both I and my hon. Friend the Member for Bradford, South have made are directed at that point. However, to put it bluntly, can we trust British Rail to do it properly, if the Bill becomes law? The letter continues:

"ii) to undertake ticket checks in a more effective manner and one that allows customer service and access to stations to be improved."

The word "effective" can hide many evils. The word means different things to different people. The Government would think it effective to close down the whole railway system and spend no public money on it at all. That is one example of an effective policy from the Government's point of view.

Ticket checks have to be made properly. I have drawn attention to the problems that ticket collectors will have to cope with on crowded InterCity trains. Ticket collectors may have a multiplicity of jobs to do, simply because tickets are not available at certain stations. What will be done to make ticket checks effective? I understand the spirit of the letter, but I need to be convinced that action will follow if the Bill becomes law. Ticket checks must also be in a manner

"that allows customer service and access to stations to be improved."

The same comments apply to that statement. I understand the spirit that lies behind it, but does it mean that customers will suffer no traumatic experiences at barriers or with guards when they try to explain why they could not obtain a ticket for their journey? If I could be convinced of that, it would remove one of the important mental obstacles that I have to the Bill. The letter continues:

[Dr. Marek]

"iii) to create conditions in which ticket examining staff have a realistic and more rewarding task, and with their security improved."

Again I agree with the spirit that lies behind that statement. Everybody wants the morale of British Rail staff to be high, but it is necessary for the staff to have a fair wage if their morale is to be high. That is a basic necessity. To improve their morale, an agreement has to be reached under which British Rail staff feel that they will receive the right remuneration for the additional jobs that they will have to do.

Of course, conditions will be created whereby ticket examining staff will have a realistic and more rewarding task but it must not be a more harassed and harrowing task in which they are liable to be assaulted. That means that those possibilities must not be in the forefront of the minds of those staff when they check tickets or permissions to travel. We need to be satisfied about that.

9.15 pm

I absolutely agree with what the director of Network SouthEast said in his letter, but we need to put a bit of flesh on the bones. The letter continued:

"You will know that we are already embarking on a substantial investment in improved ticketing facilities. We are also giving a great deal of thought to the staffing aspects of revenue protection, particularly in terms of staff training."

That is an important point which I have mentioned, and I am extremely pleased that it is included in the letter.

The letter continued:

"Staffing levels and remuneration will also be an important matter for further consideration prior to implementation of any Penalty Fares scheme. We also take most seriously the problem of staff security. It is accepted that there are conditions in which it is undesirable for ticket examining staff to work on their own. Penalty fares, by operating on a 'spot check' basis for shorter journeys (and it is only these journeys to which Penalty Fares in effect apply), will allow us to organise our ticket examiners in teams."

That is absolutely vital. I tabled an amendment providing that penalty fares can be levied only by an authorised person in the presence of another authorised person. If ticket examiners are to be organised in teams, I shall be very happy to accept that undertaking and, subject to what the hon. Member for New Forest says, I shall withdraw my amendment forthwith on that assurance.

The letter went on:

"This will enhance both their effectiveness"—

that is the ticket examiners—

"and their own security. There is an opportunity here to improve on the present arrangements in this respect, and it is one that will be lost if the Penalty Fares Bill were to fail."

I do not know whether my hon. Friend the Member for Leyton will see any other intention in the letter, and I hope that he will give it careful consideration, but, as far as I can see, there is an entirely laudable intention to carry out the aims set out in the letter.

**Mr. Cohen:** Many of the elements in that letter are laudable, particularly the suggestion that ticket examiners should work in teams because of the risks involved. After yesterday's debate when an assurance that we had been given earlier was suddenly limited so that only women in prams could go through the manual gate, when previously we had been assured that anybody would have the freedom to choose, I am worried that we will get an assurance from the sponsor of the Bill that what is in the letter stands, and

there will be teams of collectors, but later that suggestion will be thrown out the window and become worthless and staff will have to work alone in dangerous circumstances.

**Dr. Marek:** I agree with my hon. Friend. I very much hope that the attitude taken by the promoters of the LRT Bill is not the same as that taken by British Rail on this Bill. I have no letter or copy of a letter, and I do not think that any other hon. Member received an equivalent letter from London Regional Transport. I understand that no consultation took place between London Regional Transport and its employees, through the unions that represent them. But some consultation has taken place on this Bill. I shall finish discussing the letter and then I shall conclude my remarks as I know that other hon. Members wish to speak.

The letter continues:

"We appreciate that there are a number of practical matters to be resolved with staff before any Penalty Fares scheme can be introduced, but the concept is one that is, we believe, in interests of the staff, our customers and the industry. This is a view supported by the users groups."

This may be a slight question, but it would be useful if the hon. Member for New Forest could tell us which users' groups support this scheme and whether they have caveats about any aspects of it. That will probably help the House.

The last paragraph of the letter says:

"In summary, I believe Penalty Fares legislation will enable us to recover significant revenue which would otherwise be lost, to improve security for both customers and staff, and potentially offer more rewarding work. We would wish to arrange formal consultation as soon as we are able, but in the meantime I believe the possible failure of the current legislation would present a significant lost opportunity both for the industry and its staff."

Under ideal conditions, I should like to see a Bill on penalty fares introduced, but at this stage there are great hurdles to be overcome before that could be done.

Although I may have sounded a bit optimistic in the past 10 minutes, I will now bring myself down to reality. The omens are not good. Although consultation took place, it did not take place when the original consultation document was drawn up. In other areas, consultation between British Rail and its staff is perfunctory. The system of consultation between British Rail and its staff was good in the past, but it has not been used recently by British Rail management. That has been the problem. It is a great pity that the employees were not brought into the consultation from its inception so that a proper Bill could have been fashioned. After all, it is the employees who will have to operate the system and understand it. They could forewarn management of any problems.

I have already referred to the other omens that are not so good, so I shall mention them only briefly now. British Rail has much to do to convince me that it will maintain the machines properly and that the authority-to-travel machines will always be working. It has much to do to convince me that there will always be someone in the booking office and that people will always be able to buy tickets. All that requires money. In the past 10 years, finance has always been in short supply because the Government do not believe in spending money on public services. British Rail is an agent of the Government in that respect.

As a legislature, we are debating whether to give consideration to the Bill, so British Rail has a different duty. It can say that it cannot give such assurances because it has to cut down on the maintenance of machines, escalators and other areas. If it does that, the outlook will be extremely bleak. I hope that British Rail will say that it wants the Bill because it believes that the gains in terms of lower fare evasion would be worth the running costs of having proper machines in order, making arrangements for them to be properly maintained and ensuring that booking clerks were in place. British Rail could say to us, who are the legislature, that it guarantees that maintenance will be tip-top and that tickets will be available at all stations. I hope that British Rail will explain the parameters of the scheme and the way in which it will set about introducing it. It is no good British Rail saying merely that it will introduce the scheme and hope that we will be satisfied. Previous experiences have always led to disappointment. British Rail needs to say how it will carry out the scheme and what resources it will spend on the system to ensure that it will be carried out properly.

British Rail must ensure that staff have high morale, which means that they must have a fair day's pay for a fair day's work in the operation of the system. I want to be satisfied on that point. We cannot negotiate the matter here, because it is the wrong place, but I want to be satisfied on that before the Bill receives its Third Reading. There must be adequate safeguards for staff and the number of assaults should decrease. Enough equipment should be supplied and the necessary action must be taken to reduce the number of assaults.

I hope that the hon. Member for New Forest understands the apprehension that I and others feel. We would basically like the Bill if all the conditions were right. I am a little pessimistic about achieving that and I wait with interest to hear the hon. Gentleman.

**Sir Patrick McNair-Wilson:** I have listened with interest to hon. Members' speeches.

I remind the House that the Bill has been before Parliament for more than 18 months. It had an unopposed Second Reading in the other place on 2 March 1988. No petitions were deposited against it in the House of Commons and on 6 February this year it was given its Second Reading in this place. The Bill, as amended, was reported from the Unopposed Bills Committee on 19 April. It has the support of the Department of Transport. As the hon. Member for Wrexham (Dr. Marek) pointed out from a letter that he read out, consultations are taking place with the general secretary of the National Union of Railwaymen. The Bill is not new. It has been discussed over a long period. At its heart lies this simple question: do fare-paying passengers want to pay for those who cheat and go without tickets? That question must be resolved.

The hon. Member for Wrexham pointed out in the early part of his remarks that he welcomed the idea that the Bill should be considered, but he was more realistic in his closing remarks when he pointed out that that consideration would not take place this evening. I have a nasty feeling that, regardless of what I say, that will not happen.

Two options are available. One is that British Rail should collect the correct fare from fare-paying passengers. The other is that it should institute criminal proceedings against those who try to avoid payment. Those proceedings can be brought, as was made clear on Second Reading, under the Regulation of Railways Act 1889 and the attendant section 67 of the Transport Act 1962. The purpose of the Bill is to move away from those cumbersome criminal proceedings towards a penalty fare scheme which can be much quicker and avoid the time-wasting and costs of pursuing matters through the courts.

The questions which were posed tonight on the extent of fare avoidance were dealt with in detail on Second Reading in February. I remind the House of the skeleton of those figures. I corrected the hon. Member for Bradford, South (Mr. Cryer), who is not in his place now, and said that the figures for Network SouthEast alone were estimated at £36 million. There is probably a shortfall of about £50 million over the whole railway network. As has been shown, much of the avoidance takes place over comparatively short journeys. The hon. Member for Leyton (Mr. Cohen) pointed out that my constituency of New Forest comes within the scope of Network SouthEast. I assure him that my honest constituents are only too delighted to see action being taken against those who ride for nothing on the railway system.

**Mr. Snape:** Were the enormously inflated figures that the hon. Gentleman has just provided supplied to him by British Rail? If so, has it supplied him with the evidence to reinforce them?

9.30 pm

**Sir Patrick McNair-Wilson:** The figures were given to me by British Rail. May I carry the figures a little further before answering the hon. Gentleman's question? We may be talking about annual fare evasion on 20 million journeys. We are discussing short journeys, for which I have given a global figure for evasion of £50 million. Hon. Members have asked how those figures are calculated. On instruction from British Rail, inspectors take part in regular sampling. That procedure is statistically sound, but I entirely recognise the point made by the hon. Member for West Bromwich, East (Mr. Snape) that the figures are not detailed and therefore cannot be absolutely correct. Inevitably, they are round figures, but they are causing sufficient concern for British Rail's management to believe that action must be taken.

**Mr. Cohen:** What evidence has the hon. Gentleman or British Rail to show that this fraudulent behaviour occurs on short journeys? Often when people get to their destination they say, "I got on at the previous stop." That would imply longer journeys. Indeed, the huge figure for fare evasion would imply longer journeys. I appreciate the hon. Gentleman's stout defence of the honesty of his constituents, but the implication of his remarks is that they are dishonest.

**Sir Patrick McNair-Wilson** The hon. Gentleman correctly asks how we know that evasion takes place on short journeys. Longer journeys allow more time for ticket inspection, and the trains used have corridor facilities. I well remember when I had the privilege of representing the constituency of Lewisham, West from 1964 to 1966. At that time, trains consisted of single units with no connecting corridors, so obviously there was difficulty in inspecting tickets on the train.

Over the past 12 months, there have been between 3,000 and 4,000 prosecutions for fare evasion under the 1962 Act. We are dealing with a considerable problem, but the many court cases that are necessary to deal with those prosecutions, with all the work that is required to bring them to a conclusion, could be avoided by the penalty fares scheme.

**Mr. Snape:** The hon. Gentleman referred to "statistically sound" figures. Without wishing to impugn his straightforwardness in putting forward these matters, will he accept that those "statistically sound" figures perhaps were prepared by people within British Rail whose track record for preparing statistics is not the best? I am thinking of those who prepared the statistics for the estimated cost of repairing the Ribblehead viaduct on the Settle-Carlisle line, or those who prepared the figures that British Rail used to justify branch line closures in the 1960s and 1970s. Is it not a fact that all too often British Rail provides figures that are mainly invented and designed only to reinforce its somewhat specious case?

**Sir Patrick McNair-Wilson:** I listened to the hon. Gentleman's comments with interest. We are discussing one of the last of the great nationalised industries. An outside spectator might be concerned that the industry has been given a rough evening of criticism and comment. I hope that the hon. Gentleman's comments are not true. The management of British Rail is doing a good job in difficult circumstances and it is now providing an excellent service for the travelling public. However, there is always room for improvement.

I want now to consider some of the points raised by the hon. Members for Wrexham and for Bradford, South. Several of those points revolved around concerns about the facilities which will be provided to ensure that the scheme works effectively. I want to make it perfectly clear that the passage of this Bill into law will not automatically bring the scheme into operation. The scheme must be activated and British Rail has made it clear that no such activation would be requested until it was totally convinced that the right equipment and the right publicity had been provided to ensure that the travelling public understood the scheme and that the problems that have been referred to of the difficulty in obtaining tickets had been dealt with.

As I explained on Second Reading, there will inevitably be occasions when the travelling public will have difficulty in obtaining tickets. That is why new automatic machines —of which 1,000 are on order—will be brought into play and why the new deferred ticket machine which will accept all coins from 5p to £1 will also be available on station concourses. Therefore, passengers who have not been able to obtain a full ticket, perhaps because of queues, will be absolved from blame if they possess a deferred payment ticket. They will be able to pay the remainder of the ticket price later.

**Mr. Snape:** The hon. Gentleman has just raised a very important point. When we debated this on Second Reading I understood that the deferred payment machine would not be activated unless it was impossible for passengers to buy tickets at the booking office. Is that wrong, or has there been a change since Second Reading?

**Sir Patrick McNair-Wilson:** Those machines will be available for use all the time.

Safeguards for passengers who are concerned about whether they are guilty of misdemeanours are contained in clause 4. Those are far-reaching safeguards. The hon. Member for West Bromwich, East will recall that I read out a list of possible situations in which a passenger might find himself and it would be wrong of me to read it out again. However, it is important to point out that detailed training will be required of those who will be responsible for carrying out the ticket checks. People checking tickets must listen to the passenger's explanation. They will not automatically say, "You're guilty." There may be reasons why the passenger had difficulty in obtaining a ticket and there may be a sensible explanation. If it is immediately obvious that British Rail is at fault at the ticket office—and the hon. Member for West Bromwich, East has just raised this point—that will be taken into consideration before a penalty notice is issued.

If a passenger's explanation is suspect, the authorised person will begin to press for details, including the passenger's address. If he is not satisfied, he or she will report the matter to the penalty fares office with a brief statement from the passenger—the passenger still has an opportunity to make his excuse available to the final arbiter. The name and address and other details of the passenger will be checked and only then will a penalty fare notice be issued. The passenger will then be told that he has 21 days to pay. That is another safeguard. Had we had time to consider the amendments, we would have considered one tabled by the hon. Member for Wrexham on that point. It is important to make it crystal clear that no penalty fare notice will be issued until it is found that the circumstances are correct. I would not want any prospective, law-abiding British Rail traveller to feel that he was risking being forced to pay a fine.

**Mr. Pike:** There is a fear that the genuine passenger who wants to pay the fare will be worried about incurring the penalty fare. The hon. Gentleman said that the scheme cannot be activated until British Rail is satisfied that the ticket machines and staffing systems are correct. Who must the board of British Rail satisfy? Must it satisfy the Secretary of State or the House? It is important to know that.

**Sir Patrick McNair-Wilson:** The hon. Member for Burnley (Mr. Pike) has made an important point. I direct his attention to clause 8(2), which states:

"It shall be the duty of the Board to secure that the requirements of subsection (3) below with respect to warning notices are met in the case of a train service in relation to travel on which the penalty fare provisions have effect."

Clause 8(3) states:

"A warning notice stating the amount of the penalty fare shall be posted at every station at which persons may start to travel on a train service, in such a position as to be readily visible to prospective passengers and shall (however expressed) indicate the circumstances (as provided in section 4(1) or, as the case may be, 5 of this Act) in which they may be liable to pay a penalty fare."

Until those provisions are satisfied, the Secretary of State will not activate the scheme. It is certain that British Rail will not enter into a penalty fare scheme unless the board is satisfied that its passengers—its customers; those who make its profit—are sure that the scheme will work. It is important to assure the travelling public that the scheme is designed to help them and to make sure that, when they buy a ticket, they do not pay for those who travel without one.

Reference has been made to the use of automatic gates. There was a danger of comparing British Rail's automatic gates with the barriers that were discussed in last night's debate about LRT. British Rail has no plans to install automatic gates at its stations. Obviously, at a small number of stations they are in joint operational ownership with the tube service, but, as a general rule, British Rail does not intend to install them.

British Rail is opting for the type of open station that is common on the continent of Europe, both east and west. Britain remains almost the only country in Europe, east or west, with the manned barriers to which we have become accustomed. There is no danger of the travelling public being trapped in the way that the hon. Member for Bradford, South suggested.

Unfortunately, we are not likely to complete our consideration of the Bill this evening. I recognise that Opposition Members have reservations about the consultation that has taken place. The letter from the board to the general secretary which the hon. Member for Wrexham read contains answers to many of the questions that have been posed during this debate. I should like to believe that, even if we cannot complete consideration of the Bill this evening, it will be possible to do so swiftly at some other time.

It is in the interests of British Rail and the travelling public to clear up what has frankly become a millstone around the financial management of the board. It really cannot be right for those who honestly purchase a ticket for a journey to have in the back of their mind the knowledge that many of those travelling with them are doing so for nothing, and that, as a result, fares will rise and the service will become less than adequate.

I urge the House to allow the Bill to proceed and for it to pass to the statute book as soon as possible.

9.45 pm

**Mr. Peter Snape** (West Bromwich, East): As usual, the House will be grateful to the hon. Member for New Forest (Sir P. McNair-Wilson) for the able and courteous way in which he has dealt with the Bill and the other matters for which he is responsible. I would have risen before him had I realised that he was going to speak when he did. I make no complaint about that, but there are one or two points that I wish to make which have either not been dealt with or have been dealt with inadequately during this debate.

I do not wish to labour the point about statistics and how soundly based they may be, but I repeat, without criticising the principle of nationalised industries—which the hon. Member for New Forest artfully suggested I had done—that the invention of statistics to prove a case is not confined exclusively to the public sector. I am sure that he will agree with that. Many hon. Members, probably from both sides of the House, must be suspicious of the enormous sums which it is regularly alleged are being lost to British Rail through fare evasion.

The fact that fare evasion takes place is unchallengeable. Many hon. Members believe that British Rail assists the fraudulent traveller by its staffing policies and philosophies, particularly on many branch lines.

During last night's debate on London Regional Transport's equivalent of this measure, I put forward some fairly strong views about the management's attempts to justify its consistent policy of demanning the system to save money and please its political masters. The side effects of that demanning, which also apply to British Rail, actively assist those who wish to travel fraudulently. The Bill is supposed to provide a solution to the problem.

The West Midlands passenger transport authority is responsible for operating stopping trains throughout a fairly wide area, from Coventry in the south to Wolverhampton in the north, as well as the branch lines in between. The passenger transport authority was recently concerned about fare evasion and fraudulent travel and, to demonstrate its concern, had considerable and protracted correspondence with British Rail. It frequently requested British Rail to do something about the large number of stations in that area with which, for various reasons—normally staff sickness and inability to provide cover—British Rail seemed unable to deal.

So concerned was the passenger transport authority that it provided specific funds to try to rectify the problem. The funds are to provide not only extra British Transport police officers to patrol each line in the area for which it is responsible, but a squad of seven additional travelling ticket inspectors. The authority has given me some statistics demonstrating British Rail's lack of action to combat fraudulent travel.

A letter from the office of councillor Phil Bateman, chairman of the West Midlands passenger transport authority, to British Rail quotes paragraph 3 of a report which, under the heading

"Stations not staffed to schedule: 6 weeks 27 March to 7 May 1989",

lists 13 instances of unscheduled stations covering a total of 62 hours. It states:

"West Midlands stations are open for approximately 40,000 hours over a 6-week period. All instances were due to staff sickness exceeding relief cover."

The worst cases mentioned are Northfield and Perry Barr, two surburban stations in the Birmingham area.

The study undertaken by British Rail into the amount of fraudulent travel in the region came up with an estimate—accepted by the passenger transport executive—of £550,000 per annum. That is a considerable sum and many of us would wish such a large amount of fraud to be stopped, but it is nothing like the multi-million pound estimate that has been presented as a justification for the Bill.

**Mr. Cohen:** My hon. Friend has mentioned a number of stations in his patch in the west midlands. The Government have raised the spectre of privatisation out of spite, because they are trying to attack the trade unions. Would not a number of the stations to which my hon. Friend has referred be threatened with closure, and others suffer reduced services, under privatisation? Rural lines would also be affected, as would some of the less fashionable lines in London, such as the Gospel to Barking Oak line, which runs through my constituency and provides a valuable service. Would not privatisation have implications for penalty fares? Presumably it would mean higher prices and a private police force to collect the fares.

**Mr. Snape:** My hon. Friend paints a lurid scenario. I may have misheard him—I think that it is Gospel Oak to Barking rather than Barking Oak to Gospel—but, not being an expert on the North London line, I can only surmise that he may be correct.

The West Midlands passenger transport authority is paying a considerable amount to keep open the stations that I mentioned, because of the contribution that local rail services make both to the economic well-being of the west midlands and to alleviating road congestion in the region. If the PTA's contribution was withdrawn and responsibility for the stations became once more that of British Rail—as was the case before the Transport Act 1968—I have no doubt that my hon. Friend's scenario would become reality.

[*Mr. Snape*]

The hon. Member for New Forest will accept that I have cited some figures provided by British Rail and accepted on this occasion by those responsible for paying BR to operate those services. Although the sums are considerable, and we deplore the amount of fraud that takes place in the west midlands, they are not the multi-million pound sums that have been mentioned to justify the Bill.

Like their managerial counterparts in London Transport as was and London Underground Limited as it is now known, British Rail management has contributed towards the whole business of fare evasion. Indeed, when one reads the report entitled "Penalty Fares on Public Transport," to which reference has been made on numerous occasions in these debates, it is difficult to find much reference to BR.

The report, detailed though it is, was compiled almost exclusively as the result of an investigation into London Transport, although some reference is made in the report to other self-contained railways—if I might refer to them in that way—such as the Docklands light railway and the Tyne and Wear Metro. The only reference that I can find to BR to justify this amendment measure appears in paragraph 43, which says:

"In addition"

—that is in addition to the other railway routes to which I have referred, such as the Greater Manchester passenger transport authority routes, the South Yorkshire light railway and the Docklands light railway—

"British Rail are looking into the possibility of a penalty fares scheme. They are aware of the Working Group's deliberations and will be preparing their proposals in the light of this Report."

It is worrying to think that the people responsible for compiling that report evidently carried out little, if any, investigation into its impact on BR. Hon. Members who take an interest in these issues will concur with the belief of my hon. Friends and I that there is a big difference between the heavy rail system, as it is known, operated by BR and the small self-contained systems such as the Docklands light railway or the other proposed developments in Yorkshire and Manchester which, desirable though they may be, have not yet come to fruition.

The trouble with BR arises from the long-term and chronic problem of underinvestment at many railway stations. They are, because they were built a long time ago, often dingy, Victorian structures. Although creditable efforts have been made to tidy, clean up and modernise many of them, many of them remain in that dingy state.

The fact that the underlying theme of the Bill, like its London Transport counterpart, is designed to justify a further reduction in staff will mean that those dingy, dark, ill-lit stations will be even less likely to be properly manned in the future. The onus and burden of proof for those who travel without tickets will fall particularly on those who decline to loiter for a moment longer than necessary on station platforms when it is necessary to purchase tickets.

Assurances were given by the hon. Member for New Forest that where a permit to travel or authority-to-travel ticket is purchased from a machine——

**Sir Patrick McNair-Wilson** *rose in his place and claimed to move,* That the Question be now put.

*Question put,* That the Question be now put:—

*The House divided:* Ayes 104, Noes 14.

**Division No. 269]**    [10 pm

### AYES

Alexander, Richard
Amess, David
Arbuthnot, James
Arnold, Tom *(Hazel Grove)*
Atkins, Robert
Atkinson, David
Baker, Nicholas *(Dorset N)*
Bennett, Nicholas *(Pembroke)*
Bevan, David Gilroy
Boscawen, Hon Robert
Boswell, Tim
Bowis, John
Braine, Rt Hon Sir Bernard
Bright, Graham
Buck, Sir Antony
Butler, Chris
Carlisle, John, *(Luton N)*
Carlisle, Kenneth *(Lincoln)*
Carrington, Matthew
Carttiss, Michael
Chapman, Sydney
Chope, Christopher
Coombs, Anthony *(Wyre F'rest)*
Davis, David *(Boothferry)*
Devlin, Tim
Dorrell, Stephen
Dover, Den
Dykes, Hugh
Emery, Sir Peter
Fallon, Michael
Fishburn, John Dudley
Forth, Eric
Franks, Cecil
Freeman, Roger
Garel-Jones, Tristan
Gill, Christopher
Gow, Ian
Greenway, John *(Ryedale)*
Griffiths, Peter *(Portsmouth N)*
Ground, Patrick
Hague, William
Hargreaves, Ken *(Hyndburn)*
Harris, David
Hawkins, Christopher
Hogg, Hon Douglas *(Gr'th'm)*
Hordern, Sir Peter
Howarth, Alan *(Strat'd-on-A)*
Howarth, G. *(Cannock & B'wd)*
Hunt, David *(Wirral W)*
Hunt, Sir John *(Ravensbourne)*
Irvine, Michael
Janman, Tim
Johnson Smith, Sir Geoffrey
Jones, Robert B *(Herts W)*
King, Roger *(B'ham N'thfield)*

Lawrence, Ivan
Lee, John *(Pendle)*
Lightbown, David
Lilley, Peter
Lloyd, Peter *(Fareham)*
Lord, Michael
Lyell, Sir Nicholas
Macfarlane, Sir Neil
MacKay, Andrew *(E Berkshire)*
Maclean, David
McLoughlin, Patrick
Mans, Keith
Martin, David *(Portsmouth S)*
Maude, Hon Francis
Mitchell, Andrew *(Gedling)*
Mitchell, Sir David
Moate, Roger
Moss, Malcolm
Moynihan, Hon Colin
Neubert, Michael
Nicholson, David *(Taunton)*
Norris, Steve
Onslow, Rt Hon Cranley
Porter, David *(Waveney)*
Portillo, Michael
Raffan, Keith
Rhodes James, Robert
Ridsdale, Sir Julian
Roe, Mrs Marion
Sackville, Hon Tom
Shaw, David *(Dover)*
Shaw, Sir Giles *(Pudsey)*
Shaw, Sir Michael *(Scarb')*
Shepherd, Colin *(Hereford)*
Shersby, Michael
Sims, Roger
Stevens, Lewis
Stewart, Rt Hon Ian *(Herts N)*
Stradling Thomas, Sir John
Summerson, Hugo
Taylor, John M *(Solihull)*
Tebbit, Rt Hon Norman
Thorne, Neil
Thurnham, Peter
Tredinnick, David
Waddington, Rt Hon David
Wardle, Charles *(Bexhill)*
Widdecombe, Ann
Wood, Timothy

Tellers for the Ayes:
    Sir Patrick McNair-Wilson
    and
    Sir Michael McNair-Wilson.

### NOES

Banks, Tony *(Newham NW)*
Barnes, Harry *(Derbyshire NE)*
Cook, Robin *(Livingston)*
Foster, Derek
Haynes, Frank
McKay, Allen *(Barnsley West)*
Mallon, Seamus
Marek, Dr John
Nellist, Dave

Powell, Ray *(Ogmore)*
Randall, Stuart
Skinner, Dennis
Snape, Peter
Wareing, Robert N.

Tellers for the Noes:
    Mr. Peter L. Pike and
    Mr. Harry Cohen.

*Question accordingly agreed to.*

*Question,* That the Bill, as amended, be now considered, *put accordingly, and agreed to.*

*It being after Ten o'clock, further consideration of the Bill stood adjourned.*

*Bill to be further considered on Thursday 6 July.*

# Representation of the People Bill

## *[Money]*

*Queen's Recommendation having been signified—*
*Motion made, and Question proposed,*

That, for the purposes of any Act resulting from the Representation of the People Bill, it is expedient to authorise—

(a) the charging on and payment out of the Consolidated Fund of any increase attributable to the Act in the sums charged on and paid out of that Fund under any other enactment, and

(b) the payment out of money provided by Parliament of—

    (i) any increase attributable to the Act in the sums payable out of money so provided under any other enactment, and

    (ii) any administrative expenses incurred by the Secretary of State in consequence of the Act.
    —*[Mr. Douglas Hogg.]*

10.12 pm

**Mr. Harry Barnes** (Derbyshire, North-East): No price is too high for the extension of democracy. However, the Bill will mean the destruction of democracy. The poll tax has destroyed the British electorate and the Government are now prepared to spend money on replacing that electorate with expatriates who have few links with Britain. They should not spend money on the destruction of democracy. If the Government are intent on destroying democracy, they should do it on the cheap. They are not doing that in the Bill.

What is spent on electoral registration and its subsequent provisions in Britain? The explanatory and financial memorandum gives a cost of £1·72 per person for initial registration and 62p per person thereafter. What do such figures cover? Do they cover the issuing of registration forms that people are asked to complete? Will they be even simpler than my poll tax registration form, which has not yet been filled in and will not be filled in? Is there any money for advertising to encourage people to register?

The Government are very lax about encouraging people to register for electoral purposes. Last year they spent about £320,000—a little more than previously— from a total advertising budget of £100 million. It appears that the franchise is worth only 0·31 per cent. of the Government's advertising expenditure while other rubbish such as the poll tax leaflet, which costs a fortune, is dished out and used to destroy the democratic process rather than extend it.

Earlier, the Minister stated that as many as 2 million British citizens overseas could qualify for electoral registration under the provisions of the Representation of the People Bill, which has been given its Second Reading. To provide that facility will cost £3·5 million, which contrasts starkly with the £320,000 that the Government spend on stimulating the electorate in this country.

Is there any alternative to spending that £3·5 million on initial registration, and the additional £1 million required to maintain the electoral rolls of people who have little connection with this country? In many cases they have deserted this country for more than 25 years; others were taken out of this country as babes in arms but after 18 years they will qualify to vote in Britain. They will survive for at least seven years on the electoral register, probably voting in respect of constituencies that did not even exist when they were born and about which they know nothing.

[*Mr. Harry Barnes*]

No money should be spent by the Government in connection with the Representation of the People Bill. If they want to implement its provisions, they should do so off their own bat and not expect the public to pay for the destruction of democracy, of public services, and of the freedoms for which working-class people have struggled for so long.

*Question put:—*

*The House divided:* Ayes 98, Noes 5.

**Division No. 270]**	**[10.17 pm**

### AYES

Alexander, Richard
Amess, David
Amos, Alan
Arbuthnot, James
Arnold, Jacques (Gravesham)
Arnold, Tom (Hazel Grove)
Ashby, David
Atkinson, David
Baker, Nicholas (Dorset N)
Bennett, Nicholas (Pembroke)
Bevan, David Gilroy
Boscawen, Hon Robert
Boswell, Tim
Bowis, John
Braine, Rt Hon Sir Bernard
Bright, Graham
Buck, Sir Antony
Butler, Chris
Carlisle, John, (Luton N)
Carrington, Matthew
Carttiss, Michael
Chapman, Sydney
Chope, Christopher
Coombs, Anthony (Wyre F'rest)
Davis, David (Boothferry)
Devlin, Tim
Dover, Den
Emery, Sir Peter
Fallon, Michael
Fishburn, John Dudley
Forth, Eric
Franks, Cecil
Freeman, Roger
Garel-Jones, Tristan
Gill, Christopher
Gow, Ian
Greenway, John (Ryedale)
Griffiths, Peter (Portsmouth N)
Ground, Patrick
Hague, William
Hampson, Dr Keith
Hargreaves, Ken (Hyndburn)
Harris, David
Hawkins, Christopher
Hogg, Hon Douglas (Gr'th'm)
Howarth, Alan (Strat'd-on-A)
Howarth, G. (Cannock & B'wd)
Hunt, David (Wirral W)
Hunt, Sir John (Ravensbourne)
Irvine, Michael
Janman, Tim
Johnson Smith, Sir Geoffrey
Jones, Robert B (Herts W)
King, Roger (B'ham N'thfield)
Lawrence, Ivan
Lee, John (Pendle)
Lightbown, David
Lilley, Peter
Lloyd, Peter (Fareham)
Lord, Michael
Lyell, Sir Nicholas
Macfarlane, Sir Neil
MacKay, Andrew (E Berkshire)
Maclean, David
McLoughlin, Patrick
McNair-Wilson, Sir Michael
McNair-Wilson, Sir Patrick
Mans, Keith
Martin, David (Portsmouth S)
Maude, Hon Francis
Mitchell, Sir David
Moate, Roger
Moss, Malcolm
Moynihan, Hon Colin
Neubert, Michael
Nicholson, David (Taunton)
Norris, Steve
Onslow, Rt Hon Cranley
Porter, David (Waveney)
Raffan, Keith
Rhodes James, Robert
Roe, Mrs Marion
Sackville, Hon Tom
Shaw, David (Dover)
Shaw, Sir Michael (Scarb')
Shepherd, Colin (Hereford)
Shersby, Michael
Sims, Roger
Stevens, Lewis
Stradling Thomas, Sir John
Summerson, Hugo
Taylor, John M (Solihull)
Thorne, Neil
Thurnham, Peter
Waddington, Rt Hon David
Wardle, Charles (Bexhill)
Widdecombe, Ann
Wood, Timothy

Tellers for the Ayes:
Mr. Kenneth Carlisle and
Mr. Stephen Dorrell.

### NOES

Cohen, Harry
Nellist, Dave
Pike, Peter L.
Skinner, Dennis
Spearing, Nigel

Tellers for the Noes:
Mr. Harry Barnes and
Mr. Tony Banks.

*Question accordingly agreed to.*

*Resolved,*

That, for the purposes of any Act resulting from the Representation of the People Bill, it is expedient to authorise—

(a) the charging on and payment out of the Consolidated Fund of any increase attributable to the Act in the sums charged on and paid out of that Fund under any other enactment, and

(b) the payment out of money provided by Parliament of—

(i) any increase attributable to the Act in the sums payable out of money so provided under any other enactment, and

(ii) any administrative expenses incurred by the Secretary of State in consequence of the Act.

# Water Bill *[Money]* (No. 3)

*Queen's Recommendation having been signified——*

*Resolved,*

That, for the purposes of any Act resulting from the Water Bill, it is expedient to authorise the payment out of money provided by Parliament of—

(a) sums required by a Minister of the Crown for making payments to persons in respect of obligations accepted by or imposed on them in relation to land in an area designated as a nitrate sensitive area; and

(b) sums required by the Secretary of State for making any payment in respect of an indemnity given under the Act for purposes connected with increases in the fluoride content of any water.—[*Mr. Chapman.*]

## STATUTORY INSTRUMENTS, &c.

*Motion made, and Question put forthwith pursuant to Standing Order No. 101(5) (Committees on Statutory Instruments, &c.)*

### SEA FISHERIES

That the draft Fisheries Act 1981 (Amendment) Regulation 1989, which were laid before this House on 6th June, be approved.—[*Mr. Chapman.*]

*Question agreed to.*

# Northern Ireland (Elections)

*Motion made, and Question proposed,* That this House do now adjourn:—*[Mr. Chapman.]*

10.28 pm

**Mr. Seamus Mallon** (Newry and Armagh): I welcome the opportunity to introduce an Adjournment debate on the electoral affairs of Northern Ireland. It is especially relevant after today's debate, the district council elections in Northern Ireland and the European elections.

In any society it is essential that the Government and Members of Parliament keep the electoral process constantly under review. We should learn from the experience throughout the world where the majority of people do not have the right to exercise their franchise, and that right should be treasured by those of us who have a working electoral process. We must be careful, especially in a Northern Irish context, to nurture that right, rather than allow it to hang out on a limb. We all know that a solution to the problems there will not come from the bomb or the bullet, and those who advocate and use them, from Government legislation or from international arrangements. It will come through the franchise, with the people of the North of Ireland determining their future.

I believe that especially because, over the past 20 years, I have seen how the electoral process has been attacked. I have fought elections in the face of substantial boycotts, and when men with guns were standing outside the polling stations taking down the names of those who had the audacity to go in and vote. For that reason, we must be ever vigilant to ensure that we have a viable system which gives the best advantage to the people who are the most important in this matter—all those in each constituency who have the right to vote.

At present, the administrative thrust is towards making it more difficult, not easier, for people to exercise their franchise. I do not say that carpingly because I know that there is legislation to constrain everything, especially the electoral process, but I believe that an effort should be made to simplify the way in which the process operates.

A new system for the collection of registration forms has been successful, and I welcome that success. However, the system could be tidied up substantially, especially when one considers the returns and the way in which some of those appointed to handle them fell down on the job. There was a lack of returns in some areas and there was not the necessary follow-up to ensure that we had the substantial registration we all needed.

There is a tremendous gap in the postal voting system. We have inconsistencies time after time, and they derive especially from the pedantic and bureaucratic way in which the forms are framed. It is almost impossible for the ordinary person to fill in either the registration form or the postal vote application with any confidence as a result of their detailed technicalities. Those forms should be substantially simplified.

I found it disturbing in the previous two elections when the chief electoral officer ruled in effect that people with psychiatric illnesses could not vote by post. A worrying decision was made that, in effect, psychiatric illness was sufficient to disfranchise many people. We all know that psychiatric disorders are illnesses just as much as any physical illness. I am talking not about people who were confined either permanently or semi-permanently to psychiatric institutions, but about ordinary people in their

houses who were suffering from psychiatric ailments. They were prevented from voting by a decision of the chief electoral officer which I accept was based on legislation. But there must be discretion for him to deal with a substantial form of illness in the community. All Governments argue that the place for people with psychiatric illnesses is within the community where they can share the experiences and the care of the community. It seems a contradiction that they should be excluded from exercising their franchise on a legalistic point.

I apply the same argument to the way in which postal votes were allocated to the elderly. I know of two people, both 103 years old, who were denied postal votes because it was deemed that their postal vote application forms were not properly filled in. What reason had their doctor put down? Old age. I should have thought that in a society like ours a definition of old age would be sufficient to merit a postal vote for someone of 103 and to allow him or her the right to exercise the franchise. This nitpicking approach must stop.

Once postal votes are issued, responsibility should rest with the electoral office. At the moment, once the electoral office issues and hands the postal votes to the post office, its responsibility ends. I have seen at first hand the abuses that creep in. I have seen postmen who have been badgered into handing over postal votes—not one or two, but dozens—and been put into compromising situations with respect to their jobs. The Minister should closely consider a variation on the registered post theme that allows us to end that terrible abuse of the right to exercise the franchise. It is appalling that, in certain parts of the North of Ireland, some people are muscling—I use that word advisedly—elderly people out of their votes.

I am one of those who asked for, and welcomed, personal identification schemes. Given the unique circumstances in the North of Ireland, it was essential to end the wide-scale personation that took place. By and large, the process of identification has done just that, but there is much still to be desired. It is time that we considered this matter again. One of the easiest ways—probably the most effective—of improving the position would be for the Government, through the Department of Health and Social Services in the North of Ireland, to make a blanket issue of medical cards issued by the Central Services Agency. There is an anomaly in that the new medical card, which does not include a photograph or any means of identification, is acceptable, but the old medical card, which is not issued by the CSA, is not adequate. Elderly people are affected most because many do not have the CSA medical card. Such cards should be issued, and it should not be beyond the Department's ingenuity to ensure that forgeries cannot be made.

In at least the past two elections in the North of Ireland there were substantial forgeries of medical cards. They were so good that one could not tell the difference between the real card and the forgery. A doctor colleague of mine who was a candidate saw a medical card that referred to him as the doctor but had a different registration number. Because of anomalies, those who wish to cheat and to steal other people's votes can do so with the expertise at their disposal. Many people, especially the elderly, have been denied their votes because they have not yet been given the new medical cards. It is time that the Department made a blanket issue of new medical cards to everyone over 16. That would reduce the number of people who are disfranchised and cut the potential for abuse of the system.

[*Mr. Seamus Mallon*]

As long as human nature remains human nature there will be personation at elections. We must ensure that it is cut to the barest minimum. Those who assume the responsibility to stop it in the polling stations—the polling agents appointed by the political parties—are placed in an invidious position. I found myself in that position some time ago. If one challenges someone whom one knows is involved in personation, that person has clear recourse to the law and a right to legal aid. It has become a cause celebre in parts of the North of Ireland, where people who were simply trying to defend the electoral process are having to pay court costs. The political parties and those representing them are loth to make challenges because they are most vulnerable once a challenge is made. We are all aware of how people use the legal system to the detriment of not only the person and political party involved but of the electoral process.

I ask the Minister to consider closely the siting of polling stations and to impress on those responsible that that is not an excuse for a security operation but an exercise of the franchise. During the latest election we had the rather deplorable position at a polling station at St. Joseph's Creggan in Derry, where Army personnel were photographing those who were going to vote. That is a contradiction of the way in which elections should be run. I ask the Minister to ensure that that is not repeated, because it turns polling into a security operation, which stops people voting. People have stopped voting in the North of Ireland in the past for many other reasons. I remember the days of 29 and 30 per cent. turnouts in my constituency. The figure has now increased to 80 per cent., which is healthy, but we must do all that we can to ensure that that healthy position remains.

Old people in urban and rural areas must travel substantial distances across hilly terrain to polling stations. During the previous two elections, several people said to me, "If you take me to the polling station I will vote, but for heaven's sake get me back because I cannot get over the hill." I ask that the town of Newry be considered specifically because it is ridiculous to force elderly people to walk substantial distances across hilly areas, which reduces the possibility of their exercising the franchise. The siting of polling stations is reviewed every four years. I suggest that that period be reduced to one year; it should be an ongoing process rather than a four-year span.

I ask the Minister for the provision of an electoral office in Newry and Armagh. It is the only constituency west of the Bann that does not have an electoral office. We deal with an efficient and excellent electoral office that is responsible for two constituencies. I wonder why Newry and Armagh is unique among constituencies west of the Bann.

I take the opportunity of paying tribute to those involved in the running of electoral affairs in the North of Ireland, especially deputy electoral officers who, in difficult circumstances, do an excellent job. During the past 20 years, I have never experienced anything other than courtesy and co-operation.

A pedantic approach is being adopted from the top, which in many ways is constraining the most effective running of not only elections but the development of the electoral process. I ask the Minister to consider that problem.

Given the unique position in the North of Ireland, the Government should not adopt a passive role. They should adopt an active role because it is in the interests of the Government, the people and the political parties to nurture the tender plant in the North of Ireland and make it strong enough to do what it eventually will do—play a key role in solving our problems.

10.44 pm

**The Minister of State, Northern Ireland Office (Mr. Ian Stewart):** I congratulate the hon. Member for Newry and Amargh (Mr. Mallon) on obtaining an opportunity for the House to debate electoral law in Northern Ireland. I join him in his tribute to those who have been responsible for organising the electoral process, which is never an easy one to carry through, particular in the circumstances of Northern Ireland.

I pay a personal tribute to the hon. Gentleman and to other hon. Members who represent constituencies in Northern Ireland. In ways that are not always evident to those of us who represent constituencies in Great Britain, it takes a particular kind of courage and dedication to perform that democratic role. I salute the hon. Gentleman and his parliamentary colleagues from Northern Ireland for their work in maintaining the democratic process, despite the many difficulties that have been placed in its way.

The hon. Gentleman has raised several detailed points. I hope that he will understand if I am unable to respond definitively and in detail to all of them now. I shall reflect on what he has said and I shall also read the *Official Report*. If I have not covered certain points this evening, I will communicate with the hon. Gentleman about them. I assure the hon. Gentleman that I will give careful consideration to what he has said.

Some time before the recent elections, I had a meeting with the chief electoral officer because I wanted to hear at first hand from him about the arrangements being made for the forthcoming elections and to share with him the Government's concern that everything should be done to ensure that the elections were conducted in an orderly fashion without abuse or irregularity. I hope that, before too long, after he has had a chance to collect more information and analyse what has happened in the elections, I will have another opportunity to see him. I shall draw his attention to the hon. Gentleman's remarks.

As the hon. Gentleman knows, the major legislation governing the conduct of elections in Northern Ireland is contained in the Electoral Law (Northern Ireland) Act 1962 and the Representation of the People Acts of 1983 and 1985. There are, of course, differences between Northern Ireland and Great Britain because of the different electoral systems. Despite the mechanical difficulties that the hon. Gentleman has described, it is necessary to have reasonably tightly drawn rules for anything relating to elections, for the obvious reason that, if the mechanics are not well ordered or categorically stated, there are considerable opportunities for abuse. The opportunities for abuse in Northern Ireland, where intimidation and other very undesirable practices have occurred over the years, are greatly increased. The hon. Gentleman referred to a pedantic approach, but it must be set against the difficulties of not having a rather strict approach to the mechanics of the procedure. Nevertheless, I will reflect on his points.

The hon. Gentleman mentioned votes for the mentally disabled. Other hon. Members from Northern Ireland have raised that matter with me. Earlier this year, a number of people who were formerly registered as absent voters and mentally disabled were told that, in future, they would not be able to vote by post. The reason is that, throughout the country, mental disability is not and never has been a ground on which an elector becomes eligible for an absent vote.

It was formerly the case that those who applied for an absent vote on the ground of physical incapacity were not required to state the nature of the incapacity. When the chief electoral officer reviewed the list of absent votes earlier this year, he found that in a number of cases the ground for claiming an absent vote was not physical disability, but a mental one.

That is one of several points that the hon. Gentleman raised which apply equally to Great Britain and to which I will draw the attention of my right hon. Friend the Home Secretary. It would not be sensible for us to contemplate differences in matters of that kind between Northern Ireland and the rest of the United Kingdom. There is a logical reason behind that and we would not overturn it lightly. If there has been a change, it has been a change in the interpretation of the rules or a more rigid application of them rather than a change in the rules themselves. I am sure that the hon. Gentleman understands that.

The hon. Gentleman also referred to specified documents for polling purposes. I am aware that there were instances of forged medical cards which were used as documents for the purposes of personation during the elections. I understand that there has been at least one conviction and that someone else is awaiting trial in another case.

As a result of what took place in the local elections, polling staff were given additional guidance on how to minimise the risks of forgeries before the European elections on 15 June. Although I have not yet received a final report, I gather that the precautions were successful in preventing a repetition of what happened earlier. Obviously that is a matter of great concern to us. We do not want people to circumvent the safeguards introduced in the Elections (Northern Ireland) Act 1985. I assure the hon. Gentleman that we will consider whether there are other documents, or ways in which documents can be made less vulnerable to forgery, which might replace the existing medical card or be a variation of it. However, before we make any such changes, we would of course consult the political parties about any proposals for change. We have not yet reached that point. However, I accept the hon. Gentleman's point and assure him that I am as concerned about it as he is.

The hon. Gentleman referred also to the location of polling stations. As he said, the chief electoral officer is required to prepare a scheme every four years. According to the Electoral Law (Northern Ireland) Act 1962, he must

"provide for the designation of such number of polling stations in such situations as to provide for all electors in each polling district such reasonable facilities for voting as are practicable in the circumstances."

The chief electoral officer is also required to publish the scheme in draft. He can cause a local inquiry to be held on any question which arises from it and he must consider any objections or proposals that are made in relation to the draft scheme before he confirms it, either with or without qualifications.

The Polling Stations Scheme (Northern Ireland) Regulations 1972 provide for relevant sections of the draft scheme to be made available for inspection at district council offices and at the chief electoral officer's office. The regulations provide that notice of the approved scheme should be published and say when and where it can be inspected. The chief electoral officer published his scheme this year on 16 February. I gather that to avoid confusion a virtually uniform polling station scheme operated during the recent local elections and in the European elections. Comments can be made about the scheme, but relatively few have been received. I accept the hon. Gentleman's point about that. It is unlikely that it would be practicable to organise such a scheme at such frequent intervals as one year. However, I shall consider what the hon. Gentleman has said.

The hon. Gentleman also discussed the suggestion that there should be an electoral office in Newry. He knows that his constituency is covered by the offices in Banbridge and Dungannon, I think satisfactorily. These are matters for the chief electoral officer to determine. He is bound to take account of convenience, efficiency and economy. There are at present 10 electoral offices throughout Northern Ireland covering 17 parliamentary constituencies, so I do not think that the hon. Gentleman's constituency is quite as unusual as he may have suggested.

The number and location of offices was reviewed when the number of parliamentary constituencies was increased some years ago. It was then agreed that the arrangements which now exist ought to enable the chief electoral officer to carry out his responsibilities effectively. I believe that that has generally been the case, but if there are grounds for suggesting otherwise I should be ready to take them up with him. Quite a number of constituencies are served by two or more electoral offices, and they are not necessarily within the constituency. It is not for me or members of the Government to deal with that.

I said at the beginning that I hope to see the chief electoral officer before too long to hear how technical and other matters proceeded during the recent elections. That will be a suitable occasion on which to draw his attention to what the hon. Gentleman has said tonight. I imagine that, like others, the hon. Gentleman would like an electoral office in his constituency, but before such a change could be considered one would have to make out a case that the present system is not working.

Most of what the hon. Gentleman suggested is, in practice, because of the responsibilities that Parliament has delegated to the chief electoral officer, a matter of detail for him rather than me, although, on behalf of the Government, I have responsibility for ensuring that the democratic process is properly conducted in Northern Ireland. I thank the hon. Gentleman for the constructive way in which he has raised these issues. He has done so in a topical way, and soon after two elections which, while they were not without their imperfections—that would be asking quite a lot in the context of Northern Ireland—were conducted in a way which mostly embodied the best of our democratic traditions.

I endorse what the hon. Gentleman said about the importance of that democratic process, especially in

*[Mr. Ian Stewart]*

Northern Ireland, where that process, and that process alone, ought to determine the future of those whom the hon. Gentleman represents and those for whom I and fellow Ministers in the Northern Ireland Office have responsibility on behalf of the Government.

*Question put and agreed to.*

*Adjourned accordingly at two minutes to Eleven o'clock.*

# House of Commons

*Friday 30 June 1989*

*The House met at half-past Nine o'clock*

## PRAYERS

[MR. SPEAKER *in the Chair*]

## Petition

9.34 am

**Mr. Peter L. Pike** (Burnley): I wish to present a petition, which reads as follows:

"To the Honourable the Commons of the United Kingdom of Great Britain and Northern Ireland in Parliament assembled.

The Humble Petition of supporters of Burnley Football Club and members of the Burnley Football Supporters' Club, Sheweth.

That we condemn the proposed legislation to force football supporters to carry identification cards, and we believe that a system of identity cards will have little impact on the problem of football related violence, will hinder football's attempts to attract a new generation of supporters and will lead to the eventual demise of the game as a spectator sport.

Wherefore your Petitioners pray that your honourable House will urge the Government to bring forward proposals which will have the support of genuine football supporters.

And your petitioners, as in duty bound, will ever pray."

The petition is signed by 1,963 signatories and has my full support.

*To lie upon the Table.*

## BILL PRESENTED

### BLASPHEMY

Mr. Harry Greenway presented a Bill to make provision for the punishment of persons who blaspheme against certain religions: And the same was read the First Time; and ordered to be read a Second Time on Friday 7 July and to be printed. [Bill 171.]

## Listeria

**Mr. Alan Williams** (Swansea, West): On a point of order, Mr. Speaker. You will have read the reports in the newspapers of 26 babies dying because of ministerial incompetence in failing to warn expectant mothers of the risk of listeria. We expected that there would be a statement at 11 o'clock, but nothing has yet appeared on the annunciator screen. Can you say whether Ministers have asked you whether they may intervene at this stage? If they have not, may I say, through you, that we would expect such a statement at 11 o'clock?

**Mr. Speaker:** I have so far received no notification but notifications can be made at any time before 10 o'clock.

# Policing (London)

*[Relevant document: Report of the Commissioner of Police of the Metropolis (Cm. 670)].*

*Motion made, and Question proposed,* That this House do now adjourn.—*[Mr. Sackville]*

9.36 am

**The Secretary of State for the Home Department** (Mr. Douglas Hurd): I am sure that hon. Members will agree that since we last debated the policing of London the Metropolitan police have made important progress. I can speak today of continuing falls in total levels of reported crime, of better links between police and community, and of continuing measures to improve the service that the Metropolitan police deliver to the people of London.

Crime has not yet been decisively beaten; these developments are only the first glimpses of success and the Metropolitan police are clear that there is plenty of scope for further improving their performance, but I hope that throughout this debate we shall all bear in mind that we place heavy duties on our police and remember that, to carry out their duties, officers need the underlying support and positive help that they expect from the public. One of the purposes of this debate is to enable me, as police authority, to renew my pledge of that support and help.

Recorded crime figures do not tell the whole story, but they give an indication of what is happening. In his annual report for 1988, the commissioner reported a 2 per cent. decrease in recorded crime over the year. The latest figures, for the 12 months to the end of March show a 4 per cent. fall. Over the past two years, recorded crime in the Metropolitan police district has declined by 6 per cent. —a modest but very welcome reversal of earlier trends. It means, for example, that many Londoners were not burgled in 1988 who would have been burgled if the earlier trend had been maintained, although of course people do not see it that way.

This good news hides some disturbing undercurrents. Offences of violence against the person rose by 19 per cent. in 1988. The number of homicides fell by 46—23 per cent. —but violence resulting in slight or no injury—as in eight out of 10 violent offences—rose by more than 20 per cent. This includes crimes such as sexual offences and domestic violence, which are are now being reported, whereas before the victim would have kept quiet. Even so, there is a savagery and brutality in some crimes today which anger all of us and create an outward ripple of fear.

**Mr. Harry Greenway** (Ealing, North): I am sorry to interrupt my right hon. Friend so early in his speech. Does he agree that a major difficulty in overcoming public violence is the trend with new roads and the adaptation of existing roads to put in subways and remove surface crossings? Is he aware that in my constituency at the Target roundabout on the A40, which everybody knows, there have been two or three attempted rapes in a month and other serious acts of violence? Old people and young mothers are too terrified to use subways generally, and that is understandable.

**Mr. Hurd:** My hon. Friend has given an example of an important point, which is that the design of, for example, lighting and the placing of subways and crossings can be crucial in preventing or encouraging crime for years ahead. The Metropolitan police are trying to insert their skill and advice into the planning and design of projects such as the

one my hon. Friend has in mind. Without knowing more about that project, I cannot comment further. However, effective thinking about crime at the point of design is extremely important for good or ill thereafter.

**Mr. Paul Boateng** (Brent, South): I welcome the emphasis the Home Secretary puts on design in relation to crime prevention. Does he accept that design, the environment and the whole culture in which particular communities live and work have an impact on the effectiveness of crime prevention? Will he undertake to meet his right hon. Friend the Secretary of State for the Environment so that greater assistance can be given to the estates where crime is a particular problem because of design, and so that poor design features can be unravelled and the estates made more sustaining places in which to live? I am thinking especially of the Stonebridge estate in my constituency. There is also the problem of the design of some police stations. Harlesden police station, which was referred to specifically by the National Audit Office, dates back to the beginning of this century and provides the police with wholly unacceptable conditions in which to work and carry out their functions. Will the right hon. Gentleman put his money where his mouth is on this issue?

**Mr. Hurd:** The hon. Gentleman has now made his speech and I am sorry that I gave way to him. He is right on the need for the redesign of some housing estates, and the Estate Action programme of my right hon. Friend the Secretary of State of the Environment is designed to achieve that. He is also right to say that there is a long way to go before we have the well-designed and modern police stations required in the Metropolitan district.

I was talking about the outward ripple of fear caused by the savagery and brutality of some crime today. An especially threatening form of crime to many people is the street robbery of personal property after a sudden attack. In 1988, the number of those crimes was about the same as in the previous year, whereas the latest 12-month figures to the end of March show a 3 per cent. fall. The commissioner, with my full support, is determined to reduce street robberies. The campaign against street robberies in the worst affected divisions continued last year with considerable success.

One of the tactics used against street robbery is to deploy extra uniformed and plain clothes officers for set periods, targeting known trouble spots and suspects. A particularly successful example of that in 1988 was Peckham division, where that tactic, combined with posters and leaflets led to a 26 per cent. drop in street robbery and a 48 per cent. reduction in theft from the person.

Offences of violence remain a serious and growing problem. It is encouraging to see the commissioner's commitment to their reduction beginning to be reflected in the statistics. In 1988, the number of robbery offences cleared up rose by 7 per cent. and there was a 27 per cent. increase in the number of offences of violence against the person cleared up, while the clear-up rate for those offences rose from 53 to 57 per cent. I hope that those indications of growing police success in the clear-up of violent crime will help to bring about a fall in such offences. A violent offender does not offend while behind bars and the more likely he is to be caught, the less likely it is that he will try it on in the first place.

It is encouraging to see that domestic burglary continues to fall, now by 6 per cent. a year. That must in part be due to the 1·25 million households in the Metropolitan police district now involved in neighbourhood watch schemes. Theft of or from a motor vehicle has fallen by 9 per cent. Those are usually preventable crimes. It is too early to be certain, but it looks as if the message promoted by the police, Government and volunteers in the community is achieving its aim. Despite the efforts in Labour boroughs such as Lambeth to hold up this progress and to keep police and community apart. I hope that the Opposition Front Bench will show some faint sign of recognition and perhaps even of pleasure at what is being achieved.

**Mr. Simon Hughes** (Southwark and Bermondsey): Will the Home Secretary deal with two other significant areas? The commissioner's report dealt with alcohol-related offences. What is noticeable by its absence from the report are offences that have a racial element. Will the Home Secretary comment on trends in those areas?

**Mr. Hurd:** I am coming on to the matter of racial attacks. The hon. Gentleman is right to stress the heavy weight of stupid drinking and, in some cases, illegal drinking by minors, in the crime figures. As he knows, we have stiffened the law on that and we are encouraging police and magistrates to make greater use of their powers than they have done in the past.

A particularly worrying form of burglary is that in which the burglar poses as a representative of an agency or company in order to gain access to a house. The elderly are especially at risk and 3,500 such offences were recorded in London last year.

The northern area of the Metropolitan district has been concentrating resources on the investigation of these offences, in parallel with an Age Concern campaign to warn elderly people of the dangers. Arrests have been made of burglars posing as social workers, police officers and Department of Social Security officials. One man, who posed as an electricity board official, was recently convicted of 400 such offences and sentenced to 10 years' imprisonment. That is just one example, but I could have given hundreds of examples of the way in which the Metropolitan police are working hard to tackle crime better.

The reform of the police to which I referred last year has continued.

The Metropolitan police are far more decentralised than they were three years ago. Since 1986, headquarters strengths have been reduced by 400 officers. That means that more of the extra officers whom I have authorised can be deployed on divisions for operational purposes, rather than being diverted unnecessarily to desk work and administrative duties. The fruits of the policy are seen in the 1,300 additional officers now on areas and divisions and in the 23 per cent. rise in street duty hours over the past two years.

It is a better planned force. The annual strategy sets out policing priorities and major issues, and divisional objectives are published after extensive consultation with local communities. It is a better-managed force. There is a problem of attitude, in that there is a natural tendency for officers to resist being labelled as "managers", with connotations of being part of a desk-bound bureaucracy. However, there has been a growing realisation in the Metropolitan police and throughout the police service that without management skills, the police cannot make the best use of the resources they are given. These are important steps in the right direction, but we still have some way to go before we can be satisfied that value for money is being fully achieved.

In the foreword to his annual report, Sir Peter Imbert pointed out the dangers of trying to measure the efficiency of a police force as if it were a steel mill or an oil refinery. Of course he was right to do that, but I am pleased to note his commitment to applying modern business methods to the police, where they fit. Policing is not a business, but it certainly needs to be businesslike.

We are talking about a £1 billion organisation, employing over 40,000 staff, and it is not enough to rely upon the traditional policing and detective skills of the Victorian officer. The Met is a big buyer, a big caterer, a big computer organisation, a big forensic science service, a big training facility, a big vehicle fleet operator, and many other things. Each Metropolitan police officer, with the back-up services which the organisation provides, represents some £35,000 of taxpayers' and ratepayers' money each year.

There is no need to apologise for that figure, because a properly paid, adequately equipped police force costs money. Part of the job of the police authority is to make sure that resources are used to the best effect. There is now an understanding throughout the Metropolitan police force, among the officers and the civil staff, that service delivery and the delivery of value for money go hand in hand. We cannot have a good police service in 1989 without good management; nor can we accept large sums of taxpayers' and ratepayers' money without having to show that it is being used properly.

Priority continues to be given to going ahead as fast and as radically as possible with a programme of civilianisation which releases more police officers for operational duties which they alone can perform. Since May 1986 when we announced the civilianisation programme, more than 300 posts have been civilianised, releasing as many officers for operational duties. Provision is being made to civilianise another 200 posts in this financial year.

An annual programme of efficiency scrutinies, first introduced in 1985, has resulted in significant savings and management improvements. For example, the scrutiny on overtime has led to a reduction of 10 per cent. from £6 million a year, in the overtime budget, and £450,000 a year is to be saved as a result of the scrutiny of the Metropolitan police band. A recently completed scrutiny of civil staff recruitment and retention should lead to considerable improvements in the management and use of civil staff. A scrutiny of abstractions from duty, aimed at improving the proportion of time each officer spends on operations, is due to report later in the summer.

Improvements have been made in resource management. Changes were made to the system of estimating, monitoring and controlling expenditure, to enable thorough probing of all bids for expenditure. The Commissioner is committed to the development and wider use of a range of output measurements and performance indicators.

In line with other parts of the public sector, I have asked the Met to consider whether any of its functions of the organisation could be better performed if contracted out. Some 660 cleaning posts have been contracted out. The contracting out of wheelclamping has resulted in a

[*Mr. Hurd*]

fourfold increase in clamping activity. The Metropolitan police will shortly be testing the market for contracting out a part of their catering operations.

Accountancy advice has been brought into the Met finance department, and a new computerised accounting system is being introduced. Devolved budgets have been introduced on divisions in three of the eight areas of the Met, and it is planned to extend this to all areas by next year. In these and other ways, the Met is improving the use of its resources.

I have dwelt on those improvements in practical terms, giving examples, because I am a little worried and irritated when some critics of the police from all parts of society, but particularly in the quality press, write as if nothing is being done and no steps are being taken to provide value for money, and as if we are simply pouring additional money into the police without having any understanding or assurance of how it is spent. That is not so. The changes that I have mentioned are very important and are continuing. There is some way to go, but they are designed to ensure that the unprecedented increases in men and money which we have authorised in the huge organisation which is the Metropolitan police are being used for the better protection of the citizens of London.

**Mr. Simon Hughes:** Will the Home Secretary give way?

**Mr. Hurd:** No. I should like to get on. The hon. Gentleman may intervene just before I sit down.

There is still more to be done. The report by the National Audit Office, to which the hon. Member for Brent, South (Mr. Boateng), referred just now, and which was published earlier this week, drew attention to the poor condition of police stations and to the need for better planning and management of the Metropolitan police estate. My Department and the police will be examined on this by the Public Accounts Committee on Monday next.

The capital programme is now focused on operational buildings and in particular on modernising police stations. The planning and management of the estate is being improved, but a great deal needs to be done to ensure that the resources of the Metropolitan police are used to provide the efficient and effective policing which the people of London expect and which the commissioner wants to provide.

There is a role for external scrutiny—people looking from outside. I was able to report last year that for the first time, at the commissioner's invitation, Her Majesty's inspectors of constabulary had undertaken an independent inspection in the Metropolitan police. A new inspector was appointed on 1 April to help with the increased burden which inspections of the Metropolitan police will place on the inspectorate. Two inspections, one of 8 area—the City of Westminster—and the other of the use of firearms by the police in London are being undertaken during the remainder of this year. Those inspections will continue at about two each year and will augment the existing internal system of inspection in order to measure force efficiency. I can announce today that, in common with inspection reports on provincial forces, Her Majesty's inspectors' reports on the Metropolitan police will be published from next year. Like the prison service, the police service is opening itself up for public discussion and examination to an unprecedented extent. I encourage that trend and I

hope that the House will bear it in mind when it hears the next routine diatribe about the secretiveness of this Government.

The mixture of skills needed by the police makes the job of an officer difficult. The hot-blooded boldness needed to tackle a criminal—possibly armed—in mid flight might produce just the wrong result if an officer is called upon to cool the tempers of angry or frightened members of the community. The more one thinks about that and has experience of it, the less wonder it is that officers and their spokesmen sometimes complain that nowadays the public expect too many difficult things of the police and too wide a range of skills and attitudes. Anyone who is seriously acquainted with the police in London and throughout the country will sympathise with that concern, but policing must deal with a massive range of human problems. That requires a wide range of techniques if they are to be successfully resolved.

Imaginative policing is required and is carried out increasingly in London and elsewhere in the country. It is based on the partnership between the police and the community, without which crime cannot properly be controlled.

The Metropolitan police have to work with other agencies to ensure that the best possible service is provided to those who are vulnerable as victims of crime in our community. Last month my Department published the report of the interdepartmental racial attacks group. The report commended the work of the Metropolitan police in tackling racial incidents, citing in particular the best practice guidelines issued in 1986. The Met is already taking part in a project in east London in which the local agencies are working with each other and with the community to tackle racial harassment.

Women and children are also especially vulnerable as victims of crime. The Metropolitan police now have seven special victims' examination suites where women can be taken for examination, interview and, most important of all, advice and support. The Metropolitan police were also pioneers in the inter-agency investigation of child sexual abuse. Many of the techniques in joint interviewing with the social services which were developed in the special unit at Bexley are now being incorporated as part of good practice throughout England and Wales.

Hon. Members may know from recent television programmes of the initiatives to help women who are victims of domestic violence. Following the introduction of a new force order requiring a more positive response to domestic violence, a specialist unit was set up at Tottenham police station. That has now been followed by 14 other units within the Metropolitan police district. Each of those specialist units collates reports of domestic violence, even where the woman withdraws her original complaint. In every case she is offered practical advice and support. She may be referred to a refuge or given help with finding emergency accommodation for herself and her children. If she wants to pursue her complaint, she will be offered support and advice through the court proceedings and beyond if necessary.

That is all relatively new. It responds to the complaints that the police pass by on the other side and that the less they are involved in domestic violence, the more they are pleased. The traditional attitudes were understandable. It is difficult for a police officer to get involved in domestic brawlings and in accusations of sexual offences within a family. It was understandable that in the past it was thought that a fairly narrow line should be taken. However, that attitude is changing. That may produce an immediate increase in the numbers of recorded crimes, because crimes will get on to the books which previously would never have been recorded. That is a tiny price to pay, if the police are helping, with other agencies, to get people out of some morass of misery and despair in their homes.

All those initiatives show the style of policing that the Metropolitan police are seeking to develop. It must be firm in a city such as London, but it is becoming increasingly compassionate. That is not a word of which they or we should be ashamed to use in those respects. It responds to the needs of the local community, and I have given the example of domestic violence. It goes beyond the bounds of traditional policing to co-operation with other agencies in serving the needs of victims.

The Metropolitan police have joined in our Home Office safer cities initiative. That is a further example of the need and the willingness of the police to work with others. The first two London projects, in Lewisham and Tower Hamlets, are now established. I can announce today that Islington and Wandsworth boroughs have agreed to join the safer cities programme, and I wish them every success.

The press reported—it may be wrong—that the hon. Member for Huddersfield (Mr. Sheerman) was yesterday saying something in deprecation—he was almost sneering —of crime prevention activities and was accusing us of bypassing local authorities. The safer cites initiative is based on co-operation between the Home Office and local authorities. The boroughs that I have named in London, and the boroughs and cities involved in other parts of the country, show that we are not bypassing local authorities, and that local authorities controlled by the hon. Gentleman's party are coming forward and are accepting our invitations to join in.

I hope, therefore, that the Opposition Front Bench and the parliamentary Labour party will bring themselves up to date on those matters. There are things going on that are immensely helpful and useful, although there is a great deal more to be done. However, those developments correspond to the needs of their constituencies as well as to ours. There is no reason for the Opposition to be grudging, sneering or to be taking the lead from, say, the London borough of Lambeth, rather than from the interests of their own constituencies.

**Mr. Barry Sheerman** (Huddersfield): Yesterday, at the conference on crime prevention and the local authority role, I was not sneering. I was saying that the Government, who have taken billions of pounds away from local authorities and then, in the safer cities campaign, given £250,000, are not doing very much for the real demands —for example, for the modification and better lighting of high-rise buildings. We were saying that we wanted a positive partnership between local authorities, the local communities, and the police. We believe that the Government have not given a strong enough lead or the resources needed.

**Mr. Hurd:** The hon. Gentleman will know what he said. I read only a press report, according to which he accused us of indulging in simply public relations activities and bypassing local authorities. The safer cities programme refutes those accusations.

**Mr. Harry Greenway:** When the Labour party says that it wants to promote a partnership between local authorities and the police, why can boroughs such as Lambeth, which has been mentioned, and Ealing, refuse to join the established consultative police groups, which would promote more co-operation between the councils and the police than anything else?

**Mr. Hurd:** The Labour party is still living in that old world where it thinks that there is support and votes to be gained by rubbishing the police. I accept that there have been changes and developments, but that is all the more reason why people who purport to be speaking for the Labour party as a whole should not fall back into that old vocabulary. They should treat those disruptive dinosaurs in the London boroughs with the contempt that they deserve. The Leader of the Opposition lamentably neglected the chance to do that during the Vauxhall by-election.

One element of the police-public partnership that deserves particular mention is the special constabulary. The public want to help to make London's streets and the Underground safer, and that is why so many people greeted the arrival of the Guardian Angels earlier this year. I welcome the willingness to help that that shows, but I do not believe that it is sensible to build up the use of unofficial and unaccountable squads in front-line policing.

I urge all those whose interest and enthusiasm were kindled by the opportunities offered by the Guardian Angels to consider joining the special constabulary. I believe that everyone will accept that sometimes in the past the specials have felt like Cinderella. It is now pretty well acknowledged within the police service that the specials have not always been treated or deployed as well as they might have been. However, that is changing. Following an efficiency scrutiny of the Metropolitan special constabulary last year, a wide range of measures are being brought in to improve the effectiveness and the attractiveness of the Metropolitan specials. A new recruitment campaign will begin this summer, training has been improved, and divisions are being encouraged to use their special constables on a wider range of duties.

An example of what can be done is Tooting division. Between August last year, when there were 20 specials, and today, the division has tripled its number of specials. They are attached to regular police reliefs, and they play an important supporting role in policing the community. Such initiatives are being encouraged throughout London, and I hope that many more active and responsible citizens will take advantage of them.

I am aware, too, of the ideas that the commissioner is considering to harness the enthusiasm of members of the public for a range of community projects not requiring police powers. I have no objection to pilot projects along those lines, under police supervision.

**Mr. Michael Shersby** (Uxbridge): Does my right hon. Friend agree that valuable though specials can be in certain circumstances, they are no substitute for regular, full-time police officers? Does he recognise, too, that some of the proposals that have been floated in recent months by senior officers of the Metropolitan police—for such things as blue angels and similar ideas—are far from being welcomed by the regular police force in London?

**Mr. Hurd:** I know that the Police Federation has to be persuasively urged down the path that I have been

[*Mr. Hurd*]

describing, which is reasonable. My hon. Friend was right to say that the specials are not a substitute, but they can be an important supplement to the work of the regular police. That is a point that came up at the annual conference of the federation, which my hon. Friend and I recently attended. I hope that the federation will give some leadership in that direction and will not allow traditional anxieties, which I believe are now out of place, to dominate their feelings for those initiatives. All those matters need to be tested, but the example I gave of the Tooting division shows that that can be done with the support of the regular police.

**Mr. Hugh Dykes** (Harrow, East): I apologise to my right hon. Friend for missing his earlier remarks, because I was participating in a broadcast. Does my right hon. Friend believe that the specials would have a helpful supplementary role—I agree with his adjective—in dealing with the scourge of racial harassment and attacks?

**Mr. Hurd:** Yes, I think so. I see one of the possible roles of the specials as being a supplementary link between the regular force and the community. If we are increasingly successful—as the Met is—in recruiting people from the ethnic minorities, such a link in dealing with racial attacks could be especially helpful in parts of, say, the east end or the north-east of London or, for all I know, in my hon. Friend's constituency.

Any imaginative organisation committed to public service will always want more resources. There is nothing unusual about that and it is a good sign. Hon. Members, in common with me, will be familiar with the Metropolitan police officer who tells us that if he only had a few more officers, a car or a computer he could provide the community with a better service. I entirely understand that ambition and that is why we have increased the establishment of the Metropolitan police to the record level of 28,415—more than 5,000 higher than it was 10 years ago. During the same period the Met's budget has grown by 60 per cent. in real terms. There are few major public services that can show anything like that increase and it reflects the priority that we give to policing in London and elsewhere. Further increases in the Met's establishment and in the supporting resources are planned.

**Mr. Simon Hughes:** The Home Secretary has referred twice to resources and to personnel. He will be aware that one of the abiding problems faced by the Met is the retention of people in the force. One of the causes of that problem is the difficulty that people face when living in London because of house prices and the like. What does the right hon. Gentleman believe can be done this year to recruit more Londoners into the police force and to hold them, once recruited?

**Mr. Hurd:** The Met has a tradition of recruiting widely, including people from the provinces, who eventually go back to the provinces, and there is nothing wrong in that. When my hon. Friend the Parliamentary Under-Secretary replies I shall ask him to deal especially with retention of staff which, as the hon. Member for Southwark and Bermondsey (Mr. Hughes) has shown, is extremely important.

Quality of service and professionalism are the key standards by which the police are judged. It is fundamental to the professionalism of the force that the service they provide is that required by the public in all its diversity. In turn, the support of the public helps the police to provide a better service to them. But it is a process to which all of us can contribute.

Recently the Commissioner has published his "Statement of Common Purpose and Values" for the 1990s. In that statement Sir Peter tried to set out in simple and direct terms the underlying and enduring principles to which all employees of the Met should be committed. That is a difficult exercise, particularly perhaps for the commissioner of the Met. It is easy to laugh at it as an endeavour at window dressing or preaching against sin, but I believe that that statement fits. It is a brave enterprise to acknowledge and rectify the shortcomings in the service provided by the Met.

We all hear deserved compliments about the Met, but there is a steady trickle of complaints about the behaviour of Met officers. Those complaints are usually not about gross misconduct, but about discourtesy, off-handedness, a touch of arrogance or lack of interest. That kind of complaint, often trivial, can cause disillusionment among the public and it eclipses the first-class service provided by the majority of officers and makes those officers feel defensive and, at times, isolated. All Members, particularly those representing London, can do something about that.

The commissioner has established a team dedicated to converting that "Statement of Common Purpose and Values" into action. He, in common with everyone else, realises that it is by action that the programme will be judged. The staff associations of the Met, the Police Federation and the Police Superintendents Association are to be congratulated on backing up the programme. The House should do the same. It is not every organisation that, in the middle of doing a difficult and dangerous job, acknowledges its occasional faults and publicly commits itself to doing better.

The commissioner has the support of the great majority of Londoners in building on the traditions of the police to provide a service of which we can all be proud. Many problems remain, but the courage and the skill of the Met are qualities of which Londoners and the country can be proud.

10.14 am

**Mr. Barry Sheerman** (Huddersfield): The Opposition approach this important debate in a constructive and positive manner. I was slightly concerned that the Home Secretary, in an otherwise positive and thoughtful speech, saw fit once again to try to stereotype the attitude of the Labour party and Labour local authorities as being negative towards the police. It is a cheap shot to mark off one particular local authority, which represents a tiny minority, when the majority of Labour local authorities and other local authorities display a positive attitude to the police. We want to promote that constructive partnership and not to dwell on the tiny minority who choose a different path.

The citizens of London desire a police force that is efficient, corruption-free and treats the public with sensitivity and respect. They want a police force that actively promotes crime prevention and community safety, and which successfully pursues the perpetrators of crime. We believe that we have an extremely good police force in

London, but, like Sir Peter Imbert, we believe that it could be markedly improved by better management, better training and by a clear, democratic link with Londoners. The desire for such a Metropolitan police force is held by most people in the country and by the House.

We know that the Met is good, but we also know that to rest on our laurels and not to push for change means that problems will arise. It is a year since our last debate on this matter and it has been a highly significant year for the Met. We have had a swathe of reports and investigations, and 1988-89 must represent the most active period of investigation of the Met, by others and by itself. It is all good stuff and most interesting.

The Wolff Olins report, "A Force for Change" was published last autumn. It was commissioned by the Met, and, in part, it was highly critical of the force. The report referred to the Met's uncertainty about its role, to a lack of common purpose, internal division and a lack of support for those who are in contact with the public. It also referred to the need for improvement in training and management. It described the Met's wary attitude towards the world and referred to a minority of police officers

"who are too free with their language, and who adopt an aggressive attitude in their relationship with people in the street. This minority, who are rude or insensitive, create an atmosphere for the whole of the Met which deeply embarrasses the majority."

The report stated that the force's communications with the outside world were poor and, as has been mentioned already today, it said that the physical state of many police stations was run down. The report stated:

"All this contributes to an atmosphere of shabby confusion."

The report concluded that for the Met to be more effective it should first feel more united, secondly improve leadership, thirdly adopt a positive attitude towards the concept of service to the public, fourthly become less defensive and isolated, fifthly improve its communications and, lastly, improve its appearance. It emphasised the need for all in the Met to feel that they are part of a public service.

We must congratulate Sir Peter Imbert on publishing such a report. To his credit, he has worked speedily to respond to the criticisms and to bring about the change of direction proposed by it. He has introduced the Plus programme accompanied by the internal document, "Making it Happen". The commissioner has emphasised the importance of service to the public time and again on radio, television and in other media. The Plus programme is designed to produce a united force providing a quality service to the public. It recognises the importance of those who work in direct contact with the pulic and talks of introducing an effective rewards and sanctions system. It will further improve communications, buildings and equipment.

The Plus programme is designed not as a policy statement but as a mechanism to introduce and sustain change. It is a major attempt to alter the culture of the Metropolitan police. We must debate the Plus programme in depth because the crucial question is whether the changes that it proposes will take place on the ground. The criticisms made in "A Force for Change" and the attempts to change how the Metropolitan police work are not new, but will Sir Peter Imbert's determined efforts work in practice? Are local chief superintendents taking notice of them? It has been suggested that the responses from some areas have been rather bland. Does the Home Secretary

intend vigorously to ensure that the programme succeeds? Some of the remarks that he made towards the end of his speech encourage us to believe that he does. Hon. Members and the public will need to see a vigorous Home Secretary giving Sir Peter Imbert the support that he deserves in making the fundamental changes that are necessary.

The chances of the programme succeeding depend on the Metropolitan police's previous decentralisation work, much of which started under Sir Kenneth Newman. Has there been devolution of power from the centre? Has the programme been effective not only in moving bodies out of New Scotland Yard but in devolving power? The management of many commercial organisations has improved as a result of decentralisation, and if the Metropolitan police are to experience the same success the power to take decisions must be decentralised.

It is refreshing to see change and a positive commitment to change, but change should not be made for its own sake and it must be evaluated. It is no good introducing programmes for change unless they are closely evaluated. Evaluation must be part of the programmes for change so that in a year or two we can ask how effective the changes have been, but alter course or tack if they have not been so effective as we thought that they would be.

The Commissioner is to be commended on opening up the Metropolitan police to other forms of scrutiny. More information is now flowing to consultative groups and the lay visiting programme, which I believe is the most robust in the country. However, 1989 has seen the production of a highly significant document on the CID. I had hoped that the Home Secretary would make more mention of it. The document, which is known as the Crime Investigation Priority Project document, has been made available to me. It reflects uneasiness about the behaviour and attitudes of the CID, and is critical of part of it. It refers to a lack of clear purpose, inappropriate organisational structures, confusion over supervision and a lack of accountability among senior management for their juniors. If something goes wrong, the junior always seems to carry the can. The report says that more concern should be expressed for victims, and states:

"A substantial proportion of uniform officers attending as the First Officer at the scene of a routine crime are unclear as to what to do to answer either the needs of the victim or the requirement of the Force for information."

The report also states that training is inadequate and that it

"cannot be considered sufficient when only two hours were given to Constables to teach them how to investigate rather than report crimes and CID officers can receive no training for the last 20 years of their service."

The report makes 143 recommendations for change, which hardly inspires confidence in some CID activities. I hope that the Home Secretary will ensure that the proposals for change are implemented and monitored.

I ask the Home Secretary to give a little more detail about the crime reporting and information system, which he dealt with briefly. It is an important advance in technology for the police. When will the system be operated force-wide, and is he satisfied with the way in which it is currently developing? There have been reports of problems and teething troubles with it, so will he make some further comments on that?

I want to make my speech in a positive spirit, but we believe that there are problems with crime screening. It is all very well for the Home Secretary to comment on the

[*Mr. Barry Sheerman*]

slight but welcome reduction in some crimes in the Metropolitan police area, but violent crime is still increasing. According to polls, violent crime causes most concern to London residents. We understand the Home Secretary saying that the reduction in crime is welcome. However, he mentioned domestic and sexual violence— violence directed against women—and said that the number of cases being reported may have increased but suggested that it might not be the crime itself that has increased but rather the reporting of it. We understand that some of the new techniques of crime screening being used may lead to crime not being reported. The decline in burglary and some other offences may reflect the fact that crime screening is having an impact on the public. The Home Secretary looks unclear about this, so I shall be more specific. Clearly, the police must prioritise their work. No doubt screening has been going on unofficially for many years, but there is a worry that it may lead to loss of confidence in the police. The Metropolitan police estimate that only 15 per cent. of allegations will be screened. Clearly, public awareness of screening policy may lead to cynicism and could dry up the flow of information that is so vital to police work.

It appears that screening has had an effect on the number of cases reported to the police. If the public believe that nothing will be done, they will not report an incident. It will be fascinating to know how much of the drop in burglary rates in London can be attributed to the effects of screening. I therefore point out, again in a positive spirit, that screening could lead to under-reporting. It is important that individuals are handled sensitively by the police, and screening could be a problem in that regard. If an offence is screened out, the victim may be upset that positive action is not to be taken. That brings me back to the theme of behaviour of individual officers and the need to ensure that they are all sensitive to the needs of victims and the public.

From talking to senior officers, I understand that the police are unhappy about screening. The CIPP report says that screening, as currently operated, is

"discouraging first officers from investigating crimes fully; failing to provide sufficient information for a proper screening decision to be made: involving experienced detectives in the investigation of mundane crimes."

We need to take a fresh look at crime screening. Does the Home Secretary intend—or has he done so already—to ask the Home Office research unit to study screening and its effects? The results of such a study would benefit hon. Members.

The Home Secretary mentioned crime prevention and seemed to object to the positive conference that Labour Members held on crime prevention and the role of local authorities yesterday at Church house. Increasingly, crime prevention is being recognised as being of central importance to the police and the community. The Government have spoken about crime prevention at length, but we believe that their approach is deeply flawed. First, the Government's economic and social policies have had a devastating effect on inner-city areas such as those in London. Unemployment, particularly among young people, and deteriorating conditions and services have had a direct impact on offenders. Secondly, the resources put into crime prevention are woefully inadequate. We have said that to the Home Secretary many times, but he has never answered our questions.

Of course, we want safer cities campaigns, but they must be properly resourced. We estimate that the £250,000 for each campaign is the cost of modifying the front entrance doors of five high-rise blocks of flats. That is not enough in an evironment in which crime has escalated in the past 10 years. Those sums pale into insignificance when contrasted with the massive loss of resources that local authorities have experienced.

The Home Secretary should consider the French experience of the été jeunes programme in which the French authorities have recognised the growing rates of burglary and petty crime by people as young as 15. The French have recognised that resources must be invested in employment, training and creative leisure initiatives. We cannot have safer cities without greater resources flowing into the key element—the democratically elected local authorities.

**Mr. Tony Banks** (Newham, North-West): My hon. Friend is making a very apposite point about safer cities. My borough of Newham, which is the second most deprived local authority area in England and Wales and desperately needs resources, applied under the safer cities campaign and was rejected by the Government. My borough has one of the highest crime rates in London and the highest incidence of racial harassment, yet we were refused. How do the Government work that out?

**Mr. Sheerman:** It is rather mysterious. The Secretary of State chose to mention the matter two or three times. Only after some pushing from us and our discussions about why Islington had a committee promoting a safer city but no local authority representative were two people appointed to the committee.

**Mr. Jeremy Corbyn** (Islington, North): I thank my hon. Friend for referring to Islington. Islington borough council has done much to make housing estates safer and has participated closely with tenants associations and the local police in making the borough safer. The council undertook a thorough crime survey, which it published and which was used extensively by many people considering the problems caused by the misery of living in areas of great danger.

**Mr. Sheerman:** My hon. Friend is right. Islington's leadership is impressive. One of the main speakers at yesterday's conference on crime prevention was from that borough.

We do not want to have a row every time we debate this matter, but a partnership which excludes the local democratically elected element will not work. The stimulus for a positive crime prevention initiative should come from the police, local councils, the private sector and local communities working in harmony. Without the local democratically elected element, there will be problems with non-accountability, vigilantes and direct citizen action, and all the other aspects that none of us wants.

I beg the Home Secretary to consider that positive partnership, to stop slagging off the odd local authority that he does not like and to start working positively with the majority of local authorities. If he will give them a leadership role and the necessary resources, they will be able to deliver.

**Mr. Corbyn:** Before leaving this important general point, would my hon. Friend care to reflect that one problem in debates about London police and crime is that the Metropolitan police are fundamentally undemocratic? It is not satisfactory that the only public accountability of the Metropolitan police is through this debate, which happens just once a year. No vote is taken, there is no perusal of the Estimates and there is no serious discussion about force orders. All that we have is the good will, or otherwise, of the Home Secretary.

**Mr. Sheerman:** I agree with my hon. Friend. I mentioned that matter in my introduction. Labour party policy is to have a democratic link with the police.

**Mr. Shersby:** The hon. Gentleman will know from his experience as a member of the Public Accounts Committee —albeit for a short time before his elevation to the Labour Front Bench—that the Metropolitan police undergo considerable scrutiny of their expenditure and operational policing by that Committee. Scrutiny by the Public Accounts Committee, on which both sides of the House are represented, is very effective. The hon. Gentleman will know that all London Members are invited by the commissioner several times a year to discuss with him operational policing in London. That does not happen in the other police forces, so London Members of Parliament are in a uniquely privileged position.

**Mr. Sheerman:** The hon. Gentleman knows that there is no substitute for a positive link between the local community and its police force. The citizens of London should enjoy what the rest of the country enjoys.

**Mr. Hurd:** The hon. Gentleman's plea is for greater co-operation between local government and the police in preventing crime. He has glossed over the story in London. Until recently, a considerable number of boroughs have been obstructing the police and trying to make relationships between the police and the community difficult. I readily acknowledge that, under pressure, that is changing—but the change is far from complete. The efforts of the Metropolitan police, and my own efforts since I have been Home Secretary, have been directed towards taking the political poison out of the situation and creating co-operation in London and elsewhere.

Obviously, the local housing or education authorities in most parts of the country have a crucial role to play in crime prevention. That is what the safer cities campaign is about. Crime prevention requires of local London politicians a much greater sense of responsibility than some of them have hitherto shown.

**Mr. Sheerman:** The Home Secretary should stop living in the past. First, his allegations about London authorities are inaccurate. Secondly, only a tiny minority have shown a lack of co-operation. The Opposition expect the Home Secretary to look positively towards a good relationship on which to build a better future, not to keep dragging in any little item from the past that he thinks will reinforce a political stance which will impress the blue-rinse spasm at Conservative party conferences.

**Mr. Simon Hughes:** On this issue I side with the Home Secretary. I have a salient example. I spent the Vauxhall by-election in Lambeth. As of today, Labour in Lambeth does not have a representative on the police consultative committee. The former Labour Member, Stuart Holland, was not allowed to do so because he was mandated not to. I do not know whether the new Labour Member will be allowed to do so. There are authorities in London which do not allow their members to sit on the police consultative committee. Until they do, people will not be represented by the Labour party in dialogues with the police.

**Mr. Sheerman:** The local authority to which the hon. Gentleman referred has a democratic right to co-operate or not. My honest view would be to recommend any local authority to sit on police committees and have a positive partnership with the police and the other authority.

**Mr. Simon Hughes:** Does the hon. Gentleman use his influence?

**Mr. Sheerman:** Of course we use our influence, but we must recognise people's democratic rights. That is what democracy is about. Some Opposition Members, including some on the Liberal Benches or whatever they are called now, sometimes want democracy only when it produces the answers that they like. I am a realist and I know that some Labour-controlled local authorities sometimes make decisions that I do not like. That is the nature of democracy.

**Mr. Tony Banks:** The comments made by the hon. Member for Southwark and Bermondsey, (Mr. Hughes) about my good friend Stuart Holland are untrue.

**Mr. Simon Hughes:** They are not untrue.

**Mr. Banks:** I am telling the hon. Member for Southwark and Bermondsey, through my hon. Friend the Member for Huddersfield (Mr. Sheerman), that what he has just said is untrue. Stuart Holland did not sit on that committee not because he was instructed not to do so but because he thought that it was not performing its functions in the way that it should. That was his democratic right.

**Mr. Sheerman:** My hon. Friend the Member for Newham, North-West (Mr. Banks) knows more about what goes on in London than I do and I am glad that he has been able to correct a false allegation. I have given way several times, in keeping with the nature of this debate, but I hope that we can return to the main thrust of my points about crime prevention.

The involvement of local authorities in crime prevention is crucial because so much crime prevention work lies within their remit. The hostility that the Home Secretary has shown is clearly shown in the Islington experience. Initially the Home Office did not want any local councillors on the steering committee, despite Islington council's proven record in that area. It has now agreed to two local councillors on a steering committee consisting of between 12 and 15 people.

I do not want to bore the House by pursuing the theme of the need for positive partnership, but it is astounding to find when I speak to senior policemen at the level of chief constable, that they are far in advance of the Home Secretary in terms of seeking the right relationship and positive partnership with local authorities. Their best practice and the kinds of relationships that they enjoy around the country are far better and are leading the Home Secretary by example. The Home Secretary is coming around lamentably slowly to understanding the need for that partnership which the police and local authorities already recognise.

[*Mr. Sheerman*]

With regard to finance, the Comptroller and Auditor General's report on the Met's estate was published this week. That report shows an incredibly low level of financial accountability and the House must have some cause for concern about the report. The Met does not have a capital account and it does not account for the capital values of its land. Nor does it have an inventory of its properties. What do the Home Secretary and the receiver intend to do about that report?

The CPAG's report also highlights the appalling conditions of many police stations. One in five police stations is said to be so substandard and cramped as to represent a severe handicap to effective policing. Similar points were made in the Wolff Olins report and they come as no surprise to anyone who has visited Met police stations. However, the capital programme operated through the Home Office appears to be excessively bureaucratic and slow. Will the Home Secretary comment on the resources that he intends to allocate to rectify those appalling conditions, which are unacceptable for the staff and for the public? How does he intend to speed up the bureaucratic process which is becoming so notorious in his Department? Will he consider ending Crown immunity for police stations? Lay visitors say that that is a major factor behind the squalid conditions in many police stations.

The physical state of police stations is linked with an inhospitable attitude to the public in many stations. Reading between the lines in many of the reports to which I have referred this morning, it is clear that we should make police stations user and consumer friendly. The vast bulk of people do not enter police stations in handcuffs to be charged with offences. They visit as members of the public in a positive spirit wishing to help. They should be treated in a civilised fashion in a pleasant environment. They should not be intimidated by some aspects of police stations.

The Home Secretary believes strongly in civilianising certain aspects of the police. However, many of us believe that it would be a wholly retrograde step if a member of the public met a civilian instead of a uniformed police officer when he visited a police station. Many of us believe that the relationship with the police is most important and people in police stations who deal with the public should be police officers and not secretaries or clerks. The Home Secretary may disagree with that, but that is not a political view. We believe that this point should be considered thoroughly before a decision is taken. Many people in the police force would agree with that view.

The physical state of police stations could be rectified relatively quickly if the Home Secretary would put his shoulder to the wheel and support the desire for change at the head of the Met. It is also interesting to note that researchers who visited police stations recently in London and New York—we should remember that New York has a vastly different crime problem from that in London—reported that the atmosphere in New York police stations was far more relaxed and friendly with less emphasis on security than stations in the Met—[*Interruption.*] The junior Minister, the Parliamentary Under-Secretary of State for the Home Department, is doing his old Etonian act. I remind him that this is the House of Commons, not the Eton debating house. We can learn something from the United States in these matters and the Minister's snorting and carrying on at schoolboy level is quite wrong.

**Mr. Corbyn:** Public schoolboy level.

**Mr. Sheerman:** Yes, public schoolboy level.

The financing of the Met reveals Government hypocrisy about policing. We should consider the financing squarely and honestly. We hear continuously that the Government back the police and about the extra police that are provided. However, in London the slippage of expenditure away from central Government and on to local authorities has been extensive. Last year, the precept increased by 14·4 per cent. and that increase was due almost entirely to the reduction in block grant from the Government. In other words, local authorities are footing more and more of the bill for the Met and are being forced to raise their rates to compensate for that outlay. London local authorities perceive the Home Secretary to be either weak in Cabinet or the tool of the Treasury if he cannot support Met expenditure coming from central Government. He can hardly be said to be standing up for the Met now. Does he intend to continue to shift expenditure on to local authorities or will he this year match his public pronouncements on policy with the cash that is urgently needed? That reinforces our desire that the local authorities, which pay so much towards their police forces, should have a democratic voice in connection with the running of their police forces.

There are other reforms about which I want to ask the Home Secretary's views. The first reform concerns the Police Complaints Authority. The Wolff Olins report causes concern among hon. Members on both sides of the House and among the public. It refers to the complaints system as

"a major focus of dissatisfaction."

That dissatisfaction affects confidence in the police. What action does the Home Secretary intend to take about that? A close examination of how effectively the Police Complaints Authority is working is necessary. We must also consider whether it should be far more independent and powerful.

**Mr. John Wheeler** (Westminster, North): As the hon. Gentleman has referred to the independent Police Complaints Authority, I am sure that he is aware that some of his colleagues and Conservative Members in the Select Committee on Home Affairs are examining the work of that authority and will report to the House and to the Home Secretary in some detail on how we see its work progressing and how it may be further sustained.

**Mr. Sheerman:** I thank the hon. Member for Westminster, North (Mr. Wheeler) for his intervention. We hope that the Home Secretary will carefully examine the evidence submitted and the Select Committee's conclusions.

What action will the Home Secretary take to end the scandal—it is a scandal and we cannot sweep it under the carpet—of officers taking early retirement on health grounds to avoid disciplinary hearings? It is a matter of great concern. The Home Secretary should react positively to the concern being expressed by the public. It is not amusing to see on television a police officer running the London marathon or another marathon the day after taking early retirement on medical grounds. There is something wrong when many officers evade the disciplinary system by taking early retirement. The Home Secretary should concentrate his attention on that.

There is growing concern about the expansion of the private security industry, which is encroaching on areas previously the domain of the Metropolitan police. It is clear that that industry needs to be regulated, but the Government pervesely fail to take account of the views of the public and of the police. When will the Home Secretary decide that that industry will never satisfactorily regulate itself and that there should be an independent regulatory body?

What action does the Home Secretary intend to take about the growing number of immigration prisoners held on remand in police cells? Lay visitors have expressed grave concern about the matter. I do not believe that the Home Secretary has reacted positively to complaints.

Will the Home Secretary enlighten the House about where responsibility lies in the racial harassment guide distribution fiasco? We have not had a satisfactory reply. About £300,000 of public money seems to have been wasted in the non-distribution of an important booklet on racial harassment. Saatchi and Saatchi were given the contract for distribution, but many citizens have not received the booklet. When will the Home Secretary demand repayment from Saatchi and Saatchi for non-distribution of the booklet?

Traffic regulation enforcement is another matter of great public concern. Over the past few years, traffic regulation enforcement for important offences such as drink driving and speeding has decreased as a result of the rationalisation of police efforts, yet the North report showed that the public regard some of those traffic offences very seriously indeed. They are clearly related to many deaths and injuries. Opposition Members regard such matters seriously and believe that the priorities should be reversed.

There has been a lot of soul-searching by the police. The openness and honesty about the need for change have been refreshing, but will they be reflected on the ground? Will there be greater emphasis on public service? Can the Met restrain the minority of officers who can undo months of good work by one ugly incident? Will the Home Secretary end the absurdity of the capital's police force being accountable to him alone and establish a police authority for London? The open analysis and assessment of the Metropolitan police that have taken place over recent months are refreshing, but we must now press for the rigorous implementation of Sir Peter Imbert's reform throughout the force.

An answer given to my hon. Friend the Member for Islington, North (Mr. Corbyn) causes me a little concern. The danger is that if reform is too difficult or even too uncomfortable, the Government will not implement it. There would then be a temptation to resort to an even larger slice of the public relations pie, in the hope that people will be placated by the image rather than by the reality of a better service to the public. From 1979 to 1980 the Met public relations budget went from £759,000 to £3,397,000. I understand that police must have good public relations, but we want to see the very refreshing initiatives under Sir Peter Imbert resulting in a fundamental shake-up in the Met rather than greater spending on public relations.

Opposition Members agree with Sir Peter Imbert's recent comments in the *Sunday Times* that the Met must be accountable to the public, but that accountability must be based on a democratic foundation.

10.55 am

**Mr. John Wheeler** (Westminster, North): I am grateful for the opportunity to speak about the policing of London. It is a matter of concern to hon. Members who represent London constituencies, and it is also a matter of national importance.

The hon. Member for Huddersfield (Mr. Sheerman) raised several points, one of which was the accountability of the Metropolitan police. The hon. Gentleman is fundamentally wrong. He does not know the history of the police and he does not understand the character and nature of liberty and how it is preserved in this country. The Metropolitan police were established under the control of Her Majesty's principal Secretary of State, the Home Secretary, in 1829 because Parliament took the view, which it substantially still holds, that the purpose of the force is so important that it should ultimately be accountable to the House. That means that the force is accountable not only to the Home Secretary but to Committees of the House, including the Public Accounts Committee and the Home Affairs Select Committee. It is accountable also through its relationship with the 32 London boroughs, the eight outer districts that make up the Metropolitan police area, and even Her Majesty the Queen, as it is responsible for policing the royal castle at Windsor. It is responsible for policing activities outside London which are national if not international in character. For those reasons, the force has always been deemed to be a responsibility of the House and of the Home Secretary.

**Mr. Corbyn:** The hon. Gentleman is claiming that this discussion is a form of accountability of the Metropolitan police. He might have missed it on the Order Paper, but the motion is

"That this House do now adjourn."

We are debating the policing of London. There will not be a vote at the end of the debate because there cannot be. We are discussing not accountability, but consultation with the police authority in London, who happens to be the Home Secretary, who happens to be here. We want people elected by the people of London to be able to scrutinise everything that the police do and to have some power over them.

**Mr. Wheeler:** I am not sure whether the hon. Gentleman's intervention greatly adds to what I have said.

**Mr. Shersby:** Does my hon. Friend agree that the people of London elect hon. Members who are able to play their part in scrutinising the work of the Metropolitan police, through their membership of parliamentary committees such as the Public Accounts Committee, the Home Affairs Select Committee and so on? Hon. Members have every opportunity of scrutinising in minute detail the expenditure of the Metropolitan police and all their activities. They also have the opportunity to debate such matters in the House and refer them to the police authority who is here today. The hon. Member for Islington, North (Mr. Corbyn) knows that, if he wishes to vote on these matters he can participate in Committees or in debates in the House.

**Mr. Wheeler:** My hon. Friend the Member for Uxbridge (Mr. Shersby) is absolutely right. There are 84 Members of Parliament who represent London. I wonder whether the public would be greatly comforted by knowing how few of them, particularly Opposition Members, are present. Nine Members of Parliament represent the outer districts. The nature of the Metropolitan police is the concern of the whole nation. That is the principle to which I have been referring. Policing London represents a far bigger task than the size of its population would indicate. As the commissioner of Police of the Metropolis observed in his 1988 annual report, London attracts 75 per cent. of the illicit drugs market in the United Kingdom, 75 per cent. of major frauds, more than 50 per cent. of armed robberies and one third of all murders and rapes. Policing London is a matter principally, but not exclusively, for the Metropolitan police, and this debate is about policing in London. While I shall concentrate my remarks on the work of that force, we should not neglect the valuable role of those other forces that police London, including the corporation of the City of London police force, ably directed by its own commissioner—

**Mr. Alan Williams** (Swansea, West): On a point of order, Mr. Deputy Speaker. At 9.30 am I said that the Opposition expected a statement at 11 o'clock about the Government's failure to give early warning to pregnant women about the 30 per cent. fatality risk from listeriosis. No such statement seems to be forthcoming and neither of the Ministers responsible is here—I assume that they have gone into hiding for the weekend. As two Cabinet Ministers have bungled and 26 babies have died unnecessarily, the Opposition have no intention of allowing the scandal to die and will return to it on Monday.

**Mr. Wheeler:** As I was saying, the policing of London is not entirely a matter for the Metropolitan police. This House recognises the valuable work done by the other forces. I was referring to the City of London police force, under the able direction of its own commissioner, Mr. Owen Kelly. We also have the British Transport Police and the Royal Parks constabulary, which renders such valuable service in my own constituency and elsewhere in the City of Westminster.

Any view of policing in London must inevitably focus on the Metropolitan police, which is by far the largest of the United Kingdom's 52 police forces. It will cost more than £1·1 billion in national Government grants and local authority precepts in 1989-90. It controls and manages an estate valued at about £1 billion, employs more than 28,000 police officers and more than 13,000 civilians. Above all, it serves and protects a large and heterogeneous community which has the right to expect both value for money and effective policing. That provides a great challenge to the Metropolitan police and, above all others, to the commissioner, Sir Peter Imbert. I have every confidence in his ability to meet that challenge.

Today, I wish to draw attention to some matters of particular concern: the financial management of the force, the doubts expressed about the probity of some police officers, to which the hon. Member for Huddersfield (Mr. Sheerman) referred, changing levels of recorded crime, police public relations and the serious problem of drugs.

In recent years, much attention has been paid to improving the professional standing of police officers by substantial salary increases and enhanced opportunities for career development. Sadly, in the Metropolitan police district there has not been a matching allocation of resources for the police stations within which their better rewarded officers work. Moreover, the condition of many stations must have a negative impact on members of the public who may wish to seek assistance at one of the 188 police stations in the Metropolitan district.

In its recent report, the National Audit Office noted that 102 of the stations were graded in the two lowest "C" and "D" categories—either as substandard or at the end of their working life. Only 20 stations are ranked as grade "A", with first-class, long-life expectancy, modern buildings. Including the 188 police stations and other sites, the Metropolitan police force is a large London property owner. The National Audit Office found that the Metropolitan police estate occupied 1·14 million sq m of floor area and required an annual revenue and capital expenditure of nearly £100 million. As the National Audit Office correctly notes, the Metropolitan police must develop a more efficient and effective strategy for managing this estate.

Given the enormous value of property in London, there must be some scope to exploit the potential that the Metropolitan police property offers. In this context, I particularly welcome and commend to the Home Office, as the police authority for the Metropolitan police, the National Audit Office suggestion that the Metropolitan police could adopt.

"a more commercial approach to resolving their funding difficulties (which) could include joint ventures with the private sector on the development of valuable vacant sites and the construction of premises incorporating police stations as part of a wider development."

Now that these issues have been crystalised in the NAO report, I expect the report to be followed up energetically by both the Metropolitan police and the Home Office.

Steps to improve the management of the police estate in London will fit in with the trend of Metropolitan police policy. The force is endeavouring to instil a greater sense of financial accountability. Civilianisation continues to contribute to improved value for money. As my right hon. Friend the Home Secretary said, in 1988 a total of 134 posts were filled by civilian staff, releasing a similar number of police officers for operational duty. A pilot study of divisional budgeting was introduced in number 5 area in April 1988. Evaluation of the scheme indicated that it had enabled officers to exercise more effective control over the use of resources at local level, which is so important. I look forward to the introduction of divisional budgets in all eight areas in 1990 to enable financial accountability to be brought down to the lower level.

If financial affairs represent a challenge to the leadership of the Metropolitan police, fears of police partiality and incompetence provide a different, but equally important challenge. Sir Peter Imbert has provided sound leadership in this matter. Unease has been expressed, both in the House this morning and through an early-day motion, about corruption in the Metropolitan police, and one case in particular.

The Select Committee on Home Affairs, which I have the honour to chair, is conducting an inquiry into the annual report of the independent Police Complaints Authority and has examined some aspects of the problem.

There has been understandable disquiet about the premature retirement on medical grounds of an officer facing serious disciplinary charges. From the evidence that we have received from the commissioner and others, I am confident that the incident arose from the operation of the regulations and procedures relating to such cases, rather than any desire for a cover up on the part of the Metropolitan police. I am glad to be able to say that today.

I welcome the willingness of the Home Office, the Association of Chief Police Officers and the commissioner to look carefully at the relationship between the medical retirement and pending disciplinary hearings. My Committee will make representations on this point before the summer recess.

**Mr. Simon Hughes:** I have read the minutes of the Select Committee's relevant debate and the hon. Gentleman will be aware that there is more than one such case causing concern. If called to speak later, I shall allude to that. In the deliberations before his Committee completes its report, will the hon. Gentleman ensure that all the current cases of concern are thoroughly addressed so that the matter can be passed to the relevant authorities for proper investigation and, if necessary, further criminal investigation?

**Mr. Wheeler:** I am grateful to the hon. Gentleman. The Select Committee's function is not to investigate individual cases, which would be wholly wrong. We are not a final court of appeal for either side. Our function is too look at the important matter of policy and principle and seek to advise not only the House but my right hon. Friend the Home Secretary on the best way to ensure that these complicated and difficult problems are satisfactorily resolved in a way that commands the support of the general public, whose interest we serve, as well as those of the House. I beg to suggest that my Committee will seek to do that.

On an operational level the Metropolitan police have had some measure of success, as shown by the latest crime statistics for the first quarter of 1989. They show a welcome fall of 28,000 notifiable offences, or 4 per cent., over the 12 months to March 1989. This fall can be partly attributed to the work of the police and to the crime prevention initiatives which they have supported and which so many Government Departments have encouraged.

An undeniable concern to emerge from these figures is the continuing rise in the level of recorded violent crime. Even this increase, however, may reflect the success of the Metropolitan police, who have consciously set out to encourage victims—particularly female victims—to report sexual offences and domestic violence that might hitherto have gone unreported. It is encouraging to note that the clear-up rate for sexual offences against women rose by 8 per cent. and that the number of cleared-up cases of domestic violence rose by 83 per cent. in 1988.

As to the vexed question of opportunist and random violence in the street, often called mugging, it seems to me that when the police carefully target likely offenders and concentrate their forces deliberately rather than randomly they can have a remarkable impact on the extent of these crimes, which cause so much public disquiet in some parts of London. I refer especially to the welcome work done by Inspector Barry Webb in Battersea, where at one time he

achieved a 60 per cent. reduction in this sort of street crime. That is what the public want, and the police can do it when they think through the issues and plan accordingly.

Success in the fight against crime will always be the best way to improve police-public relations, but other aspects are also relevant, including police accountability, which can take many forms. In part, it can derive from debates such as this and from the work of the Committees of the House to which we have referred. It can also come from the local level. There are consultative committees in each of the 32 London boroughs, although the commissioner notes in his annual report that the majority political parties in Brent, Ealing, Hackney, Haringey and Lambeth still do not participate in those committees. This is not a political point; it is a matter of fact taken from the Commissioner's report. It is a matter of great regret that the people in these London boroughs are ill served by the Left-wing Labour councillors who persist in this old war against the police.

Community or neighbourhood policing has often been advocated as providing an important form of local police accountability. However, as is shown by the excellent report by the Police Foundation on the neighbourhood policing experiment in Notting Hill between 1981 and 1986, the Metropolitan police and the cosmopolitan populace of the capital face deep-rooted problems when forming partnerships in pro-active policing schemes. Neighbourhood policing can be effective only if the objectives to be achieved are properly and clearly defined.

The Police Foundation report raises important general questions about the management of change in this extremely large police force. Police canteen talk already refers to the eight area deputy assistant commissioners as the eight ayatollahs. The Metropolitan police need to consider carefully how the management of change can best be achieved. To serve the citizens of London well in the 1990s, some radical organisational changes may be needed.

The Police Foundation report shows how vital it is to involve all ranks in this process, from the commissioner to the newest police constable, so that the senior management in Scotland Yard is not allowed to be insulated from the realities of policing at the operational level.

A continuing menace facing the Metropolitan police is that of illicit drugs. I said earlier that 75 per cent. of the illicit drugs market in the United Kingdom is to be found in London. If that continues to be so and if the drugs market increases in line with the worst expectations, London faces a terrifying prospect in the next few years.

Last week, the Home Affairs Select Committee visited the United States, where we saw the devastating social impact of drug misuse and of the purified form of cocaine known as crack. If crack addiction develops in London the cost to the National Health Service and to local social services and the human suffering and deprivation will be enormous. In these circumstances it is better to be willing to invest now in programmes designed to limit the spread of crack in London and elsewhere in the United Kingdom. The work of the central drug squad of the Metropolitan police, of the regional crime squads and of the Customs and Excise may reduce the speed with which crack penetrates the British drug market, but the central lesson of the United States experience is that the most effective way to prevent drug trafficking is to reduce the demand for

[*Mr. Wheeler*]

drugs by education. Law enforcement may slow their spread, but it is only one part of the strategy needed to prevent crack from spreading in London.

It has been suggested that organisational change in the police is required to meet these challenges. Ideas of a British FBI have been mooted. The abiding lesson of my visit to the United States was that the multiplication of enforcement agencies does not work. I am surprised that the central drug squad is not part of the organisation of the regional crime squads, co-ordination of which is essential to law enforcement among drug dealers and importers.

The Metropolitan police continue to perform their demanding task with professionalism and commitment. They are well led and they continually strive to improve. If, for the reasons that I shall develop when my Committee has an Estimates day debate next week, there are to be organisational changes in British policing, the Metropolitan police may well offer a model for regional police forces throughout Great Britain in terms of what can be achieved by the concentration of resources and of what administrative difficulties arise in a large and complex organisation.

Those of us who serve London constituencies are rightly proud of the work of the Metropolitan police and of the other police forces that serve the people of London. They are well on course to achieve what people want—the reduction of crime—and they grow ever more confident and effective in the use of their resources, manpower and money. I am glad to say that in the House today.

11.18 am

Mr. Simon Hughes (Southwark and Bermondsey): I shall start in the vein in which the hon. Member for Westminster, North (Mr. Wheeler) ended. I pay tribute to the way in which the Metropolitan police have tried to come to grips in a new way in the past year or so, with the demands of policing the capital. I pay tribute to the Commissioner, who has got a grip on the force, to his officers in the London divisions, and to the police in my area who have consistently co-operated with my colleagues, my constituents and with me when their co-operation has been sought. There are, of course, times when the police must be criticised—they do not do everything right and the management has yet far to go, as it recognises—but if the people at the top appreciate the need for change, that filters through and attitudes and understanding are seen to be different.

I have been more grateful to the police than usual in the past year because my house has been burgled three times, and I have needed to call the police for my personal advantage. They were extremely helpful. Just in case burglars read these debates as well as police officers, I should point out that my home is now far better protected than it was a year ago and, I hope, much more secure against such intrusions.

The general improvement that has been identified and spoken about has been prompted by such initiation as the Wolff Olins report and the willingness to address the need for management change. Emphasis on service to the public has to be uppermost in the minds of all police officers and all civilians working in the police forces. There are now thankfully many more civilians doing jobs that they should always have been doing, but which, until recently, police

officers did. However, that emphasis on service is made difficult by any increase in crime, which makes the police in turn more aggressive because it means that they simply move from one tense event to another. Therefore, the continuing downward trend in crime is helpful.

The police must now be aware of the advantage in preventive activity and encouraging people to take preventive action, whether in securing homes or vehicles or in making sure that when they walk about the streets, they do not do so in a way that invites crime. That is crucial. We cannot expect the police to be our sole protectors. We have to protect ourselves and learn how to do that effectively.

In spite of the general declining trend in London crime figures, there are alarming upward trends, the most alarming of which is in violent crime. That is an extremely unsettling element of criminality in London. Increasingly, its consequence is that people have great fear of crime even if they are unlikely to be victims of it. The elderly are the obvious example, particularly the elderly on their own. Most violent crimes are committed not against them but by young people against each other outside a pub on a Friday night. However, if the perception is that violent crime is increasing, as it is, then the fear in which people live also increases.

The fear in our inner cities and on the estates is often the most debilitating feature of peoples' lives. Liberty is reduced every time someone is afraid to live their life as he or she would choose. That is the cancer at the heart of urban life. Therefore, I hope that we can counter the increases in violent crime so that those statistics go down and people gradually begin to feel more secure. I shall later look at some ways in which this can be addressed, because it involves structure and participation as well as the way in which the police carry on their activities.

I pay tribute to the noticeable fact that there are fewer complaints about inactivity or lack of responsiveness by police. These have gone down from 703 complaints in 1987 to 637 in 1988, or from 12·6 per cent. to 12 per cent. That is a gradual rather than a huge and sudden decrease, but it is important. At the same time, it is satisfying that M division in Southwark has put four more officers on the beat. Again, not an enormous change but an improvement. Fewer officers are lost to other activities away from their territory, which is encouraging. It would be helpful if more police were put on bikes. Most people can get further more quickly with a bike than on two feet, and police therefore could be more effective when they chase after criminals to catch them. Bikes also give police officers the chance to catch up with someone running away who is fitter than they are.

A good development is Pubwatch, formed by 15 Southwark licensees to help to prevent handbag snatching and other crimes in pubs and other licensed premises. There is now an initiative called Thameswatch to counter crime on the river. Another welcome initiative in Southwark is the increase in estate patrols which people on estates can call when they have a problem, such as dealing with an anti-social gang which is hanging around. These patrols consist not of the home beat officer but of a committed group of people dedicated to that task. They concentrate on an estate until it is no longer a place in which the problem persists.

I pay tribute to one scheme above all—the one developed with the Manpower Services Commission in which police have been putting decent locks on the homes of the elderly, the disabled or the vulnerable. This allows the police to be seen to be doing something positive where and when they are needed. There are fewer complaints that the home beat officer is never seen.

However, there are still management problems. The Metropolitan police are well funded, but as the Audit Commission report makes clear, they are often bad managers of their funds. For example, some initiatives that could be very good are hampered. I understand that a neighbourhood watch scheme set up by the tenants association on the Silverlock estate at Rotherhithe did not have enough money to provide the stickers for the doors and the signs for the lampposts and communal entrances. The whole purpose of neighbourhood watch schemes depends on showing that they exist. Otherwise there is no deterrent value. The idea was fine, but there were no locally available resources to implement it. Therefore, we need more resources and more staff time spent on initiatives dedicated to crime prevention, particularly in the inner city areas, where burglary, mugging and graffiti are still too prevalent, to the detriment of the environment.

I support the concern expressed by the hon. Member for Westminster, North, who speaks for London Conservative Members, about the extent of drug abuse in London. Since within a week or so of my election six years ago, I have regularly expressed concern, in many ways, about the massive amount of drug-related activity. Drug users and pushers still abound on some estates in Southwark, and there are many complaints about this. These people cause harm to the users and the often young victims, and there are all the knock-on effects. Because people need the money to buy drugs, they burgle, often stealing from their families, and a pattern of criminality develops. Local people are afraid that their youngsters will become hooked into the drug subculture. This is made worse because every day, when one walks down the street or up the staircase in an estate, one sees the evidence— silver paper, needles and sometimes people abusing drugs. Southwark has been working hard on this, across all the agencies and without party political problems, but we still need a greater emphasis on tackling the prevalence of drugs in the inner city. They are a debilitating and sad indictment of our society.

I have already referred, in an intervention in the speech of the hon. Member for Westminster, North, to the fact that another of the ways in which police service in the community and trust of that can be increased is by the police force losing its image of a private club. I pay tribute to the commissioner's antipathy to freemasonry, but there are still freemasons in the Metropolitan police and so long as they remain the effectiveness and impartiality of the force will be impaired. We need more stringent measures to stamp out freemasonry in the force. We must discourage young officers from joining the freemasons and encourage older officers who are freemasons to leave. Although there are clear indications that the most senior people are not freemasons, there are allegations— supported by evidence—that a considerable number of freemasons remain. That is not acceptable, and should be dealt with.

A similar concern has been expressed about police officers retiring, allegedly on medical grounds, when in fact there is considerable doubt about their probity. That is disgraceful. It is a matter of public record, for example, that concern has been expressed about former Superintendent Lumley.

My hon. Friend the Member for Brecon and Radnor (Mr. Livsey) has asked me to raise another matter. In March 1987, Daniel Morgan was murdered in the car park of the Golden Lion public house in Sydenham in south London. His family comes from Powys, which is why my hon. Friend has taken an interest. Daniel Morgan's brother has pursued extensive inquiries in this case. With a man called Mr. Rees, Daniel Morgan was a partner in a private detective agency. It is clear that at least one present and former police officer was and is involved in that agency —both as a serving police officer and as a recently retired police officer who even took part in the investigation of the murder complaint.

That matter has already once gone to court and has in some sense been resolved, so it is not sub-judice, but a number of unresolved matters have yet to come before the court. It is entirely unacceptable and does untold damage to the police service for any of its officers to lead that kind of double life. As I indicated, I have read the report of the Select Committee on Home Affairs and I know that the police service has admitted that fact. It is unacceptable for a police officer to be involved in a private detective agency, to retire early when something goes wrong and then to end up working for the agency full-time. I realise that the Select Committee on Home Affairs cannot deal with specific cases, but we need the most thorough investigations by the appropriate authorities of all allegations that lack of probity has led to officers retiring early.

I ask the Home Secretary as a matter of urgency to address the question of private security firms and their relationship with the police. It does the police service no good if it is thought of as a shelter for people who have been involved in such an underworld existence, and who go on to make more money out of it when they retire. The case of Daniel Morgan gives me great cause for concern. I believe that police involvement with the private security firm in this case was extremely wrong and a corrupting influence which had a direct link with the death of Daniel Morgan in south London two years ago.

Like other hon. Members, I have read the National Audit Office report, which has just been produced, which makes it clear that the police need to be moe effective in putting their own house in order. It is interesting to look back on previous debates on policing in London. We last had a debate last year and some of the points that arose then, arise again today. The Government often criticise the Inner London education authority, which is soon to be abolished as a result of the Government's decision, and London local authority social services departments for overspending. Yet the police in London spend far more per capita than those other agencies do. We should therefore get an extremely good service. Of course the costs in London of a community and social service such as policing are high, but the National Audit Office report revealed failings in management, in the use of property and revenue accounting, and so on. We need to get to grips with those failings so that all the resources can be used for proper front-line services.

At my meeting with the Home Secretary I raised the question of improving the public appearance of police stations, many of which are extremely uninviting. One often goes into a very small space to a counter and when one rings the bell someone may or may not immediately come to help. Police stations are not user-friendly and we urgently need substantial improvements.

[*Mr. Simon Hughes*]

There is another scandal. As a Southwark councillor my brother is a lay visitor of police stations. He and others with similar duties—I agree with the hon. Member for Huddersfield (Mr. Sheerman) that London's record is better than that of other areas—know well that the number of remand prisoners in police custody actually rose last year. It is no fault of the police—they do not want them there at all—but the number of people on remand in police stations in our capital city peaked at 1,296 one night last year, although it has fallen since then. Such people are often kept in appalling conditions. The cells are overcrowded and ill-ventilated and the prisoners are not given adequate exercise or washing facilities. There is no bath or shower, for example. There is often poor food or cold food and sometimes there is no food. That is not at all the fault of the police, but it is very bad news for police morale and the proper use of time and money. We need to deal very differently with the whole question of remand prisoners and where we put them rather than simply landing them on the doorstep of the police, who cannot cope.

I said earlier that I would refer to the position of the police in London. I pay tribute to the work that they have done. One area, in particular, remains on the agenda from last year. The police do not know the outcome of the cases in which they are involved. Last year I said that because prosecutions are now in the hands of the Crown prosecution service, the police officers who initiate prosecutions never know the result. That is demoralising because police officers do not know whether their efforts have brought any reward. I hope that we can make some improvements so that police officers feel more involved in the whole process from beginning to end. Perhaps if that happened and if stations were better equipped and not under such pressure from remand prisoners and had a better front-of-house atmosphere, we should not have such wastage and we should be able to recruit more people. At the moment, wastage is huge and we do not recruit nearly enough Londoners, let alone black Londoners. We are still failing to hold on to police officers and we often hear people complain that no sooner does a community get to know its new police officer than he leaves. That has a very unsettling effect on a huge force which, although it is the training ground for forces elsewhere in the country, is above all a police force for our communities, which are as much communities as those anywhere else. In London, as elsewhere, people want to live in communities. The changes that I have described would help this and be welcomed.

There is still concern that the process of police accountability depends on the goodwill and response of the police force rather than its structure. The debate has been marked by the underlying debate about the accountability of London's police. I share the view of Opposition Members who have spoken that, until we have a democratically accountable police force, we shall not have a properly accountable police force. I know the history of the Metropolitan police. It is not inconsistent to say that the Home Secretary could have special responsibility for London policing as well as there being a police authority in London, as there is everywhere else, which can look day by day into matters of cost, financing, staffing and other areas.

We may have an annual debate, but it is only a consultative exercise. We may have a meeting with the Home Secretary, which I value, but these are only consultative exercises. We may have opportunities to use the Committee system, but that does not provide the same degree of supervision—I do not use the word control, because that would be inappropriate—and the ability to render the police force in London as accountable as are forces elsewhere. It cannot be argued that the idea of a democratic police authority for London is invalid in principle simply because the Metropolitan police operate in the capital city. I know that the capital city has special characteristics, but in its ordinary activities it has the same characteristics as elsewhere.

I hope therefore, that the Government will see in due course that we must have a more properly, conventionally accountable police force in London. I also hope that Labour Members realise as the hon. Member for Huddersfield recognised, that they have a long way to go in engaging their people in the existing consultative processes from which they have so often withdrawn. There are still five boroughs in which Labour councillors do not participate in the police consultative committee and that does no good.

**Mr. Tony Banks:** Name them.

**Mr. Hughes:** I will name the boroughs. They are Brent, Ealing, Hackney, Haringey and Lambeth. The reason why the previous hon. Member for Vauxhall did not sit on the Lambeth committee was that his local Labour party asked him not to and that is on record. There may be reasons why one has complaints against the police, but that is all the more reason to participate and to voice them publicly. It is about time that the other members of the Labour party recognise that they have to play their part in consultation, as hon. Members on the Labour Front Bench do.

**Mr. Tony Banks:** The hon. Gentleman has changed his tune slightly. He said earlier that Stuart Holland was instructed. I made it clear that Stuart Holland was not instructed and he was not the sort of person who could have been instructed in those circumstances. Stuart Holland goes along with the policy of Lambeth borough council for reasons that he himself came to in consultation with his colleagues. The hon. Gentleman must understand that those councillors are elected. There are circumstances in which policing in particular parts of London is not as good as it is in other parts. Democratically elected councillors who are answerable to the people in their area are fully entitled to make a policy decision.

**Mr. Hughes:** I agree with that, but—it is an important "but"—one does not improve the performance of public servants by not talking to them. Police officers will become more alienated and less likely to be responsive. I know that because I have regularly talked to them about it. They sometimes do not feel that they are in a dialogue with people who are elected. When we are elected, we may have to talk to many people with whom we would rather not talk, but, as elected representatives, whether locally or nationally, we have a duty to have a proper dialogue with those who, on our behalf, carry out the policing of our community. I hope that the response in the next year will be that the boroughs where Labour representatives are still lagging behind will change and I hope that in return the Government will feel that we can move towards a more democratic police authority for London.

Democracy works because the police, one of its agencies, police with the consent of the people. People have to express that consent to help the police to do an even better job. The police have made substantial progress. I hope that they will continue to make that progress with full co-operation on all sides.

11.43 am

**Sir Philip Goodhart** (Beckenham): My right hon. Friend the Home Secretary opened the debate with an optimistic speech. I agree with him that the Metropolitan police are better managed, better organised, larger and better funded than they were a few years ago. However, it is sad that the commissioner's admirable report is still packed with depressing statistics. My hon. Friend the Member for Westminster, North (Mr. Wheeler) referred to the drug menace and the dire possibility that we shall be infected by the crack epidemic that is making such ravages in the United States of America. The hon. Member for Southwark and Bermondsey (Mr. Hughes) also made a largely constructive speech and concentrated on the drug problem.

I felt that the most depressing statistic in the annual report was on page 28, where the commissioner pointed out that firearms were used or fired in 2,298 crimes in London in 1988. I have looked back at the commissioner's report for 1958, which was the first full year I spent in this House. I note that in 1958, the then commissioner recorded with some alarm that there had been 35 armed robberies in London that year compared with 20 in 1957 and that there were another 14 cases in 1958 in which burglars appeared to have carried firearms, but could not be proved to have done so.

The 50-fold increase in the use of firearms in the past 30 years——

**The Parliamentary Under-Secretary of State for the Home Department (Mr. Douglas Hogg):** My hon. Friend makes a serious point, but it is a tribute to the police, as I am sure he would agree, that weapons were fired by police officers on only two occasions in 1988.

**Sir Philip Goodhart:** I support my hon. Friend's observation. The police response to the enormous increase in the use of firearms by professional criminals has been immensely restrained and they have shown great courage, as well as great restraint, in the face of that increase.

I believe that the increase has been brought about largely by the abolition of the death penalty. While that penalty existed, professional criminals did not carry or use firearms. Now, they carry firearms and are clearly prepared to use them to avoid arrest.

There has been an immense increase in serious violence and in casual violence. However, I note the astonishing fact that in the past 30 years, the streets of London have become safer for the ordinary citizen. The increase in casual violence has been matched—indeed overtaken—by a spectacular decline in the number of people killed or injured in traffic accidents in London. In 1958, a total of 765 people were killed in traffic accidents on London's roads; in 1988 that figure had dropped to 488—a decline of 277 deaths. That reduction almost exactly equals the number of people killed in the Lockerbie and Clapham

disasters. In the same 30 years, the number of people seriously injured in traffic accidents on London's roads has declined by some 2,000. I know that the hon. Member for Huddersfield (Mr. Sheerman) who, largely constructively, opened the debate for the Opposition, takes a keen personal interest in traffic safety.

All that has happened despite, or perhaps because of, the huge increase in traffic in the metropolis. As the traffic grinds to a halt, at times it becomes increasingly difficult for a motorist to build up enough speed to squash a cyclist or pedestrian. However, two Acts passed by the House in the past 30 years have contributed notably to the decline in death and injury on our roads. The first was the breathalyser Act, which has always been associated with Barbara Castle, and the second was the seat belt Act, which has also saved a great many lives and limbs.

The North report on road traffic law reform proposes to make it much easier for the police to use speed radar cameras to trap speeding offenders and drivers who tend to ignore traffic lights. I hope that in the next Session there will be no delay in presenting and passing a Bill based on that important report. I hope that the commissioner is already making plans to use those new devices as soon as he has the power to do so. If that is done, there may well be a further substantial cut in London's road toll.

Traffic congestion is also important. Too many times during the past year London has nearly come to a grinding halt when added pressure is put on our roads by strikes, demonstrations or just plain, ordinary bad weather. That problem has not been helped by the fact that the traffic warden force, controlled by the commissioner, has declined by 100 in the past year and is now 25 per cent. under strength. One of the reasons whey we do not have sufficient traffic wardens is the long-standing and unresolved argument about whether traffic wardens should be controlled by the police or by the London boroughs. If we are to resolve the traffic problems in central London, we shall have to have a sensible city wide parking policy. I believe that the control of traffic wardens in inner London must remain with the commissioner. In outer London, there is a strong case for giving additional powers to the London boroughs, but I am convinced that in inner London the commissioner must retain control.

The Treasury must agree that the money raised through fines and traffic penalties should be put back into the traffic warden force so that it can recruit adequate numbers and offer adequate pay. If we are to unclog London's traffic arteries, we must be prepared to concentrate London's traffic wardens on our main roads. I and a substantial number of Members of Parliament who represent London constituencies, particularly those who represent south London constituencies, believe that certain main roads should be classified as "red routes" and should be subjected to much higher parking penalties and much stricter enforcement. The fines should be five times heavier than normal and there should be five times the volume of enforcement so that illegal parkers on a red route would know that there was a high risk of being caught.

One of the most congested routes in London is the south circular road. The Department of Transport has commissioned a firm of consultants to produce a variety of plans for easing congestion on the south circular. Two of the proposals put forward by the consultants involve building new highways through part of my constituency.

[*Sir Philip Goodhart*]

The cost of those new highways, if either plan were adopted, could run into hundreds of millions of pounds and the dislocation would be immense.

**Mr. Jeremy Hanley** (Richmond and Barnes): Does my hon. Friend agree that not only the cost to the taxpayer, but the cost to the environment and the political cost must be taken into account?

**Sir Philip Goodhart:** I entirely agree with my hon. Friend. Some of my constituents had their homes blighted by those unnecessary schemes. I hope that the Department of Transport will soon announce that those plans will be dropped, but I also hope that parking restrictions on the south circular will be enforced.

On a Friday afternoon some weeks ago, I drove six miles from the edge of my constituency to Wandsworth bridge along the south circular road. In those six miles I saw 143 illegallly parked vehicles and not a single traffic warden. It makes no sense to spend hundreds of millions of pounds on new roads to relieve congestion on a highway which is used as an illegal parking lot. London's traffic problems can be made a great deal easier if Ministers take the essential first step of making up their minds about the control of traffic wardens and if they can persuade the Treasury to recycle the money raised through traffic penalties into providing an adequate force of traffic wardens.

Finally, I note that the debate has been particularly ill-attended. Apart from the Ministers, the Whips and the PPS, my hon. Friend the Member for Westminster, North, who made such a notable speech, my hon. Friend the Member for Uxbridge (Mr. Shersby) who has such a powerful voice in the Police Federation, and my hon. Friends the Members for Orpington (Mr. Stanbrook), for Richmond and Barnes (Mr. Hanley), for Harrow, East (Mr. Dykes) and for Faversham (Mr. Moate), hardly anyone has been present. I welcome the scant attendance in some ways because it shows that there is considerable satisfaction on the Government Benches about the way in which the commissioner is carrying out his duties. On the other hand, I noted that, apart from the hon. Members for Southwark and Bermondsey and for Huddersfield, who opened for the Opposition, the only other Back Bench Member present during the first half hour of the Minister's speech was the hon. Member for Brent, South (Mr. Boateng). I, as a citizen, am glad because that must mean that the London Labour party's assault on the Metropolitan police, which has had such a rancid effect in recent years, has come largely to an end.

As a politician, I must say that I regret that, because I believe that the anti-police antics of the London Labour party over the past years have played notably into our hands in terms of public support.

**Mr. Tony Banks:** Will the hon. Gentleman give way?

**Sir Philip Goodhart:** No, I have sat down.

12.1 pm

**Mr. Jeremy Corbyn** (Islington, North): I freely admit that I was one of those Members who were not present at the start of the debate. I was negotiating my way on my bicycle through London traffic. That should appeal to the hon. Member for Beckenham (Sir P. Goodhart), if nothing else. I thought that is was a disgusting place through which to cycle with all the dirt, danger, pollution and the abuse that one receives from motorists for having the temerity to ride a bicycle through London. I shall be returning to that subject later. Unfortunately, the Home Secretary has just left the Chamber. It must have been something that I said —unless he has gone to sort out the traffic problems of London.

**Mr. Tony Banks:** I am grateful to my hon. Friend for giving way, when the hon. Member for Beckenham (Sir P. Goodhart), who ended his speech on a highly contentious and misleading note, chose not to. My hon. Friend will have noticed that the hon. Gentleman drew the conclusion that large numbers of his colleagues were not here because they were wholly satisfied with the performance of the Metropolitan police, but he did not appear to believe that that might be the reason for the absence of Opposition Members. If, however, he had drawn such a conclusion, I would not have agreed with it. Many hon. Members do not come here for the simple reason that it is, frankly, a charade and a farce if we are trying to suggest that this is the way we hold the Metropolitan police accountable to the people of London through their Members of Parliament.

**Mr. Corbyn:** I thank my hon. Friend for that intervention. What he said was important and timely. The Opposition are as concerned as everyone else about the levels of crime. Crimes, such as street crime, harassment, violence, burglary, robbery and rape, happen not only in London, but in the communities that we all represent and in which we live. We have no interest in seeing high crime rates in London or dangers to people walking legitimately round the streets at night, but we want to see an effective police force that combats those problems in our communities. The idea that somehow we are anti the Metropolitan police and in favour of high crime rates is ridiculous and rubbish. Every year during the police debate we get the same kind of tirade from Conservative Members suggesting that we do not care about the problems in our communities.

I say sincerely to the House that my constituency suffers as much as any hon. Member's—probably more than most —from all kinds of inner-city problems and multiple deprivation, which are so often spoken about in the House. We have no interest in doing anything other than eradicating crime, making the streets, estates and playgrounds safe and our communities clean and decent places in which to live. That is what I, my local authority and our discussions with the police are committed to doing.

I want to open my speech by putting on public record my deep thanks to officers from Hornsey road police station of the Holloway division for the great bravery and courage that they showed last week, with representatives of the London fire service, when there was a terrible fire in a council flat on the Andover estate. A police car was driving by, and the two police officers saw the fire and ran into the house. They were burnt in the process and were unable to get two of the small children out. The fire service eventually went in and brought out the bodies of two children aged three and two. I attended their funerals yesterday, together with those police officers. The Andover tenants' association is shocked and horrified by the incident—as we all are—and arranged a local collection to help the family of the dead children. It wanted me to put on record my thanks to the local police for all that they did in that terrible incident. That incident has cast a pall and a blight on the entire community. It was absolutely devastated by the deaths of those children. To attend the funeral of small children is very distressing for everybody and I was grateful to the police for attending and so, too, were the family concerned. I readily put that on the record because we should be appreciative of what the police have done.

I have recieved—as presumably other hon. Members have—the local divisional reports of police station areas. I have been carefully reading through the report from the Holloway division about the area covered by the Hornsey road station. Clearly, it is situated in a mixed area with multiple problems. Many of the problems that Members of Parliament, local councils and the police have to face are not of our making, but are imposed upon us. The vast amounts of traffic flowing through my constituency are something over which the police and councils have no power, yet they are expected to solve the problems created. Likewise, Highbury stadium is in my constituency. Every fortnight during the football season it has an enormous attendance—as one would expect for the club that has just won the league championship. Obviously difficult policing decisions must be made in policing that stadium. It must be said that there has been little trouble outside Highbury stadium—apart from at the Millwall game last year— which is to the credit of many people. However, considerable disruption is caused by the presence of the stadium in my constituency.

The introduction of a membership identity card scheme will do nothing to improve the situation, but will create far more problems as everyone living around, or working near the stadium, or supporting Arsenal, knows. That is why they are so adamantly opposed to the membership scheme. I should have thought that Conservative Members, especially those representing the interests of the Police Federation, would at least recognise that the Police Federation also feels—I understand so, too, do the police generally—that the introduction of that scheme will not solve the problems of crowd violence, but will merely push those problems on to the street. I hope that those of us who represent constituencies with major stadiums in them will be recognised as having a legitimate interest in the matter and as understanding the problems.

**Mr. Harry Cohen** (Leyton): My hon. Friend will know that the Police Federation is strongly opposed to the football ID scheme. Does my hon. Friend have any idea of how the federation's representative in the House voted on that scheme.

**Mr. Corbyn:** I have examined the *Official Report* and I discovered that the hon. Member for Uxbridge (Mr. Shersby) voted according to his party Whip for the introduction of the scheme, against the express wishes of the Police Federation.

**Mr. Shersby:** The hon. Gentleman is wrong. I did not vote for the Bill against the express wishes of the Police Federation. On the contrary, I voted for it because the Police Federation, being a responsible organisation, recognises that there is a need for such a scheme. At the same time, however, it has also said that it does not believe that the scheme likely to emerge as a result of the deliberations of the Football Membership Authority will

necessarily control the problem of violence outside the ground. The hon. Gentleman made that point and it is a fair one. He should, however, take careful note of the points I made in my speech when I said that the Police Federation recognises the need for a scheme and the contribution that it could make, but that it believes it is vital for it to have an opportunity to make an input before the FMA produces the scheme. If the hon. Gentleman reads my remarks in *Hansard* he will know that I made it clear that unless the intended scheme was one which could command the support of the Police Federation I would vote against it when it comes before the House later this year.

**Mr. Corbyn:** I have noted carefully what the hon. Gentleman has just said and what he said a few days ago and I believe that he is trying to have it both ways. It is clear to me that the Police Federation is against the existing scheme, but the hon. Gentleman voted for it. It is up to him to sort out his relationship with the Police Federation, but we should remember that the hon. Gentleman voted for the introduction of the identity card scheme as proposed by his right hon. Friend the Secretary of State for the Environment.

My hon. Friends the Members for Huddersfield (Mr. Sheerman) and for Newham, North-West (Mr. Banks) have already drawn attention to the problems associated with this debate and with the accountability of the local police forces. We have had the usual tirade from the Home Secretary who claimed that London boroughs are doing nothing to consult the police, nor are they working with them locally. He knows that that is not true and that it is a lot of nonsense. If we had an effective local evening newspaper in London that was prepared to report what was going on locally instead of reporting whatever the Tory party says, it would be obvious that, in every London borough, there is some form of co-operation and consultation with the police by the local communities. That co-operation varies from borough to borough.

The Home Secretary must be aware, however, that each year the London boroughs feel a sense of frustration when they are landed with the responsibility of collecting a great deal of money to pay for the Metropolitan police without any say in how that money is spent or how the police service is administered in London. We are told by the hon. Member for Westminster, North (Mr. Wheeler) that what passes for accountability is the fact that, in 1828 when the London police force was originally established, its importance was such that it was put under the control of Parliament because it was thought to be the least corrupt body at that time and was capable of setting up that police force. It was not right then to have no elected local government in London and nor is it right not to have an elected authority in London now. That elected authority should be returned to London and it should include an elected police authority.

**Mr. Tony Banks:** My hon. Friend should bear in mind that there is one police authority in London, the City of London, which is one of the 33 London boroughs. Why does the City of London have responsibility over its police force, which the other boroughs do not?

**Mr. Corbyn:** I should imagine that it is because of the fundamentally undemocratic nature of the City of London and because it is a Tory-run authority. Responsibility for the police in the remainder of London rests with the Home

[*Mr. Corbyn*]

Secretary who represents Oxfordshire. It is not good enough to describe that as accountability. We are on a motion to adjourn the House because we happen to be talking about the police.

We are told that the Public Accounts Committee may peruse the accounts of the Metropolitan police. It can produce a report, rebuttal and critique of those accounts, but it cannot force any change of strategy or direction. The Met is not democratically accountable. All we have is the Home Secretary, as the police authority for London, being good enough to come to the House of Commons to discuss the police. He has personal control of more than £1 billion expenditure of public money. That is not a satisfactory form of accountability of the police force. The Metropolitan police must recognise that, because of the amount of money that they have spent on public relations, on the Wolff Olins report and on other matters of legitimate and genuine concern. When the Minister replies I hope that he will take note of what has been said and of disturbing matters relating to the administration of the police.

The hon. Member for Southwark and Bermondsey (Mr. Hughes) referred to freemasonry within the police force which was mentioned last year. I have read the statements made by the commissioner and by the Home Secretary and one way or another they do not support police officer membership of freemason lodges. They have not, however, eradicated freemasonry from the police force. Membership of a freemason lodge is incompatible with membership of the police force. The Minister should make it absolutely clear that police officers in London should no longer be freemasons. He can do that as he has direct control over the police force in London.

I am concerned about racial harassment and the reporting thereof to the police. The 1985-86 Home Affairs Select Committee report, "Racial Attacks and Harassment", made the following recommendations:

"1. All police forces covering areas with appreciable ethnic minorities should make clear that tackling racial incidents is regarded a one of their priority tasks . . .

3. Specific instruction concerning racial incidents should be included in police training courses . . .

6. Police forces should make it their practice always to keep victims of racial incidents informed of subsequent action".

I have read the statistics that have been prepared and submitted by the police on this matter and it is disturbing to discover that there has been an increase in the reporting of racial incidents. The difficulty is what definition is given to that racial incident when someone arrives at a police station to report it.

As I understand it, under the terms of the force order, when a victim arrives at a police station and informs the police that he believes himself to be a victim of a racially motivated assault it must be recorded as such. I wonder whether every police station is fully informed of that practice, as I believe that there is a great amount of under-reporting of racially motivated incidents. I take that matter seriously and I hope that my concern is shared by the police force.

In area 1 of the Metropolitan police, which includes my local police force, there were 334 reported racial incidents in 1987; in 1988 that figure had risen to 356. I have no way of telling whether there are many more incidents that go unreported, but I suspect that there are and I suspect that

that is the case in all parts of London. I hope that the Minister will give the assurance that a clear instruction will be issued to every police station to make it specific that a person reporting a racially motivated incident should have it reported as such. If that does not happen we will have no idea of the size of the problem.

In the Islington divisions of the Met 101 racial incidents were reported last year, but they resulted in only four arrests and 33 cases were cleared up. It is clear, therefore, that many cases are unresolved and the same pattern emerges from an examination of the statistics for London as a whole. I hope that the Minister will deal with this problem in the way intended by the Home Affairs Committee and I hope that he will ensure that such matters are followed up.

I am concerned that little progress has been made on the implementation of the domestic violence force order. Local police forces are reluctant to become involved when women report that they are being subjected to domestic violence. The police usually say, "That is a family or domestic matter." Under the calm surface of complacency, the most appalling domestic violence is occurring. To whom are the women who are the victims of domestic violence to turn? If there is a women's refuge in their community, clearly they can go there or get in touch with it. However, there are not women's refuges in every community. Many of them are over-stretched, over-burdened and unable to cope with the demands placed on them. If the police show a lack of sympathy, the plight of victims is made worse, more desperate, more dangerous and isolated.

It is difficult for men to understand the fear that many women experience when they suffer from domestic violence. The problem requires the clearest instruction and training of police officers to deal with first inquiries, in addition to counselling and follow up. If the first inquiry is not dealt with helpfully or sympathetically, the woman might ring off and not further pursue the matter. I hope that the Home Secretary will ensure that there is an improvement in the take-up of training to deal with domestic violence. I understand that only 5 per cent. of Metropolitan police officers have been trained to deal with sexual offences, which is a low figure.

**Mr. Douglas Hogg:** The hon. Gentleman will be pleased to learn that 1,556 officers have been trained in sexual offences investigation techniques.

**Mr. Corbyn:** I am pleased to learn that that number of officers have been so trained, but clearly that is a small proportion of the total number of police officers in London. I am sure that the Minister will understand that greater emphasis should be placed on such training in normal police training courses, not only in special training courses.

The hon. Member for Beckenham mentioned traffic-related offences in London. It is obvious that traffic in London is rapidly grinding to a halt because of the inadequacy of public transport, the promotion of private commuter motoring in and out of London, which blocks roads, and because of the lack of enforcement of the lorry ban and other traffic regulations.

**Mr. Cohen:** My hon. Friend mentioned the lack of enforcement of the lorry ban in London. When I and other Labour Members asked the commissioner about the police not enforcing the lorry ban, he said that the difficulty is the lack of proper road signs restricting lorries passing through residential areas at night. Is my hon. Friend aware that the Department of Transport has just issued a glossy leaflet—as it would, spending much public money—on new signs for motorists. I asked whether signs would be upgraded to enforce the Londonwide ban, and it said no. Is it not a public scandal that it has refused to take the opportunity to improve road signing so that we can have a proper lorry ban that the police can enforce?

**Mr. Corbyn:** The police did not agree with those who campaigned for the Londonwide lorry ban. They said that it would be hard to implement and pointed out all the difficulties that they foresaw. We succeeded in getting a partial lorry ban throughout London, but I see little evidence of the police enforcing it. We require the strictest possible enforcement of the ban, because it is not good enough to have 25 to 40-tonne trucks driving through London causing danger and pollution. At the heart of the problem is the profits of operators being put before the interests of London residents. I hope that the Minister will recognise that the police could contribute to the safety of Londoners by strictly enforcing the lorry ban and by absolutely strict enforcement of the bus priority measures that have been introduced. In many areas, cars are not removed from bus lanes when they should be. Any bus that is held up means that between 40 and 60 people are delayed, whereas if a car is held up only one person is delayed for a few minutes. Public transport should be the priority rather than the commuter motorist.

There is the further question of the safety of pedestrians and cyclists. The amount of traffic in London is making life more dangerous for them. I hope that the police will ensure that they protect them and strictly enforce the lorry ban.

Yet again, we are having a debate on the police force in London, which is an unsatisfactory way of dealing with police matters in London. It will fall to a Labour Government to introduce a democratically elected authority for London, so that its people can put forward their views on their city and the police direction that they want, instead of the nonsense of an annual debate without a vote or detailed perusal of estimates.

I find the commissioner's report interesting, but it lacks detailed statistical evidence. Such evidence does not appear to be available from the Vote Office. I do not know what has happened to it, but it is unsatisfactory to have a debate without the necessary information and the power radically to change anything put forward by the commissioner or the Home Secretary.

12.26 pm

**Mr. Michael Shersby** (Uxbridge): In contributing to the debate, I should declare an interest of which hon. Members are aware. I am parliamentary adviser to the Police Federation.

As my constituency is within the Metropolitan police area, I have a special interest in everything that happens within the Metropolitan police. Although Uxbridge is situated in the county of Middlesex, it falls within the London borough of Hillingdon. I hope that, with the demise of Greater London, we shall one day revert to the Middlesex borough of Hillingdon rather than the London borough of Hillingdon, which seems to be something of a misnomer.

Uxbridge is proud to be policed by the Metropolitan police, which is the largest of the 43 forces of England and Wales. We are particularly lucky to have one of the newest police stations, which was built and opened before I took up my appointment as parliamentary adviser to the Police Federation.

I welcome the debate, which on the whole has been good, but I am sorry that we were given only a week's notice of it. I suggest to the Government's business managers, who I hope will pick up this point, that longer notice should be given of these debates. When the allocation of private Members' time is being considered, perhaps notice could be given of when these debates will take place so that we have a much better turnout of London Members.

Many of the hon. Members who are absent do not lack interest in the police. I am sure that they have other pressing constituency engagements that they could not avoid.

As Members, we are fortunate in that every day we come into contact with officers of the Metropolitan police who serve in the Houses of Parliament. I pay tribute to them for the unique job that they do for all the people in the Metropolitan police area. Despite the many difficulties that they encounter daily, they have just cause to be proud of the achievements of the force during the past year. For example, there appears to be a downward trend in offences against property in London, especially burglary and car theft. There is no cause to be complacent because much progress must still be made. That trend is due, in part, to good policing, including the encouragement given by the Metropolitan police to citizens to protect their homes better. It is due also to the tremendous success of neighbourhood watch schemes throughout the Metropolitan police area. There is no doubt that there is a better clear-up rate, which is very encouraging.

On the other side, as my right hon. Friend the Home Secretary pointed out, there has been a worrying increase in crimes of violence against the person and reported sexual offences. Regrettably, this trend seems to be evident not only in London but in most of the capital cities of western Europe and North America. Some hon. Members have suggested that it may be highlighted by the greater willingness of women to report such assaults, and there is quite a lot in that. There is no doubt that women are now much more willing to report those assaults, which helps the police in dealing with this particularly horrible crime.

As the crime figures have been debated at some length and are well known to hon. Members, I shall tell the House about some of the problems of policing London as seen through the eyes of the Metropolitan police officers who are members of the Police Federation. One of the main problems that concerns the Met is the wastage of trained officers who wish to transfer to other forces. The Met loses about one third of its recruits during the first two years of service. It has been calculated that it takes seven years to recoup the cost of training a constable.

As London Members, we all know that living in or around London is expensive. The attractions of transferring to other forces in pleasant country areas are self-evident. That is why the London allowance introduced as part of the Edmund Davies formula was so important. It was intended to attract and retain recruits to the Metropolitan police. Although police pay over the past decade or so has increased in accordance with the Edmund Davies formula, there has been no increase in the London allowance for about seven years. That matter has been raised with me by officers of the Police Federation.

[*Mr. Michael Shersby*]

The forthcoming change in the rent allowance will have a significant effect on the living standards of Met officers, depending on where they live. Another big problem that the Met, and indeed every public service faces is the demographic downturn. The shortage of young people available to join in the coming decade could result in the force experiencing serious recruitment and manpower problems, as it did during the 1960s and early 1970s. We must all take account of that. It affects the police service, the National Health Service, industry and commerce alike. Great ingenuity must be deployed in dealing with that problem until more young people are available to serve in those important public services. For those and many other reasons, it is vital to maintain the Edmund Davies formula for pay, including a realistic London allowance and London weighting, if the Met is to get the manpower and womanpower that it needs.

Accommodation is another important issue. I should like to comment on some items in the report of the National Audit Office. I am in some difficulty in doing so because, as a member of the Public Accounts Committee, with my colleagues I will be taking evidence on the report on Monday next. In a way, it is a pity that this debate has taken place before the PAC has taken its evidence. However, the report exists and it is proper that I should comment on it.

Paragraph 1.42 of the National Audit Office report states:

"The National Audit Office noted that in the period 1980-87, the vacancy levels in married quarters often exceeded 15 per cent., with a peak of 26 per cent. in 1984. Vacancies in section houses show a similar pattern; actual vacancies have at times risen to double the targeted figure of 250. As at February 1988, 482 married quarters out of 3,059—16 per cent.—and 864 section house rooms out of 3,331—26 per cent.—were unoccupied."

That is serious and the Public Accounts Committee will undoubtedly want to consider it next Monday.

The need to provide housing for married and single officers arose originally from the powers of chief constables to require their officers to live in the areas that they serve to ensure rapid deployment. Operational necessity meant that officers were expected and sometimes compelled to live in police accommodation. However, better transport and communications and the general trend towards home ownership have led to the Metropolitan police gradually relaxing their requirements for officers to live close to their place of duty.

Nevertheless, the Met believes that the residential estate continues to offer a number of benefits. Those benefits are highlighted in the NAO report and include the easing of recruitment problems in high-cost housing areas; helping to retain young married officers; enabling some officers to live close to their work; and, finally, helping to resolve welfare problems.

The condition of the residential estate, as highlighted in the NAO report, is very important. I hope that the PAC will investigate that matter closely. The NAO report states:

"There was very little co-ordinated management information about the condition of the residential estate as a whole. There had been only limited surveys since the late 1970s, other than for section houses . . . the current high level of vacant properties cannot be re-let until maintenance and decoration have been completed".

Although the figures in the NAO report may be a little overstated because they include section houses that are undergoing major amelioration as well as those allocated to recruits for passing out, I believe that they are still too high. I hope that my right hon. Friend the Home Secretary and the Met will consider that problem promptly. Those very valuable quarters, whether for single or married officers, must be put to good use if we are to recruit and retain the police officers we need, particularly to work in central London.

As paragraph 2.12 of the NAO report makes clear, there is no formal strategy on the future need for and uses of headquarters accommodation. That causes me considerable concern. Paragraphs 2.22 and 2.23 of the NAO report make it clear that although attempts have been made by employing consultants to overcome the short-term difficulties, the consultants recently completed the condition survey of the operational estate at a cost of £168,875, but that did not produce significant results. No doubt it will become apparent when the PAC reports in due course that the Met must take urgent action to deal with the problem. The Wolff Olins report makes a good point about presentation. It states:

"The physical identity of the Met emerges through its buildings, vehicles, the uniforms and equipment used by its officers and so on."

The report goes on to mention the rundown state of many police stations. It states:

"The physical state of many police stations is run down. Public areas such as receptions, waiting rooms and so on, look neglected. There exists what we have described elsewhere as a 'sellotape culture' in which notices and signs are stuck up at random. All this contributes to an atmosphere of shabby confusion."

It goes on in a similar vein.

One of the most important pieces of information to emerge from the National Audit Office report is the state of police stations in London. My hon. Friend the Member for Westminster, North (Mr. Wheeler) has already referred to that. I draw the attention of hon. Members to table 2 on page 12 of the report, which makes the point that, today, 62 police stations are classed as vulnerable and 40 are classed as irrecoverable. The report clearly illustrates that 36 of the 62 vulnerable stations were built pre-1914, and that 39 of the irrecoverable stations were built pre-1914. We know that not all London police stations were purpose-built. Many of them were acquired at one time or another and had originally been designed for a quite different purpose.

The National Audit Office makes it clear that the maintenance budgets that are vital for keeping police stations in good condition have been directly raided to finance extra pay commitments. That is quite wrong. I realise that the Home Secretary has his annual problems in funding police pay awards and that difficult discussions take place with the Chancellor of the Exchequer and other Ministers, but surely it is wrong to raid the maintenance budget to finance pay awards. I hope that that will not happen again, because it has contributed to the run-down state of London's police stations.

**Mr. Tony Banks:** We have just opened a police shop in Newham. What does the hon. Gentleman think about having a police presence within the community, but not necessarily in purpose-built police stations? Whatever else one says about them, police stations are expensive to construct. There are other ways of providing a visible police presence in a consumer-friendly way, and police shops might be one of them.

**Mr. Shersby:** I am grateful for the hon. Gentleman's intervention. It is an interesting concept. I am not familiar with police shops, but I will make it my business to examine how they operate. They could point the way to more flexibility in the future.

I now refer to the size of the land bank that is presently owned by the Metropolitan police. In 1988, the Metropolitan police estimated the market value of their 29 sites at about £22 million. In some cases there have been no clear aims and objectives about the way in which such sites should be used. I do not want to pre-empt anything that the PAC may do on Monday, so I shall say nothing more about that matter. However, if, in future, the Met could make much better use of its assets, more money could be redeployed to provide better facilities and services for the force. I am encouraged to know that the Home Secretary has confirmed that new capital controls will be introduced with effect from 1 April 1990 that will provide an incentive to dispose of surplus assets by allowing free use of a specified proportion of receipts. That is a major step forward and I congratulate the Home Secretary on it. We all know from our experience of public life that there is little incentive to make better use of assets. The money goes into the common pot and those making the savings see little benefit from them. I hope that we can look forward to a completely different system.

I agree with the hon. Member for Huddersfield (Mr. Sheerman) that the commissioner's report is excellent. It deals, among other matters, with traffic. Like my hon. Friend the Member for Beckenham (Sir P. Goodhart) I am concerned that the strength of the traffic warden service declined in 1988 by almost 100 to 1,444. In addition, the reduction in the traffic division, which was carried out by a previous commissioner, is seen by many members of the Police Federation as reducing the Met's ability to combat traffic congestion.

In Uxbridge, which is in what some describe as outer London but should be described as being in the county of Middlesex, there are more cars per family than in any other London borough, and the need for traffic management schemes is urgent. When my hon. Friend the Parliamentary Under-Secretary replies to the debate, I hope that he will be able to tell my hon. Friend the Member for Beckenham and I when the Home Office working party will report. I have been tabling parliamentary questions for the past year or so trying to obtain some information about what will be done.

I understand that primary legislation is needed if local authorities are to be able to employ traffic wardens and use the income from fines to finance more off-street parking. The need for that in outer London areas such as Beckenham and Uxbridge—*[Interruption.]* My hon. Friend the Member for Richmond and Barnes (Mr. Hanley) makes the point that this also affects his constituency, and I am sure that it affects all of outer London. Action is urgently needed in all these areas.

It must be possible for local authorities to employ traffic wardens so that the chaos which becomes more evident as the weeks go by, can be dealt with. We must give some relief to the people who live in residential streets where parked cars make it almost impossible for municipal services to travel into and out of the streets.

**Mr. Tony Banks:** I entirely concur with the hon. Gentleman's point. He demonstrates that there is concern on both sides of the House. I ask him to place it on record —it is important for a Conservative Member to do so— that if borough councils become responsible for the warden schemes, they must have the resources to carry out their responsibilities efficiently and effectively. The Government frequently give more responsibility and place more duty on local authorities while at the same time taking more and more resources away from them.

**Mr. Shersby:** I take the hon. Gentleman's point. My local authority's view is that the operation could be financed from the proceeds of fines. However, it can do so only if the legislative changes to which I have referred take place. I hope that the Home Office will announce its decision before the recess because there is great agitation about this in London.

I shall refer to the sensitive and delicate issue of public order and the difficulties experienced by the Metropolitan police when handling the recent marches in opposition to the publication of "The Satanic Verses". A number of Metropolitan police officers are worried about what constitutes reasonable force when handling such a difficult matter. I am sure that hon. Members on both sides of the House will pay tribute to the way in which the Metropolitan police handled the incidents in its area, and I am equally sure that the Home Secretary will take account of the concern that exists.

The Home Secretary referred to the recruitment of specials. I should like to make it clear to him that the Police Federation is not opposed to specials; it believes that they have a role to play helping officers of the regular force, as they have done for many years. The federation does not believe that they can take over from the regular force, nor has the Home Secretary suggested that they should. The federation is worried, as my right hon. Friend knows, about the proliferation of private police forces in docks around the country, set up under the Harbours, Docks, and Piers Clauses Act 1847, under which specials can be sworn in to replace regular officers. I am grateful for the way in which my right hon. Friend listened to the federation's views on this matter and for the steps that he has taken to consult the Secretary of State for Transport on whether we need to continue creating such private forces under a Victorian Act that was never intended for that purpose.

Hon. Members have referred to the need for private security forces to be regulated. As I understand it, Government policy so far has been to rely on self-regulation by those forces, but that will need to be kept under observation—to use the favourite buzz word, we shall need to monitor the position. In shopping malls in many towns there are now private security guards who deny access to people who want to go about their usual business, and that sometimes causes anxiety. In the recent European election campaign it was made clear that the candidates were not welcome in a shopping mall which I know. That raises questions that concern us all, and the matter needs careful and sensitive treatment.

I want to put down a marker about the policing of our streets. Many hon. Members on both sides will share my firm belief that the streets should be policed by the regular officers of the police forces throughout the United Kingdom. I do not want private gated streets policed by

[*Mr. Shersby*]

private police forces. I know that the Adam Smith Institute has advocated that, but it finds no support from me.

Another matter important to every London Member is the policing of the London Underground. I pay tribute to the 80 or so Metropolitan police officers who have been seconded to help the British Transport police in this difficult task, and I welcome the support that the Metropolitan police have given. It has reassured Londoners, and I hope that, if it proves necessary to strengthen the British Transport police in the future, that need will be accommodated in the overal policing structure of London. British Transport police play a valuable role and it may be necessary at some stage to supplement their ranks.

There has been some comment in the debate on racial incidents and attacks. I was glad that the commissioner's report referred to them. There has been an increase in such cases, but of less than 2 per cent. since 1987.

I did not read only the commissioner's report; I had a look at the report on the policing of Uxbridge that was recently sent to me. In 1987, 17 racial incidents were reported, and 22 have been reported this year. Resulting from the 22 complaints, 14 people have been identified as suspects. There has been some difficulty gathering enough evidence to start prosecutions, and in other cases the victims have refused to prosecute. In eight of the incidents the suspects were not known or traced.

Not all coppers in London are brutal, racist and corrupt. They handle racial attacks very well and with great sensitivity and they should have the support of the House for the way in which they tackle those matters.

**Mr. Tony Banks:** That is a generalised statement. I assure the hon. Gentleman that the position in Uxbridge is markedly different from that in Newham. Although, according to the report, there has been only a 2 per cent. increase, that statistic masks the enormous upsurge in some areas of London—specifically, the east end—so the hon. Gentleman must be careful with it.

**Mr. Shersby:** One of the good features of a debate such as this is that one is constantly reminded of the great diversity in the population of London. I accept that there is a great difference between the hon. Gentleman's constituency and mine, but the police have made a significant contribution to dealing with this problem.

We have heard today about the community police consultative groups, one of which is in the borough of Hillingdon, in my constituency. The police in my area have drawn to my attention the difficulty in attracting young people to serve on those groups. I hope that the Home Office and the Met can do more to encourage young people to come forward so that they are constantly in touch with what is going on at local level.

I particularly welcome the paragraph in the commissioner's report dealing with victim care. I see that the force made over 100,000 referrals to victim support schemes in the past year. The hon. Member for Newham, North-West (Mr. Banks) will remember, because I recall his being in the Chamber when this matter was debated, that only a year ago we were pressing my right hon. Friend the Home Secretary for financial assistance to make such schemes possible. They give great comfort to those who have the misfortune to suffer sometimes violent attacks and who are cared for and counselled by those who work on the schemes.

I must also mention the courts and the work that the London magistrates do in complementing the Metropolitan police in the policing of our capital city. The magistrates' courts around London are experiencing serious difficulties because of the shortage of court clerks. I have raised this matter in two Adjournment debates, one in 1972 and another this year. The problem can be tackled only if my right hon. Friend the Home Secretary can persuade my right hon. Friend the Chancellor of the Exchequer to make available additional resources for the recruitment, training and retention of good court clerks. If that does not happen, courts will be closed because they cannot function properly and that will make the policing of London more difficult.

I welcome the good relations between the Police Federation and my right hon. Friend the Home Secretary and his officials. I am delighted that my right hon. Friend has shown his willingness to meet officers and the federation in Surbiton soon. I pay tribute to Sir Peter Imbert and his colleagues and all the officers of the Metropolitan police for the excellent job that they do for all Londoners. We are proud of them.

12.57 pm

**Mr. Tony Banks** (Newham, North-West): I start where the hon. Member for Uxbridge (Mr. Shersby) left off, by paying tribute to Sir Peter Imbert. I am the chairman of the London group of Labour Members of Parliament and our useful meetings with the commissioner have shown him to be courteous, co-operative and constructive. However, our complaint is that they are not frequent enough. Although the relationship between Members of Parliament and the commissioner and senior police officers is all that one would expect, unfortunately that cannot be said as one works through the ranks and sees the breakdown of relationships between our constituents and police officers, both on the beat and in the station. I am glad that we have a good relationship with Sir Peter, but I am far more concerned about the relationship between my constituents and other Londoners and the ordinary police officers. Much needs to be done to improve that relationship.

I thank the Home Secretary for his meetings with us. At least he meets us, and, although there is no great meetings of minds, we have useful exchanges.

A number of hon. Members have complained about the absence of their colleagues. I shall certainly be sending a note to my Members in the London group pointing out that I should have expected to see rather more of them. [*Interruption.*] I cannot be responsible for Conservative Members, who are not here either but, unlike Conservative Members, I do not want to make cheap party-political points. I shall save those for later.

Many hon. Members do not regard our debates on policing London as quite the useful occasions that they ought to be. There is no great exchange of views but, merely a series of speeches. We have had an opener from the Home Secretary, and the Parliamentary Under-Secretary of State for the Home Department will do some fielding and no doubt introduce his own bit of party-political venom, as he always does. There will be a lot of heat but not a great deal of light.

That is not the way to achieve accountability or a proper working relationship between Members of Parliament and the Metropolitan police. The Opposition want accountable police authorities set up in London on which elected members—MPs and local councillors—can debate and discuss and set police priorities on behalf of those whom they represent. We do not want them to control the day-to-day operations of the Metropolitan police—that is one of the grotesque caricatures that Conservative Members have drawn of our proposals for the public accountability of the police in London. We want to set police priorities, to serve the community and to allow the community through its elected representatives —with the ballot box as the arbiter—to decide exactly what should be done.

**Mr. Hurd:** The hon. Member for Newham, North-West (Mr. Banks) is contributing to a long-standing debate. He must understand that his proposal—that elected authorities should set priorities for the police—goes well beyond anything in the Police Act 1964 and well beyond the powers available to police authorities outside the capital. The hon. Gentleman seems to advocate entrusting to local authorites—to police authorities or politicians—the setting of priorities, as between public order and the policing of the right to work, for example. That amounts to domination by politicians of the operational priorities of the police, and that is a proposition that we must contest.

**Mr. Banks:** I know that there will be no agreement between us on that point. The law will be there to be enforced by the police, no matter what the law happens to be. Of course the law will be much more enlightened under a Labour Government than it is under the Conservative Administration, whose divisive, controversial and essentially anti-union laws project the police into political situations. That is one highly contentious matter. Under a Labour Government those divisive laws will not be there to put the police into situations in which they cannot win. I do not like to use this expression, because I am a vegetarian, but at present the police are very much the meat in the sandwich. They do not like that, and no responsible politican would want to impose that burden on them.

There is no reason why we should be frightened of police accountability and the setting of police priorities. The police are there to serve the community and they must be directly answerable to the community. They are not a law unto themselves. One of our great problems— especially with the Metropolitan police—is that they so often seem to be, and act as though they are, a law unto themselves. That is not acceptable to Londoners and it should not be acceptable to Members of Parliament.

The knee-jerk reaction from Conservative Members is that all police officers are wonderful and that there should be no hint of criticism. If Opposition Members say anything even mildly critical, however constructive, we are denounced as being anti-police. That grotesque caricature of our position does not serve the interests of democracy or policing.

I want the police to support the community and to have the support of the community, which is essential. I challenge any Conservative Member who talks about Labour being anti-police, because we are not. We are far more pro-police than Conservative Members are. We would give the police the necessary resources to carry out the policing priorities that we set. We are pro-police because the constituencies we represent in London are largely the areas of the greatest social and economic deprivation. We have far more of the problems on the streets, so we suport the police, but we want to ensure that the police support us.

**Mr. John Marshall** (Hendon, South): Can the hon. Gentleman tell me why, if his party is so pro-police, several Labour-controlled local authorities do not co-operate with neighbourhood watch schemes and do not encourage the police to talk to school children?

**Mr. Banks:** If the hon. Gentleman had been here a little earlier he would have heard some of those points made. Since he makes the same tedious point, which is based far more on his imagination than the truth, I must point out to him that the experience around London of the relationships between the boroughs and the local police differs markedly. Some boroughs have good working relationships whereas others do not. However, the political complexion of the boroughs where there are good relationships can be identical with those where there are bad relationships. It is not a matter of Left and Right, but of the way the police operate. The hon. Gentleman always presents the matter as if it were the fault of councillors and as if they were anti-police. He knows little about the relationships between the local authorities and the police in certain areas of London where relationships have regrettably broken down. It takes two to tango. Those democratically elected local authorities have taken decisions on their experiences. I suspect that the hon. Gentleman is speaking, as ever, far more from ignorance than knowledge. I will give way to a knowledgeable Member.

**Mr. Cohen:** My hon. Friend makes the case for accountability. The Home Secretary has now left the Chamber. As well as being scathing about Labour's policy for improved public accountability for the police, he claimed that Labour wanted to interfere with the operational requirements of the police. Will my hon. Friend confirm that that is no part of Labour policy?

The Home Secretary also implied that Conservatives do not interfere with the operational aspects of policing. Will my hon. Friend cast his mind back to the miners' strike, when we saw the police suddenly adopt a range of powers that they had not used for years, including harassing people collecting for the strikers? Was that not Conservative interference with the operational aspects of policing?

**Mr. Banks:** My hon. Friend is absolutely right. I made the point earlier that through certain pieces of legislation the Government have put the police into a high profile political position. I might add that some police officers have applied themselves to the task with far more enthusiasm than is seemly. They should beware. If they are seen to be over-enthusiastic in the way they apply partisan and divisive legislation, they will further erode the confidence of Londoners in their ability to act impartially, as they should, to enforce the law. However, police officers would do far better to say on certain areas of law that for them to enforce such a law would only lead to more trouble than letting that law go by. I expect police officers

[*Mr. Banks*]

to be able to make such judgments to the Home Secretary, but I suspect that if some did so, the Home Secretary would denounce them as being political.

**Mr. Corbyn:** Earlier, the Home Secretary said that he had a hands-off approach to the running of the police force and it was a matter for the police to carry out their policing duties. However, as my hon. Friend the Member for Leyton (Mr. Cohen) pointed out, during the miners' strike there was the greatest interference in policing and police tactics.

During the printers' dispute at Wapping there were daily statements from Ministers and from Tory Members saying what the police should be doing and encouraging them. Subsequently, Northampton police were asked to undertake an inquiry into the events at Wapping in January 1987, and as a result a number of officers have been suspended. We are still awaiting a statement about what charges will be brought and about the future of the officers involved. If there is to be any confidence in the Metropolitan police, there needs to be a clear statement of exactly what will happen to the officers involved in the disgraceful incidents at Wapping.

**Mr. Banks:** I agree with my hon. Friend. That case is another example demonstrating that the laws that the police have to enforce are socially divisive. I pay tribute to the Northampton police and Chief Superintendent Wyrko, who did a great deal of work and faced a great deal of obstruction from within the Metropolitan police in conducting his investigations.

I suspect that a cover up is going on and that there will be a whitewash. They are waiting and delaying for long enough so that the rules of evidence would point to there being no fair trial for any officers that are being accused. That is what is happening. We know precisely that that is the way in which the Government are trying to angle it. Where they are able to apply subtle pressures, no doubt they will do so. They cannot afford to allow the police officers who acted so brutally to be brought to account as that would cast doubts on the impartiality of the Metropolitan police and their actions at Wapping. It would throw into sharp relief the unpleasant nature of the legislation that involved the police in the first place and allowed people like Murdoch to sack so many good print workers and hard-working people who made a great deal of profit for that nasty little man.

I have to make progress as a number of Conservative Members still wish to speak. Turning to accountability, if we had a Grand Committee for London or a police committee sitting on a regular basis, we would not have to rely on this inadequate way of debating issues in a non-conclusive fashion. We would be able to talk to police officers and cross-examine the Home Secretary, and that would be far more satisfactory. It would not meet all the points that Labour Members have made about accountability, but it would be far better than the wholly inadequate system that operates at present.

The 9 per cent. increase in sexual crimes and sexual violence is wholly unacceptable. Although the police are handling such matters in a more sensitive manner, I suspect that they are still under-recording the incidence of sexual violence which is predominantly and overwhelmingly against women.

Crime on the Underground is getting worse. It is linked to lack of investment by the Department of Transport and by London Regional Transport in the Underground and bus services, as anyone who travels regularly around London will know.

Life in London today is more brutal and violent than it has been for many years. The social values of our society give the lead to that increasing brutality. I made the same point last Friday on the subject of litter, as these issues are linked. When the Government's philosophy is largely predicated on personal greed and selfishness, there must be a causal link between that philosophy and increasing crime, violence and brutality in our society. I blame Tory philosophy for the increasing incidence of violence in London. Public property is treated with contempt by the Conservative Government, who believe that private property is sacred but public property can be treated with contempt and abused. It is sold off or allowed to run down. That attitude spreads its disturbing way through society like an infection. People do not regard public property as theirs, because they are not encouraged to do so. They are taught by the Government, and particularly by the Prime Minister, that what is public is not good and what is private is sacred. The sense of community in London, as elsewhere, has been sorely damaged by the economic and social policies of this unpleasant and divisive Government.

The hon. Member for Uxbridge said that he did not welcome the idea of private roads and police forces, but that is inevitably the way that we will go. He might not like the idea, but I assure him that many Conservative Members do like the idea of private roads that can be shut off. Of course, those roads will be in the nicest areas and those in which the wealthiest people can afford private security guards. That is what is happening in the United States now. If hon. Members want to see what it will be like in this country in 10 years' time I suggest that they visit the United States.

The Opposition want proper policing and more resources for the police, but we want to ensure that the priorities of the police accord with the priorities of the communities that we serve. That is why, when we talk about setting police priorities, we do not mean interference with their day-to-day operational running; we mean "These are the things that you must do, but, when we will the ends, we must then will the means." My hon. Friend the Member for Huddersfield (Mr. Sheerman) will be there in the Home Office as a Minister, so he will agree that a Labour Government would ensure that the police in London have the necessary resources to meet our demands on them on behalf of the people whom we represent.

I hope that the Minister will say something about the alarming growth in civil damages paid out by the Metropolitan police in cases where police officers have been accused of ill discipline or malpractice, and the police decide to pay out rather than have the matter go to court. That strikes me as being sinister. I know that the Minister is a lawyer and, no doubt, he will tell me that the rules of evidence in civil cases are far less demanding than those in criminal cases. That may be so, but the Metropolitan police would hardly hand out hundreds of thousands of pounds to those who make complaints against the police if senior police officers and the authorities concerned did not believe that there was more than a substance of truth in the complaint.

We want to know why the amount paid in civil damages has risen so much in recent years. We also want to know what happens to the police officers after those damages are paid. It is outrageous that London ratepayers have had to shell out hundreds of thousands of pounds in civil damages for complaints against police officers, but in the end those police officers are left serving on the patches from where the complaints originated. It undermines confidence in the police to know that there is a growing number of bent coppers in the force. That is not something that one says with any great enthusiasm or pleasure, because if the confidence between the police and the community is eroded, that will damage all of us. If bent coppers are allowed to remain in the force, good policemen will also be damaged.

I would ask the Minister to comment on the Metropolitan police and the poll tax. Next year the poll tax will be introduced, but all the Home Office and the Metropolitan police receiver have said is that a set amount of the poll tax will go to the Metropolitan police. Local authorities have asked for full estimates to enable them to plan ahead, but they have not yet been given them. There could be two reasons for that. The first is that Whitehall and the police receiver have not yet got their act together and worked out the necessary sums. The second is that they might have worked out their sums, but they are keeping the figures quiet. The Government are far too frightened to release them, because of the increased costs that they will clearly impose on the London boroughs.

My borough has estimated that Newham will find that its contribution will rise from £6·4 million to more than £10 million, or perhaps as much as £12 million, for its contribution to the Metropolitan police. We demand the right to know those figures today.

I have already said that Newham has the highest police recorded level of racial attacks in London. I deeply regret to say that one in eight London incidents occur in Newham. The problem with racial attacks, as with sexual offences, is non-reporting. We estimate that, in Newham, only one in 20 incidents are reported to the police. In that context it is important to consider the quality of the police response. From 1985 to 1988 arrest rates in Newham have fallen by half and that clearly suggests why people under-report racial harassment incidents. In 1985 an arrest took place once in every eight police-reported incidents; in 1988 it had fallen to one in every 17.

I acknowledge and pay tribute to the improvements that have been made. In north Plaistow we have the country's only action project, but more resources should be made available to the police in Newham so that they can deal with this worrying and disturbing increase in racial harassment.

**Mr. Cohen:** Is my hon. Friend aware that two years ago the police undertook a pilot project in Redbridge? It lasted for six weeks and the police issued lots of extremely good leaflets about racial attacks and the need to report them. The police had a good response and the pilot project was successful. The police showed themselves to be active in the fight against racial attacks. Does my hon. Friend have any idea why that pilot project was not put into action on a permanent basis in the East End and in other areas where racial attacks are a serious problem?

**Mr. Banks:** Were I Home Secretary I might be able to answer that question, but the Minister heard it and I hope that he will respond to it later.

We need a greater commitment from the Government through action and resources rather than through words. More resources would deal with the upsurge in racial harassment in the East End.

The safer cities initiative, which is part of the action for cities programme, is aimed at crime prevention. My council applied to be one of the areas to take part in that initiative, but it recently learnt that it has not been chosen. Newham has a higher than average crime rate, one of the largest ethnic minority populations in the country and the highest incidence of racial harassment in the country. My council has a proven track record of working with the police, the Home Office and local groups to eliminate crime. Why was my council bounced? Why was it not included in the safer cities project? My council could not have been rejected because it does not work closely with the police and the community. I have already described the economic and social deprivation of my borough and the crime level. What do we need to do to prove that we have a right to get those additional resources through the safer cities initiative?

This debate has at least enabled us to raise some interesting points, but, frankly, it is not satisfactory. The Metropolitan police should be far more accountable and, if that accountability is to be through the Home Secretary alone, it is up to us here to improve the way in which it operates. A police committee in the House would not truly satisfy us, because we want proper police committees in London along the lines that I have described. I would settle for a police committee of the House, however, as the sparse attendance on both sides of the House suggests not the House's satisfaction with the Metropolitan police and the annual report, but our dissatisfaction with the wholly inadequate way in which Parliament attempts to exercise some form of accountability, through the Home Secretary, for the Metropolitan police.

1.23 pm

**Mr. Ivor Stanbrook** (Orpington): The Home Secretary was wise not to display any complacency when he talked about the crime statistics. During the past two years the overall figures may have decreased, but violent offences are still increasing—by 19 per cent. this year, I believe. Every Londoner knows that we are nowhere near getting crime and lawlessness under control. The situation is absolutely appalling. The rate of street crime, such as stealing and breaking into vehicles, is terrifying in some parts of London. Burglary is still rampant and, in addition to crimes of violence, drug misuse and drug-related crime are increasing. We are about to suffer an appalling epidemic of drug misuse due to the consumption of crack. Police resources are inadequate to deal with the problem, which will take up much police time and resources to the detriment of their other work. For London alone, we can do much more by providing more resources and more policemen on the streets. Given the scale of crime, lawlessness and the need for enforcement of law and order and public order in London, we must have more than the current 28,000 police officers. We need at least 38,000, and perhaps 48,000, police officers to look after us in London.

The current organisation of police in London could be improved. I do not understand why so many minor police forces within the Metropolitan police area are not under the operational control of the commissioner. Why should there be a separate police force for the Underground? We

[*Mr. Ivor Stanbrook*]

are all aware that it is a source of crime. To the detriment of the Metropolitan police, the Home Secretary has arranged extra officers for London Transport police. We know that the scale and fear of crime are increasing on the Underground, and it is a public disgrace that the problem is as bad as it is. There should be sufficient officers to provide at least one policeman for each Underground station in London. Why on earth are London Transport police so undermanned, and why on earth does the commissioner not have operational control? Surely the commissioner is in the best position to react tactically to day-to-day demands. Why are the Royal Parks police not under the control of the commissioner? We must consider these problems and give the commissioner greater operational control, and preferably structural control.

As a large number of hon. Members have said, Londoners are fortunate to have a police force of such quality, efficiency and integrity. The Metropolitan police are extremely well led and a high proportion of their senior ranks are well-motivated officers who are dedicated to public service. It is little wonder that they provide recruits to senior posts in provincial forces. No matter how many police officers we recruit, however, and no matter the size of the force in London, we can touch only the surface of the social malaise. The lack of respect for other people, for public or private property and for authority lies at the root of our problems. If only we could change attitudes by increasing the number of police officers in London, and if only we could instill a sense of esteem among young people who misuse drugs.

Perhaps it is not surprising that attitudes are determined not by the police or the law but by people in authority and influence, who should and could set a better example. It is no wonder that poorer people imitate people in the City, who so easily, and with so little respect for others, acquire fortunes in an afternoon and so easily buy and sell firms without regard for their employees. When the Church spends so much of its time on its own domestic problems, such as the ordination of women, and when priests use their pulpits as political platforms, it is no wonder that so many people are confused about their moral duties.

The local environment is dirty and the streets in many London boroughs are strewn with rubbish. Anyone who, like me, has a constituency in south-east London and has to drive through Peckham and Lewisham is appalled by the rubbish that lies on the streets all the time, not just after a market. It must be infinitely depressing to live in such an environment.

**Mr. Sheerman:** I have enjoyed listening to many of the hon. Gentleman's remarks, and I agree with some. I hope that he is not being too politically partisan. When I am in London I live in the City and the squalor in some parts is appalling. During the Euro-elections, I spent some time in the Ilford area. I agree that there is appalling rubbish, litter and urban decay. I hope that the hon. Gentleman accepts that this is a universal problem and not one based on the political complexion of the area through which he drives.

**Mr. Stanbrook:** I am sorry that the hon. Gentleman has introduced the element of politican partisanship into the debate. I am not talking about political parties, nor am I talking about any party that is in control in a particular

area. There are London boroughs that neglect the public collection of refuse and allow their streets to be filthy. They may be controlled by different political parties. I know of areas in Westminster that suffer from this disease. I mentioned the route from central London to south-east London because that happens to be the one I take to my constituency. One passes through two boroughs. Although they spend money on things that I do not regard as essential services, they are content to allow their citizens to live, work and travel in squalor. It is a comparatively easy, efficient and cheap exercise to keep the rubbish off their streets. Enforcement of the law in this respect is important in giving assistance to the police.

The police alone should not be responsible for enforcement of the law. They need the backing of the public and of councils. It has been said that some councils —I shall not say which political party dominates them —refuse to give police officers permission to enter schools to speak to children. It is desirable for the police to visit schools. Every school should have a police officer, preferably the local home beat officer, who drops in from time to time to take part in school activities and have chats with the children. Those authorities that refuse permission should be ashamed of themselves for not co-operating with the efforts of the police to produce a law-abiding society.

There should also be an improvement in the efforts of individuals. It should be a duty, especially for wealthy and powerful individuals, to set an example. It is disgraceful that Sir Terence Conran, a wealthy, apparently proud and arrogant man, has recently announced that his Storehouse group of firms will open on Sundays, in contravention of the Shops Act 1950. Not everyone agrees with that legislation—there have been debates in the Chamber and elsewhere about how we should amend the law—but it nevertheless remains the law. If Sir Terence Conran arranges for his shops to open, thereby deliberately setting out to break the law, not only is he setting a bad example to young people and other people who have less power and wealth than he has, but he deserves to be sent to prison until he learns to respect the law. It is disgraceful that Sir Terence Conran or anyone else, through the firms that they control, should contravene the law and encourage others to do so. How on earth can they expect humble people to respect the law and not commit petty offences when the rich and the powerful get away with it scot free?

We need more policemen in London and we need more resources. The present allocation is not adequate. Much more must be done if Londoners are to be reassured and provided with the regime of law and order that the capital deserves. Above all, we need more discipline in society, more respect for the law and more determination on the part of politicians like us and other responsible citizens to enforce the law. Only then and by giving the police the moral backing that they deserve shall we begin to redress the balance.

1.35 pm

**Mr. Harry Cohen** (Leyton): On 16 February last year the Home Secretary, in a Written Answer gave the figure for the net revenue expenditure of the Metropolitan police in 1988-89 as £1,000,004,967. For the first time, the expenditure exceeded £1 billion. Obviously, the figure will have increased substantially this year. A great deal of that burden is placed on local authorities. Their ratepayers— and in future their poll tax payers—will have to fund that sum, but they have no democratic say. I shall not repeat the detailed arguments made by my colleagues today. However, there should be a democratic, London-wide police authority. The Home Secretary cannot be accountable, as he is not even a London Member of Parliament.

This is an unsatisfactory forum in which to debate the various issues relating to police and policing in London. Speeches in this debate must include various different issues. The hon. Member for Uxbridge (Mr. Shersby), who spoke as the paid representative of the Police Federation, does not have sole claim to speak on behalf of police interests or for the protection of the police.

I want to raise a point that the hon. Member for Uxbridge did not mention. We must consider prisoners and people in police cells who might be suffering from AIDS or HIV. That is a serious problems for the police. At the moment, the police have responsibilities, but those are of a general nature. The police general orders refer to people who require medical assistance and it sets out the responsibilities and duties of police to obtain medical treatment for people brought into police stations and those already detained. Often it may not be apparent that a prisoner is suffering from an illness. Some prisoners may try to conceal their illness or they may not be aware of their condition.

Often prisoners are admitted to the Brixton prison medical wing so that extremely sick prisoners are not detained for long periods in police or court cells. However, HIV sufferers are often not considered to be extremely urgent cases. There is insufficient accommodation in prison medical wings, and prisoners are often detained in police cells, which is a problem for local police forces.

To minimise risks to police officers, there should be a high standard of hygiene in cells. According to a report that was published this week, many problems in police stations clearly reflect the lack of hygiene. The Home Secretary should institute a major programme to improve the hygiene of police cells and to give proper advice to police officers. In spite of the precautions that are taken, each year many police officers seek medical advice after contact with infected prisoners who have bitten or scratched them or pricked them with needles. There appears to be a lack of action on the part of the Home Office to produce clear regulations on treatment for AIDS prisoners and to issue guidelines to the police to establish effective training for officers and assistance for officers who contract AIDS. That important issue has not been discussed in the debate. The Home Office is also ignoring its own health officers' advice on taking effective action to stop the spread of AIDS in prisons. The same criticism applies to police cells. Police officers are at risk, and the Government are responsible.

The Police Federation has expressed concern about burglaries. That matter was not referred to by the hon. Member for Uxbridge, who is the Police Federation's representative. A recent report in "The Job" the Metropolitan police newspaper, pointed out that the police are upset about the Government's policy on burglary cases. The Director of Public Prosecutions is reluctant to prosecute burglary cases, even when the intruder's fingerprints are discovered, saying that they are not sufficient evidence. I agree that it would be difficult to rely on the fingerprints of a member of the family or a friend who visits regularly, but the fingerprints of an intruder into a burgled home are clear evidence and should

be used in court. The DPP should not make that claim about insufficient evidence as a reason why a burglary case is not taken to court. I have written a strong letter to the Attorney-General backing the Police Federation on this important matter and I hope to see some strong action by the Government.

**Ms. Diane Abbott** (Hackney, North and Stoke Newington): Will my hon. Friend join with me in congratulating our hon. Friend the Member for Islington, North (Mr. Corbyn) on his occupation of the Opposition Front Bench and hope that his tenure there will be long and happy?

In the run-up to the Notting Hill carnival, will my hon. Friend the Member for Leyton (Mr. Cohen) join with me in hoping that we have a crime-free, constructively policed carnival? Nobody wants crime and disorder at the carnival. The police have a role to play. Will my hon. Friend join with me in congratulating Mr. Frank Critchlow of the Mangrove association, who was recently acquitted of several charges? I hope that the Metropolitan police are as committed as Opposition Members are to keeping the Notting Hill carnival on the streets as a crime-free, happy and community-based event.

**Mr. Cohen:** I echo every one of my hon. Friend's words. The Notting Hill carnival is a great spectacle for Londoners. I also want it to continue to be successful and crime-free. I echo also my hon. Friend's comments about my hon. Friend the Member for Islington, North (Mr. Corbyn). It was a timely intervention.

I shall mention racial harassment, although I do not wish to make a detailed speech on it. The House will know that I introduced the first and only Bill relating to racial harassment—my Racial Harassment Bill. The majority of measures in that Bill must be implemented if we are effectively to tackle racial harassment. However, I shall leave my speech on that for another day. The Government should have a debate on that subject, because they have published their own proposals on it.

In this debate we should have answers from the Home Secretary about the debacle involving Saatchi and Saatchi and the £35,000 worth of leaflets which went down the drain. What steps have ben taken to recoup that public money and, even more important, to re-publish the leaflets and have them properly distributed? Perhaps local authorities should be invited to tender for distribution of the leaflets, because they could obviously do a better job than a private company such as Saatchi and Saatchi.

There is a tendency for police action against racial harassment to slip down the list of priorities. The Home Office must bring legislation before the House to make racial attacks and harassment specific criminal offences. Until they do so, the ability of the police to take action is hampered.

I should like an answer from the Home Secretary about the recruitment procedure of the police force and whether the ethnic minority receives equal treatment. An article in *The Independent* on 24 April stated:

"The Home Office has refused to alter a police entrance test which is known to discriminate against blacks. 70 per cent. of white applicants in London sitting the Police Initial Recruitment Test are successful, but the ethnic minority applicants have only a 40 per cent. pass rate. The principal employment officer of the Commission for Racial Equality says the test relies on the literary ability of candidates and

[*Mr. Cohen*]

requires a knowledge of English phraseology which is not so understandable to those who have not been fully educated in this country.

A Home Office spokesman, admitting that the test is biased, said it would cost £170,000 to replace it but that the money wasn't available this year."

We are talking about a budget of well over £1 billion, but the Home Office will not get rid of the test and institute a fairer one because it would cost £170,000. Clearly, the Home Office does not want equality in recruitment practices if it cannot come up with such a paltry sum. I want an answer on that point.

I raised with the Home Office the matter, of the lay visitors scheme. Waltham Forest lay visitors' panel made a number of points in its recent report which I forwarded to the Home Secretary. It talked about conditions in police stations, and said that all stations had only one wash basin for detainees. It is vital to improve hygiene standards. The panel also talked about the lack of privacy, particularly for the occasional female detainee, and hoped that the Home Office would take steps to give such prisoners the facilities to wash privately.

The panel said that Leyton police station facilities were inadequate for longer stay prisoners. Leyton divisional chief superintendent sought approval from the Home Office for the provision of a shower which, in the circumstances, should have been given immediately. It also said that there were insufficient grounds and that steps should be taken to secure an area of the station grounds so that prisoners could take outside exercise. The panel also talked about the absence of in-house food and drink facilities, particularly when people were detained in cells after 9 pm.

The response by the Home Office when I raised these points about exercise and washing facilities was:

"The Prison Service have made funds available to provide the most essential facilities, such as access to toilet and washing facilities, at stations holding Home Office prisoners. However, only limited funds are available and have to be used where the need is greatest."

Those limited funds amount to £50,000 per year, which is a pittance given the increasing need for hygiene in prison cells. The Home Office Minister must increase that amount enormously and immediately——

**The Parliamentary Under-Secretary of State for the Home Department (Mr. Douglas Hogg):** The hon. Gentleman has been talking about prisoners in police cells. He will be pleased to know that there were only 26 such prisoners in the Metropolitan area yesterday.

**Mr. Cohen:** I am pleased to know that, but we are used to that sort of information on the day before a police debate in the House. At other times the figure shoots up to well over 200. Nevertheless, I welcome the information and hope that there will be only 26 a day, a week and a year after the police debate—but somehow I doubt it.

The lay visitors also mention duty solicitors' attendance. Many people in cells do not get the chance to speak to a duty solicitor, and sometimes solicitors will deal with cases only over the telephone, which is unsatisfactory. The Home Office view is:

"the Legal Aid Office would be interested to know of any instances".

That is not good enough. The lay visitors panel has clearly identified this problem and the Home Office should tackle it.

Lay visitors are not informed of the outcome of complaints against police officers. That must be wrong, as they can then do nothing to rectify the problems. I hope that they will be notified of the outcome of such investigations in future.

The lay visitors complain about interpreting services for alleged illegal immigrants detained in cells. The visitors do not have interpreters and there is no legal requirement for the services of lay visitors to be extended to detainees of this sort. The Home Office response to this has been less than adequate—from a budget of £1 billion it will not provide the money for interpreters for lay visitors.

The debate so far has been largely devoid of statistics, which the House needs. The Prime Minister came to power pledged to restore law and order as a fact and as a concept, but her failure has been startling. Crime has undermined the standard of living of affluent Londoners. Overall, crime in London increased by 29 per cent. between 1979 and 1988 and violent offences rose by two thirds in the same period. Robberies almost trebled. There were 1,196 notified drug addicts in the capital in 1978; last year there were 3,230, and we know that the true number is between five and 10 times greater.

I want to record reported notifiable offences in London. In 1979 there were 16,194 violent offences, and in 1988 there were 27,215—an increase of 68 per cent. In 1979, 2,751 sexual offences were notified and in 1988, 4,071—an increase of 48 per cent. The figure for burglaries went up from 119,366 to 143,721—an increase of 20 per cent. Furthermore, in my constituency the clear-up rate for burglary has fallen to about 10 per cent. and the figure across London is similar. The figure for robberies went up from 6,275 to 17,929—an increase of 186 per cent. The figure for theft went up from 321,047 to 375,602—an increase of 17 per cent. The figure for fraud and forgery went up from 26,361 to 30,279—an increase of 15 per cent. The figure for criminal damage went up from 71,651 to 121,505—an increase of 70 per cent. The figure for other offences increased from 542 to 5,702—an increase of 952 per cent.

In total, the number of notifiable crimes went up from 564,187 in 1979 to 726,024 in 1988—an increase of 29 per cent. So much for restoring law and order as a fact and as a concept. The Government have a miserable criminal record, and we should get rid of them so that we can tackle crime in London and elsewhere.

1.56 pm

**Mr. Jeremy Hanley** (Richmond and Barnes): The hon. Member for Newham, North-West (Mr. Banks) criticised Conservative Members because only a few of us are present, although we well outnumber the Labour Members who are present. One reason for absences is that if Labour Members make speeches of 41, 26, 24 and 25 minutes, Conservative Members do not get a chance to contribute. I hope that in future speeches will be shorter and more to the point.

**Mr. Deputy Speaker (Mr. Harold Walker):** Order. Hon. Members from both sides of the House have made lengthy speeches.

**Mr. Hanley:** Thank you for pointing that out, Mr. Deputy Speaker. The point is that speeches from both sides of the House have been lengthy. I hope that in future debates all hon. Members will have an opportunity to take part.

Like all other hon. Members who have spoken, I represent a London constituency, and my constituents look to the Metropolitan police for their protection. Apart from two isolated cases in the past year, the relationship between my constituents and the police has been happy. There can hardly be any closer or more harmonious relationship in a London borough than that in Richmond upon Thames, with regular co-operation on crime prevention and safety for the elderly, the education of children, the maintenance of traffic control and support, financial and spiritual, to the victims of crime.

I was pleased to work with my hon. Friend the Member for Westminster, North (Mr. Wheeler) on the Select Committee on Home Affairs, which looked into the way in which society deals with the victims of crime. The victim support scheme movement largely grew from that. I pay great tribute to the victim support scheme in Richmond, which gave evidence to the Committee, and I thank my right hon. Friend the Home Secretary for his support of such schemes through the Home Office.

My knowledge of the Metropolitan police began when I was under four. I remember seeing my father, Jimmy Hanley, in a police uniform one evening. This was not because he had signed up but because he was making a well-known film, "The Blue Lamp", with the late Jack Warner, who was playing PC Dixon. Only twice in our history has somebody risen from the grave, and one of them was Jack Warner. He came back from the dead and was even promoted to sergeant in the television programme.

Many people ridicule the cosy, "Evening, all" attitude that the police were meant to have in those days, but that attitude showed how people trusted, liked and knew the local policeman and it is popular still today. Many people would like us to return to the times when the local bobby on the beat was a normal part of everyday life.

I am pleased to note that Sir Peter Imbert's excellent report for this year shows that street duty increased by 9 per cent. in 1988. That happened largely in response to public demand. Street duty enables communities to see the police and to see that, far from being remote, they are friendly individuals whose sole purpose is to protect their local community. Street duty is good for the police and good for the public, and I hope that the increase will be repeated in years ahead. The courtesy, kindness and good humour of the local bobby on the beat are something that we want to see much more in future. We should get the police out of the Panda cars, which resemble armoured cars shooting through the streets of Londonderry. That approach may be necessary in some contexts, but in London the human relationships that go with local beat police are most important, especially in encouraging good race relations.

It cannot be a complete coincidence that burglaries have fallen by 5 per cent. this year and the clear-up rate for residential burglaries has risen by 12 per cent. Even street robbery is down by 10 per cent. The presence of beat police must be partly responsible for that figure, with co-operation by local residents—which is further encouraged by good relationships with the police—also playing its part.

I fully accept what my hon. Friend the Member for Beckenham (Sir P. Goodhart) said about parking, and I agree with the comments of my hon. Friend the Member for Uxbridge (Mr. Shersby). We need more wardens to police the streets of outer London and if they could keep a share of their resources, they would have a further incentive and people would be more readily deterred from parking in antisocial and dangerous places in the streets of outer London.

Sir Peter said in his report that there hardly has to be an incident in Amritsar or Teheran or an election in El Salvador for thousands of people to take to the streets of London. Freedom of speech and the right to protest are part of our tradition, but demonstrations clog traffic and threaten—sometimes violently—innocent citizens going about their business. They can cause great disturbance and damage and they are extremely costly. I would ask those considering demonstrations to exercise self-control and to remember that their demonstration is likely to have little effect. I also ask for self-control from the media, which often attract attention to such events and make them grow in size.

In the previous Parliament I served on the Select Committee on Home Affairs and its race relations and immigration sub-committee. I attended many police courses and visited police stations to see how the police try to teach policemen at all levels awareness of the different races and cultures in our community. I addressed a conference in Manchester attended by senior police officers and I was most impressed by the care that they were taking in this matter. The racial minorities must understand what their civil rights are. It does not help matters if they believe that the police are automatically against them. Often, it is not so much the police who are responsible but the fact that the racial minorities have not been trained, as they should be, to realise what their civil and criminal rights are, or the duties of the police and the restrictions on them in dealing with civil matters. We should all help to inform the racial minorities of their rights. The police are now recognising their responsibilities in this regard, and the dramatic increase in the clear-up rate for racial crimes shows their determination.

I thoroughly agree with my hon. Friend the Member for Orpington (Mr. Stanbrook) about the London Transport police. Their independence of the Metropolitan police is an anachronism. Time dictates that I cannot expand on this matter, although I feel very strongly about it.

I pay tribute to the 1,143 specials in London, who give up much of their time. Last year, they underwent nearly 50,000 hours of training and put in nearly 250,000 hours of duty, with good humour and patience. I hope that the force will grow and that younger people will join as special cadets.

The police are being most unfairly criticised for deaths following car chases. No policeman in a car chases another car merely for fun or because the police started the chase. The chase starts because somebody has stolen a car or is suspected of having committed a criminal act. The public must support the police, who are properly trained and can avoid accidents better than the person who is trying to sprint ahead in the car in front. We should properly criticise those who cause the car chases and support the police in their efforts to protect us from individuals who have committed crimes.

We should all support the police a great deal more. In the past year, there were 5,294 complaints against the Metropolitan police, which is a reduction of 8 per cent.

[*Mr. Hanley*]

Some might think that appreciation was not readily expressed, but there were 6,278 letters of appreciation last year, an increase of 11 per cent. I am pleased that that has occurred under the stewardship of Sir Peter Imbert, to whom I could not pay greater tribute. I hope that we shall see continued good progress in the Metropolitan police and a continued excellent relationship with the people of London.

2.5 pm

**Mr. Sheerman:** By leave of the House, I shall have a second bite of the cherry and reflect quickly on the debate. We have had an interesting and constructive debate. Labour Members have framed their remarks in a constructive spirit. However frustrating, this is our one opportunity to call the Home Secretary to account in his role as the person responsible for the Metropolitan police. As many of my hon. Friends have said, it is a weak weapon of scrutiny. When we have a Labour Government after the next election, we shall move to a properly democratically accountable police authority for London.

The Home Secretary trailed many red herrings today. I remind him that we do not propose a body that would interfere with the day-to-day operational aspects of police work, as he knows well. We have made some strong suggestions about what we want to see happen and there have been some positive comments from Members of various parties. Looking to the future, I see two problems that have been expressed today only in a minor voice; I am surprised that hon. Members have not stressed those problems more.

First, there should be more emphasis on dealing with the young. I know that I tend to go on about this, but we must achieve the right responses to young offenders, not only in terms of catching them, although that is part of the process, but in deterring them in the first place and in giving them creative alternatives, which largely do not seem to exist in London at present.

The second issue that will dominate police work in the next few years, to which we shall come back more strongly this year and next, is the vulnerability of women in London and every other urban centre. Although we agree that the burglary figures and those for other crimes against property look a bit better than they did for the previous year, the figures for crimes of violence, crimes of violence against women and sexual violence against women are horrific. As my hon. Friend the Member for Newham, North-West (Mr. Banks) said, there has been a 9 per cent. increase in the most recent year. It is a disgrace that 50 per cent. of women in this city believe that they should not go out after dark. That comment is not based on only one piece of evidence. One piece of evidence after another shows that women feel unsafe walking down badly lit streets, and on London buses and the Underground at night. If women are afraid to go about their legitimate business to such an extent, the Metropolitan police, with the Government's backing, must protect women in a way that they do not protect them at present.

We have not talked much about the causes of crime, because we have tried not to be too party political today, but I must conclude by saying that policing is difficult enough in a society with a strong community that backs the police and in which people treat society as a priority.

However, in a selfish, individualistic society which has had the imprint of the Prime Minister for several years—it is a fact that the Prime Minister admires such a society—there is a breakdown in community feeling. In a society from which community spirit has disappeared, the role of the police and their job become impossible.

If we are to make the Met work as we want it to work —it is a good police force and we are trying to make it better—it will need the backing of the community. We believe that that must be a democratic relationship, but it must also be the basis for co-operation and exchange.

2.10 pm

**The Parliamentary Under-Secretary of State for the Home Department (Mr. Douglas Hogg):** We have had an interesting and important debate, the tone of which suggests that there is an ever-increasing recognition among hon. Members and people outside the House that the Metropolitan police are becoming yet more effective in carrying out their policing functions within the capital. That is a correct analysis. My right hon. Friend the Home Secretary has mentioned some of the key crime figures. They bear repeating because they demonstrate the reasons for modest optimism.

The commissioner's report for 1988 shows that overall crime figures fell by about 2 per cent. and the figures for the 12 months ending March this year show an overall fall of 4 per cent. In a two-year period there has been a welcome reduction in recorded crime of 6 per cent. The reductions have been most acute in burglary. In the 12 months ending March this year there has been a fall of nearly 6 per cent., or 25,000, in recorded cases of burglary. I must inform the hon. Member for Leyton (Mr. Cohen) that there has been a significant improvement in the clear-up rate of burglaries. The improvement in the Metropolitan police area was 7 per cent. Those reductions in the volume of committed crime have the effect of freeing officers for more operational time on the streets.

I accept that the crime statistics reflect the anxiety about violent crime. However, there are signs of modest encouragement. For example, the number of homicides fell by 46—23 per cent.—and figures for street robbery in the 12 months to the end of March this year show a 3 per cent. reduction. There are also encouraging improvements in clear-up rates. In 1988 the clear-up rate for robbery rose by 7 per cent. and for violence against the person the clear-up rate rose by 27 per cent. Those are significant improvements which are due to a variety of factors. They arise from better deployment of resources, more effective police practices and, undoubtedly, crime prevention—to which I attach very high importance—and from a substantial improvement in the resources dedicated to police work in London as a result of Government policy. We should recognise that since 1979 expenditure in the Metropolitan police area has risen by almost 60 per cent. in real terms.

The Metropolitan force is now at its record strength. Its strength is up by 5,400 and the establishment has improved by 1,826. The House will know that in April my right hon. Friend approved a further 300 police officers and 150 civilians, together with a further 100 civilians, the purpose of whom was to speed up the process of civilianisation. For Opposition Members—most notably the hon. Member for Newham, North-West (Mr. Banks)—to pretend that a Labour Government would have increased the resources over and above that which the Conservative Government have provided is frankly ludicrous. The truth is that they probably would have cut the resources. In no sense would they have matched the increase that our good management has allowed.

The hon. Member for Newham, North-West mentioned the Underground, so I shall make a specific reference to it.

**Mr. Hanley:** Is it also true that when the Labour Government left office the Metropolitan police was 4,000 under strength?

**Ms. Abbott:** Crime was falling then.

**Mr. Hogg:** My hon. Friend has made an extremely important point. Crime was rising fast, and the most striking thing about 1979 was the wholesale demoralisation of the police force. Most notable was the fact that experienced police officers, especially around sergeant level, were leaving in droves, partly because they were grossly underpaid and partly because they did not like seeing, for example, Labour Cabinet Ministers standing on picket lines supporting those who rioted and abused the police force. Let us make that entirely plain, because I am now coming to the question of accountability.

**Mr. Corbyn:** What riots?

**Mr. Hogg:** The idea that the Labour party has changed its spots on this matter is a complete illusion.

**Mr. Corbyn:** What riots?

**Mr. Hogg:** Grunwick was a riot.

**Mr. Corbyn:** Will the hon. Gentleman give way?

**Mr. Hogg:** I am not proposing to give way.

The sight of Labour Cabinet Ministers standing on picket lines is profoundly unsatisfactory. That happened not only at Grunwick. We also saw the support of the Labour Front Bench on the miners' picket lines. That is the kind of party with which we are dealing.

**Mr. Corbyn:** Will the hon. Gentleman give way?

**Mr. Hogg:** No, I will not give way.

Hon. Members will appreciate why I approach this matter with a degree of scepticism.

**Mr. Corbyn:** Will the Minister give way?

**Mr. Hogg:** No, I will not give way to the hon. Gentleman. I should have thought that I had made that entirely plain—even by his standards.

**Mr. Corbyn:** Will the Minister give way?

**Mr. Deputy Speaker:** Order.

**Mr. Hogg:** I will return to the question of accountability.

**Mr. Corbyn:** On a point of order, Mr. Deputy Speaker. Is it in order for the Minister to describe Labour Cabinet Ministers in the last Government as being involved in a riot when he knows that that is not true? He has not stated which picket line they were on or admitted that none was arrested or charged with any offence. Is it in order for the Minister to mislead the House about Labour Cabinet Ministers?

**Mr. Deputy Speaker:** I have heard much that is highly provocative, but not yet out of order.

**Mr. Hogg:** Or for that matter, Mr. Deputy Speaker, inaccurate.

**Mr. Corbyn:** On a point of order, Mr. Deputy Speaker. The Minister has claimed that what he said was not inaccurate. In that case, he must state which Cabinet Ministers, which picket line, when, who was arrested and with what offence they were charged—otherwise, he is impugning the honour of former and current Members of the House.

**Mr. Hogg:** The hon. Gentleman is showing very partial recollection of the events. If he cannot recall what happened on the Grunwick picket lines he is guilty of extraordinary self-deception.

**Mr. Corbyn:** I was there.

**Mr. Hogg:** That has been a feature of——

**Hon. Members:** He was there.

**Mr. Hogg:** I had forgotten that or I did not know that.

**Mr. Corbyn:** Further to my earlier point of order, Mr. Deputy Speaker. In replying, the Minister has impugned the honour of Members of the House concerning events that happened during the lifetime of the last Labour Government. He has clearly claimed that Labour Cabinet Ministers were on a picket line and were arrested. Unless he can substantiate——

**Hon. Members:** Involved in a riot.

**Mr. Deputy Speaker:** Order.

**Mr. Corbyn:** I beg your pardon, Mr. Deputy Speaker. They were involved in a riot. I suggest that he is impugning the honour of former Cabinet Ministers and he is not prepared to substantiate his allegation. As he is not prepared to substantiate it, because he knows it not to be true, I suggest that he be invited to withdraw his comments.

**Mr. Deputy Speaker:** General criticisms made by one side of the House about the other are usual in here, and while discourteous and distasteful, they are not out of order. It is when hon. Members identify other particular hon. Members and reflect on their honour and integrity that it becomes a matter for the Chair. I do not believe that we have quite reached that point.

**Mr. Sheerman:** On a point of order, Mr. Deputy Speaker. We were having a constructive debate until the junior Minister got to his feet and he has reduced it to his customary level. With respect, Mr. Deputy Speaker, the Minister said that Privy Councillors were involved in a riot and he specifically mentioned one incident and one strike. He must withdraw——

**Mr. Deputy Speaker:** Order. I judge what must be withdrawn——

**Mr. Hogg** *rose*——

**Mr. Deputy Speaker:** Order. So far, the Minister has not identified the matter. In referring to a particular situation and to Privy Councillors he has not gone so far

[*Mr. Deputy Speaker*]

as to identify a particular individual Member of the House. When he does so, I shall feel an obligation to reproach him.

**Mr. Sheerman:** Further to that point of order, Mr. Deputy Speaker. Everyone knows that only five Ministers were involved.

**Mr. Hogg:** After that interesting exchange, during which Opposition Members did not cover themselves with credit, I shall proceed to the question of accountability.

**Mr. Corbyn:** On a point of order, Mr. Deputy Speaker. This is a serious matter. The Minister has alleged that Cabinet Ministers of the Labour Government were involved in a riot. One of his hon. Friends was overheard to say that it was at Grunwick. The Minister clearly made that statement, but he cannot substantiate it because he knows it not to be true. Surely he must withdraw his remarks. Otherwise, if he is allowed to make statements impugning the integrity of——

**Mr. Deputy Speaker:** Order. I thought that I had made a clear statement on this matter. I hope that the hon. Gentleman will not persist, as I have ruled on this matter. I have already said that until the Minister identifies a particular Member of the House and reflects adversely on that Member's honour and integrity, then, no matter how discourteous, he is not out of order.

**Mr. Cohen:** Further to that point of order, Mr. Deputy Speaker. I invite the Minister to name the specific hon. Members involved or to withdraw his remarks.

**Mr. Deputy Speaker:** Order. I rather hope that we can get away from this matter, which is leading us in the direction of disorder. The hon. Member for Leyton (Mr. Cohen) seems intent on going down a different road. I would not advise him or the House to go in that direction. I hope that we can now get on.

**Mr. Hogg:** I must tell the House that I find the approach of the Labour party on the question of accountability profoundly unattractive. First, we must look at what is in place. The commissioner is accountable to my right hon. Friend the Home Secretary, who is the police authority. My right hon. Friend is accountable to Parliament. The commissioner submits his statutory statement to the Home Secretary for approval. The annual report containing a full statement of the year's activities is also submitted to the Home Secretary, who presents it to Parliament. We have the annual parliamentary debate, now taking place. Citizens living in the Metropolitian police districts can question Ministers in Parliament or through correspondence. The Metropolitan police fund, annual accounts and estimates are presented to Parliament as a White Paper. Metropolitan police expenditure is scrutinised by the Public Accounts Committee and their affairs may be scrutinised by the Home Affairs Select Committee.

What I have described represents a high measure of specific control. The question is whether one should go further than that. A number of hon. Members have suggested that there should be a police authority separate from that which we have been discussing. I do not commend that course of action to the House. The question

that must be asked is what responsibility the Labour party is seeking to give that police authority, but we have heard a variety of explanations.

We are told that that police authority would set the order of priority. I am not sure what that means, but, so far as I understand it to mean anything, it means telling police officers what to do. I am pleased to see that the hon. Member for Newham, North-West is back in the Chamber as he was good enough to make his views wholly plain. When talking about the relationship between the police and the police authority what he had in mind, he said:
"These are things that you must do."
It is plain that the Labour party wishes to give a police authority the power not merely to determine the police's order of priorities but to instruct them on their operational duties, or at least come close to doing so. I do not commend that course of action to the House.

**Mr. Simon Hughes:** I shall not defend the Labour party, but given that all police forces in England fall under the authority of the Home Secretary, why, uniquely, do elected local representatives in London have no say in how their police forces are run? Why are London citizens uniquely disadvantaged?

**Mr. Hogg:** I do not wish to do the hon. Gentleman an injustice, but I do not think that he was present when I went through the special methods of accountability. If he was, I apologise. The procedures that I outlined provide a different but higher degree of control than that available to most police authorities. There are consultative groups throughout the Metropolitan police district. Regrettably, a number of Labour councils—Lambeth, Ealing, Brent, Hackney and Haringey—refuse to be involved in those consultative groups. It is unattractive for people to say that they are deprived of direct input into the way in which the police conduct their affairs, yet to refrain from participating in consultative groups, who work only to their advantage. I therefore find their approach profoundly unattractive.

The points made by my hon. Friend the Member for Westminster, North (Mr. Wheeler) were of singular importance. The Select Committee on Home Affairs visited the United States. Indeed, it followed the paths that I had trodden three or four weeks previously. I entirely agree that demand reduction is the chief priority, and we are taking a variety of measures to achieve that. First, we are trying to improve the quality of demand-reduction messages in the education system. Secondly, and different but no less important, we are trying to determine an effective method of delivering demand-reduction messages in local communities. My hon. Friend believes, as I do, that demand reduction lies at the core of our policy.

Although demand reduction lies at the core of our policy, it is not our only policy; enforcement is equally important. My hon. Friend the Member for Westminster, North will be aware of the fact—I am sure that he will welcome it—that the central drugs squad has been given an additional 22 officers. He will know that the Metropolitan police have set up a team with the task of identifying and seizing the profits of drug trafficking.

The important issue of firearms was rightly raised by my hon. Friend the Member for Beckenham (Sir P. Goodhart). The figures are quite encouraging. In an intervention, I said that firearms had been discharged only twice in 1988. We are experiencing a diminution in the number of firearms-trained officers—officers are therefore more specialised—together with a reduction in the number of times that firearms are issued. In 1988, firearms were issued to Metropolitan police officers for 1,320 operations. In 1983—I use that as an idle figure for reference—firearms were issued for 2,230 operations. The number of times that firearms were issued for operational duties has been reduced substantially. There has been a substantial reduction in the numbers of authorised firearms officers. In 1988, there were 2,568—in 1983, there were 4,786. We are getting a smaller cadre of more highly trained officers who are more experienced in the use of firearms. That provides for greater public safety and more effective policing.

The hon. Member for Leyton referred to police cells. This has been a considerable worry to us all. We have introduced——

*It being half-past Two o'clock, the motion for the Adjournment of the House lapsed, without Question put.*

**Mr. Simon Hughes** (Southwark and Bermondsey): On a point of order, Mr. Deputy Speaker. My point relates to the debate for five hours—a perfectly normal debate—on policing in London. The Minister did not have an opportunity to finish what he needed to say to reply to the debate. That enhances the argument that the accountability of the police force——

**Mr. Deputy Speaker:** Order. This does not sound like a point of order for me.

**Mr. Hughes:** If I may continue, Sir.

**Mr. Deputy Speaker:** Order. The hon. Member must address himself to a point of order for the Chair.

**Mr. Hughes:** The point of order for the Chair is that the issue, the policing of London, cannot be dealt with adequately in a debate of this length. I ask you to deliberate with the other authorities so that in future we may have——

**Mr. Deputy Speaker:** Order. The Chair has no responsibility for such matters.

## PARKING BILL *[Money]*

*Queen's Recommendation having been signified—*
*Resolved,*
That, for the purposes of any Act resulting from the Parking Bill, it is expedient to authorise the payment out of money provided by Parliament of any increase attributable to that Act in the sums payable out of such money under any other Act.—*[Mr. Portillo.]*

## TELEVISING OF PROCEEDINGS OF THE HOUSE

*Ordered,*
That—
(i) the Select Committee on Televising of Proceedings of the House have power to give directions and perform other duties in accordance with the provisions of the Resolution of the House of 12th June; and
(ii) this Order, the temporary Standing Order made on 29th March 1988 and the Order made on 26th May relating to the Select Committee on Televising of Proceedings of the House be Standing Orders of the House until the end of the next Session of Parliament.—*[Mr. Garel-Jones.]*

# Ophthalmic Services (Maidstone)

*Motion made, and Question proposed,* That this House do now adjourn.—*[Mr. Garel-Jones.]*

2.31 pm

**Miss Ann Widdecombe** (Maidstone): I am grateful for the opportunity to raise this issue, which is of growing importance to my constituents. I am grateful to my hon. Friend the Minister for being present to answer the debate. This is not the first of my Adjournment debates to which he has had to respond recently. I know that he was in his constituency this morning and has had to return to answer my debate.

In criticising the ophthalmic provision available to my constituents, I am not suggesting that there is not tangible evidence in my constituency of the Government's commitment to the National Health Service. In many ways, the medical and surgical provision within the Maidstone district health authority is exemplary and reassuring to those who need it.

Following recommendations for decades, a brand new hospital was built by the Government. It will soon be expanded to include a new mass radiography unit. We have received extra money under the waiting list initiative to help in orthopaedics. In 1987, under what I still claim was plain regional mismanagement, the South-East Thames regional health authority managed to move itself, having for several years spent £600,000 on rents and rates for an empty headquarters while at the same time closing wards in Maidstone because it claimed that it did not have enough funding. At that time, the then Minister—my right hon. Friend the Member for Braintree (Mr. Newton)—was helpful in getting us the money necessary to reopen the wards. He showed extreme courtesy in meeting the delegations of our nurses and others. We have been given a fair amount of attention. Nevertheless, there is a major blot on health service provision in Maidstone and in the South-East Thames regional health authority as a whole. That blot is the inadequate ophthalmic service, especially in terms of surgery and out-patient appointments.

By contrast with the district general hospital, which is large, new and well-equipped, the ophthalmic and aural hospital is extremely old and cramped and rather dilapidated. When I visited it in a routine fashion on Christmas day last year, I was horrified to find that the traditional turkey would not have been provided if the staff had not held a collection. That was because the health authority said that there was not enough money available. If we cannot produce a turkey for the handful of patients in the hospital on Christmas day, that shows that the hospital is being severely neglected.

The real problem relates to the waiting lists for ophthalmic services prevalent in the Maidstone district health authority. For many different reasons it is not easy to travel to hospitals outside the district, let alone outside the region, if one has eye problems. Largely that is because such problems afflict the elderly disproportionately and it can be extremely difficult for an elderly person with cataracts in both eyes and no transport to make a complicated journey.

Although I have always made a point since I was elected of getting patients complaining of long waits seen outside the area, it is extremely difficult to do that for ophthalmic patients and one consultant resists making referrals outside the area because he believes that adequate

[*Miss Ann Widdecombe*]

provision should be made for patients in the district itself. Even if I am successful in getting patients referred outside the area, there are long waiting lists for ophthalmic treatment throughout south-east Kent and throughout the country generally.

Cataract patients in my constituency must now wait 19 months for an operation. An elderly patient with a blocked punctum was offered an appointment one year hence. Her husband wrote on the card which announced the appointment that the NHS must be in "a hell of a state." He then sent the card back to the surgeon. I do not agree with that sentiment. I believe that by and large the NHS is extremely healthy, but it has its black spots and the ophthalmic service is one.

Second cataracts are on a reserve list. Out-patients must wait a year for an appointment and then wait another year for surgery. That has had such an effect that in some cases treatment is given where the diagnosis is not confirmed. I received a letter late last year from a surgeon who is trying to cope with this situation: He wrote:

"Returning to outpatients and the waiting times for an appointment, we are in a situation where frequently patients are referred to us suspected of having glaucoma as diagnosed by the optician. Glaucoma is an irreversibly blinding eye condition. If I was thought to have glaucoma, I would not wait more than a few weeks. We cannot accommodate these patients in that time and they are therefore supplied with treatment on the assumption that they do have glaucoma although a definitive diagnosis has not been made. This is a practice which most doctors would say is unacceptable and morally wrong, namely that a patient is being treated for a condition that he may not have purely because he has not yet been seen by a doctor."

It is all very well for opticians in the area to ensure that they have adequate eye-testing facilities and for people like me to demand in the House that there should be health warnings where unprescribed spectacles are sold. Similarly, it is all very well to encourage the population to adopt preventive eye medicine and to have eye tests. However, if they have the tests and are found to have something as serious as glaucoma, they still cannot receive immediate appointments and must be treated on the assumption that they have that illness. It is hard to think of any other area in the NHS in which patients are treated merely on the assumption that they have a certain illness.

Efforts have been made to rectify the situation. In January 1988 a fifth consultant was appointed with a view to reducing the waiting lists. Furthermore, additional money has been made available. Once again I will try the Minister's patience by quoting a letter from Sir Peter Baldwin, the chairman of South-East Thames regional health authority. He wrote:

"We expect that an increasing elderly population will place further demands on our ophthalmology services. The attached table shows that in the main the position regarding ophthalmology across the region is far from satisfactory. We have tried to remedy this through our location of the Secretary of State's waiting list fund. In 1987-1988 a total of five districts"—

that is, within the region——

"received additional funds for their ophthalmology services, two of those schemes being specifically for cataracts, and in 1988-89 seven districts received additional money for schemes either wholly or partly connected with ophthalmology, and of those three were for cataracts."

Despite all that effort, there is still a 19-month wait for cataract operations, a year's wait for out-patient appointments and another year's wait for surgery. Elderly patients, who do not have many years in which to enjoy the fullness of their faculties and of good health, are having to go on a reserve list for a second cataract operation. They must put up with routine conditions such as blocked punctums, which although not life threatening or sight threatening, are irritating and impair the quality of life. They are expected to put up with that for a year.

Within the South-East Thames area, only Camberwell has reasonably short waiting lists. I do not know why that should be. Apart from that, there is no district health authority with a reasonable waiting list.

Despite the efforts that have obviously been made to improve matters—I am grateful for the efforts that have been made and I do not want to comment in any destructive way—ophthalmology is principally required by the elderly. The number of elderly people is increasing, and it is likely to increase as a proportion of the population for some time to come. We should look at the density of allocation of ophthalmologists throughout the NHS. In Belgium, for example, patients can be seen within five days at least to get a diagnosis, and surgery—even routine surgery such as cataract surgery—follows within six months. When we look at recruiting, and the emphasis in medical schools as people go on to train and specialise, we must question whether we have the right emphasis on a particular branch of medicine that is needed by the elderly. For years we have heard about the need to increase our orthopaedic provision, because the elderly are particularly susceptible and need hip replacements and so on, and we are doing that successfully. However, is it not time to have a similar increase in ophthalmology provision? Is there anywhere else in the country to which I could refer the fittest of our cataract patients where there are shorter waiting lists? If not, what is to be done and on what time scale?

2.42 pm

**The Parliamentary Under-Secretary of State for Health (Mr. Roger Freeman):** I congratulate my hon. Friend the Member for Maidstone (Miss Widdecombe) on securing this Adjournment debate. The frequency with which I have found myself at the Dispatch Box answering Adjournment debates in this calendar year is almost matched by the frequency with which my hon. Friend asks questions and raises important matters for her constituency and for the nation. I am well aware of her interest in and concern for the health care of her constituents. The zeal with which she looks after her constituents is an example to all hon. Members. I am sure that the constituents of Maidstone, whatever party they follow, are grateful to her as their excellent representative. My hon. Friend is also an active member of the Select Committee on Social Services, and her views are constructive and respected.

The debate is about the Kent county ophthalmic and aural hospital. I should not like this opportunity to go by without congratulating the National Health Service staff at the Maidstone health authority. The new district general hospital is a fine example of new construction in the Health Service and it is often visited by distinguished visitors to this country. It is a fine new building and the staff have a high morale. Ministers in the Department of Health and all Ministers in the Government congratulate the National Health Service staff on their thoroughly workmanlike and professional job.

Before responding to the detailed points about eye services provided by Maidstone health authority, I should say that it is the Government's policy to delegate as much responsibility as possible for the local provision of services to local management. The Government can provide resources to regional health authorities, and set priorities and guidance. It is then up to the regions to allocate the resources to the districts, and up to the districts, such as Maidstone health authority, to settle the allocation of funds and other resources to different medical specialities, for example, the provision of the hospital eye service in the authority. The Government believe strongly in the delegation of that responsibility and the White Paper "Working for Patients" carries that philosophy further by delegating tasks and making authorities more streamlined and businesslike.

At the outset of the debate my hon. Friend the Member for Maidstone talked about the move of the South-East Thames regional health authority from Croydon to Bexhill. I well understand her concern about the fact that the office premises which it left in Croydon have remained empty. However, the move has saved money because I am advised that if the authority had stayed in Croydon the rent would have risen to about £1 million per annum, which is considerably in excess of the current occupancy costs in Bexhill. Therefore, there is a saving, albeit one which hinges crucially on the assumption about the rent that would have been paid. The saving has been ploughed back into patient services.

**Miss Widdecombe:** A saving may have been made on the rent payable on the misnamed Thrift house, but is it a saving on the rent payable on Thrift house, plus the rent and rates still shelled out on the empty Croydon premises that were not disposed of? By locating itself in the wilds of Bexhill-on-Sea, the authority has created travelling inconveniences and costs for its staff that have resulted in a considerable amount of adverse comment from the district health authorities. The public and the DHAs are not convinced that the region made a cost-effective decision.

**Mr. Freeman:** I should be delighted to write to my hon. Friend and set out the precise calculations. She is perfectly right to draw this matter to the attention of the House. I have considered the matter carefully and I am convinced that a sensible decision was made. The question of where an authority locates its headquarters is a matter for the region, but I noted what my hon. Friend said. I do not find it too inconvenient to travel to Bexhill and I look forward to my next visit to the regional health authority, partly because I can follow up the outcome of this debate.

I listened very carefully to what my hon. Friend said about eye services provided at the Kent county ophthalmic and aural hospital, especially about waiting lists and waiting times. I accept that these figures are not satisfactory and the Government recognise that, despite increased activity and reduced waiting lists across the country since 1979, some patients in some areas still have to wait too long for treatment. That is why the Government set up a special waiting list initiative which over the last three years has made £86 million available to tackle the worst waiting problems. This year, Maidstone will receive almost £200,000 from this fund, of which £50,000 will enable an additional 160 ophthalmic operations to take place at Maidstone. This represents

almost 20 per cent. of the waiting list at the end of March. It will be done by appointing a locum consultant to cover the annual leave of the five existing consultant surgeons, thus preventing theatre time being lost.

I am aware that perhaps the main problem is the waiting times for a first out-patient appointment. After a significant rise since June 1987, these have improved in the last few months—the minimum wait is now 24 weeks and the maximum 52 weeks, compared with 29 and 61 weeks just three months ago. However, I entirely agree that these figures are still too high. I understand that there is a relatively high number of non-attenders at clinics—that is, people who fail to attend for their appointment—and a high ratio of repeat attenders to new attenders. Both these factors tend to lengthen waiting times for new appointments and I understand that they are being investigated. I know that health authorities are worried about the problem and the district general manager has sent me a report which includes action that is taking place to improve it.

It might help if I briefly outlined the five main sorts of action. First, a clinical assistant is being employed for six sessions a week to provide additional medical help. Secondly, a number of consultants are now referring non-Maidstone residents to out-patient clinics which they hold in Gravesend and Medway, in order to spread the load. Thirdly, there is a wide variation in referral rates to the five consultant ophthalmic surgeons, so patients and GPs are increasingly being offered the opportunity of an earlier appointment with one of the consultants whose waiting time is shorter.

I was in Sunderland on Wednesday visiting an excellent new out-patient facility for ophthalmic in-patients and out-patients. During my visit I had cause to speak to officials of the Northern regional health authority, who drew my attention to the fact that the number of patients waiting for the various consultants might not be the same. Some GPs tend to refer most of their patients to a named consultant, and junior or new consultants may have relatively small waiting lists because they are unknown. As a result, their popularity is not as great as that of other consultants. It is clearly in the interests of patients that referrals be spread more evenly between hospital consultants—that is the third step that the health authority is taking, for which I commend it.

Fourthly, revised arrangements, including more screening of patients for treatment by nurses, should be introduced to the hospital's accident unit in September to reduce the effect of that unit's work on medical time.

Fifthly, the hospital and local family practitioner committee are discussing how to ensure that, when appropriate, patients go first to their GPs rather than directly to the hospital accident unit.

Turning to waiting lists and times for in-patient admission, the district tells me that at the end of March 1989 there were 865 people on its list, the lowest number since September 1987, and that the number has gradually been falling. That is better news, and the additional patients to be treated this year from the Government's waiting list fund should significantly reduce the number. That is the fund which I said was going in part to help employ a locum consultant, to ensure that when one of the five consultants is on holiday, operations are not delayed.

I am concerned because my Department's figures show that the number of people waiting for longer than a year rose between the end of 1987 and September 1988 from 11

[Mr. Freeman]

per cent. of the total to 22 per cent. of the total—my hon. Friend referred to that. I should like that figure reduced. I hope that the attempt to equalise the waiting lists between the five consultants may go some way towards that.

I must stress that the waiting list during the past year has not resulted from any decrease in the number of patients being treated at the Kent county ophthalmic and aural hospital. Rather, it is a result of increasing demand for this specialty. A total of 21,094 out-patients were treated in 1988-89—that is, in the year ending 31 March 1989—compared with 19,500 in the previous year, an increase of 8 per cent. The figures for in-patient admissions, including day cases, was that 1,884 patients were treated, compared with 1,709 the previous year—an increase of 10 per cent.

My hon. Friend was right to say that as the population lives longer, so the need for eye surgery and treatment in hospital increases, because it is the very elderly who need corneal replacement.

An increase in resources, particularly for ophthalmic services in Maidstone, could enable more patients to be treated and reduce waiting lists. In the first instance, it must be for the health authority to decide how it will allocate resources between the competing demands. Health authorities also need to look thoroughly at how improvements can be made in the way that the existing level of resources is used in individual specialties. I know that this has been happening in Maidstone in eye surgery services. I have noted the statement by the chairman of the health authority, in a letter in January to my right hon. Friend the Member for Tonbridge and Malling (Sir J. Stanley), that until Maidstone has exhaustively looked at how the resources for eye services are used, she is not confident that it could sustain a case for extra resources that would win any arguments beyond the district. I agree with the chairman that that must be the way to proceed. I have already mentioned some of the action being taken on out-patients. On in-patients, with the help of the clinicians concerned, the authority is actively looking into the procedure for reviewing waiting lists and the most effective use of operating theatre time. The district general manager has identified limitation of theatre capacity as a major restraint to increasing patient throughput. That shows where resources might be applied once other avenues have been explored, so as to reduce waiting lists and increase patient services even more.

The Government's proposals on contract funding aim to resolve this sort of situation. In future, money will follow the patient, so there will be a financial incentive for a hospital to become increasingly efficient and obtain the contracts to treat more patients. I hope that my hon. Friend agrees that Maidstone health authority is concerned about the situation and that it is taking various actions to improve it. I shall be writing to the health authority chairman asking her to ensure that the use of resources for the provision of hospital eye services has been thoroughly investigated and to let me know, in six months, what effect these measures have had on waiting lists and waiting times.

I plan to visit Maidstone early next year, when I hope to see how the authority has coped with its problems. I hope that my hon. Friend and I can arrange a mutually convenient date so that we can make the visit on the same day not only to see the progress that I hope will have been made in eye services but to see and hear about the excellent services available at the Maidstone district general hospital.

*Question put and agreed to.*

*Adjourned accordingly at three minutes to Three o'clock.*

# Written Answers to Questions

*Monday 19 June 1989*

## PRIME MINISTER

### Test Ban Treaty

**Mr. David Nicholson:** To ask the Prime Minister what discussions took place at the recent North Atlantic Treaty Organisation summit in Brussels regarding a comprehensive test ban treaty; what is the policy of Her Majesty's Government towards negotiations with the Soviet Union on this subject; and if she will make a statement.

**The Prime Minister:** No discussions about a comprehensive test ban treaty took place at the recent NATO summit.

We welcome the bilateral negotiations between the United States and Soviet Union in Geneva aimed at the ratification of the peaceful nuclear explosions treaty and threshold test ban treaty, and hope that these two treaties will be ratified soon. Further steps to limit tests will then have to be considered. For the foreseeable future the United Kingdom's security will depend on deterrence based, in part, on the possession of nuclear weapons. That will mean a continuing requirement to conduct underground nuclear tests to ensure that our nuclear weapons remain effective and up to date.

### Sea Birds

**Dr. Godman:** To ask the Prime Minister, pursuant to her reply to the hon. Member for Greenock and Port Glasgow on 16 May, *Official Report,* column *119,* if she will outline the research being undertaken by the Nature Conservancy Council into the identification of the most important sea bird feeding and gathering grounds in the United Kingdom; when Her Majesty's Government expect to receive the findings of this research; and if she will make a statement.

**The Prime Minister:** In 1979, the Nature Conservancy Council commenced the sea birds at sea project, a research programme to study the distribution of sea bird populations most at risk from pollution, particularly oil-spill, in the North sea. The work was jointly funded by the oil and gas industry, NCC and Government Departments. A report of the studies was published in 1987.

A further phase of the project is now in progress, extending the survey to waters north and west of Scotland. The Department of the Environment expects to receive a preliminary report on the most important areas for sea birds later this year.

A final phase, due to start in 1990, will complete the geographic coverage by surveying the English channel and south-west approaches.

### European Commission

**Mr. Porter:** To ask the Prime Minister if she will raise at the next meeting of the European Council the attendance of individual commissioners at meetings of backbench Members of the national Parliaments.

**The Prime Minister:** No. Any such contacts would be a matter for Commissioners and national Parliaments.

**Mr. Porter:** To ask the Prime Minister what is her policy for negotiating proposals by the European Community Commission as between *(a)* the Commission in general and *(b)* with individual commissioners; and if she will make a statement.

**The Prime Minister:** Proposals are put forward by the Commission as a whole. Generally, they are discussed in the Council with those commissioners responsible for individual measures, rather than with the whole Commission. The same goes for bilateral contacts.

### Quasi-judicial Appointments

**Mr. Morgan:** To ask the Prime Minister (1) what restrictions are placed on the appointment of civil servants, past or present, to quasi-judicial jobs such as regulators where those civil servants may be privy to preferential information on the nature of the job;

(2) what restrictions are placed on the appointment of civil servants, temporary or permanent, to quasi-judicial jobs such as regulators;

(3) what guidelines are issued to departments for the appointment of regulators and other governmental quasi-judicial appointments.

**The Prime Minister:** In general, Ministers are free to decide who should be appointed and the manner and methods of identifying suitable candidates, subject to any statutory or constitutional requirements affecting the individual case. Full information about the job is made available as a matter of course to all those being considered for appointments.

### EC Regulations

**Mr. Teddy Taylor:** To ask the Prime Minister, pursuant to her reply of 13 June to the hon. Member for Southend, East, what information she has received concerning the proposed EC regulation on the control of concentrations and, in particular, to articles 12(1)(b), 12(1)(c) and article 13 thereof; and whether she will take steps to improve the arrangements by which she is informed of legislative proposals being submitted by the Commission.

**The Prime Minister:** I am grateful to my hon. Friend for clarifying his earlier question of 13 June. I am of course aware of the proposed regulation on the control of concentrations between undertakings which was the subject of a Commons debate on 17 May at columns 427-28 and is expected to be considered at next month's meeting of the Internal Market Council.

### Nuclear Weapons

**Mr. Flynn:** To ask the Prime Minister if, during the visit of General Jaruzelski of Poland, on 10-11 June, the issue of the fourth review conference of the nuclear non-proliferation treaty, to be held in 1990, was discussed.

**The Prime Minister:** No.

**Mr. Flynn:** To ask The Prime Minister if, during the visit of the Prime Minister of Jamaica on 14 June she discussed *(a)* initiatives to be taken to increase the number of non-aligned states which are signatory to the nuclear non-proliferation treaty in the period leading to the fourth non-proliferation treaty review conference in 1990 and *(b)* the Jamaican Government's view of the present utility of article IV of the non-proliferation treaty in regard to nuclear exports.

**The Prime Minister:** No.

**Mr. Flynn:** To ask the Prime Minister if, pursuant to her reply on representations recently received on nuclear weapons, on 26 May, *Official Report*, column *759*, she will list the organisations and individuals from whom representations were received for and against nuclear weapons; and why the information sought can be obtained only at a disproportionate cost.

**The Prime Minister:** I have nothing to add to the answer I gave the hon. Member on 26 May at column *759*.

**Mr. Flynn:** To ask the Prime Minister what discussions took place during the visit of President Bush to the United Kingdom on 31 May to 2 June on the 1990 fourth review conference of the nuclear non-proliferation treaty.

**The Prime Minister:** The 1990 non-proliferation treaty review conference was not discussed during President Bush's visit. However, preparations for the review conference are frequently discussed with the Americans at an official level.

**Mr. Flynn:** To ask the Prime Minister what is Her Majesty's Government's understanding of what percentage is represented by the word "partial" used in the communiqué issued by the North Atlantic Treaty Organisation Ministers in regard to the future revocation of land-based short range nuclear weapons in Western Europe.

**The Prime Minister:** The word "partial" was chosen deliberately to make clear that there was no question of the complete elimination of those systems.

### Power Stations (Visits)

**Mr. Flynn:** To ask the Prime Minister when she last visited *(a)* a nuclear power station *(b)* a fossil-fuelled power station and *(c)* a renewable energy project; what was the occasion of her visit; and what it cost.

**The Prime Minister:** Within the United Kingdom, the most recent visit to a nuclear power station was on Saturday 13 May 1989, when I undertook the official opening of the Torness nuclear power station in East Lothian. I have not yet visited a fossil-fuelled power station as Prime Minister. In September 1986, I visited the energy world exhibition in Milton Keynes, which contained projects involving renewable energy. Information on the precise cost of these visits is not available, since each was combined with other engagements.

### European Court

**Mr. Ron Davies:** To ask the Prime Minister if she will list those occasions in each of the last three years when the United Kingdom has been taken before the European Court, listing in each case the nature of the breach leading to action by the Commission and the court decision.

**The Prime Minister:** Proceedings commenced against the United Kingdom under article 169 of the treaty of Rome in the last three years are as follows:

| Year | Case No. | Nature of breach | Decision of courts |
|------|----------|------------------|--------------------|
| 1986 | 60/86 | Dim-dip headlamp devices: non-compliance with Council Directive 75/756 | Judgement for the Commission |
| 1987 | 93/87 | Failure to pay monetary compensatory amounts— triangular arrangements for imports for wheat | Judgement for the United Kingdom |
|      | 255/87 | Benzene in toys—failure to implement Council Directive 82/806 | Case withdrawn |
| 1988 | — — | | — |
| 1989 | — — | | — |

## HOME DEPARTMENT

### Firearms

**Mr. Maclennan:** To ask the Secretary of State for the Home Department (1) what is the average margin between the price at which firearms with a recognised value in excess of £150 have been bought in in consequence of their prohibition under the Firearms (Amendment) Act, and the price at which they have been disposed of;

(2) what is the average price at which firearms bought in at a price of £150 in consequence of their prohibition under the Firearms (Amendment) Act have been disposed of.

**Mr. Douglas Hogg:** None of the weapons surrendered under the buy-in scheme is to be disposed of by way of sale. Save for a small number of weapons of historical significance worthy of preservation for the national heritage, which will be offered to the National Museums Consortium, arrangements have been made for all weapons surrendered under the scheme to be destroyed.

**Mr. Maclennan:** To ask the Secretary of State for the Home Department what is the number of firearms which became prohibited weapons under the Firearms (Amendment) Act which have been bought in at *(a)* a cost of £150 and *(b)* a sum in excess of £150.

**Mr. Douglas Hogg:** A substantial number of claims made under the Government buy-in scheme for weapons newly prohibited by the Firearms (Amendment) Act 1988 were submitted on or shortly before the scheme finished on 30 April. Statistics on the operation of the scheme are not yet available, but we propose to publish them as soon as they are collated.

### Refugees and Soldiers

**Mr. Alex Carlile:** To ask the Secretary of State for the Home Department what up-to-date information he has about *(a)* the numbers and proportion of refugees from Nazi and other anti-semitic persecution in Europe, and of soldiers from Central Europe, who settled in the United Kingdom between 1930 and 1945, who subsequently became naturalised British subjects with a permanent right of abode in the United Kingdom and *(b)* what proportion are still resident in the United Kingdom.

**Mr. Renton:** The information is not available.

### Gartree Prison

**Sir John Farr:** To ask the Secretary of State for the Home Department if he will take steps to arrange for access to Her Majesty's prison Gartree by the media and local telvision following its regrading from category A to B.

**Mr. Douglas Hogg:** Her Majesty's prison Gartree is to change from a dispersal prison to a category B training prison in 1992. The prison service has a good record of allowing access to its establishments by the media and all such requests are carefully considered.

### Correspondence

**Mr. Nellist:** To ask the Secretary of State for the Home Department when the Parliamentary Under-Secretary of State will be in a position to give a substantive reply to the letter from the hon. Member for Coventry, South-East about Michael Patrick Brown, HMP, C58729; and if he will make a statement.

**Mr. Douglas Hogg:** I have replied to the hon. Member's letter today.

### Television Programmes

**Mr. Steel:** To ask the Secretary of State for the Home Department, pursuant to his response to the hon. Member for Clydebank and Milngavie (Mr. Worthington) of 19 May, *Official Report,* column *602,* what assessment he has undertaken of the suitability for export of television programmes produced within Scotland; and what steps he is undertaking to encourage independent Scottish television producers to export material.

**Mr. Renton:** In the exchanges to which the right hon. Member refers, I was offering a possible explanation for the point raised by the hon. Member for Clydebank and Milngavie about the relatively low proportion of programming produced by Scottish independent producers which was networked in other parts of the United Kingdom. My argument was simply that, in the end, successful programme producers will be those who respond to the demands of those who commission programmes and, ultimately, those who view them.

As to the steps being taken to encourage Scottish independent producers, the broadcasting White Paper sets out the Government's intention to require that a minimum of 25 per cent. of programmes produced for Channels 3, 4 and 5 and DBS must come from independent producers, and it will be open to Scottish producers to compete for these new opportunities that will be made available. I have also welcomed the suggestion of the chairman of the IBA that Channel 5 should be based in a production centre north of Birmingham, since the new channel can be expected to encourage and foster a new local industry in independent production.

### Mr. Roc Sandford

**Mr. Frank Field:** To ask the Secretary of State for the Home Department if he knows the current whereabouts of the wooden pipe and 1·54g of cannabis used in evidence in the prosecution of Mr. Roc Sandford at Knightsbridge Crown court in October 1985.

**Mr. Douglas Hogg:** I understand from the Metropolitan police that the pipe and cannabis used in evidence in the prosecution of Mr. Sandford were destroyed in January this year.

**Mr. Frank Field:** To ask the Secretary of State for the Home Department if he will specify the dates the various interested bodies decided to take no disciplinary action and to prefer no charges against the officers involved in the prosecution of Mr. Roc Sandford for possession of drugs at Knightsbridge Crown court in October 1985.

**Mr. Douglas Hogg:** I understand that the Crown prosecution service decided on 5 December 1986 that there was no evidence to justify criminal proceedings against the officers concerned; and that the Police Complaints Authority agreed on 30 April 1987 that no disciplinary action should be taken.

**Mr. Frank Field:** To ask the Secretary of State for the Home Department what involvement his Department had in the decision not to prosecute or discipline the officers involved on the prosecution of Mr. Roc Sandford for possession of drugs at Kinghtsbridge Crown court in October 1985.

**Mr. Douglas Hogg:** None. The decisions are the responsibility of the Crown prosecution service in respect of criminal proceedings and the Commissioner and the Police Complaints Authority in respect of disciplinary proceedings.

**Mr. Frank Field:** To ask the Secretary of State for the Home Department whether he is now in a position to release the names of the arresting officers and prosecution witnesses in the cases listed in the question of the hon. Member for Birkenhead on 6 July 1988, *Official Report,* column *596-97.*

**Mr. Douglas Hogg:** Where inquiries into allegations of impropriety on the part of the police have been investigated without evidence being forthcoming to support either criminal or disciplinary proceedings, it is not the practice for the officers or other persons involved in the cases to be identified.

**Mr. Frank Field:** To ask the Secretary of State for the Home Department who is still considering the inquiry into the circumstance under which charges were brought and proceedings conducted against Mr. Roc Sandford; and what conclusions have yet been drawn.

**Mr. Douglas Hogg:** I am informed by the Metropolitan police that, following the conclusion of the civil action taken by Mr. Sandford, additional inquiries were made and a report was submitted to the Police Complaints Authority, which indicated on 1 June 1988 that the matter should be taken no further. These further inquiries required no additional consideration by the Crown prosecution service. The inquiries are therefore considered to be complete.

**Mr. Frank Field:** To ask the Secretary of State for the Home Department why the Metropolitan police solicitor failed to give discovery of the appropriate documents during its defence against Mr. Roc Sandford's civil action for wrongful arrest, false imprisonment and malicious prosecution during the time period required by the court.

**Mr. Douglas Hogg:** I understand from the Metropolitan police solicitor that the court ordered both parties to exchange lists of documents within 28 days. As the question of the contents of the Metropolitan police's list was referred to counsel for advice, an extension was requested and was granted by Mr. Sandford's solicitors. Shortly afterwards, negotiations commenced, which eventually led to an out-of-court settlement. Because of these negotiations Mr. Sandford's solicitors did not press for the list, although it would have been open to them to do so.

## CIVIL SERVICE

### Civil Service College (Principal)

**Mr. Dalyell:** To ask the Minister for the Civil Service if he will make a statement on the appointment of the principal of the Civil Service college.

**Mr. Luce** *[holding answer 16 June 1989]:* The Civil Service college was launched as an executive agency on 6 June 1989. The current principal of the college, Mr. Roger Jackling, was appointed as its first chief executive.

Mr. Jackling, a career civil servant, has been principal for two and half years. He has maintained and improved the high teaching standards of the college and evolved the management systems which have resulted in a smooth transition to agency status. He will return to his parent department in the autumn and his successor will be recruited through an open competition run by the Civil Service Commission.

## TRANSPORT

### Excise Duty Evasion

**Mr. Warren:** To ask the Secretary of State for Transport if he will make a statement on the results of the campaign during May by the police in Surrey and Sussex with the assistance of his Department against excise duty evasion by motor vehicle owners.

**Mr. Peter Bottomley:** Nearly 2,000 motorists were reported for not having a current road fund licence on display. These cases are being investigated; where it is clear that vehicle excise duty has been evaded, those responsible will be prosecuted.

Special VED enforcement campaigns run jointly by Department of Transport and police forces form an important addition to the day-to-day VED enforcement activities. They have proved very effective in encouraging people to relicense their vehicles voluntarily as well as in catching the more determined evaders. A period of two weeks of extensive local publicity is followed by a further two weeks in which the police concentrate on identifying and reporting those who have ignored the warnings. Evaders caught during campaigns are not given the opportunity to settle out of court.

The policy find that campaigns help them to detect many other offences including lack of insurance and MOT certificates, disqualifications, unroadworthy vehicles and occasionally more serious crimes.

## London Underground

**Mr. Gerald Bowden:** To ask the Secretary of State for Transport whether he has any plans to reconsider extending the Northern Line tube to Camberwell and beyond following the omission of this option from the central London rail study.

**Mr. Portillo:** The central London rail study concluded that extending the Northern line to Camberwell could not be justified in terms of meeting that study's objectives, in particular to seek relief to central London congestion. That being so, it is for the Underground to consider whether such a link is worth while both in its own right and in relation to other priorities for improvements to the network.

## Air Traffic Control

**Mr. Bill Walker:** To ask the Secretary of State for Transport if he has any plans to privatise the training of air traffic controllers; and if he will make a statement.

**Mr. Peter Bottomley:** This is a matter for the Civil Aviation Authority and the National Air Traffic Services. I understand that training procedures are being reviewed.

## Manchester Airport (Fire)

**Sir Michael McNair-Wilson:** To ask the Secretary of State for Transport whether he will list the action taken by the Civil Aviation Authority in implementing the recommendations in the report by the Accidents Investigation Board into the fire involving a British Airways 737 at Manchester airport in 1985.

**Mr. Peter Bottomley:** These Civil aviation safety regulation issues are wholly the responsibility of the Civil Aviation Authority. The authority's current position on them is set out in its follow-up-action on accident reports (FACTAR) issued on 13 March 1989 in response to the AAIB Report on the B737 accident at Manchester, 22 August 1985. I have arranged for a copy of the FACTAR to be sent to the hon. Member. I understand that the Authority will publish shortly the initial report on the research it has undertaken into evacuation requirements.

## Water Pollution

**Mr. Malcolm Bruce:** To ask the Secretary of State for Transport how many drums or other containers containing chemicals have sunk in waters within 100 miles of the British coast in the last 30 years; how many have been recovered; how many are known to have leaked; and if he will specify the nature of the chemicals *(a)* known to have leaked, and *(b)* known to be under water and assumed not to have leaked.

**Mr. Portillo:** The information is not available.

## South Yorkshire Supertram

**Mr. Patnick:** To ask the Secretary of State for Transport when he intends to meet representatives of the South Yorkshire passenger transport authority and executive, Sheffield city council, the development corporation and the chamber of commerce, to discuss the PTE's application for grant for the South Yorkshire Supertram project.

**Mr. Portillo:** I met this morning with representatives of the South Yorkshire passenger transport authority and executive, Sheffield city council, the development corporation and the chamber of commerce. I discussed with them the application made by the PTE for grant, under section 56 of the Transport Act 1968, towards the cost of Line 1 of the proposed South Yorkshire Supertram system.

Further information and analysis will be needed on a number of important issues before it will be possible to reach a decision on grant. For example, the evaluation will have to include confirmation of the estimates of capital costs, a review of carrying capacity, and full allowance for the effects on other road users once the detailed highways arrangements have been designed. I will also expect the PTE to develop sound proposals for project management and financing, and to secure contributions from the private sector—particularly the interests along the route which will benefit from the project.

If the evaluation can be confirmed and the financing and other issues can be satisfactorily resolved, I would hope to approve a capital allocation and section 56 grant towards the capitalised cost of the expected financial deficit on Line 1. The time at which resources and grant might be made available would be determined in the light of analysis. In the meantime, I have decided to make capital allocation and 50 per cent. grant available in respect of eligible costs to be incurred in carrying out the further analysis required.

### Customs and Immigration Facilities

**Mr. Gerald Bowden:** To ask the Secretary of State for Transport what information he has on the provision of on-train Customs and immigration facilities between countries within the European Community and between Northern Ireland and the Irish Republic; whether there are to be frontier controls at Waterloo for passengers terminating in London; and if he will make a statement.

**Mr. Portillo:** I understand that on-train controls are carried out between a number of Community member states, but not everywhere. Travellers between the Republic of Ireland and Northern Ireland are not subject to immigration controls, but are subject to customs checks; passengers on express trains which travel non-stop to Belfast are cleared on disembarkation through the normal red/green customs channels, while customs clearance of stopping trains is carried out on the train while it is stationary at a point near the border. The present intention is to carry out customs checks at Waterloo for Channel tunnel rail passengers arriving in London. Immigration arrangements are under review. British Rail's choice of terminal was not dictated by frontier control considerations.

**Mr. Gerald Bowden:** To ask the Secretary of State for Transport what recent representations he has received regarding the provision of Customs and immigration facilities for the Channel tunnel rail link and those passengers disembarking in London.

**Mr. Portillo:** We receive representations from time to time about the frontier control arrangements for Channel tunnel passenger trains.

### London Regional Transport (Government Subsidy)

**Mr. Cox:** To ask the Secretary of State for Transport what has been the amount of Government subsidies given to London Regional Transport in each of the last three years.

**Mr. Portillo:** The grant paid to London Regional Transport in each of the last three years was as follows:

| Year | Amount |
|------|--------|
| 1986-87 | 295 |
| 1987-88 | 239 |
| 1988-89 | 190 |

## EMPLOYMENT

### Factory Inspectors

**Mr. Pike:** To ask the Secretary of State for Employment how many factory inspectors were employed by the health and safety inspectorate in 1979; and what is the current figure.

**Mr. Nicholls:** On 1 April 1979, 742 factory inspectors were in post in the Health and Safety Executive. On 1 June 1989, the total was 621·5.

### Labour Statistics

**Mr. Yeo:** To ask the Secretary of State for Employment which major Organisation for Economic Co-operation and Development countries had the largest rise in the number of people in employment during the last year; and if he will make a statement.

**Mr. Nicholls:** The table shows, for the United Kingdom and the major OECD countries, the increase in civilian employment in the year to the fourth quarter of 1988. The United Kingdom had the largest percentage rise.

*Increases in Civilian Employment United Kingdom and Major OECD Countries*

| | Thousands | Percentage |
|---|---|---|
| United Kingdom | 642 | 2·5 |
| Canada | 288 | 2·4 |
| United States | 2,386 | 2·1 |
| Japan | 864 | 1·5 |
| Germany (Federal Republic) | 159 | 0·6 |
| Italy | 134 | 0·6 |
| France | n/a | n/a |

n/a Not available
*Sources:*
  United Kingdom:   Department of Employment
  Other countries: OECD Labour Force Statistics, 1989/1

### Youth Opportunities Programme

**Mr. Nellist:** To ask the Secretary of State for Employment if he will estimate the value, in 1989, of the April 1978 youth opportunities programme weekly allowance for trainees if increased each year by *(a)* at a rate equal to the annual rate of price inflation and *(b)* at a rate equal to the annual average increase in wages; and if he will make a statement.

**Mr. Cope:** An allowance of £19·50 per week was paid to trainees on the youth opportunities programme in April

1978. If this allowance had been increased in line with changes in the retail price index, its value in May 1989 (based on the latest available figures) would have been £45·45. If the allowance had been updated to take account of increases in average earnings, its value in April 1989 (based on the latest available figures) would have been £58·13.

The youth opportunities programme was replaced in 1983 by YTS, which provides substantially higher quality training than YOP and incorporates structured off-the-job training. It is therefore misleading to compare the values of the YOP and YTS allowances, the the YTS allowance reflects the fact that trainees are still learning. Employers are free to supplement the minimum trainee allowance, and many do.

# ENERGY

## British Coal Corporation

**Mr. Mans:** To ask the Secretary of State for Energy if he will make a statement on the financial outlook for the British Coal Corporation for 1989-90.

**Mr. Parkinson:** As I announced on 6 February at column *479-480* the corporation is expected to make a further substantial loss in 1989-90.

The balance sheet at March 1990 will also be affected by the need to bring the corporation's accounting treatment for its concessionary coal liabilities into line with statement of standard accounting practice 24. This change will not affect the future stream of concessionary coal liabilities as already anticipated by the corporation, but will affect the way in which these liabilities are accounted for. Creating a provision in the corporation's balance sheet in respect of these liabilities will involve a prior year adjustment. This will substantially increase the accumulated deficit shown in the corporation's accounts at 31 March 1990.

The Government have given an assurance each year since 1982-83 that, subject to Parliament approving any necessary provisions, adequate funds will continue to be made available to enable the Corporation to meet its financial obligations as they fall due. A minute was laid before the House on 8 June setting out the Government's intention to extend this commitment to include the corporation's financial year ending 31 March 1990.

## Nuclear Fuel (Reprocessing)

**Dr. Kim Howells:** To ask the Secretary of State for Energy if the current British Nuclear Fuels plc offer to reprocess West German spent nuclear fuel includes any undertaking on British Nuclear Fuels plc part to retain in the United Kingdom any part of that spent fuel as remanufactured nuclear fuel.

**Mr. Michael Spicer:** BNFL's offer to reprocess West German spent nuclear fuel includes no such undertaking.

## Dounreay Reactor

**Mr. Dalyell:** To ask the Secretary of State for Energy if he will make a statement on the latest position in relation to the fast reactor site at Dounreay.

**Mr. Michael Spicer:** As my right hon. Friend said in a statement to the House on 21 July last year, the Government will continue to fund the prototype fast

reactor at Dounreay until March 1994 and the associated reprocessing plant until March 1997. The importance of Dounreay to the Caithness economy was a major factor behind the Government's decision, which gives the area the chance to develop alternative sources of employment and growth.

As far as Dounreay itself is concerned, there are a number of initiatives being taken by the Dounreay management and workforce to find additional work for the site.

Dounreay has been identified as a site where further investigations should take place to determine its potential as the site for the United Kingdom's radioactive waste repository. A decision on this, however, is still some way in the future.

## Electricity Meters

**Mrs. Fyfe:** To ask the Secretary of State for Energy if he will introduce legislation to ensure that domestic electricity consumers are not billed for electricity consumption who have been undercharged through the meter being faulty, where the meter has not been examined within the preceding 12 months; and if he will make a statement.

**Mr. Michael Spicer:** Under the Electricity Bill a public electricity supplier will be entitled to recover from a consumer any charges which are due to him and may disconnect the supply according to the procedure set out in the Bill if payment is not made, unless there is a genuine dispute over the amount. In recognition that some consumers do run into difficulty with their payments, the industry currently operates a code of practice on the payment of bills which offers a number of protections against disconnection. Under that code consumers will not be disconnected if they enter and keep to an arrangement to pay off the debt by instalments over a reasonable period. The draft public electricity supply licence requires the licensee to produce a similar code to ensure that this approach continues after privatisation.

## Euratom Safeguards Inspectors

**Mr. Flynn:** To ask the Secretary of State for Energy how many United Kingdom citizens are presently Euratom safeguards inspectors; on what grade they are; for how long each appointment has been made; and what steps he is taking to increase the number of United Kingdom safeguards experts at Euratom.

**Mr. Michael Spicer:** We have been informed by the Commission services that Euratom safeguards inspectors are recruited following standard recruitment procedures pursuant to the staff regulation of the EC. Presently there are 16 permanent EC civil servants of United Kingdom nationality in the grades A3 to B5 deployed as Euratom safeguards inspectors. It is for the Commission to initiate proposals for any staff increases.

## IAEA Safeguards Inspectors

**Mr. Flynn:** To ask the Secretary of State for Energy how many United Kingdom citizens are presently on the staff of the International Atomic Energy Agency working as safeguards inspectors; on what grade they are; for how long each appointment has been made; and what steps he is taking to increase the number of United Kingdom safeguards experts at the International Atomic Energy Agency.

**Mr. Michael Spicer:** The United Kingdom currently has five officers in the P3 and P5 grades working in the operations divisions of the International Atomic Energy Agency's safeguards department. Contracts are variously for three or five years. United Kingdom citizens also occupy a number of other professional posts in the support divisions of the safeguards department. Vacancy notices are circulated to appropriate organisations in the industry.

### Nuclear Safeguards

**Mr. Flynn:** To ask the Secretary of State for Energy if he has received a report on developments discussed at the 11th biannual symposium of the European Nuclear Safeguards Research and Development Association, held in Luxembourg on 30 May to 1 June, in so far as the issues relate to safeguards matters for which he has responsibility.

**Mr. Michael Spicer:** An official from my Department was present at the symposium.

**Mr. Flynn:** To ask the Secretary of State for Energy if the United Kingdom ambassador on the council of the International Atomic Energy Agency has received the 1988-89 safeguards implementation report from the agency.

**Mr. Michael Spicer:** The United Kingdom representative on the International Atomic Energy Agency board of governors has received the safeguards implementation report for 1988.

### Reactor Fuels Storage

**Mr. Flynn:** To ask the Secretary of State for Energy if he will seek an urgent meeting with Lord Marshall, the chairman of the Central Electricity Generating Board, concerning the problems identified by Lord Marshall in the adequacy of the wet storage facilities at British Nuclear Fuels plc., Sellafield for Magnox and advanced gas-cooled reactor fuel.

**Mr. Michael Spicer:** There are ample storage facilities at Sellafield to handle spent Magnox and advanced gas cooled reactor fuel.

### Libya (Technology Transfer)

**Mr. Flynn:** To ask the Secretary of State for Energy if there are any restrictions on United Kingdom Atomic Energy Authority technology in the area of technology transfer and assistance to Libya.

**Mr. Michael Spicer:** All exports of nuclear materials, equipment and technology are made within the guidelines set out in the statement by the then Foreign Secretary, the right hon. James Callaghan, on 31 March 1976 at columns 514-16.

### Atomic Energy Authority Technology

**Mr. Flynn:** To ask the Secretary of State for Energy what departmental representation was present at the launch of Atomic Energy Authority Technology on 16 May; and if he will make a statement on the prospects for Atomic Energy Authority Technology.

**Mr. Michael Spicer:** My right hon. Friend the Secretary of State attended the launch, as did a number of officials. I welcome the authority's initiative in marketing its R and D skills and expertise under the banner of Atomic Energy Authority Technology.

### Opencast Mining

**Mr. Malcolm Bruce:** To ask the Secretary of State for Energy if he will make a statement about the future of opencast mining; and what consideration is given to environmental impact assessment.

**Mr. Michael Spicer:** Opencast coal is an important national resource. Proposals for opencast operations need to be considered with full regard to their potential environmental effects and the scope for mitigating those effects. It is in the national interest to maximise production where that can be done in an environmentally acceptable way. To help mineral planning authorities in England and Wales strike the correct balance, the Government last year issued new, fuller guidance on the considerations to be taken into account.

Operators are expected to seek the mineral planning authorities views at an early stage on the preparation of environmental assessments appropriate to the scale of the development and the sensitivity of its location. Environmental assessments are normally required in the case of opencast mine sites of 50 hectares and above, or where they affect particularly sensitive areas. Similar requirements apply in Scotland.

## TRADE AND INDUSTRY

### Billing Computer Systems

**Mr. Cohen:** To ask the Chancellor of the Duchy of Lancaster whether the Government will introduce legislation to ensure that the police, inland revenue, Customs and Excise, and security services can obtain information that relates to telephone subscribers from the itemised billing computer systems of BT and Mercury only when they have a warrant from a court; and whether he will make a statement.

**Mr. Hurd:** I have been asked to reply.

We have no plans to amend the arrangements in the Interception of Communications Act 1985.

### Unsolicited Telephone Calls and Faxes

**Mr. Cohen:** To ask the Chancellor of the Duchy of Lancaster whether the Government will introduce legislation to control unsolicited telephone calls and unsolicited faxes by restricting the sale of telephone numbers of subscribers; and whether he will make a statement.

**Mr. Atkins:** As announced separately, my right hon. and noble Friend the Secretary of State for Trade and Industry has accepted the advice of the Director General of Telecommunications that the new branch systems general licence should contain a condition aimed at alleviating the nuisance to the users of telephone, fax, or other telecommunications systems, caused by persistent but unsolicited attempts to sell products and services.

## Interest Rates

**Mr. Roy Hughes:** To ask the Chancellor of the Duchy of Lancaster what is his latest estimate of the cumulative cost to industry of recent rises in interest rates.

**Mr. Atkins:** In 1989 so far, there has been a single one percentage point increase in bank base rates. The estimated cost to industrial and commercial companies of a one percentage point increase in bank base rates is about £0·4 billion in a full year.

## Information Technology Research

**Mr. Boswell:** To ask the Chancellor of the Duchy of Lancaster what he is doing to encourage collaboration between universities and industry in the field of information technology research.

**Mr. Forth:** Chapter 6 of the Department's White Paper on information technology (Cm. 646), published in March 1989, described the DTI's policy and programmes in support of IT collaborative research between universities and industry. Since then, the DTI and the Science and Engineering Research Council have announced support (£15 million) for a new LINK programme of collaborative research in opto-electronic systems, and increased funding (£7 million) for the information engineering advanced technology programme.

## National Engineering Laboratory

**Mr. John Evans:** To ask the Chancellor of the Duchy of Lancaster what representations he has received on his recent announcement on the future of the national engineering laboratory.

**Mr. Newton:** To date I have not received any representations on the proposals for the laboratory, which I announced on 17 May. However, the Department of Trade and Industry Council of Civil Service Unions has requested a meeting with the permanent secretary.

## Overseas Companies

**Mr. Knapman:** To ask the Chancellor of the Duchy of Lancaster how many overseas companies have set up operations in Britain; and what is his estimate of how many jobs such overseas investment has created and is sustaining.

**Mr. Atkins:** Since my Department's Invest in Britain Bureau started formally recording individual investments in 1979, there have been 2,647 inward investment projects, creating over 212,000 new jobs and, since 1983, are known to have safeguarded some 107,000 others. These figures are based upon information provided to the Department at the time the investment decisions were made and take no account of subsequent developments. They include the establishment of new businesses, the expansion or acquisition of existing businesses, and involvement in joint ventures.

## Small Businesses

**Mr. Barry Field:** To ask the Chancellor of the Duchy of Lancaster what further steps he intends taking to reduce the burden of statistical form filling in small businesses.

**Mr. Maude:** I announced the publication of a scrutiny of the collection of Depatment of Trade and Industry

statistics in reply to my hon. Friend the Member for Pembroke (Mr. Bennett) on 10 May at column 435. The recommendations of the scrutiny will be implemented over the next three years and will reduce the costs to businesses of these inquiries by about a quarter. Many of the recommendations will further help to ease the burden on the minority of small firms who are currently approached in the inquiries.

DTI Ministers will continue to press to minimise the burden of inquiries on all firms so far as it can be done without reducing the quality of statistics needed by Government. In particular, objectives to this end will be agreed with the enlarged Central Statistical Office, which will assume responsibility on 31 July for running the inquiries now conducted by DTI.

**Mr. Macdonald:** To ask the Chancellor of the Duchy of Lancaster what proportion of manufacturing employment is in businesses of approximately less than 200 employees in the current year and each of the last 10 years; and if he will also give comparative figures, where the data is available, for other European Community countries.

**Mr. Maude:** The available United Kingdom information is as follows:

*Percentage of United Kingdom manufacturing employment within local sites (factories etc.) with less than 200 employees*

|      | *Percentage* |
|------|------------|
| 1989 | 48 |
| 1988 | 47 |
| 1987 | 46 |
| 1986 | 45 |
| 1985 | 45 |
| 1984 | 43 |
| 1983 | 41 |
| 1982 | 39 |
| 1981 | n.a. |
| 1980 | n.a. |
| 1979 | 37 |

n.a. Not available
*Source:* Size Analyses of United Kingdom Businesses (PA1003).

Figures for the European Community are available for certain countries solely for 1984, and relate to enterprises (companies etc.) with employment of 20 to 99 as a percentage of all enterprises with employment of 20 or more:

|                | *Percentage* |
|----------------|------------|
| FR Germany     | 15 |
| France         | 21 |
| Italy          | 32 |
| Luxembourg     | 14 |
| Netherlands    | 29 |
| United Kingdom | 18 |

*Source:* EUROSTAT and United Kingdom census of production.

## Mail Carriers

**Mr. John Marshall:** To ask the Chancellor of the Duchy of Lancaster whether he will reduce the minimum £1 charge which private carriers of mail have to charge.

**Mr. Forth:** We keep the options under review, but we have no present plans to end the monopoly. We have, however, made it clear that the Post Office's letter monopoly is a privilege, not a right, and that in the event of a cessation or serious disruption of the letter service, we would consider suspending it.

## Cars

**Mr. Harry Greenway:** To ask the Chancellor of the Duchy of Lancaster, how many cars were *(a)* imported, *(b)* exported, *(c)* home produced and *(d)* sold in he United Kingdom in the past year, 10, 15 and 20 years ago; and if he will make a statement.

**Mr. Atkins:** I shall arrange for the figures to be included in the *Official Report*. While these show the decline the industry has suffered since the late 1960s, recent trends show an encouraging and sustained upsurge in United Kingdom production and exports.

The information is as follows:

|  | | | | *Thousands* |
|---|---|---|---|---|
|  | *1968* | *1973* | *1978* | *1988* |
| New cars imported | 102 | 505 | 801 | ¹1,349 |
| New cars exported | 677 | 599 | 466 | ¹258 |
| Cars produced in the United Kingdom | 1,816 | 1,747 | 1,223 | 1,227 |
| New cars registered in the United Kingdom | 1,145 | 1,688 | 1,592 | 2,216 |

¹ Provisional.

## Garden Products

**Mr. Alton:** To ask the Chancellor of the Duchy of Lancaster if his Department has any plans to stipulate that a sell-by date be displayed on garden products; and if he will make a statement.

**Mr. Forth:** No.

## Ferguson Shipbuilders Limited

**Dr. Godman:** To ask the Chancellor of the Duchy of Lancaster whether any progress has been made on the disposal of Ferguson Shipbuilders Limited, Port Glasgow.

**Mr. Newton** *[pursuant to the reply, 26 May, column 777]:* I understand that, although there has been a much less positive response than the HLD Group had hoped to its consultation with the work force of Ferguson Shipbuilders Limited on terms of future employment, the group regards it as just sufficient for it to be willing to enter into detailed negotiations with British Shipbuilders for the purchase of the yard.

## Ivory

**Mr. Teddy Taylor:** To ask the Chancellor of the Duchy of Lancaster if France sought the approval of the EEC Commission on its decision to ban ivory imports on 5 June; and if he will make a statement on the rights of EEC member states to impose such unilateral trade curbs.

**Mrs. Virginia Bottomley:** I have been asked to reply.
Under article 15 of the EC regulations implementing CITES in the Community, member states may take stricter measures on CITES species in certain circumstances. We had no formal notification that France intended to introduce a ban on the import of ivory before the Council of Environment Ministers on 8 and 9 June where member states were invited to do so.

## OVERSEAS DEVELOPMENT

### Black South Africans (Scholarships)

**Miss Lestor:** To ask the Secretary of State for Foreign and Commonwealth Affairs how many scholarships have been given to black South Africans for each of the last five years by *(a)* Her Majesty's Government and *(b)* the British Council.

**Mr. Chris Patten:** Following is the information. All awards listed are administered by the British Council.

|  | *Awards funded by Her Majesty's Government* | *Awards funded by British Council* |
|---|---|---|
| 1985-86 | 115 | 12 |
| 1986-87 | 235 | 14 |
| 1987-88 | 390 | 10 |
| 1988-89 | 434 | 10 |

### Malaysia

**Miss. Lestor:** To ask the Secretary of State for Foreign and Commonwealth Affairs, if he will list for the last five years gross bilateral aid given to Malaysia.

**Mr. Chris Patten:** The figures are:

|  | *£ million* |
|---|---|
| 1984 | 4·992 |
| 1985 | 7.454 |
| 1986 | 55·494 |
| 1987 | 9·402 |
| 1988 | 10·057 |

### Atlantic College

**Mr. John P. Smith:** To ask the Secretary of State for Foreign and Commonwealth Affairs if the Government have any plans to sponsor students from Soweto to attend Atlantic college.

**Mr. Chris Patten:** We are in close touch with Atlantic college about the possibility of sponsoring a limited number of students from South Africa.

## EDUCATION AND SCIENCE

### Student Loans

**Mr. Straw:** To ask the Secretary of State for Education and Science what conclusion he has reached in his discussions with the banks and financial sector on his student loans proposals; and if he will make a statement.

**Mr. Kenneth Baker:** I refer the hon. Member to the statement I made earlier today.

### Crookham Court School

**Sir Michael McNair-Wilson:** To ask the Secretary of State for Education and Science whether a notice of complaint was served on the proprietor of Crookham Court school following Her Majesty's inspector's report of 1981 and of 1988 relating *(a)* to the inspection, *(b)* to the fire precautions or *(c)* to any member of the staff.

**Mr. Butcher:** Her Majesty's inspectors carried out two full inspections of Crookham Court school, in November

1981 and in November 1987. On both occasions, a number of deficiencies were identified in the report. These deficiencies and recommendations for improvement were brought to the attention of the school in strongly worded official letters which accompanied the reports rather than through a formal notice of complaint. Recently many parents have chosen to remove their children from the school.

### Teachers (Pay)

**Mr. Fatchett:** To ask the Secretary of State for Education and Science when he expects to respond to the letter from the six teaching unions, dated 6 June, about the restoration of collective bargaining for teachers' pay and conditions; and if he will make a statement.

**Mrs. Rumbold:** I refer the hon. Member to the reply given by my right hon. Friend to my right hon. Friend the Member for Hendon, South (Mr. Marshall) on Tuesday 6 June at column *14*.

### Anderson-Fabry's Disease

**Mr. Fearn:** To ask the Secretary of State for Education and Science what research is conducted into Anderson-Fabry's disease; and what funds are provided by his Department for research into this illness.

**Mr. Jackson:** The Medical Research Council, which receives a grant in aid from this Department, is the main agency through which the Government supports medical research. The council itself determines the allocation of the funds at its disposal. In 1987-88, the last financial year for which figures are available, the council spent £37,000 on research specifically into Anderson-Fabry's disease. More generally, the council is funding a considerable amount of research on the X chromosome, some of which could contribute to an understanding of the disease. The council is always willing to consider soundly-based proposals for new research programmes, in competition with other proposals.

Additionally, university departments and medical schools support a range of research from block grants from the Universities Funding Council, some of which may be relevant to an understanding of this disease.

## NORTHERN IRELAND

### Short Bros

**Mr. John D. Taylor:** To ask the Secretary of State for Northern Ireland, pursuant to his reply to the hon. Member for Strangford of 13 June, what were his reasons for not including the oral question about Short Bros plc from the right hon. Member for Strangford on 9 March, *Official Report,* column *1018;* and whether he took account of that question in his response to the hon. Member for Strangford on 7 June, *Official Report,* column 234.

**Mr. Viggers:** In both responses referred to, no account was taken of the right hon. Gentleman's intervention which was a supplementary question rather than an oral question.

### De Lorean Motor Cars Ltd.

**Mr. Barry Field:** To ask the Secretary of State for Northern Ireland what progress he is making in recovering public funds from Mr. De Lorean.

**Mr. Viggers:** The joint receivers of the former De Lorean Motor Cars Ltd., appointed by the Government, have secured a judgment in the London High Court against Mr. John De Lorean for £30 million plus interest. Action is currently under way in the United States to enforce that judgment. In addition, the trustee of De Lorean Motor Co. in the United States bankruptcy proceedings, has recovered $9·36 million under a settlement agreement with Mr. De Lorean. The Government have a significant interest in any distributions the trustee may make.

The Government also have direct and indirect interests in the outcome of legal actions against a number of other persons in relation to the De Lorean case.

## SOCIAL SECURITY

### Family Credit (Publicity Campaign)

**Mr. Redmond:** To ask the Secretary of State for Social Security how many awards of family credit have been made to first-time claimants in the Doncaster and Mexborough areas of the county of South Yorkshire during his Department's eight-week advertising campaign; how many awards were made in the eight weeks previous to the campaign; and what percentage change of take-up by new claimants this represents since the family credit scheme began.

**Mr. Scott:** The information requested is not available on a local basis. However, we do know that at the beginning of April 1989 the number of families receiving family credit who, at the time their awards were made, were living in the areas covered by the relevant local social security offices was as follows:

|                   | *Number* |
| ----------------- | -------- |
| Doncaster (East)  | 838      |
| Doncaster (West)  | 504      |
| Wath-on-Dearne    | 211      |

This information will be updated from time to time.

### Correspondence

**Dr. Godman:** To ask the Secretary of State for Social Security (1) when the hon. Member for Greenock and Port Glasgow can expect an answer to his letter of 17 April concerning Mr. D. MacKinnon of Greenock;

(2) when he hon. Member for Greenock and Port Glasgow can expect an answer to his letter of 27 April concerning Mr. A. R. Young of Port Glasgow;

(3) when the hon. Member for Greenock and Port Glasgow can expect an answer to his letter of 27 April concerning Mr. J. O. O'Connor.

**Mr. Peter Lloyd:** Replies were sent on 22 May to the hon. Member's letter of 27 April concerning Mr. J. O'Connor, and on 14 June to the hon. Member's letters of 17 April concerning Mr. D. MacKinnon and of 27 April concerning Mr. A. Young.

## Independent Living Fund

**Mr. Alfred Morris:** To ask the Secretary of State for Social Security if he will make a statement on the progress so far of the work of the independent living fund.

**Mr. Scott:** The independent living fund is widely regarded as a success. By 30 April the fund had received 6,124 applications. Decisions had been made on 5,642 cases, of which 2,254 had been successful. The total benefit paid amounted to nearly £1·2 million.

## Grants and Loans

**Mr. Eastham:** To ask the Secretary of State for Social Security by how much Manchester offices of his Department have underspent their social fund allocations for *(a)* grant and *(b)* loans since April 1988; and what proportion of their budget for each purpose such underspending represents.

**Mr. Peter Lloyd:** Such information is available from the details held in the Library.

## Disability

**Mr. Alfred Morris:** To ask the Secretary of State for Social Security what recent representations the Minister for the Disabled has had from the British Council of Organisations of Disabled People; what reply he has sent or will be sending; if there is any action he will be taking; and if he will make a statement.

**Mr. Scott:** I recently received a letter from Mr. Richard Wood, chairman of the British Council of Organisations of Disabled People, seeking a substantial increase in the Department of Health's grant to the council. Officials have since met Mr. Wood to discuss his request. I hope to reply to his letter in the near future.

## Family Credit

**Mr. Dobson:** To ask the Secretary of State for Social Security (1) how many children he estimates would benefit if all those families eligible for family credit claimed it;

(2) what is his latest estimate of the number of families entitled to receive family credit.

**Mr. Peter Lloyd:** The latest information about the number of families eligible for family credit relates to 1988 and is contained in my right hon. Friend the Secretary of State's reply to my hon. Friend the Member for Bolton, North-East (Mr. Thurnham) on 17 March at columns *391-92*. On that basis there would have been about 1·1 million children in such families, but this does not include families not already receiving family credit where someone is self-employed.

**Mr. Dobson:** To ask the Secretary of State for Social Security how many children covered by payments of family credit are receiving sums in lieu of free school meals; and what is the average sum in lieu that each received after allowing for consequent reductions in other benefits.

**Mr. Peter Lloyd:** Each of the children's rates in family credit incorporates cash provision in place of free school meals or free welfare milk as appropriate. In March 1989 there were 392,000 children aged five or over in family credit families and for whom the cash provision might therefore be expected to be used in place of free school meals, but otherwise the information requested is not available.

## NATIONAL FINANCE

### Government Bonds

**Mr. Allen:** To ask the Chancellor of the Exchequer whether he intends to continue his policy of the early repurchasing of Government bonds.

**Mr. Lilley:** The Government will continue to operate according to the full fund rule set out in paragraph 2.23 of the 1989-90 "Financial Statement and Budget Report". The Government intend to return to a balanced budget as the norm in due course.

### Domestic Credit Control

**Mr. Allen:** To ask the Chancellor of the Exchequer if he will list European Community directives which would limit the freedom of member states to institute domestic credit control, including a deposit on the purchase of goods or a shortening of mortgage repayment schedules.

**Mr. Lilley:** No such directive has been adopted.

### PAYE

**Mr. Macdonald:** To ask the Chancellor of the Exchequer if he will make a statement on progress made on the computerisation of PAYE; and when he expects it to be in full operation.

**Mr. Norman Lamont:** The computerisation of the PAYE system was successfully completed in October 1988 when the last tax office, centre 1 in Scotland, was converted to the new system.

### Shares (Statistics)

**Mr. Macdonald:** To ask the Chancellor of the Exchequer what proportion of shares are owned by *(a)* the personal sector, *(b)* financial companies and institutions and *(c)* others.

**Mr. Norman Lamont:** Following is the information on the proportions of holdings of United Kingdom ordinary and preference shares at end 1987:

|  | *Percentage* |
| --- | --- |
| (a) Personal Sector | 29 |
| (b) Monetary Sector and Other Financial Institutions | 57 |
| (c) Industrial and Commercial Companies, Public Corporations, Central Government | 14 |

### Income Tax

**Mr. Macdonald:** To ask the Chancellor of the Exchequer what were the costs of collecting income tax in each of the previous five years; and if he will express each figure as a percentage of total income tax receipts and give comparative percentages where the data are available for other European Community countries and for Sweden and the United States of America.

**Mr. Norman Lamont:** The costs of collecting income tax in the United Kingdom, and costs as a percentage of total income tax receipts were as follows:

*Cost as percentage of total income tax receipts*

| | Cost (£ million) | Percentage |
|---|---|---|
| 1983 | 676·3 | 2·17 |
| 1984 | 730·3 | 2·25 |
| 1985 | 803·9 | 2·27 |
| 1986 | 882·9 | 2·29 |
| 1987 | 931·5 | 2·25 |

Comparable data for other countries are not available because of the differences in the tax system and the arrangements for administration and collection.

### Finance Bill (Clause 167)

**Mr. Arbuthnot:** To ask the Chancellor of the Exchequer if he will list in relation to clause 167 of the Finance Bill on instruments of variation those professional bodies or firms which have made representations *(a)* opposed to and *(b)* in favour of the principle or the detail of the clause.

**Mr. Norman Lamont:** We have received around 130 written representations, all of which were opposed to the principle or the detail of the clause.

### EC Money (Definition)

**Mr. Teddy Taylor:** To ask the Chancellor of the Exchequer if he will make a statement explaining the character and definition of Community money as referred to in paragraph 12(b) of the explanatory memorandum issued by the Paymaster General on 21 February 1989, (10449/88).

**Mr. Brooke:** The term "Community money" was used in the explanatory memorandum to refer to sums made available to the Community by member states.

### EC Finance Ministers (S'Agaro Meeting)

**Mr. Marlow:** To ask the Chancellor of the Exchequer whether any conclusions were reached at the informal meeting of European Community Finance Ministers at S'Agaro on 19 to 21 May.

**Mr. Brooke:** I refer my hon. Friend to the reply I gave to him on 12 June at column *272*.

### Small Businesses

**Mr. Aspinwall:** To ask the Chancellor of the Exchequer what the Treasury definition of a small business is for tax purposes.

**Mr. Norman Lamont** *[holding answer 15 June 1989]:* There is no specific definition. Targeting of tax reliefs for small businesses is achieved by defining the relevant qualifying conditions, taking account of the particular objective. For example, to benefit from the small companies' rate of corporation tax, a company must have profits below £100,000 or, for the purposes of the marginal relief, below £500,000. The Finance Bill contains provisions to increase these limits to £150,000 and £750,000 respectively.

### Building Society Shares

**Mr. Chris Smith:** To ask the Chancellor of the Exchequer what is his estimate of the cost to the Exchequer of the inclusion announced on 8 June of newly floated building society shares within personal equity plan portfolios; and what he expects the level of take-up to be.

**Mr. Norman Lamont** *[holding answer 12 June 1989]:* The cost to the Exchequer is expected to be negligible. The level of take-up will depend on the number of building societies converting to plc status and the extent to which personal equity plan managers offer the new facility.

### EEC Funding

**Mr. Michael Meacher:** To ask the Chancellor of the Exchequer if he will make it his policy to estimate the level of EEC funding from social and regional grants that has been lost in each of the last five years as a result of the accumulative effect each year of the reductions in the officially declared level of United Kingdom unemployment following changes in the calculation of the unemployment figures.

**Mr. Atkins** *[holding answer 12 June 1989]:* I have been asked to reply.

The question is based on a false hypothesis. Payments from the European social and regional development funds are not directly determined by unemployment levels. In so far as, following the recent reform of the funds, eligibility for grant partly depends on rates of unemployment, the relevant rates are European Commission estimates prepared on a standardised basis to eliminate any effects of differences of statistical method between Member States or at different periods.

## WALES

### In-patient Waiting Lists

**17. Dr. Marek:** To ask the Secretary of State for Wales what is the latest figure he has for in-patient waiting lists for urgent and non-urgent cases.

**Mr. Grist:** The latest figures, published on 17 May, are contained in "Welsh Hospital Waiting List Bulletin" 1989: No. 1. They show that 2,887 urgent cases and 38,362 non-urgent cases were waiting for in-patient treatment on 30 September 1988. I am pleased to note the 20 per cent. reduction in patients waiting for urgent treatment, compared to 1987, but disappointed at the 5 per cent. increase in non-urgent cases.

### Training and Enterprise Councils

**18. Mr. Ieuan Jones:** To ask the Secretary of State for Wales if he will make a statement on the progress being made in establishing training and enterprise councils in Wales.

**Mr. Peter Walker:** Good progress is being made. Employers throughout Wales are responding positively to the invitation to formulate proposals for training and enterprise councils and I expect two councils to be operational early next year with a full network across Wales during 1990.

## NHS

19. **Mr. Michael:** To ask the Secretary of State for Wales if he will publish detailed consultative documents setting out his proposals for implementation of changes in the Health Service in Wales which take account of special factors affecting the regions of Wales; and if he will make a statement.

**Mr. Grist:** I refer the hon. Gentleman to my earlier reply to the hon. Member for Brecon and Radnor (Mr. Livsey).

### Cardigan Bay

20. **Mr. Geraint Howells:** To ask the Secretary of State for Wales whether he has consulted local authorities around Cardigan bay about turning the bay into a marine nature conservation area.

**Mr. Wyn Roberts:** No. It is for the Nature Conservancy Council to apply to my right hon. Friend for the designation of a marine nature reserve after consulting relevant interested parties. However, I understand that at present it has no plans to make an application in respect of the Cardigan bay area.

### Tourism (Grants)

21. **Mr. Nicholas Bennett:** To ask the Secretary of State for Wales what representations he has received about the provision of grants for tourist projects under section 4 of the Tourism Act 1969; and if he will make a statement.

**Mr. Wyn Roberts:** My right hon. Friend and I have received representations from a number of interested organisations and individuals.

### Welsh Water Authority

23. **Dr. Kim Howells:** To ask the Secretary of State when he last met the chairman of the Welsh water authority; and what matters were discussed.

**Mr. Grist:** My right hon. Friend last met the chairman on 22 May 1989. A wide range of issues were discussed.

### Welsh Arts Council

24. **Sir Anthony Meyer:** To ask the Secretary of State for Wales when he next expects to meet the chairman of the Welsh Arts Council; and what matters he proposes to discuss.

**Mr. Wyn Roberts:** My right hon. Friend has no plans at present to meet the chairman of the Welsh Arts Council.

### Cardiff Bay Development Corporation

25. **Mr. Gwilym Jones:** To ask the Secretary of State for Wales if he will make a statement on the progress of the Cardiff Bay development corporation.

**Mr. Peter Walker:** The development corporation is making excellent progress. Some 300 acres of land has been acquired; site investigations for major land reclamation schemes are near completion; the local community has directly benefited by more than £3·5 million spent on various improvement projects. The barrage Bill can be expected to come before this House shortly, having recently been considered by a Committee in another place and approved there with one minor amendment.

The recent agreement with Associated British Ports for the development of large areas of land in the ownership of ABP will allow quicker progress to be made with the development of this important area of the bay.

I recently announced that, subject to parliamentary approval on the supplementary Estimate, I am providing a further £7 million this year to permit the corporation to acquire more land for development purposes.

### Water Pollution

**Mr. Speller:** To ask the Secretary of State for Wales if he will seek powers to require Welsh Water to seek planning permission for raw sewage outlets into the Bristol channel; and if he will make a statement on the different sources of pollution which enter this marine cul de sac.

**Mr. Grist:** No. Under part II of the Control of Pollution Act 1974, water authorities are required to obtain consents before making a discharge into the sea or water courses. Where schemes require planning permission, this is a matter for the local planning authority to determine under the Town and Country Planning Acts. With regard to sources of pollution in the Bristol channel, information on consented discharges is available on public registers held by the water authorities.

### Health Service

**Mr. Coleman:** To ask the Secretary of State for Wales what is the number of patients awaiting surgical operations in each of the Welsh district health authorities; and if he will make a statement.

**Mr. Grist:** Waiting list information is collected centrally on the basis of the number of people waiting for admission to hospital in a particular specialty and it is not known, therefore, how many are waiting for surgical operations. Information on waiting lists is published in "Welsh Hospital Waiting List Bulletin" copies of which are in the Library of the House.

**Mr. Livsey:** To ask the Secretary of State for Wales what is the average number of patients for each county in Wales per *(a)* doctor and *(b)* general practitioner practice.

**Mr. Grist:** The requested information (as at 1 October 1987) is given in the table:

| Family Practitioner Committee | Average number of patients per doctor[1] | Average number of patients per partnership[2] |
|---|---|---|
| Clwyd | 1,914 | 6,113 |
| Dyfed | 1,700 | 4,774 |
| Gwent | 1,890 | 4,930 |
| Gwynedd | 1,675 | 4,605 |
| Mid Glamorgan | 1,919 | 5,475 |
| Powys | 1,628 | 6,784 |
| South Glamorgan | 1,887 | 5,661 |
| West Glamorgan | 1,952 | 6,108 |

[1] Unrestricted principals
[2] Includes single doctor practices

### Roads

**Mr. Alex Carlile:** To ask the Secretary of State for Wales what are his current proposals for the improvement of the Shrewsbury-Aberystwyth trunk road from the Shropshire/Powys border; if any studies have been carried out to estimate increases in traffic load on the road between its present time and the year 2000; and if he will make a statement.

**Mr. Wyn Roberts:** Selective improvements of the A458/A483/A489/A470/A44 route are planned, and shown in "Roads in Wales 1989". The "National Traffic Forecasts (Great Britain) 1989" published on 18 May covers this route; a major traffic survey has recently been carried out by the Department on the A483 north of Newtown.

### Language Teaching

**Mr. Alex Carlile:** To ask the Secretary of State for Wales what assessment he has made of the level of provision for the learning of French, German, Spanish and Italian in secondary schools in Wales; and if he will make a further statement concerning his policy for the teaching of European Community languages in *(a)* primary and *(b)* secondary schools in Wales.

**Mr. Wyn Roberts:** The secondary school staffing survey conducted this year will provide information on the numbers of teachers qualified to teach these languages. The national curriculum will require all pupils aged 11 to 16 to be taught a modern foreign language, and they must all be offered the opportunity to study a European Community language. I have no plans to promote the teaching of foreign languages in primary schools.

### Village Schools

**Mr. Alex Carlile:** To ask the Secretary of State for Wales what assessment he has made of the quality of teaching and standard of educational attainment in village primary schools in Powys; and if he will make a statement concerning his policy towards village schools.

**Mr. Wyn Roberts:** Her Majesty's inspectors of schools in Wales have published a number of reports on small schools in Powys which include comments on quality of teaching and standard of educational attainment. Schools subject of reports published over the past year are:
Penrhos County Primary School, Ystradgynlais
Ysgol Pennant, Pen-y-Bont Fawr
Buttington/Trewern County Primary School
Ffynnon Gynydd Church in Wales Primary School, Glasbury
Ysgol Trefeglwys, Llanidloes
Crossgates County Primary School
In addition surveys have been carried out into various aspects of provision in Powys

Guidance on schools in rural areas is given in Welsh Office circular 20/88, a copy of which is in the Library of the House.

### Farming

**Mr. Livsey:** To ask the Secretary of State for Wales what was the average *(a)* size in hectares *(b)* average farm income *(c)* the number of farms *(d)* the average number of ewes and *(e)* the number of beef cows for upland beef and sheep farms in marginal land areas within the less-favoured areas.

**Mr. Peter Walker:** There are estimated to be 9,163 cattle and sheep farms in the less-favoured areas of Wales.

Average figures for upland beef and sheep farms are not available separately for marginal land area. Figures for all hill and upland livestock farms can be found at table 3.14 of the 1989 edition of "Farm Incomes in the United Kingdom", a copy of which is in the Library of the House.

**Mr. Livsey:** To ask the Secretary of State for Wales what was the average *(a)* size in hectares *(b)* number of dairy cows kept and *(c)* farm income for the latest period for which he has figures for an average dairy farm in Wales.

**Mr. Peter Walker:** The information requested can be found at table 3.9 of the 1989 edition of "Farm Incomes in the United Kingdom", a copy of which is in the Library of the House.

### Radioactive Waste

**Mr. Gareth Wardell:** To ask the Secretary of State for Wales if he has granted permission to Amersham International to use the Ferry road tip in the Grangetown district of Cardiff for the disposal of low-level radioactive waste.

**Mr. Grist:** An authorisation has been issued to the company to dispose of very low level solid radioactive waste at Cardiff city council's waste disposal sites at Ferry road and Lamby way.

**Mr. Ron Davies:** To ask the Secretary of State for Wales if he will list those sites within Wales that have been approved for the dumping of low level radioactive waste and state in respect of each site when approval for such use was initially granted and by which licensing authority.

**Mr. Grist:** Any waste disposal site licensed by a waste disposal authority under the Control of Pollution Act 1974 may receive a very low level radioactive waste where such a disposal method is permitted by the necessary authorisation issued by the Secretary of State under the Radioactive Substances Act 1960.

The organisations and premises specified in authorisations covering Wales are shown in the Department of the Environment/Welsh Office/Her Majesty's inspectorate of pollution publication "List of Premises in England and Wales currently authorised under the Radioactive Substances Act 1960 to dispose of Radioactive Waste" a copy of which is available in the Library of the House.

### Gwynedd Health Authority

**Mr. Wigley:** To ask the Secretary of State for Wales how many members there are of the Gwynedd health authority; how many are appointed by him; and of those so appointed, how many have their home residence in the Arfon borough area.

**Mr. Grist:** There are 17 members of Gwynedd health authority, including the chairman. The Secretary of State is responsible for appointing the chairman and 10 members, one of whom has a home residence in the Arfon borough area.

### Milk Quota

**Mr. Nicholas Bennett:** To ask the Secretary of State for Wales when the milk quota allocated to Upper Wallis farm, Ambleston, Haverfordwest, Pembrokeshire will be transferred to Mr. B. Bevan, who is due to re-occupy the farm on 30 June.

**Mr. Peter Walker** *[holding answer 16 June 1989]:* Transfers of milk quota are a matter for the parties concerned. Mr. Bevan will be able to take steps to transfer the relevant quota when he resumes occupation of Upper Wallis farm. The appropriate form is available from the milk marketing board.

## FOREIGN AND COMMONWEALTH AFFAIRS

### Namibian Refugees

**Mr. Atkinson:** To ask the Secretary of State for Foreign and Commonwealth Affairs (1) how many Namibian refugees are presently located in camps in Angola and Zambia;

(2) how many Namibian refugees were in Angola and Zambia in 1985, 1986 and 1987; and what organisations were responsible for monitoring and administering these refugees during these years;

(3) if he has made any representations concerning the discrepancy in figures published over the last three years by the United Nations High Commissioner for Refugees concerning the total number of Namibian refugees in Angola and Zambia and the most recent estimates of the United Nations High Commissioner for Refugees;

(4) when Namibian refugees, currently based in Angola and Zambia, will be returned to Namibia under the United Nations' Namibian independence plan;

(5) which non-govermental organisations are responsible under the United Nations plan for the processing and safe return of Namibian refugees from camps in Angola and Zambia to Namibia.

**Mrs. Chalker:** The United Nations High Commissioner for Refugees has responsibility for organising the repatriation of Namibian refugees. We fully support the UNHCR operation, and are in close touch with UNHCR officials.

No independent count of Namibian refugees in Angola and Zambia has been made. The UNHCR has operated its programme for Namibian refugees on the basis of estimates that there were 69,000 Namibian refugees in Angola and a further 7,000 in Zambia.

By 3 June, 41,000 returnees had registered with UNHCR for return to Namibia, though the registration process was still continuing. Not included in these figures are a large number of children who are expected to remain outside Namibia to complete their schooling and armed SWAPO units who will remain in United Nations-monitored positions north of the 16th parallel in Angola.

The repatriation operation began on 12 June and is expected to last six weeks.

### South West Africa People's Organisation

**Mr. Atkinson:** To ask the Secretary of State for Foreign and Commonwealth Affairs (1) whether Her Majesty's Government have made representations to the United Nations High Commissioner for Refugees concerning Namibians detained by the South West Africa People's Organisation; and if he will make a statement;

(2) whether Her Majesty's Government possess a list of Namibians detained by South West Africa People's Organisation; and if he will make a statement concerning the fate of Namibian refugees in Angola and Zambia;

(3) whether Her Majesty's Government will take all possible steps to ensure that all those Namibians presently detained by the South West Africa People's Organisation and accused of being South African spies are released and repatriated to Namibia at the earliest opportunity.

(4) whether he has received any representations concerning the names of those Namibians detained by the South West Africa People's Organisation accused of being South African spies; and if he will make a statement.

**Mrs. Chalker:** We are extremely concerned about the welfare of SWAPO-held detainees. Several lists of such detainees have been drawn to our attention, including one compiled by Amnesty International. We have raised the matter in our contacts with SWAPO. We have also drawn the matter to the attention of the UNHCR. The United Nations special representative for Namibia, supported by officials from the UNHCR and the International Committee of the Red Cross, has been pressing for the release of SWAPO's prisoners. Some were released last month in Angola. United Nations and ICRC staff are in contact with SWAPO to ensure that all detainees are released in accordance with the United Nations plan. We are in close touch with these organisations, and shall continue to support their efforts.

**Mr. Atkinson:** To ask the Secretary of State for Foreign and Commonwealth Affairs on how many occasions over the last two years he or Ministers from his Department have met with senior representatives from the South West Africa People's Organisation; and if he will make a statement.

**Mrs. Chalker:** We have regular official and, as appropriate, ministerial contact with representatives of SWAPO. Ministers have met senior representatives of SWAPO on three occasions in the last two years.

**Mr. Atkinson:** To ask the Secretary of State for Foreign and Commonwealth Affairs what action Her Majesty's Government have taken to ensure that the Commonwealth fellowship and training programme for Namibians will not be restricted to members of the South West Africa People's Organisation; and if he will make a statement.

**Mrs. Chalker:** We are concerned that all multilateral programmes for Namibia to which we contribute should be impartially administered and distributed. The Commonwealth programme to which my hon. Friend refers is not restricted to members of SWAPO.

### Cambodia

**Mr. Spearing:** To ask the Secretary of State for Foreign and Commonwealth Affairs what information he has concerning the action, or intention, of any Government to provide lethal aid to any group within the resistance coalition of Cambodia, within or on the borders of that country; and what reactions or representations have been made by Her Majesty's Government to any such policy.

**Mr. Eggar:** I am aware of reports that certain governments have provided, or intend to provide, lethal aid to groups resisting Vietnam's illegal occupation of Cambodia. We do not plan to make representations as long as that occupation continues.

## Malta

**Mr. Harry Barnes:** To ask the Secretary of State for Foreign and Commonwealth Affairs if he will list the agreements signed with the Government of Malta since that country's last elections.

**Mrs. Chalker:** Since the May 1987 General Elections in Malta, we have signed the following agreement with the Government of Malta: "Agreement on the development of friendly relations and co-operation". The agreement was signed in Valletta on 15 March 1989.

## Jabu Ndlovu

**Mrs. Fyfe:** To ask the Secretary of State for Foreign and Commonwealth Affairs if he will make diplomatic representations to the South African Government concerning the case of Jabu Ndlovu, whose home was attacked by Inkatha.

**Mrs. Chalker:** Jabu Ndlovu and her family were most regrettably among the latest victims of the long-running intra-communal conflict in Natal. We have made clear our hope that action will be taken to end the violence. We hope that recent contacts between the parties directly involved will lead to a lasting settlement.

## China

**Mr. Flynn:** To ask the Secretary of State for Foreign and Commonwealth Affairs if any arms or military equipment used by the Chinese People's Liberation Army in Tiananmen Square or other parts of Beijing to kill students and protestors in June were made in the United Kingdom and officially exported to the People's Republic of China.

**Mr. Eggar:** We are not aware of any British equipment having been used to kill protestors in Peking during the recent disturbances. In my right hon. and learned Friend the Secretary of State's statement to the House of 6 June, we announced a ban on arms sales to China.

## Nuclear Non-proliferation Treaty

**Mr. Flynn:** To ask the Secretary of State for Foreign and Commonwealth Affairs if he has ascertained from the Government of the People's Republic of China the terms on which they would be prepared to sign the nuclear non-proliferation treaty.

**Mr. Waldegrave:** Although we have regularly pressed the Government of the People's Republic of China to accede to the nuclear non-proliferation treaty, they have not given us any indication of the terms on which they would be prepared to do so.

**Mr. Flynn:** To ask the Secretary of State for Foreign and Commonwealth Affairs if he is aware of the conditions set by Argentina before that state will sign the nuclear non-proliferation treaty.

**Mr. Waldegrave:** To the best of our knowledge the Government of Argentina has not specified conditions under which Argentina would accede to the nuclear non-proliferation treaty.

**Mr. Flynn:** To ask the Secretary of State for Foreign and Commonwealth Affairs if he will list the last eight countries to sign the nuclear non-proliferation treaty giving the date of signature in each case.

**Mr. Waldegrave:** The last eight countries to accede to the non-proliferation treaty were Kiribati (succeeded on 18 April 1985), Malawi (acceded on 18 February 1986), Colombia (ratified on 8 April 1986), Trinidad and Tobago (ratified on 30 October 1986), Spain (acceded on 5 November 1987), Saudi Arabia (acceded on 3 October 1988), Bahrain (acceded on 3 November 1988) and Qatar (acceded on 3 April 1989).

**Mr. Flynn:** To ask the Secretary of State for Foreign and Commonwealth Affairs, if he will set out the respective dates on which *(a)* Libya, *(b)* Iraq, *(c)* Iran, *(d)* Syria and *(e)* Egypt signed the 1968 nuclear non-proliferation treaty.

**Mr. Waldegrave:** Libya ratified the nuclear non-proliferation treaty on 26 May 1975, Iraq ratified the treaty on 29 October 1969, Iran ratified on 2 February 1970, Syria on 24 September 1969 and Egypt on 26 February 1981.

**Mr. Flynn:** To ask the Secretary of State for Foreign and Commonwealth Affairs if he will set out the terms of signature communicated to Her Majesty's Government, or to the other depository states for the nuclear non-proliferation treaty, by the Republic of South Africa, before South Africa will sign the non-proliferation treaty.

**Mr. Waldegrave:** The South African Government have not set out terms to us, or, so far as we are aware, to either of the other depository Governments. On 16 August 1988, after consultations between the depository powers and South Africa had been held in Vienna, the South African Foreign Ministry stated publicly that it would sign the NPT if assured of full participation in the treaty.

**Mr. Flynn:** To ask the Secretary of State for Foreign and Commonwealth Affairs if the Government of India have indicated to the United Kingdom, or to the other two depository states for the nuclear non-proliferation treaty, the terms on which India would sign the nuclear non-proliferation treaty; and what attempts have been made by Her Majesty's Government to persuade India to sign the treaty.

**Mr. Waldegrave:** To the best of our knowledge the Government of India have not indicated terms on which India would accede to the non-proliferation treaty (NPT). However, our views on the value of the NPT are well known to the Indian Government, and we make our position clear to them whenever suitable opportunities arise.

**Mr. Flynn:** To ask the Secretary of State for Foreign and Commonwealth Affairs if, during the meeting of the North Atlantic Treaty Organisation Ministers in Brussels on 29 and 30 May, and the visit of the United State Administration executive officers to the United Kingdom on 31 May to 2 June, he raised with the United States Secretaries of Defence or State the fourth review conference of the nuclear non-proliferation treaty to be held in the summer of 1990.

**Mr. Waldegrave:** No. However, issues related to the 1990 non-proliferation treaty review conference are frequently discussed at official level.

**Mr. Flynn:** To ask the Secretary of State for Foreign and Commonwealth Affairs if, during the visit of General

Jaruzelski of Poland on 10 and 11 June, he discussed the forthcoming nuclear non-proliferation treaty fourth review conference, to be held in 1990, with members of the Polish governmental delegation.

**Mr. Waldegrave:** No.

**Mr. Flynn:** To ask the Secretary of State for Foreign and Commonwealth Affairs when the depository states for the 1968 nuclear non-proliferation treaty last held trilateral discussions on progress of the treaty.

**Mr. Waldegrave:** The non-proliferation treaty depository powers—USA, USSR, United Kingdom—last discussed the non-proliferation treaty at the first preparatory committee, held in New York from 1 to 5 May.

### Poland

**Mr. Flynn:** To ask the Secretary of State for Foreign and Commonwealth Affairs if, during the visit of General Jaruzelski and other Polish Government officials on 10 and 11 June, he discussed *(a)* the prospects of nuclear reactor and nuclear fuel cycle service sales to Poland, *(b)* the possibility of the sale of industrial air pollution control technology and fuel gas desulpherisation technology to Poland and *(c)* the possibility of the sale of combined cycle coal-gas pebble bed power plant technology to Poland.

**Mr. Waldegrave:** My right hon. and learned Friend the Secretary of State discussed none of these subjects.

### Nuclear Weapons

**Mr. Flynn:** To ask the Secretary of State for Foreign and Commonwealth Affairs what is Her Majesty's Government's policy towards the possession of nuclear weapons by the Soviet Union, the People's Republic of China, France and the United States of America.

**Mr. Waldegrave:** All four countries are recognised nuclear weapons states as defined by the non-proliferation treaty. We, therefore, recognise their right to possess nuclear weapons.

### Chemical Weapons

**Mr. Flynn:** To ask the Secretary of State for Foreign and Commonwealth Affairs what new policy initiatives were put forward by the United Kingdom ambassador to the chemical weapons disarmament negotiations when they resumed on 13 June in Geneva.

**Mr. Waldegrave:** I visited the conference on disarmament in Geneva on 15 June. As well as delivering a speech giving an overview of British policy, I tabled a paper on the United Kingdom's innovative work on "challenge inspections", a crucial part of the verification regime for a chemical weapons convention. This work involves a comprehensive programme of trial inspections at military facilities and is designed to test the concept of challenge inspection in practice to enable effective provisions to be elaborated. As far as we are aware, the United Kingdom is the first country to carry out such work which reflects the Government's practical, problem-solving approach to the achievement of a comprehensive and effectively verifiable, global ban on chemical weapons.

### Partial Nuclear Test Ban Treaty

**Mr. Flynn:** To ask the Secretary of State for Foreign and Commonwealth Affairs when the United Kingdom, United States and Soviet Union, as the depository states for the 1963 partial nuclear test ban treaty, last held trilateral discussions on progress of the treaty; and if he will make a statement on the future of the treaty.

**Mr. Waldegrave:** Several bilateral discussions between the depository Governments have taken place recently; we expect that they will meet trilaterally later this month, probably in Geneva.

### Kurdish People

**Mrs. Clwyd:** To ask the Secretary of State for Foreign and Commonwealth Affairs if Her Majesty's Government have made representations to the Iraqi embassy on the subject of the deportation of Kurds within Iraq.

**Mr. Waldegrave:** I discussed the issue most recently with the Iraqi ambassador on Wednesday 14 June. I told the ambassador that we viewed with concern the latest allegations about a policy of mass resettlement of Kurds, and pressed him to allow diplomats and journalists to visit the area in question to see for themselves what the truth is.

**Mrs. Clwyd:** To ask the Secretary of State for Foreign and Commonwealth Affairs if he has discussed with his partners in the European Community the question of deportations of Kurds within Iraq; and what action the European Community intends to take.

**Mr. Waldegrave:** The United Kingdom regularly discusses such issues within the Twelve. EC Representatives in Baghdad have prepared a report on the human rights situation in Iraq.

**Mrs. Clwyd:** To ask the Secretary of State for Foreign and Commonwealth Affairs if he has received a report compiled by the 12 European Community ambassadors in Baghdad on the subject of the deportation of Kurds within Iraq; and if he will make a statement.

**Mr. Waldegrave:** The EC ambassadors in Baghdad have produced a report on human rights in Iraq. We and our partners in the Twelve are studying it urgently.

## HOUSE OF COMMONS

### Early-day Motions

**Mr. Patrick McLoughlin:** To ask the Lord President of the Council if he will list the number of early-day motions tabled in each year since 1970.

**Mr. Wakeham:** The information requested is as follows:

| Session | Number of EDMs. |
| --- | --- |
| 1970-71 | 717 |
| 1971-72 | 474 |
| 1972-73 | 432 |
| 1973-74 | 174 |
| 1974 | 245 |
| 1974-75 | 759 |
| 1975-76 | 701 |
| 1976-77 | 473 |

| Session | Number of EDMs. |
|---|---|
| 1977-78 | 607 |
| 1978-79 | 354 |
| 1979-80 | 907 |
| 1980-81 | 631 |
| 1981-82 | 716 |
| 1982-83 | 502 |
| 1983-84 | 1,060 |
| 1984-85 | 979 |
| 1985-86 | 1,262 |
| 1986-87 | 1,000 |
| 1987-88 | 1,601 |
| 1988-89 | 984 |
| (to date) | |

# HEALTH

## Community Health Councils

**Mr. Rowe:** To ask the Secretary of State for Health if he has any plans to withdraw the guidance given to regional health authorities in circular HC(81)15 to refuse appointment to community health councils of people over 70 years of age.

**Mr. Mellor:** Members of community health councils are appointed mostly by local authorities and voluntary organisations. Only one sixth are appointed by regional health authorities. Guidance in circular HC(81)15 is that appointing bodies should not appoint people over the age of 70 unless there is a special reason—such as where the appointing organisation is concerned mainly with elderly people. We have no plans to change that guidance.

## Health Care Screening

**Mr. Allan Stewart:** To ask the Secretary of State for Health what are his Department's current priorities for screening in health care; and if he will make a statement.

**Mr. Mellor:** Priorities for screening depend upon the risk for given disorders of identifiable groups in the population.

We have established two programmes to screen women regularly for breast and cervical cancers. Women aged between 20 and 64 will be invited for a cervical smear test at least every five years and women 50 and 64 years for breast X-ray (mammogram) every three years; breast screening will also be available to women aged 65 and over on request.

Besides routine antenatal care, screening may be offered, for example, to pregnant women for foetal neural tube defects and chromosomal abnormalities (in older mothers) and, for women from certain ethnic groups, the haemoglobinopathies. There are continuing programmes for systematic screening of infants and children for sensory, physical and mental impairments. In addition, screening for single gene disorders may be appropriate for certain families.

New opportunities for worthwhile screening will undoubtedly arise as a result of the development of new technologies in for example genetics and ultra sound. We also support the cancer screening evaluation unit which provides advice on existing and possible future schemes of screening for cancer.

Screening, of course, is not the only method by which ill health can be prevented.

## Midwives

**Mr. Cox:** To ask the Secretary of State for Health what has been the amount of financial help given by his Department towards the cost of the salary regrading of midwives; and if he will make a statement.

**Mr. Mellor:** A total of £731 million was made available by the Government to meet the cost of the nurses, midwives and health visitors regrading exercise in 1988-89 in England. Including the extra £98 million announced on 21 October, this met the extra cost in full. Health authorities' own estimates provided the basis of the costing, but these were not required to be broken down between nurses, midwives and health visitors on a national basis. We do not therefore hold this information centrally.

## Remand System

**Mr. Sheerman:** To ask the Secretary of State for Health if he has any plans to fund secure accommodation for remanded juveniles from Doncaster and neighbouring areas awaiting their court appearance who because of their behaviour are unsuitable for living in normal open local authority children's homes.

**Mr. Mellor:** I refer the hon. Member to the reply given to the hon. Member for Doncaster, North (Mr. Welsh) on 16 May 1989, at column *151*.

## NHS Reform

**Mr. Winnick:** To ask the Secretary of State for Health if he will make a further statement on the procedures before any hospital opts out of the existing National Health Service management structure.

**Mr. Mellor:** Self-governing trusts will not opt out but will remain fully within the NHS. Subject to the passing of the necessary legislation, decisions on applications will rest with the Secretary of State. The application process will follow the outline in the White Paper "Working for Patients". We are issuing information about the process in connection with a national conference on self-governing hospitals on 20 June.

## NML Presentations Ltd.

**Mr. Dobson:** To ask the Secretary of State for Health what involvement NML Presentations Ltd. had in identifying doctors who favoured the proposals in the Government's National Health Service review and putting the news media in contact with them at the time of the original launch.

**Mr. Mellor:** None.

**Mr. Dobson:** To ask the Secretary of State for Health whether he assessed the success of the contributions made by NML Presentations Ltd. to the original launch of the National Health Service review before awarding them the contract for the current stage of the programme.

**Mr. Mellor:** Yes.

## Benzodiazepines

**Mr. Fearn:** To ask the Secretary of State for Health how many people were assisted by his Department to withdraw from benzodiazepines in drug and alcohol treatment centres in the last year for which figures are available; and what was the cost of this.

**Mr. Mellor:** We do not hold this information centrally.

**Mr. Fearn:** To ask the Secretary of State for Health if he will make an estimate of the cost to the United Kingdom economy, in terms of lost production and sick pay, through people addicted to benzodiazepines.

**Mr. Mellor:** We do not have the information to enable us to make such an estimate.

**Mr. Fearn:** To ask the Secretary of State for Health if his Department has carried out studies into the number of people who become epileptic after withdrawing from benzodiazepines.

**Mr. Mellor:** No.

**Mr. Fearn:** To ask the Secretary of State for Health what information he has on attempts made by the pharmaceutical industry to assist people addicted to benzodiazepines to withdraw from the drug and as to whether any compensation scheme is being considered by the industry.

**Mr. Mellor:** We have no information on attempts made by the pharmaceutical industry to assist people addicted to benzodiazepines to withdraw from the drugs.

It must be for the pharmaceutical industry to decide whether it wishes to set up its own no-fault compensation scheme.

### Social Work Staff

**Mr. Win Griffiths:** To ask the Secretary of State for Health what plans he has to overcome the national shortage of qualified social workers highlighted in the social services employment survey 1988 published by the Association of Directors of Social Services and the Local Authority Conditions of Service Advisory Board.

**Mr. Mellor:** I refer the hon. Member to my reply to the hon. Member for Newham, North-West (Mr. Banks) today.

The report of the national work force survey conducted by the Local Authority Conditions of Service Advisory Board and ADSS will be given full consideration when received. The response by local authorities to our two training support programmes targeted at staff working with elderly people and those working in the field of child care, indicates that many social service departments will be enabled to increase significantly the number of their staff seconded to social work qualifying courses.

**Mr. Hinchliffe:** To ask the Secretary of State for Health (1) if he will bring forward proposals to give financial assistance to local authorities in London to enable them to recruit social work staff;

(2) what action he is taking to deal with the nationwide shortage of 2,200 social workers identified in the recent Association of Directors of Social Services national work force survey, a copy of which he has been sent;

(3) what action he is taking to encourage people re-entering the work force to undertake professional social work training;

(4) what action he is taking to respond to the need for an additional 800 per annum social work training places

identified by the Central Council for Education and Training in Social Work in its 1987-88 annual report, a copy of which has been sent to him;

(5) what initiatives he is taking to deal with the particular problems arising in the London area as a result of the inability to recruit basic grade social workers.

**Mr. Mellor:** I refer the hon. Member to my reply to the hon. Member for Newham, North-West (Mr. Banks) today.

The Government and the Central Council for Education and Training in Social Work are taking a number of initiatives to improve the present system of social work qualifying training which will help to ensure that social work continues to attract suitable people of different ages and domestic circumstances and from a variety of social backgrounds.

The availability of places on social work courses is a matter which is currently being examined by the Department in connection with the Central Council for Education and Training in Social Work.

Our two training support programmes targeted at staff working with elderly people and those working in the field of child care have enabled many social services departments to increase significantly the number of their staff seconded to social work qualifying courses.

**Mr. Hinchliffe:** To ask the Secretary of State for Health what information he has on the age structure of those employed by local authorities as basic grade social workers.

**Mr. Mellor:** We understand that information is contained in the report of the national work force survey conducted by the Local Authority Conditions of Service Advisory Board and the Association of Directors of Social Services. We have not yet had an opportunity to study a copy of the full report.

**Mr. Tony Banks:** To ask the Secretary of State for Health (1) if he has any plans to deal with the shortage of basic social work staff in London;

(2) if he has any plans to increase finance for encouraging the recruitment of social services staff in London local authorities;

(3) what information he has about the shortage of mainstream social services professionals in London local authorities; and if he will make a statement.

**Mr. Mellor** [*holding answer 16 June 1989*]: A survey of the London social services work force was carried out by the London branch of the Association of Directors of Social Services (ADSS) with the assistance of the social services inspectorate. The results were published in April 1988. A new national work force survey, conducted by the Local Authority Conditions of Service Advisory Board and ADSS was published on 12 June 1989. Officials of the Department of Health have not had the opportunity to study the full copy of the report.

We are aware of the problems faced by some local authorities in London in attracting and retaining suitably qualified staff and of the steps they, as employers, are taking to improve the position. It is of course for individual authorities to decide how much to spend on social services from within total resources available.

Financial pressures on local authority social services, such as the need to encourage recruitment of social services staff, are taken into account in setting the overall level of central Government support to local authorities. The Government are currently considering the local authority associations' report on additional financial needs for social services departments in 1990-91 in which this issue is identified. This report, along with similar reports for other local authority services, is being discussed through the normal consultation channels under the Consultative Council on Local Government Finance.

### Occupational Therapists

**Mr. Hinchliffe:** To ask the Secretary of State for Health what action he is taking to deal with the nationwide shortage of 250 occupational therapists identified in the recent Association of Directors of Social Services national work force survey, a copy of which has been sent to him.

**Mr. Mellor:** We have taken a number of measures to overcome the shortage of occupational therapists which affects local authorities and the NHS. We are on course to increase the annual intake of occupational therapy students for three-year diploma courses by at least 100 by 1990-91. The Department is also assisting in funding shortened two-year courses for graduates in related disciplines to qualify as occupational therapists. We have also commissioned a review of the manpower, skill mix and structures within local authority and NHS occupational therapy departments, and a report is expected in August.

We are in communication with local authority representatives to encourage local authorities to make a greater contribution to the cost of training occupational therapists. We are also aware that a number of local authorities are pursuing their own local strategies to overcome staff shortages.

**Mr. Tony Banks:** To ask the Secretary of State for Health if he will state the number of occupational therapists employed by London local authorities in each of the last three years; and if he will make a statement.

**Mr. Mellor** *[holding answer 16 June 1989]:* The numbers of qualified occupational therapists employed by local authorities in London for 1985-87 (the last three years for which information is available) expressed as whole-time equivalents is given in the table. These figures reflect an increase of 24 per cent. in whole-time equivalent staff employed.

*Qualified occupational therapists employed by local authority social services departments in London, 1985-87*

| As at 30 September | Whole-time equivalents |
|---|---|
| 1985 | 256·5 |
| 1986 | 272·1 |
| 1987 | 317·6 |

*Note:* Figures for 1986 and 1987 are provisional and subject to revision.

### Botulism

**Mr. Fearn:** To ask the Secretary of State for Health (1) when each of the eight additional dairies referred to by him in *Official Report*, column *703*, 13 June, were first informed that their products were part of the investigations by his Department into the botulism outbreak;

(2) how many environmental health officers are employed by each of the public health authorities for the areas where the additional dairies mentioned in *Official Report*, column *703*, 13 June, are located; and whether each number represents the full complement;

(3) if he will state the date, time and how the public health authorities for the areas where the additional dairies he referred to in *Official Report*, column *703*, 13 June, are located, were first contacted about the botulism outbreak and informed about the connection with Young Fruits Ltd. and the dairy in their area;

(4) if he will state the day and date that environmental officers visited each of the eight dairies mentioned in *Official Report*, column *703*, 13 June, to arrange for the imediate withdrawal of hazelnut yoghurt manufactured by them;

(5) what his Department's procedures are for keeping the proprietor of Young Fruits Ltd., the 10 dairies concerned and the public informed about each stage of the investigation into suspected botulism; and if all relevant persons are immediately and fully informed of any findings.

**Mr. Mellor:** The Department keeps the public informed by means of press statements. Contact with food processing firms and dairies will normally be through environmental health departments. Other information requested is set out in the table.

| Dairy | Environmental Health Department | First DH contact with Environmental Health Department | First visit to dairy (with details of prior contact where appropriate) | Number of EHOs in post | EHO establishment |
|---|---|---|---|---|---|
| Yieldingtree Packers | Wyre Forest | 13 June, morning via Bromsgrove | 14 June, 9 am | 6 | 7 |
| Grange Farm | South Buckinghamshire | 12 June, evening | 13 June, 9.40 am | 4 | 6 |
| Battledene Farm | Cotswold | 12 June, evening | 14 June, 5.00 pm (telephone 12 June, 7.30 pm) | 8 | 8 |
| Lord Crathorne | Hambleton | 12 June, evening | 13 June, 10 am (telephone 12 June, 7 pm) | 10 | 10 |
| Stock Meadows | Staffordshire Moorlands | 12 June, evening | 13 June, 10.30 am | 9 | 9 |
| Ann Forshaws | Dibble Valley | 11 June, evening | 12 June, 11.30 am (telephone 11 June, evening) | 8 | 8 |
| Madresfield Dairy | Malvern Hills | 13 June, morning | 13 June, 11 am | 11 | 11 |
| Bodfan Foods | Chester | 13 June, evening | 13 June, 9 am[1] | 16 | 16 |

[1] A further visit was made 14 June, 9 am, following the Department's telephone call.

## NHS Staff (Upgrading)

**Mr. Nicholas Bennett:** To ask the Secretary of State for Health what is the practice of his Department on whether upgrading of National Health Service staff approved by the Whitley Council joint secretaries is backdated to the date of application; and if he will make a statement.

**Mr. Mellor** [*holding answer 16 June 1989*]*:* Cases which are, under Whitley council agreements appropriate for decision by the joint secretaries are considered on their merits.

# AGRICULTURE, FISHERIES AND FOOD

## Extensification

**Mr. Gill:** To ask the Minister of Agriculture, Fisheries and Food if he will announce his proposals for the implementation of the Community extensification scheme.

**Mr. MacGregor:** My right hon. Friends and I are today issuing to interested organisations for comment a document containing ideas for pilot extensification schemes for beef, which we are obliged to introduce this year under the terms of Community legislation and also for sheep. The concept of extensification, essentially securing lower output from the same land area, has some attractions in principle but it is extremely difficult to apply in a manner which ensures effective control and value for money for the taxpayer, particularly in the livestock sector to which, under the Community legislation, we are required to accord priority. The Government therefore consider it essential to try out extensification initially on a limited pilot basis in order to determine how, and indeed whether, extensification can best be introduced without undue cost and complexity of administration and monitoring.

I am placing copies of the consultation document in the Library. Before reaching final decisions on the nature of the pilot schemes, the Government will take account of comments, which should reach Agricultural departments by 25 August.

## Set-aside

**Mr. Ron Davies:** To ask the Minister of Agriculture, Fisheries and Food what percentage of land currently in set-aside is tenanted.

**Mr. Ryder:** Twenty-three per cent. of existing scheme participants have holdings which are wholly tenanted and a further 12 per cent. have some tenanted land. Information on the area of land concerned is not available.

## Farm Woodland Scheme

**Mr. Ron Davies:** To ask the Minister of Agriculture, Fisheries and Food if he will state the distribution by county in England and Wales and by region in Scotland of land approved for inclusion in the farm woodland scheme and the amount of such land on which forestry operations have commenced.

**Mr. Ryder:** As at 16 June 1989, our computer record shows the information for England as follows:

| County | Hectares |
| --- | --- |
| Avon | 5 |
| Bedfordshire | 16 |
| Berkshire | 27 |
| Buckinghamshire | 50 |
| Cleveland | 0 |
| Cambridgeshire | 96 |
| Cheshire | 23 |
| Cornwall | 15 |
| Cumbria | 42 |
| Derbyshire | 17 |
| Devon | 156 |
| Dorset | 85 |
| Durham | 3 |
| Essex | 54 |
| Gloucestershire | 171 |
| Hampshire | 24 |
| Hereford and Worcester | 167 |
| Hertfordshire | 6 |
| Humberside | 59 |
| Isle of Wight | 0 |
| Kent | 24 |
| Lancashire | 0 |
| Leicestershire | 24 |
| Lincolnshire | 29 |
| Greater London | 0 |
| Greater Manchester | 0 |
| Merseyside | 0 |
| West Midlands | 3 |
| Norfolk | 297 |
| Northamptonshire | 120 |
| Northumberland | 34 |
| Nottinghamshire | 25 |
| Oxfordshire | 163 |
| Shropshire | 23 |
| Somerset | 55 |
| Staffordshire | 19 |
| Suffolk | 201 |
| Surrey | 0 |
| East Sussex | 12 |
| West Sussex | 15 |
| Tyne and Wear | 0 |
| Warwickshire | 26 |
| Wiltshire | 92 |
| North Yorkshire | 87 |
| South Yorkshire | 0 |
| West Yorkshire | 0 |

No details of the area planted are yet available. The situations in Wales and Scotland are matters for my right hon. Friends the Secretaries of State for Wales and Scotland.

## Set-aside

**Mr. Ron Davies:** To ask the Minister of Agriculture, Fisheries and Food how much land currently in set-aside has been the subject of applications for planting grant from the Forestry Commission; how much has been approved for planting; and in respect of how much land grant has been paid.

**Mr. Donald Thompson:** Up to 31 March 1989, the Forestry Commission had received applications under the woodland grant scheme for the planting of 70 hectares of land under set-aside in Enland. My right hon. and learned Friend the Secretary of State for Scotland gave the information called for in the other parts of this question in his reply to the hon. Member on 15 June 1989 at column 20.

## Pesticides

**Mr. Hardy:** To ask the Minister of Agriculture, Fisheries and Food if his Department has any information on the levels in fish and eels in inland waters of dieldrin and aldrin; what are the levels of these which are safe; and if he will prohibit the use of these chemicals forthwith.

**Mr. Ryder:** I refer the hon. Gentleman to my Department's press notices of 20 October 1988 (No 409/88) and 18 May 1989 (204/89).

**Mr. Hardy:** To ask the Minister of Agriculture, Fisheries and Food if he will make it his policy to continue to prevent the use of dieldrin or aldrin in the production of daffodils.

**Mr. Ryder:** I have no plans to propose that the recent ban on the use of aldrin should be reconsidered, and I have taken steps to ensure safe disposal of unused stocks. The ban will be strictly enforced by Her Majesty's agricultural inspectorate, which reports to my right hon. Friend the Secretary of State for Employment.

### Fruit Growers

**Mr. Gill:** To ask the Minister of Agriculture, Fisheries and Food if he has received the results of the poll of growers conducted as part of the quinquennial review of the Apple and Pear Development Council.

**Mr. Donald Thompson** [*pursuant to his reply of 8 March*]: A poll held in February as part of the statutory review showed that a clear majority of apple and pear growers were opposed to the continuance of the APDC. At the request of growers' organisations, a second poll was held by them in May. It did not form part of the statutory review but was conducted in the same way and among the same growers. The poll showed that, whilst the majority of growers believed that the commercial functions of the APDC should in future be handled by the industry itself, they would support a new statutory council exercising a more limited range of functions, in particular those connected with R and D.

My noble Friend has therefore decided that the APDC should be wound up. At the same time, my noble Friend has decided a new statutory council should be set up principally to promote and finance R and D in apple and pear growing and to represent the views of growers on matters of importance to them. She will be holding further discussions with growers' representatives on the more detailed provisions and arrangements relating to this new Council. She intends that it should run for three years, after which it will be subject to statutory review. The approval of Parliament is required for these measures and a statutory instrument will be laid before both Houses once discussions with growers' representatives have been completed.

My noble Friend would like to express the Government's appreciation, which I am sure is shared by fruit growers themselves, to the chairman, Mr. Jasper Grinling, and his colleagues on the council for the unstinted services they have given to the industry.

### Wholesale Fruit and Vegetable Markets

**Mr. Bill Michie:** To ask the Minister of Agriculture, Fisheries and Food if it is intended to privatise any of the wholesale fruit and vegetable markets in Great Britain; and if he will make a statement.

**Mr. Ryder:** I announced in February that, in considering the options available on the future of Covent

Garden market, I was commissioning an independent commercial feasibility study into the possibilities of privatisation. Work on this will commence this month.

I have also received a joint discussion paper from the National Farmers' Union and the National Federation of Fruit and Potato Trades about the privatisation of local authority wholesale fruit and vegetable markets. The issues raised are extremely complex and need careful consideration. I cannot at present give any indication of the likely response.

### Salmonella

**Dr. David Clark:** To ask the Minister of Agriculture, Fisheries and Food if, pursuant to his reply of 17 May, *Official Report,* column 212-23, he is able to state whether those provisions awaiting implementation on that date have now been implemented.

**Mr. Donald Thompson:** Details of progress on the measure awaiting implementations at 17 May are as follows:
(7) Still to be implemented.
(10, 11) Implemented. The Poultry Flocks (Collection and Handling of Eggs and Control of Vermin) Order 1989 came into force on 26 May.
(17) To be introduced shortly.

**Mr. Kirkwood:** To ask the Minister of Agriculture, Fisheries and Food what plans he has to increase compensation levels for birds slaughtered due to the drop in demands for eggs after the salmonella scare.

**Mr. Donald Thompson:** Assistance for the culling of hens to reduce the size of the laying flock is no longer available. The closing date for applications under the slaughter of hens scheme was 5 January 1989. This was an exceptional short-term measure to assist the industry when the egg market suffered severe disruption at the end of last year. The market has now stabilised, and the Government have no plans for further aid.

### Irradiated Food

**Mr. Flynn:** To ask the Minister of Agriculture, Fisheries and Food if he has any plans to place a contract with an advertising agency to explain the implications to the public of food irradiation; and what information he has on present public attitudes towards irradiation treated foodstuffs.

**Mr. Ryder:** I have no such plans. I naturally ensure that I am well informed on public attitudes to all matters for which I am responsible.

### Forestry

**Mr. Ron Davies:** To ask the Minister of Agriculture, Fisheries and Food (1) how he intends to allocate the £6 million available to Britain from the new European forestry proposals adopted at the May Council of Ministers meeting;

(2) what savings will accrue to his Department by the adoption by the Council of Ministers of farm forestry proposals to make available European financed premia for the growing of trees on farmland.

**Mr. MacGregor** [*holding reply 16 June 1989*]: The amount of afforestation that takes place on agricultural land—under Forestry Commission grant schemes, their

Northern Ireland equivalent and the farm woodland scheme—will determine the scale of reimbursements that the United Kingdom will be able to claim each year from the European Community.

Parliamentary approval will be sought to appropriate the receipts in aid of the votes from which the planting grants and annual payments are funded. The receipts should therefore contribute towards the overall costs of support for forestry and agriculture.

### New Forest (Hunting Days)

**Mr. Ron Davies:** To ask the Ministry of Agriculture, Fisheries and Food what action the Forestry Commission is proposing to take in respect of the recommendations of the New Forest Review Group that there be a reduction in the number of hunting days in the New Forest.

**Mr. Ryder:** *[holding reply 16 June 1989]:* The report of the New Forest review group is still being considered. It would therefore be premature to speculate on what action the Forestry Commission might decide to take on the recommendation concerning the number of hunting days.

### Hydatid Disease

**Mr. Alex Carlile:** To ask the Minister of Agriculture, Fisheries and Food (1) how many known cases of hydatidosis in humans there were in each of the years from 1979 to 1988; and if he will make a statement concerning his policy for the eradication of hydatid disease;

(2) if he will make it his policy to introduce a system of free supply of medication for the eradication from dogs of hydatid disease; and if he will make a statement.

**Mr. Donald Thompson:** The communicable disease surveillance centre at Colindale has received reports of the following numbers of cases of hydatid disease in humans.

|      | Number |
|------|--------|
| 1979 | 5 |
| 1980 | 6 |
| 1981 | 8 |
| 1982 | 6 |
| 1983 | 22 |
| 1984 | 10 |
| 1985 | 12 |
| 1986 | 26 |
| 1987 | 20 |
| 1988 | not yet available |

My Department will co-operate with relevant health authorities to deal with hydatid disease in areas where this poses a risk to human health. I have no plans to introduce an eradication policy for this disease but would refer the hon. Member to the reply I gave to the hon. Member for Caerphilly (Mr. Davies) on 6 June, column 12-13.

### Dairy Farming

**Mr. Richard Livsey:** To ask the Minister of Agriculture, Fisheries and Food what was the average *(a)* rise in hectares, *(b)* number of dairy cows kept and *(c)* farm income for the latest period for which he has figures for an average dairy farm in England.

**Mr. Donald Thompson:** The information requested can be found in table 3.9 of the 1989 edition of "Farm Incomes in the United Kingdom", a copy of which is in the Library of the House.

### Bovine Spongiform Encephalopathy

**Mr. Ron Davies:** To ask the Minister of Agriculture, Fisheries and Food, pursuant to his answer to the hon. Member for Caerphilly on 12 June, *Official Report,* column 298, whether the suspected cases of bovine spongiform encephalopathy at markets were all identified by veterinary inspection; and how many of the cases identified at slaughterhouses were located at *(a)* European Economic Community-approved and *(b)* non-European Economic Community-approved slaughterhouses.

**Mr. Donald Thompson:** The 18 suspected cases of BSE identified at markets were inspected by Ministry veterinary staff, having been reported to the Ministry by various individuals at the markets. The information requested about the status of the slaughterhouses is not available for the period in question. Arrangements have been made to record this information in future.

**Mr. Ron Davies:** To ask the Minister of Agriculture, Fisheries and Food if he will publish in the *Official Report,* a table showing the number of confirmed cases of bovine spongiform encephalopathy for each county in England and Wales for the four-week period ended 16 June.

**Mr. Donald Thompson:** The information is given in the table:

| County | Confirmed cases |
|--------|-----------------|
| Avon | 7 |
| Bedfordshire | 1 |
| Berkshire | 4 |
| Buckinghamshire | 1 |
| Cambridgeshire | 1 |
| Cheshire | 13 |
| Clwyd | 7 |
| Cornwall | 33 |
| Cumbria | 12 |
| Derbyshire | 7 |
| Devon | 64 |
| Dorset | 45 |
| Durham | 3 |
| Dyfed | 23 |
| Essex | 1 |
| Glamorgan, Mid | 1 |
| Glamorgan, West | 1 |
| Gloucestershire | 12 |
| Gwent | 4 |
| Gwynedd | 4 |
| Hampshire | 18 |
| Hereford and Worcestershire | 11 |
| Hertfordshire | 1 |
| Isle of Wight | 3 |
| Kent | 14 |
| Lancashire | 1 |
| Leicestershire | 12 |
| Lincolnshire | 6 |
| Manchester | 1 |
| Norfolk | 4 |
| Northamptonshire | 5 |
| Northumberland | 5 |
| Nottinghamshire | 3 |
| Oxon | 5 |
| Powys | 9 |
| Salop | 16 |
| Somerset | 45 |
| Staffordshire | 5 |
| Suffolk | 3 |
| Surrey | 4 |
| Sussex, East | 4 |
| Sussex, West | 13 |
| Warwickshire | 5 |

| County | Confirmed cases |
|---|---|
| Wiltshire | 28 |
| Yorkshire, North | 6 |
| Yorkshire, West | 1 |

### Fishing Industry

**Mr. David Porter:** To ask the Minister of Agriculture, Fisheries and Food what measures he will be proposing in connection with the United Kingdom fishing industry at the Council of Ministers meeting during the current month.

**Mr. Donald Thompson:** There are a number of issues of concern to the industry which I expect to be discussed by the Council, including the state of stocks, Channel cod and other precautionary TACs, quota hopping and beam trawling within 12 miles.

## SCOTLAND

### Homelessness

**Mr. Soley:** To ask the Secretary of State for Scotland how many households were accepted as homeless by the City of Glasgow, Midlothian and Inverclyde for each quarter of 1988.

**Lord James Douglas-Hamilton:** On the basis of information thus far returned by authorities, applicant households assessed as homeless by the authorities concerned are shown in the following table.

*Applicant households assessed by local authorities as homeless: 1988*

|  | Quarter 1 | Quarter 2 | Quarter 3 | Quarter 4 |
|---|---|---|---|---|
| City of Glasgow | 335 | 271 | 313 | 184 |
| Midlothian | 30 | 31 | 18 | 26 |
| Inverclyde | 40 | 26 | 33 | 15 |

Because of different definitions and a different basis of compilation this information is not comparable with statistics of households accepted as homeless in England.

### Empty Housing

**Mr. Soley:** To ask the Secretary of State for Scotland what percentage of local authority accommodation is empty in the City of Glasgow, Midlothian and Inverclyde.

**Lord James Douglas-Hamilton:** The following table shows the percentage of local authority dwelling stock which was vacant at 31 March 1989:

|  | Percentage |
|---|---|
| City of Glasgow | 4·1 |
| Midlothian | 0·9 |
| Inverclyde | 3·0 |

These percentages include dwellings which are unavailable for letting because they are awaiting or undergoing improvement, being held to accommodate households decanted during repair, or awaiting demolition.

### RSSPCC

**Dr. Godman:** To ask the Secretary of State for Scotland if he will list the sums of money given to the Royal Scottish Society for the Prevention of Cruelty to Children in each of the past 10 years; for what purposes these sums were provided; what percentage of the RSSPCC's annual general income they represented; and if he will make a statement.

**Mr. Michael Forsyth:** Since 1979 we have provided grants to the society under the Social Work (Scotland) Act 1968 and the National Health (Scotland) Act 1968 and the National Health (Scotland) Act 1978 in support of its headquarters and regional activities, personal training and special projects such as the child sexual abuse project at Overnewton. The amounts and the percentage these represent of the Society's income are as follows:

|  | Amount of grant (£ thousand) | Percentage of income |
|---|---|---|
| 1979-80 | 80 | 15·8 |
| 1980-81 | 93 | 14·8 |
| 1981-82 | 100 | 18·0 |
| 1982-83 | 126 | 21·6 |
| 1983-84 | 133 | 22·0 |
| 1984-85 | 106 | 10·5 |
| 1985-86 | 111 | 11·0 |
| 1986-87 | 107 | 11·3 |
| 1987-88 | 108 | 10·3 |
| 1988-89 | 137 | 7·9 |

**Dr. Godman:** To ask the Secretary of State for Scotland what sums of money have been given to the Royal Scottish Society for the Prevention of Cruelty to Children for the purposes of training RSSPCC personnel in each of the past 10 years; how much money is to be provided in each of the next three years for this purpose; and if he will make a statement.

**Mr. Michael Forsyth:** The table lists payments made to the RSSPCC for training purposes between the years 1982-83 and 1987-88. Between 1979-80 and 1981-82 no specific training grant was awarded. From 1985-86 payments were made on a reducing scale in keeping with the pump priming purpose of the grant. No training grant has been given since 1987-88 and no new applications have been received.

*Training grant to RSSPCC (£)*

| Year | Amount |
|---|---|
| 1979-80 | — |
| 1980-81 | — |
| 1981-82 | — |
| 1982-83 | [1]7,000 |
| 1983-84 | 13,367 |
| 1984-85 | 17,723 |
| 1985-86 | 18,278 |
| 1986-87 | [2]11,963 |
| 1987-88 | [3]9,367 |

[1] From September.
[2] Reduced rate 75 per cent.
[3] Reduced rate 50 per cent.

### Correspondence

**Dr. Godman:** To ask the Secretary of State for Scotland when the hon. Member for Greenock and Port Glasgow can expect an answer to his letter of 29 March to the Parliamentary Under-Secretary of State with responsibility for health concerning Scottish hospices.

**Mr. Michael Forsyth:** I will write to the hon. Member very shortly.

**Dr. Godman:** To ask the Secretary of State for Scotland when the hon. Member for Greenock and Port Glasgow can expect an answer to his letter of 17 April to the Minister of State regarding Mr. James Laing and the poll tax.

**Mr. Lang:** I have replied to the hon. Member.

**Dr. Godman:** To ask the Secretary of State for Scotland when the hon. Member for Greenock and Port Glasgow can expect an answer to his letter of 3 May to the Minister of State regarding Mrs. I. Todd of Greenock.

**Mr. Lang:** I have replied to the hon. Member.

### British Nuclear Fuels

**Mr. Flynn:** To ask the Secretary of State for Scotland if any Ministers or officials in his Department attended the 30th anniversary celebration, on 12 May, of British Nuclear Fuels Chapelcross plutonium and tritium production reactors in Annan.

**Mr. Lang:** One official, from the Industry Department for Scotland, was among the guests at the function held on 12 May to celebrate the 30th anniversary of Chapelcross power station.

### Policewomen

**Mrs. Fyfe:** To ask the Secretary of State for Scotland if he will obtain a copy of the research on policewomen in Scotland carried out by Professor Roy Wilkie of the university of Strathclyde centre for policy studies for his departmental library as soon as it becomes available.

**Lord James Douglas-Hamilton:** Yes.

### Hospital Trusts

**Mr. Gordon Brown:** To ask the Secretary of State for Scotland if he will list the submissions of expressions of interest in self-governing status in the Health Service giving in each case the body or individual responsible for such expression of interest.

**Mr. Michael Forsyth:** I refer the hon. Member to the answer that I gave to the hon. Member for Roxburgh and Berwickshire (Mr. Kirkwood) on 12 June at column *343*.

# ENVIRONMENT

### Water Authorities (Land Ownership)

**Mr. Redmond:** To ask the Secretary of State for the Environment how many acres of land are in the ownership of *(a)* the Yorkshire water authority and *(b)* the Severn-Trent water authority; and, of these, how many have outline planning permission, and in respect of how many the authority is currently seeking such permission.

**Mr. Howard:** The Yorkshire water authority owns or has an interest in aproximately 70,000 acres of land. About 90 acres of this land has outline planning permission for development. Applications for outline planning permission for approximately 10 acres of land are currently outstanding. The Severn-Trent water authority owns or has an interest in approximately 44,000 acres of land. About 100 acres have outline planning permission for development. Outline planning permission is being sought for between 50 and 100 acres.

### Water Rates

**Mr. Cohen:** To ask the Secretary of State for the Environment whether, further to his answer of 19 April about average domestic water rate bills, *Official Report*, column *233*, the relevant data for 1989-90 are now available.

**Mr. Howard:** The average domestic water rate bill in the Thames water authority area for 1989-90 is £100·80; The average bill for all water authorities is £119·00. That represents a real increase of 33·6 per cent. in the average bill in the Thames area, and 45·2 per cent. nationally, since 1979-80.

### Sport and Leisure Facilities

**Mr. Redmond:** To ask the Secretary of State for the Environment, pursuant to his answer to the hon. Member for Don Valley of 2 March, *Official Report*, column *283*, what have been the results of his deliberations in respect of changes to section 19 of the Local Government (Miscellaneous Provisions) Act 1976.

**Mrs. Virginia Bottomley:** I refer the hon. Member to the reply I gave him on 12 June at column *316*.

### Non-ionising Radiation

**Ms. Walley:** To ask the Secretary of State for the Environment what research has been done into the effects of non-ionising radiation.

**Mrs. Virginia Bottomley:** Wide-ranging studies have been carried out over the last 20 years in many countries, including the United Kingdom, on the biological effects of non-ionising radiation. Currently the National Radiological Protection Board is undertaking a wide-ranging review of these studies. This review should be published before the end of the year.

### Bristol Channel (Sewage Outlets)

**Mr. Speller:** To ask the Secretary of State for the Environment if he will seek powers to require Wessex Water and South West Water to seek planning permission for raw sewage outlets into the Bristol channel; and if he will make a statement on the different sources of pollution which enter this marine cul de sac.

**Mr. Howard:** No. Under part II of the Control of Pollution Act 1974, water authorities are required to obtain consent before making a discharge into the sea or water courses. Where schemes require planning permission, this is a matter for the local planning authority to determine under the Town and Country Planning Acts. With regard to sources of pollution in the Bristol channel, I refer my hon. Friend to my reply of 6 June at column *90*.

### Leaflets

**Mr. Harry Barnes:** To ask the Secretary of State for the Environment if he will list the leaflets issued in connection with the Water Bill and the community charge, together with the print runs and costs of production of each leaflet, their main avenues of distribution and their estimated costs of distribution.

**Mr. Ridley:** I am writing to the hon. Member with the detailed information he requests.

### Sewage Works (Quality Controls)

**Mr. Harry Barnes:** To ask the Secretary of State for the Environment if he will list the proposals he has received for the relaxation of quality controls for sewage works in Derbyshire.

**Mr. Moynihan:** I refer the hon. Member to the answer my right hon. Friend the Secretary of State for the Environment gave on 11 May at column *520*. Applications for these works are being advertised in local newspapers in the areas concerned.

### Norfolk House, East Kilbride

**Mr. Ingram:** To ask the Secretary of State for the Environment if he will make a statement on his plans for Norfolk house, East Kilbride.

**Mr. Chope:** Norfolk house is still on the market for disposal.

### Green Belt (Derbyshire)

**Mr. Harry Barnes:** To ask the Secretary of State for the Environment if he has any plans to release land from the green belt in north-east Derbyshire for opencast mining or other purposes; and if he will make a statement.

**Mr. Chope:** The Government's policy on green belts is set out in the Department of the Environment's planning policy guidance note No. 2. Paragraph 15 of that guidance makes clear that minerals can be worked only where they are found. Their extraction need not be incompatible with green belt objectives, provided that high environmental standards are maintained and that the site is well restored, but each case must be considered on its merits.

### Water Quality

**Mrs. Ann Taylor:** To ask the Secretary of State for the Environment what advice his Department has given water authorities on estimating the costs of complying with the legal standards for pesticides and nitrates laid down in EC directive 80/778/EEC.

**Mr. Howard:** The Department is asking water authorities to estimate the cost of complying with the pesticides and nitrate standards in EC directive 80/778/EEC, in the context of setting initial K (the initial price-increase limit) and identifying further items of expenditure (cost pass-through). For nitrate all cost of achieving compliance will be in initial K, while for pesticides some will be in K and some in cost pass-through.

### East Beach, Shoeburyness

**Mr. Teddy Taylor:** To ask the Secretary of State for the Environment if he will seek to include east beach, Shoeburyness within the scope of the bathing water directive.

**Mr. Howard:** The range of facilities at the beach and the degree of use of the water at east beach, Shoeburyness bring this bathing water within the scope of the directive and I am pleased to announce that we have now identified it for the purposes of the directive.

### Environmental Pollution

**Mr. Wray:** To ask the Secretary of State for the Environment what is *(a)* his and *(b)* the EC's policy on involving non-EC European countries in the common measures to protect the environment against acid rain, water pollution, chlorofluorocarbons, and similar dangers; and if he will make a statement.

**Mrs. Virginia Bottomley:** It is the policy of Her Majesty's Government and of the European Community that measures to protect the environment should be taken at the most appropriate level for the problem addressed, whether by individual member states, by the Community as a whole or in a wider context. The United Kingdom and EC play a leading role in developing a common approach with other European countries in such bodies as the Organisation for Economic Co-operation and Development, the United Nations Economic Commission for Europe and the United Nations environment programme.

### Set-aside Land

**Mr. Cran:** To ask the Secretary of State for the Environment when details of the top-up payments for farmers who undertake to bring about environmental improvements on set-aside land will be announced.

**Mrs. Virginia Bottomley:** Details of the Countryside Premium for set-aside land were announced today by the chairman of the Countryside Commission. The scheme will be run by the Countryside Commission, with the help of the Nature Conservancy Council and in close co-operation with the Ministry of Agriculture, Fisheries and Food. We believe it will ensure that the set-aside scheme introduced last year by MAFF will produce positive benefits for the environment. We welcome the imaginative way this scheme has been developed.

Farmers will be invited to manage their set-aside land in ways that will benefit landscape and wildlife habitat, or provide increased recreational opportunities for the local community. Five options will be available to farmers, comprising the management of existing hedgerows or creation of new hedgerows and belts of broadleaved trees and shrubs; the creation of grassland area for the enjoyment of local people and the benefit of wildlife; the creation of habitat for suitable ground-nesting birds; the provision in selected areas of winter grazing for Brent geese; and the restoration of particularly valuable habitat in certain areas.

The scheme will be discretionary with applications assessed on their merits. Payments to farmers will range from £45 to £120 per hectare.

The scheme will initially be open to farmers in eastern England, in the counties of Bedfordshire, Cambridgeshire, Essex, Hertfordshire, Norfolk, Northamptonshire and Suffolk. This is an area in which there has been a relatively high rate of take-up for set aside, and the scope for environmental improvement under the countryside premium is that much greater.

### Community Charge

**Mr. Kirkwood:** To ask the Secretary of State for the Environment if he will estimate the number of English community charge leaflets delivered to occupants in houses in the county of Berwickshire in Scotland, on behalf of his Department.

**Mr. Gummer** [*holding answer 15 June 1989*]*:* It is not possible to provide a precise estimate. On the best information available to me, however, up to 1,450 community charge leaflets may have been delivered to addresses in the former county of Berwickshire. This arose because a postal sector and certain postal addresses are common to both England and Scotland. The mailing house involved has apologised for the mistake. The Central Office of Information, which acted as our agents in this matter, is seeking an abatement of the cost. This is however likely to have been about £500. At the same time, approximately 21 million copies of the leaflets were being delivered throughout England.

### Drug Registration Scheme

**Mr. Allen:** To ask the Secretary of State for the Environment if he has received the Association of District Councils document and letter of 2 May regarding its proposed operation of a national dog registration scheme; and if he will make a statement.

**Mrs. Virginia Bottomley** [*holding answer 9 June 1989*]: I refer the hon. Member to the statement made by my right hon. Friend, the Secretary of State for the Environment on 14 June at column 1076.

### Rottweiler Dogs

**Mr. David Young:** To ask the Secretary of State for the Environment if he will ban the importation of Rottweilers.

**Mrs. Virginia Bottomley** [*holding answer 8 June 1989*]: No. I refer the hon. Member to the statement made by my right hon. Friend the Home Secretary on 14 June in reply to my hon. Friend the Member for Plymouth, Drake (Dame J. Fookes) at column *465* on extended controls over dangerous dogs.

## DEFENCE

### Project Anchor

**Mr. Redmond:** To ask the Secretary of State for Defence if he will make a statement about project Anchor.

**Mr. Archie Hamilton:** I am not familiar with any project of that name.

### European Fighter Aircraft

**Mr. Jack:** To ask the Secretary of State for Defence when he now expects that agreement will be reached on a choice of radar and avionics systems for the European fighter aircraft; and if he will make a statement.

**Mr. Sainsbury:** As my hon. Friend knows, the choice of radar for EFA is under active consideration, and a decision will be made at the earliest opportunity. The selection of other elements of the avionics fit is being undertaken progressively.

### Low Flying

**Mr. Kennedy:** To ask the Secretary of State for Defence what agreement has been reached with his West German counterpart on further transfers of low-flying training by West German military aircraft to Britain.

**Mr. Archie Hamilton:** None.

**Mr. Kennedy:** To ask the Secretary of State for Defence what figure has been agreed with his West German

counterpart for the maximum number of low-level training flights to be conducted by the Royal Air Force over West Germany in 1989.

**Mr. Archie Hamilton:** None.

**Mr. Kennedy:** To ask the Secretary of State for Defence what proportion of low-flying training by Royal Air Force units based in Germany has been conducted in the United Kingdom in each year since 1980.

**Mr. Archie Hamilton:** I refer the hon. Member to the reply given to the hon. Member for Meirionnydd Nant Conwy (Dr. Thomas) on 10 May 1989 at column *475*.

**Mr. Kennedy:** To ask the Secretary of State for Defence what agreement has been reached with the United States authorities on the transfer of United States Air Force low-flying training from West Germany to Britain.

**Mr. Archie Hamilton:** None.

### Military Aircraft (Jettisoning)

**Mr. Kennedy:** To ask the Secretary of State for Defence what are the legislative provisions and flying regulations governing the jettisoning of *(a)* live weapons, *(b)* inert weapons, *(c)* fuel tanks and *(d)* other equipment from military aircraft in flight.

**Mr. Archie Hamilton:** Military aircraft activity over the United Kingdom and surrounding waters is carried out in accordance with comprehensive joint service regulations. These prohibit the dropping of articles over land or sea except when authorised for training or operational purposes or at the discretion of the pilot when the safety of the aircraft may be seriously endangered by not doing so.

**Mr. Kennedy:** To ask the Secretary of State for Defence if he will list all incidents since 1979 in which weapons, fuel tanks or other equipment have been inadvertently dropped, or deliberately jettisoned for safety reasons, from military aircraft over the United Kingdom, stating the date, location, type of aircraft and nature of the equipment dropped in each case.

**Mr. Archie Hamilton:** Such detailed information is not held centrally and could not be collated without disproportionate cost and effort.

### Darren Francis

**Mr. Steen:** To ask the Secretary of State for Defence when he hopes to answer the letter dated 8 March from the hon. Member for South Hams about Darren Francis of 4 Victoria place, Brixham, Devon, and his discharge from the Army.

**Mr. Neubert:** As I explained in my letter of 4 April, the case is being investigated. I shall write shortly.

### Submarines (Orkney and Shetland)

**Mr. Foulkes:** To ask the Secretary of State for Defence whether any British or allied submarines were in the area between Orkney and Shetland on 12 or 13 June; and if he will make a statement.

**Mr. Archie Hamilton:** No Royal Navy or NATO submarines were in this area at the time.

## Services (Underwear)

**Mr. Cohen:** To ask the Secretary of State for Defence how many sets of underwear are issued per week to armed services personnel.

**Mr. Neubert:** Underwear is not issued to armed services personnel for normal everyday wear. Certain items of underwear are issued to personnel engaged in some field training, operational or specialist tasks, but information on the number of issues is not readily available.

## Loan Service Personnel

**Mr. Cohen:** To ask the Secretary of State for Defence if he will list each country to which United Kingdom armed forces are currently posted as loan service personnel; and the numbers involved for each country.

**Mr. Neubert:** As of 31 March 1989, the most recent date for which comprehensive data is readily available, there were United Kingdom loan service personnel in:

| | |
|---|---|
| Australia | Lesotho |
| Bahrain | Malaysia |
| Bangladesh | Mauritius |
| Barbados | New Zealand |
| Belize | Nigeria |
| Bermuda | Oman |
| Botswana | Qatar |
| Brunei | Saudi Arabia |
| Dominica | Singapore |
| Fiji | St. Lucia |
| Gambia | St. Vincent |
| Ghana | Sudan |
| Hong Kong | Swaziland |
| Indonesia | Turks and Caicos Islands |
| Jordan | United Arab Emirates |
| Kenya | Zimbabwe |
| Kuwait | |

The number in each country is confidential between Her Majesty's Government and the Government concerned.

## Saudi Arabia

**Mr. Cohen:** To ask the Secretary of State for Defence what was the purpose, and result of the recent visit to Saudi Arabia of Marshal of the Royal Air Force, Sir David Craig.

**Mr. Sainsbury:** Sir David Craig visited Saudi Arabia soon after his appointment as chief of defence staff in order to familiarise himself with the defence relations between the two countries. The result has been to establish warm, personal contact between himself and the most senior members of the Saudi Defence Ministry and armed forces.

**Mr. Cohen:** To ask the Secretary of State for Defence when it is proposed that the first venture proposals are to be discussed with the Saudi Government offset committee; and if he will make a statement.

**Mr. Sainsbury:** The first two venture proposals developed under the Al Yamamah economic offset programme were put to the Saudi Government offset committee for its consideration in mid-May. As announced in a news release by my Department on 26 May, the first proposal is for the establishment of a missile engineering facility in the kingdom involving British Aerospace and Dowty Rotol. Secondly, British Aerospace has expressed positive interest in participation in an aluminium smelter which may be established in Saudi Arabia.

## Command and Control System

**Mr. Cohen:** To ask the Secretary of State for Defence, pursuant to his reply, *Official Report,* 27 April, column *663,* whether he will make a statement on the policy of allowing UKSL Ltd. to choose the programming languages for the IUKADGE command and control computer ICCS and this policy's relationship with the departmental policy of standardisation on the use of the programming language ADA as the means to ensure reliability and maintainability of software; and whether he will make a statement.

**Mr. Sainsbury:** The IUKADGE ICCS is a largely NATO-funded project and therefore subject to NATO policy direction; the NATO financial authorities, in approving the NATO contribution to IUKADGE ICCS costs, directed that existing NATO air defence ground environment (NADGE) software was to be re-used to the greatest extent possible. Neither the MOD nor NATO formally adopted ADA as the single preferred language standard for real-time defence computer applications until more than three years after the award of the IUKADGE ICCS contract to UKSL.

## NAAFI

**Mr. Sean Hughes:** To ask the Secretary of State for Defence if the Navy, Army and Air Force Institutes tenders for the operation of civilian staff restaurants within his Department receive any subsidy from the Department beyond that available to all other tenderers and if that part of the Navy, Army and Air Force Institutes which submits tenders produces discreet accounts to demonstrate that its activities are not receiving subsidy from other Navy, Army and Air Force Institutes activities within his Department.

**Mr. Neubert:** No. The Navy, Army and Air Force Institutes (NAAFI) is treated no differently from other contractors invited to tender for the operation of civilian staff restaurants in MOD establishments, in that premises, equipment, power and utensils are all provided at public expense. All contractors are responsible for management, staff and labour costs, food supply, preparation and serving. Cleaning of premises is arranged under separate contracts. There is no requirement for the Navy, Army and Air Force Institutes to produce separate accounts of the operation of the civilian staff restaurants, which they have been contracted to operate.

## Lightning Aircraft

**Mr. Wilson:** To ask the Secretary of State for Defence what was the total cost of the service life extension programme for RAF Lightning aircraft; and how many aircraft were involved in this programme.

**Mr. Sainsbury:** The total cost of the life extension programme for RAF Lightning aircraft was in the order of £2 million and covered 35 aircraft.

## Military Exercise (Stornoway Airport)

**Mr. Macdonald:** To ask the Secretary of State for Defence how many aircraft from the fleet requirements and air direction unit will operate from Stornoway airport during the forthcoming military exercise.

**Mr. Neubert:** No aircraft of the fleet requirement and air direction unit are planned to operate from Stornoway airport during the forthcoming military exercise.

**Mr. Macdonald:** To ask the Secretary of State for Defence (1) how many military aircraft, other than Phantoms and Tornados, and from which units, will operate from Stornoway airport during the forthcoming military exercise;

(2) how many military personnel will be deployed to Stornoway airport during the forthcoming military exercise;

(3) how many Phantom aircraft, and from which units, will operate from Stornoway airport during the forthcoming military exercise;

(4) how many Tornado aircraft, and from which units, will operate from Stornoway airport during the forthcoming military exercise;

(5) what instructions are being issued to military pilots making use of Stornoway airport in the forthcoming military exercise concerning the carrying out of run and break manoeuvres prior to landing;

(6) what is the planned number of military jet sorties to be flown into and out of Stornoway airport during the forthcoming military exercise *(a)* per day and *(b)* in total; and how many of these are planned to take place between the hours of 5 pm and 7 am;

(7) what is the stipulated circuit height for military jet aircraft using Stornoway airport during periods of military control of the airfield.

**Mr. Neubert:** From 20 June to 3 July, six Tornados from No. 11 Squadron, RAF Leeming and one Sea King from No. 202 Squadron, RAF Manston, accompanied by 175 personnel, will deploy to RAF Stornoway. During 21 to 22 June and 30 June to 3 July, support will be provided by a small number of Hercules transport sorties. Between 22 to 29 June, it is planned that the Tornados will fly some 52 sorties, normally six to eight each day. An average of two sorties each day will be between 5 pm and 10.45 pm, but there will be no flying between 10.45 pm and 7 am, and no flying at all on Sunday 25 June. The Sea King helicopter will undertake a small number of sorties as required.

All flying will be conducted in accordance with normal RAF regulations. Aircrew will be briefed fully on local conditions. The stipulated circuit height for Tornados flying the Westerly circuit at Stornoway (largely over land) is 1,100 ft; for the Easterly circuit (largely over sea) it is 800 ft. With regard to run and break manoeuvres, I refer the hon. Member to my reply of 10 March, *Official Report,* column *675.*

### Service Publications Store (Woolwich Arsenal)

**Mr. Cartwright:** To ask the Secretary of State for Defence how many publications are currently being handled by the service publications and forms store at Woolwich arsenal; how many documents are now being issued annually; and what were the comparable figures *(a)* five and *(b)* ten years earlier.

**Mr. Neubert:** The Royal Air Force and Royal Navy keep forms and publications in two separate stores at Woolwich arsenal. These, together with the Army stocks at Donnington, are to be relocated to Llangennech, Dyfed by 1991.

The Air Force currently holds about 2 million copies of publications and the Navy almost one million. Some 950,000 and 250,000 copies are issued annually from the respective stores.

Records of stock holdings and issues, five and 10 years ago, are not maintained and it would not be cost effective to research these details. Stocks of publications have, however, increased over the years and the collocation of the stores will present an opportunity to reduce stocks, rationalise systems and generally improve efficiency.

### Army (Home Owners)

**Mr. Brazier:** To ask the Secretary of State for Defence what percentage of serving members of the Regular Army are home owners.

**Mr. Neubert:** The current percentage of home ownership by serving members of the Regular Army is 26·3 per cent. This figure represents 71·4 per cent. of officers and 18·4 per cent. of other ranks.

### Army (Ages)

**Mr. Brazier:** To ask the Secretary of State for Defence what percentage of serving members of the Regular Army are over the age of 25 years; and what was the corresponding figure 20 years ago.

**Mr. Neubert:** Due to the availability of statistics, the latest figures we have are December 1988 to correspond with the figures of 20 years ago, December 1968. On this basis, the figures are as follows:

| *Regular Army over the age of 25* | |
|---|---|
| *December* | *Percentage* |
| 1988 | 51 |
| 1968 | 48 |

### Service Children (Schooling)

**Sir Michael McNair-Wilson:** To ask the Secretary of State for Defence how many boys, the sons of service personnel, have attended Crookham Court school on Ministry of Defence grants since 1974.

**Mr. Archie Hamilton:** The Ministry of Defence does not maintain past records of the numbers of children of service personnel who have attended particular boarding schools. However, at the start of the 1988-89 academic year there were 61 children of service personnel at Crookham Court school; this number has since fallen to 32.

**Sir Michael McNair-Wilson:** To ask the Secretary of State for Defence when the Service Children's Education Authority last visited Crookham Court school, Newbury, Berkshire.

**Mr. Neubert:** Crookham Court school was last visited on 8 February 1989.

**Sir Michael McNair-Wilson:** To ask the Secretary of State for Defence whether in agreeing to pay boarding school allowance for the child of service parents, his Department considers *(a)* the standard of education on offer and *(b)* the academic success achieved by a school.

**Mr. Neubert:** The criteria for the admissibility of a school for service boarding school allowance purposes were given in written answer on 9 June, at column *257*. These criteria do not take account of the academic success rate, since this is a matter for parents to consider in the light of their children's abilities. The standard of education must, however, be comparable to that available within the state system.

### Malaysia (Arms Sales)

**Miss Lestor:** To ask the Secretary of State for Defence what was the value of arms sales by the United Kigdom to Malaysia for each of the last five years.

**Mr. Sainsbury:** The value of major arms sales by the United Kingdom to Malaysia for the last five years, as reported to the Ministry of Defence, is:

| Year | £ million |
|------|-----------|
| 1984 | 4·3 |
| 1985 | nil |
| 1986 | 3·3 |
| 1987 | 2·1 |
| 1988 | 16·0 |
| Total | 25·7 |

### AWRE (Safety)

**Mr. Flynn:** To ask the Secretary of State for Defence if he will set out the environmental and safety improvements that have been instituted *(a)* at the atomic weapons research establishment at Aldermaston and *(b)* at other atomic weapons research establishment facilities since the Pochin report.

**Mr. Sainsbury:** The Pochin report related to radiological health and safety specifically at Aldermaston. Since the report, AWE has taken remedial action to deal with the deficiencies found, and has made changes including the training of staff; recruitment and deployment of specialist health and safety, engineering and support staff; continuing additions to the personnel radiation monitoring programmes as modern technology advances; and the addition of a substantial environmental monitoring programme around all AWE sites.

### Anti-Nuclear Weapons Protest Groups

**Mr. Flynn:** To ask the Secretary of State for Defence if, during the meeting of North Atlantic Treaty Organisation Defence Ministers in Brussels on 8-9 June, the views and role of anti-nuclear weapons protest groups was discussed.

**Mr. Archie Hamilton:** No.

### Toxic Waste

**Mr. Flynn:** To ask the Secretary of State for Defence what volumes of toxic wastes are present at the Ministry of Defence, atomic weapons establishment or Royal Ordnance factories at Aldermaston, Burghfield, Caerwent and HMS Vulcan; what storage and disposal facilities exist for these wastes; and what health and safety provisions cover the wastes.

**Mr. Sainsbury:** It is not the practice to give details of the quantities of radioactive and other toxic waste substances held at MOD premises. Any such wastes are held temporarily in appropriate containers and storage buildings until they can be disposed of safely in accordance with legislative commitments. While being stored, the wastes are subject to the provisions of the Health and Safety at Work, etc. Act 1974. Disposal is subject to agreement with relevant environmental regulatory departments (Her Majesty's inspectors of pollution; the Ministry of Agriculture, Fisheries and Food; and, where relevant, the Welsh Office and Her Majesty's industrial pollution inspectorate in Scotland). Transport of wastes is subject to regulatory measures of the Health and Safety Executive and the Department of Transport.

### Equestrian Activities

**Mr. Marlow:** To ask the Secretary of State for Defence if he will list those official equestrian activities which are supported by public funds.

**Mr. Neubert:** The following equestrian activities are supported from public funds:
Ceremonial and public duties
Equitation training
National and NATO service competitions.

# Written Answers to Questions

*Tuesday 20 June 1989*

## HOME DEPARTMENT

### Bail Hostels

**Mr. Andrew F. Bennett:** To ask the Secretary of State for the Home Department how many bail hostels for women will be established in the next three years; and where they will be located.

**Mr. John Patten:** To date we have agreed proposals to provide a total of 32 additional places in approved hostels for women on bail by April 1990. These will be at hostels in Basildon, Birmingham, Brighton, Cardiff and inner London. Plans for the following two years have not yet been agreed.

### Prisoners

**Mr. Cox:** To ask the Secretary of State for the Home Department how many inmates at present serving a life sentence in England and Wales are over the age of 60 years.

**Mr. Douglas Hogg:** According to records held centrally on 31 May 1989, 81 males and three females aged over 60 years were serving life sentences in prison service establishments in England and Wales.

### Deportation

**Mr. Cox:** To ask the Secretary of State for the Home Department what has been the number of people deported from the United Kingdom during each of the last five years.

**Mr. Renton:** Information on the number of persons removed from the United Kingdom under the deportation process in the years 1984 to 1988 is published in table 24 of "Control of Immigration: Statistics United Kingdom 1987" (Cm. 415) and in table 14 of Home Office Statistical Bulletin Issue 10/89 "Control of Immigration: Statistics —Fourth Quarter and Year 1988", copies of both of which are in the Library.

**Mr. Darling:** To ask the Secretary of State for the Home Department if he will list the number of persons *(a)* detained by the Metropolitan police on suspicion of being an illegal entrant and *(b)* subsequently not charged for 1988 and in each month in 1989 to the nearest available date.

**Mr. Renton:** Information is not available in the form requested.

**Mr. Darling:** To ask the Secretary of State for the Home Department (1) if he will list the numbers of illegal entrants to the United Kingdom detected in each quarter in 1988 and in each month in 1989 to the nearest available date;

(2) pursuant to his answer to the hon. Member for Edinburgh, Central, of 6 June, *Official Report,* column *51,* if he will list the total number of notices of intention to deport issued between 1986 and 1988 and in each month in 1989 to the nearest available date.

**Mr. Renton:** Information for 1986 to 1988 on the number of notices of intention to deport issued and the number of persons against whom action was commenced as illegal entrants are published in tables 13 and 14, respectively, of Home Office statistical bulletin issue 10/89 "Control of Immigration: Statistics—Fourth Quarter and Year 1988", a copy of which is in the Library. The next issue of the bulletin giving information for the first quarter of 1989 will be published around the end of the month.

**Mr. Darling:** To ask the Secretary of State for the Home Department what criteria are applied in determining whether a notice of intention to deport should be considered and signed by a member of the immigration and nationality department or by a member of the immigration service.

**Mr. Renton:** The issue of a notice of intention to deport may be authorised by designated members of the immigration service not below the rank of inspector in cases where an officer of the service, in the course of carrying out his duties, discovers a person who is liable to deportation under section 3(5)(a) of the Immigration Act 1971 as an overstayer or for working in breach of conditions. The issue of a notice in all other circumstances is authorised by members of the deportation section of the immigration and nationality department.

### Prison Visitors

**Mr. Cox:** To ask the Secretary of State for the Home Department when he plans to increase the allowance that can be paid to members of the prison board of visitors; and if he will make a statement.

**Mr. Douglas Hogg:** Allowances for travelling expenses for board members were increased on 1 January 1989, and they will shortly be notified that allowances for loss of earnings have been increased with effect from 15 May 1989. These rates are tied to those paid to justices of the peace.

Members of boards of visitors who serve on local review committees receive travelling expenses in line with Civil Service mileage allowances, which were increased with effect from 1 July 1987.

### Overseas Students

**Mr. Darling:** To ask the Secretary of State for the Home Department what representations he has received with regard to allowing female overseas students to be joined by their husbands for the duration of their studies in the United Kingdom; and if he will make a statement.

**Mr. Renton:** Two representations have been received recently on this subject: replies have been sent to both.

Although the rules make no formal provision for husbands to accompany or join their wives who are studying in the United Kingdom, entry clearance may be granted for this purpose where there are compassionate circumstances. We have considered whether the rules ought to go further, but have concluded that they should not. One of the basic purposes of immigration control is to restrict the numbers coming to live or take employment in this country. Changing the rules so that they allowed female students to be accompanied by their husbands would represent a considerable relaxation in the control, which could result in substantial additional numbers coming to work in the United Kingdom.

### Criminal Convictions

**Mr. Mullin:** To ask the Secretary of State for the Home Department how many cases of alleged miscarriage of criminal justice were considered by the C3 department of the Home Office for each year from 1980; how many of these were referred to the courts; how many of these were rejected; how many were dealt with in other ways; and how many convictions were quashed.

**Mr. John Patten:** Information in the form requested is available only from 1 October 1984, as follows:

*Representations of wrongful conviction and consequent references to the Court of Appeal under section 17(1)(a) of the Criminal Appeal Act 1968*

| Period | Number of representations considered | Number of cases referred to the Court of Appeal | Appeals allowed by the Court of Appeal | Appeals dismissed by the Court of Appeal |
|---|---|---|---|---|
| 1 October 1984 to 30 September 1985 | 770 | 2 | 1 | 1 |
| 1 October 1985 to 30 September 1986 | 773 | 4 | 1 | 3 |
| 1 October 1986 to 30 September 1987 | 784 | 6 | 3 | 3 |
| 1 October 1987 to 31 March 1988 | 274 | [2]3 | — | 2 |
| 1 April 1988[1] to 31 March 1989 | 536 | [3]2 | 1 | — |

[1] The method of collecting statistics was revised in April 1988.
[2] One case awaiting determination at 31 March 1989.
[3] One case awaiting determination at 31 March 1989.

In other cases free pardons were granted and relevant figures are given in a reply today to another question from the hon. Member.

In the other cases considered it was decided that there were no grounds in the information available for intervention in the conviction.

**Mr. Mullin:** To ask the Secretary of State for the Home Department how many criminal convictions, disregarding motoring offences, were quashed by him without reference to the Court of Appeal for each year since 1980.

**Mr. John Patten:** My right hon. Friend has no power to quash a conviction. In addition to his powers under section 17 of the Criminal Appeal Act 1968 to refer a case to the Court of Appeal, he may, in exceptional circumstances, recommend to Her Majesty the Queen that a free pardon should be granted. This course is normally followed in respect of summary convictions where there is no power to refer the case back to the courts for their consideration.

The following free pardons have been granted in the years 1980-88 (excluding motoring offences):

| | Number |
|---|---|
| 1980 | 15 |
| 1981 | 14 |
| 1982 | 10 |
| 1983 | 11 |
| 1984 | 16 |
| 1985 | 6 |
| 1986 | 7 |
| 1987 | 13 |
| 1988 | 9 |

### Mr. Wai Man Chung

**Mr. Alan Williams:** To ask the Secretary of State for the Home Department why 19 days after notifying the constituent of the right hon. Member for Swansea, West, Mr. Wai Man Chung, that entry clearance to United Kingdom from China had been granted to his wife, Mrs. Shi Jian Chung, his Department had not notified the visa section at the Foreign Office of its decision, so that it could notify the embassy in Peking.

**Mr. Renton:** A letter authorising the issue of a visa to Mrs. Chung was sent to the migration and visa department of the Foreign Office on 26 May—the same day that Mr. Chung was notified of the decision. The migration and visa department has confirmed that instructions to issue Mrs. Chung with a visa were sent to Peking on 16 June.

## ENVIRONMENT

### Local Authority Contracts (Tenders)

111. **Mr. McAllion:** To ask the Secretary of State for the Environment what steps he is taking to ensure that private sector companies tendering for local authority contracts maintain the existing employment conditions of local authority employees.

**Mr. Gummer:** None. Companies which are successful in winning local authority contracts under the compulsory competition regime will no doubt consider whether it is advantageous to employ all or some of the authority's relevant work force, but they are under no obligation to do so.

### New Towns (Developments)

**Mr. Butler:** To ask the Secretary of State for the Environment if he will ensure that a copy of the section 7(1) submission submitted to him concerning possible housing development at High Warren, Appleton is made available to the Member for Warrington, South.

**Mr. Trippier:** I have not received a submission under section 7(1) of the New Towns Act 1981 for housing development at High Warren, Appleton. I have however asked new town development corporations to ensure that they have satisfactory arrangements in place for informing hon. Members with a constituency interest of section 7(1) applications in which they have expressed an interest.

**Mr. Butler:** To ask the Secretary of State for the Environment what arrangements he intends to make to ensure that hon. Members whose constituencies were affected by new town section 7(1) submissions receive copies of such submissions as a matter of course from new town development corporations.

**Mr. Trippier:** I have asked new towns development corporations to ensure that they have satisfactory arrangements in place for informing hon. Members with a constituency interest of section 7(1) applications under the New Towns Act 1981 in which they have expressed an interest.

### Illuminated Advertisements

**Mr. Cartwright:** To ask the Secretary of State for the Environment what representations he has received from environmental organisations about his proposed relaxation of controls over illuminated advertisements; and what has been his response.

**Mr. Chope:** Joint representations opposing the introduction of "deemed consent" provisions for illuminated advertisements were made on 29 March by the Association of Conservation Officers, on behalf of 11 local authority, professional and conservation organisations. The Georgian group subsequently supported these representations. I am sending the hon. Member a copy of my reply.

### Council Housing (Tenant Initiatives)

**Mr. Fraser:** To ask the Secretary of State for the Environment what arrangements his Department has made to consult local authorities over grant funding of secondary housing co-operatives to promote tenant management co-operatives in council housing under section 16 of the Housing and Planning Act 1986; what consultation there has been over which organisations receive such funding and at what level and what steps his Department has taken to consult local authorities to co-ordinate funding on tenants' intiatives in council housing.

**Mr. Trippier:** There are no existing formal arrangements for consulting local authorities over section 16 grant funding of secondary agencies. Where necessary, the Department will discuss applications with the relevant authority.

Local authorities were invited to submit evidence on matters, including section 16, to the recent housing co-operatives review. The Government are now considering the review committee's report.

### Disabled People (Housing)

**Mr. Hannam:** To ask the Secretary of State for the Environment (1) how much money the Housing Corporation allocated in 1989-90 for the construction of wheelchair housing *(a)* in total cash terms, and *(b)* as a percentage of the total budget each year for the last six years;

(2) how much money was allocated by the Housing Corporation, to housing associations to adapt properties occupied by disabled tenants for each of the last six financial years, and how many housing associations in each of those years received money for this purpose.

**Mr. Trippier:** This information is not held by the Department. The distribution of public funds to individual housing associatons and projects is largely a matter for the Housing Corporation to determine within the broad policy framework established annually in discussion with my right hon. Friend the Secretary of State for the Environment. I have therefore asked the Housing Corporation to respond to my hon. Friend direct.

**Mr. Hannam:** To ask the Secretary of State for the Environment what percentage of local authority housing built in 1989-90 and in each of the last six previous financial years is wheelchair housing.

**Mr. Trippier:** New wheelchair dwellings completed by English local authorities as a percentage of their total new housebuilding completions are as follows:

|         | *Percentage* |
|---------|------------|
| 1983-84 | 1·0        |
| 1984-85 | 1·4        |
| 1985-86 | 1·0        |
| 1986-87 | 1·3        |
| 1987-88 | 1·3        |
| 1988-89 | 1·5        |

Information for 1989-90 is not available.

### Council House Sales

**Mr. Redmond:** To ask the Secretary of State for the Environment if he intends to introduce a scheme to convert council house rents into mortgages along the lines of that announced by the Scottish Office; and if he will make a statement.

**Mr. Trippier:** No. The Scottish scheme will entail voluntary sales to tenants of Scottish Homes. There is no organisation in England equivalent to Scottish Homes for these purposes.

### Planning Appeals

**Mr. Ron Davies:** To ask the Secretary of State for the Environment how many planning appeals were lodged with his Department in 1974, 1979, 1984 and the last full year for which figures are available; and, for each year, how many were allowed.

**Mr. Chope:** The information requested is as follows:

| Year    | Appeals Received | Appeals Allowed |
|---------|------------------|-----------------|
| 1974    | 13,324           | 2,715           |
| 1979    | 12,990           | 2,602           |
| 1984    | 16,192           | 3,773           |
| 1988-89 | 28,659           | 7,734           |

### Water Privatisation

**Mr. Wood:** To ask the Secretary of State for the Environment whether he is in a position to give further details of the share offer arrangements for employees of the privatised water authorities.

**Mr. Howard:** The Government welcome the opportunity which privatisation of the water authorities provides for employees to become shareholders in the new plcs. I can now announce the following special arrangements for eligible employees of the new water plcs and their wholly owned subsidiaries:

(i) employees will be offered free shares worth around £70 at the offer price plus about £2 of shares for every year of continuous service with their new company and the predecessor water authority up to a date close to flotation. In addition, people who were employed by the predecessor water authority on 1 April 1974, when the authority took over from bodies previously responsible for water supply and sewerage services, will be treated as having an additional five years' entitlement;

(ii) employees will also be offered two free shares for each one bought at the full offer price on a matching basis up to a maximum of £400 worth of free shares; under this element of the package, if an employee bought shares worth £200 at the offer price he would receive shares worth in total £600;

(iii) employees will be able to buy up to a maximum of £2,350 worth of additional shares at a discount of 10 per cent. from the full offer price;

(iv) employees applying for shares will be treated on a priority basis over the general public, up to an individual limit of shares worth £12,000 at the offer price; this is in addition to the free, matching and discount shares.

The free and matching shares will be available to employees who satisfy certain minimum qualification periods on length of employment and hours worked per week. The discount and priority shares will be available to all employees at a date close to the flotation date.

We have also decided that pensioners of a new water plc, its wholly owned subsidiaries or its predecessor water authority should be able to apply on a priority basis, over the general public, for shares up to an individual limit of £12,000 at the offer price.

### Property Services Agency (Vacant Buildings)

**Mr. Ingram:** To ask the Secretary of State for the Environment if he will list those buildings which are rented, leased or owned by the Property Services Agency which have lain vacant for more than the last 12 months.

**Mr. Chope** [*holding answer 13 June 1989*]: Yes. The list is as follows.

*Schedule of buildings rented, leased or owned by the PSA which have been vacant for more than 12 months as at 9 June 1989*

| Property | Local authority area |
| --- | --- |
| UBO Palmers Green, N13 | Enfield |
| Dale House, Cardinal Road, Feltham | Hounslow |
| 87 Burlington Road, New Malden, Surrey | Kingston upon Thames |
| Alpine Avenue Standard Office Buildings, Tolworth | Kingston upon Thames |
| 29 Abbotsbury Road, Morden | Merton |
| 17 Victoria Road, Strechford | Birmingham |
| 58-72 John Bright Street, Birmingham | Birmingham |
| Britannia House, Station Street, Burton on Trent | East Staffordshire |
| County Court Offices, Bank Place, Nottingham | Nottingham |
| CG Lookout, Spurn Point, Humberside | Holderness |
| Storage Depot, Tyne Mills, Hexham | Tynedale |
| 22 and 29 The Springs, Wakefield | Wakefield |
| Longworth Road, Horwich | Bolton |
| Storage Depot, Hob Lane, Dunham Hill | Chester |
| Storage Depot, Meadowview, Mickle Trafford | Chester |
| Magowan House, 11A West Street, Portadown | County Armagh |
| 116A Bradshawgate, Leigh | Wigan |
| 224-226 Queens Road, Aberdeen | City of Aberdeen |

| Property | Local authority area |
| --- | --- |
| Sheriff Court House, Castle Street, Aberdeen | City of Aberdeen |
| 276 Old Rutherglen Road, Glasgow | City of Glasgow |
| 65-87 Cowlairs Road, Glasgow | City of Glasgow |
| Norfolk House, 15 Princes Square, East Kilbride | East Kilbride |
| C and E Offices, Grange Dock North, Grangemouth | Falkirk |
| 163-165 Bank Street, Coatbridge | Monklands |
| 146-156 Main Street, Coatbridge | Monklands |
| Virginia Buildings, High Street, Buckie | Moray |
| Land at Yardie, Buckie | Moray |
| Windsor Street, Shotts | Motherwell |
| 69-73 Crossgate, Cupar | North East Fife |
| Gremista, Lerwick | Shetland Islands |
| Storage Depot, 270 Kirkintilloch Road, Bishopbriggs | Strathkelvin |
| CG Lookout, Helmsdale | Sutherland |
| Hut Number 3, Chaucer Barracks, Canterbury | Canterbury |
| 41 Medina Villas, Hove | Hove |
| Park House, Barrier Road, Chatham | Medway |
| CG Hut, Rye Harbour, Rye | Rother |
| Drakewalls, Gunnislake | Caradon |
| CG Building, South Esplanade, Burnham-on-Sea | Sedgemoor |
| Shire Hall, Shuttern, Taunton | Taunton Deane |
| Telford House, Park Gardens, Yeovil | Yeovil |
| Cold Store Depot, New Pond Road, Guildford | Guildford |
| Part Building No. 71, Bletchley Park, Bletchley | Milton Keynes |
| Stores, Shirburn Road, Watlington | South Oxfordshire |
| 35, 36, 38 and 39 Castle Street, Swansea | Swansea |

These 44 buildings represent less than 1 per cent. of the total stock held by PSA. Thirty-four of the properties have been declared surplus and are in the process of disposal and the remainder are undergoing, or being considered, for refurbishment or redevelopment to allow reoccupation by a Government Department.

### Community Charge

**Mr. Home Robertson:** To ask the Secretary of State for the Environment how many copies of his Department's leaflet "The Community Charge (The So-called 'Poll Tax'): How It Will Work For You" have been mailed to addresses in Scotland; what was the cost of distributing this material outside England; and if he will now write to those households in Scotland which received the leaflet to explain the error.

**Mr. Gummer** [*holding answer 19 June 1989*]: I refer the hon. Member to the answer which I gave to the hon. Member for Roxburgh and Berwickshire (Mr. Kirkwood) yesterday. I naturally regret the fact that a comparatively few leaflets were wrongly delivered to Scottish households, but I do not think it necessary to write to each household concerned. The mailing house concerned has apologised for the mistake.

### Set-aside Land

**Mr. Ron Davies:** To ask the Secretary of State for the Environment how many planning applications have been made to date in respect of land on which set-aside payments are being made by the Minister of Agriculture, Fisheries and Food; and, of these applications, how many have been successful.

**Mr. Chope** *[holding answer 19 June 1989]:* Only a small proportion of set-aside proposals will need planning permission. The Department does not collect information from local planning authorities in the form requested, and I understand it is not included in the records of applications for set-aside payments kept by the Ministry of Agriculture, Fisheries and Food.

### Water Quality

**Mrs. Ann Taylor:** To ask the Secretary of State for the Environment if he will publish the letter written by officials in his Department and sent to water authorities on 14 February giving advice on how to deal with the EC directive on water quality.

**Mr. Howard** *[holding answer 19 June 1989]:* No. The letter referred to was a working document on the assumptions to be made in compiling expenditure projections for the purpose of k setting (k is the initial limit on price increases to be contained in companies instruments of appointment under the Water Bill). The letter made it clear that these assumptions would be subject to review until the end of the k setting process. We will state the assumptions underlying ks once they are determined.

We have made it clear to water authorities and companies that expenditure arising from any obligations left out of initial k, for example because the costs are too uncertain for inclusion, and expenditure arising from new obligations imposed after ks are set, will be eligible for consideration in reviews of charges by the Director General of Water Services.

**Mrs. Ann Taylor:** To ask the Secretary of State for the Environment what his current estimate is for complying with EC directive 80/778/EEC in each of the water authority areas.

**Mr. Howard** *[holding answer 19 June 1989]:* The Government are fully committed to compliance with the EC drinking water directive as quickly as possible, taking account of practicalities. Water undertakers in England and Wales have drawn up improvement programmes for supplies which regularly or intermittently fail to comply with the directive in certain respects. Only when these programmes have been thoroughly assessed will it be possible to estimate the time scale for compliance with the directive.

### Environmental Assessments

**Ms. Walley:** To ask the Secretary of State for the Environment if, further to his replies of 4 May, *Official Report,* columns *247-50,* with regard to environmental assessment, he will *(a)* list those matters taken into account when determining whether environmental assessment is required, *(b)* give details of the methodology used, *(c)* specify what criteria and thresholds are used, *(d)* indicate why some extensions of mineral workings required environmental assessments and others did not, *(e)* indicate why environment assessment was required in the case of one shopping complex and not in the case of other shopping complexes and retail parks, *(f)* give details of what information was given to the relevant local authorities following these directions and *(g)* indicate what information has been given to other local authorities

subsequent to these directions in order to help them apply the Town and Country Planning (Assessment of Environmental Effects) Regulations 1988 consistently.

**Mr. Chope** *[holding answer 19 June 1989]:* In accordance with the Town and Country Planning (Assessment of Environmental Effects) Regulations 1988, environmental assessment is required of all projects of the types listed in schedule 1 to the regulations and of any project of a type listed in schedule 2 which is likely to have significant effects on the environment by virtue of factors such as its nature, size or location. Guidance on which projects are likely to have significant environmental effects so as to require environmental assessment is given in DoE circular 15/88, which also sets out indicative thresholds and criteria to which the Secretary of State has regard when considering whether to direct that assessment is required. Decisions on the need for environmental assessment turn on the facts of individual cases, and locational considerations may lead to different conclusions in respect of similar types of development. The regulations require the Secretary of State to give reasons when he directs that environmental assessment is required. Copies of decision letters are sent to the applicant and to the local planning authority, which is required to make a copy available for public inspection in the place where the planning register is kept. We are considering how best this information can be made more widely available to assist both developers and local planning authorities in the application of these regulations.

## SCOTLAND

### Scottish Enterprise

112. **Mr. Wallace:** To ask the Secretary of State for Scotland if he will make a statement on the Scottish Enterprise proposals.

**Mr. Lang:** We are currently reassessing the proposals in the Scottish Enterprise White Paper in the light of all the responses received and will announce our detailed decisions in due course.

### Population Statistics

**Mr. Ieuan Wyn Jones:** To ask the Secretary of State for Scotland what are his Department's estimates for the numbers of people aged 65 to 74 years, 75 to 79 years and over 80 years in the years 2000 and 2020 in Scotland; and what percentage increase this represents in each category over the actual figures for the last year in which they are available.

**Mr. Michael Forsyth:** The information is set out in the table.

| Age group | *Year 2000* | | *Year 2020* | |
|---|---|---|---|---|
| | *Projected population* | *Percentage change from 1988 mid-year estimate* | *Projected population* | *Percentage change from 1988 mid-year estimate* |
| 65-74 | 427,703 | −1·6 | 500,785 | 15·2 |
| 75-79 | 160,311 | 1·4 | 161,124 | 1·9 |
| 80 and over | 188,592 | 16·4 | 213,814 | 32·0 |

## Surgeries (Rural Areas)

**Mr. Maclennan:** To ask the Secretary of State for Scotland what additional funds he is making available to health boards to enable practice surgeries in rural areas to meet the requirements of the new contract.

**Mr. Michael Forsyth** *[holding answer 16 June 1989]:* Funding for general medical services following the introduction of the new contract for GPs will be determined in the course of the Government's public expenditure survey 1989. The funds will take full account of the new contract, including those aspects which relate to rural practices.

At present public expenditure on family practitioner services generally is planned to increase from £496 million in 1988-89 to £610 million in 1991-92, an increase of 23 per cent.

## DEFENCE

### Fylingdales (Equipment)

**Mr. Andrew F. Bennett:** To ask the Secretary of State for Defence what is the primary purpose of the new radar equipment at Fylingdales.

**Mr. Neubert:** The modernised radar system at RAF Fylingdales will perform the same functions as the present system, which is to provide early warning of strategic ballistic missile attack.

**Mr. Andrew F. Bennett:** To ask the Secretary of State for Defence what percentage of the cost of installing the new early warning radar equipment at Fylingdales comes from United Kingdom sources.

**Mr. Neubert:** The modernised radar system itself will be constructed by an American company, at United States Government expense. British companies will carry out all the work to be undertaken in the United Kingdom on the infrastructure for the facility, at British Government expense. This infrastructure work, for which contracts are shortly to be awarded, will amount to some 27 per cent. of the total.

### Military Communications

**Mr. Andrew F. Bennett:** To ask the Secretary of State for Defence what programmes are under way to develop protection for United Kingdom military communications satellites from anti-satellite systems.

**Mr. Sainsbury:** The potential threat to United Kingdom military communications satellites from such systems is kept under constant review.

**Mr. Andrew F. Bennett:** To ask the Secretary of State for Defence what programmes are under way to develop the use of satellite-laser systems for communications with submarines *(a)* in co-operation with the United States of America and *(b)* by the United Kingdom alone.

**Mr. Sainsbury:** It is not our practice to comment on operational matters of this kind.

### Anti-Satellite Weapons

**Mr. Andrew F. Bennett:** To ask the Secretary of State for Defence what research is currently under way concerning the development of an anti-satellite weapon programme.

**Mr. Sainsbury:** No such research is carried out by the United Kingdom.

### Low Flying

**Mr. Wilson:** To ask the Secretary of State for Defence how many complaints about low flying were received by his Department in 1988 from addresses in the Cunninghame, North constituency.

**Mr. Neubert:** In 1988 the Ministry of Defence received a total of four complaints or inquiries about military low flying from addresses in the Cunninghame, North constituency.

**Mr. Wilson:** To ask the Secretary of State for Defence (1) if he has any information on military helicopters authorised to operate at low level in Scotland on 5 May 1988, additional to that given in his reply to the hon. Member for Cunninghame, North on 27 May 1988, *Official Report,* column *391;*

(2) pursuant to his reply to the hon. Member for Cunninghame, North of 22 December 1988, *Official Report,* column *368,* whether the times of movements given for Army Air Corps Gazelle helicopter serial number XZ328 near Dalmally and at HMS Gannet on 5 May 1988 were expressed in Greenwich mean time or British summer time;

(3) pursuant to his reply to the hon. Member for Cunninghame, North of 22 December 1988, *Official Report,* column *368,* what was the point of origin of the flight to HMS Gannet by Army Air Corps Gazelle helicopter, serial number XZ328, on 5 May 1988; what route was flown by this aircraft through Argyll; and what was the purpose of the flight.

**Mr. Neubert:** Timings given for the movements of the Army Air Corps helicopter were expressed in British summer time. This helicopter, which began its sortie from RAF Leuchars, was carrying out a navigation exercise. I have nothing further to add to my reply to the hon. Member on 22 December 1988, at column *368,* or to my letter of 24 February 1989 to the hon. Member.

**Mr. Wilson:** To ask the Secretary of State for Defence, pursuant to his reply to the hon. Member for Cunninghame, North of 22 December 1988, *Official Report,* column *368,* if he will state the reasons for not listing medical establishments over which military low flying is prohibited.

**Mr. Neubert:** I have nothing further to add to my reply to the hon. Member on 22 December, at column *368.*

### ELF Transmitter

**Mr. Andrew F. Bennett:** To ask the Secretary of State for Defence when he expects the notice of proposed development relating to the proposed trial ELF transmitter at Glengarry forest to be submitted to the Highland regional council.

**Mr. Neubert:** Preparation of the notice of proposed development continues, but completion will take some time and it is not possible to say precisely when it will be submitted.

## Commissions (Sale)

**Mr. Austin Mitchell:** To ask the Secretary of State for Defence whether he has any proposals for reviving the sale of commissions as part of the Government's programme of privatisation.

**Mr. Neubert:** No.

## Historic Aircraft Collection (RAF St. Athan)

**Mr. Wilson:** To ask the Secretary of State for Defence if he will list the dates of movement and final destinations of any aircraft from the collection of historic aircraft at RAF St. Athan which have been *(a)* sold, *(b)* scrapped and *(c)* moved to other locations since 1987; and what were the reasons for any such moves.

**Mr. Neubert:** A review of the RAF's policy on historic and non-flying display aircraft resulted in a decision in early 1988 to disband the RAF St. Athan regional collection of historic aircraft. Transfers effected to date are as follows.

The remaining aircraft will be disposed of progressively over the next few months. It is not intended to scrap any, but those not required elsewhere within the service will be sold.

*Disbandment of the RAF St. Athan regional collection of historic aircraft*
*Transfers effected up to 21 June 1989*

| Year and aircraft | |
|---|---|
| **1988** | |
| Messerschmitt Me 163B | Gifted to the German Air Force |
| Auster T7 | Transferred to the regional collection at RAF Cosford, for display |
| **1989** | |
| Kawasaki | Transferred to the regional collection at RAF Cosford, for display |
| Messerschmitt Me 262A | Transferred to the regional collection at RAF Cosford, for display |
| Mitsubishi | Transferred to the regional collection at RAF Cosford, for display |
| Fiesler Storch | Transferred to the regional collection at RAF Cosford, for display |
| Percival Proctor | Transferred to the RAF museum at Hendon for display |
| Swift | Transferred to the RAF museum at Hendon for display |
| Meteor F8 | Transferred to RAF Finningley as a gate guardian |
| Spitfire Mk9E | Transferred to RAF Abingdon as a reserve for the battle of Britain memorial flight |

**Mr. Wilson:** To ask the Secretary of State for Defence if it is intended to maintain a collection of historic aircraft at RAF St. Athan.

**Mr. Neubert:** No.

## Tornado Aircraft

**Mr. Wilson:** To ask the Secretary of State for Defence what assessments were made of *(a)* current and *(b)* projected peacetime loss rates of the Tornado F2 and F3 in RAF service prior to the decision to order an additional attrition replacement batch in 1988.

**Mr. Sainsbury:** No Tornado F2s or F3s have been lost to date. The predicted peacetime attrition rate is classified.

**Mr. Wilson:** To ask the Secretary of State for Defence what consideration is being given to the placing of further attrition replacement orders for *(a)* air defence Tornados and *(b)* strike/attack/reconnaissance Tornados.

**Mr. Sainsbury:** The need for additional attrition aircraft is kept under review.

**Mr. Wilson:** To ask the Secretary of State for Defence (1) what projected peacetime attrition rate was assumed for the Tornado air defence variant in calculating the size of the original order for 165 aircraft for the Royal Air Force;
(2) what proportion of the original order of 165 Tornado air defence variants for the Royal Air Force was made up of attrition replacement aircraft.

**Mr. Sainsbury:** The information requested is classified.

## Service Cars (Argyll)

**Mr. Wilson:** To ask the Secretary of State for Defence what information he has on the presence of *(a)* Army and *(b)* Royal Navy Ford Escort estate staff cars in Argyll on 5 May 1988.

**Mr. Neubert:** The information requested is not readily available and could not be provided without disproportionate effort and cost.

## Aircraft Losses

**Mr. Wilson:** To ask the Secretary of State for Defence what percentage of the total number of Buccaneer aircraft procured for the Royal Air Force have been lost in accidents so far.

**Mr. Neubert:** Of the total number of Buccaneer aircraft taken into RAF service, 19·17 per cent. have been lost in accidents.

**Mr. Wilson:** To ask the Secretary of State for Defence what percentage of the total number of Hunter aircraft procured for the Royal Air Force have been lost in accidents over the aircraft's service life so far.

**Mr. Neubert:** Of the total number of Hunter aircraft taken into RAF service, 32·36 per cent. have been lost in accidents.

**Mr. Wilson:** To ask the Secretary of State for Defence what percentage of the total number of Jaguar aircraft procured for the Royal Air Force have been lost in accidents so far.

**Mr. Neubert:** Of the total number of Jaguar aircraft taken into RAF service, 23·76 per cent. have been lost in accidents.

**Mr. Wilson:** To ask the Secretary of State for Defence what percentage of the total number of Lightning aircraft procured for the Royal Air Force were lost in accidents over the aircraft's service life.

**Mr. Neubert:** Of the total number of Lightning aircraft taken into RAF service, 45·58 per cent. have been lost in accidents.

**Mr. Wilson:** To ask the Secretary of State for Defence what percentage of the total number of Phantom aircraft procured for the Royal Air Force have been lost in accidents so far.

**Mr. Neubert:** Of the total number of Phantom aircraft taken into RAF service, 22·54 per cent. have been lost in accidents.

### Community Charge

**Mr. Macdonald:** To ask the Secretary of State for Defence if he will publish the written guidance issued to armed service units in respect of poll tax payment.

**Mr. Neubert:** I have placed copies in the Library of the House.

### Howitzers

**Mr. Franks:** To ask the Secretary of State for Defence whether he is now able to make a statement on the procurement of 155 mm self-propelled howitzers for the Army.

**Mr. Sainsbury:** In my reply on 8 June 1988, at column *586,* to a question from my hon. Friend the Member for Berkshire, East (Mr. MacKay), I announced the award of a contract to Vickers Shipbuilding and Engineering Limited (VSEL), worth some £4 million, for further work on its AS90 self-propelled howitzer. This was to enable it to demonstrate more fully the performance of its design against the British Army's specification and to secure option prices for any subsequent production orders. In the interim period we have also closely followed the development in the United States of the M109 howitzer improvement programme.

Following a very careful and detailed evaluation of the two systems, and subject to the agreement of satisfactory terms, I have decided to place a contract with VSEL for the completion of development and a production order for 179 AS90 self-propelled howitzers. This contract, with initial spares and support, is worth some £300 million. I have also arranged an option for a further quantity of howitzers which may be exercised during the next two years.

The new weapon will replace our 105 mm Abbot guns and will significantly enhance artillery firepower. Its introduction will mark a further step in our planned programme to ensure that the armed services are equipped with up-to-date and highly capable equipment.

### Rosyth Dockyard

**Mr. Gordon Brown:** To ask the Secretary of State for Defence whether he is in a position to use a golden share over any takeover of Rosyth dockyard and under what condition.

**Mr. Sainsbury** *[holding answer 12 June 1989]:* No takeover of Rosyth dockyard is proposed. The special share held by Secretary of State is in the Rosyth Royal Dockyard plc and not the Dockyard Management Company, in which Thorn EMI currently holds a 35 per cent. shareholding. Any change in the share ownership of the management company must receive the prior written approval of the Secretary of State.

## PRIME MINISTER

### Tropical Rain Forests

105. **Mr. Corbyn:** To ask the Prime Minister what action she is taking to provide United Kingdom research into the alternatives to products of tropical rain forests.

**The Prime Minister:** The Forestry Commission has an active programme of research into the cultivation of native trees which are capable of producing wood that can be used in place of tropical timber.

### World Environment

Q22. **Mr. Leigh:** To ask the Prime Minister if she has received representations regarding the world environment.

**The Prime Minister:** I regularly receive representations about the many major environmental initiatives which this Government have taken at both the national and international level. Most recently, many nations have supported our call in the United Nations for an international framework convention on global climate change.

### China

Q89. **Mr. Bowis:** To ask the Prime Minister if she has received representations regarding recent events in China.

Q101. **Mr. Cash:** To ask the Prime Minister if she has received representations regarding recent events in China.

Q198. **Mr. Page:** To ask the Prime Minister if she has received representations regarding recent events in China.

**The Prime Minister:** Yes, I have received many representations expressing shock and outrage at recent events in China. These are of course sentiments that I and the Government share.

### EC (Voting Procedures)

Q113. **Mr. Teddy Taylor:** To ask the Prime Minister if she will raise at the next meeting of the European Council the issue of the procedures adopted in determining which directives are subject to majority vote or unanimity; and if she will make a statement.

**The Prime Minister:** I refer my hon. Friend to the replies to him of 6 and 15 June.

### Developing Countries (Debt)

Q119. **Mr. Tom Clarke:** To ask the Prime Minister what is Her Majesty's Government's policy for solving the crisis of debt repayment for developing countries.

**The Prime Minister:** The Government support the internationally agreed strategy which was reaffirmed and extended at the spring meetings of the International Monetary Fund and the World Bank on 3 and 4 April.

### Bradford

Q169. **Mr. Cryer:** To ask the Prime Minister when she next expects to pay an official visit to Bradford.

**The Prime Minister:** I have at present no plans to do so.

## Shipyards (EC Funding)

**Q216. Dr. Godman:** To ask the Prime Minister if Her Majesty's Government have any proposals to seek a revision to the list of United Kingdom shipyards with access to the European Community shipbuilding intervention fund; and if she will make a statement.

**The Prime Minister:** As the hon. Member will be aware, the intervention fund is not an EC fund but a subsidy arrangement operated by Her Majesty's Government within the term of the EC sixth directive on aids to shipbuilding. We have no plans to revise current arrangements governing access to intervention fund by individual yards.

## Electoral Registration Advertising

**Mr. Harry Barnes:** To ask the Prime Minister, pursuant to her answer to the hon. Member for Derbyshire, North-East on 12 June, *Official Report,* column *265,* if she will give the amounts spent on electoral registration advertising for each of the past seven years at current prices.

**The Prime Minister:** Expenditure on electoral registration advertising over the last seven years, revalued at 1989 prices, has been as follows:

|         | £       |
| ------- | ------- |
| 1982-83 | 123,762 |
| 1983-84 | 153,631 |
| 1984-85 | 163,240 |
| 1985-86 | 184,243 |
| 1986-87 | 356,494 |
| 1987-88 | 294,190 |
| 1988-89 | 322,833 |

## Engagements

**Mr. Barry Field:** To ask the Prime Minister if she will list her official engagements for Tuesday 20 June.

**Mr. Harry Greenway:** To ask the Prime Minister if she will list her official engagements for Tuesday 20 June.

**Mr. Stern:** To ask the Prime Minister if she will list her official engagements for Tuesday 20 June.

**Mr. Pike:** To ask the Prime Minister if she will list her official engagements for Tuesday 20 June.

**Mr. David Shaw:** To ask the Prime Minister if she will list her official engagements for Tuesday 20 June.

**The Prime Minister:** This morning I had meetings with ministerial colleagues and others. In addition to my duties in the House I shall be having further meetings later today.

## Government Information Service

**Mr. Dalyell:** To ask the Prime Minister what response her press secretary made to the Institute of Professional Civil Servants when it asked him to support a proposed code of ethics for the Government information service.

**The Prime Minister:** It is not my usual practice to publish exchanges of this kind.

## Endangered Species

**Mr. Ron Davies:** To ask the Prime Minister if she will list those gifts received in her official capacity over the last year while on foreign visits and during visits of foreign dignitaries to Britain which have required an import licence under the CITES.

**The Prime Minister** *[holding answer 13 June 1989]:* In the last year I have received three items of silver and ivory jewellery from my visit to Zimbabwe. These items have all been deposited with Her Majesty's Customs and Excise. In view of the ban on ivory imports announced by the Government on Friday 9 June, I have decided that these items should be retained by Her Majesty's Customs and Excise. Information on gifts given by foreign dignitaries during visits to Britain is a matter for them, but I am not aware of any such gifts which I have received in an official capacity which have required an import licence under the CITES.

# NORTHERN IRELAND

## Water Power Rights

**Mr. McCusker:** To ask the Secretary of State for Northern Ireland if he will list in the *Official Report* those water power rights which have been acquired by the Government as a consequence of the activities of the drainage division of the Department of Agriculture, indicating how many have been wholly and how many partially acquired.

**Mr. Viggers:** In the course of drainage division activities the Government wholly acquired water rights on two occasions, once in the upper main drainage scheme and once in Broughshane flood protection scheme. In both cases the right was expunged by removal of a weir and infill of a millrace.

## Turbines (Rivers)

**Mr. McCusker:** To ask the Secretary of State for Northern Ireland what requirement he has to determine the mean, low water and maximum flow of a river at the sites of water mills, and the capacity of any water turbine, pelton wheel, or waterwheel being installed.

**Mr. Viggers:** There is no statutory requirement to determine the mean, low water and maximum flow of any watercourse.

It may be necessary when consenting to a new installation to establish the capacity of any water turbine, pelton wheel or waterwheel being installed to ensure that it does not adversely affect the flow of water in a watercourse. It is usually the case that an existing weir or dam is used as a source of power, leaving the regime of the watercourse unchanged.

## Employment

**Mr. Thurnham:** To ask the Secretary of State for Northern Ireland what steps his Department is taking to increase employment opportunities in Northern Ireland.

**Mr. Viggers:** The Department of Economic Development, and its two industrial development agencies, the Industrial Development Board and Local Enterprise Development Unit undertake a wide range of programmes to assist the private sector to create new employment in Northern Ireland. In the year to 31 March 1989 the two agencies made financial offers to companies which could lead to the creation of 10,234 jobs. A wide range of advisory, training and other services is also available to assist firms to develop and to become more competitive. In addition it is planned to provide in the present financial year 12,400 work experience and training places to assist the long-term unemployed to re-enter the labour market and to provide 13,800 places for youth training.

### Tourism

**Mr. Baldry:** To ask the Secretary of State for Northern Ireland if he will estimate the number of new jobs created in the tourist industry in Northern Ireland in the last five years.

**Mr. Viggers:** Information on tourism-related employment as a whole is estimated only at national level. The available information for regions relates specifically to employees in employment in the hotels and catering industry. Employment in this sector in Northern Ireland increased by 1,810 (or 12 per cent.) over the last five years, to March 1989.

### Housing Executive

**Mr. William Ross:** To ask the Secretary of State for Northern Ireland if he will publish a table in the *Official Report* showing *(a)* how many void dwellings there are in the area covered by each district office of the Northern Ireland Housing Executive as at the latest available date, *(b)* how many dwellings in each such area have been void for more than three months and *(c)* the reasons for such voids or as much of such information as is available to him.

**Mr. Needham:** This is a matter for the Northern Ireland Housing Executive. I am advised by the chairman of the Housing Executive that at 1 May 1989 the number of void dwellings, that is dwellings on which the executive is not seeking to collect rent, in each district office and the number void for more than 13 weeks in each such area is as follows:

| District | Total number voids | Total number voids vacant more than 13 weeks |
|---|---|---|
| Belfast 1 | 110 | 101 |
| Belfast 2 | 396 | 333 |
| Belfast 3 | 299 | 245 |
| Belfast 4 | 525 | 468 |
| Belfast 5 | 726 | 639 |
| Belfast 6 | 264 | 218 |
| Belfast 7 | 250 | 224 |
| Belfast Total | 2,2570 | 2,228 |
| | | |
| Bangor | 52 | 30 |
| Newtownards 1 | 76 | 54 |
| Newtownards 2 | 24 | 10 |
| Castlereagh 1 | 58 | 25 |
| Castlereagh 2 | 12 | 5 |
| Lisburn 1 | 94 | 47 |
| Lisburn 2 | 30 | 21 |
| Lisburn 3 | 8 | 4 |
| Downpatrick | 178 | 116 |
| South East Total | 532 | 312 |
| | | |
| Banbridge | 69 | 50 |
| Newry 1 | 136 | 83 |
| Newry 2 | 49 | 24 |
| Kilkeel | 14 | 11 |
| Armagh | 87 | 65 |

| District | Total number voids | Total number voids vacant more than 13 weeks |
|---|---|---|
| Brownlow | 346 | 285 |
| Lurgan | 75 | 32 |
| Portadown | 89 | 70 |
| South Total | 865 | 620 |
| | | |
| Ballymena | 148 | 93 |
| Antrim | 553 | 473 |
| Newtownabbey 1 | 262 | 172 |
| Newtownabbey 2 | 89 | 66 |
| Carrick | 82 | 34 |
| Larne | 156 | 111 |
| Ballycastle | 5 | 1 |
| Ballymoney | 31 | 22 |
| North East Total | 1,326 | 972 |
| | | |
| Derry 1 | 232 | 205 |
| Derry 2 | 167 | 146 |
| Derry 3 | 22 | 12 |
| Limavady | 33 | 14 |
| Coleraine | 244 | 201 |
| Magherafelt | 14 | 5 |
| Strabane | 38 | 31 |
| North West Total | 750 | 614 |
| | | |
| Omagh | 39 | 21 |
| Cookstown | 28 | 13 |
| Dungannon | 106 | 62 |
| Fermanagh | 89 | 41 |
| West Total | 262 | 137 |
| | | |
| Northern Ireland Total | 6,305 | 4,883 |

Of the total of 6,305 void properties (3·6 per cent. of total stock):

837 are temporarily vacant awaiting allocation or have no tenant available;

1,207 are bricked up due to/or to avoid vandalism;

452 are awaiting improvements which will be completed within 12 months;

520 are bricked up and are awaiting improvements which will not be carried out within 12 months;

487 are bricked up for sale/or homesteading;

1,776 are awaiting demolition in redevelopment areas; and

1,026 are void for a variety of reasons such as decanting or security reasons.

## FOREIGN AND COMMONWEALTH AFFAIRS

### Namibia

**Mr. Atkinson:** To ask the Secretary of State for Foreign and Commonwealth Affairs (1) what recent representations he has received from the leader of the Kwanyamas tribe on behalf of eight other Namibian tribes about the role of the Namibian Council of Churches as the sole and authentic agent of the United Nations High Commissioner for Refugees in the administration of the returning South West Africa People's Organisation refugees to Namibia; and if he will make a statement;

(2) what recent representations he has received from the leader of the Kwanyamas tribe on behalf of eight other Namibian tribes about the intimidatory actions of the NANSO student organisation; and if he will make a statement;

(3) what recent representations he has received from the leader of the Kwanyamas tribe on behalf of eight other Namibian tribes about the protection of citizens in the northern and eastern territories of Namibia from the

People's Liberation Army of Namibia following the demobilisation of the South West Africa Territory Force; and if he will make a statement.

**Mrs. Chalker:** Mr. Gabriel Kautuima, senior headman of the Kwanyama tribe, met an official of the FCO on 16 June and handed over a copy of a petition submitted to the United Nations special representative for Namibia and the Administrator General of Namibia on the matters referred to in my hon. Friend's questions. Mr. Kautuima was assured of our continued commitment to the United Nations plan for Namibian independence and our support for the efforts of the United Nations Secretary General and his staff to ensure that the best possible conditions prevail for the holding of free and fair elections in Namibia.

## EDUCATION AND SCIENCE

### Russian Language

**Mr. David Nicholson:** To ask the Secretary of State for Education and Science what proposals his Department has *(a)* to promote school exchanges with the Soviet Union and *(b)* to promote the learning of the Russian language in schools; and if he will make a statement.

**Mr. Jackson:** My right hon. Friend visited the Soviet Union last October and concluded an agreement with the Soviet chairman of the State Committee for Public Education which envisaged a programme of up to 50 school exchanges on each side by the end of the 1991-92 academic year. In this, the first year of the programme, 10 school exchanges on each side have been arranged and are under way. In the next academic year, 1989-90, it is proposed that 20 school exchanges can be arranged, rising to 35 exchanges in academic year 1990-91 and 50 exchanges in academic year 1991-92. At that stage up to 2,000 pupils from each country will be involved.

The aim of the programme is to use the medium of school-to-school twinning to promote a greater degree of mutual understanding among young people of both countries through a wide programme of exchange of schoolchildren and teachers, letters, photographs, tapes and project work, for example in mathematics, science and computing. Language-based exchanges will be a significant component, but the intention is to include also the study of subjects in which the practical elements can be shared.

The national curriculum will include a modern foreign language as a foundation subject at secondary level to be studied by all pupils between the ages of 11 and 16. Russian is among those modern foreign languages specified in the Education (National Curriculum) (Modern Foreign Languages) Order 1989 as eligible to be taught as a national curriculum foundation subject. Within this framework, my right hon. Friend is encouraging schools to offer a greater diversity of languages, including Russian, and we are providing education support grants for pilot projects in some local education authorities in England to promote the preparation and implementation of plans for language diversification.

### Teachers

**Mr. Key:** To ask the Secretary of State for Education and Science if he will publish a table showing teacher

vacancies by region in January 1989, distinguishing between vacancies in *(a)* nursery and primary schools and *(b)* secondary schools.

**Mr. Butcher:** Full information on the number of teacher vacancies in maintained nursery, primary and secondary schools in England in January 1989 is not yet available. Figures for those regions where the data are complete are as follows:

| | Nursery and primary schools | Secondary schools |
|---|---|---|
| North | 92 | 62 |
| Yorkshire and Humberside | 200 | 155 |
| North West | 307 | 219 |
| East Midlands | 145 | 145 |
| West Midlands | 222 | 262 |
| East Anglia | 47 | 59 |
| Greater London | n/y/a | n/y/a |
| Other South East | 617 | 542 |
| South West | 181 | 161 |

n/y/a = Not yet available.

**Ms. Armstrong:** To ask the Secretary of State for Education and Science (1) how many teachers have resigned during the academic year 1988-89;

(2) what steps he takes to monitor the number of resignations of teachers.

**Mr. Butcher:** Information on the number of teachers resigning during the academic year 1988-89 is not yet available.

Detailed annual returns of teachers in service are made by local education authorities at 31 March, together with information on those entering and leaving service during the previous year. The returns from some authorities are subject to considerable delay, and the most recent period for which complete data are available is the year ending March 1987. The number of teachers leaving full-time service in the maintained nursery, primary and secondary sector in England in that year was 28,960, of which 2,840 were aged 60 or over.

Following a recent report by the management consultants Logica, a number of proposals are being pursued to improve the flow of teacher information to the Department. These include measures to improve the timeliness of the annual returns and the completeness of termly appointment and withdrawal notifications.

### Training Grants Scheme

**Mr. Tony Lloyd:** To ask the Secretary of State for Education and Science if he intends to introduce legislation to amend the Education Acts to bring all unpaid workers in voluntary organisations within the scope of the training grants scheme.

**Mrs. Rumbold:** All aspects of the scheme are under regular review.

### Design and Technology

**Mr. Ken Hargreaves:** To ask the Secretary of State for Education and Science when he expects his proposals for attainment targets and programmes of study in design and technology 5 to 16 to be published for consultation.

**Mr. Kenneth Baker:** My right hon. Friend the Secretary of State for Wales and I have now formulated our proposals for attainment targets and programmes of study for design and technology for pupils aged five to 16 in the light of the report from the national curriculum design and technology working group. We are very grateful to the working group for its prompt and helpful report.

I have today referred our proposals to the National Curriculum Council to start the consultations in England required by the Education Reform Act. My right hon. Friend will be initiating consultations as required by the Act in Wales. I have asked the council to report to me on the outcome of the consultations, with advice and recommendations, by 3 November 1989. I have placed a copy of our proposals and of the working group's report, with my letter to the council, in the Library.

## WALES

### Planning Applications

**Mr. Ron Davies:** To ask the Secretary of State for Wales how many planning appeals were lodged with his office in 1974, 1979, 1984 and the latest full year for which figures are available; and, for each year, how many were allowed.

**Mr. Grist:** The information is shown in the following table:

*Section 36 planning appeals*

| Year | Lodged | Allowed |
|---|---|---|
| 1974 | 676 | 127 |
| 1979 | 844 | 164 |
| 1984 | 806 | 229 |
| 1988 | 1,133 | 325 |

**Dr. Kim Howells:** To ask the Secretary of State for Wales on how many occasions during the past five years he has called in planning decisions for a final decision.

**Mr. Grist:** My right hon. Friend and his predecessor have, since June 1984, called in for their own determination 17 applications for planning permission.

### Preventive Medicine

**Dr. Kim Howells:** To ask the Secretary of State for Wales what measures he has taken to promote the cause of preventive medicine in Wales, in particular in relation to the high incidence of heart disease in the Principality.

**Mr. Grist:** The promotion of good health and the prevention of ill health has been one of the Government's major priorities for the health services in Wales for some years. Within the drive for better health we established the Welsh Health Promotion Authority in 1987 to have specific responsibility for the subject, including the operation of the Welsh heart programme—"Heartbeat Wales". This was to augment the work already being carried out by district health authorities and primary care services. Their priorities in relation to health promotion, which include action to combat heart disease, were set out in the corporate management programme for the Health Service in Wales, issued by the Department last year.

### Compact Schemes

**Mr. Ieuan Wyn Jones:** To ask the Secretary of State for Wales if he will list the companies taking part in compact schemes with schools in Wales.

**Mr. Wyn Roberts:** Many schools in Wales have links with business and industry, some of which may be along the lines of a compact, but information is not held centrally on which companies are involved.

### Community Hospitals

**Mr. Ieuan Wyn Jones:** To ask the Secretary of State for Wales if he will list the number and location of community hospitals which have been built or adapted in Clwyd and Gwynedd since 1974.

**Mr. Grist:** The information requested is as follows:
*Clwyd*
Chirk Community Hospital
Colwyn Bay Hospital
Denbigh Community Hospital
Mold Community Hospital
Prestatyn Community Hospital
Royal Alexandra Hospital, Rhyl
Ruthin Community Hospital
*Gwynedd*
Bryn beryl Hospital, Pwllheli
Dolgellau Hospital
Tywyn Hospital

### Training and Enterprise Councils

**Mr. Ieuan Wyn Jones:** To ask the Secretary of State for Wales if he will publish a list of those companies in Gwynedd which have been invited to participate in training and enterprise councils.

**Mr. Wyn Roberts:** Copies of the TEC prospectus have been sent to all employers with a work force of 20 or more. I understand that a number of different interest groups have started discussions about TECs in Gwynedd but no bid has yet been received.

### Public Bodies

**Mr. Ieuan Wyn Jones:** To ask the Secretary of State for Wales if he will publish the names of people from Gwynedd whom he has appointed to public and statutory bodies since June 1987.

**Mr. Peter Walker:** We do not collect information on where public appointees come from, but as an example the hon. Gentleman may know that the current chairman of the Welsh Development Agency came from Gwynedd.

### Population Statistics

**Mr. Ieuan Wyn Jones:** To ask the Secretary of State for Wales what are his Department's estimates for the numbers of people aged 65 to 74 years, 75 to 79 years and over 80 years in the years 2000 and 2020 in Wales; and what percentage increase this represents in each category over the actual figures for the last year in which they are available.

**Mr. Peter Walker:** Current estimates and the most recent projected figures for the age groups requested are shown in the following table:

*Elderly Population of Wales*

*Thousand*

| | | Projected Population[2] | | | |
|---|---|---|---|---|---|
| | | Year 2020 | | Year 2020 | |
| Ages | 1988 mid-year estimate[1] | Number | Percentage change 1988-2000 | Number | Percentage change 1988-2020 |
| 65-74 | 271·7 | 260 | −4·3 | 317 | +16·8 |
| 75-79 | 96·6 | 108 | +11·9 | 111 | +14·6 |
| 80 and over | 102·3 | 127 | +24·4 | 144 | +41·0 |

[1] Office of Population Censuses and Surveys.
[2] Government Actuary's Department 1987 based population projection.

### Supermarket, Holyhead

**Mr. Ieuan Wyn Jones:** To ask the Secretary of State for Wales when he expects to be able to publish the results of the application for assistance under the urban development programme in respect of a supermarket development at Holyhead.

**Mr. Grist:** Applications for urban investment grant are treated in confidence. An application for urban investment grant support towards development at Holyhead has not been made to the Department. Decisions on full appraisal of UIG grant applications are made within 10 weeks of all the appropriate information being received by the Welsh Office.

## AGRICULTURE, FISHERIES AND FOOD

### Fishing Industry

**Mr. Steen:** To ask the Minister of Agriculture, Fisheries and Food if he will now provide the information required by the European Commission for the multi-annual guidance programme, in order to unlock the grants approved for construction of new beam trawlers and other fishing vessels.

**Mr. Donald Thompson:** The Commission will continue to suspend construction aid for United Kingdom fishing vessels until we can demonstrate sufficient progress towards meeting our programme targets. We are currently considering with the industry various options for reducing fleet capacity.

### Food Irradiation

**Sir Richard Body:** To ask the Minister of Agriculture, Fisheries and Food, what research has been undertaken into the effect of food irradiation on the nutritional content of food; and with what results.

**Mr. Ryder:** I refer my hon. Friend to the report on the safety and wholesomeness of irradiated foods by the Advisory Committee on Irradiated and Novel Foods published by Her Majesty's Stationery Office in 1986, a copy of which is in the Library of the House. Chapter 7 and appendix E refer.

## TRADE AND INDUSTRY

### Book Publishing

**Mr. David Nicholson:** To ask the Chancellor of the Duchy of Lancaster what estimates he has of the proportion of the United Kingdom-based book publishing industry which is American owned.

**Mr. Atkins:** There are a number of measures of publishers' output, none of which is readily available by the nationality of the publisher. The information necessary to make an estimate could be assembled only at disproportionate cost and would be subject to qualifications.

### Merger Policy

**Mr. Teddy Taylor:** To ask the Chancellor of the Duchy of Lancaster what progress has been made in the Council of Ministers in relation to the proposed directive on merger policy; and if he will make a statement.

**Mr. Maude:** The proposed EC merger control regulation was most recently discussed in the Council of Ministers on 3 May and there was a brief follow-up discussion at the June Council. It was concluded that further consideration was needed, particularly of thresholds, criteria and the relationship of a regulation to articles 85 and 86 (EEC).

### Frag-12

**Mr. Ieuan Wyn Jones:** To ask the Chancellor of the Duchy of Lancaster whether an application has been made for a manufacturing patent for a weapon described as Frag-12.

**Mr. Forth:** An application for a patent for Frag-12 has been made, but the application has not yet been published.

### EC Technical Committees

**Mr. Cousins:** To ask the Chancellor of the Duchy of Lancaster if he will list the technical committees of the European standardisation committee, indicating in each case the country of the European Economic Community that provides the secretariat, and also the number of technical committee secretariats held by each country of the European Economic Community.

**Mr. Forth:** The latest information available is as follows:

*List of CEN technical committees as at 2 May 1989*

| | *Number* |
|---|---|
| Total number of CEN technical committees (TCs) | 138 |
| *Secretariats:* | |
| West Germany (DIN) | 51 |
| United Kingdom (BSI) | 29 |
| France (AFNOR) | 24 |
| Italy (UNI) | 8 |
| Denmark (DS) | 7 |
| Belgium (IBN) | 7 |
| Netherlands (NNI) | 4 |

|  | Number |
| --- | --- |
| Sweden (SIS) | 3 |
| Austria (ON) | 1 |
| Portugal (IPQ) | 1 |
| Norway (NSF) | 1 |
| Ireland (NSAI) | 1 |
| To be allocated (TBA) | 1 |

| CEN/TC | Title | Secretariat |
| --- | --- | --- |
| ADHOC-WG | Acoustics | DS |
| TC10 | Passenger, goods and service lifts | AFNOR |
| TC12[1] | Hoses and hose couplings for petroleum products, equipment for petroleum industry | AFNOR |
| TC15 | Inland navigation equipment | DIN |
| TC19 | Test methods and specifications for petroleum products | NNI |
| TC33 | Doors, Windows, shutters and building hardware | AFNOR |
| TC38 | Durability of wood and related materials | AFNOR |
| TC43 | Office furniture | AFNOR |
| TC44 | Household refrigerating appliances | UNI |
| TC46[1] | Oil Stoves | DIN |
| TC47 | Atomizing oil burners and their components—function—safety—testing | DIN |
| TC48 | Domestic gas-fired water heaters etc. | AFNOR |
| TC49 | Gas cooking appliances | AFNOR |
| TC50 | Lighting columns and spigots | BSI |
| TC51 | Cement and building limes | IBN |
| TC52 | Safety of toys | DS |
| TC53 | Scaffolds, falsework and mobile access towers | DIN |
| TC54 | Simple unfired pressure vessels | BSI |
| TC55 | Dental products | DIN |
| TC57 | Central heating boilers | DIN |
| TC58 | Safety and control devices for gas burners etc. | BSI |
| TC62 | Independent gas fired space heaters | BSI |
| TC63[1] | Packages for washing and cleaning powders | DIN |
| TC65 | Portable grinding machines—mechanical safety | DIN |
| TC66[1] | Tests on glass fibre reinforced plastics | IPQ |
| TC67 | Ceramic tiles | UNI |
| TC68 | Building hoists for passenger and/or materials | AFNOR |
| TC70 | Portable fire extinguishers | IBN |
| TC72 | Automatic fire detection systems | BSI |
| TC74[1] | Flanges | DIN |
| TC78[1] | Capacities of glass jars for preserved fruit, vegetables and similar products | DIN |
| TC79 | Respiratory protective devices and diving apparatus | DIN |
| TC81[1] | Capacities of metal cans for fruit, vegetables and similar products | DIN |
| TC85 | Eye protective equipment | AFNOR |
| TC87[1] | Gas fuelled smokers' lighters | AFNOR |
| TC88 | Thermal insulating materials and products | DIN |
| TC89 | Thermal performance of buildings and building components | SIS |
| TC92 | Cold water meters | AFNOR |
| TC93 | Ladders | DIN |
| TC94 | Ready-mixed concrete production and delivery | DIN |
| TC95 | Technical safety requirements for the construction of injection moulding machines for plastics and rubber | DIN |
| TC98 | Mobile elevating work platforms | DIN |
| TC99 | Wallcoverings | BSI |
| TC100 | Tactile danger warnings on packaging | DS |

| CEN/TC | Title | Secretariat |
| --- | --- | --- |
| TC101 | Steel drums | DIN |
| TC102 | Sterilizers for medical purposes | DIN |
| TC103 | Adhesives for wood and derived timber products | BSI |
| TC104 | Concrete (performance production, placing and compliance criteria) | DIN |
| TC105 | Valves and fittings to equip radiators | DS |
| TC106 | Large kitchen appliances using gaseous fuels | AFNOR |
| TC107 | Pre-fabricated district heating pipe systems | DS |
| TC108 | Homogeneous elastomers for static seals | NNI |
| TC109 | Gas-fired central heating boilers | IBN |
| TC110 | Heat exchangers | SIS |
| TC111 | Propellants for commercial ammunition | IBH |
| TC112 | Wood based panels | DIN |
| TC113 | Heat pumps and room air conditioning units | DIN |
| TC114 | Safety of machines | DIN |
| TC115 | European first aid box | DIN |
| TC116 | Bitumen sheeting | DIN |
| TC117 | Plastic and rubber sheeting for roofing and sealing | IBN |
| TC118 | Technical safety requirements for compression moulding machines for plastics and rubber | BSI |
| TC119 | Swap bodies for combined goods transport road/rail | DIN |
| TC120 | Sacks for food transport | AFNOR |
| TC121 | Welding | DS |
| TC122 | Ergonomics | DIN |
| TC123 | Lasers and laser related equipment | DIN |
| TC124 | Timber structures | DS |
| TC125 | Masonry | BSI |
| TC126 | Acoustics properties of building products and of buildings | AFNOR |
| TC127 | Fire safety in buildings | BSI |
| TC128 | Roof covering products for discontinuous laying | ON |
| TC129 | Glass in building | IBN |
| TC130 | Space heating appliances without integral heat sources | UNI |
| TC131 | Gas burners using fans | DIN |
| TC132 | Aluminium and aluminium alloys | AFNOR |
| TC133 | Copper and copper alloys | DIN |
| TC134 | Resilient and textile floor coverings | BSI |
| TC135 | Steel structures | NSF |
| TC136 | Sports, playground and other recreational equipment | DIN |
| TC137 | Assessment of workplace exposure | DIN |
| TC138 | Non-destructive testing | AFNOR |
| TC139 | Paints and varnishes | DIN |
| TC140 | In vitro diagnostic systems | DIN |
| TC141 | Industrial indicator pressure gauges | AFNOR |
| TC142 | Wood working machines—Safety | BSI |
| TC143 | Cold metal working machines—Safety | UNI |
| TC144 | Agricultural and forestry machines—Safety | AFNOR |
| TC145 | Rubber and plastics machines—Safety | DIN |
| TC146 | Packaging machines—Safety | UNI |
| TC147 | Cranes—Safety | BSI |
| TC148 | Continuous mechanical handling equipment—Safety | AFNOR |
| TC149 | Rail dependent storage and retrieval equipment—Safety | DIN |
| TC150 | Industrial trucks—Safety | BSI |
| TC151 | Construction equipment and building material machines—Safety | DIN |
| TC152 | Leisure and recreational machines/equipment—Safety | BSI |
| TC153 | Food industry machines—Safety | DIN |
| TC154 | Aggregates | BSI |

| CEN/TC | Title | Secretariat |
|--------|-------|-------------|
| TC155 | Plastic pipes | NNI |
| TC156 | Ventilation systems for buildings | BSI |
| TC157 | Non-refillable containers for liquefied petroleum gases | AFNOR |
| TC158 | Head protection | BSI |
| TC159 | Hearing protection | SIS |
| TC160 | Protection against falls from height including working belt | DIN |
| TC161 | Foot and leg protection | BSI |
| TC162 | Protective clothing including hand and arm protection and life-jackets | DIN |
| TC163 | Sanitary appliances | UNI |
| TC164 | Water Supply | AFNOR |
| TC165 | Drainage and sewerage | DIN |
| TC166 | Chimneys | UNI |
| TC167 | Structural bearings | UNI |
| TC168 | Chains, ropes, webbing, slings and accessories | BSI |
| TC169 | Lighting applications technology | DIN |
| TC170 | Ophthalmic optics | DIN |
| TC171 | Heating cost instruments based on consumption | DIN |
| TC172 | Paper, board and pulp | DIN |
| TC173 | Brushes | BSI |
| TC174 | Fruit and vegetable juices—methods of analysis | AFNOR |
| TC175 | Sawn timber and sawnlogs | AFNOR |
| TC176 | Heat energy meters | DS |
| TC177 | Prefabricated components of reinforced aerated or non-fines light-weight concrete | DIN |
| TC178 | Small paving units and kerbs | BSI |
| TC179 | Gas-fired air heaters | NNI |
| TC180 | Gas-fired overhead radiant heaters | BSI |
| TC181 | Dedicated liquefied petroleum gas appliances | NSAI |
| TC182 | Refrigerating systems—safety and environment | DIN |
| TC183 | Garbage containers | DIN |
| TC184 | High performance ceramics | BSI |
| TC185 | Threaded and non-threaded mechanical fasteners and accessories | DIN |
| TC186 | Thermoprocessing technology | DIN |
| TC187 | Refractory products and materials | BSI |
| TC188 | Conveyor belting | BSI |
| TC189 | Geotextiles and related products | IBN |
| TC190 | Foundry technology | DIN |
| TC191 | Fixed fire extinguishing systems | BSI |
| TC192 | Fire brigade equipment | BSI |
| TC193 | Adhesives | AFNOR |
| TC194 | Culinary utensils | BSI |
| TBA | Air filters for ventilation purposes | TBA |

[1] Denotes dormant committee.

## Cars (UK Content)

**Mr. Marlow:** To ask the Chancellor of the Duchy of Lancaster if he will list those makes of car which are 50 per cent. or more United Kingdom value.

**Mr. Atkins** *[holding answer 19 June 1989]:* All cars manufactured in the United Kingdom by the volume producers have over 50 per cent. United Kingdom content by value. A list of specific models would serve little purpose, since in a number of cases the United Kingdom content of the same models sold here by the multinational producers (Ford, Vauxhall and Peugeot Talbot) will depend on whether they have been produced in this country or at the companies' plants elsewhere in Europe.

## China

**Mr. David Atkinson:** To ask the Chancellor of the Duchy of Lancaster if he will discuss with his consultative committee colleagues the immediate tightening of the rules that apply to China; and if he will make a statement.

**Mrs. Chalker:** I have been asked to reply.

The United Kingdom will be discussing with its partners in the Co-ordinating Committee for Multilateral Export Control (COCOM) the implications of events in China for the present export control policy in COCOM towards China.

Amendments to the COCOM control lists, which can be agreed only by consensus, are made on strategic rather than political grounds, following an assessment of the strategic threat posed by a given country to Western security. Decisions in COCOM, including any relating to China, will be based on this criterion.

## ENERGY

### AGR Fuel Rods

**Mr. Alan W. Williams:** To ask the Secretary of State for Energy how many spent AGR fuel rods have been reprocessed at Sellafield to date; and what is the expected capacity at Sellafield for reprocessing spent AGR fuel rods for each year from 1989 to 2000.

**Mr. Michael Spicer:** To date some 18 tonnes u of AGR fuel from the Windscale AGR has been reprocessed at Sellafield. This was carried out for the United Kingdom Atomic Energy Authority in the early 1970s in a facility that was shut down in 1973.

The thermal oxide reprocessing plant is scheduled to begin reprocessing operations in late 1992. In its first 10 years of operation, BNFL has contracted to reprocess 6,000 tonnes u of fuel, of which 1,850 tonnes u is AGR fuel (some 40,000 AGR fuel assemblies) from the home generating boards and some 30 tonnes u of fuel from Windscale for the authority. It is expected that an additional 1,000 tonnes of capacity will be available during the first 10 years of the plant, so that additional capacity could be allocated to AGR fuel.

**Mr. Alan W. Williams:** To ask the Secretary of State for Energy if he will make a statement on the problem of conversion of spent AGR fuel rods in storage under water at Sellafield; what proportion are corroded; after how many years under water corrosion becomes a problem; what problems are encountered in reprocessing badly corroded AGR fuel; and how much more expensive it is to reprocess.

**Mr. Michael Spicer:** BNFL did experience problems with corrosion in one out of its three storage ponds some four years ago. The measures taken to deal with these were successful. The company estimated that only some 3·5 per cent. of the fuel pins housed there had suffered. Representative samples have been dismantled without any problems and reprocessing should proceed smoothly with no additional costs to be incurred by the generating boards.

British Nuclear Fuels plc has carried out extensive research into the storage of AGR fuel under water. I am advised that all available evidence suggests that, for fuel maintained in the correct water chemistry, no significant corrosion will occur for at least 10 years, and possibly longer.

### Nuclear Materials (Safeguards)

**Mr. Flynn:** To ask the Secretary of State for Energy on how many occasions nuclear material has been withdrawn from safeguards under article 14 of the tripartite safeguards treaty between the United Kingdom, Euratom and the International Atomic Energy Agency; and if he will list those occasions by date, facility, amount of nuclear material involved and when the withdrawal constituted a temporary change of status for operational convenience rather than use of the material for national security reasons.

**Mr. Michael Spicer:** I have nothing to add to the answer that I gave to the hon. Member on 15 June 1989, at column *486*.

**Mr. Flynn:** To ask the Secretary of State for Energy when it was agreed by *(a)* member states of the European Atomic Energy Community and *(b)* member states and the board of governors of the International Atomic Energy Agency, that the principle of fungibility should apply to consignments of civil nuclear materials in regard to application of safeguards.

**Mr. Michael Spicer:** I am advised that the existing practice regarding fungibility was formally recognised by member states of the European Atomic Energy Community by a statement of interpretation upon the adoption of Regulation 3227/76 of 19 October 1976.

### Spent Fuel Rods

**Mr. Alan W. Williams:** To ask the Secretary of State for Energy how many spent fuel rods from advanced gas-cooled reactors await reprocessing in Sellafield.

**Mr. Michael Spicer:** At 31 March 1989, some 895 tonnes u of spent AGR fuel (some 21,000 AGR fuel assemblies) and some 24 tonnes u of fuel (1,900 assemblies) from the Windscale AGR were held in storage ponds at Sellafield.

**Mr. Alan Williams:** To ask the Secretary of State for Energy how many spent Magnox fuel rods were reprocessed at Sellafield in each year from 1980.

**Mr. Michael Spicer:** Weights of individual magnox fuel rods vary considerably and it is the usual practice to give the quantities of magnox fuel reprocessed at Sellafield in tonnes u. On average there are 100 fuel rods per tonne. For the annual reprocessing tonnages from 1980, I refer the hon. Member to the answer given by my hon. Friend the Member for Eddisbury (Mr. Goodlad) to the hon. Member for Islington, South and Finsbury (Mr. Smith) on 11 December 1985 at columns *638-39*, and my reply to the hon. Member for Newport, West (Mr. Flynn) on 1 February 1988 at columns *473-74*. The figures for 1986-87 and 1987-88 were published by my Department as part of annual information on plutonium production placed in the Library of the House. The tonnage for 1988-89 was some 875 tonnes u.

### West Burton B (Power Station)

**Mr. Allen:** To ask the Secretary of State for Energy whether he has discussed the failure to commence construction of a coal-fired power station at West Burton B with the Area Electricity Board or the chair of the Central Electricity Generating Board; and if he will make a statement.

**Mr. Michael Spicer:** I refer the hon. Member to the reply that I gave the hon. Member for Ashfield (Mr. Haynes) on 15 May 1989 at column *4*.

### Sizewell B PWR

**Mr. Alan W. Williams:** To ask the Secretary of State for Energy what information he has on the outturn cost of the Sizewell B pressurised water reactor power station and as to whether the construction is on schedule.

**Mr. Michael Spicer:** This is an operational matter for the CEGB and I have asked the chairman to reply to the hon. Member.

### Sellafield

**Mr. Jack:** To ask the Secretary of State for Energy what were the total amounts of *(a)* alpha and *(b)* beta radiation discharges from Sellafield in 1978 and 1988.

**Mr. Michael Spicer:** Radioactivity in liquid discharges to the Irish sea from Sellafield in 1978 and 1987 (the latest year for which figures are available) were as follows:

|      | Alpha (terabecquerels) | Beta (terabecquerels) |
|------|------------------------|------------------------|
| 1978 | 68·0                   | 7,124                  |
| 1987 | 2·2                    | 89                     |

### Coal Industry Productivity

**Mr. Cran:** To ask the Secretary of State for Energy by what amount productivity in the coal industry has increased since 1974.

**Mr. Michael Spicer:** British Coal's productivity, measured in terms of tonnes per manshift, has risen by nearly 93 per cent. from 1973-74 to 1988-89. Between 1973-74 and 1978-79 productivity rose by just over 4 per cent. Between 1978-79 and 1988-89 it rose by some 85 per cent.

### Radioactivity

**Mr. Flynn:** To ask the Secretary of State for Energy what is the total radioactivity in curies contained *(a)* within all nuclear reactors, *(b)* within all spent nuclear fuel cooling ponds at reactor sites and *(c)* low and intermediate level radioactive waste stored at each reactor site.

**Mr. Michael Spicer:** Details of radioactivity in reactors, spent fuel and wastes stored at reactor sites are management matter for the nuclear reactor operators.

### Radioactive Waste

**Mr. Flynn:** To ask the Secretary of State for Energy what quantities of contained radioactive waste bearing plutonium traces are stored at *(a)* Sellafield, *(b)* Harwell and *(c)* Dounreay.

**Mr. Michael Spicer:** The quantities of plutonium-contaminated wastes stored at Sellafield, Harwell and

Dounreay are management matters for British Nuclear Fuels plc and the United Kingdom Atomic Energy Authority respectively.

### Nuclear Installations

**Mr. Blair:** To ask the Secretary of State for Energy what are the existing minimum emergency planning zones around nuclear installations; and if he has any plans to alter them.

**Mr. Parkinson:** The minimum emergency planning zones around nuclear installations within which detailed and pre-planned arrangements are required to ensure rapid evacuation vary from 1km and 2·4km depending on the type of installation. There are no plans to alter these minimum emergency planning zones. These arrangements also provide the basis for extending the response if required.

### Nuclear Emergencies

**Mr. Blair:** To ask the Secretary of State for Energy when the nuclear installations inspectorate and the Health and Safety Executive intend publishing their guidance on arrangements for responding to nuclear emergencies.

**Mr. Parkinson:** The Health and Safety Executive's (HSE) booklet "Emergency Plans for Civil Nuclear Installations" which was published in 1982 is being revised and updated to describe current arrangements. The HSE intends to publish the revised booklet later this year.

### Offshore Safety

30. **Mr. McAllion:** To ask the Secretary of State for Energy what steps he proposes to take to improve safety in the offshore oil and gas industry.

**Mr. Parkinson** *[pursuant to his reply, 20 March 1989, c. 412]:* I have today laid before each House the Offshore Installations (Emergency Pipe-line Valve) Regulations 1989.

Prior to the making of these regulations extensive consultations were carried out with organisations representing those persons within the offshore industry likely to be affected by them, including employers and the trade unions. They have been made on the advice of the Health and Safety Commission under the Mineral Workings (Offshore Installations) Act 1971. The regulations require emergency shutdown valves to be fitted on pipe-line risers serving offshore installations together with the periodic inspection and testing of these valves and their control systems. In addition an Order in Council was made on 13 June which has the effect of including these valves in the certification process of the installation.

These regulations represent an important step forward in securing improvements in the safety of offshore pipeline systems. I shall in due course be laying further regulations to deal with subsea isolation systems.

## NATIONAL FINANCE

### NHS Reform

**Mr. Dobson:** To ask the Chancellor of the Exchequer whether the Central Office of Information has been asked to assess the effectiveness of the original launch of the National Health Service review.

**Mr. Lilley** *[holding answer 19 June 1989]:* COI has not been involved in what is largely a staff communications exercise.

## CIVIL SERVICE

### Agencies

**Mr. Baldry:** To ask the Minister for the Civil Service if he will make a statement on whether there have been improvements in the delivery of service to the public and in labour relations in the civil service agencies established so far.

**Mr. Luce:** The main aim of the next steps initiative is to deliver Government services more efficiently and effectively, within available resources, for the benefit of taxpayers, customers and staff. Developments in service delivery and in industrial relations in individual agencies are matters for the Departments and agencies concerned, (in the light of responsibilities in each agency's framework document). Our overall policy is that each agency will account for its performance on an annual basis through a published report and accounts. We are also developing a policy evaluation framework for the initiative.

## SOCIAL SECURITY

### Vaccine Damage

**Mr. Ashley:** To ask the Secretary of State for Social Security how many vaccine damage payments were made in 1980, 1981, 1982 and 1983; and if he will categorise these according to the age of the child when the vaccination took place, the year of vaccination and the nature of the vaccination.

**Mr. Peter Lloyd:** The number of payments awarded under the provisions of the Vaccine Damage Payments Act 1979 in 1980, 1981, 1982 and 1983 were 255, 74, 43 and 42, respectively. I regret that the details requested are not available for any of those made in 1980 and only some of those made in 1981 and 1982. The details that are available are in the tables.

*Table 1*
*Vaccine damage payments scheme: awards made in 1981 by age of child at date of vaccination; year of vaccination and type of vaccination*

| Type of vaccination cited on the claim form | Age at date of vaccination (months) | Year vaccine was given |
|---|---|---|
| 1. Triple/Polio | 3 to 6 | 1966 |
| 2. Pertussis | 3 to 6 | 1959 |
| 3. Triple/Polio | 3 to 6 | 1973 |
| 4. Triple/Smallpox | 0 to 3 | 1955 |
| 5. Triple/Polio | 12 to 15 | 1970 |
| 6. Triple | 9 to 12 | 1967 |
| 7. Diphtheria/Tetanus | 6 to 9 | 1979 |
| 8. Triple | 3 to 6 | 1963 |
| 9. Triple/Polio | 3 to 6 | 1968 |
| 10. Triple/Polio | 3 to 6 | 1978 |
| 11. Triple | 3 to 6 | 1968 |
| 12. Triple | 6 to 9 | 1961 |
| 13. Measles | 2 years | 1970 |
| 14. Triple/Polio | 3 to 6 | 1979 |
| 15. Triple/Polio | 3 to 6 | 1966 |
| 16. Triple | 9 to 12 | 1961 |
| 17. Triple/Polio | 3 to 6 | 1964 |
| 18. Diphtheria/Tetanus | 6 to 9 | 1978 |

| Type of vaccination cited on the claim form | Age at date of vaccination (months) | Year vaccine was given |
|---|---|---|
| 19. Diphtheria/Pertussis | 6 to 9 | 1952 |
| 20. Triple | 6 to 9 | 1964 |
| 21. Triple | 3 to 6 | 1979 |
| 22. Triple | 6 to 9 | 1960 |
| 23. Triple | 3 to 6 | 1968 |
| 24. Diphtheria/Pertussis | 6 to 9 | 1951 |
| 25. Triple | 6 to 9 | 1979 |
| 26. Smallpox | 2 years | 1963-64 |
| 27. Tetanus/Diphtheria/Polio | 9 to 12 | 1977 |
| 28. Pertussis | 9 to 12 | 1974 |
| 29. Triple | 3 to 6 | 1965 |
| 30. Measles | 12 to 15 | 1971 |
| 31. Triple/Smallpox | 3 to 6 | 1960 |
| 32. Triple/Polio | 6 to 9 | 1975 |

*Note:* Details are not available for the remaining 42 awards made in 1981.

*Table 2*

*Vaccine damage payments scheme: awards made in 1982 by age of child at date of vaccination; year of vaccination and type of vaccination*

| Type of vaccination cited on the claim form | Age at date of vaccination (months) | Year vaccine was given |
|---|---|---|
| 1. Pertussis | 6 to 9 | 1978 |
| 2. Pertussis | 3 to 6 | 1973 |
| 3. Polio | 9 to 12 | 1960 |
| 4. Triple | 9 to 12 | 1970 |
| 5. Pertussis | 3 to 6 | 1980 |
| 6. Tetanus/Polio | 16 years | 1977 |
| 7. Pertussis | 3 to 6 | 1981 |
| 8. Measles | 15 to 18 | 1979 |
| 9. Measles | 3 to 6 | 1981 |
| 10. Triple/Polio | 6 to 9 | 1976 |
| 11. Polio | 32 years | 1979 |
| 12. Pertussis | 3 to 6 | 1978 |
| 13. Triple | 3 to 6 | 1970 |
| 14. Smallpox | 3 to 6 | 1960 |
| 15. Pertussis | 3 to 6 | 1978 |
| 16. Pertussis | 6 to 9 | 1971 |
| 17. Triple/Polio | 3 to 6 | 1978 |
| 18. Triple/Polio | 3 to 6 | 1980 |
| 19. Triple/Polio | 6 to 9 | 1976 |
| 20. Smallpox | 0 to 3 | 1961 |
| 21. * | 3 to 6 | 1965 |
| 22. Triple/Polio | 3 to 6 | 1979 |
| 23. Triple | 6 to 9 | 1976 |
| 24. Triple/Polio | 6 to 9 | 1977 |
| 25. Pertussis | 3 to 6 | 1972 |
| 26. Triple/Polio | 9 to 12 | 1968 |
| 27. Triple/Polio | 3 to 6 | 1973 |
| 28. Diphtheria/Tetanus/Polio | 2 years | 1971 |
| 29. Diphtheria/Tetanus/Polio | 2 years | 1971 |
| 30. Triple/Polio | 3 to 6 | 1973 |
| 31. Triple/Polio | 6 to 9 | 1978 |
| 32. Triple | 3 to 6 | 1972 |

*Note:* Details are not available for the remaining 11 awards made in 1982.

*Table 3*

*Vaccine damage payments scheme: awards made in 1983 by age of child at date of vaccination; year of vaccination and type of vaccination*

| Type of vaccination cited on the claim form | Age at date of vaccination (months) | Year vaccine was given |
|---|---|---|
| 1. Triple/Polio | 6 to 9 | 1979 |
| 2. Pertussis | 3 to 6 | 1981 |
| 3. Pertussis | 3 to 6 | 1980 |
| 4. Triple | 9 to 12 | 1971 |
| 5. Triple/Polio | 3 to 6 | 1971 |
| 6. Triple/Polio | 6 to 9 | 1970 |
| 7. Measles | 12 to 15 | 1980 |

| Type of vaccination cited on the claim form | Age at date of vaccination (months) | Year vaccine was given |
|---|---|---|
| 8. Triple/Polio/Measles | 6 to 9 | 1976 |
| 9. Pertussis | 3 to 6 | 1980 |
| 10. Smallpox | 21 to 24 | 1962 |
| 11. Triple/Polio | 6 to 9 | 1976 |
| 12. Triple/Polio | 9 to 12 | 1970 |
| 13. Triple | 6 to 9 | 1971 |
| 14. Triple | 3 to 6 | 1972 |
| 15. Pertussis | 6 to 9 | 1972 |
| 16. Pertussis | 6 to 9 | 1968 |
| 17. Triple | 3 to 6 | 1971 |
| 18. Triple | 3 to 6 | 1980 |
| 19. Triple/Polio | 9 to 12 | 1973 |
| 20. Polio | 3 to 6 | 1981 |
| 21. Pertussis | 3 to 6 | 1982 |
| 22. Triple/Polio | 3 to 6 | 1968 |
| 23. Pertussis | 6 to 9 | 1971 |
| 24. Pertussis | 6 to 9 | 1973 |
| 25. Measles | 2 years | 1971 |
| 26. Pertussis | 9 to 12 | 1978 |
| 27. Pertussis | 6 to 9 | 1968 |
| 28. Polio | 12 to 15 | 1959 |
| 29. Pertussis | 3 to 6 | 1967 |
| 30. Pertussis | 6 to 9 | 1975 |
| 31. Polio | 6 to 9 | 1975 |
| 32. Pertussis | 3 to 6 | 1980 |
| 33. Measles/Triple | 3 to 6 | 1981 |
| 34. Triple | 3 to 6 | 1972 |
| 35. Triple/Polio | 6 to 9 | 1969 |
| 36. Triple/Polio | 6 to 9 | 1975 |
| 37. Pertussis | 6 to 9 | 1972 |
| 38. Triple/Polio | 6 to 9 | 1965 |
| 39. Diphtheria/Polio | 3 years | 1968 |
| 40. Pertussis | 3 to 6 | 1980 |
| 41. Pertussis | 3 to 6 | 1981 |
| 42. Pertussis | 9 to 12 | 1978 |

## Mobility Allowance

**Mr. Boyes:** To ask the Secretary of State for Social Security (1) if he can state the percentage of successful claimants at each of the following stages *(a)* the examining medical practitioner/adjudicating officer, *(b)* the medical board and *(c)* the medical appeal tribunal of (i) deaf-blind and (ii) mentally handicapped claimants of mobility allowance in the survey which is being carried out by his Department; and if he will clarify the methods being used to obtain these figures:

(2) what progress has been made by his Department on the analysis that they are carrying out on a sample of deaf-blind and mentally handicapped claimants of mobility allowance; and if he will make a statement;

(3) when he expects the results of his Department's analysis of a sample of deaf-blind and mentally handicapped claimants of mobility allowance to be published.

**Mr. Scott:** Random samples of claims made by either mentally or visually handicapped people were examined, after the decision had been given, for each of the three stages of the medical adjudication system. The size of the samples and the outcome of the claims is shown as follows:

| Adjudication stage for medical questions | Sample size | Percentage successful |
|---|---|---|
| *Mentally handicapped* | | |
| Adjudication Officer | 100 | 36 |
| Medical Board | 100 | 38 |
| Medical Appeal Tribunal | 100 | 46 |
| *Visually handicapped* | | |
| Adjudication Officer | 100 | 32 |
| Medical Board | 75 | 31 |
| Medical Appeal Tribunal | 25 | 36 |

The samples of cases have been analysed by the type of claim, the availability of additional evidence, and their outcome. Further analysis has been made of the nature of the findings on behavioural and balance problems, as appropriate. In practice it has proved difficult to isolate the effect of visual or mental handicap on the individual decisions about entitlement to mobility allowance, because of the frequent incidence of multiple handicap. The results must therefore be treated with caution. We do not therefore propose to publish detailed findings, but we shall use the information which has been collected when the guidance for examining doctors is being revised.

## Pensions

**Mrs. Beckett:** To ask the Secretary of State for Social Security whether he will amend paragraph 10 of schedule 2 to the Income Support (General) Regulations 1987 to extend entitlement to the higher pension premium to men aged 60 to 64 years who satisfy the condition of paragraph 12(1)(b) that they have provided evidence of incapacity for 28 weeks.

**Mr. Peter Lloyd:** We have no plans to do so.

## HEALTH

### Drugs

**Mr. Wilson:** To ask the Secretary of State for Health if he will publish the total cost of the drug bill for the family practitioners service for the years 1978 to 1988 and the amount deducted from chemists' remuneration in respect of discounts for the same period.

**Mr. Mellor:** The basic cost of prescriptions dispensed by pharmacies in England and Wales and the amounts deducted in respect of discounts for the years 1978 to 1988 were:

| Year | Basic cost £ million | Deduction for discounts £ million |
|---|---|---|
| 1978 | 557·0 | 15·0 |
| 1979 | 636·8 | 18·3 |
| 1980 | 769·9 | 12·0 |
| 1981 | 896·4 | 33·9 |
| 1982 | 1,048·9 | 57·2 |
| 1983 | 1,176·2 | 66·1 |
| 1984 | 1,266·7 | 109·0 |
| [1]1985 | 343·2 | 21·4 |
| 1985-86 | 1,340·8 | 82·8 |
| 1986-87 | 1,505·7 | 117·2 |
| 1987-88 | 1,703·3 | 134·0 |
| 1988-89 | 1,885·0 | 154·7 |

[1] 1 January 1985 to 31 March 1985.

### Trent Regional Health Authority

**Mr. Redmond:** To ask the Secretary of State for Health how many hospital wards in the Trent regional health authority are not in use; and if he will list the reasons why in each case.

**Mr. Freeman:** I regret that the information requested is not held centrally. The hon. Member may care to write to the chairman of Trent regional health authority for the information he seeks.

**Mr. Redmond:** To ask the Secretary of State for Health if he will give details for the Trent regional health authority of each capital project costing more than £1 million *(a)* actually under construction and *(b)* at the proposal or planning stage; and if he will give the estimated date of completion for each project.

**Mr. Freeman:** The information held centrally is given in the table; estimated completion dates are not held for all the schemes at the planning stages.

*Concise 1—Developed by Department of Health*
*Health Building Directorate*
*Trent Regional Health Authority schemes*
*£1 million and over*

| Ref. | Scheme | Estimated completion |
|---|---|---|
| *Schemes under construction* | | |
| 3.67 | Bassetlaw DGH Phase 2 | 1 December 1989 |
| 3.51 | Doncaster Royal Infirmary Phase 2 Pathology Laboratory | 16 June 1989 |
| 3.15 | Glenfield DGH Phase 2 | 7 April 1990 |
| 3.41 | Kendray—Sub Phase 2B—Mental Illness Unit—ESMI | 7 August 1989 |
| 3.23 | Kings Mill DGH Phase 3 | 29 November 1991 |
| 3.11 | Leicester Royal Infirmary Phase 4B | 1 July 1990 |
| 3.76 | North Hykeham ESMI Facilities | 17 September 1989 |
| 3.54 | Northern General Renal Unit | 9 October 1989 |
| 3.70 | Notts City Replacement and Extension of X-Ray Department | 1 March 1991 |
| 3.64 | St. George's ESMI Facilities | 16 October 1989 |
| *Schemes at proposal or planning stage* | | |
| 3.46 | Bassetlaw DGH Phase 3 | August 1995 |
| 3.29 | Chesterfield and North Phase 3 Geriatric Provision | September 1993 |
| 3.114 | Derby City ESMI Day Unit | July 1992 |
| 3.112 | Derby City Hospital Mental Illness Unit | June 1992 |
| 3.47 | Derby City Hospital Paediatrics | April 1994 |
| 3.118 | Doncaster Royal Infirmary West End Redevelopment Phase 2 | October 1994 |
| 3.115 | Dukeries Community Hospital | August 1993 |
| 3.84 | Fulwood ESMI Unit | March 1993 |
| 3.73 | Gedling/Eastern Local Hospital | May 1993 |
| 3.103 | Glenfield DGH MI Department Inc ESMI | January 1994 |
| 3.28 | Glenfield DGH Phase 3 | March 1995 |
| 3.94 | Grantham and Kesteven—Phase 6 Mental Illness Department | February 1994 |
| 3.48 | Hallamshire Acute Unit for the Elderly | November 1992 |
| 3.108 | Highbury Local Hospital for the Elderly | February 1994 |
| 3.59 | Hincley Hospital Facilities for Elderly Phase 1 | December 1991 |
| 3.92 | Hinkley Development Phases 2, 3 and 4 | July 1994 |
| 3.116 | Kendray Phase 3 Mental Ilness | February 1994 |
| 3.96 | Kings Mill Phase 4 Acute Wards | |
| 3.101 | Leicester Royal Infirmary Phase 4C Post Main Phase | September 1992 |
| 3.45 | Lincoln County Phase 3A | June 1994 |

| Ref. | Scheme | Estimated completion |
|------|--------|---------------------|
| 3.110 | Mansfield Victoria Community Hospital | October 1993 |
| 3.85 | Middlewood MI Rehabilitation-Community Centre | November 1994 |
| 3.82 | North East Unit L/S Facilities for the Elderly | July 1993 |
| 3.107 | Northern General Phase 3 | February 1996 |
| 3.89 | Nottingham City Catering Department | March 1991 |
| 3.105 | Notts City ESMI Assessment Unit St. Francis Wing | November 1991 |
| 3.104 | Notts City Extension to Theatres | 2 October 1992 |
| 3.97 | Notts City Medical Unit | |
| 3.91 | Notts City Psychiatric Centre | February 1993 |
| 3.95 | Pilgrim Hospital—Phase 4 ESMI-Geriatric | June 1992 |
| 3.86 | Sheffield Genetics Etc. Department | |
| 3.44 | Sheffield Obstetric-Gynaecology-Elderly Services | |
| 3.117 | St. George's Local Community Hospital for Elderly | January 1996 |
| 3.88 | Walkley ESMI Unit | |
| 3.93 | Bassetlaw DGH Phase 2A | June 1992 |
| 3.74 | Clay Cross Community Hospital | November 1993 |
| 3.106 | Commonside ESMI Unit Sheffield | June 1992 |
| 3.100 | Doncaster Royal Infirmary West End Development Phase 1 | October 1992 |
| 3.98 | Leicester Health Authority Cook Chill Catering | April 1990 |
| 3.55 | Rotherham DGH Phase 3B—Geriatric Unit | October 1994 |
| 3.72 | Rushcliffe Hospital Development | May 1992 |
| 3.113 | Wharncliffe Long Stay Facilities for Elderly | June 1992 |
| 3.109 | Ashfield Community Hospital | November 1991 |
| 3.81 | Beighton Local Hospital for Elderly | September 1991 |
| 3.66 | Charles Clifford District Hospital New Extension | |
| 3.25 | Derby City Phase 2 Geriatrics | 30 April 1991 |
| 3.37 | Grantham and Kesteven Phase 5B | August 1991 |
| 3.26 | Lincoln County Phase 2 | October 1992 |
| 3.27 | Loughborough Phase 1 Geriatric and ESMI Provision | February 1992 |
| 3.43 | Northern General Phase 2 | February 1992 |
| 3.71 | Notts City Renal/Radiotherapy | July 1992 |
| 3.57 | Rotherham DGH Phase 3A | 15 March 1991 |

## Food Hygiene

**Mr. Robin Cook:** To ask the Secretary of State for Health when he now expects to lay before Parliament statutory instruments on standards of food hygiene.

**Mr. Freeman:** The Food Hygiene (General) Regulations 1970 already provide strict standards of food hygiene in food premises, and related regulations provide the same in respect of markets, stalls and delivery vehicles.

We are currently considering amending the regulations so as to extend temperature controls to food intended for retail sale. We anticipate that these amending regulations will be laid before Parliament in the autumn of this year.

## Bio-Plan Ltd.

**Mrs. Dunwoody:** To ask the Secretary of State for Health if he will list the extra facilities provided by Bio-Plan Ltd. to the National Health Service patients of Leighton hospital with the date of their inception and the number of patients in the National Health Service who have had access to them.

**Mr. Mellor:** We do not hold this information centrally. The hon. Member may care to contact the chairman of the Crewe health authority.

## NHS Reform

**Mrs. Dunwoody:** To ask the Secretary of State for Health what consultations will be held with (a) the staff and (b) the local authority representing the catchment area of any general district hospitals that apply to opt-out.

**Mr. Mellor:** Self-governing trusts will not opt out but will remain fully within the NHS. When a unit decides to submit an application, the RHA will seek the views of those with an interest, particularly the health authority concerned, staff at the hospital, GPs, CHCs and the local community. The Secretary of State will consider any responses alongside the application.

**Mr. David Porter:** To ask the Secretary of State for Health what representations he has had from general practitioners and others on the effects of the proposals in "Working for Patients" on rural practices; and if he will make a statement.

**Mr. Mellor** *[holding answer 19 June 1989]:* We have received a number of representations from doctors about the possible effects on rural practice of our proposal to increase to 60 per cent. the proportion of a GP's income represented by capitation payments.

A number of features of the new contract will be of benefit to GPs serving rural areas, including the new payments linked to the provision of specific services such as health promotion clinics, minor surgery and child health surveillance and the higher level of night visit fee. The new weighting of basic practice allowance will also benefit GPs with small lists including GPs in rural areas. In particular, the inclusion of home visits in the 26 hours a week availability, and the scope for GPs to fulfil this requirement over four rather than five days where the fifth day is spent on health-related activities in the public sector, will be welcomed by such GPs.

In recognition of the strength of feeling among rural GPs against our earlier proposal to introduce a new rural supplement, we agreed with the general medical services committee's negotiators on 4 May that the rural practice payments scheme will continue pending its revision by the central advisory committee on rural practice payments.

**Sir David Price:** To ask the Secretary of State for Health what change in administrative arrangements he intends to introduce for those specialised regional units in teaching hospitals where a close working relationship between the basic scientific research and developing clinical practice is common practice.

**Mr. Mellor:** The Government are still developing the details necessary for the implementation of "Working for Patients", but they recognise the value of the links between basic scientific research and developing clinical practice, and are taking these into account as their plans develop.

**Mr. Harry Greenway:** To ask the Secretary of State for Health if he will detail those points where a substantial number of general practitioners are understood to support the National Health Service White Paper; and if he will make a statement.

**Mr. Kenneth Clarke:** A substantial number of general practitioners support our proposals for:

retaining the principles on which the NHS was based;

better management in the NHS and the greater involvement of doctors in it;

clinically led medical audit;

extending resource management and better information systems so that the costs and results of decisions can be taken fully into account and so that the health service, for the first time, knows what it is doing, why, at what cost and to what standards;

the need for a comprehensive health service;

the vital role of a high standard of medical education and of an effective research programme;

the need to build on the excellent track record of the NHS to meet the changing demands of the coming decade;

the principle of money following patients; and

many general practitioners have expressed interest in practice budgets.

We are continuing discussions with representatives of the medical profession on the implementation of these and our other proposals.

## General Practitioners

**Mr. John Marshall:** To ask the Secretary of State for Health if he will make a statement about the trend in the number of general practitioners since 1979.

**Mr. Mellor:** The table gives the number of general medical practitioners in England for each year between 1979 and 1988 (the latest year for which figures are available). The figures show that the number of general medical practitioners in England has risen steadily since 1979, with an overall increase of nearly 19 per cent. between 1979 and 1988.

*Number of unrestricted principals (England)*

| Year | Number |
|------|--------|
| 1979 | 21,357 |
| 1980 | 21,812 |
| 1981 | 22,304 |
| 1982 | 22,786 |
| 1983 | 23,254 |
| 1984 | 23,640 |
| 1985 | 24,035 |
| 1986 | 24,460 |
| 1987 | 24,922 |
| 1988 | [1]25,322 |

[1] Provisional.

## NHS Scientists

**Dr. Kim Howells:** To ask the Secretary of State for Health (1) what action he intends to improve the pay and morale of medical physicists in the National Health Service;

(2) what action he intends to take to improve the pay and working conditions of scientists in the National Health Service;

(3) what action he intends to take to reduce the loss of National Health Service scientists to the private sector.

**Mr. Mellor:** The pay of medical physicists, non-medical scientists and clinical psychologists is a matter for negotiation between the management side of the Scientific and Professional Staffs Council and the staff side representing scientists employed in the NHS. Negotiations are continuing on the staff side pay claim for 1989-90. The management side has set up a working party to investigate the recuitment and retention of scientists in the NHS and is currently considering its findings.

### Toxoplasmosis

**Mr. Gerald Bowden:** To ask the Secretary of State for Health whether he has any plans to publish and distribute, through the Health Education Authority, any information and advice for pregnant women about toxoplasmosis.

**Mr. Mellor:** We are currently giving consideration to the most effective ways in which messages about toxoplasmosis can be transmitted to pregnant women.

### Immunisation

**Mr. Gareth Wardell:** To ask the Secretary of State for Health, if he will publish in the *Official Report* any preliminary figures for the uptake of measles, mumps and rubella immunisation in each health authority in England during the first three months of the measles, mumps and rubella vaccines being available.

**Mr. Freeman:** Uptake of the measles, mumps and rubella combined vaccine is being monitored monthly in selected district health authorities. Early reports suggest an increase in uptake of 10 per cent. compared to matching cohorts of children vaccinated with measles vaccine one year previously.

### Population Statistics

**Mr. Ieuan Wyn Jones:** To ask the Secretary of State for Health what are his Department's estimates for the numbers of people aged 65 to 74 years, 75 to 79 years and over 80 years in the years 2000 and 2020 in England; and what percentage increase this represents in each category over the actual figures for the last year in which they are available.

**Mr. Freeman:** The data requested are in the table.

*Population of England, thousands*
*1987-based projections*

| Age group | Mid-1987 estimates | 2000 | 2020 | Per cent change projected | |
|-----------|--------------------|------|------|------------|-----------|
| | | | | 1987-2000 | 1987-2020 |
| 65-74 | 4,218 | 4,007 | 5,112 | −5 | 21 |
| 75-79 | 1,555 | 1,657 | 1,716 | 7 | 10 |
| 80 and over | 1,634 | 2,038 | 2,281 | 25 | 40 |

### BNFL, Sellafield

**Dr. Kim Howells:** To ask the Secretary of State for Health what evidence he has of health problems, in

particular those related to tissue and blood cancers, among children living within 10 miles of the British Nuclear Fuels plc's Sellafield facility; and if he will make a statement.

**Mr. Freeman:** I refer the hon. Member to the report of the independent advisory group, chaired by Sir Douglas

Black (1), and to the published results of the birth and school cohort studies, recommended by the group and funded by Government (2). The results of the associated case-control study are expected later this year. In addition, the report on cancer incidence and mortality in the vicinity of nuclear installations in England and Wales (3) is also relevant.

(1) Investigation of the Possible Increased Incidence of Cancer in West Cumbria. Report of the Independent Advisory Group. (HMSO 1984).

(2) Gardner, M. J., et al (1987). Follow up studies of children born to mothers resident in Seascale, and those born elsewhere but attending schools in Seascale. British Medical Journal *295*, 822 and 819.

(3) Cook-Mozaffari, P. J. et al. Cancer incidence and mortality in the vicinity of nuclear installations. England and Wales 1959-80. (Office of Population, Censuses and Surveys. Studies on Medical and Population Subjects No. 51 HMSO).

## NSPCC

**Dr. Godman:** To ask the Secretary of State for Health (1) if he will list the sums of money given to the National Society for the Prevention of Cruelty to Children in each of the past 10 years; for what purpose these sums were provided by Her Majesty's Government; what percentage of the NSPCC's annual general income these sums represented; and if he will make a statement;

(2) what sums of money have been given to the National Society for the Prevention of Cruelty to Children for the purposes of training NSPCC personnel in each of the past 10 years; how much money is to be provided to the society by Her Majesty's Government in each of the next three years for this purpose; and if he will make a statement.

**Mr. Mellor** *[holding answer 19 June 1989]:* Details are provided in the table.

*Details of grants awarded to the NSPCC for each of the past 10 years*

| Year<br><br>(a) | Section 64 grants towards headquarters administrative expenditure<br><br>(b)<br>£ | Grants towards the cost of seconding NSPCC staff on to social work qualifying courses<br>(c)<br>£ | Total of columns (b) and (c)<br><br><br>(d)<br>£ | Totals in column (d) as percentage of NSPCC's total income<br><br>(e)<br>Per cent. |
|---|---|---|---|---|
| 1979-80 | 86,500 | — | 86,500 | 2·22 |
| 1980-81 | 132,450 | 25,000 | 157,450 | 3·18 |
| 1981-82 | 200,000 | 25,000 | 225,000 | 4·06 |
| 1982-83 | 168,000 | 25,000 | 193,000 | 3·14 |
| 1983-84 | 113,000 | 35,000 | 148,000 | 1·39 |
| 1984-85 | 167,000 | 35,000 | 202,000 | 1·84 |
| 1985-86 | 167,000 | 35,000 | 202,000 | 1·38 |
| 1986-87 | 167,000 | 35,000 | 202,000 | 1·10 |
| 1987-88 | 125,000 | 35,000 | 160,000 | 0·82 |
| 1988-89 | 125,000 | — | 125,000 | [1]— |

[1] Details of total income are not yet available.

The NSPCC received from the Department of Health £5,300 in the year 1987-88 and £39,198 in 1988-89 for a project it is undertaking to develop child protection training materials for child abuse consultants in local health authorities.

In addition the Prime Minister has announced that the Department of Health will be making a grant of £800,000 over three years towards the cost of the NSPCC's new national training centre in Leicester.

## Dangerous Food Products

**Dr. David Clark:** To ask the Secretary of State for Health whether he has notified the EC under the rapid notification scheme for dangerous food products about *(a)* salmonella in eggs, *(b)* bovine products and bovine spongiform encephalopathy, *(c)* listeria in cheese and *(d)* mineral hydrocarbons.

**Mr. Freeman** *[holding answer 19 June 1989]:* Yes, where appropriate the Department has notified the EC. However, questions relating to bovine products and bovine spongiform encephalopathy and mineral hydrocarbons are the responsibility of my right hon. Friend the Minister of Agriculture, Fisheries and Food.

## Tuberculosis Vaccine

**Mr. Terry Davis:** To ask the Secretary of State for Health when Evans Medical, the British supplier of tuberculosis vaccine, moved the production of this vaccine to a new site; what effect this transfer has had on the production of tuberculosis vaccine; and when he expects health authorities to be able to resume their routine school immunisation programmes.

**Mr. Freeman** *[holding answer 19 June 1989]:* Evans Medical began production of tuberculosis vaccine at its new site in November 1988 and technical difficulties emerged earlier this year. Health authorities will be advised as soon as possible when regular supplies for the routine immunisation of schoolchildren can be resumed.

## EMPLOYMENT

### Enterprise Allowance

15. **Mr. Eastham:** To ask the Secretary of State for Employment what is the most recent total number of filled enterprise training places in the Greater Manchester area, by scheme type.

**Mr. Cope:** At the beginning of June there were 578 filled enterprise training places in the Greater Manchester area. This figure comprises 413 places via enterprise training within the employment training scheme and 165 places on the business enterprise programme, outside ET.

### Health and Safety Inspectors (Sunderland)

16. **Mr. Mullin:** To ask the Secretary of State for Employment if he will make a statement on the outcome of the recent visit of health and safety inspectors to employers in Sunderland.

**Mr. Nicholls:** During the week commencing 5 June 1989 a team of inspectors from the Health and Safety Executive's north-east area office concentrated their efforts on a planned campaign of inspections to factories, construction sites and other workplaces in Sunderland. The aims were to raise employers' awareness of health and safety, to give advice to small firms, to publicise HSE's guidance and to identify firms with poor standards.

The campaign was a success. Inspectors carried out 358 inspections, giving advice on a wide range of health and safety matters. Where necessary they used their formal enforcement powers to deal with serious health and safety risks, issuing 58 enforcement notices.

### Training and Enterprise Councils

17. **Mr. Corbett:** To ask the Secretary of State for Employment how he intends to monitor the efficiency of the training and enterprise councils.

**Mr. Fowler:** Each of the training and enterprise councils will operate under a contract with my Department which will set out the specific targets that they are to achieve. Their progress in meeting these targets will be monitored by the Training Agency.

110. **Mrs. Ann Winterton:** To ask the Secretary of State for Employment if he will make a further statement on the role of training and enterprise councils in the provision of employment training.

**Mr. Cope:** Training and enterprise councils will deliver and develop employment training, YTS and other Government programmes and tailor these programmes to meet local needs. They will also stimulate enterprise and economic growth in the locality and provide practical help to local employers wishing to improve their own training efforts.

99. **Mr. Aspinwall:** To ask the Secretary of State for Employment if he will make a statement on the role of training and enterprise councils in the provision of small business counselling.

**Mr. Cope:** As TECs are established in England they will contract with the Training Agency to take responsibility for the counselling currently provided through the Training Agency's small firms service along with the appropriate share of the counselling budget. Each TEC will decide whether counselling will be provided through direct contracts with counsellors or through local enterprise agencies or other appropriate organisations. In Wales counselling for small firms will continue to be provided by the Welsh Development Agency.

95. **Sir Marcus Fox:** To ask the Secretary of State for Employment if he will make a statement on the role of training and enterprise councils in the provision of YTS.

**Mr. Cope:** Training and enterprise councils will have responsibility for the operation of YTS in their area, within the framework set out by the Secretary of State for Employment. The councils will deliver the Government's guarantee of a training place for all young people under the age of 18 who cannot find a job, and help to achieve the aim that every young person should have access to relevant education or training leading to higher levels of attainment, nationally recognised qualifications and to a job.

72. **Mr. Malcolm Bruce:** To ask the Secretary of State for Employment how many training and enterprise councils have been established; and what progress has been made in attracting two thirds board membership from the private sector.

**Mr. Cope:** Twenty-two applications have been received by the national training task force which is reviewing these proposals and will forward its recommendations to me. I will announce which TECs have been awarded development funding shortly thereafter.

The response from private sector employers has been excellent.

36. **Mr. McFall:** To ask the Secretary of State for Employment when the handbook for the training and enterprise councils will be published; and whether there will be an opportunity for the public to suggest amendments.

**Mr. Cope:** A training and enterprise council (TEC) prospectus was published in early March and circulated widely. A draft TEC operating manual for England and Wales was published in mid-April, aimed specifically at people intending to run a TEC, with the intention that it would be expanded and updated as TECs evolve. A copy of the manual was placed in the Library and copies are available to other interested parties on request. The Training Agency will take into account any comments received.

26. **Mr. Tom Clarke:** To ask the Secretary of State for Employment how many applications he has received from parties interested in setting up training and enterprise councils; and if he will make a statement.

49. **Mr. Soames:** To ask the Secretary of State for Employment which areas have put forward proposals for establishing training and enterprise councils; and if he will make a statement.

94. **Mr. Gill:** To ask the Secretary of State for Employment if he will report on progress in establishing the first training and enterprise councils; and if he will make a statement.

98. **Mr. Ieuan Wyn Jones:** To ask the Secretary of State for Employment if he will make a statement on the progress being made in establishing training and enterprise councils.

105. **Mr. Evennett:** To ask the Secretary of State for Employment how many expressions of interest his Department has received from groups of employers wishing to form training and enterprise councils; and if he will make a statement.

**Mr. Cope:** Twenty-two applications have been received by the national training task force, which is reviewing these proposals and will forward its recommendations to me. This is an excellent response. The table lists the areas from which applications have been received.

List of TECS that have applied for development funding:
    Oldham
    Dorset
    Warwickshire
    Essex
    Rochdale
    Tyneside
    North West Midlands

Sheffield
Calderdale and Kirklees
Teesside
Kingston
Devon and Cornwall
Birmingham
East Lancashire
Walsall
Milton Keynes
Hertfordshire
Isle of Wight
Hampshire
North, West and South Norfolk
South and East Cheshire
Cumbria

## Secondary Picketing

18. **Mr. Robert G. Hughes:** To ask the Secretary of State for Employment what representations he has received about secondary picketing; and if he will make a statement.

**Mr. Nicholls:** The Government receive representations on many aspects of industrial relations. In the nine years since employers were given the freedom to restrain secondary picketing by the 1980 Employment Act representations on this subject have dwindled to nothing.

## Labour Statistics

19. **Mr. Corbyn:** To ask the Secretary of State for Employment what are the latest youth unemployment figures for the Holloway travel-to-work area.

**Mr. Cope:** In the London travel-to-work area, of which Islington, North parliamentary constituency and Holloway are a part, there were about 54,500 unemployed claimants aged under 25 years.

21. **Mr. Roy Hughes:** To ask the Secretary of State for Employment what are the latest available unemployment figures for the United Kingdom and the comparable figures for 1979; and what they would have been without the changes in the method of counting unemployment.

**Mr. Cope:** In May 1989 the level of unemployment seasonally adjusted was 1,835,200, or 6·4 per cent. compared with 1,088,500 or 4·1 per cent in May 1979, on a consistent basis. It is not possible to estimate current unemployment on the basis prevailing in 1979.

106. **Mr. Neil Hamilton:** To ask the Secretary of State for Employment if he will make a statement on the reduction in long-term unemployment over the last 12 months.

109. **Mr. Andrew Mitchell:** To ask the Secretary of State for Employment by how much long-term unemployment has fallen over the past year; and if he will make a statement.

**Mr. Nicholls:** In April 1989, the number of unemployed claimants in the United Kingdom who had been unemployed for 12 months or more was 744,120 compared with 1,029,206 in April 1988, a fall of 285,086 or 27·7 per cent.

102. **Mr. Teddy Taylor:** To ask the Secretary of State for Employment what is the current number of persons unemployed in the Southend-on-Sea area; and what was the comparable total in 1979.

**Mr. Nicholls:** In May 1989 there were 3,602 unemployed claimants in Southend-on-Sea local authority area. Comparable figures are not available for 1979 on the same administrative basis and because of changes in the coverage of the count.

91. **Mr. Flannery:** To ask the Secretary of State for Employment what was the figure for unemployment in 1979; and what is the present figure.

**Mr. Nicholls:** In May 1989 the level of unemployment, seasonally adjusted, in the United Kingdom was 1,835,200 or 6·4 per cent. compared with 1,088,500 or 4·1 per cent. in May 1979, on a consistent basis.

92. **Mr. Win Griffiths:** To ask the Secretary of State for Employment in which standard planning regions in the United Kingdom there have been *(a)* increases and *(b)* reductions in employment since June 1979.

**Mr. Nicholls:** Between June 1979 and June 1988 the civilian work force in employment *(a)* increased in the south-east (including London), East Anglia, south-west, west midlands, and east midlands, and *(b)* decreased in Yorkshire and Humberside, the north-west, north, Wales, Scotland, and Northern Ireland.

89. **Mr. Holt:** To ask the Secretary of State for Employment what is the rate of fall of unemployment in the United Kingdom and in other comparable European countries; and if he will make a statement.

**Mr. Nicholls:** The table shows the fall in the unemployment rates over the past two years for the countries of the European Community. Over the past two years the rate of unemployment has fallen faster in the United Kingdom than in any other EC country.

*Unemployment, latest month compared with two years earlier*

| Country | Latest month | Percentage rate change |
|---|---|---|
| United Kingdom[1] | May 1989 | −318 |
| Belgium | March 1989 | −2·6 |
| Ireland | May 1989 | −1·6 |
| France | March 1989 | −1·5 |
| Germany | May 1989 | −0·9 |
| Portugal | March 1989 | −0·7 |
| Netherlands | December 1988 | −0·4 |
| Greece | April 1989 | −0·3 |
| Luxembourg | March 1989 | −0·3 |
| Denmark | January 1989 | 0·7 |
| Italy | February 1989 | 1·7 |

[1] Seasonally adjusted series consistent with current coverage.

83. **Mr. Dover:** To ask the Secretary of State for Employment how many people aged between 18 and 24 years were unemployed in April 1988 and April 1989, respectively; and if he will make a statement.

**Mr. Nicholls:** In April 1989, the number of unemployed claimants aged 18 to 24 years in the United Kingdom, was 530,376 compared with 697,718 in April 1988, a fall of 167,342 or 24 per cent.

78. **Mr. Andy Stewart:** To ask the Secretary of State for Employment by how many the total of persons out of work for five years or more has fallen during the past year; and if he will make a statement.

84. **Mr. Favell:** To ask the Secretary of State for Employment by how much the total out of work for five years or more has fallen since April last year; and if he will make a statement.

**Mr. Nicholls:** In April 1989 the number of unemployed claimants in the United Kingdom who had been unemployed for five years or more was 216,607 compared with 271,242 in April 1988, a fall of 54,635 or 20·1 per cent.

69. **Mr. Knapman:** To ask the Secretary of State for Employment by how much the number of people in employment rose in 1988 in the United Kingdom and in other Organisation for Economic Co-operation and Development countries; and if he will make a statement.

**Mr. Nicholls:** The table shows, for the United Kingdom and the major OECD countries, the increase in civilian employment in the year to the fourth quarter of 1988. The United Kingdom had the largest percentage rise.

*Increases in civilian employment United Kingdom and major OECD countries*

| | *Thousands* | *Percentage* |
|---|---|---|
| United Kingdom | 642 | 2·5 |
| Canada | 288 | 2·4 |
| United States of America | 2,386 | 2·1 |
| Japan | 864 | 1·5 |
| Germany (Federal Republic) | 159 | 0·6 |
| Italy | 134 | 0·6 |
| France | n/a | n/a |

n/a = not available.
*Sources:*
United Kingdom: Department of Employment.
Other countries: OECD Labour Force Statistics, 1989/1.

68. **Mr. Quentin Davies:** To ask the Secretary of State for Employment if he will make a statement on the fall in long-term unemployed in the three months to April.

**Mr. Lee:** In April 1989, the number of unemployed claimants in the United Kingdom, who had been unemployed for 12 months or more, was 744,120 compared with 821,419 in January 1989, a fall of 77,299 or 9·4 per cent.

57. **Mr. French:** To ask the Secretary of State for Employment which major Organisation for Economic Co-operation and Development country has had the sharpest fall in the rate of unemployment over the past two years; and if he will make a statement.

**Mr. Nicholls:** Over the past two years the unemployment rate has fallen faster in the United Kingdom than in any other major OECD country. The unemployment rate in the United Kingdom is now lower than the European Community average.

58. **Mr. Norris:** To ask the Secretary of State for Employment if he will make a statement on the number of people employed in the United Kingdom.

**Mr. Nicholls:** Between March 1983 and December 1988 the work force in employment in the United Kingdom increased by 2,948,000 to 26,510,000, the highest level on record. This rising trend has now continued for more than five years. The figures have been adjusted for the effects of seasonal variations. The work force in employment is the sum of employees in employment, the self-employed, Her Majesty's forces and participants in work-related Government training programmes.

52. **Mr. Amess:** To ask the Secretary of State for Employment if he will make a statement on the current level of unemployment in the United Kingdom.

**Mr. Nicholls:** In May 1989 the level of unemployment, seasonally adjusted, in the United Kingdom was 1,835,200 or 6·4 per cent. the lowest for more than eight years, on a consistent basis.

54. **Mrs. Maureen Hicks:** To ask the Secretary of State for Employment by how much long-term unemployment has fallen among the 18 to 24 age group in the past year; and if he will make a statement.

**Mr. Lee:** In April 1989, the number of unemployed claimants aged 18 to 24 years in the United Kingdom, who had been unemployed for 12 months or more, was 119,160 compared with 179,938 in April 1988, a fall of 60,778 or 33·8 per cent.

47. **Mr. Grocott:** To ask the Secretary of State for Employment when he expects unemployment in the west midlands to fall to the level it was in 1979.

**Mr. Lee:** The Department does not forecast future levels of unemployment.

48. **Mr. Robert Jones:** To ask the Secretary of State for Employment what has been the increase in the number of self-employed people in the United Kingdom since 1979; and if he will make a statement.

53. **Mr. Forman:** To ask the Secretary of State for Employment what has been the increase in the number of self-employed people in work since 1979; and if he will make a statement.

**Mr. Cope:** Between June 1979 and December 1988, the latest date for which estimates are available, there was an increase of 1,142,000, or 60 per cent., in the number of self-employed people in the United Kingdom. It is estimated that over 3 million people are now self-employed. Self-employed people now represent 11 per cent. of the work force in employment.

37. **Mr. Kirkhope:** To ask the Secretary of State for Employment what proportion of males and females are in employment in each major Organisation for Economic Co-operation and Development country; and if he will make a statement.

103. **Mr. Rowe:** To ask the Secretary of State for Employment which major Organisation for Economic Co-operation and Development countries have the highest proportion of women in employment; and if he will make a statement.

**Mr. Cope:** The latest comparative information relates to 1986 (except for Germany) and is given in the table. It shows the United Kingdom's percentage in employment to be significantly higher than those of our major European competitors, though lower than those of Japan and the United States. This country's relative position may well have become still better since 1986 as employment has increased more rapidly here than elsewhere.

*Percentage of those aged 15 to 64 in employment (including armed forces)*

| | *Males* | *Females* |
|---|---|---|
| Japan | 85 | 56 |
| United States of America | 77 | 60 |
| United Kingdom | 77 | 56 |
| Canada | 76 | 57 |
| Federal Republic of Germany[1] | 74 | 46 |

| | Males | Females |
|---|---|---|
| Italy | 74 | 35 |
| France | 70 | 48 |

[1] 1985 figures.

*Sources:*
United Kingdom: Department of Employment.
Other countries: OECD Labour Force Statistics 1966 to 1986.

**34. Mr. David Martin:** To ask the Secretary of State for Employment by how much the unemployment rate has fallen in the past two years in the United Kingdom and other European countries; and if he will make a statement.

**Mr. Nicholls:** The table shows falls in unemployment rates over the past two years for the United Kingdom and other European countries. Over the past two years unemployment has fallen faster in the United Kingdom than in any other major industrialised country.

*Unemployment, latest month compared with two years earlier*

| Country | Latest month | Percentage rate change |
|---|---|---|
| United Kingdom[1] | May 1989 | −3·8 |
| Spain | March 1989 | −2·8 |
| Belgium | March 1989 | −2·6 |
| Austria | March 1989 | −1·7 |
| Finland | February 1989 | −1·7 |
| Ireland | May 1989 | −1·6 |
| France | March 1989 | −1·5 |
| Germany | May 1989 | −0·9 |
| Sweden | March 1989 | −0·9 |
| Portugal | March 1989 | −0·7 |
| Netherlands | December 1988 | −0·4 |
| Switzerland | March 1989 | −0·3 |
| Greece | April 1989 | −0·3 |
| Luxembourg | March 1989 | −0·3 |
| Denmark | January 1989 | 0·7 |
| Italy | February 1989 | 1·7 |
| Norway | March 1989 | 2·5 |

[1] Seasonally adjusted series consistent with current coverage.

**30. Mr. Ian Bruce:** To ask the Secretary of State for Employment what is the current youth unemployment rate in the United Kingdom and in other comparable European countries; and if he will make a statement.

**Mr. Nicholls:** The table shows harmonised unemployment rates, seasonally adjusted, for those aged under 25 years, for March 1989 in the United Kingdom and other European Countries as published by the statistical office of the European Communities. The youth unemployment rate in the United Kingdom is about half the European Communities average.

*Under 25 year olds seasonally adjusted unemployment rate March 1989*

| European country | Total percentage rate |
|---|---|
| Spain | 36·7 |
| Italy | 31·9 |
| Greece | 24·4 |
| Ireland | 22·8 |
| France | 21·4 |
| Belgium | 18·7 |
| Netherlands | 16·4 |
| Portugal | 12·2 |
| Denmark | 9·6 |
| Germany | 5·2 |
| Luxembourg | 4·1 |
| United Kingdom | 9·6 |
| EC average | 18·1 |

**85. Mr. Tracey:** To ask the Secretary of State for Employment how many people are currently self-employed; and if he will make a statement.

**Mr. Cope:** In December 1988, the latest date for which estimates are available, there were, 3,048,000 self-employed in the United Kingdom. The numbers of self-employed have increased by 60 per cent. since June 1979 and currently represent 11 per cent. of the work force in employment.

**100. Mr. Stevens:** To ask the Secretary of State for Employment what was the number of people self-employed in April 1989 and April 1983, respectively.

**Mr. Nicholls:** In December 1988, the latest date for which figures are available there were 3,048,000 self-employed people in the United Kingdom and in March 1983 there were 1,906,000.

## Employment Training

**20. Mr. Nigel Griffiths:** To ask the Secretary of State for Employment how many employment training managers there are *(a)* nationally and *(b)* by standard region; and how many have been accredited with providing training of high and sustainable quality.

**Mr. Nicholls:** Nationally there are 1,251 training managers within employment training. All of them are at present undergoing examination for approved status.

The regional breakdown by standard region is as follows:

|  | Number |
|---|---|
| Scotland | 233 |
| Northern | 148 |
| Yorkshire and Humberside | 131 |
| North-West | 157 |
| West Midlands | 102 |
| East Midlands and Eastern | 106 |
| Wales | 131 |
| South-West | 69 |
| South-East | 76 |
| London | 98 |
| National total | 1,251 |

**76. Ms. Ruddock:** To ask the Secretary of State for Employment whether he has any plans to enhance payments to employment training trainees *(a)* nationally and *(b)* regionally.

**Mr. Nicholls:** At present my right hon. Friend has no plans to enhance payments to employment training trainees. However, training allowances are linked to individual benefit entitlement and so are enhanced whenever benefits are uprated. For this reason, training allowances were increased in April 1989. In addition, the levels of other payments to trainees are kept under continuous review and travel payments to trainees have been increased very recently.

**74. Ms. Mowlam:** To ask the Secretary of State for Employment how many people are on employment training in each Training Agency area; and what is the drop-out rate for each area.

**Mr. Nicholls:** Information on the number of people on employment training in each area office is given in the following table. Information on the number of leavers is not available at the area level.

*Employment Training*
*In-Training Figures at 2 June 1989*

|  | Numbers |
|---|---|
| *Northern Region* | |
| Cleveland | 6,141 |
| Durham | 5,063 |
| North Tyne | 4,259 |
| South Tyne | 6,357 |
| Total | 21,820 |
| *East Midlands* | |
| Derby | 2,861 |
| Norfolk and Suffolk | 3,141 |
| Leicestershire and Northants | 2,782 |
| Lincolnshire | 1,361 |
| Bedfordshire and Cambridgeshire | 1,699 |
| Nottinghamshire | 3,345 |

|  | Numbers |
|---|---|
| Total | 15,189 |
| *North West* | |
| Cheshire | 2,899 |
| Cumbria | 1,387 |
| Lancashire | 4,220 |
| Manchester Central | 4,022 |
| Manchester East | 2,590 |
| Manchester North | 2,624 |
| Merseyside | 8,672 |
| Total | 26,414 |
| *West Midlands* | |
| Birmingham | 7,374 |
| Coventry | 2,682 |
| Dudley | 2,889 |
| Staffordshire | 3,629 |
| Marches | 2,654 |
| Wolverhampton | 3,144 |
| Total | 22,372 |
| *South East Region* | |
| Berkshire and Oxfordshire | 1,212 |
| Essex | 1,694 |
| Hampshire and Isle of Wight | 1,992 |
| Hertfordshire and Buckinghamshire | 1,672 |
| Kent | 1,963 |
| Surrey | 445 |
| Sussex | 1,761 |
| Total | 10,739 |
| *London* | |
| Inner South | 3,309 |
| North London | 3,553 |
| East London | 2,195 |
| South London | 1,685 |
| West London | 1,197 |
| Inner North | 5,815 |
| Total | 17,754 |
| *Yorkshire and Humberside* | |
| Humberside | 5,253 |
| Leeds | 4,295 |
| Bradford | 4,540 |
| Wakefield | 5,332 |
| Sheffield | 5,342 |
| Total | 24,762 |
| *South West* | |
| Avon | 2,555 |
| Gloucester | 1,506 |
| Plymouth | 5,541 |
| Taunton | 1,868 |
| Total | 11,470 |
| *Scotland* | |
| Glasgow City | 4,525 |
| Lanarkshire | 2,534 |
| Renfrew, Dumbarton and Argyll | 2,682 |
| Ayr, Dumfries and Galloway | 2,991 |
| Lothian and Borders | 3,368 |
| Central and Fife | 2,852 |
| Grampian and Tayside | 2,583 |
| Highlands and Islands | 917 |
| Total | 22,452 |
| *Wales* | |
| Cardiff | 4,811 |
| Gwent | 2,235 |
| Swansea | 4,315 |
| Wrexham | 3,094 |

|  | *Numbers* |
|---|---|
| Total | 14,455 |

**62. Mr. Duffy:** To ask the Secretary of State for Employment how many people are currently in employment training in South Yorkshire.

**Mr. Nicholls:** On 2 June 1989, the latest date for which information is available, there were 9,083 people on employment training in South Yorkshire.

**40. Mrs. Mahon:** To ask the Secretary of State for Employment how many extra staff have been employed by the Health and Safety Executive to monitor health and safety on employment training schemes.

**Mr. Nicholls:** None. By virtue of the Health and Safety (Training for Employment) Regulations 1988, participants on employment training and similar training schemes at employers' premises are covered by the full range of statutory health, safety and welfare provisions applying to employed persons. Accordingly HSE inspectors do not, when examining conditions at workplaces, differentiate between trainees and employees.

**33. Mr. Jack Thompson:** To ask the Secretary of State for Employment how many accidents have occurred on employment training schemes since their inception.

**Mr. Nicholls:** Since the inception of employment training on the 5 September 1988, 556 accidents to ET trainees have been reported to the Training Agency.

**31. Mr. McAvoy:** To ask the Secretary of State for Employment what specific measures are taken to monitor health and safety on employment training schemes.

**Mr. Nicholls:** Health and safety arrangements for ET closely parallel those for YTS. Training managers have the prime responsibility for monitoring work placements, and they are obliged to ensure that premises are properly notified to the relevant enforcing authority, that proper insurance arrangements are available and that, in general, there is appropriate health and safety management and supervision. Training managers are also required to report and investigate accidents; to provide relevant literature, including the new booklet "Safety First in Employment Training", and to arrange for proper induction and training in health and safety matters.

The Training Agency's own staff conduct monitoring of all these requirements, by sample visits to training managers to check records and documents. They also visit work experience premises on a sample basis.

## Benefit Fraud

**22. Mr. Roger King:** To ask the Secretary of State for Employment if he will make a statement on investigations carried out by the west midlands employment fraud investigators at the Birmingham convention centre and on Operation Enterprise.

**Mr. Nicholls:** On 10 March 1989, investigators interviewed 450 building workers at the Birmingham convention site. As a result, 128 people withdrew their claims to benefit. The exercise yielded net benefit savings of approximately £98,000. Forty-four cases are being considered for prosecution.

Operation Enterprise investigated people registered with employment agencies. It commenced in July 1988 and finished in March 1989. Of the 2,350 investigations, 1,100 people withdrew their claims to benefit. The net benefit saving was approximately £800,000. A total of 147 cases are being considered for prosecution.

**87. Mr. Fishburn:** To ask the Secretary of State for Employment if he will make a statement on Operation Rag Trade carried out by employment service fraud operators in the east end of London.

**Mr. Nicholls:** Operation Rag Trade, which was carried out between October and November 1988, investigated possible benefit fraud among people engaged in the clothing industry in the east end of London. Over 1,150 investigations were undertaken with 173 people withdrawing their claims to benefit. This resulted in net benefit savings of £275,000 and five potential prosecution cases.

**38. Mr. Charles Wardle:** To ask the Secretary of State for Employment if he will report progress on tackling fraud among benefit claimants; and if he will make a statement.

**71. Mr. Brandon-Bravo:** To ask the Secretary of State for Employment if he will report on progress in tackling fraud among benefit claimants; and if he will make a statement.

**Mr. Nicholls:** During the year April 1988 to March 1989, 435,969 investigations were carried out by investigators. This resulted in 86,895 claims to benefit being withdrawn with net benefit savings of £62·55 million. In addition, 4,045 people were prosecuted for social security offences.

## Ports

**23. Mr. Thornton:** To ask the Secretary of State for Employment if he plans to meet the general secretary of the Transport and General Workers Union to discuss industrial relations in the ports; and if he will make a statement.

**Mr. Nicholls:** My right hon. Friend has no such plans. Industrial relations in scheme, and non-scheme ports are a matter for employers and their employees. The Government's proposals for the abolition of the dock labour scheme provides an opportunity for ports which evolve new arrangements to secure better industrial relations and fewer strikes.

**77. Mr. Franks:** To ask the Secretary of State for Employment how many registered dockers under the dock labour scheme are currently on the temporary unattached register; and if he will make a statement.

**Mr. Nicholls:** According to National Dock Labour Board registers for 30 May 1989 there were 130 registered dock workers then on the temporarily unattached register.

The temporarily unattached register is a product of the dock labour scheme. It maintains registered dock workers on basic pay even though they are not working and is funded by a levy on employers in scheme ports. No other industry bears the cost of such a requirement. The Government are abolishing the scheme so that scheme ports can compete on equal terms.

**73. Mr. David Nicholson:** To ask the Secretary of State for Employment what volume of Britain's overseas trade is currently handled by dockers working in ports *(a)* covered by the dock labour scheme and *(b)* those outside the scheme; and if he will make a statement.

**Mr. Nicholls:** Department of Transport port statistics for 1987 show that 51 scheme ports handled 59·73 per cent. of the volume of overseas trade, while 35 non-scheme ports handled 40·26 per cent.

Ports which bear the costs of the dock labour scheme have lost a substantial share of trade to ports outside the scheme over the past 25 years. They have also lost jobs while jobs in non-scheme ports have grown. The Government are abolishing the scheme to allow all ports to compete on equal terms and win the business needed to sustain jobs.

66. **Mr. John Townend:** To ask the Secretary of State for Employment if he will make a statement on the current industrial dispute in the ports covered by the dock labour scheme.

**Mr. Nicholls:** It is a matter for the port employers to decide how they wish to respond to unofficial strikes by a minority of registered dock workers. I hope that dock workers will look to their future, and respond to the port employers offer to negotiate locally about arrangements to be established after the dock labour scheme is abolished.

67. **Mr. Barry Porter:** To ask the Secretary of State for Employment if he has any plans to reintroduce casual labour into dock labour scheme ports after abolition of the statutory scheme.

**Mr. Nicholls:** The Government believe that there is no evidence that there can be a return to widespread casual work. Modern ports have no need of it.

Without the scheme's restrictions, non-scheme ports employ few casual workers and employers of 93 per cent. of dock workers in scheme ports have given assurances not to return to a system of casual work. They have indicated a willingness to examine this and other issues on the same port-by-port basis as already applies to other workers in scheme ports and to the one in three dock workers in ports outside the scheme.

56. **Mr. Brazier:** To ask the Secretary of State for Employment how many applications for redundancy have been received from dock workers working in ports covered by the dock labour scheme; and if he will make a statement.

**Mr. Nicholls:** My right hon. Friend has no means of knowing how many inquiries have been made to employers by registered dock workers about redundancy following the abolition of the dock labour scheme.

The Dock Work Bill which abolishes the scheme provides for the Government to contribute 50 per cent. of payments of up to £35,000 for any registered dock worker who is made redundant in the 18 months following the abolition of the scheme, and 50 per cent. of payments of up to £20,000 in the 18 months thereafter. This will provide redundancy compensation of many times normal statutory requirements and will be in addition to entitlements to early retirement pensions available under the registered dock workers occupational pension scheme from the age of 50 onwards.

41. **Mr. Jacques Arnold:** To ask the Secretary of State for Employment what representations he has received

about negotiations between dock workers and their employers in scheme ports; and if he will make a statement.

61. **Mr. Riddick:** To ask the Secretary of State for Employment what representations he has received about port-by-port negotiations between dock workers and their employers; and if he will make a statement.

97. **Mr. David Davis:** To ask the Secretary of State for Employment what representations he has received about the port-by-port negotiations between dock workers and the port employers; and if he will make a statement.

**Mr. Nicholls:** On 4 May the deputy general secretary of the Transport and General Workers Union wrote to my right hon. Friend urging negotiations with the employers about a national agreement to replace the scheme.

It is for employers and employees to decide the form of negotiations which best meets their needs. The Government note that the Transport and General Workers Union negotiates locally about terms and conditions for all other workers in Britain's ports, in and outside the dock labour scheme, and that pay rates of registered dock workers in scheme ports are also determined locally. The union, therefore, recognises that local negotiations are an appropriate response to the widely differing requirements of our ports.

The Government therefore hope that the union will lift its veto on similar local negotiations on conditions of employment for the minority of port workers who are registered dock workers.

**Mr. Couchman:** To ask the Secretary of State for Employment what plans he has to discuss dock labour schemes with the Employment Ministers of the European Community; and if he will make a statement.

**Mr. Nicholls:** I have no such plans.

It is for member states to decide their own framework for employment in ports in accordance with national needs and Community policies to minimise distortions to competition.

### Foreign Firms

24. **Mr. Ashby:** To ask the Secretary of State for Employment what proportion of foreign firms plan to increase their employment in Britain; and if he will make a statement.

**Mr. Cope:** Although the information requested is not available, I have no doubt that a strong economy and a productive work force will prove as attractive to overseas investors in the future as they have done in recent years.

### Small Businesses

25. **Mr. Bowis:** To ask the Secretary of State for Employment how many new registrations for value added tax by small firms were made in 1988; and if he will make a statement.

**Mr. Cope:** In 1987, the latest year for which figures have been published, the net increase in the number of VAT-registered businesses was 45,000, or nearly 900 a week on average. The indications are that the rate of increase during 1988 has been faster. The vast majority of VAT-registered businesses are small.

## Single Market

27. **Mr. Blunkett:** To ask the Secretary of State for Employment what plans he has to meet the training needs arising from the completion of the single European market.

**Mr. Cope:** The Government's plans for meeting future training needs, including those arising from the single European market, are set out in the White Paper "Employment for the 1990s" Cm 540.

## Skills Training

28. **Dr. Reid:** To ask the Secretary of State for Employment what steps he is taking to improve skills training in the retail sector.

**Mr. Cope:** The Government hope that employers within the retail sector will work closely with training and enterprise councils as they are established, to examine the local labour market and assess key skill needs and the adequacy of existing training arrangements.

The Government are also seeking to establish national vocational qualifications based on competence. The retail sector recently launched its new retail certificate in England and Wales and the certificate in retail distribution in Scotland. These qualifications set standards for trainees in the retail sector. The introduction of YTS and employment training into retailing provides trainees with a properly structured training programme leading to these qualifications.

It was encouraging to see that the 1988 national training award winners included winners from the retail sector, for example B & Q and J. Sainsbury.

59. **Mr. Ron Davies:** To ask the Secretary of State for Employment what help the senior management buy-out team of the Skills Training Agency have received either *(a)* financially or *(b)* professionally from his Department.

**Mr. Cope:** As I told the House on 13 March (*Official Report*, 13 March column *25*), we shall provide financial assistance to the management buy-out team towards the costs of obtaining external professional advice. No professional help has been offered from within my Department.

## Tourism

29. **Mr. Boyes:** To ask the Secretary of State for Employment when he intends to make an announcement on the future of section 4 tourism grant funding.

**Mr. Nicholls:** My right hon. Friend is still considering the future of section 4 funding in the light of the recent tourism review. He will make an announcement in due course.

86. **Ms. Armstrong:** To ask the Secretary of State for Employment what recent representations he has received (a) in favour and (b) against the continuation of section 4 grants under the Development of Tourism Act 1969.

**Mr. Nicholls:** My right hon. Friend has received representations expressing a variety of views about the section 4 scheme and will be making an announcement on the future of the scheme in due course.

75. **Mr. Atkinson:** To ask the Secretary of State for Employment if he is now in a position to make a further statement on the future of the section 4 scheme of financial assistance for tourism projects.

**Mr. Nicholls:** My right hon. Friend is still considering the future of the section 4 scheme in the light of the recent tourism review. He will make an announcement in due course.

## Business Growth Training Programme

32. **Mr. John Greenway:** To ask the Secretary of State for Employment if he will make a statement on his plans to train the self-employed on the business growth training programme.

**Mr. Cope:** On 24 January I announced that business growth training would provide training for owners and managers of very small businesses in better management and business skills in order to help them run and develop their business (*Official Report* 24 January column *550*]. This applies equally to the self-employed. Further information is available in the Library.

## Social Charter

35. **Mr. Butler:** To ask the Secretary of State for Employment if he will make a statement on the proposals put forward by the European Commission for a social charter.

**Mr. Cope:** The Government firmly believe that there is a social dimension to the single European market; because it is directed at creating new jobs, reducing unemployment and improving real standards of living. The Government do not believe that a charter of the kind proposed can contribute to achieving those goals.

## International Youth Skill Olympics

42. **Mr. Boswell:** To ask the Secretary of State for Employment what support industry and Government are giving to the international youth skill olympics to be held at the national exhibition centre in August; and if he will make a statement.

**Mr. Cope:** The Government welcome the staging of the international youth skill olympics in Birmingham. It provides a good showcase for British industry to show the skills of its young people to the rest of the world. High standards of skill through quality training are essential if we are to have continued success in the market place in the next decade.

Financial support for the international youth skill olympics is being raised primarily from industry. Sponsorship, in the form of cash, loan of machinery and materials, is expected to raise in the region of £4,000,000. The Government, through the Training Agency, provide financial support each year to the event organisers, Skill UK Ltd. During 1988-89 this amounted to £120,000 and £60,000 has been allocated for 1989-90. A contribution has also been made towards the cost of renting the national exhibition centre.

## Disabled People

43. **Mr. Wareing:** To ask the Secretary of State for Employment how many young disabled people have been

accepted for a YTS place; what percentage of them were in severity categories 1 and 2; and what percentage were in severity category 5 and above.

**Mr. Cope:** The total number of young people with disabilities in training on YTS on 31 May 1989 was 12,001. There are no figures available on the percentage of young people with disabilities by severity category.

88. **Mr. Ashley:** To ask the Secretary of State for Employment how many employers fulfil their quota of 3 per cent. disabled people on their staffs.

**Mr. Nicholls:** On 1 June 1988, the latest date for which information is available, 7,736 employers with 20 or more workers were employing their full quota of registered disabled people.

## Training

44. **Mr. Dunnachie:** To ask the Secretary of State for Employment whether he will commission further research into the support that industry is prepared to give to non-statutory training organisations.

**Mr. Cope:** A review of the progress of non-statutory training organisations on a sector-by-sector basis is due to be undertaken early next year. The review will include consideration of industry's support for these organisations.

60. **Mr. Loyden:** To ask the Secretary of State for Employment how many places have been taken on Government training schemes in the Merseyside area.

**Mr. Nicholls:** On 31 May the number of people participating in Government training schemes in the Merseyside area was as follows:

|  | *Number* |
| --- | --- |
| YTS | 14,958 |
| Employment training | 8,701 |
| Business enterprise programme | [1]236 |
| Business growth training | [1]257 |

[1] Figures for those in training are not kept for these programmes. The figures given are for starts from 1 April to 31 May.

## Strikes

45. **Mr. Watts:** To ask the Secretary of State for Employment how many working days were lost through strikes in the first five months of *(a)* 1989 and *(b)* 1979; and if he will make a statement.

**Mr. Nicholls:** The estimate for May 1989 of working days lost through stoppages of work due to industrial disputes is not yet available; but for the first four months of 1989 it is provisionally estimated that 256,000 working days were lost, compared with 7,591,000 working days lost for the corresponding period in 1979.

107. **Mr. Burt:** To ask the Secretary of State for Employment if he will introduce legislation to legalise sympathy strikes; and if he will make a statement.

**Mr. Nicholls:** No. The Green Paper "Removing Barriers to Employment", published on 20 March, states that the Government propose to make it unlawful to induce industrial action by workers of an employer not party to a trade dispute except in the case of lawful picketing.

101. **Mr. Patrick Thompson:** To ask the Secretary of State for Employment if he will make a statement on the number of working days lost through strikes in 1988.

**Mr. Nicholls:** The number of working days lost through stoppages of work due to industrial disputes in 1988 is estimated at 3,702,000. This is about a third of the annual average over the previous 10-year period.

64. **Mr. Cran:** To ask the Secretary of State for Employment when he intends to publish his proposals to limit the incidence of unofficial trade union stoppages.

**Mr. Nicholls:** The Government are reviewing the law in relation to industrial action with a view to issuing a consultative document over the next couple of months and including proposals in legislation in the autumn.

## Council for Social Aid (Manchester)

46. **Mr. Tony Lloyd:** To ask the Secretary of State for Employment if he will make a statement concerning the situation of the Council for Social Aid in Manchester.

**Mr. Nicholls:** The Council for Social Aid operated as an ET training manager through a company called Manchester Diocesan Church of England Council for Social Aid Ltd.

The directors of CSA Ltd. recently decided to put the company into voluntary liquidation when it became apparent that the company could not meet its financial obligations. The decision was a matter for the directors of the company and is not something in which I could intervene.

My right hon. Friend's major concern was to ensure that everything possible was done to minimise the disruption for trainees so that they could continue to develop their skills and improve their job prospects.

All the company's 1,011 trainees have been, or will shortly be, placed with alternative training managers.

## Picketing

51. **Mr. Redwood:** To ask the Secretary of State for Employment if he has any plans to change the law on picketing; and if he will make a statement.

**Mr. Nicholls:** The Green Paper "Removing Barriers to Employment", published on 20 March, states that the Government propose no change to the law on picketing.

## Job Share Programme

55. **Dr. Twinn:** To ask the Secretary of State for Employment how many jobs are currently shared under the job share programme; and if he will make a statement.

**Mr. Nicholls:** In the year to 30 May 1989, 166 applications were accepted under the job share programme, as a result of which 220 people have gained employment. I believe that the programme can play a useful role in helping unemployed people and encouraging more flexible patterns of work, and my right hon. Friend is considering action to give it more publicity.

## Closed Shop

70. **Mr. David Evans:** To ask the Secretary of State for Employment what estimate he has as to the number of

employees working in pre-entry closed shops; and what proportion this constitutes of the total number of employees currently working in closed shops.

**Mr. Nicholls:** Our Green Paper "Removing Barriers to Employment", which was published on 20 March, estimates the total number of people covered by all types of pre-entry closed shop arrangements in Great Britain as being of the order of 1·3 million. This constitutes half the total of around 2·6 million people estimated to be covered by all forms of closed shop arrangements. These estimates are derived from a specially commissioned survey carried out between 22 February and 6 March 1989, a summary of which has been placed in the Library.

### British Venture Capital

79. **Mr. David Shaw:** To ask the Secretary of State for Employment if he has any plans to meet the chairman of British Venture Capital to discuss the expansion of small firms; and if he will make a statement.

**Mr. Cope:** I refer my hon. Friend to my reply to my hon. Friend the Member for Surbiton (Mr. Tracey) on 16 May, *Official Report, column 175.*

### Health and Safety Inspectors

80. **Mr. Cryer:** To ask the Secretary of State for Employment if he will make a statement on the current number of health and safety at work inspectors in post.

**Mr. Nicholls:** On 1 June 1989, 1,209·5 inspectors were in post in the Health and Safety Executive. The executive plans to increase the total number of inspectors employed to 1,277 by 1 April 1990.

### Tyneside Training and Enterprise Council

81. **Mr. Cousins:** To ask the Secretary of State for Employment when he now expects to make a decision on the Tyneside training and enterprise council submission.

**Mr. Cope:** I expect to make an announcement on the application for development funding from the Tyneside prospective training and enterprise council shortly.

### National Training Task Force

82. **Dr. Goodson-Wickes:** To ask the Secretary of State for Employment when he last met the chairman of the national training task force; what matters were discussed; and if he will make a statement.

**Mr. Cope:** My right hon. Friend the Secretary of State and I last met the chairman of the national training task force on 22 May 1989 and we discussed progress on establishing training and enterprise councils. We are very encouraged by the progress made and are confident that we will have a number of high-quality TECs operational next year.

### Wages

90. **Mr. Beaumont-Dark:** To ask the Secretary of State for Employment if he will make a statement on the Government's policy on minimum wages.

**Mr. Nicholls:** A national minimum wage would raise employers' costs and destroy jobs, including the jobs of those it was designed to help.

### Co-operative Enterprises

93. **Mr. Michael:** To ask the Secretary of State for Employment whether he will make it his policy to provide adequate resources to enable the Co-operative Development Agency to consolidate and develop its work in promoting co-operative enterprises in the United Kingdom; and if he will make a statement.

**Mr. Cope:** The Co-operative Development Agency is at present largely supported by my Department under the terms of the 1984 Co-operative Development Agency and Industrial Development Act. Under this Act Government funding was increased up to an overall limit of £3 million. At current rates of spending this limit will be reached in the financial year 1990-91. In January this year my Department wrote to organisations representing the interests of the co-operative movement and consulting them on a proposal that the agency's life should not be extended. The views received are now being carefully considered and I hope to announce our conclusions and intentions in the near future.

### Wages Councils

96. **Mr. Matthew Taylor:** To ask the Secretary of State for Employment if he will make a statement on the future of wages councils.

**Mr. Nicholls:** A final decision on the council's future will be made later this year.

### Industrial Relations

104. **Mr. Dicks:** To ask the Secretary of State for Employment what information he has on the proportion of foreign firms which believe that British industrial relations have improved significantly in recent years; and if he will make a statement.

**Mr. Nicholls:** Such information is not held by my Department. There is no doubt that the last 10 years have seen major improvements in industrial relations. This is illustrated by the decline in recorded stoppages which in 1988 were at the lowest level since 1935. New jobs and employment opportunities have followed this improvement.

### Tourism and Catering

108. **Mr. Parry:** To ask the Secretary of State for Employment what steps he is taking to improve skills training in the tourism and catering industry.

**Mr. Nicholls:** I refer the hon. Gentleman to the reply given on 16 May 1989 to my hon. Friend the Member for Fylde (Mr. Jack) at columns *149-50.*

### "Perspective on the Future for Resorts"

**Mr. Fearn:** To ask the Secretary of State for Employment what action he proposes to take following the publication and submission to him by the British Resorts Association of the booklet. "Perspective on the Future for Resorts."

**Mr. Lee:** I welcome this initiative from the British Resorts Association. I am giving careful consideration to the issues raised and will be responding to the association in due course.

## Companies (Compact Schemes)

**Mr. Ieuan Wyn Jones:** To ask the Secretary of State for Employment if he will list the companies taking part in compact schemes with schools in England.

**Mr. Cope:** The number of companies taking part in compacts is growing rapidly. A list could be obtained only at disproportionate cost.

# Written Answers to Questions

*Wednesday 21 June 1989*

## SCOTLAND

### Handicapped Children

**Mr. Soley:** To ask the Secretary of State for Scotland whether he will give details of the financial aid available to send handicapped children and their parents to the Peto Institute in Hungary.

**Mr. Michael Forsyth:** Provision is included in the Self-Governing Schools Etc. (Scotland) Bill to enable education authorities in Scotland to pay all or part of the fees, travelling, maintenance and other expenses in respect of a child's attendance at an establishment which makes provision wholly or mainly for persons with pronounced, specific or complex special education needs. The Peto Institute in Hungary is such an establishment. The assistance can include, where appropriate, the expenses of parents or another accompanying person.

### Blind People

**Mr. Evennett:** To ask the Secretary of State for Scotland how many registered blind persons there are in Scotland.

**Mr. Michael Forsyth:** The provisional figure for March 1988 is 13,760.

### Environmentally Sensitive Areas

**Mr. Bill Walker:** To ask the Secretary of State for Scotland if he will publish a report on environmentally sensitive areas in Scotland.

**Mr. Michael Forsyth:** My right hon. and learned Friend is pleased to announce that a first report on environmentally sensitive areas in Scotland was published today and a copy placed in the Library. The report sets out the background to the designation of ESAs in Scotland, the main characteristics and objectives of each of the Scottish ESAs and the arrangements for monitoring the scheme.

### Forestry Commission (Wildlife)

**Mr. Ron Davies:** To ask the Secretary of State for Scotland what was the last advice he received from the Nature Conservancy Council concerning the practice of blocking of badger setts and digging of fox earths by fox hunters on Forestry Commission land.

**Lord James Douglas-Hamilton:** My right hon. and learned Friend has received no advice from the Nature Conservancy Council on this subject, although it is possible that council staff have given informal advice to the Forestry Commission on a local basis. I understand, however, that the Nature Conservancy Council is preparing a report which will include discussion of the issue.

## DEFENCE

### HMS Cambridge

**Mr. Steen:** To ask the Secretary of State for Defence when he expects to give instructions to the Property Services Agency with regard to the erection of a proposed fence around HMS Cambridge at Wembury, Plymouth.

**Mr. Neubert:** The Property Services Agency, acting on behalf of the Ministry of Defence, submitted a notification under the provisions of circular 18/84 to the South Hams district council of a proposal for the erection of new boundary fencing around the gunnery school at HMS Cambridge. The district council has objected to this proposal. No instructions will be given to the Property Services Agency for the erection of the proposed fence until the matter has been determined in accordance with normal planning procedures.

## ATTORNEY-GENERAL

### Immigration

**Mr. Cohen:** To ask the Attorney-General what is the average time from an appeal being notified to his Department from *(a)* Bombay high commission, *(b)* other Foreign Office outposts, *(c)* the Foreign Office itself, *(d)* the Home Office to (i) the date of the appeal being set and (ii) the hearing taking place.

**The Attorney-General:** This information is not recorded in the form requested. Currently, however, it is estimated that the time taken from receipt of the notice of appeal by the immigration appellate authorities in London to the despatch of the appeal papers to both parties' representative in the United Kingdom is four to eight weeks. Appeals cannot thereafter be listed for hearing until both parties' representatives indicate that they are ready to proceed: this is in the hands of the parties, and times vary from a few weeks to several months. If no response is received within nine months the appeal is automatically listed for hearing.

When both parties have indicated their readiness to proceed, the IAA are generally able to list the case for hearing within the following eight weeks, although where a party requests an expedited hearing such requests can usually be met. However, where a party seeks an adjournment, the hearing may take place more than eight weeks after the parties have indicated their readiness to proceed.

## THE ARTS

### Exhibitions (Private Funding)

**Mr. Knapman:** To ask the Minister for the Arts what contribution private funding has made to new exhibitions at national museums and galleries in the last 12 months, in addition to public funding.

**Mr. Luce:** Full details of private funding of new exhibitions are not held centrally but notable examples of such funding over the last 12 months are The British museum's "Treasures for the Nation" exhibition attracting £150,000 from British Gas. The Tate gallery successfully raised £423,000 in sponsorship for exhibitions, and the

Science museum's new "Food for Thought" gallery has attracted over £950,000 in commercial sponsorship. Such initiatives are to be encouraged.

## AGRICULTURE, FISHERIES AND FOOD

### Mechanically Recovered Meat

**Sir Richard Body:** To ask the Minister of Agriculture, Fisheries and Food if he will introduce regulations to control the use of mechanically recovered meat in food products; and if he will make a statement.

**Mr. Ryder:** Mechanically recovered meat is used in a number of meat products. The Food Labelling Regulations 1984 already require that a treatment given to a food, or food ingredient, should be shown in the appropriate place on the label if the omission of such an indication would mislead the purchaser.

### Food and Wine Exports

**Mr. Teddy Taylor:** To ask the Minister of Agriculture, Fisheries and Food what was the total amount spent by the European Economic Community and by member states in subsidising the exports of food and wine in the most recent annual period for which figures are available; and if he will include in the total the moneys spent on exporting food and wine from intervention stores.

**Mr. Ryder:** Expenditure on export refunds for food and wine in 1988 was £6,638 million (provisional), of which £165 million was for food aid.

This includes refunds on exports of commodities from the free market and from intervention stocks. The breakdown between member states is shown below.

|                | mecu  | £ million |
| -------------- | ----- | --------- |
| Belgium        | 297   | 201       |
| Denmark        | 689   | 467       |
| Germany        | 1,543 | 1,047     |
| Greece         | 76    | 52        |
| Spain          | 395   | 268       |
| France         | 2,577 | 1,748     |
| Ireland        | 317   | 215       |
| Italy          | 557   | 378       |
| Luxembourg     | 0     | 0         |
| Netherlands    | 2,698 | 1,830     |
| Portugal       | 2     | 1         |
| United Kingdom | 636   | 431       |
| TOTAL EC       | 9,787 | 6,638     |

### Less-favoured Areas

**Mr. Marland:** To ask the Minister of Agriculture, Fisheries and Food if he will make a statement about the progress on the case for extending the United Kingdom's less-favoured areas.

**Mr. Ryder:** Yesterday, my right hon. Friend, the Minister of Agriculture, Fisheries and Food, handed over to Mr. Raymond MacSharry the EC Commissioner for Agriculture a case to the EC Commission for an extension of the United Kingdom's less-favoured areas by 95,000 hectares of land in England, Wales, Scotland and Northern Ireland. This extension will require the agreement of the Commission before payment of any benefit can be considered. At this stage, I cannot say how long it will take to secure that agreement. The form of the submission follows from the initial discussions we have held with the EC Commission, which has made it clear that it will be examining our submission rigorously against the criteria on economic and demographic performance laid down in directive 75/268.

I am arranging for copies of the results of our application of these criteria, together with an illustrative map of the areas submitted to the Commission, to be placed in the Library at the House and in local Ministry offices in the areas concerned. Farmers, who made representations following the 1984 extension, will be notified individually whether their land has been included in the submission.

### Environmentally Sensitive Areas

**Mr. Hague:** To ask the Minister of Agriculture, Fisheries and Food when he will publish a report on the environmentally sensitive areas; and if he will make a statement.

**Mr. MacGregor:** The first report on the environmentally sensitive areas scheme is being published today by HMSO, meeting our obligation under section 18(8) of the Agriculture Act 1986.

The environmentally sensitive areas scheme has been warmly welcomed by conservation bodies and farmers alike. Since going to press we have received further applications from over 300 farmers wishing to bring over 9,000 hectares (22,230 acres) of their land into the scheme this year. Overall, this gives us a total of 2,708 applications and agreements covering 110,495 hectares (273,000 acres) of land in England alone since the scheme was introduced in 1987. This represents over 90 per cent. of the land which we considered likely to enter the scheme and shows overwhelmingly the farming industry's commitment to environmentally conscious farming. It points to real progress in conserving some of our most beautiful countryside.

My colleagues the Secretaries of State for Wales and Scotland have made similar announcements. The report sets out how the scheme operates in each of the designated areas and how we intend to assess its impact. I hope it will add to a wider understanding of environmentally sensitive areas and what they are designed to achieve.

Copies of this report have been placed in the Libraries of both Houses and will be available from HMSO bookshops.

### Agriculture Council

**Mr. McLoughlin:** To ask the Minister of Agriculture, Fisheries and Food if he will make a statement on the outcome of the Agriculture Council in Luxembourg on 19 and 20 June.

**Mr. MacGregor:** The main item on the agenda of this Council, at which I represented the Government, was the Commission's proposal for changes to the support arrangements for sheep. The Commission indicated ways in which it might be prepared to adjust its proposal. I emphasised the main points which would be necessary for the proposals to be acceptable to the United Kingdom including the conditions which are necessary for a unified regime. Discussion showed that major differences of view persist and the Council will return to the matter at a subsequent meeting.

The arrangements for the import of New Zealand butter into the United Kingdom, which some member states regard as closely linked to progress in the support system for sheep, were rolled forward for a further month (July) on the basis of unchanged quantities and prices.

The Council adopted a directive laying down health and hygiene standards for egg products. This will bring legislative standards for pasteurised egg in the Community as a whole up to the level of the best practices already applied by the major United Kingdom egg producers.

## HOME DEPARTMENT

### "Broadcasting in the 1990s"

**Mr. Frank Field:** To ask the Secretary of State for the Home Department when he expects to reply to the United Christian Broadcasters letter to him on the White Paper, "Broadcasting in the 1990s"; and if he will place a copy in the Library.

**Mr. Renton:** I have today placed in the Library a copy of my private secretary's reply of 8 June.

### Drugs

**Mr. Cox:** To ask the Secretary of State for the Home Department what is the policy of his Department as to the requirements of each prison in England and Wales to report the finding of drugs; and how often such reports are required to be made.

**Mr. Douglas Hogg:** All prison service establishments are required to report to their regional office every find which is made of an illicit drug. A report on each incident should be submitted as soon as possible after the find is made.

### Voting Rights

**Mr. Steel:** To ask the Secretary of State for the Home Department whether he intends to introduce legislation giving full voting rights indefinitely to Britons abroad for both United Kingdom elections and European Parliament elections, in line with the rights accorded to other European nationals.

**Mr. Greg Knight:** To ask the Secretary of State for the Home Department if he has reached any conclusions, in the light of responses to Home Department consultation papers No. 1 Representation of the People: British Citizens Overseas, issued on 29 April 1988, and No. 2 Representation of the People: Absent Voting, issued on 2 March 1989; and if he has any proposals to amend electoral law; and if he will make a statement.

**Mr. Hurd:** The Representation of the People Act 1985 brought the United Kingdom into line with most other western democracies by making provision for British citizens to vote whilst living abroad. This step was greatly welcomed by many British citizens worldwide. The detailed arrangements represented a cautious, evolutionary approach. They had the effect, amongst other things, of limiting in time the right to be registered as an overseas elector to five years from the date for which a British citizen was last registered as a United Kingdom resident; requiring the applicant to make a declaration, including a prescribed statement about residence intentions; requiring

the declaration to be attested by a consular official; and requiring the overseas elector to make a fresh declaration annually. These provisions, stricter than in many other countries, considerably restricted the numbers abroad who could have access to the franchise and imposed significant burdens on those who did. The Government made a commitment, at the time the legislation was passing through Parliament, to review the new arrangements once they were in operation, and, in particular, to reconsider the five-year time limit.

It is evident from the under-use of the franchise during its first three years of operation, and from replies to consultation paper No. 1, that the measures introduced in 1985-86 are unduly restrictive. They exclude from the franchise British citizens working on longer-term contracts abroad, often in the United Kingdom's interests, and they exclude completely anyone who left the United Kingdom before he was old enough to have been included in a register of electors. In addition, applicants are discouraged by the procedures for registration, and they are not reminded of the need to be registered annually, as are their counterparts resident in the United Kingdom.

The overseas electors' franchise deprives too many British citizens abroad of the right to vote and the existing application procedures should be simplified. I am presenting today a Representation of the People Bill to amend the law relating to overseas electors. This would extend to 25 years the period abroad during which British citizens may apply to be registered to vote in United Kingdom parliamentary and European Parliament elections. The Bill would extend the overseas franchise to include those not previously registered as electors in the United Kingdom by reason of age; and it would remove from the declaration which overseas electors must now make the statement about residence intentions. Proposals to amend the relevant representation of the people regulations, so as to simplify further the registration procedures for overseas electors, will be brought forward.

The Representation of the People Act 1985 also extended, for the first time, the right to a postal or proxy vote to any United Kingdom resident, registered as an elector, who cannot reasonably be expected to vote in person at his allotted polling station at a particular election. This reform meant that holidaymakers, people who had fallen ill, and those whose work took them away from home on polling day could nevertheless exercise their right to vote. Detailed conditions, which applicants for the new absent voting facility must satisfy, are specified in regulations. These include a requirement that applications for an absent vote at a particular election must be attested and, for the most general case, that the attester must not be related to the applicant and shall not have attested any other application in respect of the election for which the application is being made. The general election in 1987 provided the first major test of these new absent voting arrangements, and the attestation requirement gave rise to considerable difficulty with many applications being rejected as a result. We have already greatly simplified the application forms in the light of that experience, but it is clear from the response to consultation paper No. 2 that there should be some easing of the application procedures themselves. Accordingly, proposals to amend the relevant regulations will be brought before this House; it will be convenient to deal with them at the same time as the regulations relating to overseas electors.

The Bill which I am presenting seeks also to deal with a pressing difficulty which has developed over the limits on candidates' expenses at parliamentary by-elections. Electoral law makes no distinction for the purposes of such expenses between a parliamentary general election and a by-election. The character of parliamentary by-elections has changed considerably since the law on which the existing scheme is based was passed, over a century ago. They are, increasingly, national events which focus the attention of political commentators and the media and which, consequently, attract the close involvement of the various party organisations. This trend, which is unlikely to be reversed, has implications for the system of controls on candidates' expenses set out in the Representation of the People Act 1983. I propose to review these implications, in consultation with the representatives of the political parties and the returning officers who have responsibility, under the law, for conducting parliamentary elections. As a first step, I am putting in hand the preparation of a public consultation paper which will set out the background and promote consideration of the issues and options involved. Such a review will take time. In the interim it is important that the limits on candidates' expenses at parliamentary by-elections are realistic and take account of the campaigning activity which takes place. Accordingly, the Bill I am presenting today sets a new limit on candidates' expenses at parliamentary by-elections. The new limit, which is four times the one currently specified (which will continue to apply at general elections), is without prejudice to the outcome of the longer-term review I have described.

## Asylum Seekers

**Mr. Corbyn:** To ask the Secretary of State for the Home Department how many of the Kurdish asylum seekers from Turkey who have arrived since the beginning of May were refused admission at airports and removed immediately; and to which countries they went.

**Mr. Renton:** None; immigration officers are required to refer all applications for asylum to the refugee unit of the Home Office for decision.

**Mr. Corbyn:** To ask the Secretary of State for the Home Department how many asylum applications were made in 1988; and what were the nationalities of the applicants.

**Mr. Renton:** This information will be contained in the 1988 issue of the annual Home Office statistical bulletin "Refugee Statistics, United Kingdom" which will be published next month.

**Mr. Corbyn:** To ask the Secretary of State for the Home Department how many Kurdish asylum seekers from Turkey have arrived since the beginning of May; how many are currently held in *(a)* prison, *(b)* Harmondsworth detention centre and *(c)* elsewhere; and if he will list the institutions where they are being held.

**Mr. Renton:** The information is not readily available in the precise form requested since records do not identify different ethnic groupings. As of midnight on 19 June, 2,838 Turkish nationals had arrived since the beginning of May and had sought asylum; 81 were detained in prison establishments at Winchester, Dorchester, Exeter and Gloucester; 92 were detained in Harmondsworth detention centre, Gatwick beehive and Latchmere house remand centre.

**Mr. Corbyn:** To ask the Secretary of State for the Home Department how many Kurdish asylum-seekers from Turkey who have arrived in Britain since the beginning of May have been interviewed about their claim for asylum; and how many of these have been *(a)* given refugee status, *(b)* given exceptional leave to remain, *(c)* refused leave to remain and removed and *(d)* refused leave to remain and are awaiting removal.

**Mr. Renton:** By 19 June the asylum applications from 138 Turkish nationals had been considered in detail. The results of this consideration are:

12: met the criteria of the 1951 UN convention and have been recognised as refugees;

38: have been given leave to remain in the United Kingdom on an exceptional basis;

5: are receiving further consideration;

3: departed voluntarily before a final decision was reached;

61: have been notified of a provisional decision that they do not qualify for asylum and any further information/representations are awaited;

19: did not qualify for asylum or leave to enter under the immigration rules, were refused entry and have been returned to Turkey.

In addition, 128 have made voluntary departures after withdrawing their claims for asylum.

## EC Broadcasting Directive

**Mr. Teddy Taylor:** To ask the Secretary of State for the Home Department why the Council of Ministers did not approve the broadcasting directive on 14 June; and what plans the Commission has to pursue the matter.

**Mr. Renton:** The directive was not approved on that occasion because not enough member states were in a position to adopt it. It is proposed that the discussion of the Commission's re-examined proposal on the directive will continue under the French presidency.

## Immigration

**Mr. Bernie Grant:** To ask the Secretary of State for the Home Department (1) how many overseas visitors were initially refused entry to the United Kingdom in *(a)* January to May 1988, inclusive, and *(b)* January to May 1989, inclusive, and what were their nationalities;

(2) how many Jamaican citizens were initially refused entry into the United Kingdom as not being genuine visitors in *(a)* January to May, inclusive 1988 and *(b)* January to May, inclusive, 1989.

**Mr. Renton** *[holding answer 15 June 1989]:* The total numbers of passengers by nationality who were refused leave to enter and removed from the United Kingdom between January and April of 1988 and 1989 are given in the table; figures for May 1989 are not yet available. It is not possible from the information available centrally to ascertain how many sought entry as visitors.

Of the 113 Jamaican citizens removed between January and April 1988 and the 307 removed between January and April 1989, 108 and 273 respectively failed to satisfy the immigration officer that they qualified as genuine visitors under paragraph 17 of the rules. Some of the remainder may also have sought entry as visitors but have been refused for other reasons.

**Mr. Bernie Grant:** To ask the Secretary of State for the Home Department how many people were arrested as being illegal immigrants in the first five months of 1989, and in the corresponding five months in 1988; and what were their nationalities.

**Mr. Renton** *[holding answer 15 June 1989]:* The available information is of persons against whom action was commenced as illegal entrants, which is published quarterly in table 13 of Home Office statistical bulletin "Control of Immigration: Statistics", a copy of which is in the Library. The latest available figures relate to the fourth quarter of 1988 (in Bulletin 10/89). The figure for the first quarter of 1989 will be published in the next issue around the end of this month. A breakdown by nationality of the figures for the first and second quarters of 1988 is given in the following table.

*Persons against whom action was commenced as illegal entrants by nationality*

| Nationality | Number of persons 1988 | |
| | 1st Quarter | 2nd Quarter |
| --- | --- | --- |
| *Europe* | 182 | 162 |
| Austria | 3 | 2 |
| Bulgaria | 1 | — |
| Cyprus | 10 | 4 |
| Czechoslavakia | 2 | — |
| France | 5 | — |
| Federal Republic of Germany | — | 2 |
| Hungary | 2 | 4 |
| Italy | 2 | 2 |
| Malta | — | 1 |
| Netherlands | — | 1 |
| Norway | — | 1 |
| Poland | 2 | 4 |
| Portugal | 20 | 51 |
| Romania | 1 | — |
| Spain | 15 | 4 |
| Sweden | 3 | 1 |
| Switzerland | 2 | 1 |
| Turkey | 108 | 72 |
| Yugloslavia | 6 | 12 |
| | | |
| *Americas* | 51 | 55 |
| Brazil | 11 | 6 |
| Canada | 3 | — |
| Chile | — | 4 |
| Colombia | 11 | 13 |
| Jamaica | 12 | 16 |
| Mexico | 1 | 1 |
| Peru | 2 | 4 |
| Trinidad and Tobago | — | 2 |
| United States of America | 11 | 9 |
| | | |
| *Africa* | 265 | 287 |
| Algeria | 21 | 23 |
| Egypt | 4 | 10 |
| Ethiopia | 1 | 1 |
| Ghana | 93 | 112 |
| Libya | — | 3 |
| Mauritius | 5 | 3 |
| Morocco | 15 | 13 |
| Nigeria | 118 | 111 |
| South Africa | 1 | 2 |
| Sudan | 1 | 4 |
| Tunisia | 3 | 2 |
| Uganda | 1 | — |
| Zaire | 2 | — |
| Zambia | — | 3 |
| | | |
| *Asia* | 210 | 223 |
| Bangladesh | 43 | 65 |
| China | 1 | 1 |
| Hong Kong BDTC | 9 | 3 |
| India | 63 | 55 |
| Iran | 8 | 4 |
| Iraq | 1 | 4 |

| Nationality | 1988 | |
| | 1st Quarter | 2nd Quarter |
| --- | --- | --- |
| Israel | 3 | 4 |
| Japan | 8 | 2 |
| Jordan | — | 4 |
| Malaysia | 8 | 15 |
| Pakistan | 33 | 39 |
| Phillipines | 2 | 2 |
| Saudi Arabia | 1 | — |
| Singapore | 1 | 1 |
| Sri Lanka | 26 | 20 |
| Syria | 1 | 1 |
| Thailand | 2 | 3 |
| | | |
| *Australasia* | | |
| Australia | 2 | 3 |
| | | |
| Others | 30 | 38 |
| British Overseas Citizens | 4 | — |
| Other countries not otherwise specified | 14 | 27 |
| Stateless | 12 | 11 |
| | | |
| All Nationalities | 740 | 768 |

# TRANSPORT

## Radioactive Material

**Mr. McGrady:** To ask the Secretary of State for Transport if he will list year by year for the last 10 years how many tonnes of radioactive material were imported to Sellafield; what method of transport was used to convey the material to Sellafield; and from what countries the radioactive material was imported.

**Mr. Peter Bottomley:** During the past 10 years, over 2,500 tonnes of irradiated fuel have been imported for reprocessing at Sellafield from the following countries: Japan, Italy, the Federal Republic of Germany, the Netherlands, Sweden, Spain and Switzerland.

The bulk of this material has been transported by sea in BNFL's own ships with the balance being sent by rail/sea from European countries. To break this information down by individual years would involve disproportionate effort.

## Blood Testing (Motor Accidents)

**Mr. Brandon-Bravo:** To ask the Secretary of State for Transport if, in the light of the remarks by the chief constable of Gwent, echoing those by petitioners in Nottingham, of 11 May 1987, *Official Report,* column 150, he will seek to review the ban against blood testing of unconscious persons involved in motor accidents.

**Mr. Peter Bottomley:** The White Paper "The Road User and the Law" (Cmnd. 576) published in February this year recorded in paragraph 2.41 the conclusion that the case for taking blood samples from unconscious drivers was not generally yet felt to be sufficiently strong to overcome the present serious legal and ethical issues perceived to be involved.

## Bus Services (London)

**Mr. Spearing:** To ask the Secretary of State for Transport under what powers he has permitted commercial bus companies to operate in the Greater London area which are not under the auspices of London Regional Transport; and if he will state the conditions under which such services now operate.

**Mr. Portillo:** Local bus services in London other than those controlled by London Regional Transport are licensed by the metropolitan traffic commissioner under part II of the Transport Act 1985. Between October 1986 and March 1989, 101 licences for local services were granted together with 72 licences for excursions or tours. Conditions attached to licences vary according to the case, and are for the traffic commissioner to decide.

### Road Safety

**Mr. Evennett:** To ask the Secretary of State for Transport what records are maintained of accidents occurring on the public highway involving registered blind or visually handicapped persons; and if he will make a statement.

**Mr. Peter Bottomley:** Our records of injury accidents occurring on the public highway do not include details of the disabilities of people involved. The Department works closely with local authorities and with organisations of blind and partially sighted people to improve facilities available to those who are visually handicapped so that they can go out with greater safety and confidence.

### Great Central Railway Line

**Mr. Marlow:** To ask the Secretary of State for Transport if he will discuss with the chairman of British Rail the withdrawal from auction, on 6 July, of sites on the Great Central line.

**Mr. Portillo:** These are commercial matters for the British Rail property board and it would not be appropriate for Ministers to intervene.

**Mr. Marlow:** To ask the Secretary of State for Transport if he will discuss with the chairman of British Rail the action he is taking to secure the route of the Great Central line as far as Rugby as a potential route for trains from the Channel tunnel.

**Mr. Portillo:** Securing land which may be required for potential rail routes to the Channel tunnel is a matter for the proposers of the route.

## FOREIGN AND COMMONWEALTH AFFAIRS

### Pakistan (Non-proliferation Treaty)

**Mr. Flynn:** To ask the Secretary of State for Foreign and Commonwealth Affairs if he has any information on the terms and conditions set out by Pakistan that need to be met before Pakistan would sign the nuclear non-proliferation treaty.

**Mr. Eggar:** Pakistan has stated on several occasions that it will accede to the non-proliferation treaty if and when India agrees to do so.

### Hong Kong

**Mr. Canavan:** To ask the Secretary of State for Foreign and Commonwealth Affairs whether he will take steps to ensure that holders of Hong Kong British passports are given equal treatment with holders of full British passports in the matter of exit in emergency situations from the People's Republic of China; and if he will make a statement.

**Mr. Eggar:** Our policy is to give Hong Kong people holding British nationality exactly the same treatment for consular purposes as any other British national. This approach was demonstrated by the help and advice given to Hong Kong people by the British embassy in Peking and the consulate general in Shanghai during recent weeks.

## NATIONAL FINANCE

### Manufacturing Trade Deficit

96. **Mr. Graham:** To ask the Chancellor of the Exchequer what is his latest estimate of the manufacturing trade deficit in 1989.

100. **Mr. Allan Roberts:** To ask the Chancellor of the Exchequer what is his latest estimate of the manufacturing trade deficit in 1989.

**Mr. Major:** I refer the hon. Members to the reply I gave to the hon. Member for Leeds, Central (Mr. Fatchett) on 8 June at column *204*.

97. **Mr. Fearn:** To ask the Chancellor of the Exchequer what is his latest estimate of the deficit in manufactured trade for 1989-90.

**Mr. Major:** The Financial Statement and Budget Report for 1989-90 provides a forecast for trade in manufactures for calendar year 1989 only (table 3.5).

### Trade Deficit

98. **Mr. Ernie Ross:** To ask the Chancellor of the Exchequer what is his best estimate of the trade deficit in 1989.

99. **Mr. Patchett:** To ask the Chancellor of the Exchequer what is his latest estimate of the trade deficit in 1989.

**Mr. Major:** I refer the hon. Members to the reply I gave to the hon. Member for Stretford (Mr. Lloyd) on 6 June at column *115*.

### Composite Rate Investigations

**Mr. Gerald Bowden:** To ask the Chancellor of the Exchequer whether he will make an announcement on the next composite rate investigation under section 483(5) of the Income and Corporation Taxes Act 1988.

**Mr. Norman Lamont:** I have asked Inland Revenue to consult the savings institutions on arrangements for conducting a survey in respect of 1991-92.

## WALES

### Perinatal Services

**Mr. Gareth Wardell:** To ask the Secretary of State for Wales when he expects to receive the report by Professor Sir Eric Stroud on the perinatal services in Wales.

**Mr. Grist:** I understand that the expert advisory group on perinatal intensive care services in Wales, under the chairmanship of Professor Sir Eric Stroud, is presently concluding its deliberations and expects to report shortly.

### Education Authorities (Funding)

**Mr. Barry Jones:** To ask the Secretary of State for Wales (1) if he will make a special allocation of cash to local education authorities in Wales to enable them to meet their legal obligations consequent upon the enactment of the Education Reform Act;

(2) if he will make a special allocation of cash to local education authorities in Wales to enable them to meet their obligations concerning the national curriculum; and if he will make a statement;

(3) if he will make a special allocation of cash to local education authorities in Wales to enable them to meet their obligations concerning local management of schools; and if he will make a statement.

**Mr. Wyn Roberts:** LEAs' expenditure requirements arising from the Education Reform Act are considered in the context of the revenue support grant negotiations. Specific additional support for aspects of ERA implementation is provided through education support grant and the LEA training grant scheme and through direct Welsh Office funding of the Curriculum Council for Wales.

### River Pollution

**Dr. Kim Howells:** To ask the Secretary of State for Wales if he will issue a direction to the Welsh Water Authority to prosecute all alleged industrial polluters of south Wales' rivers.

**Mr. Grist:** No.

### Prescription Charges

**Mr. Michael:** To ask the Secretary of State for Wales whether he will make it his policy that when prescriptions are supplied in a combination pack of two or more items which cannot be taken in isolation and therefore are supplied only to be taken together as one course of treatment, only one prescription charge should be levied on the patient.

**Mr. Grist:** Unless the patient is entitled to exemption a prescription charge is payable in respect of each quantity of a drug prescribed and the fact that, for convenience, two or more individual preparations may be supplied in one pack does not affect the liability for payment. It would be wrong to allow manufacturers packaging arrangements to determine the amount a patient is liable to pay.

### Blind People

**Mr. Evennett:** To ask the Secretary of State for Wales how many registered blind persons there are in Wales.

**Mr. Grist:** There were, in Wales, 8,564 people registered as blind on 31 March 1988.

### Environmentally Sensitive Areas

**Mr. Gwilym Jones:** To ask the Secretary of State for Wales when he will publish a report on environmentally sensitive areas in Wales; and if he will make a statement.

**Mr. Peter Walker:** I am very pleased to say that the first report on ESAs in Wales has been published today. Copies have been placed in the Libraries of both Houses. Similar announcements are being made by my colleagues the Minister of Agriculture, Fisheries and Food and by the Secretary of State for Scotland.

The report explains the reasons for designating the Cambrian mountains and Lleyn peninsula ESAs and describes the way the schemes are operating. It sets out progress on implementation and outlines our plans to monitor the effects of the schemes.

Progress with the scheme is very encouraging. Almost two-thirds of the holdings in the original Cambrian mountains ESA have applied to join the scheme. Fifty-four per cent. (13,931 ha) of the semi-natural rough grazing in that area is already subject to management agreements, and this proportion will increase when further applications are processed. I anticipate similar success in the Cambrian mountains extended area in due course. In little more than a year, 15,403 ha (38 per cent.) of the 39,700 ha of agricultural land in the Lleyn peninsula ESA has been the subject of applications to join the scheme. This progress is a sign of considerable interest in the scheme, and of the industry's commitment to farming in an environmentally conscious way.

## NORTHERN IRELAND

### Northern Ireland Police Authority

**Mr. John D. Taylor:** To ask the Secretary of State for Northern Ireland when Mrs. Phyllis Bateson was appointed as a member of the Northern Ireland Police Authority; whether her position as a member of the authority was a matter of consultation or discussion with the Government of the Republic of Ireland under the terms of the Anglo-Irish Agreement; and what was the proposed period of her membership of the authority.

**Mr. Ian Stewart** *[holding answer 19 June 1989]:* For security reasons it is not our policy to disclose the names of members of the Northern Ireland Police Authority. Nor is it normal practice to disclose whether any views have been put forward on the composition of individual public bodies under article 6 of the Anglo-Irish Agreement.

## EDUCATION AND SCIENCE

### Community Charge

**Mr. Cohen:** To ask the Secretary of State for Education and Science whether his advice issued to local authority associations that access by community charge registration officers to the schools admissions register was not allowed because the register is under the control of school governors still applies; and if he will make a statement.

**Mrs. Rumbold:** Yes. The advice on this subject issued in a letter from the Department to the local authority associations dated 2 May, repeated in a letter dated 17 May from my hon. Friend the Parliamentary Under-Secretary of State to the hon. Member, remains valid.

### National Curriculum (Heritage)

**Mr. Strang:** To ask the Secretary of State for Education and Science what consideration has been given to the needs of archaeology and the conservation and protection of the British heritage in the development of the national curriculum.

**Mrs. Rumbold:** My right hon. Friend announced on 13 January the establishment of a working group to make recommendations on attainment targets and programmes of study for history within the national curriculum in

England and Wales. He asked the group to take into account, amongst other things, the cultural heritage of Britain; it will also consider links between history and related fields such as archaeology. The group's interim report is to be submitted to him by 30 June, and its final report by Christmas.

## Employment Training

**Mr. Wall:** To ask the Secretary of State for Education and Science (1) how many people are on employment training schemes whilst studying at college;

(2) if he will list all employment schemes, other than educational training, which are based in the further education sector; how many students are on these schemes; and how they are funded.

**Mr. Jackson:** My right hon. Friend the Secretary of State for Employment is responsible for administering and funding most training programmes. The information available for the number of students training in public further education colleges in England on 1 November 1987 (the latest year for which information is available), excluding YTS and TVEI, is as follows:

|  | Thousands |
|---|---|
| Industrial Type Training Course[1] | 7 |
| Adult Training Scheme[2] | 13 |
| Other Courses[3] | 12 |

[1] Industrial type training courses are courses at a college consisting entirely of training without a further education element, mounted at the behest of an industrial training board or employer, for which an economic charge is made.

[2] Adult training scheme, includes students enrolled under the job training scheme, training for enterprise and wider opportunities training programmes.

[3] Other courses include access to information technology and local grants to employers schemes.

## Discretionary Awards

**Mr. Wall:** To ask the Secretary of State for Education and Science how much each of the local authorities in England and Wales spend on discretionary awards as a total and as a percentage of their total budget; and what is the maximum and minimum awards given by them.

**Mr. Jackson:** The table shows provisional outturn figures for the total amount spent on discretionary awards by each local education authority in England in 1987-88; and for the percentage this represents of their total net expenditure on education in each case where the latter figure is available. Policy for discretionary awards including the amount of support which should be given in each case is for each local authority to determine in the light of its own priorities and information about the value of individual awards is not collected centrally. Expenditure on education by local authorities in Wales is the responsibility of my right hon. Friend the Secretary of State for Wales.

| Local education authority | Total expenditure on discretionary awards | |
|---|---|---|
| | (i) (£000's) | (ii) As per cent. of total net expenditure on education |
| Barking | 163 | 0·26 |
| Barnet | 561 | n.a. |
| Bexley | 264 | 0·44 |

| Local education authority | Total expenditure on discretionary awards | |
|---|---|---|
| | (i) (£000's) | (ii) As per cent. of total net expenditure on education |
| Brent | 3,342 | 3·31 |
| Bromley | 613 | 0·90 |
| Croydon | 355 | 0·42 |
| Ealing | 805 | n.a. |
| Enfield | 110 | 0·16 |
| Haringey | 385 | n.a. |
| Harrow | 237 | 0·43 |
| Havering | 192 | 0·30 |
| Hillingdon | 194 | 0·33 |
| Hounslow | 200 | n.a. |
| Kingston-upon-Thames | 155 | 0·28 |
| Merton | 179 | 0·44 |
| Newham | 389 | n.a. |
| Redbridge | 297 | 0·54 |
| Richmond-upon-Thames | 348 | 1·06 |
| Sutton | 97 | 0·25 |
| Waltham Forest | 591 | 0·79 |
| ILEA | 20,156 | 1·89 |
| Birmingham | 852 | 0·28 |
| Coventry | 350 | 0·31 |
| Dudley | 226 | 0·28 |
| Sandwell | 399 | 0·43 |
| Solihull | 212 | 0·41 |
| Walsall | 276 | 0·32 |
| Wolverhampton | 211 | n.a. |
| Knowsley | 19 | 0·03 |
| Liverpool | 30 | 0·02 |
| St. Helens | 128 | 0·22 |
| Sefton | 357 | 0·49 |
| Wirral | 1,051 | 1·15 |
| Bolton | 325 | 0·43 |
| Bury | 380 | 0·77 |
| Manchester | 878 | 0·45 |
| Oldham | 227 | 0·37 |
| Rochdale | 222 | 0·35 |
| Salford | 212 | n.a. |
| Stockport | 378 | 0·51 |
| Tameside | 201 | 0·33 |
| Trafford | 425 | 0·80 |
| Wigan | 385 | 0·40 |
| Barnsley | 578 | 0·99 |
| Doncaster | 503 | 0·58 |
| Rotherham | 193 | 0·26 |
| Sheffield | 1,016 | n.a. |
| Bradford | 1,777 | 1·15 |
| Calderdale | 394 | 0·73 |
| Kirklees | 1,023 | 0·77 |
| Leeds | 1,124 | 0·52 |
| Wakefield | 720 | 0·79 |
| Gateshead | 129 | 0·24 |
| Newcastle-upon-Tyne | 352 | 0·34 |
| North Tyneside | 235 | n.a. |
| South Tyneside | 5 | 0·01 |
| Sunderland | 798 | 0·83 |
| Isles of Scilly | 2 | 0·29 |
| Avon | 1,905 | 0·74 |
| Bedfordshire | 883 | 0·57 |
| Berkshire | 1,164 | n.a. |
| Buckinghamshire | 776 | 0·44 |
| Cambridgeshire | 1,159 | 0·69 |
| Cheshire | 3,349 | 1·26 |
| Cleveland | 1,216 | 0·63 |
| Cornwall | 390 | 0·35 |
| Cumbria | 1,558 | 1·13 |
| Derbyshire | 538 | 0·20 |
| Devon | 3,896 | 1·58 |
| Dorset | 1,479 | 1·04 |
| Durham | 381 | 0·24 |
| East Sussex | 725 | 0·46 |
| Essex | 2,251 | 0·57 |
| Gloucestershire | 2,182 | 1·64 |
| Hampshire | 4,586 | 1·16 |
| Hereford and Worcester | 1,007 | 0·62 |

| Local education authority | Total expenditure on discretionary awards | |
| --- | --- | --- |
| | (i) (£000's) | (ii) As per cent. of total net expenditure on education |
| Hertfordshire | 1,442 | 0·53 |
| Humberside | 2,500 | 0·97 |
| Isle of Wight | 330 | 1·08 |
| Kent | 3,702 | 1·06 |
| Lancashire | 2,547 | 0·65 |
| Leicestershire | 3,463 | 1·32 |
| Lincolnshire | 1,388 | 1·01 |
| Norfolk | 988 | 0·58 |
| North Yorkshire | 3,341 | 1·96 |
| Northamptonshire | 845 | 0·53 |
| Northumberland | 400 | 0·49 |
| Nottinghamshire | 1,305 | 0·43 |
| Oxfordshire | 957 | 0·65 |
| Salop | 1,202 | 1·12 |
| Somerset | 546 | 0·48 |
| Staffordshire | 1,232 | 0·43 |
| Suffolk | 1,818 | 1·20 |
| Surrey | 1,126 | 0·51 |
| Warwickshire | 1,125 | 0·90 |
| West Sussex | 364 | 0·26 |
| Wiltshire | 1,094 | 0·78 |

## Further Education

**Mr. Wall:** To ask the Secretary of State for Education and Science how much each of the local authorities in England and Wales spend on further education as a percentage of their total budget.

**Mr. Jackson:** Information in the form requested is not available. According to returns made to the Department of the Environment by local education authorities in England the percentage of the total net expenditure on Education spent on maintained establishments of further education other than polytechnics in 1987-88, the latest year for which actual expenditure is available, was as given in the table. The figures include the expenditure incurred on higher education within the other maintained establishments. Nationally, this represented some 20 per cent. of the total.

Figures for Wales are the responsibility of my right hon. Friend the Secretary of State for Wales.

*Net Expenditure on other Maintained Establishments of Further Education as a Percentage of Total Net Expenditure on Education*

| Local Education Authority | Percentage |
| --- | --- |
| Barking | 7·9 |
| Barnet | n/a |
| Bexley | 7·7 |
| Brent | 10·8 |
| Bromley | 10·7 |
| Croydon | 10·8 |
| Ealing | n/a |
| Enfield | 9·4 |
| Haringey | n/a |
| Harrow | 21·8 |
| Havering | 7·6 |
| Hillingdon | 4·4 |
| Hounslow | n/a |
| Kingston-upon-Thames | 11·1 |
| Merton | 12·1 |
| Newham | n/a |
| Redbridge | 4·1 |
| Richmond-upon-Thames | 21·4 |
| Sutton | 8·8 |
| Waltham Forest | 8·6 |
| ILEA | 12·1 |

| Local Education Authority | Percentage |
| --- | --- |
| Birmingham | 8·0 |
| Coventry | 10·2 |
| Dudley | 14·6 |
| Sandwell | 13·8 |
| Solihull | 11·4 |
| Walsall | 7·8 |
| Wolverhampton | n/a |
| Knowsley | 6·3 |
| Liverpool | 10·3 |
| St. Helens | 12·9 |
| Sefton | 9·0 |
| Wirral | 12·0 |
| Bolton | 16·2 |
| Bury | 10·2 |
| Manchester | 11·9 |
| Oldham | 9·2 |
| Rochdale | 6·0 |
| Salford | n/a |
| Stockport | 10·9 |
| Tameside | 8·6 |
| Trafford | 12·2 |
| Wigan | 13·7 |
| Barnsley | 7·0 |
| Doncaster | 9·7 |
| Rotherham | 10·7 |
| Sheffield | n/a |
| Bradford | 12·1 |
| Calderdale | 6·2 |
| Kirklees | 9·5 |
| Leeds | 7·8 |
| Wakefield | 13·2 |
| Gateshead | 7·8 |
| Newcastle-upon-Tyne | 8·9 |
| North Tyneside | n/a |
| South Tyneside | 14·6 |
| Sunderland | 6·4 |
| Avon | 10·5 |
| Bedfordshire | 13·4 |
| Berkshire | n/a |
| Buckinghamshire | 10·4 |
| Cambridgeshire | 13·2 |
| Cheshire | 11·5 |
| Cleveland | 9·5 |
| Cornwall | 11·2 |
| Cumbria | 9·9 |
| Derbyshire | 8·6 |
| Devon | 12·6 |
| Dorset | 16·0 |
| Durham | 9·6 |
| East Sussex | 9·3 |
| Essex | 10·3 |
| Gloucestershire | 14·1 |
| Hampshire | 13·5 |
| Hereford and Worcester | 14·4 |
| Hertfordshire | 12·1 |
| Humberside | 12·7 |
| Isle of Wight | 10·3 |
| Kent | 9·0 |
| Lancashire | 11·7 |
| Leicestershire | 9·0 |
| Lincolnshire | 9·2 |
| Norfolk | 10·4 |
| North Yorkshire | 8·7 |
| Northamptonshire | 11·5 |
| Northumberland | 5·5 |
| Nottinghamshire | 8·6 |
| Oxfordshire | 9·9 |
| Salop | 9·6 |
| Somerset | 14·6 |
| Staffordshire | 9·4 |
| Suffolk | 9·7 |
| Surrey | 11·1 |
| Warwickshire | 12·6 |
| West Sussex | 9·8 |
| Wiltshire | 14·3 |
| England Total | 10·8 |

**Mr. Wall:** To ask the Secretary of State for Education and Science how much was spent in England and Wales on further education in each year from 1979 to 1989.

**Mr. Jackson:** The information requested in respect of spending on further education, formerly non-advanced further education, in England, is set out in the table. The corresponding figures for Wales are a matter for my right hon. Friend the Secretary of State for Wales.

| Financial year | Cash (net) £ million |
|---|---|
| 1979-80 | 546 |
| 1980-81 | 688 |
| 1981-82 | 790 |
| 1982-83 | 878 |
| 1983-84 | 931 |
| 1984-85 | 998 |
| 1985-86 | 979 |
| 1986-87 | 1,054 |
| 1987-88 | 1,148 |
| [1]1988-89 | 1,225 |

[1] Provisional outturn spending.

**Mr. Wall:** To ask the Secretary of State for Education and Science what information he has on how many further education colleges in total and as a percentage of all further education colleges have *(a)* subsidised creche facilities for students, *(b)* free creche facilities for students, *(c)* no creche facilities for students, *(d)* subsidised meals for students, *(e)* sabbatical officers of student unions and *(f)* a student union office.

**Mr. Jackson:** No information is held centrally on the number of further education institutions providing creche facilities, subsidised meals or a student union office. Although we have no record of the total number of sabbatical officers, the DES survey of student unions suggested that it is unusual for mainstream further education colleges to have sabbatical officers.

## YTS Trainees

**Mr. Wall:** To ask the Secretary of State for Education and Science if he will list in the *Official Report* the number of YTS trainees based in further education colleges *(a)* in total at any one time, *(b)* five days a week for the duration of the academic year, *(c)* five days a week for a limited period, for example, one term, *(d)* two to three days a week for the duration of the academic year, *(e)* two to three days a week for a limited period and *(f)* one day a week on day release.

**Mr. Jackson:** My right hon. Friend the Secretary of State for Employment is responsible for administering and funding YTS programmes. The information available for the number of trainees in public further education colleges in England on 1 November 1987 (the latest year for which information is available) is as follows:

| | Thousands |
|---|---|
| Total | 141 |
| | |
| Trainees attending full-time for the duration of the course | 42 |
| Other trainees | 99 |

## University Funding

**Mr. McLoughlin:** To ask the Secretary of State for Education and Science what arrangements have been made to wind up the University Grants Committee following the assumption from 1 April of full funding responsibilities by the Universities Funding Council.

**Mr. Kenneth Baker:** The terms of office of the last members of the University Grants Committee expired on 31 March. To allow for the orderly winding-up of the UGC's affairs, the secretariat will continue to have an existence until 14 July 1989, exactly 70 years after the committee's inception. I take this opportunity to pay tribute to the way members and officers of the committee have, over that long period, discharged their responsibilities to help steer our universities steadily through periods of great change.

## SOCIAL SECURITY

### Incomes

**Mr. Lester:** To ask the Secretary of State for Social Security what are his latest estimates of the median weekly incomes, net and gross, of couples with *(a)* one child aged under five years, *(b)* single pensioners aged 75 years or over and *(c)* couples with one child under 16 years.

**Mr. Peter Lloyd:** The information is set out as follows:

*Median net and gross weekly incomes in 1986*

| | Net £ | Gross £ |
|---|---|---|
| Single pensioner aged 75 or over | 59 | 60 |
| Couples with (just) one child aged under five | 171 | 209 |
| Couples with (just) one child aged under 16 | 186 | 239 |

*Notes:*

1. Gross income is defined as income from all sources (earnings, benefits, investment and other income).

2. Net income is defined as gross income from all sources less income tax and national insurance.

3. The median is defined as the middle case in the distribution. Half the number of cases fall below the median and half above.

4. These figures are derived from the family expenditure survey. The figures may, therefore be subject to sampling errors.

5. Figures are given in cash terms rounded to the nearest £1.

### Income Support

**Mr. Sheerman:** To ask the Secretary of State for Social Security (1) what action is being taken to ensure that adjudication officers are aware of the relevant case law in relation to suspension of income support through claimant's misconduct or leaving without good cause;

(2) what guidance he issues to his officials with regard to 26 weeks being the maximum figure for disqualification from income support on the grounds of misconduct or leaving without good cause, and not the standard figure.

**Mr. Peter Lloyd:** Written guidance, which takes account of relevant case law, is given to adjudication officers by the chief adjudication officer in paragraphs 28901-28966 of the adjudication officers' guide. The adjudication officers' guide is published by Her Majesty's Stationery Office. A copy is in the Library.

**Mr. Sheerman:** To ask the Secretary of State for Social Security what is the average length of disqualification from income support for claimants who have lost their job through their misconduct, or leaving without good cause.

**Mr. Peter Lloyd:** No one is disqualified from receiving income support because they have either lost a job through their misconduct or left it voluntarily without just cause. In such cases the claimant's personal level of income support is reduced—usually by 40 per cent. but by 20 per cent. if the claimant or a member of the family is seriously ill or pregnant and the family has less than £200 in savings. The average length of such reductions could be obtained only at disproportionate cost.

**Mr. Blunkett:** To ask the Secretary of State for Social Security if he will make a statement on the rates bill estimates used to calculate the adjustments made in income support to cover claimants' 20 per cent. liability.

**Mr. Peter Lloyd:** The calculations in April 1988 were based on details of rates paid by housing benefit recipients in 1986 uprated to estimated 1988-89 levels. Income support levels were further adjusted from April this year to include help towards the minimum 20 per cent. contribution to the community charge that recipients would be expected to pay. The amounts included continue to provide help towards the minimum contribution to domestic rates for people living in England and Wales.

**Mr. Blunkett:** To ask the Secretary of State for Social Security what is the average domestic rates bill in England and Wales for 1989-90 of people in receipt of income support.

**Mr. Peter Lloyd:** I regret that this information is not available.

### Family Credit

**Mr. Hardy:** To ask the Secretary of State for Social Security what proportion of claims for family credit were approved and resulted in payment of this allowance since 1 March; and what proportion of those claims resulted in payment of £2 per week or more.

**Mr. Peter Lloyd:** A total of 58·9 per cent. of claims decided from 1 March 1989 to 16 June 1989 have been successful.

Information about the proportion of these claims where the award was £2 a week or more is not available, but 97·6 per cent. of all families receiving family credit on 18 June were receiving £2 a week or more.

## PRIME MINISTER

### Abortion

**Ms. Richardson:** To ask the Prime Minister (1) if she will publish in the *Official Report* a copy of the letter she sent to a Pro-Life group about the Government's intention to allow a clause on the upper time limit for abortion to be added when the Warnock Bill is introduced;

(2) what response she has given to the letter she was sent by a local anti-abortion group claiming that 12,000 abortion notification forms are returned each year with no medical condition recorded.

**The Prime Minister:** On the basis of the information in the questions I regret that I am not able to identify the correspondence mentioned.

### European Community Directives

**Mr. Teddy Taylor:** To ask the Prime Minister if she will outline the arrangements made for the Cabinet Office to co-ordinate the consideration of European Economic Community directives; when the arrangement was established; what existing procedures within Government have been replaced; and if he will make a statement.

**The Prime Minister:** The Cabinet Office provides support to the Cabinet and its committees on European Community issues as it does in all other key areas of Government business. A European secretariat was established in 1973 within the Cabinet Office specifically to handle Community issues and under the direction of Ministers to co-ordinate the United Kingdom's approach to the Community. Its work includes ensuring that all Community developments of importance are examined in good time; that policy is co-ordinated between the relevant Departments; and that the processes required to facilitate parliamentary scrutiny of Community legislation are properly observed by Departments.

### Rain Forests

**Mr. Dalyell:** To ask the Prime Minister pursuant to her reply of 8 June, *Official Report,* column 368, if she will give details of the beneficial measures that Her Majesty's Government are taking in relation to the rain forests.

**The Prime Minister:** Details of the Overseas Development Administration's activities to protect rain forests are given in a supplement to the December 1988 issue of "British Overseas Development", copies of which are in the Library. More recent activities were described by my hon. Friend the Minister for Overseas Development on 23 May, at columns *932-936.* Following a visit by a team of British experts my hon. Friend hopes to reach outline agreement on a package of environmental and forestry assistance when he visits Brazil in July. We are discussing the provision of technical co-operation in the forestry sector with the Indonesian Government and sent a mission on a successful visit last month.

### European Community (Contributions)

**Mr. Teddy Taylor:** To ask the Prime Minister if she will raise at the next meeting of the European Council the issue of the size of the net contributions made to the European Economic Community by the various member states; and if she will make a statement.

**The Prime Minister:** No. The review of the Community's finances concluded at the European Council in Brussels on 11-13 February 1988 confirmed the arrangements for abating the United Kingdom's contributions. The Fontainebleau mechanism remains totally intact; and it will last as long as the new own resources arrangements, reducing the United Kingdom's payments to the Community by over £1·3 billion in 1989-90.

## HEALTH

### Trent Regional Health Authority

**Mr. Redmond:** To ask the Secretary of State for Health if, pursuant to his answer of 2 March, *Official Report,* column *314,* to the hon. Member for Don Valley, he can now make an announcement as to which other hospitals in the Trent regional health authority are to be involved in the resource management initiative.

**Mr. Freeman:** I announced on 20 March the names of 50 hospitals which have been chosen to prepare for resource management in the coming months.

Those hospitals in the Trent regional health authority are listed as follows:

| Hospital | District |
| --- | --- |
| Chesterfield and North Derbyshire Royal Hospital | North Derbyshire |
| Glenfield Hospital | Leicester |
| City Hospital | Nottingham |
| Royal Infirmary | Doncaster |
| Northern General Hospital | Sheffield |
| Children's Hospital | Sheffield |

### General Practitioners

**Mr. Hind:** To ask the Secretary of State for Health whether there will be any implications for the doctor-patient relationship arising from the increased capitation element in the general practitioners' contract.

**Mr. Mellor:** By increasing the proportion of GPs' income which comes from capitation payments, we will be encouraging greater competition in the family doctor service. This will ensure a better service for patients by giving GPs a greater incentive to provide the best possible range and quality of services geared to patients' needs. As a result, the relationship between doctor and patient will be improved.

### North Western RHA

**Mr. Jack:** To ask the Secretary of State for Health when he last met the Chairman of the North Western regional health authority; and what matters were discussed.

**Mr. Kenneth Clarke:** I last met the chairmen of regional health authorities, including the chairman of the North Western regional health authority on 17 May 1989. Topics discussed included management of the service and implementation of the White Paper "Working for Patients". I have had no recent separate discussions with the chairman of the North Western regional health authority. My hon. and learned Friend the Minister for Health and my hon. Friend the Parliamentary Under-Secretary of State both met the chairman of the North Western regional health authority on 19 June, and discussed health authority appointments and a capital project issue.

### Prescription Charges

**Mr. David Nicholson:** To ask the Secretary of State for Health why applications for exemption from prescription charges are now centralised through Newcastle; when this new system was introduced; what representations he has received about its functioning; and if he will make a statement.

**Mr. Mellor:** In line with a recommendation of an efficiency scrutiny, all claims for exemption from prescription and other NHS charges on low income grounds have, since 11 April 1988, been dealt with centrally by the agency benefits unit of the Department of Social Security which administers the scheme on our behalf. Operational matters are the responsibility of that Department. On other matters the Secretary of State has received one parliamentary question, 17 letters from Members of Parliament and two letters from members of the public referring specifically to exemption from prescription charges.

### Stored Blood

**Mr. Spearing:** To ask the Secretary of State for Health what steps he is taking, what research he is supporting, and what sums from the estimates approved by Parliament for the current year are being expended in respect of the extension of the usable life of stored blood.

**Mr. Freeman:** The use of improved anti-coagulants since 1981 has extended the usable life of whole blood to 35 days under standard conditions. Experience has shown that this is adequate to ensure that most blood can be used before it reaches its expiry date. In the case of rare blood groups it is possible and worthwhile to extend the usable life further by freezing, and facilities to freeze and store red blood cells have been set up at some regional transfusion centres. The Department is not currently supporting any research on further developments to extend the usable life of stored blood.

### Consultations (Waiting Time)

**Mr. Pike:** To ask the Secretary of State for Health if his Department will undertake a study into the waiting time to see a consultant following referral by a general practitioner.

**Mr. Mellor:** We have no plans to mount a special study, although we do intend to begin to collect, for the first time, information about out-patient waiting lists and times. In and out-patient waiting times in the 22 districts with serious waiting problems are already being investigated by a team of management consultants. Under the waiting list initiative regional health authorities have been asked to agree with their district targets for reducing waiting times for out-patient treatment.

### Doncaster Community Health Council

**Mr. Redmond:** To ask the Secretary of State for Health if he will list by name and nominating organisation, the current serving members of the Doncaster community health council.

**Mr. Mellor:** We do not hold this information centrally. It is contained in Doncaster community health council's register of members which the hon. Member can inspect at all reasonable hours at thier offices.

### Hospitals (Flowers)

**Mr. Redmond:** To ask the Secretary of State for Health what has been the cost to the Trent regional health authority during the current financial year of supplying (a) plastic flowers and (b) natural cut flowers, to hospital wards and other establishments.

**Mr. Freeman:** This information is not collected centrally. I suggest that the hon. Member contacts the chairman of Trent regional health authority for the information he seeks.

## Physicists

**Mr. Hardy:** To ask the Secretary of State for Health what information he has as to which health authorities currently experience difficulties in the maintenance of services involving adequate staffing of graduate physicists.

**Mr. Mellor:** We do not hold this information centrally.

## Margaret Pyke Centre

**Sir Charles Morrison:** To ask the Secretary of State for Health if he is now in a position to make a statement about the future funding of the Margaret Pyke centre.

**Mr. Freeman:** In recognition of its role as a national centre of training family planning doctors and nurses and its work in preventing the spread of AIDS I am discussing with North East Thames regional health authority ways of making up the shortfall of £100,000 which would otherwise have arisen in its funding this financial year. These steps are being taken as an interim arrangement before the new funding arrangements proposed in "Working for Patients" comes into operation in 1991-92. There will be further discussions with the region about funding arrangements for 1990-91.

## Childhood Cancer

**Sir Michael McNair-Wilson:** To ask the Secretary of State for Health when the report by the Committee on Medical Aspects of Radiation in the Environment on the incidence of childhood cancer in the West Berkshire and North Hampshire area will be published.

**Mr. Freeman:** The report has been published today and copies placed in the Library. The committee concludes that there is a small but statistically significant increase in the incidence of childhood leukaemias and other childhood cancers in the vicinity of the atomic weapons establishments at Aldermaston and Burghfield in Berkshire. In the committee's judgment, the authorised and accidental radioactive discharges from these two sites, and from the United Kingdom Atomic Energy Authority's establishment at Harwell, Oxfordshire, are far too low to account for the observed increase in childhood cancer incidence in the area. COMARE has considered a number of possible explanations for its findings, including other mechanisms by which radiation may be involved, but the committee's view is that there is insufficient evidence to point to any one particular explanation and it is possible that a combination of factors may be involved.

More generally, the committee states that
"the findings set out in this report, taken with those in previous reports, indicate that there is a statistically significant increase in the incidence of childhood leukaemia in the vicinities of Sellafield, Dounreay and Aldermaston and Burghfield".
Although the committee cannot exclude completely the possibility that these observations are due to chance, or due to the selection of sites referred to them for consideration, it concludes that these findings warrant further investigation.

COMARE has recommended that studies of the geographical distribution of childhood cancer incidence on a nationwide basis be carried out (recommendation 4). In relation to sites not so far examined by COMARE, the committee has stated that

"We consider it unlikely that useful information will emerge from further detailed investigations of alleged childhood cancer incidence around individual nuclear installations".

COMARE has pointed out that such investigations would be difficult to interpret until the results of national studies of childhood cancer incidence, referred to in recommendation 4 of the report, are available. Once the results of these national studies are available, COMARE has recommended that it be asked to participate in a review of the evidence relating to the incidence of childhood cancer and nuclear installations (recommendation 5).

COMARE's other recommendations relate to:

The case-control study in West Berkshire and North Hampshire, which is already underway (recommendation 1);

Studies of any possible effects on the health of children of employees at the nuclear installations studied by COMARE (recommendation 2);

Improvements to the national cancer registration scheme (recommendation 3).

The Government are grateful to the committee for its comprehensive report and accepts all the recommendations made for further work. The case-control study of childhood cancer in west Berkshire and north Hampshire, is already underway and is being funded by the Department. This study will aim to identify possible factors which may have contributed to the excess incidence of childhood cancer in the area.

## Abortion Agencies

**Ms. Richardson:** To ask the Secretary of State for Health whether he will list all agencies which are currently licensed by his Department to counsel or refer women for abortions; what are the names of the owners; and whether they are run by a registered charity.

**Mr. Freeman:** The information is as follows:

| *Pregnancy Advisory Bureaux* | *Name of Proprietor* |
| --- | --- |
| British Pregnancy Advisory Service Basingstoke Branch Church Grange Health Centre Bramleys Drive Basingstoke RG21 1QN | British Pregnancy Advisory Service[1] |
| Birmingham Pregnancy Consultation Service 848 Bristol Road Selly Oak Birmingham B29 6HW | Fraterdrive (PAS) Ltd. |
| British Pregnancy Advisory Service Birmingham Branch Guildhall Buildings Navigation Street Birmingham B2 4BT | British Pregnancy Advisory Service[1] |
| Blackpool Pregnancy Testing and Counselling Centre Stanley Buildings 3 Caunce Street Blackpool | Sister Rose Ltd. |
| British Pregnancy Advisory Service Bournemouth (Pelhams) Branch Pelhams Clinic Millhams Road Bournemouth | British Pregnancy Advisory Service[1] |

| Pregnancy Advisory Bureaux | Name of Proprietor |
|---|---|
| British Pregnancy Advisory Service<br>Bournemouth (Dean Park) Branch<br>23 Ophir Road<br>Bournemouth | British Pregnancy<br>Advisory Service[1] |
| British Pregnancy Advisory Service<br>Brighton Branch<br>Wistons Site<br>Chatsworth Road<br>Brighton<br>Sussex BN1 5PA | British Pregnancy<br>Advisory Service[1] |
| British Pregnancy Advisory Service<br>Chester Branch<br>98A Foregate Street<br>Chester CH1 1HB | British Pregnancy<br>Advisory Service[1] |
| British Pregnancy Advisory Service<br>Coventry Branch<br>Coundon Health Clinic<br>Baker Butts Lane<br>Coventry | British Pregnancy<br>Advisory Service[1] |
| British Pregnancy Advisory Service<br>Doncaster Branch<br>The Bungalow<br>1a Avenue Road<br>Doncaster<br>South Yorkshire | British Pregnancy<br>Advisory Service[1] |
| Rosslyn<br>17 Rosslyn Road<br>East Twickenham<br>Middlesex<br>TW1 2AR | Pregnancy Advisory<br>Service Ltd.[1] |
| Sister Rose Pregnancy Advisory Centre<br>(Hull)<br>139 Beverley Road<br>Hull | Sister Rose Ltd. |
| British Pregnancy Advisory Service<br>Hull Branch<br>32 Beverley Road<br>Hull HU3 1YF | British Pregnancy<br>Advisory Service[1] |
| British Pregnancy Advisory Service<br>Leeds Branch<br>8 The Headrow<br>Leeds<br>Yorkshire | British Pregnancy<br>Advisory Service[1] |
| Sister Rose Pregnancy Advisory Centre<br>(Leeds)<br>4 Albion Street<br>Leeds 1 | Sister Rose Ltd. |
| Marie Stopes Centre<br>10 Queens Square<br>Leeds 2 | Population Services[1]<br>FP Programmes<br>Ltd. |
| British Pregnancy Advisory Service<br>Liverpool Branch<br>20-22 Rodney Street<br>Liverpool L1 2TQ | British Pregnancy<br>Advisory Service[1] |
| Pregnancy Advisory Service<br>Fourth Floor<br>Hepworth Chambers<br>Church Street<br>Liverpool L1 3BG | Fraterdrive (PAS) Ltd. |
| British Pregnancy Advisory Service<br>London Branch<br>7 Belgrave Road<br>London SW1 | British Pregnancy<br>Advisory Service[1] |

| Pregnancy Advisory Bureaux | Name of Proprietor |
|---|---|
| Birth Control and Pregnancy Counselling<br>10 Coptic Street<br>London WC1 | Population Services<br>FP[1] Programmes<br>Ltd. |
| London Youth Advisory Centre<br>26 Prince of Wales Road<br>London NW5 | London Youth<br>Advisory Centre |
| Metropolitan Pregnancy Control Centre<br>40 Mortimer Street<br>London W1 | Population Services<br>FP Programmes<br>Ltd.[1] |
| Pregnancy Advisory Service<br>11-13 Charlotte Street<br>London W1 | Pregnancy Advisory<br>Service Ltd.[1] |
| Preterm<br>40 Mortimer Street<br>London W1N 7RB | Population Services[1]<br>FP Programmes<br>Ltd. |
| The Well Woman Centre<br>Marie Stopes House<br>108 Whitfield Street<br>London W1 | Population Services[1]<br>FP Programmes<br>Ltd. |
| The Well Woman Centre<br>114 Whitfield Street<br>London W1 | Population Services[1]<br>FP Programmes<br>Ltd. |
| Pregnancy and Gynaecological<br>Advisory Service<br>26 Fouberts Place<br>London W1N 1HG | Detingen Ltd. |
| British Pregnancy Advisory Service<br>Luton Branch<br>3A Upper George Street<br>Luton LU1 2QY | British Pregnancy<br>Advisory Service[1] |
| British Pregnancy Advisory Service<br>Manchester Branch<br>Suite F, Ground Floor<br>Fourways House<br>57 Hilton Street<br>Manchester M1 2EJ | British Pregnancy<br>Advisory Service[1] |
| Marie Stopes<br>1 Police Street<br>Manchester M2 7LQ | Population Services[1]<br>FP Programmes<br>Ltd. |
| Pregnancy Advisory Service—Manchester<br>5th Floor<br>Newton Buildings<br>Newton Street<br>Manchester M1 2EJ | Fraterdrive (PAS) Ltd. |
| Sister Rose Pregnancy<br>Advisory Centre (Manchester)<br>Fifth Floor<br>2 St. John Street<br>Manchester 3 | Sister Rose Ltd. |
| British Pregnancy Advisory Service<br>Milton Keynes Branch<br>First Floor<br>Eaglestone Health Centre<br>Standing Way<br>Milton Keynes MK6 5AZ | British Pregnancy<br>Advisory Service[1] |
| East Midland Pregnancy Advisory<br>Service<br>The Grange<br>1 Private Road<br>Sherwood<br>Nottingham | East Midlands<br>Pregnancy<br>Advisory Service<br>Ltd. |

| Pregnancy Advisory Bureaux | Name of Proprietor |
|---|---|
| British Pregnancy Advisory Service<br>Sheffield Branch<br>160 Charles Street<br>Sheffield S1 2NE | British Pregnancy<br>Advisory Service [1] |
| 408 Young People's Consultation<br>Centre Ltd.<br>408 Ecclesall Road<br>Sheffield S11 8PJ | 408 Young People's<br>Consultation<br>Centre Ltd. |
| Pregnancy Advisory Service<br>1A George Street<br>Newcastle-under-Lyme<br>Staffordshire | Dalreagh Nursing<br>Home Ltd. |
| British Pregnancy Advisory Service<br>Swindon Branch<br>Carfax Street Health Clinic<br>Carfax Street<br>Swindon | British Pregnancy<br>Advisory Service[1] |
| British Pregnancy Advisory Service<br>Leamington Spa Branch<br>Holly Walk Welfare Clinic<br>Holly Walk<br>Leamington Spa<br>Warwickshire | British Pregnancy<br>Advisory Service[1] |
| Sister Rose Pregnancy Advisory Centre<br>(Wolverhampton)<br>Second Floor<br>19-21 Queen Street<br>Wolverhampton | Sister Rose Ltd. |
| Marie Stopes Centre<br>North London PAB<br>65 Shoot up Hill<br>London NW2 | Dr. G. Richman<br>Dr. M. Oliver<br>Dr. S. Mitchley |
| Marie Stopes Centre<br>Gosburyhill Health Centre<br>Orchard Gardens<br>Chessington<br>Surrey<br>KT9 2EU | Dr. S. V. Nathan |

| Pregnancy Advisory Bureaux | Name of Proprietor |
|---|---|
| Marie Stopes Centre<br>The Surgery<br>32 Devon Road<br>South Darenth<br>Dartford<br>Kent<br>DA4 9AB | Dr. G. Dunckley |
| Options<br>Population Control Clinic<br>45 Fitzwilliam Street<br>Huddersfield<br>HD1 5LG | Care Incorporated<br>Clinic Ltd. |
| Pregnancy Advisory Service—Blackpool<br>93A Abingdon Street<br>Blackpool<br>FY1 1PP | Fraterdrive (PAS) Ltd. |
| Pregnancy Advisory Service—Leicester<br>120A Granby Street<br>Leicester | Fraterdrive (PAS) Ltd. |
| Regents Park Clinic<br>184 Gloucester Place<br>London<br>NW1 6DS | Mrs. B. A. Binding |

[1] Registered Charities.

## Pregnancy Statistics

**Ms. Richardson:** To ask the Secretary of State for Health whether he will list *(a)* the total number and rate of pregnancies to girls aged 16, 15, 14, 13, 12, 11 and 10 years for each of the years 1970 to 1988, respectively, *(b)* the figures broken down into stillbirths, livebirths and abortions and *(c)* the total figure and rate for pregnancies to all girls aged 15 years and under for each of those years.

**Mr. Freeman:** The information requested is given in the table. All pregnancies of women usually resident in England and Wales which led to a maternity or termination by abortion under the 1967 Act are included (pregnancies which led to spontaneous abortions are not included). The latest figures which are available relate to conceptions which occurred during 1986.

| Year and age at conception | Number of conceptions | Rate per 1,000 girls in age-group | Outcome of conceptions | | | |
|---|---|---|---|---|---|---|
| | | | Maternities[3] | | | Legal abortion[4] |
| | | | Total | Live | Still | |
| *1970* | | | | | | |
| Under 11[1] | 2 | 0·0 | 1 | 1 | 0 | 1 |
| 11 | 14 | 0·0 | 8 | 7 | 1 | 6 |
| 12 | 51 | 0·1 | 24 | 22 | 2 | 27 |
| 13 | 312 | 0·9 | 160 | 157 | 3 | 152 |
| 14 | 1,446 | 4·5 | 842 | 823 | 19 | 604 |
| 15 | 5,888 | 18·4 | 4,223 | 4,181 | 42 | 1,665 |
| Total under 16[2] | 7,713 | 7·9 | 5,258 | 5,191 | 67 | 2,455 |
| 16 | 16,234 | 49·5 | 13,250 | 13,064 | 186 | 2,984 |
| *1971* | | | | | | |
| Under 11[1] | 2 | 0·0 | 2 | 1 | 1 | 0 |
| 11 | 6 | 0·0 | 2 | 2 | 0 | 4 |
| 12 | 41 | 0·1 | 17 | 17 | 0 | 24 |
| 13 | 302 | 0·9 | 158 | 157 | 1 | 144 |
| 14 | 1,763 | 5·3 | 952 | 938 | 14 | 811 |
| 15 | 6,711 | 20·5 | 4,444 | 4,390 | 54 | 2,267 |
| Total under 16[2] | 8,825 | 8·8 | 5,575 | 5,505 | 70 | 3,250 |
| 16 | 17,292 | 54·1 | 13,122 | 12,956 | 166 | 4,170 |

| Year and age at conception | Number of conceptions | Rate per 1,000 girls in age-group | Outcome of conceptions | | | |
|---|---|---|---|---|---|---|
| | | | | Maternities[3] | | Legal abortion[4] |
| | | | Total | Live | Still | |
| *1972* | | | | | | |
| Under 11[1] | 1 | 0·0 | 1 | 1 | 0 | 0 |
| 11 | 2 | 0·0 | 1 | 1 | 0 | 1 |
| 12 | 40 | 0·1 | 23 | 22 | 1 | 17 |
| 13 | 349 | 1·0 | 169 | 167 | 2 | 180 |
| 14 | 1,874 | 5·4 | 950 | 934 | 16 | 924 |
| 15 | 7,342 | 21·9 | 4,535 | 4,471 | 64 | 2,807 |
| Total under 16[2] | 9,606 | 9·3 | 5,679 | 5,596 | 83 | 3,929 |
| 16 | 17,612 | 53·5 | 12,607 | 12,476 | 131 | 5,005 |
| *1973* | | | | | | |
| Under 11[1] | 1 | 0·0 | 0 | 0 | 0 | 1 |
| 11 | 12 | 0·0 | 4 | 4 | 0 | 8 |
| 12 | 38 | 0·1 | 20 | 18 | 2 | 18 |
| 13 | 345 | 0·9 | 156 | 153 | 3 | 189 |
| 14 | 1,987 | 5·6 | 963 | 950 | 13 | 1,024 |
| 15 | 7,409 | 21·4 | 4,249 | 4,197 | 52 | 3,160 |
| Total under 16[2] | 9,792 | 9·2 | 5,392 | 5,322 | 70 | 4,400 |
| 16 | 18,034 | 53·4 | 12,419 | 12,282 | 137 | 5,615 |

[1] Rate per 1,000 girls aged 10.
[2] Rate per 1,000 girls aged 13-15.
[3] maternities which result in one or more live or still births are counted only once. Such multiple birth maternities are classified as "live" if at least one live birth is included and "still" if all the births are stillbirths.
[4] Legal terminations under 1967 Abortion Act.

| Year and age at conception | Number of conceptions | Rate per 1,000 girls in age-group | Outcome of conceptions | | | |
|---|---|---|---|---|---|---|
| | | | | Maternities[3] | | Legal abortion[4] |
| | | | Total | Live | Still | |
| *1974* | | | | | | |
| Under 11[1] | 0 | 0·0 | 0 | 0 | 0 | 0 |
| 11 | 5 | 0·0 | 4 | 4 | 0 | 1 |
| 12 | 45 | 0·1 | 24 | 24 | 0 | 21 |
| 13 | 343 | 0·9 | 157 | 155 | 2 | 186 |
| 14 | 1,922 | 5·3 | 878 | 862 | 16 | 1,044 |
| 15 | 7,056 | 19·8 | 3,780 | 3,731 | 49 | 3,276 |
| Total under 16[2] | 9,371 | 8·5 | 4,843 | 4,776 | 67 | 4,528 |
| 16 | 16,553 | 47·6 | 10,722 | 10,603 | 119 | 5,831 |
| *1975* | | | | | | |
| Under 11[1] | 1 | 0·0 | 1 | 1 | 0 | 0 |
| 11 | 6 | 0·0 | 2 | 2 | 0 | 4 |
| 12 | 45 | 0·1 | 23 | 22 | 1 | 22 |
| 13 | 349 | 0·9 | 133 | 132 | 1 | 216 |
| 14 | 1,919 | 5·1 | 837 | 831 | 6 | 1,082 |
| 15 | 6,861 | 18·8 | 3,398 | 3,359 | 39 | 3,463 |
| Total under 16[2] | 9,181 | 8·1 | 4,394 | 4,347 | 47 | 4,787 |
| 16 | 15,278 | 42·8 | 9,447 | 9,339 | 108 | 5,831 |
| *1976* | | | | | | |
| Under 11[1] | 1 | 0·0 | 1 | 0 | 1 | 0 |
| 11 | 8 | 0·0 | 2 | 2 | 0 | 6 |
| 12 | 37 | 0·1 | 14 | 14 | 0 | 23 |
| 13 | 331 | 0·8 | 136 | 134 | 2 | 195 |
| 14 | 1,898 | 4·9 | 782 | 771 | 11 | 1,116 |
| 15 | 6,916 | 18·2 | 3,363 | 3,321 | 42 | 3,553 |
| Total under 16[2] | 9,191 | 7·9 | 4,298 | 4,242 | 56 | 4,893 |
| 16 | 14,567 | 39·7 | 8,761 | 8,661 | 100 | 5,806 |
| *1977* | | | | | | |
| Under 11[1] | 1 | 0·0 | 1 | 1 | 0 | 0 |
| 11 | 7 | 0·0 | 1 | 1 | 0 | 6 |
| 12 | 37 | 0·1 | 14 | 14 | 0 | 23 |

| Year and age at conception | Number of conceptions | Rate per 1,000 girls in age-group | Outcome of conceptions | | | |
| | | | Maternities[3] | | | Legal abortion[4] |
| | | | Total | Live | Still | |
| 13 | 331 | 0·8 | 122 | 121 | 1 | 209 |
| 14 | 1,916 | 4·9 | 792 | 775 | 17 | 1,124 |
| 15 | 6,711 | 17·2 | 3,296 | 3,259 | 37 | 3,415 |
| Total under 16[2] | 9,003 | 7·6 | 4,226 | 4,171 | 55 | 4,777 |
| 16 | 14,940 | 39·1 | 8,895 | 8,7882 | 107 | 6,045 |

[1] Rate per 1,000 girls aged 10.
[2] Rate per 1,000 girls aged 13-15.
[3] Maternities which result in one or more live or still births are counted only once. Such multiple birth maternities are classified as "live" if at least one live birth is included and "still" if all the births are stillbirths.
[4] Legal terminations under 1967 Abortion Act.

| Year and age at conception | Number of conceptions | Rate per 1,000 girls in age-group | Outcome of conceptions | | | |
| | | | Maternities[3] | | | Legal abortion[4] |
| | | | Total | Live | Still | |
| *1978* | | | | | | |
| Under 11[1] | 3 | 0·0 | 2 | 2 | 0 | 1 |
| 11 | 8 | 0·0 | 1 | 1 | 0 | 7 |
| 12 | 43 | 0·1 | 18 | 18 | 0 | 25 |
| 13 | 341 | 0·8 | 142 | 140 | 2 | 199 |
| 14 | 1,822 | 4·5 | 810 | 803 | 7 | 1,012 |
| 15 | 6,886 | 17·5 | 3,439 | 3,410 | 29 | 3,447 |
| Total under 16[2] | 9,103 | 7·6 | 4,412 | 4,374 | 38 | 4,691 |
| 16 | 15,770 | 40·3 | 9,422 | 9,343 | 79 | 6,348 |
| *1979* | | | | | | |
| Under 11[1] | 7 | 0·0 | 5 | 5 | 0 | 2 |
| 11 | 16 | 0·0 | 7 | 7 | 0 | 9 |
| 12 | 39 | 0·1 | 16 | 15 | 1 | 23 |
| 13 | 319 | 0·8 | 116 | 115 | 1 | 203 |
| 14 | 1,904 | 4·7 | 760 | 756 | 4 | 1,144 |
| 15 | 6,823 | 16·8 | 3,175 | 3,153 | 22 | 3,648 |
| Total under 16[2] | 9,108 | 7·5 | 4,079 | 4,051 | 28 | 5,029 |
| 16 | 16,106 | 40·6 | 9,307 | 9,220 | 87 | 6,799 |
| *1980* | | | | | | |
| Under 11[1] | 14 | 0·0 | 11 | 0 | 11 | 3 |
| 11 | 5 | 0·0 | 2 | 0 | 2 | 3 |
| 12 | 35 | 0·1 | 13 | 0 | 13 | 22 |
| 13 | 298 | 0·8 | 99 | 0 | 99 | 199 |
| 14 | 1,714 | 4·3 | 669 | 6 | 663 | 1,045 |
| 15 | 6,513 | 16·0 | 3,140 | 3,107 | 33 | 3,373 |
| Total under 16[2] | 8,579 | 7·2 | 3,934 | 3,113 | 821 | 4,645 |
| 16 | 15,210 | 37·4 | 8,600 | 8,536 | 64 | 6,610 |
| *1981* | | | | | | |
| Under 11[1] | 3 | 0·0 | 0 | 0 | 0 | 3 |
| 11 | 11 | 0·0 | 3 | 3 | 0 | 8 |
| 12 | 65 | 0·2 | 22 | 21 | 1 | 43 |
| 13 | 356 | 0·9 | 146 | 145 | 1 | 210 |
| 14 | 1,817 | 4·6 | 684 | 682 | 2 | 1,133 |
| 15 | 6,309 | 15·8 | 2,839 | 2,811 | 28 | 3,470 |
| Total under 16[2] | 8,561 | 7·3 | 3,694 | 3,662 | 32 | 4,867 |
| 16 | 15,410 | 37·7 | 8,782 | 8,713 | 69 | 6,628 |

[1] Rate per 1,000 girls aged 10.
[2] Rate per 1,000 girls aged 13-15.
[3] Maternities which result in one or more live or still births are counted only once. Such multiple birth maternities are classified as "live" if at least one live birth is included and "still" if all the births are stillbirths.
[4] Legal terminations under 1967 Abortion Act.

| Year and age at conception | Number of conceptions | Rate per 1,000 girls in age-group | Outcome of conceptions | | | |
|---|---|---|---|---|---|---|
| | | | Maternities[3] | | | Legal abortion[4] |
| | | | Total | Live | Still | |
| *1982* | | | | | | |
| Under 11[1] | 0 | 0·0 | 0 | 0 | 0 | 0 |
| 11 | 4 | 0·0 | 2 | 2 | 0 | 2 |
| 12 | 39 | 0·1 | 15 | 15 | 0 | 24 |
| 13 | 385 | 1·0 | 121 | 120 | 1 | 264 |
| 14 | 1,868 | 4·9 | 702 | 693 | 9 | 1,166 |
| 15 | 6,703 | 17·1 | 3,035 | 3,013 | 22 | 3,668 |
| Total under 16[2] | 8,999 | 7·8 | 3,875 | 3,843 | 32 | 5,124 |
| 16 | 15,030 | 37·6 | 8,331 | 8,285 | 46 | 6,699 |
| *1983* | | | | | | |
| Under 11[1] | 0 | 0·0 | 0 | 0 | 0 | 0 |
| 11 | 3 | 0·0 | 3 | 3 | 0 | 0 |
| 12 | 29 | 0·1 | 12 | 12 | 0 | 17 |
| 13 | 335 | 0·9 | 133 | 133 | 0 | 202 |
| 14 | 2,034 | 5·4 | 790 | 781 | 9 | 1,244 |
| 15 | 6,968 | 18·3 | 3,108 | 3,085 | 23 | 3,860 |
| Total under 16[2] | 9,369 | 8·3 | 4,046 | 4,014 | 32 | 5,323 |
| 16 | 15,229 | 38·7 | 8,431 | 8,370 | 61 | 6,798 |
| *1984* | | | | | | |
| Under 11[1] | 1 | 0·0 | 0 | 0 | 0 | 1 |
| 11 | 1 | 0·0 | 1 | 1 | 0 | 0 |
| 12 | 30 | 0·1 | 15 | 15 | 0 | 15 |
| 13 | 346 | 0·9 | 135 | 135 | 0 | 211 |
| 14 | 2,018 | 5·5 | 794 | 790 | 4 | 1,224 |
| 15 | 7,253 | 19·1 | 3,333 | 3,312 | 21 | 3,920 |
| Total under 16[2] | 9,649 | 8·6 | 4,278 | 4,253 | 25 | 5,371 |
| 16 | 15,995 | 41·9 | 8,842 | 8,788 | 54 | 7,153 |
| *1985* | | | | | | |
| Under 11[1] | 0 | 0·0 | 0 | 0 | 0 | 0 |
| 11 | 1 | 0·0 | 0 | 0 | 0 | 1 |
| 12 | 22 | 0·1 | 13 | 13 | 0 | 9 |
| 13 | 302 | 0·9 | 126 | 126 | 0 | 176 |
| 14 | 2,063 | 5·5 | 836 | 828 | 8 | 1,227 |
| 15 | 7,018 | 19·1 | 3,194 | 3,169 | 25 | 3,824 |
| Total under 16[2] | 9,406 | 8·6 | 4,169 | 4,136 | 8 | 1,413 |
| 16 | 16,146 | 42·4 | 9,107 | 9,040 | 67 | 7,039 |
| *1986* | | | | | | |
| Under 11[1] | 2 | 0·0 | 2 | 2 | 0 | 0 |
| 11 | 1 | 0·0 | 1 | 1 | 0 | 0 |
| 12 | 24 | 0·1 | 10 | 10 | 0 | 14 |
| 13 | 265 | 0·8 | 107 | 107 | 0 | 158 |
| 14 | 1,980 | 5·7 | 809 | 805 | 4 | 1,171 |
| 15 | 6,922 | 18·5 | 3,293 | 3,280 | 13 | 3,629 |
| Total under 16[2] | 9,194 | 8·7 | 4,222 | 4,205 | 17 | 4,972 |
| 16 | 15,425 | 41·9 | 8,933 | 8,898 | 35 | 6,492 |

[1] Rate per 1,000 girls aged 10.

[2] Rate per 1,000 girls aged 13-15.

[3] Maternities which result in one or more live or still births are counted only once. Such multiple birth maternities are classified as "live" if at least one live birth is included and "still" if all the births are stillbirths.

[4] Legal terminations under 1967 Abortion Act.

## Maternal Deaths

**Ms. Richardson:** To ask the Secretary of State for Health whether he will list the number of maternal deaths each year from 1968 to 1988 from *(a)* all causes, *(b)* abortion, illegal, legal and spontaneous and *(c)* unknown methods of abortion; and what are the percentages for the same years of maternal death due to abortions of all types.

**Mr. Freeman:** The information for England and Wales is set out in the table.

| Year | A | B | C | D | B as per cent. of A |
|---|---|---|---|---|---|
| 1968 | 200 | 49 | 39 | 10 | 24·5 |
| 1969 | 155 | 35 | 33 | 2 | 22·6 |
| 1970 | 145 | 32 | 28 | 4 | 22·1 |
| 1971 | 132 | 26 | 22 | 4 | 19·7 |
| 1972 | 112 | 26 | 19 | 7 | 23·2 |
| 1973 | 88 | 12 | 10 | 2 | 13·6 |
| 1974 | 81 | 9 | 8 | 1 | 11·1 |
| 1975 | 77 | 8 | 7 | 1 | 10·4 |

| Year | A | B | C | D | B as per cent. of A |
|------|-----|---|---|---|------|
| 1976 | 78 | 7 | 4 | 3 | 9·0 |
| 1977 | 74 | 6 | 6 | 0 | 8·1 |
| 1978 | 68 | 5 | 5 | 0 | 7·3 |
| 1979 | 74 | 5 | 3 | 2 | 6·8 |
| 1980 | 70 | 3 | 2 | 1 | 4·3 |
| 1981 | 57 | 3 | 2 | 1 | 5·3 |
| 1982 | 42 | 3 | 3 | 0 | 7·1 |
| 1983 | 54 | 2 | 2 | 0 | 3·7 |
| 1984 | 52 | 3 | 1 | 1 | 5·8 |
| 1985 | 46 | 5 | 4 | 1 | 10·9 |
| 1986 | 45 | 1 | 1 | 0 | 2·2 |
| 1987 | 46 | 1 | 1 | 0 | 2·2 |
| 1988 | 41 | 3 | 3 | 0 | 7·3 |

A = All maternal deaths 1968-78/ICD* 630-678
    1979-88/ICD  630-676
B = All abortion deaths 1968-78/ICD 640-644
    1979-88/ICD 634-638
C = Spontaneous, illegal, legal abortion deaths
    1968-78/ICD 640-643
    1979-88/ICD 634-636
D = Unspecified abortion deaths 1968-78/ICD 644
    1979-88/ICD 637
*ICD — International Classification of Diseases 9th Revision.

### Abortion

**Ms. Richardson:** To ask the Secretary of State for Health whether he will state for each of the past five years, the cost to his Department of replying to parliamentary questions about or related to abortion.

**Mr. Freeman:** The Department does not maintain a record of expenditure on replies to parliamentary questions and any attempt at retrospective estimation would be disproportionately expensive. The cost varies widely according to the nature of the question, the availability of the information requested and, where statistics are involved, the amount of computer time required.

### Self-governing Hospitals

**Mr. Kirkwood:** To ask the Secretary of State for Health if he will define locality as it relates to the provision of core services by self-governing hospitals under the terms of his White Paper "Working for Patients."

**Mr. Mellor:** "Self-Governing Hospitals: an Initial Guide", published yesterday, gives further information about factors to be considered by DHAs in deciding what services should be core services. It explains that a decision on what is acceptable as a definition of local will vary from place to place depending on geography (especially urban versus rural), historic patterns of referral, and social factors such as travelling time and cost.

### "Working for Patients"

**Mr. Kirkwood:** To ask the Secretary of State for Health under the proposals contained in his White Paper "Working for Patients" what role patients will have in influencing the placing of contracts.

**Mr. Mellor:** Providing patients with better health care and a greater choice of service should be the overriding consideration in the placing of contracts. The ability of hospitals which are popular with patients, and in demand, to win further contracts and expand their service will be a major factor in increasing the patient-responsiveness of the NHS. It will be supported by the close involvement with GPs either as budget holders or as users of DHA contracts.

**Mr. Kirkwood:** To ask the Secretary of State for Health under the proposals contained in the White Paper "Working for Patients" what role community health councils will have in the placing of contracts.

**Mr. Mellor:** We are still considering the overall role of community health councils in relation to contract funding. They will however continue to be consulted on substantial developments or variations in health care provision.

**Mr. Kirkwood:** To ask the Secretary of State for Health what element of additional cost required for the administration of the placing of contracts he has estimated is needed to ensure that district health authorities, hospitals and doctors have the knowledge and expertise to negotiate satisfactory contracts under his White Paper proposals.

**Mr. Mellor:** The administrative cost of contract funding cannot be assessed until detailed plans for implementation have been drawn up. Over time any extra costs will be offset by the improved efficiency that contracts will bring. In the meantime the Government have made it clear that the cost of implementing the White Paper proposals will not be met at the expense of patient care. Over £82 million has been made available to cover implementation work in the current financial year.

**Mr. Kirkwood:** To ask the Secretary of State for Health what role community health councils will have in influencing the decisions of new district health authorities and the running of hospital trusts as envisaged in his White Paper "Working for Patients."

**Mr. Mellor:** Community health councils will as now have the opportunity to comment on the overall pattern of services which district health authorities will secure on behalf of their residents, including in future any provided by NHS hospital trusts.

**Mr. Kirkwood:** To ask the Secretary of State for Health what role local people will have in influencing the decisions of the new district health authorities and the running of hospital trusts as envisaged in his White Paper "Working for Patients."

**Mr. Mellor:** The non-executive members of health authorities will normally live, work or have some other connection with the area covered by the health authority. At least two of the non-executive directors of NHS hospital trusts will be drawn from the local community. Community health councils will continue to play an important role in representing the views of the local community on health service matters, while health authorities themselves will be encouraged periodically to test consumer opinion and to act on the findings. Health authority meetings will remain open to the public as now and NHS hospital trusts will be required to hold at least one public meeting a year.

**Mr. Kirkwood:** To ask the Secretary of State for Health what role patients will have in influencing the decisions of the new district health authorities and the running of hospital trusts as envisaged in his White Paper "Working for Patients."

**Mr. Mellor:** Under our proposals the role of health authorities will be enhanced as they switch from the provision of care to the identification of the health needs of their resident population and the purchase of care and services to meet that need. This enhanced role will enable them to focus on the needs of patients. Individual GPs —especially those with practice budgets—will be involved in the direct placement of contracts to meet their patients needs. This brings the provision of care closer to the level of the individual patient, whose agent the GP is. In the future patients will have more say in choosing and changing their GP.

### Hospital Trusts

**Mr. Kirkwood:** To ask the Secretary of State for Health whether any element of quality of care or accessibility of services will be built into a contract between a hospital trust and a district health authority or general practitioner's practice.

**Mr. Mellor:** "Self-Governing Hospitals: an Initial Guide" sets out the minimum contents of contracts and makes it clear that they will specify the measures of quality, relating to both the process and outcome of treatment that will be applied. District health authorities and general practitioners will be expected to use contracts to ensure that patients get the best quality of services available and that where necessary standards are raised. Among measures of accessibility waiting times in particular will be an important aspect or quality.

### NHS Policy Board

**Mr. Kirkwood:** To ask the Secretary of State for Health which members of his new policy board for the National Health Service were chosen to represent patients' interests.

**Mr. Mellor:** The policy board is not a representative body; every member will be aiming to promote patients' interests.

### Private Health Care

**Mr. Gareth Wardell:** To ask the Secretary of State for Health what representations he has received asking him to extend the proposed tax relief on insurance cover for the private health needs of over 65-year-olds to support elderly people living in their own homes purchasing supported lifelines to connect them with back-up facilities; and if he will make a statement.

**Mr. Freeman:** I am not aware of any such representations, which would be for my right hon. Friend the Chancellor of the Exchequer to consider.

### Medical Scientists

**Mr. Hardy:** To ask the Secretary of State for Health in how many relevant hospitals there are vacancies for medical scientists; and how many such vacancies existed 10 years ago.

**Mr. Mellor:** We do not collect this information centrally.

### Blind Persons

**Mr. Evennett:** To ask the Secretary of State for Health how many registered blind persons there are in England.

**Mr. Mellor:** At 31 March 1988 there were 126,828 people registered as blind with local authority social services departments in England. This figure is provisional.

## TRADE AND INDUSTRY

### Consumer Rights

**12. Mr. Boyes:** To ask the Chancellor of the Duchy of Lancaster if he now has plans to bring forward legislation affecting consumer rights.

**47. Mr. Parry:** To ask the Chancellor of the Duchy of Lancaster if he now has plans to bring forward legislation affecting consumer rights.

**Mr. Forth:** We intend to improve the protection given to consumers in a number of ways including the introduction of regulations under the Consumer Protection Act 1987 on price indications at bureaux de change and changes to other legislation affecting consumers' interests.

### Financial Services Act

**17. Mr. McCrindle:** To ask the Chancellor of the Duchy of Lancaster when he last met the chairman of the Securities and Investments Board to discuss the progress in implementation of the Financial Services Act.

**Mr. Maude:** I met the chairman of the Securities and Investments Board on 24 May. The discussion ranged widely over a number of topics concerning the regulation of financial services.

### World Trade

**18. Mr. Jim Marshall:** To ask the Chancellor of the Duchy of Lancaster which industrial countries have lost a larger share of world trade in the last 10 years than the United Kingdom.

**Mr. Forth:** The most recent information available for OECD countries is for the first three quarters of 1988. Since 1978 the Netherlands, France, Greece and Norway recorded larger reductions than the United Kingdom in their shares of world trade.

**82. Mr. Ted Garrett:** To ask the Chancellor of the Duchy of Lancaster what was the United Kingdom share of world trade 10 years ago; and what it is at present.

**Mr. Alan Clark:** The latest figures of world trade refer to the first three quarters of 1988, when the United Kingdom share of total world visible exports was 5·2 per cent. In 1979 the United Kingdom share was 5·3 per cent.

### Information Technology

**19. Dr. Moonie:** To ask the Chancellor of the Duchy of Lancaster what was the balance of trade in information technology in 1979 and 1988.

**Mr. Forth:** The United Kingdom had a trade deficit in electronics and information technology manufactured goods of £440 million in 1979. Provisional figures indicate a deficit of £2,460 million last year.

**25. Mr. McCartney:** To ask the Chancellor of the Duchy of Lancaster what further representations he has received on his response to the Select Committee on Trade and Industry's report on information technology.

**Mr. Forth:** I have received only one written representation on the White Paper.

64. **Mr. Eastham:** To ask the Chancellor of the Duchy of Lancaster if he will make a statement on progress of implementation of the Government's policy for information technology.

**Mr. Forth:** My Department continues to pursue a wide range of activities within the policy framework for IT set out in the Government's response to the Trade and Industry Select Committee report on IT (Cm 646).

New initiatives within the last two months have included:

— the launch of a programme to stimulate greater business awareness of the benefits of open IT systems
— a new LINK R&D programme in opto-electronic systems supported by £15 million of DTI and SERC funding; and
— the announcement of the £20 million second call for proposals under the information engineering advanced technology programme.

78. **Mr. Battle:** To ask the Chancellor of the Duchy of Lancaster when he expects Britain to have a trade surplus in information technology.

85. **Mr. Win Griffiths:** To ask the Chancellor of the Duchy of Lancaster when he expects Britain to have a trade surplus in information technology.

**Mr. Alan Clark:** I refer the hon. Gentleman to the reply my right hon. Friend the Chancellor of the Duchy of Lancaster gave on 19 April, at column *332* to the hon. Member for Midlothian (Mr. Eadie).

### Communications Infrastructure (Report)

21. **Mr. Turner:** To ask the Chancellor of the Duchy of Lancaster what representations he has received on the Macdonald report on communications infrastructure.

**Mr. Atkins:** My Department has received a number of representations on the communications steering group report "The Infrastructure for Tomorrow", sometimes referred to as the Macdonald report. The report sets out the conclusions of the group which was established to advise Ministers on ways in which the United Kingdom electronic communications infrastructure may be expected to develop over the next two decades. The report represents the views of the group and not necessarily those of the Government.

### National Engineering Laboratory

22. **Ms. Armstrong:** To ask the Chancellor of the Duchy of Lancaster what representations he has received on his recent proposals for the future of the national engineering laboratory.

**Mr. Newton:** To date, I have not received any representations on the proposals for the laboratory, which I announced on 17 May. However, there will shortly be a further meeting of the departmental Whitley council with the Department of Trade and Industry council of Civil Service unions to discuss the proposals.

### North East Shipbuilders

23. **Mr. Mullin:** To ask the Chancellor of the Duchy of Lancaster when he last met the chairman of British Shipbuilders to discuss the future of North East Shipbuilders.

**Mr. Newton:** I met the chairman of British Shipbuilders on 5 June. A number of matters of current interest were discussed, including the disposal of the assets of North East Shipbuilders Ltd.

### Aerospace Industry (Output)

24. **Mr. Jack:** To ask the Chancellor of the Duchy of Lancaster what, in the north-west of England, was the value of the output of the aerospace industry in 1979 and the last full year for which information is available.

**Mr. Atkins:** In 1979 the gross value added (at factor cost) by the aerospace equipment manufacturing and repairing industry in the north-west (standard region) was £276 million. The corresponding figure for 1987, the last year for which data is available, was £682 million.

### Inflation

26. **Mr. Wilson:** To ask the Chancellor of the Duchy of Lancaster what representations he has received on the effects of the level of inflation on industry.

**Mr. Atkins:** A number of representations which I receive refer to inflation. The great majority of these recognise that the control of inflation must remain the prime objective of economic policy.

### Competitiveness

27. **Mr. Tom Clarke:** To ask the Chancellor of the Duchy of Lancaster what recent representations he has received from industry on matters affecting competitiveness.

72. **Mr. Darling:** To ask the Chancellor of the Duchy of Lancaster what recent representations he has received from industry on matters affecting competitiveness.

**Mr. Maude:** Most contacts which my Department has with industry and commerce involve matters having a bearing on United Kingdom competitiveness.

### Civil Research and Development

28. **Mr. Allen McKay:** To ask the Chancellor of the Duchy of Lancaster which countries in the Organisation for Economic Co-operation and Development have reduced the share of gross domestic product spent on civil research and development between 1983 and 1986; and which countries have increased it.

**Mr. Forth:** The available information relates to gross expenditure on research and development in the fields of science, technology, social science and humanities as a percentage of gross domestic product. On this basis, of the OECD countries for which the information is available in both years only Turkey shows reduction in the percentage.

79. **Mr. Faulds:** To ask the Chancellor of the Duchy of Lancaster in which OECD countries the proportion of gross domestic product spent by Government on civil research and development has fallen since 1983.

87. **Mr. Rogers:** To ask the Chancellor of the Duchy of Lancaster in which OECD countries the proportion of gross domestic product spent by Government on civil research and development has fallen since 1983.

**Mr. Forth:** I refer the hon. Member to the answer I gave to the hon. Member for Tyne Bridge (Mr. Clelland) on 15 March at column *265*.

### Japanese Overseas Investment

29. **Mr. Raffan:** To ask the Chancellor of the Duchy of Lancaster what has been Britain's share of total Japanese overseas investment in Europe since 1979.

**Mr. Forth:** Based on information published by the Japanese Ministry of Finance on overseas investment projects notified to them, the United Kingdom received a third by value of Japanese overseas investment projects in Europe over the period 1980 to 1988 inclusive.

### Beer (Supply)

30. **Mr. Janman:** To ask the Chancellor of the Duchy of Lancaster how near he is to forming his conclusions about the Monopolies and Mergers Commission report on the supply of beer.

46. **Mr. Ashton:** To ask the Chancellor of the Duchy of Lancaster when he expects to implement the Monopolies and Mergers Commission report on the supply of beer.

48. **Mr. Riddick:** To ask the Chancellor of the Duchy of Lancaster when he expects to make a decision relating to the Monopolies and Mergers Commission report on the supply of beer; and if he will make a statement.

52. **Mr. Matthew Taylor:** To ask the Chancellor of the Duchy of Lancaster when he next expects to be able to respond to the Monopolies and Mergers Commission report on the supply of beer.

65. **Mr. Andrew MacKay:** To ask the Chancellor of the Duchy of Lancaster if he will make a further statement on the Monopolies and Mergers Commission report on the brewing industry.

83. **Mrs. Maureen Hicks:** To ask the Chancellor of the Duchy of Lancaster when he will make his response to the Monopolies and Mergers Commission report on the supply of beer.

**Mr. Maude:** We are anxious to bring this matter to a satisfactory conclusion as soon as possible. I made a statement on our preliminary intentions in a written answer on 8 June and my right hon. and noble Friend the Secretary of State for Trade and Industry developed this in a statement in another place on 14 June.

### CBI

31. **Mr. Anthony Coombs:** To ask the Chancellor of the Duchy of Lancaster when he last met the Confederation of British Industry; and what matters were discussed.

**Mr. Newton:** I last met the Confederation of British Industry on 5 June 1989 at the launch of the CBI's initiative 1992 series of seminars on information technology.

### Trade Balance

32. **Mr. Sean Hughes:** To ask the Chancellor of the Duchy of Lancaster when he now expects Britain's trade to be in balance.

54. **Mr. Geoffrey Robinson:** To ask the Chancellor of the Duchy of Lancaster when he now expects Britain's trade to be in balance.

66. **Mr. Harry Barnes:** To ask the Chancellor of the Duchy of Lancaster what forward estimate he has made of the monthly trade deficit over the next nine months.

**Mr. Alan Clark:** Forecasts of Britain's trade have been made up to the end of the first half of 1990. The results are in the Financial Statement and Budget report.

### Base Rates

33. **Mr. Livsey:** To ask the Chancellor of the Duchy of Lancaster what has been the estimated cost to industry of the rise in base rates since April 1988; and if he will make a statement.

**Mr. Atkins:** The cost to industrial and commercial companies to date of the changes in bank base rates since April 1988, compared with the cost if bank base rates had remained the same since April 1988, is estimated to be about £1·5 billion. The hon. Member should bear in mind, however, that a one percentage point increase in interest rates, even if sustained for a full year, costs companies far less than a one percentage point increase in pay settlements.

### Export Credits Guarantee Department (Report)

34. **Mr. Colin Shepherd:** To ask the Chancellor of the Duchy of Lancaster when he expects to publish his response to the Kemp report on the Export Credits Guarantee Department.

**Mr. Alan Clark:** An inter-departmental working group of officials, chaired by ECGD, has been established to provide advice to Ministers on the options examined by Mr. Kemp. This will report to Ministers as soon as possible.

### Direct Investment

35. **Mr. Bill Michie:** To ask the Chancellor of the Duchy of Lancaster what is the balance of inward and outward direct investment; and what it was 10 years ago.

70. **Mrs. Dunwoody:** To ask the Chancellor of the Duchy of Lancaster what is the balance of inward and outward direct investment; and what it was 10 years ago.

**Mr. Atkins:** In 1988, net direct investment overseas by United Kingdom residents was £15·1 billion, compared with overseas net direct investment in the United Kingdom of £7·8 billion, giving a net outflow of £7·3 billion. The corresponding figures for 1978 were £3·5 billion and £2·0 billion respectively, giving a net outflow of £1·5 billion.

### Sterling Exchange Rate

36. **Mr. Menzies Campbell:** To ask the Chancellor of the Duchy of Lancaster what advice his Department is giving to export industries regarding the exchange rate of sterling.

**Mr. Alan Clark:** Our consistent advice to exporters on exchange rates has been that they should consider protecting themselves against the risk of exchange rate fluctuations and consult experts about the best way of doing this.

## Eden Committee

**37. Mr. Illsley:** To ask the Chancellor of the Duchy of Lancaster when he proposes to introduce legislation to implement the recommendations of the Eden committee which were accepted by Her Majesty's Government.

**Mr. Forth:** Those recommendations accepted in the Government's response (Cmnd. 9850) to the report of the Eden committee which did not require primary legislation have already been implemented. It remains my Department's intention to introduce legislation to implement the remaining accepted recommendations when parliamentary time is available.

## EC Consumer Affairs Committee

**38. Mrs. Clwyd:** To ask the Chancellor of the Duchy of Lancaster if he will make a statement on the outcome of the European Economic Community Consumer Affairs Council held on 1 June.

**Mr. Forth:** As I announced to the House on 12 June, the Council reached agreement on a number of issues, including amendment to the consumer credit directive on December 1988 and continued support into 1990 for the European home and leisure accident surveillance system.

The Commission presented a proposal for a general product safety directive which was discussed for the first time by EC Ministers. Council also noted a report by the Commission on consumer education.

The United Kingdom was unable to support adoption of a draft resolution for the relaunch of consumer policy because of its proposals relating to product quality, which would constrain consumer choice without benefit in terms of additional protection.

## Goods (United Kingdom Manufacture)

**39. Sir Russell Johnston:** To ask the Chancellor of the Duchy of Lancaster what steps he is taking to encourage people to purchase goods made in the United Kingdom.

**Mr. Alan Clark:** The greatest encouragement to purchasing from United Kingdom sources is the availability of competitive United Kingdom products. My Department's policies are geared to helping businesses achieve this.

## Natural Environment

**40. Mr. Blunkett:** To ask the Chancellor of the Duchy of Lancaster whether he has any plans to require the annual publication by firms of the effects of their business on the natural environment.

**Mr. Newton:** No. We believe the emphasis should be on increasing business awareness of environmental issues and helping firms to improve their environmental standards. This is what the DTI environmental programme launched last month is designed to achieve. Details of the programme are set out in the booklet, "Your Business and the Environment", copies of which have been placed in the Vote Office and Library.

## Motor Manufacturers (Investment)

**41. Mr. Strang:** To ask the Chancellor of the Duchy of Lancaster if he will estimate the level of investments in the last financial year by indigenous motor manufacturers.

**Mr. Atkins:** The most recent reliable estimate of investment is from the annual census of production for 1987. In that year it is estimated that net capital expenditure by the United Kingdom motor industry[1] amounted to £612 million.

[1] Class 35 of the standard industrial classification, revised 1980.

## Trade Deficits

**42. Mr. Hoyle:** To ask the Chancellor of the Duchy of Lancaster which Organisation for European Economic Co-operation and Development countries are running a smaller trade deficit as a percentage of gross domestic product than the United Kingdom.

**Mr. Alan Clark:** According to the most recent OECD figures, of the 14 countries which recorded deficits on their visible trade in 1988, those of the following were smaller, as a proportion of their GDP, than that of the United Kingdom:

> Austria, Turkey, Switzerland, Iceland, United States of America, France, Italy, Norway, Australia and Belgium.

**59. Mr. Eadie:** To ask the Chancellor of the Duchy of Lancaster with which European Economic Community members Britain's trade is in deficit.

**Mr. Alan Clark:** In the 12 months to April the United Kingdom was in deficit on visible trade with Belgium/Luxembourg, Denmark, Federal Republic of Germany, France, Italy, the Netherlands and Portugal.

## Inner-city Task Forces

**43. Mr. Brandon-Bravo:** To ask the Chancellor of the Duchy of Lancaster what further progress has been made in the 16 inner-city task forces.

**51. Mr. Michael Brown:** To ask the Chancellor of the Duchy of Lancaster if he will make a statement on the progress of the inner-city task forces.

**Mr. Forth:** The inner-city task forces have continued to make good progress in meeting their objectives of securing more jobs and training for local people and encouraging local enterprise. Since the task forces began their work in 1986 they have committed about £33 million in support of nearly 1,100 projects. These generate, or safeguard, nearly 4,000 jobs, facilitate over 23,500 training places and provide support for over 2,600 businesses. Over 450 private sector companies have supported task force projects.

We have always made it clear that task forces would not be permanently located in any one inner-city area. One of their aims is to promote the long-term capability of local organisations so that eventually these bodies can take over from them, thus releasing resources for task forces to be set up in other inner city areas.

I announced on 9 March, as part of the Government's action for cities anniversary announcements, that the task forces would be withdrawing from Leicester, Wolverhampton and Preston; and that new task forces would be opening in Bradford, Granby/Toxteth in Liverpool and Deptford in Lewisham.

**49. Mr. Patnick:** To ask the Chancellor of the Duchy of Lancaster what estimate he has as to the number of firms which have now been assisted as a result of the activities of the inner-city task forces.

**Mr. Forth:** Task forces provide a variety of assistance to existing local firms and start-up businesses; for example, by providing loans through task force development funds and by supporting local enterprise agencies and other organisations offering business advice. Through these and other ways, task forces are estimated to have assisted over 2,600 businesses.

### Single Market

44. **Mr. Malcolm Bruce:** To ask the Chancellor of the Duchy of Lancaster if he will make a statement on the help which is being given to companies to enable them to take full advantage of the establishment of the internal market in 1992.

**Mr. Maude:** Our 24-hour "1992 hotline"—01-200 1992 —provides business with access to a wide range of information and advice on the single market, including detailed factsheets, booklets on standards, and an action checklist. Practical help and advice is available through our enterprise initiative; the consultancy initiatives and the export initiative are particularly relevant for firms seeking to take specific steps to prepare for the single market.

The CBI's "Initiative 1992" is a major private sector source of help on the single market; whilst a number of trade associations, Chambers of Commerce and professional bodies are providing their members with guidance on how the single market will affect their activities.

45. **Mr. David Evans:** To ask the Chancellor of the Duchy of Lancaster what steps his Department is taking to ensure that British firms are made fully aware of the opportunity to become a member of an European economic interest grouping as a means of preparing for 1992.

**Mr. Maude:** Full details on the form of a European economic interest grouping are given in our main single market booklet "The Facts" and in an article in the current edition of "Single Market News", copies of which are available through our 24-hour "1992 hotline": 01-200 1992. The rules on registering an EEIG in Great Britain are given in the statutory instrument SI 1989/638.

56. **Mr. Hague:** To ask the Chancellor of the Duchy of Lancaster if he will make a statement on progress with regard to arrangements made by his Department to assist British firms to take full advantage of the completion of the internal market in 1992.

**Mr. Maude:** Our "Europe Open for Business" information service is constantly updated and expanded to help business prepare for the single market. Recent additions include: a booklet and video on the decision-making process in Brussels ("Brussels Can You Hear Me?"); new standards booklets ("construction products", "simple pressure vessels", "directives under discussion"); a checklist on progress on single market legislation ("White Paper Checklist"). This material, together with our comprehensive single market information pack, can be obtained free of charge, through our "1992 hotline"—01-200 1992. Two new booklets—an action guide for smaller firms and a guide to public purchasing—will be available later on this summer.

57. **Mr. Livingstone:** To ask the Chancellor of the Duchy of Lancaster what recent estimates his Department have made of the effects of 1992 on each of Britain's regions.

92. **Mr. Clelland:** To ask the Chancellor of the Duchy of Lancaster what further estimates his Department has made on the effects of 1992 on each of Britain's regions,.

**Mr. Maude:** I refer the hon. Gentlemen to my reply to the hon. Member for Leicester, South (Mr. Marshall) on 19 April at column 177.

### Consumer Credit

50. **Mr. Simon Hughes:** To ask the Chancellor of the Duchy of Lancaster if he will make a statement on the level of personal consumer credit.

**Mr. Maude:** At the end of March 1989 the amount of consumer credit outstanding on the broad definition, which includes bank lending, was £43·4 billion. The vast majority of household borrowing is accounted for by mortgages.

### Sunderland Shipyards

53. **Mr. Clay:** To ask the Chancellor of the Duchy of Lancaster when he last discussed the future of the Sunderland Shipyards with the chairman of British Shipbuilders; and if he will make a statement.

**Mr. Newton:** I met the chairman of British Shipbuilders on 5 June. A number of matters of current interest were discussed, including the disposal of the assets of North East Shipbuilders Ltd.

### Toys (CE Mark)

55. **Mr. Kirkwood:** To ask the Chancellor of the Duchy of Lancaster what representations he has had recently from the toy trade about the length of time to dispose of stocks which do not have CE marks.

**Mr. Forth:** Representations have been received from various bodies about the length of time needed to dispose of stocks which do not carry the CE mark. The toy industry has sought a longer period than 1 February 1991 or that no cut-off date should be imposed. Consumer organisations are of the opinion that the proposed cut-off date in the draft regulations should not be extended. My Department will carefully consider all the representations received before making final decisions.

### Regional Selective Assistance

58. **Mr. Hind:** To ask the Chancellor of the Duchy of Lancaster if he will make a statement on the levels of regional selective assistance to applicants in the north-west of England in 1988-89.

**Mr. Atkins:** In the year 1988-89, for the DTI north-west region, offers of regional selective assistance totalled £32·1 million and payments totalled £21·8 million.

### China

60. **Mr. Gow:** To ask the Chancellor of the Duchy of Lancaster whether he will make a statement about trade with the People's Republic of China.

**Mr. Alan Clark:** In the light of the recent events in China the Government have announced the suspension of ministerial and high level military exchanges and a ban on arms sales. The ECGD is maintaining cover for the China market, but awaiting clarification of the economic position before taking decisions on respect of new businesses.

### Company Liquidity

61. **Mr. McFall:** To ask the Chancellor of the Duchy of Lancaster what is his latest estimate of company liquidity; and when it was last lower.

**Mr. Maude:** The liquidity ratio for all large industrial and commercial companies is estimated by the Department's survey to be 72 per cent. at the end of the first quarter of 1989 on a seasonally adjusted basis. It was lower at the end of the third quarter of 1982.

However, profitability of non-North sea industrial and commercial companies has risen in each year since 1981 and the sector has been a large net saver.

### Takeovers and Mergers

62. **Mr. McAvoy:** To ask the Chancellor of the Duchy of Lancaster what has been the expenditure on takeovers and mergers in the most recent year for which figures are available; and what has been the spending on research and development, training and manufacturing investment on a comparable basis.

**Mr. Maude:** Expenditure by industrial and commercial companies on acquisitions and mergers within the United Kingdom during 1988 is estimated to be £22·1 billion. During the same period gross domestic fixed capital formation by industrial and commercial companies is estimated to have been £37·4 billion. No directly comparable figures are available for spending on training or research and development.

### Shops (Closing Down Sales)

63. **Mr. Gregory:** To ask the Chancellor of the Duchy of Lancaster if he has any plans to introduce legislation to prevent shop owners from misrepresenting their closing down in order to attract customers.

**Mr. Forth:** Part III of the Consumer Protection Act 1987 makes it an offence to give misleading price indications. The code of practice for traders on price indications issued under section 25 of the Act gives guidance on good practice to help traders avoid giving misleading price indications. The code makes it clear that use of the term "sale" normally implies a price comparison and the basis for such a comparison should be made clear to the customer.

### Estate Agents

67. **Mr. Nicholas Brown:** To ask the Chancellor of the Duchy of Lancaster what progress is being made in the regulation of estate agents.

**Mr. Forth:** Over the past 11 months I have carried out an extensive review of estate agency issues. In the course of this review I have had meetings with the major bodies representing estate agents and other interested parties.

The main objective of the review was to identify ways in which the practices of estate agents could be significantly improved to provide a better service. I have concluded that the best way to achieve this is through a combination of self-regulation and statutory provision. I

have asked the Director-General of Fair Trading to discuss with the industry the introduction of a code of practice for estate agency to improve consumer protection and enhance standards of service. The code will need to include some form of disputes procedure and a system for monitoring compliance with its provisions. This should create a strong incentive, not least on commercial grounds, for estate agents throughout the industry to comply in order to attract public confidence. The director general has agreed to report to me early next year.

I have also concluded that we need to act against a number of undesirable practices identified in the review of the working of the Estate Agents Act 1979 recently published by the Director General of Fair Trading. I intend to do this by introducing an order under Section 3 of the Act which would define certain practices as "undesirable". I expect these to include, for instance, tie-in sales where the agent refuses to pass on bids unless the purchaser agrees to arrange finance or insurance with him, "bidding-up", misleading advertising and unfair or misleading contract terms. If an agent is found to be engaging in "undesirable" practices, the director general will have the power to prohibit that person from doing estate agency work. The exact wording of the order will follow from how the code of practice is set out, and I hope to lay an order soon after the director general makes his report next year.

I have also asked the director general to review the arguments for extending the Trade Description Act 1968 to misdescriptions of property.

In the course of my review discussions of the problems and potential solutions have gone wider than estate agency, and have touched on other aspects of the property transfer system. I look forward with interest to announcements by my noble and learned Friend the Lord Chancellor on the subject of competition in conveyancing, and by the Secretaries of State for Scotland and Northern Ireland on the conclusions to their reviews on the position there.

Copies of my report have been placed in the Library and the Vote Office.

### Interest Rates

68. **Mr. Jack Thompson:** To ask the Chancellor of the Duchy of Lancaster what representations he has received on the effects of current interest rates on industry.

90. **Mr. Austin Mitchell:** To ask the Chancellor of the Duchy of Lancaster what representations he has received on the effects of current interest rates on industry.

**Mr. Newton:** I have received a number of representations from business about the effects of interest rates on investment. Investment has continued to rise strongly and the DTI's June survey of investment intentions shows that a rise of 13 per cent. of total investment is expected in 1989, with a further increase in 1990.

### Brewing Industry (Report)

69. **Mr. Morgan:** To ask the Chancellor of the Duchy of Lancaster what representations he has received regarding the Monopolies and Mergers Commission report on the brewing industry.

**Mr. Maude:** I have had meetings with the Brewers Society and with a number of brewers individually. I have also met representatives of the National Licensed Victuallers Association, the Campaign for Real Ale, the Consumers Association and others. In addition, the Department has received a number of letters, representing a range of views.

### Footwear Industry

71. **Mr. Pike:** To ask the Chancellor of the Duchy of Lancaster when he last met representatives of the British footwear industry; and what issues were discussed.

**Mr. Alan Clark:** I attended, and spoke at, the British Footwear Manufacturers Federation's annual luncheon on 14 June. Various issues arose, including the EC Commission's investigation into imports of footwear from Taiwan and South Korea and United Kingdom objectives for the GATT Uruguay round.

### Mergers and Acquisitions

73. **Mr. Cox:** To ask the Chancellor of the Duchy of Lancaster what has been the percentage increase in mergers and acquisitions since 1979.

**Mr. Maude:** Expenditure on acquisitions and mergers by industrial and commercial companies within the United Kingdom in the 12 months to March 1989 is estimated to be about £19½ billion. In current prices this is about 12 times greater than the 1979 total of about £1¾ billion.

### Inward Investment

74. **Mr. Pawsey:** To ask the Chancellor of the Duchy of Lancaster what was the level of inward investment into the United Kingdom in 1988.

**Mr. Atkins:** Inward investment into the United Kingdom in 1988 was £11·4 billion of which £7·8 billion was direct investment and £3·6 billion was portfolio investment.

### Trade Statistics

75. **Mr. Orme:** To ask the Chancellor of the Duchy of Lancaster if any changes are planned in the collection of trade statistics after 1992.

76. **Mrs. Fyfe:** To ask the Chancellor of the Duchy of Lancaster if any changes are planned in the collection of trade statistics after 1992.

**Mr. Maude:** A proposal for an EC Council regulation, which sets out a revised methodology for the collection of trade statistics between member states of the European Community after 1992 to replace the current procedure based on Customs documentation, has been prepared by the EC Commission and will be considered by EC Ministers later this year.

The Government are seeking to ensure that the collection of these statistics does not impose unnecessary burdens on businesses who are involved in trade between member states and who will be required to provide the relevant data. Recently, this Department has started a consultation exercise seeking the views of trade associations and industry on the possible impact of the proposal.

Statistics of trade with countries outside the European Community will continue to be collected as at present.

### Regional Initiatives

77. **Ms. Primarolo:** To ask the Chancellor of the Duchy of Lancaster if he plans to announce any new initiatives to benefit Britain's regions.

**Mr. Atkins:** Major changes in the focus of DTI's policies were made only last year. Regional policy now operates within a framework designed to encourage enterprise and economic growth in all parts of the country but with extra help available for firms in the regions.

### Manufacturing Productivity

80. **Mr. Wood:** To ask the Chancellor of the Duchy of Lancaster what are the latest figures he has for the productivity of manufacturing industry; and what were the comparable figures one year ago.

**Mr. Atkins:** In the three months to April 1989 manufacturing productivity, as measured by output per person employed, was at a level of 119·3, based on 1985 equal to 100. This is six per cent. more than the level of 112·5 for the first quarter of 1988.

95. **Mr. Knox:** To ask the Chancellor of the Duchy of Lancaster what is the most recent figure for output in manufacturing industry; and what was the figure for the same month in 1973.

**Mr. Atkins:** In April 1989 manufacturing output was at a level of 118·5, based on 1985 equal to 100. This is 8½ per cent. more than the level of 108·8 for April 1973. But my hon. Friend will appreciate that monthly data can be erratic. A firmer based comparison would be that in the three months to April 1989 manufacturing output was 9½ per cent. higher than in the same period in 1973. Manufacturing output is now at is highest ever level.

### Postal Monopoly

81. **Mr. Bowis:** To ask the Chancellor of the Duchy of Lancaster when he last consulted the chairman of the Post Office on the lifting or easing of the postal monopoly.

**Mr. Newton:** We have not consulted the chairman of the Post Office on the lifting or easing of the postal monopoly since 1981. In 1981 the monopoly was suspended for 25 years to permit time-sensitive mail to be delivered by private carriers, provided that they charge a minimum fee of £1 per letter.

### Goods (Labelling)

84. **Mr. Flannery:** To ask the Chancellor of the Duchy of Lancaster if his Department is intending to make any new proposals for the labelling of goods.

**Mr. Forth:** Additional labelling requirements will come into force over the next year for furniture and furnishings, and toys.

### Manufacturing Output

86. **Miss Widdecombe:** To ask the Chancellor of the Duchy of Lancaster what are the latest figures he has for the output of manufacturing industry; and what was the comparable figure one year ago.

**Mr. Atkins:** In the three months to April 1989 manufacturing output was at a level of 118·0, based on 1985 equal to 100. This is 6½ per cent. more than the level of 111·0 for the first quarter of 1988.

## British Shipbuilders Ltd.

**88. Dr. Godman:** To ask the Chancellor of the Duchy of Lancaster when he last met Mr. John Lister, chairman of British Shipbuilders Ltd.; and what subjects were discussed.

**Mr. Newton:** I met the chairman of British Shipbuilders on 5 June. A number of matters of current interest were discussed.

## Japanese Market

**89. Mr. Yeo:** To ask the Chancellor of the Duchy of Lancaster what representations he has received about improving access to the Japanese market for British exporters.

**Mr. Alan Clark:** The Government continue to attach great importance to Britain's trade with Japan. Representations on market access are received from time to time and, where appropriate, we take them up vigorously with the Japanese authorities, both directly and through the European Commission. My right hon. and noble Friend the Secretary of State continued to press the Japanese Government on problems of access during his visit to Japan last month.

## Barlow Clowes

**91. Mr. Michael:** To ask the Chancellor of the Duchy of Lancaster what progress he is able to report towards achieving a satisfactory outcome for investors in Barlow Clowes in respect of *(a)* the United Kingdom-based and *(b)* the Gibraltar-based operation; what fresh initiatives he intends to take to speed up settlements; and if he will make a statement.

**Mr. Maude:** Following judgment given on 16 June in respect of the May court hearings, I understand that it has been determined that Barlow Clowes International investors are entitled to recover from Barlow Clowes Gilt Managers (the United Kingdom operation) BCGM assets representing gilts of £16·2 million to the extent that such assets can still be identified in BCGM's hands. Further judgment gives certain BCI investors, who invested after 29 February 1988, the entitlement to recover the relevant part of their investment (after expenses). I understand that the joint receivers are returning to court on 28 June to determine the basis upon which each individual BCI investor's entitlement to any distribution will be calculated.

Although the judgments do not affect those BCGM investors whose funds were placed with Lloyds Bank plc, the outstanding issue of quantification of BCGM investors' claims will be dealt with when counsel for all other categories are present. The joint liquidators have informed me that they will return to court as soon as possible to obtain direction on the outstanding issues.

## EC (Discussions)

**93. Mr. Dykes:** To ask the Chancellor of the Duchy of Lancaster when he next expects to discuss trade and industry matters with his counterparts in the other EEC member states.

**Mr. Newton:** I have just returned from a Research Council and a meeting with EC counterparts to discuss the Eureka initiative and I am planning to attend the next Industry Council on 26 September.

## Manufacturing and Service Industries (North-West)

**94. Mr. Butler:** To ask the Chancellor of the Duchy of Lancaster if he will make a statement on the health of manufacturing and service industries in the north-west.

**Mr. Atkins:** I am pleased to report that the manufacturing and service sectors in the north-west are both performing impressively.

At current prices, the north-west standard region's gross domestic product in manufacturing rose by almost 27 per cent. between 1984 and 1987 (from £8,653 million to, provisionally, £10,961 million) with financial and business services sector showing an increase of 48 per cent. over the same period (from £3,549 million to £5,268 million).

Major new investments programmes by companies such as Pilkington and ICI, the decision by the Sanwa and Fuji Banks to establish northern offices in the region, and the contract-winning performances by British Aerospace and Simon Engineering, are all evidence of the excellent health of the region's manufacturing and service sectors.

## Trade Fairs

**Mr. Arbuthnot:** To ask the Chancellor of the Duchy of Lancaster if any changes are proposed in the terms under which the Department of Trade and Industry provides support for United Kingdom companies participating in overseas trade fairs.

**Mr. Alan Clark:** My right hon. and noble Friend and I are concerned that the Department's support for exporters at trade fairs abroad should be focused more sharply on its main purpose of assisting new exporters to become established in overseas markets. We have therefore decided to raise the overall level of assistance to such exporters but to limit the number of times that a company is supported at trade fairs within any country. The total value of assistance on offer will be unchanged.

The new arrangements for assistance to firms in groups supported by the Department at overseas trade fairs will be as follows:

(i) Subject to the exceptions referred to in sub-paragraphs (iv) and (v) below, support will be limited to three participations per country. Firms which have already received assistance in three or more participations in a particular country will no longer be eligible for support in fairs in that country.

(ii) The level of support for eligible companies will be 50 per cent. of the Department's estimate of the cost of providing stands and certain services at the trade fair in question. This compares with the present level of support which varies between 60 per cent. for the first time participants to 25 per cent. for third time participants.

(iii) Support in the form of travel grants for events outside western Europe will continue for a maximum of three participations, instead of the present four.

(iv) Because it is more difficult for firms to enter the Japanese market, the limit of the number of times on which support can be given there will be five. Assistance will be at the level of 50 per cent. of costs on each occasion. Similarly, the limit on the number of times that firms qualify for travel grant will also be five.

(v) A limited number of fairs are of major international significance and are the principal event for the product sector concerned. Because these fairs are aimed at buyers from all over the world rather than the market of the country in which they are held, firms will be eligible for support in two extra participations in successive events of this sort, in addition to the three participations per country described in sub-paragraph (i) above. The level of support will be the same as in sub-paragraph (ii).

The new arrangements will come into effect for group participations in overseas trade fairs which commence after 31 March 1990, except where the Department has already made a formal offer of support.

### Telephone Systems

**Dr. Kim Howells:** To ask the Chancellor of the Duchy of Lancaster (1) what information he has on the extent of provision of leased circuits in Wales, including kilostream and megastream, on the number of towns in Wales catered for by these services and in the case of megastream, on the number of local exchanges equipped with pulse code modulation;

(2) what information he has on the extent to which and the places in which, trunk and local exchanges in Wales have been converted to digital switching and as to which areas are serviced by integrated digital access;

(3) what information he has on the number and location of packet assemblers and disassemblers in Wales.

**Mr. Atkins:** These are commercial and operational matters for British Telecommunications plc.

## EMPLOYMENT

### Small Firms (Report)

101. **Mr. Gill:** To ask the Secretary of State for Employment what consideration he has given to the conclusions of the Public Accounts Committee report on assistance to small firms.

**Mr. Cope:** The Government's response to the Public Accounts Committee's eighth report is set out in the Treasury minute dated 17 May 1989 presented to Parliament by my hon. Friend the Financial Secretary (command 697). A copy has been placed in the Library of the House.

### Training and Enterprise Councils

**Mr. Barry Field:** To ask the Secretary of State for Employment when he expects to announce the allocation of funds for training and enterprise councils by area.

**Mr. Cope:** The allocation of funds for an individual TEC will relate to the business plan that the TEC agrees with my Department and will be announced when the TEC is fully approved.

### Labour Statistics

**Mr. John Marshall:** To ask the Secretary of State for Employment if he will make a statement about the trends in unemployment in Hendon, South since 1987.

**Mr. Nicholls:** In May 1989 there were 1,343 unemployed claimants in the parliamentary constituency of Hendon, South. This compares with 2,562 in May 1987,

a fall of 1,219 or 47·6 per cent. over two years. The comparison is slightly affected by the change of coverage in the count from September 1988 due to the new benefit regulations affecting people aged under 18 years.

### Rehabilitation Service

**Mr. Strang:** To ask the Secretary of State for Employment how are the processes of assessment and rehabilitation differentiated within the work of the employment rehabilitation service.

**Mr. Nicholls:** The assessment process carried out by the employment rehabilitation service results in individual action plans being agreed with clients. For some clients the agreed action plan can include subsequent attendance on a course of employment rehabilitation which is a longer process and normally modular in form.

**Mr. Strang:** To ask the Secretary of State for Employment how many clients have passed through the assessment process of the employment rehabilitation service over the last two years; and how many through the rehabilitation process.

**Mr. Nicholls:** In 1987-88 the employment rehabilitation service helped about 16,000 people in total. About 13,400 attended assessment courses and 12,200 attended rehabilitation courses. In 1988-89 the ERS helped about 26,000 people in total. About 25,300 attended assessment courses and 11,800 attended rehabilitation courses. In each year a number of people attended both types of courses.

**Mr. Strang:** To ask the Secretary of State for Employment how many organisations other than the employment rehabilitation service have the facilities to provide residential employment rehabilitation services to disabled people such as are currently provided by Egham and Preston employment rehabilitation centres.

**Mr. Nicholls:** There are a number of organisations with facilities which potentially could be used for the provision of residential rehabilitation services as currently provided by Egham and Preston employment rehabilitation centres.

My Department has contracted with a number of residential establishments for the provision of services and is conducting negotiations with others.

**Mr. Strang:** To ask the Secretary of State for Employment how many vacancies currently exist in the employment rehabilitation service for each of the following grades *(a)* occupational psychologists, *(b)* social workers, *(c)* ERC nurses and *(d)* physiotherapists; and how many staff in each group are in post.

**Mr. Nicholls:** The information sought in the first part of the question is not available in the form required.

The number of staff in post by grade at 8 June 1989 is:

| | *Number* |
|---|---|
| (a) occupational psychologists | 63 |
| (b) social workers | 28·5 |
| (c) ERC nurses | 24 |
| (d) physiotherapists | 5 |

**Mr. Strang:** To ask the Secretary of State for Employment what publications are available which give guidance to training agents and training managers on the services provided by the employment rehabilitation service; and how training agents and managers can obtain copies of such guidance.

**Mr. Nicholls:** In addition to references in the training agents' and training managers' handbooks, the services of the employment rehabilitation service have been outlined to training agents and training managers through the Training Agency publication "Employment Training News" and through the publicity leaflets of the employment rehabilitation service.

### Disabled People

**Mr. Strang:** To ask the Secretary of State for Employment when he expects to publish the report of the ministerial review of employment provision for disabled people.

**Mr. Nicholls:** I refer the hon. Gentleman to the reply I gave to my hon. Friend the Member for Exeter (Mr. Hannam) on 8 November 1988 at column *54.*

### Student Union Fees

**Mr. Wall:** To ask the Secretary of State for Employment what percentage the Training Commission pays of student union fees of those students on Government training schemes whilst at college.

**Mr. Cope:** The Training Agency (formerly the Training Commission) is not responsible for payment of student union fees for students on Government training schemes whilst at college.

### Visually Handicapped Employees

**Mr. Evennett:** To ask the Secretary of State for Employment how many registered blind or other visually handicapped persons are employed in the United Kingdom; and if he will make a statement.

**Mr. Nicholls:** This information is not available. My Department provides a wide range of help to visually handicapped people including specialist placing, rehabilitation and training provision, a personal reader scheme, provision of special aids and equipment and sheltered employment.

We work closely with the Royal National Institute for the Blind in developing these provisions.

### Part-time Education

**Mr. Wall:** To ask the Secretary of State for Employment how many unemployed people studied part-time in further education in each year from 1979 to 1989.

**Mr. Cope:** Available estimates from labour force surveys show that the number of unemployed people (using the ILO/OECD definition) receiving part-time education in Great Britain was as follows:

| Year | Thousands |
|------|-----------|
| 1984 | 74 |
| 1985 | 68 |
| 1986 | 79 |
| 1987 | 81 |
| ¹1988 | 70 |

¹ Preliminary estimate

This includes those on a part-time course at university, polytechnic or college, including day release and block release, studying through the Open Tech, Open University or Open College, or studying on another correspondence course. The term "further education" is not specifically used in the LFS question. Data on unemployed persons receiving part-time education were not collected in labour force surveys prior to 1984, on a basis comparable with later years.

### Unique Fish (Employees' Award)

**Mr. Alan Williams:** To ask the Secretary of State for Employment why the employees of Unique Fish in Swansea have waited six months and have not yet received their protective award; and what part of the delay has been attributable to his Department transferring the administrative work from Cardiff to Birmingham and then to Manchester.

**Mr. Nicholls** *[holding answer 19 June 1989]:* Following my reply to the hon. Member on 10 April 1989, the insolvency practitioner has submitted a statement of the amount due. This has been approved by my Department's Birmingham office, and I expect payment to be made shortly by the regional finance office in Manchester. Cardiff office was closed prior to this case and was not involved.

### Council for Social Aid (ET Scheme)

**Mr. Tony Lloyd:** To ask the Secretary of State for Employment what responsibility he accepts for payment to staff on the Council for Social Aid employment training scheme for work done prior to the liquidation of the training scheme.

**Mr. Nicholls:** Wages owed to CSA Ltd's staff are the responsibility of the company and the employees concerned are its creditors. As such their interests are now a matter for the company's liquidators.

The Training Agency has provided CSA Ltd. with all the funding due under its contract, including amounts to cover wages costs up to the date the company ceased trading.

### Job Club (Walkden)

**Mr. Lewis:** To ask the Secretary of State for Employment (1) what are the circumstances which led to the decision to close the job club at the Walkden jobcentre;

(2) if there are any plans to offer alternative job club facilities in the Walkden are a consequent upon the recent closure of the job club at Walkden jobcentre.

**Mr. Nicholls** *[holding answers 16 June 1989]:* I refer the hon. Member to the reply given to my Friend the Member for Bury, North (Mr. Burt) on 27 January 1989, at column *810* in which I announced that we would be able to increase numbers helped by job clubs while streamlining the network.

The job club located in the jobcentre at Walkden closed on 28 April 1989. A second job club in Walkden remained open and had enough spare capacity to take on members from the job club which closed. There is also a job club in nearby Swinton.

## Employment Services (Privatisation)

**Mr. Alfred Morris:** To ask the Secretary of State for Employment what implications his policy of privatising employment services have on future receipts of grants for those services from the European social fund; and if he will make a statement.

**Mr. Cope** *[holding answer 14 June 1989]:* Professional and Executive Recruitment has already been privatised, and arrangements for the sale of the Skills Training Agency are well advanced. Such initiatives do not affect support under the European social fund.

# Written Answers to Questions

*Thursday 22 June 1989*

## HOME DEPARTMENT

### Kurdish Refugees

**Mr. Frank Field:** To ask the Secretary of State for the Home Department if he will place a copy of his reply to Charter 87 on the Government's treatment of Kurd refugees in the Library.

**Mr. Renton:** I hope to be able to reply shortly to Charter 87's letter of 8 June and will place a copy of that reply in the Library.

### Punishment in the Community

**Mr. Sheerman:** To ask the Secretary of State for the Home Department (1) if he will list all those organisations and individuals who responded to the Green Paper "Punishment, Custody in the Community", Cm. 424 and indicate which of them were in favour and which against *(a)* direct payment of compensation awards to victims of crime via court funds, *(b)* mediation by the probation service, *(c)* alterations of the minimum 40 hours for community service, *(d)* increasing the maximum period for attending a day centre, *(e)* greater use of tracking, *(f)* giving courts powers to require offenders to stay at home, *(g)* negative restrictions in probation orders, *(h)* judicial supervision of the proposed supervision and restriction order, *(i)* increasing the age limit for the juvenile court to 18 years, *(j)* giving magistrates or GPs the power to determine in which courts 16 to 20-year-olds should be heard, and *(k)* the setting up of a new organisation to take responsibilities for the arrangement of punishment in the community;

(2) if he will make copies of the responses of the organisations and individuals who have responded to the Green Paper "Punishment, Custody in the Community", Cm. 424 available to researchers and other interested bodies.

**Mr. John Patten:** The main organisations that responded to the Green Paper "Punishment, Custody and the Community" were set out in reply to a question from the hon. Member for St. Helens, South (Mr. Bermingham) on 2 May. It is for those who responded to decide whether to make their comments available more widely.

### Remand System

**Mr. Sheerman:** To ask the Secretary of State for the Home Department (1) if he will list all those organisations and individuals who responded to the Green Paper, "Private Sector Involvement in the Remand System" Cm. 434 and indicating which of them were in favour and which against *(a)* privately managed secure bail hostels *(b)* the privatisation of remand prisons and *(c)* the privatisation of escort services;

(2) if he will make copies of the organisations and individuals who have responded to the Green Paper, "Private Sector Involvement in the Remand System" Cm. 434 available to researchers and other interested bodies.

**Mr. Douglas Hogg:** Eighty five organisations and individuals submitted comments on the Green Paper. These are listed as follows. Copies of the responses (except that from one organisation which commented in confidence) were placed in the Library when my right hon. Friend made his statement of 1 March at columns 277-78. A wide range of views was expressed on many aspects of the issues raised in the Green Paper, and it would be misleading to attempt to summarise the responses in the form requested. The responses are available for inspection on application to the Remands Unit, Home Office, Room 723, Thames house south, Millbank SW1P 4QJ.

*Organisations and individuals who responded to the Green paper "Private Sector Involvement in the Remand System" (Cm. 434)*

1. Mr. J. Hunter, Governor, Her Majesty's Prison Highpoint
2. Mr. A. Samuels, Barrister
3. Sir Leon Radzinowicz (letter to *The Times*)
4. Mr. E. Knapman, Assistant Chief Probation Officer, Northamptonshire Probation Service
5. Correctional Medical Systems Inc. (USA)
6. Mr. P. E. Ford, Grade VI, Her Majesty's Remand Centre Feltham
7. Mr. D. Waplington, Head of New Entrant Prison Officer Training, Prison Service College, Wakefield
8. Mr. A. Booth, Grade VII, Her Majesty's Prison Gloucester
9. The Detention Corporation Limited
10. The Magistrates' Association
11. Mr. P. Turnbull and Mr. P. Quinn, Her Majesty's Remand Centre Risley
12. Northumbria Probation Service
13. Central Council of Magistrates' Courts Committees
14. Justices' Clerks' Society
15. Mrs. M. McCarey
16. Trades Union Congress
17. National Schizophrenia Fellowship
18. International Hospitals Group Limited
19. Conservative Group of Councillors on Lewisham Council
20. Dr. Keith Soothill, Member of Board of Visitors, Her Majesty's Prison Preston
21. Association of Chief Police Officers
22. Police Superintendents' Association
23. National Association for the Care and Resettlement of Offenders
24. West Yorkshire Probation Committee
25. Bedfordshire Probation Committee
26. Securicor Limited
27. National Union of Civil and Public Servants (Lord Chancellor's Department Group)
28. Berkshire Probation Service
29. Institute of Psychiatry
30. Mrs. B. Bingham, Education Officer, HMP Latchmere House
31. Professor Anthony Bottoms
32. Association of County Councils
33. Tarmac Construction
34. Standing Conference of Clerks to Magistrates' Courts Committees
35. Home Office Trade Union Side
36. Board of Visitors Co-ordinating Committee
37. The Education Department, Her Majesty's prison Holloway
38. Dr. David Wilson, Her Majesty's prison Grendon
39. National Association of Probation Officers
40. Association of Chief Officers of Probation
41. Howard League for Penal Reform
42. Her Majesty's Inspectorate of Probation
43. Mr. John Greenway MP: Selsdon Group Paper
44. Prison Reform Trust

45. The Mothers' Union
46. Prison Governors' Association
47. Mr. C. Lloyd, Member of Board of Visitors, Her Majesty's prison Sudbury
48. Mr. T. C. Newell, Governor—Her Majesty's prison and Remand centre Winchester
49. Police Federation
50. Lord Chancellor's Department Trade Union Side
51. United Kingdom Detention Services
52. The Law Society
53. London Diocesan Board for Social Responsibility
54. Metropolitan Police
55. Prison Officers' Association
56. Prison Service Chaplaincy
57. Contract Prisons PLC

*And the Boards of Visitors at the following establishments:*
58. HMYCC Aylesbury
59. HMP Bedford
60. HMP Birmingham
61. HMP Brixton
62. HMP Cookham Wood
63. HMYOI Dover
64. HMP Erlestoke
65. HMP and YCC Exeter
66. HMYCC and RC Feltham
67. HMP and YCC Grendon/HMP Spring Hill
68. HMYCC Hatfield
69. HMP Haverigg Camp
70. HMP Hindley
71. HMP Holloway
72. HMP Hull
73. HMP Latchmere House
74. HMP Lewes
75. HMP Leyhill
76. HMRC Low Newton
77. HMP Nottingham
78. HMP Preston
79. HMP Reading
80. HMRC Risley
81. HMP Sudbury
82. HMP Swaleside

83. HMP The Verne
84. HMYOI Whatton
85. HMP and RC Winchester

**Mr. Sheerman:** To ask the Secretary of State for the Home Department what action he proposes to take to ensure that 15 and 16-year-olds cease to be remanded in custody to prison department establishments.

**Mr. Douglas Hogg:** We are considering the present arrangements for juvenile remands in the light of responses to last year's consultation paper on the unruliness certification procedure and other representations.

### Hull Prison

**Mr. Sheerman:** To ask the Secretary of State for the Home Department what plans he has to improve facilities in B wing of Hull prison; and what resources are being provided for this task.

**Mr. Douglas Hogg:** A programme of work is in hand to improve conditions in B wing at Her Majesty's prison, Hull. To date, the bathing areas have been upgraded and the wing has been redecorated throughout. In addition, a library has been provided and existing classrooms extended; these are now used for association purposes in the evening. Fire precautions have also been improved, and polycarbonate windows are now being installed. The work to date has cost approximately £130,000.

### Prisons

**Mr. Sheerman:** To ask the Secretary of State for the Home Department how many (a) occupied places in open prisons, (b) unoccupied places in open prisons and (c) prisoners categorised as category D but held in closed prisons, there are in each prison department region.

**Mr. Douglas Hogg:** The information requested is as follows:

| Prison service region | Population of open prisons[1] | | Number of unoccupied places in open prisons[1] | | Number of category D prisoners in closed prisons[2][3] |
|---|---|---|---|---|---|
| | *Male* | *Female* | *Male* | *Female* | |
| Midland | 849 | — | 33 | — | 390 |
| North | 958 | 315 | 52 | 35 | 550 |
| South East | 955 | 75 | 96 | 0 | 600 |
| South West | 591 | — | 3 | — | 370 |
| TOTAL | 3,353 | 390 | 184 | 35 | 1,910 |

[1] On 9 June 1989. Open young offender institutions are not included.
[2] On 31 March 1989, the most recent date for which information is available. The figures are known to contain some inaccuracies.
[3] Males only. Females are not categorised in the same way as males.

**Mr. Sheerman:** To ask the Secretary of State for the Home Department what was (a) the average daily prison population and (b) the number of places in open prisons each year from 1966 to 1988.

**Mr. Douglas Hogg:** The information requested is published annually in the report of the work of the prison service (appendix 4 of the latest issue, for 1987-88, Cm. 516).

### Television (Scotland)

**Mrs. Ray Michie:** To ask the Secretary of State for the Home Department how much money has been raised through the ITV levy from Scottish companies for S4C in each of the years since S4C was established.

**Mr. Renton:** S4C is not funded from levy income. All ITV companies pay a fourth channel subscription to the Independent Broadcasting Authority, which is used to fund both Channel 4 and S4C. The IBA determines the proportion of this subscription to go to S4C, which may be up to 20 per cent.

Fourth channel subscription payments by Scottish ITV companies in the years since S4C was established were as follows:

| Year ending | STV | Grampian | Border | Total |
|---|---|---|---|---|
| | *£ million* | *£ million* | *£ million* | *(rounded) £ million* |
| December 1982 | 2·35 | 0·12 | 0·05 | 2·52 |
| December 1983 | 6·11 | 0·46 | 0·11 | 6·68 |
| March 1985 | 7·21 | 0·53 | 0·12 | 7·86 |

| Year ending | STV £ million | Grampian £ million | Border £ million | Total (rounded) £ million |
|---|---|---|---|---|
| March 1986 | 9·76 | 0·59 | 0·16 | 10·50 |
| March 1987 | 11·11 | 0·55 | 0·16 | 11·82 |
| March 1988 | 12·46 | 0·40 | 0·16 | 13·01 |
| March 1989 | 13·20 | 0·39 | 0·16 | 13·75 |
| Total (rounded) | 62·20 | 3·03 | 0·92 | 66·15 |

These figures do not represent the net cost of the fourth channel subscription to the ITV companies. The subscription is offset by reduced levy and tax liabilities and fourth channel advertising revenue. Precise figures on the extent of these offsets are not available.

### Drug Abuse

**Mr. Baldry:** To ask the Secretary of State for the Home Department if he will make a statement on the initiatives that he is taking to combat abuse of the drug known as crack.

**Mr. Douglas Hogg:** I refer my hon. Friend to the reply given to a question from my hon. Friend the Member for Bosworth (Mr. Tredinnick) on 15 June 1989 at column *1113*.

### Gambling

**Mr. Wilson:** To ask the Secretary of State for the Home Department (1) if he will make representations to other Governments in the European Community that they only authorise gaming competitions on conditions that invitations to forward stakes are not sent through agencies or otherwise to countries whose laws forbid such lotteries within their national territories;

(2) To ask the Secretary of State for the Home Department what representations he has made to other Governments in the European Community to prevent the unauthorised sale of foreign lottery tickets in the United Kingdom.

**Mr. John Patten:** The Foreign and Commonwealth Office has approached the authorities in the Federal Republic of Germany to explore means of stopping the posting of invitations to participate in lotteries based there to people in Great Britain, as the promotion and conduct of foreign lotteries here is unlawful under the Lotteries and Amusements Act 1976. We have no evidence of need to ask for a similar approach to be made to the authorities in any other member state of the Community, but we would certainly do so if necessary. Our understanding is that gambling legislation is a matter for each member state of the Community, as in any other country; and the means, if any, necessary to achieve respect for the law on lotteries in another country is a matter for national determination.

**Mr. Wilson:** To ask the Secretary of State for the Home Department what advice he has received from the European Commission on whether national legislation on gambling games is justified on grounds of public morality and consumer protection.

**Mr. John Patten:** None.

### Official Secrets Act 1989 and Security Services Act 1989

**Mr. Livingston:** To ask the Secretary of State for the Home Department on what date the Official Secrets Act 1989 and the Security Services Act 1989 will come into force.

**Mr. John Patten:** As soon as practicable.

### Tamil Refugees

**Mrs. Mahon:** To ask the Secretary of State for the Home Department (1) what representations he has received concerning Navaratnasingam Vathanan, a Tamil who was returned to Colombo in February 1988; and if he will make a statement;

(2) what representations he has received concerning Vythialingam Skandarajah, a Tamil who was returned to Colombo in February 1988; and if he will make a statement.

**Mr. Renton** *[holding answer 19 June 1989]:* A judicial review of our decisions to refuse refugee status to these two cases and to four other Tamils was dismissed by the House of Lords in December 1987 and they were returned to Sri Lanka in February 1988. On 13 March 1989 an adjudicator upheld appeals against refusal of leave to enter in five of these cases. My right hon. Friend sought leave to appeal to the tribunal on 22 March but on 19 April the tribunal decided that it had no jurisdiction to consider this appeal because of a clerical error in the service of the papers. On 12 May my right hon. Friend sought leave to move for judicial review of the tribunal's decision and leave was granted on 17 May. We have received a number of representations about the cases from hon. Members, organisations and individuals.

### Pop Concerts

**Mr. Dykes:** To ask the Secretary of State for the Home Department if he will urgently examine existing legislation governing the holding of mass outdoor pop concerts and similar functions to assess the need to strengthen any provisions concerning (i) sound levels and decibel controls, (ii) prior warnings to local residents and (iii) provisions against exceeding any licence terms including time limits.

**Mr. Douglas Hogg** *[holding answer 14 June 1989]:* The powers conferred on local authorities for the granting of public entertainments licences under the London Government Act 1963 and the Local Government (Miscellaneous Provisions) Act 1982 are already very wide and should, in my view, be sufficient to enable them to regulate these matters.

### PC Gerald Corley

**Mr. Mullin:** To ask the Secretary of State for the Home Department if he will ask the chief constable of Manchester to list the complaints made by members of the public against former PC Gerald Corley and the action taken in each case.

**Mr. Douglas Hogg** *[holding answer 12 June 1989]:* Responsibility for the investigation of complaints against police officers and for consideration of disciplinary action rests with the chief officer of the force concerned, subject to the provisions of part IX of the Police and Criminal Evidence Act 1984. My right hon. Friend has no part to play in these procedures.

It is not the normal practice to reveal details from a police officer's personal file. I understand from the chief constable of Greater Manchester, however, that complaints were made by members of the public against ex-PC Corley on 19 occasions from December 1977. All these complaints were fully investigated in accordance with the statutory procedures in force at the time. Where a complaint was withdrawn prior to the completion of the investigation it was reviewed by a senior police officer in accordance with force procedures.

In only two cases were complaints against Mr. Corley found to have a sufficient measure of substantiation to justify action being taken against the officer. Both concerned allegations of irregularity in procedure. On both occasions Mr. Corley was interviewed by a senior officer.

## TRADE AND INDUSTRY

### "Phones on the Move"

**Sir David Price:** To ask the Chancellor of the Duchy of Lancaster whether there has been any further developments following the publication of the discussion document "Phones on the Move" in January; and whether he will make a statement.

**Mr. Atkins:** My right hon. and noble Friend the Secretary of State for Trade and Industry has considered carefully the responses to the discussion document in the light of our wish to select at least two operators to provide personal communications networks (PCNs) in the 1990s. We have also received advice from the Director General of Telecommunications.

The director general has advised us that the capacity of Mercury Communications Ltd., a subsidiary of Cable & Wireless plc, to provide the full range of telecommunications services in competition with British Telecom is limited by the lack of a mobile radio network to compete with Cellnet, in which BT has a majority stake. We have therefore accepted his advice that a consortium led by Mercury or Cable & Wireless should be a prospective operator and in due course be offered one of the licences to operate a mobile communications network within the frequency range 1·7-2·3 GHz. This is subject to the submission of an acceptable proposal, both in regard to the consortium and in business and technical terms, by 14 September.

On the advice of the director general, we intend to identify one, or possibly two, other prospective operators by the end of the year. We are issuing notes for the guidance of applicants today. Copies of these notes have been placed in the libraries of both Houses. The closing date for applications is noon on Thursday 14 September.

Applications may be made by any company, whether or not it responded to the discussion document. The exceptions are Cellnet and Racal Vodafone, their associates and main shareholders. Since the new networks are intended to compete with these companies' existing cellular radio operations, we have decided, on the director general's advice, that they should not be able to participate in their development or operation either in their own right or as a member of a consortium. We will, however, keep

under review their needs for additional frequencies in the light of the progress they make on the pan-European cellular network and the development of competition in the United Kingdom.

We have also considered the choice of PCN technology, which will govern the appropriate technical standards. The two technologies which emerged strongly from the consultation period were those being developed for the pan-European digital cellular radio system and the digital European cordless telephone. it is our intention that the PCNs should operate according to a common technical standard, in order to ensure competition between the operators. It would be highly desirable for this to be based on a technology developed in Europe. Accordingly, we have decided that applications must be based on one or other of these technologies, and applicants may, if they wish, put in separate proposals based on each. The selected common standard will be announced when the choice of operator is made and will take account of developments in Europe.

We have also considered the major cost of linking the small radio cells needed to provide a true PCN. To aid the planning of these networks for the 1990s, we have decided that the operators will be able to provide their own radio-based network infrastructure between individual radio cells. However, the links to the public switched network, which provides the basic telecommunications service of conveying messages over fixed links, will still be provided by British Telecom or Mercury pending the outcome of the November 1990 duopoly review. In order to protect the position of the new entrants, any request by the existing cellular operators to provide similar radio links for their own networks will be considered in the light of their progress in implementing the pan-European cellular network but will in any event not be implemented until two years after both of the new PCNs have entered service, provided there are no undue delays in the introduction of the new networks.

We have been aware of the possible affect of this initiative on the four Telepoint operators we announced in January. We do not believe that the PCN initiative should significantly affect their prospects for success. The new networks will offer two-way call initiation aimed to compete with cellular radio, with its relatively expensive and sophisticated technology, and will not begin service until 1992 at the earliest. By contrast the inherently lower cost one-way Telepoint technology has already been developed and we expect it to be introduced into the marketplace well before the end of the year. We have, however, asked the director general to pay particular regard to any new ideas from the Telepoint operators themselves as to how the Telepoint concept could be further developed in the future and to advise us as necessary.

The "Phones on the Move" discussion document put forward our vision of the future in PCNs and companies responded to it with enthusiasm and imagination. We intend to maintain this momentum, and to encourage industry to make this vision a reality in the early 1990s. We do not anticipate any further major developments in new mobile telecommunications systems for some time. As a result of our announcement today and previous announcements on Telepoint, cellular radio, private mobile radio and paging, the Government have opened up new markets and provided for effective competition. We hope that all the companies involved in this field will continue to respond vigorously and to exploit the opportunities that have been created.

### Public Houses and Clubs

**Mr. Riddick:** To ask the Chancellor of the Duchy of Lancaster whether he has any evidence, in the form of comprehensive and reliable consumer surveys, on the state of consumer satisfaction or dissatisfaction with public houses and clubs in Britain.

**Mr. Forth:** I am aware of two surveys which are relevant. First the Consumers Association conducted a survey of 2,175 adults in May 1987, which formed the basis of their evidence of the Monopolies and Mergers Commission investigation into the supply of beer. A number of questions were asked which related to consumer satisfaction. According to the Consumers Association, of those respondents who said they visited pubs less often than two years previously, the largest single reason was that drinks in pubs were too expensive.

Two thirds of respondents agreed that all pubs should be allowed to sell draught bitter from more than one brewer, and 61 per cent. agreed that pub prices were too high compared with supermarkets and off-licences. More recently, Haig Whisky has published results from a MORI poll of 1,037 adults who go to the pub at least once a month, carried out in 65 constituency sampling points in the second half of May 1989. This survey was carried out to examine attitudes towards the MMC's recommendations for changes in the brewing industry. It showed a majority in favour of the Government implementing the MMC recommendations. Eighty-four per cent. said landlords (that is publicans) should have more freedom to introduce other beers. Sixty per cent. thought the quality of pubs would increase as a result of the MMC recommendations.

The Consumers Association and Haig Whisky have published documents containing the detailed results of their surveys. I am aware of recent reports that a survey commissioned by the Brewers Society comes to different conclusions, but I have not yet seen the details.

### International Organisations

**Mr. Patrick Thompson:** To ask the Chancellor of the Duchy of Lancaster what is the policy of Her Majesty's Government towards the continued location of the International Sugar Organisation and the Wheat Council in London; what is Her Majesty's Government's policy towards the anti-competitive foreign subsidies being deferred to those organisations; and if he will make a statement.

**Mr. Maude:** As my right hon. Friend the Prime Minister told the House on 25 April, the Government welcome the location of these organisations in London. They have based themselves here for many years because of the merits of London as the leading international trading centre for their products. The Government are therefore prepared to give the London chamber's proposal their full support including a financial contribution in equal partnership with the private sector. The Government will, of course, also provide the usual rates concessions to the two organisations. We shall continue to work to discourage subsidised competition so that different locations can compete fairly on their merits.

### Frag 12

**Mr. Ieuan Wyn Jones:** To ask the Chancellor of the Duchy of Lancaster in respect of which countries export licences have been applied for in respect of the weapon known as Frag 12; and what is the result of the application in each case.

**Mr. Alan Clark** *[holding answer 20 June 1989]:* No application has been received for a licence to export the Frag 12 fragmentation grenade from the United Kingdom.

## EDUCATION AND SCIENCE

### Clinical Cytogeneticists

**Mr. Amos:** To ask the Secretary of State for Education and Science if he will make a statement on the level of pay and recruitment of university clinical cytogeneticists.

**Mr. Jackson:** It is for the universities as employers to determine the level of pay and recruitment of their staff.

### English Teaching

**Mr. Jack:** To ask the Secretary of State for Education and Science when he expects his proposals for attainment targets and programmes of study for English for pupils in junior and secondary schools to be published for consultation.

**Mr. Kenneth Baker:** My right hon. Friend the Secretary of State for Wales and I have now formulated our proposals for attainment targets and programmes of study in English for pupils in key stages 2 to 4 (broadly ages eight to 16). Our proposals endorse without modification the relevant recommendations of the national curriculum English working group, and build on the provisions in the order covering English in key stage 1 laid before Parliament on 31 May. We are grateful to the group for its clear and helpful advice.

I have today referred our proposals to the national curriculum council to start the consultation in England required by the Education Reform Act. My right hon. Friend will be initiating separate consultations in Wales as required by the Act. I have placed a copy of our proposals and the working group's report, together with a copy of my letter to the national curriculum council, in the Library.

## HOUSE OF COMMONS

### Radio Broadcasting

**Mr. Spearing:** To ask the Lord President of the Council what information he has available and what information is available to hon. Members concerning the scope and extent of reportage by sound radio of proceedings in the Chamber of the House of Commons throughout its sittings.

**Mr. Wakeham:** I am not aware of any recent systematic monitoring carried out, either by the House or on its behalf, of the use to which the sound feed from the Chamber is put. So far as the broadcasters themselves are concerned, I am advised that the BBC does not collate statistics of the degree of detail implied by the hon. Gentleman's question and that to do so would be a time-consuming and costly exercise.

## Parliamentary Questions

**Mr. Ron Davies:** To ask the Lord President of the Council what guidance is issued to departmental Ministers on the criteria to be observed in determining whether to answer parliamentary questions tabled during the previous day's sitting.

**Mr. Wakeham:** Ministers are expected to follow the provisions of Standing Order No. 17.

## ENVIRONMENT

### Community Charge

**Mr. Madden:** To ask the Secretary of State for the Environment when he will publish the full set of community charge practice notes; to whom the public should apply for these notes; and when applications should be made.

**Mr. Gummer:** Community charge practice notes are published jointly by the Government and local authority associations. Nineteen notes have been issued so far and copies are available in the Library of the House. The notes are detailed, technical manuals intended for the use of local authority practitioners rather than the general public. A separate series of explanatory booklets are available to the public free of charge from Community Charge Leaflets Section PO Box 622, Bristol B599 1TR.

**Mr. Wigley:** To ask the Secretary of State for the Environment what guidelines he has issued on the evidence which is acceptable for poll tax purposes, that an individual is entitled to severe disablement allowance or to invalidity pension; and if he will make a statement.

**Mr. Gummer:** The Government have no plans to introduce a poll tax.

Detailed guidance on the evidence required to satisfy an exemption from the community charge on grounds of severe mental impairment is contained in community charge practice note No. 19, copies of which have been placed in the Library of the House.

**Mr. Cohen:** To ask the Secretary of State for the Environment how many local authorities have indicated to his Department that their costs in implementing the community charge are likely to be *(a)* less and *(b)* more than the amount granted for the purpose by Her Majesty's Government.

**Mr. Gummer:** The information we have on the revenue costs to authorities of implementation suggest that about 15 per cent. of them will be spending less than has been provided in the 1989-90 rate support grant settlement; most of the remainder intend to spend more.

**Mr. Cohen:** To ask the Secretary of State for the Environment what is his latest estimate of the proportion of total community charge implementation costs Her Majesty's Government have provided.

**Mr. Gummer:** The actual costs of implementation will not be known until next year but the figures contained in authorities' budget returns suggest that Government provision will support about half of authorities' estimated revenue expenditure on preparation. Similar figures for capital are not available. It was never the intention that resources received by individual authorities would necessarily meet in full the estimated costs of their own preferred plans. This would give no incentive to efficient implementation. We believe the resources we have made available—£110 million in the 1989-90 rate support grant settlement and capital allocations totalling £160 million —are sufficient to support reasonable levels of local authority expenditure in preparation.

**Mr. Cohen:** To ask the Secretary of State for the Environment what representations he has received that his Department arrange for a survey to be made of the costs actually incurred by all local authorities on implementation of the community charge; whether he will undertake such a survey; and if he will make a statement.

**Mr. Gummer:** We have received no such representations and have no plans to carry out such a survey. The usual financial returns from authorities to the Department will provide this information.

**Mr. Tony Lloyd:** To ask the Secretary of State for the Environment if he will seek to exempt from the provisions of the poll tax those who are mainly or wholly dependent on moneys provided to victims of Nazi persecutions.

**Mr. Gummer:** The Government have no plans to introduce a poll tax.

Individuals are exempt from the community charge if their circumstances conform to one of the categories set out in schedule 1 to the Local Government Finance Act 1988.

**Mr. Allen:** To ask the Secretary of State for the Environment how many newspapers printed his recently circulated articles on the community charge.

**Mr. Gummer:** I refer the hon. Member to the answer which my right hon. Friend, the Secretary of State gave the hon. Member for Coventry, South-East (Mr. Nellist) on 23 May at column *488*.

**Mr. Terry Davis:** To ask the Secretary of State for the Environment how many requests for community charge practice notes have been refused.

**Mr. Gummer** [*holding answer 12 June 1989*]: Community charge practice notes (which are produced jointly by the Government and the local authority association) contain guidance on technical details of the new system for the local authority staff who will be operating it. Copies of each note are provided free to all local authorities and others with a specific need for the information, and are placed in the Library of the House. Copies of the notes have not been made generally available to other bodies or the public. We have prepared a range of leaflets for that purpose.

**Mr. Strang:** To ask the Secretary of State for the Environment whether itinerant workers under the community charge will have to pay a personal charge at their permanent address and a collective charge if they are living in a designated dwelling at or near their workplace levied by their landlord.

**Mrs. Virginia Bottomley** [*holding answer 21 June 1989*]: A person registered for the personal community charge at his or her sole or main residence who stays in a property designated for the collective community charge will pay contributions towards the collective charge payable by the landlord or owner of the property.

## Sites of Special Scientific Interest

**Mr. Malcolm Bruce:** To ask the Secretary of State for the Environment how many sites of special scientific interest have been designated each year since the inception of the Wildlife and Countryside Act 1981; and how many he estimates will be created in the next 12 months.

**Mrs. Virginia Bottomley:** The Wildlife and Countryside Act 1981 provides for both renotification of sites of special scientific interest originally notified under the National Park and Access to the Countryside Act 1949 and notification of new SSSIs. The number of such sites are:

| Financial year | Number of new SSSIs notified in the year |
|---|---|
| Renotifications | |
| To 31 March 1989 | 3,187 |
| New notifications | |
| 1981-82 | 0 |
| 1982-83 | 35 |
| 1983-84 | 183 |
| 1984-85 | 268 |
| 1985-86 | 358 |
| 1986-87 | 261 |
| 1987-88 | 274 |
| 1988-89 | 282 |

In addition the Nature Conservancy Council expects to renotify 135 sites and notify a further 250 sites in the current financial year.

**Mr. Malcolm Bruce:** To ask the Secretary of State for the Environment what percentage of the total number of sites of special scientific interest have been *(a)* destroyed and *(b)* damaged since the inception of the Wildlife and Countryside Act 1981.

**Mrs. Virginia Bottomley:** No information is available prior to 1 April 1984. I am informed by the Nature Conservancy Council that since then the numbers of SSSIs which have sustained damage are as follows:

| | Number | Per cent. |
|---|---|---|
| 1984-85 | 192 | 6·77 |
| 1985-86 | 151 | 4·84 |
| 1986-87 | 205 | 6·86 |
| 1987-88 | 139 | 4·36 |

This includes damage of all kinds, whether significant or not, and to both those SSSIs notified under the 1981 Act and those notified under the National Parks and Access to the Countryside Act 1949 and not yet renotified. The number of SSSIs suffering significant damage averaged about 1 per cent. over the period.

Over this period three SSSIs were destroyed, two in 1984-85 and one in 1985-86.

Full information is provided in the NCC's annual reports copies of which are in the Library.

## Bristol Channel (Discharges)

**Mr. Speller:** To ask the Secretary of State for the Environment how many sources of industrial and trade effluent discharges there are into the Bristol channel; and where they are located.

**Mrs. Virginia Bottomley:** Responsibility for the control of discharges of industrial and trade effluent to the Bristol channel rests with the Welsh, Wessex and South West water authorities. Details of consents granted by the authorities in respect of such discharges are held on the registers maintained by each authority.

## Rating Reform

**Mr. Cohen:** To ask the Secretary of State for the Environment whether he will tabulate what a single person living in the london borough of Waltham Forest would pay *(a)* in community charge and *(b)* in a system of capital value rates plus local income tax paid in proportions of 80 to 20, respectively if the person earned *(a)* £40,000, *(b)* £80,000 and *(c)* £120,000 and lived in (i) property owned by that person worth £90,000, (ii) property owned by that person worth £120,000 and (iii) property owned by that person worth £150,000, making the same assumptions as in his reply to the hon. Member for Hornsey and Wood Green (Sir H. Rossi) on 22 March, *Official Report,* column *626.*

**Mr. Gummer:** The information requested is provided in the table.

*Illustrative annual liability in Waltham Forest under a system of capital value rates combined with local income tax, 1988-89*

| Single persons earnings | Property value £90,000 | Property value £120,000 | Property value £150,000 |
|---|---|---|---|
| £40,000 | 1,375 | 1,655 | 1,935 |
| £80,000 | 1,940 | 2,220 | 2,505 |
| £120,000 | 2,510 | 2,790 | 3,070 |

The figures are based on illustrative tax rates placed in the Library on 23 June 1988 and are for 1988-89. It is assumed that the person lives alone and taxable income is taken as earnings less £260·5, the single person's allowance, in each case. The illustrative 1988-89 community charge in Waltham Forest is £269.

## Public Rights of Way

**Ms. Walley:** To ask the Secretary of State for the Environment when he intends to introduce legislation in response to the Rubinstein case on definitive maps of public rights of way.

**Mrs. Virginia Bottomley:** The Government have announced their intention to introduce legislation to enable genuine errors in definitive maps to be corrected when there is a suitable opportunity.

## Hong Kong Citizens (Housing)

**Mr. Nicholas Bennett:** To ask the Secretary of State for the Environment whether he has received any representations to allow large scale construction of new properties in the Yeovil constituency to accommodate citizens of the colony of Hong Kong claiming right of abode in the United Kingdom.

**Mr. Trippier:** None, as yet. It would need about $1\frac{1}{4}$ million new homes to accommodate $3\frac{1}{4}$ million people.

## HOTCHA Scheme

**Mr. Hayward:** To ask the Secretary of State for the Environment when he expects to be able to announce a replacement to the HOTCHA scheme; and if he will make a statement.

**Mr. Trippier:** The Housing Corporation has published proposals to introduce an incentive scheme in 1990 to help housing association tenants to move out and buy homes on the open market. The corporation is considering the responses.

## Community Charge

**Mr. Tony Banks:** To ask the Secretary of State for the Environment if he will make a statement on the progress of student certification for the community charge in England and Wales.

**Mr. Gummer:** The Personal Community Charge (Students) Regulations 1989 were laid before the House on 17 March. They provide for certification officers in all relevant educational establishments in England and Wales, and place a duty on them to issue a certificate in the prescribed form to each person pursuing or about to pursue a full-time course of education. The regulations will come into force on 1 October 1989.

## Fossil Fuels (Pollution)

**Mr. Thurnham:** To ask the Secretary of State for the Environment what representations he has received about reducing pollution from burning fossil fuels; and if he will make a statement.

**Mrs. Virginia Bottomley:** We have received many representations on this topic. The commitments agreed by the Government under the large combustion plants and motor vehicle emissions directives of the European Community will lead to very substantial reductions in the emissions of sulphur dioxide, nitrogen oxide, hydrocarbons and carbon monoxide.

## London City Airport

**Mr. Colvin:** To ask the Secretary of State for the Environment if he has received an application to extend the runway at London City airport.

**Mr. Chope:** No.

## Nuclear Waste (Storage)

**Dr. Kim Howells:** To ask the Secretary of State for the Environment if he will make a statement on Her Majesty's Government's policy towards the development of sub-sea bed dry storage for civil nuclear waste.

**Mrs. Virginia Bottomley:** UK Nirex Ltd. has been established to identify and develop a disposal facility for low and intermediate-level radioactive waste. Nirex is currently investigating a repository in the form of a mine under the land. The Government have endorsed this programme. The possibility of investigating other locations at a later stage, or of utilising offshore options cannot be ruled out.

## Bathing Beaches

**Mr. Barry Field:** To ask the Secretary of State for the Environment what representations he has had about imposing a statutory requirement on local authorities *(a)* to clean European designated bathing beaches of litter and *(b)* to clean any beach regularly used by the public after an oil spill.

**Mr. Moynihan:** I have had no specific representations on these subjects. We have, however, announced our intention to place local authorities under a duty to keep land clean. This is one of a number of proposals for legislation on litter which my right hon. Friend intends to announce soon.

## Childhood Cancer

**Mr. Cran:** To ask the Secretary of State for the Environment what decision has been reached by the steering committee of the London School of Hygiene's small area statistics unit as to whether to proceed with an investigation into the incidence of childhood cancer in Humberside.

**Mrs. Virginia Bottomley:** I wrote to my hon. Friend on 20 June to explain that existing information is being considered by independent export members of the steering committee so that they can advise the committee when it next meets.

## Pollution (Wales)

**Mrs. Clwyd:** To ask the Secretary of State for the Environment if he will make a statement on his responsibilities for the control of environmental pollution in Wales.

**Mrs. Virginia Bottomley:** I refer the hon. Member to the Department's publication "Protecting Your Environment —A Guide" a copy of which is in the Library of the House. Pages 2 and 3 give a succinct but complete summary of the respective responsibilities of the Secretaries of State for the Environment and for Wales for environment protection.

## Rugby Union

**Mr. Canavan:** To ask the Secretary of State for the Environment when he next expects to meet representatives of rugby union; and what subjects he expects to discuss.

**Mr. Moynihan:** I have no plans at present to meet representatives of the Rugby Football Union.

## Dioxins

**Mr. Boswell:** To ask the Secretary of State for the Environment when the report on dioxins will be published; and if he will make a statement.

**Mrs. Virginia Bottomley:** The Department of the Environment has today published a report, "Dioxins in the Environment", in the pollution paper series. It is the report of an interdepartmental working group on poly chlorinated dibenzo-para-dioxins and polychlorinated dibenzofurans. The report is the culmination of work on dioxins which began two years ago. Copies have been placed in the Library.

The main purpose of the report is to make available the best information we have on dioxins from the United

Kingdom and elsewhere. There is an analysis of what this means in terms of possible human health effects and environmental impact.

Advice on the health effects of dioxins from the Department of Health's independent advisory committee on toxicity of chemicals in food, consumer products and the environment is also included in the report.

It recommends that the major sources of dioxins should be identified and appropriate measures taken to reduce inputs of dioxins to food, consumer products and the environment.

The Government welcome this advice and have already taken steps to implement the committee's recommendations.

The report has been compiled jointly by the central directorate for environmental protection in DOE, the Department of Health, the Ministry of Agriculture, Fisheries and Food, the Department of Trade and Industry and the Health and Safety Executive.

### Drinking Water

**Mrs. Ann Taylor:** To ask the Secretary of State for the Environment if he will give details of which of the standards set in the European Community drinking water directive are regularly exceeded by each of the water supplies in England which have been granted derogations.

**Mr. Howard** *[holding answer 14 June 1989]:* A list has been placed in the Library of those supplies which regularly exceed the EC drinking water directive in respect of the standard indicated and have been granted derogations by the Department under the terms of article 9 of the directive. Such derogations can be granted only where the situation is due to the nature and structure of the ground and there is no public health risk.

### Catalytic Converters

**Mr. Flynn:** To ask the Secretary of State for the Environment if, following the agreement of European Community Environment Ministers in Luxembourg on 9 June on the use of catalytic converters in small cars from December 1992, he has made an assessment of the increased contribution to the greenhouse effect that will be caused by carbon dioxide and water vapour released in exhaust gases from United Kingdom-based cars, in the period to the year 2000.

**Mrs. Virginia Bottomley** *[holding answer 19 June 1989]:* Yes. A United Kingdom fleet of 3-way catalyst cars would emit about 7·5 million tonnes per annum more carbon dioxide than a fleet of vehicles conforming to the standards of the common position reached by Environment Ministers last November. The emission of water vapour from cars does not have a significant input on the greenhouse effect.

### Chlorofluorocarbons

**Mr. Cryer:** To ask the Secretary of State for the Environment if he will make a statement on the progress on phasing out aerosols containing chlorofluorocarbon propellants; and if he expects to introduce legislation making the sale of such items illegal.

**Mrs. Virginia Bottomley** *[holding answer 21 June 1989]:* Members of the British Aerosol Manufacturers Association are well on course to meet the objective of eliminating the non-essential use of chlorofluorocarbons in their products by the end of this year. Legislation to this effect is not needed in the circumstances.

### English Heritage

**Mr. Strang:** To ask the Secretary of State for the Environment if English Heritage has any plans to commission a study of the archaeology of waterlogged urban centres.

**Mrs. Virginia Bottomley** *[holding answer 21 June 1989]:* I understand that English Heritage intends to fund a number of archaeological surveys in urban areas. These will include waterlogged sites.

### Environmental Impact Assessment

**Mr. Strang:** To ask the Secretary of State for the Environment if he has any plans to issue guidance to archaeological bodies on environmental impact assessment and monitoring.

**Mrs. Virginia Bottomley** *[holding answer 21 June 1989]:* No. The broad principle of requiring information on the effect of proposed development being available before planning applications are considered will be discussed in guidance on "archaeology and planning", which is being prepared for local authorities, developers and archaeologists.

### Repairs Grants

**Mr. Nicholas Bennett:** To ask the Secretary of State for the Environment on what date English local authorities were first informed of changes in the amount of mandatory repairs grant from 75 per cent. to 20 per cent. for landlords under sections 130 and 131 of the Housing Act 1988; and on what date they came into effect.

**Mr. Trippier:** Local authorities in England were notified of proposed changes in the rate of intermediate and mandatory repairs grants for landlords in a letter from the Department dated 14 December 1988, following consultation with the local authority associations in November. These changes were given effect by the Grants by Local Housing Authorities (Appropriate Percentage and Exchequer Contributions) Order 1989 (SI 1989 No. 72), made under sections 509 and 517 of the Housing Act 1985, which came into foce on 19 January 1989.

## ENERGY

### Fossil Fuels

**Mr. Dykes:** To ask the Secretary of State for Energy what recent disussions he has held on concepts of fossil fuel utilisation fiscal devices to enhance or reduce the consumption of such energy sources.

**Mr. Parkinson:** I have had a number of recent discussions with my officials and others about the details of the levy on fossil fuel use for power generation, provision for which is included in the Electricity Bill now before Parliament.

### Electricity Privatisation

**Mr.Campbell-Savours:** To ask the Secretary of State for Energy whether he intends to make any further appointments to regulatory posts covering the privatised electricity industry.

**Mr. Michael Spicer:** No. Under the terms of the Electricity Bill it is the Director General of Electricity Supply who will be empowered to appoint the staff of the Office of Electricity Regulation, subject to Treasury approval of their numbers and conditions of service.

## SCOTLAND

### Sheriff Courts

**Dr. Reid:** To ask the Secretary of State for Scotland when he expects publication of the report by Dr. Carol Jones of Edinburgh university on contested cases in the Scottish sheriff courts.

**Lord James Douglas-Hamilton:** Dr. Carol Jones' report on contested cases in the Scottish sheriff courts has not yet been submitted in final form. The question of publication will be considered after it has been submitted.

**Dr. Reid:** To ask the Secretary of State for Scotland when he expects publication of the report by Dr. Kenneth Miller of Strathclyde university on delays in summarising clinical cases in the sheriff courts in Scotland.

**Lord James Douglas-Hamilton:** I hope to be able to publish Dr. Kenneth Miller's report on delay in summary criminal proceedings in the sheriff courts during the summer.

### Forestry Commission Land

**Mr. Barry Jones:** To ask the Secretary of State for Scotland what is the value of sales so far of Forestry Commission land; and if he will make a statement.

**Lord James Douglas-Hamilton:** Receipts from the disposal of land and property from the start of the disposals programme in 1981 to 31 March 1989 amounted to some £124 million.

**Mr. Barry Jones:** To ask the Secretary of State for Scotland what plans he has to sell off, and over what period of time, Forestry Commission woodland; and if he will make a statement.

**Lord James Douglas-Hamilton:** I refer the hon. Member to the answer my right hon. and learned Friend gave to my hon. Friend the Member for Dumfries (Sir H. Monro) on 16 June at columns *544-45*.

### Tree Planting

**Mr. Ron Davies:** To ask the Secretary of State for Scotland if he will publish a table showing the total planting between 1 April 1988 and 31 March 1989 in England, Scotland, Wales and Northern Ireland, respectively, in each of the categories *(a)* Forestry Commission direct planting, *(b)* private planting assisted by the woodland grant scheme, *(c)* planting under the farm woodland scheme, *(d)* other assisted private planting and *(e)* other non-assisted planting.

**Lord James Douglas-Hamilton:** The information, showing new planting (NP) and restocking (R), is as follows:

|  | England NP | R | Scotland NP | R | Wales NP | R |
|---|---|---|---|---|---|---|
| *(a)* Forestry Commission direct planting | 130 | 2,890 | 3,860 | 3,980 | 60 | 1,720 |
| *(b)* Planting under woodland grant scheme | 150 | 150 | 150 | 160 | 20 | 10 |
| *(c)* Planting under farm woodland scheme | 110 | — | 10 | — | — | — |
| *(d)* Planting under other Forestry Commission grant schemes | 1,490 | 2,180 | 22,270 | 2,090 | 900 | 250 |
| *(e)* Other non-assisted | 140 | 100 | 40 | — | — | — |

*Hectares*

The figures given for categories *(b)*, *(c)* and *(d)* are the areas on which planting grant was paid by the Forestry Commission during the period 1 April 1988 to 31 March 1989.

The situation in Northern Ireland is a matter for my right hon. Friend the Secretary of State for Northern Ireland.

### Health Service

**Mr. Allan Stewart:** To ask the Secretary of State for Scotland what has been achieved as a result of competitive tendering in the National Health Service in Scotland.

**Mr. Michael Forsyth:** Since the last general election savings from competitive tendering have increased from £600,000 to £29 million from 81 contracts for ancillary services. That represents substantial additional resources for patient care in Scotland's Health Service over the next three to four years. Almost three quarters of the contracts have been won by in-house teams. The success

of the competitive tendering programme so far has encouraged health boards to press ahead with further tendering.

### Water Quality

**Mr. Malcolm Bruce:** To ask the Secretary of State for Scotland whether the water supply at Lochaber is in breach of European Community guidelines for aluminium content, or for any other additives, metals or pesticides.

**Lord James Douglas-Hamilton** *[holding answer 19 June 1989]:* Lochaber district is served by numerous public water supplies; which have differing qualities. These supplies are the responsibility of the Highland regional council from which information on any particular supply may be obtained. A number of supplies in the area contain naturally derived aluminium at concentrations which occasionally exceed the European standard but on average are below it. Work to reduce the lead content of water at consumers' taps in lead-plumbed properties is virtually complete. No supply has been found to contain other metals or pesticides in excess of the EC standards.

### Forestry Commission (Wildlife)

**Mr. Ron Davies:** To ask the Secretary of State for Scotland what was the last advice he received from the Nature Conservancy Council concerning the practice of blocking of badger setts and digging of fox earths by fox hunters on Foresty Commission land.

**Lord James Douglas-Hamilton** [*pursuant to his reply, 21 June 1989; c. 127*]: The Forestry Commission has an earth stopper's code which is designed to prevent undue interference with badger setts and fox earths.

### SOCIAL SECURITY

### Social Fund

**Ms. Mowlam:** To ask the Secretary of State for Social Security if he will publish a table, similar to the one printed on 15 May, *Official Report,* columns *76-78,* in reply to the hon. Member for Leeds, West, (Mr. Battle) but in respect of his Department's local offices at Eston, Hartlepool, Middlesbrough, Redcar and Stockton, showing reasons for social fund loan and grant refusals during the period April 1988 to March 1989.

**Mr. Peter Lloyd** [*holding answer 9 June 1989*]: The information requested is set out in the table.

The proportions have been calculated as percentages of the total number of reasons for refusal. The total number of reasons for refusal may equal or exceed the total number of refusals because the social fund officer can give more than one reason for refusing an application.

I refer the hon. Member to my pursuant reply to the hon. Member for Leeds, West (Mr. Battle) today.

*Reasons for refusal of Social Fund loans and grants 1988-89*

| | Grants | | Loans | |
|---|---|---|---|---|
| | Number of times reason given | As percent of total times reason given | Number of times reason given | As percent of total times reason given |
| OFFICE: Eston ILO | | | | |
| Savings over £500 sufficient to meet cost | 3 | 0·9 | 0 | 0 |
| Not in receipt of IS | n/a | n/a | 107 | 6·4 |
| Not in receipt of IS for 26 weeks | n/a | n/a | 300 | 17·8 |
| Not in receipt of IS and unlikely to become entitled | 30 | 8·9 | n/a | n/a |
| Excluded items | 11 | 3·3 | 81 | 4·8 |
| Excluded persons | 11 | 3·3 | 2 | 0·1 |
| Amount <£30 (not travelling expenses | 9 | 2·7 | 52 | 3·1 |
| Total debt of £1,000 | n/a | n/a | 1 | 0·1 |
| Previous application and decision for the item | 10 | 3·0 | 78 | 4·6 |
| No serious damage or risk to health or safety | n/a | | 47 | 2·8 |
| Inability to repay | n/a | | 8 | 0·5 |
| Help available from another source | 6 | 1·8 | 6 | 0·4 |
| Insufficient SF funds, priority too low | 8 | 2·4 | 929 | 55·1 |
| Suitable alternative available | 1 | 0·3 | 3 | 0·2 |
| Loan refused because CCG awarded | n/a | n/a | 31 | 1·8 |
| Other | 248 | 73·6 | 40 | 2·4 |
| | 337 | | 1,685 | |
| OFFICE: Hartlepool ILO | | | | |
| Savings over £500 sufficient to meet cost | 3 | 0·6 | 2 | 0·1 |
| Not in receipt of IS | n/a | — | 156 | 25·4 |
| Not in receipt of IS for 26 weeks | n/a | — | 434 | 24·9 |
| Not in receipt of IS and unlikely to become entitled | 72 | 13·4 | n/a | n/a |
| Excluded items | 26 | 4·8 | 81 | 4·6 |
| Excluded persons | 10 | 1·9 | 2 | 0·1 |
| Amount <£30 (not travelling expenses | 18 | 3·3 | 52 | 3·0 |
| Total debt of £1,000 | n/a | — | 1 | 0·1 |
| Previous application and decision for the item | 22 | 4·1 | 78 | 4·5 |
| No serious damage or risk to health or safety | n/a | — | 77 | 4·4 |
| Inability to repay | n/a | — | 84 | 4·8 |
| Help available from another source | 9 | — | 62 | 3·6 |

| | Grants | | Loans | |
|---|---|---|---|---|
| | *Number of times reason given* | *As percent of total times reason given* | *Number of times reason given* | *As percent of total times reason given* |
| Insufficient SF funds, priority too low | 25 | 4·6 | 583 | 33·4 |
| Suitable alternative available | 4 | 0·7 | 17 | 1·0 |
| Loan refused because CCG awarded | n/a | — | 31 | 1·8 |
| Other | 350 | 64·9 | 85 | 4·9 |
| | 539 | | 1,745 | |
| **Office: Middlesbrough ILO** | | | | |
| Savings over £500 sufficient to meet cost | 7 | 0·6 | 3 | 0·1 |
| Not in receipt of IS | n/a | — | 283 | 8·1 |
| Not in receipt of IS for 26 weeks | n/a | — | 562 | 16·1 |
| Not in receipt of IS and unlikely to become entitled | 88 | 7·1 | n/a | — |
| Excluded items | 42 | 3·4 | 180 | 5·2 |
| Excluded persons | 67 | 5·4 | 3 | 0·1 |
| Amount < £30 (not travelling expenses) | 23 | 1·9 | 103 | 3·0 |
| Total debt of £1,000 | n/a | n/a | 3 | 0·1 |
| Previous application and decision for the item | 40 | 3·2 | 132 | 3·8 |
| No serious damage or risk to health or safety | n/a | n/a | 199 | 5·7 |
| Inability to repay | n/a | n/a | 77 | 2·2 |
| Help available from another source | 8 | 0·6 | 17 | 0·5 |
| Insufficient SF funds, priority too low | 124 | 10·0 | 1,600 | 45·8 |
| Suitable alternative available | 11 | 0·9 | 38 | 1·1 |
| Loan refused because CCG awarded | n/a | — | 128 | 3·7 |
| Other | 829 | 66·9 | 163 | 4·7 |
| | 1,239 | — | 3,491 | — |
| **Office: Redcar ILO** | | | | |
| Savings over £500 sufficient to meet cost | 5 | 1·1 | 0 | 0·0 |
| Not in receipt of IS | n/a | — | 90 | 8·1 |
| Not in receipt of IS for 26 weeks | n/a | — | 273 | 24·5 |
| Not in receipt of IS and unlikely to become entitled | 56 | 12·1 | n/a | — |
| Excluded items | 30 | 6·5 | 84 | 7·5 |
| Excluded persons | 0 | — | 2 | 0·2 |
| Amount < £30 (not travelling expenses) | 14 | 3·0 | 31 | 2·8 |
| Total debt of £1,000 | n/a | n/a | 0 | 0·0 |
| Previous application and decision for the item | 8 | 1·7 | 36 | 3·2 |
| No serious damage or risk to health or safety | n/a | n/a | 40 | 3·6 |
| Inability to repay | n/a | n/a | 46 | 4·1 |
| Help available from another source | 5 | 1·1 | 19 | 1·7 |
| Insufficient SF funds, priority too low | 162 | 35·0 | 404 | 36·3 |
| Suitable alternative available | 1 | 0·2 | 1 | 0·1 |
| Loan refused because CCG awarded | n/a | n/a | 55 | 4·9 |
| Other | 182 | 39·3 | 32 | 2·9 |
| | 463 | — | 1,113 | — |
| **Office: Stockton ILO** | | | | |
| Savings over £500 sufficient to meet cost | 3 | 0·2 | 1 | ·0 |
| Not in receipt of IS | 136 | 10·5 | 265 | 10·2 |
| Not in receipt of IS for 26 weeks | n/a | n/a | 453 | 17·5 |
| Not in receipt of IS and unlikely to become entitled | n/a 136 | n/a 10·5 | — n/a | — n/a |
| Excluded items | 49 | 3·8 | 149 | 5·7 |
| Excluded persons | 260 | 20·0 | 8 | 0·3 |

| | Grants | | Loans | |
|---|---|---|---|---|
| | *Number of times reason given* | *As percent of total times reason given* | *Number of times reason given* | *As percent of total times reason given* |
| Amount < £30 (not travelling expenses) | 24 | 1·9 | 73 | 2·8 |
| Total debt of £1,000 | n/a | — | 0 | ·0 |
| Previous application and decision for the item | 65 | 5·0 | 117 | 4·5 |
| No serious damage or risk to health or safety | n/a | n/a | 134 | 5·2 |
| Inability to repay | n/a | n/a | 251 | 9·7 |
| Help available from another source | 13 | 1·0 | 39 | 1·5 |
| Insufficient SF funds, priority too low | 17 | 1·3 | 885 | 34·1 |
| Suitable alternative available | 2 | 0·2 | 10 | 0·4 |
| Loan refused because CCG awarded | n/a | — | 118 | 4·5 |
| Other | 588 | 45·3 | 91 | 3·5 |
| | 1,293 | | 2,594 | |

n/a—Not applicable.

**Mr. Battle:** To ask the Secretary of State for Social Security if, further to his reply on 4 May, *Official Report,* column *220,* he will categorise the reasons for the remaining social fund loan refusals and community care grant refusals for the year 11 April 1988 to 31 March 1989.

**Mr. Peter Lloyd** *[pursuant to his reply, 15 May 1989 c. 76-78.]:* I regret that the reply given has been found to contain an error. The information requested with the amended figures is as follows:—

*Reasons for refusal of Social Fund loans and grants 1988-89*

| | Loans | | Grants | |
|---|---|---|---|---|
| | *Number of times reason given* | *As a per cent. of all reasons for refusals* | *Number of times reason given* | *As a per cent. of all reasons for refusals* |
| Savings over £500 sufficient to meet cost | 938 | 0·3 | 2,498 | 1·7 |
| Not in receipt of IS | 35,613 | 9·6 | n/a | n/a |
| Not in receipt of IS for 26 weeks | 99,907 | 27·0 | n/a | n/a |
| Not in receipt of IS and unlikely to become entitled | n/a | n/a | 15,842 | 10·6 |
| Excluded items | 30,759 | 8·3 | 9,563 | 6·4 |
| Excluded persons | 1,094 | 0·3 | 13,734 | 9·2 |
| Amount < £30 (not travelling expenses) | 11,952 | 3·2 | 3,707 | 2·5 |
| Total debt of £1,000 | 198 | 0·1 | n/a | n/a |
| Previous application and SFO decision for this item | 14,639 | 4·0 | 5,071 | 3·4 |
| No serious danger or risk to health or safety | 24,266 | 6·6 | 0 | 0·0 |
| Inability to repay | 14,971 | 4·0 | 0 | 0·0 |
| Help available from another source | 8,281 | 2·2 | 2,136 | 1·4 |
| Insufficient SF funds, priority too low | 84,027 | 22·7 | 13,419 | 9·0 |
| Other agencies not providing back-up | n/a | n/a | 85 | 0·1 |
| Suitable alternative available | 3,978 | 1·1 | 1,177 | 0·8 |
| Loan refused—CC6 awarded | 14,725 | 4·0 | n/a | n/a |
| Other | 25,113 | 6·8 | 82,400 | 55·1 |

*Note:* Percentages may sum to more than 100 due to rounding.

### Family Credit

**Mrs. Beckett:** To ask the Secretary of State for Social Security how many new claims for family credit were made, how many were decided and how many awards resulted in each week since the beginning of April 1989; how many renewal claims, decisions and awards were made; how many existing awards expired and were not renewed; and what was the net increase in the number of current awards.

**Mr. Scott** *[holding answer 13 June 1989]:* The available information is as follows:

| | Registrations[1] | Decisions | Awards |
|---|---|---|---|
| *New Claims* Week ending:— | | | |
| 7 April | 7,639 | 7,535 | 4,383 |
| 14 April | 8,697 | 7,656 | 4,597 |
| 21 April | 16,995 | 8,554 | 4,660 |
| 28 April | 22,867 | 10,926 | 5,018 |
| 5 May | 17,881 | 10,975 | 4,191 |
| 12 May | 24,166 | 15,740 | 5,541 |
| 19 May | 26,267 | 17,141 | 6,038 |
| 26 May | 26,586 | 14,003 | 4,714 |
| 2 June | 17,803 | 12,990 | 4,150 |

| | Registrations[1] | Decisions | Awards |
|---|---|---|---|
| 9 June | 20,927 | 23,886 | 8,744 |
| 16 June | 17,014 | 21,968 | 8,391 |
| *Renewal claims* | | | |
| Week ending:— | | | |
| 7 April | 7,795 | 6,615 | 5,799 |
| 14 April | 7,600 | 7,152 | 6,394 |
| 21 April | 7,425 | 7,115 | 6,325 |
| 28 April | 6,475 | 6,912 | 6,124 |
| 5 May | 4,770 | 5,044 | 4,371 |
| 12 May | 7,705 | 5,978 | 5,207 |
| 19 May | 8,572 | 5,902 | 5,100 |
| 26 May | 9,115 | 4,652 | 4,025 |
| 2 June | 7,552 | 4,263 | 3,592 |
| 9 June | 8,713 | 8,854 | 7,662 |
| 16 June | 6,938 | 8,381 | 7,213 |

45,964 awards expired in April, and 64,345 in May, and 44,038 are due to expire in June[2].

[1] Some claims received each week were not registered until the following week. On 16 June, 1,127 claims were awaiting registration.

[2] Figures for awards expiring are available only on a monthly basis. No information is available about how many of the awards expiring were not renewed.

The number of current awards is not available on a weekly basis. At the end of March 253,500 awards were actually in payment, and at 18 June this had risen to 255,702.

**Mrs. Beckett:** To ask the Secretary of State for Social Security what was the average amount of family credit awarded in each week since the beginning of April 1989.

**Mr. Scott** *[holding answer 13 June 1989]:* I regret that the information requested is not available. The latest information relates to all awards of family credit in payment on 18 June 1989, when the average amount was estimated to be just over £25. This is broadly the same as the average amount in payment in March 1989.

### Form RR4

**Mr. Andrew Bowden:** To ask the Secretary of State for Social Security if form RR4 is available in all post offices; and if he will make a statement.

**Mr. Peter Lloyd** *[holding answer 16 June 1989]:* Leaflet RR4 "Housing Benefit—new rules" is no longer available in all post offices.

From mid-June 1988 to the beginning of April 1989 the leaflet was on display in all Crown post offices. It was removed two months ago at the time of the benefit upratings and changes in some benefit rules. In Crown post offices the four A5 format leaflet display space that the department purchases is now occupied by information on family credit, housing benefit, NHS costs, and in Scotland, community charge rebate.

In sub-post offices, whilst leaflets such as RR4 are sent to all of them, neither the Department nor the Post Office has the power to instruct that these leaflets should be displayed or given out. As independent retailers sub-postmasters/mistresses can only be requested to do so.

## TRANSPORT

### Road Accidents

**Mr. Sheerman:** To ask the Secretary of State for Transport what steps he is taking to implement recommendation 23 of the efficiency scrutiny into his Department's activities in relation to local authorities' capital expenditure on roads, published in November 1988, which would allow accident investigation and prevention schemes on local roads to be eligible for transport supplementary grant.

**Mr. Peter Bottomley:** When the efficiency scrutiny report was published last month, I said that there were seven recommendations which the Department wished to discuss with the local authority associations. Recommendation 23 is one of those.

Officials of the associations reported the views of their members on the matter at a meeting on 7 June. I expect that it will be discussed when my right hon. Friend and I meet representatives of the associations on 4 July.

### LRT (Fares)

**Mr. Spearing:** To ask the Secretary of State for Transport what are his current instructions to London Regional Transport concerning the level of fares; when they were published and in what form; which instructions or guidelines they replaced; and when he modified his instruction that fare increases should, in general, parallel changes in the cost of living index.

**Mr. Portillo:** An initial remit has been given to the new LRT chairman, Mr. Wilfrid Newton. This was set out in a written answer given by my right hon. Friend the Secretary of State to the hon. Member for Richmond and Barnes on 22 March at columns *594-95.* It asked the chairman for proposals for a management, investment and financial strategy which aims to give London safe and reliable rail and bus services; provides good value for money; and, so far as possible, transfers costs from the taxpayer to the passengers and other beneficiaries. It gives no specific instructions on fare levels. This remit replaced the objectives given to the then chairman of LRT on 20 July 1984.

### Computer Reservation Systems

**Mr. Cohen:** To ask the Secretary of State for Transport, pursuant to his reply to the hon. Member for Romsey and Waterside (Mr. Colvin) on 8 June, *Official Report,* column 219, whether he will summarise the additional requirements concerning the disclosure of personal information described in the code of conduct about computer reservation systems produced by the European Community.

**Mr. Peter Bottomley:** Subject to national legislation on security, public order and data protection, personal information concerning a consumer and generated by a travel agent may be made available by the system vendor to those not involved in the transaction only with the consent of the consumer.

### M25

**Mr. McCrindle:** To ask the Secretary of State for Transport (1) how many possible routes of the proposed motorway from the M25 to Chelmsford he has asked his officials to investigate;

(2) when he expects to appoint consultancy engineers to determine the route of the proposed motorway from the M25 to Chelmsford.

**Mr. Peter Bottomley:** We expect to appoint design agents later this year. When they have carried out preliminary investigations we shall have an indication of practicable options.

**Mr. McCrindle:** To ask the Secretary of State for Transport what environmental considerations will be taken into account in determining the route of the motorway from the M25 to Chelmsford.

**Mr. Peter Bottomley:** Choice of route is generally a balance of environmental, economic and operational considerations. Subject to that, we shall seek to adopt the route and solution which does the least environmental damage. On deciding on the options we shall as usual carry out a full environmental assessment.

### Coastal Waters (Chemicals)

**Mr. Malcolm Bruce:** To ask the Secretary of State for Transport what information he holds concerning chemicals in drums or containers which have sunk within 100 miles of the British coast in the last 30 years; and if he will make a statement.

**Mr. Michael Portillo:** On each occasion of a loss of packaged chemicals into the sea from a ship being reported to the marine pollution control unit a decision is taken on scientific advice as to whether it is necessary to relocate and recover the chemical to protect the marine environment. Where it is not, no permanent record of the incident is maintained and the location of the lost chemical is generally unknown. Accordingly, the only detailed record held by the Department stems from the only chemical salvage operation carried out by the MPCU to date. This was after the mv Perintis sank in United Kingdom waters near the channel light vessel in March, 1989. All 12 of the drums of Cypermethrin and 16 of the drums of Permethrin carried by the vessel were successfully recovered, leaving four 50 kg drums of Permethrin which could not be found. 5·8 tonnes of Lindane from the same vessel floated off from the wreck in a commercial container was subsequently lost in the approaches to Cherbourg while under tow by a French tug, and its location remains unknown.

Four tonnes of PCB contained in four electrical transformers were lost in the Piper Alpha disaster in July, 1988 and remain unlocated.

## HEALTH

### National Health Service (Reform)

**Mr. Canavan:** To ask the Secretary of State for Health how many representations he has received to date on the White Paper "Working for Patients"; and how many have been critical of the Government's proposals.

**Mr. Mellor:** We have received over 7,500 representations on the White Paper, "Working for Patients". Many ask questions, many support all or some of the proposals, some refer only to specific aspects. It is not possible to distinguish the letters in the way the hon. Member suggests.

**Mr. Adley:** To ask the Secretary of State for Health how many letters from members of the public about the proposed changes in the National Health Service, to which he has replied, have resulted in further correspondence from the writer.

**Mr. Mellor:** We have dealt with over 5,500 letters from members of the public about the White Paper "Working for Patients"; a very small number has resulted in further correspondence from the writer.

**Mr. Lofthouse:** To ask the Secretary of State for Health if he will instruct the chairman of the Wakefield family practitioner committee to arrange a meeting between the full family practitioner committee and local Members of Parliament to discuss the White Paper "Working for Patients".

**Mr. Mellor** *[holding answer 19 June 1989]:* No.

### Speech Therapy

**Mr. Win Griffiths:** To ask the Secretary of State for Health what plans he has to develop speech therapy services; and if he will make a statement.

**Mr. Mellor:** It is for individual health authorities to determine the appropriate level of provision of their speech therapy services, having regard to local circumstances, competing priorities and available resources. The number of speech therapists employed in the National Health Service in England has risen by nearly 75 per cent. since 1979 and expenditure on speech therapy services has increased by 100 per cent. in real terms over the same period.

### Census Questions

**Rev. Martin Smyth:** To ask the Secretary of State for Health what steps his Department is taking to inform the public in advance of the census; what purpose is intended in including in the census questions on educational qualifications; what use will be made of the answers to these questions; and if he will make a statement.

**Mr. Freeman:** The information requested is given in the White Paper "1991 Census of Population", Cm. 430, published on 19 July 1988, a copy of which is in the Library. Publicity and information about the census is covered in paragraphs 45 and 46 and a statement on the purpose and uses of the proposed question on higher educational and professional qualifications is given at paragraph 23.5.

### Patients (Documentation)

**Mr. David Nicholson:** To ask the Secretary of State for Health whether he has any proposals to expedite the transfer of patients' National Health Service administrative documents between general practitioner practices, when required by patients' removal, avoiding processing by family practitioner committees and the central registry in Southport; and if he will make a statement.

**Mr. Mellor:** The computerisation of the central register due in 1990 should speed up the transfer of records. In addition, where necessary, special arrangements can be made by telephone between family practitioner committees and general practitioners for records to be transferred urgently. We attach importance to speedy transfers.

### Midwives (Grading)

**Mr. Ian Taylor:** To ask the Secretary of State for Health if he will now make a statement about the recommendations from the Social Services Committee on midwives grading; and if he will provide a date for their implementation.

**Mr. Mellor:** I refer my hon. Friend to my reply to the hon. Member for Wallsend (Mr. Garrett) and my hon. Friend the Member for Batley and Spen (Mrs. Peacock) on 10 May 1989 at columns *450-51*.

### Treatment Costs

**Mr. Barry Field:** To ask the Secretary of State for Health if he will make a statement on the variations in cost of treatment between different health districts.

**Mr. Freeman:** I refer my hon. Friend to my reply to my hon. Friend the Member for Pembroke (Mr. Bennett) on 18 May, at column *283*.

### Tobacco Advisory Council

**Mr. Amos:** To ask the Secretary of State for Health if he will meet the chief executive of the Tobacco Advisory Council to discuss its recent distribution of literature to hon. Members on 13 June; and if he will make a statement.

**Mr. Mellor:** We are aware of the literature concerning environmental tobacco smoke which the Tobacco Advisory Council has sent to hon. Members, but we do not feel that a meeting with the chief executive is necessary. The Government accept the finding of the independent scientific committee on smoking and health concerning environmental tobacco smoke, that there is a 10-30 per cent. increased risk of lung cancer among non-smokers exposed to environmental tobacco smoke through most of their lives than for non-smokers not so exposed. This increase could account for several hundred deaths per year. The Tobacco Advisory Council's literature reflects the fact that it disputes this position, but the council, like all other representative organisations, is entitled to draw attention to its own viewpoint.

**Mr. Amos:** To ask the Secretary of State for Health what recent representations he has received from the Tobacco Advisory Council about smoking and health; and if he will make a statement.

**Mr. Mellor:** The Tobacco Advisory Council has recently made written representations on the draft EC recommendation on banning smoking in public places (which was adopted as a mixed resolution at the Council of Ministers on 16 May), and on the draft EC directive on the advertising of tobacco products. In addition to this, officials have had meetings with the Tobacco Advisory Council at which a range of tobacco-related issues have been discussed.

### Allocation of Resources

**Mr. Robin Cook:** To ask the Secretary of State for Health what is his estimate of what would be the allocation of resources to each regional health authority in the current year if it was done on the basis of the formula proposed in the White Paper "Working for Patients".

**Mr. Mellor** *[holding answer 25 May 1989]:* It is not possible at this stage to produce reliable estimates of notional regional allocations for the current year. Such notional figures would in any event have little meaning since the application of the new formula will be carefully phased in and will not take full effect until 1992-93.

### West Lancashire Family Practitioner Committee

**Mr. Jack:** To ask the Secretary of State for Health if he will publish in the *Official Report* details of *(a)* the numbers of general practitioners employed, *(b)* the numbers of patients registered and *(c)* the cost of the general practitioners service, in the area covered by the West Lancashire family practitioner committee for 1979 and 1988 respectively.

**Mr. Mellor** *[holding answer 15 June 1989]:* The figures for Lancashire family practitioner committee, using the latest available year, 1987-88, are:

|  | Date | Figures |
|---|---|---|
| Numbers of unrestricted principals | October 1978 | 578 |
|  | October 1987 | 673 |
| Numbers of patients registered | October 1978 | 1,395,862 |
|  | October 1987 | 1,434,464 |
| Cost of the service | 1978-79 | £10,543,000 |
|  | 1987-88 | £38,328,000 |

This represents an increase in real terms of £16,690,000, a rise of 78 per cent.

### Family Practitioner Committees

**Mr. Lofthouse:** To ask the Secretary of State for Health if he will list the circumstances in which chairmen of family practitioner committees act as agents of the Secretary of State.

**Mr. Mellor** *[holding answer 19 June 1989]:* I have nothing to add to my reply to the hon. Member for Normanton (Mr. O'Brien) on 6 June 1989 at column *105*.

**Mr. Lofthouse:** To ask the Secretary of State for Health if he will list the powers of chairmen of family practitioner committees.

**Mr. Mellor** *[holding answer 19 June 1989]:* I refer the hon. Member to the answer given to my hon. Friend the Member for Gloucester (Mr. French) on 24 January 1989 at column *538*.

**Mr. Lofthouse:** To ask the Secretary of State for Health what guidelines about their responsibilities he gives chairmen of family practitioner committees on appointment.

**Mr. Mellor** *[holding answer 19 June 1989]:* General guidance for chairmen, members and staff of family practitioner committees is issued as and when necessary in order to enable them to discharge the varied responsibilities placed upon them. The guidance takes many forms. The Department customarily invites newly appointed chairmen to a specially arranged seminar for this purpose.

## ATTORNEY-GENERAL

### Mr. Roc Sandford

**Mr. Frank Field:** To ask the Attorney-General what were the reasons for the Director of Public Prosecutions' decision not to institute criminal charges against the officers involved in the prosecution of Mr. Roc Sandford for possession of drugs in October 1985.

**The Attorney-General:** After careful consideration of the evidence the Director of Public Prosecutions concluded that it was insufficient to justify criminal proceedings against any of the officers concerned.

### Police Computers

**Mr. Cohen:** To ask the Attorney-General what is his policy on prosecuting under the Official Secrets Act unauthorised disclosures of personal data from police computers; and if he will make a statement.

**The Attorney-General:** I refer the hon. Member to my previous written answer to him on 12 May 1989.

### Immigration

**Mr. Cohen:** To ask the Attorney-General if he will publish in full in the *Official Report,* the recent correspondence between the Treasury solicitors department and immigration adjudicators concerning the application of the immigration rules in appeals tribunals.

**The Attorney-General:** No. I refer to my reply to the hon. Member for Walsall, North (Mr. Winnick) on 9 June, at column *255.*

### Sunday Trading

**Mr. Cran:** To ask the Attorney-General what information he has concerning the level of enforcement of Sunday trading laws by local authorities; and whether he has any plans to issue guidance to local authorities on the enforcement of such laws.

**The Attorney-General:** I refer to the answer of the Solicitor-General on 14 November 1988 at column *738:* and to my answer on 17 April 1989 at column *26* which I have drawn to the attention of a number of local authorities.

### Fiat Applications

**Mr. Livingstone:** To ask the Attorney-General how many applications have been made to him in each of the past 10 years for his fiat; in respect of what proceedings such applications were made; and in how many and what percentage of such cases in each such category he granted and withheld his consent, respectively.

**The Attorney-General:** Records are no longer available for the entire period. In so far as records are available, the task of collating them so as to provide the information sought by the hon. Member could be undertaken only at disproportionate cost to the taxpayer.

## PRIME MINISTER

### Government Information

Q14. **Mr. Dalyell:** To ask the Prime Minister whether she will raise during the course of her next meeting with Sir Leon Brittan, Vice-President of the European Commission, the implications for the treatment of sensitive documents pertaining to financial affairs of

companies transmitted by Her Majesty's Government to the European Commission in the light of the recently revised Cabinet Office guidance on Government Information.

**The Prime Minister:** I have no plans to do so.

### United Nations General Assembly

Q105. **Mr. Cryer:** To ask the Prime Minister when she next expects to pay an official visit to the United Nations General Assembly.

**The Prime Minister:** I have at present no plans to do so. My right hon. and learned Friend the Foreign Secretary will visit the United Nations General Assembly in September.

### NATO Summit

Q159. **Mr. John Browne:** To ask the Prime Minister if she has received representations regarding the recent North Atlantic Treaty Organisation summit.

**The Prime Minister:** No. There is a general agreement that the summit was a success for the Alliance, for the reasons I set out in my statement on 6 June.

### Poland

Q196. **Mr. Bowis:** To ask the Prime Minister if she has received representations regarding the recent elections in Poland.

**The Prime Minister:** When I met General Jaruzelski on 10 June, I told him that we welcomed the holding of the elections in Poland, and the confirmation by the Polish authorities that they would stand by the results.

### Common Agricultural Policy

Q197. **Mr. Leigh:** To ask the Prime Minister if she has received representations regarding the common agricultural policy.

**The Prime Minister:** The Government frequently receive representations about the common agricultural policy. Reform of the CAP is well under way. The measures agreed at the February 1988 European Council, particularly those dealing with budgetary discipline and stabilisation of agricultural production and expenditure, represent the most significant steps to date. The Government's policy is to build on those major reforms in EC negotiations, and to work with our GATT partners to fulfil the commitment to achieve progressive and substantial reductions in agricultural support and protection.

### Energy Conservation

Q200. **Mr. Page:** To ask the Prime Minister if she has received representations regarding energy conservation.

**The Prime Minister:** I have received a number of representations regarding energy conservation and energy efficiency.

### Community Charge

**Mr. Allen:** To ask the Prime Minister if she will pay an official visit to the Nottingham, North constituency to explain Her Majesty's Government's policy on the poll tax.

**The Prime Minister:** I have at present no plans to do so. The Government have no plans for a poll tax. The purpose and application of the community charge has been admirably explained in the leaflets published by the Department of the Environment and the Welsh Office.

### Civil Service Records

**Mr. Dalyell:** To ask the Prime Minister where personal records of Downing street civil servants covering January 1986 are to be stored on their retiral from the Civil Service.

**The Prime Minister:** Personal records of any kind are stored in accordance with instructions given in general circular GC/228 issued in February 1984.

### Heads of Government Meeting, Madrid

**Mr. Spearing:** To ask the Prime Minister if she will state the matters that are now due to be place on the agenda of the forthcoming European Council, Heads of Government meeting, in Madrid.

**The Prime Minister:** The European Council in Madrid is likely to discuss monetary co-operation; social issues; progress on the single market; frontiers; the environment; external issues and other current Community subjects.

### Engagements

**Mr. Harry Greenway:** To ask the Prime Minister if she will list her official engagements for Thursday 22 June.

**Mr Stern:** To ask the Prime Minister if she will list her official engagements for Thursday 22 June.

**Mr. David Shaw:** To ask the Prime Minister if she will list her official engagements for Thursday 22 June.

**Mr. Boswell:** To ask the Prime Minister if she will list her official engagements for Thursday 22 June.

**The Prime Minister:** This morning I presided at a meeting of the Cabinet and had meetings with ministerial colleagues and others. In addition to my duties in the House I shall be having further meetings later today, including attendance at the plenary session of the Australian-United Kingdom conference on trade and investment.

### NORTHERN IRELAND

### Security Forces (Complaints)

2. **Mr. Mullin:** To ask the Secretary of State for Northern Ireland what complaints have been received about alleged violence by members of the security forces in the Ballymurphy area during the second half of May.

**Mr. Ian Stewart:** The Royal Ulster Constabulary is currently investigating three complaints concerning the behaviour of soldiers in the Ballymurphy area of west Belfast. No complaints were made against the police.

### Licensing Law

9. **Mr. Colvin:** To ask the Secretary of State for Northern Ireland what representations he has received about the Licensing (Amendment) (Northern Ireland) Order 1989; and if he will make a statement.

**Mr. Needham:** The Government have received representations from various sources, including district councils, church bodies and trade organisations. The majority of respondents strongly supported the proposals and in particular the proposed extension of the ban on off-sales of alcohol after 9 pm. The Federation of the Retail Licensed Trade and other trade interests opposed the extension and suggested several other changes to the licensing laws.

The Government will consider very carefully all the views expressed in finalising the contents of the draft order to be laid before Parliament.

### Debt

10. **Mr. Cousins:** To ask the Secretary of State for Northern Ireland if he has any plans to repeal the payments for Debt (Emergency Provisions) Act (Northern Ireland) 1971.

15. **Mr. Michael:** To ask the Secretary of State for Northern Ireland what recent meetings he has had with groups seeking a repeal of the payments for Debt (Emergency Provisions) Act (Northern Ireland) 1971.

**Mr. Ian Stewart:** There are no current plans to repeal the Act and there have been no meetings on this subject recently. The need for the legislation is kept under review in the light of prevailing circumstances.

**Ms. Mowlam:** To ask the Secretary of State for Northern Ireland how many people were subject to deductions from *(a)* wages and *(b)* welfare benefits under the Payment for Debt (Emergency Provisions) Act (Northern Ireland) 1971 in the years 1979 to 1989 inclusive.

**Mr. Ian Stewart** *[holding answer 20 June 1989]*: The information requested is as follows:

*(a)* The number of people from whom deductions from salaries have been made in the last two years under the Payments for Debt Act is approximately as follows:

|         | Numbers |
|---------|---------|
| 1987-88 | 1,862   |
| 1988-89 | 1,809   |

These figures are the total numbers of people from whom deductions from wages or salaries have been made on behalf of Northern Ireland Electricity, the Northern Ireland gas undertakings, the Northern Ireland Housing Executive and the rating division of the DOE (NI).

Figures for 1983-84 to 1986-87 are contained in the answer given by my right hon. Friend the Member for Tonbridge and Malling (Sir J. Stanley) on 2 November 1987 (*Official Report*, column *612*). Equivalent information for the years prior to 1983 could be produced only at disproportionate cost.

*(b)* Information in relation to deductions from welfare payments is not available.

**Ms. Mowlam:** To ask the Secretary of State for Northern Ireland what total levels of debt existed in each of the years from 1979 to 1989, inclusive, in each category for which deductions were made from debtors in those years under the Payment for Debt (Emergency Provisions) Act (Northern Ireland) 1971.

**Mr. Ian Stewart** *[holding answer 20 June 1989]*: I refer the hon. Member to the answer given by my right hon.

Friend the Member for Tonbridge and Malling (Sir J. Stanley) on 12 February 1988 at column. *396.* Comparable information for 1987-88 and 1988-89 is as follows:

| | *£ million* | |
| --- | --- | --- |
| | *1987-88* | *1988-89* |
| NIHE (Rent, Rates, District Heating) | 16·8 | 18·2 |
| NIE (Electricity) | 6·5 | 6·0 |
| Rating Division | 8·5 | 8·1 |
| Belfast Gas | 2·2 | 1·9 |

### Prison Reform

11. **Mr. Battle:** To ask the Secretary of State for Northern Ireland when he last met a pressure group campaigning for a reform of the prison system.

**Mr. Ian Stewart:** My right hon. Friend and I regularly meet various bodies with an interest in prison matters. The last such occasion when prison matters were raised was during a meeting between myself and NIACRO on 12 May 1989. I have also recently invited comments on proposals to improve conditions and facilities for visitors to prisoners.

### Local Government

12. **Sir Michael McNair-Wilson:** To ask the Secretary of State for Northern Ireland whether he will now set up an inquiry into the structure of local government in the Province.

**Mr. Tom King:** I have no such plans, although I am ready to consider and discuss any proposals which elected representatives from Northern Ireland and others may wish to put to me.

### EC Funding

13. **Mr. Nigel Griffiths:** To ask the Secretary of State for Northern Ireland what steps he has taken to maximise the share of European Community structural funds assigned to Northern Ireland.

22. **Mr. Frank Cook:** To ask the Secretary of State for Northern Ireland what efforts he is making to ensure that Northern Ireland's share of European Community funding is maximised.

**Mr. Ian Stewart:** I refer the hon. Members to the answer that I gave earlier to the right hon. and learned Member for Warley, West (Mr. Archer).

### Education (Reorganisation)

14. **Mr. McGrady:** To ask the Secretary of State for Northern Ireland if he will make a statement on the proposed degree of parental consultation on current proposals for the reorganisation of state education in certain areas of Northern Ireland.

**Dr. Mawhinney:** There are statutory development procedures for school reorganisation proposals. These provide an opportunity for all interested parties—including parents—to make representation to the Department of Education. School authorities would normally consult parents before publishing a proposal.

16. **Mr. Beggs:** To ask the Secretary of State for Northern Ireland if he will make it his policy to reject any

proposals by the South Eastern education and library board to amalgamate Castlewellan Quoile and Killyleagh secondary high schools with Down high school, thereby removing grammar school status from Down high.

**Dr. Mawhinney:** No. Article 14 of the Education and Libraries (Northern Ireland) Order 1986 places a statutory obligation on the Department of Education to consider all proposals submitted by an education and library board.

### Security

17. **Mr. Flannery:** To ask the Secretary of State for Northern Ireland if he will make an assessment of the security situation in Northern Ireland.

18. **Mr. Molyneaux:** To ask the Secretary of State for Northern Ireland if he will make a statement on the security situation.

**Mr. Tom King:** I refer the right hon. Members to the answer that I gave earlier today to the hon. Member for Sheffield, Attercliffe (Mr. Duffy).

### Terrorism

19. **Mr. Ashdown:** To ask the Secretary of State for Northern Ireland how much terrorist activity has cost in terms of damage to buildings and to businesses, investment and jobs in the last year; and if he will make a statement.

**Mr. Ian Stewart:** In the financial year ended 31 March 1989 the total cost of compensation for property damaged by terrorist activity was £18·7 million. This includes £9·4 million for damage to buildings, the balance including compensation for stock and contents, consequential loss, expenses and vehicles. These figures do not include damage to property held by the Crown or other public bodies who bear their own costs. The precise information which the right hon. Member seeks on the effects of terrorism on businesses, investment and jobs is not available, but terrorist activity cannot improve the perception of Northern Ireland as a location for investment which would reduce unemployment.

23. Mr. Gow: To ask the Secretary of State for Northern Ireland what discussions he has had with Ministers in the Government of the Republic of Ireland about granting to the police and armed forces of the Republic and of the United Kingdom reciprocal rights to enter the territory of the other in pursuit of suspected terrorists.

**Mr. Tom King:** Within the framework of the Intergovernmental Conference both Governments have regular discussions about ways of improving the effectiveness of security co-operation. My hon. Friend will understand why it is not possible to go into detail on the content of those discussions.

### Labour Statistics

20. **Mr. Cryer:** To ask the Secretary of State for Northern Ireland if he will make a statement on the current level of unemployment in the Province.

**Mr. Viggers:** The latest unemployment figures, released last week, are encouraging. They show that at 11 May 1989 the seasonally adjusted level of unemployment in the Province stood at 107,200, which is its lowest level for almost six years.

### Police Authority for Northern Ireland

21. **Mr. Maginnis:** To ask the Secretary of State for Northern Ireland if he has any proposals to change the composition, and if he has assessed the level of commitment, of the Police Authority for Northern Ireland.

**Mr. Tom King:** I have no plans to change the composition of the Police Authority for Northern Ireland. I meet members of the authority on a regular basis and appreciate the commitment and courage of its members in fulfilling their responsibilities in relation to the police force in Northern Ireland.

### Security Forces (Vetting)

24. **Mr. Loyden:** To ask the Secretary of State for Northern Ireland if he will review arrangements for vetting members of the security forces in Northern Ireland.

27. **Mr. Wareing:** To ask the Secretary of State for Northern Ireland what measures he has taken to improve vetting arrangements for members of the security forces in Northern Ireland.

**Mr. Ian Stewart:** Vetting arrangements for the RUC and RUC Reserve are the responsibility of the Chief Constable, and those for the remainder of the security forces in Northern Ireland are a matter for the Secretary of State for Defence.

### Catholics (Discrimination)

25. **Ms. Short:** To ask the Secretary of State for Northern Ireland what progress has been made in reducing discrimination against Catholics in employment since 1979.

**Mr. Viggers:** Since the introduction of fair employment legislation in 1976 there have been significant increases in the proportion of Catholics employed in various sectors of employment, most notably in the public sector which accounts for 42 per cent. of Northern Ireland's working population. The proportion of Catholics employed in the public sector as a whole is now more closely in line with their representation in the population. Improvement in the position of Catholics elsewhere in employment has however been less marked and it is this problem that the radical and far-reaching legislation now before Parliament is largely designed to address.

### Assembly

26. **Mr. Bill Walker:** To ask the Secretary of State for Northern Ireland if he now has any plans to introduce a devolved assembly in Northern Ireland; and if he has considered the impact of such a proposal.

**Mr. Tom King:** I have no present plans.

### Harland and Wolff Ltd.

28. **Dr. Godman:** To ask the Secretary of State for Northern Ireland what progress has been made in the disposal of Harland and Wolff Ltd.; and if he will make a statement.

**Mr. Viggers:** Since the signing of the Heads of Agreement on 22 March significant progress has been made in preparation for the formal completion of the sale. Discussions between officials and the MEBO-Olsen team are continuing and officials have submitted the formal notification of the terms of the disposal to the European Commission. Subject to Commission approval and the satisfactory conclusion of other pre-contract conditions and procedures completion is planned for September.

### Physically Handicapped School Children

29. **Mr. William Ross:** To ask the Secretary of State for Northern Ireland what assessment he has made of the adequacy of the level of provision of boarding facilities for physically handicapped school children in Northern Ireland.

**Dr. Mawhinney:** Provision of boarding facilities for physically handicapped children at schools in Northern Ireland is a matter for the education and library boards in the first instance. I have not had any proposals from boards for any change in that provision.

### Intergovernmental Conference

30. **Mr. Alex Carlile:** To ask the Secretary of State for Northern Ireland what was discussed at the last Intergovernmental Conference; and if he will make a statement.

**Mr. Tom King:** The last meeting of the Intergovernmental Conference in Belfast on 24 May completed the review of the working of the conference provided for in article II of the Anglo-Irish Agreement. Copies of the joint statement issued after the conference and the communiqué on the review were placed in the Library.

### "Who Framed Colin Wallace"

31. **Mr. Livingstone:** To ask the Secretary of State for Northern Ireland if he will make a statement on the activities of the security services documented in the book "Who Framed Colin Wallace", by Paul Foot.

**Mr. Ian Stewart:** No.

### Planning Procedures

32. **Mr. Kilfedder:** To ask the Secretary of State for Northern Ireland if he will take steps to give objectors the right of appeal to the Planning Appeals Commission against the granting of planning permission.

**Mr. Needham:** No, Sir.

**Mr. John D. Taylor:** To ask the Secretary of State for Northern Ireland why the fencing and planting at No. 35 Ballygelagh road in the borough of Ards have not been provided in accordance with the conditions of planning permission; what proposals the Department of the Environment, planning division, has to ensure the implementation of the planning approval conditions; and if he will make a statement.

**Mr. Needham** *[holding answer 19 June 1989]*: The occupier of the new development adjacent to No. 35 Ballygelagh road submitted a planning application on 18

January 1989 for the retention of the dwelling without compliance with the condition requiring the erection of the screen fence. Since there was no reasonable ground for refusal, planning permission was granted on 23 May 1989.

## Mental Handicap

**Rev. Martin Smyth:** To ask the Secretary of State for Northern Ireland what was his Department's participation in the first European national conference for vocational training for mental handicap which took place in Maastricht, Holland, in April; what lessons have been drawn from this event; and what efforts are being made to implement the findings of the conference in the Northern Ireland context.

**Mr. Viggers:** Two officials from the Department of Economic Development attended the conference together with a representative from the Industrial Therapy Organisation in Northern Ireland. The conference provided an opportunity to learn how other countries are dealing with this particular disability group and the experience gained will be valuable in the planning of future provision in Northern Ireland.

## Turbines (Rivers)

**Mr. McCusker:** To ask the Secretary of State for Northern Ireland if, further to his written answer to the hon. Member for Upper Bann, 25 April, *Official Report*, column 483, he will list the principal statutory responsibilities of the Northern Ireland Departments of Agriculture, Environment and Economic Development, for installations affecting the flow in a particular water course for water abstractions and for health and safety at work considerations arising from the operation of such turbines.

**Mr. Ian Stewart:** The information requested is as follows:

(i) If the installation of any structure is likely to affect the flow of water in any particular watercourse, the consent of the Department of Agriculture is required in accordance with article 32 and schedule 6 of the Drainage (NI) Order 1973. The Fisheries Act (NI) 1966 contains requirements to provide and maintain fish passes in dams constructed, re-built, reinstated or heightened since 1842; and to close mill sluices for 24-hour periods at weekends or when mills are not in use.

(ii) The Department of the Environment for Northern Ireland has power under section 14 of the Water Act (NI) 1972 to make regulations to control the abstraction of water from waterways if it is considered expedient to do so. No such regulations have yet been made.

(iii) Where turbines form part of an undertaking for which the Department of Economic Development is the enforcing authority for health and safety at work legislation, the principal health and safety enactments which apply to the operation of turbines are the Health and Safety at Work (NI) Order 1978 and the Factories Act (NI) 1965.

## Social Security

**Mr. McGrady:** To ask the Secretary of State for Northern Ireland (1) how many people awarded transitional protection as a result of the implementation of the new social security legislation from 11 April 1988 at each of the social security offices in South Down are no longer entitled to such a payment; (2) how many people were awarded transitional protection as a result of the implementation of the new social security legislation from 11 April 1988 at each of the social security offices in South Down.

**Mr. Needham:** This information is not readily available and could be provided only at disproportionate cost.

## Prisoners

**Mr. Andrew F. Bennett:** To ask the Secretary of State for Northern Ireland how many prisoners in Northern Ireland, who were under 20 years of age when convicted, have now served 10 or more years in prison.

**Mr. Ian Stewart:** Forty-two. Of these, 16 are Secretary of State's pleasure cases. The remaining 26 are life sentence prisoners.

## Housing Executive

**Mr. William Ross:** To ask the Secretary of State for Northern Ireland if he will publish a table in the *Official Report* showing the number of persons recruited and employed in the headquarters, and in each regional and district office of the Northern Ireland Housing Executive in each of the last two years, broken down as far as possible into the various departments of the organisation, or as much of such information as is available to him.

**Mr. Needham** *[holding answer 20 June 1989]:* The information requested in so far as it can be readily provided is set out in the following tables. The figures shown for industrial and non-industrial staff represent permanent staff in post and do not take account of temporary staff as the numbers of such staff could not be disaggregated between various locations except at disproportionate cost. The figures for temporary non-industrial staff at 31 March 1988 and 31 March 1989 were 193 and 145 respectively. The figures for temporary industrial staff at 31 March 1988 and 31 March 1989 were 207 and 487 respectively.

Information on the composition by departments of non-industrial staff at district office level and figures for recruitment of industrial staff cannot be provided except at disproportionate cost.

*Table 1: Non industrial staff at headquarters and regions at 31 March 1988 and 31 March 1989*

| | At 31 March | Housing and planning | Technical services and direct labour organisation | Finance | Personnel and management services and information technology | Information and Secretariat | Total |
|---|---|---|---|---|---|---|---|
| Belfast | 1988 | 494 | 253 | 23 | 56 | 3 | 829 |
| | 1989 | 516 | 262 | 23 | 49 | 3 | 853 |
| North East | 1988 | 277 | 84 | 12 | 23 | 1 | 397 |
| | 1989 | 281 | 91 | 11 | 19 | 1 | 403 |
| North West | 1988 | 278 | 95 | 9 | 25 | 2 | 409 |
| | 1989 | 269 | 88 | 12 | 27 | 2 | 398 |
| South | 1988 | 258 | 97 | 13 | 28 | 2 | 398 |

| At 31 March | Housing and planning | Technical services and direct labour organisation | Finance | Personnel and management services and information technology | Information and Secretariat | Total |
|---|---|---|---|---|---|---|
| 1989 | 255 | 103 | 12 | 27 | 2 | 399 |
| South East  1988 | 288 | 103 | 10 | 24 | 2 | 427 |
| 1989 | 296 | 103 | 13 | 22 | 1 | 435 |
| West  1988 | 130 | 71 | 6 | 22 | 4 | 233 |
| 1989 | 149 | 63 | 7 | 19 | 2 | 240 |
| Headquarters  1988 | 62 | 139 | 206 | 153 | 19 | 579 |
| 1989 | 53 | 118 | 205 | 165 | 19 | 560 |
| Total staff in post  1988 | 1,787 | 842 | 279 | 331 | 33 | 3,272 |
| 1989 | 1,819 | 828 | 283 | 328 | 30 | 3,288 |

Table 2: Non Industrial Staff in Post at Regional and District Offices at 31 March 1988 and 31 March 1

| Region and Regional Head quarters and District Office | Staff in Post at 31 March 1988 | Staff in Post at 31 March 1989 |
|---|---|---|
| *Belfast* | | |
| Regional Head quarters | 457 | 464 |
| Belfast 1 | 45 | 47 |
| Belfast 2 | 54 | 55 |
| Belfast 3 | 56 | 59 |
| Belfast 4 | 47 | 52 |
| Belfast 5 | 52 | 52 |
| Belfast 6 | 45 | 46 |
| Belfast 7 | 73 | 78 |
| Sub Total | 829 | 853 |
| *North East* | | |
| Regional Head quarters | 164 | 165 |
| Antrim | 43 | 46 |
| Ballycastle | 15 | 15 |
| Ballymena | 41 | 41 |
| Ballymoney | 22 | 23 |
| Carrickfergus | 28 | 30 |
| Larne | 23 | 23 |
| Newtownabbey 1 | 31 | 30 |
| Newtownabbey 2 | 30 | 30 |
| Sub Total | 397 | 403 |
| *North West* | | |
| Regional Head quarters | 181 | 169 |
| Coleraine | 41 | 41 |
| Limavady | 27 | 27 |
| Londonderry 1 | 38 | 40 |
| Londonderry 2 | 33 | 33 |
| Londonderry 3 | 29 | 29 |
| Magherafelt | 25 | 24 |
| Strabane | 35 | 35 |
| Sub Total | 409 | 398 |
| *South* | | |
| Regional Head quarters | 197 | 193 |
| Armagh | 29 | 32 |
| Banbridge | 27 | 27 |
| Craigavon | 25 | 24 |
| Kilkeel | 10 | 10 |
| Lurgan | 27 | 27 |
| Newry 1 | 30 | 32 |
| Newry 2 | 28 | 29 |
| Portadown | 25 | 25 |
| Sub Total | 398 | 399 |
| *South East* | | |
| Regional Head quarters | 192 | 188 |
| Bangor | 35 | 36 |
| Castlereagh 1 | 27 | 27 |
| Castlereagh 2 | 21 | 21 |
| Lisburn 1 | 32 | 36 |
| Lisburn 2 | 20 | 21 |

| Region and Regional Head quarters and District Office | Staff in Post at 31 March 1988 | Staff in Post at 31 March 1989 |
|---|---|---|
| Lisburn 3 | 20 | 21 |
| Newtownards 1 | 27 | 30 |
| Newtownards 2 | 19 | 18 |
| Downpatrick | 34 | 37 |
| Sub Total | 427 | 435 |
| *West* | | |
| Regional Head quarters | 131 | 133 |
| Cookstown | 20 | 20 |
| Dungannon | 26 | 29 |
| Enniskillen | 31 | 32 |
| Omagh | 25 | 26 |
| Sub Total | 233 | 240 |
| Total | 2,693 | 2,728 |

Table 3: Recruitment of non-industrial staff during years 1987-88 and 1988-89

| | 1987-88 | 1988-89 |
|---|---|---|
| Belfast Regional Office | 34 | 38 |
| District Offices | 8 | 33 |
| North East Regional Office | 1 | 6 |
| District Offices | 2 | 12 |
| North West Regional Office | 3 | 9 |
| District Offices | 0 | 2 |
| West Regional Office | 1 | 4 |
| District Offices | 0 | 5 |
| South Regional Office | 3 | 12 |
| District Offices | 1 | 6 |
| South East Regional Office | 9 | 8 |
| District Offices | 0 | 16 |
| Headquarters (including Linenhall Street and Carlton House) | 20 | 30 |
| Totals | 81 | 184 |

Table 4
Industrial staff in post at Regions and depots at 31 March 1989

| Depots | 31 March 1988 | 31 March 1989 |
|---|---|---|
| *West Region* | | |
| Cookstown | 28 | 22 |
| Dungannon | 40 | 35 |
| Enniskillen | 37 | 33 |
| Omagh | 37 | 32 |
| Total | 142 | 122 |

| Depots | 31 March 1988 | 31 March 1989 |
|---|---|---|
| *South Region* | | |
| Amargh | 39 | 39 |
| Banbridge | 21 | 17 |
| Carn | 61 | 59 |
| Kilkeel | 13 | 13 |
| Newry | 56 | 54 |
| Total | 190 | 182 |
| *North West* | | |
| Pennyburn | 59 | 56 |
| Drumahoe | 47 | 41 |
| Strabane | 42 | 40 |
| Coleraine | 36 | 34 |
| Limavady | 19 | 14 |
| Castledawson | 28 | 28 |
| Total | 231 | 213 |
| *Belfast* | | |
| Gardiner Street | 114 | 105 |
| Grosvenor Road | 98 | 87 |
| Paulette Avenue | 85 | 85 |
| Total | 297 | 277 |
| *North East* | | |
| Ballycastle | 11 | 13 |
| Ballyclare | 31 | 44 |
| Ballymena | 37 | 52 |
| Ballymoney | 26 | 27 |
| Total | 105 | 136 |
| *Grounds Maintenance Staff* | | |
| Belfast | 33 | 27 |
| South East | 29 | 29 |
| North East | 32 | 28 |
| South | 28 | 28 |
| West | 29 | 29 |
| North West | 37 | 36 |
| Total | 188 | 177 |
| *Ancilliary Staff* | | |
| Housing centre | 51 | 42 |
| Belfast | 96 | 92 |
| South East | 28 | 30 |
| North East | 32 | 30 |
| South | 31 | 31 |
| West | 16 | 17 |
| North West | 34 | 30 |
| Total | 288 | 272 |
| Total staff in post | 1,441 | 1,379 |

### Population Statistics

**Mr. Ieuan Wyn Jones:** To ask the Secretary of State for Northern Ireland what are his Department's estimates for the numbers of people aged 65 to 74 years, 75 to 79 years, and over 80 years in Northern Ireland in the years 2000 and 2020; and what percentage increase this represents in each category over the actual figures for the last year in which they are available.

**Mr. Needham** [*holding answer 19 June 1989*]: The information requested is as follows:

| Age groups | 1988 Mid-year estimates | Year 2000 | Percent-age change | Year 2020 | Percent-age change |
|---|---|---|---|---|---|
| 65-74 | 113,000 | 110,000 | − 2·7 | 135,000 | +19·5 |
| 75-79 | 41,000 | 41,000 | 0·0 | 46,000 | +12·2 |
| 80 and over | 39,000 | 47,000 | +20·5 | 54,000 | +38·5 |

## EMPLOYMENT

### Tourist Industry

**Mr. Meacher:** To ask the Secretary of State for Employment if he will now publish the report of the review committee into the tourist industry which he established in July 1988.

**Mr. Lee:** I have no plans to publish the report.

### Employment Training

**Mr. Meacher:** To ask the Secretary of State for Employment if he will publish in the *Official Report (a)* the number of ET starts *(b)* the number of people who have left the scheme and finished their courses, *(c)* the number and percentage of those leaving and finishing who obtained a nationally recognisable qualification and *(d)* the qualifications obtained for the latest available date.

**Mr. Nicholls:** To 9 June, the latest date for which information is available, 317,800 people had started on employment training. Information broken down as requested about trainees who have left the programme is not available.

### Training

**Mr. Clelland:** To ask the Secretary of State for Employment if he will make a statement on the sources for the figures for the number of single parents on employment training schemes at December 1988, given by his Department to the Gateshead metropolitan borough council's special programmes committee on 25 January.

**Mr. Nicholls:** [*holding answer 15 May 1989*]: The information provided to the special programmes committee of the Gateshead metropolitan borough council about the number of single parents joining employment training was provided by the Department's officials from the normal management information system. It relates only to those people who entered the programme under the special arrangements for lone parents in receipt of income support on an order book through the Department of Social Security. In addition, lone parents may enter under other eligibility conditions, including the main one of being unemployed for six months or more.

The information I provided on 7 April about single parents on employment training to the hon. Member in my reply to his previous question is correct; there is no information presently available about the total number of single parents on the programme.

## FOREIGN AND COMMONWEALTH AFFAIRS

### China

**Mr. Harry Greenway:** To ask the Secretary of State for Foreign and Commonwealth Affairs if he will make a statement on the application for asylum by a member of the Chinese educational mission in Middlesex.

**Mr. Renton:** I have been asked to reply. An official of the Chinese embassy walked into Ealing police station on 11 June and asked for political asylum. The application is under consideration.

## WALES

### Derelict Land (Shotton)

**Mr. Barry Jones:** To ask the Secretary of State for Wales if he will call a conference on Clwyd county council, Alyn and Deeside council and Deeside town and community councils with a view to discussing how 7,000 new jobs might be created on the derelict industrial land adjacent to Shotton steelworks; and if he will make a statement.

**Mr. Peter Walker:** Clwyd has clearly benefited from the success of the Government's policies to revitalise industrial and economic performance in Wales. Unemployment in the county has fallen by 4,860 in the last 12 months. Regional aid approvals since January 1988 are associated with capital investment of £590 million, including £200 million inward investment, forecasting some 11,300 new jobs.

I am confident that this progress will be maintained and I see no reason to convene a meeting along the lines proposed.

### Broadcasting

**Mr. Barry Jones:** To ask the Secretary of State for Wales how many times he has had formal talks with the chairman of the Welsh Fourth Channel S4C; and what plans he has for further meetings.

**Mr. Wyn Roberts:** My right hon. Friend has visited S4C twice since becoming Secretary of State, most recently last month. He has had informal discussions with the chairman and members of the authority, as well as with senior staff, on both occasions.

### Radiation

**Dr. David Clark:** To ask the Secretary of State for Wales whether he now intends to conduct an aerial survey for radioactivity in the restricted area of North Wales; and if he will make a statement.

**Mr. Peter Walker:** No.

**Mr. Ron Davies:** To ask the Secretary of State for Wales if he will list those sites for which he has given authorisation for the disposal of low-level radioactive waste during the last five years.

**Mr. Grist:** A list of current authorisations for the disposal of low-level radioactive waste issued in the last five years is as follows:

*Clwyd*

North East Wales Institute of Higher Education
Kelsterton College
Connahs Quay

Wales Gas Board
Maelor Works
Marchwiel
Wrexham

Clwyd Health Authority
Maelor General Hospital
Croesnewydd Road
Wrexham

Clwyd Health Authority
Ysbyty Glan Clwyd
Bodelwyddan

Porton Products Ltd.
Unit 9
Ash Road
Wrexham Industrial Estate
Wrexham

Pilkington PE Ltd.
Glascoed Road
St. Asaph

*Dyfed*

West Wales General Hospital
Glangwili
Carmarthen

Penglais Estate
University College
Aberystwyth

Welsh Plant Breeding Station
Plas Gogerddan
Aberystwyth

Animal Health Research Unit
Peithyll
Capel Dewi
Aberystwyth

Withybush General Hospital
Haverfordwest

*Gwent*

Nevill Hall Hospital
Brecon Road
Abergavenny

ReChem International Ltd.
Pontyvelin Industrial Estate
New Road
Panteg
Pontypool

Royal Gwent Hospital
Newport

St. Woolos Hospital
Newport

Allt-Yr-Yn Hospital
Newport

BT Consumer Electronics Ltd.
Cwmcarn Factory
Cross Keys
Newport

Mayer Cohen Industries Ltd.
Newtown Industrial Estate
Cross Keys
Newport

Monsanto plc.
Corporation Road
Newport

*Gwynedd*
University College of North Wales
Department of Marine Science
Menai Bridge
Anglesey

Gwynedd Health Authority
Gwynedd Hospital
Penrhosgarnedd
Bangor

*Mid Glamorgan*
Simbec Research Limited
Merthyr Tydfil Industrial Park
Cardiff Road
Merthyr Tydfil

Mid Glamorgan Health Authority
East Glamorgan General Hospital
Church Village
Pontypridd

Mid Glamorgan Health Authority
Aberdare General Hospital
Aberdare

Mid Glamorgan Health Authority
Bridgend General Hospital
Bridgend

Perkin-Elmer Limited
Llantrisant Trading Estate
Pontyclun

Miles Limited
Western Avenue
Bridgend Industrial Estate
Bridgend

Prince Charles Hospital
Merthyr Tydfil

Princess of Wales Hospital
Bridgend

*South Glamorgan*
South Glamorgan County Council
South Glamorgan Institute of Higher Education
Western Avenue
Llandaff
Cardiff

University of Wales College of Cardiff
Cathays Park
Cardiff

South Glamorgan Health Authority
University Hospital of Wales
Heath Park
Cardiff

South Glamorgan Health Authority
South Wales Radiotherapy and Oncology Centre
Velindre and Whitchurch Hospitals
Cardiff

South Glamorgan Health Authority
Llandough Hospital
Penarth

Welsh Regional Blood Transfusion Centre
Rhydlafar
St. Fagans
Cardiff
  Dow Corning Ltd.
  Cardiff Road

Barry

University of Wales College of Cardiff
King Edward VII Avenue
Cathays Park
Cardiff

University of Wales College of Cardiff
Aberconway Building
Colum Drive
Cardiff

University of Wales College of Cardiff
School of Pure and Applied Biology
Newport Road
Cardiff

Biotal Ltd.
5 Chilton Close
Ty Glas Industrial Estate
Llanishen
Cardiff

RSR Ltd.
Avenue Industrial Park
Pentwyn
Cardiff

South Glamorgan Health Authority
Prince of Wales Hospital
Rhydlafar
St. Fagans
Cardiff

The Public Health Laboratory Service
Cardiff Royal Infirmary
Newport Road
Cardiff

The Public Health Laboratory Service
Public Health Laboratory
University Hospital of Wales
Heath Park
Cardiff

Cardiff City Council
Environmental Health Department
City Analysts Laboratory
Roath
Cardiff

Amersham International plc
Cardiff Laboratories
Forest Farm
Whitchurch
Cardiff

South Glamorgan Health Authority
Cardiff Royal Infirmary
Newport Road
Cardiff

*West Glamorgan*
West Glamorgan Health Authority
Neath General Hospital
Neath

West Glamorgan Health Authority
Singleton Hospital
Sketty
Swansea

West Glamorgan Health Authority
Morriston Hospital
Swansea

British Steel Corporation
Welsh Laboratory
Port Talbot

## Labour Statistics

**Mr. Barry Jones:** To ask the Secretary of State for Wales (1) how many people aged 18 to 25 years have been unemployed for six months or more in Wales; and in each of the parliamentary constituencies of Wales; and if he will make a statement;

(2) how many people aged 18 to 25 years are unemployed in each of the parliamentary constituencies of Wales.

**Mr. Peter Walker:** The latest available figures are shown in the following table. This includes figures for two years earlier. I am sure the hon. Gentleman will join me in welcoming the substantial fall in the number of unemployed young people over the last two years.

*Unemployed person aged 18 to 24 years[1]*

| Parliamentary constituency areas | Total all durations | | Total over six months[2] | |
|---|---|---|---|---|
| | April 1987 | April 1989 | April 1987 | April 1989 |
| Alyn and Deeside | 1,141 | 640 | 595 | 225 |
| Clwyd North West | 1,696 | 1,027 | 934 | 448 |
| Clwyd South West | 1,144 | 704 | 571 | 292 |
| Delyn | 1,221 | 629 | 668 | 213 |
| Wrexham | 1,341 | 823 | 721 | 311 |
| Carmarthen | 1,050 | 633 | 534 | 283 |
| Ceredigion and Pembroke North | 1,107 | 629 | 513 | 264 |
| Llanelli | 1,353 | 793 | 682 | 290 |
| Pembroke | 1,785 | 1,150 | 833 | 498 |
| Blaenau Gwent | 1,489 | 1,108 | 756 | 493 |
| Islwyn | 1,011 | 724 | 512 | 285 |
| Monmouth | 876 | 484 | 438 | 182 |
| Newport East | 1,434 | 830 | 813 | 357 |
| Newport West | 1,634 | 960 | 951 | 426 |
| Torfaen | 1,503 | 1,107 | 767 | 479 |
| Caernarfon | 969 | 733 | 487 | 335 |
| Conwy | 1,175 | 765 | 623 | 304 |
| Meirionnydd Nant Conwy | 563 | 275 | 275 | 108 |
| Ynys Môn | 1,287 | 944 | 728 | 434 |
| Bridgend | 1,042 | 633 | 505 | 233 |
| Caerphilly | 1,609 | 1,019 | 944 | 402 |
| Cynon Valley | 1,228 | 953 | 636 | 408 |
| Merthyr Tydfil and Rhymney | 1,562 | 1,248 | 766 | 560 |
| Ogmore | 1,161 | 794 | 650 | 322 |
| Pontypridd | 1,368 | 886 | 740 | 392 |
| Rhondda | 1,648 | 1,087 | 989 | 506 |
| Brecon and Radnor | 701 | 340 | 360 | 127 |
| Montgomery | 511 | 221 | 234 | 64 |
| Cardiff Central | 2,017 | 1,189 | 1,195 | 591 |
| Cardiff North | 684 | 352 | 363 | 137 |
| Cardiff South and Penarth | 1,559 | 924 | 987 | 444 |
| Cardiff West | 1,709 | 1.046 | 998 | 476 |
| Vale of Glamorgan | 1,346 | 883 | 709 | 371 |
| Aberavon | 1,265 | 713 | 613 | 274 |
| Gower | 1,016 | 626 | 577 | 267 |
| Neath | 1,171 | 751 | 825 | 302 |
| Swansea East | 1,542 | 1,098 | 838 | 499 |
| Swansea West | 1,794 | 1,201 | 1,111 | 551 |
| WALES | 48,772 | 30,922 | 26,056 | 13,153 |

[1] Specific totals for the age group 18 to 25 are not available.
[2] Data quoted do not include persons unemployed for up to and including six months.

**Mr. Barry Jones:** To ask the Secretary of State for Wales if he will list in the *Official Report* the number of long-term unemployed people, male and female, indicating in each instance how many are under the age of 25 years in Wales and in each of the parliamentary constituencies of Wales; and if he will make a statement.

**Mr. Peter Walker:** The latest available information, for April 1989, is shown in the table. This includes figures for two years earlier. I am sure that the hon. Gentleman will join me in welcoming the substantial fall in the number of long-term unemployed over the last two years.

*Parliamentary constituency areas*

| | All | | Male long-term unemployed[1] Less than 25 years[2] | |
|---|---|---|---|---|
| | April 1987 | April 1989 | April 1987 | April 1989 |
| Alyn and Deeside | 1,152 | 496 | 205 | 58 |
| Clwyd North West | 1,557 | 794 | 344 | 145 |
| Clwyd South West | 932 | 519 | 182 | 69 |
| Delyn | 1,573 | 567 | 261 | 64 |
| Wrexham | 1,400 | 696 | 294 | 78 |
| Carmarthen | 986 | 650 | 129 | 85 |
| Ceredigion and Pembroke North | 1,031 | 525 | 123 | 61 |
| Llanelli | 1,301 | 695 | 210 | 85 |

| | All | | Male long-term unemployed[1] Less than 25 years[2] | |
| | April 1987 | April 1989 | April 1987 | April 1989 |
|---|---|---|---|---|
| Pembroke | 1,483 | 1,082 | 219 | 142 |
| Blaenau Gwent | 1,857 | 1,236 | 286 | 175 |
| Islwyn | 1,236 | 702 | 206 | 95 |
| Monmouth | 844 | 433 | 121 | 53 |
| Newport East | 1,634 | 810 | 352 | 121 |
| Newport West | 1,892 | 965 | 400 | 154 |
| Torfaen | 1,584 | 845 | 258 | 138 |
| Caernarfon | 1,094 | 656 | 167 | 104 |
| Conwy | 996 | 617 | 169 | 85 |
| Meirionnydd Nant Conwy | 422 | 213 | 64 | 30 |
| Ynys Mon | 1,527 | 840 | 275 | 122 |
| Bridgend | 1,019 | 539 | 160 | 62 |
| Caerphilly | 2,079 | 964 | 422 | 122 |
| Cynon Valley | 1,524 | 1,034 | 277 | 133 |
| Merthyr Tydfil and Rhymney | 1,847 | 1,211 | 367 | 215 |
| Ogmore | 1,689 | 868 | 314 | 120 |
| Pontypridd | 1,523 | 943 | 325 | 158 |
| Rhondda | 1,822 | 1,033 | 456 | 205 |
| Brecon and Radnor | 581 | 280 | 94 | 32 |
| Montgomery | 480 | 140 | 52 | 12 |
| Cardiff Central | 2,073 | 1,139 | 447 | 212 |
| Cardiff North | 782 | 380 | 150 | 43 |
| Cardiff South and Penarth | 2,034 | 1,116 | 419 | 171 |
| Cardiff West | 2,245 | 1,260 | 434 | 200 |
| Vale of Glamorgan | 1,321 | 753 | 236 | 105 |
| Aberavon | 1,154 | 515 | 227 | 83 |
| Gower | 897 | 420 | 183 | 46 |
| Neath | 986 | 552 | 151 | 79 |
| Swansea East | 2,103 | 1,174 | 385 | 197 |
| Swansea West | 2,180 | 1,284 | 516 | 197 |
| Wales | 52,840 | 28,946 | 9,880 | 4,256 |

*Parliamentary constituency areas*

| | All | | Female long term unemployed[1] Less than 25 years[2] | |
| | April 1987 | April 1989 | April 1987 | April 1989 |
|---|---|---|---|---|
| Alyn and Deeside | 360 | 173 | 97 | 24 |
| Clwyd North West | 525 | 243 | 194 | 43 |
| Clwyd South West | 375 | 185 | 113 | 44 |
| Delyn | 428 | 155 | 113 | 23 |
| Wrexham | 380 | 198 | 102 | 45 |
| Carmarthen | 387 | 219 | 116 | 42 |
| Ceredigion and Pembroke North | 411 | 195 | 109 | 31 |
| Llanelli | 421 | 193 | 143 | 36 |
| Pembroke | 547 | 308 | 192 | 74 |
| Blaenau Gwent | 401 | 235 | 123 | 49 |
| Islwyn | 276 | 161 | 77 | 24 |
| Monmouth | 343 | 174 | 110 | 31 |
| Newport East | 465 | 236 | 155 | 49 |
| Newport West | 537 | 252 | 180 | 55 |
| Torfaen | 451 | 273 | 139 | 59 |
| Caernarfon | 300 | 177 | 85 | 33 |
| Conwy | 323 | 205 | 110 | 41 |
| Meirionnydd Nant Conwy | 177 | 102 | 44 | 14 |
| Ynys Môn | 534 | 381 | 192 | 85 |
| Bridgend | 292 | 137 | 66 | 21 |
| Caerphilly | 392 | 176 | 138 | 34 |
| Cynon Valley | 305 | 190 | 107 | 38 |
| Merthyr Tydfil and Rhymney | 369 | 229 | 140 | 64 |
| Ogmore | 273 | 141 | 83 | 21 |
| Pontypridd | 359 | 183 | 124 | 38 |
| Rhondda | 398 | 233 | 160 | 56 |
| Brecon and Radnor | 256 | 118 | 73 | 15 |
| Montgomery | 208 | 65 | 49 | 15 |
| Cardiff Central | 540 | 293 | 211 | 84 |
| Cardiff North | 198 | 118 | 45 | 17 |
| Cardiff South and Penarth | 387 | 209 | 152 | 60 |
| Cardiff West | 456 | 243 | 186 | 56 |
| Vale of Glamorgan | 447 | 243 | 134 | 57 |
| Averavon | 311 | 100 | 106 | 23 |
| Gower | 310 | 137 | 88 | 32 |
| Neath | 359 | 167 | 109 | 39 |

| | All | | Female long term unemployed[1] Less than 25 years[2] | |
| --- | --- | --- | --- | --- |
| | April 1987 | April 1989 | April 1987 | April 1989 |
| Swansea East | 444 | 236 | 158 | 65 |
| Swansea West | 509 | 275 | 185 | 76 |
| Wales | 14,454 | 7,558 | 4,708 | 1,613 |

*Source:* Employment Department.

[1] Data quoted are for claimants who have been unemployed for more than 52 weeks.

[2] Claimants aged 16-24 years.

### Welsh Language

**Mr. Barry Jones:** To ask the Secretary of State for Wales if he proposes to allow children whose first language is Welsh to take national curriculum testing at seven through the medium of Welsh; and if he will make a statement.

**Mr. Wyn Roberts:** Yes. Children taught through the medium of Welsh will be assessed in Welsh. Organisations contracted to develop standard assessment tasks are preparing them in both English and Welsh.

**Mr. Barry Jones:** To ask the Secretary of State for Wales if he proposes to publish a Welsh Language Bill; and if he will make a statement.

**Mr. Peter Walker:** I have made clear to the chairman of the Welsh Language Board that I will consider very carefully any specific proposals that the board might make.

The strategy document that the board has published today makes clear the board's view that all those with an interest should have the opportunity to shape future policy in support of the Welsh language. The strategy document is the starting point in that process and the board will be consulting on it widely.

**Mr. Barry Jones:** To ask the Secretary of State for Wales if he will list the representations he has received concerning national curriculum testing of pupils at the ages of seven and 11 years and whose first language is Welsh; and if he will make a statement.

**Mr. Wyn Roberts:** A number of the respondents to the consultation exercise on proposals for attainment targets and programmes of study in English 5-11 commented on assessment and testing; most of these supported the Secretary of State's proposals. I shall write to the hon. Gentleman to list the respondents and to list those who subsequently responded to the consultation on the proposal to exempt pupils taught in Welsh from assessment against the attainment targets for English.

**Mr. Barry Jones:** To ask the Secretary of State for Wales if he will meet the county councils of Wales to discuss his Department's proposals to enhance the status of the Welsh language; and if he will make a statement.

**Mr. Wyn Roberts:** My right hon. Friend has no plans at present to meet the Welsh county councils to discuss the Welsh Language Board's proposals in relation to the Welsh language. The Welsh Language Board will however be consulting all those organisations with an interest.

**Mr. Barry Jones:** To ask the Secretary of State for Wales what is his policy under the national curriculum on testing in English of pupils whose first language is Welsh at 11 years; and if he will make a statement.

**Mr. Wyn Roberts:** Pupils who are taught through the medium of Welsh will be assessed in Welsh. At the age of 11 all pupils, whether taught in Welsh or English, will be assessed against the same attainment targets for English.

**Mr. Barry Jones:** To ask the Secretary of State for Wales whether he proposes to meet the Welsh Language Board to discuss the board's suggestion concerning the possible contents of a Welsh Language Bill.

**Mr. Wyn Roberts:** My right hon. Friend regularly meets the chairman of the Welsh Language Board to discuss any proposals that they make.

**Dr. Thomas:** To ask the Secretary of State for Wales if he will list those district councils in Wales which have published *(a)* bilingual poll tax forms, *(b)* English-only forms with a reference to provision of Welsh language forms if requested and *(c)* English-only forms with no such statement.

**Mr. Grist:** This information is not held centrally. A welsh translation of the model community charge canvass form circulated in practice note 8 was sent to all district councils in Wales. Camera-ready copy of this translation was also made available on request.

### Language Teachers

**Mr. Barry Jones:** To ask the Secretary of State for Wales (1) if he will call a conference in Wales of local education authorities, teachers unions, parent-teacher associations, trades unions and employers organisations to discuss the shortage in Wales's high schools of teachers of modern languages; and if he will make a statement;

(2) if he will call an all-Wales conference to discuss the shortage of Welsh language teachers with the local education authorities of Wales; and if he will make a statement;

(3) what initiatives he plans to end the difficulties of recruiting to the high schools of Wales sufficient numbers of Welsh language teachers; and if he will make a statement;

(4) what plans he has to enable the recruitment in the high schools of Wales of sufficient teachers of *(a)* German, *(b)* French and *(c)* Spanish before 1992; and if he will make a statement;

(5) what steps he has taken to ensure that there are sufficient numbers of teachers of the Welsh language to meet the requirements of the national curriculum in *(a)* local education authority secondary schools and *(b)* private secondary schools.

**Mr. Wyn Roberts:** There are no immediate plans to call a national conference to discuss shortages either of Welsh language or of other modern language teachers. The Department will shortly be consulting each of the Welsh local education authorities about the number of teachers needed, including teachers of Welsh and other modern languages, to meet the requirements of the national curriculum and to discuss how the demand can be met.

Officials are also in close touch with the training institutions and we intend to promote liaison between the Department, the Wales Advisory Body and the Universities Funding Council, over the distribution of initial teacher training places within Wales, to ensure that targets are set as high as demand requires and realistic recruitment expectation justifies. Measures to encourage recruitment both from traditional and non-traditional sources have already been taken in conjunction with the Department of Education and Science. The teaching as a career unit has developed a specific programme to attract more Welsh language and Welsh-medium students.

We have no plans to ensure the supply of teachers to private schools but, in setting overall targets of teacher demand, full account is taken of the numbers of trained teachers expected to transfer to or directly enter the private sector.

However, encouraging teacher recruitment, either direct from training or of teachers returning to the profession, represents only part of our strategy for staffing schools to deliver the national curriculum. A very large part of the demand will need to be met by the re-training of teachers already in service. A framework for delivering the necessary in-service training is in place under the local education authority training grant scheme. My right hon. Friend has made expenditure provision for £223,000 under the scheme in 1989-90 for Welsh language training and a further £2·8 million for other training related to the national curriculum, including that necessary for modern languages. A further allocation of £582,000 for school management is intended to help heads and senior staff to manage the changes arising from the Education Reform Act.

We again expect to give a high priority to these training categories when the scheme allocations for 1990-91 are announced later this summer.

### Education Reform

**Mr. Barry Jones:** To ask the Secretary of State for Wales (1) if he will convene a conference of the local education authorities of Wales to discuss with directors of education and chairmen of local education authorities the (i) financial and (ii) professional consequences to the schools service of local management of schools and the national curriculum;

(2) if he will visit each of the local education authorities in Wales to discuss with them the (i) financial and (ii) professional consequences of local management of schools and the national curriculum; and if he will make a statement.

**Mr. Wyn Roberts:** No request has been made to my right hon. Friend by local education authorities to meet and discuss the consequences of the implementation of the Education Reform Act 1988. At official level discussions on these issues continue to take place through working groups on which all local education authorities are represented.

**Mr. Barry Jones:** To ask the Secretary of State for Wales if he will list in the *Official Report* all Government documents issued to *(a)* local education authorities and

*(b)* schools as a consequence of the Education Reform Act listing both the number of pages and the cost of the document; and if he will make a statement.

**Mr. Wyn Roberts:** The following documents have been issued by the Welsh Office to local authorities and schools as a direct result of the passing of the Education Reform Act 1988. Most of these documents were produced within the Department and costs cannot be separately identified. I am ensuring that copies are available in the Library of the House.

Length and Control of School Sessions: Draft Circular
Admission of pupils to County and Voluntary Schools: Circular 47/88
Charges for school activities: Circular 4/89
Religious Education and Collective Worship: Circular 6/89
Grant Maintained Schools: Circular 49/88
Local Management of Schools: Circular 36/88
Statutory Approval of Qualifications: Circular 33/89
National Curriculum Mathematics and Science Orders: Circular 14/89
The School Curriculum and Assessment: Circular 15/89
Local Arrangements for the Consideration of Complaints made under Section 23: Circular 26/89
Modern Foreign Languages in the National Curriculum: Circular 32/89
Governance of Maintained Further and Higher Education Institutions: Circular 37/88
Local Management of Further and Higher Education Institutions: Planning and Delegation of Schemes and Articles of Government: Circular 38/88
Local Management of Further and Higher Education Colleges: Circular Letter

*Mathematics for Ages 5–16:*
*Proposals of the Secretaries of State 1988*
Education (National Curriculum) (Attainment Targets and Programmes of Study in Mathematics) Order 1989

"Mathematics in the National Curriculum" (Associated document to above).

*Science for Ages 5–16:*
*Proposals of the Secretaries of State 1988*
Education (National Curriculum) (Attainment Targets and Programmes of Study in Science) Order 1989

"Science in The National Curriculum" (Associated document to above).

*Design and Technology for Ages 5–16:*
*Proposal of the Secretaries of State 1989*
National Curriculum Implementation: Circular Letter to Headteachers

National Curriculum: Draft Statutory Regulations— Exemptions from English at Key Stage 1: Consultation Letter

National Curriculum Temporary Exceptions for Individual Pupils: Draft Regulations and Circular

LEA Training Grants Scheme and ESG—National Curriculum Development Plans: Guidance Note

National Curriculum: Task Group on Assessment and Testing (TGAT): Report
Education Reform: The Government's Proposals for Schools: Booklet
School Governors: How to Become A Grant Maintained School: Booklet
School Governors: A New Role: Booklet
Shouldn't You Become A School Governor: Booklet
School Governors: A Guide to the Law for County and Controlled Schools: Booklet
English for Ages 5–11: Booklet
English in the National Curriculum Key Stage 1: Booklet

### Cancer Patients

**Mr. Barry Jones:** To ask the Secretary of State for Wales when he proposes to make public his plans to improve the facilities in north wales for cancer patients; and if he will make a statement.

**Mr. Grist:** Central funds have been made available to Clwyd and Gwynedd health authorities to improve facilities for cancer patients. A comprehensive study of cancer treatment services in north Wales, commissioned by the Welsh Office, is nearing completion and I will wish to consider it carefully, with the health authorities involved, in planning the further development of services.

### Bovine Spongiform Encephalopathy

**Mr. Ron Davies:** To ask the Secretary of State for Wales how many cases of BSE infected cattle at EEC-approved slaughterhouses in Wales have been identified.

**Mr. Peter Walker:** Two.

### Environmental Pollution

**Mrs. Clwyd:** To ask the Secretary of State for Wales if he will make a statement on his responsibilities for the control of environmental pollution in Wales.

**Mr. Grist:** I refer the hon. Lady to the reply given today by my right hon. Friend the Secretary of State for the Environment.

### Forestry Commission

**Mr. Barry Jones:** To ask the Secretary of State for Wales (1) what is the current acreage of the Forestry Commission in Wales;

(2) what is the estimated acreage in Wales of Forestry Commission land planted with (i) broadleaves, and (ii) conifers; and if he will make a statement.

**Mr. Peter Walker:** At 31 March 1989 the Forestry Commission managed the following areas of land in Wales:

|  | Hectares |
| --- | --- |
| Broadleaved woodland | 6,000 |
| Conifer woodland | 124,000 |
| Other land | 13,000 |
| Total | 143,000 |

**Mr. Barry Jones:** To ask the Secretary of State for Wales what is the estimated value of the assets of the Forestry Commission in Wales.

**Mr. Peter Walker:** The estimated value of the Forestry Commission's fixed assets in Wales at 31 March 1988 was as follows:

Plantations (land, roads and timber) £440 million.

Other tangible assets (land, buildings, machinery, plant and equipment) £11 million.

## AGRICULTURE, FISHERIES AND FOOD

### Scrapie

**Sir Geoffrey Johnson Smith:** To ask the Minister of Agriculture, Fisheries and Food (1) if he will ban food stuffs made from scrapie-infected sheep for all fowls, animals and fish following the Southwood report's recommendation of a ban on such feeds for ruminants;

(2) whether only ruminants were being fed with scrapie-infected feed when the Southwood report recommended banning it.

**Mr. Donald Thompson:** The Southwood working party was aware of the fact that protein derived from ruminants was fed to types of animal other than ruminants, and recognised the fact. The working party endorsed the action that the Government had already taken in banning the feeding of ruminant-based protein in ruminant rations. There are no plans to include feed for other types of animal in this ban.

### Fur Farming

**Mr. Flynn:** To ask the Minister of Agriculture, Fisheries and Food what representations the British Government has made and will be making to the Council of Europe concerning its current discussions on fur farming.

**Mr. Donald Thompson:** My officials attend these meetings at which recommendations for the welfare of fur-bearing animals are being elaborated. They are seeking to negotiate the most suitable recommendations for the welfare of these animals bearing in mind the Farm Animal Welfare Council's view that there is not enough evidence to set specific cage sizes and that further research is needed into some aspects of fur farming.

### Whales

**Mr. Cohen:** To ask the Minister of Agriculture, Fisheries and Food if he will raise at the next meeting of the European Community Council of Fisheries Ministers the continual slaughtering of whales by the whaling fleets of certain maritime nations; and if he will make a statement.

**Mr. Donald Thompson:** The European Community does not have competence on whaling matters as such, but those members with an interest in whaling are members of the IWC and we consult them in that forum. At the recent 41st annual meeting of the International Whaling Commission, the commission passed resolutions asking Japan, Iceland and Norway to reconsider their scientific research whaling programmes and rejected Japan's request for its small coastal whaling boats to take 320 minke whales off Japan. I welcome those decisions.

### Rabbits

**Mr. Colvin:** To ask the Minister of Agriculture, Fisheries and Food (1) if there have been any reports in the last year of viral haemorrhagic disease in rabbits in the United Kingdom; and if he will make a statement;

(2) what steps he is taking to prevent viral haemorrhagic disease in rabbits entering the United Kingdom.

**Mr. Donald Thompson:** There have been no reports of viral haemorrhagic disease in rabbits in this country. Imported rabbits are subject to six months quarantine and this is an effective safeguard against the introduction of the disease.

**Mr. Colvin:** To ask the Minister of Agriculture, Fisheries and Food if he will publish in the *Official Report* figures for the importation into the United Kingdom of frozen rabbit meat and live rabbits, and the countries of origin, for the last five years.

**Mr. Donald Thompson:** Data on imported rabbit meat are not available for the years prior to 1988. For 1988, imports of frozen rabbit meat were not separately identified. But imports for 1988 of all presentations of rabbit meat (fresh, chilled, frozen and edible offal) were:

| Country | Rabbit meat and offal (kg) |
| --- | --- |
| France | 113,800 |
| Poland | 1,700 |
| China | 2,314,100 |

Imports of live domestic rabbits and countries of origin for the last five years were:

| Country | Live rabbits (kg) |
| --- | --- |
| *1984* | |
| France | 1,076 |
| Irish Republic | 3,000 |
| | |
| *1985* | |
| France | 720 |
| | |
| *1986* | |
| France | 412 |
| | |
| *1987* | |
| USA | 490 |
| | |
| *1988* | |
| USA | 3,362 |

### Food Labelling

**Mr. McLoughlin:** To ask the Minister of Agriculture, Fisheries and Food whether he is yet in a position to make an announcement about the outcome of his consultation on the proposed guidelines by the Food Advisory Committee on the use of the word "natural" and similar terms in the labelling and advertising of food; and whether he will make a statement.

**Mr. Ryder:** We have received a large number of comments on the proposed guidelines from consumer, trade and enforcement bodies and from others with an interest in the proposals. I am pleased to say that there has been general support for the principle of the FAC's guidelines and for the voluntary approach proposed. However, concern has been expressed about the detail of certain parts of the guidance and some clarification has also been requested. In view of this, I asked the FAC to consider all the responses received and advise whether, in the light of these, they wished to amend their guidance.

My colleagues and I have now received the committee's further advice. After careful consideration the committee has reaffirmed its recommendation for voluntary self regulation, in the first instance, in this area of labelling. The committee has also agreed some important revisions to the text of the statement, which I believe directly address many of the concerns raised by respondents, generally by clarifying or expanding on certain principles in the statement to ensure that they are as clear and unambiguous as possible. My colleagues and I consider the committee's revised statement to be a sensible basis from which answers to problems in this area of labelling might be developed.

I am sending the FAC's advice out to all interested parties in the United Kingdom with a firm suggestion that in future, when considering food labelling, they observe and adopt the principles that the Food Advisory Committee has set out. I shall watch carefully to see whether this voluntary approach achieves the desired results, and will consider whether further action would be appropriate.

The FAC has also reaffirmed its advice that an advisory group of interested parties, to which cases of doubt could be referred, would ease adoption of the principles proposed. The committee has emphasised that it is not their intention that such a group should in any way circumvent the legal process but simply assist in interpretation of the guidance for particular cases. I cannot see, however, how such a group could operate effectively without becoming involved in matters of legal interpretation which are the responsibilities of the courts. I shall therefore not pursue this idea, but I shall ask my officials to inquire from the various interested parties, in 12 months' time, how the FAC's guidelines are working out in practice.

I have also written to the European Commission enclosing the FAC's advice, and commending this approach to them in formulating their own policies for Community rules in this area of labelling.

### Fisheries Council

**Mr. Marland:** To ask the Minister of Agriculture, Fisheries and Food what was the outcome of the Fisheries Council in Luxembourg on 20-21 June; and if he will make a statement.

**Mr. Donald Thompson:** Together with my right hon. colleague, Lord Sanderson, Minister of State, Scottish Office, I attended the Council of Fisheries Ministers in Luxembourg on 21 June 1989.

We secured agreement to an important amendment to restriction on beam trawl lengths that would have applied on 1 July. This will assist our inshore beam fleet and allow them to continue their operations without incurring costly modification. This is most welcome.

We also secured in the negotiations a commitment from the Commission to review urgently this year's total allowable catch for Channel cod and other precautionary TAC's.

After a difficult discussion the Council adopted a regulation laying down common marketing standards for preserved sardines. I ensured that our traditional sardine pastes and pates could continue to be marketed to the benefit of consumers.

On quota-hopping, I stresed the Community-wide nature of the problem and expressed my hope that the Commissioner will come forward urgently with a Community solution. I received strong support from five other member states, and the Commissioner undertook to examine the problem and present the proposals to the Council. The Commissioner also undertook to ensure that in enforcing Community rules there would be no discrimination between member states.

As we requested last December, the Commission reported on recent scientific advice reviewing the TACs for

North sea cod and haddock. We have to accept that there is no case for increasing these this year if we are to safeguard the future of these stocks.

### Set-aside Scheme

**Mr. Harry Greenway:** To ask the Minister of Agriculture, Fisheries and Food how much land he expects to be taken out of agricultural production under the set-aside scheme; and if he will make a statement.

**Mr. Yeo:** To ask the Minister of Agriculture, Fisheries and Food how much land has been set aside under the set-aside scheme.

**Mr. Ryder:** United Kingdom arable farmers who joined the scheme for the 1988-89 crop year have set aside some 55,000 hectares of land. The scheme is open until 31 July 1989 for applications from farmers wishing to join for the 1989-90 crop year. The amount of additional land entered for the scheme, in this and future years, will depend on the decisions of farmers in the light of their own circumstances and the continuing reductions in support for arable crops under the stabiliser system.

### Multi-annual Guidance Programme

**Mr. Wallace:** To ask the Minister of Agriculture, Fisheries and Food what progress has been made by the United Kingdom and other European Economic Community countries towards meeting the targets set in the fisheries multi-annual guidance programme.

**Mr. Donald Thompson:** A number of member states are deemed by the Commission to have made sufficient progress towards meeting their programme targets. The United Kingdom is currently considering with industry representations various options for reducing fleet capacity.

### Bovine Spongiform Encephalopathy

**Mr. Ron Davies:** To ask the Minister of Agriculture, Fisheries and Food what is the largest number of cases of BSE recorded on a single farm; what is the average number of cases per affected herd; what is the proportion of affected herds which have had a single case; and what is the proportion of all dairy herds that have had one or more cases.

**Mr. Donald Thompson:** The information is as follows:
—largest number of confirmed BSE cases on a single farm—18
—average number of cases per infected herd—1·5
—proportion of affected herds having a single case—71 per cent.
—proportion of all dairy herds having one or more cases—6·5 per cent.

**Mr. Ron Davies:** To ask the Minister of Agriculture, Fisheries and Food, pursuant to his answer to the hon. Member for Caerphilly of 19 June, when he intends to introduce recording of the information concerning the incidence of BSE at EEC approved and non-approved slaughterhouses.

**Mr. Donald Thompson:** This is already in hand. The results will be collected each quarter beginning with the period April-June 1989.

### Tuberculosis

**Mr. Ron Davies:** To ask the Minister of Agriculture, Fisheries and Food what are the public policy considerations which underlie the decision to operate a slaughter with compensation scheme for cattle infected with tuberculosis but not for deer infected with tuberculosis.

**Mr. Donald Thompson:** I announced on 16 June at column *563*, in reply to my right hon. Friend the Member for Westmoreland and Lonsdale, (Mr. Jopling) my intention to introduce a slaughter with compensation scheme for deer suffering from tuberculosis.

### Animal Disease

**Mr. Ron Davies:** To ask the Minister of Agriculture, Fisheries and Food in respect of which notifiable animal disease he operates a slaughter without compensation scheme; and if he will list such schemes together with details of the appropriate authority.

**Mr. Donald Thompson:** None.

### Divisional Headquarters

**Mr. Ron Davies:** To ask the Minister of Agriculture, Fisheries and Food if he will list the divisional headquarters offices of his Department.

**Mr. Donald Thompson:** My department's regional and divisional Offices are situated in the following locations in England:

*Eastern Region*
Regional office:
Cambridge

Divisional offices:
Chelmsford
Huntingdon
Lincoln
Norwich

*Midlands and Western Region*
Regional office:
Wolverhampton

Divisional offices:
Crewe
Nottingham
Preston
Worcester

*Northern region*
Regional office:
Leeds

Divisional offices:
Beverley
Carlisle
Newcastle-upon-Tyne
Northallerton

*South Eastern region*
Regional office:
Reading

Divisional offices:
Guildford
Maidstone
Oxford

*South Western region*
Regional office:
Bristol

Divisional offices:
Exeter
Gloucester
Taunton
Truro

Staff of my Department's Agricultural Development and Advisory Service are also located in Wales, but the Welsh Office is responsible for their accommodation.

## Price Fixing

**Dr. David Clark:** To ask the Minister of Agriculture, Fisheries and Food with which organisations he or his ministerial colleagues had meetings to discuss the price fixing of agricultural produce prior to their agreement in Brussels in 1988.

**Mr. MacGregor:** In 1989, as in 1988 and previously, Agriculture Ministers and senior officials held meetings with a number of organisations to discuss the Commission's price fixing proposals. In 1989 these discussions involved, in particular, the following bodies:

Agricultural and Allied Workers National Trade Group of the Transport and General Workers Union

Consumers in the European Community Group

National Farmers Union, Scottish National Farmers Union, Ulster Farmers Union

Farmers Union of Wales

Food and Drink Federation

A number of other organisations were offered invitations to attend meetings to discuss the Commission's price proposals but declined to do so.

## Environmentally Sensitive Areas

**Dr. David Clark:** To ask the Minister of Agriculture, Fisheries and Food whether he intends to designate all the areas on the original list submitted to him by the Countryside Commission and Nature Conservancy Council as environmentally sensitive by the end of 1990; and if he will make a statement.

**Mr. Ryder:** I have no plans at present to designate any further ESAs. All the areas shortlisted for ESA status in England by the Countryside Commission and the Nature Conservancy Council have been designated. These schemes are being monitored and I plan to carry out a full review of ESA policy before the first agreements terminate in 1992.

## Farm Diversification Grants

**Dr. David Clark:** To ask the Minister of Agriculture, Fisheries and Food if he will list the number of grants approved under the farm diversification grants scheme; and the number that were rejected on environmental grounds.

**Mr. Ryder:** During 1988, 669 applications for capital grant were approved under the farm diversification grant scheme; 137 applications were rejected but none were on environmental grounds.

Between 1 January and 31 May 1989, 332 applications were received and 87 were rejected. I regret that information on the reasons for rejections during this period is not readily available.

## Hedgerows

**Dr. David Clark:** To ask the Minister of Agriculture, Fisheries and Food (1) if he will list the names of all grant schemes available to farmers for planting hedgerows, giving their date of introduction, when they ceased; and whether they are still available, since 1959;

(2) if he will list the names of all grant schemes available to farmers for renewing hedgerows, giving their date of introduction, when they ceased, and whether they are still available, since 1959.

**Mr. Ryder:** Grant was available under the following schemes for the provision, replacement or improvement of hedges:

| Name of Scheme | Date Introduced | Date Closed to Applications |
|---|---|---|
| Farm improvement scheme | 1 September 1957 | 31 December 1970 |
| Horticulture improvement scheme | 14 April 1960 | 31 December 1973 |
| Hill land improvement scheme | 14 August 1967 | 31 December 1970 |
| Farm capital grant scheme | 1 January 1971 | 30 September 1980 |
| Horticulture capital grant scheme | 1 January 1974 | 30 September 1980 |
| Farm and horticulture development scheme | 1 January 1974 | 30 September 1980 |
| Agriculture and horticulture development scheme | 1 October 1980 | 30 September 1985 |
| Agriculture and horticulture grant scheme | 1 October 1980 | 9 July 1985 |
| Agriculture improvement regulations | 1 October 1985 | 28 November 1988 |
| Agriculture improvement scheme | 1 October 1985 | 29 November 1988 |

The closing dates quoted are those for the receipt of new applications. Expenditure incurred before the closing date could be claimed subsequently and where the applicant held an approved plan of investments, the expenditure too could be incurred after the closing date. Claims are still being accepted from holders of approved plans under the agriculture and horticulture development scheme and the Agriculture Improvement Regulations.

Grants of 50 per cent. in the less favoured areas and 40 per cent. elsewhere for the provision, replacement or improvement of hedges are currently available under the farm and conservation grant scheme which was introduced on 20 February 1989.

## Training Courses

**Dr. David Clark:** To ask the Minister of Agriculture, Fisheries and Food if he will give the number of training courses given on protectiing rivers and streams from agricultural pollution by the agricultural development advisory service officers on *(a)* a national basis and *(b)* a regional basis; and if he will make a statement.

**Mr. Ryder:** ADAS provides routine training for new entrants and specialist and general advisers on pollution avoidance and control measures. The training is undertaken at national and regional level as an integrated part of discipline training, but records are not available of the precise number of courses held.

**Dr. David Clark:** To ask the Minister of Agriculture, Fisheries and Food if he will give the number of training courses given on conservation of wildlife and landscape by the agricultural development advisory service offices on *(a)* a national basis and *(b)* a regional basis in each year since 1981; and if he will make a statement.

**Mr. Ryder:** Since 1981, 35 national training courses have been held by ADAS on conservation of wildlife and landscape involving approximately 900 advisory officers. Information on regional training over the same period is not available, but since 1987 more than 20 conservation courses have been held in regions. Conservation is also included as an integral part of discipline training for new entrants and ADAS advisers.

### Planning Applications

**Dr. David Clark:** To ask the Minister of Agriculture, Fisheries and Food (1) how many planning applications he has commented on *(a)* within national parks and *(b)* outside national parks since 1986; and in each category how many were opposed;

(2) how many planning applications he has commented on *(a)* within environmentally sensitive areas and *(b)* outside environmentally sensitive areas since 1987; and in each category how many were opposed;

(3) how many planning applications he has commented on *(a)* within areas of outstanding natural beauty and *(b)* outside areas of outstanding natural beauty since 1986; and in each category how many were opposed.

**Mr. Ryder:** The statistics on consultations with MAFF by planning authorities about development involving agricultural land are not kept in the format requested. The information is, therefore, not readily available.

## DEFENCE

### Territorial Army (Vetting)

33. **Mr. Allen McKay:** To ask the Secretary of State for Defence if he has any proposals to improve the arrangements for vetting members of the Territorial Army in Northern Ireland.

**Mr. Neubert:** The procedures aimed at ensuring members of paramilitary or extremist organisations are excluded from service in the Territorial Army in Northern Ireland or any other part of the armed forces are kept under constant review.

### Photonics

**Mr. Andrew F. Bennett:** To ask the Secretary of State for Defence if any research programmes are under way concerning the use of photonics for communicating with Royal Navy submarines.

**Mr. Neubert:** It is not our practice to comment on operational matters of this kind.

### Transmitters

**Mr. Andrew F. Bennett:** To ask the Secretary of State for Defence if he will list the sites of all current and proposed extremely low frequency, very low frequency and low frequency transmitters in the United Kingdom.

**Mr. Neubert:** I am not prepared to comment on security grounds, beyond acknowledging the proposed trial of an extremely low frequency transmitter at Glengarry, which has been the subject of several previous answers to the hon. Member.

**Mr. Andrew F. Bennett:** To ask the Secretary of State for Defence (1) what plans his Department has to increase the number of low frequency transmitters in the United Kingdom;

(2) what plans his Department has to increase the number of VLF transmitters in the United Kingdom.

**Mr. Neubert:** I am not prepared to comment for security reasons.

### Submarine Communications

**Mr. Andrew F. Bennett:** To ask the Secretary of State for Defence (1) what plans his Department has to increase the number of systems available for communicating with the Trident submarine fleet;

(2) what water space management agreements exist to ensure that United States and United Kingdom SSBNs do not encounter each other whilst on patrol.

**Mr. Neubert:** It is not our practice to comment on operational matters of this kind.

### Submarines (Communications)

**Mr. Andrew F. Bennett:** To ask the Secretary of State for Defence if he will list the reasons why a TACAMO-type system of very low frequency communication with submarines was rejected for the Royal Navy.

**Mr. Neubert:** No.

**Mr. Andrew F. Bennett:** To ask the Secretary of State for Defence if there are any plans to equip Royal Navy submarines in order to receive Oscar or Lasercom signals.

**Mr. Neubert:** It is not our practice to comment on operational matters of this kind.

### Tornado Aircraft (Storage)

**Mr. Wilson:** To ask the Secretary of State for Defence how many Tornado aircraft are currently held in storage at RAF Leeming.

**Mr. Neubert:** None.

**Mr. Wilson:** To ask the Secretary of State for Defence how many Tornado aircraft are currently held in storage at RAF Coningsby.

**Mr. Neubert:** No Tornados are held in storage at RAF Coningsby. However, as the RAF's receiving point for new Tornado F3s, at any one time a small number of aircraft may be held there in reserve while awaiting allocation to their operational squadrons.

**Mr. Wilson:** To ask the Secretary of State for Defence (1) how many Tornado GR 1 aircraft were held in storage on 1 April in each year since 1981;

(2) what is the average length of time for which individual Tornado GR1 aircraft have been held in storage since 1981.

**Mr. Neubert:** No Tornado GR1s were held in storage on 1 April of any year since 1981 with the exception of

1983 and 1984. Although detailed records are no longer held, it is estimated that seven and 18 Tornado GR1s were held in storage on 1 April 1983 and 1984 respectively, while awaiting allocation to their operational squadrons. The average period in storage of each aircraft is estimated to have been between six to nine months.

### RAF St. Athan (Aircraft Storage)

**Mr. Wilson:** To ask the Secretary of State for Defence what has been the *(a)* average and *(b)* peak total number of aircraft held in storage at RAF St. Athan in each year since 1980.

**Mr. Neubert:** RAF St. Athan is a major maintenance depot and is used routinely for storing attrition aircraft and aircraft awaiting servicing. Records of the number of aircraft held in storage are not kept in the form requested. However, it is estimated that, on average, about 50 aircraft of various types and ages are held at RAF St. Athan.

### Land (Cunninghame, North)

**Mr. Wilson:** To ask the Secretary of State for Defence what plans exist for acquisition of additional land by his Department in the Cunninghame, North constituency.

**Mr. Neubert:** There are at present no such plans.

### Nuclear Deterrent

**Mr. Redmond:** To ask the Secretary of State for Defence, pursuant to his answer to the hon. Member for Don Valley of 2 March, *Official Report,* columns *253-54,* if he will make a statement as to what factors Her Majesty's Government consider to be the essential constituents of a fully effective, reliable and survivable deterrent.

**Mr. Neubert:** I refer the hon. Member to the second memorandum submitted by the Ministry of Defence to the Foreign Affairs Committee on 11 May 1988, which was published on pages 35 to 37 of the minutes of evidence in its third report of the 1987-88 Session (HC280). Paragraphs 6 to 8 in particular contain the information he seeks.

### Sea-based Nuclear Weapons

**Mr. Flynn:** To ask the Secretary of State for Defence whether Her Majesty's Government have any plans to *(a)* withdraw some of the sea-based tactical nuclear weapons on Royal Navy vessels and *(b)* re-evaluate the utility to United Kingdom national defence of sea-based nuclear weapons.

**Mr. Neubert:** As part of the studies related to modernising the United Kingdom's theatre nuclear weapons capability, consideration is being given to the replacement of the full spectrum of United Kingdom tactical nuclear weapons, including sea-based systems. However, no decisions have yet been taken.

### F111 Aircraft

**Mr. Boyes:** To ask the Secretary of State for Defence how many United States Air Force F111 aircraft were withdrawn from bases in England in 1988; and what was the reason for their withdrawal.

**Mr. Neubert:** None.

### "Who Framed Colin Wallace?"

**Mr. Livingstone:** To ask the Secretary of State for Defence if he will make a statement on allegations concerning the forging of CIA documents used by former serving army officers and civil servants reported in the book "Who Framed Colin Wallace?" by Paul Foot.

**Mr. Neubert:** The hon. Member made allegations as to the forging of CIA documents during the Adjournment debate of 20 June last year, but they are not repeated in Mr. Foot's book. I have nothing to add on this matter to the many answers the hon. Member has already received, for example in the letter sent to him on 15 August 1988 by my predecessor, a copy of which was placed in the House of Commons Library.

### Reserve Establishments

**Mr. Nellist:** To ask the Secretary of State for Defence if he will list the locations of all Royal Naval Reserve and Royal Marines Reserve establishments in the United Kingdom.

**Mr. Neubert:** Not all Naval reservist units have their own establishments; some are accommodated with other service units. The following is a list of all Royal Naval Reserve and Royal Marines Reserve units with their locations:

*RNR*
HMS Calliope, Tyne and Wear
HMS Cambria, Cardiff
HMS Camberdown, Dundee
HMS Caroline, Belfast
HMS Ceres, Leeds
HMS Claverhouse, Edinburgh
HMS Dalriada, Greenock
HMS Dragon, Swansea
HMS Eaglet, Liverpool
HMS Essex, Shoeburyness
HMS Ferret, Ashford
HMS Flying Fox, Bristol
HMS Forward, Birmingham
HMS Graham, Glasgow
HMS Hallam, Sheffield
HMS Mercia, Coventry
HMS Northwood, Northwood
HMS Palatine, Preston
HMS Paragon, Middlesbrough
HMS Pellew, Exeter
HMS President, London
HMS Salford, Manchester
HMS Scotia, Pitreavie
HMS Sherwood, Nottingham
HMS Southwick, Fareham
HMS Sussex, Brighton
HMS Vivid, Plymouth
HMS Wessex, Southampton
HMS Wildlife, Chatham

*RMR*
RMR City of London, Bermondsey, with detachments in:
  Chatham
  Portsmouth
  Henley (being established)
RMR Scotland, Glasgow, with detachments in:
  Grangemouth
  Greenock
  Dundee
RMR Bristol, Bristol, with detachments in:
  Cardiff
  Lympstone
  Plymouth
  Poole

RMR Merseyside, Liverpool, with detachments in:
    Manchester
    Birmingham
RMR Tyne, Newcastle upon Tyne

### Recruitment Offices

**Mr. Nellist:** To ask the Secretary of State for Defence if he will list those cities and towns in the United Kingdom which have recruitment offices for *(a)* the Army, *(b)* the RAF and *(c)* the Royal Navy.

**Mr. Neubert:** The information requested is given in the following tables.

The Royal Navy have recruiting offices in the following towns:

*England*
  Barnsley
  Birmingham
  Blackburn
  Brighton
  Bristol

  Cambridge
  Canterbury
  Carlisle
  Chatham
  Chelmsford
  Coventry

  Derby
  Dorchester

  Exeter

  Guildford

  Hartlepool
  Hull

  Ilford
  Ipswich

  Leeds
  Leicester
  Lincoln
  Liverpool
  London
    Central
    Blackheath
    Croydon
  Luton

  Manchester
  Milton Keynes

  Newcastle Upon Tyne
  Northampton
  Norwich
  Nottingham

  Oxford

  Peterborough
  Plymouth
  Portsmouth
  Preston

  Reading

  St Helens
  Scunthorpe
  Sheffield
  Shrewsbury
  Southampton
  Stoke on Trent
  Sunderland
  Swindon

  Truro

  Watford
  Wolverhampton
  Worcester

  York

*Scotland*
  Aberdeen
  Dundee
  Edinburgh
  Inverness

*Wales*
  Cardiff
  Swansea
  Wrexham

*Northern Ireland*
  Belfast

The Army have recruiting offices in the following towns:

*England*
  Aldershot
  Andover
  Ashford
  Ashington
  Banbury
  Barnsley
  Barnstaple
  Basingstoke
  Bath
  Bedford
  Birkenhead
  Birmingham
  Bishop Auckland
  Blackburn
  Blackpool
  Bolton
  Bootle
  Boston
  Bournemouth
  Bradford
  Brighton
  Bristol
  Burnley
  Burton on Trent
  Bury St. Edmunds

  Cambridge
  Cannock
  Canterbury
  Carlisle
  Chatham
  Chelmsford
  Cheltenham
  Chester
  Chesterfield
  Chichester
  Colchester
  Corby
  Coventry
  Crewe

  Darlington
  Derby
  Doncaster
  Dover
  Durham

  Exeter

  Gloucester
  Grantham
  Grimsby
  Guildford

  Halifax
  Harlow

Hartlepool
Hastings
Hereford
High Wycombe
Horden
Horsham
Huddersfield
Hull

Ipswich

Kettering
Kings Lynn

Leeds
Leicester
Lincoln
Liverpool

London
  Central
  Acton
  Blackheath
  Camberwell
  Crayford
  Edmonton Green
  Finchley
  Forest Gate
  Holloway
  Norbury
  Penge
  Romford
  Surbiton
  Wandsworth
  Wembley
Lowestoft
Luton

Maidstone
Manchester
Middlesbrough
Milton Keynes

Newcastle Upon Tyne
Newport (IOW)
Northampton
Norwich
Nottingham
Nuneaton
Oldham
Oxford

Peterborough
Plymouth
Portsmouth
Preston

Reading
Redruth
Rochdale

St. Albans
St. Helens
Salisbury
Scunthorpe
Sheffield
Shrewsbury
Slough
South Shields
Southampton
Southend
Stockport
Stoke on Trent
Sunderland
Swindon

Taunton
Telford
Torquay
Tunbridge Wells

Wakefield
Warrington
Warwick
Watford
Weston Super Mare
Wigan
Wolverhampton
Worcester
Workington
Worksop

York

*Scotland*
Aberdeen
Ayr
Bathgate
Dumbarton
Dumfries
Dundee
Dunfermline
Edinburgh
Elgin
Galashiels
Glasgow
Glenrothes
Greenock
Hamilton
Inverness
Irvine
Keith
Maryhill
Paisley
Perth
Springboig
Stirling
Wick

*Wales*
Bangor
Cardiff
Llanelli
Merthyr Tyfil
Newport
Pembroke Dock
Pontypridd
Rhyl
Swansea
Wrexham

*Northern Ireland*
Belfast
Coleraine
Omagh
Portadown

*Channel Islands*
Jersey

The Royal Air Force have recruiting offices in the following towns:

| *England* | |
| --- | --- |
| Bedford | Gloucester |
| Birmingham | Grimsby |
| Blackpool | Guildford |
| Bournemouth | |
| Bradford | Huddersfield |
| Brighton | Hull |
| Bristol | |
| | Ilford |
| Cambridge | Ipswich |
| Canterbury | |
| Carlisle | Leeds |
| Chatham | Leicester |
| Coventry | Lincoln |
| | Liverpool |
| Darlington | London (Central) |
| | Luton |
| Exeter | |
| | Manchester |
| | Middlesbrough |

| | Taunton |
|---|---|
| Newcastle Upon Tyne | Truro |
| Norwich | |
| Nottingham | Wolverhampton |
| | |
| Oldham | York |
| Oxford | |
| | *Scotland* |
| Peterborough | Aberdeen |
| Plymouth | Ayr |
| Portsmouth | Dundee |
| Preston | Edinburgh |
| | Glasgow |
| Reading | Inverness |
| | |
| St Helens | *Wales* |
| Sheffield | Bangor |
| Shrewsbury | Cardiff |
| Southampton | Newport |
| Southend | Swansea |
| Stoke on Trent | Wrexham |
| Sunderland | |
| Swindon | *Northern Ireland* |
| | Aldergrove |

### Nuclear Depth Bombs

**Mr. Nellist:** To ask the Secretary of State for Defence what increase there has been since 1980 in the number of Royal Naval helicopters capable of dropping nuclear depth bombs; what plans are in existence or under consideration to increase this capability; and if he will make a statement.

**Mr. Neubert:** The number of helicopters capable of dropping nuclear depth bombs has remained broadly constant since 1980. Our plans in this area, as in all others, are kept under regular review.

### NATO (Report)

**Mr. Flynn:** To ask the Secretary of State for Defence if he has received a copy of the report "New Directions for NATO: Adapting the Atlantic Alliance to the Needs of the 1990s" by the Institute for Resource and Security Studies and the Institute for Peace and International Security.

**Mr. Neubert:** Yes.

### BAOR (Security)

**Mr. O'Neill:** To ask the Secretary of State for Defence how many service personnel are involved in the maintenance of security at the British Army of the Rhine base at Osnabruck.

**Mr. Neubert:** A range of measures, including the use of service personnel, is taken to maintain security at the base but, for security reasons, I am not prepared to disclose details.

**Mr. O'Neill:** To ask the Secretary of State for Defence how many service personnel are involved in the maintenance of security at British Army of the Rhine bases.

**Mr. Neubert:** For security reasons it is not our policy to divulge such details.

**Mr. O'Neill:** To ask the Secretary of State for Defence what information he has about the reported bombing of Quebec barracks at the British Army of the Rhine base at Osnabruck; and if he will make a statement.

**Mr. Neubert:** At 0130 hours on 19 June 1989 an explosion took place at Quebec barracks at Osnabruck. The attack involved five high explosive devices, only one of which exploded. Shortly before the explosion, an unidentified intruder was challenged by a German civilian employee. The intruder was armed and a shot was fired. The German civilian was then struck in the face by the intruder, sustaining minor injuries. As a result of the shot being fired, the occupants of a nearby accommodation block were roused, the alarm was raised and several suspected devices were discovered outside the accommodation block. The building was successfully evacuated before one of the devices exploded. There were no casualties. Police inquiries are in progress in Germany and elsewhere.

It is worth noting that, like the failed attack on Clive barracks at Tern hill on 20 February this year, the terrorists' intention of causing significant casualties was thwarted by the vigilance and prompt action of on-duty personnel. In the case of Quebec barracks I would like to pay tribute to the action of the German employee who, though unarmed, challenged the intruder.

**Mr. O'Neill:** To ask the Secretary of State for Defence (1) what was the annual expenditure on physical security arrangements for British Army of the Rhine bases in each of the last five years;

(2) what was the annual expenditure on physical security at the British Army of the Rhine base at Osnabruck for each of the last five years.

**Mr. Neubert:** It would require disproportionate cost and effort to identify such figures.

**Mr. O'Neill:** To ask the Secretary of State for Defence when the last co-ordinated test and evaluation of security at the Osnabruck British Army of the Rhine base was carried out.

**Mr. Neubert:** A co-ordinated test and evaluation of security at Quebec barracks was last carried out on 9 June 1989.

**Mr. O'Neill:** To ask the Secretary of State for Defence whether any civilian workers at British Army of the Rhine bases have any involvement in the maintenance of security at those bases.

**Mr. Neubert:** For security reasons it is not our policy to disclose this information.

### Blind Take-off Manoeuvres

**Mr. Nellist:** To ask the Secretary of State for Defence what is the purpose of the practice of blind take-off manoeuvres; how frequently this manoeuvre is carried out by *(a)* RAF aircraft based in the United Kingdom and *(b)* United States Air Force aircraft based in the United Kingdom; and if he will make a statement.

**Mr. Neubert:** Take-off manoeuvres by aircraft of the Royal Air Force or the United States Air Force stationed in this country are not carried out "blind".

# Written Answers to Questions

*Friday 23 June 1989*

## HOME DEPARTMENT

### Harp Seals

**Dr. Kim Howells:** To ask the Secretary of State for the Home Department what is his policy towards the culling of baby harp seals.

**Mr. Douglas Hogg:** Since there are no harp seals which are native to the United Kingdom, the question of culling does not arise in this country.

### Prisoners (Transfers)

**Mr. Burt:** To ask the Secretary of State for the Home Department on what basis his Department considers requests by prisoners to serve the remainder of their sentences in another United Kingdom jurisdiction.

**Mr. Hurd:** My Department, in conjunction with the Scottish and Northern Ireland Offices, has recently reviewed the policy governing requests by prisoners to be transferred to another jurisdiction in the United Kingdom. Any inmate in England and Wales, Scotland or Northern Ireland who applies to be transferred to either of the other jurisdictions to serve the rest of his or her sentence will normally be transferred, provided that (1) the inmate would have at least six months left to serve in the receiving jurisdiction before his or her date of release; (2) the inmate was ordinarily resident in the receiving jurisdiction prior to the current sentence; or his or her close family currently reside there and there are reasonable grounds for believing that it is the inmate's firm intention to take up residence there on release; and (3) both Departments concerned are reasonably satisfied that the inmate will not, if transferred, disrupt or attempt to disrupt any prison establishment, or otherwise pose an unacceptable risk to security.

Even if these conditions are met, however, transfer may be refused if it is considered that the inmate's crimes were so serious as to render him or her undeserving of any degree of public sympathy or to make it inappropriate that the inmate should benefit from a substantial reduction in time left to serve, if that would be a consequence of transfer. Similarly, transfers may be refused if there are reasonable grounds for believing that the inmate's primary intention in making the application is to secure a reduction in the time left to serve. On the other hand, an application that does not meet these conditions may nevertheless be granted where there are strong compassionate or other compelling grounds for transfer.

### Students (Immigration)

**Mr. Hannam:** To ask the Secretary of State for the Home Department whether the new immigration rule which prevents visitors switching to student status whilst in the United Kingdom will be applied to visa nationals only; and if he will make a statement.

**Mr. Renton:** Yes. The generous provisions in the current rules have been abused by some who are not students but whose aim is to take work or to remain here permanently. Many of these enter as visitors and subsequently switch to student status, but have no intention whatsoever of pursuing genuine study here. The "no-switching" provision is designed to prevent this abuse and has been confined to visa nationals because the available evidence suggests that passengers from visa countries are the major source of the abuse. Hence, while in recent years visa nationals have made up only about 20 per cent. of those admitted to the country as students, they have constituted 60 per cent. of grants of extensions of stay as a student to those originally admitted as visitors. Further, two exercises conducted by the immigration service and the police against suspect educational establishments revealed that, of some 6,000 alleged students on the books of these establishments, 95 per cent. were visa nationals and 95 per cent. of these had been orginally admitted as ordinary or business visitors. The educational facilities offered were adequate for only a fraction of the number on the books.

The change is therefore necessary to ensure the effective operation of the visa system. It would be wasteful of resources and unnecessary to extend it to non-visa nationals; in particular such an extension would require the needless issue of over 100,000 additional entry clearances worldwide each year. Visa nationals will still be able to come to the United Kingdom for study, even if they have been unable to finalise all the arrangements beforehand, provided that they make their intentions clear and obtain the necessary visa in advance. Genuine visitors will not be affected in any way.

## NORTHERN IRELAND

### Social Security (South Down)

**Mr. McGrady:** To ask the Secretary of State for Northern Ireland what was the number of claimants who made application, were awarded and accepted *(a)* social fund loans, *(b)* community care grants at each of the social security offices in South Down for the financial year 1988-89.

**Mr. Needham:** The information for the period 11 April 1988 to 31 March 1989 is given in the table.

| Social Security Office | Budgeting loans | | Crisis loans | | Community care grants | |
|---|---|---|---|---|---|---|
| | Number of applications | Number of awards | Number of applications | Number of awards | Number of applications | Number of awards |
| Downpatrick | 1,155 | 678 | 433 | 375 | 446 | 238 |
| Newcastle | 465 | 309 | 169 | 143 | 202 | 134 |
| Kilkeel | 164 | 146 | 33 | 32 | 165 | 133 |
| Ballynahinch | 204 | 141 | 84 | 73 | 168 | 109 |
| Newry | 2,011 | 1,496 | 392 | 352 | 956 | 548 |
| Banbridge | 744 | 493 | 210 | 158 | 420 | 289 |

The balance of applications in each category were refused, withdrawn by the applicant or were still to be decided at the end of March 1989.

**Mr. McGrady:** To ask the Secretary of State for Northern Ireland how many pensioners at each of the social security offices in South Down no longer qualify for housing benefit as a result of the recent pension increase.

**Mr. Needham:** The information requested is not readily available and could be obtained only at disproportionate cost.

**Mr. McGrady:** To ask the Secretary of State for Northern Ireland what proportion of the total social fund expenditure has been written off as unrecoverable for the financial year 1988-89.

**Mr. Needham:** Total social fund expenditure in the period 11 April 1988 to 31 March 1989 was £18,485,998. It was not practicable to pursue recovery of funeral payments of £934,665 and loans of £1,952. These figures are provisional.

### Kincora Boys' Home

**Mr. Livingstone:** To ask the Secretary of State for Northern Ireland, pursuant to his reply of 18 April, *Official Report,* column *130,* to the hon. Member for

Brent, East, on what date the three claims were settled; and when he expects the eight other claims to be processed by.

**Mr. Needham** *[holding answer 22 June 1989]:* One claim was settled on 15 April 1988, the other two on 5 April 1989. It is not possible to give any indication of when the eight other claims will be processed.

### Housing (Armagh City)

**Mr. John D. Taylor:** To ask the Secretary of State for Northern Ireland how many units of accommodation there are in each Housing Executive estate within Armagh city; how many units are currently unoccupied at each estate; how many units of each estate are presently vandalised or boarded up; and how many new units of accommodation does the executive propose to construct in Armagh city in each of the next five years.

**Mr. Needham** *[holding answer 15 June 1989]:* This is a matter for the Northern Ireland Housing Executive. I am advised by the chairman that at 1 May 1989 the number of units of accommodation, the number of units unoccupied and the number of units vandalised or boarded up in each estate in Armagh city are as follows:

| Armagh city estate | Number of executive owned units | Number of units unoccupied | Number of units vandalised/ boarded up |
|---|---|---|---|
| Emania Terrace | 12 | — | — |
| Banbrook/Brookhill/Railway Street | 122 | — | — |
| Callanbridge Park | 140 | 8 | 3 |
| Callan Street/Crescent | 40 | 4 | 3 |
| Cregagh/Mullanstown Primates Cottages | 59 | — | — |
| Culdee/Upper Irish Street | 102 | — | — |
| Daires Willows | 19 | — | — |
| Dalton | 66 | — | — |
| Druid's Villas | 28 | — | — |
| Drumarg | 126 | 1 | — |
| Drumbreda | 112 | — | — |
| Duke's Grove | 39 | 3 | — |
| Legarhill Park | 56 | — | — |
| Longstone | 94 | — | — |
| Mullacreevie | 187 | — | — |
| Navan Street/Terrace/Niall's Crescent | 60 | — | — |
| Windmill | 42 | — | — |
| Alexander | 60 | — | — |
| Ardmore Drive | 75 | — | — |
| Ballinahone | 62 | — | — |
| Barrack Street/Gaul Square/Woodford Place | 27 | — | — |
| Bridge House | 17 | — | — |
| Folly | 154 | 7 | — |
| Gough Avenue/Barrack Hill | 87 | — | — |
| Lisanally Gardens/Villas | 54 | — | — |
| Lonsdale Gardens | 14 | — | — |
| Newry Road | 4 | — | — |
| Orangefield Drumadd | 156 | — | — |
| Victoria Park | 13 | — | — |
| Total | 2,014 | 23 | 6 |

The number of units of accommodation planned in Armagh City in each of the next five years are as follows:

| Year | Number of units |
|---|---|
| 1989-90 | 21 |
| 1990-91 | [1]16 |
| 1991-92 | [2]— |
| 1992-93 | [2]— |
| 1993-94 | [2]— |

[1] Joint scheme with SHSSB. Includes six dwellings to be allocated for mentally handicapped.
[2] No schemes as yet programmed.

## NATIONAL FINANCE

### Government Bonds

**Mr. Allen:** To ask the Chancellor of the Exchequer what is the value of the early repurchases of Government bonds since the April Budget.

**Mr. Lilley:** Q2 figures will be published in the August *Bank of England Quarterly Bulletin*. Net transactions, including redemptions, for March and April are published in table F of the Bank of England's monthly monetary statistics.

### Value Added Tax

**Rev. Martin Smyth:** To ask the Chancellor of the Exchequer if he will make a statement about the operation of the value added tax cash accounting scheme; and whether he has any plans *(a)* to adjust the turnover level of £250,000 to take into account changes to the retail prices index and *(b)* to review the level of the threshold.

**Mr. Lilley:** The cash accounting scheme was introduced on 1 October 1987 and is available to businesses with an annual taxable turnover not exceeding £250,000. It is used by about 60,000 businesses. Customs and Excise have recently consulted representative bodies and small businesses to consider all aspects of the scheme with the aim of improving take-up. The views of those who responded are currently being considered and the outcome of the consultation will be announced in due course. The existing turnover limit is significantly higher than that originally proposed and required the formal agreement of the European Commission. Any further increase would also have to be approved by the Commission.

### Privatisation (Debt Repayment)

**Mr. Allen:** To ask the Chancellor of the Exchequer if he will list the individual amounts of debt repayments written off in each of the privatisations and sale of Government assets since 1979 and the aggregate of these write-offs.

**Mr. Norman Lamont:** The normal practice on privatisation of a nationalised industry or company wholly or majority owned by Government is to repay, rather than write off, debt. This repayment may be financed from the company's existing resources, the injection of new equity or new debt finance. In some cases the Government have provided the finance to repay debts, for example, by an equity injection.

National loans fund debt has been written off only in the cases listed in the table, totalling £3,014,662,728. These write-offs had no direct effect on public expenditure since they represented a reconstruction of the balance sheets of the industries concerned. In each case, having had NLF debt written off, the successor company issued new equity or debt securities to be held by the Secretary of State as assets on the consolidated fund pending realisation.

| Year and Company | Amount £ |
| --- | --- |
| 1980-81 | |
| National Freight Corporation (under Section 45 of the Transport Act 1980) | 100,000,000 |
| 1982-83 | |
| British Transport Docks Board (under Section 6(1) of the Transport Act 1981) | 81,293,616 |
| 1984-85 | |
| British Telecom (BT Extinguishment of Loans Order 1982) | 2,789,865,772 |
| 1986-87 | |
| BAA (under section 3 of the Airports Act 1986) | 43,503,340 |

## TRANSPORT

### Rail Electrification (Birmingham)

**Mr. Snape:** To ask the Secretary of State for Transport if he has received a letter dated 16 May from the chairman of the West Midlands passenger transport authority seeking a meeting between him and a delegation of members of the authority to discuss the electrification of the Birmingham cross-city railway line; and if he will meet such a delegation in the near future.

**Mr. Portillo:** I have agreed to meet the chairman of the West Midlands PTE when I have had BR's formal submission on this scheme.

### Pedestrian Safety

**Mr. Sheerman:** To ask the Secretary of State for Transport what is the annual cost of the major research programme designed specifically to help identify further ways of reducing pedestrian casualties to which he refers in his pedestrian safety proposals published in April.

**Mr. Peter Bottomley:** The cost of the research programme referred to in the Department's leaflet on pedestrian safety is roughly £1·6 million in the current year. It is likely to increase next year.

Over 40 per cent. of the current figure is being spent on research aimed primarily at pedestrian safety. The remainder will benefit pedestrians along with other road users.

### Fast Rail Link

**Mr. Dunn:** To ask the Secretary of State for Transport if he will publish in the *Official Report* the terms of reference and time scale to which private interests will need to work in order to bring about the construction of British Rail's proposed fast rail link from the Kent coast to London.

**Mr. Portillo:** These are matters for British Rail to discuss with the private interests concerned.

### Birmingham North Orbital Route

**Mr. Richard Shepherd:** To ask the Secretary of State for Transport if he will list those private companies who have approached his Department in connection with alternative methods of finance for the Birmingham north orbital route; and the date of their first approach.

**Mr. Portillo:** Some approaches have been made but these must remain commercially confidential.

### MV Majestic

**Mr. Foulkes:** To ask the Secretary of State for Transport, pursuant to his answer of 16 June, *Official Report,* column *550,* to the hon. Member for Carrick,

Cumnock and Doon Valley relating to MV Majestic, what futher details he has of the nature of the underwater obstruction referred to.

**Mr. Portillo:** The investigation is continuing. It is known that the nets caught on an obstruction on the sea bottom but the nature of the obstruction has not been determined.

### Road Traffic Law

**Mr. Knox:** To ask the Secretary of State for Transport when he proposes to bring forward legislation to implement his proposals in "The Road User and the Law".

**Mr. Peter Bottomley:** Legislation will be brought forward as soon as parliamentary time is available.

## HOUSE OF COMMONS

### Timetable Motions

**Mr. Richard Shepherd:** To ask the Lord President of the Council if, further to his reply of 16 March, *Official Report,* column *311,* he will list the further occasions on which the Government have introduced the guillotine this Session.

**Mr. Wakeham:** The information requested is as follows:

*Allocation of time order*

| Bill | |
|---|---|
| Self-Governing Schools Etc. (Scotland) | 3 May 1989 |
| Dock Work | 8 May 1989 |

## WALES

### Medical Physicists

**Dr. Kim Howells:** To ask the Secretary of State for Wales what action he intends to take on the problem of medical physicists leaving National Health Service hospitals in south Wales.

**Mr. Peter Walker:** The number of medical physicists —whole-time equivalents—employed by health authorities in Wales over the past four years is given in the table. The management side of the Scientific and Professional Staffs Council is currently investigating the recruitment and retention of scientists, including medical physicists, within the NHS generally.

In Wales, medical physicists have been included in staff groups designated for detailed scrutiny as part of the 1989 manpower resource planning exercise being undertaken by all district health authorities under the auspices of the manpower steering group, established by my Department, with the intention of examining manpower requirements over the next 10 years. Those plans will also examine wastage and recruitment rates for the purpose of identifying potential staffing difficulties and to enable action to be taken at the local or all-Wales level to forestall problems. Work is also in hand by the manpower steering group on a study of medical physics and bio-engineering in the NHS in Wales, which will address the question of staff retention, particularly in the area of equipment management.

| Health Authority | WTE as at 30 September | | | |
|---|---|---|---|---|
| | 1985 | 1986 | 1987 | 1988 |
| Clwyd | 5·0 | 4·0 | 4·0 | 3·0 |
| East Dyfed[1] | — | — | — | — |
| Gwent[1] | — | — | — | — |
| Gwynedd | 2·0 | 2·0 | 4·0 | 3·0 |
| Mid Glamorgan[1] | — | — | — | — |
| Pembs[1] | — | — | — | — |
| Powys[1] | — | — | — | — |
| South Glamorgan | 37·0 | 37·0 | 34·0 | 32·0 |
| West Glamorgan | 11·0 | 10·8 | 12·8 | 15·7 |
| Wales | 55·0 | 53·8 | 54·8 | 53·7 |

[1] Medical physics services for these authorities are provided by the relevant departments in the four authorities which do employ medical physicists.

### Water Shortages

**Mr. Barry Jones:** To ask the Secretary of State for Wales (1) if he will list in the *Official Report* the outstanding capital projects and their estimated cost throughout Wales proposed by the Welsh water authority which plan to alleviate dry weather water shortages; and if he will make a statement;

(2) if he will list in the *Official Report,* for each of the years since 1979 and giving their cost, all those capital projects of the Welsh water authority which have been initiated to guard against water shortages as a consequence of dry weather;

(3) if he will list those areas in Wales where water supply levels give cause for concern; and if he will make a statement;

(4) if he will make a statement concerning water shortages in Wales consequent upon the current heat wave and the Welsh water authority's banning of water hoses and sprinklers in all areas.

**Mr. Peter Walker:** No. This is a matter for the Welsh water authority.

## ENVIRONMENT

### Unleaded Petrol

**Mr. Colvin:** To ask the Secretary of State for the Environment what information he has about the effectiveness of the Government television advertising campaign on unleaded petrol.

**Mrs. Virginia Bottomley:** In a survey conducted during the week commencing 21 April, 60 per cent. of those interviewed, when prompted, were aware of the advertisement. This put it in the top 10 TV advertisements most remembered by the public.

The advertisements ran from 1 to 14 April and were shown on all commercial TV stations in the United Kingdom. It is estimated that 76 per cent. of all adults had the opportunity to see them at least once and 33 per cent. at least four times. On average the target audience of all motorists responsible for purchasing petrol had four opportunities to see the advertisement.

The unleaded petrol share of the market has increased dramatically from 6·4 per cent. in March to 19·3 per cent. in May.

### Teesside UDC (Jobs)

**Mr. Bell:** To ask the Secretary of State for the Environment how many jobs have been created within the Teesside urban development corporation zone since its inception; how many jobs were created as a consequence of the direct intervention of the corporation; and what has been the cost per job.

**Mr. Trippier:** Comprehensive figures on the total number of jobs created within the Teesside development corporation area since its inception are not readily available. The corporation estimates, however, that up to the end of March 1989, 1,459 permanent jobs had been created within the UDA, in projects assisted by the corporation, at a cost per job of £984. The Government also have two task forces and an action team contributing to the regeneration of inner cities on Teesside, and unemployment in the 15 wards within the Teesside DC zone has fallen by over one third in the two years since May 1987.

### All Souls Burial Ground, Halifax

**Mrs. Mahon:** To ask the Secretary of State for the Environment when he intends to reply to queries about the closure of All Souls burial ground raised by the parochial church council of All Souls Living Church council, Haley hill, Halifax, on 3 May 1988, 23 September 1988, 14 March 1989 and 16 May 1989; and why it is still waiting for a reply.

**Mrs. Virginia Bottomley:** The Department replied on 22 June. I very much regret the long delay in replying due to an oversight which has now been rectified.

### Community Charge

**Mr. Terry Davis:** To ask the Secretary of State for the Environment what is the estimated cost of the minority language versions of the community charge leaflet, "The Community Charge (The So-called Poll Tax): How It Will Work For You."

**Mr. Gummer:** Translations in eight languages are being produced, in initial print runs of 10,000 each. The total cost is estimated at £40,000 approximately.

**Mr. John Evans:** To ask the Secretary of State for the Environment if he will make a statement on progress on the implementation of poll tax registration by local authorities, with reference to support facilities provided by his Department.

**Mr. Gummer:** Community charges registration officers (CCROs) have until 1 December 1989 to compile their registers. I believe that most CCROs are making good progress. To assist CCROs and authorities with implementation generally, the Department has issued 18 practice notes, and laid the regulations as soon as was practicable after the enactment of the primary legislation.

**Mr. Blunkett:** To ask the Secretary of State for the Environment (1) whether he intends to issue any further advice to community charge registration officers on the information which can be properly sought through community charge registration forms;

(2) if he intends to issue a leaflet to every household in England and Wales informing potential poll tax payers of their precise rights and duties in completing registration forms;

(3) if he will make a statement on action that should be taken by individuals who are asked by community charge registration officers to answer non-statutory questions on their community charge registration forms;

(4) what steps he is taking to monitor the information being requested by community charge registration officers as a part of the registration process in England and Wales.

**Mr. Gummer** *[holding answer 19 June 1989]:* The Department has given clear and explicit advice to local authorities and community charges registration officers on this matter, and, in conjunction with the local authority associations, issued a model registration form last autumn. It is for registration officers to ensure that their requests for information comply with their statutory powers and the Data Protection Act.

Registration officers may require only such information as is necessary for them to carry out their statutory functions, which are to compile and maintain the register. Advice on the information that needs to be sought from the public in order to compile the register was provided to registration officers in community charge practice note number 3. Advice on the requirements of the Data Protection Act is contained in community charge practice notes numbers 4 and 10 which deal specifically with the data protection aspects of registration, and the need to register as a data user. Practice note number 8 contains the model registration form, and advises registration officers to ensure that any requests for information additional to that needed for registration purposes should be clearly indicated, so that people would know that they did not have to supply it. Practice note number 16, on joint and several liability, specifically points out that joint and several liability is not a registration matter, and advises against including questions on relationships on registration forms.

### Birds

**Mr. Ron Davies:** To ask the Secretary of State for the Environment what representations he has made to his counterpart Ministers in the EEC concerning the shooting and trapping of protected bird species during migration; and if he will seek to persuade them to enforce in full the provisions of the appropriate European legislation.

**Mrs. Virginia Bottomley** *[holding answer 22 June 1987]:* The EC directive 79/409 EEC on the conservation of wild birds requires all member states to protect migratory and other birds. The Government fully support the directive and its enforcement. It is the responsibility of the EC Commission to ensure that adequate measures are taken.

## TRADE AND INDUSTRY

### Barlow Clowes

**Mr. Michael:** To ask the Chancellor of the Duchy of Lancaster what assessment he has made of the effect on recovery by Barlow Clowes investors in the United Kingdom of last Friday's High Court ruling authorising the transfer of funds from the British-based to the Gibraltar-based operation.

**Mr. Maude:** It is too soon to make any such assessment.

**Mr. Michael:** To ask the Chancellor of the Duchy of Lancaster when he expects to be able to provide sufficient information about the Barlow Clowes collapse to make a full statement to the House.

**Mr. Maude:** The Parliamentary Commissioner for Administration is currently considering the role of my Department in this matter. In addition, there are a number of actions before the courts. It is too soon to say when all these matters will be resolved.

**Mr. Michael:** To ask the Chancellor of the Duchy of Lancaster whether there are any outstanding requests from the ombudsman to his Department in connection with the cases currently under investigation by him arising out of the Barlow Clowes collapse.

**Mr. Maude:** My Department is co-operating fully with the Parliamentary Commissioner for Administration and endeavours to respond to all his inquiries as quickly as possible.

# FOREIGN AND COMMONWEALTH AFFAIRS

## Antarctic (Protection)

**Mr. Barry Field:** To ask the Secretary of State for Foreign and Commonwealth Affairs, pursuant to his answer of 14 March, *Official Report,* column *143,* what appraisal he has made of the possible effects on the ecology of the Antarctic as a result of the passage of the Antarctic Minerals Bill.

**Mr. Eggar:** We believe that the Antarctic minerals convention provides protection of the Antarctic environment of a very high order. Its entry into force will protect the Antarctic environment against uncontrolled minerals exploitation. We are proceeding with the Antarctic Minerals Bill to enable the United Kingdom to ratify the Convention.

**Mr. Barry Field:** To ask the Secretary of State for Foreign and Commonwealth Affairs, pursuant to his answer of 14 March, *Official Report,* column *143,* what steps he is taking to negotiate specific treaty obligations to protect the Antarctic in the event of an oil spill or blowout.

**Mr. Eggar:** Control of marine pollution and therefore of oil spills in Antarctica is on the agenda of the XV Antarctic treaty consultative meeting in Paris in October.

There can be no oil exploration in Antarctica, and therefore no blowouts, until the Antarctic minerals convention comes into force and a liability protocol has been negotiated and has itself entered into force. The convention contains strict safeguards for the protection of the Antarctic environment, and requires that no minerals activity can take place until the capacity exists to respond effectively to accidents.

## Cambodia

**Mr. Frank Field:** To ask the Secretary of State for Foreign and Commonwealth Affairs if he will detail the moves, in which the United Kingdom is participating being taken to oppose a return of the Khmer Rouge army in Cambodia.

**Mr. Eggar:** The surest way to prevent the Khmer Rouge returning to power by force is a political settlement under which Cambodians can freely elect a Government of their choice. We are actively involved in international efforts to achieve such a settlement, both multilaterally and in bilateral contacts with those most closely concerned.

## DNA Testing

**Mr. Madden:** To ask the Secretary of State for Foreign and Commonwealth Affairs what are the projected public expenditure savings arising from the introduction of a central DNA testing scheme for those seeking entry clearance to the United Kingdom; and if he will identify the savings to his Department.

**Mr. Eggar:** We need practical experience of the numbers who will be processed under the scheme to judge what, if any, resource savings may be achievable. The scheme will be voluntary and take-up will vary from post to post. The position will be closely monitored.

## Foreign Service Staff (Children's Education)

**Sir Michael McNair-Wilson:** To ask the Secretary of State for Foreign and Commonwealth Affairs (1) how many independent boarding schools are accepted by his Department as suitable to receive grant payment for the education of children employed by the foreign service; how many children are currently in receipt of this financal assistance; how often members of his Department visit the schools to satisfy themselves about the education and the welfare provided for young people; and how often financial assistance has been withdrawn because a school has failed to meet the required criteria,

(2) what criteria are used for judging the quality and academic achievements of independent boarding schools before agreeing to provide finance for members of the foreign service wishing to have their children educated at these schools.

**Mr. Eggar:** As I explained in my written answer of 16 June at column *562,* diplomatic service staff may receive an allowance to send their children to any registered independent boarding school in the United Kingdom, provided it offers the full range of subjects normally offered by a state day school and in a form generally available in the state system. Within that broad range parents accept responsibility for choosing a school whose record of accomplishments appears to suit the requirements and capabilities of their children. All such schools will have been approved by the Department of Education and Science and will be inspected periodically by one of Her Majesty's inspectors. We have neither the expertise nor the resources to duplicate the work of that Department.

Allowances are currently paid in respect of 881 children attending a total of 355 schools. There has never been a case of allowances being withdrawn as a result of a school's performance.

## Entry Clearance

**Mr. Madden:** To ask the Secretary of State for Foreign and Commonwealth Affairs when instructions were sent to the British embassy in Islamabad to issue a visa to Mr. Zahood Ahmed to enter the United Kingdom; when Mr. Ahmed, whose date of birth is 22 July 1967 and whose Home Office reference is A412361, first applied for entry clearance; when Mr. Ahmed's appeal against refusal to grant him a visa was upheld; and if he will make a statement.

**Mr. Eggar** *[pursuant to his reply, 12 June 1989 c. 310]:* In accordance with the recent guidelines on the handling of representations by Members of Parliament in immigration cases, issued to Members on 14 December 1988, I have referred the question to the correspondence unit of migration and visa department of the Foreign and Commonwealth Office. The hon. Member will receive a reply from the unit in due course.

**Mr. Madden:** To ask the Secretary of State for Foreign and Commonwealth Affairs when Mr. Afzal Kahn, whose date of birth is 18 November 1969, and whose reference is IMM 92807, applied for entry clearance to the United Kingdom at Her Majesty's embassy in Islamabad; when his application was refused; and when an explanatory statement setting out the detailed grounds of refusal was despatched to Mr. Khan or his representation.

**Mr. Eggar** *[pursuant to his reply, 12 June 1989, c. 310]:* Mr. Khan applied for an entry clearance at the embassy in Islamabad on 18 November 1987. His application was refused on 25 September 1988 and the embassy received an appeal from him on 10 November 1988. I regret that due to pressure of work at the embassy the explanatory statement has not yet been despatched. It is, however, nearing completion and will be forwarded to the appellate authority very shortly.

## PRIME MINISTER

### European Community

**Mr. Redmond:** To ask the Prime Minister what benefits have been brought to *(a)* Doncaster and *(b)* South Yorkshire from membership of the European Community.

**The Prime Minister:** The European regional development fund has made grants during the last four years of some £53 million to South Yorkshire, of which about £11 million went to Doncaster. Low interest loans worth £750,000 for Doncaster and £13 million for South Yorkshire have been obtained from the European Coal and Steel Community. In the last three years the European social fund made grants of some £1·65 million to Doncaster, within £11·4 million for South Yorkshire as a whole.

### Ivory

**Mr. Ron Davies:** To ask the Prime Minister, pursuant to her answer of 20 June *Official Report,* column *78,* when she returned from Zimbabwe; when the articles were deposited with Her Majesty's Customs and Excise; whether an import licence under CITES was applied for in respect of these items; when she decided that they should be retained by Her Majesty's Customs and Excise; on what date and by what means she informed Her Majesty's Customs and Excise of her decision; if she will describe the three items of silver and ivory jewellery and state a valuation of each item; and whether she took any steps to determine the origin and the legality of the ivory contained in the ivory jewellery.

**The Prime Minister:** I returned from Africa on 2 April 1989. I deposited the articles with Her Majesty's Customs

and Excise as soon as I was informed that the requirements for importation had not been completed. I have nothing further to add to the reply which I gave to the hon. Member on 20 June.

### Israel

**Mr. Marlow:** To ask the Prime Minister whether at her recent meeting with the Israeli Prime Minister she asked him whether he accepted Security Council restriction 242.

**The Prime Minister:** During my talks with Mr. Shamir, I stressed that, to be successful, negotiations on a middle east settlement must be held on the basis of territory for peace as called for in resolution 242. Mr. Shamir has not so far given any commitment on this point.

### Malaysia

**Miss. Lestor:** To ask the Prime Minister who indicated on behalf of Her Majesty's Government that they would consider a request from the Malaysian Government for overseas aid, contained in correspondence concerning the sale of arms to Malaysia that preceded the signing of the memorandum of understanding in 1988; and what period of time elapsed before Her Majesty's Government stated that it would not be acceptable to link aid with the defence sales package.

**The Prime Minister** *[holding answer 22 June 1989]:* The Government made clear to the Malaysian Government on a number of occasions in 1988 that we were most willing to consider Malaysian requests for aid. However, as indicated in the answer given to the hon. Member on 13 June by my hon. Friend the Parliamentary Under-Secretary of State for Defence Procurement, my right hon. Friend the Secretary of State for Defence made it clear in his letter to the Malaysian Finance Minister of 28 June 1988 that the provision of overseas aid as an integral part of a negotiated agreement on the defence package was not possible.

## SOCIAL SECURITY

### AIDS

**Mr. Alfred Morris:** To ask the Secretary of State for Social Security (1) what advice he has received concerning the cost of a recommended diet for people with AIDS or HIV infection; and if he will make a statement;

(2) what is his estimate of the current underprovision of benefit for a person on income support who has been recommended a diet for someone with AIDS or HIV infection who *(a)* does and *(b)* does not qualify for a disability premium;

(3) what is his estimate of the double provision a person on supplementary benefit before April 1988 would have received if he had been awarded the full cost of a recommended diet for someone with AIDS or HIV infection; and if he will make a statement.

**Mr. Scott:** The supplementary benefit scale rates did not include a specific amount for food. It was for individuals to decide how best to spend their money in the light of their own needs and preferences. The same is true of income support. The estimates requested cannot therefore be made.

I am aware that people with AIDS are frequently advised to follow a high protein, high calorie diet. I have been advised that a diet giving 150 per cent. of normal protein and calorie requirements can be devised to meet the needs of individual patients. Such a diet was costed at £14·19 per week (1986 prices) in an article by MacDonald and Forsythe from St. James' university hospital, Leeds, which was published in "Human Nutrition: Applied Nutrition" in 1986.

I am also aware that people with HIV infection, but who are otherwise healthy, are advised to follow a healthy eating plan which is simply a normal balanced diet. Such a diet was costed by Macdonald and Forsythe in their article at £9·46 for a moderately active man.

### State Pensions

**Mr. Marlow:** To ask the Secretary of State for Social Security what is the normal level of state pension available to *(a)* a single male and *(b)* a married couple in each European Community country for those aged 60, 65, 70, 75 and 80 years who have no private resources or pension including social security payments unrelated to living condition, but related to age subsequent to the increases in benefit about to be made available.

**Mr. Lloyd:** I refer my hon. Friend to the Department's publication "Tables of Social Benefit Systems in the European Communities (Position at 1 January 1988)", a copy of which is in the Library. These tables set out the levels of pension in the national currencies together with the sterling equivalent converted according to the OECD's purchasing power parity figures as shown in the introduction to the tables.

### Community Care Grants

**Ms. Harman:** To ask the Secretary of State for Social Security what is the success rate in obtaining community care grants in the offices covering the Peckham constituency for applicants *(a)* assisted and *(b)* not assisted by an advice worker.

**Mr. Peter Lloyd:** I regret that the information requested is not available.

### Social Fund

**Ms. Harman:** To ask the Secretary of State for Social Security why the budget for social fund loans and grants in the offices covering the Peckham constituency was not increased in the current financial year.

**Mr. Peter Lloyd:** A note explaining the basis of allocation of social fund budgets to local offices for 1989-90 is in the Library. The allocation formula was applied in exactly the same way to all local offices.

## HEALTH

### NHS Beds (Occupation)

**Mr. Rowe:** To ask the Secretary of State for Health what proportion of National Health Service beds are occupied by people over 70 years of age.

**Mr. Freeman:** The information available centrally is that in 1987-88, 53 per cent. of NHS beds were occupied by patients aged 65 years and over, and 34 per cent. by patients aged 75 years and over.

### Bristol Channel (Bathing Waters)

**Mr. Speller:** To ask the Secretary of State for Health what information he has received about illness caused to individuals from bathing in coastal waters on either side of the Bristol channel.

**Mr. Freeman:** I am not aware at present of any reports of any adverse effects to health caused by bathing in coastal waters in the Bristol channel.

### Liver and Kidney Transplants

**Mr. Dalyell:** To ask the Secretary of State for Health if he will make a statement on the latest position in relation to the shortage of blood for liver and kidney transplants.

**Mr. Freeman:** There was a temporary shortage of blood following the late May bank holiday. There has now been an excellent response from donors, and national stocks are again sufficient for all operations to go ahead.

### Abortions

**Mr. Amess:** To ask the Secretary of State for Health if he has any plans to instigate any new studies into the nature and incidence of post-abortion syndrome; and if he will make a statement.

**Mr. Freeman:** We await the report of a joint Royal College of General Practitioners/Royal College of Obstetricians and Gynaecologists study "Attitudes to Pregnancy". A large body of data from this United Kingdom study, which was funded by the Department, is currently undergoing careful analysis. I understand that the report should be available later this year.

**Mr. Amess:** To ask the Secretary of State for Health if he will publish in the *Official Report* a table showing the number of non-National Health Service abortions performed in each gestational week according to licensed clinic in 1987 and 1988.

**Mr. Freeman:** The table shows the readily available data. Details relating to numbers performed by individual licensed clinics cannot be released for reasons of confidentiality.

*Number of abortions performed in non-NHS premises by gestation week to usual residents of England and Wales, 1987 and 1988*

| Gestation weeks | 1987 Non-NHS | [1]Of which agency | 1988 Non-NHS | [1]Of which agency |
|---|---|---|---|---|
| Under 9 | 38,879 | 2,283 | 42,387 | 2,709 |
| 9-12 | 35,637 | 4,346 | 42,544 | 5,096 |
| 13-14 | 4,493 | 539 | 4,940 | 597 |
| 15-16 | 2,430 | 258 | 2,795 | 277 |
| 17-18 | 2,659 | 384 | 3,237 | 436 |
| 19-20 | 1,446 | 189 | 1,766 | 196 |
| 21-22 | 779 | 31 | 1,007 | 27 |
| 23-24 | 413 | 9 | 510 | 15 |
| 25+ | 2 | — | — | — |
| Not stated | 11 | 2 | 9 | 4 |
| Total | 86,749 | 8,041 | 99,195 | 9,357 |

[1] These figures represent the operations carried out in the private sector on NHS patients.

**Mr. Amess:** To ask the Secretary of State for Health what advice his Department gives to women about the risks of abortion to their mental and physical health; and if he will make a statement.

**Mr. Freeman:** This is a matter for the clinical judgment of the medical staff involved in the light of all the relevant facts about the woman's condition.

**Mr. Amess:** To ask the Secretary of State for Health what is the latest medical evidence available to him as to the earliest gestation age at which an unborn child may be capable of being born alive; and if he will make a statement.

**Mr. Freeman:** The 22nd gestational week is considered by doctors to be the earliest time that there is the slightest possibility of a foetus being born alive, since before then the lungs are not mature enough to function even if ventilated. Between the 22nd and 24th week of gestation the chance of being born alive and the chance of surviving afterwards increase, but up to 24 weeks both are rare. Whether or not any particular foetus is capable of being born alive must be a matter for the clinical judgment of the doctor concerned in the full knowledge of the circumstances of the particular case.

**Mr. Amess:** To ask the Secretary of State for Health what is the procedure adopted by his Department in checking and approving abortion notification forms.

**Mr. Freeman:** All operating doctors are required to notify the chief medical officer, within seven days, of each abortion they perform. The detailed information in these forms is scrutinised by staff authorised by the chief medical officer to ensure that they do not indicate any contravention of the abortion law.

**Mr. Amess:** To ask the Secretary of State for Health what representations he received in 1987 and 1988, respectively, on *(a)* abortion and *(b)* human embryo experimentation; how many were hostile to each of these practices; and what percentage the latter represents of the former.

**Mr. Freeman:** In 1987 and 1988 we received some 9,000 representations about abortion issues and 500 about human embryo experimentation. Most were from members of the public and the views expressed varied widely. Any analysis on the lines requested would involve disproportionate cost.

### Blood Transfusion Service

**Mr. Spearing:** To ask the Secretary of State for Health if he will make a statement concerning the circumstances in the national blood transfusion service that has caused the recent cancellation of operations and on the action he is now taking to prevent a repetition of such circumstances.

**Mr. Freeman:** The recent shortage of blood which led to the postponement of a small number of operations in some regions arose primarily because blood donors were not coming forward in sufficient numbers to maintain supplies.

The fine weather, bank holidays, and transport strikes contributed to the fall in numbers of donations.

The national directorate of the blood transfusion service will be improving its monitoring of blood stocks and donor attendances so that timely steps can be taken to encourage donors to attend blood donor sessions in the future.

The temporary shortage of blood following the late May bank holiday has now been corrected.

### SERCO/Capita plc

**Mrs. Mahon:** To ask the Secretary of State for Health (1) if he or his Department have had any representations from, or meetings with, SERCO plc; and if he will make a statement;

(2) what recent meetings he or his Department had with Capita plc; and if he will make a statement.

**Mr. Freeman:** The director of NHS procurement, Mr. Tom Critchley, has had two meetings in March and May with the director of Capita Health Care group to discuss the services which that company, in collaboration with SERCO plc, is prepared to offer by way of facilities management or technical and non-clinical support services to the NHS. The meetings were part of a wider series of meetings which Mr. Critchley and officials from the NHS procurement directorate have had with a number of service companies able and ready to bid for NHS site management contracts covering a range of different support services. By way of explanation I refer the hon. Member to paragraph 9.11 of the White Paper "Working for Patients".

### Venereal Disease

**Sir Michael McNair-Wilson:** To ask the Secretary of State for Health if he will give the latest figures for venereal disease as a total and then disease by disease; and if he will give an indication of the trends in this group of diseases.

**Mr. Freeman:** The available information is given in the table. This relates to new cases seen at NHS genito-urinary medicine clinics over the last 10 years. Not all patients seen at clinics have conditions which are sexually transmitted, and some do not require treatment. Some patients have more than one condition, and are counted under each condition found. Discernible trends over the last ten years are:

*(a)* The total number of new cases seen in clinics has been increasing steadily in recent years until 1987, when it fell by over 25,00 compared with 1986. This was the first time since 1962 that the number had declined. The main components of the increase were non-specific genital infection, herpes, wart virus, and candidiosis in women. However, cases of syphilis and gonorrhoea have been declining.

*(b)* Since 1977 the incidence of syphilis has declined by 64 per cent. and gonorrhoea by 57 per cent. Gonorrhoea has been declining more rapidly, particularly among males aged 35 to 44, since about 1982, but there was a very marked fall in both male and female cases between 1986 and 1987. This is probably due to changes in sexual behaviour following the publicity about AIDS.

*(c)* The number of new cases of herpes increased rapidly until 1985, but declined slightly in 1986 and again in 1987.

*(d)* The number of new cases of genital warts has continued to increase at a rapid rate and now accounts for 12 per cent. of all new cases seen.

*New cases seen at NHS genito urinary medicine clinics, England, 1977 to 1987, 1987-88*

| | 1977 | 1978 | 1979 | 1980 | 1981 | 1982 | 1983 | 1984 | 1985 | 1986 | 1987 | 1987-88 |
|---|---|---|---|---|---|---|---|---|---|---|---|---|
| Syphilis | 4,266 | 4,375 | 4,001 | 4,059 | 3,810 | 3,564 | 3,327 | 2,933 | 2,404 | 1,932 | 1,538 | 1,463 |
| Gonorrhoea | 58,734 | 56,673 | 55,062 | 54,433 | 52,200 | 52,156 | 48,393 | 47,662 | 46,314 | 40,705 | 25,265 | 22,884 |
| Chancroid | 43 | 52 | 42 | 54 | 91 | 125 | 80 | 40 | 61 | 47 | 39 | 44 |
| Lymphogranuloma venereum | 34 | 26 | 30 | 28 | 40 | 30 | 36 | 30 | 30 | 42 | 15 | 16 |
| Granuloma inguinale | 17 | 11 | 30 | 20 | 25 | 15 | 21 | 19 | 17 | 20 | 27 | 22 |
| Non specific genital infection | 95,491 | 98,390 | 102,390 | 114,306 | 120,018 | 128,197 | 134,079 | 139,352 | 149,524 | 157,792 | 131,383 | 125,973 |
| Non specific genital infection with arthritis | 496 | 457 | 456 | 544 | 583 | 501 | 462 | 428 | 487 | 504 | 533 | 571 |
| Trichomoniasis | 20,051 | 19,781 | 19,511 | 20,641 | 20,224 | 20,162 | 18,274 | 16,751 | 15,381 | 14,041 | 10,658 | 9,889 |
| Candidiasis | 38,090 | 39,564 | 39,700 | 44,604 | 46,947 | 52,404 | 57,876 | 59,668 | 60,517 | 63,108 | 59,768 | 58,817 |
| Scabies | 2,185 | 2,186 | 2,076 | 2,288 | 2,145 | 2,044 | 2,192 | 2,043 | 2,015 | 1,742 | 1,365 | 1,224 |
| Pubic lice | 6,058 | 6,778 | 7,478 | 7,966 | 8,718 | 9,799 | 9,093 | 10,183 | 9,859 | 9,333 | 6,920 | 6,628 |
| Herpes simplex | 7,722 | 8,406 | 8,854 | 10,043 | 11,147 | 13,653 | 16,534 | 18,301 | 18,935 | 18,800 | 16,699 | 16,510 |
| Warts | 22,766 | 24,136 | 24,490 | 28,176 | 29,704 | 33,343 | 37,899 | 44,050 | 52,177 | 67,068 | 74,542 | 74,655 |
| Molluscum contagiosum | 930 | 964 | 968 | 1,153 | 1,212 | 1,378 | 1,574 | 1,928 | 2,195 | 2,820 | 3,228 | 3,140 |
| Other treponemal diseases | 1,107 | 1,080 | 1,086 | 923 | 878 | 833 | 745 | 658 | 592 | 526 | 532 | 471 |
| Other conditions requiring treatment | 42,437 | 46,431 | 49,555 | 59,963 | 67,842 | 79,019 | 90,817 | 100,213 | 109,318 | 119,460 | 111,667 | 108,172 |
| Other conditions not requiring treatment | 95,537 | 99,268 | 99,813 | 107,123 | 111,407 | 117,127 | 121,900 | 120,951 | 130,162 | 143,092 | 168,556 | 155,527 |
| Other conditions referred elsewhere | 1,749 | 2,133 | 2,242 | 2,655 | 2,933 | 3,318 | 4,135 | 4,718 | 5,318 | 6,327 | 7,531 | 7,719 |
| Grand total, all conditions | 397,713 | 410,711 | 417,784 | 458,979 | 479,924 | 517,668 | 547,437 | 569,928 | 605,306 | 647,359 | 620,266 | 593,725 |

## EMPLOYMENT

### Social Measures (EC)

**Mr. Teddy Taylor:** To ask the Secretary of State for Employment, pursuant to the reply to the hon. Member for Southend, East on 14 June, *Official Report,* column *909,* if he will list the issues which the Commission proposes to deal with in social measures related to the European Economics Community and the draft directives issued to date; and if he will seek the guidance of the Commission on what social issues it will be presenting directives on the basis of majority voting.

**Mr. Cope** *[holding answer 21 June 1989]:* The European Commission has put forward a preliminary draft proposal for a "Community charter of fundamental social rights", which it proposes should be adopted as a solemn declaration of the 12 heads of state and Government. The preliminary draft proposal invites the Commission to draw up a programme of work by June 1990. A copy of the preliminary draft has been deposited in the Library, and an explanatory memorandum has been provided to the Select Committee on European Legislation. The preliminary draft is not based on any article of the treaty and is proposed as a political statement.

The following draft legislation proposals, which have not yet been agreed, have been issued to date:
    draft directive on procedures for informing and consulting employees in complex undertakings;
    draft directive concerning temporary work;
    draft directive on voluntary part-time work;
    draft recommendation on the reduction and reorganisation of working time;
    draft directive on parental leave and leave for family reasons;
    draft directive on the burden of proof in the area of equal pay and equal treatment for men and women;
    draft directive amending directive 68/360/EEC on the abolition of restrictions on movement and residence within the Community for workers of member states and their families.
    draft directive concerning the minimum health and safety requirements for work with visual display units.
Whether the voting arrangements for specific proposals are based on simple majority, qualified majority or unanimity depends on the subject matter and the article(s) of the treaty of Rome on which they are based. The proposed treaty base is indicated on draft legislation.

In addition, in the area of health and safety at work, there are:
    draft directive concerning the minimum health and safety requirements for the workplace;
    draft directive on the approximation of the laws of the member states relating to machinery;
    draft directive on the approximation of the laws of the member states relating to personal protective equipment;
    draft directive on the minimum health and safety requirements for handling heavy loads when there is a risk of back injury for workers.

## DEFENCE

### Type 23 Frigate

**Mr. Duffy:** To ask the Secretary of State for Defence if he will make a statement on progress on the new command system for the type 23 frigate programme.

**Mr. Sainsbury:** I refer the hon. Member to the answer I gave to the hon. and learned Member for Fife, North-East (Mr. Campbell) on 6 June at column *124.*

# Written Answers to Questions

*Monday 26 June 1989*

## SCOTLAND

### East Kilbride (Transport)

**Mr. Cartwright:** To ask the Secretary of State for Scotland how many homes would have to be demolished to make way for British Rail's proposed extension to East Kilbride town centre.

**Lord James Douglas-Hamilton:** Until detailed studies have been commissioned it is impossible to say how many homes would have to be demolished, but it is established public policy to keep such numbers to an absolute minimum, consistent with the technical requirements of any development proposal.

**Mr. Cartwright:** To ask the Secretary of State for Scotland if he intends to hold an inquiry into British Rail's proposal to build a rail extension into East Kilbride town centre.

**Lord James Douglas-Hamilton:** If British Rail is unable to satisfy the petitioner against the relevant provisional order deposited under the Private Legislation Procedure (Scotland) Act 1936, the provisions of the Act require that the Secretary of State shall direct an inquiry by commissioners.

**Mr. Cartwright:** To ask the Secretary of State for Scotland what consideration has been given to improving the existing 'park and ride' facilities serving East Kilbride town centre.

**Lord James Douglas-Hamilton:** This is a matter for Strathclyde passenger transport executive to consider in consultation with East Kilbride development corporation and ScotRail. I understand that the existing park and ride facilities are to be retained.

**Mr. Cartwright:** To ask the Secretary of State for Scotland what is the estimated cost of the proposed British Rail proposed extension to East Kilbride town centre.

**Lord James Douglas-Hamilton:** A preliminary estimate published with the provisional order gave a total cost of £8·295 million. However East Kilbride development corporation stresses that any such estimates are somewhat speculative until detailed design studies have been concluded particularly in this case as some tunnelling would be necessary and in the absence of detailed knowledge of local geological conditions.

### Forestry

**Mr. Lord:** To ask the Secretary of State for Scotland what effect changes in taxation relating to the forestry industry made in the 1988 budget have had on that industry; and if he will make a statement.

**Lord James Douglas-Hamilton:** It is too early to say precisely what effect the 1988 Budget changes will have on the forestry industry. We do, however, expect that there will be some temporary reduction in the amount of new planting as the industry adjusts to the new arrangements.

### Glasgow School of Art

**Mr. Wray:** To ask the Secretary of State for Scotland what are the total grants given to the Glasgow school of art by his Department for each year since 1981 in 1989 money; and what is the planned grant for 1990-91.

**Mr. Michael Forsyth:** The information is set out in the table.

*Glasgow school of art recurrent and non-recurrent grants (£ million financial year)*

| Financial year | Recurrent | Non-recurrent | Total grants |
| --- | --- | --- | --- |
| 1981-82 | 3·376 | 0·306 | 3·682 |
| 1982-83 | 3·767 | 0·420 | 4·187 |
| 1983-84 | 3·823 | 0·128 | 3·951 |
| 1984-85 | 3·867 | 0·391 | 4·258 |
| 1985-86 | 3·832 | 0·249 | 4·081 |
| 1986-87 | 3·957 | 0·034 | 3·991 |
| 1987-88 | 4·059 | 0·493 | 4·552 |
| 1988-89 | 3·889 | 0·761 | 4·650 |

*Note:* The figures have been expressed at 1989-90 prices, using the latest GDP deflator.

For 1989-90, an offer of £3·795 million grant-in-aid for recurrent expenditure has been made, subject to parliamentary approval; the value of non-recurrent grant (for capital items) has not yet been determined. Firm plans have not yet been made for 1990-91; decisions will be made towards the end of this year in the light of the school's institutional plans, resources available for the grant-aided college sector as a whole, and the Government's proposals to shift the balance of funding for universities and colleges such as Glasgow school of art from grant-in-aid towards students' tuition fees with effect from the academic year 1990-91.

**Mr. Wray:** To ask the Secretary of State for Scotland what steps he is taking to ensure that the Glasgow school of art remains open.

**Mr. Michael Forsyth:** I have every confidence that the school will continue. My recent decision to abolish quotas on student intakes will encourage the school to increase student numbers and generate more income.

Departmental officials are in close touch with the school about the preparation of its institutional plan for 1990-91 and beyond, and decisions on the allocation of grant-in-aid for 1990-91 will be taken later this year in the light of that. I am also considering proposals for major capital expenditure to improve physical facilities at the school.

### Epilepsy Centre

**Mrs. Ray Michie:** To ask the Secretary of State for Scotland (1) if he will list the reasons why the support rate for epilepsy centre clients in Strathclyde increased at a lower rate than actual running costs in the period between 1 April 1987 and 1 April 1989;

(2) what is his Department's policy towards the provision of support rate for epilepsy centre clients; and if he will make a statement.

**Mr. Michael Forsyth:** The level of financial support for day care and residential centres provided by voluntary bodies or for those attending them is at the discretion of the regional council. My right hon. and learned Friend has no power to intervene in their decisions.

## Common Services Agency

**Mr. Wray:** To ask the Secretary of State for Scotland (1) if doctors will continue to have the same choice when they purchase orthopaedic appliances following the Common Services Agency's takeover of the allocation of contracts from health boards;

(2) what advice was taken from doctors regarding the decision to transfer the purchasing of orthopaedic apliances from the health boards to the Common Services Agency;

(3) what savings he expects will be made following the Common Services Agency's takeover of the allocation of contracts for the purchase of orthopaedic appliances.

**Mr. Michael Forsyth:** The purchasing of orthopaedic appliances continues to be the responsibility of the relevant health boards. The supplies division of the Common Services Agency acts on their behalf in the arrangement of contracts for the supply of orthopaedic appliances, as for many other commodities bought by the Health Service. The new contracts arranged by the Common Services Agency, which come into effect on 1 July, were entered into on the advice of a panel of health board experts including a consultant orthopaedic surgeon from Greater Glasgow health board. The contracts give doctors access to the same range of items as at present and each health board has a choice of suppliers for most items.

The contracts include special clauses designed to ensure that the appliances are of good quality and it is expected that patient satisfaction will be improved as a result. The main purpose of the new contracts is to improve quality, but they will also make significant savings compared with current costs. The precise amount will depend on the number of appliances of various types which are bought under the new contracts but is provisionally estimated at approximately £1 million.

## ATTORNEY-GENERAL

### Immigration Appeals (Scotland)

**Mr. Wray:** To ask the Attorney-General what is the number of immigration appeals heard in Scotland for each year since 1976.

**The Attorney-General:** The number of appeals heard by immigration adjudicators in each year since 1976 is as follows:

|      | *Number* |
|------|--------|
| 1976 | 96 |
| 1977 | 86 |
| 1978 | 97 |
| 1979 | 129 |
| 1980 | 119 |
| 1981 | 92 |
| 1982 | 116 |
| 1983 | 163 |
| 1984 | 148 |
| 1985 | 164 |
| 1986 | 149 |
| 1987 | 116 |
| 1988 | 160 |

## Legal Aid

**Mr. Hardy:** To ask the Attorney-General what is the average payment received by solicitors and by barristers acting for the defence in legal aid cases considered by the Crown court and in which the standard fee applies.

**The Attorney-General:** The average standard fee received by solicitors for preparation of the brief for counsel and other matters including attendance at court in legal aid cases in the Crown court was £258·67 in the financial year 1988-89. In the same year the average standard fee received by barristers for preparing for trial and providing representation in the Crown court in legal aid cases was £209·10.

### Killan Fach Farm, Swansea

**Mr. Alan Williams:** To ask the Attorney-General if he will outline the action he has taken, and the reasons for that response, on the application to him from the City of Swansea Council to authorise a prosecution under the Agricultural Land (Removal of Soil) Act 1953 against the owner of Killan Fach Farm, Swansea.

**The Solicitor-General:** I refused my consent to a prosecution since the time limit for commencing proceedings expired before the council presented me with any information to enable me properly to consider the case.

## FOREIGN AND COMMONWEALTH AFFAIRS

### Cambodia

**Mr. Frank Field:** To ask the Secretary of State for Foreign and Commonwealth Affairs if the Government will be attending the Paris peace conference on Cambodia in July.

**Mr. Eggar:** The French Government plan to host an international conference on Cambodia in August. In principle, we expect to attend.

### Ivory

**Mr. Steel:** To ask the Secretary of State for Foreign and Commonwealth Affairs, pursuant to his reply to the hon. Member for Bosworth (Mr. Tredinnick), *Official Report*, 7 June, column *138*, what information he has on the Hong Kong Government's urgent review of its position on trading in ivory; and if he will make a statement.

**Mr. Eggar:** The Hong Kong Government announced on 9 June their support for a ban on trade in new ivory. Pending the outcome of the meeting of the convention on international trade in endangered species in October 1989, they have suspended the issue of licences for imports of raw ivory from all sources.

### Human Rights

**Mr. Spearing:** To ask the Secretary of State for Foreign and Commonwealth Affairs if he will list those members of the European Economic Community who have acceded to the United Nations and Council of Europe conventions on human rights, respectively; and what is the policy of Her Majesty's Government concerning any similar declarations by the European Community.

**Mr. Eggar:** All members of the European Community except Ireland and Greece have ratified the international covenant on civil and political rights; all but Ireland have ratified the international covenant on economic, social and cultural rights. These are the two major United Nations human rights instruments. The position on other United Nations conventions varies. All EC members have ratified the European convention on human rights.

The United Kingdom is signatory to the 1977 joint declaration, by the European Parliament, the Council and the Commission, of fundamental rights. Protection of human rights forms an important part of EC law.

**Ms. Abbott:** To ask the Secretary of State for Foreign and Commonwealth Affairs whether he will ensure that the United Kingdom delegate to the 41st session of the United Nations human rights sub-commission due to sit in Geneva this summer makes a definitive and strong statement about gross violations of human rights in Ethiopia, and a demand for a direct response.

**Mrs. Chalker:** The British member of the United Nations human rights sub-commission is an independent expert and does not take instructions from Her Majesty's Government.

### Rain Forest

**Dr. David Clark:** To ask the Secretary of State for Foreign and Commonwealth Affairs (1) if he will make a statement on the environmental damage caused by British companies to the Amazon rain forest;

(2) whether he will have discussions with the chairman of *(a)* British Petroleum, *(b)* Barclays, *(c)* Shell and *(d)* British American Tobacco about reducing the environmental damage caused by them to the Amazon rain forest; and if he will make a statement;

(3) whether he will sek a meeting with representatives of the Brazilian Government to discuss ways of regulating the activities of foreign companies to prevent the destruction of the Amazon rain forest; and if he will make a statement;

(4) whether he will have discussions with British Petroleum about reducing the environmental damage caused to the Amazon rain forest by that company; and if he will make a statement.

**Mr. Eggar:** My right hon. Friend the Minister for Overseas Development will be visiting Brazil, including the Amazon region, from 4 to 9 July. During his visit, he will be discussing with Brazilian Ministers and officials our efforts to identify effective ways of helping them with a wide range of environmental problems, including rain forest conservation. He will also be meeting representatives of British companies operating in Brazil with whom he hopes to discuss their role in environmental protection.

The hon. Member will be aware of recent media reports alleging involvement by United Kingdom companies in rain forest destruction. We are studying these, but I understand that the companies claim that these press reports contain important errors of fact, and that they themselves operate significant environmental protection programmes in their projects in Brazil.

### Human Rights (Australia)

**Mr. Vaz:** To ask the Secretary of State for Foreign and Commonwealth Affairs how many representations he has made complaining about the denial of human rights in the last five years in Australia.

**Mr. Eggar:** None.

### Human Rights (Kenya)

**Mr. Vaz:** To ask the Secretary of State for Foreign and Commonwealth Affairs how many representations he has made complaining about the denial of human rights and the use of torture in the last five years in Kenya.

**Mrs. Chalker:** We have made a number of representations about human rights to the Kenyan authorities over the last five years, but the precise information requested is not readily available and could only be provided at disproportionate cost. We welcome the recent release of all political detainees.

### Executions (China)

**Mr. Foulkes:** To ask the Secretary of State for Foreign and Commonwealth Affairs what representations he has made in connection with the continuing executions of protestors in China: and if he will make a statement.

**Mr. Eggar:** Representations have been made in Peking to the Chinese authorities on behalf of all 12 EC members appealing for clemency. We have made it clear that we deeply deplore the recent executions and have renewed our appeal to the Chinese authorities not to persecute those campaigning for their democratic rights.

### Deportations (Iraq)

**Mrs. Clwyd:** To ask the Secretary of State for Foreign and Commonwealth Affairs if he will make representations to the Government of Iraq about the forced deportation of 100,000 people from the town of Qaladiza which began on Monday 12 June; and if he will make a statement.

**Mr. Waldegrave:** I summoned the Iraqi ambassador on 14 June and repeated our concern about renewed reports of mass resettlement of Kurdish people within northern Iraq. We view these stories with considerable concern. We shall continue to press the Iraqis to allow foreign diplomats and journalists access to the areas in question to see for themselves.

**Mrs. Clwyd:** To ask the Secretary of State for Foreign and Commonwealth Affairs if he will raise the matter of the Iraqi programme of forced deportations of its Kurdish minority in the context of European Economic Community political co-operation, as well as in other appropriate international meetings.

**Mr. Waldegrave:** We discuss this issue regularly with our partners in the Twelve, as well as in other international meetings, and shall continue to do so.

**Mrs. Clwyd:** To ask the Secretary of State for Foreign and Commonwealth Affairs what representations he has made to the Government of Iraq about its campaign of forced deportation of its Kurdish citizens; if he will protest strongly against this breach of Iraq's obligations under the international human rights conventions; and if he will make a statement.

**Mr. Waldegrave:** I summoned the Iraqi ambassador on 14 June to repeat our concern at renewed reports of the mass resettlement of Kurds from northern Iraq. The Iraqi authorities are under no illusion that we expect them to fulfil their obligations under the human rights conventions to which they are a signatory.

## Immigration

**Mr. Flynn:** To ask the Secretary of State for Foreign and Commonwealth Affairs how many applications for residency in the United Kingdom from all people in *(a)* Hong Kong, *(b)* Pakistan, *(c)* India and *(d)* Soviet Union have been (i) accepted and (ii) rejected in each year since 1979 for each respective country.

**Mr. Renton:** I have been asked to reply.

I would refer the hon. Member to the reply given to him on 8 May columns *286-88,* which gave the information available for the numbers granted settlement in the United Kingdom, and for the numbers of applications received, granted and initially refused for entry clearance for settlement and for a certificate of entitlement to the right of abode in the United Kingdom. The available information on refusals of applications for settlement made on arrival in the United Kingdom and after admission for a limited period are given in the following tables:

*Table 1*

*Persons[1] seeking settlement in the United Kingdom on arrival who were refused leave to enter and removed from the United Kingdom, by certain nationalities*

| 1979-88 | | | | Number of persons |
|---|---|---|---|---|
| | [2] Hong Kong | Pakistan | India | Soviet Union |
| 1979 | 3 | 45 | 42 | — |
| 1980 | 4 | 35 | 22 | — |
| 1981 | 1 | 25 | 32 | 1 |
| 1982 | 1 | 41 | 30 | — |
| 1983 | 3 | 47 | 51 | — |
| 1984 | 1 | 34 | 30 | — |
| 1985 | 1 | 26 | 17 | — |
| 1986 | 2 | 63 | 50 | — |
| 1987 | 6 | 54 | 22 | — |
| 1988 | 5 | 31 | 31 | — |

[1] Includes those seeking settlement on grounds of marriage.
[2] British Dependent Territory citizens.

*Table 2*

*Refusals[1] of applications for settlement made in the United Kingdom following initial admission for a limited period, by certain nationalities.*

| 1986-88 | | | | Number of persons |
|---|---|---|---|---|
| | [2] Hong Kong | Pakistan | India | Soviet Union |
| 1986 | 20 | 140 | 210 | — |
| 1987 | 30 | 150 | 210 | — |
| 1988 | 20 | 100 | 150 | — |

[1] Includes refusals of applications for settlement on grounds of marriage.
[2] British Dependent Territory citizens.

## Political Asylum

**Mr. Foulkes:** To ask the Secretary of State for Foreign and Commonwealth Affairs what arrangements his Department is making to deal with requests for political asylum from people in China who fear persecution.

**Mr. Renton:** I have been asked to reply.

In accordance with our normal practice, we will look carefully at any entry clearance application made in China from a Chinese national claiming to be in immediate danger who has links with the United Kingdom.

## EDUCATION AND SCIENCE

### Research Biologists

**Mr. Cousins:** To ask the Secretary of State for Education and Science if he will set up an inquiry into the future supply of research biologists.

**Mr. Jackson:** No.

### Student Loans

**Mr. Spearing:** To ask the Secretary of State for Education and Science what further information he has received or new decisions he has made since 19 June in respect of his scheme for students' loans.

**Mr. Jackson:** Following my right hon. Friend's statement on 19 June at columns 21-22, we have set in hand continued discussions with the financial institutions on the arrangements for the top-up loans scheme. We shall announce further details of those arrangements in due course.

### Public Relations

**Mr. Blair:** To ask the Secretary of State for Education and Science which public relations firms his Department has employed and at what cost, for each year since 1979.

**Mrs. Rumbold:** The consistent practice of successive Governments has been to avoid the use of public relations firms or other firms outside government for public relations work, apart from their use by some Departments in the special circumstances of privatisation work.

### University Teachers (Outside Earnings)

**Mr. Dalyell:** To ask the Secretary of State for Education and Science if he will make a statement on his latest discussions with the university authorities about the optimum level of outside earnings of university teachers.

**Mr. Jackson:** I have not had any formal meeting with the university authorities on this topic but I have discussed it, like many others, in my frequent contacts with the academic world.

### Student Loans

**Mr. Andrew Smith:** To ask the Secretary of State for Education and Science, further to his reply of 19 June, *Official Report,* column 33, if he will publish a revised version of annex E to the White Paper on student loans to include estimates of administrative costs, interest subsidy, default and write off costs, on the assumption of *(a)* 80 per cent. take-up, *(b)* 90 per cent. take-up and *(c)* 100 per cent. take-up.

**Mr. Jackson:** I refer the hon. Member to my previous answer of 21 March at columns *497-99,* which showed the effect of various take-up assumptions on the estimates in annex E of Cm. 520. Those estimates made allowance for the cost of an illustrative 10 per cent. default rate, and of writing off debts in cases of death or of deferment beyond the age of 50. Those estimates also allowed for the cost of the zero real interest rate, which has the effect, as compared with a higher interest rate, of reducing the size of repayments. The administrative costs mentioned in my right hon. Friend's statement on 19 June at columns 21-22 were based on there being 1·15 million accounts in 1995. It is estimated that the scheme will grow eventually to some 2·5 million accounts in the second decade of the next century, but it is not expected that administrative costs will increase in proportion.

### Chinese Students

**Mr. Foulkes:** To ask the Secretary of State for Education and Science if he will list the number of Chinese students presently enrolled in each educational institution in the United Kingdom.

**Mr. Jackson:** Details for individual institutions are confidential. In 1987-88, there were 1,200 full-time and part-time students in further and higher education in the United Kingdom from the People's Republic of China.

### Educational Institutions (China)

**Mr. Foulkes:** To ask the Secretary of State for Education and Science what information he has about current cultural and educational links between educational institutions in the United Kingdom and China.

**Mr. Jackson:** This Department keeps no record of links between educational institutions in this country and China. The British Council, with funds from the Foreign and Commonwealth Office and the Overseas Development Administration, administers a variety of cultural and educational programmes. A list of current activity under the academic links with china scheme (ALCS) is as follows:

*Main links and projects supported under academic links with China scheme (ALCS)—April 1989*

| Year ALCS support ends | Chinese Institution | United Kingdom Institution | Subject | Main contact |
| --- | --- | --- | --- | --- |
| 1990-91 | China National Research Centre for Science and Technology for Development (CNRCSTD) CHI/992/14 | Science Policy Research Unit (SPRU) Sussex University | Science Policy Research | Professor C. H. G. Oldham |
| 1990-91 | Shanghai Medical University CHI/992/24 | Middlesex Hospital Medical School | Medical Biochemistry | Professor P. N. Campbell |
| 1990-91 | Nanjing Agricultural College CHI/992/32 | Rothamsted Experimental Station | Plant Virus Research | Dr. A. J. Cockbain |
| 1990-91 | Foreign Affairs College Beijing CHI/992/38 | Queen Elizabeth House Oxford | International Relations | Mr. N. Maxwell |
| 1990-91 | Nanjing College of Pharmacy CHI/992/39 | Strathclyde University | Pharmaceutics | Professor J. Midgley |
| 1990-91 | Dalian Institute of Technology CHI/992/44 | University of Liverpool | Engineering Optimization | Dr. A. B. Templeman |
| 1989-90 | People's University of China, Beijing CHI/992/56 | University of Sussex | Economics and Comparative/ International Politics | Dr. R. Benewick and Dr. R. White |
| 1990-91 | Institute of Soviet and East European Studies/Institute of Contemporary International Relations CHI/992/60 | Glasgow University | Soviet and East European Studies | Professor W. V. Wallace |
| 1990-91 | Tongji University, Shanghai CHI/992/61 | Sheffield University | Petroleum Geology | Professor C. D. Curtis |
| 1988-89 | Nanjing University CHI/992/66 | Leeds University | Quantitative Economics Management of Enterprise | Dr. A. D. Pearman |
| 1990-91 | University of Science and Technology of China (USTC) CHI/992/74 | Imperial College/UMIST | Computational Combustion | Professor D. B. Spalding Professor B. E. Launder |
| 1989-90 | University of Beijing/National Cancer Hospital, Beijing CHI/992/79 | Glasgow University | Oral and Maxillo-facial Surgery | Mr. K. Moos |
| 1989-90 | Institute of Mechanics, Beijing CHI/992/80 | Oxford University | Engineering Science | Dr. C. Ruiz |
| 1988-89 | Nanjing Institute of Posts and Telecommunications CHI/992/81 | Chelmsford College of Higher Education | Telecommunications | Dr. J. P. Sumner |
| 1989-90 | Gansu University of Technology CHI/992/83 | Strathclyde University | Electrical Engineering | Dr. K. Lo |
| 1990-91 | Institute of High Energy Physics CHI/992/89 | Southampton University | Hard X-Ray Astronomy | Dr. D. Ramsden |
| 1990-91 | Beijing Agricultural Engineering University CHI/992/90 | Silsoe (Agricultural) College (part of Cranfield Institute of Technology) | Agriculture | Professor B. May |

| Year ALCS support ends | Chinese Institution | United Kingdom Institution | Subject | Main contact |
|---|---|---|---|---|
| 1990-91 | Institute of Economic Research Beijing University CHI/992/96 | University of Cambridge Faculty, Board of Economics and Politics | Development Economics | Dr. A. Hughes |
| 1990-91 | Beijing College of Commerce CHI/992/97 | Lancashire Polytechnic | Business and Management Education | Mr. N. Maynard |
| 1990-91 | Xiamen University CHI/992/90 | City University | Electrochemistry | Professor A. C. Tseung |
| 1989-90 | Shanghai Fisheries College CHI/992/101 | Humberside College of Education | Fisheries Education and Research | Mr. R. Blair |
| 1989-90 | Ministry of Urban and Rural Construction and Environmental Protection (MURCEP) CHI/992/102 | Strathclyde University (ABACUS) | Building Design | Professor T. Maver |
| 1988-89 | University of International Business and Economics (UIBE), Beijing CHI/992/106 | Lancaster University | Management Education Methods | Mrs. M. E. McClintock |
| 1989-90 | Chinese Commission for Integrated Survey of Natural Resources CHI/992/107 | Institute of Terrestrial Ecology | Natural Resources | Mr. J. N. R. Jeffers |
| 1989-90 | Central South Institute of Technology, Changsha CHI/992/110 | UMIST | Metallurgy and Materials | Professor E. Smith and Dr. R. Taylor |
| 1989-90 | Beijing Institute of Labour Protection | Queen Mary College | Coal Combustion and Power Plant Design | Dr. J. Sharpe |
| 1989-90 | Institute of History, Chinese Academy of Social Sciences (CASS) CHI/992/112 | School of Oriental and African Studies | Chinese History | Dr. D. Pollard |
| 1988-89 | Chengdu University of Science and Technology CHI/992/114 | Dundee University | Civil Engineering | Professor A. Vardy |
| 1989-90 | Beijing Academy of Agricultural and Crop Protection and Plant Biotechnology CHI/992/115 | Rothamsted Experimental Station | Forestry Sciences | Dr. T. Lewis |
| 1989-90 | Shanghai Jiaotong University CHI/992/116 | Birmingham University | English Language Teaching | Professor J. Sinclair |
| 1990-91 | Xian University CHI/992/119 | St. Mary's Hospital Medical School, London and Trinity College, London | Medical Science and Clinical Medicine | Professor P. Richards and Dr. C. Seymour |
| 1989-90 | Zheijiang Agricultural University CHI/992/121 | University of Newcastle upon Tyne | Soil Science Studies | Professor K. Syers |
| 1989-90 | Institute of West Asian and African Studies, CASS CHI/992/122 | Exeter University | Middle Eastern Studies | Dr. T. C. Niblock |
| 1990-91 | Institute of Philosophy, Beijing CHI/992/124 | Royal Institute of Philosophy | Philosophy | Dr. M. Tiles |
| 1989-90 | Beijing Normal University and Hangzou CHI/992/125 | University of Sussex | Education | Dr. K. Lewin |
| 1990-91 | Tianjin University of Science and Technology CHI/992/126 | Manchester University | Internal Combustion Engine | Professor D. E. Winterbone |
| 1989-90 | Shenzhen and Chongsha University CHI/992/127 | Manchester University | Polymer Chemistry | Dr. C. Booth |
| 1990-91 | Tongji University CHI/992/128 | Bradford University | Mathematics Modelling (of Flow and Pollution Transport) | Professor R. A. Falconer |
| 1990-91 | Xian Jiaotong University CHI/992/130 | Strathclyde University | Institutional Link (Business Studies) | Mr. R. L. Crawford |
| 1990-91 | Northern Jiaoton University CHI/992/131 | Oxford Polytechnic | Town Planning | Mr. T. E. Mervyn-Jones |
| 1990-91 | East China Petroleum Institute CHI/992/132 | Herriot-Watt University | Petroleum Engineering | Professor Stuart |
| 1990-91 | Shanghai University of Technology CHI/992/133 | Manchester University | Fluid Mechanics | Dr. J. Turner |

| Year ALCS support ends | Chinese Institution | United Kingdom Institution | Subject | Main contact |
|---|---|---|---|---|
| 1990-91 | Shanxi Agricultural University CHI/992/134 | UCw Aberystwyth | Agricultural Sciences | Mr. G. Brown |
| 1990-91 | Institute of Quantitative Economics, CASS, Beijing CHI/992/135 | Herriot-Watt University | Economics | Professor Hare |
| 1990-91 | Nanjing Institute of Meteorology CHI/992/136 | Edinburgh University | Meteorology | Dr. Weston |
| 1990-91 | Lanzhao and Xinjiang University CHI/992/137 | Liverpool, Institute of Tropical Medicine | Tropical Medicine | Dr. New |
| 1990-91 | Zhejiang Academy of Fine Arts CHI/992/138 | Slade School of Fine Art | Fine Arts | Professor George Cohen |
| 1990-91 | People's University, Beijing CHI/992/139 | Aston University | Management Education | Professor J. Child |
| 1990-91 | State Science and Technology Commission, Beijing CHI/992/140 | Aston University | Science Policy | Dr. F. Steward |
| 1990-91 | Tianjin College of Finance and Economics CHI/992/141 | North East London Polytechnic | Management Economics | Mr. G. Minshaw |
| 1990-91 | China Research Academy for Environmental Sciences, Beijing CHI/992/142 | Liverpool University | Environmental Sciences | Professor Dix |
| 1991-92 | Beijing University of Iron and Steel Technology CHI/992/143 | Lancaster University | Higher Education Administration | Dr. P. Summerfield |
| 1991-92 | Hauzhong Normal University CHI/992/145 | South Bank Polytechnic | Information and Technology | Dr. J. G. Taylor |
| 1991-92 | East China Normal University CHI/992/146 | University of London Institute of Education | Education | Professor A. Taylor |
| 1991-92 | Shanghai Jiatong University CHI/992/147 | Queen Mary College | Mechanical Engineering | Professor W. A. Woods |
| 1991-92 | Institute of Scientific and Technical Information CHI/992/148 | Ealing College of Higher Education | Information Science | Mr. James Shearer |
| 1991-92 | Nanjing University CHI/992/149 | Edinburgh University | History | Professor Dickinson |
| 1991-92 | Chongqing University CHI/992/150 | Leicester University | Space Physics | Dr. J. Beynon |
| 1991-92 | Dalian University of Technology CHI/992/152 | Hydraulics Research Ltd. | Hydraulics Research | Dr. E. P. Hart |
| 1991-92 | Beijing University Applied Mathematical Studies CHI/992/153 | Leeds University | — | Professor D. B. Inghare |
| 1991-92 | Fudan University CHI/992/154 | University of Essex | International Politics | Professor A. King |
| 1991-92 | North China Institute of Electrical Power CHI/992/155 | Queens University, Belfast | Electrical Engineering | Mr. B. W. Hogg |

In addition, it is estimated that there are currently about 3,000 Chinese students in this country, under a variety of award schemes. The British Government provide approximately 1,000 of these awards.

There is also a small programme involving Chinese teachers who come to the United Kingdom to work with local education authorities for up to one academic year. In the current year, 10 Chinese teachers are attached to LEAs. Four United Kingdom teachers have visited China under this programme this year. Some administrative support for this programme is provided by the central bureau, a body grant-aided by this Department.

## Teachers (Salaries)

**Mr. Evennett:** To ask the Secretary of State for Education and Science, pursuant to the reply to the hon. Member for Erith and Crayford of 8 May, *Official Report*, column *299*, if he will now publish a table based on the 1987 database of teacher records data showing the distribution of teachers across the salary scales at March 1987, distinguishing between primary and secondary sectors; whether the numbers of teachers in each sector on scale 3, scale 4 or senior teacher scales agrees with the projections made by his Department based on the March

1985 database of teacher records data for the purposes of salary assimilation in September 1987; and if he will make a statement.

**Mrs. Rumbold** *[holding answer 14 June 1989]:* The information is as follows:

*Distribution of teachers by salary scale: March 1987*

| | Nursery and primary schools[1] | | Secondary schools[1] | |
|---|---|---|---|---|
| Scale 1 | 55,920 | — | 59,120 | — |
| Scale 2 | 63,240 | — | 59,470 | — |
| Scale 3 | 14,360 | (16,000) | 56,490 | (53,000 |
| Scale 4 | 300 | (0) | 29,950 | (28,500) |
| Senior teacher | 50 | (0) | 7,280 | (6,500) |
| Deputy head | 18,680 | — | 10,310 | — |
| Head | 21,740 | — | 4,990 | — |
| TOTAL | 174,280 | — | 227,610 | — |

[1] The figures in brackets are the numbers forecast in 1987 on the basis of the 1985 database of teacher records.

# NATIONAL FINANCE

## Entertainers and Sportsmen

**Mr. Nicholas Baker:** To ask the Chancellor of the Exchequer how much revenue has been earned by Her Majesty's Inland Revenue under the entertainers and sportsmen's rules introduced by the Finance Act 1986 and now contained in chapter III of part XIII of the Income and Corporation Taxes Act 1988.

**Mr. Norman Lamont:** The special scheme for deducting tax at source from payment to non-resident entertainers and sportsmen yielded £6·9 million net (after repayments) in the period 1 May 1987 (when it took effect) to 31 March 1988 and £12·4 million net in 1988-89.

## Housing Costs

**Mr. Chris Smith:** To ask the Chancellor of the Exchequer if, further to the reply by the Economic Secretary to the hon. Member for Islington, South and Finsbury on 16 June, *Official Report,* column *549,* he will indicate what percentage proportion of *(a)* the Italian consumer price index, and *(b)* the United Kingdom retail prices index is represented in each case by the lists of housing costs contained in his reply.

**Mr. Lilley:** The information is as follows:

*Weight given to housing costs in the United Kingdom RPI and Italian consumer price index.*

*(All items = 100)*

| | United Kingdom | Italy |
|---|---|---|
| *Owner occupier costs* | | |
| MIPs | 6·0 | 0·0 |
| *Rental costs* | | |
| Rent | 3·2 | 4·5 |
| *Other costs* | | |
| Rates | 4·2 | 0·0 |
| Water and other charges | 0·7⎱ | |
| Repair and maintenance charges | 0·9⎰ | 0·4 |
| Dwelling insurance and ground rent | 0·8 | 0·0 |
| Do it yourself materials | 1·7 | 0·0 |
| *Total housing costs* | 17·5 | 4·9 |

## Interest Rates

**Mr. McLeish:** To ask the Chancellor of the Exchequer if he will give an estimate of the increased costs to British industry of each 0·5 per cent. increase in interest rates.

**Mr. Lilley:** The cost to industrial and commercial companies of a 0·5 per cent. increase in United Kingdom short-term interest rates maintained for a full year is estimated to be about £0·2 billion.

## Economic and Finance Council

**Miss Widdecombe:** To ask the Chancellor of the Exchequer if he will make a statement on the outcome of the latest meeting of the European Community's Economic and Finance Council.

**Mr. Lilley:** The ECOFIN Council met in Luxembourg on 19 June. I represented the United Kingdom.

The Council adopted a regulation re-weighting the ecu.

The Council reached substantive agreement on a common position, subject to some further procedural details, on the draft second banking co-ordination directive and on the solvency ratios directive; and reached agreement on a common position on the insider trading directive.

The Council reached agreement on a common position on a revised financial regulation. The Council adopted the 18th VAT directive.

The Council had a further discussion of the Commission's proposals on fiscal frontiers.

The Council discussed proposals for the three company tax measures to encourage cross-border co-operation.

The Council heard a progress report on the latest proposals for anti-fraud measures, supported the useful progress made since the March ECOFIN, and endorsed the need to continue progress.

## Public Service Management

**Miss Widdecombe:** To ask the Chancellor of the Exchequer if he will place in the Library a copy of his recent Audit Commission lecture on public service management.

**Mr. Major:** I have already done so.

## Capital Gains Tax

**Mr. Nicholas Brown:** To ask the Chancellor of the Exchequer if he will give the estimated gain to the Exchequer in 1988-89 and 1989-90 of reducing capital gains tax exemptions from £5,000 to *(a)* £1,000 and *(b)* £2,000; and what would be the number of people who would have chargeable gains on this basis.

**Mr. Norman Lamont** *[holding answer 19 June 1989]:* I regret that precise estimates are not possible, but the figures for gains realised in each of these years could be of the order of:

| Annual exempt amount | Increase in revenue | Increase in number of taxpayers |
|---|---|---|
| | *£ million* | *'000* |
| £1,000 | 300 | 500 |
| £2,000 | 200 | 200 |

**Mr. Nicholas Brown:** To ask the Chancellor of the Exchequer if he will give the estimated gain to the

Exchequer in 1990-91 of reducing capital gains tax exemptions from £5,000 to *(a)* £1,000 and *(b)* £2,000 and the number of people who would have chargeable gains on this basis allowing for the impact of independent taxation.

**Mr. Norman Lamont** *[holding answer 19 June 1989]:* I regret that no sufficiently firm estimate can be made.

### Water Privatisation

**Mrs. Ann Taylor:** To ask the Chancellor of the Exchequer if he gave specific approval for additional moneys to the water authorities for pre-flotation advertising.

**Mr. Norman Lamont** *[holding answer 20 June 1989]:* The Government allowed for expenditure on the water authorities' current corporate awareness advertising campaigns when approving the water authorities' overall financing limits.

## PRIME MINISTER

### NATO (Weapons Deployment)

**Dr. Thomas:** To ask the Prime Minister if she will make a statement on what is meant in terms of length of time by the phrase, "for the foreseeable future," in regard to the need for a continued mix of conventional and nuclear weapons in Europe deployed by NATO.

**The Prime Minister:** This agreement was reached by 16 Governments. It is not for any one Government to vary the normal meaning of the words.

### Australian Prime Minister

**Dr. Thomas:** To ask the Prime Minister if, during her meeting with the Prime Minister of Australia on his forthcoming visit to Europe, she has any plans to raise *(a)* initiatives to be taken to strengthen the nuclear non-proliferation treaty in the lead up to the 1990 non-proliferation treaty review conference, and *(b)* the arrangements for safeguards on uranium imported to the United Kingdom from Australia.

**The Prime Minister:** We discussed non-proliferation matters. The answer to the second part of the question is no.

**Dr. Thomas:** To ask the Prime Minister if, during the forthcoming visit of the Prime Minister of Australia, she plans to raise *(a)* the amendment conference for the 1963 partial nuclear test ban treaty and *(b)* the French nuclear testing programme in the Pacific and its effect on the treaty of Rarotonga.

**The Prime Minister:** Nuclear testing in the Pacific was discussed.

### Conventional Force Cuts, Europe

**Dr. Thomas:** To ask the Prime Minister what is the basis for her statement at the NATO press conference in Brussels on 30 May that President Bush's plan for conventional force cuts in Europe within six months to a year is a very optimistic timetable.

**The Prime Minister:** The practical details (such as definitions, counting rules and verification arrangements)

of a negotiation as complex as this are daunting. Negotiating satisfactory arrangements within the time-table we have set ourselves will be hard work, but we have made a good start.

### Apartheid

**Mr. Cartwright:** To ask the Prime Minister if she will use the opportunity of her planned discussions with Mr. F. W. de Klerk to urge the South African Government to negotiate an end to apartheid.

**The Prime Minister:** Yes. We want to see the peaceful abolition of apartheid through negotiation.

### Rain Forests

**Mr. Dalyell:** To ask the Prime Minister if she will make a statement on her discussions on rain forest issues with Dr. Ghillean Prance during her official visit to Kew gardens.

**The Prime Minister:** During my visit to the Royal botanical gardens at Kew on 16 June, I spoke to a number of experts with whom I discussed, among many other things, the problems of tropical reafforestation which follow the destruction of natural habitats.

**Dr. Clark:** To ask the Prime Minister whether she will host a conference in Britain for private companies to enable discussions to take place in order to reduce the damage caused to rain forests throughout the world; and if she will make a statement.

**The Prime Minister:** I share the widespread concern about the depletion of the tropical rain forests, and this was among the subjects discussed at the seminar which I held at Downing street on 26 April which involved individuals from the world of science and of business. I have no present plans for a further conference.

### Ministerial Meetings

**Mr. Wray:** To ask the Prime Minister if she will list, for each year since 1986, all the ministerial talks and meetings held by her or other Ministers with Ministers or representatives of the Governments of *(a)* Guatemala, *(b)* Haiti, *(c)* Honduras, *(d)* El Salvador and *(e)* South Africa.

**The Prime Minister:** The following table lists those meetings at ministerial level of which we have records. Ministers have had additional informal bilateral meetings in the margins of international conferences.

In addition to these formal and informal meetings with their opposite numbers, Ministers in London regularly see the ambassadors of these countries in the course of their normal duties.

| Country | Date | |
|---------|------|---|
| *1986* | | |
| El Salvador | None | |
| Guatemala | 7 May | Lady Hooper met President Cerezo at inauguration of President Arias in San José |
| | 17 November | Lady Young met President Cerezo at Miami Conference |
| Haiti | November | Lady Young met General Henri Namphy (then President) at Miami Conference |

| Country | Date | |
|---|---|---|
| Honduras | 17 November | Lady Young met President Azcona at Miami Conference |
| | 15 December | Lady Young met Foreign Minister Lopez Contreras in London |
| South Africa | 23 July | Foreign Secretary met State President PW Botha and Foreign Minister Pik Botha in South Africa |
| | 27 July | Foreign Secretary met Foreign Minister Pik Botha and Minister of Trade and Industry de Villien |
| | 29 July | Foreign Secretary met Foreign Minister Pik Botha, Finance Minister du Plessis and State President PW Botha |
| | October | Chancellor of The Exchequer met Finance Minister du Plessis |
| *1987* | | |
| El Salvador | 11-12 May | Foreign Minister Acevedo Peralta met Foreign Secretary and Lady Young in London |
| Guatemala | 11 February | Lady Young met President Cerezo and Foreign Minister Quiñones in Guatemala |
| | 21 September | Foreign Secretary met President Cerezo in New York |
| | 20 October | Mr. Eggar met Minister of Economy Lizardo Sosa Lopez in London |
| Honduras | None | |
| South Africa | 28 November | Mrs. Chalker met Deputy Foreign Minister Kobus Meiring in South Africa |
| *1988* | | |
| El Salvador | 9 March | Mr. Eggar met Foreign Minister Acevedo Peralta in London |
| Guatemala | 8 March | Foreign Secretary and Mr. Eggar met Vice-President Carpo Nicolle in London |
| | December | Mr. Eggar met President Cerezo in Miami |
| Honduras | 27-28 April | Foreign Secretary and Mr. Eggar met Foreign Minister Lopez Contreras in London |
| South Africa | 1 November | Mrs. Chalker met Deputy Foreign Minister Kobus Meiring in South Africa |
| *1989* | | |
| El Salvador | 1 June | Mr. Alan Howarth, Whip, attended inauguration of President Cristiani as a Ministerial Representative, saw members of incoming administration |
| Guatemala | 2-3 March | Mr. Eggar met Vice-President Carpo Nicolle, Foreign Minister Palencia and Interior Minister Valle Valdizán in Guatemala City |
| Haiti | February | Mr. Eggar met Foreign Minister Serge Charles at inauguration of President Perez of Venezuela |
| Honduras | 27 February | Mr. Eggar met Minister of Health in Honduras |

| Country | Date | |
|---|---|---|
| South Africa | 15 March | Foreign Minister Pik Botha met Prime Minister and Foreign Secretary in London |
| | 1 April | Foreign Minister Pik Botha met Prime Minister in Namibia |
| | 24-25 April | Prime Minister and Foreign Secretary met Finance Minister du Plessis in London |
| | 23 June | Prime Minister and Foreign Secretary met Minister of National Education de Clerk |

### Economic Assistance

**Mrs. Clwyd:** To ask the Prime Minister if she will ensure that the principle of making economic assistance and trade credits conditional on an improvement in democratic and human rights is applied in the case of Iraq as well as in that of Poland.

**The Prime Minister:** We regularly make clear to the Iraqi Government our concerns over their human rights record, but we do not believe that unilateral economic measures would be effective in ending human rights abuses. Only by maintaining a working relationship can we hope to achieve changes. I announced a number of steps on 10 June following my meeting with General Jaruzelski to support progress towards democracy and a market economy, including the contribution of £5 million a year for five years towards a "Know How" fund. Our policy on export credit guarantees for Poland is governed by economic considerations.

### China

**Mr. Cox:** To ask the Prime Minister if she will ensure that the current events in China and the repression by the Chinese authorities will be discussed as a matter of urgency at the EEC summit in Madrid; and if she will make a statement.

**The Prime Minister:** I can assure the hon. Member that the current repression by the Chinese authorities will be discussed at the forthcoming Madrid European Council.

**Mr. Cox:** To ask the Prime Minister if Her Majesty's Government will protest to the Chinese ambassador to the United Kingdom on the executions now taking place in China; and if she will make a statement.

**The Prime Minister:** My right hon. and learned Friend the Foreign Secretary told the House on 6 June that he had summoned the Chinese chargé d'affaires to make clear our attitude to the violent suppression of peaceful protest in Peking. As I made clear in the House on 22 June, I was among the first to condemn the recent executions in China, about which representations have also been made to the Chinese authorities by the 12 EC member states.

## SOCIAL SECURITY

### Disability Benefits

**Mr. Wigley:** To ask the Secretary of State for Social Security if, in the light of the Social Security Advisory Committee's report, "Benefits for Disabled People: A Strategy for Change", he plans to increase spending on disability benefits.

**Mr. Scott:** Current expenditure plans, Command 615, provide for spending on benefits for the sick and disabled to increase by over £3 billion by 1991-92. We shall give careful consideration to the report of the Social Security Advisory Committee when we reach conclusions on the implications of the results of the surveys of disability carried out by the Office of Population Censuses and Surveys. It is too soon to say how this will affect existing expenditure plans.

### Social Fund

**Mr. Cohen:** To ask the Secretary of State for Social Security which of his Department's offices in the Greater London area have spent more than 100 per cent. of their profile allocation for social fund loans and social fund grants for (i) April 1989 and (ii) May 1989.

**Mr. Peter Lloyd:** The information is as follows:

*Loans*
April 1989
    Balham
    Barking
    Canning Town
    Cricklewood
    Ealing
    Edgware
    Greenwich Park
    Kennington Park
    Paddington
    Poplar
    Romford
    Shoreditch
    Southwark
    Walthamstow
    Wood Green

May 1989
    Bexley
    Brixton
    Camberwell
    Canning Town
    Croydon
    Crystal Palace
    Ealing
    Edmonton
    Eltham
    Greenwich Park
    Harlesden
    Highgate
    Hounslow
    Kensington
    Oval
    Paddington
    Peckham
    Poplar
    Southwark
    Thames North
    Tottenham
    Walthamstow
    Woodgrange Park
    Wood Green
    Woolwich

*Community care grants*
April 1989
    Barking
    Barnet
    Canning Town
    Cricklewood
    Crystal Palace
    Ealing
    Edgware
    Eltham
    Euston
    Finsbury Park
    Harrow
    Hither Green
    Kennington Park

    Kensington
    Neasden
    Oval
    Paddington
    Peckham
    Poplar
    Romford
    Southwark
    Stoke Newington
    Twickenham
    Wood Green
    Woolwich

May 1989
    Balham
    Barking
    Bexley
    Camberwell
    Canning Town
    Croydon
    Ealing
    Euston
    Finsbury Park
    Greenwich Park
    Harrow
    Hendon
    Kensington
    Leytonstone
    Oval
    Peckham
    Shoreditch
    Walthamstow
    Wood Green

**Mr. Cohen:** To ask the Secretary of State for Social Security which of his Department's offices in the Greater London area have spent between 90 per cent. and 100 per cent. of their profile allocation for social fund loans and social fund grants for (i) April 1989 and (ii) May 1989.

**Mr. Peter Lloyd:** The information is as follows:

*Loans*
April 1989
    Bexley
    Chelsea
    Croydon
    Edmonton
    Euston
    Hackney
    Highgate
    Hoxton
    Mitcham
    Peckham
    Tottenham
    Wandsworth
    Wimbledon
    Woodgrange Park
    Woolwich

May 1989
    Barnet
    Finsbury Park
    Hackney
    Kingston
    Leytonstone
    Mitcham
    Notting Hill
    Stepney
    Streatham
    Stoke Newington
    Sutton

*Community Care Grants*
April 1989
    Balham
    Battersea
    Bexley
    Bloomsbury
    Brixton
    Camberwell
    Chelsea

Croydon
Greenwich Park
Hackney
Harlesden
Hendon
Highgate
Hoxton
London City
Plaistow
Stepney
Sutton
Tottenham
Walthamstow
Wandsworth
Westminster
Woodgrange Park

May 1989
Acton
Barnet
Battersea
Brixton
Bromley
Chelsea
Crystal Palace
Edgware
Hackney
Highgate
Mitcham
Neasden
Notting Hill
Romford
Stepney
Streatham
Westminster
Woodgrange Park

**Mr. Malcolm Bruce:** To ask the Secretary of State for Social Security how many decisions made by social fund officers are overturned by social fund inspectors.

**Mr. Peter Lloyd:** The social fund commissioner has advised me that in the period from 11 April 1988 to 31 March 1989 social fund inspectors reviewed 2,499 cases. A total of 1,109 were referred back to social fund officers to redetermine and in 96 cases the social fund inspector substituted his own decision.

### Hostels

**Mr. Wallace:** To ask the Secretary of State for Social Security what grants are available for the establishment of hostels.

**Mr. Peter Lloyd:** Grants can be made under schedule 5 of the Supplementary Benefit Act 1976, as amended, to voluntary organisations and/or local authorities. These would be to set up facilities for those people without a settled way of life with a view to influencing them to lead a settled way of life. However, such grants are currently being restricted to organisations that provide hostels which form part of an approved scheme to replace resettlement units.

### Public Relations

**Mr. Blair:** To ask the Secretary of State for Social Security which public relations firms his Department has employed, and at what cost, for each year since 1979.

**Mr. Peter Lloyd:** Apart from the special circumstances of privatisation work, the consistent practice of successive Governments has been to avoid the use of public relations firms or other firms outside Government for public relations work.

### Housing Benefit

**Ms. Quin:** To ask the Secretary of State for Social Security if he will give the numbers of people receiving housing benefit rent allowances in May 1986, May 1987, and May 1988.

**Mr. Peter Lloyd:** The information requested is as follows. The figures represent the estimated average number receiving benefit in the year.

*Estimated numbers receiving housing benefit rent allowances*

| | *Million* |
|---|---|
| 1986-87 | 1·18 |
| 1987-88 | 1·20 |
| 1988-89 | 0·93 |

**Ms. Quin:** To ask the Secretary of State for Social Security if he will list the numbers of people who are currently receiving rent allowance via housing benefit.

**Mr. Peter Lloyd:** The latest available estimate for 1989-90 is 1·04 million.

### Community Charge

**Mr. Harry Barnes:** To ask the Secretary of State for Social Security if he will list the categories of information held in his Department that are available for use by community charge registration officers.

**Mr. Peter Lloyd:** The information that may be passed to community charge registration officers is prescribed in the Community Charges (Information Concerning Social Security) (Scotland) Regulations 1988 and the Community Charges (Information Concerning Social Security) Regulations 1989. It is confined to the name and address of any person aged over 18, and of any partner he or she may have aged over 18, who has been awarded income support and who, prior to 1 April 1989 in Scotland and prior to 1 April 1990 in England and Wales, has not claimed housing benefit, or who, after 1 April 1989 in Scotland and after 1 April 1990 in England and Wales, has not claimed a community charge rebate. In Scotland the information may also include the date of birth of any such person.

### Pensioners

**Mr. McAllion:** To ask the Secretary of State for Social Security what is his estimate of the number of pensioners in *(a)* Scotland and *(b)* the United Kingdom whose only source of income is the basic national insurance retirement pension.

**Mr. Peter Lloyd:** In 1986, just under 20 per cent. of United Kingdom pensioners' sole source of income was from state benefits.
*Source:* Family Expenditure Survey 1986.
*Notes:* The data cannot be broken down further to provide the proportion of pensioners' income derived from the basic state pension.
It is not possible to provide information for Scotland because the Scottish sample size in the FES is too small to be statistically significant in answering this question.

**Mr. McAllion:** To ask the Secretary of State for Social Security what is his estimate of the number of pensioners in *(a)* Scotland and *(b)* the United Kingdom who are in receipt of housing benefit for each year since 1981.

**Mr. Peter Lloyd:** The available information for Great Britain is as follows. Figures for Scotland and the United Kingdom are not available in the form requested. Housing Benefit did not come into full operation until April 1983.

Estimated number of pensioners receiving Housing Benefit 1983-4—1988-9.

|        | Million |
|--------|---------|
| 1983-4 | 4·105   |
| 1984-5 | 4·110   |
| 1985-6 | 4·120   |
| 1986-7 | 4·030   |
| 1987-8 | 4·045   |
| 1988-9 | 2·850   |

### War Widows

**Sir Michael McNair-Wilson:** To ask the Secretary of State for Social Services how many war widows are receiving war widows pensions because their husband left the services before 31 March 1973; and what would be the total cost of uprating their pensions to £5,000 per person.

**Mr. Peter Lloyd:** At 31 March approximately 56,000 pre-1973 war widows were in receipt of a pension under the war pensions scheme. We estimate that the total extra cost of uprating their pensions to £5,000 per person would be about £100 million per annum.

### Territorial Army

**Mr. Soames:** To ask the Secretary of State for Social Services what are the regulations governing the treatment of earnings from the Territorial Army for unemployed males receiving benefit.

**Mr. Peter Lloyd:** Unemployed people receiving earnings from the Territorial Army are most likely to be in receipt of unemployment benefit, income support and housing benefit. The main provisions dealing with the treatment of these earnings in each benefit are as follows.

The regulation governing the effect on unemployment benefit of earnings specifically from the Territorial Army is regulation 3(3) of the Social Security (Computation of Earnings) Regulations 1978. Under this regulation no account is taken of annual bounty and payment in respect of attendance at the first 16 authorised drill nights each year. Further payments are subject to regulation 7(1)(g)(i) of the Social Security (Unemployment, Sickness and Invalidity Benefit) Regulations 1983, under which a day is not treated as a day of unemployment if earnings for that day exceed £2.

For unemployed reservists receiving income support or housing benefit, the weekly amount of the earnings and the period for which they are to be taken into account are determined by reference to regulations 29, 31 and 32 of the Income Support (General) Regulations, and regulations 21 and 25 of the Housing Benefit (General) Regulations. Payments made in respect of income tax, class 1 national insurance contributions and half of any sum paid by an employee towards an occupational or personal pension scheme are disregarded under regulation 36(3) of the Income Support (General) Regulations 1987 and regulation 29(3) of the Housing Benefit (General) Regulations 1987. The first £15 of weekly earnings is also disregarded under paragraph 7(1) of schedule 8 to the income support regulations and paragraph 6(1) of schedule 3 to the housing benefit regulations.

The annual bounty paid to reservists is treated as capital under Income Support (General) Regulation 48 and Housing Benefit (General) Regulation 40(1) and does not affect entitlement as long as the total capital held does not exceed £3,000.

For income support only, reservists attending annual training camp are normally treated as being in remunerative work and are not entitled to benefit in accordance with regulation 5 of the Income Support (General) Regulations. Earnings arising from this period are ignored completely on reclaiming benefit under the provision of paragraph 1 of schedule 8 to the regulations.

### Community Care Grants

**Ms. Harman:** To ask the Secretary of State for Social Security whether in addition to any provision in the Acts and regulations, there is any *(a)* guidance to all Departments of Social Security offices and *(b)* internal guidance within the offices covering the Peckham constituency on the amounts to be awarded to people in different categories who are given community care grants.

**Mr. Peter Lloyd:** Guidance has been issued in the social fund manual on suggested maximum amounts which may be awarded to applicants who need a start-up grant, a clothing grant and minor structural repairs to the home. The decision on how much to award in an individual case rests with the social fund officer.

**Ms. Harman:** To ask the Secretary of State for Social Security whether there is any *(a)* guidance to all Departments of Social Security offices and *(b)* internal guidance within the offices covering the Peckham constituency on the priority for community care grants as between homeless women in refuges, people coming out of mental institutions, children leaving care, and others.

**Mr. Peter Lloyd:** Guidance on the national priorities for community care grants has been issued in the social fund manual. Local office managers have issued guidance to social fund officers on local priorities.

### Benefits

**Mr. Sheerman:** To ask the Secretary of State for Social Security what level of state benefit income an unemployed family consisting of mother, father, and two children aged 12 and 5 years received in 1979; and what benefit they would receive today if 1979 benefits had been increased to match inflation if the benefits were paid on the same basis as in 1979.

**Mr. Peter Lloyd:** There is no prescribed procedure for uprating supplementary benefit or housing benefit— different elements of these schemes have been uprated in different ways and by different indices at different times.

**Sir Ian Gilmour:** To ask the Secretary of State for Social Security if he will publish figures showing the number of families with children: *(a)* entitled to and *(b)* receiving supplementary benefit/income support in each year since 1970, distinguishing between one and two-parent families.

**Mr. Peter Lloyd** *[holding answer 3 May 1989]:* The available information is as follows:

*Families with children receiving supplementary benefit/income support and estimated eligible non-recipient families by family status*

| | Total in receipt (000s) | One parent families in receipt (000s) | One parent families eligible but not in receipt (000s) | Two parent families in receipt (000s) | Two parent families eligible but not in receipt (000s) |
|---|---|---|---|---|---|
| 1970 | 364 | 218 | — | 146 | — |
| 1971 | 436 | 246 | — | 190 | — |
| 1972 | 433 | 259 | — | 175 | — |
| 1973 | 373 | 257 | 60 | 116 | 80 |
| 1974 | 405 | 269 | — | 136 | — |
| 1975 | 502 | 296 | — | 206 | — |
| 1976 | 556 | 323 | — | 233 | — |
| 1977 | 553 | 326 | 50 | 227 | — |
| 1978 | 535 | 339 | — | 196 | — |
| 1979 | 488 | 322 | 60 | 166 | 60 |
| 1980 | 581 | 336 | — | 245 | — |
| 1981 | 794 | 392 | 50 | 402 | 150 |
| 1982 | 929 | 441 | — | 488 | — |
| 1983 | 975 | 475 | 40 | 500 | — |
| 1984 | 1,057 | 518 | — | 539 | — |
| 1986 | 1,172 | 606 | — | 565 | — |
| 1987 | 1,181 | 664 | — | 517 | — |

*Notes:*

1. Sources: Annual statistical enquiries 1970 to 1987 for those families with children in receipt of benefit. For eligible non-recipient families appropriate Family Expenditure Survey data.
2. The two columns can not be added to give a total figure of those claiming and not claiming. Recipient families are identified on a 'snapshot basis'. Take-up estimates are based on an average caseload over the year and exclude the institutional population and from 1983 to 1987 Housing Benefit Supplement recipients.
3. All estimates, but especially of eligible non-recipients, are subject to sampling error.
4. One parent familes exclude those temporarily separated.

**Sir Ian Gilmour:** To ask the Secretary of State for Social Security if he will publish figures showing the estimated number of families *(a)* entitled to and *(b)* receiving family income supplement/family credit in each year since 1971, distinguishing between employed, self-employed, one-parent and two-parent families, and including a case-load estimate for its current year.

**Mr. Peter Lloyd** *[holding answer 3 May 1989]:* The information is as follows:

*Families with dependent children receiving family income supplement/family credit and eligible non-recipient families with dependants by family and employment status*

| | Employed[10] | | | Self-employed[10][11] | |
|---|---|---|---|---|---|
| | One parent (000s) | Two parent (000s) | Estimated eligible non-recipients (one or two parents)[3][9] (000s) | One parent (000s) | Two parent (000s) |
| Family income supplement[1] | | | | | |
| August 1971 | 15 | 30 | — | [8]— | 1 |
| April 1972 | 27 | 51 | — | [8]— | 3 |
| April 1973 | 35 | 44 | — | 1 | 3 |
| April 1974 | 39 | 33 | — | 1 | 3 |
| April 1975 | 30 | 22 | — | 1 | 3 |
| April 1976 | 30 | 25 | — | 1 | 4 |
| April 1977 | 36 | 42 | — | 1 | 5 |
| April 1978 | 40 | 49 | [4]75 | 1 | 5 |
| April 1979 | 37 | 36 | — | 1 | 4 |
| April 1980 | 49 | 33 | — | 1 | 5 |
| April 1981 | 53 | 45 | [5]130 | 1 | 7 |
| April 1982 | 63 | 66 | — | 2 | 11 |
| April 1983 | 76 | 92 | [6]150 | 3 | 18 |
| April 1984 | 78 | 100 | — | 3 | 23 |
| April 1985 | 80 | 95 | — | 3 | 25 |
| April 1986 | 79 | 92 | — | 4 | 26 |
| April 1987 | 87 | 97 | — | 4 | 31 |
| | | | | | |
| Family credit | | | | | |
| April-December 1988 | n.a. | n.a. | [7]250 | n.a. | n.a. |
| March 1989[2] | 100 | 139 | — | 8 | 35 |

[1] *Source:* 10 per cent. sample of Family Income Supplement awards.

[2] 1989 Family Credit figures derived from Family Credit statistical system and North Fylde Central Ofice load. Earlier figure on comparable terms are not available.

[3] Eligible non-recipients from Family Expenditure survey.

[4] 1978-79 FES.

[5] 1981-82 FES.

[6] 1983-84 FES.

[7] April-December 1988 FES. Around 50 per cent. of eligible population of 500,000 employees.

[8] Under 500.

[9] Columns for claimants and eligible non-claimants cannot be added to give a precise total figure of those claiming and not claiming. Recipient families are identified on a 'snapshot basis'.

Take-up estimates are usually based on an average caseload over two years. For Family Credit, the take-up estimate is based on 9 months of Family Expenditure Survey data.

[10] All estimates, especially those for eligible non-recipients, are subject to sampling error.

[11] No estimates are available for self-employed eligible non-recipients. Separate estimates of eligible non-recipient one parent and two parent employed cases would be subject to large sampling errors.

## Benefits (Children)

**Sir Ian Gilmour:** To ask the Secretary of State for Social Security how many English children depended on *(a)* SB/IS and *(b)* FIS/FC in each year since 1978-79 (i) in total and (ii) as a percentage of all English children.

**Mr. Peter Lloyd** *[holding answer 4 May 1989]:* The latest available information is set out in the following tables.

*Dependent children in families in England in receipt of supplementary benefit*

| Year | Number of children[1] in families receiving supplementary benefit[2] Thousands | Proportion of all children in England[3] Per cent. |
|---|---|---|
| 1978 | 894 | 7·8 |
| 1979 | 784 | 6·9 |
| 1980 | 937 | 8·4 |
| 1981 | 1,294 | 11·7 |
| 1982 | 1,495 | 13·8 |
| 1983 | 1,573 | 14·8 |
| 1984 | 1,704 | 16·3 |
| 1986 | 1,870 | 18·2 |
| 1987 | 1,880 | 18·4 |

[1] Dependent children aged under 19.
[2] *Source:* Annual Statistical Enquiries 1978 to 1987.
[3] Based on the Child Benefit recipient population.

*Children in families in England receiving Family Income Supplement*

| Year | Children in families receiving FIS[1] Thousands | Proportion of all children in England[2] Per cent. |
|---|---|---|
| 1978-79 | 169 | 1·5 |
| 1979-80 | 151 | 1·3 |
| 1980-81 | 154 | 1·4 |
| 1981-82 | 193 | 1·7 |
| 1982-83 | 267 | 2·5 |
| 1983-84 | 338 | 3·2 |
| 1984-85 | 354 | 3·4 |
| 1985-86 | 340 | 3·3 |
| 1986-87 | 367 | 3·6 |
| 1987-88 | 376 | 3·7 |

[1] *Source:* 10 per cent. sample of Family Income Supplement awards and Social Security Statistics for those receiving Child Benefit.
[2] Based on Child Benefit recipient population.

**Sir Ian Gilmour:** To ask the Secretary of State for Social Security how many Scottish children depended on *(a)* SB/IS and *(b)* FIS/FC in each year since 1978-79 (i) in total and (ii) as a percentage of all Scottish children.

**Mr. Peter Lloyd** *[holding answer 4 May 1989]:* The available information is as follows:

*Children in families in Scotland in receipt of supplementary benefit*

| Year | Number of children[1] in families receiving supplementary benefit[2] Thousands (000) | Proportion of all children in Scotland[3] Percentage |
|---|---|---|
| 1978 | 122 | 9·3 |
| 1979 | 112 | 8·7 |
| 1980 | 122 | 9·6 |
| 1981 | 159 | 12·8 |
| 1982 | 187 | 15·5 |
| 1983 | 181 | 15·3 |
| 1984 | 202 | 17·4 |
| 1986 | 219 | 19·6 |
| 1987 | 225 | 20·5 |

[1] Dependent children aged under 19.
[2] *Source:* Annual Statistical Enquiries 1978 to 1987.
[3] Based on the Child Benefit recipient population.

*Children in families in Scotland receiving family income supplement*

| Year | Children in families receiving family income supplement[1] Thousands (000) | Proportion of all children in Scotland[2] Percentage |
|---|---|---|
| 1978-79 | 24 | 1·8 |
| 1979-80 | 20 | 1·6 |
| 1980-81 | 24 | 1·9 |
| 1981-82 | 28 | 2·3 |
| 1982-83 | 37 | 3·0 |
| 1983-84 | 38 | 3·2 |
| 1984-85 | 50 | 4·3 |
| 1985-86 | 48 | 4·2 |
| 1986-87 | 51 | 4·5 |
| 1987-88 | 53 | 4·8 |

[1] *Source:* 10 per cent. sample of FIS awards and Social Security Statistics for those receiving Child Benefit.
[2] Based on the Child Benefit recipient population.

## Grants and Loans

**Mr. Nellist:** To ask the Secretary of State for Social Security what percentage of *(a)* budgetary loans and *(b)* community care grants were awarded to each of the 15 client groups defined by his Department for the midlands region in the financial year 1988-89.

**Mr. Peter Lloyd** *[holding answer 19 June 1989]:* The table shows the figures for the midlands region for the period 11 April 1988 to 31 march 1989.

*Budgeting loans and community care grants for midlands region Percentage by client group—1988-89*

| Client group | Budgeting loans | Community care grants |
|---|---|---|
| Unallocated or unidentified | 0·34 | 0·21 |
| Over 80—with income support higher pensioner premium | 0·35 | 5·19 |
| Aged 60-79—disabled with higher pensioner premium | 0·49 | 4·03 |
| Aged 60-79—with ordinary pensioner premium, or over 60 without pensioner premium | 4·10 | 16·59 |
| Lone parent with income support disability premium | 0·30 | 0·82 |
| Family with disability premium | 3·28 | 3·00 |
| Other with disability premium | 2·67 | 9·48 |
| Lone parent without disability premium | 43·90 | 25·13 |
| Signs at UBO quarterly with income support family premium | 0·85 | 0·51 |

| Client group | Budgeting loans | Community care grants |
|---|---|---|
| Signs at UBO quarterly without family premium | 2·29 | 1·34 |
| Signing unemployed or with training allowance with family premium | 18·39 | 8·51 |
| Signing unemployed or with training allowance without family premium | 18·55 | 16·67 |
| Others with family premium | 0·92 | 2·14 |
| Others without family premium | 3·55 | 5·72 |
| Involved in trade dispute | 0·01 | 0·00 |
| Applicant not in receipt of income support—not applicable for budgeting loans | n/a | 1·00 |

# HEALTH

## NHS Reform

**Mr. Yeo:** To ask the Secretary of State for Health what is the latest figure for the number of hospitals which have expressed interest in becoming self-governing institutions within the National Health Service.

**Mr. Mellor:** A total of 179 expressions of interest in self-governing status have been received. Some are for non-hospital facilities and others include more than one hospital.

**Mr. Win Griffiths:** To ask the Secretary of State for Health what plans he has to ensure that his proposals for hospitals opting-out of the National Health Service management structure will be supported by the staff responsible for providing all services to hospital patients.

**Mr. Mellor:** Self-governing hospitals will not opt out, but will remain fully within the NHS. When a unit decides to submit an application for self-government, the relevant regional health authority will seek the views of those with an interest including staff at the hospital. My right hon. and learned Friend the Secretary of State will consider any responses alongside the application, although no group will have a veto on any proposals.

**Mr. Harry Barnes:** To ask the Secretary of State for Health if he will list the leaflets issued in connection with proposals to reform the National Health Service together with the print runs and costs of production for each leaflet, their main avenues of distribution and their estimated costs of distribution.

**Mr. Mellor** *[holding answer 19 June 1989]:* The following leaflets have been issued in connection with proposals to reform the National Health Service:

| Leaflet | Print run | Production cost £ | Distribution Avenue | Cost £ |
|---|---|---|---|---|
| *Working for Patients:* | | | | |
| Management summary | 350,000 | 109,250 | RHAs; DHAs; CHCs; FPCs; GPs | 15,500e |
| Popular leaflet HSR1 | 3,000,000 | 117,050 | RHAs; DHAs; Post Offices; Libraries; Pharmacies | [2]22,255e |
| *Self Governing Hospitals:* | | | | |
| Staff leaflet HSR2 | 250,000⎫ | 23,000e | RHAs⎫ | [1]2,706 |
| Local public leaflet HSR3 | 250,000⎭ | | RHAs⎭ | |

[1] Estimated cost.
[2] Excludes Post Office distribution costs covered by an annual contract.
RHA Regional Health Authority.
DHA District Health Authority.
CHC Community Health Council.
FPC Family Practitioner Committee.
GP General Medical Practitioner.

## Private Health Care

**Mr. Campbell-Savours:** To ask the Secretary of State for Health what representations he has received from the Health Service unions on the question of private health provision.

**Mr. Mellor:** None.

## Crown Indemnity

**Sir Gerald Vaughan:** To ask the Secretary of State for Health when he proposes to implement a scheme of Crown indemnity for doctors and dentists working in National Health Service hospitals and community health services, as outlined in the reply to the hon. Member for Newbury (Sir. M. McNair-Wilson), on 7 April, *Official Report*, column *304*; and if he will make a statement.

**Mr. Mellor:** We are currently considering the responses to the consultation exercise which finished in May. An announcement will be made as soon as possible.

## Public Relations

**Mr. Blair:** To ask the Secretary of State for Health which public relations firms his Department has employed and at what cost, for each year since 1979.

**Mr. Mellor:** None. The consistent practice of successive Governments has been to avoid the use of public relations firms or other firms outside government for public relations work.

## Waiting Lists

**Mr. Cousins:** To ask the Secretary of State for Health if he will list the waiting list for each district health authority as at 31 March and indicate the rank order of each district in size of its waiting list.

**Mr. Mellor:** We do not yet have available figures of the number of people waiting for hospital treatment in each district health authority at 31 March 1989.

## "Working for Patients"

**Mr. Cousins:** To ask the Secretary of State for Health if he will state the distribution by National Health Service region, by spending head and by spending head within each National Health Service region of the extra £40 million so far announced for the implementation of the proposals in "Working for Patients".

**Mr. Mellor:** A total of £32 million of the additional £40 million is for the hospital and community health services and has been distributed as shown in the table. The remainder is to meet the administrative costs incurred by the Department of Health in implementing the review.

*Distribution of £32 million additional funding for the hospital and community health services 1989-90*

*(£ million)*

|  | [1]*Personnel function* | [1]*Finance function (staff)* | [2]*Capital charging* | [3]*Medical audit* | *Total allocated* |
|---|---|---|---|---|---|
| Northern | 0·366 | 0·634 | 0·865 | 0·051 | 1·916 |
| Yorkshire | 0·411 | 0·711 | 0·920 | 0·053 | 2·095 |
| Trent | 0·512 | 0·887 | 0·946 | 0·064 | 2·409 |
| East Anglian | 0·220 | 0·381 | 0·460 | 0·031 | 1·092 |
| North West Thames | 0·427 | 0·739 | 0·865 | 0·051 | 2·082 |
| North East Thames | 0·526 | 0·910 | 1·062 | 0·063 | 2·561 |
| South East Thames | 0·463 | 0·801 | 0·959 | 0·060 | 2·283 |
| South West Thames | 0·374 | 0·648 | 0·800 | 0·044 | 1·866 |
| Wessex | 0·307 | 0·532 | 0·643 | 0·042 | 1·524 |
| Oxford | 0·247 | 0·427 | 0·518 | 0·048 | 1·240 |
| South Western | 0·364 | 0·631 | 0·738 | 0·044 | 1·777 |
| West Midlands | 0·587 | 1·016 | 1·288 | 0·077 | 2·968 |
| Mersey | 0·294 | 0·509 | 0·601 | 0·036 | 1·440 |
| North Western | 0·502 | 0·869 | 1·108 | 0·067 | 2·546 |
| All RHAs | 5·600 | 9·695 | 11·773 | 0·731 | 27·799 |
| London post-graduate SHAs | 0·100 | 0·174 | 0·227 | 0·019 | 0·520 |
| Total RHAs and SHAs | 5·700 | 9·869 | 12·000 | 0·750 | [4]28·319 |

[1]Total allocated pro rata to initial revenue cash limits.
[2]Comprises a basic allocation of £13,000 per RHA/SHA plus £25,000 per district (excluding Peterborough, Chester and Calderdale health authorities which have attracted separate funding as capital asset pilot sites), with the remainder allocated pro rata to initial revenue cash limits.
[3]Total allocated pro rata to number of medical consultants in each RHA/SHA.
[4]Total excludes sums held back for later allocation for example:

|  | £ million |
|---|---|
| Internal markets: | |
| training | 0·771 |
| Medical audit: | |
| regional implementation | 0·750 |
| methodology development | 0·500 |
| Finance function: | |
| training initiatives | 1·660 |
| Total | 3·681 |

## Psychiatric Services (Children)

**Mr. Gale:** To ask the Secretary of State for Health how many children under the age of 16 years were seen for assessment of treatment by child and adolescent psychiatric services in 1986-87 and 1987-88; how many of these children were severely or profoundly deaf; what proportion used sign language; and what proportion used spoken language as their main method of communication.

**Mr. Mellor:** We do not hold this information centrally.

## Hospitals (Cleaning)

**Mr. Gale:** To ask the Secretary of State for Health what assessment he has made of the implications of the incidence of occasions, since the award of private cleaning contracts at the Kent and Canterbury hospital, the Thanet district hospital and the Royal Seabathing hospital, upon which payments for specific cleaning areas have been suspended; and what action he proposes to take to deal with such occurrences.

**Mr. Freeman:** The issues raised are contractual matters between the relevant contractor and the Canterbury and Thanet district health authority. Ultimately both parties have the sanction of terminating the contract if there are continuing and serious breaches of its terms. Usually, however, mutually satisfactory arrangements are achieved without the need for drastic action.

## Blood Transfusion Service

**Mr. Harry Barnes:** To ask the Secretary of State for Health if he will list the terms and conditions under which blood is transferred from the blood transfusion service to organisations outside the National Health Service.

**Mr. Freeman:** Blood from the national blood transfusion service is supplied to non-NHS hospitals in England and Wales according to the terms of health circular HC(89)14 a copy of which is in the Library. A handling charge is made for blood supplied in this way to cover items such as the costs of collection, testing and processing. No charge is made for the freely donated blood itself.

## Rotherham Health Authority

**Mr. Hardy:** To ask the Secretary of State for Health what financial provision has been made for the Rotherham Health Authority in 1989-90; and what was the comparable provision in the previous two years.

**Mr. Freeman:** Allocations to individual district health authorities are a matter for the regional health authority concerned. I suggest the hon. Member contacts the chairman of Trent regional health authority for the information he seeks.

**Mr. Hardy:** To ask the Secretary of State for Health what is the financial provision per capita for the Rotherham health authority in 1989-90; what is the average provision for health authorities on a per capita basis; and what significant progress will be made this year in the resources allocation working party context.

**Mr. Freeman:** Allocation of resources to district health authorities is a matter for the relevant regional health authority. The national average provision for health authorities in England in 1989-90 is £264 per capita.

The allocations for 1989-90 announced on 21 December 1988 allow every regional health authority to benefit to the maximum extent from the additional resources available. As the White Paper makes clear, the Government now intend to move on from RAWP to a simpler and fairer approach.

## Benzodiazepines

**Mr. Fearn:** To ask the Secretary of State for Health what instructions relating to deprioritising the benzodiazepine issue he has issued to health authorities or other bodies.

**Mr. Mellor:** None. On the contrary in guidance issued to health and local authorities we continue to give a high priority to the development and expansion of services for drug misusers including those dependent on benzodiazepines. This high priority is emphasised by the allocation by the Department of nearly £15 million in 1989-90 to regional health authorities specifically for the development of these services. The Department will also continue to encourage doctors to prescribe benzodiazepines only in accordance with current guidelines, as contained in the Committee on Safety of Medicines "Current Problems" No. 21 and in the British National Formulary.

## Foster Parents (Insurance)

**Mr. Hinchliffe:** To ask the Secretary of State for Health if his Department's boarding out of children regulations require agencies arranging placements to make provision for the insurance of foster parents.

**Mr. Mellor:** Agencies are required under the Boarding-Out of Children (Foster Placement) Regulations 1989 to inform foster parents of the agency's arrangements for meeting any legal liabilities of a foster parent arising by reason of the placement. We expect that agencies will make effective arrangements: A number of options are suggested in the handbook of guidance issued in association with the regulations.

## Dystonia

**Sir Michael McNair Wilson:** To ask the Secretary of State for Health (1) if he will make a grant to the Dystonia Society under section 64;

(2) what action his Department is taking to make dystonia better understood by medical professionals, to improve hospital facilities for dystonia sufferers and to enable them to obtain their drugs fee of prescription charge.

**Mr. Mellor:** The Dystonia Society was included as a candidate for funding from the RPI error money which was announced by my right hon. Friend the Minister for Social Security on 9 February. They were awarded £10,000 towards the cost of providing a nurse practitioner at the national Hospital for Nervous Diseases to give advice and counselling to sufferers of dystonia. This project, which is scheduled to run for three years, will offer the opportunity to evaluate whether this ensures a better service for dystonia sufferers with a view to introducing it into other NHS hospital neurological departments, if appropriate.

Unfortunately it was not possible to award a section 64 core grant to the society in the current financial year since the number of applications for funding exceeded the level of funds available for grant awards.

Undergraduate and postgraduate medical education is, primarily, a matter for medical schools and postgraduate medical institutions. Measures to increase doctors' knowledge of dystonia and movement disorders is more appropriate for these bodies and the medical profession.

Because of the existing wide-ranging provisions for exemption from prescription charges and particularly those for persons on low incomes, we have no plans to include dystonia in the list of medical conditions which confer exemption from prescription charges.

## Prescriptions

**Mr. Sayeed:** To ask the Secretary of State for Health when his Department decided to set up a new discount inquiry for products dispensed under National Health Service prescriptions; when he expects it to come into force; when was the last inquiry; and what kind of discounts are currently available.

**Mr. Mellor:** We consider the need for discount inquiries annually in consultation with the pharmaceutical services negotiating committee (PSNC). The next discount inquiry will be based on purchases of drugs made during April 1989. The results of the inquiry will be implemented from April 1990 or such earlier date as may be agreed between the Department and the PSNC. The last inquiry was undertaken in respect of April 1986 purchases. The price differences taken into account include discounts for volume and early settlement, special lines, the ordering of supplies by computer, free offers and lower prices for parallel imported and other products.

## Abortions

**Mr. Amess:** To ask the Secretary of State for Health if he will publish in the *Official Report* a breakdown of the reasons for abortions performed under ground two of the Abortion Act 1967 for 1987 and 1988.

**Mr. Freeman** *[holding answer 23 June 1989]*: The information is shown in the table.

*Abortions performed under ground 2[1] (alone) of the 1967 Abortion Act: numbers by principal medical condition, England and Wales 1987-88*

| ICD[2] and Condition | Number 1987 | 1988 |
|---|---|---|
| All legal abortions | 154,627 | 163,624 |
| With mention of a medical condition | 144,687 | 154,542 |
| Without mention of a medical condition | 9,940 | 9,082 |
| 638 Failed attempted abortion | 1 | — |
| 640 Haemorrhage in early pregnancy | — | 1 |
| 641 Antepartum Haemorrhage, abruption placentae and placenta praevie | — | — |
| 642 Hypertension complicating pregnancy, childbirth and puerperium | 49 | 98 |
| 643 Excessive vomiting in pregnancy | 16 | 28 |
| 646 Other complications in pregnancy, not elsewhere classified | 15 | 17 |
| 647 Infective and parasitic conditions in the mother classified elsewhere | 11 | 8 |
| 648 Mental disorders | 144,046 | 153,907 |
| Neurotic disorder | 100,688 | 105,769 |
| Depressive disorder not elsewhere classified | 43,036 | 47,789 |
| Other | 322 | 349 |
| 654 Abnormality of organs and soft tissue of pelvis | 41 | 25 |
| 655 Known or suspected foetal abnormality affecting management of mother | 116 | 64 |
| 656 Other foetal and placental problems affecting management of mother | 4 | 2 |

[1] The continuance of the pregnancy would involve risk of injury to the physical or mental health of the pregnant woman greater than if the pregnancy were terminated.

[2] International Classification of Diseases (ICD) code, 9th revision.

**Mr. Amess:** To ask the Secretary of State for Health how many incomplete abortion notification forms were accepted by his Department in 1984, 1985, 1986, 1987 and 1988 where no medical reason was given for the operation.

**Mr. Freeman** *[holding answer 23 June 1989]:* The table shows the number of abortions performed in England and Wales during 1984-88 where no medical reason for the operation was given on the notification form. This does not mean, however, that these notification forms were incomplete; on a number of occasions, notifications are received where, quite properly, no existing medical condition has been recorded.

Such notifications refer to situations where there is an implied future risk to the mother were the pregnancy to continue, rather than to an existing medical condition. The Abortion Act 1967 allows an abortion to be performed if two registered medical practitioners are of the opinion formed in good faith that

"the continuance of the pregnancy would involve risk of injury to the physical or mental health of the pregnant woman greater than if the pregnancy were terminated."

Most of the cases without mention of medical condition are terminations performed under this ground.

There are also a small number which are accounted for by those notified on the grounds that

"the continuance of the pregnancy would involve risk or injury to the physical or mental health of any existing child(ren) in the family of the pregnant woman greater than if the pregnancy were terminated"
(Ground 3 of the 1967 Abortion Act).

*Legal abortions performed without mention of medical condition, England and Wales, 1984-88*

| Year | Total |
|---|---|
| 1984 | 12,533 |
| 1985 | 12,815 |
| 1986 | 13,166 |
| 1987 | 13,645 |
| 1988 | 12,177 |

## HOME DEPARTMENT

### Passports

81. **Mr. Harry Barnes:** To ask the Secretary of State for the Home Department when he last met representatives of the trade unions; and whether the subject of the issue and renewal of passports was discussed.

**Mr. Renton:** Officials at the Passport Department last met representatives of the Civil and Public Services Association and the National Union of Civil and Public Servants on 16 June in the course of efforts to resolve the current dispute over staffing levels at the passport offices. An offer was made to increase numbers of permanent staff in return for greater flexibility in working practices and co-operation in a number of management initiatives to improve the efficiency of the Passport Department. We expect this will lead to a return to work by striking staff at the Liverpool office tomorrow and a resumption of normal working at the other passport offices. The first priority will then be to clear the current backlog of applications and to provide an improved service to the public.

### Sunday Trading

**Mr. Michael Morris:** To ask the Secretary for State for the Home Department whether he has any proposals to increase the fines available to the courts for traders who break the Sunday trading laws.

**Mr. Renton:** Not at present.

### Road Traffic Law Review

**Mr. Knox:** To ask the Secretary of State for the Home Department when he last met (a) the Association of Chief Police Officers and (b) the Magistrates Association to discuss some of the recommendations for improving traffic regulation enforcement made by the road traffic law review.

**Mr. Douglas Hogg:** My right hon. Friend last met the Association of Chief Police Officers to discuss road traffic matters on 24 October 1988. He has not met the Magistrates Association to discuss this subject. Home Office officials are involved in continuing discussions with representatives of the police service and the magistrates courts about implementation of the proposals set out in the White Paper "The Road User and the Law" (Cm. 576).

## United Kingdom Immigrants Advisory Service

**Mr. Wray:** To ask the Secretary of State for the Home Department what is the financial support given to the United Kingdom Immigrants Advisory Service for each year since 1976 in 1989 money.

**Mr. Renton:** The total Home Office grant-in-aid to the United Kingdom Immigrants' Advisory Service in each of the financial years from 1976-77, expressed at assumed 1989-90 prices by use of the GDP deflator, is given in the table:

|  | £ |
| --- | --- |
| 1976-77 | 755,000 |
| 1977-78 | 692,000 |
| 1978-79 | 909,000 |
| 1979-80 | 850,000 |
| 1980-81 | 891,000 |
| 1981-82 | 993,000 |
| 1982-83 | 1,026,000 |
| 1983-84 | 1,058,000 |
| 1984-85 | 1,038,000 |
| 1985-86 | 1,086,000 |
| 1986-87 | 1,060,000 |
| 1987-88 | 1,087,000 |
| 1988-89 | 1,062,000 |

## Political Asylum

**Mr. Cartwright:** To ask the Secretary of State for the Home Department how many applications for political asylum in the United Kingdom are currently being received each month; and from what nationalities.

**Mr. Renton:** Information is not available in the form requested. A provisional breakdown by nationality of all applications made in each quarter is supplied by the United Nations High Commissioners for Refugees, one quarter in arrears. Copies are placed in the Library. Statistics for the first quarter of 1989 will be available at the beginning of July. We know that there has recently been a large increase in the number of Turkish nationals applying for asylum on arrival at ports. There have been over 3,000 such applications since the beginning of May.

**Mr. Cartwright:** To ask the Secretary of State for the Home Department (1) how many applications for political asylum in the United Kingdom he expects to be granted on the basis of his Department's backlog criteria;

(2) in what circumstances applications for political asylum in the United Kingdom are to be granted in order to reduce the current backlog of such cases and to release staff to deal with new applications.

**Mr. Renton:** Asylum applications continue to be decided under the criteria of the 1951 convention. There is no question of granting refugee status in cases which do not qualify under the convention in order to reduce the backlog of outstanding applications. Efforts are being made to reduce the backlog and staff are encouraged to identify and resolve more quickly through the grant of exceptional leave cases which do not qualify under the convention but in which outright refusal is likely to be inappropriate or impractical. Cases continue to be resolved on their individual merits and we can make no estimates of the likely outcomes.

**Mr. Cartwright:** To ask the Secretary of State for the Home Department how many applications for political

asylum in the United Kingdom are currently awaiting a decision; and how many of these have been delayed for 12 months or longer.

**Mr. Renton:** Information on the number of applications for refugee status in the United Kingdom awaiting a decision at the end of the year is published annually in Home Office Statistical Bulletin "Refugee Statistics, United Kingdom". The 1988 volume of this bulletin will be published next month. The latest available volume is for 1987 (Issue 16/88), a copy of which is in the Library. Of the estimate of a total of 8,300 applications recorded as awaiting a decision at the end of 1987, approximately 4,200 were recorded as outstanding for 12 months or more. However, these figures are maxima which overstate the position, because of under recording of decisions made earlier.

**Mr. Cartwright:** To ask the Secretary of State for the Home Department how many immigration officers are currently dealing with applications for political asylum in the United Kingdom; and what were the comparable figures one, three, five and 10 years previously.

**Mr. Renton:** The information centrally available does not distinguish the number of immigration officers who, as part of their duties, may currently be dealing with asylum applications, or might in the past have been so engaged. But the arrival of substantial numbers of Turkish asylum applications this year has significantly increased the demands on the resources of the immigration service.

## Immigration Appeals

**Mr. Wray:** To ask the Secretary of State for the Home Department what information he has as to the average length of time which immigration appeal cases in Scotland take to be prepared and presented.

**Mr. Renton:** The information is not available in the form requested. The time that it takes to hear an individual appeal varies greatly from case to case because of both the number of stages involved and the differing lengths of time that each stage can take. I am aware however that the time between the lodging of an appeal and the hearing commonly exceeds one year for cases heard in Scotland.

**Mr. Wray:** To ask the Secretary of State for the Home Department what new measures of support he is taking to help the United Kingdom Immigrants Advisory Service in Scotland to deal with immigration appeals.

**Mr. Renton:** The Home Office makes an annual grant-in-aid to the United Kingdom Immigrants Advisory Service, under section 23 of the Immigration Act 1971, as the basis for the provision of a nationwide service of advice and assistance to persons who have rights of appeal under the Act. The grant in 1988-89 was £1,007,000 and is reviewed annually. It is for the service to decide how to allocate these moneys to the various aspects of its work.

## C3 Division

**Mr. Mullin:** To ask the Secretary of State for the Home Department how many people are employed by the C3 Division and at what cost.

**Mr. John Patten:** Forty-eight people are currently employed in C3 Division of the Home Office at an annual cost of £756,000. Of these, 18 are employed in dealing with work associated with alleged miscarriages of justice and the exercise of the royal prerogative of mercy, at an annual cost of £275,500.

### Immigration Rules

**Mr. Madden:** To ask the Secretary of State for the Home Department whether he proposes to hold an inquiry into the leaking of the memorandum from G. N. Stadlen, of B2 division, dated 9 June headed "Immigration Rules Changes and DNA Announcement" including a draft letter to the Lord President for signature by the Home Secretary; and if he will make a statement.

**Mr. Hurd:** Yes: any suggestion that an unauthorised disclosure of information has occurred is investigated.

### Sinn Fein

**Mr. Dalyell:** To ask the Secretary of State for the Home Department what formal representations he has received from the British Broadcasting Corporation about the banning of the appearance of Sinn Fein on television and radio; and if he will make a statement.

**Mr. Renton:** None. When the directions were issued, the BBC and the IBA undertook to implement them, although they requested that the need for them should be kept under close review.

### Mr. Ning Hong Shan

**Mr. Mullin:** To ask the Secretary of State for the Home Department if a decision has been reached regarding the request for asylum by Mr. Ning Hong Shan; and if he will make a statement.

**Mr. Tim Renton:** The application is under consideration.

### Mr. Abbas Karbassian

**Mr. Nellist:** To ask the Secretary of State for the Home Department why his Department refused leave to remain for Mr. Abbas Karbassian of 14 Bromwich close, Ernesford Grange, Coventry, reference K296103; whether the criteria for the granting of indefinite leave to remain on the basis of length of residence in the United Kingdom have changed since his reply to the hon. Member for Islington, North (Mr. Corbyn) of 17 March 1986, *Official Report,* column *9;* and if he will make a statement.

**Mr. Renton:** Mr. Karbassian's application for leave to remain on the basis of his marriage to a British citizen was refused because the couple had subsequently separated. An earlier application to remain as a student was refused because the Secretary of State was not satisfied that Mr. Karbassian intended to leave the United Kingdom at the end of his studies. Mr. Karbassian's application for settlement on the basis of his lengthy residence in the United Kingdom was considered on its merits but it was decided not to exercise discretion in his favour.

The criteria for the grant of indefinite leave to remain on the basis of length of residence were set out more fully in the reply of 5 November 1987 at column *833* to a question from the hon. Member for Norwood (Mr. Fraser). They remain as stated.

### Broadcasting Licences

**Mr. Wray:** To ask the Secretary of State for the Home Department what response he is giving to representations against the proposed auction of broadcasting licences to the highest bidder and to calls for the protection of quality of television programmes.

**Mr. Renton:** The case for allocating television licences by competitive tender and the steps which we propose to preserve quality programming are set out in our White Paper "Broadcasting in the '90s: Competition, Choice and Quality". In the statement my right hon. Friend made to the House on 13 June on the future of commercial television at columns *710-15* he announced further ways in which quality would be safeguarded, notably by strengthening the quality threshold which all applicants for licences would have first to satisfy; by giving the Independent Television Commission power in exceptional circumstances not to accept the highest bid; and by requiring the successful applicant to post a substantial performance bond which would be liable to forfeiture if programme quality requirements are not met. Taken together these proposals represent substantial safeguards for the delivery of quality programmes.

### Media Supervision

**Mr. Wray:** To ask the Secretary of State for the Home Department whether he has any plans to establish an independent body composed of representatives of television producers, journalists, actors, musicians and playwrights to supervise quality control and anti-monopolistic practices in television and the press.

**Mr. Renton:** No.

### Passports (Chinese Nationals)

**Mr. Cox:** To ask the Secretary of State for the Home Department if he will consider his policy towards Chinese students and nationals whose passports may expire in the near future; and if he will make a statement.

**Mr. Renton:** Chinese nationals who, for good reason, are unable or unwilling to approach their own authorities for documentation, and who wish to travel may apply to the Home Office, Travel Document Section, Lunar house, Croydon CR9 2BY for a travel document.

### Work Permits

**Mr. Cox:** To ask the Secretary of State for the Home Department if he will make it his policy to look sympathetically at applications for work permits from Chinese students who are able to obtain employment towards the payment of their college fees and expenses; and if he will make a statement.

**Mr. Renton:** We will look sympathetically at any applications from Chinese students who, because of the situation in China, seek permission to take employment to help with their expenses.

## HOUSE OF COMMONS

### WEU

**Sir Russell Johnston:** To ask the Lord President of the Council if he will make available reports of plenary debates of the Western European Union in the Library and Vote Office on the day following the debate.

**Mr. Wakeham:** It is not possible to give this undertaking since the availability of these reports is not a matter under the control of the House. The Library and the Vote Office will make them available to hon. Members as soon as possible after their publication.

### THE ARTS

#### Public Libraries

**61. Mrs. Golding:** To ask the Minister for the Arts what information he has on the purchasing power of public libraries' expenditure on books over the past 10 years.

**Mr. Luce:** Information for the last 10 years is not available. In the 10 years from 1977-78 to 1986-87 public libraries expenditure on books fell by 1·7 per cent. in real terms, but it has increased by 14 per cent. between 1981-82 and 1986-87.

**66. Mr. Haynes:** To ask the Minister for the Arts how many public libraries are open for more than 45 hours a week.

**Mr. Luce:** In 1987-88, the most recent period for which statistics are available, returns from 98 authorities show that 630 service points in England were open for more than 45 hours per week.

#### Greater London Arts

**62. Mr. Tony Banks:** To ask the Minister for the Arts when he last met the chairman and director of Greater London Arts to discuss the future of arts administration in London.

**67. Mr. Chris Smith:** To ask the Minister for the Arts when he last met the chairman of Greater London Arts to discuss the future funding and administration of the arts in London.

**Mr. Luce:** I met the director of Greater London Arts at a sponsorship launch on 12 April.

#### Departmental Funding

**63. Mr. Jessel:** To ask the Minister for the Arts what have been the increases in the funding of his Department over the last five years, and those announced for future years.

**Mr. Luce:** This year my Department is spending £439 million, an increase of 63 per cent. over the corresponding cash programme for 1984-85. My plans are for expenditure of £450 million in 1990-91 and £480 million in 1991-92.

#### Theatres (London)

**64. Mr. Goodlad:** To ask the Minister for the Arts what information he has as to attendances at theatres in London.

**Mr. Luce:** According to the PSI publication "Cultural Trends" there were nearly 10 million paid admissions at theatres in London in 1987. This a 6 per cent. increase on 1986.

#### Disabled People (Access Arrangements)

**65. Mr. Greg Knight:** To ask the Minister for the Arts what steps he is taking to improve access for the disabled to arts venues.

**Mr. Luce:** On 20 December last year I announced a contribution of £150,000 towards a fund to improve access to arts venues for the disabled, to be set up by the Carnegie trust.

#### Mappa Mundi

**68. Mr. Colin Shepherd:** To ask the Minister for the Arts what representations he has received in the last four weeks as to the future of the Mappa Mundi.

**Mr. Luce:** I have received no representations as to the future of the Mappa Mundi in recent weeks. However, I wish the Dean and Chapter every success with their appeal to raise funds without resorting to the sale of the map. I understand that the Dean and Chapter have been in touch with the national heritage memorial fund to arrange a meeting to discuss the position.

#### Trade Balance

**69. Mr. Jack:** To ask the Minister for the Arts what assessment he has made of the contribution of the arts to Britain's overseas trade balance.

**Mr. Luce:** An assessment made by the Policy Studies Institute last year, using a broad definition of the arts, put overseas earnings in this field at £4 billion.

#### National Museums (Maintenance)

**70. Dr. Marek:** To ask the Minister for the Arts when he plans to meet the chairman of the Museums and Galleries Commission to discuss the repairs and maintenance needs of national museums.

**Mr. Luce:** I meet the chairman of the Museum and Galleries Commission quite frequently and on a wide range of subjects which have included matters raised in the Commission's May 1988 report on the national museums.

#### Merseyside Arts

**71. Mr. Wareing:** To ask the Minister for the Arts when he plans to meet the chairman of Merseyside Arts to discuss the future of arts administration on Merseyside.

**Mr. Luce:** I have no plans to do so.

#### Independent Museums

**72. Mr. Butler:** To ask the Minister for the Arts if he will make a statement on the development of the independent museum sector.

**Mr. Luce:** The independent museums sector represents over half of the 2,000 or so museums and galleries in the United Kingdom. Independent museums give great pleasure to the visiting public, and I am delighted to see their continued successful development.

## Museums and Historic Properties

**73. Mr. Simon Coombs:** To ask the Minister for the Arts what information he has as to visits to local museums and historic sites and houses in the most recent year for which he has information, and for the two previous years.

**Mr. Luce:** The Museums Association estimates that the number of visitors to museums and galleries in the United Kingdom increased from 73 million in 1986 to 80 million in 1988. This figures is expected to rise to 100 million during 1989, which has been designated Museums Year. The English Tourist Authority has estimated the number of visitors to historic properties as 55·5 million in 1986, 57·3 million in 1987 and 59 million in 1988.

## Theatre Museum

**Mr. Maclennan:** To ask the Minister for the Arts what discussions he has had with the director of the Victoria and Albert museum about the future of the theatre museum.

**Mr. Luce:** I have not had discussions with the director of the Victoria and Albert museum about the theatre museum, but I meet the chairman of the board of trustees and the director quite frequently when a wide range of issues is covered.

## NORTHERN IRELAND

### Census Questions

**Rev. Martin Smyth:** To ask the Secretary of State for Northern Ireland what representations have been made through the Anglo-Irish Intergovernmental conference regarding the inclusion of Irish language questions in the 1991 census.

**Mr. Tom King:** The Irish Government have indicated to us on a number of occasions in the conference that they would welcome the inclusion of a question on knowledge of the Irish language in the 1991 census, in line with the language questions asked elsewhere in the United Kingdom.

## TRADE AND INDUSTRY

### Insider Dealing

**Mr. Cousins:** To ask the Chancellor of the Duchy of Lancaster how many prima facie cases of insider dealing have been referred to his Department by the Stock Exchange insider dealing group.

**Mr. Maude:** About 180 cases of possible insider dealing offences have been referred by the Stock Exchange to my Department since insider dealing became a criminal offence in June 1980. Of those cases 76 have been referred since Royal Assent to the Financial Services Act 1986.

**Mr. Cousins:** To ask the Chancellor of the Duchy of Lancaster in how many cases of prima facie insider dealing prosecutions have resulted since the passing of the Financial Services Act.

**Mr. Maude:** Since the Financial Services Act 1986 received Royal Assent in November 1986 six prosecutions for insider dealing offences have been instituted and completed, and proceedings have begun in a further eight cases. Seven out of those 14 prosecutions followed reports from inspectors appointed under section 177 of the Financial Services Act.

**Mr. Cousins:** To ask the Chancellor of the Duchy of Lancaster in how many cases of prima facie insider deals the Government have appointed inspectors to investigate using their powers under the Financial Services Act.

**Mr. Maude:** Inspectors have been appointed under section 177 of the Financial Services Act 1986 to investigate 31 cases of possible insider dealing offences.

## China

**Mr. Foulkes:** To ask the Chancellor of the Duchy of Lancaster what is the total value of trade between the United Kingdom and China for 1988 and 1989 to the latest available date.

**Mr. Alan Clark:** United Kingdom trade with China in 1988 was valued at imports £443·7 million and exports £411·6 million.

In the period January to April 1989, the latest for which information is available, imports were £158·3 million and exports £140·7 million.

## Iraq

**Mrs. Clwyd:** To ask the Chancellor of the Duchy of Lancaster what changes have taken place in the provision of export credits to Iraq in the past year; what proposals he has to make further changes; and if he will make a statement.

**Mr. Alan Clark:** The United Kingdom/Iraq joint commission on trade and economic co-operation which was held in Baghdad in November 1988 resulted in a further £340 million of United Kingdom export credit support for Iraq. To date three loan agreements have been signed comprising:

> a £65 million buyer credit to finance a contract for four turbine generators for the Al-Shemal power station
> a £75 million line of credit for pharmaceutical and humanitarian products
> a £100 million line of credit for capital goods and projects

The balance of £100 million has not yet been allocated under any specific facility but will be used to finance United Kingdom capital goods and projects. No drawings have yet been made under the above loans.

There will be a further United Kingdom/Iraq joint commission in London later this year but it is too early to anticipate what further United Kingdom export credit facilities might be made available to Iraq for 1990.

### Business Development Consultancy Initiative

**Mr. McLeish:** To ask the Chancellor of the Duchy of Lancaster if he will give the number of applications *(a)* received and *(b)* approved for business development consultancy initiatives from 1 April 1988 to the most recent date for which information is available and *(c)* what was the total amount of expenditure involved in each of the regions of his Department, Scotland and Wales and *(d)* for assisted areas, urban programme areas and non-assisted areas.

**Mr. Newton:** In the period from 1 April 1988 to 31 May 1989 24,291 applications were received for the business development consultancy initiatives. In the same period 17,740 applications were approved for assisted consultancy. The Department's contribution to the cost of completed consultancies totalled £16·8 million. It is estimated that those consultancies not completed by 31 May 1989 will cost the Department £26·4 million. I am unable to provide a breakdown of expenditure between assisted areas, urban programme areas and non-assisted areas but 55·5 per cent. of applications approved for consultancy have been from assisted and urban programme areas. A breakdown of numbers and cost of consultancy projects for each DTI region and for Scotland and Wales is as follows:

| DTI Region/Country | (a) Number of applications received | (b) Number of applications approved for assisted consultancy | (c) DTI expenditure on completed consultancies (£ thousand) | (d) Estimated expenditure on outstanding consultancies (£ thousand) |
|---|---|---|---|---|
| North East | 1,194 | 924 | 784 | 1,315 |
| North West | 3,538 | 2,894 | 3,166 | 4,762 |
| Yorkshire and Humberside | 2,293 | 1,698 | 1,880 | 2,711 |
| West Midlands | 2,562 | 1,830 | 1,855 | 3,319 |
| East Midlands | 1,483 | 1,154 | 1,091 | 1,897 |
| South West | 2,335 | 1,434 | 1,069 | 2,112 |
| South East: | | | | |
| Cambridge | 1,893 | 1,097 | 766 | 1,567 |
| London | 2,929 | 2,066 | 1,694 | 2,070 |
| Reading | 1,433 | 1,098 | 823 | 1,220 |
| Reigate | 1,415 | 1,064 | 753 | 1,325 |
| Scotland | 1,789 | 1,475 | 1,908 | 2,463 |
| Wales | 1,427 | 1,006 | 1,106 | 1,613 |
| Total | 24,291 | 17,740 | 16,805 | 26,374 |

**Mr. McLeish:** To ask the Chancellor of the Duchy of Lancaster if he will list the consultancy firms involved in the business development consultancy initiative for each of the regions of his Department, Scotland and Wales.

**Mr. Newton:** It is not our practice to detail the consultancy firms used by scheme contractors to undertake enterprise initiative assisted consultancy projects. This is to avoid the risk of such a list being seen as a form of Government approval or endorsement, to the unfair disadvantage of practices no less competent but which for one reason or another are not associated with the scheme; and also to avoid the risk of consultancies being exposed to pressures which could compromise the independence and impartiality of their advice to clients.

**Mr. McLeish:** To ask the Chancellor of the Duchy of Lancaster if he will give the estimated expenditure in the business development consultancy initiative in each of the years 1988-89, 1989-90, 1990-91 and 1991-92.

**Mr. Newton:** We estimate that the total amount of expenditure on the business development consultancy initiatives in 1988-89 was £43·1 millions. The Estimates provision for 1989-90 is £91 millions. The level of provision for future years will depend upon public expenditure decisions yet to be taken: however, planned provision is £107 millions in 1990-91 and £109 millions in 1991-92.

### Bio-ethics

**Rev. Martin Smyth:** To ask the Chancellor of the Duchy of Lancaster what representation will attend the first symposium on bio-ethics in December from the United Kingdom.

**Mr. Mellor:** I have been asked to reply.

The United Kingdom will be invited to the Council of Europe's first symposium on bio-ethics to be held on 5-7 December 1989. No decision has yet been taken on who will attend on behalf of the United Kingdom. Participation is by invitation only.

**The Rev. Martin Smyth:** To ask the Chancellor of the Duchy of Lancaster if he will list in the *Official Report* all the members of the Council of Europe's ad-hoc committee of experts on bio-ethical issues together with the method by which they were appointed and the research disciplines from which they came.

**Mr. David Mellor:** I have been asked to reply.

The members of the Council of Europe's ad-hoc committee of experts on bioethics (CAHBI) are currently:

*Austria:* Dr. Renate Kausek

*Belgium:* M. Armand Andre *(Vice Chairman)*; Mme. Isabella Hamer

*Cyprus:* Mrs. Frosso Parrisiadou; M. Jorgen Falck Larsen; Mme. Linda Taudaz

*Denmark:* Mr. Ulrich Horst Petersen

*France:* M. Christian Byk; Mme. Colette Moyse

*Federal Republic of Germany:* Mrs. Helga Seibert

*Greece:* Mrs. Panagiota Dalla-Vorgia

*Ireland:* Dr. Niall Tierney

*Italy:* M. Umberto Bigozzi; M. Salvatore Puglisi

*Luxembourg:* M. Arsene Betz

*Malta:* Rev. Prof. Charles G. Vella

*Netherlands:* Mrs. Johanna H. W. Kits Nieuwenkamp

*Norway:* Mr. Kare Berg; Mrs. Trine Fernsjo; Mrs. Julie Skjaraasen; Mrs. Grete Gjertsen

*Portugal:* M. Luis Mendes Graca

*Spain:* Dr. Octavi Quintana-Trias

*Sweden:* Ms. Ann-Christin Filipsson

*Switzerland:* M. Pierre A. Widmer; M. Hansjakob Mueller; M. Franz Furger

*Turkey:* M. Turgay Yucel

*United Kingdom:* Dr. Jeremy S. Metters *(Chairman)*; Mr. Edwin Robert Moutrie.

Members are appointed by nomination of the member states of the Council of Europe. The research disciplines of the members are not known to Her Majesty's

Government. Detailed inquiries of this nature might more properly be addressed to the Council of Europe via the Parliamentary Assembly.

### Ulburghs Report

**Rev. Martin Smyth:** To ask the Chancellor of the Duchy of Lancaster what has been the response of the British Government to Resolution A.2-78/88 of the European Parliament on harmonisation of medico-ethical questions, the Ulburghs report.

**Mr. Mellor:** I have been asked to reply.

Resolution A.2-78/88 was adopted by the European Parliament on 12 September 1988 by the narrow margin of 82 in favour, 79 against and four abstentions. No proposals based upon the report have yet been submitted by the European Commission to the British Government for consideration.

### EC Recommendation 1100

**Rev. Martin Smyth:** To ask the Chancellor of the Duchy of Lancaster what has been the British Government's response to the Council of Europe Parliamentary Assembly Recommendation 1100.

**Mr. Mellor:** I have been asked to reply.

Recommendation 1100 of the Parliamentary Assembly is still being considered within the Council of Europe's internal consultative machinery and has not yet been submitted to Her Majesty's Government for their response.

### Rothley and Casini Reports

**Rev. Martin Smyth:** To ask the Chancellor of the Duchy of Lancaster what has been the response of the British Government to resolution A.2-327/88 of the European Parliament on genetic engineering, Rothley report, and resolution A.2-372/88 on artificial insemination, the Casini report.

**Mr. Mellor:** I have been asked to reply.

We do not consider that a response to these two resolutions—A.2-237/88 and A.2-372/88—would be appropriate at this juncture. We intend to introduce legislation during this current Parliament on human fertilisation and embryology, and there will be a free vote in Parliament on questions of embryo research.

## OVERSEAS DEVELOPMENT

### South America

**Mr. Sheerman:** To ask the Secretary of State for Foreign and Commonwealth Affairs if he will list the level of overseas aid to South America in each of the last 15 years.

**Mr. Chris Patten:** The information is as follows:

| Country | Year | | | | | | | | | | | | | | £ thousand |
|---|---|---|---|---|---|---|---|---|---|---|---|---|---|---|---|
|  | 1974 | 1975 | 1976 | 1977 | 1978 | 1979 | 1980 | 1981 | 1982 | 1983 | 1984 | 1985 | 1986 | 1987 | 1988 |
| Argentina | 124 | 124 | 61 | 24 | 15 | 5 | 30 | 2 | 2 | — | — | — | — | — | — |
| Bolivia | 353 | 376 | 620 | 1,471 | 1,062 | 888 | 1,158 | 1,052 | 988 | 1,199 | 1,182 | 1,421 | 1,953 | 1,748 | 2,953 |
| Brazil | 1,850 | 3,348 | 2,263 | 1,213 | 719 | 1,022 | 1,002 | 632 | 9,960 | 5,574 | 7,780 | 4,014 | 880 | 766 | 1,443 |
| Chile | 451 | 324 | 943 | 2,073 | 1,079 | 2,131 | 2,021 | 1,452 | 675 | 442 | 257 | 334 | 373 | 261 | 306 |
| Colombia | 902 | 2,552 | 1,312 | 1,229 | 863 | 1,242 | 848 | 765 | 617 | 635 | 460 | 838 | 1,018 | 762 | 1,822 |
| Ecuador | 718 | 1,195 | 4,838 | 2,037 | 1,795 | 1,897 | 945 | 762 | 1,046 | 783 | 916 | 909 | 836 | 2,560 | 1,514 |
| Falkland Islands | 1,179 | 1,376 | 1,493 | 1,115 | 2,121 | 915 | 1,015 | 1,058 | 4,025 | 9,053 | 6,016 | 10,700 | 10,252 | 8,165 | 4,257 |
| Guyana | 1,460 | 1,741 | 1,402 | 895 | 6,395 | 2,606 | 2,356 | 2,475 | 1,724 | 1,555 | 419 | 354 | 487 | 635 | 521 |
| Paraguay | 41 | 103 | 123 | 164 | 226 | 267 | 270 | 219 | 3,263 | 1,281 | 207 | 51 | 221 | 277 | 497 |
| Peru | 664 | 1,610 | 1,125 | 3,570 | 820 | 882 | 950 | 973 | 676 | 4,427 | 476 | 928 | 1,214 | 1,012 | 1,363 |
| Surinam | — | — | — | — | — | — | — | — | 1 | — | — | — | — | — | 11 |
| Uruguay | 28 | 24 | 43 | 39 | 27 | 35 | 37 | 9 | 11 | 16 | 14 | 7 | 13 | 38 | 18 |
| Venezuela | 112 | 48 | 7 | 6 | 4 | — | — | — | 2 | 3 | — | 1 | 10 | 24 | 10 |
| Unallocated | — | — | — | — | — | — | 15 | −11 | −239 | −327 | 25 | 34 | 56 | 51 | — |
| Total | 7,882 | 12,821 | 14,230 | 13,836 | 15,126 | 11,890 | 10,645 | 9,386 | 22,752 | 24,643 | 17,755 | 19,591 | 17,313 | 16,299 | 14,715 |

### Overseas Aid (Charities)

**Mr. Thurnham:** To ask the Secretary of State for Foreign and Commonwealth Affairs what proposals he has for an increased role for charities in the provision of overseas aid.

**Mr. Chris Patten:** The British voluntary agencies working in developing countries are independent charities who determine their own role. I have a high regard for their work; and I have increased the aid funds available for jointly funding their development projects by 43 per cent. to £16 million this year. I have also increased our support for the volunteer sending agencies by 20 per cent. to £13 million this year.

### Andean Countries

**Mr. Sheerman:** To ask the Secretary of State for Foreign and Commonwealth Affairs if he will list the level of overseas aid to the Andean group of countries in each of the last 15 years.

**Mr. Chris Patten:** The information is as follows:

£ thousand

| Country | 1974 | 1975 | 1976 | 1977 | 1978 | 1979 | 1980 | Year 1981 | 1982 | 1983 | 1984 | 1985 | 1986 | 1987 | 1988 |
|---|---|---|---|---|---|---|---|---|---|---|---|---|---|---|---|
| Bolivia | 353 | 376 | 620 | 1,471 | 1,062 | 888 | 1,158 | 1,052 | 988 | 1,199 | 1,182 | 1,421 | 1,953 | 1,748 | 2,953 |
| Chile[1] | 451 | 324 | 943 | — | — | — | — | — | — | — | — | — | — | — | — |
| Columbia | 902 | 2,552 | 1,312 | 1,229 | 863 | 1,242 | 848 | 765 | 617 | 635 | 460 | 838 | 1,018 | 762 | 1,822 |
| Ecuador | 718 | 1,195 | 4,838 | 2,037 | 1,795 | 1,897 | 945 | 762 | 1,046 | 783 | 916 | 909 | 836 | 2,560 | 1,514 |
| Peru | 664 | 1,610 | 1,125 | 3,570 | 820 | 882 | 950 | 973 | 676 | 4,427 | 476 | 928 | 1,214 | 1,012 | 1,363 |
| Venezuela | 112 | 48 | 7 | 6 | 4 | — | — | — | 2 | 3 | — | 1 | 10 | 24 | 10 |
| Total | 3,200 | 6,105 | 8,845 | 10,386 | 5,623 | 7,040 | 5,922 | 5,004 | 4,004 | 7,489 | 3,291 | 4,431 | 5,404 | 6,367 | 7,968 |

[1] Chile withdrew from the Andean Group in January 1977.

### Cambodia

**Mr. Wigley:** To ask the Secretary of State for Foreign and Commonwealth Affairs what representations he has received from Oxfam in relation to the situation in Cambodia.

**Mr. Chris Patten:** Over the past 12 months, I have received a number of representations from OXFAM on different aspects of United Kingdom aid policy towards Cambodia. I discussed Cambodia with OXFAM staff most recently on 8 June.

### Rain Forest

**Dr. David Clark:** To ask the Secretary of State for Foreign and Commonwealth Affairs what urgent action he proposes to take to protect the rain forests throughout the world; and if he will make a statement.

**Mr. Chris Patten:** I refer the hon. Member to the answer which my right hon. Friend the Prime Minister gave the hon. Member for Linlithgow (Mr. Dalyell) on 21 June, at column 148.

### Tibet (Technology)

**Mr. Livingstone:** To ask the Secretary of State for Foreign and Commonwealth Affairs if he will allocate moneys from the Overseas Development Administration for the funding of the appropriate technology for Tibetans.

**Mr. Chris Patten:** Her Majesty's Government have received no official request for the provision of appropriate technology for Tibetans.

### Aid (Iraq)

**Mrs. Clwyd:** To ask the Secretary of State for Foreign and Commonwealth Affairs what has been the total amount of aid provided to Iraq in each of the past two years; and what funds have been disbursed under the aid and trade provision for projects in Iraq since the ending of the Gulf war.

**Mr. Chris Patten:** No British bilateral aid, including funds from the Aid and Trade Provision, has been provided for Iraq for many years.

## EMPLOYMENT

### Employment Training Managers

**Mr. Tony Lloyd:** To ask the Secretary of State for Employment how his Department monitors the performance of employment training managers in terms of financial viability and efficiency.

**Mr. Nicholls:** Employment training managers are monitored in terms of financial viability under the financial appraisal and monitoring (FAM) procedures which have their origins in the recommendations of the 1984 Coopers and Lybrand report on financial controls for YTS and the community programme. The arrangements introduced for ET were modelled on those for YTS. The FAM system centres on *(a)* an annual financial viability assessment of the degree of risk which a provider represents to public money; *(b)* an appraisal of the providers' administrative and financial systems to ensure the proper handling of public money and the reasonableness of providers' financial claims; and *(c)* financial monitoring visits linked to the degree of risk.

**Mr. Tony Lloyd:** To ask the Secretary of State for Employment how his Department initially satisfies itself that a training manager is competent to run employment training.

**Mr. Nicholls:** Potential training managers are asked by the Department's area office to submit a formal training proposal outlining what experience and capability they have in operating as training providers. These proposals are appraised by the area office staff to ensure, so far as is practicable, that the organisation has the knowledge and professional ability to deliver training of the appropriate quality and has adequate resources including premises and equipment, to deliver it effectively.

**Mr. Tony Lloyd:** To ask the Secretary of State for Employment what percentage of training managers by Training Agency area are receiving subsidies.

**Mr. Nicholls:** In addition to the basic grant for employment training, training managers, a range of other grants is available to purchase training. No subsidies are offered to ET training managers.

**Mr. Tony Lloyd:** To ask the Secretary of State for Employment what subsidies are offered to ET training managers above the basic grant per trainee.

**Mr. Nicholls:** ET training managers do not receive subsidies. Grants are available to purchase training.

**Mr. Tony Lloyd:** To ask the Secretary of State for Employment what audit procedures the Training Agency undertakes with respect to ET managers.

**Mr. Nicholls:** Claims for training grants submitted by ET training managers are subject to financial checks both within Training Agency area offices and at the training managers' premises. Training managers' claims are also subject to audit by the Training Agency internal audit branch and the National Audit Office on a sample basis.

**Mr. Tony Lloyd:** To ask the Secretary of State for Employment how many training mangers have *(a)* withdrawn or *(b)* been withdrawn from employment training; and how many employment training places have been lost as a result.

**Mr. Nicholls:** The information requested could be provided only at disproportionate cost.

### Council for Social Aid (Manchester)

**Mr. Tony Lloyd:** To ask the Secretary of State for Employment what steps have been taken to ensure that confidential information on trainees, formerly with the Council for Social Aid, Manchester, will remain confidential following the transfer of this information to the liquidators.

**Mr. Nicholls:** Immediately after being notified that the company had ceased trading, the Training Agency took into safe custody the personal files of trainees, including their action plans.

**Mr. Tony Lloyd:** To ask the Secretary of State for Employment when the Training Agency last received audited accounts from the Council for Social Aid, Manchester.

**Mr. Nicholls:** Audited accounts from the Council for Social Aid were last received by the Training Agency in February 1989. These accounts related to the Council for Social Aid's community programme agency contract which ran from April 1987 to September 1988.

**Mr. Tony Lloyd:** To ask the Secretary of State for Employment how many places the Council for Social Aid, Manchester, originally contracted for, and how many employment training places were filled, by month from September 1988 until its demise in May 1989.

**Mr. Nicholls:** The Council for Social Aid originally contracted to provide 2,557 employment training places. The following table lists how many places were filled, by month, from September 1988.

| Month (1988-89) | Council for Social Aid Number filled places |
| --- | --- |
| September | 1,818 |
| October | 1,695 |
| November | 1,792 |
| December | 1,632 |
| January | 1,410 |
| February | 1,223 |
| March | 1,024 |
| April | 1,045 |
| May | 1,011 |

### Employment Training

**Mr. Tony Lloyd:** To ask the Secretary of State for Employment how many filled employment training places there are in the Greater Manchester area; and what percentage this represents of the original departmental projections.

**Mr. Nicholls:** At 16 June 1989, the latest date for which information is available, there were 9,300 people on employment training. In Greater Manchester this represents 47 per cent. of the total number of places originally contracted.

**Mr. Tony Lloyd:** To ask the Secretary of State for Employment how many training managers have reduced their original number of contracted employment training places *(a)* nationally and *(b)* by training agency area.

**Mr. Nicholls:** The information is not available in the form requested and can be provided only at disproportionate cost.

### C.V. Carpets, Batley

**Mr. Madden:** To ask the Secretary of State for Employment whether he has been notified by Coats Viyella of the closure of C. V. Carpets, Greenhill Mills, Batley; if he will estimate the cost to public funds of making the work force redundant; and what representations he has received concerning this closure.

**Mr. Nicholls:** Notifications of proposed redundancies under section 100 of the Employment Protection Act 1975 are confidential to my Department.

### TRANSPORT

### Road Traffic Studies

**Sir Barney Hayhoe:** To ask the Secretary of State for Transport whether traffic studies, funded by public funds, in recent years have revealed evidence linking increased road capacities with increased traffic and worsening traffic congestion; and whether he will make a statement.

**Mr. Peter Bottomley:** The Department is currently undertaking a feasibility study into whether a before and after study of an urban trunk road scheme could detect the size of various changes in travel patterns, such as generation of new trips, changes in destination of journey time, and changes in mode of travel.

We are all asking the independent standing advisory committee on trunk road assessment to review the evidence on these effects. The Department has not recently carried out any traffic studies specifically addressed at identifying the effects of increased road capacity on the level of traffic.

For all new trunk road schemes, the Department monitors actual traffic flow a year after opening, for the purpose of making comparisons with the scheme forecasts. The evidence from this monitoring supports the Department's assumption in traffic forecasting that the general inter-urban road improvements do not generate significant additional traffic. The main effect is on choice of route.

### Bridge Street (Hole)

**Mr. Cohen:** To ask the Secretary of State for Transport if he will take urgent steps to mend the hole at the north-west corner of the Bridge street/Victoria embankment junction, so as to remove the cause of pedestrians being splashed on emerging from or entering the pedestrian subway at that point.

**Mr. Bottomley:** These local roads are the responsibility of Westminster city council.

### Single Tracking

**Mr. Worthington:** To ask the Secretary of State for Transport if he will make a statement on the Monopolies and Mergers Commission inquiry into the running of British Rail's provincial services with regard to the issue of single tracking, with particular reference to the Westerton to Milngavie railway lines.

**Mr. Portillo:** My right hon. Friend will in due course present to Parliament British Rail's response to the report, along with the Government's observations. It would not be appropriate to comment on individual aspects of the report in advance of the Government's formal response.

**Mr. Worthington:** To ask the Secretary of State for Transport what action his Department is taking with regard to ScotRail's proposals to single track the railway line from Westerton to Milngavie.

**Mr. Portillo:** This is an operational matter for British Rail.

### Breath Tests

**Mr. Day:** To ask the Secretary of State for Transport what proportion of respondents favoured the introduction of random breath testing in the last public opinion survey on this subject carried out by his Department's Transport and Road Research Laboratory.

**Mr. Peter Bottomley:** A survey carried out for TRRL in March 1989 asked 750 respondents whether they were in favour of random breath testing being introduced to discourage drinking and driving. The results were:

|                          | *Percentage* |
|--------------------------|--------------|
| Strongly in favour       | 48           |
| In favour                | 29           |
| Undecided                | 10           |
| Against                  | 8            |
| Strongly against         | 2            |
| Don't know/No answer     | 2            |

This was part of a survey into attitudes to a wide variety of road safety counter-measures. It did not explain the implications of random breath testing. The results reflect the strength of public opinion against drinking and driving.

A summary of the results of this survey will be published later this year.

### British Rail (Complaints)

**Mr. David Porter:** To ask the Secretary of State for Transport how many complaints about the performance of British Rail he has received in the past two years; and how he has responded to the complaints.

**Mr. Michael Portillo:** The Department does not keep statistics by subject matter of the letters we receive from members of the public about rail services. Unless they raise wider policy issues that are properly a matter for the Government, complaints are usually referred either to the British Railways board, which is responsible for operating the railway, or to local transport users consultative committees, which exist to represent the views of all users and can often help in resolving particular problems.

### Motor Cycles

**Mr. David Porter:** To ask the Secretary of State for Transport if he intends to bring forward any proposals to control queue jumping by motor cycle riders; and if he will make a statement.

**Mr. Peter Bottomley:** There may be no fully effective way of controlling queue jumping by any class of travellers.

Queue jumping by motor cycle riders when unsafe is covered by the existing offences of careless or reckless driving. We have no proposals to make it a specific offence. Proposals have already been announced to introduce mandatory training of new riders before they are allowed to ride unsupervised. This training will include safe practice when riding on the road. In October a new more arduous driving test for motorcyclists will be introduced. The tester will follow the candidate on another motorcycle and will thus be more able to assess ability to ride safely in traffic.

### British Rail (Compensation)

**Mr. David Porter:** To ask the Secretary of State for Transport (1) if he will discuss with the Chairman of British Rail a voluntary scheme for compensating travellers for British Rail's failure to supply an agreed service, along the lines of British Telecom's voluntary scheme;

(2) if he will give consideration to introducing a statutory compensation scheme for cases where British Rail fails to deliver an agreed level of service.

**Mr. Portillo:** British Rail's conditions of carriage already allow for refunds to be considered in cases where timetabled connections cannot be made or where services have been altered, withdrawn or suspended for any reason. I have no present plans for legislation.

### British Rail (Privatisation)

**Mr. David Porter:** To ask the Secretary of State for Transport if he will make a statement on progress of discussions by his officials with interested parties on the privatisation of British Rail.

**Mr. Portillo:** The work which is currently being undertaken on the possible privatisation of British Rail has been discussed fully with British Rail. In addition a small number of representations has so far been received from interested organisations. My right hon. Friend expects to consult widely in due course if a decision is made to privatise.

## Crash Barriers

**Mr. David Porter:** To ask the Secretary of State for Transport what progress is being made on installing crash barriers on central reservations of dual carriageways; and what plans he has for such barriers on future dualling works.

**Mr. Peter Bottomley:** Substantial progress is being made.

It is the Department's policy to install central reserve safety fencing on all new dual carriageway schemes as part of the construction works.

## HGVs (Exhaust Emissions)

**Mr. David Porter:** To ask the Secretary of State for Transport what plans he has further to curb exhaust emissions from heavy goods vehicles; and if he will make a statement.

**Mr. Peter Bottomley:** We are urging the European Commission to bring forward the most stringent standards that are technically and economically feasible. A further strengthening of these standards and the addition of a particulate standard is now being discussed in Europe.

Regulations are being prepared to enforce, from 1 October 1990, Community standards on the emissions of carbon monoxide, oxides of nitrogen and hydrocarbons from new vehicles over 3·5 tonnes gross vehicle weight.

## Buses Monopolies

**Mr. Wray:** To ask the Secretary of State for Transport what steps he is taking to prevent the formation of buses monopolies in the United Kingdom.

**Mr. Portillo:** The Office of Fair Trading has the appropriate powers to investigate the formation of monopolies in the bus industry. I have made clear that, in giving consent to the sale of public transport companies, one of our main objectives is to promote fair and sustained competition in the bus industry. Local authorities have been advised to consult the Department of Transport at an early stage where a sale seems likely to result in one company gaining a dominant and substantially unchallenged position in the local market.

## Traffic Lights

**Mr. David Porter:** To ask the Secretary of State for Transport if he has carried out any assessment of the efficiency of the French traffic light system of having additional lights at car driver level, with a view to implementing such a system in the United Kingdom.

**Mr. Peter Bottomley:** The Department discusses issues relating to the safety and efficiency of traffic signals with its French counterpart. The operation of the United Kingdom system of traffic lights provides drivers with the same information as that of the French system. No assessment of the kind referred to has therefore been made.

## China (Contacts)

**Mr. Foulkes:** To ask the Secretary of State for Transport whether he has any plans to visit China; and whether any of his officials are involved in or planning contacts with, or visits to, China.

**Mr. Peter Bottomley:** All ministerial visits to and from China have been suspended. No visits to China by my officials are planned.

**Mr. Foulkes:** To ask the Secretary of State for Transport what information his Department has about current contacts or contracts with China in the transport field.

**Mr. Peter Bottomley:** These are commercial matters for the companies involved.

## Civil Aviation (Privatisation)

**Mr. Bill Walker:** To ask the Secretary of State for Transport what advice or direction he has given to the Civil Aviation Authority and National Air Traffic Services on competitive tendering and privatisation within their organisations.

**Mr. Peter Bottomley:** The authority is subject to the same guidelines and rules on procurement that apply to all nationalised industries. Some years ago the authority considered, at the Government's request, privatising its Highlands and Islands airports, but this did not prove to be feasible.

## ENVIRONMENT

### Football Membership Scheme

**Mr. Cohen:** To ask the Secretary of State for the Environment, pursuant to his reply, *Official Report*, 25 May, column *673*, whether he will seek to amend the Football Supporters Bill so that police, security services, Inland Revenue and Customs and Excise cannot obtain personal data from the football membership scheme for purposes unconnected with the operation of the scheme.

**Mr. Moynihan:** No. The Data Protection Registrar has advised that section 28(3) of the Data Protection Act 1984 provides for the disclosure of information where the data user concerned is satisfied that this is necessary for crime prevention or tax collection purposes. As I explained to the hon. Member on 25 May at column *673*, I cannot envisage circumstances in which the Football Membership Authority—as the data user—would be asked to disclose information about members of the national membership scheme for purposes unconnected with the scheme. I do not therefore see a case for amending the Football Spectators Bill as the hon. Member suggests.

### World Student Games

**Mr. Patnick:** To ask the Secretary of State for the Environment if he will give financial aid to the arena in Sheffield required for the world student games in 1991; and if he will reconsider the decision on the funding of Hyde park flats, Sheffield, to be used as student accommodation for the games.

**Mr. Trippier:** I have from the outset made it clear to Sheffield that the Government cannot provide any special additional funding for the world student games. I have said, however, that we are prepared to consider assisting though existing programmes any schemes which meet the normal programme criteria and provide good value for money.

We have been in close discussion with the promoters of the arena project in the lower Don valley and I am very hopeful that we shall be able to give the necessary support for the project to get under way. I have also recently agreed to consider a scheme for estate action funding of work on the Hyde park flats as part of a joint development programme involving the Housing Corporation and a private developer.

I am sure that both schemes would be a major boost to development in Sheffield and, as a by-product, would assist the city council's efforts in preparing for the world student games.

## Rating Reform

**Mr. Cohen:** To ask the Secretary of State for the Environment whether he will tabulate what a single person living in the London borough of Waltham Forest would pay *(a)* in community charge and *(b)* in a system of capital value rates plus local income tax paid in proportions of 80 to 20, respectively, if the person earned *(a)* £10,000, *(b)* £15,000, *(c)* £20,000, *(d)* £25,000 and *(e)* £30,000 and lived in (i) rented accommodation, (ii) property owned by that person worth £60,000, and (iii) property owned by that person worth £90,000, making the same assumptions as in his reply to the hon. Member for Hornsey and Wood Green (Sir H. Rossi) on 22 March *Official Report,* column 626.

**Mr. Gummer:** The information requested is provided in the table.

*Illustrative annual liability in Waltham Forest under a system of capital value rates combined with local income tax, 1988-89*

| Single persons earnings £ | (i) + (ii) Property Value £60,000 £ | (iii) Property Value £90,000 £ |
|---|---|---|
| *(a)* 10,000 | 665 | 945 |
| *(b)* 15,000 | 740 | 1,020 |
| *(c)* 20,000 | 810 | 1,090 |
| *(d)* 25,000 | 880 | 1,160 |
| *(e)* 30,000 | 950 | 1,230 |

The liability of a person in rented accommodation would be the same as for a person living in property owned by that person of the same value. The figures are based on the illustrative tax rates placed in the Library on 23 June 1988 and are for 1988-89. It is assumed that the person lives alone and has no entitlement to rebates. Taxable income is taken as earnings less £2,605, the single person's allowance, in each case. The illustrative 1988-89 community charge in Waltham Forest is £269.

## Land Register (Sites)

**Mr. Steen:** To ask the Secretary of State for the Environment how many homes he estimates could be built on the 7,900 sites currently on the Land Register.

**Sir Hal Miller:** To ask the Secretary of State for the Environment how many homes he estimates could be built on the 7,900 sites currently on the Land Register.

**Mr. Trippier:** It is not possible to estimate the number of homes that could in practice be built on such sites. At 31 May 1989, approximately 2,100 sites on the register had a planning indication for residential use.

## Lindane

**Mr. Graham Allen:** To ask the Secretary of State for the Environment if he will introduce controls on the use of Lindane.

**Mrs. Virginia Bottomley:** The Food and Environment Protection Act and the Control of Pesticides Regulations 1986 provide comprehensive controls over the sale, supply, storage, advertisement and use of pesticides, including wood preservatives. Products containing Lindane are currently permitted for agricultural and wood preservative use. It is an offence to use them in any way other than that stated on the label. The uses of Lindane are currently under review by the Advisory Committee on Pesticides.

Lindane is also present in some veterinary medicines used to control ectoparasites on animals. These are currently being reviewed as part of the overall review of veterinary medicines by the Ministry of Agriculture, Fisheries and Food in accordance with the requirements of the European Community.

## Local Authorities (Sports Facilities)

**Mr. Heddle:** To ask the Secretary of State for the Environment when he intends to lay the orders relating to the contracting out of local authority sports facilities.

**Mr. Moynihan:** Soon.

## National Parks (Planning Appeals)

**Mr. Ron Davies:** To ask the Secretary of State for the Environment what was the number of planning appeal decisions which were *(a)* allowed, *(b)* dismissed, *(c)* withdrawn and *(d)* undetermined in each of the English national parks in 1974, 1979 and 1984; and if he will express the numbers allowed and dismissed as a percentage of those determined.

**Mr. Chope:** The information available is given in the following table.

*Year: 1 April 1984—31 March 1985*

| National Park | Allowed Number | Allowed Per cent. | Dismissed Number | Dismissed Per cent. | Withdrawn |
|---|---|---|---|---|---|
| Peak District | 6 | 26·1 | 17 | 73·9 | 3 |
| Exmoor | 4 | 57·1 | 3 | 42·9 | 0 |
| Northumberland | 0 | — | 2 | 100·0 | 0 |
| Dartmoor | 6 | 18·8 | 26 | 81·2 | 2 |
| Lake District | 6 | 35·3 | 11 | 64·7 | 1 |
| Yorkshire Dales | 7 | 31·8 | 15 | 68·2 | 2 |
| North Yorkshire Moors | 8 | 28·6 | 20 | 71·4 | 3 |

## Planning Applications

**Mr. Stern:** To ask the Secretary of State for the Environment if he has any plans to allow potential developers to buy out potential objectors' rights to object in advance of a disputed planning application.

**Mr. Chope:** No. There are no proposals to change the fundamental basis of United Kingdom land-use planning under which planning applications must be determined on their merits having regard to all material considerations.

## Grappenhall Heys and Appleton Thorn

**Mr. Butler:** To ask the Secretary of State for the Environment (1) whether, in his consideration of the 7(1) development submissions for Grappenhall Heys and Appleton Thorn, he will take into account the importance of maintaining an adequate easement for the Shell pipeline traversing the area;

(2) whether, in his consideration of the 7(1) development submissions for Grappenhall Heys and Appleton Thorn, he will take into account the preservation of overflight paths for civilian light aircraft.

**Mr. Trippier:** In reaching a decision on these submissions I will take into account all material considerations.

## North Sea Pollution

**Mr. Greg Knight:** To ask the Secretary of State for the Environment what proportion of pollution in the North sea comes from Britain.

**Mr. Ridley:** Rivers are the most important source of contaminant substances in the sea and United Kingdom rivers generally account for only about 20 per cent. of contaminents in the North sea.

## London Assessment Studies

**Sir Barney Hayhoe:** To ask the Secretary of State for the Environment what advice or information has been supplied to his Department to those undertaking the London assessment studies.

**Mr. Ridley:** My Department has been kept in touch with the progress of the studies since their inception. Recent discussions with the Department of Transport have covered the inter-relationship between the studies and strategic planning guidance for London.

## Tyneside Enterprise Zone (Rates)

**Mr. Cousins:** To ask the Secretary of State for the Environment how much has been paid to *(a)* Newcastle and *(b)* Gateshead Council in respect of rates otherwise payable to them in respect of properties within the Tyneside enterprise zone in each year since the enterprise zone's declaration; and if he will distinguish between classes of property in each case.

**Mr. Trippier:** The amounts paid to Newcastle city council and Gateshead metropolitan borough council in respect of rate revenue forgone in each year are given in the following table. The payments cannot be broken down by class of property.

*Rate revenue foregone in Tyneside enterprise zone*

|  | Gateshead £ million | Newcastle £ million |
|---|---|---|
| 1981-82 | 0·9 | 0·5 |
| 1982-83 | 1·8 | 1·1 |
| 1983-84 | 2·0 | 1·0 |
| 1984-85 | 2·1 | 1·1 |
| 1985-86 | 2·6 | 1·4 |
| 1986-87 | 5·5 | 1·4 |
| 1987-88 | 7·8 | 1·3 |
| 1988-89 | 9·1 | 1·4 |

## Water Meters

**Mr. Churchill:** To ask the Secretary of State for the Environment, further to his reply to the hon. Member for Davyhulme of 6 March, what is his best estimate of *(a)* the average cost per household and *(b)* the overall cost of installing individual water meters in each dwelling in England and Wales.

**Mr. Howard:** The programme of installing meters in the large-scale metering trials on the Isle of Wight is not expected to be completed until the end of March 1990. So it is still too early to draw any reliable conclusions on the cost of installing meters on a wide scale in England and Wales which will depend on a number of factors including the number of joint supplies and the siting of meters.

## Water Charges

**Mr. Churchill:** To ask the Secretary of State for the Environment what consideration has been given to the imposition of a standard per capita charge in respect of domestic water supplies, analogous to the community charge.

**Mr. Howard:** It will be for each of the new water services companies to decide what method of charging to adopt as a replacement for rateable value-based charges. Metering and a flat rate charge, possibly with extra charges for hose pipes and sprinklers, are the main options currently being considered by the industry.

**Mr. Churchill:** To ask the Secretary of State for the Environment what estimate he has made of the cost of water to the average domestic consumer in England and Wales in the current year, assuming that water undertakings had already been privatised and metering of individual households had been introduced.

**Mr. Howard:** None. It remains to be seen what efficiency savings the privatised companies can achieve over time and it is too early to assess the cost and long-term benefits of large-scale metering.

**Mr. Churchill:** To ask the Secretary of State for the Environment what plans he has to introduce rebates following water privatisation to assist low-income families with their water bills; and what estimate he has made of this as a charge on public funds.

**Mr. Howard:** There are no plans to introduce water charge rebates. Water undertakers operate budget payment plans to help customers pay their bills and the proposed conditions of appointment for the new companies will give additional encouragement to this practice. Income support is the appropriate way of helping those on low incomes to meet their outgoings, including water charges.

## Environment-friendly Products

**Mr. Tredinnick:** To ask the Secretary of State for the Environment whether he proposes to introduce a green label scheme for products which are friendly to the environment; and what assessment he has made of the extent to which such a scheme would encourage consumers to buy such products and organically grown food.

**Mrs. Virginia Bottomley:** We have no present plans to introduce a national scheme of environmental labelling, although we are keeping the idea under review in the light of views expressed by consumers, retailers and producers. We welcome efforts by producers and retailers to give consumers information about the environmental effect of products. The impact of any national scheme on consumers' purchasing decisions would depend, among other things, on its scope. A system of environmental labelling—the Blue Angel scheme—has operated in the Federal Republic of Germany since 1978, but food products are excluded from its scope. As for organically grown food, the United Kingdom Register of Organic Food Standards, set up at the instigation of my right hon. Friend the Minister of Agriculture, Fisheries and Food, announced on 2 May national standards and a national symbol relating to the production of organic foods.

## Rent Arrears

**Mr. Patnick:** To ask the Secretary of State for the Environment what arrangements he proposes for the financial management by local authorities of their arrears of rents and other income; and if he will make a statement.

**Mr. Gummer:** The Local Government and Housing Bill provides that from 1 April 1990 local authorities will be able to cover their arrears of rents and other income by borrowing for six months after the end of the year in which the arrears arose. Having carefully considered the representations of the local authority associations, my right hon. Friends the Secretary of State and the Secretary of State for Wales now propose to extend this period to 12 months, but thereafter authorities must make provision in their budgets for any arrears remaining outstanding. We also propose that housing rent arrears will fall within the ring-fenced housing revenue account, and hence if not collected within the 12-month period will have to be paid for by the other tenants.

For the transition we propose that housing rent arrears outstanding at 31 March 1990 should be dealt with outside the ring-fenced HRA and hence if uncollected will be a charge on community chargepayers. We recognise that if these arrangements were immediately applied in full to those few authorities which have irresponsibly allowed their arrears to escalate to very high levels, this could put very great burdens on their chargepayers. Accordingly, we are also proposing that an authority with high outstanding arrears at 31 March 1990 may apply to my right hon. Friends to enable them to spread over three to five years any budgetary provision for writing off these arrears.

We intend to bring forward in another place appropriate amendments to the Local Government and Housing Bill to give effect to these proposals.

It is each authority's responsibility to collect efficiently the sums due to it. We believe that our proposals, including the transitional arrangements, are fair to housing tenants and chargepayers, and will mean that in future authorities in both England and Wales have greater incentives for efficient collection of their income.

## Housing Management

**Mr. Matthew Taylor:** To ask the Secretary of State for the Environment whether his Department has, during the last five years, including the current financial year, ever awarded less than a full year's funding, excluding start-up costs, under its grant-making powers contained in section 16 of the Housing and Planning Act 1986 and section 73 of the Housing Act 1985.

**Mr. Trippier:** Yes. In 1987-88, the first year in which grants under section 16 were available, they were awarded for the latter part of that year. In 1988-89, some section 16 grants were for less than a full year. In the period in question, with the exception of the current year, grants under section 73 have all been for a full year.

## Empty Council Properties

**Mr. Soley:** To ask the Secretary of State for the Environment (1) how many local authority properties have been vacant for *(a)* less than six months and *(b)* more than six months in (i) Greater Manchester metropolitan county, (ii) Westminster, (iii) Suffolk, Coastal and (iv) the Isles of Scilly;

(2) if he will list the numbers of local authority properties which have been empty *(a)* for up to a year and *(b)* for more than a year in (i) Greater Manchester metropolitan county, (ii) Westminster, (iii) Suffolk, Coastal and (iv) the Isles of Scilly.

**Mr. David Trippier** *[holding answer 19 June 1989]:* Based on the information provided by the authorities in their housing investment programme returns, HIP1 for April 1988 the figures are as follows:

*Local authority empty dwellings at April 1988*

| | Six months or less | More than six months | Number of dwellings empty for: All empty dwellings | A year or less | More than a year | All empty dwellings |
|---|---|---|---|---|---|---|
| Greater Manchester metropolitan council[1] | 8,716 | 3,547 | 12,263 | 10,471 | 1,792 | 12,263 |
| Westminster | 332 | 561 | 893 | 535 | 358 | 893 |
| Suffolk Coastal | 70 | 12 | 82 | 81 | 1 | 82 |
| Isles of Scilly | 1 | 0 | 1 | 1 | 0 | 1 |

[1] Comprises the 10 metropolitan districts of Bolton, Bury, Manchester, Oldham, Rochdale, Salford, Stockport, Thameside, Trafford and Wigan.

### Aldrin and Dialdrin

**Mr. Hardy:** To ask the Secretary of State for the Environment what advice he is now giving about the continuing use of aldrin and dialdrin.

**Mrs. Virginia Bottomley** [*holding answer 20 June 1989*]: Aldrin and Dialdrin can no longer be legally supplied or used.

### Property Revaluation

**Dr. Cunningham:** To ask the Secretary of State for the Environment when he proposes to *(a)* announce the special provisions for non-domestic rating from 1990 onwards, following his consultation paper on the effects of revaluation of non-domestic property, and *(b)* inform individual non-domestic ratepayers of the new rateable values of their properties from 1 April 1990 following the revaluation of non-domestic property; and if he will make a statement.

**Mr. Ridley** [*holding answer 21 June 1989*]: I shall announce the Government's final proposals for phasing in the effect of the uniform business rate and the non-domestic revaluation as soon as we have completed our consideration of the responses to the consultation paper.

The Valuation Office will deposit with charging authorities draft lists showing new rateable values by 31 December 1989.

### Public Works Contracts

**Dr. Cunningham:** To ask the Secretary of State for the Environment if he will seek to amend section 17 of the Local Government Act 1988 to co-ordinate procedures for the award of public works contracts as set out in the European Community draft directive on public works contracts (COM(89)141); and if he will make a statement.

**Mr. Ridley** [*holding answer 22 June 1989*]: The implications of the agreement reached in the internal market council on 14 June on a directive to amend the EC public works directive are currently being examined, but it would not appear at this stage that an amendment to section 17 of the Local Government Act 1988 is required.

### Community Charge

**Dr. Cunningham:** To ask the Secretary of State for the Environment what is his estimate of the level of community charge for spending at needs assessment which would apply in 1989-90 if the proposed local government finance system were in operation; and what assumptions are made to arrive at that answer.

**Mr. Ridley** [*holding answer 22 June 1989*]: The estimate is £240 per adult. This figure is calculated by deducting rate support grant, and the assumed yield of non-domestic rates from total grant-related expenditure, leaving the amount to be raised by the community charge. This figure underlay the information placed in the Library on 1 March.

### Water and Sewerage

**Mr. Tim Boswell:** To ask the Secretary of State for the Environment when he intends to publish a Model Instrument of Appointment under the Water Bill for the water and sewerage undertakers.

**Mr. Howard** [*pursuant to his reply, 20 December 1988, c. 195*]: I am today placing copies of the latest draft of the model instrument of appointment for water and sewerage undertakers in the Library of both Houses, together with copies of a note of the main changes since the December model, also in the Library, and an explanatory note on interim determination of K, condition B, part IV.

## ENERGY

### Greenhouse Effect

7. **Mr. Wallace:** To ask the Secretary of State for Energy what assessment he has made of the effect of the price of carbon fuels on the production of greenhouse gases and the implications for Government policy.

**Mr. Parkinson:** Discussion of the problem of global warming is proceeding at international level. The effect of changes in the price of carbon fuels depends on the particular fuel considered, the way in which it is used and the availability of alternatives.

44. **Dr. Goodson-Wickes:** To ask the Secretary of State for Energy what is his estimate of the quantities of greenhouse gases which would be released into the atmosphere if all the United Kingdom's current nuclear electricity generation was replaced by coal-fired stations.

**Mr. Michael Spicer:** If the electricity that was generated by nuclear power in the United Kingdom in 1987 had been generated by fossil fuel power stations an estimated additional 45 million tonnes of carbon dioxide would have been released into the atmosphere.

**Mr. Win Griffiths:** To ask the Secretary of State for Energy what potential he has identified for the reduction of the generation of greenhouse gases via improved energy efficiency.

**Mr. Peter Morrison:** In addition to the continuing work of the Energy Efficiency Office to identify and bring to the attention of users cost-effective energy efficiency measures, my Department is making an assessment of the potential for further reduction of greenhouse gases via improved energy efficiency in the context of the work of the intergovernmental panel on climate change and of the European Community's energy programme. Energy efficiency is likely to be only one element of any response to the threat of climate change; it will require a combination of technologies and other measures to meet the challenge posed by $CO_2$ and other greenhouse gases.

### Exploration Drilling

15. **Sir Geoffrey Johnson Smith:** To ask the Secretary of State for Energy what is the level of exploration drilling for 1989, and what were the comparable figures in the two previous years.

**Mr. Peter Morrison:** Fifty-two exploration wells, of which eight are onshore, had been started by mid-June this year. This figure is already greater than that for the first halves of 1988 and 1987 when 40 and 36 wells were drilled respectively.

## Central Electricity Generating Board

16. **Mr. Patchett:** To ask the Secretary of State for Energy when he next expects to meet the chairman of the Central Electricity Generating Board; and what matters he expects to discuss.

**Mr. Parkinson:** I meet the chairman of the Central Electricity Generating Board whenever that is necessary to discuss matters of common interest.

## Energy Efficiency

18. **Mr. Tony Banks:** To ask the Secretary of State for Energy what incentives are made available through his Department for energy efficiency schemes.

**Mr. Peter Morrison:** The programmes and initiatives of the Energy Efficiency Office are all designed to draw to the attention of energy users the financial and other benefits of cost-effective energy efficiency measures.

## Energy Efficiency

28. **Ms. Quin:** To ask the Secretary of State for Energy whether he has proposals to devote more time and resources to promoting energy efficiency and conservation.

**Mr. Peter Morrison:** The Energy Efficiency Office will continue to promote energy efficiency vigorously. Furthermore, the Government's proposals for electricity privatisation will break new ground in promoting efficiency both within the industry and with consumers. Arrangements have also been agreed for close co-operation between the EEO and the Office of Electricity Regulation.

29. **Mr. Martlew:** To ask the Secretary of State for Energy what plans he has to encourage the use of energy-efficient electric appliances.

**Mr. Peter Morrison:** Manufacturers and consumer associations already publish energy consumption data for electrical appliances. My Energy Efficiency Office is considering how best to publish further information in order to draw attention to the energy consumption of appliances and thereby promote the selection of the most efficient.

42. **Mr. McAvoy:** To ask the Secretary of State for Energy whether his Department has assessed the effectiveness of domestic and commercial electrical appliance efficiency standards such as those recently introduced in the United States of America.

**Mr. Peter Morrison:** My Energy Efficiency Office will be assessing the applicability of standards as part of a general survey of the energy efficiency of electrical appliances in the United Kingdom and elsewhere.

## Electricity (Carbon Dioxide Emissions)

19. **Mr. Rost:** To ask the Secretary of State for Energy if he has any plans to bring forward amendments to the Electricity Bill, strengthening the obligation to promote energy efficiency in the supply and use of electricity, as a contribution to the reduction of $CO_2$ release.

**Mr. Parkinson:** The Government are fully committed to energy efficiency. The Electricity Bill breaks new ground in promoting energy efficiency both within the industry and by those who use electricity.

## North Sea Oil

20. **Mr. Hind:** To ask the Secretary of State for Energy how many jobs are supported by the North sea oil industry; and what number are based in *(a)* Scotland and *(b)* the north-east.

**Mr. Peter Morrison:** The Department of Employment estimated that 25,400 persons were directly employed in the oil and gas industry in June 1989. There are no official figures on the much larger total number of jobs supported by the North sea oil industry.

## AGR Fuel Rods

21. **Mr. Frank Cook:** To ask the Secretary of State for Energy what evidence he has that corroded AGR fuel rods stored at nuclear sites are not creating a public safety hazard.

**Mr. Michael Spicer:** The storage of AGR fuel rods at power stations is subject to stringent safety checks by the nuclear installations inspectorate which is satisfied that these arrangements are fully adequate.

31. **Mr. Menzies Campbell:** To ask the Secretary of State for Energy whether he has received any proposals for investment for the construction of any dry storage bunkers for spent nuclear fuel rods.

**Mr. Michael Spicer:** I am aware of the electricity industry's interest in constructing a dry buffer store for spent AGR fuel at Heysham. I understand that the industry is currently carrying out site investigations and has yet to submit a planning application for the dry store.

## Coal Privatisation

22. **Mr. Gow:** To ask the Secretary of State for Energy when he expects to complete the privatisation of the coal industry.

**Mr. Parkinson:** We intend to privatise the coal industry as soon as possible after the next general election. The precise timing will depend on the decisions reached on the future structure of the industry and the terms under which operators will be able to mine coal.

## British Coal (Electricity Purchases)

23. **Mr. Hardy:** To ask the Secretary of State for Energy what is his latest estimate of the tonnage level of purchases from British Coal by *(a)* National Power and *(b)* Power Gen in the calendar year 1990.

**Mr. Parkinson:** My Department makes no such estimates. This is a matter for negotiation between British Coal and the generators.

## Hinkley Point C Inquiry

24. **Mr. Stern:** To ask the Secretary of State for Energy what is the total cost to public funds, to the latest available date, of the Hinkley C inquiry.

**Mr. Michael Spicer:** There is no net cost to public funds of running the Hinkley Point C public inquiry, because all such costs are either met directly by the CEGB or recovered from it.

**Mr. Flynn:** To ask the Secretary of State for Energy if his Department was consulted by the Central Electricity

Generating Board in the preparation of the reply by Mr. R. J. Tivey to the Hinkley C inquiry secretariat on plutonium accounting dated 25 April 1989, inquiry code number S 3481 part 2.

**Mr. Michael Spicer:** Officials in my Department were aware of the terms of Mr. Tivey's letter.

### Power Plant Construction

25. **Ms. Mowlam:** To ask the Secretary of State for Energy what information he has on the power plant construction projects planned by the private sector.

**Mr. Michael Spicer:** My Department is aware of some 20 proposed private generation projects with a total capacity of around 7 GW. Details of individual projects are commercially confidential until companies announce them.

### Nuclear Power Stations (Decommissioning)

26. **Mr. Batiste:** To ask the Secretary of State for Energy what would be *(a)* the total cost and *(b)* the effect on jobs of decommissioning all United Kingdom nuclear power stations by the year 2000.

**Mr. Michael Spicer:** No estimate has been made of the total cost or the effect on jobs of decommissioning all United Kingdom nuclear power stations by the year 2000. Although some existing nuclear power stations will be taken out of service by the year 2000, many will continue to operate well into the next century, as will those now under construction or planned. After the existing nuclear power stations are taken out of service the power station operators propose to delay the final stage of decommissioning for a period of the order of 100 years to take the benefit of the process of radioactive decay in the reactor core.

### Vector Fuel (Sellafield)

27. **Mr. Alan W. Williams:** To ask the Secretary of State for Energy if he will make a statement on the backlog of spent advanced gas-cooled vector fuel at Sellafield, the corrosion problems being encountered and the implications for electricity supplies in the 1990s.

**Mr. Michael Spicer:** British Nuclear Fuels plc has ample pond space at Sellafield to receive the projected quantities of deliveries of spent AGR fuel from the home generating boards and their successors. BNFL's extensive research into the storage of AGR fuel under water suggests that, for fuel maintained in the correct water chemistry, no significant corrosion will occur for at least 10 years, and possibly longer.

### Office of Electricity Regulation

30. **Ms. Armstrong:** To ask the Secretary of State for Energy what guidance he has given to the director general-designate of the Office of Electricity Regulation on the best means of defending the interest of consumers.

**Mr. Michael Spicer:** The Electricity Bill sets out the Director General of Electricity Supply's duties in relation to the protection of consumers' interests. It will create many new rights for the consumer, including an improved right to an electricity supply, protection for consumers who get their electricity from a landlord, protection for the elderly and disabled, help for those having difficulty paying bills and a new system of guaranteed standards of performance with automatic compensation for failures to meet these standards. The director general will have a statutory duty to protect the interests of the consumer and the new regional consumers committees will provide him with lay advice on consumer issues.

**Mr. Murphy:** To ask the Secretary of State for Energy what guidance he has given to the director general-designate of the Office of Electricity Regulation on the regulator's independence from political interference.

**Mr. Parkinson:** The director general's powers and duties are set out clearly in the Electricity Bill. The Government believe that Professor Littlechild will be a strong, effective and independent regulator.

### Pressurised Water Reactors

32. **Mr. Flynn:** To ask the Secretary of State for Energy what is his latest estimate of the number of pressurised water reactor nuclear power stations in the small family which the Central Electricity Generating Board intends to build.

**Mr. Michael Spicer:** I understand that it is the CEGB's wish that the small family should consist of Sizewell B, which is currently under construction, and Hinkley Point C, Wylfa B and Sizewell C, in respect of which they have made applications for my right hon. Friend's consent.

36. **Mr. Matthew Taylor:** To ask the Secretary of State for Energy what is the number of pressurised water reactors which he expects to be in operation in the United Kingdom by 2010.

**Mr. Michael Spicer:** Decisions to apply for consent to construct new power stations are a matter for the electricity supply industry. So far my right hon. Friend has received applications for his consent to the construction of a further three PWR nuclear power stations which are similar in design to that being constructed at Sizewell B.

### Combined Heat and Power

33. **Mr. Clelland:** To ask the Secretary of State for Energy, when he expects the first full-scale combined heat and power project to be commissioned in the United Kingdom.

**Mr. Peter Morrison:** Full-scale combined heat and power plants have been operated successfully by United Kingdom industry for many years.

My Department has been active in promoting novel applications of CHP industry and commerce through its energy efficiency demonstration scheme where 25 projects have been supported. The Government have also encouraged the economic development of urban combined heat and power/district heating schemes under its lead city programme and contributed towards studies in Belfast, Edinburgh and Leicester. Other work to examine the feasibility of major CHP/DH schemes and to develop proposals has been taken forward without Government support. In addition to the lead city studies and subsequent development of the Leicester scheme, my Department is aware of work being done by groups in Newcastle, Sheffield and south-east London. The commissioning date of new schemes is, however, a commercial matter for the promoters.

The Government are also taking measures under the provisions of the Electricity Bill to enable CHP operators to compete with the established utilities. In this regard we are giving licensed CHP operators power to break streets to lay cables and heat mains.

### British Coal

34. **Mr. Janner:** To ask the Secretary of State for Energy when he last met the chairman of British Coal; and what matters were discussed.

**Mr. Michael Spicer:** My right hon. Friend and I meet the chairman of British Coal regularly to discuss all aspects of the coal industry.

### Electricity Privatisation

35. **Mr Meale:** To ask the Secretary of State for Energy what is the total cost incurred to date by his Department on advice on financial aspects of the privatisation of the electricity supply industry.

52. **Mr. Bill Michie:** To ask the Secretary of State for Energy if he will state the total cost incurred to date by his Department on advice on legal aspects of the privatisation of the electricity supply industry.

**Mr. Michael Spicer:** The total cost to my Department of all advisers working on electricity privatisation amounted to £0·8 million in 1987-88 and £5·5 million in 1988-89. In addition, a provision of £26·5 million has been sought to cover relevant expenses in 1989-90. More detailed expenditure surrounding contracts of advisers working on electricity privatisation is commercially confidential.

45. **Mr. Cummings:** To ask the Secretary of State for Energy what is his latest estimate of the advertising costs of privatising the electricity supply industry in *(a)* the current and *(b)* next financial year.

**Mr. Michael Spicer:** I refer the hon. Member to the answer I gave to the hon. Member for Cynon Valley (Mrs. Clwyd) earlier today.

48. **Mrs. Currie:** To ask the Secretary of State for Energy what assessment he has made of the expected level of competition following the privatisation of the electricity supply industry.

**Mr. Michael Spicer:** The new structure for the electricity industry will introduce competition into generation and supply and will provide an environment in which more will develop.

For example, the generation market will include National Power, Power Gen, supplies from Scotland and France, and existing and potential independent generators. We are currently aware of about 20 proposed independent generation projects. The substantial requirement for new generation capacity in the next 10 years will provide further opportunities for competition.

53. **Mr. Buckley:** To ask the Secretary of State for Energy whether he has reassessed his view of 6 March 1988 that the Government's plans for electricity will cut electricity bills.

**Mr. Michael Spicer:** Nothing has changed my view that privatisation will mean that prices will be lower than if electricity remains nationalised.

### Spent Nuclear Fuel (Sellafield)

37. **Mr. Malcolm Bruce:** To ask the Secretary of State for Energy what is the most recent assessment made by the nuclear installations inspectorate of storage facilities for spent fuel at Sellafield.

**Mr. Michael Spicer:** All the storage facilities for spent fuel at Sellafield are subject to constant review and assessment by the Health and Safety Executive's nuclear installations inspectorate as part of the routine inspections which it carries out.

### Gas-powered Turbines

38. **Mr. Hayward:** To ask the Secretary of State for Energy how many projects his Department is aware of involving electricity generation from gas-powered turbines.

**Mr. Michael Spicer:** Almost all the major independent projects known to my Department are proposing to use gas-powered turbines. In addition, the National Power and Power Gen divisions of the CEGB has each recently applied for my consent to construct two gas-fired stations.

### Fossil Fuel Combustion Tax

39. **Mr. Lofthouse:** To ask the Secretary of State for Energy what recent discussions he has had on proposals to levy a fossil fuel combustion tax.

**Mr. Michael Spicer:** The Government have no proposals for a tax on the use of fossil fuel.

### National Power (Contracts)

40. **Dr. Moonie:** To ask the Secretary of State for Energy what provision he is making for National Power to renegotiate contracts signed with British Nuclear Fuels plc before electricity privatisation.

**Mr. Michael Spicer:** The CEGB is currently in discussion with BNFL concerning contracts for fuel services which will continue post privatisation and will take account of the powers that the Government are seeking under clause 93 of the Electricity Bill. The Government's aim is that these contracts should be fair as between BNFL and the electricity supply industry.

### Coal Production

41. **Mr. Michael Brown:** To ask the Secretary of State for Energy what is British Coal's record of productivity in coal production since 1985; and what information he has on comparable figures for other major international coal producers.

**Mr. Michael Spicer:** British Coal's productivity rose by over 30 per cent. from 2·72 tonnes per manshift in 1985-86 to 3·62 tonnes in 1987-88. In Australia productivity rose from 12·32 tonnes in 1984-85 to 13·96 tonnes in 1986-87 (the latest period for which figures are available), a rise of 13 per cent., and in the United States of America productivity (measured in short tons) rose from 14·69 to 18·18 tons between the calendar years 1985 to 1987, a rise of 23 per cent. Since then, British Coal's productivity has increased further to 4·14 tonnes per manshift in 1988-89; I understand that there have also been substantial productivity gains in Australia and the United States of America since 1987.

## Nuclear Agencies (Memorandum of Understanding)

**43. Mr. Dykes:** To ask the Secretary of State for Energy if he will make a statement on the joint memorandum of understanding signed by the World Association of Nuclear Operators and the International Atomic Energy Agency on 6 June.

**Mr. Michael Spicer:** A joint memorandum of understanding between the World Association of Nuclear Operators (WANO), and the International Atomic Energy Agency (IAEA) was signed at the agency's headquarters in Vienna on 6 June. The agreement was signed by Lord Marshall of Goring, who is chairman of WANO's governing board, and Dr. Hans Blix, Director General of the IAEA. The memorandum provides for the open exchange of information covering technical reports and reviews of operational experience, as well as extending to participation in meetings of mutual benefit to both organisations.

## Longannet (Output)

**46. Mr. Douglas:** To ask the Secretary of State for Energy if he will make a statement on the current state of negotiations between British Coal and the South of Scotland electricity board relating to output from the Longannet complex.

**Mr. Michael Spicer:** The Government have made it quite clear that they regard the negotiations between British Coal and the South of Scotland electricity board as a commercial matter for the two parties, but we see no reason why a mutually satisfactory settlement cannot be reached. In the meantime, I understand that the SSEB is taking supplies from British Coal at a rate of 2 million tonnes a year.

## Sellafield (Storage Ponds)

**47. Mr. Kirkwood:** To ask the Secretary of State for Energy what proposals for the development of storage ponds at Sellafield he has received from British Nuclear Fuels plc.

**Mr. Michael Spicer:** I have received no such proposals. British Nuclear Fuels plc has ample storage capacity at Sellafield.

## Coal-fired Electricity Generation

**49. Mr. Patrick Thompson:** To ask the Secretary of State for Energy what level of thermal efficiency is currently being achieved in coal-fired electricity generation.

**Mr. Michael Spicer:** I am advised that the thermal efficiency of the CEGB's coal-fired power stations for 1988-89 was 35·52 per cent.

## Plutonium

**50. Mr. Simon Hughes:** To ask the Secretary of State for Energy what is his policy for the continuation of civilian reprocessing capability and the extraction of plutonium in the United Kingdom.

**Mr. Michael Spicer:** Reprocessing is a proven and safe technology for which there is a continuing demand. It is for the owners of the spent fuel to decide on safety, technical and economic grounds whether to reprocess spent fuel.

**Mr. Flynn:** To ask the Secretary of State for Energy what evidence his Department has that plutonium created in Central Electricity Generating Board Magnox nuclear reactors up to 31 March 1969, and subsequently, put into the United Kingdom Atomic Energy Authority military stockpile has not been used in nuclear warhead production subsequently.

**Mr. Michael Spicer:** Plutonium created in the CEGB Magnox reactors and purchased by the UKAEA prior to 31 March 1969, was consigned to the United States before 1971 under the mutual defence agreement. The United States authorities have said that none of this plutonium has been used in weapons and that this continues to be their policy. For the civil uses to which this plutonium has been put in the United States, I refer the hon. Member to the reply given by my right hon. Friend the Member for Croydon, Central (Mr. Moore) to my hon. Friend the Member for Erewash (Mr. Rost) on 27 July 1982 at column *438*.

## Petrol Prices

**51. Mr. Yeo:** To ask the Secretary of State for Energy what recent representations he has received regarding the price of petrol.

**Mr. Peter Morrison:** We have received a number of letters from the public, and from Members on behalf of their constituents, expressing concern at increases in the prices of petrol. I have had no further representations since prices fell more recently.

## Druridge Bay

**54. Mr. Beith:** To ask the Secretary of State for Energy what is his latest assessment of the likelihood that the Druridge bay site will be used for a nuclear power station in the foreseeable future.

**Mr. Michael Spicer:** The CEGB plan to build four PWRs between now and the year 2000. Druridge bay has not been nominated by the CEGB as one of the sites for these reactors.

## Spent Fuel Rods

**Mr. Alan W. Williams:** To ask the Secretary of State for Energy how many spent Magnox fuel rods await reprocessing *(a)* in storage tanks at Sellafield and *(b)* in cooling ponds at Britain's nuclear power stations.

**Mr. Michael Spicer:** At 31 March 1989, some 940 tonnes uranium (u) of spent Magnox fuel were held at Sellafield awaiting reprocessing and some 350 tonnes u held by the generating boards at power stations. On average there are 100 fuel rods per tonne.

**Mr. Alan W. Williams:** To ask the Secretary of State for Energy what is the total storage capacity for spent advanced gas-cooled reactor fuel rods at Sellafield and at nuclear power stations for each year from 1989 to 2000.

**Mr. Michael Spicer:** Space for storage of a minimum of some 2,700 tonnes uranium (u) of AGR fuel (some 60,000

AGR fuel assemblies) has been allocated in ponds on the Sellafield site. This will be more than sufficient to meet operational requirements for the THORP project. The total pond capacity at the AGR stations operated by the generating boards is some 390 tonnes u (some 9,400 assemblies).

## Severn Barrage

**Mr. Speller:** To ask the Secretary of State for Energy if he will report on progress with and make a statement on current Severn barrage proposals.

**Mr. Michael Spicer:** No new information on Severn barrage studies has become available since I replied to my hon. Friend the Member for Bristol, North-West (Mr. Stern) on 12 June (at column *267*) on this subject. I refer my hon. Friend to that answer.

## Nuclear Reprocessing Industry

**Dr. Kim Howells:** To ask the Secretary of State for Energy (1) if, following the decision to withdraw major funding for the fast reactor programme at Dounreay, the Government will reconsider their continuing support for the nuclear reprocessing industry;

(2) if, following the recent announcement by the West German Government that they are to abandon their projected nuclear reprocessing facility at Wackersdorf for financial and environmental reasons, the Government will reconsider their continued support for the nuclear reprocessing industry.

**Mr. Michael Spicer:** Reprocessing is a proven and safe technology for which there is a continuing demand. BNFL has contracts with overseas customers for reprocessing in THORP worth some £2·77 billion in total. Additional contracts worth some £1·6 billion are being negotiated with utilities in the Federal Republic of Germany. It is for the owners of the spent fuel to decide on safety, technical and economic grounds whether to reprocess spent fuel.

## Low-level Radioactive Waste

**Mr. McGrady:** To ask the Secretary of State for Energy what representations he has received about the proposed Nirex recommendations to store low-level radioactive waste at Sellafield and Dounreay.

**Mr. Michael Spicer:** My right hon. Friend the Secretary of State for the Environment announced on 21 March that the Government had accepted Nirex's recommendation that further investigatory work should be carried out to assess the potential of Sellafield and Dounreay as possible sites for a deep repository for radioactive waste. Since that time I have received two representations expressing concern about these proposals.

## Transfers (Approval)

**Mr. Cohen:** To ask the Secretary of State for Energy which countries have been the destination of transfers of nuclear technology, reprocessing and waste management which have been subject to Government approval since June 1988; and if he will provide details of all such transfers.

**Mr. Michael Spicer:** No new transfer of technology has been approved since June 1988.

## Non-fossil Fuel Levy

**Mr. Blair:** To ask the Secretary of State for Energy what is his current estimate of the non-fossil fuel levy for the year 1989-90 under his privatisation plans.

**Mr. Parkinson:** The initial rate of the fossil fuel levy will depend on the outcome of contract negotiations for fossil and non-fossil generating capacity which are currently under way. The rate will be announced towards the end of this year.

## Oil and Gas Reserves

**Mr. Thurnham:** To ask the Secretary of State for Energy what representations he has received about reserves of oil and gas in the United Kingdom.

**Mr. Peter Morrison:** My Department's latest estimates of oil and gas reserves were given in my right hon. Friend's report on the development of the oil and gas resources of the United Kingdom ("The Brown Book") published in April. I have received no representations about the estimates, other than views expressed by the companies concerned in the course of their preparation.

## Radioactive Material

**Mr. Hardy:** To ask the Secretary of State for Energy what discussions he has had during the last six months with the Central Electricity Generating Board and with British Nuclear Fuels plc in regard to the storage and reprocessing of radioactive material.

**Mr. Michael Spicer:** My right hon. Friend and I regularly meet both chairmen to discuss a range of matters.

## Oil Exploration

**Mr. Hayward:** To ask the Secretary of State for Energy (1) how many civil servants currently employed in his Department are involved with exploration, development and extraction of oil from the North sea;

(2) if he has had any discussions with any of the oil companies involved in the North sea concerning the possible relocation of the Department's civil servants responsible for exploration, development and extraction of the North sea outside London;

(3) what consideration has been given to relocating those civil servants responsible for exploration, development and extraction of oil within the Department of Energy away from London;

(4) what impact the decision of Conoco to concentrate its exploration operations division at Aberdeen and Shell and BP's increased emphasis on exploration and operations in Scotland has had on his policy in relation to the location of the Department's operations;

(5) what saving would be made by relocation of all the Department of Energy's civil servants dealing with exploration, development and extraction of oil from the North sea, from London to Glasgow;

(6) what saving would be made by the relocation of all the Department of Energy's civil servants dealing with exploration, development and extraction of oil from the North sea, from London to Aberdeen;

(7) what saving would be made by the relocation of all the Department of Energy's civil servants dealing with exploration, development and extraction of oil from the North sea, from London to Edinburgh.

**Mr. Peter Morrison:** There are 174 staff currently employed in my Department's petroleum engineering division, which is responsible for ensuring as far as possible the maximum economic and safe recovery of the United Kingdom's petroleum resources. Of these 16 staff, concerned with offshore safety, are already located in Aberdeen. Following a review in 1987 it was decided that a move of the division as a whole outside London was not feasible. It was estimated that no financial savings would arise from such a move. Moreover the division is very much involved in providing advice to Ministers and has day-to-day discussions with the headquarters of the companies in the oil and gas industry, most of whom remain located in London. If further consideration is given in the future to the relocation of staff in the division, the location of the companies' operations will be a relevant factor, though only one of a number of factors. No specific discussions have been held with the companies on this issue. Moreover of the 90 or so staff in the Department's Offshore Supplies Office, which is responsible for the promotion of the United Kingdom offshore supplies industry on the United Kingdom continental shelf and worldwide, some 80 are based in Scotland.

### Redundant Mineworkers (Pensions)

**Mr. Barron:** To ask the Secretary of State for Energy what is the number of ex-mineworkers who are currently receiving payments under the redundant mineworkers pension scheme for the years 1978-79, 1979-80, 1980-81, 1981-82, 1982-83, 1983-84, 1984-85, 1985-86 and 1986-87.

**Mr. Michael Spicer:** The number of ex-mineworkers who are currently receiving payments under the redundant mineworkers payments schemes by year of redundancy is as follows:

| Year of redundancy | Beneficiaries as at 1 April 1989 |
|---|---|
| 1979-80 | 8 |
| 1980-81 | 149 |
| 1981-82 | 1,268 |
| 1982-83 | 2,183 |
| 1983-84 | 13,332 |
| 1984-85 | 5,457 |
| 1985-86 | 21,036 |
| 1986-87 | 16,758 |
| Total payees | 60,191 |

### Power Stations (Desulphurisation)

**Mr. Butler:** To ask the Secretary of State for Energy what progress has been made to date in the desulphurisation of power stations.

**Mr. Michael Spicer:** Work on retrofitting flue gas desulphurisation equipment to Drax power station is proceeding well. I expect to receive an application for the next retrofit during the course of this year.

### Continental Shelf

**Mr. Robert G. Hughes:** To ask the Secretary of State for Energy what progress has been made in explorations on the United Kingdom continental shelf so far in the current year.

**Mr. Peter Morrison:** Up to mid-June, 43 exploration wells had been started on the United Kingdom continental shelf since the beginning of the year.

Nine significant discoveries have been announced.

### Depleted Uranium Exports

**Dr. Thomas:** To ask the Secretary of State for Energy what depleted uranium from *(a)* British Nuclear Fuels Ltd. stockpiles and *(b)* United Kingdom Atomic Energy Authority stockpiles has been exported from the United Kingdom and used in anti-tank shells, tank protective armour and other non-nuclear military uses; when and to which countries.

**Mr. Michael Spicer** *[holding answer 13 June 1989]:* Since 1979, one such export has been authorised for the specific purposes mentioned. Details are commercially confidential.

### Orimulsion

**Mr. Blair:** To ask the Secretary of State for Energy (1) what information he has on the sulphur content of orimulsion;

(2) how many tonnes of orimulsion were imported into Britain in the current calendar year; and whether there are any plans to introduce a policy to encourage the conversion of power stations to orimulsion.

**Mr. Parkinson:** The sulphur content of orimulsion varies between 2·2 per cent. and 2·8 per cent. by weight. Twenty six thousand tonnes have been imported so far this year. Decisions on the conversion of power stations to this fuel are a matter for the commercial judgment of the CEGB.

### Fuel Reprocessing

**Mr. Alan W. Williams:** To ask the Secretary of State for Energy what information he has on the consideration given by the Central Electricity Generating Board to cancellation of contracts with British Nuclear Fuels Ltd. for reprocessing spent AGR fuel at Sellafield.

**Mr. Michael Spicer:** I have no such information.

### Thermal Oxide Reprocessing

**Mr. Hardy:** To ask the Secretary of State for Energy for how long spent fuel rods can safely be stored before thermal oxide reprocessing.

**Mr. Michael Spicer:** I refer the hon. Member to my reply to the hon. Member for Carmarthen (Mr. Williams) on 20 June 1989 at columns *90-91.*

### Electricity Supply (Computer Systems)

**Mr. Tony Blair:** To ask the Secretary of State for Energy what is the cost of installing the new computer systems to be introduced into the electricity supply industry as a result of privatisation.

**Mr. Parkinson:** This is a matter for the electricity supply industry. I have asked the chairman of the Electricity Council to write to the hon. Member.

## Energy Conservation

**Mr. David Tredinnick:** To ask the Secretary of State for Energy what representations he has received about the conservation of energy; and whether he proposes to act on any of those representations.

**Mr. Peter Morrison:** I have received a number of representations regarding energy conservation and energy efficiency all of which have been taken into account in reviewing the programmes of the Energy Efficiency Office as well as the Government's proposals for the privatisation of the electricity supply industry.

## CEGB (Disabled Staff)

**Mr. Blair:** To ask the Secretary of State for Energy what information he has as to what percentage of the work force employed by the Central Electricity Generating Board are registered as disabled.

**Mr. Parkinson:** This is a matter for the Central Electricity Generating Board. I shall ask the chairman of the CEGB to write to the hon. Member.

## DEFENCE

## BNFL (Open Day)

**Mr. Flynn:** To ask the Secretary of State for Defence if any Ministers or officials in his Department attended the thirtieth anniversary open day celebration of the opening of British Nuclear Fuels plutonium and tritium production reactors at Chapelcross in Annan on 13 May.

**Mr. Sainsbury:** Yes.

## Tornado (Accidents)

**Mr. Boyes:** To ask the Secretary of State for Defence (1) how many Royal Air Force Tornado major accidents have been caused by teething problems with the introduction of the aircraft;

(2) if he will list all major accidents to Royal Air Force Tornado aircraft since its entry into service, specifying the cause of each accident.

**Mr. Neubert:** The information requested is given in the following table:

*Major accidents to RAF Tornados*

| Date | Accident | Location | Category | Cause |
|---|---|---|---|---|
| 12 May 1982 | Accident on landing | RAF Conningsby | 4 | Not positively identified |
| 27 September 1983 | Accident on descent | Wolferton | 5 | Technical fault |
| 28 October 1983 | Accident on descent | Off North Norfolk Coast | 5 | Not positively identified |
| 14 November 1983 | Heavy landing | RAF Honington | 4 | Air crew error |
| 6 February 1984 | After Lightning strike, unnecessary ejection | Federal Republic of Germany | 5 | Air crew error |
| 12 July 1984 | Mid air collision | Off Sheringham (Norfolk coast) | 5 | Air crew error |
| 18 July 1984 | Flap failure | Goose Bay, Canada | 5 | Technical fault |
| 8 November 1984 | Unnecessary command ejection | Federal Republic of Germany | 5 | Air crew error |
| 12 December 1985 | Flew into Sea | Flamborough Head | 5 | Not positively determined |
| 2 December 1986 | Damage to electrical systems | Near Diss | 5 | Not positively determined |
| 10 December 1986 | Mid air collision (2 Tornados) | Near Thorney | 5 / 4 | Air crew error |
| 30 March 1987 | Failure of locking mechanism | Federal Republic of Germany | 5 | Technical fault |
| 3 June 1987 | Failure of mechanical and electrical systems | Manby, 5 nm East of Louth | 5 | Technical fault |
| 17 June 1987 | Mid-air collison | 3 nm South East Keswick | 5 | Operational |
| 27 July 1987 | Hydraulic system failure | Fadmoor, Near Pickering | 5 | Technical fault |
| 30 March 1988 | Accident on exercise | Nevada Desert | 5 | Air crew error |
| 10 May 1988 | Flew into ground | Federal Republic of Germany | 5 | Air crew error |
| 9 August 1988 | Mid-air collision (2 Tornados) | Appleby, Cumbria | 5 / 5 | Still under investigation |
| 13 January 1989 | Mid-air collision | Federal Republic of Germany | 5 | Still under investigation |

*Notes:*

1. Category 4 Damage not repairable on site.

2. Category 5 Aircraft is damaged beyond repair or is missing.

The accidents on 27 September 1983, 18 July 1984 and 2 December 1986 were attributed to teething problems with the aircraft.

**Mr. Boyes:** To ask the Secretary of State for Defence (1) what figures he can provide for the rate of major accidents per 10,000 flying hours for Tornado aircraft in Italian air Force service, excluding the Tornado tri-national training establishment;

(2) what figures he can provide for the rate of major accidents per 10,000 flying hours for Tornado aircraft in German air force service and German navy service excluding the Tornado tri-national training establishment.

**Mr. Neubert:** The public release of national aircraft accident statistics is a matter for the respective Government.

**Mr. Boyes:** To ask the Secretary of State for Defence what has been the overall rate of major accidents per 10,000 hours for Royal Air Force Tornado GR1 aircraft, excluding those assigned to the Tornado tri-national training establishment; and if he will provide a breakdown of this figure into annual major accident rates for each year since 1981.

**Mr. Neubert:** It is not our policy to publish such information.

## Anti-tank Weapons and Artillery

**Mr. Boyes:** To ask the Secretary of State for Defence if he will list all changes in the definitions used to calculate the numbers of North Atlantic Treaty Organisation and Warsaw pact *(a)* anti-tank weapons and *(b)* artillery, between those used to compile the tables in chapter six of the "Statement on the Defence Estimates 1988", and those used to compile the tables in chapter six of the "Statement on the Defence Estimates 1989".

**Mr. Archie Hamilton:** Until 1988, United Kingdom definitions were used to calculate these figures, but in the interests of consistency within the Alliance figures 8 and 9 in chapter 6 of the "Statement on the Defence Estimates 1989", Cm. 675-I, were compiled according to the definitions and counting rules used by NATO. The changes involved the transfer of anti-tank guns from the artillery to the anti-tank weapons category; the exclusion of armoured infantry fighting vehicles and helicopters equipped with anti-tank guided missiles from the anti-tank weapons category; and the inclusion of mortars with a calibre size equal to or exceeding 100 mm in the artillery category.

**Mr. Boyes:** To ask the Secretary of State for Defence if he will make a statement on the reasons for the change in his Department's assessment of the numbers of anti-tank guided weapons deployed by the Warsaw pact in the central region, portrayed in figure 15 on page 61 of the "Statement on the Defence Estimates 1988" and figure 9 on page 47 of the "Statement on the Defence Estimates 1989".

**Mr. Archie Hamilton:** In the "Statement on the Defence Estimates 1988", Cm. 344-I, the figure for the number of anti-tank guided weapons deployed by the Warsaw pact in the central region was based on the United Kingdom definition and counting rules. In the "Statement on the Defence Estimates 1989", Cm. 675-I, NATO definitions and counting rules are used, in the interests of consistency within the Alliance.

**Mr. Boyes:** To ask the Secretary of State for Defence if he will provide figures for the number of anti-tank weapons held by the Warsaw pact in the central region in late 1988, counting crew-served systems and helicopter or vehicle-mounted systems, but excluding those that may be fired through the gun barrel of Soviet tanks.

**Mr. Archie Hamilton:** The overall number of anti-tank weapons held by the Warsaw pact in the central region in late 1988, excluding those that may be fired through the gun barrel of tanks, is assessed to be 13,700.

### Chemical Weapons

**Mr. Boyes:** To ask the Secretary of State for Defence (1) if he will list those Warsaw pact countries which were formerly producing chemical warfare agents but which have now ceased production;

(2) which Warsaw pact countries are currently manufacturing chemical warfare agents.

**Mr. Archie Hamilton:** The Soviet Union is the only member of the Warsaw pact to have admitted producing chemical warfare agents, and it has also claimed that such production has ceased. The other Warsaw pact countries have stated that they do not produce such agents, but none has provided any evidence to support its claims.

All the non-soviet Warsaw pact countries have chemical industries with the capability to produce chemical warfare agents and we believe that some have produced chemical weapons. The details of our assessments of individual countries' programmes are classified.

**Mr. Boyes:** To ask the Secretary of State for Defence in what year the Soviet Union first deployed chemical weapons in any non-Soviet Warsaw pact country; and whether *(a)* Soviet chemical warfare agents, *(b)* Soviet chemical weapons and *(c)* unfilled Soviet chemical munitions are currently deployed in any Warsaw pact country other than the Soviet Union.

**Mr. Archie Hamilton:** In spite of Soviet claims, we have good reason to believe that the Soviet Union has stationed chemical weapons in Eastern Europe. I am not prepared to comment in detail for security reasons, but there is an obvious need for the Soviet Union to make available much more information about its chemical warfare capabilities.

**Mr. Boyes:** To ask the Secretary of State for Defence what information he has on the supply of *(a)* chemical warfare agents and *(b)* precursors for chemical warfare agents by Warsaw pact countries to non-Warsaw pact countries.

**Mr. Archie Hamilton:** We have no evidence that in recent years any Warsaw pact country has supplied chemical warfare agents to any non-Warsaw pact country.

The Warsaw pact countries have very large chemical industries whose products are exported worldwide. Many of the precursors for chemical warfare agents are common chemicals which have a variety of legitimate uses. These are traded widely by many countries, including those of the Warsaw pact. The Warsaw pact countries have stated that they impose export controls on a number of the immediate precursors to chemical warfare agents, and we have no evidence that controls are being contravened.

### Warsaw Pact (Aircraft)

**Mr. Boyes:** To ask the Secretary of State for Defence if he will make a statement on the portrayal of information in current and past editions of the "Statement on the Defence Estimates" on the numbers of embarked and shore-based aircraft assigned for naval operations in the Warsaw pact's *(a)* northern fleet, *(b)* Baltic fleet and *(c)* Black sea fleet; and if he will publish figures showing the numbers of aircraft in these categories in each fleet for each year since 1979.

**Mr. Archie Hamilton:** Revised figures for embarked and shore-based aircraft, fixed-wing and helicopters, assigned for naval operations in the Warsaw pact's Northern, Baltic and Black sea fleets from 1979 to 1989 are approximately as follows:

| | Northern Fleet | Baltic Fleet | Black Sea Fleet |
|---|---|---|---|
| 1979 | 350 | 270 | 260 |
| 1980 | 360 | 290 | 270 |
| 1981 | 370 | 270 | 300 |
| 1982 | 400 | 280 | 300 |
| 1983 | 400 | 280 | 320 |
| 1984 | 420 | 280 | 330 |
| 1985 | 400 | 270 | 300 |
| 1986 | 450 | 300 | 300 |
| 1987 | 425 | 270 | 300 |
| 1988 | 425 | 270 | 300 |
| 1989 | 425 | 270 | 280 |

Since 1985, the definitions of the type of aircraft included have altered and, as is the case with all estimates, the figures published in previous Statements on the Defence Estimates are subject to revision as new material becomes available.

**Mr. Boyes:** To ask the Secretary of State for Defence if the figures for Warsaw pact aircraft deployed west of the Urals on page 51 of the "Statement on the Defence Estimates 1989" include aircraft from front-line units which are undergoing maintenance and modification in addition to mission-ready aircraft.

**Mr. Archie Hamilton:** The aircraft figures quoted reflect the complete strength of the unit, which includes those undergoing maintenance and modification.

**Mr. Boyes:** To ask the Secretary of State for Defence what are the reasons for the decline between late 1986 and late 1987 in the numbers of Warsaw pact SRINF aircraft deployed west of the Urals, as depicted in figure 16 on page 68 of the "Statement on the Defence Estimates 1987" and figure 19 on page 67 of the "Statement on the Defence Estimates 1988".

**Mr. Archie Hamilton:** The change in deployment numbers is the result of the reorganisation of the Soviet air and air defence forces. A number of air regiments were transferred from tactical aviation forces, which have a nuclear role, to the strategic air defence force which does not have a nuclear attack role.

**Mr. Boyes:** To ask the Secretary of State for Defence what are the reasons for the differences between the figures for Warsaw pact SRINF aircraft as at the end of 1988 provided in *(a)* the reply from the hon. Member for Romford (Mr. Neubert) to the right hon. Member for Bethnal Green and Stepney (Mr. Shore) of 2 March, *Official Report,* column *254,* and *(b)* figure 12 on page 51 of the "Statement on the Defence Estimates 1989", volume 1.

**Mr. Archie Hamilton:** The figures given in the answer on 2 March 1989 by my hon. Friend the Member for Romford (Mr. Neubert) at column *254* did not include the Frogfoot aircraft. This type of aircraft was included in figure 12 of the "Statement on the Defence Estimates 1989", Cm. 675-I, following a further assessment of its possible roles.

**Mr. Boyes:** To ask the Secretary of State for Defence what assessment he has made of the reasons for the change in the numbers of Warsaw pact long-range INF aircraft between the end of 1987 and the end of 1988, as depicted in figure 18 on page 66 of the "Statement on the Defence Estimates 1988" and figure 12 on page 51 of the "Statement on the Defence Estimates 1989".

**Mr. Archie Hamilton:** The reduction in the numerical strength of Warsaw pact LRINF medium bombers between 1987 and 1988 is due to the modernisation programme that has been undertaken by the Warsaw pact, with the continuing introduction of the Backfire

supersonic dual-capable bomber. With the deployment of this superior weapon system, the Warsaw pact has been able to retire an increasing proportion of their ageing and obsolescent Badger medium bombers. Therefore, although the overall size of the aircraft component of the LRINF is gradually being reduced, its overall operational capability is being improved.

**Mr. Boyes:** To ask the Secretary of State for Defence what was the number of *(a)* Badger, *(b)* Blinder and *(c)* Backfire aircraft deployed by the Warsaw pact west of the Urals at the end of each year since 1979, excluding those with a primary maritime role.

**Mr. Archie Hamilton:** The approximate numbers were as follows:

|      | Badger | Blinder | Backfire | Totals |
|------|--------|---------|----------|--------|
| 1979 | 420    | 160     | 40       | 620    |
| 1980 | 450    | 160     | 70       | 680    |
| 1981 | 450    | 160     | 70       | 680    |
| 1982 | 450    | 160     | 80       | 690    |
| 1983 | 420    | 160     | 100      | 680    |
| 1984 | 410    | 160     | 100      | 670    |
| 1985 | 410    | 160     | 120      | 690    |
| 1986 | 350    | 160     | 130      | 640    |
| 1987 | 290    | 160     | 150      | 600    |
| 1988 | 290    | 150     | 160      | 600    |
| 1989 | 210    | 150     | 180      | 540    |

### HMS Chatham and HMS Norfolk

**Mr. Boyes:** To ask the Secretary of State for Defence if he will make a statement on the portrayal of the operational status of the Royal Navy vessels HMS Chatham and HMS Norfolk in annex A of volume 1 of the "Statement on the Defence Estimates 1989".

**Mr. Archie Hamilton:** HMS Chatham and HMS Norfolk are due to be accepted into service later this year, as is made clear at paragraph 324 of the Statement on the Defence Estimates 1989, Cm 675-I. As such, they should have been marked by an asterisk in annex A. Unfortunately they were not, due to a printing error.

### Warsaw Pact (Weapons)

**Mr. Boyes:** To ask the Secretary of State for Defence if he will publish in the *Official Report* a table updating the information contained in the table entitled "Weapons Production for Warsaw Pact Forces" on page 62 of the "Statement on the Defence Estimates 1988;" and if he will include in the North Atlantic Treaty Organisation figures the production of weapons by France and Spain.

**Mr. Archie Hamilton:** Estimated total production between 1979 and 1988 is as follows:

|                                               | Soviet Union | Non-Soviet Warsaw Pact | Total Warsaw Pact | Total NATO |
|-----------------------------------------------|--------------|------------------------|-------------------|------------|
| Main Battle Tanks                             | 26,000       | 5,400                  | 31,400            | 11,000     |
| Other Armoured Vehicles                       | 48,000       | 6,300                  | 54,300            | 20,800     |
| Field Artillery, Mortars and Rocket Launchers | 25,000       | 6,500                  | 31,500            | 5,800      |
| Tactical Combat and Interceptor Aircraft      | 7,300        | 1,200                  | 8,500             | 6,400      |

| | Soviet Union | Non-Soviet Warsaw Pact | Total Warsaw Pact | Total NATO |
|---|---|---|---|---|
| Major Surface Warships | 83 | 23 | 106 | 175 |
| Attack Submarines | 64 | 2 | 66 | 59 |

*Note:*

The above table is taken from the United States Secretary of Defence's Annual Report to Congress for Fiscal Year 1990. French and Spanish production is not included.

### Backfire Bombers

**Mr. Boyes:** To ask the Secretary of State for Defence if the figures for the numbers of Backfire bombers in his answer to the right hon. Member for Bethnal Green and Stepney (Mr. Shore) of 2 March, *Official Report,* column 255, included maritime-assigned Backfires; and if he will provide figures showing the numbers of Backfire aircraft deployed in operational units in each year since 1985, excluding those with a maritime role.

**Mr. Archie Hamilton:** The figures given in the answer on 2 March by my hon. Friend the Member for Romford (Mr. Neubert) at column 255 include maritime-assigned aircraft. The number of Backfire aircraft deployed in operational units in each year since 1985, excluding those with a maritime role, are approximately as follows:

| | Numbers |
|---|---|
| 1985 | 120 |
| 1986 | 130 |
| 1987 | 150 |
| 1988 | 160 |
| 1989 | 180 |

### LRINF Aircraft

**Mr. Boyes:** To ask the Secretary of State for Defence if the numbers of North Atlantic Treaty Organisation LRINF aircraft listed in military balance tables in successive editions of the "Statement on the Defence Estimates" since 1984 include all aircraft deployed in Europe; and if he will make a statement.

**Mr. Archie Hamilton:** The number of aircraft presented in the Statement on the Defence Estimates covers all NATO's operational LRINF aircraft permanently based in Europe. As the tables show, these consist entirely of F-111 aircraft. There are also a further 12 EF-111 based in Europe, which would operate only in the electronic warfare role. Similarly, the figure presented for Warsaw pact LRINF aircraft does not include around 100 aircraft of the same types which it is believed would operate in non-nuclear, supporting roles. The final two sentences of paragraph 618 of the Statement on the Defence Estimates 1989, Cm. 675-I, apply only to SRINF aircraft.

**Mr. Boyes:** To ask the Secretary of State for Defence what trends have been observed in the numbers of long-range INF aircraft deployed by the Warsaw pact since the end of 1988.

**Mr. Archie Hamilton:** The Warsaw pact continues to modernise its long-range INF air forces, as it replaces the obsolescent Badger medium bomber with the modern variable-geometry supersonic Backfire. The overall number of medium bombers has decreased, and will continue to do so as the Badger is withdrawn from service.

However, within the next five years the aircraft component of the Warsaw pact's long-range INF force will consist of an all-supersonic force of Backfire and Blinder aircraft.

### Frogfoot

**Mr. Boyes:** To ask the Secretary of State for Defence in what year the Su-25 Frogfoot entered service with the Warsaw pact.

**Mr. Archie Hamilton:** Production of the Su-25 Frogfoot began in 1980. We assess that the first units became operational in the conventional role in the USSR in 1981. Subsequently, the aircraft was used operationally in Afghanistan.

**Mr. Boyes:** To ask the Secretary of State for Defence in what year the Su-25 Frogfoot is assessed to have acquired a nuclear capability.

**Mr. Archie Hamilton:** All Soviet ground-attack aircraft have a potential nuclear delivery capability. The Su-25 Frogfoot entered operational service in 1981 in the conventional role, but was not assessed by NATO to have acquired a nuclear capability until 1988.

### Flanker

**Mr. Boyes:** To ask the Secretary of State for Defence in what year the Su-27 Flanker entered service with the Warsaw pact.

**Mr. Archie Hamilton:** The Su-27 Flanker entered service with the Soviet strategic air defence force in 1985.

**Mr. Boyes:** To ask the Secretary of State for Defence in what year the Su-27 Flanker is assessed to have acquired a nuclear capability.

**Mr. Archie Hamilton:** Some Su-27 Flanker aircraft have the primary mission of air superiority in the central region. In fulfilling this role, the aircraft is equally likely to attack targets in the air or on the ground. The Flanker is capable of both nuclear and conventional ground-attack operations, and is assessed to have been so since 1987.

### Conventional Forces (Balance)

**Mr. Boyes:** To ask the Secretary of State for Defence what consideration is being given to the diversion of military personnel to non-military tasks such as public works and environmental restoration in the event of achievement of a conventional force balance in Europe at force levels lower than those currently maintained by the North Atlantic Treaty Organisation.

**Mr. Archie Hamilton:** NATO is committed to seeking an agreement on conventional forces in Europe which will lead to a stable and secure balance at lower levels, but at this stage it would be premature to speculate on which military units might be affected. It is unlikely that the Ministry of Defence would be responsible for redeploying service personnel to non-military tasks.

### Warsaw Pact (Arms Production)

**Mr. Boyes:** To ask the Secretary of State for Defence what independent British national capability exists for assessment and calculation of Warsaw pact arms production levels.

**Mr. Archie Hamilton:** This capability is provided by the defence intelligence staff, whose responsibilities include the assessment of Warsaw pact arms production levels.

### Ammunition Propellant

**Mr. Boyes:** To ask the Secretary of State for Defence what proportion of the North Atlantic Treaty Organisation ammunition propellant is manufactured in Czechoslovakia.

**Mr. Archie Hamilton:** Logistics matters, including the procurement of ammunition propellant, are a national responsibility. I am not aware of any instance where propellant manufactured in Czechoslovakia has been used in Ministry of Defence ammunition.

### Soviet Naval Activity

**Mr. Boyes:** To ask the Secretary of State for Defence what trends have been observed in Soviet naval activity in the eastern Atlantic since the publication of the "Statement on the Defence Estimates 1988".

**Mr. Archie Hamilton:** Since the publication of the Statement on the Defence Estimates 1988, Soviet naval activity in the eastern Atlantic has remained virtually constant at the reduced level observed in 1987.

### Soviet Defence Spending

**Mr. Boyes:** To ask the Secretary of State for Defence what will be the implications for British defence policy of the announced halving of Soviet defence spending by 1995.

**Mr. Archie Hamilton:** We welcome the recent announcement by the Soviet Prime Minister of plans to reduce the proportion of national income devoted to defence, but the implications for the future Soviet defence programme are far from clear, and we await further details with interest. In the meantime, the Soviet Union and its allies in the Warsaw pact continue to have a massive superiority in many types of conventional armaments in Europe. Our commitment to the mutual defence provided by NATO, and to NATO's policy of strength in defence combined with readiness for dialogue and co-operation with the East, will remain the foundation of our defence policy.

### Departmental Property

**Mr. Soley:** To ask the Secretary of State for Defence how many properties are leased by his Department from the local authority in *(a)* Greater Manchester metropolitan county, *(b)* Westminster, *(c)* Suffolk Coastal and *(d)* Isles of Scilly.

**Mr. Neubert:** The answers are as follows: *(a)* Six (three office properties and three separate areas of land on which

MOD have subsequently had built a total of 37 residential properties); *(b)* None; *(c)* None; *(d)* One, a small fuel store of approximately 22 sq m.

### Ptarmigan

**Mr. Rogers:** To ask the Secretary of State for Defence if he has any plans to increase the number of Ptarmigan mobile trunk modes currently in service with the British Army.

**Mr. Sainsbury:** No decision has yet been taken on further orders for trunk modes for the Ptarmigan system.

### Buccaneer

**Mr. Rogers:** To ask the Secretary of State for Defence what consideration has been given to replacing the Buccaneer maritime strike aircraft.

**Mr. Sainsbury:** We are now carefully studying the need to replace the Buccaneeer in due course.

### IUKADGE Command and Control System

**Mr. Rogers:** To ask the Secretary of State for Defence what consideration was given to using one common computer software language for the improved United Kingdom air defence ground environment command and control system when its specifications were originally determined.

**Mr. Sainsbury:** During the nationally funded project definition stage of the IUKADGE CCS in 1977-78, consideration was given to the use of a single preferred software language, CORAL 66, and the codes of software practice extant at that time. However, a subsequent decision to seek maximum return from the NATO common infrastructure budget resulted in the United Kingdom having to abide by the rules of NATO international competitive bidding, ICB, existing at the time, which precluded the specification of a single software language. In addition, the NATO financial authorities directed that existing NATO Air Defence Ground Environment, NADGE software was to be re-used to the greatest extent possible.

**Mr. Rogers:** To ask the Secretary of State for Defence (1) what is the current estimate of the date on which the improved United Kingdom air defence ground environment command and control system will be declared fully operational;

(2) when the improved United Kingdom air defence ground environment command and control system was intended to be fully operational when it was first ordered.

**Mr. Sainsbury:** The improved United Kingdom air defence ground environment, IUKADGE, is being progressively introduced over a number of years, in accordance with a plan that takes account of the need to maintain a continuous operational capability as the transition from the old to the new is accomplished. Some elements of the system are already in service use. The element known as the IUKADGE command and control system has been delayed and, with the agreement of the prime contractor, UKADGE Systems Ltd., is currently subject to an independent audit and review. It would be premature to comment further before the outcome of that audit has been assessed.

## NFR 90

**Mr. Rogers:** To ask the Secretary of State for Defence when the project definition phase for the NFR 90 programme will be completed.

**Mr. Sainsbury:** The contract for the project definition study is due to complete early in 1991.

There will then follow a period in which the results will be assessed and decisions taken with the other Governments involved.

**Mr. Rogers:** To ask the Secretary of State for Defence which British companies have been consulted as part of the project definition phase for the NFR 90 programme.

**Mr. Sainsbury:** Regular contact is maintained with British industry through several mediums including the Defence Contracts Bulletin, the Defence Industries Council, the NFR United Kingdom Industrial Advisory Panel, made up of the principal defence trade associations and interested companies, and with the nine member companies of Supermarine Consortium Ltd., the United Kingdom shareholder in the international joint venture company undertaking the project definition study.

## EH 101 Helicopter

**Mr. Rogers:** To ask the Secretary of State for Defence when the project definition phase for the tactical support variant of the EH 101 helicopter will be completed.

**Mr. Sainsbury:** The formal project definition phase is being undertaken in two stages, the first of which will run for one year from April this year, although the essential analysis of alternatives will be available at the end of December this year. No timetable has been set for the second stage of project definition.

## Nuclear Submarines

**Mr. Rogers:** To ask the Secretary of State for Defence whether design work on the next generation of nuclear-powered submarines has been completed.

**Mr. Sainsbury:** Design work on SSN 20, the first of class of the next generation of nuclear-powered fleet submarines, is at an early stage.

## Z-berths

**Mr. Martyn Jones:** To ask the Secretary of State for Defence what is the present state of negotiations between local authorities and his Department on the proposed Z-berths at Swansea.

**Mr. Archie Hamilton:** After our initial discussions with local authorities, a feasibility study was carried out, and this is now under consideration within the Ministry of Defence. If the results prove favourable, further discussions will take place.

**Mr. Martyn Jones:** To ask the Secretary of State for Defence what is the present state of negotiations between local authorities and his Department on the proposed Z-berth at Tilbury.

**Mr. Archie Hamilton:** I have nothing to add to the answer that I gave to the hon. Member for Bow and Poplar (Ms. Gordon) on 5 May at column *277*.

## Housing (Dunoon-Sandbank)

**Mr. Wilson:** To ask the Secretary of State for Defence how many additional houses for United States navy personnel are planned in the Dunoon-Sandbank area; what is the estimated cost of their construction; and what military functions will be performed by the occupants of the additional housing.

**Mr. Neubert** *[holding answer 22 June]:* I understand that the United States navy is in the process of leasing up to 50 buildings in the Dunoon-Sandbank areas to house United States naval and civilian personnel involved in maintaining support for the ships and facilities in Holy loch. Some work will be required to bring the buildings up to the required standard and to facilitate use of United States domestic appliances. The United States navy also intends to investigate the possibility of leasing a further 44 houses. The details and costs of this programme are a matter for the United States Government.

44. **Sir Michael McNair-Wilson:** To ask the Secretary of State for Defence how many boys, the sons of service personnel, have attended Crookham Court School on Ministry of Defence grants since 1974.

**Mr. Archie Hamilton** *[pursuant to his reply, 19 June 1989, c. 59, and the reply, 12 June 1989, c. 321]:* There are presently six children of service parents at Crookham Court school.

# CIVIL SERVICE

## Mr. Bernard Ingham

80. **Mr. Dalyell:** To ask the Minister for the Civil Service if he will arrange for Mr. Bernard Ingham to give a lecture at the Civil Service college.

**Mr. Luce:** In February this year, Mr. Ingham gave an informal talk to senior civil servants on a top management course, run by the Office of the Minister for the Civil Service, held at the college in Sunningdale.

# WALES

## National Museum of Wales

55. **Mrs. Clwyd:** To ask the Secretary of State for Wales if he has any plans to visit the national museum of Wales.

**Mr. Peter Walker:** I hope to visit the national museum of Wales later this year.

## Water Pollution

**Dr. Kim Howells:** To ask the Secretary of State for Wales how many inspections of waste outfalls from factories were carried out on the Ely and Glyn rivers in Mid Glamorgan by Welsh water authority inspectors or bailiffs over the past 12 months.

**Mr. Grist:** This is a matter for the Welsh water authority.

### Rivers (Fish Loss)

**Dr. Kim Howells:** To ask the Secretary of State for Wales what information he has on the causes of the recent loss of stocked fish in the rivers Ely and Glyn in Mid Glamorgan.

**Mr. Grist:** This is a matter for the Welsh water authority.

### European Parliament

**Mr. Barry Jones:** To ask the Secretary of State for Wales when he next proposes to visit the European Parliament; and if he will make a statement.

**Mr. Peter Walker:** I have no immediate plans to do so.

### Epilepsy Association

**Mr. Wigley:** To ask the Secretary of State for Wales how much assistance his Department intends to give to the Wales Epilepsy Association for 1989-90; and if he will make a statement.

**Mr. Grist:** I refer the hon. Gentleman to the reply I gave him on 26 May 1989 at column *762*.

### Valleys Initiative

**Mr. Michael:** To ask the Secretary of State for Wales if he will list the projects and their costs funded by his Department as part of the Valleys initiative.

**Mr. Barry Jones:** To ask the Secretary of State for Wales if he will list the projects and their costs funded by his Department as part of the Valleys programme; and if he will make a statement.

**Mr. Peter Walker:** A full list of the very many projects taking place in the Valleys could only be provided at a disproportionate cost. I shall be making a progress statement on the Valleys programme shortly.

**Mr. Michael:** To ask the Secretary of State for Wales what was the starting date of the Valleys initiative.

**Mr. Barry Jones:** To ask the Secretary of State for Wales what was the starting date of the Valleys programme of his Department, and if he will make a statement.

**Mr. Peter Walker:** The Valleys programme was formally launched on 14 June 1988.

### NHS Reform

**Mr. Barry Jones:** To ask the Secretary of State for Wales (1) what consultations will be held with *(a)* the staff and *(b)* the local authority representing the catchment area of any general hospitals that apply for self-governing status; and if he will make a statement;

(2) what consultations will be held with local communities in the catchment area of any general hospitals in Wales that apply for self-governing status; and if he will make a statement.

**Mr. Grist:** Any application for self-governing status will be the subject of consultation with interested parties, including in particular health authorities concerned, staff at the hospital, general practitioners, community health councils and the local community. My right hon. Friend will consider any responses alongside the application.

# Written Answers to Questions

*Tuesday 27 June 1989*

## TRANSPORT

### Road Safety

**Mr. Knox:** To ask the Secretary of State for Transport what contribution he expects the proposals in "Road Users and the Law" to make towards his target for reducing casualties in his policy document, "Road Safety: The Next Steps."

**Mr. Peter Bottomley:** In 1987 we set the target of reducing casualties by one third by the year 2000. That means a reduction of some 100,000 deaths and injuries. Our priority must be the deaths and serious injuries.

In 1988 we made good progress towards this. Deaths decreased by 2 per cent. compared with 1987, and were 10 per cent. down compared to the baseline of our target. Serious injuries were down by 1 per cent. compared with 1987, −15 per cent. compared with the target baseline. This represents good progress, particularly as traffic volumes continue to rise.

Publication of the North report, and the White Paper "The Road User and the Law", (Cm. 576) has helped considerably to increase the awareness of the need for action to cut road casualties, and to give such action much higher priority. The proposals in the White Paper are an important part of the Government's overall package of measures which, by changing public attitudes, improving enforcement and adopting improved road engineering techniques are together designed to achieve the target.

### Road Traffic Law

**Mr. Knox:** To ask the Secretary of State for Transport if he will make a statement on any progress made in implementing some of the non-legislative recommendations of the road traffic law review which he accepted.

**Mr. Peter Bottomley:** The White Paper "The Road User and the Law" sets out the Government's proposals for taking forward the non-legislative recommendations accepted from the road traffic law review.

We have received many positive and helpful comments from interested organisations. We will now be discussing with them how best to take forward, jointly, the non-legislative aspects of the White Paper. We shall also be adding a number of projects to our research programme to follow up those aspects of the North report which require further research.

### Rail Freight (Barnes Bridge)

**Sir Barney Hayhoe:** To ask the Secretary of State for Transport what information he has on the average weekly amount of rail freight transported over Barnes bridge and its average journey length; and what assessment has been made of the equivalent number of average road freight vehicle miles this represents.

**Mr. Peter Bottomley:** This information is not known to the Department.

### Roads (Liverpool)

**Mr. Alton:** To ask the Secretary of State for Transport how much his Department has given for road building and improvement in Liverpool; and if he will list the Liverpool city council plans it was allocated for, for each of the last five years.

**Mr. Peter Bottomley:** There are no trunk roads in Liverpool. We support expenditure on the city council's more important roads through the transport supplementary grant system. The information requested is:

| Year | Amount of TSG given (£ million) (including minor works) |
| --- | --- |
| 1985-86 | 12·083 |
| 1986-87 | 2·702 |
| 1987-88 | 2·267 |
| 1988-89 | 1·235 |
| 1989-90 | 1·762 |

1 (to Merseyside County Council).

| Major Schemes accepted for TSG 1985-1990 | Years TSG allocated |
| --- | --- |
| Liverpool Inner Ring Road | 1985-86, 1986-87, 1987-88 |
| Garston Bypass | 1985-86, 1986-87, 1987-88 |
| Access to Lime Street Station | 1985-86, 1986-87, 1987-88 |
| Great George Street | 1985-86, 1986-87, 1987-88 |
| Everton Valley Improvement | 1985-86, 1986-87, 1987-88, 1988-89 |

**Mr. Alton:** To ask the Secretary of State for Transport what representations he has received about road building and upgrading plans in Liverpool; and if he will make a statement.

**Mr. Peter Bottomley:** We have recently received representations about the Park road relief road from the chairman of the Merseyside development corporation and the hon. Member. My right hon. Friend the Member for Wallasey (Mrs. Chalker) wrote to me about motorway communications on Merseyside and in Liverpool.

## NATIONAL FINANCE

### EAGGF (Commitment Appropriations)

**Mr. Teddy Taylor:** To ask the Chancellor of the Exchequer if he will make a statement explaining the procedures under which one quarter of all EAGGF commitment appropriations were made available to the Commission in January of recent years when provisional twelfths applied.

**Mr. Brooke** *[holding answer 19 June 1989]:* In 1980, 1985, 1987 and 1988, when provisional twelfths have applied, one quarter of all EAGGF commitment appropriations have been made available to the Commission, on its request, in accordance with article 204 of the Rome treaty and article 8 of the financial regulation. The Commission has used these commitments to meet EAGGF payments, which tend to fall disproportionately in the early part of the year.

## THE ARTS

### Disabled People

**Mr. Janner:** To ask the Minister for the Arts how many and what percentage of persons employed in his Department are registered as disabled.

**Mr. Luce:** None.

## ENVIRONMENT

### Greenhouse Effect

**Mr. Rost:** To ask the Secretary of State for the Environment if he will give the carbon dioxide emissions recorded for 1987 and 1988 related to public sector energy use, broken down into *(a)* central Government offices, by individual Departments of State, *(b)* local government, *(c)* health authorities and *(d)* other public sector bodies.

**Mrs. Virginia Bottomley:** Estimates of carbon dioxide emissions in the United Kingdom have been published in the "Digest of Environmental Protection and Water Statistics, Number 11", copies of which have been placed in the Library of the House. Emissions due to fossil fuel use in the public sector are included in the source category "Commercial/Public Service": in 1987 these amounted to 32 million tonnes of $CO_2$, which was 5 per cent. of the total United Kingdom annual emissions. Data for 1988 are currently being prepared. It would involve disproportionate cost to provide emission estimates in the categories requested.

**Mr. Allan Roberts:** To ask the Secretary of State for the Environment what specific proposals his Department has put forward for consideration and enactment, in order to reduce greenhouse gas emissions such as carbon dioxide and methane, since the seminar on the greenhouse effect held by the Prime Minister on 26 April.

**Mrs. Virginia Bottomley** *[holding answer 26 June 1989]:* At the first meeting of parties to the Montreal protocol, held in Helsinki in May, my right hon. Friend the Secretary of State gave the full support of the United Kingdom to the European Community's call for a reduction in the production and consumption of chlorofluorocarbons by 85 per cent. as soon as possible with a view to phasing them out by the end of the century.

At the Council of EC Environment Ministers, held in Luxembourg 9-10 June, my noble Friend the Minister of State for Housing, the Environment and Countryside, successfully pressed for the Commission to report back to Council on measures that can be taken to combat carbon dioxide emission from cars.

### Ivory

**Mr. Harris:** To ask the Secretary of State for the Environment what consideration has been given to the payment of compensation for firms whose business will be destroyed by a ban on trade in new ivory.

**Mrs. Virginia Bottomley:** It is not normal practice to pay compensation to firms whose trade is adversely affected by import restrictions imposed for the purposes of conserving endangered species.

### Community Charge

**Mr. Harry Barnes:** To ask the Secretary of State for the Environment what guidance has been issued to community charge registration officers concerning the obtaining of addresses from telecommunications operators.

**Mr. Gummer:** Community charge practice note No. 3, published in August last year, gave guidance to registration officers on those bodies from whom they have power to require information. These do not include telecommunications operators.

### River Pollution

**Mr. Redmond:** To ask the Secretary of State for the Environment if any rivers in South Yorkshire are known to be polluted by the use of tributyl tin by boat owners; and if he will make a statement.

**Mr. Howard:** The main freshwater rivers affected have been those carrying large numbers of pleasure craft, which were treated with tributyl tin antifouling paints before the Government banned their sale and supply in 1987. The rivers of South Yorkshire do not fall into this category and so have not been monitored.

**Mr. Alton:** To ask the Secretary of State for the Environment how many companies have deemed consent to discharge into the River Mersey.

**Mr. Howard** *[holding answer 26 June 1989]:* I understand from the North West water authority that 27 companies currently have deemed consents under the terms of part II of the Control of Pollution Act 1974 to discharge effluent into the River Mersey.

The number of extant deemed consents is being progressively reduced as they are reviewed by the North West water authority and either revoked or replaced by a positively determined consent. Following privatisation, the National Rivers Authority will take responsibility for this work.

**Mr. Alton:** To ask the Secretary of State for the Environment if he will name the establishment on Merseyside that is exempt from the Control of Pollution Act 1974.

**Mr. Howard** *[Holding answer 26 June 1987]:* There are no establishments exempt from the provision of part II of the Control of Pollution Act 1974 other than those which are subject to Crown immunity. In such cases, it is the general policy of the Government that the standards of pollution control applied should, wherever possible, be no lower than that for other establishments.

### Rainfall

**Mr. Redmond:** To ask the Secretary of State for the Environment what are the most recent figures and those for five and 10 years ago on the levels of acidification in rainfall *(a)* in Doncaster, *(b)* the three counties of Yorkshire and Humberside and *(c)* nationally.

**Mrs. Virginia Bottomley:** The data requested are provided only for 1988 in the table. Prior to 1986 no data are available for the region and there are insufficient to calculate a representative United Kingdom average. The Doncaster value has been interpolated from nearby rural stations which may not be representative of an urban area.

| Annual mean precipitation weighted acidity in rainfall in u eq H+/litre | | |
|---|---|---|
| Data region | u eq H+/litre | pH |
| United Kingdom | 25 | 4·6 |
| Yorkshire and Humberside | 58 | 4·2 |
| Doncaster | 73 | 4·1 |

## Grants (South Yorkshire)

**Mr. Redmond:** To ask the Secretary of State for the Environment what grants have been, or are due to be made by the Rural Development Commission, for the county of South Yorkshire during 1989-90; and if he will list them.

**Mrs. Virginia Bottomley:** Under the 1989 rural development programme for South Yorkshire the Rural Development Commission has agreed in principle to support six projects:

Rural Development Area Project Officer
Sports hall extension
Church Street/Bridge Street infrastructure link
Resource centre
Market extension
Workspace

Bids for other specific projects will also be considered as they arise. Formal approval and timing of projects will depend on the availability of resources and consideration of detailed applications. The commission also offers grants within the rural development area for the conversion of redundant buildings.

## Public Relations

**Mr. Blair:** To ask the Secretary of State for the Environment which public relations firms his Department has employed and at what cost, for each year since 1979.

**Mr. Ridley:** Apart from the special circumstances of privatisation work, the consistent practice of successive Governments has been to avoid the use of public relations firms or other firms outside Government for public relations work.

Since July 1988 my Department, jointly with the Water Authorities Association, has employed Dewe Rogerson Ltd. as marketing and public relations advisers in connection with the forthcoming privatisation of the water authorities. I am unable to reveal the costs of its work for reasons of commercial confidentiality.

## Dioxin

**Mr. George Howarth:** To ask the Secretary of State for the Environment when he intends to publish the findings of an investigation commissioned by his Department into the extent and effects of dioxin contamination.

**Mrs. Virginia Bottomley:** I refer the hon. Member to the reply I gave on 22 June to my hon. Friend the Member for Daventry (Mr. Boswell) [at columns 202-3], when I announced publication of pollution paper No. 27, entitled "Dioxins in the Environment". A copy is in the Library.

## Housing Co-operatives

**Mr. George Howarth:** To ask the Secretary of State for the Environment when he intends to publish the report of his Department's working party on housing co-operatives.

**Mr. Trippier:** I welcome the report of the committee which has carried out the review of housing co-operatives

in England and which has been published today. The committee has responded positively to its terms of reference and confirmed that co-ops and other tenant control arrangements are popular with tenants, are effective, and are able to justify the grant support which has already been provided for them.

The committee recommends several important measures to increase the involvement of tenants in the management of their homes, and extra support for tenants' groups to help them form housing co-operatives and the other types of tenant control considered in the review.

I am delighted to accept the committee's recommendations and to endorse its view that an expansion of co-operatives and other tenant-led initiatives is now needed. This mirrors the Government's belief that real choices must be available for tenants.

This expansion must be accompanied by further work, linked to research recently carried out and soon to be published by the Department, to refine our understanding of the value for money that tenant-led management can offer and to monitor progress. In the meantime, I am happy to announce that:

we will provide a significant build-up for additional support for the promotion and development of new housing co-operatives and alternative forms of tenant control in the local authority stock;

my Department will urgently discuss with interested bodies training opportunities for both tenants and development workers and ways of improving them;

we will make £2 million available in 1990/91 to provide start-up support for new tenant initiatives and the promotion of new co-operatives in the housing association stock;

a new promotional unit will be set up at the Housing Corporation to increase opportunities for participation among housing association tenants;

we will ensure effective monitoring arrangements are established to ensure progress is made with tenant involvement using these newly increased resources;

we will discuss with interested parties possible ways of improving the coverage of sources of advice and assistance for tenants by secondary co-operatives and other local organisations;

we will invite local authorities to discuss proposals for the decentralisation of a major part of whole of their stock to local management organisations. We intend to develop a small number of pilot projects to test cost-effectiveness and service delivery.

Copies of the report have today been placed in the Libraries of both Houses.

## Domestic Property (Compensation)

**Mr. Heddle:** To ask the Secretary of State for the Environment when he proposes to publish regulations to deal with the basis of compensation payable under part 2 of the Landlord and Tenant Act 1954.

**Mr. Trippier:** It is hoped that consultations with the relevant bodies will take place towards the end of the year and that proposals will be laid before Parliament thereafter.

## Brodsworth Hall, Doncaster

**Mr. Redmond:** To ask the Secretary of State for the Environment what representations he has received about the future of Brodsworth hall, near Doncaster; and if he will make a statement.

**Mrs. Virginia Bottomley:** My right hon. Friend the Secretary of State gave his agreement on 5 April to English

Heritage opening negotiations with the National Heritage Memorial Fund and with the owners of Brodsworth hall on the acquisition of the hall and its contents. No representations have been received since then.

### Bradford West End Scheme

**Mr. Cryer:** To ask the Secretary of State for the Environment if he will list the occasions when his officials had discussions with the developer for the Bradford "west end" scheme for a city grant; and if he will make a statement.

**Mr. Trippier:** Members of the Department's team of professional appraisers and other officials have had a number of discussions on the proposals for "west end". For reasons of commercial confidentiality it is not our practice to comment on individual city grant proposals.

### Water Supplies

**Dr. Cunningham:** To ask the Secretary of State for the Environment if he will list the number of private drinking water supplies in England and Wales and the number of people served by those supplies.

**Mr. Howard:** Local authorities collect and hold information on private supplies in their respective areas. Precise information is not held centrally. However, we estimate that there are 80,000 to 100,000 private supplies in the country serving approximately 1 per cent. of the population.

### North West Water Authority (Contracts)

**Mr. Hoyle:** To ask the Secretary of State for the Environment what information he has on (i) the length and nature of the contracts given by North West water authority to *(a)* Mr. Archie Ramsay and *(b)* Miss Dora McCabe and (ii) their current responsibilities.

**Mr. Howard** *[holding answer 23 June 1989]:* Mr. Ramsay has been appointed by the Secretary of State as an executive member of North West water authority on terms similar to those in his original contract with the authority. His present salary is £65,000. Miss McCabe's appointment as an officer remains a matter for the authority. They continue to fill the posts of financial director and corporate affairs manager respectively.

### Set-aside Land

**Mr. Ron Davies:** To ask the Secretary of State for the Environment how many applications for development on set-aside land have been submitted since the scheme was launched.

**Mr. Chope** *[holding answer 23 June 1989]:* I refer the hon. Member to the reply I gave him on 20 June, at column 68-9.

### Blood Sports

**Mr. Hinchliffe:** To ask the Secretary of State for the Environment what advice has been given by his Department to the Nature Conservancy Council regarding the pursuance of blood sports on land purchased by conservancy bodies with grant-aid.

**Mrs. Virginia Bottomley** *[holding answer 26 June 1989]:* Traditional country rights and uses should be interfered with only where they are in conflict with conservation interests.

## ATTORNEY-GENERAL

### "A Few Scientific Statements on Racial Difference"

**Mr. Cartwright:** To ask the Attorney-General what representations he has received about the British Voice publication, "A Few Scientific Statements on Racial Difference," which has been circulated through the post to residents of south-east London, urging prosecution of those responsible for its distribution under section 5a of the Public Order Act; and if he will make a statement.

**The Solicitor-General:** The Attorney-General has received representations from Greenwich borough council about the publication. The Director of Public Prosecutions has been asked to request the police to make inquiries concerning its publication and distribution. Section 5a of the Public Order Act 1936 has been repealed and replaced by part 3 of the Public Order Act 1986.

## SCOTLAND

### NHS Reform

72. **Mr. Marlow:** To ask the Secretary of State for Scotland if he will make a further statement on his proposals for the reform of the Health Service.

**Mr. Michael Forsyth:** Following publication of the White Paper (Cm. 555) and our working papers a large number of responses have been received. These responses, which include a number of generally positive and constructive comments, will be considered before final decisions are taken on the implementation of our proposals for improving the NHS in Scotland.

### Management Consultants

**Mr. Worthington:** To ask the Secretary of State for Scotland how much money was spent in 1988-89 and in the first quarter of 1989-90 on management consultants brought in from outside the National Health Service.

**Mr. Michael Forsyth:** £192,336 was spent centrally in 1988-89 and £36,595 in the first quarter of 1989-90.

### Consultancy Fees

**Mr. Galbraith:** To ask the Secretary of State for Scotland if he will give for each health board the amount spent on consultancy fees in the year 1988-89 and the first quarter of 1989-90.

**Mr. Michael Forsyth:** Information available from the annual accounts of health boards relates to the total of fees paid to management consultants, to legal firms (other than for legal expenses connected with compensation claims) and to work study consultants. The amounts for each health board for 1988-89 are shown in the table.

| Health Board | 1988-89 £ |
| --- | --- |
| Argyll and Clyde | 68,429 |
| Ayrshire and Arran | 32,084 |
| Borders | 15,562 |

| Health Board | 1988-89 £ |
|---|---|
| Dumfries and Galloway | 61,258 |
| Fife | 61,810 |
| Forth Valley | 67,789 |
| Grampian | 42,576 |
| Greater Glasgow | 257,258 |
| Highland | 106,072 |
| Lanarkshire | 26,570 |
| Lothian | 172,797 |
| Orkney | 17,499 |
| Shetland | 5,405 |
| Tayside | 14,738 |
| Western Isles | 28,534 |
| Total | 978,381 |

Information relating to the current financial year is not yet available centrally.

### Ambulance Service

**Mr. Galbraith:** To ask the Secretary of State for Scotland if he will give for each year since 1980 the number of emergency call-outs by the Scottish ambulance service both in absolute terms and as a percentage of the 1980 figure.

**Mr. Michael Forsyth:** The information requested is as follows:

| Year | Number of emergency calls | Percentage of 1980 total |
|---|---|---|
| 1980 | 129,201 | 100·0 |
| 1981 | 131,219 | 101·6 |
| 1982 | 132,672 | 102·7 |
| 1983 | 138,229 | 107·0 |
| 1984 | 146,302 | 113·2 |
| 1985 | 145,383 | 112·5 |
| 1986 | 154,018 | 119·2 |
| 1987 | 161,822 | 125·2 |
| 1988 | 165,956 | 128·4 |

## WALES

### Sewage

**Mr. Ron Davies:** To ask the Secretary of State for Wales if he will publish details of Welsh Water's proposals for investment in sewage treatment works in Rhymney valley necessary to ensure compliance with the relevant European directive; and if he will indicate in respect of each works the projected time scale for completion.

**Mr. Grist:** There is no European directive concerning the performance of sewage treatment works. However, Welsh Water is engaged upon a programme of improvements to provide for full compliance with discharge consent conditions at poorly performing works.

**Mr. Michael:** To ask the Secretary of State for Wales if he will list the precise location of each of the applications for derogation of sewage discharges in Wales advertised by his Department on 21 June; and if he will also list all other derogations currently in force in a similar way.

**Mr. Grist:** No applications for derogation of sewage discharges in Wales have been advertised by the Department.

Details of the Welsh Water applications for time-limited variations of consent conditions, including the national grid reference of the location of discharge, were advertised by the authority in the *London Gazette* and *Western Mail* on 21 June. A copy of the applications may be inspected at the regional rivers division of Welsh Water, St. Mellons, Cardiff.

**Mr. Michael:** To ask the Secretary of State for Wales if he will state for each sewage discharge derogation site currently approved in Wales or currently under consideration by his Department (a) whether he has approved a programme of works to improve the effluent at each specific site, (b) when each programme of work is due to start and finish and (c) to what level each programme of works is designed to improve the effluent at that point of discharge.

**Mr. Grist:** All Welsh Water sewage treatment works for which applications for time-limited consents have been received are included in a programme of capital improvements designed to ensure future compliance. Details of the consent parameters applied for are included in the detailed applications which are available for inspection at the regional rivers division of Welsh Water at St. Mellons, Cardiff.

**Mr. Michael:** To ask the Secretary of State for Wales what justification for a request for derogation in respect of a sewage discharge has been given to him by Welsh Water in each case where a derogation is in force in Wales or is currently under consideration by his Department.

**Mr. Grist:** In making an application for a time-limited variation to an existing discharge consent, Welsh Water must satisfactorily define its plans for investment to improve the performance of the works.

**Mr. Michael:** To ask the Secretary of State for Wales what monitoring arrangements he has made in respect of each of the derogations of sewage in force in Wales; and what arrangements he will make for each of those currently under consideration by his Department.

**Mr. Grist:** There are no derogations of sewage treatment works consent conditions currently in force in the Principality. The water authority is currently responsible for monitoring all its own discharges; subject to enactment of the Water Bill, the National Rivers Authority will assume this duty.

### River Pollution

**Dr. Kim Howells:** To ask the Secretary of State for Wales (1) pursuant to the reply to the hon. Member for Pontypridd of 21 June, if he will list the nature and results in terms of judgments and fines, of prosecutions brought against polluters of south Wales rivers over the past 10 years;

(2) pursuant to the reply to the hon. Member for Pontypridd of 21 June, if he will list the recorded incidents of pollution of the rivers and streams of south Wales over the past 10 years, on a year-by-year basis, including specific dates, locations, effects and, where known, polluters.

**Mr. Grist:** This is a matter for the Welsh water authority.

**Dr. Kim Howells:** To ask the Secretary of State for Wales, pursuant to the reply to the hon. Member for

Pontypridd of 21 June, how the Government intend to enable the National Rivers Authority to prosecute polluters of Welsh rivers, including those companies which release raw sewage into those rivers, after the privatisation of the water authorities.

**Mr. Grist:** Under the provisions of the Water Bill the National Rivers Authority will have the power to institute criminal proceedings. How it uses that power will be a matter for the authority.

**Dr. Kim Howells:** To ask the Secretary of State for Wales, pursuant to the reply to the hon. Member for Pontypridd of 21 June, whether the Government intend to allow the Welsh water authority to continue to discharge raw sewage into Welsh rivers after the privatisation of that company.

**Mr. Grist:** The consenting of Welsh Water discharges after privatisation will be matter for the National Rivers Authority, subject to enactment of the Water Bill.

### Water Supplies

**Mr. Michael:** To ask the Secretary of State for Wales what arrangements he has made for monitoring by his Department or on behalf of his Department of derogations of water supplies granted by him under article 9 of the EC drinking water directives 80/778/EEC.

**Mr. Grist:** Monitoring of the quality of all drinking water supplies within Welsh Water's area is carried out by that authority and regular reports are submitted to the Department.

## DEFENCE

### Nuclear Weapons

**Mr. Snape:** To ask the Secretary of State for Defence if there has been any modernisation of Britain's nuclear depth bomb capability since 1980; and if there are any plans in existence or under consideration to modernise this capability.

**Mr. Archie Hamilton:** There has been no modernisation of Britain's nuclear depth bomb capability since 1980. As part of the studies related to modernising United Kingdom tactical nuclear weapons capability, consideration is being given to the replacement of the full spectrum of United Kingdom tactical nuclear weapons, including sea-based systems. However, no decisions have yet been taken.

**Mr. Corbett:** To ask the Secretary of State for Defence whether there has been any increase or decrease in Britain's stockpile of nuclear depth charges since 1980; and whether there is any current consideration of increasing the numbers held.

**Mr. Archie Hamilton:** For security reasons it is not our policy to comment on the size of the nuclear stockpile. However, it is the policy of the British Government to maintain the stockpile at the minimum level possible to provide a credible, effective deterrent.

**Mr. Corbett:** To ask the Secretary of State for Defence whether there has been any modernisation of Royal Navy helicopters capable of delivering nuclear depth bombs since 1980; and whether there is any current consideration of modernisation of these helicopters.

**Mr. Archie Hamilton:** Nuclear depth bombs would be deployed from Royal Navy ASW helicopters. These helicopters have been modernised in various ways since 1980, and will continue to be modernised as required. Work carried out to date has not been directly related to the helicopters' nuclear weapon delivery capabilities.

### Trident Programme

**Mr. Corbett:** To ask the Secretary of State for Defence whether he will publish in the *Official Report* a list of those parliamentary constituencies which will benefit from contracts as a result of the Trident programme, detailing for each constituency the name of the contractor and the value and general nature of the contract.

**Mr. Sainsbury:** The information can be provided only at disproportionate cost.

### Royal Ordnance Factory plc

**Mr. Straw:** To ask the Secretary of State for Defence what estimate he makes of the value which would have been put on the Royal Ordnance factory, Blackburn, when the Royal Ordnance Factory plc was sold to British Aerospace if full account had been taken of the factors listed in the recent report by the Comptroller and Auditor General.

**Mr. Sainsbury:** Our surveyors took full account of all the significant factors relevant to the existing use and alternative use valuations of each site as at the date of the valuation. There are no additional factors mentioned in the Comptroller and Auditor General's report which would have affected the valuations made.

**Mr. Straw:** To ask the Secretary of State for Defence what value was put on the Royal Ordnance factory, Blackburn, when the Royal Ordnance Factory plc was sold to British Aerospace.

**Mr. Sainsbury:** As with all the sites owned by Royal Ordnance plc, ROF Blackburn was valued on both an existing use and an alternative use basis, as at 31 December 1985. These valuations were £4,400,000 and £400,000 respectively. Only the higher, existing use, valuations were made available to prospective purchasers of Royal Ordnance.

**Mr. Straw:** To ask the Secretary of State for Defence whether *(a)* the potential development value of the site of the Royal Ordnance factory Blackburn, and *(b)* the proximity of the site to the extension of the M65 motorway to the M6 were included in the value placed upon the factory when Royal Ordnance Factory plc was sold to British Aerospace.

**Mr. Sainsbury:** All the significant circumstances relevant to the alternative use valuation of ROF Blackburn as at the date of the valuation were taken into account.

## OVERSEAS DEVELOPMENT

### Rain Forests

**Mr. Mans:** To ask the Secretary of State for Foreign and Commonwealth Affairs if he has any new proposals to assist preservation of the Brazilian rain forests.

**Mr. Chris Patten:** An Overseas Development Administration environmental mission, led by my chief forestry officer and including the director of the Royal Botanic Gardens, Kew, visited Brazil last month to identify proposals for a new programme of environmental assistance to the Brazilian Government, particularly in rain forest conservation. This mission was very successful and has come back with a number of specific proposals for technical co-operation projects in sustainable forest management, genetic resource exploration and conservation, and environmental monitoring which we hope can be finalised within the next few months. I shall make the details available as soon as they are settled. During my own visit to Brazil next week I hope to be able to sign a memorandum of understanding with the Brazilian Government to establish the framework for this new environmental programme. I also hope to visit Amazonia and talk to some of the Brazilian bodies actively involved in trying to protect the rain forest.

## ENERGY

### Uranium

**Mr. Flynn:** To ask the Secretary of State for Energy what quantities of depleted uranium owned by *(a)* British Nuclear Fuels Ltd, *(b)* United Kingdom Atomic Energy Authority, and *(c)* foreign customers are currently stored at Sellafield, Chapelcross and Dounreay sites, respectively.

**Mr. Michael Spicer:** Stocks of civil depleted uranium held under safeguards and resulting from the reprocessing of civil magnox fuel or the operation of enrichment plants by British Nuclear Fuels plc are held at a number of sites. The total quantities are:

|  | Uranium tonnes |
| --- | --- |
| Sellafield | 100 |
| Chapelcross | 5,000 |
| Dounreay | 50 |

A further 18,400 tonnes u of such material are held at Capenhurst and 6,200 tonnes u at Springfields.

Some 20 per cent. of the stocks held at BNFL sites are owned by BNFL and some 5 per cent. by its overseas customers. The BNFL stocks include some 50 tonnes u owned by the authority. Almost all the material held at Dounreay is owned by the UKAEA.

### Electricity Disconnections

**Mr. Barry Jones:** To ask the Secretary of State for Energy if he will give the number of domestic customer disconnections in 1979 and for the latest date in *(a)* Wales and *(b)* each electricity board in England and Wales, and the percentage change in each case.

**Mr. Michael Spicer:** I refer the hon. Member to the answer I gave to the hon. Member for Sedgefield (Mr. Blair) on 9 December 1988, at column 377, setting out the total figures for disconnections in each of the years 1979-1980 to 1987-88. The number of disconnections in England and Wales in 1988-89 was 75,230.

Detailed figures for disconnections in each area board are a matter for the electricity supply industry and I have asked the chairman of the Electricity Council to write to the hon. Member with the requested information.

### Berkeley Nuclear Power Station

**Mr. Cohen:** To ask the Secretary of State for Energy whether, following the removal of fuel at Berkeley nuclear power station, the cores will be vented by atmospheric air throughout the period before final dismantling; and if he will make a statement.

**Mr. Michael Spicer:** This is an operational matter for the Central Electricity Generating Board. I have asked the chairman to write to the hon. Member.

### Efficiency Campaign

**Mr. Rost:** To ask the Secretary of State for Energy what targets he has set for the initial 12 months of his public sector energy efficiency campaign launched in January; and if he will make a statement.

**Mr. Peter Morrison:** Details of the campaign are still under consideration.

### Office of Electricity Regulation

**Mr. Rost:** To ask the Secretary of State for Energy whether the office of electricity regulation staff is to be restricted entirely to personnel from the Department of Energy, and the electricity supply industry.

**Mr. Michael Spicer:** No.

### Hinkley C (Inquiry)

**Dr. Thomas:** To ask the Secretary of State for Energy when a witness from his Department is next expected to appear at the Hinkley C nuclear public inquiry; how many support officials will accompany the witness; on what topic he will give evidence; and whether the witness will be permitted to answer questions on the merits of Government policy.

**Mr. Michael Spicer:** The Department's official witness will return to the inquiry, at the inspector's request, on 20 July to give further evidence on the progress of the Electricity Bill and any other developments in Government policy relevant to the inquiry since the date of his previous appearance. He will be supported by other officials from the Department as necessary. As I told the hon. Member on 27 October 1988, at column 318, it is not customary for an official representative of a Government Department to answer questions as to the merits of Government policy and I continue to see no reason for the Department's witness to do so.

### Public Relations

**Mr. Blair:** To ask the Secretary of State for Energy which public relations firms his Department has employed and at what cost, for each year since 1979.

**Mr. Parkinson:** Apart from the special circumstances of privatisation work, the consistent practice of successive Governments has been to avoid the use of public relations firms or other companies outside Government for public relations work.

My Department has used the following companies in connection with privatisation:

Charles Barker in 1982 for Britoil
Streets Financial in 1983 for Enterprise Oil

Dewe Rogerson in 1985 for British Gas.

In addition, I appointed Lowe Bell Communications in 1988, jointly with the area boards, and Valin Pollen International in 1989, jointly with the CEGB, to draw up marketing strategies for the offers for sale of the electricity distribution companies and generating companies respectively.

The amounts paid are commercially confidential.

# FOREIGN AND COMMONWEALTH AFFAIRS

## Cambodia

**Mr. Wigley:** To ask the Secretary of State for Foreign and Commonwealth Affairs if he will make a statement on progress of the United Kingdom's participation in efforts to secure a peaceful and democratic future for Cambodia.

**Mr. Eggar:** Both through bilateral contacts and through multilateral action in the United Nations' Security Council, and in the run-up to the Paris international conference in August, we are playing our full part in the search for a peaceful and durable settlement to the conflict in Cambodia.

## China

**Mr. Wigley:** To ask the Secretary of State for Foreign and Commonwealth Affairs on what date he has had discussions with the ambassador of the People's Republic of China, with regard to the recent troubles in China and their implications for United Kingdom students in China; and if he will make a statement.

**Mr. Eggar:** I refer the hon. Member to the reply given to my hon. Friend the Member for Christchurch (Mr. Adley) on 16 June, at column *560*.

## Turks and Caicos Government

**Mr. Allason:** To ask the Secretary of State for Foreign and Commonwealth Affairs how many Ministers in the Turks and Caicos Government have been convicted of drug offences or corruption since 1984.

**Mr. Eggar:** Three Turks and Caicos Ministers were convicted on drugs charges in the United States of America in 1985.

There have been no further convictions since we suspended ministerial government in the Turks and Caicos Islands in 1986. A new constitution came into effect with the return of ministerial government in March 1988.

## Western European Union

**Sir Russell Johnston:** To ask the Secretary of State for Foreign and Commonwealth Affairs if he is satisfied with the availability of Western European Union documents to hon. Members in view of the process of reactivation.

**Mr. Waldegrave:** Given the limitations imposed by the fact that most documents produced by the Council of the Western European Union are classified, I am satisfied with their availability to hon. Members. Documents produced by the Assembly of the Western European Union are distributed to all Members of the British delegation to the Assembly, who have not so far asked that they be made more widely available.

## Antarctic Treaty

**Mr. Dalyell:** To ask the Secretary of State for Foreign and Commonwealth Affairs if he will make a statement on his latest discussions with the United Kingdom's co-signatories to the Antarctic treaty.

**Mr. Eggar:** The Antarctic treaty consultative parties met in Paris in May in preparation for the XV Antarctic treaty consultative meeting in October. A full agenda for the ATCM was provisionally adopted. Items for discussion will include comprehensive measures for the protection of the Antarctic environment, marine pollution, promotion of international scientific co-operation, Antarctic tourism, charting of Antarctic waters, and air safety.

## Rain Forests

**Mr. Dalyell:** To ask the Secretary of State for Foreign and Commonwealth Affairs if he will make a statement on his discussions with Sir Peter Walters, chairman of BP about their mining operation in the Brazilian rain forest.

**Mr. Eggar:** I refer the hon. Member to my reply to the hon. Member for South Shields (Dr. Clark) of 26 June, at column *287*. My officials are in contact with BP on this issue.

**Mr. Allen McKay:** To ask the Secretary of State for Foreign and Commonwealth Affairs what action the Government are taking to stop *(a)* BP and *(b)* other British companies contributing to the destruction of rain forests around the world.

**Mr. Eggar:** My right hon. Friend the Minister for Overseas Development will be visiting Brazil including the Amazon region from 4-9 July. During his visit he will be discussing with Brazilian Ministers and officials our efforts to identify effective ways of helping them with a wide range of environmental problems including rainforest conservation. He will also be meeting representatives of British companies operating in Brazil with whom he hopes to discuss their role in environmental protection.

The hon. Member will be aware of recent media reports alleging involvement by United Kingdom companies in rain forest destruction. We are studying these, but I understand that the companies, including BP, claim that these press reports contain important errors of fact, and that they themselves operate significant environmental protection programmes in their projects in Brazil.

More generally, Britain is a leading supporter of the tropical forestry action plan and the International Tropical Timber Organisation which aim to help countries conserve their forests and manage them sustainably.

## Universal Postal Union

**Mr. Bowis:** To ask the Secretary of State for Foreign and Commonwealth Affairs how many of his officials will attend the congress of the Universal Postal Union in Washington DC in the current year; and what percentage of these would normally be employed in Her Britannic Majesty's embassy at Washington DC.

**Mr. Eggar:** The British delegation will consist largely of officials from the Department of Trade and Industry and the Post Office. It is anticipated that there will be one representative from the Foreign and Commonwealth Office in London. As this is a major international conference taking place in Washington, we expect that there will be some involvement on the part of embassy staff, depending on requirements as they arise.

### Human Rights

**Mr. Vaz:** To ask the Secretary of State for Foreign and Commonwealth Affairs how many representations he has made complaining about the denial of human rights and the use of torture in the last five years in China.

**Mr. Eggar:** We have made a number of representations about human rights to the Chinese authorities over the last five years, but the precise information requested is not readily available and could be provided only at disproportionate cost.

**Mr. Vaz:** To ask the Secretary of State for Foreign and Commonwealth Affairs how many representations he has made complaining about the denial of human rights and the use of torture in the last five years in Brazil.

**Mr. Eggar:** In November 1988 I discussed allegations in Amnesty International's report entitled "Brazil, Authorized Violence in Rural Areas" with the then Brazilian Justice Minister. I refer to the answer given on this subject by my hon. Friend the Minister of State to the hon. Member for Stoke-on-Trent North (Ms. Walley) on 21 April 1989, at columns *313-14*.

We have not otherwise made any representations to the Brazilians on human rights since democracy was restored in 1985.

**Mr. Vaz:** To ask the Secretary of State for Foreign and Commonwealth Affairs how many representations he has made complaining about the denial of human rights and the use of torture in the last five years in the United States of America.

**Mr. Eggar:** None.

### EC Directives

**Mr. Teddy Taylor:** To ask the Secretary of State for Foreign and Commonwealth Affairs if he will make a statement setting out the powers which are available to member states if they consider that the Commission has presented directives which are outside the competence of the Commission and the Community, or if the directive is presented on the basis of majority voting without good reasons; and if he will list the occasions on which Her Majesty's Government have made use of these powers.

**Mr. Eggar:** Proposals requiring unanimity may be defeated by a single vote against. Those requiring a qualified majority may be defeated by a blocking minority of 23 votes, or amended by unanimity. In addition, member states may challenge measures, after adoption, in the European Court of Justice. The United Kingdom has challenged the Council in the court over treaty base issues for hormone growth producers in animals (1986); minimum standards for battery hens (1986); youth training (1988) and COMETT II (1989).

### EC Social Charter

**Mr. Michael Morris:** To ask the Secretary of State for Foreign and Commonwealth Affairs whether it is the United Kingdoms Government's intention to accept in the future any of the articles of the Council of Europe's social charter which currently rejects articles 2(1), 4(3), 7(1), 7(4), 7(7), 8(2), 12(2), 12(3) and 12(4).

**Mr. Cope:** I have been asked to reply.

At the present time the Government have no plans to accept articles 2(1), 4(3), 7(1), 7(4), 7(7), 8(2), 12(2), 12(3) and 12(4) of the Council of Europe's European social charter. However, the situation is kept under review.

### Programmes and Schemes (Finance)

**Mr. Spearing:** To ask the Secretary of State for Foreign and Commonwealth Affairs if he will list in the *Official Report* all those programmes or schemes for research, development, co-operation or exchange of information on associated activity for which financial provision is made within the current budget of the European Economic Community, listed under the relevant Department of the United Kingdom Government with official title, or where allocated, an acronym, and showing for each project the date of its inception, the authorisation and amounts of funding and the principal participants or beneficiaries within the United Kingdom.

**Mr. Newton** *[holding answer 6 June 1989]:* I have been asked to reply.

The Community's 1987-91 framework programme for research and development covers several areas of R and D. The Cabinet Office is responsible for overall co-ordination of the United Kingdom's interests in the framework programme, while individual Departments are responsible for United Kingdom interest in specific sub-programmes. I represent Her Majesty's Government at meetings of the Community Council of Ministers (Research) at which the implementation of the framework programme is agreed. A wide range of research co-operation, exchanges of information and associated activity also takes place outside the framework programme. The information requested is therefore not readily available and could be provided only at disproportionate cost.

A breakdown of R and D programmes within the framework programme is as follows. Of the programmes listed, seven (radiation protection, FLAIR, MAST, DOSES, MONITOR, VALUE and an extension to EUROTRA) were adopted at the most recent Research Council on 20 June. The Council also adopted common positions on a further four programmes (which will probably be formally adopted before the end of the year):

— STEP (science and technology for environmental protection) and EPOCH (European programme on climatology and natural hazards) are two programmes intended to improve the scientific base of environmental policy. Over a period of four years STEP will receive funding of 75 million ecu (£50 million) and EPOCH 40 million ecu (£27 million).

— BRIDGE (biotechnology research for innovation, development and growth in Europe) will receive Community funding of 100 million ecu (£67 million) over four years

— The research and technological development programme in the field of raw materials and recycling will receive Community funding of 45 million ecu (£30 million) over three years.

The Research Council also adopted a resolution reaffirming its support for the COST framework for European collaboration in R and D involving both EC and non-EC countries, and held a preliminary policy debate on the mid-term review of the 1987-91 framework programme.

| Name of Programme | United Kingdom lead Department | Duration of programme | Authorisation | Community Funding |
|---|---|---|---|---|
| Medical and Health Research | Department of Health | 1987–1991 | Council Decision 17 November 1987 | 65 million ecu (£43 million) |
| Radiation Protection | Department of Health | 1990–1991 | Council Decision 20 June 1989 | 21·2 million ecu (£14 million) |
| ESPRIT II (European Strategic Programme for Research and Development in Information Technologies) | Department of Trade and Industry | 1987–1992 | Council Decision 11 April 1988 | 1,600 million ecu (£1,067 million) |
| RACE (Research and Development in Advanced Communications technologies in Europe) | Department of Trade and Industry | 1987–1992 | Council Decision 14 December 1987 | 550 million ecu (£367 million) |
| DELTA (Development of European Learning through Technological Advance) | Department of Employment | 1988–1990 | Council Decision 29 June 1988 | 20 million ecu (£13 million) |
| DRIVE (Dedicated Road Infrastructure for Vehicle safety in Europe) | Department of Transport | 1988–1991 | Council Decision 29 June 1988 | 60 million ecu (£40 Million) |
| AIM (Advanced Informatics in Medicine in Europe) | Department of Health | 1988–1990 | Council Decision 4 November 1988 | 20 million ecu (£13 million) |
| BRITE/EURAM (Basic Research in Industrial Technology/Advanced Materials) | Department of Trade and Industry | 1989–1992 | Council Decision 15 December 1988 | 499 million ecu (£333 million) |
| BCR (Community Bureau of Reference) | Department of Trade and Industry | 1988–1992 | Council Decision 29 June 1988 | 59·2 million ecu (£39·5 million) |
| ECLAIR (European Collaborative Linkage of Agriculture and Industry through Research) | Ministry of Agriculture, Fisheries and Food | 1988–1993 | Council Decision 23 February 1989 | 80 million ecu (£53 million) |
| FLAIR (Food linked agro-industrial research) | Ministry of Agriculture, Fisheries and Food | 1989–1993 | Council Decision 20 June 1989 | 25 million ecu (£17 Million) |
| Controlled Thermonuclear fusion —JET and general programme | Department of Energy | 1988–1992 | Council Decision 25 July 1988 | 735 million ecu (£490 million) |
| Joint Research Centre's programme of activities for 1988-1991 (covering Quality of Life, modernisation of industrial sectors and energy) | Cabinet Office | 1988–1991 | Council Decisions 29 October 1988 | 700 million ecu (£467 million) |
| JOULE (Joint Opportunities for Unconventional or Long-Term Energy supply) | Department of Energy | 1989–1992 | Council Decision 15 December 1987 | 122 million ecu (£81 million) |
| Science and Technology for Development | Overseas Development Administration | 1987–1991 | Council Decision 14 December 1987 | 80 million ecu (£53 million) |
| Fisheries programme | Ministry of Agriculture, Fisheries and Food | 1988–1992 | Council Decision 19 December 1987 | 30 million ecu (£20 million) |
| SCIENCE (Co-operation and exchanges between scientists and laboratories) | Department of Education and Science | 1988–1992 | Council Decision 29 June 1988 | 167 million ecu (£111 million) |
| SPES (Stimulation Plan for Economic Science) | Department of Education and Science | 1989–1992 | Council Decision 17 November 1988 | 6 million ecu (£4 million) |
| Large Scale Scientific Facilities (Community support plan to facilitate access to large-scale scientific facilities of European interest) | Department of Education and Science | 1988–1992 | Council Decision 14 March 1989 | 30 million ecu (£20 million) |
| MONITOR (strategic analysis, forcasting and evaluation in science and technology) | Department of Trade and Industry | 1988–1992 | Council Decision 20 June 1989 | 22 million ecu (£15 million) |
| Extension to EUROTRA (machine translation system) | Department of Trade and Industry | 1989–1990 | Council Decision 20 June 1989 | 7 million ecu (£4·6 million) |
| DOSES (Development of Statistical Expert systems) | Department of Trade and Industry | 1989–1992 | Council Decision 20 June 1989 | 4 million ecu (£2·6 million) |
| VALUE (dissemination and utilisation of S & T results) | Department of Trade and Industry | 1989–1992 | Council Decision 20 June 1989 | 38 million ecu (£25 million) |

# HOME DEPARTMENT

## Road Traffic Law Review

**Mr. Knox:** To ask the Secretary of State for the Home Department what research projects have been initiated by his Department in line with the recommendations in the road traffic law review which he accepted.

**Mr. Douglas Hogg:** The Home Office is undertaking a study of how traffic policing resources are organised and targeted. We hope to undertake a research project on the level of driving while disqualified later this year or early next year.

## Public Relations

**Mr. Blair:** To ask the Secretary of State for the Home Department which public relations firms his Department has employed and at what cost, for each year since 1979.

**Mr. Douglas Hogg:** None.

## "The Satanic Verses"

**Mr. Cryer:** To ask the Secretary of State for the Home Department if he is satisfied that members of the Iranian embassy are not involved in financing or assisting in any way organised violence connected with the campaign centred on the book "The Satanic Verses"; and if he will make a statement.

**Mr. Hurd:** Iran closed its embassy in London and withdrew all its diplomats on 28 February 1989 at the Government's request, following the threats issued by the Iranian leadership to the lives of Mr. Salmon Rushdie and his publishers. The Government have made it plain that the promotion of organised violence in the United Kingdom will not be tolerated, and all necessary measures will continue to be taken against it.

**Mr. Cryer:** To ask the Secretary of State for the Home Department if he will ask for a report from the chief constable of West Yorkshire police on the rioting during and following a meeting organised by the Council of Mosques in Bradford on Saturday 17 June, and in particular whether any Iranian students were involved on an organised basis in the disruption, and the level of policing available from the start of the meeting at 11 am, and if he will make a statement.

**Mr. Douglas Hogg:** I understand from the chief constable of West Yorkshire police that around 3,000 Moslems, including, it is believed, a small number of Iranian students, took part in the demonstration. The organisers and stewards co-operated fully with the police and the meeting itself was conducted in an orderly manner. After the meeting some 200 youths ran through the centre of Bradford jostling bystanders and causing some damage to cars and other property. A small number of police officers and members of the public were hurt. At the meeting there were initially six officers present with larger numbers in reserve nearby. During the disturbances lasting around 90 minutes some 200 police officers were deployed.

### Blasphemy

**Mr. Cryer:** To ask the Secretary of State for the Home Department if he will now introduce legislation to repeal the law relating to blasphemy; and if he will make a statement.

**Mr. John Patten:** We have no plans to change the law on blasphemy.

### Cocaine

**Mr. Corbett:** To ask the Secretary of State for the Home Department how many samples of freebase cocaine or crack have been submitted to the forensic science laboratories and the laboratory of the Government chemist in each of the last three years.

**Mr. Douglas Hogg:** In 1986, 1987 and 1988 there were zero, five and 15 samples confirmed as crack submitted to these laboratories. A further 12 samples have been confirmed as crack in the first five months of this year. In addition over the same three-year period five, seven and 13 samples had features of crack with a further 10 identified this year.

**Mr. Corbett:** To ask the Secretary of State for the Home Department what in each of the last three years for which figures are available, have been the number of deaths in which cocaine in any form has been a cause or contributory factor.

**Mr. Douglas Hogg:** The Home Office collects information on the deaths by overdose of drug misusers. The number of such deaths in which cocaine in any form was recorded as a cause or contributory factor in the three years to 31 December 1987, the latest for which figures are available, is given in the following table:

|      | Number |
|------|--------|
| 1985 | 1 |
| 1986 | 7 |
| 1987 | 9 |

**Mr. Corbett:** To ask the Secretary of State for the Home Department whether he will place a document in the Library listing by name all the medical and scientific authorities on whom he relies for his statements about the harmful effects of crack, the smokeable, base-form of cocaine.

**Mr. Douglas Hogg:** "Drug Misuse—a basic briefing" prepared by the Institute for the Study of Drug Dependency includes, among the harmful effects of cocaine, the following: misusers may develop a strong psychological dependence; misuse can lead to an extreme state of agitation, anxiety, paranoia and perhaps hallucination; continued misuse may cause a state of mind similar to paranoid psychosis; although rare, excessive doses can cause death from respiratory or heart failure. It also states that smoking cocaine is a more potent method of administration than "snorting" and that the effects are felt more immediately. I am placing a copy of the booklet in the Library.

Cocaine smoked in the form of crack is a recent phenomenon, but experience from the United States suggests that because crack acts more rapidly it poses a much greater risk of addiction. The ministerial group on the misuse of drugs has instituted a review of the available medical and scientific literature on the effects of crack.

### EC Social Charter

**Mr. Teddy Taylor:** To ask the Secretary of State for the Home Department if he will seek to establish from the European Commission whether the directive on the harmonisation of conditions of residence, as proposed in the Community "Charter for Fundamental Social Rights" Com. 89-248-final, will fall to be presented to the Council on the basis of majority voting.

**Mr. Renton:** The voting arrangements for a particular proposal depend on the substance of the proposal and on the specific article(s) of the treaty of Rome, as amended by the Single European Act, appropriate to this. Until a draft proposal is agreed by the Commission it is not possible to know on which article the Commission will be basing its proposals.

### Police Complaints Authority

**Mr. Wheeler:** To ask the Secretary of State for the Home Department whether he has reached his decisions on the recommendations contained in the report of the Police Complaints Authority "Triennial Review 1985-1988.

**Mr. Hurd:** Yes. I announced on 14 November 1988 that a consultation document on the recommendations was being sent to the police representative bodies, the local authority associations, the Director of Public Prosecutions and the Police Complaints Authority. The document was also being made available to anyone else on request. I have given further consideration to the recommendations in the light of the comments received.

I have decided to accept 11 of the authority's recommendations in whole or in part.

Of these 11 recommendations, three have been or will be dealt with by administrative action by my Department as follows:

I intend that recommendation (4) should be met by making available to the authority information which chief officers currently supply to Her Majesty's chief inspectorate of constabulary.

I have accepted the following recommendations which will be implemented by amendments to regulations. I have asked my officials to bring forward the necessary amendments as quickly as possible.

> (3) that "complaint . . . about the conduct" should be enlarged to embrace all such matters arising out of or in the course of the incident complained of as the authority may determine by investigation or otherwise (paragraph 1.8);
>
> (4) that chief officers be under an obligation to provide us with such information on the informal resolution procedure as we may reasonably require to enable us to fulfil the mandate of section 97(4) (paragraph 1.14);
>
> (7) that the police authority be required to deal with complaints against senior officers through a small disciplinary sub-committee, enjoined to a proper judicial approach to the task (paragraph 1.26).
>
> (5) That the words "or informally resolved" should be added to those conditions necessary for dispensation under regulation 3 on the ground that the complaint is repetitious (paragraph 1.17);
>
> (15) that the authority be given an equivalent discretionary power and propose that it be done by way of amendment of the Police (Anonymous, Repetitious Etc. Complaints) Regulations 1985, to include words such as "or vexatious, oppressive, or an abuse of the complaints system" in the description of complaints for which we can grant a dispensation from investigation (paragraph 2.29);
>
> (16) that there should be a time limit of 12 months from the date of the incident, or the latest incident, giving rise to the complaint within which to bring it to notice. There should be the usual safeguard to enable us to exercise discretion to extend the time limit where good reason for delay is shown and no injustice is likely to be caused (paragraph 2.30).

It will not be possible to give direct effect to the third of these recommendations by regulation. But I intend to bring forward amendments to regulations which will achieve the purpose sought by the authority.

I have also accepted five recommendations for action at the next legislative opportunity.

> (9) That the language of sections 90 and 92 be amended to make it clear beyond doubt what is intended (paragraph 1.41);
>
> (10) that the Act be amended to enable the authority to give its reasons for preferring charges at the stage of recommendations, when the chief officer must be consulted (paragraph 1.42);
>
> (11) that an alternative composition of a disciplinary tribunal should be considered (paragraph 1.45);
>
> (13a) that section 98 be restructured so as to provide: that the authority has discretion to publish such information as is reasonably necessary to inform the public of the outcome of investigations, without derogation from the principle of confidentiality between the authority, complainants and those who provide information (paragraph 2.11);
>
> (17) that the authority be granted a discretion to dispense with supervision in cases where it is satisfied on proper evidence that the injury sustained is minor, notwithstanding the definition in section 87(4), whether this is apparent from the start or becomes so only in the course of the investigation (paragraph 2.31).

The purpose of the first two of these recommendations will be achieved by administrative action pending legislation.

I propose to review the case for the following two recommendations when next contemplating legislation on the complaints procedures.

> (1) That there should be a definition of complaint in the Act which distinguishes between categories of complaint (paragraph 1.5);
>
> (6) that the authority should be able to satisfy itself in suitable cases that a complaint has been withdrawn by an entirely voluntary and well-informed consent (paragraph 1.17).

I have asked my officials to hold further discussions with the Police Complaints Authority and the police on two recommendations before I come to a final decision:

> (12) That steps be taken, perhaps by regulation, to lay down a time scale within which the various procedures necessary to bring about a disciplinary hearing are to be completed (paragraph 1.47);
>
> (13b) that section 98 be restructured so as to provide: that chief officers be restricted in the use of their copy of a report of a supervised investigation, to the purpose for which they receive their copy under the Act and that they publish no part of it (paragraph 2.11).

I have decided not to accept four of the authority's recommendations:

> (2) That the last word about recording or de-recording a complaint should be with the independent authority rather than with the police (paragraph 1.6)
>
> (8) that the powers described in section 88 of the Act should be extended to the authority in those cases where it appears to them that by reason of their gravity or exceptional circumstances the investigations should be supervised even if there is no complaint (paragraph 1.34);
>
> (14) that we ought to have the right to exercise the power to require the production of documents in our own name, which right is at present in doubt (paragraph 2.15);
>
> (18) that all incidents in the course of which a firearm is discharged, whether accidentally or deliberately, should be mandatorily referable to us. This would enable there to be an independent presence at the examination of the circumstances surrounding those incidents which understandably give rise to public anxiety (paragraph 2.33).

Finally, I have noted the authority's comment that the question of a lower level of summary disciplinary hearings is worthy of further discussion (paragraph 3.20).

I have been heartened by the positive response to the consultation document on the authority's recommendations and I am satisfied that the action I have outlined above will further enhance the operation of the procedures for dealing with complaints against the police.

### Summer Time

**Dr. Michael Clark:** To ask the Secretary of State for the Home Department when the consultation document on summer time arrangements is to be published.

**Mr. Hurd:** A Green Paper entitled 'Summer Time—A Consultation Document', Cm. 722, is published by HMSO today. The document seeks views on three options for future summer time arrangements with a closing date for responses of 29 September 1989.

### Fixed Penalties

**Mr. Greg Knight:** To ask the Secretary of State for the Home Department what steps he has taken to review the operation of the extended fixed penalty system introduced on 1 October 1986 under the provisions of part III of the Transport Act 1982, now part III of the Road Traffic Offenders Act 1988; and if he will make a statement.

**Mr. Hurd:** A working group comprising representatives of the Home Office, Department of Transport, the police service and the courts was formed early in 1988 to review the operation of the extended penalty system. I have received its report, a copy of which has been placed in the Library.

The report concludes that the new procedures are broadly meeting their objectives which were:

   (i) to improve the efficiency and effectiveness of road traffic law enforcement;

   (ii) to improve police-public relations in road traffic encounters;

   (iii) to reduce the burden of prosecution for the police, the Crown prosecution service and the courts; and

   (iv) to improve the level of compliance as compared with the previous fixed penalty system.

The working group has, however, identified a number of areas where some "fine tuning" is required.

While the extension of the fixed penalty system to a far wider range of less serious road traffic offences has produced a substantial drop in the number of court proceedings, there has been a significant increase in the numbers of fixed penalty notices issued. This has placed a considerable burden on the courts and the police in registering and enforcing unpaid fixed penalties.

The new arrangements whereby unpaid fixed penalties are enhanced by 50 per cent. and registered and enforced as fines has led to some improvement in early payment rates, particularly in London where, under the previous system, the problem of unpaid fixed penalties was most acute. However, there is still scope for improvement and the working group has identified a number of administrative measures to reduce the number of cases reaching the fine enforcement stage and, for those which do, to ensure that fine recovery is achieved as effectively and efficiently as possible.

The working group recommends that the fixed penalty levels should be increased. The levels were set in 1986 at £12 for non-endorsable offences and £24 for endorsable offences. The report recommends that these should be increased to £15 and £30 respectively with effect from 1 January 1990. As required by section 88 of the Road Traffic Offenders Act 1988, I shall be consulting representative organisations about these proposed increases. I shall also be seeking views about those of the working group's other recommendations which would involve primary legislation.

### War Crimes

**Mr. Wheeler:** To ask the Secretary of State for the Home Department whether he has yet received the report of the war crimes inquiry; and whether he intends to publish it.

**Mr. Hurd:** I have received the inquiry's report. I am examining it, first with a view to publication subject to the need to avoid prejudicing the position of individuals or any proceedings which might take place.

## EMPLOYMENT

### Jobcentres and Benefit Offices

**Mr. Andrew F. Bennett:** To ask the Secretary of State for Employment if he will make a statement on the progress of pilot schemes for integration between jobcentres and unemployment benefit offices.

**Mr. Lee:** I refer the hon. Member to the reply I gave to him on 10 May, at column *441*.

### Departmental Expenditure

**Mr. Leighton:** To ask the Secretary of State for Employment what are the changes in the planned figures for his Department's expenditure for 1989-90 and subsequent years in Cm. 607 from the plans for those years in Cm. 288; and for what reasons.

**Mr. Cope:** The plans for the years 1989-90 and 1990-91 in Cm. 607 show a decrease of £232 million and £340 million respectively from the plans in Cm. 288. This was mainly because the rapid growth in the economy and fall in unemployment allowed a decrease in planned expenditure on employment and training programmes.

**Mr. Leighton:** To ask the Secretary of State for Employment what are the reasons for any differences between the 1988-89 public expenditure plans for his Department published in Cm. 288 and the latest 1988-89 estimated outturn; and how much of any increase is attributable to use of the Reserve.

**Mr. Cope:** The estimated outturn for 1988-89 is 22 per cent. lower than the 1988-89 public expenditure plans published in Cm. 288. This is due mainly to training volumes being lower than planned for adult and youth training because of the rapid growth of the economy and decrease in unemployment.

**Mr. Leighton:** To ask the Secretary of State for Employment what new commitments have been undertaken which will involve spending by his Department after 1991-92 since the publication of Cm. 288.

**Mr. Cope:** Since the publication of Cm. 288 the Department has entered into the following new commitments which will involve spending in the years after 1991-92: Employment training, business growth training, training and enterprise councils, compacts, enterprise in higher education and Seville expo 92. In addition, as announced in the *Official Report*, 27 October 1988, column 318, from 1 April 1990 the Health and Safety Commission will take over the Department of Energy's responsibility for contracting research programmes related to the safety of established thermal nuclear power stations.

### Social Fund

**Mr. Harris:** To ask the Secretary of State for Employment when the guidelines for programmes under the European social fund for the next three years will be available to local authorities.

**Mr. Cope:** The European Commission published its guidelines concerning European social fund intervention in respect of action against long-term unemployment and occupational integration of young people in the *Official Journal* of the European Communities on 24 February 1989. My Department circulated these guidelines, the new European social fund regulations and its own guidance to all past fund applicants and representatives of the local authority associations on 11 April 1989. My Department also circulated to them on 21 June 1989 its own guidance on how to complete the European Commission's form for operational programmes, "Application For Assistance From The European Social Fund".

## Labour Statistics

**Mr. Redmond:** To ask the Secretary of State for Employment what was the total number of unfilled vacancies and the unemployment figure in Doncaster and Mexborough, for April of each year from 1979 to 1989.

**Mr. Lee:** The following is the available information, which is also in the Library. The table shows the number of unfilled vacancies at jobcentres covering the area most closely corresponding to the Doncaster travel-to-work area, together with the number of unemployed claimants in the Doncaster travel-to-work area, for April of each year from 1984 to 1989. Unemployment figures are affected by changes in the coverage of the count. Corresponding figures for 1979 to 1983 are not available.

*Unemployment and unfilled vacancies in Doncaster travel-to-work area for April 1984 to 1989*

| | Number of unemployed claimants | Number of unfilled vacancies |
|---|---|---|
| 1984 | 18,555 | [1]156 |
| 1985 | 19,575 | [1]128 |
| 1986 | 21,897 | 178 |
| 1987 | 20,692 | 352 |
| 1988 | 17,491 | 382 |
| 1989 | 13,327 | 462 |

[1] Number of unfilled vacancies given are for the month of March as April data are not available.

## Training

**Mr. Leadbitter:** To ask the Secretary of State for Employment if he will list the training schemes sponsored by his Department, the total numbers targeted for those schemes, the actual numbers attending, the costs, and the payments made to trainees in each of the last five years.

**Mr. Lee:** Figures for total numbers targeted and payments made to trainees can be calculated only at disproportionate cost.

The following table shows the numbers of people in Great Britain who started on an adult or youth training scheme, sponsored by the Training Agency (formerly Training Commission, formerly Manpower Services Commission), for each year from 1984-85 to 1988-89 and the cost.

| F/Y ended March | Adult Training (000's) | Cost £ million | YTS (000's) | Cost £ million |
|---|---|---|---|---|
| 1985 | 183 | 265·2 | 397 | 780·7 |
| 1986 | 328 | 261·9 | 406 | 809·8 |
| 1987 | 534 | 302·8 | 420 | 861·0 |
| 1988 | 619 | 341·5 | 398 | 991·0 |
| [1]1989 | 640 | 626·3 | 397 | 993·8 |

[1] Starts for 1988-89 are subject to revision and costs figures have not been audited.

## Skilled Labour

**Mr. Leadbitter:** To ask the Secretary of State for Employment (1) what response he has made to the Confederation of British Industry industrial trends survey suggesting a shortage of skilled labour;

(2) what response he has made to the survey published by the Institute of Directors suggesting nearly half the companies questioned said it had become more difficult to recruit skilled employees.

**Mr. Cope:** I am aware of the results of these surveys. The Government are continuing to encourage employers to define and tackle their own skill needs particularly through the introduction of training and enterprise councils and business growth training. The Government are also helping young people and the unemployed to learn new skills through YTS and employment training.

## EC Social Charter

**Mr. Teddy Taylor:** To ask the Secretary of State for Employment if he will seek to establish from the European Commission whether the directives on a minimum wage, on trade union rights, on employee participation and on holiday entitlement and rest period for part time workers as proposed in the "Community charter for fundamental social rights" Com. 89-248-final, will fall to be presented to the Council on the basis of majority voting.

**Mr. Cope:** The voting arrangements for a particular proposal depend on the substance of the proposal and on the specific article(s) of the Treaty of Rome, as amended by the Single European Act, appropriate to this. Until a draft proposal is agreed by the Commission it is not possible to know on which article the Commission will be basing its proposals.

## Council for Social Aid, Manchester

**Mr. Tony Lloyd:** To ask the Secretary of State for Employment how much public money from the Training Agency has been given to the Council for Social Aid, Manchester, and on what dates.

**Mr. Nicholls** *[holding answer 26 June 1989]:* Money advanced by the Training Agency to the Council for Social Aid was in accordance with the terms of the council's contract with the Training Agency. The precise terms of this contract are confidential to the parties involved.

## Health and Safety (Sunderland)

**Mr. Mullin:** To ask the Secretary of State for Employment if he will list the companies in Sunderland recently served with enforcement notices by the Health and Safety Executive.

**Mr. Nicholls** *[holding answer 26 June 1989]:* Information on enforcement notices is not published except in the minority of cases where notices have implications for the safety of the public and details of these are available at the Health and Safety Executive's local area offices.

# PRIME MINISTER

## Disabled People

**Q16. Mr. Tom Clarke:** To ask the Prime Minister when she expects to meet Mencap and other organisations representing the disabled to discuss the Disabled Persons (Services, Consultation and Representation) Act 1986 and its implementation; and if she will make a statement.

**Mr. Wakeham:** I have been asked to reply.

My right hon. Friend the Prime Minister has no plans to do so. the implementation of the Disabled Persons (Services, Consultation and Representation) Act 1986 is a matter for my right hon. and learned Friend the Secretary of State for Health.

## Heavy Commercial Vehicles

Q18. **Mr. Alexander:** To ask the Prime Minister if she has received representations regarding the use of heavy commercial vehicles.

Q144. **Sir Anthony Grant:** To ask the Prime Minister if she has received representations regarding the use of heavy commercial vehicles.

**Mr. Wakeham:** I have been asked to reply.

My right hon. Friend the Prime Minister has received about a dozen such representations this year. They have concerned a variety of subjects, such as general environmental and safety issues, accidents involving dangerous goods, improved facilities for lorry drivers, and the possibility of transferring freight from road on to rail.

## Hong Kong

Q24. **Mr. Leigh:** To ask the Prime Minister if she has received representations regarding the people of Hong Kong.

**Mr. Wakeham:** I have been asked to reply.

My right hon. Friend the Prime Minister has received many representations about Hong Kong following the recent appalling events in China. My right hon. Friend met Dame Lydia Dunn, Senior Member of the Executive Council and Mr. Allan Lee, Senior Member of the Legislative Council on 23 June. She listend to their concerns and reaffirmed the Government's determination to work for a secure and prosperous future for Hong Kong, as provided for in the Sino-British joint declaration.

## Whales

Q28. **Dr. Godman:** To ask the Prime Minister if, in the light of the recommendations made at the 41st annual meeting of the International Whaling Commission which took place in San Diego, California, from 12 June to 16 June 1989, Her Majesty's Government will recommend to the European Commission that concerted action be taken against those nations which continue to slaughter whales and which claim that they need to acquire dead whales for research purposes.

**Mr. Wakeham:** I have been asked to reply.

The European Community does not have any competence on whaling matters. Those member states with an interest in whaling are already members of the International Whaling Commission and we consult them in that relevant forum. At its recent annual meeting the IWC adopted resolutions which were jointly sponsored by the United Kingdom, calling upon Japan, Norway and Iceland to reconsider their whaling research plans.

## Economic and Monetary Union

Q41. **Mr. Cash:** To ask the Prime Minister if she has received representations regarding the disadvantage of economic and monetary union in the European Economic Community.

**Mr. Wakeham:** I have been asked to reply.

My right hon. Friend the Prime Minister has received a number of representations on this subject.

## Malpas, Newport

Q65. **Mr. Flynn:** To ask the Prime Minister if she is planning to visit the Malpas area of Newport, Gwent.

**Mr. Wakeham:** I have been asked to reply.

My right hon. Friend the Prime Minister has at present no plans to do so.

## British Medical Association

Q103. **Mr. Favell:** To ask the Prime Minister if she has had any recent representations from the British Medical Association.

**Mr. Wakeham:** I have been asked to reply.

My right hon. Friend the Prime Minister has received a copy of a letter which I understand has been sent to all right hon. and hon. Members.

## Higher Education

Q138. **Mr. Bowis:** To ask the Prime Minister if she has received representations regarding higher education.

**Mr. Wakeham:** I have been asked to reply.

My right hon. Friend the Prime Minister receives many representations on education matters, including the Government's policies for higher education, which have helped secure a 27 per cent. increase in student numbers over the last decade.

## Unleaded Petrol

Q140. **Mr. Page:** To ask the Prime Minister if she has received representations regarding unleaded petrol.

**Mr. Wakeham:** I have been asked to reply.

Yes, my right hon. Friend the Prime Minister has received many representations about unleaded petrol.

The Government have taken many steps to promote unleaded petrol. We played a major role in securing agreement in 1985 for the future introduction of unleaded petrol within the European Community. The unleaded petrol directive requires that member states should ensure the availability and balanced distribution of the fuel by October of this year. Regulations have been adopted which will require all new cars on sale in the United Kingdom to run on the fuel by October of next year.

My right hon. Friend the Chancellor of the Exchequer has progressively increased the duty differential in favour of unleaded petrol over a three-year period and this has resulted in the fuel being now on sale about 10p a gallon cheaper at the pumps than 4-star leaded petrol. A successful Government-funded advertising campaign was shown on television during April to motivate motorists to have their cars adjusted and to use the fuel. Numerous other initiatives have been implemented with considerable assistance offered by the private sector. The Motability lead-free campaign has been very successful in obtaining support from major companies to promote the fuel.

The success of these measures can now be seen in the rapid uptake of the fuel, which is now accounting for over 19 per cent. of the market. Unleaded petrol is readily available; at least 50 per cent. of petrol stations now stock it.

### Mr. Lech Walesa

Q119. **Mr. Cox:** To ask the Prime Minister if, in view of the election results in Poland on 4 June, she will now extend an official invitation to visit the United Kingdom to Mr. Lech Walesa.

**Mr. Wakeham:** I have been asked to reply.

Mr. Walesa already has an official invitation to visit the United Kingdom. We hope he will take it up as soon as possible. Meanwhile, my right hon. Friend the Prime Minister saw another Solidarity leader, Professor Geremek, when he was in London last week at our invitation.

### Postal Services

**Mr. Bowis:** To ask the Prime Minister whether, pursuant to her reply to the hon. Member for Hendon, South (Mr. Marshall), *Official Report,* 6 June, column 15, she will make a further statement on the postal monopoly and competition.

**Mr. Wakeham:** I have been asked to reply.

I have nothing to add to the reply that my right hon. Friend the Prime Minister gave to my hon. Friend the Member for Hendon, South (Mr. Marshall) on 6 June, at column 15.

### Rain Forests

**Mr. Allen McKay:** To ask the Prime Minister what action will she take in order to stop the destruction of the rain forests in the Brazilian national park by BP; and if she will take steps to oblige BP to reforest the 250,000 acres it has destroyed.

**Mr. Wakeham:** I have been asked to reply.

My right hon. Friend the Minister for Overseas Development will be visiting Brazil, including the Amazon, from 4-9 July. During his visit he will be discussing with Brazilian Ministers and officials our efforts to identify effective ways of helping them with a wide range of environmental problems including rain forest conservation. He will also be meeting representatives of British companies operating in Brazil, with whom he hopes to discuss their role in environmental protection.

The hon. Member will be aware of recent media reports alleging involvement by United Kingdom companies in rain forest destruction. We are studying these, but I understand that the companies, including BP, claim that these press reports contain important errors of fact.

More generally, Britain is a leading supporter of the tropical forestry action plan and the International Tropical Timber Organisation, which aim to help countries conserve their forests and manage them sustainably.

### EC Social Charter

**Mr. Teddy Taylor:** To ask the Prime Minister if she intends to sign the Community "Charter for Fundamental Social Rights", Com. 89-248-final, at the Madrid meeting of the European Council.

**Mr. Wakeham:** I have been asked to reply.

My right hon. Friend the Prime Minister will make a statement in due course.

### Engagements

**Mr. Canavan:** To ask the Prime Minister if she will list her official engagements for Tuesday 27 June.

**Mr. Harry Greenway:** To ask the Prime Minister if she will list her official engagements for Tuesday 27 June.

**Mr. David Shaw:** To ask the Prime Minister if she will list her official engagements for Tuesday 27 June.

**Mr. Stern:** To ask the Prime Minister if she will list her official engagements for Tuesday 27 June.

**Mr. Barry Field:** To ask the Prime Minister if she will list her official engagements for Tuesday 27 June.

**Mr. Win Griffiths:** To ask the Prime Minister if she will list her official engagements for Tuesday 27 June.

**Mr. Boswell:** To ask the Prime Minister if she will list her official engagements for Tuesday 27 June.

**Mr. Tredinnick:** To ask the Prime Minister if she will list her official engagements for Tuesday 27 June.

**Mr. Wakeham:** I have been asked to reply.

My right hon. Friend the Prime Minister is attending the European Council in Madrid.

## TRADE AND INDUSTRY

### Public Relations

**Mr. Blair:** To ask the Chancellor of the Duchy of Lancaster which public relations firms his Department has employed, and at what cost, for each year since 1979.

**Mr. Forth:** Apart from the special circumstances of privatisation work, the consistent practice of successive Governments has been to avoid the use of public relations or other firms for public relations work. The following firms were retained to advise on privatisations:

Charles Barker Lyons, 1981
Dewe Rogerson, 1984 and 1988
Streets Financial, 1985
Valin Pollen, 1986

Details of such contracts, including their cost, are commercially confidential.

### Television Advertising

**Mr. Grocott:** To ask the Chancellor of the Duchy of Lancaster what is the total cost of the television advertising campaign on the enterprise initiative; and what is the cost expressed in terms of expenditure for each successful application received.

**Mr. Forth:** Expenditure on television advertising for the Enterprise Initiative since January 1988 has been about £13 million. Up to 2 June 1989, over 26,500 firms had successfully applied for assisted EI consultancies. It is not appropriate, however, to express one in terms of the other since the advertising has been concerned with the Enterprise Initiative as a whole and not just the six EI consultancy initiatives.

### Steel Industry

**Mr. Henderson:** To ask the Chancellor of the Duchy of Lancaster (1) what is the total employment in the steel industry for every year since 1959 in the United Kingdom;

(2) what is the total steel production in million tonnes for every year since 1959 in the United Kingdom.

**Mr. Atkins:** The information is as follows:

*Steel Production and Employment in the United Kingdom*

| Year | Crude steel (million tonnes) | Employment (thousands, end year) |
|------|------|------|
| 1959 | 20·5 | n.a. |
| 1960 | 24·7 | n.a. |
| 1961 | 22·4 | n.a. |
| 1962 | 20·8 | n.a. |
| 1963 | 22·9 | n.a. |
| 1964 | 26·6 | n.a. |
| 1965 | 27·4 | n.a. |
| 1966 | 24·7 | n.a. |
| 1967 | 24·3 | n.a. |
| 1968 | 26·3 | n.a. |
| 1969 | 26·8 | n.a. |
| 1970 | 28·3 | n.a. |
| 1971 | 24·2 | n.a. |
| 1972 | 25·3 | n.a. |
| 1973 | 26·6 | 198·5 |
| 1974 | 22·3 | 196·9 |
| 1975 | 20·1 | 184·4 |
| 1976 | 22·3 | 182·3 |
| 1977 | 20·4 | 178·9 |
| 1978 | 20·3 | 165·4 |
| 1979 | 21·5 | 156·6 |
| 1980 | 11·3 | 112·1 |
| 1981 | 15·6 | 88·2 |
| 1982 | 13·7 | 74·5 |
| 1983 | 15·0 | 63·7 |
| 1984 | 15·1 | 61·9 |
| 1985 | 15·7 | 59·0 |
| 1986 | 14·7 | 55·9 |
| 1987 | 17·4 | 54·9 |
| 1988 | 19·0 | 55·1 |

Employment on European Coal and Steel Community Treaty activities, only.
*Source:* Iron and Steel Statistics Bureau.
n.a.: not available.

## Postal Services

**Mr. Bowis:** To ask the Chancellor of the Duchy of Lancaster (1) if he has received a copy of the Post Office's reply to the couriers' complaint to the European Commission about anti-competitive postal practices; and if he will make a statement;

(2) if he will discuss with the European Commission the complaint by the courier services about remail;

(3) what discussions his Department has had with the European Commission about the formal complaint made by private courier services about anti-competitive practices by postal administrations; and if he will raise the matter in future discussions.

**Mr. Forth:** The question of the couriers' complaint is a matter between the European Commission and the postal administrations concerned, in our case the Post Office. I have not received a copy.

**Mr. Bowis:** To ask the Chancellor of the Duchy of Lancaster if he has received the CEPT working party's proposal for a European postal monopoly; and if he will make a statement.

**Mr. Forth:** No. As far as I am aware, no such proposal exists although many postal administrations have argued that they need some form of monopoly to support the cost of their social obligations.

**Mr. Bowis:** To ask the Chancellor of the Duchy of Lancaster if he will list in the *Official Report (a)* all overseas visits made in 1988 and 1989 by officials in his Department in connection with the ITU, CEPT and UPU, *(b)* the cost of each visit, *(c)* the length of each visit, *(d)* the purpose of each visit and *(e)* the number and duration of visits which are planned in the current financial year.

**Mr. Forth:** This information is not readily available and could be assembled only at disproportionate cost.

**Mr. Bowis:** To ask the Chancellor of the Duchy of Lancaster if he will refer the Post Office letter post service to the Monopolies and Mergers Commission.

**Mr. Forth:** No.

**Mr. Bowis:** To ask the Chancellor of the Duchy of Lancaster (1) what discussions he has had with officials in New Zealand regarding their intention to liberalise the postal monopoly.

(2) what discussions he has had with postal officials in Gibraltar regarding their intention to integrate the private sector into public postal services.

(3) what discussions he has had with the European Commission about European postal services from 1993.

**Mr. Forth:** None.

**Mr. Bowis:** To ask the Chancellor of the Duchy of Lancaster what plans he has received from Post Office Counters Ltd. for future private investment.

**Mr. Forth:** Details of such plans would be commercially confidential.

**Mr. Bowis:** To ask the Chancellor of the Duchy of Lancaster what plans he has received from Post Office Parcels Ltd. for private investment in the parcels network.

**Mr. Forth:** Details of such plans would be commercially confidential.

**Mr. Bowis:** To ask the Chancellor of the Duchy of Lancaster what steps he will take to ensure freepost election communications are not delayed by industrial action.

**Mr. Forth:** Post Office industrial relations are the responsibility of the board. However, I understand that the Post Office discusses arrangements for the delivery of election communications both nationally and locally in advance, to minimise the possibility of disputes when such deliveries are pending.

**Mr. Bowis:** To ask the Chancellor of the Duchy of Lancaster what was the cost to the British Overseas Trade Board of the recent report it commissioned from the Institute of Logistics and Distribution Management; and what were its terms of reference.

**Mr. Alan Clark:** The Department agreed to pay for the cost of preparation of this report up to £54,000.

The terms of reference were for a study of the United Kingdom express goods services markets for destinations in mainland Europe, North America and the far east.

**Mr. Bowis:** To ask the Chancellor of the Duchy of Lancaster when he will discuss the options for change in the letter monopoly with the Association of International Courier and Express Services.

**Mr. Forth:** I have no plans for such a meeting.

**Mr. Bowis:** To ask the Chancellor of the Duchy of Lancaster when his Department will meet interested parties to discuss the report prepared for the British Overseas Trade Board on the market for express goods services between the United Kingdom and Europe, North America and the far east.

**Mr. Alan Clark:** My Department has discussed the report with the Association of International Courier and Express Services, and is ready to meet other interested parties who may wish to present views.

**Mr. Bowis:** To ask the Chancellor of the Duchy of Lancaster when his Department will next meet the Institute of Logistics and Distribution Management, and what issues he expects to discuss.

**Mr. Alan Clark:** My Department is keeping in contact with the institute on how it is seeking to encourage United Kingdom industry to respond further to the growing opportunities in the express freight market demonstrated in the recent report on the subject prepared by the institute.

**Mr. Bowis:** To ask the Chancellor of the Duchy of Lancaster whether all non-monopoly services are wholly independent of the Post Office's letter service.

**Mr. Forth:** While the Post Office businesses are financially independent, they are not operationally independent but charge at commercial rates for services to each other. Letters costing over £1, and so outside the monopoly limit, are not carried separately from letters below £1.

### Post Office Board

**Mr. Bowis:** To ask the Chancellor of the Duchy of Lancaster what increase in remuneration was awarded to each member of the Post Office board on 1 April.

**Mr. Forth:** Information about board members' remuneration is published in the Post Office's annual accounts for the year in question.

## EDUCATION AND SCIENCE

### Grant-maintained Schools

**Mr. Tredinnick:** To ask the Secretary of State for Education and Science how many schools have now opted for grant-maintained status; and if he will make a statement.

**Mrs. Rumbold:** My right hon. Friend has so far approved proposals for grant-maintained status from 19 schools. A further 24 have published proposals, or voted to do so, and he will determine these on their merits in due course.

### Special Educational Provision

**Mr. John Evans:** To ask the Secretary of State for Education and Science what initiatives are planned by his Department to improve special educational provision in secondary schools.

**Mr. Butcher:** Special educational provision in secondary schools is primarily a responsibility of LEAs. The introduction of the national curriculum is a major initiative which will enable LEAs and schools to improve educational provision for all children, not least those who require special educational provision. The in-service training of teachers in ordinary schools with a designated responsibility for pupils with special educational needs is a national priority area in the Department's local education authority training grants scheme.

### Postgraduate Students

**Sir William Shelton:** To ask the Secretary of State for Education and Science what was the number of United Kingdom students enrolled in postgraduate studies in the United Kingdom in each year since 1979.

**Mr. Jackson:** The numbers of home students enrolled in postgraduate studies in United Kingdom public institutions are as follows (thousands).

|  | Number (Thousands) |
|---|---|
| 1979-80 | 81·5 |
| 1980-81 | 84·8 |
| 1981-82 | 85·0 |
| 1982-83 | 84·6 |
| 1983-84 | 87·1 |
| 1984-85 | 91·0 |
| 1985-86 | 90·7 |
| 1986-87 | 100·2 |
| 1987-88 | 103·7 |

These figures exclude the Open University (1,300 in 1986-87).

### School Governors

**Mr. Cartwright:** To ask the Secretary of State for Education and Science what evidence he has of the extent to which places for parents' representatives on school governing bodies are being filled by parents who are teachers employed at other schools; and if he will make a statement.

**Mrs. Rumbold:** The Government have commissioned the National Foundation for Educational Research to conduct a survey of a sample of school governing bodies, and their membership. One of the questions concerns the occupational background of governors.

**Mr. Cartwright:** To ask the Secretary of State for Education and Science what steps he is taking to ensure that appropriate training is available to school governors in the light of their increased responsibilities under local management schemes.

**Mrs. Rumbold:** Local education authorities have a duty to make any necessary training available to school governors. The Government are paying education support grant on nearly £5 million of local authority expenditure on school governor training in England this year. Government funds have supported the production of national training materials on the local management of schools. We are discussing with LEAs and others the scope for further national initiatives.

## First Aid and Fire Safety

**Mr. Cartwright:** To ask the Secretary of State for Education and Science what steps he has taken to establish the existence of effective fire safety and first aid arrangements in schools and colleges; and with what result.

**Mr. Butcher:** Responsibility for fire safety and first aid arrangements in maintained schools and colleges rests with the local education authorities.

Guidance on fire safety is contained in the Department's "Building Bulletin No. 7", and in September 1987 the Department issued a note of guidance on arrangements for first aid provision in schools and colleges to all authorities.

## University Staff (Pay)

**Mr. Franks:** To ask the Secretary of State for Education and Science if he will make a statement on the recent pay agreement between the management and staff sides in the universities.

**Mr. Kenneth Baker:** The Government have today accepted proposals put forward by the university employers and staff sides for salary increases for non-clinical academic staff in 1989-90. I am pleased that these provide for greater flexibility and differentiation in the salaries of lecturers and professors to take account of merit and market conditions. The Government have agreed that an extra £37 million should be made available for university staff pay this year, with corresponding sums in future years.

The universities have also provided evidence of satisfactory progress with the appraisal of their staff. I have accordingly authorised the Universities Funding Council to release to universities the £67 million which was conditional on the production of that evidence.

## EDUCATION AND SCIENCE

### Teachers (Re-entrants)

**Mr. Thornton:** To ask the Secretary of State for Education and Science if, further to his reply to the hon. Member for Crosby 13 April, *Official Report,* columns *629-30,* he will publish a similar table for the year ended March 1987 showing *(a)* re-entrants to maintained nursery, primary and secondary schools by sector, *(b)* re-entrants to maintained secondary schools by graduate status and degree subjects and *(c)* re-entrants to maintained secondary schools by sex and age.

**Mr. Kenneth Baker** *[holding answer 13 June 1989]:* Figures for the year ending March, 1987 (and also revised figures for 1986) of qualified teachers re-entering full-time service in maintained nursery, primary and secondary schools in England are as follows:

| | Year ending 1986 | 1987 |
|---|---|---|
| *Re-entrants to maintained nursery, primary and secondary schools by sector* | | |
| Re-entrants to nursery and primary schools | | |
|   number | 8,150 | 8,650 |

| | Year ending 1986 | 1987 |
|---|---|---|
|   as a percentage of all entrants to these schools | 64 | 62 |
| Re-entrants to secondary schools | | |
|   number | 6,880 | 6,770 |
|   as a percentage of all entrants to these schools | 49 | 48 |
| Re-entrants to nursery, primary and secondary schools | | |
|   number | 15,030 | 15,420 |
|   as a percentage of all entrants to these schools | 56 | 55 |
| *Re-entrants to maintained secondary schools by graduate status and degree subject* | | |
| Graduate re-entrants | 3,680 | 3,600 |
| Of which, number whose degree subject is: | | |
|   Mathematics | 240 | 230 |
|   Physics | 110 | 90 |
|   Other Sciences | 520 | 550 |
|   Geography | 210 | 200 |
|   Economics and other social sciences | 280 | 290 |
|   English | 550 | 550 |
|   History | 280 | 280 |
|   Modern languages | 430 | 420 |
|   Other subjects | 1,060 | 990 |
| Non-graduate re-entrants | 3,210 | 3,170 |
| *Re-entrants to maintained secondary schools by sex and age* | | |
| Men re-entrants | 1,430 | 1,510 |
| Of which, number aged: | | |
|   less than 30 | 300 | 240 |
|   30-34 | 340 | 350 |
|   35-39 | 310 | 350 |
|   40-44 | 190 | 250 |
|   45-49 | 140 | 150 |
|   50 or over | 150 | 160 |
| Women re-entrants | 5,460 | 5,260 |
| Of which, number aged: | | |
|   less than 30 | 670 | 520 |
|   30-34 | 1,180 | 1,040 |
|   35-39 | 1,860 | 1,710 |
|   40-44 | 1,020 | 1,110 |
|   45-49 | 430 | 550 |
|   50 or over | 300 | 320 |

### Teachers

**Mr. Thornton:** To ask the Secretary of State for Education and Science (1) how many full-time teachers in maintained secondary schools in England left full-time service in the maintained sector at or beyond normal retirement age in the year to March 1987;

(2) if, further to his reply to the hon. Member for Crosby of 27 April, *Official Report,* columns *619-20,* he will publish a similar table for the year ended March 1987 showing an analysis by age and sex of leavers below normal retirement age;

(3) if, further to his reply to the hon. Member for Crosby, 13 April, *Official Report,* columns *630-32,* he will publish a similar table for the year ended March 1987 showing full-time teachers in maintained secondary schools leaving full-time service before normal retirement age; and if he will estimate the number of teachers retiring early in that year.

**Mr. Kenneth Baker** *[holding answer 13 June 1989]:* Figures for the year ending March 1987 (and also revised and corrected figures for 1984-86) of full-time teachers in maintained secondary schools in England leaving full-time service in the maintained sector are as follows:

| | *Year ending March* | | | |
| | *1984* | *1985* | *1986* | *1987* |
| --- | --- | --- | --- | --- |
| All leavers aged 60 or over | 1,900 | 1,800 | 1,630 | 1,310 |
| All leavers aged under 60 | 13,750 | 15,070 | 15,750 | 14,490 |
| Men leavers under 60 | 4,810 | 5,520 | 6,080 | 5,550 |
| of which, number aged: | | | | |
| less than 30 | 1,060 | 1,060 | 1,200 | 1,060 |
| 30-34 | 820 | 900 | 940 | 900 |
| 35-39 | 590 | 730 | 890 | 870 |
| 40-44 | 330 | 440 | 480 | 480 |
| 45-49 | 340 | 360 | 370 | 380 |
| 50-54 | 600 | 780 | 860 | 780 |
| 55-59 | 1,070 | 1,250 | 1,340 | 1,080 |
| Women leavers under 60 | 8,950 | 9,550 | 9,680 | 8,940 |
| of which, number aged: | | | | |
| less than 30 | 3,140 | 3,070 | 2,700 | 2,370 |
| 30-34 | 2,110 | 2,200 | 2,210 | 2,110 |
| 35-39 | 1,050 | 1,210 | 1,410 | 1,330 |
| 40-44 | 600 | 680 | 810 | 850 |
| 45-49 | 430 | 520 | 590 | 590 |
| 50-54 | 690 | 810 | 900 | 820 |
| 55-59 | 930 | 1,060 | 1,060 | 870 |
| Graduate leavers under 60 | 8,050 | 9,050 | 9,620 | 9,110 |
| of which, number whose degree subject is: | | | | |
| Mathematics | 630 | 650 | 750 | 640 |
| Physics | 260 | 290 | 310 | 260 |
| Other sciences | 1,250 | 1,450 | 1,460 | 1,330 |
| Geography | 480 | 580 | 550 | 550 |
| Economics and other social sciences | 670 | 760 | 750 | 690 |
| English | 1,160 | 1,270 | 1,230 | 1,060 |
| History | 610 | 690 | 690 | 600 |
| Modern languages | 1,050 | 1,170 | 1,150 | 970 |
| Other subjects | 1,930 | 2,210 | 2,720 | 3,030 |
| Non-graduate leavers under 60 | 5,710 | 6,020 | 6,140 | 5,370 |

The figures for leavers under 60 in the years ending March 1986 and 1987 include about 3,800 and 3,100 early retirements respectively.

## SOCIAL SECURITY

### Family Credit

**Mr. Cohen:** To ask the Secretary of State for Social Security (1) how many families in receipt of family credit also receive a local authority rent rebate and a rate rebate;

(2) how many families in receipt of family credit also receive a local authority rate rebate.

**Mr. Peter Lloyd:** Provisional information suggests that in May 1988, 62,000 families receiving some form of housing benefit were also receiving family credit. Further information is not available.

**Mr. Cohen:** To ask the Secretary of State for Social Security how many of the families receiving family credit are estimated to be entitled to *(a)* a rent rebate and*(b)* a rate rebate.

**Mr. Peter Lloyd:** Information from the 1985-86 family expenditure survey (FES), updated to 1988-89, suggests

that of the families receiving family credit 7·4 per cent. would be entitled to a rent rebate or rent allowance only; 17·6 per cent. to a rate rebate only; and 5 per cent. to both a rent rebate-allowance and rate rebate.

### Departmental Agencies

**Mr. David Nicholson:** To ask the Secretary of State for Social Security how his Department's agencies will improve service to the public.

**Mr. Jack:** To ask the Secretary of State for Social Security how the Department of Social Security agencies will improve service to his social security customers.

**Mr. Peter Lloyd:** The establishment of agency status for Social Security operations will enable us to carry forward and strengthen our existing strategy for improving service to the public.

In particular agencies will ensure:
delegation of decision-making to the lowest possible level giving a quicker, more sensitive response to local needs;
clear objectives for the quality of service to be achieved, expressed as performance targets, and;
effective performance measurement to ensure that those targets are met.

### Mobility Allowance

**Mr. Cran:** To ask the Secretary of State for Social Security what plans he has to undertake a full review of the regulations concerning the payment of mobility allowance; and if he will make a statement.

**Mr. Scott:** We shall look at mobility allowance, in common with other benefits for people with disabilities, in the light of the findings of the OPCS surveys of disability.

### Children

**Mr. Redmond:** To ask the Secretary of State for Social Security how many children in the Don Valley constituency are dependent upon *(a)* income support and *(b)* family income supplement or family credit for the latest year he has figures (i) in total, and (ii) as a percentage of all children in South Yorkshire.

**Mr. Peter Lloyd:** I regret that this information is not available.

### Availability for Work

**Mr. Redmond:** To ask the Secretary of State for Social Security (1) if he will list *(a)* the number of claimants of all supplementary benefits, *(b)* the number of claimants of supplementary pensions, *(c)* the number of claimants of supplementary allowances and *(d)* the numbers of claimants of supplementary benefits required to be available for work, in respect of his Department's local offices in Doncaster, and the Mexborough area, for April of each year from 1979 to 1989;

(2) if he will list *(a)* the total number of claimants receiving income support, *(b)* claimants of income support receiving pensioner premiums and *(c)* the number of claimants of income support required to be available for work, in respect of his Department's local offices in Doncaster, and the Mexborough area, for April of each year from 1979 to 1989;

**Mr. Peter Lloyd:** The information is as follows:

*Number of claimants receiving supplementary benefit income support by statistical category*

| Local office | | ¹May 1979 | May 1980 | May 1981 | May 1982 | May 1983 | May 1984 | May 1985 | May 1986 | May 1987 | May 1988 | ²May 1989 |
|---|---|---|---|---|---|---|---|---|---|---|---|---|
| | E | 1,631 | 1,647 | 2,758 | 4,020 | 4,914 | 4,989 | 5,298 | 5,328 | 5,181 | 4,002 | 3,765 |
| Doncaster East | A | 1,449 | 1,383 | 1,582 | 1,903 | 2,212 | 2,910 | 3,111 | 3,270 | 3,629 | 3,013 | 3,210 |
| ILO | P | 2,686 | 2,683 | 2,744 | 2,751 | 2,889 | 2,889 | 2,899 | 2,904 | 3,059 | 3,131 | 3,143 |
| Total | | 5,766 | 5,713 | 7,084 | 8,674 | 10,015 | 10,788 | 11,308 | 11,502 | 11,869 | 10,146 | 10,118 |
| | E | 1,652 | 1,942 | 3,560 | 5,127 | 6,131 | 6,501 | 6,672 | 7,061 | 6,676 | 5,249 | 4,734 |
| Doncaster West | A | 1,964 | 2,007 | 2,157 | 2,630 | 2,900 | 3,607 | 3,920 | 3,961 | 4,621 | 4,153 | 4,209 |
| ILO | P | 3,531 | 3,536 | 3,528 | 3,876 | 3,600 | 3,760 | 3,551 | 3,495 | 3,644 | 3,516 | 3,452 |
| Total | | 7,147 | 7,485 | 9,245 | 11,633 | 12,631 | 13,868 | 14,143 | 14,517 | 14,941 | 12,918 | 12,395 |
| | E | 1,036 | 1,225 | 1,958 | 2,856 | 3,344 | 3,416 | 3,695 | 3,905 | 3,488 | 3,067 | 3,054 |
| Wath-on-Dearne | A | 1,236 | 1,186 | 1,365 | 1,495 | 1,771 | 2,228 | 2,392 | 2,476 | 2,595 | 2,355 | 2,618 |
| AO | P | 1,904 | 1,864 | 1,878 | 1,990 | 2,079 | 2,052 | 2,016 | 1,983 | 2,000 | 1,844 | 1,815 |
| Total | | 4,176 | 4,275 | 5,201 | 6,341 | 7,194 | 7,696 | 8,103 | 8,364 | 8,083 | 7,266 | 7,487 |

¹ E = claimants required to be available for work.
   A = claimants not required to register for work.
   P = pensioners.
² 1989 data are provisional and subject to amendment.
*Source:* 100 per cent. count of cases in action; this will include a number of cases where benefit payments have ceased but other action is continuing.

## Late Claims

**Mr. Galbraith:** To ask the Secretary of State for Social Security if he will give *(a)* the number of claims for income support where entitlement has been recognised but the claim has been disallowed on the grounds of late submission, *(b)* the total value of these claims, *(c)* the number of such claims appealed against with the number successful and *(e)* the cost of dealing with these claims and appeals.

**Mr. Peter Lloyd:** The information requested is not readily available and could be obtained only at a disproportionate cost.

## Benefits

**Mr. Canavan:** To ask the Secretary of State for Social Security what was the total number of recipients of supplementary benefit or supplementary pension or income support for each year from 1969 to the present.

**Mr. Peter Lloyd:** The information is as follows:

| Supplementary Benefit | All claimants | Supplementary pensioners¹ | Other claimants |
|---|---|---|---|
| November 1969 | 2,688,000 | 1,875,000 | 813,000 |
| November 1970 | 2,738,000 | 1,902,000 | 836,000 |
| November 1971 | 2,909,000 | 1,919,000 | 990,000 |
| November 1972 | 2,911,000 | 1,909,000 | 1,002,000 |
| November 1973 | 2,675,000 | 1,844,000 | 831,000 |
| November 1974 | 2,680,000 | 1,807,000 | 872,000 |
| December 1975 | 2,793,000 | 1,679,000 | 1,113,000 |
| December 1976 | 2,960,000 | 1,687,000 | 1,274,000 |
| November 1977 | 2,991,000 | 1,738,000 | 1,253,000 |
| November 1978 | 2,932,000 | 1,738,000 | 1,195,000 |
| November 1979 | 2,855,000 | 1,723,000 | 1,132,000 |
| December 1980 | 3,118,000 | 1,694,000 | 1,423,000 |
| December 1981 | 3,723,000 | 1,738,000 | 1,895,000 |
| December 1982 | 4,267,000 | 1,781,000 | 2,486,000 |
| December 1983 | 4,350,000 | 1,651,000 | 2,699,000 |
| December 1984 | 4,609,000 | 1,683,000 | 2,926,000 |
| February 1986 | 4,938,000 | 1,717,000 | 3,221,000 |
| May 1987 | 4,896,000 | 1,727,000 | 3,169,000 |

| Income Support | All claimants | Pensioners² | Other claimants |
|---|---|---|---|
| May 1988 | ³4,352,000 | ³1,719,000 | ³2,632,000 |

*Source:* Annual Statistical Enquiries.
¹ Claimants over pension age (65 for men, 60 for women).
² Claimant, or any partner, aged 60 or over.
³ Latest available estimates.
There was no Annual Statistical Enquiry in 1985: the one due in December that year was deferred until February 1986.

## EC Social Charter

**Mr. Teddy Taylor:** To ask the Secretary of State for Social Security if he will seek to establish from the European Commission whether the directives on a Euro-pension for the elderly and for a minimum entitlement for unemployment benefit, as proposed in the Community "Charter for Fundamental Social Rights" 89-248-final, will fall to be presented to the Council on the basis of majority voting.

**Mr. Peter Lloyd:** The voting procedure for Commission proposals depends on the articles of the treaty of Rome on which they are based. The articles which cover social security require unanimity.

## HEALTH

## Cochlear Implants

15. **Mr. Ashley:** To ask the Secretary of State for Health what steps he proposes to take to ensure that cochlear implants are readily provided by the National Health Service for those profoundly deaf patients who could benefit from them.

**Mr. Mellor:** Provision of cochlear implants is a matter for health authorities in the light of their assessment of local needs and priorities. This is an important new development and I have asked officials to review the position to see whether some form of additional help from the centre would be possible. Given the complexity of the funding issues involved, no early decision will be possible.

## NHS Reform

17. **Mr. Amos:** To ask the Secretary of State for Health if he will make a statement on the future provision of resources for teaching and training of doctors under the proposals in the White Paper, "Working for Patients."

**Mr. Kenneth Clarke:** In the White Paper we emphasised the Government's continuing commitment to maintaining the quality of medical education. We recognised that hospitals in which teaching and research take place incur higher costs as a result, and said that we had decided to accept that the service increment for teaching—(SIFT)—should be enhanced. More recently, I announced in a written reply to my hon. Friend the Member for Staffordshire, Moorlands (Mr. Knox) on 6 June that we have agreed to improve means for the distribution of SIFT. We have also stressed the importance we continue to attach to the postgraduate training of doctors, and our intention is that hospitals should not be placed at an unfair disadvantage or advantage in the distribution of resources by undertaking such training.

18. **Mr. Anthony Coombs:** To ask the Secretary of State for Health if he will make a statement on the intended effects of the increased capitation element in the new general practitioners' contract for patient care.

**Mr. Mellor:** By increasing the proportion of general practitioners' income which comes from capitation payments we will be encouraging greater competition in the family doctor service. This will ensure a better service for patients by giving GPs a greater incentive to provide the best possible range and quality of service to all patients.

20. **Dr. Michael Clark:** To ask the Secretary of State for Health how patient care will be affected by the proposals to allow large general practitioner practices to hold their own budgets.

32. **Mr. Waller:** To ask the Secretary of State for Health what are the implications for patient care of the proposals for general practitioners' practices to operate their own budgets.

**Mr. Mellor:** The introduction of practice budgets, in common with our other proposals for the National Health Service, will lead to even higher standards of service and better quality of care for patients. General practitioners who choose to have budgets will for the first time hold the purse-strings to finance the treatment of their patients which falls within the scope of the budget. This will mean that hospitals will become more responsive to the needs of GPs and their patients. Practice budget holders will also be able to transfer funds between the different elements of the budget which will provide them with greater flexibility in meeting the individual needs of their patients. Greater freedom in managing their own budgets will enhance the clinical freedom of the doctors involved.

22. **Dr. Twinn:** To ask the Secretary of State for Health how the proposals in the White Paper "Working for Patients" on medical audit will affect patient care.

**Mr. Mellor:** The objectives of developing a comprehensive system of medical audit as proposed in the White Paper is to enhance the overall quality of care given to patients in the National Health Service.

23. **Mrs. Gillian Shephard:** To ask the Secretary of State for Health what are the intended effects of the changes in composition of the family practitioner committees proposed in the White Paper "Working for Patients".

**Mr. Mellor:** I refer my hon. Friend to the reply given to my hon. Friend the Member for Gillingham (Mr. Couchman) on 23 May 1989, at columns *482-83*.

25. **Mr. Sumberg:** To ask the Secretary of State for Health how many requests for information he has now received from hospitals inquiring about the possibility of obtaining self-governing status.

**Mr. Kenneth Clarke:** People or groups interested in self-governing status have been advised to direct inquiries in the first instance to their regional health authority. RHAs have so far notified my Department of a total of 179 expressions of interest, including a number of units which feature more than one hospital.

27. **Mr. Gill:** To ask the Secretary of State for Health how the proposals to allow hospitals to become self-governing National Health Service hospitals will affect patient care.

70. **Mr. Hannam:** To ask the Secretary of State for Health if he will explain the effects of the proposals to allow hospitals to become self-governing.

**Mr. Mellor:** Self-governing hospitals will remain firmly within the NHS and there will be safeguards to ensure that essential local services continue to be provided locally. But they will have far more freedom to take their own decisions on the matters which affect them most without detailed supervision from above. This will give patients more choice, produce a better quality service and encourage other hospitals to do even better in order to compete.

29. **Mr. Hayes:** To ask the Secretary of State for Health what will be the benefits for patient care of the indicative drug budgets proposed in the National Health Service White Paper.

48. **Mrs. Maureen Hicks:** To ask the Secretary of State for Health how much account has been taken under the proposals for prescribing budgets of the needs of patients in receipt of drugs on a long-term basis.

66. **Mr. French:** To ask the Secretary of State for Health how patient care will be affected by the proposals in the White Paper "Working for Patients", for indicative drug budgets.

**Mr. Mellor:** Indicative prescribing budgets will provide a further incentive to general practitioners to examine their prescribing patterns critically and in particular to avoid excessive and unncessary prescribing. This is very much in the best interests of patients and more economical prescribing will release money for other forms of patient care in the NHS,. We have made it clear that the amount allocated to a practice for its indicative prescribing budget will take into account the presence on the practice's list of patients, such as the elderly or chronically sick, who need drugs on a longer-term basis. All patients will always get the drugs they need.

30. **Mr. Livsey:** To ask the Secretary of State for Health what percentage of consultants' contract hours he expects to be devoted to administrative work as a result of the proposals in the White Paper on the National Health Service.

**Mr. Mellor:** We are not making any estimate of the time consultants will spend in administrative work, but we expect—and would wish to see—consultants taking an increasing management role, as "Working for Patients" makes clear, through the devolution of managerial responsibility, the extension of resource management, and the establishment of self-governing hospitals.

36. **Mr. Raffan:** To ask the Secretary of State for Health what representations he has received concerning the proposals contained in the White Paper "Working for Patients", relating to medical audits.

**Mr. Mellor:** The proposal to develop a comprehensive system of medical audit in the NHS has been widely welcomed and the medical profession supports the concept of audit and consider it a central part of the doctor's obligation to his patient.

38. **Mr. Conway:** To ask the Secretary of State for Health whether he has received any expressions of interest from general practitioners' practices about operating their own practice budgets.

**Mr. Mellor:** Although we have not yet asked GPs to register formally their interest in becoming budget holders, we are encouraged by the level of interest from eligible practices.

39. **Mr. McLoughlin:** To ask the Secretary of State for Health what effect the proposals in the National Health Service White Paper will have on the distance that patients will have to travel for treatment.

**Mr. Mellor:** Surveys suggest that many people are willing to travel for better and quicker treatment. In setting contracts for services district health authorities will take full account of the wishes of patients and there will be no question of patients being expected to travel unreasonable distances.

43. **Mr. Flannery:** To ask the Secretary of State for Health what are the conditions which have to be fulfilled before the authorities in a National Health Service hospital apply to be self governing; and if he will make a statement.

**Mr. Mellor:** The main criteria were set out in the White Paper "Working for Patients" and working paper (1) "Self-governing Hospitals". Further details are given in the document "Self Governing Hospitals: An Initial Guide" published last week and copies are available in the Library.

44. **Mr. Gregory:** To ask the Secretary of State for Health how the additional £40 million to assist with the implementation of the National Health Service reforms will be allocated.

49. **Mr. Franks:** To ask the Secretary of State for Health if he will give further details of the recently announced extra £40 million for the implementation of the health service reforms.

**Mr. Mellor:** I refer my hon. Friends to my reply to the hon. Member for Newcastle upon Tyne, Central (Mr. Cousins) on 26 June, at columns *315-16*.

46. **Mr. Rooker:** To ask the Secretary of State for Health what is the cost to the latest date of the promotion and information relating to his White Paper "Working for Patients".

**Mr. Kenneth Clarke:** I am introducing into the NHS a system of regular direct communications with the staff which I believe is necessary for any large organisation and certainly for one which employs over 1 million people. It is misleading to compare this with public advertising or political promotion campaigns of the kind being conducted by the BMA and other interest groups. The cost of the communications exercise to inform the staff and management of the NHS about the White Paper proposals is approximately £1·25 million.

Estimated expenditure on the next stage of information for NHS staff about self-governing hospitals will be some £750,000.

The only expenditure on material aimed at the public included in these sums is the cost of:

(a) a leaflet for the public on the White Paper proposals, costing £117,000;

(b) a further leaflet to be made available to the general public on request in the local areas of units which have expressed an interest in becoming self governing, costing £13,000.

47. **Mr. David Davis:** To ask the Secretary of State for Health whether he has any plans to privatise self-governing hospitals.

**Mr. Mellor:** No.

50. **Mr. Michael Brown:** To ask the Secretary of State for Health how patients' choice will be affected by the proposals in the White Paper "Working for Patients".

56. **Mr. Burt:** To ask the Secretary of State for Health if he will make a further statement on the implications for patient choice of the proposals in the White Paper "Working for Patients."

**Mr. Mellor:** A fundamental aim of the White Paper proposals is to make the Health Service more responsive to the needs of patients. We will stimulate better services to patients by encouraging suitable hospitals to apply for self-governing status, by delegating responsibility to local level and by allowing money for patients' treatment to cross administrative borders. GPs will be able to improve the service they offer their patients by applying for their own budgets. Patients will be able to choose their GPs on the basis of the services they offer. We intend to raise the performance of all hospitals and GPs to that of the best. The reformed Health Service will offer a better quality of service and better value for money.

52. **Mr. Macdonald:** To ask the Secretary of State for Health what further representations he has received in respect of his proposals to cash-limit general practitioners' budgets.

**Mr. Mellor:** I refer the hon. Member to the reply I gave earlier today to the hon. Member for Oxford, East (Mr. Smith).

53. **Mr. Latham:** To ask the Secretary of State for Health whether he will make a statement on the outcome of his consultations to date on the White Paper "Working for Patients".

**Mr. Kenneth Clarke:** Consultations are continuing and have been useful. In particular, I have held many meetings with members of the medical profession and have established that, despite some remaining important disagreements, there is a substantial area of agreement.

There is almost universal agreement with the aims of the White Paper to produce a better NHS for patients giving medical treatment free at the point of delivery regardless of means and financed largely as now out of general taxation.

I also judge that the great majority of doctors accept the need for a framework of quality control, in the form of medical audit; the distribution of resources in a way which ensures that "money follows the patient"; and improved systems of financial management using modern information technology. The BMA has told me in meetings that it accepts these three proposals but it has fundamental disagreements with the details of our proposed reforms to implement them. Unfortunately, it and the great majority of doctors have no alternative proposals of their own. The BMA has been discouraging its members from putting constructive alternative proposals to me.

**58. Mr. Carttiss:** To ask the Secretary of State for Health how the proposals in the White Paper "Working for Patients" will affect general practitioners' freedom to refer patients for treatment.

**Mr. Kenneth Clarke:** The new arrangements will enable general practitioners to play a more direct part in deciding which hospitals will provide services for their patients. GP practice budget holders will be able to refer patients to hospitals which provide the best care and shortest waiting times irrespective of administrative boundaries. Those practitioners who do not hold budgets will be consulted extensively before DHAs place contracts with hospitals based on GPs' wishes and there will be provision for GPs to make extra-contractual referrals.

**61. Mr. Norris:** To ask the Secretary of State for Health how patients will be affected by the proposals in the White Paper," Working for Patients"; and if he will make a further statement.

**68. Mr. Irvine:** To ask the Secretary of State for Health if he will make a statement on the intended effects on patient care of the proposals in the White Paper, "Working for Patients".

**Mr. Mellor:** Our proposals will produce a better quality of care for all NHS patients, including elderly and chronically sick people. We intend to bring all services up to the standard of the very best and to make certain that taxpayers' money is used to best effect from the patient's point of view. The proposals reflect our strong commitment to the principles on which the NHS was founded and will ensure that it is more than ready to face the rapidly changing and rising demands upon it as medical science progresses and the average age of the population rises.

**65. Mr. Michael:** To ask the Secretary of State for Health what steps he has taken to *(a)* sponsor adequate research and *(b)* undertake pilot projects to an adequate level on the likely effects of the White Paper proposals on the effectiveness of the National Health Service.

**Mr. Mellor:** Many of our proposals are evolutionary in nature and we will learn from the experience gained. We are quite satisfied that the NHS needs reform on the lines proposed to improve its management and to improve the service to patients.

**69. Mr. Key:** To ask the Secretary of State for Health whether he proposes that self-governing hospitals will be required to retain core services.

**Mr. Mellor:** Before self-governing status is granted to a hospital the initial arrangements for provision of core services will have to be approved by my right hon. and learned Friend the Secretary of State. Thereafter self-governing hospitals will be expected to continue to provide these services subject to review at the request of either the hospital or the DHA concerned or, in the event of disagreement, the Secretary of State's further approval.

**Mr. Malcolm Bruce:** To ask the Secretary of State for Health if he will make a statement on the current situation with regard to the new contract for general practitioners.

**Mr. Kenneth Clarke:** On the 4 May I reached agreement with the negotiators of the General Medical Services Committee on all the major outstanding issues in the new contract. The negotiators undertook to commend this agreement to the annual conference of local medical committee representatives on 21 June. This conference voted to reject the agreement reached by the negotiators, and there will be a ballot of all GPs in the country.

I am disappointed that the conference has rejected the contract which its own leadership commended to it. The contract negotiations were long and hard—over 100 hours of discussion spread over more than a year. The resulting agreement was hard fought and I made a number of important concessions which I would not have made but for my desire to reach an agreement if possible. Both sides agreed on the need for a new contract which rewarded good performance. I believe this contract does meet that need and I see no sensible basis upon which negotiations could be reopened. My task is to raise the quality of primary health care within the NHS and, in order to pursue that, I aim to have in place by 1990 a contract which rewards doctors who provide the highest standards of care for their patients and encourages the rest to match the performance of the best.

Recent research by York university's centre for health economics has demonstrated the wide range of quality of service to patients provided in different parts of the country under the old contract. I shall be laying regulations before Parliament later this year to bring a new contract into effect by 1990.

**Ms. Harman:** To ask the Secretary of State for Health if he will give an estimate of what percentage of a district health authority's budget would be for contractual referrals for hospital care and what percentage would be for extra-contractual referrals under his White Paper.

**Mr. Mellor:** District health authorities will make provision, within their budgets, for the possibility of referrals which were not foreseen when they placed their contracts. The size of this contingency fund will be a matter for them. However, in deciding the pattern of contracts DHAs will be required to take account of the views of all local GPs and place contracts to secure the referral patterns which local GPs wish to see in place unless there are compelling reasons for not doing so. In this way the need for a contingency fund will be minimised.

**Mr. Kirkwood:** To ask the Secretary of State for Health how many general practitioners budget holders practices he intends to approve to begin operating in 1991.

**Mr. Mellor:** Applications to participate in the practice budget scheme will be made to, and approved by, regional health authorities. It is too early to estimate the likely numbers which will be in operation from 1 April 1991, but there have been an encouraging number of preliminary inquiries.

**Mr. Kirkwood:** To ask the Secretary of State for Health if he will make a statement on the effects of his White Paper "Working for Patients", especially relating to self-governing hospitals, on supra-regional services including poisons units.

**Mr. Mellor:** The NHS review White Paper has stated that
"some central funding will be necessary for the development of supra-regional services".
A working party is currently considering the implications of this for these services. The NHS management executive will discuss with regional health authorities the detailed application to specialist services of the new funding arrangements proposed. It is, however, too early to say how individual units will be affected.

**Mr. Kirkwood:** To ask the Secretary of State for Health if, under his plans for capital valuation of self-governing hospitals, he will offset the cost of any backlog on building or equipment maintenance against the capital valuation.

**Mr. Freeman:** The valuation of the property occupied by self-governing hospitals will be on the basis of open market value for existing use. This valuation takes account of the age and condition of the buildings.

**Mr. Kirkwood:** To ask the Secretary of State for Health what mechanism and estimate of cost exists for separating the cost of treatment from research and training in order that self-governing teaching hospitals have the necessary information to operate effectively.

**Mr. Mellor:** We have developed a method for estimating the excess service costs arising from teaching and research at hospitals where at least 5 per cent. of student teaching is undertaken. This is used in the calculation of the service increment for teaching (SIFT). Regions and districts as appropriate to local circumstances will contract with hospitals (including self-governing hospitals) to provide service facilities for teaching in return for SIFT payments.

**Mr. Kirkwood:** To ask the Secretary of State for Health (1) whether he plans to introduce a system of cross charging for accident and emergency work under his proposals for self-governing hospitals where a hospital is situated near a major travel point or in a major commuter area;
(2) whether, in those inner-city areas where patients are more likely to use accident and emergency services rather than a general practitioner, he has any plans either to allow a hospital to curtail such services or to cross charge a general practitioner or family practitioner committee for costs incurred.

**Mr. Mellor:** All hospitals which provide accident and emergency treatment will do so under a block contract with the health authority in whose district they are located. District health authorities will be responsible for securing sufficient accident and emergency services in their district irrespective of the place of residence for all patients who are present. There is no intention that family practitioner committees or GPs should be charged.

**Mr. Kirkwood:** To ask the Secretary of State for Health whether he will postpone his plans to introduce general practitioners' budgets if all hospitals are not operating the necessary management and accounting systems needed to work out the nature of various contracts by April 1991.

**Mr. Mellor:** We are quite sure that district health authorities and GP practice budget holders will be able to manage the contractual process by April 1991.

**Mr. Kirkwood:** To ask the Secretary of State for Health whether the capital valuation of a self-governing hospital or unit is to be based on a value for present use or on the current market value of the site.

**Mr. Freeman:** The valuation of the property occupied by self-governing hospitals will be on the basis of open market value for existing use.

**Mr. Kirkwood:** To ask the Secretary of State for Health whether, if a hospital offers an integrated hospital and community midwifery service, he will ensure that the service continues if the hospital has opted out.

**Mr. Mellor:** Self-governing hospitals will not opt out but will remain fully within the NHS. The NHS will continue to provide integrated hospital and community services.
Where maternity services are designated by a district health authority as "core services" my right hon. and learned Friend the Secretary of State will approve the initial arrangements for provision of such services on establishment of a self-governing hospital. The detailed arrangements will be set out in contracts between the hospital and health authority. Subsequent changes in provision will have to be either by agreement between the district health authority and self-governing hospital or have my right hon. and learned Friend the Secretary of State's approval.

**Mr. Kirkwood:** To ask the Secretary of State for Health (1) whether comprehensive care services will be provided at all self-governing hospitals;
(2) whether emergency and outpatient facilities will be provided at all self-governing hospitals.

**Mr. Mellor** *[holding answer 21 June 1989]:* We are prepared to consider all hospitals and a variety of other units as potentially eligible for self-governing status. Comprehensive core services or particular services need not necessarily be provided by each one.

### British Medical Association

19. **Mr. Andrew MacKay:** To ask the Secretary of State for Health when he last met the British Medical Association; and what issues were discussed.

**Mr. Kenneth Clarke:** I last met the British Medical Association on 14 June and it confirmed that it shared the aims of the Government to create a better National Health Service, as set out in the foreword to the White Paper.

The BMA also confirmed that it agrees on the desirability of introducing better financial control, and quality control in the form of medical audit in the service. It also agreed on the need to make money follow the patient, and to make patient service the prime objective of the service.

It did not, however, agree with some of the major proposals in the White Paper such as self-governing hospitals, about which many people in the NHS have expressed interest. These proposals are crucial to delivering the better service which both I and the BMA want. It did not put forward any new proposals of its own to achieve those aims. It did agree to further discussions.

I intend to reform the NHS to make it more able to provide an improved service to patients. I made it clear to the BMA that I would welcome a constructive contribution from it to that process of reform whenever it felt able to make one.

**33. Mr. David Nicholson:** To ask the Secretary of State for Health what matters were discussed at his last meeting with representatives of the British Medical Association.

**45. Dame Jill Knight:** To ask the Secretary of State for Health when he last met the British Medical Association representatives to discuss the Health Service review; and if he will make a statement.

**62. Mr. Patrick Thompson:** To ask the Secretary of State for Health when he last met the chairman of the British Medical Association; and what matters were discussed.

**67. Mr. Favell:** To ask the Secretary of State for Health when he last met the representatives of the British Medical Association; and what was discussed.

**Mr. Mellor:** I refer my hon. Friends to the reply my right hon. and learned Friend the Secretary of State gave to my hon. Friend the Member for Berkshire, East (Mr. MacKay) today.

### Head Inspections

**21. Mr. Hinchliffe:** To ask the Secretary of State for Health what is his policy on head inspections in schools by health authority nursing staff.

**Mr. Freeman:** Responsibility for the control of headlice infection among pupils rests with the individual health authorities through the school health service. It is for them to determine the policy for dealing with this problem in the light of local circumstances.

### Food (Health Risks)

**24. Mr. Loyden:** To ask the Secretary of State for Health what steps he intends to take to reduce or eliminate the risks to health in the food chain.

**Mr. Freeman:** The Government have introduced a range of measures designed to reduce the risk of food contamination and, with industry, are continuing to consider what further action is necessary.

Both primary and secondary legislation are under review. We recently announced the intention to consult on changes in the food hygiene regulations, and the Government are presently considering the results of consultation on a wide-ranging review of the Food Act.

The Committee on the Microbiological Safety of Food has commenced work under the chairmanship of Sir Mark Richmond.

Meanwhile we shall continue to act promptly to contain outbreaks of food poisoning which occur, and I refer the hon. Member to the statement my right hon. and learned Friend the Secretary of State made on 13 June, at columns 703-9.

### Student Midwives

**26. Mr. Colvin:** To ask the Secretary of State for Health whether he will review the grading structure for qualified nurses who became student midwives prior to 1 April 1988; and if he will make a statement.

**Mr. Mellor:** We will be responding shortly to the Social Services Committee's report on midwives' regrading, which raises this issue.

### Capital Programmes (Yorkshire)

**28. Mr. Riddick:** To ask the Secretary of State for Health what has been the average annual expenditure on capital programmes in the area covered by the Yorkshire regional health authority between 1979 and 1989; what was the equivalent annual figure for the years between 1974 and 1979; and if he will make a statement.

**Mr. Freeman:** Following are figures derived from the annual accounts of the health authorities comprising the Yorkshire region:

*Average annual total capital expenditure*

| Period | £000 (Cash) |
|---|---|
| 1974-75 to 1978-79 (5 years) | 22,837 |
| 1979-80 to 1987-88[1] (9 years) | 54,508 |

[1] Latest year available.

The average figure for the later period represents an increase in real terms (measured at 1987-88 prices) of almost 10 per cent. on that for the earlier period.

### Heart Disease

**31. Mr. Tim Smith:** To ask the Secretary of State for Health what steps he is taking to prevent coronary heart disease.

**Mr. Mellor:** Together with the Health Education Authority, the Department launched the "Look After Your Heart" campaign in April 1987 as an ongoing initiative to combat the high level of coronary heart disease. This initiative aims to increase awareness about the risk of heart disease and how it may be avoided, and to provide practical help to people in making the necessary changes to their lifestyle. It is doing this through publicity campaigns and special promotions, provision of detailed advice about smoking, nutrition and exercise, and funding of local initiatives. It has developed a very successful workplace element. These activities are currently being expanded, and other areas of work, such as with primary health care and in schools, are being developed.

Much other work is also going on. The Government are taking specific action to discourage smoking, which is a key factor in causing heart disease, and excessive consumption of alcohol. The Standing Medical Advisory Committee has been asked to look at the cost-effectiveness of cholesterol screening in relation to the prevention of coronary heart disease. Under changes to general practitioners' terms of service, they will be required to offer patients regular check-ups, including measurement of blood pressure. We believe that this important development will provide an opportunity for GPs to give personal advice to patients, particularly those most at risk of heart disease, about steps they can take to lessen this risk.

### Hospital Food

34. **Mr. Simon Hughes:** To ask the Secretary of State for Health if he will make a statement about the quality of food served in hospitals.

**Mr. Freeman:** It is health authorities' responsibility to determine the standard and quality of food to meet the needs of patients and staff in their hospitals.

### Hospitals (Harrow)

35. **Mr. Dykes:** To ask the Secretary of State for Health what recent representations he has received from all sources concerning the possible transfer to self-governing status of the Northwich Park hospital and the Royal National orthopaedic hospital in the Harrow district health authority area.

**Mr. Mellor:** Expressions of interest in self-governing status have been received from both Northwick Park hospital and the Royal National orthopaedic hospital. My right hon. and learned Friend the Secretary of State has received a number of representations on the latter. Should this interest, in either case, proceed to an application, I can assure my hon. Friend that all the main interests— including staff and the local community—will have an opportunity to express their views when detailed proposals have been worked out.

### GPs (Patient Time)

37. **Mr. Madel:** To ask the Secretary of State for Health what information he has as to the average amount of time per week that general practitioners now spend seeing patients; and if he will make a statement.

**Mr. Mellor:** The available information is taken from the general medical practitioners workload survey carried out in 1985-86 by the Health Departments and the British Medical Association. it shows that in an average working week GPs spend 26 hours seeing patients. This comprises 18 hours in surgery, six hours in home visits and two hours in clinics.

### NHS Policy Board

40. **Mr. Stevens:** To ask the Secretary of State for Health if he will make a statement on the role of the recently announced National Health Service policy board.

**Mr. Mellor:** The role of the NHS policy board is to advise my right hon. and learned Friend the Secretary of State on the formulation of policy for and the strategic oversight of the NHS. It sets objectives for the NHS management executive and monitors their achievement.

### Consultants

41. **Mr. Patnick:** To ask the Secretary of State for Health how many additional posts for consultants he estimates will be created over the next three years.

**Mr. Mellor:** We estimate that about 1,000 new medical and dental consultant posts will be created in England between 1989 and 1992, including the 100 posts announced in "Working for Patients".

### Cancer Screening

42. **Rev. Martin Smyth:** To ask the Secretary of State for Health if he will make a statement about the number of medical screening units and future demand for screening.

**Mr. Mellor:** We have established two programmes to screen women regularly for cervical and breast cancers. Most of the cervical smears performed each year are taken by general practitioners. Breast cancer screening is organised by regional health authorities and is carried out in specifically equipped centres.

I refer the hon. Member to my reply to the hon. Member for Glasgow, Maryhill (Mrs. Fyfe), on 14 June, at columns 429-30 for information about those breast screening centres in England which are operational and to my reply to my hon. Friend the Member for Eastwood (Mr. Stewart), on 19 June, at column 35, for information about screening in health care.

Information on screening in the other parts of the United Kingdom is the responsibility of my right hon. Friends the Secretaries of State for Wales and Northern Ireland and my right hon. and learned Friend the Secretary of State for Scotland.

64. **Ms. Richardson:** To ask the Secretary of State for Health whether he has issued guidelines to National Health Service hospitals on *(a)* the information they provide on breast cancer screening and *(b)* levying charges for breast cancer screening.

**Mr. Mellor:** The Health Education Authority has produced a leaflet which can accompany a woman's invitation letter to explain what happens at a breast screening centre. Additional material has been produced to inform staff involved in health education and primary care about the screening programme. A general information leaflet on breast screening is also due to be published shortly. The guidance to health authorities concerning the provision of breast cancer screening referred to in the reply my hon. Friend the Parliamentary Under-Secretary of State for Health gave to the hon. Member on 21 February, at columns *606-7,* drew attention to the role the Health Education Authority would play in supporting health authorities' education programmes for women.

Guidance issued to health authorities in March on income generation HN(89)9 states that the Department should be consulted where proposals for income generation clearly involve national policy,
"for example breast and cervical cancer screening".

### Community Care

51. **Mr. Fearn:** To ask the Secretary of State for Health when he intends to announce his Department's plans for the provision of community care in response to "An Agenda for Action".

**Mr. Mellor:** We have been giving very thorough consideration to all the available options for the future organisation and management of community care, taking account of the many representations and views we have received. We hope to be able to announce our proposals shortly.

## Hospital Waiting Lists

54. **Mr. David Evans:** To ask the Secretary of State for Health how much the Government spent in 1988-89 on measures designed to help reduce the length of hospital waiting lists.

**Mr. Mellor:** We allocated £30 million from the central waiting list fund in 1988-89 as part of the Government's drive to reduce hospital waiting lists and times. This money enabled over 117,000 additional in-patients and day cases and over 92,000 extra out-patients to be treated from the waiting lists.

## Queen's Medical Centre, Nottingham

55. **Mr. Allen:** To ask the Secretary of State for Health if he will hold a ballot of all staff at the Queen's medical centre, Nottingham on opting out.

**Mr. Mellor:** No.
Self governing trusts will not opt out but will remain fully within the NHS.
If an application is made for QMC Nottingham to become self-governing, Trent regional health authority will ensure that all those with an interest have the opportunity of expressing their views but a ballot will not be required. My right hon. and learned Friend the Secretary of State will consider any responses alongside the application.

## Medical Scientists

57. **Mr. Hardy:** To ask the Secretary of State for Health if he will take steps to ensure that the salaries of medical scientists employed within the National Health Service are sufficient to ensure that there are no critical shortages of such staff.

**Mr. Mellor:** The pay of non-medical scientists is a matter for negotiation between the management side of the Scientific and Professional Staff Council and the staff side representing scientists employed in the NHS. Negotiations are continuing on the staff side pay claim for 1989/90. The pay of medically qualified staff is decided after taking into account recommendations of the doctors and dentists review body.

## Blood Shortages

59. **Mr. Matthew Taylor:** To ask the Secretary of State for Health what plans he has to correct the shortage of blood available for transfusion; and if he will make a statement.

**Mr. Freeman:** I refer the hon. Member to my reply to the hon. Member for Linlithgow (Mr. Dalyell) on 23 June, at column *278*.

## Patients (Statistics)

60. **Sir Michael McNair-Wilson:** To ask the Secretary of State for Health what is the average number of patients per general practitioner at the current date; and what was the figure in 1979.

**Mr. Mellor:** The information is as follows:

*England—Average list size*

|  | Number |
| --- | --- |
| 1 October 1979 | 2,286 |
| 1 October 1987 | [1]2,020 |

[1] Latest available figure.

## "Perinatal, Neonatal and Infant Mortality"

63. **Miss Lestor:** To ask the Secretary of State for Health when the Government will be responding to the Social Services Select Committee report "Perinatal, Neonatal and Infant Mortality".

**Mr. Mellor:** Very soon.

## Nurses

71. **Mr. Hardy:** To ask the Secretary of State for Health how many appeals have been submitted in regard to salary grading by members of the nursing profession; and what are the numbers that have yet to be determined.

**Mr. Mellor:** We do not hold this information centrally.

**Mr. Kirkwood:** To ask the Secretary of State for Health (1) where nurse education is organised across more than one hospital, what are the implications for such education where one hospital opts out;
(2) whether the budget for nurse education currently with the district health authority will devolve to a hospital which opts out which is currently operating or partly operating a school of nursing.

**Mr. Mellor:** There will be a further working paper on education and training next month which will address these issues.

## Northern Regional Health Authority

**Mr. Bell:** To ask the Secretary of State for Health (1) if he has discussed the future of Middlesbrough and South Cleveland hospitals with the Northern regional health authority; and if he will make a statement;
(2) what agreements have been entered into with the planning authorities for the development of sites at Poole and South Cleveland hospitals in the event of their sale to the private sector; and if he will make a statement;
(3) what discussions have taken place between the Northern regional health authority and the Teesside development corporation concerning the replacement of the Middlesbrough general and South Cleveland hospitals by a new medical complex on Teesside; and if he will make a statement;
(4) what funding he will make available for the construction of a new medical centre on Teesside; over what period of time; when any final decision will be made and by whom; and if he will make a statement;
(5) what proposals he has received from the Northern regional health authority concerning the creation of a private health company to run any new medical complex on Teesside; and if he will make a statement;
(6) what proposals he has received from the Northern regional health authority concerning the siting of a new medical complex to be built on a site presently containing chemical storage tanks; what feasibility studies in relation to safety have been carried out; by whom and when; and if he will make a statement;

(7) what proposals he has received from the Northern regional health authority concerning the transfer of capital allocations presently earmarked for health schemes in South Tees to a new medical complex on Teesside; and if he will make a statement;

(8) what proposals he has received from the Northern regional health authority for the creation of a private health care sector within any new medical complex on Teesside; and if he will make a statement;

(9) what proposals he has received from the Northern regional health authority for the closure of North Riding infirmary and the transfer of its facilities to a new medical complex on Teesside; and if he will make a statement;

(10) what proposals he has received from the Northern regional health authority concerning alternative funding arrangements in respect of the plant and equipment in any new medical facility on Teesside; and if he will make a statement;

(11) what proposals he has received from the Northern regional health authority concerning a joint development between the regional health authority and college of Durham university concerning a new medical complex on Teesside; and if he will make a statement;

(12) what reports he has received from the Northern regional health authority concerning the involvement of management consultants, Richard Ellis Venture Consultants Ltd. and Peat Marwick McLintock in the proposed new scheme for a medical complex on Teesside, and the cost at which the management consultants have been retained, and who is paying; and if he will make a statement;

(13) what representations he has received from the Northern regional health authority concerning a proposed new medical complex on Teesside; and if he will make a statement.

**Mr. Freeman:** The hon. Member is aware that Northern regional health authority is considering the possibility of a new NHS medical complex in Teeside. The proposal is at an early stage of consideration and its feasibility is currently being appraised. The outcome will be considered in conjunction with the results of a strategic review of the provision of hospital services in South Tees, which is nearing completion. Specialist advice has been commissioned by the Northern RHA from two firms of management consultants, whose fees will be payable by the RHA. No formal proposals have yet been submitted to the Department, but officials are being kept informed as the exercise progresses. Any firm plans that may result from the studies would be aimed at providing a modern, high quality hospital service within the NHS. Such a development would involve rationalisation of existing services, resulting in a significant improvement in the quality of care available locally. The proposals would not envisage the closure of existing modern facilities at South Cleveland hospital. Northern RHA is known to be in touch with the various interested parties, including Teeside development corporation and relevant local authorities, but details of such contacts are not held centrally. The hon. Member may wish to seek any additional information from the chairman of Northern regional health authority.

**Mr. Bell:** To ask the Secretary of State for Health what are the present National Health Service capital allocations for South Tees; for what they are earmarked; and if he will make a statement.

**Mr. Freeman:** This information is not held centrally. Allocation of resources to South Tees health authority is the responsibility of Northern regional health authority and the hon. Member may wish to contact the chairman for the information.

**Mr. Bell:** To ask the Secretary of State for Health (1) what proposals he has received from the Northern regional health authority for the sale of land at Poole and south Cleveland hospitals;

(2) what proposals he has received from the Northern regional health authority to sell sites that the Northern region considers to be surplus to requirements, including land at Middlesbrough maternity hospital, south Cleveland and Poole hospitals; what approvals are required for such sales; when approval is likely to be forthcoming; and if he will make a statement;

(3) what proposals he has received from the Northern regional health authority concerning estate rationalisation within the South Tees area health authority; how many surplus sites are proposed to be sold; what is proposed to happen to the funds; and if he will make a statement.

**Mr. Freeman:** We have received no proposals from Northern regional health authority. Once NHS sites are declared surplus to requirements by health authorities they may be disposed of in accordance with the procedures set out in the NHS handbook on land transactions and the proceeds retained locally.

**Mr. Bell:** To ask the Secretary of State for Health when the last new facilities were opened at south Cleveland hospital; by whom; and what reasons have been advanced by the Northern regional health authority to have these closed and removed to a new medical complex on Teesside.

**Mr. Freeman:** The new maternity unit was officially opened by HRH The Princess of Wales on 6 October 1988. We are not aware of there being any intention to close or transfer this facility.

### Health Care (Purchase)

**Mr. Tredinnick:** To ask the Secretary of State for Health if he will explain the intended effects of the proposals to allow health authorities to purchase health care from hospitals.

**Mr. Freeman:** All National Health Service hospitals, whether run by health authorities or self-governing, will be free to offer their services to different health authorities and to the private sector. Consequently, a health authority will be better able to discharge its duty by using its available funds to secure a comprehensive service, including emergency services, to obtain the best service it can whether from its own hospitals, from another authority's hospitals, from NHS hospital trusts or from the private sector.

### NHS Policy Board

**Sir David Price:** To ask the Secretary of State for Health what reply he has sent to the Royal College of Nursing in response to its complaint that the chief nursing officer has been excluded from membership of the National Health Service policy board.

**Mr. Mellor:** On 14 June my right hon. and learned Friend the Secretary of State met the Royal College of

Nursing to discuss this issue and a copy of the statement made after that meeting is in the Library. The fact that Mrs. Poole has not been appointed to the board has in no way altered her position and authority as the Government's chief nursing officer, nor does it imply that the Government no longer have a high regard for the nursing profession.

## Eye Tests

**Mr. Hinchliffe:** To ask the Secretary of State for Health what information he supplied to opticians as to his Department's definition of a near relative of glaucoma sufferers in his criteria for free eye tests.

**Mr. Mellor** *[holding answer 26 June 1989]:* A free sight test is available to all people aged 40 or over who are either the parent, brother, sister or child of a diagnosed glaucoma patient. Information on eligibility was circulated to opticians through a family practitioner notice in March 1989. Poster SB54 and leaflet G11, which are currently being distributed, also draw attention to the special entitlement of this group of people.

# NORTHERN IRELAND

## Census Questions

**Rev. Martin Smyth:** To ask the Secretary of State for Northern Ireland what information he has as to whether the inclusion of more questions in the census than previously has reduced the numbers responding.

**Mr. Needham:** None. The census is compulsory by law, and everyone is obliged to respond to it. However, the census is based on the principle that it should be generally acceptable to the public, and limited in its overall demands.

**Rev. Martin Smyth:** To ask the Secretary of State for Northern Ireland what percentage of respondents to the census of 1961, 1971 and 1981 did not answer the question concerning religion; and if he will make a statement.

**Mr. Needham:** The information is as follows:

|      | Percentage |
|------|-----------|
| 1961 | 1·9       |
| 1971 | 9·4       |
| 1981 | 18·5      |

A question on religion has traditionally been included in Northern Ireland censuses for answer on a voluntary basis. The Government propose to retain a religion question on the same basis in the 1991 census.

**Rev. Martin Smyth:** To ask the Secretary of State for Northern Ireland what purpose is intended in including in the census questions on educational qualifications; and what use will be made of the answers to these questions.

**Mr. Needham:** The information derived from these questions will be used, together with information from other questions, to show the number of people with higher qualifications in different industries and occupations. Regional variations in the proportions of people with higher qualifications will be used in planning education and training. It will also show the reserves of qualified people among, for example, housewives and the out of work, including those not currently seeking work.

## Census

**Rev. Martin Smyth:** To ask the Secretary of State for Northern Ireland what steps his Department is taking to inform the public in advance of the census.

**Mr. Needham:** In due course, the census office will arrange publicity to explain the purpose of the census, convey assurances of confidentiality and deal with other aspects of public concern. The office will also arrange the distribution of appropriate leaflets and posters to libraries and other public places, issue an explanatory leaflet about the census and set up a telephone service to deal with inquiries from the public.

## Sites of Special Scientific Interest

**Mr. John D. Taylor:** To ask the Secretary of State for Northern Ireland if, in view of the imminence of the summer holiday period, he will extend the period for the submission of objections to the proposed Strangford lough (part III) area of special scientific interest beyond the present proposed date of 22 August.

**Mr. Needham:** Notification of the declaration of Strangford lough (part III) area of special scientific interest was issued on 21 April 1989. As required by article 24 of the Nature Conservation and Amenity Lands (Northern Ireland) Order 1985 the notification stated the period within which representations and objections could be made. It is not possible under the provisions of the order to extend the period beyond 22 August since this was the closing date stipulated in the notification.

**Mr. John D. Taylor:** To ask the Secretary of State for Northern Ireland what is the largest area of special scientific interest by area identified so far in Northern Ireland; and how many landowners there are within this area of special scientific interest.

**Mr. Needham:** The largest area of special scientific interest (ASSI) so far declared is Strangford lough (parts I, II and III) with a total area of 4,108 hectares. There are some 300 landowners and occupiers.

## Planning Procedures

**Mr. John D. Taylor:** To ask the Secretary of State for Northern Ireland whether Ringhaddy avenue, Bowtown road, Newtownards was given planning approval as a cul-de-sac; whether the existing right-of-way through the steel fence at Ringhaddy avenue conforms with the planning approval; and what proposals he has to provide access from the Abbots road estates to Newtownards town centre consistent with existing approvals under the roads and planning legislation.

**Mr. Needham** *[holding answer 22 June 1989]:* Ringhaddy avenue was determined and constructed as a cul-de-sac. Following representations from a resident, a pedestrian link was provided through the steel fence. Planning approval was not necessary.

The Department of Environment for Northern Ireland currently has no plans to provide access from the Abbots road estate to Newtownards town centre.

**Rev. Martin Smyth:** To ask the Secretary of State for Northern Ireland, if he will list all appointments of chairmen and members of public and non-governmental bodies made by him since he took up office, together with the names of those appointed, the salaries and expenses paid to them and the method by which their appointment was made.

**Mr. Ian Stewart** *[holding answer 5 May 1989]:* The information requested is set out in the table:

*Northern Ireland since 4 September 1985*

| Name of body and Member's names | Salary | Expenses | Method of appointment |
|---|---|---|---|
| Queen's University Senate |  |  |  |
| F. A. Mackle OBE (Member) | Nil | Nil | Nominees suggested by CAU and QUB |
| J. J. Sheil (Member) | Nil | Nil |  |
| Miss A. E. A. Lambe (Member) | Nil | Nil |  |

| Name of body and Member's names | Salary | Expenses | Method of appointment |
|---|---|---|---|
| Rev. J. Dunlop (Member) | Nil | Nil | |
| C. T. Hurst OBE (Member) | Nil | Nil | |
| **Planning Appeals Commission** | | | |
| Brian Alexander Moore Banks (Professional Commissioner) | £19,810 | Nil | Recommendations submit to Secretary of State arising from a nationwide recruitment competition. |
| John Allen OBE (Deputy Chief Commissioner) (part-time) | £123 for each appeal £123 for each report | Travel and subsistence payable at Civil Service rates | Recommendations made to the Secretary of State from list supplied by CAU |
| Mrs. Colette Quigley (Commissioner) (part-time) | £98 for each appeal £98 for each report | | |
| Ronald H. A. Blackburn (Commissioner) (part-time) | £98 for each appeal £98 for each report | | |
| Noel Baxter (Commissioner) (part-time) | £98 for each appeal £98 for each report | | |
| Norman Drummond (Commissioner) | £98 for each appeal £98 for each report | | |
| Mrs. I. Marie Campbell (Commissioner) | £98 for each appeal £98 for each report | | |
| Mrs. J. Hennessy (known as Ms. J. O'Dempsey) (Commissioner) | £98 for each appeal £98 for each report | | |
| **Technology Board for Northern Ireland** | | | |
| D. V. McCaughan (Chairman) | Nil | Expenses paid at normal Civil Service rates. To date £3,405 | Letter of Appointment from Secretary of State |
| **Council for Professions Allied to Medicine** | | | |
| C. Dallat (Member) | Nil | A matter for the Council | Recommended by the Minister responsible DHSS |
| **Health and Personal Social Services Tribunal Medicine Practitioners** | | | |
| Dr. J. D. Boyd MB BCh MRCGP (Member) | Nil | Nil | Nominations are sought from relevant professional organisations and appointments made from the nominees |
| Dr. R. M. Shearer MB Bch MD (Deputy) | Nil | Nil | |
| **Health and Personal Social Services Tribunal Dental Practitioners** | | | |
| Mr. M. O'Farrell LDS (Member) | Nil | Nil | Nominations are sought from relevant professional organisations and appointments made from the nominees |
| Mr. H. Morrow OBE BOS (Deputy) | Nil | £393·08 | |
| **Health and Personal Social Services Tribunal Ophthalmic Medical Practitioners** | | | |
| Dr. E. A. McWilliams MB BCH DO (Member) | Nil | Nil | Nominations are sought from relevant professional organisations and appointments made from the nominees |
| Dr. C. Flynn MB (Deputy) | Nil | Nil | |
| **Health and Personal Social Services Tribunal Ophthalmic Opticians** | | | |
| Dr. Anderson FBOA (Member) | Nil | Nil | Nominations are sought from relevant professional organisations and appointments made from the nominees |
| Mr. S. J. Barbour BSC, FBCD (Deputy) | Nil | Nil | |
| **Health and Personal Social Services Tribunal Pharmacists** | | | |
| R. G. Dillon MPSNI (Member) | Nil | Nil | Nominations are sought from relevant professional organisations and appointments made from the nominees |
| J. Chambers BSc MPSNI (Deputy) | Nil | Nil | |
| **Law Reform Advisory Committee for Northern Ireland** | | | |
| The Hon. Mr. Justice Carswell (Chairman) | Nil | Travelling and accommodation expenses are paid at normal Civil Service rate | Appointments were made by Secretary of State from nominations received from the Lord Chief Justice of Northern Ireland, the Executive Committee of the Inns of the Court of Northern Ireland, the Law Society of Northern Ireland and the QUB |
| His Hon. Judge Gibson QC (Member) | Nil | | |
| Patrick Coghlin QC (Member) | Honorarium of £2,000 per annum | | |
| J. B. Garrett (Member) | Honorarium of £2,000 per annum | | |
| Ms. Siobhan Grant (Member) | Honorarium of £2,000 per annum | | |
| Professor Desmond Greer (Member) | Honorarium of £2,000 per annum | | |
| Patrick Markey QC (Member) | Honorarium of £2,000 per annum | | |
| John Meehan (Member) | Honorarium of £2,000 per annum | | |

| Name of body and Member's names | Salary | Expenses | Method of appointment |
|---|---|---|---|
| **Board of the International Fund for Ireland** | | Travelling and accommodation expenses are paid at normal Civl Service rate | Appointments to the board are made jointly by the United Kingdom and Irish Governments |
| Mr. C. E. B. Brett (Chairman) | £2,000 | | |
| Sir E. Bell | £1,000 | | |
| Sir G. Booth | £1,000 | | |
| Mr. M. Canavan | £1,000 | | |
| Mr. J. Craig | £1,000 | | |
| Mr. G. Dempsey | £1,000 | | |
| Mr. J. Doherty | £1,000 | | |
| Dr. A. McGuckian | £1,000 | | |
| Mr. N. McCann | £1,000 | | |
| **Northern Ireland Economic Council** | | | Following consultation with Northern Ireland Permanent Secretaries, Head of Northern Ireland Civil Service making recommendation to Secretary of State |
| Professor C. M. Campbell (Chairman) | £12,745 | Actual cost basis | |
| N. W. Shaw | £2,560 | Nil | |
| Dr. V. Furness OBE | £2,560 | Nil | |
| J. Stanley | £2,560 | Nil | |
| Professor Sue Birley | £2,560 | Actual cost basis | |
| J. McCusker | £2,560 | Nil | Nominated by NIC/ICTU |
| R. Jeary | £2,560 | Nil | |
| M. Dummigan | £2,560 | Nil | |
| R. Gibson | £2,560 | Nil | Nominated by CBI/NICC |
| W. McCourt | £2,560 | Nil | |
| A. MacLaughlin | £2,560 | Nil | |
| **Police Authority for Northern Ireland** The names of Authority members are not disclosed for security reasons | Chairman £22,950 Vice-Chairman honorarium £11,475 Members honorarium £3,000 | Attendance allowance of £9·12 for meetings of not more than 4 hours or £18·25 for meetings of more than 4 hours. Travel and subsistence expenses are paid at Civil Service rates | The present Secretary of State has appointed the Chairman, Vice-Chairman and 18 members. Membership is determined by the Secretary of State after consultation with local authorities, the legal profession, trade unions, and other interested groups, including voluntary organisations |
| **Independent Commission for Police Complaints** | | Travel and subsistence expenses are paid at Civil Service rates | Appointments made by Secretary of State after an assessment of the qualifications and experience of those who have indicated an interest in public service against the requirements of the positions available |
| James Grew (Chairman) | £16,405 | | |
| Lady Carswell (Deputy Chairman) | £11,110 | | |
| Brian Garrett (Deputy Chairman) | £5,555 | | |
| James Gardner (Member) | £4,625 | | |
| Mrs. Denise Kennedy (Member) | £4,625 | | |
| Mr. Kevin Murnaghan (Member) | £4,625 | | |
| Brian Reid (Member) | £4,625 | | |
| Mrs. Brenda Sheil (Member) | £4,625 | | |
| **Probation Board for Northern Ireland** | | Up to 4 hours including travelling time, £17·47. Over 4 hours including travelling time, £34·98 | Appointments are made by the Secretary of State from nominations received through the CAU. The present Secretary of State has appointed the Chairman, Deputy Chairmen and 27 members |
| James Grew (Chairman) | £7,605 | | |
| Thomas Millar (Chairman) | £7,605 | | |
| John V. Simpson (Chairman) | £7,605 | | |
| Thomas Millar (Deputy Chairman) | Nil | | |
| Edward Barry (Deputy Chairman) | Nil | | |
| Lawrence J. McArdle (Deputy Chairman) | Nil | | |
| Mr. B. Brotherston (Member) | Nil | Up to 4 hours inclusive of travelling time £13·10. Over 4 hours including travelling time £26·23. | |
| Mr. R. Clarke (Member) | Nil | | |
| Ms. E. M. Donnelly (Member) | Nil | | |
| Mr. H. Taggart (Member) | Nil | | |
| Ms. M. Glass (Member) | Nil | For all members: travel expenses range from 17·6p per mile to 21·3p per mile depending on size of vehicle. Subsistence rates are £4-£12 according to length of absence. Overnight subsistence within United Kingdom (excluding London and the Republic of Ireland) £50·50. London rate is £57·60 | |
| Mr. R. E. Carroll (Member) | Nil | | |
| Mr. H. M. Cunningham (Member) | Nil | | |
| Ms. T. Greeves (Member) | Nil | | |
| Mr. F. Wheeler (Member) | Nil | | |
| Ms. J. A. Hayes (Member) | Nil | | |
| Mr. L. A. McArdle (Member) | Nil | | |
| Ms. J. Douglas (Member) | Nil | | |
| Mr. J. P. Graham (Member) | Nil | | |
| Ms. C. Cunningham (Member) | Nil | | |
| Mr. O. Gibson (Member) | Nil | | |
| Ms. R. Gregg (Member) | Nil | | |
| Mr. D. J. H. McGuinness (Member) | Nil | | |
| Mr. M. J. Curran (Member) | Nil | | |
| Ms. B. B. McIvor (Member) | Nil | | |
| Mr. T. D. Banford (Member) | Nil | | |
| Mr. J. H. Baird (Member) | Nil | | |
| Ms. J. Beveridge (Member) | Nil | | |
| Ms. E. A. Ferguson (Member) | Nil | | |
| Mr. E. Rainey (Member) | Nil | | |
| Ms. M. F. Skillington (Member) | Nil | | |
| Mr. Aidan P. McNamee (Member) | Nil | | |

| Name of body and Member's names | Salary | Expenses | Method of appointment |
| --- | --- | --- | --- |
| Mr. M. J. McIvor (Member) | Nil | | |
| Rathgael and Whiteabbey Training Schools Management Board | | | |
| Mr. M. G. Brown (Chairman) | £100 per annum | Travel expenses paid at various rates depending on length of journey and size of car—from 18·8p to 52·8p per mile. | The present board was appointed from nominations received from various interested bodies. The new board to take office from 1 August 1989 will be comprised of persons nominated from the CAU and a number of persons re-appointed from the present Board. |
| Rev. H. D. McMorran (Deputy Chairman) | Nil | | |
| Mr. G. S. Shaw (Member) | Nil | | |
| Mr. J. Donaghy (Member) | Nil | | |
| Rev. M. Elizabeth Hewittan (Member) | Nil | Chairman of sub-committees may claim necessary telephone expenses, which amount to not more than £2 per person per month. | The present Secretary of State has appointed the Chairman, Deputy Chairman and 13 members |
| Mr. L. Shanks (Member) | Nil | | |
| Mr. G. J. Ginn (Member) | Nil | | |
| Mr. M. J. McIvor JP (Member) | Nil | | |
| Lady M. A. Porter (Member) | Nil | | |
| Mrs. A. E. Cullen (Member) | Nil | | |
| Mr. W. Keown (Member) | Nil | | |
| Mrs. M. Sandford DL JP (Member) | Nil | | |
| Mr. P. Patrick (Member) | Nil | | |
| Mr. S. M. Hamilton (Member) | Nil | | |
| Mr. R. Doran (Member) | Nil | | |
| Boards of Visitors and Visiting Committees Names are not disclosed for security reasons | Nil | Travelling expenses are paid. Details not readily available | Appointments are made after nominations are received from various public groups and bodies which are representative of the community as a whole. Fifty appointments have been made by the present Secretary of State |
| Standing Advisory Commission on Human Rights | | | |
| Mr. James O'Hara (Chairman) | £6,216 | Travel and subsistence expenses are paid at Civil Service rates | The present Secretary of State has made 17 appointments and re-appointments in accordance with section 20 of the Northern Ireland Constitution Act 1973 |
| Sir Oliver Napier (Chairman) | £6,216 | | |
| Mr. P. Girvan QC (Member) | Daily attendance fee of £72·00 | | |
| Professor T. Hadden (Member) | | | |
| Professor J. Darby (Member) | | | |
| Mrs. D. Field (Member) | | | |
| Mrs. J. McCrum (Member) | | | |
| Mr. A. H. MacLaughlin (Member) | | | |
| Dr. J. C. McCrudden (Member) | | | |
| Mr. R. A. Ferris (Member) | | | |
| Mr. T. Carlin (Member) | | | |
| Mrs. J. Brett (Member) | | | |
| Mr. T. H. Kernohan (Member) | | | |
| Mr. D. Stevens (Member) | | | |
| Dr. P. J. Cosgrove (Member) | | | |
| Sister Genevieve O'Farrell (Member) | | | |
| Mrs. D. Tennis (Member) | | | |
| Parliamentary Boundary Commission for Northern Ireland | | | No appointments to the Commission have been made by the present Secretary of State |

## AGRICULTURE, FISHERIES AND FOOD

### Greenhouse Effect

**Dr. David Clark:** To ask the Minister of Agriculture, Fisheries and Food what are the current estimates of greenhouse gas emissions, such as nitrous oxide, methane and carbon dioxide, from the agricultural sector in the United Kingdom; and what are his proposals to reduce these emissions.

**Mr. Donald Thompson:** Agriculture both produces and consumes carbon dioxide, and net emissions are likely to be small. Annual emissions of methane and nitrous oxide from agriculture are very tentatively and approximately estimated at 1·4 million tonnes and 0·06 million tonnes (as N) respectively.

**Dr. David Clark:** To ask the Minister of Agriculture, Fisheries and Food what specific proposals his Department has put forward for consideration and enactment, in order to reduce greenhouse gas emissions such as nitrous oxide, methane and carbon dioxide, since the seminar on the greenhouse effect held by the Prime Minister on 26 April.

**Mr. Donald Thompson:** My Department participates in the work of the Intergovernmental panel on climate change, and we have drawn its attention to a number of schemes in the United Kingdom which encourage farmers to protect the environment, and which help to reduce greenhouse gas emissions.

### Food Irradiation

**Dr. David Clark:** To ask the Minister of Agriculture, Fisheries and Food whether he intends to have a period of public consultation on his proposals to lift the ban on food irradiation and on his report of a working policy on the introduction of food irradiation in the United Kingdom; and if he will make a statement.

**Mr. Donald Thompson:** There will be full public consultation when detailed proposals are put forward.

**Mr. Warren:** To ask the Minister of Agriculture, Fisheries and Food if he will make arrangements to label all food which has been irradiated; and if he will make a statement.

**Mr. Ryder:** The Council of the European Communities agreed on 14 June to amend the food labelling directive to provide for specific indication on the label of foodstuffs that have been irradiated. This requirement will be implemented into United Kingdom food labelling legislation in due course.

**Mr. Home Robertson:** To ask the Minister of Agriculture, Fisheries and Food if he will list the micro-organisms which are not destroyed by food irradiation.

**Mr. Donald Thompson:** Populations of all micro-organisms in food are reduced to a greater or lesser extent by food irradiation. The process has been shown to be effective in dealing with vegetative micro-organisms such as salmonella, camphylobacter and listeria, but is not effective in the reduction of micro-organisms that produce spores—in particular clostridium botulinum.

**Mr. Home Robertson:** To ask the Minister of Agriculture, Fisheries and Food if he will list the countries in which food irradiation is approved, giving the nature of the approval and details of the type of food covered for each country.

**Mr. Donald Thompson:** The list is as follows:

WORLD TAKE-UP OF FOOD IRRADIATION BY COUNTRY WITH FOODS FOR WHICH IRRADIATION APPROVED

P = Provisional     C = Conditional     U = Unconditional

**EC**

*Belgium*
- Potatoes (P)
- Strawberries (P)
- Onions (P)
- Garlic (P)
- Shallots (P)
- Black, White Pepper (P)
- Paprika Powder (P)
- Arabic Gum (P)
- Spices (P)
- (Semi)-Dried Vegetables (P)

*Denmark*
- Spices (U)
- Herbs (U)

*France*
- Potatoes (P)
- Onions (P)
- Garlic (P)
- Shallots (P)
- Spices (U)
- Aromatic Substances (U)
- Gum Arabic (U)
- Muesli-like Cereal (U)
- Dehydrated Vegetables (U)
- Mechanically Deboned Poultry Meat (U)
- Dried Fruits (U)
- Dried Vegetables (U)

*Germany (Dem. Rep)*
- Onions (U)
- Enzyme Solutions (U)

- Spices (P)

*Italy*
- Potatoes (U)
- Onions (U)
- Garlic (U)

*The Netherlands*
- Mushrooms (U)
- Potatoes (U)
- Chicken (U)
- Spices (P)
- Onions (U)
- Frozen Frog Legs (P)
- Rice and Ground Products (P)
- Rye Bread (P)
- Frozen Shrimp (P)
- Malt (P)
- Boiled and Cooled Shrimp (P)
- Frozen Fish (P)
- Egg Powder (P)
- Dry Blood Protein (P)
- Dehydrated Vegetables (P)

*Spain*
- Potatoes (U)
- Onions (U)

**REST OF EUROPE**

*Finland*
- Dry and Dehydrated Herbs and Spices (U)
- All Foods for Patients requiring a Sterile Diet (U)

*Hungary*
- Onions (U)
- Sour Cherries Canned(C)
- Black Pepper (C)
- Spices (U) and (C)

*Norway*
- Spices (U)

*Poland*
- Potatoes (P)
- Onions (P)

*Yugoslavia*
- Cereals (U)
- Legumes (U)
- Onions (U)
- Garlic (U)
- Potatoes (U)
- Dehydrated Fruits and Vegetables (U)
- Dried Mushrooms (U)
- Egg Powder (U)
- Herbal Teas, Tea Extracts (U)
- Fresh Poultry (U)
- Spices (U)

**NORTH AMERICA**

*United States*
- Wheat and Wheat Flour (U)
- White Potatoes (U)
- Spices and Dry Vegetable Seasonings (38 Commodities) (U)
- Dry or Dehydrated Enzyme Preparations (Including Immobilised Enzyme Preparations) (U)
- Pork Carcases or Fresh Non-Heat Processed Cuts of Pork Carcases (U)
- Fresh Foods (U)
- Food (U)
- Dry or Dehydrated Aromatic Vegetable Substances (U)

*Canada*
- Potatoes (U)
- Onions (U)
- Wheat Flour, Wholewheat (U)
- Spices and Certain Dry Vegetable Seasonings (U)
- Onion Powder (U)

ELSEWHERE

*Argentina*

    Strawberries (U)
    Potatoes (U)
    Onions (U)
    Garlic (U)
    Cocoa Powder (U)
    Spinach (U)

*Bangladesh*

    Chicken (U)
    Papaya (U)
    Potatoes (U)
    Wheat and Ground Wheat Products (U)
    Fish (U)
    Onions (U)
    Frog Legs (P)
    Shrimp (P)
    Mangoes (U)
    Pulses (U)
    Spices (U)
    Rice (U)

*Brazil*

    Rice (U)
    Potatoes (U)
    Onions (U)
    Beans (U)
    Maize (U)
    Wheat (U)
    Wheat Flour (U)
    Spices (13 different products) (U)
    Papaya (U)
    Strawberries (U)
    Fish and Fish Products (Fillets, Salted, Smoked, Dried, Dehydrated) (U)
    Poultry (U)

*Chile*

    Potatoes (U)
    Papaya (U)
    Wheat and Ground Wheat Products (U)
    Strawberries (U)
    Chicken (U)
    Onions (U)
    Rice (U)
    Teleost Fish and Fish Products (U)
    Cocoa Beans (U)
    Dates (U)
    Mangoes (U)
    Pulses (U)
    Spices and Condiments (U)

*China*

    Potatoes (U)
    Onions (U)
    Garlic (U)
    Peanuts (U)
    Grain (U)
    Mushrooms (U)
    Sausage (U)
    Apples (U)

*Cuba*

    Potatoes
    Onions

*India*

    Potatoes (U)
    Onions (U)

*Indonesia*

    Dried Spices (U)
    Tuber and Root Crops (Potatoes, Shallots, Garlic and Rhizomes) (U)
    Cereals (U)

*Israel*

    Potatoes (U)
    Onions (U)
    Poultry and Poultry Sections (U)
    Onions (U)
    Garlic (U)
    Shallots (U)
    Spices (36 different products) (U)
    Fresh Fruits and Vegetables (U)
    Grains, Cereals, Pulses, Cocoa and Coffee Beans, Nuts, Edible Seeds (U)
    Mushrooms and Strawberries (A)

    Spices and Condiments, Dehydrated and Dried Vegetables, Edible Herbs
    Poultry Feeds

*Japan*

    Potatoes (U)

*New Zealand*

    Herbs and Spices (P)

*Philippines*

    Potatoes (P)
    Onions (P)
    Garlic (P)

*Republic of Korea*

    Potatoes (C)
    Onions (C)
    Garlic (C)
    Chestnuts (C)
    Fresh and Dried Mushrooms (C)
    Garlic Powder (C)

*South Africa*

    Potatoes (U)
    Dried Bananas (P)
    Avocados (P)
    Onions(U)
    Garlic (U)
    Chicken (U)
    Papaya (U)
    Mango (U)
    Strawberries (U)
    Bananas (U)
    Litchis (U)
    Pickled Mango (Achar) (U)
    Frozen Fruit Juices (U)
    Green Beans (U)
    Tomatoes (U)
    Brinjals (U)
    Soya Pickle Products (U)
    Ginger (U)
    Vegetable Paste (U)
    Bananas (Dried) (U)
    Almonds (U)
    Cheese Powder (U)
    Yeast Powder (U)
    Herbal Tea (U)
    Various Spices (U)
    Various Dehydrated Vegetables (U)

*Thailand*

    Potatoes, Onions, Garlic (U)
    Dates (U)
    Mangoes, Papaya (U)
    Wheat, Rice, Pulses (U)
    Cocoa Beans (U)
    Fish and Fishery Products (U)
    Stawberries (U)
    Nam (U)
    Moor Yor (U)
    Sausage (U)
    Frozen Shrimps (U)
    Chicken (U)
    Spices and Condiments, Dehydrated (U)
    Onions and Onion Powder (U)

*USSR*
    Potatoes (U)
    Grain (U)
    Dried Fruits (U)
    Dry Food Concentrates Buckwheat Mush, Gruel, Rice
        Pudding
    Onions (U)

*Uruguay*
    Potatoes (U)

## Pesticides

**Mr. Ron Davies:** To ask the Minister of Agriculture, Fisheries and Food if he will list the research sponsored by his Department into alternatives to pesticides for pest control.

**Mr. Donald Thompson:** The following research projects on alternatives to pesticides for pest control are currently being carried out for and by my Department.

1. *Integrated control of pests on outdoor crops*
The use of natural enemies, chemical and cultural methods to control aphid pests in cereals.

2. *Biology and ecology of pests, pathogens and beneficial organisms*
    (a) The development of new methods of insect management using non-polluting chemicals affecting behaviour.
    (b) The development of methods using natural predators and pesticides in integrated control systems for pests of arable crops.
    (c) To determine the effects of straw incorporation and cultivation techniques on populations of pest aphids and beneficial insects, and to assess the implications for future pesticide usage.

3. *Control of diseases in cereals*
To develop methods, involving biological control, agrochemicals, host resistance and husbandry practices to minimise the harmful effects of takeall.

4. *Development of oats and diseases resistant cereals*
To evaluate new sources of disease resistance and to incorporate new resistant germplasm into high yielding winter and spring oat varieties.

5. *Disease and pest management in agro-ecosystems harmonised with the environment*
    (a) To rationalise the development of resistant varieties by understanding the mechanisms underlying genetic host resistance, its specificity with regard to pathogen variation, its relationship with non-host resistance and the corresponding implications for its durability.
    (b) To identify and conserve genetically resistant germplasm of currently important crops and minor alternative crops. Characterisation and determination of the durability of such resistances and their deployment in disease management systems using reduced pesticide inputs.
    (c) To develop an holistic approach to the deployment of genetic resistance in the field with special reference to grassland cereal farming and farm forestry in de-intensified systems.
    (d) To integrate the use of natural biocides, particularly *Bacillus thuringiensis* toxin, genetic resistance and systemic pesticides in the management of crop pests and diseases.

6. *The improvement of dry peas*
To define an optimum model for composition of storage compounds in a pea seed by understanding genetic variation and storage product accumulation in embryos, to improve the quality of peas for use as food and feed, and to improve disease resistance in the pea crop.

7. *Pests of non-cereal crops*
To develop methods for the containment of soil, dwelling nematodes by the integrated use of crop rotations, reliable resistant cultivars and efficiently-used, safely-formulated nematicides, thereby delaying selection of virulent nematode pathotypes and minimising cost and risks to operatives and the environment. Particular attention is paid to potato cyst nematodes and to other nematodes of forage and grain legumes. Problems of nematode attack in oilseed rape and other alternative crops such as sunflower and lupin are being investigated. Studies on the nature of host tolerance to nematode attack and the complex interactions between nematode host races and culture resistance are contributing to the development of integrated control measures.

8. Bird damage assessment and development of control techniques.

9. The biology of storage arthropods and development of physical and biological control strategies.

10. Laboratory and field evaluation of novel methods of pest control.

11. Control of storage pests using modified atmospheres.

12. Cereals: soil-borne fungal diseases.

13. Control of specific weeds and headland weed control.

14. Alternative cropping systems. Includes work on milling wheat production under organic farming systems.

15. Novel methods of pest control.

16. *Field Vegetable Breeding*
    Genetic improvement of lettuce. Work to find new sources of genetic resistance to downy mildew, lettuce root aphid and important viral diseases.
    Genetics of host resistance to disease and development of resistant breeding material for important fungal and viral diseases.

17. *Field Vegetable Pests*
    Resistance of vegetables to insect pests, including biochemical methods of screening plant material for resistance, and pest-host plant interactions.

18. *Field Vegetable Diseases*
    Biology, resistance and control of diseases of composites, crucifers and legumes. Methods of control through resistance, including durability of single gene resistance.
    Screening for resistance to cucumber mosaic virus in marrow.

19. *Field Vegetable Weeds*
    Development of novel programmes for weed control in vegetable crops, including cultural and other techniques for controlling weeds with less reliance on herbicides.

20. *Top Fruit Breeding*
    To breed and select apple, pear, cherry, plum scion varieties and rootstocks which, amongst other attributes, are resistant to pests and diseases.

21. *Top Fruit Protection*
    In vitro techniques for selection for resistance to fireblight.
    In vitro techniques for testing for resistance to bacterial canker in cherry.
    Biology, ecology and control of apple and pear pests, including regulation of spider mite in apples by predatory mites, regulation of *P. pyncola* on pears by predators.

22. *Soft Fruit Breeding*
    Breeding and selection of strawberries and raspberries which, amongst other attributes, are resistant to pests and diseases.

23. *Soft Fruit Protection*
    To elucidate the biology of wilt disease of strawberries and to improve control through biological means; select and exploit plant resistance for wilt control.

To study the biology, ecology and pest/damage relationships for several pest species, together with the development of control strategies.

24. *Hop Production and Protection*
Evaluation of wilt resistance in breeding material of hops.
Control of damson-hop aphids by introducing or encouraging the migration to hop gardens of natural predators.
Study of factors affecting the sexual activity and migration of damson-hop aphids to identify weak points in its life cycle.
Evaluation of biological agents for controlling the two-spotted spite mite.

25. *Glasshouse Crop Pests*
Biological control of major glasshouse pests (whitefly and red spider mite), secondary pests (especially aphids and thrips) and newly-established non-indigenous pests.

26. *Glasshouse Crop Diseases*
Integrated control of bacterial and fungal pathogens, utilising biological agents.

27. *Evaluation of biological and other novel methods for pest control in greenhouse crops*
Improvement in efficiency of Bacillus thuringiensis for arthropod pest control.
Use of fungi for control of arthropod pests.
Use of insect viruses for control of phytophagous pests.
The diagnosis of pathogens in invertebrate pest populations.
Use of insect parasite nematodes for pest control of glasshouse and mushroom pests.

28. *Mushroom Protection*
Novel control methods for mushroom pests, including behaviour-modifying chemicals, antagonists, repellants, and insect-parasite nematodes.
Biological control of bacterial blotch disease.

29. *Hardy Ornamental Nursery Stock-Protection*
Control of disease in the propagation of container-grown nursery stock, including biological control.

30. *Bulb Breeding*
Use of induced mutations and conventional methods to breed disease resistant Narcissus cultivars.

31. *Bulb Protection*
Control of fungal diseases of ornamental bulbs and corms, including screening for genetic resistance and biological control methods.

32. Development of integrated control methods for Western Flower Thrips.

33. Control of Narcissus basal rot by antagonists.

34. *Influence of pests and diseases on grassland agriculture, and their control by biological means*
(a) To develop non-polluting methods of controlling pests and diseases in newly-sown grassland with emphasis on legumes.
(b) To determine the magnitude of losses of grassland legumes to pests and diseases and, thereby, the potential for application of biocontrol methods to grassland.
(c) To determine the potential of endophytic fungi in ryegrass as a means of biocontrol of grassland pests.

35. *Diseases and pests of forage grasses and legumes*
(a) Host: nematode relationships in forage grasses.
(b) Host: nematode relationships in forage legumes.
(c) Host: fungus relationships in forage grasses.
(d) Host: fungus relationships in forage legumes.
(e) Host: virus relationships in graminaceous and legume species. Mechanisms of host resistance.

(f) Identification of genetically resistant germ plasm in grasses and forage legumes.
(g) Relationships between endophytic fungi and their grass hosts.

36. *Exploit genetic variability in forage grasses*
(a) Develop selection criteria and produce new gene combinations in perennial ryegrass.
(b) Enhancement of new germplasm created by hybridising Italian and perennial ryegrass and development of new gene combinations in Italian ryegrass.
(c) Develop and evaluate ryegrass/fescue hybrids with new potentials for coping with climatic change.

37. *Develop techniques and exploit genetic variation to improve legumes*
Exploit genetic variation to improve yield, reliability of yield persistency and seed yield in white clover.

38. *Field boundaries: biological components influencing invertebrate predator overwintering*
(a) To create overwintering habitats on farmland which favour the development of high numbers of polyphagous predators by modifying existing boundaries and by creating new ones.
(b) To monitor the accumulation of predators in autumn and winter in these new habitats together with their dispersal, distribution and predation rate in the crop in spring and summer.
(c) to convert the date into 'packaged' advice which could be made available via Videotex methods with ADAS co-operation.

39. *Exploitation of predatory beetles and parasitic wasps resident in field margins, hedgerows and shelter belts around grassland*
To enhance the number and variety of predators and parasitic invertebrates present by increasing the size, stability and diversity of the flora in hedgerows, field margins and shelter belts around grassland and to investigate ways of how this may best be achieved.

40. *Epidemiology and inter-relationships between clover viruses of pasture crops and field boundary ecosystems*
To determine the field host range and interactions of the major viruses and their vectors that infect white clover, relating this to the ecology of hosts in field boundaries and in grassland crops. To identify for development resistant genotypes in white clover and related species and genera.

**Mr. Ron Davies:** To ask the Minister of Agriculture, Fisheries and Food what arrangements exist to ensure the competence of farm workers to apply pesticides; how these requirements differ according to the pesticide in use; and what are the different categories of such pesticides.

**Mr. Donald Thompson:** All people using pesticides have to be competent in their usage. Employees, and the self-employed, must have had adequate instruction and guidance in safe and efficient use. Additionally, people may not use certain pesticides unsupervised unless they hold an appropriate certificate of competence, or are working on their own or their employer's land, or are exempted by age. The arrangements are set out in the Ministers' consent to use pesticides (C(i)) published in the *Gazettes* on 20 January 1989 and in "Reference Book 500 (Pesticides 1989)".

The pesticides attracting certification as a result of consent C(i) are each identified in "Reference Book 500". In brief, these are the pesticides approved for professional cultivation of crops and management of weeds. Certification thus extends beyond farm workers, but does not cover all their activities. Pesticides approved for use as, for instance, rodenticides, or for the protection of stored products do not attract certification.

**Mr. Jack:** To ask the Minister of Agriculture, Fisheries and Food what steps have been taken to improve his Department's methods of responding to any public concerns on particular pesticide use or residues.

**Mr. Ryder:** My Department responds promptly to all new information on pesticide safety. It also provides the public with information on the government's very extensive controls on pesticides and pesticide residues, and on the widescale monitoring of residues in food and the environment which it undertakes.

### Parliamentary Questions

**Mr. Ron Davies:** To ask the Minister of Agriculture, Fisheries and Food if he will list those written parliamentary questions answered by his Department which had been tabled during the previous day's sitting during the last 12 months indicating the hon. Member asking each such question.

**Mr. Donald Thompson:** This information is not readily available within the Department but the hon. Member may be able to obtain some information from House of Commons records.

### Tripe

**Mr. Ron Davies:** To ask the Minister of Agriculture, Fisheries and Food (1) whether he had plans to extend the ban on bovine offals for human consumption to include tripe;

(2) whether he has any evidence that tripe carries the infective agent responsible for bovine spongiform encephalopathy.

**Mr. Donald Thompson:** The potential for tripe to carry the BSE agent is currently being studied. A decision on whether to ban its use for human consumption will be taken when the results of this study and the views of interested parties are known and have been evaluated.

### Product Licences

**Mr. Ron Davies:** To ask the Minister of Agriculture, Fisheries and Food whether he has any information on the commercial sale and use of products for use in treating animals or fish which have not been granted a product licence.

**Mr. Donald Thompson:** Information on the commercial sale and use of veterinary medicinal products is not required for the purposes of the Medicines Act 1968 and is not collected by my Department.

### Sheepmeat

**Mr. Macdonald:** To ask the Minister of Agriculture, Fisheries and Food if he will make a further statement on the future of the European Community sheepmeat regime.

**Mr. Donald Thompson:** Discussions on the EC Commission's proposals for a revised sheepmeat regime took place at the Agriculture Council on 19 and 20 June. Major differences of view persist amongst member states and the Council will return to this matter at a subsequent meeting.

### Animal Welfare

**Mr. Allen McKay:** To ask the Minister of Agriculture, Fisheries and Food when he last met representatives of Compassion in World Farming to discuss animal welfare.

**Mr. Donald Thompson:** I last met Compassion in World Farming on 3 April and my officials last met them on 21 June.

### Potato Marketing Board

**Mr. John Marshall:** To ask the Minister of Agriculture, Fisheries and Food when he expects to make an announcement about the future of the Potato Marketing Board.

**Mr. Ryder:** I refer my hon. Friend to the reply given to the Member for Roxburgh and Berwickshire (Mr. Kirkwood) on 14 June at column *411*.

### Coastal Defence Works

**Mr. Barry Field:** To ask the Minister of Agriculture, Fisheries and Food if he will list those authorities which have made representations to him about coastal defence and repair works during the last year.

**Mr. Ryder:** There is continuing correspondence with various authorities on matters relating to coastal defences. During 1988-89 the following authorities made comments on policy or submitted proposals for coast protection or sea defence work:

Allerdale District Council
Alnwick District Council
Arun District Council
Blackpool Borough Council
Bournemouth Borough Council
Brighton Borough Council
Canterbury City Council
Carrick District Council
Castle Morpeth District Council
Chichester District Council
Christchurch Borough Council
Cleethorpes Borough Council
Dover District Council
Easington District Council
Eastbourne Borough Council
East Yorkshire Borough Council
Gosport Borough Council
Great Yarmouth Borough Council
Hartlepool Borough Council
Hastings Borough Council
Havant Borough Council
Holderness Borough Council
Kerrier District Council
Lancaster City Council
Langbaurgh Borough Council
Lewes District Council
New Forest District Council
North Cornwall District Council
North Norfolk District Council
Penwith District Council
Poole Borough Council
Portsmouth City Council
Purbeck District Council
Rother District Council
Scarborough Borough Council
Shepway District Council
South Hams District Council
South Lakeland District Council
South Wight District Council
Suffolk Coastal District Council
Sunderland Borough Council
Swale Borough Council
Tendering District Council

Thanet District Council
Torridge District Council
Wansbeck District Council
Waveney District Council
West Dorset District Council
West Somerset District Council
Weymouth and Portland Borough Council
Wirral Borough Council
Worthing Borough Council
Wyre Borough Council
Mappleton Parish Council
Anglian Water Authority
Southern Water Authority
Aldeburgh Town Council
Orford and Gedgrave Parish Council
Mablethorpe and Sutton Town Council

## Common Agricultural Policy

**Mr. Allen:** To ask the Minister of Agriculture, Fisheries and Food if he will review British participation in the Common Agricultural Policy.

**Mr. MacGregor:** The treaty establishing the European Economic Community provides specifically for a common agricultural policy (CAP). The Government's policy is to participate fully in negotiations on the CAP, pressing for reform to continue, in order to increase market-orientation, control expenditure and bring supply into better balance with demand. Substantial progress has been made in this direction, though more remains to be done.

## Hedgerows

**Mr. Andrew F. Bennett:** To ask the Minister of Agriculture, Fisheries and Food, pursuant to his answer to the hon. Member for Denton and Reddish of 16 March, *Official Report,* column *346,* if he can now estimate how many miles of hedgerow were re-layed in the 1988-89 winter in the United Kingdom with grant-in-aid assistance.

**Mr. Ryder:** Figures for the full 1988-89 winter period are not yet available. In the period October-December 1988, grants were paid in the United Kingdom under the agriculture improvement scheme for the planting and laying of some 260 miles of hedgerows.

**Mr. Greg Knight:** To ask the Minister of Agriculture, Fisheries and Food when he expects the review of the demand for veterinary surgeons to be completed.

**Mr. Donald Thompson:** I have asked for the report to be prepared by the end of this year.

## Public Relations

**Mr. Blair:** To ask the Minister of Agriculture, Fisheries and Food which public relations firms his Department has employed and at what cost, for each year since 1979.

**Mr. Donald Thompson:** It is not my Department's policy to employ public relations firms.

## Food Poisoning

**Mr. Canavan:** To ask the Minister of Agriculture, Fisheries and Food how many complaints about food poisoning he has dealt with in the past year; and what steps he is taking as a result.

**Mr. Ryder:** Incidents of food poisoning are generally handled by local authorities in the first instance, and the oversight of epidemiological information is the responsibility of my right hon. and learned Friend the Secretary of State for Health. However, I receive a number of representations on related matters. In the last 12 months I have, for example, introduced a comprehensive set of measures to deal with salmonella in eggs, and set in hand research on a wide range of related issues, including the susceptibility of listeria to temperatures applied in storage or cooking.

With my right hon. and learned Friend I have also issued a food hygiene leaflet entitled "Food Safety A Guide From Her Majesty's Government", and set up a committee, under the chairmanship of Professor Sir Mark Richmond, to make recommendations on the microbiological safety of food.

## Unpasteurised Milk

**Mr. Wigley:** To ask the Minister of Agriculture, Fisheries and Food how many letters he has received expressing opposition to the limiting of availability of unpasteurised milk; and if he will make a statement.

**Mr. Donald Thompson:** I refer the hon. Member to the reply my right hon. Friend gave to the hon. Member for Ludlow (Mr. Gill) on 13 June at column *353.*

# Written Answers to Questions

*Wednesday 28 June 1989*

## DEFENCE

### Low Flying

**Mr. Snape:** To ask the Secretary of State for Defence how many low-flying sorties were flown over the United Kingdom by United States Air Force aircraft based in the United Kingdom in 1987 and 1988.

**Mr. Neubert:** A total of 21,869 low-flying sorties were flown over the United Kingdom during 1987 by United States Air Force aircraft based in the United Kingdom and 22,050 during 1988.

### Lead-free Petrol

**Mr. Menzies Campbell:** To ask the Secretary of State for Defence how many motorised vehicles in his Department and in the armed forces run on lead-free petrol; if he has any plans to increase the use of lead-free petrol by vehicles run by his Department and the armed forces; and if he will make a statement.

**Mr. Neubert:** The majority of my Department's current vehicle fleet uses and will continue to use diesel fuel. We have already implemented, for petrol-engined staff cars, vans and minibuses, a policy of purchasing vehicles capable of running on unleaded petrol. The remainder of the current fleet of petrol-engined vehicles, which can be technically and cost-effectively adapted to run on unleaded petrol, is being converted during routine servicing.

### Surface Fleet

**Mr. Menzies Campbell:** To ask the Secretary of State for Defence if he will list in the *Official Report* the names of the destroyers and frigates of the surface fleet, available for service at 24 hours' notice on 1 June 1988, 1 January 1989, and 1 June 1989.

**Mr. Archie Hamilton:** Details of ships available for operations at precise periods of notice are classified. However, the names of the destroyers and frigates that were available for operational deployment immediately or within a short period for each of the dates requested are as follows:

| 1 June 1988 | 1 January 1989 | 1 June 1989 |
| --- | --- | --- |
| HMS Achilles | HMS Achilles | HMS Achilles |
| HMS Active | HMS Active | HMS Active |
| HMS Alacrity | HMS Alacrity | HMS Alacrity |
| HMS Amazon | HMS Amazon | HMS Amazon |
| HMS Ambuscade | HMS Ambuscade | HMS Ambuscade |
| HMS Andromeda | HMS Andromeda | HMS Andromeda |
| HMS Apollo | HMS Arethusa | HMS Argonaut |
| HMS Arethusa | HMS Avenger | HMS Ariadne |
| HMS Avenger | HMS Beaver | HMS Arrow |
| HMS Battleaxe | HMS Birmingham | HMS Avenger |
| HMS Beaver | HMS Boxer | HMS Beaver |
| HMS Birmingham | HMS Brave | HMS Birmingham |

| 1 June 1988 | 1 January 1989 | 1 June 1989 |
| --- | --- | --- |
| HMS Boxer | HMS Brazen | HMS Boxer |
| HMS Brave | HMS Brilliant | HMS Brave |
| HMS Brazen | HMS Bristol | HMS Brilliant |
| HMS Bristol | HMS Broadsword | HMS Bristol |
| HMS Charybdis | HMS Cardiff | HMS Broadsword |
| HMS Cleopatra | HMS Charybdis | HMS Campbeltown |
| HMS Cornwall | HMS Cleopatra | HMS Cardiff |
| HMS Danae | HMS Cornwall | HMS Charybdis |
| HMS Edinburgh | HMS Coventry | HMS Cleopatra |
| HMS Euryalus | HMS Cumberland | HMS Cornwall |
| HMS Exeter | HMS Danae | HMS Coventry |
| HMS Gloucester | HMS Edinburgh | HMS Cumberland |
| HMS Hermione | HMS Euryalus | HMS Danae |
| HMS Juno | HMS Gloucester | HMS Edinburgh |
| HMS Jupiter | HMS Hermione | HMS Gloucester |
| HMS Liverpool | HMS Juno | HMS Hermione |
| HMS London | HMS Jupiter | HMS Jupiter |
| HMS Manchester | HMS Liverpool | HMS Liverpool |
| HMS Minerva | HMS London | HMS London |
| HMS Newcastle | HMS Manchester | HMS Manchester |
| HMS Nottingham | HMS Newcastle | HMS Newcastle |
| HMS Penelope | HMS Nottingham | HMS Nottingham |
| HMS Phoebe | HMS Penelope | HMS Penelope |
| HMS Scylla | HMS Phoebe | HMS Phoebe |
| HMS Sheffield | HMS Scylla | HMS Scylla |
| HMS Sirius | HMS Sheffield | HMS Sheffield |
| HMS Southampton | HMS Sirius | HMS Sirius |
| HMS York | HMS York | HMS York |

### Electro-Magnetic Propulsion

**Mr. O'Neill:** To ask the Secretary of State for Defence what expenditure has been incurred by the British Government on research and development work on the electro-magnetic propulsion of projectiles.

**Mr. Sainsbury:** It is not our practice to give details of funding of particular projects. However, I can say that such funding represents only a very small proportion of the defence research programme.

**Mr. O'Neill:** To ask the Secretary of State for Defence what work has been carried out by the royal armament research and development establishment on the electro-magnetic propulsion of projectiles.

**Mr. Sainsbury:** The royal armament research and development establishment has been undertaking research into electro-magnetic propulsion of projectiles since the early 1980s. It is not our practice to go into details of particular projects. However, it has a wide-ranging potential application for land, sea and air-based weapons.

**Mr. O'Neill:** To ask the Secretary of State for Defence whether any injuries have been caused as a result of research or development work into the electro-magnetic propulsion of projectiles.

**Mr. Sainsbury:** I am not aware of any injuries caused as a result of research or development work into electro-magnetic propulsion of projectiles undertaken in the United Kingdom.

**Mr. O'Neill:** To ask the Secretary of State for Defence whether the Ministry of Defence has received any funding from the United States Department of Defence to carry out research or development work into the electro-magnetic propulsion of projectiles.

**Mr. Sainsbury:** Yes, in December 1986 for a period of three years.

### Strategic Defence Initiative

**Mr. O'Neill:** To ask the Secretary of State for Defence what work has been carried out at the royal armament research and development establishment on behalf of the United States Government strategic defence initiative programme.

**Mr. Sainsbury:** Such a programme of work has been in hand at the royal armament research and development establishment since December 1986 with the purpose of achieving a greater understanding of electro-magnetic launcher capabilities.

## TRADE AND INDUSTRY

### Unichem Ltd.

**Mr. Oppenheim:** To ask the Chancellor of the Duchy of Lancaster what action he proposes to take following the publication last month of a proposed order to prohibit UniChem Ltd. from continuing to operate its share scheme as recommended by the Monopolies and Mergers Commission in its report published on 17 May.

**Mr. Maude:** I have today laid before the House the UniChem Limited (Allotment of Shares) Order 1989 which will come into force on 19 July. Except for a minor technical amendment, this will follow the draft order published in May.

## FOREIGN AND COMMONWEALTH AFFAIRS

### Mr. T. Gizaw

**Mr. Andrew Bowden:** To ask the Secretary of State for Foreign and Commonwealth Affairs if, in view of the libellous statements made about Mr. Louis Fitzgibbon of Portland place, Brighton by Mr. T. Gizaw, the Ethiopian press counsellor, he will take steps to expel Mr. Gizaw from the United Kingdom.

**Mr. Eggar:** No. The Foreign and Commonweath Office maintains an impartial stance in this private libel action, where the facts are disputed.

### Students (China)

**Mr. Sedgemore:** To ask the Secretary of State for Foreign and Commonwealth Affairs if he has made any representations to the Chinese embassy in Britain concerning the protection of the lives and interests of students from China who are studying in Britain; and if he will make a statement.

**Mr. Eggar:** I refer the hon. Member to my reply to my hon. Friend the Member for Chislehurst (Mr. Sims) on 16 June, at columns *559-60*.

## NATIONAL FINANCE

### Tax Liability

**Mr. Chris Smith:** To ask the Chancellor of the Exchequer if he will indicate, for each fiscal year since 1979, the total amount of taxation income forgone by Her Majesty's Treasury as a result of extra-statutory decisions on tax liability.

**Mr. Norman Lamont:** Extra-statutory concessions are operated locally and it would be disproportionately expensive, for the Departments and taxpayers, to collect the detailed information needed to determine precise annual costs. Most concessions are made to deal with what are, on the whole, minor or transitory anomalies under the legislation or to meet cases of hardship at the margins of the tax code. They generally apply to relatively few people and usually involve small amounts of tax in individual cases. There are, however, some exceptions—where the numbers of taxpayers benefiting from a concession and the amounts of tax involved in individual cases are larger.

The Inland Revenue has been able to estimate, in terms of broad orders of magnitude, the current annual revenue costs of most concessions appearing in its published booklet (IR1). The details are given in the table—references are to the numbers that appear in the booklet. The five largest concessions are all practices of long standing—A1, A5 and A67 date from the 1940s, A63 from the 1960s and A65 from the start of North sea oil exploration.

| Revenue Cost—£ million | Inland Revenue (Booklet IR1) | |
|---|---|---|
| 250 | : A63 | External training course—expenses borne by employer. |
| 200 | : A5 | Expenses allowances and benefits in kind (mainly removal expenses and bridging loan costs borne by employers). |
| 50-100 | : A67 | Payments to employees moved to higher cost housing areas. |
| 10-50 | : A65 | Workers on offshore oil and gas rigs or platforms—free transfers from or to mainland. |
| | : A1 | Flat rate allowances for cost of tools and special clothing.. |
| 3-10 | : A2 | Meal vouchers. |
| | : A6 | Miners: free coal and benefits in kind. |
| | : A19 | Arrears of tax arising through official error. |
| | : A22 | Long service awards. |
| | : A27 | Mortgage interest relief: temporary absences from mortgaged property. |
| | : D2 | Residence in the United Kingdom: year of commencement or cessation of residence. |
| | : D22 | (CGT) Relief for the replacement of business assets: expenditure on improvements to existing assets. |
| | : D24 | (CGT) Relief for the replacement of business assets: assets not brought immediately into trading use. |
| | : D26 | (CGT) Relief for exchange of joint interests. |
| | : I2 | Direct exports from tanker-loading fields. |
| | : I5 | Petroleum Revenue Tax instalments. |

Of the remaining 181 Inland Revenue concessions currently in operation, which include about 40 that are obsolescent and a further eight that are being legislated this year and/or are likely to become obsolescent as a result of legislation this year, the relevant revenue costs are thought to be:

| Revenue Cost—£ million | Number of Concessions |
|---|---|
| 0·5-3 | 13 |
| 0·1-0·5 | 30 |
| below 0·1 | 85 |

This leaves 53 for which the costs are not known, although the majority of these are thought unlikely to involve significant amounts of tax.

Customs and Excise concessions are published in notice 748. They have 39 concessions currently in operation, of which nine are being legislated this year. They estimate that at least 10 of these—and almost certainly more—involve minimal negligible cost in terms of tax forgone.

### War Loans

**Mr. Allen:** To ask the Chancellor of the Exchequer if he will redeem the $3\frac{1}{2}$ per cent. war loans; and if he will make a statement.

**Mr. Lilley:** There are no plans to redeem $3\frac{1}{2}$ per cent. war loan.

### EC Finance Ministers

**Mr. Adley:** To ask the Chancellor of the Exchequer when he next intends to meet his EC counterparts; and what he intends to discuss.

**Mr. Brooke:** EC Finance Ministers meet on a regular basis. The next Ecofin Council will take place in Brussels on 10 July 1989.

## HOME DEPARTMENT

### European Elections

**Mr. David Nicholson:** To ask the Secretary of State for the Home Department whether he has received any representations about enabling EEC nationals, long resident in the United Kingdom to vote for United Kingdom Members of the European Parliament; what is his policy on this; and if he will make a statement.

**Mr. Douglas Hogg:** We receive, from time to time, representations that citizens of other European Community states should be able to vote in European Parliament elections held here. It is for the European Parliament to make any recommendation for such a system to be adopted by the member states and none has as yet been forthcoming.

### Unconvicted Juveniles

**Mr. Sheerman:** To ask the Secretary of State for the Home Department whether he is seeking alternative accommodation to B wing of Hull prison for unconvicted juveniles; and whether he is considering the former detention centre at Gringley-on-the-Hill as a possible alternative.

**Mr. Douglas Hogg:** There is at present no practicable alternative accommodation for the unconvicted juvenile prisoners who are held in B wing of Hull prison. The accommodation at the former detention centre at Gringley is unsuitable for those prisoners. However the Department of Health and the local authority have reviewed the need for secure accommodation for 15 and 16-year-old boys in the region and plans for a new unit for the Yorkshire and Humberside region are well advanced with a target date for opening in early 1991. A 300-place remand centre is also planned to open on Humberside in 1991. Meanwhile a programme of action has been put in hand to improve conditions in Hull B wing.

### Mr. Albert Baker

**Mr. Livingstone:** To ask the Secretary of State for the Home Department, pursuant to his reply to the hon. Member for Brent, East, 6 April, *Official Report,* column *239,* if he will make a further statement as to the case of Mr. Albert Baker.

**Mr. Douglas Hogg:** Mr. Baker was refused leave to move for judicial review of the Government's decision not to transfer him to Northern Ireland. His petitions remain under consideration and a reply will be sent to him as soon as possible.

### DNA Testing

**Mr. Madden:** To ask the Secretary of State for the Home Department what are the projected public expenditure savings arising from the introduction of a central DNA testing scheme for those seeking entry clearance to the United Kingdom; and if he will identify the savings to his Department and also the appellate authorities.

**Mr. Renton:** We do not anticipate any reduction in Home Office expenditure from the introduction of a central DNA testing scheme into the entry clearance process overseas. The administration of the immigration appeals system is the responsibility of my noble and learned Friend the Lord Chancellor.

### Chinese Students

**Mr. Sedgemore:** To ask the Secretary of State for the Home Department if he is taking any special steps to protect the lives and interests of students from China who are studying in Britain; and if he will make a statement.

**Mr. Renton:** If any Chinese student feels at risk in the United Kingdom he or she should contact the police.

**Mr. Sedgemore:** To ask the Secretary of State for the Home Department (1) if he will allow all students from China who are studying in Britain to extend their stay during the current crisis; and if he will make a statement;

(2) if he will estimate the number of students from China studying in Britain.

**Mr. Renton:** I refer the hon. Member to the reply I gave on 16 June to questions from the hon. Members for Leyton (Mr. Cohen), for Leeds, West (Mr. Battle) and for Tooting (Mr. Cox) at column *566.*

## PRIME MINISTER

### Nuclear Non-proliferation Treaty

**Dr. Thomas:** To ask the Prime Minister if, during the visit of the Prime Minister of Spain on 19 June, she raised the nuclear non-proliferation treaty and prospects for new initiatives to be developed with North Atlantic Treaty Organisation allies in the lead up to the fourth review conference on the nuclear non-proliferation treaty in 1990.

**The Prime Minister:** No, but the nuclear non-proliferation treaty and related matters are regularly discussed with Spain at official level.

**Dr. Thomas:** To ask the Prime Minister if, during her meeting with the President-Designate of the Republic of South Africa, Mr. de Klerk, on 23 June, she raised the prospects of South Africa joining the nuclear non-proliferation treaty.

**The Prime Minister:** No, but the issue was raised by my right hon. and learned Friend the Secretary of State for Foreign and Commonwealth Affairs during his talks with Mr. de Klerk.

## EDUCATION AND SCIENCE

### Environmental Research

**Mr. Michael:** To ask the Secretary of State for Education and Science what plans he has to increase his Department's budget for sponsoring research into environmental matters and ensuring that the findings of such research are readily available to inform policy making at a national and local level.

**Mr. Jackson:** The findings of research into environmental matters sponsored by this Department are published in national and international scientific journals. The Natural Environment Reseach Council publishes an annual report which is laid before the House; copies of the latest report, for 1987-88, are available in the Library. The NERC also issues an annual corporate plan, annual reports of each of its institutes, and other publications detailing strategies in individual areas of science; copies of these are available direct from the NERC. The other research councils have similar arrangements. The Government review their expenditure plans each year after they have received advice from the Advisory Board for the Research Councils.

### Parents

**Mr. Gill:** To ask the Secretary of State for Education and Science what assessment he has made of the contribution of parents to the life and work of schools.

**Mrs. Rumbold:** My right hon. Friend and I view the contribution of parents to the life and work of schools as having the utmost importance, and many of our policies are designed to extend parental choice and influence. The Department has funded a major research project to examine the involvement of parents in their children's schooling. The report on the project is due later this year.

### Teacher Recruitment

**Mr. John Marshall:** To ask the Secretary of State for Education and Science what proposals he has to ease the problems of teacher recruitment *(a)* in shortage subjects and *(b)* in regions of high living costs.

**Mr. Butcher:** Action to tackle teacher shortages has been aimed in particular at London and the south-east where recruitment is hindered by the cost of housing. We have in place a series of measures which have cost £50 million over the last three years. The education support grant programme for 1990-91 includes support for expenditure of £2 million on local recruitment activity.

### Teachers

**Sir William Shelton:** To ask the Secretary of State for Education and Science what was the number of teachers in *(a)* higher education and *(b)* postgraduate studies in each year since 1979; and what has been their average real earnings in each such year.

**Mr. Jackson:** Data are not readily available in the form requested. However, the following may be helpful. The number of teachers in *(a)* universities and *(b)* polytechnics, and average salaries for each group are shown in the following tables.

*Table A Universities*

| Year | Number of Lecturers | Average Salary £ | Real Terms |
|------|---------------------|------------------|------------|
| 1979 | 18,585 | 8,458 | 100·0 |
| 1980 | 18,757 | 9,979 | 96·9 |
| 1981 | 18,409 | 11,187 | 97·0 |
| 1982 | 17,406 | 11,936 | 94·6 |
| 1983 | 17,200 | 12,543 | 95·5 |
| 1984 | 16,504 | 13,342 | 96·6 |
| 1985 | 16,970 | 13,964 | 94·6 |
| 1986 | 16,959 | 14,242 | 93·6 |
| 1987 | 16,479 | 16,592 | 104·6 |

*Note*

1. These figures relate to lecturers' *salaries* and exclude other staff including professors, readers and senior lecturers for whom data are not readily available. Information on total *earnings* is not collected.
2. The figures relate to full-time, non-clinical academic staff at universities in Great Britain.
3. The Real Terms column is indexed using the Retail Prices Index as at April, with 1979 taken as 100.

*Table B*

| Polytechnics | Number of Staff | Average Salary | Real Terms |
|--------------|-----------------|----------------|------------|
| 1979 | 16,854 | 7,462 | 100·0 |
| 1980 | 17,042 | 9,016 | 92·2 |
| 1981 | 16,824 | 11,399 | 112·0 |
| 1982 | 16,250 | 12,359 | 111·0 |
| 1983 | 15,883 | 13,152 | 113·5 |
| 1984 | 15,642 | 13,842 | 113·6 |
| 1985 | 15,490 | 14,481 | 111·2 |
| 1986 | 15,548 | 15,453 | 115·1 |
| 1987 | 15,299 | 16,291 | 116·4 |

*Note*

1. The figures for polytechnics relate to all grades up to and including Principals and to England and Wales only.
2. The Real Terms column is indexed as for universities.

### Further and Higher Education

**Mr. Andrew F. Bennett:** To ask the Secretary of State for Education and Science, how many people stayed on in full-time education after 16 for each of the last five years.

**Mr. Robert Jackson:** The information is as follows:

*Participation in full-time education: England. Percentage of age group*

| | Age at previous 31 August | | |
| | 16 | 17 | 18 |
| --- | --- | --- | --- |
| 1984 | 45 | 31 | 17 |
| 1985 | 45 | 31 | 17 |
| 1986 | 45 | 32 | 17 |
| 1987 | 45 | 32 | 17 |
| 1988 | 47 | 33 | 18 |

### Examination Dates

**Mr. Fry:** To ask the Secretary of State for Education and Science what discussions he has had with education authorities and examination bodies over the possibility of moving the main dates for the General Certificate of Secondary Education and A-levels from the summer.

**Mrs. Angela Rumbold:** None.

### Teacher Morale

**Mr. Barry Jones:** To ask the Secretary of State for Education and Science when he proposes to answer the letter of 17 March concerning teacher morale, sent to him by the hon. Member for Alyn and Deeside, acknowledged 20 March, Ref. 55 JB/0525/0076; and if he will make a statement.

**Mr. Butcher:** I replied to the hon. Member for Alyn and Deeside on 26 June.

## WALES

### Cynon Valley (Pollution)

91. **Mrs. Clwyd:** To ask the Secretary of State for Wales if he will make a statement on environmental pollution at the Phurnacite plant in the Cynon valley.

**Mr. Grist:** The hon. Lady will know from discussions and correspondence with my right hon. Friend that he is fully aware of local feelings about pollution from the Phurnacite plant. Coal Products Ltd's applications for planning permission for proposed developments at the plant to replace the outdated disticoke batteries with a mild heat treatment process are being considered by the local planning authority, Cynon Valley borough council. If planning permissions are given, Her Majesty's inspectorate of pollution will need to be satisfied that the process is designed to meet current emission control standards before it is allowed to operate.

### Liver Disease

**Mr. Barry Jones:** To ask the Secretary of State for Wales how many people died in Wales of cirrhosis of the liver in each of years 1975 to 1988; and if he will make a statement.

**Mr. Grist:** The numbers of deaths of residents of Wales where the underlying cause of death was recorded as cirrhosis of the liver were as follows:

| Year | Deaths |
| --- | --- |
| 1975 | 139 |
| 1976 | 123 |
| 1977 | 121 |
| 1978 | 111 |
| [1]1979 | 147 |
| 1980 | 130 |
| 1981 | 165 |
| 1982 | 128 |
| 1983 | 149 |
| 1984 | 138 |
| 1985 | 177 |
| 1986 | 151 |
| 1987 | 165 |
| 1988 | 164 |

[1] Prior to 1979: Cirrhosis of Liver ICD 571 8th revision; from 1979 onwards: Chronic liver disease and cirrhosis ICD 571 9th revision.
*Source:* Office of Population Censuses and Surveys.

## AGRICULTURE, FISHERIES AND FOOD

### Irradiated Food

**Mr. Home Robertson:** To ask the Minister of Agriculture, Fisheries and Food if he will place in the Library copies of any reports on the health effects of food irradiation which indicate that irradiated food might be unsafe.

**Mr. MacGregor:** A full review of the health effects of irradiation was carried out in the United Kingdom by the independent scientific Advisory Committee on Irradiated and Novel Foods, whose report contains an extensive bibliography. Copies of this report are in the Library. Similar reviews have also been carried out by the World Health Organisation, the Food and Agriculture Organisation and scientists of the EC Scientific Committee for Food. All have concluded that irradiated food is both safe and wholesome.

**Mr. Home Robertson:** To ask the Minister of Agriculture, Fisheries and Food if he will make a statement on the Government's policy for the labelling of irradiated food, in the wholesale, retail and catering sectors, respectively.

**Mr. MacGregor:** The Council of the European Communities agreed on 14 June to amend the food labelling directive to provide for specific indication on the label of foodstuffs that have been irradiated. This requirement will be implemented into United Kingdom food labelling legislation in due course. Wholesale and retail sales are covered by the directive, as are sales to caterers, but not sales by caterers. The question of such labelling in the catering sector will therefore need to be given detailed consideration, bearing in mind my clear commitment to informed consumer choice in this matter.

**Mr. Home Robertson:** To ask the Minister of Agriculture, Fisheries and Food if he will list the studies which have been conducted into the effects on human and animal health of food irradiation.

**Mr. MacGregor:** A full list could not be collated without undue expenditure of time and effort since research has been undertaken in a number of countries over a period of more than 40 years. References to the main studies will be found in appendix G to the report on the safety and wholesomeness of irradiated foods by the Advisory Committee on Irradiated and Novel Foods. A copy of this report is in the Library.

**Mr. Home Robertson:** To ask the Minister of Agriculture, Fisheries and Food if he will list the radiolytic products which have been identified in irradiated food.

**Mr. MacGregor:** Most of the known radiolytic products in irradiated food are found either naturally in some foods or are formed as a result of cooking or other methods of preservation. The lack of unique radiolytic products is also reflected in the absence of a detection test for irradiated food. Extensive research has so far failed to find a radiolytic product which could be used as the basis of such a test.

**Mr. Home Robertson:** To ask the Minister for Agriculture, Fisheries and Food if he will list the nutrients and vitamins in food which may be adversely affected by irradiation.

**Mr. MacGregor:** Some destruction of nutrients, including vitamins, occurs with cooking, storage and processing of all foods. In the case of proteins, carbohydrates and minerals, studies in general reveal no detectable effect through irradiation at the low levels of dose contemplated. The small reduction in some vitamins noticed in some studies would not produce any adverse dietary effects, and nutritional losses through irradiation are not considered to be significant in the diet as a whole. Nevertheless the nutrient content of irradiated food will be monitored under the existing arrangements for monitoring the nutrient content of all foods.

**Mr. David Young:** To ask the Minister for Agriculture, Fisheries and Food if he will list the commercial organisations that wrote to or lobbied him in favour of irradiation of food.

**Mr. MacGregor:** No commercial organisation has lobbied me on the irradiation of food. Support has, however, been publicly expressed by the Food and Drink Federation, the Spice Trade Association and the Institute of Cereals Manufacturers.

### Farm Animal Welfare

**Mr. Dunnachie:** To ask the Minister for Agriculture, Fisheries and Food if he will introduce legislation to safeguard the welfare of animals on farms.

**Mr. Donald Thompson:** Part I of the Agriculture (Miscellaneous Provisions) Act 1968 already makes it an offence to cause unnecessary pain or distress to farm livestock. In addition, regulations on farm animal welfare and welfare codes have been made under the Act. I hope soon to lay before the House draft regulations that will make some of the welfare code provisions mandatory.

### Abattoirs

**Mr. Mullin:** To ask the Minister of Agriculture, Fisheries and Food what action he has taken following recent reports that local authorities are failing to enforce regulations for abattoirs relating to hygiene, safety and humane killing.

**Mr. Donald Thompson:** Recent reports in the media have criticised conditions in some slaughterhouses without identifying the establishments concerned. It is the responsibility of all, including those who produce such reports, to draw to the attention of the appropriate local authority any breaches in the law which they may have witnessed.

Local authorities take their enforcement responsibilities very seriously and I am confident that none would hesitate to take appropriate action if abuses were reported.

Officers of the state veterinary service visit all slaughterhouses to monitor hygiene and welfare standards and give advice to enforcement authorities.

### National Fruit Collection

**Mr. Dalyell:** To ask the Minister of Agriculture, Fisheries and Food what action he is taking to prevent the dispersal of the national fruit collection and archives at Brogdale.

**Mr. Donald Thompson:** We have made clear our intention to ensure that the national fruit collection and its associated records are preserved, and we are considering what arrangements should be made in the event that Brogdale experimental horticulture station is closed.

### Torry Research Station

**Mr. Buchanan-Smith:** To ask the Minister of Agriculture, Fisheries and Food what are his plans for Torry research station; and if he will make a statement.

**Mr. Donald Thompson:** Torry research station is one of the world's leading research institutes in the area of fish safety, hygiene and quality. It carries out a programme costing over £2 million per annum in support of Government policies for food safety and quality. In accordance with the high priority which the Government attach to these policies, this work, which includes important underpinning research, is to continue.

In addition, there is work at Torry research station which is mainly concerned with product and process development. We have consulted the fishing and related industries about their readiness to fund near-market work in these areas. However, the industries have shown very little readiness to fund such work. Accordingly we are now setting in train the necessary steps to concentrate the research at Torry on those areas of work which are required in support of our policies for food safety and quality. This will mean stopping about one third of Torry's current programme. About 30 posts at the laboratory will be lost, although we will endeavour to keep the number of compulsory redundancies to a minimum. Naturally, if between now and the completion of this exercise, any new industry funding is forthcoming we will be ready to try to retain the necessary expertise and facilities to meet the proposed research contracts. In any event, I expect Torry research station to continue to attract significant outside funding for analytical services and consultancies as it has done in recent years.

### Forestry

**Mr. John Evans:** To ask the Minister of Agriculture, Fisheries and Food what representations he has received concerning the decline in commercial forestry planting levels in England and Wales.

**Mr. MacGregor:** During the last six months I have received nine representations about the possible effects on planting levels of the forestry taxation changes introduced in the 1988 Budget. Some of these were general comments, while others referred to the problems of woodland maintenance and the difficulties faced by forest nurseries. None of the representations referred specifically to a decline in commercial forestry planting levels in England.

The situation in Wales is a matter for my right hon. Friend the Secretary of State for Wales.

## Monofilament Gill Nets

**Dr. Godman:** To ask the Minister of Agriculture, Fisheries and Food (1) if he is able to estimate how many fishing vessels registered in English ports deploy monofilament gill nets, where they normally fish and for which species;

(2) if he is able to estimate the number of fishing vessels registered at ports in Wales which deploy monofilament gill nets, where they normally fish and for which species.

**Mr. Donald Thompson** [*holding answer 15 June 1989*]: Data collected by my Department in 1988 of the landings of seafish made by registered vessels over 10 metres show that 251 vessels in England and six vessels in Wales used gill or enmeshing nets, the majority of which would have been of monofilament construction. Comparable data are not collected for landings made by vessels under 10 metres, but we estimate that some 1,000 craft under 10 metres in England and 200 craft in Wales would have used gill or enmeshing nets. some of these boats will also be licensed to fish salmon and sea trout. An illustrative map showing the location of the main gill net fisheries off England and Wales and the principal species caught has been placed in the Library of the House.

## HEALTH

### Cook-chill Food

**Mr. Hinchliffe:** To ask the Secretary of State for Health (1) what assessment he has made of the implications for the food consumer of vitamin losses which occur during the cook-chill process;

(2) what evaluation of the nutritional content of cook-chill food has been undertaken in the United Kingdom;

(3) what information his Department has collected on whether foods which are high in polyunsaturated acids are suitable for use in the cook-chill process.

**Mr. Freeman:** After a thorough review of the available data the working group of independent experts concluded that wherever food is heated and/or stored there will be nutrient losses. Where food is to be stored, consideration at the menu planning stage should be given to the reduction in the amount of foods with high levels of polyunsaturated fatty acids as they are particularly prone to rancidity during storage.

The expert group considered that the nutritional loss in a properly managed cook-chill catering system were no more than in any other large-scale catering system.

### Listeria

**Mr. Hinchliffe:** To ask the Secretary of State for Health what is the latest information his Department has received regarding the levels of heat resistance of listeria in food.

**Mr. Freeman:** The Department has received copies of the MAFF-sponsored research carried out by the Camden Food and Drink Research Association.

## Dental Laboratories

**Mr. Allen:** To ask the Secretary of State for Health (1) what encouragement his Department gives to general dental practitioners to use the certification scheme for dental laboratories;

(2) what involvement his Department has with the certification scheme for dental laboratories; and if he will make a statement.

**Mr. Freeman:** At present there is no certification scheme for dental laboratories. The Dental Laboratories Association (DLA) has taken the initiative in the formation of an independent body known as the Certification Authority for Dental Laboratories and Suppliers (CADLAS), which plans to commence operation from October 1989.

The Department's NHS procurement directorate was approached by the DLA on this matter in November 1987. Since then the directorate's technical staff have encouraged, advised and held discussions with the DLA about CADLAS, in terms of participating in a series of seminars arranged by the DLA throughout the United Kingdom, sending an observer to the first two meetings of the CADLAS council and advising CADLAS on quality assurance requirements and the draft good manufacturing practice (GMP) standard.

The Department accepts the need for a recognised system of quality assurance in this field and is confident that CADLAS is equipped to fulfil this role. Its ultimate success will, however, depend on its acceptance and recognition by dental practitioners who have the prime responsibility for the quality of dental prosthetics.

## Midwives

**Mr. Hayes:** To ask the Secretary of State for Health when he will lay before the House the Government's response to the fourth report of the Select Committee on Social Services, HC 289, Session 1988-89, on midwives' regrading.

**Mr. Mellor:** My right hon and learned Friend has done so today.

The Government welcome the Committee's interest in this matter, and have carefully studied its report and recommendations. The Government wish to take this opportunity of emphasising the importance that they attach to the role of the midwifery profession within the National Health Service and their recognition of the skilful and dedicated contribution that midwives make to the welfare of mothers and babies.

The Government followed the principle set out in the Committee's fourth recommendation—that future regrading exercises for NHS staff be separated from assimilation to the new pay scales—when implementing the new grading structure for nursing and midwifery educational staff, but for the reasons given in their response are unable to accept the remaining recommendations.

In the Government's view, it is important that the Committee's report should be considered in the wider context. Since March 1988 alone, midwives' pay has increased by over 28 per cent. on average, and the pay of midwives, like that of nurses and health visitors, is now at its highest-ever level in real terms. For the nine out of 10 staff midwives graded E or above in the new clinical grading structure, and the three out of four midwifery sisters graded G, pay levels are now 50 per cent. higher in real terms than they were in 1979. Moreover, the new structure gives midwives, like nurses and health visitors, better clinical career prospects than ever before.

# EMPLOYMENT

## Public Relations

**Mr. Blair:** To ask the Secretary of State for Employment which public relations firms his Department has employed and at what cost, for each year since 1979.

**Mr. Cope:** Apart from the special circumstances of privatisation work, the consistent practice of successive Governments has been to avoid the use of public relations firms or other firms outside government for public relations work. The Department has not employed any.

## Employment Training

**Ms. Short:** To ask the Secretary of State for Employment how much his Department paid out in advance funding to employment training agents and managers; how much has been recouped; and if he will make a statement.

**Mr. Nicholls:** The information requested is not available except at disproportionate cost.

All employment training (ET) training agents and training managers other than local authorities were entitled to 100 per cent. advance funding in the first three months of ET. Advances will be recouped where appropriate up to August 1989.

**Mr. Wilson:** To ask the Secretary of State for Employment if he will state *(a)* the production cost, *(b)* the amount spent on television advertising so far and *(c)* the projected campaign budget, in respect of the current commercial for employment training.

**Mr. Nicholls:** The information required is as follows:
(a) The production cost of the commercial was £494,500. This included producing both the 60 and 40 second versions.
(b) The amount spent on television advertising up to 21 June 1989 is £2,024,000 excluding production costs.
(c) The projected budget for the current TV campaign excluding production costs is £3,795,000.
All figures are inclusive of value added tax.

**Mr. Hannam:** To ask the Secretary of State for Employment to what extent extended introduction is being made available to people with disabilities on employment training; and whether its uptake is monitored by training agents, training managers and the employment rehabilitation service.

**Mr. Nicholls:** Disabled people form part of the client group which extended introduction is designed to help. Opportunities to join extended introduction are available in all the Department's Training Agency's areas. Statistics are not available on the number of disabled people entering extended introduction. However, training managers work to remove any obstacles such as premises constraints which could make it difficult for disabled people to take advantage of extended introduction.

**Mr. Hannam:** To ask the Secretary of State for Employment what measures are being taken to inform disablement resettlement officers of the residential training provision available to disabled people wishing to take part in the employment training programme.

**Mr. Lee:** The initial training of disablement resettlement officers includes information about residential training provision and incorporates a visit to a residential training college. While in post, they receive further information through written instructions and guidance, as well as through newsletters and information packs which detail the residential training available. Disablement resettlement officers have also taken part in Training Agency workshops about employment training, including residential provision for trainees.

**Mr. Hannam:** To ask the Secretary of State for Employment what percentage of trainees currently taking part in the employment training programme are registered as disabled under the Disabled Persons (Employment) Act 1944.

**Mr. Nicholls:** Information is not presently available in the form requested. However, people who identified themselves as having a disability or long-term health problem which affects the work they can do make up 12 per cent. of entrants to employment training.

**Mr. Hannam:** To ask the Secretary of State for Employment what proportion of the disabled trainees who entered the employment training programme by the end of February, are currently training with an employer on a work placement.

**Mr. Nicholls:** The information requested is not available.

## Training Bonuses

**Ms. Short:** To ask the Secretary of State for Employment if he will make a statement about his future policy on paying training bonuses in 1991-92, and when employment training is run by training and enterprise councils.

**Mr. Nicholls:** The policy for payment of training bonuses remains unchanged.

## Business on Own Account Scheme

**Mr. Hannam:** To ask the Secretary of State for Employment how many applications for the business on own account scheme were received for each of the last five years for which figures are available; how many were approved; and what were the total grants made in each year.

**Mr. Lee:** The information requested about the business on own account scheme is given in the table:

|  | Number of applications | Number of approvals | Expenditure on grants £ |
|---|---|---|---|
| 1984-85 | 15 | 7 | 26,272 |
| 1985-86 | 14 | 5 | 42,506 |
| 1986-87 | 12 | 1 | 4,211 |
| 1987-88 | 9 | 6 | 22,012 |
| 1988-89 | 16 | 8 | 30,454 |

The future development of my Department's special schemes for people with disabilities, including the business on own account scheme is being considered as part of our internal review of services for people with disabilities.

# SOCIAL SECURITY

## Pensioners

**Mr. Win Griffiths:** To ask the Secretary of State for Social Security if he will list the messages he has received from pensioner organisations *(a)* agreeing and *(b)* disagreeing with the sentiments of his recent speech to Age Concern.

**Mr. Peter Lloyd:** I assume that the hon. Member is referring to the recent speech of my right hon. Friend the Secretary of State at the sheltered housing conference on 5 June. We have received no messages from pensioner organisations relating to the speech made on that occasion.

## Social Fund

**Mrs. Beckett:** To ask the Secretary of State for Social Security in what proportion of applications to social fund inspectors the applicant is represented.

**Mr. Peter Lloyd:** The social fund commissioner has advised me that the information requested is not collected.

**Mr. Cartwright:** To ask the Secretary of State for Social Security how much his Department's Woolwich office have been allocated for *(a)* social fund loans and *(b)* social fund grants in 1989-90; and what were the comparable figures in the preceding year.

**Mr. Peter Lloyd:** The information requested is available in the Library.

## Independent Living Fund

**Mr. Allen:** To ask the Secretary of State for Social Security how many civil servants and at what grade run the independent living fund.

**Mr. Scott:** Thirty-two, ranging in grade from administrative assistant to senior executive officer, working under the direction of the trustees of the fund.

**Mr. Allen:** To ask the Secretary of State for Social Security if he will brief local social security offices about the independent living fund; and if he will make appropriate forms available at those offices.

**Mr. Scott:** Guidance on the independent living fund has been issued to all local offices. Posters and explanatory leaflets publicising the fund, and explaining how an application form may be obtained, have also been issued.

**Mr. Allen:** To ask the Secretary of State for Social Security what is the budget for the independent living fund for each of the years for which figures are available.

**Mr. Scott:** Up to £5 million was made available for the first year of the independent living fund. A further £5 million has been made available for the current year, but this figure is under continuous review.

**Mr. Allen:** To ask the Secretary of State for Social Security what are the criteria for deciding how much money an applicant gets from the independent living fund.

**Mr. Scott:** The amount payable is decided by the trustees and is based on the cost of reasonable care which cannot be met from other sources.

**Mr. Allen:** To ask the Secretary of State for Social Security what items of guidance, by topic, his Department has issued to local authorities on the independent living fund.

**Mr. Scott:** The director of the independent living fund is writing to all local authority directors of social services, bringing the fund to their attention, and explaining what help it can give to severely disabled people.

**Mr. Allen:** To ask the Secretary of State for Social Security what steps he is taking to advertise the independent living fund to potential claimants.

**Mr. Scott:** Publicity for the independent living fund has been mainly through the specialist press and organisations representing disabled people. The trustees are responsible for publicity and are continuing to use various methods to make the fund even more widely known.

## Housing Benefit

**Mr. Robin Cook:** To ask the Secretary of State for Social Security what is the estimated cost per successful application for housing benefit transitional payments made by the Glasgow unit of his Department.

**Mr. Peter Lloyd** *[holding answer 12 June 1989]:* The work of the transitional payments unit (TPU) involves the processing of applications and correspondence from applicants and local authorities, making awards and payments to successful applicants, liaising with local authorities, producing leaflets and claim forms, and maintaining a free advice line. Both capital and manpower costs were heavily concentrated in the unit's first year of operation; administrative costs have fluctuated according to the level of activity in the unit and will decline significantly in future years. It is not possible to apportion the costs of the TPU between the activities undertaken, nor to produce a cost per claim. However, the full administrative costs of the unit in 1988-89 amounted to 21p in every pound of expenditure on the transitional payments scheme in that year.

## Transitional Protection Unit

**Mr. Cohen:** To ask the Secretary of State for Social Security (1) if he will publish his Department instructions issued to the transitional protection unit and place a copy in the Library;

(2) whether the instructions issued by his Department to the transitional protection unit includes a restriction on the amount of housing benefit transitional protection which can be paid because a local authority is rate-capped; and if he will make a statement.

**Mr. Peter Lloyd** *[holding answer 19 June 1989]:* The housing benefit transitional payments scheme is intended to provide help to vulnerable groups of claimants who experienced reductions in their housing benefit as a result of changes introduced by the Government in April 1988. Because the method of calculating transitional payments involves a comparison between housing benefit in payment before and after 4 April 1988, some applicants who lived in an area whose local authority was rate-capped and which reduced its domestic rates and who were therefore entitled to a lesser amount of housing benefit may well have received a transitional payment for this reason and not because of the Government's changes to the housing benefit scheme. The procedural instructions to the transitional payments unit (TPU) do not provide for a different assessment in these cases, but some cases (less than 100) were incorrectly assessed and transitional payment was reduced on account of rate capping. If the hon. Member is aware of any such cases and will supply the Department with details, the transitional payment will be reassessed and arrears paid.

In view of the proximity of the closing date for applications (30 June) and the transitory nature of the scheme there are no current plans to publish the TPU instruction manual.

## TRANSPORT

### Trunk Roads (London)

**Sir William Shelton:** To ask the Secretary of State for Transport what was the total capital expenditure invested in trunk roads in London in 1988-89.

**Mr. Peter Bottomley:** Capital expenditure on motorways and trunk roads in 1988-89 amounted to nearly £74 million. Of that total, just over £12 million was spent on capital maintenance.

### Light Dues

**Mr. Patrick Thomson:** To ask the Secretary of State for Transport what was the amount of light dues paid by fishing vessels during the year 1987-88; and what was the original estimate.

**Mr. Portillo:** I refer my hon. Friend to the answer I gave to the hon. Member for Moray (Mrs. Ewing) on 16 February at column *285*. The general lighthouse authorities have now received some £191,000 in light dues paid for United Kingdom-registered fishing vessels for the financial year 1987-88. A similar sum is estimated to have been received in light dues paid by non-United Kingdom registered fishing vessels, but disproportionate effort would be required to establish a precise figure.

### Ports

**Mr. Patrick Thompson:** To ask the Secretary of State for Transport how much public subsidy is given to British ports; and what is the situation in EEC countries.

**Mr. Portillo:** The only grants that the Government make to British ports are for fishing harbour projects and severance payments to surplus registered dock workers. A few local authorities fund the losses of ports which they own. In some other member states public funds meet a large proportion of the cost of port infrastructure developments. Certain ports in all parts of the Community may also receive grants from the European regional development fund.

**Mr. Patrick Thomson:** To ask the Secretary of State for Transport if he will list by *(a)* volume and *(b)* value the amount of trade handled by British ports in each year since 1979.

**Mr. Portillo:** Her Majesty's Customs and Excise data on the volume and value of imports and exports through the seaports of the United Kingdom from 1979 to 1988 (excluding imports of oil and gas by pipeline from the Norwegian sector of the North sea) are as follows:

*Trade through United Kingdom sea ports*

|  | Volume (million tonnes) | | Value (billion pounds) | |
|  | Imports | Exports | Imports | Exports |
|---|---|---|---|---|
| 1979 | 156·0 | 89·3 | 38·1 | 31·7 |
| 1980 | 130·9 | 93·0 | 38·1 | 37·0 |
| 1981 | 121·0 | 116·5 | 40·7 | 40·4 |
| 1982 | 120·8 | 115·7 | 45·7 | 43·9 |
| 1983 | 117·6 | 121·5 | 51·8 | 47·2 |
| 1984 | 137·7 | 127·2 | 61·3 | 53·8 |
| 1985 | 142·3 | 133·1 | 66·9 | 59·7 |
| 1986 | 147·9 | 137·6 | 67·8 | 53·6 |
| 1987 | 149·9 | 136·0 | 74·5 | 58·3 |
| [1]1988 | 160·6 | 123·1 | 82·7 | 59·0 |

[1] Provisional.

**Mr. Patrick Thompson:** To ask the Secretary of State for Transport how many passengers, cars and coaches passed through Britain's ports in each year since 1979.

**Mr. Portillo:** Information on car, coach and international passenger movements through the seaports of Great Britain, up to 1987, is published in "Transport Statistics Great Britain 1977-1987" (tables 1.9 and 4.11) copies of which are in the Library. Car and coach figures include domestic movements except those to the Isle of Wight. Corresponding figures for 1988 are 4,234,000 cars, including 262,000 by hovercraft services, 170,000 buses and coaches, and 24,867,000 passengers.

### Road Traffic Studies

**Sir Barney Hayhoe:** To ask the Secretary of State for Transport whether those undertaking the London assessment studies have been asked to include consideration of road pricing, area licensing and other methods of road traffic restraint in arriving at their conclusions and recommendations.

**Mr. Peter Bottomley:** The consultants will carry out sensitivity tests on a range of options within the study areas. These tests will assess the effects of road traffic restraint measures on the options.

**Sir Barney Hayhoe:** To ask the Secretary of State for Transport whether he has received any representations from individuals or organisations in the Chiswick area in favour of the new road proposals through Chiswick and Grove Park contained in the west London assessment study published in 1988; and whether he will give summary details of such representations.

**Mr. Peter Bottomley:** We have received a large number of representations from individuals and organisations in the Chiswick area on different aspects of the west London assessment study. It would not be practicable to analyse them in the way requested.

**Sir Barney Hayhoe:** To ask the Secretary of State for Transport when he expects to publish the results of stage 2B of the west London assessment study; and whether he proposes a period of public consultation before the announcement of the Government's response.

**Mr. Peter Bottomley:** We expect to receive the consultants report on their assessment of options later in the summer. They will be published as soon as possible thereafter. There will be an opportunity for public comment before decisions are taken.

## Aircraft Noise

**Sir Eldon Griffiths:** To ask the Secretary of State for Transport if, following the report of the inter-departmental land compensation working party, he will state the Government's policy in regard to insulation and compensation for injurious affection of schools and hospitals that are subjected to military aircraft noise exceeding 70 dba.

**Mr. Peter Bottomley:** The general position is that compensation for injurious affection arising from the use of public works including airfields is limited to owners and owner-occupiers of residential property, owner-occupiers of agricultural property and owner occupiers of hereditaments not exceeding a rateable value of £2,250. There are no proposals to extend this eligibility.

The land compensation working party set up a sub-group to look at the Noise Insulation Regulations 1975 and regulations governing certain civil airports with a view to their possible extension to buildings other than dwellings. It is expected that the sub-group's report will be submitted in July.

Buildings near military airfields are not covered by these statutory provisions. However, the Ministry of Defence deals with them on analogous basis. Their noise compensation scheme would reflect any change to the statutory provisions.

## Public Transport (South-East London)

**Mr. Gerald Bowden:** To ask the Secretary of State for Transport what forecast demand studies have been made for future public transport requirements in south-east London.

**Mr. Portillo:** I know of no recent specific studies of public transport demand in south-east London, but the consultants working on the south London and south circular assessment studies are considering whether public transport options might help to solve the problems which those studies are addressing.

## Night Flights

**Mr. Goodlad:** To ask the Secretary of State for Transport how many night flights have (a) been authorised and (b) taken place in the current year and last year at (i) Gatwick, (ii) Heathrow and (iii) Manchester airports.

**Mr. Peter Bottomley:** Quota and actual movement information for the three airports is as follows:

| | Gatwick | | Heathrow | | Manchester | |
|---|---|---|---|---|---|---|
| | Quota | Actual | Quota | Actual | Quota | Actual |
| 1988 Summer | 4,430 (60) | 4,430 (57) | 2,750 (60) | 1,830 | 6,760 | 6,723 |
| 1988-89 Winter | 2,025 (30) | 2,040 (11) | 2,982 (30) | 3,002 (30) | — | 1,464 |
| 1989 Summer | 4,580 (60) | 1,281 ( 5) | 2,750 (60) | 802 (39) | 7,098 | 2,179 |

*Notes:*
1. 1989 summer 'actual' figures are given to 17 June.
2. Figures in brackets are delayed noisy movements subject to special quota.
3. Figures for Manchester airport provided by Manchester Airport plc who are responsible for setting the monitoring quotas at that airport. Winter night jet operations at Manchester are not subject to quota restrictions.
4. The current summer season does not end until 24.00 hours on 28 October.
5. At Gatwick and Heathrow the night noise restrictions permit the airport manager to disregard flights from the restrictions if they are delayed by widespread and prolonged disruption of air traffic or in other exceptional circumstances. In the summer season of 1988 Gatwick Airport Limited disregarded for quota purposes 1,598 movements and Heathrow Airport Limited disregarded 97. In the winter season 1988-89 Gatwick disregarded 95 movements while Heathrow disregarded 56 movements. At Manchester whilst restrictions were temporarily suspended for the same reason there were 961 night flights. All these flights are additional to the figures already mentioned.
6. The quota of 3,000 movements for winter 1988-89 at Heathrow was reduced to 2,982 because 18 infringements of the maximum permitted noise level were recorded prior to 31 January.

## Noisy Aircraft

**Mr. Goodlad:** To ask the Secretary of State for Transport (1) what progress he has made in international negotiations towards the phasing out of noisy aircraft including the BAC 1-11 and the B727; and if he will make a statement;

(2) what progress he has made internationally in developing controls over aeroplanes certificated to ICAO's annex 16, volume 1, chapter 2 standards; and if he will make a statement.

**Mr. Peter Bottomley:** Internationally the Government have been actively pursuing their objective, first stated in the 1985 White Paper on airports policy (para 8.5), of securing the phasing out of chapter 2 aeroplanes such as the BAC1-11 and B727. Since aircraft have long operational lives, the replacement of chapter 2 by chapter 3 aircraft will be a long and expensive process, but a start has been made with the decision, supported by the United Kingdom, of the European civil aviation conference that from 1 October 1990 no further chapter 2 aircraft should be added to member states' registers. The issue of the eventual banning of operations of chapter 2 aircraft is one of the main topics to be discussed at the International Civil Aviation Organisation's general assembly in the autumn.

## Manchester Airport

**Mr. Goodlad:** To ask the Secretary of State for Transport if he is satisfied that Manchester airport plc has consulted adequately in conformity with section 35 of the Civil Aviation Act 1982 with representatives from local authorities affected by excessive aircraft noise.

**Mr. Peter Bottomley:** This is a matter between Manchester Airport plc and the local authorities in the neighbourhood of the airport.

**Mr. Goodlad:** To ask the Secretary of State for Transport if he will make a statement on the designation of Manchester airport under sections 78 and 79 of the Civil Aviation Act 1982.

**Mr. Peter Bottomley:** My right hon. Friend is considering the various representations he has received about designation.

**Mr. Goodlad:** To ask the Secretary of State for Transport (1) if he has any plans to lower the maximum permissible take-off noise levels at Manchester airport;

(2) if he has any plans to seek an improvement in the monitoring of noise levels in the vicinity of Manchester airport.

**Mr. Peter Bottomley:** These are both matters for Manchester Airport plc.

## London Underground

**Mr. Gerald Bowden:** To ask the Secretary of State for Transport (1) what representations he has received regarding the provision of an extension of the Northern line of the tube into south-east London to Camberwell and beyond since January 1989;

(2) what assessment has been made of the socio-economic effects of an extension of the Northern line of the Underground to Camberwell and beyond, with particular reference to the effects of improving transport links to areas of higher employment in attracting new enterprise into the area;

(3) what assessment has been made of the effects of an extension of the Northern line of the Underground to Camberwell and beyond on overcrowding in the Victoria area;

(4) what assessment has been made of the effects of an extension of the Northern line of the Underground into south-east London to Camberwell and beyond on congestion on the roads of south-east London;

(5) if, following the publication of the central London rail study in January 1989 and subsequent representations, he intends to provide for an extension of the Northern line to Camberwell and beyond; and if he will make a statement.

**Mr. Portillo:** The Department has received 17 letters supporting the extension of the Underground to Camberwell. The central London rail study concluded that such an extension would not achieve the study's objectives. It is now for London Underground Limited and London Regional Transport to consider in the first instance whether a line to Camberwell is worthwhile in its own right and how it compares with the many competing schemes for improvements to the Underground network.

## Banbury Trunk Relief Road

**Mr. Baldry:** To ask the Secretary of State for Transport when he expects to announce his decision in respect of the inspector's report relating to the compulsory purchase, side roads and bridge orders concerning the Banbury trunk relief road, stages II and III.

**Mr. Peter Bottomley:** Within the next few weeks.

## Driver and Vehicle Statistics

**Mr. John Marshall:** To ask the Secretary of State for Transport if he will detail the number of vehicle first registrations, and of replacement driving licences issued by the Driver and Vehicle Licensing centre, Swansea in each of the past 10 years.

**Mr. Peter Bottomley:** The numbers of first vehicle registrations and replacement driving licences issued have increased by some 15 per cent. and 100 per cent.

respectively since 1979-80. The tables provide the year-on-year information (the volumes include commercial vehicles and motorcycles, as well as cars):

*Vehicle First Registrations 1978-80/1980-89*

| Year | Volume |
| --- | --- |
| 1979-80 | 2,386,868 |
| 1980-81 | 2,038,140 |
| 1981-82 | 2,004,335 |
| 1982-83 | 2,211,126 |
| 1983-84 | 2,306,742 |
| 1984-85 | 2,253,508 |
| 1985-86 | 2,277,893 |
| 1986-87 | 2,365,901 |
| 1987-88 | 2,554,442 |
| 1988-89 | 2,736,327 |

*Replacement Driving Licences 1979-80/1980-89*

| Year | Volume |
| --- | --- |
| 1979-80 | 1,469,295 |
| 1980-81 | 1,576,957 |
| 1981-82 | 1,354,354 |
| 1982-83 | 1,869,745 |
| 1983-84 | 1,972,378 |
| 1984-85 | 2,035,602 |
| 1985-86 | 2,295,228 |
| 1986-87 | 2,808,782 |
| 1987-88 | 2,920,831 |
| 1988-89 | 2,930,869 |

## Privatisation

**Mr. Gerald Bowden:** To ask the Secretary of State for Transport what plans he has for any future privatisation programme; and if he will name the financial advisers employed to advise on such a programme.

**Mr. Portillo:** My right hon. Friend keeps the options for further privatisation under constant review. A study of the long-term options for British Rail is in progress, including the feasibility of transfer to the private sector.

As part of that work Deloitte, Haskins and Sells was appointed to carry out a factual study of the structural options, National Economic Research Associates to advise on regulation and Samuel Montagu to provide financial advice.

# ENVIRONMENT

## Dogs

13. **Mr. Knapman:** To ask the Secretary of State for the Environment what measures he proposes to deal with the problem of dog fouling.

**Mrs. Virginia Bottomley:** As my right hon. Friend announced in the House on 14 June, we propose to place on local authorities a duty to clear up dog mess in public places. This will be enforced through a code of practice to which local authorities will be required to adhere.

65. **Mr. McAllion:** To ask the Secretary of State for the Environment if his Department uses a definition of domestic pet in relation to the keeping of dogs in private homes.

**Mrs. Virginia Bottomley:** No. The Dangerous Wild Animals Act 1976 lists those animals for which licences are required if kept on domestic premises.

44. **Mr. Bradley:** To ask the Secretary of State for the Environment what discussions has he had with local authority associations concerning dogs and public health.

**Mrs. Virginia Bottomley:** No formal discussions have taken place recently. We shall, however, be consulting the local authority associations and other interested organisations shortly about the proposal that my right hon. Friend the Secretary of State announced on 14 June to place on local authorities a duty to deal with strays and clear up dog faeces in public places.

### Dogs (Registration)

16. **Mr. Janner:** To ask the Secretary of State for the Environment how many representations he has received in the last month concerning the registration of dogs.

**Mrs. Virginia Bottomley:** We have received a large number of representations on this matter. My right hon. Friends the Secretary of State and the Home Secretary announced on 14 June a package of measures to deal with the problems caused by irresponsible dog ownership—dog attacks, straying and fouling. Registration is not the answer to these problems.

69. **Mr. Ashton:** To ask the Secretary of State for the Environment what would be the estimated cost of a compulsory dog registration scheme.

**Mrs. Virginia Bottomley:** We have made no such estimate. A recent report by the London school of economics on behalf of the RSPCA estimates that the cost of administering and keeping up to date a national dog registration scheme would be about £20 million annually. We do not believe that dog registration addresses the real problems caused by dogs.

### Council House Sales

17. **Mr. Dunn:** To ask the Secretary of State for the Environment whether he will take measures to penalise local authorities which are inefficient in processing council house sale applications.

31. **Sir George Young:** To ask the Secretary of State for the Environment when he implemented the provision in the Housing Act 1988 for council tenants to set aside rent against mortgage payments in the event of delays by councils in processing their applications to buy their homes.

48. **Miss Widdecombe:** To ask the Secretary of State for the Environment what measures he proposes to speed up the processing of council house sale applications.

51. **Mr. Rowe:** To ask the Secretary of State for the Environment when he implemented the provision in the Housing Act 1988 for council tenants to set aside rent against mortgage payments in the event of delays by councils in processing their applications to buy their homes.

60. **Sir Hal Miller:** To ask the Secretary of State for the Environment whether he will take measures to penalise local authorities which are inefficient in processing council house sale applications.

**Mr. Robert G. Hughes:** To ask the Secretary of State for the Environment what measures he proposes to speed up the processing of council house sale applications.

**Mr. Trippier:** As I announced in my answer of 10 March to my hon. Friend the Member for Harrow, West (Mr. Hughes) at column *699,* section 124 of the Housing Act 1988 came into force on that date. It enables tenants whose applications are delayed by the landlord to have rent payments set against the purchase price of their homes.

68. **Mr. Knox:** To ask the Secretary of State for the Environment how many council houses have been sold to sitting tenants in England since May 1979.

**Mr. Trippier:** From April 1979 to March 1989 about 1,040,000 tenants bought their homes from English local authorities and new towns.

41. **Mr. Gow:** To ask the Secretary of State for the Environment what proposals he has to extend the opportunities of council tenants to become owner-occupiers.

**Mr. Trippier:** I refer to the answer I gave my hon. Friend on 24 May at columns *591-92.*

### River Don (Pollution)

18. **Mr. Flannery:** To ask the Secretary of State for the Environment what steps he is taking to ensure that sufficient measures are being taken to prevent further pollution of the River Don where it flows through Sheffield and South Yorkshire.

**Mr. Moynihan:** The river objective for the River Don, set by Yorkshire water authority is for fair quality-class 2. This should be achieved shortly for the Don upstream of Sheffield with the implementation of the final stages of the Don valley interceptor sewer. A major programme for upgrading and extending Sheffield's sewage treatment works and sewerage system, combined with improved trade effluent discharges, should result in 63km of the River Don downstream of Sheffield reaching this standard by 1995.

### Empty Properties

19. **Mr. Hinchliffe:** To ask the Secretary of State for the Environment if he will make it his policy to ensure the efficient and urgent use of empty properties before allowing green belt land to be used for property development; and if he will make a statement.

**Mr. Trippier:** There are already stringent controls on development in the green belts. They should ensure that all opportunities for meeting development needs elsewhere are fully considered.

### Unleaded Petrol

20. **Mr. Anthony Coombs:** To ask the Secretary of State for the Environment what was the level of demand for unleaded petrol in March.

29. **Mr. Patnick:** To ask the Secretary of State for the Environment what proportion of total petrol sales in the United Kingdom are now accounted for by the sale of unleaded petrol.

**Mrs. Virginia Bottomley:** In the month to mid-March, unleaded petrol accounted for 6·4 per cent. of the market.

Uptake more than doubled in the following month to 14·4 per cent. The latest figure for the month to mid-May is 19·3 per cent., which shows that the switch to unleaded fuel is rapidly gaining momentum. The rate of progress is very encouraging as the average for the whole of 1988 was a mere 1·1 per cent. This can be attributed to the Chancellor's Budget incentive, the successful national television advertising campaign and many other Government and private sector promotional initiatives.

66. **Mr. Mans:** To ask the Secretary of State for the Environment what percentage of refuellings now take place at garages which stock unleaded petrol.

**Mrs. Virginia Bottomley:** The United Kingdom Petroleum Industry Association advises us that approaching two out of three refuellings now take place at petrol stations where unleaded fuel is available.

### Empty Council Properties

21. **Mr. Squire:** To ask the Secretary of State for the Environment if he will supply the latest estimate of empty council properties in the Greater London area.

**Mr. Trippier:** London boroughs reported some 23,300 empty council properties in their housing investment programme returns for April 1988.

### Football Membership Scheme

22. **Mr. Harry Barnes:** To ask the Secretary of State for the Environment when he last met the Professional Footballers Association to discuss the proposed football membership scheme.

**Mr. Moynihan:** I have yet to meet representatives of the Professional Footballers' Association formally to discuss the national membership scheme, but I hope to do so shortly.

34. **Mr. Cox:** To ask the Secretary of State for the Environment when he last met officials from the Football Leagues to discuss the proposed football membership scheme.

**Mr. Moynihan:** My right hon. Friend and I last discussed the Football Spectators Bill with the chairman of the Football Association and the President of the Football League on 24 May.

### EC Water Directives

23. **Mr. Win Griffiths:** To ask the Secretary of State for the Environment when he now expects to submit to the European Community proposals to meet the requirements of the European Commission bathing water directive and the drinking water directive in full.

**Mr. Ridley:** I expect to be able to present proposals to meet the requirements of the EC bathing water and drinking water directives to the European Commission shortly.

### Unified Business Rate

24. **Mr. Baldry:** To ask the Secretary of State for the Environment what estimate he makes of the level of the unified business rate in Oxfordshire.

**Mr. Gummer:** We estimate that if the uniform business rate had taken effect this year it would have been of the order of 35p in the pound in England.

### Local Authority Services

25. **Mrs. Gillian Shephard:** To ask the Secretary of State for the Environment what measures he proposes to introduce greater efficiency into the provision of local authority services.

**Mr. Gummer:** We have introduced a number of measures to secure greater efficiency into the provision of local authority services. The Audit Commission we established is responsible for reviewing value for money in local government. Local authorities are being required to put seven services out to competitive tender, and the community charge and our proposals for the new capital finance system and ring fenced housing revenue account will lead to greater accountability and increased efficiency in the provision of services.

### Street Cleaning

26. **Mr. Patrick Thompson:** To ask the Secretary of State for the Environment whether he proposes to seek to place a duty on local authorities to keep their local streets clean.

**Mrs. Virginia Bottomley:** A duty on local authorities to keep land clean, and to have regard to a code of practice, is one of a number of proposals for legislation on litter which my right hon. Friend intends to announce soon.

### Competitive Tendering

27. **Mr. Charles Wardle:** To ask the Secretary of State for the Environment what he estimates would have been the additional costs so far incurred if services currently put out to competitive tender had not been so treated.

**Mr. Gummer:** Research carried out by the Audit Commission and published in its report "Preparing for Compulsory Competition" suggests that savings of at least 20 per cent. can be made on previous contract costs, irrespective of whether a private contractor or the in-house organisation wins the work. Figures relating to competition under the Local Government Act 1988 are not yet generally available.

**Mr. John Marshall:** To ask the Secretary of State for the Environment if he will make a statement about the latest estimate for the savings from competitive tendering by local authorities.

**Mr. Gummer:** The Department will be asking authorities to supply information on the first round of tendering shortly. Earlier research into the voluntary competition indicated that savings of 20 to 30 per cent. were available on an expenditure of some £3,000 million.

### Community Charge

28. **Ms. Mowlam:** To ask the Secretary of State for the Environment if he will make a statement on the medical advice he has received on the exemption of severe dementia sufferers from the community charge.

**Mr. Gummer:** My right hon. Friend receives medical advice on these matters from the Department of Health.

**Dr. Cunningham:** To ask the Secretary of State for the Environment if the leaflet, "The Community Charge (The So-Called Poll Tax): How It Will Work For You" delivered to all households in England has been reprinted with amendments.

**Mr. Ridley:** Neither amendments nor reprints have been necessary.

88. **Mr. Grocott:** To ask the Secretary of State for the Environment what is his latest estimate of the cost of implementing the poll tax.

**Mr. Gummer:** The Government have no plans to introduce a poll tax.

In advice that the Department commissioned from Price Waterhouse, the current cost of preparing for the community charge in 1989-90 was estimated to be between £99 million and £122 million, and the capital costs in 1989-90 was estimated to be between £125 million and £175 million. These estimates were at November 1987 prices.

81. **Mrs. Mahon:** To ask the Secretary of State for the Environment whether he has any plans to issue further guidance to community charge registration officers on the questions being asked on community charge registration forms.

**Mr. Gummer:** Clear and explicit advice on these matters has already been issued to community charge registration officers, as well as a model community charge registration form. It is for registration officers to ensure that their requests for information comply with the statutory requirements.

58. **Mr. McLoughlin:** To ask the Secretary of State for the Environment which three counties would on the current figures levy the highest community charge; and which party controls each of them.

**Mr. Gummer:** In the illustrative community charge figures published for 1988-89, the three shire counties with the highest over-spend per adult were Cleveland, Cumbria and Derbyshire, Cleveland and Derbyshire were Labour-controlled in April 1988, but no party had overall control in Cumbria.

47. **Mr. Amess:** To ask the Secretary of State for the Environment what information he has received so far regarding campaigns to encourage the non-payment of the community charge.

**Mr. Gummer:** The Government are aware of the actions of a number of bodies and individuals whose aim is to encourage people to evade their legal responsibilities in relation to the community charge. Such actions are irresponsible and undemocratic.

## New Settlements

30. **Mr. Haynes:** To ask the Secretary of State for the Environment if he will make a statement on his policy for the siting of new settlements in the south of England.

**Mr. Chope:** Current policy on new settlements is set out in paragraph 11 of planning policy guidance note 3, which makes it clear that proposals must be subject to normal planning procedures and must be considered within the framework of existing planning policies.

## African Elephant

32. **Mr. Michael Brown:** To ask the Secretary of State for the Environment what steps he is taking to safeguard the future of the African elephant.

77. **Mr. William Powell:** To ask the Secretary of State for the Environment whether he will now recommend that the African elephant become an appendix I protected animal at the next meeting of CITES in October.

**Mrs. Virginia Bottomley:** We have introduced an immediate ban on the import of ivory into the United Kingdom pending the introduction of a Community wide ban, and have asked our European colleagues to support the case for transferring the African elephant from appendix II to appendix I of the convention on international trade in endangered species of fauna and flora (CITES). We shall play a full part in the discussions on this difficult and complex issue at the forthcoming conference of the parties to CITES.

## Schools (Sport)

33. **Mr. Frank Cook:** To ask the Secretary of State for the Environment what estimate he has made of the number of school children participating in sport and recreation; and what action his Department is taking to ensure adequate facilities are available for outside school sports facilities.

**Mr. Moynihan:** I have no detailed information on which to base an estimate of the number of school children participating in sport and recreation. The Sports Council provides grant-aid towards the provision of sports facilities and this year has earmarked nearly £9 million from its allocated budget of £41 million for this purpose.

## Urban Development Corporations

35. **Mr. Bill Michie:** To ask the Secretary of State for the Environment if he will give a breakdown of the money provided to each urban development corporation up to March 1989; and if he will make a statement.

**Mr. Trippier:** The total provision to 31 March 1989 was as follows:

| UDC | Provision £ million |
|---|---|
| Black Country | 25·4 |
| Bristol | 0·3 |
| Central Manchester | 2·5 |
| Leeds | 2·7 |
| London Docklands | 514·5 |
| Merseyside | 189·2 |
| Sheffield | 8·0 |
| Teesside | 26·0 |
| Trafford Park | 26·0 |
| Tyne and Wear | 28·0 |

## Litter

36. **Mr. Andrew MacKay:** To ask the Secretary of State for the Environment if he will make a statement about future initiatives to combat litter.

50. **Mr. David Nicholson:** To ask the Secretary of State for the Environment what further measures he proposes to deal with the litter problem.

**Mrs. Virginia Bottomley:** My right hon. Friend will shortly be announcing a number of proposals for legislation designed to ensure more effective action to be taken against litterers and litter; to set clear standards for cleanliness in public places; and to ensure that those standards are met.

59. **Mr. Andrew Mitchell:** To ask the Secretary of State for the Environment whether the Government plan to bring forward legislation to enable local authorities to issue fixed penalty tickets for litter offences; and whether he will make a statement.

**Mrs. Virginia Bottomley:** The Government are considering fixed penalty schemes for littering as one of a range of options for improving legislation to combat litter, which my right hon. Friend intends to announce soon.

### Sporting Events

37. **Mr. Steinberg:** To ask the Secretary of State for the Environment what efforts are being made to attract major sporting events to this country.

**Mr. Moynihan:** It is for the national governing bodies of sport to seek to attract major sporting events to this country. I have no doubt that, as in the past, we can look forward to many major sporting events being staged in the United Kingdom.

70. **Mr. Sumberg:** To ask the Secretary of State for the Environment on how many occasions in the past 10 years Britain has been the venue for international sporting events; and what discussions are currently taking place on the possibility of future events being held within the United Kingdom.

**Mr. Moynihan:** This information is not held centrally. It is for the national governing bodies of sport to decide whether to bid to host international sporting events. I have no doubt we can look forward to many future international sporting events being held in this country.

### Environmental Research

38. **Mr. Michael:** To ask the Secretary of State for the Environment whether he will make it his policy to increase his Department's sponsorship of environmental research projects with particular reference to all matters of public interest for which his Department has some responsibility.

**Mr. Ridley:** The scale of my Department's expenditure on environmental research is assessed on the needs to inform decisions, guide policy, and monitor the achievement of environmental goals. It is planned to increase from £31·5 million in 1988-89 to £35·8 million in this financial year.

### Environmental Statements

39. **Mr. Matthew Taylor:** To ask the Secretary of State for the Environment if he will make it his policy to recommend the environmental statement by Wyre Forest district council as a model for other local authorities.

**Mrs. Virginia Bottomley:** No. Local authorities have a range of important environmental responsibilities, such as the collection and disposal of waste and the control of certain sources of air pollution. We look to them to ensure that they discharge these responsibilities effectively, as well as taking informed purchasing decisions, which is a main concern of Wyre Forest district council's statement.

### Urban Programme

40. **Mr. David Evans:** To ask the Secretary of State for the Environment how many projects in inner city areas have now been assisted by grants provided through the Government's urban programme.

**Mr. Trippier:** Since 1979-80, when the enhanced urban programme was introduced, an estimated total of some 43,500 projects have been assisted. This includes projects supported under the former traditional urban programme.

### Rivers

42. **Sir Peter Blaker:** To ask the Secretary of State for the Environment what information he has as to which European Community member states had more rivers in good or fair condition than the United Kingdom at the latest date for which figures are available.

**Mr. Howard:** The 1985 river quality surveys indicated that about 95 per cent. of river lengths in the United Kingdom were classifed as being of good or fair quality. Comprehensive information on a comparable basis for other EC member states is not available. However, a study published in 1988 by the Water Research Centre, in reviewing classification schemes in member states, showed that on the basis of comparisons made using the United Kingdom river classification scheme, no other member state had a greater proportion of "good" or "fair" quality rivers, although our position was matched by that of the Netherlands. A summary of these results is published in the Water Authorities' Association publication "Water Facts 1988".

### Homelessness

43. **Mr. Cartwright:** To ask the Secretary of State for the Environment whether he will give his Department's latest estimate of the number of families accepted as being homeless for inner London; and if he will make a statement.

**Mr. Trippier:** Latest estimates of households accepted as homeless in inner London appear in table 1(a) of "Local authorities' action under the homelessness provisions of the 1985 Housing Act: England. Results for the first quarter of 1989, Supplementary Tables", which are in the Library.

### Structure Plans

45. **Mr. Adley:** To ask the Secretary of State for the Environment if he will make a statement about the future of structure plan procedures.

**Mr. Howard:** Our proposals were published last January in the White Paper on the future of development plans, Cm. 569. The counties will continue to have a key role in the planning process, but will be expected in future to concentrate on those planning issues which genuinely need to be considered on a county-wide basis. Structure plans will be replaced by statements of county planning policies—SCPPs—dealing with a specified range of topics. Each district planning authority will be required to have regard to the SCPP and to ensure that its district development plan is consistent with the SCPP.

Each county will be responsible for adopting its own SCPP, and for conducting the public examination of the draft statement. My right hon. Friend will continue to appoint the chairman of the panel, and the inspector member, but the statement will not be subject to his formal approval, unless reserve powers are invoked.

### Business Rates (Northumberland)

**46. Mr. Amos:** To ask the Secretary of State for the Environment if he will make a statement on the estimated level of rates on businesses in Northumberland in 1990-91.

**Mr. Gummer:** The report of a preliminary survey carried out by the Inland Revenue of the effects of the uniform business rate and the 1990 revaluation of business property, which is available in the Library, suggests that rate bills for businesses in the northern region could fall by some £50 million a year once the transition to the new system is complete.

Separate figures on the effects of revaluation in Northumberland are not available. However, if the uniform business rate had been introduced this year the effect would have been to reduce the rate poundage paid by businesses in Northumberland by between 15 and 24 per cent. depending on the district council area concerned.

### Nature Reserves

**49. Mr. Archer:** To ask the Secretary of State for the Environment when he will respond to the Nature Conservancy Council report, "Towards a Strategy for National Nature Reserves".

**Mrs. Virginia Bottomley:** I refer the right hon. and learned Member to the statement made by my noble Friend the Minister for Housing, Environment and Countryside in another place on 3 May.

### Rural Housing

**52. Mr. Gill:** To ask the Secretary of State for the Environment what is his latest estimate of the deficit of affordable housing in rural areas.

**Mr. Trippier:** It is not practicable to make a meaningful, reliable estimate of the sort suggested.

**76. Mr. Redmond:** To ask the Secretary of State for the Environment what further proposals he has to increase the supply of low-cost houses for rent in rural and urban areas; and if he will make a statement.

**Mr. Trippier:** The Government have taken a variety of measures to encourage supply of affordable rented housing, including the deregulation of private letting, the encouragement of private investment in housing associations and an 80 per cent. increase in funding for the Housing Corporation.

**74. Mr. Barron:** To ask the Secretary of State for the Environment if he has plans to advise planning authorities to make land available in urban and rural areas for *(a)* rented accommodation and *(b)* affordable housing; and if he will make a statement.

**Mr. Chope:** My right hon. Friend's statement on 3 February—*Official Report,* column *433*—set out the Government's policy on the role of the planning system in

securing the release of land for low-cost housing to meet local needs in rural areas. Planning policy guidance note 3 stresses that the planning system should cater effectively for the demand for land both for owner occupation and for rented housing. This applies to urban and to rural areas.

**64. Mr. Yeo:** To ask the Secretary of State for the Environment what recent representations he has received regarding the need for low-cost housing in rural areas.

**Mr. Trippier:** My right hon. Friend receives many representations on the housing problems of both rural and urban areas from hon. Members, from interest groups, and from members of the public. The Government's policy on rural housing was set out in his statement of 5 July 1988, and amplified in statements of 3 and 7 February, copies of which are in the Library.

### Council Works (Contracts)

**53. Mrs. Maureen Hicks:** To ask the Secretary of State for the Environment if he is satisfied with the procedure of local authorities in awarding contracts for council works to the private sector.

**Mr. Gummer:** We are concerned about the high incidence of complaints to the Department about alleged anti-competitive behaviour by authorities in introducing competition under the Local Government Act 1988. My right hon. Friend the Secretary of State has strong sanction powers under the Act and he will not hesitate to use them when necessary.

### District Plans

**54. Mr. Colin Shepherd:** To ask the Secretary of State for the Environment how many district councils in England have not yet completed their district plan; and if he will make a statement.

**Mr. Chope:** Figures for November 1988 show that 243 of the 296 non-metropolitan districts in England do not have local plans on deposit or adopted which fully cover their areas. Planning policy guidance note 12 urged authorities to extend local plan coverage, and current indications are that most authorities intend to complete draft plans for the whole of their districts within the next two years. The proposals set out in "The Future of Development Plans" (Cm. 569) will ensure that these plans can, where appropriate, be incorporated into the new district development plans which all authorities will be required to prepare.

### Water Privatisation

**55. Mr. Rooker:** To ask the Secretary of State for the Environment if he will make a statement on progress of publication of the prospectus for water privatisation.

**Mr. Howard:** It is expected that the prospectus will be published in November this year.

### Sea Water

**56. Mr. Lord:** To ask the Secretary of State for the Environment what steps he is taking to improve the quality of the sea water around the beaches of the United Kingdom; and if he will make a statement.

**Mr. Howard:** Water authorities are currently spending about £100 million a year on improvements to bathing waters.

In 1988, a total of 6 per cent. of bathing waters in England, Wales and Northern Ireland met the mandatory coliform bacteria standards of the EC bathing water directive. I have asked water authorities to draw up programmes with the aim of bringing the remaining waters up to these standards by the mid-1990s.

### Planning Decisions

**Mr. Allen McKay:** To ask the Secretary of State for the Environment if he is now in a position to provide the information referred to in his answer of 22 March, *Official Report,* column *635* relating to planning decisions; and if he will make a statement.

**Mr. Chope:** I wrote to the hon. Member on 5 April with a list of the cases concerned. I am sending him a further copy of my letter.

### Vacant Land

61. **Mr. Nicholas Baker:** To ask the Secretary of State for the Environment how many homes he estimates could be built on the 49,900 acres of land currently vacant, unused and surplus to requirements and owned by local authorities; and what progress he is making in putting such vacant land to good use.

**Mr. Trippier:** It is not possible to estimate how many homes could in practice be built on such land. At 31 May 1989 approximately 14,700 acres of local authority land on the land register had a planning indication for residential use. It is for authorities to dispose of surplus land and make effective use of what they retain. By 31 May 1989 some 17,000 acres of local authority land had been removed from the register, mainly disposed of or brought into use. My right hon. Friend's powers to direct disposals will continue to be used where appropriate. By 31 May use of these powers had been initiated in respect of some 1,500 acres of local authority land.

### Nuclear Waste

62. **Mr. Kirkwood:** To ask the Secretary of State for the Environment if he will make a statement about the importing of nuclear waste.

**Mrs. Virginia Bottomley:** No nuclear waste is imported into the country.

### Land Register

63. **Mr. Bevan:** To ask the Secretary of State for the Environment how many homes he estimates could be built on the 7,900 sites currently on the land register.

**Mr. Trippier:** I refer my hon. Friend to the answer I gave on 26 June to my hon. Friends the Members for South Hams (Mr. Steen) and for Bromsgrove (Sir H. Miller).

### Housing Defects

67. **Mr. Meale:** To ask the Secretary of State for the Environment what additional allocations he intends to make in the current year's housing investment programme for local authorities who have difficulties in meeting their housing defects obligations; and if he will make a statement.

**Mr. Trippier:** Local authorities are normally expected to be able to meet their housing defects obligations from within their general housing programme resources, but to help authorities with particular difficulties with designated defective properties, we distributed an extra £15 million of resources this year.

### Water Quality

71. **Mr. Illsley:** To ask the Secretary of State for the Environment whether he has received any recent representations about the quality of water in the Barnsley area.

**Mr. Moynihan:** The hon. Member for Barnsley, West and Penistone (Mr. McKay) has written to my right hon. Friend, and I have replied. The director of administration, Barnsley metropolitan borough council, has also written to the Department and a reply has been sent.

### London City Airport

72. **Mr. Grylls:** To ask the Secretary of State for the Environment when he next hopes to meet the chairman of the London Docklands development corporation to discuss the London City airport site and its surrounds.

**Mr. Trippier:** My right hon. Friend the Secretary of State has no plans to do so at present.

### EC Ministers

73. **Ms. Quin:** To ask the Secretary of State for the Environment when he next expects to meet his European Community counterparts; and what matters will be discussed.

**Mr. Ridley:** The European Community's Environment Council, which is usually attended by my noble Friend the Minister for Housing, Environment and Countryside, will next meet on 19 September. It will be for the French presidency to decide the agenda.

### Basthby Thorpe (Methane)

75. **Mr. Vaz:** To ask the Scretary of State for the Environment if he has received any representations concerning the accumulation of methane in the Basthby Thorpe area landfill site; and if he will make a statement.

**Mrs. Virginia Bottomley:** I discussed this case with the hon. Member and representatives from the local residents' association on 12 June. No other representations have been received.

### Sea Water Pollution (Southend)

78. **Mr. Teddy Taylor:** To ask the Secretary of State for the Environment if he will make a statement on the pollution levels in the sea water at Southend-on-Sea.

**Mr. Howard:** At Southend-on-Sea, the Anglian water authority recently brought into use an extension to an existing outfall at a cost of £5 million. While this has brought about significant improvements in water quality, it is clear that further measures are needed. In response to a request from my right hon. Friend the Secretary of State, the Anglian water authority is developing proposals for satisfactory long-term arrangements for sewage disposal at Southend.

However, as a temporary measure, the water authority is disinfecting sewage with peracetic acid prior to discharge through the outfall. This has enabled the identified bathing waters at Thorpe bay and Westcliff bay consistently to meet the bathing water directive's mandatory coliform standards so far during the 1989 bathing season.

East beach, Shoeburyness, which was recently identified as a bathing water under the EC bathing water directive, already meets those mandatory standards.

### Gleneagles Agreement

79. **Mr. Robert Hughes:** To ask the Secretary of State for the Environment what advice his Department is giving to the organisation of the Henley regatta to ensure that both the spirit and the letter of the Gleneagles agreement are observed at this year's regatta.

**Mr. Moynihan:** The organisers of the Henley royal regatta are well aware of the terms of the Gleneagles agreement and of the Government's continuing commitment to it.

87. **Mr. Tony Banks:** To ask the Secretary of State for the Environment when he last discussed the Gleneagles agreement with the chairman of the Sports Council.

**Mr. Moynihan:** I have not discussed the Gleneagles agreement formally with the newly-appointed chairman of the Sports Council. As chairman of the council, Mr. Yarranton issued a statement expressing his support for the agreement on 12 June.

### Housing Action Trust, Lambeth

80. **Mr. Fraser:** To ask the Secretary of State for the Environment if he is now able to announce a timetable for a ballot on a housing action trust for the Angell and Loughborough estates in Lambeth.

**Mr. Trippier:** I refer the hon. Member to the answer I gave to him on 24 May 1989, concerning ballots in the proposed housing action trust areas.

### Planning Proposals (Consultation)

82. **Mr. Madel:** To ask the Secretary of State for the Environment whether he is considering a more important role for district health authorities in the consultative process of planning proposals at district council level in his forthcoming planning Bill; and if he will make a statement.

**Mr. Howard:** The White Paper "The Future of Development Plans" (Cm. 569) set out the Government's proposals for reform of the development plan system. Under the new arrangements district planning authorities will, when preparing their draft plans, be required to consult any statutory bodies likely to be affected. There will continue to be provision, as there is now, for local public inquiries to be held by an inspector appointed by my right hon. Friend to hear objections to deposited plans. It will be up to district health authorities to make appropriate use of those procedures.

### Marine Nature Reserves

83. **Mr. Geraint Howells:** To ask the Secretary of State for the Environment if he will make a statement about the progress of consultations on marine nature reserves.

**Mrs. Virginia Bottomley:** The first statutory marine nature reserve around Lundy island was established on 21 November 1986. The Nature Conservancy Council has formally submitted proposals for a second reserve at Skomer island —Marloes peninsular—to my right hon. Friend the Secretary of State for Wales. A decision is awaited from the South Wales sea fisheries committee on a proposed byelaw controlling fishing before further progress can be made.

The NCC published a consultation paper on Menai Straits in September 1988 and is considering the 175 responses it has received.

### Energy Conservation

84. **Mr. Lofthouse:** To ask the Secretary of State for the Environment, what advice and help with grants for repairs and so on, his Department is giving to people on low incomes to conserve energy in their homes; and if he will make a statement.

**Mr. Trippier:** The homes insulation scheme, administered by housing authorities and funded by my Department, provides 90 per cent. grant for loft insulation in qualifying dwellings whose householders are recipients of income support, family credit or housing benefit. A departmental booklet for scheme applicants, distributed to all authorities, includes detailed guidance to those who wish to carry out the work themselves. Discretionary aid for energy conservation measures may also be available via home improvement grants, usually as part of a wider package of improvements. Advice to householders is contained in the Department's housing booklet No. 14.

### Rating Revaluations

85. **Mr. Riddick:** To ask the Secretary of State for the Environment what would be the effect of a rating revaluation on the level of rates payable on a typical terraced house with a current rateable value of £40 in the area covered by Kirklees council; and if he will make a statement.

**Mr. Gummer:** Under the Local Government Finance Act 1988 domestic rates are to be replaced from 1 April 1990 by the community charge. No revaluation of domestic rateable values is therefore to be made. Such a revaluation would in any event now be very difficult to undertake because of lack of evidence of market rents for domestic property.

### Surrey Structure Plan

86. **Mr. Ian Taylor:** To ask the Secretary of State for the Environment what representations he has received in response to his proposed revised modifications to the first alteration to the Surrey structure plan; and if he will make a statement.

**Mr. Howard:** The Secretary of State has so far received three responses to the proposed revised modification which was formally advertised by the county council on 18 May. Six weeks are allowed for representations, the closing date for which will be 10 July.

The Secretary of State will then complete his consideration of the proposed revised modification, and his approval of the first alteration to the Surrey structure plan will follow as soon as possible afterwards.

### Stonehenge

89. **Mr. Key:** To ask the Secretary of State for the Environment if he will make a statement on the future of Stonehenge.

**Mrs. Virginia Bottomley:** English Heritage is responsible for managing Stonehenge on behalf of my right hon. Friend. As my hon. Friend knows, it has plans for a new visitor centre and other major improvements in the way Stonehenge is presented to the public. Critical to the success of these plans is the choice of access route to the visitor centre. This has taken time to resolve because of the conflicting interests of adjoining landowners, and questions of archaeology and military security. However, discussions are taking place, and I hope that the matter will be resolved soon.

### Derelict Land

90. **Mr. Hardy:** To ask the Secretary of State for the Environment if he will take further steps to discourage development outside the conurbations and provide additional incentives to secure reclamation of derelict land within them.

**Mr. Trippier:** The Government are already firmly committed to the preservation of the countryside and the maximum use of urban land for new development. Under the derelict land grant, priority is given to reclaiming derelict sites in urban areas and city grant and urban programme grants are also available to reclaim derelict land and facilitate development. In addition, the 10 urban development corporations now established in England are making a significant impact on the derelict land in their areas.

Nevertheless, the latest household projections make it clear that some land for housing will continue to be needed in the foreseeable future on new sites outside urban areas. Such sites will have to be identified with an eye to all material planning considerations.

### Playing Fields

**Mr. Harry Greenway:** To ask the Secretary of State for the Environment what measures he is taking to prevent building development by housing associations, local councils and other public bodies on school and other playing fields; and if he will make a statement.

**Mr. Chope:** Local planning authorities are responsible for determining development proposals in the first instance. As I indicated in reply to the hon. Member for Durham, North (Mr. Radice) on 24 May, we have urged authorities to take account of the wider needs of the community and to consult local sports and recreational interests when considering proposals for the development of recreational land.

### Waste Disposal

**Mr. Paice:** To ask the Secretary of State for the Environment what representations he has received from Cambridgeshire county council on his consultation paper regarding the role and function of waste disposal authorities, and what was the nature of their representations.

**Mrs. Virginia Bottomley:** I have received detailed comments from Cambridgeshire county council. These, along with many others, are being given careful consideration.

### Rents into Mortgages Scheme

**Mr. French:** To ask the Secretary of State for the Environment if he has received any representations on the introduction of a rents into mortgages scheme for council tenants in England, similar to the one proposed for Scotland.

**Mr. Trippier:** My hon. Friend and a small number of members of the public have made such representations. The scheme announced on 11 May is confined to tenants of Scottish Homes and does not extend to local authority tenants.

### Rent and Rate Arrears

**Mr. Nicholas Bennett:** To ask the Secretary of State for the Environment what representations he has received concerning *(a)* local authority members who are tenants of the same authority in arrears with their rents and *(b)* such members in arrears with their rates; and whether he has any proposals to deal with the rent or rate arrears by councillors.

**Mr. Trippier:** I have received various representations. It is obviously destructive to effective rent collection if those elected to local authorities do not set an example by not getting in arrears. I am considering whether it would be desirable to introduce arrangements whereby any allowances due to a councillor could be offset against significant sums that that councillor may owe to the authority.

### Sports Council

**Mr. Meale:** To ask the Secretary of State for the Environment when he last met the chairman of the Sports Council.

**Mr. Moynihan:** I refer the hon. Member to the answer which I gave earlier today to the hon. and learned Member for Fife, North-East (Mr. Campbell).

### Hostels

**Mr. Randall:** To ask the Secretary of State for the Environment how much has been spent by his Department since 1981 on hostels which are financed and managed through the Department of Social Security system.

**Mr. Peter Lloyd:** I have been asked to reply.

Before 31 March 1985 the Department's accounting system did not specifically identify expenditure on its hostels (known as resettlement units). Also, up to 31 March 1987, most of the resettlement units were jointly run with the Department's re-establishment centres. Therefore, separate expenditure details for resettlement units are available only from 1987-88 after the closure of the re-establishment centres. Gross expenditure including that paid to PSA for certain maintenance work was as follows:

| | £ million |
|---|---|
| 1985-86 | [1]12·5 |
| 1986-87 | [1]11·5 |
| 1987-88 | 12·1 |
| 1988-89 | [2]12·5 |

[1] Includes expenditure on re-establishment centres.
[2] Forecast.

# SCOTLAND

## Electricity

**Mr. Steel:** To ask the Secretary of State for Scotland whether he intends to ensure that independent electricity producers in Scotland will be allowed equal access with the North of Scotland Hydro-Electric Board and the South of Scotland Electricity Board to the distribution network after privatisation.

**Mr. Lang:** Yes. There will be use of system arrangements which will ensure that independent power producers have access to the transmission and distribution systems of the Scottish utilities on an equitable basis. The principles for providing access and the structure of charging will be set out in the licences granted to the successor companies of the Scottish electricity boards and will be overseen by the Director General of Electricity Supply.

## Forests (Privatisation)

**Mr. Stern:** To ask the Secretary of State for Scotland if he has any plans to extend private ownership of forests in Scotland.

**Lord James Douglas-Hamilton:** I refer the hon. Member to the reply that my right hon. and learned Friend gave to my hon. Friend the Member for Dumfries (Sir H. Monro) on 16 June 1989 at columns *544-45*.

## Community Charge

**Mr. Allen:** To ask the Secretary of State for Scotland how many people in Scotland have paid the community charge; and how many have not.

**Mr. Lang:** The information requested is not available at present.

## Nature Conservancy Council

**Mr. Maclennan:** To ask the Secretary State for Scotland if he will list by region the number of land agents employed by the Nature Conservancy Council.

**Lord James Douglas-Hamilton** *[holding answer 27 June 1989]:* The Nature Conservancy Council has advised me that the number of land agents currently employed by the council in its Scottish regions is as follows:

| | Number |
|---|---|
| North West region | 2 |
| North East region | 0 |
| South West region | 1 |
| South East region | 1 |

The land agency complement in Scotland is 10 and efforts are being made to recruit the balance.

## Sites of Special Scientific Interest

**Mr. Maclennan:** To ask the Secretary State for Scotland if he will list by region the number of management agreements made between the Nature Conservancy Council and landowners in 1988 and each of the preceding two years.

**Lord James Douglas-Hamilton** *[holding answer 27 June 1989]:* The Nature Conservancy Council has advised me that the numbers of management agreements made in its Scottish regions in the years 1986-87 to 1988-89 were as follows:

| | *1986-87* | *1987-88* | *1988-89* |
|---|---|---|---|
| North West region | 13 | 17 | 12 |
| North East region | 16 | 15 | 18 |
| South West region | 10 | 25 | 9 |
| South East region | 9 | 19 | 5 |

**Mr. Maclennan:** To ask the Secretary State for Scotland what is the average time taken between notification by the Nature Conservancy Council of its intention to place a restriction on certain farming activities on a site of special scientific interest and the reaching of a management agreement with the landowner.

**Lord James Douglas-Hamilton** *[holding answer 27 June 1989]:* The notification of land as a site of special scientific interest by the Nature Conservancy Council does not restrict existing farming activities. Where such activities are damaging to the special interest, they may be restricted only under a voluntary management agreement. Where a farmer proposes changes in activity he is obliged to serve notice on the NCC which if it wishes to restrict such activities will, within four months, offer to negotiate a management agreement. For the length of time taken to negotiate a management agreement I would refer the hon. Member to the answer given by my hon. Friend the Parliamentary Under-Secretary of State for the Environment on 14 February 1989 to the hon. Member for the Isle of Wight (Mr. Field), column *189*.

# NORTHERN IRELAND

## Dogs

**Sir Michael McNair-Wilson:** To ask the Secretary of State for Northern Ireland whether the dog registration scheme in the Province, set up under the Dogs (NI) Order 1983, is enforced by dog wardens; how many stray dogs are collected annually; how many dogs have been put down annually since the order was introduced.

**Mr. Viggers** *[holding answer 19 June 1989]:* The provisions of the Dogs (NI) Order 1983 are enforced by Northern Ireland's 26 district councils, each of which employs dog wardens. The other information requested is as follows:

| | *Stray dogs collected* | *Dogs put down (including at owners' expense)* |
|---|---|---|
| 1984 | 8,297 | 7,828 |
| 1985 | 11,306 | 10,567 |
| 1986 | 10,833 | 10,384 |
| 1987 | 10,520 | 10,575 |
| 1988 | 11,888 | 11,907 |

**Sir Michael McNair-Wilson:** To ask the Secretary of State for Northern Ireland how many dogs are licensed by district councils under the Dog (NI) Order 1983; what have been the totals in 1984, 1985, 1986, 1987 and 1988; and if he will state *(a)* the amount of revenue generated by the scheme annually and *(b)* the cost of administration.

**Mr. Viggers** *[holding answer 19 June 1989]:* The number of dog licences issued under the Dogs (NI) Order 1983 and the revenue generated from licences is as follows:

|       | Number of dog licences issued | Licence revenue £ |
|-------|-------------------------------|-------------------|
| 1984  | 84,137                        | 419,000           |
| 1985  | 70,001                        | 348,000           |
| 1986  | 69,046                        | 343,000           |
| 1987  | 64,847                        | 320,000           |
| 1988  | 70,315                        | 348,000           |

The number of licences issued includes block licences (for three or more dogs). Information on the costs of administration is not collected centrally.

# HOUSE OF COMMONS

## Early-day Motions

**Mr. Amess:** To ask the Lord President of the Council how many early-day motions were tabled in each Session since 1966; and how many were subsequently debated on the floor of the House.

**Mr. Wakeham:** The information requested for the sessions 1966-67 to 1969-70 is as follows:

| Session | Number of EDMs |
|---------|----------------|
| 1966-67 | 640            |
| 1967-68 | 446            |
| 1968-69 | 443            |
| 1969-70 | 300            |

For information about subsequent sessions, I refer my hon. Friend to the reply I gave to my hon. Friend the Member for Derbyshire, West (Mr. McLoughlin) on Monday 19 June, *Official Report,* column *34.*

The information requested in the second part of the question is not held in the form requested and could be provided only at disproportionate cost.

**Mr. Amess:** To ask the Lord President of the Council (1) if he will publish a list of early-day motions, other than prayers, debated on the Floor of the House in parliamentary time provided by the Government in each Session since 1966.

(2) if he will publish in the *Official Report* a list of early-day motions, other than prayers, debated on the Floor of the House since 1966.

**Mr. Wakeham:** I regret that this information is not held in the form requested and could be provided only at disproportionate cost.

## Private Members' Bills

**Mr. Amess:** To ask the Lord President of the Council if he will publish in the *Official Report* a list of private Members' Bills where a division took place on Second Reading and where the Bill received the Royal Assent in each Session since 1966.

**Mr. Wakeham:** Since the 1966-67 Session, the following private Members' Bills have received Royal Assent having previously been read a Second time on a Division:

|                          | Year    |
|--------------------------|---------|
| Divorce Reform Bill      | 1968-69 |
| Conservation of Seals Bill | 1969-70 |

**Mr. Amess:** To ask the Lord President of the Council if he will seek to amend Standing Order No. 90 so as to provide that, for private members' Bills, not fewer than 20 hon. Members rising in their places shall be required to constitute objection; and if he will make a statement.

**Mr. Wakeham:** I have no plans to do so.

## Procedure Committee Reports

**Mr. Amess:** To ask the Lord President of the Council what representations he has received concerning the Procedure Committee's reports on use of time on the Floor of the House and private Members' time; how many supported the implementation of these reports; and how many expressed an opposite view; and what percentage the latter represents of the former.

**Mr. John Wakeham:** Since my reply to a similar question by my hon. Friend on 23 May at column *509,* I have received one further letter which was in support of the recommendations in the two reports so far as they relate to private Members' time.

# Written Answers to Questions

*Thursday 29 June 1989*

## NORTHERN IRELAND

### Tourism

**Mr. Kilfedder:** To ask the Secretary of State for Northern Ireland if he is now able to announce the result of the review of tourism policy in Northern Ireland which was commissioned in October.

**Mr. Viggers:** Following the recent review, a statement of the Government's proposals for tourism is being published today, and copies of the document "Tourism in Northern Ireland—A View to the Future" are available in the House of Commons Library.

The review concludes that tourism in Northern Ireland has not prospered in line with its opportunities. One feature of difficulty in the promotion of tourism in Northern Ireland is its image, but that does not reflect the full picture, and should not prevent the implementation of change in the marketing of the product.

The Government intend to create a body which will have responsibility for both marketing and product development, bringing together the present promotional role of the Northern Ireland tourist board, and the grant-aiding functions of the Department of Economic Development.

Implementation of the proposed changes will require legislation in due course.

### Irish Language

**Rev. Martin Smyth:** To ask the Secretary of State for Northern Ireland how many pupils passed *(a)* O-level and *(b)* A-level Irish language in the years 1985 to 1988.

**Dr. Mawhinney:** The information is as follows:-

*Passes in Irish language*

|  | O-level | A-level |
|---|---|---|
| 1985 | 1,221 | 230 |
| 1986 | 1,208 | 209 |
| 1987 | 1,072 | 223 |
| 1988 | 1,046 | 203 |

*Notes:*
O-level passes for 1985-87 comprise CSE Grade 1 and GCE Grades A-C. In 1988, GCSE replaced GCE and CSE: figure given is for GCSE Grades A-C.
A-level passes comprise grades A-E.

### Post-graduate Awards

**Mr McCusker:** To ask the Secretary of State for Northern Ireland what are the principal differences in the granting of post-graduate awards between Northern Ireland and Great Britain; and how many such awards have been granted in Northern Ireland during the past five years.

**Dr. Mawhinney:** The principal differences between Northern Ireland and Great Britain in the granting of post-graduate awards are (a) in Northern Ireland the Department of Education is responsible for making awards to Northern Ireland students for those areas of study which in Great Britain are the responsibility of the science and engineering, the natural environment, and the economic and social research councils, the British Academy, the Department of Education and Science and the Scottish Education Department;

(b) the Department of Education offers up to 20 postgraduate distinction awards each year to enable graduates from anywhere in the United Kingdom who have gained first-class degrees to undertake research at the two Northern Ireland universities.

New awards made in each of the last five years are as follows:-

|  | Studentships | Bursaries |
|---|---|---|
| 1984-85 | 311 | 131 |
| 1985-86 | 307 | 131 |
| 1986-87 | 311 | 134 |
| 1987-88 | 311 | 133 |
| 1988-89 | [1]337 | 133 |

[1] Includes 20 Distinction Awards.

### Police Complaints (Report)

**Mr. Jessel:** To ask the Secretary of State for Northern Ireland if he will arrange for copies of the first annual report of the Independent Commission for Police Complaints for Northern Ireland to be laid in the House.

**Mr. Tom King:** I have arranged to do so today. This is the first report of the commission which I set up in February last year and, therefore, relates to a settling-in period. However the report clearly demonstrates that the commission has established a very firm foundation for the thorough and impartial consideration of complaints against members of the Royal Ulster Constabulary. As the new commission develops its role I have every confidence that it will make a material contribution to strengthening good relations between the RUC and the whole community in Northern Ireland.

### Human Rights

**Mr. French:** To ask the Secretary of State for Northern Ireland if he has received the 14th report of the Standing Advisory Commission on Human Rights; and if he will make a statement.

**Mr. Tom King:** The report has been published today, and copies have been laid before Parliament. It covers the period 1 November 1987 to 31 March 1989.

The report covers a wide range of matters which the commission has considered during the period under review. These include fair employment, the Criminal Evidence (Northern Ireland) Order 1988, electoral law, broadcasting restrictions, emergency legislation, the draft Police and Criminal Evidence (Northern Ireland) Order and education.

Copies of my response to the commission's report and of the report itself have been placed in the Library.

## THE ARTS

### Museums (Repairs)

**Mr. Devlin:** To ask the Minister for the Arts, what is the estimated cost of necessary repairs and fabric at the national gallery, the national portrait gallery, the Victoria and Albert museum, the Tate gallery and the natural history museum; and what is the estimated cost of modernising the plumbing at each of the above-named institutions.

**Mr. Luce:** The maintenance and repair of these historic buildings is a continuous process which will always require a rolling programme of expenditure. Major maintenance projects are in hand at all of these institutions, but I accept that further investment is necessary. I have allocated £72 million in the current three-year funding period for the building and maintenance programmes at these institutions and hope to announce further allocations later in the year.

### Horniman Museum and Library

**Mr. Fraser:** To ask the Minister for the Arts when he will appoint a shadow board of trustees for the Horniman museum and library; and when he will announce what resources there are available for the institution.

**Mr. Luce:** I hope that some members of the 'shadow' board of trustees for the Horniman museum and library will be appointed this autumn. I will announce in due course the financial provision which will be made for the museum from the arts programme.

## NATIONAL FINANCE

### Child Car Restraints

**Mr. Gregory:** To ask the Chancellor of the Exchequer what is his estimate of the revenue from value added tax on child car seat restraints for the current year; and if he will make a statement.

**Mr. Lilley:** I regret that the information requested is not available.

## ENVIRONMENT

### Community Charge

**Mr. Cohen:** To ask the Secretary of State for the Environment whether he has taken legal advice to test whether the community charge registration form produced by Trafford council is ultra vires; and whether he will make a statement.

**Mr. Gummer:** It is not for the Department to test whether the registration forms issued by community charge registration officers (CCROs) are intra vires. We have issued detailed guidance on community charge registration and a model registration form. If CCROs use the model form and follow the guidance, I am confident that they will be acting intra vires.

**Mr. McAllion:** To ask the Secretary of State for the Environment if he will make a statement on the effects of his policy on community charge exemptions on the future of care in the community.

**Mr. Gummer:** The Government have provided a number of exemptions from the community charge including those for certain residential care workers and those for severely mentally impaired people. These, combined with rebate arrangements and uprated income support, ensure that our policy on community care is unaffected.

### Sewage Treatment Works

**Mr. Redmond:** To ask the Secretary of State for the Environment what ministerial permission has *(a)* been requested and *(b)* been granted, for relaxation of sewage treatment works discharge consents for Yorkshire water authority; and what period of time they cover.

**Mr. Howard:** Lists of sewage treatment works for which applications have been made by water authorities for time-limited relaxations to discharge consents have been placed in the Libraries of both Houses. Details of the applications, including the period for which the temporary variation has been requested, may be obtained from the public register maintained by Yorkshire water authority. The duration of any time-limited relaxation granted will, within the constraints set out in my announcement of 7 December 1988, *Official Report* column *199* reflect the expected time scale of the capital improvements to be carried out. None of the applications from the authority has yet been granted.

### Sport

**Mr. Pendry:** To ask the Secretary of State for the Environment when he will respond to those parts of the report "Sport and Young People, Partnership and Action" produced by the school sport forum in July 1988 which relate to his departmental responsibilities.

**Mr. Moynihan:** My right hon. Friends the Secretaries of State for the Environment and for Education and Science will issue their joint response to the report "Sport and Young People, Partnership and Action" shortly.

### Domestic Property (Compensation)

**Mr. Heddle:** To ask the Secretary of State for the Environment, further to his answer to the hon. Member for Mid-Staffordshire, 17 January *Official Report,* column *149,* if he is now in a position to publish his proposals for dealing with the compensation code for domestic property which, under current legislation, is based either upon gross, net annual or rateable values for implementation on 1 April 1990, under the Local Government Finance Act 1988.

**Mr. Chope:** Paragraphs 7 and 8 of the Department's consultation paper on land compensation and compulsory purchase legislation issued on 7 March, include proposals for amendments to the method of calculating home loss payments when domestic rateable values are abolished on 1 April 1990. I am sending my hon. Friend a copy of the consultation paper to which we have received many interesting responses which we are now considering.

### Valuation and Community Charge Tribunals

**Mr. Redmond:** To ask the Secretary of State for the Environment if he will list the selected valuation and community change tribunal offices where he proposes to use his Department's valuation office staff for user computer support; and if he will make a statement.

**Mr. Gummer:** The valuation and community charge tribunal offices proposed as regional centres for computer user support are:

    Cleveland and Durham
    Essex North and South
    Greater London (South Eastern)
    Greater Manchester North
    Greater Manchester South
    Hereford and Worcester
    and Kent

**Mr. Redmond:** To ask the Secretary of State for the Environment if he will list the valuation and community charge tribunal offices that received in January an interim pay award to its staff of *(a)* three increments and *(b)* one increment; and if he will make a statement as to why there was a differential pay award.

**Mr. Gummer:** Staff in 16 offices set out in list (a) received an interim pay award equivalent to three increments while the staff of the remaining 26 offices in list (b) received one increment. The award to offices in list (a) reflected local market factors affecting recruitment retention of staff. Since January 1989 a further seven offices indicated by an asterisk in list (b) have been added to list (a) in the light of evidence of similar market factors.

*List (a)*

    Central London, Holborn
    London North East, Ilford
    London North West, Harrow
    London South East, Croydon
    London South West, Hounslow
    Avon and Gloucestershire, Cheltenham
    Befordshire and Hertfordshire, Hertford
    Berkshire, Wokingham
    Coventry, Solihull and Worcestershire, Leamington Spa
    Essex North and South, Chelmsford
    Hampshire South and Isle of Wight, Southampton
    Hampshire North and Wiltshire, Winchester
    Kent, Maidstone
    Leicestershire, Northamptonshire and Nottinghamshire, Nottingham
    Surrey, Woking
    West Sussex, Chichester

*List (b)*

    Buckinghamshire, Aylesbury*
    Cambridgeshire, Peterborough
    Cheshire, Chester
    Cleveland and Durham, Darlington
    Devon, Cornwall and Isles of Scilly, Plymouth*
    Cumbria, Whitehaven
    Derbyshire, Chesterfield
    Dorset and Somerset, Yeovil
    Hereford and Worcester, Worcester
    Humberside, Bridlington
    Lancashire, Preston
    Lincolnshire, Horncastle
    Merseyside, Liverpool
    Manchester, North, Bolton
    Manchester South, Chorlton-Cum-Hardy, Manchester*
    West Midlands West, Dudley
    Birmingham, Birmingham
    Norfolk, Norwich*
    Northumberland, Tyne and Wear, North Shields
    Oxfordshire, Oxford
    Staffordshire and Shropshire, Stafford
    Suffolk, Ipswich*
    East Sussex, Eastbourne*
    North Yorkshire, Middlesbrough*
    South Yorkshire, Doncaster
    West Yorkshire, Leeds

**Mr. Redmond:** To ask the Secretary of State for the Environment why his Department proposes to use valuation office staff for user computer support and place them in selected valuation and community charge tribunal offices; and if he will make a statement.

**Mr. Gummer:** Computer systems in 42 valuation and community charge tribunal offices become operational in September this year. By then a fully effective support system must be in place to help the offices overcome any problems. We propose to achieve this by seconding experienced computer staff from the Inland Revenue to selected tribunal offices within easy reach of other offices.

### Water Stocks

**Mr. Hayward:** To ask the Secretary of State for the Environment if he has any further information in relation to impounded water stocks following his answer to the hon. Member for Kingswood, 8 June, *Official Report,* column *87.*

**Mr. Howard:** There are some impounded stocks below normal in the Southern and South West water authorities areas.

### Wild Birds

**Mr. Stern:** To ask the Secretary of State for the Environment if he will list, by reference to site location, the occasions since 1 December 1981 when the European Commission has initiated inquiries with his Department concerning development proposals or other activities which may have an adverse impact on areas qualifying for special protection under article 4 of EC directive 79/409 on the conservation of wild birds.

**Mrs. Virginia Bottomley:** Such inquiries are confidential between the European Commission and Her Majesty's Government, and details are not normally made public.

**Mr. Stern:** To ask the Secretary of State for the Environment, pursuant to his answer of 6 June, *Official Report,* column *89,* what additional legal protection to that given under section 28 of the Wildlife and Countryside Act 1981 is given to areas which meet the criteria for designation under article 4 of EC directive 79/409 on the conservation of wild birds or wetlands of international importance under the Ramsar convention.

**Mrs. Virginia Bottomley:** I refer my hon. Friend to the last paragraph of my reply to him on 6 June at column *89* in respect of SPAs. Ramsar sites are a further subset of SSSIs. The fact of designation in accordance with this international convention would influence decisions on development proposals affecting these areas; the factors to be taken into account when considering development proposals are set out in detail in DOE circular 27/87— "Nature Conservation".

**Mr. Stern:** To ask the Secretary of State for the Environment when he next intends to announce the designation of an area either as a site under the Ramsar convention on the conservation of wetlands of international importance or as a special protection area under EC directive 79/409 on the conservation of wild birds, or both.

**Mrs. Virginia Bottomley:** A number of proposals are currently being considered by my right hon. Friend the Secretary of State and my right hon. and learned Friend the Secretary of State for Scotland. The next classification of a site will be announced as soon as the necessary consultations have been satisfactorily completed.

## Shopping Developments

**Mr. Tony Lloyd:** To ask the Secretary of State for the Environment if he will give details of any organisation or individuals to which his decision about some or all of the applications for out-of-town shopping developments have been communicated.

**Mr. Howard:** It is my right hon. Friend's invariable practice to notify applicants and others concerned of his decisions on planning appeals and called-in applications when they are finalised, and not before. Decisions on the group of appeals and called-in planning applications for major retail developments in Greater Manchester and north-east Cheshire have not yet been finalised.

## North West Water

**Mr. Straw:** To ask the Secretary of State for the Environment what is the cost of advertising by North West Water in the current year and each of the previous four years.

**Mr. Howard:** This is a matter for the authority.

## Ivory Imports

**Mr. Ron Davies:** To ask the Secretary of State for the Environment how many appeals he has received during the last 12 months against the refusal to grant an import licence under CITES; how many of these appeals he granted; and whether any were in respect of ivory earrings or other ivory jewellery.

**Mrs. Virginia Bottomley:** I refer the hon. Member to the answer I gave him on 15 June 1989 at column *540*.

## National Park Planning Boards

**Mr. McLoughlin:** To ask the Secretary of State for the Environment if he will list how many members of each national park planning board live within the area of that park as a percentage of the total numbers on each board.

**Mrs. Virginia Bottomley:** The information for the seven English national parks is as follows:

| Park | Members | Number living within Park | Percentage of total number Per cent. |
|------|---------|---------------------------|--------------------------------------|
| Dartmoor | 21 | 7 | 33 |
| Exmoor | 21 | 4 | 19 |
| Lake District[1] | 30 | 10 | 34 |
| Northumberland | 27 | 2 | 7 |
| North York Moors | 27 | 4 | 15 |
| Peak District | 34 | 10 | 29 |
| Yorkshire Dales | 24 | 11 | 46 |

[1] 29 members are in place and there is currently one vacancy on the Lake District Board.

## Tenants' Choice Ballots

**Mr. Bowis:** To ask the Secretary of State for the Environment when he will make available the model contract which a tenants' choice applicant landlord must use when employing an independent teller to conduct the ballot of tenants' views.

**Mr. Trippier:** A model contract setting out detailed obligations on applicant landlords and independent tellers

when consulting tenants in a tenants' choice ballot was issued by the Department and the Housing Corporation today. It has been drawn up in consultation with the Electoral Reform Society.

The applicant landlord is required to use this contract as a condition of his approval to apply to acquire the property. The contract is a rigorous document designed to ensure as far as possible that every tenant eligible to do so is able to return a fully informed vote within the consultation period.

Copies of the contract have been placed in the Libraries of both Houses and are available from the Housing Corporation.

## River Pollution

**Mr. Clay:** To ask the Secretary of State for the Environment (1) if he will list all discharges into the River Wear which are controlled by the sewage treatment effluent consent standards by maximum admissible concentrations, the number of occasions when these standards have been breached and action taken to enforce compliance;

(2) if he will list the number of occasions the Northumbria water authority has been found to be in breach of the Control of Pollution Act 1974 *(a)* river by river in the authority's area, *(b)* the substances involved in each incident, *(c)* the source of the contravention, and *(d)* on coastal outfalls and the substances involved;

(3) if he will list the number of times that Northumbria water authority has been in breach of the sewage effluent consent standards on the River Wear since 1987; which sewage treatment works were involved in each incident; and what action was taken to enforce compliance.

**Mr. Howard** *[holding answer 21 June 1989]:* Details of the consents to discharge into the River Wear, including those for sewage effluent, and information about breaches of these consents are held on registers maintained by the Northumbrian water authority and are available for public inspection, free of charge, at all reasonable hours. This information is not held centrally.

In considering what action to take to enforce compliance, Her Majesty's inspectorate of pollution pay particular attention to the following factors: whether the sewage treatment works is persistently or grossly non-compliant; whether the breach has had a detrimental effect on the receiving water quality; and whether there are plans for improvement either through capital investment, by better maintenance or by improved operational control.

## Street Lighting

**Ms. Walley:** To ask the Secretary of State for the Environment if he will make an allocation to each local authority to enable a survey to be carried out to assess the need for the repair and replacement of street lighting; and if he will make available to local authorities adequate funding to finance a rolling programme to improve street lighting.

**Mr Peter Bottomley:** I have been asked to reply.

No. The repair and renewal of street lighting on local roads is a local highway authority responsibility. Local authorities finance them from within their general resources for roads expenditure. If individual authorities have special needs they may wish to highlight them in their transport policies and programme submissions to the Department.

## FOREIGN AND COMMONWEALTH AFFAIRS

### West Bank (Schools)

**Mr. Fraser:** To ask the Secretary of State for Foreign and Commonwealth Affairs what representations have been made to the Government of Israel about the closure of schools in the West Bank.

**Mr. Waldegrave:** We have repeatedly made clear our view that the closure of schools is not justified by Israel's security concerns, and called on the Israeli authorities to allow the schools to reopen—most recently in the European Council declaration on the middle east of 27 June.

### Mohammed Nazak and Jurida Begum

**Mr. Nellist:** To ask the Secretary of State for Foreign and Commonwealth Affairs when the hon. Member for Coventry, South-East can expect a substantive reply to his letter of 27 January to the Parliamentary Under-Secretary, concerning the case of Mohammed Nazak and Jurida Begum and the appeal lodged in Abu Dhabi on 1 May 1988; and if he will make a statement.

**Mr. Eggar:** I refer the hon. Member to my letter of 20 February 1989 in reply to his letter of 27 January. I will be sending the hon. Member another copy.

## ATTORNEY-GENERAL

### Mr. Colin Wallace

**Mr. Livingstone:** To ask the Attorney-General on what date the chief constable of the Sussex police consulted the Director of Public Prosecutions concerning correspondence between the hon. Member for Brent, East and the chief constable of the Sussex police regarding the circumstances surrounding Mr. Colin Wallace's conviction for manslaughter.

**The Attorney-General:** I take the hon. Member's question to refer to his letter to the chief constable of the Sussex police dated 24 February 1989. It was referred to the Director of Public Prosecutions by letter dated 7 March 1989.

## ENERGY

### Windscale

**Mr. Cohen:** To ask the Secretary of State for Energy (1) what monitoring systems are installed at No. 2 pile at Windscale to safeguard against a release of Wigner energy; and if he will make a statement;

(2) whether any attempt was made to anneal or remove the stored Wigner energy in the No. 2 pile at Windscale; and if he will make a statement.

**Mr. Michael Spicer:** Controlled releases of Wigner energy were made at intervals while Windscale No. 2 pile was in operation, but none has been attempted since 1957

when it was closed down and defuelled. This energy could be released in significant quantity only by substantial heating of the pile; there are no credible circumstances in which such heat could be generated inadvertently. Nevertheless, temperatures are monitored continuously using instruments positioned in the outlet ducts.

### Disconnections

**Mr. Barry Jones:** To ask the Secretary of State for Energy if he will make it his policy to collect statistics on the numbers of domestic credit customers disconnected in each region of British Gas during (i) 1979 and (ii) the most recent full year for which figures are available.

**Mr. Peter Morrison:** It is for the Gas Consumers Council to monitor disconnections figures and take up any issues arising from them. The GCC published a report on disconnections in February of last year when disconnections were still rising. Subsequently British Gas modified its procedures on debt and disconnections, in agreement with the Office of Gas Supply, and in the latest 12-month period for which figures are available the number of disconnections has fallen by 35 per cent.

### Sellafield (Radioactive Chimneys)

**Mrs. Mahon:** To ask the Secretary of State for Energy what measures have been taken to protect the Cumbrian population during the dismantling of the two radioactive chimneys associated with the 1957 fire at Windscale (Sellafield); and what plans are under way for the examination of children and pregnant women during this period.

**Mr. Michael Spicer:** BNFL is currently decommissioning one of the two original Windscale pile chimneys. All necessary safety precautions will be taken during the decommissioning and this will ensure that no member of the public will be at risk from exposure to radioactive contamination.

### Oil and Gas Revenues

**Mr. Churchill:** To ask the Secretary of State for Energy what has been the cumulative total of benefit to the Exchequer from North sea oil and gas since May 1979 to date in respect of *(a)* licence fees and other revenues, and *(b)* taxation.

**Mr. Peter Morrison:** The cumulative total of licence fees attributable to United Kingdom oil and gas production over the fiscal years 1979-80 to 1988-89 is £545 million. Receipts from the gas levy over the same period were £3·8 billion. Total royalty revenues over the period are estimated at £13·6 billion, and total tax revenues at £51·6 billion. Further details are contained in the Report of the Secretary of State for Energy to Parliament of April 1989 (the "Brown Book").

### Petroleum Licensing

**Mr. McLoughlin:** To ask the Secretary of State for Energy whether he is ready to announce the results of the 11th offshore petroleum licensing round.

**Mr. Peter Morrison:** I am pleased to be able to tell the House that I am today making conditional offers of 105 licence awards.

The round has been a great success. Virtually all the major companies involved on the United Kingdom continental shelf have made applications. Overall there were 414 applications for individual blocks, many more than in most previous rounds, and representing an average of 3·6 applications for each block applied for.

The high quality of the work programmes on offer was a particular feature of this round, which was evident both by the willingness of many applicants to evaluate prospects at many different geological layers, and by the average of 2·38 firm or conditional wells per block offered by the successful applicants, which is a far higher average than in any previous round.

This round was intended to give the industry the chance to make up lost ground after the difficulties occasioned by low oil prices at the time of the 10th round. These results show that our confidence in launching the round was entirely justified. The industry has responded magnificently, and its commitment will ensure that the UKCS continues to be a major international oil province well into the 21st century.

Before offering particular blocks my Department undertook extensive consultations with fishing, environmental, shipping and defence interests, and where appropriate other particular interests in the area. Special conditions, tailored to the precise circumstances of the block in question, will be included in the licences to ensure that these concerns are taken into account when undertaking operations. I have also ensured that all operators for the newly licensed blocks will be capable of meeting the necessary safety standards.

I am pleased to see that British independents have been well represented in this round. As a result of the awards some British independents will be taking on offshore operatorships for the first time. This demonstrates that our own independent sector is alive and well, and I hope that these opportunities will encourage the further growth of this sector.

A copy of the list of awards has been placed in the Libraries of both Houses.

### British Coal (Licensing)

**Sir John Stanley:** To ask the Secretary of State for Energy if he will list the operators of private coal mines currently licensed by British Coal.

**Mr. Michael Spicer:** This is a matter for the British Coal Corporation and I have asked the chairman to write to my right hon. Friend.

**Sir John Stanley:** To ask the Secretary of State for Energy (1) what principles he expects to be reflected in British Coal's statement of its licensing policy and practice in relation to the private mining sector referred to in his reply to the right hon. Member for Tonbridge and Malling on 3 November, *Official Report,* column *708;*

(2) when British Coal's statement on its licensing policy and practice in relation to the private mining sector referred to in his reply to the right hon. Member for Tonbridge and Malling on 3 November, *Official Report,* column *708,* will be finalised;

(3) whether he will place in the Library a copy of British Coal's statement on its licensing policy and practice in relation to the private mining sector when it is finalised.

**Mr. Michael Spicer:** British Coal's statement of licensing policy and practice has now been finalised, and I am today arranging for a copy to be placed in the Library of the House.

The statement represents the furthest that the corporation considers it can go towards greater flexibility and transparency towards the licensed sector within the constraints imposed by the Coal Industry Nationalisation Act 1946. It describes the criteria the corporation will use for assessing licence applications, and sets the target of processing applications within three months and of indicating objections at an earlier stage if possible. In addition, although a system of external appeal against licence rejection would not be consistent with the 1946 statute, British Coal is instituting internal arrangements along the same lines.

British Coal has reaffirmed its undertaking to set royalties at levels that will permit efficiently managed operations to develop their business profitably, and to reduce royalties for new licences in any case where accounting evidence is provided which demonstrates that profit expectations would otherwise be cut to unreasonably low levels. The corporation has also offered to discuss an increase in the licence period, which may facilitate licensees' mine planning and financial arrangements.

The statement confirms that it is not British Coal's policy to refuse a licence solely on the ground that it is already adequately supplied. It recognises the importance to licensed mines of reasonably assured markets for their coal, and supports the endeavours of licensed operators supplying on a continuing basis to obtain terms which properly reflect this.

British Coal has agreed to prepare annual reviews of developments in the licensed sector, together with brief summaries each six months. I will ensure that copies of these reviews will be placed in the Library of the House.

### UKAEA

**Mr. John Browne:** To ask the Secretary of State for Energy what financial targets and external finance limits have been set for the United Kingdom Atomic Energy Authority for 1989-90.

**Mr. Parkinson:** I have set a financial target of 4 per cent. return on capital employed defined as current cost profits before long-term interest and extraordinary items on the current cost value of the authority's assets. The external finance limit is £1·2 million, as published in the public expenditure White Paper (Cm. 606).

### WALES

### Low-Cost Housing

**Mr. Barry Jones:** To ask the Secretary of State for Wales what initiatives he will take to encourage the provision of low-cost starter homes; and if he will make a statement.

**Mr. Grist:** We have made record provision for housing associations in Wales, not least because they are in a good position to provide starter homes. The Housing for Wales programme for 1989-90 itself allows for significant investment in new low-cost home ownership schemes. I shall be in touch with local authorities and other interests very soon as regards planning considerations for houses in rural areas.

**Mr. Barry Jones:** To ask the Secretary of State for Wales what initiatives he will take to provide low-cost rented accommodation in conjunction with (i) housing associations, (ii) local authorities and (iii) the private sector; and if he will make a statement.

**Mr. Grist:** We welcome the hon. Gentleman's interest in mixed funding. We have encouraged housing associations and local authorities to work together to provide homes for rent as well as for shared ownership. Some £15 million of private investment in social housing is expected to be attracted to Wales in 1989-90 on top of the publicly funded programme of over £70 million.

### Health Service

**Mr. Barry Jones:** To ask the Secretary of State for Wales what representations he has received from general practitioners and others on the effects of the proposals outlined in the National Health Service White Paper, "Working For Patients", on practices in *(a)* the south Wales valleys and *(b)* rural areas; and if he will make a statement.

**Mr. Grist:** Information is not available in the form requested and could be provided only at disproportionate cost.

### Social Workers

**Mr. Barry Jones:** To ask the Secretary of State for Wales if he will take measures to increase the number of social workers in Wales; and if he will make a statement.

**Mr. Grist:** It is for individual local authorities to determine the appropriate number of social workers required to meet their statutory obligations and provide an adequate range and depth of services. Rate support grant provision to local authorities for 1989-90 was 14·5 per cent. higher than that for 1988-89. My right hon. Friend will be announcing the rate support grant for 1990-91 in the autumn.

**Mr. Barry Jones:** To ask the Secretary of State for Wales what is his estimate of the number of social workers employed by each of the county authorities of Wales; what is his estimate of the number of fully qualified social workers; and if he will make a statement.

**Mr. Ian Grist:** The information requested is given in the table. Details of qualifications are available centrally only for full-time staff.

| Local Authority | Number of full-time social workers at 30 September 1988 | |
| | Total[1] | Qualified[2] |
| --- | --- | --- |
| Clwyd | 168 | 144 |
| Dyfed | 148 | 117 |
| Gwent | 208 | 175 |
| Gwynedd | 111 | 71 |
| Mid Glamorgan | 245 | 204 |
| Powys | 41 | 27 |
| South Glamorgan | 188 | 170 |
| West Glamorgan | 167 | 106 |

*Notes:*
[1] Senior social workers, social workers and community workers.
[2] Holding the certificate of qualification in social work of the CCETSW or equivalent.

### Sewage Outfalls

**Mr. Win Griffiths:** To ask the Secretary of State for Wales if he will publish a list indicating the position of all sewage outfalls, whether into rivers or the sea, and the daily average volume of effluent released by each outfall.

**Mr. Grist:** No. This information is already available on public registers maintained by water authorities.

### Postgraduate Medical and Dental Education

**Mr. Gwilym Jones:** To ask the Secretary of State for Wales what arrangements he intends to make for postgraduate medical and dental education in Wales following the abolition of the Council for Postgraduate Medical Education in England and Wales; and if he will make a statement.

**Mr. Peter Walker:** Following extensive consultation by officials of my Department, I have concluded that a separate Welsh Council for Postgraduate Medical and Dental Education would be appropriate and will be established with effect from 1 July 1989, with the following terms of reference:

To advise the Secretary of State for Wales and make provision on his behalf for the delivery of postgraduate and continuing medical and dental education in Wales, taking into account both the standards promulgated by professional bodies and the potential difficulties of reconciling service and training needs; to identify particular problems and to develop realistic solutions to these in consultation with relevant interests; and to report regularly.

The chairman of the council will be Mr. E. M. W. Griffith CBE, chairman of Clwyd health authority. Members have been selected so as to cover the widest range of educational, professional and service interests. The setting up of this new body, after extensive consultation with professional and educational interests in Wales, reflects the Government's commitment to maintaining and enhancing the standards of medical and dental education in Wales.

## TRADE AND INDUSTRY

### Licensed Premises

**Mr. Heddle:** To ask the Chancellor of the Duchy of Lancaster if, pursuant to this reply to the hon. Member for Cambridgeshire, South-West (Sir A. Grant) on 8 June, *Official Report*, column *229*, he will make a statement on his proposals to amend the Landlord and Tenant Act 1954 in so far as it affects the security of tenure of tenants of licensed premises.

**Mr. Maude:** The Government will bring forward legislation to amend the Landlord and Tenant Act 1954 in relation to the security of tenure of licensed premises as soon as parliamentary time permits.

### Wolverhampton and Dudley Brewery

**Mr. John Marshall:** To ask the Chancellor of the Duchy of Lancaster in which petty sessional divisions Wolverhampton and Dudley Brewery has over 33 per cent. of the public house licences.

**Mr. Maude:** In 1986, which is the most recent year for which detailed figures are available, Wolverhampton and

Dudley Breweries owned 33 per cent. or more of the full on-licensed premises in the following petty sessional divisions: Dudley, Kidderminster, Stourbridge, Bewdley Borough.

### Faulty Cars

**Mr. Nicholas Baker:** To ask the Chancellor of the Duchy of Lancaster if he will consider introducing into United Kingdom law, laws similar to the United States Lemon laws giving a right to consumers to reject faulty cars.

**Mr. Forth:** The Sale of Goods Act 1979 provides for the consumer, if he acts within a reasonable time, to reject goods which are not of merchantable quality. Subject to minor clarifying amendments, the Government intend to implement the Law Commissions' recommendations (Cm. 137) for changes which would strengthen and clarify consumers' rights, in particular by replacing the old requirement of "merchantable" quality with a more up-to-date definition. However there are no plans to introduce legislation similar to United States Lemon laws.

### Iraq

**Mrs. Clwyd:** To ask the Chancellor of the Duchy of Lancaster what British trade missions have visited Iraq in the past year; and if he will ensure that any future missions are briefed by the Government on the Iraq Government's war against its Kurdish minority.

**Mr. Alan Clark** *[holding answer 26 June 1989]:* In the 12 months ended 31 May 1989 the DTI sponsored four trade missions to Iraq led by:

British Water Industries Group
Engineering Industries Association
Association of British Healthcare Industries
British Electro-technical and Allied Manufacturers Association

The addition my Department is aware of three missions led by:

Nottingham Chamber of Commerce
Coventry Chamber of Commerce
Manchester Chamber of Commerce

Officials from my Department normally brief officially sponsored missions and those unsponsored missions they are invited to address. Such briefing concentrates on commercial relations and aspects of doing business in the country. Officials in the United Kingdom and commercial staff abroad are always willing to brief trade delegations on political developments.

### Human Genome Analysis

**Rev. Martin Smyth:** To ask the Chancellor of the Duchy of Lancaster what advice has been given by the British Government to the European Communities regarding the Commission of the Communities proposal for a programme in human genome analysis.

**Mr. Mellor** *[holding answer 26 June 1989]:* The European Commission's proposal for a new research programme in predictive medicine is concerned with human genome analysis. An explanatory memorandum on this programme was submitted to the Committees of the House concerned with European legislation by the Department of Health on 28 September 1988. Discussion on the programme is still taking place in a working group of the European Council in which the British Government participated.

## SCOTLAND

### Nephrops

71. **Mr. Dunnachie:** To ask the Secretary of State for Scotland if he has any proposals to add the nephrops fisheries in areas IV and VI to the current United Kingdom pressure stock licensing scheme; and if he will make a statement.

**Mr. Michael Forsyth:** In view of the fact that nephrops in area IV are not subject to a quota, and that catches of nephrops in areas Vb and VI have been on average only 70 to 80 per cent. of the United Kingdom's total allowable catch in recent years, I do not consider that the designation of these stocks as pressure stocks would be justified. However, fisheries departments continue to monitor these stocks closely and have the ability to restrict their uptake if necessary.

### Regional Grants

**Mr. McLeish:** To ask the Secretary of State for Scotland (1) if he will give the total amount of expenditure in regional development grant between 1 April 1988 and 31 March 1989 and for each of the region and island authorities;
(2) if he will give the total amount of expenditure on enterprise grants between 1 April 1988 and 31 March 1989 and for each of the region and island authorities;
(3) if he will give the total amount of expenditure on regional selective assistance between 1 April 1988 and 31 March 1989 and for each of the region and island authorities.

**Mr. Lang:** Comprehensive figures in the form requested are not available for expenditure under the old regional development grant scheme. Expenditures on each of the revised regional development grant (RDG2) scheme, regional enterprise grants (REG) and regional selective assistance (RSA) in the period 1 April 1988 to 31 March 1989 are given in the table.

| Region | Regional development grants £ million | Regional enterprise grants £ million | Regional selective assistance £ million |
|---|---|---|---|
| Borders | — | — | * |
| Central | * | * | 2·0 |
| Dumfries and Galloway | * | — | 0·8 |
| Fife | * | — | 3·7 |
| Grampian | — | — | * |
| Lothian | — | — | * |
| Highland | 4·9 | * | 6·8 |
| Strathclyde | 41·6 | 0·2 | 22·4 |
| Tayside | 4·0 | * | 1·8 |
| TOTAL | 50·8 | 0·3 | 38·0 |

*Notes:*

(i) Regional development grants and regional enterprise grants are available in development areas. Regional selective assistance is available in development and intermediate areas.

(ii) Starred entries are suppressed to avoid disclosure of information relating to individual businesses.

**Mr. McLeish:** To ask the Secretary of State for Scotland (1) if he will give the total number of applications *(a)* received and *(b)* approved for regional development grants between 1 April 1988 and 31 March 1989 and for each of the region and island authorities;

(2) if he will give the total number of applications *(a)* received and *(b)* approved for enterprise grants between 1 April 1988 and 31 March 1989 and for each of the region and island authorities;

(3) if he will give the total number of applications *(a)* received and *(b)* approved for regional selective assistance between 1 April 1988 and 31 March 1989 and for each of the region and island authorities.

**Mr. Lang:** Comprehensive figures in the form requested are not available for the old regional development grant scheme. The revised regional development grant (RDG2) scheme closed to new applications on 31 March 1998. Figures for RDG2 approvals and for applications and offers of regional enterprise grants (REG) and regional selective assistance (RSA) in the period 1 April 1988 to 31 March 1989 are given in the table:

| Region | RDG2 Approvals | REG Applications | Offers | RSA Applications | Offers |
|---|---|---|---|---|---|
| Central | * | * | * | * | * |
| Dumfries and Galloway | 6 | — | — | * | * |
| Fife | * | * | * | 29 | 24 |
| Highland | — | — | — | * | * |
| Lothian | 176 | 29 | * | 27 | 26 |
| Strathclyde | 2,742 | 394 | 195 | 152 | 131 |
| Tayside | 218 | 31 | 15 | 29 | 24 |
| Western Isles | — | — | — | * | * |
| Location undecided | — | * | — | — | — |
| Total | 3,148 | 481 | 226 | 255 | 221 |

Notes: (i) RDG2 and REG are available in development areas. RSA is available in development and intermediate areas.

(ii) Starred figures are suppressed to avoid disclosure of information relating to individual businesses.

## HOME DEPARTMENT

### Bail Hostels

**Mr. Andrew F. Bennett:** To ask the Secretary of State for the Home Department what proposals for new bail hostels he has received from the Greater Manchester area; and what steps he is taking to encourage proposals.

**Mr. John Patten:** Following a meeting between officials and representatives of the Greater Manchester probation service on 1 December 1988 capital provision of £550,000 was allocated to provide about 50 new bail hostel places in Manchester by April 1990. On 9 March 1989 officials visited the Greater Manchester probation service to discuss their proposals which will involve two new bail hostels and additional places at two existing hostels.

### Criminal Injuries Compensation Board

**Mr. Campbell-Savours:** To ask the Secretary of State for the Home Department (1) what is the average time taken between an applicant to the Criminal Injuries Compensation Board applying for an appeal hearing and the appeal taking place;

(2) what is the average length of time taken between receipt of a claim and its single member adjudication by the Criminal Injuries Compensation Board.

**Mr. John Patten:** Information is not available in the form requested, but the percentage of cases resolved by the Criminal Injuries Compensation Board within certain periods of registration, either by single member adjudication or hearings determination, is shown at paragraphs 6 and 11 of the board's latest annual report (Cm. 536), a copy of which is in the Library.

**Mr. Campbell-Savours:** To ask the Secretary of State for the Home Department (1) how many claims to the Criminal Injuries Compensation Board are awaiting single member adjudication; and, of those, how many have been awaiting adjudication for over one year, two years, three years, four years and five years, respectively;

(2) what is the longest period that has been taken to reach single member adjudication in any claim to the Criminal Injuries Compensation Board;

(3) what plans there are to speed up the processing of claims to the Criminal Injuries Compensation Board; and if he will make a statement.

**Mr. John Patten:** The board does not keep detailed information about the length of time for which cases have awaited determination by a single member. On 1 June 1989, 69,480 applications were awaiting final determination by a single member. Interim assessments of compensation had been made in 2,828 of these cases.

To speed up the processing of claims the board's complement has been increased from 220 in 1987 to 320 now and a new office has been opened in Glasgow where recruitment is expected to be easier and turnover lower than in London. The board's new chairman is reviewing administrative procedures with the aim of reducing the time taken to resolve claims.

**Mr. Campbell-Savours:** To ask the Secretary of State for the Home Department (1) how many members of staff are employed by the Criminal Injuries Compensation Board;

(2) how many staff vacancies at the Criminal Injuries Compensation Board are presently being advertised;

(3) what is the present level of staff shortages as a percentage of the recommended full staff complement at the Criminal Injuries Compensation Board.

**Mr. John Patten:** On 23 June 1989 the board had the equivalent of 317 whole-time staff, 0·9 per cent. below its complement of 320, including 36 temporary staff engaged as part of the phased relocation of about 180 posts from London to Glasgow. The vacancies are being filled by interdepartmental trawl.

**Mr. Campbell-Savours:** To ask the Secretary of State for the Home Department what is the average length of time taken between the receipt of an appraisal by single member adjudication and receipt of a formal Criminal Injuries Compensation Board decision and the notification of the outcome to the applicant.

**Mr. John Patten:** Notification of a decision by a single member of the board is usually dispatched within two weeks of the date of the decision. Applicants whose claims are decided following a hearing are usually advised of the decision at the conclusion of the proceedings.

### Seat Belt Offences

**Mr. Amess:** To ask the Secretary of State for the Home Department (1) if he will publish in the *Official Report* a table showing the number of *(a)* males and *(b)* females (i) charged and (ii) convicted of failure to wear a seat belt in 1987 and 1988;

(2) if he will publish in the *Official Report* a table showing the number of *(a)* males and *(b)* females (i) 16 to 18, (ii) 19 to 21, (iii) 22 to 24, (iv) 25 to 30 and (v) 30 years and over who were *(aa)* charged and *(bb)* convicted of failure to wear a seat belt in 1987 and 1988.

**Mr. John Patten:** The latest available information is shown in the table. Information on the age of persons proceeded against for summary offences is not generally collected for those aged 21 and over. Since 1 October 1986, the police have been able to issue fixed penalty notices for seat belt offences as an alternative to prosecution. Further information is given in Home Office statistical bulletin issue 32/88, table 13 of which suggests that in 1987 there was a large rise in the enforcement of this legislation. Figures for 1988 will be published in the autumn.

*Proceedings at magistrates' courts for seat belt offences*

England and Wales 1987                                                                    *Number of offences*

| Age group | Males Proceeded against | Found guilty | Females Proceeded against | Found guilty |
|---|---|---|---|---|
| Under 16 | 16 | 13 | — | — |
| 16 to 18 | 341 | 285 | 29 | 26 |
| 19 to 20 | 655 | 555 | 49 | 43 |
| 21 and over | 7,497 | 6,094 | 563 | 488 |
| Total | 8,509 | 6,947 | 641 | 557 |

### Parties (Police Powers)

**Dr. Glyn:** To ask the Secretary of State for the Home Department (1) if he plans to seek further powers to enable the police to deal with large-scale party-style events held on private property;

(2) if he will call for a report from the Chief Constable of the Thames Valley on the events at White Waltham industrial estate on Saturday 24 June, and on the outcome of police inquiries into these events.

(3) if he will take steps to ensure that police and local authorities are aware in advance of the planned location of the large-scale party-style events planned for July.

**Mr. Hurd:** I have just received from the Chief Constable of Thames Valley a report on the incident at White Waltham on 24 June and I will consider the need for any further action in the light of his assessment of events. The police have been aware of the growth of these parties and, insofar as there may be a breach of the law or a risk to public safety, have taken action to prevent them where possible. I understand that the Metropolitan Police have been able to prevent in advance or shut down some 75 such parties so far this year.

In addition to continuing police action, those involved in these events should be aware that they may be in breach of existing public entertainment law. The controls exist to ensure that the local authority, police and fire services are given advance notice of events, that there are proper control and safety arrangements, and to minimise nuisance to the local community. It is already an offence to provide public entertainment involving music and dancing without a licence. The maximum penalty in Greater London is a fine of up to £2,000 plus imprisonment of up to three months. Outside Greater London, the fine is the same but imprisonment is not available.

There are also controls over nuisance caused by noise, for which the maximum penalty is a fine of up to £2,000.

We are satisfied that the existing law on the misuse of drugs is strong and adequate. At large gatherings of young people there is always the risk of drugs being used or supplied. The police attach high priority to drugs enforcement and action will be taken where necessary.

Those who hire out large premises would be well advised to exercise caution to establish the true purpose of the activity and inform the police if they are suspicious. Regular use of premises for purposes for which planning permission had not been obtained may result in enforcement action.

There is in being a comprehensive set of controls, backed up by offences, and penalties for those who commit them, to keep events within proper grounds.

I am considering whether there are any gaps in the law, but it is clear that the main need is for citizens who have advance knowledge of any party at which the law may be broken to give timely information to the police so that the law can be enforced.

### Prisons

**Mr. Vaz:** To ask the Secretary of State for the Home Department how many prisoners there were in Leicester prison as at *(a)* 26, *(b)* 23, *(c)* 16, *(d)* 9 and *(e)* 2 June, and *(f)* 26 *(g)* 19 and *(h)* 12 May 1989.

**Mr. Douglas Hogg:** The information requested is as follows:

| | *Numbers* |
|---|---|
| 26 June 1989 | 362 |
| 23 June 1989 | 365 |
| 16 June 1989 | 369 |
| 9 June 1989 | 389 |
| 2 June 1989 | 374 |
| 26 May 1989 | 381 |
| 19 May 1989 | 388 |
| 12 May 1989 | 379 |

## Immigration

**Mr. Madden:** To ask the Secretary of State for the Home Department when a decision is to be taken on the application of Mr. G. M. Tinwala—reference: T204490—to settle in the United Kingdom.

**Mr. Renton:** The British deputy high commission in Bombay was notified on 27 June that entry clearance may be issued to Mr. Tinwala.

**Mr. Nellist:** To ask the Secretary of State for the Home Department when the hon. Member for Coventry, South-East can expect to hear from his Department on the case of Mohammed Nazak and Miss Jurida Begum, reference N. 158192, whose papers were forwarded by the Foreign and Commonwealth Office to his Department on 6 February; and if he will make a statement.

**Mr. Renton:** I have replied to the hon. Member's letter of 6 June today.

## Road Accidents

**Mr. Nicholas Bennett:** To ask the Secretary of State for the Home Department what instructions are given to chief constables in relation to the inspection of tachographs and their charts following road accidents involving vehicles which are required to carry them.

**Mr. Douglas Hogg:** None. This is a matter for individual chief officers of police.

## Crime Prevention

**Mr. Maclennan:** To ask the Secretary of State for the Home Department if he has proposals to review the effectiveness of prison sentences in controlling crime; and if he will make a statement.

**Mr. John Patten:** Our views were set out in the Green Paper "Punishment, Custody and the Community" (Cm. 424), published in July last year.

## Commission for Racial Equality

**Mr. Bernie Grant:** To ask the Secretary of State for the Home Department (1) how many men from the ethnic groups *(a)* Afro-Caribbean or African, *(b)* Asian and *(c)* white have been appointed in the principal, director and chief executive grades of the Commission for Racial Equality;

(2) how many women from the ethnic groups *(a)* Afro-Caribbean or African, *(b)* Asian and *(c)* white have been appointed in the principal, director and chief executive grades of the Commission for Racial Equality.

**Mr. John Patten:** The information requested is as follows:

| | Chief Executive | Director | Principal |
|---|---|---|---|
| *Men* | | | |
| a. Afro-Caribbean and African | — | — | 1 |
| b. Asian | — | 1 | 5 |
| c. White | 1 | 1 | 7 |
| *Women* | | | |
| a. Afro-Caribbean and African | — | — | — |
| b. Asian | — | — | — |
| c. White | — | 2 | 2 |

## Prisoners (Rule 43)

**Mr. Cox:** To ask the Secretary of State for the Home Department how many people were on rule 43 in prisons in England and Wales on 1 June.

**Mr. Douglas Hogg** *[holding answer 14 June 1989]:* The latest readily available information is given in the table.

*Prisoners held in prison service establishments in England and Wales under prison rule 43 and young offender institution rule 46: by type of segregation, age group and sex, 30 April 1989*

| | Own protection | Good order or discipline |
|---|---|---|
| Aged under 21 | | |
| Males | 185 | 55 |
| Females | 17 | 3 |
| Adults | | |
| Males | 2,065 | 178 |
| Females | 35 | 9 |

# TRANSPORT

## Greenhouse Effect

**Ms. Ruddock:** To ask the Secretary of State for Transport if he has taken account of the implications for the greenhouse effect of his Department's forecast increase in vehicle miles of 83-142 per cent. by the year 2025 in his recent White Paper, "Roads for Prosperity" (Cm. 693);

(2) what account has been taken of environmental degradation including atmospheric pollution in his recent White Paper, "Roads for Prosperity" (Cm. 693).

**Mr. Peter Bottomley:** Road congestion is bad for the environment. It increases atmospheric pollution whereas free-flowing traffic cuts down on emissions and saves fuel.

The proposals in "Roads for Prosperity" will also have a major impact in improving the environment by taking traffic away from communities and off unsuitable roads. The emphasis in our programme on increasing the capacity of existing routes will help minimise its environmental impact. Protecting and enhancing the environment will continue to be a major feature of our road building plans.

I have sent the hon. Member a copy of the press notice No. 291 (28 June) which illustrates how exhaust fumes at the 1979 levels would be possible if economic driving and efficient maintenance were widespread.

**Ms. Ruddock:** To ask the Secretary of State for Transport what proposals his Department has put forward for reducing greenhouse gas emissions such as carbon dioxide and tropospheric ozone from road transport since the Prime Minister's seminar on the greenhouse effect on 26 April.

**Mr. Peter Bottomley:** At the Council of Environment Ministers held in Luxembourg on 8 and 9 June my noble Friend the Minister for Housing, Environment and Countryside supported tighter new limits on gaseous emissions from small cars. These gases are the precursors of tropospheric ozone. He was also successful in pressing the Commission to report back to the Council on measures that can be taken to combat carbon dioxide emissions from cars.

### Orange Badges

**Mr. David Porter:** To ask the Secretary of State for Transport whether he sought advice from organisations representing disabled people before deciding that eligibility for orange badges should not automatically be extended to those with upper limb disabilities.

**Mr. Peter Bottomley:** The decision that badges should continue to be restricted to people with severe mobility problems was made in the light of representations from the statutory disabled persons transport advisory committee (DPTAC).

The committee's constituent organisations include: the joint committee on mobility for the disabled, the Disabled Drivers Association, the Royal Association for Disability and Rehabilitation and the Disabled Drivers Motor Club. The majority of DPTAC's members are people with disabilities. We have accepted DPTAC's advice. We are taking medical advice on the mobility problems specific to Thalidomide victims. We are also in touch with the Thalidomide Trust and the Thalidomide Society.

Any individual who has a severe mobility problem may qualify for a badge, regardless of the medical cause of the problem.

### Channel Tunnel Rail Link

**Mr. Gerald Bowden:** To ask the Secretary of State for Transport what assessment he has made of *(a)* the effects of private sector involvement in the building of the Channel tunnel rail link and *(b)* whether the private sector has a role in appraisal of the design; and what financial advisers are employed by his Department to advise on private sector investment in building the Channel tunnel rail link.

**Mr. Portillo:** Our assessment will depend on the outcome of British Rail's current discussions with a number of private sector interests. The Department has not as yet appointed financial advisers on this matter.

### Aircraft (Near-Misses)

**Mr. Rhodes James:** To ask the Secretary of State for Transport whether he will ask the Air Accident Investigation Branch for an urgent report on the near-miss over Heathrow airport at approximately 07.30 hours on Saturday 26 June involving an Air Canada flight from London to Nice and another aircraft; and if he will make a statement.

**Mr. Peter Bottomley:** The Civil Aviation Authority which has statutory responsibility for the safety regulation of civil aviation within the United Kingdom, has no record of any near-miss incident occurring over Heathrow airport at the time specified on either Saturday 24 June or Monday 26 June.

### Severn Crossing

**Mr. Roy Hughes:** To ask the Secretary of State for Transport whether he will make arrangements for an exhibition at Westminister similar to the one currently on

display in venues in Gwent, together with a briefing by officials, in order for hon. Members on both sides of the Bristol channel to be fully informed of the proposals for the second Severn crossing.

**Mr. Peter Bottomley:** The exhibition—which explains proposed changes to the route of the approach roads to the second Severn crossing—is already being held at venues on both sides of the Bristol channel—at Caldicot 26 to 28 June; at Rogiet 29 June to 1 July; at Pilning 3 to 5 July; and at Avonmouth 7 and 8 July. Officials will be on hand throughout to respond to queries.

Hon. Members with a constituency interest were told in advance about the exhibition. Any hon. Member unable to attend should write to me; it may be possible to arrange a separate viewing for them of the display material at a later date.

### Unleaded Petrol

**Dame Jill Knight:** To ask the Secretary of State for Transport what information he has on whether car engines deteriorate more quickly when only lead-free petrol is used in them.

**Mr. Peter Bottomley:** Most of the information available to the Department comes from the United States, where there is more than a decade of experience with running on unleaded petrol. It has been found that components of the drivetrain, such as spark plugs and exhaust systems may last longer with unleaded petrol. There is no indication of damage from unleaded petrol when engines are designed for its use.

Using unleaded petrol in a vehicle for which it is not designed could result in serious damage.

### British Rail (Safety)

**Mr. Patchett:** To ask the Secretary of State for Transport (1) if he will list *(a)* the number of reports he has received from the railways inspectorate, *(b)* the number recommending prosecutions, and *(c)* the number of prosecutions taken up and the outcome for each of the past 10 years;

(2) if he will list *(a)* the number of deaths on British Rail premises each year in the last 10 years and *(b)* the number of prosecutions for such deaths and the outcome of the prosecutions.

**Mr. Portillo:** The number of deaths on British Rail premises during the period 1979-88 is in table A. Table B shows the number of prosecutions arising from incidents involving fatalities and the outcome. The decision to go ahead with prosecutions under the Health and Safety at Work etc. Act 1974 is a matter solely for the chief inspecting officer of railways. He does not consult my right hon. Friend before proceeding. Details of all prosecutions, and their outcome, during the period 1980-1988 were set out in my answer of 4 May 1989, at column *118* to the hon. Member for Southwark and Bermondsey (Mr. Hughes) There were no prosecutions in 1979.

*Table A*
*Fatal Accidents on BR Premises 1979-1988*

| Year | Passengers | Staff | Other Persons | Total |
|------|-----------|-------|---------------|-------|
| 1979 | 52 | 43 | 12 | 107 |
| 1980 | 26 | 32 | 11 | 69 |
| 1981 | 39 | 27 | 10 | 76 |

| Year | Passengers | Staff | Other Persons | Total |
|------|-----------|-------|--------------|-------|
| 1982 | 20 | 27 | 10 | 57 |
| 1983 | 29 | 28 | 12 | 69 |
| 1984 | 39 | 25 | 12 | 76 |
| 1985 | 33 | 25 | 16 | 74 |
| 1986 | 32 | 16 | 24 | 72 |

| Year | Passengers | Staff | Other Persons | Total |
|------|-----------|-------|--------------|-------|
| 1987 | 68 | 16 | 20 | 104 |
| 1988 | [1] | [1] | [1] | [1] |

[1] Figures for 1988 not yet available.

*Table B*
*Prosecutions involving fatalities 1979-1988*

| Prosecution in respect of incident at | Number of fatalities involved | Date of first proceedings | Outcome |
|---|---|---|---|
| Denham Station | 3 | 25 April 1983 | Not Guilty. |
| Barking Station | 1 | 3 December 1984 | Guilty, fined £1,000 plus £500 costs (BRB appealed successfully and costs awarded against HSE). |
| Birmingham International | 1 | 10 September 1984 | Absolute discharge. |
| Coquet Viaduct | 2 | 23 September 1985 | Guilty, fined £1,250 plus £1,100 costs. |
| Glasgow Central Station | 1 | 2 July 1985 | Company, which was in liquidation, received an admonition. |
| Liverpool Street Station | 1 | 13 January 1987 | Guilty, fined £5,000 plus £900 costs. |

## Street Lighting

**Ms. Walley:** To ask the Secretary of State for Transport how much money has been spent by each county council highways authority on street lighting in 1988-89 and 1989-90; and what percentage that money is of the total amount spent on roads, by each county.

**Mr. Peter Bottomley:** Figures for local authority spending on street lighting are not yet available for the years in question.

## Capital Expenditure

**Sir William Shelton:** To ask the Secretary of State for Transport what was the capital expenditure invested in *(a)* Rail Network SouthEast and *(b)* London Underground in 1988-89.

**Mr. Portillo:** This information will be published in the 1989-90 annual report and accounts for British Rail and London Regional Transport. Both documents will be published shortly.

## M3

**Mr. Hanley:** To ask the Secretary of State for Transport what information he has on the state of the surface of the M3 between junctions 4 and 2, London-bound; and when repairs are scheduled to take place.

**Mr. Peter Bottomley:** This length of motorway is in need of surface maintenance. The necessary work is planned for early next year.

## Highways

**Ms. Walley:** To ask the Secretary of State for Transport what allocation each county council highways authority has made in 1988-89 and 1989-90 for non-major schemes.

**Mr. Peter Bottomley:** No figures are available yet for 1989-90. The counties' 1988-89 budgets for capital expenditure on schemes costing less than £1 million were as follows:

*1988-89 budgets for capital expenditure on schemes costing under £1 million*

| Authority | (£'000) |
|---|---|
| Avon | 2,399 |
| Bedfordshire | 1,549 |
| Berkshire | 3,887 |
| Buckinghamshire | 1,729 |
| Cambridgeshire | 1,660 |
| Cheshire | 4,720 |
| Cleveland | 1,990 |
| Cornwall | 1,381 |
| Cumbria | 1,995 |
| Derbyshire | 8,693 |
| Devon | 2,758 |
| Dorset | 2,848 |
| Durham | 1,884 |
| East Sussex | 4,335 |
| Essex | 3,339 |
| Gloucestershire | 2,173 |
| Hampshire | 6,490 |
| Hereford and Worcestershire | 2,098 |
| Hertfordshire | 2,445 |
| Humberside | 1,921 |
| Isle of Wight | 1,894 |
| Kent | 8,010 |
| Lancashire | 2,553 |
| Leicestershire | 2,740 |
| Lincolnshire | 4,210 |
| Norfolk | 3,586 |
| Northamptonshire | 2,546 |
| Northumberland | 1,219 |
| North Yorkshire | 3,098 |
| Nottinghamshire | 8,013 |
| Oxfordshire | 2,351 |
| Shropshire | 467 |
| Somerset | 3,524 |
| Staffordshire | 3,374 |
| Suffolk | 2,474 |
| Surrey | 2,946 |
| Warwickshire | 2,812 |
| West Sussex | 1,700 |
| Wiltshire | 1,782 |

## Docklands (Traffic Delays)

**Mr. Sheerman:** To ask the Secretary of State for Transport (1) for how long the hon. Member for Enfield, Southgate (Mr. Portillo) was delayed in traffic on his visit to Luciano Pavarotti's concert in docklands; what representations he has received on traffic delays in the docklands area; and if he will increase planned expenditure on road links between central London and docklands;

(2) if, given the considerable traffic delays encountered by those attending last Sunday's London Arena concert by Luciano Pavarotti, he will speed up work on *(a)* roads and *(b)* communications generally for the London docklands.

**Mr. Portillo** *[holding answer 26 June 1989]:* It took me just over an hour from Westminster to the Arena, which is about the time I allow for journeys to major events at Earls Court, Wimbledon and so on. It was perhaps a pity that more people did not choose to travel by docklands light railway, which was operated especially for the Pavarotti concert.

The Department and the London Docklands development corporation have very large road programmes which are being pursued with all possible urgency. On the A13 trunk road in Tower Hamlets and Newham, over £60 million of schemes will provide interim and permanent improvements to every major junction and bridge over the next seven years. These schemes form part of the Department's £600 million programme for trunk roads in east London of which the Sidcup bypass, South Woodford to Barking relief road, Rochester way relief road and Beckton flyover tidal flow are already complete, and others in hand include the A406 Chingford road to Hale End road improvement, the A12 Hackney Wick to M11 link road and the proposed east London river crossing, on the design of which we hope to make an announcement shortly. With refurbishment of the Blackwall tunnel south bore now nearing completion, we hope to tackle the north bore in offpeak periods over the two years from September. We have also invited tenders for a new traffic control and communications system for east London to be located at Blackwall.

The London Docklands development corporation's £550 million programme of access roads includes schemes already complete in the Surrey docks and under way at the Royal docks. Work will start later this year on a new crossing over the lower Lea, and the compulsory purchase order has now been made for the proposed 1·5 km dual two-lane cut-and-cover tunnel from The Highway to Westferry road and Poplar, known as the Limehouse link.

The Department is working closely on co-ordination of streetworks with the utilities, developers, the police and the LDDC which has commissioned a study into extending the controlled parking zone to docklands.

On public transport, the reliability of the docklands light railway is being improved with an urgent programme of remedial measures. Capacity will be trebled on completion of the extension to Bank, and the Bill for a link to Beckton is now completing its parliamentary passage. I am about to receive the report of the east London rail study recommending extension of the Jubilee line through Surrey docks, Canary wharf and the Greenwich peninsula to Stratford, for which we shall be seeking contributions from developers. Subject to satisfactory contributions, LRT could deposit the necessary Bill in Parliament in November. British Rail is introducing longer trains in October on its north London link, where capacity will be increased by a tunnel refurbishment to be funded by LDDC. The new network of docklands minibus routes usefully complements London Regional Transport's improved docklands bus services, and Thamesline riverbus services are being extended to Greenland and Greenwich piers.

My chairmanship of a steering group comprising operators, boroughs, utilities, developers, the police and the LDDC enables me to help keep the momentum up and to intervene whenever necessary to facilitate action.

I am satisfied that the docklands transport programmes are appropriate and are being progressed as fast as possible.

## PRIME MINISTER

### Water Privatisation

Q13. **Mr. Leigh:** To ask the Prime Minister if she has received representations regarding water privatisation.

Q105. **Mr. Goodlad:** To ask the Prime Minister if she has received recent representations regarding water privatisation.

**The Prime Minister:** I receive many representations about water privatisation, which provides the best framework and conditions for achieving even higher standards of water quality.

### United States of America

Q71. **Mr. Malins:** To ask the Prime Minister if she has received representations regarding relations with the United States of America.

**The Prime Minister:** No.

### Berlin Wall

Q83. **Mr. Cash:** To ask the Prime Minister if she has received representations regarding the Berlin wall.

**The Prime Minister:** There is widespread concern in Britain about the Berlin wall and the shootings which took place there earlier this year. Such barriers to freedom have no place in Europe today. We look forward to the day when the wall is torn down.

### Competition Policy

Q89. **Mr. Page:** To ask the Prime Minister if she has received representations concerning competition policy.

**The Prime Minister:** I receive many and varied representations about the Government's policies which seek to extend competition and opportunity.

### Peterstene Wentlooge

Q95. **Mr. Flynn:** To ask the Prime Minister whether she intends to pay an official visit to the Peterstene Wentlooge area of Newport, West.

**The Prime Minister:** I have at present no plans to do so.

### Small Businesses

Q98. **Mr. William Powell:** To ask the Prime Minister if she has received representations regarding the performance of small businesses.

**The Prime Minister:** No specific representations have been received. The small firms sector is flourishing in the beneficial climate the Government have created for businesses. Estimated, unadjusted figures for last year are already showing a record rate of new business formation, net of closures, of 1,300 new businesses a week.

### Self-employment

Q100. **Mr. Marland:** To ask the Prime Minister if she has received representations regarding self-employment.

**The Prime Minister:** I receive many letters from people who have become self-employed or who are thinking of setting up their own businesses. Many refer to the satisfaction they have found in setting up in business, having taken advantage of the improved climate for enterprise in this country. This improvement is reflected in the increase by 1 million in the number of self-employed people in the United Kingdom since this Government came into office.

### City of London

Q101. **Sir Anthony Grant:** To ask the Prime Minister if she has received representations regarding the performance of the City of London.

**The Prime Minister:** I regularly discuss the performance of the City which makes an important contribution to our economic prosperity.

### Environment Protection

Q102. **Sir Hugh Rossi:** To ask the Prime Minister if she has received representations regarding the protection of the environment.

**The Prime Minister:** I have received a number of representations regarding the environment. The Government have undertaken a great many measures to improve the quality of the environment. We intend to bring forward further legislative proposals shortly.

### National Heritage

Q104. **Mr. Alexander:** To ask the Prime Minister if she has received representations regarding the national heritage.

**The Prime Minister:** My right hon. Friends and I receive representations frequently. The national heritage is vital to the quality of life.

### Ozone Layer

Q107. **Mr. Bowis:** To ask the Prime Minister if she has received recent representations regarding the ozone layer.

**The Prime Minister:** I have received many representations regarding the ozone layer.

### Yorkshire and Humberside

Q149. **Mr. Cryer:** To ask the Prime Minister when she next expects to pay a visit to Yorkshire and Humberside.

**The Prime Minister:** I have at present no plans to do so.

### British Rail (Land)

**Mr. Adley:** To ask the Prime Minister if she will make it her policy not to require British Rail to dispose of railway land from which railway services have been withdrawn.

**The Prime Minister:** I understand that before British Rail declare unused railway land non-operational, they normally take account of possible future railway requirements.

### Family Problems

**Mr. Boswell:** To ask the Prime Minister if she will co-ordinate action to tackle current problems of the family.

**The Prime Minister:** The present arrangements for co-ordination between Government Departments ensure that full consideration is given to all matters affecting the family.

### Rain Forests

**Mr. Dalyell:** To ask the Prime Minister whether Commissioner Carla Ripa Di Meana had any consultations with Her Majesty's Government before arranging *(a)* to meet representatives of the Green party and *(b)* to make contact with non-governmental organisations concerned with the rain forest in Britain; and if she will make a statement.

**The Prime Minister:** No. I understand that the European Commission is prepared to listen to the views of all bodies with an interest in the environment, including Opposition parties and non-governmental organisations. They are not obliged to consult the Governments of member states of the European Community before doing so. Her Majesty's Government have had regular and detailed discussions with the Commissioner on a wide range of environmental issues since he took up his post in January of this year.

### Import Licences

**Mr. Ron Davies:** To ask the Prime Minister if she will list all those gifts received by her or her Ministers during the past five years which have required an import licence under the conventions on international trade in endangered species; and how many such applications were *(a)* initially granted, *(b)* granted on appeal and *(c)* refused.

**The Prime Minister:** This information is not readily obtainable and could be provided only at disproportionate cost.

### Community Charge

**Mr. Patchett:** To ask the Prime Minister if she will make an official visit to South Yorkshire and the Barnsley, East constituency to explain Government policy on the poll tax.

**The Prime Minister:** I have at present no plans to do so. The Government have no plans for any poll tax. The Government policy on and implications of the community charge have been fully set out in the excellent leaflets published by the Department of the Environment and the Welsh Office.

### Malaysia

**Miss Lestor:** To ask the Prime Minister, pursuant to her answer of 23 June, *Official Report,* column 276, whether any of the clarifications by which the Government made clear to the Malaysian Government, on a number of occasions in 1988, that they were willing to consider Malaysian requests for aid were contained in correspondence which also related to the arms sales package, the memorandum of understanding of which was they were signed in 1988.

**The Prime Minister:** The contents of Government-to-Government correspondence are confidential. As the hon. Member will be aware from the reply of my right hon. Friend the Minister for Overseas Development to her earlier question on 19 June at column *18* we have been giving grant aid to Malaysia since well before negotiations on the defence sales package began.

### Engagements

**Mr. Barry Field:** To ask the Prime Minister if she will list her official engagements for Thursday 29 June.

**Mr. Stern:** To ask the Prime Minister if she will list her official engagements for Thursday 29 June.

**Mr. David Shaw:** To ask the Prime Minister if she will list her official engagements for Thursday 29 June.

**Mr. Harry Greenway:** To ask the Prime Minister if she will list her official engagements for Thursday 29 June.

**Mr. Win Griffiths:** To ask the Prime Minister if she will list her official engagements for Thursday 29 June.

**Mr. Tredinnick:** To ask the Prime Minister if she will list her official engagements for Thursday 29 June.

**The Prime Minister:** This morning I presided at a meeting of the Cabinet and had meetings with ministerial colleagues and others. In addition to my duties in the House I shall be having further meetings later today.

## DEFENCE

### Port Calls

**Mr. Snape:** To ask the Secretary of State for Defence if he will list all the dates of port calls by Royal Naval vessels to foreign ports in 1987, 1988 and 1989; and what are the dates of planned port calls up to 1990.

**Mr. Archie Hamilton:** It is not our normal practice to disclose planned port visits by Royal Navy vessels, but I will write to the hon. Member about the first part of his question.

**Mr. Snape:** To ask the Secretary of State for Defence what importance the Government attach to visits by Royal Naval vessels to foreign ports; and what is the Government's policy regarding port calls.

**Mr. Archie Hamilton:** The Government attach great importance to visits to foreign ports by Her Majesty's ships. Port calls help to forge and maintain links with other countries and navies and, by providing opportunities for rest and recreation, play a prominent part in maintaining crew morale. Visits are also made for operational reasons, such as to take on supplies and fuel, and can offer opportunities to display British technology which can be of direct benefit to United Kingdom industry.

It is our policy to encourage Royal Navy visits to foreign ports and, where appropriate, to reciprocate by welcoming foreign naval vessels to United Kingdom ports.

### Public Relations

**Mr. Blair:** To ask the Secretary of State for Defence which public relations firms his Department has employed and at what cost, for each year since 1979.

**Mr. Archie Hamilton:** Apart from the special circumstances of privatisation work, the consistent practice of successive Governments has been to avoid the use of public relations firms or other firms outside Government for public relations work.

### Low Flying

**Ms. Short:** To ask the Secretary of State for Defence if he will list all the areas in the United Kingdom where low flying at 250 ft is permitted and where ultra low flying at 100 ft is permitted; and which of these areas is used by naval aircraft or aircraft assigned to naval operations.

**Mr. Neubert:** Since the introduction of the revised United Kingdom low flying system in 1979, the whole of Great Britain has, in principle, been open to low flying down to 250 feet except for major conurbations, danger zones and certain areas such as civil and military air traffic zones, airports and glider sites. Flying down to 100 feet is permitted only in three sparsely populated areas in northern Scotland, central Wales and the Borders. The United Kingdom low flying system as a whole is available for use by Royal Navy aircraft where their role makes such training necessary.

**Ms. Short:** To ask the Secretary of State for Defence what percentage of low flying sorties over the United Kingdom were flown by naval aircraft or aircraft assigned to naval operations in 1987 and 1988.

**Mr. Neubert:** Central records are not held in a form that would allow this information to be provided.

**Mr. Alan Williams:** To ask the Secretary of State for Defence when he first received information from the right hon. Member for Swansea, West about a low-flying Royal Air Force aircraft's simulated attack on Swansea airport; when he intends to let him know the outcome of the Department's inquiries into the allegation of low flying; and if he will give detailed reasons for the delay.

**Mr. Neubert:** As the right hon. Member will recall, I met him on the evening of Monday 30 January to discuss several alleged low flying incidents in the west Swansea area. I wrote to the right hon. Member on 1 February with full details of the incident involving a simulated attack on Swansea airport by a Royal Air Force aircraft. I also wrote to the right hon. Member on 19 May about a separate incident on 24 January. I hope to be able to write to the right hon. Member shortly about another incident in the Swansea area on 20 January, into which the RAF police investigation has not yet been concluded, but I am not aware that either of these incidents involved Swansea airport.

### Ministry Houses, Barton Stacey

**Sir David Mitchell:** To ask the Secretary of State for Defence how many houses the Ministry of Defence owns at Barton Stacey; and, of these, how many were empty on 31 March in each year from 1986 to 1989.

**Mr. Neubert:** The Army's stock of married quarters and vacancies at 31 March for each of the years 1986 to 1989 was as follows:

|  | *Stock* | *Vacancies* |
|---|---|---|
| 31 March 1986 | 161 | 29 |
| 31 March 1987 | 161 | 86 |
| 31 March 1988 | 138 | 35 |
| 31 March 1989 | 138 | 27 |

Of the 27 vacancies at 31 March this year, seven were already allocated to nominated incomers, one was awaiting repair and 10 were already being processed for disposal and will shortly be advertised under the discounted sale to service men scheme.

### Nuclear Weapons

**Mr. Cartwright:** To ask the Secretary of State for Defence what agreement has been concluded with the United States Government relating to the development of a stand-off nuclear missile to replace the WE177 free-fall nuclear bomb.

**Mr. Archie Hamilton:** We are still studying a number of procurement options for possible replacement of the WE177 free fall nuclear bomb, but no decisions have yet been taken.

### Nuclear Submarines (Swansea)

**Mr. Alan Williams:** To ask the Secretary of State for Defence what approvals are required for a nuclear submarine berth to be established at the port of Swansea; and which approvals have been obtained so far.

**Mr. Archie Hamilton:** All berths for nuclear-powered submarines require the approval of the nuclear-powered warships safety committee, an independent committee whose members include national experts on nuclear safety matters. The nuclear-powered warships safety committee reports to the Secretary of State for Defence on all public safety aspects of the use of a berth by nuclear-powered warships. If a berth is approved by the nuclear-powered warships safety committee, a final decision on its use is taken by this Department, in consultation with local and port authorities.

Since I replied to the hon. Member for Clwyd, South-West (Mr. Jones) on 26 June at column *371,* the nuclear-powered warships safety committee has given its approval for a berth at Swansea to be used by nuclear-powered submarines: further discussions between Ministry of Defence officials and local and port authorities will follow.

### Trucks Supply

**Sir Hal Miller:** To ask the Secretary of State for Defence when the result of the competition to supply 4-tonne trucks to the services will be made known.

**Mr. Sainsbury:** Detailed appraisal of the results of demanding and comprehensive user and evaluation trials of vehicles supplied by the three competing companies— AWD Ltd, Leyland DAF and Volvo (GB) Ltd.—has now been completed. This, together with a comparative assessment of the three companies' commercial proposals in terms of both capital purchase and whole life costs make it clear that the Leyland DAF vehicle is the one giving best value for money. I am pleased to anounce, therefore, that we shall shortly be placing an order with Leyland DAF for the supply of 4-tonne trucks to meet the services'

requirements over the period 1990-91 to 1994-95. I should add that the competition provided an excellent example of the effectiveness of our procurement policy. It was hard fought between three very good companies, any one of whose vehicles would have met the services' requirements.

## EDUCATION AND SCIENCE

### Food Research

69. **Mr. Tom Clarke:** To ask the Secretary of State for Education and Science if he will make a statement about the future of the institutes of food research in Reading, Norwich and Bristol.

**Mr. Jackson:** The AFRC has taken the decision, consistent with the policy outlined in its corporate plan, to consolidate the work of the Institute of Food Research at the Reading and Norwich sites and to secure the future of the laboratories. The restructured institute will allow for greater emphasis on key areas such as food safety. The laboratory at Langford, Bristol will cease to be part of the institute by the end of 1990.

70. **Mr. Cryer:** To ask the Secretary of State for Education and Science how many research workers will be made redundant by the closure of the food research centre at Bristol; and if he will make a statement.

**Mr. Jackson:** Although there will be redundancies arising from the withdrawal of AFRC funding from the Bristol laboratory of the Institute of Food Research, it is not possible at this stage to state precisely the number of research workers involved. The detailed implementation of staffing changes for the institute as a whole, following the restructuring plan announced by AFRC, is now being determined; every effort will be made to keep compulsory redundancies to a minimum. With respect to the Bristol laboratory, there will be opportunities for the redeployment of some of its scientists, to new scientific posts and other vacancies within the remaining institute laboratories at Reading and Norwich, within the agricultural and food research service and elsewhere.

### Sport

**Mr. Pendry:** To ask the Secretary of State for Education and Science when he will respond to those parts of the report "Sport and Young People, Partnership and Action" produced by the school sport forum in July 1988 which relate to his departmental responsibilities.

**Mrs. Rumbold:** My right hon. Friends the Secretaries of State for Education and Science and for the Environment will issue a joint response shortly.

### City Technology Colleges

**Mr. Dykes:** To ask the Secretary of State for Education and Science if he will give an updated report on progress so far with the establishment of various city technology colleges.

**Mr. Butcher:** I refer my hon. Friend to the reply that my right hon. Friend gave on 6 June to my hon. Friend the Member for Wyre Forest (Mr. Coombs) *Official Report,* column *10.*

**Mr. Straw:** To ask the Secretary of State for Education and Science if he will publish a table in the *Official Report* in respect of city technology colleges, giving, in respect of each city technology college or proposed or planned city technology college, information as to *(a)* name, site, and local authority, *(b)* numbers of pupils, *(c)* total cost, *(d)* maximum amount of Exchequer contribution by way of (i) grant and (ii) loans, *(e)* amount of sponsors' contributions whether in cash or kind and names of principal sponsors, *(f)* the nature of any contracts for the supply of goods or services awarded to sponsors, or close associates of sponsors, and their names, *(g)* whether closure of an existing school is involved, *(h)* whether any ballot of parents has been held and (i) what level of teachers' salaries are paid.

**Mr. Kenneth Baker:** The information requested by the right hon. Member is as follows:

| | Kingshurst | Gateshead | Bradford | Dartford | The British school for performing arts and technology | Nottingham | Teesside |
|---|---|---|---|---|---|---|---|
| Name | Kingshurst CTC | Tyneside CTC | Bradford CTC | Dartford CTC | The British School for Performing Arts and Technology | Djanogly CTC | Macmillan College |
| Site | Former Kingshurst School site | St. John Fisher School site | Part of Newby Square site | Downs School site | Share of site currently occupied by Selhurst Tertiary Centre | Site of the former Players Warehouse, Sherwood Rise, Nottingham | St. Michael RC School site, Dunstable Road, Middlesbro |
| LEA | Solihull | Gateshead | Bradford | Kent | Croydon | Nottingham-shire | Cleveland |
| Planned number of pupils | 1,000 | 900 | 980 | 1,250 | 720 | 990 | 1,050 |
| Total cost[1] | £9·65 million | To be determined | To be determined | To be determined | To be determined | £9·05 million | £7·5 million |
| Exchequer contribution i) grant ii) loans | £7·55 million | To be determined | To be determined | To be determined | To be determined | £7·655 million | £5·625 million |
| Sponsors' contribution i) cash[2] ii) in hand | £2·1 million | £1·13 million[3] | £1 million[3] | £1·2 million | To be determined | £1·4 million | £1·875 million |
| Principal sponsors | Hanson's plc, Lucas plc and over 70 supporting sponsors | Group of local businessmen —Peter Vardy, Albert Dicken, John Laing plc and Argyle Group plc | Dixons plc | G. Leigh of Allied London Properties, Wellcome Foundation | The British Record Industry Trust | Mr. Harry Djanogly, Boots, W. H. Smith | BAT Industries, Cameron Hall Develop-ments, British Steel, Davy Corporation |
| Contracts awarded to sponsors or close associates and names | None | Building contract— Laings Northern | None | None | None | None | None |
| Is closure of an existing school involved | No | No | No | Yes | No | No | No |
| Has a ballot of parents been held and with what result | No | No | No | No[4] | No | No | No |

[1] This covers only the initial capital costs of establishing the CTC. It does not include revenue costs.

[2] Sponsors' contribution to date. Funding raising continues in each project. This includes contributions in kind which are as yet uncosted.

[3] Confirmed sponsorship to date.

[4] Public consultations were held by Kent on its proposals to close the Downs school. One statutory objection containing 62 signatures was made to the section 12 proposal subsequently published.

In addition sponsors have announced plans for the establishment of CTCs in the premises of the Sylvan school, Croydon, the Haberdashers' Aske's schools, Hatcham, and the Bacon's school, Bermondsey. These all involve the closure or discontinuance of the existing schools under the provisions of either section 12 of the 1980 Education Act or section 14 of the 1944 Education Act. I have made clear that any such proposals which come to me will be treated strictly on their merits and it would be inappropriate to comment further. CTCs are independent schools and it will be for their governors to determine what level of salaries are paid to their staff. However, my recurrent grant to CTCs will be comparable to what LEAs spend on maintained schools in similar areas, including expenditure on staff salaries.

### Higher Education (Consultative Paper)

**Mr. Menzies Campbell:** To ask the Secretary of State for Education and Science what representations he has received in relation to his consultative paper, "Shifting the Balance of Public Funding of Higher Education to Fees."

**Mr. Jackson:** We have received more than 150 almost wholly favourable responses.

### Crack

**Mr. Butler:** To ask the Secretary of State for Education and Science if he will list the 15 inner-city areas targeted by education co-ordinators in a campaign to persuade teenagers to say no to crack; and if he will make a statement.

**Mr. Butcher:** The Government believe that it would be counterproductive to identify particular localities. Local education authorities' drugs education co-ordinators are intensifying their efforts and collaborating with other agencies and the wider local communities in all areas where crack appears to them to be an actual or potential problem. The Government are ready to support local efforts of this sort, and are in touch with local agencies about appropriate means of doing so.

### Expenditure

**Mr. Churchill:** To ask the Secretary of State for Education and Science what has been the cumulative total of his Department's expenditure since May 1979 to date over and above the expenditure level prevailing in May 1979.

**Mrs. Rumbold:** The total programme of the Department of Education and Science in 1979 and each subsequent financial year is given in the table below:

| Expenditure (outturn) | |
|---|---|
| *Financial year* | *£ million* |
| 1979-80 | 8,945 |
| 1980-81 | 10,899 |
| 1981-82 | 11,841 |
| 1982-83 | 12,741 |
| 1983-84 | 13,421 |
| 1984-85 | 13,940 |
| 1985-86 | 14,410 |
| 1986-87 | 15,659 |
| 1987-88 | 17,081 |
| 1988-89 | [1]18,412 |
| 1989-90 | [2]19,571 |

[1] Estimated outturn.
[2] Plans.

### School Closures

**Mr. Straw:** To ask the Secretary of State for Education and Science how many proposals for *(a)* closure and *(b)* reorganisation of schools he has received during the current academic year; how many school places these represent; how many such closures and reorganisations he has approved and how many school places these decisions represent; what was the target for the year; and if he will give comparable figures for each academic year since 1979.

**Mr. Kenneth Baker:** The information is not available in the form requested. The available data is summarised in the following table.

| Calendar year | Number of proposals decided | Number of places to be taken out of use by proposals in column 2 | Number of proposals in column 2 approved | Number of surplus places to be taken out of use as a result of approved proposals |
|---|---|---|---|---|
| *(1)* | *(2)* | *(3)* | *(4)* | *(5)* |
| 1983 | 366 | 104,174 | 330 | 85,606 |
| 1984 | 292 | 85,862 | 270 | 77,590 |
| 1985 | 205 | 101,097 | 185 | 88,218 |
| 1986 | 172 | 81,663 | 147 | 62,828 |
| 1987 | 159 | 55,116 | 134 | 45,326 |
| 1988 | 145 | 64,256 | 116 | 27,170 |

The Government's national targets for the removal of surplus places cannot be directly compared with the figures in column 5 since the former also include places taken out of use as a result of the rationalisation of split sites, mothballed classrooms and the removal of temporary accommodation. In 1987-88 a total of 124,000 places were taken out of use against the national target of 139,000.

### Teachers' Resignations

**Mr. Straw:** To ask the Secretary of State for Education and Science how many teachers had submitted resignations by 31 May 1989.

**Mr. Kenneth Baker:** This information is not available. The latest data are for the year ending March 1987, when 28,960 teachers left full-time service in the maintained nursery, primary and secondary sector in England. Of these, 1,760 transferred to full-time service elsewhere in the maintained sector in England and Wales and 2,900 to part-time service in the maintained sector. A further 8,500 retired and 450 died.

### Foreign Languages

**Mr. Straw:** To ask the Secretary of State for Education and Science if he will publish a progress report on his drive to improve the teaching of foreign languages announced on 16 June 1986.

**Mr. Kenneth Baker:** The Government attach great importance to improving the nation's skills in modern foreign languages. That is reflected in our policy on modern foreign languages in the school curriculum was set out in the January 1988 policy statement "Modern Languages in the School Curriculum", and in the inclusion among the national curriculum foundation subjects of a modern foreign language to be studied by all pupils between the ages of 11 and 16.

From this autumn, pupils will have to study a modern foreign language for a reasonable time in the first three years of secondary schooling. This requirement will be extended to the last two years of compulsory schooling later. My right hon. Friend the Secretary of State for Wales and I published on 19 May the Education (National Curriculum) (Modern Foreign Languages) Order 1989 under section 3(2)(b) of the Education Reform Act 1988, specifying those languages eligible to be taught as the national curriculum foundation subject.

Within this framework, and to implement the 1988 policy statement, I am encouraging schools to offer a greater diversity of languages and I am providing education support grants for pilot projects in some local education authorities in England to promote the preparation and implementation of plans for language diversification. Schools will be free to offer a second foreign language during the 11 to 16 phase or in the sixth form in addition to meeting the national curriculum requirements. I hope that greater numbers studying a language to the age of 16 will result in an increase in those continuing with language learning not only in the sixth form but in post-school education.

Changes in examinations at 16 and 18 will improve standards of oral and written communication.

I shall shortly be announcing the establishment of a national curriculum working group on modern foreign languages with a view to beginning to implement the first attainment targets and programmes of study in schools from autumn 1992.

### Students

**Mr. Straw:** To ask the Secretary of State for Education and Science what are the number of *(a)* full-time students, *(b)* part-time students expressed as full-time equivalents, in first degree courses, for each year since 1979 to date in *(a)* universities, *(b)* polytechnics and *(c)* other institutions of higher education.

**Mr. Kenneth Baker:** The readily available information is shown in the following table:

*First degree students in Great Britain*

Thousands

| | 1979 | 1980 | 1981 | 1982 | 1983 | 1984 | 1985 | 1986 | 1987 |
|---|---|---|---|---|---|---|---|---|---|
| | | | | *Academic year beginning in* | | | | | |
| *Full-time* | | | | | | | | | |
| University | 241·2 | 247·8 | 250·2 | 246·9 | 240·8 | 237·8 | 238·3 | 241·1 | 245·6 |
| Polytechnics and colleges | 127·5 | 130·8 | 147·2 | 161·0 | 171·3 | 178·0 | 181·0 | 186·9 | 195·3 |
| *Full-time equivalent of part-time*[1] | | | | | | | | | |
| Open University | 21·4 | 21·0 | 22·1 | 23·2 | 23·4 | 23·6 | 23·2 | 23·8 | 25·0 |
| Other universities | 0·9 | 1·0 | 1·1 | 1·2 | 1·3 | 1·5 | 1·6 | 1·6 | 1·8 |
| Polytechnics and colleges | 5·8 | 5·9 | 6·3 | 6·6 | 7·0 | 7·3 | 7·8 | 8·3 | 8·8 |

[1] For consistency between sectors all part-time students have been counted as 0·35 FTE.

### Teacher Shortages (Tower Hamlets)

**Mr. Straw:** To ask the Secretary of State for Education and Science what proposals he has for securing the education of children in Tower Hamlets who are presently unable to attend school as a consequence of teacher shortages.

**Mr. Kenneth Baker:** The staffing of schools in Tower Hamlets is a matter for the Inner London education authority and, from 1 April 1990, the borough of Tower Hamlets. I welcome the fact that both authorities are now taking specific steps to ensure that schools are adequately staffed.

I had a constructive meeting on 13 June with the Inner London education authority, accompanied by the right hon. Member for Bethnal Green and Stepney (Mr. Shore); further discussions are being held at official level to explore ways of tackling the situation.

### Secondary Schools Staffing Survey

**Mr. Straw:** To ask the Secretary of State for Education and Science (1) when he will publish the full results of the secondary schools staffing survey;

(2) when, and in what form, the secondary schools staffing survey was published; and whether *(a)* any press notice was issued to accompany it and *(b)* any briefing for the press by Ministers or officials was held.

**Mr. Kenneth Baker:** Key results from the 1988 secondary school staffing survey were placed in the Library of the House on 2 May, and issued under a press notice on 3 May. The results included summary analyses of teachers by age and qualification by subject, their deployment on subject teaching, the percentages of secondary pupils studying different subjects in each year group of compulsory schooling and information on teacher absences. I drew attention to the main findings in a speech in the House on 2 May. No press conference was held about the results.

A full set of analyses from the survey will be published shortly.

### Higher Education

**Mr. Butler:** To ask the Secretary of State for Education and Science what proportion of working-class children go on to higher education in Great Britain; and if he will make a statement.

**Mr. Jackson:** Results from the youth cohort study show that in the academic year 1987-88 5 per cent. of 18-year-olds in socioeconomic groups 3 (manual), 4 and 5 in England and Wales entered higher education. Given that these young people amount to more than 60 per cent. of the age group, this is clearly not enough. The Government's policies for schools and higher education will help to increase their participation.

# SOCIAL SECURITY

## Lone Parents

**Mr. Robert G. Hughes:** To ask the Secretary of State for Social Security by how much the average living standards of lone parents have increased since 1979.

**Mr. Peter Lloyd:** From 1979 to 1985, the average living standards of lone parents improved by 10 per cent. This improvement is larger than for couples without children or single people. Both these groups had improvements in their living standards of 6 per cent.

## Claim Forms

**Mr. Speller:** To ask the Secretary of State for Social Security if he will take steps to simplify the forms used to claim benefit; and if he will make a statement.

**Mr. Peter Lloyd:** Steps are taken in the production of forms to ensure that they are as simple and as easy to use as they can be. The Department is committed to research and testing as part of a continuing programme in the designing and writing of new and existing forms.

## Housing Benefit

**Ms. Quin:** To ask the Secretary of State for Social Security what are the estimates of the numbers of people who would be eligible to claim housing benefit rent allowances if rents were to be increased nationally by *(a)* 1 per cent., *(b)* 3 per cent., *(c)* 5 per cent. and *(d)* 8 per cent.

**Mr. Peter Lloyd:** The estimated increases in the rent allowance caseload for 1989-90 if rents were to increase nationally are as follows:

| Rent increase (per cent.) | Increase in caseload |
| --- | --- |
| *(a)* 1 | 1,000 |
| *(b)* 3 | 2,000 |
| *(c)* 5 | 5,000 |
| *(d)* 8 | 10,000 |

*Notes:*

1. The estimates allow for differential take-up, taking account of increased incentives at higher levels of entitlement, and for a time lag in take-up.

2. Rent figures used derive from the Department's projections based on the family expenditure survey data.

## Pensioners (Savings)

**Mr. Greg Knight:** To ask the Secretary of State for Social Security what percentage of pensioners have savings.

**Mr. Peter Lloyd:** In 1986, 70 per cent. of all pensioners and 85 per cent. of recently retired pensioners had income from savings and investment.

## Disability

**Mr. Barry Jones:** To ask the Secretary of State for Social Security what was the number of people in Wales receiving (i) attendance allowance, (ii) industrial disablement benefit, (iii) mobility allowance, (iv) invalid care allowance, (v) invalidity benefit and (vi) severe disablement benefit for the latest available date.

**Mr. Scott:** I regret that some of the information requested is not available and could be obtained only at disproportionate cost. The information which is available is as follows:

Recipients of invalidity benefit in Wales at 2 April 1988 —126,900 (statistical estimate).

Recipients of severe disablement allowance in Wales at 31 May 1981—17,948.

**Mr. Alfred Morris:** To ask the Secretary of State for Social Security if, pursuant to his reply to the right hon. Member for Manchester, Wythenshawe of 19 June, *Official Report,* column *21,* about the representations that the Minister for the Disabled has had from the British Council of Organisations of Disabled People, he will publish his reply to the chairman in the *Official Report.*

**Mr. Scott:** I have placed a copy of my reply in the Library.

**Mr. Hannam:** To ask the Secretary of State for Social Security when the fifth report by the Office of Population Censuses and Surveys on disability in Great Britain will be published.

**Mr. Scott:** The Office of Population Censuses and Surveys (OPCS) has today published the fifth report on the findings of the surveys of disability in Great Britain carried out between 1985 and 1988. The report covers the financial circumstances of families with disabled children living in private households.

The report contains detailed information about the effect of a child's disability on a family's income and expenditure. It does not however take account of the financial value of services received by families with a disabled child. The final report in the series, which will be published next month, will provide information about the use of services, transport and education by disabled children.

The report's findings relate to 1985 when the data was collected. Since then the social security reforms and this year's uprating have targeted increased help on families. More than 10,000 families with disabled children now receive specific help through the disabled child's premium as well as the family premium which is paid to all families receiving income support and housing benefit. This year's uprating targeted further help on families by adding an extra 50p to child allowances in income support, family credit and housing benefit.

We welcome comments on this report, as we have on the four reports already published.

## Benefit Rules

**Mr. Madden:** To ask the Secretary of State for Social Security when changes in the housing benefit rules, enabling under-18s to be paid the same rate as over-18s, are to be introduced; what publicity is being issued to explain the changes; and if he will make a statement.

**Mr. Peter Lloyd:** From 10 July 1989, single people under 18 will be entitled to the same housing benefit personal allowances as those aged 18 to 24, as set out in the Housing Benefit (General Amendment No. 3) Regulations 1989 (SI 1989 No. 1017)). An information note for claimant advisers is in preparation.

## Community Charge

**Mr. Nellist:** To ask the Secretary of State for Social Security if he will list by each charging authority in the west midlands the income level at which *(a)* a single person aged under 25 years, *(b)* a single person aged over 25 years, *(c)* a single pensioner, *(d)* a pensioner couple, and *(e)* a couple with two children all with no savings would lose entitlement to a community charge rebate, assuming the most recent safety-netted community charge figures.

**Mr. Peter Lloyd:** I refer the hon. Member to my reply to the hon. Member for Sheffield, Brightside (Mr. Blunkett) on 19 May 1989 at columns *327-8*.

## Transitional Payments

**Mr. Andrew Bowden:** To ask the Secretary of State for Social Security (1) how many claims had been made for housing benefit transitional payments by 8 June; and how many claims had been successful;

(2) if he will extend the deadline for housing benefit transitional payments beyond 30 June;

(3) if he will state the total number of successful claims as a proportion of the number of households estimated to be entitled to housing benefit transitional payments;

(4) what further steps he is taking to publicise the availability of housing benefit transitional payments.

**Mr. Peter Lloyd** *[holding answer on 16 June 1989]:* Housing benefit transitional payments are intended to provide help to vulnerable groups of people who experienced reductions in their housing benefit as a result of changes introduced by the Government in April 1988. Two national press publicity campaigns were undertaken, more than 8 million leaflets RR4 "Housing Benefit New Rules" were made available and posters were displayed in post offices. Further publicity is not considered necessary.

The closing date for the receipt of applications was originally 31 March 1989 but this was extended by a full three months to 30 June to ensure optimum take-up. As the scheme was intended to assist people only during the transition to the new scheme in April 1988 it would be inappropriate to extend the deadline any further.

It was originally estimated that up to 300,000 people might be eligible for payment. Up to 8 June 477,687 applications had been received and 198,916 awards made but some 26,000 applications have yet to be decided pending return of inquiry forms for housing benefit details from local authorities. Final figures will not, therefore, be available until all applications have been received and processed. Given the uncertainty which attaches to the original estimate it is not possible to calculate meaningful take-up estimates.

## HEALTH

### Contraception

**Ms. Ruddock:** To ask the Secretary of State for Health if he will indicate what steps are being taken to prevent prescription, in Britain, of the Copper 7 IUD and other contraceptive devices by drug companies wishing to test such products before making them available on the United States market; and if he will make a statement.

**Mr. Mellor:** There is no question of pharmaceutical companies or manufacturers, whether based in the United Kingdom or overseas, themselves prescribing licensed products for patients. Medical treatments, including the use of devices such as IUDs, can be prescribed only by qualified medical practitioners on the basis of their clinical judgment of the patient's individual needs.

All clinical trials of IUDs in the United Kingdom are now subject to the provisions of the Medicines Act 1968 in which a clinical trial certificate, or exemption from holding a clinical trial certificate, must be obtained by the manufacturer, unless a registered medical practitioner has initiated the trial, in which circumstances he takes full responsibility for its conduct.

### Family Practitioner Committees

**Mr. Turner:** To ask the Secretary of State for Health if he will publish a table showing for 1983, 1985, 1987 and 1989, the number of family practitioner comittee chairmen who were contractors, distinguishing between general practitioners, dentists, pharmacists and opticians.

**Mr. Mellor:** The information for 1985, 1987 and 1989 is contained in the table. Before 1 April 1985 family practitioner committee chairmen were not appointed by the Secretary of State and the information requested is not available centrally.

| | 1 April 1985 | 1 April 1987 | 1 April 1989 |
|---|---|---|---|
| General Medical Practitioners | 18 | 12 | 7 |
| General Dental Practitioners | 5 | 2 | 1 |
| Ophthalmic Opticians | 3 | 1 | — |
| Pharmacists | 1 | 1 | — |

**Mr. Turner:** To ask the Secretary of State for Health under what powers he is allowing regional health authorities to implement the proposal contained in "Working for Patients" to replace family practitioner committee administrators with general managers or chief executives.

**Mr. Mellor:** We have not asked regional health authorities to implement our intention that general managers should be appointed in all family practitioner committees, although we have asked them to provide a complete service to FPCs, through the personnel directorates, for the process of recruitment and appointment. The responsibility of shortlisting and selection falls to a panel led by the FPC chairman, subject to approval by the National Health Service management executive.

### Self-Governing Hospitals

**Mr. Michael Welsh:** To ask the Secretary of State for Health when Doncaster royal infirmary made a decision as to whether to seek self-governing status; whether medical or other staff were consulted on this decision; how many employees at the infirmary supported seeking self-governing status; how many employees in the infirmary are also employed on private health treatment; and under whose signature the letter expressing an interest in self-governing status was sent.

**Mr. Redmond:** To ask the Secretary of State for Health when Montagu hospital made a decision as to whether to seek self-governing status; whether medical or other staff were consulted on this decision; how many employees at the hospital supported seeking self-governing status; how many employees in the hospital are also employed on private health treatment; and under whose signature the letter expressing an interest in self-governing status was sent.

**Mr. Mellor:** We have recieved an expression of interest in self-governing status for the Doncaster royal infirmary, Montagu Hospital, Mexborough and from Trent regional health authority. We were not privy to the internal discussions on the matter. Those with an interest will have an opportunity to express their views at a later stage if those expressing interest decide to proceed with an application.

### NHS Reform

**Ms. Harman:** To ask the Secretary of State for Health who will pay the contract fee when a general practitioner budget holder refers a woman to a hospital for maternity services under his White Paper proposals.

**Mr. Mellor:** Inpatient maternity services fall outside the scope of the general practitioner practice budget scheme and therefore district health authorities will be responsible for securing such services through contracts.

**Ms. Harman:** To ask the Secretary of State for Health (1) who will pay the contract fee when an employee of the local education authority refers a child for psychiatric services under the proposals of his White Paper;

(2) who will pay the contract fee when a social worker refers a child patient for care at a psychiatric hospital under the proposals of his White Paper.

**Mr. Mellor:** Under the proposals in the White Paper "Working for Patients" contracts for hospital and community health services will be between NHS bodies. We do not propose that agencies outside the NHS such as social services departments or education authorities should enter into contracts or be charged for services.

The responsibility for arranging the provision of psychiatric services, including those to which social workers or education authority employees refer children, remains that of district health authorities, which will in future secure this provision by placing appropriate contracts.

**Mr. Cartwright:** To ask the Secretary of State for Health what discussions have taken place between his Department and the Greenwich health authority about the possibility of hospitals in the area being run as self-governing trusts.

**Mr. Mellor:** None, so far.

**Mr. Fearn:** To ask the Secretary of State for Health how many of the units which expressed interest in self-governing status include or provide maternity services.

**Mr. Mellor** *[holding answer 28 June 1989]:* We understand that about 90 of the units which have expressed an interest in self-governing status include or provide maternity services.

### Cot Deaths

**Mr. John Morris:** To ask the Secretary of State for Health, further to his answer of 21 April, *Official Report,* columns *343–44,* what progress has been made in his Department's discussion with the Medical Research Council on the funding of further work on the usefulness and effectiveness of temperature monitors and alarms to reduce the number of cot deaths.

**Mr. Freeman:** The position on research into sudden infant death was discussed at a meeting between the Department and the Medical Research Council (MRC) on 17 April. Subsequently the Department asked the MRC to commission a critical review of the literature, including that on the relationship between sudden infant deaths and infant temperature. The MRC has specifically been asked for advice on the type of device which would reliably monitor infant temperature changes and the value of an intervention study designed to test the effectiveness of such a device in monitoring changes and preventing "cot deaths".

### Pharmaceutical Prices

**Mr. Sayeed:** To ask the Secretary of State for Health what is the average discount under the current pharmaceutical price regulation scheme; and how much it is estimated to have saved the National Health Service during 1987 and 1988.

**Mr. Mellor:** Discounts do not feature in the pharmaceutical price regulation scheme. The amount deducted from payments to pharmacies in respect of discounts is on average some 8·3 per cent. of the basic price of medicines. As regards the resulting savings I would refer my hon. Friend to my reply to the hon. Member for Cunninghame, North (Mr. Wilson), on 20 June at column *97.*

**Mr. Sayeed:** To ask the Secretary of State for Health what was the cost to the National Health Service of brand name drugs dispensed by retail pharmacy contractors during the calendar year 1987.

**Mr. Mellor:** Based on a one in 200 sample of prescriptions, the net ingredient cost of named drugs dispensed by retail pharmacists during the calendar year 1987 is estimated to have been £1·3 billion, without taking account of other factors such as pharmacists' fees and container allowances.

### "Working for Patients"

**Mr. Patchett:** To ask the Secretary of State for Health how many representations he has received to date on the White Paper "Working for Patients" from Yorkshire; and how many have criticised the Government's proposals.

**Mr. Mellor:** We have received many comments on the White Paper proposals, covering a wide range of issues from differing viewpoints. We are taking these carefully into account as the implementation process goes forward. It would not be possible, except at disproportionate cost, to identify separately those received from Yorkshire.

### Competitive Tendering

**Mr. Patchett:** To ask the Secretary of State for Health what has been achieved in Yorkshire as a result of competitive tendering in the National Health Service.

**Mr. Freeman:** In respect of domestic services, catering and laundry the costs of services within Yorkshire regional health authority were reduced by an average of 19 per cent. as a result of the competitive tendering initiative, giving net savings of £8·75 million which could be ploughed back into improved patient care. Additional benefits have been the setting of clearer performance standards, introduction of more flexible and innovative services, and more systematic monitoring of service provision.

### Food Poisoning

**Ms. Harman:** To ask the Secretary of State for Health how many cases of food poisoning of people living in Southwark have been notified in each of the last 10 years; and if he will specify what sort of poisoning.

**Mr. Freeman:** The table shows the number of notifications of food poisoning received for the London borough of Southwark from 1979 to 1988. Information about the suspected food involved in each case is not readily available.

| Year | Number of Cases |
|------|-----------------|
| 1979 | 46 |
| 1980 | 44 |
| 1981 | 45 |
| 1982 | 75 |
| 1983 | 58 |
| 1984 | 83 |
| 1985 | 91 |
| 1986 | 83 |
| 1987 | 78 |
| 1988 | 156 |

### Waiting Times

**Sir John Farr:** To ask the Secretary of State for Health what is the average waiting time for an orthopaedic operation *(a)* at the Leicester general hospital, *(b)* in Trent region and *(c)* nationally.

**Mr. Mellor** *[holding answer 28 June 1989]:* We do not have information on average waiting times for those awaiting admission to hospital centrally. The numbers on the waiting list are analysed by time waited and a percentage distribution based on this information is provided in the published statistics. The figures for England, the Trent region and Leicestershire district are given in the booklet "Hospital In-Patient Waiting Lists —England at 30 September 1988", a copy of which is in the Library. We do not collect information by individual hospital.

### Regional Health Authorities

**Mr. Cousins:** To ask the Secretary of State for Health if he will place in the Library copies of all letters and circulars sent to regional health authorities about the streamlining of regional health authorities' operations and services and of the preliminary replies from regional health authorities due in by 5 May.

**Mr. Mellor** *[holding answer 26 June 1989]:* The chief executive of the National Health Service wrote to regional general managers on 22 March about the delegation of regional health authority functions in line with the Government's proposals set out in chapter 2 of "Working for Patients". Copies of his letter (EL(89)MB/59) have been placed in the Library. The preliminary replies from

regional health authorities are statements of general intention which are subject to further discussion within authorities, with their staff-side interest, and within the Department. It would not be appropriate to publish these, or correspondence relating to them at this stage. However, authorities' final proposals, due on 30 September 1989, will be public documents.

## AGRICULTURE, FISHERIES AND FOOD

### Organic Farming

16. **Mr. Kirkwood:** To ask the Minister of Agriculture, Fisheries and Food what financial incentives are made available for farmers wishing to transfer to organic farming methods; and if he will make a statement.

**Mr. MacGregor:** No financial incentives are available specifically to assist with conversion to organic farming. However, farmers wishing to convert may be able to take advantage of the provisions for fallowing under the set-aside scheme. In addition, I am considering the possibility of organic options under the European Communities extensification scheme.

### Fur Farming

17. **Mr. Corbyn:** To ask the Minister of Agriculture, Fisheries and Food whether he has discussed fur farming in the European Community Council of Ministers; and if he will make a statement.

**Mr. Donald Thompson:** I refer the hon. Member to the reply I gave earlier to the hon. Members for Pontypridd (Dr. Howells), for Halifax (Mrs. Mahon) and for Bristol, South (Ms. Primarolo).

### Battery Hens

18. **Mr. Livsey:** To ask the Minister of Agriculture, Fisheries and Food if he will make a statement about battery caged poultry.

**Mr. Donald Thompson:** Our legislation on battery hens is based on the EC directive which is due for review in 1993. My Department has asked the Farm Animal Welfare Council to consider what practical welfare improvements we could press for at that time.

### Irradiated Food

19. **Mr. McAllion:** To ask the Minister of Agriculture, Fisheries and Food what research he has carried out into the nutritional effects of irradiation on food.

**Mr. MacGregor:** I refer the hon. Member to the reply of my hon. Friend the Parliamentary Secretary to my hon. Friend the Member for Holland with Boston (Sir R. Body) on 22 June at column *85.*

29. **Mr. Kirkhope:** To ask the Minister of Agriculture, Fisheries and Food what representations he has received from consumer groups in favour of the principle of food irradiation.

**Mr. MacGregor:** A number of consumer groups have recognised that, with proper controls, this technology has benefits for consumers.

43. **Mr. Foulkes:** To ask the Minister of Agriculture, Fisheries and Food whether he has met the British Medical Association to discuss food irradiation.

**Mr. MacGregor:** My officials, together with officials from the Department of Health, have recently met representatives of the British Medical Association to discuss food irradiation.

52. **Mr. David Marshall:** To ask the Minister of Agriculture, Fisheries and Food what consultations he is having with consumer organisations about the introduction of food irradiation.

63. **Sir Hal Miller:** To ask the Minister of Agriculture, Fisheries and Food what action he has taken to ensure that consumer interests are considered and protected in any decision on food irradiation.

**Mr. MacGregor:** There is always full consultation with consumer organisations over food safety policies. Both Ministers and officials have been involved in recent discussions with organisations over food irradiation, and there will be plenty of opportunity for further consultations given that both the primary legislation and the legislation thereafter will have to be discussed and approved by Parliament.

58. **Mr. Conway:** To ask the Minister of Agriculture, Fisheries and Food whether he will make a statement on the proposals of the working group established to devise a control framework for food irradiation in the United Kingdom.

**Mr. MacGregor:** I refer my hon. Friend to the statement I made in the debate on food safety, research and health on 21 June 1989 at columns 347-59. A copy of the report of the working group of officials is in the Library of the House.

### Food Legislation

20. **Mr. Rogers:** To ask the Minister of Agriculture, Fisheries and Food what consultations he is having with interested organisations about changing the legislation on food.

**Mr. MacGregor:** Officials in my Department have undertaken extensive consultations with interested consumer, enforcement and trade organisations on possible changes to our food legislation. We shall introduce new legislation as soon as the parliamentary timetable permits.

27. **Dr. Marek:** To ask the Minister of Agriculture, Fisheries and Food if he will make a statement about his plans to introduce legislation on food.

**Mr. MacGregor:** Work on the detailed preparation of new food legislation, which we announced in October 1987, is well advanced. The Government will introduce proposals for new legislation as soon as the parliamentary timetable permits.

60. **Mr. Waller:** To ask the Minister of Agriculture, Fisheries and Food if he will make a statement about the progress of his consultations on changes to food law.

**Mr. MacGregor:** Officials of my Department and that of my right hon. and learned Friend the Secretary of State for Health, have undertaken consultations with a very large number of interested consumer, enforcement and trade organisations. Work on the preparation of new primary food legislation is well advanced and we shall introduce new legislation as soon as the parliamentary timetable permits.

### Farm Woodland Scheme

21. **Mr. Lord:** To ask the Minister of Agriculture, Fisheries and Food how many farmers have expressed an interest in participating in the farm woodland scheme; and if he will make a statement.

**Mr. MacGregor:** In the first eight months of the farm woodland scheme, nearly 900 farmers have applied to participate in the scheme. I regard this as a very encouraging start to this new scheme.

64. **Mr. Devlin:** To ask the Minister of Agriculture, Fisheries and Food if he will indicate the uptake of the farm woodland scheme.

**Mr. MacGregor:** In the first eight months of the farm woodland scheme nearly 900 farmers have applied to plant about 6,200 hectares of trees during the next three years throughout the United Kingdom.

### Organic Farming

22. **Mr. Malcolm Bruce:** To ask the Minister of Agriculture, Fisheries and Food whether he has any proposals for bringing about an increase in organic farming methods.

30. **Mr. Flynn:** To ask the Minister of Agriculture, Fisheries and Food what new initiatives he will take to increase the percentage of organically grown food.

**Mr. MacGregor:** The Government are encouraging in various ways the development of organic farming in response to consumer demand, for example through its strong support for the United Kingdom register of organic food standards.

### Country Landowners Association

23. **Mr. Favell:** To ask the Minister of Agriculture, Fisheries and Food when he last met the president of the Country Landowners Association; and what matters were discussed.

51. **Mr. Fatchett:** To ask the Minister of Agriculture, Fisheries and Food when he last met representatives of the Country Landowners Association to discuss land value.

**Mr. MacGregor:** I last met the president of the Country Landowners Association on 9 June when a wide range of issues was discussed.

### Whaling

24. **Mr. Tony Banks:** To ask the Minister of Agriculture, Fisheries and Food if he is in a position to outline his Ministry's reaction to the recommendations made at the 41st annual meeting of the International Whaling Commission; and if he will make a statement.

**Mr. Donald Thompson:** The major decisions of the International Whaling Commission concerned the adoption of resolutions co-sponsored by the United Kingdom calling upon Japan, Iceland and Norway to reconsider their plans to take whales for scientific reseach purposes, and rejection of Japan's request for a catch quota of 320 minke whales for its small coastal whaling boats. I strongly welcome these decisions as upholding the spirit of the present moratorium on commercial whaling. These and the preparatory work for the comprehensive assessment needed for the review of the moratorium next year are essential to protect and enhance the status of the world's depleted whale stocks.

### Aujesky's Disease

25. **Mr. Alexander:** To ask the Minister of Agriculture, Fisheries and Food if he will endeavour to ensure that the European Economic Community gives Aujesky's disease category 1 protection in order to protect the British pig industry against future outbreaks of the disease.

**Mr. Donald Thompson:** I refer my hon. Friend to the answer given on 2 May to my hon. Friend the Member for Harborough (Sir J. Farr) at column *81.*

### Environmentally Sensitive Areas

26. **Mr. Janman:** To ask the Minister of Agriculture, Fisheries and Food what proportion of eligible land has been entered into the environmentally sensitive areas scheme.

**Mr. MacGregor:** The proportion of eligible land which has been entered into the ESA scheme in England is 93 per cent.

46. **Mrs. Gillian Shephard:** To ask the Minister of Agriculture, Fisheries and Food if he will give details of the total land area covered by environmentally sensitive areas.

**Mr. MacGregor:** The total land area covered by ESAs in England is 333,470 hectares split as follows:

|  | Total area of ESA (Ha) |
| --- | --- |
| Broads | 29,870 |
| Pennine Dales | 15,960 |
| Somerset Levels | 26,970 |
| South Downs | 53,340 |
| West Penwith | 7,210 |
| Breckland | 94,030 |
| North Peak | 50,250 |
| Shropshire Borders | 21,000 |
| Suffolk River Valleys | 32,150 |
| Test Valley | 2,690 |

### Animal Health

28. **Mr. Colin Shepherd:** To ask the Minister of Agriculture, Fisheries and Food what recent discussions he has had with the European Community Commission over the proposals for harmonised animal health rules in respect of both intra-Community trade and imports from third countries.

**Mr. Donald Thompson:** I met Commissioner MacSharry on 20 June. I said that, in the context of the single market, the Government supported the Commission's objective of achieving a uniformly high animal health status throughout the Community and that we also agreed on the need for common high standards for imports from third countries. I said that our view

remained that until serious diseases such as foot and mouth disease were eradicated, effective controls on movements of animals and animal products from affected parts of the Community to parts which are free would be required to prevent disease spread, including an appropriate level of checking by member states of destination and quarantine where necessary.

### Beef Cows

31. **Mr. Gill:** To ask the Minister of Agriculture, Fisheries and Food what is the latest forecast of beef cow numbers in the United Kingdom for June 1990.

**Mr. Donald Thompson:** The future herd size depends upon a number of factors, not all of which can be foreseen, and it is not our practice to publish forecasts.

### Agricultural Research Centres

32. **Sir Michael McNair-Wilson:** To ask the Minister of Agriculture, Fisheries and Food how many agricultural research centres are funded by his Ministry.

**Mr. MacGregor:** Agricultural research is commissioned within my Department at 11 experimental husbandry farms, eight experimental horticultural stations, the farm building development centre, the field drainage experimental unit and the feed evaluation unit plus the ADAS central science laboratories and the central veterinary laboratories. My Department also commissions agricultural research externally with the eight institutes of the Agricultural and Food Research Council plus short-term contracts with a large number of universities, colleages, polytechnics and other establishments.

### Fishing

33. **Mr. Robert Hicks:** To ask the Minister of Agriculture, Fisheries and Food if he has any plans to improve the fishing opportunities currently available to south-west England fishermen; and if he will make a statement.

**Mr. Donald Thompson:** I am very much aware of the difficulties faced by fishermen in the south-west of England. At the Fisheries Council on 21 June we secured an important amendment to restrictions on beam length that will greatly assist our inshore beam fleet, and we secured a commitment from the Commission to review urgently the 1989 total allowable catch for Channel cod and other precautionary TACs. I have already taken steps to deal with the problem of quota hopping.

### Straw Burning

34. **Mr. Key:** To ask the Minister of Agriculture, Fisheries and Food what is his policy on the control of the burning of straw and stubble.

**Mr. Donald Thompson:** My Department's policy is to reduce the level of straw and stubble burned in the field by encouraging farmers to adopt alternative disposal methods where practicable, while at the same time reminding those farmers who continue to employ burning to observe the NFU code and local byelaws. Our annual straw survey indicates that, between 1983 and 1988, the proportion of straw disposed of by burning fell from 37·7 per cent. to 23·8 per cent., and there has also been a substantial reduction in complaints and prosecutions.

## Farming (Employment)

35. **Mr. Home Robertson:** To ask the Minister of Agriculture, Fisheries and Food if he will make a statement on the trend in regular full-time employment in the farming industry since 1978.

**Mr. Donald Thompson:** Between June 1978 and June 1988 the number of all those engaged in agriculture on a regular full-time basis in the United Kingdom declined by just under 21 per cent. or nearly 85,000. Within this total the number of full-time workers declined by nearly 31 per cent. (almost 61,000) of whom about 53,300 were hired workers and 7,400 family workers, while the number of full-time farmers, partners and directors fell by some 24,000 or just over 11 per cent.

## NFU

36. **Mr. Boswell:** To ask the Minister of Agriculture, Fisheries and Food when he last met the president of the National Farmers Union to discuss means of improving farmers' returns.

50. **Mr. David Nicholson:** To ask the Minister of Agriculture, Fisheries and Food when he last met the president of the National Farmers Union; and what matters were discussed.

**Mr. MacGregor:** I last met the president of the National Farmers Union on 21 June when we discussed various agricultural matters.

## Potato Marketing Board

37. **Mr. Hunter:** To ask the Minister of Agriculture, Fisheries and Food if he will make a further statement on the future of the Potato Marketing Board;

40. **Mr. Hague:** To ask the Minister of Agriculture, Fisheries and Food when he expects to announce a decision about the future of the Potato Marketing Board.

**Mr. Nicholas Bennett:** To ask the Minister of Agriculture, Fisheries and Food whether he is yet in a position to make a statement on the outcome of the review of the Potato Marketing Board.

**Mr. MacGregor:** I refer my hon. Friends to the reply given to the hon. Member for Roxburgh and Berwickshire (Mr. Kirkwood) on 14 June at column *411*.

56. **Mr. Hind:** To ask the Minister of Agriculture, Fisheries and Food when he last met the chairman of the Potato Marketing Board; what matters were discussed; and if he will make a statement.

**Mr. MacGregor:** I last met the chairman of the Potato Marketing Board on 8 March 1989, to discuss the board's response to the Government's consultation paper on future potato market policy.

## Apple Sprays

38. **Mr. Menzies Campbell:** To ask the Minister of Agriculture, Fisheries and Food when he next intends to review the safety of apple sprays.

**Mr. MacGregor:** A programme for the review of approved active ingredients was announced on 16 March. Pesticides used on apples will be covered in the review of each relevant active ingredient.

## Small Farmers Association

39. **Mr. Amess:** To ask the Minister of Agriculture, Fisheries and Food when he last met the chairman of the Small Farmers Association, and what matters were discussed.

**Mr. Donald Thompson:** My right hon. Friend has not met the chairman recently. But he is kept regularly in touch with the Small Farmers Association's views.

## EC Sheep Regime

41. **Mrs. Ray Michie:** To ask the Minister of Agriculture, Fisheries and Food what information he has about discussions on the European Economic Community's sheep regime; and if he will make a statement.

**Mr. MacGregor:** At the Agriculture Council on 19 and 20 June, discussions on the reform of the sheepmeat regime revealed that major differences of view continue to persist among member states. The Council will return to this subject at a subsequent meeting.

62. **Mr. Stevens:** To ask the Minister of Agriculture, Fisheries and Food when he expects the renegotiation of the sheepmeat regime to be concluded.

**Mr. MacGregor:** Discussions on this subject at the last Agriculture Council revealed that major differences of views continue to persist among member states. Negotiations may, therefore, be protracted.

## Dairy Farming

42. **Mr. Knox:** To ask the Minister of Agriculture, Fisheries and Food when he is next due to meet the chairman of the Milk Marketing Board to discuss the dairy sector.

**Mr. Donald Thompson:** My right hon. Friend and I have regular contacts with the chairman of the Milk Marketing Board to discuss various issues affecting the dairy industry.

## Research

44. **Mr. Michael:** To ask the Minister of Agriculture, Fisheries and Food whether he will make it his policy to increase the resources devoted by his Department to scientific research into those aspects of *(a)* environmental concerns and *(b)* food production which come within the scope of his Department's responsibilities.

**Mr. MacGregor:** My Department has been increasing the resources devoted to environmental and food safety research, based on a number of considerations including the advice of the priorities board for research and development in agriculture and food.

## Cold Storage (Audits)

45. **Mr. Dykes:** To ask the Minister of Agriculture, Fisheries and Food if he will take steps to ensure that the Reading, Berkshire Intervention Board for Agricultural Produce cold storage audited figures are properly audited by independent accounting officers.

**Mr. Donald Thompson:** All the intervention board's expenditure is subject to independent audit by the National Audit Office.

## Torry Research Station

47. **Mr. Robert Hughes:** To ask the Minister of Agriculture, Fisheries and Food when he last visited the Torry research station; and what subjects were discussed.

**Mr. Donald Thompson:** I last visited Torry research station on 31 August 1988 and discussed the work of the station.

## Forestry Commission

48. **Mrs. Gorman:** To ask the Minister of Agriculture, Fisheries and Food when he last met the chairman of the Forestry Commission; and what matters were discussed.

**Mr. MacGregor:** I last met the chairman of the Forestry Commission on 14 June when a wide range of forestry matters was discussed.

## Fisheries Council

49. **Mr. Harris:** To ask the Minister of Agriculture, Fisheries and Food if he will make a statement on the latest Fisheries Council meeting.

**Mr. Donald Thompson:** I refer my hon. Friend to the reply I gave to my hon. Friend the Member for Gloucestershire, West (Mr. Marland) on 22 June at columns *248-49*.

## Royal Society for the Protection of Birds

53. **Mr. Hanley:** To ask the Minister of Agriculture, Fisheries and Food when he last met representatives of the Royal Society for the Protection of Birds; and what matters were discussed.

**Mr. MacGregor:** My hon. Friend the Parliamentary Secretary and I had a meeting with the chairman and other representatives of the Royal Society for the Protection of Birds on 17 November last year. We discussed several topics of mutual interest.

## Nature Conservancy Council

54. **Mr. Gwilym Jones:** To ask the Minister of Agriculture, Fisheries and Food when he last met the chairman of the Nature Conservancy Council; and what matters were discussed.

**Mr. Donald Thompson:** My hon. Friend the Parliamentary Secretary met the chairman of the Nature Conservancy Council on 7 November last year when they discussed a wide range of subjects.

## National Institute for Agricultural Botany

55. **Mr. Cousins:** To ask the Minister of Agriculture, Fisheries and Food if he will take steps to ensure that voluntary premature retirement schemes are offered to staff at the National Institute for Agricultural Botany.

**Mr. MacGregor:** We are considering this question.

## Forestry

57. **Mr. Martyn Jones:** To ask the Minister of Agriculture, Fisheries and Food when he last met representatives of the Association of Professional Foresters to discuss forestry in England and Wales.

**Mr. MacGregor:** I have not had the opportunity to meet representatives of the Association of Professional Foresters.

## Council for the Protection of Rural England

59. **Mr. Latham:** To ask the Minister of Agriculture, Fisheries and Food when he last met the Council for the Protection of Rural England; and what matters were discussed.

**Mr. Donald Thompson:** My hon. Friend the Parliamentary Secretary met representatives, including the chairman, of the Council for the Protection of Rural England on 22 March, when they discussed a number of issues of mutual concern.

## Poultry

61. **Mr. Geraint Howells:** To ask the Minister of Agriculture, Fisheries and Food if he will make a statement on the poultry section of the agricultural industry.

**Mr. Donald Thompson:** The market for poultry meat weakened in the early part of this year, but chick placings for table poultry have fallen in recent months; and due to this and to other factors, the market has now firmed again, with wholesale prices now at or above the levels of a year ago.

## Tenant Farmers

65. **Mr Ken Hargreaves:** To ask the Minister of Agriculture, Fisheries and Food when he last met the chairman of the Tenant Farmers Association; and what matters were discussed.

**Mr. Donald Thompson:** I last met the chairman of the Tenant Farmers Association on 31 May when we discussed various matters relating to the tenanted sector.

## Staging Posts

66. **Mr. George Howarth:** To ask the Minister of Agriculture, Fisheries and Food what is his Department's view of the increasing use of staging posts to enable livestocks to be transported long distances prior to slaughter.

**Mr. Donald Thompson:** EC legislation requires that animals in international transport should be offered food and water at suitable intervals and should not be left for more than 24 hours without being fed and watered.

Under our legislation exporters are required to provide details of arrangements made for feeding and watering animals on long international journeys. The staging points used for this purpose are authorised by the United Kingdom and the country in question.

## Set-aside Scheme

67. **Mr. Doran:** To ask the Minister of Agriculture, Fisheries and Food if he will make a statement on the use of set-aside land for forestry.

**Mr. Donald Thompson:** In the first year of the scheme, about 800 hectares of land have been set aside to woodland, either directly or through the farm woodland scheme. I recently invited applications for the second year of set-aside, and since farmers have now had more time to plan for tree planting, I expect enhanced interest in this option. I welcome increased planting of trees on arable land as a contribution to the reduction of surpluses, to the enhancement of the landscape and to helping to meet our timber requirements in the longer term.

## Women's Farmers Union

68. **Mrs. Ann Winterton:** To ask the Minister of Agriculture, Fisheries and Food when he last met the president of the Women's Farmers Union; and what matters were discussed.

**Mr. MacGregor:** I refer my hon. Friend to the reply given on 25 May to my hon. Friend the Member for Maidstone (Miss Widdecombe) at column *740*.

## Nitrates

**Mr. Tredinnick:** To ask the Minister of Agriculture, Fisheries and Food what representations he has received recently concerning nitrates in water supplies; what action he has taken; and if he will make a statement.

**Mr. MacGregor:** I refer my hon. Friend to the reply I gave earlier today to my hon. Friend the Member for Beverley (Mr. Cran).

## Waste Dumping (British Coal)

**Sir John Stanley:** To ask the Minister of Agriculture, Fisheries and Food what is his policy on the dumping by British Coal of solid sludge and liquid waste into the sea and on the development of alternatives to sea dumping; and whether he will make a statement.

**Mr. Donald Thompson:** Licences for the disposal at sea of colliery waste are granted only where practical land-based means of disposal are not available. In particular, the sea disposal of spoil by tipping on Durham beaches creates an environmental problem and I am anxious to see it stopped as soon as possible. As a condition of the sea disposal licence issued by the Ministry, British Coal has reassessed the availability and cost of disposal of this waste on land in the area, by analysing a range of options.

I am now asking British Coal to study in more detail the land-based options already analysed which appear to merit further work, and to report to me. I intend this to provide the Ministry with a basis for a final decision on whether a practicable and environmentally preferable alternative to sea disposal exists.

Liquid colliery waste which is discharged to sea across Durham beaches is subject to control by the Northumbrian water authority. I consider, with the support of the authority, that it would be in the interests of protection of the land and marine environments for British Coal's more detailed studies to incorporate an assessment of the scope for disposal of these tailings on land in an environmentally satisfactory way. I am pleased that British Coal is prepared to take on this further assessment.

## Horticultural Trades Association

**Mr. Patchett:** To ask the Minister of Agriculture, Fisheries and Food when he last met representatives of the Horticultural Trades Association; and what matters were discussed.

**Mr. Donald Thompson:** My noble Friend the Parliamentary Secretary in another place met representatives of the horticultural industry including the Horticultural Trades Association (HTA) on 31 May to discuss research and development.

# OVERSEAS DEVELOPMENT ADMINISTRATION

## Greenhouse Effect

**Mr. Foulkes:** To ask the Secretary of State for Foreign and Commonwealth Affairs what specific proposals his Department has put forward for consideration and enactment, in order to hold down and reduce greenhouse gas emissions in developing countries, since the seminar on the greenhouse effect held by the Prime Minister on 26 April.

**Mr. Chris Patten:** The Government proposed a global climate convention, applicable to all countries, at the United Nations in New York on 8 May. At the Helsinki review meeting of the Montreal protocol on 3 May my right hon. Friend the Secretary of State for the Environment outlined the support we could offer developing countries which are trying to avoid the use of CFCs. My Department has stepped up efforts to increase aid for forestry and is examining the scope for more support for energy efficiency.

### Non-governmental Organisations

**Sir John Stanley:** To ask the Secretary of State for Foreign and Commonwealth Affairs if he will list the non-governmental organisations associated with overseas development which received financial support from his Department in 1988-89, and the sum received by each organisation in that year.

**Mr. Chris Patten:** Figures for 1988-89 are not yet available. I shall let my right hon. Friend know when they are.

# EMPLOYMENT

### Remploy

**Mr. McAvoy:** To ask the Secretary of State for Employment if he will give the amount of the subvention paid to Remploy in the years 1975, 1979, 1984 and 1989.

**Mr. Lee:** The subvention paid to Remploy Ltd. for current expenditure in the following financial years was:

|  | £ |
|---|---|
| 1974-75 | 10,114,000 |
| 1978-79 | 22,530,000 |
| 1983-84 | 44,572,000 |
| 1988-89 | 53,714,000 |

**Mr. McAvoy:** To ask the Secretary of State for Employment what information he has about plans by the Remploy company to close a number of its factories.

**Mr. Lee:** Other than Rutherglen, I am not aware of plans to close specific Remploy factories.

**Mr. McAvoy:** To ask the Secretary of State for Employment what proportion of the cost of employing disabled people employed by Remploy was provided by the Government and what proportion by the company in the years 1985, 1986, 1987, 1988 and 1989 to date.

**Mr. Lee:** The proportion of the cost of employing people with disabilities at Remploy provided by the Government in each of the following financial years was:

|  | *Percentage* |
|---|---|
| 1984-85 | 100 |
| 1985-86 | 100 |
| 1986-87 | 94 |
| 1987-88 | 87 |
| 1988-89 | 90 |

The remainder was provided by the company from its trading surplus.

### Disabled People

**Mr. McAvoy:** To ask the Secretary of State for Employment what responsibility the Government have to provide employment for disabled people in local areas.

**Mr. Lee:** The Secretary of State approves facilities which local authorities set up to provide employment for people with severe disabilities ordinarily resident in their areas. He also has powers to direct local authorities in the extent of this provision. My Department is using local labour market information to allocate its resources for providing employment for people with severe disabilities with the aim of producing an equitable distribution of resource, although this will take some time to achieve. We are planning in the future to pay closer attention to geographical provision as well as to the needs of individuals.

### Labour Statistics

**Mr. Patchett:** To ask the Secretary of State for Employment if he will list in the *Official Report* the number of long-term unemployed people, male and female, indicating in each instance how many are under the age of 25 years in Yorkshire and in each of the parliamentary constituencies of Yorkshire; and if he will make a statement.

**Mr. Lee:** The information is available from the Library. The following table shows for Yorkshire and for each parliamentary constituency of Yorkshire the total number of unemployed claimants in April 1989, who had been unemployed for over 12 months, analysed by sex and separately identifying those aged under 25 years. In the year to April 1989 long-term unemployment fell by an average of 28·1 per cent. in the parliamentary constituencies concerned.

*Long-term unemployment in Yorkshire parliamentary constituencies April 1989*

| | Number of unemployed claimants | | | |
|---|---|---|---|---|
| | Male | | Female | |
| Parliamentary constituency | Total | Of which under 25 years | Total | Of which under 25 years |
| Harrogate | 241 | 21 | 94 | 13 |
| Richmond | 391 | 39 | 187 | 22 |
| Ryedale | 333 | 22 | 149 | 14 |
| Scarborough | 739 | 88 | 252 | 40 |
| Selby | 380 | 41 | 191 | 25 |
| Skipton and Ripon | 242 | 21 | 135 | 15 |
| York | 1,045 | 142 | 309 | 62 |
| Barnsley Central | 1,730 | 215 | 287 | 62 |
| Barnsley East | 1,461 | 198 | 259 | 70 |
| Barnsley West and Penistone | 1,378 | 158 | 304 | 69 |
| Don Valley | 1,581 | 181 | 388 | 84 |
| Doncaster Central | 1,836 | 217 | 501 | 115 |
| Doncaster North | 1,875 | 264 | 458 | 86 |
| Rother Valley | 1,322 | 131 | 338 | 83 |
| Rotherham | 1,554 | 241 | 357 | 100 |
| Sheffield Central | 2,628 | 513 | 665 | 231 |
| Sheffield Attercliffe | 1,267 | 205 | 324 | 88 |
| Sheffield Brightside | 1,969 | 366 | 466 | 156 |
| Sheffield Hallam | 797 | 181 | 334 | 104 |
| Sheffield Heeley | 1,582 | 303 | 476 | 123 |
| Sheffield Hillsborough | 1,053 | 177 | 403 | 97 |
| Wentworth | 1,485 | 177 | 311 | 63 |
| Batley and Spen | 844 | 121 | 244 | 48 |
| Bradford North | 1,614 | 232 | 383 | 92 |
| Bradford South | 1,149 | 184 | 297 | 51 |
| Bradford West | 1,753 | 241 | 409 | 106 |
| Calder Valley | 502 | 61 | 213 | 35 |
| Colne Valley | 483 | 69 | 206 | 55 |
| Dewsbury | 748 | 100 | 229 | 74 |
| Elmet | 502 | 49 | 179 | 33 |
| Halifax | 913 | 128 | 268 | 59 |
| Hemsworth | 1,289 | 144 | 218 | 42 |
| Huddersfield | 752 | 120 | 284 | 57 |
| Keighley | 561 | 55 | 243 | 33 |

| | Number of unemployed claimants | | | |
|---|---|---|---|---|
| | Male | | Female | |
| Parliamentary constituency | Total | Of which under 25 years | Total | Of which under 25 years |
| Leeds Central | 1,792 | 320 | 434 | 109 |
| Leeds East | 1,517 | 275 | 408 | 112 |
| Leeds North East | 860 | 157 | 266 | 68 |
| Leeds North West | 617 | 90 | 207 | 47 |
| Leeds West | 1,020 | 160 | 347 | 70 |
| Morley and Leeds South | 822 | 111 | 242 | 37 |
| Normanton | 709 | 67 | 213 | 29 |
| Pontefract and Castleford | 1,409 | 159 | 259 | 56 |
| Pudsey | 364 | 45 | 157 | 21 |
| Shipley | 429 | 46 | 148 | 18 |
| Wakefield | 1,043 | 104 | 270 | 54 |

*Long-term unemployment in Yorkshire, April 1989*
*Number of unemployed claimants*

| | Male | | Female | |
|---|---|---|---|---|
| County | Total | Of which under 25 years | Total | Of which under 25 years |
| North Yorkshire | 3,371 | 374 | 1,317 | 191 |
| West Yorkshire | 21,692 | 3,042 | 6,142 | 1,306 |
| South Yorkshire | 23,518 | 3,527 | 5,871 | 1,531 |
| Yorkshire | 48,581 | 6,943 | 13,312 | 3,028 |

**Mr. Teddy Taylor:** To ask the Secretary of State for Employment how many new jobs have been created over the past five years in *(a)* the United Kingdom, *(b)* the rest of the European Economic Community and *(c)* the European Free Trade Area; and what assessment he has made of the reasons for the differences in these figures.

**Mr. Lee:** The latest available information is given in the following table. The EFTA unemployment rates are not directly comparable with those for the United Kingdom and the EEC because of differences in the definitions, methods of compilation and timing of the statistics.

The unemployment rate in the United Kingdom remains lower than that of the majority of our European partners.

| | Unemployment rate Per Cent. |
|---|---|
| United Kingdom (Apr) | 6·9 |
| EEC (Apr) | 9·3 |
| EFTA[1] | 2·8 |

[1] Excluding Iceland, Liechtenstein.

*Note:* Rates for United Kingdom and the EEC are seasonally adjusted comparable rates produced by the Statistical Office of the European Communities.

The rate for the EFTA is based on unadjusted unemployment for the latest available month for each country.

The Government have placed great stress on creating the right economic conditions in which enterprise can flourish and jobs can be created. Since 1980 the United Kingdom economy has been the fastest-growing major economy in Western Europe and we are now well into our eighth successive year of sustained growth. As a result of this, growth in employment over the past five years has been better than any other European country.

### Council for Social Aid

**Mr. Tony Lloyd:** To ask the Secretary of State for Employment on what date consideration was first given to withdrawing the contract for the Council for Social Aid, Manchester, as an ET manager; and when the final decision to cancel the contract was made.

**Mr. Nicholls** *[holding answer 26 June 1989]:* The full extent of CSA's financial position became clear on 3 May with a report released by its accountants. Between that date and 18 May CSA Ltd. made unsuccessful efforts to raise additional funds. The decision to terminate the contract was made on 19 May.

# Written Answers to Questions

*Friday 30 June 1989*

## EDUCATION AND SCIENCE

### University Lecturers

**Mr. Andrew Smith:** To ask the Secretary of State for Education and Science how many university lecturers are at each level of the promotion scale, expressed in total numbers and percentages; and if he will give the same information for each of the past 10 years.

**Mr. Jackson:** Information is not immediately available in the form requested. Information which is available is listed in the table.

| Salary range £ | Number of Lecturers | Percentage of Lecturers |
|---|---|---|
| *1984* | | |
| under 6,600 | 42 | 0·25 |
| 6,600-7,054 | 116 | 0·68 |
| 7,055-7,519 | 110 | 0·65 |
| 7,520-7,979 | 81 | 0·48 |
| 7,980-8,449 | 300 | 1·77 |
| 8,450-8,919 | 172 | 1·01 |
| 8,920-9,389 | 304 | 1·79 |
| 9,390-9,859 | 385 | 2·27 |
| 9,860-10,329 | 580 | 3·42 |
| 10,330-10,719 | 498 | 2·94 |
| 10,720-11,204 | 568 | 3·35 |
| 11,205-11,674 | 625 | 3·68 |
| 11,675-12,149 | 674 | 3·97 |
| 12,150-12,634 | 877 | 5·17 |
| 12,635-13,119 | 839 | 4·95 |
| 13,120-13,624 | 884 | 5·21 |
| 13,625-14,134 | 884 | 5·21 |
| 14,135-14,924 | 944 | 5·56 |
| 14,925 and above | 8,028 | 47·32 |
| Not known | 53 | 0·31 |
| Totals | 16,964 | 99·99 |
| *1985* | | |
| under 6,865 | 52 | 0·31 |
| 6,865-7,339 | 109 | 0·64 |
| 7,340-7,819 | 115 | 0·67 |
| 7,820-8,299 | 130 | 0·76 |
| 8,300-8,789 | 317 | 1·86 |
| 8,790-9,279 | 342 | 2·00 |
| 9,280-9,764 | 19 | 0·11 |
| 9,765-10,254 | 662 | 3·88 |
| 10,255-10,744 | 523 | 3·07 |
| 10,745-11,149 | 595 | 3·49 |
| 11,150-11,654 | 568 | 3·33 |
| 11,655-12,144 | 874 | 5·13 |
| 12,145-12,639 | 808 | 4·74 |
| 12,640-13,139 | 116 | 0·68 |
| 13,140-13,644 | 935 | 5·49 |
| 13,645-14,169 | 699 | 4·10 |
| 14,170-14,699 | 790 | 4·64 |
| 14,700-15,524 | 8,012 | 47·00 |
| 15,525 and over | 1,333 | 7·82 |
| Not known | 45 | 0·26 |
| Total | 17,044 | 99·98 |

| Salary range £ | Number of Lecturers | Percentage of Lecturers |
|---|---|---|
| *1986* | | |
| under 7,055 | 74 | 0·44 |
| 7,055-7,529 | 68 | 0·40 |
| 7,530-8,019 | 114 | 0·67 |
| 8,020-8,504 | 61 | 0·36 |
| 8,505-8,999 | 303 | 1·78 |
| 9,000-9,494 | 131 | 0·77 |
| 9,495-9,879 | 271 | 1·60 |
| 9,880-10,374 | 364 | 2·14 |
| 10,375-10,864 | 422 | 2·49 |
| 10,865-11,274 | 448 | 2·64 |
| 11,275-11,789 | 552 | 3·25 |
| 11,790-12,279 | 611 | 3·60 |
| 12,280-12,779 | 631 | 3·72 |
| 12,780-13,289 | 802 | 4·72 |
| 13,290-13,799 | 652 | 3·84 |
| 13,800-14,334 | 773 | 4·55 |
| 14,335-14,869 | 791 | 4·66 |
| 14,870-15,699 | 1,223 | 7·20 |
| 15,700 and above | 8,634 | 50·86 |
| Not known | 53 | 0·31 |
| Total | 16,978 | 100·00 |
| *1987* | | |
| under 8,185 | 72 | 0·44 |
| 8,185-8,734 | 57 | 0·34 |
| 8,735-9,304 | 143 | 0·87 |
| 9,305-9,864 | 66 | 0·40 |
| 9,865-10,439 | 280 | 1·69 |
| 10,440-11,014 | 124 | 0·75 |
| 11,015-11,459 | 258 | 1·56 |
| 11,460-12,034 | 330 | 2·00 |
| 12,035-12,604 | 382 | 2·31 |
| 12,605-13,079 | 396 | 2·40 |
| 13,080-13,674 | 454 | 2·75 |
| 13,675-14,244 | 644 | 3·90 |
| 14,245-14,824 | 532 | 3·22 |
| 14,825-15,414 | 798 | 4·83 |
| 15,415-16,009 | 644 | 3·90 |
| 16,010-16,629 | 661 | 4·00 |
| 16,630-17,249 | 742 | 4·49 |
| 17,250-18,209 | 861 | 5·21 |
| 18,210 and above | 9,034 | 54·67 |
| Not known | 45 | 0·27 |
| Total | 16,523 | 100·00 |

**Mr. Andrew Smith:** To ask the Secretary of State for Education and Science how many university lecturers have been at the top point of the promotion scale for *(a)* five years or more and *(b)* 10 years or more.

**Mr. Jackson:** This information is not readily available.

### Pupil-Teacher Ratio

**Mr. Yeo:** To ask the Secretary of State for Education and Science what is the most recent available figure for the pupil-teacher ratio nationally.

**Mr. Butcher:** In January 1988 the overall pupil-teacher ratio in maintained schools in England was 17·0.

## HOME DEPARTMENT

### Firearms Offences

**Mr. Bellingham:** To ask the Secretary of State for the Home Department (1) how many and which notifiable offences involving firearms have been committed by licensed possessors of shotguns;

(2) how many and which notifiable offences involving firearms have been committed in which licensed pistols have been used;

(3) how many and which notifiable offences involving firearms have been committed in which licensed rifles have been used.

**Mr. Douglas Hogg:** The police do not report to the Home Office whether or not firearms used in crime are held legally. The available information is published annually in table 3.6 of "Criminal Statistics, England and Wales", and most recently in the issue for 1987, Cm 498; corresponding information for 1988 will be published in the autumn.

### Litter

**Mr. Amess:** To ask the Secretary of State for the Home Department (1) how many people were *(a)* charged and *(b)* convicted of litter offences in 1987 and 1988;

(2) how many people were *(a)* charged and *(b)* convicted of litter offences in the Basildon area in 1987 and 1988.

**Mr. John Patten:** The information requested is in the table.

Information for 1988 is not yet available.

*Persons proceeded against or convicted of litter offences: England and Wales 1987*

| | England and Wales | [1] Billericay |
|---|---|---|
| Prosecutions for litter offences | 1,888 | 2 |
| Total found guilty | 1,694 | 2 |

[1] Data is not collected centrally for Basildon alone but for the whole of the Billericay petty sessional division.

### Murder and Manslaughter

**Mr. Amess:** To ask the Secretary of State for the Home Department how many people were *(a)* charged and *(b)* convicted of (i) murder and (ii) manslaughter in each year since 1982.

**Mr. John Patten:** The information requested in respect of England and Wales is published annually in volumes 1 and 2 of the "Criminal Statistics, England and Wales", supplementary tables, copies of which can be found in the Library. Information for 1988 is not yet available.

### Football Matches (Public Order)

**Mr. Amess:** To ask the Secretary of State for the Home Department if he will publish in the *Official Report* a table showing the number of persons *(a)* charged and *(b)* found guilty of public order offences at football matches in the following age groups (i) 10 to 14, (ii) 15 to 18, (iii) 19 to 24, (iv) 25 to 30 and (v) 30 years and over in 1987 and 1988.

**Mr. John Patten:** The information requested is not available from the records held centrally.

### Holloway Prison

**Mr. Bermingham:** To ask the Secretary of State for the Home Department if he will list existing facilities for the treatment of prisoners who are psychiatrically ill or known to be drug dependent at Her Majesty's prison, Holloway; and if he will make a statement.

**Mr. Douglas Hogg:** Most of the psychiatrically disturbed inmates of Holloway prison are remanded there

for the purpose of assessment for the courts. Their care during this time is provided by the prison medical and nursing staff. Four of the five medical officers are registered under section 12 of the Mental Health Act 1983 or possess a diploma in psychiatric medicine. Over one third of the 65 nurses in post are psychiatrically qualified. The future arrangements for housing such inmates are being assessed.

If on reception at Holloway a person is identified as having a history of drug misuse she is offered the treatment that the medical officer, in her individual clinical judgement, considers necessary. In reaching her judgment the medical officer would have full regard to the possible merit of substitution or other therapies. Such an inmate would be located in one of the medical units until free of symptoms. Counselling and group therapy would be available in the medical unit and continue on normal location. Where indicated, individual psychotherapy with a visiting consultant psychotherapist would also be available.

**Mr. Bermingham:** To ask the Secretary of State for the Home Department what is the total number of permanent medical staff currently employed at Her Majesty's prison Holloway; and if he will make a statement.

**Mr. Douglas Hogg:** The total number of permanent medical staff currently employed at Her Majesty's prison Holloway is as follows:
1 Principal Medical Officer
1 Senior Medical Officer
3 Medical Officers
46·5 Nurses
2 Hospital Officers
A further two hospital officers are attached to the prison hospital as supernumeraries and will join the permanent staff on successful completion of a four-week induction course. A drive to recruit additional nurses is well advanced, and Holloway is one of the priority establishments for the deployment of newly recruited hospital officers with suitable nursing qualifications.

**Mr. Bermingham:** To ask the Secretary of State for the Home Department (1) what was the prison population at Her Majesty's prison, Holloway, for the latest date available; and if he will make a statement;

(2) what was the total number of women being held on C wing at Her Majesty's prison, Holloway, for the latest date available; and if he will make a statement.

**Mr. Douglas Hogg:** At unlocking on Thursday 29 June the population at Her Majesty's prison Holloway was 466, including 137 in C wing.

**Mr. Bermingham:** To ask the Secretary of State for the Home Department (1) what was the total number of incidents of self-inflicted injury which have been recorded at Her Majesty's prison, Holloway, in *(a)* 1987, *(b)* 1988 and *(c)* current figures for 1989; and if he will make a statement;

(2) what was the total number of suicides which have occurred at Her Majesty's prison, Holloway, in each of the last five years for which figures are available; and if he will make a statement.

**Mr. Douglas Hogg:** No suicides have occured at Her Majesty's prison Holloway during the last five years. The available information on numbers of incidents of non-fatal self-injury relates to financial years and is as follows:

| | Number |
|---|---|
| 1986-87 | 149 |
| 1987-88 | 209 |
| 1988-89 | 85 |

## Welford Road Prison (Moves)

**Mr. Vaz:** To ask the Secretary of State for the Home Department how many prisoners were moved from Welford Road prison to *(a)* Stafford prison, *(b)* Ashwell prison, *(c)* Winson Green prison and *(d)* Littlehey prison for the weeks ended (i) 12 May, (ii) 19 May, (iii) 26 May, (iv) 9 June, (v) 16 June and (vi) 23 June; and what were the reasons for the moves.

**Mr. Douglas Hogg:** The information requested is as follows:

*Numbers of prisoners moved from Her Majesty's prison Leicester to:*

| | Stafford | Her Majesty's prisons Ashwell | Birmingham | Littlehey |
|---|---|---|---|---|
| *Week ending:* | | | | |
| 12 May | 10 | — | — | 4 |
| 19 May | — | 4 | — | — |
| 26 May | — | 2 | — | — |
| 9 June | 7 | 3 | — | — |
| 16 June | 8 | 5 | — | — |
| 23 June | 9 | — | 10 | — |

All these transfers comprised normal allocations to training prisons except for the 10 who were sent to Her Majesty's prison Birmingham to relieve overcrowding at Leicester.

## Drugs

**Mr. Cox:** To ask the Secretary of State for the Home Department how many reported drug finds there were in each of the prisons in England and Wales during the last 12 months.

**Mr. Douglas Hogg** *[holding answer 23 June 1989]*: The following numbers of finds made in prisons of drugs or of substances believed to be drugs have been notified for the year up to 31 May 1989:

| | Drug finds |
|---|---|
| Her Majesty's Prison Acklington | 19 |
| Her Majesty's Prison Albany | 51 |
| Her Majesty's Prison Aldington | 5 |
| Her Majesty's Prison Ashwell | 24 |
| Her Majesty's Prison Askham Grange | 2 |
| Her Majesty's Prison Bedford | 9 |
| Her Majesty's Prison Birmingham | 62 |
| Her Majesty's Prison Blantyre House | 2 |
| Her Majesty's Prison Blundeston | 13 |
| Her Majesty's Prison Bristol | 54 |
| Her Majesty's Prison Brixton | 212 |
| Her Majesty's Prison and Young Offender Institution Bullwood Hall | 15 |
| Her Majesty's Prison Camp Hill | 21 |
| Her Majesty's Prison Canterbury | 9 |
| Her Majesty's Prison Cardiff | 27 |
| Her Majesty's Prison Channings Wood | 15 |
| Her Majesty's Prison Chelmsford | 47 |
| Her Majesty's Prison Coldingley | 25 |
| Her Majesty's Prison Cookham Wood | 6 |
| Her Majesty's Prison Dartmoor | 22 |
| Her Majesty's Prison Dorchester | 11 |
| Her Majesty's Prison and Young Offender Institution Drake Hall | 5 |

| | Drug finds |
|---|---|
| Her Majesty's Prison Durham | 26 |
| Her Majesty's Prison and Young Offender Institution East Sutton Park | 8 |
| Her Majesty's Prison Erlestoke | 9 |
| Her Majesty's Prison Exeter | 27 |
| Her Majesty's Prison Featherstone | 19 |
| Her Majesty's Prison Ford | 77 |
| Her Majesty's Prison Frankland | 49 |
| Her Majesty's Prison Full Sutton | 12 |
| Her Majesty's Prison Garth | 13 |
| Her Majesty's Prison Gartree | 18 |
| Her Majesty's Prison Gloucester | 20 |
| Her Majesty's Prison Grendon-Spring Hill | 10 |
| Her Majesty's Prison Haverigg | 20 |
| Her Majesty's Prison Highpoint | 29 |
| Her Majesty's Prison Holloway | 46 |
| Her Majesty's Prison Hull | 16 |
| Her Majesty's Prison Kingston | 4 |
| Her Majesty's Prison Kirkham | 39 |
| Her Majesty's Prison Lancaster | 8 |
| Her Majesty's Prison Leeds | 11 |
| Her Majesty's Prison Leicester | 22 |
| Her Majesty's Prison Lewes | 24 |
| Her Majesty's Prison Leyhill | 12 |
| Her Majesty's Prison Lincoln | 26 |
| Her Majesty's Prison Lindholme | 36 |
| Her Majesty's Prison Littlehey | 27 |
| Her Majesty's Prison Liverpool | 67 |
| Her Majesty's Prison Long Lartin | 42 |
| Her Majesty's Prison Maidstone | 18 |
| Her Majesty's Prison Manchester | 76 |
| Her Majesty's Prison Morton Hall | 6 |
| Her Majesty's Prison and Young Offender Institution New Hall | 10 |
| Her Majesty's Prison Northeye | 42 |
| Her Majesty's Prison North Sea Camp | 5 |
| Her Majesty's Prison Norwich | 38 |
| Her Majesty's Prison Nottingham | 2 |
| Her Majesty's Prison Oxford | 3 |
| Her Majesty's Prison Parkhurst | 34 |
| Her Majesty's Prison Pentonville | 60 |
| Her Majesty's Prison Preston | 9 |
| Her Majesty's Prison Ranby | 16 |
| Her Majesty's Prison Reading | 12 |
| Her Majesty's Prison Rochester | 47 |
| Her Majesty's Prison Rollestone | 5 |
| Her Majesty's Prison Rudgate | 17 |
| Her Majesty's Prison Send | 15 |
| Her Majesty's Prison Shepton Mallet | 7 |
| Her Majesty's Prison Shrewsbury | 5 |
| Her Majesty's Prison Stafford | 51 |
| Her Majesty's Prison Standford Hill | 47 |
| Her Majesty's Prison Stocken | 14 |
| Her Majesty's Prison and Young Offender Institution Styal | 9 |
| Her Majesty's Prison Sudbury/Foston Hall | 16 |
| Her Majesty's Prison Swaleside | 9 |
| Her Majesty's Prison Swansea | 9 |
| Her Majesty's Prison Thorp Arch | 12 |
| Her Majesty's Prison The Verne | 18 |
| Her Majesty's Prison Wakefield | 19 |
| Her Majesty's Prison Wandsworth | 266 |
| Her Majesty's Prison Wayland | 39 |
| Her Majesty's Prison Winchester | 43 |
| Her Majesty's Prison Wormwood Scrubs | 214 |
| Her Majesty's Prison Wymott | 9 |

Cannabis represented about 92 per cent. of the above finds.

## NORTHERN IRELAND

### Tourism

**Mr. Amos:** To ask the Secretary of State for Northern Ireland what is the outcome of the review of tourism policy in Northern Ireland, commissioned last October.

**Mr. Viggers:** I refer my hon. Friend to the answer that I gave on Thursday 29 June to the hon. Member for North Down, (Mr. Kilfedder) *Official Report,* Vol. 155, col. *499.*

## TRADE AND INDUSTRY

### RENAVAL Programme

**Ms. Quin:** To ask the Chancellor of the Duchy of Lancaster if he will list the applications which have been submitted by the Department of Trade and Industry to the European Commission for funding under the RENAVAL programme for assistance to shipbuilding areas.

**Mr. Atkins:** The Government have made applications to the Commission under article 3(2) of the RENAVAL regulation, EEC regulation No. 2506/88, for Plymouth, Gibraltar and Strathclyde.

### Shipbuilding (Redundancies)

**Ms. Quin:** To ask the Chancellor of the Duchy of Lancaster what was the total number of redundancies in the shipbuilding and shiprepair industries in Tyne and Wear during the period 1 January 1979 to 31 December 1988.

**Mr. Atkins:** Information about redundancies in the shipbuilding and shiprepair industries in Tyne and Wear is not available. However, information provided to the Department of Trade and Industry suggests that employment in these industries in Tyne and Wear fell by some 19,000 between 1 January 1979 and 31 December 1988. This figure is likely to be an overestimate of the number of redundancies.

**Ms. Quin:** To ask the Chancellor of the Duchy of Lancaster what was the total number of redundancies in the shipbuilding and shiprepair industries in Merseyside during the period 1 January 1987 to 31 December 1988.

**Mr. Atkins:** Information about redundancies in the shipbuilding and shiprepair industries in Merseyside is not available. However, information provided to the Department of Trade and Industry suggests that employment in these industries in Merseyside has risen by about 600 between 1 January 1987 and 31 December 1988.

### Coats Viyella

**Mr. Madden:** To ask the Chancellor of the Duchy of Lancaster whether Coats Viyella has made any application for financial or other assistance in transferring production from C. V. Carpets, Greenhill Mills, Batley, to Northern Ireland; and what representations he has received concerning this transfer of production; and if he will make a statement.

**Mr. Atkins** *[holding answer 26 June 1989]:* No; none.

## TRANSPORT

### Rail Workers (Remuneration)

**Mr. Meacher:** To ask the Secretary of State for Transport if he will give the average pay for each of the main grades of workers on the railways, London Underground and bus services over each of the last 10 years, the percentage increase each year and the percentage increase in the retail price index and in national average earnings for each of those years.

**Mr. Portillo:** I regret that the information requested is not available.

### European Tourism Year

**Mr. Fearn:** To ask the Secretary of State for Transport whether the Government have any plans to increase investment in transport and, in particular, rail to coincide with an anticipated influx of visitors in European Tourism Year 1990.

**Mr. Portillo:** It is for British Rail to make plans for rail investment. If it thinks that European Tourism Year will result in additional traffic that is profitable for it, I am sure that it will take that into account.

### Severn Bridge

**Mr. Roy Hughes:** To ask the Secretary of State for Transport if he has now received the report of the inspector who conducted the inquiry into the Government's proposals to increase toll charges on the Severn bridge.

**Mr. Peter Bottomley:** Yes. It is being considered.

### Humber Bridge

**Mr. Roy Hughes:** To ask the Secretary of State for Transport if he has now reached a decision on the inspector's report following last year's inquiry into toll charges on the Humber bridge; and if there have been any discussions with the bridge authorities concerning the oustanding debt.

**Mr. Peter Bottomley:** The decision was issued on 28 May. Discussions with the bridge board about its debt will be arranged.

### Industrial Action

**Mr. Dalyell:** To ask the Secretary of State for Transport if he will make a statement on the implications for British Rail's investment plans of industrial action on the railways.

**Mr. Portillo:** Industrial action can only damage the revenue of the railway and the confidence of its customers. It is for the board to decide how to meet its external financing limit in view of the revenue losses.

### Roads (Liverpool)

**Mr. Alton:** To ask the Secretary of State for Transport how much his Department has given for road building and improvement in Liverpool; and if he will list the Liverpool city council plans it was allocated for, for each of the last five years.

**Mr. Peter Bottomley** *[pursuant to his reply 27 June 1989, c. 376]:* The following should be added to the table:

| Major schemes accepted for TSG 1985-90 | Years TSG allocated |
|---|---|
| Hunter Street improvement | 1985-86, 1986-87, 1987-88, 1988-89, 1989-90 |
| Urban Traffic Control | 1988-89, 1989-90 |
| Park Road Relief Road | 1988-89, 1989-90 |

# WALES

## Voluntary Organisations

**Mr. Wigley:** To ask the Secretary of State for Wales what is the total available funding for 1989-90 for supporting voluntary organisations in Wales in the social services field under section 64 of the Health Service and Public Health Act 1968; and what was the corresponding figure in each of the previous three years.

**Mr. Grist:** The information is as follows:

| | £ |
|---|---|
| 1986-87 | 1,126,202 |
| 1987-88 | 1,145,680 |
| 1988-89 | 1,133,998 |
| 1989-90 | 1,696,653 |

Funds for voluntary organisations in the social services field are also available under section 26 of the Development of Rural Wales Act 1976. The figures are as follows:

| | £ |
|---|---|
| 1986-87 | 594,616 |
| 1987-88 | 725,049 |
| 1988-89 | 811,527 |
| 1989-90 | 965,245 |

## Cervical Smears

**Mr. Nicholas Bennett:** To ask the Secretary of State for Wales what is the average time taken by each Welsh health authority to process cervical smear tests and provide the results for the patient and her general practitioner; and if he will make a statement.

**Mr. Grist:** Information for 1988-89 is currently being collected by the Department from Welsh health authorities. I shall write to my hon. Friend once the results have been collated.

## Bovine Spongiform Encephalopathy

**Mr. Ron Davies:** To ask the Secretary of State for Wales how many cases of bovine spongiform encephalopathy infected cattle, at non-European Economic Community-approved slaughterhouses in Wales, have been identified.

**Mr. Peter Walker:** Four cases have been reported of which two proved positive and one negative; on the other one the result of testing is still awaited.

# HEALTH

## Abortion

**Mr. Amess:** To ask the Secretary of State for Health how many babies were born alive in 1987 and 1988 and to date in 1989 at 21, 22, 23, 24, 25, 26, 27, 28, 29, 30 and 31 weeks' gestation.

**Mr. Freeman:** The information requested is not available. Gestation period is recorded at the registration of still births but not live births.

**Mr. Amess:** To ask the Secretary of State for Health (1) if he will publish in the *Official Report* the dates of implementation of the nine recommendations contained in the Select Committee on the Abortion (Amendment) Bill 1974-75; and if he will make a statement;

(2) if he will publish in the *Official Report* those recommendations contained in the Select Committee on the Abortion (Amendment) Bill 1974-75 which were implemented *(a)* in part and *(b)* in full; and if he will make a statement.

**Mr. Freeman:** The information is as follows:
*Select Committee recommendation with implementation and date*
1. Counselling of women
   In full in July 1977 (HC(77)26)

*Select Committee recommendation with implementation and date*
2. Examination of the Women
   In part in March 1976 (SI 1976 No. 15)

3. Certification and Notification
   In part in March 1981 (SI 1980 No. 1724)

4. Disclosure of Information
   In full in March 1976 (SI 1976 No. 15)

5. Private Sector Arrangements
   In part in September 1975 through the system of "assurances" which proprietors of approved places are required to give to the Secretary of State

6. Foreign Women
   In part in December 1975

7. National Health Service—Termination after the 20th week
   Discussed with Regional Medical Officers in 1975 and 1983

8. Referral Agencies
   In full in March 1977

9. The Use of Foetuses and Foetal Material for Research (the Peel Report)
   The Peel Code of Practice issued in 1972 was voluntarily accepted by the professions. The Department ensures that arrangements for supply of foetal material for research from private sector places carrying out abortions comply with the Code of Practice.

**Mr. Amess:** To ask the Secretary of State for Health if he will seek to obtain for his departmental library a copy of the hearings and report from the United States Judiciary Committee on the Human Life Bill of the 97th Congress; and if he will make a statement.

**Mr. Freeman:** The Department is obtaining a copy of this report.

**Mr. Amess:** To ask the Secretary of State for Health what information he has as to the medical circumstances which created the need for abortions to be performed in emergencey to save the life of the mother in those cases which have arisen in 1986, 1987 and 1988; and if he will indicate the number of times each of those conditions has been the relevant factor.

**Mr. Freeman:** There were two abortions performed in England and Wales in 1986 with mention of ground 5 of the 1967 Abortions Act, which allows an abortion to be performed in emergency in order to save the life of the pregnant woman, on the notification form. In 1987 there were three such abortions, and in 1988 there were six.

Further details relating to the medical circumstances which created the need for these abortions to be performed cannot be released for reasons of maintaining confidentiality.

**Mr. Amess:** To ask the Secretary of State for Health what were the reasons for the two non-National Health Service abortions in 1987 over 25 weeks gestation.

**Mr. Freeman:** The informatin requested cannot be released for reasons of maintaining confidentiality.

### Voluntary Organisations

**Mr. Stevens:** To ask the Secretary of State for Health if he will list the grants awarded in 1988-89 to voluntary organisations under his Department's general scheme of section 64 grants.

**Mr. Freeman:** Our section 64 general scheme provides both core grants, to assist national voluntary organisations with their administrative costs, and project grants, which are experimental or innovative. In 1988-89, 237 organisations were awarded grants. These are listed in the table.

*Grants to voluntary organisations under S64 of the health services and Public Health Act 1968—general scheme (subhead D2(1)A) 1988-89 outturn*

| | £ |
|---|---:|
| Access Committee (England) | 91,000 |
| Action on Smoking and Health | 230,000 |
| Adfam | 21,200 |
| Advance | 33,000 |
| Age Concern | 252,000 |
| Age Exchange Theatre Company | 5,000 |
| AIDS Ahead | 17,800 |
| Alcohol Concern | 580,000 |
| Alzheimer's Disease Society | 130,000 |
| Amnesia Association | 5,000 |
| Anorexic Family Aid | 51,500 |
| Assoication for Research into Restricted Growth | 13,000 |
| Association for Spina Bifida and Hydrocephalus | 26,250 |
| Association of Breastfeeding Mothers | 5,000 |
| Association of Professions for the Mentally Handicapped | 7,000 |
| Association of Residential Communities for the Retarded | 8,000 |
| Association to Combat Huntington's Chorea | 10,000 |
| Asthma Society | 10,000 |
| Babylife Support Systems | 8,000 |
| Bacup | 15,000 |
| Breakthrough Trust | 35,000 |
| Breastcare and Mastectomy Association of Great Britain | 15,000 |
| Brendoncare Foundation | 550 |
| Bridge | 60,000 |
| British Agencies for Adoption and Fostering | 285,000 |
| British Association for Services to the Elderly | 12,000 |
| British Association of Immediate Care | 10,000 |
| British Association of the Hard of Hearing | 39,564 |
| British Council of Organisations of Disabled People | 13,000 |
| British Fluoridation Society | 30,000 |

| | £ |
|---|---:|
| British Institute of Industrial Therapy | 25,000 |
| British Institute of Mental Handicap | 35,000 |
| British Kidney Patient Association | 35,000 |
| British Organ Donor Society | 5,000 |
| British Red Cross Society | 10,000 |
| Brittle Bones Society | 6,000 |
| Brook Advisory Centres | 53,500 |
| Campaign for the Mentally Handicapped | 24.205 |
| Cancer Link | 10,000 |
| Carers National Association | 77,000 |
| Catholic Child Welfare Council | 1,500 |
| Catholic Marriage Advisory Council | 40,000 |
| Centre for Policy on Ageing | 9,200 |
| Centre on Environment for the Handicapped | 38,500 |
| Chest Heart and Stroke Association | 23,000 |
| Child Accident Prevention Trust | 93,500 |
| Child Care | 115,500 |
| Child Line | 83,200 |
| Child Poverty Action Group | 17,000 |
| Children's Legal Centre | 38,000 |
| Children's Society | 25,750 |
| Chinese Health Information Centre | 30,000 |
| Christian Concern for the Mentally Handicapped | 11,000 |
| Coeliac Society | 14,500 |
| Community Service Volunteers | 50,452 |
| Compassionate Friends | 15,000 |
| Contact | 30,000 |
| Contact a Family | 64,969 |
| Cope | 72,000 |
| Coronary Prevention Group | 80,000 |
| Council for the Advancement of Communication with Deaf People | 78,000 |
| Crossroads Care Attendant Scheme Ltd | 80,000 |
| Cruse | 134,931 |
| Cry-Sis | 4,000 |
| Demand | 10,500 |
| Dial UK | 40,000 |
| Disability Alliance | 20,000 |
| Disabled Living Foundation | 313,000 |
| Disabled Living Services Manchester | 7,000 |
| Disablement Income Group | 37,000 |
| Dr. Barnardo's | 240,000 |
| Ethnic Study Group | 33,827 |
| Exploring Parenthood | 9,000 |
| Extend | 25,000 |
| Family Holiday Association | 7,000 |
| Family Planning Association | 146,620 |
| Family Policy Studies Centre | 125,000 |
| Family Rights Group | 36,000 |
| Family Service Units | 160,000 |
| Family Welfare Association | 96,450 |
| First Key | 91,000 |
| Foundation for the Study of Infant Deaths | 10,000 |
| Foundation for Women's Health Research and Development (Forward) | 20,000 |
| Friends for the Young Deaf | 10,000 |
| Gingerbread | 78,000 |
| Good Practice in Mental Health | 94,973 |
| Haemophilia Society | 35,000 |
| Headway Association | 40,000 |
| Herpes Association | 5,000 |
| Holiday Care Service | 10,000 |
| Home Start Consultancy | 45,000 |
| Homes for Homeless People | 48,000 |
| Horticultural Therapy | 52,000 |
| Housing Campaign for Single Homeless | 34,800 |
| Institute for the Study of Drug Dependence | 317,207 |
| International Social Service | 47,500 |
| In Touch | 2,500 |
| Iris Fund | 2,500 |
| Joint Committee on Mobility for the Disabled | 900 |
| La Leche League of Great Britain | 7,000 |
| Landmark South London HIV Centre | 69,500 |
| L'Arche Ltd. | 12,000 |
| London Black Womens Health Action Project | 3,000 |
| London Lighthouse | 207,986 |
| MacFarlane Trust | 100,000 |
| Manic Depression Fellowship | 2,500 |

| | £ |
|---|---:|
| Marie Curie Memorial Foundation | 10,000 |
| Maternity Alliance | 37,000 |
| McIntyre Schools (Shipton) | 2,000 |
| Medical Commission on Accident Prevention | 7,000 |
| Mencap | 220,000 |
| Menieres Disease Society | 5,000 |
| Mental After Care Association | 50,000 |
| Mental Health Film Council | 55,000 |
| Mental Health Foundation | 27,000 |
| Mildmay Mission Hospital | 256,000 |
| Miscarriage Association | 4,000 |
| Mobility Information Service | 5,000 |
| Motor Neurone Disease Association | 10,000 |
| Myalgic Encephalomyelitis Association | 5,000 |
| Nafsiyat | 5,000 |
| National Aids Trust | 113,919 |
| National Association for Maternal and Child Welfare | 10,000 |
| National Association for Mental Health (Mind) | 415,000 |
| National Association for Patient Participation | 4,730 |
| National Association for the Care and Resettlement of Offenders | 300,000 |
| National Association for the Childless | 33,000 |
| National Association for the Limbless Disabled | 15,000 |
| National Association for the Welfare of Children in Hospital | 90,000 |
| National Association of Leagues of Hospital Friends | 24,000 |
| National Association for Voluntary Hostels | 5,250 |
| National Association of Young People in Care | 32,000 |
| National Back Pain Association | 21,000 |
| National Childbirth Trust | 77,682 |
| National Childminding Association | 105,000 |
| National Children's Bureau | 322,506 |
| National Childrens Home (Leeds) | 17,500 |
| National Citizens Advocacy | 11,250 |
| National Community Health Resource | 89,421 |
| National Council for One Parent Families | 150,000 |
| National Council for Voluntary Organisations | 112,500 |
| National Eczema Society | 5,000 |
| National Federation of Kidney Patients | 10,000 |
| National Foster Care Association | 100,000 |
| National Information Forum | 1,000 |
| National Institute for Social Work | 172,000 |
| National Organisation for Counselling Adoptees and Parents (NORCAP) | 8,000 |
| National Osteoporosis Society | 20,000 |
| National Out of School Alliance | 77,000 |
| National Playbus Association | 51,500 |
| National Schizophrenia Fellowship | 91,000 |
| National Society for the Prevention of Cruelty to Children | 125,000 |
| National Stepfamily Association | 10,000 |
| National Toy Libraries | 45,000 |
| National Youth Bureau | 74,000 |
| New Horizons Trust | 10,000 |
| Newcastle upon Tyne Council for the Disabled | 4,500 |
| Northern Schizophrenia Fellowship | 27,500 |
| North Lambeth Day Centre Ltd | 16,000 |
| North Regional Association for the Blind | 53,169 |
| North West Fellowship | 20,000 |
| Ockenden Venture | 104,000 |
| One to One | 1,500 |
| Organisation for Sickle Cell Anaemia Research | 11,250 |
| Outset | 25,000 |
| Overseas Doctors Association | 15,000 |
| Pain Relief Foundation | 8,000 |
| Parent to Parent Information on Adoption Services | 6,500 |
| Parentline Opus | 38,000 |
| Parents Against Injustice (PAIN) | 18,000 |
| Parents for Children | 48,500 |
| Parkinsons Disease Society | 15,000 |
| Partially Sighted Society | 10,000 |
| Patients Association | 12,500 |
| Phobic Action | 8,000 |
| Phobics Society | 5,000 |
| Physically Handicapped and Able Bodied | 30,000 |
| Pre-School Playgroups Association | 410,000 |
| Prince of Wales Advisory Group on Disability | 15,000 |

| | £ |
|---|---:|
| Queen Elizabeth Foundation for the Disabled | 32,500 |
| Rape Counselling and Research Project | 25,000 |
| Rathbone Society | 20,000 |
| Raynauds' Association Trust | 6,000 |
| Research Council for Complementary Medicine | 40,000 |
| Research Institute of Consumers Association | 8,000 |
| Research Trust for Metabolic Diseases | 5,000 |
| Richmond Fellowship | 97,000 |
| Royal Association for Disability and Rehabilitation (RADAR) | 237,000 |
| Royal National Institute for the Blind | 270,000 |
| Royal National Institute for the Deaf | 66,380 |
| Samaritans | 155,000 |
| Save the Children Fund | 423,489 |
| Scoliosis Association UK | 1,000 |
| Sense (NADBRH) | 45,000 |
| Sequal | 41,000 |
| Sexual and Personal Relationships of the Disabled | 33,500 |
| Shape | 1,050 |
| Sickle Cell Society | 15,000 |
| Society of Voluntary Associates | 15,900 |
| South Regional Association for the Blind | 106,702 |
| Spinal Injuries Association | 25,000 |
| St. Christopher's Hospice Information Service | 5,711 |
| St. John Ambulance | 10,000 |
| St. Katherine Housing Trust | 18,000 |
| Standing Committee on Sexual Abuse of Children | 12,000 |
| Standing Conference on Drug Abuse (SCODA) | 236,000 |
| Stillbirth and Neonatal Death Association | 22,000 |
| Tacade | 19,248 |
| Tay Sachs and Allied Diseases Association | 1,000 |
| Terence Higgins Trust | 400,000 |
| Thalassamenia Society | 15,000 |
| Tibble Trust | 500 |
| Tripscope | 4,000 |
| Tuberous Sclerosis Association | 1,500 |
| Turning Point | 100,00 |
| Twins and Multiple Births Association | 3,000 |
| Vitiligo | 4,000 |
| Vocal | 15,000 |
| Voice for the Child in Care | 3,500 |
| Voluntary Council for Handicapped Children | 40,000 |
| Voluntary Organisations Liaison Committee for Under Fives | 37,650 |
| Volunteer Centre | 12,500 |
| Vortex | 12,500 |
| Walsingham Community Homes | 10,000 |
| Wessex Rehabilitation Association | 24,000 |
| Westminster Pastoral Foundation | 66,000 |
| West Yorks Youth Association | 25,000 |
| Widows Advisory Trust | 25,000 |
| Winged Fellowship Trust | 15,000 |
| Women's Aid Federation (England) | 121,961 |
| Women's Health Concern | 17,500 |
| Women's National Cancer Control Campaign | 74,500 |
| Womens Therapy Centre | 5,000 |
| Working Mothers Association | 15,950 |
| Young Minds | 3,000 |
| £ for £ Scheme | 19,855 |
| | |
| Total paid | 13,517,507 |

## THE ARTS

### Museums (Fire Alarms)

**Mr. Devlin:** To ask the Minister for the Arts how many and which national museums do not have adequate fire alarms _(a)_ at their main gallery and _(b)_ at any storage warehouse; what proposals he has to remedy this defect; how many do not currently meet fire regulations; when they were last inspected for safe electrical wiring; and what was the result of these inspections.

**Mr. Luce:** All national museums and galleries have fire alarm and precaution systems which, since the institutions untied from the Property Services Agency, are subject to inspection by the appropriate local authority fire officer. Fire alarm systems, which are often combined with security systems, are upgraded and updated as and when necessary, in consultation with the fire officer. A completely new fire and security system is being installed in the National gallery to coincide with the opening of the Sainsbury wing and the British museum is also planning to replace and upgrade its present system.

Institutions carry out regular inspections of their wiring, and replace it when necessary. Work is in progress, for example, on a major new high voltage ring main system serving all three of the South Kensington museums.

Directors very rightly treat these basic safety matters as of high priority.

## NATIONAL FINANCE

### Supply-side Measures

**Mr. Leighton:** To ask the Chancellor of the Exchequer what have been the Government's main supply-side measures over the last 10 years; and what have been their practical results.

**Mr. Major:** The Government have undertaken a very wide range of measures over the past decade which have contributed to freer and more flexible markets and have improved the competitiveness of the economy. These include the privatisation programme, deregulation, liberalisation of financial markets, tax reform, improved incentives, promotion of enterprise and reforms in housing, education, and industrial relations. The cumulative result has been a positive transformation in our economic performance and prospects, with buoyant investment, profitability, and output and employment growth.

### Personal Savings

**Mr. Allen:** To ask the Chancellor of the Exchequer what he is doing to improve the savings ratio.

**Mr. Lilley:** The rise in interest rates over the past year will encourage higher saving and lower borrowing.

### Pound Coins and Notes

**Mr. Canavan:** To ask the Chancellor of the Exchequer what estimate he has of the number of pounds sterling coins and notes which are in circulation *(a)* in Scotland and *(b)* in the United Kingdom.

**Mr. Lilley:** The total number of £1 coins in circulation in the United Kingdom is estimated at 842 million. There are no statistics available on the number of £1 coins in circulation in Scotland. At the end of February 1989 there were 102 million Bank of England £1 notes recorded as outstanding, but none of these is in active circulation anywhere in the United Kingdom. Certain Scottish and Northern Irish banks retain a privilege to issue their own bank notes; the numbers of each denomination of their notes in circulation is a matter for them.

### Finance Bill

**Dr. Godman:** To ask the Chancellor of the Exchequer when the hon. Member for Greenock and Port Glasgow can expect an answer to his letter, dated 12 May, regarding clause 167 of the Finance Bill and the Royal National Lifeboat Institution.

**Mr. Norman Lamont:** Shortly.

### Investment

**Mr. Gordon Brown:** To ask the Chancellor of the Exchequer whether he will show for 1988 the total level of fixed investment by industrial and commercial companies in *(a)* plant and machinery, *(b)* dwellings, *(c)* company cars, *(d)* other vehicles, *(e)* other new buildings and works, *(f)* purchases less sales of land and existing buildings and *(g)* all fixed assets.

**Mr. Major:** Total fixed investment by industrial and commercial companies in 1988 is estimated at £37,461 million. The analysis by type of asset is not yet available. An analysis will be published in the 1989 edition of the "United Kingdom National Accounts" in September, but will not distinguish between company cars and other vehicles.

**Mr. Jack:** To ask the Chancellor of the Exchequer what are the latest projections for the growth of manufacturing investment in 1989.

**Mr. Major:** The latest Department of Trade and Industry investment intentions survey published in June projected manufacturing investment in constant prices to rise by 15 per cent. in 1989 on a year earlier. The latest CBI quarterly trends survey published in April confirms this buoyant outlook.

### Italian Consumer Price Index

**Mr. Chris Smith:** To ask the Chancellor of the Exchequer if, further to the reply by the Economic Secretary to the hon. Member for Islington, South and Finsbury on 26 June, he will indicate what local government taxation costs are included in the Italian consumer price index.

**Mr. Lilley** *[holding answer 29 June 1989]:* I refer the hon. Member to my reply to his question of 26 June, at column *297,* which stated that the Italians do not include rates or their equivalent in their consumer price index.

### Ivory

**Mr. Ron Davies:** To ask the Chancellor of the Exchequer what action Her Majesty's Customs and Excise proposes to take in respect of the ivory earrings deposited with them by the Prime Minister after her visit to Africa.

**Mr. Lilley** *[holding answer 29 June 1989]:* Customs and Excise use articles made from parts and derivatives of endangered species for educational, publicity and display purposes. The goods deposited by the Prime Minister have been added to the pool of items from which they may draw.

# FOREIGN AND COMMONWEALTH AFFAIRS

## Human Rights

**Mr. Vaz:** To ask the Secretary of State for Foreign and Commonwealth Affairs (1) how many representations he has made complaining about the denial of human rights in the last five years in West Germany;

(2) how many representations he has made complaining about the denial of human rights in the last five years in Canada.

**Mr. Eggar:** None.

**Mr. Vaz:** To ask the Secretary of State for Foreign and Commonwealth Affairs how many representations he has made complaining about the denial of human rights and the use of torture in the last five years in Ethiopia.

**Mr. Eggar:** We have made many representations about human rights to the Ethiopian authorities over the last five years. The latest occasion was my right hon. Friend's meeting with the Ethiopian Foreign Minister on 20 June. However, the precise information requested is not readily available and could be provided only at disproportionate cost.

## People-to-People Relations

**Mr. John Hughes:** To ask the Secretary of State for Foreign and Commonwealth Affairs what is the Government's policy towards people to people links between citizens in the United Kingdom and those abroad and, in particular, links with people in the Soviet Union and the countries of the eastern bloc; and what measures are being taken to encourage people-to-people relations.

**Mr. Waldegrave:** We are strongly committed to increasing direct contacts between people in this country and those in the Soviet Union and eastern Europe. The success of this policy depends, however, on the approach adopted by the other countries involved. In some cases direct contacts are developing rapidly as east European Governments lift longstanding restrictions on their citizens. But in other cases little or no progress has been made because the Governments concerned still prevent their own people from travelling abroad and discourage Western visitors.

## Council of Ministers

**Mr. Tredinnick:** To ask the Secretary of State for Foreign and Commonwealth Affairs if he will make a statement on the forthcoming business in the European Community Council of Ministers.

**Mr. Eggar:** The usual forecast was deposited in the House earlier today. At present five meetings of the Council of Ministers are planned for July.

The Economic and Finance Council will meet on 10 July to consider the Commission's second quarterly review of the economic situation in the Community.

The Foreign Affairs Council meets on 17 and 18 July. It will discuss issues relating to the current renegotiation of the Lomé convention, and receive reports from the Commission on EC relations with the United States and the Gulf Co-operation Council. It is also likely to discuss the draft broadcasting directive. The Council may also discuss relations with Eastern Europe, in particular the negotiation of a trade and co-operation agreement with Poland.

The Internal Market Council in 18 July will discuss a number of measures relevant to the completion of the single market.

The Agriculture Council will meet on 24 and 25 July to discuss reform of the sheep regime, New Zealand butter and sheep, and adaptation of agricultural structures policy (Objective 5(A)). It may also discuss bovine somatotropine compound feedingstuffs and pesticide residues.

The Budget Council on 28 July will give a first reading to the 1990 Community Budget.

## International Coffee Agreement

**Mr. Mans:** To ask the Secretary of State for Foreign and Commonwealth Affairs what is the current state of negotiations on a new international coffee agreement.

**Mrs Chalker:** The international coffee agreement (1983) expires on 30 September 1989. Intensive discussions have taken place since mid-1988 but have failed to result in a consensus on the content of a new agreement. On 3 July the International Coffee Council will consider two draft resolutions for extension with economic provisions. If neither resolution obtains the required majority, the Council may adopt a resolution providing for the 1983 agreement to be extended without economic provisions. With its Community partners the United Kingdom has supported the principle of extension of the 1983 agreement as part of a transition to a new agreement.

It has been the practice to lay the text of any agreed resolution for extension of an international commodity agreement before Parliament for 21 sitting days before the United Kingdom deposits an instrument of acceptance with the United Nations. Given the parliamentary recess, there will not be 21 sitting days between 3 July and 1 October. We cannot wait until Parliament sits again in the autumn, because under the terms of article 68 of the current ICA, contracting parties who have not notified the United Nations of their acceptance by 1 October 1989 will cease to be members of the ICA.

I have therefore decided to place in the Library of the House today copies of the two draft resolutions to be considered by the Council on 3 July. Once the final text of the Council resolution is known, I will ensure that it is laid before Parliament for as much of the usual 21-day period as possible.

# ENVIRONMENT

## Community Charge

**Mr. David Nicholson:** To ask the Secretary of State for the Environment if community charges are payable by a single person who is a resident member of staff in a boarding school during term time and who also rents a home elsewhere which is only occupied out of term time.

**Mr. Gummer:** All adults, unless they are exempt, will pay a personal community charge to the charging authority in which they have their sole or main residence. Individuals with more than one home will pay a personal community charge to the authority where they mainly live and may be liable to a separate standard charge on any other domestic property they own or lease if it is no other person's main residence.

## Environmental Assessment

**Ms. Walley:** To ask the Secretary of State for the Environment when he expects the booklet on guidance for developers and others on environmental assessment to be published.

**Mr. Howard:** We hope to send this booklet to the printers shortly.

## Rose Theatre

**Mr. Fisher:** To ask the Secretary of State for the Environment what information he has about the title to the site of the Rose theatre held by Imry Merchant Ltd.

**Mrs. Virginia Bottomley:** The hon. Member may approach the developers, Imry Merchant Developers plc for the details.

**Mr. Fisher:** To ask the Secretary of State for the Environment what sums his Department has paid to the developers Imry Merchant Ltd. in compensation for any delays experienced at the site of the Rose theatre.

**Mrs. Virginia Bottomley:** None so far.

## Water Purity

**Mrs. Ann Taylor:** To ask the Secretary of State for the Environment, further to his reply to the hon. Member for Dewsbury of 14 June, *Official Report,* column *417,* if he will publish his response to the reasoned opinion of 14 April.

**Mr. Howard:** Both the European Commission and the Government regard the detailed, formal correspondence on infraction proceedings as confidential. To publish the United Kingdom response to the Commission's reasoned opinion would be a breach of that confidentiality.

## Council House Sales

**Mr. Cartwright:** To ask the Secretary of State for the Environment if he will set out the number of appeals to the district valuer against right-to-buy valuations made in each London borough during *(a)* 1988 and *(b)* the first quarter of 1989, indicating the numbers resulting in reductions.

**Mr. Trippier:** The information requested is as follows:

*Determinations under section 128 of the Housing Act 1985*

| | Period 1 January-31 December 1988 | | | Period 1 January-31 March 1989 | | |
|---|---|---|---|---|---|---|
| | Requests received | Reports issued | Valuations reduced | Requests received | Reports issued | Valuations reduced |
| *Borough* | | | | | | |
| Barking and Dagenham | 70 | 68 | 22 | 26 | 16 | 5 |
| Barnet | 72 | 72 | 17 | 16 | 10 | 1 |
| Bexley | 5 | 5 | 0 | 2 | 2 | 2 |
| Brent | 9 | 7 | 3 | 19 | 9 | 8 |
| Bromley | 7 | 7 | 6 | 2 | 2 | 0 |
| Camden | 293 | 293 | 275 | 152 | 144 | 129 |
| Croydon | 51 | 28 | 20 | 25 | 5 | 0 |
| Ealing | 35 | 35 | 18 | 11 | 6 | 3 |
| Enfield | 9 | 9 | 5 | 3 | 3 | 1 |
| Greenwich | 369 | 369 | 360 | 213 | 150 | 149 |
| Hackney | 49 | 49 | 22 | 29 | 21 | 14 |
| Hammersmith and Fulham | 44 | 40 | 25 | 26 | 8 | 6 |
| Haringey | 58 | 54 | 46 | 24 | 22 | 18 |
| Harrow | 5 | 5 | 1 | 1 | 1 | 1 |
| Havering | 46 | 45 | 9 | 22 | 9 | 2 |
| Hillingdon | 21 | 21 | 13 | 0 | 0 | 0 |
| Hounslow | 75 | 71 | 57 | 25 | 3 | 2 |
| Islington | 267 | 267 | 111 | 120 | 79 | 30 |
| Kensington and Chelsea | 8 | 8 | 4 | 12 | 8 | 3 |
| Kingston upon Thames | 5 | 5 | 3 | 2 | 2 | 0 |
| Lambeth | 39 | 38 | 22 | 21 | 19 | 11 |
| Lewisham | 47 | 42 | 40 | 26 | 11 | 11 |
| Merton | 19 | 19 | 2 | 15 | 13 | 3 |
| Newham | 26 | 24 | 17 | 35 | 3 | 2 |
| Redbridge | 15 | 15 | 14 | 10 | 10 | 5 |
| Richmond upon Thames | 61 | 60 | 10 | 8 | 8 | 5 |
| Southwark | 125 | 106 | 74 | 40 | 31 | 12 |
| Sutton | 12 | 4 | 3 | 6 | 1 | 0 |
| Tower Hamlets | 195 | 195 | 73 | 36 | 8 | 1 |
| Waltham Forest | 33 | 33 | 29 | 25 | 24 | 22 |
| Wandsworth | 102 | 102 | 36 | 50 | 50 | 38 |
| City of Westminster | 155 | 131 | 50 | 24 | 20 | 4 |
| City of London | 14 | 14 | 12 | 1 | 1 | 1 |

## Planning Authority Membership

**Mr. McLoughlin:** To ask the Secretary of State for the Environment if he will list the planning authorities on which members of those authorities *(a)* do not have a requirement to live or work in the area in which those

authorities have planning jurisdiction and *(b)* do not have to live within the area of their planning jurisdiction as a result of their election.

**Mr. Chope** *[holding answer 29 June 1989]:* Except in areas covered by the Peak District and Lake District national parks, the Broads Authority and the English urban development corporations, the planning authority is the local authority. Section 79(1) of the Local Government Act 1972 requires that candidates for election to office as a member of a local authority should *(a)* be a local government elector for the area of the authority or *(b)* have occupied as owner or tenant land or premises in the area for the whole 12 months preceding the election or *(c)* have worked in the area during the preceding 12 months or *(d)* have lived in the area during the whole of the preceding 12 months.

# DEFENCE

## NATO Naval Exercises

**Ms. Short:** To ask the Secretary of State for Defence if there has been any change in Soviet naval responses to NATO naval exercises since President Gorbachev announced changes in Soviet military strategy towards defensive defence.

**Mr. Archie Hamilton:** The reduced Soviet response to NATO naval exercises, which was evident before the announced change in military doctrine towards "defensive defence", has since continued.

## Soviet Naval Forces

**Ms. Short:** To ask the Secretary of State for Defence if there have been any changes in the deployment of Soviet naval forces since President Gorbachev announced changes in Soviet military strategy towards defensive defence.

**Mr. Archie Hamilton:** The lower level of Soviet naval activity worldwide, evident before the announced change in Soviet military strategy towards "defensive defence", has since continued.

## British and French Ships (Docking)

**Mr. McFall:** To ask the Secretary of State for Defence if reciprocal insurance arrangements exist for British/French ships docking at British/French bases.

**Mr. Neubert:** No. Any claims arising from the activities of a vessel of either navy visiting the other country would be dealt with in accordance with well-established international procedures.

## Soviet Submarines

**Ms. Short:** To ask the Secretary of State for Defence what was the number of incidents of detection of Soviet submarines in the vicinity of *(a)* the United States navy base at Holy Loch and *(b)* British naval bases in 1978; and whether the frequency of such incidents has increased since President Gorbachev announced changes in Soviet military strategy towards defensive defence.

**Mr. Archie Hamilton:** I presume that the hon. Member intended to refer to 1987. The answer is *(a)* nil; *(b)* nil. Since the announced change in Soviet military strategy towards "defensive defence" there have been no such detections.

## Nuclear Submarines

**Mr. John Evans:** To ask the Secretary of State for Defence if he will make a statement on the progress of research into radiation and nuclear submarine personnel.

**Mr. Archie Hamilton:** There is no research specifically being undertaken into radiation and nuclear submarine personnel. The study to which I presume the hon. Member refers is part of the general study being undertaken by the Medical Research Council environmental epidemiological centre at Southampton univerity into mortality and morbidity among all submariners in the machine-manufactured submarine environment. The study, which began in 1988, is due to finish next year. It is too early to comment on any possible findings.

## Rosehearty Range

**Mr. Salmond:** To ask the Secretary of State for Defence how many bombing and firing runs have been made on Rosehearty range in each year since 1979.

**Mr. Neubert:** Bombing and firing runs have been made on Rosehearty range as follows:
    1979 to 1986—No records available.
    1987—8,332 passes.
    1988—8,547 passes.
    1989 (to May)—4,363 passes.

**Mr. Salmond:** To ask the Secretary of State for Defence what increases in the hours of aerial bombing and firing activity at Rosehearty bombing range are planned for the month of July; on which dates these activities will take place; how many and what types of aircraft will take part; and what is the purpose of the additional activity.

**Mr. Neubert:** From 8 to 23 July, while Tain range is closed for maintenance work, the operating hours at Rosehearty range will be as follows:
    Monday 0900-1630 and 1730-2200 (normally 0830-1200 and 1300-1630)
    Tuesday 0900-1700 (normally 0830-1200 and 1300-1630)
    Wednesday 0900-1630 and 1730-2200 (normally 0830-1200 and 1300-1630)
    Thursday 0900-1700 (normally 0830-1200 and 1300-1630)
    Friday 0900-1700 (normally 0830-1200 and 1300-1630)
    The range will close for maintenance from 24 July until 11 August (except for 2 and 3 August).
    Aircraft types using the range will be Jaguar, Buccaneer, F111, Tornado and Hawk. It is not possible to say in advance the numbers of aircraft involved, but the range utilisation is not expected to be greater than normal.
    A local press release about the evening opening will be made during the week beginning 3 July.

## Low Flying

**Mr. Salmond:** To ask the Secretary of State for Defence if he will make a statement on the special procedures to be followed by military pilots in low flying area 14C.

**Mr. Neubert:** Special procedures apply to aircraft operating in the coastal area between Aberdeen and Rattray Head because of intensive civilian helicopter activity in the area.

## ROF Enfield

**Mr. John Hughes:** To ask the Secretary of State for Defence whether he was aware of British Aerospace's proposals to close the former Royal Ordnance factory at Enfield at the time when the factory was sold to Britsh Aerospace.

**Mr. Sainsbury:** No.

### Tornado Aircraft

**Mr. Wilson:** To ask the Secretary of State for Defence when the decision was taken to divert aircraft off the Royal Air Force Tornado production line in order to meet orders from Saudi Arabia and Oman; and what has been the impact on the timing of deliveries of Tornado aircraft to the Royal Air Force of these changes.

**Mr. Sainsbury** *[holding answer 14 June 1989]:* Details of the decision to divert a small number of Tornado aircraft to meet orders from Saudi Arabia were announced during the RAF debate on 26 February 1986 at column 960. As the House has been informed, the diversion will have a temporary effect on the build up of the RAF's Tornado force.

I understand that Oman's order for Tornados has been postponed for the time being; the question of a consequent possible delay in the delivery of aircraft to the RAF does not, therefore, arise.

### United States Warships (Visits)

**Mr. John Evans:** To ask the Secretary of State for Defence if he will list United States foreign naval warship visits to British ports from June 1987 to the present date, the time at which they visited, and the type of vessel involved.

**Mr. Archie Hamilton** *[holding answer 26 June 1989]:* The following United States naval warships have visited British ports since June 1987:

| Port | Ship | Type | Dates |
|------|------|------|-------|
| Thurso | McCoy | Frigate | 13 to 15 July 1987 |
| Leith | Capondanno | Frigate | 25 to 28 September 1987 |
| Portsmouth | Augusta | Submarine | 19 to 22 February 1988 |
| Portsmouth | Mendel Rivers | Submarine | 22 to 25 April 1988 |
| Plymouth | Portland | Dock Landing Ship | 13 to 15 June 1988 |
| Glasgow | Portland | Dock Landing Ship | 17 to 21 June 1988 |
| Leith | Portland | Dock Landing Ship | 30 June to 6 July 1988 |
| Portsmouth | Mississippi | Cruiser | 4 to 7 July 1988 |
| Loch Ewe | King | Destroyer | 5 to 6 July 1988 |
| Portsmouth | Se Morrison | Frigate | 7 to 12 July 1988 |
| Leith | Elrod | Frigate | 11 to 15 August 1988 |
| Faslane | Baton Rouge | Submarine | 12 to 15 August 1988 |
| Liverpool | Elrod | Frigate | 2 to 6 September 1988 |
| Scapa Flow | Puget Sound | Destroyer Tender | 8 to 10 September 1988 |
| Portsmouth | Ly Spear | Submarine Tender | 16 to 22 September 1988 |
| Portsmouth | Semmes | Destroyer | 23 to 27 September 1988 |
| Portsmouth | Forrestal | Aircraft Carrier | 24 to 27 September 1988 |
| Newcastle | Portland | Dock Landing Ship | 28 September to 2 October 1988 |
| Newport | Annapolis | Frigate | 30 September to 2 October 1988 |
| Portsmouth | Mt Whitney | Amphib Command Ship | 2 to 6 October 1988 |
| Leith | Grapple | Salvage Ship | 8 to 13 October 1988 |
| Rosyth | Hayler | Destroyer | 25 October to 2 November 1988 |
| Faslane | Phoenix | Submarine | 1 to 9 November 1988 |
| Portsmouth | Alberquerque | Submarine | 3 to 8 February 1989 |
| Southampton | Dahlgren | Destroyer | 19 to 22 March 1989 |
| Plymouth | Hayler | Destroyer | 19 to 22 March 1989 |
| Fairlie | McInery | Destroyer | 16 to 18 April 1989 |
| Portsmouth | Preble | Destroyer | 19 to 23 May 1989 |

### Nuclear Weapons

**Ms. Short:** To ask the Secretary of State for Defence if there has been any increase in the number of the Royal Navy's tactical nuclear weapon capable ships since 1980; and if there are any plans in existence or under consideration to increase this capability.

**Mr. Archie Hamilton:** No; I refer the hon. Member to the answer I gave to the hon. Member for West Bromwich, East (Mr. Snape) on 27 June at column 385.

## AGRICULTURE, FISHERIES AND FOOD

### Atlantic Salmon

**Mrs. Golding:** To ask the Minister of Agriculture, Fisheries and Food what amounts of Atlantic salmon have been imported into *(a)* Great Britain, and *(b)* the United Kingdom in the last five years.

**Mr. Donald Thompson:** Atlantic salmon are not distinguished from other types of salmon in the statistics on overseas trade. The tonnages of all types of salmon imported, including prepared or preserved salmon, are shown in the table:

| | Imported into: | |
|---|---|---|
| | *Great Britain Tonnes* | *United Kingdom Tonnes* |
| 1984 | 27,770 | 28,107 |
| 1985 | 25,472 | 26,096 |
| 1986 | 33,978 | 34,482 |
| 1987 | 31,695 | 32,075 |
| 1988[1] | 25,684 | 25,975 |

[1] The figures for 1988 are not precisely comparable with those for earlier years due to the introduction of a revised classification for overseas trade statistics.

### Shell Fish

**Mr. Pike:** To ask the Minister of Agriculture, Fisheries and Food what steps his Department intends to take to assess the possible effects of the proposed long sea outfall from Rossall point to the Lune Deep on shell fish in Morecombe bay and adjacent coastal areas.

**Mr. Donald Thompson:** My Department has already assessed the design dilution and dispersion characteristics of the proposed outfall. We will maintain our routine monitoring of the contaminent levels in fish and shell fish in the eastern Irish Sea. In addition, information will be obtained as appropriate on the quality of shell fish in Morecombe bay from work undertaken by other relevant organisations.

**Mr. Pike:** To ask the Minister of Agriculture, Fisheries and Food (1) what information his Department holds on the chemical quality of shell fish harvested in Morecombe bay and adjoining coastlines with particular reference to compounds identified as black, grey or red list; and if he will make a statement;

(2) what information is held by his Department on the bacteriological quality of shell fish harvested in Morecombe bay and adjoining coastlines; and if he will make a statement;

(3) what information is held by his Department on the virological quality of shell fish harvested in Morecombe bay and adjoining coastlines; and if he will make a statement.

**Mr. Donald Thompson:** I refer the hon. Member to the reply that I gave on 20 February to the hon. Member for Bootle (Mr. Roberts) at column *534*.

### Hill Livestock Compensatory Allowances

**Mr. Macdonald:** To ask the Minister of Agriculture, Fisheries and Food how many individual farmers or landowners receive annually in hill livestock compensatory allowance payments more than £25,000, £50,000, £100,000 and £200,000.

**Mr. Donald Thompson:** The information requested is not readily available and could be provided only at disproportionate cost.

**Mr. Macdonald:** To ask the Minister of Agriculture, Fisheries and Food if he will estimate the total loss to United Kingdom farmers of limiting hill livestock compensatory allowance payments to 90 livestock units; and at what stock level a farmer would be less well off under such a restriction than under the present system.

**Mr. Donald Thompson:** If HLCA payments to producers were limited to 90 livestock units per holding, we estimate that the total loss to United Kingdom farmers would be about £30 million per year under the existing scheme arrangements. The producers disadvantaged by any such limitation would be those with more than 90 beef cows or 600 breeding ewes (or a combination of cows and ewes in excess of 90 livestock units). Producers below these limits would be unaffected.

## SCOTLAND

### Alloa Sheriff Court

**Mr. Worthington:** To ask the Secretary of State for Scotland what is the average delay in bringing cases to trial in Alloa sheriff court.

**Lord James Douglas-Hamilton:** The present period between the pleading diet and the trial diet in summary criminal cases at Alloa sheriff court is 15 weeks.

## EMPLOYMENT

### "New Life for Urban Scotland"

**Mr. Salmond:** To ask the Secretary of State for Employment when he intends to answer the written question tabled by the hon. Member for Banff and Buchan on Tuesday 13 June, relating to the New Life for Urban Scotland programme.

**Mr. Fowler:** I have replied to the hon. Member today.

### Inner Cities

**Mr. Salmond:** To ask the Secretary of State for Employment what plans he has to introduce a scheme, as part of the New Life for Urban Scotland programme, whereby long-term unemployed people will be asked to work for employers on a benefit-only basis; what guarantee of employment will be attached to such arrangements; and if he will make a statement.

**Mr. Fowler:** On 9 March, in my reply to my hon. Friend the Member for Wyre Forest (Mr. Coombs) *Official Report,* column *616,* I announced that my Department will be piloting a scheme for employers to guarantee to interview long-term unemployed people in return for help in selecting and preparing them for jobs. As part of the scheme, unemployed people will have the option, on an entirely voluntary basis, of trying out a job for a short period of time while they are still drawing benefit. I shall be announcing full details of this scheme shortly.

# INDEX TO THE

# PARLIAMENTARY DEBATES

## OFFICIAL REPORT

**SIXTH SERIES**

SESSION 1988–89

**VOLUME 155**

*19th June—30th June 1989*

## SCOPE OF THE INDEX, ARRANGEMENT AND ABBREVIATIONS

This index is derived from the House of Commons Library's Parliamentary On-Line Information System (POLIS), and the subject terms used are based on those used in POLIS. There are often changes in column numbering, etc, between the daily part or weekly Hansard (which simply collects together the daily parts without revision) and the bound volume. The index for the bound volume is revised to take account of these changes.

### Scope and arrangement of the Index

Oral and Written Parliamentary Questions are indexed under subject headings and the names of Members asking and Ministers replying to them. Questions are not listed under the names of Departments replying. Departmental listings can be arrived at indirectly by looking under the names of the Minister(s) of that Department. There are, however, the headings 'Northern Ireland', 'Scotland', and 'Wales' under which one can find not only most Questions answered by the Northern Ireland Office, Scottish Office, Welsh Office but also Questions about these areas of the United Kingdom which are answered by other Departments. Ministerial statements are indexed under subject headings, under 'Ministerial statements' and the names of Ministers making them and Members speaking on them. General debates are indexed under broad subject headings and under the names of all Members and Ministers taking part. Debates on legislation (Bills, Orders, Regulations etc.) are indexed under the name of the Bill, Statutory Instrument etc, under subject headings and under the names of those taking part.

Rulings and Statements by Mr. Speaker and his deputies are brought together under the heading Speaker's rulings and statements.

Other contributions by Mr. Speaker and his deputies appear under the heading Speaker.

Opposition Day Debates, Estimates Day Debates and Standing Order No. 10 applications are listed under those respective headings and under subject headings too.

The date of each item except Parliamentary Questions is inserted immediately before the reference.

Members' names are given in the form by which they prefer to be known and are printed in bold italics. Under their names, entries are arranged under one of the two headings *Debates etc* (to include interventions on statements, points of order and so on) or *Questions*.

### Abbreviations

*Bills* 1R = first reading, 2R = second reading, Money res = money resolution, Com = Committee stage, Rep = Report stage, 3R = third reading, amendt/amendts = amendment/amendments, * = matter taken formally, without debate.

Column numbers followed by the letter W refer to Written Questions. These appear at the end of each daily part or volume with their own sequence of column numbers printed in italics.

**Betting & gaming duties**
Greyhound racing (21:06:89) 339-41

**Bevan, Mr David Gilroy**
*Questions*
Vacant land registers, Housing construction 491w

**Bilateral aid**
Iraq 335w
Malaysia 18w

**Bill of rights**
Northern Ireland 479-81

**Billericay**
565w

**Bilston Glen Colliery**
Compensation 686-7

**Biology**
Scientists 292w

**Bioplan Holdings**
Leighton Hospital 101-2w

**Birds**
Nature conservation 1w, 274w
Special protection areas 506w

**Birmingham**
Railway electrification 270w

**Birmingham relief road**
Road construction 270w

**Blackburn**
Royal ordnance factories 388w

**Blackburn, Dr John G**
*Debates etc.*
Civil liberties (19:06:89) 109

**Blair, Mr Tony**
*Debates etc.*
Coal mining (26:06:89) 756-60, 761, 763-4, 791
*Questions*
Central Electricity Generating Board, Disabled workers 363w
Electricity supply industry, Computers 362w
Electricity supply industry, Privatisation 360w
Energy conservation 690
Nuclear accidents, Emergency planning 95w
Nuclear power stations, Emergency planning 95w
Orimulsion, Imports 362w
Public relations, Dept of Education & Science 292w
Public relations, Dept of Employment 471w
Public relations, Dept of Energy 390-1w
Public relations, Dept of Health 316w
Public relations, Dept of Social Security 307w
Public relations, Dept of the Environment 381w
Public relations, Dept of Trade & Industry 408w
Public relations, Home Office 395-6w
Public relations, Ministry of Agriculture Fisheries & Food 456w
Public relations, Ministry of Defence 532w

**Blaker, Rt Hon Sir Peter**
*Questions*
River pollution, EC countries 488w

**Blasphemy**
397w

**Blasphemy Bill 1988/89**
*Debates etc.*
1R (30:06:89) 1211

**Blind**
167-8w
Disabled workers 185w
Road accidents 139w

**Blind**—*continued*
Scotland 129w
Wales 141w

**Blood**
Medical research 152w

**Blood sports**
Environment protection 383-4w
New Forest 47w

**Blood tests**
Immigration controls 276w, (21:06:89) 468-74
Road accidents 138w

**Blood transfusion services**
431w
Private health services 318-9w
Surgery 281-2w
Transplant surgery 280w

**Blunkett, Mr David**
*Debates etc.*
Local Government & Housing Bill, 3R (21:06:89) 395, 430-3
*Questions*
Community charge, Computer privacy 963
Community charges register, Computer privacy 273-4w
EC internal trade, Training 121w
Income support, Community care 149w
Industry, Environment protection 173w
Rates & rating, Social security recipients 149w

**BMA**
see British Medical Association

**BNFL**
see British Nuclear Fuels

**Board of Inland Revenue**
see Inland Revenue

**Boarding schools**
Community charge 580w

**Boarding-out of Children (Foster Placement) Regulations 1988**
*Questions*
319w

**Boards of trustees**
Horniman Museum 503w

**Boateng, Mr Paul**
*Debates etc.*
Immigration rules (20:06:89) 302-5
Police, Greater London (30:06:89) 1214

**Body, Sir Richard**
*Questions*
EC social charter 143-4
Irradiated food, Nutrition 87w
Meat, Processed food 131w

**Boeing 727**
477-8w

**Bombings**
BAOR 263-4w

**Bonsor, Sir Nicholas**
*Debates etc.*
Immigration rules (20:06:89) 290, 292-3, 294, 295, 296

**Border Television**
191-3w

**Boswell, Mr Tim**
*Debates etc.*
Food hygiene (21:06:89) 343, 368-70
*Questions*
Dioxins 204-5w
Families 530w
Information technology, Research 15w
National Farmers' Union, Farm incomes 553w
Official engagements 223w, 408w
Water supply industry, Privatisation 349-50w
Youth Skill Olympics 122w

**Bottomley, Mr Peter**, *Under-Secretary of State for Transport*
*Debates etc.*
Road Traffic (Driver Licensing & Information Systems) Bill (HL), Rep (26:06:89) 797, 800, 802
*Questions*
Air accidents, Manchester Airport 8w
Air traffic control, Training 8w
Air transport, Contracts for services 342w
Air travel, Computer privacy 216w
Aircraft noise, Manchester Airport 478-9w
Aircraft noise, Military aircraft 477-8w
Aircraft noise, Treaties 477-8w
Airmisses, Heathrow Airport 523w
Breathalysers 339w
Exhaust emissions, Greenhouse effect 522-3w
Handicapped drivers 523w
Humber bridge, Road tolls 570w
Lead free petrol, Motor vehicle parts 524w
London assessment studies, Road traffic control 476w
London assessment studies, West London 476w
Lorries, Exhaust emission controls 341w
M3, Repairs & maintenance 525w
M25, Road construction 216-7w
Manchester Airport, Aircraft noise 478w
Ministers' visits abroad, China 341-2w
Motor vehicle registration 479-80w
Motorcycles, Driving offences 340w
Night flying, Airports 478w
Pedestrians, Road safety 270w
Railway freight transport, Barnes bridge 377-8w
River Severn, Road construction 523-4w
Road accidents, Blind 139w
Road accidents, Blood tests 138w
Road construction, Banbury 479w
Road construction, Liverpool 378w, 570-1w
Road safety 377w
Road safety, Transport supplementary grants 215-6w
Road safety barriers, Dual carriageways 341w
Road tax, Tax evasion 7w
Road traffic 338w, 377w
"Road User & the Law White Paper" 271w
Road works, City of Westminster 339w
Roads, Capital investment 525-6w
Roads, Greater London 475w
Severn bridge, Road tolls 570w
Street lighting, Local government expenditure 525w
Street lighting, Repairs & maintenance 508-9w
Traffic lights, France 341w
Transport, China 342w
Transport of radioactive materials, Sellafield 138w

**Bottomley, Mrs Virginia**, *Parliamentary Under-Secretary of State, Dept of the Environment*
*Debates etc.*
Litter (23:06:89) 663-8
*Questions*
Acid rain, Doncaster 380-1w
Archaeological sites, Environmental impact assessment 206w
Archaeological sites, Urban areas 206w
Birds, Nature conservation 274w
Blood sports, Environment protection 383-4w
Brodsworth Hall 382-3w
Carbon dioxide, Air pollution 379w
Cemeteries, Halifax 273w
Child health, Humberside 204w
Chlorofluorocarbons, Air pollution control 205-6w
Community charge, Transient people 200-1w
Dioxins 204-5w, 381w
Dog registration scheme 481w
Dog registration scheme, Association of District Councils 55w
Dog registration scheme, Costs 481w

9

**Davies, Mr Ron**—*continued*
Skills Training Agency, Buy outs 121w
Tree planting, Government grants 208w
Veterinary drugs, Licensing 453w

**Davis, Mr David**
*Debates etc.*
Self-governing Schools etc (Scotland) Bill,
Rep & 3R (20:06:89) 261
*Questions*
Dock labour scheme 120w
Self-governing hospitals, Privatisation 422w

**Davis, Mr Terry**
*Questions*
Community charge, Departmental
publications 200w
Community charge, Ethnic minorities 273w
Tuberculosis, Vaccination 105-6w

**Day, Mr Stephen**
*Questions*
Breathalysers 339w
Family doctors, Contracts of employment
815

**Day nurseries**
Further education colleges 147w

**DE**
see Dept of Employment

**De Lorean**
20w

**De Lorean, John**
20w

**Death**
British Rail 524-6w
Narcotics 397w

**Debt collection**
Northern Ireland 224w

**Debts**
Developing countries 78w
Humber bridge 570w

**Debts written off**
Privatisation 269-70w

**Deer**
Tuberculosis 251-2w

**Defamation**
Ethiopia 459w

**Defective housing**
Housing investment programmes 491-2w

**Defence**
Nuclear weapons 828

**Defence contracts**
Artillery 77w
Military vehicles 533-4w
Parliamentary constituencies 388w
Saudi Arabia 57w
Trident 388w

**Defence equipment**
Uranium 362w

**Defence expenditure**
USSR 371w

**Defence procurement**
Tornado aircraft 75-6w
Warsaw Pact 368-71w

**Defence research**
Guided weapons 458w
Strategic defence initiative 459w
USA 458w

**Delors Report**
(21:06:89) 335-6, (29:06:89) 1109-24

**Delyn enterprise zone**
9

**Demolition**
East Kilbride 285w

**Demonstrations**
Iran 397w

**Dental Laboratories Association**
470w

**Dental services**
Certification 470w
Laboratories 470w

**Dept of Education & Science**
Public relations 292w

**Dept of Employment**
Public expenditure 402w
Public relations 471w

**Dept of Energy**
390w
Civil service dispersal 360-1w
Public relations 390-1w

**Dept of Health**
Public relations 316w

**Dept of Social Security**
541w
Civil service agencies 416w
Personal records 308w
Public relations 307w

**Dept of Social Security local offices**
Social Fund 305-7w

**Dept of the Environment**
Public relations 381w

**Dept of Trade & Industry**
175w
Civil service dispersal 317-8
Departmental records 320-1
Public relations 408w

**Dept of Transport**
341-2w, 480w

**Departmental correspondence**
Administrative delays 20w
British Council of Organisations of
Disabled People 542w
Broadcasting 133w
NHS Review 217-8w

**Departmental forms**
Social security claims 541w

**Departmental leaflets**
Community charge 52w, 54-5w, 70w, 273w,
485w
Housing benefits 215w
Independent Living Fund 473w
Water supply industry 52w

**Departmental publications**
Air force 59-60w
Community charge 200w
Education Reform Act 1988 245-6w
Employment rehabilitation 184-5w
Environmental impact assessment 581w
Navy 59-60w
NHS Review 316w
Welsh Office 245-6w

**Departmental records**
Dept of Trade & Industry 320-1

**Departmental responsibilities**
Pollution control 204w

**Deportation**
63-4w
Illegal immigrants 63-4w
Iraq 34w, 290-1w

**Derbyshire**
Greenbelt 53w
Sewage 53w

**Derelict land**
Shotton 235w
Urban areas 495w

**Derelict land grants**
495w

**DES**
see Dept of Education & Science

**Design & Technology Working Group**
see National Curriculum Design &
Technology Working Group

**Design Right (Semiconductor Topographies)
Regulations 1989**
*Debates etc.*
(22:06:89) 595

**Deterrence theory**
Nuclear weapons 257w

**Developing countries**
Debts 78w

**Devlin, Mr Tim**
*Debates etc.*
Community care (26:06:89) 713
Self-governing Schools etc (Scotland) Bill,
Rep & 3R (20:06:89) 255
*Questions*
Employment opportunities, North East
region 132
Farm woodland scheme, Take-up 550w
Museums & galleries, Fire alarms 576-7w
Museums & galleries, Repairs &
maintenance 503w
Sea pollution, North Sea 957

**Devolution**
Northern Ireland 227w

**Dewar, Mr Donald**
*Debates etc.*
Housing Benefit (Community Charge
Rebates) (Scotland) Amendment
Regulations 1989 (21:06:89) 443-8, 450,
451-2
Scotland, European Communities
(28:06:89) 987, 993, 1000-6
Self-governing Schools etc (Scotland) Bill,
Rep & 3R (20:06:89) 188-9, 192-3, 266,
272
*Questions*
Wang Laboratories, Factory closures 833-4

**DH**
see Dept of Health

**Dickens, Mr Geoffrey**
*Debates etc.*
Business questions intervention (22:06:89)
500
Litter (23:06:89) 639, 648, 668-9
*Questions*
Business statements 497
Coal mining, Dismissal 682
Energy conservation, Electricity
consumption 690
Redundant mineworkers' payments scheme
139

**Dicks, Mr Terry**
*Debates etc.*
Football Spectators Bill (HL), 2R &
instruction to Com (27:06:89) 851
*Questions*
Industrial relations 126w

**Dieldrin**
44-5w, 349w

**Diets**
AIDS 278-9w

**Dioxins**
204-5w, 381w

**Diplomatic service**
China 391w
Private education 276w

**Dir75/268/EEC**
131-2w

**Dir79/409/EEC**
274w

**Dir80/778/EEC**
53w, 71w, 205w, 387w, 582w

**Director General of Electricity Supply**
Public appointments 682

**Disabled child premium**
542w

**Disabled Persons (Employment) Act 1944**

**Dunwoody, Mrs Gwyneth**
  *Questions*
  Foreign investment in UK 172w
  Leighton Hospital, Bioplan Holdings 101-2w
  Self-governing hospitals 102w
  Vaccination, Tuberculosis 827-8

**DVLC**
  see Driver & Vehicle Licensing Centre

**Dykes, Mr Hugh**
  *Debates etc.*
  Police, Greater London (30:06:89) 1221
  *Questions*
  City technology colleges 534w
  Community charge 963
  EC internal trade 181-2w
  Electricity supply industry, Retail trade 685
  Fossil fuels, Energy consumption 206w
  Intervention Board, Audit 554w
  Pop festivals, Noise control 194w
  Self-governing hospitals, Harrow Health Authority 429w
  World Association of Nuclear Operators, International Atomic Energy Agency 357w

**Dystonia**
  Medical treatments 320w

**Dystonia Society**
  Government grants 320w

**Eadie, Mr Alexander**
  *Questions*
  Balance of trade, EC countries 174w
  Coal mining, Redundancy 691
  Redundant mineworkers' payments scheme 139

**EAEC**
  see Euratom

**EAGGF**
  see European Agricultural Guidance & Guarantee Fund

**Ear nose & throat**
  Wales 12

**Early day motions**
  34-5w
  House of Commons debates 17-8, 499-500w
  Speaker's rulings & statements (26:06:89) 702

**Early retirement**
  National Institute of Agricultural Botany 556w

**Earned income**
  University teachers 292w

**East Anglia**
  Social security abuse 129

**East Kilbride**
  Demolition 285w
  Park & ride schemes 285w
  Railway network 285w

**East Midlands**
  Social Fund 314-5w
  Unemployment 112w

**East West relations**
  579w
  Berlin 528w

**Eastham, Mr Ken**
  *Questions*
  Employment Training, Greater Manchester 106w
  Information technology 169w
  Social Fund, Manchester 21w

**EC action**
  Broadcasting 325
  Dock labour scheme 120w
  Fishing vessels 251w
  Food hygiene 105w

**EC action**—*continued*
  Genetics 515w
  Ivory 17w
  Marginal land 131-2w
  Mergers 2w, 88w
  Postal services 409w
  Science & technology research 394-6w

**EC Agriculture Council**
  132-3w, 453w

**EC budget**
  23w

**EC budget contributions**
  UK contributions to EC budget 150w

**EC Commission**
  see European Commission

**EC Consumer Affairs Council**
  173w

**EC countries**
  Balance of trade 174w
  Harmonisation of standards 88-91w
  Industry 181-2w
  Manufacturing industries 16w
  Pensions 279w
  River pollution 488w
  Unemployment 110w, 139-40
  Youth unemployment 113-4w

**EC Draft 8066/88**
  (22:06:89) 506

**EC Economic & Finance Council**
  see EC Finance Council

**EC Energy Council**
  Greenhouse effect 686

**EC Environment Council**
  492w
  Ivory 969

**EC environmental policy**
  Pollution control 53-4w

**EC external relations**
  Kurdistan 290w

**EC external trade**
  Textiles 325
  Trade barriers 324-5

**EC Finance Council**
  23w, 300w, 461w

**EC Fisheries Council**
  49w, 250-1w, 555w

**EC framework programme**
  394-6w

**EC grants & loans**
  Doncaster 277w
  Fishing vessels 87w
  Forestry 46-7w, 1096-7
  Northern Ireland 225w, 476-8
  Shipbuilding 79w, 569w
  South Yorkshire 277w
  Unemployment 24w

**EC internal trade**
  181-2w
  Advisory services 175w
  Economic regions 175-6w
  North East region 132
  Publicity 331-2
  Statistics 179w
  Training 121w

**EC Labour & Social Affairs Council**
  120w

**EC labour policy**
  283-4w

**EC law**
  78w
  Antidumping duties (28:06:89) 1085-90
  Banks 489
  Broadcasting 136w
  Cabinet Office 149-50w

**EC law**—*continued*
  Credit controls 22w
  Environment protection 144
  Voting methods 393w
  Water pollution 53w, 71w, 483w

**EC social charter**
  143-4, 407w, 491-2, (29:06:89) 1109-24
  Employment 122w
  Industrial democracy 140
  Right of abode 398w
  Voting methods 404w, 418w
  Women's employment 488-9

**EC social policy**
  283-4w

**ECOFIN**
  see EC Finance Council

**Economic policy**
  577w, 828-9
  Employment level 829
  Unemployment 131-2

**Economic regions**
  EC internal trade 175-6w
  Regional planning & development 180w

**Economic sanctions**
  China 488

**Eden Committee**
  see Weighing & Measuring Machines Review Committee

**Edinburgh University**
  (26:06:89) 701-3

**Edinburgh University Dental School**
  Standing Order No 20 applications (26:06:89) 701-3

**Education**
  Arts 692
  Expenditure 537-8w

**Education & industry**
  Norfolk (26:06:89) 807-10
  Wales 86w

**Education (National Curriculum) (Attainment Targets & Programmes of Study in England) Order 1989**
  *Debates etc.*
  (29:06:89) 1139

**Education (National Curriculum) (Modern Foreign Languages) Order 1989**
  *Debates etc.*
  (29:06:89) 1139

**Education Reform Act 1988**
  *Questions*
  Departmental publications 245-6w

**Education (School Hours & Policies) (Information) Regulations 1989**
  *Debates etc.*
  (29:06:89) 1139

**Education support grants**
  412w, 538-9w

**Educational benefits**
  Conductive education 129w

**Educational exchanges**
  China 294-8w

**Educational finance**
  Further education 145-7w
  Higher education 537w

**Educational health services**
  Head lice 427w

**Educational policy**
  Languages education 538-9w
  Northern Ireland 225w

**Educational population**
  464-5w

**Educational qualifications**
  Census of population 218w, 437w
  Publicity 218w

**Prosecutions**—*continued*
Insider trading 329-30w
Litter 565w
Railway Inspectorate 524-6w
River pollution 386-7w
Safety belts 519-20w

**Protection of Residents in Retirement Homes Bill 1988/89**
*Debates etc.*
2R order read (23:06:89) 670

**Protest movements**
Nuclear weapons 62w

**Provisional Sinn Fein**
see Sinn Fein

**PSA**
see Property Services Agency

**Ptarmigan**
Army 372w

**Public appointments**
Civil servants 2w
Civil Service College 7w
Community health councils 35w
Director General of Electricity Supply 682
Electricity supply industry 207w
Family practitioner committees 544w
Gwynedd 86w
Gwynedd Health Authority 28w
National parks 507w
North West Water Authority 383w
Police Authority for Northern Ireland 142w
Wakefield Family Practitioner Committee 220w

**Public bodies**
Northern Ireland 438-44w

**Public contracts**
Local authorities 349w

**Public expenditure**
Dept of Employment 402w
Wales 11-2

**Public houses**
Consumers 197w
Wolverhampton & Dudley Breweries 514-5w

**Public inquiries**
Hinkley Point C 352-3w, 390w

**Public libraries**
Expenditure 327w
Opening hours 328w

**Public order offences**
Football 565w

**Public petitions**
Burnley Football Club (30:06:89) 1211
Gypsies (28:06:89) 1083-4
Road construction (23:06:89) 607
Student loans (28:06:89) 1083
Western environmental improvement route (28:06:89) 1084

**Public Places (Hygiene) Bill 1988/89**
*Debates etc.*
1R (21:06:89) 147-8

**Public relations**
Dept of Education & Science 292w
Dept of Employment 471w
Dept of Energy 390-1w
Dept of Health 316w
Dept of Social Security 307w
Dept of the Environment 381w
Dept of Trade & Industry 408w
Home Office 395-6w
Ministry of Agriculture Fisheries & Food 456w
Ministry of Defence 532w

**Public Safety Information Bill 1988/89**
*Debates etc.*
2R order read (23:06:89) 670

**Public sector**
Energy conservation 390w

**Public sector housing**
Government grants 348w

**Public transport**
London Docklands 526-8w
South London 478w

**Publicity**
Botulism 42w
Community charge 199w
EC internal trade 331-2
Educational qualifications 218w
Electoral register 79w
Independent Living Fund 474w
Irradiated food 46w
Lead free petrol 272w
NHS Review 821-2

**Publishing**
Racial incitement 384w
Training & enterprise councils 108w
USA 87-8w

**"Punishment Custody & the Community Consultation Paper"**
189w

**Pupil-teacher ratios**
564w

**Quality control**
Manufactured goods 323

**Queen Mary & Westfield College Bill (HL) 1988/89**
*Debates etc.*
2R order read (28:06:89) 955, (29:06:89) 1091

**Queen's Medical Centre Nottingham**
Self-governing hospitals 431w

**Quin, Ms Joyce**
*Debates etc.*
European Council (29:06:89) 1117
*Questions*
EC Environment Council 492w
Energy conservation 351w
Estate agents, Codes of practice 334
Rent allowances, Social security claims 541w
Rent allowances, Social security recipients 308w
Shipbuilding, EC grants & loans 569w
Shipbuilding, Merseyside 569w
Shipbuilding, Tyne & Wear 569w

**Quota of disabled workers**
123w

**Rabbits**
Animal diseases 248w
Imports 249w
Meat 249w

**Racial discrimination**
491

**Racial incitement**
Publishing 384w

**Radar**
European fighter aircraft 55w
RAF Fylingdales 73w

**Radiation hazards**
AWE Aldermaston 61w
Children 103-5w
Leukaemia 153-4w
Nuclear submarines 583-4w

**Radio**
House of Commons broadcasting 198w

**Radio engineering**
Glengarry forest 74w
Radio frequencies 255-6w
Submarines 256w

**Radio frequencies**
Radio engineering 255-6w

**Radioactive waste disposal**
Cardiff 28w
Electricity supply industry 684

**Radioactive waste disposal**—*continued*
Seas & Oceans 203w
Wales 28w, 235-8w

**Radioactive wastes**
Dounreay 359w
Imports 138w, 491w
Plutonium 94-5w
Sellafield 94w, 359w

**Radioactivity**
94w
North Wales 235w

**RAF Coningsby**
Tornado aircraft 257w

**RAF Fylingdales**
Radar 73w

**RAF Leeming**
Tornado aircraft 256w

**RAF St Athan**
75w
Military aircraft 257w

**RAF Stornoway**
Military aircraft 58-9w
Military exercises 59w

**Raffan, Mr Keith**
*Questions*
A55, Clwyd 6
Delyn enterprise zone 9
Foreign investment in UK, Japan 171w
Medical audit 421w

**Railway electrification**
Birmingham 270w

**Railway freight transport**
Barnes bridge 377-8w

**Railway industry**
Industrial disputes 570w
Investment 570w

**Railway Inspectorate**
Prosecutions 524-6w

**Railway network**
Channel tunnel 139w, 270w
East Kilbride 285w
Greater London 479w
Scotland 339w

**Railway property**
Auctions 139w

**Railway transport**
Management 339w
Strikes 1105

**Railway travel**
Compensation 340w
Complaints 339-40w
Customs 9w

**Railway workers**
Pay 570w

**Rain**
Air pollution 380-1w

**Rain forests**
302w
Brazil 150w, 388-9w, 407w
British Petroleum 392w
Environment protection 530w
Forest protection 302w, 392w
Overseas aid 150w, 335w
Tree felling 964
UK companies abroad 289w
Wood 78w

**Raison, Rt Hon Timothy**
*Questions*
Local government reform 959

**Ramsar Convention**
506w

**Randall, Mr Stuart**
*Debates etc.*
Representation of the People Bill, 2R & Money res (29:06:89) 1144, 1145-9, 1150, 1163

**Winnick, Mr David**
  *Debates etc.*
Local Government & Housing Bill, 3R
  (21:06:89) 422-4
Representation of the People Bill, 2R &
  Money res (29:06:89) 1143, 1155-7
Student loans (19:06:89) 32
  *Questions*
Business statements 495-6
Cabinet, Ministers 830
House of Commons chamber 17
Self-governing hospitals, NHS
  administration 36w

**Winterton, Mrs Ann**
  *Debates etc.*
Community care (26:06:89) 731
Football Spectators Bill (HL), 2R &
  instruction to Com (27:06:89) 903
  *Questions*
Training & enterprise councils,
  Employment Training 108w
Women's Farmers' Union 557w

**Winterton, Mr Nicholas**
  *Debates etc.*
Community care (26:06:89) 715, 723-6
Peak district national park, Floods
  (22:06:89) 598-602
  *Questions*
Doctors' list of patients 816
Ivory, International trade 969-70

**Wolverhampton**
Employment Training 137
Lead free petrol 965

**Wolverhampton & Dudley Breweries**
Public houses 514-5w

**Women's employment**
EC social charter 488-9
OECD countries 112w

**Women's Farmers' Union**
557w

**Wood**
Rain forests 78w

**Wood, Mr Timothy**
  *Questions*
Defence, Nuclear weapons 828
Electricity generation, Carbon dioxide 688
Hard core unemployed 130
Manufacturing industries, Productivity
  180w
Water authorities, Privatisation 68-9w

**Woodland grant scheme**
44w, 208w, 1095

**Woolwich**
Social Fund 473w

**Woolwich Arsenal**
59-60w

**Work permits**
China 326w

**Work sharing**
Employment schemes 124w

**Working class**
Higher education admission 540w

**"Working for Patients White Paper"**
425w, 513w, 819
Costs 422w

**World Association of Nuclear Operators**
International Atomic Energy Agency 357w

**World Student Games**
Sheffield 342-3w

**Worthington, Mr Tony**
  *Debates etc.*
Community care (26:06:89) 713-4, 717
Self-governing Schools etc (Scotland) Bill,
  Rep & 3R (20:06:89) 176
  *Questions*
Management consultants, NHS 384w
Railway network, Scotland 339w
Railway transport, Management 339w
Scottish courts, Administrative delays 588w

**Wray, Mr Jimmy**
  *Questions*
Broadcasting, Broadcasting controls 326w
Broadcasting licences, Broadcasting
  controls 326w
Bus services, Monopolies 341w
Common Services Agency, Orthopaedics
  287w
EC environmental policy, Pollution control
  53-4w
Glasgow School of Art 286w
Glasgow School of Art, Government
  grants 286w
Immigration, Advisory services 323w
Immigration appeals, Scotland 287w, 324w
Ministers' visits abroad, Central America
  302-4w
Retirement pensions, Poverty 1104-5

**Wrightington Hospital**
NHS hospital trusts 827

**Written questions**
Ministry of Agriculture Fisheries & Food
  453w

**Wyre Forest District Council**
Environment protection 487-8w

**Yeo, Mr Tim**
  *Questions*
Employment level, OECD countries 10w
Environment protection, EC law 144
Export promotion, Japan 181w
Housing, Rural areas 490w
Petrol, Prices 358w

**Yeo, Mr Tim**—*continued*
Pupil-teacher ratios 564w
Self-governing hospitals 315w
Set-aside schemes, Agricultural land 251w

**Yeovil**
202-3w

**Yorkshire & Humberside**
529w
European Regional Development Fund
  321-2
Hard core unemployed 560-1w
NHS Review 546w
Self-governing hospitals 816-7

**Yorkshire Regional Health Authority**
Capital investment 428w
Contracts for services 546-7w

**Yorkshire Water Authority**
Planning permission 51w
Sewage 504w

**Young, Mr David**
  *Questions*
Irradiated food 467w
Rottweilers, Imports 55w

**Young, Sir George**
  *Questions*
Council house sales, Administrative delays
  481-2w

**Young Fruits**
42w

**Young offenders**
36w
Doncaster 36w
Hull Prison 461-2w

**Young people**
Abortion 158-64w
Housing benefits 542w
Pregnancy 158-64w
Remand in custody 192w

**Youth opportunities programme**
Training allowances 10-1w

**Youth Skill Olympics**
122w

**Youth training programme**
80-1w

**Youth training scheme**
Further education colleges 147w
Handicapped 122-3w
Training & enterprise councils 108w

**Youth unemployment**
EC countries 113-4w
Holloway 109w